ENCYCLOPEDIA OF

RELIGION

SECOND EDITION

ENCYCLOPEDIA OF RELIGION

12

SECOND EDITION

RNYING MA PA SCHOOL
•
SOUL

LINDSAY JONES
EDITOR IN CHIEF

MACMILLAN REFERENCE USA
An imprint of Thomson Gale, a part of The Thomson Corporation

THOMSON
GALE

Detroit • New York • San Francisco • San Diego • New Haven, Conn. • Waterville, Maine • London • Munich

THOMSON
GALE™

Encyclopedia of Religion, Second Edition

Lindsay Jones, Editor in Chief

For more information, contact
Macmillan Reference USA
An imprint of Thomson Gale
27500 Drake Rd.
Farmington, Hills, MI 48331-3535
Or you can visit our Internet site at
http://www.gale.com

LIBRARY OF CONGRESS CATALOGING-IN-PUBLICATION DATA

Encyclopedia of religion / Lindsay Jones, editor in chief.— 2nd ed.
p. cm.
Includes bibliographical references and index.
ISBN 0-02-865733-0 (SET HARDCOVER : ALK. PAPER) —
ISBN 0-02-865734-9 (V. 1) — ISBN 0-02-865735-7 (v. 2) —
ISBN 0-02-865736-5 (v. 3) — ISBN 0-02-865737-3 (v. 4) —
ISBN 0-02-865738-1 (v. 5) — ISBN 0-02-865739-X (v. 6) —
ISBN 0-02-865740-3 (v. 7) — ISBN 0-02-865741-1 (v. 8) —
ISBN 0-02-865742-X (v. 9) — ISBN 0-02-865743-8 (v. 10)
— ISBN 0-02-865980-5 (v. 11) — ISBN 0-02-865981-3 (v. 12) — ISBN 0-02-865982-1 (v. 13) — ISBN 0-02-865983-X (v. 14) — ISBN 0-02-865984-8 (v. 15)
1. RELIGION—ENCYCLOPEDIAS. I. JONES, LINDSAY, 1954-

BL31.E46 2005
200'.3—dc22 2004017052

This title is also available as an e-book.
ISBN 0-02-865997-X
Contact your Thomson Gale representative for ordering information.

Printed in the United States of America
10 9 8 7 6 5 4 3 2

EDITORS AND CONSULTANTS

Harvard Forum on Religion and Ecology
Ecology and Religion

JOSEPH HARRIS
Francis Lee Higginson Professor of English Literature and Professor of Folklore, Harvard University
Germanic Religions

URSULA KING
Professor Emerita, Senior Research Fellow and Associate Member of the Institute for Advanced Studies, University of Bristol, England, and Professorial Research Associate, Centre for Gender and Religions Research, School of Oriental and African Studies, University of London
Gender and Religion

DAVID MORGAN
Duesenberg Professor of Christianity and the Arts, and Professor of Humanities and Art History, Valparaiso University
Color Inserts and Essays

JOSEPH F. NAGY
Professor, Department of English, University of California, Los Angeles
Celtic Religion

MATTHEW OJO
Obafemi Awolowo University
African Religions

JUHA PENTIKÄINEN
Professor of Comparative Religion, The University of Helsinki, Member of Academia Scientiarum Fennica, Finland
Arctic Religions and Uralic Religions

TED PETERS
Professor of Systematic Theology, Pacific Lutheran Theological Seminary and the Center for Theology and the Natural Sciences at the Graduate Theological Union, Berkeley, California
Science and Religion

FRANK E. REYNOLDS
Professor of the History of Religions and Buddhist Studies in the Divinity School and the Department of South Asian Languages and Civilizations, Emeritus, University of Chicago
History of Religions

GONZALO RUBIO
Assistant Professor, Department of Classics and Ancient Mediterranean Studies and Department of History and Religious Studies, Pennsylvania State University
Ancient Near Eastern Religions

SUSAN SERED
Director of Research, Religion, Health and Healing Initiative, Center for the Study of World Religions, Harvard University, and Senior Research Associate, Center for Women's Health and Human Rights, Suffolk University
Healing, Medicine, and Religion

LAWRENCE E. SULLIVAN
Professor, Department of Theology, University of Notre Dame
History of Religions

WINNIFRED FALLERS SULLIVAN
Dean of Students and Senior Lecturer in the Anthropology and Sociology of Religion, University of Chicago
Law and Religion

TOD SWANSON
Associate Professor of Religious Studies, and Director, Center for Latin American Studies, Arizona State University
South American Religions

MARY EVELYN TUCKER
Professor of Religion, Bucknell University, Founder and Coordinator, Harvard Forum on Religion and Ecology, Research Fellow, Harvard Yenching Institute, Research Associate, Harvard Reischauer Institute of Japanese Studies
Ecology and Religion

HUGH B. URBAN
Associate Professor, Department of Comparative Studies, Ohio State University
Politics and Religion

CATHERINE WESSINGER
Professor of the History of Religions and Women's Studies, Loyola University New Orleans
New Religious Movements

ROBERT A. YELLE
Mellon Postdoctoral Fellow, University of Toronto
Law and Religion

ERIC ZIOLKOWSKI
Charles A. Dana Professor of Religious Studies, Lafayette College
Literature and Religion

ABBREVIATIONS AND SYMBOLS USED IN THIS WORK

abbr. abbreviated; abbreviation
abr. abridged; abridgment
AD *anno Domini,* in the year of the (our) Lord
Afrik. Afrikaans
AH *anno Hegirae,* in the year of the Hijrah
Akk. Akkadian
Ala. Alabama
Alb. Albanian
Am. *Amos*
AM *ante meridiem,* before noon
amend. amended; amendment
annot. annotated; annotation
Ap. *Apocalypse*
Apn. *Apocryphon*
app. appendix
Arab. Arabic
'Arakh. *'Arakhin*
Aram. Aramaic
Ariz. Arizona
Ark. Arkansas
Arm. Armenian
art. article (pl., arts.)
AS Anglo-Saxon
Asm. Mos. *Assumption of Moses*
Assyr. Assyrian
A.S.S.R. Autonomous Soviet Socialist Republic
Av. Avestan
'A.Z. *'Avodah zarah*
b. born
Bab. Babylonian
Ban. Bantu
1 Bar. *1 Baruch*
2 Bar. *2 Baruch*
3 Bar. *3 Baruch*
4 Bar. *4 Baruch*
B.B. *Bava' batra'*
BBC British Broadcasting Corporation
BC before Christ
BCE before the common era
B.D. Bachelor of Divinity
Beits. *Beitsah*
Bekh. *Bekhorot*
Beng. Bengali
Ber. *Berakhot*
Berb. Berber
Bik. *Bikkurim*
bk. book (pl., bks.)
B.M. *Bava' metsi'a'*
BP before the present
B.Q. *Bava' qamma'*
Brāh. *Brāhmaṇa*
Bret. Breton
B.T. Babylonian Talmud
Bulg. Bulgarian
Burm. Burmese
c. *circa,* about, approximately
Calif. California
Can. Canaanite
Catal. Catalan
CE of the common era
Celt. Celtic
cf. *confer,* compare
Chald. Chaldean
chap. chapter (pl., chaps.)
Chin. Chinese
C.H.M. Community of the Holy Myrrhbearers
1 Chr. *1 Chronicles*
2 Chr. *2 Chronicles*
Ch. Slav. Church Slavic
cm centimeters
col. column (pl., cols.)
Col. *Colossians*
Colo. Colorado
comp. compiler (pl., comps.)
Conn. Connecticut
cont. continued
Copt. Coptic
1 Cor. *1 Corinthians*
2 Cor. *2 Corinthians*
corr. corrected
C.S.P. Congregatio Sancti Pauli, Congregation of Saint Paul (Paulists)
d. died
D Deuteronomic (source of the Pentateuch)
Dan. Danish
D.B. Divinitatis Baccalaureus, Bachelor of Divinity
D.C. District of Columbia
D.D. Divinitatis Doctor, Doctor of Divinity
Del. Delaware
Dem. *Dema'i*
dim. diminutive
diss. dissertation
Dn. *Daniel*
D.Phil. Doctor of Philosophy
Dt. *Deuteronomy*
Du. Dutch
E Elohist (source of the Pentateuch)
Eccl. *Ecclesiastes*
ed. editor (pl., eds.); edition; edited by

'Eduy. *'Eduyyot*
e.g. *exempli gratia,* for example
Egyp. Egyptian
1 En. *1 Enoch*
2 En. *2 Enoch*
3 En. *3 Enoch*
Eng. English
enl. enlarged
Eph. *Ephesians*
'Eruv. *'Eruvin*
1 Esd. *1 Esdras*
2 Esd. *2 Esdras*
3 Esd. *3 Esdras*
4 Esd. *4 Esdras*
esp. especially
Est. Estonian
Est. *Esther*
et al. *et alii,* and others
etc. *et cetera,* and so forth
Eth. Ethiopic
EV English version
Ex. *Exodus*
exp. expanded
Ez. *Ezekiel*
Ezr. *Ezra*
2 Ezr. *2 Ezra*
4 Ezr. *4 Ezra*
f. feminine; and following (pl., ff.)
fasc. fascicle (pl., fascs.)
fig. figure (pl., figs.)
Finn. Finnish
fl. *floruit,* flourished
Fla. Florida
Fr. French
frag. fragment
ft. feet
Ga. Georgia
Gal. *Galatians*
Gaul. Gaulish
Ger. German
Giṭ. *Giṭṭin*
Gn. *Genesis*
Gr. Greek
Ḥag. *Ḥagigah*
Ḥal. *Ḥallah*
Hau. Hausa
Hb. *Habakkuk*
Heb. Hebrew
Heb. *Hebrews*
Hg. *Haggai*
Hitt. Hittite
Hor. *Horayot*
Hos. *Hosea*
Ḥul. *Ḥullin*
Hung. Hungarian
ibid. *ibidem,* in the same place (as the one immediately preceding)
Icel. Icelandic
i.e. *id est,* that is
IE Indo-European
Ill. Illinois
Ind. Indiana
intro. introduction
Ir. Gael. Irish Gaelic
Iran. Iranian
Is. *Isaiah*
Ital. Italian
J Yahvist (source of the Pentateuch)
Jas. *James*
Jav. Javanese
Jb. *Job*
Jdt. *Judith*
Jer. *Jeremiah*
Jgs. *Judges*
Jl. *Joel*
Jn. *John*
1 Jn. *1 John*
2 Jn. *2 John*
3 Jn. *3 John*
Jon. *Jonah*
Jos. *Joshua*
Jpn. Japanese
JPS Jewish Publication Society translation (1985) of the Hebrew Bible
J.T. Jerusalem Talmud
Jub. *Jubilees*
Kans. Kansas
Kel. *Kelim*
Ker. *Keritot*
Ket. *Ketubbot*
1 Kgs. *1 Kings*
2 Kgs. *2 Kings*
Khois. Khoisan
Kil. *Kil'ayim*
km kilometers
Kor. Korean
Ky. Kentucky
l. line (pl., ll.)
La. Louisiana
Lam. *Lamentations*
Lat. Latin
Latv. Latvian
L. en Th. Licencié en Théologie, Licentiate in Theology
L. ès L. Licencié ès Lettres, Licentiate in Literature
Let. Jer. *Letter of Jeremiah*
lit. literally
Lith. Lithuanian
Lk. *Luke*
LL Late Latin
LL.D. Legum Doctor, Doctor of Laws
Lv. *Leviticus*
m meters
m. masculine
M.A. Master of Arts
Ma 'as. *Ma'aserot*
Ma 'as. Sh. *Ma' aser sheni*
Mak. *Makkot*
Makh. *Makhshirin*
Mal. *Malachi*
Mar. Marathi
Mass. Massachusetts
1 Mc. *1 Maccabees*
2 Mc. *2 Maccabees*
3 Mc. *3 Maccabees*
4 Mc. *4 Maccabees*
Md. Maryland
M.D. Medicinae Doctor, Doctor of Medicine
ME Middle English
Meg. *Megillah*
Me 'il. *Me'ilah*
Men. *Menaḥot*
MHG Middle High German
mi. miles
Mi. *Micah*
Mich. Michigan
Mid. *Middot*
Minn. Minnesota
Miq. *Miqva'ot*
MIran. Middle Iranian
Miss. Mississippi
Mk. *Mark*
Mo. Missouri
Mo'ed Q. *Mo'ed qaṭan*
Mont. Montana
MPers. Middle Persian
MS. *manuscriptum,* manuscript (pl., MSS)
Mt. *Matthew*
MT Masoretic text
n. note
Na. *Nahum*
Nah. Nahuatl
Naz. *Nazir*
N.B. *nota bene,* take careful note
N.C. North Carolina
n.d. no date
N.Dak. North Dakota
NEB New English Bible
Nebr. Nebraska

Ned. *Nedarim*
Neg. *Nega'im*
Neh. *Nehemiah*
Nev. Nevada
N.H. New Hampshire
Nid. *Niddah*
N.J. New Jersey
Nm. *Numbers*
N.Mex. New Mexico
no. number (pl., nos.)
Nor. Norwegian
n.p. no place
n.s. new series
N.Y. New York
Ob. *Obadiah*
O.Cist. Ordo Cisterciencium, Order of Cîteaux (Cistercians)
OCS Old Church Slavonic
OE Old English
O.F.M. Ordo Fratrum Minorum, Order of Friars Minor (Franciscans)
OFr. Old French
Ohal. *Ohalot*
OHG Old High German
OIr. Old Irish
OIran. Old Iranian
Okla. Oklahoma
ON Old Norse
O.P. Ordo Praedicatorum, Order of Preachers (Dominicans)
OPers. Old Persian
op. cit. *opere citato,* in the work cited
OPrus. Old Prussian
Oreg. Oregon
'Orl. *'Orlah*
O.S.B. Ordo Sancti Benedicti, Order of Saint Benedict (Benedictines)
p. page (pl., pp.)
P Priestly (source of the Pentateuch)
Pa. Pennsylvania
Pahl. Pahlavi
Par. *Parah*
para. paragraph (pl., paras.)
Pers. Persian
Pes. *Pesahim*
Ph.D. Philosophiae Doctor, Doctor of Philosophy
Phil. *Philippians*
Phlm. *Philemon*
Phoen. Phoenician
pl. plural; plate (pl., pls.)
PM *post meridiem,* after noon
Pol. Polish
pop. population
Port. Portuguese
Prv. *Proverbs*
Ps. *Psalms*
Ps. 151 *Psalm 151*
Ps. Sol. *Psalms of Solomon*
pt. part (pl., pts.)
1Pt. *1 Peter*
2 Pt. *2 Peter*
Pth. Parthian
Q hypothetical source of the synoptic Gospels
Qid. *Qiddushin*
Qin. *Qinnim*
r. reigned; ruled
Rab. *Rabbah*
rev. revised
R. ha-Sh. *Ro'sh ha-shanah*
R.I. Rhode Island
Rom. Romanian
Rom. *Romans*
R.S.C.J. Societas Sacratissimi Cordis Jesu, Religious of the Sacred Heart
RSV Revised Standard Version of the Bible
Ru. *Ruth*
Rus. Russian
Rv. *Revelation*
Rv. Ezr. *Revelation of Ezra*
San. *Sanhedrin*
S.C. South Carolina
Scot. Gael. Scottish Gaelic
S.Dak. South Dakota
sec. section (pl., secs.)
Sem. Semitic
ser. series
sg. singular
Sg. *Song of Songs*
Sg. of 3 *Prayer of Azariah and the Song of the Three Young Men*
Shab. *Shabbat*
Shav. *Shavu'ot*
Sheq. *Sheqalim*
Sib. Or. *Sibylline Oracles*
Sind. Sindhi
Sinh. Sinhala
Sir. *Ben Sira*
S.J. Societas Jesu, Society of Jesus (Jesuits)
Skt. Sanskrit
1 Sm. *1 Samuel*
2 Sm. *2 Samuel*
Sogd. Sogdian
Soṭ. *Soṭah*
sp. species (pl., spp.)
Span. Spanish
sq. square
S.S.R. Soviet Socialist Republic
st. stanza (pl., ss.)
S.T.M. Sacrae Theologiae Magister, Master of Sacred Theology
Suk. *Sukkah*
Sum. Sumerian
supp. supplement; supplementary
Sus. *Susanna*
s.v. *sub verbo,* under the word (pl., s.v.v.)
Swed. Swedish
Syr. Syriac
Syr. Men. *Syriac Menander*
Ta' an. *Ta'anit*
Tam. Tamil
Tam. *Tamid*
Tb. *Tobit*
T.D. *Taishō shinshū daizōkyō,* edited by Takakusu Junjirō et al. (Tokyo,1922–1934)
Tem. *Temurah*
Tenn. Tennessee
Ter. Terumot
Ṭev. Y. *Ṭevul yom*
Tex. Texas
Th.D. Theologicae Doctor, Doctor of Theology
1 Thes. *1 Thessalonians*
2 Thes. *2 Thessalonians*
Thrac. Thracian
Ti. *Titus*
Tib. Tibetan
1 Tm. *1 Timothy*
2 Tm. *2 Timothy*
T. of 12 *Testaments of the Twelve Patriarchs*
Ṭoh. *ṭohorot*
Tong. Tongan
trans. translator, translators; translated by; translation
Turk. Turkish
Ukr. Ukrainian
Upan. *Upaniṣad*
U.S. United States
U.S.S.R. Union of Soviet Socialist Republics
Uqts. *Uqtsin*
v. verse (pl., vv.)
Va. Virginia
var. variant; variation
Viet. Vietnamese

viz. *videlicet,* namely
vol. volume (pl., vols.)
Vt. Vermont
Wash. Washington
Wel. Welsh
Wis. Wisconsin
Wis. *Wisdom of Solomon*
W.Va. West Virginia
Wyo. Wyoming
Yad. *Yadayim*
Yev. *Yevamot*
Yi. Yiddish
Yor. Yoruba
Zav. *Zavim*
Zec. *Zechariah*
Zep. *Zephaniah*
Zev. *Zevaḥim*

* hypothetical
? uncertain; possibly; perhaps
° degrees
+ plus
– minus
= equals; is equivalent to
× by; multiplied by
→ yields

Q–R
CONTINUED

RNYING MA PA (NYINGMAPA) SCHOOL. The expression "Rnying ma (Nyingma) pa school" may be used to refer to the Rnying ma (Nyingma) pa order of Tibetan Buddhism, as well as to the broad range of lineages claiming to derive their authority from the early transmission of Buddhism in Tibet during the seventh through ninth centuries. A common mytho-historical view of the origins of their tradition, as well as adherence to similar doctrinal and ritual foundations, serve to distinguish the Rnying ma pa from the other major trends in Tibetan Buddhism. At the same time, elements of Rnying ma pa ritual and contemplative practice play a role, sometimes an important one, within the non-Rnying ma pa orders.

The Rnying ma pa stand in a distinctive relationship to all other traditions of Tibetan religion. As their name, which literally means the "ancients," suggests, the school maintains that it uniquely represents the ancient Buddhism of Tibet, introduced during the reigns of the great kings of Tibet's imperial age. Fundamental to the distinctions informing Tibetan views of religious adherence is a broad division between the "ancient translation tradition" (*snga 'gyur rnying ma*) and the "new *mantra* traditions" (*gsang sngags gsar ma*), where *mantra* refers to Buddhist esotericism, or Tantrism, as it is called in the West, in general. The former includes all of those lines of teaching that eventually came to be grouped together under the rubric Rnying ma pa. Their identity, however, was formed only after the tenth century, when the proponents of the newly introduced esoteric systems began to attack the older traditions as corrupt, or as outright Tibetan fabrications. In response, the adherents of the earlier traditions argued that their esoteric teachings and practices were derived from the texts and instructions transmitted during the time of the Tibetan monarchs of the seventh through ninth centuries, Khri Srong lde btsan (Trisong detsen, r. 755–c. 797) above all. The post tenth-century Rnying ma pa came to hold that the Buddhist cultural heroes of that age—in particular, the Indian masters Padmasambhava and Vimalamitra and the Tibetan translator Vairocana, but many others as well—had introduced a purer, more refined and elevated form of esotericism than that which

Clockwise from top left corner. Qur'ān written in Nashki script. *[The Art Archive/Private Collection/Eileen Tweedy]*; Pre-Toltec Quetzalcoatl in the form of the morning star. Ethnologisches Museum, Staatliche Museen zu Berlin. *[©Werner Forman/Art Resource, N.Y.]*; Etruscan bronze capitoline she-wolf, c. fifth century BCE, with twins added later by Antonio Pollaiuolo. Musei Capitolini, Rome. *[©Timothy McCarthy/Art Resource, N.Y.]*; Cathedral of Saint Basil in Moscow. *[©Corbis]*; Fifteenth-century illustration by Marco dell'Avogadro of Ruth at work during the harvest, from the *Bible of Borso d'Este.* Biblioteca Estense, Modena. *[©Scala/Art Resource, N.Y.]* .

characterized the teaching transmitted in Tibet from the late-tenth century on. During this period in which a distinctive Rnying ma pa identity took form, the lineages involved were often familial lines of lay priests, not monks, and it is impossible to think of them as yet forming a cohesive order. In later times, the Rnying ma pa tended to rely on the renewed revelation of texts and teachings that were held to be spiritual "treasures" (*gter ma*) inspired by, but not derived in a direct line from, the traditions of the early masters. The proliferation of large numbers of new *gter ma* lineages further undercut the unity of the Rnying ma pa.

In contradistinction to the organized Bon religion, the Rnying ma pa identify themselves as purely Buddhist, whereas, over and against the other Tibetan Buddhist schools and in harmony with the Bon, they insist upon the value of an autochthonous Tibetan religious tradition, expressed and exalted within a unique and continuing revelation of the Buddha's doctrine in Tibet in the form of "treasures" (*gter*). The following features of Rnying ma pa Buddhism are particularly noteworthy: The primordial Buddha Samantabhadra (Tib., Kun tu bzang po [Küntuzangpo], the "Omnibeneficent"), iconographically most often depicted as a naked Buddha of celestial blue-color in embrace with his consort, is regarded as the supreme embodiment of buddhahood (shared with Bon). The highest expression of and vehicle for attaining that Buddha's enlightenment (which is equivalent to the enlightenment of all buddhas) is the teaching of the "Great Perfection" (Rdzogs chen [Dzogchen], also shared with Bon). The paradigmatic exponent of this teaching, and indeed of all matters bearing on the spiritual and temporal well-being of the Tibetan people, is the immortal Guru Padmasambhava, the apotheosis of the Indian Tantric master remembered for playing a leading role in Tibet's conversion to Buddhism during the eighth century, and who is always present to intercede on behalf of his devotees. Moreover, the teachings of the latter are continually renewed in forms suitable to the devotee's time, place, and circumstances, the agents for such renewal being "discoverers of spiritual treasure" (*gter ston/ bton*), thought to be embodiments of, or regents acting on behalf of, Padmasambhava.

While the Rnying ma pa adhere, as do other Tibetan Buddhists, to Tantric forms of ritual and contemplative practice, their Tantric canon is altogether distinctive, incorporating a great quantity of literature whose "authenticity" is challenged by some adherents of the other Tibetan Buddhist schools, as is the authenticity of their special teaching of the Great Perfection. Hence, from relatively early times, their unique standpoint created for the Rnying ma pa a remarkable justificatory problem, which has generated an elaborate apologetical literature, much of which is historical in character.

In their thinking about the history of their own tradition, the Rnying ma pa have come to identify three phases in the lineage through which their special doctrines have been transmitted: the "lineage of the conquerors' intention" (*rgyal ba dgongs brgyud*); the "symbolic lineage of the awareness-holders" (*rig 'dzin brda brgyud*); and the "aural lineage of human individuals" (*gang zag snyan brgyud*). The first of the "three lineages" is related to the primordial origination and disclosure, in the domain of the Buddha's enlightenment, of the doctrine, especially that of the Great Perfection. The third concerns the successive transmission of that doctrine through a line of human individuals, related each to the next as master to disciple, and always thought to be placeable, datable persons, though the specifics may be sometimes debated. The second lineage explains the beginnings of the transmission in the human world, the stages whereby a doctrine belonging to the timeless inexpressible realm of awakening came to be expressed in time.

HISTORICAL DEVELOPMENT. Although a clear Rnying ma pa identity was formed only in reaction to the criticisms of early Tibetan Tantrism that became current from the late tenth century on, certain of the characteristic features of later Rnying ma pa teaching are already evident in documents from Dunhuang dating to the ninth to tenth centuries, as well as in the works of relatively early writers such as Bsnubs chen Sangs rgyas ye shes (Nupchen Sangye Yeshe, late ninth to early tenth centuries). These works make it clear that two of the key elements of the Rnying ma pa ritual and contemplative tradition were already emerging: the Mahāyoga (Great Yoga) system of Tantric ritual, and the Rdzogs chen (Great Perfection) approach to meditation, emphasizing abstract contemplation. By the eleventh century some adherents of the old lineages began to defend their tradition against its detractors and at the same time to elaborate its doctrine and codify its ritual. The prolific scholar and translator Rong zom Chos kyi bzang po (Rongzom Chözang) and the ritual masters of the Zur lineage exemplify these trends.

In 1159 the monastery of Kaḥ thog was founded in far Eastern Tibet by Dam pa Bde gshegs (Dampa Deshek, 1122–1192). This soon emerged as an important center of scholarship, where a distinctively Rnying ma pa exegetical tradition based on the system of nine progressive vehicles (*theg pa rim pa dgu*) was elaborated. The influence of Kaḥ thog was widely felt throughout southeastern Tibet, penetrating even neighboring areas in Yunnan. During the same period, Rnying ma pa traditions were reinvigorated by the discoveries of treasure-doctrines (*gter chos*). Some of the foremost promulgators of the newly revealed teachings included Nyang ral Nyi ma 'od zer (Nyangrel Nyima Özer, 1124–1192) and Guru Chos dbang (Guru Chöwang, 1212–1270), and, sometime later, the discoverer of the so-called *Tibetan Book of the Dead*, Karma gling pa (Karma Lingpa, fourteenth century), as well as Rig 'dzin Rgod ldem can (Rikdzin Gödemcen, 1337–1408), whose Northern Treasure (Byang gter) spread throughout the Tibetan world.

The contemplative teachings of the Great Perfection, too, were greatly refined, syncretically absorbing and reinterpreting elements of the new Tantric traditions. The Seminal Essence (Snying thig) system, in particular, which placed great emphasis on visionary experience, developed through a series of revelations spanning some two centuries and came to be regarded as the culminating synthesis of Rnying ma pa teaching. Klong chen pa Rab 'byams pa (Longcen Rabjampa, 1308–1363), a poet and philosopher of unusual depth and refinement, codified the textual corpus of the Seminal Essence in four parts (*snying thig ya bzhi*), and in his own expansive writings—the *Mdzod bdun* (Seven treasuries), *Ngal gso skor gsum* (Trilogy of rest), and *Mun sel skor gsum* (Trilogy removing darkness), among others—he set forth an encyclopedic summation of the entire Buddhist path, which has remained the definitive Rnying ma pa doctrinal formulation. He was later believed to have been reborn as Padma gling pa (Pema Lingpa, 1450–1521), a treasure-discoverer whose revelations played a special role in the emergence of the Himalayan kingdom of Bhutan.

During the seventeenth century, a period of intensive civil war and sectarian conflict, the Rnying ma pa were fortunate to find a patron in the person of the fifth Dalai Lama (1617–1682), himself a revealer of treasures. With the encouragement of the "Great Fifth," a renewed monastic movement emerged among the Rnying ma pa, which had formerly been situated primarily in lay lineages, local temples, and individual adepts. Six preeminent monastic centers eventually came to be recognized: Rdo rje brag (representing the Northern Treasure tradition) and Smin grol gling in Central Tibet; and Kaḥ thog, Dpal yul, Rdzogs chen and, somewhat later, Zhe chen, all in far Eastern Tibet. Smin grol gling, in particular, enjoyed very close ties with the fifth Dalai Lama, so that its hierarchs were recognized as the official heads of Rnying ma pa order. The writings of its two great luminaries, the brothers Gter bdag gling pa (Terdak Lingpa, 1646–1714) and Lo chen Dharmaśrī (1654–1717), offer a uniquely influential synthesis of Rnying ma pa ritual traditions. Their efforts, however, were impeded by the 1717 invasion of Central Tibet by the Dzungar Mongols, which was accompanied by grievous sectarian persecution. Rnying ma pa establishments and adherents were among the Dzungar's victims, and Dharmaśrī and many other leading teachers perished in the onslaught. Smin grol gling was later revived by the efforts of Gter bdag gling pa's daughter, Mi 'gyur dpal sgron (Mingyur Paldrön, 1699–1769), whose career marks the beginning of a notable succession of female teachers.

Rnying ma pa resurgence in Central Tibet continued with the revelation by 'Jigs med gling pa (Jikme Lingpa, 1730–1798) of a new cycle of treasures, the Seminal Essence of the Great Expanse (Klong chen snying thig), inspired in part by the writings of Klong chen Rab 'byams pa. These teachings enjoyed a remarkable success and were soon studied and practiced throughout Tibet. They remain perhaps the most widely practiced Rnying ma pa Tantric ritual system at the present time. His successors came to play a notable role in the eclectic or universalist movement (*ris med*) in nineteenth-century Khams. 'Jam dbyangs Mkhyen brtse'i dbang po (Jamyang Khyentse, 1820–1892), thought to be his incarnation, was a particularly prominent exponent of the nonpartisan perspective and encouraged one of his most talented disciples, Mi pham rgya mtsho (Mipham Gyatso, 1846–1912) to extend the insights of characteristically Rnying ma pa teaching to the interpretation of Buddhist doctrine generally. The copious commentarial writings of Mi pham on all aspects of Buddhist thought and practice have enjoyed considerable prestige and are regarded as second only to the writings of Klong chen Rab 'byams pa as definitive expressions of Rnying ma pa thought. During the twentieth century the leading exponents of the Rnying ma pa order have mostly represented Mi pham's outlook, though some dissenters have criticized him for laying too much stress on the cataphatic doctrines of buddha-nature and pure awareness, and so perhaps compromising the radical emptiness associated with Madhyamaka thought.

Following the exile of large numbers of Tibetans in 1959, a number of leading Rnying ma pa teachers became established in South Asia and began to attract Western students. Two heads of the order, Bdud 'joms Rin po che 'Jigs bral ye shes rdo rje (Dudjom Rinpoche, 1904–1987) and Dil mgo Mkhyen brtse Rin po che (Dilgo Khyentse Rinpoche, 1910–1991), particularly inspired the spread of Rnying ma pa instruction in the West.

CHARACTERISTIC DOCTRINES. The Rnying ma pa adhere to the same canon of Kanjur and Tanjur as do other Tibetan Buddhists, but they supplement these with uniquely Rnying ma pa textual collections to which they accord a similar canonical status. Foremost in this regard is the *Rnying ma rgyud 'bum* (Collection of the ancient Tantras), which exists in many differing versions, but is always held to represent the body of Tantras translated into Tibetan prior to the tenth century. The Tantric rites of the Rnying ma pa, those for which a continuous lineage extending back to the imperial period is claimed, are gathered in the *Rnying ma bka' ma* (Oral tradition of the ancients). Though each particular lineage among the Rnying ma pa adheres to its own favored treasure-doctrines, during the nineteenth century a master of the universalist movement, 'Jam mgon Kong sprul Blo gros mtha' yas (Jamgön Kongtrül, 1813–1899), assembled a grand anthology of treasure-texts in over sixty large volumes, which has been widely promulgated since.

The Rnying ma pa teaching is generally organized according to the progression of nine sequential vehicles (*theg pa rim pa dgu*): those of (1) *śrāvakas*, (2) *pratyekabuddhas*, and (3) *bodhisattvas*, which are the three "causal vehicles" (*rgyu'i theg pa*); followed by (4) Kriyā Tantra, (5) Caryā Tantra, and (6) Yoga Tantra, which are the three outer vehicles among the "fruitional vehicles" of *mantra* (*'bras bu'i theg pa sngags phyi pa*); and culminating with (7) Mahāyoga, (8) Anuyoga, and (9) Atiyoga, which are the inner *mantras* (*sngags nang pa*). Atiyoga is also called Rdzogs chen, the Great Perfection. The first six vehicles are shared with the other traditions of Tibetan Buddhism and so require no special treatment here. The last three, though finding parallels in the

Tantric teachings of the "new" schools, are, in their precise formulation, distinctively Rnying ma pa.

Mahāyoga ("Great Yoga") emphasizes the creative visualization of the divine *maṇḍala* and the elaborate rites, including collective feast assemblies (*tshogs 'khor*; Skt. *gaṇacakra*) and ritual dance-drama (*'cham*), that are associated with it. The feast assembly, in particular, plays an important role in Rnying ma pa ritual life, and in most communities, whether monastic or lay, assemblies are held on the tenth day of the lunar month, consecrated to the *guru* (i.e., Padmasambhava), and on the twenty-fifth, consecrated to the Ḍākinī (Tib., Mkha' 'gro ma), the goddess embodying enlightenment. As a subject of study and reflection, the focal point of the Mahāyoga is the *Guhyagarbha Tantra*, which has generated an enormous commentarial literature.

Anuyoga ("Subsequent Yoga") is explained generally as emphasizing the internal manipulation of the energies (*rlung*; Skt., *vāyu*) and seminal essences (*thig le*; Skt., *bindu*) that flow through the channels (*rtsa*; Skt., *nāḍī*) of the subtle body. However, it is at the same time a complete system, which in its most elaborate forms embraces the entire teaching of the nine vehicles. In this respect, it is primarily associated with a vast Tantric compendium, the *Mdo dgongs pa 'dus pa* (The sūtra that gathers the [Buddha's] intentions), said to have been translated into Tibetan from the Burushaski language during the tenth century. It is possible that this work reflects developments in the Śaiva traditions of Kashmir during the period of its composition.

The highest pinnacle among the nine vehicles is the Atiyoga ("Highest Yoga"), or Rdzogs chen (Great Perfection). Kong sprul explains it as follows:

> "Great Perfection" is derived from the term *mahāsandhi*: it is "great concentration," [*mahāsamādhi*], or "great absorption" [*mahādhyāna*]. It therefore has the significance of "unsurpassed pristine cognition," in which all the phenomena of *saṃsāra* and *nirvāṇa* naturally arise in the expanse of the unique abiding nature of reality, surpassing the intellectualized doctrinal systems of the eight lower vehicles. . . .The Great Perfection has three classes according to their relative degrees of profundity whereby the naturally emergent pristine cognition itself functions as the path. Among them, the exoteric Mental Class [*sems sde*] is liberated from the extreme of renunciation, for one has realized that all phenomena have transcended causal and conditional effort and attainment in the play of mind-as-such alone. . . .The esoteric Spatial Class [*klong sde*], free from activity, is liberated from the extreme of antidotes, for one has realized that, because all phenomenal manifestations neither arrive in nor depart from the space of Omnibeneficent Mother [Kun tu bzang mo], there is no getting away from the expanse of the naturally present three bodies [*sku gsum*; Skt., *trikāya*]. . . .The secret and profound esoteric Instructional Class [*man ngag sde*] is free from the extremes of both renunciation and antidote, for one has realized that particularly characterized mode of being wherein the significance of all phenomena—ground, path, and result—is the indivisible union of primordial purity and spontaneous presence. . . .So it is that the objects adhered to in the sūtras and in the inner and outer *mantras*, up to and including Anuyoga, are all merely tenets grasped by the intellect. For this reason, [the Great Perfection] clearly teaches the particular ways whereby one falls into the error of not seeing the original abiding nature of reality just as it is. The pristine cognition of the Great Perfection transcends the eight aggregates of consciousness, including thought and speech, cause and result. It is that great freedom from elaboration, in which all mind and mental events attain to peace in the expanse of reality. Because the naturally emergent reality of awareness, free from activity, the natural disposition of the great transcendence of intellect, itself abides in its self-possession and is otherwise uncontrived, the appearance of its expressive power as ephemeral taint passes away, naturally dissolving into the natural expanse. For these reasons, this way is particularly superior to all of the lower philosophical and spiritual systems.

The adepts who have mastered this path, realizing its highest goals in the progressive disclosure of visions emerging from the revelation of the innermost nature of mind, are believed to transcend the boundaries of ordinary human mortality, and so pass away by vanishing into light in the attainment of a rainbow body (*'ja' lus*).

SEE ALSO Buddhism, article on Buddhism in Tibet; Buddhism, Schools of, article on Tibetan and Mongolian Buddhism.

BIBLIOGRAPHY

Achard, Jean-Luc. *L'essence perlée du secret: Recherches philologiques et historiques sur l'origine de la Grande Perfection dans la tradition rNying ma pa.* Turnhout, Belgium, 1999. On the development of the Great Perfection during the early second millennium.

Blezer, Henk. *Kar gliæ źi khro: A Tantric Buddhist Concept.* Leiden, 1997. Study of the *Tibetan Book of the Dead.*

Boord, Martin J. *The Cult of the Deity Vajrakīla.* Tring, U.K., 1993. On the "vajra-spike," a principle divinity of the Rnying ma pa tradition.

Cuevas, Bryan J. *The Hidden History of the Tibetan Book of the Dead.* New York, 2003. On the spread and reception in Tibet of the famous book.

Dudjom Rinpoche, Jikdrel Yeshe Dorje. *The Nyingma School of Tibetan Buddhism: Its Fundamentals and History.* Translated by Gyurme Dorje and Matthew Kapstein. 2 vols. Boston, 1991. Compendium of Rnying ma pa historical and doctrinal traditions.

Ehrhard, Franz-Karl. "*Flügelschäge des Garuḍa*": *Literar- und ideengeschichtliche Bemerkungen zu einer Liedersammlung des rDzogs chen.* Stuttgart, Germany, 1990. Study and translation of a popular Great Perfection manual by Zhabs dkar, a major nineteenth-century master.

Germano, David. "Architecture and Absence in the Secret Tantric History of rDzogs Chen." *Journal of the International Association for Buddhist Studies* 17, no. 2 (1994): 203–335. On the evolution of the Great Perfection systems of teaching.

Guenther, Herbert V. *Kindly Bent to Ease Us: From the Trilogy of Finding Comfort and Ease.* 3 vols. Emeryville, Calif., 1975–1976. Translation of Klong chen pa's *Trilogy of Rest.*

Gyatso, Janet. *Apparitions of the Self: The Secret Autobiographies of a Tibetan Visionary.* Princeton, 1998. Study of 'Jigs med gling pa's autobiographies, and of the Rnying ma pa tradition of "treasures."

Kapstein, Matthew T. *The Tibetan Assimilation of Buddhism: Conversion, Contestation, and Memory.* New York, 2000. Includes studies of some key Rnying ma pa myths.

Kapstein, Matthew T. "The Strange Death of Pema the Demon-Tamer." In *The Presence of Light: Divine Radiance and Religious Experience,* edited by Matthew T. Kapstein. Chicago, 2004. On the "rainbow body."

Karmay, Samten Gyaltsen. *The Great Perfection: A Philosophical and Meditative Teaching of Tibetan Buddhism.* Leiden and New York, 1988. Provides the early documents of the Great Perfection as known from Dunhuang.

Karmay, Samten Gyaltsen. *Secret Visions of the Fifth Dalai Lama: The Gold Manuscript in the Fournier Collection.* London, 1988. The revealed treasures of the fifth Dalai Lama.

Kohn, Richard. *Lord of the Dance: The Mani Rimdu Festival in Nepal and Tibet.* Albany, N.Y., 2001. Detailed documentation of a major Rnying ma pa ritual dance-drama.

Padmakara Translation Committee. *The Words of My Perfect Teacher.* San Francisco, 1994; 2d ed., Boston, 1998. Lucid translation of the most widely studied introductory manual of Rnying ma pa practice.

Pettit, John. *Mipham's Beacon of Certainty: Illuminating the View of Dzogchen, the Great Perfection.* Boston, 1999. On Mi pham's approach to Madhyamaka philosophy.

Ricard, Matthieu, et al., trans. *The Life of Shabkar: The Autobiography of a Tibetan Yogin.* Albany, N.Y., 1994. Memoirs of a leading nineteenth-century Rnying ma pa master.

Thondup Rinpoche, Tulku. *Hidden Teachings of Tibet: An Explanation of the Terma Tradition of the Nyingma School of Buddhism,* edited by Harold Talbott. London, 1986. A Rnying ma pa view of the "treasure" traditions.

Williams, Paul. *The Reflexive Nature of Awareness: A Tibetan Madhyamaka Defence.* Surrey, U.K., 1998. Focuses on Mi pham's reflections on reflexivity.

MATTHEW T. KAPSTEIN (2005)

ROBERTSON SMITH, WILLIAM SEE SMITH, W. ROBERTSON

ROHDE, ERWIN

ROHDE, ERWIN (1845–1898) was German philologist. Rohde served as professor of classical philology at several universities; appointed to a chair at Kiel in 1872, he moved to Jena four years later and to Tübingen in 1878, followed by a very short stay in Leipzig in 1886, from where he went to Heidelberg.

Rohde's major study on the Greek novel, *Der griechische Roman und seine Vorläufer,* appeared in 1876. Its second edition (1900), prepared by Fritz Scholl, contains as an appendix an address given by Rohde in 1875, in which he suggests the desirability of further study of the book's tentative thesis: that the animal fables and many other tales from India and other parts of Asia originated in Greece and, much later, found their way back to the West, where speculations about their Asian origin began. A third edition of this work was published in 1914, prepared by Wilhelm Schmidt, and a fourth was released in 1961, reflecting an ongoing interest in the study.

Rohde's name, however, is associated primarily with *Psyche, Seelencult und Unsterblichkeitsglaube der Griechen* (1890–1894). In 1897 the author completed his preparations for the second edition of this work, which went through several later editions and was translated into English as *Psyche: The Cult of Souls and Belief in Immortality among the Greeks* (1925). The author stresses that the cult of the souls, discussed in part 1 of the book, is a notion clearly distinct from and to some extent in contrast with belief in immortality, to which the second part is devoted. The most succinct formulation of this distinction is found in chapter 8: "The continued life of the soul, such as was implied in and guaranteed by the cult of souls, was entirely bound up with the remembrance of the survivors upon earth, and upon the care, the cult, which they might offer to the soul of their departed ancestors." Belief in the immortality of the soul, in contrast, sees the soul as "in its essential nature like God," a notion in radical conflict with "the first principle of the Greek people," namely that of an absolute gulf between humanity and divinity (pp. 253–254).

Tracing the belief in the divinity and immortality of the soul back to its Thracian context, Rohde elaborates his thesis of the formative impact on Greek life and thought of, on the one hand, the religion of paramount gods of the Homeric poems and, on the other hand, the worship of Dionysos, a Thracian deity whose cult was "thoroughly orgiastic in nature." These two forces explain the two opposing features of the Greeks, an "extravagance of emotion combined with a fast-bound and regulated equilibrium." (p. 255). His description of "the awe-inspiring darkness of the night, the music of the Phrygian flute . . . , the vertiginous whirl of the dance," which could lead people to a state of possessedness, conveys vividly his own vision of the cult. "Hellenized and humanized," the Thracian Dionysos found his place beside the other Olympian gods, and continued to inspire, not least in the field of the arts: "the drama, that supreme achievement of Greek poetry, arose out of the choruses of the Dionysiac festival" (p. 285).

Much of Rohde's language has been adopted by later researchers. At the scholarly level, his thesis of the Dionysian origin of the Greek belief in immortality is now widely rejected, following the criticism of, among others, Martin P. Nilsson, and his interpretation of *psuche* was largely abandoned after Walter F. Otto's study of 1923. But whatever criticisms have been raised, there is still widespread agreement that Rohde's *Psyche* is one of the most significant books in the field because of its remarkable erudition, the clarity of its methodology, and the tremendous impact it has had in circles beyond those professionally engaged in the study of the classical Greek world. The work is in its own right a "classical" expression of the belief in "the imperishable spirit of Hellas."

BIBLIOGRAPHY

In addition to works cited in the text of the article, Rohde's *Kleine Schriften,* 2 vols. (Tübingen, 1901), bears mention. Biographical resources on Rohde include Otto Crusius's *Ein biographischer Versuch* (Tübingen, 1902) and Friedrich Nietzsche's posthumously published *Friedrich Nietzsches Briefwechsel mit Erwin Rohde,* edited by Elizabeth Forster-Nietzsche and Fritz Scholl (Leipzig, 1923).

New Sources

Cancik, Hubert. "Erwin Rohde—ein Philologe der Bismarckzeit." In *Semper Apertus, Sechshundert Jahre Ruprecht-Karl-Universität Heidelberg,* edited by Wilhelm Doerr, vol. 2, pp. 436–505. Berlin, 1985.

Hofmiller, Josef. "Nietzsche und Rohde." In *Versuche.* Munich, 1909.

Seillière, Ernest. *Nietzsches Waffenbruder Erwin Rohde.* Berlin, 1911.

Vogt-Spira, Gregor. "Erwin Rohdes Psyche: eine verpaßte Chance der Altertumswissenschaften?" In *Mehr Dionysos als Apoll. Antiklassizistische Antike-Rezeption um 1900,* edited by Achim Aurnhammer and Thomas Pittrof, pp. 159–180. Frankfurt am Main, 2002.

WILLEM A. BIJLEFELD (1987)
Revised Bibliography

RÓHEIM, GÉZA. Géza Róheim (1891–1953) was born in Budapest and died in New York City. He immigrated to the United States from Hungary in 1938. Of Jewish descent, he was the only child of prosperous bourgeois parents. At an early age he developed an abiding interest in folklore, and he later chose to study ethnology in Leipzig and Berlin. It was during his time in Germany that he discovered the works of Sigmund Freud and his followers, which he embraced with great enthusiasm. Róheim is mainly remembered as a pioneer of psychoanalytic anthropology.

In 1915 and 1916 Róheim was analyzed by his compatriot and a member of Freud's inner circle, Sándor Ferenczi. With his wife Ilonka Róheim, he undertook fieldwork in various locations around the world between 1928 and 1931, including Somaliland, Normanby Island (now part of Papua New Guinea), and Arizona. However, Róheim's most significant ethnographic work was done with Arrernte, Luritja, and Pitjantjatjara Aborigines in central Australia, where he stayed for nine months in 1929. Róheim was the first properly psychoanalytically trained ethnographer and the first anthropologist to apply rigorous Freudian methods in his research and writing. He was a prolific writer, with his many books and papers having their primary focus on religion, magic, and folklore.

In 1925 Róheim published *Australian Totemism,* a large volume that scoured the ethnographic literature on Australian Aborigines for evidence to support and extend Freud's primal horde theory of the origins of religion and morality, put forward in *Totem and Taboo* (1913). Like Freud, Róheim understood Australian Aborigines to be "stone age savages" and thus a suitable testing ground for an evolutionist explanation of totemism as the primal religious form. Hence *Australian Totemism* followed Freud's lead in being a form of psychohistory, taking the vast array of Aboriginal myths, rituals, and related phenomena to be so many complex symbolic transformations that, through analysis, could be used to reconstruct the prehistoric transition from nature to culture. It fundamentally confirmed Freud's idea that totemism, as the primal religion, took a properly human form through the projection of "the father" into totemic species but also suggested that it had a prior, protohuman form that relied on the projection of maternal symbolism into the environment.

Róheim's appreciation of "primitive" life and religion altered somewhat as a result of his fieldwork experiences. Between 1932 and the end of his life he produced a number of works that were ethnographically rich and theoretically innovative. In particular he began to pay less attention to Freud's primal horde story and more openly interrogated its assumption that phylogenetic memory underlay the symbolic resolution of the Oedipus complex. While he never gave up his interest in psychohistory, Róheim devoted much of his attention to functionalist explanations, formulating what he called "the ontogenetic interpretation of culture." He argued that human societies differed culturally to the extent that they had evolved different "type traumata" giving rise to peculiarly distinctive adult character types (later known as "modal personalities"), together with systemically reproduced forms of defense mechanism and sublimation.

Whereas this theory was an account of culture in general, a specific interpretation of religion lay within its ambit. The totemic gods of Aboriginal Australia, for example, were said to have their origins in the demonic projections that arise in children as a result of anxieties prompted by the primal scene, demons being "bad" parents projected into the environment in the name of ego integrity. But these very demons are the basis of totemic religion, in the sense that they are transformed into authentic gods (totemic heroes) in the passage into adult life. Initiation into the male cult reverses the earlier trends of ego protection and fosters development of the superego. Concomitantly the demons that once gave rise to anxiety are transmuted, introjected, and dutifully revered as ancestral protectors of the law. Róheim believed that the religious emblems of this law (sacred objects representing the ancestors) took symbolic forms organically related to the demonic projections of childhood.

Róheim never wavered in his allegiance to Freud and rarely explicitly challenged any of the fundamentals of the primal horde theory of religious origins. Even as he rejected the Freudian idea of a "group mind," his originality lay more in the manner in which he extended the insights of *Totem and Taboo* and brought new emphases to bear on its scope. Like Freud, Róheim believed that religion had its origins in ancestor worship and that the psychoanalytic problem of "the father" was central to the symbolic creation of deities. Also like Freud, he understood the deification of ancestors to be symptomatic of the very process of cultural transmission itself. But unlike Freud, Róheim maintained an abiding interest in pre-oedipal development and hence with the problem of "the mother." His genius lay in giving due attention to feminine principles in the origin and function of religion and wedding this broader psychoanalytic program to an up-to-date anthropological methodology based on fieldwork and cultural relativism. Freud never directly encountered "primitive religion," but Róheim witnessed it in the flesh. This may be one reason why Róheim was not, like his master, quick to patronize "the primitive" or dismiss religion per se as a neurotic illusion.

See Also Australian Indigenous Religions; Psychology, article on Psychotherapy and Religion; Totemism.

BIBLIOGRAPHY

Dadoun, Roger. *Géza Róheim et l'essor de l'anthropologie psychanalytique.* Paris, 1972. A non-Hungarian book exclusively about Róheim's life and work.

Róheim, Géza. *Australian Totemism: A Psycho-Analytic Study in Anthropology.* London, 1925. Róheim's first major anthropological study. An encyclopedic account of the Australian ethnographic literature confirming Freud's psychohistory of the primal horde. Also develops a sequence of phases in Aboriginal religious development.

Róheim, Géza. *Animism, Magic, and the Divine King.* London, 1930. A psychoanalytic meditation on anthropological questions originally framed by Edward Burnett Tylor and James Frazer.

Róheim, Géza. "Psycho-Analysis of Primitive Cultural Types." *International Journal of Psycho-Analysis* 13, nos. 1–2 (1932): 1–224. Róheim's main published field report covering his findings from Australia, Normanby Island, and Somaliland. Includes a chapter on totemic ritual in central Australia.

Róheim, Géza. *The Riddle of the Sphinx; or, Human Origins.* Translated by R. Money-Kyrle. London, 1934; reprint, New York, 1974. Róheim's first major post-fieldwork book. Discusses the idea of "the primal religion" in relation to central Australian totemism and interprets the material in terms of "the ontogenetic interpretation of culture." Reprint includes an introductory essay, "Róheim and the Beginnings of Psychoanalytic Anthropology," by Werner Muensterberger and Christopher Nichols.

Róheim, Géza. *The Origin and Function of Culture.* New York, 1943. The most succinct summation of Róheim's mature theoretical position.

Róheim, Géza. *The Eternal Ones of the Dream: A Psychoanalytic Interpretation of Australian Myth and Ritual.* New York, 1945. The main post-fieldwork update of Róheim's original views on Australian totemism.

Róheim, Géza. *The Gates of the Dream.* New York, 1952. Considers the role of dreaming and regression in connection with animism, shamanism, folklore, and mythology.

Róheim, Géza. *The Panic of the Gods and Other Essays.* Edited by Werner Muensterberger. New York, 1972. A collection of papers from the *Psychoanalytic Quarterly* on religion. Also includes an introductory essay by the editor reappraising Róheim's theory of the origins of religion.

Róheim, Géza. *Children of the Desert,* vol. 1: *The Western Tribes of Central Australia.* Edited by Werner Muensterberger. New York, 1974. First part of a major ethnographic manuscript prepared before Róheim's death. Carries an introductory essay by the editor on Róheim's pioneering fieldwork.

Róheim, Géza. *Children of the Desert,* vol. 2: *Myths and Dreams of the Aborigines of Central Australia.* Edited by John Morton and Werner Muensterberger. Sydney, Australia, 1988. Second part of a major ethnographic manuscript prepared before Róheim's death. Carries an introductory essay by John Morton on Róheim's contribution to Australian ethnography.

Voigt, Vilmos, ed. "Psychoanalytic Studies in Honor of Géza Róheim." *Acta Ethnographica Hungarica* 38, nos. 1–3 (1993): 1–67. A collection of essays in English and French about or inspired by Róheim's work.

John Morton (2005)

ROMAN CATHOLICISM [FIRST EDITION].

The first question in defining the scope of Roman Catholicism has to do with the term itself. There are Catholics who object to the adjective *Roman* because the community encompassed by the designation "Roman Catholicism" includes those who do not regard themselves as Roman. These are the so-called Uniate Catholics, the name given to former Eastern Christian or Orthodox churches that have been received under the jurisdiction of the church of Rome and retain their own ritual, practice, and canon law. They are the Melchite Catholics, the Maronites, the Ruthenians, the Copts, and the Malabars, among which there are six liturgical rites: Chaldean, Syrian, Maronite, Coptic, Armenian, and Byzantine.

There are, on the other hand, Christians who consider themselves Catholic but who do not accept the primatial authority of the bishop of Rome. This group insists that the churches in communion with the see of Rome should call themselves Roman Catholic to distinguish them from those Catholic churches (Anglican, Orthodox, Oriental, and some Protestant) not in communion with Rome. For some Protestants in this group, the Roman Catholic church did not begin as a church until the time of the Reformation. Indeed, in their eyes, Roman Catholicism is no less a denomination than Presbyterianism or Methodism, for example.

Protestantism is usually defined negatively, as the form of Western Christianity that rejects obedience to the Roman papacy. But this definition encounters the same difficulty described above. There are also non-Roman Christians who reject the papacy but who consider themselves Catholic rather than Protestant. For that reason alone it would be inadequate to define Catholicism by its adherence to papal authority.

Roman Catholicism refers both to a church (or, more accurately, a college of churches that together constitute the universal Catholic church) and to a tradition. If one understands the body of Christ as the whole collectivity of Christian churches, then the Roman Catholic church is a church within the universal church. And if one understands Christian tradition to embrace the full range and pluralism of doctrinal, liturgical, theological, canonical, and spiritual traditions, then the Roman Catholic tradition is a tradition within the one Christian tradition. For Roman Catholicism, however, the Catholic church and the Catholic tradition are normative for other Christian churches and traditions (as expressed in the Dogmatic Constitution on the Church, no. 14, issued by the Second Vatican Council).

As a church, Roman Catholicism exists at both the local level and the universal level. In the canon law of the Roman Catholic church, the term "local church" (more often rendered as "particular church") applies primarily to a diocese and secondarily to a parish. The term "local church" has a wider meaning in Catholic theology than in canon law. It may apply to provinces (regional clusters of dioceses within a country) and to national churches (all the dioceses within a country), as well as to parishes and individual dioceses. A diocese is a local church constituted by a union, or college, of other local churches known as parishes. Each diocese is presided over by a bishop, and each parish by a pastor. The universal Roman Catholic church, on the other hand, is constituted by a union, or college, of all the local Catholic churches throughout the world. There are more than one-half billion Catholics worldwide, by far the largest body of Christians. Apart from other important doctrinal, liturgical, theological, canonical, and spiritual links, what holds these various churches and individual members in solidarity is the bond each has with the diocese of Rome and with its bishop, the pope.

As a tradition Roman Catholicism is marked by several different doctrinal and theological emphases. These are its radically positive estimation of the created order, because everything comes from the hand of God, is providentially sustained by God, and is continually transformed and elevated by God's active presence within it; its concern for history, because God acts within history and is continually revealed through it; its respect for rationality, because faith must be consonant with reason and reason itself, fallen and redeemed, is a gift of God; its stress on mediation, because God, who is at once the First Cause and totally spiritual, can have an effect on us only by working through secondary causes and material instruments, for example, the humanity of Jesus Christ, the church, the sacraments, the things of the earth, other people; and, finally, its affirmation of the communal dimension of salvation and of every religious relationship with God, because God has created us a people, because we have fallen as a people, because we have been redeemed as a people, and because we are destined for eternal glory as a people.

The very word *catholic* means "universal." What is most directly opposed to Catholicism, therefore, is not Protestantism (which, in any case, has many Catholic elements within it) but sectarianism, the movement within Christianity that holds that the church is a community of true believers, a precinct of righteousness within and over against the unredeemed world of sin, pronouncing judgment upon it and calling it to repentance but never entering into dialogue with it, much less collaboration on matters of common social, political, or religious concern. For the sectarian, dialogue and collaboration are invitations to compromise.

The contrast between Catholicism and sectarianism is nowhere more sharply defined than in their respective approaches to the so-called social question. Catholic social doctrine acknowledges the presence and power of sin in the world, but insists that grace is stronger. Catholic social doctrine underlines the doctrines of creation, providence, the incarnation, redemption, and sanctification through the Holy Spirit. Christians are called to collaborate with God in Christ, through the power of the Holy Spirit, to bring the entire fallen and redeemed world to the perfection of the kingdom of God, "a kingdom of truth and life, of holiness and grace, of justice, love and peace" (Vatican Council II, Pastoral Constitution on the Church in the Modern World, no. 39).

HISTORY. What are the origins of Roman Catholicism? What events and personalities have shaped it? How is it presently being transformed?

Peter and the Petrine ministry. If one insists that Roman Catholicism is not a denomination within Christianity but is its original expression, one faces at the outset the historical fact that the earliest community of disciples gathered in Jerusalem and therefore was Palestinian rather than Roman. Indeed, the see, or diocese, of Rome did not exist at the very beginning, nor did the Roman primacy.

If, on the other hand, one holds that the adjective *Roman* obscures rather than defines the reality of Catholicism, Catholicism does begin at the beginning, that is, with Jesus' gathering of his disciples and with his eventual commissioning, probably following the resurrection, of Peter to be the chief shepherd and foundation of the church. Therefore, it is not the Roman primacy that gives Catholicism its distinctive identity within the community of Christian churches but the Petrine primacy.

Peter is listed first among the Twelve (*Mk.* 3:16–19, *Mt.* 10:1–4, *Lk.* 6:12–16) and is frequently their spokesman (*Mk.* 8:29, *Mt.* 18:21, *Lk.* 12:41, *Jn.* 6:67–69); he is the first apostolic witness of the risen Christ (*1 Cor.* 15:5, *Lk.* 24:34); he is prominent in the original Jerusalem community and is well known to many other churches (*Acts* 1:15–26, 2:14–40, 3:1–26, 4:8, 5:1–11, 5:29, 8:18–25, 9:32–43, 10:5, 12:17, *1 Pt.* 2:11, 5:13). Peter's activities after the council of Jerusalem are not reported, but there is increasing agreement that he did go to Rome and was martyred there. Whether he actually served the church of Rome as bishop cannot be known with certainty from the evidence at hand.

For the Catholic tradition, the classic primacy texts are *Matthew* 16:13–19, *Luke* 22:31–32, and *John* 21:15–19. The fact that Jesus' naming of Peter as the Rock occurs in different contexts in these three gospels does raise a question about the original setting of the incident. Did it occur before the resurrection, or was it a postresurrection event, subsequently "retrojected" into the accounts of Jesus' earthly ministry? In any case, the conferral of the power of the keys clearly suggests an imposing measure of authority, given the symbolism of the keys as instruments for opening and shutting the gates of the kingdom of heaven. On the other hand, special authority over others is not clearly attested, and indeed Peter is presented in the *Acts of the Apostles* as consulting with the other apostles and even being sent by them (8:14), and he and John act almost as a team (3:1–11, 4:1–22, 8:14).

But there seems to be a trajectory of images relating to Peter and his ministry that sets him apart within the original company of disciples and explains his ascendancy and that of his successors throughout the early history of the church. He is portrayed as the fisherman (*Lk.* 5:10, *Jn.* 21:1–14), as the shepherd of the sheep of Christ (*Jn.* 21:15–17), as an elder who addresses other elders (*1 Pt.* 5:1), as proclaimer of faith in Jesus, the Son of God (*Mt.* 16:16–17), as receiver of a special revelation (*Acts* 1:9–16), as one who can correct others for doctrinal misunderstanding (*2 Pt.* 3:15–16), and as the rock on which the church is to be built (*Mt.* 16:18).

The question to be posed on the basis of recent investigations of the New Testament is therefore whether the subsequent, postbiblical development of the Petrine office is consistent with the thrust of the New Testament. The Catholic church says "Yes." Some other Christian churches are beginning to say "Perhaps."

The biblical images concerning Peter continued in the life of the early church and were enriched by additional ones: missionary preacher, great visionary, destroyer of heretics, receiver of the new law, gatekeeper of heaven, helmsman of the ship of the church, co-teacher and co-martyr with Paul. By the latter half of the second century, the church had accommodated itself to the culture of the Greco-Roman world, particularly the organizational and administrative patterns that prevailed in areas of its missionary activity. Accordingly, the church adopted the organizational grid of the Roman empire: localities, dioceses, provinces. It also identified its own center with that of the empire, Rome. Moreover, there was attached to this city the tradition that Peter had founded the church there and that he and Paul were martyred and buried there.

In the controversy with Gnosticism, defenders of orthodoxy appealed to the faith of sees (local churches) founded by the apostles, and especially to the faith of the Roman church, which was so clearly associated with Peter and Paul. During the first five centuries, the church of Rome gradually assumed preeminence among all the churches. It intervened in the life of distant churches, took sides in theological controversies, was consulted by other bishops on doctrinal and moral questions, and sent delegates to distant councils. The see of Rome came to be regarded as a kind of final court of appeal as well as a focus of unity for the worldwide communion of churches. The correlation between Peter and the bishop of Rome became fully explicit during the pontificate of Leo I (440–461), who claimed that Peter continued to speak to the whole church through the bishop of Rome.

Constantine and Constantinian Catholicism. One of the major events during this early period was the conversion of the Roman emperor Constantine I (306–337) in the year 312. Constantine subsequently pursued a vigorous campaign against pagan practices and lavished money and monuments upon the church. Roman law was modified to reflect Christian values more faithfully, and the clergy were accorded privileged status. For some, the conversion of Constantine provided the church with extraordinary opportunities for proclaiming the gospel to all nations and for bringing necessary order into the church's doctrinal and liturgical life. It also allowed the church to be less defensive about pagan culture and to learn from it and be enriched by it. For others, however, the event marked a dangerous turning point in the history of the church. For the first time, the church enjoyed a favored place in society. Christian commitment would no longer be tested by persecution, much less by death. The community of disciples was on the verge of being swallowed up by the secular, and therefore anti-Christian, values of the state and the society, which now embraced the church. Indeed, there is no word of greater opprobrium laid upon Catholic Christians by sectarian Christians than "Constantinian."

Monasticism. The first protest against Constantinianism, however, came not from sectarians but from Catholic monks. The new monastic movement had an almost immediate impact upon the church. Bishops were recruited from among those with some monastic training. For example, Athanasius (d. 373) was a disciple of Antony of Egypt (d. 355), generally regarded as the founder of monasticism. One historian has argued that the strong missionary impetus, the remarkable development of pastoral care, the effort to christianize the Roman state, and above all the theological work of the great councils of the fourth and fifth centuries would have been inconceivable without monasticism. On the other hand, when monks were appointed bishops they tended to bring with them some of their monastic mores, particularly celibacy and a certain reserve toward ordinary human experiences. As a result, there developed a separation between pastoral leaders and the laity, based not only upon the exercise of power and jurisdiction but also upon a diversity in spiritualities.

Imported into the West from the East, monasticism reached its high point in the middle of the sixth century with the founding of Monte Cassino by Benedict of Nursia (d. 547). Monks were directly involved in the missionary expansion of the church in Ireland, Scotland, Gaul, and England between the fifth and the seventh century. This missionary enterprise was so successful that, in the eighth century, English missionaries had a prominent role in evangelizing the more pagan parts of Europe.

In spite of its simple purposes of work and prayer, Western monasticism would serve as the principal carrier of Western civilization during the Middle Ages. No other movement or institution had such social or intellectual influence. With the restoration of some political stability to Europe by the middle of the eleventh century, monks tended to withdraw from temporal and ecclesiastical affairs to return to their monasteries, and a renewal of monasticism followed. The foundings of the Franciscans, Dominicans, Cistercians, and Jesuits were among the major effects of this renewal, as were the rich theological and spiritual writings that emerged from these communities by, for example, Thomas Aquinas (d. 1274) and Bonaventure (d. 1274).

Doctrinal controversies. At the heart of the Catholic faith, as at the heart of every orthodox expression of Christian faith, is Jesus Christ. In the fourth and fifth centuries there was a preoccupation with dogmatic controversies about the relationship between the one God, the creator of all things, and Jesus Christ, the Son of God and redeemer of humankind, and then about the relationship of the Holy Spirit to both. Arianism (Christ was only a creature, greater than humans but less than God) was opposed by the Council of Nicaea (325); Apollinarianism (Christ had no human soul), by the First Council of Constantinople (381); Nestorianism (the man Jesus was separate from the divine Word, or Logos; the two were not united in one person), by the Council of Ephesus (431); and monophysitism (Christ's human nature was completely absorbed by the one divine person), by the Council of Chalcedon (451). Jesus is at once divine and human. The divine and the human are united in one person, "without confusion or change, without division or separation" (the definition of the Council of Chalcedon). This stress on theological and doctrinal balance has been an abiding feature of the Catholic tradition.

The same balance was preserved in the great Western debate about nature and grace. Pelagianism had argued that salvation is achieved through human effort alone. Augustine of Hippo (d. 430) insisted on the priority of grace, without prejudice to human responsibility. Indeed, the church would later condemn quietism, Pelagianism's opposite, in the constitution *Caelestis pastor* of Innocent XI (d. 1689). Moral effort *is* essential to the spiritual life, although such effort is always prompted and sustained by grace. Grace, in turn, builds on nature, as the Scholastics would put it.

Structure and law. By the beginning of the fifth century, German tribes began migrating through Europe without effective control. This movement has been called, somewhat inaccurately, the barbarian invasions. It was to last some six hundred years and was to change the institutional character of Catholicism from a largely Greco-Roman religion to a broader European religion. The strongly militaristic and feudal character of Germanic culture influenced Catholic devotion, spirituality, and organizational structure. Christ was portrayed as the most powerful of kings. The place of worship was described as God's fortress. Monks were perceived as warriors of Christ. The profession of faith was understood as an oath of fidelity to a kind of feudal lord. Church office became more political than pastoral. Eventually a dispute arose about the appointment of such officers. Should they be appointed by the church or by the state? This led to the so-called investiture struggle, which was resolved in favor of the church through the leadership of Gregory VII (d. 1085).

When, at the beginning of the eighth century, the Eastern emperor proved incapable of aiding the papacy against the Lombards in northern Italy, the pope turned for help to the Franks. This new alliance led eventually to the creation of the Holy Roman Empire, climaxed in 800 with the crowning of Charlemagne (d. 814). The line between church and state, already blurred by Constantine's Edict of Milan some five hundred years earlier, was now practically erased. When the Carolingian empire collapsed, however, the papacy was left at the mercy of an essentially corrupt Roman nobility. The tenth and part of the eleventh centuries were its dark ages. Only with the reform of Gregory VII was the papacy's luster restored. Gregory attacked three major abuses: simony (the selling of spiritual goods), the alienation of church property (allowing it to pass from ecclesiastical hands to private hands), and lay investiture (granting the power of church appointment to secular authorities). Papal prestige was even more firmly enhanced during the pontificate of Innocent III (1198–1216), who fully exploited the Gregorian teaching that the pope has supreme, even absolute, power over the whole church.

Canon law was codified to support the new network of papal authority. The church became increasingly legalistic in its theology, moral life, and administration of the sacraments, especially marriage, which was regarded more as a contract than as a covenant based on mutual love. By the middle of the thirteenth century the classical papal-hierarchical concept of the church had been securely established. Newly elected popes were crowned like emperors, a practice observed for centuries until suddenly discontinued by John Paul I (d. 1978). Emphasis on the juridical aspects of the church did not subside until the Second Vatican Council (1962–1965), which declared that the church is first and foremost the people of God and a mystery (i. e., a reality imbued with the hidden presence of God) before it is a hierarchical institution. Indeed, that principle must be kept firmly in mind, lest this historical overview be read only from the top down. The story of the Catholic church always remains the story of Catholic people.

Divisions in the church. Through a series of unfortunate and complicated political and diplomatic maneuvers, the historical bond between the church of Rome and the church of Constantinople came apart. In 1054 the patriarch of Constantinople, Michael Cerularios (d. 1058), was excommunicated by papal legates, but it was the Fourth Crusade (1202–1204) and the sack of Constantinople by Western knights that dealt the crucial blow to East-West unity.

By the beginning of the fourteenth century, other events had introduced a period of further disintegration, reaching a climax in the Protestant Reformation of the sixteenth century. First, there was the confrontation between Boniface VIII (d. 1303) and Philip the Fair (d. 1314) over the latter's power to tax the church. The pope issued two bulls asserting his own final authority: *Clericis laicos* (1296) and *Unam sanctam* (1302), the latter having been described as the most theocratic doctrine ever formulated. But Philip arrested Boniface, and the pope died a prisoner.

Then there was the proliferation of financial abuses during the subsequent "Babylonian Captivity" of the papacy at Avignon, France (1309–1378). There followed a rise in nationalism and anticlericalism in reaction to papal taxes. Theological challenges mounted against the recent canonical justifications of papal power, especially in the advocacy by Marsilius of Padua (d. 1343) of a conciliar rather than a monarchical concept of the church. The Western schism of 1378–1417—not to be confused with the East-West schism involving Rome and Constantinople—saw at one point three different claimants to the papal throne. Finally, the Council of Constance (1414) turned to the principle of conciliarism (i. e., a general council of the church, not the pope, is the highest ecclesiastical authority) and brought the schism to an end. The three claimants were set aside (one was deposed, a second resigned, and a third eventually died), and Martin V (d. 1431) was elected on Saint Martin's Day, 11 November 1417.

There were, of course, more immediate causes of the Reformation: the corruption of the Renaissance papacy of the fifteenth century; the divorce of piety from theology, and of theology from its biblical and patristic roots; the debilitating effects of the Western schism; the rise of the national state; the too-close connection between Western Catholicism and Western civilization; and the vision, experiences, and personalities of Luther (d. 1546), Zwingli (d. 1531), and Calvin (d. 1564).

The Reformation itself took different forms: on the right, it retained essential Catholic doctrine but changed certain canonical and structural forms (Lutheranism and Anglicanism); on the left, it repudiated much Catholic doctrine and sacramental life (Zwinglianism and the Anabaptist movement); nearer to the center, it modified both Catholic doctrine and practice but retained much of the old (Calvinism).

The Council of Trent and post-Tridentine Catholicism. The Catholic response was belated but vigorous. Known as the Counter-Reformation, it began at the Council of Trent (1545–1563) and was conducted especially under the leadership of Paul III (1534–1549). The council, which was perhaps the single most important factor in the shaping of Catholicism from the time of the Reformation until the Second Vatican Council, a period of some four centuries, articulated Catholic doctrine on nature and grace, following a middle course concerning doctrines of salvation between Pelagianism, which emphasizes human effort, and Protestantism, which emphasizes God's initiative. The council also defined the seven sacraments, created the Index of Forbidden Books, and established seminaries for the education and formation of future priests. At the heart of the Catholic Counter-Reformation was the Society of Jesus (Jesuits), the strongest single force in helping the church regain its lost initiative on the missionary, educational, and pastoral fronts.

By and large, the post-Tridentine Catholic church continued to emphasize those doctrines, devotions, and institutions that were most vehemently attacked by the Protestants: veneration of the saints, Marian piety, eucharistic adoration, the authority of the hierarchy, and the essential role of priests in the sacramental life of the church. Other important elements received less emphasis, perhaps because they were perceived as part of the Protestant agenda: the centrality of Christ in theology and spirituality, the communal nature of the Eucharist, and the responsibility of the laity in the life and mission of the church.

With the Reformation, Catholic missionary activity was reduced in those countries where Protestant churches began to flourish, but Catholicism was carried abroad by Spain and Portugal, who ruled the seas. New gains were sought to offset losses in Europe. Dominicans, Franciscans, and the newly formed Jesuits brought the Catholic faith to India, China, Japan, Africa, and the Americas. The Congregation for the Propagation of the Faith was founded in 1622 to supervise these new missionary enterprises.

By the beginning of the seventeenth century, the Catholic church faced yet another challenge from within: Jansenism, a movement in France that drew much of its inspiration from Augustine. Augustine had always stressed the priority of grace over nature, but Jansenism seemed to take his emphasis many steps further, portraying nature as totally corrupt and promoting a theory of predestination. From such principles there emerged a form of Catholic life that was exceedingly rigorous and even puritanical. When Rome moved against Jansenism, many in the French church saw Rome's action as a threat to the independence of French Catholicism. Gallicanism thus emerged as an essentially nationalistic rather than theological movement, asserting that a general council, not the pope, has supreme authority in the church. Consequently, all papal decrees would be subject to the consent of the entire church, as represented in a general council. Gallicanism was condemned by the First Vatican Council

(1869–1870), which declared that infallible teachings of the pope are irreformable, that is, not subject to the consent of any higher ecclesiastical body or authority.

The Enlightenment. One cannot easily underestimate the impact of the Enlightenment on modern Catholicism, although it influenced Protestantism sooner and much more profoundly. Characterized by a supreme confidence in the power of reason, an optimistic view of human nature, and an almost inordinate reverence for freedom, the Enlightenment exhibited a correspondingly hostile attitude toward the supernatural, the notion of revelation, and authority of every kind, except that of reason itself. The Enlightenment affected Catholicism primarily in the Catholic states of Germany, where it stimulated advances in historical and exegetical methods, improvements in the education of the clergy, the struggle against superstition, liturgical and catechetical reform, and the promotion of popular education. However, much Catholic theology before the Second Vatican Council remained largely untouched by the Enlightenment.

The French Revolution. If the Enlightenment marked the beginning of the end of unhistorical, classicist Catholic theology, the French Revolution (1789) marked the definitive end of medieval Catholicism. The feudal, hierarchical society that had been so much a part of medieval Catholicism disappeared, but the French Revolution had other effects as well. It was so extreme that it provoked counterreaction among some European intellectuals, who returned with new enthusiasm to the basic principles of Catholicism (see "Romanticism," below). The Revolution also destroyed Gallicanism by uprooting the clerical system upon which it had been based. The clergy were compelled to look to Rome and the papacy for support and direction. Finally, the French Revolution gave the Catholic church the "grace of destitution." It no longer had much to lose, and so it was free once again to pursue the mission for which it was originally founded.

Romanticism. In France and Germany the French Revolution generated an opposite phenomenon, romanticism, which extolled Catholicism as the mother of art and the guardian of patriotism. Thousands who had been alienated from the Catholic church returned. With the notable exception of Cardinal John Henry Newman (d. 1890), theology at this time was restorative rather than progressive. What was restored, however, was not the witness and wisdom of sacred scripture and the ancient Christian writers but the literal content of a renewed scholastic philosophy and theology. There developed in France a rigid traditionalism, characterized by integralism and fideism, which was distrustful of all rational speculation and critical thinking in theology. The practitioners of such theology looked "beyond the mountains," the Alps, to Rome for papal direction (thus, the movement's name, ultramontanism). The popes of this day, Gregory XVI (d. 1846) and Pius IX (d. 1878), set themselves stubbornly against the winds of change and modernity. Nowhere was their defiant attitude more sharply formulated than in Pius's *Syllabus of Errors* (1864), which proclaimed that the pope "cannot and should not be reconciled and come to terms with progress, liberalism, and modern civilization."

Although Pius IX successfully persuaded the First Vatican Council to define papal primacy and papal infallibility, he lost the Papal States (September 1870) and with them his remaining political power. Not until the Lateran Treaty of 1929 (renegotiated in 1983) were the pope's temporal rights to the Vatican territory acknowledged.

Catholic social doctrine. The nineteenth century also witnessed the rapid development of industrialism, and with it a host of new social problems, not least of which was the worsening condition of workers. Marxism stepped into the gap. The workers found themselves alienated not only from the fruits of their labor but from their Catholic heritage as well. The Catholic church responded, albeit belatedly, in 1891 with Leo XIII's encyclical *Rerum novarum*, which defended the right of workers to unionize and to enjoy humane working conditions and a just wage.

Catholic social doctrine was further refined by Pius XI (d. 1939) in his *Quadragesimo anno* (1931); by Pius XII (d. 1958) in his various Christmas, Easter, and Pentecost messages; by John XXIII (d. 1963), in his *Mater et magistra* (1961) and *Pacem in terris* (1963); by the Second Vatican Council's Pastoral Constitution on the Church in the Modern World, known also as *Gaudium et spes* (1965); by Paul VI (d. 1978), in his *Populorum progressio* (1967) and *Octagesima adveniens* (1971); by the *Iustitia in mundo* (1971) of the Third International Synod of Bishops; and by John Paul II's *Redemptor ho-minis* (1979) and *Laborem exercens* (1981). The twin pillars of Catholic social doctrine, as articulated in these documents, are the infinite dignity of each and every human person, and the responsibilities all persons, agencies, and nations have to the common good.

Modernism. Just as the Catholic church could not ignore various social, economic, and political developments initiated in the nineteenth century, neither could it ignore corresponding intellectual developments. As these developments began to make some impact on Catholic scholars, there emerged a new ecclesiastical phenomenon known as modernism. Modernism was not a single movement but a complex of movements. It assumed many different forms, some orthodox and some unorthodox. But distinctions were rarely made, and the term *modernist* was usually employed in early-twentieth-century discussions as one of opprobrium.

Modernists were those who refused to adopt a safely conservative standpoint on all debatable matters pertaining to doctrine and theology. Modernism was condemned by Pius X (d. 1914) through the Holy Office decree *Lamentabili* (1907) and the encyclical *Pascendi* (1907). Much of pre-Vatican II twentieth-century Catholic theology was written under the shadow of modernism. Deviations from the main lines of neoscholastic theology during this period were regarded as reductively modernist. Theologians, pastors, and others were required to swear to an antimodernist oath.

Some of the positions once denounced as modernist, however, were later reflected in the teachings of Vatican II and even in certain decrees of the Curia Romana, for example, regarding the historical truth of sacred scripture and the development of dogma. The modernists had argued that dogmatic truths, as well as truths contained in sacred scripture, are not absolute and unchanging but are affected by historical conditions and circumstances. Official Catholic teaching at first condemned this view but gradually accommodated itself to it, particularly in the Congregation for the Doctrine of the Faith's *Mysterium ecclesiae* (1973), which noted that "even though the truths which the Church intends to teach through her dogmatic formulas are distinct from the changeable conceptions of a given epoch and can be expressed without them, nevertheless it can sometimes happen that these truths may be enunciated by the Sacred Magisterium in terms that bear traces of such conceptions."

Between the World Wars (1918–1939). The period before Vatican II was not without its progressive movements (otherwise Vatican II itself would be inexplicable). The liturgical movement bridged the gap between altar and congregation by emphasizing the nature of worship and by stressing the Thomistic principle that sacraments are signs of grace as well as causes of grace. As signs, sacraments must be understandable, in terms of both language and ritual. The biblical movement carried forward the work of critical interpretation without provoking additional papal condemnations. But Catholic biblical scholars labored under a cloud until Pius XII issued the so-called Magna Carta of Catholic biblical scholarship, *Divino afflante Spiritu* (1943). The social action movement continued to apply the teachings of the social encyclicals, particularly in support of the labor union movement. The lay apostolate movement under Pius XI and Pius XII sought to involve larger numbers of laity in the work of the church (a movement also known as Catholic Action). The ecumenical movement had a more difficult path, given the negative tone of Pius XI's encyclical *Mortalium animos* (1927), but pioneers like Yves Congar were preparing the way for Vatican II. Meanwhile, the missionary movement, which had experienced a major revival in the nineteenth century, with as many as 8 million converts, was increasingly liberated from undue colonial and European influence. Both Pius XI and Pius XII stressed the importance of establishing native clergies and native hierarchies in mission lands.

Pope John XXIII and the Second Vatican Council. No other persons or events have had so profound an impact on modern Catholicism as John XXIII and the Second Vatican Council he convoked. When elected in 1958, John insisted that his was "a very humble office of shepherd" and that he intended to pattern his ministry after that of Joseph in the Old Testament story, who greeted the brothers who had sold him into slavery with the compassionate and forgiving words, "I am Joseph, your brother." When the new pope ceremonially took possession of the Lateran Basilica in Rome, he reminded the congregation, which included cardinals, archbishops, bishops, and assorted ecclesiastical dignitaries, that he was not a prince surrounded by the outward signs of power but "a priest, a father, a shepherd." He visited the sick in the Roman hospitals, the elderly in old-age homes, the convicts at Regina Coeli prison.

John XXIII first announced his council on January 25, 1959 and officially convoked it on December 25, 1961. In his address at the council's solemn opening on October 11, 1962, he revealed again his spirit of fundamental hope. He complained openly about some of his closest advisers, who "though burning with zeal, are not endowed with much sense of discretion or measure. In these modern times they can see nothing but prevarication and ruin." He called them "prophets of gloom, who are always forecasting disaster, as though the end of the world were at hand." He believed instead that "Divine Providence is leading us to a new order of human relations." He had not called the council to preserve doctrine. "The substance of the ancient doctrine . . . is one thing, and the way in which it is presented is another." This was not the time for negativism. The most effective way for the church to combat error would be by "demonstrating the validity of her teaching rather than by condemnations." The purpose of the council, therefore, would be the promotion of "concord, just peace and the brotherly unity of all."

Although John XXIII died between the first two sessions of the council, his successor, Paul VI, carried his program to fulfillment:

1. Vatican II taught that the church is the people of God, a community of disciples. The hierarchy is part of the people of God, not separate from it. Authority is for service, not for domination. Bishops are not merely the delegates of the pope, and laity are not merely instruments of their bishops. (See the Dogmatic Constitution on the Church.)
2. The church must read the signs of the times and interpret them in the light of the gospel. The church is part of the world, and its mission is to serve the whole human family in order to make the history of the human race more human. (See the Pastoral Constitution on the Church in the Modern World.)
3. Christian unity requires renewal and reform. Both sides were to blame for the divisions of the Reformation; therefore both sides have to be open to change. The body of Christ embraces more than Catholics (Roman or otherwise). (See the Decree on Ecumenism.)
4. The word of God is communicated through sacred scripture, sacred tradition, and the teaching authority of the church, all linked together and guided by the Holy Spirit. The sacred realities are always open in principle to a growth in understanding. (See the Dogmatic Constitution on Divine Revelation.)
5. The church proclaims the gospel not only in word but

also in sacrament. Since the whole people of God must actively participate in this worship, the signs, that is, language and rituals, must be intelligible. (See the Constitution on the Sacred Liturgy.)

6. No one is to be forced in any way to embrace the Christian or the Catholic faith. This principle is rooted in human dignity and the freedom of the act of faith. (See the Declaration on Religious Freedom.)
7. God speaks also through other religions. The church should engage in dialogue and other collaborative efforts with them. The Jews have a special relationship to the church. They cannot be blamed as a people for the death of Jesus. (See the Declaration on the Relationship of the Church to Non-Christian Religions.)

After four sessions the Second Vatican Council adjourned in December 1965. The story of Catholicism since the council—through the pontificates of Paul VI (1963–1978), John Paul I (1978), and John Paul II (1978–)—has been shaped largely, if not entirely, by the church's efforts to come to terms with the various challenges and opportunities which that council presented: specifically, how can the church remain faithful to its distinctively Catholic heritage even as it continues to affirm and assimilate such modern values as ecumenism, pluralism, and secularity?

CATHOLIC VISION AND CATHOLIC VALUES. Catholicism is not an isolated reality. The word *Catholic* is not only a noun but also an adjective. As an adjective, it modifies the noun *Christian.* The word *Christian,* too, is both a noun and an adjective. As an adjective, it modifies *religious.* The word *religious* also functions as an adjective and a noun. As an adjective, it modifies the word *human.* Thus the Catholic church is a community of persons (the fundamentally *human* foundation of Catholic identity) who believe in and are committed to the reality of God and who shape their lives according to that belief and in fidelity to that commitment (the *religious* component of Catholicism). The church's belief in and commitment to the reality of God is focused in its fundamental attitude toward Jesus Christ (the *Christian* core). For Catholics, as for every Christian, the old order has passed away, and they are a "new creation" in Christ, for God has "reconciled us to himself through Christ" (*2 Cor.* 5:17, 5:19). "Catholic," therefore, is a qualification of "Christian," of "religious," and of the human. To be Catholic is to be a kind of human being, a kind of religious person, and a kind of Christian.

To be Catholic is, before all else, to be human. Catholicism is an understanding and affirmation of human existence before it is a corporate conviction about the pope, or the seven sacraments, or even about Jesus Christ. But Catholicism is also more than a corporate understanding and affirmation of what it means to be human. Catholicism answers the question of meaning in terms of ultimacy. With Dietrich Bonhoeffer (d. 1945), Catholicism confirms that there is more to life than meets the eye, that there is "a beyond in our midst." With Paul Tillich (d. 1975), Catholicism affirms that there is a ground of all being which is being itself. With Thomas Aquinas, Catholicism affirms that all reality is rooted in the creative, loving power of that which is most real (*ens realissimum*). Catholicism answers the question of meaning in terms of the reality of God. In brief, Catholicism is a religious perspective, and not simply a philosophical or anthropological one.

But Catholicism is not some undifferentiated religious view. Catholicism's view of and commitment to God is radically shaped by its view of and commitment to Jesus Christ. For the Christian, the ultimate dimension of human experience is a triune God: a God who creates and sustains, a God who draws near to and identifies with the human historical condition, and a God who empowers people to live according to the vocation to which they have been called. More specifically, the God of Christians is the God of Jesus Christ.

But just as Jesus Christ gives access to God, so, for the Catholic, the church gives access to Jesus Christ. However, the church itself is composed of many churches, as noted above. The church universal is the communion of local churches, and the body of Christ is composed of denominations (for want of a better term). Thus the noun "church" is always modified: the Catholic church, the Methodist church, the Orthodox church, the Lutheran church, and so forth. Moreover, even those modifiers can themselves be modified: the Lutheran Church-Missouri Synod, the Lutheran Church of America, the American Lutheran Church, and so forth.

There are many churches, but one body of Christ. Within the community of churches, however, there is one church that alone embodies and manifests all the institutional elements necessary for the integrity of the whole body. In Catholic doctrine and theology, that one church is the Catholic church. As ecumenical as the Second Vatican Council certainly was, it did not retreat from this fundamental Catholic conviction:

> They are fully incorporated into the society of the Church who, possessing the Spirit of Christ, accept her entire system and all the means of salvation given to her, and through union with her visible structure are joined to Christ, who rules her through the Supreme Pontiff and the Bishops. This joining is effected by the bonds of professed faith, of the sacraments, of ecclesiastical government, and of communion. (Dogmatic Constitution on the Church, no. 14)

Since Vatican II, however, much has happened to suggest that the traditional lines of distinction have been blurred. It is more evident now that, in spite of the distinctiveness of the Catholic claims for the papal office, Catholic identity is rooted in much broader and richer theological values. Specifically, there is a configuration of characteristics within Catholicism that is not duplicated anywhere else in the community of Christian churches. This configuration of characteristics is expressed in Catholicism's systematic theology; its body of doctrines; its liturgical life, especially its Eucharist; its variety of spiritualities; its religious congregations and lay apostolates; its official teachings on justice, peace, and human rights; its exercise of collegiality; and, to be sure, its Petrine ministry.

Roman Catholicism is distinguished from other Christian traditions and churches in its understanding of, commitment to, and exercise of the principles of sacramentality, mediation, and communion. Differences between Catholic and non-Catholic (especially Protestant) approaches become clearer when measured according to these three principles.

Sacramentality. In its classical (Augustinian) meaning, a sacrament is a visible sign of an invisible grace. Paul VI provided a more contemporary definition: "a reality imbued with the hidden presence of God." A sacramental perspective is one that "sees" the divine in the human, the infinite in the finite, the spiritual in the material, the transcendent in the immanent, the eternal in the historical. Over against this sacramental vision is the view, strengthened by memories of past excesses in the sacramental vision, that God is so "totally other" that the divine reality can never be identified with the human, the transcendent with the immanent, the eternal with the historical, and so forth. The abiding Protestant fear is that Catholics take the sacramental principle to a point just short of, if not fully immersed in, idolatry.

The Catholic sacramental vision "sees" God in and through all things: other people, communities, movements, events, places, objects, the world at large, the whole cosmos. The visible, the tangible, the finite, the historical—all these are actual or potential carriers of the divine presence. Indeed, for the Catholic, it is only in and through these material realities that we can even encounter the invisible God. The great sacrament of our encounter with God, and of God's encounter with us, is Jesus Christ. The church, in turn, is the key sacrament of our encounter with Christ, and of Christ with us; and the sacraments, in turn, are the signs and instruments by which that ecclesial encounter with Christ is expressed, celebrated, and made effective for the glory of God and the salvation of men and women.

The Catholic, therefore, insists that grace (the divine presence) actually enters into and transforms nature (human life in its fullest context). The dichotomy between nature and grace is eliminated. Human existence is already graced existence. There is no merely natural end of human existence, with a supernatural end imposed from above. Human existence in its natural, historical condition is radically oriented toward God. The history of the world is, at the same time, the history of salvation.

This means, for the Catholic, that authentic human progress and the struggle for justice, peace, freedom, human rights, and so forth, is part of the movement of and toward the kingdom of God (Vatican Council II, Pastoral Constitution on the Church in the Modern World, no. 39). The Catholic, unlike Luther, espouses no doctrine of the two kingdoms. The vast body of Catholic social doctrine, from Leo XIII in 1891 to John Paul II a century later, is as characteristic of Catholic Christianity as any element can be. In virtue of the sacramental principle, Catholics affirm that God is indeed present to all human life and to history. To be involved in the transformation of the world is to be collaboratively involved in God's own revolutionary and transforming activity.

For the Catholic, the world is essentially good, though fallen, because it comes from the creative hand of God. And for the Catholic, the world, although fallen, is redeemable because of the redemptive work of God in Jesus Christ. And for the Catholic, the world, although fractured and fragmented, is capable of ultimate unity because of the abiding presence of the Holy Spirit, who is the "first fruits" of the final kingdom of God.

Mediation. A kind of corollary of the principle of sacramentality is the principle of mediation. A sacrament not only signifies; it also causes what it signifies. Indeed, as the Council of Trent officially taught, sacraments cause grace precisely insofar as they signify it. If the church, therefore, is not a credible sign of God's and Christ's presence in the world, if the church is not obviously the "temple of the Holy Spirit," it cannot achieve its missionary purposes. It "causes" grace (i. e., effectively moves the world toward its final destiny in the kingdom of God) to the extent that it signifies the reality toward which it presumes to direct the world.

On the other hand, sacraments are not only signs of faith, as Protestants affirmed at the time of the Reformation. For the Catholic, God is not only present in the sacramental action; God actually achieves something in and through that action. Thus, created realities not only contain, reflect, or embody the presence of God, they also make that presence effective for those who avail themselves of these realities. Encounter with God does not occur solely in the inwardness of conscience or in the inner recesses of consciousness. Catholicism holds, on the contrary, that the encounter with God is a mediated experience, rooted in the historical and affirmed as real by the critical judgment that God is truly present and active here or there, in this event or that, in this person or that, in this object or that.

Again, the Protestant raises a word of caution. Just as the principle of sacramentality edges close to the brink of idolatry, so the principle of mediation moves one along the path toward magic. Just as there has been evidence of idolatry in some Roman Catholic piety, so there has been evidence of a magical view of the divine-human encounter in certain forms of Catholic devotional life. Some Catholics have assumed that if a certain practice were performed a given number of times in an unbroken sequence, their salvation would be guaranteed. A magical worldview, of course, is not a solely Catholic problem, but it is an inherent risk in Catholicism's constant stress on the principle of mediation.

Catholicism's commitment to the principle of mediation is evident, for example, in the importance it has always placed on the ordained ministry of the priest. God's dealings with us are not arbitrary or haphazard. God is present to all and works on behalf of all, but there are also moments and actions wherein God's presence is specially focused. The function of the priest, as mediator, is not to limit the encounter between God and the human person but to focus it more clearly for the sake of the person, and ultimately for the community at large.

The principle of mediation also explains Catholicism's historic emphasis on the place of Mary, the mother of Jesus Christ. The Catholic accepts the role of Mary in salvation on the same ground that the Catholic accepts the role of Jesus Christ. God is present in, and redemptively works through, the humanity of Jesus. This is the principle of mediation in its classic expression. The Catholic understands that the invisible, spiritual God is present and available to us through the visible and the material, and that these are made holy by reason of that divine presence. The Catholic, therefore, readily engages in the veneration (not worship) of Mary, not because Catholicism perceives Mary as some kind of goddess or supercreature or rival of the Lord himself, but because she is a symbol or image of God. It is the God who is present in her and who fills her whole being that the Catholic grasps in the act of venerating yet another "sacrament" of the divine.

Communion. Finally, Catholicism affirms the principle of communion: the human way to God, and God's way to humankind, is not only a mediated but a communal way. Even when the divine-human encounter is most personal and individual, it is still communal, in that the encounter is made possible by the mediation of a community of faith. Thus there is not simply an individual personal relationship with God or Jesus Christ that is established and sustained by meditative reflection on sacred scripture, for the Bible itself is the church's book and the testimony of the church's original faith. There is no relationship with God, however intense, profound, or unique, that dispenses entirely with the communal context of every relationship with God.

And this is why, for Catholicism, the mystery of the church has always had so significant a place in its theology, doctrine, pastoral practice, moral vision, and devotion. Catholics have always emphasized the place of the church as the sacrament of Christ, which mediates salvation through sacraments, ministries, and other institutional elements and forms, and as the communion of saints and the people of God. It is here, at the point of Catholicism's understanding of itself as church, that one comes to the heart of the distinctively Catholic understanding and practice of Christian faith. For here, in Catholic ecclesiology, one finds the convergence of those three principles that have always been so characteristic of Catholicism: sacramentality, mediation, and communion.

The Protestant again raises a word of caution. If one emphasizes too much the principle of communion, do we not endanger the freedom of individuals? If sacramentality can lead to idolatry, and mediation to magic, the principle of communion can lead to a collectivism that suppresses individuality, and an authoritarianism that suppresses freedom of thought.

But stress on the individual also has its inherent weakness, just as there are inherent weaknesses in the historic Protestant insistences on the otherness of God (over against the Catholic sacramental principle) and on the immediacy of the divine-human encounter (over against the Catholic principle of mediation). Some important Protestant theologians like Paul Tillich and Langdon Gilkey have come to acknowledge these inherent problems in Protestantism and the corresponding truth of the Catholic sacramental vision. According to Gilkey, the Catholic principle of symbol or sacramentality "may provide the best entrance into a new synthesis of the Christian tradition with the vitalities as well as the relativities of contemporary existence" (Gilkey, 1975, p. 22).

THEOLOGY AND DOCTRINE. The principles of sacramentality, mediation, and communion frame Catholic thinking and teaching about every significant theological question. The following is not an exhaustive list, and some overlapping with the above discussion is inevitable.

Revelation and faith. Catholics share with other Christians the conviction that God has somehow communicated with humankind in the history of Israel; supremely in Jesus Christ, the Son of God; then through the apostles and evangelists; and, in a different way, through nature, human events, and personal relationships. Some Roman Catholics have tended to restrict revelation to the teachings of the church, just as some Protestants have tended to limit revelation to the Bible. But fundamentally, all Christians, conservative and liberal alike, are united in the belief that Jesus Christ, as both person and event, provides the fullest disclosure of God. Christian faith is the acceptance of Jesus Christ as the Lord and Savior of the world and as the great sacrament of God's presence among us.

Roman Catholics, however, have always been insistent that such faith is reasonable, not arbitrary or blind. The First Vatican Council (1869–1870) taught that faith is "consonant with reason." Roman Catholics, therefore, exclude fideism, on the one hand, and rationalism, on the other. Faith is neither beyond intellectual support nor fully open to intellectual scrutiny. It is neither rational nor irrational. It is reasonable. That is, we can identify solid motives for believing, and we can show that one need not surrender intellectual integrity in order to be a Christian.

The most celebrated Roman Catholic exponent and practitioner of this view has been Thomas Aquinas. For centuries Thomism and Catholicism have been identified in many minds. Accordingly, some Protestants have thought that Catholics are too analytical and too rational about their faith. And some Catholics have assumed that the "truth" of Roman Catholic claims is so demonstrably clear that any open-minded person would have to accept them once he or she examined the "evidence."

While Roman Catholic apologetics has moved away from its earlier rational, almost rationalistic, orientation, it remains committed to the notion that Christian faith does have a "content," that it is, for example, more than the personal acceptance of Jesus Christ or a feeling of absolute dependence upon God.

Creation and original sin. Roman Catholics adhere to the ancient Christian creeds, which professed their belief in one God, the Almighty Creator, who made the heavens and the earth, and all things visible and invisible. And they adhere as well to the later councils of the church, which added that God freely created the world from nothing at the beginning of time in order to share his own goodness, to manifest his own glory, and to sanctify humankind. Jesus Christ is not only the head of the whole human race but also is himself the summit of all creation. He is the Second Adam through whom all else came into being (*Col.* 1:15). Because of their understanding of creation, Roman Catholics have always had an essentially positive attitude toward the world.

But the specific origins of men and women have posed a more thorny problem. The councils of the church (specifically Lateran IV in 1215 and Vatican I in 1869–1870) had taught that all people owe their existence to the creative action of God. Although humankind was specially favored by God in the beginning, we sinned and thereby suffered both physical and spiritual losses (Council of Trent, 1545–1563). But how exactly did this original sin occur, and who "committed" it? Present Catholic scholarship, both biblical and theological, argues that there is no necessary connection between monogenism (the theory that the whole human race sprang from one set of parents) and the integrity of Catholic doctrine. What is clearly maintained is that humankind comes from the creative hand of God. This creative action, however, could have been an evolutionary process just as likely as a one-time event. And so, too, the entrance of human sin could have been evolutionary in character. Some would argue, therefore, that sin gradually spread through the human race until it became truly universal in the sin that was the rejection of Christ. But there are problems with this view, and many Catholic theologians continue to insist that the original sin be traced to a primal fault that immediately affected the entire race.

Nonetheless, original sin has a meaning that goes beyond the personal decisions of Adam and Eve. It is the state in which all people are born precisely because they are members of the human race. As such, we are situated in a sinful history that affects our capacity to love God above all and to become the kind of people God destined us to be. What is important to remember, Catholics insist, is that we came forth from the hand of God essentially good, not essentially evil. Sin has rendered our condition ambiguous, at best and at worst. Unlike some Protestants, Roman Catholics have been less inclined to paint the human scene in dark and ominous colors, several examples to the contrary notwithstanding. Humankind is redeemable because men and women are radically good.

Nature and grace. The question of grace raises one of the sharpest issues that have historically divided Protestant from Roman Catholic. How is humankind justified and eventually saved? By our own efforts? By God's alone? Or by a combination of both? Appearances to the contrary, Roman Catholics have never endorsed the view that people are saved by their own power. That position, known as Pelagianism, has been condemned consistently by the councils of the church, especially by Trent, and by Augustine in particular. Catholics, however, regard the second view as equally objectionable, namely, that human beings contribute nothing at all to salvation, because it is so totally the work of God. Such a belief, Catholics have always argued, undermines human freedom and human responsibility and encourages a passive, quietist approach to the Christian life. We are saved neither by faith alone nor by works alone, but by a living faith that overflows in works befitting a "new creature" in Christ (*Gal.* 6:15).

To be in the state of grace means to be open to the presence of God, and of the Holy Spirit in particular. This indwelling of the Spirit really transforms us. Our sins are not merely "covered over." They are obliterated by an act of divine forgiveness and generosity, on the sole condition that we are truly sorry for having offended God in the first place. The graced person is still liable to sin, of course, and so in this sense he or she may be said to be both just and sinful (*simul iustus et peccator*). But that gives a different meaning to the expression than some of the reformers assigned it. They would have been less prepared than Catholics to stress the internal transformation by grace.

Jesus Christ and redemption. Roman Catholics share with other Christians the central conviction of Christian faith that Jesus of Nazareth is the Lord of history (*Phil.* 2:5–11), that he was crucified for our sins, was raised from the dead on the third day, was exalted as Lord of all, is present to history now in and through the church.

Jesus Christ is both human and divine in nature, yet one person. "Born of a woman" (*Gal.* 4:4), he is like us in all things save sin (*Heb.* 4:15). At the same time, he is of the very being of God, Son of the Father, the light of God in the world. He is, in the words of the Second Vatican Council, "the key, the focal point, and the goal of all human history" (Pastoral Constitution on the Church in the Modern World, no. 10).

While Roman Catholic piety has often emphasized the divinity of Christ at the expense of the humanity ("God" died on the cross; "God" dwells in the tabernacle, etc.), Roman Catholics have sometimes suspected some Protestants of reversing the emphasis in favor of Jesus' humanity. Whatever the exaggerations on either side of the Reformation divide, official Roman Catholic doctrine has always maintained a balance, without confusion, between the human and divine natures.

Roman Catholics believe, of course, in the centrality and absolute necessity of Jesus Christ for personal salvation and the salvation of all the world, but they do not believe that one must be an explicit Christian, confessing the lordship of Jesus, before one can be saved. People of good will who lead exemplary lives are just as likely to enter the heavenly banquet as professed Christians. Catholics have called this "baptism by desire." Conversely, Roman Catholics also acknowledge that professed Christians can be damned, their fervent appeal to the lordship of Jesus notwithstanding. "Not everyone who says to me, 'Lord, Lord,' shall enter the kingdom of heaven, but he who does the will of my Father who is in heaven" (*Mt.* 7:21).

Neither do Roman Catholics readily identify with the evangelical Protestant stress on the propitiatory nature of the crucifixion of Jesus, even though this view has durable roots in history, particularly in the writings of Anselm of Canterbury (d. 1109). Jesus did not die in order to pay off a debt coldly demanded by his Father. He was executed because his person and his message were threatening to the political and religious establishments of his day. By accepting death, he demonstrated that love and freedom are more powerful than apathy and fear. The crucifixion was the will of God in the sense that God wills the personal fulfillment of every man and woman, and specifically God willed that Jesus should confront and challenge the network of sin in human society even though such a confrontation and challenge would surely polarize all the forces of sin against him.

In any case, for Catholics the redemption was accomplished by the whole paschal mystery, that is, Christ's passing over to his Father through a life of suffering servanthood, his obedient death on the cross, and his resurrection, ascension, and exaltation at the right hand of God. The redemptive act is not limited to the crucifixion alone.

Holy Spirit and Trinity. The Holy Spirit is God's self-communication as love and as the power of healing, reconciliation, and new life. The divinity of the Holy Spirit was defined by the First Council of Constantinople in 381. The Spirit has the same divine essence as the Father and the Son and yet is distinct from them both. Within the Trinity, the Spirit proceeds from the Father *through* the Son. Despite the bitter East-West dispute on this point, the Council of Ferrara-Florence (1438–1440) did allow for the preposition "through" as a legitimate alternative to the preferred conjunction "and." The God who created us, who sustains us, who will judge us, and who will give us eternal life is not a God infinitely removed from us (i. e., God the Father). On the contrary, God is a God of absolute proximity: a God who is communicated truly in the flesh, in history, within the human family (i. e., God the Son), and a God who is present in the spiritual depths of human existence as well as in the core of unfolding human history, as the source of enlightenment and community (i. e., God the Holy Spirit). The mystery and doctrine of the Trinity is the beginning, the end, and the center of all Christian and, therefore, all Catholic theology.

Mary. Whatever the popular exaggerations in the past, Roman Catholic doctrine does not say that Mary is coequal with Christ. However, she is the mother of Jesus, and her motherhood is what roots Christ in our humanity. Indeed, Mary's name was involved in the earliest christological controversies. If Jesus was not divine, then of course it would have been wrong to call her the Mother of God. But the Council of Ephesus condemned the Nestorians in 431, and Mary was proclaimed *theotokos* (Mother of God)—which effectively meant that Jesus was proclaimed as true God as well as true man.

Controversy has continued to surround Mary, especially since the middle of the nineteenth century: first in 1854 with the promulgation of the dogma of the Immaculate Conception (that she was conceived without original sin), then in 1950 with the dogma of the Assumption (that she was taken up bodily into heaven after her death). Mary has also been called the Mediatrix of all graces (i. e., by the will of Christ, all the grace he earned for us is channeled through her), co-Redemptrix (i. e., she shares somehow in the redemptive work of her Son, without prejudice to the supreme saving power of his own death and resurrection), and Mother of the church (i. e., she has a certain priority in the church, as chief among the saints, and is the prototype of the church, a sign of the church's call to obedience and fidelity to God's word). Controversy has been rekindled, too, in the matter of the Virgin Birth (i. e., Mary conceived Jesus by the power of the Holy Spirit alone, without benefit of a human partner), while reports of Marian appearances in Guadalupe (1531), Lourdes (1858), and Fatima (1917) have generated both skepticism and fervor.

Devotion to Mary is a characteristically Catholic phenomenon in that it expresses the three fundamental principles of Catholic theology and practice:

1. The principle of sacramentality, which affirms that the invisible and spiritual God is present through the visible and the material, and that these are in turn made holy by that presence. This includes Mary, in whom God is very specially present.
2. The principle of mediation, which affirms that grace is a mediated reality, first through Christ and secondarily through the church and other human instruments, including Mary.
3. The principle of communion, which affirms that the saving encounter with God occurs not only personally and individually but also corporately and ecclesially. To be in the church, that is, to be in communion with other Christians, is to be in and with Christ. Mary is the preeminent member of this communion of saints. Our unity with her is an expression of our unity in and with Christ.

Church, kingdom of God, and sacraments. For the Catholic, the church is the whole body, or congregation, of persons who are called by God the Father to acknowledge the lordship of Jesus, the Son, in word, in sacrament, in witness, and in service, and, through the power of the Holy Spirit, to collaborate with Jesus' historic mission for the sake of the kingdom of God. The mission of the church, as also Jesus' mission, is focused on the kingdom of God. By kingdom of God is meant the redemptive presence of God actualized through the power of God's reconciling Spirit. Literally, the kingdom of God is the reign, or rule, of God. The kingdom happens whenever and wherever the will of God is fulfilled, for God rules where God's will is at work. And since God's will is applicable to the cosmos, to nature, to objects, to history, to institutions, to groups as well as overarching as the claims and scope of the divine will itself.

The mission of the church is unintelligible apart from the kingdom of God. The church is called, first, to proclaim in word and in sacrament the definitive arrival of the kingdom of God in Jesus of Nazareth; second, to offer itself as a test case or sign of its own proclamation, that is, to be a people transformed by the Holy Spirit into a community of faith, hope, love, freedom, and truthfulness; and third, to enable and facilitate the coming of the reign of God through service within the community of faith and in the world at large.

For the Catholic, the church does God's work because God is present and at work within it. To speak of the church as the presence and instrument of God is to speak of it sacramentally. Just as Christ is the sacrament of God, so the church is the sacrament of Christ. Because the church is a sacrament, it acts sacramentally. In the course of its history, the Catholic church has identified seven specific acts as sacraments in the strictest sense of the term: baptism, confirmation, and Eucharist (which together constitute the rite of Christian initiation), and marriage, holy orders, reconciliation (or penance), and the anointing of the sick. The sacraments, individually and collectively, are signs of faith, causes of grace, acts of worship, and signs and instruments of the unity of the church and of Christ's presence in the world.

The relationship between sign and cause, however, has provoked the most serious sacramental controversy, particularly at the time of the Reformation. The Council of Trent rejected two extreme notions of causality: the one that reduced sacraments to magical actions, and the other that robbed sacraments of their inner spiritual reality and efficacy. The sacraments cause grace, not because of the faith of the recipient but because of the working of God within the sacraments themselves (*ex opere operato*). On the other hand, God does not force the human will. Faithfully reflecting the teaching of Thomas Aquinas, the Council of Trent recognized that the recipient must have the right disposition if the sacrament is to be spiritually fruitful: interior conversion, faith, and devotion. Finally, the validity of a sacrament does not depend on the holiness of the minister, although some sacraments can be validly celebrated only by certain authorized ministers (bishops in the case of holy orders; bishops and delegated priests in the case of confirmation; priests in the case of the Eucharist, the anointing of the sick, and penance; priests and deacons in the case of the sacrament of marriage, which the couple themselves administer to each other; and a priest or deacon in the case of baptism, although in principle anyone can administer baptism.

Catholic morality. For Catholicism, morality is a matter of thinking and acting in accordance with the person and the community one has become in Christ. It is therefore a matter not only of obeying the rules but also of being faithful to the spirit as well as to the letter of the gospel. Since human agents are free to accept or reject Christ and his gospel, Catholicism contends with the reality of sin. But the church's moral vision and its approach to the moral demands of Christian life are qualified always by its confidence in the power of grace and by its readiness to expect and understand the weaknesses and failures rooted in original sin. And so Catholicism is a moral universe of laws but also dispensations, of rules but also exceptions, of respect for authority but also freedom of conscience, of high ideals but also minimal requirements, of penalties but also indulgences, of censures and excommunications but also absolution and reconciliation.

Catholic morality, therefore, is characterized by a both/and rather than an either/or approach. It is not nature *or* grace, but graced nature; not reason *or* faith, but reason illumined by faith; not law *or* gospel, but law inspired by the gospel; not scripture *or* tradition, but normative tradition within scripture; not faith *or* works, but faith issuing in works and works as expressions of faith; not authority *or* freedom, but authority in the service of freedom; not the past *versus* the present, but the present in continuity with the past; not stability *or* change, but change in fidelity to stable principle, and principle fashioned and refined in response to change; not unity *or* diversity, but unity in diversity, and diversity that prevents uniformity, the antithesis of unity.

This both/and approach to morality also explains the so-called seamless-garment approach of U. S. Catholic bishops to contemporary issues such as nuclear warfare, capital punishment, aid to the handicapped, abortion, human rights, and the like. And the Catholic church's beliefs about the universality of grace and the capacity of all persons, Catholic or not, to come to an understanding of the law of God written in every human heart (*Rom.* 2:15) explains its conviction that Catholic moral teachings about such matters as nuclear warfare and abortion are also universally applicable, and not restricted to Catholics alone.

The last things. Catholic teaching and belief about life after death applies to individuals, the church, and the human community as a whole. Everyone and everything is destined for the kingdom of God, but there is no guarantee of universal salvation. The separation of the sheep and the goats (*Mt.* 25) will occur at both the general judgment (i. e., at the end of human history) and at the particular judgment (i. e., at the end of each individual's life). Some will join God forever in heaven; some may be separated eternally from God in hell; others may find themselves in a state of merely natural happiness in limbo; and others will suffer in purgatory some temporary "punishment" still required of sins that have already been forgiven. Such "punishments" can be partially or fully remitted through the application of indulgences.

Each individual is destined for the beatific vision (heaven, eternal life) and the resurrection of the body. Purgatory is an intermediate state between heaven and hell, reserved for those who, at the moment of death, are not yet ready to see God "face to face" (*1 Cor.* 13:12). Catholic tradition holds that it is possible for the living (the church militant) spiritually to aid "the souls in purgatory" (the church suffering). All members of the church, living and dead, are bound together as a communion of saints. Just as the prayers of the living may benefit those in purgatory, so the prayers of the saints in heaven (the church triumphant) may benefit those on earth who make intercession to them.

Although the church has defined that certain persons are in heaven (canonized saints), it has never defined that anyone is actually in hell. Thus, a Catholic is required to believe in hell as a real possibility for those who utterly reject the grace of God, but the Catholic is not required to believe that anyone has actually been consigned to hell. The destiny of the unbaptized infant or young child, on the other hand, has, since the Middle Ages, been linked with a state called limbo, a condition of "natural happiness," where the individual is free of punishment but deprived of the vision of God. However, belief in limbo and teaching about limbo has declined as the hope of universal salvation has gradually increased since the Second Vatican Council.

POLITY. According to its own official teachings, the Roman Catholic church is neither a monarchy nor an oligarchy nor a democracy. Its governance is of a unique kind because the church has a "unique essence" (Rahner and Ratzinger, *The Episcopate and the Primacy,* 1962, p. 33). The universal church is a college of local churches. The supreme jurisdictional power of this universal church is vested at one and the same time in the pope and in an ecumenical council, over which the pope presides and of which he too is a member. Indeed, the universal church is itself a kind of ecumenical council convoked by some human agent (today the pope, in the past popes and emperors alike). The papacy is the highest pastoral office in the Roman Catholic church because of the pope's status as bishop of the diocese of Rome. As such, he is head of the college of bishops, and is called the Vicar of Christ (more accurately, the Vicar of Peter) and pastor of the universal church on earth.

According to the legal tradition of the Roman Catholic church, however, the church seems closer to an absolute monarchy. The Code of Canon Law accords the pope "supreme, full, immediate and universal ordinary power in the Church, which he can always freely exercise" (canon 331). Therefore, there is "neither appeal nor recourse against a decision or decree of the Roman Pontiff" (canon 333, no. 3). The only way a pope can lose such authority is through death or resignation.

Just as the universal church is composed of an international college of local churches, so the universality of the church is expressed through the collegial relationship of the bishops, one to another. The bishop of Rome serves as the head and center of this collegial network. Even the Code of Canon Law of the Roman Catholic church acknowledges that the church is not a strict monarchy, for the college of bishops, which always includes the pope, "is also the subject of supreme and full power over the universal Church" (canon 336), a power that it exercises solemnly in an ecumenical council. Bishops also participate in the governance of the church through synods. A synod of bishops is a group of bishops who have been chosen from the different regions of the world to discuss matters of general interest to the church and to make recommendations for pastoral action. Since the Second Vatican Council, international synods of bishops have met in Rome every two, and then every three, years. An extraordinary synod of bishops was called by John Paul II in 1985.

The college of cardinals constitutes a special college of bishops within the larger episcopal college. There were lay cardinals until 1918, when the Code of Canon Law specified that all cardinals must be priests. Pope John XXIII decreed in 1962 that all cardinals must be bishops. The responsibility of the college of cardinals is to provide for the election of a new pope and to advise the pope when and if he seeks its counsel on matters pertaining to the governance of the universal church. In its present form, the college of cardinals dates from the twelfth century. Earlier the title had been bestowed on deacons and priests of the leading churches of Rome and on bishops of neighboring dioceses. The title was limited, however, to members of the college in 1567. The number of cardinals was set at seventy in 1586 by Sixtus V, and that limit remained in force until the pontificate of John XXIII, who gradually increased it. Paul VI limited the number of cardinals eligible to vote in papal elections to 120.

The Curia Romana is the administrative arm of the papacy. It consists of the Secretariat of State, the Council for the Public Affairs of the Church, and various congregations, tribunals, and other institutions, whose structure and competency are defined in special law. There are ten congregations (Doctrine of the Faith, Oriental Churches, Bishops, Discipline of the Sacraments, Divine Worship, Causes of Saints, Clergy, Religious and Secular Institutes, Catholic Education, and the Evangelization of Peoples, or Propagation of the Faith); three tribunals (Sacred Apostolic Penitentiary, Apostolic Signatura, and the Sacred Roman Rota); three secretariats (one for Christian Unity, one for Non-Christians, and one for Non-Believers); and a complex of commissions, councils, and offices, which administer church affairs at the central executive level (e.g., Theological Commission, Council of the Laity, and Central Statistics Office). The terms *apostolic see* or *holy see* apply not only to the pope but also to the Secretariat of State, the Council for the Public Affairs of the Church, and other institutions of the Curia.

The Code of Canon Law also stipulates that the pope "possesses the innate and independent right to nominate, send, transfer and recall his own legates to particular churches in various nations or regions, to states and to public authorities; the norms of international law are to be observed concerning the sending and the recalling of legates appointed to states" (canon 362). These legates are usually called nuncios and have ambassadorial rank. Those without full ambassadorial rank are called apostolic delegates.

The polity of the Roman Catholic church is not limited to the organizational structure and operation of its Rome base. In Eastern-rite churches that are in union with the Holy See, there are patriarchs and patriarchates that have "existed in the Church from the earliest times and [were] recognized by the first ecumenical synods" (Vatican Council II, Decree on Eastern Catholic Churches, no. 7). A patriarch is a bishop who has jurisdiction over all bishops, clergy, and people of his own territory or rite. "The Patriarchs with their synods constitute the superior authority for all affairs of the patriarchate, including the right to establish new eparchies [dioceses] and to nominate bishops of their rite within the territorial bounds of the patriarchate, without prejudice to the inalienable right of the Roman Pontiff to intervene in individual cases" (no. 9).

At the diocesan level there are bishops, auxiliary bishops, vicars general, chancellors, marriage courts, diocesan pastoral councils, and the like. At the parish level there are pastors, associate pastors, pastoral ministers, extraordinary ministers of the Eucharist, parish councils, and the like. The Second Vatican Council substantially expanded the participation of the laity in the governance of the church, particularly through its teaching that the church is the people of God (Dogmatic Constitution on the Church, nos. 30–33).

SPIRITUALITY AND ETHOS. As the name itself suggests, Catholicism is characterized by a radical openness to all truth and to every authentic human and spiritual value. One finds in it, in varying degrees, all the theological, doctrinal, spiritual, liturgical, canonical, structural, and social diversity and richness that are constitutive of Christianity as a whole. Catholicism is the very antithesis of a sect, and it is not inextricably linked with the culture of a particular nation or region of the world. It is in principle as Asian as it is European, as Slavic as it is Latin, as Mexican as it is Nigerian, as Irish as it is Polish.

There is no list of Catholic fathers or mothers that does not include the great figures of the period before as well as after the division of East and West and the divisions within the West. Gregory of Nyssa is as much a Catholic father as is Augustine or Thomas Aquinas. Nor are there schools of theology that Catholicism excludes. Catholicism embraces Ignatius of Antioch and Clement of Alexandria, Athanasius and Cyril of Jerusalem, Gregory of Nazianzus and Augustine of Hippo, Anselm of Canterbury and Bernard of Clairvaux, Abelard and Hugh of Saint Victor, Thomas Aquinas and Bonaventure, Roberto Bellarmino and Johann Adam Möhler, Karl Rahner and Charles Journet, as well as John and Luke, Peter and Paul. Nor are there spiritualities that Catholicism excludes. It is open to *The Cloud of Unknowing* and the *Introduction to the Devout Life*, to the way of Francis of Assisi and that of Antony of Egypt, to Ignatius Loyola and John of the Cross, to Abbott Marmion and Thomas Merton, to Catherine of Siena and Dorothy Day, to Teresa of Ávila and Mother Teresa.

Catholicism is not just a collection of beliefs and practices but a community of persons. Catholicism is, and has been, composed of martyrs and ascetics, pilgrims and warriors, mystics and theologians, artists and humanists, activists and outsiders, pastors and saints. Catholicism is in Dante Alighieri, Michelangelo Buonarroti, Blaise Pascal, Erasmus, Joan of Arc, Julian of Norwich, Thomas More, Thérèse of Lisieux, and many others. "The splendour of saints, the glory of cathedrals, the courage of reformers, the strangeness of myth and marvel, the soaring ecstasies of mystics and the sorrows of the poor—all these are the home of the Catholic enterprise" (Haughton, 1979, p. 249).

SEE ALSO Apostles; Atonement; Baptism; Biblical Literature, article on New Testament; Basilica, Cathedral, and Church; Canon; Christian Ethics; Christianity; Christian Liturgical Year; Church, article on Church Polity; Cistercians; Constantinianism; Councils, article on Christian Councils; Creeds, article on Christian Creeds; Cult of Saints; Death; Dominicans; Eucharist; Evil; Fall, The; Franciscans; Gallicanism; Grace; Heresy, article on Christian Concepts; Humanism; Iconography, article on Christian Iconography; Incarnation; Jesuits; Jesus; Kingdom of God; Mary; Merit, article on Christian Concepts; Ministry; Missions, article on Christian Missions; Modernism, article on Christian Modernism; Monasticism, article on Christian Monasticism; Music, article on Religious Music in the West; Papacy; Peter the Apostle; Pilgrimage, articles on Roman Catholic Pilgrimage in Europe and Roman Catholic Pilgrimage in the New World; Priesthood, article on Christian Priesthood; Redemption; Reformation; Religious Communities, article on Christian Religious Orders; Sacrament, article on Christian Sacraments; Schism, article on Christian Schism; Scholasticism; Sin and Guilt; Trent, Council of; Trinity; Ultramontanism; Vatican Councils, article on Vatican II; Worship and Devotional Life, article on Christian Worship.

BIBLIOGRAPHY

Adam, Karl. *Das Wesen des Katholizismus.* Tübingen, 1924. Translated by Justin McCann as *The Spirit of Catholicism* (New York, 1954). Translated into many languages, including Chinese and Japanese, this work represents the best of pre-Vatican II Catholic theology, formulated in reaction to a prevailing neoscholasticism that tended to reduce Catholicism to a system of doctrines and laws. On the other hand, the text does reflect the exegetical, ecumenical, and ecclesiological limitations of its time.

Cunningham, Lawrence S. *The Catholic Heritage.* New York, 1983. Conveys the heart of Catholicism through certain ideal types, for example, martyrs, mystics, and humanists, including "outsiders" like James Joyce and Simone Weil.

Delaney, John, ed. *Why Catholic?* Garden City, N. Y., 1979. A collection of essays by various American Catholic figures on their understanding of the meaning of Catholicism and on their own personal appropriation of that meaning. Contributors include Andrew Greeley, Abigail McCarthy, and Archbishop Fulton Sheen.

Gilkey, Langdon. *Catholicism Confronts Modernity: A Protestant View.* New York, 1975. Chapter 1, "The Nature of the Crisis," is particularly useful because it identifies what the author regards as the essentially positive characteristics of Catholicism: sacramentality, rationality, tradition, and peoplehood.

Happel, Stephen, and David Tracy. *A Catholic Vision.* Philadelphia, 1984. The approach is historical and the thesis is that Catholicism emerges progressively and processively as it encounters new forms of life that it constantly attempts to understand and transform. Jointly authored, the book may lack the necessary clarity and coherence that a less sophisticated inquirer would require.

Haughton, Rosemary. *The Catholic Thing.* Springfield, Ill., 1979. An original approach that portrays Catholicism as a reality shaped by an enduring conflict between what the author calls "Mother Church" (the more traditional, institutional side) and "Sophia" (the more unpredictable, communal side). In this regard, the book is similar to Cunningham's (above).

Hellwig, Monika K. *Understanding Catholicism.* New York, 1981. Covers some of the doctrinal and theological territory treated in my more comprehensive *Catholicism* (below), but without so much attention to historical and documentary detail.

Lubac, Henri de. *Catholicisme.* Paris, 1938. Translated by Lancelot C. Sheppard as *Catholicism: A Study of the Corporate Destiny of Mankind* (New York, 1958). As its English subtitle suggests, the book underlines the essentially social nature of Catholicism—in its creeds and doctrines, in its sacramental life, and in its vision of history. It draws heavily on patristic and medieval sources, excerpts of which are provided in an appendix.

McBrien, Richard P. *Catholicism.* Rev. ed. 2 vols. in 1. Minneapolis, 1981. The most comprehensive, up-to-date exposition of Catholic history, theology, and doctrine available. Its main lines are reflected in this article.

Rahner, Karl, and Joseph Ratzinger. *Episkopat und Primat.* Freiburg im Bresgau, 1962. Translated by Kenneth Barker and others as *The Episcopate and the Primacy* (New York, 1962). An important corrective to exaggerated notions of papal authority, and at the same time a significant contribution to the literature on the meaning of collegiality. Its ideas, written before Vatican II, were essentially adopted by the council.

RICHARD P. MCBRIEN (1987)

ROMAN CATHOLICISM [FURTHER CONSIDERATIONS] A significant theme recurs in Roman Catholic studies at the turn of the twenty-first century: before nominally indicating a church or adjectivally describing a belief, Roman Catholicism denotes action. It is what people do with spiritual sensibilities redolent of the Christian God and tutored in traditions of Roman Catholic memory. Terrence Tilley's 2000 study of Roman Catholicism as a religious tradition is representative, illustrating Roman Catholicism as the *act* of handing something on *(traditio)* as much as the *things (tradita) passed down.*

This focus on human action belies the oversimplified image of Roman Catholicism as a hierarchical, authoritarian church of immutable beliefs and acquiescent believers. It reveals a much more complex phenomenon: a church hierarchical in form, yet materially diverse in its religious actions and insights. Roman Catholics variably control and contest the practice of their religious sensibilities; practices formed as much by aesthetic sensibilities as by dogmatic pronouncement. What emerges from this scholarship is a Christianity not reckoned by a plurality, but expressive of a surprising pluralism. Sociologists of religion such as Kevin Christiano strike a common note: "many people—not excluding Catholics themselves—think that the Catholic Church is unitary in addition to universal, monolithic as well as monumental, and immutable as much as it is inimitable. Nothing could be farther [sic] from the truth (2002)."

Attending to what Roman Catholics do, contemporary research mines the everyday world of time and space. Uncovered in such work are previously unrecognized changes in Roman Catholicism over time, as well as locally distinct religious practices shaped by the geographic and social spaces within which Roman Catholics find themselves. Eamon Duffy's 1992 work *The Stripping of the Altars: Traditional Religion in England c.1400–c.1580* illustrates this trend. Duffy scrutinizes daily life in late medieval England and discovers lay Roman Catholic religious practices that are surprisingly vibrant and changing. Overturning the standard view of the period, Duffy unearths a popular religiosity that seems scarcely moribund or decadent enough to seed an English Reformation.

Other historical investigations apply this method to spaces beyond the Eurocentric limits of earlier Roman Catholic scholarship. Gauvin Bailey (1999), for example, analyzes art on the Jesuit missions in Asia and South America from the sixteenth to the eighteenth centuries.

Kathleen Myers and Amanda Powell (1999) edit and translate the seventeenth-century journal of Mexican nun Madre María de San Jose. Austen Ivereigh (2000) edits essays on Roman Catholic religious politics in nineteenth-century Central and South America. These and more examinations outside Europe further disclose the variable impact of time and space on lived Roman Catholicism.

Regard for historicity and contextuality also marks present Roman Catholic theology. Ethnically and regionally focused theologies have proliferated, drawing on Roman Catholic behaviors and convictions particular to nearly every region of the world. There are African and Asian Catholic theologies, European-American, Hispanic-American, and African American Catholic theologies, as well as theologies differentiating many national cultures of Central and South America. Robert Schreiter summarizes this development in his 1985 book *Constructing Local Theologies:* "there is now a realization that all theologies have contexts, interests, relationships of power, special concerns—and to pretend that this is not the case is to be blind."

Allied to this fascination with action in time and space is scholarly concentration on Roman Catholic group activity. Between the microscopic level of personal religious practice and the macroscopic level of hierarchical church authority lies a "mesoscopic" layer of group and organizational action. From parish ladies' guilds and food-drive committees, through regional ethnic associations and right-to-life groups, across diocesan social justice offices and marriage preparation conferences, to national lay organizations and Marian devotion assemblies, Roman Catholicism is replete with mesoscopic religious action. In his historical-analytical investigation of this fact, Ad Leys (1995) observes both the practical ubiquity of Roman Catholic group life and the theoretical expression it is given in the social-moral principle of subsidiarity.

Recent explorations attend to important, but previously unexamined, groups and organizations. Especially poignant are studies of women's religious orders, the unheralded creators of vast school, orphanage, poorhouse, hospital, and social service networks around the world since the early nineteenth century. Like the African American Oblate Sisters of Providence described by Diane Batts Morrow (2002), many of these heroic women's groups struggled against not only social discrimination, but also the disregard of their own church leadership. To this day, a push-pull relationship with church authority persists for some women's religious orders. Characteristic of Roman Catholicism, two national organizations of women religious, representing contrasting responses to this relationship, evolved in the United States after the Second Vatican Council (1961–1965): the Leadership Conference of Women Religious and the Council of Major Superiors of Women Religious.

Heightened strain on the quality and funding of public schools at the end of the twentieth century has called attention to another previously neglected mesoscopic organization: the Catholic school. Though many schools have closed and enrollment has declined over the past twenty-five years, the remaining 120,000 Roman Catholic elementary and secondary schools and their fifty million students around the world still play a vital role in many societies. Analysts Anthony Bryk, et al. (1993) and Gerald Grace (2002) are particularly fascinated with the loose federation, relative autonomy, and commitment to inner-city, non-Catholic children that is emblematic of many Roman Catholic schools—organizations ironically nested within their church's centralized, authoritarian structure.

Bryk observes another irony in the operation of Roman Catholic high schools. Teachers and students still grant the (typically lay) Roman Catholic school principal a greater degree of power and deference than is generally given principals in public schools. But today, this vestige of religious order, authoritarian empowerment, is used as much for encouraging parental involvement and local, decentralized school control as for maintaining discipline. From an international perspective, Grace (2003) explains how schools employ this power in relation to church authority, from those that are largely compliant (e.g., in Australia and Ireland), through moderately challenging (e.g., in England, Scotland, and the United States), to boldly resistive (e.g., in Brazil, Chile, and South Africa).

Research on women religious orders and Catholic schools parallels the new scholarly concentration on the parish, the place where the micro-, meso-, and macroscopic levels of religious life intersect for most Roman Catholics. Andrew Greeley captures this reality when he writes that "it is the parish where people do their living and dying, their loving and their quarreling, their doubting and their believing, their mourning and their rejoicing, their worrying and their praying" (1990). James Davidson, et al., communicate the point statistically: 78 percent of parish-affiliated Roman Catholics in the United States consider parishes "very important" organizations, as do 50 percent of those no longer affiliated with a parish (1997).

While a Roman Catholic's sacramental life cycle surely accounts for much of this affiliation, Mark Kowalewski's research offers an additional reason. As a member of a church with largely distant, ostensibly unchanging authority, a lay Roman Catholic's typical contact with approachable and flexible religious leadership is the parish priest. When such person-to-person leadership is effective, Roman Catholics receive help not only in managing their sacramental lives through the upheavals of contemporary economic, familial, and cultural existence, but also in coping with these hard realities on a day-to-day basis. Parish priests, says Kowalewski, are "not simply bearers of the official directives of the organization, they also exercise their ministry in the context of individual pastoral experience—an experience which often calls for compromise and negotiation" (1993).

As they do with school principals, Roman Catholics frequently defer to their parish priests. The common result is a parish milieu mirroring the priest's style of response toward church authority. Today, Roman Catholics worldwide popularly categorize parishes as conservative, liberal, or radical.

In the United States, however, the prerogatives granted to parish priests have come under intense scrutiny, ever since numerous disclosures of clerical sexual abuse of children occurred in the 1980s and subsequent decades. This priest-pedophilia tragedy has been compounded immeasurably by the delinquency of church authority. Schooled in habits of hierarchical, authoritarian arrogance, few bishops initially felt compelled to respond compassionately to the victims of past abuse or to safeguard potential future victims. Instead, their first instincts were to protect predator priests, by reassigning them to other parishes without notice or simply by denying that the abuse ever took place. Not surprisingly, lay Roman Catholics have reacted by creating multiple protest groups. The Voice of the Faithful collaborates with bishops on church reform, while the Survivors' Network of those Abused by Priests (SNAP) is less inclined to participate in such collaboration.

These examples display the plural, mesoscopic ways in which Roman Catholics practice and perceive their everyday religiosity, and how they relate this religiosity to the power and instruction issued from hierarchical church authority. Scholars regularly model this relationship on a conservative, liberal, and radical scale. Mary Jo Weaver and Scott Appleby (1995) add further complexities to this scale. At each point, a Roman Catholic congregation may articulate comparatively "right" and "left" orientations, approaches that are often additionally nuanced by a group's unique regional history.

This complex combination affects the many Roman Catholic groups in the Americas that are devoted to improving society. Responding to prevailing public policies, as well as to church authority, groups on the conservative-right, such as Catholics United for the Faith, exist alongside those on the conservative-left, such as the North American neoconservative movement. Simultaneously, liberal-right groups like the St. Egidio communities work differently from liberal-left organizations such as the social-justice lobby, Network. Added to this mix are radical-right groups, such as those sustaining Dorothy Day's Catholic Worker legacy, and radical-left groups, such as those inspired by the earlier Latin American *comunidades eclesiales de base* movement.

Some Roman Catholics deride this variety as the undesirable byproduct of "cafeteria Catholics"—people who select only those items in Roman Catholicism they like and pass over items they dislike. If this phenomenon did not exist, critics argue, Roman Catholic thought and action would more uniformly replicate the instruction of hierarchical church authority. But as Dean Hoge points out, "Catholicism includes an amazing collection of teachings, symbols, rituals, devotions, and practices, which has grown up over the centuries." Accordingly, it is not transparently obvious to Roman Catholics which elements are core and which are peripheral. "Catholics today are faced with the question," says Hoge, "of sorting out core and periphery in their rich, many-stranded tradition." Hence, "everyone is, to some degree, a cafeteria Catholic" (2002).

This is not a new phenomenon. Thomas Bokenkotter (1998), Marvin Krier Mich (1998), Paul Misner (1991), and others map an analogous range of Roman Catholic dispositions dating as far back as the French Revolution. Eighteenth- and early nineteenth- century conservative Catholics include the autocratic *caudillos* in South America on the right and German romantic traditionalists like Adam Müller on the left. Liberal Catholics can be found supporting Frédéric Ozanam's St. Vincent de Paul societies on the right and Félicité Lamennais' *L'Avenir* republicanism on the left. Similarly, some radical-right Catholics support communitarian experiments inspired by the earlier Jesuit reductions in Paraguay, while other radical-left Catholics embrace Philippe Buchez's Christian socialism.

Frank recognition of Roman Catholic pluralism, past and present, invites assessment of how this compound Christian religiosity sustains itself over time. Drawing on the thought of Félix Guattari, Renée de la Torre offers a "transversalized institution" model. In such institutions, multiple horizontal axes of popular practice intersect a single vertical axis of hierarchical authority. As in Roman Catholicism, this vertical axis of objective law meets multiple, horizontal "group aspirations and strategies which cross it from different points—within and without, above and below." As these lateral activities crisscross the axis of the hierarchical authority, "spaces of conflict that traverse and penetrate the institution" are produced (2002).

In transversalized institutions, therefore, vertical and horizontal axes operate in tensive, but mutually beneficial, ways. This model suggests that Roman Catholicism persists in its formal religious structure and dizzying array of material religiosity by "the continuance, rather than the dissolution, of contradictions" (2002). For de la Torre, Roman Catholicism not only is, but also *must be,* a site of religious contestation.

The functionality of this control-contest interaction can be further elucidated using Paul Connerton's (1989) and Ann Swidler's (2001) investigations of social memory. With its protracted and geographically diffuse history, Roman Catholicism possesses more religious memory than it can express at any given time. By selecting and communicating a manageable portion of this memory, church authorities perform an important control function for a Roman Catholic's religious identity.

But Roman Catholic lay people contribute to corporate identity formation as well. They also select and communicate religious memory, primarily to meet the practical challenges of day-to-day economic, familial, and cultural life. Church authority tutors most, but not all, of this lay religious memory. Some religious memories may include personally and locally cherished practices and perceptions that were never known, long forgotten, or once silenced by church authority. Other memories may recall searing family crises resolved by untutored, customized religious insights unavailable or even contrary to the letter of formal church teaching.

Sometimes, the institutionally unknown, novel, and contested religious memories alive in 98 percent of the Roman Catholic population rejuvenate the 2 percent of Catholics who exercise church authority. Though such memories may first appear divisive to church leaders, often their long-term effect is to lessen, if not prevent, arthritis in the vertical axis.

Thomas Reese's (1989, 1992, 1996) in-depth research on the structures and processes of Roman Catholic church authority indicates that religious *ressourcement* may also originate within the vertical axis itself. Reese tracks the often covert interplay of control and contest among popes, cardinals, and bishops. Though infrequent, inside reform may sometimes be overt, as in Pope John XXIII's 1959 call for an ecumenical council.

Michael McCallion and David Maines (1999) explore intra-institutional transformation in Roman Catholicism by taking up sociological "frame analysis" and social movement research. In particular, they look at change in religious liturgy. Since the Second Vatican Council, a class of professional liturgists has appeared; these practitioners are committed to a relatively egalitarian "People of God" theology inspired by conciliar documents. Through variously inserting this ideological "frame" into patterns of worship, these "oppositional insiders" press against the formally asymmetric relationship between priest and people.

The seemingly impressive power of adaptation detailed in these examinations has not sheltered Roman Catholicism from defection of worshippers, however. Statistical surveys in Europe and the Americas demonstrate that Mass attendance has not noticeably rebounded from the precipitous decline during the 1960s and 1970s. More Roman Catholics have converted to evangelical forms of Protestant Christianity. Fewer young people get married in the Roman Catholic Church, and an even smaller number become priests or nuns. The large population of divorced Roman Catholics typically leaves the church, alienated by what they perceive to be an arcane, duplicitous annulment process.

Disaffection with church authority also registers high in survey research. As more and more people around the world expect and demand operational transparency from the institutions that affect their lives, the procedures of the Roman Catholic hierarchy remain shrouded in secrecy. At a time when official church teaching encourages democratic forms of participation and oversight in worldwide political and cultural institutions, no formal structure allows lay people to check and balance the hierarchical, authoritarian power of their leadership. Coincidentally, these same church leaders use secular rational-legal systems to protect their own clergy—and themselves—from civil lawsuits.

Despite all this, most Roman Catholics stay in their church. Michele Dillon (1999) cites this seeming anomaly in her discussion of women. As profound as the work of women's religious orders has been, nothing matches the contribution women have made to the practical, day-to-day survival of Roman Catholic Christianity. From quietly praying with newborns and herding families to Mass, through organizing liturgies and planning parish fund-raisers, from handing out food baskets and editing church bulletins, to laundering altar linens and making coffee after Mass, women perform most of the practices which preserve everyday, local Roman Catholicism. Yet women continue to be excluded from priestly ordination and are largely prevented from holding positions of decision-making power in parishes and dioceses.

The glue Dillon finds securing women—whether conservative, liberal, or radical—to Roman Catholicism is the rich melange of symbols, stories, devotions, and rituals they claim as their own. When linked to memory, says Dillon in a 1998 book, these traditions remind most women that "their genealogy is entwined with a historically continuous church rather than a history of sectlike divisions. There is a disposition therefore to stay, rather than to leave, and to work towards transformation from within the tradition."

Dillon's observation touches on a growing theme in contemporary Roman Catholic research: the centrality of aesthetic resources for the understanding and exercise of Roman Catholic religiosity. Important to this renewed theological interest in beauty has been the English translations of Hans Urs von Balthasar's five-volume theological aesthetics, *The Glory of the Lord.* Critical too has been increased theological focus on culture. Works such as Roberto S. Goizueta's *Caminemos Con Jesús: Toward a Hispanic/Latino Theology of Accompaniment* (1995) show how attention to aesthetics discloses heretofore hidden theological resources in the cultural practices of the Roman Catholic laity.

Greeley points this out in terms of narrative when he insists that "religion is story before it is anything else and after it is everything else" (2000). Writtings such as John Shea's popular *Stories of Faith* (1980) have highlighted the role narrative plays in Roman Catholic religiosity.

Greeley signals another topic of current exploration when he observes that "religious sensibility is passed on by storytellers, most of whom are not aware that they are telling stories because their narratives reside more in who they are and what they do than in what they say" (2000). Several Roman Catholic investigations today probe the transmission of religiosity through such aesthetic embodiment, correcting for an earlier overemphasis on religious faith as a predominantly cognitive matter. Characteristically, Aidan Nichols comments that "nothing is in the intellect that is not first in the senses" (1996).

Interest in aesthetics and bodily senses has likewise created interest in the role of affectivity in the play of Roman Catholic Christianity. Important advances have been made, for example, in understanding how affections influence the moral life, as William C. Spohn explains in *Go and Do Likewise: Jesus and Ethics* (2000). This focus has also added novel twists to the much-explored field of Roman Catholic sacramentality. In *Extravagant Affections: A Feminist Sacramental Theology* (1998), Susan Ross creatively enjoins these dynamics, inviting one to consider the sacramentality of such actions as giving birth, cooking meals, mediating conflicts, and tending to the sick.

With this attention to Roman Catholicism as action, this overview of Roman Catholic studies returns to where it began. The focus on action in Roman Catholic research has lead scholars in many fresh directions, only a few of which have been outlined here. The overall effect of this quarter century of research has been to heighten appreciation for the rich complexity of Roman Catholicism. As its population center continues to shift from the Northern to the Southern Hemisphere, away from the comforts of middle-class existence to the soul-testing conditions of hunger and disease, the challenges confronting this multifaceted religious community will continue to be great indeed.

BIBLIOGRAPHY

Bailey, Gauvin Alexander. *Art on the Jesuit Missions in Asia and Latin America 1542–1773.* Toronto, 1999.

Bokenkotter, Thomas. *Church and Revolution: Catholics in the Struggle for Democracy.* New York, 1998.

Bryk, Anthony S., Valerie E. Lee, and Peter B. Holland. *Catholic Schools and the Common Good.* Cambridge, Mass., 1993.

Christiano, Kevin J., William H. Swatos, Jr., and Peter Kivisto. *Sociology of Religion: Contemporary Developments.* Walnut Creek, Calif., 2002.

Connerton, Paul. *How Societies Remember.* Cambridge, U.K., 1989.

Davidson, James D., Andrea S. Williams, Richard A. Lamanna, Jan Stenfenftenagel,

De la Torre, Renée. "The Catholic Diocese: A Transversalized Institution." *Journal of Contemporary Religion* 17 (2002): 303–316.

Dillon, Michele. *Catholic Identity: Balancing Reason, Faith, and Power.* New York, 1999.

Driskel, Paul Michael. *Representing Belief: Religion, Art and Society in Nineteenth- Century France.* University Park, Pa., 1992.

Duffy, Eamon. *The Stripping of the Altars: Traditional Religion in England c. 1400–c. 1580.* New Haven, Conn., 1992.

Goizueta, Roberto S. *Caminemos con Jesús: Toward a Hispanic/Latino Theology of Accompaniment.* Maryknoll, N.Y., 1995.

Grace, Gerald. *Catholic Schools: Mission, Markets, and Morality.* London, 2002.

Greeley, Andrew M. *The Catholic Myth: The Behavior and Beliefs of American Catholics.* New York, 1990.

Greeley, Andrew M. *The Catholic Imagination.* Berkeley, Calif., 2000.

Hoge, Dean R. "Core and Periphery in American Catholic Identity." *Journal of Contemporary Religion* 17 (2002): 293–302.

Ivereigh, Austin, ed. *The Politics of Religion in the Age of Revival: Studies in Nineteenth Century Europe and Latin America.* London, 2000.

Kowalewski, Mark R. "Firmness and Accommodation: Impression Management in Institutional Roman Catholicism." *Sociology of Religion* 54 (1993): 207–217.

Leys, Ad. *Ecclesiological Impacts of the Principle of Subsidiarity.* Kampen, Netherlands, 1995.

McCallion, Michael J., and David R. Maines. "The Liturgical Social Movement in the Vatican II Catholic Church." *Research in Social Movements, Conflicts and Change* 21 (1999): 125–149.

Mich, Marvin L. Krier. *Catholic Social Teaching and Movements.* Mystic, Conn., 1998.

Misner, Paul. *Social Catholicism in Europe: From the Onset of Industrialization to the First World War.* New York, 1991.

Morris, Charles. *American Catholic: The Saints and Sinners Who Built America's Most Powerful Church.* New York, 1997.

Morrow, Diane Batts. *Persons of Color and Religion at the Same Time: The Oblate Sisters of Providence, 1828–1860.* Chapel Hill, N.C., 2002.

Myers, Kathleen A., and Amanda Powell, eds. and trans. *A Wild Country Out in the Garden: The Spiritual Journals of a Colonial Mexican Nun.* Bloomington, Ind., 1999.

Nichols, Aidan. *Epiphany: A Theological Introduction to Catholicism.* Collegeville, Minn., 1996.

Reese, Thomas J. *Archbishop: Inside the Power Structure of the American Church.* San Francisco, 1989.

Reese, Thomas J. *A Flock of Shepherds: The National Conference of Catholic Bishops.* Kansas City, Mo., 1992.

Reese, Thomas J. *Inside the Vatican: The Politics and Organization of the Catholic Church.* Cambridge, Mass., 1996.

Ross, Susan A. *Extravagent Affections: A Feminist Sacramental Theology.* New York, 1998.

Schreiter, Robert J. *Constructing Local Theologies.* Maryknoll, N.Y., 1985.

Schreiter, Robert J. *The New Catholicity: Theology between the Global and the Local.* Maryknoll, N.Y., 1997.

Schuck, Michael J. *That They Be One: The Social Teaching of the Papal Encyclicals 1740–1989.* Washington, D.C., 1991.

Shea, John. *Stories of Faith.* Chicago, 1980.

Spohn, William C. *Go and Do Likewise: Jesus and Ethics.* New York, 2000.

Swidler, Ann. *Talk of Love: How Culture Matters.* Chicago, 2001.

Tilley, Terrance W. *Inventing Catholic Tradition.* Maryknoll, N.Y., 2000.

Weaver, Mary Jo, and R. Scott Appleby, eds. *Being Right: Conservative Catholics in America.* Bloomington, Ind., 1995.

Weigert, Kathleen Maas, William J. Whalen, and Patricia Wittberg. *The Search for Common Ground: What Unites and Divides Catholic Americans.* Huntington, Ind., 1997.

MICHAEL J. SCHUCK (2005)

ROMAN RELIGION

This entry consists of the following articles:

THE EARLY PERIOD
THE IMPERIAL PERIOD

ROMAN RELIGION: THE EARLY PERIOD

HISTORY OF SCHOLARSHIP. Although Roman religious institutions had been studied earlier (by, for example, Barnabé Brissonius, 1583), the differentiation between Greek and Roman religion within antique "heathendom" or "polytheism" was the work of nineteenth-century scholars. Concentrating on literary sources and on origins as described by ancient historiographers and critically reviewed by contemporary historians, the studies by J. A. Hartung (1836), Rudolph H. Klausen (1839), and J. A. Ambrosch (1839) marked the beginning of a scientific reconstruction of the religion of the city of Rome (and, marginally, of the religions of Italy). Under the impact of the extensive collection of inscriptions and the systematization of Roman law and the Roman "constitution" assembled by Theodor Mommsen (1817–1903), German scholars, especially Georg Wissowa (1859–1931), reconstructed authentic Roman religion as a body of sacral law and conservative ritualism informed by legal conceptions of deities. The Roman calendar, projected into the regal period as a document of early systematization, and the lost "books of the priests" (*libri sacerdotum*), transmitted in occasional antiquarian quotations only, formed the basis of the reconstruction.

Wissowa's handbook (1902/1912), with its detailed account of deities, temples, and rituals, dominated factual research in the twentieth century. Less successful were the more experiential or expressive interpretations of Roman rituals (e.g., Fowler, 1899 and 1911) and the attempts of Hermann Usener's school and James George Frazer to elucidate these rituals by ethnographic comparison, opening classical material to late-nineteenth-century evolutionary schemes (late resonances in Bailey [1932] and Wagenvoort [1947]). Drawing on comparative linguistics and mythology, Georges Dumézil interpreted Roman deities within an Indo-European framework of three basic "functions" (sovereignty, warfare, and agriculture). Dumézil's impact remained limited, but his attention to a mythology present in the guise of Roman historiography re-enlarged the objects of studies.

The quest for origins and "Wesen" (spiritiual substance) led to a neglect of the interaction with Hellenic culture (an important exception was Altheim, 1930), visible already in the archaeology of early Rome (Foro Boario), and with Italian religions that were increasingly subjected to Roman domination and increasingly present in Rome. Thus the reinterpretation of public Roman religion within the framework of a more skeptical and more sociological image of the history of Roman political institutions (see Beard et al., 1998) must be supplemented by intensified research in Italian imagery and architecture (e.g., Wiseman, 1995, 2000; Coarelli, 1987), as well as a new look at late republican literature (e.g., Feeney, 1998; Barchiesi, Rüpke, and Stevens, 2004) and extra-urban inscriptions.

SOURCES. Any attempt at a historical reconstruction of republican Roman religion has to rely on a critical reading of early Augustan historiography (late first century BCE). With a few exceptions (e.g., Plautus's comedies from the early second century BCE, Cato the Elder, some inscriptions), contemporary literary evidence is lacking before the intensively documented first century. The most important antiquarian source, Marcus Terentius Varro (116–27 BCE), is mostly known through quotations from imperial times and late antiquity (Augustine, Servius) only. Although the calendar, including information on many temple foundation days, is known from a wall painting from shortly before the Julian calendar reform in 45 BCE, an extended epigraphical culture did not begin until the reign of Augustus (r. 27 BCE–14 CE). Temple structures and fragments of architectural decor have been excavated, but the archaeological record of altars, reliefs, and statues is entirely dominated by the imperial rebuilding of Rome. However, a unique coinage features individual religious motifs from the late second century BCE onward.

Major advances have been made in locating, documenting, and interpreting new archaeological and epigraphic sources outside Rome. Major findings of votive objects at different sites in Italy allow the reconstruction of the production, usage, local variations, and overarching trends, and help put the Roman material (mostly recovered from the Tiber) into context. Local archaeological research in the Roman colonies and a new edition and commentary on republican laws and statues (Crawford, 1996) have clarified the processes of expansion and Romanization. In addition, new archaeological methods used at excavations at Osteria dell'Osa (Bietti Sestieri, 1992) and other sites have added to the collections of funerary ware and provided insights into the formation and changes of early Italian pre-urban societies.

A history of Roman religion is impossible for any period before the fifth century BCE, even though the archaeological record attests important religious sites and enables a reconstruction of the history of the early Forum Romanum (an unhesitatingly optimistic stance is taken by Carandini, 1997). Structurally, Rome has to be seen as a Latin city under Etruscan domination, increasingly establishing direct commercial and cultural relationships with (Italian) Greek and Punic cities.

ROMAN AND ITALIAN RELIGION. "Roman religion" is an analytical concept that is used to describe religious phenomena in the ancient city of Rome and to relate the growing variety of cults to the political and social structure of the city. Although Rome gradually became the dominant power in Italy during the third century BCE, as well as the capital of an empire during the second century BCE, its religious institutions and their administrative scope only occasionally extended beyond the city and its nearby surroundings (*ager Romanus*). Nothing is known about the religious structure of the early Roman colonies in Italy. The establishment of towering Capitolia (replicas of the threefold temple on the Roman Capitoline hill, dedicated to Jupiter [*Iuppiter*], Juno [*Iuno*], and Minerva) had no structural necessity, but represented infrequent individual efforts to acquire prestige and demonstrate loyalty. Intense contacts led to manifold processes of exchange, the direction of which could hardly be ascertained. From the second century BCE onward, intense urbanization led municipal elites to the reception of Roman models of administration and representation. The most visible effect of this process was the parallel Hellenization of the cities and townships.

The resulting similarities were due to competition among the cities, as well as adaptation from the cultural centers, including Rome, Athens, and Alexandria. The resulting Mediterranean *koiné* remains an object for further research. The process itself intensified in imperial times. The religious profile of Pompeii during the first centuries BCE and CE is neither Oscan nor Roman, but rather a local variant of Mediterranean polis religion. The pantheon of the Umbrian town of Iguvium contained a grouping of three gods parallel to the Roman Capitoline triad: Iou, Mart, and Vofiono, all bearing the common epithet Grabovio (its meaning is obscure). This similarity between the two pantheons is all the more apparent since *Vofiono* is the exact linguistic equivalent of *Quirinus,* even to its adjectival form *-no-,* derived from a nominal root. Yet the *tabulae Iguvinae,* the Iguvine tablets from the second and first centuries BCE, are not an independent attestation of an Indo-European structure, but rather the religious product of a city with confederate status from the first half of the third century BCE onward. That is not to deny the importance of local and translocal cultures independent of or even superior or opposed to Rome (e.g., the religious conceptions and symbols of the Etruscan elites and the Greeks of Magna Graecia, located to the south of the Volturno River). The Roman solar calendar did not even replace middle Italian and Etruscan lunisolar calendars until the first century BCE. And yet the Iguvine documents in Oscan language use Latin letters in their later section, and they attest an interest in documenting rituals that cannot be separated from the cultural developments of the whole peninsula, subjected to Roman rule.

Basic concepts. The idea of obligation lies at the very root of the Romans' attitude toward the gods, and it is expressed in the word *religio.* If the modern languages of the Western world (both Romance and Germanic) have failed to translate this word and have settled on a simple copy thereof (*religion, religione*), the reason lies in the fact that this idiom is untranslatable. Indeed, in the ancient world there was no Greek equivalent. All the expressions that one can bring to mind by analogy—*sebas* (respect for the gods), *proskunesis* (adoration), *eulabeia* (reverential fear), *threskeia* (cult)—fall far short of filling the semantic range of *religio.* Careful examination shows that the Latins, who were not concerned with philological rigor, connected *religio* more with the verb *religare* (to tie), alluding to the bonds between gods and humans, than with the verb *relegere* (to take up again with care). Such as it is, *religio* expresses a fundamental preoccupation manifested in two complementary ways: the care taken to avoid divine wrath, and the desire to win the benevolence and favor of the gods. It was the Romans' inner conviction that without the accord of the gods they could not succeed in their endeavors. This explains the solemn declaration of Cicero (106–43 BCE) proclaiming the Roman people to be "the most religious in the world" (*De natura deorum* 2.3).

This preoccupation is evident throughout the history of Livy (59 BCE–17 CE). Roman accomplishments rise and fall in complete rhythm with the disfavor or favor evinced by the gods. A revealing example is furnished in the Romans' desperation following the sack of Rome by the Gauls (in 390 BCE by Varronian chronology, but probably, according to a Polybian synchronism, to be dated to 387/6). Overwhelmed, they were nearly resolved to abandon the ruins of their city, at the instigation of their tribunes, in order to emigrate to Veii. It was then that M. Furius Camillus, the predestined leader (*dux fatalis)* and dictator who conquered Veii in 396, and now the restorer of the situation in Rome, lit upon the decisive argument that inspired the mood reversal of the assembly: to abandon Rome, many times endowed with heavenly blessings since its origins, would be to commit sacrilege. In the course of his address, Camillus called to mind this permanent lesson for the benefit of his listeners: "Consider the events of these last years, whether successes or reversals. You will find that everything succeeded when we followed the gods, and everything failed when we scorned them" (Livy, 5.51.4).

Ideas as *religio* were not reflected upon before the very end of the Republic. It was under the influence of Greek philosophy that some Roman authors (usually at the end of their political career) started to systematically reflect upon their own religious tradition in order to clarify concepts. Cicero is the foremost exponent, realizing in his books *On the Nature of the Gods, On Divination,* and *On Fate* a multivolume theological project. However, his reflections on religion did not arrive at a unified concept: *religio* was a feeling of obligation; *pietas* (piety), a corresponding attitude; and *sacra* (rituals) and *caerimonia* (forms of veneration), were the way to put *religio* and *pietas* into practice.

Because a general concept of religion as a system of actions and ideas was lacking, no corresponding concept of "sacred law" could exist. There were rules to be followed in matters of divine property, divination, and priests, but they did not add up to a *ius sacrum,* a phrase that did not exist in antiquity. And even these rules were flexible, matters of debate, traditions frequently fixed only under the impact of the encounter with Greek critical thought. The term *Roman religion,* therefore, encompasses what belongs to our modern concept of religion.

Early Iron Age Latium. It is not before the beginning of the first millennium BCE (between the end of the Bronze Age and the beginning of the Iron Age) that it becomes possible to identify traits of a Latin material culture attesting to an ethnogenesis in the plain south of the lower course of the Tiber, a territory that was bordered on the northwest by the Tiber and the hills north of it, and on the northeast by the (later) Sabine mountainous area. On the east this area was bound by the Alban chain from the mountains of Palombara, Tivoli (Tibur), Palestrina (Praeneste), and Cori (Cora) as far as Terracina (Anxur) and Circeo (Circei), and to the west was the shore of the Tyrrhenian Sea. Small settlements formed in this area within a population that was melted together from (probably) local people and immigrants from the north and northeast. Scholars know nothing of their religion apart from the tombs attesting inhumation, as well as cremation. At Rome traces of earlier presences of humans have been found, but continuous settlements on places like the Palatine started around the tenth century. From around 830 BCE onward, smaller settlements took shape at privileged places of the plain, a proto-urban phase.

It is possible to give some detail of the conditions of life in these population centers. They drew their sustenance mainly from animal husbandry and from the exploitation of natural resources (salt, fruit, and game). Their inhabitants progressively took up agriculture in pace with the clearing of the woods and the draining of the marshes, at the same time making pottery and iron tools. Their language belonged to the Indo-European family. The first document in the Latin language may be an inscription on a golden brooch from Praeneste, dated to the end of the seventh century: "manios med fhefhaked numasioi" (in classical Latin: "Manius me fecit Numerio" ["Manius made me for Numerius"]). However, the authenticity of this inscription is doubtful.

The placing and the contents of tombs attest to growing social differentiation and the formation of gentilician groups; urns in the form of oblong huts are characteristic. At Osteria dell'Osa of the ninth century, cremation served as a social marker that separated outstanding male warriors—recognizable by miniature weapons—from the rest of the population.

Social differentiation was certainly furthered by the presence of Greeks in Italy from 770 BCE onward who could serve as traders and agents in long-distance contacts with the southern and eastern part of the Mediterranean. The Orientalizing period (c. 730–630 BCE) is present in the form of luxury tombs, princely burials with highly valuable and prestigious objects in sites around Rome (Praeneste, Ficana, Castel di Decima [= Politorium?]), though not in Rome itself. Social power offered the possibility of acquiring wealth and long-distance contacts; such contacts and goods served to further prestige.

Early Rome. The urbanization of Rome could be inferred from the paving of the Forum and the removal of preceding huts around 650 BCE to form a central and common space soon to be enlarged and surrounded by a growing number of stone buildings from 600 onward. A site adjacent to the Comitium paved with black stones (*lapis niger*) probably marked an open sanctuary to the god Vulcan. Another building that at least later on served as a cultic center, the Regia (king's palace), was built during the sixth century. It should be noted that Greek influence is visible in the arrangement of the central "political" space, as it is in archaeological details. The archaeological remnants of the earliest temples of the Forum Boarium (San Omobono), the cattle market on the border of the Tiber, are decorations by Greek artisans.

The most impressive testimony to early Rome's relation to the Mediterranean world dominated by the Greeks is the building project of the Capitoline temple of Jupiter Optimus Maximus (Jove [*Iove*] the Best and Greatest), Juno, and Minerva, dateable to the latter part of the sixth century. By its sheer size the temple competes with the largest Greek sanctuaries, and the grouping of deities suggests that that was intended. The investment in the quality of the terracotta statuary (Varro in Pliny the Elder, *Historia naturalis* 35.157) points to the same intention. The actual size of the late-sixth-century city remains debated, but even as a larger city with international contacts, as shown by the treaty with Carthage, Rome was but one of the Latium townships. The conquests attributed to regal Rome in the Roman annalistic tradition were made up from a painful series of conflicts that ended with the Latin wars in 340 to 338 BCE. The Latin league was dissolved and the Latins were incorporated into the Roman community.

Parallel to the central investment of resources, the luxury of individual tombs—unlike in Etruscan centers—receded. Yet it would be erroneous to assume a highly centralized state. During republican times, even warfare was an enterprise frequently organized on a gentilician basis, as the institutions of the *fetiales* (legates that established the involvement or disinvolvement of the community as a whole into predatory conflicts) and the *lapis Satricanus* demonstrate. This dedicatory inscription from around 500 BCE, found at Satricum (northeast of Antium), accompanied a dedication to the warrior god Mars by followers *(sodales)* of a certain Poplios Valesius.

Religion of the early period. Our image of the early period is far drier than the colorful narratives of late republican and Augustan times, transmitted especially by the historians Livy and Dionys of Halikarnassos. The earliest phase was organized narratively in the form of a diptych: the "providential" passage from the "savage" state to the "civilized" state. The narrative by Cicero follows this form (*De republica* 2.4). He first evokes the divine origin of the twins Romulus and Remus, born of the god Mars and the Vestal Virgin Rhea Silvia. Romulus and Remus were left exposed on the banks of the Tiber by their granduncle Amulius, king of Alba Longa, but were then miraculously saved by the intervention of a nursing wolf. The author draws a contrast between the pastoral phase, which saw the assertion of the authority of Romulus (the elimination of Remus is passed over in silence), and the civilizing phase of the city's founder.

Within the succession of seven kings, Romulus, the founder, and Numa, the second king, shared in the establishment of important institutions like central cults and priesthoods. Yet the picture of the net of traditions is complex: Numa is said to be a pupil of the southern Italian philosopher Pythagoras; King Tullius was killed in his attempts to manipulate flashes in secret rites.

As stated above, the archaeological record of temples remains meager. Nevertheless the statues of the temples of San Omobono belie later reconstructions of pure origins. A remark by Varro (*Antiquitates rerum divinarum* frg. 18, Cardauns, quoted by Augustine, *De civitate Dei* 4.31) deserves attention: "For more than 170 years, the Romans worshiped their gods without statues. If this custom had prevailed, the gods would be honored in a purer fashion." This reference to a lost state of purity (*castitas*) is an indirect criticism of the Hellenic anthropomorphism that attributed human passions and vices to the gods, as in Homer's *Iliad* or in Hesiod's *Theogony.*

Rituals can be hypothetically reconstructed only on the basis of much larger attestations that try to account for social changes and external influences. Despite the probable short presence of Etruscan rule in the sixth century, symbols of power and some public rituals seem to have been heavily influenced by Etruscan models, perhaps indicating "self-Etruscanization" rather than conscious implantation by Etruscan tyrants. Etruscan influence is evident in the central position of the monthly festival of the full moon, the ides (*eidus*), dedicated to Jupiter (Macrobius, *Saturnalia* 1.15.14–16). Etruscan influence is also probable for the processional ritual and the chariot races of such old games as the Equirria. Chariots had been aristocratic prestige objects since the Orientalizing period, and they were no longer in use in middle Italian warfare by the end of the sixth century BCE.

Religion and topography. Late republican tradition and religious practice included festivals related to topographical situations that might date back to regal or early republican times. The topographical grid that corresponds to the feast of the Septimontium, celebrated on December 11, reflects already an extended township. The three knolls of the Palatine region (Palatium, Cermalus, Velia) are joined with the three knolls of the Esquiline group (Fagutal, Oppius, Cispius), along with the Subura (the Caelius was added later to this list of seven names). These are the stages of the procession that the abridger Sextus Pompeius Festus outlines for this feast, but in a different order, probably in line with the liturgical itinerary. The list is borrowed, as is known, from the scholar M. Verrius Flaccus: Palatium, Velia, Fagutal, Subura, Cermalus, Oppius, Caelius, Cispius.

At a later stage of topographical development the city was divided into four regions: Palatina, Esquilina, Suburana, and Collina, the last comprising the Quirinal and the Viminal. Surrounding walls were constructed. Tradition attributes these initiatives to the next-to-last king, Servius Tullius. Recent archaeological discoveries have verified a notable territorial extension of the city during the sixth century. As for the ramparts, if the date of the wall made by Servius in *opus quadratum* should be advanced to the fourth century, after the burning of Rome by the Gauls, the existence of walls in the sixth century is nonetheless established by the vestiges of an *agger* found on the Quirinal. The discovery at Lavinium of a rampart in *opus quadratum* dating from the sixth century leads, analogously to the Roman situation, to the same conclusion.

A comparison of different cults gives profile to the development—again hypothetically, for contemporary evidence is lacking and the possibility of archaizing constructions of rituals cannot be ruled out. The latter is illustrated by the ritual of the declaration of war that is described by Livy (1.32) and was performed by Octavianus before the war against Cleopatra and Antonius. The antiquarian account supposes a fetial priest throwing a spear across the border of the hostile territory. The spear is made of cornel wood hardened by fire, without an iron point. This account forms the backdrop of the same rite being performed by Octavian in 32 BCE in the city of Rome (Dio, *Roman history* 50.4.4–5), allegedly on "hostile" territory ritually set apart for that purpose (Servius, *Ad Aeneidum* 9.52). The new ritual made the observers forget that they were witnessing the opening of a major civil war, turning a ritual gesture, earlier attested for the general leading his army, into an archaized priestly activity: the late use of iron was part of Roman historical knowledge.

The Lupercalia, celebrated on February 15, delimited the very cradle of the city. On that date "the old Palatine stronghold ringed by a human flock" (Varro, *De lingua Latina*) was purified by naked Luperci (a variety of wolf-men, dressed in loincloths), who, armed with whips, would flog the public. Everything about this ceremony—the "savage" rite (see Cicero, *Pro Caelio* 26) and the territorial circumscription—demonstrates its extreme archaism.

The feast of Septimontium on December 11 designated, as its name suggested, a more extended territory. It involved no one except the inhabitants of the *montes* (mountains). These seven mountains (which are not to be confused with the seven hills of the future Rome) are the following: the knolls of the Palatium, the Germalus, the Velia (which together would make up the Palatine), the Fagutal, the Oppius, the Cespius (which three would be absorbed by the Esquiline), and the Caelius (Sextus Pompeius Festus, while still asserting the number of seven *montes,* adds the Subura to this list). This amounted, then, to an intermediary stage between the primitive nucleus and the organized city. One will note the use of the word *mons* to designate these knolls, as opposed to *collis,* which would be reserved for referring to the northern hills.

The feast of the Argei, which required two separate rituals at two different times (on March 16 and 17, and on May 14), marks the last stage. It involved a procession in March in which mannequins made of rushes (Ovid, *Fasti* 5.621) were carried to the twenty-seven chapels prepared for this purpose. On May 14 they were taken out of the chapels and cast into the Tiber from the top of a bridge, the Pons Sublicius, in the presence of the pontiff and the Vestal Virgins. There are different opinions on the meaning of the ceremony. Wissowa saw in it a ritual of substitution taking the place of human sacrifices. (A note by Varro, *De lingua Latina* 7.44, specifies that these mannequins were human in shape.) However, Kurt Latte prefers to compare these mannequins of rushes to *oscilla* (figurines or small masks that were hung from trees), which absorbed the impurities that were to be purged from the city. The itinerary of the procession shows that it corresponds to the final stage of the city's development, the Rome of the *quattuor regiones* (four regions). Varro outlined the procession as follows: it proceeded through the heights of the Caelius, the Esquiline, the Viminal, the Quirinal, and the Palatine, and encircled the Forum—henceforth located in the heart of the city.

An important line, at least legitimated by religious arguments in later times, was the *pomerium*, separating the area of *domi* (at home, at peace) and *militiae* (the area of warfare and the unlimited power of the war leader). What was this *pomerium*? According to Varro (*De lingua Latina* 5.143), it was a circle within the surrounding wall marked by stones and describing the limit inside of which urban auspices had to be taken. Rome included sectors outside the pomerial zone that were still part of the city: the Aventine Hill, which had been outside the city of the four regions (its incorporation into the city was attributed by tradition sometimes to Romulus and sometimes to Ancus Marcius), remained outside the pomerial zone until the time of Claudius (first century CE), even though it was surrounded by what was called "Servius's wall."

The same extrapomerial status held true for the Field of Mars, which owed its name to the military exercises that were conducted on its esplanade. Yet here there occurs a further practice that lies at the root of Roman law. On this emplacement there was an altar consecrated to Mars from time immemorial. It is mentioned by the "royal" law of Numa in relation to the distribution of the *spolia opima* (spoils taken from an enemy's general slain by one's own army commander) and was completed later by the erection of a temple in 138 BCE. The assemblies of military centuries (*comitia centuriata*) were also held there. In addition, every five years the purification of the people (*lustrum*) was celebrated on the Field of Mars by the sacrifice of the *suovetaurilia,* the set of three victims—boar, ram, and bull—that had been paraded beforehand around the assembly of citizens. The presence of the old Mars outside the *pomerium* (similarly, another temple of Mars, constructed in 338 BCE to the south of Rome outside the Porta Capena, was also outside the pomerial zone) was in strict conformity with the distinction established between the *imperium domi,* the jurisdiction of civil power circumscribed by the pomerial zone, and the *imperium militiae* that could not show itself except outside this zone. This is why it was necessary to take other auspices when one wanted to go from one zone to another. If one failed to do so, every official act was nullified. This misfortune befell the father of the Gracchi, T. Sempronius Gracchus, during his presidency of the *comitia centuriata.* While going back and forth between the Senate and the Field of Mars, he forgot to take the military auspices again; as a result, the election of consuls that took place in the midst of the assemblies when he returned was rejected by the Senate (see Cicero, *De divinatione* 1.33 and 2.11). The delimitation of Roman sacral space by the pomerial line explains the distribution of the sanctuaries. Vesta, the goddess of the public hearth, could only be situated at the heart of the city within the *pomerium,* whereas a new arrival, such as Juno Regina, originating in Veii, was received, as an outsider, in a temple built on the Aventine (in 392 BCE).

Early festivals and priests. The calendar of festivals reflected and conventionalized temporal rhythms. The preparation for warfare finds ritual reflection in some festivals and in the ritual activities of the priesthood of the Salii in the month of March, the opening month of the year. Mars is the god presiding over warfare; the Salians performed dances clad in archaic warrior dress and cared for archaically formed shields in the shape of an eight. Agricultural and pastoral festivals could be found in the month of April, the Parilia with their lustration of cattle being probably the oldest one (April 21). Fordicidia, the killing of pregnant cows (April 15); the Cerialia (April 19), named after the goddess of cereals; the Vinalia, a wine festival (April 23); and the Robigalia, featuring the sacrifice of a dog to further the growing of the grain (April 25), might denote old rituals, too. Series of festivals in August and December, addressed to gods related to the securing of the harvest and abundance, might have produced other foci of communal and urban ritualizing of the economic activities of farmsteads. The subordination of the festival listed to the monthly—originally empirical, later fictitious—lunar phases of the developed calendar warns of the assumption of complex festival cycles, too easily postulated by scholars like Dumézil. The same warning holds true for the postulation of complex cycles of initiation rites (Torelli, 1984). Sociologically, Rome was not a tribal society, but a precarious public of gentilician leaders and their followers and an increasingly incoherent urban population. What looks like initiatory phenomena are rites reserved mostly for young aristocrats organized as representative priesthoods.

The concept of priesthood, however, is far from clear for the early period. At least from the late fourth century BCE onward, the public priesthoods underwent a process of politicization, adapting these lifelong roles and the modes of accession to the model of annual magistracies. The preceding phase might have been one of a sacralization of ousted political positions that once combined political and religious authority. Such an interpretation is particularly plausible for the figures of the *rex* and the *regina sacrorum* (king and queen of the rites), who took care of important routine rites in the course of the month and year, but did not have any significant political or even religious competence in historical times. The Regia on the Forum Romanum formed one of the centers of their cult activities; it must have been part of a complex that embraced the *atrium* and *aedes Vestae* as well. Here, the Vestal Virgins, six in number, resided and performed. Under the direction of a *virgo maxima,* their essential mission was to maintain the public hearth in the *aedes Vestae.* Their service lasted thirty years and enjoyed great prestige (Cicero, *Pro Fonteio* 48). Their liturgical importance is confirmed by two significant points. Once a year, they would make their way to the king in order to ask him: "Are you vigilant, king? Be vigilant!" On another solemn occasion, the *virgo maxima* mounted the Capitolium in the company of the *pontifex maximus* (Horace, *Carmina* 3.30.8).

Drawing on the legendary figure of the seer Attus Navius, it might be asked whether a slow integration of charismatic religious figures into an organized public college of *augurs* would also be a possible line of development. In either case, the shift from regal to consular rule, from kingdom to Republic, would have been of the utmost importance.

Private worship is attested by votives from early on; Lavinium features dedications from the seventh century BCE. Like several larger sanctuaries in the surroundings, it might have drawn clients from the city. Migrant artisans offered their services at the sanctuaries on a temporal basis; mass production, not individual expression, forms the economic basis of this form of material documentation of piety, even in lower social strata.

The regional context. *Latium Vetus*, or *Latium Antiquum*, was augmented later on by the *Latium Adiectum*, or *Latium Novum* (New Latium), formed by the territories won from the Volsci, the Aequi, the Hernici, and the Aurunci by conquests or federations (see Pliny the Elder, *Historia naturalis* 3.68–70). Traditionally, the Latins are called *populi Latini* (Latin peoples) or by the collective noun *nomen Latinum* (Latin nation). In the historical epoch, older structures, including those around the sanctuary of Jupiter Latiaris on Mons Albanus and those surrounding the sanctuary of Diana Aricina located in "the sacred grove" of Aricia (Nemus Dianae), were preserved by religious federations based on common cults.

Another federal cult would play an important role in history because it held privileged ties with the Romans. This cult was centered at Lavinium, which Varro (*De lingua Latina* 5.144) identifies as the religious metropolis of Rome: "Lavinium:. . .ibi di Penates nostri" ("Lavinium:. . . there are our household gods"). Excavations have uncovered the site, which includes a necropolis dating back to the tenth century BCE. There are also ruins of ramparts dating from the sixth century, the vestiges of a house of worship flanked by thirteen altars, and a mausoleum (it could be a *heroion* in memory of Aeneas) that houses an archaic tomb from the seventh century BCE. Thousands of votives attest the appeal of a healing sanctuary for several centuries. In the imperial period, the religious existence of the city was preserved in the form of a symbolic community, whose offices were assigned like priesthoods to members of the Roman equestrian class.

The integration of federal cults into Roman dominance could follow different routes. The Romans' capacity for adaptation to different circumstances is evident here in an especially remarkable way, as illustrated by the following three cases.

One of the most ancient federal cults presupposes the original preeminence of the ancient city of Alba Longa: the *Feriae Latinae* (Latin holidays) were celebrated at the summit of the Alban Hills in honor of Jupiter Latiaris. In earlier times, the Latins had been granted an equal share of the sacrifice, which consisted of a white bull (this detail, coming from Arnobius in *Adversus nationes* 2.68, would show that the ordinary rule, which provided a castrated victim for Jupiter, did not apply here). Once the consecrated entrails *(exta)* were offered to the god, all in attendance would share the meat, thus demonstrating their bonds of community. After the destruction of Alba Longa, Rome quite naturally picked up the thread of this tradition by incorporating the *Feriae Latinae* as a movable feast into its liturgical calendar. Still, the attitude of the Romans was selective: even though they transferred the entire Alban population to Rome itself, they kept the Alban celebrations in their usual locations. They simply built a temple to Jupiter Latiaris where previously there was only a *lucus*, a sacred grove. During the historical epoch, the Roman consuls, accompanied by representatives of the state, would make their way to the federal sanctuary shortly after assuming their responsibilities and would preside there over the ceremonies. The *Feriae Latinae* had come under Roman control.

The conduct of the Romans was very different with regard to the federal cult of Diana. Tradition places this cult at Aricia near Lake Nemi, which is known as the *speculum Dianae*, "mirror of Diana" (Servius, *Ad Aeneidem* 7.515). An archaic rite determined that the priest of Diana's sacred grove, called the *rex nemorensis*, could hold office there until he was killed by his successor in single combat (the point of departure of J. G. Frazer's *Golden Bough)*. During the historical period, this odd priesthood attracted only fugitive slaves. The federal altar had been consecrated to Diana by the Latin dictator Egerius Laevius, a native of Tusculum. Tusculum was the center of a federation of Latin towns, established perhaps after the disappearance of Alba Longa. When the cult came under Roman authority, it was transferred into the city on the extrapomerial hill of the Aventine. It had nothing there at first except an altar, then a temple that Varro acknowledges as having federal status: *commune Latinorum templum*. Yet this status was only one of appearance, since no assembly of Latin cities is recorded as ever having occurred on the Aventine during the Roman period, any more than at Aricia. Another point is significant: the anniversary of the temple fell on the ides of August and bore the name *Dies Servorum* (slaves' day). Whatever interpretation one gives to this designation, the fact remains that the cult of Diana was not of concern either on the Aventine or in Aricia. This time Rome had reduced a federal cult to a suitable level. In contrast with Jupiter Latiaris, Diana, whose name is a semantic homologue of *Jupiter* (since both names were formed from the root **diu;* she signified nocturnal light, just as he signified the light of day), was doomed to fade gradually away. Identified with Artemis, she would be invoked in Horace's *Carmen saeculare* as the sister of Apollo.

The relations that Rome held with Lavinium were very different. In the Roman mind, Lavinium had the same resonance as the Alban Hills, judging from the discourse that Livy attributes to the dictator Camillus. Camillus did not hesitate to put these two high places on the same level: "Our ancestors entrusted to us the celebration of religious ceremonies on Mount Alban and in Lavinium." In reality, the latter ranked higher than the former. Varro (*De lingua Latina* 5.144) specifies it as the source of Roman lineage and the cradle of the Roman *penates.* Lavinium benefited from a continual deference on the part of the Romans after the treaty that tradition traced back to the time of T. Tatius (Livy, 1.14.2). This deference was evident in the ritual processions of higher magistrates to the *penates* and to Vesta as they entered their office and as they left it. The deference was likewise evident in the annual pilgrimages by the pontiffs and the consuls to the sanctuary of Aeneas Indiges, which Ascanius is reputed to have built for his divinized father. If one considers that Lavinium was also the cradle of the religion of Venus, who was understood according to Trojan legend to be the *Aeneadum genetrix* ("mother of the descendants of Aeneas"), one can imagine that this exceptional site exerted in every way a great attraction for the Romans.

Archaeology has recently made an important contribution concerning the territory of Lavinium by bringing to light, among other things, a *heroion* (temple) from the fourth century BCE, constructed upon an archaic tomb (which its discoverer, Paolo Sommella, identifies as the mausoleum of Aeneas) and a set of thirteen altars, of which twelve were in use in the middle of the fourth century. They may have served a new Latin federation presided over by Rome. Indeed, Rome did not stop at destroying the Latin confederation in 338 BCE, but also reinforced the privileges of Lavinium. For Lavinium, as Livy points out (8.11.15), had added to its titles the merit of loyalty by refusing to join the Latin revolt. It brought even more renown upon itself as a pilgrimage center. Thus Rome's attitude toward federal cults was definitively shown under three very different aspects: sometimes Rome assumed them (Alba Longa), sometimes Rome restricted them (Aricia), and sometimes Rome exalted them (Lavinium).

Conceptions of the divine. The Latin word designating divinity has an Indo-European origin. *Deus,* which phonetically comes from the ancient *deivos* (just as *dea* comes from *deiva*), means "heavenly being." In line with this etymology, *deus* and *dea* represent for the Latins powers in relation to the luminous sky *(divum),* in opposition to humans *(homo),* who are bound to the earth *(humus), homo* itself being a derivative of an Indo-European word meaning "earth." One immediate consequence of this is the fact that the Latin noun is distinguished from its Greek homologue *theos,* which takes its meaning from a different etymology: *theos* probably is connected with the prototype **thesos,* which refers to the sphere of the sacred (Émile Benveniste), though no one has been able to specify the limits of its meaning. We note, however, that this difference of vocabulary between the Latin and the Greek in naming the divinity fades at the level of the supreme god: *Iuppiter (*Iou-pater,* with **Iou-* deriving from **dyeu-*) and *Zeus (*dyeus)* both go back to the same Indo-European root. It also follows that the Latins represented the divinity as an individual and personal being. This linguistic fact at once discredits the "animist" or pre-animist notion that would postulate a pre-deist phase in Rome which would have preceded the advent of the personal divinity.

And yet, compared to the gods of Homer's Greek pantheon, the Roman gods lack in personality. They lack the embellishments of a mythology that is more or less abundant with picturesque variations. They were mainly defined by their specific competence, far from any tie with the human condition. Wissowa (1912) observed that there was no marriage or union between gods and goddesses at Rome. This fact is particularly verified by the existence of many divinized abstractions, such as Fides, the goddess of good faith, who received each year the common homage of three major priests. They would come in an open chariot to her chapel to ask her to preserve harmonious relations within the city. Also, Ceres, the etymology of whose name places her in charge of growth (especially of grains), appears as the background to the feast of the Cerialia, which was celebrated annually on April 19. These, then, are not minor divinities, nor is Consus, the god of grain storage (*condere,* "to store"), who was celebrated at the time of the Consualia on August 21, as well as at the time of the Opiconsiva on August 25, when he was in association with Ops, the goddess who watched over abundance. As for Janus (*Ianus*), god of beginnings and of passages, and Vesta, the goddess of the sacred fire, their importance in the Roman liturgy was such, as reported by Cicero (*De natura deorum* 2.67), that the former shared in the beginning of every religious ceremony, while the latter was invoked at the end.

Did this tendency toward divinized abstraction lend itself to excesses? One readily cites the example of the minor specialist gods that assisted Ceres in her functions, according to Fabius Pictor (quoted by Servius Danielis, *Ad Georgica* 1.21): Vervactor (for the plowing of fallow land), Reparator (for the renewal of cultivation), Imporcitor (for marking out the furrows), Insitor (for sowing), Obarator (for plowing the surface), Occator (for harrowing), Sarritor (for weeding), Subruncinator (for hoeing), Messor (for harvesting), Convector (for carting the harvest), Conditor (for storage), and Promitor (for distribution). Another group of minor divinities gave Augustine of Hippo occasion for sarcastic comments in detailing its list. This group included lesser divine entities who were regarded as aiding the husband on his wedding night: Virginensis (to loosen the belt of the young virgin), Subigus (to subdue her), and Prema (to embrace her). "And what is the goddess Pertunda [from *pertundere,* "to penetrate"] doing here? Let her blush, let her flee! Let her leave the husband something to do! It is really a disgrace that someone else besides himself is fulfilling the duty that this goddess's name embodies" (*De civitate dei* 6.9.264–265).

What can be said about all this? Whatever the merit of these lists of specialized divinities (the first one, transmitted by Servius, is guaranteed by the quality of the source: Fabius Pictor, the author of books on pontifical law, contemporary with Cato the Elder), one can observe that they name only secondary entities that are served by no particular priest (even though the Roman institution recognized the *flamines minores,* the "lesser priests"). Nor did they appear in the liturgical calendar. Moreover, these entities moved in the wake of top-level divinities. This trait is expressly brought out by the list of lesser specialists who gravitate toward Ceres: the *flamen* (priest) of this goddess invokes them when he offers, during the Cerialia, the sacrifice to Tellus (earth) and to Ceres. Everything indicates that the same applies to the list drawn up by Augustine: all those names fit easily within the circle of Juno Pronuba, protector of marriages. They demonstrate the analytic abilities of pontifical experts and their concern for accompanying each phase of an activity with a religious factor. Finally, this tendency to divine miniaturization corresponds to a kind of luxuriant manifestation of the inclination of Roman pontiffs toward abstract analysis. At the same time it should not be forgotten that the Romans started to put their religion into writing from the third century BCE onward. It is difficult to ascertain which degree of systematization had been reached before the writing process began.

These divine abstractions exist in both masculine and feminine forms, without any interference between the two. The apparent exceptions are only illusory. Thus it is that Faunus has no feminine counterpart. (His name's meaning is uncertain; it has sometimes been compared by the ancients with *fari,* "to talk," as in Varro, *De lingua Latina* 7.36, and sometimes with *favere,* "to be favorable," as in Servius Danielis, *Ad Georgica* 1.10; this god had been assimilated to the Greek Pan, as is confirmed by the location of his temple, erected in 194 BCE on the Isle of the Tiber, in the extrapomerial zone.) Indeed, Fauna seems to be an artificial construction of syncretic casuistry that attempted to associate her with Faunus as either wife or sister or daughter (Wissowa, 1912). Her name was later confused with Fatua and with Bona Dea (an appellation also used in turn by Damia, a goddess originating in Tarentum).

The same holds true for Pales, the goddess whose feast, the Parilia, occurred on April 21, the anniversary of the foundation of Rome. (In contrast, two Pales appear on the date of July 7 on the pre-Julian calendar of the town of Antium. Nothing prevents us from considering these as two goddesses liable for distinct tasks, the protection of different categories of animals: small and large livestock.) The god Pales, mentioned by Varro (quoted by Servius, *Ad Georgica* 3.1), belongs to the Etruscan pantheon and has no liturgical place in Rome.

How then is one to understand the expression "sive deus sive dea" ("whether god or goddess"), which is found in many prayers? It does not reflect uncertainty about the gender of a possibly epicene divinity but rather uncertainty about the identity of the divinity that one is addressing. In Cato's example the peasant, careful not to make a mistake in the form of address when pruning a *lucus,* where he does not know the protective divinity, envisions the two possibilities: he thus invokes either a god or a goddess.

The same prudence is evident in the precautionary formula inserted by the pontiffs, cited by Servius (*Ad Aeneidem* 2.351): "Et pontifices ita precabantur: Iupiter Optime Maxime, sive quo alio nomine te appellari volueris" ("And the pontiffs uttered this prayer: Jupiter, Best and Greatest, or whatever be the name by which you choose to be called"). This formula is all the more instructive in that it provides for the case in which Jupiter, while well identified by his Capitoline titles, might by chance desire some other name.

Since a Roman divinity is essentially defined by its action, even a single manifestation of this action suffices for the existence of the divinity to be acknowledged. Such would be an exceptional, but significant, case. In vain a voice once called out on the Via Nova in the silence of the night to announce the approach of the Gauls. The Romans later reproached themselves for their culpable negligence and erected a sanctuary to the voice under the name of Aius Locutius ("he who talks, he who tells"; Livy, 5.32.6; 50.5; 52.11). Similarly, a *fanum* (shrine) was constructed outside of the Porta Capena to the god Rediculus. This was because Hannibal in his march on Rome had retreated, overcome by apparitions, from that place.

Changes in hierarchy. As noted above, the Capitoline triad of Jupiter, Juno, and Minerva dominated the republican self-image of the city's pantheon. Wissowa (1912) pointed to the importance in Roman religion of another configuration, the triad of Jupiter-Mars-Quirinus, which appears at the point of convergence of several factors and proceeds from the ancient priestly hierarchy as transmitted by Festus, who set down the following hierarchy: the king, the *flamen Dialis,* the *flamen Martialis,* the *flamen Quirinalis,* and the *pontifex maximus.* Framed by the king and the grand pontiff, the three major *flamines* (the *flamines maiores*) bring into relief the gods to which they are respectively attached: Jupiter, Mars, and Quirinus. Their close union is emphasized by the ritual in which, once a year, they would go together to the chapel of Fides, to venerate the goddess of good faith.

The same triad is manifest in the interior arrangement of the Regia, which under the Republic became the official seat of the pontifical college. Indeed, this building housed three different cults in addition to the cults of Janus and Juno, who were honored respectively as ushers of the year and of the month: the routine cult of Jupiter, associated with all the *nundinae* (market days); that of Mars, in the *sacrarium Martis;* and, in another room, the cult of Ops Consiva (abundance personified) in conjunction with Consus, the god of the storage *(condere)* of grains. This last goddess belongs to the group of agrarian divinities headed by Quirinus (whose *flamen* could act in related cults, too: thus, in Ovid's *Fasti* 4.910 we learn that the *flamen Quirinalis* officiated in the ceremonies of Robigus, or Robigo, the divinity invoked against mildew in grains). These deities are involved in what has been described as a group of festivals accentuating the rhythm of agrarian activities in the city of Rome.

The same triad of Jupiter, Mars, and Quirinus is found after Janus, the god of passage, and before the divinities invoked by reason of particular circumstances in the old hymn of the *devotio* (Livy, 8.9.6) that a Roman general uttered in order to consecrate himself, at the same time as the enemy army, to the *di manes.* The triad also appears in the regulations provided by the ancient royal law of Numa Pompilius for the distribution of the *spolia opima.* The first of these spoils were offered to Jupiter Feretrius, the second to Mars, the third to Janus Quirinus (Plutarch, *Life of Marcellus* 8.5; Servius, *Ad Aeneidum* 6.859). The ternary scheme is clearly supported by the document, despite some difficulties of interpretation. The meaning of *Feretrius* (derived from *ferire,* "to smite," or from *ferre,* "to carry") is not certain. As for the expression *Ianus Quirinus,* Robert Schilling has offered the explanation that the presence of Janus comes from his role as the initiator of the peacemaking function of Quirinus in opposition to the fury of Mars Gradivus. The tertiary scheme appears finally in the threefold patronage of the college of Salian priests ("who are under the protection of Jupiter, Mars and Quirinus"; Servius, *Ad Aeneidum* 8.663).

This archaic triad had been interpreted by Dumézil as corresponding, in an Indo-European world, to three diversified functions. Jupiter embodies sovereignty in its magical and juridical aspects, which in Vedic India belong respectively to Varuṇa and Mithra; Mars embodies power (his physical and military attributes are similar to Indra in India); Quirinus (**Couirio-no,* the god of the community of citizens in time of peace) is connected with fruitfulness and with prosperity in its pastoral and agrarian forms. This triad would show the survival of the characteristic tripartite ideology of the Indo-European world, which considered the hierarchical structuring of these three complementary functions to be indispensable for the prosperity of society. Despite a later evolution that would progressively fossilize their offices as the pantheon was opened to new gods, the three major *flamines* would remain the unimpeachable witnesses of this Indo-European heritage in Rome. However, such an interpretation is highly problematical with regard to the postulation of a historical Indo-European society that would be attested in but a few words and conceptual configurations. For Rome, it supposes a hierarchical structuring of the pantheon, which is visible only in an antiquarian attempt at systematization (the Augustan scholar Verrius Flaccus as quoted by Festus). The dedication of the calends to Juno and the ides to Jupiter, and the acting of the *rex* and *regina sacrorum* as priests to these two, suggest an early importance of Juno. The pantheon of Roman gods was never fully hierarchized, but is characterized by different, incoherent, and very partial internal configurations. When the Romans presented for the first time several gods and goddesses in the necessarily hierarchical order of a banquet within the ritual of *lectisternium* (see below), they fall back on undeniably Greek principles of grouping.

Given this background, the establishment of the Capitoline triad by dedicating a temple to Jupiter, Juno, and Minerva at the end of the sixth century BCE was no revolution. The project being associated with an unclear form of temporary Etruscan dominance toward the end of the sixth century (tradition named three kings who were of Etruscan origin: Tarquin the Elder, Servius Tullius, and Tarquin the Proud) transformed the masculine triad into a new triad in which Jupiter's masculine associates were replaced by two goddesses. That these goddesses were none other than Juno and Minerva can be explained not only by the fact that their Etruscan homologues, Uni and Mernva, held respectable places in their pantheon, but by reference to important Greek cultic centers as well. Schilling offered an even larger sociological interpretation. Juno, the patroness of *iuniores* (especially of youth available for battle), succeeded Mars, the god of war; Minerva, the protector of artisans and crafts, succeeded Quirinus, the god overseeing economic activity. The keystone of the triad remained immovable, even though Jupiter took on the traits of Tinia, as illustrated by the Etruscan artist Vulca of Veii, who produced the cult statue.

Tradition associated the temple built on the Capitoline Hill in honor of the new triad of Jupiter, Juno, and Minerva with the transition from the royal to the republican period. According to tradition, the construction of the Capitoline temple was begun under the Tarquins, while the dedication was performed by the consul M. Horatius Pulvillus in the first year of the Republic (509 BCE, a constructed synchronism).

Yet, it has to be stressed again: the political change from lifelong monarchs to an annual consul (the collegiality of two consuls might be a later development) did not provoke any religious upheaval. The Capitoline triad was not called into question, in spite of its strong Etruscan connotation. Instead, Jupiter more and more dominated the representation of the *res publica,* the "common affair," of the family leaders. If there was a conscious demythologization of the Roman pantheon, it was, as Carl Koch has demonstrated, focused on the figure of this god. None of the competing aristocrats could claim descent from this god (and hence superiority); even references to divine offspring—although present in nearby sanctuaries—were removed from Roman cults. At the end of the Republic, it was the second-rank families that claimed divine ancestors, as they were not able to claim a sufficient number of consular forefathers, Caesar and the *gens Iulia* offering a splendid example. The attempt of Scipio Africanus to associate himself with Jupiter by frequent presence and prayer in his temple was highly suspicious.

The title of king was maintained on the religious level. On that account, the official designation from then on was *rex sacrorum* or *rex sacrificulus*—in other words, a king limited to his liturgical functions but stripped of his political privileges. This point of prudence is explained by observing the care that the Romans took to avoid irritating their gods with untimely interventions in the realm of the sacred.

Mythology. Throughout its history, Rome was a city on the margin of Greek culture. Influence was both indirect and direct. It was indirectly influenced by the Etruscans, to the extent that Etruscan culture, its script as well as its material culture and pantheon, was itself Hellenized. It was directly influence by the nearness of Magna Graecia. All the parties involved took it for granted that, within a horizon of benevolent ethnography, deities of the other culture could be interpreted as the deities known to one's own society. *Interpretatio graeca* or *romana* was practiced by travelers, diplomats, and ethnographers, and put to use by artisans and storytellers. Thus, the large body of Greek mythology and imagery (itself already enriched by even more ancient Middle Eastern traditions) was available and attractive for middle Italian, Etruscan, and Roman reception and consumption.

A Greek ceramic fragment, showing Hephaistos, under the earliest layer of the Volcanal, the sanctuary for the Italian god Vulcan, offers an early example for equations. The sanctuary at San Omobono featured a statue group of Athena and Herakles (Minerva and Hercules), thus attesting the presence of whole narratives; the grouping would probably show the story of the apotheosis of the hero-god. The archaic sanctuary of Anna Perenna, a new year and fluvial deity venerated on the shore of the Tiber to the north of the city, contained a tile decoration of the Greek fluvial deity Achelous. If a continuity of the cult at that place (down to late antiquity) is admitted, the seemingly abstract and popular (rather than public) deity Anna Perenna was inserted into narrative patterns from Greek mythology. Instead of remaining an abstract concept of "creative" force *(creare),* Ceres was more or less identified with a Demeter in human form and enhanced by a moving legend (Demeter in search of her daughter Kore, abducted by Pluto). This "new" Ceres was made into a statue which, according to Pliny the Elder, was "the first bronze statue made in Rome." Consequently, she gained a "house," the temple built in 493 BCE to the triad near the Circus Maximus. The temple was decorated with the paintings and sculptures of Damophilos and Gorgasos, two celebrated Greek artists.

Patricians and plebeians. Other cults reflect, so to speak, the specific aspirations of the two classes that formed the basis of Roman society, the patricians and the plebeians. One observes an antagonism between the two classes that is evident not only on economic, social, and political levels, but also on the religious level. Until 300 BCE only the patricians were allowed to discharge as an official function the great traditional priesthoods, such as the pontificate and the augury. At that date a kind of religious equality was established by a law (the *Lex Ogulnia*), which, in providing members for these two colleges, reserved half of the seats for plebeians. Nevertheless, the patricians kept for themselves the privilege of admittance to the archaic priesthoods: the *rex sacrorum,* the three major *flamines,* and the Salii. The question of the origin of the differentiation of the two "orders" remains a matter of debate and has been dated to the regal, as well as early republican, period.

This rivalry between the two classes explains diverse cult initiatives that are nonetheless not necessarily mutually exclusive. In the critical phases of the city's history, they were able to coexist in a way that was satisfactory to both parties. A particularly convincing example comes to us from the beginning of the fifth century, when one individual strove to balance the two tendencies. It was the time when, according to Livy (2.18.3), "a coalition of thirty tribes" was formed against Rome. The situation induced the Romans to name a dictator, Aulus Postumius, who was vested with full powers, in place of the two consuls.

Aulus Postumius had two problems to resolve: stabilizing the food supply, which had been disrupted by war, and confronting the enemy in decisive combat. He successfully accomplished his twofold mission. The victory he won over the Latins (in 499 BCE) near Lake Regillus is celebrated in the annals. This battle entered a critical phase when the infantry failed to hold its ground. On that account, the dictator decided to send in the Roman cavalry and, at the same time, made a vow to build a temple dedicated to Castor. He thus combined, according to Livy's expression, "human and divine" means. He did so because this god, of Greek origin, was the patron of horsemen. Before going into the campaign, the dictator took another step toward easing the difficulties surrounding the food supply: he made a vow to build a temple to the Roman triad of Ceres-Liber-Libera, the names of which barely disguised the Greek divinities Demeter-Dionysos-Kore.

The victory enabled Castor to become a Roman god and to acquire a temple above the Forum: the *aedes Castoris* (dedicated in 484 by the dictator's son; Pollux was not to join his brother until the beginning of the Empire, and even then the name *aedes Castorum* recalled the original primacy of Castor). Since the harvests were abundant, Aulus Postumius also fulfilled his vow to the triad of Ceres-Liber-Libera by dedicating a sanctuary. This was a source of great satisfaction for the plebeians, for the sanctuary was entrusted to their charge and served as a meeting place for *aediles* (plebeian officials). Thus, circumstances had moved Aulus Postumius to achieve a skillful balance by the concomitant foundation of a patrician cult and a plebeian cult. Only the placement of the sanctuaries revealed a difference of status: Castor was installed inside the *pomerium,* in the heart of the Forum, while Ceres and her associates had to be located outside of the *pomerium,* near the Circus Maximus.

The codification of law of the Twelve Tables, which made law an (ever more) important instrument in dealing with social conflicts, is said to have entailed regulation of the calendar. Whereas such an exact dating remains questionable, it is certain that during the fifth century the commonly used lunisolar calendar was replaced by a purely solar calendar with fixed lengths of month, a civil calendar without parallel in the Mediterranean world. Thereafter, the lunar cult was kept but became fossilized, and observation of the lunar phases were declamatory only. It is perhaps a consequence of this change that astronomical deities did not gain in importance until the Italian reception of astrological practices beginning in the late second century BCE.

THE MIDDLE REPUBLIC: SOCIAL AND RELIGIOUS CHANGES. It is not before the fourth century BCE that we reach surer ground for historical reconstruction. Even then, the processes leading to the formation of a new patricio-plebeian elite in the second half of the century remain obscure in their details and sequence. The closing of the mainly religiously defined patriciate, marked by the interdict on intermarriage in the law of the Twelve Tables (around 450 BCE), and their monopolization of political roles gave way to a balance between patrician and plebeian office holders (the *leges Liciniae Sextia* are traditionally assigned to 367 BCE). The result was the formation of a new elite that channeled their competition into office holding and military success as public Roman generals.

Rituals were important in giving profile to achievements. The *pompa imaginum,* the funerary procession that paraded living statues—actors wearing masks representing the ancestors—to give a summary of all the achievements of the deceased's family in terms of higher offices held, was perhaps the most characteristic expression of the new culture. Ancestors who had not performed any higher magistracy did not participate and were not commemorated in the speech *(laudatio funebris)* that explained the file of ancestors on display in the Forum, the pinnacle of the procession (Polybios, 6.53). As Harriet Flower has shown, this ritual must have originated in the latter part of the fourth century.

Wealth was not eliminated as an instrument to gain prestige, but its legitimate spending depended on electoral success and the attainment of offices that offered the opportunity to stage attractive rituals. Praetorships and especially consulates provided opportunities to greatly enlarge one's wealth through successful warfare and the acquisition of booty. The contribution of such gains into the public fund was expected, but the share was never regulated. A victory enlarged the general's *clientela* by adding the legionaries who had sworn on his name. The festival of return consisted of impressive processions (the triumph), ever more attractive games, and occasionally temple dedications.

The proliferation of games was the most important religious innovation of the period. The combination of processional rituals parading gods and actors through the city of Rome and the competitions in circuses or the presentation of dramas on temporary stages brought religion into the central public space and enabled the participation of larger shares of the populace as spectators. Thus, the rituals gave information about foreign affairs and culture, they offered space for communication between the various social groups seated in an orderly arrangement in the theater or circus, and they produced a feeling of common identity—a victorious Roman identity.

Divination. The checks and balances developed in the formation of the new political elite entailed an exceptional use of divination in politics. Despite the usually distanced relationship to their gods, every important act of the higher magistrates was subjected to the prior assent of the gods, in particular Jupiter. Religious legitimation of the elected magistrates was not given once and for all, but in a piecemeal manner. To this end, there existed an indigenous institution especially charged with this mission: auspicy. On the morning of the action planned, the magistrate had to observe the cries and the flight of birds, checking them against the rule specified by himself concerning what would count as divine assent. A large number of forms eventually became standard. At least from the third century BCE onward, the *tripudium,* the observation of the hens picking fodder in cages, was the usual form. Such a technique was open to manipulation, but the lack of empirical input did not devaluate the system in the eyes of contemporaries. The duty to read auspices was at some points of the political process an opportunity to question the validity of the legitimation, or to announce the observation of adverse signs *(obnuntiatio).* Augurs were specialists of the techniques; they had an individual right to observe contrary signs in the context of popular assemblies, but the normal right to the observation *(spectio)* was held by the magistrates.

Other techniques, borrowed from Rome's neighbors in Etruria or Magna Graecia and employed collectively or individually included *haruspicinae disciplina* (lore of the haruspex) and the consultation of the Sibylline Books. This accumulation of divination methods is explained by the desire to benefit from new techniques, which were all the more seductive when they appeared to offer independent access to the will of the gods. Whereas *auspicia* indicated Jupiter's assent for the very day of the procedure only, Etruscan soothsayers boasted of being able to foretell the future, either by examining the entrails of sacrificed animals (*libri haruspicini*), by observing lightning (*libri fulgurales*), or by interpreting marvels (*libri rituales*). The first method, divining by examination of entrails, was especially popular. It featured, among the *exta* (entrails) used, the liver, which was considered a microcosm of the world. Every lesion detected in some part of the former allowed an inference on the fate of the latter.

The Sibylline Books, which had been introduced, according to tradition, in regal times under Tarquin the Proud, purported to contain prophetic verses. These books, kept in the temple of Capitoline Jupiter (they would later be transferred by Augustus to the sanctuary of Apollo Palatine), could be consulted, upon order of the Senate, by persons specialized in that office, the *X,* later *XV viri sacris faciundis.* Usually, the announcement of bad signs *(monstra, prodigia)* instigated an examination of their significance and measures to placate the gods. The measures advocated (often the introduction of new divinities) were evaluated by the Senate, which would make the final decision. The sibyl did not enjoy a liberty comparable to that of the oracle of Delphi: Her responses were always subject to senatorial censorship. There is no need to stress further the benefit that the Romans hoped to gain from these divination techniques of foreign origin. This cluster of methods is instructive, moreover, to the extent that it reveals a fundamental trait of Roman polytheism. Founded upon a conservative tradition, it was always open to enrichment and renewal.

New divinities and temples. The Senate controlled claims to triumph and the selection of sites for new temples, and probably also the date of their dedication. The erection of permanent theaters was delayed until the very end of the Republic when Pompey built a theater on the Campus Martius. Initiative, however, rested with individuals, and the introduction of a new god into the pantheon of Rome generated more attention than, for example, the restoration of an old temple. Rome's loosely organized polytheism lent itself to this sort of openness when the traditional gods proved to be inadequate in critical situations. Circumstances, perhaps family practices or local practices of significant places, inspired the Romans' attitude. An early example is demonstrated by the entry of Castor into Rome, described above.

There were other ways for foreign gods to be introduced into Rome. When the Romans had trouble with an enemy city, they resorted to the *evocatio,* which consisted of a kind of abduction of divine power at the adversary's expense and to Rome's benefit. A famous case (and also unique in the annals) occurred in the siege of Veii in 396 BCE. The war against that Etruscan city seemed endless (it was to last ten years, as long as the Trojan war). Finally, the dictator M. Furius Camillus directly addressed the city's protective divinity, Uni (the Etruscan homologue of Juno): "Juno Regina, who resides now in Veii, I pray that you will follow us after our victory into our city, which will soon be yours; you will there have a temple worthy of your majesty" (Livy, 5.21.3). In this way Juno Regina acquired a temple on the Aventine, as a divinity of outside origin, while continuing to sit, as a national divinity, on the Capitolium at the side of Jupiter. The practice is still attested in the late Republic, even if the cult offered to the tutelary deity of Isaura vetus in Asia minor was realized on the spot (*Année épigraphique* 1977, 816).

There was another procedure for introducing foreign gods into Rome: the capture, pure and simple, of a foreign divinity. This arrogant approach may seem strange on the part of a people imbued with "religious" respect toward the supernatural world. By way of explaining the *evocatio,* Macrobius (in *Saturnalia* 3.9.2) advanced precisely this reason: "Quod. . .nefas aestimarent deos habere captivos" ("they regarded it as sacrilege to make prisoners of the gods"). However, the seizure of Falerii in 241 BCE resulted in captivity for its goddess, who was then given a small shrine in Rome at the foot of the slope of Caelius, under the name of Minerva Capta (Ovid, *Fasti* 3.837). During the campaigns of the second century, most gods from the eastern part of the Mediterranean entered Rome only as artistic valuables, and, as such, they were not offered cults but were given a place in a villa or a public colonnade.

For the third century before the start of the second Punic War (218), the following temples were established: Bellona (296), Venus Obsequens (295), Iuppiter Victor (295), Iuppiter Stator (294), Fors Fortuna (293), Aesculapius (292), Hercules Invictus (292), Portunus (292), Summanus (276), Consus (272), Tellus (268), Pales (267), Vortumnus (264), Minerva (263/2), Ianus (260), Tempestates (Storms, 259), Spes and Fides (258/7), Volcanus (252), Ops Opifera (250), Neptunus (257), Iuturna (242/1), Iuno Curritis (241), Fortuna Publica (241), Flora (240), Honos (233), Fons (231), Feronia (225), Hercules Magnus custos (223), and Honos et Virtus (222). Further temples to Flora, Hercules, Honos, Hora Quirini, Lares, Luna, Penates, Sol et Luna, Sol Indiges, Tiberinus, Vica Pota, Iuppiter Fulgur, and Ops cannot be dated with certainty (Ziolkowski, 1992, pp. 187–188).

The list is remarkable in its incoherency. In the long run, the popularity of the gods invoked was very divergent. The temple of Asklepios, for example, introduced as a filiation of the great healing sanctuary of Epidaurus, flourished as a center of private devotion, a healing cult in the Greek manner. Thus, the specter of shrines that could be addressed for personal needs (as Minerva Medica) was significantly enlarged. It should not be forgotten that the importance of public religion did not stop or diminish private cult activities and traditional ways of dealing with personal crises. Individual religion was taken seriously: one could legitimately, for example, temporarily defer the military draft if one had to care for private cults and auspices (Cincius in Gellius, *Attic Nights* 16.4.4–5).

Influences of Hellenism. The military expansion gradually intensified cultural contacts. As discussed earlier, Rome was from its beginning within reach of direct and indirect Greek influence. The Dionysian cult that was fought in 186 BCE (see below), was, despite perhaps some recent organizational changes, a long-established private cult in Italy. During the third century, Rome came in direct contact with the southern Italian *Magna Graecia,* and during the second century the Romans installed themselves in continental Greece and Asia Minor. The speed of imports and the quality of the reaction changed.

Some gods of the Greek world had particularly attractive features. Aesculapius has already been mentioned, and Apollo, whose introduction was due to an epidemic, was equally appealing to the Romans. Indeed it was not the god of the Muses, nor the sun god, nor the prophet god who would later become the patron of the Sibylline Books (these titles would appear in the *Carmen saeculare* by Horace during the time of Augustus) and to whom the Romans had appealed for aid at the beginning of the fifth century; rather, this Apollo was the healing god. His temple, voted "pro valetudine populi" ("for the people's health") in 433, was dedicated in 431 in the Flaminian Meadows at the southwest of the Capitol, within a sector that already bore the name Apollinare ("Apollo's enclosure"; Livy, 4.25.3, 40.51.4). The oldest invocation used in the prayers of the Vestals was directed to the "physician": Apollo Medice, Apollo Paean (Macrobius, *Saturnalia* 1.17.15).

New rituals. The introduction of the *lectisternia* ritual had been recommended by the Sibylline Books, which were consulted upon orders of the Senate by the *II viri sacris faciundis* in the face of an alarming pestilence. This ritual would be used more and more, and, as a result, the Romans became very familiar with this new form of devotion, which had more significance on the emotional level than was usual in Roman worship. The standard Roman sacrificial ritual consisted essentially of a canonical prayer followed by the slaughtering of an animal and the offering of consecrated entrails (the *exta*) to the divinity (the distinction between *exta*—comprising the lungs, heart, liver, gall bladder, and peritoneum—and the *viscera,* flesh given over for profane consumption, is fundamental in Roman ritual). The sacrificial ceremony was celebrated by qualified magistrates or priests on private initiative around an altar placed in front of the temple. In the new ritual, however, statues of the deities reposing on cushions *(pulvinaria)* were displayed within the temples on ceremonial beds *(lectisternia).* Men, women, and children could approach them and offer them food and prayers in fervent supplication (see Livy, 24.10.13; 32.1.14), often presided over by the *II* or *X viri sacris faciundis* (cf. Livy, 4.21.5).

The first *lectisternium,* which was allegedly celebrated in 399 BCE, joined in heterogeneous pairs Apollo and Latona, Hercules and Diana, and Mercury and Neptune (Livy, 5.13.4–6). Outwardly, half of the names were of purely Greek origin (Apollo, Latona, Hercules), and the other half of Latin origin. In fact, even these Latin names applied to Hellenic divinities: Diana/Artemis, Mercury/Hermes, Neptune/Poseidon. The healing god Apollo, accompanied by his mother Latona, was at the head of the list during this period of epidemic.

Much more dramatic circumstances—Hannibal at the walls of Rome—instigated in 217 BCE the last and most celebrated *lectisternium* in the history of the Republic (Livy, 22.10.9). On this occasion, the Romans for the first time adopted the Greek plan of a set of twelve deities divided into six couples in the following order: Jupiter and Juno, Neptune and Minerva, Mars and Venus, Apollo and Diana, Vulcan and Vesta, and Mercury and Ceres. This ceremony would remain unique (one cannot regard as a parallel the merry parody organized by Augustus during a *cena* where the twelve dinner companions disguised themselves as gods and goddesses; see Suetonius, *Life of Augustus* 70). Without a doubt, the Greek inspiration is evident in this list in the presentation of pairs of gods and goddesses (the idea of grouping twelve principal deities would be repeated later by the installation of gilded bronze statues of the *di consentes* in the niches located below the Portico at the foot of the Capitolium).

Yet it is necessary to avoid misunderstanding the meaning of the coupling here. The Greek model appeared in outline after the first four couples: Zeus-Hera, Poseidon-Athena; Ares-Aphrodite, Apollo-Artemis. It could suggest a conjugal meaning for Jupiter and Juno and an erotic meaning for Mars and Venus, but nothing of the kind would apply to the association of Neptune and Minerva (which evokes the rivalry of Poseidon and Athena in giving a name to Athens), nor for Apollo and Diana/Artemis, who were brother and sister. One can also wonder if the Romans were not still more heedful of the representative value of these divine pairs. Only a functional bond makes sense for the two last couples, in Rome as well as in Greece: fire for Vulcan and Vesta, economic activity (commerce and grain) for Mercury and Ceres. As for the couples that seemed most to bear the stamp of Hellenism, they were explained perfectly in accord with Roman norms. Thus Jupiter and Juno were associated here, just as they had been in the Capitoline cult since the sixth century. Nor did Venus and Mars form a couple in Rome in the strict sense of the term. Mars, father of Romulus, is the old Italic god, while Venus, mother of Aeneas, appeared as the protector of the Romans-Aeneades. In a word, Rome knew how to utilize the Greek plan to its own ends without in turn submitting to it. Rome joined together the two essential personages of its history: Aeneas, founder of the nation, and Romulus, founder of the city.

Putting the Mediterranean to use. The example described above makes manifest a constant attitude. Nothing is more significant in this connection than the introduction of the cult of Venus Erycina. Once again the circumstantial cause was the imperative need for supplementary divine aid, this time during the Second Punic War (218–210) after the disaster of Trasimene in 217 BCE. Named as dictator, Q. Fabius Maximus (who would bear the surname *Cunctator,* or "delayer") obtained from the Senate a consultation with the Sibylline Books, which prescribed, among other measures, a promise to provide a temple dedicated to Venus Erycina (Livy, 22.9.7–11). This choice becomes clear when one recalls that, at the time of the First Punic War, the consul Lucius Junius had "recognized" Venus, the mother of Aeneas, in the Aphrodite of Mount Eryx, which he had succeeded in occupying from the start (248 BCE) till the victorious finish. Thus Q. Fabius Maximus, who was struggling with the same enemy (the Carthaginians), vowed to give the same goddess—as a pledge of victory—a temple, which was dedicated in 215 on the Capitolium. It was the "Trojan light" that earned for Venus Erycina, "mother of the Aeneades," this majestic entry to the summit of the Capitolium, which was included at that date within the pomerial zone.

Some ten years later, the Oriental goddess Cybele was introduced on the same basis, and marvels impressed religious awareness: "two suns were seen; intermittent flashes had streaked through the night; etc." (Livy, 29.14.3). An oracle drawn from the Sibylline Books had predicted "the day when an enemy of foreign race would bring war to Italian soil, he could be defeated and banished from Italy, if the Mater Idaea were carried from Pessinus to Rome" (Livy, 29.10.5). In this way the Magna Mater (alias Cybele), honored as a "Trojan" ancestor, was solemnly received in Rome in 204 BCE and was installed on the Palatine. Until the building of her own temple, which was dedicated in 191 BCE, she was provisionally lodged in the temple of Victoria.

The entry of these two goddesses, understood in terms of the "Trojan light," is instructive on another account as well. In spite of the considerable honors that Rome accorded them (far from treating them as outsiders, they were installed on the prestigious hills of the Capitoline and the Palatine), Rome did not neglect to subject their cults to discreet censorship. Venus Erycina was treated in two ways. In the temple on the Capitoline (dedicated in 215) Rome venerated her as a Roman goddess. However, in the extrapomerial temple, built later outside of the Porta Collina and dedicated in 181, Rome considered her to be a foreign goddess, covered by the statute of the *peregrina sacra* (foreign rites), which allowed for tolerance of certain original customs. The temple of Venus Erycina outside the Porta Collina admitted, as an extension of the one on Mount Eryx, the presence of prostitutes in imitation of the sacred courtesans on the Sicilian mountain. The restraints were even stricter for the Mater deum Magna Idaea. Her routine cult could be practiced only by the Galli, the eunuch-priests, positions from which Roman citizens were excluded, and the cult was placed under the surveillance of the urban praetor. Still, the aristocrats did not hesitate to institute mutual visits and banquets during the goddess's festival. Her games were among the most splendid public rituals in the Roman festival list of the late Republic.

The *supplicatio* (organized in 207 BCE, following a miracle) in honor of Juno Regina of the Aventine make a particularly memorable impression with an innovation: twenty-seven girls sang a hymn composed especially for the occasion by the poet Livius Andronicus (Livy, 27.37.7–15)

Public worship. The aim of public worship (the *sacra publica*) was to assure or to restore the "benevolence and grace of the gods," which the Romans considered indispensable for the state's well-being. Annually returning rituals dominated public cultic activity. The feasts were fixed *(stativae)* or movable *(conceptivae)* or organized around some particular circumstance *(imperativae).* The *feriae,* a special class of days given to the gods as property (and hence free from every mundane activity) were marked as a special class of *dies nefasti* (days not to be used), namely as a group of days whose violation made piacular sacrifices necessary (hence marked by the letters *NP* and abbreviations of the festival names). Many of these festivals go back to the early Republic or an even earlier period. Usually, they were coordinated with the days that structured each month. The *calendae,* often marked by festivals to Juno, were the first day of the month, the *nonae,* were the ninth day before the ides (accordingly the fifth or seventh day) and the *idus* fell on the thirteenth or the fifteenth, respectively, according to whether they were ordinary months or March, May, July, or October. The idus were usually dedicated to Jupiter, but the same day staged other important festivals, too.

To that end, the calendar days were divided into profane days *(dies profesti)* and days reserved for the gods (*dies festi* or *feriae*), and thus for liturgical celebrations. However, if one looks at a Roman calendar, one observes that the list of days contains other signs. When the days are profane, they are marked by the letter *F (fasti);* when they pertain to the gods, by *N (nefasti).* This presentation does not call into question the division of "profane" and "sacred" times. It simply changes the perspective as to when "divine" becomes "human." Indeed, for the Romans, the day is *fastus* when it is *fas* (religiously licit) to engage in profane occupations, *nefastus* when it is *nefas* (religiously prohibited) to do so, since the day belongs to the gods. In reality, the analytical spirit of the pontiffs came up with yet a third category of *C* days *(comitiales),* which, while profane, lent themselves in addition to the *comitia,* or "assemblies." Furthermore, there are other rarely used letters, such as the three *dies fissi* (half *nefasti,* half *fasti*). The *dies religiosi* (or *atri*) are outside these categories: they are dates that commemorate public misfortunes, such as July 18, the *Dies Alliensis* (commemorating the disaster of the battle of Allia in 390 BCE).

The republican calendar (called *fasti*) divided the ferial days over the course of twelve months. Each month was marked by the *calendae* (the first day), the *nonae,* and the *idus* (the last two fell respectively on the fifth or seventh, and the thirteenth or the fifteenth, according to whether they were ordinary months or March, May, July, or October). The feasts were fixed *(stativae)* or movable *(conceptivae)* or organized around some particular circumstance.

The Roman liturgy developed in line with an order of feasts consecrated to particular deities. An overlap was therefore possible: since the ides, "days of full light," were always dedicated to Jupiter. The sacrifice of the Equus October (horse of October) on October 15 coincided with the ides.

This ritual sequence was punctuated by the rhythm of seasons for the agrarian celebrations (especially in April and in July and August) and by the schedule of training for military campaigns. Thus it is interesting to note that the month of March contained several feasts marking the opening of martial activities. There was registered on the calendars a sacrifice to the god Mars; the blessing of horses on the Equirria on February 27 and March 14; and the blessing of arms on the Quinquatrus and of trumpets on the Tubilustrium on March 19. In addition, there was the Agonium Martiale on March 17. The Salii, carrying lances *(hastae)* and shields *(ancilia),* roamed the city performing martial dances. Apart from the feriae and connected ritual sequences, many commemoration days of the dedication of temples filled the calendar. The annual sacrifice in front of the temple sometimes gave rise to very popular festivals.

Besides the liturgical feasts, it is also necessary to cite the *ludi,* games consisting essentially of chariot races. They went back to an old tradition represented by the Equirria. The new *ludi* replaced the *bigae,* teams of two horses, with the *quadrigae,* teams of four, for the races in the Circus Maximus and included various performances: riders leaping from one horse to another, fights with wrestlers and boxers. (The gladiator fights, which were Etruscan in origin, appeared in 264 BCE for private funeral feasts, but they did not become part of the public games until the end of the second century BCE.) These competitions were soon complemented by other spectacles: pantomimes and dances accompanied by the flute. The principal ones were the *Ludi Magni* or *Ludi Romani*, celebrated from the fifteenth through the eighteenth of September after the ides that coincided with the anniversary of the temple of Jupiter Capitoline. Considered to have been instituted by Tarquin the Elder (Livy, 1.35.9), they became annual events starting in 367 BCE, which is the date that saw the creation of the curule magistracy *(aediles curules).* The *Ludi Plebei*, a kind of plebeian reply to preceding games, were instituted later: they are mentioned for the first time in 216 BCE (Livy, 23.30.17). They took place in the Circus Flaminius, involved the same kind of games as the *Ludi Romani*, and were celebrated around the ides of November. It is also noteworthy that the *Ludi Romani* and the *Ludi Plebei* were both held around the ides (of September or November) and dedicated to Jupiter, to whom a sacrificial meal, the *Epulum Iovis*, was offered.

The priesthood. Priests were not necessary for private cult. An *aedituus*, a guardian of a temple, would have to open a temple that was normally closed or provide items necessary for the cult (water, for example). However, much of private ritual was performed on private ground. Neither prayer nor animal sacrifice was in need of a cultic specialist other than the *pater familias*, the head of the family, a person in charge of a farm, or the president of an association. The same holds true for public rituals. Many were led by the chosen magistrates, who gave the order to kill an oxen or start a horse race. A pontiff might assist in reciting a prayer that the magistrate uttered aloud, but it was the magistrate who performed, for example, the dedication of a new temple.

By the late Republic, certain priests who were dedicated to special cults—functioning, perhaps, but one or two times a year—were hardly important or prestigious. Few of these twelve *flamines minores* are known by name. The same type of specialized priesthood, but more to the fore, was represented by the *rex sacrorum* and the three major *flamines* of Jupiter (Dialis), Mars (Martialis) and—already a lesser figure—Quirinus (Quirinalis). The *flamines minores* oversaw a number of central, but routine, rituals that probably took place without a large public audience, and their priestly role was not more than a part-time job. They were, however, subjected to rules that limited their opportunities for entering a political career—a subject frequently leading to conflict. On the other hand, they were recruited at a comparatively young age, in their early twenties during the late Republic (and later), which is more than fifteen years before a consulate would take office. The wives of the *rex* and the *flamines minores* supplemented their ritual tasks as *regina sacrorum* (with a separate range of cults) or *flaminica*.

The only exception to the latter characterization were the six Vestal Virgins, who had to live in celibacy in the *atrium Vestae* on the Forum Romanum, adjacent to the Regia and the *aedes Vestae*, a circular sanctuary accessible to nobody else. "Caught," as the technical expression was, by the *pontifex maximus* at a minimum age of six years, their period of service was said to last for thirty years, although no case of a Vestal who left after that period is known. Instead, the role of the *Vestalis maxima*, the eldest one, was one of utmost authority and sanctity in the eyes of the public.

The predominant priests from perhaps the fourth century BCE onward were those organized as *collegia sacerdotum.* They were responsible for certain procedures and areas of religious regulation, but were—as a rule—not dedicated to the cult of specific deities. The mode of their recruitment and the persons recruited were increasingly adapted to the rules and personal reservoirs of the political magistrates. Although election was not implemented for most of them before 104 BCE *(Lex Domitia)*, they came from the leading families only, being appointed shortly before the consulate or even afterward in the case of "new men" risen from nonconsular families. These colleges had no special building for their meetings, but regularly (probably monthly) met at their private homes. Holding their offices as lifetime appointments, they formed powerful networks within the political elite.

The most important and most politicized position was held by the *pontifex maximus.* He presided over the pontifical college, to which the *flamines* and *Vestales* (both "caught" by him), as well as the *rex sacrorum*, were attached. Jurisdictional competence and participation in large public rituals led to an enlargement or, even better, differentiation of the college. Its scribes were given the title "minor pontiffs" and the status of priests; a second college, the three (later seven) "men for Jupiter's banquets" *(Septemviri epulonum)*, was split off in 196 BCE and ascended to nearly equal dignity under the Empire. In particular, it was their duty to organize the sacrificial supper, the *Epulum Iovis*, at the *Ludi Romani* and the *Ludi Plebei*, the Roman and Plebeian games on the ides of September and November. They numbered three at first, then seven, and finally (without a change of name) ten. The pontiffs were early specialists of Roman public and private law; the realm of religious property rights—divine property, tombs *(locus religiosus)*, the juridical and religious quality of the time, and intercalation were in their hands. The college, originally recruited from patricians only, grew—always in parallel to the augural college—to nine members by the *Lex Ogulnia* of 300 BCE, then to fifteen by the *Lex Cornelia* of 82 BCE (opening prestigious positions for Sulla's supporters in the Civil war), and finally to sixteen by Caesar's *Lex Julia* of 46 BCE.

The augurs made up the second college. Their competence encompassed divination and the change of sacral status. Thus, it fell upon them to inaugurate both persons (the *rex sacrorum* and the three *flamines maiores*) and space *(templa)*; in the ritual of the *augurium maximum* they even checked for the status of a ritual; that is, they asked for Jupiter's consent to have the ritual performed. As a college, and in certain functions as individuals, they served as experts for everything concerning the *auspicia,* the divination by means of the observation of birds regularly performed by magistrates. Being able to question or invalidate auspicial legitimation, they were highly political figures, and the regulations concerning the college were at pains to ensure the independence of its members, who would not loose their priesthood even if they were condemned or exiled.

The *Duo viri sacris faciundis* (men in charge of the celebration of sacrifices) were responsible for safeguarding and for consulting the Sibylline Books by order of the Senate. There were at first two of them, then ten (*Decemviri,* beginning in 367 BCE), and finally—equating them to the other colleges—fifteen *(quindecimviri).*

The electoral procedures for the members of these priestly colleges, probably enacted for the first time in the second half of the third century, show how carefully Roman procedures regulated the religious realm. Only a minority (seventeen chosen by lot) of the thirty-five "tribes," originally regional voting units, selected among the candidates nominated by the surviving priests. The successful candidate was than formally adrogated by the college, thus continuing the practice of *cooptatio* (cooptation) that remained the rule for all the other, politically less important priestly groups. Even priests elected in a popular assembly were not installed by majority vote.

In addition to the four *collegia,* it is worth mentioning the fraternities that confirm the preference in Rome for priestly specialization and the division of religious authority. The twenty Fetiales saw to the protection of Rome in foreign relations, especially with regard to declarations of war and conclusion of peace treaties. The twenty-four Salii (twelve *Salii Palatini* and twelve *Salii Collini,* from Augustus onward) were dancer-priests who opened the season of war in March and who were the youngest aristocratic priests; female Salians are mentioned only once (Servius, *Ad Aeneiden* 8.285). The twenty-four Luperci (twelve *Fabiani* and twelve *Quinctiales*) acted only in the rites of the Lupercalia on February 15. The twelve Arval Brethren were in charge of the cult of the agrarian deity Dea Dia, whose sanctuary was located outside the city in the fields *(arva).* The function of the *Sodales Titii* (perhaps likewise twelve men) remains unknown; perhaps they continued a regal heroic cult. It is characteristic of the reduced political importance of these priesthoods that hardly any member is known, or rather the membership of those who are known was rarely made explicit. In contrast, between one- and two-thirds of the members of the major colleges are known for most years from the Second Punic War onward. By way of a unique ensemble of marble inscriptions from their sanctuary, the *fratres Arvales* are the best documented priesthood of the Empire.

Private worship. Religion as organized by the nobility, the political elite, and paid for by state funds—hence *religio publica*—offered a space for religious activities for the aristocracy and the framework for various collective or individual activities on the part of ordinary citizens or simply inhabitants of Rome. The *sacra publica,* publicly financed ritual, were not restricted to activities of the city as a whole. Territorial subdivisions, such as the *curiae* or the neighborhoods of the *compitalia* (crossroad sanctuaries), offered space for ritual interaction and communication. The *curio maximus* was the second priesthood to be included into the procedure of popular election, more than one hundred years before the augurs and the other pontiffs. In imperial times, the *vicomagistri* who presided over *compitalician* cult were given the right to wear the *toga praetexta,* togas with a purple strip distinguishing Roman magistrates, during their services.

We do not know much about gentilician cult, but much is known about family and household cult from literary and archaeological sources,which serve as a helpful corrective against poetic or antiquarian idealization. Rented Roman flats lacked built-in altars, and the ancestor cult of deceased relatives simply dumped into the extra-urban pits might have been limited.

The cult within the *familia,* the extended Roman family placed under the unrestricted authority of the *pater familias,* may be regarded in a biographical perspective. The day of birth *(dies natalis)* and the day of purification (*dies lustricus:* the ninth day for boys, the eighth for girls, when the infant received its name) were family feasts. In the atrium of the family home, the infant would acquire the habit of honoring the household gods (the *lar familiaris* and the *di penates*). The allusion made in the *Aulularia* (v. 24s) by Plautus to a young daughter who every day would bring "some gift such as incense, wine, or garlands" to the *lar familiaris* shows that personal devotion was not unknown in Rome. Livy (26.19.5) cites a more illustrious example of this kind about P. Cornelius Scipio, the future conqueror of Hannibal. "After he received the *toga virilis,* he undertook no action, whether public or private, without going right away to the Capitolium. Once he reached the sanctuary, he remained there in contemplation, normally all alone in private for some time." (It is true that a rumor attributed divine ancestry to Scipio, something he very carefully neither confirmed nor denied; see above).

The taking of the *toga virilis,* or *pura* (as opposed to the *toga praetexta,* bordered with a purple ribbon and worn by children), generally took place at age seventeen during the feast of the Liberalia on March 17. Before this point, the *puer* (boy) offered his *bulla* (a golden amulet) to the *lar familiaris.* From then on, he was a *iuvenis,* and he would go to the Capitolium to offer a sacrifice and leave an offering in the sanctuary of the goddess Juventus (*Iuventas*). Girls would offer dolls and clothing on the day of their wedding. Another family feast honored the father of the family on his birthday; for reasons of convenience the commemoration and party seems to have frequently been moved to the next calends or ides. A warm atmosphere brought together the whole family, including the servants, at least twice a year. On March 1, the feast of the Matronalia, mothers of families would make their way up the Esquiline to the temple of Juno Lucina, whose anniversary it was. Together with their husbands they prayed "for the safeguarding of their union" and received presents. They then prepared dinner for their slaves. Macrobius (*Saturnalia* 1.12.7), who mentions this custom, adds that on December 17, the feast of the Saturnalia, it was the masters' turn to serve their slaves, unless they preferred to share dinner with them (*Saturnalia* 1.7.37). It is characteristic of the gendered perspective of the Romans that the "male" Saturnalia developed into a carnival lasting for several days, characterized by an exchange of gifts, as well as excessive drinking.

At the end of life, the *Feriae Denecales* (*denecales* or *deni-*, perhaps from *de nece,* "following death") took place. The purpose was to purify the family in mourning, for the deceased was regarded as having defiled his or her family, which thus became *funesta* (defiled by death). To this end, a *novemdiale sacrum* was offered on the ninth day after burial. As for the deceased, the body, or a finger thereof kept aside *(os resectum)* in the case of cremation, was buried in a place that become inviolable *(religiosus).* The burial was indispensable in order to assure the repose of the deceased, who from then on was venerated among the *di parentes* (later the *di manes*). If there were no burial, the deceased risked becoming one of the mischievous spirits, the *lemures,* which the father of the family would expel at midnight on the Lemuria of May 9, 11, and 13.

During the *Dies Parentales,* from February 13 to 21, the family would go to the tombs of their dead in order to bring them gifts. Since the period ended on February 21 with a public feast called the Feralia, the following day, February 22, reverted to a private feast, the Caristia or Cara Cognatio, in which the members of the family gathered and comforted one another around a banquet. This explains the compelling need in an old family for legitimate offspring (either by bloodline or by adoption). In their turn, the duty of the descendants was to carry on the family worship and to calm the souls of their ancestors. Foundations or donations to associations could serve the same purpose.

Religious associations. The sacrifice and banquet framed family festivals and organized social space for secondary groups as well. The Romans believed that their associations dated back to the early regal period. Common economic interest and sociability usually went together, formally united by the cult of a suitable deity. Bakers, for example, venerated Vesta, the goddess of the hearth. In addition, slaves of large households were known to have organized themselves into associations during imperial times. Given the weak economic position of many individuals and families, associations might provide funeral services as well.

The multifunctional form of the association *(collegium)* often opened them to criticism and suspicion. For example, associations of venerators of the goddess Isis, originally stemming from Egypt but present at Rome from the second century BCE onward, were regarded as political troublemakers and organizers of popular unrest in the last decennium of the Republic. Even the territorially organized groups of the *compitalia* were subject to suspicion, and they eventually dissolved. The most famous and best documented conflict between a religious organization and Roman officials is the persecution of the Italian Bacchanalia in 186 BCE.

The affair is known from Livy's extensive narrative (39.8–18) and from a bronze copy of the final decree of the Senate, which enforced the Roman sanctions of the cult within the whole of Italy, or at least the Roman territories *(Senatusconsultum de Bacchanalibus).* The cult of Dionysos had a long history and was widespread throughout Italy. Accordingly, the Senate's action was not directed against the god Bacchus or his cult in principle. Following a denunciation, alarm had been created by the secret gatherings (Livy, 39.8.3) that reeked of scandals involving both men and women. The bacchants were accused of taking part in criminal orgies in a milieu marked by "the groans of victims amid debaucheries and murders." The prohibition was dictated out of a concern for public order. The reaction involved draconian sanctions, including the death penalty for some leading figures. The cult however, was not suppressed. If restricted to five persons or fewer and to female priests and a majority of female members, and with the renunciation of a associative framework (money, officers), the cult could continue—everything else had to be explicitly requested and permitted by the Senate.

The Bacchanalian affair illustrates the Roman approach of honoring the religious obligations of subjects as the city itself fulfilled the religious obligations that had arisen in the long course of history *(religiones).* The gods would be helpful and would not interfere, if they were given their due. In this process there was an acceptable range of behavior, but any excess would be superstitious *(superstitio).* In founding new colonies and regulating their affairs, Roman officials were forced to address the religious basics and put them into legal terms: that was part of the *ius publicum.* With regard to such decisions, the most important source is the *Lex Coloniae Iuliae Genetivae Ursonensis,* a law written in 44 BCE for a Spanish colony founded by C. Julius Caesar, which survived in fragmentary form in a copy from the end of the first century CE (Crawford, 1996). The basics are few: a college of augurs and pontiffs had to be installed (without specifying their tasks); their succession was to be regulated; and the (low) pay of the haruspices was specified. Games had to be held for the Capitoline triad and Venus, the tutelary deities. The introduction of every other cult was left to the city council, as was probably the calendar. It was made certain that the colony was able to pay for the cults and the religious obligation it had taken up: the coordination of contracts with suppliers of victims and organizers of games was the first topic in the city council every year.

SEE ALSO Indo-European Religions, overview article.

BIBLIOGRAPHY

Altheim, Franz. *Griechische Götter im alten Rom.* Giessen, Germany, 1930.

Altheim, Franz. *A History of Roman Religion.* Translated by Harold Mattingly. London, 1938.

Ambrosch, Jul[ius] Athanas[ius]. *Studien und Andeutungen im Gebiet des altrömischen Bodens und Cultus.* Breslau, 1839.

Bailey, Cyril. *Phases in the Religion of Ancient Rome.* Berkeley, 1932.

Beard, Mary, John North, and Simon Price. *Religions of Rome,* vol. 1, *A History;* vol. 2, *A Sourcebook.* New York and Cambridge, U.K., 1998.

Barchiesi, Alessandro; Jörg Rüpke; Susan Stephens, ed. *Rituals in Ink: A Conference on Religion and Literary Production in Ancient Rome, Held at Stanford University in February 2002.* Stuttgart, Germany, 2004.

Belayche, Nicole Andreas Bendlin, et al. "Forschungsbericht römische Religion." *Archiv für Religionsgeschichte* 2 (2000): 283–345; 5 (2003): 297–371.

Bernstein, Frank. *Ludi publici: Untersuchungen zur Entstehung und Entwicklung der öffentlichen Spiele im republikanischen Rom.* Stuttgart, Germany, 1998.

Bietti Sestieri, Anna Maria. *The Iron Age Community of Osteria dell'Osa: A Study of Social-Political Development in Central Tyrrhenian Italy.* Cambridge, U.K., 1992.

Bispham, Edward, and Christopher Smith, eds. *Religion in Archaic and Republican Rome and Italy: Evidence and Experience.* Edinburgh, 2000.

Borgeaud, Willy Alfred. *Fasti Umbrici: Études sur le vocabulaire et le rituel des Tables eugubines.* Ottawa, Ont., 1982.

Brissonius, Barnabé. *De formulis et solennibus populi Romani verbis libri VIII.* Paris, 1583.

Carandini, Andrea. *La nascita di Roma: Dèi, Lari, eroi e uomini all'alba di una civiltà.* Turin, Italy, 1997.

Champeaux, Jacqueline. *La religion romaine.* Paris, 1998.

Coarelli, Filippo. *I santuari del Lazio in età repubblicana.* Studi N I S archeologia 7. Rome, 1987.

Cornell, T. J. *The Beginnings of Rome: Italy and Rome from the Bronze Age to the Punic Wars (c. 1000–264 BC).* London, 1995.

Crawford, Michael H., ed. *Roman Statutes.* 2 vols. London, 1996.

Devoto, Giacomo. *Tabulae Iguvinae.* 3d ed. Rome, 1962.

Dumézil, Georges. *La religion romaine archaïque.* 2d ed. Paris, 1974. Translated from the first edition by Philip Krapp as *Archaic Roman Religion,* 2 vols. Chicago, 1970.

Egelhaaf-Gaiser, Ulrike, and Alfred Schäfer, eds. *Religiöse Vereine in der römischen Antike: Untersuchungen zu Organisation, Ritual und Raumordnung.* Tübingen, Germany, 2002.

Erskine, Andrew. *Troy between Greece and Rome: Local Tradition and Imperial Rome.* Oxford, 2001.

Feeney, Denis. *Literature and Religion at Rome: Cultures, Contexts, and Beliefs.* Cambridge, U.K., 1998.

Flower, Harriet I. *Ancestor Masks and Aristocratic Power in Roman Culture.* Oxford, 1996.

Fowler, W. Warde. *The Roman Festivals of the Period of the Republic: An Introduction to the Study of the Religion of the Romans.* 1899; reprint, Port Washington, N.Y., 1969.

Fowler, W. Warde. *Religious Experience of the Roman People: From Earliest Times to the Age of Augustus.* 1911; reprint, Totowa, N.J., 1971.

Graf, Fritz. ed. *Mythos in mythenloser Gesellschaft: Das Paradigma Roms.* Stuttgart, Germany, 1993.

Hartung, J. A. *Die Religion der Römer nach den Quellen dargestellt.* Erlangen, Germany, 1836.

Klausen, Rudolph H. *Aeneas und die Penaten: Die italischen Volksreligionen unter dem Einflusse der griechischen dargestellt.* 2 vols. Hamburg, Germany, 1839.

Koch, Carl. *Der römische Juppiter.* Frankfurt, Germany, 1937.

Latte, Kurt. *Römische Religionsgeschichte.* Munich, 1960.

Linderski, Jerzy. "The Augural Law." In *Roman Questions: Selected Papers.* Stuttgart, 1995.

Marquardt, Joachim. *Le culte chez les Romains.* 2 vols. Paris, 1889–1890.

Massa-Pairault, Françoise-Hélène, ed. *Le mythe grec dans l'Italie antique: Fonction et image.* Paris, 1999.

Mommsen, Theodor. *Römisches Staatsrecht* (1871–1888). 3 vols. Basel, Switzerland, 1952.

North, J. A. *Roman Religion.* Oxford, 2000.

Orlin, Eric M. *Temples, Religion, and Politics in the Roman Republic.* Leiden, 1997.

Pailler, Jean-Marie. *Bacchanalia: La répression de 186 av. J.-C. à Rome et en Italie, vestiges, images, tradition.* Rome, 1988.

Rawson, Elisabeth. *Intellectual Life in the Late Roman Republic.* London, 1985.

Rüpke, Jörg. *Domi militiae: Die religiöse Konstruktion des Krieges in Rom.* Stuttgart, Germany, 1990.

Rüpke, Jörg. *Kalender und Öffentlichkeit: Die Geschichte der Repräsentation und religiösen Qualifikation von Zeit in Rom.* Berlin, 1995.

Rüpke, Jörg. *Die Religion der Römer: Eine Einführung.* Munich, 2001.

Scheid, John. *La religion des Romains.* Paris, 1998. Translated by Janet Lloyd as *An Introduction to Roman Religion.* Bloomington, Ind., 2003.

Scheid, John. *Religion et piété à Rome.* 2nd ed. Paris, 2001.

Schilling, Robert. *Rites, cultes, dieux de Rome.* Paris, 1979.

Simón, Francisco M. *Flamen dialis: El sacerdote de Júpter en la religión romana.* Madrid, 1996.

Torelli, Mario. *Lavinio e Roma: Riti iniziatici e matrimonio tra archeologia e storia.* Rome, 1984.

Turcan, Robert. *Religion romaine.* Leiden, 1988.

Versnel, H. S. *Triumphus: An Inquiry into the Origin, Development, and Meaning of the Roman Triumph.* Leiden, 1970.

Wagenvoort, H. *Roman Dynamism: Studies in Ancient Roman Thought, Language, and Custom.* Oxford, 1947.

Wiseman, Timothy Peter. *Remus: A Roman Myth.* Cambridge, U.K., 1995.

Wiseman, Timothy Peter. "Liber Myth, Drama and Ideology in Republican Rome." In *The Roman Middle Republic: Politics, Religion, and Histography c. 400-133 B.C.,* edited by Christer Bruun, pp. 265–299. Rome, 2000.

Wissowa, Georg. *Religion und Kultus der Römer.* 2d ed. Munich, 1912.

Ziolkowski, Adam. *The Temples of Mid-Republican Rome and Their Historical and Topographical Context.* Rome, 1992.

ROBERT SCHILLING (1987)
JÖRG RÜPKE (2005)

ROMAN RELIGION: THE IMPERIAL PERIOD

The Roman state's extraordinary and unexpected transformation from one that had hegemony over the greater part of Italy into a world state in the second and first centuries BCE had implications for Roman religion that are not easy to grasp. After all, Christianity, a religion wholly "foreign" in its origins, arose from this period of Roman ascendancy. To begin, then, to understand the religious system of imperial Rome, it is best to confine the discussion to some elementary and obviously related facts.

First, the old Roman practice of inviting the chief gods of their enemies to become gods of Rome (*evocatio*) played little part in the new stage of imperialism. *Evocatio* played some role in Rome's conquests in the middle Republic, but the practice had been transformed. The last temple to be built in Rome to house a deity "evoked" from an enemy of Rome was that of Vortumnus (264 BCE). A version of the ritual was probably used to "evoke" the Juno of Carthage in the 140s BCE, but no temple was built to her in Rome. The extent of the transformation is shown by the fact that in 75 BCE a Roman conqueror of Isaura Vetus (in Asia Minor) took a vow (in language reminiscent of the *evocatio*), which seems to have resulted in the foundation of a new local cult of the patron deity of Isaura Vetus. The old procedures of *evocatio* are not found in the imperial period. Instead, the cults of Rome's subjects continued to form the basis for their local religious system.

Second, while it was conquering the Hellenistic world, Rome was involved in a massive absorption of Greek language, literature, and religion, with the consequence that the Roman gods became victorious over those of Greece while their old identification with Greek gods became more firmly established. Because the gods were expected to take sides and to favor their own worshipers, this could have created some problems. In fact, from the middle Republic onward, the Romans respected the gods of the Greeks. As early as 193 BCE the Romans replied to the city of Teos (in Asia Minor) that they would "seek to improve both honors towards the god [Dionysos, the patron deity of Teos] and privileges towards you," on the grounds that Roman success was due to her well-known reverence towards the gods (Sherk, 1969, pp. 214–216). In other words, the Romans accepted that the Greek god Dionysos was included among the gods that favored Rome. In consequence, the Greeks felt no pressure to modify their ancestral cults, and traditional Greek cults remained vibrant throughout the imperial period.

Third, the conquest of Africa, Spain, and Gaul produced the opposite phenomenon of a large, though by no means systematic, identification of Punic, Iberian, and Celtic gods with Roman gods. This, in turn, is connected with two opposite aspects of the Roman conquest of the West. On the one hand, the Romans had little sympathy and understanding for the religion of their Western subjects. Although occasionally guilty of human sacrifice, they found the various forms of human sacrifices that were practiced more frequently in Africa, Spain, and Gaul repugnant (hence their later efforts to eliminate the Druids in Gaul and in Britain). On the other hand, northern Africa (outside Egypt) and western Europe were deeply Latinized in language and Romanized in institutions, thereby creating the conditions for the assimilation of native gods to Roman gods.

Yet the Mars, the Mercurius, and even the Jupiter and the Diana seen so frequently in Gaul under the Romans are not exactly the same as in Rome. The individuality of the Celtic equivalent of Mercurius has already been neatly noted by Caesar (*Gallic War* 6.17). Some Roman gods, such as Janus and Quirinus, do not seem to have penetrated Gaul. Similarly, in Africa, Saturnus preserved much of the Baal Hammon with whom he was identified. There, Juno Caelestis (or simply Caelestis, destined to considerable veneration outside Africa) is Tanit (Tinnit), the female companion of Baal Hammon. The assimilation of the native god is often revealed by an accompanying adjective (in Gaul, for example, Mars Lenus and Mercurius Dumiatis). An analogous phenomenon had occurred in the East under the Hellenistic monarchies: native, especially Semitic, gods were assimilated to Greek gods, especially to Zeus and Apollo. The Eastern assimilation went on under Roman rule (as seen, for example, with Zeus Panamaros in Caria).

Roman soldiers, who became increasingly professional and lived among natives for long periods of time, played a part in these syncretic tendencies. A further consequence of imperialism was the emphasis on Victory and on certain gods of Greek origin (such as Herakles and Apollo) as gods of victory. Victoria was already recognized as a goddess during the Samnite Wars; she was later associated with various leaders, from Scipio Africanus to Sulla and Pompey. Roman emperors used an elaborate religious language in their discussions of Victory. Among Christians, Augustine of Hippo depicted Victory as God's angel (*City of God* 4.17).

These transformations are part of the changing relationship between the center (Rome) and the periphery (the Empire). By the early Empire, Italy fell wholly under the authority of Rome: in 22 CE the senate decided that "all rituals, temples, and images of the gods in Italian towns fall under Roman law and jurisdiction" (Tacitus, *Annals* 3.71). The provinces were different and not subject to Roman jurisdiction in the same way. However, Roman governors of the imperial period were required to watch over religious life in their province. They were concerned that religious life proceed in an orderly and acceptable manner, and the governors' official instructions included the order to preserve sacred places. They also ensured that the provincials took part in the annual performance on January 3 of the Roman ritual vows of allegiance to the emperor and the Empire.

Roman practices were celebrated in certain specific contexts throughout the Empire. Roman *coloniae*, settlements consisting of Roman citizens (ex-soldiers and landless poor from Rome), were established in the provinces in the late Republic and early Empire. Such settlements were privileged clones of Rome in a sea of mere subjects of Rome. Their public religious life had a strongly Roman cast, despite much variation from place to place. Many *coloniae* had their own Capitolium, priesthoods (pontifices and augures), and rituals based on those of Rome.

The Roman army also followed overtly Roman rules. Military camps had at their center a building that housed the legionary standards and imperial and divine images (sometimes including images of Romulus and Remus). The importance of the building is reflected in the fact that in 208 CE it is even called a Capitolium (*Année épigraphique*,1989, no. 581, from Aalen in Germany). From the early Empire all legionary soldiers (who were Roman citizens) and later all auxiliary soldiers (who were originally not Roman citizens) celebrated religious festivals modeled on those of Rome. They celebrated festivals on the Roman cycle (e.g. Vestalia or Neptunalia); they performed imperial vows to the Capitoline triad on January 3; and they celebrated imperial birthdays and other events.

Towns with the status of *municipia* (where local citizens had the so-called Latin right and some even full Roman citizenship) shared some of the Roman religious features of *coloniae*; their principal priesthoods, for example, were named after and modeled on Roman institutions—*pontifices*, *augures*, and *haruspices*. And from the second century CE onward, *municipia* in North Africa also began to build their own Capitolia. Overtly Roman practices served as part of the process of competitive emulation that marked civic life in many parts of the Empire. The original Caesarian regulations for the *colonia* of Urso in southern Spain, which constitute our fullest single document of this process, remained sufficiently important to Urso for them to be reinscribed a hundred years later, at a time when other Spanish communities had just received the (lesser) status of the Latin right (Crawford, 1996, pp. 393-454). Throughout the Empire, whatever the technical status of the community, there were publicly organized and celebrated religious rites. For example, the Greek city of Ephesus (Gr., Ephesos) proudly commemorated the fact that Artemis was born at Ephesus and voted to extend the period of her festival "since the god Artemis, patron of our city, is honored not only in her native city, which she has made more famous than all other cities through her own divinity, but also by Greeks and barbarians, so that everywhere sanctuaries and precincts are consecrated for her, temples are dedicated and altars set up for her, on account of her manifest epiphanies" (*Die Inschriften von Ephesos* no. 24, c. 163 CE). Individuals took part in such festivals and also sacrificed incense on small altars outside their houses when processions in honor of the Roman emperor passed by. This is not to say that piety towards the gods existed only in public contexts or indeed was constituted primarily through civic channels. Individuals formed private religious associations, either simply to worship a particular deity or to form a society that would ensure the proper burial of its members. They also made private prayers and vows to the appropriate god and set up votive offerings to the god in his or her sanctuary.

IMPERIAL ATTITUDES TOWARD AND USES OF RELIGION. Augustus and his contemporaries thought, or perhaps in some cases wanted other people to think, that the preceding age (roughly the period from the Gracchi to Caesar) had seen a decline in the ancient Roman care for gods. Augustus himself stated in the public record known as the *Res gestae* that he had restored eighty-two temples and shrines (in one year, 28 BCE). He revived cults and religious associations, such as the Arval Brothers and the fraternity of the Titii, and appointed a *flamen dialis*, a priestly office that had been left vacant since 87 BCE. This revivalist feeling was not entirely new: it was behind the enormous collection of evidence concerning ancient Roman cults, the "divine antiquities," that Varro had dedicated to Caesar about 47 BCE in his *Antiquitatum rerum humanarum et divinarum libri*; the rest of the work, the "human antiquities," was devoted to Roman political institutions and customs. Varro's work codified Roman religion for succeeding generations, and as such it was used for polemical purposes by Christian apologists.

The Romans also turned certain gods of Greek origin into gods of victory. As early as 145 BCE, L. Mummius dedicated a temple to Hercules Victor after his triumph over Greece. After a victory, generals often offered 10 percent of their booty to Hercules, and Hercules Invictus was a favorite god of Pompey. Apollo was connected with Victory as early as 212 BCE. Caesar boosted her ancestress Venus in the form of Venus Victrix. But it was Apollo who helped Octavian, the future Augustus, to win the Battle of Actium in September of 31 BCE.

It is difficult to do justice both to the mood of the Augustan restoration and to the unquestionable seriousness with which the political and military leaders of the previous century tried to support their unusual adventures by unusual religious attitudes. Marius, a devotee of the Mater Magna (Cybele), was accompanied in his campaigns by a Syrian prophetess. Sulla apparently brought from Cappadocia the goddess Ma, soon identified with Bellona, whose orgiastic and prophetic cult had wide appeal. Furthermore, he developed a personal devotion to Venus and Fortuna and set an example for Caesar, who claimed Venus as the ancestress of the *gens* Julia. As *pontifex maximus* for twenty years, Caesar reformed not only individual cults but also the calendar, which had great religious significance. He tried to support his claim to dictatorial powers by collecting religious honors that, though obscure in detail and debated by modern scholars, anticipate later imperial cults.

Unusual religious attitudes were not confined to leaders. A Roman senator, Nigidius Figulus, made religious combinations of his own both in his writings and in his practice: magic, astrology, and Pythagoreanism were some of the ingredients. Cicero, above all, epitomized the search of educated men of the first century BCE for the right balance between respect for the ancestral cults and the requirements of philosophy. Cicero could no longer believe in traditional divination. When his daughter died in 45 BCE, he embarked briefly on a project for making her divine. This was no less typical of the age than the attempt by Clodius in 62 BCE to desecrate the festival of Bona Dea, reserved for women, in order to contact Caesar's wife (he escaped punishment).

The imperial age inclined toward distinctions and compromises. The Roman *pontifex maximus* Q. Mucius Scaevola (early first century BCE) is credited with the popularization of the distinction, originally Greek, between the gods of the poets as represented in myths, the gods of ordinary people to be found in cults and sacred laws, and finally the gods of the philosophers, confined to books and private discussion. It was the distinction underlying the thought of Varro and Cicero. No wonder, therefore, that in that atmosphere of civil wars and personal hatreds, cultic rules and practices were exploited ruthlessly to embarrass enemies, and no one could publicly challenge the ultimate validity of traditional practices.

The Augustan restoration discouraged philosophical speculation about the nature of the gods: Lucretius's *De rerum natura* remains characteristic of the age of Caesar. Augustan poets (Horace, Tibullus, Propertius, and Ovid) evoked obsolescent rites and emphasized piety. Vergil interpreted the Roman past in religious terms. Nevertheless, the combined effect of the initiatives of Caesar and Augustus amounted to a new religious situation.

For centuries the aristocracy in Rome had controlled what was called *ius sacrum* (sacred law), the religious aspect of Roman life, but the association of priesthood with political magistracy, though frequent and obviously convenient, had never been institutionalized. In 27 BCE the assumption by Octavian of the name Augustus implied, though not very clearly, permanent approval of the gods (*augustus* may connote a holder of permanent favorable auspices). In 12 BCE Augustus assumed the position of *pontifex maximus*, which became permanently associated with the figure of the emperor (*imperator*), the new head for life of the Roman state. Augustus's new role resulted in an identification of religious with political power, which had not existed in Rome since at least the end of the monarchy. Furthermore, the divinization of Caesar after his death had made Augustus, as his adopted son, the son of a *divus*. In turn, Augustus was officially divinized (*apotheosis*) after his death by the Roman Senate. Divinization after death did not become automatic for his successors (Tiberius, Gaius, and Nero were not divinized); nevertheless, Augustus's divinization created a presumption that there was a divine component in an ordinary emperor who had not misbehaved in his lifetime. Divinization also reinforced the trend toward the cult of the living emperor, which had been most obvious during Augustus's life. With the Flavian dynasty and later with the Antonines, it was normal for the head of the Roman state to be both the head of the state religion and a potential, or even actual, god.

As the head of Roman religion, the Roman emperor was therefore in the paradoxical situation of being responsible not only for relations between the Roman state and the gods but also for a fair assessment of his own qualifications to be considered a god, if not after his life, at least while he was alive. This situation, however, must not be assumed to have applied universally. Much of the religious life in individual towns was in the hands of local authorities or simply left to private initiative. The financial support for public cults was in any case very complex, but many sanctuaries (especially in the Greek world) had their own sources of revenue. It will be enough to mention that the Roman state granted or confirmed to certain gods in certain sanctuaries the right to receive legacies (Ulpian, *Regulae* 22.6). In providing a local shrine with special access to money, an emperor implied no more than benevolence toward the city or group involved.

Within the city of Rome, however, the emperor was in virtual control of the public cults. As a Greek god, Apollo had been kept outside of the *pomerium* since his introduction into Rome: his temple was in the Campus Martius. Under Augustus, however, Apollo received a temple inside the *pomerium* on the Palatine in recognition of the special protection he had offered to Octavian. The Sibylline Books, an ancient collection of prophecies that previously had been preserved on the Capitol, were now transferred to the new temple. Later, Augustus demonstrated his preference for Mars as a family god, and a temple to Mars Ultor (the avenger of Caesar's murder) was built. It was no doubt on the direct initiative of Hadrian that the cult of Rome as a goddess (in association with Venus) was finally introduced into the city centuries after the cult had spread outside of Italy. A temple to the Sun (Sol), a cult popular in the Empire at large and not without some roots in the archaic religion of Rome, had to wait until Emperor Aurelian in 274 CE, if one discounts the cult of the Ba'al of Emesa, a sun god, which came and went with the emperor Elagabalus in 220–221 CE. Another example of these changes inside Rome is that Emperor Claudius found the popularity of these alien cults partially responsible for the neglect of the art of haruspicy among the great Etruscan families, and he took steps to revive the art (Tacitus, *Annals* 11.15, 47 CE).

A further step in the admission of "Oriental gods" to the official religion of Rome was the building of a temple to Isis. In the late Republic, the cult was formally suppressed, only for the triumvirs to vow a shrine to the goddess in 43 BCE, and official action was taken once more against the cult under Augustus and Tiberius. At some point between then and the fourth century CE, festivals of Isis entered the official

Roman calendar, possibly under the emperor Gaius Caligula. From at least the second century CE, the main Roman sanctuary of Isis on the Campus Martius was architecturally related to the east side of the Saepta, or official voting area, and to other public monuments in this area, which suggests its integration into the official landscape of Rome. It was, however, the only new foreign sanctuary, so far as can be discovered from the surviving fragments, to be represented on the third-century CE official map of the city of Rome. Jupiter Dolichenus, a god from northern Syria popular among soldiers, was probably given a temple on the Aventine in the second century CE.

There is some evidence that the Roman priestly colleges intervened in the cults of *municipia* and *coloniae* (in relation to the cult of Mater Magna), but on the whole it is unreasonable expect the cults of Rome herself to remain exemplary for Roman citizens living elsewhere. For example, Vitruvius, who dedicated his work on architecture to Octavian before the latter became Augustus in 27 BCE, assumes that in an Italian city there should be a temple to Isis and Sarapis (*De architectura* 1.7.1), but Isis was kept out of Rome in those years. Emperor Caracalla, however, presented his grant of Roman citizenship to the provincials in 212 CE in hope of contributing to religious unification: "So I think I can in this way perform a [magnificent and pious] act, worthy of their majesty, by gathering to their rites [as Romans] all the multitude that joins my people" (*Papyrus Giessen* 40). Although the cult of Zeus Kapetolios appears three years later at the Greek city of Ptolemais Euergetis in Egypt, the general results of Caracalla's grant were modest in religious terms.

Coins and medals, insofar as they were issued under the control of the central government, provide some indication of imperial preferences in the matter of gods and cults, as well as when and how certain Oriental cults (such as that of Isis, as reflected on coins of Vespasian) or certain attributes of a specific god were considered helpful to the Empire and altogether suitable for ordinary people who used coins. But because as a rule it avoided references to cults of rulers, coinage can be misleading if considered alone. Imperial cult and Oriental cults are, in fact, two of the most important features of Roman religion in the imperial period. But it is crucial to take into consideration popular, not easily definable trends; the religious beliefs or disbeliefs of the intellectuals; the greater participation of women in religious and in intellectual life generally; and, finally, the peculiar problems presented by the persecution of Christianity.

MAGIC AND DIVINATION. A striking development of the imperial period was that the concept of magic emerged as the ultimate *superstitio*, a system whose principles were parodic of and in opposition to true *religio*. The definition of magic is contentious and hotly debated. In the nineteenth and earlier part of the twentieth century, many theorists (especially Sir James Frazer, the author of *The Golden Bough*) defined "magic" as an inferior and prior form of religion: whereas religion had a complex cognitive significance, magical actions were purely instrumental, believed to have a direct causal effect on the world; or, in an alternative formulation, the magician coerced the deities, whereas the priest of religion entreated them in prayer and sacrifice. Such theories still underlie widely held conceptions of magic. But this grand developmental scheme, in which magic is seen as the precursor of "true religion," has become increasingly discredited, along with the nineteenth-century evolutionary views of human society and development of which it is a part. Besides, the definition of magic as coercive and instrumental as against the (essentially Christian and partisan) view of "real" religion as noninstrumental and noncoercive does not often match (or help us to classify) the varieties of ritual, worship, or religious officials in the ancient world. A better starting point is the discussions of magic (and its relation to religion) in the writings of the Romans themselves. For example, according to the encyclopedia of Pliny the Elder, magic, which originated in Persia, was a heady combination of medicine, religion, and astrology that met human desires for health, control of the gods, and knowledge of the future. The system was, in his view, totally fraudulent (*Natural History* 30.1-18; cf. Lucan's *Pharsalia* 6.413-830). Such views of magic as a form of deviant religious behavior should also be related to the developing concepts and practices of Roman law in the imperial period. The speech by Apuleius (*De magia*) defending himself against a charge of bewitching a wealthy heiress in a North African town is particularly important.

The relationship of this stereotype to the reality of magical practice is, however, complex. Magic was an important part of the fictional repertoire of Roman writers, but it was not only a figment of the imagination of the elite; and its practice may have become more prominent through the principate—a consequence perhaps of it too (like other forms of knowledge) becoming partially professionalized in the hands of literate experts in the imperial period. So, for example, the surviving Latin curses (often scratched on lead tablets, and so preserved) increase greatly in number under the Empire, and the Greek magical papyri from Egypt are most common in the third and fourth centuries CE. Roman anxieties about magic may, in part, have been triggered by changes in its practices and prominence, as well as by the internal logic of their own worldview.

Divination had been central to republican politics and to the traditional religion of the Roman state. For example, before engagement in battle or before any meeting of an assembly the "auspices" were taken—in other words, the heavens were observed for any signs (such as the particular pattern of a flight of birds) that the gods gave or withheld their assent to the project in hand. These forms of divination changed in Rome under the principate. The traditional systematic reporting of prodigies, for example, disappeared in the Augustan period: these seemingly random intrusions of divine displeasure must have appeared incongruous in a system where divine favor flowed through the emperor; such prodigies as were noted generally centered on the births and deaths of emperors. There were many other forms of divination. Some of them (such as astrology) involved specific foretelling of the future. Some (such as dream interpretation) were a private, rather than a public, affair. Some could even be practiced as a weapon against the current political order—as when casting an emperor's horoscope foretold his imminent death.

The practitioners of divination were as varied as its functions. They ranged from the senior magistrates (who observed the heavens before an assembly) and the state priests (such as the *augures* who advised the magistrates on heavenly signs) to the potentially dangerous astrologers and soothsayers. These people were periodically expelled from the city of Rome and under the principate were subject to control by provincial governors. The jurist Ulpian included in his treatise on the duties of provincial governors a section explaining the regulation of astrologers and soothsayers; a papyrus document survives from Roman Egypt, with a copy of a general ban on divination issued by a governor of the province in the late second century CE (on the grounds that it led people astray and brought danger); and at the end of the third century CE the emperor Diocletian issued a general ban on astrology. Consultation of diviners that threatened the stability of private families or the life of the emperor himself were obvious targets for punishment.

The Imperial Cult. The imperial cult was many things to many people. Indeed, it can be said that there was no "imperial cult;" instead, there were many "imperial cults," as appropriate in many different contexts. The emperor never became a complete god, even if he was considered a god, because he was not requested to produce miracles, even for supposed deliverance from peril. Vespasian performed miracles in Alexandria soon after his proclamation as emperor, but these had no precise connection to his potential divine status; he remained an exception in any case. Hadrian never performed miracles, but his young lover Antinous, who was divinized after death, is known to have performed some (Dörner, 1952, p. 40, no. 78).

Apotheosis, decided by the Senate, was the only official form of deification valid for everyone in the Empire and was occasionally extended to female members of the imperial family (Drusilla, the sister of Gaius, who received apotheosis in 38 CE, was the first such honorand.) It had its precedent, of course, in the apotheosis of Romulus. Ultimately, the cult of the living emperor mattered more. It was the result of a mixture of spontaneous initiative by provincial and local councils (and even by private individuals) and promptings from provincial governors and the emperor himself. It had precedents not only in the Hellenistic ruler cult but also in the more or less spontaneous worship of Roman generals and governors, especially in the Hellenized East. Though it is unlikely that temples were built to provincial governors, Cicero had to decline such worship when he was governor of Cilicia (*Ad Atticum* 5.21.7).

The cult of Roman provincial governors disappeared with Augustus, to the exclusive benefit of the emperor and his family. When he did not directly encourage the ruler cult, the emperor still had to approve, limit, and occasionally refuse it. Although he had to be worshiped, he also had to remain a man in order to live on social terms with the Roman aristocracy, of which he was supposed to be the *princeps.* It was a delicate balancing act. It is probably fair to say that during his lifetime the emperor was a god more in proportion to his remoteness than his proximity, and that the success (for success it was) of the imperial cult in the provinces was due to the presence it endowed to an absent and alien sovereign. His statues, his temples, and his priests, as well as the games, sacrifices, and other ceremonial acts, helped make the emperor present; they also helped people to express their interest in the preservation of the world in which they lived.

The imperial cult was not universally accepted and liked. Seneca ridiculed the cult of Claudius, and Tacitus spoke of the cult in general as Greek adulation. In the third century the historian Dio Cassius attributed to Augustus's friend Maecenas a total condemnation of the imperial cult. Jews and Christians objected to it on principle, and the acts of the Christian martyrs remind us that there was an element of brutal imposition in the imperial cult. But its controversial nature in certain circles may well have been another factor in the cult's success (conflicts help any cause). There is even evidence that some groups treated the imperial cult as a mystery religion in which priests displayed imperial images or symbols.

Schematically, it can be said that in Rome Augustus favored the association of the cult of his life spirit (genius) with the old cult of the public *lares* of the crossroads (*lares compitales*). Such a combined cult was in the hands of humble people (especially ex-slaves). Similar associations developed along various lines in Italy and the West and gave respectability to the ex-slaves who ran them. Augustus's birthday was considered a public holiday. His genius was included in public oaths between Jupiter Optimus Maximus and the *penates.* In Augustus's last years Tiberius dedicated an altar to the *numen Augusti* in Rome; the four great priestly colleges had to make yearly sacrifices at it. *Numen,* in an obscure way, implied divine will.

In the West, central initiative created the altar of Roma and Augustus outside Lyons, to be administered by the Council of the Three Gauls (12 BCE). A similar altar was built at Oppidum Ubiorum (Cologne). Later temples to Augustus (by then officially divinized) were erected in Western provinces. The key episode occurred in 15 CE, the year after the official deification of Augustus in Rome, when permission was given to the province of Hispania Tarraconensis for a temple to Divus Augustus in the *colonia* of Tarraco. Its priests were drawn not just from Tarraco but from the whole province, and Tacitus (*Annals* 1.78), reporting the decision of 15 CE, notes that the temple set a precedent for other provinces. In the East, temples to Roma and Divus Julius (for

Roman citizens) and to Roma and Augustus (for Greeks) were erected as early as 29 BCE. There, as in the West, provincial assemblies took a leading part in the establishment of the cult. Individual cities were also active: priests of Augustus are found in thirty-four different cities of Asia Minor. The organization of the cult varied locally. There was no collective provincial cult of the emperor in Egypt, though there was a cult in Alexandria. And any poet, indeed any person, could have his or her own idea about the divine nature of the emperor. Horace, for example, suggested that Augustus might be Mercurius (*Odes* 1.2).

Augustus's successors tended to be worshiped either individually, without the addition of Roma, or collectively with past emperors. In Asia Minor the last individual emperor known to have received a personal priesthood or temple is Caracalla. In this province—though not necessarily elsewhere—the imperial cult petered out at the end of the third century. Nevertheless, Constantine, in the fourth century, authorized the building of a temple for the *gens* Flavia (his own family) in Italy at Hispellum, but he warned that it "should not be polluted by the deceits of any contagious *superstitio*"—whatever he may have meant by this (Hermann Dessau, *Inscriptiones Latinae Selectae* 705, lines 46-48, 337 CE).

It is difficult to say how much the ceremonies of the imperial court reflected divinization of the emperors. Domitian wanted to be called *dominus et deus* (Suetonius, *Domitian* 13.2), but this is anomalous and broke the normal convention that the emperor should present himself to the Roman elite as *primus inter pares* (first among equals). In the third century a specific identification of the living emperor with a known god seems to be more frequent (for instance, Septimius Severus and his wife, Julia Domna, with Jupiter and Juno). When the imperial cult died out, the emperor had to be justified as the choice of god; he became emperor by the grace of god. Thus Diocletian and Maximian, persecutors of Christianity, present themselves not as Jupiter and Hercules but as Jovius and Herculius, that is, the protégés of Jupiter and Hercules. It must be added that during the first centuries of the Empire the divinization of the emperor was accompanied by a multiplication of divinizations of private individuals, in the West often of humble origin. Such divinization took the form of identifying the dead, and occasionally the living, with a known hero or god. Sometimes the divinization was nothing more than an expression of affection by relatives or friends. But it indicated a tendency to reduce the distance between men and gods, which helped the fortunes of the imperial cult (Wrede, 1981).

In at least the "civilized" parts of both East and West, the principal social change that accompanied these religious changes was the role of local elites in the service of Rome. Holders of the local offices of the imperial cult received prestige in their local communities, as they did for holding other offices or priesthoods, and they might be able to use such offices to further the status of themselves or their families. In the West, ex-slaves with Roman citizenship (who formed a significant upwardly mobile group) could aspire to a public status that articulated their position in the framework of the Roman Empire.

"Oriental" Influences. It has long been standard to employ the category "Oriental religions" in discussing the new religious options in imperial Rome. This category was first widely used, if not invented, by the Belgian scholar Franz Cumont in the early years of the twentieth century in his pioneering studies of Roman religion. For Cumont, the key to understanding the religious history of the period lay in the influx into Rome of a group of Eastern religions that shared a number of common characteristics setting them apart from traditional civic cults—and paving the way, eventually, for the rise of Christianity. However, these religions cannot be neatly pigeonholed as "Oriental." Several of the cults did proclaim an Eastern "origin" for their wisdom, but it is often clear that a Roman version of the cult differed substantially from its (notional) Eastern ancestor. Above all, the "Orient" itself was hardly the homogeneous category that modern scholars (and the Romans, no doubt) often try to make it: different cults came from quite different religious backgrounds—the religious traditions of the home of Mithras in Persia, for example, had little in common with the Egyptian traditions in the worship of Isis and Sarapis.

The issue of whom the new cults attracted is difficult. Did the different "messages" appeal more to some sections of the inhabitants of Rome than to others? Were the poor more commonly to be found among the adherents than the rich? Women more commonly than men? Did these alternative religions attract those who had only a small role to play in the traditional civic cults and the political order that those cults sustained? Were they, in other words, "religions of disadvantage?" There is no simple answer to those questions. There was enormous variety within the population of Rome, which had no single axis between privilege and disadvantage. In a society where some of the richest and most educated members were to be found outside (and indeed ineligible for) the ranks of the elite, it makes no sense to imagine a single category of "the disadvantaged." Besides, it is very hard now (and no doubt always was for most outside observers) to reconstruct accurately the membership of any particular cult; for apparently casual references to a cult's adherents in the writing of the period are often part and parcel of an attack on that cult—deriding a religion as being, for example, the business of women and slaves. But it is clear that male members of the senatorial order were conspicuously absent from the new cults. No senators are attested as initiates of Jupiter Dolichenus, Jupiter Optimus Maximus Heliopolitanus, Isis, Mithras, or (probably) Christianity before the mid-third century CE.

New cults claiming an "Oriental" origin penetrated the Roman Empire at various dates, in different circumstances, and with varying appeal, although on the whole they seem to have supplemented religious needs in the Latin West more than in the Hellenized East. They tended, though not in equal measure, to present themselves as mystery cults: they often required initiation and, perhaps more often, some religious instruction.

Cybele, the first Oriental divinity to be found acceptable in Rome since the end of the third century BCE, was long an oddity in the city. As the Mater Magna (Great Mother), she had been imported by governmental decision, she had a temple within the *pomerium*, and she was under the protection of members of the highest Roman aristocracy. Yet her professional priests, singing in Greek and living by their temple, were considered alien fanatics even in imperial times. What is worse, the goddess also had servants, the Galli, who had castrated themselves to express their devotion to her.

Under the emperor Claudius, Roman citizens were probably allowed some priestly functions, though the matter is very obscure. Even more obscure is how Attis became Cybele's major partner. He is so poorly attested in the republican written evidence for the cult of Cybele that scholars used to believe that he was introduced to the cult only in the first century CE (they saw Catullus 63 as a purely "literary" text). However, excavations at the Palatine temple of Mater Magna discovered a major cache of statuettes of Attis dating to the second and first centuries BCE. The find hints that religious life in republican Rome was more varied than the written record suggests. A new festival, from March 15 to 27, apparently put special emphasis on the rebirth of Attis. Concurrently, the cult of Cybele became associated with the ritual of the slaying of the sacred bull (taurobolium), which the Christian poet Prudentius (*Peristephanon* 10.1006–1050) interpreted as a baptism of blood (though his depiction of the ritual is deeply suspect, forming part of a fierce and late anti-pagan polemic). The taurobolium was performed for the prosperity of the emperor or of the Empire and, more frequently, for the benefit of private individuals. Normally it was considered valid for twenty years, which makes it highly questionable whether it was meant to confer immortality on the baptized.

Although Isis appealed to men as well as to women—and indeed her priests were male—it seems clear that her prestige as a goddess was due to the unusual powers she was supposed to have as a female deity. The so-called aretalogies (description of the powers) of Isis insist on this. Thus the earliest aretalogy, found at Maroneia in Thrace, tells of Isis as legislator and as protector of the respect of children for their parents (*Supplementum Epigraphicum Graecum* 26, no. 821). The text from Kyme (in West Turkey) declares that she compelled husbands to love their wives (H. Engelmann, ed., *Inschriften von Kyme* 41, 1.97), and the hymn from Oxyrhynchus (Egypt) in her honor explicitly states that she made the power of women equal to that of men (Oxyrhynchus Papyri 11.1380). No god or goddess of Greece and Rome had achievements comparable with those of Isis. The girlfriends of the Augustan poets Tibullus and Propertius were captivated by her. In association with Osiris or Sarapis, Isis seems to have become the object of a mystery cult in the first century CE; she appears as such in Apuleius's *Metamorphoses.*

Late in the first century CE, Mithraism began to spread throughout the Roman Empire, especially in the Danubian countries and in Italy (in particular, as far as can be known, in Ostia and Rome). A developed mystery cult, it had ranks of initiation and leadership and was—though this has been disputed—reserved for men, a clear difference from the cult of Isis. It was practiced in subterranean shrines rather than in temples; the rooms were ritual versions of the cave in Persia where Mithra had once slain a bull. The environment of the Mithraic cult, as revealed in numerous extant shrines, was one of darkness, secrecy, and dramatic lighting effects.

What promise Mithra held for his devotees cannot be known for certain. The cult seems to have encouraged soldierly qualities, including sexual abstinence. It certainly presented some correspondence between the degrees of initiation and the levels of the celestial spheres, which probably implies an ascent of the soul to these spheres. The killing of the bull (different from the taurobolium and perhaps without any implication of baptism) was apparently felt to be a sacrifice performed not for the god but by the god. The initiates reenacted this sacrifice and shared sacred meals in a sort of communal life. The progressive transformation of the soul of the initiate in this life, on which much of the cult focused, was probably conceived to continue after death. Tertullian considered Mithraism a devilish imitation of Christianity, but the Neoplatonist Porphyry found in it allegorical depths.

The cult of Sabazios may have been originally Phrygian, but later was known also as an "ancestral" deity of Thrace. Sabazios appears in Athens in the fifth century BCE as an orgiastic god. He was known to Aristophanes, and later the orator Aeschines may have become his priest. There is evidence of mysteries of Sabazios in Lydia dating from the fourth century BCE. In Rome the cult was already known in 139 BCE. It may at that time have been confused with Judaism, but Sabazios was often identified with Jupiter or Zeus, and there seems to be no clear evidence of syncretism between Sabazios and Yahweh. Sabazios was most popular in the second century CE, especially in the Danubian region. In Rome his cult left a particularly curious document in the tomb of Vincentius, located in the catacomb of Praetextatus. The document includes scenes of banquets and of judgment after death. Whether this is evidence of mystery ceremonies or of Christian influence remains uncertain (Hermann Dessau, *Inscriptiones Latinae Selectae* 3961; see Goodenough, 1953, p. 45 for a description) The tomb of Vincentius appears to belong to the third century, when, judging by the epigraphic evidence, there seems to have been a decline of the cult of Sabazios and, indeed, of all mystery cults. Although a shortage of inscriptions does not necessarily imply a shortage of adepts, it leaves the impression that by then Christianity was seriously interfering with the popularity of Oriental cults.

Another popular Oriental god occupies a place by himself. This is Jupiter Dolichenus, who emerged from Doliche in northern Syria in the first century CE and who has over six hundred monuments. His cult is known mostly in Rome and along the Rhine-Danube border zone. Of the Oriental gods, he seems to have been the least sophisticated and to have disappeared earliest (in the third century). Christian polemicists ignored him. While he circulated in the Empire, he preserved his native attributes: he is depicted as a warrior with Phrygian cap, double ax, and lightning bolt, standing erect over a bull. In the Roman interpretation, the goddess Juno Regina often accompanied him. Twins, identified with the Castores, followed him; their lower parts were unshaped, and they were probably demons. Soldiers seem to have loved the cult of Jupiter Dolichenus. Its priests were not professional, and the adepts called each other brother. Admission to the cult presupposed instruction, if not initiation.

Religious Pluralism? There is a constant danger of either overrating or underrating the influence of these Oriental cults on the fabric of the Roman Empire. If, for instance, Mithraists knew of the Zoroastrian deity Angra Mainyu, what did he mean to them? How did this knowledge affect the larger society? At a superficial level these cults can be seen as an antidote to the imperial cult, an attempt to retreat from the public sphere of political allegiance to the private sphere of small, free associations. The need for small loyalties was widely felt during the imperial peace. Distinctions between social, charitable, and religious purposes in these multiform associations are impossible. Tavern keepers devoted to their wine god and poor people meeting regularly in burial clubs are examples of such associations (*collegia*). Ritualization of ordinary life emerged from their activities. Nor is it surprising that what to one was religion was superstition to another (to use two Latin terms that ordinary Latin speakers would have been hard-pressed to define). Although allegiance to the local gods (and respect for them, if one happened to be a visitor) was deeply rooted, people were experimenting with new private gods and finding satisfaction in them. Concern with magic and astrology, with dreams and demons, seems ubiquitous. Conviviality was part of religion. Aelius Aristides has good things to say about Sarapis as patron of the symposium. Pilgrimages to sanctuaries were made easier by relative social stability. Several gods, not only Asclepius (Gr., Asklepios), offered healing to the sick. (Here again, Aelius Aristides is chief witness for the second century.) Hence miracles, duly registered in inscriptions; hence also single individuals, perhaps cranks, attaching themselves to temples and living in their precincts.

The real difficulties in understanding the atmosphere of paganism in the Roman Empire perhaps lie elsewhere. It remains a puzzle how, and how much, ordinary people were supposed to know about official Roman religion. The same problem exists concerning the Greeks in relation to the religions of individual Greek cities. But in Greek cities the collective education of adolescents, as *epheboi*, implied participation in religious activities (for instance, singing hymns in festivals) that were a form of religious education. In the Latin-speaking world, however, there is no indication of generalized practices of this kind. People who tell us something about their own education, such as Cicero, Horace, and Ovid, do not imply that it included a religious side. The situation does not seem to have changed in later times, as illustrated, for instance, in Tacitus's life of Agricola. Children at school no doubt absorbed a great deal from classical authors, but, whether they read Homer or Vergil, they did not absorb the religion of their own city. Temples carried inscriptions explaining what was expected from worshipers as well as the qualities of the relevant god. Cultic performances, often in a theater adjoining the temple, helped to explain what the god was capable of. However, a distinct line cannot be drawn between cultic performances, perhaps with an element of initiation, and simple entertainment. More puzzling still is the question of what general idea of "Roman religion" (if, by that, is meant the religious institutions and practices of the capital) the population of towns in Italy and *coloniae* in the provinces would have had. One possible channel is Varro's *Divine Antiquities.* This treatise remained even under the Empire the only general work on the Roman religious system. That provincials did turn to it for inspiration is suggested by the effective (polemical) use made of it by the Christian Tertullian, writing in North Africa. But even Varro's book is difficult to apply to particular local issues.

Another element difficult to evaluate is the continuous, and perhaps increased, appeal of impersonal gods within Roman religion. There is no indication that Faith (Fides) and Hope (Spes) increased their appeal (they came to play a different part in Christianity by combining with Jewish and Greek ideas). At best, Fides gained prestige as a symbol of return to loyalty and good faith during the reign of Augustus. But Fortuna and Virtus were popular; the typology of Virtus on coins seems to be identical with that of Roma. Genius was generalized to indicate the spirit of a place or of a corporation. Strangely, an old Latin god of the woods, Silvanus, whose name does not appear in the Roman calendar, became important, partly because of his identification with the Greek Pan and with a Pannonian god, but above all because of his equation with Genius. The god as protector of Roman barracks was called Genius Castrorum, Silvanus Castrorum, or Fortuna Castrorum. Victoria, too, was often connected with individual emperors and individual victories (Victoria Augusti and Ludi Victoriae Claudi, for example).

A third complication is syncretism, which means two different things. One is the positive identification of two or more gods; the other is the tendency to mix different cults by using symbols of other gods in the sanctuary of one god, with the result that the presence of Sarapis, Juno, and even Isis was implied in the shrine of Jupiter Dolichenus on the Aventine in Rome. In either form, syncretism may have encouraged the idea that all gods are aspects, or manifestations, of one god. In most cases of identification of two or more gods, there is only the record of a mixed divine name, so it is left to guesswork what that name meant, which deity (Roman or native) was uppermost in the minds of the worshippers, or whether the two had merged into a new composite whole (a process often now referred to as *syncretism*). There is no way to know, in other words, how much of the process was an aspect of Roman take-over (and ultimately obliteration) of native deities, how much it was a mutually respectful union of two divine powers, or how much it was a minimal, resistant, and token incorporation of Roman imperial paraphernalia on the part of the provincials. Signs of syncretism, then, always need to be interpreted. For example, to understand why most deities in the eastern part of the Empire did not merge with Roman counterparts but retained their individual personalities and characteristics, whereas in the western part pre-Roman gods acquired Roman names, or non-Roman and Roman divine names were linked, it is necessary to investigate the nature of Roman religion outside Rome and attend to the agenda of all those groups involved in developing a new Roman imperial worldview.

A related issue is monotheism. According to a Christian writer of the second century CE, the Greeks had 365 gods. For the proponent of one (Christian) god this alleged fact demonstrated the absurdity of Greek religion. Modern scholars also sometimes assume the nobility and superiority of one supreme god (monotheism) as against the proliferation of little gods (polytheism). But the number of the Greek gods (not as great as 365) does not mean that those gods lacked significance any more than does the multiplicity of gods in the Hindu tradition. In addition, proponents of monotheism (whether Jewish, Christian, or Islamic) are often not ready to note the disruptive consequences of monotheistic intolerance or the extent to which alleged monotheisms contain plural elements. Within Christianity, what about the Trinity, the Blessed Virgin Mary, or the saints? In fact the categories *monotheism* and *polytheism* do not promote historical understanding. Some scholars have sought to "rescue" polytheism by arguing for an element of monolatry (or henotheism), in which the power of one god in the pantheon is proclaimed as supreme. But this maneuver is conditioned by a Judaeo-Christian evaluation of monotheism, and the tendency to monolatry in antiquity is much overstated. The terms *polytheism* and *monotheism* are best left to the theologians.

Interest in an abstract deity was encouraged by philosophical reflection, quite apart from suggestions coming from Judaism, Christianity, and Zoroastrianism. Some have therefore thought it legitimate to consider the cult of Sol Invictus, patronized by the emperor Aurelian, as a monotheistic or henotheistic predecessor of Christianity. But believers would have had to visualize the relation between the one and the many. This relation was complicated by the admission of intermediate demons, either occupying zones between god (or gods) and men or going about the earth and perhaps more capable of evil than of good. Even those (such as Plutarch) who could think through, in some depth, the idea of one god were still interested in Zeus or Isis or Dionysos, whatever their relation to the god beyond the gods. Those educated people in late antiquity who liked to collect priesthoods and initiations to several gods, in pointed contrast with Christianity, evidently did so because they did not look upon the gods concerned as one god only. The monuments of the leading pagan senator Vettius Agorius Praetextatus are an example of this tendency. In the face of a Christianity that was gaining the upper hand, he and those like him sought to gather together all that could be saved from the traditional cults (*Corpus Inscriptionum Latinarum*, Berlin, 1863, vol. 6, no. 1778, 387 CE; Hermann Dessau, *Inscriptione Latinae Selectae* 1259, tombstone).

This is not to deny the convergence of (or at least striking parallels between) certain beliefs and experiences. For example, the mystical experience of ascension to heaven was shared by Paul, Jewish rabbis, Gnostics such as the author of the *Gospel of Truth*, Plotinus, and the author of the "Mithras liturgy" (preserved in the Great Magical Papyrus of Paris).

ROLE OF WOMEN. Gender had always been a factor in the organization of cults. It is important to consider how the appeal of the various cults to different genders determined the membership of new religions. The official civic cults of Rome were principally in the control of men—though there were some exceptions (e.g. Vestal Virgins). Some cults and festivals demanded the participation of women. According to tradition, The temple of Fortuna Muliebris, "the Fortune of Women," was dedicated by senatorial wives in 493 BCE and served as the focus for their religious activities. In the imperial period, the temple was restored by Augustus's wife, Livia (and again by Emperor Septimius Severus, along with his two sons and his wife, Julia Domna). Formal involvement of women in the official cults of Rome was largely restricted to women of senatorial families.

In general, although the attendance of women at most religious occasions (including games) was not prohibited, women had little opportunity to take an active religious role in state cults. Even occupational or burial associations generally did not include women; only in the purely domestic associations of the great households were women normally members. Much more fundamentally, women may have been banned—in theory, at any rate—from carrying out animal sacrifice; and so prohibited from any officiating role in the central defining ritual of civic religious activity.

These limited roles may have been satisfying to some women, but almost certainly not to all. How far then did women find in the new cults a part to play that was not available to them in civic religions? Some women no doubt found an opportunity within these cults for all kinds of religious expression not available within the civic cults of Rome. For some women, it may even have been precisely that opportunity which first attracted them to an alternative cult. On the other hand, there is no evidence to suggest that women were particularly powerful within these cults in general or that they dominated the membership in the way suggested by the conventional stereotype of the literature of the period. In the cult of Isis, men held the principal offices, and the names of cult members recorded in inscriptions do not suggest that women predominated numerically.

The literary stereotype, in other words, almost certainly exaggerates the number and importance of women in the cults by representing them effectively as "women's cults." Why is this? In part the explanation may lie in the exclusively elite vision of most of the literary sources. Even if women did not dominate the new religions, it seems certain that upper-class women were involved in these cults before their male counterparts. Wives of senators, that is, were participating in the worship of Isis at a period when no senator was involved in the cult; and wives of senators are attested as Christians from the late second century CE, before any Christian senator. Thus, the literary stereotype may reflect a (temporary) difference between the involvement of elite men and women that did not necessarily apply at other levels of society. Much more fundamentally, however, the claims of female fascination with foreign religion are embedded in the vast literary and cultural traditions of Greco-Roman misogyny. And, at the same time, foreign peoples and places were denigrated in specifically female terms. In traditional Roman ideology, "Oriental" cults would inevitably raise questions of gender.

Women's participation in new cults is one aspect of the active part they played in the religious life of the imperial period. Women, especially wealthy women, experienced considerable freedom of movement and could administer their own estates. Roman empresses of Eastern origin (Julia Domna, wife of Septimius Severus, and Julia Mamaea, mother of Severus Alexander) contributed to the diffusion outside Africa of the cult of Caelestis, who received a temple on the Capitol in Rome. The wife of a Roman consul, Pompeia Agrippinilla, was priestess of an association of about four hundred devotees (all members of her household) of Liber-Dionysos in the Roman Campagna in the middle of the second century CE (Moretti, 1968, no. 160). In the Greek world, women served as priestesses (as they had always done) but received new public honors. In the city of Thasos in the third century CE, a woman, Flavia Vibia Sabina, was honored by the local council "as a most noteworthy high priestess . . . the only woman, first in all times to have honors equal to those of the councilors" (Pleket, 1969, no. 29). Women could be asked to act as *theologoi,* that is, to preach about gods in ceremonies even of a mystery nature. It is revealing that the emperor Marcus Aurelius declared himself grateful to his mother for teaching him veneration of the gods.

The intellectual and religious achievements of women become more conspicuous in the fourth century CE. Women such as Sosipatra, described in Eunapius's account of the lives of the Sophists, and Hypatia of Alexandria are the counterparts (though apparently more broadly educated and more independent in their social actions) of Christian women such as Macrina, sister of Gregory of Nyssa (who wrote her biography), and the followers of Jerome.

Dedications of religious and philosophical books by men to women appear in the imperial period. Plutarch dedicated his treatise on Isis and Osiris to Clea, a priestess of Delphi. Diogenes Laertius dedicated his book on Greek philosophers (which has anti-Christian implications) to a female Platonist. Philostratus claims that Julia Domna encouraged him to write the life of Apollonius of Tyana. What is more, according to the Christian writer Eusebius, Julia Mamaea (mother of the emperor Alexander Severus) invited Origen to visit her in Antioch, allegedly to discuss Christianity.

EVIDENCE. Epigraphy and archaeology are the starting point for analysis of the religious history of the Roman Empire. Both types of evidence are the actual products of religious adherents of the period, designed to promote or support their religious actions and beliefs. The interpretation of the iconography of objects, the design of buildings, and the formulation of dedications is absolutely critical. This evidence does, however, need to be used with care. Inscriptions have to be treated not simply as texts (which is how they are often presented in modern books), but as texts with particular relationships to the objects on which they were written. In addition, texts painted on walls (*dipinti*) or written on material other than stone or bronze rarely survive. But the sheer number of religious dedications tempts one to treat the variations in their numbers over time as an index of the varying popularity of the deity concerned. This is a mistake, as the variation in the number of religious dedications parallels the variations in the number of inscriptions in general. In other words, religious inscriptions share in the variations in the "epigraphic habit."

A further point to note is that not all religious groups embedded their practices in material form. Jewish and Christian groups in the early Empire are largely invisible from either archaeological or epigraphical evidence (in Rome, for example, there are no remains of synagogues and no secure evidence of churches before Constantine).

In addition to epigraphy and archaeology, the religions of the Roman Empire survive mainly through writings in Latin, Greek, Syriac, and Coptic (not to speak of other languages), such as biographies, philosophical disputations, epic poems, antiquarian books, exchanges of letters, novels, and specific religious books. Most of the authors speak only for themselves. But taken together, they convey an atmosphere of sophisticated cross-questioning that would have prevented minds from shutting out alternatives. For example, the Stoic Lucan in his *Pharsalia,* a poem on the civil wars, excludes the gods but admits fate and fortune, magic and divination. Two generations later, Silius Italicus wrote an optimistic poem describing Scipio as a Roman Heracles supported by his father, Jupiter. More or less at the same time, Plutarch was reflecting on new and old cults, on the delays in divine justice, and (if the work in question is indeed his) on superstition.

In the second part of the second century Lucian passed from the caricature of an assembly of gods and from attacks against oracles to a sympathetic description of the cult of Dea

Syria; he abused such religious fanatics as Peregrinus, as well as Alexander of Abonuteichos, the author of a new cult, whom he considered to be an impostor. Perhaps what Lucian wanted to give is, in fact, what readers get from him—the impression of a mind that refuses to be imposed upon. Fronto's correspondence with Marcus Aurelius confirms what can be deduced from other texts (such as Aelius Aristides's speeches): preoccupation with one's own health was a source of intense religious experience in the second century CE. In his *Metamorphoses,* also known as *The Golden Ass,* Apuleius offers a (partially satirical) account of the mysteries of Isis that may be based on personal experience. But Apuleius's *Golden Ass* is only one of the many novels that were fashionable in the Roman Empire. The appeal of such works probably resided in their ability to offer readers vicarious experiences of love, magic, and mystery ritual.

The variety of moods and experiences conveyed by these texts, from the skeptical to the mystical, from the egotistic to the political in the old Greek sense, gives us an approximate notion of the thoughts of educated people on religious subjects. These books provide the background for an understanding of the Christian apologists who wrote for the pagan upper class. How much of pagan religious thinking was conditioned by the presence of Jews and, even more, of Christians in the neighborhood? The anti-Jewish attitudes of a Tacitus or of a Juvenal offer no special problem; they are explicit. The same can be said about the anti-Christian polemics of Celsus. The problem, if any, is that the text is lost and inferences have to be made from the reply given in changed circumstances by the Christian Origen. But there are far more writers who seldom or never refer to Christianity yet who can hardly have formulated their thoughts without implicit reference to it.

How much Lucian or Philostratus (in his life of Apollonius of Tyana) was trying to put across pagan points of view in answer to the Christian message is an old question. Nicomachus Flavianus, a pagan leader, translated the biography of Philostratus into Latin in the late fourth century. Another author who may know more about Christianity than his silence about it would indicate is Diogenes Laertius. In his lives of philosophers, he pointedly refuses to admit non-Greek wisdom and enumerates all the Greek schools, from Plato to Epicurus, as worthy of study and admiration. With the renascence of Neoplatonic thought in the third and fourth centuries and the combination of Platonism with mystical and magical practices (the so-called *theurgy*) in the circles to which Julian the Apostate belonged, the attempt to erect a barrier to Christianity is patent but, even then, not necessarily explicit.

The most problematic texts are perhaps those that try to formulate explicit religious beliefs. Books such as the Chaldaean Oracles (late second century, or third century CE) or the Hermetic texts, composed in Greek at various dates in Egypt (and clearly showing the influence of Jewish ideas), make it difficult to decide who believed in them and to what extent. Such texts present themselves as revealed: they speak of the human soul imprisoned in the body, of fate, and of demonic power with only a minimum of coherence. They are distantly related to what modern scholars call Gnosticism, a creed with many variants that was supposed to be a deviation from Christianity and, as such, was fought by early Christian apologists. Today, much more is known about the Gnostics, thanks to the discovery of the Nag Hammadi library, which supplemented, indeed dwarfed, previous discoveries of Coptic Gnostic texts. Assembled in the fourth century from books mainly translated from Greek, the Nag Hammadi library represents an isolated survival. It points to a previous, more central movement thriving in the exchange of ideas. What was the impact of the Gnostic sects when they placed themselves between pagans and Christians (and Jews) in the first centuries of the Empire?

State Repression and Persecution. The Roman state had always interfered with the freedom to teach and worship. In republican times, astrologers, magicians, philosophers, and even rhetoricians, not to speak of adepts of certain religious groups, had been victims of such intrusion. Under which precise legal category this interference was exercised remains a question, except perhaps in cases of sacrilege. Tacitus writes that Augustus considered adultery in his own family a crime against *religio* (*Annals* 3.24). Whatever the legal details, Druid cults and circles were persecuted in Gaul and Britain in the first century. Augustus prohibited Roman citizens from participating in Druid cults, and Claudius prohibited the cult of the Druids altogether. Though it is not clear what the consequences were for participating, there is little recorded of the Druids from this time on. Abhorrence of their human sacrifices no doubt counted for much. But Augustus also did not like the practice of foretelling the future, for which the Druids were conspicuous, and he is credited with the destruction of two thousand prophetic books (Suetonius, *Augustus* 31). The Druids were also known to be magicians, and Claudius condemned to death a Roman knight who had brought to court a Druidic magic egg (Pliny, *Natural History* 29.54).

Roman action against the Druids is an example of Roman action against practices deemed to be noxious *superstitio.* It is often said that the Roman government only exceptionally acted in this way: existing cults might or might not be encouraged, but they were seldom persecuted; even Jews and Egyptians were ordinarily protected in their cults. This view of a general liberal Roman state is false. The Romans acted whenever need arose against *superstitio.* In 19 CE two scandals in Rome brought the cults of Isis and Judaism to the attention of emperor and Senate. The outcome, according to Tacitus, was that the Senate banished four thousand ex-slaves to a labor camp in Sardinia and expelled those of higher status from Italy "unless they gave up their profane rites before an appointed day" (*Annals* 2.85; cf. Josephus, *Jewish Antiquities* 18.65–84). The principles of religious coercion were firmly in place before the emergence of Christianity.

The long-standing conflict between the Christians and the Roman state has to be set against this background. As with actions against other troublesome people, persecution was desultory and instigated from below, until the mid-third century. However, there are some unique aspects, mostly as a result of Christian rather than of imperial behavior. First, the Christians obviously did not yield or retreat, as did the Druids. Indeed they were believed actively to seek conversions, even without the knowledge or approval of the head of the household. Second, the Christians hardly ever became outright enemies of, or rebels against, the Roman state. The providential character of the Roman state was a basic assumption of Christianity. The workings of providence were shown, for Christians, by the fact that Jesus was born under Roman rule, while the Roman state had destroyed the Temple of Jerusalem and dispersed the Jews, thus making the church the heiress to the Temple. Third, the Christians were interested in what can be called "classical culture." Their debate with the pagans became, increasingly, a debate within the terms of reference of classical culture; the Jews, in contrast, soon lost their contact with classical thought and even with such men as Philo, who had represented them in the dialogue with classical culture. Fourth, Christianity and its ecclesiastical organization provided what could alternatively be either a rival or a subsidiary structure to the imperial government. The Roman government under Constantine chose the Church as a subsidiary institution (without quite knowing on what conditions).

The novelty of the conflict explains the novelty of the solution—not tolerance but conversion. The emperor had to become Christian and to accept the implications of his conversion. It took about eighty years to turn the pagan state into a Christian state. The process took the form of a series of decisions about public non-Christian acts of worship. The first prohibition of pagan sacrifices seems to have been enacted in 341 (*Codex Theodosianus* 16.10.2). Closing of the pagan temples and prohibition of sacrifices in public places under penalty of death was stated or restated at an uncertain date between 346 and 354 (*Codex Theodosianus* 16.10.4).

Even leaving aside the reaction of Julian, these measures cannot have been effective. The emperor remained *pontifex maximus* until Gratian gave up the position in 379 (Zosimus, 4.36.5). Gratian was the emperor who removed the altar of Victoria from the Roman Senate and provoked the controversy between Symmachus and Bishop Ambrose, the most important controversy about the relative merits of tolerance and conversion in late antiquity. Then, in 391, Theodosius forbade even private pagan cults (*Codex Theodosianus* 16.10.12). In the same year, following riots provoked by a special law against pagan cults in Egypt, the Serapeum of Alexandria was destroyed. The significance of this act was felt worldwide. The brief pagan revival of 393, initiated by the usurper Eugenius, a nominal Christian who sympathized with the pagans, was soon followed by other antipagan laws. Pagan priests were deprived of their privileges in 396 (*Codex Theodosianus* 16.10.4), and pagan temples in the country (not in towns) were ordered to be destroyed in 399 (*Codex Theodosianus* 16.10.16)—though in the same year, festivals that appear to have been pagan were allowed (*Codex Theodosianus* 16.10.17).

Rome in the fourth century CE remained for some people a city characterized by the worship of the ancient gods. The pagan historian Ammianus Marcellinus, when describing the visit of the emperor Constantius II to Rome in 357 CE, depicted the (Christian) emperor admiring the temples and other ancient ornaments of the city (16.10.13–17). This account tendentiously suppresses any mention of Christianity or Judaism in Rome.

The traditional monuments of the city were duly restored in the course of the fourth century CE by the prefectus urbi (prefect of the city). Even after the reforms of Gratian, when the responsibility of the prefect of the city was redirected toward the Christian buildings instead of the traditional temples, the imperial authorities did not entirely neglect the monuments of pagan religion. Under Emperor Eugenius (392–394 CE) some temples were again restored, and as late as the 470s a prefect of the city restored an image of Minerva.

The traditional religious practices of Rome were not mere fossilized survivals. They did not incorporate elements of Christianity or Judaism, but there were continuing changes and restructuring through the fourth century. For example, in the Calendar of 354 CE, games in honor of the emperor continued to be remodeled and adjusted to the new rulers, and the cycle of festivals in honor of the gods was also reworked.

The process of change is also visible in cults long established in Rome, which sometimes received new and heady interpretations. In the fourth century the cult of Mater Magna placed a new emphasis on the practice of the *taurobolium.* Inscriptions from the sanctuary in the Vatican area record that some worshippers repeated the ritual after a lapse of twenty years—one claimed that he had been thereby "reborn to eternity," which seems to have been a radically new significance. The reinterpretation of the *taurobolium* in what was by now an ancient cult of Rome shows clearly how even such ancestral religions could still generate new meanings—in this case, a new intensity of personal relationship with the divine.

The process of incorporation of once foreign cults into the "official" religion is most visible in the priesthoods held by members of the senatorial class. Until the end of the fourth century, senators continued to be members of the four main priestly colleges, but there were, in addition, priests of Hecate, Mithras, and Isis. For senators to associate themselves with these cults in Rome was an innovation of the fourth century. The change should be seen as a trend toward assimilating into "traditional" paganism cults in Rome that had not previously received senatorial patronage. Faced with the new threat posed by imperial patronage of Christianity, senators redefined (and expanded) their ancestral heritage.

After the fall of Eugenius, Theodosius's ban on sacrifices was more effectively applied, and the implications of the old calendar for public life were revised. Traditional public festivals were not banned, but they were officially marginalized in favor of Christian festivals. The last pagan senatorial priests are attested in the 390s, the series of dedicatory inscriptions from the sanctuary of Mater Magna in the Vatican area runs from 295 to 390 CE, and the last dated Mithraic inscription from Rome is from 391 CE (slightly later than from elsewhere in the Empire). Some Christians went on the offensive, destroying pagan sanctuaries, including sanctuaries of Mithras. The sanctuary of the Arval Brothers was dismantled from the late fourth century onward.

But traditional religious rites were very tenacious, and their demise cannot be assumed from the ending of dedicatory inscriptions. Emperors through the fifth and into the sixth century elaborated Theodosius's ban on sacrifices—presumably in the face of the continuing practice of traditional sacrifice, for a pagan writer traveling up from Rome through Italy in the early fifth century observed with pleasure a rural festival of Osiris. At around the same time the old ways were revived during the siege of Rome by the Goths (408–409 CE). When Christianity was not obviously helping, the prefect of the city, after meeting diviners from Etruria, attempted to save the city by publicly celebrating the ancestral rituals with the Senate on the Capitol. The economic independence and traditional prestige of local pagan aristocrats, especially in Rome, allowed them to survive for a time and to go on elaborating pagan thought. Around 430 CE the Roman writer Macrobius sought to recreate in his *Saturnalia* the religious learning and debate of the age of Symmachus, a generation before. Most striking (given the date of its composition) is the complete exclusion of Christianity—an exclusion that sought (in vain) to align classical culture and traditional religion. The Neoplatonists of Athens had to be expelled by Justinian in 529.

Even at the end of the fifth century CE, the Lupercalia was still being celebrated in Rome. The bishop of Rome found it necessary both to argue against the efficacy of the cult and to ban Christian participation. Hopes that the pagan gods would come back excited the Eastern provinces during the rebellion against the emperor Zeno in about 483, in which the pagan rhetorician and poet Pampremius had a prominent part (Zacharias of Mytilene, *Vita Severi*, in *Patrologia Orient.* 2.1.40; M.-A. Kugener, ed., Paris, 1903, repr. Turnhout 1993). The peasants (*rustici*), about whom Bishop Martin of Bracara in Spain had so many complaints, gave more trouble to the ecclesiastical authorities than did the philosophers and the aristocrats of the cities. Sacrifices, because they were generally recognized as efficient ways of persuading the gods to act, were at the center of Christian suspicion. According to a widespread opinion shared by the apostle Paul (but not by all the church fathers) pagan gods existed—as demons.

SEE ALSO Apotheosis; Constantinianism; Druids; Emperor's Cult; Gnosticism, article on Gnosticism from Its Origins to the Middle Ages; Hellenistic Religions; Hermetism; Isis; Mithra; Mithraism; Mystery Religions; Sabazios.

BIBLIOGRAPHY

General

Georg Wissowa, *Religion und Kultus der Römer*, 2d ed. (Munich, 1912) and Kurt Latte, *Römische Religionsgeschichte* (Munich, 1960) are basic works of reference. They are supplemented by Martin P. Nilsson, *Geschichte der griechischen Religion*, vol. 2, 3d. ed. (Munich, 1974), for the Eastern side of the Roman Empire. Mary Beard, John North, and Simon Price, *Religions of Rome*, 2 vols. (Cambridge, U.K., 1998) offer a synthesis of newer approaches (vol. 1 is an analytic history, vol. 2 a sourcebook of texts in translation and monuments, with commentary; a full bibliography appears in both volumes). See also Arthur Darby Nock, *Conversion: The Old and the New in Religion from Alexander the Great to Augustine of Hippo* (Oxford, 1933) and *Essays on Religion and the Ancient World*, 2 vols., edited by Zeph Stewart (Oxford, 1972). Current research is surveyed in *Archiv für Religionsgeschichte* 2 (2000): 283–345 and 5 (2003): 297–371.

Other useful general books include Jean Beaujeu, *La religion romaine à l'apogée de l'empire*, vol. 1, *La politique religieuse des Antonins, 96–192* (Paris, 1955); Jean Bayet, *Histoire politique et psychologique de la religion romaine* (Paris, 1969); E. R. Dodds, *Pagan and Christian in an Age of Anxiety* (Cambridge, U.K., 1965); Clara Gallini, *Protesta e integrazione nella Roma antica* (Bari, 1970); J. H. W. G. Liebeschuetz, *Continuity and Change in Roman Religion* (Oxford, 1979); Martin Goodman, *Mission and Conversion: Proselytizing in the Religious History of the Roman Empire* (Oxford, 1994); Denis C. Feeney, *Literature and Religion at Rome: Cultures, Contexts, and Beliefs* (Cambridge, UK, 1998); John North, *Roman Religion.* Greece and Rome New Survey 30 (Oxford, 2000); and John Scheid, *An Introduction to Roman Religion* (Edinburgh, 2003). Clifford Ando, ed., *Roman Religion* (Edinburgh, 2003) republishes some useful articles.

Roman Temples

See Amanda Claridge, *Rome* (Oxford, 1998). For a full analyses, consult E. Margareta Steinby, ed., *Lexicon Topographicum Urbis Romae*, 6 vols. (Rome, 1993–1999).

Roman Images

See Inez Scott Ryberg, *Rites of the State Religion in Roman Art* (Memoirs of the American Academy at Rome 23; New Haven, 1955); Robert Turcan, *Religion romaine*, 2 vols, (Iconography of Religions 17; Leiden, 1988).

Rituals and Calendar

On Roman sacrifice see *Le sacrifice dans l'antiquité* (Entretiens Fondation Hardt 27; Geneva, 1981) and John Scheid, *Romulus et ses frères. Le collège des frères Arvales, modèle du culte public romain dans la Rome des empereurs* (Rome, 1990). For information about the calendar, see Jörg Rüpke, *Kalender und Öffentlichkeit. Die Geschichte der Repräsentation und religiösen Qualifikation von Zeit in Rom.* (Berlin and New York, 1995).

Epigraphic Texts

Epigraphic texts cited in the text include Michael H. Crawford, ed., *Roman Statutes*, vol. 1 (London, 1996), pp. 393–454;

F. K. Dörner, *Denkschriften der Wiener Akademie* 75 (Vienna, 1952) p. 40, no. 78; Luigi Moretti, *Inscriptiones Graecae Urbis Romae* I (Rome, 1968), no. 160; H. W. Pleket, *Texts on the Social History of the Greek World* (Leiden, 1969), no. 29; Robert K. Sherk, *Roman Documents from the Greek East* (Baltimore, 1969), pp. 214–216.

Cults outside Rome

On cults outside of Rome see Marcel Leglay, *Saturne africaine* (Paris, 1966); Javier Teixidor, *The Pagan God: Popular Religion in the Greco-Roman Near East* (Princeton, 1977); Ramsay MacMullen, *Paganism in the Roman Empire* (New Haven, 1981); and Martin Henig, *Religion in Roman Britain* (London, 1984). See also the following articles by Louis Robert: "De Cilicie à Messine et à Plymouth avec deux inscriptions grecques errantes," *Journal des Savants* 1973, pp. 161–211 (repr. in his *Opera Minora Selecta* [*OMS*] 7: 225–275); "Trois oracles de la Théosophie et un prophète d'Apollon," *CRAI* 1968: pp. 568–599 (repr. in *OMS* 5: 584–615); "Un oracle gravé à Oenoanda," *CRAI* 1971: pp. 597–619 (repr. in *OMS* 5: 617–639); "Le serpent Glycon d'Abônouteichos à Athènes et Artémis d'Ephèse à Rome," *CRAI* 1981: 513–535 (repr. in his *OMS* 5: 749–769); and "Une vision de Perpétue martyre à Carthage en 203," *CRAI* 1982: 229–276 (repr. in his *OMS* 5: 791–839). See Robin Lane Fox, *Pagans and Christians* (Harmondsworth and New York, 1986), on Greek civic cults of the imperial period. Also of interest are Paul Veyne, *Did the Greeks Believe in their Myths?* (Chicago and London, 1988); James B. Rives, *Religion and Authority in Roman Carthage* (Oxford, 1995); Hubert Cancik and Jörg Rüpke, eds., *Römische Reichsreligion und Provinzialreligion* (Tübingen, 1997); chapter 7 of Mary Beard, John North, and Simon Price, *Religions of Rome*, 2 vols. (Cambridge, U.K., 1998); Ton Derks, *Gods, Temples, and Ritual Practices: the Transformation of Religious Ideas and Values in Roman Gaul* (Amsterdam, 1998); David Frankfurter, *Religion in Roman Egypt: Assimilation and Resistance* (Princeton, 1998); Simon Price, *Religions of the Ancient Greeks* (Cambridge, U.K., 1999); William van Andringa, *La religion en Gaule romaine* (Paris, 2002); Ted Kaizer, *The Religious Life of Palmyra* (Stuttgart, 2002); and Simon Price, "Local Mythologies in the Roman East," in Chistopher Howgego, Volcker Heuchert and Andrew Burnett (eds), *Coinage and Identity in the Roman Provinces* (Oxford: Oxford University Press, 2005), pp. 115–124. Volumes 2.16 (Rome and Imperial Cults) and 2.17 (Rome and Oriental Cults), 2.18 (Provinces), 2.19–21 (Judaism), and 2.23–27 (Christianity) of *Aufstieg und Niedergang der römischen Welt* (Berlin and New York, 1978–) vary in quality but include some useful studies. A searchable index is available from http://www.uky.edu/AS/Classics/biblio/anrw.html.

Magic and Divination

See Frederick H. Cramer, *Astrology in Roman Law and Politics* (Philadelphia, 1954); David S. Potter, *Prophets and Emperors: Human and Divine Authority from Augustus to Theodosius* (Oxford, 1994); Fritz Graf, *Magic in the Ancient World* (Cambridge, Mass., 1997); chapter 5 of Mary Beard, John North and Simon Price, *Religions of Rome*, 2 vols. (Cambridge, U.K., 1998); Daniel Ogden, *Magic, Witchcraft, and Ghosts in the Greek and Roman Worlds: a Sourcebook* (Oxford, 2002); James B. Rives, "Magic in Roman Law: the Reconstruction of a Crime," *Classical Antiquity* 22 (2003): 313–339; and S. R. F. Price, "The Future of Dreams: from Freud to Artemidorus," in *Studies in Ancient Greek and Roman Society*, edited by Robin Osborne, pp. 226–59 (Cambridge, U.K., 2004).

The Imperial Cult

See Louis Robert, "Le culte de Caligula à Milet et la province d'Asie." *Hellenica* 7 (Paris, 1949): 206–238; Louis Robert, "Recherches épigraphiques V–VI," *REA* 62 (1960), pp. 285–324 (repr. in his *Opera Minora Selecta* [Amsterdam, 1969–1990]), 2: 801–840); Louis Robert, "Théophane de Mytilène à Constantinople." *Comptes Rendus de l'Académie des Inscriptions* (repr. in his *Opera Minora Selecta* 5: 561–83); Stefan Weinstock, *Divus Julius* (Oxford, 1971); Willem den Boer, ed., *Le culte des souverains dans l'empire romain* (Geneva, 1973); J. Rufus Fears, *Princeps a diis electus: The Divine Election of the Emperor as a Political Concept at Rome* (Rome, 1977); Simon R. F. Price, *Rituals and Power: The Roman Imperial Cult in Asia Minor* (Cambridge, U.K., 1984); Simon R. F. Price, "Gods and Emperors: The Greek Language of the Roman Imperial Cult," *Journal of Hellenic Studies* 94 (1984): 79–95; Simon R. F. Price, "From Noble Funerals to Divine Cult: The Consecration of Roman Emperors," in *Rituals of Royalty: Power and Ceremonial in Traditional Societies*, edited by David Cannadine and Simon R. F. Price, pp. 56–105 (Cambridge, U.K., 1987); Duncan Fishwick, *The Imperial Cult in the Latin West*, 3 vols. (Leiden, 1987–2004); Alastair Small, ed., "Subject and Ruler: The Cult of the Ruling Power in Classical Antiquity," *Journal of Roman Archaeology*, Supp. 17 (1996); and Ittai Gradel, *Emperor Worship and Roman Religion* (Oxford, 2002). See also Lellia Cracco Ruggini, "Apoteosi e politica senatoria nel IV sec. d. C.," *Rivista storica italiana* (1977): 425–489; and Keith Hopkins, *Conquerors and Slaves* (Cambridge, U.K., 1978), pp. 197–242. Henning Wrede, *Consecratio in formam deorum* (Mainz, 1981) examines "private" deifications.

Oriental Cults

On Oriental cults, the publications by Franz Cumont remain influential. See, for instance, *Astrology and Religion among the Greeks and Romans* (New York, 1912); *After Life in Roman Paganism* (New Haven, 1922); *Les religions orientales dans le paganisme romain*, 4th ed. (Paris, 1929); *Recherches sur le symbolisme funéraire des Romains* (Paris, 1942); and *Lux Perpetua* (Paris, 1949). Robert Turcan's *The Cults of the Roman Empire* (Oxford, 1996) is a synthesis on Oriental cults. For more recent approaches see Ugo Bianchi and Maarten J. Vermaseren, ed., *La soteriologia dei culti orientali nell'impero romano* (EPRO 92; Leiden, 1982); Walter Burkert, *Ancient Mystery Cults* (Cambridge, Mass., 1987) and chapter 6 of Mary Beard, John North and Simon Price, *Religions of Rome*, 2 vols. (Cambridge, U.K., 1998). On Mater Magna (Cybele) see Maarten J. Vermaseren, *Cybele and Attis* (London, 1977); Philippe Borgeaud, *La mère des dieux: de Cybèle à la vierge Marie* (Paris, 1996). On Isis see: Friedrich Solmsen, *Isis among the Greeks and Romans* (Cambridge, Mass., 1979); F. Dunand, *Le culte d'Isis dans le bassin oriental de la Méditerranée*, 3 vols. (EPRO 26; Leiden, 1973); Henk S. Versnel, *Inconsistencies in Greek and Roman Religion I: Ter Unus* (Leiden, 1990), pp. 39–95 and chapter six of Stephen J. Harrison, *Apuleius, A Latin Sophist* (Oxford, 2000) for a discussion of the problems of reading *Metamorphoses* 11. On Mithras see Reinhold Merkelbach, *Mithras* (Königstein, 1984); Richard L. Gordon, *Image and Value in the Graeco-Roman World* (Aldsershot, U.K., and Brookfield, Vt., 1996); and Manfred Clauss, *The Roman Cult of Mithras* (Edinburgh, 2000).

Gnosticism

Giovanni Filoramo, *A History of Gnosticism* (Oxford and Cambridge, Mass., 1990); Christoph Markschies, *Gnosis: An Introduction* (London, 2003); and Karen L. King, *What Is Gnosticism?* (Cambridge, Mass., 2003) are the best introductions. An examination of revelation can be found in James D. Tabor, *Things Unutterable: Paul's Ascent to Paradise in Its Greco-Roman, Judaic and Early Christian Contexts* (Lanham, Md., and London, 1986); and also see Simon Price, "The Mithras Liturgy," in Andreas Bendlin, ed., *Religion and Society: Aspects of Religious Life in the Eastern Mediterranean under Roman Rule* (Tübingen, 2005).

Relations between Pagans, Jews, and Christians in the First Three Centuries

See Erwin R. Goodenough, *Jewish Symbols in the Graeco-Roman Period*, 13 vols. (New York, 1953–1968); Ramsay MacMullen, *Christianizing the Roman Empire, A. D. 100–400* (New Haven, 1984); Jonathan Z. Smith, *Drudgery Divine: On the Comparison of Early Christianities and the Religions of Late Antiquity* (London and Chicago, 1990); L. Michael White, *Building God's House in the Roman World* (Baltimore and London, 1990); Paul R. Trebilco, *Jewish Communities in Asia Minor* (Cambridge, U.K., 1991); Judith Lieu, John North, and Tessa Rajak, eds., *The Jews among Pagans and Christians* (London and New York, 1992); Leonard V. Rutgers, *The Jews in Late Antique Rome* (Leiden, 1995); Judith Lieu, *Image and Reality: The Jews in the World of the Christians in the Second Century* (Edinburgh, 1996); Martin Goodman, ed., *Jews in a Graeco-Roman World* (Oxford, 1998); Mark Edwards, Martin Goodman, and Simon Price, eds., *Apologetics in the Roman Empire* (Oxford, 1999); Erich S. Gruen, *Diaspora: Jews amidst Greeks and Romans* (Cambridge, Mass., 2002). See also Morton Smith's article "Prolegomena to a Discussion of Aretalogies, Divine Men, the Gospels and Jesus," *Journal of Biblical Literature* 90 (June 1971): 174–199.

Transition to Christianity

See Bernhard Kötting, *Peregrinatio religiosa: Wallfahrten in der Antike und das Pilgerwesen in der alten Kirche* (Münster, 1950); Arnaldo Momigliano, ed., *The Conflict between Paganism and Christianity in the Fourth Century* (Oxford, 1963); Peter Brown, *Religion and Society in the Age of Saint Augustine* (London, 1972); Lellia Cracco Ruggini, "Simboli di battaglia ideologica nel tardo ellenismo," in *Studi storici in onore di Ottorino Bertolini*, pp. 117–300 (Pisa, 1972); Lellia Cracco Ruggini, "Il paganesimo romano tra religione e politica, 384–394 d. C.," *Memorie della classe di scienze morali, Accademia Nazionale dei Lincei*, 8.23.1 (Rome, 1979), 3–141; Lellia Cracco Ruggini, "Pagani, ebrei e cristiani: Odio sociologico e odio teologico nel mondo antico," in *Gli ebrei nell'Alto Medioevo*, Settimane di studio del Centro italiano di studi sull'alto Medioevo 26 (Spoleto, 1980): 13–101; Sabine G. MacCormack, *Art and Ceremony in Late Antiquity* (Berkeley, 1981); Peter Brown, *Society and the Holy in Late Antiquity* (Berkeley and London, 1982); Robert A. Markus, *The End of Ancient Christianity* (Cambridge, U.K., 1990); Michelle Salzmann, *On Roman Time: The Codex-Calendar of 354 and the Rhythms of Urban Life in Late Antiquity* (Berkeley, 1990); Averil Cameron, *Christianity and the Rhetoric of Empire: The Development of Christian Discourse* (Berkeley, 1991); Ramsay MacMullen, *Christianity and Paganism in the Fourth to Eighth Centuries* (New Haven, 1997); chapter 8 of Mary Beard, John North, and Simon Price, *Religions of Rome*, 2 vols. (Cambridge, U.K., 1998); John Curran, *Pagan City and Christian Capital: Rome in the Fourth Century* (Oxford, 2000); Peter Brown, *The Rise of Western Christendom: Triumph and Diversity, AD 200–1000*. 2d ed. (Oxford, 2003).

ARNALDO MOMIGLIANO (1987)
SIMON PRICE (2005)

ROSENZWEIG, FRANZ (1886–1929), German-Jewish philosophical theologian, writer, translator of Jewish classical literature, and influential Jewish educational activist. Generally regarded as the most important Jewish philosophical theologian of this century, Rosenzweig also became a model of what the Jewish personality in the twentieth-century West might be.

He was born into an old, affluent, and highly acculturated German-Jewish family in Kassel, in which the sense of Jewishness, though lively, had shrunk to a matter of upper middle-class formalities. He studied at several German universities, ranging over multiple disciplines, and finished as a student of Friedrich Meinecke, the important German political and cultural historian. During those years he also had intense conversations on religion in the modern world, especially with close relatives and friends, several of whom had converted to Christianity. Having already adopted a strong German nationalist outlook, Rosenzweig also tried to sort out his own religious convictions at the very time that he was writing his Ph.D. dissertation (on Schelling and Hegel) and his first important book (*Hegel und der Staat*, 2 vols., 1920). In a night-long conversation on July 7, 1913 with his cousin, the physiologist Rudolf Ehrenberg (who had become a Christian theologian), and his distant relative Eugen Rosenstock-Huessy (later the influential Protestant theologian, also a convert), Rosenzweig decided that he, too, ought to become a Christian; however, he would take this step "as a Jew," not "as a pagan," and he would, therefore, briefly return to the synagogue. His experience there during the High Holy Days that year, however, changed Rosenzweig's mind completely: he would instead turn himself from a nominal into a substantial Jew, and he would devote his life to Jewish values. He studied with and became a close friend to the Neo-Kantian philosopher Hermann Cohen, who was then living in Berlin in retirement but was still very active with Jewish writing and teaching. Rosenzweig immediately began to write on Jewish subjects.

During World War I, Rosenzweig served in various, mainly military, capacities. He continued, however, to correspond with Rosenstock-Huessy on theological matters

(Rosenstock-Huessy, *Judaism despite Christianity*, Alabama, 1968) and with Cohen and others on Jewish matters. He also wrote and published essays on historical, political, military, and educational subjects. Assigned to eastern Europe and the Balkans, he experienced some of the full-blooded life of the Jewish communities there. Above all, he began on postcards to his mother the composition that he finished on returning home from the war—his magnum opus, *Der Stern der Erlösung* (Frankfurt, 1921; translated as *The Star of Redemption*). An injury he sustained during the war may have been the cause of his severe and eventually fatal postwar illness.

The Star of Redemption is a complex, difficult, and ambitious work, in some ways comparable to Hegel's *Phenomenology of Spirit.* The introduction to the first part argues that the fundamental and ineluctably individualistic fact of human death breaks up all philosophy *qua* monism, idealistic or materialistic, into the three realities of human experience: man, God, and the world. (Metaphysical empiricism is thus an apt name for what Rosenzweig also calls "the new thinking.") In the first part, he philosophically "constructs" these three realities very much in the manner of the later Schelling, as logico-mathematical and metaphysical entities. In this condition man, God, and the world constitute the "pagan" universe: they exist without interrelationships, as three unconnected points.

In the second part, the three realities enter into relationships with one another through "revelation," that is, by continuously revealing themselves to each other. God reveals his love to man and thus becomes available to human prayer, and the world is revealed as divine creation, available to human transformation. Speech is the operative force in this dimension of the world. Three points have formed a triangle. The final part of the book establishes the second triangle of the "star of redemption" when the individual relations between man, God, and the world are transformed into collective, historical forces, specifically, Judaism and Christianity. (Two interlocking triangles form the hexagram that is the Magen David, the Star of David, symbol of redemption.) Judaism is "the fire in the star"; that is, Israel is "with God/the truth," outside of history, in eternity. Christianity is the rays from the star on pilgrimage through the world and history toward God/the truth, in order to conquer the kingdom of God's eventual universal realm. In this dimension of the world, collective speech—liturgy and hymn—is the operative force. Judaism and Christianity are the two valid covenants—Sinai for Jews and Calvary for the rest of mankind, to be unified only when the road to truth has brought the Christian world to the Jewish domicile in truth. In the meantime loving acts of believers are to "verify" the love of revelation and prepare the eschatological verity of God as "the all in all." (Truth is thus Hegelian-existentialist "subjectivity," and the three parts of *The Star* explicate the basic theological triad of creation, revelation, and redemption.)

After the war Rosenzweig wanted to translate his beliefs and his pronounced educational interests into action. He settled in Frankfurt, where he entered into close relationships with Nehemiah Nobel, the Orthodox rabbi of the community; with Martin Buber; with a younger generation of German Jews; and with eastern European Jews on their way west. He founded what became famous as the Free Jewish House of Learning (Lehrhaus), in which teachers and students together sought out classic Jewish sources and, translating and publishing them, tried them out on the modern world. Rosenzweig and Buber were joined as teachers by well-known chemists, physicians, sociologists, and activists, and such influential contemporary Jewish scholars as S. D. Goitein, Ernst Simon, Gershom Scholem, Hans Kohn, Erich Fromm, and Nahum N. Glatzer.

Rosenzweig married in 1920 and fathered a son just before coming down with a disease so grave that he was expected to die within months. Instead he lived for six years, so paralyzed, however, that ultimately he could communicate only by blinking an eyelid to the recitation of the alphabet. Nevertheless his associates flocked to his side and spread his influence. Rosenzweig continued to write philosophical and religious essays and conducted a large correspondence. He edited the *Jüdische Schriften* (Jewish Writings) of Hermann Cohen (3 vols., Berlin, 1924) and, in an extensive introduction, reinterpreted Cohen's posthumous philosophical theology as having laid the basis for a proto-existentialist doctrine. He continued to study Jewish sources. He translated, among other things, the Hebrew poetry of Yehudah ha-Levi and supplied it with extensive commentaries. In 1924 he joined with Martin Buber to produce a new German translation of the Hebrew Bible, and in the process the two also developed a sophisticated theory of translation, language, and textuality. Their position was that the full meaning of a text develops through what has since come to be called "reception history." Thus the Bible is divinely revealed not as a matter of Orthodox dogma or in opposition to Bible-critical history but in terms of its effects over time. Translation must not adjust the text to a new culture but must confront the new culture with the text's own authenticity. This confrontation takes place on the ground of the universal, Adamite human speech embedded in the literary forms of both languages. When Rosenzweig died at the age of forty-three, the Bible translation had progressed to *Isaiah.* (Buber finished it in the 1950s.)

Rosenzweig's basic tenets led to some new and promising positions in modern Jewish life. Between the Orthodox belief in the Sinaitic revelation and the Liberal critical historicism regarding the Bible, his "postmodernist" view made it possible to take all of Torah with revelatory seriousness and punctiliousness, while neither rejecting modern scholarship nor committing oneself to a fideistic view. This coincided with and influenced the biblical work of such scholars as Buber, Benno Jacob, Yeḥezkel Kaufmann, and Umberto Cassuto. It also laid the basis for much subsequent renewed Jewish traditionalism among the acculturated in Germany and elsewhere. Rosenzweig's outlook, beyond the established fronts of Orthodoxy and Liberalism, also offered help with respect to Jewish law (*halakhah*). In opposition to Buber's subjectivistic, pietistic antinomianism, Rosenzweig called for an open-minded, receptive confrontation with Jewish law to embrace it "as much as I can" in terms of one's own preparation and honesty. His "two-covenant doctrine" serves as a strong foundation for Jewish-Christian dialogue, although it can easily be abused in an "indifferentist" spirit and although it suffers inherently from Rosenzweig's pervasive europocentrism (e.g., his total blindness to Islam) and his antihistoricism (cf. Hegel's "absolute spirit" after "the end of history"). Unlike his friend Buber, Rosenzweig rejected the notion of a Jewish state (which would bring Israel back into history); on the other hand, he naturally preferred Jewish self-reauthentification in language, ethnicity, culture, and religion to liberalistic acculturation in gentile societies. With the rise of Nazism, Rosenzweig's educational ideology, along with that of Buber, spoke to German Jewry so aptly and powerfully that the Lehrhaus pattern of highly cultured and acculturated teachers and students in community spread throughout the country and produced an "Indian summer" of German-Jewish creativity of a high order in the 1930s.

The impact of Rosenzweig's thought continues to be strong, philosophically and religiously. The interconnections between him and Martin Heidegger, whom Rosenzweig praises in his last essay ("Vertauschte Fronte," 1929; in *Gesammelte Schriften*, vol. 3, pp. 235–237), are increasingly being crystallized. Heideggerian existentialist phenomenologism, with Jewish-Rosenzweigian modifications, has further left its significant marks on diverse movements of thought—the Frankfurt School (of Hegelian neo-Marxists) on the one hand, and Emmanuel Levinas, who goes beyond Heidegger and Husserl in philosophy and takes Buberian-Rosenzweigian dialogism yet closer to historical Judaism, on the other. Rosenzweig's sophisticated traditionalism comprises ethnicity, language, and religion (though still without "land") and shows the way back from European high culture to Jewish self-definition.

BIBLIOGRAPHY

The most extensive collection of Rosenzweig's writing and study of his life is *Franz Rosenzweig, der Mensch und sein Werk: Gesammelte Schriften*, 6 vols. (Dordrecht, 1976–1984). In English, see *Franz Rosenzweig: His Life and Thought*, 2d rev. ed., edited by Nahum N. Glatzer (New York, 1961), and my *Franz Rosenzweig, 1886–1929: Guide of Reversioners* (London, 1961).

Rosenzweig's magnum opus, *The Star of Redemption*, has been translated by William W. Hallo (New York, 1971). It is discussed in Else-Rahel Freund's *Franz Rosenzweig's Philosophy of Existence: An Analysis of The Star of Redemption*, translated by Stephen L. Weinstein and Robert Israel and edited by Paul R. Mendes-Flohr (The Hague and Boston, 1979); it is also the subject of my book review in *The Thomist* (October 1971): 728–737.

New Sources

Batnitzky, Leora. *Idolatry and Representation: The Philosophy of Franz Rosenzweig Reconsidered.* Princeton, N. J., 2000.

Cohen, Richard A. *Elevations: The Height of the Good in Rosenzweig and Levinas.* Chicago, 1994.

Gibbs, Robert. *Correlations in Rosenzweig and Levinas.* Princeton, N. J., 1992.

Hollander, Dana. "On the Significance of the Messianic Idea in Rosenzweig." *Cross Currents* 53 (Winter 2004): 555–566.

Mack, Michael. "Franz Rosenweig's and Emmanuel Levinas's Critique of German Idealism's Pseudotheology." *Journal of Religion* 83 (January 2003): 56–79.

STEVEN S. SCHWARZSCHILD (1987)
Revised Bibliography

RO'SH HA-SHANAH AND YOM KIPPUR,

holy days prominent in the Jewish religious calendar, mark the beginning of the new year and set off the special period traditionally designated for self-scrutiny and repentance. They are referred to as Yamim Nora'im ("days of awe"), the time when the numinous aspect of Judaism comes into its own.

RO'SH HA-SHANAH. Ro'sh ha-Shanah ("head of the year," i. e., New Year) is the name given in postbiblical times to the biblical festival of the first day of the seventh month (counting from the spring month of the Exodus from Egypt) and described (*Lv.* 23:23–25, *Nm.* 19:1–6) as a day of blowing the horn. The postbiblical name is based on Talmudic teachings that on this day all humanity is judged for its fortunes in the coming year. For this reason Ro'sh ha-Shanah is also called Yom ha-Din ("day of judgment"). Biblical scholars, exploring the origins of the festival, have noted the parallels with ancient Near Eastern agricultural festivities in the autumn and the enthronement ceremonies of the king as the representative of the god Baal or Marduk. According to the critical view, references to the festival occur in sections of the Pentateuch known as the Priestly code, which is post-exilic and hence could well have been influenced by Babylonian practices. Such theories remain, however, conjectural. In *Nehemiah* 8:1–8 there is a vivid description of the dramatic occasion when the Israelites who had returned from Babylonian captivity renewed their covenant with God. Ezra read from the Torah on this first day of the seventh month; the people, conscious of their shortcomings, were distressed at hearing the demands of the Law, but Nehemiah reassured them: "Go your way, eat the fat, and drink the sweet and send portions unto him for whom nothing is prepared; for this day is holy unto our Lord; neither be ye grieved, for the joy of the Lord is your strength" (*Neh.* 8:10). These are the antecedents of the festival as it later developed (held on the first and second days of the autumnal month of Tishri), a day of both joy and solemnity. The day also became known as Yom ha-Zikkaron ("day of remembrance") because on it God remembers his creatures.

The themes of God as king and judge of the universe and the need for repentance all feature prominently in the Ro'sh ha-Shanah liturgy. The special additional prayer consists of three groups of verses and prayers: (1) *malkhuyyot* ("sovereignties," in which God is hailed as king), (2) *zikhronot* ("remembrances," in which God is said to remember his creatures), (3) *shofarot* ("trumpet sounds," which refer to the blowing of the horn). A popular medieval interpretation of these three is that they represent the three cardinal principles of the Jewish faith: belief in God, in reward and punishment (God "remembers" humankind's deeds), and in revelation (the horn was sounded when the Law was given at Sinai, as stated in *Exodus* 19:16). Another prayer of the day looks forward to the messianic age, when the kingdom of heaven will be established and all wickedness will vanish from the earth. In a hymn recited on both Ro'sh ha-Shanah and Yom Kippur, continuing with the judgment theme, God is spoken of as the great shepherd tending his flock. He decides on Ro'sh ha-Shanah, and sets the seal on Yom Kippur, "who shall live and who shall die; who shall suffer and who shall be tranquil; who shall be rich and who poor; who shall be cast down and who elevated." At various stages in the liturgy of Ro'sh ha-Shanah and Yom Kippur there are prayers to be inscribed in the Book of Life, based on a Talmudic passage stating that the average person whose fate is in the balance has the opportunity during the period from Ro'sh ha-Shanah to Yom Kippur to avert the "evil decree" by repentance, prayer, and charity. These days, including Ro'sh ha-Shanah and Yom Kippur, are consequently known as the Ten Days of Penitence, the period for turning to God and for special strictness in religious observances. The verse "Seek ye the Lord while he may be found" (*Is.* 55:6) is applied especially to this time of the year.

The central ritual of the Ro'sh ha-Shanah festival is the ceremony of blowing the shofar. Although the shofar may be fashioned from the horn of several kosher animals, a ram's horn, reminiscent of the ram sacrificed by Abraham in place of Isaac, is preferred. Many attempts have been made to explain the significance of the rite; Maimonides' is typical:

> Although it is a divine decree that we blow the shofar on Ro'sh ha-Shanah, a hint of the following idea is contained in the command. It is as if to say: "Awake from your slumbers, you who have fallen asleep in life, and reflect on your deeds. Remember your Creator. Be not of those who miss reality in the pursuit of shadows, who waste their years seeking vain things that neither profit nor deliver. Look well to your souls, and improve your actions. Let each of you forsake his evil ways and thoughts." (*Code of Law,* Repentance 3.4)

The shofar is sounded a number of times during the synagogue service. The three basic notes are *teqi'ah* (a long, drawn-out note, signifying hope and triumph), *shevarim* (a broken set of short notes), and *teru'ah* (a set of even shorter notes that, like *shevarim,* represents weeping). First, the *teqi'ah* suggesting firm commitment to God's laws is sounded followed by the two weeping sounds as humanity reflects on his sins and failings, and finally a second *teqi'ah* is blown signifying confidence in God's pardon where there is sincere repentance.

At the festive meal on Ro'sh ha-Shanah it is customary to dip bread in honey and to eat other sweet things while praying for "a good and sweet year." In some places the celebrants eat fish to symbolize the good deeds they hope will proliferate like fish in the sea in the year ahead. An ancient custom is to go to the seaside or riverside on the afternoon of the first day of Ro'sh ha-Shanah, there to cast away the sins of the previous year. This is based on *Micah* 7:19, a verse that speaks of God casting away the sins of the people into the depths of the sea.

YOM KIPPUR. Yom Kippur ("day of atonement") is the culmination of the penitential season, the day of repentance and reconciliation between humanity and God and between people and their neighbors. It is the most hallowed day in the Jewish year and is still observed by the majority of Jews, even those who are otherwise lax in religious practices. In Temple times, elaborate sacrificial and purgatory rites, described in *Leviticus* 16, were carried out. The high priest entered the Holy of Holies in the Temple, where no other person was allowed to enter under pain of death, to make atonement for his people. A whole tractate of the Mishnah (*Yoma'*) describes in greater detail the Temple service on Yom Kippur. The Mishnah was compiled over one hundred and fifty years after the destruction of the Second Temple, but at least some of the material does represent the actual practice in the Second Temple period. After the destruction of the Temple in 70 CE, the day became one of prayer and worship. The reference to "afflicting the soul" (*Lv.* 16:29) on this day is understood as an injunction to fast. No food or drink is taken from sunset on the ninth of Tishri until nightfall on the tenth. Other "afflictions" practiced are abstaining from marital relations, from wearing leather shoes, and from bathing.

The ninth of Tishri, the day before Yom Kippur, is devoted to preparation for the fast. On this day, festive meals are eaten both for the purpose of gaining strength for the fast and to celebrate the pardon Yom Kippur brings. In Talmudic teaching, Yom Kippur does not bring atonement for offenses against other human beings unless the victims have pardoned the offenders. It is the practice, consequently, for people to ask forgiveness of one another on the day before the fast. The custom of *kapparot* ("atonements") is carried out in the morning. The procedure is to take a cockerel, wave it around the head three times, and recite "This shall be instead of me," after which the cockerel is slaughtered and eaten. Many medieval authorities disapproved of the practice as a pagan superstition, but it is still followed by some Jews. Others prefer to use money instead of a cockerel, and then to distribute it to the poor. Another custom still observed by some is that of *malqot* ("flagellation"), in which the beadle in the synagogue administers a token beating with a strap as atonement for sin. Many pious Jews, in preparation for the fast, immerse themselves in a *miqveh* (ritual bath) as a purification rite. Before leaving for the synagogue, as the fast begins, parents bless their children.

In the majority of synagogues, services are several hours long on Yom Kippur night, and continue without pause during the day from early morning until the termination of the fast. The evening service begins with the Kol Nidrei ("all vows"), a declaration in Aramaic to the effect that all religious promises that will be undertaken in the year ahead are hereby declared null and void. This was introduced as a means of discouraging such vows since a promise made to God had dire consequences if broken. Throughout the day hymns and religious poems composed over many centuries are chanted. These consist of praises, supplications, martyrologies, and, especially, confessions of sin. A prominent feature of the additional service (Musaf) is the remembering of the Temple service on Yom Kippur. At the stage that relates how the high priest would utter the divine name and the people would then fall on their faces, the members of the congregation kneel and then prostrate themselves. This is the only occasion nowadays when there is prostration in the synagogue. At the late-afternoon service, *Jonah* is read as a lesson that none can escape God's call and that he has mercy even on the most wicked if they sincerely repent. The day ends with Neʿilah ("closing"), a special service signifying that the gates of heaven, open to prayer all day, are about to close. At this particularly solemn time of the day, the worshipers make an urgent effort to be close to God, many standing upright for the hour or so of this service. As the sun sets, the congregation cries out aloud seven times: "The Lord he is God." Then the shofar is sounded to mark the termination of the fast.

White, the color of purity and mercy, is used on Yom Kippur for the vestments of the scrolls of the Torah and the ark in which the scrolls are kept as well as for the coverings in the synagogue. Traditional Jews wear white robes; in fact, these are shrouds to remind humanity of its mortality. This tradition serves a main theme of Yom Kippur: human life is frail and uncertain, but one can place trust in God and share in God's goodness forever. Since the festival of Sukkot falls a few days after Yom Kippur, it is advised that as soon as the worshipers return home from the synagogue and before breaking the fast, they should make some small preparation for the erection of the Sukkot booths and so proceed immediately after the day of pardon to do a good deed.

See Also Atonement, article on Jewish Concepts.

Bibliography

Norman H. Snaith's *The Jewish New Year Festival* (London, 1947) considers the views of the myth and ritual school that Ro'sh ha-Shanah had its origin in enthronement ceremonies. Two useful little books of my own are *A Guide to Rosh Ha-Shanah* (London, 1959) and *A Guide to Yom Kippur* (London, 1957). A good survey of the liturgical themes of Ro'sh ha-Shanah and Yom Kippur is Max Arzt's *Justice and Mercy* (New York, 1963). The anthology by S. Y. Agnon has been translated into English as *Days of Awe* (New York, 1948). Two anthologies with comprehensive bibliographies are Philip Goodman's *The Rosh Hashanah Anthology* (Philadelphia, 1970) and *The Yom Kippur Anthology* (Philadelphia, 1971).

Louis Jacobs (1987)

ROSICRUCIANS.

Although the secrecy pledged by members necessarily limits knowledge of Rosicrucian fraternities and their legendary founder, Christian Rosencreutz (whose surname means "rose cross"), documents published in the early seventeenth century and specific historical allusions to the Rosicrucians from that time on both provide basic information on these fraternities and adumbrate their significance within the esoteric traditions that arose in early modern Europe. The story of Christian Rosencreutz was promulgated through the publications *Fama Fraternitatis* (1614) and *Confessio Fraternitatis* (1615), which recounted his life and teachings and described the fraternity he founded. A third document, the *Chymische Hochzeit Christiani Rosencreutz* (Chemical Wedding; 1616), portrayed an alchemistic initiatory process, the representation of which was based in part on the actual wedding of Frederick V, Elector Palatine, and Princess Elizabeth, daughter of James I of England.

History. According to the story recounted in these documents, Christian Rosencreutz was a German scholar born in 1378. He lived to be 106. One hundred and twenty years after his death, his followers, obeying his instructions, opened his tomb; they heralded this event as the "opening" of a new era in Europe. The tomb purportedly contained Rosencreutz's uncorrupted body, various artifacts, and texts summarizing his teachings. In his quest for wisdom, Rosencreutz had traveled to the Holy Land, Egypt, Morocco, and Spain; his teachings reflected the influences of alchemy, Alexandrian Hermetism, Christian gnosticism, Jewish mysticism (Qabbalah), and the Paracelsian medical tradition. Following his own preparation and study, Rosencreutz, with three companions, established the Society of the Rose Cross. This fraternity was to have no other profession than (in the manner of Paracelsus) to attend to the sick for free. Members were also required to travel in order to gain and to disseminate knowledge, to report yearly by letter or in person to the center Rosencreutz had founded (called the Home of the Holy Spirit), to wear no distinctive garb, to seek worldly successors, and to employ the rose cross as their seal and symbol.

Significantly, both the publication of the aforementioned Rosicrucian documents and the purported opening of Rosencreutz's tomb occured in the early seventeenth century, thus placing Rosicrucianism directly in the context of Reformation and Counter-Reformation currents. Further, the documents originally appeared in Bohemia, which at the time was a haven for alchemists, freethinkers, millenarians, and adherents of diverse religious traditions. The authorship of the three key texts has been attributed to Johann Valentin Andreae (1586–1654), a Lutheran theologian and mystic. Andreae later described the history of the Rosicrucians up to his time as pure fabrication; at their publication, however, his texts met with a receptive and enthusiastic audience. With the collapse in 1620 of the brief reign in Bohemia of Frederick and Elizabeth and the onset of the Thirty Years War, Rosicrucianism became associated with Protestantism and "heretical teachings." As part of their campaign against

Rosicrucianism, the Jesuits even penned their own Rosicrucian-style document, the *Rosa Jesuitica* (c. 1620).

During the seventeenth century, Rosicrucian figures such as the "Great Hermeticist" Michael Maier (1568–1622) and the physician Robert Fludd (1574–1637) were instrumental in the spread of Rosicrucian thought and influence on the European continent and in England, respectively. The antiquarian Elias Ashmole (1617–1692) is believed to have brought the Rosicrucian current into speculative Freemasonry. What linked these writers, as well as numerous minor figures, was less an identifiable Rosicrucian brotherhood than an adherence to Rosicrucian beliefs. The claims of Descartes and Leibniz—that, the secrecy of the Rosicrucian order notwithstanding, their efforts to meet a live Rosicrucian were in vain—support the contention that Rosicrucianism existed mainly as a religious and intellectual approach to life rather than as an actual association. In this connection, the question of whether Francis Bacon was a Rosicrucian is unimportant, for he certainly was influenced by, and a participant in, the Rosicrucian trends affecting European intellectual life.

Following a period of relative quiescence in the eighteenth and early nineteenth centuries, Rosicrucianism was revived. The Societas Rosicruciana in Anglia, founded in the latter part of the nineteenth century by Robert Wentworth Little (d. 1878), played an important role in the renewal and spread of Rosicrucianism. This was not, however, the only strain. Here, polemic concerns of divers Rosicrucian groups obscure the already uncertain history of interactions among European currents and the introduction of Rosicrucianism into America. In the mid-1980s, two major Rosicrucian societies exist in the United States: the Society of Rosicrucians, or Societas Rosicruciana in America, founded in New York City and presently located in Kingston, New York, and the Ancient and Mystical Order of Rosae Crucis, based in San Jose, California. The Societas Rosicruciana publishes the *Mercury* quarterly; the first issue appeared in 1916. The Ancient and Mystical Order issues the *Rosicrucian Digest,* which began publication as the *Triangle* in 1921.

In addition to the establishment of Rosicrucian organizations, the late nineteenth century witnessed Rosicrucianism's strong influence upon Western esotericism. Rosicrucian traditions took form in the Order of the Golden Dawn, a Hermetic society whose initiates practiced a spiritual discipline that they claimed was based upon principles of occult science and the magic of Hermes Trismegistos. At various times, the order numbered William Butler Yeats and Aleister Crowley among its members. Rosicrucianism's influence was also felt in the artworks of an idealist renaissance fostered by the occult aestheticism of Joséphin Peladan's Salons de la Rose + Croix in Paris and in the work of Rudolf Steiner and the Anthroposophical Society.

DOCTRINES. From its beginnings, Rosicrucianism spread a message of general reformation, preached a new enlightenment, promised a new Paradise, and taught a combination of religious illumination, evangelical piety, and magic. Rosicrucian "science" comprised a system of mathematics and mechanics for the lower world, celestial mathematics for the higher world, and angelic conjuration for the supercelestial world. In principle, the angelic sphere could be penetrated by the use of Rosicrucian technique, and, thus, the essence of all reality was graspable. The initiates were offered insight into the nature of all life. The Hermetic axiom "As above, so below," typical of Rosicrucian teaching, had a profound effect on early modern scientific thought, and Rosicrucianism—like other occult paths—has been credited with having helped to prepare the way for the rise of modern science.

The *Chymische Hochzeit* depicts the initiatory aspects of Rosicrucianism. Echoing themes of the *Fama* and the *Confessio,* its story recounts Christian Rosencreutz's participation in the celebration of a royal wedding. Called on the eve of Easter from his preparation for Communion, Rosencreutz journeys to a magical castle full of treasures. There he joins the wedding party, and over the course of the Christian Holy Week he views many marvels and becomes initiated into chivalric orders. This romance stands as a spiritual allegory both of Rosencreutz's inner transformation and of the transformation of the Rosicrucian elect.

The esoteric dimension of the transformation is rendered in alchemical symbols. Union of bride and bridegroom represents a mystical marriage of the soul, and this spiritual image is bound to an alchemic metaphor of elemental fusion. Likewise, the theme of spiritual death and rebirth is tied to the alchemy of elemental transmutation. The symbolic components of the rose cross may further evidence the importance of the alchemical tradition to Rosicrucian spiritual discipline: Within the alchemical lexicon, *ros,* or dew, is the solvent of gold, and *crux,* the cross, is the equivalent of light.

The emblem, however, clearly draws on other symbolic traditions as well. Rosicrucianism's roots in chivalric traditions are revealed in certain aspects of the rose cross. The "chemical wedding" leads to Christian Rosencreutz's initiation as a Red Cross knight, and the initiation he experiences in the allegorical tale is similar to that actually undergone by Frederick V (at the time of his marriage) into the English Order of the Garter, whose heraldric symbol is the Red Cross of Saint George.

The symbol of the rose and the cross also evokes mystical images of the rose of the Virgin and the death of Christ. (Coincidentally, the rose cross was one of Luther's emblems.) For contemporary Rosicrucians, the interpretation of the rose cross centers in the maxim "No cross, no crown," that is, the belief that one comes to the rose (signifying the divine) through mortal suffering.

SEE ALSO Anthroposophy; Freemasons; Paracelsus; Steiner, Rudolf.

BIBLIOGRAPHY

Arthur E. Waite's *Real History of the Rosicrucians* (London, 1887) is the standard account of Rosicrucianism. *The Secret Doc-

trine of the Rosicrucians (Chicago, 1918), by Magus Incognito (pseudonym for Clifford Edward Brooksmith), is a partisan study of teachings and symbols. The best recent account, particularly of the cultural, intellectual, and political milieu in which Rosicrucianism emerged, is Frances A. Yates's *The Rosicrucian Enlightenment* (London, 1972). This book draws upon the full range of recent scholarship. *A Christian Rosenkreutz Anthology,* edited by Paul M. Allen and Carlo Pietzner (Blauvelt, N.Y., 1968), offers a useful compilation of traditional texts as well as essays by Rudolf Steiner and others associated with Anthroposophy. Francis King's *Magic* (London, 1975) explores Rosicrucian influences on Western magic.

New Sources

Åkerman, Susanna. *Rose Cross over the Baltic: The Spread of Rosicrucianism in Northern Europe.* Boston, Mass, 1998.

Melton, J. Gordon, ed. *Rosicrucianism in America.* New York, 1990.

Mulvey Roberts, Marie. *Gothic Immortals: The Fiction of the Brotherhood of the Rosy Cross.* New York, 1990.

McKintosh, Christopher. *The Rose Cross and the Age of Reason: Eighteenth-Century Rosicrucianism in Central Europe and Its Relationship to the Enlightenment.* New York, 1992.

McKintosh, Christopher. *The Rosicrucians: The History, Mythology, and Rituals of an Esoteric Order.* York Beach, Me., 1997.

HARRY WELLS FOGARTY (1987)
Revised Bibliography

ROUSSEAU, JEAN-JACQUES (1712–1778) was a Geneva-born author, social and educational theorist, and advocate of a nondogmatic religion of nature. Rousseau was a prolific writer; however, his mature religious thought is encapsulated in a comparatively short section, "The Profession of Faith of the Savoyard Vicar," of *Émile* (1762), his treatise in support of experientially based educational methods. The straightforward, somewhat serene tone of this famous statement stands in marked contrast to the complex, turbulent pattern of its author's life history.

Amid the natural beauties of the Alps, Rousseau's vicar, a simple, unpretentious country priest, recounts his efforts to resolve his doubts, stemming from the diversity of competing beliefs. Dissatisfied with the philosophers, of whom he says he is not one, he has found a basis for certitude and optimism in his own experience. This has convinced him, ultimately, of the presence of order in the universe, which is only explicable by the existence of a powerful, intelligent, and beneficent God. He further asserts the immortality of the immaterial soul and the natural goodness of human beings. Evil stems from ignoring the "heavenly voice" of conscience, which teaches a sociable sympathy for others and rejects self-interest as the basis of right conduct. The vicar concludes that the adherent of natural religion may in good conscience follow the prescribed religious customs of the jurisdiction in which he or she happens to live, as he himself does in Roman Catholic Savoy.

The vicar's views are unquestionably Rousseau's own. Of equal importance with his positive beliefs is his rejection of, as unanswerable and, practically speaking, unimportant, many of the traditional central questions of metaphysics and theology, such as the meaning of "creation," the alleged eternal punishment of the wicked, and the status of "revelation." Although Rousseau, an admirer of the scriptural Jesus, considered himself a Christian, he refused, consistently with his natural religion, to endorse claims that Jesus' alleged miracles were proof of his divinity.

These religious views were central to Rousseau's entire outlook. In his autobiographical *Confessions* (completed in 1770 but published posthumously, in two parts, in 1782 and 1789) and elsewhere, he speaks rather positively of his early moral upbringing in Calvinist Geneva, although he had left there at the age of sixteen in search of wider horizons. Within a brief time, he had declared himself a convert to Catholicism in Turin. He next established some reputation as a music teacher and theorist, traveling to various Swiss and French cities before settling in Paris. There he made the acquaintance of Thérèse Levasseur, a working-class woman who became his lifelong companion, and of the social circle surrounding the *philosophes,* notably Diderot. He eventually contributed to their *Encyclopedia.*

An incident in the autumn of 1749, known as "the illumination of Vincennes," shaped Rousseau's subsequent career. Stopping along the road to rest, he glanced at a journal announcement of a prize essay contest on the question of whether the renaissance of the sciences and arts had contributed to the purification of morals. The insight that, on the contrary, civilization and progress had brought about degeneration from the more natural earlier state of humanity struck him forcefully. His *Discourse on the Sciences and Arts* (1750), which elaborates on the consequences of this degeneration, won the prize. In his *Discourse on the Origins of Inequality* (1755), he imaginatively reconstructs humanity's development from a happy but unenlightened early state of nature through successive stages leading to the establishment of private property, government, and ultimately despotism. But he also insists that an attempt to return to the primitive state would be unrealistic. His *Social Contract,* published in the same year (1762) as *Émile,* aims to show how a free community structured in accordance with the general will of its citizens could claim moral legitimacy. It concludes with the chapter "On Civil Religion," in which Rousseau proposes to combine the principles of natural religion with the state's need for religious reinforcement: a new doctrine affirming the "sacredness of the social contract and the laws" is the result.

Rousseau's work of 1762, particularly the "Profession of Faith," was attacked by Catholics, Protestants, and *philosophes* alike. He was forced to flee France to avoid arrest and was also condemned by the authorities of Geneva, whose citizenship and religion he had proudly readopted eight years earlier. Subsequent forced displacements and isolation led him to suspect the existence of a large conspiracy against him. But by the time of his death, Rousseau's ideas—especially, perhaps, as popularized in his romantic novel, *The New Heloise* (1761)—had won many adherents. His name later came to be associated with the French Revolution; Robespierre was a great admirer of Rousseau's, as was Kant, who took Rousseau's ideal of societal self-government—obedience to a law that one has prescribed for oneself—as his formula for moral autonomy.

Subsequent uses and interpretations of Rousseau's thought have been equally disparate. Was he a rationalist or a proponent of the purest sentimentality? A totalitarian or a democrat? A conservative or a protosocialist? A sympathetic portrayer of female heroines or a blatant sexist? A Pelagian, a Deist in spite of himself, or a consistent exponent of the fundamental ideas of the Reformation? Textual evidence exists for these and many other incompatible, ardently defended interpretations of Rousseau. What is correct in any case is that Rousseau had a keen sense for dialectical paradoxes in the human condition, and that he was a pioneer in exploring the complex tensions and ambivalences of the human psyche, beginning with his own.

BIBLIOGRAPHY

One complete English translation of *Émile* in current circulation is Barbara Foxley's (1903; reprint, London, 1966), and there is another of the *Profession of Faith of the Savoyard Vicar,* translated by Arthur H. Beattie as *Creed of a Priest of Savoy* (New York, 1956). Multiple translations of other major Rousseauean writings exist, the most numerous being those of *The Social Contract.* Particularly distinguished, in terms of scholarship, is Roger D. Masters and Judith R. Masters edition of *The First and Second Discourses* (New York, 1964). Ronald Grimsley has edited a collection entitled *Religious Writings* (Oxford, 1970). Among the numerous secondary works, Grimsley's *Rousseau and the Religious Quest* (Oxford, 1968) is perhaps the most useful introduction to this topic in English, although it cannot compare in comprehensiveness to Pierre Maurice Masson's *La Religion de Jean-Jacques Rousseau,* 3 vols. in 1 (1916; reprint, Geneva, 1970). Among more general English-language studies, Charles Hendel's two-volume *Jean-Jacques Rousseau, Moralist* (1934; reprint, New York, 1962), remains an especially lively and readable classic.

WILLIAM LEON MCBRIDE (1987)

ROY, RAM MOHAN (1772–1833), important early nineteenth-century reformer of Indian religion and society, founder of the Brāhmo Samāj. Roy's lasting influence has earned him the epithet "father of modern India."

Ram Mohan Roy was born into an orthodox Hindu *brahman* family on May 22, 1772, in Radhanagar, a small town in modern West Bengal. He was sent at an early age to Patna, then a center of Islamic learning, to study Persian and Arabic, the languages of social and political advancement at that time. At Patna, Roy became acquainted with Islamic thought, particularly Islamic monotheism and views on Hindu image worship, which was to have a lasting influence on his own religious beliefs. His new ideas and subsequent criticism of Hinduism caused such conflict with his parents that he left their home to travel around northern India, perhaps venturing as far as Tibet, to study the religions of those areas firsthand. Encouraged by his mother, he then settled down in Banaras (Varanasi) for a few years to study Sanskrit and the Hindu scriptures. At this time he also began to study English, which eventually enabled him to secure an appointment in Bengal under the East India Company in 1803.

Success as an administrator and an assured income from landed estates permitted Roy to retire at the age of forty-two and settle permanently in Calcutta, then the political and intellectual capital of India. There he launched an active career calling for reforms in Indian religion and society. There too he began to develop close ties with the Unitarian missionaries of Calcutta. Roy was attracted to the Unitarian doctrine of divine unity, and for a time (1824–1828) he regularly attended Unitarian services and considered himself a "Hindu Unitarian." Later, he and his followers rejected Unitarianism as unsuited to their views and principles; in 1828 they founded their own movement, which came to be known as the Brāhmo Samāj, a society organized to provide for the proper worship of *brahman,* whom Roy considered to be the one true God of the Hindu scriptures. In 1830 he set sail for England to realize a long-held dream of visiting Europe, the land of the scientific rationalism to which he had become so attracted. He was, unfortunately, never to return to India, for his life was cut short by a serious illness; he died at Bristol on 22 September 1833.

Roy's first work of major importance was the *Tuḥfat al-muwāḥḥidīn* (A gift for the monotheists). This work, written in Persian and Arabic at an early date but not published until 1804, argues that, by natural reason, all human beings believe in one being who is the source and governor of creation, but by habit and training at the hands of deceitful religious leaders, they stray from this virtuous belief. In 1815 Roy published a major study of Hindu Vedanta, *Vedāntagrantha* (also abridged as *Vedāntasāra*), and from 1816 to 1819 he published translations of five major Upaniṣads in both Bengali and English. He hoped to show by these efforts that the belief in and worship of the one *brahman* was the only sensible religious practice for Hindus. Roy published *The Precepts of Jesus* in 1820, which presented Christianity as a simple, virtuous moral code, avoiding mention of miracles and opposing the doctrine of the Trinity in favor of the unity of God. This publication upset both the orthodox Hindu community and the Baptist missionaries of Calcutta.

The two primary tenets of Roy's religious reform were the establishment of a Hindu monotheism and the abolishment of what he called Hindu "idolatry." He wrote in his English introduction to the *Vedāntasāra*:

> My constant reflections on the inconvenient or, rather, injurious rites introduced by the peculiar practice of Hindoo idolatry, which, more than any other pagan worship destroys the texture of society, together with compassion for my countrymen, have compelled me to use every possible effort to awaken them from their dream of error; and by making them acquainted with their scriptures, enable them to contemplate, with true devotion, the unity and omnipresence of nature's God. (de Bary, 1958, p. 575)

Roy believed that the pure Hinduism of an earlier age had become encrusted with degrading customs, of which it had to be purged. Although his appreciation of monotheism began with his exposure to Islamic thought and was strengthened by Christian Unitarianism, Roy was born a Hindu and would not be satisfied until he had found approval for his monotheistic ideas in the Hindu scriptures. He found this confirmation in his study of Vedantic thought, particularly that of the Upaniṣads. The Upaniṣadic *brahman,* according to Roy, is not a static absolute but rather the sole "author and governor of the universe." As for Hindu image worship, he contended that the scriptures recommend it only for the feebleminded and he therefore declared it inferior and unworthy of practice.

Much of what Roy criticized in Hinduism was precisely what was condemned by the Christian missionaries in Calcutta. His reform program had two essential purposes: to convince the Hindus that many of their beliefs and practices were not sanctioned by their own scriptures and to demonstrate both to the adherents of other religions and to the British rulers that, contrary to common understanding, the Hindu scriptures did not advocate polytheism and idolatry but in fact contained a lofty and rational message. These efforts, of course, caused deep resentment and outrage among many orthodox Hindus.

Roy also campaigned vigorously for certain social reforms. He promoted modern education and struggled ceaselessly for women's rights. Roy's influence was particularly conspicuous in the official British proscription of *satī* (the self-immolation of a widow on her husband's funeral pyre) in 1829.

Many scholars place Roy at the head of a reformation of Indian religion and society that was to change Indian culture significantly in the nineteenth and twentieth centuries. The most important and lasting event in his career was the establishment of the Brāhmo Samāj. Through this religious society, which nurtured such figures as Rabindranath Tagore and Keshab Chandra Sen, Roy's continuing influence was assured. Roy shaped the Brāhmo Samāj with his ideas, and many scholars will argue that it was the Brāhmo Samāj that shaped modern Indian culture.

SEE ALSO Brāhmo Samāj.

BIBLIOGRAPHY

A reliable source for the life of Ram Mohan Roy is the first chapter of Sivanath Sastri's *History of the Brāhmo Samāj,* 2d ed. (Calcutta, 1974). Two recent biographies are B. N. Dasgupta's *The Life and Times of Rajah Rammohun Roy* (New Delhi, 1980) and M. C. Kotnala's *Raja Ram Mohun Roy and Indian Awakening* (New Delhi, 1975). *The English Works of Raja Rammohun Roy,* 6 vols., edited by Kalidas Nag and Debajyoti Burman (Calcutta, 1945–1951), is the sourcebook of Roy's works for the English reader. A good study of Roy's religious ideas is Ajit Kumar Ray's *The Religious Ideas of Rammohun Roy* (New Delhi, 1976). For the lasting influence of Ram Mohan Roy and the Brāhmo Samāj, see David Kopf's *The Brahmo Samaj and the Shaping of the Modern Indian Mind* (Princeton, 1979).

Extracts from Roy's introduction to the *Vedāntasāra,* including the quotation that appears above, can be found in *Sources of the Indian Tradition,* edited by Wm. Theodore de Bary (New York, 1958), pp. 573–575.

New Sources

Datta, Bhabatosha. *Resurgent Bengal: Rammohun, Bankimchandra, Rabindranath.* Calcutta, 2000.

Mazumder, Durga Prasad. *Dimensions of Political Culture in Bengal, 1814–1857: With Special Reference to Raja Rammohun Roy.* Calcutta, 1993.

Mitra, Saroj Mohan, ed. *The Golden Book of Rammohun Roy.* Calcutta, 1997.

Robertson, Bruce Carlisle. *Raja Rammohan Ray: The Father of Modern India.* Delhi, 1995.

DAVID L. HABERMAN (1987)
Revised Bibliography

ṚTA (Skt., "cosmic order") represents the Vedic notion of an impersonal and powerful force upon which the ethical and physical worlds are based, through which they are inextricably united, and by which they are maintained. *Ṛta* is the universal truth that gives effective strength to Vedic ritual practices, that serves as the foundation for proper social organization, and that preexists even the Vedic gods themselves, who find in it the very source and essence of their power. In many ways, *ṛta* stands as the Vedic antecedent for the notion of *dharma* (the established order of things, proper behavior, fitting truth), a concept of central importance not only to the various forms of Hinduism but also to the teachings of Buddhism, Jainism, and other South Asian religious systems.

The term *ṛta* is based on the Sanskrit verbal root *ṛ* ("go, move"), which itself reflects the Indo-European verbal root **ar* ("fit together properly"). Thus *ṛta* signifies the cosmic law that allows the universe to run smoothly, the dynamic structure in which every object and all actions have their proper place and in which all parts support and strengthen the whole in a flowing symbiosis. The word is related through **ar* to the Greek *harmos,* from which the English *harmony* derives, and to the Latin *ars* ("skill, craft"), the source of the English *art* and *artist.* Accordingly, the term *ṛta* connotes the experience of a "finely tuned" universe whose laws can give creative power to those gods and cultic specialists who understand its structures.

The *Ṛgveda* (c. 1200 BCE) commonly assigns to the gods such epithets as "he who possesses *ṛta*," "he who grows according to *ṛta*," or "he who is born of *ṛta*," descriptions representing the Vedic notion that the gods derive their strength from their adherence to cosmic law. If they—or humans, for that matter—were to go against the structures of *ṛta*, they would then be said to be *anṛta*, a common synonym for *vṛjina* ("crooked, wrong") and even *asatya* ("untrue"). Thus even the gods must obey the laws of *ṛta*. The principles of *ṛta* (like those of the Zand Avestan *asha*, a Zoroastrian notion to which *ṛta* is linguistically and conceptually related) function in eternal opposition to any principle of disjunctive or disintegrative power (*druh;* Av., *druj*) as well as to those personal demons and humans who seek to disrupt impersonal cosmic order by means of harmful magical practices (*yātu*).

Throughout the Vedic period *ṛta* was understood to be an impersonal law and was never personified or hypostatized into a deity. Characteristically, the primary agent or guardian of the laws of *ṛta* is the god Varuna, who—in Vedic times at least—was an ethical sky god whose omniscient judgment the Vedic cult admired and feared.

As the impersonal source of cosmic and ethical order, *ṛta* includes important creative aspects. The gods find their ability to create the world precisely in their ability to recognize the principles of *ṛta*. These creative dimensions appear frequently in Vedic salutatory depictions of natural processes. Thus the wonderful facts that the sun rises in the east every morning and that water runs downhill are trustworthy cosmic events because they reflect the truth of cosmic harmony (see *Ṛgveda* 1.105.12). Furthermore, Vedic tradition held that the very structures of *ṛta* allow the human community access to the powers that drive the universe itself. This is most apparent in the performance of the ritual: since proper cultic activity embodies the structures and processes of cosmic law, the incorrect performance of the ritual would signal the collapse of cosmic order and would be as devastating to the Vedic community as it would be if the sun were not to rise or rivers not to flow.

SEE ALSO Dharma, article on Hindu Dharma.

BIBLIOGRAPHY

The most complete study of *ṛta* continues to be Heinrich Lüders's *Varuṇa,* vol. 2, *Varuṇa und das Ṛta* (Göttingen, 1959). Shorter discussions may be found in Hermann Oldenberg's *Die Religion des Veda* (Berlin, 1894), pp. 195–221; Edward Washburn Hopkins's *Ethics of India* (New Haven, 1924), pp. 2ff., 40–44; and F. Max Müller's *Lectures on the Origin and Growth of Religion* (London, 1879), pp. 237–250.

WILLIAM K. MAHONY (1987)

RUDRA is a Vedic god and precursor of the great Hindu divinity Śiva. The name *Rudra* derives from the verbal root *rud* ("to howl, to roar"), from which he takes the epithet "the howler." The root *rud* also connotes "red" (as in English *ruddy*), suggesting that the earliest concept of the divinity was inspired by red storm clouds or the sound of thunder. Rudra has no correlates in other Indo-European mythologies.

Some scholars believe that the earliest prototype of Rudra may be traced to an Indus Valley seal in which four animals surround a seated figure. This seal, and some Vedic texts, suggest Rudra's connection with animals. As the Lord of Animals (Paśupati), he is their protector as well as their destroyer, an ambivalence common in many mythologies. The animal most frequently associated with Rudra is the bull, a symbol of rain and fertility. Typically, the figure in the Indus Valley seals is seated in a posture later associated with yogic meditation, leading some to postulate a non-Aryan origin of his post-Vedic role as the ascetic mendicant *par excellence.*

Rudra's wife is Pṛśni, whose name denotes a leather water bag, clearly an association with rainwater. This association is strengthened by references in the *Ṛgveda* to Rudra as the bringer of fertilizing rain. Rudra is invoked in only four hymns of the *Ṛgveda,* although he also figures in the later Saṃhitās and in the Brāhmaṇas. The Ṛgvedic hymns describe him as a well-dressed god riding in a chariot, carrying a bow and arrows. These hymns seek to avert the wrath of a fearsome and destructive god who hurls his lethal arrows at random upon men and beasts. In addition to the wind gods, Vāyu-Vātāḥ, Rudra's Vedic associates are the Rudras and the Maruts, who share his benign and chthonic traits respectively. The word *marut,* derived from the root *mṛ* ("to die"), seems to signify a spirit of the dead. Cultic worship of Rudra also confirms his close connection with Yama, the god of death, with spirits of the dead, and with the dark goddess Nirṛti. His oblations and the venue and manner of offering them are characteristic of a chthonic god. Rudra's later Vedic consort was Rudrāṇī, or Mīḍhuṣī. The latter, like Pṛśni, signifies Rudra's function as the "pourer," and indirectly connects him with fertility, a trait incipient from the Indus Valley period. This perhaps explains the worship of Rudra in the phallic emblem, which later almost completely replaced his anthropomorphic representation.

In the Vedic literature Rudra is intimately connected with Agni and Soma. Indeed, in his power, brilliance, and destructive capacity he is almost an alter ego of Agni. Like Soma, he dwells on a mountaintop, especially Mount Mūjavat, the abode of Soma in later literature. But from the *Yajurveda* onward, a syncretism begins in which the Ṛgvedic Rudra merges with other gods evidently of indigenous origin, reflecting the fusion of Aryan and non-Aryan peoples. In that text Rudra is invoked as the god of burglars, highwaymen, night rovers, and cheats. His benign characteristics persist, but dark and malevolent traits now appear, and his chthonic character is henceforth established. In later Vedic literature Rudra assumes such new names as Bhava, Śarva, Ugra, Mahādeva, and Śiva. Some of these figures are clearly of regional origin, while others are still unspecified but may be indigenous gods of non-Vedic origin. Both the *Yajurveda* and the Brāhmaṇas record the progress of Rudra's syncretism with other gods until he finally merges into Śiva, his mythological successor. The complex "Rudra-Siva" is thus often used by students of the tradition to designate the mythological and cultic fusion of Śiva and his Vedic precursor.

Because of the fairly early syncretism with other indigenous regional and tribal gods, Rudra becomes a conglomerate of disparate traits. His evident ambivalence toward the sacrifice bears testimony to this. In the subsequent Śaiva mythological cycle, the sacrifice flees from him, or he is denied a share in Dakṣa's sacrifice. Infuriated, he destroys the sacrifice, killing men and injuring gods. These anti-Vedic traits continue to multiply until the Ṛgvedic god who granted boons, forgave sins, and blessed his devotees assumes a dual personality combining benign and malevolent traits.

See Also Śiva.

Bibliography

Agarwala, Vasudeva S. *Śiva Mahādeva, the Great God.* Varanasi, 1966.

Bhandari, V. S. "Rudra as the Supreme God in the Yajurveda." *Nagpur University Journal* 16 (October 1965): 37–42.

Bhattacharji, Sukumari. *Indian Theogony: A Comparative Study of Indian Mythology from the Vedas to the Puranas.* Cambridge and New York, 1970. Includes chapters on Rudra-Śiva.

Dange, Sadashiv Ambadas. "Tryambaka." *Journal of the Oriental Institute* (University of Baroda) 19 (1969): 223–227.

Machek, Václav. "Origin of the Gods Rudra and Pūṣan." *Archiv orientalni* 22 (1954): 544–562. A perceptive article.

Mayrhofer, Manfred. "Der Gottesname Rudra." *Zeitschrift der Deutschen Morgenländischen Gesellschaft* 103 (1953): 140–150. An original article on the import of the god's name.

O'Flaherty, Wendy Doniger. *Ascetism and Eroticism in the Mythology of Śiva.* London, 1973.

Pisani, Vittore. "Und dennoch Rudra 'Der Rote.'" *Zeitschrift der Deutschen Morgenländischen Gesellschaft* 104 (1954): 136–139. Seeks to trace the god's identity from the derivation of his name.

Sukumari Bhattacharji (1987)

RŪMĪ, JALĀL AL-DĪN

(AH 604–672/1207–1273 CE), Muslim mystic and poet. No Ṣūfī poet has exerted a vaster influence on Muslim East and Christian West than Jalāl al-Dīn, called Mawlānā, or Mawlawī, "our master." His Persian works are considered the most eloquent expression of Islamic mystical thought, and his long mystico-didactic poem, the *Mathnavī*, has been called "the Qur'ān in the Persian tongue" by the great fifteenth-century poet Jāmī of Herat.

Life. Muḥammad Jalāl al-Dīn was born in Balkh, now Afghanistan; the Afghans therefore prefer to call him "Balkhī," not "Rūmī," as he became known after settling in Anatolia, or Rūm. Although the date of his birth seems well established, he may have been born some years earlier. His father, Baha' al-Dīn Walad, a noted mystical theologian, left the city some time before the Mongol invasion of 1220 and took his family via Iran to Syria, where Jalāl al-Dīn studied Arabic history and literature. They then proceeded to Anatolia, an area that had not yet been reached by the Mongol hordes and thus offered shelter to numerous mystics and scholars from the eastern lands of Islam. They enjoyed the liberal patronage of the Seljuk Sulṭān ʿAlā' al-Dīn Kaykōbād. After Bahā' al-Dīn's family settled in Laranda (now Karaman), Jalāl al-Dīn married, and in 1226 his first son, Sulṭān Walad, was born. The aged Baha' al-Dīn was invited to Konya (ancient Iconium), the capital of the Anatolian Seljuks, to teach in one of the city's numerous theological colleges. After his death in early 1231, Jalāl al-Dīn succeeded him in the chair.

A disciple of Rūmī's father, Burhān al-Dīn Muḥaiqqiq, reached Konya in the early 1230s and introduced Jalāl al-Dīn into the mystical life and to the ideas of his father, whose *Maʿārif,* a collection of sermons and a spiritual diary, were later to form an important source of inspiration for Rūmī. He also studied the Persian poetry of Ḥakim Sanā'ī of Ghazna (d. 1131), the first poet to use the form of *mathnavī,* "rhyming couplets," for mystical instruction. Rūmī may have visited Syria in the 1230s, but nothing definite is known. His teacher later left Konya for Kayseri (Caesarea), where he died about 1242.

Shams al-Dīn. After ʿAlā' al-Dīn's death in 1236, the Mongols invaded Anatolia, and the internal situation deteriorated owing to the incompetence of his successors. In the midst of the upheavals and troubles in eastern and central Anatolia Jalāl al-Dīn underwent an experience that transformed him into a mystical poet. In October 1244 he met the wandering dervish Shams al-Dīn, "Sun of Religion," of Tabriz, and, if the sources are to be believed, the two mystics spent days and weeks together without eating, drinking, or experiencing any bodily needs. The discussions of Rūmī and Shams, who must have been about the same age, led Jalāl al-Dīn into the depths of mystical love but also caused anger and jealousy among his students and his family. Shams left Konya, and in the pangs of separation, Mawlānā suddenly turned into a poet who sang of his love and longing while whirling around to the sound of music. He himself could not understand the secret of this transformation and expressed his feelings in ever-new verses, declaring that it was the spirit of the beloved that made him sing, not his own will. There was no question of seeking a fitting rhyme or meter—they came to him spontaneously, triggered by a casual sound, a word, or a sight. The poems of this early period, which excel in their daring paradoxes and sometimes eccentric imagery, do not mention the name of the beloved but allude to it with frequent mention of the sun, which became Rūmī's favorite symbol to express the beautiful and destructive but always transforming power of love. In addition to classical Persian, he sometimes used the Turkish or Greek vernacular as it was spoken in Konya.

When news reached Konya that Shams al-Dīn had been seen in Damascus, Mawlānā's elder son, Sulṭān Walad, traveled there and succeeded in bringing his father's friend back. As Sulṭān Walad says in his poetical account of his father's life, "They fell at each other's feet, and no one knew who was the lover and who the beloved." This time, Shams stayed in Mawlānā's home, married to one of the young women there, and the intense spiritual conversation between the two mystics continued. Again jealousy built up, and Shams disappeared in December 1248. It seems certain that he was assassinated with the connivance of Mawlānā's younger son. Rūmī knew what had happened but refused to believe it; his poetry expressed the certitude that "the sun cannot die," and he even went to Syria to seek the lost friend. But eventually he "found him in himself, radiant as the moon," as Sulṭān Walad says, and most of his lyrical poetry came to be written in the name of Shams al-Dīn.

Friends and disciples. After reaching complete annihilation (*fanā'*) in Shams, who had claimed to have attained the stage of being "the Beloved" and who appeared as the true interpreter of the secrets of the Prophet, Mawlānā found spiritual peace in his friendship with Ṣalāḥ al-Dīn, an illiterate goldsmith with whom he had long-standing relations through his own spiritual teacher, Burhān al-Dīn. Ṣalāḥ al-Dīn became, as it were, Rūmī's mirror; in his pure simplicity he understood the friend without questioning. To cement the relationship, Mawlānā married Sulṭān Walad to Ṣalāḥ al-Dīn's daughter, and his letters to his beloved daughter-in-law are beautiful proofs of his humanity.

The number of disciples that gathered around Rūmī grew steadily. They came from different layers of society, for he was a friend of some of the powerful ministers who, for all practical purposes, ruled the country; but there were also greengrocers and craftsmen among them. A number of women belonged to his circle, some of whom arranged musical sessions for him in their homes. Outstanding in piety and obedience among his disciples was the youthful Ḥusām al-Dīn Chelebī, who now became Rūmī's third source of inspiration.

A poem dated November 1256 reveals the moment when Ḥusām al-Dīn first assumed his new role. About that time, he had asked the master to compose a mystical *mathnavī* for the benefit of his students so that they would no longer need to go back to the epics of Sanā'ī and 'Aṭṭar. Rūmī began by reciting the famous "Song of the Reed," the eighteen introductory verses of the *Mathnavī,* which express the soul's longing for home, and from that time Ḥusām al-Dīn wrote down whatever inspirational teaching came from the master. The composition of the *Mathnavī* was interrupted in 1258 when Ṣalāḥ al-Dīn died after a protracted illness and Ḥusām al-Dīn lost his wife; the poems attributed to the next four years are usually didactic in character though lyrical in form. The dictation of the *Mathnavī* resumed in 1262, when Ḥusām al-Dīn was designated as Rūmī's spiritual successor (*khalīfah*), and continued almost to the master's death on December 17, 1273. His death was lamented not only by the Muslims but also by the numerous Christians and Jews of Konya, for he had friendly relations with all of them (and his verse at times shows a remarkable awareness of Christian thought and ritual).

Ḥusām al-Dīn, his first successor, died in 1284; then Sulṭān Walad, the obedient son, assumed the leadership of the disciples and shaped them into a Ṣūfī fraternity proper. He institutionalized the mystical dance, *samā'*, in the form that has remained current through the centuries. By the time he died in 1312, the Mevlevi order (called Whirling Dervishes in the West) was firmly established and continued to exert great influence on Turkish culture, particularly music and poetry. The order was abolished, like all mystical fraternities, in 1925 by Kemal Atatürk; but since 1954 the anniversary of Rūmī's death is again being celebrated in Konya, and the performers of the *samā'* have toured Western countries under the label of a "tourist attraction."

WORKS. Mawlānā's writings can be divided into two distinct parts: the lyrical poetry that was born out of his encounter with Shams and is collected in the more than thirty-six thousand verses of the so-called *Dīvāni Shams-i Tabrīz,* and the didactic *Mathnavī-yi ma'navī* with about twenty-six thousand verses, written in a simple meter that had already been used for similar purposes by 'Aṭṭar. Mawlānā's "table talks" have been collected under the title *Fīhi mā fīhi;* these prose pieces sometimes supplement the poetry, since the same stories are used at times in both works. More than a hundred letters, written to dignitaries and family members, have also survived; they show that Mawlānā was also practically-minded and looked well after those who entrusted themselves to him.

Dīvān-i Shams. The *Dīvān* is a remarkable piece of literature in that it translates the author's ecstatic experiences directly into poetry. The form is the traditional *ghazal* with its monorhyme. The rhythm is strong, and often the verses invite scanning by stress rather than by the rules of quantitative classical Persian prosody, although Rūmī uses the traditional meters most skillfully. He is also a master of rhetorical plays, puns, and unexpected ambiguities, and his allusions show that he had mastered Arabic and Persian classical literatures and history as well as religious writings completely. In some poems one can almost follow the flow of inspiration: Beginning from a seemingly trivial event, such as a strange sight in the street, the mystic is carried away by the music of the words and the strength of his rapture until, at least in some longish poems, the inspiration tapers off even though the rhyme continues to carry him through some more (not too good) verses.

Mathnavī. As the *Dīvān* was largely born out of an ecstatic experience that was expressed in unusual and extremely rich imagery, it is difficult to analyze. The *Mathnavī* is somewhat more accessible, and it has been a source for mystical instruction ever since it was written. For the Western reader, the book is still not easy to understand, for stories grow out of stories to lead to a mystical adage or a highly lyrical passage, and after long digressions the poet may return to the original anecdote only to be carried away by a verbal association or, as we may surmise, by the interruption of a listener who set him on a different train of thought. The *Mathnavī* is a storehouse not only of Ṣūfī lore but also of folklore, proverbs, and sometimes very crude, even obscene stories that, again, turn into surprising symbols of spiritual experiences. The book contains so little technical terminology of the Ṣūfīs and so few theoretical discussions of "stages," "states," and so forth that some listeners objected to the master's simple "storytelling," as becomes evident from scattered remarks in the *Mathnavī* itself.

Content. The subject of Mawlānā's work is always love, the true moving power in life. Those verses in the *Dīvān* that can be assigned with some certainty to the early years (c. 1245–1250) use especially strong images to describe the mystery of love, the encounter between lover and beloved, the secrets of seeking and finding, of happiness in despair. They carry the reader away even though the logical sequence is not always very clear. Love is personified under different guises—Rūmī sees it as a police officer who enacts confiscation of humanity's goods or as a carpenter who builds a ladder to heaven, as a ragpicker who carries away everything old from the house of the heart, or as a loving mother, as a dragon or a unicorn, as an ocean of fire or a white falcon, to mention only a few of the images of this strongest power of life. God's preeternal address to the not-yet-created souls, "Alastu bi-rabbikum" ("Am I not your Lord?" Qur'ān 7:171), is interpreted as the first music, which caused creation to dance out of not-being and to unfold in flowers, trees, and stars. Everything created participates in the eternal dance, of which the Mevlevi ritual is only a "branch." In this ritual, the true mystery of love, namely "to die before dying," of sacrificing oneself in order to acquire a new spiritual life, is symbolized by the dervishes casting off their black gowns to emerge in their white dancing dresses, symbols of the luminous "body of resurrection." For the idea of suffering and dying for the sake of transformation permeates all of Rūmī's work, and he expresses it in ever-new images: not only the moth that casts itself into the candle, or the snow that melts when the sun enters the sign of Aries, but even the chickpeas that are boiled in order to be eaten, and thus to reach a higher level of existence in becoming part of the human body, speak of this mystery of transformation, as does the image of the treasure that can only be found in ruins; for the heart must be broken in order to find in itself the "hidden treasure," which is God.

Most interpreters, including the leading European expert, Reynold A. Nicholson, have understood Rūmī's work almost exclusively in the light of Ibn al-ʿArabī's theosophy. Although on friendly terms with Ibn al-ʿArabī's stepson and foremost interpreter, Ṣadr al-Dīn Qunawī, Mawlānā was not fond of the "great master's" theoretical approach and his ingenious systematization. To explain everything in the *Mathnavī* in the light of *waḥdat al-wujūd,* "unity of being," as systematized by Ibn al-ʿArabī, would be wrong. Of course, Rūmī was deeply convinced, as is every true Muslim, that the multiplicity of phenomena is a veil before the absolute Divine Unity: God's creative command, "Kun!" ("Be!"), with its two letters (*kn*), is like a two-colored rope that makes people forget the unity of God who created it. The end of the ascending ladder of manifestations through which the creatures have to pass in their constant attempt to return to their beginning (symbolized by the reed bed out of which the complaining flute was once cut) lies in *ʿadam,* "positive nothingness," the divine essence that is absolutely hidden and beyond any qualifications. But Rūmī's experience of unity is not based on mere speculations of a gnostic approach to life; rather, it develops out of the experience of love, for the lover believes that everything he sees, hears, or feels merely points to the one Beloved with whom he experiences an ever-growing proximity until his own "I" has been burned away in the fire of separation, and he feels that only the Friend exists, who has taught him that "there is no room for two I's in the house."

This loving relationship is also expressed in prayer. Among all Muslim mystics, Rūmī has expressed the mystery of prayer most eloquently: Prayer is the language of the soul, and the poor shepherd's prayer in which he offers his beloved God "to sweep his little room, to comb his hair, to pick his lice, and to bring him a little bit of milk" is more acceptable to God than learned words uttered without feeling or with pride, for it is the expression of true love. More importantly, prayer is a gift of God: The man who called "God" ever so long and was finally seduced by Satan to refrain from calling is informed by God himself that "in every 'O God' of yours there are a hundred 'Here am I' of mine." Without divine grace, people would not be able to pray—how could a rose grow out of mere dust?

It was out of this life of constant prayer that Mawlānā was able to teach and to inspire later generations. But one must not forget that he was well aware of this world, even though he considered it "like the dream of a sleeping person." Yet, the actions that occur in this dreaming life will be interpreted in the "morning light of eternity," and Mawlānā never tired of teaching his disciples that, as the Prophet had stated, "this world is the seedbed of the other world," for each action—rather, each thought—brings its fruits for spiritual development. Death, therefore, is the true mirror that will show everyone his real face.

This awareness of the world makes Rūmī's poetry especially powerful. There is nothing abstract in his verse, and he does not shun to mention the lowliest manifestations of life, since for him everything turns into a symbol of some higher reality. Spring is the time of resurrection, when the frozen material world suddenly becomes a paradise thanks to the thunder's "trumpet of Isrāfīl," and the trees, donning green paradisical garments, dance in the spring breeze of eternal love. Animals and plants, the arts and crafts of the citizens of Konya (sewing, weaving, calligraphy, pottery, and the like), and the skills of gypsy rope dancers inspired him as much as the legends of the Ṣūfī saints of yore, or the traditions of the Prophet. Allusions to and quotations from the Qur'ān form the warp and woof of his work. Just as the sun, according to Eastern folklore, is able to transform pebbles into rubies, so too Rūmī, touched by the "Sun of Tabrīz," who was for him the locus of manifestation of the divine sun of love, was able to transform everything into a poetical symbol. It goes without saying that not all his verse is on the same level, but the spirit is the same everywhere. Even though Rūmī, in a moment of anger, claimed that he thoroughly disliked poetry, he knew that he was forced by the mystical Friend:

> I think of rhymes, but my Beloved says: "Don't think
> of anything but of my face!"

The allusions to philosophical problems in some of the later lyrics, and especially in the fourth book of the *Mathnavī,* show that during the mid-1260s Rūmī developed some interest in more theoretical aspects of Sufism, but this period apparently did not last long.

Mawlānā's life can be seen as the ideal model of the mystic's progress: After the experience of the love of Shams, which, like a high-rising flame, burned him to complete annihilation, there followed a period of comparative quietude in his relationship with the goldsmith, a time of finding his transformed self. Finally, in the descending semicircle of his life, he returned to the world and its creatures by teaching Ḥusām al-Dīn the mysteries he had experienced through the medium of the *Mathnavī.* This sequence explains the stylistic differences between the *Dīvān* and the *Mathnavī;* it also explains why the *Mathnavī* became the centerpiece of mystical education wherever Persian was understood, from Ottoman Turkey to the borders of Bengal.

Legacy. In the East, the *Mathnavī* has been translated into many languages, and hundreds of commentaries have been composed; it has been a source of inspiration for mystics and kings alike. In the West, Rūmī's work was studied from about 1800 onward and inspired poets such as Rückert in Germany, whose free adaptations of some *ghazals* are still the best introduction to Rūmī's style and thought. Through Rückert, Hegel learned of "the excellent Rūmī," in whom he saw a distant forerunner of his own thought. Numerous partial translations of Mawlānā's lyrics exist, but to do full justice to him is next to impossible because of the multicolored imagery of his verse, and the innumerable allusions would require a running commentary. Simple prose translations, again, cannot convey the delight that the reader feels when carried away by the rhythmical flow of these poems, which mark the high point of mystical verse in Islam.

See Also Sufism.

Bibliography

The most important Rūmī scholarship in the West has been carried out by Reynold A. Nicholson, whose *Selected Poems from the Dīvān-i Shams-i Tabriz* (1898; reprint, Cambridge, 1952) is the first major study of the *Dīvān* with useful notes, even though the tendency toward a Neoplatonic interpretation is somewhat too strong. Nicholson edited and translated *The Mathnawi of Jalalu'ddin Rūmī* (London, 1925–1940) in six volumes with two additional volumes of a most welcome commentary.

The *Dīvān,* which has been published often in the East, was critically edited in ten volumes by Badiʿ al-Zaman Furuzanfar (1957; reprint, Tehran, 1977). *Fihi ma fihi,* Mawlānā's prose work, is likewise available in several Eastern editions and in a translation by A. J. Arberry as *Discourses of Rūmī* (London, 1961). Arberry has published other translations of Rūmī's work, including *Tales from the Masnavi* (London, 1961) and *Mystical Poems of Rūmī* (Chicago, 1968, selections 1–200; Boulder, 1975, selections 201–400). Earlier translations of parts of the *Mathnavī* by James W. Redhouse, *The Mesnevi* (London, 1881), and E. H. Whinfield, *Masnavi i ma'navi* (1887; reprint, London, 1973), may be used for reference.

Afzal Iqbal's *The Life and Thought of Mohammad Jalālud-Dīn Rūmī* (Lahore, 1956), enlarged in later editions, provides an introduction to Rūmī's life and work, as does William Chittick's excellent book *The Sufi Path of Love* (Albany, N.Y., 1983). Most valuable are the studies of the Turkish scholar Abdülbâki Gölpinarli, who has not only written a fine biography of Rūmī, *Mevlânâ Celâlettin, hayati, felsefesi, eserlerinden seçmeleri* (Istanbul, 1952), and a history of the Mevlevi order, *Mevlânâ'dan sonra Mevelivīlik* (Istanbul, 1953), but has also translated the *Dīvān* (*Divan-i kebir,* 7 vols., Istanbul, 1957–1960) and the letters (*Mevlânâ'nin mektuplari,* Istanbul, 1963) into Turkish. For a general survey, with emphasis on the poetical aspects of Rūmī's work, see my study *The Triumphal Sun* (London and The Hague, 1978), with extensive bibliography.

One of the oldest biographies of Mawlānā, his friends, and his family, Shams al-Dīn Aḥmad Aflākī's two-volume *Manāqib al-ʿārifīn,* was published in the Persian original by Tahsin Yazici (Ankara, 1959–1961) and translated by him into Turkish (*Âriflerin menkibeleri,* Ankara, 1964). The French version by Clément Huart, *Les saints des derviches tourneurs* (Paris, 1918–1922), is not very reliable.

There is a considerable literature on Rūmī, and (partly very free) translations of his poems, in German, the latest ones being *Aus dem Diwan* (Stuttgart, 1963) and *Rumi: Ich bin Wind und du bist Feuer* (Cologne, 1982) by me and *Licht und Reigen* (Bern, 1974) by J. Christoph Bürgel. Important for the serious scholar are Helmut Ritter's numerous studies, including "Philologika XI: Maulānā Ǧalāladdīn Rūmī und sein Kreis," *Der Islam* 26 (1942): 116–158, 221–249, and "Neuere Literatur über Maulānā Calāluddīn Rūmī und seinen Orden," *Oriens* 13–14 (1960–1961).

Annemarie Schimmel (1987)

RUNES [FIRST EDITION].

The modern English word *rune* (Dan., *rune;* Swed., *runa;* Icel. pl., *rúnar;* Ger.,

Rune) signifies any character in the ancient Germanic, and especially Scandinavian, alphabet. The word is seemingly derived from a hypothetical Germanic form, **runo-*, meaning "secret" (cf. modern Ger. *raunen*, "whisper"; Icel. *rýna*, "speak confidentially"; Goth. *rûna*, "secret"; AS *rún*, "rune, secret whispering"). The Finnish word *runo*, meaning "song," is an early borrowing from Germanic.

Comprising the earliest known form of writing in any Germanic tongue, runic inscriptions can be documented for as early as 200 CE. What is known of cultural, and especially linguistic, development in general leads to the supposition that runes must have been in existence for some generations by the time the earliest preserved inscriptions were carved. Numerous theories concern the date of their creation, the tribal identity of their inventors, and the models by which they were inspired. Much discussed also is the original purpose or purposes of the runes: were they invented and used initially to serve religious (and magical) ends or were they primarily conceived of as a mode of communication? It is attested that during the period of their employment—for a millennium and longer—they served both these purposes.

The geographical distribution of the earliest brief inscriptions points strongly to early Denmark as the primary center for the first important use of runes. From Denmark the loci of early Germanic inscriptions radiate outward to southern Norway and Sweden, to northern Germany, Poland (Rozwadów), and the Ukraine (Kowel), and ultimately to Hungary (Szabadbattyán) and Romania (Pietroassa). Later the runes spread to England, undergoing in time characteristic modifications and additions and eventually awakening the interest of monks and bishops.

The geographical evidence for a centralized origin of the runes is reinforced by a linguistic consideration. From the outset, as evidenced by all known examples, there was no faltering or sign of experimentation: whether created by an individual genius or by a group, the runes were made full-blown, not only in their graphic and phonetic values but in their unique order and arrangement. Made up of twenty-four characters divided into three groups of eight, the runic "alphabet" is now known, after its first six characters, as the *futhark*. During the Viking age, commencing around 800, and through a second act of decisive linguistic creativeness, the Scandinavian *futhark* was shortened to sixteen characters, still arranged in three groups. This took place first in Denmark, then in Norway and Sweden.

The earliest inscriptions, from 200 CE or so, appear on small objects such as spearheads, buckles, amulets, and horns, apparently as marks of ownership. Their angular shape indicates the practice of carving onto wooden tablets. By the fourth century they were being chiseled into stone, particularly in Norway where rocks are plentiful. With that step, the runes acquired additional scope and permanence, chiefly as memorial inscriptions, which frequently have historical value of note. The oldest of this new type, dating from 350–400, is the brief inscription of Einang, Norway, reading "[I, Go-]dagastiz painted the rune" (i.e., carved the inscription). The longest inscription (720 runes) is that of Rök, which is partly versified and is filled with mythological and semihistorical allusions. The westernmost, and northernmost, inscription is the fourteenth-century carving from Kingiktorsoaq, Greenland, far above the Arctic circle.

Of five thousand known inscriptions, more than three thousand are Swedish, most of which were carved before 1100. Lacking a cursive form and hence unhandy for manuscript use, and imperiled after 1100 by the spread of Latin letters, the runes nevertheless persisted, especially in Sweden, for several centuries. Ultimately, they fell into disuse save as an occasional pastime or for such limited purposes as marking the calendar or, recapitulating their earliest use, indicating ownership. In Sweden a form of runic shorthand enjoyed a limited vogue.

Conflicting theories derive the runes, via some early Germanic-speaking tribe, from the Greek alphabet, the Roman alphabet, or from North Italic (Etruscan); even Celtic influence has been posited. Suggested intermediaries are the Goths around the Black Sea and the Marcomanni, who were resident in Bohemia until their destruction at Vercellae in 18 CE. But the Gothic alphabet of Bishop Ulfilas (fourth century) itself shows runic influence, and the Marcomanni or their fellow Germans would simply have adopted the Latin alphabet entirely. The greatest number of similarities is between runic and Latin, and that accords well with the intense early relations between Rome and (pre-Danish) Jutland, "the long-time heartland of Germania" (Haugen, 1976).

Some early rune masters, however, had no doubt of the origin of the runes. It is explicitly stated on the Noleby Stone (Sweden, 450 CE), on the Sparlösa Stone (Sweden, 800), and in the Old Norse *Hávamál* (st. 80; cf. ss. 138–144) that the runes derived from the gods. Whether or not the runes were originally created for religio-magical purposes, they were certainly no less adaptable to such use than were the classical alphabets that preceded and coexisted with them. Early inscriptions repeatedly contain the word *alu*, meaning "protection, magic, taboo"; on the Stone of Nordhuglo (Norway, 425) the rune master proudly refers to himself as the *gudija* (priest) "protected against magic."

In time, Christian notions succeeded traditional Germanic conceptions. Inscriptions in the younger *futhark*, often carved within traditional serpentine patterns, came to be decorated with Christian crosses as well; the serpents were retained partly out of tradition and convenience as line markers and occasionally out of residual resentment or defiance of the "new faith." But as Christianity gained sway in the north, runic incantations, maledictions, and appeals to the Germanic gods yielded to such phrases as "So-and-so made this thing (e.g., built this bridge) for his soul." Late inscriptions are sometimes mixed with Latin phrases; the hammer of Þórr (Thor) is paired with a Christian cross; the Virgin Mary is mentioned.

In the British Isles runes were adroitly drawn into the service of the church. One of the finest examples of this is the splendid Ruthwell Cross (Dumfriesshire, c. 800), adorned with evangelical pictures and containing portions of *The Dream of the Rood.* The tenth-century Jelling Stone (No. 2), that huge royal Danish monument erected by King Harald Bluetooth in honor of his parents and himself, is aggressively Christian; on it, Harald claims credit for having christianized the Danes. Many rune stones have been transported to churchyards and even immured in church walls, as a rule with the inscribed face obscured, a practice that points rather to economic than to religious considerations.

In the sixteenth century the study of runes became a learned preoccupation in Sweden, whence it spread to Denmark, and by the nineteenth century the subject was being pursued to some effect in Germany and Great Britain. In the twentieth century much energy has been devoted to such topics as runic cryptography, speculative theories of Germanic uniqueness, and efforts to derive the runes from early conceptual signs (*Begriffszeichen*). Little of this has borne fruit, but the systematic study of runology during the past hundred years or so has brought forth works of great distinction.

BIBLIOGRAPHY

The important task of photographing, systematizing, and interpreting the great corpus of inscriptions is going forward in several countries. Notable names in modern runological research are, for Denmark, Ludvig Wimmer, Lis Jacobsen, Erik Moltke, and Karl-Martin Nielsen; for Iceland, (the Dane) Anders Baeksted; for Norway, Sophus Bugge, Magnus Olsen, Carl J. S. Marstrander, and Aslak Liestøl; for Sweden, Sven Söderberg, Erik Brate, Otto von Friesen, Elias Wessén, Elisabeth Svärdström, and Sven B. F. Jansson; for Finland, Magnus Hammarström; for Germany, Wilhelm Krause, Helmut Arntz, Hans Zeiss, and Hertha Marquardt; and for Great Britain, R. W. V. Elliott and R. I. Page. Excellent orientations and bibliographies can be found in the following works.

Derolez, R. *Runica Manuscripta: The English Tradition.* Ghent, 1954.

Düwel, Klaus. *Runenkunde.* Stuttgart, 1968.

Elliott, R. W. V. *Runes: An Introduction.* New York, 1959.

Haugen, Einar. *The Scandinavian Languages.* Cambridge, Mass., 1976.

Jansson, Sven B. F. *The Runes of Sweden.* Stockholm, 1962.

Musset, Lucien. *Introduction à la runologie.* Paris, 1965.

Page, R. I. An *Introduction to English Runes.* London and New York, 1973.

ERIK WAHLGREN (1987)

RUNES [FURTHER CONSIDERATIONS].

The first edition's article on "Runes" has held up well, although some updates are necessary. First, the Noleby stone is now believed to be from c. 600 CE. Second, the word *alu,* found frequently in runic inscriptions from the third to the eighth centuries, is no longer interpreted as "amulet" (cf. Gothic *alhs,* "temple"). Instead, a connection with Hethitic *alwanzahh* (to charm) and Greek *alúein* (to be beside oneself) suggests a meaning of "ecstasy" or "magic." Third, the continued use in the Christian era of serpentine patterns to contain a series of runes is now considered to be due to tradition rather than as signalling pagan defiance. Finally, it should be pointed out that the Ruthwell Cross inscription (now dated c. 627–725 CE) quotes an Old English poem that in the mid-ninth century was reworked into another Old English poem called *The Dream of the Rood.*

Early scholarship on runes assumed that this system of writing was essentially magical, and despite considerable skepticism about that view, many early inscriptions (second–eighth centuries CE) do appear magical in nature. But whether magical, religious, or secular, runic inscriptions provide much contemporary evidence regarding Germanic paganism. The Glavendrup (c. 900–925 CE) and Snoldelev (early ninth century) inscriptions on stone monuments refer to priests. Their formula "Þórr consecrate these runes" attests to a belief in this god, and the monuments themselves show the importance of commemoration of the dead. The Rök inscription (early ninth century) contains riddling allusions to obscure legends. The rune-master raised the stone in memory of his dead son, but evidently the father was a priest, and the stone appears to have a second purpose of testing a person's knowledge of ancient lore. Runes also appear on cult objects such as bracteates (medal-like gold jewelry) and drinking horns. An inscription on a secular item of jewelry, the south German "Nordendorf fibula" (c. 600–650 CE), refers to *Wodan* and *Wigiþonar* (Hallowing-Thor), making it one of the few sources that record the south Germanic belief in the Germanic pantheon.

Another aspect of Germanic paganism was the belief in the magical properties of runes. Each rune represented not only a sound but also the word that was its name. For example, the f-rune was named *fé* (cattle, or wealth), and the t-rune was named for Týr, god of victory, and was often carved on weapons. A rune could be repeated in an inscription to emphasize its concepts, as could magical words. Migration Age bracteates were inscribed with the words *laukaR laukaR laukaR* (leek, leek, leek) to invoke the particularly effective medicinal and magical powers of this plant. The healing power of runes is explained in the eddic poem *Sigrdrífumál,* and another eddic poem calls runes the antidote for misfortune (*Hávamál,* sts. 138–141). The þ-rune was sometimes called *þurs* (giant) and could be used in black magic; the eddic poem *Skírnismál* (st. 6) says that carving it three times will bring disgrace, madness, and restlessness to its victim. Yet another eddic poem (*Rígsþula,* st. 41) includes runic lore among the cultural gifts divinely transmitted to the nobility, along with the aristocratic pastimes of swimming and the chess-like game of "tables."

After the demise of paganism, runes were widely used in Christian contexts. On the Isle of Man, which developed Christianity from Irish sources but was later settled by Scandinavians, Celtic high crosses were carved with runic inscriptions and dedications like those on continental Scandinavian monuments. That Manx Scandinavians assimilated the Cross as a warrior standard and implement of power—akin to the weapons of the pagan gods—is seen from the tenth-century slate cross fragment at Kirk Andreas. On the right side of the cross, Óðinn with his spear and raven treads on the jaw of a wolf; on the left, Jesus or a saint, armed with cross and book, treads on a serpent, flanked by a fish (cf. *Gen.* 3:15). To either side of the upper member of the cross are runic inscriptions. The Danish Jelling Stone (c. 965–987 CE), raised by a king to commemorate his role in the conversion of Denmark, displays a simple cross surrounded by interlace and a serpentine runic inscription. A fashion for somewhat similar memorials left thousands of eleventh-century rune stones in Sweden, where memorial stones with runic inscriptions continued to be erected until around 1100. The custom died out not due to the introduction of Christianity per se (many of the later stones are definitely Christian), but perhaps due to the new custom of burying the dead in churchyards. Pieces of wood with runic inscriptions of mythological poetry, found in the Bryggen section of Bergen, Norway, show that this medium as well as this material had an enduring life in an Christian, urban, non-clerical environment as late as the twelfth to fourteenth centuries. Runes in Bergen could be used for magical purposes—in love charms, for example, or as something like a curse ("Ími heated the stone so that the hearth would smoke! Never shall the food be cooked! Out with heat! In with cold! Ími heated the stone!")—but usually they had secular purposes, acting as ownership tags for merchandise, accounting records, packing slips, and other kinds of ordinary, everyday communication. The knowledge of runic writing was evidently widespread from the eleventh century on, and some 10 percent of all medieval (c. 1050–1500) runic inscriptions are in Latin and have religious content. Some are prayers; others are charms. Churches and ecclesiastical furniture such as baptismal fonts, bells, and censers were inscribed with runes.

See Also Eddas; Germanic Religion, overview article.

Bibliography

Blandade runstudier. Runrön: Runologiska bidrag utgivna av Institutionen för nordiska språk vid Uppsala universitet. 2 vols. Uppsala, Sweden, 1992 and 1997.

DuBois, Thomas A. *Nordic Religions in the Viking Age.* Philadelphia, 1999.

Düwel, Klaus. *Runenkunde.* 2d ed. Stuttgart, Germany, 1983.

Düwel, Klaus, ed. *Runeninschriften als Quellen interdisziplinärer Forschung: Abhandlungen des Vierten Internationalen Symposiums über Runen und Runeninschriften in Göttingen vom 4.–9. August 1995.* Berlin, 1998.

Herteig, Asbjørn, ed. *The Bryggen Papers.* Supplementary Series 2. Oslo, 1988.

Lönnroth, Lars. "The Riddles of the Rök-Stone: A Structural Approach." *Arkiv för Nordisk Filologi* 92 (1977): 1–57.

Page, R. I. *Runes.* Reading the Past 4. London and Berkeley, Calif., 1987.

Page, R. I. *Runes and Runic Inscriptions: Collected Essays on Anglo-Saxon and Viking Runes.* Woodbridge, U.K., 1995.

Elizabeth Ashman Rowe (2005)

RUSSIAN ORTHODOX CHURCH.

Vladimir I, grand prince of Kiev (960–1015) was the first Christian ruler of Russia. Having sent ambassadors to investigate the religions of his day, Vladimir was persuaded to embrace Greek Christianity when, according to the Russian *Primary Chronicle,* his envoys reported that at the liturgy in Constantinople they did not know whether they were in heaven or on earth. Vladimir's marriage to the Byzantine princess Anna and his economic dealings with the empire also played a significant part in his decision to align his principality with the imperial Church of Byzantium. Vladimir was baptized in 988.

Kievan Christianity. After the baptism of the Kievan peoples by prince Vladimir, Orthodox Christianity flourished in the lands of Rus'. Before the Tatar devastations in the thirteenth century, Kiev was a cosmopolitan city with commercial and cultural ties with Europe and the East. Its spiritual center was the Kievan Monastery of the Caves founded by Anthony of Kiev (d. 1072) and Theodosius (d. 1074). The monastery provided the first literary and historical as well as religious writings in the Russian lands; for centuries it served as the theological and spiritual center of Russian church life. In the early years of Christian Kiev, several remarkable churches were constructed, such as the Cathedral of Holy Wisdom (Hagia Sophia, 1037); these churches conformed to Byzantine patterns of architecture, iconography, and mosaic decoration. The leader of church life was the bishop of Kiev, often a Greek by nationality, who had the title *metropolitan.*

The city-republics of Novgorod and Pskov to the north also developed vibrant Christian societies after their conversions, boasting wonderful architectural and iconographic achievements that early began to show independence and originality. Spared attacks by the Tatars, these areas were threatened by crusading Christians from the West who desired to enforce Latin Christianity in the region. Grand Prince Aleksandr Nevskiy (d. 1263) led the Russians in their defeat of the invading Swedes (1240) and the Teutonic Knights (1242), thus preserving the Orthodox faith. He also managed to maintain peace with the Tatars through skillful diplomacy accomplished by extensive visits to the khans, to whom he paid homage and tribute.

Muscovite Christianity. After the devastation of Kiev by the Tatars in 1240, the center of Russian political and ecclesiastical life shifted to Moscow. The Muscovite princes succeeded in bringing the rival cities of the region into submission, and with the final defeat of the Tatars by Grand Prince Dmitri Donskoi in 1380, their city reigned supreme among the Russians. The ascendancy of Moscow could not have occurred without the efforts of church leaders, particularly the metropolitans, such as Alexis (d. 1378), who for a time served as governing regent, and the abbot Sergiy of Radonezh (d. 1392).

Sergiy is considered by many to be Russia's greatest saint and the "builder" of the nation. A simple monk who became famous for his ascetic labors and mystical gifts, he was appointed abbot of the Saint Sergius Trinity Monastery, which he founded in the wilderness north of Moscow. The monastery soon became the center of social and economic as well as religious and spiritual life in the region. Its members and their disciples provided Russia over the centuries with hundreds of bishops, abbots, missionaries, thinkers, artists, and secular leaders, many of whom were canonized saints of the church. One such figure was the monk-iconographer Andrei Rublev (c. 1360–1430), whose painting of the Trinity in the form of three angels who visited Abraham is among the great masterpieces of Russian art. Closed after the 1917 revolution, the monastery was reopened after World War II; it attracts thousands of pilgrims annually and houses the Moscow Theological Academy and Seminary.

THE IMPERIAL PERIOD. In the fifteenth century, with the fall of Constantinople to the Turks (1453), the theory developed that Moscow was the "third Rome," the last center of true Christianity on earth. Job, the metropolitan of Moscow, was elected patriarch. This election was confirmed by Jeremias II of Constantinople in 1589, thus giving the Russian Church a status of self-governance and honor equal to that of the ancient patriarchates of the Christian empire: Rome, Constantinople, Alexandria, Antioch, and Jerusalem. The patriarchate existed in Russia de facto until 1700, de jure until 1721, when Peter the Great (1672–1725) issued the Ecclesiastical Regulation, which created a synodical form of church government patterned after that of the Protestant Churches of Europe. The patriarchate was restored to the Russian Church only in 1918, when the All-Russian Church Council, the first such assembly allowed since before Peter's rule, elected Tikhon Belavin (d. 1925), a former archbishop of the North American mission, to the office.

In the seventeenth century Patriarch Nikon (d. 1681) attempted to reform the Russian Church according to the practices of the Church of Constantinople. He corrected the liturgical service books and instituted Greek forms of ritual, such as the practice of making the sign of the cross with three fingers instead of two, as was the practice among the Russians. Nikon's reform was taken as an assault on the "third Rome" theory because it radically questioned any special calling of the Russian Church and nation. Its result was not only the resignation of the unyielding patriarch but the schism of great numbers of "old ritualists" from the established church.

During the time of the westernization of Russia under Peter the Great and subsequent czars, the Russian Church became the virtual captive of the state. The patriarchate was abolished and replaced by the Holy Synod, consisting of bishops, presbyters, and laypeople. Church councils were forbidden, ecclesiastical properties were appropriated and secularized, and church schools began to teach in Latin. The clergy were alienated from the people, particularly the intellectuals, and the church structure was bureaucratized, with the lay government official for ecclesiastical affairs, the Oberprocuror of the Holy Synod, at its head.

LATINIZATION IN THE UKRAINE. From the end of the fifteenth century the church in the Kievan area, by now a part of the Polish-Lithuanian Kingdom, was canonically attached to the patriarchate of Constantinople and not to Moscow. In 1596 in Brest-Litovsk, the metropolitan of Kiev signed an act of union with the Church of Rome, a move opposed by some bishops and most leading laypeople. Great numbers of believers in the territories of these bishops became Uniates at this time and, over the centuries, developed into strongly committed members of the Catholic Church. In the early twenty-first century the Ukrainian and Ruthenian Eastern Rite Churches remain staunchly anti-Russian and anti-Orthodox.

The defense of Eastern Orthodoxy during this period was led by the Orthodox metropolitan of Kiev, Petr Moghila (d. 1647). Though violently anti-Catholic, Petr was himself trained in the West and became responsible for bringing many Latin doctrines and liturgical practices into the Orthodox Church through his publications and the school he founded in Kiev, which influenced not only the whole Russian Church but the entire Orthodox world. In addition to the theological school in Kiev, higher faculties of theological study specializing in preparing missionaries for the Eastern regions were established in Moscow, Saint Petersburg, and Kazan.

RUSSIAN MISSIONARY ACTIVITY. In the eighteenth and nineteenth centuries the missionary efforts of the Russian Church were extensive. The Scriptures and services of the church were translated into many Siberian languages and Alaskan dialects as the eastern regions of the empire were settled and evangelized. Russian missionaries reached the Aleutian Islands in Alaska in 1794, thus beginning the history of Russian Orthodoxy in the New World. The monk Herman (d. 1830), a member of the original missionary party, was canonized a saint of the church in 1970 by both the Russian Church and the Orthodox Church in America. The latter, formerly the Russian missionary diocese in North America, was recognized in the same year by the Russian Church as the fifteenth autocephalous (self-governing) Orthodox Church in the world.

Joining Herman in the Orthodox calendar of saints were two other great missionaries. Innokentiy Veniaminov (d. 1879) was a young married priest who traveled extensively through Siberia and North America, reaching as far as San

Francisco. He created several Alaskan alphabets, translated many texts, wrote many books, and converted countless people before becoming head of the Russian Church as metropolitan of Moscow, which post he occupied until his death. Nikolai Kasatkin (d. 1912) was the first Orthodox archbishop of Tokyo and the founder of the now autonomous Orthodox Church of Japan. In addition to contributing to the conversion of thousands, he translated Scriptures and services into Japanese and built the cathedral of Nikolai-Do in Tokyo.

SPIRITUAL REVIVAL OF THE EIGHTEENTH AND NINETEENTH CENTURIES. The eighteenth and nineteenth centuries also saw a revival of traditional Orthodox ascetical and mystical life, uninfluenced by the westernizing tendencies of the ecclesiastical institutions. Paisiy Velichkovskiy (d. 1794) brought the hesychast method of mystical prayer, rooted in the invocation of the name of Jesus, into the Ukraine and Russia from Mount Athos, an important monastic center in northern Greece. He translated into Church Slavonic many ancient texts, including the anthology of writings on the spiritual life by the church fathers titled the *Philokalia (Dobrotoliubie).* (Church Slavonic, the language created for the Slavs by the Greek brothers Cyril and Methodius in the ninth century, is still used liturgically in the Russian Church.) Bishop Feofan Govorov (d. 1894) translated into modern Russian many of the same works, including several contemporary Greek and Latin spiritual classics. Feofan also wrote many treatises on the spiritual life that continue to exercise wide influence in the Orthodox Church. He accomplished this task after retiring as bishop and spending twenty-five years as a monastic recluse. Another retired bishop canonized for his ascetic life and spiritual writings was Tikhon of Zadonsk (d. 1783), who inspired the Russian novelist Fyodor Dostoevsky (1821–1881) to name after him a character in *The Possessed.*

During this same period there emerged in Russia a tradition of spiritual eldership (*starchestvo*), the most famous center of which was the hermitage of Optina, where such elders (*startsy*) as Leonid, Macarius, and Ambrose spent several hours each day instructing and counseling people of all classes, including many philosophers, intellectuals, and statespeople, among whom were Leo Tolstoy (1828–1910), Dostoevsky, Vladimir Soloviev (1853–1900), and Konstantine Leontiev (1831–1891).

The most famous saint of the time, however, was an elder from the Sarov monastery, the priest-monk Serafim (d. 1833), whose teachings on the Christian life understood as the "acquisition of the Holy Spirit" still have great influence among the Orthodox. Ioann of Kronstadt (d. 1908), a parish priest from the port town of Kronstadt near Saint Petersburg, also was acclaimed at this time throughout the nation as an "all-Russian pastor." He is glorified in the church as a man of prayer and preaching who called the people to spiritual and sacramental renewal on the eve of the Russian revolution, which both he and Serafim had predicted.

The beginning of the twentieth century also saw a revival of patristic studies and a recapturing of the authentic Orthodox theological and liturgical tradition in the ecclesiastical schools as well as a religious renaissance on the part of a significant number of Russian intellectuals, many of whom either perished in Joseph Stalin's prison camps, like Pavel Florenskiy (d. 1937), or who were exiled to the West. Among the latter group were the philosopher Nikolai Berdiaev (d. 1948) and the theologian Sergei Bulgakov (d. 1944), who served as dean of the émigré Russian Orthodox Theological Institute of Saint Serge in Paris. The institute educated scores of pastors and church workers and sent scholars, such as George Fedotov (d. 1951), Georges Florovsky (d. 1979), Alexander Schmemann (d. 1983), and John Meyendorff (d. 1992), to Saint Vladimir's Seminary in New York.

THE ERA OF PERSECUTIONS. When the Bolsheviks came to power in Russia in October 1917, one of the main points on their ideological program was the war against all manifestations of religion. This battle turned into full-fledged genocide in the 1920s and 1930s: the repressive wave of militant atheism spared nobody—neither bishops, priests, monks, nuns, nor laypeople. The bitter fate of persecuted clergy was shared by their wives and their children, who were declared "children of the enemies of the people" and placed in special boarding schools, where they were raised in an antireligious spirit. People from all religions—Christians (Orthodox, Catholics, Protestants), Muslims, Jews, and Buddhists—suffered equally from the persecutions. All of this took place while slogans of the struggle for freedom, equality, and fraternity, inherited from the French Revolution, were proclaimed.

The notion of freedom had a limited meaning when it came to religion. The Stalinist constitution of 1929 allowed the freedom to exercise a religious cult and to propagate atheism. It was therefore possible to promote only atheism, because the preaching of religion was officially forbidden. In practice mere membership in a church was seen as a threat to the entire Soviet society and almost inevitably led to dismissal from one's job and the loss of social status. In many cases, especially during the bloody 1920s and 1930s, to be a believer meant risking one's life and the lives of one's loved ones.

During the twenty years of revolutionary terror that began during Vladimir Lenin's (1870–1924) time and continued during the rule of Joseph Stalin (1879–1953), the church was almost totally annihilated. By 1939 all monasteries and theological schools were closed, and tens of thousands of churches were either blown up or shut down. Of the more than 60,000 prerevolutionary churches, only about a hundred remained open; of the more than 150 bishops serving before the revolution only 4 remained free. The overwhelming majority of the clergy and monastics (whose number before the revolution exceeded 200,000) were either shot to death or tortured in concentration camps.

The catastrophic course of combat at the beginning of World War II forced Stalin to mobilize all the national resources for defense, including the Russian Orthodox Church as the people's moral force. Some churches were opened for services, and some bishops and priests were released from prisons. The Russian Church did not limit itself to giving spiritual and moral support to the country in danger. It also rendered material aid by providing funds for all kinds of things, including army uniforms. This process, which can be described as a rapprochement between church and state in a "patriotic union," culminated in Stalin's receiving Patriarchal Locum Tenens Metropolitan Sergiy (Stragorodsky) and Metropolitans Alexy (Simansky) and Nikolay (Yarushevich) at a meeting on September 4, 1943.

From that historic moment a thaw began in relations between church and state. Later in September 1943 in Moscow, with the permission of state authorities, a Bishops' Council convened and elected Metropolitan Sergiy (Stragorodsky) patriarch of Moscow and All Russia. His successor was Metropolitan Alexy (Simansky), elected patriarch in 1945. During and after World War II some theological schools and monasteries were reopened, and some churches were restored. The church, however, remained always under state control, and any attempts to spread its work outside its walls were met with strong rebuffs, including administrative sanctions.

The 1960s, when Nikita Khruschev (1894–1971) was in power, brought a new wave of repressions, when thousands of churches throughout the Soviet Union were closed "for ideological reasons." State control over the church affairs continued under Leonid Brezhnev (1906–1982), when Patriarch Pimen (1971–1990) was the primate of the church. One of the leading hierarchs of that time was Metropolitan Nikodim of Leningrad (d. 1978), who invested great efforts into the struggle for better understanding between the church and the state and greater independence of the former from the latter.

Until the end of the 1980s it was impossible to confess one's faith openly and at the same time occupy any more or less significant position in society. The entire activity of the church was under the strictest control of the authorities, the number of churches and clergy was severely regulated, and missionary, educational, and charitable work was forbidden.

In the last years of the Soviet era the Russian Orthodox Church in the U.S.S.R. had the legal right to hold church services in buildings authorized by the state for such purposes. A council of twenty laypeople was needed to petition for the use of a church. Because few churches and monasteries were functioning at that time, church services were normally crowded. The church had no right to teach, preach, or pray outside of these buildings, because "religious propaganda" was still expressly forbidden by Soviet law. Admission to the three operating theological schools was strictly monitored by the state. There were no church schools for children and laypeople, who received daily instruction in Marxist-Leninist doctrines with accompanying antireligious propaganda that was legally supported and officially enacted by the state.

RUSSIAN ORTHODOX CHURCH IN THE TWENTY-FIRST CENTURY. The situation changed drastically after the collapse of the Soviet regime. In the 1990s millions of people returned to their faith and were baptized, and thousands of churches, hundreds of monasteries, and dozens of theological schools were opened. The number of bishops more than doubled and by 2004 was approximately 150, and the number of priests and deacons and their parishes more than quadrupled and in 2004 stood at about 30,000. The growth statistics of monasteries and church educational institutions was particularly impressive: in 1988 there were eighteen monasteries in the jurisdiction of the Russian Church, and by 2004 there were over six hundred; and the number of theological schools during this period grew from three to approximately one hundred.

According to 2003 statistics, about 70 percent of Russians think of themselves as belonging to the Russian Orthodox Church. The majority of believers in the Ukraine, Belarus, and Moldova belong to the Russian Church, and most Orthodox Christians in the Baltic (Estonia, Latvia, Lithuania) and Central Asian countries (Kazakhstan, Kyrgyzstan, Tadzhikistan, Turkmenistan, Uzbekistan) count themselves members of the Russian Church. The total number of faithful of the Russian Orthodox Church living in Russia, the above-mentioned countries, and elsewhere (particularly in western Europe) comprises over 150 million.

This unprecedented quantitative growth in the 1990s was accompanied by radical changes in the church's sociopolitical situation. After more than seventy years the church once again became an integral part of society in all the countreis of the former Soviet Union and was recognized as a highly authoritative spiritual and moral power. And after many centuries the church acquired the right to define independently its place in society and its relations with the state without any interference from secular authorities.

This change in the church's status required from it tremendous efforts in overcoming the "ghetto mentality" that had formed during the many years of forced isolation. Previously clergy had associated only with their parishioners, but now they had to confront a great number of people unfamiliar with the church's teaching and practices and whose knowledge of religion was either rudimentary or nonexistent. Previously priests did not preach outside the walls of their churches, but now they had opportunities to appear on television, on radio, and in print. Previously society and the church had followed their own separate courses, but now the church was drawn into society's discussions of the fundamental questions of human existence.

Ten years of intensive work in understanding and analyzing the contemporary issues were crowned with the adoption of a document titled *The Bases of the Social Concept of the Russian Orthodox Church* at the Bishops' Council of 2000. The significance of this document is conditioned by the fact that it reflects the church's position on questions involving church-state relations and contemporary society in general. The document is intended to serve as a spiritual and moral guide for the entire Russian Orthodox Church—not just for the clergy but in no lesser way for the laity as well.

CHURCH AND STATE RELATIONS. Orthodoxy was the state religion of Russia for many centuries, which meant the church not only enjoyed a respected position in society and a substantial income but also was totally dependent on the government. During the synodal period (1700–1917) the church was essentially part of the bureaucratic system; consequently its freedom was violated, and its activities were limited. During Soviet times it was even more enslaved to the state, and although the principle of separation of church and state had been proclaimed, it worked only in favor of the authorities: the church received nothing from the government, whereas the latter interfered in the affairs of the church and controlled its workings.

On account of the persecutions in the twentieth century, the Russian Orthodox Church, when it became free from government control, categorically declined to be associated with the government and to become a state church. In 2000 in the *Bases of the Social Concept* the church declared both its loyalty to and its independence from the state and reserved for itself the right, if necessary, of civil disobedience. Cases of such civil disobedience can be of either a personal or a general nature:

> The Christian, following the will of his conscience, can refuse to fulfil the commands of state forcing him into grave sin. If the church and her holy authorities find it impossible to obey state laws and orders, after a due consideration of the problem, they may take the following action: enter into direct dialogue with the authorities on the problem, call upon the people to use democratic mechanisms to change the legislation or review the authority's decision, apply to international bodies and world public opinion and appeal to her faithful for peaceful civil disobedience.

The *Bases of the Social Concept* is the first document in the history of world Orthodox Christianity that includes an official statement on the possibility of disobedience to the state. The document also maintains that

> the state should not interfere in the life of the church or her government, doctrine, liturgical life, spiritual guidance of her flock, etc., or the work of canonical church institutions in general, except for those aspects where the church is supposed to operate as a legal entity obliged to enter into certain relations with the state, its legislation and governmental agencies. The church expects that the state will respect her canonical norms and other internal statutes.

According to the *Bases of the Social Concept,* the Russian Orthodox Church can effect its participation in state affairs by cooperating in those areas that touch upon its sphere of interests, such as peacemaking at the international, interethnic, and civil levels, fostering mutual understanding and cooperation among peoples, nations, and states; concern for the moral state of society; spiritual, cultural, moral, and patriotic education; works of mercy and charity and the development of joint social programs; the protection, restoration, and development of the historical and cultural legacy, including the care of historical and cultural monuments; dialogue with organs of state government of any kind and at all levels on questions significant to the church and society, including those involving the creation of relevant legislation, decrees, and decisions; pastoral care for soldiers and law-enforcement personnel and their spiritual and moral education; crime prevention and pastoral care for prisoners; scholarship, including research in the area of humanities; health; culture and creative activities; the work of church and secular mass media; activities for the conservation of the environment; economic activity for the benefit of the church, state,and society; supporting the institution of the family, motherhood, and childhood; and opposing the activities of pseudo-religious organizations harmful for the individual and society.

CHURCH GOVERNANCE. The Russian Orthodox Church (which is also known officially as the Moscow Patriarchate) has a hierarchical structure of governance. The supreme bodies of church authority and governance are the Local Council, the Bishops' Council, and the Holy Synod, which is chaired by the patriarch of Moscow and All Russia.

The Local Council consists of the bishops and representatives of the clergy, monastics, and laity. It interprets the teaching of the Orthodox Church, preserving the doctrinal and canonical unity with the local Orthodox Churches. It also deals with internal matters of church life, canonizes saints, elects the patriarch of Moscow and All Russia, and establishes the procedure of such elections.

The Bishops' Council, which is convened every four years, consists of the diocesan bishops and those assistant bishops who direct synodal departments and theological academies, or have canonical jurisdiction over parishes in their charge. The Bishops' Council is responsible for, among other things, preparation for convening a Local Council and monitoring the implementation of its decisions. It also adopts and amends the Statute of the Russian Orthodox Church; resolves basic theological, canonical, liturgical, and pastoral issues; canonizes saints; adopts liturgical offices; gives competent interpretation to church regulations; expresses pastoral concern for contemporary problems; defines the nature of relations with governmental bodies; maintains relations with local Orthodox Churches; establishes, reorganizes, and dissolves self-governed churches, exarchates, dioceses, and synodal institutions; and approves ecclesiastical awards.

The Holy Synod, chaired by the patriarch of Moscow and All Russia, is the governing body of the Russian Orthodox Church between Bishops' Councils. It is convened several times a year. Apart from the patriarch, it includes seven permanent and five temporary members. The permanent members of the synod are the metropolitans of Kiev and All Ukraine, of Minsk and All Belorussia, of Kisineu and All Moldova, of Krutitsy and Kolomna, and of Saint Petersburg and Ladoga as well as the chancellor of the Moscow Patriarchate and the chairman of the Department for External Church Relations. Temporary members of the Holy Synod are invited by rotation from among diocesan bishops to each session.

The patriarch of Moscow and All Russia is the first in honor among the bishops of the Russian Orthodox Church. He governs the Russian Orthodox Church together with the Holy Synod, which he chairs. The patriarch is elected by the Local Council from among those bishops who are at least forty years old; enjoy a good reputation and confidence among the bishops, clergy, and people; are higher theological school graduates; have sufficient experience of diocesan governance; are distinguished by their commitment to the canonical order; and "have a good report of them which are without" (*1 Tm.* 3:7). The patriarch is elected for life. In 2004 the primate of the Russian Orthodox Church was His Holiness Alexy II (Ridiger), patriarch of Moscow and All Russia, who in 1990 succeded Patriarch Pimen.

The synodal institutions are executive bodies under the patriarch and the Holy Synod. There are a Department for External Church Relations, a Publishing Board, an Education Committee, a Department for Catechism and Religious Education, a Department for Charity and Social Service, a Mission Department, a Department for the Co-Operation with the Armed Forces and Law-Enforcement Bodies, and a Youth Department. The chancellery is also part of the Moscow Patriarchate with the status of synodal institution.

Internal Organization. The Russian Orthodox Church is divided into dioceses, which are local churches headed by a bishop and uniting diocesan institutions, deaneries, parishes, monasteries, church representations, theological educational institutions, brotherhoods, sisterhoods, and missions. Some dioceses of the Russian Orthodox Church are consolidated in exarchates. This consolidation is based on the national-regional principle. In 2004 the Russian Orthodox Church had the Byelorussian exarchate located in the Republic of Belarus and headed by the metropolitan of Minsk and Slutsk, patriarchal exarch for All Belarus.

The Moscow patriarchate incorporates autonomous and self-governed churches. Self-governed churches function on the basis of and within the limits provided by the patriarchal tomos issued by the decision of the Local Council or the Bishops' Council. In the early twenty-first century the self-governed are the Latvian Orthodox Church (primate—the metropolitan of Riga and All Latvia), the Orthodox Church of Moldova (primate—the metropolitan of Kishinev and All Moldova), and the Estonian Orthodox Church (primate—the metropolitan of Tallinn and All Estonia).

The Ukrainian Orthodox Church is a self-governed church with the right of broad autonomy. Its primate is the metropolitan of Kiev and All Ukraine.

The three Russian Orthodox dioceses in the Republic of Kazakhstan are united into one metropolia headed by the metropolitan of Astana and Alma-Ata. The parishes in Kyrgyzstan, Tadzhikistan, Turkmenistan, and Uzbekistan belong to the diocese of Tashkent and Central Asia headed by the metropolitan of Tashkent and Central Asia.

The Russian Orthodox Church has eight dioceses "in the distant abroad": Argentine and South America, Berlin and Germany, Brussels and Belgium, Budapest and Hungary, the Hague and the Netherlands, Korsun (in France, Spain, Italy, Portugal, Switzerland), Sourozh (in the United Kingdom and Ireland), and Vienna and Austria. The patriarchal parishes in the United States and Canada are consolidated into deaneries governed by assistant bishops.

The Russian Orthodox Church has representations to the European Institutions in Brussels, to the World Council of Churches in Geneva, to the United Nations in New York, to the Patriarchate of Alexandria in Cairo, to the Patriarchate of Antioch in Damascus, to the Patriarchate of Serbia in Belgrade, to the Patriarchate of Bulgaria in Sofia, and to the Church of Czech Lands and Slovakia in Prague. The Russian Orthodox Church also has representations in Dusseldorff, Strasbourg, Bari, Dublin, and in some other cities as well as the ecclesiastical mission in Jerusalem.

The Japanese Autonomous Orthodox Church and the Chinese Autonomous Orthodox Church are independent churches free in their internal affairs and linked with Universal Orthodoxy through the Russian Orthodox Church. The primate of the Japanese Autonomous Orthodox Church is the archbishop of Tokyo, metropolitan of All Japan. The primate is elected by the Local Council of the Japanese Autonomous Orthodox Church, and his nomination is approved by the patriarch of Moscow and All Russia. In the early twenty-first century the Chinese Autonomous Orthodox Church consists of several communities of believers who because of political circumstances are deprived from permanent pastoral care.

The so-called Russian Orthodox Church Outside of Russia is a self-governed metropolia headed by its first hierarch, the metropolitan of New York and Eastern America. It separated from the Moscow Patriarchate in the 1920s for political reasons. In the early twenty-first century it is not recognized as canonical either by the Moscow Patriarchate or by any other local Orthodox Church. However, the process of its rapprochement with the Moscow Patriarchate is underway, which may eventually lead to restoration of full communion between it and the world Orthodoxy.

See Also Uniate Churches.

Bibliography

Arseniev, Nicholas. *Russian Piety.* 2d ed. Crestwood, N.Y., 1975.

Bolshakoff, Serge. *Russian Mystics.* Kalamazoo, Mich., 1980.

Bulgakov, Sergei. *The Orthodox Church.* Revised translation by L. Kesich. Crestwood, N.Y., 1988.

Ellis, Jane. *The Russian Orthodox Church: A Contemporary History.* London and Sydney, Australia, 1986.

Fedotov, George P. *The Russian Religious Mind,* vol. 1: *Kievan Christianity: The Tenth to the Thirteenth Centuries,* vol. 2: *The Middle Ages: The Thirteenth to the Fifteenth Centuries (1946–1966).* Belmont, Mass., 1975.

Fedotov, George P. *A Treasury of Russian Spirituality.* Belmont, Mass., 1975.

Kovalevsky, Pierre. *Saint Sergius and Russian Spirituality.* Crestwood, N.Y., 1976.

Lossky, Vladimir. *The Mystical Theology of the Eastern Church.* Cambridge, U.K., 1957.

Meyendorff, John. *The Orthodox Church.* Crestwood, N.Y., 1981.

Pospielovsky, Dimitri. *The Russian Church under the Soviet Regime, 1917–1982.* 2 vols. Crestwood, N.Y., 1984.

Ramet, Petra, ed. *Eastern Christianity and Politics in the Twentieth Century.* Durham, N.C., and London, 1988.

Ramet, Sabrina. *Nihil Obstat: Religion, Politics, and Social Change in East-Central Europe and Russia.* Durham, N.C., and London, 1998.

Schmemann, Alexander. *The Historical Road of Eastern Orthodoxy.* Crestwood, N.Y., 1977.

Struve, Nikita. *Christians in Contemporary Russia.* New York, 1967.

Ware, Bishop Kallistos. *The Orthodox Church.* New York, 1993.

Zernov, Nicolas. *The Russian Religious Renaissance of the Twentieth Century.* New York, 1963.

Zernov, Nicolas. *The Russians and Their Church.* New York, 1964.

THOMAS HOPKO (1987)
HILARION ALFEYEV (2005)

RUTH AND NAOMI have long enjoyed favored status in Jewish and Christian tradition. Ruth is often portrayed as a paragon of virtue and a model for religious conversion. However, feminist scholars have tended to replace idyllic interpretations with more complex understandings of the scriptural narrative that bears Ruth's name.

THE *BOOK OF RUTH*. *Ruth,* one of two Hebrew Bible books titled after women, is a beautifully crafted tale consisting of eighty-five verses divided into four chapters. More than half the verses feature dialogue among main characters. Naomi, Ruth, and Boaz are leading figures in *Ruth.* Orpah and an unnamed relative/redeemer play key roles near the beginning and end. Bethlehem's women and (male) elders also figure importantly in the story. The narrative is framed by the death of three men and the birth of one child. The basic plot is as follows:

In chapter 1, Elimelech and Naomi, with sons Mahlon and Chilion, journey from famine-stricken Bethlehem (meaning "house of food") to Moab for survival. After Elimelech's unexplained death, the two sons marry Orpah and Ruth (both Moabite). Ten years pass. Mahlon and Chilion die, leaving the three women alone. Naomi begins a journey back to Bethlehem and instructs her daughters-in-law to return to their mothers' houses. Orpah departs with a kiss, but Ruth clings to Naomi with a pledge. The two arrive in Bethlehem at harvest. Naomi publicly laments her emptiness.

In chapter 2, at her own initiative, Ruth obtains food and protection by gleaning in the fields of Boaz, a relative of Elimelech. Boaz, an upstanding citizen, is generous with the women, and Naomi blesses him in her words to Ruth.

In chapter 3, Ruth seeks out a satiated, sleeping Boaz on the threshing floor one night. Adapting Naomi's scheme, Ruth uncovers his "legs" and lies beside him. When Boaz awakes, Ruth asks him to claim her and to act as redeemer of Naomi and Elimelech's land. Boaz praises Ruth's character and agrees to her requests, but acknowledges the existence of a closer relative/redeemer. Ruth returns secretly with food to Naomi.

In chapter 4, Boaz publicly approaches the closer relative and manipulates him into waiving his right of redemption. Boaz receives a blessing from the elders and claims Ruth as his wife. Together, they produce an heir to Elimelech's estate. Neighbor women bless the Lord, praise the boy's mother, and ascribe him to Naomi. They name the child Obed, the future grandfather of King David.

The *Book of Ruth* concludes with a genealogy that may be read either as integral to the story or as an external addition. The genealogy makes Ruth an ancestress of David and, therefore, of a Davidic messiah. The Christian *Gospel of Matthew* includes Ruth in a genealogy of Jesus (*Mt.* 1:5).

ORIGINS AND IMPLICATIONS. Some scholars have concluded from the Obed genealogy that the *Book of Ruth* was written to foster support for the Davidic dynasty. Others have emphasized Ruth's Moabite heritage (reiterated frequently in the text) and have suggested *Ruth* was written in opposition to Ezra's and Nehemiah's post-exilic policy forbidding marriage to outsiders. Both claims are speculative.

The story itself, based on a folk-tale model, offers sparse evidence about historical matters such as date and circumstance of origin. This tale (or separate Ruth and Naomi traditions) may have circulated orally before becoming written text. The most scholars have said with certainty is that the *Book of Ruth* achieved its final form no earlier than the time of David. Name etymologies attributed to the characters in *Ruth* are historically suspect at best. *Ruth* also provides little reliable information about actual Israelite practices concerning levirate marriage (which this technically is not), redemption of land, legal procedures, or religious acts.

God is mentioned as the agent of blessing and the source of Naomi's complaint. Many readers understand God to be a silent but active character in the story. The *Book of Ruth* portrays ordinary people bringing about extraordinary events. The *Ruth* scroll is read and celebrated annually during the Jewish festival of Shavu'ot (Pentecost).

The authorship of the *Book of Ruth* is unknown. Some scholars have proposed that, unlike most Hebrew scriptures, this narrative speaks with a "woman's voice." The author could be a woman, a community of women, or a man or men sensitive to and influenced by women's experience. But this is pure speculation and is more relevant to reading and interpreting than to making historical or literary claims.

The pledge of Ruth to Naomi is commonly recited at weddings, even though the original context is not marriage, but two women whose fates are joined by an oath that remains intact even when one of them marries someone else: "Do not press me to leave you or to turn back from following you! Where you go, I will go; where you lodge, I will lodge; your people shall be my people, and your God my God. Where you die, I will die—there will I be buried. May the LORD do thus and so to me, and more as well, if even death parts me from you!" (*Ru.* 1:16–17). Naomi responds to Ruth with silence, which leads some commentators to suggest that the pledge is more of a threat (or at least an expression of determination) than a promise.

Feminist scholars have pondered the implications of the *Book of Ruth*. On the one hand, it may be read as a positive story of strong women who work together to obtain security in a man's world. Scholars who have taken this view have compared Ruth to Tamar in *Genesis* 38. Tamar is also a strong woman who obtains justice and security from her father-in-law (Judah) through extraordinary means. On the other hand, *Ruth* may be read as a story of assimilation where the title character gains then loses her individual identity. When Naomi arrives in Bethlehem, she speaks to the women of "emptiness," although Ruth, having pledged her presence, presumably stands nearby. Ruth gains an identity (in Naomi's eyes as well as the reader's) while interacting with Boaz. Yet in the end, Ruth's child becomes Naomi's, and neither woman is named in Obed's genealogy, where the child is attributed to Boaz. According to this reading, Ruth the independent Moabite woman is transformed into a servant of patriarchal interests concerning land and lineage.

Some feminist scholars have dismissed Ruth and found in Orpah the better role model. As Naomi's words reveal, both daughters-in-law have shown *chesed*, meaning "kindness" or "loyalty" (*Ru.* 1:8). Orpah loves Naomi and honors her by following instructions. In returning to her mother's house, Orpah remains loyal to her own family, her own national identity (Moabite), and her own gods. Whether read traditionally or nontraditionally, the *Book of Ruth* and its characters are rich with meaning.

SEE ALSO Shavu'ot.

BIBLIOGRAPHY

Influential commentaries include Jack M. Sasson's *Ruth: A New Translation with a Philological Commentary and a Formalist-Folklorist Interpretation* (Baltimore, 1979) and Edward F. Campbell Jr.'s *Ruth*, vol. 7 of the Anchor Bible (Garden City, N.Y., 1975). A commentary that takes feminist critique into account is Katharine Doob Sakenfeld's *Ruth*, in the Interpretation Series (Louisville, Ky., 1999). Danna Nolan Fewell and David Miller Gunn offer a self-described subversive reading in *Compromising Redemption: Relating Characters in the Book of Ruth* (Louisville, Ky., 1990). Feminist readings are also available in works edited by Athalya Brenner: *A Feminist Companion to Ruth* (Sheffield, U.K., 1993) and *Ruth and Esther: A Feminist Companion to the Bible*, second series (Sheffield, U.K., 1999). Visual images linked to feminist commentary on Ruth are available at http://womensearlyart.net/ruth/.

SUSANNA W. SOUTHARD (2005)

RUUSBROEC, JAN VAN (1293–1381) was a Flemish Christian mystic, known as "the Admirable." Born in Ruusbroec, near (or in) Brussels, he was educated for the priesthood in both lower and higher studies under the care of his kinsman Jan Hinckaert, canon of Saint Gudule collegial church in Brussels. He was ordained a priest at age twenty-four and became influential in the theological and spiritual currents of the church and of the tradition of Middle Netherlandic (Netherlandic-Rhenish) mysticism. He led a devout life in the circle of friends around Hinckaert and Vrank van Coudenberch. Aware of the need to bring doctrinal teaching to the people in their own language, Ruusbroec wrote in the Brabant vernacular.

In 1343, impelled by a longing for silence and a richer spiritual life, Ruusbroec and his companions withdrew to the solitude of Groenendael, near Brussels. A few years later their association developed into a monastery of canons regular under the Augustinian rule of order. His gentleness gained him the epithet "the good prior," and his spiritual wisdom earned him the title "Doctor Admirabilis." He wrote four extensive treatises and seven shorter works; only seven of his letters have been preserved. His reputation for holiness was ratified when the church declared him "blessed" on December 2, 1908.

In Ruusbroec's doctrine, human being is fundamentally oriented toward the triune God. He sees God as at once indivisibly one and threefold, in constant tension between activity and essence. Essence enjoys itself quietly in modelessness. Activity is fecund. The Father, in knowing himself, creates relationships; he brings forth and expresses himself in his Son, the Word of God. In the reciprocal beholding of Father and Son, the Holy Spirit flows forth as the mutual bond of active love. Turning inward in essential love, they enjoy the unity of essence, which drives them afresh toward activity.

In turning outward, God creates according to the image of his Son and in the power of the Holy Spirit. The human creature in its selfhood is irrevocably distinct from the transcendent God. At the same time, however, the creature is in relation with and directed toward God because human being is created in the unity of God's likeness and image.

Ruusbroec sees humanity as structured in a threefold way, according to three interacting unities. The body and the lower faculties of the soul are under the heart and form the unity of the heart. The higher faculties of the soul, oriented to the highest human powers, form the unity of spirit, which in activity is receptive to God's essence. In these two lower unities, by the grace of God, the creature attains likeness to God in active (outer) life and in inner life ("unity by means"). According to the third unity, the creature attains its oneness with God's image in the contemplative life ("unity without means," or "unity without difference").

In Christ (the God-man) humanness is realized in the fullness of likeness and unity-of-image in himself, and this fullness is communicated to and in humankind. The ascent in likeness and unity is realized in Christ and in human beings: on earth, characterized by mortality, in the likeness of grace; in heaven, characterized by immortality and irradiated by the *lumen gloriae,* in the likeness of glory. Ruusbroec's grandiose view provides a balanced synthesis of God's outflowing transcendent love and of humankind's potentiality for harmonious ascent to union with God.

BIBLIOGRAPHY

Works by Ruusbroec

Ruusbroec, Jan van. *Werken.* 2d ed. 4 vols. Antwerp, 1944–1948. In original Dutch.

Wiseman, J. A., ed. *John Ruusbroec: The Spiritual Espousals and Other Works.* New York, 1985.

Works about Ruusbroec

Ampe, Albert. *Kernproblemen uit de leer van Ruusbroec.* 4 vols. Tielt, 1950–1957.

Ampe, Albert. "Jean Ruusbroec." In *Dictionnaire de spiritualité,* vol. 8. Paris, 1974.

Dupré, Louis. *The Common Life: The Origins of Trinitarian Mysticism and Its Development by Jan Ruusbroec.* New York, 1984.

Mommaers, Paul. *The Land Within: The Process of Possessing and Being Possessed by God according to the Mystic Jan van Ruysbroeck.* Chicago, 1975.

Mommaers, Paul, and Norbert de Paepe, eds. *Jan van Ruusbroec: The Sources, Content and Sequels of His Mysticism.* Louvain, 1984.

ALBERT AMPE (1987)

S

SAʿADYAH GAON (882–942), properly Saʿadyah ben Yosef al-Fayyumī, was a Jewish theologian, jurist, scholar, and gaon ("head, eminence") of the rabbinic academy at Sura, Babylonia. Saʿadyah was born in Dilaẓ (modern Abu Suwayr) in the Faiyūm district of Upper Egypt. Virtually nothing is known about his family and early education. By age twenty-three, however, he had corresponded with the noted Jewish Neoplatonist Yitsḥaq Israeli (c. 855–955), published the first Hebrew dictionary (*Sefer ha-agron*), and composed a polemic against the Karaite schismatic ʿAnan ben David (fl. 760). After leaving Egypt, Saʿadyah spent time in both Palestine and Syria but eventually, in 921 or 922, settled in Babylonia. There he championed the cause of the Babylonian rabbis in a dispute with Palestinian authorities over fixing the religious calendar and published his views in two treatises, *Sefer ha-zikkaron* and *Sefer ha-moʿadim.* Recognizing his ability, the exilarch, or hereditary leader of the Jewish community, awarded Saʿadyah with an academic appointment in 922 and subsequently elevated him to the gaonate of Sura. Soon afterward, in 930, a legal dispute between the two developed into a bitter political struggle in which each deposed the other from office. Saʿadyah was driven into formal retirement in Baghdad, but, ultimately, reconciliation led to his reinstatement in 937.

A versatile and prolific author, Saʿadyah pioneered in many areas of Jewish scholarship. He translated the Hebrew Bible into Arabic, wrote commentaries on most of its books, assembled the first authorized *siddur,* or Jewish prayerbook, and composed numerous other works in the fields of jurisprudence, grammar, lexicography, liturgical poetry, and theology. His most famous work, *Sefer emunot ve-deʿot* (933; *The Book of Beliefs and Opinions,* 1948), was the first systematic exposition and defense of the tenets of Judaism and contains a detailed account of his views.

The Book of Beliefs and Opinions reflects both the cosmopolitanism and the sectarian rivalries characteristic of tenth-century Baghdad. Saʿadyah indicates that the intense competition between adherents of the various religious and philosophical creeds had produced an atmosphere of spiritual confusion in which believers were either mistaken or in doubt about the inherited doctrines of their religion, whereas unbelievers boasted of their unbelief. Seeking to dispel such doubt and establish a common basis for achieving religious

Clockwise from top left corner. Sixteenth-century illuminated miniature of dancing dervishes, from the "Sessions of the Lovers." *[©Bodlein Library, University of Oxford]*; South torana at the Great Stupa at Sāñcī, India. *[©Adam Woolfitt/Corbis]*; Eleventh-century Śiva Naṭarāja from Southern India. Musée Guimet, Paris. *[©Giraudon/Art Resource, N.Y.]*; The "Wedded Rocks" at Futamigaura in Ise, Japan. *[©Werner Forman/Art Resource, N.Y.]*; Angkor Vatt, Cambodia. *[Dave G. Houser/Corbis]*.

certainty, Saʿadyah adopted the methods of *kalām* (Islamic speculative theology) current in his day. He aimed to defend the doctrines of his faith and to refute errors by using rational arguments that could convince any reasonable person. Thus, from mere acceptance of traditional doctrines, itself always open to doubt, the reader would arrive at rationally established beliefs or convictions, just as the book's title suggests.

To facilitate this transition, Saʿadyah begins by identifying the causes of error and doubt. He then analyzes three sources of truth and certainty and illustrates their proper use: (1) sense perception, (2) rational intuition of self-evident principles, and (3) valid inference. To these he adds a fourth source based on the other three, reliable tradition, which is both indispensable to civilized life and the medium in which God's revelation to the prophets is transmitted. While Saʿadyah confidently believes human speculation can arrive at the truth of everything disclosed in prophecy, revelation is still necessary to teach the truth to those incapable of speculation and to guide the fallible inquiries of those who are capable, since only God's knowledge is complete. Because verification of revealed truths confirms faith, Saʿadyah considers such verification a religious obligation.

Saʿadyah's organization of the rest of the treatise likewise reflects *kalām,* especially the preoccupation of the Muʿtazilī school with establishing God's unity and justice. To prove the existence of the one God, Saʿadyah employs four standard *kalām* arguments showing that the world was created and must therefore have a creator.

(1) Since the world is spatially finite, the power within it that maintains it in existence must also be finite. But then the world's existence over time must likewise be finite, indicating that it was created.

(2) Everything composite is created by some cause. Since the whole world displays skillful composition, it must have been created.

(3) All bodies in the world are inseparably linked to accidental characteristics that are created in time. But whatever is inseparably linked to something created is itself created.

(4) If the world were eternal, an infinite period of time would have to have elapsed for the present to be reached. But since an infinity cannot be traversed and the present has been reached, the world must have existed for only a finite period after being created.

Saʿadyah offers further arguments to show that the world could only have been created out of nothing and by a single deity.

Saʿadyah's discussion of God's nature and attributes traces the implications of his being a creator. For God to have created a world such as ours at a point in the past, he must be alive, powerful, and wise. But insofar as God is creator and not creature, he cannot possess the characteristics of creatures. Hence, he must be incorporeal and absolutely simple in nature. Moreover, the essential attributes of life, power, and wisdom should not be understood as separate features of God's nature but as identical with it. Only a deficiency of language necessitates speaking about distinct attributes. Similarly, reason dictates that whenever scripture depicts God with creaturely characteristics, these terms should be understood metaphorically.

In accounting for God's relation to his creatures, Saʿadyah takes up various questions about divine justice. By creating the world out of nothing, God wished to endow creatures with the gift of existence. He further sought to provide them with the means for attaining perfect bliss by giving them the commandments of the Torah. By thus requiring human effort to attain happiness rather than bestowing it by grace, God assured that such happiness would be all the greater. The commandments themselves fall into two classes: rational commandments, such as the prohibitions against murder and theft, and traditional commandments, such as the dietary and Sabbath laws. The authority of the former lies in reason itself, while that of the latter lies in the will of the commander. God revealed both types of law, because without revelation not even perfectly rational men would agree on the precise application of the rational laws, much less discover the traditional laws, on both of which their salvation depends.

For Saʿadyah, the fact of revelation is confirmed by the occurrence of publicly witnessed miracles, announced in advance, that could have been performed only by God's omnipotence. They are to be accepted as proof of the authenticity of the revelation, unless the revealed teaching is contrary to reason.

Once God holds humanity responsible for fulfilling his commandments, justice requires that people be able to choose to obey or disobey. Saʿadyah argues that sense experience attests to this ability in us and that reason shows that God does not interfere with its exercise. While God foreknows exactly what one shall choose, his knowledge in no way causes one's choices. One can always choose otherwise, although he would foreknow that choice too.

Rewards and punishments are determined according to the majority of one's actions, and for Saʿadyah the suffering of the righteous and the prosperity of the wicked also conform to this rule. For either such experiences represent immediate retribution in this world for the minority of one's evil or good actions (with eternal reward or punishment for the rest to follow in the world to come), or they are temporary trials whereby God may increase one's reward in the hereafter. These latter are "sufferings of love," and bearing them bravely counts as a righteous act deserving reward. Indeed, Saʿadyah's commentary on *Job* interprets it as a debate designed to show that undeserved suffering really is a trial. For Job erroneously thought that God's justice consists simply in doing as he wishes, a position reminiscent of the rival Ashʿarī school of *kalām,* while the friends mistakenly supposed all suffering is a penalty. Only Elihu claims that Job's afflictions are a trial that divine justice will repay, and God confirms this by reasserting his providence over all creation and restoring Job's material fortunes prior to rewarding his soul in the hereafter.

Sa'adyah defines the soul as a pure, luminous substance that can act only through the body. Because the body and the soul are jointly responsible for one's behavior, God's justice requires that retribution affect both together. Accordingly, he will resurrect the bodies of Israel's righteous from the dust with the same power he used to create them *ex nihilo.* This event heralds Israel's messianic age and universal peace. It occurs either when all Israel repents or when God's foreordained end arrives, whichever is first. However, when God finishes creating the appointed number of souls, there will be a general resurrection and judgment, and a new heaven and earth. In this final retribution, the righteous will bask, and the wicked will burn, in the light of a miraculous divine radiance.

Sa'adyah concludes the treatise by describing the kind of conduct worthy of reward. Since humans are composite creatures with many conflicting tendencies, they should not devote themselves to one above all others. Rather, they should strive for a balance and blending of preoccupations determined by reason and Torah.

Aside from offering the first systematic exposition of Judaism in rational terms, Sa'adyah laid the foundation for all later medieval Jewish philosophy by asserting the complete accord of reason and revelation. Although Sa'adyah was far more confident than his successors about what reason could prove, his commitment to investigation and proof in all areas of Jewish scholarship gave rationalism a legitimacy in Judaism that it might not otherwise have enjoyed. He is rightly recalled as "the first of those who speak reason in every area."

Bibliography

Still the best general survey of Sa'adyah's life and oeuvre is Henry Malter's *Saadia Gaon: His Life and Works* (1921; reprint, Philadelphia, 1978). The only complete English translation of Sa'adyah's main theological work is Samuel Rosenblatt's *Saadia Gaon: The Book of Beliefs and Opinions* (New Haven, 1948), with an analytical table of contents and a useful index. An abridged translation of the same work with an excellent introduction and notes is Alexander Altmann's *Saadia Gaon: Book of Doctrines and Beliefs,* available in *Three Jewish Philosophers,* edited by Hans Lewy et al. (New York, 1960). The most comprehensive discussion in English of Sa'adyah's entire worldview is Israel I. Efros's "The Philosophy of Saadia Gaon," in his *Studies in Medieval Jewish Philosophy* (New York, 1974), since it draws from a variety of Sa'adyah's works. A shorter but still valuable discussion remains Julius Guttmann's "Saadia Gaon," in *Philosophies of Judaism* (New York, 1964). A basic resource for understanding Sa'adyah's relation to *kalām* is Harry A. Wolfson's *The Repercussions of the Kalam in Jewish Philosophy* (Cambridge, Mass., 1979). Useful individual studies of Sa'adyah's communal activities as well as different aspects of his literary, scholarly, and theological work may still be found in the *Saadia Anniversary Volume,* edited by Boaz Cohen for the American Academy for Jewish Research (New York, 1943); Abraham Neuman and Solomon Zeitlin's *Saadia Studies* (Philadelphia, 1943); and Steven T. Katz's *Saadiah Gaon* (New York, 1980).

New Sources

Aizenberg, Yehudah. *Ha-Derekh li-shelemut: e-mishnato shel Rav Se'adyah Ga'on.* Jerusalem, 1985.

Eisen, Robert. "Job as a Symbol of Israel in the Thought of Saadiah Gaon." *Daat* 41 (1998): 5–25.

Simon, Uriel. *Four Approaches to the Book of Psalms: From Saadiah Gaon to Abraham Ibn Ezra.* Translated by Lenn J. Schramm. Albany, N.Y., 1991.

Weiss, Roslyn. "Saadiah on Divine Grace and Human Suffering." *Journal of Jewish Thought & Philosophy* 9 (2000): 155–171.

Zewi, Tamar. "Biblical Hebrew Word Order and Saadya Gaon's Translation of the Pentateuch." *Ancient Near Eastern Studies* 38 (2001): 42–57.

Barry S. Kogan (1987)
Revised Bibliography

SABAZIOS, a god of the Thracians and the Phrygians, is also known from Greek and Latin sources as Sabadios, Sauazios, Saazios, Sabos, Sebazios, Sabadius, and Sebadius. His name is related to the Macedonian word *sauâdai,* or *saûdoi,* meaning "satyrs" (Detschew, 1957, p. 427). According to some scholars (e.g., Lozovan, 1968), he was a Thracian mountain god whose cult was carried by Phrygian emigrants from Thrace to Anatolia.

Greek sources from the fifth century BCE onward mention Sabazios as a Thracian or Phrygian god. In Athens, his cult's initiation ceremonies took place by night, and the adepts were purified by being rubbed with mud. A sacramental drink was also involved. The identification of Sabazios with Dionysos, which occurs regularly in Hellenistic sources, is unquestionable. However, Phrygian inscriptions relate him to Zeus, and in North Africa, where his cult is attested as early as the fourth century BCE, he might have had the features of a heavenly god; hence he was later identified with the Semitic god Baal, both of them receiving the Greek epithet *hupsistos* ("highest, supreme"). He was probably worshiped in Thrace under other local names, such as Athyparenos, Arsilenos, Batalde Ouenos, Eleneites, Mytorgenos, Ouerzel(enos), and Tasibastenus.

Sabazios's name has been connected with the Indo-European **swo-,* meaning "[his] own," and with the idea of freedom, which occurs frequently among the epithets of Dionysos. Franz Cumont has suggested a relationship with the Illyrian *sabaia,* or *sabaium,* identifying a beer extracted from cereals (see Russu, 1969, p. 241). More recently, Gheorghe Muşu has translated *Sabazios* as "sap god," from the Indo-European roots **sap-* ("taste, perceive") and **sab-* ("juice, fluid"). This translation corresponds well to the pattern of Dionysos/ Sabazios, who was the divinity of humidity and as such was connected with both vegetation and intoxication (see Muşu, in Vulpe, 1980, pp. 333–336).

The Jews of Syria and Anatolia identified Sabazios with Sabaoth. Under the Roman rulers Sabazios was worshiped in Thrace, where he was more often known as Sebazios or, in Latin, Sabazius, Sabadius, or Sebadius and where he received such epithets as *epekoos* ("benevolent"), *kurios* ("lord"), *megistos* ("greatest"), and so forth. In Crimea, probably under Jewish-Anatolian influence, he was called *hupsistos.* He was constantly identified with both Zeus and the sun. Motifs of hands making the votive gesture of *benedictio Latina* are among the distinctive features of his cult. According to several Christian writers (Clement of Alexandria, Arnobius, and Firmicus Maternus), the most impressive rite of initiation into the mysteries of Sabazios consisted of the adept's contact with a snake (*aureus coluber*) that was first put over his breast (*per sinum ducunt*) and then pulled down to his genitals.

No less enigmatic than Zalmoxis, Sabazios was worshiped as early as the fourth century BCE both as a chthonic and as a heavenly god. Scholars have too often tried to solve this riddle by supposing a borrowing from Jewish religion, but Jewish influence was not relevant in Anatolia before the third century BCE. One should rather consider that chthonic features determined the character of the Thracian Sabazios, whereas the Phrygian Sabazios was probably connected with the sky.

BIBLIOGRAPHY

Bianchi, Ugo, and Maarten J. Vermaseren, eds. *La soteriologia dei culti orientali nell'impero romano.* Leiden, 1982. See the index, s. v. *Sabazios.*

Detschew, Dimiter. *Die thrakischen Sprachreste.* Vienna, 1957.

Lozovan, Eugen. "Dacia Sacra." *History of Religions* 7 (February 1968): 209–243.

Russu, I. I. *Ilirii istoria, limba şi onomastica romanizarea.* Bucharest, 1969.

Vulpe, Radu, ed. *Actes du Deuxième Congrès International de Thracologie,* vol. 3, *Linguistique, ethnologie, anthropologie.* Bucharest, 1980.

New Sources

Bodinger, Martin. "Le dieu Sabazios et le Judaisme." *Archaeus* 6 (2002): 121–139.

Corpus Cultus Iovis Sabazii (CCIS). Vol. I: *The Hands.* Vol. II: *The Other Monuments and Literary Evidence.* Vol. III: Conclusions, edited by Maarten J. Vermaseren and Eugene N. Lane. Leiden, 1983–89.

Giuffré Scibona, Concetta. "Aspetti soteriologici del culto di Sabazio." In *La soteriologia dei culti orientali nell'impero romano. Atti del Colloquio Internazionale (Roma 24–28 Settembre 1979),* edited by Ugo Bianchi e Maarten J. Vermaseren, pp. 552–561. Leiden, 1982.

Johnson, Sherman E. "The Present State of Sabazios Research." In *Aufstieg und Niedergang der Römischen Welt* 2.17.3, pp. 1583–1613. Berlin and New York, 1984.

Lane, Eugene. "Sabazius and the Jews in Valerius Maximus: A Reexamination." *Journal of Roman Studies* 69 (1979): 35–38.

Lane, Eugene. "Towards a Definition of the Iconography of Sabazius." *Numen* 27 (1980): 9–33.

Taceva-Hitova, Margarita. "Wesenzüge des Sabatioskultes in Moesia Inferior und Thracia." In *Hommages à Maarten J. Vermaseren,* edited by M. B. de Boer and T. A. Edridge, vol. III, pp. 1217–1230. Leiden, 1978.

Tassignon, Isabelle. "Sabazios dans les pantheons des cités d'Asie Mineure." *Kernos* 11 (1998): 189–208.

IOAN PETRU CULIANU (1987)
CICERONE POGHIRC (1987)
Revised Bibliography

SABBATEANISM SEE SHABBETAI TSEVI

SABBATH, JEWISH SEE SHABBAT

SACRAMENT

This entry consists of the following articles:

SACRAMENT: AN OVERVIEW

The meaning of the term *sacrament* is heavily determined by Christian usage. This circumstance presents both important opportunities and certain difficulties for the scientific study of religion. On the one hand, the familiarity of the term and of the rituals to which it refers in Christianity makes possible, at least for the Western student of religion, progression from the known to the less known with the aid of developed categories used for comparative purposes. On the other hand, there is the danger that the derivation of the category of sacrament from Christianity will result in a distortion of other religions, unduly emphasizing cognates or analogies while ignoring or dismissing distinctive features of other traditions.

In order to both make good on the comparative opportunities provided by the term and to overcome the limitations of too heavy a reliance upon the perspective that has determined its customary meaning, this article will first indicate some of the antecedents to the standard Christian view of sacrament. A consideration of parallels or cognates to Christian sacraments will be followed by a brief consideration of the possibility of a more strictly formal definition of the category.

HELLENISTIC SACRAMENTS. While classical Christian usage has largely determined the understanding of *sacrament* that the student of comparative religion employs in the study of religion, it is important to have some awareness of the pre-Christian understanding of *sacrament* and its Greek antecedent, *mustērion.* Three antecedents to the classical use of the term will be considered: the mystery cults, the apocalyptic mystery, and the mystical, or gnostic, tradition.

The mystery cults. The Greek *mustērion* is of uncertain etymology but is most probably associated with *muein,* meaning "to close" (the mouth), and thus "to keep secret." Certainly it was this connotation of secrecy that dominated the technical usage of the term to designate the Hellenistic cults, especially those associated with Eleusis, which are accordingly known as "mystery cults" or simply as "mysteries" (*musteria*). The term *mustērion* designates the sharp dividing line between initiates, for whom the secret history of the god (his birth, marriage, or death and rebirth, depending on the cult) is dramatically reenacted, thus binding their fate to the god's, and noninitiates, who cannot participate in this kind of salvation.

If the term were to be employed in this, its earliest technical religious sense, for phenomenological and comparative purposes, its application would necessarily be restricted to esoteric initiation rites of cult societies such as those found among the indigenous peoples of the Americas (for example, the Snake and Antelope societies of the Hopi). A somewhat more flexible usage might include those rites of passage that stress the esoteric character of the knowledge imparted.

Such usage, however, would be unwieldy for two reasons: (1) it would exclude many rituals for which the term *sacrament* has become standard—Christian and Hindu rituals in particular—and (2) it would duplicate existing terminology of initiatory rituals and rites of passage.

Apocalyptic usage. In the New Testament, *mustērion* is used in a way that is grounded in apocalyptic rather than cultic sensibility. Here *mustērion* refers to the disclosure of God's ultimate, or eschatological, intention. The term is used quite widely to designate anything that prefigures the final consummation of the divine will or plan. Thus Christian proclamation, biblical typology, and the inclusion of Jew and gentile in divine election could all be referred to as *mustērion* (which becomes *sacramentum* in Latin). Significantly, the term was not used in a specifically cultic sense at all in this period.

If this sense of the term, derived from late Jewish and early Christian apocalyptic writings, were to be decisive for phenomenological or comparative approaches to the study of religion, then the term's application would be restricted to those groups that have a strong orientation to future fulfillment. The Ghost Dance of the indigenous peoples of the North American Plains and the elaborate baptismal rites of the African independent churches are illustrations of ritual enactments of such eschatological expectations.

Gnostic usage. Deriving from the theory and practice of the mystery cults, certain mystical and especially gnostic philosophical traditions of the Hellenistic world used *mustērion* to apply to the quest for transcendental insight. While they dispensed with outward forms of ritual or cult, they nevertheless sought by knowledge a saving union with the divine.The religious tradition that best exemplifies this sense of *mustērion*/sacrament is the Hinduism of the Upaniṣads and of yoga. While these movements do not reject the ritual or cult but seek to give it a more pure, interior, and "noetic" significance, other reform movements—most notably Buddhism—reject this connection to the Vedic rites in the quest for ultimate insight. In the Western Christian tradition examples of sacramental mysticism often approximate the pattern of the yogic or gnostic transformation of external ritual into interior discipline. While these parallel phenomena demonstrate the way in which the bodily action of ritual may become paradigms for an interior praxis, it is with sacrament as a species of bodily action that the phenomenology of religion must be most concerned.

EMERGENCE OF THE CLASSICAL PERSPECTIVE. The Latin *sacramentum* was generally employed as a technical term for a military oath, the vow of a soldier. The initiatory function of this vow understood in relation to the vow of secrecy associated with the Greek mysteries made possible the appropriation of the term *sacramentum* for those activities (especially baptism) in which the Christian confession of faith (which, like the vow of soldiers, placed one in mortal danger) played an important role. Thus, despite the typically exoteric character of Christian doctrine and practice, ideas and practice associated with the Greek mysteries were used to interpret Christian rituals. *Sacramentum* gradually lost its wider, apocalyptic meaning, was increasingly used to refer to baptism and eucharist, and then was extended by analogy to apply to related ritual actions including confession and penance, confirmation, marriage, ordination, and unction. The earlier Latin sense of "vow" can still be discerned in baptism, confirmation, marriage, and ordination, but the oldest Greek associations with cultic participation in salvation predominate. Thus sacrament comes to be exclusively identified with a set of ritual actions that are understood to be both necessary to and efficacious for salvation.

COGNATE SACRAMENTS. Since the scientific study of religion is a discipline that has arisen within the culture most heavily influenced by Christianity, it is natural that much of its terminology is borrowed from Christianity. (Just as, *mutatis mutandis,* Christianity has borrowed its terminology from the cultures in which it has taken root.)

If sacrament is defined ostensively, by reference to the set of rituals that bear that name in Christianity, then one is confronted with the question of whether to restrict this discussion to the two sacraments accepted by most Protestants (baptism and eucharist) or to include the additional five sacraments (confirmation, penance, marriage, ordination, and extreme unction) accepted by Catholics. Clearly, eucharist and baptism have a place of singular importance in all Christian traditions; a phenomenological approach, however, will seek the widest possible range of data and so provisionally accept the more inclusive enumeration.

There are two sorts of such sacraments, those that deal with transitional moments and so are not repeated and those that are regularly repeated.

Sacraments of transition. The earliest and most important of the transitional sacraments is baptism. In early Christianity this ritual signified the movement from the worldly to the eschatological reality, or, under influence from the Greek mysteries, from the profane to the cultic sphere of participation in the fate of the god. This type of transitional rite is analogous to the initiation into cult societies of, for example, the indigenous peoples of the North American Plains. It is also characteristic of the African independent churches of central and southern Africa.

As Christianity became more or less coextensive with culture and society, the transition came more and more to be identified with birth or early infancy (a development contingent upon the understanding of penance and eucharist as supplementing the forgiveness of sins and transformation of life originally associated with baptism). As a ritual associated with infancy, it took the place of the Jewish rite of circumcision, except that it applied equally to female infants. It is thus similar in function to the Hindu sacrament of Namakarana, in which the child receives a name.

As baptism became "infant baptism," the catechetical aspect of the ritual that inaugurated persons into full membership in the cult society became fixed in the form of confirmation. Insofar as confirmation is associated with adolescence, it could enter into homology with rites of tribal initiation—a species of ritual that is exceedingly widespread and well developed among the indigenous peoples of the Americas, Africa, and Australia. In Africa and Australia the sacrament of initiation takes the form of segregating a cohort of adolescent males and placing them under great stress (often including circumcision) so that distinctions among them are erased. The loss of social identity and the violation of bodily integrity is accompanied by esoteric instruction and rites of great emotional force that frequently involve symbolism of death and birth. A significant number of groups, for example, the Bemba of Africa, have initiation rites (Chisungu) of similar intensity for adolescent females. Among North American aboriginal peoples, the young males (and, rarely, females) undertake the highly individualized dream or vision quest, which may entail a rigorous journey, fasting, and other ordeals. This individualized initiation contrasts sharply with the corporate initiation of African and other groups.

A further extension of transitional sacrament occurs with the development of extreme unction, the anointing of the sick. This sacrament may assume the form of a viaticum, by means of which the recipient is enabled to make the transition from this life to the world beyond. Insofar as the Christian sacrament of unction has the intention of healing (as in the anointing of the sick), it becomes repeatable and homologous to the healing rites found in virtually all religious traditions. Collections of incantations for this same purpose constitute the Egyptian *Book of Going Forth by Day,* and in ancient Iran the whispering of formulas to the dying person was accompanied by the administration of *haoma,* the sacred beverage.

Unlike baptism, confirmation, and unction, which traditionally have been required of all Christians, two other sacraments of transition, ordination and marriage (traditionally thought of as mutually exclusive), have developed. Rites of ordination are found in virtually all societies in which a priestly caste is drawn from the society as a whole. (In a number of societies the priesthood is hereditary, and rites associated with accession to cultic authority may be coterminous with accession to adulthood. This appears to be largely true of the brahmanic class of Hinduism, for example.) Marriage rites are obviously quite widespread although only those that have a clearly sacred or religious character are directly comparable. Often these have the added dimension of rites to ensure fertility.

Perhaps the most highly developed system of sacraments of transition is to be found in Hinduism. The term *saṃskāra,* which generally translated as "sacrament," refers to any rite of transition, of which several hundred may have been performed. In modern Hinduism the number of reduced (to between ten and eighteen). These sacraments begin with conception (*Garbhādhāna*) and continue through pregnancy (Puṃsavana, Simanta, Jātakarman). In addition to the naming ceremony (Nāmakaraṇa), which occurs a few days after birth, there are sacraments to mark the first appearance of the infant outside the home, the child's first solid food, the tonsure, and the piercing of the child's ears. Sacraments that mark the progress of the male child's education include Upanayana and Vedārambha. The completion of these studies requires a further sacrament (Samāvartana). Marriage (Vivāha) is the only sacrament permitted to *śūdras* or lower castes. The final transition of death is marked by the sacramental rites of Antyeṣṭi.

These sacraments generally involve sacrifices, ceremonies of fire and water, ritual washings, recitation of appropriate mantras and prayers, and so on. Both individually and collectively these Hindu sacraments are far more elaborate than the comparable set of Christian rituals and so may provide the student of religion with a more adequate set of categories for studying sacraments of transition.

Repeatable sacraments. While sacraments of transition are in principle nonrepeatable (with the possible and limited exceptions of marriage and extreme unction), two sacraments of great importance in traditional Christianity, penance and eucharist, do require repeated performance.

In the Christian tradition penance is related to baptism as the restoration of baptismal purity and to the Eucharist as the necessary preparation for participation. The confession of sin has a place of central importance in the religion of Handsome Lake practiced by contemporary Iroquois in the United States and Canada. Individual confession to a priest was of great importance in Central and South America, among the Inca and Maya, as is confession to a shaman among, for example, the Inuit (Eskimo).

The ritual that is most often associated with sacramentality is the Eucharist, Mass, or Communion of the Christian community. The selection of comparable rituals from the history of religions will depend upon the degree of emphasis placed upon one of three aspects: thanks giving or offering, communal meal, or sacrifice of the divine victim.

Certainly for much of Western history the last aspect has been especially emphasized. The most dramatic instances are the human sacrifices, which include the Greek *pharmakos,* a number of African rites, and practices belonging to the high civilizations of the Americas, especially the Aztec. Among the latter the sun god, Tezcatlipoca, was impersonated by the prisoner of war most honored for beauty and bravery, who received homage for a full year before being sacrificed. Many of the human sacrifices, including those to Huitzilopochtli, the god of war, were subsequently eaten as a form of ritual cannibalism.

Substitutions for the flesh of the divine victim are also found, including the eating of a dough image of Huitzilopochtli, which first was shot with an arrow, and a similar ritual involving the dough image of the tree god, Xocotl.

The communal meal is a common feature of many sacrifices. A vegetable, animal, or cereal offering is presented to the god and is subsequently shared by all participants, much as in the Christian Communion the bread and wine is first offered in thanksgiving and then shared by the participants. Where these rites are associated with first-fruits festivals or with harvest, the element of thanksgiving (eucharist) is especially pronounced. These rites are found not only in agrarian societies. Common among hunters and gatherers are rituals involving a communal meal in which the sacralized game animal is both praised and eaten. An example from the Pacific coast of North America is the ritual surrounding the first salmon catch. Among circumpolar peoples such rites are performed after successful bear hunts.

Here too should be mentioned the preparation of sacred substances whose consumption makes for unity with the divine. The *haoma* of Iran, the *soma* of India, and the hallucinogenic substances so important to the indigenous peoples of the Americas are illustrations. Members of the Native American Church, which includes many of the aboriginal peoples of North America, use peyote as a sacramental element within a liturgical setting in order to acquire union with the divine.

FORMAL DEFINITIONS OF SACRAMENT. The procedure that has just been illustrated, of finding material cognates to the sacraments of the Christian tradition in the field of religious studies, while illuminating in certain respects, may tie the term too closely to the Christian tradition to be genuinely serviceable for phenomenological purposes. Accordingly, one may attempt to acquire a more formal definition of *sacrament,* a definition that can be employed for comparative purposes.

Since Christian theology has devoted considerable energy to the development of such a formal definition, one may look first to the theological definitions. When this is attempted, however, it becomes clear that these are either of such an *ad hoc* nature that they devolve to disguised ostensive definitions or are so broad as to identify virtually any ritual action. If, for example, *sacrament* is defined in accordance with the principle of *ex opere operatum* ("what the action signifies it also accomplishes"), any ritual thought by its practitioners to be efficacious (including, of course, all forms of magic) will be covered. If, on the other hand, only those ritual actions positively commanded by Jesus are said to be sacraments, this proves to be an ostensive definition (which, moreover, is usually applied in an arbitrary manner—so as to exclude ritual foot washing, for example). The same is true of definitions of *sacrament* that insist on the conjunction of matter and form. According to this view, *form* designates the crucial pronouncement whereas *matter* may refer, for example, to the water of baptism, the oil of unction, or the bread and wine of the Eucharist. Moreover, this notion of matter may be arbitrarily extended to apply also to the sacraments of penance (the sin of the believer) and marriage (the love between spouses).

If a formal definition is required, it appears that theology will not be of much help. It does seem possible, however, to propose a more strictly phenomenological definition. On this basis *sacrament* may be defined as "a ritual that enacts, focuses, and concentrates the distinctive beliefs, attitudes, and actions of any religious tradition." While any ritual may perform this function to some degree, it will usually be possible to discriminate within the ritual complex of a tradition as a whole that ritual (or group of rituals) that functions as a paradigm for other ritual action and so may be said to have a privileged and normative relationship to the articulated system as a whole. Usually these sacraments will be found within the prescribed corporate ritual or liturgy.

In this definition the initiation rites of the mystery religions, the Christian Eucharist, the Ghost Dance and peyote ritual of the North American Indians, and many other rituals already mentioned would be included. But the principle of inclusion is not their resemblance to specific Christian rituals but their location and function within the religious tradition of which they are a part.

In addition, rituals that are not material cognates to Christian sacraments and so are necessarily overlooked on the basis of an ostensive definition of sacrament now acquire a sacramental character. Thus the Shalako ceremony of the Zuni Indians of New Mexico, which displays the vigor and values of the Zuni while inviting the participation and blessings of the gods, is a sacrament in the form of a dance (to which there are no Christian but many other religious cognates). While regular occasions for prayer do not have a sacramental character in Christianity, they may well have this character in Islam, which is generally suspicious of ritual and of Christian sacraments in particular. Finally, the Buddhist practice of *zazen,* which consists of periods of sitting and breathing punctuated by periods of walking, may have a place of importance and function similar to the Christian Eucharist.

The further refinement of a phenomenological definition of *sacrament* in tandem with its use in the analysis of the place and function of particular rituals within the wider ritual complex of which they are a part is an important agenda for the study of religion.

SEE ALSO Gnosticism; Human Sacrifice; Initiation; Mystery Religions.

BIBLIOGRAPHY

For concise historical background, see the article on *musterion* by Günther Bornkaum in *Theological Dictionary of the New Testament,* edited by Gerhard Kittel and Gerhard Friedrich (Grand Rapids, 1964–1976), and the article "Mystery," in the *Encyclopedia of Theology,* edited by Karl Rahner (New York, 1975).

The classic treatment of rites analogous to sacraments of transition is Arnold van Gennep's *Les rites de passage* (Paris, 1909), translated by Monika B. Vizedom and Gabrielle L. Caffee as *The Rites of Passage* (Chicago, 1960). Victor Turner's *The Ritual Process* (Chicago, 1969) is a major contribution to the understanding of these rituals. A useful source for the Hindu sacraments is Raj Bali Pandey's *Hindu Samskaras: A Socio-Religious Study of the Hindu Sacraments,* 2d rev. ed. (Delhi, 1969). Ake Hultkrantz's *Religions of the American Indians,* translated by Monica Setterwall (Los Angeles, 1979), contains important information and an excellent bibliography. Ronald L. Grimes's *Beginnings in Ritual Studies* (Washington, D. C., 1982) suggests the relationship between *zazen* and the Eucharist.

New Sources

Davis, Richard H. *Ritual in an Oscillating Universe: Worshiping Siva in Medieval India.* Princeton, N.J., 1991.

Vahanian, Gabriel. "Word and Sacrament: The Religious Dialectic of Nature and Culture." In *Natural Theology Versus Theology of Nature,* pp. 140–149. Berlin; New York, 1994.

THEODORE W. JENNINGS, JR. (1987)
Revised Bibliography

SACRAMENT: CHRISTIAN SACRAMENTS

In the Christian community sacraments are acts of worship that are understood by the worshipers to give access to an intimate union with the divine and to be efficacious for salvation. The term *sacraments* is sometimes used in a very broad sense for places, persons, things, ceremonies, and events that mediate, or are intended to mediate, the presence and power of the divine. In this broad sense, Christians acknowledge sacraments in other religious traditions and also in the particular circumstances of the lives of individuals and groups. A simple illustrative story in the Hebrew scriptures (the Old Testament of Christians) is that of Jacob setting up a stone in the desert and calling the place Bethel, house of God (*Gn.* 28:10–22).

More usually the term *sacraments* refers to a limited number of ancient rituals understood to be the acts of Jesus Christ carried out through the continuing ministry of the church. The Eastern Christian and Roman Catholic churches enumerate these rituals as seven: baptism, confirmation (or chrismation), eucharist, penance (sacrament of reconciliation), matrimony, ordination (or holy orders), and the anointing of the sick (extreme unction). Protestant churches usually enumerate the sacraments (in the narrower sense of the term) as only two, namely, baptism and eucharist, because these two are clearly identified in the New Testament.

The word *sacrament* derives from Latin *sacramentum,* meaning "oath," "pledge," or "bond." As a Christian term applied to rituals of worship, it is found no earlier than the third century, when it came into use in Western churches as a translation of the Greek term *mustērion,* which had the religious connotation of effecting union with the divine, even before Christians used the term in that sense. When the word *sacrament* is used in the singular without contextual specification, it may be assumed to mean the Eucharist.

JEWISH ROOTS. At the time of Jesus of Nazareth the people of Israel, the Jewish community, enjoyed a rich accumulation of symbolism and ritual. Jesus and his early followers participated in that heritage and followed the observances. Characteristically, Christian rituals were shaped not only out of the immediate experience of the early Christian community but also out of the stories, imagery, and ritual observances of their Jewish tradition. This influence can be seen in Christian perceptions of sacred space and sacred time, and it also appears in the configuration of sacred actions.

The core of the Christian sacramental system is the Eucharist, also known as the Divine Liturgy, the Lord's Supper, the Communion service, and the Mass. The ritual is based directly on the table grace of Jewish observance as solemnized in the Passover Seder. There are several common elements: the community is gathered to respond to God's call and to fulfill a commandment; the gathering is at a ritual meal at which prescribed foods are blessed, shared, and consumed; the accompanying prayers and ceremonies ritually reenact a past saving event so that the present worshipers become part of that past event and it becomes present in their experience; the doing of this anticipates a fulfillment that still lies in the future; the ritual (though not it alone) constitutes the participants as God's holy people. In the Jewish understanding and also in the Christian, the ritual is not effective in isolation from the community's daily life; on the contrary, it is effective precisely in its reshaping of the imagination and sense of identity of the worshipers, bringing about a transformation of individual and social life.

Other sacramental rites that have clear antecedents in Jewish observances are baptism in water as a ritual of spiritual regeneration, the imposition of hands in blessing, and the action of anointing to confer an office or mission. Beyond the direct influence of ritual actions of Jewish life, there is the much more extensive and pervasive indirect influence of stories, prayers, and symbols from the Hebrew scriptures. Thus, baptism is not easily understood without knowledge of the Hebrew stories of creation and sin, of the Deluge, and of the passing through the waters of the Red Sea at the Exodus and through the waters of the Jordan River as Israel took possession of the Promised Land. Similarly, confirmation (chrismation) is not readily understood without reference to the theme of the breath of God, which runs through the Hebrew scriptures.

EARLY HISTORY. Although there are references to sacramental activity in the New Testament, and these are accompanied by a sacramental theology (e.g., *1 Cor.*), little is known about the form of early Christian ritual except through late second-century sources. By the fourth century most of the rituals were elaborate and well established in the patterns that were to endure, though they were not numbered explicitly as seven until the twelfth century in the West and the seventeenth century in the East.

Early Christian rites. The central sacrament has always been the Eucharist. From early times it has consisted of a ritual meal of small amounts of bread and wine, commemorating the farewell supper of Jesus before his death and extending the presence and friendship of Jesus to his followers through the ages. The celebration begins with readings from the Bible, prayers, usually a sermon on the biblical texts read, and sometimes, hymns. Then follows a great prayer of praise and thanksgiving, recited by the one who presides over the ritual; in this context the story of the farewell supper is recited and reenacted. The bread and wine are consecrated, the bread is broken and distributed to the worshipers, who consume it immediately, and the wine is likewise consumed. This eating and drinking is known as "communion."

Admission to the community formed around the Eucharist is by baptism and confirmation. In the early centuries baptism was by total immersion of the candidate, preferably in running water, accompanied by a formula of profession of faith. This going through the water symbolizes a death and a spiritual rebirth. Baptism was surrounded by lesser ritual elements: a divesting of old clothes and donning of a new white robe (which was worn for about one week), an anointing, and the receiving of a lighted candle. The ritual was generally preceded by a fast of some days and an all-night vigil. A further step of the initiation into the community was a confirmation of the baptism by the bishop (the leader of the local church) with a laying on of hands, a further anointing, and a prayer that the Holy Spirit (the breath of God that was in Jesus) might descend upon the candidate.

In the early centuries, there were also many reconciliation (penance, repentance) rituals: the recitation of the Lord's Prayer was one. However, there was also a more formal ritual of reconciliation, later modified radically, that applied to those excommunicated from the Eucharist and the company of the faithful for some grave offense. A period of exclusion, accompanied by the wearing of a special garb and the performance of prescribed works of repentance that were supported by the prayers of the community, was concluded by a ceremony in which the bishop led the penitents back into the worship assembly to readmit them to the Eucharist.

The custom was established in the early centuries of the laying on of hands not only in confirmation but also in the designation of persons to certain ministries or offices in the life and worship of the community. Such laying on of hands symbolized the passing on of authorization understood to come in a continuous line from Jesus and his earliest followers. It was performed in the context of a worship assembly and was accompanied by prayers and solemnity.

From the fourth century onward there is evidence of the blessing of marriages, at least in certain cases, by bishops, although the ritual of marriage was otherwise performed according to local civil custom. Of the anointing of the sick there is, despite the injunction found in the New Testament (*Jas.* 5:14), no clear evidence from the early centuries of the church.

Theology of the rites. Christian sacraments are based on the understanding that human existence in the world as human beings experience it is not as it is intended by God, its creator; hence they stand in need of salvation (redemption, rescue, healing). If all were in the harmony of God's creation, all things would speak to humanity of God and would serve its communion with God. However, because of a complex legacy of the misuse of human freedom (a legacy known as original sin), the things of creation and the structures of human society tend to betray humans, turning them away from their own true good. Jesus Christ is seen as the savior (redeemer and healer) in his life, actions, teachings, death, and resurrection. The sacraments are understood as continuing his presence and redeeming power.

In the New Testament and the other writings extant from the earliest period of Christian history, known as the patristic period, the community dimension of the sacraments is inseparable from the communion with God that they offer. Sacraments are redemptive because they draw people into the fellowship in which salvation is found. Baptism is the outreach of God through Jesus in his community whereby it is possible for a person to turn (convert) from the ways and society of a world gone astray to the ways and society of the community of the faithful. That this is the meaning of baptism is evident in the New Testament in the early chapters of the *Acts of the Apostles* and in the instructions given in the early community, for instance, in the *Didache*. Similarly, the Eucharist is seen as fashioning worshipers into "one body" with Jesus Christ, which has far-reaching consequences for their lives and their relationships (as the apostle Paul explains in *1 Corinthians*, chapters 11–13).

In the patristic period, the theology of the sacraments was more inclusive and less specific than it later became, because the terms *musterion*, among Greek writers, and *sacramentum*, among Latin writers, were being used rather generally for all Christian rituals, symbols, and elements of worship. But the emphasis is clearly on the Eucharist and the initiation into the fellowship of the Eucharist, with the understanding that it constitutes a dynamic in history. Not only does it commemorate the past event of the death and resurrection of Jesus, and put the worshiper in intimate communion with that event, but it anticipates a glorious fulfillment of all the biblical promises and hopes in the future, and puts the worshiper into intimate communion with that future, thereby transforming the quality of life and action within the historical present.

SACRAMENTS IN THE ORTHODOX CHRISTIAN TRADITION. The sacramental practice and theology of the Orthodox churches is in direct continuity with the Greek patristic writings, emphasizing wonder and reverence in the presence of the holy.

Orthodox rites. Besides the seven sacraments enumerated above, Eastern Christianity recognizes a wide range of ritual considered sacramental in a broader sense: the anointing of a king; the rite of monastic profession; burial rites; blessing of water on the feast of the Epiphany; and blessings of homes, fields, harvested crops, and artifacts. These are not, however, all of equal importance.

Although, since the seventeenth century, the Orthodox churches have accepted the Western enumeration of seven rites, the manner of celebration of Orthodox sacraments does not correspond closely to the Western celebrations. The first sacramental participation of an Orthodox Christian is that of initiation, usually in infancy. The children are baptized by total triple immersion with an accompanying formula invoking the triune God. This is followed immediately by the chrismation (anointing) of forehead, eyes, nostrils, mouth, ears, breast, hands, and feet, with words proclaiming the seal of the gift of the Holy Spirit. As soon as possible thereafter, the infant is given Communion (either a small taste of the wine, or both bread and wine). This initiation is performed by a bishop or a priest.

The Eucharist, also known as the Divine Liturgy, is ordinarily celebrated daily, though the community as a whole is more likely to participate on Sundays, special feasts, and weekdays of Lent. It is performed in a highly elaborated way with processions, candles and incense, congregational singing, and the wearing of special vestments by the celebrating clergy.

The ordinary ritual of repentance and reconciliation is not a public ceremony as in the early church but a private conversation between a Christian and a priest who acts in the name of the church. The penitent, the person seeking forgiveness and reconciliation through the ministry of the church, ordinarily stands or sits before a cross, an icon (sacred image) of Jesus Christ, or the book of the Gospels. The priest, who stands to one side, admonishes the penitent to confess his or her sins to Christ, because he, the priest, is only a witness. Having heard the confession, and having perhaps given advice, the priest lays his stole (a type of scarf used as a ritual vestment) on the head of the penitent, lays his hand on it and pronounces a prayer of forgiveness. Besides this ritual of repentance, which can be repeated many times by the same person, the anointing of the sick is available to all who are ill, whether or not they are in danger of death. Anointing of the sick has the double purpose of prayer for healing from illness and forgiveness of sin.

The Orthodox churches ordain men only to their ministries, as bishops, priests, deacons, subdeacons, and readers. Ordinations are performed by a bishop during the Liturgy, and the consecration of a bishop is normally performed by three bishops. Essentially the rite is that of imposition of hands, but this is preceded by an acclamation of the congregation in which the faithful approve the candidate and consent to his ordination. The candidate is then brought to the altar to kiss its four corners and the hands of the bishop. The bishop lays hands on the candidate with a prayer invoking God's blessing.

The Orthodox marriage ceremony, celebrated by a priest, has two parts, the Office of Betrothal and the Office of Crowning, and includes the blessing and exchange of rings, the crowning of the bride and groom, and the sharing of a cup of wine by the couple.

Theology of the rites. Orthodox liturgy is concerned with making the beauty of the spiritual an element of experience, even a haunting element of experience. Liturgy is "heaven on earth," an anticipation of the glorious future. The fundamental sacramental principle is that in Jesus Christ a process of divinization has begun that continues in the sacramental mysteries and draws the worshipers in. Christ himself is the first sacramental mystery, continuing to live in the church, whose sacred actions reach forward to a glorious fulfillment in the future. The sacramental actions are the realization or becoming of the church as heavenly and earthly community. Therefore, they establish communion with the redemptive events of the past, communion among persons, and communion with the heavenly realm.

In the theology of the Orthodox church there is a strong sense of the organic wholeness, continuity, and pervasive presence of the redemption in the world, and therefore an unwillingness to draw some of the sharp distinctions that the West has been willing to draw concerning the sacramental mysteries.

WESTERN DEVELOPMENTS UP TO THE SIXTEENTH CENTURY. In the West, the sacraments underwent more change than in the East. This was caused by many factors, such as the large-scale conversions of European peoples, the cultural discontinuity resulting from the dissolution of the Roman empire, the problem of the difference in languages, a poorly educated clergy in the medieval period, and some other characteristics of Western traditions in church organization and theology.

Western rites. In the practice of the sacraments as received from the early church, there were some modifications. In the initiation, which was almost always conferred on children in the medieval period, baptism, confirmation, and first participation in the Eucharist were separated. The custom grew up of baptizing not by immersion but by pouring water over the forehead of the child. Confirmation, being the prerogative of the bishop, might be considerably delayed, and Communion was delayed out of a sense that infants might "desecrate" the holy.

The Eucharist became something that the priest did; the people had little part in it and little understanding of it. Its symbolism had become rather obscure and overlaid with additions and the Latin language, which had been adopted because it was the vernacular in the West in earlier centuries, was retained long after ordinary people no longer understood it. Communion by the laity became rare at this time, and even then it was restricted to the bread alone, the priest being the only one who received from the cup. Many ordinary Christians sought their real inspiration and forms of worship outside the liturgy of the Eucharist and the sacraments, and thus a great variety of other devotional practices arose.

As in the East, the old solemn and public form of reconciliation gave way to a far more private one embodied in a conversation between penitent and priest. This had originated in a tradition of voluntary individual spiritual guidance given by a wise and spiritual person who was not necessarily a priest. However, by the thirteenth century it had become obligatory for all people to confess, at least once a year, "all their grave sins" to their own parish priest, and the ceremony was constructed rather like a judicial procedure. By a subtle shift of usage in the twelfth century, the prayer that God might forgive had become a declaration that the priest forgave by the power the church had vested in him. There were also some changes in the other sacraments. The anointing of the sick became, in effect, the sacrament of the dying. Ordination was restricted not only to men, but to celibate men, and the consent of the faithful was not sought, even as a ritual formality. Effectively, the ranks of the clergy were reduced to two: bishop and priest. Men were ordained to the other ranks (deacon, subdeacon, minor orders) only as an intermediate step to the priesthood.

There seems to have been no obligatory religious ritual for a marriage until the eleventh century, although there was a custom of celebrating a Eucharist at which a canopy was placed over the bride and groom and a special blessing was pronounced. After the eleventh century, weddings were performed at the church door with the priest as witness and were followed by a Eucharist at which the marriage was blessed. Essential to the ceremony was the exchange of consent by the couple. A ring was blessed and given to the bride.

Theology of the sacraments. The Western theology of the sacraments is heavily indebted to Augustine, bishop of Hippo (d. 430), though the Scholastic theology of the West in the Middle Ages elaborated Augustine's teachings much more. Key ideas in Scholastic teaching are concerned with the validity, the necessity, and the efficacy or causality of the sacraments.

Validity is a legal concept, and this gave a different direction to Western sacramental theology from that of the East. Sacraments are valid if the rite is duly performed by a duly authorized minister, quite independently of the spiritual goodness or worthiness of that minister, because essentially they are the acts of Christ performed through the mediation of his church. Therefore a Eucharist correctly celebrated by someone who has gone into schism from the church or who is wicked would nevertheless be a true Eucharist.

According to the Scholastics, the necessity of baptism, and of sacraments in general, for salvation is grounded in the universal involvement of the human race in the heritage of sinfulness and disorientation. This led to much speculation in medieval times concerning the fate of people who were not baptized because the opportunity had not been presented to them. The Scholastics found an acceptable compromise in postulating, besides the "baptism of blood" of martyred converts who had not yet been initiated, a "baptism of desire" granted to those who lived in good faith by the light that God had given them.

There was strong emphasis in this theology on the efficacy of the sacraments because they were the acts of Christ. Their efficacy is to bestow grace, that is, an elevation of human existence to a privileged intimacy with God leading to salvation. Augustine's teaching tended to emphasize the gratuity of God's gifts so strongly that it gave the impression to some that the human response of faith and surrender was not a constituent of the sacramental encounter. Augustine and the medieval theologians taught that the salvific effect of (or the grace bestowed by) a sacrament was not dependent on the virtue of the one who administered the sacrament. Unfortunately, this was sometimes popularly understood as meaning that sacraments are also not dependent for their efficacy on finding faith in the recipient.

SACRAMENTS IN POST-REFORMATION ROMAN CATHOLIC TRADITION. The Council of Trent (1545–1563), while correcting many abuses, substantially reaffirmed both the practice and the theology of the sacraments as they had been received from the medieval period. It was not until the twentieth century, and particularly until the Second Vatican Council (1962–1965), that substantive developments occurred.

Roman Catholic rites. The most significant and pervasive changes in the sacramental rites following Vatican II were the restoration of a more extensive and careful use of scripture and of preaching on the biblical readings; a reconstruction of rites to emphasize the communal character of the sacraments and the full and active participation of the laity; and a simplification and clarification of the symbolism of the rites, effected by stripping away accretions and rediscovering the classic forms from the heritage of the early church, and also by introducing some cautious and modest contemporary adaptations.

In the case of adults, initiation has been restored to its ancient form with some adaptations. As in the primitive church, the culminating ceremonies are placed at the conclusion of a leisurely time of preparation known as *catechumenate.* In the case of infants, baptism has been simplified and made more clearly a community action and commitment.

The Eucharist, like the other sacraments, is now celebrated in the vernacular. Even in large congregations, the presiding priest now faces the community across the altar rather than facing away from the people. More people now have active roles in the ceremony. It is usual, not exceptional, for all to communicate, that is, to partake of the bread, and, on special occasions, also of the wine. The whole community at every Eucharist, not only the clergy on certain solemn occasions, exchanges a ritual "kiss of peace" (which is actually more usually a handshake).

The anointing has been reinstated as a sacrament of the sick rather than the dying. But perhaps the greatest changes have occurred in the structures for the sacrament of reconciliation, which now has not only an individual rite, but also a communal one and a mixed one. The individual form remains much as before but is enriched by scripture readings, while the focus of the rite has shifted from the judicial function to spiritual guidance in a progressive Christian conversion. The communal form consists of an assembly in which scripture is read; a sermon is preached; there are hymns and prayers including a common, generic confession of sin and repentance; and a general absolution, given in the name of the church. In the mixed form a similar service is held, but a pause is made during which individuals can go aside to make a personal and specific confession of sins to a priest out of earshot of the congregation, and an individual absolution is given.

The significant change in holy orders is not in the ceremony but in the fact that the Catholic church once again ordains permanent deacons (thereby restoring a third rank of clergy), who, moreover, may be married men. Marriages are more usually celebrated with an exchange of rings, rather than a ring for the bride only, and both partners receive the nuptial blessing. It is still understood that the partners themselves confer the sacrament on each other; the priest serves as witness.

Theology of the sacraments. The Catholic theology of the sacraments after Vatican II has returned to closer affinity with the patristic and Eastern understanding. The fundamental sacrament is Jesus Christ, who is made present in the sacrament of the church, which in turn is realized as a sacrament in its own sacramental actions and assemblies. But sacramentality is pervasive in Christian experience and not restricted to the seven special moments. The liturgy (especially that of the Eucharist) is the peak or summit of Christian life in that everything should lead to it and everything should flow from it. That is to say, life for the Christian community should be progressively transformed in the grace of Christ, in lifestyle, in relationships, and in community structures and values by the repeated immersion of the community in the eucharistic moment.

A distinct but related aspect of the renewed theology of the sacraments after Vatican II is the rediscovery of the link that was seen so clearly in the early church between Christian sacraments and social justice. The very ceremonies and symbols of the sacraments are seen as presenting a radical challenge to many of the existing structures of the world. Under the influence of biblical renewal and patristic scholarship, there is a consistent effort in contemporary Catholic sacramental theology to correct a former bias by constant remembrance that the sacraments are not simply acts of Christ but also of the community, are not only channels of grace but also acts of faith and worship.

SACRAMENTS IN THE PROTESTANT TRADITION. Although Protestant churches cannot simply be taken as a unity when discussing the sacraments, they do have one factor in common: They define themselves by their discontinuity with the medieval church tradition. Positively they also define themselves by a special emphasis on scripture and on personal faith.

Protestant rites. In general, the Protestant churches acknowledge as sacraments, in the strict sense of the term, only baptism and the Lord's Supper. Although other rites are celebrated, they are ordinarily not called sacraments because Protestants generally find no evidence of their institution by Jesus Christ. Some Christian groups of the Western church that are traditionally grouped with Protestants do not acknowledge sacraments at all; examples are the Society of Friends (Quakers), Unitarians, and Christian Scientists.

Among those Protestant churches that practice baptism, some insist on the "believer's baptism" and therefore will not baptize infants because they are not capable of a response of faith. Such, for instance, are the Baptists, the Disciples of Christ, and the Mennonites. These groups practice baptism by immersion. Most Protestant groups, however, do baptize infants and consider the pouring (sometimes the sprinkling) of water over the head as sufficient, accompanied by the recital of a formula usually invoking the triune God.

Protestant churches in general do not celebrate the Eucharist (Lord's Supper) as frequently as do the Catholic and Orthodox churches. Even a weekly celebration is not customary in most cases, though a monthly Communion service is quite usual. Although there is a variety of rites in the various churches, the central elements remain: the blessing and breaking of bread and its distribution to the worshipers to eat, accompanied by the biblical words of and about Jesus at his farewell supper; the blessing and distribution of the cup of wine (in some cases nonalcoholic grape juice) to be drunk by the worshipers, also accompanied by the appropriate biblical formula; biblical readings and meditation; and some expression of fellowship in the community. In general the Eucharist as celebrated by the Protestant churches is marked by a certain austerity of ritual expression and elaboration when compared with the celebrations of the Catholic and Orthodox churches.

Most Protestant churches celebrate some or all of the other rites that the Catholic and Orthodox churches enumerate as sacraments, although Protestants do not accord the rites that designation. There is a variety of rites of reconciliation, ranging from private confession of specific sins to an ordained minister, through such other forms as mutual confession between laypersons or stylized, generic formulas in which the whole congregation acknowledges sinfulness and need of forgiveness, to the characteristic Mennonite rite of foot washing (commemorating the action of Jesus related in the *Gospel of John* 13:2–10).

Anointing of the sick and other anointings have traditionally been practiced in some churches and have become far more common under the influence of the charismatic and Pentecostal movements. Marriages are commonly celebrated with some religious ceremony that includes bestowal of a ring or exchange of rings, exchange of marriage vows, and an exhortation in the context of community worship. Although most Protestant churches have some type of ordination of ministers, the ceremonies for such conferral reflect the different ways in which ministry and the role and status of the minister are understood.

Theology of the rites. Common to the Protestant churches is the insistence on the primacy of the Bible and on faith in salvation. Generally the efficacy of sacraments is not emphasized, while the role of the faith of the individual participant is stressed. This emphasis, combined with a strong sense of the priesthood of all believers, means that there is less concern over the "validity" of sacraments, and especially over the "validity of orders" of presiding ministers than in the Catholic and Orthodox traditions.

A major concern in celebrating the two great sacraments is obedience to the command of Jesus to do so, as that command is read in the New Testament. However, a significant difference exists between the Lutheran and the Calvinist understanding. In the former an act of God in the sacrament is effective when it encounters faith in the participant. In the latter a sacrament is a sign of God's grace but does not confer that grace.

ECUMENICAL ISSUES. The sacraments raise some ecumenical questions among Christians of different churches. One of these is the question of "intercommunion," that is, whether Christians of one church may receive communion at the Eucharist of another. Most churches allow this practice, at least in some circumstances. Another question is whether Christians transferring from one church tradition to another should be baptized again. With some exceptions, the churches do not confer baptism a second time, because they consider the first baptism valid. The question of accepting the ordination to ministry of other churches has proved far more controversial.

SEE ALSO Ablutions; Atonement; Baptism; Confession of Sins; Eucharist; Grace; Hands; Initiation; Justification; Marriage; Ministry; Ordination; Passover; Priesthood, article on Christian Priesthood; Repentance; Rites of Passage, article on Jewish Rites; Water; Worship and Devotional Life, article on Jewish Worship.

BIBLIOGRAPHY

The most inclusive single-volume introduction to sacraments in the Western tradition is Joseph Martos's *Doors to the Sacred* (New York, 1981). The biblical themes that underlie the symbolism of the sacraments are discussed briefly in my book *The Meaning of the Sacraments* (Dayton, Ohio, 1972). A detailed account of the historical development of the symbolism is given in Jean Daniélou's *The Bible and the Liturgy* (Notre Dame, Ind., 1966). What is known of the origins of the Christian rites in apostolic times is summarized in Ferdinand Hahn's *The Worship of the Early Church* (Philadelphia, 1973). The development of the rites through the patristic period is described in Josef A. Jungmann's *The Early Liturgy to the Time of Gregory the Great* (Notre Dame, Ind., 1959). The rites of the Orthodox tradition and their theological explanations are described in part 2 of Timothy Ware's *The Orthodox Church* (Baltimore, 1963). A further presentation of contemporary Orthodox sacramental theology is available in Alexander Schmemann's *Sacraments and Orthodoxy* (New York, 1965). A Protestant discussion of the rites and their theology, written from a Reform perspective but discussing the Lutheran tradition also, is G. C. Berkouwer's *The Sacraments,* translated from the Dutch by Hugo Bekker (Grand Rapids, Mich., 1969). Another Protestant account, written from the perspective of the Disciples of Christ, is J. Daniel Joyce's *The Place of the Sacraments in Worship* (Saint Louis, 1967). A detailed history of the rites from the point of view of the Episcopal church is Marion J. Hatchett's *Sanctifying Life, Time and Space: An Introduction to Liturgical Study* (New York, 1976). The Catholic theological understanding of the sacraments prior to Vatican II is succinctly presented in Bernard Piault's *What Is a Sacrament?* (New York, 1963). The Catholic understanding of the sacraments in the light of Vatican II is very clearly presented in Bernard Cooke's *Sacraments and Sacramentality* (Mystic, Conn., 1983). Karl Rahner's *The Church and the Sacraments* (London, 1963) is a short but highly technical reformulation of the older Roman Catholic sacramental theology in the light of a renewed ecclesiology. Edward Schillebeeckx's *Christ: The Sacrament of the Encounter with God* (Mission, Kans., 1963), an epoch-making book in its time, is a similar reformulation linking traditional sacramental theology to a renewed Christology. Bernard Cooke's *Ministry to Word and Sacraments: History and Theology* (Philadelphia, 1976) is a lengthy study showing the historical development of the sacraments in relation to changing perceptions of priesthood. A series of essays on the ecumenical questions relating to the sacraments is collected in *The Sacraments: An Ecumenical Dilemma,* edited by Hans Küng (New York, 1967), and *The Sacraments in General: A New Perspective,* edited by Edward Schillebeeckx and Boniface Willems (New York, 1968). Technical and detailed bibliographies are given in each of these volumes.

New Sources

Boswell, John. *Same-Sex Unions in Pre-Modern Europe.* New York, 1994.

Fahey, Michael. A., ed. *Catholic Perspective on Baptism, Eucharist and Ministry.* Lanham, Md., 1986.

Gorringe, Timothy J. *The Sign of Love: Reflections on the Eucharist.* London, 1997.

Guernsey, Daniel P., ed. *Eucharistic Texts and Prayers throughout Church History.* San Francisco, 1999.

Limouris, Gennadios, and N. M. Vaporis, eds. *Orthodox Perspectives on Baptism, Eucharist, and Ministry.* Brookline, Mass., 1985.

Mitchell, Nathan. *Eucharist as Sacrament of Initiation.* Chicago, 1994.

O'Malley, William J. *Sacraments: Rites of Passage.* Allen, Tex., 1995.

Primavesi, Anne. *Our God Has No Favorites: A Liberation Theology of the Eucharist.* Tunbridge Wells, U.K., and San Jose, Calif., 1989.

Reumann, John Henry Paul. *The Supper of the Lord: The New Testament, Ecumenical Dialogues, and Faith and Order on Eucharist.* Philadelphia, 1985.

Shurden, Walter B. *Baptism and the Lord's Supper.* Macon, Ga., 1999.

White, James F. *The Sacraments in Protestant Practice and Faith.* Nashville, Tenn., 1999.

MONIKA K. HELLWIG (1987)
Revised Bibliography

SACRED AND THE PROFANE, THE. When referring to the sacred and the profane and distinguishing between them, the languages of modern scholarship are indebted to Latin, even though they may have equivalent or synonymous terms for both that have been derived from their own linguistic traditions. To the Roman, *sacrum* meant what belonged to the gods or was in their power; yet when referring to *sacrum* one was not obliged to mention a god's name, for it was clear that one was thinking of cult ritual and its location, or was primarily concerned with the temple and the rites performed in and around it. *Profanum* was what was "in front of the temple precinct"; in its earlier usage, the term was always applied solely to places. Originally, *profanare* meant "to bring out" the offering "before the temple precinct (the *fanum*)," in which a sacrifice was performed. *Sacer* and *profanus* were therefore linked to specific and quite distinct locations; one of these, a spot referred to as *sacer,* was either walled off or otherwise set apart—that is to say, *sanctum*—within the other, surrounding space available for profane use. This purely spatial connotation adheres to the two terms to this day, and implies that it represents a definition of them, or at least of their more important features. It makes sense wherever the church still stands next to the town hall, the cult site alongside the village council chamber, and wherever an assembly of Buddhists or Muslims is something other than an assembly of professional economists or athletes.

If one clings to the spatial aspect of these terms, however, and attempts to use it as a means of distinguishing not only between the two of them but also between religion and nonreligion, one is led astray. This occurs if one posits the sacred as a special category of religion in the way that the correct or the true has been made a category of cognition theory, the good a category of ethics, and the beautiful a category of aesthetics. The sacred is then what gives birth to religion, in that humanity "encounters" it; or it functions as the essence, the focus, the all-important element in religion. Of course it is possible to define the sacred in such a way if one determines that a single attribute is sufficient for an all-encompassing statement about religion. But when one is forced to find attributes that suggest religion's links to altogether different concepts, aside from those having to do with the quality of lying beyond a specific boundary, one discovers that the attribute of sacrality is no longer enough, even if one views its original spatial aspect as a transcendental or metaphysical one. And today, confronted with definitions advanced by critics of ideology, sociologists, psychoanalysts, and others, it indeed necessary to find such attributes. Any definitions, even simple descriptions of the sacred and the profane, are affected by these as well; they also depend, in turn, on the manifold factors one has to muster when identifying the concept of religion.

Yet it is not necessary to discard the ancient Roman distinction between *sacer* and *profanus,* for the idea that they exist side by side represents a fundamental paradigm for making distinctions in general. It therefore has a certain heuristic value, though admittedly only that and nothing more.

The relationship between the sacred and the profane can be understood either abstractly, as a mutual exclusion of spheres of reality, or cognitively, as a way of distinguishing between two aspects of that reality. The former approach necessarily presupposes that such exclusion is recognizable; the latter, that one is dealing with ontic factuality. Even if one assumes a transsubjective reality, the boundary between the two spheres may prove to be movable or even fictitious, and even if one confines oneself to the fact of subjectivity, one may at times conclude that transcendence conditions the individual psychologically. Thus, when asking whether the sacred and the profane "exist," and how humans "experience" them, one encounters even greater difficulties than when inquiring after being and its various modes. Even though this article contains primarily the most important information about the various ways in which the sacred has been perceived in the history of religions, these difficulties of meaning must be borne in mind. It is necessary to suppress one's own conclusions about how and in what dimensions the sacred might exist, and about what it "is," in favor of the numerous theories that have been advanced on the question; according to these, conclusions may only be drawn case by case, in the light of the data and the theoretical arguments presented, and may well come out differently in every instance. Only with such reservations in mind can one consider the nature of the sacred and the profane.

MEANS OF IDENTIFICATION. In selecting evidence of the sacred and its relationship to the profane one must be limited to two approaches: Either it is tacitly perceived as something real, or it assumes some kind of symbolic form. In order to establish tacit perception, one requires proofs that silence is maintained for the sake of the sacred. These proofs suffice not only for the mystic, for example, who could speak but prefers to maintain silence, but also for persons who have spoken, but whose language is unknown: namely, the people of prehistory and early historical times.

Symbolic forms may be specifically linguistic or of a broader cultural nature. If they are linguistic, the historian of religions must distinguish between the language spoken by the people who are the objects of study ("object language") and the one spoken by the scholar, though naturally the two will have shadings and terms in common. One can best make this distinction by keeping one's own definition of what is sacred or profane separate from the definition that is given by the culture under scrutiny itself ("self-definition"). Each definition naturally identifies the sacred and profane in a different way. The self-definition is part of those languages in which religious and nonreligious documents have come down to us; in terms of methodology, these are the same as object languages. The definitions the historian develops must arise not only out of the categories of language, but also out of those of modern sociology, psychology, aesthetics, and possibly other disciplines as well, categories employed in an attempt to understand the sacred and profane without resorting to the concepts one customarily translates with *sacred* and *profane;* in terms of methodology, this amounts to a metalanguage.

If the symbolic forms are not of a linguistic nature, there is no self-definition at all. The definitions given from outside to which one must restrict oneself, in this case to relate to language, are not metalinguistic in nature, for the object area is not expressed merely in language, but rather through social behavior, anthropological data, or works of art.

Whether considered a linguistic or a nonlinguistic expression, the definition given from outside can assume an affirmative character, and in so doing turn into the self-definition of the scholar who identifies himself with a given artifact, be it in a text, a specific event, a psychic configuration, or a work of art. The researcher compiling a definition can thus identify himself with both its sacredness and profaneness.

As a rule, one should give neither of these means of identification precedence over the other. It is for purely practical reasons that this article now turns its attention first to those methods relying on linguistic evidence.

Philological methods. It is an axiom in the logic of criticism that one can declare the use of a concept of sacredness in a source to be false. However, the conclusions of the modern scholar, no matter how subtly they might not only deny phenomena of sacredness within religions but also manage to demonstrate them outside of religions, are constantly in need of correction by object-language traditions.

Seen in terms of the history of scholarship, the first object-language tradition to contain the terms for *sacred* and *profane* (upon which the terminology of the medieval precursors of modern scholarly languages was based) was the Latin of the Roman classical writers and church fathers, including, among the texts of the latter, the Vulgate and the harmony of its gospel texts represented by Tatian's *Diatessaron* in the Codex Fuldensis. Equating words resulted in the double presentation of terms in the vernacular, as can still be seen from various contextual, interlinear, and marginal glosses, and in the translations of the *Abrogans,* an alphabetical dictionary of synonyms, and the *Vocabularius Sancti Galli,* in which the terms are arranged by subject. Bilingualism, resulting from the rechristianization of Spain, was also responsible for the earliest translation of the Qurʾān by Robertus Ketenensis and Hermannus Dalmata, for the unfinished *Glossarium Latino-Arabicum,* and for some important translations from Hebrew, which not only reflect the Jews' skill as translators throughout the Diaspora, but also represent active endeavors on the part of the medieval mission among the Jews. Terms for the sacred and its opposites could thus be translated into the vernaculars directly out of Hebrew, Latin, and Catalan, and out of the Arabic by way of Latin. They also became available from Greek, once the early humanists, the forerunners of the modern scholars, had rediscovered the Greek classics through the Latin ones, and the original text of the New Testament and the Septuagint by way of the Vulgate. At the Council of Vienne, in 1311–1312, it was decided to appoint two teachers each of Greek, Arabic, Hebrew, and Chaldean at each of five universities; thenceforth Latin emerged once and for all as a metalanguage with respect to the terminologies of these languages (including Latin itself, now considered as an object language), and in so doing came to stand fundamentally on the same footing as the European vernaculars.

In order to avoid short-circuiting self-confirmations within the terminology of sacredness, it is best to consider this complex as an independent one transmitted to modern scholarship not from the Middle Arabic of the Islamic traditionalists, nor from the Middle Hebrew of the Talmudists, but solely from the Middle Latin of the Christian scholars. It must be distinguished from a later complex that resulted from the use of the European vernaculars in missionary work and in colonization. These were able to reproduce certain word meanings from the native languages, but more often led to interpretations dependent on the terminology of sacredness from the former complex, rather than congenial translation. Moreover, true bilingualism was only present in the work of a few explorers and missionaries. More recently, of course, translation has been accomplished increasingly in accordance with methods taken from the study of the early oriental languages, of Indo-European, and of comparative philology, as well as from linguistic ethnology; only in the twentieth century did all of these achieve independence from interpretations provided by classical antiquity and by Judeo-Christian-Islamic tradition.

Philologia classica sive sacra. The relationship between *sacer* and *profanus* can be called a contradictory opposition, if one understands *sacer* as the object-language expression of something true and *profanus* as its logical negation. In the rich cultic vocabulary of Latin *sacer* is of prime importance. Rites such as those of the *ver sacrum*—the sacrifice of all animals born in the spring and the expulsion from the community and cult congregation of all grown people about to establish their own domestic state (for the purpose of securing the support of Mars, who worked outside communal boundaries)—or the *devotio*—the offering of an individual life as a stand-in for an enemy army, so that Mars will destroy it as well—serve as prime examples of the characteristic relationship between the *sacrum*'s liability and certain kinds of human behavior. It follows that all cult objects and sites included in ritual acts can also be *sacra*. This meaning gives rise to derivations such as *sacrare, sacrificare, sancire, sacramentum, sacerdos*. Of these, *sancire* ("to set aside as *sacer*"; later also "to designate as being *sacer*," or, even more generally, "to establish with ceremony") is the most fertile, for its participle *sanctus* would ultimately come to characterize everything appropriate to the *sacrum*. *Sanctus* could thus assume a multitude of meanings, including those of cult infallibility and moral purity. Accordingly, it was an ideal translation for the Greek *hagios* of the New Testament and the Septuagint, and, by way of the latter, for the Hebrew *qadosh* as well. When used in such a Judeo-Christian context, *sacer* was then restricted in meaning to "consecrated," and this tended to fix a change in meaning that had begun already in the Latin of the writers of the Silver Age, as *sacrum* ceased to have an almost innate quality and came to depend on the act of consecration to a deity. A new formation such as *sacrosanctus* ("rendered *sanctum* by way of a *sacrum*") attests to this difference, as well as to the continuing similarity between the two meanings.

The basic meaning of *profanus* may also be discovered within the context of human actions, for the spatial connotation, which is always at its root, doubtless first derived from the use made of the area outside the *sacrum*. Originally, perhaps, this space may even have been used for rites, for the fact that even here one is dealing not with banal functions but with special ones is shown by legal arguments about how assets owned by a god or in the estate of a deceased citizen can be used "profanely."

Along with *profanus*, there is also another concept that is the opposite of *sacer*, namely that of *fas*. This designates, in a purely negative way, the sphere in which human affairs may take place. *Fas est* means that one *may* do something without any religious scruples, but not that one *must* do so. It first appears as a qualifier for a permitted act, then for a condition as well, and accordingly was used through all of the literature of the Roman republic only as a predicate concept. Livy, who also used the term *sacrosanctus* with some frequency, was the first to employ the concept as a subject as well. Specific times came to be distinguished by the activities appropriate to them. *Dies fasti* were days on which civil, political, commercial, or forensic activities were *fas*, or permitted by the religious institutions; *dies nefasti* were those on which such activities were *nefas*, that is, not permitted, or sacrilegious.

The meaning of *fas* does not accord with that of *fanum*, then—nor are they related etymologically; *fas* is related to *fatum*—as though *fas* is "what is appropriate to the *fanum*." Here it is rather the profane sphere that is the positive starting point. *Fas* is the utterance (from *fari*, "speak") of the responsible secular praetor who permits something; *nefas* is that which the priest responsible in the *fanum* finds unutterable, which constitutes sacrilege on those days over which his institution has control. When one recognizes that what is here accepted as natural and immutable passes over into what has been fixed by humans and is therefore subject to change, and which can be objectively false just as its opposite can, then one can speak of the opposition between *fanum/sacer* and *fas* as a contrary one.

Sacer thus has a contradictory opposite (*profanus*) and a contrary one (*fas*). In addition, finally, there is a dialectical opposition contained within the concept of *sacer* itself. This comes from the ambivalence produced when, as with *fas*, the extrasacral sphere is assumed as the positive starting point in one's appraisal. *Sacer* is thus what is venerated, to be sure, but also something sinister; or, to put it another way, it is both holy and accursed. Consecration to a god is perceived by humans as a blessing, whereas being possessed by a god is perceived as a misfortune. One must not make this dialectical contrast into an actual one by construing possession and misfortune as a fatal consecration to an underworld deity inimical to humans, for in so doing one destroys an ambiguity that is part of the basic structure of every religious experience. Positively, *sacer esto* simply means that a person is handed over to a deity; negatively, it implies that he is excluded from the community. The negative side of the dialectic may extend as far as demonization. If damnation or demonization is manifest on the historical level, then one is dealing with something other than profanation, and, outside the holy, still another sphere is revealed in addition to the profane. The dialectical relationship with this sphere comes about only through humanity's limited capacity for experience, and must not be enhanced by philologically setting up some finding related to *sacer*; that is, it must not be turned into an essential contrary working inside the nature of a *numen* or a deity.

The types of contrasts between the terms designating the sacred and the profane are less fundamental in Greek than in Latin, even though elements of ambivalent background experience may also be recognized in *hagios* and *hieros*. For the most part, the expressions have the character of a primary positing dependent on premises other than those relating to the differences between inclusion in or exclusion from a given precinct, or between ritual and nonritual behavior. As a rule, the antithesis was only created belatedly, through the use of the alpha privative, as in *anhieros, anosios, amuetos*, or *asebes;* the only term that appears to relate to an original negative concept, namely the opposite of *hieros,* is *bebelos,* which can be translated as "profane," while *koinos* can function as the opposite of practically all the concepts of sacredness. In a survey of the latter, then, the contrary concepts may be easily imagined, even though not specifically named.

From Mycenaean times on, the decisive concept is that designated as *hieros.* Behind it, most likely, is a sense of force altogether lacking in the early Roman term. *Hieros* functions almost exclusively as a predicate, both of things and of persons: offerings, sacrificial animals, temples, altars, votive gifts (even including money), the road leading to Eleusis, the wars engaged in by the Delphic amphictyony, and priests, initiates in the mysteries, and temple slaves. Only very rarely did anyone go so far as to call a god or a goddess *hieros;* Greek-speaking Jews and Christians were forced to resort to the term *hagios.* Traces of some experiential ambivalence are apparent when a *hieros logos,* or cult legend, is regarded as *arreton* ("unspeakable") and a shrine as *aduton* or *abaton* ("unapproachable"). It is nonetheless striking that in Homer and the older Greek literature a whole range of things may be called *hieros:* cities, walls, hecatombs, altars, temples, palaces, valleys, rivers, the day and the night, the threshing floor, bread and the olive tree, barley and olives, chariots, guard and army units, individual personality traits, mountains, letters, bones, stones used in board games. Here it is rare to find *hieros* used with any connection to the gods, as when grain and the threshing floor, for example, are spoken of as the gifts of Demeter. On the whole it is tempting to speak of a certain profanation due to literary redundancy, though in fact a complete reversal of meaning is never produced.

Hagnos, which also encompasses what is pure in the cultic sense, is even more profound in its meaning than *hieros;* it relates to *hazesthai* ("to avoid in awe, to fear, to venerate") in the same way that *semnos* ("solemn, sublime, holy"—i. e., lacking the component of purity) relates to *sebesthai* ("to be afraid, to perceive as holy"). *Hagnos* is more frequently used than *hieros* when referring to the gods (Demeter, Kore, Persephone, Zeus, Apollo, Artemis), but in that they are elements that can purify, water and fire can also be *hagnos,* as can sky, light, and ether. Because of this connotation, *hagnos* can be used not only for things and persons in the same way as *hieros,* but may also designate rites and festivals or the conditions of sexual purity and of freedom from the contamination of blood and death, as, for example, when applied to bloodless offerings (*hagna thumata*). *Hagnos* can even extend to the whole conduct of one's life outside the cult, though the connotation "sacred" never entirely disappears; it is only in Hellenistic Greek that it comes to mean "purity of character." Whether one is justified in calling this a profane use or not depends upon one's judgment of the nature of post-classical religiosity in general. In any case, the only clearly contradictory opposite of *hagnos* is *miaros* ("polluted, disgusting").

From the root *hag-,* from which *hagnos* derives, the adjective *hagios* was also created. This does not limit, but rather emphasizes (hence, too, its superlative *hagiotatos*), and is used especially of temples, festivals, and rites, though only rarely of the reverent attitudes of men. In classical Greek and the pagan Greek of Hellenistic times it is used only relatively rarely. Precisely for this reason its clear religious connotation was preserved, and this is what recommended the term to Hellenistic Jewry as a virtually equivalent translation for the Hebrew *qadosh,* whereas from the *hieros* group of words one finds only *hiereus* as a possible rendering of the Hebrew *kohen* ("priest"), and *hieron* to designate a pagan shrine. The New Testament develops even further the sense given to *hagios* in the Septuagint—though unlike the Septuagint it can also use *hieron* when referring to the Temple in Jerusalem—and thereby transmits this sense to the Greek of the church fathers and the Byzantine church. Secular modern Greek continues to use *hagios* as the standard term for "sacred" to this day.

The word *hosios* designates behavior that conforms to the demands of the gods. Accordingly, it can be applied to human justice just as properly as to a correctly performed cult ritual. Both are carried out on the profane level. Though one cannot translate *hosios* with "profane," one must think of it as a contrary opposite of *hieros:* If money belonging to the gods is *hieron,* that means one cannot touch it, but the rest, which is *hosion,* may be freely used. The Septuagint never uses *hosios* as a translation for *qadosh* but generally does for *ḥasid* ("pious"). The Vulgate, however, renders *hosios* unaffectedly with *sanctus,* whether applied to humans or to God.

Sebesthai ("to shrink back from a thing, to be awestruck") has no parallel in the Semitic languages, and hence the word is important solely in the classical Greek tradition. The related adjective *semnos* implies exaltedness or sublimity when used of gods; when applied to speeches, actions, or objects (a royal throne, for example) it suggests that they command respect. It appears only infrequently in the Greek Bible for various terms, just as does the important classical concept *eusebēs,* which is chosen in a few instances to render *tsaddiq* ("the just one"), which in turn may also be translated with *dikaios.* The Vulgate has difficulty with both adjectives, and makes do with approximations or circumlocutions.

In the Hebrew Bible the all-important concept is *qadosh.* If its root is in fact *qd* ("to set apart"), its fundamental meaning is not unlike the Roman *sacer.* But it is also possible that its root is *qdsh,* as in the Akkadian *qadashu* ("to become pure"), which would point to a cultic connection. Nothing is *qadosh* by nature, however; things only become *qadosh* by being declared so for, or by, Yahveh Elohim. All of creation is potentially eligible: persons, especially priests; places, especially the city of Jerusalem; festivals, especially the Sabbath; buildings, especially the Temple; adornments, especially the priest's crown and robe; bodies of water; plants; and animals, especially sacrificial ones. The prophets—assisted by a trend that emerged from the reading of God's law at the Israelite feast of covenantal renewal and culminated in the establishment of the Holiness Code (*Lv.* 17–26)—managed to transfer the attribute "holy" almost exclusively to Yahveh Elohim. As a result, only a very few of the above-mentioned categories of objects and activities continued to be accorded the attribute of holiness in the actual target language of Hebrew. In large part, reference to holy places, times, actions, and objects is metalanguage interpretation. It is not factually wrong, for even a holiness accorded by God on the basis of his own holiness is deserving of the name. Nevertheless, one must be aware of the special quality of having been created by him that is typical of such holiness; this is in distinct contrast, for example, to the Greek concept of nature. And it affects the designation of what is profane in Israel. An important thesis of secularization theory asserts that the desacralization of the world, especially of nature and its wonders as it was accomplished in the Israelite theology of holiness, and later transmitted by Christianity, was one of the fundamental preconditions for the worldliness of the modern era. If one does not regard this basic precondition as a *conditio sine qua non,* it is doubtless correctly identified. It would be possible to view the realm of created things in the Israelite concept of the world as profane, just as one might view secularity as a legitimizing criterion for what constitutes the modern era, but that profaneness would be altogether different in kind from that of Rome or Greece. Given this situation, it is understandable that in the Old Testament languages (Hebrew and Septuagint/Vulgate translations) the "profanity" of the world is expressed in quite dissimilar fashion and only fragmentarily, depending upon whether it is mentioned in the cult context of pure and impure or in prophetic preaching about obedience and sin. As a clear contradiction to *qadosh* is thus found, in only a few instances, the adjective *ḥol,* which is rendered by the Septuagint with *bebēlos* and by the Vulgate with *profanus* (*ṭame',* "impure," becomes *akathartos* and *pollutus,* respectively; *ṭaher,* "pure," becomes *katharos* and *mundus*). *Ḥol* designates only something that is accessible and usable without ritual, while the verb *ḥalal* suggests a genuine desecration by means of an abomination.

The grateful use of created things, which God makes holy, by people who are likewise holy because God is, is not the same thing as the Greeks' and Romans' removal of things from profane use. The closest parallel to the latter in Israel is the practice of bans. Translated etymologically, *ḥerem* ("the banned object") means what has been set apart. The difference not only between this practice and profane use of a holy object but also between it and the sacrifice of an object lies in the fact that the purpose for the setting apart is the object's destruction. The Septuagint quite correctly expresses the term's identity with the idea of damnation by using *ana(te)thema(tismenos),* while the Vulgate makes do with *consecratum* or *votum.*

In Arabic, at least since the appearance of the Qur'ān, words with the root *ḥrm* take on the central importance that *qdsh* and its derivatives have in Hebrew. At the same time, the Arabic *qds* and its offshoots (*muqaddas,* "holy") continue to survive with more general meaning. This switch in the relative values of the two may have occurred simply because all of the concepts of sacredness having to do with rites and sacrifices were concentrated on a specific precinct. It is as though the Israelite concept of holiness, bound as it was to the ideas of sacrifice and consecration, were multiplied by the Roman concept, with its original link to a well-defined location. The city of Mecca is a *ḥarīm,* a circumscribed, inviolable spot. The strip of land that surrounds and protects it is known as *al-ḥarām.* In the city's center lies *al-masjid al-ḥarām,* the "forbidden mosque," so named because it may not be entered by those who have not performed an *iḥrām,* or consecrated themselves. In the center of its inner courtyard, *al- ḥarām al-sharīf* (the "noble precinct"), lies the *aedes sacra,* the Kaʿbah, *al-bayt al-ḥarām* (the "forbidden house"). Everything outside this complex is known as *ḥill,* where, just as in the *profanum,* except during a period of three months, everything is *ḥalāl* ("permitted") that is prohibited in the sacred sites. The Arabic *ḥalāl* is thus close in meaning to the Hebrew *ḥol,* but quite different from *ḥalāl.*

Linguistica externa. Regarding the problem of "the holy," a number of groups of terminologies have to be located between the Latin/Greek/Hebrew/Arabic ensemble and the modern scholarly languages influenced by them, terminologies that can suggest things similar to those existing in the gap between those object languages and these metalanguages. Semantic antinomies that can remain unrecognized in the latter should certainly not influence this terminology. There are three ways of attempting to establish meanings here: through etymological "translation," through synonyms, and through analysis of the context and its cultural background. The first of these, especially favored in the case of the Indo-European and Semitic languages, is altogether worthless. Reliable checks are only provided by context analysis. In this way one can discover "synonyms"—though not always synonyms in the strict sense—which more or less approximate what the meta-languages define as sacred/holy and profane.

The Sanskrit term *iṣira* has the same root as the Greek *hieros,* but contextually it means "strong, robust, impetuous." Sanskrit does not even have a separate word for "holy," though there are numerous adjectives applied to objects and persons in the religious sphere, such as *puṇya* for a geographical location, *tīrthaka* for a ford, or the crossing or passageway to a pilgrimage shrine, or substantives such as *muni* for a seer or an ascetic. Related etymologically to the Greek *hazesthai/hagios* are the Sanskrit *yaj* and Avestan *yaz.* These two also mean "to hold in awe," but their usage is limited to the sense of "bestow, present," as when one brings a gift to a deity (Skt. *ijyā,* Av. *yasna,* "the offering"), and there is no connotation, as in the Greek *hagios,* of an otherworldly essence from which the earthly is thought to have derived. For this latter sense Avestan has the word *spenta,* to which are related the Slavic *svętu* and Lithuanian *šventas.* These latter two are used in Christian contexts for *sacer,* but their root meaning originally lay somewhere between "supernaturally powerful" and "especially favorable, extremely useful." Pahlavi translations render *spenta* with *abzōnig* ("overflowing, bursting with power"). The cultural background is the world of plants and animals, which in its abundant energy has the miraculous ability to bring forth new life and set it to work in its own cause.

The Germans have translated *spenta* with *heilwirkend* ("producing well-being" or "prosperity") employing a root that means "whole, sound, intact," and that gave rise to the German *heilig* ("holy"). Gothic *hails* meant "healthy"; Old Icelandic and Old High German *heil* is "a good omen" or "good fortune." Runic *hailag* means roughly "gifted with good fortune [by a god]," but also, conversely, "consecrated [to a god]." This becomes equal to the Gothic adjective *weihs* and its related active verb *weihan,* medial verb *weihnan,* and abstract noun *weihitha,* which appear in the Gothic translation of the Bible in place of the Greek *hagios, hagiazein, hagiazesthai,* and *hagiasmos,* respectively. All in all, the German *heil-* words connote a physical integrity with distinct religious significance. Possession of such integrity is a boon that can be given. The god who bestows it thereby becomes one to whom one gives veneration (Ger., *weiht*). Accordingly, even in Gothic the two concepts *weihs* and *hails* (which can also develop to *hailigs*) are interchangeable, and the situation in other Germanic languages is similar.

In general the synonyms in the Indo-European languages for what the metalanguages imply with their contrast between profane and sacred boil down to a qualitative exaggeration, intensification, or concentration of aspects of nature.

Among the ancient peoples of Asia Minor, to whose ideas the mythology of the Hittites in part attests, there appears to have been no special word for mysteries, such as the amazing magnetic force of stones or the destruction of creation by the creator himself. Yet a Hittite adjective, *parkui,* refers to the state of purity required in preparation for contact with the gods, and another, *shuppi,* designates such contact itself. Among the Sumerians, for reasons whose elaboration would go beyond the scope of this article, one must assume from earliest times a well-defined pantheon that predated all ritual. The basic polytheistic structure is of a more general character than anything that has been defined to demonstrate a consistent background world beyond the differentiations into socially and functionally limited deities. Yet even the world of the gods is permeated by a single, unifying element that one can only call "the divine." This is the *me,* which is met with in compounds like *melam* ("divine radiance, divine majesty"). Mythical people and kings can also exhibit it, in which case they are god-men. The gods pronounce *me* and exclude it from the framework of fate, which they in fact subordinate to the *me.* Humanity is required to bring itself into conformity with this *me* so as to be able to realize it in the world. There are numerous adjectival terms corresponding to this concept, the most important being *kug, mah,* and *zid.* In Babylonian, *kug* is translated with *ellu* ("[ritually] pure, bright, free"), *mah* with *siru* ("first-rank, exalted"), and *zid* with *imnu* ("right-hand") or *kanu* ("to be firm"). Alternatives to *ellu* in Babylonian spells are the terms *namru* ("clear, radiant") and *quddushu* ("purified, [made] perfect"), the latter having the same root as the Hebrew *qdsh.* Moreover, the Babylonian creation epic *Enuma elish* attests to a primordial cosmogony in a preexistent world. For the relationship between what the metalanguages call the sacred and the profane one finds *analogies* in the relationship between human and animal forms of deities, as well as between their constructive activity (including Marduk's creation of the world) and the social organization of gods and human beings.

In Egypt, whose language became accessible by way of Greek (through the Rosetta Stone), temples and necropolises especially were set apart from the everyday world, and, in connection with them, so were gods and specific objects. This sense of being separate did not have to be concentrated in a specific term, but from the first to twentieth dynasties this was frequently done with the word *dsr. Dsr* means, first of all, a kind of vibrating motion, but it can also designate a defense against a rush of attackers or, more generally, a clearing resulting from the settling of a whirlwind. These have in common a sense of thrusting away that amounts to the establishment of distance. The word came to be used, in an increasingly abstract sense, for such distance when an appropriate attribute was required to describe the location of a cult statue in a necropolis, a shrine, the eternal body of the god Re, the space in which bulls were sacrificed, the realm of the gods, and the underworld paths reserved for the dead once they had become Osiris. It is simplest to conceive of the relationship of such places and objects to the everyday world as the subsequent removal of the distance at which they have been placed. Something of this sort happens when texts used in the context of religious institutions become the models for secular literature; the most important ancient Egyptian narrative, the *Story of Sinuhe,* for example, poses as a copy of an autobiographical tomb inscription.

Western knowledge of the Chinese and Japanese languages is due in general to the presence of Jesuit missionaries in China and Japan in the sixteenth century. Deeper understanding of the vocabulary of East Asian religions comes most of all from Chinese translations of Buddhist texts originally written in Indian dialects, and already known through other channels; and, later, from the study of Japanese renderings of the better-known Chinese. The first bilingual (i. e., Chinese- or Japanese-European) dictionaries finally appeared in the nineteenth century. Whether or not there are precise equivalents for *sacred* and *profane* is largely a matter of each individual lexicographer's interpretation. The Chinese *shensheng,* which some gloss as meaning "holy," is held by others to mean, roughly, "extremely right," "highly exalted," or "doubtless as it must be." Of course, it is possible to interpret an ecstatic act such as submersion into the totality of the Tao as the attainment of holiness; however, the foundation in physical nature that is discovered to be a basic principle of the mystical experience is so much more magical here than in other religions that a difference in quality results. The relationship between the sacred and the profane would thus be roughly the same as that between alchemy and hygiene, both of which are practiced within Taoism as a means of attaining "not-dying."

The Shintō concept of nature is doubtless both more spiritual and more mythological. The *kami,* or nature and ancestral deities, are profane or sacred to the precise degree in which they do or do not belong organically to the everyday world of the living. The monks (*shidosō*) and wandering *hijiri* who carried the rites and concepts of the popular and even more magical esoteric Buddhism out into the provinces, and thereby contributed greatly to its fusion with Shintō, can rightly be called "holy men"—whatever that may imply about the charismatic leaders of new religions in the present day, who take them as their models.

The metalanguage expressions *sacred* and *profane* and their equivalents are only synonyms for all of the views derived from the various terminologies discussed here. If one proceeds from the roots of their subject matter and not from an all-inclusive hermeneutics, they are not complete synonyms but only partial ones, of a conceptual rather than a stylistic nature.

Metalanguage meanings. The modern scholarly languages for the most part presuppose the changes of meaning that the classical vocabulary ultimately experienced as a result of being put to Christian use, in part after certain non-Christian usages that prepared the way. These changes of meaning are characterized by the fact that a clear distinction exists between the quality of God in the beyond and the quality of creation in the here and now; and the terms are distributed accordingly. This distinction must not be thought of as static, however, for it can be suspended in either direction, that is to say, both by God's communication with humans and by humans' consecration of things to God.

In the first sense, the Latin term *sanctus* had ultimately come to mean a primarily divine quality; and consequently there is now the French *saint* and the Italian and Spanish *santo.* The Germanic languages, on the other hand, perpetuate the root that in the language's earliest stages had meant "intact, healthy, whole," represented by the English *holy* (related to *whole;* synonyms: *godly, divine*), by the German and Dutch *heilig,* and by the Swedish *helig.* And the Slavic languages preserve a root that had meant "efficacious" in the early stage of the language: the Russian *sviatoi,* for example, or Polish *święty.*

In the second sense, that is, for the quality attained by dedication to God, Latin had preserved the term *sacer,* which was linked to places, objects, and situations. Later, though relatively early, *sacer* existed alongside *sanctus,* which, confusingly enough, could also be used to refer to this mode of transformation. *Sacer* could be exchanged for the clearer form *sacratus,* and it is from this that the French *(con)sacré,* the Italian *sacro* (synonym: *benedetto*), and the Spanish *(con)sagrado* derive. For this meaning English employs the Romance word *sacred,* while German and Dutch make use of the ancient root **ueik-* (possibly a homonym; "to set apart" or "to oppose oneself to someone") with the forms *geweiht* and *gewijd.* In addition, German also substitutes for this a form from the former word group, using *geheiligt* in the sense of *geweiht,* a situation that gives rise to constant misunderstanding. This misunderstanding had been prepared for by the double direction of Gothic *weihs/hailigs,* and it was strengthened by imitating the biblical wording. For the sake of clarity, some careful speakers therefore prefer the form *dargeheiligt* to mean "consecrated." This substitution also occurs in Swedish, which uses only *vigd* and *helgad.* In the scholarly Slavic language ambiguity is avoided through incorporation of the simple form into a composite, as in the case of the Russian *sviaschchennyi* and the Polish *świątobliwy.*

In Latin, *profanus* had continued to be the opposite of both *sanctus* and *sacer,* the latter in its broader, classical Roman sense as well as its more limited Judeo-Christian meaning. Accordingly, the Romance languages and Romance-influenced English still use the term, while the strictly Germanic languages have it only as a loan word. In all of them there are synonyms with the meaning "secular," or something similar. Synonyms of this type have completely replaced the Latin form in the Slavic languages; Russian has *svetskii* or *zemnoi,* Polish *świecki* or *światowy.*

It is most important to notice the metalanguage nature of these terms as they are used to translate expressions from the linguistic complex Latin/Greek/Hebrew/Arabic, as well as from other languages. Scholars have frequently failed to do so, and this has led to a great number of semantic antinomies that were not recognized as such and therefore became, often enough, the cause of premature or totally false identifications.

Sociological methods. For the examination of symbolic forms of a nonlinguistic nature, the methods of sociology are the most effective. Of such nonlinguistic forms, the most important are, of course, rites. Much would suggest that rites were in fact the very earliest forms of religious expression. This article shall here assume stereotypings to be next in importance, forms that are even more hypothetical and that serve, among other things, as the rationale for institutionalizations. The two scholars who have analyzed these forms most profoundly are Émile Durkheim and Max Weber, and this article shall draw on their findings. In so doing their identifications are accepted, by and large, though not their theories regarding the ultimate origin of religion(s).

Neither Durkheim's nor Weber's method is correct in itself, but together they may well be so. Durkheim's idea that, in contrast to individual reality, society is of the nature of a thing, and Weber's idea that social reality is made up of continuous human action, inclusive of theorizing, are complementary. It is true of both, as for most of the other sociological approaches, that they strive to work with pure designations, but that these are also more or less stamped by metalanguage usage and by concepts from classical and church tradition. This often tends to compromise the accuracy of translation from native languages; but, on the other hand, this is what permits at least an approximate understanding of unfamiliar terms.

The nature of the sacred and profane in the objectivity of social reality. In *The Elementary Forms of the Religious Life* (New York, 1915), Émile Durkheim points out that all religious beliefs share one characteristic in common. They presuppose, he notes,

> a classification of all things, real and ideal, of which men think, into two classes or opposed groups, generally designated by two distinct terms which are translated well enough by the words *profane* and *sacred* (*profane, sacré*). . . . By sacred things one must not understand simply those personal beings which are called gods or spirits; a rock, a tree, a spring, a pebble, a piece of wood, a house, in a word, anything can be sacred. A rite can have this character; in fact, the rite does not exist which does not have it to a certain degree. . . . The circle of sacred objects cannot be determined, then, once for all. Its extent varies infinitely, according to the different religions. . . . We must now show by what general characteristics they are to be distinguished from profane things. One might be tempted, first of all, to define them by the place they are generally assigned in the hierarchy of things. They are naturally considered superior in dignity and power to profane things. . . . It is not enough that one thing be subordinated to another for the second to be sacred in regard to the first. . . . On the other hand, it must not be lost to view that there are sacred things of every degree. . . . But if a purely hierarchic distinction is a criterium at once too general and too imprecise, there is nothing left with which to characterize the sacred in its relation to the profane except their heterogeneity. However, this heterogeneity is sufficient to characterize this classification of things and to distinguish it from all others, because it is very particular: *it is absolute.* In all the history of human thought there exists no other example of two categories of things so profoundly differentiated or so radically opposed to one another. The traditional opposition of good and bad is nothing beside this. . . . In different religions, this opposition has been conceived in different ways. Here, to separate these two sorts of things, it has seemed sufficient to localize them in different parts of the physical universe; there, the first have been put into an ideal and transcendental world, while the material world is left in possession of the others. But howsoever much the forms of the contrast may vary, the fact of contrast is universal. (pp. 52–54)

These words express the most strictly sociological theory of all those that have been advanced regarding the concept of the sacred and the profane. Durkheim argues that it is society that continuously creates sacred things. The things in which it chooses to discover its principal aspirations, by which it is moved, and the means employed to satisfy such aspirations—these it sets apart and deifies, be they men, objects, or ideas. If an idea is unanimously shared by a people, it cannot be negated or disputed. This very prohibition proves that one stands in the presence of something sacred. With prohibitions of this kind, cast in the form of negative rites, humanity rids itself of certain things that thereby become profane, and approaches the sacred. By means of ritual deprivations such as fasts, wakes, seclusion, and silence, one attains the same results as those brought about through anointings, propitiatory sacrifice, and consecrations. The moment the sacred detaches itself from the profane in this way, religion is born. The most primitive system of sacred things is totemism. But the totem is not the only thing that is sacred; all things that are classified in the clan have the same quality, inasmuch as they belong to the same type. The classifications that link them to other things in the universe allot them their place in the religious system. The idea of class is construed by men themselves as an instrument of thought; for again it was society that furnished the basic pattern logical thought has employed. Nonetheless, totemism is not merely some crude, mistaken pre-religious science, as James G. Frazer supposed; for the basic distinction that is of supreme importance is that between sacred and profane, and it is accomplished with the aid of the totem, which is a collective symbol of a religious nature, as well as a sacred thing in itself. Nor does a thing become sacred by virtue of its links through classification to the universe; a world of profane things is still profane even though it is spatially and temporally infinite. A thing becomes sacred when humans remove it from ordinary use; the negative cult in which this happens leads to taboo. A person becomes sacred through initiation. Certain foodstuffs can be forbidden to the person who is still profane because they are sacred, and others can be forbidden to the holy person because they are profane. Violation of such taboos amounts to desecration, or profanation, of the foodstuffs in the one case, of the person in the other, and profanation of this kind can result in sickness and death. In the holy ones—that is to say, both the creatures of the totem species and the members of the clan—a society venerates itself.

The meaning of sacred and profane in the context of subjective religious action. Max Weber states in *Wirtschaft und Gesellschaft* (Tübingen, 1922) that the focus for sociology is the "meaning context" of an act. In order to interpret an act with understanding, the sociologist

> has to view [social] structures as simply the consequences and connections of specific action on the part of *individual* persons, since for us these are the only representatives of meaningful action we can comprehend. . . . Interpretation of any action has to take notice of the fundamentally important fact that [the] collective structures . . . belonging to everyday thought are *conceptions* of something in part existing, in part desired to be true in the minds of actual persons

> . . . conceptions on which they *base* their actions; and that as such they have a most powerful, often virtually dominating causal significance for the manner in which actual persons conduct themselves. (pp. 6–7)

The same also applies to religiously (or magically) motivated communal action, which can only be comprehended from the point of view of the subjective experiences, conceptions, and goals of the individual, that is, from the point of view of its meaning. According to Weber, such action is at bottom oriented to the here and now. It gradually attains a wealth of meanings, ultimately even symbolic ones. Trial and adherence to what has been tried are of particular importance, since deviation can render an action ineffective. For this reason, religions are more tolerant of opposing dogmatic concepts than they are of innovations in their symbolism, which could endanger the magical effect of their actions or rouse the anger of the ancestral soul or the god. Hence there is encountered in all cultures religious stereotyping, in rites, in art, in gestures, dance, music, and writing, in exorcism and medicine. The sacred thus becomes specifically what is unchangeable. By virtue of it, religious concepts also tend to force stereotypes upon behavior and economics. Any actions intended to introduce change have to be correspondingly binding. The ones most likely to fulfill this requirement are specific contracts. The Roman civil marriage in the form of *coemtio* was, for example, a profanation of the sacramental *confarreatio.*

Anthropological methods. At times humans reveal themselves in situations that appear to be of a different quality than ordinary ones. The latter form the basis for comparison either as the sum of their normal behavior or as a social cross section. For the moment, comparisons demonstrating the specific differences between a possibly sacred condition and a profane one, or showing social appraisal of a specific human type as sacred in contrast to the profane average person, are best relegated to categories of a historical anthropology, for as yet no historical psychology exists that might penetrate still further. A culture may choose to identify any number of unusual individual conditions or situations as sacred or profane. The most important of these warrant closer examination.

Ecstasy and trance. Even in terms of ethology, one could probably establish a similarity between humans and animals in the way they concentrate on an opponent, holding their breath in silence and maintaining a tense calm from which they can instantly switch into motion. Presumably this has its roots in the moment when the first hunter found himself confronting his prey. As far as humans are concerned, the perpetuation and further development of this primeval behavior is a history of self-interpretations that presuppose continuously changing social contexts. This was probably first apparent in shamanism, and continues to be so wherever it persists. Contributing to the Greek concept of *ekstasis* was the idea that man is capable of "standing outside himself." Specifically, from the fifth century BCE on, it was believed that one could physically step out of one's normal state; and from the first century BCE, that one's essential being, the soul, the self or perceiving organ, could take leave of the body. The notion of ecstasy is found throughout the history of the human psyche and human culture. It may seize a person for no apparent reason or be induced through meditation, autohypnosis, fasting, drugs, fixing the eyes on specific objects, or extended ritual repetition of certain words or motions. Ecstasy is not necessarily sacred; it can also be profane, though quite often specific manifestations, such as intoxication, glossolalia, receptivity to visions and voices, hyperesthesia, anesthesia, or paresthesia, are identical. In technologically poor cultures, profane ecstasies may accompany initiations, rites of passage, and preparation for war, or may be reactions to specific defeats or social setbacks. Examples of profane ecstasies in literary cultures are those of the Corybantes and Maenads of Greece, of the dancers and flagellants who appeared in the wake of the Black Death in the fourteenth century, of Shakers and Quakers, of individual psychopaths, and of social outcasts. Ecstasy is only sacred in the context of historical religion and is never the primal germ of any religion. Nevertheless, ecstasy can be experienced within a religion as the basic source of its particular variety of mysticism.

It then passes over into trance, of which possession has already been recognized as the hyperkinetic primal form. When the being by which one is possessed, or—to put it more mildly—inspired, is held to be a god who has replaced the extinguished consciousness, classical Greek already spoke of *enthousiasmos.* By definition, such possession is sacred. Profane trances, on the other hand, are those accompanied by visions of distant events, or past or future ones.

Sexuality and asceticism. Sex, especially female sexuality, is considered sacred. It stands as the positive condition contrary to both infertility and asexuality. If a woman was infertile, it probably meant above all that she was malnourished, and starvation is always profane when not undertaken in deliberate fasts as a means of conquering the physical self. (The sacredness of the mother must certainly have been enhanced when, in the Neolithic period, agriculture was first developed—a new science made possible by Mother Earth.)

Sexuality, especially active sex, is also held to be the contrary of asexuality, the profane sign either of the normal condition of both sexes as the result of danger, cold, or constant labor, or of the lesser capacity for frequent orgasm on the part of the male.

The importance in archaic societies of dominant goddesses, especially mother goddesses, is solely dependent on the sacredness of their sexuality and is not a result of their given character as either the otherworldly representatives of matriarchal societies or the polar referents in patriarchal ones. From the role of a great goddess alone it is impossible to draw any conclusions about a given social order. Such goddesses are frequently of a dual nature, both helpful and cruel, both givers and destroyers of life, and this ambiguity is altogether a part of their sacredness.

Asceticism is not the profanation of sexuality but rather a transcendence over the normal human condition into a perfection that lies in the opposite direction. The ascetic practices self-denial with regard to all aspects of life, including eating and drinking. In suppressing his sexuality, he is to a certain extent both acknowledging its sacred dimension and claiming that sacredness for himself.

Innocence and wisdom. Since Vergil's fourth *Eclogue,* perhaps since the prophecies of Isaiah, or even earlier, the innocence of the messianic child has been seen as sacred. Mere babbling childishness, on the other hand, is profane. Yet one can hardly conclude from the innocence of the messianic child how sinful or jaded the society that hopes for him actually considers itself.

Wisdom can be the sacredness of old age, as in the case of the Hindu guru, the mystagogue of late antiquity, or the *tsaddiq* in Jewish Hasidism, who only after long experience is able, through their own example, to help their fellow people find communion with God. Feebleness on the part of the elderly is widely considered to be profane, and when it poses a burden on the young they tend to segregate themselves from it socially. In extreme cases the old are sent off into the wilderness, as in some cultures of ancient India, or are left behind in an abandoned campsite, a practice of some nomadic peoples. The aged exile only avoids being profane by seeking his own salvation, and that of the others, through a curse, rather than through wisdom.

Charismatic and magical gifts. The relationship between these is complex, especially since subsequent explanation of a magical or miraculous act frequently shifts the accent or undertakes to reevaluate it, and since modern interpretation is bound to suspect an element of trickery in the majority of miracles.

A miracle worker was often thought of as a sacred person, as were Origen's pupil Gregory Theodoros of Sykeon and others who were given the epithet *Thaumaturgus.* But not all of the figures canonized as saints by the Catholic Church, for example, were miracle workers—unless, of course, one considers it miraculous that anyone could have fulfilled absolutely the commandment to love God, his neighbor, and his enemy. Conversely, it is also possible for a miracle worker *not* to be recognized as a saint or be held to have been so according to religious scholarship—as were Jean-Baptiste-Marie Vianney and Giovanni Melchior Bosco—and still not count as a charlatan like Cagliostro or Rasputin (who were, in fact, probably neither totally profane nor demonic). Here profaneness is easier to define: That person is profane who is simply incapable of controlling sicknesses, natural forces, or his or her own feelings of animosity. One also hears of "false prophets," as, for example, in ancient Israel or in Lucian's satire on the pseudoprophet Alexander—though it cannot be discerned whether these were simply instances of certain holy people winning out over others. In late antiquity it was possible for charismatic persons to rise to "sainthood," for better or for worse, by taking over the control of cities or towns in which the elected administration or leading landholders had been rendered powerless by social or religious upheavals (see Brown, 1982). Similarly, magic can be either sacred or profane, as can seen if it is examined from the perspective of history.

Sacred and Profane History. Related to the anthropological approach is the historical. In terms of history, qualities of objects, modes of conduct, events, relationships, and persons in part define themselves as sacred or profane, and insofar as they do one may either accept them or criticize them. In part, however, it is up to the scholar to establish and define them. In either case it is quite possible that the sacred is truly metaphysical, eternal, and transhistorical and manifests itself only fragmentarily and partially in a continuing succession of historical objects. It is equally possible in either case that the sacred is constantly forming itself anew out of certain symbol-making forces inherent in the historical processes, by transcending even the objectifications of such forces.

In the history of religions there are numerous examples of belated creation of the sacred out of the profane. The sacred may initially have been only a catchall concept for specific desires and may have later become genuine; or it may have come into being by means of true consecration, or sanctification, in both senses of the term, as have been identified above. One thinks, for example, of the sanctification of actions that were originally only ethical, of the evolution of the gift (Marcel Mauss's term) into the offering, of the emergence of gods from humans by way of the intermediate stage of the hero, and so forth.

Related to this is the problem of whether the sacred and profane should be viewed as having come into being simultaneously, or one before the other. All three possible theories have been advanced. Unfortunately, however, the findings of religious phenomenology and the history of religions permit no sure pronouncements about the very earliest religious manifestations. Even the basic assumption that religion came into being along with the appearance of man, though most likely correct, provides no solution to the problem of priority. For even if one makes such an assumption, one still cannot know whether religion once encompassed the whole of life, or whether there was not from the very beginning a profane worldview alongside the religious one, with its knowledge of the sacred.

Origins. The sacred may be an integral part of religion, but when studying its history it is necessary to treat it as quite independent. According to one possible view, the sacred and the profane came into being simultaneously. Another theory has it that the sacred was a later elevation of the profane. Still a third presupposes a kind of primal pansacrality, claiming that the sacred was once a totality that encompassed or unified the entire world. Even the magical was not yet detached from it. And the profane, whether magical or not, only gradually developed through a kind of primal secularization.

The primal polarity and homogeneity of the sacred and profane. For this thesis one can point to caves and grottoes from the middle Paleolithic (the Drachenloch and the Wildenmannlisloch in the Swiss canton of Saint Gall; Petershöhle in Middle Franconia, in Germany), others from the late Paleolithic (Altamira, Lascaux, Trois Frères, Rouffignac), and numerous Neolithic ones. Their special nature fulfills only the two criteria for holiness: (*a*) spatial detachment from the settings of everyday life and (*b*) unusualness; but these are sufficient to justify calling them sanctuaries. These caves are difficult to reach, they are located either at a great height or far below the surface, access to them is either narrow or hard to find, and they are too low or too dark for everyday activities. They contain artworks sequestered away from day-to-day viewing as well as deposits of bones and skulls that cannot be merely the remains of meals. These facts indicate that here, in addition to the profane area (namely, the sitting, sleeping, and eating space near the cave entrance), there was also a sacred room. The question of whether the deposits were offerings or not, and whether they were meant for a single god or several, remains unanswered. But it is virtually certain that the caves were used for sacred activities, in many cases for initiation rites. Entering them, one proceeded out of the *profanum* into the *sacrum.* It is not known what other relationships may have been maintained between these two, but it is clear that they did exist side by side. It is then altogether probable that each had come into being as distinct from the other, and that at no earlier date did the two occupy a single space that was predominantly only one or the other.

The priority and homogeneity of the profane and subsequent appearance and heterogeneity of the sacred. This thesis accords with the one that supposes that there was once a time when humankind was as yet without religion. It is based primarily on ethnological theories, and in part also on psychoanalytical ones. It claims, with James G. Frazer, that magic as a prescientific science proved wanting, and humans therefore had to seek refuge in religion.

In the formula of dogmatic Marxism, the primeval human's social existence was so primitive that his or her consciousness was wholly absorbed with practical matters and was incapable of giving birth to religious abstractions. Only when magic became necessary to assist in the attainment of food through hunting and agriculture did religion evolve along with it, and its function was then further bolstered by the appearance of hierarchical social structures.

According to Wilhelm Wundt and others, the sacred had its origins in notions of impurity. Taboo, the instilling of a reluctance to touch, was common to both (and still continues to be so), whereas the everyday sphere is profane and pure. At some point this reluctance entered the religious sphere and split into awe in the presence of the sacred and loathing for the demonic; everything that was displeasing to the sacred deity was now held to be impure, that is, profane, and the sacred was pure. Gradually, the impure has come to function as the opposite of the sacred, and between the two lie the pure and the ordinary—now seen as profane, that is, as the realm of what is permissible.

In Freud's view, the central taboo is the one against incest; it derives from the will of the primal father. After he has been killed, one's relationship to him becomes ambivalent and finds its synthesis in the idea of sacredness. The reason behind his murder is the primal father's castration of his sons, which is replaced symbolically by circumcision. It is the circumcision performed on the male progeny of Israel, for example, that represents the actual sanctification of that people.

René Girard argues that the sacred arose out of sacrifice, which, as the ultimate form of killing and bloodletting, brings to an end the chain of force and counterforce that constitutes the profane history of humankind. Since the ultimate use of force that cancels out everything can no longer be arbitrary, it comes to be circumscribed and restrained through rituals. Once the resultant sacred act is correctly identified as such and distinguished from profane action, the roles of the sacred and profane in society are truly segregated. If the sacred and the profane come to be indistinguishable, a sacrificial crisis ensues; this is at the same time a confusion of roles and brings on a social crisis. The force required to restore stability is applied both by individuals and by the collective: by individuals in the form of asceticism, self-discipline, and other actions against the self, through which they attain sacredness; and by the collective, through deflection onto a scapegoat, which protects society from the threat that groups within it will destroy each other. (See Girard, [1972] 1977.)

Some of these theses can point to changes that have actually occurred in the relationship between the sacred and profane through the course of history, and even Freud's theory, though otherwise impossible, contains an element of truth in the fact that the exercise of religion can actually become a compulsive act. Girard's thesis is doubtless the most realistic in its incorporation of the nature of man, and the nature of his socialization, within the primary constitution of sacrifice (to the extent to which the latter exists at all). But none of this is of any use toward a valid reconstruction of prehistory.

The priority and homogeneity of the sacred and heterogeneity of the profane. All of the things now distinguished as religion, magic, and science; as religious worship, sorcery, and medicine; as prophecy, law-giving, and ethics; and as priests, kings, and shamans, were once united in a sacral unity. Such is the widespread, fundamental view derived from the thesis of a primal monotheism, as propounded by thinkers from Andrew Lang to Wilhelm Schmidt; derived, too, from the theologoumena of a primal revelation advanced by Johann Tobias Beck and Adolf Schlatter, the elements of E. B. Tylor's animism theory, the *mana-orenda* identification from the period between R. H. Codrington and Gerardus van der Leeuw, and the preanimism or dynamism theory promulgated from R. R. Marett to Konrad T.

Preuss. One can say that the profane becoming independent is the result of a process of differentiation out of primal sacrality only if one ignores the synonymity between the very definition of the sacred and the naming of the phenomena on which these theories are based.

Temporal existence. Since it is impossible to verify any theory of origins or development, it is advisable to do without one altogether, and to adopt the approach of Mircea Eliade, who for historical consideration sees the sacred as an element in the structure of consciousness, rather than as a stage in the history of its development. Regardless of the similarity of religious phenomena throughout cultures, it is the cultural-historical context that at the same time lends an immeasurable novelty to their various manifestations. As for the phenomena of the sacred and the profane, the following temporal aspects are of fundamental importance.

Unchangeableness. The sacred is absolutely unchangeable only if one has extrahistorical reasons for treating it as a metaphysical, eternal, or transhistorical reality. As understood by Max Weber, it is not unchangeable. On the historical plane, unchangeableness and constancy are evident to the degree that in everything that the religious phenomenologies identify as sacred—persons, communities, actions, writings, manifestations of nature, manufactured objects, periods, places, numbers, and formulas—not only are situations, motive, and conditions expressed, but an ancient type remains operative, or makes a reappearance. Once delineated, such types can reappear at any moment, and they persist through great periods of time. Notwithstanding, genuine changes also take place.

Metamorphoses. These appear as either transcendence over the profane or secularization—now no longer considered primary, as it was above—of the sacred. The former occurs in initiations, sacraments, and baptisms, in the use of stones for shrines or of animals as offerings, in the blessing of an object, an act, or a person. The latter is evident on a large scale in world-historical processes. On a small scale it is present whenever a sacred function is simulated, when a myth is transformed from the fact that it *is* into a reporting of facts, when a sacred text is read for entertainment, or whenever someone's behavior swerves from his vows to God, without his actually sinning. The ultimate form of secularization is the destruction of the sacred while the profane continues to exist; the greatest possible transcendence is the restitution of the sacred together with a fundamental skepticism regarding the profane.

Destruction. The destruction of religion is not the same thing as the destruction of the sacred. The destruction of a religion occurs most clearly when it is confined to institutions, as these can simply be abolished. It is less apparent when a religion ceases to have its original function, but this too can finally be ascertained. The sacred, on the other hand, increasingly tends, in industrial society, to be transformed from the active element it once was into a kind of unexpressed potentiality. It then decays in social intercourse and such intercourse becomes wholly profane. Nevertheless, its archetype persists in the human spirit, and is always capable of restoring the religious feeling to consciousness, if conditions are favorable.

Just what sort of conditions these have to be, no one can say. It may be that they are altogether unfavorable when a civil religion is established of the type envisioned by Jean-Jacques Rousseau at the end of his *Social Contract;* it may also be that they are indeed favorable when no organized religion continues to play any role.

Restoration. It is possible to try to secure once more the place for the sacred in society that it lost thanks to the disappearance of the distinction between it and the profane that once existed. This is what motivates the scholarship of the Collège de Sociologie. Every community that is intact and wishes to remain so requires a notion of the sacred as *a priori.* Archaic societies that provided sufficient room for the sacred kept it socially viable in secret fraternities or through magicians or shamans. Modern societies can achieve the same by means of public events such as festivals, which generate social strength, or by the establishment of monastic, elitist orders, or the creation of new centers of authority.

DETERMINING THE RELATIONSHIPS. The relationships between the sacred and the profane occur both on the level of their expression in language and on a (or *the*) level of existence that is characterized by various different ontological qualities. The relationships between these two levels themselves are of a more fundamental nature. Since only the *homo religiosus* is capable of bearing witness to the manner of such existence, and not the scholar, one can speak of it only in formal categories that reveal both the conditions of one's possible perception of the sacred and the transcendental prerequisites of its mode of being.

The epistemological approach. Non-Kantian religious thinkers and scholars have always restricted themselves to their inner experience. What they have found there could easily be rediscovered in history. The experiential method, which tends toward psychology, was therefore always superbly compatible with the historical-genetic method. On the other hand, it is also possible to apply a logical, analytical, transcendental method, and in fact this can be used in investigating the possibilities of both inner experience and historical perception. Heretofore, discussion of these alternatives has been most productive toward determining the position of the philosophy of religion, and therefore religion itself, within the overall scheme of culture and scholarship. At the same time, it has tended to curtail any elucidation of the religious phenomenon in general and the phenomenon of the sacred and its relation to the profane in particular. Perhaps one could take it further.

A priori and a posteriori. In his book *Kantisch-Fries'sche Religionsphilosophie und ihre Anwendung auf die Theologie* (Tübingen, 1909), Rudolf Otto took a rational approach to the *a priori* concept and applied it to the idea of God. God is not an object alongside or superior to other objects, and he cannot be placed in one of the various standard relationships. He is able to transcend space and time as well as every particular relationship. Accordingly, it must be possible to imagine the sacred as standing in a transcendental primal relationship to things. One way or the other, the *a priori* concept is rational.

Rationality and irrationality. When writing *Das Heilige* (1917), Otto abandoned his transcendental philosophical position. He did not give up the *a priori* concept, however, but rather reinterpreted it with a psychological slant. In this way, the transcendentality of the rational applied to the *a priori* concept becomes the capacity of thought to be rational. This capacity can then be opposed to the irrational. The rational concepts of absoluteness, necessity, and essential quality, as well as the idea of the good, which expresses an objective and binding value, have to be traced back to whatever lies in pure reason, independent of experience, whereas the irrational element of the sacred must be traced back to the pure ideas of the divine or the numinous. Here, from the point of view of irrationality, "pure" becomes the attribute of something psychically given, and the *a priori* becomes emotional.

On the other hand, as Anders Nygren argues, just as one questions the validity of perception, using the *a priori* of cognition theory, it becomes necessary to question the validity of religion, using the religious *a priori* concept. Further, Nygren and Friedrich Karl Feigel suggest, it becomes necessary to comprehend the sacred as a complex category *a priori*, not so as to be able to experience it in itself, but rather so as to identify the sacred in experience and cognition, even in the course of history.

The ontological approach. Links exist not only between the sacred and the profane, each of which has its own complexity, but also between the sacred and the demonic, the profane and the evil, the profane and the demonic, and the sacred and the evil. The first and second links have ontological implications, the third and fourth have ethical ones, and the fifth has both. One obscures the demonic aspect when one asks the question whether one can have an ethic that can deal with the awesome potential powers at modern humanity's disposal without restoring the category of the sacred, which was thoroughly destroyed by the Enlightenment. In Hans Jonas's view, these powers continue to accumulate in secret and impel humankind to use them, and only respectful awe in the face of the sacred can transcend calculations of earthly terror. But it is not the task of this article to enter into a discussion of ethical implications; the reader must be content to consider the ontological ones.

Ambivalence. Otto described the positive aspect of the sacred by using the numinous factor *fascinans* and various subordinate factors of the numinous factor *tremendum.* He characterized its negative aspect by way of a subordinate factor of the latter that he called "the awesome." In so doing he provided countless studies with the suggestion of an ambivalence that truly exists and is not to be confused with the dialectic of the hierophanies. However, Otto was referring primarily to the essence of the sacred in itself. Such an approach is logically possible only if one begins consistently and exclusively from "above." Since Otto declares both aspects to be factors of the same numinousness, his methodological starting point becomes, *de facto,* if not intentionally, Judeo-Christian theocentricity. This is certainly extremely productive, but it also exhibits one of the limits of scholarly study of religion: namely its continual orientation, only seeming to overcome the theological *a priori,* at the starting point of historical scholarship, namely recognition of the ambivalence in the ancient Roman notion of the *sacrum.*

Dialectics. Eliade has concentrated the links between the complexes of the sacred and the profane on the plane of appearances, introducing the inspired concept of hierophany. A hierophany exposes the sacred in the profane. Since there are numerous hierophanies (though the same ones do not always appear everywhere), he sets up a dialectic of hierophanies to explain why an object or an occurrence may be sacred at one moment but not at another. Such an approach makes it possible to examine every historical datum and identify it as sacred or profane—and in so doing to write a new history of religions within profane history. In addition, one can draw conclusions about the objectivity of the sacred, which is satiated with being and therefore has the power, functioning through the hierophanies (including even their profane element), to become apparent. Eliade does both. The former demonstrates a historical phenomenology, and points toward an as yet unrealized historical psychology of religion. The latter is subject to the same criticism as the ontological proof of God.

IDEOGRAMMATICS AND HERMENEUTICS. The sacred remains closely bound to the modalities of its names. One cannot do without the testimony revealed in language, but one must not restrict the sacred to the terms language provides. In addition to such testimony, one has to discover the sacred in experience. The sum of linguistic testimony and descriptions of such experience can serve both as a check on each other and as mutual confirmation.

Deciphering the sacred. Using this approach, one can only speak of the sacred ideogrammatically. Classical phenomenology of religion is content to present the sacred as revealed in so-called phenomena that corroborate each other within a larger context. However, this kind of evidence obscures the ambivalence that permits one to experience a sacred phenomenon simultaneously with a profane one. Therefore, one can only understand the phenomenon of the sacred, whether evidenced with the aid of language or writing or not, as something like the Greek *idea,* and accordingly regard the forms of the sacred accessible to description and investigation as its ideograms. However, these can also be understood as "tautograms," that is, as designations that withhold immanence, but at the same time one cannot call them profane merely because they lack the connotation of transcendence into the sacred. Otto's book on the holy was already in large part an ideogrammatics of the sacred.

Understanding the sacred. At the heart of the findings from the study of synonyms that have provided reasons for speaking of both the sacred and the profane in the singular are certain basic attributes, such as separateness, power, intensity, remoteness, and otherness. Cognition theory has less difficulty identifying the sacred when it examines larger systems, within which such fundamental attributes are mutually complementary. In doing so, one cannot only recognize the ideograms of the sacred in texts but also treat the sacred as though it were explained. Eliade's work represents just such a hermeneutics of the sacred as distinguished from the profane.

See Also Hierophany; Holy, Idea of the; Purification; Sacred Space; Sacred Time; Secularization.

Bibliography

The most influential modern book on the subject is Rudolf Otto's *Das Heilige* (Breslau, 1917; often reprinted), translated by John W. Harvey as *The Idea of the Holy* (Oxford, 1923). The most important earlier contributions (Wilhelm Windelband, Wilhelm Wundt, Nathan Söderblom), subsequent ones (Joseph Geyser, Friedrich Karl Feigel, Walter Baetke, et al.), and various specific philological studies are collected in *Die Diskussion um das Heilige,* edited by Carsten Colpe (Darmstadt, 1977). A new epoch began with the work of Mircea Eliade, and one could cite a great number of monographs by him. As the most relevant, one might single out his *Traité d'histoire des religions* (Paris, 1949), translated by Rosemary Sheed as *Patterns in Comparative Religion* (New York, 1958), and *Das Heilige und das Profane* (Hamburg, 1957), translated by Willard R. Trask as *The Sacred and the Profane* (New York, 1959).

Hans Joachim Greschat has provided a study of the classical late nineteenth-century theme in his *Mana und Tapu* (Berlin, 1980). Examples from an African people are provided by Peter Fuchs in *Kult und Autorität: Die Religion der Hadjerai* (Berlin, 1970) and by Jeanne-Françoise Vincent in *Le pouvoir et le sacré chez les Hadjeray du Tchad* (Paris, 1975). Exemplary philological investigation of linguistic usage and concepts among the Greeks, Romans, Jews, and early Christians is found in the article "Heilig" by Albrecht Dihle in the *Reallexikon für Antike und Christentum,* vol. 13 (Stuttgart, 1987); similar study of late antiquity appears in Peter Brown's *Society and the Holy in Late Antiquity* (London, 1982). The same subject matter, expanded to include the ancient Orient and India, is found in the important work edited by Julien Ries et al., *L'expression du sacré dans les grandes religions,* 3 vols., (Louvain, 1978–1986), for which there is a separate introduction by Julien Ries, *Le sacré comme approche de Dieu et comme ressource de l'homme* (Louvain, 1983). Supplementing this with respect to Egypt is James Karl Hoffmeier's *"Sacred" in the Vocabulary of Ancient Egypt: The Term DSR, with Special Reference to Dynasties I–XX* (Freiburg, 1985).

Theoretical implications are investigated by Ansgar Paus in *Religiöser Erkenntnisgrund: Herkunft und Wesen der Apriori-Theorie Rudolf Ottos* (Leiden, 1966) and by Georg Schmid in *Interessant und Heilig: Auf dem Wege zur integralen Religions-wissenschaft* (Zurich, 1971). Important sociological investigation of ritual is found in Jean Cazeneuve's *Sociologie du rite* (Paris, 1971) and of the history of force, counterforce, and sacrifice in René Girard's *La violence et le sacré* (Paris, 1972), translated by Patrick Gregory as *Violence and the Sacred* (Baltimore, 1977). Additional ethical implications are considered by Bernhard Häring in *Das Heilige und das Gute, Religion und Sittlichkeit in ihrem gegenseitigen Bezug* (Krailling vor München, 1950). On the disappearance of the sacred through secularization and its reappearance in times of crisis, see Enrico Castelli's *Il tempo inqualificabile: Contributi all'ermeneutica della secolarizzazione* (Padua, 1975) and Franco Ferrarotti and others' *Forme del sacro in un'epoca di crisi* (Naples, 1978). Summaries from various points of view include Roger Caillois's *L'homme et le sacré* (1939; 3d ed., Paris, 1963), translated by Meyer Barash as *Man and the Sacred* (Glencoe, Ill., 1959); Jacques Grand'Maison's *Le monde et le sacré,* 2 vols. (Paris, 1966–1968); and Enrico Castelli and others' *Il sacro* (Padua, 1974).

New Sources

Anttonen, Veikko. "Sacred." In *Guide to the Study of Religions* edited by Willi Braun and Russell T. McCutcheon, pp. 271–282. London and New York, 2000. An attempt to connect the cognitive and the cultural.

Borgeaud, Philippe. "Le couple sacré/prophane. Genèse et fortune d'un concept 'opératoire' en histoire des religions." *Revue de l'histoire des religions* 211, no. 4 (1994): 387–418. Important novel assessment by an historian of religions.

Cazelles, Henri. "Sacré et sainteté dans l'Ancien Testament." In *Dictionnaire de la Bible. Supplément 10,* pp. 1393–1432. Paris, 1985.

Colpe, Carsten. *Über das Heilige.* Frankfurt am Main, 1990. The idea of holy in philosophy and in today's world.

Colpe, Carsten. "Heilig (sprachlich)" and "Das Heiliege." In *Handbuch religionswissenschaftlicher Grundbefriffe,* vol. 3, edited by H. Cancik, B. Gladigow and K.-H. Kohl. Stuttgart, 1993. The definitive synthetic appraisal by the foremost scholar of the sacred.

Courtas R., and F. A. Isambert. "La notion de 'sacré'. Bibliographie thématique." *Archives de sciences sociales des religions* 22 (1977): 119–138.

Idinopulos, Thomas A., and Eward A. Yonan. *The Sacred and its Scholars: Comparative Methodologies for the Study of Primary Religious Data.* Leiden, 1996. Historiographical, methodological and idiographic studies in a cross-disciplinary perspective. Select bibliography.

Mol, Hans J. *Identity and the Sacred.* Oxford, 1976. The sacred in social scientific perspective.

Morani, Moreno. "Lat. *sacer* e il rapporto uomo-dio nel lessico religioso latino." *Aevum* 55 (1981): 30–46.

Morani, Moreno. "Le parole del 'sacro in Grecia." In *Atti del secondo incontro internazionale di linguistica greca,* edited by Emanuele Banfi, pp. 175–193. Trento, Italy, 1997.

Morani, Moreno. "La terminologia del 'sacro' in lingue indoeuropee antiche: riflessioni e problemi." In *Pensiero e istituzioni del mondo classico nelle culture del Vicino Oriente,* edited by R. Bianca Finazzi and A. Valvo, pp. 165–196. Alessandria, Italy, 2001. A novel assessment of this issue in historical-linguistic perspective.

Ries, Julien. "Sacré." In *Dictionnaire des religions*, 3d ed., Paris, 1993. A remarkable synthesis with an account of the historiographical debate.

Santi, Claudia. *Alle radici del sacro. Lessico e formule di Roma antica.* Rome, 2004. A refreshingly novel approach to the issue of the relationship sacer / sanctus in its ancient Roman background. Extensive bibliography.

Schilling, Robert. "Sacrum et profanum. Essay d' interprétation." *Latomus* 30 (1971): 953–969. A classical study by a distinguished scholar of Roman religion.

Segal, Robert A., et al. "Symposium on the Sacred." *Method and Theory in the Study of Religion* 3 (1991): 1–46. Methodological.

Webb, Eugene. *The Dark Dove: The Sacred and Secular in Modern Literature.* Seattle, 1975. The author is an expert in both comparative literature and comparative religion.

York, Michael. "Toward a Proto-Indo-European Vocabulary of the Sacred." *Word* 44 (1993): 235–254.

CARSTEN COLPE (1987)
Translated from German by Russell M. Stockman
Revised Bibliography

SACRED SPACE. A sacred place is first of all a defined place, a space distinguished from other spaces. The rituals that a people either practice at a place or direct toward it mark its sacredness and differentiate it from other defined spaces. To understand the character of such places, Jonathan Z. Smith has suggested the helpful metaphor of sacred space as a "focusing lens." A sacred place focuses attention on the forms, objects, and actions in it and reveals them as bearers of religious meaning. These symbols describe the fundamental constituents of reality as a religious community perceives them, defines a life in accordance with that view, and provides a means of access between the human world and divine realities.

As meaningful space, sacred space encompasses a wide variety of very different kinds of places. It includes places that are constructed for religious purposes, such as temples or *temenoi,* and places that are religiously interpreted, such as mountains or rivers. It includes spaces that can be entered physically, as the outer geography of a holy land, imaginatively, as the inner geography of the body in Tantric yoga, or visually, as the space of a *maṇḍala.* Sacred space does not even exclude nonsacred space, for the same place may be both sacred and nonsacred in different respects or circumstances. In traditional Maori culture, for example, the latrine marks the boundary between the world of the living and that of the dead. As such, it is the ritual place at which an unwanted spirit can be expelled or the help of the spirits obtained. Therefore, it is sacred. And it is still a latrine. Similarly, a house is a functional space, but in its construction, its design, or the rites within it, it may be endowed with religious meaning. A shrine that is the focus of religious activity on certain occasions may be ignored at other times. In short, a sacred place comes into being when it is interpreted as a sacred place.

This view of sacred space as a lens for meaning implies that places are sacred because they perform a religious function, not because they have peculiar physical or aesthetic qualities. The tradition articulated by Friedrich Schleiermacher and developed by Rudolf Otto links the perception of holiness to religious emotion. Originally or authentically, therefore, sacred places ought to have had the power to evoke an affective response. And many sacred places do precisely that: The sacred mountains of China, the Gothic cathedrals of Europe, and the sources and the estuaries of India's holy rivers have a beauty and a power that are elements of their religious dimension. But such qualities of place are not inevitable. Many sacred places, even places that are central in the religious life of the community, are unimpressive to someone outside the tradition. The form of the place, without a knowledge of what and how it signifies, may not convey any religious sense whatever. Ṛddhipur, for example, is the principal pilgrimage place of the Mhānubhāvs, a Kṛṣṇaite Maharashtrian sect. It is the place where God lived in the incarnate form of Guṇḍam Rāül, where he deposited divine power, and where he performed acts that revealed his divine nature. It is the place visited by another divine incarnation, Cakradhar, who founded the Mhānubhāv community. But Ṛddhipur itself is completely unexceptional, and the places where Guṇḍam Rāül performed his deeds are indicated only by small stone markers. There is nothing there that gives rise to a sense of awe or mystery, and yet the village is revered and protected by religious restrictions. The place is not aesthetically profound, but it is nonetheless religiously powerful.

ESTABLISHMENT OF SACRED SPACE. Both the distinctiveness of sacred space and its reference to the ultimate context of a culture are often expressed in the conviction that sacred space is not arbitrary. Objectively, and not only subjectively, a sacred place is different from the surrounding area, for it is not a place of wholly human creation or choice. Rather, its significance is grounded in its unique character, a character that no purely human action can confer on it.

In traditional societies, the whole land of a culture is normally sacred, and this sacredness is often communicated in the narratives of its foundation. Sometimes the land is uniquely created. The *Kojiki* and *Nihongi* record the traditions of the age of the *kami* when Japan and its way of life were established. According to these texts, the divine pair, Izanagi and Izanami, looked down upon the waters of the yet unformed earth and dipped a jeweled spear into the ocean. From the brine that dripped from the spear the first island of Japan was formed. The divine couple later gave birth to other deities, among them the sun goddess, Amaterasu, whose descendants rule over Japan. Thus, Japan is different from all other places: It is the first land, and the land whose way of life is established by the gods. Or a land may become sacred because it is given by a god, like the land of Israel. Or again, a land may be established by ritual. According to an early Indian tradition in the *Śatapatha Brāhmaṇa,* the land lying to the east of the Sadanira River was unfit for habitation by *brahmans.* It became fit when the sacrificial fire was carried across the river and established in the land.

Similarly, a sacred structure or place within a holy land possesses something—a character, a significance, or an object—that sets it apart. The traditions of the greater Hindu temples and pilgrimage places declare that they are intrinsically, not ascriptively, sacred. The holiest images of the Śaiva tradition are the *svayambhūliṅga*s, images of Śiva that are not human creations but self-manifestations of the god. Similarly, the holiest places of the goddess are the *pīṭha*s, the places where the parts of her body fell after her suicide and dismemberment. In other cases, not an object but the very ground itself fixes the worship of a divinity to a particular spot. According to the traditions of the temple at Śrīraṅgam, the shrine originated in heaven. From there it was brought to earth, to the city of Rāma. Rāma then gave it to a pious demon, who wished to take it with him to his home in Sri Lanka. On the way, however, he put it down near a ford on the Kāverī (Cauvery) River, and when he tried to pick it up again he could not move it. The god of the temple then appeared to him and told him that the river had performed austerities to keep the shrine within her bounds and that the god intended to stay there (Shulman, 1980, p. 49). The current location of the temple is therefore where the god, not any demon or human, chose it to be.

The gods may also communicate the special sanctity of a place through signs. Animals often serve as messengers of divine choice. So, for example, the Aztec city of Tenochtitlán was founded at the place where an eagle landed on a blooming cactus, and Aeneas followed a pregnant sow to the place where it farrowed and there founded Alba Longa. The search for such signs could develop into a science of divination. Chinese geomancy is just such an attempt to sort out the objective qualities of a place by studying the contours of the land and the balance of waters, winds, and other elements.

In other cases, a location becomes holy because of religiously significant events that have occurred there. From the time of Muḥammad, Jerusalem has been a holy place for Islam. Although various traditions were attached to the city, it was above all the Prophet's journey there that established its sanctity. One night Muḥammad was brought to Jerusalem and to the rock on the Temple mount, and from there he ascended through the heavens to the very presence of God. The mosque of the Dome of the Rock and the establishment of Jerusalem as a place of pilgrimage both expressed and intensified the sanctity of the city. That sanctity was heightened by the discovery of tokens of Muḥammad's journey: his footprints on the rock, the imprint made by his saddle, and even the place where the angel Gabriel flattened the rock before the Prophet's ascent. And it was further intensified by bringing other religiously significant events into connection with it. The stories of Abraham and Isaac, of Melchizedek, king of Salem, and of Jacob's ladder were among the other biblical and nonbiblical narratives set there. As this example illustrates, a sacred place can draw a variety of traditions to itself and thereby become even more powerfully sacred.

Places may also be made sacred through the relics of holy beings. A grave may sanctify a place, for the tomb marks not only the separation of the living from the dead but also the point of contact between them. In early Christianity, for example, tombs of martyrs became places of communion with the holiness of the deceased. Later, beginning about the sixth century, the deposition of relics became the center of rites for the consecration of a church. These sanctified the church and, within the church, the sanctuary where they were installed.

Finally, the form of a place may give it meaning and holiness. In different cultures, various kinds of places suggest the presence of deities. As has been seen, the land of Japan is holy because it is created and protected by the *kami.* Within Japan there are particular places where the *kami* are manifestly present: Mountains, from Mount Fuji to the hills of local shrines, for example, may be tokens of the presence of the *kami.* In India, rivers and confluences are sacred, for purifying waters and meeting streams suggest places where gods are present and approachable. In these cases, the shape of the land suggests meanings to which the sacredness of the place draws attention.

At the beginning of this section, it was stated that sacred places are typically not arbitrary. But there are places of religious activity that are meaningful precisely because they are arbitrary. If the tendency to institute sacred places is universal, so also is the tendency to deny the localization of divinity. The Indian devotional tradition, like other religious traditions, is pulled in two directions: one toward divinities located in specific places, the other toward the denial that divinity should be sought in any place other than within. "Why bow and bow in the mosque, and trudge to Mecca to see God? Does Khuda live in the mosque? Is Ram in idols and holy ground?" asks Kabīr (Hess and Singh, 1983, p. 74).

Mosque architecture shows the tension between the sanctification of a place and the denial of any localization of divine presence. The mosque carries values typical of other sacred places. The interior is oriented toward a holy center: The *miḥrāb* (prayer niche) directs worship toward the sacred city of Mecca. The space of the mosque is differentiated from other kinds of spaces: Persons must leave their shoes at the entrance. Within the area of the mosque, the holiest area, the sanctuary (*ḥaram*), is clearly marked from the courtyard (*ṣaḥn*). Some mosques are pilgrimage places because they are burial sites of holy men or women who endow them with spiritual power. The most prominent of these is the mosque at Medina built over the tomb of the Prophet.

At the same time, the architecture can be read quite differently as the meaningful negation of sacred space. The primary function of the mosque is to serve as a space for common prayer. It has significance in Islam because the community gathers and worships there, not because of the character of the place. "All the world is a *masjid,*" a place of prayer, says one tradition (cf. Kuban, 1974, p. 1). In Islamic lands the mosque often does not stand out from secondary buildings or call attention to itself as a holy place. Even the dome, which typically surmounts it and which recalls the arch of heaven, has a generalized meaning of power or place of assembly and does not necessarily designate a sacred place. Neither is that symbolism of the sky pursued within the mosque, nor does it have liturgical significance. While the sanctuary is oriented toward Mecca, the remaining parts of the building do not have any inherent directional or axial structure. Even the *miḥrāb,* which might be a place of particular holiness, is kept empty, emphasizing that the deity worshiped is not to be located there or anywhere. All this accords with the Islamic view that while God is the creator of the world, he is above it, not within it. The mosque is sacred space according to the definition of sacred space as a place of ritual and a place of meaning. But it is expressive, meaningful space because it denies the typical values of sacred places.

Similar negations of localization occur in Protestant architecture, particularly in the Protestant "plain style." During the Reformation in Holland, for example, larger Gothic churches were not destroyed but were re-created into places of community prayer and preaching. Sculptural ornament was removed, clear glass was substituted for stained glass, the high altar was removed, and the chancel was filled with seats. In short, all the visible signs of the sacredness of a specific location were eliminated. The architecture made positive statements as well, but statements that again located sanctity elsewhere than in place. A high pulpit was centrally situated and became a focal point, but the pulpit was not itself a place of divine power or presence. Rather it pointed to the holiness of the word of God, which was read and preached there. Again, these churches are sacred places by being visible denials that the holiness of divinity is mediated through the symbolism of space.

FUNCTIONS OF SACRED SPACE. The symbols that give a place meaning typically refer to the religious context in which a people lives. This section examines the ways in which sacred space acts to fix this context and to create interaction between the divine and human worlds. Three roles of sacred space are especially significant, for they are widely attested in religious systems and fundamental to their purposes. First, sacred space is a means of communication with the gods and about the gods. Second, it is a place of divine power. And third, it serves as a visible icon of the world and thereby imparts a form to it and an organization to its inhabitants.

Places of communication. First, sacred spaces are places of communication with divinity, places where people go to meet the gods. This function is often indicated by symbols that represent a link between the world of humans and transcendent realms. Such symbols might be vertical objects that reach from earth toward heaven, such as mountains, trees, ropes, pillars, and poles. North Indian temples, for example, connect the realm of heaven, symbolized by the *amṛtakalaśa* ("jar of the elixir of deathlessness") atop the temple, with the plane of earth. The spires of these temples are also architectural recapitulations of mountains, which are the dwelling places of the gods. The Kailāsa temple, for example, bears not only the name of the mountain on which Śiva dwells, but even its profile. But symbols that express the intersection of realms can be of other forms as well. In Byzantine churches, to walk from the entrance toward the altar is to move from the world of humans toward that of divinity. The doorway between these realms is the iconostasis, the screen between the chancel and sanctuary. As they pass through the doors of the iconostasis, priests become angels moving between realms. The icons themselves provide visual access to heaven. In general, "the iconostasis is not a 'symbol' or an 'object of devotion'; it is the gate through which this world is bound to the other" (Galavaris, 1981, p. 7).

Another way of joining gods and humans is through symbols of the gods. A sacred place may include images of the gods or other tokens that make their presence manifest. A Hindu temple is a place of meeting because it contains a form in which the god has graciously consented to dwell. The Ark of the Covenant in the Holy of Holies of the Temple in Jerusalem was the throne of Yahveh, a visible sign of his presence or of the presence of his name. Shintō shrines are dwelling places for the *kami,* whose material form is a sacred object called a "divine body" or "august-spirit substitute." It is housed within the innermost chamber of the shrine, kept from sight by doors or a bamboo curtain, but its presence invests the shrine with the presence of divinity. Similarly, a Japanese home becomes a sacred place when it has a *kamidana,* which enshrines symbols of the *kami,* and a *butsudan,* an altar that holds both Buddha images and ancestor tablets.

Even without explicit symbols of communication or tokens of the gods, a place may be understood as a point of contact between gods and humans. Islam strongly resists localization or visible symbols of divinity. Although the Kaʿbah is the center toward which worship is directed, it does not house an image of God, nor is it the dwelling place of God. Nonetheless, Islamic interpretation occasionally characterizes it as a place of particular access to divinity. A medieval tradition describes the Black Stone embedded in the Kaʿbah as God's right hand, "which he extends to his servants (who kiss it), as a man shakes hands with his neighbors," and a 1971 newspaper article urges: "When you touch the black stone and kiss it—you place your love and your yearnings in it and turn it into a mailbox from which your love is delivered to the creator of this world whom eyes cannot see" (Lazarus-Yafeh, 1981, pp. 120, 123). As these cases suggest, the deity is not exactly present, yet the Kaʿbah does become the point of communication between God and humanity.

As a place of communication with divinity, a sacred space is typically a place of purity because purity enables people to come in contact with the gods. There, the imperfections and deficiencies, the "messiness" of normal life, are reduced. The sacred place reveals the ideal order of things, which is associated with the perfect realm of divinity, with life and vitality among humans, or with the values to which people should aspire. The Shintō shrine is a place of purity, for it is a place of the *kami* and it is a place that excludes pollution, for pollution is decay and death. The shrine's purity is expressed in the rites of approach to it. Traditionally, an open pavilion with a stone basin provides water for rinsing the hands and mouth, and three streams spanned by bridges lead to a shrine, so that worshipers purify themselves as they cross these streams. Its purity also is expressed in clarity of definition. *Torii* (Shintō gateways), fences, enclosed spaces, and bridges mark distinct areas and signal the approach to the deity. Other sacred places mark the movement from a zone of impurity to one of purity by defining an intermediate space for rites of purification. Some churches, synagogues, and mosques have such an area at the entrance to the principal space of the sacred precincts.

A sacred place can be a place of communication not only with divinity but also about divinity. For example, a central paradox of religion is that if divinity is everywhere, then it must be somewhere. Even if the whole world is "full of God's glory," that glory must be manifest in some place. This paradox is reflected in the Temple at Jerusalem, which contained the Ark of the Covenant, symbolizing the throne of Yahveh, but which enshrined no image of Yahveh. Similarly, in Deuteronomic theology, Yahveh has made his name but not his person to be present at the Temple. In their different ways, therefore, both the Temple and the text sought to mediate the paradox of the simultaneous localization and universality of Yahveh. Larger Hindu temples, on the other hand, normally have a variety of images of deities. Typically, worshipers will see other gods and goddesses or other forms of the central divinity of the shrine, or they will worship at shrines to other divinities in preparation for their approach to the central deity. A Hindu temple thus reflects Indian views of a divine hierarchy, which culminates in a particular divine being. Or, again, in Renaissance churches architectural balance and harmony reflect divine beauty and perfection. In all these instances, the form of the place expresses the nature of the deity worshiped there.

Places of divine power. Because it is a place of communication with divine beings, the sacred place is also a locus for divine power, which can transform human life. The nature of this transformation varies according to the religious tradition and reputation of the sacred space. According to a Hindu tradition, pilgrimage places provide *bhukti* ("benefit") and *mukti* ("salvation"). Typically, one benefit is healing. In medieval Christianity, for example, many pilgrimages were inspired by a desire to witness or to experience miraculous cures. Pilgrimage was so closely associated with healing, in fact, that a young man of Warbleton refused to go to Canterbury, "for I am neither dumb nor lame and my health is perfectly sound." Another person argued, "I am in excellent health. What need have I of St. Thomas?" (Sumption, 1972, p. 78). Lourdes remains a place of pilgrimage for millions seeking miraculous cures, though the Catholic church has certified few healings as true miracles. A place may even specialize in its cures. As the location of a manifestation of the god Śiva, the mountain Arunācala heals especially lung disease and barrenness, and two Ṣūfī shrines in the Punjab help leprosy and leukoderma (Bharati, 1963). The power of divinity encountered at sacred places may also secure more general goals of physical and material well-being. Success in business or in school, the birth of children, or simply the blessing of the deity may all be reasons to visit a sacred place.

Salvation can also be attained at sacred places. According to various Hindu traditions, to die at Banaras, to be cremated there, or to disperse the ashes of the dead in the Ganges at Banaras assures salvation for the deceased. Often salvation is directly related to the purity of a sacred place and its ability to purify those within it. An English reformer, Hugh Latimer, lamented that the sight of the blood of Christ at Hailes was convincing pilgrims that "they be in clean life and in state of salvation without spot of sin" (Sumption, 1972, p. 289). The sacred place as an access to divinity thus also becomes a way to the perfection of human life.

Places as icons of the world. Sacred space is often a visual metaphor for a religious world. The connection between the ordering of space and the ordering of human life is a natural one. A life without purpose or meaning is often expressed in spatial metaphors: It is to be "lost," "disoriented," and "without direction." Because they are defined spaces, sacred places are natural maps that provide direction to life and a shape to the world. They order space—often geographic space, always existential space—and by ordering space, they order all that exists within it. The Lakota sweat lodge provides a good example of the ordering of space in the image of a sacred place. The outer perimeter of the lodge is a circle. Its frame is created by bending twelve to sixteen young willows from one quadrant of the circle across to the opposite quadrant. According to Black Elk, "the willows are set up in such a way that they mark the four quarters of the universe; thus the whole lodge is the universe in an image, and the two-legged, four-legged, and winged peoples, and all the things of the world are contained in it." A round hole, which will hold heated rocks for making steam, is dug in the center of the lodge. This center "is the center of the universe, in which dwells Wakantanka [the Great Spirit], with his power which is the fire" (Brown, 1971, p. 32). The center belongs to Wakantanka, for he is the summation of all divine powers.

The sweat lodge, therefore, encompasses physical space and draws the other realities of the Lakota world into its form. Its center becomes an ultimate point of reference in which space, all beings, and all powers finally converge.

Another spatial metaphor closely connected with sacred places is orientation. The sacred place focuses attention on a symbolically significant region by being itself turned, or turning those within it, toward that region. Sacred places show a variety of orientations and values of direction. First Coptic and Eastern churches, and later Western churches, were oriented toward the rising sun, which was the symbol of the resurrected Christ. Hindu temples face various directions for various reasons. For example, the temple of Taraknatha at Tarakeswar faces north. The head of the monastic community at the temple has explained that north is particularly auspicious, first, because it is the opposite of south, the direction of the world of the dead; second, because it is the direction of Mount Kailash, the home of Śiva; and third, because by beginning in the north, circumambulation of the inner shrine first proceeds east, the direction of the sun and of the light of knowledge (Morinis, 1984, p. 291). The abbot's explanations show the restless logic of sacred space, which finds significance in its every facet. In other traditions, the cardinal directions are not the basis for orientation: Synagogues traditionally are oriented toward Jerusalem, and mosques toward Mecca. These places are similar not because they express similar systems of orientation but because they all make direction meaningful.

Sacred places also create actual and functional divisions of geographic space, divisions that are at the same time metaphors for different ways of life. In ordering the world, they may be not only centers on which the world converges but they may also mark boundaries between realms. These may include both boundaries between visible and invisible realities and geographic boundaries. The Maori latrine mentioned above formed the border between the world of humans and that of the dead, which was associated with excrement. But the world of the dead was also the world of the gods. A ritual of biting the latrine beam opened up communication across this boundary. Those who wished to expel an unfriendly spirit bit the beam to send the spirit back to its realm. Those who wished to obtain the help of the gods bit it in order to establish contact with the gods. The border formed by the latrine was thus open in both directions.

Boundaries created by sacred spaces can also define the limits of the visible world or create distinctive spaces within it. In a northern Thai tradition, for example, a series of twelve pilgrimage shrines created a system of nested spaces. Beginning from the innermost and smallest area, this system encompassed successively larger concentric areas and defined the successively broader communities to which the people at the center belonged. These communities were seen from the perspective of the Ping River valley, in which four of the twelve shrines were located. These four shrines and four other shrines associated with the major northern Thai principalities outside the Ping River valley defined the second community, that of the Lanna Thai people. The third community included all adherents of northern Thai and Lao Buddhism, which were perceived as closely related. This community was defined through the addition of a shrine in northeastern Thailand sacred to the Lao peoples of Thailand and Laos. Fourth, the addition of the Shwe Dagon shrine in Rangoon, Burma, identified Thai Buddhism with that of the peoples of lower Burma, to whom the Shwe Dagon shrine was especially sacred. Fifth, the shrine at Bodh Gayā, where the Buddha gained enlightenment, joined Northern Thai and Burmese Buddhism to the community of all Buddhists. The last shrine was in the Heaven of the Thirty-three Gods. This location is still within the sphere of the worlds governed by *karman,* and thus it defines the community of all sentient beings in heaven and earth who are subject to death and rebirth. In this way, the sacred shrines both distinguished and integrated the various spaces and beings of the world to which the people of the Ping River valley were related.

Similarly, in South Asia the traditional pattern of city planning created a series of concentric spaces around a central temple in the urban heart of a region. This pattern occurs, for example, in Kathmandu. The city is surrounded by twenty-four shrines of the Mātṛkās, the eight mother goddesses. A ritual of sequential worship at these shrines arranges them into three sets of eight, which form three concentric circles around Kathmandu. The widest circle encompasses the area traditionally under the kings of Kathmandu. The second encloses the valley of Kathmandu, which includes surrounding villages and areas familiar to the urban population. The third defines the city itself. The central part of the city was laid out in twelve rectangular wards centered on the temple to Taleju, a goddess closely connected with the Malla kings. The geometric clarity of the city distinguished it from the surrounding areas and marked it as the most sacred area in which the realization of divine order was most perfectly articulated. In this way, the shrines define different levels of sanctity extending from the sacred center of the city to the entire kingdom.

ENCODING OF SACRED SPACE. The functions of sacred space are, in their different ways, aspects of its essential function: to identify the fundamental symbols that create the patterns of life in a culture. This section will sketch some of the symbolic systems that make sacred space meaningful. These systems are superimposed on the structure of a place and thereby joined to one another and to the manifest form of that place. A space can encompass, among many other things, the human body, the cosmos, the stages in the creation of the cosmos, the divisions of time, the sacred narratives of a tradition, and the various spheres of human life. The more central a place is in the religious life of a culture, the more numerous the systems to which it refers.

Body. The human body is a primary system—if not *the* primary system—through which people order and interpret the world. It is itself a space, sometimes even a sacred space—

as in forms of Tantric yoga, in which the body becomes the field for the transformations effected by yoga. It also can be a correlate of external spaces, to which it imparts a shape and character. In many instances that correlation between body and place is explicit. The horizontal plan of Gothic churches represented not only Christ on the cross but the human form more generally. In the symbolism of the Byzantine church, the nave represented the human body, the chancel the soul, and the altar the spirit. In South Asian culture areas, body symbolism of sacred places is pervasive. Hindu temples, for example, are explicitly recapitulations of the body. The symbolic blueprint of a temple is the Vāstupuruṣa Maṇḍala, a diagram drawn on its future site. This diagram incorporates the directions, the lunar mansions, the planets, the gods, and the human body and symbolically transmits their forms to the temple rising above it. Indian architectural manuals explicitly liken the temple to the body: The door is the mouth; the dome above the spire is the head. Just as the human skull has a suture, from which the soul at death departs to heaven, so also the dome is pierced with a finial; and the inner sanctum of the temple is the place of the soul within the human body. "The temple," summarizes the *Śilparatna,* "should be worshiped as the cosmic man" (cf. Kramrisch 1946, vol. 2, p. 359).

A variety of meanings is invested in such correspondence of place and body. Both the Gothic church and the Hindu temple are images of the cosmos as well as the body, and thereby both portray the sympathy and parallelism between microcosm and macrocosm. The Gothic church signifies the body of Christ, who is the whole Christian church, who is the incarnate deity, and upon whom the world and history center. The correspondence of the church and the body of Christ thus gives visible expression to the centrality of Christ in the world and his presence in the life of the community. Because the Hindu temple represents a human body, the journey into the temple is also a journey within oneself. Contact with the image of divinity in the heart of the temple is the symbolic replication of the meeting of divinity within the center of one's being. Thus, while the shape of the body generally imparts meaning to space, the specific meaning is developed in the context of individual religious traditions.

Cosmos. Sacred space often imparts form to the world by taking the form of the world. According to Mircea Eliade's paradigm of sacred space, the major vertical divisions of the world intersect at the sacred place and are represented in it. These divisions are frequently the upperworld, the earth, and the underworld. David D. Shulman has found this pattern in the temples of Tamil Nadu, which contain not only symbols that rise from earth upward but also symbols of a *bilādvara,* a doorway to the underworld. Other structures express more unique cosmological conceptions. At Wat Haripuñjaya in Thailand, for example, the *ceitya,* which is the central structure of the sacred complex, vertically encompasses the three fundamental realms of the Buddhist world: the sensuous, the formed, and the formless. The *ceitya* not only represents these different spheres but also the possibility of ascent to full enlightenment.

Sacred places may represent not only the vertical realms of the world but one or another of its layers. As noted, the sacred place is often the place where humans enter the realm of the gods or, conversely, the place where the gods are among humans. In either case, it becomes the place of the presence of divinity and therefore an image of the realm of divinity. Through its use of simple geometric forms, proportionality, and light, for example, the Gothic cathedral was imagined as the image of the heavenly city. The holy cities of Jerusalem and Banaras have heavenly prototypes, according to Christian and Hindu traditions, and hence they are the forms of heaven.

Heaven may be not only the realm of the gods but also the exemplar of divine order and regular progression. The sacred place may be a heaven on earth, which transposes the eternal and sanctified order of heaven onto the plane of earth. At the founding of cities within the Roman world, for instance, the augur drew a circle quartered by lines running east-west and north-south. This diagram replicated the heavenly order and thereby established it on earth. Through ritual formulas, the diagram was then projected onto the whole tract of land to be encompassed by the city, so that the periphery of the city reproduced the boundary of the universe. The east-west line represented the course of the sun; the north-south line, the axis of the sky. The augur and the city thus stood at the crossing point of these two lines and hence immovably and harmoniously at the center of the universe.

Cosmogony. Sacred space may also reproduce the successive steps through which the world came into being. Again, according to Eliade's paradigm, because the sacred place is the center around which the world is ordered and the point of intersection with the realm of the divine, it is also the point of origin. Creation began there and from there it extended. That symbolism is apparent in the architecture of the Hindu temple. In the innermost shrine of the temple is the dark center from which emerge the forms of the world, portrayed on the walls or gateways of larger temples. The naturalness of this symbolism can be illustrated by its secondary attachment to places whose primary meaning lies elsewhere. According to *Midrash Tanḥuma',* Qedoshim 10, for example, Jerusalem and the Temple are holy because the Holy Land is the center of space and the Temple is the center of the Holy Land: "Just as the navel is found at the center of a human being, so the Land of Israel is found at the center of the world . . . and it is the foundation of the world. Jerusalem is at the center of the Land of Israel. The Temple is at the center of Jerusalem. The Holy of Holies is at the center of the Temple. The ark is at the center of the Holy of Holies, and the Foundation Stone is in front of the ark, which spot is the foundation of the world." Such symbolism conveys the primacy of the place, for what is first in time is naturally first in significance.

Time. The divisions of time may also be represented in the sacred space, especially when time is ordered or governed by the rites performed there. For example, the sides of the *mingtang*, the Chinese calendar house, represented the seasons. Each side was further divided into three positions representing the months of one season. The rituals enacted at the place guaranteed the orderly progression of these cycles of time. They also guaranteed that the movement of time, and thus the fate of all living beings, depended upon the emperor, who carried out these rites. A different kind of temporal symbolism was connected with the brick altars created in particular Vedic rites. The layers and bricks of the altar represented the seasons, the months, the days and nights, and finally the year, which was the symbol of the totality of time. The completion of the rite was the consolidation of time and ultimately the attainment of immortality for the sacrificer.

Sacred narratives. Sacred space may not only bear the imprint of the natural world but also of sacred narratives. A particular place may be a reminder of events said to have occurred there, or it may contain tokens or depictions of sacred narratives which recall them to memory and reflection. At Wat Haripuñjaya in Thailand, the walls of the *vihāra* (monastic compound) are adorned with illustrations that tell the lives of the Buddha in his earlier incarnations and express the basic moral values of Buddhism. Similarly, Christian churches of both the East and the West contain paintings and sculptures depicting the history of salvation. In Eastern churches, for example, the upper part of the iconostasis contains depictions of the twelve great events in the life of Jesus, which are celebrated in the great feasts of the Christian year. Other icons might depict scenes from the Bible or from the lives of saints and martyrs, all of which recall the history of God's work in the world. Or again, the rites of the *ḥājj* move within a space that reminds the pilgrim of two critical moments in Islamic sacred history: the time of Abraham, who built the Kaʿbah and who established monotheistic worship there; and the time of the Prophet, whose final pilgrimage is recalled in rites at the plain of Arafat. In this last instance, the sacred place not only recalls an event but is also the location of the event, for the Prophet gave his last sermon during his farewell pilgrimage at Arafat. The place removes the physical distance between the worshiper and the event, and in doing so, it also mitigates the temporal distance between the time of the Prophet and the present. By thus collapsing space and time, it endows the event with an imposing reality.

Spheres of human life. In their form or function, sacred places organize human life and activity. Grounding the precarious and fluid structures of social organization in these places imparts to them a sense of conformity to a system that is not arbitrary but intrinsic to the very nature of things. The sacred place often creates a vivid parallelism between the objective order of the universe, the eternal realm of the gods, and the constructs of human relationships.

This aspect of the sacred place has been investigated in an extraordinary work by Paul Wheatley, *The Pivot of the Four Quarters*. In it, Wheatley discusses the ceremonial complexes that were the seed and integrating center of ancient urbanism. These ceremonial centers "were instruments for the creation of political, social, economic, and sacred space, at the same time they were symbols of cosmic, social, and moral order" (Wheatley, 1971, p. 225).

In Wheatley's description, the ancient Chinese city functioned in just this way to anchor the human order in the divine. The city was laid out as an image of the universe: It possessed cardinal orientation and a major north-south axis corresponding to the celestial meridian. The center of the city was the most sacred spot, corresponding to the polestar, the axis around which the sky turned. And in the center was the royal palace. The city, therefore, re-created the celestial order on earth and its pivot in the ruler. As the heavens eternally moved around the polestar, so the state revolved around the emperor. The political order was firmly established in the objective order of the universe, which was made plain in the sacred images of space.

The ceremonial complex as cosmic center also helped make it an economic center. In Mesopotamia, for example, agricultural labor was apparently under the centralized control of the temple officials. The preeminent economic function of the ceremonial center lay in its role as an instrument of redistribution. This could imply either storage and reapportionment of goods or merely rights of disposal. The ancient cities of Sumer, the temple cities of Cambodia, and Tenochtitlán, the capital of the Aztec Empire, are all examples of cities whose sacredness confirmed the economic control they exercised.

A sacred area may also project the image of the social order. The villages of the Boróro of Mato Grosso, Brazil, for example, were laid out in a cosmological image. The houses formed a rough circle around the men's house, and this circle was divided into quarters by axes running north-south and east-west. But these divisions also governed the social life of the village and its systems of kinship and intermarriage (cf. Lévi-Strauss, 1973, pp. 227ff.). A sacred space may be the center of a system of social prestige that divides and structures society. In the South Indian temple town of Srirangam, the two innermost ring roads closest to the temple are inhabited almost exclusively by *brahmans*. Other, less prestigious, castes live farther toward the periphery.

In one way or another, sacred space orders space in a socially meaningful way. Because a sacred place is both visible and comprehensible, it lends concreteness to the less visible systems of human relationships and creates an identifiable center of social and political organization.

CONCLUSION. This article began with the assumption that if a place is the location of ritual activity or its object, then it is sacred. To designate a place as sacred imposes no limit on its form or its meaning. It implies no particular aesthetic or religious response. But if sacred places lack a common content, they have a common role. To call a place sacred asserts that a place, its structure, and its symbols express fundamental cultural values and principles. By giving these visible form, the sacred place makes tangible the corporate identity of a people and their world.

See Also Architecture; Basilica, Cathedral, and Church; Caves; Center of the World; Cosmology; Geography; Geomancy; Human Body; Mosque, article on Architectural Aspects; Mountains; Orientation; Relics; Rivers; Sacred Time; Temple.

Bibliography

For recent scholarship, the agenda for the study of sacred space has been largely set by Mircea Eliade. His paradigm of the form and meaning of sacred space is presented in a number of his works, especially *The Sacred and the Profane: The Nature of Religion* (New York, 1959), pp. 20–67; *Patterns in Comparative Religion* (New York, 1958), pp. 367–387; and "Centre du monde, temple, maison," in *Le symbolisme cosmique des monuments religieux,* edited by Giuseppe Tucci (Rome, 1957), pp. 57–82.

A number of scholars have made significant contributions to the discussion of the symbolism of space by opening up or refashioning elements of Eliade's paradigm. Among the most thoughtful are Jonathan Z. Smith's *Map Is Not Territory: Studies in the History of Religions* (Leiden, 1978), esp. pp. 88–146, and *Imagining Religion: From Babylon to Jonestown* (Chicago, 1982), esp. pp. 53–65. The final chapter in Paul Wheatley's *The Pivot of the Four Quarters: A Preliminary Enquiry into the Origins and Character of the Ancient Chinese City* (Chicago, 1971), titled "The Ancient Chinese City as a Cosmomagical Symbol," pp. 411–476; Davíd Carrasco's "Templo Mayor: The Aztec Vision of Place," *Religion* 11 (July 1981): 275–297; Benjamin Ray's "Sacred Space and Royal Shrines in Buganda," *History of Religions* 16 (May 1977): 363–373; and Kees W. Bolle's "Speaking of a Place," in *Myths and Symbols: Studies in Honor of Mircea Eliade,* edited by Joseph M. Kitagawa and Charles H. Long (Chicago, 1969), pp. 127–139, are case studies that also advance the discussion of sacred space in this general line.

For other approaches to the meaning of architectural space, see the essays in *Traditional Concepts of Ritual Space in India: Studies in Architectural Anthropology,* edited by Jan Pieper, "Art and Archaeology Research Papers," no. 17 (London, 1980), and *Shelter, Sign, and Symbol,* edited by Paul Oliver (London, 1975). Kent C. Bloomer and Charles W. Moore's *Body, Memory, and Architecture* (New Haven, 1977) is an especially clear introduction to meaning in architecture and the role of the body in establishing meaning.

Studies of the religious significance of urban space include Joseph Rykwert's *The Idea of a Town: The Anthropology of Urban Form in Rome, Italy and the Ancient World* (Princeton, 1976); Diana L. Eck's *Banaras: City of Light* (New York, 1982); and the previously cited work by Wheatley. This essay also utilized Niels Gutschow's "Ritual as Mediator of Space: Kathmandu," *Ekistics* 44 (December 1977): 309–312, and Jan Pieper's "Three Cities of Nepal," in Paul Oliver's *Shelter, Sign, and Symbol* (cited above), pp. 52–69.

For pilgrimage places and the religious definition of space, see E. Alan Morinis's *Pilgrimage in the Hindu Tradition: A Case Study of West Bengal* (Oxford, 1984); Jonathan Sumption's *Pilgrimage: An Image of Mediaeval Religion* (London, 1972); Charles F. Keyes's "Buddhist Pilgrimage Centers and the Twelve-Year Cycle: Northern Thai Moral Orders in Space and Time," *History of Religions* 15 (1975): 71–89; Agehananda Bharati's "Pilgrimage in the Indian Tradition," *History of Religions* 3 (Summer 1963): 135–167; Anne Feldhaus's *The Deeds of God in Ṛddhipur* (Oxford, 1984); and Hava Lazarus-Yafeh's *Some Religious Aspects of Islam: A Collection of Articles* (Leiden, 1981). The last has three excellent essays on both popular and classical traditions concerning Jerusalem, the *ḥajj,* and the Kaʿbah.

Study of the places of worship is an engaging entry into the subject of sacred space and into history of religions generally. For Hinduism, the fundamental work has long been Stella Kramrisch's *The Hindu Temple,* 2 vols. (Calcutta, 1946). The temple is analyzed from the ground up and placed within the tradition of Brahmanic thought. David D. Shulman's *Tamil Temple Myths: Sacrifice and Divine Marriage in the South Indian Śaiva Tradition* (Princeton, 1980) draws on localized traditions that explain the origins and power of shrines.

In Buddhism, one of the most richly symbolic structures is Borobudur in central Java, and the classic study is Paul Mus's *Barabudur: Esquisse d'une histoire du bouddhisme fondée sur la critique archéologique des textes,* 2 vols. (Hanoi, 1935). For more recent interpretation, see *Barabuḍur: History and Significance of a Buddhist Monument,* edited by Luis O. Gómez and Hiram W. Woodward, Jr. (Berkeley, 1981). Borobudur is both a *maṇḍala* and a stupa. For the former, see Giuseppe Tucci's *The Theory and Practice of the Maṇḍala,* translated by Alan H. Brodrick (London, 1969), and for the latter, *The Stupa: Its Religious, Historical and Architectural Significance,* edited by Anna Libera Dallapiccola, Beiträge zur Südasienforschung Südasien-Institut Universität Heidelberg, vol. 55 (Wiesbaden, 1980). Donald K. Swearer's *Wat Haripuñjaya: A Study of the Royal Temple of the Buddha's Relic, Lamphun, Thailand* (Missoula, Mont., 1976) shows the expression of the moral, spiritual, cosmic, and social orders in the symbol systems of a Buddhist religious complex.

For the interpretation of Islamic architecture, Dogan Kuban's *Muslim Religious Architecture: The Mosque and Its Early Development* (Leiden, 1974) provides a brief introduction and a useful bibliography. See also *Architecture of the Islamic World: Its History and Social Meaning,* edited by George Michell (London, 1978).

The Gothic cathedral illustrates one expression of Christianity in architecture, and its symbolism has been luminously explored in Otto von Simson's *The Gothic Cathedral: Origins of Gothic Architecture and the Medieval Concept of Order* (New York, 1956). Harold W. Turner's *From Temple to Meeting House: The Phenomenology and Theology of Places of Worship* (The Hague, 1979) interprets the history of church architecture as the tension between buildings that localize the presence of divinity and those that serve for congregational worship. The sanctity of Eastern Christian churches is communicated largely through its icons. See, for example, George Galavaris's *The Icon in the Life of the Church: Doctrine, Liturgy, Devotion* (Leiden, 1981).

The interpretation of the Maori latrine presented in this essay follows F. Allan Hanson's "Method in Semiotic Anthropology, or How the Maori Latrine Means," in his edited volume, *Studies in Symbolism and Cultural Communication,* University of Kansas Publications in Anthropology, no. 14 (Lawrence, Kans., 1982), pp. 74–89. For Black Elk's description of Lakota rites and places, see *The Sacred Pipe: Black Elk's Account of the Seven Rites of the Oglala Sioux,* edited by Joseph Epes Brown (1953; Baltimore, 1971). The analysis of the Boróro village is found in Claude Lévi-Strauss's *Tristes tropiques,* translated by John Weightman and Doreen Weightman (New York, 1973).

Kabīr is only one of the many saints of various traditions who had little use for the sacred places. For Kabīr as iconoclast, see *The Bījak of Kabīr,* translated by Linda Hess and Shukdev Singh, edited by Linda Hess (San Francisco, 1983).

New Sources

Alcock, Susan E., and Robin Osborne. *Placing the Gods: Sanctuaries and Sacred Space in Ancient Greece.* Oxford, 1994.

Apostolos-Cappadona, Diane. "Religion and Sacred Space." In *The Religion Factor: An Introduction to How Religion Matters,* edited by William Scott Green and Jacob Neusner; pp. 213–226. Louisville, Ky., 1996.

Brockman, Norbert C. *Encyclopedia of Sacred Places.* Santa Barbara, 1997.

Chidester, David, and Edward Tabor Linenthal, eds. *American Sacred Space.* Bloomington, Ind., 1995.

Eckel, Malcolm David. *Buddhism: Origins, Beliefs, Holy Texts, Sacred Place.* New York, 2002.

Gordon, Matthew. *Islam: Origins, Practices, Holy Texts, Sacred Persons, Sacred Places.* New York, 2002.

Kelly, Klara B., and Harris Francis. *Navajo Sacred Places.* Bloomington, 1994.

Littleton, C. Scott. *Shinto: Origins, Rituals, Festivals, Spirits, Sacred Places.* New York, 2002.

Oldstone-Moore, Jennifer. *Confucianism: Origins, Beliefs, Practices, Holy Texts, Sacred Places.* New York, 2002.

Prawer, Joshua, B. Z. Kedar, and R. J. Zwi Werblowsky. *Sacred Space: Shrine, City, Land.* New York, 1998.

JOEL P. BRERETON (1987)
Revised Bibliography

SACRED TIME. Pichugi having just given birth, Chachugi prepared his bow for the hunt. Like all Guayaki men, Chachugi was a hunter, but that was not why he headed into the forest on this cold morning in 1963. As father of the child, he had to go hunting because Pichugi, "letting fall" this new life, had made him *bayja,* one who attracts living creatures. It was a dangerous state, *bayja,* but a propitious and sacred time. Dangerous, because if he failed to return today with the prey for which man and jaguar always competed, he was most at risk of becoming the prey of jaguar. Propitious, because animals would be drawn to him despite the cold, leaping into the arc of his arrows. Sacred, because *bayja* and the hunt were as much a part of the ritual of birth as the taking of a bamboo knife to the umbilical cord and the lifting up of the infant from the cold earth to the warmth of a human breast. Walking into the Paraguayan forest, Chachugi knew that he had to recompose his own life in the wake of the birth of another. "In reality," observed the anthropologist Pierre Clastres in his *Chronicle of the Guayaki Indians* (1998, p. 37), Chachugi was "walking ahead of himself, in quest of his own self, his own substance."

In 1881, a man wrote to the *Christian Neighbor* of South Carolina in celebration of the thirtieth anniversary of his silver watch, a watch so thick some called it a turnip. The turnip had been faithful to him, and he in turn was faithful to the turnip, which he would never exchange for some thin modern gold watch. "When I do, you may set me down for a barbarian! Not the best gold and jewelled 'Hunter' in existence would tempt me to swap. That watch marked the time when my children were born, and the record is set down in the family Bible." The ticking turnip had taken his family through births and illnesses, had "marked the time when the doctor's medicines were to be given," and had intimated at what lay beyond death and the "many records that are fast sealed up, to be opened only when another time comes." Mark M. Smith, who happened upon this letter while writing *Mastered by the Clock* (1997, p. 51), adds that African Americans of the same era placed clocks in their burial grounds, clocks that had been stopped at death, as former slave Elizabeth Bunts explained (p. 147): "I would not stay in a house that would not stop the clock the minute the person dies, for every minute that clock runs takes the soul that much longer to cross the valley of the shadow of death alone, and if the clock is stopped he makes the crossing swiftly and unafraid."

When Jesuit missionaries brought European clocks to China in the seventeenth century, the mandarins were impressed by the intricate mechanisms but unmoved by the tightly wound chronology that came attached. As Erik Zürcher notes in *Time and Space in Chinese Culture* (1995, pp. 148–149), the Christian arithmetic of time seemed unwarrantably narrow to the more expansive Chinese. "Saying that 7000 years ago there was no world amounts to saying that there is a today but not a yesterday," argued the lay Buddhist scholar Hsü Ta-shou, skeptical of a Creation dated no farther back than biblical genealogies would allow, while his fellow Buddhists operated comfortably within a cosmology that extended across millions of years. "They only [use such a story] to intimidate the ignorant rabble, calling [the act of Creation] something 'beyond human imagination'—but this is like telling young children that there is a ghost in a dark room."

A ghost in a dark room: Not only is time differently experienced within and across religious traditions, it is also differently conceived and formatted. These differences, debated openly within traditions and operating tacitly at crossroads between traditions, reflect the richness of the human architecture of time. If by *sacred* is meant that which marks or secures a connection with what lasts beyond an individual life and manifests powers beyond human agency, there is no equally brief synopsis of *time*, a subject that engages physicists and philosophers, novelists and neurobiologists, historians and theologians, economists and environmentalists, poets and prophets. The conjoining of *time* with the *sacred* is especially contested because much about being human—possibility and purpose, faithfulness and forgetting, nostalgia and regret, mortality and immortality—is at stake. In order to make clear the salience and liveliness of a topic that could seem forbiddingly abstruse, it is best to begin with a review of different senses of sacred time, breaking from encyclopedic formality into a style that embodies the heat and heart of those differences.

SHARING IN THE CONVERSATION. Here then are a dozen definitions, in the colloquial, with brief examples.

1. Time itself is sacred. All time is sacred time, there's not a minute to waste, make the seconds count. Each moment must be cherished, for life is a precarious gift.

So medieval Roman Catholic bishops decried the lending of money at daily, weekly, monthly, or yearly interest rates, since those who profited from loans were poaching on God's gift, the time of our lives; so the early Muslim scholar and ascetic Hasan al-Basri wrote, "There is not a single day which is ushered in by its morning twilight except it calls out, 'O son of Adam! I am a new creature, and I am a witness over your deeds. Therefore take your provision out of me, for if I pass away, I shall not recur to the Day of Resurrection.'"

2. The sacred must be timeless. Since what's sacred must be what's true and what's true must be unchanging, only what stands apart from time can be truly sacred. There's no such thing as sacred time. There's a sacred timelessness of which we all have inklings, but time drags everyone into the muck of the profane: age, accidents, illness, nightmares, loss, death, decay. Don't confuse the hours you spend at prayer, meditation, or confession with sacred time; those are just hours spent in pursuit, honor, or awe of something eternal that's never within reach. Eternal is what we aren't; you and I, we're bastards of time, and time, to be blunt, is trauma.

So the French philosopher Maurice Merleau-Ponty (1908–1961) backed into a discussion of time in his *Phenomenology of Perception* through the experience of the phantom limb, an amputee's continuing trauma of presence-in-absence; so early Daoists struggled with the paradox of a cosmos whose origins lay in chaos, *hun-tun*, and whose nature was infinitely chaotic, but which amounted at last to something more revealing than confusion, so long as, according to the *Zhuangzi*, "The sage steers by the touch of chaos and doubt"; so the Christian theologian Origen (c.185–c.245), calling time a natural reality, resisted any imputation of sacredness to time.

3. Sacred time is the experience of the transcendent. A belief in some sort of soulfulness can be found nearly everywhere on the globe, and with it a conviction of times of transcendence. Sacred time must be that time during which people experience their lives as unbounded: during which they commune with ancestors or other worlds; during which they are alert to voices and figures that call and dance beyond our human confines; during which they learn how they too can escape those confines.

So, in the throes of divine possession among the Danhom of West Africa, Brazilian Candomblé, and Caribbean vodou, worshippers petition Legba, spirit of the open and unforeseeable, to refrain from interrupting, but Legba's help must also be solicited as translator of messages from other gods, for transcendence is as tricky as it is thrilling; so English Quakers of the late seventeenth century, German Pietists of the eighteenth century, and North American Swedenborgians and Spiritualists of the nineteenth century developed rules of discernment by which to know what voices were speaking to or through them, what was inspiration and what was aspiration.

4. Sacred time is ritual time. We're all mortal and vulnerable, and unless we're saints we can't go around all day feeling transcendent. If the sacred has to do only with the unbounded, then it's sheer escapism. Most days are going to be humdrum, that's just how it is. The sacred is the ordinary lifted into the extraordinary, which makes for a democracy of inspiration. Birth, puberty, coupling, death, those are the transfiguring times that everyone shares, and each society creates rituals around them, and also for such significant recurring events as new moons, solstices, first rains, first fruits.

So, in the uncreated, vast but finite universe contemplated by the Jaina community of mendicant teacher-ascetics and lay followers, for whom the soul is reborn in a succession of bodies bound by the karma of past deeds and the state of mind at the instant of death, Jains perform a funeral ritual in which a new body is shaped out of symbolic balls of rice that stand as guarantors of a swift and positive reincarnation for the departing soul, lest it be stuck in a sacred limbo.

5. Sacred time is epiphanous. It seems oxymoronic to rely upon a regular series of rituals to invite the extraordinary. Rather than exalting repetition, shouldn't sacred time be the time that I hold dear precisely because it surprises me, yielding sudden revelations? Sacred time should be like a bolt of lightning, a moment that I keep holy through an ongoing archive of those rare and astonishing insights by which I have come to know myself more acutely in this world.

So the ninth-century Persian Ṣūfī, Sahl At-Tustarī, had theophanies, pre-visions of Allah, consistent with a theology that saw life unfolding as an unbroken series of instantaneous, divinely-sustained events; so among the Campa of Peru and the Waiwai of the Brazilian Amazon, it is through song and music, at once ephemeral and memorable, that the sacred enters the world of mortals.

6. Time becomes sacred through neural patterning. If the sacred is worth its salt, it has to be about more than suddenness and the self. Listen instead to cognitive scientists, who tell us that humans are hard-wired to notice quantity, periodicity, and causality. Time as before/after and time as repetition are built into our brains, hence into philosophy and theology. Is the sacred built in too? Well, we are also wired to locate patterns in our environment. Let's hypothesize that the sacred is basically an antique expression of the inborn conviction that everything we encounter is ultimately assimilable to an overarching pattern. Sacred time, then, may simply be the moment of the discovery or confirmation of such a pattern, when opiates are released in our brains and we enjoy what we call an "otherworldly" satisfaction.

So, argued the neurophilosopher Paul Churchland in *The Engine of Reason, the Seat of the Soul* (1995, pp. 17–18), the doctrine that human cognition resides in an immaterial soul or mind looks, "to put if frankly, like just another myth, false not just at the edges, but to the core," but in the crafting of "a proper theory of brain function" he hoped for a conceptual revolution that would "allow us to achieve a still higher level of moral insight and mutual care."

7. Sacred time is sacred because unique and inexplicable. What hubris, to think that sacred time is just a field of synapses sparkling with chemically bonded ecstasy! It has to be clear to the most bleary-eyed neuroanatomist that experiences of sacred time are triggered by what is not assimilable to, or which exceeds our capacity for, pattern. Even should we accept the materialist slant of neurobiology, there is little evidence that our opiate receptors are more indulged by perceptions of pattern than by delightful encounters with the new and unique. Scientists themselves relish anomaly; grand patterns are usually the projects of paranoiacs and megalomaniacs. The sacred need be neither surprising nor instantaneous; it must, like the best art, be irreproducible. Sacred time is misunderstood because by nature it's indefinable and, like any unique event, can be approached only by way of inadequate analogy. Trying to explain sacred time head-on is liking trying to explain to inveterate gamblers why odds of a trillion-to-one make it unlikely that they will be the one.

So in Chinese and Japanese Chan (Zen) Buddhism, masters and students approach revelation obliquely, their sacred time spent "sitting straight, without any thought of acquisition, without any sense of achieving enlightenment" (from the thirteenth-century conversations of Dōgen, recorded by his disciple Ejō in the *Shōbū genzō zuimonki,* pp. 98–99). In this way they prepare for the puzzle of a *koan* which liberates the mind from time-bound logic, as in this eleventh-century verse appended to *The Recorded Sayings of Layman P'ang* by Master Fo-Jih Ta-Hui:

> The Birthless is basically wordless;
> To speak is to fall into words.
> Kindred gather in a happy family circle;
> A tiger watches the water-mill turn.

8. Sacred time is divine time. The problem with gamblers and riddlers is that they mystify the accidents of chance and personalize fortune, which leads to mystifying and personalizing everything unique and inexplicable. But the unique and inexplicable, that's the divine, and the divine, though manifested as miracle or marvel, is hardly mystifying and never exclusive to an individual. Ditto for sacred time: it's simply the time instituted for us all by the divine, intervals during which we are enabled and inspired. It's forgivable that people confuse the time they make for the sacred with the time the divine has made for them; it's reprehensible to forget that our lives and times are always at the pleasure of the divine.

So after six days of offering tributes at the temples, "On the Seventh day as the sun declines the day is desacralized; at sunset the king is desacralized," according to Ugaritic Instructions for the Ritual Calendar of the Month of Vintage (1500–1200 BCE), as translated by Nick Wyatt (1998, p. 354). "Seven times, with all his heart, the king shall speak: As the sun declines the day is desacralized, at sunset the king is desacralized. Then they shall array him in fine clothes and shall wash his face. They shall return him to his palace, and when he is there, he shall raise his hands to heaven."

9. Sacred time is cosmic. Beware turning sacred time into stultifying obligation or authoritarian imposition, in much the same fashion as secular society, making time machinable and merchandisable, poisons the gift of time by turning it into chores and stock futures. There has to be an appreciable gravity to sacred time that makes it worthy, comprehensible, and memorable. Sacred time must be that time during which people individually and collectively bear the weight and fate of the cosmos. Neither that weight nor that fate can be long sustained by any one person; it must therefore be presented within a sacred theater of sacrifice and renewal, atonement and attunement, that is undeniably momentous. Each of us, for the well-being of the planet and our posterity, needs to bear the weight and fate of the cosmos, if only for the briefest moment, for in that moment we learn what the universe requires of us lifelong.

So Hindi men and women throughout northern India at the end of the rainy season move back and forth between participation and spectatorship in the epic play cycle of the Ramlila, lasting some places as long as thirty days, reenacting the life of the god Rāma, his victory over the demon king Rāvaṇa and his shattering of the great cosmic bow of Śiva, the god of devouring time; so the Mayan ball games with their deadly ritual replay of the motions of the heavens, and so the human sacrifices on the Mexica (Aztec) pyramids, where the years were bound together in spirals of death and rebirth that encompassed people, plants, cities, kings, and the gods themselves, eaten up by time.

10. Sacred time is time out. Must we resort to grandiloquence or terror to prevent sacred time from being cheapened? If we all had to wait upon a cosmic connection to claim sacred time, this entire entry might as well be blank. That's not a bad idea. . . . What's sacred about sacred time is that it's set aside from our usual course. It can be a time of rest or ecstasy, of silence or drumming, of solitude or communion, as long as its rhythm is unusual and it alludes to forces that ride above everyday turmoil. Other definitions suffer from a subtle arrogance with regard to the sacred or to time, as if we humans had a hand in running the universe. All we have it in our hands to do, now and then, is to pause, dedicating those pauses to something beyond the immediate.

So Plato in his *Laws* called a religious holiday an *anapaula*, a breathing space, and whether as a Sabbath, a carnival, a festival, a jubilee, or days added at the end of the year to keep a calendar aligned with the seasons, most cultures recognize a time out; so, warned Gary Eberle more than two millennia later in *Sacred Time and the Search for Meaning* (2003, p. xiii), when we don't do justice to a sabbatical, we end up in an impermanent world, "untouched by anything we might call eternity." Whoso would know sacred time, let them stop counting the hours.

11. Sacred time is spiritually receptive time. An aphorism whose latitude erodes its attitude. Leisure time should not be mistaken for sacred time, lest the supramundane become another species of the mundane. Those who take time out to meditate, to go on pilgrimage, to fast and contemplate, or to study scripture put themselves in a receptive frame of mind, a heightened attention that has nothing in common with idle relaxation. Released from the daily grind, one ignores the pricklings of the personal in order to support profound insights.

So the Jewish qabbalist Moses ben Jacob Cordovero of sixteenth-century Safed wrote in his *Or Ne'erav*: "the time that is most conducive to understand matters in depth is during the long nights, after midnight; or on the Sabbath, for the Sabbath itself lends predisposition to it; and similarly on the eve of the Sabbath, commencing after midnight"; so Shintō ceremonies incorporate the Japanese principle of *ma*, interval, which opens up time as well as space, allowing for the entrance of spirits on which the worshipper waits with expectant stillness.

12. Experiencing the sacred, time is discovered to be an illusion. You have to realize that the closer you come to the sacred, the weaker is time's grip on you, until at last time is totally unhinged, since it is a vise of your own making with nothing absolute about it. A better aphorism might be: Sacred time is what you make of time when time is made out to be none of your own. Once you get beyond your attachments to this world, time no longer has any attachment to you, and the illusion drops away.

So in the Yoga Vāsiṣṭha, one Hindu philosophical school argues from the relativity of time—how, according to one's mental state, an instant may feel like an eon or vice versa—that the object of yogic practices is to get beyond the conceit of time, at best a vehicle for reincarnation, at worst a self-deception; so Buddhists of the Śūnyavāda school insist that time is merely a set of subjective conventions, and the wheel of time, the *kālachakra*, at best a teaching tool, at worst a prison.

GETTING SERIOUS. There's a deadline for this essay, and that's no illusion, so I'd better get cracking. But that very "get cracking" has been at the crux of the debate over sacred time between Aristotle and Augustine, the former certain of the reality of time as a measure of motion and substrate of potentiality, the latter uncertain of its reality, given the flickering of human horizons and the frailty of human comprehension. For both of them, though, sacred time is the bottom line.

LEARNING WHAT'S AT STAKE. Drama inheres in beginnings and endings. What lies between is as much the province of Sacred Time as creation or conclusion, and what is thought to lie before or beyond (the Uncreated, the Prime Mover, Eternity, the Infinite) works in tandem with each calculus of the quotidian. How religions handle the less climactic intervals is key to the spiritual framing of that ongoing dailiness by which human life is ordinarily lived.

If time has to do with instantiation, duration, sequence, causality, and change, then sacred time has to do with the implicit issues that make time of particular moment: presence, continuity, consequence, story, and transformation. Variably fraught and freighted, these issues may be expressed at a personal level in terms of self-identity, trust, generational bonds, memory, and hope. Either way, time is fully implicated in notions and experiences of the sacred, whether time is depicted as the primal ground of being or as the presiding force that sustains and destroys each world; as that which is set in motion through a cosmic act of sacrifice or as that which must be overcome on the path to enlightenment; as the slow revealer of truth, which must withstand all storms, or as the swiftness of revelation, which proves itself by the very storm of its truth; as the implacable enemy of all illusions, eroding all disguises, or as the archetypal illusion.

Without time in its manifold senses, the experience of the sacred would lack a sense of occasion (timing), urgency (timeliness), momentum (time-after-time), resolution (timefullness) or relief (timelessness). The secular world, of course, may also be driven by time to such an extent that people of no avowed faith upbraid themselves for "worshipping the clock" and efficiency experts, bankers, taxi dispatchers, journalists, and air traffic controllers unite in a secular priesthood of timekeepers, but these are customs and clerisies of the immediate, where time "saved" is hardly, in the long run, redemptive. Those who deal in the long run—astronomers, mythographers, folksingers, tombstone carvers—owe their professions rather to religion, to stories of cosmic origin and evolution by which time is installed in the sacred and the sacred instilled with time.

Folded into cosmology, rituals of renewal, calendars of festivals, images of a future state heavenly or hellish, time becomes sacred. This at least would be the weak explanation, granting time and the sacred separate tracks with culturally variable crossings. A stronger claim would be that time makes the sacred possible, since without it believers would be at a loss to embrace the holy in past, present, future, memory or dream. The counterclaim here would be that the sacred is time's contractor, and that it is the first job of every religion and spiritual tradition to enable time. The strongest claim would be that time and the sacred are congenital, given that humans are temporal beings whose humanity is manifested through an intrinsic awareness of mortality and an intrinsic desire to bridge each mortal span. The strongest counterclaim would be that time and the sacred are accidental categories that obscure the ultimate insignificance of human life, the realization of which can be the only respite from suffering.

The stronger claims, speculative though they may seem, have exercised many a theologian and religious philosopher, since agreement on sacred time appears to be vital to the conduct of ceremonies and refinement of liturgies that hold communities together through the years. Even for those who do not bundle time into neat parcels of past, present, and future, or whose sagas swallow the eons in great gulps, sacred time must still be reckoned, and reckoned with. Although the Ainu off the coast of Northeast Asia told no tales of the future and counted their present not by years or months but by two irregular seasons and the daily barking of sled dogs at dawn, noon, and dusk, yet (through at least the 1960s) they understood the winter, the morning, and the first half of each lunar period as times for prayer, contact with good spirits, ceremonies for the bear, and mediations with the goddess of the moon.

EXPLORING POSSIBILITIES. In general, each religious group determines the borders and meanings of night and day, the seasons, childhood and adulthood, life and death. Each group then establishes nodes of tension and relaxation along these divides, such that the quotidian round is structured through periods of preparation, consummation, and relaxation whose coincidence with cycles fixed by human and celestial bodies is notable but distinct. That is, the universals of breath and digestion, of sex and death, of sunset and moonfall, are differently incorporated into each society and differently experienced through its set of observances acknowledging, praising, appraising, or acceding to sacred time.

Specifically, sacred time is shaped by five acts of definition that, separately or in complex conjunction, engage the supernal. These five acts define the nature, origin, spectrum, power, and rhythm of time in relation to the sacred.

Where, at one extreme, time is understood as an independent ordering principle, time may be deified (Brahmanic Hinduism, Iranian Zurvanism, Aztec and Mayan cosmology) and the five acts of definition may together constitute a theology; where, at the other extreme, moments are experienced as parts of an indeterminate flux (early Daoism, modern pantheism), the five acts of definition may together constitute a radical phenomenology in which the sacred becomes that alone which survives from moment to moment. Most spiritual traditions plot time between the extremes of paramount coherence and particular incoherence, risking thereby logical and psychological inconsistencies—inconsistencies that, theoretically and experientially, are in turn projected onto time, which is then seen as imbued with conundrum and felt as happily contradictory, neutrally brutal, or fatally enigmatic. The nature of time may be as passionately disputed within as between traditions, giving rise to schools of thought (most forcefully in Neoplatonic, Hindu, Chinese Buddhist, and Protestant circles) at odds over ostensibly minor points that actually feed major divergences in approaches to the role of ancestors, the virtue of sociopolitical action, the chronology of grace or redemption. If, as in the Sikh tradition in India, time began with the divine creation of an existential reality that leads through an irreversible, dynamically evolutionary process to the spiritual union of human beings with God, then history, and a believer's place in history, may be active and sometimes revolutionary. If, as in the Qumran community near the Dead Sea, all events have been prepared by God as the "master of time," then one's responsibility is to honor God's decrees with the utmost purity and ceremonial precision, isolated from the disruptions of larger society, "for your mighty deeds we will extol your splendor at every moment, and at the times indicated by your eternal edicts, at the onset of day and at night at the fall of evening and at dawn. For great is the plan of your glory" (War Scroll, 1QM xiv 13–14).

Given that time would, *prima facie*, make origins imaginable, and given that many cultures consider the original *ipso facto* sacred, the sacredness of time might seem overdetermined, especially where primitivist strains (as in Anabaptist, Puritan, Methodist, and Iroquois revitalization movements) strongly encourage a return to an earlier and uncorrupt or incorruptible era. However, the origin of time can be untwinned from its essence in those traditions where time is solicited primarily to initialize aging and mortality (as with the Iraqw of Tanzania, who have no origin or creation myths) or to stand as guarantor for an inherent immortality (modern Theosophy). Time may even be circumscribed at both ends, serving primarily as a measure for the precise execution of rituals geared fiercely to the present or to the immediate presence of ancestors (Ruist Confucianism, Shintō). In cases where a culture has constructed a tight nexus between space and time (Incan cult, Tibetan Buddhist *maṇḍala,* Icelandic saga, the longhouses of the Pirā-paranā Indians of the northwest Amazon), the origin of time and of the universe may be so entwined that each act of memory is a sacred emplacement.

The spectrum of time refers to the variety of phenomena scaled by time. For some cultures, and for industrial society, maturity, adulthood, legal rights, social rank, economic standing, and attributed wisdom are all etched by year counts, which also guide such religious ceremonies as baptism, conversion, confirmation, circumcision, and weddings; here the spectrum of time is short, dense, and finely notched—and would be further inflected with arrows of upswing and downswing. For other cultures (as with the Komo of Zaire), time as age or clock-count has little to do with rank, rights, or respect, but time as seasonality does demand attention for plantings or migrations and may track some rites of passage; here the spectrum of time is thin and marked at relatively long intervals—and the very notion of a spectrum of time would be alien. For many cultures, beyond the obvious biological, climatic, agricultural, and riverine cycles that act upon human beings, acts of prophecy, witch-detection, mediumship, healing, and clairvoyance demonstrate one's intimacy with, if not also mastery of, time; here the spectrum of time is long and complexly indexed—and would be reconceived in non-Euclidean intersecting parallel lines.

Power is a tortured subject. The question is, what can time do? Of course, time's nature provides part of the answer: if time is a god, it may have diverse powers; if time is a force, it may have one sphere of influence; if time is an illusion, it deceives. But the question is at root comparative: What can time do that cannot be done elsewise or undone? What are its unique powers? Is time the sole prompter of change, or is change what prompts a sensitivity to time? Does time devour all, or do human beings fear time as a devourer because they are flawed and fall short on their promises? Is fate another face of time and are human fortunes inscribed between time's eyes, or is time in its expansiveness the best assurance of free will, for otherwise an awareness of time would be nothing but torture for all those shunted along a predestined path toward hell, karmic demotion, or the wrong kind of oblivion. Is time itself a master, a mistress, or a liberator?

Everywhere, people dance to the rhythm of day and night, lunations and tides, equinoxes and solstices. These may be celestial phenomena, but rarely are they merely astronomical, considering how much they are seen to influence living things through their powerfully regular rhythms. Their repetitions and syncopations, widely taken as intimations of the divine, are refracted in human arts of time: storytelling, fortune-telling, music-making, star-tracing, trance-dancing. The rhythms are captured with more subtlety in the extensions and compressions of sacred calendars and their punctuation by solemn Sabbaths or mortal games, in the accordion of swift and slow motions throughout a complex ritual, in the staccato or fluid discourse of the bewitched or inspired, in all of the rhythms that build beyond the thumping of the heart.

Call and Response. Nature, origin, spectrum, power, rhythm: these are analytic categories that no tradition would acknowledge in this particular pen-tangle, but they do assist in the unpacking of "sacred time," a phrase with much baggage. They do not, unfortunately, keep the study of sacred time from being knocked for a loop by a number of methodological problems common to international baggage-handling.

First, perhaps foremost, among the problems is the abstraction of Time, which for this paragraph appears alone in the upper case to emphasize that in this Case abstraction simultaneously hypostatizes. That is to say, it is hard to write about Time without ascribing to Time an independent existence. Not all groups welcome or understand the abstracting of Time (indeed, degrees of abstraction or concretion are at the nub of a controversy about notions of Time among Africans and Native Americans); few societies have hypostatized Time as thoroughly as have the countries of the industrialized North Atlantic ecumene. The problem of abstraction should have become evident through the initial quicktime of competing definitions, some of which deny Time substance or independent action, but Time has moved paragraph by paragraph to reclaim that autonomy which often is its preeminent claim upon the Sacred.

So now the Sacred demands the upper case, as if the Sacred were a book. Among religions that rely upon scripture, Sacred time seems bound up with language and efforts toward the permanent inscription of truths. For religions in which the word, oral or written, is held to be creative and instrumental, the syntax of expression would seem to define both the scope and processes of time, even as it makes strenuous any clarification of time aside from language. Sociolinguists and anthropologists have sought to infer from a language's tenses, aspects, and moods that language-group's experience of time. A highly conjugated matrix of predicates that finely parses the past, the progressive, the habitual, the punctual, the perfective, the future, the optative, and the conclusive would indicate a culture whose concept of time is highly articulated and important enough to keep company with the Sacred, which must inevitably address difficult issues of persistence and loss, order and disorder, origin and end. A meager inventory of temporal markers would indicate a culture in which time is not key to the consideration of those elements of life that are believed to give it depth or enduring significance. At least two perilous assumptions come into play here: assuming what (for most South American and many Asian traditions) remains to be proven, that time is a human construct rooted in language; assuming that concepts of time, especially Sacred time, cannot be fully developed through nonlinguistic processes such as painting, sculpture, music, and dance (as in the "dreaming" and paintings of Australian aborigines, the Lion Mask dances of Korean animism, the rock art of the San of southern Africa, or the *gamelan* music accompanying Javanese Hindu-Buddhist plays).

This second problem has had a graphic companion in a third and more widespread problem: the frisking of religions for signs of linear as opposed to cyclical time. Like the desire to differentiate a tribal god of judgment from a catholic god of love, the desire to differentiate the "cyclical" time of archaic hunter-gatherer or agrarian societies from the "linear" time of urban or industrial societies stemmed from Protestant historians desperate to give a universal footing to their sense of civilization's moral advance. Denizens of "cyclical" time were supposedly caught in a maze of their own making, resilient but condemned to traditionalist pieties and a pervasive fatalism, anxious for each year to be renewed in the image of the old and reluctant to plan a better world. Denizens of linear time, in contrast, were supposedly politically engaged, driven by a past that betokens a brilliant, if often apocalyptic, future, which explains why they become reformers, looking ever for improvement. That binary set, whether in the blatant stereotype sketched here or in more sinuously seductive versions, still rules public conversation, although it has been shown to be historically groundless by Jonathan Z. Smith for the ancient Near East, Pierre Vidal-Naquet for ancient Greece, Sacha Stern for ancient Judaism, and Nancy Farriss for the Mayan world.

The same binary set, with value signs reversed, was adopted in the 1990s by cultural critics deploring a frenzied busyness that was "bleeding meaningful time out of our lives," as the American philosopher Jacob Needleman had it in his *Time and the Soul* (2003, p. 2). People need some of that old-time cycling, he wrote, to catch their breaths and find their true selves. But nearly every religious system gambols between the cyclical and the linear, because human beings, familiar with recurrence and adept at repetition, are also fascinated by novelty and blessed with inventiveness. The best one can do with the mountain of words on cyclical and linear time is to note that priestly forms of religion lean toward the cyclic just enough to protect the temple and its servitors from violent shifts of direction, while demotic forms lean toward the linear just enough to keep possibilities open, to make for immediate second chances, to rescue the downtrodden from persecution, forced conversion, slavery.

There may be more advantage to a complementary set of terms that has been applied to Sacred Time (both now momentarily in the upper case) in cultures far removed from their roots in Greece and the eastern reaches of Neoplatonism and early Christianity: *aion, kairos,* and *chronos. Aion* is time understood as a principle, and principal, of infinite, undifferentiable, unceasing time, sometimes pictured as an ouroboros, a serpent swallowing its own tail, an Egyptian symbol of renewal. *Kairos* is time felt and depicted as the knife's edge, a pregnant moment on which all hangs in suspense or, as Tukanoan tribes of the northwest Amazon mean by their verb *~su? husé*, that instant in which all conditions are propitious for conception. *Chronos* is time enumerated, the sequence of event following event, from which proceed schedules, chronologies, chronometers, and the raw data of history, but which may also mount up to a long-anticipated total, the Aztec calendar round of 52 years, the Qumran cycle of 294 years, the Mayan long count of 1,872,000 days, the allotted 6,000 years of Jewish messianism and Western Christian apocalyptics, the 7,000 years of Eastern Orthodox eschatology, or the 432,000 years of the Hindu *kaliyuga,* last and least of the four ages of the 28th of 71 mah(yugas (four-age cycles) in the 7th of 14 overarching manvantaras in the first kalpa or eon of the second half of the life of Brahman. The virtue of the three terms is that they are neither culturally nor mutually exclusive; although *aion* has special potency in analyses of Orphism, Mithraism, and Siberian shamanism, *kairos* in Christian soteriology, and *chronos* in ancient Egyptian royal cults and modern secularization, none of the terms insists upon the subservience of the others. Rather, one can see how, as in sixteenth-century Andean syntheses of local cults and colonial Catholicism or in the South African Xhosa cattle-killing movement of 1856–1857, communities handle crises through a complex manipulation of *aion, kairos,* and *chronos.*

A fourth methodological problem in the study of sacred time (back to the lower case) derives from a misplaced devotion to *chronos.* Much of the scholarly corpus makes the "time before" sacred to investigations of sacred time, seeking intact cores of religious belief that have resisted the influence of foreign raiders and invaders, colonial powers with their resident armies and missionaries, tourists, journalists, and anthropologists. Why expect sacred times to be unswerving or uncontested? As the anthropologist Johannes Fabian and ethnographer Nicolas Thomas have pointed out, Western researchers have tended to regard non-Western societies (read: non-white, or tribal, nomadic, primitive, even "stone age") as relics. Whereas all peoples going about their business on any given day are effectively coevals, once regarded as relics they become reliquaries, appearing to hold up to the world valuable remnants of ancient truths. Because sacred times and their train of ceremonies and rites of passage are presumed to be at the core of religious life, researchers have looked as much to fragments of sacred times as to ruins of sacred spaces to establish what that tradition had in mind before the incursions of strangers.

Within and without, of course, sacred times have long been subject to renegotiation, as in the shift of Manichaean cosmology and ecclesiology under the impact of Buddhism in northwestern China, or the mixed discourse of Cree heaven and Methodist Sabbath in the program of the Cree prophet Abishabis in Ontario (Canada) in the 1840s. To expect of any religion a resolute invariance and coherence in its construct of sacred time is to make two idealizing mistakes, imposing both a system and a stasis that would have turned such a religion into a museum piece from the start, in the name of an anthropological "eternal" that has proven as difficult to shake as the Ptolemaic astronomy of beautifully eternal epicycles.

Which unearths the archeological eternal. Digging through "layers of time" and walking the stone circles of Neolithic peoples or tunneling through underground burial chambers, archaeologists have found not only prehistoric time-keeping but prehistoric ritual, and through prehistoric ritual, prehistoric sacred time. Or is it vice versa: from sacred time, ritual? Their arguments are themselves elegantly circular, implying that there is something irretrievably human and visceral to the keeping of time which, because it is inexplicably human and visceral, must be numinous. Rather than couching sacred time in a culture's myths of origin, archeologists and archaeo-astronomers have often devised their own origin myths of sacred time for Iron and Bronze Age cultures in England and Israel, for Old Kingdom Egypt, for Shang China, for the prehistoric Mayans—origin myths that are then embraced and elaborated by resurgent spiritual groups (Druids, Hermeticists, Wiccans, Neopagans) strongly invested in the sacredness of an elemental or "natural" time.

The flip side of the archaeological eternal is "real time." A mischievous phrase, "real time" has come to be associated as much with unmanipulated media as with the honestly existential. "Real time" is what is happening "as we speak"; what has not been edited, prerecorded, or reenacted; what, in short, has not been tampered with. It is easy to see how the premise of "real time" can result in an implicit promise of sacred time, if one takes sacred time to be inviolate time, a pure time "delivering the goods," the good, the gods. Electronically infused with event, contemporary society further conflates *aion, kairos,* and *chronos,* identifying the eternally valid with the constant repercussions of breaking news. "Real time" is integral to utopian premises that those who live relatively unalarmed lives (i.e., those in preindustrial, "precontact" or monastic societies) enjoy greater access to the sacred. "Real time" is prominent in dystopian premises that those not "in touch" with what is going on "under their own eyes" (because isolated, illiterate, impoverished, disabled, or senile) cannot appreciate the meanings of their actions and are, to put it cruelly, cut off from the sacred. "Real time" informs the documentarist premise that taking cognizance of any segment of life automatically unveils the sacred, as if a "respectful" approach to the passage of time is all that one needs to access "the holy."

RETURNING TO "REAL LIFE" BY WAY OF HUMILITY. The bristling quotation marks of the paragraph above are signs of overprotectiveness regarding "time" and "the sacred." With or without seven thousand seven hundred words that less than one-thousandth of one percent of the billions of humankind will ever read, people will surely conceive, experience, and reconceive sacred time in their own fashion.

AFFIRMATION AND DEPARTURE. What then is the point of an article on sacred time? Why am I still writing? Why are you still reading? Wouldn't everyone's time be more valuably spent in working to eliminate poverty, feed the starving, comfort the suicidal?

These are not rhetorical questions. Whether in the form of a liturgical calendar through which a people's traumatic memories of persecution, enslavement, and devastation are at once condensed and transmuted (Jewish, Sikh, Cuban Santería, the Nation of Islam); or as a formal period of waiting (in exile, hospital, asylum, prison) through which fantasies and frustrations may merge and emerge in spiritual transformation; or as an active pursuit of the holy through fasting, initiation, hallucinogenic retreat, vision quest, pilgrimage, or prolonged mourning, sacred time is that time during which the contingency of human life is confronted and one must decide, again and again, how to spend one's life and give of one's time. A philosopher of language, Jacques Derrida, argued that time, belonging to no one, cannot possibly be given but is always the object of human desires to give of—and beyond—oneself, a cogent postmodern reformulation of sacred time. Clearly in this mode, Alfred L. Roca of the Laboratory of Genomic Diversity at the National Cancer Institute in Maryland, together with seven collaborators around the world, meant in 2004 to give a small animal, the highly-endangered solenodon, the gift of time literally and twice over. Demonstrating the origins of this shrew-like mammal in a genetic divergence that occurred seventy-six million years ago, they hoped thereby to persuade Cuban and Hispaniolan authorities to act to prevent the extinction of a species whose lineage, older than most mammalian orders, is ancestral to, and perhaps coterminous with, our own.

SEE ALSO Aion; Apocalypse, overview article; Birth; Calendars, overview article; Chronology; Consciousness, States of; Cosmology, overview article; Death; Eschatology, overview article; Eternity; Funeral Rites, overview article; Heaven and Hell; Initiation, overview article; Inspiration; Meditation; Memorization; Millenarianism, overview article; Miracles, overview article; Morality and Religion; Phenomenology of Religion; Prophecy, overview article; Rites of Passage, overview article; Sacred Space; Seasonal Ceremonies; Secularization.

BIBLIOGRAPHY

A full-fledged bibliography on sacred time might begin with a quotation from the first volume of *Remembrance of Things Past* (1913–1927), where Marcel Proust, as he is leaving church, genuflects before the altar and suddenly feels the fragrance of almonds steal toward him through the blossoms of a hawthorn bush. "Despite the heavy, motionless silence of the hawthorns," (C. K. Scott Moncrieff's translation, New York, 1924, p. 87), "these gusts of fragrance came to me like the murmuring of an intense vitality, with which the whole altar was quivering like a roadside hedge explored by living antennae, of which I was reminded by seeing some stamens, almost red in color, which seemed to have kept the springtime virulence, the irritant power of stinging insects now transmuted into flowers." That intensity of sensation so common to sacred time, that flow of memory into presence and presence into passion, resonated with the work of Proust's cousin-in-law Henri Bergson, son of a Jewish musician and himself a philosopher alive to issues of tempo and temporality, beginning with his first book, *Essai sur les donnés immédiates de la conscience (Time and Free Will,* Paris, 1889), which made of time a rich, indivisible flow. The task of religion, wrote Henri Hubert in 1905, using Bergson as a springboard, was to endow such uncut time with a definite rhythm of interruptions by which the sacred could be told from the profane. In his *Étude sommaire de la représentation du temps dans la religion* (Paris, 1905), available as *Essay on Time,* translated by Robert Parkin and Jacqueline Redding (Oxford, 1999). The young Hubert was also an obvious disciple of the sociologist Émile Durkheim, whose *Les formes élémentaires de la vie religieuse* (*The Elementary Forms of the Religious Life,* Paris, 1912) informed most subsequent European analyses of the sacred. After the First World War and its killing time in the trenches, sacred time itself suffered from a kind of shellshock to which Rudolf Otto's war-stricken *Das Heilige (The idea of the holy,* Breslau, 1917) was incomplete antidote. It was left to Martin Heidegger, a disciple of the German philosopher Edmund Husserl (an exact contemporary of Bergson's), to put sacred time into phenomenological perspective in his short lecture, *Begriff der Zeit* (1924), translated by William McNeill as *The Concept of Time* (Oxford, 1992). Writing in Parisian exile in 1945 with the ruins of the Second World War splayed before him, the Romanian erotic novelist and scholar of Indian religions Mircea Eliade chose history over fiction as a vehicle for reviewing and renewing the options of sacred time in *Le mythe de l'éternel retour: archétypes et répétition* (Paris, 1949), translated by Willard R. Trask as *Cosmos and History: The Myth of the Eternal Return* (Princeton, 1954).

Since then, many of the central works have not been monographs but wide-ranging anthologies of essays, drawn often from conferences on the topic of time in religion or the broader topic of time across cultures. These began with Henry Corbin and others, *Man and Time,* vol. 3 of *Papers from the Eranos Yearbooks* (Princeton, N.J., 1957), but it was J. T. Fraser, founder of the International Society for the Study of Time in 1966 and organizer of *The Voices of Time: A Cooperative Survey of Man's Views of Time as Expressed by the Sciences and by the Humanities* (New York, 1966), who etched the template with *The Study of Time (1972–),* a series of conference volumes on which he collaborated over two decades with a number of co-editors, eventually relinquishing the series to other hands, as with vol. 11, *Time and Uncertainty,* edited by Paul Harris and Michael Crawford (Leiden, the Netherlands, 2004). Publication of similar collections accelerated in the years leading up to 2001: Paul Ricoeur and others, *Les cultures et le temps: études préparées pour l'UNESCO* (Paris, 1975); Tommy Carlstein and others, eds., *Timing Space and Spacing Time,* 3 vols. (London, 1978); Dorian Tiffeneau, ed., *Mythes et représentations du temps* (Paris, 1985); Dorothea M. Dooling, ed., "Time and Presence," *Parabola* 15 (spring, 1990), entire issue; John Bender and David E. Wellbery, eds., *Chronotypes: The Construction of Time* (Stanford, Calif., 1991); Anindita N. Balslev and J. N. Mohanty, eds., *Religion and Time* (Leiden, the Netherlands, 1993); Etienne Klein and Michel Spiro, eds., *Le temps et sa flèche* (Luisant, France, 1994); Diane Owen Hughes and Thomas R. Trautman, eds., *Time: Histories and Ethnologies* (Ann Arbor, Mich., 1995); Kurt Weis, ed., *Was Ist Zeit?,* 2 vols. (Munich, 1996); Yasuhiko Nagano, ed., *Time, Language and Cognition* (Osaka, 1998); Jeremy Butterfield, ed., *The Arguments of Time* (Oxford, 1999); John B. Brough and Lester Embree, eds., *The Many Faces of Time* (Dordrecht, the Netherlands, 2000); Deutschen Religionsgeschichtlichen Studiengesellschaft, *Zeit in der Religionsgeschichte* (Münster, Germany, 2001); and Vincianne Pirenne-Delforge and Őhnan Tunca, eds., *Représentations du temps dans les religions* (Geneva, 2003, essays solicited in 2001). Meanwhile, Samuel Macey, who had published at length on time and mythology, enlisted a growing community of scholars in the creation of an *Encyclopedia of Time* (New York, 1994), many of whose articles set a bead on the sacred. Two new journals were also launched: *Time and Society* (London, 1992–) and *KronoScope: Journal for the Study of Time* (Leiden, 2001–). During the centurial years 1999–2001, academic journals often mounted special issues on time; among those most focused on sacred time were the *American Historical Review* 104, no. 5 (1999), *Ethnohistory* 47, no. 1 (2000), and *International Review of Sociology* 11, no. 3 (2001).

By the late twentieth century, time had been so enlarged as a field of study that methodological critiques began to seem urgent. Time had already been problematized in physics, vividly in Thomas Gold, ed., *The Nature of Time* (Ithaca, N.Y., 1967), recording the rambunctious speculations of physicists toying with a phrase coined by the English physicist Arthur Eddington in 1928, the "arrow of time"—a phrase further problematized by Stephen Jay Gould in *Time's Arrow, Time's Cycle: Myth and Metaphor in the Discovery of Geological Time* (Cambridge, Mass., 1987) and by Huw Price in *Time's Arrow and Archimedes' Point: New Directions for the Physics of Time* (New York, 1996). In this context, respected models for the investigation of sacred time, such as E. E. Evans-Pritchard's *Nuer Religion* (Oxford, 1956) and Clifford Geertz's *The Religion of Java* (New York, 1960), were taken to task by other anthropologists: Johannes Fabian, *Time and the Other: How Anthropology Makes Its Object* (New York, 1983); Nancy Munn, "The Cultural Anthropology of Time: A Critical Essay," *Annual Review of Anthropology* 21 (1992): 93–123; and Nicholas Thomas, *Out of Time: History and Evolution in Anthropological Discourse,* 2d ed. (Ann Arbor, 1996). Ruling assumptions about cyclical and linear time were also undermined, as anticipated by Edmund R. Leach in two brief essays, "Cronus and Chronos," *Explorations* 1 (1953): 15–23, and "Time and False Noses" *Explorations* 5 (1955): 30–35, reprinted with revisions in his *Rethinking Anthropology* (London, 1961), pp. 124–136. The critique was deepened by Pierre Vidal-Naquet, "Divine Time and Human Time," in *The Black Hunter: Forms of Thought and Forms of Society in the Greek World,* translated by Andrew Szegedy-Maszak (Baltimore, Md., 1986), pp. 39–60; Nancy M. Farriss, "Remembering the Future, Anticipating the Past: History, Time and Cosmology among the Maya of the Yucatan," *Comparative Studies in Society and History* 29, 3 (1987): 566–593; Jonathan Z. Smith, *To Take Place: Toward Theory in Ritual* (Chicago, 1987); Anthony Aveni, *Empires of Time: Calendars, Clocks, and Cultures* (New York, 1989); and Alfred Gell, *The Anthropology of Time: Cultural Constructions of Temporal Maps and Images* (Oxford, 1992).

Given such momentum, challenges were issued as well to dominant theories about particular religious systems—Sassanid Persia's worship of Zurvan, originary god of time (according to R. C. Zaehner), Africa's futurelessness (according to John S. Mbiti), Hopi ritual atemporality (according to Benjamin Lee Whorf), the ultimate unsustainability of Hindu cosmology (according to G. W. von Hegel)—by such scholars as Shaul Shaked, "The Myth of Zurvan: Cosmogony and Eschatology," in *Messiah and Christos,* edited by Ithamar Gruenwald and others (Tübingen, Germany, 1992), pp. 219–240; Peter R. McKenzie, "Sacred Time," in his *Hail Orisha! A Phenomenology of a West African Religion in the Mid-Nineteenth Century* (Leiden, 1997), pp. 154–208; Ekkehart Malotki, *Hopi Time: A Linguistic Analysis of the Temporal Concepts in the Hopi Language* (Berlin, 1983); and Gayatri Chakravorty Spivak, "Time and Timing: Law and History," in *Chronotypes: The Construction of Time,* edited by Bender and Wellbery (Stanford, Calif., 1991), pp. 99–117.

Debate continues, with a vehemence equal to that of Hubert (who with Durkheim's nephew Marcel Mauss published in 1899 a seminal study of sacrificial rites), concerning the degree to which sacred time originates in, or is primitively defined by, blood sacrifice as a psychic strategy of re-creation or as a means of collective renewal. On this, see Georges Bataille, *Theory of Religion,* translated by Robert Hurley (New York, 1992); Raimundo Panikkar, "Time and Sacrifice: The Sacrifice of Time and the Ritual of Modernity," *The Study of Time III,* edited by J. T. Fraser (New York, 1978), pp. 683–727; Kay A. Read, whose *Time and Sacrifice in the Aztec Cosmos* (Bloomington, Ind., 1998) is also sensitive to the gendered aspects of sacred time, as is Johan Normark, *Genderized Time and Space in Late Classic Maya Calendars,* Museion Occasional Paper No. 1 (Göteborg, Sweden, 2000). Elsewhere too, attention has been called to gender: Warren L. d'Azavedo, "Gola Womanhood and the Limits of Masculine Omnipotence," in *Religion in Africa,* edited by Thomas D. Blakely and others (London, 1994), pp. 342–362; Fatima Mernissi, "The Muslim and Time," in *The Veil and the Male Elite,* translated by Mary Jo Lakeland (Reading, Mass., 1991), pp. 15–24; Susan Starr Sered, "Gender, Immanence and Transcendence: The Candle-Lighting Repertoire of Middle-Eastern Jews," *Metaphor and Symbolic Activity* 6, no. 4 (1991): 293–304; Sarah Lund Skar, "Andean Women and the Concept of Space/Time," in *Women and Space, Ground Rules and Social Maps,* edited by Shirley Ardener, revised edition (Oxford, 1993), pp. 31–45; and numerous contributors to *Nature Religion Today: Paganism in the Modern World,* edited by Joanne Pearson and others (Edinburgh, 1998). For a woman theologian's perspective, see Carol Ochs, *The Noah Paradox: Time as Burden, Time as Blessing* (Notre Dame, Ind., 1991).

In addition to the works already mentioned, see the following for specific geohistorical settings:

East Asia: Robert Eno, *The Confucian Creation of Heaven: Philosophy and the Defense of Ritual Mastery* (Albany, N.Y.,1990); N. J. Girardot, *Myth and Meaning in Early Taoism: The Theme of Chaos (hun-tun)* (Berkeley, Calif., 1983); Chun-Chieh Huang and Erik Zürcher, eds., *Time and Space in Chinese Culture* (Leiden, the Netherlands, 1995); David N. Keightley, *The Ancestral Landscape: Time, Space, and Community in Late Shang China (ca. 1200–1045 BC)* (Berkeley, Calif., 2000); Emiko Ohnuki-Tierney, "Sakhalin Ainu Time Reckoning," *Man* 8 (1973): 285–299; Richard Pilgrim, "Intervals (*Ma*) in Space and Time: Foundations for a Religio-Aesthetic Paradigm in Japan," *History of Religions* 25, no. 3 (1986): 255–277; and Ruth Fuller Sasaki and others, trans., *A Man of Zen: The Recorded Sayings of Layman P'ang* (New York, 1971).

Southeast Asia: Janet Hoskins, *The Play of Time: Kodi Perspectives on Calendars, History and Exchange* (Berkeley, Calif., 1993); Robert McKinley, "Zaman dan Masa, Eras and Periods: Revolutions and the Permanence of Epistemological Ages in Malay Culture," in *The Imagination of Reality in Southeast Asian Coherence Systems,* edited by A. L. Becker and Aram A. Yengoyam (Norwood, N.J., 1979), pp. 303–324; Geoffrey Samuel, "The Religious Meaning of Space and Time in South and Southeast Asia and Modern Paganism," *International Review of Sociology* 11, no. 3 (2001): 395–418.

South Asia: Jasabir Singh Ahluwalia, "Time, Reality, and Religion," in his *The Doctrine and Dynamics of Sikhism* (Patiala, India, 1999), pp. 29–50; Maitreyee R. Deshpande, *The Concept of Time in Vedic Ritual* (Delhi, 2001); Werner Herzog's film, *Rad der Zeit* (Wheel of Time) (Germany, 2003, eighty minutes); Padmanath S. Jaini, *Collected Papers on Jaina Studies* (Delhi, 2000); Hari Shankar Prasad, ed., *Time in Indian Philosophy* (Delhi, 1992); Alexander von Rospatt, *The Buddhist Doctrine of Momentariness* (Stuttgart, 1995); Geshe Lhundub Sopa and others, *The Wheel of Time: The Kālachakra in Context,* edited by Beth Simon (Ithaca, 1991); Thomas R. Trautman, "Indian Time, European Time," in *Time: Histories and Ethnologies,* edited by Hughes and Trautman (Ann Arbor, 1995), pp. 167–197; Peter Van Der Veer, "Ayodhya and Somnath: Eternal Shrines, Contested Histories," *Social Research* 59, no. 1 (1992): 85–109.

Central Asia: Mary Boyce, *A History of Zoroastrianism: I. The Early Period* (Leiden, the Netherlands, 1996); Hans-Joachim Klimkeit, trans. and comp., *Gnosis on the Silk Road* (San Francisco, 1993); Samuel N. C. Lieu, *Manichaeism in Central Asia and China* (Leiden, the Netherlands, 1998); John Walbridge, *Sacred Acts, Sacred Space, Sacred Time* (Oxford, 1996) on Baha'i.

Western Asia and the Mediterranean Littoral: Petro B. T. Bilaniuk, "*Chronos* and *Kairos*: Secular and Sacred Time in Relation to the History of Salvation and Eternity," *Studies in Eastern Christianity* 5 (Munich, 1998) pp. 3–7; Gerhard Böwering, *The Mystical Vision of Existence in Classical Islam* (Berlin, 1980); Paul F. Bradshaw and Lawrence A. Hoffman, eds., *Passover and Easter: The Symbolic Structuring of Sacred Seasons* (Notre Dame, Ind., 1999); Gershon Brin, *The Concept of Time in the Bible and the Dead Sea Scrolls* (Leiden, the Netherlands, 2001); Barry M. Gittlen, ed., *Sacred Time, Sacred Place: Archaeology and the Religion of Israel* (Winona Lake, Ind., 2002); Sylvie Anne Goldberg, *La clepsydre: essai sur la pluralité des temps dans le juda(sme* (Paris, 2000); L. E. Goodman, "Time in Islam," in *Religion and Time,* edited by Balslev and Mohanty (Leiden, the Netherlands, 1993), pp. 138–162; Richard D. Hecht, "The Construction and Management of Sacred Time and Space: *Sabta Nur* in the Church of the Holy Sepulcher," in *NowHere: Space, Time, and Modernity,* edited by Roger Friedland and Deirdre Boden (Berkeley, Calif., 1994), pp. 181–235; Yūsuf al-Qaradāwī, *Time in the Life of a Muslim,* translated by Abu Maimounah Ahmad ad bin Muhammad Bello (London, 2000); Samuel Sambursky and Shlomo Pines, *The Concept of Time in Late Neoplatonism* (Jerusalem, 1971); Sacha Stern, *Time and Process in Ancient Judaism* (Oxford, 2003); Robert Taft, "A Tale of Two Cities: The Byzantine Holy Week Triduum as a Paradigm of Liturgical History," in *Time and Community,* edited by J. Neil Alexander (Washington, D.C., 1990), pp. 21–42; Panagiōtēs Tzamalikos, *The Concept of Time in Origen* (New York, 1991); James C. VanderKam, *Calendars in the Dead Sea Scrolls: Measuring Time* (London, 1998); Nick Wyatt, *Religious Texts from Ugarit* (Sheffield, U.K., 1998); Nick Wyatt, *Space and Time in the Religious Life of the Near East* (Sheffield, U.K., 2001).

Europe: Guido Alliney and Luciano Cova, eds., *Tempus Aevum Aeternitas: La concettualizzazione del tempo nel pensiero tardomedievale* (Florence, Italy, 2000); Eamon Duffy, *The Stripping of the Altars: Traditional Religion in England, c.*

1400–c.1580 (New Haven, Conn., 1992); Alex Gibson and Derek Simpson, eds., *Prehistoric Ritual and Religion* (Thrupp, U.K., 1998); Jacques Le Goff, *Your Money or Your Life: Economy and Religion in the Middle Ages,* translated by Patricia Ranum (New York, 1988); Paul Ricoeur, *Time and Narrative,* translated by Kathleen McLaughlin and David Pellauer, 3 volumes (Chicago, 1984–1988), with much on Aristotle and St. Augustine; David G. Roskies, *Against the Apocalypse: Responses to Catastrophe in Modern Jewish Culture* (Cambridge, Mass., 1984); Tamar M. Rudavsky, *Time Matters: Time, Creation, and Cosmology in Medieval Jewish Philosophy* (Albany, N.Y., 2000); Richard Sorabji, *Time, Creation, and the Continuum: Themes in Antiquity and the Early Middle Ages* (Ithaca, N.Y., 1983); and Yosef H. Yerushalmi, *Zakhor: Jewish History and Jewish Memory* (New York, 1989).

Africa: Thomas O. Beidelman, *Moral Imagination in Kaguru Modes of Thought* (Washington, D.C., 1993); Thomas D. Blakely and others, eds., *Religion in Africa* (London, 1994); Pierre Bourdieu, "The Attitude of the Algerian Peasant toward Time," in *Mediterranean Countrymen,* edited by Julian Pitt-Rivers (Paris, 1973), pp. 55–72; James W. Fernandez, *Bwiti: An Ethnography of Religious Imagination in Africa* (Princeton, N. J., 1982); David Frankfurter, ed., *Pilgrimage and Holy Space in Late Antique Egypt* (Leiden, the Netherlands, 1998); Steven Kaplan, "Te'ezza Sanbat: A Beta Israel Work Reconsidered," in *Gilgul: Essays on Transformation, Revolution, and Permanence in the History of Religions,* edited by Shaul Shaked and others (Leiden, 1987) on the Ethiopian Sabbath; Wauthier de Mahieu, "Le temps dans la culture komo," *Africa* 43 (1973): 2–17; John S. Mbiti, *African Religions and Philosophy,* 2d revised edition (Oxford, 1990); J. B. Peires, *The Dead Will Arise: Nongqawuse and the Great Xhosa Cattle-Killing Movement of 1856-7* (Johannesburg and Bloomington, Ind., 1989); John Parratt, "Time in Traditional African Thought," *Religion* 7 (autumn, 1977): 117–126; Robert J. Thornton, *Space Time and Culture among the Iraqw of Tanzania* (New York, 1980).

Africans in the Americas: Joseph N. Murphy, *Working the Spirit: Ceremonies of the African Diaspora* (Boston, 1994); Anthony B. Pinn, *Varieties of African American Religious Experience* (Minneapolis, Minn., 1998); Albert J. Raboteau, *Slave Religion: The "Invisible Institution" in the Antebellum South* (New York, 1978).

South America: Brian S. Bauer and Charles Stanish, *Ritual and Pilgrimage in the Ancient Andes* (Austin, Tex., 2001); Pierre Clastres, *Chronicle of the Guayaki Indians,* translated by Paul Auster (New York, 1998); Christine Hugh-Jones, *From the Milk River: Spatial and Temporal Processes in Northwest Amazonia* (Cambridge, 1979); Sabine MacCormack, *Religion in the Andes: Vision and Imagination in Early Colonial Peru* (Princeton, 1991); Gerardo Reichel-Dolmatoff, *Yuruparí: Studies of an Amazonian Foundation Myth* (Cambridge, Mass., 1996); Frank Salomon and George L. Urioste, eds. and trans., *Huarochirí Manuscript* (Austin, Tex., 1991); Lawrence E. Sullivan, "Sacred Music and Sacred Time," *World of Music* 26, no. 3 (1984): 33–51, examples primarily from South America; William Sullivan, *The Secret of the Incas: Myth, Astronomy, and the War Against Time* (New York, 1996).

Mesoamerica: Anthony Aveni, "Time, Number, and History in the Maya World," *KronoScope* 1, nos. 1–2 (2001): 29–62; David Carrasco, *Quetzalcoatl and the Irony of Empire: Myths and Prophecies of the Aztec Tradition,* revised edition (Boulder, Colo., 2000); Barbara Tedlock, *Time and the Highland Maya,* revised edition (Albuquerque, N. Mex., 1992); E. Michael Whittington, ed., *The Sport of Life and Death: The Mesoamerican Ballgame* (New York, 2001).

North America: Melissa Axelrod, *The Semantics of Time: Aspectual Categorization in Koyukon Athabaskan* (Lincoln, Nebr., 1993); Edmund S. Carpenter, "The Timeless Present in the Mythology of the Aivilik Eskimos" in *Eskimos of the Canadian Arctic,* edited by Victor F. Valentine and Frank G. Vallee (Toronto, 1968), pp. 39–42; Richard T. Hughes and C. Leonard Allen, *Illusions of Innocence: Protestant Primitivism in America, 1630–1875* (Chicago, 1988); Randall A. Lake, "Between Myth and History: Enacting Time in Native American Protest Rhetoric," *Quarterly Journal of Speech* 77, no. 2 (1991): 123–151; Mark M. Smith, *Mastered by the Clock: Time, Slavery, and Freedom in the American South* (Chapel Hill, N.C., 1997); Stanley Walens, "The Weight of My Name Is a Mountain of Blankets: Potlatch Ceremonies," in *Celebration: Studies in Festivity and Ritual,* edited by Victor Turner (Washington, D.C., 1982), pp. 178–189.

Oceania and Australia: Bruce Chatwin, *The Songlines* (New York, 1987); Frederick H. Damon, "Time and Values," in *From Muyuw to the Trobriands: Transformations along the Northern Side of Kula Ring* (Tucson, Ariz., 1990), pp. 16–53; Hans Peter Duerr, *Dreamtime,* translated by Felicitas D. Goodman (Oxford, 1985); Barbara Glowczewski, *Du rêve à la loi chez les aborigines* (Paris, 1991); Lynne Hume, *Ancestral Power: The Dreaming, Consciousness, and Aboriginal Australians* (Carlton South, Victoria, Australia, 2002); Karen Sinclair, *Maori Times, Maori Places* (Lanham, Md., 2003); Marilyn Strathern, "Artefacts of History: Events and the Interpretation of Images," in *Culture and History in the Pacific,* edited by Jukka Siikala (Helsinki, 1990), pp. 25–44; Tony Swain and Garry Trompf, *The Religions of Oceania* (London, 1995).

For social-theoretical contributions, see Barbara Adam, *Time and Social Theory* (Philadelphia, 1990); Sylviane Agacinski, *Time Passing: Modernity and Nostalgia,* translated by Jody Gladding (New York, 2003); Éric Alliez, *Capital Times: Tales from the Conquest of Time,* translated by Georges Van Den Abbeele (Minneapolis, Minn., 1996); James A. Beckford, "Doing Time: Space, Time, Religious Diversity, and the Sacred in Prisons," *International Review of Sociology* 11, no. 2 (2001): 371–382; Lawrence W. Fagg, *The Becoming of Time: Integrating Physical and Religious Time* (Durham, N.C., 2003); Richard K. Fenn, *Time Exposure: The Personal Experience of Time in Secular Societies* (Oxford, 2001); Krzysztof Pomian, *L'ordre du temps* (Paris, 1984); Barry Schwartz, *Queueing and Waiting: Studies in the Social Organization of Access and Delay* (Chicago, 1975).

For philosophical works cited, see Paul Churchland, *The Engine of Reason, the Seat of the Soul* (Cambridge, Mass., 1995); Jacques Derrida, *Given Time: I. Counterfeit Money,* translated by Peggy Kamuf (Chicago, 1992); Gary Eberle, *Sacred Time and the Search for Meaning* (Boston, 2003); Jacob Needleman, *Time and the Soul* (San Francisco, Calif., 2003).

For more on the solenodon, see Alfred L. Roca and others, "Mesozoic Origin for West Indian Insectivores," *Nature* 429 (June 10, 2004): 649–651.

HILLEL SCHWARTZ (2005)

SACRIFICE [FIRST EDITION].

The term *sacrifice,* from the Latin *sacrificium* (*sacer,* "holy"; *facere,* "to make"), carries the connotation of the religious act in the highest, or fullest sense; it can also be understood as the act of sanctifying or consecrating an object. *Offering* is used as a synonym (or as a more inclusive category of which sacrifice is a subdivision) and means the presentation of a gift. (The word *offering* is from the Latin *offerre,* "to offer, present"; the verb yields the noun *oblatio.)* The Romance languages contain words derived from both the Latin words. The German *Opfer* is generally taken as derived from *offerre,* but some derive it from the Latin *operari* ("to perform, accomplish"), thus evoking once again the idea of sacred action.

Distinctions between sacrifice and offering are variously drawn, as for example, that of Jan van Baal: "I call an offering every act of presenting something to a supernatural being, a sacrifice an offering accompanied by the ritual killing of the object of the offering" (van Baal, 1976, p. 161). The latter definition is too narrow, however, since "killing" can be applied only to living beings, human or animal, and thus does not cover the whole range of objects used in sacrifice as attested by the history of religions. A truly essential element, on the other hand, is that the recipient of the gift be a supernatural being (that is, one endowed with supernatural power), with whom the giver seeks to enter into or remain in communion. Destruction, which can apply even to inanimate objects, is also regarded as essential by some authors but not by all; thus, according to the *Encyclopaedia Britannica,* a sacrifice is "a cultic act in which objects were set apart or consecrated and offered to a god or some other supernatural power" (1977, vol. 16, p. 128b). On the other hand, it is indeed essential to the concept that the human offerer remove something from his own disposal and transfer it to a supernatural recipient. The difference between the broad concept of offering and the narrower concept of sacrifice may be said to reside in the fact that a rite, a more or less solemn external form, is part of sacrifice.

Sacrifice differs from other cultic actions. The external elements of prayer are simply words and gestures (bodily attitudes), not external objects comparable to the gifts of sacrifice. Eliminatory rites, though they may include the slaying of a living being or the destruction of an inanimate object, are not directed to a personal recipient and thus should not be described as sacrifices. The same is true of ritual slayings in which there is no supernatural being as recipient, as in slayings by which companions are provided for the dead (joint burials) or that are part of the dramatic representation of an event in primordial time.

According to some theories, the conception of sacrifice as gift-giving is the result of a secondary development or even of a misunderstanding of rites that originally had a different meaning. (On this point, see "Theories of the Origin of Sacrifice," below.)

MORPHOLOGY (TYPOLOGY) OF SACRIFICE. The various forms of sacrifice show some common elements that respond to the following questions: (1) Who offers the sacrifice? (2) What is offered? (3) What external forms belong to the act of offering? (4) In what places and at what times are sacrifices offered? (5) Who is the recipient of the sacrifice? (6) For what reasons are sacrifices offered? The classifications implied by these questions often overlap (e.g., the type of material used for the sacrifice may determine the rite).

The sacrificer. Most religions allow not only sacrifices offered by a group or community but also individual sacrifices for entirely personal reasons; in unstratified societies, therefore, everyone is in principle able to offer sacrifices. In fact, however, such purely personal sacrifices are rare, and as soon as sacrifices become connected with a group, however small, not every member of the group but only a representative may offer them. The sacrificer may be the head of a family or clan, an elder, or the leader of a band of hunters; in matrilinear societies, the sacrificer may be a woman. This is true especially of hunting and food-gathering cultures as well as nomadic pastoral cultures; even when these include individuals with specific ritual functions (medicine men, sorcerers, soothsayers, shamans), the function of offering sacrifice is not reserved to them. (In pastoral cultures we can sometimes see that only at a secondary stage do shamans replace family heads for certain sacrifices.) Food-planting cultures, on the other hand, commonly have cultic functionaries to whom the offering of sacrifice is reserved (e.g., the "earth-chiefs" in West African cultures). In sacrifices occasioned by some public endeavor or concern (e.g., an epidemic, or before or after a military campaign) the head of the tribe or larger group is the natural offerer of sacrifice. In archaic high cultures the function often goes with the kingly office; frequently, however, it decreases in importance in the course of further development and is then discernible only in vestigial form.

The more fully articulated the divisions in a society, the more often there is a class of cultic ministers to whom the offering of sacrifice is reserved. In this situation, tensions and changing relations of power can arise between king and priests, as in ancient Egypt. When a special priestly class exists, membership is either hereditary or must be earned through a consecration that is often preceded by lengthy training, or both may be required: descent from a certain family, class, or caste and training that leads to consecration. The consecrated functionary who is an offerer of sacrifice often must then submit to further special preparation (through purificatory rites, etc.) before exercising his office. A priest may have other cultic or magical functions in addition to that of offering sacrifice; he may, for example, act as oracle, exorcist, healer, or rainmaker, he may be a source of tradition and knowledge, and he may have noncultic functions as well.

Myths sometimes speak of the gods themselves as offering sacrifice. Sacrifice by human beings is then simply an imitation of the primal sacrifice that played a role in the establishment of the cosmic order.

Material of the oblation. Scholars often generalize, as for example: "If we look about in the history of religion, we find there are very few things that have not, at some time or in some place, served as offering" (van Baaren, 1964, p. 7). Others will say that everything which has a value for human beings can be the material of sacrifice; the value may be symbolic and not necessarily inherent (as seen, for example, in the firstlings sacrifices of food-gatherers). Perhaps we may say that originally what was sacrificed was either something living or an element or symbol of life; in other words, it was not primarily food that was surrendered, but life itself. Yet inanimate things were also included in the material for sacrifice. (But do not archaic cultures regard a great deal as living that to the modern scientific mind is inanimate? Some scholars emphasize not the life but the power of the object.) Only by including inanimate objects is it possible to establish a certain classification of sacrificial objects, as for example, on the one hand, plants and inanimate objects (bloodless offerings), and, on the other, human beings and animals (blood offerings). But such a division is not exhaustive, since a comprehensive concept of sacrifice must include, for example, a bloodless consecration of human beings and animals.

Bloodless offerings. Bloodless offerings include, in the first place, vegetative materials. Thus food-gatherers offer a (symbolic) portion of the foodstuffs they have collected. Cultivators offer to higher beings (whom they may regard as in need of nourishment) sacrifices of food and drink: fruits, tubers, grains, and the foods that are made from these plants (meal, baked goods, oil), along with drinks, especially beer and other alcoholic beverages, that are poured out as libations. Among herders milk and milk products (e.g., koumiss, a drink derived from milk and slightly fermented, used in Inner Asia) play a similar role, especially in firstlings sacrifices (see below). In the ritual pouring (and especially in other ritual uses) of water, the intention is often not sacrifice but either some other type of rite (lustration, purification, or expiation) or sympathetic magic (e.g., pouring water in order to bring on rain). The offering of flowers or of a sweet fragrance otherwise produced (as in the widespread use of incense, or, among the American Indians, of tobacco smoke) also serves to please the gods or other higher beings.

Inanimate objects used in sacrifice include clothing, jewelry, weapons, precious stones and precious metals, sacrificial vessels made of metal, and, in more advanced civilizations, coins (especially as substitutes). Also used in sacrifice are all sorts of objects that are offered as votive gifts and are kept in a sanctuary, though it is possible that sympathetic magic also plays a role here, as for instance when one seeks deliverance from illnesses by depositing likenesses of the diseased organs.

Blood offerings. When animals or human beings serve as the sacrificial gift, the shedding of blood may become an essential part of the sacrificial action. Thus *ritual* slaying makes its appearance among cultivators and herders. (The practice is generally not found in hunting cultures, where a small but symbolically important part of the animal slain during the hunt is offered; thus the slaying is not part of the sacrificial action but precedes it. The slaying by the Ainu of a bear raised for the purpose is perhaps not really a sacrifice but a "dismissal" rite.)

The most extensive development of ritual slaying is found among cultivators. Here blood plays a significant role as a power-laden substance that brings fertility; it is sprinkled on the fields in order to promote crop yield. Head-hunting, cannibalism, and human sacrifice belong to the same complex of ideas and rites; human sacrifice is also seen as a means of maintaining the cosmic order. The combination of blood rites with magical conceptions of fertility is found more among tuber cultivators than among grain cultivators (but it is also found among maize growers, as in Mesoamerica). The assumption that all blood sacrifices originated among food cultivators and then were adopted at a later stage by nomadic herders is one-sided; ritual slaying probably made its appearance independently among the latter.

Blood sacrifices consist primarily of domesticated animals: among cultivators, sheep, goats, cattle, pigs, fowl; among nomads, also reindeer, horses, and camels (whereas pigs are regarded as unclean animals and not used, while fowl would not usually be kept). Dogs too may serve as sacrificial animals; they are especially sacrificed to provide companions for the dead. The offering of fish, birds other than domesticated fowl or doves, and wild animals is rarer. The characteristics of the sacrificial animal are often determined by the recipient; thus brightly colored animals are offered to the divinities of the sky, black animals to the divinities of the underworld and the dead or to feared demonic beings.

Sacrificial animals are not always killed by the shedding of their blood; they are sometimes throttled (especially in Inner Asia) or drowned in water or a bog. Furthermore, there is also the bloodless consecration of an animal, in which the animal is not killed but transferred alive into the possession of the divinity or other higher being, after which it often lives out its life in a sacred enclosure. Such animals can best be described as offerings, not as victims.

Substitutes. Blood sacrifices, especially those in which human beings were offered, were often replaced at a later stage by other sacrificial gifts, as, for example, "part-for-the-whole" sacrifices, like the offering of fingers, hair, or blood drawn through self-inflicted wounds. Some authors would thus classify so-called chastity sacrifices and include under this heading very disparate and sometimes even opposed practices such as, on the one hand, sexual abandon (sacral prostitution) and, on the other, sexual renunciation, castration, and circumcision.

Animal sacrifices can replace human sacrifices, as seen in well-known examples from Greek myth, epic, and history and in the Hebrew scriptures (Old Testament; *Gn.* 22:1–19). This shift may also be due to the suppression of an older religion (e.g., of the Bon religion of Tibet by Buddhism) or to measures taken by a colonial regime (e.g., the British rule in India) against human sacrifice. Substitute gifts for human beings or animals may also be of a vegetative kind (e.g., sacrificial cakes) or may consist of payments of money. Another form of substitution is that by representations, such as the clay figure substitutes for human beings that were buried with a high-ranking dead person and sent into the next world with him. Such figurines accompanying the dead are known from ancient Egypt and China; however, it is not certain that the practice was preceded by actual human sacrifices in these countries or that these practices are best described as sacrifices. Other kinds of pictorial representations have also been used, including objects cut from paper. Many votive offerings should probably be listed under this heading.

That human sacrifices were replaced by other kinds of sacrifices is certain in many instances, as in the late stage of Punic religion, when under Roman rule human sacrifices were replaced by other gifts (for example, lambs), as is attested by votive inscriptions; in other instances it is simply a hypothesis that certain rites replaced human sacrifice. Thus the so-called hair sacrifice is often a rite of initiation, sacralization, or desacralization (a rite of passage) in which the hair is not really a sacrificial gift and need not have replaced any human sacrifice. Sacral prostitution may also be understood as a magical rite of fertility or as a symbolic act of union with a divinity, rather than as a substitute for human sacrifice.

Divine offerings. In the examples given under the previous heading, a sacrificial gift is replaced by another of lesser value. The opposite occurs when the sacrificial gift itself is regarded as divine. This divine status may result from the idea that the sacrificial action repeats a mythical primordial sacrifice in which a god sacrificed either himself or some other god to yet a third god. In other cases the sacrificial object becomes divinized in the sacrificial action itself or in the preparation of the gifts. Thus among the Aztec the prisoner of war who was sacrificed was identified with the recipient of the sacrifice, the god Tezcatlipoca; moreover images of dough, kneaded with the blood of the sacrificed human, were identified with the sun god Huitzilopochtli and ritually eaten. In the Vedic religion divinity was assigned to the intoxicating drink *soma,* and in Iranian religion to the corresponding drink *haoma* or to the plant from which it was derived. For Christians who regard the celebration of the Eucharist as a rendering present of Christ's death on the cross, Christ himself is both offerer and sacrificial gift.

Rite (manner and method) of sacrifice. Sacrifice involves not only a visible gift but an action or gesture that expresses the offering. This may consist of a simple deposition or a lifting up of the gift, without any change being effected in the object. The external form of the offering is already determined in many cases by the material of sacrifice; in the case of fluids, for example, the natural manner of offering them is to pour them out (libation), which is a kind of destruction. If the gift is a living being (animal or human), the destruction takes the form of killing. It is doubtful, however, whether destruction can be regarded as an essential element of any and every sacrificial rite. It is true that in many sacrifices the offering is in the form of slaughter or ritual killing; in others, however, the slaughter is only a necessary presupposition or technical requirement for the act of offering as such. Thus, among the Israelites, Levitical law prescribed that the slaughtering not be done by the priest; the latter's role began only after the slaughtering and included the pouring of sacrificial blood on the altar.

When food as such is in principle the real object offered, slaughter is a necessary first step if the animal sacrificed is to be in a form in which it can be eaten. When it is thought that the divinity (or, more generally, the recipient) does not eat material food but simply receives the soul or life of the sacrificial animal, burning may be used as a way of letting the soul rise up in the form of smoke ("the odor of sacrifice"; see also, on the burning of incense, below). When blood in particular is regarded as the vehicle of life, the pouring out of the blood, or the lifting up of bleeding parts of the victim, or even the flow of blood in the slaughtering may be the real act of offering. Another category of blood rites serves to apply the power in the blood to the offerers, their relatives, and the sphere in which they live their life (dwelling, property); this application may take the form of, for example, smearing.

The conception that the offerers have of the recipient and of his or her location also helps determine the form of the rite. If the recipient is thought to dwell in heaven, then the smoke that rises from a burning object becomes an especially appropriate symbol. The offerers will prefer the open air and will choose high places, whether natural (mountains, hills) or artificial (roofs, temple towers), or else they will hang the sacrificial gift on a tree or stake. Sacrifices to chthonic or underworld beings are buried, or the blood is allowed to flow into a hole. For water divinities or spirits the sacrifice is lowered into springs, wells, streams, or other bodies of water (although the interpretation of prehistoric burials in bogs as "immersion sacrifices" is not undisputed), or the offerers fill miniature boats with sacrificial gifts. Sacrifices offered to the dead are placed on the graves of the latter, or the blood of the victims is poured onto these graves.

Finally, the intention of the offerers or the function of the sacrifice also influences the form of the rite. If the sacrifice establishes or renews a covenant or, more generally, if it promotes the communion or community of recipient and offerer, then a sacrificial meal is usually an indispensable part of the rite. This meal can be understood as sharing a meal with the god or, the recipient, or more rarely, as ingesting the god; in this second case, the communion has a mystical character. In the first case, acceptance by the recipient removes the sacrificial gift from the profane sphere and sanctifies it; the recipient now becomes a host and celebrates a banquet with the offerer, who thereby receives back the sacrificial gift (or at least a part of it) as a vehicle now laden with higher powers. Thus understood, the sacrificial meal can be called a sacrament. The meal also establishes or strengthens the communion of the offerers with one another when it is a group that makes the offering. More rarely, people have believed that they eat the god himself in the flesh of the sacrificial animal (as in some Greek mysteries) or in images of dough (which were sometimes mixed with the blood of sacrificed human beings, as among the Aztec). (For the Christian conception of the Eucharist as a sacrificial meal, see below.)

Other rituals also express communion. For example, part of the sacrificial blood is poured on the altar, while the participants are sprinkled with the rest (as in the making of the covenant at Sinai, according to *Ex.* 24: 3-8). Or a person walks between the pieces of a sacrificial animal that has been cut in half.

In other cases the victim is completely destroyed, as in a burnt offering, or holocaust, which may express homage or complete submission to the divinity on which the offerers consider themselves dependent. Total destruction often also characterizes an expiatory sacrifice, in which a sacrificial meal is antecedently excluded by the fact that the sacrificial animal becomes the vehicle of sin or other uncleanness and must therefore be eliminated or destroyed (e.g., by being burned outside the camp).

The ritual of sacrifice can take very complicated forms, especially when professionals (priests) do the offering; part of their training is then the acquisition of a precise knowledge of the ritual. The sacrificial action is in stages: the sacrificial animal is often chosen some time in advance, marked, and set aside; before the sacrificial act proper, it is ritually purified and adorned; next comes the slaughter of the animal, then the offering proper or consecration or transfer from the profane to the sacred sphere or condition. At times, signs are heeded that are thought to show acceptance of the gift by the recipient. The division of the sacrificed animal can take various forms: an uncontrolled tearing apart of the victim by the participants, in imitation of a dismemberment reported in myth, or a careful dissection, as when the condition of specific organs yields omens (divination). In some sacrifices the bones may not be broken. A special form of division is cutting in two, which is practiced not only in sacrifices proper but also in rites of purification and expiation. (See Henninger, 1981, pp. 275–285.) A sacrificial meal may conclude the sacrifice, but there may also be special concluding rites for releasing the participants from the realm of the sacred. It is sometimes also prescribed that nothing is to be left of the sacrificial gift and nothing carried away from the sphere of the sacred; any remnants must be buried or burned (though this last action is not the same as a burnt offering).

Place and time of sacrifice. The place of offering is not always an altar set aside for the purpose. Thus sacrifices to the dead are often offered at their graves, and sacrifices to the spirits of nature are made beside trees or bushes, in caves, at springs, and so on. Artificial altars in the form of tables are relatively rare; they become the normal site of sacrifice only in the higher civilizations, where they are usually located in a temple or its forecourt and are sometimes specially outfitted, as for example with channels to carry away the sacrificial blood. Far more frequently, natural stones or heaps of stones or earthen mounds serve as altars. A perpendicular stone is often regarded as the seat of a divinity, and sacrifice is then offered in front of the stone, not on it. Flat roofs and thresholds can also be preferred locations for sacrifice.

With regard to time, a distinction must be made between regular and extraordinary (occasional or special) sacrifices. The time for regular sacrifices is determined by the astronomical or vegetative year; thus there will be daily, weekly, and monthly sacrifices (especially in higher cultures in which service in the temple is organized like service at a royal court). Sowing and harvest and the transition from one season to the next are widely recognized occasions for sacrifice; in nomadic cultures this is true especially of spring, the season of birth among animals and of abundance of milk. The harvest season is often marked by first-fruits sacrifices that are conceived as a necessary condition for the desacralization of the new harvest, which may only then be put to profane use. The date of the New Year feast is often established not astronomically but in terms of the vegetative year. In the life of the individual, birth, puberty, marriage, and death are frequently occasions for sacrifices. The annual commemoration of a historical event may also become a set part of the calendar and thus an occasion for sacrifice.

Extraordinary occasions for sacrifice are provided by special occurrences in the life of the community or the individual. These occurrences may be joyous, as, for example, the erection of a building (especially a temple), the accession of a new ruler, the successful termination of a military campaign or other undertaking, or any event that is interpreted as a manifestation of divine favor. Even more frequently, however, it is critical situations that occasion extraordinary sacrifices: illnesses (especially epidemics or livestock diseases) and droughts or other natural disasters. Many expiatory sacrifices also have their place in this context, whether offered for individuals or the community (see below).

Van Baal (1976, pp. 168–178) distinguishes between low-intensity and high-intensity rites; the former occur in normal situations, the latter in disasters and misfortunes, which are taken as signs that relations with higher beings have been disturbed. This division is to a great extent the same as that between regular and extraordinary sacrifices, but it pays insufficient heed to the fact that joyous occasions may also lead to extraordinary sacrifices.

Recipient of sacrifice. Many definitions of sacrifice specify divine beings (in either a monotheistic or a polytheistic context) as the recipients of sacrifice, but this is too narrow a view. All the many kinds of beings to whom humans pay religious veneration, or even those whom they fear, can be recipients of sacrifice. Such recipients can thus be spirits, demonic beings, and even humans, although sacrifice in the proper sense is offered to humans only when they have died and are considered to possess a superhuman power. The dead to whom sacrifice is offered include especially the ancestors to whom is attributed (as in Africa and Oceania) a decisive influence on human beings. Care for the dead (e.g., by gifts of food and drink) need not always indicate a cult of the dead; a cult exists only when the dead are regarded not as helpless and in need (as they were in ancient Mesopotamia), but rather as possessing superhuman power.

Intentions of sacrifice. Theologians usually distinguish four intentions of sacrifice: praise (acknowledgment, homage), thanksgiving, supplication, and expiation; but several or even all four of these intentions may be combined in a single sacrifice. From the standpoint of the history of religions this schema must be expanded somewhat, especially with regard to the third and fourth categories.

Praise (homage). Pure sacrifices of praise that express nothing but homage and veneration and involve no other intention are rarely found. They occur chiefly where a regular sacrificial cult is practiced that resembles in large measure the ceremonial of a royal court.

Thanksgiving. Sacrifices of thanksgiving are more frequent. According to the best explanation of firstlings sacrifices, these, in the diverse forms they have taken in various cultures, belong to this category. (For divergent interpretations, see "Theories of the Origin of Sacrifice," below.) Votive sacrifices likewise belong here, insofar as the fulfillment of the vow is an act of thanksgiving for the favor granted.

Supplication. Yet more commonly found are sacrifices of supplication. The object of the petition can range from purely material goods to the highest spiritual blessings (forgiveness of sins, divine grace). The line of demarcation between these sacrifices and sacrifices of expiation and propitiation is often blurred.

Sacrifices of supplication include all those sacrifices that, in addition to establishing or consolidating the link with the world of the sacred (which is a function of every sacrifice), are intended to have some special effect. Such effects include the maintenance of the cosmic order; the strengthening of the powers on which this order depends (e.g., by the gift of blood, as in the human sacrifices of the Aztec); and the sacralization or consecration of places, objects, and buildings (construction sacrifices, dedication of boundary stones, idols, temples), of individual human beings, and of human communities and their relationships (ratification of treaties). Construction activities are often thought to be an intrusion into the sphere of superhuman beings (spirits of earth and water, or divinities of earth and water) who may resent them; for this reason, scholars speak in this context of sacrifices intended to appease or placate. These come close to being expiatory sacrifices (in the broadest sense of the term), insofar as the offerers intend to forestall the anger of these higher beings by a preventive, apotropaic action (protective sacrifices).

Sacrifices are also offered for highly specialized purposes, for example, in order to foretell the future by examining the entrails of the sacrificial animal.

Expiation. In the narrow sense, expiatory sacrifices presuppose consciousness of a moral fault that can be punished by a higher being who must therefore be placated by suitable acts on the part of the human beings involved. But the concept of expiation (purification, lustration) is often used in a broader sense to mean the removal or prevention of every kind of evil and misfortune. Many authors assume that the ethical concept of sin was a late development and therefore consider rites of purification and elimination for the removal of all evils (in which no relation to higher personal beings plays a part) to be the earliest form of expiation. Furthermore, when there is a human relationship to personal beings, a distinction must be made. These beings (spirits, demons, etc.) may be regarded as indifferent to ethical considerations, unpredictable, and capricious, or even malicious, envious, cruel, and bloodthirsty. In this case expiation means simply the removal of what has roused (or might rouse) the anger of these beings, so that they will leave humans in peace; no relationship of goodwill or friendship is created or sought. On the other hand, the higher beings may be regarded as inherently benevolent, so that any disturbance of a good relationship with them is attributed to a human fault; the normal good relationship must therefore be restored by an expiatory sacrifice or other human action; in these cases we speak of atonement, conciliation, or propitiation. The human fault in question may be moral, but it may also be purely ritual, unintentional, or even unconscious.

Certain facts, however, render questionable the overly schematic idea of a unilinear development from a non-ethical to an ethical conception that is connected with general theories on the evolution of religion. Even very "primitive" peoples have ideas of higher beings that approve and keep watch over moral behavior. Furthermore, not only in the high cultures but in primitive religions as well, expiatory sacrifice is often accompanied by a confession of sins. A more highly developed form of the ideas underlying expiatory sacrifice may be linked to the concept of representation or substitution, especially when the role of substitute is freely accepted (self-sacrifice). This, however, is not the proper context for speculative theories (developed especially by James G. Frazer and those inspired by him) on the ritual slaying of the king, who may be replaced by a substitute; Frazer is speaking of the magical influence of the king in his prime on the general welfare of the community, and not of disturbances of the communal order by faults for which amends must be made.

THEORIES OF THE ORIGIN OF SACRIFICE. Very different answers have been given to the question of which of the various forms of sacrifice presented above is to be regarded as the oldest and the one out of which the others emerged either by development to a higher level or by degeneration. In each case, theories of sacrifice have been heavily influenced by their authors' conceptions of the origin and development of religion. Scholars today generally approach all these explanations with some skepticism. A brief review of the various theories is nonetheless appropriate, since each emphasizes certain aspects of the phenomenon and thus contributes to an understanding of it.

Sacrifice as gift. Before the history of religions became an independent discipline, the conception of sacrifice as gift was already current among theologians; it was therefore natural that the history of religions should initially make use of this concept. In this discipline, however, the conception acquired two completely different applications: the sacrificial gift as bribe and the sacrificial gift as act of homage.

The gift as bribe. The gift theory proposed by E. B. Tylor (1871) supposes that higher forms of religion, including monotheism, gradually developed out of animism as the earliest form. Since the spirits resident in nature are indifferent to moral considerations and have but a limited sphere of power, they can be enriched by gifts and thereby influenced; in other words, they can be bribed. Sacrifice was therefore originally a simple business transaction of *do ut des* ("I give so that you will give in return"), an activity without moral significance. Sacrifice as homage and as abnegation or renunciation developed only gradually out of sacrifice as bribe; but even when it did, the *do ut des* idea continued to be operative for a long time in the later stages of religion, especially wherever sacrifice was conceived as supplying the recipient with food.

Critics of this view have stressed that in archaic cultures the giving of a gift, even between human beings, is not a purely external transaction but at the same time establishes a personal relation between giver and recipient. According to some scholars, the giving of a gift also involves a transfer of magical power for which, in a very generalized sense, they often use the term *mana.* This personal relation is even more important when a gift is presented to superhuman beings. Thus it is understandable that sacrificial gifts of little material value can be quite acceptable; such gifts need not be interpreted as efforts to circumvent the higher beings and their influence. In light of this consideration, later theories of sacrifice gave the *do ut des* formula a deeper meaning and regarded the commercial understanding of it as a degenerate version.

The gift as homage. Wilhelm Schmidt (1912–1955, 1922) understood the sacrificial gift in a way completely different from Tylor. He took as his point of departure the principle that the original meaning of sacrifice can be seen most clearly in the firstlings sacrifices of primitive hunters and food-gatherers. These are sacrifices of homage and thanksgiving to the supreme being to whom everything belongs and who therefore cannot be enriched by gifts—sacrifices to the giver of foods that human beings do not produce but simply appropriate for themselves through hunting and gathering. These sacrifices consist in the offering of a portion of food that is often quantitatively small but symbolically important. In nomadic herding cultures this sacrifice of homage and thanksgiving takes the form of an offering of the firstlings of the flocks (young animals) or of the products of the flocks (e.g., milk). In food-growing cultures the fertility of the soil is often attributed to the dead, especially the ancestors; they, therefore, become the recipients of the first-fruits sacrifice. When this happens, however, the character of the sacrifice is altered, since the recipients now have need of the gifts (as food) and can therefore be influenced. According to Anton Vorbichler (1956), what is offered in firstlings sacrifices is not food but life itself, but since life is seen as deriving from the supreme being as creator, the basic attitude of homage and thanksgiving remains unchanged.

Schmidt's historical reconstruction, according to which firstlings sacrifices are the earliest form of sacrifice, has not been sufficiently demonstrated. From the phenomenological standpoint, however, this kind of sacrifice, in which the gift has symbolic rather than real value and is inspired by a consciousness of dependence and thanksgiving, does exist and must therefore be taken into account in any general definition of sacrifice.

Sacrifice as a (totemic) communal meal. W. Robertson Smith (1889) developed a theory of sacrifice for the Semitic world that he regarded as universally applicable. He saw the weakness of Tylor's theory, which paid insufficient heed to the sacral element and to the function of establishing or maintaining a community. Under the influence of J. F. McLennan, who had done pioneer work in the study of totemism, Smith proposed a theory of sacrifice whereby the earliest form of religion (among the Semites and elsewhere) was belief in a theriomorphic tribal divinity with which the tribe had a blood relationship. Under ordinary circumstances, this totem animal was not to be killed, but there were rituals in which it was slain and eaten in order to renew the community. In this rite, recipient, offerer, and victim were all of the same nature; sacrifice was thus originally a meal in which the offerers entered into communion with the totem. As a vivid example of such a ceremony, Smith cites a story told by Nilus of a camel sacrifice offered by the bedouin of the Sinai. It was the transition to a sedentary way of life and the social changes effected by this transition that gave rise to the conception of sacrifice as a gift comparable to the tribute paid to a sovereign, the latter relationship being taken as model for the relation to the divinity. The burnt offering, or holocaust, was likewise a late development.

Smith's theory is valuable for its criticism of the grossly mechanistic theory of Tylor and for its emphasis on the communion (community) aspect of sacrifice; as a whole, however, it is unacceptable for a number of reasons. First, the idea of sacrifice as gift is already present in the firstlings sacrifices offered in the egalitarian societies of primitive hunters and food-gatherers; it does not, therefore, presuppose the model of the offering of tribute to a sovereign. Second, it is doubtful that totemism existed among the Semites; furthermore, totemism does not occur universally as a stage in the history of human development, as was initially supposed in the nineteenth century when the phenomenon was first discovered, but is rather a specialized development. Third, the *intichiuma* ceremonies (increase ceremonies) of central Australian tribes are magical rites aimed at multiplying the totem animal species. They were used by early theorists of totemism, but they do not in fact match the original model of sacrifice postulated by Smith. Finally, the supposed account by Nilus is not a reliable report from a hermit living in the Sinai Peninsula but a fiction whose author is unknown; it shares with the late Greek novel certain clichés used in depicting barbarians and cannot be regarded as a reliable historical source (see Henninger, 1955). Smith's theory of sacrifice also contributed to Freud's conception of the slaying of the primal father, which Freud saw as the origin of sacrifice and other institutions, especially the incest taboo; this conception is therefore subject to the same criticisms.

A link between the profane and sacral worlds. Henri Hubert and Marcel Mauss (1899) rejected Tylor's theory because of its mechanistic character. They also rejected Smith's theory because it arbitrarily chose totemism as a universally applicable point of departure and reconstructed the development of the forms of sacrifice solely by analogy and without adequate historical basis and, further, because offering is an essential element in the concept of sacrifice. Hubert and Mauss themselves begin with an analysis of the Vedic and Hebraic rituals of sacrifice and, in light of this, define sacrifice as "a religious act which, by the consecration of a victim, modifies the condition of the moral person who accomplishes it, or that of certain objects with which he is concerned" (*Encyclopaedia Britannica,* 1977, vol. 16, p. 129a). The victim is not holy by nature (as it is in Smith's theory); the consecration is effected by destruction, and the connection with the sacral world is completed by a sacred meal. Implied here is the view (which goes back to Émile Durkheim) of the French sociological school that the sacral world is simply a projection of society. "Gods are representations of communities, they are societies thought of ideally and imaginatively. . . . Sacrifice is an act of abnegation by which the individual recognizes society; it recalls to particular consciences the presence of collective forces, represented by their gods" (Evans-Pritchard, 1965, p. 70).

The objection was raised against this explanation that conclusions universally valid for the understanding of sacrifice as such, especially in "primitive" societies, cannot be drawn from an analysis of two highly developed forms of sacrifice, even if the two differ among themselves. Thus E. E. Evans-Pritchard, having called the work of Hubert and Mauss "a masterly analysis of Vedic and Hebrew sacrifice," immediately adds: "But masterly though it was, its conclusions are an unconvincing piece of sociologistic metaphysics. . . . They are conclusions not deriving from, but posited on a brilliant analysis of the mechanism of sacrifice, or perhaps one should say of its logical structure, or even of its grammar" (Evans-Pritchard, 1965, pp. 70–71).

Sacrifice as magic. Hubert and Mauss considered the recipient of sacrifice to be simply a hypostatization of society itself. Other authors have gone even further, regarding the idea of a recipient as not essential to the concept of sacrifice. They more or less explicitly presuppose that the idea of an impersonal force or power, to which the name *mana* is given more frequently than any other, is older than the idea of soul or spirit as understood in animism. For this reason, the idea of sacrifice as a purely objective magical action (the triggering of a magical force that is thought to be concentrated especially in the blood), accomplished by destruction of a sacrificial gift (e.g., the slaying of an animal), must be the basic form, or at least one of the basic forms, of sacrifice. Sacrifices of this kind are said to be "predeistic." Expressions such as this, which imply a temporal succession, are also used by phenomenologists, who claim in principle to be simply describing phenomena and not asserting any kind of development. In this view the concept of sacrifice as gift is a secondary development in which gifts to the dead played an important role (Loisy, 1920). According to Gerardus van der Leeuw (1920–1921), sacrifice conceived as gift constitutes a transfer of magical force; the *do ut des* formula describes not a commercial transaction but the release of a current of force (*do ut possis dare,* "I give power to you so that you can give it back to me"). The recipient is strengthened by the gift; the two participants, deity and human beings, are simultaneously givers and receivers, but the central role belongs to the gift itself and to the current of force that it sets in motion. This theory, then, combines to some extent the gift theory and the communion theory, but it does so from the standpoint of magic.

There do in fact exist rituals of slaying and destruction in which no personal recipient is involved and that are regarded as operating automatically; there is no evidence, however, that such rituals are older than sacrifice in the sense described earlier. The examples constantly adduced come to a very great extent from high cultures (e.g., Roman religion). An especially typical form occurs in Brahmanic speculation, where sacrifice is looked upon as a force that ensures the continuation of a cosmic process to which even the gods are subject. Other examples come from food-growing peoples. When human beings contribute by their own activity to the production of food, their consciousness of dependence on higher powers is less than in an economy based on the appropriation of goods not produced by humans. Thus it is easier to adopt the idea that the higher powers can be influenced and even coerced by sacrifices and other rites. For this reason, the firstlings sacrifices of hunters and food-gatherers do not fit in with speculations that give priority to magic, nor do such speculations take account of such sacrifices, and thus the full extent of the phenomenon of sacrifice is lost from view. Sacrifice and magic should rather be considered as phenomena that differ in nature; they have indeed influenced each other in many ways, but neither can be derived from the other. The personal relation that is established by a gift is fully intelligible without bringing in an element of magic (see van Baal, 1976, pp. 163–164, 167, 177–178).

Sacrifice as reenactment of primordial events. According to Adolf E. Jensen (1951), sacrifice cannot be understood as gift; its original meaning is rather to be derived from certain myths found in the cultures of cultivators, especially in Indonesia and Oceania. These myths maintain that in primordial time there were as yet no mortal human beings but only divine or semi-divine beings (*dema* beings); this state ended with the killing of a *dema* divinity from whose body came the plants useful to humans. The ritual slaying of humans and animals, headhunting, cannibalism, and other blood rites are ceremonial repetitions of that killing in primordial time; they affirm and guarantee the present world order, with its continuous destruction and recreation, which would otherwise be unable to function. Once the myth had been largely forgotten or was no longer seen to be connected with ritual, rites involving slaying were reinterpreted as a giving of a gift to divinities (who originally played no role in these rites, because the primordial divine being had been slain); blood sacrifices thus became "meaningless survivals" of the "meaningful rituals of killing" of the earlier food-growing cultures. Magical actions are likewise degenerate fragments of the originally meaningful whole formed by the mythically based rituals of killing.

This theory has some points in common with Freud's theory of the murder of the primal father and with the theory according to which sacrifice originated in the self-sacrifice of a divine being in the primordial time of myth. The common weakness of all these theories is that they take account only of blood sacrifices. These, however, developed only in food-growing and even later cultures, whereas in the firstlings sacrifices of hunters and food-gatherers there is no ritual killing, and bloodless offerings are widespread in many other cultures as well.

Sacrifice as anxiety reaction. In the theories discussed thus far, except for the theory of sacrifice as a gift in homage, firstlings sacrifices receive either inadequate attention or none at all. Vittorio Lanternari (1976), on the other hand, provides a formal discussion of these, but gives an interpretation of them that is completely different from that of Schmidt. Lanternari's point of departure is the analysis of a certain form of neurosis provided by some psychologists; according to this analysis, this kind of neurosis finds expression in the undoing of successes earlier achieved and is at the basis of certain religious delusions. Lanternari maintains that a similar psychic crisis occurs among "primitives" when they are confronted with success (hunters after a successful hunt, food cultivators after the harvest) and that this crisis leads them to undertake an at least symbolic destruction of what they had gained. For Lanternari, then, a firstlings sacrifice is the result of anxiety, whereas for Schmidt it is an expression of gratitude. Hunters feel the slaying of the animal to be a sacrilege, which explains the rites of Siberian peoples that seek a reconciliation with the slain animal and a repudiation of the killing. For cultivators the sacrilege consists in the violation of the earth, which is the dwelling of the dead, by the cultivation of the soil; they feel anxiety at the thought of the dead and worry about future fertility, even if the harvest is a good one. It is a secondary matter whether the symbolic destruction of the gain is accomplished by offering food to a higher being or by simply doing away with a portion of it.

Critics of the psychopathological explanation have pointed out the essential differences between the behavior of neurotics and the religious behavior exhibited in firstlings sacrifices. In the psychically ill (those who are defeated by success), efforts at liberation are purely individual; they are not part of a historical tradition, are not organically integrated into a cultural setting, and do not lead to inner deliverance. In religious life, on the contrary, efforts to surmount a crisis are organically inserted into tradition and culture, tend to restore psychic balance, and in fact achieve such a balance. For this reason the "primitive" peoples in question are not defeated by life, as neurotics are; on the contrary, their way of life has stood the test of ages. Whatever judgment one may pass on the value or nonvalue of the underlying religious views and modes of behavior of these peoples, one cannot characterize them as pathological; for this reason a psychopathological explanation of sacrifice must also be rejected. This is not to deny that fear or anxiety plays a significant part in certain forms of sacrifice; such feelings result primarily from the ideas of the offerers about the character of the recipient in question (see Henninger, 1968, pp. 176–180).

Sacrifice as a mechanism for diverting violence. Whereas Jensen derived rituals involving killing, which were subsequently reinterpreted as "sacrifices," from certain myths of food-growing cultures, René Girard (1977, 1978) has proposed a more comprehensive theory that explains not only sacrifice but the sacred itself as resulting from a focusing of violent impulses upon a substitute object, a scapegoat. According to Girard, the peaceful coexistence of human beings cannot be taken for granted; when the desires of humans fasten upon the same object, rivalries arise and with them a tendency toward violence that endangers the existing order and its norms. This tendency can be neutralized, however, if the reciprocal aggressions are focused on a marginal object, a scapegoat. The scapegoat is thereby rendered sacred: it is seen as accursed but also as bringing salvation. Thus the focusing of violence on an object gives rise to the sacred and all that results from it (taboos, a new social order). Whereas the violence was originally focused on a randomly chosen object, in sacrifice the concentration takes a strict ritual form; as a result, internecine aggressions are constantly being diverted to the outside and cannot operate destructively within the community. At bottom, therefore, sacrifice lacks any moral character. Eventually it was eliminated by the critique of sacrifice that began in the Hebrew scriptures and, most fully, by the fact that Jesus freely made himself a "scapegoat" and in so doing transcended the whole realm of sacrifice. Girard supports his thesis by appealing to the phenomenon of blood sacrifice, which (especially in the form of human sacrifice) is a constant in the history of religions, and by citing the evidence of rivalry and violence, leading even to fratricide, that is supplied by the mythical traditions (especially myths of the origin of things) and also by history (persecution of minorities as scapegoats, etc.).

A critique of this theory can in part repeat the arguments already advanced against Jensen. Apart from the fact that it does not distinguish between sacrifice and eliminatory rites, Girard's concept of sacrifice is too narrow, for he supports it by reference solely to stratified societies and high cultures. It could at most explain blood sacrifices involving killing, but not sacrifice as such and certainly not the sacred as such, since the idea of the sacred exists even among peoples (e.g., in Australia) who do not practice sacrifice. As was pointed out earlier, firstlings sacrifices (of which Girard does not speak) have intellectual and emotional presuppositions far removed from Girard's key concepts of "primal murder" and "scapegoat mechanism."

The value of the theories here reviewed is that each of them highlights a certain aspect of sacrifice. It is unlikely that we will ever have a sure answer to the question of whether there was a single original form of sacrifice or whether, on the contrary, various forms developed independently.

Sacrifice in History. It will never be possible to write a complete history of sacrifice. In any case, sacrifice is found in most of the religions known to us. The extent to which the human mind has taken the phenomenon of sacrifice for granted is clear, for example, from the role it plays in many myths dealing with primordial time. Probably to be grouped with these sacrifices is the sacrifice that Utanapishtim, the hero of the Mesopotamian flood story, offers after the flood, as well as the one that Noah offers in the biblical flood story (*Gn.* 9:20–21). Even earlier, the Bible tells of the sacrifices offered by Cain the farmer and Abel the shepherd (*Gn.* 4:3–5); these are expressly said to be firstlings sacrifices. Aristotle, too, was of the opinion that the sacrifice of firstlings (of field and flock) is the oldest form of sacrifice. As we know today, these sacrifices were also performed by peoples—hunters and food-gatherers—whose economy was of a purely appropriative kind.

Archaic cultures. Scholars disagree on whether there are unambiguous indications of sacrifice in the Paleolithic period. On the basis of a comparison with the practices of more recent hunting peoples, various authors have interpreted the burial of the skulls and long bones of cave bears as part of firstling sacrifices; this view, however, has met with strong criticism. Nonetheless, Hermann Müller-Karpe (1966, pp. 224–229) insists that there is clear evidence of sacrifice in the early Paleolithic period. There is undisputed evidence of sacrifice in the Neolithic period (Müller-Karpe, 1968, pp. 334–348; see also pp. 348–371 on the treatment of the dead).

Sacrifice is also found in all the types of nonliterate cultures made known to us by ethnologists. It is not detectable, however, among some primitive hunters and food-gatherers, for example, in Australia; whether it was present there at an earlier time is uncertain. On the other hand, it is amply attested among nomadic shepherds in both Asia and Africa, and among food-growing peoples, from primitive tuber cultivators down to the most highly developed grain growers, who themselves mark a transition to the high cultures (as for instance the ancient rice-growing cultures of Japan and China). It is typical of many food-growing cultures (e.g., in Africa) that, while they believe in a supreme creator god, they assign him hardly any role in cult. Sacrifices are offered primarily or even exclusively to lesser divinities, spirits of nature, and ancestors who in some instances are regarded as mediators and intercessors with the supreme creator god.

Historical high cultures. In Shintō, the ancient nature religion of Japan, sacrifices were offered to the divinities of nature and to the dead; these were in part regularly recurring sacrifices determined by the rhythm of the agricultural year and in part sacrifices of supplication or sacrifices in fulfillment of vows made under extraordinary circumstances. While originally offered simply by individuals, sacrifice eventually became the concern of the community and was therefore offered by the emperor or by priests commissioned by him. Human sacrifices also occurred.

In China the sacrifice that the emperor offered to heaven and earth at the time of the winter solstice had an important function. In addition to sacrifices determined by the agricultural year, sacrifices especially to the ancestors played a large part in the life of the people. These were offered at the graves of the dead, in the clan's hall of the ancestors, or before the family's ancestral tablets. The emperor sacrificed to his ancestors in temples erected especially in their honor.

For ancient Egypt, the archaeological, epigraphical, and literary evidence points to a strictly ritualized sacrificial cult, administered by a highly organized priesthood and including daily sacrifices in the temples, where the divinity was treated like a sovereign in his palace.

The same was true of ancient Mesopotamia, where the Sumerians already had a professional priesthood and a rather full calendar of feasts with accompanying obligatory sacrifices. Both priesthood and calendar were to a very large extent taken over and developed still further by the invading Semites. The ritual and therefore the sacrificial cult of the Hittites were strongly influenced by the pre-Indo-European population of Anatolia (whose language also continued to be largely used in ritual), but were also influenced by Mesopotamia. Mythological and ritual texts from Ugarit give evidence of a sacrificial cult that in part was influenced by Mesopotamia and in part showed peculiarly Canaanite characteristics; some of the terms connected with sacrifice are related to Hebrew terms.

The evidence for the other Semites is sketchy. In the high cultures of southern Arabia, which are known to us from inscriptions dating from as far back as the first millennium BCE, the sacrificial cult was administered by a professional priesthood and was offered mainly to the three major astral divinities (Sun, Moon, Venus). Documentation for northern and central Arabia begins at a later time; apart from rock inscriptions containing scattered details about religion, the chief sources are literary, mostly from the Islamic period, and provide rather sparse information about pilgrimages to the shrines of local divinities and the sacrifices offered there.

In Vedic and later Hindu religion, sacrifice, which was controlled by the brahmans, was ritualized down to the smallest detail and given a comprehensive speculative theological explanation. In the horse sacrifice (the Aśvamedha) and in other cultic practices, as, for example, the sacrifice of butter and of the sacred intoxicating drink *soma,* there are elements common to the Indo-Iranian world, but after the immigration of the Aryans into India, these were to some extent amalgamated there with pre-Aryan rites. Buddhism, on the other hand, rejected sacrifice in principle; tendencies to a spiritualization of sacrifice and its replacement by asceticism are also found in some currents of Hinduism.

Animal sacrifices were also practiced in the oldest form of Iranian religion, where they were inherited from the Indo-Iranian period. During his reform, Zarathushtra (Zoroaster) abolished these practices. In later times such sacrifices again made their appearance to some extent; they were offered, however, not to Ahura Mazdā but to subordinate heavenly beings. Bloodless sacrifices, involving especially the sacred intoxicating drink *haoma,* remained especially important.

Historical Greek religion combined the religion of the Indo-European invaders with that of the pre-Indo-European population; the same combination marked the sacrificial cult. There were bloodless sacrifices of food and drink. In blood sacrifices a distinction was made, as far as objects and ritual were concerned, between those offered to the ouranic gods *(hiereia, thusiai),* which culminated in a sacrificial meal, and those offered to the chthonic gods *(sphagia),* in which there was no sacrificial meal and the victim was often completely cremated or buried (sacrifices of destruction). Pigs and cattle were sacrificed to the ouranic gods, while inedible animals (horses, asses, dogs) were the chief offerings to the chthonic gods. Human sacrifice was later replaced by other sacrifices. The sacrificer was the ruler in the earliest period; later on there were professional priests.

In its earliest form, before intensive contact with Greek religion, Roman religion was pronouncedly agrarian. Occasions for sacrifices were therefore determined primarily by the agricultural year, and only later by special occasions in civic life. Etruscan influence shows in the divination *(haruspicia)* that was connected with sacrifice; the animals sacrificed were chiefly pigs, sheep, and cattle *(suovetaurilia).* Like Roman religion generally, the sacrificial cult had a marked juridical character.

The sacrifices known from the Hebrew scriptures (Old Testament) are, in their external form, largely the same as those found in the surrounding world, especially among the Canaanites. As far as ritual was concerned, a distinction was made chiefly between the burnt offering, or holocaust *(ʿolah),* in which the sacrificial animal was completely burned up, and the sacrifice of salvation or peace *(zevaḥ shelamim).* In the latter, only certain parts of the sacrificial animal were burned; the blood, regarded as the vehicle of life and therefore not to be consumed by humans, was poured out (in many sacrifices it was smeared on the altar), and the rite ended with a sacrificial meal. Expiatory sacrifices constituted a special category comprising *asham,* "guilt sacrifice," and *ḥaṭʾaṭ,* "sacrifice for sin," the distinction between which is not entirely clear. In these sacrifices the animal had to be burned up, probably because it had become the vehicle of impurity. *Minḥah* meant a bloodless sacrifice (of vegetables), but the term was also used in a broader sense. There were, in addition, incense sacrifices and libations. The sacrificial cult was ritualized in great detail, especially in the period after the Babylonian exile. In this ritual the three major feasts, those involving a prescribed pilgrimage to the central sanctuary, were marked by extensive sacrifices. In addition, there were daily sacrifices in the temple. There were also individual occasions for sacrifice, some of them prescribed, others inspired by freely made vows. After the destruction of the Second Temple in 70 CE, the sacrificial cult ceased and was replaced by other religious activities.

Islam is in principle opposed to sacrifice. "It is not their flesh and blood [i.e., that of sacrificial animals] that reaches God but the piety of your heart" (Qurʾān, surah 22:38). Sacrifice thus has no place in official worship. Pre-Islamic blood sacrifices live on, in external form, in the great slaughters that take place as part of the pilgrimage ritual at Mount Arafat near Mecca, and similarly in almost all the countries of the Islamic world, on the tenth day of the month Dhū al-Ḥijjah. These are interpreted, however, as commemorations of the sacrifice of Abraham and as almsgiving, inasmuch as the flesh is given to the poor or to anyone who wants it. Blood sacrifices (and bloodless ones as well) are also part of popular piety, especially of veneration of the saints; but these are not sanctioned by orthodox Islam.

According to New Testament teaching, which is developed especially in the letter to the Hebrews, the sacrifices of the Old Testament were only provisional and had to cease under the new covenant. The self-giving of Jesus in his death on the cross is understood as the definitive and perfect sacrifice that has the power in itself to effect expiation and redemption and that therefore makes all earlier sacrifices superfluous. In the Roman Catholic church and the Eastern churches the celebration of the Eucharist is regarded as a rendering present (not a repetition) of the sacrifice of the cross, and therefore itself constitutes a real sacrifice in which Jesus Christ the high priest, using the ministry of the ordained priests who represent him, offers himself as the perfect sacrificial gift. The sixteenth-century reformers rejected the official priesthood and the sacrificial dimension of the Eucharist (Calvin took the most radical position on this point); the celebration of the Lord's Supper thus became simply a commemoration of Jesus and, though a sacrament, had no sacrificial character. In recent times, there has been a tendency in the Lutheran church to confer to some degree a sacrificial character on the Lord's Supper. Even more explicit however is the emphasis placed on the sacrificial character of the Lord's Supper by the Anglican church. In Protestantism generally the term *sacrifice* refers to a purely interior attitude.

CONCLUSION. In the course of its history, which can be traced through several millennia, sacrifice has undergone many changes, and this in all its aspects: changes in the material of sacrifice (occasioned by economic changes but also by ethical considerations, e.g., in the suppression of human sacrifice); changes with regard to place and time (centralization of cult, regulation of feasts and thereby of the occasions for sacrifice); changes in the offerer (the rise of classes of official sacrificers); and changes in ritual and motivation. These developments do not, however, reflect a one-directional "advance." Egoistic and magical motives were not always eliminated by higher motives; in fact, they often asserted themselves even more strongly in connection with manifestations of religious degeneration. In the same context a quantitative increase in sacrifices is also often to be seen; thus in some late cultures the number of human sacrifices became especially extensive (e.g., among the Punics and the Aztec).

Disapproval and criticism of sacrifice might spring from a skeptical, antireligious attitude that condemned sacrifice as meaningless waste. However, it could also be motivated by a more profound reflection on the meaning of sacrifice in the light of religious interiority, leading to an emphasis on inner conviction, the self-giving of the human being to the divinity, which finds symbolic expression in sacrifice, and without which the external rite has no religious value. This cast of mind could lead to the complete abolition of the external rite, but also to a consciously established accord between external action and interior attitude.

Tendencies to the spiritualization and ethicization of sacrifice were already present in Indian religion, where they produced a mysticism of sacrifice; in the philosophers of classical antiquity, who regarded ethical behavior as of highest value; and above all in the biblical religions. Early in the Hebrew scriptures the idea was expressed that obedience to God's commandments is better than sacrifice (*1 Sm.* 15:22), and the prophetic criticism of sacrifice was directed at an outward cult unaccompanied by interior dispositions and ethical behavior. The wisdom literature, too, repeatedly stresses the superior value of religious dispositions and moral behavior. This outlook became even more pronounced in postbiblical Judaism, once the destruction of the Second Temple in 70 CE had put an end to the sacrificial cult. From the beginning, Christianity emphasized not only the continuance of cultic sacrifice in the celebration of the Eucharist but also the necessity of a self-surrender that finds external expression in other ways as well; thus, even in the New Testament, prayers, hymns of praise, good works, and especially love of neighbor are described as "sacrifices." These tendencies became particularly strong in Protestantism, which no longer acknowledged the Eucharist to be a sacrifice.

Finally, the idea of renunciation, which is connected with the offering of a gift, was especially emphasized in Christianity, so that every kind of asceticism and self-abnegation came to be called sacrifice (there is a similar development in Buddhism). A one-sided emphasis on this aspect led finally to a very broad and metaphorical use of the term *sacrifice.* Thus an abandonment of possessions and a personal commitment to an idea or to the attainment of certain goals, especially if this commitment demands costly effort, is described as sacrifice in the active sense of the term. We also speak of the victims of wars, epidemics, natural disasters, and so on with a sense that they are, in a passive sense, sacrificial victims. Thus the word *sacrifice* ultimately became very much a secular term in common usage; yet the origins of sacrifice in the religious sphere remain evident.

SEE ALSO Atonement; Blood; Cannibalism; Gift Giving; Human Sacrifice; Magic; New Year Festivals; Scapegoat; Seasonal Ceremonies.

BIBLIOGRAPHY

Baal, Jan van. "Offering, Sacrifice and Gift." *Numen* 23 (December 1976): 161–178.

Baaren, Th. P. van. "Theoretical Speculations on Sacrifice." *Numen* 11 (January 1964): 1–12.

Bertholet, Alfred. *Der Sinn des kultischen Opfers.* Berlin, 1942.

Closs, Alois. "Das Opfer in Ost und West." *Kairos* 3 (1961): 153–161.

Evans-Pritchard, E. E. *Theories of Primitive Religion.* Oxford, 1965.

Faherty, Robert L. "Sacrifice." In *Encyclopaedia Britannica.* 15th ed. Chicago, 1974.

Girard, René. *Violence and the Sacred.* Translated by Patrick Gregory. Baltimore, 1977.

Girard, René. *Des choses cachées depuis la fondation du monde.* Paris, 1978.

Gray, Louis H., et al. "Expiation and Atonement." In *Encyclopaedia of Religion and Ethics,* edited by James Hastings, vol. 5. Edinburgh, 1912.

Heiler, Friedrich. *Erscheinungsformen und Wesen der Religion.* Vol. 1 of *Die Religionen der Menschheit.* Stuttgart, 1961.

Henninger, Joseph. "Ist der sogenannte Nilus-Bericht eine brauchbare religionsgeschichtliche Quelle?" *Anthropos* 50 (1955): 81–148.

Henninger, Joseph. "Primitialopfer und Neujahrsfest." In *Anthropica.* Studia Instituti Anthropos, vol. 21. Sankt Augustin, West Germany, 1968.

Henninger, Joseph. *Les fêtes de printemps chez les Sémites et la Pâque israélite.* Paris, 1975.

Henninger, Joseph. *Arabica Sacra: Aufsätze zur Religionsgeschichte Arabiens und seiner Randgebiete.* Fribourg, 1981.

Hubert, Henri, and Marcel Mauss. "Essai sur la nature et la fonction du sacrifice." *L'année sociologique* 2 (1899): 29–138. An English translation was published in 1964 (Chicago): *Sacrifice: Its Nature and Function.*

James, E. O. *Sacrifice and Sacrament.* London, 1962.

James, E. O., et al. "Sacrifice." In *Encyclopaedia of Religion and Ethics,* edited by James Hastings, vol. 11. Edinburgh, 1920.

Jensen, Adolf E. *Myth and Cult among Primitive Peoples.* Translated by Marianna Tax Choldin and Wolfgang Weissleder. Chicago, 1963.

Kerr, C. M., et al. "Propitiation." In *Encyclopaedia of Religion and Ethics,* edited by James Hastings, vol. 10. Edinburgh, 1918.

Lanternari, Vittorio. *'La Grande Festa': Vita rituale e sistemi di produzione nelle società tradizionali.* 2d ed. Bari, 1976.

Leeuw, Gerardus van der. "Die *do-ut-des*-Formel in der Opfertheorie." *Archiv für Religionswissenschaft* 20 (1920–1921): 241–253.

Leeuw, Gerardus van der. *Religion in Essence and Manifestation* (1938). 2 vols. Translated by J. E. Turner. Gloucester, Mass., 1967.

Loisy, Alfred. *Essai historique sur le sacrifice.* Paris, 1920.

Müller-Karpe, Hermann. *Handbuch der Vorgeschichte.* 2 vols. Munich, 1966–1968.

Le sacrifice, I–V. Nos. 2–6 of *Systèmes de pensée en Afrique noire.* Ivry, France, 1976–1983.

Schmidt, Wilhelm. *Der Ursprung der Gottesidee.* 12 vols. Münster, 1912–1955. See especially volume 6, pages 274–281, 444–455; volume 8, pages 595–633; and volume 12, pages 389–441, 826–836, and 845–847.

Schmidt, Wilhelm. "Ethnologische Bemerkungen zu theologischen Opfertheorien." In *Jahrbuch des Missionshauses St. Gabriel,* vol. 1. Mödling, 1922.

Smith, W. Robertson. *Lectures on the Religion of the Semites: The Fundamental Institutions* (1889). 3d ed. Reprint, New York, 1969.

Tylor, E. B. *Primitive Culture* (1871). 2 vols. Reprint, New York, 1970.

Vorbichler, Anton. *Das Opfer auf den uns heute noch erreichbaren ältesten Stufen der Menschheitsgeschichte: Eine Begriffsstudie.* Mödling, 1956.

Widengren, Geo. *Religionsphänomenologie.* Berlin, 1969.

Additional literature is found in the works cited in the article, especially those by Hubert and Mauss, Loisy, Schmidt, Bertholet, van der Leeuw, Henninger, Lanternari, Heiler, James, and Widengren, as well as in *Le sacrifice,* especially volume 1.

JOSEPH HENNINGER (1987)
Translated from German by Matthew J. O'Connell

SACRIFICE [FURTHER CONSIDERATIONS]. Since Joseph Henninger's outstanding summary of the literature and practices of sacrifice in world religions, scholars have continued to explore the sacrificial practices, meanings, and conundrums of these types of violent, symbolic practices. New studies of human sacrifice, bloodletting, biblical sacrifices, animal sacrifices, and the role of women and gender in sacrifice have been carried out. The rise in terrorism with its various forms of martyrs has also led to new reflections on the meaning of sacrifice. As one scholar, concerned about whether the origin of violence in human beings is to be located in biology or culture, writes, "The one thing that cannot be denied is that violence is ubiquitous and tenacious and must be accounted for if we are to understand humanity" (Hamerton-Kelly, 1987, p. vi). In what follows, we will review a handful of more recent studies on sacrifice that have tried to "account" for the ubiquity, tenacity, and mystery of ritual violence and its creative and destructive powers in human society.

One of the most fascinating studies of sacrifice has come from the historian of Greek religion, Walter Burkert, in his *Homo Necans: The Anthropology of Ancient Greek Sacrificial Ritual and Myth* (1972). Burkert sought to understand the persistence of archaic survivals of religion, especially sacrifice, in Greek culture. Noticing on the one hand that sacrificial myth and ritual accompanied many major religious dimensions of Greek culture (e.g., oracles, games, cults, mysteries, drama, funerals, and royal ceremonies), while on the other that the handling of bones of animal victims mirrored that of the practices of Paleolithic hunters, the author developed a theory of religion and ritual, based in large part on the hunt. In his view, the hunt was a supremely collective, dramatic experience that demanded disciplined behavioral codes (rituals) which channeled unwieldy human aggressions toward new definitions and practices of shared territory, food distribution, mating, and reproduction. Critical in his view was the capacity of the hunting cultures to ritualize immense human aggressions by focusing them away from other humans and refocusing them onto the prey, which became a kind of organizing symbol that opened up new social possibilities as a result of the kill. In Burkert's view, the dramatic scenes and emotions associated with the killing of animals after careful planning and intense physical and mental exertions resulted in new processes of perception and reflection or the creation of mythologies about the events. The kill, the planning and the success of the hunters, and the body, power, and beauty of animals stimulated the human capacity for ritual and myth into a creative nexus or religion. In other words,

> The hunting ritual gave rise to the full range of articulations that we understand to be mythic or symbolic, articulations characteristic of religion. The naming of the 'Master of the Animals', the songs and 'prayers' that address the prey, the gestures surrounding the kill, the care of the bones, the narration of the ritualized hunt as a sequence of events (myth), and the eventual articulation of social codes and honors, including honors due the Master of the Animals ('worship'), all are found to be generated by the complex experience of the act of killing. Thus a theory of the ritualization of the hunt

> becomes a theory of the origin of religion. (Mack, 1987, p. 26.)

In this theory of religion and sacrifice, the effectiveness and emotionality of the kill, as well as its intense planning and coordination, is not only the dramatization of a new social ordering—it actually restructures society for the satisfaction of basic human needs.

A new, evocative approach to sacrifice was put forth by Nancy Jay in her *Throughout Your Generations Forever: Sacrifice, Religion, and Paternity* (1992), which surveys Greek, Israelite, Roman, Nuer, Hawaiian, Lugbara, and Ashanti sacrifice. Jay's work also looks at the Christian Eucharist as sacrifice and proceeds from two powerful observations, almost always ignored by other scholars. First, "in no other major religious institution is gender dichotomy more consistently important, across unrelated traditions, than it is in sacrifice." The exclusion of women and the repeated father-son relations in sacrificial rituals have gone largely unremarked upon, and Jay's work illuminates this lacuna and begins to fill it up with new meanings. Her second observation is that the literature reveals a consistent opposition between blood sacrifice and childbirth or between male sacrificers and childbearing women. She notes that while women sometimes participate in sacrifices, mothers never do and she wants to know why.

Jay's work brought gender and feminist studies into the scholarship on sacrifice by making two claims that have recently undergone critical examination and appreciation. She states that sacrifice is "at home," that is, sacrifice thrives and has historical continuity in social settings that require intergenerational continuity to facilitate inheritance of power, property, and prestige. This means that sacrifices serve to assist in the selective continuity between males and not females. In other words, "ancestor worship" involves sacrifices designed to favor one gender of ancestors. Secondly, Jay argues that sacrifices are valuable because of their unexpected social achievement. Sacrifices give to males the mysterious powers that are akin to those that women have in childbirth. Just as women bring new beings into the world in childbirth, males recreate their lines of descent as authoritative social structures through sacrifice. Descent through males is not naturally given but socially achieved through ritual violence.

Jay's work is worth attention for at least two reasons. It is the first study to place a broad range of scholarship about ritual violence under serious feminist scrutiny and interpretation. Secondly, it applied rigorous anthropological interpretations to biblical texts about violence and then placed them in a fresh comparative perspective by looking at other cultures with similar practices.

Other works that have made their mark include Valerio Valeri's *Kingship and Sacrifice: Ritual and Society in Ancient Hawaii* (1985), Peggy Reeves Sanday's *Divine Hunger: Cannibalism as a Cultural System* (1986), Jon Levenson's *The Death and Resurrection of the Beloved Son: The Transformation of Child Sacrifice in Judaism and Christianity* (1993), Davíd Carrasco's *City of Sacrifice: The Aztec Empire and the Role of Violence in Civilization* (1999), and *The Cuisine of Sacrifice Among the Greeks* (1989), edited by Marcel Detienne and Jean-Pierre Vernant. Valeri's detailed anthropological work gives new emphasis to the significance of social and cosmological hierarchies associated with royal sacrifices that serve as mirrors of the major concepts of pre-Western Hawaiian society. Sanday's work takes up the difficult topic of ritual cannibalism in a number of tribal societies and shows how cultural "selves," cosmological order, and a cannibalistic consciousness combined to control the vitality of the world and the reproduction of human society. Levenson shows how the story of the miraculous liberation of a beloved son from the sacrificial knife is a powerful, shared theme in both Christianity and Judaism, which sets the stage for new kinds of comparisons. Carrasco argues that sacrifices, and especially human sacrifices, become social forces largely through the construction of monumental ceremonial centers that function as theatres for the remembering and re-experiencing of both mythic episodes and other human sacrifices. The work of Detienne and Vernant, emerging from the Center for Comparative Studies of Ancient Societies in Paris, is a multidisciplinary and detailed analysis of how the sacrifice, cooking, and eating of animals functioned in Greek society to tie humans to the gods but also to insure that social relatedness on all political levels was rejuvenated. As one author states, "political power cannot be exercised with sacrificial practice" (Detienne and Vernant, 1989, p. 3).

While new studies of sacrifice and its social, religious, cultural, and political significance continue to be produced, perhaps the best model for real dialogue, theoretical advance, and understanding appeared in *Violent Origins: Walter Burkert, René Girard, and Jonathan Z. Smith on Ritual Killing and Cultural Formation.* This book, edited by Robert Hamerton-Kelly and published in 1987, came from a conference that involved papers, conversations, and responses from Girard, Burkert, Smith, Renato Rosaldo, and Burton Mack. Interested readers will see how this event and its publication explored the tantalizing possibility that understanding human violence against animals and other humans is one major source for developing persuasive theories about the nature of religion and culture. In this constructive sense, Burkert's claim and invitation seem highly relevant to the contemporary situation. "More can be said for the thesis that all orders and forms of authority in human society are founded on institutionalized violence."

BIBLIOGRAPHY

Burkert, Walter. *Homo Necans: The Anthropology of Ancient Greek Sacrificial Ritual and Myth.* Translated by Peter Bing. Berkeley, 1983.

Carrasco, Davíd. *City of Sacrifice: The Aztec Empire and the Role of Violence in Civilization.* Boston, 1999.

Detienne, Marcel, and Jean-Pierre Vernant, eds. *The Cuisine of Sacrifice Among the Greeks.* Translated by Paula Wissing. Chicago, 1989.

Hamerton-Kelly, Robert G., ed. *Violent Origins: Walter Burkert, René Girard, and Jonathan Z. Smith on Ritual Killing and Cultural Formation.* Stanford, Calif., 1987.

Jay, Nancy. *Throughout Your Generations Forever: Sacrifice, Religion, and Paternity.* Chicago, 1992.

Levenson, Jon. *The Death and Resurrection of the Beloved Son: The Transformation of Child Sacrifice in Judaism and Christianity.* New Haven, 1993.

Mack, Burton. "Introduction: Religion and Ritual." In *Violent Origins: Walter Burkert, René Girard, and Jonathan Z. Smith on Ritual Killing and Cultural Formation,* edited by Robert G. Hamerton-Kelly, pp. 1–72. Stanford, 1987.

Robbins, Jill. "Sacrifice." In *Critical Terms for Religious Studies,* edited by Mark C. Taylor, pp. 285–297. Chicago, 1998.

Sanday, Peggy Reeves. *Divine Hunger: Cannibalism as a Cultural System.* Cambridge, U.K., 1986

Valeri, Valerio. *Kingship and Sacrifice: Ritual and Society in Ancient Hawaii.* Translated by Paula Wissing. Chicago, 1985.

DAVÍD CARRASCO (2005)

SACRILEGE is typically defined as "violation or theft of the sacred." It originates from the Latin *sacrilegium* or *sacer* (sacred) and *lego* (to gather or to steal). In addition to the literal theft of sacred objects or the violation of sacred places, *sacrilege* connotes violation of sacred practices (orthopraxy) and sacred beliefs (orthodoxy). Because the concept of sacrilege is founded upon the distinction between *sacred* and *profane,* this entry will begin with a brief overview of the academic distinction between those two terms and their relationship to sacrilege. An overview of different religious approaches to the problem of sacrilege and transgression will follow.

Émile Durkheim (1858–1917) argued that sacred and profane are distinct categories defined only by their absolute opposition. The sacred is that unique category circumscribed by boundaries that differentiate it from ordinary, or profane, reality. However, Durkheim claimed, the sacred is a category created by humans and not unique in and of itself: anything can potentially be set aside and distinguished as sacred. Mircea Eliade (1907–1986), on the other hand, argued that the sacred was an essential experiential category. From his perspective, the sacred is qualitatively different from ordinary, profane reality. While a sacred object may be physically identical to a profane object, they are not interchangeable because the sacred object has a special quality that the profane object does not have. Physically identical profane objects, on the other hand, are also qualitatively identical and interchangeable. Mary Douglas (1921–), argues that the distinction between sacred and profane is a distinction between order and disorder. From her perspective, sacrilege means disturbing or disrupting the established order of the sacred. Contemporary scholars of religion, such as Jonathan Z. Smith (1938–), argue that the definitions put forth by Durkheim, Eliade, and Douglas, while helpful, are too rigid and do not accurately describe religious realities. The sacred and profane are flexible, fluid categories that frequently overlap, distort, and transform. For Smith, a central religious problem is adapting sacred ideals to the messy reality of lived experience. Thus sacrilege is also a situational interpretive frame that must continually adapt to its context. What is clear, however, is that sacrilege is essentially concerned with the boundaries of the sacred.

The sacred is constituted by a perimeter, a differential limit. Sacrilege is the violation or rupture of sacred boundaries. "Theft from the sacred" and "violation of the sacred" are reciprocal actions. They consist of either bringing the profane into or the taking the sacred out of its established limits. In either case the sacred comes into contact with the profane and the order and purity of the sacred is disturbed. There are two distinct forms of sacrilege: interreligious and intrareligious. Violations committed by religious outsiders, or interreligious violations, are frequently described as "desecration" and will be discussed in the section below. Sacrilege typically refers to intrareligious violations, or violations by religious insiders, which will be the focus of the remainder of this section.

Although its etymological roots are in pagan Rome, sacrilege, particularly in its connotation of unorthodoxy, is a Christian concept (and to a lesser degree an Abrahamic concept) whose greatest cultural impact occurred during the Middle Ages and continued throughout the eighteenth century. Since the eighteenth century, its theological importance has waned, as a subject search in any academic library clearly demonstrates. Its Christian context is important because wide application of the concept requires the type of hierarchical organizational structure that was characteristic of Christendom during that period. Broad accusations, prosecutions, and actions of sacrilege require the broad agreement upon definitions of orthodoxy and unorthodoxy that only a hierarchical religious organization can bring to bear. When localized religious subgroups control definitions and consequences of sacrilege, its coercive power is significantly diminished. The definition of sacrilege is thus conceptually constrained in Jewish and Islamic communities, where the local community by and large sets its own criteria for transgressive behavior.

If sacredness is inherently dualistic, in that its definition requires the profane, then sacrilege or transgression are also inherent and essential to sacredness. However, this dualistic boundary can be drawn more or less boldly. The more absolute and impermeable the boundary is between the sacred and the profane, the more rigid and inflexible the concept and consequences of transgression will be. In the Abrahamic traditions, dualism is essential to creation, good and evil are irreconcilable, and the boundary between the two is conceptually impermeable. Non-Abrahamic traditions, such as Buddhism and Hinduism, on the other hand, conceive of an underlying unity behind duality. Consequently, the boundary between sacred and profane is more lightly drawn, and both traditions include antinomian sects that employ transgression as a means of transcending duality and dissolving the boundary between sacred and profane.

Sacrilege and transgression are problematic because the sacred and profane inevitably come into contact during the messy reality of lived experience. Absolute conceptual and physical limits invite and require human transgression. The heart of the sacred lies at its edges, not at its center. It is in the encounter with boundaries, and their transgression, that we experience the sacred. The Abrahamic concept of sacrilege calls for retribution in so far as it maintains rigid boundaries. As rigid hierarchical boundaries lessen so too does the need for retributive sacred justice. The transgression of boundaries understood as sacred does not destroy the sacred, rather, it heightens awareness of those sacred boundaries where human desire for the sacred meets the mortal, transgressive reality of human life.

DESECRATION. Interreligious sacrilege consists of actions by members of one religious group that violate the sacred boundaries of another religious group. Such destruction or damage by outsiders inflicted upon temples, shrines, and other sacred places, as well as upon sacred objects or beings, is commonly characterized as desecration, in contradistinction to intrareligious, or insider, sacrilege. In the case of sacred violation resulting from sectarian disputes, either term may apply, although sectarian conflicts inherently redefine former insiders as outsiders.

While intentional desecration has a long history, it is a particularly pressing issue at the beginning of the twenty-first century. Because of the increasing religious plurality of many societies in the so-called global village, and the resulting contact between members of different religious traditions, interreligious friction and tension with the potential for sacred violation and violence will continue to increase. The sacred boundaries, both physical and ideological, of multiple religions can be, and frequently are, coextensive. When sacred boundaries overlap in physical, ideological, or social spaces, competing sacred claims can result in volatile confrontations from which desecration may result.

Most acts of desecration are the result of interreligious contestation over sacred territory. It is an assertion of the primacy of one territorial claim over conflicting sacred claims. Desecration disrupts, destroys, and denies the claims of other religious communities to the sanctity of their sacred territory. As such it is an inherent attack upon the validity of those sacred claims and the very identity of the competing religious group.

The Ayodhyā dispute is one example of contested claims to sacred space that led to desecration. In 1992, Hindu demonstrators destroyed the 464-year-old Babri Masjid Mosque located in Ayodhyā, India, about one hundred miles north of Banares. The territorial dispute can be traced to 1528, when a Hindu temple on the site was destroyed to make way for the mosque. The earlier Hindu temple was constructed on the site because according to Hindu belief the site was the birthplace of Rāma, the iconic hero of the 2,500-year-old Hindu epic, the *Rāmāyaṇa.* A new temple honoring Rāma was begun immediately after the destruction of Babri Masjid. Rather than an isolated incident, the Ayodhyā dispute is but one symptom of centuries-old tensions between Hindu and Muslim communities in northern sections of the Indian subcontinent. While the 1947 partition of India and Pakistan was an attempt to resolve such longstanding Hindu-Muslim conflicts, at the beginning of the twenty-first century relations have arguably deteriorated to the lowest level since partition.

Desecration is frequently directed at sacred sites such as temples and cemeteries, but can also include sacred texts and ritual objects. Like the Ayodhyā incident, desecration is not simply the result of conflicting claims to coextensive sacred territory. In most cases, including seemingly inadvertent desecration (discussed below), it is a strike against the legitimacy of the particular religious identity itself. Desecration occurs within the context of complex social, economic, and political tensions. Because religion and its demarcations of sacrality are so closely tied to individual and community identity, desecration is frequently linked to intolerance and hatred of religio-ethnic groups. Desecration is a symbolic negation of the targeted religious group.

Surprisingly, seemingly inadvertent desecration can also be understood as religious intolerance and negation. In 1990 the Native American Graves Protection and Repatriation Act (NAGPRA) was signed into U.S. law. The NAGPRA was an attempt to address Native American concerns about the historic and ongoing collection of native remains. Since death and the disposal of human remains are the object of intensive religious activity, disturbance of the dead constitutes desecration, particularly when it involves intentional abuse of the burial site or remains. Because many contemporary Native Americans experience collection and disturbance of ancestral remains as desecration, archeological excavation of historically remote but potentially native remains has emerged as a serious controversy.

Is it fair to use the term *desecration* when actions do not appear to intentionally target religious identity? After all, the object of collecting native remains is scientific knowledge, not the violation of sacred space. However, the historical context tells a different story. Anthropological study of Native American culture during the nineteenth century led to a frenzied collection of human remains, ritual objects, and secret ceremonial practices of those supposedly dying cultures. The alienation of remains and ritual objects, as well as the revelation of ritual knowledge, was, and is, a literal theft of the sacred. Most of the collection was illegitimate because objects and ceremonies were sold by native individuals who had no right to sell communal property, and others were simply taken without permission. All of these actions were desecration because they inevitably denied and negated Native American control of sacred possessions and, ultimately, the religious identity of those communities.

Such seemingly inadvertent desecration results from an underlying conflict over the right and ability of competing communities to designate sacrality itself. While there are clearly cases of errant violations of sacrality, apparent ignorance of the designation "sacred" more frequently results from an underlying challenge to the legitimacy of that designation. One community simply asserts and forcibly imposes its values or desires upon another community, irrespective of the second community's sacred designations. The inherent statement is that those other religious values do not matter and are unworthy of recognition. Like intentional desecration it is a symbolic (and actual) negation of the religious identity of the other community.

Because religious claims, by definition, supercede all other claims, interreligious contact can potentially lead to acts of desecration whenever two or more religious claims are in opposition. Since secular values tend to dismiss the ultimacy of religious claims, particularly when those claims are made by a less powerful or minority community, contact between secular and religious communities can also potentially lead to acts of desecration. The twentieth century, like previous centuries, witnessed horrible acts of desecration. The twenty-first century will be no different, unless or until individual religious communities find other means to live coextensively with other communities whose religious claims and values conflict with their own religious claims and values.

Jewish Sacrilege. In order to understand sacrilege in the Jewish tradition, it is first necessary to appreciate the significance of the fact that, for Jews, God is the sole genesis of all that exists. Because all of creation originates from God, all of creation must be considered of divine origin and, therefore, sacred. Moreover, the first humans were created in the image of God and became living beings only when God breathed life into them. Thus all of creation, including human beings, is of divine origin and is sacred. However, even though humans are made in the image of god, they are formed out of the earth, and this earthly component, insofar as it is derivative of God, is the impure, transgressive quality that leads to human mortality. Insofar as creation and humans find their genesis in God, they are sacred, but insofar as creation and humans become separate and independent from God, they are profane. Transgression, from this perspective, is simply separation and independence from God.

But God made a covenant with Abraham that was sealed by Moses and that bound the Hebrew people to God. Or, to put it a little differently, the purpose of the covenant was and is to bind the Hebrew people to God. How does it accomplish this? The covenant is the means by which God's chosen people are to honor and remember the sacred genesis of creation and themselves. For example, the keeping of the Sabbath is nothing less than the ritual remembrance of the divine origin of creation. Keeping the covenant involves maintaining connection to and awareness of the sacredness of God's creation. Failure to keep the covenant is a transgression against God; it is a sacrilege.

In the Jewish tradition the chosen people maintain the sacredness of creation through the keeping of the covenant. Without deliberate human action, the sacred aspect of creation and humans is profaned. The sacred is sustained through intentional human action. When humans fail to keep the covenant, they lose sight of the divine origin of creation. The material world becomes simply the material world, and human beings become simply flesh and blood. When the divine origin of creation is forgotten, God's creation is stolen from God. Keeping the Torah requires remembering that creation is more than simply the world we see; it means awareness that behind what we see is the sacred mystery of God. In the Jewish tradition sacrilege is stealing the creation from its source and reducing it to merely the dirt of materiality.

Jews who profane the sacred origin of creation lose their claim to the world to come. Only a life lived with full awareness for the divine aspect of humanity and its environment is worthy of the immortal life of the human spirit. A life governed by the covenant is one that continually reflects upon the fact that humans are created in the image of God. Sacrilege amounts to renouncing the knowledge of the divine breath that sparks human life and thereby cutting oneself off from God. Sacrilege is the grave loss suffered by those who lose sight of their intimate connection to the divine creative force inherent to all that exists. Moreover, the failure to recognize the image of God in others is equally problematic. All creation, including oneself and other humans, should be understood as an inherently sacred aspect of God's continually unfolding creation.

The sum result of profaning the sacred is to lose one's claim to the world to come. Full awareness of having been created in the image of God is necessary to claim immortal life for the spirit. Sacrilege means cutting oneself off from the image of God and thereby forfeiting an intimate connection to God. God established the Torah to promote consciousness of the sacred, divinely created aspect of humanity and the rest of the physical world. Transgression is essentially any violation of the Torah. There are consequences for this, but reconciliation is always possible with sincere atonement. Because of our earthly aspect, humans are naturally transgressive. Orthopraxis (correct practice) brings humans into union with God, as partners in the maintenance of the sacred essence of creation. God created the Torah because it makes it possible to mitigate or manage human transgression.

In the Jewish tradition the primary transgression is idolatry. Idolatry violates the entire Torah because it negates God's genesis of creation and renders it profane. Public profaning of God's name can result in excommunication. However, other than violation of the Torah, there is no uniform code of transgression in the Jewish tradition. Transgression and its consequences are determined by the local community to which one belongs. Different communities establish different standards and may not recognize the determinations of other communities. Thus it is apparent that the Torah creates and maintains the worldwide Jewish community as a sacred community. Following the Torah sets Jews apart from the surrounding secular community. The community is differentiated through its self-conscious spiritual identity. For example, the laws of purity situate the community as having a different orientation than surrounding communities. Transgression of these laws separates the individual from both God and the community. Maintaining the Torah establishes one's life and community within a world that is sacred through an intentional acknowledgement of the givenness of God throughout all creation. Sacrilege is turning one's back on the sacred and thereby dwelling in the world of the undifferentiated profane.

Christian Sacrilege. The history of heresy, inquisition, and witchcraft in the Christian church has been the subject of an enormous body of scholarship. The picture presented here is far from complete, and the reader should be on guard against easy or fashionable generalizations. In the history of the concept and pattern of sacrilege in Europe, one is confronted with striking paradoxes: it is often the case that sacrilege was neither invented nor spread by those one would have at first suspected. Sometimes the very forces that were responsible for the prosecution of sacrilege were the ones that prevented such prosecution from being effective. If trials for sacrilege finally came to an end, this did not happen according to any known law of human progress. A thorough investigation of this phenomenon, as of any other phenomenon in history, will show that whenever human consciousness, reflection, and intentionality are involved, things are far from being simple.

The Roman Empire. In the Roman Empire, sacrilege was considered to be a crime carrying the penalty of death, and torture was sometimes used to extort confession. The persecution of Christians, in particular, was justified by a pattern of defamation: besides their sacrilegious practices, the Christians were represented as murderers of infants and as engaged in promiscuous sexual intercourse.

This basic pattern of defamation, analyzed historically by Norman R. C. Cohn in his influential book *Europe's Inner Demons* (1975), was then taken over by the victorious church and applied to several of its enemies, both external and internal. The revival of Roman criminal law in the eleventh century provided the legal procedures for the conduct of the Christian Inquisition. These procedures were in turn copied by the lay authorities of Europe at the time of the witch craze of the sixteenth and seventeenth centuries. By this time the Inquisition itself had adopted a skeptical attitude that in some cases prevented abuses by the secular powers.

The eleventh to thirteenth century. The revival of Roman criminal law in the eleventh century seems to have been accompanied by a revival of the ancient Roman pattern of the defamation of Christians, used this time, however, by the Christians themselves against enemies of their own. This was not entirely new. Augustine had used these tactics against the Manichaeans, and John of Odzun had used them against the Armenian Adoptionists in 719. Now the target was the heretics of Orleans (1022), who were said to recite a litany of demons, renounce Christ, spit upon his image, engage in sexual orgies, sacrifice children, and practice cannibalism. At the end of the century (1076–1096), the priest Alberic of Brittany was convicted of sacrilege for having smeared the crucifix with excrement and poured animal blood upon the altar. He was further accused of selling this blood to the people as relics.

By 1150 to 1160, a group of heretics in Germany had been accused of offering solemn sacrifices to the Devil, practicing incestuous intercourse, and ridiculing the celebration of the nativity on Christmas Eve when, in mockery of the Christian kiss of peace, their priest allegedly uncovered his backside to be kissed by the congregation. This is perhaps the earliest testimony concerning the *osculum infame* (kiss of infamy). In 1182, Walter Map mentioned the kiss of infamy as being practiced upon the backside, the genitals, or the paw of a huge cat. Down to the mid-fifteenth century, the new conventicles of the alleged worshipers of Satan were called *synagogues* (later *sabbat,* a term also used in reference to witches), a clear reference to a group to whom sacrilegious activities of the most extreme kind were attributed, namely the Jews. Sexual intercourse with the Devil is mentioned for the first time in 1275, when a woman in Carcassonne, France, was burned at the stake for this sacrilege.

Inquisitorial and criminal procedure to the fourteenth century. The relationship between ecclesiastic and criminal justice forms one of the most fascinating chapters in the history of European civilization. Without some knowledge of this relationship, it is impossible to understand such a fundamental phenomenon as the witch craze. It is important to establish two facts: first, that this relationship underwent constant changes; second, that it varied from country to country.

In the early Middle Ages, religious offenses in Germany were prosecuted by the secular authorities. The accusation had to be proved, and thus the accuser risked greater damages than the accused. In Spain under the Visigoths, by contrast, religious offenses were, according to the juridical formula, *mixti fori,* that is, they belonged both to the ecclesiastical and to the lay authorities. In Italy, according to Langobardic law, the crime of *maleficium* fell under secular jurisdiction. In northern Italy, under French influence, the episcopal inquisition was in place after 800. Indeed, in the Frankish Empire, justice in religious matters was assured by episcopal visitation and inquisition (Latin *inquisitio,* "investigation"), the bishop being supported by the landlord as *defensor ecclesiae* (this is the oldest form of local justice, the *justice seigneuriale*). After the fall of the Frankish Empire, however, the institution of royal justice became increasingly important, having been taken as a model by the local landlords.

The procedures of the episcopal inquisition were introduced by the church in 1184. A further step was taken by

Gregory IX (1227–1241), who created the papal Inquisition as a central institution staffed by the Dominicans and the Franciscans and directed from Rome. Torture, sporadically employed since the eleventh century, was expressly recommended for inquisitorial procedures against heretics by Innocent IV in 1252. The death penalty, in accordance with Roman law, had been applied since the eleventh century in the French and German territories, but not in southern Europe. Starting in 1197, the death penalty for heretics upon relapse was decreed in Aragon, France, Lombardy, Sicily, and Germany. In 1232 it became effective for the entire Holy Roman Empire. In 1198, Innocent III had recommended execution upon relapse in instances when excommunication had proved ineffective. By the fifteenth century, witches were burned as heretics upon first conviction rather than after a relapse.

Islamic Sacrilege. Because the Islamic tradition does not have a central hierarchical authority structure, the generally accepted definition of sacrilege is relatively narrow. Transgression of the first and foundational pillar of Islam, the Shahādah, is the tradition's only unforgivable sin. While a Muslim is obligated to fulfill all the five pillars of Islam, sincere and devout recitation of the Shahādah is the sole requirement for becoming a Muslim. The Shahādah is the deceptively simple statement: "There is no God but Allāh, and Muḥammad is his prophet." The first of two assertions in the statement is that there is no God but Allāh (*Lā ilāha illā Allāh*). There is only one God, and that God is known as Allāh. The Arabic word translated as God, *ilāh,* means one who is worshiped, one who has the greatness and power worthy of worship. It also implies the Islamic principle of *tawḥīd,* the absolute oneness and unity of God. The first principle of Islam is a radical, or absolute, monotheism. Allāh is one all-powerful harmonious being. Allāh is not and cannot be a multiplicity.

In addition to the unity of Allāh, the statement "there is no God but Allāh" necessarily requires that Allāh is not a physical being. Allāh is the powerful and mysterious being behind all other powers in creation. As such, Allāh cannot possibly be a physical being. *Shirk,* idolatry, is the worship of anything less than the all-encompassing unity of Allāh. Allāh is the limitless power concealed beyond the human or material world, indeed Allāh is beyond human understanding altogether. Focusing one's care and attention upon any worldly power, such as wealth, fame, sex, and even nature, is *shirk,* just as much as the worship of an idol is *shirk.* Both the denial of the unity of Allāh and idolatry are sacrilege in the sense that they lessen and thereby violate the essential sacred qualities of Allāh.

Like idolatry, apostasy is a transgression against Shahādah. Abandonment or renunciation of the Islamic faith amounts to the repudiation of the Shahādah. Like religious conversion, apostasy repudiates the divinity and unity of Allāh. Thus, either apostasy or conversion amount to transgressions against the sacrality of Allāh.

The second assertion of the Shahādah is "Muḥammad is his prophet." (*Muḥammad rasūl – Allāh*). This statement legitimizes Muḥammad as a prophet among other prophets of the Abrahamic traditions. It is also understood to establish Muḥammad as the final prophet, the last of Allāh's messengers, who seals, or completes, all revelations from God to humans. As the last prophet, the message revealed to Muḥammad supercedes all other prophets, including both Moses and Jesus. As a result of having brought divine revelation to an end, worship of Allāh in a consecrated temple is no longer necessary. Muḥammad's message includes the revelation that the entire earth can now be a place of worship and purification. This is relevant to discussion of sacrilege because sacred space is transformed. Prayer in a state of impurity simply makes the prayer invalid. Pollution of sacred space is of lesser concern than the ritual purity of the individual who offers prayer to Allāh. After Muḥammad brings the revelation, violation of sacred space is no longer universally understood as sacrilege. Prayer that takes place within a polluted context is simply invalid.

Muḥammad is the preeminent human, but human nonetheless. His humanity and mortality are essential because he in absolutely no way resembles the singular divinity of Allāh. On the other hand, Muḥammad is the foremost exemplar of human behavior. His speech and character are models of perfection. Thus the *sunnah,* the historical record of Muḥammad's words and deeds, is considered the second most sacred text in Islam. Because of Muḥammad's unique exemplary status, he is worthy of obedience and the utmost respect. Any statements or action that impugn Muḥammad in any way are without a doubt sacrilegious. Salmon Rushdie's *Satanic Verses* (1988) was condemned by the Islamic community precisely because it characterized the prophet in derogatory and offensive ways. Rushdie's book provoked outrage because it profaned the sacred name and character of the prophet.

The divine origin of the Qurʾān is implicit in the statement that Muḥammad is Allāh's prophet. Islamic tradition understands the genealogy of the Qurʾān as having been transmitted directly from Allāh to the angel Gabriel, who brought Allāh's message to Muḥammad. The Qurʾān is nothing less than the divine speech of Allāh. The Qurʾān, in its original Arabic, is not created nor interpreted by Muḥammad or any other human. Because it is an exact replication of divine speech, the Qurʾān is unique among all other texts. Both the oral recitation and the written text (in Arabic) are considered sacred and should be treated reverently. Consequently, physical mistreatment, misrepresentation, or mockery of the Arabic Qurʾān is considered extremely sacrilegious. Questioning the validity or truth of the Qurʾān is equally transgressive. Scholarly investigation of the literary and historical origin of the Qurʾān, in itself, would amount to sacrilege precisely because it undercuts its foundational claim to authority by presupposing human authorship.

Hindu Sacrilege. There are two areas in Hinduism where concerns similar to the Abrahamic concept of sacrilege arise.

One area of primary concern would be *nāstika*, unorthodox interpretation of the Vedas. Religions derived from Hinduism, such as Buddhism and Jainism in particular, constitute the unorthodox insofar as they are a rejection of the authority of the Vedas. For example, rejection of the principle of saṃsāra, the ongoing cycle of rebirth, would be an extreme form of unorthodoxy worthy of censure. The second concern is the so-called laws of purity. While purity concerns vary by caste, there are general principles governing purity and pollution. The near universal prohibition against sexual contact with menstruating women also holds in the Hindu tradition. Intercaste sex or marriage, like all intercaste contact, is also subject to regulation. Included in such prohibitions would be objects and food handled by those of a low caste. Finally, contact with excrement and dead animals or humans, as in many cultures, is a source of pollution that must be ritually regulated.

Vāmācāra, left-handed conduct, refers to ritual Tantric practice of traditionally prohibited behavior involving sex, alcohol, dead bodies, and so on. *Savism* is the best known form of Hindu Tantrism; it refers the ritual practices of devotees of the deity Śiva. Śiva is the destroyer, but he is also a creator, in that he destroys the cosmos at the end of its cycle, making way for creation anew. A common depiction is of Śiva dancing within a ring of fire. The fire represents both the destruction of ignorance and the fire of cremation. Śiva is the first of all yogis, demonstrating sensual experience and the freedom of nondualistic awareness. Śiva exists in the particular and subsumes all duality—creation and destruction, good and evil, bodily eroticism and supreme consciousness.

Left-handed *Savism* exploits the embodied, erotic aspect of Śiva in order to attain to the nonduality of Śiva. Like all Hindu gods, Śiva is powerless without Śakti, the feminine power that animates all things. Śiva and Śakti together are the combination of consciousness and power. The union of Śiva and Śakti is the model for Tantric sexual ritual. Through sexual union with the active principle of the woman, the pure consciousness of the male yogi is liberated from the oppositions of the material world. The devotee becomes oblivious to everything but divine unity. At this point, the categories of purity and impurity are also destroyed. Tantric ritual also employs other ostensibly sacrilegious practices, such as contact with death or prohibited castes, in order to merge the Śakti power of impurity with yogic consciousness. Such legitimized sacrilegious behavior is powerful precisely because it transgresses the opposition of purity and impurity, exposing them as products of dualistic consciousness, and thereby paving the way to liberation from the body and to unified consciousness beyond opposition. This is an example of when ostensibly sacrilegious behavior is legitimized within a sect but condemned by the orthodox tradition.

BUDDHIST SACRILEGE. The Buddhist perspective is that all transgressions arise from one source: fundamental ignorance about the nature of the self and the world. *Anātman* (no permanent self) is a foundational principle of Buddhist thought. While the precise meaning and implications of *anātman* are beyond the scope of this entry, the general idea is that wrong actions stem from the normal human illusion of possessing a permanent self. From this illusion, self-serving and self-interested behaviors necessarily follow. The Buddhist view is that the individual self is impermanent in the sense that it is in a constant state of flux. Furthermore, duality, the perception of self and other as discrete entities, is also an illusion that leads to actions harmful to both self and other. Because the two are inextricably linked through the chain of causality, self-interested actions that negatively impact the other will inevitably impact the self negatively.

Because Buddhism understands that duality and wrong action are illusions, sacrilege is both the result of individual illusions and, ultimately, also an illusion itself. However, there are boundaries of moral transgression. There are five moral precepts that all Buddhists are expected to uphold: no killing, no stealing, no sexual misconduct, no mistruth, and no intoxication. Violations of these precepts (or the violation of any other vow) constitute the primary "sins" of Buddhism. During the lifetime of the Buddha, members of the *saṃgha* (the religious community) could also be expelled for lying about spiritual achievements. During this time, the five worst transgressions were patricide, matricide, killing a monk, wounding the Buddha, and causing dissent in the community. Even so, when the Buddha's cousin, Devadatta, tried to kill the Buddha several times and sought to undermine his leadership, the Buddha reacted to these grave transgressions with equanimity and compassion, and Devadatta was never punished for his actions. The Buddha's action, or more accurately, nonaction, set the precedent that transgressions should be handled with compassion precisely because the transgressors are already enduring the suffering that inevitably arises from the illusion of self and other.

Buddhist Tantrism was derived from Hindu Tantrism; both are widely known antinomian traditions. Tantra (to weave) refers to ritual instructions opposed to sūtra, a discourse of the Buddha. Originating from Bengal, Buddhist Tantra developed within the Vajrayāna tradition (diamond vehicle) of Tibet in the tenth and eleventh century CE. The Tantras are ritual instructions and practices for visualizing buddhas and *bodhisattvas* with the express intent of bringing the practitioner into transcendent union. The goal is to remove karmic defilements and the illusion of self, and thereby experience the supreme reality of nonduality that underlies the perceptual world. The goal is nothing less than achieving the union of *saṃsāra* and *nirvāṇa*; that is, to experience nonduality while still living within the illusionary world of suffering and duality.

Tantrism is best known in the West for the practice of imagining or actually engaging in sexual union as the culmination of disciplined spiritual practice. The underlying premise is that the lesser pleasure of sexual union is linked to the superior pleasure of the transcendental union that occurs when the illusion of duality is overcome. This premise is based on three observations. First, sexual union gives rise to desire and is extremely pleasurable. Second, sexual union is the union of the male-female dyad, and thus an experience of nonduality. Third, the pleasure of sexual union is a minute fraction of the pleasure of transcendental union. The Tantric insight is that sexual desire can be employed as the means to overcome the desires that bind one to the duality of saṃsāra.

The Tantra adept is supervised by a *gurū* who has mastered the Tantric rituals and teachings. While Tantrism is thought to be the fast way to enlightenment, traditional Buddhist practices, such as meditation, must be mastered prior to Tantric practice. When the *gurū* determines the adept has demonstrated the spiritual discipline needed to experience transcendental union, the practitioner is instructed to focus upon the previously cultivated experience of nonduality during sexual intercourse, rather than upon sexual desire. It is thought that the pleasure of sexual union will be experienced as inferior to the much greater ecstasy of the spiritual union of opposites. Sexual desire will in turn be diminished because it will be eclipsed by the desire to experience complete nonduality, rather than the experience of limited nonduality of sexual union.

Other Tantric practices include the eating of meat, sex with low-caste women, and meditation in cemeteries or upon corpses. All of these practices are intended to overcome saṃsāra in its most polluted form so as to experience the blissful spiritual reality that underlies it. Intimate contact with a corpse, for example, is an experiential lesson in the transitory nature of bodily life. Tantric practice seeks to exploit transgression by putting it into direct relationship with the transcendental union of opposites. In this sense, Tantric practice articulates and explores the boundaries of Buddhist transgression. Tantrism exaggerates and underscores the very behaviors that transgress the boundaries of traditional Buddhist mores; as such it provides an inverted image of Buddhist sacrilege.

Zuni People and Sacrilege. The concept of sacrilege is not indigenous to the Zuni people; however, actions and things that do not conform to their conservative social and religious norms make the problem of transgression a central concern. Traditional Zuni society is highly structured, as it is among other tribes in the Pueblo cultural group. Membership in Zuni society brings specific rights, privileges, and duties. All Zuni are expected to actively participate in religious societies and perform the accompanying ceremonial duties. Their ceremonies are organized according to a rigid agricultural cycle, and individual participants are often required to undergo exacting preparations and ritual restrictions. Failure to perform ceremonies to traditional standards or individual failure to carry out ritual privations brings great danger to both individuals and the group. The ceremonial responsibilities of the Zuni are among the most exacting in the world.

Individual behavior is closely monitored, and conformity to group values—including hard work, good manners, and social conservatism—is expected. At the heart of the Zuni value system is conformity to traditional mores. The individual is taught from an early age to avoid either deviation or notoriety. Public display of inappropriate behavior is highly censored. Expressions of sexuality, such as kissing or touching; smoking (for women); or any hint of immoderation or disrespect is considered deeply disgraceful. Secrecy, not only in relation to people outside the pueblo but also in regard to intra-Zuni behavior, is therefore highly regarded and always an ideal. For the Zuni, transgressions of such traditional mores, and of prescribed ritual responsibilities and restrictions, are treated seriously and subject to a range of social and ritual sanctions.

During many Zuni rituals, divine beings arrive at Zuni and dance in the plaza at the center of town. These divine beings, *kachinas*, are present in the form of masked members of Zuni religious societies. During *kachina* dances the plaza exists within sacred space and time, and it represents the idealized spiritual life. However, in the midst of the ritual dance, masked clowns inevitably arrive and disrupt the proceedings with antics that transgress proper social and sacred behavior. These ritual clowns may engage in simulated copulation, sex-role reversal, gluttony, backward behavior, smearing of ashes (associated with witchery and death), and other disgraceful behaviors, including mockery of either audience members or the *kachinas* themselves. What do these ritual clowns, who are brought into divine presence and sacred space and time, teach about the transgression of the sacred?

The actions of Zuni ritual clowns draw attention to and reflect upon the progress of the *kachina* ritual. When the clowns disrupt the ritual, the contrast between sacred and profane behavior heightens. The actions of the clowns clearly delineate the boundary and distance between the clowns and the *kachinas*. The role of the clown is to stand in and act as the agent of the ordinary human members of the audience. The clowns remind the Zuni that in the face of the sacred all humans are transgressive, all humans are clowns who cannot control themselves and who do everything backward. The clowns are funny and entertaining, but they also prod the people to reflect upon the incongruence of their own behavior with their spiritual aspirations.

The ritual clowns' bodily humor and mockery of spiritual solemnity during sacred rituals is often perplexing to Euro-American observers. However, the clowns perform a profoundly moral role in Zuni cosmology. The clowns, in fact, are one manifestation of the Zuni attempt to mediate duality. The clowns, continually "in process," weave together the sacred and the profane, the people and the deities, such that the ritual performance brings bodily, material life into the realm of eternal truth. Rather than profaning the sacred, the ritual clowns express the sacred potential of the profane. Through attention to these two essential, but opposite, poles, the delicate balance of cosmic duality is maintained and affirmed.

The clowns remind the Zuni people that the ideal spiritual life is ultimately incongruent with their everyday profane lives. And yet their spiritual aspirations require that they bring their transgressiveness into the presence of the *kachinas'* sacred dance. The ritual clowns dissolve the absolute distinction between sacred and profane, creating a permeable boundary that welcomes human contradictions and transgressions into the sacred dance of life. However, the tension between human transgressions and spiritual ideals is heightened, not erased, especially when the clowns are eventually disciplined by the *kachinas* for their behavior. Here then is what the clowns teach: that human appetites and desires, and the transgressions to which they give rise, need not be eliminated prior to contact with the sacred. When transgression is recognized as the place where the human and sacred meet, incongruity is not eliminated but does become manageable.

SEE ALSO Blasphemy; Heresy, overview article; Inquisition, The, article on The Inquisition in the Old World; Taboo.

BIBLIOGRAPHY

Ahsan, M. M., and A. R. Kidwai. *Sacrilege Versus Civility: Muslim Perspectives on the "Satanic Verses" Affair.* Leicester, U.K., 1991; rev. ed., 1993.

Barber, Malcolm. *The Trial of the Templars.* Cambridge, U.K., 1978.

Blackman, Philip, ed. and trans. *Tractate Avoth: Ethics of the Fathers.* New York, 1964.

Caldor, Norman. "The Limits of Islamic Orthodoxy." In *Intellectual Traditions in Islam,* edited by Farhad Daftary, pp. 66–86. London, 2000.

Chanchreek, K. L., and Saroj Prasad. *Crisis in India.* Delhi, 1993.

Churchill, Ward. *Indians Are Us? Culture and Genocide in Native North America.* Monroe, Maine, 1994.

Cohn, Norman R. C. *Europe's Inner Demons: An Enquiry Inspired by the Great Witch-Hunt.* New York, 1975.

Denny, Frederick M. *An Introduction to Islam.* New York, 1985; 2d ed., 1994

Douglas, Mary. *Purity and Danger: An Analysis of the Concepts of Pollution and Taboo.* New York, 1966.

Durkheim, Émile. *The Elementary Forms of the Religious Life.* Translated by Joseph Ward Swain. New York, 1965.

Eliade, Mircea. *The Sacred and the Profane: The Nature of Religion.* Translated by Willard R. Trask. New York, 1959.

Gibb, H. A. R., et al. *The Encyclopedia of Islam.* New ed. London, 1960.

Grimes, Ronald L. "Desecration of the Dead: An Inter-Religious Controversy." *American Indian Quarterly* 10, no. 4 (1986): 305–318.

Handleman, Don. "The Ritual Clown: Attributes and Affinities." *Anthropos* 76 (1981): 321–370.

Heib, Louis A. "Meaning and Mismeaning: Toward an Understanding of the Ritual Clown." In *New Perspectives on the Pueblos,* edited by Alfonzo Ortiz, pp. 163–195. Albuquerque, N. Mex., 1972.

Kristeva, Julia. *Powers of Horror: An Essay on Abjection.* Translated by Leon S. Roudiez. New York, 1982.

Maimonides, Moses. *The Guide for the Perplexed.* Translated by M. Friedlander. New York, 1904.

Malkani, K. R. *The Politics of Ayodhya and Hindu Muslim Relations.* New Delhi, India, 1993.

Muller-Ortega, Paul E. "Aspects of Jivanmuki in the Tantric Savia Traditions." In *Living Liberation in Hindu Thought,* edited by Andrew Fort and Patricia Y. Mumme, pp. 187–217. Albany, N.Y., 1996.

Neusner, Jacob; Alan J. Avery-Peck; and William Scott Green; eds. *Encyclopedia of Judaism.* 3 vols. New York, 1999.

Ortiz, Alfonzo. *New Perspectives on the Pueblos.* Albuquerque, N. Mex., 1972.

Ray, Reginald A. *Secret of the Vajra World: The Tantric Buddhism of Tibet.* Boston, 2001.

Russell, Jeffrey Burton. *Witchcraft in the Middle Ages.* Ithaca, N.Y., 1972.

Smith, Jonathan Z. *Map Is Not Territory: Studies in the History of Religions.* Leiden, Netherlands, 1978.

Stallybrass, Peter, and Allon White. *The Politics and Poetics of Transgression.* Ithaca, N.Y., 1986.

Taussig, Michael. "Transgression." In *Critical Terms for Religious Studies,* edited by Mark C. Taylor, pp. 349–364. Chicago, 1998.

Tigunait, Pandit Rajmani. *Śakti: The Power in Tantra, a Scholarly Approach.* Honesdale, Pa., 1998.

Trungpa, Chogyam. *Journey without Goal: The Tantric Wisdom of the Buddha.* Boston, 1981.

Valiaveetil, Chacko, S. J. "Living Liberation in Saiva Siddhant." In *Living Liberation in Hindu Thought,* edited by Andrew Fort and Patricia Y. Mumme, pp. 219–246. Albany, N.Y., 1996.

Walker, D. P. *Unclean Spirits: Possession and Exorcism in France and England in the Late Sixteenth and Early Seventeenth Centuries.* Philadelphia, 1980.

Wilcox, Michael. "The Collectors." In *Spirit Wars: Native North American Religions in the Age of Nation Building,* edited by Ronald Niezen, pp. 161–189. Berkeley, Calif., 2000.

PETRU CULIANU (1987)
CRAIG A. BURGDOFF (2005)

SADDUCEES. The Sadducees were one of the main Jewish political and religious groups (usually termed "sects") of the Second Temple period. By about the reign of John Hyrcanus I (135–104 BCE), they were a recognizable aristocratic group. Most of them were apparently priests or members of the families that had intermarried with the high priestly families. They tended to be moderate Hellenizers whose primary loyalty was to the religion of Israel but whose culture was greatly influenced by Hellenism. The Sadducees derived their name, Greek *Saddoukaioi,* Hebrew *ṣāddūqim,* from that of Zadok, the high priest of the Jerusalem Temple in the time of Solomon. In *Ezekiel* 40–48, the priestly duties were assigned exclusively to this clan. This family of high priests served throughout First and Second Temple times, except when foreign worship was brought into the Temple and when the Hasmoneans took control of the high priesthood. Sources mentioning the Sadducees are Josephus, the New Testament, rabbinic literature, and the Dead Sea Scrolls; there are no primary sources written by the Sadducees themselves.

The Sadducees rejected the "tradition of the fathers" that the Pharisees considered as law. For this reason the later rabbinic sources picture them as rejecting the oral law. The notion of some Church Fathers that the Sadducees accepted only the Torah as authoritative, rejecting the prophets and the emerging corpus of writings, is unsubstantiated by any earlier sources. The New Testament maintains that Sadducees did not believe in resurrection. Josephus writes that they rejected personal immortality, reward and punishment after death, and determinism, but that they believed strongly in absolute free will.

The Sadducees differed in matters of Jewish law from the Pharisees, according to rabbinic sources. The Sadducees required compensation for injuries done by a person's servant, whereas the Pharisees required it only in the case of one's animals, according to their interpretation of *Exodus* 21:32, 35–36. The Sadducees required that false witnesses be executed only when the accused had already been put to death because of their testimony (*Dt.* 19:19–21). The Pharisees imposed this penalty only when the accused had not been executed. The Sadducees criticized the inconsistencies in Pharisaic interpretations of the purity laws, and the Pharisees regarded Sadducean women as menstrually impure. In general, the Sadducees saw the purity laws as referring to the Temple and its priests, and saw no reason for the extension of these laws into the daily life of all Israel, a basic pillar of the Pharisaic approach.

A fundamental question is why the Sadducees disagreed so extensively with the Pharisaic tradition. Later Jewish tradition claimed that all differences revolved around the Sadducean rejection of the oral law. Based on this assumption, modern scholars argued that the Sadducees were strict literalists who followed the plain meaning of the words of the Torah only. Yet such an approach would not explain most of the views regarding legal matters attributed to the Sadducees.

Recent discoveries from the Dead Sea caves have illuminated Sadducean law. One particular text (4QMMT), written in the form of a letter purporting to be from the founders of the Dead Sea sect (who were apparently closely related to the Sadducees) to the leaders of the Jerusalem establishment, lists some twenty-two matters of legal disagreement. Comparison of these matters with the Pharisee-Sadducee disputes recorded in rabbinic literature has led to the conclusion that the writers of this "letter" took the view attributed to the Sadducees while their opponents in the Jerusalem priestly establishment held the views attributed later to the Pharisees. Examination of this document and related materials leads to the conclusion that Sadducees had their own methods of biblical exegesis and accordingly derived laws that were different from those of the Pharisees and their supporters.

The Sadducean party cannot be said to have come into being at any particular point. The priestly aristocracy, which traced its roots to First Temple times, had increased greatly in power in the Persian and Hellenistic periods, since the temporal as well as spiritual rule of the nation was in their hands. Some of these priests had been involved in the extreme Hellenization leading up to the Maccabean revolt, but most of the Sadducean lower clergy had remained loyal to the Torah and the ancestral Jewish way of life.

In the aftermath of the revolt, a small and devoted group of these Sadducean priests probably formed the group that eventually became the Dead Sea sect. They were unwilling to tolerate the replacement of the Zadokite high priest with a Hasmonean in 153–152 BCE, and they disagreed with the Jerusalem priesthood regarding matters of Jewish law. Soon after the Hasmonean takeover of the high priesthood, this group repaired to Qumran on the shore of the Dead Sea. The Dead Sea Scrolls refer to the early leaders of the sect as "sons of Zadok," testifying to some connection with the Sadducean tradition. Other moderately Hellenized Sadducees remained in Jerusalem, and it was they who were termed Sadducees in the strict sense of the term by Josephus in his descriptions of the Hasmonean period and by the later rabbinic traditions. They continued to be a key element in the Hasmonean aristocracy, supporting the priest-kings and joining, with the Pharisees, in the gerousia. After dominating this body for most of the reign of John Hyrcanus I and that of Alexander Janneus, the Sadducees suffered a major political setback when Queen Salome Alexandra (r. 76–67 BCE) turned thoroughly to support the Pharisees. Thereafter the Sadducees returned to greater power in the Herodian era, when they made common cause with the Herodian dynasty. In the end, it would be a group of lower Sadducean priests whose decision to reject the sacrifice offered for the Roman emperor set off the full-scale revolt of the Jews against Rome in 66 CE.

Closely allied to the Sadducees were the Boethusians. Most scholars ascribe the origin of the Boethusians to Simeon ben Boethus, appointed high priest by Herod in 24 BCE so that he would have sufficient status for Herod to marry his daughter Mariamne (II). This theory is completely unproven, and certain parallels between Boethusian rulings and material in the Dead Sea Scrolls argue for a considerably earlier date. There certainly were some differences between the Sadducees and the Boethusians, but the latter appear to have been a subgroup or an offshoot of the Sadducean group.

The most central of the disputes recorded in rabbinic literature as having separated the Boethusians from the Pharisees was that of the calendar. The Boethusians held that the first offering of the Omer (*Lv.* 23:9–14) had to take place on a Sunday, rather than on the second day of Passover. Such a calendar, similar to that known from the Dead Sea sect and the Book of Jubilees, was based on both solar months and solar years. If so, the Sunday in question would be that after the seventh day of Passover (most interpreters have taken it as referring to the intermediate Sunday of the festival). Following this calendar, the holiday of Shavuot (Pentecost) would always fall on a Sunday. While this approach seemed to accord better with the literal interpretation of the words "on the morrow of the Sabbath" (*Lv.* 23:11), the Pharisees could accept neither this innovative calendar (the biblical calendar was based on lunar months) nor the interpretation on which it was based. To them, "Sabbath" here meant festival. (Attribution of this Boethusian calendric view to the Sadducees by some scholars results from confusion in the manuscripts of rabbinic texts.)

The approach of the Sadducees certainly had a major impact on the political and religious developments in Judaism of the Second Temple period, including the formation of the Dead Sea sect. There is evidence that some Sadducean traditions remained in circulation long enough to influence the medieval literalist sect of the Karaites that arose in the eighth century CE. Yet otherwise, with the destruction of the Temple in 70 CE, the Sadducees ceased to be a factor in Jewish history. The sacrificial system in which they played so leading a role was no longer practiced. Their power base, the Jerusalem Temple, was gone, and their strict constructionism augured poorly for the adaptation of Judaism to its new circumstances.

SEE ALSO Dead Sea Scrolls; Jerusalem, overview article.

BIBLIOGRAPHY

LeMoyne, Jean. *Les Sadducéens.* Paris, 1972.

Schiffman, Lawrence W. *Reclaiming the Dead Sea Scrolls: The History of Judaism, the Background of Christianity, the Lost Library of Qumran.* Philadelphia, 1994. See pages 83–89.

Schürer, Emil. *The History of the Jewish People in the Age of Jesus Christ* (175 BC–AD 135). Edinburgh, 1979. See pages 404–414.

LAWRENCE H. SCHIFFMAN (2005)

SĀDHUS AND SĀDHVĪS. The term *sādhu* (feminine, *sādhvī*) derives from the Sanskrit root *sādh* (meaning "accomplish") and also has the general sense of "a good or virtuous person." More specifically, within the Hindu religious tradition a *sādhu* or *sādhvī* (a *sādhvī* is also referred to as *mai* and "Mātājī") is someone who, under a *guru*, has undergone a ritual of renunciation known as *saṃnyāsa* and formally abandoned family life and conventional worldly means for making a livelihood. The *saṃnyāsa* rite, which is preceded by a preliminary initiation rite, is usually performed at a Kumbha Melā, the preeminent festival for *sādhus*. The rite is assisted by a *guru* and several Brahmin *paṇḍits*, thereby relieving the initiate's family of any future responsibility in that regard. *Sādhus* are usually buried in a seated position when they die, in distinction from the traditional Hindu practice of cremation.

The Hindu religious explanation for taking *saṃnyāsa* and becoming initiated as a *sādhu* is to "realize God" or obtain liberation (*mokṣa*), an objective considered to be difficult in worldly life. While some *sādhus* claim to have experienced a direct religious calling to renounce—occasionally in old age—others become *sādhus* to escape legal, financial, personal, or family problems. In some instances an orphan is adopted and raised by *sādhus*, and *sādhvīs* are not infrequently bereaved. Renunciate practices range from a primarily devotional approach to liberation—through reciting *mantras* or chanting and singing the names and praises of a personal deity—to a path of austerities and asceticism (*tapas*, literally "heat") that may involve meditation and yoga. Within the Hindu mythological world, the practice of asceticism, which may range from dietary restrictions to extreme forms of mortification, is also believed to produce powers (*siddhis*) of a supernatural kind, which are feared and considered to be real at a popular level. *Sādhus* are revered almost as forms of a deity in some areas of north India.

After performing the *saṃnyāsa* rite, the lifestyle of the *sādhu* is, traditionally, thereafter that of a wandering mendicant. However, the rite also simultaneously constitutes an initiation into the renunciate sect to which the initiating *guru* belongs. An initiate receives a new name, a new religious identity, and enters the network of an alternative social world, with its own hierarchies and implicit codes of behavior. The names of renunciates are usually recorded by an official from the sect into which the candidate is initiated. Although most *sādhus* live simply—some in remote places—from alms or local produce, an initiate into a renunciate order also has potential access to a network of *āśramas* and *maṭhas* (monasteries), which can be extensive for the larger sects. These institutions often provide food and shelter for both resident *sādhus* and those on pilgrimage to holy places. Many of even the largest *āśramas* have developed over time from a simple dwelling constructed by a *sādhu* who settled somewhere, frequently after traveling for many years on pilgrimage throughout the Indian subcontinent.

There are currently around sixty Hindu (or semi-Hindu) renunciate sects of *sādhus* in India and Nepal. Orders of *sādhus* (or their equivalent) are also a constituent of several of the other religious traditions currently represented in India. They are to be found amongst Muslims, where, according to some schemata, there are fourteen orders of Sūfīs (also referred to as *fakīr*); amongst Sikhs (in the Udāsin and Nirmala orders); and also amongst Jains, where *sādhvīs* significantly outnumber *sādhus*. Within the Jain tradition there is a closer relationship between the *sādhu* and lay communities than in other Indian renunciate traditions. Buddhist monks, who are not very numerous in India, are represented in a few regions, but they are almost exclusively attached to monasteries.

All renunciate sects trace their origin to a revered founding *guru*, the sectarian identity of members being exhibited by a variety of means. These include specific ash or paste marks on the face and body, the kinds of beads or seeds used for a necklace (*mālā*), accoutrements (such as a particular kind of staff), and also the type and color of clothing, which is frequently scant. *Sādhus* of some orders, particularly *nāgās* (who are traditionally naked, fighting ascetics), cover their entire body with ashes. *Sādhus* have their head fully shaved during initiation, but some subsequently grow dreadlocks.

Amongst Hindus, while there are several relatively small sects of Tantric/*śākta sādhus*, whose main deity is a form of the goddess (*devī*), most Hindu renunciate sects are primarily *vaiṣṇava* or *śaiva* in orientation, and their main deity is a form of, respectively, Viṣṇu or Śiva. The two largest sects of *sādhus*—with several hundred thousand initiates—are the *vaiṣṇava* sect of Rāmānanda (known as Rāmānandīs or *vairāgīs*) and the *śaiva* sect of *saṃnyāsīs* (or Daśanāmīs, meaning "ten names"), founded, according to their respective traditions, by Rāmānanda in the fourteenth century and the *advaita* (nondual) philosopher Śaṅkarācārya in the ninth century.

According to traditional Brahmanical norms, women are ineligible for *saṃnyāsa*. However, there is considerable historical evidence of ascetic women renunciates, and some women ascetics may be found in nearly all renunciate sects. Currently, more than 90 percent of *sādhus* are men, though government census data from the early twentieth century indicate that at that time women *sādhvīs* comprised up to 40 percent of the renunciate population in some areas of India. It is not uncommon for women renunciates to have suffered bereavement and to have become *sādhvīs* to escape the difficult circumstances often experienced by widows in South Asia.

In most instances, women renunciates are initiated by male preceptors and do not have their own institutions wherein there is a lineage of authority transmitted from a female *guru* to a female successor. However, in a few orders there are branches that have their own female *gurus*. For example, amongst Daśanāmīs—nominally an orthodox sect—there is a division of around a thousand *mais* who are *nāgā* and are affiliated to the Jūnā *akhāḍā* (see below) but live entirely separately from their male counterparts. Similarly, there are two communities of women renunciates (the Śrī Śāradā Maṭha and the Śāradā Rāmakṛṣṇa [Ramakrishna] Mission) who are devotees of the nineteenth-century Bengali saint, Rāmakṛṣṇa Paramahaṃsa, and his wife, Śāradā Devī. However, unlike the Daśanāmī *nāgā* women who occasionally travel to pilgrimage sites and attend festivals such as the Kumbha Melā, the women renunciates of the orders affiliated to the Rāmakṛṣṇa Mission reside most of the time in monastic institutions. As most renunciate orders have an ambivalent attitude toward female ascetics, it is also not uncommon for women renunciates to become independent *gurus*, some of whom attract a considerable lay following.

According to the traditional Hindu ideal, renunciates undertake austerities of some kind or other to purify the mind and body, food is collected by begging, and celibacy is maintained. However, a wide range of practice is evident both between and within the various renunciate sects. Being a renunciate does not necessarily entail asceticism, and limited regimens of asceticism are not infrequently practiced by householders. Some sects—notably those of the *vaiṣṇava* devotees of Vallabha (1479–1531 CE), Caitanya (1486–1533 CE), and Dādū (1544–1604 CE)—have both celibate and married initiates. Managers of one of the larger *sādhu āśramas* have significant responsibilities for the maintenance of buildings, observance of temple activities, the welfare of visitors, and administrative affairs, which may include income derived from land-holdings. There is generally a hierarchy of authority and responsibility within the renunciate orders, with posts for cooks, security officers, secretaries, and property managers. Titular heads of monasteries may wield considerable influence, not only locally but even at the national level, as in the case of the Śaṇkarācāryas, who head the Daśanāmī order. There are also instances of renunciates taking political office, a prominent example being Ūma Bhāratī, a *saṃnyāsin* who became a politician, and who was subsequently sworn in, on December 8, 2003, as the first woman chief minister of the state of Madhya Pradesh. While, at one end of the spectrum, *sādhus* may be strict vegetarians who avoid all forms of intoxication, at the other end of the spectrum, some few *sādhus* of the most radical orders, the Aghorīs, and some Nāths and Tantrics, may inhabit graveyards and exhibit extreme antinomian behavior, eating from human skulls and even consuming human flesh. *Sādhus* of the more radical orders often consume alcohol and also large quantities of cannabis, which is either smoked with tobacco, or eaten or drunk in the form of *bhāṅg*, a prepared form of the leaves of the plant.

Scholars still do not agree on when ascetic renunciates first emerged on the religious landscape of South Asia. Some believe that semi-shamanic ascetics date back to the Indus Valley civilization (2500–1800 BCE) or even earlier, and may be seen as the *yati* or *muni*, semi-mythological characters who appear in the *Ṛgveda* (c. 1200–1400 BCE). This characterization is disputed by other scholars, who maintain that during the so-called axial age (fifth–sixth centuries BCE), economic and social developments provided the context for the development of a new worldview, the notion of renunciation, and the institution of renunciate religious sects, such as the Ājīvika, Jain, and Buddhist orders. One of the earliest available reports of a foreigner visiting India is that of Megasthenes (fourth century BCE), who like many other visitors, records the activities of ash-covered philosophers (gymnosophists), some of whom were capable of extreme feats of endurance. Around this time were produced the earliest Sanskrit texts to include sections detailing the way of life of the renunciate *saṃnyāsin* as being within the scope of the *dharma* (religious rules and practices) of orthodox Brahmanical culture. Several of these texts, the *Dharma-sūtras*, provide rules and procedures for those wishing to take *saṃnyāsa*, and renounce Brahmanical ritual life and the daily religious activities—based on the *Veda*—incumbent upon all members of ancient Brahmanical society. Whatever the origins of Brahmanical religious asceticism, by around the beginning of the Common Era, *saṃnyāsin* had become the term generally used by the Brahmanical tradition to designate those who had renounced ritual life, preferably in the fourth and last stage (*āśrama*) of life.

However, it appears that it was not only older people who had retired from Brahmanical ritual life who became ascetic renunciates. Perhaps the earliest reference to sectarian asceticism in South Asia is by the grammarian Pāṇini (fourth century BCE), who refers to *śaiva* ascetics. These ascetics were most probably Pāśupatas, renowned for their antisocial behavior. They are the earliest known sect of "Hindu" ascetics, who survived into the fourteenth century. The earliest known monasteries (*maṭha*) for Hindu renunciate orders date from the eighth century CE, and were of *śaiva* orders, namely the Kāpālikas (the predecessors of the Aghorīs) and the (less radical) Kālāmukhas, both of which superseded the Pāśupatas. *Maṭhas* of the influential Śaiva-Siddhānta order appear to have been first founded in the tenth century. Śaṇkarācārya is reputed to have founded the first order of orthodox Brahmanical ascetics, the *śaiva* Daśanāmī-Saṃnyāsīs, though recent research casts some doubt on this. Several of the most important orthodox *vaiṣṇava* orders, which also have renunciate initiates, have preceptors dating to the early centuries of the first millennium CE: the Śrī *sampradāya* (order/sect) of the devotional philosopher Rāmānuja (traditionally dated to 1017–1137 CE), and the *sampradāyas* of Madhva (1238–1317 CE) and Nimbārka (twelfth century). Several more *vaiṣṇava sampradāyas* with both householder and renunciate initiates arose during the next few centuries. A number of sects were also established that have a partially *vaiṣṇava* religious culture, but whose adherents worship a formless (*nirguṇī*) god. One of the best known of these sects is the *panth* (sect) of Kabīr (c. 1450–1525 CE). In distinction from nearly all *śaiva* and most *vaiṣṇava sādhus*, renunciates of some *vaiṣṇava* sects do not perform the *saṃnyāsa* rite, but undergo a parallel rite whereby a special relationship is established between the renunciate and the deity of the sect.

Besides the monastic traditions of the renunciate sects, which have produced innumerable scholars and philosophers, *sādhus* have also been periodically engaged in significant military and mercenary activities. Although as early as the eighth century Pāśupata ascetics were armed by guilds to protect trade, it was during the late sixteenth and seventeenth centuries that *nāgā* (naked) ascetics from the Nāth, Daśanāmī-Saṃnyāsī (also called *gosain*), Vairāgī (Bairāgī), Dādū-*panth*, Nimbārkī (Nīmāvat), and Rādhavallabhī sects first became organized as fighting units (*akhāḍā*, literally "wrestling ring"), primarily owing to state patronage. Initiation as a *nāgā* into an *akhāḍā* is nearly always performed subsequent to the *saṃnyāsa* rite. During the latter half of the eighteenth and early nineteenth centuries—a time of great political instability in north India—*nāgās* were employed in many instances as part of a regularly paid standing army of several thousand troops in service to *māharājās* of Jodhpur, Jaipur, Jaisalmer, Bikaner, Udaipur, Baroda, Marwar (western Madhya Pradesh), and Bhuj (the capital town of Kacch, Gujarat). At the height of their careers in the late eighteenth century, three prominent Daśanāmī *nāgā saṃnyāsīs*, namely Rajendra Giri Gosain (d. 1753 CE) and his *celās* (disciples), the brothers Anūp Giri Gosain (Himmat Bahādūr, 1730–1804 CE) and Umrao Giri Gosain (b. 1734 CE), commanded forces of up to forty thousand horse and foot soldiers. They were highly regarded by the British as a fighting force, ranked alongside the Afghans and Sikhs, and were particularly renowned for their nighttime guerrilla operations. These *nāgās* fought many campaigns, mostly on behalf of Mughal regents, but changed allegiances several times over the decades.

There are currently thirteen *akhāḍās* extant in India; seven are Daśanāmī, three are Rāmānandī, and three are Sikh-related, namely the Nirmala and two Udāsin *akhāḍās*. The *nāgā* members of the *akhāḍā* still train for fighting, but after the imposition of British rule in India their military operations were almost entirely curtailed. As a consequence of their mercenary activities many *gosains* became wealthy, acquiring substantial property and trading enterprises. By the 1780s *gosains* had become the dominant moneylenders and property-owners in Allahabad, Banaras, Mirzapur, Ujjain, and Nagpur, and they were major brokers in Rajasthan and the Deccan at places such as Hyderabad and Pune. Their influence declined during the nineteenth century, and since the beginning of the twentieth century, nearly all renunciate institutions, including most of the *akhāḍās*, have been actively engaged in educational and social welfare programs throughout India. Being Hindu institutions, renunciate sects have also been periodically vocal in the politics of India. This was particularly evident during the 1990s, when the leaders of several renunciate institutions became more closely involved with the ruling, nationalist Bharatiya Janata Party.

In several regions of South Asia there are castes of Saṃnyāsīs, Nāths, and other renunciate sects, who exhibit some of the customs of the sect to which their ancestors were members, but having married and settled, are otherwise integrated into worldly society amongst a general hierarchy of castes.

SEE ALSO Asceticism; Ashram; Gurū; Kabīr; Kumbha Melā; Madhva; Moksa; Nimbārka; Nuns, overview article; Ordination; Rāmānuja; Saivism, overview article; Saṃnyāsa; Śaṅkara; Sārāda Devī; Vaiṣṇavism, overview article.

BIBLIOGRAPHY

Although a considerable number of articles related to specific renunciate sects have been published, relatively few general studies of *sādhus* and *sādhvīs* have appeared since the late 1970s.

Burghart, Richard. "Renunciation in the Religious Traditions of South Asia." *Man* (New Series) 18 (1983): 635–653. This article provides a useful critique of a still prevalent anthropological notion of a "lone" casteless ascetic, illustrating hierarchies and marriage status amongst various renunciant sects.

Clementin-Ojha, Catherine. "Feminine Asceticism in Hinduism: Its Tradition and Present Condition." *Man In India* 61, no. 3 (1981): 254–285. Having surveyed the historical situation of women *saṃnyāsinīs*, Clementin-Ojha presents three women renunciate *gurus* who have followers and *āś ramas* in Banaras.

Gross, Robert Lewis. *The Sadhus of India: A Study of Hindu Asceticism.* Jaipur, India 1992.

Hartsuiker, Dolf. *Sādhus: Holy Men of India.* 2d ed. London, 1993. Hartsuiker's book contains many excellent photos and a good introductory account of *sādhus*.

Khandelwal, Meena. *Women in Ochre Robes: Gendering Hindu Renunciation.* Albany, N.Y., 2004. This is one of the few studies on Hindu women renunciates. It focuses primarily on two Daśanāmī women living in Haridwar, and relates their daily lives.

Lester, Robert C. "The Practice of Renunciation in Śrivaiṣṇavism." *Journal of Oriental Research, Madras* (*Dr. S. S. Janaki Felicitation Volume*) 1986–1992, vols. 61–72 (1992): 77–95. Lester's article is an informative survey of the history and practices of the renunciate sect whose preceptor is Rāmānuja.

Lorenzen, David N. "Warrior Ascetics in Indian History." *Journal of the American Oriental Society* 98, no. 1 (1978): 61–75. This article provides a compact, general survey of the topic.

Miller, David M., and Dorothy C. Wertz. *Hindu Monastic Life: The Monks and Monasteries of Bhubaneswar.* Montreal, 1976. This study examines twenty-two monasteries of various sects in the city.

Olivelle, Patrick, ed. and trans. *Saṃnyāsa Upaniṣads: Hindu Scriptures on Asceticism and Renunciation.* New York, 1992. A comprehensive historical introduction to the development of the Brahmanical institution of *saṃnyāsa* precedes Olivelle's translation of a corpus of texts on asceticism and renunciation produced during the first millennium CE.

Olivelle, Patrick, ed. and trans. *Rules and Regulations of Brahmanical Asceticism:* Yatidharmasamuccaya *of Yādava Prakāśa.* Albany, N.Y., 1995. Olivelle provides a useful introduction and a translation of the earliest-known Brahmanical text (twelfth century CE) devoted exclusively to renunciation.

Sinha, Surajit, and Baidyanath Saraswati. *Ascetics of Kashi.* Vārāṇasī, India, 1978. Based on anthropological fieldwork carried out in Banaras in the 1970s, this book (somewhat difficult to obtain), on the various *sādhu* sects and institutions of the city, is one of the most generally informative.

Thiel-Horstmann, Monika. "On the Dual Identity of Nāgās." In *Devotion Divine: Bhakti Traditions from the Regions of India,* edited by Diana L. Eck and Françoise Mallison, pp. 255–272. Groningen, Germany, and Paris, 1991. This article surveys the history and religious practices of *nāgās* of the Dādū *panth.*

Tripathi, B. D. *Sadhus of India: The Sociological View.* Bombay, 1978. Tripathi was initiated into both Daśanāmī and Nimbārkī sects, and secretly undertook surreptitious sociological fieldwork in the state of Uttar Pradesh in the 1960s. He gives an insider's view and some interesting, though perhaps partial, statistics.

White, David Gordon. *The Alchemical Body: Siddha Traditions in Medieval India.* Chicago, 1996. This book provides a comprehensive account of Nāths/*siddhas* in the medieval period, illustrating their complex roles in society.

MATTHEW CLARK (2005)

SAʿDĪ (AH 597?–690/1200?–1291 CE), pen name of Abū ʿAbd Allāh Musharrif (al-Dīn) ibn Muṣliḥ al-Dīn Saʿdī-yi Shīrāzī, Islamic Persian belletrist, panegyrist, and popularizer of mystically colored poetry. His exact name (other than the universally used *nom de plume*) and his precise birth and death dates have been much disputed, and he has often been credited with longevity of well over a century. He was born and died in the south Iranian capital of Shiraz, but allegedly spent some half of his life elsewhere, partly perhaps to escape the Mongol invasions and the constant petty warfare within Iran itself. His wanderings fall into three categories: study, most importantly at Baghdad; pilgrimages to the holy cities of Islam (Mecca and Medina); and general drifting, as he claims, all over the Islamic world and beyond.

At one point, so he relates, he was a prisoner of war of the Crusaders and was set to hard labor until ransomed into an unfortunate marriage. Some time around the second and major Mongol invasion of the Middle East in the late 1250s, he seems finally to have retired to his native city—Shiraz was somewhat off the beaten track for the Mongols, as it proved—and established himself as a man of letters and a sort of court-holding sage. The detailed facts of Saʿdī's life are almost as much disputed as his full name and dates, for most of the information derives from, or depends heavily on, his own avowedly "poeticized" writings. However, along with his acknowledged stature as a writer, certain features of his career are hardly open to doubt: his hard-won erudition, his urbane and even cynical world experience, and his familiarity with all aspects of the dervish way of life, both practical and theoretical.

Saʿdī's writings, most of which are poetry, fall into various categories and are often published in one large volume as *Kullīyāt* (Collected works). Once again, there is much controversy as to the period of his life to which some items belong, but the two longest and most significant can be fairly specifically dated. These are the *Būstān* (Herb garden), completed at some time in late autumn of 1257, and the *Gulistān* (Rose garden), published in the spring of 1258. In the few months between these two dates there occurred one of the most traumatic events, at least from the psychoreligious point of view, in the history of Islamic society: the sacking of the capital city of Baghdad and the extinction of the venerable Abbasid caliphate. Yet if the onrushing storm is nowhere presaged in the former work, its aftermath—at only some eight hundred kilometers' distance—is equally passed over in silence in the latter. There could be several plausible reasons to account for this idyllic detachment on the part of one of Iran's great commentators on life: one is that (other arguments notwithstanding) Saʿdī might have been a Shīʿī, and no sorrier than Naṣīr al-Dīn Ṭūsī to see the symbol of perceived Sunnī usurpation so drastically defaced. Certainly, despite one or two brief and formal elegies elsewhere on the passing of the old order, he would soon come to offer panegyrics to the new rulers.

The *Būstān* is a work of some 4,100 lengthy couplets, divided into ten unequal sections, the rich content of which is only approximately indicated by such general titles as "On Humility," "On Contentment," and so forth. Though clearly grounded in a rather humane, mystically tinged Islamic, and even pre-Islamic, tradition, it is ethical, moralistic, and edifying rather than religious in any strict sense. An element of entertainment, rarely missing from such works in Persian at any time, is provided by frequent variation of matter, style, and pace, and by the inclusion of some 160 illustrative stories (some quite short and not designated as such). At the same time, the poem is not merely exhortatory, but reflective and in places almost ecstatic. Yet if it achieves a beneficial moral effect, it does so primarily through its incomparable style and narrative power: at virtually all points throughout its lengthy sweep, it is fluent, elegant, graphic, colorful, witty, paradoxical, and above all epigrammatic.

The *Gulistān*, Saʿdī would have us believe, is a hasty compound of material left over from the *Būstān*. Superficially, it is certainly quite similar in subject matter, but it is much more obviously a work of art and light entertainment. Arranged in eight main sections, again of considerable vagueness as to central theme, it is primarily a collection of stories, told in exemplary (often rhyming) Persian prose with verse embellishments in both Persian and Arabic. The general tone is much less lofty than that of the *Būstān*; indeed, it is frequently quite worldly, even cynical and flippant. Despite this, it has always been the more popular of the two in both East and West, though manuscripts and editions of both have been reproduced beyond counting, so quintessentially Persian are they held to be.

Apart from a few prose essays, the rest of Saʿdī's writings consists largely of monorhyming poems of two kinds: the long *qaṣīdah* (some forty double lines or more) and the shorter, more lyrical *ghazal* (of a dozen double lines or so). These poems are usually classified in various arbitrary ways having little or nothing to do with their essential character. Quite a few are circumstantial and panegyric, and some (not included in most editions) are downright obscene. Excepting a few in Arabic, nearly all of them are in Saʿdī's native Persian, and the great majority anticipate Ḥāfiẓ (d. 1389?) in ambiguously using the language of earthly love for mystical statement or vice versa. Saʿdī was a complex character, clearly vain of his own literary skill and disingenuous about his loyalties, and his allegedly religious utterances, however sublime, can rarely be taken at simple face value. Indeed, he often warns his readers against taking any of his words too literally. His supreme achievement was to speak with the voice of his age and his culture, and his writings are religious only in the sense that the age was (and the culture still is) deeply permeated by the matter of religion.

BIBLIOGRAPHY

The literature on Saʿdī is enormous, but most of it (apart from articles in the standard histories of Persian literature and similar reference works) is still not available in Western languages, and nearly all of it is long out of print. The standard monograph, which reviews virtually everything worthwhile prior to its own date, is Henri Massé's *Essai sur le poète Saadi* (Paris, 1919).

Editions of Saʿdī's works in Persian are countless; practically none of them are in any sense critical. As to translations, few of the individual poems have been satisfactorily rendered into any Western languages. There are, however, reliable and recent English renderings of the two major works: the *Būstān*, which I have translated with an introduction and notes as *Morals Pointed and Tales Adorned* (Toronto, 1974), and *The Gulistān or Rose Garden of Saʿdī*, translated by Edward Rehatsek (1888), which I have revised with an introduction (New York, 1965). Both of these contain further bibliographical information.

New Sources

Daniel, Marc. "Arab Civilisation and Male Love." In *Reclaiming Sodom*. Edited by Jonathan Goldberg. New York, 1994.

Murray, Stephen O., and Will Roscoe, eds. *Islamic Homosexualities: Culture, History, and Literature.* New York, 1997.

Roth, Norman. "Fawn of My Delights: Boy-Love in Hebrew and Arabic Verse." In *Sex in the Middle Ages,* edited by Joyce E. Salisbury. New York, 1991.

Schmitt, Arno, and Jehoeda Sofer, eds. *Sexuality and Eroticism among Males in Moslem Societies.* New York, 1991.

Wilson, Peter Lamborn. *Scandal: Essays in Islamic Heresy.* New York, 1988.

G. M. WICKENS (1987)
Revised Bibliography

ṢADR AL-DĪN SHĪRĀZĪ SEE MULLĀ ṢADRĀ

SAGAS are long prose narratives in Old Norse written primarily in Iceland between approximately 1180 and 1500. They are generally categorized by their subject matter. The kinds of sagas important for the study of Norse paganism are the *kings' sagas*, which are biographies of Scandinavian kings (related sagas are about the Scandinavian earls of the Orkneys and the Faeroes); *family sagas* (or "sagas of the Icelanders"), which recount the histories of Iceland and Greenland from their settlement in the ninth and tenth centuries up to about 1030 (a related text is *Landnámabók* [Book of the Land-Takings], an account of the settling of Iceland, which began around 870); and *mythical-heroic sagas*, which describe adventures taking place in Scandinavia before the settlement of Iceland. All three groups of texts contain material relating to Scandinavian paganism, mythology, and other non-Christian beliefs and practices.

The kings' sagas about Olaf Tryggvason and Olaf Haraldsson describe their efforts to convert Norway and Iceland to Christianity in the period from 995 to 1030, including their encounters with pagan gods, temples, idols, and believers. The legendary history of the early kings presents the Swedish royal family as the descendants of Freyr and worshippers of Óðinn. It also includes myths not found elsewhere, some of which (such as the story that the giantess Skaði married Óðinn after she separated from Njörðr) may be medieval inventions. Family sagas contain characters who are pagan priests, seeresses, witches, and sorcerers, and they describe rituals such as fortune-telling, "baptism," funerals, sanctifications of land and temples, oath-taking, and sacrifices. Mythical-heroic sagas, some of which draw on pagan myth and legend, treat all of the above, although their setting in the legendary past and their cast of heroes, gods, and monsters make their accounts of paganism seem less realistic than those of the other kinds of sagas, which tend to a more factual-seeming style.

Although this material may possibly be accurate, somehow preserved by oral tradition, the saga authors are generally writing long after the fact and are interpreting (if not inventing) the tale for reasons of their own and according to their Christian worldview. For example, authors of the family sagas often wanted to show that the beliefs and social institutions of pagan Icelanders prefigured those of a fully Christian society. A later saga author could also borrow from an earlier saga, so the existence of some element of paganism in more than one saga is not necessarily proof of its origin in the shared pagan heritage. It is just as likely to derive from vague memories and popular tradition, deliberate antiquarian reconstruction, or the writer's own suppositions as to what the old religion was like. For instance, the account in the family saga *Hrafnkels saga* (Saga of Hrafnkell) of a sacred horse shared by the hero with the god Freyr, which he swore that no man should ride, on pain of death, is now generally recognized as a late and fictitious presentation of heathen beliefs and practices unlikely to have been part of pagan culture. Similarly, the description of a heathen temple in the family saga *Eyrbyggja saga* (Saga of the People who Lived at Eyr) is now considered a learned reconstruction. Nonetheless, traces of the old heathen religion and its rituals are preserved in the sagas, and increasingly reliable the lower the religious plane, as simple magical practices that surely continued to be performed into the Christian era.

The sagas attest to a belief in *landvættir* (land spirits), who can bring luck in farming and fishing, and they depict pagans devoting themselves to Þórr (a protector against bad weather at sea and the god who supports order in the community), Óðinn (a sower of strife but also the god who endows poets with the valuable power over words), and Freyr (the bringer of good harvests). *Eyrbyggja saga* chronicles the arrival from Norway of Þórólfr, a devout worshipper of Þórr who settles in western Iceland. He is shown choosing his land at the prompting of the god, setting up pillars brought from Þórr's shrine in Norway, marking his boundaries with fire, and building a new temple near his home. The association of Þórr with the land, with the choice of a sacred field for the Law Assembly, and the taking of oaths on a sacred ring appears authentic. The mythical-heroic saga *Gautreks saga* (Saga of Gautrek) describes Starkaðr the Old, a famous warrior renowned for the talents Óðinn bestowed on him. His mother dedicated him to the god before birth in return for help in a brewing contest, and when he grew to manhood, Óðinn was compelled by Þórr's curse to cause Starkaðr to commit terrible deeds, such as the sacrificial death (by hanging and stabbing with a spear) of the king he served. One version of the king's saga about Olaf Tryggvason includes a tale about a fugitive Icelander who joined the priestess of Freyr as she traveled from farm to farm in Sweden in a chariot with a statue of Freyr; this was believed to bring good harvests. The young man soon substituted himself for the statue, and when the priestess became pregnant the people took it as a sign of divine favor. Although this episode is probably intended to mock paganism, the practice it describes is confirmed from other sources, such as Tacitus's description of the procession of Nerthus.

Two priestesses are mentioned in *Landnámabók;* these Icelandic women are also distinguished by being related to the local chieftains. One was the wife of Þorvaldr Koðránsson, and the story goes that, during the efforts to spread Christianity in Iceland, Þorvaldr was assisting in the preaching at the Assembly but his wife remained at home, offering a sacrifice at a temple. When considering such a report, it must be remembered that medieval Christianity associated the male with the spiritual and the female with the carnal, and the sagas therefore contain many episodes in which a woman promoting or defending paganism is defeated by a man's efforts to promote Christianity. In the family saga *Njáls saga* (Saga of Njál), it is a woman who forcefully defends the pagan faith and even attempts to convert King Olaf Tryggvason's missionary, the priest Þangbrandr. The king's saga about Olaf Haraldsson includes a tale in which a farmwife has her household worshipping a preserved horse's penis; when King Olaf hears of this, he travels to their remote district and preaches Christianity to them in person. Another female-led ritual practice that occurred within the household was *seiðr*, a kind of divination that, according to myth, was taught by Freyja, the Vanir goddess of love. It could be used for black magic, but its purpose in several sagas is to predict the future and men's fates. A famous description of it is in the family saga *Eiríks saga rauða* (Erik the Red's Saga), where a famine in Greenland prompts one of the leaders of the community to invite a seeress to a feast. She wears special clothing and is fed special food. The next day she obtains the help of another woman who knows the right chant; this draws many spirits to the circle of women, and the seeress is able to forecast the end of the famine, predict famous progeny for the woman who sang, and answer questions put by various individuals.

In contrast to the mythic origin of this practice, *Landnámabók* and the king's saga about Harald Fairhair of Norway refer to *seiðr* and magic being learned from the Sámi or Lapps in northern Norway. (Not quite a saga is the Norwegian *Historia Norwegiae* [History of Norway], written circa 1178 to 1220, which gives a Latin account, purportedly based on the testimony of a Christian eyewitness, of two Sámi shamans who attempt to retrieve the missing life-soul of a woman struck unconscious by an unknown adversary.) Like the category of the female, the Sámi are generally deployed in the sagas as a "cultural other," that is, a group that is used to define Norse society by being the group that the Norse are not. Thus, both women's magic and Sámi shamanism can, from the perspective of the sagas, easily be interpreted as witchcraft and sorcery, although witchcraft, strictly speaking, is a phenomenon of Christian Europe. *Eiríks saga*'s account of the seeress's garb includes the detail of her cat-fur gloves, which is more reminiscent of European witchlore than Finno-Ugric shamanism. The saga authors probably saw little difference between the *seiðr* of the past and thirteenth-century notions of witches.

The biases just described, however, were not universal, and several Icelandic men of good reputation are depicted as involved in divination and manipulative magic. The king's saga about Olaf Tryggvason includes a tale about an Icelander who can see the future, including the imminent death of his best friend's son, soon to be killed by malevolent *dísir*, female spirits associated with his family, who are angry that the family will abandon them for a new faith. The family saga *Egils saga Skallagrímssonar* (Saga of Egill, Son of Bald Grímr) describes one incident in which Egill cures a woman who was sickened by the improper use of runes, which had been cut into a stick that was then put into her bed. Because the carver of the runes was incompetent, his runes made her ill instead of infatuated. Egill cuts away the runes, burns the shavings, and cuts new runes into the stave that restores the woman to health.

Another aspect of Germanic paganism that does not involve the gods is a belief that the dead were conscious inhabitants of their graves. A related belief, documented in *Landnámabók* as well as *Eyrbyggja saga*, held that the dead spent the afterlife with their ancestors in a nearby mountain. The latter says that the Þórr-worshipper Þórólfr brought the tradition with him from Norway, and he and his son Þorsteinn are said to retire after their death to a certain mountain, where they feast in the company of their ancestors. Helgafell ("Holy Mountain"), the familial mountain in western Iceland, is guarded from being defiled by bloodshed or excrement, and no one is allowed to look at it without being washed. (Interestingly, Helgafell became a thriving monastic center by the thirteenth century.) *Landnámabók* notes that the descendents of Auðr, a Christian settler of Iceland, reverted to Holy Mountain worship after her death.

Pagan Germanic cultures varied widely, from the warrior tribes known to the Romans through the kingdoms of Scandinavia and Anglo-Saxon England, with their well-developed towns and trade routes, to the unique North Atlantic society of Iceland, which for its first four hundred years was a commonwealth of farm-based chieftains, with neither king nor any urban center. The religion and rituals of these cultures also varied, as do the reflexes of them found in the sagas. In addition to the beliefs and practices that the sagas depict as beliefs and practices, there are also episodes that appear to derive from rituals, although the saga author seems to be unaware of their special nature. These are found in mythical-heroic sagas based on Migration Age legends, such as *Völsunga saga* (Saga of the Völsungs) and *Hrólfs saga kraka* (Saga of Hrólf Kraki). Primarily they involve initiation ceremonies used to mark (or make) the change of boys into young warriors.

A thousand years later, these tribal practices had faded from memory, but knowledge of the Old Norse mythic world was still a cultural resource of the Icelanders, and without it the sagas cannot be fully understood. It was not the only cognitive category they possessed—Christianity was another—but it was one means by which they could communicate a wide range of concepts and ideas that were integral to their culture. Nonetheless, the saga authors and audiences were Christians, and their use of paganism as a theme and the old myths as narrative patterns was, on the largest scale, subsumed within a Christian worldview in one of several ways—for example, by considering the age of paganism to be the Scandinavian equivalent of the "old dispensation" (the period before the old law of the Jews was replaced by the new law of Christ). Paganism and pagan associations, such as Odinic characters, are deployed according to the Christian author's view of the past or agenda for his history. Snorri Sturluson (1179–1241) emphasizes the Odinic allegiances of Earl Hákon, who is the opponent and pagan counterpart of King Olaf Tryggvason, the Christian who must assert political control over his new kingdom and begin its conversion. The family saga *Víga-Glúms saga* (Saga of Killer-Glúmr) describes an Icelandic intercult rivalry between Freyr and Óðinn. The author implies that such a proud and vengeful society can only escape its failings by accepting Christianity. Pagan behaviors are thus shown to be embodiments of Christian sin. *Eyrbyggja saga*'s Þórólfr establishes the authority of his temple through demanding tributes from neighboring farms, and similar characteristics are found in the figure of Hrafnkell, who is deeply affectionate towards the stallion he has dedicated to Freyr and is kind to his own supporters, though he forces others to become his supporters and does not treat them fairly. In these sagas, the oppression exercised by these priests probably signifies the spiritual burden and evil nature of paganism.

BIBLIOGRAPHY

Many sagas are available in English translation from Penguin. *The Complete Sagas of Icelanders*, 5 vols., edited by Viðar Hreinsson (Reykjavík, 1997), contains all the family sagas and many related medieval tales. Stephen A. Mitchell provides a list of English translations of the mythical-heroic sagas on pages 188–190 of his *Heroic Sagas and Ballads* (Ithaca, N.Y., 1991). Lee M. Hollander translated Snorri Sturluson's *Heimskringla: History of the Kings of Norway* (Austin, Tex., 1964; reprint, 1991). For a survey of scholarship on the sagas, see *Old Norse—Icelandic Literature: A Critical Guide*, edited by Carol Clover and John Lindow (Ithaca, N.Y., 1985). Further references are found in John Lindow's *Scandinavian Mythology: An Annotated Bibliography* (New York, 1988). Margaret Clunies Ross treats the Norse myths and their reception in medieval Iceland in the two volumes of *Prolonged Echoes: Old Norse Myths in Medieval Northern Society* (Odense, Denmark, 1994 and 1998). Thomas A. DuBois's *Nordic Religions in the Viking Age* (Philadelphia, 1999) investigates the dynamic relationship between Christianity, Norse paganism, and the Balto-Finnish and Sámi religions. The use of saga information about pagan rituals is discussed by Jens Peter Schjødt and Margaret Clunies Ross in *Old Norse Myths, Literature and Society*, edited by Margaret Clunies Ross (Odense, Denmark, 2003), pp. 261–299.

ELIZABETH ASHMAN ROWE (2005)

SAHAK PARTHEV

SAHAK PARTHEV (d. 439) was chief bishop of Armenia from circa 387 to 439. Sahak, son of Nerses the Great, is surnamed Parthev, or Part'ew ("the Parthian"), because of his descent from Gregory the Illuminator and the Armeno-Parthian Arsacid dynasty. There is very little information about his early years and the first two decades of his pontificate. The fifth-century Armenian historians Koriwn and Lazar of P'arpi speak for the most part about his role in the cultural movement at the time of the invention of the Armenian alphabet in 404 CE. Sahak, who presided over the Persian sector of Armenia, patronized the educational, missionary, religious, and literary activities of Mesrop Mashtots', the inventor of the Armenian alphabet. Sahak was instrumental in the spread of literacy in the royal central provinces of Armenia; he personally revised the Armenian version of the scriptures on the basis of the Septuagint and translated several works of the Fathers from Greek, a language in which he was proficient.

In 420 Sahak went to the Persian court in Ctesiphon (near present-day Baghdad), where he intervened on behalf of the Persian Christians who were being persecuted. In 428, when the Sasanids put an end to the Arsacid dynasty of Armenia, Sahak was removed from office, since he was of Arsacid lineage. He was replaced by southern and Syriac bishops, but evidently continued to exercise authority in spiritual matters.

Sahak is well known for his correspondence with Patriarch Proclus of Constantinople (434–446) and Bishop Acacius of Melitene concerning the "heretical" teachings of Theodore of Mopsuestia. Contact with these bishops led Sahak to banish Theodore's works from Armenia. A part of Sahak's letter to Proclus was officially read during one of the sessions of the Second Council of Constantinople in 553.

In the mid-430s, while Sahak was still alive, the canons of the councils of Nicaea and Ephesus were brought to Armenia and translated into Armenian, probably by Sahak himself. There are also canons attributed to Sahak that are probably not authentic that are from a later period predating the eighth century.

Koriwn states that Sahak translated and adapted the Greek liturgical texts for practical use. The exact nature of his influence on the present-day liturgical books has still not been carefully studied. There are also hymns ascribed to him that bear the stylistic marks of later centuries. The earliest translations of the Fathers, however, were made under his supervision, according to the trustworthy testimony of Koriwn.

Sahak died on September 7, 439, and was buried in Ashtishat. Soon thereafter a martyrium was built over his grave, and he was venerated as a saint. In his youth he had married and fathered a daughter, who became the mother of Vardan Mamikonian, the commander-in-chief of the Armenian army. Sahak was the last of the bishops of Armenia who were of the lineage of Gregory the Illuminator. He is greatly venerated by the Armenians as a saint and honored, with Mesrop Mashtots', as the cofounder of the Armenian literary tradition.

BIBLIOGRAPHY

Conybeare, F. C. "The Armenian Canons of Saint Sahak Catholicos of Armenia." *American Journal of Theology* 2 (1898): 828–848.

Garitte, Gérard, ed. *La narratio de rebus Armeniae.* Louvain, 1952.

Koriwn. *Vark' Mashtots'i.* Yerevan, 1941. Translated into English by Bedros Norehad as *Koriun: The Life of Mashtots* (New York, 1964).

Lazar of P'arpi. *Patmut'iwn Hayots* (1763). Tbilisi, 1904. Translated into French by P. S. Ghésarian as "Lazare de Pharbe, Histoire d'Arménie," in *Collection des Historiens de l'Arménie,* edited by Victor Langlois, vol. 2 (Paris, 1869).

Tallon, Maurice. *Livre des lettres.* Beirut, 1955.

KRIKOR H. MAKSOUDIAN (1987)

SAI BABA MOVEMENT

SAI BABA MOVEMENT. The Sai Baba movement is perhaps the most popular modern South Asian religious movement. It owes its origin to Shirdi Sai Baba (d. 1918). Through one of the inheritors of his charisma, Sathya Sai Baba (b. 1926), the movement became a transnational phenomenon in the late twentieth century.

While most of the available literature is hagiographical in nature, scholars have studied some aspects of the movement, including the figures of Shirdi Sai Baba and Sathya Sai Baba, the middle-class constituency of Sathya Sai Baba, and the movement's pedagogical innovations. In addition, Shirdi Sai Baba has been identified with certain Ṣūfī orders in Maharashtra and Karnataka (Shepherd, 1985), the medieval figure of Kabīr (Rigopoulos, 1993), and the protean Indian deity, Dattātreya (Rigopoulos, 1998). Rigopoulos points out that the "syncretistic quality of Kabīr's life and teachings" seems to have been Sai Baba's model (1993, p. 305), and that on one occasion Shirdi Sai Baba stated that his "religion" was Kabīr. Dattātreya's "interreligious eclecticism" is found in the Sai Baba movement: Shirdi Sai Baba was believed by his devotees to be an incarnation of Dattātreya, and Sathya Sai Baba has presented himself as an incarnation of the same figure (Rigopoulos, 1998, p. 251). An early ethnographic study of the Sathya Sai Baba movement by Lawrence Babb (1986) focuses on miracles as central moments that make the world of the devotee seem like an enchanted place. While the miracles of both Shirdi Sai Baba and Sathya Sai Baba (healing; appearing in dreams to foretell the future or provide guidance; producing substances, such as ash, that have sacred and salutary effects; etc.) are certainly significant, this entry examines specific institutions, processes, texts, and practices in the growth of the Sai Baba movement.

The authoritative account of Shirdi Sai Baba's life, *Shri Sai Satcharita,* states that he arrived as a tall lad of about sixteen in Shirdi, a small village in Maharashtra, India (Gunaji, 1972, p. 20). The majority of the population there were Hindu peasants, and Muslims worked mainly as artisans or agricultural laborers. He stayed for three years in Shirdi, then disappeared, only to return in 1858 when he began to reside in a dilapidated mosque, his belongings limited to a pipe, tobacco, a tin pot, a long white robe, and a staff. He sat in front of a sacred fire *(dhuni)* to ward off the cold. He never used his own name but was referred to by others as "Sai Baba." Rigopoulos suggests that *Sai* means "holy one" or "saint," while *Baba* literally means "father" (1993, p. 3). Shirdi Sai Baba often used the term *mendicant* (*fakir* or *faqir*) when referring to either himself or God. Initially, few people came to him: the incident that transformed him almost overnight from a mad mendicant to a holy saint was a miracle in which he apparently converted water to oil.

Shirdi Sai Baba adopted modes of oral and scriptural instruction for his followers. To some, he recommended the reading of such scriptures as the *Rāmāyaṇa* and the *Bhagavadgītā,* or he recommended simply chanting the sacred names of Rāma, Viṣṇu, or Allāh. He sent other followers to various temples, with gifts to other saints, and explained to them the meaning of certain sacred verses, concepts, or texts, either personally or in dreams. At first, Shirdi Sai Baba was worshiped through individual offerings of sandal paste and flowers. With Baba's permission, around 1897, one of his devotees (who had been blessed with a child through his intervention) began the practice of holding a festival commemorating the death of a Muslim saint (*urs*) in Shirdi. Towards the end of the nineteenth century, Shirdi Sai Baba began the practice of collecting sacrificial fees (*dakshina*) from the hundreds who began to flock to Shirdi. The complement of this was the sacred ash (*udi*) that Baba collected from burning logs in his sacred fire, for use in all manner of cures.

About 1908, other devotees transformed the early individual worship of Shirdi Sai Baba into a congregational form along the lines of the worship at Pandharpur in Maharashtra, one of the most important pilgrimage centers of Hindu devotionalism in the region. Around this time, Shirdi Sai Baba gave up begging, and the food brought by his devotees would be distributed after he blessed it. In 1912, certain devotees decided to hold a *Rāma Navami* festival (to celebrate the birth of the Hindu deity, Rāma) along with the *urs,* and this became an annual festival at Shirdi, with Shirdi Sai Baba actively participating. In 1918, Baba had an attack of fever and passed away. A dispute arose as to where he should be buried. The Muslim devotees wished to lay their saint in an open piece of land in Shirdi, while the Hindu worshipers wished him to be buried in a building where a Kṛṣṇa image was to have been placed. Eventually a plebiscite settled the matter in a way favorable to the Hindus.

By 1918, Shirdi Sai Baba's constituency had become increasingly urban and his Ṣūfī practices became more overlaid with those identified with sectarian Hinduism. When Baba passed away, he had no property, while all the paraphernalia of worship came to be vested in the Sai Sansthan trust in 1922. The Sai Sansthan today is a vast organizational network, with hotels, rooms for pilgrims, a magazine, and other publications to cater to thousands of devotees. The sacred fire still burns in Shirdi, a site that links devotees to the memory of Shirdi Sai Baba and his life, and sacrificial fees are often collected at the temple where his tomb lies, dominated by his imposing white marble image. Shirdi is on the pilgrimage route for many Hindus and Muslims who regard him as a saint who still speaks from the tomb. Today, the devotion of Shirdi Sai Baba is a national and transnational phenomenon with devotees around the world. There are temples dedicated to Shirdi Sai Baba in virtually every major city in India and in many overseas; several popular films about his life have been made; and while traveling in autorickshaws in India, one comes across pictures of Shirdi Sai Baba pasted near the handlebars of the vehicle, alongside those of other deities, the Qur'ān, and movie stars.

Shirdi Sai Baba's reassurances that even after his death he would continue to help his devotees led to the belief among some that he would be reincarnated. While a number of persons subsequently posed as Baba reborn, the most famous claim of reincarnation is that of Sathya Sai Baba, born on November 23, 1926, as Sathyanarayana Raju to a peasant family in Puttaparthi, a village in a drought-prone region of Andhra Pradesh. Sathya seems to have had a fairly normal early life, although biographers and oral accounts claim a number of mysterious events at the time of his birth, including a snake lying under his bed (interpreted as an indication of the deity Śiva's presence) and the sound of musical instruments playing. As a child, Sathya would produce countless articles from a bag for his playmates, and he also seems to have possessed intuitive powers. In his early teens he went through a prolonged period of "illness" and erratic behavior after apparently being stung by a black scorpion. He refused to speak for long periods and would break into weeping and song, sometimes reciting Sanskrit verses. The family took him to various doctors and even an exorcist, but to no avail. According to the official biography by N. Kasturi, on May 23, 1940, Sathya announced his spiritual genealogy to be in the lineage of two Indian sages, Āpastamba and Bhāradvaja, and declared that he was Sai Baba (Kasturi, 1968, pp. 42–43). A few months later, he cast off his school books and said that his devotees were calling him.

At first, Sathya Sai Baba resided in the garden of an excise inspector's bungalow and taught what is considered his first devotional song (*bhajan*), singing that meditating on one's spiritual preceptor (*gurū*) could take one across the difficult sea of existence. He lived in the house of a Brahman woman named Subbamma till about 1944 or 1945, and then he relocated to a building constructed for him by a group of devotees. By 1950 a hermitage called Prasanthi Nilayam was completed on the outskirts of Puttaparthi. Witnesses carefully recorded the details of his maturing ministry: he performed miracles, granted boons to devotees who gravitated towards Puttaparthi, and visited towns and cities in south India. The appearance of Sathya Sai Baba in dreams, the appearance of sacred ash and honey on photographs of Sathya Sai Baba and other holy figures in homes, reports of healings, and so on, formed an ever-growing fund of folklore; Sathya Sai Baba himself has referred to these as his "calling cards." The watershed in his career occurred in 1957, when he left for his first tour of northern Indian cities and sacred sites; thereafter his public role came to be voiced distinctly. He spoke at gatherings of devotees and at temples, hospitals, schools, and language associations, sharing platforms with government ministers, educators, and other religious leaders.

Sathya Sai Baba has categorized his life in terms of three time periods. He stated as far back as 1953 (Sathya Sai Baba, 1999, p. 3) that the first sixteen years of his life were a period of childhood miracles and divine sport. The second period witnessed the centrality of divine miracles, and after his thirty-second year the task was spiritual instruction and the guiding of humanity back to the path of truth (*sathya*), righteousness (*dharma*), peace (*shanthi*), and love (*prema*). Sathya Sai Baba was using the term *incarnation* (*avatar*) at least as early as 1955 to describe himself and his mission to reform humanity. He also declared a disinterest in creating a new religious path, for the divine had a million names and forms leading to God. The giant architectural symbol of this universalism is the Sarva Dharma Stupa, an enormous pillar in his hermitage with symbols from five "world" religions—Hinduism, Christianity, Islam, Buddhism, and Zoroastrianism.

Although Sathya Sai Baba had earlier indicated that he was the incarnation of Shirdi Sai Baba, on Gurū Pūrṇimā day in 1963 he made the startling announcement that he was the divine bi-unity of Śiva and Śakti (male and female principles of divinity). He also announced that a third Sai Baba would be reborn a few years after his passing away. The recasting of the memory of Shirdi Sai Baba and the prediction of another incarnation, Prema Sai Baba, signaled the beginning of a massive organization and a pan-Indian and international role for Sathya Sai Baba. The first all-India conference of Sai organizations was held in Madras in 1967, and the first world conference at Bombay in 1968. Sathya Sai Baba left for a tour of East Africa, his first and only foreign trip, the same year. The year 1968 was important in other ways: Sathya Sai Baba established an arts and sciences college for women in Anantapur in Andhra Pradesh (a similar institution was founded in 1969 in Bangalore for men). In 1981 Sathya Sai Baba established the Sri Sathya Sai Institute of Higher Learning, which eventually achieved university status. He later inaugurated two "super-specialty" medical institutes in Puttaparthi (1990–1991) and Bangalore (2000). One of the most ambitious of Baba's projects provides drinking water for Anantapur district in Andhra Pradesh—a project completed in 1996, after only one year of work.

Apart from the central hermitage in Puttaparthi, there is a second center of the Sathya Sai Baba movement in Bangalore called Brindavan, and Baba also maintains residences in Hyderabad, Chennai, and Mumbai. Four main festivals have been celebrated at these centers since the early years: Sathya Sai Baba's birthday, Śivaratri in February/March (dedicated to Śiva), Gurū Pūrṇimā in July (dedicated to one's spiritual preceptor), and a nine-day autumn festival called Dasara. Today, a number of other holidays—for example, Christmas, Buddha's birthday, New Year festivals, and so on—have been added to the list, and the older festivals have become more elaborate. Thousands travel to Puttaparthi to celebrate Sathya Sai Baba's birthday and to participate in other festivals.

There is a vast and growing corpus of literature on Sathya Sai Baba. Apart from accounts of devotees' experiences, the official biography, and publications of the Sathya Sai Central Trust, Baba's own discourses and works are central to the movement. The first category within them is a set of books that are discourses called "streams" (*vahini*) on specific themes, such as meditation, peace, knowledge, and so on, aimed at the clarification of spiritual truths. The second category includes his exegeses on different scriptures. Sathya Sai Baba is an indefatigable public speaker—he speaks mainly in Telugu—and he gives lectures to devotees, students, villagers, and other religious organizations. *Summer Showers in Brindavan* are speeches given by him to college students during courses held for them. The newsletter, *Sanathana Sarathi* ("The eternal charioteer," a reference to Kṛṣṇa), devoted to the moral and spiritual awakening of humanity, was inaugurated in 1958. Many of Sathya Sai Baba's speeches find their way into *Sanathana Sarathi.* Others have been collected in more than thirty volumes titled *Sathya Sai Speaks.*

A central aspect of the Sathya Sai Baba movement is the casting of the relationship between ancient values and modernity in terms of the Sai golden age, a millenarian process in which all followers have a role to play. The path laid down by Sathya Sai Baba for devotees comprises three sets of activities: (1) spiritual activities, including devotional singing, study circles of Sai teachings, and meditation; (2) educational activities, including a program in human values for children; and (3) service activities, including the organizing of medical camps, blood donations, the feeding of the poor, emergency relief, and adoption of underdeveloped villages. The devotional songs are essentially utterances of the names of God, and they form the spiritual center of the movement and a devotee's everyday life. Every week, men and women may gather to sing for about an hour in front of pictures of Sathya Sai Baba (and sometimes, Shirdi Sai Baba, Jesus, Buddha, and others, depending on the constituency) and an empty chair that signifies his presence. The Human Values program for children is meant to create a firm spiritual basis for future society by focusing on the moral education of children. Members are also enjoined to engage in service to society, a reflection of Baba's philosophy that devotion and service are intertwined practices and that the body is the site for realizing the self. Practices such as devotional singing, meditation, or social service become the path by which the self is realized.

The Sathya Sai centers, or *samitis,* were instituted by Sathya Sai Baba to be the main venue for these activities. The first was registered in 1965 in Mumbai. By 2002 there were 8,447 centers in India and about 9,000 in other parts of the world. The main function of the centers is to undertake spiritual, educational, and service activities under the inspiration and guidance of Sathya Sai Baba and the Sri Sathya Sai Seva Organization's 1981 charter. The organization is meant for all and does not recognize any distinctions based on religion, caste, color, or creed. Its fundamental objective is to awaken the awareness of inner divinity by propagating through practice and example the basic principles emphasized by Sathya Sai Baba.

BIBLIOGRAPHY

Babb, Lawrence A. *Redemptive Encounters: Three Modern Styles in the Hindu Tradition.* Berkeley, Calif., 1986.

Gokak, V. K. *Bhagwan Sri Sathya Sai Baba: An Interpretation.* New Delhi, 1989.

Gunaji, N. V. *Shri Sai Satcharita.* Adapted from the original by Govind Raghunath Dabholkar. 6th ed. Shirdi, India, 1972.

Kasturi, N. *Sathyam Sivam Sundaram.* Part I. 7th ed. Prasanthi Nilayam, India, 1968.

Kasturi, N. *Sathyam Sivam Sundaram.* Part II. Prasanthi Nilayam, India, 1968.

Kasturi, N. *Sathyam Sivam Sundaram.* Part III. Bombay, 1972.

Kasturi, N. *Sathyam Sivam Sundaram.* Part IV. Prasanthi Nilayam, India, 1980.

Klass, Morton. *Singing with Sai Baba: The Politics of Revitalization in Trinidad.* Boulder, Colo., 1991.

Rigopoulos, Antonio. *The Life and Teachings of Sai Baba of Shirdi.* Albany, N.Y., and Delhi, 1993.

Rigopoulos, Antonio. *Dattātreya, the Immortal Guru, Yogin, and Avatāra: A Study of the Transformative and Inclusive Character of a Multi-Faceted Hindu Deity.* Albany, N.Y., 1998.

Sathya Sai Baba. *Sathya Sai Speaks,* vol. 1: *1953–1960.* Prasanthi Nilayam, India, 1999.

Shepherd, Kevin. *Gurus Rediscovered: Biographies of Sai Baba of Shirdi and Upasni Maharaj of Sakori.* Cambridge, U.K., 1985.

Srinivas, Smriti. "The Brahmin and the Fakir: Suburban Religiosity in the Cult of Shirdi Sai Baba." *Journal of Contemporary Religion* 14, no. 2 (1999): 245–261.

Srinivas, Smriti. "The Advent of the Avatar: The Urban Following of Sathya Sai Baba and Its Construction of Tradition." In *Charisma and Canon: Essays on the Religious History of the Indian Subcontinent,* edited by Vasudha Dalmia, Angelika Malinar, and Martin Christof, pp. 293–309. Delhi, 2001.

Swallow, D. A. "Ashes and Powers: Myth, Rite, and Miracle in an Indian God-Man's Cult." *Modern Asian Studies* 16 (1982): 123–158.

White, Charles. "The Sai Baba Movement: Approaches to the Study of Indian Saints." *Journal of Asian Studies* 31 (1972): 863–878.

SMRITI SRINIVAS (2005)

SAICHŌ (767–822), also known by his posthumous title Dengyō Daishi; founder of Japanese Tendai, a sect derived from the teachings and practices of the Chinese Tiantai school.

LIFE. Saichō was born into a family of devout Buddhists. At the age of twelve he went to study at the provincial temple in Ōmi. There he studied under Gyōhyō (722–797), a disciple of Daoxuan (702–760), the Chinese monk who had brought Northern School Chan, Kegon (Chin., Huayan) teachings, and the *Fanwang* precepts to Japan in 736. Saichō's studies of meditation and Kegon "one-vehicle" (Skt., *ekayāna*; Jpn., *ichijō*) doctrines during this period influenced his lifelong doctrinal predilections. Shortly after he was ordained in 785, he decided to climb Mount Hiei. He remained there for approximately a decade to meditate and study. During his retreat, Saichō read about Chinese Tiantai meditation practice in Kegon texts and managed to obtain several Tiantai texts that had been brought to Japan by Jianzhen (Ganjin, 688–763) in 754 but had subsequently been ignored by Japanese monks.

The capital of Japan was moved from Nara to Nagaoka in 784, and then to Kyoto in 795. Mount Hiei was located to the northeast of Kyoto, a direction considered dangerous by geomancers, but Saichō's presence on the mountain protected the new capital and brought him to the attention of the court. In addition, the court was interested in reforming Buddhism by patronizing serious monks without political aspirations and by supporting those teachings that would bridge the traditional rivalry between the Hossō (Yogācāra) and Sanron (Madhyamaka) schools. Soon various court nobles, especially those of the Wake clan, began to show an interest in Saichō. With court support, Saichō traveled to China in 804 to obtain Tiantai texts and to study with Chinese teachers. During his eight months there, he received initiations into a variety of Buddhist traditions, including the Tiantai school, Oxhead Chan, the *Fanwang* precepts (a set of fifty-eight Mahayana disciplinary rules), and Esoteric Buddhism.

Upon his return to Japan in 805, Saichō discovered that his brief studies of Esoteric Buddhism attracted more attention than his mastery of Tendai teachings. Saichō's major patron, Emperor Kammu (r. 781–806), was ill, and Saichō used Esoteric rituals in an attempt to restore Kammu's health. Shortly before Kammu died the court awarded Saichō two yearly ordinands, one in Tendai and one in Esoteric Buddhism. This event marked the formal establishment of the Tendai school.

Saichō spent the next few years studying Esoteric Buddhism, but his efforts were overshadowed by the return of Kūkai (774–835) from China in 806. Kūkai's knowledge of Esoteric Buddhist practice and doctrine was clearly superior to that of Saichō. Although Saichō and some of his disciples went to study with Kūkai and borrowed Esoteric texts from him, by 816 irreconcilable differences on doctrinal issues, a dispute over the loan of certain Esoteric texts, and the defection of Taihan (778–858?), one of Saichō's most able disciples, ended Saichō's hopes of mastering Esoteric Buddhism.

During the years that Saichō studied Esoteric Buddhism, more than half of the Tendai yearly ordinands left Mount Hiei. Many of them defected to the Hossō school; others departed in order to study Esoteric Buddhism with Kūkai or to support their ailing mothers. It became clear that if Tendai were to survive, Saichō would have to retain many more of his students on Mount Hiei. During the last five or six years of his life, Saichō strove to secure the place of Tendai within Japanese Buddhism, and in the process composed almost all of his major works.

Saichō's activities during this period can be divided into two categories. First, he defended Tendai doctrines and meditation practices against attacks by the Hossō monk Tokuitsu (d. 841?). Two of Saichō's major works, the *Shugo kokkaishō* (Essays on protecting the nation) and the *Hokke shūku* (Elegant words on the *Lotus Sūtra*) were written during this period. Saichō argued that everyone could attain Buddhahood and that many could do so in their present lifetime through Tendai and Esoteric practices. He firmly rejected the Hossō argument that the attainment of Buddhahood required aeons of practice and that some people would never be able to attain it. Second, Saichō proposed major reforms in the Tendai educational system, in monastic discipline, and in the ordination system. Saichō suggested that Tendai monks be ordained on Mount Hiei, where they would be required to remain for the next twelve years without venturing outside the monastery's boundaries. Ordinations were to be supervised by lay administrators *(zoku bettō)* who also held important positions at court. Two texts, the *Sange gakushō shiki* (Rules for Tendai students) and the *Kenkairon* (Treatise elucidating the precepts) concern Saichō's proposals on administration and monastic discipline.

In addition, Saichō criticized the *Sifenlu* (*Dharmaguptaka Vinaya*) precepts, which traditionally had been conferred at ordination in China and Japan. He argued that the *Sifenlu* were Hīnayānist rules that would cause the recipient to retrogress, not progress, in his religious practice. The *Sifenlu* precepts were to be replaced with the *Fanwang* precepts, a set of Mahayana precepts traditionally used in East Asia to inculcate Mahayana attitudes in monks, nuns, and lay believers, but not to ordain laypeople as monks or nuns. The adoption of the *Fanwang* precepts was intended to strengthen monastic discipline on Mount Hiei by providing the monks with a more relevant guide to conduct than the *Sifenlu* precepts. After the yearly ordinands had completed their twelve years on Mount Hiei, many of them were to receive official appointments as administrators of monastic affairs in the provinces. During their terms, they were to devote much of their time to projects that would benefit the populace. Saichō expected these activities to contribute to the spread of Tendai influence.

Saichō's proposals were vehemently opposed by the Hossō and other Nara schools because their approval would have entailed implicit recognition of Saichō's criticisms of Hossō doctrine and practice. In addition, the proposals would have removed Tendai monks from the supervision of the Office of Monastic Affairs (Sogo). The court, not wishing to become involved in disputes between schools, hesitated to act on Saichō's proposals. As a result, Saichō died without seeing his reforms approved; however, one week after Saichō's death the court approved the proposals as a posthumous tribute.

THOUGHT. Most of Saichō's works were polemical and designed either to prove that Tendai doctrine and practice were superior to that of any of the other schools of Japanese Buddhism or to argue that the Tendai school should be free of any supervision by other schools. In his defense of Tendai interests, Saichō discussed a number of issues that played important roles in later Japanese religious history.

Saichō had an acute sense of the flow of Buddhist history. The teachings of the *Lotus Sūtra,* the text that contained the Buddha's ultimate teaching according to the Tendai school, had been composed in India and then transmitted to China. Japan, Saichō believed, would be the next site for the rise of the "one-vehicle" teachings propagated by Tendai. Saichō was conversant with theories on the decline of Buddhism and believed that he was living at the end of the Period of Counterfeit Dharma (*zōmatsu*), described as an era in which many monks would be corrupt and covetous.

Although Saichō believed major changes were needed in Japanese Buddhism, he did not use theories on the decline of Buddhism to justify doctrinal innovations, as did some of the founders of the Kamakura schools. Rather, Saichō argued that because Buddhism in the capital had declined, monks should retreat to the mountains to practice assiduously.

Many of Saichō's doctrinal innovations were based on his belief that the religious aptitude of the Japanese people as a whole had matured to the point where they no longer needed any form of Buddhism other than the "perfect teachings" *(engyō)* of the Tendai school. Earlier Buddhist thinkers had also been interested in the manner in which the religious faculties of people matured, but had usually discussed the process in terms of individuals rather than Religious training for people with "perfect faculties" (*enki,* i. e., those whose religious faculties respond to the "perfect teachings") was based on the threefold study (*sangaku*) of morality, meditation, and doctrine. Saichō believed that Tiantai teachings on meditation and doctrine were adequate, although they could be supplemented by Esoteric Buddhism. However, he was dissatisfied with the traditional Tiantai position on morality, which maintained that a monk could follow the *Sifenlu* precepts with a Mahayana mind. Saichō argued that adherence to the *Sifenlu* would cause a monk to retrogress toward Hīnayāna goals. Tendai practices could be realized only by using the Mahayana *Fanwang* precepts for ordinations and monastic discipline.

Chinese Tiantai had been a syncretistic tradition, particularly at the Tiantai Yuquan monastery. Chinese monks had been interested in Chan and Esotertic Buddhism as well as in the *Sifenlu* and *Fanwang* precepts. Saichō inherited this tradition, but developed certain aspects of it in innovative ways. For example, Saichō considered Esoteric Buddhism to be essentially the same as Tendai (*enmitsu itchi*) and thus awarded Esoteric Buddhism a more central place in the Tendai tradition than it had been given by most Chinese monks. Like Kūkai, Saichō emphasized the importance of striving for enlightenment as an immediate goal to be attained in this existence (*sokushin jōbutsu*). Tendai and Esoteric practices, he felt, provided a direct path *(jikidō)* to enlightenment, whereas the teachings of the Nara schools required aeons to bring the practitioner to enlightenment.

The Chinese Tiantai systems for classifying teachings (*kyōhan*) developed by Zhiyi (538–597) had been designed to demonstrate how the "perfect teachings" of the *Lotus Sūtra* revealed the ultimate meaning of all other Buddhist traditions and could be used to unify and interpret various Buddhist doctrines. Later, as the competition between Tiantai and other schools intensified, Tiantai scholars such as Zhanran (711–782) developed classification systems that demonstrated the complete superiority of the *Lotus Sutra* over other teachings. Saichō's rejection of Hossō doctrine and the *Sifenlu* precepts was based on the later Tiantai classification systems. Saichō also developed his own systems, which emphasized the importance of relying on the Buddha's words from such texts as the *Lotus Sutra,* rather than on the commentaries (*śāstras*) used by the Hossō and Sanron schools. In addition, he stressed the importance of matching teachings to the faculties of the religious practitioner so that enlightenment could be rapidly attained.

SEE ALSO Mappō; Shingonshū; Tendaishū.

BIBLIOGRAPHY

Saichō's works have been collected in *Dengyō Daishi zenshū,* 5 vols. (1926; reprint, Tokyo, 1975). Important collections of Japanese scholarship are *Dengyō Daishi kenkyū,* 5 vols. (Tokyo, 1973–1980), and Shioiri Ryōdō's *Saichō* (Tokyo, 1982). For studies in English, see the following:

Abé, Ryūichi. "Saichō and Kūkai: A Conflict of Interpretations." *Japanese Journal of Religious Studies* 22.1–2 (1995): 103–137.

Groner, Paul. *Saichō: The Establishment of the Japanese Tendai School.* Honolulu, 2000.

Groner, Paul. "The *Lotus Sūtra* and Saichō's Interpretation of the Realization of Buddhahood with This Very Body." In *The Lotus Sūtra in Japanese Culture,* edited by George Tanabe and Willa Tanabe, pp. 53–74. Honolulu, 1989.

Tamura, Kōyū. "The Doctrinal Dispute Between the Tendai and the Hossō Sects." *Acta Asiatica* 47 (1984): 48–81.

PAUL GRONER (1987 AND 2005)

SAID, EDWARD W. (1935–2003) is best known as the author of the influential and widely read *Orientalism* (1978), a study of the modes of thought and writing which have created a Manichean and essentialist divide between "the Orient" and "the Occident" since the eighteenth century. In his introduction to the book Said argues that one must grasp the remarkable consistency of thought and method which underpins Western representations of the Arab Muslim world across the centuries if one is to understand properly "the enormously systematic discipline by which European [and later American] culture was able to manage—and even produce—the Orient politically, sociologically, militarily, ideologically, scientifically, and imaginatively during the post-Enlightenment period" (p. 3). No other single work has had a greater formative influence than *Orientalism* on debates about the representation of non-Western cultures within the discourses of the West, on the historical and theoretical understanding of the dynamics of culture and power between center and periphery in colonial and postcolonial contexts, or, more specifically, on the ways in which knowledge of Islam and the Arab Muslim world has been shaped or misshaped in Europe and America.

But Said's writing career was a long and productive one and his intellectual interests were marked by a rare and impressive range. He wrote with authority and passion on literature, politics, and Western classical music; and he worked with equal ease and effectiveness in academia as well as in the world of the popular media. Diverse as the books, collections of essays, newspaper articles, reviews, and interviews are, a number of common threads tie them together. Said was concerned throughout his career with the nature and function of secular criticism (and so also with its religious opposite), with the relationship of knowledge to power, of culture to imperial histories, with the experience of exile and diaspora within modernity, and above all with the role of the intellectual in the contemporary world. His forceful defense of secular humanism and of the public role of the intellectual, as much as his trenchant critiques of Orientalism and his unwavering advocacy of the Palestinian cause, made Said one of the most internationally influential cultural commentators writing out of the United States in the last quarter of the twentieth century.

Said was born into an extremely well-to-do Christian family in Jerusalem in 1935. His father, Wadie, a Protestant, had immigrated to the United States before the First World War and had returned to the Middle East with American citizenship after volunteering for service in France. Upon his return he had married the daughter of a Baptist minister. *Out of Place* (1999), a memoir of Said's years of childhood in Palestine, Cairo, and Lebanon, describes his sense of distance from his disciplinarian father and his lonely retreat into the world of novels and classical music. The Cairo School for American Children and Victoria College were among the schools Said attended as a boy. When he was expelled from Victoria College in 1951, his parents decided to send him to Mount Hermon, a preparatory school in the United States.

Said was an accomplished student and pianist and spoke several languages. He went on to graduate from Princeton, to gain a Ph.D. from Harvard, and, in 1963, to join the faculty at Columbia University in New York, where later he became a professor of English and comparative literature. Though he seemed confidently embarked on what promised to be a successful career as a literary scholar, Said was jolted by the Arab-Israeli war in 1967, the Arab defeat, and what he saw as the almost universal pro-Israeli stance in the United States, into a newly politicized sense of his own Palestinian and exilic identity and of Palestinian and Arab history. However, as important as 1967 proved to be, one should not forget that the focus of Said's Ph.D. is Joseph Conrad (1857–1924), himself an exile and among the most incisive analysts of the imperial project in modern literature—and a touchstone for Said throughout his career.

Said's first book was *Joseph Conrad and the Fiction of Autobiography* (1966), and his second major work was *Beginnings* (1975), an ambitious attempt to examine the notion of the point of departure in literature. Later works on literature developed more political and historical perspectives. *Culture and Imperialism* (1993), a sequel of sorts to *Orientalism*, examines the constitutive role of empire in major works of Western literature and music. *The World, the Text, and the Critic* (1983), which outlines some key theoretical foundations of Said's work, insists on the worldliness of the text, and argues for the necessity of a properly "secular criticism"—which is to say a criticism free from the priestly specializations of academic discourse and the dangers of ideological certainties. As William D. Hart has pointed out in his important *Edward Said and the Religious Effects of Culture* (2000), Said's defense of secular criticism is necessarily haunted by the specter of the religious, understood in both the literal and the figurative senses. Quoting Said himself, Hart notes that "the object of Said's critique, and what he holds to be distinctive of religious discourse, is the appeal to 'the extrahuman, the vague abstraction, the divine, the esoteric and the secret'" (p. 10). Just as some critics have rightly argued that *Orientalism* has a tendency to create a monolithic version of Western discourse lacking an adequate sense of historical and individual variation, so Hart is also right to suggest that Said has a tendency to slip into antireligious cliché and that he does not fully acknowledge the ways in which religious practices can become "a site of hegemonic struggle by subaltern classes (the ruled) against the ruling class" (p. 37).

If the idea of the religious was a constitutive deep structure in Said's thought, the actual religion of Islam, the culture that it has produced, and the reception of that culture in the West also preoccupied Said. Of central importance here is the trilogy of books which perhaps more than any others define the key concerns and methods of Said's post-1967 career: *Orientalism*, *The Question of Palestine* (1979), and *Covering Islam* (1981; revised 1997). Where *Orientalism* provides a sweeping literary and cultural survey, *The Question of Palestine* is concerned with the immediacy of contemporary politics and attempts to offer an account of the emergence of Palestinian nationhood in its confrontation with Zionism and Israel. *Covering Islam* offers yet another perspective on the relationship of the Arab Muslim world and the West by providing a scorching account of the representation of Islam and the Muslim world in the Western media. It is the argument of *Covering Islam* that the indiscriminate use of the label "Islam" to explain almost everything that happens in the Arab world is a violent but persistent simplification. This label of "Islam," writes Said in the revised edition, "defines a relatively small proportion of what actually takes place in the Islamic world, which numbers a billion people, and includes dozens of countries, societies, traditions, languages, and, of course, an infinite number of different experiences" (p. xvi). For Said, the label also obscures the fact that it is "secularism, rather than fundamentalism" which has "held Arab Muslim societies together" (p. xxvi). It was Said's aim to use "the skills of a good critical reader to disentangle sense from nonsense" and to ask "the right questions": "At that point humanistic knowledge begins and communal responsibility for that knowledge begins to be shouldered" (p. lix). Few intellectuals have done more to advance this project.

Edward Said died at the age of sixty-seven on September 25, 2003.

See Also Orientalism.

BIBLIOGRAPHY

Selected works by Said

Beginnings: Intention and Method. New York, 1975.

Orientalism. New York, 1978.

The Question of Palestine. New York, 1979.

Covering Islam: How the Media and the Experts Determine How We See the Rest of the World. New York, 1981; revised 1997.

The World, the Text, and the Critic. Cambridge, Mass., 1983.

Musical Elaborations. New York, 1991.

Culture and Imperialism. New York, 1993.

The Politics of Dispossession: The Struggle for Palestinian Self-Determination, 1969–1994. London, 1994.

Representations of the Intellectual: The 1993 Reith Lectures. London, 1994.

Peace and Its Discontents: Essays on Palestine in the Middle East Peace Process. New York, 1996.

Out of Place: A Memoir. New York, 1999.

The End of the Peace Process: Oslo and After. New York, 2000.

Reflections on Exile and Other Literary and Cultural Essays. London, 2000.

Power, Politics, and Culture: Interviews with Edward W. Said. New York, 2001. An important collection of interviews.

Humanism and Democratic Criticism. New York, 2004.

Selected works on Said

Ansell-Pearson, Keith, Benita Parry, and Judith Squires, eds. *Cultural Readings of Imperialism: Edward Said and the Gravity of History.* New York, 1997.

Aruri, Naseer, and Muhammad A. Shuraydi, eds. *Revising Culture, Reinventing Peace: The Influence of Edward W. Said.* New York, 2001.

Ashcroft, Bill, and Hussein Kadhim, eds. *Edward Said and the Post-Colonial.* Huntington, N.Y., 2001.

Ashcroft, Bill, and Pal Ahluwalia. *Edward Said: The Paradox of Identity.* London, 1999; revised 2001. A useful short introduction to Said's career.

Barsamian, David. *Culture and Resistance: Conversations with Edward W. Said.* London, 2003.

Bové, Paul A., ed. *Edward Said and the Work of the Critic: Speaking Truth to Power.* Durham, N.C., 2000.

Hart, William D. *Edward Said and the Religious Effects of Culture.* Cambridge, U.K., 2000. A serious and sustained examination of the place of the religious in Said's thought; wide-ranging and balanced in its contextualization of Said.

Hussein, Abdirahman A. *Edward Said: Criticism and Society.* London, 2002. A full-length biography arguing for an intellectual unity in Said's diverse body of work.

Kennedy, Valerie. *Edward Said: A Critical Introduction.* London, 2000.

Marrouchi, Mustapha. *Edward Said at the Limits.* Albany, N.Y., 2004.

Sprinker, Michael. *Edward Said: A Critical Reader.* Oxford, 1992.

Walia, Shelley. *Edward Said and the Writing of History.* Cambridge, U.K., 2001.

SHAMOON ZAMIR (2005)

SAINTHOOD.

SAINTHOOD. *Saint* is a designation that Christianity has used to recognize individuals deemed to have lived lives of heroic virtue and who, as a result, dwell eternally with God. They therefore may be venerated in a public cult. Historians of religion have liberated the category of sainthood from its narrower Christian associations and have employed the term in a more general way to refer to the state of special holiness that many religions attribute to certain people. The Jewish *ḥasid* or *tsaddiq,* the Muslim *walīy,* the Zoroastrian *fravashi,* the Hindu *ṛṣi* or *guru,* the Buddhist *arahant* or *bodhisattva,* the Daoist *shengren,* the Shintō *kami,* and others have all been referred to as saints.

THE CATEGORY OF SAINTHOOD. The problem for the historian of religions is whether the term *sainthood* so broadly applied retains any meaning. Can a category that grows out of one religion be properly and usefully extended cross-culturally? William James described universal saintliness in psychological terms, while Joachim Wach defined the saint as a particular type of religious authority alongside the founder, the reformer, the priest, the prophet, and others. But sainthood may embrace persons of diverse psychological constitutions and religious offices. Fundamentally, then, sainthood may be described as a religion's acclamation of a person's spiritual perfection, however that perfection is defined. Persons so acclaimed exemplify the religion's highest values and thus function as models for others to follow. At the same time, the special holiness that inheres in such people endows them with supernatural powers that their devotees may call upon in their own spiritual quests. These figures may serve as wonder-workers, helpmates, or intercessors. In other words, saints are recognized by their religions as both subjects for imitation and objects of veneration. The tension between imitability and inimitability, between likeness to humans and otherness than humans, lies at the core of the saint's identity. While the extent to which particular saints or classes of saints are either emulated or worshiped varies greatly within and among religions, all saints attract some measure of both imitation and veneration.

Usually sainthood is a posthumous phenomenon. While recognition and proclamation of a person's exemplary virtues and exceptional powers may begin during his or her lifetime, a saint is one who stands the test of time. Indeed, a saint's exemplariness and powerfulness must transcend his or her death and be available to those who did not know him or her in the flesh. Thus, those who function as saints after their deaths may have been priests or prophets, activists or ascetics, rulers or the simple pious during their lifetimes. Sainthood, so understood, may embrace the holders of any number of religious offices but depends more on personal charisma than on religious status. Some religions even sponsor mythical saints, legendary people who lived long ago or dwell anonymously in the present world but who function for their followers much the same as do the historical human beings more commonly deemed saints.

Saints, however, should probably be distinguished from founders, the initiators of religious insights and religious communities. While founders may also be imitated and venerated posthumously, as are, for instance, Jesus of Nazareth and Gautama Buddha, they occupy a position of uniqueness in the structure of their religions that no saint can claim. Saints often imitate a founder, devoting themselves to living in his or her image. They may "translate" the founder's life and teachings for their own time and place. Saints come in quantity, collectively mapping out a topography of holiness that renders accessible the founder's example and power.

Sainthood in Major World Religions. Sainthood, as here typified, does not exist universally. Not all religious communities acclaim holy individuals as both paradigms to be imitated and intercessors to be venerated. Classic rabbinic Judaism, for instance, stressed the redemption of the entire Jewish people rather than individual salvation. Thus personal intercessors had little function in the religion. Furthermore, Judaism forbids the worship of human beings. Protestant Christianity, while emphasizing individual salvation, repudiated the Catholic cult of saints, finding in God's grace alone the key to redemption. Yet some forms of both Judaism and Protestantism recognize saints: The Besht (Yisra'el ben Eli'ezer), spiritual leader of Hasidism, and Mary Baker Eddy, founder of the Christian Science church, for example, are given the status of sainthood by their followers. Archaic and primitive religions tend to associate holiness more with certain offices, such as shaman or medicine man, than with unique individuals.

Christianity. The recognition of the special holiness of certain people began early in the history of Christianity. Under the Roman persecution that began in the first century, many Christians gave up their lives rather than renounce their faith. These martyrs became the first persons to be given the title *hagios* ("saint"), though earlier the word had been used in the plural to designate the faithful in general. A martyr's willing renunciation of life demonstrated to other Christians his or her superhuman strength and convinced them that this person had conquered death. By the third century, commemorations in Rome marked the anniversaries of these deaths and celebrated the martyrs' rebirth into heavenly lives. Meanwhile the power of dead martyrs in drawing the faithful to their cemeteries had attracted the attention of the bishops, who made altars of their tombs and claimed them as their heavenly patrons. Christian officialdom thus embraced the popular veneration of martyrs and made it the cornerstone of ecclesiastical power.

At first the martyrs were remembered primarily as witnesses, examples to encourage others in times of persecution: Other Christians were urged to follow their model of imitating Christ by submitting to death. But at the same time, because they had transcended death and dwelled in heaven, martyrs possessed extraordinary powers, which the faithful could summon. At martyrs' tombs one could pray for cures of ills, for forgiveness of sins, or for protection from enemies. Indeed, after the establishment of Christianity as the state religion in the fourth century diminished persecution, the martyr was seen less as a paradigm and more as a hierophant.

With martyrdom on the wane, confessors, those who suffered but did not die for the faith, joined the ranks of the saints, as did ascetics, solitaries, and monks. By suffering voluntarily these saints imitated Christ and separated themselves from the world in order to know God better. They renounced food, money, marriage, human company, and even their own free will in order to discipline themselves for the contemplative life. In Eastern Orthodox Christianity the life of contemplation came to be the quintessential model of holiness. In the West in the thirteenth century, the mendicant orders, such as the Franciscans and Dominicans, promoted the contrasting saintly ideal of active service in the world. The image of Francis of Assisi overflowing with love for all creation balances the specter of pathological self-torture attributed to so many other Christian saints.

Although martyrdom was clearly believed to transport a person to heaven and sainthood, other forms of superlative piety required the evidence of miracles to substantiate posthumous heavenly domicile. Thus the miraculous element in the lives of the saints was increasingly stressed: Saints healed, exorcised, prophesied, and mastered the elements of nature. Although the Roman Catholic church insists upon the moral quality of a candidate for sainthood, only miracles constitute absolute proof that the candidate is in heaven and thus can intercede for those on earth.

Saints, especially monks and royal figures, are also central to the piety of Eastern Orthodox Christianity. Saints are venerated in icons, elaborated and stylized pictures, not only found in churches but also prominently displayed in homes. These pictures aim to show the power that emanates from union with Christ and to depict graphically the unity of the church by linking the dead with the living.

In the sixteenth century Martin Luther attacked the Catholic cult of saints, which then included a huge traffic in relics. He ridiculed the veneration of saints as idolatry, for like the old pagan gods, many saints had special realms of expertise and particular places from which they could be invoked. While maintaining a belief in the exemplary value of some saints, Luther denied their intercessory efficacy. Protestant Christianity on the whole follows his lead, although some groups, such as the Mormons and the Christian Scientists, tend to revere their founders as saints.

Islam. The monotheistic religion preached by Muḥammad and exhibited in the Qurʾān abhorred and forbade the association of anything or anyone with God. Even Muḥammad himself was seen only as God's spokesman. The Arabic term generally translated as "saint," *walī* (pl., *awliyāʾ*), is used in the Qurʾān to refer both to God and to God's "friends," that is, pious people in general. Those who obey God are *awliyāʾ* and God acts as *walī* to them. Nevertheless, popular Islam came to understand the *walī* as a particular kind of friend of God, one whose special closeness to divinity mediated between the ordinary faithful and that all-powerful and distant deity. Islam embraced and sanctified charismatic sons and daughters in its vast empire as vehicles for the popular transmission of the scriptural faith. These *awliyā'* personalized and localized the stern and austere faith of Muḥammad.

No formal canonization process, as exists in Roman Catholicism, determines who is to be *walī*. According to Islamic beliefs, a saint is made not by learning, asceticism, or piety but rather through a spontaneous enrapturing by God. Saints know who they are and may even proclaim their own sainthood. Together they form a single hierarchy headed by the *quṭb*, the pillar or axis, a legendary figure who dwells at the center of the universe and sustains it. Despite their power, saints occupy a lower spiritual rank than prophets, persons who bear special messages from God. Islamic theologians and jurists were forced by popular consensus to recognize saints and to acknowledge their miracles, but they did protest against pilgrimages to saints' graves and the practice of cultic activities there.

The figures who best illustrate the saint as imitated and venerated holy person are the Ṣūfī masters. Sufism, the general term for Islamic mysticism, traditionally traces its origins to Muḥammad himself, for his reception of revelation is seen as a mystical experience. Ascetic tendencies among individuals who sought to interiorize their Islamic faith had led by the twelfth century to the formation of Ṣūfī brotherhoods. In these associations disciples were expected to submit to the way of the master like, it was said, a corpse in the hands of an undertaker. The Ṣūfī shaykh modeled the mystical path for his disciples and guided them along its stages. The stages of this path are epitomized in a Turkish saying:

> *Sharī'ah* ("law"): Yours is yours and mine is mine.
> *Tarīqah* ("way"): Yours is yours and mine is yours too.
> *Mā'rifah* ("gnosis"): There is neither mine nor thine.

Veneration of a Ṣūfī master continued posthumously at his tomb, especially on the anniversary of his birth. In Tanta, Egypt, for instance, the autumn *mawlid* ("birthday") of Sidi Aḥmad, the founder of a Ṣūfī order, is celebrated as a huge agricultural fair. The present head of the order, the caliph, bestows Sidi Aḥmad's blessings during a long parade to the tomb-mosque complex, where prayers, sermons, and circumcision rituals take place. Relics of Ṣūfī saints, such as their clothes and utensils, are often preserved by their orders.

Not all Muslim saints are Ṣūfīs, however. Even an outspoken opponent of the cult of saints, the jurist Ibn Taymīyah (of the thirteenth to fourteenth century), who championed the equal access of all Muslims to superlative piety, was venerated after his death by those who sought his intercession and *barakah* ("spiritual power"). In Morocco, marabouts (warrior-saints), who claim descent from the Prophet and possession of thaumaturgic powers, are believed to preside after death over the territory around their tombs and bestow blessings through their descendants, some of whom will in turn become saints. Through the marabout, it is believed, the *barakah* of the Prophet directly touches the common person.

If saints play an important but unofficial role in Sunnī Islam, they lie at the very heart of Shī'ī orthodoxy. In Shī'ī Islam the term *wilayāh* denotes not sainthood in general but rather the position of authority of the imam who claims direct descent from the Prophet. This imam alone knows the esoteric interpretation of the Qur'ān, and he alone sustains the world. For one group of Shī'īs, the Twelvers, the last imam went into occultation (hiding) centuries ago but continues to exert cosmic influence. For another group, the Isma'iliyah, the contemporary Aga Khan IV is the latest in an unbroken chain of imams who embody holiness for their followers.

Judaism. Although classic rabbinic Judaism gave no sanction to hagiography or hagiolatry, it revered a whole galaxy of exemplary figures. Biblical heroes such as Abraham and Moses, rabbinic sages such as Hillel and Me'ir (of the first and second centuries, respectively), and martyrs such as 'Aqiva' ben Yosef (also of the second century) all displayed imitable virtues commended to the faithful in the legends of the Talmud and Midrashic literature. Martyrs were especially sacred to a people so often persecuted; their sacrifices were believed to atone for the community's sins, and as a group they were remembered in various liturgies. Generally speaking, however, rabbinic Judaism honored above all others the scholar who through learning, righteousness, and piety sanctified himself and the community at large.

If the rabbis of the Talmud never countenanced the veneration of human beings alive or dead, popular sentiment was often otherwise. Reputed graves of biblical and rabbinic worthies, for instance, were the objects of pilgrimages in ancient and medieval days, and among Middle Eastern Jews they still are. Mystical groups have been especially prone to lionize their founders. Yehudah ben Shemu'el, leader of a medieval German ascetic and pietistic movement, was transformed into a wonder-worker in later legends, while among Spanish qabbalists the second-century rabbi Shim'on bar Yoḥ'ai was considered a patron saint. The sixteenth-century mystic Isaac Luria, of Safad, Palestine, called a *tsaddiq* ("just man") by his followers, saw himself as a reincarnation of Shim'on bar Yoḥ'ai and "discovered" the graves of other ancient sages, with whom he communed. His teachings and habits were reverently preserved by his disciples and had great influence on later Jewish mysticism.

In eighteenth-century Poland the pietist wonder-worker Yisra'el ben Eli'ezer, called the Besht—an acronym of Ba'al Shem Tov (Master of the Name [of God])—initiated the modern revivalist movement of Hasidism, which focused on the intercessory powers of the *tsaddiqim*. This movement appealed to Jews who were repelled by rabbinic elitism and learning. The *tsaddiqim*—the Besht, certain of his disciples, and certain of their descendants—functioned for their followers as living, personal embodiments of Torah (law). In the "court" of the *tsaddiq* the *ḥasid* (disciple) found a warm and fervent piety and a man who understood his innermost thoughts and needs. The *tsaddiq* could intercede with God on behalf of his followers and raise them to higher spiritual achievement. Thus the *tsaddiq* represents the clearest specimen of contemporary Jewish sainthood.

Hinduism. The boundary between humanity and divinity is far more fluid in Hinduism and in Eastern religions generally than it is in the monotheistic faiths. Thus devotees do not always distinguish human saints from divine incarnations. Hindu deities are regularly described anthropomorphically, and highly spiritual humans manifest divinity. The god Kṛṣṇa, for instance, appears in the *Bhagavadgītā,* Hinduism's most popular text, as both instructor and object of devotion to the young warrior Arjuna, while the sixteenth-century Bengali teacher Caitanya is sometimes deified by his followers as an incarnation of the same Kṛṣṇa.

Classic Vedic religion focused on the elaborate priestly performance of the sacrifice rather than on individual personalities; yet the ancient *ṛṣis,* legendary composers of Vedic hymns and renowned wonder-workers, and *śramaṇas,* self-mortifying ascetics, were highly revered. As the Vedic heritage was criticized and reinterpreted, human exemplars came more to the fore. The first famous historical model and teacher was Śaṅkara (788–838), whose monist philosophy revitalized orthodoxy and in the twelfth century provoked the dualist response of the equally revered Ramanuja.

But it was the *bhakti* ("devotion") movements, focused on the worship of theistic gods, principally Viṣṇu and Śiva, in which the *guru* ("preceptor") as saint became prominent. In literature as early as the Upanisadic texts the *guru* was seen not only as a teacher of the Vedas but also as a model whose daily habits pointed the way to spiritual liberation. The student not only learned from his master but also served him by attending to his sacred fire, his cattle, and his other priestly needs. In the *bhakti* tradition, however, the *guru* was honored not because of his knowledge or birth but because of the wholehearted devotion to his god that he manifested. The *guru's* experience of liberation (*mokṣa*) became his disciples' goal. The tenth-century poet Jñanesvara described the total fulfillment that he experienced in the worship of his *guru* Nivritti to be like bathing in all the holy waters of the world. In the Vaiṣṇava and Śaiva sects the *gurus* were considered divine incarnations and were worshiped with incense and offerings.

In modern times *gurus* have continued to be an important force in Hindu religion, and some have found substantial followings beyond India. The gentle and sensitive Ramakrishna Paramahamsa (1836–1886) came to the attention of the West through the efforts of his disciple Vivekenanda, who spread his teaching worldwide. Similarly, the teachings of Caitanya are continued in the International Society for Krishna Consciousness. The most famous modern Hindu saint, Mohandas Gandhi (1869–1948), exemplified ancient Indian religious ideals and employed them to work for the cause of Indian nationalism. In so doing he became a "guru" for social justice movements in the West.

Buddhism. The two major divisions of Buddhism, Theravāda and Mahāyāna, have different understandings of sainthood. The Theravāda, whose adherents live primarily in Sri Lanka and Southeast Asia, acclaim the *arahant* as the acme of human perfection. The *arahant* achieves the final stage of the monastic quest for release from suffering and rebirth. The seeker begins by renouncing the householder's life in favor of homelessness and then passes countless lifetimes pursuing the "three trainings" in higher morality, higher concentration, and higher wisdom. At the end the *arahant* achieves the destruction of the *asavas,* the wrong mental states that bind one to *kamma* (Skt., *karman*) and rebirth. He declares, "Destroyed is rebirth, lived is the higher life, done is what is to be done; there is no further becoming for me." The numerous legends of the *arahants* in the Pali canon complement the descriptions of the path by relating stories about the previous lives of the *arahants,* the ways they attain wisdom, their virtues, and their miraculous powers.

Remote from the ordinary person, the *arahant* provokes veneration rather than imitation. Indeed, few *arahants* have been recognized since the time of Gautama Buddha. Yet a person can and should imitate the developing *arahant* as he is portrayed in the stories about his previous lives. By making offerings at pagodas containing the *arahants'* relics, the householder purifies his own mind and earns merit. Moreover, by providing food, clothing, and housing to monks, laymen enable them to pursue enlightenment while, at the same time, accruing merit for themselves.

While Theravāda Buddhism idealizes the world-renouncing saint who follows the Buddha's reported last words to "seek your *own* salvation with diligence," Mahāyāna schools, dominant in East Asia, stress the power of saints to aid ordinary laymen to attain enlightenment. The *bodhisattva* (lit., "Buddha-to-be") is a saint who has postponed his complete enlightenment in order to help others along the path. He emulates the compassion of the Buddha by nurturing the seeds of enlightenment that are present in all beings.

The *bodhisattva* path is open to all people. Those who after many lifetimes have reached the stage of "arousing the thought of enlightenment" (*bodhicitta*) resolve to work for the welfare of others. Through the practice of the six perfections (*pāramitās*)—giving, morality, patience, vigor, meditation, and wisdom—*bodhisattvas* overcome their self-motivated behavior. By imitating the virtues of a *bodhisattva* and having faith in his compassion, a person can be assured of eventual enlightenment. The *bodhisattva* is capable of transferring his own merit to the sincere seeker and thus directly speeding his progress.

The most advanced *bodhisattvas* are mythical figures who became venerated as divine saviors. Closely related are the celestial Buddhas, counterparts of Gautama Buddha existing in other worlds. In China and Japan devotion to the Buddha Amitābha, for instance, assures one of rebirth in the Pure Land. There the hindrances on the way to enlightenment are far fewer than they are in this world.

Tibetan Buddhists venerate the lama ("preceptor"), who may be either a scholar-monk or a wonder-worker like the most popular lama, Mi la ras pa (Milarepa) (1040–1123). The most famous saints of Tibet are the Dalai Lamas, incarnations of the celestial *bodhisattva* Avalokiteśvara. Upon the death of a Dalai Lama, the incarnation passes to an infant born forty-nine days later, who must be discovered and properly raised for his exemplary and yet inimitable role.

Confucianism. As one of the several religious components of precommunist China, Confucianism offers a distinct notion of sainthood. For Confucius (551–479 BCE, as recorded in the *Analects,* the ideal humans were the sage-kings, the legendary ancient rulers who disclosed the ways of Heaven to humans and ruled in accord with those ways. Mengzi, a late fourth-century BCE follower of Confucius, did not restrict the *sheng* ("sage") to antiquity but recognized the ongoing possibility of such exemplars. For Mengzi the sage was by nature the same as other people, so through learning and self-cultivation anyone could aspire to sagehood.

The Neo-Confucians worked out the ways to this goal. The school of Principle stressed the effort and discipline necessary to investigate *li,* the moral order in oneself and other things, while the school of Mind insisted that the highest good is waiting within to be uncovered and brought to fruition. For both, sagehood consists of the full realization of one's nature or mind and the sense of oneness with all things. A sage can be recognized by his peacefulness, warmth, honesty, and empathy for all beings. Sagehood thus became a reachable even if rarely realized goal.

As saint the sage is not only exemplary but also venerated. When, during the Han dynasty (206 BCE–220 CE), Confucianism became the official state religion, temples devoted to Confucius and noteworthy Confucians proliferated. Even in modern times the Wenmiao (Temple of Learning) was the site of sacrificial rites to Confucius. Such devotion arose out of respect for Confucian teaching, however, and not from the desire to seek intercession from Confucian masters. In the official religion the heroes were not deified. Yet in more popular circles Confucius was taken up as a deity in family shrines, along with ancestors, Buddhas, and popular gods.

PATHS TO SAINTHOOD. Recalling that the most diverse types of people have been acclaimed as saints, as individuals both imitable and inimitable, one can nonetheless identify three broad paths to sainthood: moral, intellectual, and emotional.

The moral path is followed by those who seek to control and purify their will in order to do but one thing well: Serve their god or realize ultimate truth. The spiritual soldier is one who cultivates discipline in order to do his duty. Frequently that duty demands asceticism: By denying himself the ordinary pleasures of life, the ascetic reaches for extraordinary bliss. Among Christian saints chastity divided the world of spirit from the world of flesh. Eradicating bodily desires and mortifying the flesh, the Christian ascetic sought to remove the impediments that blocked his or her total communion with God. Similarly, for the Theravāda Buddhist monk the renunciation of the household life and the taking up of the begging bowl represent sacrifice of self-interest in the pursuit of enlightenment. Martyrdom represents the most extreme form of volitional control, a sure path to heaven in Christianity and Islam.

Other saints pursue an intellectual road to sanctity. Exercising the mind to know deeply oneself, the world, and ultimate reality has often been deemed a saintly vocation. The Confucian sage seeks the correlation between his inner self and the structure of the world outside, while the Jewish mystical sage aims to discover in Torah, God's revelation, the secrets of creation itself. For both, the mind is the road to truth. Judaism and Islam especially emphasize mastery of the written divine law as the prerequisite for further spiritual pursuits. On the other hand, education alone cannot make a saint. Religions typically emphasize supernatural intellectual qualities such as intuition, clairvoyance, and prophecy when elaborating sagely wisdom. The saint in this category rarely rests in his wisdom but reaches out instead as a teacher to share his wisdom with others. The master or preceptor type of saint, the Muslim *shaykh* or the Hindu *guru,* for instance, aims to guide others. Less by communicating objective knowledge than by teaching a way to live, the master exemplifies wisdom for his disciples.

The third path to sainthood is the way of the emotions, the perfecting of the heart to love unqualifiedly. Mystics of all religions are great lovers, and those acclaimed as saints have expressed that love in ways that inspire others to love. The Christian saint Bernard of Clairvaux and the Muslim saint Rābi'ah al-'Adawīyah did not hesitate to express their love for God in frankly erotic terms. Perfected love overflows into love for other human beings; thus saints are acclaimed for their healing and redeeming actions. The modern Jewish Ḥasid who experiences the love of his *tsaddiq* is elevated to new levels of holiness and feels all his earthly cares melt away in the master's presence. The typical *walī* can be depended on to listen to the prayers of barren women, paralytics, and the poverty-stricken and to respond compassionately. The quintessential lovers are the *bodhisattvas*, who aid their fellow creatures on the road to enlightenment. By assuming the sufferings of others they advance all beings toward final peace.

Finally, special note must be taken of the woman's path to sainthood, for it often varies from that of her male coreligionists. In general women have not had equal access to sainthood, especially in Judaism, Hinduism, and Confucianism. Still, the cults of Hindu goddesses such as Kālī and popular Chinese heroine-goddesses such as Mazi are likely functional equivalents to the veneration of established, male saints. Elsewhere, the ways to sainthood for women seem more rigid than those for men. In Roman Catholicism women are far more dependent upon supernatural powers to establish their holiness than are men and, as female nurturers, constitute a high proportion of the helping and healing saints. Their stories also typically feature penitential acts especially aimed at obliterating their debilitating sexuality. The Mahāyāna *bodhisattva* ideal, although asexual, requires of women, more so than men, a purge of their sexuality. In many cases a woman must undergo a sexual transformation in either this or a future life in order to become a *bodhisattva,* although some celestial *bodhisattvas* do retain their femininity.

SEE ALSO Bodhisattva Path; Cult of Saints; Hasidism; Imamate; Martyrdom; Merit; Miracles; Perfectibility; Sufism.

BIBLIOGRAPHY

A fine survey using sainthood as a category in world religions is provided by the essays in *Sainthood: Its Manifestations in World Religions,* edited by George D. Bond and Richard Kieckhefer (Berkeley, Calif., 1988). Very different in approach is the suggestive philosophical analysis of three models of spiritual perfection by Robert C. Neville, *Soldier, Sage, Saint* (New York, 1978).

For a classic psychological perspective on saintliness, see William James's *The Varieties of Religious Experience* (New York, 1902). Brief taxonomical discussions of the saint are found in Gerardus van der Leeuw's *Religion in Essence and Manifestation: A Study in Phenomenology,* 2 vols., translated by J. E. Turner, incorporating additions of the 2d German ed. (Gloucester, 1967), and Joachim Wach's *Sociology of Religion* (1944; reprint, Chicago, 1962).

To explore sainthood in more depth one must consult works on the specific religions. The novelty and centrality of Christian sainthood in the context of late antiquity is the subject of Peter Brown's masterful work, *The Cult of the Saints* (Chicago, 1981). A fascinating sociological study of Christian saints is Donald Weinstein and Rudolph M. Bell's *Saints and Society: The Two Worlds of Western Christendom, 1000–1700* (Chicago, 1982). For a critique and reappraisal of the meaning of Christian sainthood for today, see Lawrence S. Cunningham's *The Meaning of Saints* (San Francisco, 1980). Of the many studies on Islamic saints, the classic is Ignácz Goldziher's "Veneration of Saints in Islam," in *Muslim Studies,* vol. 2, edited by S. M. Stern and C. R. Barber (Chicago, 1973). Most valuable on Sufism is Annemarie Schimmel's *Mystical Dimensions of Islam* (Chapel Hill, N. C., 1975). Some discussion of Jewish mystical saints is found in Gershom Scholem's *Major Trends in Jewish Mysticism* (1941; reprint, New York, 1961). A summary of the role of the *guru* in Hinduism is Joel D. Mlecko's "The Guru in Hindu Tradition," *Numen* 29 (July 1982): 33–61. For Buddhism, a standard introduction with a good discussion of the *bodhisattva* is Richard H. Robinson and Willard L. Johnson's *The Buddhist Religion: A Historical Introduction,* 2d ed. (Encino, Calif., 1977). On women saints in Buddhism, see Diana Y. Paul's *Women in Buddhism: Images of the Feminine in Mahayana Tradition* (Berkeley, Calif., 1979).

New Sources

Abou-El-Haj. *The Medieval Cult of Saints: Formations and Transformations.* Cambridge, U.K., 1997.

Blumenfeld-Kosinski, Renate, and Timea Szell, eds. *Images of Sainthood in Medieval Europe.* Ithaca, N.Y., 1991.

Cushing, Kathleen. "Events that Led to Sainthood: Sanctity and the Reformeo in the Eleventh Century." In *Belief and Culture in the Middle Ages.* Edited by Richard Gameson and Henrietta Leyser. New York, 2001.

Dempsey, Corinne. *Kerala Christian Sainthood: Collisions of Culture and Worldview in South India.* New York, 2001.

Ewing, Katherine. *Arguing Sainthood: Modernity, Psychoanalysis, and Islam.* Durham, N.C., 1997.

Kieckhefer, Richard. "The Holy and the Unholy: Sainthood, Witchcraft, and Magic in Late Medieval Europe." *Journal of Medieval and Renaissance Studies* 24 (fall 1994): 355–385.

Schulenberg, Jane Tibbets. *Forgetful of their Sex: Female Sanctity and Society ca. 500–1100.* Chicago, 1998.

Sticco, Sandro, ed. *Saints: Studies in Hagiography.* Medieval and Renaissance Texts and Studies series. Binghamton, N.Y., 1996.

ROBERT L. COHN (1987)
Revised Bibliography

ŚAIVISM

This entry consists of the following articles:

AN OVERVIEW
ŚAIVA SIDDHĀNTA
VĪRAŚAIVAS
NĀYAṈĀRS
KRAMA ŚAIVISM
TRIKA ŚAIVISM
ŚAIVISM IN KASHMIR
PRATYABHIJÑĀ
PĀŚUPATAS
KĀPĀLIKAS

ŚAIVISM: AN OVERVIEW

Śaivism and Vaiṣṇavism form the two principal religious currents of classical and modern Hinduism. Śaivism centers on the worship of the god Śiva and Vaiṣṇavism on that of Viṣṇu. In classical Hindu mythology Śiva is the god of destruction, generally portrayed as a yogin who lives on Mount Kailāsa in the Himalayas. His body is smeared with ashes, his hair piled up in matted locks. He wears an animal skin and carries a trident. A cobra often serves as his garland and the crescent moon as his hair ornament. He has a third eye, kept closed, in the middle of his forehead. He may be surrounded by his beautiful wife, Pārvatī, and their two sons, the six-faced Skanda and the elephant-headed Gaṇeśa.

The migration of bands of people called Aryans into the northwest of the Indian subcontinent initiates the Vedic period (c. 1200–600 BCE), known through the religious texts called Vedas, Brāhmaṇas, and Upaniṣads. In them the minor god Rudra serves as a prototype of the later Śiva. The two gods, each with his own varied forms and names, are identified with each other in the classical Hindu tradition represented by the Sanskrit texts known as the *Mahābhārata* (300 BCE–300 CE) and the Purāṇas (200–1300 CE). Beginning in about the second century of the common era, a number of important Śaiva sects appear, each with its own texts and doctrines. Many worshipers of Śiva belong to such sects, but the majority simply count themselves as Hindus who believe in this god over all others.

Discussions of Śaivism traditionally begin with an examination of the so-called proto-Paśupati seals of the ancient pre-Aryan civilization centered in the Indus Valley of Pakistan. The most interesting of these seals depicts an anthropomorphic and apparently ithyphallic figure seated on a low dais in a yogalike position with his heels meeting in the perineal region, the hands of his extended and braceleted arms resting on his knees, and his head—which may or may not be triple-faced and/or bovine—bearing a horned headdress. Surrounding this figure are small representations of a rhinoceros, a buffalo, a tiger, and an elephant. Under the dais are two goats or deer. The seal also bears a seven-sign inscription.

Starting from the hypothesis of the archaeologist George Marshall, most scholars have accepted the identification of this figure as the precursor of the god Śiva in his Paśupati, or Lord of Animals, form. The most important dissent from this consensus was made by D. D. Kosambi, who pointed out that the horns of the figure were those of a buffalo and not of a bull (the latter being the animal most closely associated both with the Vedic Rudra and the later Śiva). Kosambi further proposed a historically improbable identification of the proto-Paśupati figure with the buffalo demon named Mahiṣāsura (which dates at least 1,500 years later) and through this demon back to Śiva. Until further evidence or an accepted reading of the Indus script becomes available, it seems best to suspend judgment on the whole problem.

Still, the discussion clearly bears directly not only on the question of the historical origins of Śiva, the god of Śaivism, but also on that of the transition from the minor Vedic god Rudra to the major post-Vedic Śiva. Among the varied hypotheses on these questions, several basic tendencies can be distinguished. A. B. Keith (1925) suggests that the attempt to distinguish Aryan and non-Aryan elements in Rudra-Śiva is basically fruitless. The character of the god develops through a constant process of accretion resulting from the identification of other minor gods, both Aryan and non-Aryan, with the Vedic Rudra. Jan Gonda (1970) prefers to see a fundamental continuity between the Vedic Rudra and post-Vedic Śiva, and between Vedic and post-Vedic religion in general. He regards the lack of reference to many aspects of the god in Vedic literature as due in large part to the class bias of the priestly authors, who ignored or excluded many of the god's more popular traits. Louis Renou (1953), on the other hand, suggests that there was a decisive break between Vedism and Hinduism. He notes the absence of any obvious connection between the Veda and the earlier Indus civilization and accepts the possibility of some connection between Indus religion and later Hinduism. With less caution, R. N. Dandekar (1967, 1971) speaks of the religion of the Vedas as an "interlude" between protohistorical and historical Hinduism. However this case may be, Dandekar also makes the important observation that Vedic mythology is an "evolutionary mythology," one that evolves in accordance with the ethos of a historical period and with the changing conditions of life.

It is now clear that there was a gap of five hundred years or more between the end of the mature phase of the Indus Valley civilization (c. 1800 BCE) and the hymns of the *Ṛgveda* (c. 1200 BCE). It is also evident that Hinduism, as opposed to Vedism, grew up—together with Buddhism, Jainism, and other non-Vedic cults—in the Ganges River valley (Uttar Pradesh and Bihar). The rise of these new movements corresponds to the transition from an economy based on pastoralism mixed with shifting cultivation to one based on sedentary grain production, and to the political transition from migratory tribal oligarchies to kingships with clearly demarcated territories. These historical changes imply the existence of dramatic cultural and religious changes as well, changes that did not derive from the influence of the ancient and distant civilization of the Indus Valley. Elements of the new religions may ultimately be traced to that civilization—and to the little-known culture of the early non-Aryan inhabitants of the Ganges Valley—but the new religions as systems should be considered new creations arising in conjunction with the new and radically changed economic and political conditions.

The Vedic Rudra is a fierce and terror-inspiring god of storms, disease, and the untamed aspects of nature. He is exclusively invoked in only four of the 1,028 hymns of the *Ṛgveda,* although he is frequently mentioned in it as the father of the Maruts, gods of the winds, and as one of the *viśvadevas,* or All-Gods. The hymns contain only brief allusions to the mythology of Rudra, but the epithets he receives and the attitude with which he is invoked give a clear picture of his basic character. The name *Rudra* itself is traditionally derived from the known root *rud,* meaning "cry" or "howl," and is evidently related to his association with storms. An alternative derivation from a postulated root **rud,* meaning "be red" or "shine," can be connected with a proposed derivation for the name *Śiva* ("auspicious") from a Dravidian word meaning "red." In the hymns the poets implore Rudra to be "compassionate" and "easy to invoke," not to kill cows or men, and to keep men "prosperous and free from disease." He is frequently described as a "bull," as being "brown," and as "terrible." He possesses a "sharp weapon," a "thunderbolt," and "swift arrows." He wears "braided hair" (*kapardin*) and brings a "cooling [?] medicine." Although in two hymns he is associated with Soma, god of the intoxicating sacrificial drink, his principal association in Vedic literature as a whole is with Agni, the god of fire, with whom he is already identified once in the *Ṛgveda* and several times in the Brāhmaṇas.

In the *Yajurveda* Rudra is invoked at length in the section called the *Śatarudriya.* Among the noteworthy epithets he receives in this text are "mountain dweller," "lord of cattle" (*paśūnāṃ patiḥ*), "wearer of an animal hide," "blue-necked," "ruddy," and the names or seminames Kapardin, Śarva, Bhava, Śambhu, Śaṅkara, and Śiva. His prowess as an archer is repeatedly mentioned, as is his association with the untamed aspects of nature and with hunters, thieves, and brigands.

An important passage in the *Atharvaveda* (15.5.1–7) closely associates seven apparently independent gods, all of whom early become identified as names or forms of Rudra-Śiva, with the enigmatic *vratyas*, a class or group of religious officiants who were only partly aryanized. These gods are Bhava, Śarva, Paśupati, Ugra, Rudra, Māhadeva, and Īśāna. Each is associated with a particular region. Quite similar lists appear in the Brāhmaṇas and other later Vedic texts, with the addition of an eighth name, Aśani or Bhīma (and in one text the names Hara, Mrda, Śiva, and Śaṅkara as well). In post-Vedic Hindu texts the same eight names of Śiva are sometimes listed, but more important are the five forms or faces of the god: Sadyojāta, Vāmadeva, Aghora, Tatpuruṣa, and Īśāna.

A key theme that first appears in later Vedic literature is the god's rather ambiguous relation to the sacrificial oblations and offerings. Originally Rudra seems to have been at least partly excluded from orthodox Vedic sacrifices and thus has to demand his share of the offerings, sometimes described as the share that is "left over" (*ucchiṣṭa*). In the classical mythology of Hinduism, this theme is incorporated into Śiva's conflict with his father-in-law, the brahman named Dakṣa, whose sacrifice Śiva destroys because he was not invited to it. Śiva beheads Dakṣa and then replaces the head with that of a goat, the sacrificial animal. This myth again suggests popular, nonhieratic origins for the god.

The god Rudra-Śiva appears for the first time as the object of monotheistic devotion rather suddenly in the *Śvetāśvatara Upaniṣad,* a text often described as a Śaiva *Bhagavadgītā.* The *Śvetāśvatara* is one of the later of the early Upaniṣads, possibly dating from about the sixth century BCE, and clearly illustrates how these texts mark the historical transition from Vedism to Hinduism. It refers explicitly to important aspects of Sāṃkhya metaphysics and Yoga practice. Its own metaphysical position is not entirely consistent, but it bears some resemblance to the later system of "qualified monism" (*viśiṣṭādvaita*) propounded by Rāmānuja (twelfth century). In the Upaniṣad, Rudra is described as the "one God" (*eka deva*), the ruler and cause of all, the *brahman* itself, and he is addressed as Hara, Īśa, Mahāpuruṣa, Īśāna, Bhagavat, Śiva, and Maheśvara.

Between the Upaniṣads and the *Mahābhārata* epic, chronologically the next major source for knowledge of Śiva, there appears to be a gap of several hundred years in the course of which Vedism is replaced by an already mature Hinduism. In recent years the classical mythology of Śiva in the *Mahābhārata* and in the later Purāṇas has been extensively analyzed by Wendy O'Flaherty, Stella Kramrisch, J. Bruce Long, and others, using methodologies influenced by the theories of Mircea Eliade and Claude Lévi-Strauss. The resulting emphasis on symbolic archetypes and on thematic structures and motifs has provided a clearer idea of the mental structures and contents of the myths, but it has also tended to exaggerate their consistency and to isolate them from their sociohistorical contexts.

In classical Hindu mythology Brahmā, Viṣṇu, and Śiva are linked together as the gods of creation, preservation, and destruction, respectively. In the varied Śaiva versions of the myths, however, Śiva is generally portrayed as the one God over all, who is ultimately responsible for creation and preservation as well as destruction. Vaiṣṇava versions do the same for Viṣṇu. This informal monotheism takes more systematic forms in the theological works of the Śaiva and Vaiṣṇava sects.

Many of the main episodes in the Śaiva myth cycle revolve around the dynamic tension between Śiva as the god equally of asceticism and eroticism, a master of both yogic restraint and sexual prowess. This tension is frequently expressed in terms of the image of castration: the real castration of the god himself and symbolic castrations (loss of eyes or teeth, beheading) of his opponents.

Śiva destroys Kāma, the god of erotic love, with the fire from his third eye when Kāma attempts to disturb his ascetic trance. Subsequently Pārvatī, daughter of the Himalaya, wins Śiva's love through her own ascetic penance and persuades him to revive Kāma in disembodied form. For his visit to the pine forest Śiva wears the guise of a naked, ash-smeared ascetic, but he uses the occasion to seduce, or to attempt to seduce, the wives of the forest sages. As a result either of the sages' curse or of his own action, Śiva is castrated and his phallus, or *liṅga,* becomes fixed in the earth. The stylized stone *liṅga,* mounted on an equally stylized vulva, or *yoni,* has become the central image of Śaiva worship and serves as the dual symbol of the god's creative and ascetic power.

By chopping off the fifth head of the god Brahmā, Śiva is charged with the major sin of the murder of a brahman and must undertake the penance, or Great Vow (*māhavrata*), of the Skull-Bearer (*kapālin*), an ascetic who wanders about with a skull as a begging bowl. This Great Vow becomes the archetypal basis of the ascetic sect of the Kāpālikas or Mahāvratins, who are equally noted for their indulgence in orgiastic rites of Tantric character.

The complicated myth of the birth of the six-faced Skanda, a son of Śiva, exists in a number of very different versions. In part, Skanda is the son of Śiva and Pārvatī, but he is at the same time the son of Agni and of the six Kṛttikas. His role is to destroy the terrible demon Tāraka. In South India, the Dravidian god Murukaṉ was early identified with Skanda and contributed to the historical development of his mythology.

The three sons of Tāraka later establish the mighty triple city of the demons, which Śiva eventually destroys with a single arrow from his bow, Pināka. Another demon, named Andhaka, the blind son of Śiva and/or of the demon Hiraṇyākṣa, lusts after Pārvatī but is defeated and reformed by Śiva. Śiva beheads his son Gaṇeśa, whom he has never met, when Gaṇeśa tries to prevent the apparent stranger from entering the room of Pārvatī, Śiva's wife and Gaṇeśa's mother. Śiva then replaces his son's head with that of an elephant with one broken tusk, just as he once replaced Dakṣa's head with that of a goat. Historically, Gaṇeśa was perhaps originally an independent elephant god. As part of Śiva's family he serves as the god of obstacles and hence of luck, to be invoked at the beginning of any undertaking.

The existence of an extensive mythology of Śiva in the *Mahābhārata* suggests the existence of an important cult dedicated to the god by about the beginning of the common era. Unfortunately, direct historical evidence for the cult before that date is not plentiful. Megasthenes, a Greek ambassador to the court of Candragupta Maurya (c. 324–300 BCE), mentions the presence in India of worshipers of Herakles and Dionysos. These two gods are usually identified as Kṛṣṇa and Śiva, respectively. The early grammarian Patañjali (c. 150 BCE) mentions Śiva Bhāgavatas who carry iron lances. These must be Śaiva ascetics. The earliest example of a Śiva *liṅga* seems to be the large, realistic stone *liṅga* from Guḍimallam in southeastern India, estimated by some to date from the first or second century BCE.

Coins and inscriptions that give evidence of Śaiva worship are plentiful from the period of the Kushans (first and second centuries CE) and, more important, that of the Guptas (300–550 CE). Although the Gupta emperors mostly preferred Vaiṣṇavism, they also sponsored temples of Śiva. The kings of the contemporary Vākāṭaka dynasty were mostly followers of Śiva, as were those of the slightly later Maukhari dynasty. From about the seventh century, Śaivism became the dominant religious current in the south, largely replacing the Jains and Buddhists and competing successfully with the Vaiṣṇavas. The southern dynasties of the Pallavas, Cōḻas, and Cālukyas were all patrons of Śaivism.

The age of the Guptas seems to mark the beginning of distinct Śaiva sects. Except for the Pāśupatas these sects do not appear in the *Mahābhārata,* but they become prominent in the Purāṇas. The sects are made up chiefly of ascetics but also have some sort of lay following. The Pāśupata sect was founded by Lakulīśa, who was born near Broach in western India about the beginning of the second century. Lakulīśa is already regarded as an incarnation of Śiva in several Purāṇas, and the Pāśupata sect became important, particularly in southern India, from about the seventh to the fourteenth century. The Kālamukhas, a closely related sect, were influential in the Karnataka region of the south during much the same period. Another early Śaiva sect, of considerable symbolic interest but uncertain historical importance, was that of the Kāpālikas.

A fourth early sect is that of the Śaiva Siddhāntins, often simply called Śaivas. This sect grew out of a devotional movement centered in the Cauvery River basin of the southeast and led by the Śaiva Nāyaṉārs (Nāyaṉmār), poet-saints of the seventh to tenth centuries whose devotional hymns composed in Tamil even today occupy a central place in Śiva worship in this region. The sect is still active and has produced, or appropriated to itself, an extensive literature in both Sanskrit (the twenty-eight Śaivāgamas) and Tamil (the twelve Tirumuṟai and the fourteen Meykaṇṭaśāstras).

The Pāśupatas, Kālāmukhas, and Śaiva Siddhāntins all maintain monotheistic theological systems in which the grace (*prasāda*) of God and devotion (*bhakti*) to him play essential roles in attaining personal salvation. All accept an ontological distinction between God (*pati*), the individual person (*paśu*), and mundane existence (*pāśa*).

The Pāśupata and Kālāmukha sects are now extinct. In the Karnataka region they gave way to another Śaiva sectarian movement known as the Vīraśaivas or Liṅgāyats. This sect, especially in its initial stages, has been noted for its advocacy of social reforms, including attacks against casteism and the subjugation of women. Its metaphysics is less dualistic than that of the other southern sects, though it also stresses the importance of devotion and God's grace. The most important literature of the sect consists of devotional hymns composed in Kannada by various inspired devotees beginning with Basava (c. 1150), often considered the founder of the sect. Many of the hymns are collected in the *Śunyasaṁpādane.*

In the north, the Śaiva sect known as the Trika or Kashmiri school became important from about the ninth century. It incorporated Tantric and Buddhist influences and adopted a monistic metaphysical position similar to that of nondualist (*advaita*) Vedānta. The extensive literature of the sect is divided into the categories of Āgama Śāstra, Spanda Śāstra, and Pratyabhijña Śāstra. Its greatest thinker was Abhinavagupta (c. 1000).

Tantric influences have been strong in Śaivism since about the end of the Gupta period, when this religious current first became important. Tantrism blended with yoga, particularly *haṭhayoga,* forms the doctrinal basis of the medieval Śaiva sect of the Nāths, also called Siddhas and Kānphaṭa Yogis. This group emphasizes yogic control over mind and body, including the winning of magical powers (*siddhis*), and aims at spiritual enlightenment through the domination of the inner "serpent power" *(kuṇḍalini),* which lies trapped within the veins or nerves (*nāḍīs*) and centers, or ganglia (*cakras*), of a supraphysical yogic anatomy. A few Nath Yogis still exist, although the influence of the sect continues mainly through the diffusion of *haṭhayoga* into the mainstream of Hinduism and beyond.

During the past few centuries the worship of Viṣṇu and his *avatāras* has proved to be more adaptable to the emotional devotionalism of modern Hinduism than has the worship of Śiva. Śaivism, however, still claims many millions of devotees. Most of them are not followers of specific sects, nor even necessarily exclusively devoted to Śiva. They patronize Śiva temples and make offerings of flowers, sweets, coconuts, and money to the god and his priests. The holy city of the Hindus, Banaras, is the city of Śiva, and the temple of Śiva Viśveśvara there is one of the chief pilgrimage sites of all India. Similarly, in Hindu mythology the holy river Ganges is portrayed as a goddess who descends to earth through Śiva's matted hair.

The priests of Śiva temples often belong to the nonsectarian, orthodox tradition of the Smārtas, who practice the worship of five shrines (*pañcāyatana-pūjā*) dedicated to the gods Viṣṇu, Śiva, Sūrya, Gaṇeśa, and Dūrgā. This Smārta tradition is compatible with a variety of metaphysical positions, but is often linked with the nondualist (*advaita*) theology derived principally from Śaṅkarācārya (c. 700–750).

According to tradition, Śaṅkarācārya was a devotee of Śiva and composed a number of devotional hymns dedicated to this god. Although his authorship of these hymns has often been disputed, the orthodox monastic sect of the Daśanāmīs, which he is said to have founded, retains this Śaiva influence. Today the monks (*samnyasins*) and abbots of the Daśanāmī monasteries are the dominant arbiters of theological orthodoxy and socioreligious tradition (*varṇāśrama-dharma*). Through them Śiva has come full circle from his role as the heretical outsider of Dakṣa's sacrifice to that as the patron deity of Hindu orthodoxy.

BIBLIOGRAPHY

The most useful general survey of Śaivism is still R. G. Bhandarkar's *Vaiṣṇavism, Śaivism and Minor Religious Systems* (1913; reprint, Varanasi, 1965). It has been partly superseded by Jan Gonda's *Viṣṇuism and Śivaism* (London, 1970). A well-documented summary of the "proto-Paśupati" controversy, expressing a view similar to Kosambi's, is Alf Hiltebeitel's "The Indus Valley 'Proto-Śiva,'" *Anthropos* 73 (1978): 767–797. For Śaiva mythology, the best work is Wendy Doniger O'Flaherty's *Śiva: The Erotic Ascetic* (London, 1981), a reprint of *Asceticism and Eroticism in the Mythology of Śiva* (1973); but most should find the treatment in her *Hindu Myths* (Baltimore, Md., 1975) entertaining and sufficient. A very personal interpretation, packed with information, is Stella Kramrisch's *The Presence of Śiva* (Princeton, N.J., 1981). My own study *The Kāpālikas and Kālāmukhas* (Berkeley, 1972) can be consulted on these sects and on the Pāśupatas. Mariasusai Dhavamony's *Love of God According to "Śaiva Siddhānta"* (Oxford, 1971) is essential for that sect. No really satisfactory work exists on the Viraśaivas or on Kashmir Śaivism, but some Viraśaiva hymns have been beautifully translated by A. K. Ramanujan in *Speaking of Śiva* (Harmondsworth, 1973). For Tantrism, Yoga, and the Naths, the best source is the classic of Mircea Eliade, *Yoga: Immortality and Freedom,* 2d ed. (Princeton, 1969). Discussions of the evolution of Rudraśiva can be found in Arthur Berriedale Keith's *The Religion and Philosophy of the Veda and Upanishads,* 2 vols. (1925; reprint, Westport, Conn., 1971), in Louis Renou's *Religions of Ancient India* (London, 1953), in R. N. Dandekar's *Some Aspects of the History of Hinduism* (Poona, 1967), and in Dandekar's "Hinduism," in *Historia Religionum,* edited by C. Jouco Bleeker and Geo Widengren, vol. 2, *Religions of the Present* (Leiden, 1971), pp. 237–345.

New Sources

Chitgopekar, Nilima. *Encountering Sivaism: The Deity, the Milieu, the Entourage.* New Delhi, 1998.

Tagare, Ganesh Vasudeo. *Saivism, Some Glimpses.* New Delhi, 1996.

DAVID N. LORENZEN (1987)
Revised Bibliography

ŚAIVISM: ŚAIVA SIDDHĀNTA

Śaiva Siddhānta is an important medieval system of Śaiva thought. The term technically refers to a set of Śaiva theologies written in Sanskrit and Tamil in South India, although this classification need not be considered a rigid one. While Śaiva Siddhānta differs in many ways from the theologies presented by Kashmir Śaivism (most particularly in its assertion that the world and individual souls are real entities and that final release depends on the grace of Śiva, in contrast to Kashmiri idealistic and monistic ontologies and soteriologies), both schools accept as canon the Vedic Saṃhitas and Upaniṣads as well as the twenty-eight Sanskrit Śaiva and Raudra Āgamas, which date to the seventh century CE. The Śaiva Siddhānta distinguishes itself from other Śaiva systems, however, in that along with these literatures it accepts as scriptural authority the twelve Tirumuṟai and the fourteen Meykaṇṭaśāstras.

The Tirumuṟai consist of devotional poems written in Tamil in South India by Śaiva mystics and gathered in the latter part of the tenth century by Nampi Āṇṭār Nampi. The Meykaṇṭaśāstras are doctrinal works written in Tamil in the thirteenth and early fourteenth centuries by Śaiva theologians, the most influential of whom was Meykanta Tevar (Meykantar), a *śūdra* who lived to the north of Madras in the thirteenth century. Meykaṇṭa Tēvar's important work known as *Civañaṉāpōtam* (Instructions on the knowledge of Śiva) consists of Tamil translations of twelve *sūtras* from the *Raurava Āgama,* a seventh-century Sanskrit Śaiva work, to which he added Tamil commentaries and analogic interpretations. The system he taught became known as the Śaiva Siddhānta, the "doctrine of the followers of Śiva."

The Śaiva saints portray a vivid personal experience of God (Śiva), the fundamental theme of which is expressed by Tirumūlar: "The ignorant say that God and love are different; when they know that love and God are the same, they rest in God's love." Elsewhere Tirumūlar writes, "They have no love for God who have no love for all mankind." Appar (seventh century) speaks of the man who has unshakable belief in God's mercy and love. Śiva indwells every creature in a subtle form and manifests himself to his devotees. All that is required to be saved is to attune one's mind to Śiva and to be intent on his love and service. Inward and spiritual worship is the essence of religion, according to Appar. Without love for Śiva, the knowledge of scriptures, external rituals, and asceticism are of no avail for salvation. Campantar (seventh century) and Cuntarar (ninth century) stress the need of *bhakti* (love of God) in order to be freed from fetters. The mystic formula "Namo Śivāya," which represents the essence of the four Vedas and the essence of Śiva's name, when pronounced with true devotion, saves even nonmystics. Māṇikkavācakar (ninth century) describes in his *Tiruvācakam* the progress of a soul out of the bondage of ignorance and passion to the liberty of light and love. The main themes of this work are strong monotheism; infinity of bliss in Śiva alone; the purification, by grace, of the soul from delusion, as a preparation for eternal fellowship and communion with Śiva; prayers for forgiveness of sin; and enthusiastic love of God. Great prominence is given to the working of divine grace in Śaiva Siddhānta. *Aruḷ* (grace) is the remedy against *iruḷ* (ignorance). The illuminating grace takes the form of divine and mystical knowledge by which the soul, liberated from darkness, realizes its oneness with Śiva.

According to the Śāstras, there are three eternal and real substances: God *(pati)*, souls (*paśu*), and bondage (*pāśa*). God (Śiva) is immanent in everything and yet transcends everything. He is pure being, pure consciousness, and pure bliss. He is the efficient cause, and his *śakti,* composed of knowledge, action, and desire, is the instrumental cause of the world and of souls. He stands in relation to the universe as the soul to the body. As eyes cannot see but for the light of the soul, the soul cannot know but for the light of God. God and souls are one in the sense that they cannot be disjoined; they exist and function together. *Advaita* means inseparability, not identity; hence souls preserve their distinct character even in the final state of liberation.

Souls are endowed with knowledge, volition, and the ability to act, but they are bound by the fetters of *āṇava* (ignorance), *karman* (the effects of action), and *māyā* (changing reality), and therefore they experience themselves as independent of God. Śiva imparts to the soul instruments of empirical knowledge when it is in the *kevala* state (the state of the soul only with *āṇava*) and illuminating knowledge when it is in the *sakala* (embodied) state. Empirical knowledge leads to good and evil acts, and the result is the rebirth of the soul in different states. The three paths of salvation are those of service (*caryā*), worship (*kriyā*), and meditation (*yoga*), all of which should be animated by the love of God. All these ways dispose the soul to receive gratuitously from Śiva divine knowledge (*patijñāna*), by which is realized perfect union with Śiva in supreme love. This divine knowledge is imparted to souls either directly through intuition in the case of advanced souls or through a *Śivaguru* to the less advanced.

SEE ALSO Māṇikkavācakar; Meykaṇṭār; Umāpati Śivācārya; Tamil Religions.

BIBLIOGRAPHY

Devasenapathy, V. A. *Śaiva Siddhānta as Expounded in the Śivajñāna-Siddhiyar and Its Six Commentaries.* Madras, 1960.

Dhavamony, Mariasusai. *Love of God According to Śaiva Siddhānta: A Study in the Mysticism and Theology of Śaivism.* Oxford, 1971.

Nallaswami Pillai, J. M. *Studies in Saiva Siddhanta.* Dharmapura Adhinam, 1962.

Paranjoti, Violet. *Śaiva Siddhānta.* 2d ed. London, 1954.

Piet, John H. *A Logical Presentation of the Śaiva Siddhānta Philosophy.* Madras, 1952.

Schomerus, H. W. *Der Çaiva-Siddhānta, eine Mystik Indiens.* Leipzig, 1912.

New Sources

Gangadharan, S. *Saiva Siddhanta with Special Reference to Sivaprakasam.* Madurai, 1992.

Nandimath, S. C. *Theology of the Saivagamas: A Survey of the Doctrines of Saiva Siddhanta and Veerasaivism.* Thiruvananthapuram, 2001.

Schomerus, Hilko Wiardo. *Saiva Siddhanta: An Indian School of Mystical Thought Presented as a System and Documented from the Original Tamil Sources.* Delhi, 2000.

Singaravelu, C. N. *Glimpses of Saiva Siddhanta.* Madras, 1992.

Soni, Jayandra. *Philosophical Anthropology in Saiva Siddhanta: With Special Reference to Sivagrayogin.* Delhi, 1989.

MARIASUSAI DHAVAMONY (1987)
Revised Bibliography

ŚAIVISM: VĪRAŚAIVAS

The Indian religious movement of the Vīraśaivas ("heroic Śaivas")—also known as Liṅgāyats ("bearers of a *liṅgā*")—appeared as a reformist Śaiva sect in Hinduism probably in the middle of the twelfth century in the border regions of Maharashtra and Karnataka. Its founder is said to have been a brahman named Basava or Basavanna (1106–1167), though the main reformist role may have been that of Ekantada Ramayya, a contemporary of Basava. The Vīraśaiva doctrine was probably further elaborated in the following centuries.

The sect now has about six million adherents, mostly in Karnataka, where, though officially classified as "backward," they are a not unimportant group. Vīraśaivism may have appeared as a reaction of Dravidians against Brahmanic (and therefore Aryan) domination. Temple worship, sacrifice, and pilgrimages are condemned as useless. The caste system is rejected, the sexes are declared equal, child marriage is forbidden, and widows are allowed to remarry. Caste distinctions tended, however, to reappear in the course of time. There are, for instance, hereditary priests, the *jaṅgamas,* while the sect itself is regarded as a caste.

All Vīraśaivas must belong to a group connected with one of the sect's five main religious centers or *maṭhas* (Kedarnath, Śrīsaila, Balehalli, Ujjain, Varanasi). All must have a *guru,* undergo initiation, and carry a small *liṅgā* in a tube fastened to the neck or arm (hence the name Liṅgāyat). The sect mark is a white dot on the forehead. The dead are buried, not cremated.

Though they condemn all ritual, Vīraśaivas still admit some rites, but these are performed by *jaṅgamas,* not *brāhmaṇas,* the main rite being initiation (*dīkṣā*) of male children. They must also pay homage at least twice per day to the small *liṅgā* they wear. Fundamental to their religion and deemed indispensable for salvation are the so-called eight covers (*aṣṭāvaraṇa*): the *guru,* who is even more revered than God; the *liṅgā;* the *jaṅgamas;* holy water (*padodaka*); returned offerings (*prasāda*); holy ashes (*vibhūti*); the rosary (*rudrākṣa*); and the *mantra* "Namaṇ Śivāya." Vīraśaivas believe in reincarnation, except for those who attain a certain degree of holiness in this life.

The metaphysical creed of the Vīraśaivas is "qualified dualism" (*viśeṣādvaita*), a Śaiva variant of Rāmānuja's doctrine, from which it may derive. Śiva acts through his energy (*śakti*), which divides itself into the Lord as manifested in the *guru* and the *liṅgā* and into all individual souls (*aṅgas*). *Māyā* is the cause and origin of the material world. Liberation from this world is gained by devotion to God and through a sixfold practice, the six phases (*sthalas*) of which will eventually bring the devotee to union with Śiva (united with Śakti), a union that is not, however, complete identity with God.

The literature is in Sanskrit, Kannada, and Telugu. That in Sanskrit is mostly doctrinal; some Āgamas include Vīraśaiva elements. The most important and popular texts are in Kannada, the main part being made up of *vacanas* ("sayings"). These are sermons, poems, and mystical utterances of the great Vīraśaiva saints and masters (Basava, Kasimayya, Mahādēviyakka, Allamaprabhu). This literature, in which *bhakti* and Tantric elements combine to form a very remarkable synthesis, is often of great poetic beauty.

See Also Rāmānuja.

Bibliography

For the doctrine and practices of the Vīraśaiva, and historical facts, any of the good histories of Indian religions may be consulted, for instance Jan Gonda's *Die Religionen Indiens,* vol. 2, *Der jüngere Hinduismus* (Stuttgart, 1963). The best introduction to the subject is probably *Speaking of Śiva,* translated with an introduction by A. K. Ramanujan (New York, 1973), a short but excellent anthology with very useful and perceptive commentaries. A vast collection of *vacanas* in the original text and English translation, *Śūnyasampādane,* 5 vols., edited and translated by S. S. Bhoosnurmath et al. (Hubli-Dharwar, 1965–1972), is interesting but difficult to find.

New Sources

Nandimath, Sivalingayya Channabasavayya. *Theology of the Saivagamas: A Survey of the Doctrines of Saiva Siddhanta and Veerasaivism.* Thiruvananthapuram, 2001.

André Padoux (1987)
Revised Bibliography

ŚAIVISM: NĀYAṈĀRS

The sixty-three Nāyaṉārs (c. 500–750 CE) are the early leaders (Tam., *nāyaṉār,* "lord, leader"; pl., *nāyaṉmār*) and canonized saints of the Tamil Śaivas, a Hindu sect that commands a large following in the Tamil linguistic area of South India. Along with the Vaiṣṇava Āḻvārs, the Nāyaṉārs were among the first saints of a regional, vernacular *bhakti* (devotional) tradition in Hinduism.

Preeminent among the Nāyaṉārs are Ñāṉacampantar (also called Tiruñāṉacampantar or Campantar; c. 650), Tirunāvukkaracar (also called Appar; c. 580–670) and Cuntaramūrtti (also called Nampi Ārūrar; seventh to eighth century), authors of the Tamil hymns of the *Tēvāram,* which form the first seven books of the Tamil Śaiva canon, and are sung during temple rituals. Māṇikkavācakar, author of the *Tiruvācakam* (c. ninth century), is revered as the fourth saint-teacher (*camayakuru*) of the tradition, although he is not included among the Nāyaṉārs. Next in popularity to the four poet-saints are the woman hymnist Kāraikkāl Ammaiyār (c. 550–600), Tirumūlar (c. eighth century), author of the mystical text *Tirumantiram,* and the legendary figures Kaṇṇappar and Caṇṭēcar.

The contributions of Ñāṉacampantar, Appar, and Cuntaramūrtti are embodied in their hymns, which Tamil Śaivas consider equal to the Vedas, holiest of Hindu scriptures. In the Tamil hymns—the first vernacular religious texts in Hinduism—the saints eloquently express emotional love for a personal God (Śiva), a form of religiosity new to Hinduism. The three Nāyaṉārs traveled to 260 shrines of Śiva in Tamil country and celebrated his presence in these places. The saints' emphasis on Tamil cultural elements, such as emotional love in the setting of particular places, endeared their religion to the Tamils. The *Tēvāram* helped to drive Buddhism and Jainism out of the Tamil region and to establish Tamil Śaivism as the national religion of the Tamils, patronized by the kings and practiced by the masses.

In his Tamil work *Periyapurāṇam* (The great history), the hagiographer Cēkkiḻār (c. 1135) narrates the lives of Cuntaramūrtti and the sixty-two historical and legendary saints named in a hymn (*Tēvāram* 7.39). The Nāyaṉārs came from all segments in Tamil society. The majority were from the upper castes and classes—kings, brahmans, cultivators—but the list also includes a hunter, a low-caste musician, and even an untouchable. In contrast to the traditional Hindu caste hierarchy, the saints formed an ideal society, a spiritually egalitarian community of devotees of Śiva. The extreme acts of Kaṇṇappar, who dug out his own eyes to replace the miraculously bleeding eyes of the *linga* image of Śiva that he was worshiping, and of Ciṟuttoṇṭar, who upon request cooked and served his own son to a Śaiva devotee, are dramatic yet typical examples of the pattern of the saints' lives. At the end of such episodes, Śiva reveals himself, commending the saint as an exemplary "servant" (*aṭiyār*). The lives of the Nāyaṉārs articulate the Tamil Śaiva view of devotion as love of God expressed with intensity; as emotional poetry; and as ritual service (*toṇṭu*) to God and service to his devotees, rendered with total and selfless love. To this day, Tamil Śaivas celebrate the saints by worshiping their images, singing their hymns, and retelling their lives.

SEE ALSO Māṇikkavācakar; Poetry, article on Indian Religious Poetry; Tamil Religions.

BIBLIOGRAPHY

There is no comprehensive work on the Tamil Śaiva Nāyaṉārs. Translation of the major texts relating to these saints—the *Periyapurāṇam,* the *Tēvāram* and the *Tirumantiram*—remains a desideratum, as does a systematic study of the role of the sixty-three saints in the tradition.

Among the few translations available of the *Tēvāram* hymns, Francis Kingsbury and Godfrey E. Phillips's *Hymns of the Tamil Śaivite Saints* (New York, 1921) remains the best to date; though only 79 of the 8,273 verses in the *Tēvāram* have been translated in this book, the selections are representative, accurate, poetic, and readable. H. W. Schomerus's *Śivaitische Heiligenlegenden, Periyapurāṇa und Tiruvātavūrar Purāṇa: Aus dem Tamil übersetzt* (Jena, 1925) contains a careful translation of the excellent prose summary of the *Periyapurāṇam* hagiography done by the Jaffna Tamil scholar Āṟumukanāvalar (1822–1879). M. A. Dorai Rangaswamy's *The Religion and Philosophy of Tēvāram, with Special Reference to Nampi Ārūrar* (*Sundarar*), 4 vols. in 2 (Madras, 1958–1959), is a comprehensive study of the life and hymns of Cuntaramurtti, and also includes a general discussion of Tamil Śaiva devotion and the lives of the sixty-three Nāyaṉārs. The sheer bulk and detail of this erudite study render it more useful to the scholar than to the general reader. Kamil Zvelebil has provided a stimulating and insightful analysis of the lives of the Nāyaṉārs and of the hymns of the four poet-saints as religious literature in *The Smile of Murukaṉ: On Tamil Literature of South India* (Leiden, 1973), chap. 12, "Śaiva Bhakti: Two Approaches," pp. 185–206. Two other recent essays of interest are George W. Spencer's "The Sacred Geography of the Tamil Shaivite Hymns," *Numen* 17 (December 1970): 232–244, and my article "Singing of a Place: Pilgrimage as Metaphor and Motif in the *Tēvāram* Songs of the Tamil Saivite Saints," *Journal of the American Oriental Society* 102 (January–March 1982): 69–90. The former explores the political, cultural and historical dimensions of the travels of the saints, while the latter offers translations of hitherto untranslated *Tēvāram* hymns and assesses the contribution of each of the three poet-saints to Tamil religion and culture.

New Sources

Dehejia, Vidya. *Slaves of the Lord: The Path of the Tamil Saints.* New Delhi, 1988.

INDIRA VISWANATHAN PETERSON (1987)
Revised Bibliography

ŚAIVISM: KRAMA ŚAIVISM

The term *Krama Śaivism* refers to a number of closely related mystical cults of the goddess Kali and her emanations, which, originating in Uḍḍiyāna (Swat) and Kashmir before the ninth century, propagated an idealist metaphysics that exerted a decisive influence on the Trika and thence on the Śrīvidyā. The Krama rituals and their wild, skull-decked, often theriomorphic deities place them within the Kāpālika culture of the cremation grounds.

The branch of Krama scriptures that originated in Uḍḍiyāna (of these, manuscripts survive of the *Devīpañcaśataka, Kramasadbhāva, Devīdvyardhaśatikā,* and *Yonigahvara Tantra*) has assimilated Kaulism and so professes to have distanced itself from this Kāpālika background. Nonetheless, several Krama *gurus* in Kashmir, though they followed these scriptures, were Kāpālika ascetics, while in the other major scriptural source of the Krama, the Kashmirian *Jayadrathayāmala,* the reforming influence of Kaulism is absent and the Kāpālika context of the Krama is vividly described. Here it is seen that the Krama arose within a tradition of Kali worship principally concerned with Kāpālika rites of spontaneous and controlled possession. The concept of possession developed into that of an enlightenment in which social individuality, with its constituent belief in a world of external powers and in the objectivity of Brahmanical criteria of purity, is displaced by the radiant expansion of Kālī from within as an impersonal, value-free, and infinite power of consciousness that projects and resorbs the universe within itself.

All forms of the Krama ritual are designed to induce this liberating intrinsicism through assimilative worship of Kālī (the true Self) in and as a "sequence" (*krama*) of sets of divine powers. This "sequence" embodies all the phases through which this cyclical dynamism manifests itself in the microcosm of the individual's cognition, as it fills and empties itself from moment to moment in the flux of experience. Thus in its commonest form the Krama ritual culminates in the worship of a sequence of deities that successively encodes the projection of content, immersion in content, retraction of content into the state of latent impression within the subject, and finally the dissolution of these subjective impressions in the implosion of consciousness into its pristine, nondiscursive potentiality. In some traditions, pure luminosity (*bhāsā*) is worshiped as a fifth phase englobing these four as its creative vibrancy. Fortifying this gnostic ritual with the expansive joy of caste-free sexual union and the consumption of wine, flesh, and the impurities of the body, the initiate penetrates through the inhibition of external values and the rebirth-generating bondage of self-awareness that this inhibition entails, thereby attaining the conviction that his individualized consciousness is but the spontaneous play of these universal powers. No longer enslaved by the appearance of subjection to the not-self in consciousness, he achieves liberation within the very flow of extroverted cognition.

This neo-Kāpālika mysticism of the Krama reached its highest theoretical and liturgical coherence in Kashmir in the preceptorial lineage of Jñānanetranatha (fl. c. 850–900). Emerging out of the Krama of Uḍḍiyāna, the outstanding works of this Kashmirian tradition are three texts, each entitled *Mahānayaprakāśa* (Illumination of the Great Doctrine), one anonymous (between 1000 and 1200) and the others by Arṇasiṃha (fl. c. 1050–1100) and Śitikaṇṭha (fifteenth century?). While remaining a distinct sectarian tradition, the

Krama strongly influenced the Trika, the other major Śaiva soteriology in Kashmir. Krama deities were incorporated into the core of the Trika pantheon in the second phase of Trika, and in its third phase the *gurus* who propagated the Pratyabhijñā (in the tenth century) took initiations in the lineage of Jñananetranātha. It is probable that this Krama background inspired their idealist nondualism. Among them Abhinavagupta contributed to the literature of the independent Krama, while his better-known exegesis of the Trika attempts to show that the Trika's categories contain the Krama as their essence. The independent Krama, influenced in turn by the Pratyabhijñā, spread in the twelfth century to the Śaiva centers of the far South. Of this phase there are the *Mahārthamañjarī* (Flower-cluster of the Great Doctrine) by Maheśvārananda of Cidambaram (fl. c. 1175–1225) and the *Cidgaganacandrikā* (Moonlight of the sky of consciousness) by Śrīvatsa, probably of Śucīndram (between 1075 and 1150).

Apart from these Kashmirian and southern developments, forms of the Krama flourished outside Kashmir as the basis of the cult of the goddess Guhyakālī. The earliest and richest work of this tradition is the *Kālīkulakramārcana* of Vimalaprabodha (before 1000), drawing on both the tradition of Uḍḍiyāna and that of the *Jayadrathayāmala.* Many liturgical texts of this branch of the Krama survive in the Kathmandu valley, where the cult of Guhyakālī (often identified with Guhyeśvarī, the principal local goddess) has continued into modern times. It is also to the Śaiva Newars of Nepal that is owed the preservation of manuscripts of the Krama scriptures, which are mentioned and quoted by the early authors of Kashmir but have not survived there.

See Also Abhinavagupta.

Bibliography

Rastogi, Navjivan. *The Krama Tantricism of Kashmir,* vol. 1. Delhi, 1979.

Silburn, Lilian, trans. *Hymnes aux Kāli: La roue des énergies divines.* Publications de l'Institut de Civilisation Indienne, fasc. 40. Paris, 1975.

Silburn, Lilian, trans. *La Mahārthamañjarī de Maheśvarānanda, avec des extraits du Parimala.* Publications de l'Institut de Civilisation Indienne, fasc. 29. Paris, 1968.

Alexis Sanderson (1987)

ŚAIVISM: TRIKA ŚAIVISM

The Śaivas of the Trika tradition were the principal propagators of the nondualist idealism that flourished in Kashmir from about 900 CE. Although all the known exegetical literature of the Trika is Kashmirian or inspired by Kashmirian authors, there are reasons to doubt that the tradition was Kashmirian in origin. The earliest and probably pre-Kashmirian phase of its development is seen in the *Siddhayogeśvarīmata Tantra,* the *Mālinīvijayottara Tantra,* and the *Tantrasadbhāva Tantra.* These Tantras lack the exegetes' doctrine that the world is the projection in and of consciousness, and their liturgies and yogic systems share the absence of the goddess Kālī/Kālasaṃkarṣiṇi, whose cult was later central to the Trika.

In the earlier period (probably before 800 CE) Trika Śaivism is defined by a system of ritual whose goal is the assimilation of the power of a "triad" (*trika*) of goddesses, Parā, Parāparā, and Aparā, the first benevolent, the other two wild and terrifying, garlanded with skulls and brandishing the *khatvāṅga,* the skull-topped staff of the Kāpālikas. Associated with the cult of these sect-defining deities was that of the eight mother goddesses and their embodiments in "clans" (*kula*) of *yoginīs*. The latter are both supernatural apparitions and human females considered to be permanently possessed by the mother goddesses. They were to be invoked and/or placated with offerings of blood, flesh, wine, and sexual fluids by power-seeking adepts whose affinity with one or other of these clans was divined at the time of initiation.

This cult of supernatural power through the manipulation of impurity incorporated Kālī in the second phase of its development, first alone, as the transcendental goddess immanent in the original three as her emanations (this is seen in the *Devyāyāmala Tantra* and in parts of the *Jayadrathayāmala Tantra*), and then accompanied by the pantheon of Krama Śaivism's cycle of cognition, as in the *Trikasadbhāva Tantra* and *Trikahṛdaya Tantra.* Since the Krama originated in the far Northwest, it is probable that this second phase of the Trika developed in Kashmir.

The third phase of the Trika (from c. 900 CE), represented principally by the *Tantrāloka, Mālinīvijayavārtika,* and *Parātriṃśikāvivaraṇa* of Abhinavagupta, shows the tradition competing with the Śaiva Siddhānta for authority within the mainstream of Kashmirian Śaivism. Equipped in the Pratyabhijñā with a respectable metaphysics, it distanced itself from the visionary, power-orientated world of the early Trika. Its sect-defining rituals are directed inward to self-contemplation in unmotivated performance, so that in principle they can be abandoned when gnostic self-cultivation no longer requires their support.

Behind this level of Tantric ritual, which gave the sect its broad base in the Śaiva community, this phase of the Trika preserved, as the cult of the virtuosi, a variety of the erotico-mystical Kaulism associated with the perhaps mythical saint Macchanda (also known as Matsyendranātha). This tradition had its roots in the cult of the clans of the eight mother goddesses seen in the first phase of the Trika, in related Śaiva cults (e.g., that of the *Picumatabrahmayāmala Tantra*), and in Buddhist adaptations in the Heruka Tantras, but broke away from this substratum by rejecting the external aspects of the culture of the cremation grounds. This trend toward mystical interiorization is extremely marked in the Trika Kaulism of Abhinavagupta, who propagated a meta-aesthetics in which orgasm with the consecrated female partner or "messenger" (*dūtī*)—the key moment of higher Kaula practice—was to reveal the all-containing dynamism of the absolute self radiating in blissful consciousness as the reality embodied and less directly perceived in the structure of its divine powers worshiped by lesser adepts in the Tantric and preliminary Kaula rituals.

Distinctive of the third phase of the Trika are (1) the doctrine of the co-essentiality of the "triad" (*trika*) of the individual (*aṇu* or *nara*), cosmic power (*śakti*), and the ground of *śakti*, Śiva; (2) the equation of the worship of the three goddesses in their Kali-ground with liberating awareness of the unity in pure consciousness of (a) precognitive impulse, cognition, and action, (b) object, medium, and agent of cognition, and (c) projection of, immersion in, and retraction of content in consciousness; (3) the ascent through the three means of salvation: the *āṇava* (through action, both ritual and yogic), the *śākta* (through the gradual intensification of a purely intellectual representation of reality toward its self-transcendence in nondiscursive revelation), and the *śāmbhava* (self-realization unmediated by thought, in the inner vibrancy of the precognitive impulse); (4) the hierarchy of seven levels of the contraction of the self, from the Śiva-mode to that of the individual; and (5) the claim to catholicity: The third phase of the Trika claims to be the summation of and key to all Śaiva traditions, both "orthodox" (i.e., Śaiva Siddhānta) and "heterodox" (i. e., the Bhairavatantras, Kaulism, and the Krama). After Abhinavagupta and his pupil Kṣemarāja, the third phase of the Trika spread to the Tamil country. There it provided the theoretical basis for and influenced the form of the cult of Śrīvidya.

See Also Abhinavagupta.

Bibliography

Abhinavagupta. *Tantraloka.* Translated by Raniero Gnoli as *Luce delle sacre scritture—Tantraloka.* Turin, 1972.

Abhinavagupta. *Tantrasara.* Translated by Raniero Gnoli as *Essenza del Tantra.* Turin, 1979.

Padoux, André. *Recherches sur la symbolique et l'énergie de la parole dans certains textes tantriques.* Publications de l'Institut de Civilisation Indienne, fasc. 21. Paris, 1963.

Sanderson, Alexis. "Maṇḍala and Agamic Identity in the Trika of Kashmir." In *Mantras et diagrammes rituels dans l'hindouisme,* edited by André Padoux. Paris, 1986.

Alexis Sanderson (1987)

ŚAIVISM: ŚAIVISM IN KASHMIR

From the second half of the ninth century CE, Tantric Śaivism in Kashmir advanced in various forms into the front line of Brahmanical thinking. Learned authors superimposed upon roughly homogenous groups of scriptural traditions uniform systems of metaphysics and soteriology that could be defended not only against each other but also against the major non-Śaiva doctrines of the time. By the tenth century the Śaiva scene was dominated by the confrontation of two radically opposed schools: on the one hand, a group of nondualistic traditions, principally the Trika and the Krama, and on the other, the dualistic Śaiva Siddhānta. The nondualists, upholding the doctrine that the world and persons are no more than the play of the power of a universal consciousness-self, operated from within transgressive cults "tainted" by the Kāpālika culture of the cremation grounds and the erotico-mystical soteriology of the Kaulas. The Kashmirian Śaiva Siddhānta sealed itself off from these "impure," visionary traditions. It sustained a "pure" cult of Śiva, based on the twenty-eight Āgamas, with a soteriology that subordinated gnosis to the ritual praxis of indissolubly individual agents, claiming, moreover, that this praxis was entirely compatible with orthodox Brahmanical duty and caste purity.

The outstanding authors of this conservative Śaivism were Nārāyaṇakaṇṭha (fl. c. 950–1025 CE) and his son Rāmakaṇṭha. The most outstanding work is the latter's *Nareśvaraparīkṣāprakāśa.* The rise of the nondualist theology that opposed the Śaiva Siddhānta began with Vasugupta and his pupil Kallaṭa (fl. c. 850–900), was philosophically refined by Somānanda (fl. c. 900–950) and his pupil Utpaladeva, and culminated in the monumental works of Abhinavagupta and his pupil Kśemarāja (fl. c. 1000–1050). This tradition also sought to accommodate orthodox life, but by a different route. While the dualists adapted Śaivism to the orthodox view of the castebound ritual agent, the nondualists offered the initiate an esoteric self concealed within his perceived individuality, a blissful, transindividual consciousness which, being the cause and substance of all phenomena, could be seen as freely assuming the appearance of his limitation by an "outside world" and its values, as though it were an actor playing a role. Behind this outer conformity the Śaiva householder initiated into the Trika could experience the power of transcendence through contemplative worship that involved not only consumption of meat and wine but—in the case of the elite of *vīra*s ("heroes")—sexual intercourse.

This nondualistic tradition with its relatively sect-neutral metaphysics has generally been called Kashmir Śaivism. This term, however, obscures the fact that in the tenth and eleventh centuries, the period of most of the existing Śaiva literature, it was the Śaiva Siddhānta that was the dominant Śaiva doctrine (*jñāna*) in Kashmir, whereas the principal Śaiva cult in that region was then, as it has remained, neither that of the Śaiva Siddhānta nor that of the Trika or Krama. Rather it was the worship of Svacchandabhairava and his consort Aghoreśvarī, a form of Śaivism that falls between these two extremes. Naturally, the two schools competed for authority over this middle ground. The Śaiva Siddhānta had propagated a dualistic and socially conservative exegesis of its principal scripture, the *Svacchanda Tantra,* which Kśemarāja countered from within the newly consolidated nondualism in his own, subsequently authoritative commentary.

The new nondualism also entered the Kaula cult of the goddess Tripurasundarī, or Śrīvidyā, which rose to eminence in Kashmir during the eleventh century. This Kashmirian tradition of the Śrīvidyā, which by the twelfth century had spread to the Tamil country, came to be adopted in Trika circles with the result that the Trika became less a system of Tantric worship than a matrix of metaphysics and soteriological theory. Outstanding representatives of this Trika-based Śrīvidyā in Kashmir were Jayaratha (fl. c. 1225–1275), Sāhib Kaula (b. 1629), Śivopādhyāya (fl. c. 1725–1775), and Harabhaṭṭa (1874–1951). The cult of Tripurasundarī also permeated the worship of the local family goddesses of Kashmir (Jvālāmukhī, Śārikā, Rājñī, Bālā, etc.). Indeed, she was generally seen as the archetype and source of all the goddesses enshrined in the valley.

Although Trika ritual seems largely to have been replaced by that of the Śrīvidyā, that of the Krama retained its vigor, being preserved in such late texts as the *Mahānayaprakāśa* of Śitikaṇṭha, the *Chummasaṃpradāya,* and the *Śivarātrirahasya* of Nityasvatantra, in which Krama ritual is seen to play an important role in the annual Śivarātri festival. It is also probable that a related tradition based on the *Mādhavakula* of the *Jayadrathayāmala Tantra* and worshiping Kālī as the consort of Narasiṃha, the man-lion incarnation of Viṣṇu, survived into the late Middle Ages. At present, nondualist Śaiva doctrine and some techniques of meditation continue to be accessible to the brahmans of the valley, but the tradition of Tantric ritual maintained by the priests (*gōrini*) through the centuries of Muslim rule has declined to such an extent that it faces imminent extinction.

See Also Abhinavagupta; Tantrism.

Bibliography

Abhinavagupta. *Tantrāloka.* Translated by Raniero Gnoli as *Luce delle sacre scritture—Tantrāloka.* Turin, 1972.

Pandey, Kanti Chandra. *Abhinavagupta: An Historical and Philosophical Study.* 2d ed., rev. & enl. Varanasi, 1963.

Sanderson, Alexis. "Purity and Power among the Brahmans of Kashmir." In *The Category of the Person,* edited by Michael Carrithers, Steven Collins, and Steven Lukes. Cambridge, 1986.

New Sources

Dehejia, Harsha V. *Parvatidarpana: An Exposition of Kasmir Saivism through the Images of Siva and Parvati.* Delhi, 1997.

Muller-Ortega, Paul Eduardo. *The Triadic Heart of Siva: Kaula Tantricism of Abhinavagupta in the Non-Dual Shaivism of Kashmir.* Albany, 1989.

Pandita, Balajinnatha. *History of Kashmir Saivism.* Srinagar, Kashmir, 1989.

Alexis Sanderson (1987)
Revised Bibliography

ŚAIVISM: PRATYABHIJÑĀ

The Pratyabhijñā system of thought is part of what is called Kashmir Śaivism, a name applied to nondualist forms of Śaivism that flourished approximately between the ninth and thirteenth centuries in Kashmir and other parts of northern India but also elsewhere. The importance of the Pratyabhijñā in nondualist Śaivism is underscored by the fact that Mādhava (fourteenth century), in the *Sarvadarśanasaṃgraha,* a classical work on Indian religious and philosophical systems, describes this school as Pratyabhijñā. The doctrine was first formulated systematically by Somānanda (ninth century?) in his *Śivadṛṣṭi,* then by his disciple Utpaladeva in the *Īśvarapratyabhijñākārikā* (Verses on the Recognition of God) and in a subsequent commentary (*Vṛtti*) on them. It was further elaborated by Abhinavagupta (tenth to eleventh century) in two important commentaries, the *Īśvarapratyabhijñā Vimarśinī* and the *Īśvarapratyabhijñā Vivṛttivimarśinī.* Abhinavagupta's disciple Kṣemarāja gave a short and clear exposition of this doctrine in the *Pratyabhijñāhṛdaya.* These treatises, all from Kashmir, rank among the main Indian philosophical works.

The term *pratyabhijñā* is usually translated as "recognition." The word has been explained as knowledge (*jñāna*) of an object to which one turns back (*prati*) and which then faces (*abhi*) the knower. It is the knowledge regained of the identity of the individual self and of the world with the Supreme Source of all.

For this school, to quote Kṣemarāja, "it is the divine Consciousness alone, self-shining absolute free will, that flashes forth in the form of the multitudinous universe": It is the unique cause, the inner reality and the substratum of cosmic manifestation, which it projects as a shining forth (*ābhāsa*) on itself as on a screen. This consciousness, Śiva, is the one absolute reality. The world is insubstantial—though not illusory, for it is, in its ultimate nature, of the same stuff as consciousness, from which it has evolved and with which it remains merged. But this identity is hidden because of the action of *māyāśakti,* the limiting and obnubilating power of Śiva. The world, in such a vision, exists only as a kind of cosmic oblivion of reality, hence the role of recognition through which the "forgotten" truth is rediscovered. *Pratyabhijñā* is not remembrance, however. It does not result from memory, despite the important metaphysical role of remembrance—*smaraṇa*—in nondualist Śaivism, but from a synthetic activity of the mind that destroys the misconceptions veiling the real nature of the supreme Self and finally brings one to realize the truth: "I am Śiva, the only true consciousness, omniscient, the only active power of the universe."

This knowledge, brought about by intense spiritual concentration (*bhāvanā*) and with the necessary help of God's grace (*anugraha* or *śaktipāta,* the "descent of divine energy"), is attained by the yogin after having reached the state of *samādhi,* where the yogin experiences a merging with (*samāveśa*) or a unifying contemplation of (*samāpatti*) the Supreme. It is said to shine as an intuitive vision (*pratibhā*), destroying all illusion. When this state becomes permanent, the yogin is freed from all bondage and is totally identified with Śiva, master of the whole cosmic process. The highest cosmic bliss (*jagadānanda*) is then experienced while one is still in life (*jīvanmukti*); it is a state in which empirical awareness and perfect transcendental consciousness coincide.

SEE ALSO Abhinavagupta.

BIBLIOGRAPHY

A short and useful book on the subject is Kṣemarāja's *Pratyabhijñāhṛdayam, Saṃskṛta Text with English Translation and Notes,* 2d ed., edited and translated by Jaideva Singh (Delhi, 1977). Abhinavagupta's *Īśvarapratyabhijñāvimarśinī* has been translated "in the light of the Bhāskarī"—that is, in the spirit of a later commentary, by one Bhāskara—by Kanti Chandra Pandey in *Bhāskarī,* vol. 3 (Lucknow, 1954).

ANDRÉ PADOUX (1987)

ŚAIVISM: PĀŚUPATAS

The Pāśupatas were possibly the earliest, and certainly one of the most influential, of the Hindu religious sects dedicated to the god Śiva. The probable founder of this sect was called Lakulīśa, meaning "the lord [*īśa*] with the club [*lakula*]." According to several of the Purāṇas, and other sources as well, Lakulīśa was an incarnation of Śiva, who entered a human body in the village of Kāyāvataraṇa or Kāyārohaṇa, located in western India near the city of Broach. He had four disciples named (with variants) Kuśika, Gārgya, Kauruṣa, and Maitreya. Each of them established an important genealogy of religious preceptors. An inscription from Mathura of 380 CE mentions a Śaiva *guru* who was tenth in descent from Kuśika. Assuming that this Kuśika was his direct disciple, Lakulīśa must have lived in about the first half of the second century.

The Pāśupata sect seems to have died out by about the end of the fifteenth century. Nonetheless, its doctrines and practices are reasonably well known from two surviving Pāśupata texts: the *Gaṇakārikā,* attributed to Haradatta, with a commentary attributed to Bhāsarvajña (tenth century), and the *Pāśupata Sūtra,* with the commentary of Kauṇḍinya. Both of these texts are cited by Sāyaṇa-Mādhava (fourteenth century) in the chapter on this sect in his *Sarvadarśanasaṃgraha.* The influence of the Pāśupatas is evident in several Śaiva Purāṇas and in the late *Atharvaśiras Upaniṣad,* but the Pāśupata doctrines and practices described in these works differ considerably from those of the *Gaṇakārikā* and *Pāśupata Sūtra.*

The Pāśupatas were quite influential over much of South India from about the seventh to fourteenth centuries. The Kālamukhas, a closely related sect that also traced its foundation to Lakulīśa, controlled many temples and monasteries in the Karnataka region of the South during much of the same period. The ascetics of both sects actively participated in the revival of Śaivism that virtually eliminated Jainism and Buddhism from South India and competed successfully with the rival Hindu Vaiṣṇavas as well. As a result, even today Śiva remains the principal god of the Hindus of this region.

According to the *Pāśupata Sūtra,* the doctrine of the sect is based on the analysis of five major topics: effect (*kāraṇa*), or the created universe; cause (*kārya*), namely God; union (*yoga*), the purposeful association of the individual soul with God; observance (*vidhi*), ascetic and devotional practice; and end of sorrow (*duḥkhānta*), or salvation. The *Gaṇakārikā* describes five different stages (*avasthā*) in the adept's spiritual progress, each connected with a particular place, strength, impurity, purification, procedure, attainment, and aspect of initiation. In the first, "marked" (*vyakta*) stage, the adept stays with his *guru* in a temple. In an act typical of Śaiva ascetics he daily "bathes" in ashes and offers six different acts of worship dedicated to Śiva. In the second, "unmarked" (*avyakta*) stage, he leaves the temple to live among ordinary people and engages in the curious practices called "doors" (*dvāra*), the aim of which is to earn the active contempt of the uninitiated populace. These practices include walking about as if sick or crippled, making "amorous" gestures toward women, and acting and talking as if without any wits. The ascetics thereby pass their own bad *karman* to their unsuspecting revilers while at the same time absorbing these revilers' good *karman.* The remaining three stages are basically progressive levels of spiritual enlightenment unrelated to external behavior.

As in the possibly related doctrine of the Saiva Siddhantins, the Pāśupatas make an ontological distinction between the individual soul (*paśu*), God (*pati*), and the fetters of this world (*pāśa*). Their basic metaphysical position is thus both dualist and monotheistic. The grace of God is believed to be essential for salvation, which is conceived of as an intimate association of the soul with Śiva (*Rudrāsayujya*). Several Pāśupata theologians were renowned as logicians (*naiyāyikas*).

BIBLIOGRAPHY

A documented review of modern scholarship on the Pāśupatas is found in my study *The Kāpālikas and Kālāmukhas: Two Lost Śaivite Sects* (Berkeley, Calif., 1972). See also *The Pāśupata-sūtram with Pañchārtha-Bhāṣya of Kauṇḍinya,* translated by Haripada Chakraborti (Calcutta, 1970). The critical translation by Minoru Hara of the Pāśupata chapter of Sāyaṇa-Mādhava's *Sarvadarśanasaṃgraha* in *Indo-Iranian Journal* 2 (1958): 8–32, is excellent on Pāśupata doctrine and practice.

New Sources

Hara, Minoru. *Pasupata Studies.* Publications of the De Nobili Research Library v. 30. Vienna, 2002.

DAVID N. LORENZEN (1987)
Revised Bibliography

ŚAIVISM: KĀPĀLIKAS

In the South Indian text *Periya Purāṇam* by Cekkilar (c. 1100), a Śaiva ascetic visits the home of a seventh-century householder-saint, one of the sixty-three Nāyaṉārs, and demands to be fed with the flesh of the saint's only son. With limitless devotional zeal, the saint promptly beheads his young son, helps his wife prepare a curry of their son's flesh, and finally agrees even to join the ascetic in the gruesome feast. At the last moment the cruel guest disappears and the sacrificed son returns to life. The ascetic reveals himself to be none other than the god Śiva come to test his devotee. This legend is typical of those associated with the Kāpālikas, or Bearers of the Skull (*kapāla*), a heterodox Śaiva sect often accused of both necrophilic and orgiastic practices.

The true character of the Kāpālika sect is difficult to determine since it is known almost exclusively from the text of its opponents, especially from dramatic works such as the *Prabodhacandrodaya* of Kṛṣṇamiśra (c. 1050–1100) and the *Mattavilāsa* of Mahendravarman (c. 600–630), and from the hagiographies of the great theologian Śaṅkarācārya written by Mādhavācārya (c. 1700?), Anantānandagiri (c. 1400?), and others. It is even possible to suppose that the Kāpālika sect has been created by these authors to personify the varied groups of unorthodox and Tantric ascetics who worshiped the god Śiva. There does, however, exist sufficient evidence to indicate the probable historical reality of a specific Kāpālika sect between about the fifth and fifteenth centuries CE.

First, the Kāpālikas, sometimes also called Kapālins or Mahāvratins, are frequently mentioned as one of the four principal religious sects dedicated to the god Śiva. The historical existence and importance of the others—the Pāśupatas, Kālāmukhas, and Śaiva Siddhāntins—is beyond doubt. Second, two inscriptions from western India, dating from the seventh and eleventh centuries, record donations to what must have been Kāpālika ascetics. In the first inscription the recipients of the gifts are described as Mahāvratins who reside in the temple of Kāpāleśvara, Lord of the Kāpālas; in the second the recipient is described as a Mahāvratin ascetic who is "like the Kapālin Śaṅkara in bodily form." This Kapālin is none other than Śiva in the form of a Kāpālika ascetic. The myth of Śiva-Kapālin is the third and most important basis for supposing the existence of a specific Kāpālika sect, since this myth evidently serves as the archetypal model for the religious practices of the ascetic members of the sect. The myth is not clearly referred to in texts earlier than the Purāṇas (c. 200–1300), but it is indirectly linked to the early Vedic myth of the conflict between the gods Prajāpati and Rudra and to the *Mahābhārata* myth of Rāma Rāghava and the sage Mahodara.

The Puranic myth of Śiva-Kapālin begins with an argument between Śiva and the creator god, Brahmā. The upshot of the dispute is that Śiva removes one of the five heads of Brahmā and thereby is afflicted with the sin of *brahmahatyā*, the killing of a brahman. To free himself from this sin, symbolically represented by the skull of Brahmā sticking to his left hand, Śiva must undertake a twelve-year penance, wandering about in the guise of a Kāpālika ascetic who uses the skull as a begging bowl. This penance is known as the Great Vow (*mahāvrata*), and Śiva consequently becomes a Mahāvratin (Follower of the Great Vow). The penance is eventually completed in Banaras, the holy city of Śiva, at the sacred bathing place (*tīrtha*) on the Ganges called Kapālamocana, where the skull finally falls from his hand.

The descriptions of human Kāpālika ascetics likewise conform to those of the Kapālin form of Śiva. They wander about with a skull begging-bowl, their bodies smeared with ashes, wearing bone or skull ornaments and loincloths of animal skin, with their hair in matted locks. They sometimes carry a special club called a *khaṭvāṅga,* consisting of a skull mounted on a stick.

In none of this is there any suggestion of orgiastic behavior. Nonetheless, the more heterodox Śaiva sects generally are associated with the religious current known as Tantrism, which does feature rites that break, either symbolically or in fact, orthodox socioreligious injunctions concerning both food and sex. The best known of such rites is that of the five *ma* sounds (*pañcamakāra*) in which the devotee partakes of liquor (*madya*), meat (*māṃsa*), fish (*matsya*), parched grain (*mudrā*), and coition (*maithuna*). Kāpālika ascetics are frequently regarded as libidinous hypocrites who practice the Tantric reversals of conventional morality on a daily basis.

In Tantric cults, salvation (*mukti*) is often imagined as a state of bliss homologous to the bliss of the sexual union of Śiva and Pārvatī. The doctrine of the Kāpālikas is usually called Soma Siddhanta, a term that is traditionally explained as the doctrine (*siddhānta*) of Śiva united with his wife Uma (*sa-umā*).

BIBLIOGRAPHY

My study *The Kāpālikas and Kālāmukhas: Two Lost Saivite Sects* (Berkeley, Calif., 1972) attempts a full reconstruction of Kāpālika history, practice, and doctrine. An excellent treatment of the myth of Śiva-Kapālin is found in Wendy Doniger O'Flaherty's *The Origins of Evil in Hindu Mythology* (Berkeley, Calif., 1976).

DAVID N. LORENZEN (1987)

SAKA RELIGION SEE SCYTHIAN RELIGION

ŚAKTI SEE KUṆḌALINĪ; TANTRISM

SAKYA PAṆḌITA (SA SKYA PAṆḌITA)

(1182–1251). The religious culture of Tibet came to be characterized, from the thirteenth century on, by a remarkable emphasis not just upon Buddhist thought and practice, but also upon a broad range of Indian learning sometimes only indirectly related to the study of Indian Buddhism *per se.* The broadening of Tibetan cultural horizons that this entailed may be traced directly to the considerable influence of the renowned monastic scholar Sa skya Paṇḍita.

HIS LIFE. Sa skya Paṇḍita (the "*paṇḍit* from Sa skya"), whose proper name was Kun dga' rgyal mtshan (Kunga Gyaltsen), was born in 1182 as the son of Dpal chen 'od po, a scion of the ruling 'Khon family of the principality of Sa skya in southwestern Tibet. During the preceding century, his forebears had already established a reputation for Sa skya as an important seat of Buddhist learning and a major center for the promulgation of the esoteric system of the Tantras. He was accordingly educated in these traditions under the tutelage of his uncle, Grags pa rgyal mtshan (Trakpa Gyaltsen, 1147–1216), a renowned lay scholar and adept. During his mid-teens, he came to be regarded as a master of the familial legacy and, advised by his uncle, left Sa skya to continue his studies under a variety of masters of the major Indian Buddhist philosophical and doctrinal treatises, concentrating in particular upon epistemology and Madhyamaka dialectical thought.

In 1204 the Kashmiri master Śākyaśrībhadra (d. 1225) arrived in Tibet accompanied by an entourage of Indian scholars. Sa skya Paṇḍita was one of a number of up-and-coming Tibetan clerics who were inspired by this opportunity to learn directly from knowledgeable Indian teachers and he invited one of them, Sugataśrī, to return with him to Sa skya. For a period of three years (1205–1207), Sa skya Paṇḍita applied himself to mastering Sanskrit grammar and other aspects of Sanskrit linguistic and literary learning, a training that would lend a notably "Indological" perspective to his scholarship in later years. In 1208 he again met Śākyaśrībhadra and received the full monastic ordination of a *bhikṣu* from him, an event that traditionally is held to mark the inception of the Sa skya pa as a properly monastic order. For the next five years he continued to study a broad range of Buddhist textual traditions under Śākyaśrībhadra and the other members of his entourage. Following the death of his uncle Grags pa rgyal mtshan in 1216, Sa skya Paṇḍita came to be recognized as the leading successor within the religious tradition of Sa skya.

For the three decades that follow, the exact chronology of Sa skya Paṇḍita's life is obscure, though it is clear that it was during this time that he was most active as a teacher and author, achieving widespread fame in Tibetan learned circles. At some point—it remains unclear just when—he traveled to the Tibet-Nepal frontier, where he is said to have engaged in debate and soundly defeated a Hindu ascetic named Haranandin. The story of their dispute, though only thinly documented in early sources, later became a popular tale of magical warfare in which Sa skya Paṇḍita had to call upon the services of a Rnying ma (Nyingma) pa sorcerer in order to vanquish his opponent, who was about to fly miraculously into Tibet.

A real threat to Tibet, however, did emerge during the last years of Sa skya Paṇḍita's life: the Mongol descendants of Chinggis Khan, having conquered much of Eurasia, began to direct their armies toward Tibet, where an incursion was made in 1239. Sa skya Paṇḍita's preeminence came to the attention of the Mongol ruler Godan Khan not long after this, and in 1244 the latter summoned him to the court, effectively to negotiate Tibet's submission. Traveling with his young nephews, 'Phags pa (Phagpa, who would later become the preceptor of Khubilai Khan) and Phyag na, he arrived in Liangzhou (in modern Gansu) in 1246 and met the Khan early the following year. Tibet, as a result, became one of the few lands to enter into the Mongol empire through negotiation, without subjection to the horrors of invasion, the Sa skya pa emerging as Tibet's rulers for the century that followed. These developments, however, occurring gradually over roughly two decades, were not the immediate outcome of Sa skya Paṇḍita's mission to Godan Khan, which nevertheless provided a precedent for the Sa skya pa-Mongol alliance.

Sa skya Paṇḍita passed away in Liangzhou in 1251. Besides the fame he enjoyed among later generations of Tibetans, the Mongolian peoples have also honored him as one of the first Buddhist masters to introduce them to the faith that in later times they adopted.

MAJOR WRITINGS. Sa skya Paṇḍita's writings are known today primarily through the standard, Sde dge (Derge) xylographic edition of his collected works in three volumes, published during the mid-1730s and containing a total of over one hundred individual texts ranging from short poems to extended systematic treatises. Though by no means a large corpus for an important Tibetan author, Sa skya Paṇḍita's oeuvre is nevertheless noteworthy for the diversity of the subjects treated, as for the unusual influence his major writings have had throughout much of Tibetan intellectual and literary history. Recent Tibetan bibliographical scholarship has revealed some additional works preserved only in manuscript that may be securely attributed to Sa skya Paṇḍita's authorship, while at the same time a number of texts included in the Sde dge edition have been shown to be pseudepigraphical. Most notorious among the latter is a substantial work, the *Gzhung lugs legs bshad* (Excellent exposition of textual traditions), that appears to have been inserted in the standard edition on the mistaken assumption that it was to be identified with Sa skya Paṇḍita's still lost treatise on Buddhist philosophical systems.

Among the many notable writings that are presently available, it is the *Mkhas pa 'jug pa'i sgo* (Scholar's gate) that comes closest to setting forth a general program representing Sa skya Paṇḍita's ideals of Sanskritic learning. He presents here the exposition of a trivium based upon the mastery of composition, rhetoric, and debate, and in the first chapter, on composition, he supplies a series of short, fine surveys of the elements of grammar and poetics, including the theory of designation and meaning, and a relatively detailed introduction to the topics of aesthetic sentiment and poetic ornament. His promulgation in Tibet of Indian literary conventions is further represented by his *Legs bshad rin chen gter mdzod* (Jewel mine of aphorisms), perhaps his most famous work, a collection of short verses, many of which were culled from Indian books of ethical and political admonition. Sa skya Paṇḍita's pithy Tibetan renditions have achieved proverbial status and even today are frequently cited from memory.

Indian traditions of logic and epistemology (*pramāṇa*) figured prominently among his major concerns. Among his key contributions here was the final redaction of the Tibetan translation of Dharmakīrti's masterwork, the *Pramāṇavārttika,* henceforth the basis for all Tibetan scholarship in this field. His own synthesis of Indian Buddhist epistemology, the *Tshad ma rigs gter* (Treasury of epistemic reason), enjoys a singularly extensive commentarial tradition in later Tibetan scholasticism and is said to have been the sole Tibetan philosophical work ever translated into Sanskrit (though no proof of this has so far emerged).

Sa skya Paṇḍita's Buddhist doctrinal writings are represented by his *Thub pa dgongs gsal* (Clarification of the sage's intention), providing a comprehensive guide to the path of the *bodhisattva* according to the major scriptures and treatises of the Indian Mahāyāna. His *Sdom gsum rnam dbye* (Analysis of the three vows) is perhaps his most controversial work, in which he sets forth trenchant criticisms of doctrinal and exegetic developments in Tibet, organized according to the three major Buddhist ethical and disciplinary codes, those of the monastic Vinaya, the path of the *bodhisattva,* and the esoteric Tantras. His foremost target, considered in others of his writings as well, was the notion of an "immediate entry" (*cig car 'jug pa*) into enlightenment, which he often characterized as the "Chinese Great Perfection" (Rgya nag Rdzogs chen), referring to the Chan traditions attributed to the eighth-century Heshang Moheyan. His remarks about this, together with his frequent critical asides, have earned Sa skya Paṇḍita something of the reputation of a pugnacious author of polemics. Nevertheless, given the restraint and the aesthetic refinement characterizing much of his writing, such an assessment appears overly to exaggerate the importance of just one aspect of his work.

The diversity of Sa skya Paṇḍita's interests is reflected by his *Rol mo'i bstan bcos* (Treatise on music), a rare example of musicological writing by a Tibetan Buddhist author. Its discussions of the Buddhist ritual use of the drum may offer some insights into now otherwise lost Indian Buddhist liturgical music. Others among his works offer contributions to Sanskrit lexicography and poetic meter, Tantric ritual and meditation, as well as several epistles responding to particular queries on the part of Tibetan contemporaries.

INTELLECTUAL LEGACY. Sa skya Paṇḍita influenced the later development of Tibetan culture significantly. His studies of Sanskrit and Indian linguistic and literary learning convinced him, on the one hand, that there was an intrinsic value to such studies, which formed the basis of a classical Indian education. On the other hand, he believed that the Tibetans frequently erred in their understanding of Indian Buddhist works in Tibetan translation precisely because they had lost site of the cultural and linguistic context of the originals. Sanskritic learning, in short, was to be valued for its roles both in the cultivation of personal refinement and in the hermeneutics of the Buddhist religion. With variations, these guiding ideas would be taken up by later generations of Tibetan scholars, so that, for the most part, Tibetan learning from the late thirteenth century on distinctly bears Sa skya Paṇḍita's imprint.

Specifically, his interest in Sanskrit poetics provoked a virtual revolution in Tibetan literary style. Following the Tibetan translation by his disciple, Shong ston Rdo rje rgyal mtshan (Shongtön Dorje Gyaltsen, fl. late thirteenth century), of such Sanskrit literary classics as Kālidāsa's famed *Meghadūta* (Cloud messenger) and Daṇḍin's *Kāvyādarśa* (Mirror of poetics), the stylistic emulation of Sanskrit poetic ornament became a fundamental feature of Tibetan composition. Though contemporary critics have sometimes lamented the privileging of such work over and against more characteristically indigenous Tibetan modes of expression, echoes of Sa skya Paṇḍita's Sanskritizing voice may be found even among today's young Tibetan authors.

The emphasis on the full range of Indian learning that Sa skya Paṇḍita's project entailed found perhaps its greatest exemplification in the work of the Great Fifth Dalai Lama (1617–1682) and his regent Sde srid Sangs rgyas rgya mtsho (1653–1705), whose extensive efforts to codify in detail the full range of the arts and sciences (*rig gnas*; Skt., *vidyāsthāna*) known in Tibet explicitly acknowledge the contributions of Sa skya Paṇḍita as their precedent.

BIBLIOGRAPHY

Bosson, James. *Treasury of Aphoristic Jewels.* Bloomington, Ind., 1969. Annotated translation of the Tibetan and Mongolian versions of Sa skya Paṇḍita's renowned collection of gnomic verse.

Canzio, Ricardo. "On the Way of Playing Drums and Cymbals Among the Sakyas." In *Tibetan Studies in Honour of Hugh Richardson,* edited by Michael Aris and Aung San Suu Kyi, pp. 62–72. Warminster, U.K., 1980. Includes remarks on the *Rol mo'i bstan bcos.*

Jackson, David. *The Entrance Gate for the Wise (Section III): Sa skya Paṇḍita on Indian and Tibetan Tradition of Pramāṇa and Philosophical Debate.* 2 vols. Vienna, 1987. Textual study, introduced with important surveys of Sa skya Paṇḍita's life, work, and legacy.

Jackson, David. "Sa-skya Paṇḍita the 'Polemicist': Ancient Debates and Modern Interpretations," *Journal of the International Association of Buddhist Studies* 13, no. 2 (1990): 17–116. On the contestatory dimension of Sa skya Paṇḍita's work.

Jackson, David. *Enlightenment by a Single Means.* Vienna, 1994. On the Tibetan debates concerning immediate realization, with particular reference to Sa skya Paṇḍita's contributions.

Kapstein, Matthew T. *The Tibetan Assimilation of Buddhism: Conversion, Contestation, and Memory.* Oxford, 2000. Includes an analysis of Sa skya Paṇḍita's methods of argument as represented in the *Tshad ma rigs gte.*

Kapstein, Matthew T. "The Indian Literary Identity in Tibet." In *Literary Cultures in History: Reconstructions from South Asia,* edited by Sheldon Pollock, pp. 747–802. Berkeley, Calif., 2003. Surveys his contributions to Sanskrit literary culture in Tibet.

Petech, Luciano. *Central Tibet and the Mongols: The Yüan-Sa-skya Period of Tibetan History.* Rome, 1990. Places Sa skya Paṇḍita's mission to the Mongol in its proper historical and political context.

Rhoton, Jared, trans. *A Clear Differentiation of the Three Codes: Essential Distinctions Among the Individual Liberation, Great Vehicle, and Tantric Systems.* Albany, N.Y., 2002. Annotated translation of the controversial treatise on the "three vows," with selected shorter writings.

Ruegg, David Seyfort. *Ordre spirituel et ordre temporel dans la pensée bouddhique de l'Inde et du Tibet.* Paris, 1995. Discusses in detail Tibetan views regarding the ordering of knowledge and the branches of learning.

Van der Kuijp, Leonard W. J. "On the *Lives* of Śākyaśrībhadra (?–?1225)." *Journal of the American Oriental Society* 114, no. 4 (1994): 599–616. A review of the available Tibetan biographies of Sa skya Paṇḍita's foremost Indian teacher.

MATTHEW T. KAPSTEIN (2005)

SALANTER, YISRA'EL (1810–1883), born Yisra'el Lipkin, Lithuanian rabbinic scholar and leader, founder of the Musar movement. Yisra'el Lipkin, the son of a rabbi and an exceptionally educated woman, showed scholarly promise at an early age. At the age of twelve he traveled to the town of Salant to continue his studies under the tutelage of the noted scholar Tsevi Hirsh Braude. From his stay of some fifteen years in Salant derives Rabbi Yisra'el's usual designation, Salanter.

The young Yisra'el came under the influence of the charismatic but reclusive rabbi, Yosef Zundel of Salant. Characteristic of the latter's approach were an intense concern with the moral aspects of Jewish law and the development of psychological techniques meant to heighten moral sensitivity and inspire righteous action. Yisra'el Salanter's discipleship under Zundel also put him in a direct line of discipleship from Zundel's teacher Ḥayyim of Volozhin to Ḥayyim's master, Eliyyahu ben Shelomoh Zalman (the "Vilna Gaon," 1720–1797), the most revered figure in the Lithuanian rabbinic tradition.

Salanter's public career began upon his arrival in Vilna (modern Vilnius) in 1840. He first served as the head of a major *yeshivah* in the city but soon left to found his own academy in a Vilna suburb. During this period Salanter began his efforts to set up a mass movement dedicated to individual ethical improvement. He addressed audiences of all social classes, arranged for the reprinting of classical ethical tracts, established the *musar-shṭibl,* a place for the study of moral works, and formed a nucleus of disciples who would spread the Musar doctrine.

Salanter was a widely revered figure known for his scholarship, his personal saintliness, and his concern for the suffering of others. His independent spirit and his moral authority in the community are illustrated by an incident in which Salanter suspended the Yom Kippur fast during a cholera epidemic in 1848. That same year government officials offered him the post of Talmud instructor in a newly opened modern rabbinical seminary, but Salanter, who opposed cooperation with government-sponsored Enlightenment programs or with *maskilim* ("enlightened" Jews), instead took up residence in Kovno (modern Kaunas).

In Kovno, Salanter forged the model of the Musar *yeshivah,* where the study of ethical works and the practice of self-contemplation became regular parts of the curriculum. From Kovno, Salanter sent letters to his followers outlining aspects of his Musar doctrine. These letters, later collected and printed in numerous editions, constitute the greater part of Salanter's written legacy.

In 1857, seeking medical treatment for depression and nervous disorders, Salanter moved to Germany, where he remained the rest of his career. In 1860 he published one of the first Orthodox periodicals, *Tevunah,* and in 1877 founded an advanced *yeshivah* in Kovno for married students. In Germany he met with university students, proposed a project to translate the Talmud into other languages, and asked that Talmud study be accepted as part of the university curriculum. He helped organize religious institutions for eastern European immigrants in Memel (modern Klaipeda, Lithuania), Paris, and other cities. Throughout his later years Salanter maintained correspondence with and influence over his disciples in Lithuania.

SEE ALSO Musar Movement.

BIBLIOGRAPHY

The best historical study of Salanter and his movement is Immanuel Etkes's *R. Yisra'el Salanter ve-re'shitah shel tenu'at ha-Musar* (Jerusalem, 1982), which, however, as its title indicates, does not cover all of Salanter's career. The only full-length study of Salanter and his disciples remains Dov Katz's hagiographic *Tenu'at ha-Musar,* 5th ed., 5 vols. (Jerusalem, 1974), which must be consulted with caution. Volume 1 of Katz's work has been translated by Leonard Oschry as *The Musar Movement: Its History, Leading Personalities and Doctrines* (Tel Aviv, 1977). On the development of Salanter's thought, see Hillel Goldberg's highly detailed study *Israel Salanter: Text, Structure, Idea* (New York, 1982), which includes a comprehensive bibliography of works by and about Salanter. In *Kitvei R. Yisra'el Salanter* (Jerusalem, 1972), Mordecai Pachter presents most of Salanter's writings with explanatory notes and a long, insightful introduction. An English translation of Salanter's key "Letter on Mussar" appears in Menahem Glenn's *Israel Salanter: Religious-Ethical Thinker* (New York, 1953). For an early short survey of Salanter's life and teachings, see Louis Ginzberg's *Students Scholars and Saints* (New York, 1928), pp. 145–194.

GERSHON C. BACON (1987 AND 2005)

ṢALĀT. The *ṣalāt* is a ritually prescribed prayer in the Islamic faith. Although the Qurʾān mentions *ṣalāt* many times, the specific details of how, when, where, and under what conditions to perform the ritual prayer are not minutely described in the Qurʾān. Rather, the early Muslim community formalized the ritual on the basis of the Prophet Muḥammad's example, or *sunnah.* Such matters as the exact postures, times, conditions, and recitations of the *ṣalāt* were arrived at thanks to the early community's recollections of the prophet's practice. Inspired by the Qurʾanic decree to emulate Muḥammad as their most beautiful model (*uswa al-ḥasana*), oral reports called *ḥadīth* recalling what Muḥammad said or did began to circulate soon after his death. As many spurious *ḥadīth* also proliferated, eventually they had to be sifted in terms of their reliability on the basis of criteria developed by *ḥadīth* scholars. In the century after Muḥammad's demise, Muslims sought to consolidate their faith and identity in institutional, legal, and theological terms. To this end, scholars (*ʿulamāʾ*) and jurists (*fuqahā*) devoted considerable attention to debating and determining the religious duties of Muslims. What it meant to be a Muslim in terms of doctrines and practices was still in a state of flux, and *ṣalāt* was part of this process of discovery and construction of identity.

PRAYER IN THE QURʾĀN. Prayer is of central significance in Islam. At the core of Islamic faith is the act of submission to God expressed in the first place through worship (ʿībādat). The Qurʾān repeatedly emphasizes the necessity of prayer, especially in the form of praise and self-surrender: "Establish regular prayer, enjoin what is just, and forbid what is wrong; and bear with patient constancy" (31:17); "And be steadfast in prayer; practice regular charity; and bow down your heads with those who bow down [in worship]" (2:43). Indeed, faith without prayer is simply meaningless in Islam. The Qurʾān uses several terms connoting prayer, including supplication (*duʿāʾ*), remembrance (*dhikr*), repentance (*istighfār*), glorification (*tasbīḥ*), litany (*wird*), and ritual (*ṣalāt*). Worship in Islam thus encompasses a wide variety of expressions, and the *ṣalāt* must be seen within this broader context.

The Qurʾān places the origin of forms of worship under divine guidance and declares that all the prophets established ritual prayers that were divinely inspired. For instance, Abraham begged God to bless him and his descendants with the privilege of performing worship (*ṣalāt*): "O Lord! Make me one to establish proper worship, and some of my posterity [also] and Lord accept Thou my prayer!" (14:40). In Islam, the primary sense of worship and devotion is to fulfill God's will. This is conveyed by the term *ʿībādat,* which is derived from the root *ʿabada,* meaning "to serve."

ETYMOLOGY OF *ṢALĀT.* The delineation of *ṣalāt* as a specific form of ritual prayer and as a distinct religious obligation (*farḍ*) was part of the historical development of *sharīʿah*, or Islamic law. The word *ṣalāt* is not found in pre-Islamic sources. Most likely, the term entered Arabic usage through monotheists in Arabia, notably Christians and Jews living in Muḥammad's time. The ritual of *ṣalāt* has several formal features that suggests it drew inspiration from contemporary Jewish services. The Arabic term *ṣalāt* was probably derived from the Aramaic word *ślotā.* In Aramaic, the root *ś-l-ʾ* means "to bow, bend, stretch"; *ślotā* is the act of bending or bowing. The Arabic verb *ṣallā* means to perform *ṣalāt.*

The form and content of *ṣalāt* evolved even during Muḥammad's lifetime. For instance, in the earliest Meccan revelations, the term *ṣalāt* was used in the sense of worship or prayer in general: "Those will prosper who purify themselves, and glorify the name of the Lord and pray" (87:14–15). *Ṣalāt* as a ritual with specific formal elements occurs more frequently in the Medinan revelations during the formation of Islam as an institutional religion. For example, the Qurʾān gives guidance on how to conduct prayers under special circumstances, such as while traveling or in battle: "And when you travel through the land, there is no blame on you to shorten your prayers if you fear that those who disbelieve may attack you" (4:101–103). It is clear, given its use in the Qurʾān in both the general sense of prayer and the specific sense of formal ritual performed by Muḥammad, that the word *ṣalāt* had a wider meaning at the beginning of Islam. However, it is this latter, more specific usage that became the basis of the codified and obligatory ritual consisting of certain prescribed gestures and acts by which the *ṣalāt* is known today. It should also be noted that from Turkey to India, the Persian word for *ṣalāt, namāz,* is commonly used to designate the obligatory ritual prayer.

DIVERSITY OF INTERPRETATION. Influenced by historical events, political interests, theological approaches, and exposure to other faiths and cultures, Muslims had already begun to diversify into communities of interpretation in the first centuries after Muḥammad's life (570–532 CE). One of the most important questions on which the earliest generation of Muslims differed was how much emphasis to give to the authority of ʿAli (598–661 CE), Muḥammad's cousin and son-in-law, as his interpreter and successor. Difference of opinion led to the formation of many groups in Islam, of which the two major movements are the Shīʿah and Sunnī.

***ḤADĪTH, FIQH,* AND THE PILLARS OF ISLAM.** Although *ṣalāt* has remained fairly uniform since Muḥammad's time, slight variations in practice do exist between various Muslim groups. Shīʿah and Sunnī schools appeal to different sources of authority to ascertain and establish the fundamentals of Muslim faith and practice. All Muslims turn to the Qurʾān as the primary source of authority in religious matters. Next in authority for the Shīʿah are the memory of prophetic example (*sunnah*) inscribed in the collections of *ḥadīth,* and the teachings of the *imāms.* The Sunnī give greater emphasis to the *sunnah,* and consider the *ḥadīth* collections of al-Bukhārī (d. 870) and al-Muslim (d. 875) to be the two most trustworthy ones (*as-ṣaḥīhan*). The Shīʿah have their own *ḥadīth* compilations which give priority to traditions narrated by ʿAli, Muḥammad's daughter Fatimah, and the hereditary *imāms.* Authoritative Shīʿah collections include those of al-Kulaynī (d. 939), Ibn-Bābūya (d. 991), and al-Ṭusī (d. 1067), and great importance is given to ʿAli's sermons in *Najhul Balāgha* and the teachings of Imām Jaʿfar al-Ṣādiq (d. 765). In addition to the Qurʾān, the teachings of the *imāms,* and the *ḥadīth,* of great practical importance are the writings of scholars and jurists of the different schools of law which form the day-to-day basis of *sharīʿah,* or Islamic law. Muslim religious practices are anchored in different schools of Islamic jurisprudence called *madhāhib al-fiqh,* whose authority is founded upon the law books and manuals written by such famous jurists as Mālik ibn Anas (d. 795), al-Shāfiʿī (d. 820), Aḥmad Ḥanbal (d. 855), and Abū Ḥanīfah (d. 767) for Sunnī jurisprudence, and Imām Jaʿfar aṣ-Ṣādiq, ʿAllāma al-Ḥillī (d. 1325), and Qāḍī an-Nuʿmān (d. 974) for Shīʿah jurisprudence.

Fiqh, or Islamic jurisprudence, is the summation of rules and regulations formulated by the leader of the *madhhab,* or law school, according to its own methodology. The part of Islamic law (*sharīʿah*) dealing with rites and rituals is called *fiqh al-ʿībādat.* The canonical collections of *ḥadīth* (both among the Shīʿah and Sunnī) begin with the requirements of worship, or ʿībādat, and include the pillars of Islam (*arkān al-dīn*). Although they are not mentioned in the Qurʾān, by the time the essential doctrines had been articulated in the ninth century, all branches of Islam accepted the fundamental tenets or requirements expressed in shorthand as the five pillars, which include the *shahādah* (testifying to the oneness of God and Muḥammad as God's messenger), *ṣalāt* (five daily ritual prayers), *zakāt* (alms for the poor), *ṣawm* (fasting during Ramadan), and *ḥājj* (pilgrimage to Mecca once in one's lifetime). The Shīʿah have additional pillars, including *wilāyah* (devotion to the *imāms* of the *ahl al-bayt*) and *jihād* (defending one's faith; striving for moral and spiritual perfection).

The *ṣalāt* was legally the most important pillar after the *shahādah* (which it included), and rules regarding conditions of prayer occupy a vast volume of *ḥadīth* and *fiqh* literature. Thus, it can be surmised that the *ṣalāt* and its details were crystallized once the major *ḥadīth* were compiled in the ninth century. That there was vigorous discussion and interpretation of the sources prior to this time can be seen from the fact that numerous slight distinctions in *ṣalāt* performance were adopted and justified by the different *madhhabs* in their legal texts (for example, whether to say *āmīn* silently or loudly after the opening Qurʾanic verse *al-Fātiḥah*). Obviously, the final conclusions regarding the details of worship were shaped by the different methods and historical situations of the jurists. Generally speaking, the Sunnī schools of law have shown considerable tolerance for each other's differences. For the most part, however, they have contested or rejected the legitimacy of the Shīʿah *madhhabs.*

DESCRIPTION, VARIATIONS, AND REQUIREMENTS OF *ṢALĀT.*

We now turn to a discussion of the requirements and description of the *ṣalāt.* The *ṣalāt* is obligatory when one attains the age of reason, usually deemed to be seven years of age, but certainly once one has reached the age of puberty. An individual must be of sound mind to perform *ṣalāt,* which is an act of personal choice and self-conscious submission to God's will. There are both obligatory (*farḍ*) and voluntary (*nafl*) *ṣalāt.* The obligatory *ṣalāt* is one of the five (or seven) pillars of Islam and the foundation of faith. Punctuating the day and night with deliberate prayer acts as a reminder that life is a gift from God and that time itself is sacred. All schools are in agreement that the obligatory *ṣalāt* must be performed in Arabic, a regulation which was essential in preserving the identity and solidarity of the early Arab Muslim communities in the context of the new lands and cultures in which they lived.

Conditions for *ṣalāt.* In addition to being clean and sober, proper clothing must be worn during *ṣalāt.* Shoes or sandals are removed, although some *imāms* wear special slippers in the mosque. The earliest regulations on dress were primarily concerned with decency, humility, and sobriety. This applied to men and women, both of whom are equally obliged to perform the *ṣalāt* and other pillars. In Muḥammad's time, it is clear that women prayed alongside men and participated fully in the religious and political life of the community. However, numerous *ḥadīth* linking women to the concept of disorder, or *fitnah,* came into circulation after Muḥammad died, partly as a result of historical events (such as Muḥammad's youngest wife ʿĀʾishah's battle against ʿAli, which started the first civil war between Muslims) and partly in reaction against Muḥammad's reforms to improve women's status. These *ḥadīth* have been used to discourage women from praying in public spaces. Arguing that the very presence of women is disruptive because they arouse sexual desire in men, Sunnī jurists in particular have allowed women permission to attend mosques only under strict conditions: they may not wear perfume; they must be fully covered; they may not interact with men; they must sit separately or at the back of the mosque; they must ask permission from their husbands or male guardians to attend prayers. Additionally, women are not allowed to pray or fast during menstruation. Generally, among the Shīʿah and Sufis, women have had greater latitude to engage actively in communal prayers and religious life. Muslim women's actual participation in the mosque and the practice of segregation and seclusion, however, has varied in different historical periods and regions of the world. In contemporary times, patriarchal restrictions on women's full religious participation have been called into question by both Muslim men and women, but normative gender roles and practices remain relatively unchanged.

Place for *ṣalāt.* Ṣalāt may be recited individually or in congregation. It is recommended that the ritual prayer be performed collectively if possible, although nonobligatory *ṣalāt* (*nafl*) may be offered individually. Congregational prayers are led by a leader (*imām*) selected from the assembly by virtue of his piety and religious knowledge. If a male is not present, a woman may lead a group of only women in prayer. Although all schools of law permit women to attend mosque, in practice they are encouraged to pray at home. Ṣalāt can be performed anywhere as long as the place is clean. Usually, if a mosque is accessible, Muslim men pray there, but if they are on the street or elsewhere at the prescribed time for prayer, they roll out prayer rugs to perform the *ṣalāt.* The word *masjid* means, literally, a "place of prostration." A key requirement when performing the *ṣalāt* is to face in the direction of Mecca. A typical mosque has a *qiblah* wall with an arched recess or prayer niche called *miḥrāb* which indicates the direction facing Mecca. Worshipers make straight rows behind the *imām* facing the *qiblah.* Mosques may also have a pulpit, or *mimbar,* to the right of the *miḥrāb* where the *imām* gives his *khuṭbah,* or sermon; a minaret from which the call to prayer (*adhān*) is recited; a fountain or other public facility for ablutions (*wuḍū*ʾ); and a central prayer hall. Mosques do not have chairs of pews and seldom have figural images and murals on the walls. Instead, the interior and exterior of mosques are usually decorated with delicate geometric designs and inscribed with Qurʾanic verses rendered in the splendid styles of Islamic calligraphy.

Times for *ṣalāt*: Qurʾān and *sunnah*. The five times of *ṣalāt* in current practice are not named in the Qurʾān. Rather, the number of times to perform *ṣalāt* was established and given legal force by the *sharīʿah.* The rich vocabulary used in reference to times of day for prayer in the Qurʾān indicates that such matters were still at an evolutionary stage during Muḥammad's life. The Qurʾān mentions three essential times for *ṣalāt,* to which a middle prayer was added in the Medinan period. Verses describing the three times of prayer include: "And establish prayer at two ends of the day and the first hours of the night" (11:114); "Establish prayers at the setting of the sun till the darkness of night, and the recital of the Qurʾān at dawn. Verily, the morning recital is witnessed" (17:78). Nightly prayers and vigils (*tahajjud*) were closely associated with the first Muslim community in Mecca: "Truly, the vigil by night is most keen and most certain for words [of prayer]" (73:6). In the Medinan period, emphasis upon the nocturnal prayer appears to have decreased, but a midday prayer, possibly influenced by the practice of the Jews, was added: "So glorify God in the evening and the morning; to Him be praise in the heavens and the earth at the sun's decline and at midday" (30:17–18).

In addition to the Qurʾān, jurists drew on *ḥadīth* to settle upon the requirement for performing *ṣalāt* five times a day. According to tradition (*sunnah*), the divine injunction to pray five times was received during Muḥammad's famous night journey, the *Miʿrāj.* The original account is very terse and is tied to the Qurʾānic verse 17:1–2, which refers to a journey from the holy sanctuary to the further mosque (later interpreted to be the Kaʿbah in Mecca and Dome of the Rock in Jerusalem). Tradition and the Muslim literary imagination has furnished details and embellished the story over the centuries. Muḥammad is depicted as being transported to Jerusalem (*isrāʾ*) and thence on to the heavens (*miʿrāj*) by the angel Gabriel on a winged beast called Burāq. During his ascension to heaven, he meets the biblical prophets Abraham, Moses, and Jesus. Upon reaching the summit, God commands Muḥammad that his community must perform fifty *ṣalāt* every day. When Moses hears this he tells Muḥammad to return to God, make a plea of mercy, and beg for a lighter obligation. Muḥammad goes back and forth between God and Moses several times until God reduces the number of obligatory prayers to five. The traditions offer an origin for the *ṣalāt* while at the same time linking it to the biblical prophets, and establishing a heavenly bond between the Peoples of the Book (*ahl alkitāb*). The symbolism connecting the Kaʿbah, Jerusalem, biblical prophets, and the throne of God to the *ṣalāt* anchors it in an ancient genealogy of monotheism. The five-times prayer thus acquires the quality of a fixed duty.

The five *ṣalāt*. The five daily prayers have specific requirements. The dawn prayer (*ṣalāt al-subh or al-fajr*) is performed between daybreak and the actual rising of the sun, and requires two cycles of prostration (*rakaʿāt*). The noonday prayer (*ṣalāt al-ẓuhr*) is performed anytime from midday until afternoon, and requires four *rakaʿāts.* The late afternoon prayer (*ṣalāt al-ʿaṣr*) must be performed between the *ẓuhr* prayer and sunset, and requires four *rakaʿāts.* The evening prayer (*ṣalāt al-maghrib*) is performed after sunset and before dusk, and requires three *rakaʿāts.* The night prayer (*ṣalāt al-ʿishaʾ*) is performed after darkness sets in but before the middle of the night, and requires four *rakaʿāts.* A missed prayer can be made up at a later time. The Shīʿah perform the five obligatory prayers thrice a day by joining the noon and late afternoon prayers and the evening and night prayers. As noted earlier, the three times of prayer are mentioned in the Qurʾān, and this practice was prevalent in Muḥammad's time as well.

Call to prayer: adhān and iqāmah. Each prayer time is announced by the call to prayer (*adhān*) from a mosque. About fifteen minutes before the *ṣalāt* begins, a muezzin ascends the minaret—a tower adjoining the mosque—or stands at the door of the mosque to recite the call. These days, the *adhān* is often recorded and broadcast over loudspeakers located atop the minaret or mosque dome. Muslims living outside Islamic countries can also use electronic *ṣalāt* clocks which announce prayer times. These "global Bilals" (named after the first muezzin in Medina, known for his powerful voice) display the *ṣalāt* times and play the *adhān* before each *ṣalāt.* Some timepieces also come equipped with compasses showing the *qiblah,* or direction to Mecca. Just prior to starting the *ṣalāt,* another call to prayer (*iqāmah*) is repeated, ending with the phrase, "the prayer has begun." The text of the *adhān* in translation is as follows:

> God is Great! [recited four times]; I bear witness there is no God but God; I bear witness that Muḥammad is God's messenger; [after this phrase, the Shīʿah add: "I bear witness that ʿAli is the friend of God and the

> prophet's viceregent"]; Come to prayer [twice]; Come to salvation [twice]; [the Shīʿah say: "Come to the best of deeds"]; God is Great [twice]; There is no God but God. [Sunnīs add, "And prayer is better than sleep" prior to the *takbīr* in the early morning *adhān*.]

The slightly different phrasing of the *adhāns* helps to differentiate between a Shīʿah and Sunnī mosque.

Preparations for *ṣalāt*: ablutions. Ritual purity (*ṭahārah*) is a prerequisite for prayer. To perform *ṣalāt,* one must be clean. An oft-quoted *ḥadīth* reports that Muḥammad said "Purity is half of faith." Before touching the Qurʾān, performing *ṣalāt,* going on pilgrimage, and participating in religious festivals, a Muslim must be ritually clean. As with other faiths, concepts of purity and impurity play a role in many areas of Islamic life. There are two types of purification rituals; their use depends upon the degree of one's impurity. Major impurities require a complete bath (*ghusl*) to wash the whole body. The *wuḍūʿ* (lesser ablution) is performed to remove minor impurities. To indicate which is required, *wuḍūʿ* or *ghusl,* the *sharīʿah* specifies in great detail various actions that cause minor and major impurity. Opinions vary on what constitutes major and minor pollution among the different schools of law. Major impurities generally include sexual intercourse, menstruation, ejaculation, childbirth, and contact with a corpse. Any emission from the body, exposure to death and decay, loss of blood, and sexual activity is ritually polluting. Minor impurities include touching one's private parts, visiting the toilet, touching a person of the opposite sex, and intoxication. In general, *wuḍūʿ* is performed in the mosque before prayer.

The washing ritual draws inspiration from Qurʾanic verses such as the following: "O ye who believe! When you rise up for prayer, wash your faces and your hands up to the elbows; and lightly rub your heads and your feet up to your ankles. And if you are unclean, purify yourselves. And if you are sick or on a journey, or one of you comes from the toilet, or you have had contact with women, and you find not water, then take some clean earth or sand and rub your faces and your hands with it" (5:6). The *wuḍūʿ* ritual is quite brief and economical, and involves a sequence of cleansing acts: washing the hands; rinsing the mouth and nose; washing the face; washing the arms and elbows; washing the feet and ankles; and wiping the ears, neck, and head. The Shīʿah usually wipe or rub their feet rather than wash them. The washing routine is repeated thrice. Mosques often have fountains and basins in their courtyards for this purpose. If water is not available, a Muslim may use sand or dust to wash using the same gestures; this is called *tayammum. Tayammum* is also permitted for those who are sick or are traveling. The *wuḍūʿ* is preceded by making an intention, or *nīyah,* to perform it, and is concluded with a short prayer.

Mental preparation for *ṣalāt*: intention. Repetitive rituals can become habitual and lifeless. The *sharīʿah* addresses this problem by requiring that deliberate intention (*niyyah*) precede any act of worship. Before the *ṣalāt* is performed, one must make a *niyyah,* that is, one must declare one's intention to pray. Whether the intention is to be pronounced audibly or made silently depends on the school of law one follows. Some schools of law argue that *niyyah* is an action of the heart, not the tongue, so it should be made silently. Others say it should be softly pronounced. Nevertheless, there is consensus that *niyyah* must accompany worship. Just as purification with water or sand before *ṣalāt* cleanses the body for prayer, so also intention prepares the mind and heart to pay attention during *ṣalāt.* Expressed as a decision or goal, *niyyah* is an act of recognition that one is about to do something. Thus, it gathers the mind's energies to focus on the act of obedience and worship. As an exercise of the will, it also signifies a personal choice to surrender one's destiny to God. *Niyyah* brings mindfulness and self-awareness to the performance of *ṣalāt.*

Performance of *ṣalāt*. The actual prayer ritual is quite simple and short. Each *ṣalāt* consists of two or four cycles of bowing, called *rakʿah.* A *rakʿah* (pl. *rakaʿāt*) is a cycle of movements accompanied by certain recitations. A minimum of seventeen *rakaʿāts* must be completed in the course of the five daily prayers. After making the *niyyah,* the worshiper goes through a series of steps, with slight variations according to the *madhhab.* The words of the prayer must be recited from memory.

Standing with feet slightly apart, one raises the hands to the ears palms facing outwards and recites aloud the *takbīr*: "Allāhu akbar!" ("God is Great"). In this standing position, called *qiyām,* with the hands either brought back down to the sides (Mālikī and Shīʿā) or clasped above the navel (Ḥanafī), above the heart (Shāfiʿī), or at the center of the chest (Hanbalī), the first *sūrah* of the Qurʾān, *al-Fātiḥah,* is recited. The Sunnī say "āmīn" after the *Fātiḥah,* but the Shīʿah do not. This is followed by reciting (*qirāʾah*) another passage from the Qurʾān. The Sunnī may recite any portion of a *sūrah* after the *Fātiḥah*; the Shīʿah require a complete *sūrah* to be recited, and most often it is *sūrah al-Ikhlāṣ* (112:1–4). This is then followed by a *takbīr.*

One then bows with hands placed on the knees (*rukūʿ*) and says silently three times, "Glory be to God!" (the Shīʿah add, "And praise be to God"). Standing erect again in a position called *wuqūf,* one says, "God hears one who praises Him," followed by "O Lord, Praise be to you!" and then recites another *takbīr,* "God is Great!" Then, one prostrates oneself (*sujūd*), touching the forehead to the ground with the palms flat on the ground, and silently says three times "Praise be to God Almighty, the most High!" The Shīʿah place a tiny tablet of clay from one of the holy Shīʿī shrines (Kerbala, Mashad, or Najaf) on the spot where the forehead touches the ground and add the phrase, "Glory be to God!" Then one raises oneself and says *takbīr.*

In this seated position, called *julūs,* one asks for forgiveness (Ḥanafīs), says nothing (Mālikīs), or offers petitions, or duʿāʾ, called *qunūt.* Then another *takbīr* is recited. The exact sitting posture varies: Sunnīs sit with toes touching the floor but heels upright; Shīʿah sit with their feet folded. One completes the *rakʿah* by making a second prostration and returning to the sitting position. Then one stands and the cycle is repeated again. At the end of the second cycle (or third or fourth, depending on the time of prayer), a formal greeting (*taḥiyyah*) calling for God's blessings on Muḥammad and God's servants is recited, followed by the *tashahhud* (literally, "witnessing"), in which the *shahādah* (testimony of faith) is pronounced. While reciting the *tashahhud*, it is common among Sunnī *madhhabs* to point the forefinger and move it in circles; however, this is not permitted by the Shīʿah. The text of the *tashahud* differs based on the *madhhab*; the Shīʿah add to the *shahādah* the phrase attesting to ʿAli's special position. A final prayer for peace, called *taslīm*, is said; while turning the head right and left one declares, "Peace be upon you" ("as-salāmu alaykum"). Again, there are slight variations in words among the different schools. After the *ṣalāt*, worshipers may remain seated to offer duʿāʾ, or superarogatory prayers. The Shīʿah recite duʿāʾ to keep alive the memory of their *imāms* and their spiritual link with them through devotional prayers.

Friday Prayer and Other Festivals. Although the *ṣalāt* may be performed individually, there are numerous *ḥadīth* stressing the excellence of communal prayer. A famous *ḥadīth* says: "Prayer which a man performs in congregation is worth twenty-five times the prayer performed at home or the market place." Several Qurʾanic verses provide scriptural basis for communal prayer service held on Friday. For instance: "O ye who believe! When the call to prayer is proclaimed on the day of assembly, hasten to remember God and cease your business. This is best for you if you understand" (62–9). The congregational prayer (*ṣalāt al-jumʿah*) held on Fridays is obligatory for males in most *madhhabs*. Attending Friday services is not compulsory for women and, in fact, women are not encouraged to participate. Major Muslim cities have huge congregational mosques called *jumʿah masjid* to accommodate large gatherings. *Jumʿah* is performed at the time of the noonday prayer, which it replaces. Upon entering the mosque, worshipers perform two *rakaʿāts*. Then, the *imām* ascends to the pulpit (*minbar*) and gives two short sermons (*khuṭbah*), after which he leads the *jumʿah ṣalāt*. Generally, the sermons explain an Islamic ethical principle or practice on the basis of a Qurʾanic verse. In Islamic countries, sermons provide a means to mobilize the faithful; therefore, the ruler or state frequently maintains close control over *jumʿah* mosques. Major Muslim festivals are also held in the *jumʿah masjids*, where the whole community gathers to celebrate and offer special prayers. These festivals include the feasts that follow the end of the fast during the month of Ramaḍān (ʿĪd al-Fiṭr), and the end of the *ḥājj*, or pilgrimage to Mecca (ʿĪd al-Aḍḥā).

Significance of Ṣalāt. In conclusion, the *ṣalāt* is a focal point of Muslim religious life. At the eve of Islam, the *ṣalāt* played a crucial formative role in the transformation of religious identity, for both pre-Islamic Arabs and those who adopted Islam as it spread. Undoubtedly, the *ṣalāt* demands discipline, and the question remains as to what degree Muslims do, in fact, observe the five prayers. Over the course of Islamic history, the *ṣalāt* has enjoyed different interpretations ranging from esoteric to exoteric. Esoteric interpretations look upon *ṣalāt* as an act leading to a spiritual encounter and relationship with God, a method of transformation of individual consciousness through the disciplined practice of continual submission and self-surrender. Exoteric interpretations tend to emphasize *ṣalāt* as primarily an act of ritual observance and submission to God's law. In the former case, emphasis on *ṣalāt* performance may diminish or take on symbolic import, whereas in the latter case, faithful performance of *ṣalāt* is always essential. The two views are not mutually exclusive. They have influenced each other but also been suspicious of one another for excesses of liberalism or literalism, as the case may be. The majority of Muslims, however, affirm that *ṣalāt* is a means of purification and submission of the body, mind, and soul, and that it embodies total surrender of the human being to God's will.

See Also Dhikr; Postures and Gestures; Prayer.

Bibliography

Bābūya, Muḥammad ibn ʿAlī. *A Shiʿite Creed*, translated by Asaf A. Fyzee. Oxford, 1942.

Bowen, John R. "Salat in Indonesia: The Social Meaning of an Islamic Ritual." *Man* 24 (1989): 600–619.

Brohi, Allahbakhsh K. "The Spiritual Dimension of Prayer." In *Islamic Spirituality: Foundations*, edited by Seyyed H. Nasr, pp. 131–143. New York, 1987.

Fyzee, Asaf A. A., trans. *The Pillars of Islam: Daʿaʿ im al-Islam of al-Qadi alNuʿman*, revised and annotated by Ismail K. Poonawala. Oxford, 2002.

Goitein, Solomon D. "Prayer in Islam." In *Studies in Islamic History and Institutions*, edited by Solomon D. Goitein, pp. 73–89. Leiden, 1966.

Muhsin Khan, Muḥammad, trans. *Ṣaḥiḥ al-Bukhārī*. Chicago, 1976.

Siddiqui, Abdul Hameed, trans. *Ṣaḥiḥ al-Muslim*. Lahore, Pakistan, 1971.

Von Grunebaum, Gustave E. *Muḥammadan Festivals*. London, 1992.

Watt, W. Montgomery. *Faith and Practice of Al-Ghazālī*. London, 1953.

Wensinck, A. J. " Ṣalāt." In *Shorter Encyclopedia of Islam*, edited by H.A.R. Gibb and J.H. Kramer, pp. 491–499. Ithaca, N.Y., 1953.

Yusuf Ali, Abdullah, trans. *The Meaning of the Holy Qurʾan*. Beltsville, Md., 1995.

Muzammil H. Siddiqi (1987)
Tazim R. Kassam (2005)

SALT has been a necessary additive to humanity's diet from the time people began cooking meat. The use of salt as a preservative and condiment became so important that it soon acquired a truly astonishing variety of symbolic meanings.

The Egyptians and Greeks used salt in certain sacrifices, but it is not clear with what intent. In Brahmanic sacrifices, in Hittite rituals, and during the New Moon festivals of Semites and Greeks, salt was thrown on fire to produce a crackling sound that may have had symbolic significance. This interesting multicultural custom, however, does not seem to be related to Mark's enigmatic saying: "Everyone must be salted with fire" (*Mk.* 9:49).

The Hebrews had a "covenant of salt" with Yahveh (*Nm.* 18:19, *2 Chr.* 13:5) and sprinkled their sacrifices with the "salt of the covenant" (*Lv.* 2:13). Though this practice probably developed from the use of salt as a preservative, for these Semites salt signified the fellowship of the table and the shared meal, just as it did for the Greeks and Romans. This association of salt (which was served as a separate dish) with the communal meal is also mentioned in *Ezra* (4:14). The Samaritans invoked their sharing of salt with the king of Persia as proof of friendship. In medieval Europe, it was considered wrong to harm someone with whom salt had been shared. Even today, Arabs offer salt to visitors as a sign of hospitality.

Furthermore, in the *Acts of the Apostles* (1:4), the Greek word *sunalizomenos,* usually translated "eating together," means literally "taking salt together." This word was adopted in the Clementine homilies (*Patrologia Graeca,* vol. 2, cols. 332, 345), and its meaning was similarly understood by the Greeks and Romans.

A very ancient ritualistic use of salt occurred in exorcisms. Some exegetes understand Elisha's throwing of salt in the bitter waters as a form of exorcism (*2 Kgs.* 2:20–22). This concept was borrowed by the church fathers, and salt was used for its apotropaic qualities in the Roman liturgy. Salt drives out the devil, according to a number of prayers for catechumens and the making of holy water that are found in the *Gelasian Sacramentary* (sixth century). This symbolic use of salt derived from its ability to preserve meat from corruption.

Similar reasoning has applied to the rubbing of salt on newborn babies, a custom among Semites, Persians, and ancient Greeks, still practiced today by such varied peoples as the Toda of South India and the Lao of Southeast Asia. Even though salt was applied primarily for medicinal purposes, its use often involved ritual to ward off evil. In fact, this apotropaic quality of salt is found in the folklore of societies all over the world. Salt is considered to have power over demons in Southeast Asia, over witches in Germanic traditions, and over the evil eye in Arab lands.

The practical use of salt to enhance the flavor of foods has evoked a number of taste-related symbolisms. The words for "tasteless" or "insipid" in Hebrew, Greek, and Latin also mean "foolish." Salt, therefore, confers wisdom, according to the rite for catechumens in the Roman liturgy. This play on words is likewise evident in the saying of Jesus: "If salt loses its savor [becomes foolish], with what will it be salted?" (*Mt.* 5:13). An extension of this theme was developed by the church fathers, who interpreted salt as God's word, spiritual discourse, and preaching. Paul thus exhorted Christians to season their language with salt (*Col.* 4:16). For the Athenians and Romans, salt stood for wit.

Especially in the Roman liturgy, salt symbolized spiritual health, unquestionably because salt was an ingredient in many medications (cf. Pliny, *Natural History* 31.102). The delicate but vital role that salt plays in the human metabolism was implicitly acknowledged in ancient times when the Roman legions were given their ration of salt and, at a later date, a *salarium* ("salary") with which to buy their own salt.

As with most other symbols, salt also has a negative aspect. In *Judges* (9:45), salt was sown on a destroyed city to signify sterility. The practice was followed by the Assyrians and Hittites and was later adopted by Attila at Padua and Frederick Barbarossa at Milan. A curse could produce a salt marsh (*Ps.* 107:34), a salt pit (*Zep.* 2:9), or a land of brimstone and salt (*Dt.* 29:23).

Salt has many other meanings that appear, for example, in Brahmanic and early Hindu literature. In the Upaniṣads, a grain of salt dissolved in water is a symbol of the reabsorption of the ego in the "universal self." In other Brahmanic texts, salt refers to cattle, seed, and the sacrificial essence of sky and earth.

References to salt among indigenous Americans are rare except in the context of ritual fasting and sacred fire. There was, however, an Aztec goddess of salt, Huixtocihautl.

The purifying and protecting virtue of salt is evoked in Japanese Shintō ceremonies. Izanagi, during the creation, constituted the first central island of Onogorojima with the help of salt extracted from the primordial waters.

In alchemy, salt had more to do with a basic principle than with actual substance. In hermetic symbolism, salt is the product and the equilibrium of the properties of its components, sulfur and mercury.

Bibliography

Latham, James E. *The Religious Symbolism of Salt.* Paris, 1982. A study of the symbolism of salt from earliest times until the end of the sixth century CE. Special consideration is given to an analysis of texts from the Bible, from Roman liturgy, and from the writings of the early church fathers.

Trumbull, H. Clay. *The Covenant of Salt as Based on the Significance and Symbolism of Salt in Primitive Thought.* New York, 1899. A questionable thesis that sees salt and blood as interchangeable in their symbolic natures, qualities, and uses.

New Sources

Kurlansky, Mark. *Salt: A World History.* New York, 2003.

Laszlo, Pierre. *Salt: Grain of Life.* New York, 2002.

James E. Latham (1987)
Revised Bibliography

SALUTATIONS are more or less formally ordered expressions acknowledging the presence of another. They occur generally upon meeting but also upon departure from the person met. Salutations include an enormous variety of oral and ritual forms that differ significantly in length and elaborateness and that express a range of emotions from kindness to humility or dread. Among these are bows, prostrations, ritual attack and defense, the firing of arms, the baring of the head, the clasping of hands, embracing, weeping, kissing, and smelling, as well as the utterance of short to very lengthy verbal prescriptions. The form of salutation appropriate in one civilization is very often offensive or ludicrous in another, and in any particular civilization the salutation varies with context. Most research on salutations has attempted to account for the relative elaborateness or simplicity of traditional greetings by seeing the relation of these to other aspects of religion and culture.

Ceremonial Greetings. While the salutation has been largely neglected in the study of religion and culture, it has been observed that salutations between equals tend to be brief and simple while those offered to sovereigns by their subjects or to higher ranking persons by lower ranking persons tend to be more ceremonious. Early visitors to such regions as Melanesia, Thailand, and parts of Africa reported that visitors to a chief approached him crawling on hands and knees. Ancient Egyptian and Mesopotamian sculptures show the lowly prostrations of subject kinds before a conquering monarch. Subjects, advisers, even the wives of kings of ancient Israel (*1 Sm.* 24:8; *2 Sm.* 24:20; *1 Kgs.* 1:23, 1:31) did obeisance to them with face to the ground, as did ancient personalities to God, his emissary, or his prophet (*Gn.* 17:3, 18:2; *2 Kgs.* 1:13). In the Hindu tradition, the person of inferior caste is expected to salute his superior, but the superior is not to acknowledge the greeting. On the other hand, as the historian Herodotus (485?–425? BCE) observes, in the ancient Near East the kiss was common between equals, a form of greeting that Paul recommends among the brethren of the church at Corinth (*1 Cor.* 16:20).

The above observations, of themselves, help little toward an understanding of ceremonial greetings involving the reception of visitors whose status may not be known. An early European traveler to Pemba, an island off the coast of Tanzania, observed that the otherwise friendly king ordered his musketeers to fire their arms upon his arrival in order to expel evil spirits. An early visitor to Africa reported being received with what he called war dances. Among the Maori of New Zealand, ritualized combat was performed at the arrival of visitors. In the Tonga Islands near Fiji, presents were offered to new arrivals as well as to natives who had been away. At the same time, the newcomer could be challenged by anyone to a mock fight that the rules of protocol forbade him to decline.

Material such as this evoked the view that the stranger, like the divine king, chief, or priest, was regarded as being replete with magical power that could discharge itself upon anyone with whom he came in contact. Just as taboo acts performed with respect to the king were designed to preserve his contagious spiritual force, the formalized greetings offered to strangers, according to James G. Frazer, were precautionary observations—an elementary dictate of savage prudence—intended to guard against the stranger's possibly baneful influence. Because such magical influence could infect anyone who traveled to strange and distant lands, the same observations would naturally accompany the arrival of a villager who had been traveling a distance from his home. Acknowledging this insight, Arnold van Gennep, in 1909, drew the conclusion that ceremonial greetings to strangers are rites of incorporation intended to reinforce the social cohesion of the group to whom the stranger is introduced. The length of greeting, then, understandably varies according to the extent to which the person arriving is a stranger.

These conclusions, however, do little to explain the lengthy and elaborate greeting ceremonies between persons of equal status who may even be acquainted. In ancient China such a ceremony began with the arrival of the visitor, carrying, in winter, a freshly killed pheasant, in summer, a dried one, held up by both hands, with the bird's head facing left. The visitor begins: "I have desired an interview for some time, but have had no justification for asking for it; but now his honor So-and-so orders me to an interview." To this the host replies: "The gentleman who introduced us has ordered me to grant you an interview. But you, sir, are demeaning yourself by coming. I pray your honor to return home, and I shall hasten to present myself before you." The guest replies: "I cannot bring disgrace on you by obeying this command. Be good enough to end by granting me this interview." This ceremony (which continues for several similar self-deprecating exchanges, accompanied by specified bows, and ends finally with the reception of the guest and the gift) is described in *The Book of Etiquette and Ceremonial* (c. 100 BCE), one of three ancient Chinese texts that deal with the subject of *li,* known to be the warp and woof of heaven and earth and consisting of the rules of propriety and politeness according to which all human relationships ought to be governed. The foundation of *li,* according to the Confucian tradition, is the heart that is willing to defer.

Greetings Prescribed by Law. The context that determines the relative length and elaborateness of the salutation evidently reflects the view of reality perpetuated by the tradition in which it occurs. For example, an ancient formulation of Hindu law, the *Āpastamba Dharmasūtra* (c. 500 BCE), provides that every day and after any absence, a student is to salute his parents, his grandparents, and his teachers with a kneeling embrace of the feet. The same salutation is to be observed for elder siblings in order of their seniority. Upon meeting an officiating priest, a father-in-law, or an uncle (even one younger than himself), the student is to offer this salutation or the salutation normally prescribed for his caste. *Brāhmaṇas* are to salute by extending their right hand on a level with their eye; *kṣatriyas* by extending the hand on a level with their breast; *vaiśyas* by extending it on a level with their waist. *Śūdras* are to salute bending forward, their joined hands held low. These salutations are performed standing with shoes off, with empty hands, and with head uncovered. On the other hand, in a state of impurity students are to salute no one. They is not to salute anyone who is impure, and the impure person is not to return a salute.

GREETINGS AS TOOLS OF SPIRITUAL ACHIEVEMENT. The salutations prescribed in this system of laws reflect not only the social system that they support but attitudes underlying the social system. In ancient India, the salutation is an act productive of merit toward earthly weal, heavenly bliss, and final liberation. The person of high caste, especially the teacher, is regarded as replete with vital power, the result of the accumulated merit of present and former lives. The higher the age and caste, the greater the store of power. The higher the vital power of the person one salutes the greater the merit achieved. In this respect, a *brāhmana* of ten years and a *kṣatriya* of one hundred stand to each other as parent to child, the ten-year-old *brahmana* as the parent. Another text, the *Laws of Manu* (c. 200 BCE), states that the vital airs of a young person mount upward to leave the body when an elder approaches. By rising to meet and salute the elder, the vital powers are recovered.

The powers achieved through the merit of worthy acts, however, must constantly be guarded against depletion, since they are inclined to flow, as it were, downhill from the person of higher prestige to the person of lower prestige. A salutation to a lower-caste person or an unclean person, the acknowledgment of his salute, or an unnecessary conversation with him, can result in the loss of vital force. If conversation with a lower-caste person is necessary, one must assume a posture of psychic neutrality in order to prevent such dissipation of power. Hindu salutations also reflect the fear of the evil eye, whose untoward effects can be invited even by a careless word. In traditional Hindu society, one does not comment upon another's pleasing appearance, the attractiveness of his or her children, even the pleasantness of the day. Whatever is offhandedly declared to be good is likely to attract inauspicious elements, tempting disaster. Against this, meticulous precautions are taken.

In contrast, the salutations found in the early Buddhist tradition reflect the elevation of spiritual achievement above hereditary status and an absence of occult concerns. "No brahman is a brahman by birth; no outcaste is an outcaste by birth." This shift is neatly expressed in the story of the meeting of the Buddha with the five ascetics with whom he had spent the years prior to his enlightenment. Upon seeing the Buddha walking toward them, the five agreed not to rise in salutation, because he had abandoned his former vows and given up ascetic practice. Yet as he approached, they involuntarily rose, and in spite of their resolution they greeted him and offered the customary refreshments, although in addressing him they employed his family name. To this the Buddha responded that he was indifferent as to whether he was treated with respect, but that it was rude and careless so to address a person (i. e., by his family name) who looks with equal kindness upon all living beings: Buddhas bring salvation to the world, therefore they ought to be treated with the respect that children pay to their fathers (Aśvaghoṣa, *Buddhacarita,* vv. 1229ff.). In Theravāda Buddhist countries, the act of prostration before the image of the Buddha or the pagoda (his principal symbol) is an integral part of worship. To perform this act the worshiper kneels, places his clasped hands to his forehead, and three times touches his forehead to the ground. Similar acts are performed by a layperson upon coming into the presence of a monk, by younger monks in the presence of their senior, by young children when they meet their parents, and by adults when on prescribed holy days they visit their parents' homes to pay them special respect.

Over and against all of this, the salutations prescribed in the Muslim tradition reflect a belief in the sovereignty of God and the equality of all humanity. The Qur'ān commands: "When you are greeted with a salutation, reply with a better one, or at least return it" (surah 4:86). In the Islamic world the usual greeting is "Al-salām ʿalaykum" ("Peace be upon you"). The appropriate reply is "Wa-ʿalaykum al-salām" ("And upon you be peace"); or to this may be added "Wa-rah-mat Allāh wa-barakātuhu" ("And God's mercy and blessings"). This, according to Islamic tradition, is the greeting with which Adam was commanded to greet a group of angels when he was created. His and their reply was to be the greeting for all of his descendents. The *ḥadīth* specifies particular situations in which the salutation ought to be offered and who is to initiate it. The younger person should greet the older person. The person riding should salute the person walking. The person passing should salute the person sitting. The smaller group should greet the larger group. Regardless of the circumstances, the greeting remains the same. While forms of the peace greeting are found in other documents of the ancient Near East (e.g., *Gn.* 43:23, *Jgs.* 19:20, *1 Sm.* 25:6, *1 Chr.* 12:18), it is significant that in this tradition the act of prostration to the ground, also found in the ancient Near East, is reserved for the worship of God.

Salutations, then, seem to express and perpetuate values and sentiments about the person greeted that are appropriate to the conception of reality of the culture or tradition in which they occur and serve to preserve such sentiments and values from subversion, thereby supporting the solidarity and continuity of the culture or tradition in question. Even when it is not explicit in the prescribed words of greeting, the sentiment that is communicated in traditional salutations is often of a religious nature. To an outsider, "Al-salām ʿalaykum" uttered by a Muslim may not express any specifically religious idea. To another Muslim, however, the relation of peace, as earthly well-being, to submission to God is understood. In *Nuer Religion* (London, 1956), E. E. Evans-Pritchard observes that the most common greeting among the Nuer people of eastern Sudan is a phrase that translates as "Have you slept?" What he thinks is implied, however, is something like "Are you at ease?" This interpretation is confirmed by the question that follows, "Are you well?" implying "Are you at peace?" That this is understood to be related to the peace that comes from God is implied by the further question, "Have you prayed?" and the next, "Does smoke rise from your hearth?" which is to say, "Is everything well at home?" A final question sometimes asked is "Has it dawned?" implying "Is it well for you?" When the answers are affirmative they convey the picture of easy sleep, contentment, prayer, a person at peace with God, his neighbor, and himself.

SECULARIZATION OF SALUTATIONS. It has also been observed that salutations tend to be longer and more elaborate in ancient, primitive, and traditional societies, shorter and simpler in modern industrial civilization. Salutations reflect the processes of cultural interpenetration and secularization occurring in many parts of the world at the present time. Words and gestures of salutation are perhaps among the most commonly borrowed of customs. In India, the gesture of touching the breast, the lips, and the forehead with the fingertips, as well as the bow with the right hand over the breast, are forms of the Muslim *salām* greeting introduced to India during the Mughal empire (1526–1857), from which influence came also the custom of the close embrace. It is interesting that the *salām,* which is normally used among Muslims to greet fellow believers, but not the infidel, is sometimes used by Hindus as a form of greeting for strangers. In India, as well as in Buddhist countries, the Muslim world, and elsewhere where Western influence has been felt, the handshake is growing in acceptance despite opposition, although in rural areas it remains less adopted. Among the most striking evidence of Western influence is the recent spread of the use of the greeting card for the exchange of good wishes on occasions that would once have required a visit. This phenomenon, which suddenly grew to a grand scale in England and America in the middle of the twentieth century, is now being employed for the exchange of greetings at Jewish holidays and also on the occasion of the great annual Islamic festivals. In general, where cultural borrowing occurs, it is the simpler, shorter, and less ceremonious custom that is appropriated by persons outside the tradition, and in the exchange the more subtle religious sentiments are likely to be lost.

The effect of secularization upon salutations is evident in the presence in modern greetings of the relic of a religious sentiment. The Namaskāra, perhaps the most general of salutations in India in the early twenty-first century, was originally a *śūdra* salute. The two open hands held together accompanied by the word "Namas" or "Namaste" was originally an exclamation of homage meant for the deity. Likewise, in modern European salutations like the French "Adieu" (lit., "to God"), the Spanish "Adios" (from "Vaya con Dios," meaning "Go with God"), the remains of the religious sentiment, now barely intended, can still be seen. In others, like the French "Bonjour" and "Au revoir" or the German "Auf Wiedersehen" and "Guten Morgen," the relic is perhaps more deeply submerged. In English the word *goodbye* is taken by most etymologists as a derivative of "God be wi' ye" (i. e., "God be with you"), which appears in Shakespeare as "God buy you" (*Twelfth Night* 4.2). Likewise, "Good morning" is taken as a short form of "God be with you this morning," or "God give you a good morning." In general, the secularization process abbreviates the originally religious salutation as the religious conception within it is no longer seriously intended. As scholarship has focused upon those aspects of religion that pertain to the more enduring of institutions and social structures, salutations have been far from the center of attention. With increasing interest in aspects of religion that pertain to social and cultural change, these eminently changeable cultural forms may prove to be an important subject of research.

BIBLIOGRAPHY

An impressive record of greeting ceremonies in primitive societies as first seen by modern Western observers is found in James G. Frazer's monumental work *The Golden Bough,* 3d ed., rev. & enl., vol. 3 (London, 1911), chap. 3, now recognized as deficient in its theories. Relevant greeting ceremonies of China are found in two texts of classical Chinese literature: *The I-Li, or, The Book of Etiquette and Ceremonial,* 2 vols., translated by John Steele (London, 1917), and *Li Chi: Book of Rites,* 2 vols., translated by James Legge (Oxford, 1885). The latter constitutes volumes 27 and 28 of the series "Sacred Books of the East," edited by F. Max Müller (Oxford, 1879–1910). Noah Edward Fehl's *Li, Rites and Propriety in Literature and Life: A Perspective for a Cultural History of Ancient China* (Hong Kong, 1971) is an excellent study of the nature of *li.* Justus Doolittle discusses everyday greeting customs in modern China in *The Social Life of the Chinese, with Some Account of Their Religious, Governmental, Educational, and Business Customs and Opinions,* 2 vols. (New York, 1868). Hindu salutations are prescribed in a number of ancient texts, several of which are collected in *The Sacred Laws of the Aryas,* "The Sacred Books of the East," vols. 2 and 14, translated by Georg Bühler (Oxford, 1879–1882). Traditional greeting customs and their changing contemporary forms in India are discussed in *The Hindu World: An Encyclopedic Survey of Hinduism* by George Benjamin Walker (New York, 1968), pp. 341ff. Buddhist rules of etiquette are found in *The Vinaya Texts,* translated by T. W. Rhys Davids and Hermann Oldenberg, "Sacred Books of the East," vols. 13, 17, and 20 (Oxford, 1881–1885). The relation of Buddhist ritual salutations to their social and cultural context is explored in Melford E. Spiro's *Buddhism and Society: A Great Tradition and Its Burmese Vicissitudes,* 2d ed. (Berkeley, 1982), chaps. 8–11. A concise discussion of greeting customs in the Jewish tradition is found in "Greetings," in *The Encyclopedia of the Jewish Religion,* edited by R. J. Zwi Werblowsky and Geoffrey Wigoder (New York, 1966). For the Muslim tradition, see Thomas P. Hughes's "Salutations," in *A Dictionary of Islam* (Delhi, 1973).

GEORGE ALFRED JAMES (1987 AND 2005)

SALVATION SEE ENLIGHTENMENT; ESCHATOLOGY; JUSTIFICATION; REDEMPTION; SOTERIOLOGY

SALVATION ARMY. The Salvation Army is described in its official mission statement as an "international movement" and "an evangelical part of the universal Christian Church." Its "message is based on the Bible," its "ministry is motivated by the love of God," and its "mission is to preach the Gospel" and to "meet human needs" without discrimination. In 2001 the organization operated in 108 countries and had 17,341 active clergy (officers) and 1,028,691 active members (soldiers). Members of any rank are called Salvationists.

Salvationists are officially required to subscribe to eleven doctrines, which are fundamentalist, evangelical, and Protestant. The army's theological position is based on that of John Wesley (1703–1791), the founder of Methodism, and is a restatement of the orthodox belief that love is the single motive for all true Christian endeavor: as God loved his children and sent his Son to die for them, so his children desire to love God and to show love to each other and to all people, especially the unsaved. Salvationists show this love through aggressive evangelism and a broad range of social welfare activities. Except for the omission of sacramental observances, the doctrinal beliefs of the Salvation Army have excited little controversy.

HISTORY AND AIMS. The doctrinal positions, objectives, and military structure of the Salvation Army have not changed since its beginning in 1878, and in many aspects even its methods of operation have changed surprisingly little. The movement was the brainchild of William Booth (1829–1912), an English evangelist, and his wife Catherine Booth (1829–1890). Members of their immediate family held important positions of leadership until the Booths' daughter Evangeline Booth (1865–1950) retired in 1939. The founders' influence over the modern army has remained strong.

The forerunner of the Salvation Army was the Christian Mission, which the Booths established in the East End of London in 1865 to evangelize the urban poor. Booth and his associates believed that this segment of the population had been ignored by the organized religious bodies of their day. While this was not true, Booth's efforts developed into the first systematic and large-scale program to reach London's poor with the gospel. A degree of social conscience was characteristic of the Christian Mission almost from the beginning. Efforts to relieve the destitution of those who attended their religious services were a natural outgrowth of the missionaries' evangelical zeal: kindness and generosity were commanded by Christ, and, on the practical level, hunger and cold kept many potential converts from paying proper attention to the gospel message. By 1867, four small-scale charitable activities, including a soup kitchen, were listed in the mission's annual report.

The military structure, by which the Christian Mission was transformed into an army, seemed to be the inspiration of a moment, although Booth and his closest associates had been dissatisfied with the conference system of governing the mission for some time. While preparing the mission's annual report for 1878, Booth deleted the term *volunteer army* in describing the work and substituted *Salvation Army.* The effect was electric. Booth became the "General"; full-time mission workers became "officers" and adopted a variety of military titles; converts and members became "soldiers." Brass bands, long popular with the English working class and especially well suited to the army's open-air evangelism, were added in 1879, along with a weekly devotional and news publication suitably called the *War Cry.* In 1880 the first regulation uniform was issued to George S. Railton (1849–1913) as he departed for the United States to establish the army's first official overseas mission. Comrades who died were "promoted to Glory," and children born into army families were hailed as "reinforcements." Since 1890, soldiers have been required to subscribe to the "Articles of War," a statement of doctrine, allegiance, and zeal for the "salvation war."

The new Salvation Army grew rapidly. Booth and his officers were driven by an overpowering sense of urgency—not to change the social structure but to save souls by any means. The great work was not revolution but rescue, while time yet remained. The army's most frequent self-portrayal, which appeared in posters, on the *War Cry* covers, and in songs, was as a lifeboat or a lighthouse, with eager Salvationists shown snatching the lost from the waves of drunkenness, crime, and vice. The thrill of losing oneself in a triumphant crusade, the military pomp, and a constantly expanding scheme of social relief proved irresistible to large numbers of the poor and to many working- and middle-class persons as well. Despite legal obstructionism from municipal authorities and ridicule from the movement's opponents, by 1887 there were a thousand corps (local units) in Great Britain, and by the end of the decade work had been started in twenty-four other countries and British colonies.

DOCTRINES AND PRACTICES. The Salvation Army held its converts at least partly on the clarity and simplicity of its doctrines, which were formally established by an act of Parliament in 1878. The army's doctrinal statement proclaims, on the one hand, both the atonement of Christ and the necessity of radical conversion and, on the other hand, the "privilege of holiness." In Salvation Army terms, *holiness* means that the sincere believer can live for love, in adoration of Christ, in joyful fellowship within the ranks of the army, and in kindly service to a dying world. Pioneer Salvationists saw religious questions in stark and simple terms; anything that was not deemed absolutely essential to salvation or helpful to evangelism, or that was regarded as inherently confusing to unlettered converts was simply jettisoned. It was partly for these reasons that the Booths abandoned sacramental observances; in addition, they had committed their movement almost from the start to the temperance (abstinence) crusade, which would not allow the use of sacramental wine.

As appealing as the doctrines of the Salvation Army may be, however, they are neither original nor unique, and they only partly explain its strength as a religious movement. The rest of the explanation has been the use to which the army puts its members, its system of discipline, and its social relief program. Converts are put promptly to work giving testimony about their own conversions, distributing the *War Cry,* praying, singing, playing a band instrument at indoor and outdoor religious meetings, or visiting the elderly, sick, and needy. Soldiers expect a lifetime of such service, and occasional natural disasters add to the ordinary demands on local army personnel. In addition, a number of entertaining and useful programs have been developed to utilize the energy of young people. Parades, military regalia, and an effective use of music augment, where they do not actually create, joy and pride in being part of the "Army of God." The Salvation Army has always made its appeal as broad as possible and is intentionally multicultural.

Salvationists are comfortable within the army's autocratic structure, which emphasizes obedience, loyalty, and efficiency. The system has changed more in practice than in spirit since 1878. The most important alteration in the absolute autocracy established by William Booth came in 1929, when the general's privileges of serving for life and naming his own successor were abolished. The generalship became an elective office at the disposal of a council of all territorial commanders, and the leader so chosen serves only until a certain age. Once a general is installed, however, his or her powers differ little in theory from those of the founder. Every subordinate officer is expected to obey without question the orders of a superior, and much the same is required of the soldiers. In practice, the principle of unquestioning obedience is tempered by many considerations. There is a growing commitment to a more consultative management style.

The army offers a "balanced ministry," which consists of its evangelistic program and a vast system of social welfare activities. There were important beginnings in the 1880s in England, the United States, and elsewhere, but the turning point in the development of the army's social welfare program came in 1890 with the publication of General Booth's manifesto titled *In Darkest England and the Way Out.* The book and the scheme it offered for relieving the sufferings of the "submerged tenth" of Victorian society attracted considerable publicity and support. An immense and varied program, marked by a quick delivery of services at the point of need, has developed. The army has sponsored food and shelter depots, industrial rehabilitation centers, rescue homes for converted prostitutes, hospitals for unwed mothers, orphanages, day-care centers, halfway houses for released convicts, programs for alcoholics and drug addicts, camping trips for poor city children, a variety of family relief and counseling services, and abuse shelters.

The Salvation Army's greatest strength is in English-speaking countries. Just over 50 percent of all active officers and 85 percent of all lay employees are in five countries: the United States, Great Britain, Canada, Australia, and New Zealand. Although the international headquarters remains in London, the American branch is by far the largest in terms of social programs, whereas the largest numbers of active members are found in Africa, India, and Pakistan.

The army in the United States is divided into four territorial commands, each with its own headquarters and training school. The territorial leaders report to the national commander, whose headquarters is in Alexandria, Virginia. In 2003, two-thirds of the 3,647 Salvation Army officers in the United States were serving as ministers to the 1,369 local congregations (called corps), while also directing the numerous social services that flow from these local units. Other officers serve in staff and educational appointments or as administrators of the army's many social institutions. The Adult Rehabilitation Command, which offers residential alcoholic rehabilitation to both men and women, is particularly well developed.

See Also Booth, William.

Bibliography

The amount of written material produced by the Salvation Army since its beginning is enormous; it is of uneven quality, but an acquaintance with at least some of it is indispensable to an understanding of the movement. Early issues of the *War Cry* (London, 1879–; New York, 1881–) portray the zeal and colorful activities of the pioneers. The serious student should begin with *Chosen to Be a Soldier: Orders and Regulations for Soldiers of the Salvation Army* (London, 1977 [earlier editions were written by the founder]) and *Salvation Army: Salvationist Handbook of Doctrine* (London, 1998). A useful and informative *Salvation Army Yearbook* (London, 1903–) is published annually. The best full-scale history of the army is a long-range project by senior officers, Robert Sandall, Arch R. Wiggins, and Frederick Coutts, and Henry Gariepy, *The History of the Salvation Army,* 8 vols. (London and New York, 1947–1994). The most comprehensive history of the army in the United States is still Edward H. McKinley, *Marching to Glory: The History of the Salvation Army in the United States of America, 1880–1992,* 2d rev. ed. (Grand Rapids, Mich., 1995), but the serious student should consult the growing body of new scholarly works on the army. Notably useful is Diane H. Winston, *Red-Hot and Righteous: The Urban Religion of the Salvation Army* (Cambridge, Mass., 1999). The army's international, U.S., and territorial headquarters maintain copious websites that are continually updated.

Edward H. McKinley (1987 and 2005)

SAMĀʿ is an Arabic term for the music or listening parties arranged by Muslim mystics in the belief that music serves as spiritual nourishment (*qūt-i rūhānī*) and attunes one's heart to divine communion. The word *samāʿ*, which literally means "hearing," does not occur in the Qurʾān but was used in ancient Arabic in the sense of "singing." ʿAlī ibn ʿUthmān al-Hujwīrī (d. AH 469?/1076? CE) thought that through *samāʿ* the last of the veils between man and God could be lifted. Abū Ḥāmid al-Ghazālī (d. 1111) and others after him believed that mystics who devoted most of their time to austere practices such as penitences, vigils, and fasts needed listening parties to relieve the heart's boredom, to infuse it with fresh energy and vigor, and above all, to channel, rather than annihilate, emotion. Criticism of this institution by orthodox theologians, however, obliged the mystics to lay down elaborate rules and conditions for its organization. As a result, the legality of *samāʿ* became contingent upon the fulfillment of four conditions: (1) the singer should not be a youth or a woman but an adult man; (2) the audience should be continuously in divine contemplation alone; (3) no obscene verses should be recited; and (4) no musical instruments should be used.

Al-Hujwīrī laid down even more detailed rules with regard to *samāʿ*: (1) it should be practiced seldom and only in response to an inner craving for it; (2) the spiritual mentor should be present at the listening party; (3) no person unfamiliar with the mystic path should be permitted to join the assembly; (4) the singer should be a like-minded person; (5) the audience should cleanse its heart of all worldly thoughts; (6) the emotions aroused by the music should not be checked; (7) a beginner should not be allowed to attend *samāʿ*; and (8) women should not look at the dervishes from house-tops.

Shaykh Abū al-Najīb ʿAbd al-Qāhir Suhrawardī (d. 1167), the founding saint of the Suhrawardī order, distinguished three groups who listen to mystical music: (1) those who are with their creator while listening to songs and who attain the vision (*mushāhadah*) of God, (2) those who listen to music with their hearts fully absorbed in it and achieve the benefits of spiritual seclusion (*murāqabah*), and (3) those who listen with their lower self (*nafs*) involved in it and need spiritual penitence (*mujāhadah*) to achieve their objective, because *samāʿ* is "for one whose heart is alive and whose *nafs* is dead." Suhrawardī considered music a means of igniting the fire of love in the heart of a mystic. Like al-Hujwīrī, he made the legality of *samāʿ* conditional. *Samāʿ*, he said, is like rain: it fertilizes the productive land but has no effect on barren fields. He also quoted Mimshad-i Dinawar (d. 911), who was told by the Prophet in a dream that there was nothing objectionable if the *samāʿ* meetings began and ended with the recitation of the Qurʾān. Suhrawardī considered that in music heart, soul, and the lower self (*nafs*) are all involved. Its effect, however, varies from individual to individual; it is spiritual nourishment or medicine for some and poison for others. The early Islamic mystic Dhū al-Nūn al-Miṣrī (d. 861) used to say, "Audition is a divine influence which stirs the heart to seek God: those who listen to it spiritually attain unto God, and those who listen to it sensually [*bi-nafs*] fall into heresy." For perfect spiritual enjoyment through *samāʿ*, the Iranian mystic Rūzbihān (d. 1209) considered three things to be essential: fine odor, a beautiful face to look at, and a lovely voice. He regarded the beauty of the singer as a prerequisite for spiritual happiness.

Saints of the Chishtī, Bektāshī, and other Ṣūfī orders constructed *samāʿ khānahs* (music halls) in their *khānqāhs* (lodges) for the exclusive purpose of holding listening parties. While listening to music, mystics often fell into ecstacy and stood up to dance, weep, and cry. Sometimes they gave everything they possessed, including the clothing they wore, to the musician. According to the rules pertaining to such ecstatic conditions, if any verse stirred up the emotions of a listener, the singer was expected to continue reciting the same couplet until the emotional storm had passed. It was said that Shaykh Quṭb al-Dīn Bakhtiyār Kākī (d. 1235) listened to a verse of Aḥmad Jām for several days and finally gave up the ghost while the verse was still being recited.

Mystics have adopted special types of behavior in *samāʿ*. Some of them have controlled their emotions in such a way that, except for fleeting expressions on their faces and tears trickling down their cheeks, there is no physical movement. By contrast, however, the Ṣūfīs belonging to the Mevlevi order of Jalāl al-Dīn Rūmī dance with amazing abandon. In India, disciples of Shaykh Burhān al-Dīn Gharīb (d. 1337?), who came to be known as Burhānīs, also danced in a special manner. Ibn Baṭṭūṭah, the renowned world traveler of the fourteenth century, refers to the *samāʿ* of the Rifāʿī dervishes which had its own unique features.

The Arab jurist and theologian Ibn Taymīyah (1263–1328) was a bitter critic of the institution of *samāʿ*, and under his influence contemporary and later generations of religious scholars (*ʿulamāʾ*) severely criticized the practice. The followers of Muḥammad ibn ʿAbd al-Wahhāb (1703–1787), founder of the Wahhābī movement in Arabia, were equally vehement in their opposition to this practice. Though some of the mystic orders, such as the Qādirīyah and the Naqshbandīyah, did not take to *samāʿ*, they rarely joined the *ʿulamāʾ* in their criticism of it. Shaykh Bahāʾ al-Dīn Naqshband (1317–1389) is reported to have remarked about *samāʿ*: "Neither do I practice it nor do I refute it." This remained the general attitude of those mystics who did not themselves arrange *samāʿ* meetings. However, Shāh Walī Allāh (1703–1762), a leading Naqshbandī saint of Delhi, went a step further and arranged *samāʿ* in his religious college, or *madrasah*, for the visit of the famous Chishti saint Shāh Fakhr al-Dīn (1714–1785).

The mystics who advocated *samāʿ* defended their position by referring to the Qurʾanic verses that attribute a sonorous voice to the prophet Dāʾūd (34:10; 21:79; 38:18–19, as explained by Mawdūdī in light of the traditions of the Prophet), to the tradition of the Prophet in which he is reported to have listened to the songs of girls on the eve of his return from a victorious campaign, and to the tradition that the Prophet did not allow people to disturb girls who were singing on a feast day. In the fourteenth century, Mawlānā Fakhr al-Dīn Zarrādī wrote a brochure, *Uṣūl al-samāʿ* (Principles of *Samāʿ*) to refute the arguments of the *ʿulamāʾ* at the court of the Indian ruler Ghiyāth al-Dīn Tughlaq.

While there could be no method of testing the subjective state of a mystic's mind when listening to music, the other, outward conditions were strictly enforced and deviations sternly dealt with. Shaykh Niẓām al-Dīn Awliyāʾ of Delhi (1238–1325) reprimanded those who used musical instruments, and Ḥāfiẓ Muḥammad ʿAlī of Khayrabad (d. 1849) expressed his condemnation of mystics who allowed recitation of verses by women.

However, these restrictions were not always kept in mind by the mystics, especially during the later centuries when the mystic orders lost their centralized structure and many of them became specific to their geographic setting. A corollary to this process was the trend through which saints, using mystic channels and idiom to convey their message to the common people, failed, unlike their predecessors, to check the reverse flow of popular superstitions, distortions, and accretions to their own ways. *Samāʿ* was no exception to this tide, and conditions regulating it were flouted. The orthodox criticism of *Samāʿ*, which had never really subsided, only became more poignant.

BIBLIOGRAPHY

Works in Arabic

Hujwīrī, ʿAlī ibn ʿUthmān al-. *Kashf al-maḥjūb.* Edited by Muḥammad Shafi. Lahore, 1967. An abridged translation of the *Kashf al-maḥjūb* was made by Reynold A. Nicholson in 1911 (2d ed., 1936; reprint, London, 1976).

Qushayrī, Abū al-Qāsim ʿAbd al-Karīm. *Al-risālah al-qushayrīyah fi ʿilm al-taṣawwuf.* Cairo, 1959.

Sarrāj, Abū Naṣr al-. *Kitāb al-lumaʾ fī al-taṣawwuf.* Edited by Reynold A. Nicholson. Leiden, 1914.

Suhrawardī, Shihāb al-Dīn Abū Ḥafṣ ʿUmar al-. *ʿAwārif al-maʿārif.* Beirut, 1966.

Zarrādī, Fakhr al-Dīn. *Uṣūl al-samāʿ.* Delhi, n. d.

Works in other languages

Macdonald, D. B. "Emotional Religion in Islam as Affected by Music and Singing, Being a Translation of a Book of the *Iḥyaʾ ʿulūm ad-dīn* of al-Ghazzali." *Journal of the Royal Asiatic Society* (1901): 195–252, 705–748; (1902): 1–28.

Meier, Fritz. "Der Derwisch-Tanz." *Asiatische Studien* 8 (1954): 107–136.

Molé, Marijan. "La danse extatique en Islam." *Sources orientales* 6 (1963): 145–280.

Ritter, Helmut. "Der Reigen der tanzenden Derwische." *Zeitschrift für vergleichende Musikwissenschaft* 1 (1933).

Schimmel, Annemarie. *Mystical Dimensions of Islam.* Chapel Hill, N. C., 1975. See discussion of *samāʿ* on pages 178–186.

New Sources

Amnon, Shiloah. *Music in the World of Islam: A Socio-Cultural Study.* Detroit, Mich., 1995.

KHALIQ AḤMAD NIZAMI (1987)
Revised Bibliography

SAMĀDHI. The Sanskrit term *samādhi* (from *sam,* "together," the intensifying particle *ā,* and the verbal root *dha,* "place, put") literally means "placing together." It hints at the merging of subject and object, the essential characteristic of the mystical state of unification to which it refers. It is most frequently rendered by *ecstasy,* but because of the emotive charge of that Greek loanword, the neologism *enstasy*—from the Greek for "standing in [oneself]"—was suggested (Eliade, 1969) and is gaining increasing acceptance.

The earliest mention of *samādhi* is in the Buddhist Pali canon, where it stands for "concentration." Buddhist authorities define it as "mental one-pointedness" (*cittasya ekāgratā;* see, e.g., Buddhaghosa's *Aṭṭhasālinī* 118). This is not, however, the sporadic concentration of the conventional mind, but the creative yogic process of abstracting attention from external objects and focusing it upon the inner environment.

Slightly later than the Buddhist references is the mention of *samādhi* in the *Bhagavadgītā* (2.44, 53, 54) in the sense of one-pointedness as communion with the divine being. This enstatic and transformative experience of the divine is said to be fostered through strict meditational practices (see, e.g., *Bhagavadgītā* 6.12–15), but also through disinterested action (see, e.g., *Bhagavadgītā* 12.10) and simple devotion to the personal God (see, e.g., *Bhagavadgītā* 12.11). Prior to these usages is the employment of the past participle *samāhita* ("collected") in reference to mental concentration (see, e.g., *Bṛhadāraṇyaka Upaniṣad* 4.4.23).

As "perfect concentration" *(samyaksamādhi),* the term figures in Hinayana Buddhism as the last limb of the Eightfold Path of the Buddha. As such it comprises all the techniques of meditative introversion known as *dhyāna* (Pali, *jhāna*), of which eight stages of progressive simplification of the contents of consciousness are distinguished. The first four stages pertain to the category of "meditation with form" (*rūpa dhyāna*), the last four to that of "formless meditation" (*arūpa dhyāna*). Beyond these mystical realizations lies the unconditional, transcendental reality, *nirvāṇa.*

The most elaborate metapsychology of *samādhi* states, modeled in part on the Buddhist schema, is found in the literature of classical Yoga. According to the *Yoga Sūtra* (2.11), *samādhi* ensues when the five types of fluctuations (*vṛtti*)—perceptual or inferred knowledge, error, conceptualization, sleep, and memory—are perfectly suspended. That suspension (*nirodha*) is achieved by means of sensory inhibition (*pratyāhāra*), concentration *(dhāraṇā),* and meditation (*dhyāna*), even though the state of suspension is only a sufficient, not a necessary, condition for the occurrence of the enstatic consciousness (grace motif).

In classical Yoga, *samādhi* designates the *technique* of mystical identification with the intended object, whereas the underlying *process* is more properly expressed by the term *samāpatti* ("coincidence"), which is reserved in Buddhism for the four states of formless meditation. Similarly, the expressions *dhāraṇā* and *dhyāna* represent types of yogic technique, while their essential processes are more accurately referred to as *ekāgratā* ("one-pointedness") and *ekatānatā* ("one-flowingness"), respectively.

The *Yoga Sūtra* (1.42–44) mentions four levels of enstatic coincidence: (1) *savitarka samāpatti,* or "cogitative coincidence"; (2) *nirvitarka samāpatti,* or "transcogitative coincidence"; (3) *savicāra samāpatti,* or "reflexive coincidence"; and (4) *nirvicāra samāpatti,* or "transreflexive coincidence." The first two levels are practiced in relation to an intended object pertaining to the "coarse" dimension, whereas in the latter two the yogin's consciousness merges with a "subtle" (psychic, unmanifest) object. These four progressively "higher" stages belong to the category of *saṃprajñāta samādhi,* or "enstasy with [object-]consciousness."

In the *Yoga Bhasya* (1.17) two further levels are mentioned: (5) *ānanda samāpatti,* or "blissful coincidence" (according to Vācaspati Miśra's *Tattvavaiśāradī* 1.17, the intended object is here a sense organ), and (6) *asmitā samāpatti,* or "coincidence with the sense of individuation." Vācaspati Miśra makes a further distinction between (7) *nirānanda samāpatti,* or "coincidence beyond bliss," and (8) *nirasmitā samāpatti,* or "coincidence beyond the sense of individuation," but the existence of these types is adamantly denied by Vijñānabhikṣu in his *Yoga Vārttika* (1.17).

The evidence of the *Yoga Sūtra* itself suggests that the highest form of enstasy associated with object-consciousness is *nirvicāra vaiśāradya,* or "autumnal-lucidity in the transreflexive (state)." In this condition the transcendental Self (*puruṣa*) is intuited over against the nonself or ego-mechanism of nature (*prakṛti*). When even that "vision of discernment" (*viveka khyāti*) is suspended, there occurs a sudden, unpredictable switch-over into *asaṃprajñāta samādhi,* the enstasy devoid of object-consciousness in which only subconscious activators (*saṃskara*) are operative. As this state is cultivated over a period of time, these activators neutralize each other, ultimately leading to *dharmamegha samādhi,* the "enstasy of the cloud of *dharma* [constituent, truth]." That condition is nowhere clearly defined, but it appears to be the terminal phase of *asaṃprajñāta samādhi,* being responsible for the cessation of the five causes of affliction (*kleśas*) and all *karman* (see *Yoga Sūtra* 4.30), thus giving rise to final emancipation (*apavarga, kaivalya*).

The dualist ontology and metapsychology of classical Yoga suggest that emancipation coincides with the demise of the finite body-mind. This goal of "disembodied liberation" (*videhamukti*) contrasts with the ideal, in nondualist traditions like Advaita Vedanta, of "liberation in life" (*jīvanmukti*). Whereas the abovementioned forms of enstasy represent realizations based on the introversion of attention, the enstasy associated with liberation in life is founded on the transcendence of attention itself. It is known as *sahajasamādhi* or "spontaneous [i. e., natural] enstasy"—the enstasy "with open eyes" (Da Free John, 1983), transcending all knowledge and experience, both secular and esoteric.

See Also Yoga.

Bibliography

Albrecht, Carl. *Psychologie des mystischen Bewusstseins.* Bremen, 1951. A profound phenomenological investigation of the meditative state preceding ecstasy/enstasy, with some fundamental observations about the nature of subject-object transcendence.

Conze, Edward. *Buddhist Meditation.* New York, 1969. A useful reader.

Da Free John. *Enlightenment and the Transformation of Man.* Edited by Georg Feuerstein. Clearlake, Calif., 1983. A compilation of published and unpublished materials with special reference to *sahaja samādhi.*

Dasgupta, Surendranath. *The Study of Patañjali.* Calcutta, 1920. An early study of classical Yoga containing useful materials on the enstatic state.

Eliade, Mircea. *Yoga: Immortality and Freedom.* 2d ed. Princeton, 1969. There are several relevant sections in this standard work on Yoga; see especially pages 76ff. and 167ff.

Feuerstein, Georg. *The Philosophy of Classical Yoga.* Manchester, 1980. The different stages of enstatic unification are given a fresh examination, especially on pages 81ff.

Feuerstein, Georg. *The Bhagavad Gītā: Its Philosophy and Cultural Setting.* Wheaton, Ill., 1983. See especially the chapter on the yogic path, pages 126–146.

Jarrell, Howard R. *International Meditation Bibliography, 1950–1982.* ATLA Bibliography Series, no. 12. Metuchen, N.J., and London, 1985. An extensive, if still incomplete, bibliography listing over one thousand books and more than nine hundred articles on the subject of meditation.

Koelman, Gaspar M. *Pātañjala Yoga: From Related Ego to Absolute Self.* Poona, 1970. The enstatic state is given careful attention on the basis of the commentarial literature on the *Yoga Sūtra,* especially on pages 187ff.

Langen, Dietrich. *Archaische Ekstase und asiatische Meditation.* Stuttgart, 1963. A comparative study of ecstatic/enstatic techniques in relation to contemporary psychotherapeutic-medical methods of relaxation and hypnosis.

Oberhammer, Gerhard. *Strukturen yogischer Meditation.* Vienna, 1977. The most detailed Indological study of yogic meditation and enstasy, with particular reference to Sāṃkhya, the *Mṛgendra Tantra,* and classical Yoga.

New Sources

Biermann, Derek. *Samādhi: Personal Journeys to Spiritual Truth.* Boston, 2000.

Georg Feuerstein (1987)
Revised Bibliography

SAMARITANS. The Samaritans are an ethno-religious group in Palestine and in Israel. Their religious center is Mount Gerizim in the vicinity of Nablus. Half of the community lives on the mountain, half lives in Ḥolon, a southern suburb of Tel Aviv. In the early twenty-first century the community comprises approximately 660 members. The Samaritan religion is an outgrowth of the Israelite-Jewish religion as it existed around the beginning of the common era. It therefore has many features in common with Judaism, above all the belief in the first five books (the Pentateuch) of the Bible. As opposed to Judaism, though, the Samaritans never developed the institution of the rabbinate but are led by priests and a high priest.

HISTORICAL SIGNIFICANCE. As a group the Samaritans have always lived in Palestine; that is, from their inception in antiquity to the present there have been Samaritans in the Holy Land. Their numbers have varied from tens or even hundreds of thousands in the early period to barely over one hundred in the nineteenth century. For this reason it has often been assumed that they preserved biblical traditions that were lost in Judaism. Although it can be shown that certain elements of Samaritanism go back to antiquity, such as the recitation of the Torah, not all their beliefs and practices necessarily continued unbroken from antiquity to modern times; each case has to be judged on its own merits. Due to the lack of sources for long stretches of Samaritan history, it cannot be ruled out that certain rituals were revived by going back to the text of the Torah. Nevertheless, Samaritanism represents an important nonrabbinic tradition of ancient biblical religion.

MAJOR THEORIES OF THE ORIGIN OF THE SAMARITANS. According to traditional Samaritan beliefs (as expressed in chapters 9 and 10 of the chronicle of Abū al-Fath and in chapter 43 of the Samaritan *Book of Joshua*; see below), their origin goes back to a schism in the time of Eli, a priest at Shiloh during the period of the Judges (*1 Sam.* 1:9, 2:11). Eli is said to have left the sanctuary on Mount Gerizim and erected a schismatic sanctuary in Shiloh that ushered in the Era of Divine Disfavor, or *Pnwth* (pronounced Fanūta)—God turned away (Aramaic, *pny*) his face from his people. The Samaritans consider themselves to be those Israelites who remained faithful to Gerizim. In Judaism it was believed—beginning with Josephus (*Antiquities* 9:288–291) and up to modern times—that the Samaritans originated in the pagan or the mixed population (Israelite and pagan) of the northern kingdom, Israel, after the Assyrian conquest in 721 BCE, as told in *2 Kings* 17:24–41. On the basis of this account, Jewish sources then pejoratively called the Samaritans "Kutim" after one of the peoples settled in Israel by the Assyrians. Since the Samaritan religion contains no traces of syncretism, and since not all inhabitants of the northern kingdom were deported by the Assyrians, it is thought by some modern authors that the Israelites that were left in the country are the ancestors of the Samaritans.

Another view of the origin of the Samaritans is the assumption that the Samaritans developed from dissident Jews of the southern kingdom, Judah, breaking away from Judaism in the fifth or fourth century BCE, a belief based on certain passages in the Bible (*Ezra* 4:1–5; *Neh.* 13:28) and in Josephus (*Antiquities* 11:302–347). The discoveries in Qumran and recent archaeological excavations (those undertaken since 1984), however, suggest a different reconstruction. It is now virtually common opinion among scholars of Samaritanism that the origin of the Samaritans as a distinct religion has to be sought in Maccabean times. The tensions between the YHWH-worshiping northern Israelites and the Judeans that surfaced after the Babylonian Exile resulted in a break between the two groups in the second century BCE. In the time before the break the northern Israelites who worshiped YHWH can be called proto-Samaritans—Israelites from Samaria who were in the process of developing into a religious community independent from Judeans. Decisive for the split was the rejection of Jerusalem as a relevant place of worship and the establishment of Gerizim as the only legitimate sacred place by the northern Israelites (or proto-Samaritans) who thus became the Samaritans. Both form and recitation of the Samaritan Pentateuch, the oldest extant Samaritan writing, reflect precisely this time period.

EVIDENCE FOR THE COMMUNITY'S HISTORY. There are no early Samaritan sources relating their own history. The most important extant Samaritan chronicle was written by Abū al-Fath ibn Abī al-Hasan al-Sāmirī al-Danafī in the fourteenth century, the *Kitāb al-Tarīkh.* Although Abū al-Fath used older sources for his compilation, it is only to a limited extent that his work can be used for the reconstruction of Samaritan history. In the main it is necessary to rely on non-Samaritan sources, such as Josephus, Greek and Roman authors, early Christian authors, rabbinic writings, Byzantine laws, Muslim sources, travel accounts, and archaeology. For any reconstruction the origin and *Tendenz* (or bias) of the writings must of course be taken into account. In the case of the rabbinic literature the different layers of redaction and the chronology must be established to arrive at a proper interpretation. Furthermore, there is the question of how far rabbinic passages concerning the Samaritans are reflections of actual situations or attempts at Jewish self-definition vis-à-vis others. Mutatis mutandis such criteria are to be applied to all literary sources. Archaeology of Samaritan sites, in particular on Mount Gerizim, as well as the excavations of several synagogues have come to play an increasingly vital role in the exploration of early Samaritan history.

HISTORY OF THE SAMARITANS. As mentioned above, the Samaritans originated in the Maccabean period. A crucial event in the relations between northern Israelite YHWH worshipers and Judeans was the destruction of the Samaritan sanctuary on Mount Gerizim by John Hyrcanus I (134–104 BCE) at the end of the second century BCE. According to Josephus, the temple on Mount Gerizim was built at the beginning of the Hellenistic period. Josephus's account, however, must be treated with caution. Excavations on the top of Mount Gerizim have unearthed a large city with an extensive, fortified sacred precinct in the center, dated by the excavator, Yitzhak Magen, to the Hellenistic period. In the center of the sacred precinct stood (most likely) a sanctuary. According to Josephus (*Antiquities* 11:310, 13:256), this was a temple similar to the one in Jerusalem. But some scholars think it may well have been an open-air sanctuary with an altar as described in *Exodus* 24–40. The archaeological finds, on the other hand, convinced the excavator that it was in fact a temple building. Due to Roman and Byzantine building activities on the very spot, however, many of the earlier installations have been destroyed. The Hellenistic sanctuary appears to have been preceded by a sanctuary from the Persian period built, according to the excavator, in the first half of the fifth century BCE. Mount Gerizim was certainly a holy place from ancient times on (see *Deut.* 11:29, 27:11–13; *Josh.* 8:33–35; *John* 4:20). Definite judgments about the buildings on the mountain can only be made after all the excavated material has been assessed. The Samaritan tradition is silent on the city as well as on the temple except for a few scattered passages in medieval chronicles that briefly refer to a temple (Abū al-Fath, *Kitāb* 63, 79, 80, 102, 183; Stenhouse, 1985).

Despite the breach between Jews and Samaritans in Maccabean times, the two communities continued to interact. This becomes clear from the discussions in rabbinic literature that presuppose such relations and from archaeological excavations that have brought to light *miqva'ot* (ritual baths) and synagogues just like those of the Jews. In the Middle Ages the Samaritans incorporated Jewish *midrashim* into their own compositions and even adopted (with adaptations) whole Jewish writings.

Early in their history as a distinct religion, Samaritans experienced the rise of divisions. It seems that the Samaritan heresiarch Dositheus arose in the first century CE and still had followers, the Dositheans, in later centuries. The third and fourth centuries CE were a period of religious reform and literary creativity. The person credited with this reform, Baba Rabba, is known only from later Samaritan sources. He strengthened the lay element and reorganized the Samaritans by establishing a "Council of Elders" and installing leaders who, together with priests, presided over newly established districts into which he divided the area inhabited by the Samaritans. During Baba Rabba's lifetime lived some of the greatest poets and writers of the Samaritans, including Amram Dāre and Mårqe, both authors of many hymns. Mårqe is also author of the Samaritan *midrashic* work *Memar Marqah* (*Mīmār Mårqe*), or *Tībåt Mårqe.* The Samaritan sources also ascribe the building of synagogues to Baba Rabba.

The fortunes of the Samaritans sharply declined over the course of the Byzantine period. The Byzantine emperors persecuted them more than they persecuted the Jews, as becomes clear from Byzantine legislation. This maltreatment at the hands of the Christian authorities provoked the Samaritans into several uprisings during the fifth and sixth centuries CE described in Christian sources. The revolts left the Samaritans weak and severely decimated at the end of the period. A great number perished, and some converted, genuinely or otherwise, to Christianity. In the wake of the first revolt in 484 CE, Emperor Zeno built a church to the Virgin Mary on the site of the former Samaritan sanctuary, the ruins of which are still visible. The church's enclosure was reinforced by Emperor Justinian I (527–565 CE) after the Samaritan revolt of 529 CE. Little wonder that the Samaritans, like other populations repressed by the Byzantines, were ready to cooperate with the conquering Muslims in the seventh century CE, although the Byzantines forced them to fight the Muslims. While the Umayyad rulers (661–750 CE) treated the local population well, the situation changed under the Abbasids (750–1258). Higher taxes and cruel local rulers made life difficult for the Samaritans and other non-Muslims. Extreme economic hardships imposed by Muslim rulers caused many families to convert to Islam. Thus the numbers of Samaritans decreased further in the Muslim period. From the eleventh century on, Arabic was used for their writings, and there is even an Arabic translation of the Pentateuch.

During the crusader period (1099–1291) the Samaritans seem to have suffered less, although some Samaritan buildings were destroyed. A note by the Jewish traveler Benjamin of Tudela from approximately 1170 indicates that in all of Palestine there lived fifteen hundred Samaritans (or Samaritan families), one thousand of whom lived in Nablus. There were also small numbers of Samaritans in Damascus and in Egypt. Although, similar to the other local population of Palestine, the Samaritans were of inferior social status, they were allowed to continue their cult on Mount Gerizim and to regulate their own affairs. They did suffer, though, from Muslim violence.

The crusaders were driven from their last Syrian and Palestinian possessions in 1291 by the Mamluks. For the Samaritans the following period was one of relative calm, and in fact the fourteenth century saw a Samaritan renaissance with many new writings, among them the chronicle of Abū al-Fath. Samaritans continued to live in Nablus, Gaza, Cairo, and Damascus. Their numbers, however, dwindled further, until they counted only a few hundred. In 1517 the Mamluks were overthrown by the Ottomans when Sultan Selim I (1512–1520) defeated their troops in Syria and in Egypt. Palestine was now governed by Turkish officials. Despite their small numbers and persecutions by Muslims in the seventeenth century, the Samaritans survived and even experienced a flowering of religious literature. Toward the end of the sixteenth century European scholars obtained Samaritan manuscripts and began a long correspondence with the Samaritans. Gradually, Samaritan communities outside of Nablus, in particular in Cairo, Gaza, and Damascus, ceased to exist, and the one in Nablus counted barely two hundred individuals. This number dropped further until the mid–nineteenth century, when there were only slightly more than one hundred Samaritans left. Late in that same century some Samaritans began to marry Jewish women, and the numbers of the Samaritans increased. This trend continued into the twenty-first century. Around 1900, Samaritans began to settle outside Nablus again. Eventually the Samaritans living in Israel concentrated in Ḥolon, so that two Samaritan centers, Kiryat Luza (the Samaritan settlement on Mount Gerizim) and Ḥolon, developed.

Beliefs and Practices. The foundation of Samaritan beliefs and practices lies in the Pentateuch that the Samaritans have in common with the Jews. Thus the basic monotheistic outlook of Samaritanism is the same as in Judaism. Specific to the Samaritans is the belief, based on a slight difference in the text of the Samaritan Pentateuch, that the place chosen by God for his worship is Mount Gerizim rather than Jerusalem; it is on this mountain that the only legitimate sanctuary was to be built. The only prophet was, according to the Samaritans, Moses. He is the subject of extraordinary praise and admiration in Samaritan literature. In the end-times a prophet like Moses (*Dt.* 18:15, 18:18), the Taheb (the "returning one," from the Aramaic *twb*), will appear and bring back the Era of Divine Favor, or *Rhwth*—God will again be pleased (Aramaic *rd' y*) with his people. The concept of the Taheb underwent a development in the course of Samaritan history from a prophetic to an eschatological figure.

Samaritan eschatology also underwent changes, in particular the idea of the resurrection of the body. Early Christian as well as rabbinic sources accuse the Samaritans of not believing in resurrection. The rabbinic tractate *Massekhet Kutim* even makes the acceptance of resurrection by the Samaritans one of two conditions on which the latter will be "taken back" by the Jews, the second being the renunciation of Mount Gerizim and the acceptance of Jerusalem. A gradual change began in the eleventh century and was completed by the fourteenth century, so that modern Samaritans believe in resurrection. The concept of the Day of Vengeance and Recompense, on the other hand, has existed in all epochs of Samaritan religion. Its basis in the Samaritan Bible is *Deuteronomy* 32:35. Whereas the Jews read "vengeance is mine," the Samaritan Pentateuch (as well as the Septuagint) reads "for the day of vengeance." It is the day of the final judgment.

Samaritan practices, like their beliefs, have much in common with those of the Jews. Samaritans celebrate the feasts based in the Pentateuch but not festivals introduced into Judaism later, such as Purim and Ḥanukkah. The feast of Passover is observed by the Samaritans as it is described in *Exodus* 12—that is, sheep are slaughtered, roasted, and eaten on Mount Gerizim. Three times a year—at Pesaḥ-Massot, Shavuʿot, and Sukkot—the Samaritans make a pilgrimage (*Ex.* 23:14–19) to the top of Mount Gerizim. In the course of the pilgrimage they visit a number of sacred sites on the mountain, including the place where Abraham was to sacrifice Isaac, and conclude the pilgrimage on the so-called Eternal Hill, a flat rock that the Samaritans associate with the most significant events in their religious history. For the festival of Sukkot, or Tabernacles, the Samaritans build *succot* within their houses, using the "four species" mentioned in the Bible (*Lv.* 23:40) to make roofs, a custom that may date from the period of Byzantine persecutions.

The liturgy, other than the pilgrimage, is held in synagogues. Women attend synagogues on Yom Kippur only; at other times, including the Sabbath, they pray and read the Scripture at home. The leaders of the community are the priests, headed by a high priest, now the oldest priest. Circumcision is always performed on the eighth day after the birth of a boy. Sabbath is strictly observed through prayers and abstention from work; prepared food can only be kept warm in thermo dishes. Men perform the Sabbath prayers in the synagogue. Samaritan synagogues have no pews, so the worshipers pray on carpets spread on the floor; shoes are left at the entrance. A special Sabbath dress, a long striped robe, is worn by men during Sabbath; the prayer shawl of a long, white cloth is worn over the Sabbath dress in the synagogue. Men's heads must be covered during prayer.

LITERATURE. The oldest and most important writing is the Pentateuch. Except for a small number of readings specific to the Samaritan version and variations in spelling, it is the same text that the Jews have. The oldest extant copies date from the tenth or eleventh century. The most revered Torah scroll is the so-called Abisha Scroll, believed by the Samaritans to have been written by the great-grandnephew of Moses. In the third or fourth century CE the Samaritans translated the Hebrew Bible into Aramaic, the Samaritan Targum. Numerous liturgical compositions date from the fourth century CE to the present. One of the major works is *Tībåt Mårqe* by the third- or fourth-century Samaritan poet and scholar Mårqe, mentioned above. It is a *midrashic* work in six books on passages of the Pentateuch. Samaritan scholars also wrote *halakhic* works, the oldest extant compilations dating from the eleventh century; no authoritative collections similar to those in Judaism were made. In the twelfth century Munajja b. Sadaqa authored a *halakhic* compendium that outlines the differences between Samaritan and Jewish *halakhah.*

There are a number of so-called chronicles, that is, accounts of events in Samaritan history, sometimes ranging from the creation of the world to the time of the author or copyist. They were written in Hebrew, Aramaic, and Arabic. The earliest chronicle is called *Tūlīda* (Chronicle). Its oldest part dates from the twelfth century, although the main portion of the text was written in the fourteenth century, and it was continued by later scribes until 1859. In the thirteenth century the Samaritan Arabic *Book of Joshua* was written or compiled from earlier sources, originally covering the time from the death of Moses to Alexander the Great; it too was later expanded.

There is also a list of Samaritan high priests, the so-called *Shalshāla* or Chain of the High Priests, whose date of origin is unknown. It extends from Adam to the compiler, Jacob b. Aaron, in the nineteenth century. The oldest complete chronicle is Abū al-Fath's chronicle, the *Kitāb al-Tarīkh.* Composed in 1355 CE, it is the most important Samaritan source for their history. A *Continuatio* of this chronicle is a firsthand source of the impact of early Islam (seventh to tenth centuries) on the Samaritans. A more recent chronicle is the *Chronicle Adler,* so named after its publisher, Elkan Nathan Adler. In addition to the above literature, Samaritans also wrote grammatical, lexical, and exegetical works.

THE SAMARITANS IN THE IDEOLOGY AND SELF-IMAGE OF JUDAISM AND CHRISTIANITY. From the time of Josephus, Judaism applied *2 Kings* 17 to the Samaritans, seeing in them a semipagan group that was only superficially close to Judaism. Rabbinic writings were ambiguous, sometimes admitting that the Samaritans are scrupulous observers of the law, sometimes considering them as outright Gentiles, and sometimes placing them somewhere in between Jews and non-Jews. In 1985–1986 the Israeli chief rabbinate and rabbinical courts declared that the Samaritans are Gentiles. Contemporary Jewish scholars, on the other hand, are divided. Some see the Samaritans as a branch of the Jewish people, others underline the introduction of foreigners into Samaria in biblical times. The state of Israel regards the Samaritans as a branch of the Jewish people and applies the Law of Return to those Samaritans who want to move from Nablus to Israel.

Christian authors of antiquity saw the Samaritans as a sect of Judaism. Later Christianity lost sight of the Samaritans until they were rediscovered in the sixteenth century. In the seventeenth century the first copy of the Samaritan Pentateuch was acquired and published. It was subsequently used in disputes between Catholics and Protestants; the former thought it supported the Septuagint version against the Masoretic text favored by the Protestants. Most Christians associate Samaritans primarily with the New Testament parable of the Good Samaritan (*Luke* 10:29–37).

BIBLIOGRAPHY

Alan David Crown, ed., *A Bibliography of the Samaritans* (Philadelphia, 1993), is a helpful reference work. Comprehensive sources are Alan David Crown, ed., *The Samaritans* (Tübingen, Germany, 1989); and Alan David Crown, Reinhard Pummer, and Abraham Tal, eds., *A Companion to Samaritan Studies* (Tübingen, Germany, 1993). Also important are James D. Purvis, *The Samaritan Pentateuch and the Origin of the Samaritan Sect,* Harvard Semitic Monographs 2 (Cambridge, Mass., 1968); Hans G. Kippenberg, *Garizim und Synagoge: Traditionsgeschichtliche Untersuchungen zur samaritanischen Religion der aramäischen Periode,* Religionsgeschichtliche Versuche und Vorarbeiten 30 (Berlin and New York, 1971); R. J. Coggins, *Samaritans and Jews: The Origins of Samaritanism Reconsidered,* Growing Points in Theology (Oxford, 1975); and Reinhard Pummer, *The Samaritans,* Iconography of Religions 23, 5 (Leiden, 1987).

Modern editions and translations of Samaritan texts include Abraham Tal, *The Samaritan Pentateuch, Edited according to MS 6 (C) of the Shekhem Synagogue,* Texts and Studies in the Hebrew Language and Related Subjects 8 (Tel Aviv, 1994); Abraham Tal, *The Samaritan Targum of the Pentateuch,* Texts and Studies in the Hebrew Language and Related Subjects 4–6 (Tel Aviv, 1980–1983); Mosheh Florentin, ed. and trans., *The Tūlīda: A Samaritan Chroncile* (Jerusalem, 1999 [in Hebrew]); Paul Stenhouse, trans., *The Kitāb al-Tarīkh of Abū 'l-Fath,* Studies in Judaica 1 (Sydney, 1985); Milka Levy-Rubin, ed. and trans., *The Continuatio of the Samaritan Chronicle of Abū l-Fath al-Sāmirī al-Danafī,* Studies in Late Antiquity and Early Islam 10 (Princeton, N.J., 2002); Ze'ev Ben-Hayim, ed. and trans., *Tībåt Mårqe* (Jerusalem, 1988). Josephus's texts in Greek and English can be found in Ralph Marcus, ed. and trans., *Josephus, VI: Jewish Antiquities, Books IX-XI* (Cambridge, Mass., 1966). A summary report in Hebrew on the excavations on Mount Gerizim by Yitzhak Magen is in *Qadmoniot* 120 (2000)—the whole issue, in fact, is devoted to the excavations on Mount Gerizim; the individual articles are as follows: Yitzhak Magen, "Mt. Gerizim—A Temple City" (pp. 74–118); Ephraim Stern and Yitzhak Magen, "The First Phase of the Samaritan Temple on Mt. Gerizim—New Archaeological Evidence" (pp. 119–124); Yitzhak Magen, Levanah Tsfania, and Haggai Misgav, "The Hebrew and Aramaic Inscriptions from Mt. Gerizim" (pp. 125–132); Yitzhak Magen, "Mt. Gerizim during the Roman and Byzantine Periods" (pp. 133–143). For earlier English reports see Frédéric Manns and Eugenio Alliata, eds., *Early Christianity in Context,* Studium Biblicum Franciscanum, Collectio Maior, 38 (Jerusalem, 1993). On synagogues see Reinhard Pummer, "Samaritan Synagogues and Jewish Synagogues: Similarities and Differences," in *Jews, Christians, and Polytheists in the Ancient Synagogue,* edited by Steven Fine, Baltimore Studies in the History of Judaism (London and New York, 1999), pp. 118–160.

For contemporary Samaritan life, see the biweekly newspaper *A.B.: Samaritan News* (1969–). Since 1984 the "Société d'Études Samaritaines" has organized international congresses at regular intervals and has published their proceedings.

REINHARD PUMMER (2005)

SAṂGHA

This entry consists of the following articles:

SAṂGHA: AN OVERVIEW

Saṃgha (or *saṅgha)* is a common noun meaning "multitude" or "assemblage" in Sanskrit, Pali, and the various prakrit languages. Buddhists have adopted the word to describe their religious community; followers of Jainism and other contemporary religious groups also use the term in this sense.

The Buddhist saṃgha consists of four "assemblies" (Skt., *pariṣad;* Pali, *parisā);* they are the monks *(bhikṣu;* Pali, *bhikkhu),* the nuns *(bhikṣuṇī;* Pali, *bhikkhunī,* the male lay followers *(upāsaka),* and the female lay followers *(upāsikā).* Jain sources also include a similar wider understanding of the term "fourfold *saṃgha."* In the narrower sense of the word, *saṃgha* refers to the community of monks and nuns only.

The first Buddhist *saṃgha* was established by the Buddha himself, Siddhārtha Gautama (c. 563–c. 483 BCE), when he accepted as his disciples five men before whom he had preached his first sermon in a park near Vārāṇasī. During his lifetime, the community grew considerably, and the Buddha is credited with having regulated its life and organization in a rather detailed manner.

SOURCES OF RULES. The first part of the Buddhist scriptures forms the law book for the Buddhist *saṃgha.* This collection, called the Vinaya Piṭaka (Basket of monastic discipline), or Vinaya, has been handed down in a number of different recensions, each belonging to a particular "school" *(nikāya)* of early Indian Buddhism. The rather close similarity of the main parts of these texts clearly points to a common source. The complete text of the Vinaya Piṭaka of the Mahāvihāra (the main tradition of the Theravāda school of Buddhism in Sri Lanka and Southeast Asia) has been preserved in Pali. Most other versions were originally composed in Sanskrit, but only parts of the original texts have been preserved. Several complete recensions are available in Chinese translation, and the Mūlasarvāstivāda version is available in Tibetan translation. Chinese translations exist of nearly complete manuscripts of the Vinaya Piṭakas of the Sarvāstivāda, Mūlasarvāstivāda, Dharmaguptaka, Mahīśāsaka, and Mahāsāṃghika schools. Parts of the Vinaya texts of the Lokottaravāda, Kāśyapīya, and Sammatīya schools are also extant.

Most versions of the Vinaya Piṭaka consist of three main sections: the *Vibhaṅga* (Pali, *Vibhaṅga* or *Suttavibhaṅga)* or *Vinayavibhaṅga* (in certain traditions, *Prātimokṣavibhaṅga),* the *Skandhaka* (Pali, *Khandhaka)* or *Vinayavastu,* and the *Parivāra* (partly corresponding with *Kṣudrakavastu, Muktaka Prakīrṇaka* sections in other versions of the Vinaya collection). The essential part of the *Vibhaṅga* is represented by the group of rules known as the *Prātimokṣa* (Pali, *Pātimokkha),* injunctions regulating the behavior of monks and nuns; all of these rules are believed to have been issued by the Buddha himself. Their number is slightly different for each of the various early Buddhist schools, ranging from 218 rules for the Mahāsāṃghikas to 263 rules for the Sarvāstivādins. These rules are also handed down as a separate work serving as the confession formula to be recited at the regular confessional ceremonies of the *saṃgha.* In the *Vinayavibhaṅga,* all these rules are listed, along with an account of the occasion upon which the Buddha issued each one, with casuistry and additional explanations. The work is divided into two parts, the first of which lists regulations for monks and the second gives rules for nuns. Since each rule is an injunction whose transgression is followed by a particular sanction, the *Prātimokṣa* and *Vibhaṇga* represent a compendium of the penal laws of the *saṃgha.*

The *Skandhaka,* or *Vinayavastu,* functions as the procedural law of the *saṃgha.* This section describes regulations for admission to the order, the confessional ceremony, and various aspects of monastic life, such as the behavior prescribed for monks and nuns during the rainy season, what possessions they are permitted to own, the use of medicines, and so forth. Most versions of these Vinaya texts contain as an appendix an account of the first two Buddhist councils *(saṅgīti* or *saṅgāyanā).* The *Parivāra* contains additional material in the form of mnemonic summaries, explanations, and so on.

RULES AND PROCEDURES IN THE LAWS OF THE *SAṂGHA.* The term *saṃgha* may be used in a general sense denoting "the *saṃgha* of the four directions" (i.e., the Buddhist monastic communities as a whole), but in the context of the juridical prescriptions of the Vinaya Piṭaka, it designates the saṃgha of a particular place that may perform a "Vinaya act" *(vinayakarma* or *saṅghakarma)* within an established "boundary" *(simā)* in accordance with the regulations of Buddhist law.

Admission to the *saṃgha* by the Buddha himself was a rather informal process, but detailed formalities were prescribed in the Vinaya for the admission by the monastic community after the Buddha's death. Two steps are required in the complete transformation of a lay person to a fully ordained monk or nun. The first step is *pravrajyā* (Pali, *pabbajjā),* the "going forth" by which a candidate becomes a novice *(śrāmaṇera;* Pali, *sāmaṇera).* The second step is *upasaṃpad* (Pali, *upasampadā),* the "obtaining" of ordination, whereupon the novice is admitted as a *bhikṣu,* a full-fledged member of the *saṃgha.* Admission as a *śrāmaṇera* requires a minimum age of eight years. The novice remains under the guidance of a preceptor and a spiritual master even after ordination, for which the minimum age is twenty years. *Śrāmaṇeras* and *bhikṣus* are expected to follow the respective rules of monastic discipline *(vinaya).* The novice obeys ten precepts *(śikṣāpada;* Pali, *sikkhāpada),* whereas a *bhikṣu is* expected to obey all injunctions listed in the *Prātimokṣa.* These regulations are divided into seven groups according to the seriousness of offenses against them. Violation of the four *pārājika* injunctions, which forbid sexual intercourse, theft, the intentional taking of human life, and falsely or self-interestedly claiming superhuman powers, is cause for permanent expulsion from the *saṃgha.* A monk who transgresses the rules of the second group is subject to temporary demotion in the *saṃgha.* For minor offenses, confession is considered a sufficient punishment.

Further procedures of the *saṃgha* include the *poṣadha* (Pali, *uposatha),* or confessional ceremony, which is held on the days of the new moon and the full moon, during which time the *Prātimokṣa* is to be recited. All procedures must strictly follow the established rules in order to be valid. They must be performed by a complete saṃgha within an established boundary *(sīmā)* by using the particular *karmavācanā* (Pali, *kammavācā),* or prescribed formula. All monks living within a particular place defined by such boundaries that have been fixed by a formal act of the *saṃgha* must meet and act together. The minimum number of monks who may perform valid acts of Vinaya is four, but for particular legal acts, a larger number of monks must be present; for example, ten monks are required for the performance of an ordination in India, but only five are required in the borderlands. For most formal acts, a unanimous decision is necessary; for less important decisions, a majority vote may be permissible.

In order to be valid, an ordination must go back in an uninterrupted succession to an ordination obtained from the Buddha himself and all ordinations in this lineage must be valid. If this is not the case, the particular person may not be considered a Buddhist monk or nun. He or she may still join the Buddhist community, however, as an *upāsaka* or *upāsikā.*

As mentioned before, the Buddha also admitted women to be members of the *saṃgha.* Therefore, the nuns have similar rules, viz. the *Bhikṣuṇīvibhaṅga* (Pali, *Bhikkhunīvibhaṅga).* The particular procedural laws for the *bhikṣuṇis* in the Theravāda tradition are formulated in a particular section of the *Cullavagga* (second part of the *Vibhaṅga),* whereas the texts of some other schools contain separate collections of regulations for nuns.

In nearly all Buddhist traditions, the lineage of the ordination of nuns has been uninterrupted; the only exception is in the tradition of the Dharmaguptaka school. Most Buddhist nun communities demonstrate great vitality, particularly in Taiwan and Korea. Recently, engaged Buddhist women undertook reestablishing the *saṃgha* of nuns in the Theravāda tradition, but as of the early twenty-first century, most Buddhist monks had not accepted their claim.

If the *saṃgha* of a particular place fails to assemble in full, or if it cannot agree, *saṃgha bheda* (division in a *saṃgha*) has occurred; such a schism is considered a grave offense. Devadatta, the adversary of the Buddha, created the first *saṃgha bheda* by unsuccessfully trying to replace the Buddha and make himself the head of the Buddhist community.

LIFE OF THE MONKS. Early *saṃghas* were communities of mendicants. The tradition states that, upon leaving worldly life, the candidate must give up all possessions and thenceforth depend on the laity for his or her subsistence. The number of requisites he or she owns is prescribed. Members live on the food that is placed in their begging bowls during the daily alms round. They are allowed to accept personal invitations for meals, but not to eat after midday.

As a community, however, the *saṃgha* may accept most kinds of donations, including property, and generous contributions to the *saṃgha* by laity are considered highly meritorious acts. In this way, some monastic communities became wealthy, and the way of life of their members came to differ from original doctrinal and canonical ideals. Therefore, the application of the formal rules of monastic discipline grew more imperative, and the degree of strictness in the fulfillment of these regulations was considered a measure of the moral standard of a Buddhist monastic community.

The original *saṃgha* had practically no hierarchical organization. During his lifetime, the Buddha was the highest authority, but he declined to appoint a successor, saying that his doctrine alone should guide his followers. The only hierarchical principle accepted by the early *saṃgha* was that of seniority, counting from the day of ordination. An elder monk is called *sthavira* (Pali, *thera).* In principle, all monks have equal rights and equal obligations. In practice, however, the *saṃgha* elects particular monks to serve in various roles, including dispute resolution, ecclesiastical jurisdiction determinations, and various administrative duties in the monastery. As the *saṃghas* evolved from groups of mendicants into residential monastic units, the importance of these responsibilities grew.

THE PLACE OF THE *SAṂGHA* IN THE TEACHING OF THE BUDDHA. The structure of the saṃgha as described above characterizes it as a legal system with formal regulations. The Buddha, however, stressed that he proclaimed all of his teachings for the exclusive purpose of guiding his disciples on their way to final enlightenment. The texts make it clear that monastic discipline and the *saṃgha* represent only the outer form, created in order to allow people to abandon their secular responsibilities and worldly connections in order to concentrate on enlightenment. Monastic discipline is the formal aspect of morality *(śīla;* Pali *sīla),* which is the right mode of mind and volition and, as such, the first foundation of the way to liberation. Morality in this sense is practiced through self-restraint; thus, the observance of the Vinaya is an integral part of the spiritual training of the Buddha's disciples.

In relation to the laity, a member of the *saṃgha* is legitimized as a disciple of the Buddha by his adherence to the laws of Vinaya. The *saṃgha* is worthy of respect and donations because it follows and perpetuates the Buddha's law, thereby embodying the "highest field of merit." On the other hand, the existence of the saṃgha is a precondition for the continuation of Buddhism, inasmuch as it hands down the teaching of the Buddha. The Buddha ordered his monks to preach his *dharma,* but in a decent, restrained manner, and only if asked to do so.

HISTORY OF THE *SAṂGHA.* Immediately after the death of the Buddha, a first "council" *(saṃgīti* or *saṃgāyanā)* of Buddhist monks assembled in Rājagṛha and collected the words of the Buddha, thereby compiling the Buddhist scriptures. Although the extant scriptures are of later origin, the ancient record seems to reflect an historical event. It is likely that the earliest version of the Prātimokṣa and the most important sermons of the Buddha were collected during this meeting. A second council assembled at Vaiśāli one hundred years later to resolve certain disputes on monastic discipline. The division of the Buddhist tradition into various schools or groups *(nikāyas),* which are often wrongly termed "Buddhist sects," began at this time. In the first period, the formation of these groups was based mainly on the geographic diversification of local *saṃghas* and on different views about details of monastic discipline. The texts were handed down orally; their written codification began only in the first century BCE. In most cases, the formation of the "schools" took place in such a way as to avoid the formal violation of the above-mentioned injunction against *saṃgha bheda.*

The *nikāyas* handed down separate recensions of the scriptures, and they also organized additional councils or convocations to collect and correct them. These collections of the scriptures arose in different parts of India and were originally transmitted in Middle Indo-Aryan dialects. Most of them were translated later into Sanskrit, with the exception of the scriptures of the Theravāda school, which remained in Pali, a dialect originating from central India.

Historical accounts of several schools contain traditions on a third council, held during the reign of King Aśoka (272–231 BCE), but from the rather contradictory accounts it becomes clear that the diversification of the schools was already far advanced by that time.

Mahāyāna Buddhism came into existence around the beginning of the common era, yet its presence did not affect the organization of the early *nikāyas*, precisely because the *nikāyas* differed by their acceptance of a particular version of the Vinaya texts and not by dogmatic opinions. Therefore, in some instances, monks who held Hīnāyāna views could live together and perform *vinayakarmas* together, along with followers of Mahāyāna. In contrast, monks belonging to different *nikayas* rarely formed a common *saṃgha*, though they might accept similar dogmatic views. In the course of time, new *nikāyas* emerged on the basis of dogmatic dissensions. Each Buddhist monk, regardless of school, accepts and (at least theoretically) follows one particular recension of the Vinaya Piṭaka; consequently, each monk can be connected with one of the *nikāyas* of early Buddhism.

THE *SAṂGHA* IN THERAVĀDA BUDDHISM. As mentioned above, the validity of a monk's ordination depends on an uninterrupted line of valid ordinations going back to the Buddha himself. Since *pārājika* offenses incur mandatory expulsion from the *saṃgha*, the validity of an ordination can be assured only if the monks who belong to the particular *saṃgha* lead an irreproachable life. Whenever the discipline in the *saṃgha* deteriorated, its legal existence was in danger, whether or not the transgressors continued to wear the monks' robes.

Originally, the Buddhist *saṃgha* was an autonomous body; its original laws did not permit interference by the laity. In this respect, the Jain order was different; there, the laity exercised a considerable degree of control over the *saṃghas*. King Aśoka, however, acted in order to achieve a purification of the Buddhist *saṃgha* in conformity with Vinaya rules. This tradition shaped the history of Theravāda Buddhism in Sri Lanka from the time of its introduction during the reign of King Aśoka. Several purifications of the Sinhalese *saṃgha* under royal patronage occurred. Later, additional law books, termed *katikāvata*, regulated the affairs of the saṃgha, supplemented by a hierarchical system. Parallel developments occurred in the history of the *saṃgha* of the other Theravāda communities in Burma, Thailand, Laos, and Cambodia. Buddhism in these countries introduced ordination traditions from other countries that were deemed superior to the local tradition on the occasions of *saṃgha* purification. Moreover, royal patronage of the monastic institutions went far beyond that of ancient Indian rulers; in fact, in some countries, such as Thailand, the administration of the monasteries developed into a kind of government department. After the breakdown of royal patronage of the *saṃgha* in Burma and Sri Lanka, monks in these two countries interfered in secular affairs during the colonial and postcolonial eras. Since 1978, however, the people of Burma (now called Myanmar) have attempted to form an autonomous hierarchical organization of the *saṃgha* under the patronage of the government.

Theravāda countries continue to support the old tradition that the *saṃgha* should be devoted solely to its spiritual aims. To this end, monks in these areas formed groups of forest dwellers *(araññavāsm)*. Eventually, the forest dwellers were integrated into the structure of the official *saṃgha* organization; other monks decided to leave the established ways of fully organized monasticism and retreat into solitude. Membership in the *saṃgha* always implies, of course, minimal relationships with other monks in order to perform the prescribed *vinayakarmas*.

New schools *(nikāyas)* of Thervāda have emerged at various times. In ancient Sri Lanka, the Abhayagirivihāravāsin formed a separate *nikāya* in the first century BCE, as did the Jetavanavihāravāsin in the fourth century CE. In the twelfth century, King Parākramabāhu I ordered the three *nikāyas* to reunite and declared the Mahāvihāra tradition authoritative. Since the beginning of the nineteenth century, however, the *saṃgha* of Sri Lanka has again split into a considerable number of *nikāyas*. In Burma, the first great schism arose about 1165 CE when Chapaṭa and his disciples established the *Sīhaḷa saṅgha* (based on a tradition of ordination introduced from Sri Lanka), in contrast to the local *Mrammasaṅgha*. From the early eighteenth century, until a royal decision that was issued in 1784, the Burmese *saṃgha* was divided over the correct way of wearing the monastic robes. During the nineteenth century, a number of new *nikāyas* were established there. In Thailand and in Cambodia, the *saṃgha* currently comprises the Mahānikāya and the reformist Dhammayuttikanikāya (founded in 1864 by King Mongkut while he was still a *bhikkhu)*. These divisions prevent monks belonging to different *nikāyas* from performing *vinayakarmas* together, but they do not prevent them from cooperating in many other ways, including performing other rituals. Most of these divisions have arisen, not from dissensions about dogma, but from controversies about the validity of *vinayakarmas*. For the Buddhist laity, such divisions are largely irrelevant.

Naturally, the *saṃgha* became involved with communal life in many ways, particularly in areas where nearly everyone identified with Buddhism. The study of the holy scriptures *(pariyatti)* and the realization of the road to salvation *(paṭipatti)* remained the traditional tasks of the monks, but religious practice largely concentrated on the gaining of merit, which is accomplished through the cooperation of monks and lay people. The everyday relationship between *saṃgha* and laity is characterized by copious gifts from ordinary people to the monks and monasteries, and invitations to the monks to participate in important functions, such as funerals. The monks give religious addresses, readings of sacred texts, and ceremonial recitations of *paritta*, texts from the Buddhist scriptures providing protection from evil forces and disaster. Until the creation of modern school systems, monks also acted as teachers, giving general education to the laity in their monasteries. A highly sophisticated system of monastic schools and ecclesiastical examinations and titles still functions in Sri Lanka, Burma, and Thailand.

As mentioned above, there have always been monks who have concentrated almost exclusively on asceticism and meditation, and a living tradition of meditation masters still exists in a number of Burmese and Thai monasteries. In recent years, famous monk-teachers have opened meditation centers to instruct laity interested in the practice.

THE *SAṂGHA* IN MAHĀYĀNA BUDDHISM. Many of the ancient *nikāyas* survived in India until the final destruction of Buddhism by Islamic conquerors. The Buddhist monasteries housed both Hīnāyāna and Mahāyāna monks; the situation was similar in eastern Turkestan. Mahāyāna Buddhism prevailed in China, Korea, Japan, and Tibet, but the *saṃgha* as an institution continued to be based on one of the old Vinaya traditions. The Chinese monks follow the Vinaya of the Dharmaguptaka school, and this tradition has been adopted in other countries where Buddhism was introduced from China, including Vietnam. The Tibetans follow the Mūlasarvāstivāda tradition, and this version of the *Prātimokṣa* is still recited today in their monasteries. Mahāyāna and Vajrayāna Buddhism encompass other forms of religious initiation, and religious communities outside the structures of traditional monasticism have come into existence. The histories of Chinese and Tibetan Buddhism recount several successful efforts to revive the ancient monastic discipline, and, as a rule, the formal distinction between monks and laity is still observed. This, however, does not apply to all forms of Central Asian and East Asian Buddhism. Particularly in Japan, the ancient monastic tradition has lost much of its original importance, and a majority of Buddhist communities there no longer form monastic institutions.

THE *SAṂGHA* AND THE INTERNATIONAL BUDDHIST MOVEMENT. Buddhist monks played a leading role in the formation of the international Buddhist movement, which was created in order to bring together Buddhists of all schools and of all countries. Although the movement began at the end of the nineteenth century, an international *saṃgha* organization did not come into being until 1966. The World Buddhist Sangha Council met that year in Colombo, created by delegates from the following countries: Sri Lanka, Vietnam, Malaysia, Taiwan, Hong Kong, Nepal, Cambodia, Korea, Pakistan, India, Singapore, Thailand, England, and Laos, and a special delegation of the Tibetan *saṃgha* in exile. In a declaration made at its third congress (Taipei, 1981), this organization stated that more than one million Buddhist monks practice their faith in the world today.

SEE ALSO Councils, article on Buddhist Councils; Monasticism, article on Buddhist Monasticism; Priesthood, article on Buddhist Priesthood.

BIBLIOGRAPHY

The Theravāda Vinaya Piṭaka in Pali was edited by Hermann Oldenberg as *The Vinaya Piṭakaṃ,* 5 vols. (London, 1879–1883), and has been translated by I. B. Horner as *The Book of the Discipline,* 6 vols., "Sacred Books of the Buddhists," vols. 10–14, 20, and 25 (London, 1938). For a complete bibliography of the Vinaya literature of other Buddhist schools published before 1978, see Yūyama Akira's *Vinaya-Texte* (Wiesbaden, 1979). The most recent relevant publications are: *Prātimokṣasūtra der Sarvāstivādins,* ed. Georg von Simson, part 2 (Göttingen, 2000); Ann Heirman's *"The Discipline in Four Parts"–Rules for Nuns according to the Dharmaguptakavinaya,* 3 vols. (Delhi, 2002; with translation). An excellent study of the growth of Vinaya texts is Erich Frauwallner's *The Earliest Vinaya and the Beginnings of Buddhist Literature* (Rome, 1956). Further information on the early Buddhist *saṃgha* and early Buddhist schools is provided in the relevant chapters of the standard work by Étienne Lamotte, *Histoire du bouddhisme indien: Des origines à l'ère śaka* (Louvain, 1958); English translation: *History of Indian Buddhism from the Origins to the Śaka Era,* transl. Sara Webb-Boin (Louvain-la-neuve, 1988). On *karmavācanā,* see Herbert Härtel's *Karmavācanā: Formulare für den Gebrauch im buddhistischen Gemeindeleben* (Berlin, 1956); on the problem of *saṃgha bheda* and *nikāyabheda* and Aśoka's reform of the *saṃgha,* see Heinz Bechert's essay "The Importance of Aśoka's So-Called Schism Edict," in *Indological and Buddhist Studies: Volume in the Honour of Professor J W. de Jong,* edited by L. A. Hercus and others (Canberra, 1982). A survey of all available versions of the *Prātimokṣa* is found in Wang Pachow's *A Comparative Study of the Prātimokṣa* (Shantiniketan, 1955); a translation of six versions of the *Prātimokṣa* rules for nuns was provided by Chatsumarn Kabilsingh, *The Bhikkhunī Pātimokkha of the Six Schools* (Delhi, 1998). Earlier monographs on the Buddhist *saṃgha* and several recent studies mainly concentrate on historical and sociological aspects, such as the books by Sukumar Dutt, *Early Buddhist Monachism* (London, 1924), Gokuldas De, *Democracy in Early Buddhist Sangha* (Calcutta, 1955), Patrick Olivelle, *The Origin and the Early Development of Buddhist Monachism* (Colombo, 1974), Rabindramath Bijay Barua, *The Theravāda Buddhist Sangha* (Dacca, 1978), and Gunaratne Panabokke, *History of the Buddhist Sangha in India and Sri Lanka* (Colombo, 1993). The application of the Vinaya rules in Thailand is dealt with by Vajirañanavarorasa, *The Entrance to the Vinaya, Vinayamukha,* 3 vols. (Bangkok, 1969–83) and *Ordination Procedure* (Bangkok, 1973). Recently, important aspects of the structure of the *saṃgha* and details of the relevant regulations have been extensively dealt with by several authors, including Petra Kieffer-Pülz, *Die Sīmā* (Berlin, 1992), Haiyan Hu- von Hinüber, *Das Poṣadhavastu, Vorschriften für die buddhistische Beichtfeier* (Reinbek, 1994), Ute Hüsken, *Die Vorschriften für die buddhistische Nonnengemeinde* (Berlin, 1997), Jin-il Chung, *Die Pravāraṇā* (Göttingen, 1998). For the *saṃgha* in China and its more recent history, see Holmes Welch's *The Practice of Chinese Buddhism,* 2d ed. (Cambridge, Mass., 1973), *The Buddhist Revival in China* (Cambridge, Mass., 1968) and Marcus Günzel's *Die Taiwan -Erfahrung des chinesischen Saṅgha* (Göttingen, 1998). Important sources from Sri Lanka are edited and translated by Nandasēna Ratnapāla in his *The Katikāvatas: Laws of the Buddhist Order of Ceylon from the*

Twelfth Century to the Eighteenth Century (Munich, 1971). For the relation between *saṃgha* and state in later Theravāda Buddhism, see relevant titles in the second part of this article, Saṃgha and Society. See also H. Bechert's *Buddhismus, Staat and Gesellschaftin den Ländern des Theravāda Buddhismus,* new enlarged ed., 2 vols (Göttingen, 1998–2000); Ruth-Inge Heinze, *The Role of the Sangha in Modern Thailand* (Taipei, 1977). For *saṃgha* in Jainism, see Shantaram Bhalachandra Deo's *Jaina Monastic Jurisprudence* (Varanasi, 1960) and his *History of Jaina Monachism, from Inscriptions and Literature* (Poona, 1956).

HEINZ BECHERT (1987 AND 2005)

SAṂGHA: SAṂGHA AND SOCIETY IN SOUTH AND SOUTHEAST ASIA

The Sanskrit word *saṃgha* (Pali, *sangha*) denotes the Buddhist monastic order, although in its early usage (c. 500 BCE) in North India the word referred to the gatherings of the tribal republics of the time. The *saṃgha*'s relationship to society can best be prefaced with a consideration of its historical origins. Because the *saṃgha*'s significance is inseparable from that of Buddhist thought and philosophy, this will include a consideration of the social origins of that philosophy as well.

The details of ancient Indian history are controversial, but the major outlines are generally accepted. Accordingly, this article can focus on the material and social background immediately preceding the rise of Buddhism in the region of its birth, the area known as the Middle Country (*madhyadeśa*), in northeastern India. The eastward-moving Aryans, who entered India around 1500 BCE, seem to have established themselves in the region by the sixth century BCE, the time of the Buddha's birth. The demographic picture, however, is far from simple, for the area also seems to have been populated by people who were of Tibetan and Burmese extraction. This period was one of extensive development of settled agriculture, a change from the nomadic type of existence ascribed to the predominant Aryans. Along with other developments such as crafts and industry, this economic progress led to surpluses, the rise of cities, and changes in political organization from ancient tribal republics to monarchies. Six great cities figure prominently in the Buddhist texts: Sāvatthī (Śrāvastī), Sāketa, Kosambi (Kauśāmbī), Kāsī (modern Vārāṇasī), Rājagaha (Rājagṛha), and Champa (Campā). Smaller cities such as Kapilavastu, Mithilā, Vesālī (Vaiśālī), and Gayā are also mentioned frequently. The cities seem to have had high population densities and to have developed a complex division of labor.

The replacement of the collective rule of the tribal republics by a monarchial form of rule reflected the centralization of power in one person, the rise of cities, and the division of labor, which emphasized the worth of the individual specialist. These factors are understood by some scholars to be indicative of a fundamental change in the evaluation of the individual within society. From a status of submergence in the group the individual gradually achieved a relative independence somewhat analogous to that of the individual in the modern West. Furthermore, many hold that the rise of the individual during this period, with the complementary need to competitively foster that individuality, set in motion potentially anomic forces that tended to minimize traditional social values of mutuality in favor of an egoistic construction of the self.

It therefore comes as no surprise that Buddhism, a tradition that is conspicuous for its early association with urbanism, should conceive of the problem of existence as one caused by an exaggerated notion of the ego or "self." The visible, tangible misery caused by excessive individualism in the realm of politics or economics (or wherever competitiveness and the display of egoism are dominant) is easily translated into the sphere of the transcendental as the idea that the malaise of the individual being is the exaggeration of the ego or the individual self. According to this analysis, the source of tranquillity must be sought in a devaluation of that self. This step is accomplished by the philosophical formulation that the self is an illusion. It is not that those who adopt this view attempt to reduce Buddhist philosophy, in particular its central doctrine of *anātman* (Pali, *anatta,* "no-self"), to a sociological phenomenon; rather, what is suggested is merely a correspondence.

If humanity's suffering stems fromits exaggerated perception of an ego and from clinging to its desires, then suffering can be alleviated only by the denial of that ego and its desires. Just as the ego grew out of all proportion within the social context, the same social mechanism can be used to vitiate it, to realize that there is no immutable soul, but only process created by the perceiving aggregates. This realization must ultimately be a personal one, but it is facilitated by social organization. That facilitating social organization is the *saṃgha,* a unique idea in Indian religious thought. Groups of wandering ascetics existed before and after the founding of the Buddhist *saṃgha,* but none was so organized and institutionally complex. Unlike previous groups, the *saṃgha* was structured around a sophisticated code of discipline and monastic etiquette, the Vinaya. Although the pursuit of mental cultivation by withdrawal to the forest or cave persisted, it appears that this "rhinoceros [i.e., solitary] ideal" was a survival from pre-Buddhist practice. Religious quest within a well-organized social group, the *saṃgha,* was a specifically Buddhist innovation. Although the ideals of the *saṃgha* were spiritual, its nonegoistic, socialistic, and republican features made it a model for a secular society at peace with itself, just as the uncompromising commitment of the renouncer was a virtue to be emulated by the individual layperson.

THE ECONOMIC LIFE OF THE SAṂGHA. Although some Western interpreters have maintained that Buddhism is concerned with the salvation of the individual renouncer, from its inception the tradition also clearly had a ministerial component. The Buddha's instruction to the seekers who heard his message was to carry it far and wide "for the good of the many, the comfort of the many." Yet alongside this purely missionary function grew functions of a pedagogic and parish nature arising out of the *saṃgha*'s scholastic bent and the instructional needs of the laity. Thus in the *saṃgha* two divisions grew, the "bearing of contemplation" (*vipassanā dhura*), or meditative development of one's own spirituality, and the "bearing of the books" (*gantha dhura*), the scholastic and parish functions. Eventually, the latter would gain in valuation, indicating the close relation the *saṃgha* was expected to maintain with society. At the same time, society took on the obligation to support and maintain the *saṃgha*. This arrangement, however, can be considered a consequence, albeit an early and a necessary one, of the rise of Buddhism within a social context.

There was a more basic reason why the economic life of the *saṃgha* could not exist apart from the munificence of the laity. An individual member of the *saṃgha*, the *śramaṇa* (f., *śramaṇā*), or renouncer, renounced what belonged to him or her in order to tread the path of purity and spiritual release. Providing such renouncers with their needs was an excellent opportunity for those who must remain within the bounds of household life to gain stores of merit (*puñña*) that would bear them fruit in the form of good fortune and good future births. The poverty of the *saṃgha* thus perfectly suited a laity in search of opportunities to perform good deeds (*puñña kamma;* Skt., *puṇya karman*), for it was held that no deed was so good in its potential for generating merit as the support of the *saṃgha*. The *saṃgha*'s economic dependence on the laity for subsistence is, therefore, no mere necessity, but, as more than one scholar has observed, an outward token of the renouncer's abandonment of personal resources to depend on those of the community that he serves. Thus, early in the development of Buddhism, the renouncer's needs were confined to the *catu paccaya* ("four requisites"), namely food, clothing, shelter, and medication. An individual monk ideally owns nothing privately but the *aṭṭha parikkhāra* ("eightfold items"), robes, begging bowl, and other basic personal accoutrements.

During the historical development of Buddhism, especially in the Buddhist kingdoms of Sri Lanka, Thailand, and Burma, the economic life of the *saṃgha* went through radical transformations. Extensive monastic properties grew, paradoxically arising from the sacred poverty of the *saṃgha*. Similarly, it was the fundamentally nonhierarchical nature of the *saṃgha*, among other reasons, that led to its being closely allied with the political order. In Sri Lanka, Buddhism was established as the state religion from its very inception: According to tradition, the king was the first Buddhist. Thus it was incumbent upon the king to endow the *saṃgha* generously, as did successive kings of all Buddhist polities, to bring under the purview of the *saṃgha* vast properties in the form of land. The king's act was exemplary and was followed by his patrimonial bureaucracy, down to the petty chiefs. Thus, paralleling the political hierarchy grew a hierarchy of monasteries owning vast stretches of property. The ideal of monastic poverty, however, was never abandoned, even though individual monks may have had access to considerable economic resources. This ideal was maintained in two ways. First, although land grants were made to the monasteries, their administration was separated from them and entrusted to lay officials. Second, lands granted to the monasteries, especially by the king, could in theory be taken away, although in fact this hardly ever occurred. However, in Sri Lanka sectarian schisms occasionally prompted monarchs to transfer properties of one monastic sect to another. The policy of making large-scale land grants contributed enormously to the longevity of the *saṃgha* and to its ability to survive economic adversity. In those agricultural societies that depended on the vagaries of rainfall for the cultivation of crops, especially the staple rice, prosperity could not be taken for granted, and often war and famine made it difficult for the laity to continue unbroken their pious donations. Indeed, the Sinhala term for famine, *durbhikṣa*, literally means the "absence of shares [i.e., food given as alms]." Thus the wealth of the monasteries can be considered to have played no small role in the viability of the *saṃgha* in the Buddhist polities of South and Southeast Asia.

The king's munificence toward the *saṃgha* served a politically legitimizing function. In addition, the land grants had a more direct political use, arising from the king's choice of their location. The king in Sri Lanka, for example, sometimes donated areas of property located in a province too distant for his immediate control (and hence potentially rebellious) and placed it under the control of a loyal subordinate. The tract of land thus demarcated, often extensive in size, essentially constituted a pocket of royal authority that acted as a counterforce to the threat posed by the provincial ruler.

A related point of great interest is the argument that monastic properties gave rise to monastic social structures. This intriguing theory has an important kernel of truth, especially when viewed in the context of the absence of hierarchical organization in the *saṃgha*. It can plausibly be argued that certain monastic social structures are indeed a function of the management of properties. The weakness of the theory lies in its very limited explanatory potential. Monastic properties, although in theory granted to an idealized *saṃgha* unbounded by time and space, are in fact granted to actual worldly institutions. It is in the context of particular space- and time-bound social structures that such properties must be understood. Even here it is doubtful whether the holding of property preceded evolution of the social structure, for the simple reason that it was an existing institution that received the property, an institution whose sociological structure could, of course, be modified by virtue of the new acquisition. At the broadest levels, and in the long run, it is difficult to maintain the materialist view that social structures are the product of property relations, although certain dynamic interrelations between the two are undeniable.

SAṂGHA AND POLITICAL AUTHORITY. One of the striking contrasts presented by early Buddhism is that whereas the *saṃgha* was ordered according to the political principles of the ancient tribal republics of India, its preferred political ally was clearly the monarchy. This may be explained by several factors. As has been indicated, Buddhism has been viewed as a reaction to a spirit of individualism that it perceived as the cause of social and individual suffering. Because the rise of the monarchical principle epitomizes that same individualism, it would seem appropriate for the *saṃgha* to organize itself on nonindividualist, nonmonarchical, nonhierarchical lines. However, Buddhism, always realistic in spirit, seems to have accepted the likelihood that the propagation of its message would be better facilitated by good relations with the monarchy. It must not be supposed, however, that this was a one-way process. The benefits were mutual. As Buddhism was from its very inception a movement that appealed most to urban strata, the task of controlling the powerful urban centers and sub-centers was rendered easier for the political authority, the monarch, once he espoused the religious ideology of the socially and economically dominant urban strata.

The affinity of Buddhism and its *saṃgha* to kingship is expressed in diverse ways, including myths and symbols of Buddhist kingship. Buddhist literature and lore have elevated the Buddha's father, the Sakyan ruler of a small kingdom, to the status of a monarch of imperial stature. The close relations between the Buddha and the kings of the Middle Country such as Kośala and Bimbisāra are no doubt characterized by some literary embellishment, but the historicity of the Buddha's affinity with contemporary monarchs of the region cannot be doubted. The most elaborate correlations between Buddhism and kingship are perhaps those in the symbolic sphere, in particular the identity between the Buddha and the *cakravartin* ("wheel turner"), the universal monarch. The auspicious bodily marks of the Buddha and the *cakravartin* are considered in Buddhist lore to be the same. The *cakravartin* turns the wheel of political conquest while the Buddha turns the wheel of the Dharma, the philosophy of Buddhism as well as its moral law of righteousness. The obsequies of the Buddha are considered in Buddhist literature to be those appropriate to a *cakravartin.*

The absence of hierarchy in the *saṃgha* has already been noted. Although this does not by any means make the *saṃgha* a democracy in the modern political sense—distinctions of senior and junior, teacher and pupil, ordained and novice are definitely observed—the *saṃgha* had no effective encompassing organization with laws, edicts, and codes smoothly flowing down a hierarchy of *saṃgha* officials. Because the *saṃgha* had no effective coercive authority within the bounds of its own organization, it had to look elsewhere for the sustenance and objectification of its moral and political integrity and for the adjudication of its conflicts. The preeminent repository of these functions was the king. Thus the *saṃgha* was politically as well as economically dependent on the king. This dependence most often took the form of "purification of the order" (*śāsana viśodhana;* Pali, *śāsana visodhana*), that is, by the staging of periodic purges of the *saṃgha* to free it from monks who violated the code of discipline. In addition, the purifications signified public reaffirmation of the *saṃgha*'s purity, on which depended its high esteem in society. The general public welcomed the purges because they guaranteed a virtuous and exemplary *saṃgha,* donations to which surpassed, in popular belief, all other acts of merit. The purifications were thus generally beneficial to all parties. Hence it is possible that these were regularly staged in Buddhist polities, as the historical record illustrates, whether or not an objective purificatory need existed. Apart from purifications, the king's organizational role in relation to the *saṃgha* was also manifest in the codification of doctrine and other acts that would enhance the *saṃgha*'s collective integrity. Historically, then, the king was indispensable to the *saṃgha.* Today, in Buddhist societies bereft of monarchy, this role is performed by the state.

Often, the integration of the *saṃgha* was historically effected by a hierarchy, imposed on it by the king, a hierarchy that duplicated the hierarchy of his secular patrimonial bureaucracy. The effectiveness of such imposed hierarchy, however, depended on the king's firm exercise of authority. At such times, the *saṃgha* may be considered to have had a more-than-usual political integration. In fact, it is more accurate to say that at all other times the *saṃgha* was merely a collection of politically disparate and inarticulate local communities. A king, however, was only able to integrate the *saṃgha* if he were an able ruler who integrated the secular polity itself, which in these systems was in a chronic state of tension between centripetality and centrifugality. Thus the king's integration of the *saṃgha* by the imposition of a hierarchy was no more than an extension of the integration of his secular power. Paradoxically, when the *saṃgha* was most politically integrated, and therefore most powerful, it was most dominated and regulated by the secular authority. At the same time, the king, while dominating the *saṃgha,* dared not alienate the monastic order lest it strike at the source of his legitimacy. Acceptance by the *saṃgha* was politically crucial for the king. It was part of the general cultural ideology of the Buddhist polity that the religion was the true sovereign over the land. Thus in Sri Lanka, kingship was described as being conferred by the *saṃgha* in order to maintain the religion. Kings periodically enacted symbolic abdication in favor of the Three Jewels (Buddha, Dharma, and Sangha), and the *saṃgha* "in keeping with custom" restored the kingship to the king, accepting in return a token of its overlordship, such as a land grant made on the occasion by the king.

One of the fundamental dilemmas of the association between kingship and the *saṃgha* is their respective ideal representation of two divergent realms, the temporal and the spiritual. The tension between the two spheres becomes reality when, as is the case with the Buddhist polity, righteousness is declared the foundation of the state. Statecraft necessitates not only the maintenance of internal law and order ultimately backed by coercive means but also the suppression of external enemies by bloodshed, not to mention more covert Machiavellian (or, the Indian context, Kautilyan) acts by means of which the state's ends are maintained. Such practices are far from "righteous."

Two resolutions of this dilemma are discernible in the history of Buddhist polities. First, the ruler's reign is divided into two periods, an unrighteous period followed by a righteous period, with the implication that the sins of the former are washed away by the pure waters of the latter. The empirical prototype of such a king, and indeed of all Buddhist kingship, is Aśoka (268–231 BCE), who, as Caṇḍāśoka ("Aśoka the cruel"), ruthlessly expands the empire bequeathed him by his Mauryan ancestors; his reign climaxed in the bloody conquest of Kalinga. Later, as Dharmāśoka ("Aśoka the righteous"), he proclaims the end of conquest by the sword and the dawn of the reign of *dharma* alone. The emperor's inner transformation thus serves as the resolution of the might-versus-right conflict.

The second resolution of the king's dilemma, like the first, is initiated by the personal remorse of the conqueror, although the process takes a less ethicized form. Apprehensive of the moral retribution that may befall him in future lives, the conqueror grows afraid of the demerit of bloody conquest overtaking the merit column of his moral balance sheet. The resolution of this conflict involves a diminution of the universal perspective, for it takes the form of personal reassurance granted the conqueror that the bloodshed he caused was for the purpose of protecting from alien threat the *dharma* and maintaining its dominance. Thus in the Sri Lankan chronicle *Mahāvaṃsa,* the hero Duṭṭhagāmaṇī is assured by the *saṃgha* that of the thousands massacred during the conquests, the number of human beings killed amounts to a mere one and a half (the rest being heathen whose extinction has little consequence for the king's moral state). This second resolution, in which elements less than universalist are apparent, can be further evaluated as ethically inferior in its relative valuation of human life (believers are truly human, heathens fit for slaughter).

This tension between the ideals of the *saṃgha* and those of the king are meaningfully characterized precisely because the two are in relation. Had they been fully and completely separate from each other, as in the case of a hypothetical fully secular king and an equally hypothetical forest-dwelling ascetic having no relations with the society of people, there would be no occasion for this dilemma to arise. However, in the actual world, the spiritual and the temporal, though ideally separate, are in fact coexistent. In the case of the Buddhist polity this "dialectical tension," as Stanley J. Tambiah has called it, is generated by the location of the *saṃgha* in society even while the *saṃgha* is not of the society. Such tension is based not so much on any social relationship between king and *saṃgha* or on the king's role as conqueror and converter of the heathen as on the indistinguishability of the spiritual and the temporal in the office of the sovereign as conceived in the Buddhist notion of kingship. Furthermore, this indistinguishability forces on the king the paradoxical obligation to deal with schisms in the *saṃgha.* This obligation involves the use of force against members of the *saṃgha* who are deemed offenders against orthodox purity. But such a judgment can by no means be objectively assured. Not infrequently in the history of the Buddhist polities "purges" of the *saṃgha* constitute a "unification" of the church, the meaning as well as durability of which may be dubious. Yet at least at the time of its accomplishment the act itself would appear to represent a victory both for the king and the section of the *saṃgha* he supported, and, in its "unified" sense, for the *saṃgha* as a whole. In principle, the king, now armed with the force of a purified and unified *saṃgha,* gains important political and religious prestige through his action, although such action presupposes considerable political power in the first place.

The relationship between kingship, that is, political authority, and the *saṃgha* has been so close in Buddhist polities that it is sometimes said that the existence of the *saṃgha* presupposes Buddhist kingship. The functional complementarity of the two parties centers around the *saṃgha's* dependence on the king for economic and organizational sustenance and the king's need of the *saṃgha* to legitimize his authority. *Saṃgha*-society relations are, however, broader than *saṃgha*-king relations, for the whole of society includes a third crucial party that makes up the whole, the mass of the lay population. Thus, it has been observed that the Buddhist polity consists of a triadic relation between *saṃgha,* king, and people. In time, such a polity could develop a strong identity fortified further by a common language and a real or imagined common ethnicity. Such an entity could grow to possess considerable integrative potential submerged in its chronic tension between centripetality and centrifugality. This potential could manifest itself with vigor at times of crisis, such as the external threat of some alien religion, language, and/or ethnic group. At such times, an ordinarily dormant and structurally vague *saṃgha* might awaken, assume formidable solidarity, and inspire the people to heightened states of patriotic fervor. Characteristically, it would return to its structural somnolence at the abatement of the crisis. The Buddhist polity is thus capable of producing two remarkable phenomena: (1) a unification of the *saṃgha* from within, inconceivable during normal times, when unification is achieved only by state imposition, and (2) a sense of political unity and identity, rare in the traditional world, which becomes historically ubiquitous only with the rise of the modern nation-state. Clearly, this crisis-triggered phenomenon represents neither a true unification of the *saṃgha* nor political centralization.

SAṂGHA SECTS AND SECTARIANISM. It is sometimes observed that there are no doctrinally differentiated sects in Buddhism. Yet Theravāda and Mahāyāna can both be considered sects in this sense. So can the numerous schools that developed within Theravāda in the early period of Buddhism. But throughout most of the history of Buddhist kingdoms, sects in this sense did not survive. As the schisms, purifications, and unifications show, however, differences of opinion and their corresponding social manifestations as sects (*nikāya*) were an integral part of the history of Buddhist kingdoms.

It is possible to posit two kinds of sects as ideal types. First are those sects that have as their basis some doctrinal difference. Ideology here determines the social categorization. Second are *saṃgha* sects derived from or influenced by secular social organization. The term *ideal type* is used because empirically neither type is found in pristine form. The ideologically determined sects have social factors contributing to their genesis; the socially determined ones often have ideological differences (however hairsplitting they may be), or at least cover the social origins of their differences in ideological apparel.

Present in both modern times and antiquity are sects that express the tension in the *saṃgha* between eremitical and cenobitic ideals, forest dwelling and village dwelling, "bearing of contemplation" and "bearing of the books." Although Buddhist liberation is an act of personal endeavor, it has been noted above that from its inception Buddhism conceived of the greater facility with which this end can be reached within a community framework; hence the vast importance in Buddhism of the *saṃgha* as the "third jewel." At the same time, the pre-Buddhist orthodox means of salvation by resorting to solitary confinement in forest or cave, the rhinoceros ideal, continued to be followed by some, if only a minority. Perhaps because the very solitariness of the search suggested greater purity and commitment, free from any obligations either to fellow members of the *saṃgha* community or to the laity, the solitary ideal was always held in high esteem. Sects or breakaway groups in the history of the *saṃgha* that were founded on doctrinal differences exemplify the ascetic/monastic tension and have invariably proclaimed their departure from the fold of orthodoxy as a movement toward greater purity and a renunciation of the comforts and social involvement of monasticism. Undoubtedly, such proclamations are idealizations; the true picture is more complex and allied with less lofty causal variables. Nevertheless, in terms of the renouncing group's own conceptualizations, movements toward asceticism can be viewed as purifications generated within the *saṃgha* itself, as opposed to those imposed upon it by the political authority.

In the history of the *saṃgha* such rebel movements, often inspired by and centered upon charismatic leadership, have in time succumbed to the very monastic organizational structures (and their secular economic, political, and adulatory accompaniments) that they denounced to begin with. Eventually, they have been lured back to the fold of worldly monasticism within which they may either rejoin the original parent group, remain within it as a distinct subgroup, or form a new sect altogether. Whichever of these forms the newly returned group assumes, its organizational form will normally be identical with that of the established sects. This "routinization of charisma" is neatly expressed in microcosmic form in the rite of ordination, in which the neophyte takes extreme vows of asceticism and, at the end of the ceremony, emerges with a higher status in the monastic establishment. Just as the rite of ordination is no more than a reaffirmation of high and pure ascetic ideals, so ascetic movements are periodic reminders of the true path of renunciation.

When confronted with cases in which elements of the secular social order have played a decisive role in the formation of Buddhist sects (as was true of the role of the Sinhala caste structure in the formation of certain nineteenth- and twentieth-century sects), some sociological observers have seen no more in these movements than the intrusion of society into the *saṃgha.* While this view is not wholly without merit, to assert it unequivocally is to reduce to social form phenomena that are ideologically autonomous and irreducible to social or other causal factors. To have recourse to this deterministic view is also to ignore the role of symbolic classification in the generation of sects. The evidence from Sri Lanka in particular suggests that certain sectarian divisions followed successive binary differentiations.

SECTS, SAINTS, AND MILLENNIAL BUDDHISM. The forest dwellers, a group that either came into being as a result of the self-purifying tendency within the *saṃgha* or arose anew from the laity (a less likely possibility), symbolically represent physical distance from the established secular order. They also typify a politically peripheral status in their habitation of the traditional sanctuary of the politically rebellious, namely the untamed forest. Hence, their appeal to the established political center can be vast. Furthermore, forest dwelling is synonymous with virtue and purity, and in the Buddhist polities of East Asia in particular, forest dwellers are often attributed great miraculous powers. As Tambiah's study of Thai Buddhism illustrates, the forest saints not only exemplify true asceticism as described in the classic text on the subject, the *Visuddhimagga,* but are also sometimes considered by the laity to have actually reached liberation by achieving "the winning of the stream" in the voyage to *nirvāna* (Pali, *nibbāna*). The politically central personalities—kings, prime ministers, generals—are thus forced by both spiritual and temporal interests to recognize and pay homage to them, a task that temporarily forces them out of their central fortresses to make uneasy journeys to the physical and political periphery where saints coexist with rebels. In general the saints are not interested in politics; their concern is spiritual commitment and the spiritual welfare of their immediate disciples and votaries. Nor is it possible for the political center to devote its sole energy to the veneration of the saints. In Thailand a happy medium is struck in medallions and amulets blessed with the saint's miraculous powers. In these cultic metal objects, which are made available to those who inhabit and control the political center, spiritual and temporal interests are welded together in much the same way as they are in the saint of the forest, whose path of purification also leads to the cosmic mountain symbolic of world conquest.

Today as in the past, a group surrounding such a forest saint is a potential threat to the political center, a threat to which the latter typically reacts in either of two ways. First, as already observed, it can make peaceful and devoted overtures and invoke the power of the miraculous objects blessed by the saint. Second, if the group surrounding the saint turns hostile, the center may resort to military action, against which the rebels, armed more with millennial expectations than military hardware, are no match. The forest saint's implicit premise that the established *saṃgha* and polity are corrupt may become the rallying point of rebellion, although this need not necessarily be so. In the established realm, *saṃgha* and political authority are separate but bound in reciprocity and mutuality, whereas in millenarianism, one possible rallying point of which is the forest-dwelling exemplar, the roles of renouncer and ruler tend to fuse together. This brings back full cycle, however fragile and illusory, the ideal unification of world renunciation and world conquest.

SEE ALSO Aśoka; Buddhism, overview article, and article on Buddhism in Southeast Asia; Buddhism, Schools of, article on Tibetan and Mongolian Buddhism; Cakravartin; Duṭṭhagāmaṇī; Kingship; Monasticism, article on Buddhist Monasticism; Priesthood, article on Buddhist Priesthood.

BIBLIOGRAPHY

A concise yet lucid source of the social and ideological background of Buddhism and the incipient *saṃgha* is Trevor O. Ling's *The Buddha* (London, 1973). Further details on this early period and developments up to about 1200 CE, with more focus on the *saṃgha* than on the wider society, are found in Sukumar Dutt's two works, *Early Buddhist Monachism,* 2d ed. (Bombay, 1960), and *Buddhist Monks and Monasteries of India: Their History and Their Contribution to Indian Culture* (London, 1962). E. Michael Mendelson's *Sangha and State in Burma: A Study of Monastic Sectarianism and Leadership,* edited by John P. Ferguson (Ithaca, N.Y., 1975), discusses several aspects of *saṃgha* relations with society, including the tension between the *saṃgha* and the political order. Kitsiri Malalgoda's *Buddhism in Sinhalese Society, 1750–1900* (Berkeley, Calif., 1976) discusses the response of the *saṃgha* to colonial domination in nineteenth-century Sri Lanka and relates sectarianism to caste competition generated by the dynamism of the period. The economic basis of monastic social structures is argued with forceful subtlety by R. A. L. H. Gunawardhana in his *Robe and Plough: Monasticism and Economic Interest in Early Medieval Sri Lanka* (Tucson, 1979), a work notable for its painstaking scholarship. The *saṃgha*'s preeminent position in society and polity in ancient Sri Lanka is described in Walpola Rahula's *History of Buddhism in Ceylon* (Colombo, 1956). The towering achievement in the study of *saṃgha*-society relations remains Stanley J. Tambiah's trilogy based on Thai material. *Buddhism and the Spirit Cults in North-East Thailand* (Cambridge, 1970), *World Conqueror and World Renouncer* (New York, 1976), and *The Buddhist Saints of the Forest and the Cult of Amulets* (Cambridge, 1984). The first work illustrates the transformation of the *saṃgha* in the process of meeting village-level society. The second is a grand view of the relations between *saṃgha* and polity. As Tambiah demonstrates, while in the decentralized kingdoms of Sukhōthai, Ayutthayā, and early Bangkok the *saṃgha*'s relations with the polity were loosely articulated, in the centralized Thai polity dating from the mid-nineteenth century the *saṃgha* became a systematized order actively participating in and regulated by the polity. This work also traces the path of achievement available to monks, from the rural monastery to the metropolis. The third of the trilogy examines the polity's relations with the nonestablished *saṃgha,* the forest-dwelling saints. The high esteem in which the political center holds this peripheral order, and the issue of millennialism lurking in its shadow, are discussed with authority and insight. All three works display vast learning and contain excellent bibliographies. Among the modern masters of social thought, Max Weber alone dealt with Buddhism in *The Religion of India,* translated and edited by Hans H. Gerth and Don Martindale (1958; reprint, New York, 1967), where he characteristically constructs an ideal type of the early *saṃgha* as separate from society yet in time transforming itself to accommodate lay religious needs. Although many of Weber's views are disputed, most forcefully by Tambiah, whose sociological imagination and expository style are reminiscent of Weber's own, there is still a great deal of potency and suggestiveness in his observations. Bardwell Smith has edited two volumes, *Religion and Legitimation of Power in Thailand, Laos and Burma* and *Religion and Legitimation of Power in Sri Lanka* (both Chambersburg, Pa., 1978), that contain several useful articles on the subject.

The Mahāyāna monastic orders of Japan and Tibet are vastly different from the Theravāda *saṃghas* of Sri Lanka, Thailand and Burma, which constitute data for the analysis presented in this article. For Tibet, there is little scholarly focus from a social science point of view, the bulk of the work being textual and religio-philosophical. Authoritative though brief discussions on Tibetan monasticism ("Lamaism") are found in Giuseppe Tucci's *The Religions of Tibet* (Berkeley, Calif., 1980) and Rolf A. Stein's *Tibetan Civilization* (Stanford, Calif., 1972). Daigon and Alicia Matsunaga's *Foundations of Japanese Buddhism,* 2 vols. (Los Angeles and Tokyo, 1978), deals with, among other things, the development of scholastic Buddhism as a magical agent of the Ritsuryo government, and the generalization of Buddhism from an aristocratic religion to one embracing all strata, and suggests the cyclically regenerative and reinterpretive nature of Japanese Buddhism. For a historically based discussion of the relationship of church and state in early Chinese Buddhism, see Erik Zürcher's *The Buddhist Conquest of China,* 2 vols. (Leiden, 1972).

H. L. SENEVIRATNE (1987)

SAṂGHA: SAṂGHA AND SOCIETY IN TIBET

In general, monasticism is based on the creation of a form of life separate from the confusion of the world to allow for the full expression of the religious vocation. In the Indian context, this monastic separation finds its standard expression in the phenomenon of world renunciation (*saṃnyāsa*). However, this analysis of monasticism as based on an ideal of world transcendence intended for virtuosi does not come close to capturing the historical reality of Buddhist monasticism. Even ideal-typically, Buddhist monks and nuns are not just virtuosi renouncers who live the homeless life prescribed by the Vinaya. They also play the role of priests, operating as the functionaries of the cult for the service of lay people to whom they provide ritual services in exchange for support. It is difficult to say when this priestly function developed, but it is clear that it started very early on, perhaps even earlier than the reign of Aśoka (c. 270–230 BCE). This transformation of the monastic ideal has affected all Buddhist traditions, and in this respect Tibet is not very different. This is not to say, however, that Tibetan monasticism does not have particularities of its own. In order to understand those, it may be helpful to start with a brief historical overview of the development of monasticism in Tibet and its relation to society before examining its institutional structures.

THE HISTORY OF THE TIBETAN *SAṂGHA*. Traditional Tibetan and modern scholars agree that the first Tibetan *saṃgha* was established during the second half of the eighth century. Prior to that period, there had been Buddhist monks in Tibet, mostly from Central Asia, but no indigenous *saṃgha*. This changed when the great Indian thinker Śāntarakṣita (c. 725–790) was invited to Tibet by the emperor Tri Song Detsen (740–798) to establish the first monastery at Bsam yas (Samye). Since at first it was not clear whether Tibetans would take to the monastic life, Śāntarakṣita ordained a trial group of seven Tibetans representing some of the prominent families. The trial was successful and other ordinations followed. Thus the *saṃgha* developed rapidly during the late period of the Tibetan empire, receiving the backing of some of the more important families and gaining the ability to exercise political influence over the court. During Tri Ralpacen's (817–838) reign, monks seem to have received further marks of favor from the ruler and to have increased their power, assuming even ministerial functions. It is also during this time that the first system of taxation was set up to support monks and monasteries. It is this situation that seems to have created a strong opposition leading to Ralpacen's assassination and his replacement by his brother, Lang Darma, the (in)famous last emperor. Traditional historians describe him as a persecutor of Buddhism, but modern scholars have argued that his target was less Buddhism than the sociopolitical influence of the *saṃgha*. Regardless, it is clear that his reign, and the events that followed his assassination by a Buddhist monk in 842, created a very confused situation that ultimately led to the disintegration of the empire.

As is often the case in Buddhist history, the demise of central power created considerable difficulties for the *saṃgha*, which seems to have disappeared from Central Tibet. A handful of monks found refuge in Kham in Eastern Tibet. There a young man, later known as Lhacen Gompa Rabsel, asked for ordination, but the five fully-ordained monks required for the ordination ritual could not be found until two Chinese monks agreed to participate. Several people were then ordained, and this allowed this lineage of ordination, which traces its source to Śāntarakṣita, to survive and later reestablish itself in Central Tibet, particularly among some of the Bka' gdams (Kadam) monasteries, such as Snar thang (Narthang).

This reestablishment of monasticism in Central Tibet took place during the second diffusion of Buddhism, particularly between the end of the tenth century and the beginning of the thirteenth century. It is during this period that the new schools (*gsar ma*), which take the second diffusion as their point of reference, emerged in opposition to the old school (*rnying ma*), which focuses on the earlier transmission. During this period, two other lineages of ordination came to Tibet, the first from Western Tibet, initiated by the king of Purang, Lha Lama Yeshe Öd, who, after ordaining himself, decided to seek a more proper ordination lineage from two Indians, Dharmapāla (963–1058) and Prajñāpāla. This line of ordination later spread to some Bka' gdams and Sa skya (Sakya) monasteries and included Rendawa and Gyeltsap. The last line of ordination to come to Tibet was brought by the famous scholar Śākya Śrībhadra (c. 1127–1225), who ordained his student, Sa skya Paṇḍita (1182–1251). This lineage became popular, and it came to include the great scholar Tsong kha pa (1357–1419) and most of his disciples. All three lineages derive from the Mūlasarvāstivāda and have been considered equally valid by Tibetan Vinaya masters. Belonging to a different school of ordination (Mahāsaṃghika), Atīśa (982–1054), the great Indian teacher whose synthesis of exoteric and esoteric traditions provides the basic structure of Tibetan Buddhism, decided not to participate in any ordination to avoid splitting the *saṃgha* in Tibet.

The monasticism of this later period, however, developed differently from that of the earlier period, in large part due to the historical circumstances. Whereas during the earlier period the authority of the state had been strong and relatively stable, the later period was marked by the collapse of such authority and the proliferation of local hegemonies. This political vacuum contributed to many of the characteristics of Tibetan monasticism, particularly the large intra- and intersectarian differences between monasteries and the role of non-ordained practitioners. It also partly explains the large political role that monastic groups have played in Tibetan history.

It is mostly among the new traditions that monasticism first redeveloped. The first school was the Bka' gdams school, which was established by Atīśa's disciple Drom dön ba (1005–1064), who, though himself a lay person, emphasized monasticism and the practice of the exoteric aspects of Buddhism. This emphasis on monasticism was imitated by other groups, such as the Sa skya and several Bka' brgyud (Kagyu) traditions, which were then forming. These schools followed some of the Bka' gdams ideas but also emphasized the importance of esoteric Buddhism. It was also during this period that Tibetan monasteries started to create their own indigenous scholastic culture. During the earlier period, Bsam yas had been a scholastic center, but it had fallen apart with the disintegration of the empire. From the end of the eleventh century, new centers started to emerge, the most famous being Sangpu, created in 1073 and further developed by Ngok Lotsawa and Chaba Chöki Sengge during the next hundred years. Many others, such as Sagya, Snar thang and Kathog, followed, introducing an important intellectual component within Tibetan monasticism.

Monasticism received a spectacular boost from Tsong kha pa, who after training in the monastic centers of his time, proposed his own synthesis. His approach strongly stressed the role of monasticism and emphasized the value of scholastic training. In 1409, Tsong kha pa founded the monastery of Dga' ldan (Gaden), followed by two powerful monastic centers, 'Bras pung (Drepung) and Se ra. Together they constitute the three monastic seats (*gdan sa*) and have come to play a central role in Tibetan monasticism, particularly in the last three centuries.

SAṂGHA AND SECTARIAN DEVELOPMENTS. The rise to prominence of these three monastic seats was the result of the spectacular growth among Tsong kha pa's followers. Although this group was initially well accepted as one among many, the situation quickly changed. Tsong kha pa's views became the target of numerous criticisms, and his followers gradually came to see themselves as forming a separate tradition, the Dge lugs (Geluk). The sectarian process was further strengthened by the political climate of the time, particularly the power struggle between the forces of Gtsang (Tsang) supported by the Sa skya and Bka' brgyud, and the forces from Central Tibet supported by the Dge lugs. This struggle lasted until the forces of Central Tibet, with Mongol support, won and established their hegemony in 1642, imposing their leader, the fifth Dalai Lama, as the supreme authority in Tibet. Under the protection of his government, the Dge lugs school became the most powerful, and its monasteries grew exponentially, particularly 'Bras pung, Dga' ldan, and Se ra. At the same time, restrictions were imposed on other schools. Some monasteries were converted, while others were limited in their scholarly activities and the range of material that monks could study. Not all non-Dge lugs schools, however, were equally affected. The Rnying ma (Nyingma), which remained separate, flourished during this period, creating monasteries and thus starting a move toward monasticism. This move gained impetus during the second half of the nineteenth century, when under the guidance of several nonsectarian teachers, all three non-Dge lugs schools started a revival, revitalizing their monastic centers and recreating their scholarly culture.

It is during this period of intense sectarian confrontation that two features of Tibetan monasticism became well established. The first is the role of reincarnated lamas, or *tulkus,* as leaders of monastic communities. The first example of such a unique Tibetan institution seems to have been the third Karma pa, Rang byung rdo rje (Rangjung Dorje, 1284–1339), who presented himself as the reincarnation of his illustrious predecessor, Karma pakshi (1204–1283). But prior to the fifteenth century, this mode of transmission of authority remained limited to a few lamas. The number and role of *tulkus* started to grow during the fifteenth century, a time of intense sectarian confrontation. This phenomenon is clear in the Dge lugs school, where authority over the tradition was at first transmitted following monastic lines of succession. But the effective leadership of the school gradually shifted to *tulkus,* particularly to the Dalai Lamas, who emerged during the sixteenth century as the de facto leaders of this tradition. This preeminent role was reinforced by the victory of 1642, which propelled the Dalai Lama to the rulership of the country. Henceforth, Tibet was going to be ruled, at least nominally, by a Buddhist monk, a unique occurrence in the history of Buddhist monasticism.

The rule of the Dalai Lama did not mean that monks held all the power, but it did imply that monasteries had a preeminent place and that their support became a governmental priority. As a result, starting from the seventeenth century, the number of monks and nuns grew, leading to what Melvyn Goldstein has aptly described as *mass monasticism*—the inclusion of a significant proportion of the population in the monastic order. Some estimate that before the invasion of Tibet by the People's Republic of China in 1950, up to 20 percent of the population may have been ordained, a proportion that appears to be without historical precedent. The consequence of this increase was the lowering of monastic standards. Monasteries placed few severe restrictions on comportment and allowed their monks extensive freedom to chose their lifestyle. This was particularly true of larger monasteries, where one could find a variety of monastic vocations, from that of great scholars and meditators to that of monks involved in trade and politics, or even that of punk monks (*ldab ldob*), who maintained order, collected taxes from recalcitrant payers, and defended monastic officials during their travels.

THE TIBETAN MONASTIC INSTITUTION. It would be wrong, however, to exaggerate the consequences of mass monasticism, for the lowering of standards did not affect all monasteries equally. In fact, when one surveys pre-1950 Tibetan monasticism, one fact dominates: the enormous diversity of organizational forms, disciplinary strictness, and institutional structures.

One of the intriguing aspects of this diversity is that monasticism in Tibet is not the only form of renunciate religiosity. Since the early period, there have been many nonordained *tantrikas* (*lngags pa*), often forming smaller communities that could compete with monasteries for resources. During the early stages of the second diffusion, these wandering or home-based practitioners often came into conflict with monks, who advocated a more established and exoteric form of Buddhism. A solution to this conflict developed gradually, starting with Atīśa's synthesis of Mahāyāna ideals and Tantric practices. This synthesis received further institutional implementation with the development of the Sa skya and Bka' brgyud schools, where Tantric rituals became integrated within monasticism. In this by now prevalent model, the community abides by the monastic discipline but practices Tantric rituals. It is often led by a lama, reincarnated or hereditary, who acts as the Tantric master and guides the community. This formula has allowed monasteries to provide the kind of rituals requested by the laity and thus successfully compete with non-ordained practitioners.

There were also major differences in disciplinary strictness among monasteries. Some monasteries were extremely lax in the enforcement of discipline, with monks often staying only occasionally in the monastery and spending most of their time working with their families. But other monasteries maintained very strict discipline. In the Tantric Monastery of Higher (Lhasa), for example, monks had to follow fairly strict Vinaya rules. They also had to spend the first three years of their careers in difficult conditions under close supervision. Even within a single monastery, variations existed. In general, the large central monasteries tended to be much stricter than the smaller local monasteries. Among those, there were also significant differences according to location. Monasteries in central areas tended to be stricter than those in more marginal areas. This diversity in monastic discipline is typical of a traditional society where the normalizing power of the state is limited. But such diversity seems to have been more accentuated in Tibet, in part due to the geography of the country, which makes communication difficult, but mostly because of the persistent weakness of the state throughout the formative period of Tibetan monasticism.

This diversity is enshrined in the local monastic constitution (*bca' yig*) of each monastery. This is, in fact, the central normative document of Tibetan monasteries, where life is less regulated by the canonical Vinaya than by the local constitution. Each monastery has its own (written or oral) constitution, a condensed body of customs, oral lore, and traditional documentation woven together with aspects of the Vinaya. This constitution addresses the governance of the monastery; the duties, responsibilities, and dress of monastic officers; the order of priority among members; the judicial procedures through which decisions are made; and the calendar for ritual observances. Thus, the role of the Vinaya became greatly reduced. Instead of providing the socio-juridical basis of monasticism, it became reduced to the definition of the monastic ethical code.

The monastic constitution also defines the monastery as a corporate entity, an association of the individual monks (or nuns) who are parts of the monastery, and who own and govern it in accordance with the rules prescribed by the constitution. Hence, a Tibetan monastery is not just a residence for monks or nuns, but a corporate body whose identity is maintained across generations and is enmeshed in politico-economical relations that can involve complex bureaucratic structures, mandatory activities, and onerous duties. As such, a monastery in pre-1950 Tibet often had considerable land holdings with a significant number of tenants. It was to manage this socio-economical involvement that monasteries were set up as associations.

Since a monastery is typically an association, to reside in that monastery as an ordained person is not enough to qualify as a member. A monk must be formally accepted by the monastic authorities after fulfilling the criteria for admission, which varies from monastery to monastery, the basic requirement being the ability to read and memorize the monastery's rituals. After being admitted, a member acquires certain rights and privileges. He has, for instance, the right to partake in the resources distributed by the monastery and to participate in the decisions governing the life of the community. Together with these rights come certain duties. He must attend the rituals of the monastery, and he may be appointed by the association to any of the monastic offices, tasks that can be at times extremely demanding.

One of the central activities of such an association is the practice of rituals. It is not an exaggeration to say that Tibetan monasteries are first and foremost ritual communities, which reflect the priestly role that monks have assumed throughout the history of the tradition. Even in large monasteries that have fostered the growth of a scholastic culture, life revolves around the practice of rituals, which take precedence over any other activity, studies included. Moreover, each monastery is identified by its own ritual material, which differentiates it from other monasteries. The monastic rituals of most monasteries are, however, similar, ranging from the ceremonies prescribed by the Vinaya to elaborate Tantric practices, often done at the request of sponsors.

INSTITUTIONAL STRUCTURES AND ECONOMIC LIFE. The diversity of Tibetan monasticism is also evident in its institutional structures. Some monasteries are very small, with perhaps as few as the four monks necessary to form a *saṃgha*, often staffed by monks who live at home. Others are large institutions with thousands of permanent residents and hundreds of highly trained scholars. To make sense of this variety it may be helpful to distinguish heuristically between local and central monasteries. Local monasteries are devoted almost exclusively to the practice of ritual and provide little training to their members. Or at least they do not function as training centers for monks from other monasteries. This is the role of central monasteries, where monks of a particular tradition can receive scholastic training.

Each school of Tibetan Buddhism has its own central monasteries, which also function as political, social, and economical centers. Each central monastery is at the heart of an extended network of affiliated local monasteries, which may be regional or may cover all of Tibet. This network brings the central monastery considerable resources, extending its pool of supporters and sponsors, and ensuring considerable influence. Although the difference between local and central monasteries is not always clear and has changed historically, it is usually accepted that there are six central monasteries in the Dge lugs tradition: the three seats (Dga' ldan, 'Bras pung, and Se ra), Tashi Lhunpo (bkra shis lhun po) in Shigatse, and Tashi Gomang (bkra shis sgo mang) and Kumbrum (sku 'bum) in Amdo. In the Rnying ma six monasteries function as centers: Mingdröling (smin grol gling) and Dorje Drak (rdo rje brag) in Central Tibet, plus Ka-thok (ka thog), Dzokchen (rdzogs chen), Payül (dpal yul), and Zhechen in Kham. Each of these large central monasteries has its own institutional structure. Since Dga' ldan, 'Bras pung, and Se ra are the largest monasteries ('Bras pung is said to have had more than ten thousand monks), a glimpse at their complex structures gives us some idea of the Tibetan premodern monastic institution.

First, the three seats each consisted of several monasteries, sometimes mislabeled in the secondary literature as "colleges." For example, 'Bras pung had four monasteries: Loseling, Gomang, Ngakpa (i.e., Tantric Monastery), and Deyang. Each of these entities was a monastery (*gwra tshang*), with its own assembly hall, administrative and disciplinary structures, economic basis, monastic constitution, scholastic manuals, and internal subdivisions into regional houses. The monastic seat was administered by a council composed of the representatives of the monasteries and regional houses, the present and former abbots of each monastery (the seat did not have an abbot), and important monastic officials. The council was in charge of deciding questions of discipline, arbitrating conflicts between monasteries, and relating to the outside world. Its decisions were implemented by two head disciplinarians whose authority was backed up by considerable disciplinary resources. The council and the head disciplinarians had no say, however, in the religious activities of each monastery.

Each monastery had its own administrative, disciplinary, and religious structure. It was administered by a council composed of the abbot, the representatives of each of the regional houses of the monastery, and important monastic officials. The religious activity of the monastery was directed by the abbot, who headed the monastery. Discipline was enforced by the disciplinarian, who had considerable authority, though less than the seat's head disciplinarians. A prayer leader led the monastic assembly in its ritual performances, and the director of studies oversaw aspects of the scholastic routine.

At the lowest level were the regional houses (*khang tshan*), where monks from the different regions were grouped. Each monastery had several regional houses. For example, in 'Bras pung, Gomang had sixteen regional houses, and Loseling had twenty-three. The regional houses were ruled by a council, which appointed a house teacher to administer the house. He was in charge of the discipline of the house, and of making sure that the schedule was respected, that young monks memorized their texts, that scholars went to debates, and so on. The house administrator also ensured that monks did not keep knives in their rooms, a reminder of the heteroclite nature of the monasteries, where the best scholar could lived side by side with the worst punk. As with the other monks in charge of monastic discipline, the house administrator could not be criticized while in office, even by the house's council. However, once he had stepped down after a fixed term (often a year), he could be criticized, and even penalized, by the council for his actions as house teacher. This system allowed officers to have sufficient authority over a large group of people who were often rowdy and difficult to control. It also provided checks and balances, since the officers were retroactively accountable for their actions and had to be mindful not to overstep their authority.

This description of the monastic chain of command does not even begin to communicate the complexity of the bureaucracies involved in the administration of the three seats. Each corporate entity (i.e., the seat, the monasteries, and the regional houses) was managed financially by a complex administration headed by several stewards. Even a single regional house had at least one steward and several grainkeepers and treasurers in charge of commercial transactions. Each corporate entity also had large estates where its subjects (*mi gser*) lived, bound to the land. The stewards and their administration would collect taxes (paid in the form of grain or butter rather than money) from these tenants. 'Bras pung (the seat, not the monasteries) is said to have had 185 estates with twenty thousand subjects, three hundred pastures, and sixteen thousand nomads. These resources would then be used by monastic officials to engage in a variety of trade and lending operations. For instance, grain might be lent to the peasants and collected back with a yearly interest as high as 20 percent. Butter would be sold, either on the market or as barter against other goods.

The administration of these monastic entities in Tibet required real political, administrative, and financial skill in the hands of monks who devoted their lives to these tasks. There was a kind of *cursus honorum* for those interested in the politico-administrative side of monastic life. Monks moved from lower to higher echelons, reaching important jobs that were a source of honor and considerable power. Often, but not always, the important jobs were monopolized by monks from aristocratic backgrounds, or by those belonging to one of the large households (*shag tshang chen mo*) of the monastery, which functioned like small dynasties of monastic administrators.

This administrative system illustrates the evolution of monasticism in Tibet, exemplifying the corporate nature of monasteries and their socioeconomic involvement. But it should be remembered that this system is not only a Tibetan development, but is also the result of an evolution within the overall trajectory of Buddhist monasticism. The existence of large monastic centers was made possible by the transformation of the role of monks, who were not just renouncers, but also performed priestly duties. It is this basic transformation that is reflected in the very structure of Tibetan monasteries, which are corporate entities organized in large part around the performance of this priestly function.

SEE ALSO Buddhism, article on Buddhism in Tibet; Buddhist Books and Texts, article on Canon and Canonization—Vinaya; Dalai Lama; Karma pas; Rnying ma pa (Nyingmapa) School; Tsong kha pa.

BIBLIOGRAPHY

Cabezón, José Ignacio. "The Regulations of a Monastery." In *Religions of Tibet in Practice,* edited by Donald Lopez Jr., pp. 335–351. Princeton, 1997.

Dreyfus, Georges. *The Sound of Two Hands Clapping: The Education of a Tibetan Buddhist Monk.* Berkeley, 2003.

Ellingson, Ter. "Tibetan Monastic Constitutions: The *bCa Yig.*" In *Reflections on Tibetan Culture: Essays in Memory of Turrell V. Wylie,* edited by Lawrence Epstein and Richard Sherburne, pp. 204–230. Lewiston, N.Y., 1990.

Goldstein, Melvyn. "A Study of the *ldab ldob.*" *Central Asiatic Journal* 9 (1964): 123–141.

Goldstein, Melvyn, and Paljor Tsarong. "Tibetan Buddhist Monasticism: Social, Psychological, and Cultural Implications." *Tibet Journal* 10, no. 1 (1985): 14–31.

Goldstein, Melvyn, and Matthew Kapstein. *Buddhism in Contemporary Tibet: Religious Revival and Cultural Identity.* Berkeley, 1998.

Gyatso, Lobsang. *Memoirs of a Tibetan Lama.* Ithaca, N.Y., 1998.

Kvaerne, Per. "Continuity and Change in Tibetan Monasticism." In *Korean and Asian Religious Tradition,* edited by Chai-Shin Yu. Toronto, 1977.

Kyongla Rato Rinpoche. *My Life and Lives: The Story of a Tibetan Incarnation.* New York, 1977.

Strøm, A. "The Dynamics and Politics of Institutional Continuity: Tibetan Monastic 'Colleges' in India." Ph.D. diss., Oslo University, 2000.

Tarab, Tulku. *A Brief History of Tibetan Academic Degrees in Buddhist Philosophy.* Copenhagen, 2000.

Wallace, B. Alan. *The Life and Teaching of Geshé Rabten: A Tibetan Lama's Search of Truth.* London, 1980.

GEORGES DREYFUS (2005)

SAMI RELIGION. The term *Sami* is an ethnonym used by the Sami people to describe themselves. They are also known by the term *Lapp,* which refers to their nomadic way of life, not to ethnicity, in accordance with the Swedish phrase "leva som lapp," which translates as "to live in the Lapp (i.e., nomadic) way," but the Sami find this expression to be pejorative. The Sami are popularly called "the people with four countries" because they make up an ethnic unit inside the borders and under the jurisdiction of four countries: Norway, Sweden, Finland, and Russia. From the Greek and Roman historians of antiquity to scholars of the present day, the Sami (also called Fenni and Finner) have excited the interest of historians (from the Greeks and Romans of antiquity to scholars of the present day), by virtue of the Old Norse sagas and as the people of Ultima Thule, occupying most northern territories of Northern Europe.

Within the Uralic language family, the Sami belong to the Finno-Ugric group, and are thus linguistically related to many of the peoples who live on the southern and eastern borders of their territories (e.g., the Baltic Finns: Finns, Karelians, and Estonians). Anthropologically, however, they are quite distinct from all but the Ob Ugric peoples (the Khanty and Mansi) and the Samoyed speakers who live at approximately the same latitude on either side of the Uralic Mountains in Russia. This kind of linguistic and anthropological diversity has given rise to a lively but as yet inconclusive scholarly debate as to the location of their original homeland. Present theories based on interdisciplinary research in archaeology, philology, anthropology, ethnography, and comparative religion suggest that the ancestors of contemporary Sami people probably came from diverse backgrounds and they spoke several different languages. Some of these ancestral languages must have died out without ever having been written down, so that now their cultures can only be hypothesized from archaeological evidence and their oral traditions, as well as through genetic analysis of blood types and other molecular research.

Today there remain about nine distinct Sami languages. These may be classified into two main groups. The Eastern group includes Inari, Skolt, Akkala, Kildin, and Ter; the Western group includes Mountain or Norwegian Sami, and includes the languages of Lule, Pite, and southern Sami dialects. The Sami languages share the same basic structure but are otherwise quite distinct; so much so that Sami speakers—many of whom are not only bilingual but rather tri- or even quin-lingual—must often resort to Finnish, Swedish, or Russian to understand each other. The linguistic situation is further complicated by the fact that a variety of competing orthographies have been employed to render the languages in written form.

Since the medieval era, from the twelfth century onwards, the Sami-occupied territories have been the most northerly point at which the Eastern and Western branches of Christianity meet. Beginning at that time and continuing until the seventeenth century, missionaries of the Russian Orthodox Church made converts among the Skolt, Akkala, Kildin, and Ter Sami of Kola peninsula and neighboring areas in North Russia. The Sami peoples in the West, on the other hand, had their earliest contacts with the Roman Catholic Church, but in the seventeenth and eighteenth centuries most of these were baptized into the Evangelical Lutheran Churches supported by the states in which they lived: Denmark (including Norway), and Sweden (including Finland). The earliest written document, the *Historia Norwegiae* from the twelfth century, describes an early encounter between Kristiani (Christians) and the "heathen" Sami *noaiddi.*

Most written texts that deal with non-Christian Sami religion date to the seventeenth and eighteenth centuries. These texts concentrate primarily on the beliefs of the nomadic reindeer breeders of Finland and Scandinavia (other Sami groups are less well represented). Many of the texts were written by clergy and missionaries, and often take the form of "confessions of heathenism" that were held in front of ecclesiastical courts. From the Sami of the east we have only ethnographic and linguistic notes dating to the nineteenth and twentieth centuries. By this time, the native religion had already been relegated to "the old custom" or "memories," and belief in the old gods had fallen away. However, there are good reasons to suppose that there existed, and still exists, a set of shared structures of belief, common to the whole Sami area, in which shamanism and ritual sacrifice are the dominant characteristics.

RELATIONS BETWEEN HUMANS AND ANIMALS. As is common among many of the peoples of the arctic and sub-arctic regions, the earliest Sami economies were based on hunting and fishing. Consequently, their most important rituals revolved around the hunting, killing, and burial of animals. They developed an elaborate conceptual, mythical, and ritual world in which animal spirits and divinities, that is supernatural beings whose zoomorphic forms and features have been taken from the animal kingdom, figure prominently.

The Sami in Finland called these spirits *haldi* (from the Finnish *haltija*, derived from an old Germanic word meaning "to own, to control, to protect"). They believed that all animals, as well as certain important geographical locales such as lakes, had their own protective *haldi*, and that people were obliged to show their respect for these spirits through such tokens as sacrificial offerings.

Of all the animals of the sub-polar region, the bear was regarded as the most sacred animal, and the rites connected with the bear hunt clearly reflect the reverence people felt for these special animals and for all other living creatures. Pehr Fjellström (writing in 1755) and Lars Levi Laestadius (a clergyman writing in the mid-1800s) provide detailed descriptions of the ceremonies performed at the start of a bear hunt. When someone found a hibernating bear, he led the rest of his group in a procession to the den. A ritually important person known as "the drummer" followed immediately behind him, after whom came the hunters, arrayed in a predetermined order. Once the animal had been killed, the hunters sang songs of thanks both to the bear and to the *Leibolmai* (alder-tree man), who is described as the god of the hunt or the lord of the animals. This divinity may be described by the German concept "Herr der Tiere," since his most important role was as the lord of the species of the bears and the largest representative of the zoomorphic world, with control and guardianship over all prey animals.

In their songs the hunters assured the bear that they had not intended to cause him any suffering. Indeed, they sometimes tried to shift the blame from themselves to others. In some of their songs they sang that "men from Sweden, Germany, England, and all foreign lands" had caused the bear's death, and when they returned home from the hunt their waiting women welcomed them as "men from all foreign lands." The meat was prepared by the men in a special place and brought into the *kota* ("tent" or "hut") through a special door. This was the *boassio-raikie*, the holy back door situated opposite the ordinary door. Arrayed in festive dress, the women sat waiting inside and spit chewed alder bark at the men as the meat was carried in. This custom of spitting should probably be regarded as a purification rite. Once the meat was eaten, all the bones were collected and buried in the order in which they are found in the body. The bear was thus given a proper funeral so that it could migrate to its celestial domain as the Great Bear (*Ursa major*). In accordance with Arctic astral mythology, the individual bear was regarded as the representative of its entire species, with the primordial mother of the clan as his spouse; by showing it due respect, the hunters hoped to secure the good will of all bears. This good will would work to their advantage during the next hunt.

The skeletons of other animals were occasionally treated with the same reverence. At certain times of the year, for example, all the bones of a reindeer were placed before a holy image at the place of sacrifice after the assembled men had eaten the meat (women were permitted to participate in the holy meal only on special occasions). The idol was smeared with the blood and grease of the sacrificial animal. It was believed that the god to whom the reindeer was offered would then resurrect the animal in his kingdom and derive benefit from it there.

IDOLS AND HOLY SITES. The word *seite*, or *siei'di* (also spelled *sieidi*), identifies a central phenomenon in Sami religion. In scholarly usage it has become a standard term for designating a phenomenon defining a particular type of sacred landscape found throughout the Sami area. A *seite* was a naturally formed stone found on a place that was regarded as *passe* ("sacred," "holy") and to which sacrifices were made by a clan, a reindeer herding community called *siida*, or a family. An unusual cliff could have the same function, and a whole mountain, called Ailigas, of which there are several throughout the Laplands (from Scandinavian *helig*, meaning holy), may have been regarded as a *seite*. Although we do not know their exact symbolism, we do know that *seite*-places were situated at certain points along Sami migration routes between different territories and that, as they passed such markers, people laid sacrificial offerings to bring them luck with their reindeer. There were also *seite*-stones or wooden idols with anthropomorphic forms at the good fishing spots on the shores of many lakes, and presumably sacrifices were made there to ensure good fishing.

SOUL CONCEPTIONS AND LAPP *NOAIDDI*; SAMI EXPRESSIONS ON SHAMANISM. The Sami notion that animals have guardian beings that must be respected by humans is based on the idea that every living being has at least two souls: a corporeal soul and a "free" soul. The free soul can manifest itself outside the body, and is regarded as a guardian spirit and a manifestation of a dual personality. Animals are regarded as the equal of humans and are treated as such. In dreams or in trancelike states such as ecstasy, the human free soul can leave the body and assume a concrete form.

Occasionally, a malicious being captures a soul, posing a mortal threat to the bearer. It was believed, for example, that serious illness occurred when someone, perhaps a dead relative, wanted to summon the ailing person to the realm of the dead, and had therefore captured the soul of the afflicted. In such cases the *noaiddi* (shaman) intervened. Shamans underwent a long and painful period of apprenticeship, and were believed to possess extraordinary psychic powers. As a result, the *noaiddi* could enter a state of ecstasy and, under this trance, send his soul to the home of the dead (*Jabme-aimo*), to negotiate with the dead or the goddess of the dead (called *Jabme-akka* in certain places) about the return of the soul. Sometimes the soul could be recovered through the promise of a sacrifice, in which case the sick person got well. One finds similar beliefs that the dead influence the well-being of the living among other peoples of the sub-polar region, with the shaman cast in a similar redemptive role.

The main role of the *noaiddi* is that of a mediator. However, he could not undertake his journeys to *Jabme-aimo* unassisted. During his apprenticeship he acquired relationships with supernatural beings who could aid him when necessary. Paramount among these helpers were the sacred animals: birds, fish (or snakes), and bull reindeer. The *noaiddi* recruited his assistants from *Sájva-ájmuo*, the dwelling place of the holy spirits. (*Sájva-ájmuo* corresponds to *Bâsse-Passevare*, the sacred mountains in the northern Sami territory.) Other spirits could also help the *noaddi* in the performance of his office. Legends tell of deceased *noaiddi* who provide a new *noaiddi* advice or provide other assistance.

The *noaiddi*'s ability to go into an ecstatic trance made him a general intermediary between human beings, who lived in the middle world, and the supernatural beings of the other (upper and nether) worlds. This belief in the triadic division of the universe has been shared with many peoples of northern Siberia who practiced shamanism. In addition to regulating relations between the middle world and the divinities and spirits of the other worlds, the *noaddi* also regulated the relationship between people and the powers of nature.

DEITIES. The Sami were not only aware of their dependence upon the rulers of places and animals; they also worshipped heavenly and atmospheric divinities. These superterrestrial beings had no part in immediate, everyday concerns, but rather they were powers to be reckoned with and were given sacrifices on special occasions. Among the eastern Sami, there was the popular divinity, *Tiermes*, who manifested himself in thunder and has been linked to the Ob-Ugric god of the sky, *Num-Turem*, and to the Samoyed god of the sky, *Num*. Among the western Sami, *Radien* (or *Rariet*: the ruler) was chief of the gods. In some places he was also called *vearalden Olmai* (man of the world, or cosmos) and *Mailman Radien* (the ruler of the world). The cult dedicated to him was primarily concerned with furthering reindeer breeding, but he was also the god who sustained the world. This was symbolized by a pillar, known among some of the Sami as the world's *stytto*, which was erected beside the ruler's idol at the sacrificial site. It was believed that the North Star was attached to the uppermost point of the pillar.

The mighty thunder god *Horagalles*, also known as *Attjie* (father), and *Bajjan* (he who is above), could demolish the mountains with his hammer and scatter and injure the reindeer. Sacrifices were offered to him in appeasement. The sun, *Beivie*, was vital to plant life, and sacrifices were made to him to ensure good grazing for the reindeer and rich vegetation in general. One observer writes that offerings to *Beivie* were burned to symbolize the heat of the sun. *Beivie* was also believed to help in curing mental illness. The moon, *Aske* or *Manno*, also received sacrifices, particularly during midwinter. *Bjiegg-Olmai* (wind man), also known as *Ilmaris*, controlled the winds and weather and was worshipped throughout the Sami region. The Sami celestial sphere, which was painted on drums, was centered around the Sun and the Moon, the Polar Star, the Great Bear and its Hunter (Orion) as well as the horned elk or reindeer (*Perseus* constellation) on their route to the Milky Way.

In traditional Sami beliefs and practice, women were under the special protection of the goddess *Madder-Akka* ("old woman of the tribe") and her three daughters, *Sarakka*, *Ugsakka*, and *Juksakka*. These goddesses were considered to be intimately connected with the household and domestic life.

SEE ALSO Finno-Ugric Religions.

BIBLIOGRAPHY

Source materials on Lapland and the Sami traditions begin to accumulate as early as the mid-seventeenth century, when Christian priests and missionaries reported to their superiors on all aspects of Sami culture, including religion and folklore. Some of these materials, focusing exclusively on Swedish Lapland, were published by Johannes Scheffer in his *Lapponia* (Frankfurt, 1673). Scheffer, a scholar from Elsass, was appointed Professor of Rhetorics in Uppsala by the kingdom of Sweden to counter prevailing rumors that the Sami used witchcraft on behalf of Sweden during its wars throughout Europe. The work was immediately translated into other European languages, including English (*The History of Lapland*, Oxford, 1694). Another translation appeared in 1736.

Eighteenth-century missionary reports contain greater details on the religious beliefs of the Scandinavian Saami, but few of them are available in a major language. Exceptions are Pehr Högström's *Beschreibung des der crone Schwweden gehörenden Lapplanders* (Copenhagen and Leipzig, 1748) and translations of Knud Leem's *Beskrivelse over Finmarkens Lapper, deres tungemaal, Leve-maade og firrige Afgudsdyrkelse* (*A Description of the Finnmark Lapps, Their Language, Customs, and Former Idolatry*, Copenhagen, 1767).

Lars Levi Laestadius published a valuable manuscript *Fragmenter i lappska Mythologien* that provides an ethnographical survey on Sami mythology. Written in five parts from 1840 to 1845, it was published by Juha Pentikäinen in Swedish in 1997, Finnish in 2000, and in English in 2002.

More recent and valuable sources dealing with the Sami of Finland and Russia include Arvid Genetz's *Wörterbuch der Kolalappischen Dialekte nebst Sprachproben* (Helsinki, 1891), a survey of traditional religion among the Russian Sami. Also important is Toivo Immanuel Itkonen's *Heidnische Religion und späterer Aberglaube bei den finnischen Lappen* (Helsinki, 1946), a collection of accounts of earlier beliefs among the Sami of Finland. Nickolai Kharuzin's *Russkie Lopari* (Moscow, 1890) contains extensive materials on myths, but the cult he describes derives largely from the materials of Scheffer and Högström—that is, from Scandinavia.

The Sami religion has mainly attracted Scandinavian scholars, and the first surveys were published in one or another of the Nordic languages. Such scholars as Uno Holmberg (Harva after 1927) in *Lappalaisten uskonto* (Porvoo, Finland, 1915), and Rafael Karsten, in *The Religion of the Samek* (Leiden, Netherlands, 1955), were strongly influenced by the evolutionism popular at the time, which they supplemented with theories on cultural borrowings. Holmberg's later survey of Finno-Ugric and Siberian mythology in *The Mythology of All Races*, vol. 4 (Boston, 1927), is methodologically much more modern. The most recent survey is Åke Hultkrantz's "Die Religion der Lappen," in *Die Religionen Nordeurasiens und der amerikanischen Arktis*, edited by Ivar Paulson et al. (Stuttgart, Germany, 1962). Among more recent scholars on Sami religion and mythology may be mentioned Louise Bäckman, Hans Mebius, Juha Pentikäinen and Håkan Rydving. *Sami Folkloristics* (2000) is an example of cooperation between Sami and non-Sami scholars and a model of a new approach to Sami studies that seeks to understand and interpret the oral and written sources on Sami folklore and folk belief.

There are some eighty preserved shaman drums in the museums around Europe, the oldest dating from the mid-seventeenth century. These have been described in detail by Ernst Mauritz Manker in *Die lappische Zaubertrommel*, vols. 1-2 (Stockholm, 1938–1950).

Various aspects of Sami religion, such as the bear ceremony, sacrifices, the shaman, rites of the dead, conceptions of the soul, the sun cult, the notion of the lord of animals, and the origin of the Saami, have also received extensive scholarly treatment.

LOUISE BÄCKMAN (1987)
JUHA PENTIKÄINEN (2005)

ŚAṂKARA SEE ŚAṄKARA

SĀṂKHYA, a Sanskrit word meaning "enumeration," "categorization" is derived from the substantive *saṃkhyā* ("number") and is the name of one of the earliest Hindu philosophical schools.

THE TEACHINGS OF THE SCHOOL. As the name implies, the Sāṃkhya school relies on distinct and recognizable patterns of enumeration as methods of inquiry. The different patterns of enumeration can be grouped into three main separate divisions according to their overall function in the system: the principles of twenty-five (constitutive), the dispositions of eight (projective), and the categories of fifty (effective).

Basic to an understanding of the Sāṃkhya school is the importance it places on the distinction between contentless consciousness *(puruṣa)* and materiality *(prakṛti)*, two completely different principles. Nothing exists apart from these two principles. This distinction caused the Sāṃkhya school to be labeled "dualistic." Contentless consciousness is the opposite of materiality in that it is inactive, yet conscious, and therefore not subject to change. Materiality, on the contrary, is potentially and actually active, but unconscious. Materiality is both unmanifest and manifest. The unmanifest materiality may also be called the "original materiality" because it is from this that the whole manifest universe emerges.

The universe undergoes cycles of evolution and absorption. During absorption, the original materiality is dormant, and the three constituents of materiality (the *guṇas*: *sattva*, *rajas*, and *tamas*) are in a state of equilibrium. On disturbing this equilibrium of the three constituents, the original materiality starts to reproduce itself. Unmanifest transforms into manifest materiality and keeps on transforming from one principle to the other until the original materiality has manifested itself in twenty-three principles. This is the constitutive pattern of enumeration, which is an extension of the fundamental duality. According to some accounts, the first principle to emerge is "the large one" (*mahat*); other accounts maintain that intellect (*buddhi*) emerges first. Either of these two principles produces ego (*ahaṃkāra*). Ego, in turn, produces ten faculties: five sense faculties (*buddhīndriya*) and five action faculties (*karmendriya*); ego also produces the mind (*manas*) and the five subtle elements (*tanmātra*). These subtle elements produce five gross elements (*bhūta*). Figure 1 (fashioned after the Sāṃkhya classic, the *Sāṃkhyakārikā* of Īśvarakṛṣṇa) gives an overview of the twenty-five principles that constitute the universe: the twenty-three produced principles and the two basic principles, contentless consciousness and original materiality.

All twenty-three principles of manifest materiality are a transformation of one thing, namely, the original materiality. These principles, in fact, are not new products or effects; their effects already exist in their causes. The essence of this theory of causality (*satkāryavāda*) is that an effect must be connected to preexisting necessary conditions, otherwise anything could be a cause of anything else; in other words, there must be a dependent relation between cause and effect, such that milk alone, for example, and not water, produces yogurt.

The Sāṃkhya school postulates that materiality is one, and that the evolution of a number of things out of that one materiality is understood as causation. The numerous things in this world are different from the original materiality, and yet they are the same. The things of everyday reality, ourselves, our minds, egos, and intellects are materiality. Mental functions are transformations, too. Contentless consciousness itself gets mixed up, as it were, with these transformations, although in reality contentless consciousness is merely a witness to them. But since contentless consciousness does not undergo any change and does not produce any activity, this confusion must be rooted in materiality. If anything is

Contentless Consciousness *(puruṣa)*		(1)
Original Materiality *(prakṛti)*		(1)
The Large One *(mahat)*/Intellect *(buddhi)*		(1)
Ego *(ahaṃkāra)*		(1)
Ear, Skin, Eye, Tounge, Nose	Five sense faculties *(buddhīndriya)*	(5)
Voice, Hand, Foot, Anus, Genitals	Five action faculties *(karmendriya)*	(5)
Mind *(manas)*		(1)
Sound, Touch, Color, Taste, Smell	Five subtle elements *(tanmātra)*	(5)
Air, Wind, Fire, Water, Earth	Five gross elements *(bhūta)*	(5)
		(25)

FIGURE 1. The Constitutive Pattern: The twenty-five principles that constitute the universe.

to be effected, it has to happen in materiality. It is not clear from Sāṃkhya literature how the two basic entities interact, if indeed they do.

It is here that metaphysics and epistemology merge. The confusion of contentless consciousness with materiality gives ground to epistemology. How does one remove this confusion, this ignorance that keeps the world in the repeating cycle of existence? Bondage in the cycle of lives is contingent upon ignorance of the distinction between materiality and contentless consciousness. The removal of confusion and ignorance is achieved by particular knowledge which differentiates or discriminates contentless consciousness from materiality. By means of this knowledge, one wins liberation. Thereby one ceases transmigrating from life to life.

Intellect, ego, mind, the five sense faculties, the five action faculties, and the five subtle elements together form the subtle body. This subtle body is attachable to, and detachable from, the gross body; by attaching itself to the gross body, it animates it. On the other hand, by detaching itself from the gross body at the time of death, the subtle body transmigrates. This subtle body includes the eight dispositions inherent in the intellect that form the projective pattern of enumeration, shown in figure 2. With respect to liberation, the left-hand column lists four dispositions that are constructive, and the right-hand column lists four dispositions that are destructive. Their composition changes depending on which disposition is predominant.

The effective pattern of enumeration results from the interaction between the eight dispositions of the intellect (the projective pattern) and the twenty-five principles that constitute the universe (the constitutive pattern). This effective pattern lists fifty categories of creations of the intellect: five misconceptions; twenty-eight incapacities of the sense, action, and mental faculties; nine contentments; and eight spiritual attainments.

These categories have still further subdivisions. At the same time, this pattern is interpreted in terms of four created forms of life: plants, animals, gods, and humans.

Patterns of enumeration were designated as a scholarly system that employs methodological devices (*tantrayukti*) based on a careful enumeration of subjects, features, and topics of things organized according to the different disciplines of the intellectual tradition in ancient India. These devices developed in various branches of learning, such as medicine and statecraft. According to the *Yuktidīpikā*, a commentary of the Sāṃkhya school of the latter half of the first millennium CE, the list of methodological devices of the scholarly system begins with mnemonic verses, followed by the instruments of knowledge, the members of inference, the complete set of the sixty topics of the Sāṃkhya system, doubt and proof, brief and detailed explanation, the order of topics as known in the evolution of the universe, and the description of things by name.

As is apparent from this enumeration of methodological devices, there is an emphasis on philosophical devices. These were employed to establish knowledge of things as they are, for the purpose of acquiring knowledge to attain liberation. Knowledge must be acquired by proper devices or methods of knowing, namely, perception, inference, and verbal testimony. The Sāṃkhya school gives special attention to inference since it is through inference that one can know the two principal entities: contentless consciousness and original materiality, both are beyond immediate sensory perception.

HISTORICAL OVERVIEW. The Sāṃkhya school grew out of naturalistic concerns. In the earliest articulation of Sāṃkhya ideas in the Upaniṣads (600 BCE to the first centuries of the common era), the most prominent ideas were often those characterized by the enumeration of various principles, such as elements of nature.

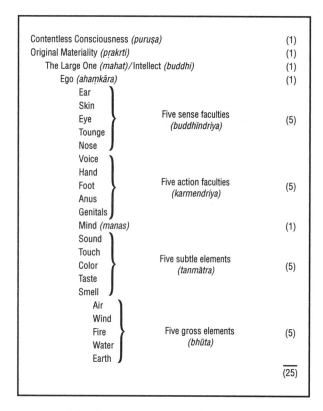

The *Bṛhadāraṇyaka Upaniṣad* and the *Chandogya Upaniṣad*, two of the oldest Upaniṣads, contain numerous explanations of the world in terms of sets of three constituents (*guṇas*), sometimes in the form of colors (black, white, and red), basic necessities of life (food, water, and heat), or seasons (summer, rains, and harvest), and so on. Obviously these oldest Upaniṣads represent layers of various thought structures. There seemed to be two elements, opposites, beneath the triple system: black and white, food and water, summer and rains, and so on. By adding a third element, such as the color red, the necessity of heat, or the season of harvest, the tension between the opposites was removed; and thus the triad lent itself to endless combinations. These triplings form the origins of the three constituents of materiality.

The analysis can continue by breaking this triad down into a dyad and the dyad into a single thing (the first Being). This process recalls the one-by-one involution of the twenty-three principles of the manifest materiality into the unmanifest original materiality at the time of reabsorption of the universe.

The polarity of contentless consciousness and materiality is characterized by the tension inherent in opposites. These two things cannot be combined. At most, they appear to interact; and in order to describe their relationship the Sāṃkhya teachers gave figurative illustrations. For example, a lame man can be of use to the blind man, and vice versa.

At the beginning of the common era, syncretism found its way into most intellectual environments. The names *Sāṃkhya* and *Yoga* might not refer at this time to philosophical schools. *Sāṃkhya* may be a name for any set of ideas explaining metaphysics, the knowledge of which leads to liberation. *Yoga* may be a name for meditative and postural practices that also were employed for spiritual advancement toward liberation.

Sāṃkhya and Yoga are often considered sibling schools, yet it is not clear whether their origins were symbiotic. Their origins are obscure. Both exhibit ideas of dissent from the Vedic sacrificial tradition which have been fully articulated in the anti-Vedic śramaṇic traditions, such as that of the Buddhists. In fact, Yoga was a practice of breathing, meditation, and postures used by a variety of religious traditions, yet not identified by any one in particular. Thus Yoga often existed alongside the newly formulated ideas that constituted the beginnings of the Sāṃkhya teachings. Since both, Sāṃkhya and Yoga, were some of the most extensively articulated teachings of the time, both found acceptance. The tendency toward interrelatedness of Sāṃkhya and Yoga was reflected in such works as the *Bhagavadgītā* (most prominently in the second chapter) and the *Mokṣadharma*, both of which are parts of the great epic the *Mahābhārata* (compiled in the period between the last centuries BCE and the first centuries CE). The adoption of Yoga in varied environments is echoed by Sāṃkhya in that that the Sāṃkhya doctrines became a substratum to many intellectual endeavors since the Upaniṣadic times for about one and half millennium. It can be said that where the Vedic tradition could not support new ideological developments, it was Sāṃkhya which paralleled as an alternative system to provide a base to intellectual activity. This substratum is evident in the medical treatises, such as *Caraka Saṃhitā* as well as in aesthetic compendia, such as the *Bhāratīya Nāṭyaśāstra*, not to omit later the Tantra movement where Sāṃkhya tenets provided the ontological, metaphysical, and ethical basis.

Constructive	Destructive
Merit	Demerit
Knowledge	Ignorance
Nonattachment	Attachment
Power	Impotence

FIGURE 2. The Projective Pattern: The eight dispositions of the intellect.

The time of syncretism was also clearly marked by theistic tendencies. References to the Sāṃkhya school indicated two directions, one theistic, the other atheistic, despite the fact that the school of Sāṃkhya, unlike that of Yoga, explains the creation and the existence of the universe in the absence of God. In discussions of Sāṃkhya and Yoga, reference to "the theistic school" usually means Yoga. Historically, Sāṃkhya and Yoga were closest to each other during the period of syncretism. It seems that from this time the two schools went their respective ways until the medieval period, when they again merged.

There is no independent work of the Sāṃkhya school's teachings from the first centuries of the common era. In later philosophical literature, there are references to *ṣaṣṭitantra* as a system of Sāṃkhya teachings. Again, it is not clear whether *ṣaṣṭitantra* was originally a name for a system of teachings or the title of a written work. When the fourteenth-century Jain scholar Guṇaratna mentions a revision of the *Ṣaṣṭitantra*, he is presumably referring to a work of the Sāṃkhya school. Apparently, just as Sāṃkhya and Yoga originally were names for teachings and only later became the designations of the schools, so also *ṣaṣṭitantra* was likely first a name for a system of teachings and only later a title of a work.

As the name indicates, *ṣaṣṭitantra* refers to "sixty topics" of a system. These topics are the ten basic topics characterizing the two entities (contentless consciousness and materiality) and the fifty categories mentioned above as intellectual creations. The date and authorship of the *Ṣaṣṭitantra*, either the original or the revised work, are difficult to verify. Estimated dates range between the first and fourth centuries CE. Authorship is attributed variously to Pañcaśikha or Vṛṣagaṇa or sometimes to the founder of the Sāṃkhya school, Kapila.

The list of Sāṃkhya teachers points to a rich intellectual heritage; unfortunately, none of their works has survived. One of these teachers, Vindhyavāsin, won a reputation as an ardent opponent of the Buddhists. He is also renowned for his statement that the mind is the sole instrument of the cognitive processes, as opposed to the assertion of the mainstream Sāṃkhya school that cognitive processes result from the internal instruments of intellect, ego, and mind. Vindhyavāsin thus expressed the understanding of the Yoga school, that is, the idea of only one internal instrument, the mind. Another Sāṃkhya teacher, Madhava, diverged from the mainstream of the Sāṃkhya school by interpreting the three constituents in terms of atoms, quite likely under the influence of the Vaiśeṣika school.

LITERATURE. The first extant independent written work of the Sāṃkhya school is the *Sāṃkhyakārikā* of Īśvarakṛṣṇa. This work has been variously dated but will be best placed at c. 500 CE. The *Sāṃkhyakārikā* is a sort of codification of the Sāṃkhya teachings; it deals with the various patterns of enumeration and sets forth the purpose of the teaching, that is, liberation through discrimination between contentless consciousness and materiality. This work marked the Sāṃkhya school with a philosophical emphasis because its goal, which can be described as religious experience, is accomplished through a cognitive process employing logic and epistemology.

A number of commentaries were written about this classic work over subsequent centuries: the *Suvarnasaptati* (preserved in the Chinese translation of Paramartha), *Sāṃkhyavṛtti*, *Sāṃkhyasaptativṛtti*, *Gauḍapādabhāṣya*, *Māṭharavṛtti*, *Jayamangalā*, *Yuktidīpikā*, and *Sāṃkhyatattvakaumudī*. With the exception of the *Yuktidīpikā* and the *Sāṃkhyatattvakaumudī*, the commentaries are mostly rephrasings and glossings on the mnemonic verses of the *Sāṃkhyakārikā*.

The *Yuktidīpikā*, which was made available in its first published edition in 1938, is the main source of information on many aspects of the Sāṃkhya teachings that have not been accessible otherwise. The *Yuktidīpikā*'s date and authorship are unclear. Moreover, Albrecht Wezler has shown that it contains two types of commentaries. One commentary, the *Rājavārttika*, is written in concise nominal statements (*vārttika*); the other is a commentary on these concise statements rather than on the *Sāṃkhyakārikā* itself. Thus it will be necessary to determine the dates and authors of the *Rājavārttika* and the *Yuktidīpikā*, respectively. The *Yuktidīpikā* proper deals with philosophical issues of the Sāṃkhya school in an argumentative style. The author presents a series of challenges posed by opponents (primarily Buddhist) and uses them to explain and prove the Sāṃkhya position.

The *Sāṃkhyatattvakaumudī*, a commentary written by Vācaspati Miśra I (c. eighth to ninth century CE), was the most important commentary on the *Sāṃkhyakārikā* before the discovery of the *Yuktidīpikā*. After this, there was no significant work until the sixteenth century, when the Sāṃkhya teacher Vijñānabhikṣu wrote the *Sāṃkhyapravacanabhāṣya* and the *Sāṃkhyasāra*. The *Sāṃkhyapravacanabhāṣya* is a commentary on the *Sāṃkhyasūtra*. Vijñānabhikṣu's interpretation of the Sāṃkhya teachings was influenced by the Vedānta school, at that time the most widespread philosophical school. This work represents the fusion of Sāṃkhya and Yoga.

The Sāṃkhya teachers continued into modern times to write commentaries on earlier Sāṃkhya works. Of the twentieth-century commentaries, the one of Bālarāma Udāsīna on the *Sāṃkhyatattvakaumudī* called *Vidvattoṣiṇī* is considered by the traditional scholars of India to be a fresh and lucid explanation of the Sāṃkhya teachings. The twentieth-century Sāṃkhya ascetic and teacher Hariharānanda Āraṇya followed the example of the old teachers: he spent most of his life meditating in solitude, only occasionally emerging to teach or to write such works as *The Sāṃkhyasūtras of Pañcaśikha* and *The Sāṃkhyatattvāloka*. Finally, the late Pandit Ram Shankar Bhattacharya, a Sāṃkhya teacher and scholar, has reedited significant old Sāṃkhya works and contributed articles to various journals.

SEE ALSO Indian Philosophies; Yoga.

BIBLIOGRAPHY

The most comprehensive work on the Sāṃkhya school is *Sāṃkhya: A Dualist Tradition in Indian Philosophy*, edited by Gerald J. Larson and Ram Shankar Bhattacharya (Princeton and Delhi, 1987), a volume in the *Encyclopedia of Indian Philosophies*, edited by Karl H. Potter. It has a detailed and up-to-date introduction to the different theories of the Sāṃkhya school; the larger part of the volume is given to the summaries of the Sāṃkhya works from early to modern times. The volume is a result of collaboration of Indian and Western scholars. Gerald J. Larson's *Classical Sāṃkhya: An Interpretation of Its History and Meaning*, 2d ed. (Santa Barbara, 1979) traces the origins of the school and also supplies the Sanskrit text of the *Sāṃkhyakārikā* with an English translation. The second edition differs from the first (Delhi, 1969) by a few additions to the original body of chapters. Michael Hulin's slim volume *Sāṃkhya Literature*, in *A History of Indian Literature*, edited by Jan Gonda, vol. 6, fasc. 3 (Wiesbaden, 1978), gives a survey of the Sāṃkhya writings. A lucid presentation of Sāṃkhya theory appears in Surendranath Dasgupta's *A History of Indian Philosophy*, vol. 1 (Cambridge, 1922), although his understanding is influenced by the medieval teacher Vijñanabhikṣu, whose interpretation of the Sāṃkhya is tinged in turn by Vedānta theory. A readable and thorough history of the Sāṃkhya school is in Erich Frauwallner's *Geschichte der Indischen Philosophie*, vol. 1 (Salzburg, 1953), translated by V. M. Bedekar as *History of Indian Philosophy*, vol. 1 (Delhi, 1973). One of the earlier works of good scholarship, but somewhat outdated, is Arthur Berriedale Keith's *The Sāṃkhya System*, 2d ed. (Calcutta, 1949). On the historical origins, see E. H. Johnston's *Early Sāṃkhya: An Essay on Its Historical Development according to the Texts* (1937; reprint, Delhi, 1974).

New Sources

Connolly, Peter. *Vitalistic Thought in India: A Study of the Prana Concept in Vedic Literature and Its Development in the Vedanta, Samkhya and Pancaratra Traditions.* Columbia, Mo., 2003.

Gopla, Lallanji. *Retrieving Samkhya History: An Ascent from Dawn to Meridian.* New Delhi, 2000.

Jacobsen, Knut A. *Prakrti in Samkhya-Yoga: Material Principle, Religious Experience, Ethical Implications.* Delhi, 2002.

Kesavan Nampoothiri. *The Concept of Apovarga in Samkhya Philosophy.* Delhi, 1990.

Larson, Gerald James. *Classical Samkhya: An Interpretation of Its History and Meaning.* Delhi, 2001.

Perrett, Roy W. "Computationality, Mind and Value: The Case of Samkhya Yoga." *Asian Philosophy* 11 (March 2001): 5–15.

Weerasinghe, S. G. M. *The Samkhya Philosphy: A Critical Evaluation of Its Origins and Development.* Delhi, 1993.

EDELTRAUD HARZER (1987 AND 2005)

SAṂNYĀSA. The Sanskrit term *saṃnyāsa* commonly means "renunciation of the world." It refers both to the initiatory rite at which a renouncer (*saṃnyāsin*) formally breaks all his ties with society and to the way of life into which he is so initiated. The term is absent from the Vedic texts and from the Buddhist and Jain literature. It is used exclusively in the Brahmanic tradition and the Hindu sectarian traditions deriving from the medieval period; it refers to renunciation as practiced only within these traditions. The word entered the Brahmanic vocabulary probably around the second century BCE.

RENUNCIATION AND BRAHMANISM. There is no consensus among scholars regarding the origin of world renunciation in India. Given the fragmentary nature of the evidence, this is an issue that is likely to remain unresolved. Recent scholarship, however, has shown that the claim once made that the renunciatory ideal originated exclusively among the non-Brahmanic or even the non-Aryan population is unfounded. The earliest available evidence shows that by the sixth century BCE the institution of world renunciation formed an important part of the entire spectrum of religious traditions and sects of North India, including Brahmanism. Renunciation, nevertheless, questioned the value of major Brahmanic institutions such as marriage, sacrificial rites, and the social hierarchy of castes. Because it proclaimed the path of renunciation, divorced from ritual and society, as the acme of religious life, the way of renunciation posed a special challenge to the society-centered Vedic religion, which recognized only one socioreligious role for adult men, that of the married householder with his social, procreative, and ritual obligations. The Brahmanic tradition, however, has always demonstrated the ability to absorb the new without discarding the old. Attempts were made to find theoretical legitimations for the lifestyles of both the renouncer and the householder, the most significant of which was the system of the four *āśramas* (orders of life). Renunciation was sometimes redefined to accommodate life in society. The devotional traditions *(bhakti)*, for example, considered true renunciation to be the inner quality of detachment from the world and from the results of one's actions rather than the physical separation from society. Some of these traditions defined renunciation as surrender to God. Despite such efforts at synthesis, a tension between these two ideals has continued to exist within Brahmanism.

LIFESTYLE AND GOAL. The main features of the renunciant life are substantially the same in all sects at least within the ideal rules presented in the textual traditions. Renouncers are homeless. Except for the four months of the rainy season (June through September), they are required to wander constantly. Their ideal residence is the foot of a tree. Renouncers shave their heads and either go naked or wear an ocher robe. They practice celibacy and poverty, obtaining their food and the other few necessities of life by begging. Several terms for a renouncer, such as *parivrājaka* ("wanderer") and *bhikṣu* ("mendicant"), reflect these aspects of his life. All these features, moreover, need to be understood not merely as ascetic practices but as symbolic rejections of social customs and institutions. A significant feature of the renouncers' style of life is the abandonment of fire. It symbolizes their separation from Vedic society and religion, and in a special way their rejection of the Vedic sacrifice. Though it is present in all renouncer traditions, the abandonment of fire occupies a central position in Brahmanic renunciation, which is often defined as the abandonment of all ritual actions. The absence of fire gave rise to two other customs. Unable to cook for themselves, renouncers beg cooked food daily. After death they are not cremated like other people but are buried either on land or in water, for cremation is performed with the sacred fires of the deceased and constitutes his last sacrifice (*antyeṣṭi*). The greatest transformation of renunciation occurred in early Buddhism with the establishment of permanent monastic communities and the consequent abandonment of the itinerant lifestyle. Monastic orders were not organized within Brahmanism until a much later period. The best known among them is the Order of Ten Names (Daśanāmis), reputedly founded by the Advaita philosopher Śaṅkara (788–820 CE). In spite of the reality of settled monastic living, however, it was never accepted either as law or as ideal. The rule of homeless wandering was maintained at least theoretically both within and outside Brahmanism. Although lower goals, such as attaining a heavenly world, are often mentioned, liberation (*mokṣa*) from the constant cycle of births and deaths (*saṃsāra*) is considered the goal of renunciation. Many sects regard it as a precondition for liberation. Saṃnyāsa, therefore, is often referred to as *mokṣāśrama* or simply as *mokṣa.* Brahmanism establishes a hierarchy among renouncers based on the degree of their removal from the world and from social norms. The lowest is called a *kuṭīcaka.* He lives a life of retirement in a hut and receives food from his children. The next is a *bahūdaka,* who begs for food and adopts a wandering life. A *haṃsa* carries a single staff, and is thus distinguished from the first two, who carry three staffs tied together. The fourth and highest type of renouncer is a *paramahaṃsa.* He breaks all social ties, discarding the sacrificial thread and the tuft of hair on the crown, the two basic symbols of his former ritual and social status.

INITIATION. All renouncer sects devised some form of initiation, and Brahmanism was no exception. In fact, one of the earliest usages of the term *saṃnyāsa* was with reference to the Brahmanic rite of renunciation. No uniform rite, however, evolved within Brahmanism, and even the medieval handbooks give different versions. On the major features, nevertheless, there is agreement. The rite takes two days, although most of the major ceremonies are performed on the second. On the first day the candidate performs nine oblations for the dead (Śrāddha), the last of which he offers for himself. The following day he performs his last sacrifice and gives away all his worldly goods. He then symbolically deposits his sacred fires within himself by inhaling their smoke, burns his sacrificial utensils, and extinguishes his sacred fires. The abandonment of fire and ritual is interpreted as an internalization; a renouncer carries the fires within himself in the form of his breaths (*prāṇa*) and offers an internal sacrifice in these fires every time he eats. He then utters three times the Praisa, or renunciatory formula: "I have renounced" ("Saṃnyastaṃ mayā"), and gives the "gift of safety" (*abhayadāna*) to all creatures with the promise never to injure any living being. He is now a renouncer. He ceremonially takes the requisites of a renouncer, such as staff and begging bowl, the emblems of his new state (*yatiliṅga*).

QUALIFICATION. The rite of renunciation results in the ritual abandonment of all rites. Paradoxical as this seems, it enabled the socioritual norms of Brahmanism to control the entry into the very state that aims at transcending them. The question of qualification precedes any discussion of a ritual action, including the rite of renunciation. Only the three twice-born classes (*varṇas*) are qualified to perform rites, and, therefore, to renounce. Opinion, however, is sharply divided as to whether only brahmans or all three upper classes are so qualified. A person, moreover, has to pass through the *āśramas* of student, householder, and forest hermit before renouncing, although with the obsolescence of the hermit's state this rule was interpreted to mean that a person should be free from the three debts incurred at birth, namely Vedic study, sacrifice, and procreation, which are paid by fulfilling the obligations of the first two *āśramas.* One view, however, holds that these provisions apply only to ordinary people; one who is totally detached from the world may renounce immediately. The position of women is also ambiguous. Orders of nuns exist in Buddhism, in Jainism, and in some medieval Hindu sects. Female renouncers are referred to frequently in Sanskrit literature, and their position is recognized in Hindu law. Brahmanic authorities generally deny the legitimacy of female renunciation, although occasionally dissenting voices are heard in this regard.

RITUAL AND LEGAL EFFECTS. The renunciatory rite is regarded as the ritual death of the renouncer. Although dead, he is nevertheless visibly present among the living and occupies an ambivalent position within Brahmanism. He is excluded from all ritual acts. His status as far as ritual purity is concerned is unclear. Although theologically he is often considered the acme of purity, within ritual contexts his presence is feared as a cause of impurity. In Hindu law, the renouncer's ritual death constitutes also his civil death. The renunciation of the father, like his physical death, is the occasion for the succession of his heirs. It also dissolves his marriage, and some authorities, such as the *Nāradasmṛti* (12.97), would permit his wife to remarry. Renouncers, moreover, cannot take part in legal transactions and are released from previous contractual obligations and debts. They are not even permitted to appear as witnesses in a court of law. Renunciation is considered an irreversible state, both ritually and socially. A renouncer who reverts to lay life (*ārūḍhapatita*) becomes an outcaste (*cāṇḍāla*) and is excluded from all ritual and social contact.

CONCLUSION. Renunciation was one of the most significant developments in the history of Indian religions. It influenced the post-Vedic worldview based on the central concepts of *saṃsāra* and *mokṣa.* The founders of almost all major Indian religions and sects were renouncers. The mentality of the renouncer influenced even the religious life and the value system of people within society. The society-centered and the world-renouncing ideologies represented by the householder and the *saṃnyāsin* continued to exist side by side within Brahmanism. As Dumont (1960) observes, "The secret of Hinduism may be found in the dialogue between the renouncer and the man-in-the-world" (pp. 36–37). Hinduism in general and Brahmanism in particular cannot be understood adequately if the researcher ignores either of these two poles and their interaction.

SEE ALSO Bhakti; Mokṣa; Monasticism, article on Buddhist Monasticism; Rites of Passage, article on Hindu Rites; Śaivism, articles on Kāpālikas, Pāśupatas; Saṃsāra.

BIBLIOGRAPHY

Dumont, Louis. "World Renunciation in Indian Religions." *Contributions to Indian Sociology* 4 (1960): 33–62. A seminal study on the role of renunciation in the historical development of religion in India.

Ghurye, G. S. *Indian Sadhus.* 2d ed. Bombay, 1964. Somewhat outdated, but still the most comprehensive account of the ascetical sects within Hinduism.

Heesterman, Jan C. "Brahmin, Ritual and Renouncer." *Wiener Zeitschrift für die Kunde Süd- und Ostasiens* 8 (1964): 1–31. Attempts to demonstrate that renunciation was the logical outcome of the inner dynamic of Brahmanism.

Kane, Pandurang Vaman. *History of Dharmasastra,* vol. 2. 2d ed., rev. & enl. Poona, 1974. Part 2, pp. 930–975, provides the most comprehensive account of *saṃnyāsa* in the Dharmasastra literature.

Miller, David M., and Dorothy C. Wertz. *Hindu Monastic Life: The Monks and Monasteries of Bhubaneswar.* Montreal, 1976. A good description of Hindu monks and monasteries in a major monastic center in modern India.

Olivelle, Patrick. "Contributions to the Semantic Development of Saṃnyāsa," *Journal of the American Oriental Society* 101 (1981): 265–274. The only study on the early uses of the term *saṃnyāsa.*

Olivelle, Patrick. *Saṃnyāsa Upaniṣads: Hindu Scriptures on Asceticism and Renunciation.* New York, 1992.

Olivelle, Patrick, ed. and trans. *Vasudevasrama Yatidharmaprakasa.* 2 vols. Delhi and Vienna, 1976–1977. A medieval handbook that shows how renunciation was understood and practiced within Brahmanism.

Sharma, Har Dutt. *Contributions to the History of Brahmanical Asceticism (Saṃnyāsa)*. Poona, 1939. An early but still useful study based on the law books and the *Saṃnyāsa Upaniṣads.*

Sprockhoff, Joachim Friedrich. *Saṃnyāsa: Quellenstudien zur Askese im Hinduismus.* Wiesbaden, 1976. A detailed examination of the *Saṃnyāsa Upaniṣads.* The best overall study of Brahmanic renunciation.

PATRICK OLIVELLE (1987 AND 2005)

SAMOYED RELIGION. The Samoyeds are the indigenous peoples of the tundra, taiga and mountainous territories in northern Eurasia who speak a systematically related set of languages. Most live in western Siberia, in the region extending from the Yamal and Taimyr peninsulas at the Arctic Ocean in the north along the waterways of the Yenisei River to the Sayan Mountains in the south; a few live in northeasternmost Europe on the Kola Peninsula and near the Pechora River. As a linguistic group, Samoyed is related to Finno-Ugric; together they form the Uralic language family.

Currently numbering about thirty-five thousand, the Samoyed peoples are broadly divided into the northern Samoyeds and the southern Samoyeds. Northern Samoyed groups include the Nentsy (also called the Yurak Samoyeds or the Yuraks), who, with approximately thirty thousand members, are by far the largest Samoyed group, extending their territory from the Kola Peninsula crossing the Urals and over the Yamal Peninsnula to the Yenisei; the Nganasani (or Tavgi), with about 800–1000 members at the Taimyr Peninsula; and the Entsy (or Yenisei Samoyeds), with about 200–400 members. Of the southern Samoyeds, only one group survives, the Selkup (formerly called the Ostiak Samoyeds), with some 3,500 members.

Some extinct southern Samoyed groups, such as the Kamassians, the Koibal, the Motor, and the Taigi are now known only from notes and records made by such scholars as M. A. Castrén and Kai Donner. The Kamas language became extinct in 1991 with the death of its last speaker and singer, Klaudia Plotnikova, who lived in Krasnoyarsk on the Yenisei River.

Before the formation of the present Samoyed languages and groups, a proto-Samoyed group presumably existed some 3,500 years ago, when it seceded from the larger proto-Uralic parent group.

The neighbors of the Samoyed are, or have been in the course of history, the Khanty and the Komi at the Ob River, the Sami and the Komi on the Kola Peninsula (Finno-Ugric peoples), various Siberian Turkic peoples, the Evenki (a Tunguz people), the Ket (sometimes classified as a Paleosiberian group), and most recently the Russians. After the colonialization of the Soviet period from the 1920s and the intensive gas production of the 1960s, the Samoyeds had the whole multitude of peoples from the former Soviet Union as their neighbors.

Samoyed traditional culture is based primarily on hunting for fur-bearing animals, gathering, fishing, and reindeer breeding. Collectivization was introduced into the Samoyed economy by the Soviet government in the 1920s.

THE SPIRIT WORLD. The principal Nentsy deity is Num, the creator of the world, of human beings, and of inanimate objects. His role is ambiguous: in general he distances himself from human beings and abstains from interference in their affairs except when they call on him explicitly for help in the struggle against Nga, the god of evil, death, and hell. In Nenets religion, Nga is Num's son, but this father-son duality is not found among other Samoyed groups, in which the high benevolent gods and their opposites are considered to be independent of one another. Sacrifices are made to Num twice a year, at the beginning of winter and again in the spring. These sacrifices are either bloody, involving the killing of dogs or reindeer; or bloodless, involving the offering of money, clothing, and food.

Another inhabitant of the spirit world is Ilibemberti; in Nenets religion he is reported variously as a spirit who grants good fortune in the pursuit of reindeer and foxes and alternately as a protector of reindeer. He does not have the status of a god, which is reserved for Num and Nga. Freely translated, the name Ilibemberti means "the spirit that gives riches or sustenance (in reindeer or game)." The significance of this supernatural personality lies in the fact that Ilibemberti is involved in the concrete here and now, and is as such opposed to Num, the highest god and creator, who is shapeless and transcends time. The Samoyeds also recognize an earth mother deity who is sympathetic to humans, especially to women in childbirth.

The Nentsy are reported to worship stones and rocks. Properly speaking, this finding means that certain mountains and rocks, as well as some rivers and lakes, were considered to have individual spirits deserving reverence. The Nganasani are said to have believed that some artifacts of human manufacture could understand human language. The Nganasani grouped supernatural beings into a hierarchy of three classes: benevolent master spirits associated with fire, water, forests, hunting, and fishing; evil anthropomorphic spirits; and the shaman's auxiliary spirits, who were mostly zoomorphic. Among the Selkup, the master spirits were sometimes considered repositories of good fortune. In general, the spirits were regarded as intermediaries between Num and humans, and as being in contact with shamans. Each person was thought to have a corresponding star in the heavens—a belief that brings people closer to Num than Num's disinterested attitude mentioned earlier would suggest.

SAMOYED RITUALS. Besides the cyclic sacrifices to Num mentioned above, other sacrifices are made at specific sacred sites, where wooden or stone representations of certain spirits are erected. Among the Selkup these sites are phratrilocal. Of the rites of passage celebrated by the Samoyed groups, the most important are the shaman's initiation, rites after childbirth that primarily involve purification of the tent, and ritual ceremonies for the dead.

It is believed that the dead continue to live as shadow souls—varieties of lower spirits—in the underworld. Among the Entsy, the deceased person is left in the tent, wrapped in hides for a number of days, while family life continues unchanged. After a sacrifice involving bread placed in a pot with a lid, brick tea, and some of the belongings of the deceased, the corpse is transported to the burial site and placed in a coffin constructed with iron nails, with the corpse's feet pointing north. Before the coffin is lowered into the freshly dug grave, it is loaded with the gifts that have been prepared earlier, as well as with utensils used in the processing of animal hides. The nearest surviving relative chants laments. Later, sticks are placed over the footprints leading to the burial site while the mourning party, pointing to the north, exhorts the deceased not to return.

The Nentsy also deposit a dead man's broken sledge near his grave and slaughter reindeer on the occasion of the funeral ritual. Infants who die soon after birth are wrapped in bundles and suspended from trees or poles. After the death of an adult male, his wife makes a wooden amulet or doll-effigy in the shape of her husband; she clothes and feeds it, and sleeps with it for six months after his death; she may not remarry during this period. Among some groups this amulet is kept for three years. Amulets are generally kept on a specially designated shelf in the rear part of the tent, which is considered sacred.

Specialized rites among the Samoyeds include tent-cleaning ceremonies (in February among the Nganasani). Among the Nentsy, loon skins are burned to ensure good weather, or locks of someone's hair or clippings of his fingernails are burned in order to cause that person misfortune.

Relations between Human Beings and Animals. Only one animal is expressly singled out as evil among the Samoyed: the wolf, which is the reindeer's most dangerous foe. Some fish, such as the pike, are revered. The reindeer is regarded as a pure animal; white reindeer, in particular, are associated with the sun and considered sacred. As elsewhere in Siberia, the bear is accorded special respect. Bear meat must be chewed in a prescribed manner and may not be consumed at all by women. Women are also forbidden to eat the heads of reindeer or of certain fish, such as pike or raw sturgeon.

Certain Samoyed clans associate their origins or ancestors with specific clan-protector spirits envisaged as animals. Such beliefs are usually defined by historians of religion as totemistic. These beliefs govern specific attitudes and behavior patterns (especially taboos) in regard to particular animals. As has already been implied, many taboos were traditionally engendered by attitudes toward women. Because women were considered unclean, they were forbidden to step over hunting equipment.

Shamanhood. Broadly speaking, the Samoyed shaman's functions and roles in society are quite similar to those in other societies in the long shamanistic belt that stretches geographically over northern Eurasia from Scandinavian Lapland to the Kamchatka Peninsula. The Nganasan concept of a shaman, *öt*, was later replaced by the non-Nganasan term *cacäpä*. According to Janhunen (2004), *cacäpä* is a noun derived from the otherwise unattested verbal stem *cacä-* and possibly refers to the act of shamanizing. The shaman has been the prime religious functionary in various Samoyed cultures. He mediates between human beings and the supernatural: he treats the ailing (disease is considered the temporary absence of the soul from the body); predicts the future; summons protection and help in hunting and fishing; finds objects that have disappeared; and officiates at funeral rites. The shamans are ranked in native concepts in accordance with their expertise and skills. There are three categories of Nenets shamans: the most powerful, who can work miracles on all three levels of the Samoyed universe; an intermediate class; and "small" or lesser shamans. (There is also a class of soothsayers, but these are not, properly speaking, shamans. They have no shamanic power, but even natives often confuse them with shamans.)

The shaman's office is passed down from one generation to the next along clan lines as well as on a spiritual basis. Traditionally, each kin group (clan or phratry) had its own shaman who tried to transmit his office to a successor in a traditional ritual of instruction and initiation, usually during his own lifetime. The shamanic séance was a collective act led by the shaman, who was usually a male, although he was often accompanied by his wife or another elderly woman who led the singing and fed the spirits with whom he communicated. Female shamans, however, are said to have existed among the Samoyed of the Turukhan area in the south.

Reports on the Samoyed shaman's initiation vary. Essentially, the shaman-to-be—who might be a boy of fifteen—is selected and trained by an older kinsman. Training may involve such ordeals as blindfolding and beating, and the candidate may declare that he has had dreams in which he has traveled to distant forests and settlements or communicated with supernatural beings. It is believed that during the process of selecting a new shaman all of the ancestor-shamans' spirits, as well as such other spirits as those of water and earth, are present. These spirits are asked to assist the candidate in his future office.

The shaman officiates during a séance when, as one of them has reported, he sees "a road to the north." Another report equates the séance with a trip to the south. The shaman is accompanied by his assistant spirits during the journey; his locomotion is provided by an animal, generally a reindeer. During the séance, the shaman addresses questions to Num, and if contact is established, he reports Num's answers. His primary accessories are his drum—round, broad-rimmed, covered with skin on one side, from thirty to fifty centimeters in diameter—and his drumstick. The noise that results from the drumming represents both the voyage to the other world and the shaman's interaction with Num and his assistants. During the séance the shaman's eyes may be covered with a kerchief so that he may concentrate on the journey more effectively.

Shamans' costumes have survived among most Samoyed groups, although not among the Nentsy. Nganasan shamans each have three costumes because it is believed that shamans are born three times. The name of the Selkup shaman's headgear is said to have been borrowed from the Tunguz; this fact suggests relatively recent cultural contacts in the sphere of religion. It is also known that Nenets shamans occasionally visit Evenk shamans.

Payments for the services of a shaman range from a pair of mittens to a deerskin or several reindeer. If a shaman's successor has already been chosen at the time of his death, the shaman is buried in his everyday clothes. After the death of a Nenets shaman, a wooden replica of a reindeer is made and is wrapped in the hide of a reindeer calf; the reindeer represents the shaman's assistant spirits.

Samoyed Religion in Transition. The Russians, in their expansion toward the east, reached the Yenisei River in 1603 and brought about a gradual revolution in the economic and spiritual life of the Samoyeds. Although there was planned missionary activity, it was superficial. Samoyed Christianity was quite nominal, and autochthonous beliefs survived. Contact with Europeans brought the Samoyeds new weapons, tools, and goods in exchange for furs, but it also introduced alcohol, syphilis, and smallpox. Thus the Samoyeds developed an ambiguous relationship with the Europeans. Although in one sense traditional religion was weakened, in another it was strengthened because it served as a rallying point for ethnic self-awareness and survival. This contradiction is inherent in the general cultural history of Siberia's native populations.

A second radical change came with the Russian Revolution of 1917, but even this change preserved and perpetuated the older contradiction in a new garb. On the one hand, the ideology of the new Soviet regime dictated a protective attitude toward the natives, guaranteeing the right of tribal self-assertion, which had been inhibited or stifled during tsarist rule. Thus the Nenets and Selkup languages were systematically reduced to writing for practical everyday purposes after 1917. An institute for the study of the peoples of the North was founded in Leningrad and provided higher education for young natives. On the other hand, the new government was explicitly committed to atheism and therefore to the destruction of the social apparatus that underlay the native religion. The natives were again caught in the proverbial middle.

This ambiguous situation has continued, with one or the other tendency prevailing at a particular point in time. During the last quarter of the twentieth century, Soviet ethnographers, benefiting from a tolerant attitude on the part of their government, uncovered many aspects of shamanism (such as séances, with texts and music) that had been thought extinct. Shamanic repertoires by Turbyaky Kosterkin, a Nganasan Shaman from Taimyr District, with his wife Valentina Kosterkina, were recorded and studied by Lennart Meri, the President of Estonia from 1991 to 2003, Eugene A. Helimski, and other scholars.

See Also Castrén, Matthias Alexander; Donner, Kai; Finnish Religions; Num; Shamanism, overview article; Taboo; Totemism.

Bibliography

Concrete factual information, much of it based on the field experiences of some of the authors, can be found in three collective works: *Popular Beliefs and Folklore Tradition in Siberia,* edited by Vilmos Diószegi (The Hague, Netherlands, 1968), *Shamanism in Siberia,* edited by Vilmos Diószegi and Mihály Hoppál (Budapest, Hungary, 1978), and *Shamanism in Eurasia,* 2 vols., edited by Mihály Hoppál (Göttingen, Germany, 1984). Compact synopses are provided in Péter Hajdú's *The Samoyed Peoples and Languages* (Bloomington, Ind., 1963) and in *The Peoples of Siberia,* edited by M. G. Levin and L. P. Potapov (Chicago, 1964). Kai Donner's *Among the Samoyed in Siberia,* translated by Rinehart Kyler and edited by Genevieve A. Highland (New Haven, Conn., 1954), is a record of personal experiences and observations, while Toivo Lehtisalo's *Entwurf einer Mythologie der Jurak-Samojeden* (Helsinki, 1924) is a synthesis based on both older sources and personally collected data. Ivar Paulson's chapter on Siberia in *Die Religionen Nordeurasiens und der amerikanischen Arktis,* edited by Ivar Paulson, Åke Hultkrantz, and Karl Jettmar (Stuttgart, Germany, 1962), is thematically arranged, as is Uno Holmberg's treatment in *The Mythology of All Races,* vol. 4, *Finno-Ugric, Siberian* (Boston, 1927). Of Marie A. Czaplicka's contributions to this field of study, two deserve to be singled out, although by now they have mostly historical value: *Aboriginal Siberia* (Oxford, 1914) and the article "Samoyed," in the *Encyclopaedia of Religion and Ethics,* edited by James Hastings, vol. 11 (Edinburgh, 1920). The most recent studies written by Eugene Helimski, Jarkko Niemi, Timo Leisiö, and others have been published in Juha Pentikäinen's collections: *Shamanism and Northern Ecology* (Berlin and New York, 1996); *Shamanhood–Symbolism and Epic* (Budapest, Hungary, 2001); and *Shamanhood, An Endangered Language* (Oslo, Norway, 2004).

Robert Austerlitz (1987)
Juha Pentikäinen (2005)

SAṂSĀRA is a Sanskrit word meaning "to wander or pass through a series of states or conditions." It is the name for the theory of rebirth in the three major indigenous Indian religions, Hinduism, Buddhism, and Jainism. *Saṃsāra* is the beginningless cycle of birth, death, and rebirth, a process impelled by *karman.* Taken together, *Saṃsāra* and *karman* provide Indian religions with both a causal explanation of human differences and an ethical theory of moral retribution.

The term *saṃsāra* is also applied to phenomenal existence in general to indicate its transient and cyclical nature.

Saṃsāra is the conditioned and ever changing universe as contrasted to an unconditioned, eternal, and transcendent state (*mokṣa* or *nirvāṇa*). In all three Indian religions, the soteriological goal is defined as liberation from *saṃsāra,* that is, as release from bondage to the cycle of rebirth through rendering the process of *karman* inoperative.

The origins of the theory of rebirth in India are disputed. Some scholars trace the belief to the ancient Aryan religion of fire sacrifice known as Vedism. The Vedic view that a sacrificial act produces a future result is regarded as the precursor to the *karman* theory, and the Vedic notion of "redeath" in heaven (*punar mṛtyu*) is seen as the forerunner of "return" (*punar avṛtti*) to new life on earth. Other scholars believe that the rebirth doctrine had its origin among the non-Aryan tribal peoples of ancient India. Still others think it was produced by one or another of the mendicant and anti-Vedic groups of the ancient Gangetic regions. In any case, by the sixth century BCE, the time of the rise of early Buddhism and Jainism on the one hand and of the Upaniṣads on the other, the theory of rebirth was nearly universally accepted. Since then all Indian religions, sects, and philosophies, save only the Cārvākas or materialists, have assumed the doctrine of *karman* and rebirth.

There is no one all-embracing view of the nature of *saṃsāra* and the process of rebirth. Each religion has a distinctive position and within each religion there will be sectarian variations. Some generalities, however, may be stated. In general, all traditions concur in characterizing *saṃsāra* by suffering and sorrow, as well as by impermanence. The source of those intentional acts leading to perpetual rebirth is usually found in desire (and especially the desire for continued individual existence) and in ignorance of the true nature of reality. One may be reincarnated in various heavens, as a human or an animal on earth, or in hells of one sort or another, depending on one's *karman.* Some traditions also claim that rebirth as an insect, a plant, or even a rock is possible, though obviously not desirable.

The predominant theory of Hindu traditions regards the rebirth process as similar to the movement of a caterpillar from one blade of grass to another. The eternal and universal self (*ātman*) is totally unaffected by *karman* and rebirth. The transmigrating entity is the individual self (*jīva*), which is endowed with a "subtle body" and encumbered with karmic residues that determine the direction it takes as it leaves the body at death. There are three possible paths it may take. The "way of the gods" leads to the highest heaven, equated with final liberation, from which there is no further rebirth. The "way of the ancestors" leads to the moon, where the soul is converted to rain and brought back down to earth, where it attaches itself to a plant. When eaten by a human or animal, the transmigrating soul is then transformed into semen, which subsequently brings new life to the individual self. The third possible course results in rebirth in hell or on earth as a small animal, insect, or plant.

Buddhist theories of rebirth are distinguished from others in that they postulate no enduring entity that moves from one existence to another. The problem that has exercised the minds of Buddhist philosophers over the ages is how to explain "transmigration" in light of the central teaching of "no-self" (*anātman*). The Pudgalavādins, or Personalists, came very near to contradicting the *anātman* doctrine with their concept of a personal entity (*pudgala*). Other schools posited an "intermediate being" (*antara bhāva*) that, impelled by *karman,* goes to the location where rebirth is to take place and attaches itself at the juncture of its future parents' sexual organs. The Theravādins, however, strongly denied the existence of the "intermediate being," preferring to identify consciousness with its karmic dispositions as the link between death and rebirth. There is not a transmigration of consciousness but only a causally connected series of discrete moments. To illustrate this notion, Buddhist writers often rely on similes. The rebirth process is likened to the lighting of one lamp with the flame of another, the lamp representing the body and the flame standing for consciousness, or to the transformation of fresh milk to curds. The milk is not the same as the curds (i.e., there is no enduring essence), but the latter are produced out of the former (as one existence is karmicly related to its predecessor).

Saṃsāra, artistically represented as a "wheel of life," is analyzed into its twelve preconditions (the doctrine of "dependent origination," or *pratītya samutpāda),* which express the Buddhist law of cause and effect and explain on what suffering depends and the points at which the chain may be broken. In Theravāda Buddhism the conditioned realm of *saṃsāra* is opposed to *nirvāṇa,* while in Mahāyāna and Vajrayāna Buddhism the two are ultimately equated, both considered equally "empty" (*śunya*) of essence.

Jainism is centered around the belief in an originally pure and perfect soul *(jīva)* that is trapped in *saṃsāra* because of the *karman* that accumulates on it. *Karman,* here regarded as a kind of substance, forms itself into a "body" that is constantly attached to the soul until liberation. There are four categories of *karman* responsible for the mechanism of rebirth. *Nāmakarman* determines different aspects of the future body, including its class (human, animal, or other) and its sex. *Gotrakarman* produces the spiritual quality of the new life. *Vedanīyakarman* determines the pleasant or unpleasant tone of that life, and *āyuḥkarman* its duration. Jain texts do not explain how the soul enters the womb but emphasize that there is no interval between death and rebirth. Reincarnation occurs instantaneously after death as the karmic body conveys the soul to its predetermined destination.

Although all three religions officially declare *saṃsāra* to be bondage and recommend the cultivation of knowledge in order to attain liberation from it, in practice many followers engage in what has been called "samsaric" forms of religion, that is, good works designed to procure a better birth in the next life. Gift giving, acts of devotion, vows of austerity, and other methods of merit making are designed not to obtain release from the cycle of rebirth but rather to achieve a better position within it.

SEE ALSO Karman; Mokṣa; Reincarnation.

BIBLIOGRAPHY

For a collection of recent articles on *saṃsāra* in the three principal religions of India by leading authorities, consult *Karma and Rebirth in Classical Indian Traditions,* edited by Wendy Doniger O'Flaherty (Berkeley, Calif., 1980). Paul Yevtic's *Karma and Reincarnation in Hindu Religion and Philosophy* (London, 1927) remains a useful survey. For a comparative study of the classical views on *saṃsāra* in Hinduism and Buddhism, see Noble Ross Reat's "Karma and Rebirth in the *Upaniṣads* and Buddhism," *Numen* 24 (December 1977): 163–185.

New Sources

Narayana Prasad, Muni. *Karma and Reincarnation: The Vedantic Perspective.* New Delhi, 1994.

Wayman, Alex. *The Vedic Gandharva and Rebirth Theory.* Pune, 1997.

BRIAN K. SMITH (1987)
Revised Bibliography

SAMSKĀRAS SEE RITES OF PASSAGE, *ARTICLE ON* HINDU RITES

SAMSON,

or, in Hebrew, Shimshon; legendary Israelite hero who flourished, according to tradition, circa the twelfth century BCE. The thirteenth to sixteenth chapters of the *Book of Judges* recount the adventurous life of Samson, a charismatic leader, or "judge," of the tribe of Dan. His name, *Shimshon,* means "one of the sun." Endowed with superhuman strength, an impetuous nature, and a penchant for verbal wit, Samson delivered the Israelites from their enemies to the west, the Philistines, in a series of personal vendettas. While biblical traditions may have crystallized around an actual figure, the present narrative is encrusted with mythological (especially solar), folkloristic, and literary motifs and patterns that obscure whatever historical facts underlie the story.

Samson was born to a childless Israelite couple. His birth was announced by a messenger from God in the manner of other traditional heroes. He performed a number of feats, all of them paralleled by such heroes of the ancient world as the Mesopotamian Gilgamesh and the Greek Herakles. Samson ripped apart a lion with his bare hands, burned Philistine fields by unleashing three hundred foxes with torches fastened to their tails, slew a thousand Philistines with the jawbone of an ass, and hoisted the city gates of Gaza. He succumbed to a lust for Philistine women three times. The third woman, Delilah, tricked him into revealing the secret of his strength—his unshorn hair—and sold him to his Philistine adversaries. In the end, blinded by his captors, he collapsed the temple of the Philistine god Dagon upon himself and upon a crowd of the enemy who were taunting him and the God of Israel.

As the primitive saga took on its biblical shape, the unshorn Samson was transformed into a Nazirite, a person dedicated to God by vows, chief among which was abstention from cutting or shaving one's hair (see *Nm.* 6:2–6). His story follows the pattern of the people Israel as described in *Judges:* bound to God by vows, enjoying the divine spirit, he broke vow after vow and lost divine favor, but in a final moment of returning to God, he regained his strength.

BIBLIOGRAPHY

For a fairly comprehensive discussion of the Samson story, highlighting its literary elements, see James L. Crenshaw's *Samson: A Secret Betrayed, a Vow Ignored* (Atlanta, 1978). A close literary reading of the story with discussion of its literary history is Yair Zakovitch's *The Life of Samson (Judges 13–16): A Critical-Literary Analysis* (in Hebrew; Jerusalem, 1982). The solar interpretation of Samson is summarized by Abram Smythe Palmer in *The Samson-Saga and Its Place in Comparative Religion* (1913; reprint, New York, 1977). Hermann Gunkel's "Simson," in *Reden und Aufsätze* (Göttingen, 1913), pp. 38–64, sees Samson as the Israelite "nature man," in conflict with the Philistine civilization. The parallel between the stories of Samson and the people Israel is drawn most extensively in my own "The Riddle of Samson," *Prooftexts: A Journal of Jewish Literary History* 1 (September 1981): 237–260. For a folkloristic analysis, see Susan Niditch's "Samson as Culture Hero, Trickster, and Bandit: The Empowerment of the Weak," *Catholic Biblical Quarterly* 52 (1990): 608–624.

EDWARD L. GREENSTEIN (1987 AND 2005)

SAMUEL

(twelfth century BCE), or, in Hebrew, Shemu'el, was a judge and prophet of Israel. The story of Samuel's birth and the account of his youth present him as a Nazirite, dedicated to God's service through his mother's vow and raised in the sanctuary at Shiloh to be a priest (*1 Sm.* 1–2). While still a youth in this priestly service he is called to be a prophet to deliver a message of judgment to the house of Eli, and in one scene (*1 Sm.* 19:18–24) he appears as the head of an ecstatic band of prophets and the protector of David in his flight from Saul. The prophetic role predominates in the rest of the narratives about him. In addition, however, Samuel is considered by the author of *1 Samuel* to be a judge and is included in his scheme of a succession of judges—charismatic leaders—who ruled in Israel before the rise of the monarchy (*1 Sm.* 7:15–17, *Jgs.* 2:16–19). As such Samuel is depicted as a transitional figure, the last of the old order and the one who consecrates the new. This variety of roles in the tradition makes it difficult to reconstruct his historical role in early Israelite society.

The story of Samuel's birth follows a common folktale pattern of explaining a hero's name and future destiny from the circumstances of his birth. Yet because the story seems to involve a wordplay upon the name Saul (see Ackroyd, 1971 and McCarter, 1980) it has often been taken as a story about the birth of Saul that was later transferred to Samuel.

The difficulty with this view is that none of the story's details fits with Saul's known origins, nor does the birth announcement presage a royal destiny. Instead, the announcement leads directly into the account of Samuel's youth, so that *1 Samuel* 1–3 must be taken together. In this *vita* of Samuel's birth, dedication, and prophetic calling, the historian marks out Samuel as one of the major figures of his history.

In *1 Samuel* 7, Samuel is a spokesman of religious reform, calling the people to repentance. At the same time, as judge he saves the people from their enemies, not by feats of military prowess but by intercessory prayer and sacrifice. When the people raise with Samuel their desire for a king to replace the institution of judgeship (*1 Sm.* 8), the author of the book uses the speeches of Samuel to express his own feelings of ambivalence about the monarchy, both as a source of social and religious sins (*1 Sm.* 8, 12) and as a divinely instituted political order (*1 Sm.* 10:17–27, 11:12–15).

In the folktale of Saul's search for his father's donkeys (*1 Sm.* 9–10:16) Samuel is only a local seer with clairvoyant powers. But the historian has transformed his role by adding an account of the secret anointment of Saul by Samuel, identifying him as the divinely chosen king in anticipation of his later public acclamation. In a similar fashion, Samuel anoints David (*1 Sm.* 16:1–13) and thus assures his destiny.

Samuel is also a prophet of judgment to Saul. The scene of Saul's secret anointment is linked directly to an act of disobedience in which Samuel announces God's rejection of Saul's kingship in favor of another, David (*1 Sm.* 13:8–15; cf. *1 Sm.* 10:8). In a second episode (*1 Sm.* 15), in which Samuel commands Saul to exterminate the Amalekites, Samuel again declares God's rejection of Saul, this time for not completely carrying out all of the prophet's instructions; this episode leads directly to the account of the secret anointment of David as Saul's replacement. This rejection scene also anticipates the final episode of Samuel's appearance, as a ghost (*1 Sm.* 28), at which point rejection is reinforced and Saul's imminent death along with that of his sons is predicted.

Bibliography

Two important studies that deal with major parts of the Samuel tradition are Bruce C. Birch's *The Rise of the Israelite Monarchy: The Growth and Development of 1 Samuel 7–15* (Missoula, Mont., 1976) and Artur Weiser's *Samuel: Seine geschichtliche Aufgabe und religiöse Bedeutung* (Göttingen, 1962). Two helpful commentaries are Peter R. Ackroyd's *The First Book of Samuel,* "The Cambridge Bible Commentary" (Cambridge, 1971), and P. Kyle McCarter, Jr.'s *I Samuel,* vol. 8 of the Anchor Bible (Garden City, N.Y., 1980). See also my book *In Search of History: Historiography in the Ancient World and the Origins of Biblical History* (New Haven, 1983).

New Sources

Brenner, Althalya, ed. *Samuel and Kings.* Sheffield, U.K., 2000.

Dietrich, Walter. *Samuel.* Neukirchen-Vluyen, 2003.

Evans, Mary J. *1 and 2 Samuel.* Peabody, Mass., and Carlisle, U.K., 2000.

John Van Seters (1987)
Revised Bibliography

SAMUEL THE AMORA See SHEMU'EL THE AMORA

SANCTIFICATION See BLESSING; GRACE; JUSTIFICATION

SANCTUARY.

As etymology suggests, a sanctuary is a sacred place, a place set apart from the space of ordinary existence (LL, *sanctuarium,* from *sanctus,* "sacred, holy," by analogy with *sacrarium,* "shrine," from *sacer*). Thus, the term implies a distinction between "the sacred" and "the profane" that may not be universal; consequently, "sanctuaries" may, strictly speaking, be found only in a limited if significant number of religious traditions.

Virtually any place can serve as a sanctuary. It is essential, however, that a sanctuary be marked off, that is, that the distinction between sacred and profane be perceptibly indicated, whether by natural means (e.g., a cave) or by artificial means. The latter may range from the technologically simple (a ring of stones) to the technologically elaborate (ornate Buddhist stupas). In addition, the shapes that a sanctuary's construction assumes generally carry symbolic meanings appropriate to notions of the sacred found in the community by which the sanctuary has been constructed. European cathedrals have taken the form of a cross, Mesopotamian ziggurats represent the sacred mountain, and so on.

But the term *sanctuary* usually carries one (or both) of two more specific meanings, one cultic, the other social. In the first case, it denotes a place of worship. The place where the sacred dwells or manifests itself becomes the place where human beings encounter it. Such a sanctuary may be used by groups of varying size, from individual dwelling units (e.g., shrines in Nuer dwellings, the *pūjā* room in Hindu households) to large communities (e.g., city temples). If it stands separately, it may be called, somewhat ethnocentrically, a *domus dei* ("house of god"). Harold W. Turner isolates four dimensions of the *domus dei:* It is the center with reference to which life is oriented, the point at which heaven and earth meet, the microcosm of the heavenly realm, and the locus of the divine presence, often signaled by a cult object or image.

The sanctuary as *domus dei* invites a great deal of specialization and elaboration. The result may be large buildings and complexes of buildings containing areas of varying sanctity, including one or more sanctuaries in a more specialized sense: particularly isolated areas or chambers where the sacred is most powerfully present, such as the "Holy of Holies" in the Jerusalem Temple or the *aduton* of Greek temples. Access to this sanctuary is limited, often to only the highest religious functionaries (e.g., the chief priest) at very specific, cultically significant times.

Besides the *domus dei,* there is another sort of religious sanctuary, not the place where the sacred dwells but the place where the religious community (itself sacred) worships. This type, which lacks the four dimensions of the *domus dei* isolated by Turner, may be designated by the parallel term *domus ecclesiae* ("house of the gathered assembly"). Its paradigmatic form is the Jewish synagogue, on which the Muslim mosque and various Christian houses of worship are patterned (such as the meetinghouse of the Society of Friends).

In the social sense, a sanctuary is a place of refuge or asylum, a place set apart from the regulations of ordinary social intercourse. Places of refuge are found widely in conjunction with religious sanctuaries. For example, in Greek mythology Orestes was safe from the Erinyes (the Furies) so long as he remained in contact with the *omphalos* ("navel"), a sacred stone at Delphi. Just as entire cities can be set aside as religious sanctuaries (e.g., Kasi/Banaras in India), so too entire cities have been set aside as social sanctuaries, as were the cities of refuge in ancient Israel. In the West, the right of sanctuary was formulated by law as early as the end of the fourth century, and in time specific provisions became quite complex. But movements to curb rights of sanctuary began in the early modern period (sixteenth century), and by the end of the eighteenth century such rights had virtually disappeared in western Europe.

The sanctuary as legal asylum finds an intriguing antitype in an institution that arose as the right of sanctuary disappeared: the penitentiary. As it developed in religiously valorized form in the early nineteenth century, the penitentiary, too, was a place set apart from ordinary social intercourse. But in the penitentiary the guilty were not protected from punishment by the presence of the sacred. Instead, the guilty had to come to terms with themselves and their misdeeds. That is, they had to repent (hence the name) and "convert"—convicts were forced to listen to sermons—before emerging from confinement as new persons.

See Also Ḥaram and Ḥawṭah.

Bibliography

For a general discussion of sacred space, see Mircea Eliade's *Patterns in Comparative Religion* (New York, 1958), especially chapter 10, "Sacred Places." Harold W. Turner's *From Temple to Meeting House* (The Hague, 1979) discusses both the *domus dei* and the *domus ecclesiae* at length, but in a context that eventually leads to theological reflection. On sanctuary as asylum, Edward A. Westermarck's article "Asylum," in the *Encyclopaedia of Religion and Ethics,* edited by James Hastings, vol. 2 (Edinburgh, 1909), is a treasure-store of cross-cultural information that, however, must be used critically today. For a more detailed study limited to one particular culture, see John Charles Cox's *Sanctuaries and Sanctuary Seekers of Medieval England* (London, 1911). A provocative history of the penitentiary is provided by Michel Foucault in *Discipline and Punish:* The Birth of the Prison, translated by Alan Sheridan (New York, 1977).

New Sources

Evans, Nancy A. "Sanctuaries, Sacrifices and the Eleusinian Mysteries." *Numen: International Review for the History of Religions* 49 (2002): 227–255.

Gregory D. Alles (1987)
Revised Bibliography

SANHEDRIN, a Hebrew and Jewish-Aramaic loanword from the Greek *sunedrion,* is believed to be the name of the supreme autonomous institution of the Jews of Palestine during the Roman and early Byzantine periods (63 BCE to the fifth or sixth century CE). The generally accepted view of the Sanhedrin is as follows. Composed of seventy or seventy-one members, it possessed administrative, judicial, and quasi-legislative powers that were also recognized by the Jews of the Diaspora. Until 70 CE the Sanhedrin met in the precincts of the Jerusalem Temple. Following the destruction of the Temple in that year, a reconstituted Sanhedrin met at various sites in Palestine.

Historical Evidence. The historicity of the Sanhedrin is the subject of much disagreement in modern scholarship. The disagreement results from inconsistencies among the sources used to reconstruct the history of the institution. Strictly speaking, the Sanhedrin is mentioned only in Hebrew and Aramaic sources, of which the most important is the rabbinic literature of the first five centuries CE. In addition, scholars adduce evidence from references to the word *sunedrion* in Greek sources relating to the Jews of Roman Palestine. The most important of these are the writings of the Jewish historian Josephus Flavius (37–c. 100 CE) and the Gospels and *Acts of the Apostles* in the New Testament. The use of the Greek sources poses two problems. First, the word *sunedrion* exhibits a variety of meanings: "place of assembly, session, assembly, council, court." Thus not every mention of the word in Josephus or in the New Testament necessarily refers to *the* Sanhedrin. Second, even when *sunedrion* seems to refer to the supreme Jewish institution, that institution is rather different from the Sanhedrin of rabbinic sources. The latter is an assembly of Torah scholars presided over by the leader of the Pharisees. The Jerusalem *sunedrion* of the Greek sources is an aristocratic council presided over by the high priest. The attempt to resolve this inconsistency has produced three basic approaches. Some simply reject one set of sources, usually the rabbinic, as unhistorical. A second approach posits the existence of two Sanhedrins in Jerusalem. The Greek sources describe a political Sanhedrin closely associated with the Roman provincial authorities, while the rabbinic sources describe a purely religious Sanhedrin that dealt with issues of Jewish law. Since none of the sources hints at the simultaneous existence of two supreme assemblies, a third approach attempts to harmonize the sources by less radical means. Some argue that the composition and competence of the Sanhedrin varied over time. Others suggest that it comprised subcommittees, each with its own chairman, that dealt with different types of issues. All three approaches appear in current scholarship. In the following sections this article shall summarize the evidence of each set of sources in the light of historical criticism.

Evidence in rabbinic literature. Since relatively few rabbinic traditions explicitly mention the Sanhedrin, they may be supplemented by other traditions, more numerous and more detailed, that use the Hebrew term *beit din* (pl., *batei din*), meaning "court." These two sets of traditions, one referring to the Sanhedrin and one to the *beit din,* overlap in many details and appear side by side in rabbinic documents. That the terms *Sanhedrin* and *beit din* refer to the same institution emerges clearly from the overlap of their function and structure recorded in rabbinic literature. According to these traditions, each town with a certain minimum population could establish a "small Sanhedrin" or *beit din* of twenty-three scholars, competent to try even capital cases. Matters that the local institutions could not resolve were referred to the "Great Sanhedrin" or "Great Beit Din" (*beit din ha-gadol,* i.e., "great court") of seventy-one members. This latter body, meeting in the Chamber of Hewn Stone in the Jerusalem Temple, would resolve the matter on the basis of precedent or by majority vote. Some traditions that speak of the *beit din* describe a "four-tier" system, interposing two additional bodies of three members each between the local and supreme bodies (e.g., Tosefta *Ḥag.* 2.9; *Sheq.* 3.27, San. 11.2–4). Membership in a lower body was a prerequisite for appointment to a higher one. The supreme body, whether called the Great Beit Din as in Tosefta *Ḥagigah* 2.9 or the Great Sanhedrin as in Mishnah *Middot* 5.4, had authority over the priesthood. It possessed political as well as religious powers: declaring offensive wars, playing a role in the appointment of kings, and so forth. The sources also allude both to Sanhedrins and to *batei din* of the tribes (e.g., *San.* 1.5; cf. *Hor.* 1.5) and to the possibility of small Sanhedrins outside of Palestine (Tosefta *San.* 1.5). The most important feature of the rabbinic account of the Sanhedrin is that it describes an idealized and admittedly distant past, which will be renewed only with the full restoration of the Israelite polity. The tradition of the four levels of courts (Tosefta *Ḥag.* 2.9) relates how at first this system prevented dissension by resolving all questions of law. But then, in the generation after Hillel and Shammai, dissension was rampant. Thus, the source implies that the system had broken down by the beginning of direct Roman rule in 6 CE, for Hillel and Shammai are generally considered contemporaries of King Herod. Further, the rabbinic account is replete with details that concern things the sources admit did not exist in the Roman period, such as the tribal system and prophecy. Moreover, rabbinic traditions on events from the Roman conquest (63 BCE) onward assign no role whatsoever to the Great Sanhedrin or Great Beit Din. By contrast, rabbinic literature does mention Sanhedrins of the biblical period, from the time of Moses to the Babylonian exile. In sum, the rabbinic sources on the Sanhedrin make no claim to describe an institution of the Roman period.

Evidence in Josephus Flavius. Jewish literature in Greek from before 70 CE never mentions a supreme Jewish institution called the *sunedrion.* The word does occur, but only in the general sense of "assembly, council, court." The same situation prevails in the writings of Josephus. In almost every case Josephus uses the word to denote what the Romans called a *consilium.* This was an ad hoc assembly of friends and advisers convened by an official to assist in policy decisions or in trying a case. In only three instances does Josephus use *sunedrion* to designate a formally constituted ongoing institution. In one instance he refers to the leadership of the Jewish revolt against Rome in 66 CE as "the *sunedrion* of the Jerusalemites" (*The Life 62*). But elsewhere (in *The Life* and in *The Jewish War*) he designates this body by a variety of names, most commonly *koinon* ("corporation, community"). Hence, *sunedrion* was not the formal or usual name. More apropos is the second instance, concerning Aulus Gabinius, the Roman governor of Syria in 57 BCE. Gabinius stripped the high priest John Hyrcanus II of his political powers and divided the Jewish state into five districts, each ruled by what Josephus calls a *sunodos* in one place (*War* 1.170) and a *sunedrion* in another (*Jewish Antiquities* 14.96). One of these bodies sat in Jerusalem. This recalls the measures taken by Rome in Macedonia in 168 BCE. The latter kingdom was divided into four regions, each administered by a council of senators that Livy calls a *synhedros* (Annals 45.32.2). In any case, Gabinius's arrangements lasted no more than ten years, for in 47 BCE Julius Caesar restored Hyrcanus to nationwide political power. The third instance of Josephus's mention of the term is the closest parallel to the rabbinic Sanhedrin. His *Jewish Antiquities* (14.158–184) reports the trial of the future king Herod before "the *sunedrion*" in Jerusalem in 47/6 BCE. From this account it emerges that the latter was an ongoing institution with nationwide jurisdiction and unique competence in capital cases. However, in a parallel account of these events in his earlier history, *The Jewish War* (1.204–215), as well as in a brief reference to them in *Jewish Antiquities* (15.3–4), Josephus does not mention the *sunedrion.* The version in *Antiquities* 14 has a close parallel in rabbinic literature (B.T., *San.* 19a–b), but with no mention of the Sanhedrin. The *sunedrion* as described in *Antiquities* 14 does not reappear in the writings of Josephus. Given the rabbinic parallel (one of several in *Antiquities*) and the fact that the hero of the story is a Pharisee, it appears that Josephus transmits here a Pharisaic version of the trial of Herod—a version whose historicity is not certain. Josephus also mentions three judicial or administrative bodies of seventy members each, all from around 66 CE, but does not call any of them a *sunedrion.* These are (1) the assembly established by Josephus himself when he assumed command of Galilee in the revolt against Rome, (2) the deputation of the leading men of the colony of Babylonian Jews in Batanaea, and (3) a jury convened in the Jerusalem Temple to try a charge of treason. Josephus's arrangements in Galilee reflect his interpretation of *Deuteronomy* 17:8–9 in *Antiquities* 4.214–218, where he calls the assembly of priests,

Levites, and the judiciary a *gerousia* (council of elders). The number seventy obviously derives from the seventy elders assembled by Moses according to *Numbers* 11:16. But aside from the regional *sunedrions* (or *sunodoses*) established by Gabinius and the *sunedrion* that tried Herod (according to a unique version of this event), Josephus does not mention any continuing institution by this name.

Evidence in the New Testament. The New Testament includes several instances of the word *sunedrion,* usually translated as "council" (RSV). In a few cases the word refers to local Jewish courts (certainly in *Mark* 13:9 and parallels in *Matthew* 10:17 and possibly in *Matthew* 5:21). However, in the accounts of the passion of Jesus and the trials of the apostles, *sunedrion* seems to designate the supreme Jewish institution in Jerusalem. Closer analysis reveals several uncertainties. The Synoptic Gospels and *Acts of the Apostles* frequently allude to the Jewish leadership as composed of "the chief priests, elders, and scribes" or the like. As is generally agreed, this means the priestly and lay aristocracies along with a professional class of experts in Jewish law. In certain passages these three elements constitute some sort of *sunedrion.* In some of these passages, the term *sunedrion* can be interpreted in its general meaning of "assembly" or "session." This is the case in *John* 11:47 (cf. *Mk.* 11:48 and *Lk.* 19:47), *Luke* 22:66 (cf. *Mk.* 15:1 and *Mt.* 27:1), and *Acts* 4:15. In other instances *sunedrion* appears to be a proper name. Thus in *Mark* 14:55 and *Matthew* 26:59, "the chief priests and the whole council [*sunedrion*]" conduct a formal trial of Jesus on the night following his arrest. In *Mark* 15:1 (but not *Mt.* 27:1; cf. *Lk.* 22:66–23:1) "the chief priests, with the elders and scribes, and [Gr., *kai*] the whole council [*sunedrion*]" reconvene the following morning. Presumably, here the *kai* is explanatory, to be translated as "that is." *Acts,* attributed to the author of *Luke,* refers to the *sunedrion* in connection with the second arraignment of Peter and the arraignments of Stephen and Paul (e.g., *Acts* 5:21, 6:12, 23:1). But the terminology of *Luke* and *Acts* is not consistent. According to *Luke* 22:66, the consultation on the morning following the arrest of Jesus was attended by "the assembly of the elders of the people [*presbuterion*] . . . , both chief priests and scribes." Similarly, in *Acts* 22:5 Paul calls on "the high priest and the whole council of elders [*presbuterion*]" to attest his earlier persecution of the believers in Jesus. And *Acts* 5:21 has Peter brought before "the council [*sunedrion*] and [*kai*] all the senate [*gerousia*] of Israel." The word *kai* here may be explanatory, or it may reflect the author's belief that the *sunedrion* was more exclusive than the *gerousia.* It may be noted in passing that only *Mark* and *Matthew* report a trial of Jesus before the *sunedrion. Luke* reports only a morning consultation of the *presbuterion,* chief priests and scribes. And *John* merely has "the Jews" accuse Jesus before Pontius Pilate. In the present context one can ignore the much-debated questions of whether the trial is a Markan invention and whether *Luke* or *John* relies on independent sources. What is consistent in the Synoptic Gospels and *Acts* is the characterization of the Jewish leadership in Jerusalem as composed of the priestly and lay aristocracies and the scribes. This much is confirmed by Josephus, as is the New Testament picture of these groups consulting and acting in consort. But the institutionalization of these consultations and joint actions in the form of a regularly meeting assembly called the *sunedrion* is not clear from the New Testament evidence itself. And Josephus, who was born in Jerusalem within a decade of the crucifixion of Jesus and still lived there during the troubles of Paul, makes no mention of the *sunedrion* as an ongoing body in his account of this period.

THE SANHEDRIN AFTER 70 CE. Some scholars posit the existence of a Sanhedrin at Yavneh after 70, at Usha (in the Galilee) after 135, and still later at other locations. Whatever the nature of the institutions that existed at these places, they are never called Sanhedrins in the ancient sources. In fact, two second-century traditions refer to the Sanhedrin as a thing of the past: Mishnah *Sotah* 9.11 explicitly and *Makkot* 1.10 implicitly. A single post-70 reference to a contemporary "Great Court," at Tosefta *Ohalot* 18.18, is probably only rhetorical. A relatively late and probably non-Palestinian tradition in the Babylonian Talmud (*R. ha-Sh.* 31a–b, with parallel at *Gn. Rab.* 97) lists a number of towns, mostly in Galilee, as consecutive sites of post-70 Sanhedrins. This tradition probably reflects the fact that these towns served as the residence of Jewish patriarchs (sg., *nasi'* and the site of rabbinical conclaves. The sources do mention groups of rabbis meeting together to resolve questions of law, fix the calendar, and make similar decisions, but these meetings are never called Sanhedrins. (See, for example, *Shabbat* 1.4, *Ohalot* 18.9, *Yadayim* 4.1; Tosefta *Ohalot* 18.18; B.T., *Berakhot* 63 b; J.T., *Ḥagigah* 3.1, 78d; *Song of Songs Rabbah* 2.5.) The reference in a law of Theodosius II from 429 to "the *sunedrions* of the two Palestines" probably refers to local Jewish courts and reflects New Testament usage. Finally, a Babylonian source, perhaps from the eighth century, mentions a Sanhedrin in Tiberias in 520, but this source probably misconstrues an earlier text that does not mention this institution.

CONCLUSION. The accounts of the Sanhedrin in these sources neither overlap chronologically nor confirm one another. Moreover, each account is problematic. The rabbinic is idealized, and the New Testament is inconsistent. Josephus describes in one case a short-lived system imposed by the Romans, and in the other case his own parallel accounts know nothing of the *sunedrion.* So there is no unequivocal historical evidence for the Sanhedrin. What is probably in the Greek sources are the historical realities from which the rabbinic account of the Sanhedrin was created: an aristocratic council (*gerousia* or *presbuterion*), judicial or administrative bodies of seventy, and possibly a municipal council (*boulē*) in Jerusalem. One should also note that unlike other Greek administrative terms borrowed in the Semitic vernaculars of the Roman East, *sunedrion* is a loanword only in Hebrew and Jewish-Aramaic (apart from a very few instances in Syriac, probably from writers who knew Greek). This unique borrowing, especially as a term for an important Jewish institution, suggests that some Jewish body of Roman times was called *sunedrion* in Greek. But as has been seen, the evidence does not establish what that body was. Thus the existence of a supreme governing body in Jerusalem called the Sanhedrin cannot be proven by the sources, and if it existed, it cannot be described.

See Also Pharisees.

Bibliography

The best treatment of the problem of the Sanhedrin is Yehoshua Efron's Hebrew article "The Sanhedrin as an Ideal and as Reality in the Period of the Second Temple," in *Doron,* edited by S. Perlman and B. Shimron (Tel Aviv, 1967). An English summary appears under the same title in *Immanuel* 2 (1973): 44–49. Efron's differentiated and consistently critical survey of almost all the relevant sources manages to transcend the stagnant debate still prevailing in the scholarly literature. His method and conclusions have greatly influenced this article.

The two major studies in English both adopt the theory of two Sanhedrins. They are Sidney B. Hoenig's *The Great Sanhedrin* (New York, 1953) and Hugo Mantel's *Studies in the History of the Sanhedrin* (Cambridge, Mass., 1961). Mantel presents detailed summaries of the scholarly debate and a very full bibliography. For a recent, sophisticated version of this theory, see Ellis Rivkin's "Beth Din, Boulé, Sanhedrin: A Tragedy of Errors," *Hebrew Union College Annual* 46 (1975): 181–199.

Other recent surveys adopt variations of the moderate harmonistic approach. Most useful are Edmund Lohse's "Sunedrion," in *Theological Dictionary of the New Testament,* edited by Gerhard Kittel, vol. 7 (Grand Rapids, Mich., 1971), pp. 860–867; Samuel Safrai's "Jewish Self-Government," in *The Jewish People in the First Century,* edited by Samuel Safrai and Menachem Stern, vol. 1 (Assen, 1974), pp. 379–400; and Emil Schürer's *The History of the Jewish People in the Age of Jesus Christ,* a new English version revised and edited by Géza Vermès et al., vol. 2 (Edinburgh, 1979), pp. 199–226.

New Sources

Albeck, Shalom. *Bate ha-din bi-yeme ha-Talmud.* Ramat-Gan, Israel, 1980.

Boyarin, Daniel. "A Tale of Two Synods: Nicaea, Yavneh, and Rabbinic Ecclesiology." *Exemplaria* 12 (2000): 21–62.

Efron, Joshua. *Studies on the Hasmonean Period.* Leiden and New York, 1987.

Graff, Gil. "Priests, Sages and the Jurisdiction of the High Court, 50–100 C.E.: A Note on the Demotion of Rabban Gamaliel." *Shofar* 8 (1990): 1–7.

Hezser, Catherine, ed. *Rabbinic Law in Its Roman and Near Eastern Context.* Tübingen, 2003.

Kee, Howard Clark. "Central Authority in Second-Temple Judaism and Subsequently: From Synedrion to Sanhedrin." *Annual of Rabbinic Judaism* 2 (1999): 51–63.

Livingstone, Reuven. "Beyond Reasonable Doubt: In Search of a Just Justice." *Le'ela* 40 (1995): 23–27.

David Goodblatt (1987)
Revised Bibliography

ŚAṄKARA

ŚAṄKARA (c. 700 CE), also known as Saṃkara or Śaṅkarācārya, was a Hindu metaphysician, religious leader, and proponent of Advaita Vedānta. Śaṅkara is generally acknowledged to be the most influential of all Hindu religious thinkers. The many modern interpretations and popularizations of his uncompromisingly intellectual metaphysics represent the dominant current of contemporary Hindu religious thought. For scholars of Sanskrit his compositions, above all his famous commentary (*bhāṣya*) on the *Brahma Sūtra* of Bādarāyaṇa, serve as models of philosophical and literary excellence.

Śaṅkara's dates remain a matter of scholarly controversy. Many accept the traditional dates 788–820; in recent years, however, several scholars have argued for a longer life span centered around the beginning of the eighth century. The considerable number of Sanskrit hagiographical accounts of the life of Śaṅkara all appear to be comparatively recent compositions. It is difficult to judge to what extent they embody factual historical traditions. The most influential of these hagiographies is the *Śaṅkaradigvijaya* or *Saṅkṣepa Śaṅkarajaya* of Mādhava, composed sometime between 1650 and 1800 and possibly reworked about the middle of the nineteenth century. This is a composite text that includes verses taken from a number of somewhat earlier works, notably those of Vyāsācala and Tirumalla Dīkṣita. The *Śaṅkaravijaya* of Anantānandagiri is another important hagiography representing an independent tradition associated with the Advaita center at Kanchipuram, Tamil Nadu.

According to Mādhava, Śaṅkara was born to a brahman family of the brahman village of Kālaṭi in Kerala, South India. Mādhava states that his parents had long been childless, but that the god Śiva finally agreed to become incarnate as their son to reward their devotion and penances. This son, Śaṅkara, was a miraculously precocious student: By his sixth or seventh year he had already resolved to bypass the householder stage of life (*gṛhasthāśrama*) and become a religious ascetic (*saṃnyāsin*). With the reluctant consent of his widowed mother he left home and became a disciple of a Govindanātha or Govindapāda somewhere on the river Narmada. In some of his own works Śaṅkara identifies his guru's guru (*paramaguru*) as Gauḍapāda, and tradition claims that Govindanātha was a disciple of this earlier Advaita thinker. Govindanātha later sent Śaṅkara to Varanasi (Banaras), where he acquired his first important disciple, Sanandana, later called Padmapāda. After some time Śaṅkara moved on to Badarī in the Himalayas, where he wrote (at the age of twelve, according to Mādhava) his famous *Brahma-sūtra-bhāṣya.* While at Badarī he also composed commentaries on various Upaniṣads and on the *Bhagavadgītā,* and produced other commentaries and independent treatises such as the *Upadeśasāhasrī.* The rest of his life he spent traveling from place to place defending the views of Advaita Vedānta against opponents from a variety of different religious sects and philosophical schools.

Where Śaṅkara spent his final days is disputed by his biographers. Mādhava says that toward the end of his short life Śaṅkara was afflicted with a debilitating rectal fistula occasioned by the evil magic of Abhinavagupta, a Tantric opponent. Śaṅkara was allegedly cured of this ailment but died not long afterward at Kedarnath in the Himalayas. Anantānandagiri places his death at Kanchipuram, while other sources mention still other locations.

According to traditions not preserved by either Mādhava or Anantānandagiri, Śaṅkara established four or five monastic centers for the spread of Advaita Vedānta: one at Badarī in the Himalayas (north); one at Dvāraka in Gujarat (west); one at Puri in Orissa (east); one at Śṛngerī in Karṇataka (south); and another, not considered to be of equal status by some, at Kanchipuram. Through these centers an extensive network of Advaita teachers and monasteries was organized that did much to establish the dominance of Advaita over rival sects and schools. The religious ascetics who belong to this network are divided into ten (*daśa*) monastic orders, the members of each order taking a distinct final name (*nāma*). For this reason they are collectively called Daśanāmīs.

The study of the enormous number of Advaita works attributed to Śaṅkara has long been handicapped by the inability of critical scholarship to distinguish his genuine compositions from works falsely attributed to him. Recently, however, Paul Hacker, Mayeda Sengaku, and others have established criteria that have largely resolved this problem. They conclude that the works that may be reliably attributed to Śaṅkara are (1) the *Brahmasūtra-bhāṣya;* (2) the commentaries on the *Bṛhadaraṇyaka, Taittirīya, Chāndogya, Aitareya, Īśa, Kaṭha, Kena* (two), *Muṇḍaka,* and *Praśna* Upaniṣads; (3) the commentary on the *Bhagavadgītā;* (4) the commentaries on the *Māṇḍūkya Upaniṣad* with the *Gauḍapādīyakārikā;* and (5) the *Upadeśasāhasrī.* All other works, including the many devotional hymns attributed to Śaṅkara, are probably compositions of later authors.

In these works Śaṅkara generally subordinates philosophizing to the goal of liberation (*mokṣa*) from the bonds of transmigratory existence (*saṃsāra*), which arise from the consequences of one's action (*karman*). Unlike some of his more scholastic successors, Śaṅkara often prefers to leave certain perplexing, and perhaps insolvable, philosophical problems unanswered. In his view, the sole means to achieve this liberation is right knowledge (*jñāna*) leading to an instantaneous spiritual illumination that somehow dissolves all except the residual effects of past deeds (*prārabdhakarman*). After death, liberation is complete and final. The alternative religious paths of devotion (*bhakti*) and moral or religious works (*karman*) may lead to a better rebirth either in this world or in the world of the gods, but they are of no use whatsoever for the illumination that is absolute liberation. For this the sole prerequisites are nonattachment to the things of this world; mental and emotional restraint and tranquillity; a suitable guru; and the study, under his supervision, of the "knowledge portion" (*jñānakāṇḍa*) of the Vedas, especially the Upaniṣads. Since this last prerequisite is permitted only to members of the higher castes, *śūdras* are explicitly ineligible for this illumination.

The word *advaita* means "non-dual." In contrast to the rival school called Sāṃkhya, which assigns a separate but full reality to both spirit (*puruṣa*) and matter (*prakṛti*), Advaita Vedānta asserts that absolute (*paramārthika*) reality, called *brahman,* is non-dual. The manifold visible world around one (*saṃsāra*) has merely a functional (*vyāvahārika*) reality. It is considered to be a transformation (*pariṇāma*) or, more commonly in Advaita, a mere appearance (*vivarta*) that somehow arises from *brahman.*

A central doctrine of Śaṅkara's thought claims that from the point of view of the supreme truth (*paramārthataḥ*) one's inner self or soul (*ātman*), the essence of consciousness (*cit*), is identical with the essence of being (*sat*), *brahman* itself. This doctrine, Śaṅkara believes, cannot be fully established by rational discourse alone. In the final analysis its truth rests on revelation, namely the texts called Upaniṣads, which form the "end of the Vedas" (*vedānta*). The Upaniṣads, the *Brahma Sūtra,* and the *Bhagavadgītā* constitute the threefold scriptural foundation of all schools of Vedānta. Although each school interprets these texts in often radically different senses, the texts do establish definite parameters within which the discussion must operate. These include the ideas that *ātman* and *brahman* are entities somehow closely related to each other and to individual living beings (*jīvas*) and to God (Īśvara) respectively, and that these living beings are subject to *karman* and the pains of transmigratory existence until they somehow manage to win liberation.

How and why does *saṃsāra* make its appearance? According to Śaṅkara it is ignorance (*avidyā*), sometimes called illusion (*māyā*), that occasions the appearance of *saṃsāra* through a process known as superimposition (*adhyāsa*). Through this process *ātman-brahman* becomes reflected as many individual conscious beings (*jīvas*) on the one hand and as God (Īśvara) on the other. God in turn becomes the cause, both efficient and material, of the physical universe, which evolves indirectly from a primal "substance" called "name-and-form" *(nāma-rūpa).* In this psychophysical cosmology, liberation is nothing but the removal of ignorance, the deep realization that from the point of view of the ultimate truth *ātman* and *brahman* are identical and represent the only reality, the very substance of being and consciousness. All else—the physical universe, one's individual self, even God—are things conditioned by ignorance and hence ultimately unreal.

But how does this process of superimposition operate? On this subject Śaṅkara elaborates a series of sophisticated and often controversial epistemological arguments based in part on a set of analogies drawn from everyday experience. The most famous is that of the rope and the snake. When in a dim light one mistakes a rope for a snake, one is making a superimposition of false attributes derived from memory.

Once one realizes the error, the real object, the rope, eliminates and replaces one's false perception of a snake. In an analogous way one superimposes false attributes on *ātman-brahman.* If one eliminates ignorance, this superimposition is dissolved and *ātman-brahman* alone shines forth. Transmigratory existence and one's bondage to it are immediately broken. One becomes liberated. It is as simple, and as difficult, as that.

SEE ALSO Avidyā; Bādarāyaṇa; Bhagavadgītā; Brahman; Jñāna; Māyā; Sāṃkhya; Upaniṣads; Vedānta.

BIBLIOGRAPHY

Most of the traditional "biographies" of Śaṅkara remain untranslated, but a complete English translation of Mādhava's *Śaṅkaradigvijaya* by Swami Tapasyananda has been published (Madras, 1979). A thematic analysis of this text is attempted in my "The Life of Śaṅkarācārya," in *The Biographical Process,* edited by Frank E. Reynolds and Donald Capps (The Hague, 1976). For the understanding of Śaṅkara's thought, two recent publications contain long introductions that are models of clarity and perspicacity: *Advaita Vedānta up to Śaṃkara and His Pupils,* edited and with an introduction by Karl H. Potter, vol. 3 of his *Encyclopedia of Indian Philosophies* (Delhi, 1981), and *A Thousand Teachings: The Upadeśasāhasrī of Śaṅkara,* translated by Mayeda Sengaku (Tokyo, 1979). For Śaṅkara's famous *Brahmasūtra-bhāṣya,* the 1904 translation of George Thibaut, *The Vedānta Sūtra, with the Commentary by Śaṅkara,* in "Sacred Books of the East" (reprint; New York, 1962) is still basic, as is Thibaut's introduction.

New Sources

Bader, Jonathan. *Conquest of the Four Quarters: Traditional Accounts of the Life of Sankara.* New Delhi, 2000.

Isaeva, N. V. *Shankara and Indian Philosophy.* Albany, 1993.

Marcaurelle, Roger. *Freedom through Inner Renunciation: Sankara's Philosophy in a New Light.* Albany, 2000.

Victor, P. George. *Life and Teachings of Adi Sankaracarya.* New Delhi, 2002.

DAVID N. LORENZEN (1987)
Revised Bibliography

SAN RELIGION SEE KHOI AND SAN RELIGION

ŚĀNTARAKṢITA (c. 725–788 CE), an Indian Buddhist scholar and monk also known as Śāntirakṣita and the Great Abbott Bodhisattva, was renowned for his synthesis of diverse streams of Mahāyāna Buddhist philosophical thought and for his seminal role in the early transmission of Buddhism to Tibet. Scholarly consensus and Tibetan tradition maintain that Śāntarakṣita made two visits to Tibet, both during the lifetime of the Tibetan king Khri srong lde btsan (c. 740–798). There, Śāntarakṣita supervised the construction of Bsam yas, the first Buddhist monastery in Tibet, where he ordained the first Tibetan Buddhist monks and taught Buddhist meditation, ethics, and reasoning to the king and his entourage. According to tradition, when the king and his court converted to Buddhism, local Tibetan spirits were upset and caused floods and other calamities throughout Tibet. Śāntarakṣita advised the king to invite an Indian Buddhist Tantric adept, Padmasambhava, to pacify the spirits. Padmasambhava arrived, and through his great spiritual power summoned the troublesome gods and demons, taught them the Buddhist doctrine of karma and rebirth, converted them to Buddhism, and bound them with oaths to protect the new state religion. As a result, King Khri srong lde btsan, the Great Abbot Bodhisattva Śāntarakṣita, and the Precious Guru Padmasambhava are very often depicted together as protectors of Buddhism in the monasteries and temples of Tibet.

Little is known of Śāntarakṣita's earlier life in India. Tibetan sources indicate that he was from Zahor—a locale identified variously by modern scholars with sites in Bengal, Bihar, and Pakistan—and that he had been the abbot of the famous Nālandā monastic university. Although this cannot be confirmed, there is no doubt that Śāntarakṣita was a remarkably erudite scholar who was deeply versed in a wide range of Indian dialectical traditions. The lengthy citations and refutations of non-Buddhist as well as Buddhist positions on epistemological, logical, and metaphysical topics in the verse treatise *Tattvasaṃgraha* (Collection of Realities), Śāntarakṣita's major work preserved in Sanskrit, reveals the extent of his learning. Drawing on the theories of his predecessors, Dignāga and (especially) Dharmakīrti, Śāntarakṣita in this work attempts to lead his readers through a series of arguments designed to whittle away at philosophical notions of essence or intrinsic identity (*svabhāva*). To accomplish this aim, Śāntarakṣita employs the "sliding scale of analysis" (a technique used earlier by Dharmakīrti) whereby under certain conditions a philosopher may be rationally justified in arguing from diverse and even contradictory metaphysical premises within the confines of a single work. In brief, this technique allows for the construction of provisional arguments aimed at particular audiences with the understanding that certain premises of the arguments may be subsequently challenged at a higher level of philosophical analysis.

Most of the arguments in the *Tattvasaṃgraha* are adduced at the lowest level of analysis, identified by Śāntarakṣita's disciple Kamalaśīla in his commentary as Sautrāntika. This level of analysis operates with an ontology in which causally functioning real particulars, some of which exist outside the mind, produce mental images that are then known by awareness. Śāntarakṣita uses this level of analysis to advance arguments against various versions of intrinsic identity, including the notions of an unchanging creator God, a permanent self or soul, irreducible substance, and intrinsically existent relations. He also stays mostly on this level of analysis when explicating his interpretation of inference and perception, the two instruments of correct knowledge (*pramāṇa*) accepted in the Buddhist epistemological tradition.

The shift to the next level of analysis occurs only once Śāntarakṣita has judged the reader to have been convinced of some basic Buddhist truths, namely, that all things are impermanent, that there is no creator god nor any soul, that words cannot refer directly to real things, and that viable religious teachings must be demonstrable through inference and perception. This next level of analysis, identified by Kamalaśīla as the Vijñānavāda or Yogācāra, operates with an ontology in which real particulars do not exist outside the mind. Images arise in awareness due to the causal functioning of an imprint or "seed" contained within the beginningless mind itself. The shift from the Sautrāntika to the Vijñānavāda is rationally justified because one can demonstrate that it is impossible to know particulars outside the mind.

A third level of analysis, the Madhyamaka, operates in an important sense with no ontology, in that neither the particular known nor the awareness that knows is held to be intrinsically real. Although this level remains only nascent in the *Tattvasaṃgraha*, it is fully developed in Śāntarakṣita's other famous work, the *Madhyamakālaṃkāra* (Ornament of the Middle Way) together with his own commentary on it. Here, Śāntarakṣita uses the sliding scale of analysis to integrate the Madhyamaka perspective he may have inherited from his reputed teacher, Jñānagarbha, with his logical and epistemological training, so as to create a place for philosophical analysis within a larger path that ultimately denies the validity of all instruments of knowing.

Later Tibetans classify Śāntarakṣita and Kamalaśīla as followers of Yogācāra-Svātantrika-Madhyamaka. This classification indicates, first, that Śāntarakṣita and Kamalaśīla accept as an accurate description of conventional reality the basic Yogācāra position that objects of knowledge do not exist outside the mind, and second, it indicates that, unlike the followers of the allegedly superior Prāsaṅgika-Madhyamaka of Candrakīrti, they fully endorse the logical apparatus of the Buddhist epistemological tradition, especially the so-called autonomous (*svatantra*) inferences. For many Tibetans, this second element of their philosophical thought renders Śāntarakṣita and Kamalaśīla inferior proponents of Madhyamaka, because it obliges them to accept a measure of intrinsic identity, even if they deny doing so. Despite this censure, however, many Tibetans, such as the nonsectarian (*ris med*) scholar Mi pham rgya mtsho (1846–1912), have upheld Śāntarakṣita as a brilliant philosopher, model Buddhist, and national hero.

See Also Buddhism, article on Buddhism in Tibet; Buddhism, Schools of, article on Tibetan and Mongolian Buddhism; Kamalaśīla; Padmasambhava; Tibetan Religions, overview article.

Bibliography

Blumenthal, James. *The Ornament of the Middle Way: A Study of the Madhyamaka Thought of Śāntarakṣita.* Ithaca, N.Y., 2004. Translation, edition, and study of Śāntarakṣita's *Madhyamakālaṃkāra*, together with a Tibetan commentary by rGyal tshab dar ma rin chen (1364–1432) of the Dge lugs pa school of Tibetan Buddhism.

Doctor, Thomas, trans. *Speech of Delight: Mipham's Commentary on Śāntarakṣita's Ornament of the Middle Way.* Ithaca, N.Y., 2004. Translation and edition of the *dBu ma rgyan gyi nam bshad* of Mi pham rgya mtsho (1846–1912) of the nonsectarian (*ris med*) movement of Tibetan Buddhism.

Dreyfus, Georges B. F., and Sara L. McClintock, eds. *The Svātantrika-Prāsaṅgika Distinction: What Difference Does a Difference Make?* Boston, 2003. Collection of articles on the Svātantrika-Prāsaṅgika distinction, with several contributions touching on the Madhyamaka philosophy of Śāntarakṣita and Kamalaśīla.

Jha, Ganganatha, trans. *The Tattvasaṅgraha of Shāntarakṣita with the Commentary of Kamalashīla.* 2 vols. Baroda, India, 1937; Reprint, Delhi, 1986. The only complete translation of the encyclopedic *Tattvasaṃgraha* and its commentary; although valuable for gaining a sense of the work's overall structure and arguments, the work should be used with caution as the translation is at points deeply misleading.

Kajiyama, Yūichi. "Later Mādhyamikas on Epistemology and Meditation." In *Mahāyāna Buddhist Mediation: Theory and Practice,* edited by Minoru Kiyota, pp. 114–43. Honolulu, 1978. This useful article presents a synopsis of the arguments in the *Madhyamakālaṃkāra,* Śāntarakṣita's primary Madhyamaka treatise.

López, Donald S. Jr. *A Study of Svātantrika.* Ithaca, N.Y., 1987. Exploration of the category of Svātantrika-Madhyamaka based principally on Tibetan (especially Dge lugs pa) sources.

Wangdu, Pasang, and Hildegard Diemberger. *dBa' bzhed: The Royal Narrative Concerning the Bringing of the Buddha's Doctrine to Tibet.* Vienna, 2000. Annotated translation, study and facsimile edition of one version of an early Tibetan account of the arrival of Buddhism in Tibet, the construction of Bsam yas monastery, the ordination of the first Tibetan monks, and the famous debate at Bsam yas.

Sara L. McClintock (2005)

SANTERÍA is a religious tradition of African origin that developed in Cuba and that was spread throughout the Caribbean and the United States by exiles from the revolution of 1959. Santería began in the nineteenth century when hundreds of thousands of men and women of the Yoruba people, from what are now Nigeria and Benin, were brought to Cuba to work in the island's booming sugar industry. Despite brutal conditions, some were able to reconstruct their religious lives through a fusing of the traditions remembered from their homeland and from their encounter with the folk piety of the Roman Catholic church.

The Cuban Yoruba often used the iconography of Catholic saints to express their devotions to Yoruba spirits called *orishas.* The name *Santería,* "the way of the saints," is the most common Spanish word used to describe these practices, and the word *santero* (m.) or *santera* (f.) indicates an initiated devotee. Later generations of *santeros* would construct elaborate systems of correspondences between *orishas* and saints, leading observers to see this Caribbean religion as a model for understanding religious syncretism and cultural change. Despite the frequent presence of Catholic symbols in Santería rites and the attendance of *santeros* at Catholic sacraments, Santería is essentially an African way of worship drawn into a symbiotic relationship with Catholicism.

Santeros believe that every individual, before he or she is born, is given a destiny, or road in life, by the Almighty. It is the responsibility of the individual to understand his or her destiny and to grow with it rather than to be a victim of it. *Santeros* recognize a pantheon of *orishas* whose aid and energy can bring devotees to a complete fulfillment of their destinies. The basis of Santería is the development of a deep personal relationship with the *orishas,* a relationship that will bring the *santero* worldly success and heavenly wisdom. Devotion to the *orishas* takes four principal forms: divination, sacrifice, spirit mediumship, and initiation.

For the ordinary devotee, Santería serves as a means for resolving the problems of everyday life, including problems of health, money, and love. Divination can reveal the sources of these problems, and it points the way to their resolution. Santería has preserved several Yoruba systems of divination in a hierarchical ranking according to their reliability and the amount of training required to master them. The most complex system of divination in Santería, Ifa, can be "read" only by male priests called *babalawos.* In response to a querent's problem, a *babalawo* will throw a small chain *(ekwele)* that has eight pieces of shell, bone, or other material affixed to it. Each piece is shaped so that, when thrown, it lands either concave or convex side up. This arrangement results in 256 possible combinations, each representing a basic situation in life. The combination that falls at any particular time is the purest expression of fate, and thus of the God-given destiny of the querent. Most of the patterns refer to stories that tell of the problems faced by the *orishas* and heroes in the past, and that relate the solutions that were found. These solutions become the archetypes used by the querent to resolve the problem that he or she has brought to Ifa.

Nearly all problems are resolved by deepening the devotee's relationship with the *orishas.* There is no firmer way for the devotee to show this relationship than through the symbolism of shared food—that is, through sacrifice. The *orishas,* like all living things, must eat in order to live. Although they are immensely powerful, they are by no means immortal, and for continued life they depend on the sacrifice and praise of human beings. Each *orisha* enjoys certain special foods, ranging from cakes to stews, fruits, or drinks. If an *orisha* requests, *santeros* will sacrifice fowl, sheep, or other animals. The slaughter is always performed quickly and cleanly according to ritual rules, and the flesh is nearly always cooked and consumed by the congregation as part of the *orisha's* feast.

The most dramatic form of devotion to the *orishas* is ceremonial spirit mediumship. At certain ceremonies called *bembes, guemileres,* or *tambores,* a battery of drums calls the *orishas* to join the devotees in dance and song. If an *orisha* so chooses, he or she will "descend" and "seize the head" of an initiate. In this state the incarnated *orisha* may perform spectacular dances that the human medium would be hard put to imitate in ordinary consciousness. More important, an incarnated *orisha* will deliver messages, admonitions, and advice to individual members of the community, bringing their heavenly wisdom to bear on their devotees' earthly problems.

As a devotee grows in these ways of devotion, one particular *orisha* may begin to assert itself as the devotee's patron, and the love of this *orisha* will provide the devotee with his or her basic orientation in life. When this *orisha* calls for it, the devotee will undergo a demanding and irrevocable initiation into the mysteries of the patron *orisha.* The initiation ceremony is carried out with great solemnity and care in the home of an initiate of long experience. During a lengthy period of isolation and instruction, the devotee is brought to a spiritual rebirth as a true child of the *orisha.* During this ceremony the *orisha* is "enthroned in the head" of the devotee, seated and sealed as a permanent part of the devotee's personality.

As the initiate grows in this new level of devotion, his or her relationship with the seated *orisha* becomes increasingly fluid. The sacrificial exchange between them comes to be seen as the outward manifestation of an inner process. Thus Santería culminates in a mysticism of identity between human and divine, where the road of life is the way of the *orishas.*

Santería continues to grow in the late twentieth century. Its popularity in Cuba seems to have been little affected by the socialist revolution, and thanks to nearly one million Cuban exiles, it is thriving in Venezuela, Puerto Rico, and the United States. The number of full initiates is difficult to determine because of the tradition of secrecy that *santeros* have maintained in order to survive a history of oppression and misunderstanding. The presence of Santería in a given neighborhood may be gauged by the profusion of *botánicas,* small retail stores that sell the herbs and ritual paraphernalia of Santería ceremonies. In 1981, there were at least eighty *botánicas* in Miami, Florida, and more than a hundred in New York City.

See Also Afro-Brazilian Religions; Journalism and Religion; Vodou; Yoruba Religion.

Bibliography

A limited literature exists on Santería in English. The finest presentation of the symbolism of the *orishas* is Robert F. Thompson's *Flash of the Spirit: African and Afro-American*

Art and Philosophy (New York, 1981). Migene González-Wippler has written three books on the subject. *Santería: African Magic in Latin America* (Garden City, N. Y., 1975) is a disorganized introduction that borrows freely from Spanish sources. *The Santería Experience* (Englewood Cliffs, N. J., 1982) is a detailed, well-written, first-person account of the author's experience with Santería in New York. *Rituals and Spells of Santería* (New York, 1984) presents source materials on Santería liturgy and magic. William R. Bascom has written two articles on Santería in Cuba; reflecting his wide experience as an anthropologist among the Yoruba in Nigeria, these articles are "The Focus of Cuban Santeria," *Southwestern Journal of Anthropology* 6 (Spring 1950): 64–68, and "Two Forms of Afro-Cuban Divination," in *Acculturation in the Americas,* edited by Sol Tax (Chicago, 1952), pp. 169–184.

Among Spanish sources, pride of place belongs to the works of Fernando Ortiz. Between 1906 and his death in 1969, he published hundreds of pieces on all aspects of Afro-Cuban culture. The work that deals most directly with Santería is perhaps *Los bailes y el teatro de los negros en el folklore de Cuba* (Havana, 1951). The most widely available works in Spanish in the United States are those of the great exiled folklorist Lydia Cabrera. Among her many books in print on Afro-Cuban themes, *El monte* (Miami, 1968) and *Koeko iyawo: Pequeño tratado de regla Lucumi* (Miami, 1980) are considered authoritative by practitioners and observers alike. Two books by anthropologically trained scholars provide excellent surveys of the tradition: Julio Sánchez's *La religión de los orichas* (Hato Rey, Puerto Rico, 1978) and Mercedes Cros Sandoval's *La religion afrocubana* (Madrid, 1975). Sandoval's book makes use of Pierre Verger's classic *Notes sur le culte des Orisa et Vodun à Bahia* (Dakar, 1957), which traces the connections between the religion of the *orishas* in Africa and that in Brazil and includes invaluable texts of prayers to the *orishas* as well as excellent photographs.

JOSEPH M. MURPHY (1987)

ŚĀNTIDEVA (seventh and eighth centuries CE) was an Indian Buddhist monk and scholar at the great Buddhist monastic center of Nālandā in northern India. He was a follower of Mahāyāna Buddhism and has been traditionally associated with the Mādhyamika philosophical lineage, especially that of the Prāsaṅgikas, although his precise philosophical affiliation remains a matter of debate among scholars. Śāntideva is famous for his eloquent Sanskrit treatises on the Mahāyāna bodhisattva ideal.

Sanskrit and Tibetan biographies portray Śāntideva as both a Mahāyāna monk renowned for the composition of erudite texts and a Tantric *siddha* noted for performing miracles. For this reason, some scholars have speculated that his biography may represent an amalgamation of two different persons. According to his biographies, Śāntideva was a crown prince and devotee of Mañjuśrī or Mañjughoṣa, a bodhisattva associated with wisdom who appeared to Śāntideva in visions and dreams. Upon his father's death, Śāntideva fled the kingdom in order to pursue religious practice. Śāntideva became a monk at Nālandā, where he was called Bhusuku, a name indicating that he appeared to do nothing but eat, sleep, and stroll about for the sake of his digestion. Some biographies, however, state that Śāntideva secretly composed Buddhist treatises and contemplated the teachings he had received from Mañjuśrī. Śāntideva was threatened with expulsion from Nālandā because he appeared unable to memorize any sūtras. When put to the test, Śāntideva asked those assembled whether they wanted to hear something they already knew or something new. Asked for something new, Śāntideva astounded the assembly by reciting his most famous composition, the *Bodhicaryāvatāra.* Demonstrating both his erudition and supernormal powers, Śāntideva rose into the air and disappeared when he reached the ninth chapter (on wisdom). His voice, however, could still be heard reciting the text to its conclusion. Thereafter Śāntideva left monastic life. His biographies recount the performance of numerous miracles, such as restoring sight, bringing animals back to life, feeding the hungry, and converting heretics.

Sanskrit and Tibetan biographies credit Śāntideva with three Sanskrit works: the *Śikṣāsamuccaya* (Compendium of training), the *Bodhicaryāvatāra* (Understanding the way to awakening), and the *Sūtrasamuccaya* (Compendium of scriptures). The *Sūtrasamuccaya* does not appear to have survived. A work of this title, extant in Tibetan and Chinese, has been attributed by most modern scholars to another Indian Mahāyāna scholar-monk named Nāgārjuna, whom scholars have variously placed between the late first and third centuries CE. The *Bodhicaryāvatāra,* of which there are two recensions of differing length, is written entirely in verse. The *Śikṣāsamuccaya,* which quotes extensively from approximately one hundred Buddhist sources, combines verse and prose.

The *Bodhicaryāvatāra* and the *Śikṣāsamuccaya* provide a broad overview of Indian Mahāyāna beliefs and practices, particularly from a male monastic perspective. Both texts describe the path of a bodhisattva, a being who has generated the *bodhicitta,* or aspiration for buddhahood. Bodhisattvas embody the Mahāyāna twin ideals of compassion and wisdom because their aspiration for buddhahood is motivated by a desire to help others. The cultivation of *bodhicitta* and its accompanying compassion are among the most important themes in Śāntideva's works, because these define the path to buddhahood as one of compassionate service to others. Another important theme is that of emptiness (*śūnyatā*), a Mahāyāna philosophical concept used to describe the ultimate nature of reality. The wisdom a bodhisattva seeks is the ability to perceive all phenomena as lacking, or empty of, intrinsic, independent, and permanent existence. The ninth chapter of the *Bodhicaryāvatāra,* on wisdom, contains Śāntideva's most famous discussion of emptiness. In this chapter, which reflects a well-established tradition of scholastic debate in medieval India, Śāntideva asserts the correctness of his view of ultimate reality over and against those of other Buddhist and non-Buddhist philosophical schools.

For all their erudition, Śāntideva's works were intended as practical handbooks for religious practitioners committed to the bodhisattva ideal. Thus his works also contain extensive instruction on Mahāyāna ethics and ritual. Key ethical concerns include cultivating the six perfections (*pāramitās*) of generosity, morality, forbearance, vigor, concentration, and wisdom; eradicating the defilements (*kleśa*) of greed, anger, and delusion, which bind living beings to *saṃsāra*, or the cycle of rebirth; and generating the mindfulness (*smṛti*) and awareness (*saṃprajanya*) needed to refrain from committing sinful deeds.

Śāntideva's works prescribe a wide range of rituals known in his day; however, the two most commonly associated with him are a liturgy called the supreme worship and a meditation called exchanging self and other. The supreme worship (*anuttara-pūjā*) is a complex liturgy that includes, among other practices, praise and worship of buddhas and bodhisattvas, confession of sinful deeds, and dedication of merit to other living beings. Its purpose is to cultivate *bodhicitta* and merit. Exchanging self and other is another means of cultivating *bodhicitta.* The meditation begins with the reflection that all living beings are fundamentally alike because they share the same desire for happiness and the same fear of suffering. Hence there is no reason to privilege one's own concerns above those of others. As the meditation progresses, one comes to reflect that, because others are infinite in number, their concerns, taken as whole, should matter more than one's own. By performing this meditation, bodhisattvas increase their compassionate regard for living beings and their commitment to attaining buddhahood for the sake of others.

Śāntideva holds an important place in Indian Mahāyāna history. His works have been studied and commented upon by many Indian and Tibetan Buddhist scholars. Śāntideva's influence remains particularly strong in Tibetan Buddhism. His works continue to inform the beliefs, practices, and teachings of leading contemporary Tibetan Buddhist figures, such as the Dalai Lama.

SEE ALSO Mādhyamika.

BIBLIOGRAPHY

Abhayadatta. *Buddha's Lions: The Lives of the Eighty-Four Siddhas.* Translated by James B. Robinson. Berkeley, Calif., 1979. Translation of *Caturaśīti-siddha-pravṛtti.*

Gyatso, Tenzin (Fourteenth Dalai Lama). *A Flash of Lightning in the Dark of Night: A Guide to the Bodhisattva's Way of Life.* Boston, 1994.

La Vallée Poussin, Louis de, ed. *Prajñākaramati's Commentary to the Bodhicaryāvatāra of Śāntideva.* Calcutta, 1901–1914.

Pezzali, Amalia. *Śāntideva: Mystique bouddhiste des septième et huitième siècles.* Florence, Italy, 1968. Readers should also consult the review of this book: J. W. de Jong, "La Légende de Śāntideva," *Indo-Iranian Journal* 16 (1975): 161–182.

Śāntideva. *Śikshāsamuccaya: A Compendium of Buddhistic Teaching (1897–1902).* Edited by Cecil Bendall. Osnabrück, Germany, 1970.

Śāntideva. *Śikṣā Samuccaya: A Compendium of Buddhist Doctrine* (1922). Translated by Cecil Bendall and W. H. D. Rouse. Delhi, India, 1981.

Śāntideva. *The Bodhicaryāvatāra.* Translated by Kate Crosby and Andrew Skilton. Oxford, U.K., 1996. Crosby and Skilton introduce each chapter of the text by explaining and contextualizing the ideas and practices described therein. The translation also includes a general introduction to Śāntideva and his world by Paul Williams.

SUSANNE MROZIK (2005)

SAOSHYANT. The Avestan term *saoshyant* ("future benefactor"; MPers., *sōshans*) designates the savior of the world, who will arrive at a future time to redeem humankind. The concept of the future savior is one of the fundamental notions of Zoroastrianism, together with that of dualism; it appears as early as in the *Gāthās.* Zarathushtra (Zoroaster), as prophet of the religion, is himself a Saoshyant, one who performs his works for the Frashōkereti, the end of the present state of the world, when existence will be "rehabilitated" and "made splendid."

Later Zoroastrian tradition developed this notion into a true eschatological myth and expanded the number of Saoshyants from one to three. All the saviors are born from the seed of Zarathushtra, which is preserved through the ages in Lake Kansaoya (identified with present-day Lake Helmand, in Seistan, Iran), protected by 99,999 *fravashis*, or guardian spirits. The greatest of the awaited Saoshyants, the victorious Astvatereta ("he who embodies truth"), the son of the Vīspataurvairī ("she who conquers all"), is the third, who will make existence splendid; he appears in *Yashts* 19. Upon his arrival humankind will no longer be subject to old age, death, or corruption, and will be granted unlimited power. At that time the dead will be resurrected, and the living will be immortal and indestructible. Brandishing the weapon with which he kills the powerful enemies of the world of truth (that is, the world of the spirit, and of *asha*), Astvatereta will look upon the whole of corporeal existence and render it imperishable. He and his comrades will engage in a great battle with the forces of evil, which will be destroyed.

The name *Astvatereta* is clearly the result of theological speculation (Kellens, 1974), as are those of his two brothers, *Ukhshyatereta,* "he who makes truth grow," and *Ukhshyatnemah,* "he who makes reverence grow"; the names of the three virgins (*Yashts* 13) who are impregnated with the seed of Zarathushtra when they bathe in Lake Kansaoya and give birth to the Saoshyants, are equally speculative. Each of these Saoshyants will arrive in the last three millenia, initiating a new age and a new cycle of existence; Astvatereta will appear in the third and final millennium to save humankind.

The doctrine of the future savior had already taken shape in the Achaemenid period (sixth to fourth centuries BCE). It was not, perhaps, the principal element in the formation of the messianic idea, but it was certainly a determining factor, one that enjoyed great success in the Hellenistic period beyond the confines of the Iranian world. A similar concept, that of the future Buddha, Maitreya, was most likely indebted to it, and Christian messianism can trace its roots to the same source.

SEE ALSO Frashōkereti.

BIBLIOGRAPHY

Boyce, Mary. *A History of Zoroastrianism*, vol. 1. Leiden, 1975.

Duchesne-Guillemin, Jacques. *La religion de l'Iran ancien*. Paris, 1962.

Herzfeld, Ernst. *Zoroaster and His World*. Princeton, 1947.

Kellens, Jean. "Saošiiaṇt-." *Studia Iranica* 3 (1974): 187–209.

Messina, Giuseppe. *I Magi a Betlemme e una predizione di Zoroastro*. Rome, 1933.

Molé, Marijan. *Culte, mythe et cosmologie dans l'Iran ancien*. Paris, 1963.

Nyberg, H. S. *Irans forntida religioner*. Stockholm, 1937. Translated as *Die Religionen des alten Iran* (1938; 2d ed., Osnabrück, 1966).

Widengren, Geo. *Die Religionen Irans*. Stuttgart, 1965. Translated as *Les religions de l'Iran* (Paris, 1968).

Widengren, Geo. "Leitende Ideen und Quellen der iranischen Apokalyptik." In *Apocalypticism in the Mediterranean World and the Near East*. Tübingen, 1989.

GHERARDO GNOLI (1987)
Translated from Italian by Roger DeGaris

ŚĀRADĀ DEVĪ (1853–1920) was the wife of Śri Ramakrishna Paramahamsa (1836–1886), a highly regarded Hindu spiritual master from Bengal, India. She is called the Holy Mother (*Śrima*) by the followers of Ramakrishna, who worship her along with her husband as a manifestation of the divine. By the end of Ramakrishna's life, his followers included some leading Bengali intellectuals. As he wished, Śāradā Devī became the chief source of spiritual and emotional support for his disciples after his death, when they began to establish a spiritual order in his name. Up to this point she had led her life in accordance with the Indian cultural ideal of a quiet and dutiful wife; however, she played a pivotal role in the burgeoning order with her piety, pragmatism, and motherly qualities. In the early twenty-first century Śāradā Devī receives the highest degree of honor in the order's many centers throughout the world, along with Ramakrishna himself and his most famous disciple Swami Vivekananda (1863–1902).

Śāradā Devī was born to a poor Brahmin family in Jayrambati, a tiny village in West Bengal, in 1853. As a child Śāradā—then known as Saradamani—was fascinated by Indian folklore and Hindu narratives. She did not receive any formal education but learned to serve others as she helped her mother run a large household. During the terrible famine of 1864, Śāradā worked ceaselessly as her family served food to hungry people. Service to others remained her chief occupation throughout life. At the age of six she was married to Gadadhar Chattopadhaya—who later took the name of Ramakrishna—from a neighboring village. Chattopadhaya, who was eighteen years her senior, was the priest of Kālī's temple in Dakshineshwar, a town near Calcutta, and engaged in intense spiritual practices. His frequent ecstasies and unorthodox ways of worship led some onlookers to doubt his mental stability. Śāradā joined her husband on her own accord when she was eighteen, after hearing these rumors about his mental health. She found her husband to be a kind and caring person; however, he never consummated the marriage. Instead, he began to give her spiritual instruction. Śāradā complied with her husband's wish to lead the life of a celibate spiritual seeker.

Even while leading the life of a married virgin at Dakshineshwar, Śāradā Devī served her husband, who was now also her *gurū*, her living god. Except for her hours of meditation, most of her time was spent in cooking for Ramakrishna and the growing number of his devotees. While Śāradā Devī remained completely in the background, her unassuming but warm personality attracted some female devotees to become her lifelong companions. She also welcomed in her circle some women of low status and questionable character whom her husband had admonished. Ramakrishna then declared that Śāradā was the Mother of the Universe and performed an elaborate ritual of worship for her. He also asked his disciples to address her as the Holy Mother. While this exalted status fulfilled Śāradā Devī's maternal dreams in some ways, it did little to change her daily work routine, which became even more grueling when Ramakrishna was diagnosed with terminal cancer.

After Ramakrishna died in 1886, Śāradā Devī moved to his village of Kamarpukur and bravely endured poverty verging on starvation for a year. When Devī was invited to return to Calcutta by Ramakrishna's disciples, who had begun to form the Ramakrishna order, her spiritual ministry began in earnest. She did not lead the secluded life of a traditional Hindu widow after 1887. Moving back and forth between Jayrambati and Calcutta, she initiated disciples with *mantras*, advised them in spiritual and practical matters, and provided the community with motherly warmth. Her ministry was markedly different from that of Ramakrishna. While the latter instructed his disciples in the intricacies of meditation and mystical experiences, she taught them devotion to the master, simplicity in living, and loving service to others through her own example. Following Vivekananda's visit to America, his Western followers also came to regard her as the Holy Mother.

Śāradā Devī was among the earliest Hindu spiritual personalities to have Western devotees. She accepted the divine status accorded to her and the adoration of the devotees without much concern. Even with her changed status, she continued to cook for and feed her disciple-children and took care of her younger siblings' families. She welcomed low-caste devotees and showed a special concern for women. Though uneducated herself, she advocated education for women. Her contemporary devotees emphasize the theme of forgiveness in her teachings. Her saying, "No one is a stranger. The whole world is your own," is considered her most valuable message to the world. When Devī died in 1920, the growing circle of Ramakrishna's followers around the world regarded her as the Holy Mother in her own right, a manifestation of God's maternal love.

Unfolding during the heyday of British rule in India, Śāradā Devī's life demonstrated the strength of simplicity and motherly affection—a quality that was considered a distinctive characteristic of Mother India in the nationalist discourse of the early twentieth century. In Devī's ability to combine traditional values with a liberal outlook and to transform mundane work into spiritual practice through selfless service, she provided a model of inspiration for modern Indian women. Even though some contemporary critics of Ramakrishna view Śāradā Devī as a helpless victim of exploitation and imposed spirituality, her quintessential motherly qualities and piety made her the leader of one of the most successful spiritual orders of modern India that has attracted followers around the world.

See Also Gender and Religion, article on Gender and Hinduism; Hinduism; Ramakrishna.

Bibliography

Her Devotee Children. *The Gospel of the Holy Mother Sri Sarada Devi.* Madras, 1984.

Kripal, Jeffrey J. *Kali's Child: The Mystical and the Erotic in the Life and Teachings of Ramakrishna.* Chicago, 1995.

Mandavia, Chetna. "Sri Sarada Devi: An Ideal for Modern Women." *Prabuddha Bharat* 45 (1990): 500–506.

Nikhilananda, Swami. *Holy Mother: Being the Life of Sri Sarada Devi, Wife of Ramakrishna and Helpmate in Mission.* 3d ed. New York, 1997.

Nivedita, Sister (Margaret Noble). *Letters of Nivedita.* Edited by Sankari Basu. 2 vols. Calcutta, 1982.

Sil, Narasingha P. *Divine Dowager: Life and Teachings of Saradamani the Holy Mother.* Selinsgrove, Pa., and London, 2003.

Tapasyananda, Swami. *Sri Sarada Devi the Holy Mother: Her Life and Conversations.* Madras, 1977.

Neelima Shukla-Bhatt (2005)

SARAH was the wife of Abraham and mother of Isaac. Abraham's self-serving presentation of her as his sister when they were visiting foreign lands (*Genesis* 12:11–13 and 20:2) may be an attempt to justify his self–serving statement, "And Abraham said of Sarah his wife, She [is] my sister" (*Genesis* 20:2). According to the Bible, Sarah was originally called Sarai until her name was changed as part of God's blessing to Abraham, formerly Abram. The two forms are generally regarded as dialectal variants of the same name, probably meaning "princess"; however, their rendering in the Septuagint (*Sara* and *Sarra*) does not conform to the traditional Hebrew pronunciation. Sarah was married to Abraham in Mesopotamia and migrated with him to Canaan, where they wandered until her death at the age of 127; she was buried in the cave of Machpelah, near Hebron.

The narratives of Genesis focus on Sarah's beauty and infertility. Sarah's beauty is also praised in rabbinic literature and greatly elaborated in the *Genesis Apocryphon,* a pre–Christian text found among the Dead Sea Scrolls. Twice the Bible recounts Abraham's fear that her desirability would lead foreign kings to have him killed so they could marry Sarah. To avoid this fate, Abraham presents Sarah as his sister (*Gn.* 12:10–20, 20:1–18). Documents from fifteenth–century Nuzi (modern-day Yorghan Tepe) have sometimes been interpreted as suggesting that especially honored wives in this North Mesopotamian culture were granted the title "Sister;" however, these texts can be interpreted in other ways, and this theory has come to be generally regarded as unlikely.

Sarah's infertility is noted the first time she is mentioned in the Bible (*Gn.* 11:30). In accordance with a widespread ancient Near Eastern practice, attested in both Nuzi documents and the Code of Hammurabi, Sarah gave Abraham her slave girl Hagar with the intention that the offspring of this union be credited to her as owner of the slave. However, it is clear in Genesis that the chosen line was to proceed through Sarah, a point the New Testament emphasizes (*Gal.* 4:21–31). When, in accordance with God's promise, Sarah herself conceived and bore Isaac, she insisted that Hagar and her son Ishmael be expelled from their home (*Gn.* 21); another version of this incident suggests that Hagar fled while still pregnant because of mistreatment at Sarah's hands (*Gn.* 16).

Rabbinic tradition ascribes prophetic powers to Sarah and identifies her with Iscah, Abraham's niece (*Gn.* 11:29), perhaps because the Bible provides no explicit genealogy. In the New Testament, Sarah is regarded as a symbol of faith (*Heb.* 11:11) and wifely submissiveness (*1 Pt.* 3:6).

Bibliography

An excellent survey of the patriarchal narratives is Nahum M. Sarna's *Understanding Genesis* (New York, 1966); his treatment of the wife–sister theme should, however, be qualified by the summary of information in John Van Seters's *Abraham in History and Tradition* (New Haven, Conn., 1975). Louis Ginzberg has collected rabbinic traditions in *The Legends of the Jews,* 7 vols., translated by Henrietta Szold and Paul Radin (1909–1938; reprint, Philadelphia, 1937–1966; 2nd edition, in 2 vols., Philadelphia, 2003); refer to the index s.v. Sarah.

Frederick E. Greenspahn (2005)

SARASVATĪ is a goddess of pan-Indian importance best known as the patron of learning and the fine arts. Her name means "flowing, watery," and indeed, she first appears in the

Ṛgveda as a sacred river. Since Ṛgvedic times Sarasvatī has been associated with knowledge and learning, and quite early she developed a special connection with music, as is shown iconographically by the lute (*vīṇā*) that she often holds. In texts beginning with the Yajurveda she is identified with Vāc, a female personification of sacred speech.

Sarasvatī's primary mythic association is as the wife (or sometimes the daughter) of the god Brahmā; as his cult waned, she came increasingly to be represented, along with Lakṣmī, as a spouse of Viṣṇu. Although she has been assimilated in this way to various deities of the Brahmanic tradition, her primary religious importance is as a goddess in her own right. Thus, in spite of her frequent consort status, she is popularly viewed as unmarried, and she is commonly worshiped alone. Images characteristically portray her as fair, wearing white garments and many ornaments, sitting with one leg pendant, and playing the *vīṇā* with two of her four arms while holding one or more other objects, such as a manuscript, a white lotus, a rosary, or a water vessel. A ruddy goose or swan (*haṃsa*), her usual mount (*vāhana*) and emblem, is often represented at her feet; less commonly, she has been depicted with a ram.

MYTHOLOGY. From the *Ṛgveda* onward, Sarasvatī's mythic associations have been various and complex. As one form of the sacrificial fire, she is conceived of as the wife of Agni, whose mount is also a ram. In the Āprī hymns of the *Ṛgveda* she is praised together with Iḷā and Bhāratī as the triple tongue of the sacrificial fire. Yet her closest Vedic associations are with Indra and with the twin Aśvins, the physicians of the gods. Vedic accounts portray her as healing, refreshing, and giving strength to Indra, either as a river or by the power of her speech, and she is sometimes said to be Indra's wife and sometimes the wife of the Aśvins. Her banks were considered the most sacred place for sacrifices, and her waters alone were deemed capable of purifying humans from that most heinous of crimes, brahmanicide.

In the later tradition, Sarasvatī's river aspect gradually diminished, perhaps at the same time that the actual river by that name receded and eventually disappeared; certain epic and Puranic myths do, however, retain a sense of her earlier identity. In a *Mahābhārata* story she preserves the Vedas during a twelve-year drought by feeding her son Sārasvata on her fish when other brahmans have become too weak to remember the sacred texts; she is also praised in the Purāṇas and in inscriptions for bearing the virulent Aurvā fire to the sea. Yet increasingly she is conceived of as an anthropomorphic goddess, whose beauty and quick temper cause problems for those around her. In a Puranic elaboration of a Vedic kernel, Brahmā so desires to keep his lovely daughter in view as she circumambulates him that he grows a face in every direction. Other Purāṇas tell of a quarrel among the three wives of Viṣṇu—Sarasvatī, Lakṣmī, and Gaṅgā—which becomes so fierce that Viṣṇu gives Sarasvatī to Brahmā and Gaṅgā to Śiva.

Although Sarasvatī has continued to be associated with Brahmā, she early developed connections not only with Lakṣmī and Viṣṇu but also with Durgā and Śiva. Images of Viṣṇu from the ninth century CE or earlier in eastern India represent her, together with Lakṣmī, at Viṣṇu's side. In Bengal, Sarasvatī and Lakṣmī are popularly viewed as the daughters of Śiva and Durgā, and their rivalry is proverbial. In certain Purāṇas and images Sarasvatī is herself assimilated to the great goddess Durgā and is provided with Durgā's mount, a lion.

CULT. Although the worship of Sarasvatī has been as various as her mythology, there are notable points of continuity. The ram, the he-goat, and the ewe are prescribed in Vedic texts as sacrificial offerings to her, and this custom has continued into the twentieth century in the district of Dacca, Bangladesh, where a ram fight has also served as entertainment on the day of her worship. Rice and barley, which are also among her offerings from Vedic times, suggest a connection with fertility, as does early spring, the season of her festival in Bengal. Prosperity and cure, as well as success in marriage and procreation, are chief among the boons requested of her since ancient times.

Sarasvatī's continuing importance for scholars is attested to by her prominence in the invocatory (*maṅgala*) verses of Sanskrit manuscripts, in which she appears more frequently than any other deity except Gaṇeśa. Her role as the goddess of learning is prominent in her worship in homes, where students place their books before her image on her festival day. On that day, too, the family priest puts chalk in the hand of the youngest child and guides the child's hand in writing his or her first letters. Musicians, especially in South India, place their instruments before her shrine and worship them—with fruits, coconut, cloth, incense, and lighted oil lamps—as the very body of the goddess.

BUDDHIST AND JAIN TRADITIONS. Sarasvatī as the goddess of learning has also figured prominently in both the Jain and the Buddhist traditions. She has been worshiped by the Jains since ancient times as Śrutadevatā, the deity who presides over the sacred teachings, and in later Vajrayāna Buddhism she became the female counterpart and consort of Mañjuśrī, the *bodhisattva* of wisdom. Through Indian Vajrayāna her cult spread to Nepal, Tibet, and Mongolia, as well as China and Japan, and it has remained popular among Buddhists of those lands.

SEE ALSO Ganges River; Goddess Worship, article on The Hindu Goddess; Indian Religions, article on Mythic Themes; Rivers.

BIBLIOGRAPHY

There is no single comprehensive study of Sarasvatī. Most works treating her have focused almost entirely on texts or images, rarely combining the two approaches. Among textual studies are Manisha Mukhopadhyay's "Lakṣmī and Sarasvatī in Sanskrit Inscriptions" and A. K. Chatterjee's "Some Aspects of Sarasvatī," both included in *Foreigners in Ancient India and Lakṣmī and Sarasvatī in Art and Literature,* edited by D. C. Sircar (Calcutta, 1970). The earlier and more comprehensive article of Haridas Bhattacharyya, "Sarasvatī the Goddess of Learning," in *Commemorative Essays Presented to Professor Kashinath Bapuji Pathak* (Poona, 1934), pp. 32–52, goes beyond these two in giving brief but suggestive accounts of popular conceptions and practices. Sushila Khare's *Sarasvatī* (Varanasi, 1966) provides a useful compendium in Hindi of Vedic, epic, and Puranic sources for understanding the goddess. Although Khare includes a chapter treating the various directions for making Sarasvatī's images as found in Hindu, Jain, and Buddhist treatises, her work is largely limited to the elite Brahmanic tradition and takes little or no account of popular conceptions or contemporary practice. Still more specialized is the richly detailed monograph by Jan Gonda, *Pūṣan and Sarasvatī* (Amsterdam, 1985), in which he attempts through a close study of Vedic literature to determine the early history of the conceptions of these two deities.

The almost exclusively textual approach of the above studies of Sarasvatī requires correction by a careful examination of her extant images. T. A. Gopinatha Rao's *Elements of Hindu Iconography,* 2 vols. (1914–1916; 2d ed., New York, 1968), treats her briefly, showing certain simple correlations between descriptive and prescriptive texts and selected images. The studies of Nalini Kanta Bhattasali and Jitendra Banerjea offer fuller analyses and more imaginative interpretations of the data. Bhattasali's landmark work, *Iconography of Buddhist and Brahmānical Sculptures in the Dacca Museum* (Dacca, 1929), is unique in its effective juxtaposition of textual and iconographic evidence, especially regarding the connection of Sarasvatī with Viṣṇu. In *The Development of Hindu Iconography,* 2d ed. (Calcutta, 1956), Banerjea shows the influence of popular iconographic types—represented by terracotta figurines from the Maurya and Śuṅga periods—on early images of the goddess. Curt Maury's provocative *Folk Origins of Indian Art* (New York, 1969) provides evidence that Sarasvatī is a regional variant of an ancient lotus goddess, called also Śrī and Lakṣmī.

Art-historical studies are themselves incomplete without a knowledge of the contexts in which the images have been used. In the case of Sarasvatī, these contexts have not been sufficiently explored. Also needed is a close investigation of her contemporary cult, especially in the villages. It is likely that further research will identify other indigenous elements that have coalesced with the more readily traceable Brahmānical ones to form her composite character. A thorough historical study of the interplay among popular and literary conceptions and practices should thus yield a more accurate and balanced view of the religious significance of this major Indian goddess.

DONNA MARIE WULFF (1987)

SARMATIAN RELIGION. The Sarmatians were Iranian-speaking nomadic tribes that formed in the middle of the first millennium BCE in the southern Urals. In the last centuries before the common era they spread from there in a westward direction—to the lower Volga region, the Ciscaucasus, and the northern Black Sea shore—where they were still dominant in the first centuries CE. In language and culture, the Sarmatians were close to the Scythians. Their ethnonym is similar to that of the Sauromatians, who inhabited the left bank of the Lower Don in the middle of the first millennium BCE. Classical tradition often treated both these names as identical, but in contemporary scholarship the question of the degree of relationship between the Sauromatians and the Sarmatians remains debatable.

The Sarmatians' lack of a written language has severely limited the scope of available data about their religion. The only evidence about their pantheon is the indication by a writer of the fifth century CE that in the language of the Alani (a tribe of the Sarmatian group) the name of the town Feodosia in the Crimea was Ardabda ("seven gods"). This is a reflection of the tradition, common among the ancient Indo-Iranians, of worshiping seven gods, a practice also characteristic of Scythian religion. The actual makeup of this Sarmatian pantheon is unknown. Perhaps it was about one of the gods of this pantheon that Ammianus Marcellinus (31.2.23) wrote, comparing him to the Roman Mars and relating that the Alani worshiped him in the form of an unsheathed sword driven into the ground. This ritual may be interpreted as the erection of the *axis mundi,* which joins the world of people with the world of the gods. Such an interpretation is confirmed by information about the Scythians, who had a similar ritual; but the Scythians performed it on special stationary altars, whose complete absence among the Sarmatians (and of all other monumental religious structures as well) was specifically noted by the classical writers. Hence the religious practices of the Sarmatians had a more nomadic character, entirely suited to their mobile way of life.

The ancient writers also indicate that the tribes living along the Don worshiped that river (the ancient Tanais) as a god and that, moreover, they called the Sauromatians "fire worshipers." The worship of fire and water as gods is an ancient tradition of all Iranian peoples, and it may be assumed that the deities of these elements were part of the Sarmatian pantheon of seven gods, as was the case among the Scythians.

These sparse data constitute the sole written evidence on the religion of the Sarmatians. To some extent they have been correlated with archaeological findings, the basic sources for the reconstruction of this religion. It is true that, owing to the nomadic character of the Sarmatian way of life, the only monuments left by them are burial mounds. Thus they reflect only those aspects of Sarmatian religion that focus on Sarmatian burial practices. For example, data on Sarmatian fire-worship have something in common with their extensive use of fire in one form or another in their burial practices. The Sarmatians did not practice cremation of the dead or the burning of the grave construction, but quite often they covered the graves with the remnants of the ritual bonfire, which sometimes led to the combustion of the grave's wooden covering and even to the scorching of the corpse. The earth tempered by such fires was sometimes spread in a ring around the grave or was admixed with the soil from which the burial mound covering the grave was formed. Traces of such fires are often found in the burial mound itself, not far from the grave. It is not clear whether the fire in these rituals was considered as an element to which the dead person was consigned or only as a purifying principle.

Also connected with the worship of fire are the stone or ceramic censers, used for burning aromatic substances, that have frequently been found in Sarmatian graves. Archaeologists also consider fragments of a red mineral dye, realgar, often found in Sarmatian graves, to be a substitute for fire in a burial. The same interpretation for chalk—another mineral commonly found in Sarmatian graves—is more debatable. But its purifying function is completely obvious. Chalk was either put in the grave in pieces or strewn on the bottom of the grave. The latter custom, like the tradition of laying grass under the burial, was evidently meant to prevent the corpse from coming into direct contact with the earth and thus being defiled. This custom was a prominent characteristic of Zoroastrian burial practice, which developed from ancient Iranian beliefs.

The Sarmatian custom of placing burial mounds around one of the oldest mounds may be interpreted as evidence of the worship of ancestor graves and, in the final analysis, of an ancestor cult. In some burial mounds in which persons of high social rank were interred, there have also been found the bodies of people who were deliberately killed—servants, swordbearers, and so forth—indicating that the Sarmatians practiced human sacrifice. Far more widespread was the custom of placing in the graves food for the dead, in the form of parts of the carcass of a horse or a sheep. A typically Sarmatian feature is the placing in the grave of a specially broken mirror, or of its fragments, perhaps indicating that the Sarmatians regarded the mirror as the person's "double," who died together with him.

There is no doubt that animal-style art, widespread in Sarmatian culture, is connected with the religio-mythological concepts of the Sarmatians. Zoomorphic motifs were used to decorate ritual objects and to adorn the trappings of horses and warriors. However, no study has yet been made of the Sarmatian animal style, and the iconography remains obscure.

Among the objects most frequently decorated with zoomorphic images are the Sauromato-Sarmatian portable altars—small stone dishes with or without supporting feet—used for grinding chalk and realgar, for igniting fires, and, probably, for other ritual activities. The small size of these altars again bears witness to the mobile nature of Sarmatian religious practice, which had been adapted to a nomadic way of life. An interesting feature of these altars is that they are found exclusively at female burials. Evidently, the rituals connected with them were the monopoly of priestesses. This fact is usually related to the information from Herodotus and other classical authors about the high position of women in Sauromato-Sarmatian society. It is not by chance that ancient authors connected the origins of these people with the Amazons, and even called them "woman-ruled."

The rather sparse data cited here on the Sauromato-Sarmatian religion are constantly being supplemented with archaeological investigations of the monuments of this people. In time these will enable a much more detailed and well-grounded reconstruction of the Sarmatian religion.

SEE ALSO Inner Asian Religions; Prehistoric Religions, article on The Eurasian Steppes and Inner Asia; Scythian Religion.

BIBLIOGRAPHY

Up to the present, no monographs have been devoted to the Sarmatian religion. For general information on the history of the Sarmatians, see János Harmatta's *Studies in the History and Language of the Sarmatians,* vol. 13 of "Acta Universitatis de Attilla Jozsef Nominatae: Acta Antiqua et Archaeologica" (Szeged, 1970). A fuller summary of archaeological data on the Sauromatians, including information on their religious antiquities, is in K. F. Smirnov's *Savromaty: Ranniaia istoriia i kul'tura sarmatov* (Moscow, 1964). On Sarmatian monuments of the Ural region, see K. F. Smirnov's *Sarmaty na Ileke* (Moscow, 1975). As for works devoted exclusively to the Sarmatian religion, there is only a short article, K. F. Smirnov's "Sarmaty-ognepoklonniki," in the collection *Arkheologiia Severnoi i Tsentral'noi Azii* (Novosibirsk, 1975), pp. 155–159.

New Sources

General studies on the Sarmatians include, after the pioneering inqury by Mikhail Rostovtzeff, *Iranians and Greeks in South Russia* (Oxford, 1922); Tadeusz Sulimirski, *The Sarmatians* (New York, 1970); *Antiquités d'Eurasie de l'époque scytho-sarmate,* edited by M.G. Moškova (Moskva, 1984). M. A. Ocir-Gor'ajeva, *La culture sarmate de la Basse Volga du VI au V siècle avant notre ère* (Leningrad, 1988); V. V. Fedotov, "La typologie des caractéristiques historico-géographiques des Sarmates et des Alains dans les sources antiques." In *La culture matérielle de l'Orient,* pp. 54–68. Moskva, 1988; John Joseph Wilkes, "Romans, Dacians and Sarmatians in the first and early second centuries." In *Rome and Her Northern Provinces. Papers Presented to S. Frere in Honour of His Retirement from the Chair of Archaeology of the Roman Empire,* edited by Brian Hartley and John Wacher, pp. 255–289. Gloucester, 1983.

Bibliographic hints are offered by Alexander Haeusler, "Beiträge zum Stand der Sarmatenforschung." *Zeitschrift für Archäologie* 17 (1983): 159–194.

Mikhail I. Rostovtzeff, "L'État, la religion et la culture des Scythes et des Sarmates." *Vestnik Drevnej Istorii* 188 (1989): 192–206 deals with religion in a general perspective.

On funerary customs see: K. F. Smirnov, "Les sépultures sarmates en catacombes découvertes dans les régions méridionales pré-ouraliennes et transvolgiennes et leurs rapports aux catacombes du Caucase du Nord." *Sovietskaja Archeologija* 1 (1972): 73–81; I. I. Marcenko, *Les Sarmates des steppes de la rive droite du Bas Kouban de la 2 moitié du IV siècle avant notre ère au III siècle de notre ère (d'après les sépultures en tumuli)* (Leningrad, 1988).

D. S. Raevskii (1987)
Translated from Russian by Mary Lou Masey
Revised Bibliography

SARTRE, JEAN-PAUL (1905–1980), French philosopher and man of letters, is generally regarded as the chief exponent of the atheistic branch of existentialism. Soon after World War II, Sartre wrote in *Existentialism and Humanism* (London, 1948): "Atheistic existentialism, of which I am a representative, declares . . . that if God does not exist there is at least one being whose existence comes before its essence, a being which exists before it can be defined by any conception of it. That being is man" (pp. 27–28). Sartre's existentialism, given its most sophisticated expression in *Being and Nothingness: An Essay on Phenomenological Ontology* (New York, 1956), is a philosophy of human reality that views human beings without recourse to any divine creator, that is, without appeal to God. Neither a virulent nor a polemical atheist, Sartre is not interested in the traditional philosophical or theological proofs for the existence of God. It would be more precise to say that Sartre is concerned with other matters, for, according to him, even if God did exist, his existence would be irrelevant to Sartre's fundamental project: to draw the final conclusions of a view of reality in which human beings define themselves through the choices that they make of their lives and that form the portraits of their being. In *Existentialism and Humanism* Sartre quotes Dostoevskii's statement that "if God did not exist, everything would be permitted" and adds: "that, for existentialism, is the starting point" (p. 33). Whether or not God does exist, it might be said, in Sartrean terms, "everything is permitted"—and that means that human beings are the source of value, choice, and responsibility. At the same time, Sartre holds that the individual's choice is not a solitary event but a moment of responsibility in which the chooser chooses an image of existence for everyone

Although Sartre considers the existence of God irrelevant, he "finds it extremely embarrassing that God does not exist, for there disappears with Him all possibility of finding values in an intelligible heaven" (*Existentialism and Humanism,* p. 33). That "embarrassment" is explored more cautiously and profoundly in *Being and Nothingness,* where Sartre maintains that the basic polarities of being, the "For-itself" and the "In-itself," are incapable of synthesis. The For-itself, or the human reality, is understood as consciousness (both pre-reflective and reflective), a continually nihilating movement of temporality that arises, absurdly, from being In-itself. The In-itself is simply that which it is: an opaque plenum. The In-itself is underivable from God or from any divine act of creation; in its utter density, the In-itself, according to Sartre, "is never anything but what it is" (*Being and Nothingness,* p. lxviii). The For-itself is empty and seeks to fill itself, to ground itself in the fullness of the In-itself. But a paradox ensues: The more human beings endeavor to become "something," stable, fixed, assured in their status, the more they are In-itself-like, the more they lose their freedom and choose "bad faith," a negation of human authenticity. Yet the primordial ontological project of the For-itself is to achieve a stable synthesis with the In-itself. That synthesis, for Sartre, would be God. "To be man means to reach toward being God. Or, if you prefer, man fundamentally is the desire to be God" (*Being and Nothingness,* p. 566). What Sartre calls the "passion" of the human being to unite itself with the plenum of being In-itself and become For-itself-In-itself is from the ontological outset doomed to defeat. Sartre writes:

> Every human reality is a passion in that it projects losing itself so as to found being and by the same stroke to constitute the In-itself which escapes contingency by being its own foundation, the *Ens causa sui,* which religions call God. Thus the passion of man is the reverse of that Christ, for man loses himself as man in order that God may be born. But the idea of God is contradictory and we lose ourselves in vain. Man is a useless passion. (*Being and Nothingness,* p. 615)

The striking feature of Sartre's atheism is that it remains so closely in touch with—even in ontological terms—the concept of God. The anguish of human beings, ultimately, is that they cannot be God and that in consequence they are forced back upon themselves—utterly and without recourse. But it is evident that however "religiously unmusical" Sartre's writings may be, there is not only in *Being and Nothingness* but in later works, such as his book on Genet and his study of Flaubert, the intransigent recognition that fellow human beings *believe.* The faith of others haunts the human reality. In his autobiographical study *Words* (London, 1964), Sartre explores the complex religious background of his childhood. The harsh and thorough repudiation he has given his Protestant-Catholic heritage has negated its essentials; but he has not succeeded altogether in ridding religious nuances from his writing: "I depend only on those who depend only on God, and I do not believe in God. Try and sort this out" (ibid., pp. 172–173). Sartre's atheism is not a state of being or a fixed condition. Rather it is a provocative affirmation that "*becoming-an-atheist* is a long and difficult undertaking" ("The Singular Universal," in *Kierkegaard: A Collection of Critical Essays,* Garden City, N.Y., 1972, p. 264).

In contrast to Camus, a writer whose honey of the absurd has attracted many theistic readers—that is, believers—Sartre's bitter gift to the faithful and the theologians is a replication of Hegel's "unhappy consciousness" (see Sartre, *Being and Nothingness,* p. 90). Viewed in religious terms, Sartre is an aberrant supplicant to a shattered God.

Bibliography

Bibliographies

Contat, Michel, and Michel Rybalka, comps. *The Writings of Jean-Paul Sartre,* vol. 1, *A Biographical Life.* Evanston, Ill., 1974.

Lapointe, François H., with the collaboration of Claire Lapointe. *Jean-Paul Sartre and His Critics: An International Bibliography, 1938–1980.* 2d ed., annot. & rev. Bowling Green, Ky., 1981.

Wilcocks, Robert. *Jean-Paul Sartre: A Bibliography of International Criticism.* With a preface by Michel Contat and Michel Rybalka. Edmonton, 1975.

Secondary Sources

Desan, Wilfred. *The Tragic Finale: An Essay on the Philosophy of Jean-Paul Sartre.* Cambridge, 1954.

Grene, Marjorie. *Sartre.* New York, 1973.

Hartmann, Klaus. *Sartre's Ontology.* Evanston, Ill., 1966.

Jeanson, Francis. *Sartre and the Problem of Morality.* Bloomington, Ind., 1980.

Jolivet, Régis. *Sartre: The Theology of the Absurd.* Westminster, Md., 1967.

King, Thomas M. *Sartre and the Sacred.* Chicago, 1974.

Natanson, Maurice. *A Critique of Jean-Paul Sartre's Ontology* (1951). Reprint, The Hague, 1973.

Schilpp, Paul A., ed. *The Philosophy of Jean-Paul Sartre.* La Salle, Ill., 1981.

New Sources

Aronson, Ronald. *Camus and Sartre: The Story of a Friendship and the Quarrel that Ended It.* Chicago, Ill., 2004.

Dobson, Andrew. *Jean-Paul Sartre and the Politics of Reason: A Theory of History.* New York, 1993.

Wider, Kathleen Virginia. *The Bodily Nature of Consciousness: Sartre and Contemporary Philosophy of Mind.* Ithaca, N.Y., 1997.

MAURICE NATANSON (1987)
Revised Bibliography

SARVĀSTIVĀDA.

The school of Sarvāstivāda was one of the so-called Eighteen Schools (*nikāya, ācariyavāda*) of early Buddhism. The term *Sarvāstivāda* is also used to designate the body of doctrine and literature associated with this community. The sociological nature of the group, however, remains unknown.

HISTORICAL DEVELOPMENT. Although it is customary to refer to the Sarvāstivāda as a Hīnayāna "sect," it seems evident that it was primarily a monastic and intellectual movement—thus the term *sect* might be inappropriate. The term *Hīnayāna* is equally problematic, and in this case it must be taken to establish only a definition by exclusion—"that which is not Mahāyāna." The Sarvāstivāda was one of the parent lines in the genealogic tree of the Eighteen Schools, consistently identified in traditional doxography as one of the earlier Sthavira groups. From the Sarvāstivāda arose in turn, according to most accounts, the schools of the Sautrāntika and the Mūlasarvāstivāda, and perhaps that of the Dharmaguptaka.

Existing knowledge of the history and teachings of the early schools is based on late sources, and there is little agreement among scholars as to the true affiliation of the sects mentioned in these sources. It is not clear, for instance, whether the Mahīśāsaka school should be classified under the Sarvāstivāda or under "mainline" Sthaviras. There is, nevertheless, agreement among the classical sources on the derivation of the Sarvāstivāda from a main Sthavira trunk, most probably after the great schism that separated the early Sthavira from the Mahāsāṃghika. The separation of Sarvāstivāda from its trunk of origin is supposed to have taken place at the Third Buddhist Council, held under King Aśoka. They separated from the Sthaviras according to some accounts, from the Mahīśāsaka, according to others.

It is known from inscriptional evidence that the area of greatest strength of the Sarvāstivāda was the Northwest, from Mathura to Afghanistan and the Central Asian desert. But they also were known in East and South India. Their influence extended to Indonesia, and, indirectly, to China.

The Sarvāstivādins received the royal patronage of Kaniṣka (second century CE). According to tradition, the Tripiṭaka of this school was finally closed during his reign. But it is not clear whether this legend is due to a confusion between the writing of their Abhidharma and the compilation of the canon. It is more likely that most of the Sarvāstivādin Tripiṭaka was redacted earlier, and that by the second century CE Sarvāstivādin scholars were engaged in exegetical work. This was the time for the major systematic works, and the beginning of the work of synthesis such as would develop into the *Mahāvibhāṣā.*

As a school of philosophy Sarvāstivāda was gradually absorbed by the Sautrāntika and the Mahāyāna. But it remained a strong monastic institution, especially in the Northwest. Sarvāstivāda survived at least into the ninth century CE through the Mūlasarvāstivāda subschool. By counting Mūlasarvāstivādin texts as works of Sarvāstivādin imprint, one can form an approximate idea of the greater part of the Tripiṭaka of this school. The combined literature of both groups almost constitutes a complete canon, preserved mostly in Chinese and Tibetan translation, but also in several Sanskrit fragments from central Asia. This body of literature is an important source for the study of the so-called Hīnayāna schools, eclipsed in this respect only by that of the Theravāda tradition.

LITERATURE. The Sarvāstivādin canon is a Tripiṭaka only in the sense that it was conceived as having three parts. But it is characteristic of this canon that in addition to the three traditional Piṭakas (Sūtra, Vinaya, and Abhidharma), it eventually developed a Kṣudraka Piṭaka to accommodate miscellaneous works of late origin. Also characteristic of this canon was the exclusion of texts such as the *Dharmapada* (considered paracanonical) and the composition of extensive commentaries on the Abhidharma Piṭaka.

A good part of the Sarvāstivādin canon survives in Chinese translation. The *Madhyama Āgama* found in the Chinese canon is definitely Sarvāstivādin; some scholars also regard the Chinese translation of the *Saṃyuktāgama* as of Sarvāstivāda origin, although this collection is probably a Mūlasarvāstivāda work. The Dharmaguptaka *Dīrghāgama* may be quite similar to the corresponding Sarvāstivāda collection, now lost. The Sarvāstivāda Vinaya is also preserved in Chinese in several versions, including a short, early version, and an expanded version accompanied by a commentary, the *Vinaya-vibhāṣā.* This last text became the Mūlasarvāstivādin Vinaya, which is also preserved in Tibetan. Another recension has been recovered in Sanskrit manuscripts from Gilgit and Afghanistan. The Abhidharma of the Sarvāstivāda is preserved in its entirety in the Chinese canon (some books in more than one translation). Only fragments remain in the original Sanskrit.

Fragments of the Sarvāstivādin canon have been found in Central Asia (the Tarim Basin). These Sanskrit manuscripts include parts of the Vinaya, the *Bhikṣu-* and *Bhikṣuṇī-prātimokṣa,* and the Sūtra Piṭaka. The same region has yielded several manuscripts of the *Udānavarga* (a collection similar to the Pali *Dhammapada*). One of the seven books of the Sarvāstivāda Abhidharma, the *Abhidharmasaṃgītiparyāya,* has been found in Afghanistan (Bamiyan). A Sanskrit manuscript of a postcanonical work of Sarvāstivādin Abhidharma, the *Abhidharmadīpa,* was recovered in Tibet. It is believed that this is the work of Saṃghabhadra (fourth century) or one of his disciples.

The greater part of the remaining Sanskrit works of the school belong to the *avādana* literature and are for the most part late compositions or redactions. The *Lalitavistara,* for instance, a biography of the life of the Buddha (up to his enlightenment), shows strong Mahāyāna influence. Two other important works of this genre, the *Avadānasataka* and the *Divyāvadāna,* are probably associated with the Mūlasarvāstivādin subsect. To this same group belongs the Vinaya discovered at Gilgit and some of the fragments from Turfan (e.g., the *Mahāparinirvāṇa Sūtra*).

THE SARVĀSTIVĀDIN ABHIDHARMA. The Sarvāstivādin Abhidharma Piṭaka is divided into six treatises and a seventh work of synthesis ("the six feet and the body" of Abhidharma): (1) *Prakaraṇapada,* (2) *Vijñānakāya,* (3) *Dharmaskandha,* (4) *Prajñāptiśāstra,* (5) *Dhātukāya,* (6) *Saṃgītiparyāya,* and (7) *Jñānaprasthāna.* Each of the works has a putative author, but sources vary on their attribution (e.g., Mahākauṣṭhila or Śāriputra for the *Saṃgītiparyāya,* Śāriputra or Maudgalyāyana for the *Dharmaskandha*). However, the last (and latest) of these seven books, the *Jñānaprasthāna,* is consistently attributed to Kātyāyanīputra; his authorship is generally accepted as factual, although the *Mahāvibhāṣā* claims that he was merely the redactor of the text and that its real author was the Buddha. Three of the works in the Sarvāstivādin Abhidharma reflect the style and content of earlier catechistic (*mātṛkā*) and cosmological sūtras, found in the Sūtra Piṭaka of other schools. In all probability these form the original core of the Abhidharma and explain the Sarvāstivādin claim that the Abhidharma was also the word of the Buddha (*buddhavacana*).

The most influential text of the school was the fruit of its dedication to Abhidharma studies, a collective work of exegesis, the *Mahāvibhāṣā* (150–200 CE), purporting to be a commentary to Kātyāyanīputra's *Jñānaprasthāna.* But this work is more than a commentary; it provides invaluable information on the earlier traditions of Abhidharma (e.g., the doctrines of the "four great masters," Vasumitra, Dharmatrāta, Ghoṣa, and Buddhadeva), and on rival schools, including some non-Buddhist philosophical schools (e.g., Sāṃkhya). Apart from its value as a major source of information on Buddhist scholastic traditions, this work influenced the development of other schools, including the Mahāyāna. Even when criticized (as in the *Abhidharmakośa* of the Sautrāntika philosopher Vasubandhu, or in the *Mahāprajñāpāramitā-upadeśa Śāstra* of the Mahāyānist pseudo-Nāgārjuna), the *Mahāvibhāṣā* continued to provide the basic model for intellectual order and spiritual typologies. Moreover, the two above-mentioned critical works contributed to the diffusion of Sarvāstivādin ideas in East Asia. Because of the central role of this text in defining Sarvāstivādin orthodoxy, mainline Sarvāstivādins are sometimes known as Vaibhāṣikas, that is, followers of the (*Mahā*) *Vibhāṣā.*

CHARACTERISTIC DOCTRINES. A characteristic doctrine of this school, the one from which the school derives its name, is the theory of time. According to this doctrine—summarized in the phrase *sarvam asti* ("everything exists")—all of the three dimensions of time (past, present, future) exist; that is, the present continues to exist when it becomes the past, and so forth. This doctrine seems to have been developed as a way to protect the laws of causality (especially as they apply to karmic or moral retribution) from the potentially undermining effect of the doctrine of impermanence.

Dharma theory. Another means of insuring continuity and order in the philosophical world of Sarvāstivāda was the doctrine of *dharmas.* According to the Sarvāstivāda understanding, although all things are impermanent, the basic building blocks of reality including even some attributes and relations, are substantial and real. These substantial entities (*dravyasat*) are known as *dharmas.* With the exception of three elements of reality, all things are compounds of *dharmas*; they can be broken into their component parts and are in that sense impermanent. Some compounds and the *dharmas* that compose them are pure, others impure. Only *nirvāṇa* is both pure and permanent (as well as uncompounded). There are, however, two other *dharmas* that are uncompounded: cessation without conscious discrimination, and space.

Karman and no-self. The Sarvāstivāda theory of *karman* is based on the *dharma* theory. All actions resulting from human intention affect the constituents of the personality—that is, they change its *dharma* composition. This effect of action is made possible by a relational *dharma* called "appropriation" or "acquisition" (*prāpti*). *Prāpti* was a key concept in the attempt to establish the rationality of moral responsibility in an impermanent world; that is, it was meant to account for karmic continuity in the absence of an agent, or self. But the key term used in formulating a rational account of the element of continuity in the empirical self was *santāna* ("series"). The term *self* was considered a misnomer for a series of *dharmas*. With no lasting element or underlying substance, this series is held together only by the laws of causality. The doctrine of *prāpti* was criticized by the Sautrāntikas—mainly in the work of Vasubandhu (c. fourth century CE)—but the concept of *santāna* remained a central tool of philosophical explanation in later Buddhist philosophy.

Buddhology. In soteriology and in their theory of the Path, the Sarvāstivāda developed perhaps the most complex and complete of the Buddhist maps of spiritual growth. They were concerned with the path of the *bodhisattva* as well as that of the *arhat,* although they still perceived the former as a rare occurrence. Their Abhidharma literature considers the goal of arhatship the only ideal to which one could aspire, but the *avādana* literature (possibly of late Mūlasarvāstivādin composition) gives numerous legendary accounts of faithful taking the vows to "become a buddha" in a future life. In the same way, although the Sarvāstivāda had a doctrine of the "perfections" (*pāramitā*) of a *bodhisattva,* a theory of the two bodies of the Buddha (*rūpakāya* and *dharmakāya*), and a belief in the Buddha's "great compassion" (*mahākaruṇā*), and although they accepted the mythology of the vow and the prophecy (*vyākaraṇa*) in the career of the Buddhas, they do not seem to have developed these ideas as possible models for religious life.

SECTARIAN OUTGROWTHS. A number of important subgroups appear to be related to the Sarvāstivāda. Unfortunately, the sources offer contradictory information. Two movements are definitely derivative schools: the Sautrāntikas and the Mūlasarvāstivādins, both of which were especially active in Central India. The Dharmaguptaka school may also be derived from Sarvāstivāda, although this case is more problematic than the other two. They were concentrated in South India. Another important subgroup of the Sthaviras, the Mahīśāsaka, must be related to the Sarvāstivādins; but the nature of the relationship remains unclear. They had monasteries in the Punjab and Andhra.

Tradition has it that after the council at Pāṭaliputra a Sarvāstivādin scholar by the name of Madhyāntika took the teachings of the school to Kashmir, where it flourished. He is believed to belong to the spiritual lineage of Ānanda and to have been originally from Mathurā. The latter region was the missionary province of Upagupta. Both locations were important cultural centers in the empire of the Kushans and provided the base for imperial patronage of the Sarvāstivāda under Kaniṣka. The Chinese pilgrim Xuanzang, who visited India between the years 629 and 645, reported the existence of Sarvāstivādin monasteries only in the Northwest and in the upper Ganges River valley. Another pilgrim, Yijing, who was himself a Sarvāstivādin, visited India half a century later (671–695) and reported a much wider distribution of monasteries under Sarvāstivādin influence. Although he found Sarvāstivādins in almost all parts of India, they were the dominant group only in Northwest India and in the Indonesian archipelago.

Sautrāntikas. A subgroup of the Sarvāstivādins, the Dārṣṭāntikas—followers of Kumāralāta's *Dṛṣṭāntapaṅki*—gave rise to a new movement in reaction to Sarvāstivādin emphasis on the Abhidharma. Whereas the Sarvāstivādins were of the opinion that the Buddha had preached the Abhidharma at Sravasti, this new group maintained that the Abhidharma was not the word of the Buddha. Only the sūtras had canonical authority for them. They claimed that the term *Abhidharma Piṭaka* could refer only to those sūtras belonging to the *mātṛkā* genre. Therefore, they called themselves Sautrāntikas ("followers of the sūtra or *sūtrānta*"). Their first great master was Śrīlāta, a disciple of Kumāralāta (both from around the first century BCE). But their most distinguished scholar was the independently minded Vasubandhu (fourth to fifth century), whose major Abhidharmic work, the *Abhidharmakośa,* championed certain Sautrāntika doctrines. Vasubandhu's work, however, had its critics, among whom the most famous was Saṃghabhadra, whose *Abhidharmanyāyānusāra* was written as a polemic against the *Abhidharmakośa.*

The Sautrāntikas opposed the Sarvāstivādin belief in substantial entities and what they saw as surreptitious ways of retaining notions of permanence. They denied that the unconditioned or uncompounded *dharmas* have any existence, preferring instead to regard them as bare nonexistence or absence (*abhāva*). They asserted that some of the *dharmas* of the Sarvāstivāda are mere denominations or conceptual constructs (*prajñāpti*). Among the *dharmas* whose reality they criticized in this way was the concept of appropriation (*prāpti*). In order to explain the process of *karman,* the Sautrāntikas brought to prominence an old concept shared by most Buddhist schools, the concept of karmic seeds (*bīja*). These Sautrāntika theories were first proposed by Śrīlāta and developed by Vasubandhu. The doctrine of *bīja* became one of the cornerstones of Mahāyāna idealistic philosophy.

The Sautrāntikas also formulated a radical theory of impermanence known as the doctrine of *kṣaṇikavāda* ("momentariness"). This doctrine denied the Sarvāstivādin theory of the displacement through time of a permanent entity or essence (*svabhāva*). It also contributed to the development of a theory of knowledge that would have a major impact on the formation of Mahāyāna epistemology. They proposed that the senses cannot apprehend an object directly (among other reasons, because of its momentary existence); accordingly, perception is the arising of mental images or representations that are only analogical or coordinated with their objects (*sārūpya*). In this way the Sautrāntikas became the first Buddhist phenomenalists, perhaps the first in the history of world philosophy. Their influence continued to be felt in the Buddhist logicians and in the metaphysics of Mahāyāna idealistic philosophy until the end of Buddhist monasticism on Indian soil; it continues today in Tibetan philosophical speculation.

Mūlasarvāstivādins. This school seems to have been a late development in the Sarvāstivāda tradition. It was dominant in North India from the seventh to the ninth century and became the main source of non-Mahāyāna texts for the Tibetan canon. The Mūlasarvāstivādin Vinaya is preserved in Tibetan translation (early ninth century, now incorporated into the Bka' 'gyur) and has also been recovered in a Sanskrit manuscript from Gilgit. Some scholars would consider this Vinaya an early compilation, but others believe the work is late.

Although their doctrines do not seem to have differed significantly from those of the Sarvāstivādins, their literature—at least what remains of it—contains some materials that must derive from non-Sarvāstivāda sources. In addition to their Vinaya, several works from their *avādana* literature have survived; these include the *Divyāvadāna, Avadānaśataka,* and *Aśokāvadāna.*

Dharmaguptakas. It is not clear whether the Dharmaguptakas should be regarded as a subset of the Vibhajyavādins (through the Mahīśāsaka line) or a subset of the Sarvāstivādins. They tended to emphasize Vinaya and Sūtra more than Abhidharma. Their Vinaya is preserved in Chinese translation (the *Sifen Lü*) and became the model for monastic rules in China. Another work of great importance for the study of early Abhidharma, the *Sāriputrābhidharmaśāstra,* is of Dharmaguptaka provenance. This text also shows strong influence from the Mahāsāṃghika school. The connection of this school with the development of Mahāyāna is confirmed not only by the eclectic nature of this text but also by their frank criticism of the limitations of the *arhat* ideal, by their addition of Bodhisattva and Dhāraṇī Piṭakas to their canon, and by their role in the formation of Chinese monasticism, the connection of which to Mahāyāna thought owes much to the exegesis of the Chinese monk Daoxuan (596–667), founder of the Southern Mountain (Nanshan) tradition of Chinese Vinaya (Lü) studies.

INFLUENCE. The geographical expansion of Sarvāstivāda represents only one of the aspects of its influence, for the sophistication and maturity of its philosophy clearly won many followers, even among those who disagreed with its basic presuppositions. Sarvāstivāda Abhidharma was a standard element in the classical curricula of Indian universities, not only at their centers in Puruṣapura (Peshawar) and Valabhī (Kathiawar), but in Mahāyāna centers of learning as well.

Sarvāstivāda as Hīnayāna. The study of Sarvāstivāda as the representative doctrine of Hīnayāna philosophy continued in India long after the school had declined. Vasubandhu's *Abhidharmakośa* became the standard textbook and was the object of numerous commentaries (those of Guṇamati, Sthiramati, Vasumitra, and, above all, the *Sphuṭārtha-abhidharmakośa-vyākhyā* of Yaśomitra). Buddhist and Hindu doxography to this day recognizes four main schools of Buddhist philosophy, among which Sarvāstivāda and Sautrāntika are the only representatives of non-Mahāyāna philosophy. This is still the basic model even among contemporary scholars in Japan and the West, where the *Abhidharmakośa* continues to be required reading for the Buddhist scholar.

The Sarvāstivāda school also provided the model for Hīnayāna in the Far East. In China, it was transmitted mainly as part of the Jushe (Abhidharmakośa) school. Of Sautrāntika inspiration, this school was the main competitor of the other two Abhidharmic schools, the Chengshi (Satyasiddhi) school (perhaps Bahusrutiya), and the Faxiang (*dharmalaksana,* that is, the Mahāyāna Yogacara school, which has Mahīśāsaka roots).

As a source for Mahāyāna. The evident role of the Mahāsāṃghika school in the formation of Mahāyāna tends to eclipse the contribution of other Hīnayāna schools. The Sarvāstivāda in particular was a decisive element in the formation of the higher doctrines and philosophy of Mahāyāna. The first developments in the *bodhisattva* theory—especially as it is supposed to fit in the map of the Path—were probably those found in Sarvāstivādin literature. The basic structures of Mahāyāna soteriology and Abhidharma are clearly derived from Sarvāstivāda and Mahīśāsaka sources, and so is much of their philosophical terminology. The Sarvāstivāda also contributed, through Vasubandhu and the Sautrāntikas, the underpinnings for Mahāyāna epistemology.

SEE ALSO Buddhism, Schools of; Buddhist Philosophy; Dharma, article on Buddhist Dharma and Dharmas; Indian Philosophies; Sautrāntika; Soul, article on Buddhist Concepts; Vasubandhu.

BIBLIOGRAPHY

Anacker, Stefan. *Seven Works of Vasubandhu.* Delhi, 1984. Includes Vasubandhu's logical work *Vadavidhi,* two of his Sautrāntika works, as well as four of his Mahāyāna treatises.

Aung, Shwe Zan, and C. A. F. Rhys Davids, trans. *Points of Controversy.* London, 1915. The most important Theravāda source on the early schools.

Banerjee, Anukul Chandra. *Sarvāstivāda Literature.* Calcutta, 1957. This is a catalog of works; although somewhat dated, it is still useful.

Bareau, André. "Les origines du Çāriputrābhidharmaçāstra." *Le Muséon* 63 (1950): 69–95. In this work Bareau, the modern scholar who has devoted most time and sound research to the question of the origin of Buddhist sects, has studied one of the most influential Dharmaguptaka texts. He collected data on the "unconditioned" *dharmas* from all the schools in his *L'absolu en philosophie bouddhique: Évolution de la notion d'asaṃskrta.* (Paris, 1951). His studies on the Abhidharma of the schools and the classical sources, "Les sectes bouddhiques du Petit Véhicule et leurs Abhidharmapiṭaka," *Bulletin de l'École Française d'Extrême-Orient* 50 (1952): 1–11, and "Trois traités sur les sectes bouddhiques attribués à Vasumitra, Bhavya et Vinītadeva," *Journal asiatique* 242 (1954): 229–266 and 244 (1956): 167–200, respectively, were part of the spadework for his two major contributions on the subject: *Les premiers conciles bouddhiques* (Paris, 1955) and *Les sectes bouddhiques du Petit Véhicule* (Saigon, 1955).

Bechert, Heinz. "Zur Frühgeschichte des Mahāyāna-Buddhismus." *Zeitschrift der Deutschen Morgenländischen Gesellschaft* 113 (1963): 530–535.

Demiéville, Paul. "L'origine des sectes bouddhiques d'après Paramārtha." In *Mélanges chinois et bouddhiques,* vol. 1, pp. 15–62. Brussels, 1931–1932. See also his "À propos du concile de Vaiśālī," *T'oung pao* 40 (1951): 239–296.

Dutt, Nalinaksha. *Early History of the Spread of Buddhism and the Buddhist Schools* (1925). Reprint, New Delhi, 1980. See also Dutt's *Aspects of Mahāyāna Buddhism and Its Relation to Hīnayāna* (London, 1930) and "The Second Buddhist Council," *Indian Historical Quarterly* 35 (March 1959): 45–56. Some of the author's early (1930–1940) articles on the subject were collected (without significant revisions) in his *Buddhist Sects in India* (Calcutta, 1970).

Glasenapp, Helmuth von. "Zur Geschichte der buddhistischen Dharma-Theorie." *Zeitschrift der Deutschen Morgenländischen Gesellschaft* 92 (1938): 383–420. See also his "Der Ursprung der buddhistischen Dharma-Theorie," *Wiener Zeitschrift für die Kunde des Morgenlandes* 46 (1939): 242–266.

Hirakawa Akira. "The Rise of Mahāyāna Buddhism and Its Relationship to the Worship of Stūpas." *Memoirs of the Research Department of the Toyo Bunko* 22 (1963): 57–106.

Jaini, Padmanabh S. "The Vāibhaṣika Theory of Words and Meanings," "The Sautrāntika Theory of *bīja,*" and "Origin and Development of the Theory of *viprayukta-saṃskāras.*" *Bulletin of the School of Oriental and African Studies* 22 (1959): 95–107, 236–249, and 531–547. These are brief, in-depth studies of Sarvāstivāda and Sautrāntika philosophy. Jaini also edited the *Abhidharmadīpa* (Patna, India, 1959); his introduction contains valuable information on the Sarvāstivāda school.

Lamotte, Étienne. *Histoire du bouddhisme indien des origines à l'ère Śaka.* Louvain, 1958. See pages 547–549, 576–606, and 662–694. The most compact of the scholarly surveys on the history of the early sects, this should be supplemented with Bareau's *Les sectes,* since the two authors disagree both in approach and detail. Lamotte has also translated an important Sautrāntika treatise that summarizes and criticizes the Sarvāstivādin theory of *karman,* "Le traité de l'Acte de Vasubandhu: Karmasiddhiprakaraṇa," in *Mélanges chinois et bouddhiques,* vol. 4 (Brussels, 1935–1936), pp. 151–288. An English translation of this text is contained in Anacker (1984).

La Vallée Poussin, Louis de. "Sautrāntikas." In *Encyclopaedia of Religion and Ethics,* edited by James Hastings, vol. 11. Edinburgh, 1920. This Belgian scholar was one of the pioneers of Buddhist studies, especially of the Abhidharma tradition. His extensive scholarly contribution to our understanding of Sarvāstivāda includes "La controverse du temps et du Pudgala dans le *Vijñanakāya,*" *Études asiatiques publiées à l'occasion du vingt-cinquième anniversaire de l'École Française d'Extrême-Orient* (Paris, 1925), vol. 1, pp. 343–376; "Les deux nirvanas d'après la Vibhāṣā," *Académie Royale de Belgique, Bulletin de la classe des lettres et des sciences morales et politiques* 15 (1929): 367–374; "Documents d'Abhidharma: Textes relatifs au Nirvana," *Bulletin de l'École Française d'Extrême-Orient* 30 (1930): 1–28, 247–298; and "Documents d'Abhidharma," in *Mélanges chinois et bouddhiques,* vol. 1 (Brussels, 1932), pp. 65–109. La Vallée Poussin also translated the most influential work of Abhidharma, *L'Abhidharmakośa de Vasubandhu,* 6 vols. (1923–1931; reprint, Brussels, 1971).

Masuda Jiryō. "Origins and Doctrines of Early Indian Buddhist Schools." *Asia Major* 2 (1925): 1–78. A translation of Vasumitra's treatise on the Eighteen Schools.

Mizuno Kogen. "Abhidharma Literature." In *Encyclopaedia of Buddhism,* edited by G. P. Malalasekera, vol. 1. Colombo, 1963.

Prebish, Charles S. "A Review of Scholarship on the Buddhist Councils." *Journal of Asian Studies* 33 (February 1974): 239–254. See also his *Buddhist Monastic Discipline: The Sanskrit Prātimokṣa Sūtras of the Mahāsāṃghikas and Mūlasarvāstivādins* (University Park, Pa., 1975).

Stcherbatsky, Theodore. *The Central Conception of Buddhism and the Meaning of the Word "Dharma"* (1923). 4th ed. Delhi, 1970. This is the classic study on the *dharma* theory of the Sarvāstivādins. Although it is dated and at times obscure, it is still the only comprehensive discussion accessible to general readers who cannot read French or German.

Takakusu Junjirō. "On the Abhidharma Literature of the Sarvāstivādins." *Journal of the Pāli Text Society* 14 (1904–1905): 67–146. In this essay Takakusu surveyed the Sarvāstivāda Abhidharma preserved in the Chinese canon. Dated, but still useful if studied in conjunction with more recent studies, is his article "Sarvāstivādins," in the *Encyclopaedia of Religion and Ethics,* edited by James Hastings, vol. 11 (Edinburgh, 1920).

Wayman, Alex. "Aspects of Meditation in the Theravāda and Mahīśāsaka." *Studia Missionalia* 25 (1976): 1–28.

New Sources

Chung, Jin-Il. *Die Pravāranā in den kanonischen Vinaya-Texten der Mulasarvāstivādin und der Sarvāstivādin.* Göttingen, 1998.

Cox, Collett. *Disputed Dharmas, Early Buddhist Theories on Existence: An Annotated Translation of the Section on Factors Dissociated from Thought from Sanghabhadra's Nyāyānusāra.* Tokyo, 1995.

Frauwallner, Erich. *Studies in Abhidharma Literature and the Origins of Buddhist Philosophical Systems.* Translated by Sophie Francis Kidd under the supervision of Ernst Steinkellner. Albany, N.Y., 1995.

Hirakawa Akira. *A History of Indian Buddhism: From Śākyamuni to Early Mahāyāna.* Translated and edited by Paul Groner. Honolulu, 1990.

La Vallée Poussin, Louis de. *Abhidharmakośabhāṣyam.* Translated by Leo M. Pruden. 5 vols. Berkeley, 1988–1990.

Potter, Karl, ed. *Encyclopedia of Indian Philosophies, vol. 9, Buddhist Philosophy from 350 A.D.* Delhi, 1999.

Willemen, Charles, Bart Dessein, and Collett Cox. *Sarvāstivāda Buddhist Scholasticism.* Leiden, 1998.

Williams, Paul, with Anthony Tribe. *Buddhist Thought: A Complete Introduction to the Indian Tradition.* London, 2000. See Chapter 4.

LUIS O. GÓMEZ (1987)
Revised Bibliography

ŚĀSTRA LITERATURE. The Sanskrit term *śāstra* means, first, "precept, command, rule"; hence, a treatise in which precepts on a particular topic have been collected; and, finally, any branch of technical lore. *Vāstuśāstra,* for example, refers both to a treatise on *vāstu* ("architecture") and to the science of architecture generally; *Cikitsāśāstra* indicates both a treatise on medicine and the science of medicine; and so forth.

This article will be primarily concerned with the *śāstras* connected with the three goals (*trivarga*) that a Hindu is supposed to pursue during life: *dharma* ("spiritual obligations"), *artha* ("material welfare"), and *kāma* ("pleasure, enjoyment"). It is worth noticing that the texts in each of these three categories, to a greater or lesser extent, also recognize the importance of pursuing the other two goals. In fact, a harmonious pursuit of the *trivarga* is a necessary condition to reach a Hindu's ultimate goal: *mokṣa,* final liberation from the cycle of deaths and rebirths (*saṃsāra*).

Most important—and most voluminous—are the Dharmaśāstras. They basically cover the same material as the Dharmasūtras, but they are more detailed and better organized, are mostly in verse (the thirty-two syllable *anuṣṭubh,* or *śloka*), and are considered to be more recent. Like the Dharmasūtras, they are attributed to ancient sages or "seers" (*ṛṣi*), the most important of whom was Manu. The date of the *Manava Dharmaśāstra* (Laws of Manu) is uncertain, but falls somewhere between about 200 BCE and 100 CE. It was followed, probably in this order, by the Dharmaśāstras attributed to Yājñavalkya, Viṣṇu, Nārada, Bṛhaspati, Kātnāyana, and others.

The Dharmaśāstras, together with the *sūtras*, constitute what is known as the *smṛti* (from the root *smṛ,* "to remember"); hence the titles *Manusmṛti* (the *Mānava Dharmaśāstra*), *Yājñavalkyasmṛti,* and so forth. The *smṛti* is considered to be a form of revelation based on the Vedas, which in turn form the *śruti* (from the root *śru,* "to hear"). The *śruti* is the only more authoritative body of writings than the *smṛti;* the *śāstras* themselves state that, in case of a conflict between *śruti* and *smṛti,* the former shall prevail. Although all *smṛtis* theoretically have equal authority, in practice the *Manusmṛti* is recognized as being superior to the others.

The *Manusmṛti* represents the Indian ideal of a Dharmaśāstra. After an introductory section on the creation, the text devotes five chapters to the description of the *saṃskāras*, that is, those ritual performances that mark off the successive periods in a Hindu's life, and of the duties to be performed in each of the four principal stages (*āśramas*). The next three chapters concentrate on the *dharma* of one individual: the king. He is to protect those among his subjects who adhere to their own *dharma* against those who do not. The section on the king's *dharma* (*rājadharma*) naturally includes those passages for which the text first became known to Westerners, those on Hindu law. (Hence the title *Laws of Manu.*) Among the miscellaneous topics treated in the last three chapters are the duties and occupations of the different castes (*varṇa*) including "mixed castes," expiations of sins, and the rules governing specific forms of rebirth.

The beginning of this century witnessed the discovery—and publication—of the text of the *Arthaśāstra* attributed to Kauṭilya (or Kauṭalya; occasionally Cāṇakya or Viṣṇugupta). Even though minor Arthaśāstra texts had been known before that time, and even though some Arthaśāstra materials also appear in the Dharmaśāstras, until 1905 the text called *Arthaśāstra* was known from a few quotations only. Kauṭilya, unlike the composers of the Dharmaśāstras, is a historic figure. If he was indeed a minister of the Maurya king Candragupta, he must have lived at the end of the fourth century BCE. Some scholars, however, do not believe in Kauṭilya's authorship; based on detailed comparisons of elements in the *Arthaśāstra* with their appearance in various other works of Sanskrit literature, they assign the text later dates, down to the fourth century CE.

The *Arthaśāstra,* in prose occasionally mixed with verse, is a manual for the king and for the successful administration of his kingdom. It provides detailed prescriptions on the various administrative departments, the duties of their heads, and their internal organization. Perhaps the text has become even better known for its ideas on foreign policy. Each king is considered a potential world conqueror (*cakravartin*), and the *Arthaśāstra* provides him with various ways to achieve that goal. Kauṭilya's view that one's neighbor is, by definition, one's enemy who must be defeated with the support of his neighbor (who is, again by definition, a temporary ally), and his ruthless instructions on how to use spies and secret agents, are some of the reasons why he has been labeled "the Indian Machiavelli."

Within the area of Kāmaśāstra literature the principal text is undoubtedly the *Kāma Sūtra* attributed to Vatsyayana. The *Kāma Sūtra* shares a number of important characteristics with the *Arthaśāstra:* The *Kāma Sūtra* is also mostly in prose, interspersed with verses; like Kauṭilya, Vātsyāyana repeatedly quotes the opinions of predecessors, some of whom are the same as those named by Kauṭilya; and most important, both texts exhibit a number of passages that correspond, word for word. There seems to be general agreement that Vātsyāyana lived after Kauṭilya; his date, therefore, varies according to the individual scholar's opinion on the age of the *Arthaśāstra.*

The *Kāma Sūtra* instructs the *nāgaraka,* the prosperous citizen, on how to enjoy life to its fullest. Even though this involves, to a certain extent, the *nāgaraka*'s relationship with women—including married women and courtesans—the

Kāma Sūtra also treats numerous other topics that shed light on the way of life and worldview of one section of ancient Indian society.

The true nature and purpose of the Indian *śāstras* is still the object of much discussion among scholars. Contrary to the early belief of Westerners—which led to the adoption, in 1772, of "the shaster" as the main source of Hindu family law in British India—it was soon recognized that, at least as far as the Dharmaśāstras are concerned, they may very well have painted an ideal picture that did not necessarily correspond to real life situations. Hence the high expectations on the occasion of the discovery of the *Arthaśāstra;* scholars believed, and wrote at length, on the extent to which a book on *artha* was bound to provide a more realistic description of classical Indian society. The author of this article prefers to look upon the *śāstras* as—no doubt highly stylized and systematized—compendia of existing customs and practices. They provided the overall theoretical framework that authorized each individual—mostly groups of individuals—to engage in the practice (*prayoga*) of their traditionally recognized ways of behavior.

SEE ALSO Cakravartin; Dharma, article on Hindu Dharma; Law and Religion; Manu; Mokṣa; Saṃsāra; Sūtra Literature.

BIBLIOGRAPHY

The most encyclopedic treatment of Dharmaśāstra is P. V. Kane's *History of Dharmaśāstra,* 5 vols. (Poona, 1930–1962). For a brief survey, see J. D. M. Derrett's *Dharmaśāstra and Juridical Literature* (Wiesbaden, 1973). The *Manusmṛti* has been translated in volume 25 of the "Sacred Books of the East" (Oxford, 1886); other translations in this series are the *Viṣṇusmṛti* in volume 7 (Oxford, 1880) and the *Nāradasmṛti* and *Bṛhaspatismṛti,* both in volume 33 (Oxford, 1889). The most recent edition and translation of the *Arthaśāstra* is R. P. Kangle's *The Kauṭilīya Arthaśāstra,* 3 vols. (Bombay, 1960–1965); that of the *Kāma Sūtra* is S. C. Upadhyaya's *Kāma Sūtra of Vatsyāyāna* (Bombay, 1961). For a bibliography on this subject, see Ludwik Sternbach's *Bibliography on Dharma and Artha in Ancient and Mediaeval India* (Wiesbaden, 1973).

New Sources

Boesche, Roger. *The First Great Political Realist: Kautilya and His Arthashastra.* Lanham, 2002.

Goyala, Srirama. *The Kautilya Arthasastra: Its Author, Date, and Relevance for the Maurya Period.* Jodhpur, 2000.

Kamasutra of Vatsyayana Mallanaga. Translated by Wendy Doniger and Sudhir Kakar. Oxford; New York, 2002.

Sastri, Manabendu Banerjee, ed. *Occasional Essays on Arthasastra.* Calcutta, 2000.

LUDO ROCHER (1987)
Revised Bibliography

SATAN. Although the name *Satan* sometimes has been connected with the Hebrew verb *suṭ,* which means "to roam" (perhaps suggesting that Satan acts as God's spy), it is more commonly derived from the root *saṭan,* which means "to oppose, to plot against." The word thus basically connotes an adversary. Its use in the Hebrew scriptures (Old Testament) covers three types of beings as opponents: (1) a human being, as in *2 Samuel* 19:22, (2) an angelic being, as in *Numbers* 22:22–35, and (3) a particular adversary, as in *Zechariah* 3:1–2, where *saṭan* functions as a common rather than a proper noun and does not refer to "the Satan," but where the idea of a being having a distinct personality is still conveyed. This supernatural being not only acts as an adversary: his name itself means "an obstructor" (Russell, 1977, p. 190). In the New Testament, Satan as the Devil is called the "great dragon" and "ancient serpent" (*Rv.* 12:9). However, while echoes of a Canaanite myth of God's conflict with the dragon and the sea may be found in the Old Testament, Satan is not associated with these references but is clearly mentioned in three contexts (except for *Psalms* 109:6, in which he is inferred). The first of these contexts is in the *Book of Job,* where Satan belongs to the court of God and, with God's permission, tests Job. By contrast, in a second occurrence (*Zec.* 3), Satan, on his own initiative, opposes Joshua. The third passage in the Old Testament in which Satan figures (*1 Chr.* 21:1) is, according to George A. Barton (1911),

> A further witness to the fact that Satan is now held to be responsible for evil. The chapter gives an account of David's census and of the punishment for it, and is dependent on 2 Samuel 24; but whereas it is said in Samuel that Jahweh said to David, "Go, number Israel" because he was angry with the people, it is said in Chronicles that Satan "moved David to number Israel." Satan is clearly a development out of the group of spirits which were in earlier days thought to be from Jahweh's court, members of which were sent upon errands of disaster to men. (p. 598)

Scholars seems somewhat divided on the question of the extent to which evil may be associated with Satan in the Old Testament. It has been argued that Satan "was not evil but became evil by identification with his functions" in the course of time (Robbins, 1966, p. 130). One might distinguish here between two approaches toward Satan in the Old Testament. According to one approach, represented by Giovanni Papini, Jeffrey Burton Russell, John Noel Schofield, Gustav Davidson, and others, Satan is still not quite God's adversary, only his minion. Other scholars, such as Edward Langton and Ronald S. Wallace, see a more definite movement toward an association of evil with Satan. But the transition from the *saṭan* of the Old Testament, which pre-figures the Devil in some way, to the *Satanas* of the New Testament, who *is* the Devil, is clear enough.

The figure of Satan in noncanonical Hebrew literature intensifies his identification with evil. He not only emerges as an adversary of God, but, as such apocalyptic works as *Jubilees,* the *Testament of Reuben,* the *Book of the Secrets of Enoch (2 Enoch),* and the Qumran documents show, he is also the leader of the fallen angels. It should be noted, however, that although Satan comes to stand for evil, in "Hebrew thought in the Old Testament there is no suggestion of any dualism, whether temporal, spatial or ethical. . . any philosophy of evil culled from the Bible must find room for evil within the concept of God and within his purpose." This also holds true for much apocalyptic literature; signs of temporal, spatial, and ethical dualism begin to emerge only in later Judaism. At the temporal level, the view is developed that history consists of two ages. The present age is marked by the Devil's power, which will be nullified at the end of the present age when the divine age is ushered in. At the spatial level, the kingdoms of the Lord and Satan are contrasted as being in cosmic opposition; at the ethical level, humans are seen as being affected by sin, which will be overcome in a divine denouement. Persian influence has been traced in this movement toward dualism. But Hebrew and Christian thought stopped short of specifying that the Devil is entirely evil in essence. This tension between explicit monotheism and implicit dualism became characteristic of Judaism and Christianity, as contrasted with Zoroastrianism, Manichaeism, and gnosticism. "The Devil," as Luther said, "is God's Devil."

Christianity synthesized Greek and Jewish concepts of the Devil. The word *devil* is actually derived from the Greek *diabolos*, which has the dual sense of "accuser" and "obstructor." If the Old Testament, according to later tradition, implicates Satan in the fall of humankind, the New Testament refers clearly to the fall of Satan himself in *2 Peter* 2:4 and in *Revelation* 12:7–9. Again, in contrast with the Old Testament, the power of the Devil is often mentioned (e.g., *Lk.* 4:6). He is also identified with other names: *Beelzebul* ("lord of flies"), *Beelzebub* ("lord of dung"), and, with somewhat less critical certainty, *Lucifer.*

In the ministry of Jesus Christ, "there is a constant campaign against Satan from the temptation after Jesus' Baptism until his death on the cross, and, in each act of healing or exorcism, there is anticipated the ultimate defeat of Satan and the manifestation of the power of the new age," as is the case of Mark's gospel, the central part of which calls upon Jesus' disciples "to participate through suffering in his own confrontation with the power of Satan" (Davis, 1984, p. 952). Indeed, Mark and Paul are more inclined to use the name *Satan*; other New Testament writers prefer other forms. Nevertheless, the motif of both the original (*Rom.* 16:20) and the ultimate and eschatological fall of Satan (*Rv.* 20:2, 7–10) undergirds the New Testament, though the latter is more prominent. The Devil is the lord of both *aion* and *kosmos*, words used in the context of sinful human society and probably suggestive of the dichotomy of spirit and matter in Greek thought. Russell summarized the chief characteristics of the Devil in the New Testament as follows (1977, p. 256): (1) he is the personification of evil; (2) he physically attacks or possesses humans; (3) he tempts people to sin in order to destroy them or recruit them in his struggle against God; (4) he accuses and punishes sinners; (5) he leads a host of evil spirits, fallen angels, or demons; (6) he has assimilated many evil qualities of ancient destructive nature spirits or ghosts; (7) he will rule this world until the coming of the kingdom of God, and in the meantime will be engaged in constant warfare against Christ; (8) he will be defeated by Christ at the end of the world. Above all, he is identified with temptation and death, like his counterpart Māra in Buddhism.

In early Christianity it was believed that the death of Jesus redeemed humankind from the Devil, who had been overcome in his own house by Christ's descent into hell (*Mt.* 12:29). Thus, although the idea of the final conquest of evil or the Devil is not unique to Christianity but is also present in Zoroastrianism and Judaism, "the unique note in the Christian message is the announcement that Satan is already being defeated in Christ" (Ling, 1961, p. 102). Despite this general picture, however, Russell notes that the position of the Devil remains anomalous in the New Testament, and the "elements of cosmic dualism in the synoptic gospels are much stronger in Luke than in Mark and Matthew and stronger in John than in any of the synoptics" (1977, p. 232).

Satan's name appears as *Shayṭān* in the Qurʾān, although it is not clear whether the name is Arabic or not. Shayṭān shares certain functions of the Judeo-Christian Satan, such as leading people astray (4:83), but there is a significant extension of this view in that Satan is accused of tampering with divine verbal revelation (22.52). However, it is in his role as Iblīs (2:34, etc.) that al-Shayṭān is most striking (Watt, 1970, p. 155). He is deposed for refusing to bow before man as the other angels had done, but is allowed, after his refusal, to tempt mortals. According to an established tradition, "Satan sits in the blood of Adam's children" and thus "could be equated with *nafs*, the lower principle, the flesh" (Schimmel, 1975, p. 193). In Islam, the figure of Satan achieves a mystical dimension not found in Judaism and Christianity, where the devil is more or less exclusively associated with evil and the underworld. This association may help "account for the Western tradition that Satan is not only Lord of evil and of death but is also associated with fertility and sexuality, a trait evident in the witches' orgy and in the horns the Devil often wears" (Russell, 1977, p. 64).

Satan plays an important role in the folklore of Judaism, Christianity, and Islam. Already by the end of the apocalyptic period he had been identified with the following mythological themes in Jewish demonology and folklore: darkness, the underworld, and the air, sexual temptation and molestation, the goat, the lion, the frog or toad, and the serpent or dragon. In rabbinic folklore, Satan is not linked with the legend of Lilith, but he appears to Eve as a beautiful angel, and tempts Rabbi ʿAqivaʾ (ʿAqivaʾ ben Yosef, first-second century CE) in the form of a woman. According to the Talmud he was created on the sixth day of creation. His great rival was Michael, the leader of the angels. Satan was deemed capable of assuming any form, and there are accounts in hagiographic literature of his grappling physically with Christian saints.

Both similarities and differences may be noted between Christian and Islamic perceptions regarding Satan. One difference, according to A. J. Wensinck (1971, p. 669) lies in the fact that "Muslim thought remains undecided as to whether he was an angel or a *djinn* and does not pronounce an opinion on the possibility of his being 'a fallen angel.'" A similarity is found in Satan's characteristic ability of assuming any shape, or none at all. His ability to appear as an angel, the dreaded "midday Devil" of the *Psalms*, was what made Mary fearful at the Annunciation. As a *hātif* (one who is heard but not seen), Satan similarly almost beguiled ʿAlī into not washing the body of the Prophet, until ʿAli was corrected by another *hātif*. Thus the imperative of distinguishing between good and bad spirits due to Satan's operations is common to both Christianity and Islam.

The serpent or snake is perhaps the best-known symbol associated with Satan. *Genesis* (3:1ff.) mentions the serpent but not Satan; in *Romans* (16:20), however, Paul suggests that the serpent was Satan, an association already made in apocalyptic literature. This would imply that Satan tempted Adam, but the consensus of early Christina tradition was that Satan fell after Adam (Russell, 1977, p. 232). There may be good reason for believing that not until Origen in the third century CE was it clearly established that Satan's sin was pride, that he fell before Adam's creation, and that he was the serpent in the garden of Eden. Agobard of Lyons (ninth century) saw him as becoming the serpent. In a Jewish text, the *Apocalypse of Moses*, it is written that the serpent who tempted Eve was merely the tool of Satan, who, as a sinning angel, tempted the serpent to share his envy of Adam and Eve. In later Jewish literature, the identities of Satan and the serpent coalesce, or are closely associated with one another.

Satan is referred to by two different names in the Qurʾānic account of creation: he is called Iblīs when he refuses to bow down before Adam, and *al-Shayṭān* ("the demon") when he is the tempter (Wensinck, 1971, p. 669). Although there is no allusion to the serpent in the creation account in the Qurʾān, the term *shayṭān* was probably applied by the Arabs to serpents (Lagton, 1969, p. 9). Once Satan had been identified with *nafs*, or a human's lower appetites, according to Annemarie Schimmel, the *nafs* was seen as taking the form of a snake. "This serpent can be turned into a useful rod, just as Moses transformed serpents into rods. More frequent, however, is the idea that the power of the spiritual master can blind the snake; according to folk belief, the snake is blinded by the sight of an emerald (the connection of the pīr's spiritual power with the green color of the emerald is significant). Thus, his influence renders the *nafs*-snake harmless" (Schimmel, 1975, p. 113). The contrast with the *kuṇḍalinī* in some forms of yoga is very striking.

Satan is persistently, if not consistently, associated with the serpent. Leaving aside the question of the actual nature of Satan as formulated by the Council of Toledo (447), or the tendency to consider him an imaginative personification of evil, the association with the serpent needs to be accounted for. Several views have been advanced. At a homiletic level, the serpent has been taken to represent cunning. At a psychoanalytic level, the serpent has been associated with emergent sexuality. From a broader, history of religions approach "the serpent is the symbol of the Gods of vegetation; without being the representative of sex as such, he represents the temptations of the divinities that sacralize sex" (Ricoeur, 1967, p. 249). But perhaps in the end one inclines toward the hermeneutic suggested by Ricoeur that the serpent

> Represents the aspect of evil that could not be absorbed into the responsible freedom of man, which is perhaps also the aspect that Greek tragedy tried to purify by spectacle, song, and choral invocation. The Jews themselves, although they were well armed against demonology by their intransigent monotheism, were constrained by truth, as Aristotle would say, to concede something, to concede as much as they could without destroying the monotheistic basis of their faith, to the great dualisms which they were to discover after the Exile. The theme of the serpent represents the first landmark along the road of the Satanic theme which, in the Persian epoch, permitted the inclusion of a near-dualism in the faith of Israel. Of course, Satan will never be another god; the Jews will always remember that the serpent is a part of the creation; but at least the symbol of Satan allowed them to balance the movement toward the concentration of evil in man by a second movement which attributed its origin to a prehuman, demonic reality. (Ricoeur, 1967, pp. 258–259)

Although Satan has come to symbolize evil so closely as to become synonymous with it, he has also been associated with some positive concepts. He was worshipped in certain Gnostic circles for enabling knowledge to be brought forth. The Ṣūfī tradition has tended at times to see in him the ultimate monotheist who would bow down before naught but God, even in defiance of God's own command. It is also worth noting that there is no such fixed focus of moral evil as Satan in Hinduism (but see O'Flaherty, 1976), notwithstanding its shared cultural matrix with Buddhism, which did produce the figure of Māra. Despite the nuances of difference in Jewish, Christian, Greek, and Islamic conceptualizations of Satan, they may all share a common heritage.

Interest in Satan has intensified in the past decade, even before President Bush began to speak of the "axis of evil." Elaine Pagels (1995), who phenomenologically brackets the question of the existence of Satan, has carefully delineated the rise of Satan as it were in her works, drawing special attention to how the cosmological split implied by his existence also became a social split in the hands of sectarian groups like the Essenes between "Sons of Light" and "Sons of Darkness," which then runs like a dividing line throughout the history of Christianity in which enemies, both within and without, are identified as "agents of Satan," with Ayotollah's characterisation of U.S.A. as "the Great Satan" representing the inversion of this legacy. Others, such as Whitney S. Bodman (2003) have probed more deeply the sublimely positive role Satan comes to enjoy in Islamic mysticism at times, far beyond Rābiʿah's refusal to denounce him because she was too preoccupied with praising God.

See Also Antichrist; Devils; Dualism; Evil; Job; Māra; Theodicy; Witchcraft, article on Concepts of Witchcraft.

Bibliography

Awn, Peter J. *Satan's Tragedy and Redemption: Iblis in Sufi Psychology.* Leiden, 1983.

Barton, George A. "Demons and Spirits (Hebrew)." In *Encyclopaedia of Religion and Ethics,* edited by James Hastings, vol. 4. Edinburgh, 1911.

Bodman, Whitney S. "The Poetics of Iblīs: Narrative Theology in the Qur'ān." Doctoral dissertation. Harvard Divinity School, 2003.

Boyd, James W. *Satan and Māra: Christian and Buddhist Symbols of Evil.* Leiden, 1975.

Davis, H. Grady, et al. "Biblical Literature." In *The New Encyclopaedia Britannica,* Macropaedia, vol. 2. Chicago, 1984.

Day, John. *God's Conflict with the Dragon and the Sea.* Cambridge, 1985.

Langton, Edward. *Essentials of Demonology.* London, 1949.

Ling, T. O. *The Significance of Satan.* London, 1961.

O'Flaherty, Wendy Doniger. *The Origins of Evil in Hindu Mythology.* Berkeley, 1976.

Pagels, Elaine. *The Origin of Satan.* New York, 1995.

Ricoeur, Paul. *The Symbolism of Evil.* Translated by Emerson Buchanan. Boston, 1967.

Robbins, Rossell Hope. *The Encyclopedia of Witchcraft and Demonology.* New York, 1966.

Russell, Jeffrey Burton. *The Devil: Perceptions of Evil from Antiquity to Primitive Christianity.* Ithaca, N.Y., 1977.

Schimmel, Annemarie. *Mystical Dimensions of Islam.* Chapel Hill, N.C., 1975.

Wallace, Ronald S. "Devil." In *New International Dictionary of the Christian Church,* rev. ed., edited by J. D. Douglas. Grand Rapids, Mich., 1978.

Watt, W. Montgomery. *Bell's Introduction to the Qur'ān.* Edinburgh, 1970.

Wensinck, A. J. "Iblīs." In *The Encyclopaedia of Islam,* new ed., vol. 3. Leiden, 1971.

Arvind Sharma (1987 and 2005)

SATANISM has assumed a variety of forms through human history. Allegations of organized worship of Satan can be traced to Europe during the Middle Ages. Fears of Satan worship surfaced during the fifteenth-century witch-hunts, and Christian manuals were produced for depicting and combating Satanism, most notably the *Malleus maleficarum* (c. 1486) and *Compendium maleficarum* (c. 1620). Historians suggest the existence of a satanic cult in the royal court of Louis XIV that conducted "Black Masses" to mock the Catholic Mass. There were also a few practicing satanists in Europe during the late nineteenth century, triggering Satanism fears. In America, colonial-era New England experienced a period of witchcraft allegations and witch-hunting. Beyond the colonial witchcraft episode, satanic imagery has been perpetuated throughout American history by conservative Christian groups that believe that Satan is an active, personal presence in human affairs. Satan serves the function of explaining evil and misfortune, identifying heretical faiths, and bolstering Christian solidarity. This essay describes the more recent incarnations of Satanism, the 1960s countercultural satanic churches, and the 1980s Satanism scare by reviewing the history and organization of satanic churches, the current outbreak of satanic subversion fears, and the relationship between them.

Churches. Satanic churches began forming, first in California and then gradually spreading across the United States and to Europe, during the late 1960s. These churches achieved popularity in the 1970s as part of the counterculture movement of that period. The Church of Satan and Temple of Set are the largest and most visible existing satanic churches. A number of other satanic churches also appeared, but most were small and short-lived organizations that originated as schismatic offshoots of the Church of Satan. Although the Church of Satan claimed hundreds of thousands of members during its heyday, the total active membership of all the satanic churches never exceeded a few thousand. The Church of Satan is the more significant of the two groups; it is the first contemporary church devoted to the worship of Satan, it gave rise to most other satanic churches, and practicing satanists typically trace their beliefs to Anton LaVey's thought. Interest in satanic churches, although not Satanism, declined dramatically with the demise of the counterculture.

The Church of Satan was founded in San Francisco in 1966 by Anton Szandor LaVey (1930–1997), born Howard Stanton Levey. The details of LaVey's life remain contested, but evidence has mounted that most published accounts are in error and that major elements of LaVey's life were fabricated by sympathetic biographers who created a legendary persona for LaVey. In the legendary account, LaVey's grandmother was a Transylvanian gypsy who introduced him to the occult as a child. LaVey then ran away from home at age sixteen and worked successively in jobs such as an oboe player in the San Francisco Ballet Orchestra, lion tamer with the Clyde Beatty Circus, stage hypnotist, nightclub organist, and police department photographer. He also claimed romantic affairs with Marilyn Monroe and Jayne Mansfield. Most of this colorful personal history has now been challenged. Nonetheless, LaVey did become something of a celebrity during the 1960s when he pronounced himself the Black Pope, officiated at both the first satanic wedding and the first satanic funeral, and conducted a satanic service at which a nude woman served as the altar. His persona included a shaven head and black robe, a coroner's van as a car, and a pet Nubian lion.

LaVey's version of Satanism is presented in *The Satanic Bible* (1969), whole sections of which were drawn rather directly from several other writers' works. The iconoclastic philosophy contained in *The Satanic Bible* is decidedly hedonistic and is premised on self-preservation as the most basic instinct of human beings. LaVey inverts traditional Christian values, such as sexual constraints, pride, and avarice, and he elevates their opposites, such as indulgence, self-assertion, and sexual freedom, as satanic virtues. For LaVey, Satan is not an anthropomorphic being but a source of power that humans can control and that, once unleashed, can make humans gods. The major rituals conducted at Church of Satan "grottoes"—sex magic, help and healing, and destruction—reflect satanic values. LaVey's thought has been more influential than the small church membership might suggest; his *Satanic Bible* has sold hundreds of thousands of copies in a number of languages and it continues to serve as the primary scriptural source for satanists.

The Temple of Set was founded by Michael Aquino (b. 1946), who holds a Ph.D. in political science from the University of California at Santa Barbara and who rose to the rank of lieutenant colonel in the army before his retirement in 1994. Aquino and his wife joined the Church of Satan in 1969, and Aquino quickly rose in the leadership ranks. Over the next several years the relationship between LaVey and Aquino deteriorated, however, and Aquino, along with several dozen Church of Satan leaders and members, left to form the Temple of Set. Aquino served as high priest of the Temple of Set from its inception in 1975 to his retirement in 1996.

Aquino reports that he invoked Satan during his 1975 dispute with LaVey and received a visitation from Set, the Egyptian god of night. According to Aquino, Set is a metaphysical being formerly known under the Hebrew misnomer *Satan.* Set has used his power over the millennia to alter the genetic makeup of humans and to produce a species possessing an enhanced, nonnatural intelligence and potential. Although humans are not destined for immortality, they have the potential to achieve it through Setian beliefs and practices. The objective of the Temple of Set is to realize full human potential through self-creation and empowerment. In their quest for self-creation, initiates can progress through the following six degree levels: Setian, Adept, Priest or Priestess of Set, Master of the Temple, Magnus, and Ipsissimus. Total membership in the Temple of Set's local chapters ("pylons") has never exceeded several hundred.

SATANIC CULTS AND THE SATANISM SCARE. The "Satanism scare" swept the United States, Canada, and Europe during the 1980s. Satanic cults were thought to exist in an underground network that was involved in a variety of nefarious activities, including ritual sacrifice of children. According to the groups that mobilized to combat satanists, the outbreak of Satanism was simply the latest in a series of incursions by evil forces through human history. The incursion was inevitable, it was argued, even if its timing and form were not predictable. Because putative satanists operate underground, it was believed that they were able to penetrate major social institutions and engage in considerable destructive activity before their presence was detected. By some estimates, satanists were ritually sacrificing fifty to sixty thousand children annually in the United States alone during the 1980s. Satanists allegedly are motivated by a quest for personal power, which they seek to enhance by appropriating the life energy of children at the moment of their deaths in ritual sacrifices.

Proponents of satanic cult theory claim that Satanism is organized at four levels, with involvement often beginning at lower levels and subsequently graduating to higher-level activity. At the lowest level are "dabblers," typically adolescents who are lured into Satanism through experimentation with heavy metal music and fantasy games containing embedded satanic themes. More sinister are the "self-styled satanists" who employ satanic imagery in committing antisocial activity and are thought to be members of satanic cults. The public face of Satanism belongs to "organized satanists," consisting of the satanic churches, which publicly engage in the worship of Satan. Orchestrating the entire range of satanic activity are the "traditional satanists," who are organized into an international, secret, hierarchically structured, tightly organized cult network that engages in ritual abuse and sacrifice of children. Satanists procure children through abduction of missing children, purchase of children on the black market, and control over child-care institutions. Some children are abused, some sacrificed, and others raised as "breeders" to produce babies for later rituals. Intimidation, drugs, hypnosis, and brainwashing are employed to maintain power over children in satanists' hands and prevent them from revealing the existence of the satanic cults. Outsiders rarely discover well-concealed, secret satanic activity; those who do are intimidated into silence by satanists in positions of power.

A variety of evidence was offered in the 1980s to demonstrate the existence and active operation of satanic groups. There were widespread reports of mutilated animal remains that were thought to have been killed for body parts used in satanic rituals. Communities across the country mobilized to repel satanic cult incursions upon discovering satanic graffiti or rumors of impending satanic abductions of children for ritual sacrifice. Satanic churches, such as the Church of Satan, were cited as evidence of the public presence of satanists. Several high-profile criminals, such as Richard Ramirez ("The Night Stalker") who committed a series of murders in Los Angeles and San Francisco before being captured in 1985, openly flaunted satanic loyalties. Most compelling were the horrific personal testimonies of young children and adults who recalled satanic abuse in the course of therapeutic treatment. Therapists reported threats to their safety if they revealed the accounts of their clients.

In response to these various occurrences public opinion began to reflect heightened concern with Satanism. Mass media reports of satanic activity burgeoned, therapists treating individuals diagnosed as ritual abuse victims warned of the catastrophic impact of the abuse on their clients, special training and therapeutic procedures were developed for law enforcement and mental health professionals, police excavated the sites where ritual abuse victims were believed to be buried, and child protection agencies investigated preschools where child abuse allegedly occurred. In addition, legislatures conducted hearings on Satanism and passed laws facilitating the testimony of ritual abuse victims, and a number of high-profile trials resulted in the conviction of individuals on child-abuse charges.

The extraordinary claims of satanic cult subversion gradually were discredited, however, as evidence of satanic networks was challenged. Investigations of unexplained animal deaths led to the conclusion that they were the product of roadkills, trapping, disease, poisoning, and predators. Local panics over impending satanic abductions of adolescents turned out to be instances of urban legends with a satanic theme. Graffiti with satanic symbolism was found to be the work of isolated, alienated adolescents. No cases of satanic messages embedded in heavy metal music were documented. No connection between satanic churches or sociopathic criminals and a satanic cult network was ever established. Nor was any trace of the satanic cults themselves produced: no organizational records, documents containing doctrines or rituals, physical implements or equipment, meeting places, or defectors. Repeated official investigations of purported ritual sites yielded no supporting evidence. Most compellingly, not a single death attributable to a ritual sacrifice was documented. By contrast, disconfirming evidence steadily mounted.

The primary evidence supporting the existence of satanic cults was the testimony of children and adults who recalled abuse while in therapeutic treatment. However, the validity of these accounts was undermined by discoveries that biographical accounts by individuals claiming to be ritual abuse victims were fraudulent and that satanic material was introduced by therapists rather than raised by clients. A succession of reports by scholars, investigative journalists, police agencies, and governmental commissions unanimously concluded that there was no plausible support for the satanic cult claims.

CONCLUSIONS. The social creation of satanic forces has a long history in Western societies. In contemporary Western societies, Satanism has assumed two marginally related forms. The satanic churches constituted one element of the 1960s countercultural rebellion in which Satanism represented a rejection of traditional Christian morality in favor of hedonistic, individualistic values. The Church of Satan in particular was more culturally significant than its small peak membership might suggest. Many thousands of individuals held brief memberships in the church, and *The Satanic Bible* became the primary scriptural source for countercultural satanists who never maintained any organizational affiliation. While the Church of Satan and Temple of Set were swept up in the Satanism scare of the 1980s, no connection between these churches and underground satanic cults was ever produced. The Satanism scare of the 1980s was a reaction to rapid social changes that reconstituted home and workplace relationships in North America and Europe. Satanism symbolically represented a widely experienced sense of vulnerability and danger by American families. The threat was symbolically constructed as satanic cults, organizations that exploited the vulnerability of American families by so abusing and terrorizing young children as to permanently impair their capacity for full expression of selfhood. What the satanic churches and Satanism scare had in common, then, was the creation of social evil symbolized in satanic forms, one reacting against historical Christian morality and the other the emerging individuation of modern and postmodern society.

SEE ALSO Anticult Movements.

BIBLIOGRAPHY

Bromley, David. "Satanism: The New Cult Scare." In *The Satanism Scare,* edited by James Richardson, Joel Best, and David Bromley, pp. 49–74. Hawthorne, N.Y., 1991. A theoretical analysis of the Satanism scare from a sociological perspective. Bromley treats the Satanism scare as one of a number of subversion episodes that have occurred through American history and links it to societal changes that produced widespread fears of child endangerment.

Hicks, Robert. *In Pursuit of Satan: The Police and the Occult.* Buffalo, N.Y., 1991. A critical analysis of the Satanism scare from the perspective of a law enforcement official. Hicks meticulously debunks claims of an underground satanic cult network and provides information critical to law enforcement officers confronted by alleged satanic incidents.

Kahaner, Larry. *Cults That Kill: Probing the Underworld of Occult Crime.* New York, 1988. Kahaner is a journalist who in this book lays out the case for an underground satanic cult engaged in horrific crimes.

La Fontaine, Jean. *The Extent and Nature of Organized and Ritual Abuse: Research and Findings.* London, 1994. La Fontaine conducted a governmental investigation of satanic activity in England. The report debunks claims of an underground satanic network engaged in ritual sacrifice or other crimes.

Lanning, Kenneth. "Satanic, Occult, Ritualistic Crime: A Law Enforcement Perspective." *Police Chief* 56 (1989): 62–83. An analysis of satanic and occult crime reports by an official in the Federal Bureau of Investigation. Lanning finds no evidence of organized, satanic ritual crime.

LaVey, Anton Szandor. *The Satanic Bible.* New York, 1969. The best-known and most influential statement of satanic theology. This book contains precepts of Satanism that underpinned the Church of Satan as well as a number of other satanic groups.

Nathan, Debbie, and Michael Snedeker. *Satan's Silence: Ritual Abuse and the Making of a Modern American Witch Hunt.* New York, 1995. Nathan is a journalist and Snedeker an attorney. Together they trace the emergence of child abuse as a problem, the unquestioned acceptance of children's abuse testimony, and the resulting national hysteria about ritual sexual abuse of children.

Ofshe, Richard, and Ethan Watters. *Making Monsters: False Memories, Psychotherapy, and Sexual Hysteria.* Berkeley, Calif., 1994. This book examines the process through which pseudo-memories are implanted by therapists. One of the cases deals with purported satanic ritual abuse.

Pulling, Patricia. *The Devil's Web: Who Is Stalking Your Children for Satan?* Lafayette, La., 1989. Pulling was one of the more vocal, public advocates of the existence of an organized satanic cult engaged in ritual abuse. She sought restrictions on fantasy games, such as Dungeons and Dragons, which she claimed constituted one means by which youth were lured into satanic cults.

Richardson, James, Joel Best, and David Bromley, eds. *The Satanism Scare.* Hawthorne, N.Y., 1991. An interdisciplinary, academic collection of essays on the Satanism scare. The contributors debunk the Satanism scare by examining the history of Satanism, the construction of the satanic threat to children, the role of therapists and police in promoting the scare, and the circulation of rumors of satanic activity.

Smith, Michelle, and Lawrence Pazder. *Michelle Remembers.* New York, 1980. A biographical account of alleged satanic ritual abuse by Michelle Smith, written with her therapist, Lawrence Pazder. The therapeutic relationship led to a romantic relationship as Smith and Pazder both left their spouses and were married. Publication of this book is widely regarded as the immediate event that triggered the Satanism scare. Smith's claims were subsequently discredited.

Stratford, Lauren. *Satan's Underground: The Extraordinary Story of One Woman's Escape.* Eugene, Ore., 1988. A biographical account of alleged satanic ritual abuse by Laurel Wilson writing under a pseudonym. For a time Wilson was influential in spreading satanic ritual abuse claims, recounting horrific stories from her childhood. Her claims were ultimately discredited, and the book was withdrawn from circulation by the publisher.

DAVID G. BROMLEY (2005)

SATI. The difficulties encountered in the study of sati—the death of a woman on her husband's funeral pyre, or on a separate pyre soon afterwards—are reflected in the terminology used. The term coined by the British in India (*suttee*) suggests the oppression of widows and the woman as victim, both reinforced by the term *widow-burning.* The same word in its original Sanskrit (*satī*, a feminine noun derived from *sat*, meaning "goodness" or "virtue") denotes not the practice but the practitioner: the "good woman" who, by choosing to join her husband in death, refuses to become an inauspicious widow. In its traditional context, the term *satī* conveys supreme virtue, personal strength, and religious autonomy. The most common Sanskrit terms for the practice are *sahagamana* ("going with"), *anugamana* ("going after"), and *anumaraöa* ("dying after"). In this article, the practice is denoted by the modern term *sati*, and the Sanskrit word *satī* ("good woman") is reserved for the person. (There is no parallel notion of the "good man" who chooses to burn on the pyre of his dead wife, a fact that suggests that this one-sided practice is rooted in the male desire to control the sexuality of women; by contrast, the widower is encouraged to remarry.)

Outside India, sati was practiced in one form or another (that is, not always by fire) by the ancient Greeks, Germans, Slavs, Scandinavians, Egyptians, and Chinese. Although there is evidence of the custom in the Indo-European period, by the time the Indo-Aryan language reached India, only traces of an archaic practice remained. The earliest indisputable reference to sati in a Sanskrit text is found in the *Mahābhārata*, the great epic which evolved between 400 BCE and 400 CE, reaching its present form by the sixth or seventh century. An account is also given by the Greek author Diodorus Siculus (first century BCE) in his history of the Panjab in the fourth century BCE. Physical evidence in the form of "sati stones," memorials to women who died as *satīs*, is found in many parts of India, dating from as early as 510 CE. In the Muslim period, the tenth to the eighteenth centuries, the Rajputs practiced a form of collective ritual suicide termed *jauhar* (denoting a construction made of combustible materials for the purpose of burning people alive); that is, to avoid dishonor at the hands of the (Muslim) enemy and to encourage their menfolk to fight, Rajput women burned themselves before their husbands' expected death in battle (as, for example, in the three celebrated occasions of the mass suicides of women at Chitorgarh in Rajasthan in 1303, 1535, and 1568). In the medieval period in general, the hardships experienced by Hindu widows (such as severe restrictions on diet and dress, and the stigma of inauspiciousness) probably encouraged the spread of sati. The further increase in the practice among the brahmins of Bengal, especially during the period from 1680 to 1830, is ascribed by some scholars to the fact that the system of law prevailing there gave inheritance rights to widows: although some widows enjoyed the powers this conferred, others succumbed to a greater familial pressure to die. Other scholars argue that, by destabilizing traditional Hindu values, the British were partly responsible for the increase.

Although the number of women who died as *satīs* is statistically small, the ideal is revered throughout traditional India even today. The ideology behind this belief is debated in the texts of Sanskrit religious law (*dharmaśāstra*) in the section devoted to the proper behavior of women (*strīdharma*). The issue is usually raised in the context of widowhood: some texts (such as *Manusmṛti*) describe only the duties of the widow for the woman whose husband has died; some allow a choice between widowhood and sati; few recommend sati. The standard objection is that sati is a form of suicide, and suicide is prohibited; the standard riposte is that ritual death is not suicide. Other objections include that ritual death, appropriate in the legendary period of ancient India, no longer applies in the "degenerate era" (*kaliyuga*) of recorded history; that sati, traditionally a warrior or Rajput custom, is prohibited to brahmin women; and that the ritual applies only rarely and only to exceptionally virtuous women. The arguments in favor of sati focus on the rewards accruing to the "good woman," further evidence that this form of ritual death was optional; that is, the ritual is open to those women who actively seek the rewards described. By about 700 CE, however, the merit bestowed by sati was so great that it cut across the usual implications of *karma* for both wife and husband. The *satī* is credited with the power to rescue even a bad husband from hell, taking them both (and, according to some sources, seven generations of ancestors on either side) to heaven. There is even some scriptural justification for persuading, even forcing, a "bad" woman to burn herself: whatever her reasons for joining her husband on his pyre, her sacrifice purified them both.

Ethnographic evidence is somewhat different. Among traditional communities in Rajasthan even today, the *satī* is no longer a woman: she is worshiped as a goddess, a deified eternal wife. According to belief, the pyre ignites solely by the power of the *satī*, that is, by the inner heat of *sat*, the force of virtue at her core. Fire is thus not so much the cause of her death but the essence of her being. There are three stages in the life of the *satī*: as a married woman, she is the devoted wife (*pativratā*); when she takes a vow to become a *satī*, she is termed a *satīvratā*; when she ends her life in spontaneous combustion, she has become a "*satī*-mother" (*satīmātā*). The paradoxical notion of the "living *satī*" is applied to saintly women who are believed to be possessed by *sat*, who have taken the vow to become *satī*s, but who are unable to fulfill those vows because sati is illegal. Such women are worshiped as liminal beings, living on the cusp of the human and divine realms.

There has always been resistance to sati, even within orthodox and traditional Hinduism; hence the debates in Sanskrit and vernacular texts. The Mughal rulers Humayun and Akbar both tried to abolish the practice. In the British colonial period, a vigorous campaign against sati—headed by the governor-general of India, Lord William Bentinck, and supported by Hindu reformers such as Rammohun Roy—culminated in the Suttee Regulation Act of 1829. When the British left India, the independent Indian government reaffirmed the illegality of sati. Despite the efforts of both British and Indian governments, however, instances of sati continued to occur, and the respect and devotion paid to the memories of those women remained unchanged.

The reemergence of sati in north India since the 1970s—including the celebrated sati of Roop Kanwar in Deorala, Rajasthan, in 1987—has prompted renewed interest in the topic among activists (both for and against sati) and commentators. As early as 1983, for example, the Rani Sati Sarva Sangh (largely funded by the Marwari community) launched a campaign to popularize sati, to administer sati shrines, and to promote the building of additional sati temples. Pro-sati activism of this kind is consistently met by anti-sati campaigns, both giving rise to a complex debate among students of Indian religion, political and cultural commentators, and Indian and Western feminists.

SEE ALSO Gender and Religion, article on Gender and Hinduism.

BIBLIOGRAPHY

Anand, Mulk Raj, ed. *Sati: A Write-Up of Raja Ram Mohan Roy about the Burning of Widows Alive.* Delhi, 1989. Published soon after the death of Roop Kanwar in Deorala in 1987, this volume juxtaposes the key texts of Ram Mohan Roy's anti-suttee campaign in the early nineteenth century and a range of responses to the Deorala sati in the late 1980s.

Datta, V. N. *Sati: Widow-burning in India. A Historical, Social and Philosophical Enquiry into the Hindu Rite of Widow Burning* [sic]. Delhi, India, 1988.

Fisch, Jörg. *Tödliche Rituale: Die Witwenverbrennung und andere Formen der Totenfolge.* Frankfurt, Germany, 1998. A comprehensive study of ritual death outside India and "widow-burning" in India.

Harlan, Lindsey. *Religion and Rajput Women: The Ethic of Protection in Contemporary Narratives.* Berkeley, Calif., 1992. An account of Rajput women's conceptions of what it is to be a good Rajput woman. In this context, the term *satīmātā* embraces both the woman who dies on her husband's funeral pyre and the "living *satī*"; in each case, the ideal of wifely devotion (*pativratā*) is central.

Hawley, John Stratton, ed. *Sati, the Blessing and the Curse: The Burning of Wives in India.* New York, 1994. This collection of essays by Indian and Western scholars, written in response to the sati of Roop Kanwar in Rajasthan in 1987, attempts to clarify the multiple realities of sati from the distant past to the present day.

Leslie, Julia. "A Problem of Choice: The Heroic *Satī* or the Widow-Ascetic." In *Rules and Remedies in Classical Indian Law,* edited by Julia Leslie, pp. 46–61. Leiden, 1991. Rulings for the widow and the *satī* are compared with those for the male renouncer with a view to examining the traditional idea that widowhood is a valid path of renunciation for women.

Leslie, Julia. "Suttee or *Satī*: Victim or Victor?" In *Roles and Rituals for Hindu Women,* edited by Julia Leslie, pp. 175–191. London, 1991. An analysis of four different discourses on sati: the British colonial, the radical feminist, the orthodox Hindu text, and contemporary Indian experience.

Mani, Lata. "Contentious Traditions: The Debate on Sati in Colonial India." In *Recasting Women: Essays in Colonial History,* edited by Kumkum Sangari and Sudesh Vaid, pp. 88–126. Delhi, 1989. A feminist critique of official, native and missionary writings on sati in colonial India between 1780 and 1833, this important study draws attention to the blindness of the patriarchies on both sides of the colonial divide to the physical agonies of the women under discussion.

Mani, Lata. *Contentious Traditions: The Debate on Sati in Colonial India.* Berkeley, Calif., 1998. The 1989 article expanded to book length.

Sharma, Arvind, ed., with Ajit Ray, Alaka Hejib, and Katherine K. Young. *Sati: Historical and Phenomenological Essays.* Delhi, 1988. Twelve essays on sati in the context of the colonial and Hindu-Christian encounter, as well as in terms of orthodox Hinduism.

Van den Bosch, Lourens P. "A Burning Question: Sati and Sati Temples as the Focus of Political Interest." *NUMEN* 37, no. 2 (December 1990): 174–194.

Weinberger-Thomas, Catherine. *Cendres d'immortalité: La crémation des veuves en Inde.* Paris, 1996. Translated by Jeffrey Mehlman and David Gordon White as *Ashes of Immortality: Widow-Burning in India* (Chicago, 1999). An experiential and psychoanalytic account of ritual self-sacrifice in South Asia based on fifteen years of fieldwork in north India, drawing on both Sanskrit and vernacular texts.

JULIA LESLIE (2005)

SATIRE SEE HUMOR AND RELIGION

SAUL, or, in Hebrew, Sha'ul, son of Kish, a Benjaminite, was the first king of Israel (c. 1020 BCE). The beginning of the monarchy under Saul, and with it the creation of a national state out of a loose association of tribes and clans, is attributed in the tradition to external threats from east and west. Saul's kingship is presented in *1 Samuel* as a transition from the time of the judges, temporary charismatic leaders of individual tribes or regions, to that of a more unified and permanent military rule.

Saul's ability to rally support from the Israelite tribes in order to relieve Jabesh-gilead from the Ammonite siege and achieve a victory for the Transjordanian tribes (*1 Sm.* 11) was the actual occasion in the oldest tradition for making him king. In subsequent military activity his forces also had some success against the Philistine garrisons in the central hill country (*1 Sm.* 13–14), but in a major encounter between the two armies Saul and his sons lost their lives in battle (*1 Sm.* 31).

The length of Saul's reign (cf. *1 Sm.* 13:1) and the exact extent of his domain are not known. His authority probably did not include Judah. His residence, in Gibeah of Benjamin, did not include an elaborate court. Yet he did much to pave the way for David's later success (*1 Sm.* 14:47–51).

The older traditions about Saul's monarchy, including a folktale about his youth (*1 Sm.* 9–10:16), have been expanded by the historian of *Samuel* and *Kings* in order to depict the prior divine election and designation of Saul as king (*1 Sm.* 9:15–17, 10:1, 17–27) and his later rejection (*1 Sm.* 13:8–15; cf. *1 Sm.* 15) through the prophet Samuel. The author also expresses his ambivalence about the monarchy as both a divinely sanctioned institution and a possible source of religious waywardness, injustice, and corruption (*1 Sm.* 8, 12). Finally, in his account of David's rise to power, the rejected Saul is used as a foil for the virtues of David, God's chosen successor.

SEE ALSO David; Samuel.

BIBLIOGRAPHY

For the history of Saul's reign, see John Bright's *A History of Israel,* 3d ed. (Philadelphia, 1981). For a discussion of the text of *Samuel* with a review of the critical problems, see P. Kyle McCarter, Jr.'s *I Samuel,* vol. 8 of the Anchor Bible (Garden City, N.Y., 1980). A more detailed treatment of my own views can be found in my book *In Search of History: Historiography in the Ancient World and the Origins of Biblical History* (New Haven, Conn., 1983), chap. 8.

New Sources

Nicholson, Sarah. *Three Faces of Saul: An Intertextual Approach to Biblical Tragedy.* Sheffield, U.K., 2002.

JOHN VAN SETERS (1987)
Revised Bibliography

SAULE. Written historical sources about the pre-Christian religion of the ancient Latvians are fragmented and often unreliable, but concur in condemning it as pagan idolatry and the worship of natural phenomena. In 1199 this attitude was consecrated in a papal bull from Pope Innocent III, who had conferred upon the conquest and Christianization of the Baltic region the status of a crusade.

Nature worship was attributed to the ancient Baltic tribes in a variety of historical documents, many of which were compiled and analyzed by Wilhelm Mannhardt in his impressive *Letto-Preussische Götterlehre* (left unfinished at his death in 1870, and only published in Riga in 1936). The earliest is a 1326 chronicle by the Christian knight Peter von Duisburg, in which he pithily states that Baltic peoples worshipped the sun, the moon, the stars, and four-legged animals. Later documents include occasional observations by travelers to the region, but mostly consist of records of witch trials or reports of ecclesiastical inspections, aimed at eliminating pre-Christian rites and beliefs—which seem to have survived many centuries of merciless persecution by both the Catholic and Protestant churches. The Romantic movement caused a radical reversal in attitude by kindling scholarly interest in popular antiquities and in oral traditions containing archaic elements.

Evidence of a cult of the *saule* ("sun"; pron. *sow-leh*) as part of an archaic nature religion, as well as prehistoric cosmogonic concepts linked to the sun may be found in Latvian folk legends, magical formulae, traditions, and beliefs, but most of all in the hundreds of thousands of variants of lyrical folk-song, or *daina,* texts.

Within the most recent and complete collection of over 4,000 *daina* texts (Vīķe-Freibergaand Freibergs, 1988) containing words with the root form for "sun," around 2,500 texts refer literally to the sun as a celestial body or physical phenomenon, either in its chronological or its meteorological aspect (Vīķe-Freiberga, 1999; 2002). But even this physical sun—which shimmers, glitters, glimmers, glares, blazes, shines forth, and conveys its presence in a dozen more ways for which there are Latvian words but no English equivalent—has a profoundly magical and beneficial influence on all aspects of human life. Thus, for a man to be born in the summer while the sun is shining ensures that his rye will grow tall, his barley will thrive, and his bay horses will breed vigorous and strong.

Around 1,500 numbered *type-songs* (some having over 100 variants) refer to the clearly personified, feminine figure of Saule, and contain motifs that are both mythological and cultic in nature. This mythical Saule appears as a resplendent, richly dressed, generous, compassionate, and also playful being: she dances "on a silver mountain, with golden slippers on her feet," she "strums her psaltery *[kokles],* while sitting in the East," she plays with golden apples. Saule rides in her chariot across the Hill of Heaven or sails in a boat that she leaves behind after setting into the sea. She sits on a hill, with golden reins in her hand, while her horses bathe in the sea.

Finally, a few hundred texts are "cosmological" in the sense of reflecting a "mental model" of the universe, both in its structural and in its dynamic aspects (Vīķe-Freiberga, 1997). The sun is a major point of reference in the spatial bisection of the Cosmos along the vertical plane between above and below, in which the world (the earth and everything on it) is *pasaule,* literally "the place under the sun." The sun also governs the temporal opposition between the brief limited span of a human life on earth *(mūžs)* and eternity as expressed in the concept of the "life span of the sun" *(saules mūžs).* Finally, a third cosmological dimension combines temporal with spatial aspects in distinguishing between temporal life in "this sun" *(šī saule)* and eternal life in "that sun" *(viņa saule).* The "other sun" or "nether sun" is the realm in which the sun sleeps at night. Each new dawn demonstrates anew that the sun has not been destroyed by darkness, but has only retired for a while into a different plane of existence, for "Does the sun rise in the same spot where it has set?" By being reborn every day, Saule becomes not just a symbol of immortality, but also the main mediator between Life and Death. Saule is the one who knows the path of transition between them, passing through double gates on the horizon, each marked by a verdant tree. The red tree of sunrise is the tree of life, youth, health, and beauty, and magically projects these qualities unto the East:

> The sun rises every morning In a scarlet tree; Young lords grew old While seeking that tree. (Saules dainas, p. 175, song nr. 33786)

The other Sun Tree grows at the gate through which the sun exits at the end of her daily path, entering the "other sun" of night and death:

> Stately grows the oak tree At the end of *Sun's path;* There Saule hangs up her belt Each evening at sunset. (*Saules dainas,* p. 186, song nr. 33827v4)

The setting sun has lost the hale hues of morning and has grown pale, wan, and tired, just like a person who in old age has lost the rosy bloom and vigor of youth. As she leaves our world, Saule takes along with her everything that has fulfilled its mission in this world and has come to the end of its cycle. As shown in magical formulae and incantations, the setting sun takes with her our sighs and our sorrows, our mishaps and misfortunes; she carries away blight, illness, disintegration, and decay. Most important of all, the main task of the setting sun is to bring along with her the souls of all those whose mortal bodies have been lain to rest that day:

> My dear mother has left Along with the sun. I called out, but she couldn't hear, I ran after her, but in vain. (*Saules dainas,* p. 91, song nr. 4110)

Several texts stress the importance of completing burials before sunset, for Saule carries away the keys to the gates to the World of the Shades, which then become locked for the night. Saule (just like the ancient Greek god Hermes) is thus clearly a *psychopompos* or leader of the souls of the dead. For this reason, the period just after sunset each day had to be celebrated by interrupting all work in honor of the sacred "path of the Sun," "under-the-sun's steps," or the "grey hour." Women in labor (and their husbands), however, also pray to Saule not to take away the keys. This suggests that Saule may hold the entrance key to "this sun" as well as the exit keys.

In many texts the Sun Tree that stands at the entrance gate between the worlds has clearly become the World Tree, or *Axis Mundi.* It grows on a stone in the middle of the sea—the Cosmic ocean—or, paradoxically, it may be a mere reed on which the sun rests at night. Or again, the live tree is replaced by the axle of a celestial hand-mill:

> Whose is this waxen mill At the crown of a clear oak? The son of Dievs is the owner, The daughter of Saule the miller. (*Saules dainas,* p. 181, song nr. 33796)

Each night the constellations make a full circle around the pole star, the only one to remain in a fixed position, as if it marked the tip of a cosmic axis around which everything turns. The sons of Dievs (the supreme deity and sky god) are linked (among other things) to the constellations. The daughter of Saule acting as a miller, turns the axle of a heavy, stone hand-mill like those formerly used by women on Latvian farms. Yet a vision of the Sun Tree may also refer to a purely subjective state, acting as the symbol of a moment of spiritual revelation. A number of longer songs describe a marvelous oak tree suddenly discovered on a holy morn, with its roots of copper, golden branches, and silver leaves. This tree becomes a symbol of the dual nature of mankind: with the roots of its physical existence deriving from Mother Earth, the human soul in its evolution grows with arms stretched up like the branches of a tree, with fingers like leaves reaching for the sky.

The status of Saule as a cult object becomes evident in such motifs as that of the goddess in the tree, the numerous variants of which interchangeably describe Saule or Laima (the goddess of fate) or Māra (a form of the earth goddess) as sitting in a tree (willow, apple tree, or other), and bestowing gifts upon humans (on the tree and gift-giving, see Bynum, 1978). Saule as benefactor is also a rich godmother, "Reaching out her hands across the river, All fingers of both hands Covered with gold spiral rings" (*Saules dainas*, p. 228, song nr. 33932). In her generosity, Saule (just like Dievs and Laima) singles out the dispossessed and the needy, and even stands in for her dead mother at the wedding of an orphan girl, just like Mēness (the Moon) stands in for her father. In contrast, the maiden crown (i.e. the coronet that was the traditional head-gear of unmarried women) of a girl who had died was to be hung to bleach in a tree on the grave as a sort of offering to Saule.

A major function of Saule is to produce vegetal fruitfulness, which is the central focus of the numerous all-night rituals of Jāņi, the celebration of the midsummer solstice. The bright vernal sun is not just an icon of growth and general fertility; like the Greek goddess Demeter and the Roman Ceres, Saule is also the special patroness of grain crop fertility:

> What shines, what shimmers, Back yonder field? It's Saule sowing silver Among stumps in the clearing. (*Saules dainas*, p. 183, song nr. 54924)

The gray cloud of pollen hovering over a rye field in bloom becomes a manifestation of Saule in her aspect as provider of fruitfulness:

> Saule walks over the rye field, Wearing her grey skirts. Oh Saule, lift up your hem, Take care of the blossoms. (*Saules dainas*, p. 212, song nr. 32532v6)

As the primal cause of the fertility of the earth, Saule best embodies the boundless generosity of the Cosmic, scattering her gifts over the earth as from a bottomless cornucopia: "Dear Mother Saule, What are you doing in the granary?— I'm sifting silver, I'm filling the bins" (*Saules dainas*, p. 231, song nr. 16566).

As inhabitants of a cool and frequently damp climate, the Latvians feel an especial affinity with the sun as giver of warmth, who lightens the burden of all those who have to labor in the open, exposed to the elements. To the young children sent out at dawn to herd the flocks, the sun that dries the morning dew and dissipates the mists is just like a human mother who comforts her child by drying its tears and warming it on her lap. Shepherd children and orphans become a metonym for the dispossessed and the destitute in general, who have only Dear Mother Saule as their patroness and protector:

> Saule, dearest mother, Wearing your golden cloak! Take pity on all orphans, Dry (all) their tears. (*Saules dainas*, p. 230, song nr. F17,28624)

With its measured and rhythmical daily and yearly course across the vault of heaven, the sun serves not just as a heavenly timepiece, but also becomes a visible embodiment of divine law, order, regularity, and justice. On the social plane, these are translated as norms of social equity, fairness, and justice. Any transgression against these social norms then becomes a contravention of divine law as well, a threat to the harmonious equilibrium of the Cosmos. Thus, brutal masters, who require their serfs to work in the fields even past sundown, represent an abomination in both a social and a cosmic sense. The consequences of such transgressions are symbolized by the Black Snake that grinds its grain on a stone in the middle of the sea. Evildoers are meant to taste of this bitter meal of divine retribution, for the white Sun is also the all-seeing eye and ever-present witness. One turns to Saule with a prayer for help both in suffering and with regard to social injustice:

> Dear, white Saule in your course, Please "even out" this earth: The rich are quite ready To bury the poor alive. (*Saules dainas*, p. 226, song nr. 31244)

The solar myth of the celestial wedding is not a narrative fixed in any canonical form, but rather a large corpus of variants on a number of wedding themes. Either Saule herself or her daughter is enjoined to dress in silver, for their drivers have come with "water horses, a stone carriage, a silvery sleigh," or with "Dievs' carriage, the horses of the wind." The link of myth to metaphor can best be seen in the motif in which Saule as the bride's mother distributes gifts *(veltīdama)* from her daughter's dowry by handing patterned mittens or a woven belt to the oak tree, a woolen cloak to the linden tree, and golden or green copper rings to the slim alders, just as the setting sun simply gilds *(zeltīdama)* the treetops in other song variants. The Daughter of Saule *(Saules meita)* is variously described as being courted by the Sons of Dievs *(Dieva dēli;* clear analogues of the Vedic *Ashvins* and the Greek *dioskuroi*), by Auseklis (the Morning Star, or by Pērkons (Thunder). Many poetic texts picture the Sons of Dievs as looking at the daughter of the sun through blossoms or branches, as heating the bathhouse for her (think of mists swirling on summer evenings), as tangling up the golden cloth that they are weaving in the sky, or as teasing her or even doing her violence. A separate motif involves the wrath of Pērkons over the abduction of the Daughter of Saule; he strikes the Sun Tree standing at the gate and smashes it to pieces. Saule weeps for three years while picking up the pieces and only picks up the tip of the tree during the fourth year. In other variants, Pērkons as the heavenly smith is forging a golden brooch or belt for the dowry of the Daughter of Saule.

In parallel to the purely celestial wedding, another motif has the sun shining during rainfall as a sign that the Daughter of Saule is getting married. But rather than coming from heaven, her suitor comes from the land of the dead: "my brother died young, he is now taking a bride." This motif ties in with the concept of Saule as the gatekeeper to the land of the dead.

SCHOLARLY DEBATES. In spite of the richness and diversity of oral materials about Saule, no major study on the Latvian Sun-myth is available in the English language. The first serious study of the Latvian Sun-myth is to be found in Wilhelm Mannhardt's monograph of 1875, in which he analyses a corpus of ninety Latvian Sun-songs. Mannhardt points to the numerous analogies with the folklore and mythology of other peoples found in Latvian Sun-songs, which he terms a "rich treasure trove of mythological poetry" (*reiche Schatzkammer mythologischer Poesie*). Referring to the then popular theories of Adalbert Kuhn, Mannhardt concludes that the Latvian folk songs contain genuine fragments of the original Indo-European Nature religion in its still nascent, "precrystallized" form. Eduard Zicāns (1936) has expanded this approach by analyzing the motif of the solar wedding in the *dainas,* along with its Indo-European parallels. A fascination with the Indo-European Sun-myth culminated in the nineteenth century with the wildly popular scholarship of Max Müller, who came to see solar motifs or a "solar hero" in practically every myth and tale ever recorded. After decades of unbridled enthusiasm, however, the mid-twentieth century (at least in North America) saw not just "an eclipse of solar mythology" (Dorson, 1955), but also a veritable scholarly taboo on interest in the Sun-myth as well as in Indo-European studies.

The thread was picked up again within the Swedish sociological school of religious studies by Haralds Biezais (1972), in an extensive and detailed study of Saule as a member of *"Die himmlische Gőtterfamilie der alten Letten"* (The Heavenly Family of God of the Ancient Latvians). Biezais stresses the "sociological background" of gods or mythological figures, whereby their functions are expressed mainly in terms of the family relationships among them. The feminine Saule is presented as a heavenly farm wife *(die himmlische Hausfrau),* married to the masculine Mēness (Moon) and living in what is essentially the projection upon the Hill of Heaven of a prosperous Latvian farmhouse, with all its tools and implements. Similarly, under the influence of Émile Durkheim and the Swedish school of interest dominance among historians of religion, the German scholar Bauer, in his 1972 doctoral dissertation, stresses the importance of "technomorph concepts" in Baltic (i.e., Latvian and Lithuanian) mythology.

The concrete objects and activities linked to Saule in the Latvian *dainas* are certainly such as would be known from the singers' everyday life experiences and circumstances, only richer and shinier. Saule has servants who have to mow silver meadows and plough golden mountains. She has silken skirts which she puts out to air in the evening. The Daughters of the Sun *(Saules meitas)* in turn, may be washing tankards, bleaching cups, scrubbing linden tables, knitting mittens, weaving shirts, herding cows, sweeping paths, grinding meal, cooking dinner, and altogether as busily engaged in womanly tasks as any farmer's daughter ever could be. But do these poetic images derived from the "poorly differentiated life of the Latvian peasants" reflect a religious experience that is equally undifferentiated, narrow, limited, and obtuse, when it is not outright incoherent and irrational (Biezais, 1972, p. 391; Bauer, 1972, p. 194)? I would argue that they do not.

Along a different line of thought, some scholars have argued that the Latvian *dainas* contain little of what could be called "mythical" in the narrow sense of the word (adopted by Mircéa Eliade, among others): that is to say they do not form a coherent, solemn narrative about the birth, life struggles, and adventures of gods or superhuman heroes. By taking *narrative* as a central defining characteristic of what is mythical, Albert Lord (1989), for example, concludes that we should not talk of "mythical" *dainas* just because they refer to a god or mythological figure, but should treat them instead as courting, wedding, funeral, or other kinds of songs, according to their content or performance context.

Yet the very principle that narrative is a major defining characteristic of myth may be seriously questioned. Narrative involves character as well as plot, like two sides of the same coin, while lyrical poetry puts the accent on characterization. In his seminal work of 1875, Mannhardt offers a useful, broader definition of myth, proposing to treat "hymns, songs of praise, adoration and respectful prayers" as genuine mythical materials. In other words, the attitude expressed toward the mythological figure should be a crucial component of our understanding of its significance.

With respect to the Latvian Saule, Ludis Adamovičs (1956, pp. 567–568) has noted that, along with undeniably mythic and cultic elements in the Latvian materials, there are evident nature metaphors that may be merely the subjective products of poetic fantasy. This implies a questionable dichotomy between myth that is "real," that has some literal meaning in the prosaic sense, and poetic imagery or metaphor that is an "unreal" product of the imagination. In the same vein, the Lithuanian folklorist Jonas Balys (1953, pp. 7–9) claims that Latvians tend to overestimate the importance of their own songs for mythological studies. According to Balys, folk poetry is much more unreliable than prose narrative in that regard, and he quotes with approval an assertion by Emil N. Setälä (1934) that poetry, after all, is only poetry, and contains precious little of religion in the proper sense of that word. But if religion should be prosaic in order to be taken seriously, one wonders what to make of so many books of the Old Testament?

Along the same lines, the famous Finnish scholar K. F. Karjalainen (1921, pp. 20–21) has criticized the studies of Bernát Munkácsi on Vogul mythology (based on Vogul folk poetry), claiming that the corpus examined by Munkácsi needed a serious weeding out of images of poetic fantasy and random contributions by individual singers before such a "song religion" could be placed on an equal footing with "true" (prosaic?) folk beliefs. Even Biezais, who unconditionally accepts Saule as part of the "heavenly enlarged family" of ancient Latvian divinities, sees the poetic fantasy aspect as a sort of contamination in the otherwise valuable and rich source of materials of the Latvian *dainas.* Poetic images are said to appear without "rationally meaningful" motivation (Biezais, 1972, p. 264) or details that are difficult to interpret are treated as the meaningless products of poetic fantasy, due to confusion (or worse) on the singers' part (Biezais, 1972, pp. 270–271).

To proponents of the sociological school of religion, the fact that the personified Saule appears dressed and equipped in gold and silver is sufficient proof "that she belongs to the celestial realm and is divinised" (Biezais, 1972, p. 214). This, however, cannot be the sole criterion, since such ornamental or "focusing" epithets (Vīķe-Freiberga, *Mosaic* 6, 1973) are applied to everything in the *dainas,* starting with the humblest blade of grass. The metaphorical personification of a natural phenomenon is a legitimate step in its divinization, but not the ultimate one. The personified mythological figure must also have divine powers and functions attributed to it and must be linked to metaphysical and cultic concepts. In the case of the Latvian materials, where sociological reductionism would see Saule and her entourage as a projection unto the Hill of Heaven of the ordinary ancient farmstead, one could argue for the very contrary psychological process. Personified nature metaphors, in this view, are the expressions of individual subjective experiences of the numenous, of epiphanies linked to moments of religious revelation or of Cosmic illumination. The mythopoetic metaphor is an attempt to express the inexpressible by encoding it in images derived from everyday experience. In the Latvian *dainas,* the whole of nature and its phenomena are seen as manifestations of divine forces, as the incarnation of the divine spirit in matter. It is the divine or the spiritual that is projected downward into matter, not the sociological or the meteorological that is projected upward. One could go even further and claim that a nature divinity such as Saule is seen as consubstantial with its analogue in physical nature.

See Also Baltic Religion, overview article; Sun.

Bibliography

Adamovičs, Ludis. "Senlatviešu mitologija." In *Latviešu tautas dziesmas,* edited by Arvēds Švābe, Kārlis Straubergs, and Edīte Hauzenberga-Šturma, vol. 11, pp. 557–568. Copenhagen, 1956.

Balys, Jonas. "Parallels and Differences in Lithuanian and Latvian Mythology." In *Spiritus et Veritas,* edited by Auseklis, Societas theologorum Universitatis Latviensis, pp. 7–9. Eutin, Germany, 1953.

Bauer, Gerhard. "Gesellschaft und Weltbild im baltischen Traditionsmilieu." Ph.D. dissertation, Ruprecht-Karls-Universität, Heidelberg, 1972.

Biezais, Haralds. *Die himmlische Götterfamilie der alten Letten.* Uppsala, Sweden, 1972.

Bynum, David E. *The Dæmon in the Wood: A Study of Oral Narrative Patterns.* Cambridge, Mass., 1978.

Dorson, Richard M. "The Eclipse of Solar Mythology." *Journal of American Folklore* 68 (1955): 393–416. Reprinted in *The Study of Folklore,* edited by Alan Dundes, pp. 53–83. Englewood Cliffs, N.J., 1965.

Eliade, Mircéa. *Cosmos and History: The Myth of the Eternal Return.* New York, 1959.

Karjalainen, K. F. "Die Religion der Jugra-Völker. I." *Folklore Fellows Communications* 8, no. 41 (1921): 1–204. See especially pages 20–21.

Lord, Albert B. "Theories of Oral Literature in the Latvian *Dainas.*" In *Linguistics and Poetics of Latvian Folk Songs,* edited by Vaira Vīķe-Freiberga [Vaira Vīķis-Freibergs], pp. 35–48. Montreal and Kingston, Ontario, 1989.

Mannhardt, Wilhelm. "Die lettischen Sonnenmythen." *Zeitschrift für Ethnologie* 7 (1875): 73–104; 209–329.

Mannhardt, Wilhelm. *Letto-preussische Götterlehre.* Riga, Latvia, 1936.

Setälä, Emil N. "Das rätsel vom Sampo." *Finnisch-ugrische Forschungen* 22 (1934): 177–203.

Vīķe-Freiberga, Vaira [Vaira Vīķis-Freibergs]. "Myth and Metaphor in Latvian *Dainas.*" In *Baltic Literature and Linguistics,* edited by A. Ziedonis Jr., J. Puhvel, R. Šilbajoris, and M. Valgemae, pp. 127–134. Columbus, Ohio, 1973a.

Vīķe-Freiberga, Vaira [Vaira Vīķis-Freibergs]. "The Poetic Imagination of the Latvian *Dainas.*" *Mosaic* 6, no. 4 (1973b): 209–221.

Vīķe-Freiberga, Vaira [Vaira Vīķis-Freibergs], and Imants Freibergs. *Saules dainas.* Montreal, 1988.

Vīķe-Freiberga, Vaira. *Trejādās saules: I. Kosmoloģiskā saule.* Riga, Latvia, 1997. An analysis of the themes in Latvian folksongs about the sun.

Vīķe-Freiberga, Vaira. *Trejādās saules: II. Hronoloģiskā saule.* Riga, Latvia, 1999.

Vīķe-Freiberga, Vaira. *Trejādās saules: III. Meteoroloģiskā saule.* Riga, Latvia, 2002.

Zicāns, Eduard. "Die Ewigkeitsahnung im lettischen Volksglauben." *Studia Theologica* II (1940): 41-63.

Vaira Vīķe-Freiberga (2005)

SAURA HINDUISM is the branch of Hinduism in which the sun is worshiped as the principal deity. The first clear evidence of sun worship in India comes from the Vedas, the collections of ritual hymns produced by the Aryans who entered India around 1500 BCE. Several *devas* ("powers" or "deities") praised in the Vedas had solar qualities, and the sun was also a *deva* in his own right as Sūrya or Āditya, the visible sun, and as Savitṛ, the stimulator of life. Vedic ritual practice honored the sun with daily recital of the Gayātrī *mantra* to Savitṛ and sacrifices to Sūrya. Despite this recognition, however, the sun was never considered the most important *deva* during the Vedic period.

Vedic sacrificial religion was basically aniconic. The only visible solar *deva,* Sūrya was represented in some Vedic rituals by symbols such as a twelve-petaled lotus, a wheel, or a golden disc, but the first anthropomorphic images of the sun god were stone reliefs of Sūrya in a one-wheeled chariot from Buddhist sites at Bodh Gayā and Bhaja in the first century BCE. These images indicate the emergence of Sūrya as a popular, but subsidiary, deity, a status that he maintained throughout southern India. In the North, however, Sūrya worship was transformed by foreign influence into Saura Hinduism.

The context of this transformation was the conquest of northern India late in the first century CE by the Indo-

Scythian empire of the Kushans, which extended from Central Asia through Bactria to its capital at Mathura. Contact with the neighboring Parthian empire opened the way for Iranian as well as Scythian influences during the century and a half of Kushan rule. Together, these influences changed the earlier solar religion into a popular theistic sect with distinctive foreign features.

The first change was the iconographic remodeling of Sūrya to look like a Kushan ruler with a close-fitting Scythian tunic and boots, an iconography that was preserved in all subsequent images of Sūrya in northern India. The second development, as described in the main text of Saura Hinduism, the *Sāmba Purāṇa,* was the creation of a major center of Sūrya worship at Multan in the Punjab by Sāmba, a son of Vāsudeva Kṛṣṇa, who also brought magi from Iran to serve as priests. A major concern of the *Sāmba* was thus not only to exalt the worship of Sūrya as savior but to justify the use of magi as brahmans in the cultic ritual.

There was already a major temple at Multan by the time the oldest portion of the *Sāmba* was written early in the sixth century; the text mentions further centers of Sūrya worship in Mathura and Orissa. Expansion continued throughout northern India for many centuries, but the sect went into rapid decline after the fifteenth century. The temple at Multan has not survived, and most Sūrya temples show the effects of long neglect. The eighth-century Sūrya temple at Martand in Kashmir and the eleventh century temple at Modhera in Gujarat, however, show the range of Saura influence, and the great thirteenth-century Sun Temple at Konarak in Orissa proves the grandeur of its vision.

SEE ALSO Sun.

BIBLIOGRAPHY

The qualities of all of the solar *devas* that appear in the Vedic hymns are described in detail in A. A. Macdonell's *Vedic Mythology* (Strassburg, 1897; reprint, New York, 1974). The evolution of Sūrya images is comprehensively traced and explained in Jitendra Nath Banerjea's *The Developement of Hindu Iconography,* 2d ed., rev. & enl. (Calcutta, 1956). The historical and cultural context of the early Sūrya sect is provided in John M. Rosenfield's *The Dynastic Arts of the Kushans* (Berkeley, Calif., 1967). The history, contents, and significance of the *Sāmba Purāṇa* are given careful scholarly treatment in R. C. Hazra's *Studies in the Upapurāṇas,* vol. 1, *Saura and Vaisnava Upapurāṇas* (Calcutta, 1958). Descriptions and illustrations of the extant Sūrya temples are provided in Percy Brown's *Indian Architecture,* vol. 1, *Buddhist and Hindu Periods,* 5th ed. (Bombay, 1965). A brief but interesting description of the Sūrya temple at Multan in 641 CE is given in the accounts of the Chinese Buddhist pilgrim Xuanzang in Samuel Beal's *Si-yu-ki, Buddhist Records of the Western World* (London, 1884; reprint, Delhi, 1981).

New Sources

Mahapatra, Sitakant. *Tribal Wall Paintings of Orissa.* Bhubaneswar, 1991.

Patnaik, N., ed. *The Saora.* Bhubaneswar, 1989.

THOMAS J. HOPKINS (1987)
Revised Bibliography

SAUTRĀNTIKA. Most available sources agree that the Sautrāntika school separated from the Sarvāstivāda perhaps some four centuries after the death of Śākyamuni Buddha. Its followers were called Sautrāntika, meaning those who take the sūtras as the last word, because although they accepted the two main parts of the Buddhist canon (the Tripiṭaka), namely, the Vinaya and the Sūtras, as the true word of the Buddha, they rejected the third part, the Abhidharma of the Sarvāstivāda tradition, considering it later philosophical disquisition, which for them had no binding authority. However, the Sautrāntikas must have remained effectively a branch of the Sarvāstivāda, as they continued to follow the same Vinaya, or monastic discipline, and their differences remained not so much practical as philosophical. They are sometimes referred to by such variant names as *Sūtrāntavādins* or *Sūtrapramāṇikas* (meaning the same as *Sautrāntika*), or as *Saṃkrāntivādins,* referring to their theory of rebirth or transmigration (*saṃkrānti*). Names such as *Saurodayika* ("like the sunrise," perhaps a reference to one of their famous teachers) and *Dārṣṭāntika* ("users of similes") are also applied to them. As a philosophical movement deriving from the Sarvāstivāda school, they distinguished themselves primarily from the Vaibhāṣikas, namely, those who adhered to the *Vibhāṣa* (Philosophical disquisition), a text based upon the (Sarvāstivāda) Abhidharma literature, and who maintained the reality of *dharmas* in all three times: past, present, and future.

According to the Chinese monk Xuanzang, who visited India between the years 627 and 645, the Sautrāntika recognized Ānanda, the closest disciple of Śākyamuni, as their chief master. According to another Chinese scholar their founder was called Uttara. Some Tibetan sources say that this school was called Uttarīya ("superior") in recognition of its superiority with regard to Dharma. Bhavya relates that the Saṃkrāntivāda was also called Uttarīya and that its founder, Uttara, seceded from the Sarvāstivāda. Tāranātha maintains that the names Saṃkrāntivāda, Uttarīya, and Tāmraśatīya all referred to the same school. A Chinese source asserts that one Pūrṇa, who propagated the Vinaya and Abhidharma teachings, encountered opposition from some monks who thereupon took Ānanda, the master of the Sūtras, as their patron. Vasumitra believes that the Sautrāntika and the Sarvāstivāda held similar teachings, but Vasubandhu and Saṃghabhadra concentrate mainly on the polemics between these two schools. In the Abhidharma literature there are references to four people who are said to have been the "four suns" of the Sautrāntikas: Kumāralābha, reputed as the founder of this school, Dharmatrāta, Buddhadeva, and Śrīlābha. Some modern scholars assert that such well known Buddhist thinkers as Vasubandhu, Dignāga, or even

Dharmakīrti were adherents or sympatizers of the Sautrāntikas.

Like the teachings of several other early Buddhist schools whose writings have been lost, Sautrāntika theories are known mainly from the surviving literature of other philosophical schools, Hindu as well as Buddhist, who most often refer to the Sautrāntikas in the process of refuting views at variance with their own. Although such references are bound to be partisan, it is nonetheless possible to gain a fair idea of Sautrāntika doctrines from them. In that these doctrines clearly serve as a link between the realistic atomizing theories of the earlier schools and the "mind only" (*cittamātra*) theories of the Yogācāra tradition, such an endeavor is all the more rewarding.

While the Sautrāntika adhere to the fundamental Buddhist "dogma" of *anātman* ("no-self," i.e., no transmigrating element) they reinterpret the earlier theory of *dharmas* (elemental particles), of which the five components (*skandhas*) of individual personality are said to be composed. Individual personality is essentially a nonentity (a "no self"), definable as a constant flux of elemental psychophysical particles, momentarily composing themselves under the effect of *karman* as form or matter (*rūpa*), feelings *(vedanā),* perceptions *(saṃjñā),* impulses *(saṃskāra),* and consciousness *(vijñāna),* namely as the five components. The main point at issue between the Vaibhāṣikas and the Sautrāntikas concerns the operation of *karman* upon the elemental particles resulting in a new interpretation of their nature. According to the Sarvāstivāda, all elements exist in past, present and future; hence their name, coined from *sarvāsti* ("everything exists"). An individual personality is therefore an ever-changing flow of real elements, the components of which vary from moment to moment in accordance with its *karman.* The Sarvāstivāda argue that every action projects its eventual effect upon the fluctuating stream of elements in the form of a fresh type of elemental particle known as *prāpti,* literally "acquisition" or "appropriation." Although itself of momentary existence like all other particles, *prāpti* continues to remanifest itself in the general stream of elements until an appropriate combination with other elements, themselves the effects of subsequent actions, produces the "fruit" or retribution of that particular action. Thus, *prāpti* may be regarded as the force that acts within a particular stream of elements (i.e., an individual personality) keeping it united as a seemingly coherent entity, not only within a single life-stream but also in the passage from one life to the next.

Since personality is also regarded under the threefold aspect of body, speech, and mind, action (*karman*) is definable as physical, vocal, or mental. Probably all Buddhists agree that mind or thought predominates in some way, but the extent and manner of its predominance presented a major area of discussion and disagreement among the early schools. Applying the theory of real elemental particles to everything, the Sarvāstivāda identified mental action as "volition" *(cetanā),* while vocal and physical action, treated as an "expression" (*vijñapti*) of volition, were classed as elements within form or matter (*rūpaskandha*). Thus, mental action would cause the arising of vocal or physical action according to the normal process of *karman* throughout past, present, and future, and all elements in the process remain equally "real." The Vatsīputriyas, on the other hand, argued that vocal and physical acts are not real elements or "things in themselves" but a mere "process" or "motion" *(gati)* provoked by mental *karman* or volition, which receives expression *(vijñapti)* thereby.

The Sautrāntikas rejected the concept of action as operative in the past, present, and future; thus, strictly speaking, an action cannot result in an effect in the future, since neither past nor future can exist simultaneously with the present. The past *has* existed and the future *will* exist in relationship to the ever passing present, but only the present can actually exist and its existence is momentary (*kṣaṇika*). Thus bodily and vocal action resulting from mental action (i.e. thought) cannot exist in the manner envisaged by the Sarvāstivāda or Vaibhāṣika, and their concept of *prāpti* as a holding force can have no meaning. Likewise, *vijñapti* as the "expression" of thought has no real existence in itself; indeed, it is only the mental action as volition that exists, possessing moral value as good, bad, or indifferent. The Sautrāntikas analyze volition under three aspects: "deliberation" (*gaticetanā*), "decision" (*niścayacetanā*), and "impulsion" (*kiraṇacetanā*). It should be noted that all three terms include *cetanā,* "mentation," or the process of thinking. The first two constitute the "action of thinking" (*cetanākarma*), which in effect is volition, manifest as mental reflection (*manaskāra*) or thoughts (*caitta*). They both represent the "action of thought" (*manaḥkarma*). The third aspect, "impulsion" (*kiraṇacetanā*), is twofold: that which impels bodily movement and that which impels speech. This explanation reduces the actions of body and speech, conceived by the Vaibhāṣikas as realities (classed within the *rūpaskandha*) that succeed mental action throughout a time process, to mere aspects of volition, which alone is a reality, manifesting itself momentarily in what is always effectively the present. It is thus thought alone that has moral value as good, bad, or indifferent.

The Sautrāntikas claim that the maturing of *karman* as the "fruit" or effect of morally qualifiable volition can be explained by the manner in which the mental series evolves. An action, being a thought associated with a particular volition, is momentary (*kṣaṇika*). It disappears the very moment it is committed (and thus has no real duration as explained by the Sarvāstivāda) but it impregnates (*vāsanā*) the mental series (*cittasaṃtāna*) of which it forms a starting point with a particular potentiality (*śaktiviśeṣa*). The impregnated series undergoes an evolution (*pariṇāma*) of varied periods of time and culminates in the final transformation-moment (*viśeṣa*), which constitutes the state of retribution. The evolution of the series is compared to a seed and its gradual transformational growth until it matures as a fruit.

The Sautrāntikas had to answer certain objections as to what happens when the series is interrupted, as for instance in suspended meditation. A primitive interpretation, as represented by the Dārṣṭāntika view, assumed the theory of two simultaneous series, one mental, constituted by the six consciousnesses, and one material, constituted by the corresponding sense organs. When the mental series is interrupted it resumes in due course its evolution from its seeds or germs (*bīja*) that are preserved in the material series. Similarly, the material series, when it is interrupted (in death or in the meditative trances of the *ārūpyadhātu),* becomes reborn from its seeds preserved by the mental series. But where, it may be asked, is the continuity of the series as such? How are the germs retained? The answer of the Sautrāntikas is to assert the existence of a subtle thought (*sūkṣmacitta*) underlying the mental series and constituting its continuity.

Subtle thought was defined by the Sautrāntika thinkers in two different ways: some said it was mental consciousness (*manovijñana*) free of concepts (*saṃjñā*) and feeling (*vedanā*); others envisaged it as mental consciousness (*citta*) free of mentations (*caitta*). Both groups agreed that its objective sphere (i.e., its real nature) is "imperceptible" (*asaṃvidita*). This subtle consciousness was known by such other names as *ekarasaskandha* ("aggregate[s] of one flavor or nature"), *mūlāntikaskandha* ("origin and cause of the five *skandhas*"), and *paramārthapudgala* ("true and real person"). Later, the nature of "subtle consciousness" was explained by distinguishing two kinds of thought: a multiple or complex mind (*nānacitta*) as represented by the six kinds of active consciousnesses, and a store or subtle thought (*ācayacitta*). The complex mind and the elements (*dharmas*), all of which evolve simultaneously, impregnate the subtle thought with their seeds or germs.

The complex mind functions through different objects (*ālambana*), aspects (*ākāra*), and modalities (*viśeṣa*). The Sautrāntikas argued that when these functions of complex mind are absent, as in, for instance, a state of suspended meditation, the state is deprived of thought in the sense that the series is interrupted, but that in fact this absence does not indicate total interruption because subtle thought continues to exist, serving as a repository of all the seeds (*sarvabīja*) deposited by the complex mind. As the series evolves, the seeds mature and produce their "fruit" (retribution), which consists of a new (good or bad) complex mind and elements. As the subtle consciousness is the sustainer of these new or matured seeds, it is also called the "consciousness of retribution" (*vipākaphalavijñāna*). From the time of birth until the moment of death the subtle mind constitutes the continuity of the series and it transmigrates (*saṃkrāmate*) from one existence to the next, assuming different manifestations (reincarnations). Once it reaches the moment of passing into *nirvāṇa* (final retribution or deliverance) it is cut off and completely extinguished. This interpretation was criticized but also adopted with modifications by the Vijñānavāda and Mādhyamika schools.

The Sautrāntika rejected the existence of the unconditioned elements (*asaṃskṛta*). For them, these elements were not real or distinct entities but represented mere denomination of absence. Thus, space (*ākaśa*) represented an absence of tangible bodies (*spṛṣṭavya*) and *nirvāṇa* denoted the nonmanifestation of passions and adverse psychophysical elements. They also denied the reality of the fourteen "unassociated" elements (*cittaviprayuktasaṃskāra*), among which origination, duration, decay, and impermanence in particular were viewed not as entities but as mere denominations of the flux of the elements.

The Sautrāntika maintained that the objects of the external world are not really perceived because, being momentary, they disappear before they can be perceived. Thus, the object of cognition, being already passed as soon as it appears, is not perceived directly; it leaves behind an image that is reproduced in the "act of cognition." Such a process gives the impression that it exists, while in fact it only did so in the now nonexistent past.

In opposition to other schools, which maintained that only a person who was advanced on the path toward arhatship might possess the potentiality (*anāsravaskandha*) of liberation, the Sautrāntika maintained that ordinary people (*pṛthagjana*) had the same potentiality. Finally, they also asserted that apart from the Noble Eightfold Path (*āryāṣṭāṅgamārga*) there was no other way to destroy the *skandhas*; meditation and other practices can suppress the passions (*kleśas*) but cannot eradicate them completely.

SEE ALSO Buddhism, Schools of; Buddhist Philosophy; Dharma, article on Buddhist Dharma and Dharmas; Indian Philosophies; Sarvāstivāda; Soul, article on Buddhist Concepts; Vasubandhu; Yogācāra.

BIBLIOGRAPHY

No single work treats the Sautrāntika school as whole. Our chief source of information on the tradition is Vasubandhu's *Abhidharmakośa* (and *bhāṣya)* and works composed in reference to it, especially Yaśomitra's *Abhidharmakośa sphuṭārthavyākhyā*. The references listed below are sources of further information.

Lamotte, Étienne, ed. and trans. "Le traité de l'acte de Vasubandhu: Karmasiddhiprakaraṇa." *Mélanges chinois et bouddhiques,* vol. 4, pp. 151–288. Brussels, 1935–1936.

Masuda, Jiryo. "Origin and Doctrines of Early Indian Buddhist Schools." *Asia Major* 2 (1925): 1–78.

Mimaki Katsumi. "Le chapitre de Blo gsal grub mtha' sur les Sautrāntika, un essai de traduction." *Memoirs of the Research Institute for Humanistic Studies* (Kyoto) 16 (1979): 143–172.

New Sources

Cox, Collett. "On the Possibility of a Nonexistent Object of Consciousness: Sarvāstivādin and Dārṣṭāntika Theories." *Journal of the International Association of Buddhist Studies* 11, no. 1 (1988): 31–87.

Cox, Collett. *Disputed Dharmas, Early Buddhist Theories on Existence: An Annotated Translation of the Section on Factors Dissociated from Thought from Sanghabhadra's Nyāyānusāra.* Tokyo, 1995.

Klein, Anne, trans. *Knowing, Naming, and Negation: A Sourcebook on Tibetan Sautrāntika.* With oral commentary by Geshe Belden Drakba. Ithaca, N.Y., 1991.

La Vallée Poussin, Louis de. *Abhidharmakośabhāṣyam.* Translated by Leo M. Pruden. 5 vols. Berkeley, 1988–1990.

Williams, Paul, with Anthony Tribe. *Buddhist Thought: A Complete Introduction to the Indian Tradition.* London, 2000. See Chapter 4.

TADEUSZ SKORUPSKI (1987)
Revised Bibliography

SAVONAROLA, GIROLAMO (1452–1498), was a Dominican preacher, reformer, and prophet. Savonarola was born in Ferrara, Italy, and under the eye of his grandfather, the distinguished court physician Michele Savonarola, was educated in religious and liberal studies before going on to medicine. A story that he was disappointed in love, and his early poem *De ruina mundi* give some insight into his decision to enter the Order of Friars Preachers in 1475. In Bologna he completed his novitiate and attended the Dominican Studium Generale. In 1482 he went to Florence as reader in the Observant Dominican convent of San Marco. The recently rediscovered Borromeo Codex, containing Savonarola's sermon notes, poetry, and other writings from this period, shows a young reformer in process of development rather than the born prophet portrayed by his hagiographers. The moralizing, ascetic sermon drafts contain none of the spectacular visionary themes, still less the millenarian themes, of Savonarola's later preaching. Still under the influence of Scholastic homiletics with its labored, allegorical exegesis, he was just beginning to find a more personal and direct, if as yet unflamboyant, style.

In 1484, ruminating on the wickedness of the world, he conceived "on the basis of scripture" that the church had imminently to be scourged and reformed, and he announced his new apocalyptic reading of scripture in his Lenten sermons in San Gimignano in 1485 and again in 1486. He was appointed *magister studiorum* in Bologna in 1487, and in the next few years he gained attention as a preacher in various north Italian cities. In 1490 he was reassigned to San Marco at the request of Lorenzo de' Medici, unofficial ruler of Florence, who may have been prompted by Giovanni Pico della Mirandola, one of the friar's admirers. Elected prior, he briefly considered taking his friars into the woods of a nearby mountain valley, but instead he concentrated upon reforming San Marco and preaching in the city. He began to criticize tyrants as corrupters of the people, and he warned of coming tribulations. He was aware that he might share the fate of other preachers, most recently Bernardino da Feltre, who had been expelled from Florence for stirring up unrest; but the city's rulers made no effort to pluck this latest thorn from the flesh of the body politic, perhaps because they were pleased by Savonarola's fruitful efforts to create a new Tuscan congregation of Dominican houses with San Marco at its center, perhaps because they knew it would be difficult to dislodge him without scandal among his widespread following. With Piero de' Medici, who succeeded Lorenzo in 1492, he seems to have been on good terms.

By the 1490s rumbles of the earthquake that was to destroy Italy's facade of collective security were beginning to be heard. Charles VIII (1483–1498) was heralded as the new Charlemagne, who would restore French imperial glory, cross the sea to conquer "the Infidel," and convert the world into a single sheepfold under one shepherd. To Savonarola he was the *flagellum Dei* who would scourge the church and carry the children of Israel into captivity. Florence, that den of iniquity, would suffer with the rest. In the fall of 1494 Charles invaded Italy, and his opposition melted away as he marched to the frontiers of Tuscany. A frightened Piero de' Medici hurried to the king's camp and surrendered the key Florentine strongholds. Returning to Florence, Piero encountered a city in revolt, and he fled. After sixty years of Medici domination Florence had recovered its liberty.

Savonarola's standing as a popular champion and prophet gave him unrivaled authority. Holding no civic office, he exercised his influence through preaching (now supported by visions), through meetings with civic leaders, and through political allies in the city's councils. He charted a course between direct democracy and narrow oligarchic reaction, the chief feature of which was a new Great Council with hereditary qualifications for admission and sovereign powers on the model of Venice. In the city's religious institutions he changed little, but he sought to introduce a spiritual revolution through moral reform. Ascetic conduct was urged from pulpits and enjoined by new laws and by youthful vigilantes organized from San Marco. Religious processions replaced secular festivals; bonfires of "vanities" consumed the tokens of "worldliness"; specially written lauds celebrated the millennial glories of a spiritually revitalized Florence. The Jews, tolerated by the Medici regime, were expelled, and a public loan fund (Monte di Pietà), advocated by Franciscan preachers, was set up. Ignoring his earlier warnings of tribulation and doom, Savonarola now envisioned Florence as the New Jerusalem, center of liberty and virtue, from which would radiate the new era, when Florence would be "richer, greater, more powerful than ever."

Inevitably, however, Savonarola's insistence that the French king was Florence's divinely elected champion led to the city's political isolation in Italy, and the longer Charles put off his return, the lower Savonarola's credit dropped. His avoidance of the pope's summons to Rome and his disobedience to a command of silence led to his excommunication, and a papal interdict for harboring him threatened the city. All this created a situation that Savonarola's enemies could exploit. He was unable to block a Franciscan's challenge to a trial by fire, and he bore the brunt of the blame when this eagerly awaited test failed to take place. A mob attacked San Marco, and Savonarola and two other friars were imprisoned, interrogated, and tortured. Altered versions of Savonarola's confession to false prophecy and political conspiracy were published. On May 23, 1498 the three friars were hanged and burned on a specially constructed scaffold in Florence's main civic square.

The Savonarolan republic survived until 1512, when the Medici were restored by Spanish troops. It was revived by a revolt in 1527, in which *piagnone,* or Savonarolan, ideology played a fundamental role. Once again revolutionary millenarianism and puritanical republicanism flowed from San Marco. Once again the Jews were expelled. Prostitutes were banned. Pro-Medicean utterances were made a capital offense. Enemies of the regime were exiled. Blasphemers and sodomites were put to death. Such uncompromising fanaticism alienated republican moderates and strengthened the hand of the Medici, who came back to the city in 1530. As a political movement "piagnonism" was finished, although the cult of Savonarola thrived and has been revived periodically up to the present day. Its traces can be discerned in the Risorgimento biography by Pasquale Villari, the Catholic modernist life by Joseph Schnitzer, and the cinquecentennial biography by Roberto Ridolfi. Hagiography apart, Savonarola's sermons and devotional works continued to be printed and read in Italy, Spain, France, and Germany. Savonarolan piety, with its emphasis upon individual religious experience, charity, and the way of the cross of Christ, was admired by Martin Luther. A statue of the Dominican was erected in Wittenberg, although Savonarola surely belongs more to the Catholic than to the Protestant reformation.

BIBLIOGRAPHY

Cattin, Giulio. *Il primo Savonarola: Poesie e prediche autografe dal Codice Borromeo.* Florence, 1973.

Polizotto, Lorenzo. "The Piagnoni and Religious Reform, 1494–1530." Ph. D. diss., University of London, 1975.

Ridolfi, Roberto. *The Life of Girolamo Savonarola.* Translated by Cecil Grayson. New York, 1959.

Schnitzer, Joseph. *Savonarola: Ein Kulturbild aus der Zeit der Renaissance.* 2 vols. Munich, 1924.

Weinstein, Donald. *Savonarola and Florence: Prophecy and Patriotism in the Renaissance.* Princeton, N. J., 1970.

DONALD WEINSTEIN (1987)

ṢAWM in Islam signifies fasting, an act of worship that consists of religiously intended abstention from eating, drinking, and sexual intercourse from dawn until dusk. Muḥammad introduced it in AH 1 (622 CE) by fasting and asking his followers to fast on ʿĀshūrāʾ, the tenth day of the month of Muḥarram, in deference to the Jewish practice. The following year came the Qurʾanic revelation (surah 2:183ff.) whereby the ʿĀshūrāʾ fast was replaced by the fast of Ramaḍān.

The Qurʾān indicates that fasting is an inalienable part of the religious life of people, since it was prescribed for Muslims as well as "for those before you," in order "that you become pious" (2:183). The earmarking of Ramaḍān, the month in which "the Qurʾān was sent down" (2:185), for fasting seems to be a recognition of the centrality of the Qurʾān in Muslim religious life and an attempt to reinforce it. In Muslim understanding, fasting is a means of fostering piety, of celebrating the glory of God, and of thanking him for revealing the Qurʾān, "a guide for mankind, and clear signs for guidance, and judgment" (2:185).

Except for a very few days of the year, Muslims may fast whenever they wish to as an act of supererogation. Fasting is so meritorious that in addition to obligatory fasting pious Muslims frequently observe voluntary fasting (*ṣawm al-taṭawwuʿ*), seeking self-purification and spiritual growth. Certain days and months have been specially recommended for voluntary fasting.

Fasting is obligatory for anyone who makes a vow to fast. In certain circumstances fasting has been prescribed as an alternative means of atonement. In addition, those who miss any days of the Ramaḍān fast (apart from the elderly or incurably sick) must make up the fast at a later date.

RAMAḌĀN. As one of the "Five Pillars" of Islam, the fast of Ramaḍān has a special position in Muslim religious life. All Muslims who have attained puberty and are in full possession of their senses are obliged to fast. Persons who are sick or traveling, and pregnant or nursing women, are exempted. Women in their periods of *ḥayḍ* ("menstruation") or *nifās* ("bleeding on the childbed") are not allowed to fast, although they are required to make up later for those days missed. The elderly and the incurably sick are totally exempted from fasting, but for every day of fasting missed they should feed one poor person.

Each day's fast commences when "the white thread of dawn appears to you distinct from the black thread" (2:187), and fasting restrictions remain applicable until sunset. This poses a problem in the polar regions, where days and nights are sometimes indistinguishable; it has been suggested, therefore, that the times of sunrise and sunset at the forty-fifth parallel be considered standard for determining times for fasting for places lying between the forty-fifth parallel and the pole.

It is recommended that those who fast should have a meal (*saḥūr*) before dawn, preferably as late as possible. Likewise, it is highly recommended that after sunset one should hasten *ifṭār,* the breaking of the fast. Any food or beverage may be taken for *ifṭār,* although dates or water is preferred. *Ifṭār* is usually a light meal and is taken hastily, since the *maghrib* ("sunset") prayer is performed minutes after sunset. It is considered highly meritorious to provide *ifṭār* to others, especially to the poor. It is common among Muslims to have *ifṭār* together in the neighborhood mosque and to invite friends, relatives, and neighbors to *ifṭār* parties.

Infractions of fasting such as eating, drinking, smoking, sexual intercourse, or indulgence in love play leading to seminal emission invalidate the fast. Such infractions variously necessitate *qāḍā'* ("restitution") alone, or *qāḍā'* and *kaffārah* ("atonement"). *Qāḍā'* consists of fasting one day for each day of invalidated fasting, whereas *kaffārah* necessitates the liberation of one Muslim slave, two months of consecutive fasting, or the feeding of sixty of the poor. Both *qāḍā'* and *kaffārah* are necessary when the fast of Ramaḍān is deliberately and voluntarily broken without extenuating reasons such as travel or sickness. The jurists are agreed that sexual intercourse necessitates both *qāḍā'* and *kaffārah*. In cases of eating and drinking, the Shāfiʿī and Ḥanbalī schools prescribe only *qāḍā'*, whereas the Ḥanafī and Māliki schools prescribe *qāḍā'* and *kaffārah*.

Ramaḍān is a month of concentrated worship and charity. Muslims have been urged to perform special prayers in the evening called *tarāwiḥ*. These consist, according to most Muslims, of twenty *rakʿahs*, or prayer sequences; they are generally performed in congregation, with the whole of the Qur'ān recited over the month. The last ten days of Ramaḍān, especially the nights, are considered highly blessed, since one of them is Laylat al-Qadr, the Night of Power, which is "better than a thousand months," the night in which "angels and the spirits descend and it is peace till the rising of the dawn" (97:4–6). Devout Muslims spend the better part of these nights praying and reciting the Qur'ān. It is also recommended that Muslims observe *iʿtikāf* ("withdrawal") during Ramaḍān, especially in its last ten days. *Iʿtikāf* consists of withdrawing to a mosque and devoting oneself exclusively to worship. Moreover, following the example of the Prophet, whose charitableness and philanthropy were heightened during Ramaḍān, Muslims show much greater propensity to charity at this time.

The end of Ramaḍān, signaled by the sighting of the new moon, is celebrated in the ʿĪd al-Fitr (the festival marking the end of fasting). The religious part of the ʿĪd consists of two *rakʿahs* of prayers in congregation and payment of a fixed charity, *ṣadaqat al-fiṭr*. The ʿĪd, however, also has an important social dimension. Muslim cities and villages take on a festive look, people usually wear their best clothes, and friends, relatives, and neighbors meet in mosques or on streets, congratulating, embracing, and kissing each other. The exchange of visits is also quite common.

SIGNIFICANCE AND INNER DIMENSION OF ṢAWM. The legal minutiae associated with *ṣawm* sometimes prevent appreciation of its religious significance and inner dimension. Religiously sensitive Muslims are not satisfied merely with observance of the outward rules, which serve as an assurance against the invalidity of the fast but not of its acceptance by God. The Prophet is reported to have said that "he who does not abandon falsehood and action in accordance with it, God has no need that he should abandon his food and drink." The desire to make one's fasting acceptable to God has led devout Muslims to emphasize the qualitative aspect of fasting. Al-Ghazālī (d. 1111), for instance, emphasized that abstention from food, drink, and sexual satisfaction is only the elementary level of fasting. At a higher level fasting means keeping one's ears, eyes, tongue, hands, and feet free from sin. And at a still higher level fasting means a withdrawal of the heart and mind from unworthy concerns and worldly thought in total disregard of everything but God.

A major object of fasting, in al-Ghazālī's view, is for humans to produce within themselves a semblance of the divine attribute of *ṣamadīyah*, freedom from want. Another scholar, Ibn Qayyim al-Jawzīyah (d. 1350), viewed fasting as a means of releasing the human spirit from the clutches of desire, thus allowing moderation to prevail in the carnal self. Shāh Walī Allāh (d. 1762), one of the most famous South Asian theologians, viewed fasting as a means of weakening the bestial and reinforcing the angelic element in humans. A contemporary Muslim thinker, Sayyid Abū al-Aʿlā Mawdūdī (d. 1979), emphasized that fasting "for a full month every year trains a man individually, and the Muslim community as a whole, in piety and self-restraint; enables the society—rich and poor alike—to experience the pangs of hunger; and prepares people to undergo any hardship to seek the pleasure of God."

SEE ALSO Islamic Religious Year; Worship and Devotional Life, article on Muslim Worship.

BIBLIOGRAPHY

No comprehensive monograph on fasting is available. For relevant materials, see the notes on the Qur'anic verses 2:183–187 in the major works of *tafsīr* (Qur'anic exegesis) and the chapters on *ṣawm* or *ṣiyām* in the major *ḥadīth* collections and works of *fiqh*. Al-Bukhārī's and Muslim's collections of *ḥadīth* are available in English translation: See *The Translation of the Meanings of Ṣaḥīḥ al-Bukhārī*, 4th ed., 9 vols., translated by Muḥammad Muḥsin Khān (Chicago, 1977–1979), and *Ṣaḥīḥ Muslim*, 4 vols., translated by Abdul Hameed Siddiqui (Lahore, 1971–1975). See also Muḥammad ibn ʿAbd Allāh al-Khaṭib al-Tibrīzī's *Mishkāt al-maṣābīḥ*, 4 vols., translated by James Robson (Lahore, 1963–1965). For useful works in English with full chapters on *ṣawm*, see *Inner Dimensions of Islamic Worship* (Leicester, 1983), a partial translation by Muhtar Holland of al-Ghazālī's *Iḥya' ʿulūm al-dīn*; Abulhasan Alī Nadvī's *The Pillars of Islam*, translated by Mohammad Asif Kidwai (Lucknow, 1972); and G. E. von Grunebaum's *Muḥammadan Festivals* (New York, 1951).

The impact of *ṣawm* on the lives of people, especially the ways in which Ramaḍān has been and is being observed in different Muslim lands, is a subject worth exploring. Good sources are travel accounts written by Muslims as well as outsiders.

ZAFAR ISHAQ ANSARI (1987)

SAXO GRAMMATICUS

SAXO GRAMMATICUS (c. 1150–after 1216) was a Danish historian whose writings (*Gesta Danorum*) constitute one of the few important early sources on Germanic mythology and religion. Saxo studied in France and later became secretary to the Danish archbishop Absalon, who suggested that he write a history of Denmark. By 1200 he had completed seven books covering the monarchy from Harald II (known as Bluetooth) to Knut IV (a period from c. 950–1086.) During the next decade, he wrote nine more books on the mythical traditions of antiquity prior to Harald II. He drew upon all available sources, both oral and written, and wrote excellent Latin, including verse in various classical meters. He was well acquainted with Norse saga traditions, which he had either heard as a boy or learned from Icelandic poets. He wove the legendary material into a continuous narrative, taking liberties as he pleased. Book 3 contains the earliest mention of the Hamlet story.

Saxo's importance is threefold. Much of his material provides corroboration of other mythological documentation, in particular the works of Snorri Sturluson. Furthermore, some of Saxo's material is all that exists on certain topics, because of the loss of original texts. Finally, his legendary tales demonstrate his euhemeristic method of transforming myths into history. A fine example of all three points is the saga of Hadingus (*Gesta Danorum* 1.5–8). The main character, Hadingus, is none other than the god Njǫrđr transformed into a hero. The parallels are striking. Both figures have two relationships with women. The earlier relationship in each case is incestuous (Njǫrđr with his sister and Hadingus with the giantess Harthgrepa, who had nurtured him as a child). The later relationship for each comes about when the woman uses a special method of selecting her mate (Skađi chooses Njǫrđr on the basis of his beautiful feet, while Regnilda picks out Hadingus by his legs). In this saga, Saxo corroborates the information provided by Snorri on Njǫrđr. Like Njǫrđr, Hadingus is a master of the ocean, having power over the winds and familiarity with the seas. Saxo provides copious detail on how Hadingus acquired this mastery; such detail in respect to Njǫrđr is completely lacking in other sources. There are many other examples of Saxo's euhemerization of the Norse pantheon, such as his transformation of Freyr to Frothi, Baldr to Balderus, and Skađi to Høtherus. Saxo and Snorri used the same sources, but Snorri's rendition of the old myths is more adept.

SEE ALSO Germanic Religion; Njǫrðr; Snorri Sturluson.

BIBLIOGRAPHY

An English translation of Saxo's *Gesta Danorum* is Hilda R. Ellis, ed., *The History of the Danes,* vol. 1 (Cambridge, 1979), translated by Peter Fisher; Fisher and Ellis wrote the commentary that makes up volume 2 (Cambridge, U.K., 1980). A recent collection on Saxo is Carlo Santini, ed., *Saxo Grammaticus: Tra storiografia e letteratura* (Rome, 1992); see especially the articles by Teresa Paroli, Anatoly Liberman, Mats Malm, Regis Boyer, and Margaret Clunies Ross. See also Karsten Friis-Jensen, *Saxo Grammaticus As Latin Poet: Studies in the Verse Passages of the Gesta Danorum* (Rome, 1987). Georges Dumézil's *From Myth to Fiction: The Saga of Hadingus* (Chicago, 1973) is a work on Saxo and his importance for Indo-European myth and religion. Dumézil's *Gods of the Ancient Northmen* (Berkeley, Calif., 1973), edited by Einar Haugen, contains his tripartite structure of Indo-European religion as reflected in the Germanic branch. Jan de Vries, *Altnordische Literaturgeschichte,* 2d ed. (2 vols., Berlin, 1964–1967), contains much useful information on Saxo.

JOHN WEINSTOCK (1987 AND 2005)

SAYERS, DOROTHY L. (1893–1957) was a writer whose theology found expression through many literary genres. Sayers began her education in languages at the age of seven when her father, a Church of England clergyman, began teaching her Latin. She gained first-class honors at Somerville College, Oxford, in 1915, and in 1920 was among the first group of women allowed to take their B.A. and M.A. degrees from Oxford. She earned her living as an advertising copywriter while establishing herself as a poet and as a writer of detective fiction, inventing her character Lord Peter Wimsey. Her novel *Gaudy Night,* published in 1935, is both a detective story and an unabashed defense of academic and intellectual work as undertaken by women, for whom she was a provocative advocate throughout her life. In her detective fiction she explored the emotional cost to Wimsey and others of establishing the truth about the circumstances of the various deaths of her fictional characters, and she also explored the mediation of impartial divine justice through the relatively imperfect procedures of the rule of law in the society of her day.

Thoroughly familiar with the Book of Common Prayer and the Authorized Version of the Bible, and with her beliefs formed and framed by the demanding theology of the Church of England's matins and evensong, Sayers made outstanding contributions to the development of religious drama, from works written for radio broadcast to plays written for performance in cathedrals. Outstanding were her twelve radio plays—the first broadcast on December 21, 1941—collectively titled *The Man Born to Be King.* These broke new ground in having the portrayed voice of Jesus of Nazareth "on the air," and Sayers thus helped to open the door to depicting the Gospel in various ways on stage and screen.

In 1941 Sayers published a significant (and unjustly neglected) work on Trinitarian theology, *The Mind of the Maker,* elaborating her conviction that human creativity provides clues to divine creativity, and exploring the analogy of human and divine creativity via the concepts of "Creative Idea," "Creative Energy," and "Creative Power." Sayers also gave valuable stimulus to thinking again about the integrity of the arts and about their neglect in her day, despite their roots in Christian tradition. Her work was of considerable interest to authors as different as T. S. Eliot (1888–1965), C. S. Lewis (1898–1963), and Charles Williams (1886–1945).

Sayers owed a particular debt of gratitude to Williams, himself a writer and editor of poetry, novels, essays, and theology. In 1943 he published *The Figure of Beatrice,* which plunged Sayers back into reading Dante Alighieri's *Divine*

Comedy in its original Italian. She and Williams exchanged an ecstatic series of letters during what turned out to be the last nine months of Williams's life. Sayers found in Dante someone whose love for and recollection of a living human person, Beatrice, enabled him to symbolize the full humanity of women, for Dante's Beatrice was a mistress of philosophy and science as well as of theology. He represented her as the perfect integration of the intellectual, the emotional, and the bodily in her own great beauty, supremely well fitted for teaching Dante whatever he needed to know, as well as being for him the sacramental mediator of grace and salvation.

The reading and appreciation of Dante reinvigorated Sayers's own theology, and through her lectures and publications on Dante she brought theology to a wide audience. Her translation and commentary in 1949 of *Cantica I: Hell*, the first section of *The Divine Comedy*, led to the only academic honor she accepted after her first degrees: a doctorate of letters given to her in 1950 by England's University of Durham. After Sayers's unexpected death in 1957, Barbara Reynolds completed Sayers's translation of *Cantica III: Paradise*—a tribute to years of collaboration with her.

BIBLIOGRAPHY

Dante Alighieri. *The Comedy of Dante Alighieri the Florentine. Cantica I: Hell; Cantica II: Purgatory; Cantica III: Paradise.* Translated by Dorothy L. Sayers. Harmondsworth, Middlesex, England, 1949, 1955, 1962. The first two volumes include Sayers's theological introduction, notes, and commentary on her translation; the third volume required completion of the translation by Barbara Reynolds, and appropriate notes and commentary.

Loades, Ann. "The Sacramentalist's Agenda: Dorothy L. Sayers." In *Feminist Theology: Voices from the Past* by Ann Loades, pp. 167–192. Oxford and Malden, Mass., 2001. This chapter assesses Sayers's critique of the deficiencies of Christian anthropology so far as women are concerned, and the resources she found for her critique in the work of Dante.

Reynolds, Barbara. *The Passionate Intellect: Dorothy L. Sayers' Encounter with Dante.* Kent, Ohio, 1989.

Reynolds, Barbara. *Dorothy L. Sayers: Her Life and Soul.* London, 1993. Major biography by Sayers's collaborator, who also edited the letters of Sayers, published in four volumes between 1995 and 2000.

Sayers, Dorothy L. *The Mind of the Maker.* London, 1941.

Sayers, Dorothy L. *Introductory Papers on Dante.* London, 1954.

Sayers, Dorothy L. *Further Papers on Dante.* London, 1957.

Sayers, Dorothy L. *Spiritual Writings.* Selected and introduced by Ann Loades. London, 1993. A selection, with introductions to each section, of Dorothy L. Sayers's theological work in a variety of literary genres.

ANN LOADES (2005)

SCANDINAVIAN RELIGION

SEE GERMANIC RELIGION

SCAPEGOAT.

Scapegoat rituals are among the oldest known rituals. A more rudimentary form is already found in two texts from Ebla dating to the later third millennium BCE, but the first full-fledged descriptions come from outlying parts of the Hittite empire, Kizzuwadna, Hapalla, and Arzawa (i.e., city-states in southeast Anatolia and northern Syria). The prescription of Ashella, a man of Hapalla, which dates to the thirteenth century BCE, reads:

> When evening comes, whoever the army commanders are, each of them prepares a ram—whether it is a white ram or a black ram does not matter at all. Then I twine a cord of white wool, red wool, and green wool, and the officer twists it together, and I bring a necklace, a ring, and a chalcedony stone and I hang them on the ram's neck and horns, and at night they tie them in front of the tents and say: "Whatever deity is prowling about (?), whatever deity has caused this pestilence, now I have tied up these rams for you, be appeased!" And in the morning I drive them out to the plain, and with each ram they take 1 jug of beer, 1 loaf, and 1 cup of milk (?). Then in front of the king's tent he makes a finely dressed woman sit and puts with her jar of beer and 3 loaves. Then the officers lay their hands on the rams and say: "Whatever deity has caused this pestilence, now see! These rams are standing here and they are very fat in liver, heart, and lions. Let human flesh be hateful to him, let him be appeased by these rams." And the officers point at the rams and the king points at the decorated woman, and the rams and the woman carry the loaves and the beer through the army and they chase them out to the plain. And they go running on to the enemy's frontier without coming to any place of ours, and the people say: "Look! Whatever illness there was among men, oxen, sheep, horses, mules, and donkeys in this camp. And the country that finds them shall take over this evil pestilence." (Cited in Gurney, 1977, p. 49)

The ritual is clearly an ad hoc purification performance and not tied to the calendar. It is applied in times of pestilence, combines both a decorated human and an adorned animal, and finally, it is offered by the king and the army commanders to the hostile deity who has caused the pestilence. Interestingly, the ritual was appropriated from northern Syria by both the Greeks and the Israelites, each in a specific manner that fitted their own particular religion.

THE GREEK UNDERSTANDING. In the Greek world, the rituals surface for the first time in the writings of the sixth-century Ionian poet Hipponax of Colophon, a city on the western coast of modern Turkey, where Anatolian religious influence is well attested. According to Hipponax, somebody was thrown down on a meadow and whipped with fig branches and squills "like a scapegoat" to purify the city. The scapegoat also received dried figs, bread, and cheese and even reappears in the context of the Thargelia, a two-day festival of first-fruit offering and seasonal renewal. According to other descriptions, especially from Athens and Massilia, the scapegoats were often people of low standing in the community but temporarily treated very well and dressed up in nice clothes. At a certain day they were led out of the city—sometimes carrying food, such as loaves and beer or dried figs, bread, and cheese—in a procession in which probably the whole of the population had to take part and during which pipers played a specific, undoubtedly unharmonious tune.

Origen (c. 185–c. 254) even compared the Greek scapegoats with Jesus: "They [the apostles] not only dared to show to the Jews from the words of the prophets that he was the prophesied one, but also to the other peoples that he, who had been recently crucified, *voluntarily* died for mankind, like those who died for their fatherland, to avert plague epidemics, famines, and shipwreck" (*Contra celsum* 1.31). Voluntariness of a victim was an important part of Greek sacrificial ideology, which stressed that a victim was pleased to go up to the altar, sometimes could even hardly wait to be sacrificed. This voluntariness is also stressed in Greek scapegoat rituals.

Finally, the scapegoats were expelled from the city through stoning and pelting. Yet it is clear (whenever sufficient information is available) that they were not killed. However, the effect must have been a social death and the corresponding myths always speak of a real death, which classical scholars long, if erroneously, translated into a former human sacrifice. The myths, especially as given shape in the tragedies of Euripides (c. 480–406 BCE), often mention a cult for those scapegoats whose death had saved the city. In other words, those who had given their lives for the community also received a special honor from that community. Finally, the location of the scapegoat ritual on the Thargelia shows that the Greeks had incorporated the ritual into their festival calendar, but as pestilences always strikes unexpectedly, they also performed the ritual if need arose.

In these Greek scapegoat rituals, there is a clear difference with those of the Hittites. Whereas among the latter the king and the army commanders play the main role in the ritual, in Greece it is the city that needs to be cleansed, as is stated by Hipponax. This element gained in importance in the classical period, when the polis became the center of a Greek's life. Strikingly, the city is reportedly saved by girls, perhaps in their capacity as the more expendable parts of the household. In these myths, the element of purifying, which was so prominent in the ritual, has receded, whereas the saving effect has come to the foreground. Although the ritual probably stopped being performed in the fourth century, this aspect stayed alive through the telling of the myths, just like the expendable quality of the scapegoats: Several of the terms to denote the victim (e.g., *pharmakos*, *perikatharma*, or *peripsema*) long remained in use as insults.

THE JEWISH INTERPRETATION. Whereas several notices from all over Greece exist about the scapegoat ritual, knowledge of ancient Israel is limited to chapter 16 of the *Book of Leviticus*, which describes the day of atonement. The date of the final redaction of the chapter is much debated, but it seems safe to date it to the postexilic era before the arrival of Alexander the Great (356–323 BCE). The chapter is a complicated mixture of several rituals. There is first the expiation for the sins of the high priest, Aaron, and his house through the sacrifice of a young bull (*Lev.* 16:3). Regarding the scapegoat proper, Aaron had to select two goats (*Lev.* 16:5), the cheapest of the domesticated animals. After a lottery, one of them was assigned to Yahweh, and the other was meant for Azazel, a still obscure deity or demon (*Lev.* 16:7–10). Second, Aaron then had to transfer the sins of the Israelites onto the goat by laying his hands on the goat (*Lev.* 16:21), an archaic means of transfer that could still derive from the Hittite rites but that is absent from the Greek material. Finally, somebody (not further specified) had to take the goat to the desert (*Lev.* 16:21), which was clearly structurally similar to the enemy in the Hittite texts or the area beyond the borders in the Greek traditions. As was the case with the Greek scapegoats, the Israelite goat apparently escaped with its life, which gave it its English name, (e)scapegoat, whereas the German Reformer Martin Luther wanted to emphasize the transfer of the sins and therefore introduced the word *Sündebock* (sin-goat) into the German language.

The day of atonement also occurs in the Dead Sea Scrolls from Qumran dated to the period around the times of Jesus, even though the ideas about atonement in the Qumran community have not yet been satisfactorily studied. The beginning of the ritual is related in an *Apocryphon of Moses* (4Q375), but the *Temple Scroll* (11Q19 25) mentions an expansion of the initial sacrifices. Instead of the bullock as sin-offering and the ram as burnt-offering, it describes a burnt-offering for Yahweh consisting of a bullock, a ram, and seven yearling lambs; a sin-offering of a goat; and a burnt-offering of two rams for the high priest with the house of his father (and presumably for the people, but the text is corrupt at this place). Further details are given about the exact treatment of the various parts of the offerings and the catching of their blood in a golden sprinkling bowl, but the expulsion of the scapegoat resembles that of *Leviticus.*

A few additional details can be gleaned from the Mishnah treatise *Joma*, even though it was written after the destruction of the Temple. According to the text, the position of the high priest within the ritual had become more important, because his role was dramatized: The preparations had been intensified (*Joma* I) and instead of linen clothes, he now wore golden ones (*Joma* III 4a). Also noted is the participation of members of the Sanhedrin (*Joma* I 3a) and the aristocracy of Jerusalem (*Joma* VI 4b)—apparently, the upper class of Israel had deemed it necessary to become visibly involved in its most important religious ritual. The goat was adorned with a crimson thread around its head (*Joma* IV 2a, VI 6a), very much like the Hittite scapegoat.

Evidently, Israel had also appropriated the Anatolian scapegoat ritual, although the date and route of derivation are still totally unclear. However, like the Greeks, the Israelites did not take over the ritual unchanged. Whereas the Hittites used both animals and humans as scapegoats, the Greeks only selected humans and the Israelites, only animals. Moreover, in the postexilic period at the latest, they had integrated the ritual into the temple service and thus fixed it at a specific date, even though its archaic origin still remains visible.

Early Christian Understanding. An intriguing problem remains the influence of the scapegoat ritual on the birth of the early Christian idea of the atonement. Clearly, Jesus himself did not yet interpret his coming death as an atoning sacrifice for the salvation of humanity. Moreover, attempts at finding a Jewish background for the doctrine have also been unsuccessful. This does perhaps suggest an influence from the Greek mythological tradition as inspired by the scapegoat ritual, because only here do people voluntarily die to save the community from a catastrophe. Unfortunately, the exact road along which the early Christians came to this interpretation has remained obscure, but Palestine was already highly Hellenized in Jesus' time and Euripides' tragedies, which often treat the theme of the saving human sacrifice, were also well known to educated Jews. Still, there is much uncertain here, and no consensus has been reached in this field.

The notice of Origen quoted previously suggests that scapegoat rituals could also be performed at sea. Undoubtedly, he thought in this connection of the story told in the homonymous *Book of Jonah.* The prophet Jonah is en route to Nineveh when storms threaten to engulf his ship. The crew concludes that one man is culpable and should be thrown into the sea. Jonah is saved only by a great fish (traditionally known as a whale), which spits him out after three days. The story exemplifies the principle that the death of one person can save the whole of the community. It is undoubtedly an old principle. The Babylonian epic of creation *Enuma elish* already mentions in a sentence of a guilty god: "He alone shall perish that mankind shall be fashioned." And indeed, parallels from all over the world show that this principle (i.e., to give up one or a few persons to save the group) is very widespread and seems to be part of the human makeup. It was sometimes even ritualized in a very similar manner to the scapegoat rituals previously discussed (e.g., in Tibet).

Scapegoat as Social Phenomenon. On a more general level, it is clearly also a very widespread phenomenon that people consider that crises (economic, political, social) have been caused by a specific person or minority. As a rule, people do not like to blame themselves and would rather accuse others. This mechanism is already in place in the great European witch-hunts from the fourteenth to seventeenth centuries. Here the culprits were especially looked for among old women (a very vulnerable group in earlier times), free masons, Jews, and heretics. As these people must be considered guilty of some act, normally in these cases they are accused of the most horrific crimes, such as incest, sodomy, or the killing of children. Such accusations were even put into writing as in the notorious nineteenth-century anti-Semitic fake *The Protocol of the Elders of Zion* and used to legitimate the murder of the Jews by the Nazis. As the elimination of the scapegoats often goes concomitant with the restoration of some social order, the link between the two processes can be easily argued, and thus the scapegoat mechanism perpetuates itself. Politicians who take the blame in a crisis may even receive special praise and return to the political stage at a later date. In other words, the mechanisms of the scapegoat pattern are observable in contemporary society.

These observations led the French literary critic René Girard (b. 1923) to formulate a theory about the scapegoat that was enormously influential in the last decades of the twentieth century. Girard noted the elements that have been previously mentioned: (1) a crisis, (2) the selection of victims not because of real crimes but because they belong to a social (e.g., Jews, heretics, old women) or physical (e.g., disabled) minority, (3) the restoration of the social order through the violence against the scapegoats. In this process, the community lets one member—preferably an outsider so that there will be no revenge and the violence perpetuated—die for the whole. Girard has long been fascinated by the problem of violence, and his views have to be seen against this background. According to him, society is driven by a mimetic desire: People long to have what other people long to have. These desires often result in violence, and the death of the scapegoat that can eliminate this violence. Only religion is able, according to Girard, to keep a lid on human violence by its disciplining character. Girard's work is very stimulating, and his anthropological insights illuminating. Yet he evidently often confuses mythical stories and history, and his grand theory should be taken as an incitement to reflect about violence rather than as a resolution of a problem that plagues human existence.

See Also Atonement; Sacrifice; Violence.

Bibliography

For general studies, see Walter Burkert, *Structure and History in Greek Mythology and Ritual* (Berkeley, Calif., 1979), pp. 59–77, 168–176; Jan N. Bremmer, "The Scapegoat between Hittites, Greeks, Israelites and Christians," in *Kult, Konflikt und Versöhnung,* edited by Rainer Albertz, pp. 175–186 (Münster, Germany, 2001). For Jonah-type stories see Lutz Röhrich, *Gesammelte Schriften zur Volkslied- und Volksballadenforschung,* pp. 113–154 (Münster, Germany, 2002). For the Eblaite origin, see Ida Zatelli, "The Origin of the Biblical Scapegoat Ritual: The Evidence of Two Eblaite Texts," *Vetus Testamentum* 48 (1998): 254–263. The Hittite rituals are easily accessible in Oliver R. Gurney, *Some Aspects of Hittite Religion,* pp. 47–52 (Oxford, 1977). For the Greek ritual, see Robert Parker, *Miasma,* pp. 258–280 (Oxford, 1983); Jan N. Bremmer, "Scapegoat Rituals in Ancient Greece," in *Oxford Readings in Greek Religion,* edited by Richard Buxton, pp. 271–93 (Oxford, 2000).

For the Israelite ritual, see Bernd Janowski and Genrot Wilhelm, "Der Bock, der die Sünden hinausträgt," in *Religionsgeschichtliche Beziehungen zwischen Kleinasien, Nordsyrien und dem Alten Testament,* edited by Bernd Janowski, Klaus Koch, and Gernot Wilhelm, pp. 109–169 (Freiburg, Germany, 1993). The origin of the Christian idea of the atonement is much discussed. See especially Jan N. Bremmer, "The

Atonement in the Interaction of Jews, Greeks, and Christians," in *Sacred History and Sacred Texts in Early Judaism,* edited by Jan N. Bremmer and F. García Martínez, pp. 75–93 (Kampen, Germany, 1992) and Cilliers Breytenbach, "'Christus starb für uns.' Zur Tradition und paulinischen Rezeption der sogenannten 'Sterbeformeln,'" *New Testament Studies* 49 (2003): 447–475. For the ideas of Girard, see especially René Girard, *Des choses cachées depuis la fondation du monde* (Paris, 1978) and *Le bouc émissaire* (Paris, 1982).

JAN N. BREMMER (2005)

SCARIFICATION SEE BODILY MARKS

SCHECHTER, SOLOMON

SCHECHTER, SOLOMON (c. 1847–1915), was a Talmud scholar and educator. A product of four distinct European cultural ambiences, Solomon Schechter came to New York in 1902 to lead a reorganized Jewish Theological Seminary of America. During the thirteen years of his presidency he exerted a formative influence on an emergent American Judaism by facilitating the gradual transfer of the academic study of Judaism from the old to the new world and by creating the institutions, leaders, and rhetoric of a movement for Conservative Judaism.

Born in the still largely traditional Jewish society of eastern Romania, Schechter came to Vienna in his mid-twenties with a formidable mastery of classical Jewish texts. A four-year stay in the 1860s at the rabbinical school founded by Adolf Jellinek gave him rabbinic ordination, command of the new Western methods of Jewish scholarship, and a lasting affection for his teacher, Meir Friedmann. In 1879 Schechter moved on to Berlin to continue his training as a Jewish scholar at the recently opened Hochschule für die Wissenschaft des Judentums, where he came under the influence of Israel Lewy, the outstanding critical Talmudist of his generation. In 1882 he received an invitation from Claude Montefiore, whom he had befriended at the Hochschule, to come to England as Montefiore's tutor in rabbinic literature. Five years later he gave resounding evidence of his scholarly abilities with a model critical edition of an early homiletical rabbinic text, *Avot de Rabbi Natan.* Dedicated to Montefiore, it combined Friedmann's love of *midrash* with Lewy's critical method.

By 1890 Schechter had achieved academic respectability, though not financial security, with a lectureship (later a readership) in rabbinics at Cambridge University. During the next decade he moved quickly to the forefront of a lackluster generation of Jewish specialists ensnared by the pulpit and polemics. His scholarship was marked by a sweep, competence, and originality usually associated with the polymaths who had founded the *Wissenschaft des Judentums.* Prior to his departure for America, Schechter published the first fruits of his eventual synthesis of rabbinic theology (1894–1896), a collection of popular essays on Jewish history and literature (1896), a good part of the Hebrew original of *Ben Sira* (1899), and the first volume of a large Yemenite *midrash* on the Pentateuch (1902). Of still greater consequence was Schechter's dramatic foray in January 1897 into the long-abandoned *genizah* of Cairo, where he was compelled "to swallow the dust of centuries" in order to exhume and bring to Cambridge an inexhaustible trove of manuscripts from ancient and medieval sources related to Jewish society and culture.

A scholar of international renown, a superb expositor of Judaism in English, a charismatic personality, a religious moderate, and a man of culture—these were the qualities that made Schechter so attractive to the plutocracy of American Jews of German descent who were eager to revitalize the Jewish Theological Seminary. For his part, Schechter wished to escape the growing burdensomeness of his religious isolation and inadequate salary at Cambridge.

Once in New York, Schechter moved to replicate the academic model pioneered in Breslau, Vienna, Berlin, and Budapest: a nonpartisan rabbinical school free of outside rabbinic control whose graduates would be immersed in the academic study of Judaism. Schechter insisted that every applicant have the B.A. degree, "bearing evidence of his classical training," and recruited a young, largely European-trained faculty of great promise to challenge the often unsympathetic Christian scholarship on Judaism.

Religiously, Schechter articulated an inchoate conception of Judaism that was anti-Reform, pro-Zionist, while remaining open to all historical expressions of Judaism, all-embracing, and responsive to change. He rejected Reform's excessive rationalism, eagerness to "occidentalize" Judaism, preoccupation with Judaism's mission, and minimal commitment to the Hebrew language. His own broad embrace is best documented in his inimitable three-volume *Studies in Judaism* (London, 1896, 1908; Philadelphia, 1924), which cherishes every historical expression of Judaism. Choice and change are ultimately effected "by the collective conscience of Catholic Israel," and history supplements scripture as a medium of revelation. Despite the implicit historicism of this view, Schechter failed to enunciate a procedure for sanctioning change and, indeed, dedicated most of his energy to defending what the past had sanctified. In 1906 he dared to defy his own benefactors, the wealthy and anti-Zionist Jews who had brought him to the United States, by avowing Zionism as an antidote to the erosion of Jewish identity.

The persistent weakness of the seminary forced Schechter by the end of his first decade of leadership to consider building a congregational base that would provide additional support. After protracted deliberations, the United Synagogue of America was founded in 1913 with Schechter as its first president. The occasion, however, did not provide for further ideological clarification. The omission of any reference to "Conservative" in the organization's preamble epitomized the reluctance of Schechter and his associate Cyrus

Adler to form a "third party in Israel." The coalescence of a religious movement was to be the achievement of others during the interwar period, after Schechter's death.

SEE ALSO Conservative Judaism.

BIBLIOGRAPHY

Ben-Horin, Meir. "Solomon Schechter to Judge Mayer Sulzberger." *Jewish Social Studies* 25 (1963): 249–286, 27 (1965): 75–102, and 30 (1968): 262–271.

Bentwich, Norman De Mattos. *Solomon Schechter.* Philadelphia, 1948.

Millgram, Abraham E., and Emma G. Ehrlich. "Nine Letters from Solomon Schechter to Henrietta Szold." *Conservative Judaism* 32 (Winter 1979): 25–30.

Oko, Adolph S. *Solomon Schechter: A Bibliography.* Cambridge, 1938.

Parzen, Herbert. *Architects of Conservative Judaism.* New York, 1964.

Rosenblum, Herbert. "The Founding of the United Synagogue of America, 1913." Ph. D. diss., Brandeis University, 1970.

New Sources

Karp, Abraham J. *Jewish Continuity in America: Creative Survival in a Free Society.* Tuscaloosa, Ala., 1998.

Montefiore, Claude Goldsmid. *Lieber Freund: The Letters of Claude Goldsmid Montefiore to Solomon Schechter, 1885–1902.* Edited by Joshua B. Stein. Studies in Judaism. Lanham, Md., 1988.

Starr, David Benjamin. "The Importance of Being Frank: Solomon Schechter's Departure from Cambridge." *Jewish Quarterly Review* 94 (2004): 12–18.

ISMAR SCHORSCH (1987)
Revised Bibliography

SCHELER, MAX

SCHELER, MAX (1874–1928). German philosopher. Scheler was born in Munich on August 29, 1874, and died, after a dramatic life filled with personal misfortunes, in Frankfurt on May 19, 1928. He taught philosophy at the universities of Jena, Munich, and Cologne.

His thought is divided into two periods. In the first, up to 1921, he concentrated on value ethics and the strata of human emotions; in the second, he was occupied with metaphysics, sociology, and philosophical anthropology. Both periods are characterized by numerous studies in religion, culminating in the thought of the "becoming" Deity that is realizing itself in human history.

The first period centered on three major works: *Wesen und Formen der Sympathie* (1913), *Der Formalismus in der Ethik und die materiale Wertethik* (1913–1916), and *Vom Ewigen im Menschen* (1921). It is characterized by Scheler's phenomenology and, extrinsically, by Roman Catholicism, to which he had been converted in his early life. Scheler's phenomenology is distinct from Husserl's in that (1) Scheler, unlike Husserl, did not conceive consciousness to be absolute but, rather, dependent on the "being of person," and also because (2) for Scheler all regions of consciousness through which entities are given in their particular nature (e.g., as animate or inanimate, etc.) are ultimately based in the region of the absolute, in which each person relates to what he holds to be absolute. This made Scheler the forerunner of phenomenology of religion.

In *Vom Ewigen im Menschen* and other works Scheler showed how this region of the absolute can be "filled" by various gods, fetishes, or even nihilism. Therefore, he posed a basic question: What is it that gives itself adequately—and how does it accomplish this—in this region of the absolute of human consciousness? His answer: God as person. For Scheler, God is experienceable only through "love" of divine personhood, not through rational acts. Love itself is an emotive act and prior to perception and knowledge. Love reveals an order *(ordo amoris)* in which values are "felt." The highest value is the "holy." The human heart, as the seat of love, has its own "logic" (as Pascal held). In the heart, and not in knowledge, God as person is phenomenologically "given."

In his second period, Scheler abandoned this form of theism, without however abandoning the primacy of love. He now conceived the deity as unperfected, becoming, and in strife with itself. He explained this process in terms of two opposite divine attributes: urge (*Drang*) and spirit (*Geist*). Scheler reached his conclusion about the deity through a "transcendental elongation" of humanity's own nature, that is, by setting humanity's own vital urge, which posits reality, in opposition to the human mind, which bestows ideas on reality. The vital urge is humanity's self-moving, self-energizing life center in which the deity's urge also pulsates. Without urge and drives the mind would remain "powerless" and "unreal." There is no mind unless it is "in function" with the self-propulsion of life. Hence, God's spirit also requires divine urge for its realization. The theater of this divine process is human and cosmic history, in which deity "becomes" as it struggles for its realization. Humanity is called upon to "co-struggle" with this divine becoming.

Scheler died without resolving the question whether or not the theogenetic process would ever reach completion. He held, however, that the uncreated process of the becoming of human, world, and deity had reached a "midpoint" toward both spiritualization and divinization of both humanity and life. In 1926, Scheler envisioned the future as a new, long, and perilous "world era of adjustment" between the too-intellectual and active West and the more passive East. The future, thought Scheler, would reflect gradual balance and less struggle between spirit and urge; history will become "less historical" as God ever more "becomes" in it.

BIBLIOGRAPHY

The best introductory reading of Scheler's first period of philosophy of religion remains his own *Vom Ewigen im Menschen,* 6th ed., in his *Gesammelte Werke,* vol. 5 (Munich, 1968). The English translation by Bernard Noble, *On the Eternal in*

Man (London and New York, 1960), is not always an acceptable rendition of the German original. It should be read in conjunction with part 2 of Scheler's *Der Formalismus in der Ethik und die materiale Wertethik,* 6th ed., vol. 2 of his *Gesammelte Werke* (Munich, 1980), translated as *Formalism in Ethics and Non-Formal Ethics of Values* (Evanston, Ill., 1973) by myself and Roger L. Funk. Scheler's *Wesen und Formen der Sympathie* (Bonn, 1931) has been translated by Peter Heath as *The Nature of Sympathy* (London, 1954). Recommended as general introductions are *Process and Permanence in Ethics: Max Scheler's Moral Philosophy,* by Alfons Deeken, S.J. (New York, 1974); and *Max Scheler,* by Eugene Keely (Boston, 1977); as well as my own book, *Max Scheler: A Concise Introduction into the World of a Great Thinker* (Pittsburgh, 1965). Scheler's thought of the second period is available in his *Erkenntnislehre und Metaphysik,* in his *Gesammelte Werke,* vol. 11 (Munich, 1979). *Metaphysik des einen und absoluten Seins* (Meisenheim am Glan, 1975) by Bernd Brenk, and my study "Gott und das Nichts: Zum Gedenken des fünfzigsten Todestages Max Schelers," *Phänomenologische Forschungen* 6/7 (1978): 118–140. A list of currently available English translations of Scheler's works can be found in the *Journal of the British Society for Phenomenology* 9 (October 1978): 207–208.

MANFRED S. FRINGS (1987)

SCHELLING, FRIEDRICH

SCHELLING, FRIEDRICH (1775–1854), German philosopher. Born at Leonberg in Württemberg, Friedrich Wilhelm Joseph Schelling received his early education at the preparatory seminary at Bebenhausen, where his father, a Lutheran minister, was professor of Old Testament studies. From an early age, Schelling was exposed both to Lutheranism and to the Swabian mystical pietism of Bengel and Oetinger. Precociously entering the University of Tübingen at fifteen, he enthusiastically espoused (with his comrades G. W. F. Hegel and Friedrich Hölderlin) the ideas of the French Revolution and the philosophy of Kant. At the time of his first professorship in 1798, at Jena, Schelling had met J. G. Fichte, had published in significant journals, and had offered a synthesis of the new philosophy and the new natural sciences.

Schelling's philosophical career unfolded in four major periods: Fichtean transcendentalism (to 1796); systems synthesizing the history of consciousness and nature (to 1806); explorations of the ground of freedom and consciousness in the mode of mysticism (to 1820); and the final system, whose second and third parts describe the unfolding of idealism in the history of religion (1827–1843). Because of the years of friendship with Hegel at Jena after 1800 and their years of enmity after Hegel's first publications, we can only suspect Schelling's creative influence in ideas that today are associated with Hegel.

Of the great philosophers of the early nineteenth century, Schelling remains comparatively little known, and his thought is usually falsely presented as a sterile, unwieldy structure of mental forms drawn from his early works. Despite his youthful break with church and orthodoxy, Schelling's philosophy by 1802 had reexamined religion; his move first to Würzburg and then to Munich was crucial, for these cities placed him in contact with Franz von Baader, the rehabilitator of Meister Eckhart and Jakob Boehme, and with the vigor and sacramental mysticism of the Bavarian renaissance under Ludwig I. Stimulated particularly by Boehme, Schelling, in his important *Essay on Human Freedom* (1809), led German philosophy from the consideration of structures of consciousness to the enterprise of will. Beyond necessity and freedom, good and evil, a ground of the divine being in its longing for its own identity sets in motion an exoteric process. This process realizes itself in a triad of powers that guides the universe, human history, and God's own life.

After some years at the University of Erlangen, Schelling returned to join Baader, Joseph von Görres, Johann von Döllinger, and Johann Möhler at the new University of Munich. There, in 1827, he announced his final system, one that was not an exploration of transcendental concepts but a presentation of the birth of God in a trinitarian dialectic: a vast but real extension of dialectic into history, into religion, and then into the incarnation and kenosis of Christ. Although Schelling presented this system for over fifteen years, the final section on the age of the Holy Spirit and the church—the synthesis in the Johannine church of the dynamics of both Peter (Catholic) and Paul (Protestant)—was never developed beyond a few pages.

Theologically, Schelling was influenced by Neoplatonism, Lutheran Christianity, and forms of mysticism; he read extensively in the theological writings, Protestant and Catholic, of his time. From 1798 to 1830 he was the mentor of progressive Catholic theologians in the south, while Protestant theologians such as Karl Daub were initially impressed with his work. Schelling influenced Russian philosophy and theology and, through Coleridge, English culture; although rejected by the young Kierkegaard and Engels, in thinkers such as Paul Tillich and Gabriel Marcel the existentialism of his final thought touched the twentieth century. The centenary year of his death, 1954, began a new interest in Schelling, while the 1970s saw mature works on him as well as the initiation of a critical text.

BIBLIOGRAPHY

Complete bibliographies on Schelling's writings and secondary literature on him do not reach beyond the 1970s: Guido Schneeberger's *Vriedrich Wilhelm Joseph von Schelling: Eine Bibliographie* (Bern, 1954); Hans Jörg Sandkühler's *Friedrich Wilhelm Joseph Schelling* (Stuttgart, 1970); and my "F. W. J. Schelling: A Bibliographical Essay," *Review of Metaphysics* 31 (December, 1977): 283–309.

On Schelling and Christianity see the two dissertations by Paul Tillich available in English translations; Walter Kasper's *Das Absolute in der Geschichte: Philosophie und Theologie der Geschichte in der Spätphilosophie Schellings* (Mainz, 1965); my *Romantic Idealism and Roman Catholicism: Schelling and the Theologians* (Notre Dame, Ind., 1982). Emilio Brito has published large studies on Schelling and religious themes as has Marc Maesschalk. Xavier Tilliette's two-volume work, *Schelling: Une philosophie en devenir* (Paris, 1970), led to a number of volumes of essays in this field—some touch on the "speculative Christology" of German idealism—and ends with the magisterial study, *Schelling: Biographie* (Paris, 1999).

Work on the critical text is reaching the writings done after 1800, and the previous volumes have been accompanied by a series of specialized studies on areas touching the volumes published by Frommann-Holzboog in Stuttgart. The basic text of Schelling was republished by the Wissenschaftliche Buchgesellschaft in 1976. There are some recent translations into English, including four early works translated by Fritz Marti, three works published by Thomas Pfau including the "Stuttgart Seminars," a translation of *Die Weltalter* by Judith Norman, and one by Victor Hays of segments of the philosophies of myth and revelation.

THOMAS F. O'MEARA (1987 AND 2005)

SCHENIRER, SARAH (1883–1935), was a pioneer in religious education for Jewish females and founder of Baiš Ya'aḳov educational institutions. Born to a Belzer Hasidic family in Kraków, descendant of rabbinic scholars, Schenirer was a devout Jew who worked as a seamstress by day and spent her evenings in the private study of biblical texts and rabbinic legends, a discipline begun in her youth. This was unusual for a woman in her times and even as a child she was affectionately teased as "the little pious one."

In 1914, inspired by a sermon, Schenirer conceived the idea of Jewish classes for women. Until that time, Jewish education in eastern Europe was designed exclusively for men, inasmuch as rabbinic tradition interpreted the commandment to study Torah as incumbent upon males only. But Schenirer's religious fervor and love of sacred texts, combined with her fear of the inroads of cultural assimilation, secular Zionism, and Polish feminism, led her to radical innovation: the creation of a school that would both increase the knowledge and strengthen the faith of young Jewish women.

Despite initial setbacks, Schenirer persisted. Securing the blessings of the influential *rebe* of the Belzer Ḥasidim, in 1918 she opened her first school in her home, with two young aides whom she sent off after a year to establish schools in other communities. In 1919, the Orthodox Agudat Yisra'el movement adopted and expanded the network of Baiš Ya'aḳov (Yi., House of Jacob). By 1925, twenty schools were operating, including several high schools. In combining religious studies with secular and professional training, Baiš Ya'aḳov represented a synthesis of Polish Hasidic piety and Western enlightenment.

Schenirer soon relinquished executive duties but remained a central figure in the movement, a role model and personal source of inspiration to the students. She also founded the Baiš Ya'aḳov Teachers' Seminary and established the Bnoš (Daughters) Youth Organization for religious females.

Little is known of her personal life. Her first marriage ended in divorce; a primary factor in the couple's incompatibility was that her husband was less religiously committed and observant than she. She had no children and died of cancer at the age of fifty-two.

The Baiš Ya'aḳov movement suffered a terrible blow in the Holocaust. Most of the students and teachers who had been involved with Baiš Ya'aḳov between 1918 and 1939 did not survive. After the war, Baiš Ya'aḳov and Bnoš were reestablished and expanded in the United States, Israel, and Europe—with more of an eye, however, to conserving tradition than to bridging tradition and modernity, as was its aim in Schenirer's lifetime.

SEE ALSO Agudat Yisra'el.

BIBLIOGRAPHY

The most sophisticated analysis of Baiš Ya'aḳov as a religious, cultural, and political movement, and of Schenirer's role in it, is Deborah Weissman's "Baiš Ya'aḳov: A Historical Model for Jewish Feminists," in *The Jewish Woman: New Perspectives,* edited by Elizabeth Koltun (New York, 1976), pp. 139–148. A more personal portrait of the woman and the movement is drawn by Judith Grunfeld-Rosenbaum, a former teacher in the Baiš Ya'aḳov institutions in Poland, in her article "Sarah Schenierer," in *Jewish Leaders, 1750–1940,* edited by Leo Jung (New York, 1953), pp. 405–432. The most valuable source of information is *Em be-Yisra'el: Kitvei Sarah Shenirer,* 4 vols. (Tel Aviv, 1955–1960), a collection of Schenirer's writings translated into Hebrew from the original Yiddish, including her diary, stories, and plays, as well as articles she wrote for the *Baiš Ya'aḳov Journal.*

New Sources

Teller, Hanoch. *Builders: Stories and Insights of Three Primary Builders of the Torah Renaissance.* New York, 2000.

BLU GREENBERG (1987)
Revised Bibliography

SCHIMMEL, ANNEMARIE. Annemarie Schimmel (1922–2003) was a German Orientalist and historian of religions. Born in Erfurt to a Protestant family, she started learning Arabic at the age of fifteen and studied Arabic, Persian, and Turkish beginning in 1939 in Berlin, where she completed her Ph.D. in 1941 at the age of nineteen, with a doctoral thesis on "Calif and Cadi in Late Medieval Egypt [i.e., in the late Mamluk period]." Schimmel then prepared her *Habilitation* on the military class in Mamluk Egypt and finished it, after World War II, in Marburg in 1946. While teaching Islamic languages and literature she prepared another thesis in *Religionswissenschaft* under the guidance of Friedrich Heiler, and she completed the newly established doctor of science in religion degree in 1951 with a thesis on the concept of love in Islamic mysticism. Although Schimmel was not a Muslim, she was given a five-year appointment as full professor of history of religions in the Islamic theological faculty of Ankara University in Turkey, a position she held from

1954 to 1959. She later taught Islamic languages at the universities of Marburg (1959–1961) and Bonn (1951–1967) and at Harvard University (1967–1992), where she was given the newly founded Chair of Indo-Muslim Cultures.

Schimmel lectured in Bonn after her retirement from Harvard in 1992, and continued there until shortly before her death. She also lectured in universities around the world, addressing audiences of all levels in Asia, Europe, and America. The various prestigious posts she held included serving on the editorial board of Mircea Eliade's *Encyclopedia of Religion* (1987) and as president of the International Association for the History of Religions (1980–1990). Schimmel also received many honorary doctorates and was highly decorated by academic and cultural institutions in both Western and Islamic countries. Among her many awards was the 1995 Peace Prize of the German Book Trade, which caused some political controversy due to a television interview in which she expressed some sympathy with the Muslims who were offended by Salmon Rushdie's *Satanic Verses.* Because of this episode, and because of meetings she had with Pakistan's Zia lu-Haq and other dictatorial Muslim leaders, this award was criticized. Though reports often circulated in the Islamic world about her conversion to Islam, in her will she requested a Protestant funeral, which was held in Bonn.

Schimmel's work concentrates on Islamic mysticism (*Mystical Dimensions of Islam,* 1975); on mystic poetry (*As Through a Veil,* 1982; *A Two-Colored Brocade,* 1992); on individual mystic writers (*I Am Wind, You Are Fire: The Life and Work of Rumi,* 1992; *Gabriel's Wing: A Study into the Religious Ideas of Sir Muhammad Iqbal,* 1963); on forms of Islamic veneration (*And Muhammad Is His Messenger,* 1983); on everyday Muslim practice (*Islamic Names,* 1989); and on other cultural expressions, such as calligraphy (*Islamic Calligraphy,* 1970; *Calligraphy and Islamic Culture,* 1984); as well as on surveys on specific literatures (*Islamic Literatures of India,* 1973; *Sindhi Literature,* 1974; *Classical Urdu Literature from the Beginning to Iqbal,* 1975) and on Islam in India and Pakistan (*Islam in the Indian Subcontinent,* 1980; *Islam in India and Pakistan,* 1982).

In the phenomenology of religion, Schimmel's inspiring Gifford Lectures, "Deciphering the Signs of God: A Phenomenological Approach to Islam" (1994), attempt to apply Heiler's categories of "Erscheinungsformen und Wesen der Religion" (Forms of manifestations and the essence of religion) to a specific religion, and to thus present a phenomenological introduction to a religion. The main thesis of her book *Wie universal ist die Mystik? Die Seelenreise in den grossen Religionen der Welt* (How universal is mysticism? The journey of the soul in the world's great religions, 1996) is that behind all the dogmatic differences in religious teachings there is a common ground accessible through mystic experience. These works explain why Schimmel distanced herself more and more from *Religionswissenschaft,* for which methodological approaches from such human sciences as the sociology of religion or the psychology of religion were more important than sympathy with religious experience.

In the field of Islamic mysticism, Schimmel follows the German tradition represented by Hellmut Ritter, Fritz Meier, and Richard Gramlich, and she used the vocabulary of German Christian mysticism as the prototype for translation of Islamic terms. Schimmel was one of the few representatives of this type of research. Along with Friedrich Max Müller, Schimmel was an important pioneer on research into the Indo-Muslim and Sanskrit Indian context. In the phenomenology of religion she was loyal to Heiler's approach, despite the development of new approaches in the study of religions.

Schimmel's numerous books and articles show a remarkably wide range of knowledge in all kinds of cultural phenomena, both Islamic and Western. Her works are equally appreciated by both Muslim and non-Muslim academics. She is one of the rare non-Muslims whose work has found uncontested acceptance in the world of Islam, and her writings have helped make Muslim thought known across Islamic cultures. The fact that Schimmel quotes from Sindhi, Pashto, Punjabi, Urdu, Persian, Turkish, and Arabic sources allowed her to widen the horizons of Muslims, as well as non-Muslims, to the great variety of religious expression within the Islamic world. Since she translated many of her books herself from her native German into English, and vice versa, most of her work is available in both languages. Moreover, she published works in several other languages (Asian and Western) so that her research could be understood in various linguistic contexts. In addition, many of her works have been translated into countless languages around the globe.

BIBLIOGRAPHY

For Schimmel's English-language works on Islamic mysticism, see *Mystical Dimensions of Islam* (Chapel Hill, N.C., 1975). On mystic poetry, see *As Through a Veil: Mystical Poetry in Islam* (New York, 1982); and *A Two-Colored Brocade: The Imagery of Persian Poetry* (London and Chapel Hill, N.C., 1992). On individual mystic writers, see *I Am Wind, You Are Fire: The Life and Work of Rumi* (Boston, 1992); and *Gabriel's Wing: A Study into the Religious Ideas of Sir Muhammad Iqbal* (Leiden, 1963). On forms of Islamic veneration, see *And Muhammad Is His Messenger: The Veneration of the Prophet in Islamic Piety* (London and Chapel Hill, N.C., 1983). On everyday Muslim practice, see *Islamic Names* (Edinburgh, 1989). On calligraphy, see *Islamic Calligraphy* (Leiden, 1970); and *Calligraphy and Islamic Culture* (New York, 1984). For surveys on specific literatures, see *Islamic Literatures of India* (Wiesbaden, Germany, 1973); *Sindhi Literature* (Wiesbaden, Germany, 1974); and *Classical Urdu Literature from the Beginning to Iqbal* (Wiesbaden, Germany, 1975). On Islam in India and Pakistan, see *Islam in the Indian Subcontinent* (Leiden, 1980); and *Islam in India and Pakistan* (Leiden, 1982).

Besides the English-language works listed above, several of Schimmel's German publications deserve mentioning. For Islamic mysticism, see "Sufismus und Volksfrömmigkeit" in *Der Islam,* vol. 3, *Islamische Kultur-Zeitgenössische Strömungen-Volksfrömmigkeit* (Stuttgart, Germany, 1990); *Meine Seele ist eine Frau: Das Weibliche im Islam* (Munich, 1995); *Jesus und Maria in der islamischen Mystik* (Munich, 1996); and *Sufismus: Eine Einführung in die islamische Mystik* (Munich, 2000). For Islamic literature, see *Nimm eine Rose und nenne sie Lieder: Poesie der islamischen Völker* (Cologne, Germany, 1987); *Aus dem goldenen Becher: Türkische Gedichte aus sieben Jahrhunderten* (Cologne, Germany, 1993); *Rumi: Sieh! Das ist Liebe, Gedichte* (Basel, Switzerland, 1993); and *Die schönsten Gedichte aus Pakistan und Indien: Islamische Lyrik aus tausend Jahren* (Munich, 1996). For cultural topics, see *Die orientalische Katze* (Cologne, Germany, 1983); *Das Mysterium der Zahl: Zahlensymbolik im Kulturvergleich* (Cologne, Germany, 1984); *Friedrich Rückert: Lebensbild und Einführung in sein Werk* (Freiburg, Germany, 1987); "Künstlerische Ausdrucksformen des Islam" and "Europa und der islamische Orient" in *Der Islam,* Vol. 3, *Islamische Kultur-Zeitgenössische Strömungen-Volksfrömmigkeit* (Stuttgart, Germany, 1990); *Die Träume des Kalifen: Träume und ihre Deutungen in der islamischen Kultur* (Munich, 1998); *Im Reich der Grossmoguln: Geschichte, Kunst, Kultur* (Munich, 2000); *Kleine Paradiese: Blumen und Gärten im Islam* (Freiburg, Germany, 2001); and *Das islamische Jahr: Zeiten und Feste* (Munich, 2001).

For autobiographical information, see *A Life of Learning: Charles Homer Haskins Lecture* (Washington, D.C., 1993); *Morgenland und Abendland: Mein west-östliches Leben* (Munich, 2002); and *Auf den Spuren der Muslime: Mein Leben zwischen den Kulturen,* edited by Hartmut Bobzin and Navid Kermani (Freiburg, Germany, 2002).

PETER ANTES (2005)

SCHISM

This entry consists of the following articles:

AN OVERVIEW
CHRISTIAN SCHISM

SCHISM: AN OVERVIEW

Schism is the process by which a religious body divides to become two or more distinct, independent bodies. The division takes place because one or each of the bodies has come to see the other as deviant, as too different to be recognized as part of the same religious brotherhood. Often disputes over doctrine or organization brew for years before some triggering incident incites the final break. During that preparatory period, groups of adherents slowly come to understand their procedures and convictions as being fundamentally different from those of the opposing group. The psychological and sociological process of separation is often complete before an organizational break occurs.

TYPES OF SCHISMS. One way to classify schisms is to look at who defines whom as deviant. Either the parent group or the departing group, or both, may see the other as having diverged from the true faith. In the first instance, when the parent group defines the schismatic group as deviant, the charge against it (or more often against its leader) is usually heresy. Ironically, such heretics do not usually set out to leave the parent body. Rather, they have new ideas about how the faith should be practiced or how the religious body should be organized; but in the course of promulgating their ideas, these reformers are found intolerable by the parent body and forced out. Such a process was most visible in the Protestant Reformation of the sixteenth century. But it also occurred within Protestantism as, for instance, when Puritan dissidents such as Anne Hutchinson and Roger Williams were cast out of the Massachusetts Bay Colony as heretics, forcing them to form new schismatic groups. Although reformers may declare the current leadership and practice of their body to be corrupt, in this kind of schism the body itself is not usually condemned until the separation is imminent.

In the second instance, schism may occur when a departing group declares the parent body to be illegitimate, and the parent body seeks to retain the schismatics within the fold. Such an occurrence is most common when the schism parallels clear political or ethnic divisions. The parent body seeks to retain a broad definition of itself and its power, and the schismatics seek more local, independent control. For instance, the Philippine revolution of 1897–1898 was followed in 1902 by a schism of many local churches away from the Roman Catholic hierarchy. Because the church had become a symbol of imperial rule, religious schism followed political independence. Throughout their history, the Sikhs of the Punjab have claimed that their way of life should be both politically and religiously independent of Hindu India, whereas India has taken a more inclusive (some would say imperialistic) stance. In the United States, various nineteenth-century Protestant schisms resulted from ethnic and cultural differences introduced by immigrants. As in the 1963 split in the (American) Serbian Orthodox church, these schismatic groups came to see the parent body as unresponsive to their needs and probably irredeemable. Schisms took place despite protests from the parent group.

The third kind of schism is probably the most common. Here each side comes to see the other as having deviated from the true path. Although each may try for a time to convert the other, their final separation is a recognition that they can no longer work and worship together. This pattern has been typical for American Protestantism, from the regional divisions of the mid-nineteenth century to the fundamentalist departures of the 1920s. Since no single Protestant body monopolizes religious authority, charges of heresy can be made by almost anyone. When the charge has found fertile ground in popular discontent, Protestant doctrinal disputes have often led to schism.

IDEOLOGICAL FACTORS. Religious schism, of course, by definition is an ideological matter. Differences in belief and practice are almost always at stake. In Eastern cultures, the scale is likely to tip toward differences in religious practice as the source of division, whereas in Western society, dogma assumes a more central role. The ultimate values of most groups are vague enough to allow for differences in practical interpretation. In religious groups those practical differences can create divergent paths to salvation and opposing definitions of good and evil, with each side nevertheless seeking to justify its beliefs in terms of the same core of sacred values.

Even organizational and political disputes, when they occur within religion, are infused with sacred meaning. In *The Religion of India* (1958), Max Weber argues that the original division between Hinayānā and Mahāyāna Buddhism was more organizational than dogmatic. The Mahāyāna tradition began to allow more leniency in relationships to worldly affairs, the laity, and money. Today, leaders of religious organizations are not just subject to accusations of inefficiency and poor administration but to charges of violating a sacred trust. When dissidents seek to reform a religious organization, they often charge that those in power have corrupted the true ideals of the group. Typical bureaucratic intransigence can become proof of evil intent. The battle cries of religious conflict originate in arguments about ultimate truth, and for that reason they must be taken seriously as factors in the divisions that occur from time to time.

SOCIAL FACTORS. It is, however, impossible to treat religious schism exclusively as a theological matter. The ideas over which believers fight and divide make sense only as a part of the lives of people in a given time, place, and social position. When social change occurs, people's understanding of the religious life changes as well. Separation occurs not only because people come to hold incompatible views about salavation but because those views are born of different life experiences. The kinds of social differences that can lead to religious schism fall into three broad, interrelated categories.

Economic differences. H. Richard Niebuhr claims that "the division of the churches closely follows the division of men into the castes of national, racial, and economic groups" (1929, p. 6). Although class divisions are rarely a perfect predictor of religious schism, they often play an important role. Niebuhr's argument is that sects (that is, schismatic groups) arise as the socially disinherited seek a religion that more nearly meets their needs. They are more concerned with emotion, informality, ethical purity, and the coming new age than more established, well-to-do believers either need or wish to be.

More recently, Dean R. Hoge (1976) has demonstrated that the class base for current divisions is not so much in objective differences in income, occupation, or region as in the degree to which individuals perceive middle-class values to be threatened by change. At a theological level, the differences are seen in disagreements over the dualistic nature of humanity. At an organizational level, the two parties differ on how the church should order its priorities. The result is an incipient schism across American Protestantism that pits the traditional conservatism of the upper class and of the lower middle class against the innovation of those in the upper middle class who are neither so entrenched nor so insecure as to feel threatened by change.

Beyond these divisions within advanced capitalist societies, changes in the world economic order as a whole can also create a climate for schism. When either masses or elites find themselves in a new economic context, displayed from old loyalties, living in a world that operates by different rules, religious revolutions are possible. In medieval Japan, political and economic chaos provided the setting in which the Pure Land and Nichiren sects were formed within Buddhism. It was no accident that the Protestant Reformation occurred in the context of declining feudalism and rising nationalism. It is also no accident that the independent churches in Africa today have arisen with the decline of imperialism. Again in Japan, cultural change since the middle of the nineteenth century has been enormous, and there has been a parallel proliferation of new religious movements. Changes in the economic and political order create new religious questions and leave spaces into which new religious solutions can fit.

Modernization. Much of the social change that leaves people open to religious reorganization and schism can be seen as part of the longterm process of modernization. To be modernized is, among other things, to learn new skills for encountering and manipulating the world, among the most important being literacy. Having personal knowledge of sacred texts often distinguishes a schismatic group from its parent body. As early as the fourteenth century, reformers such as John Wyclif were teaching their followers to read and thereby sowing the seeds of the revolt from Catholicism that would follow. More recently, David B. Barrett (1968) has demonstrated that African independent churches are springing up most predictably in the areas where the Christian scriptures are available in the vernacular. Having personal access to scripture is part of a climate of individualism that is neither necessary nor possible in an unmodernized world. It is also part of the social process of religious schism.

Modernization not only creates social dislocation and encourages individualism, it also creates a world in which there are multiple versions of truth, in which there is pluralism. Ironically, one of the factors most important in predicting schism is a preexisting state of division. Where differences are already an everyday fact of life, religious schism is more likely and more easily accomplished. For this reason, it is not surprising that in the Philippines, Protestantism was most successful in precisely the same areas that had first experienced schism from the Roman church as part of the development of the Philippine Independent Church. When Islam began to dominate India in the fifteenth century, one of the responses to its spread was new religious differentiation within Hinduism. Likewise, Barrett has documented that schism in Africa is more likely where independent African churches have been established in neighboring tribes, where the culture is not dominated by Islam, and where there is a relatively large Christian population. Where monolithic religious authority is absent and examples of divison are at hand, schism is more likely.

Political differences. Religious schisms also occur because religious life cannot be separated from the political circumstances in which people exist. The Donatist schism, among the earliest divisions in the Catholic church, happened in part as a result of political tensions between North Africa and Rome. Later, during the Middle Ages, the formal schism between the Eastern and Western churches had its greatest practical reality in places like Russia, where religious schism followed the lines of political animosity between Russians and Poles. The Protestant Reformation might have taken very different form but for the rivalries among various heads of state and between them and Rome. Likewise, the shape of Protestantism in America has been undeniably affected by divisions among ethnic and immigrant groups, divisions over slavery, and divisions between frontier and city, local and cosmopolitan.

In most of Asia, religion and communal life have been so inextricably intertwined that political change has, by definition, meant religious change, and vice versa. The nineteenth-century Daibing rebels in China adopted a religious synthesis of Christian and Confucian thought that propelled them into military conflict with the Manzhu rulers. Today, religious divisions often parallel political ones within the Indian subcontinent. The prejudices and divisions of everyday life are more often reflected in religious separation than overcome by religious unity.

ORGANIZATIONAL DYNAMICS OF SCHISM. All of the theological, cultural, economic, and political factors that give rise to schism are necessary causes, but they are not sufficient causes in themselves. They cannot explain why one missionized culture experiences schism and another does not, why some ethnic groups share a religious heritage, and others see each other as religiously alien. To explain those differences, one must take into account the organizational structures in which divisions are encountered. Some organizations make schism likely, whereas others prevent division from occurring. Those who have studied social movements have identified various ingredients in organizations that may make schism possible. The factors they list may be divided into two broad categories.

Conditions in the parent body. Most basically, conditions that produce cohesiveness also inhibit schism. If there are strong incentives of loyalty and reward binding people to the parent body, splinter groups will have difficulty forming. Likewise, when the members have few competing ties to other organizations, their religious commitments are more central and less likely to be disturbed.

However, since conflict is always a possibility in the application of religious values to everyday life, organizations that learn to control conflict can avoid schism. Often this means simply hearing and responding to grievances. It may mean establishing structures in which disagreements can be contained and made useful (e.g., the establishment of monastic orders in Catholicism). When organizational hierarchies are too authoritarian to change or to allow diversity, they may be confronted by schism.

Conversely, organizations that have too little dogma, too loose an identity, are equally vulnerable. The incredible diversity of Hinduism can in part be accounted for by the lack of concrete dogma, organized clergy and congregations, or any central group giving it limits of belief and practice.

Equally important, the form of authority in the organization provides the raw materials out of which schisms can occur. The more democratic the group's polity and the more autonomous its constituent units, the more it is susceptible to division. As authority is dispersed, it is more easily claimed and protected by dissident groups. Schism is, after all, at least in part a struggle for organizational power. It is an attempt to impose one group's views on the whole. That imposition can take place only as long as the instruments of power are also under the group's control. Decentralized religious organizations provide niches of power that can be used by dissidents mobilizing a revolt.

An implication of the foregoing is that parent bodies with effective means of social control are less likely to experience schism. When organizational hierarchies know what their members are doing and are able to apply effective sanctions, dissidents are less able to mobilize. Heretics who are banished or burned only occasionally become the inspiration for later schisms.

Conditions in the dissenting body. To achieve a successful withdrawal from a parent body, dissenters must mobilize a variety of resources. They must make it rewarding for people to participate in their movement by offering them opportunities to lead, to be recognized, and to feel they are defending important values. Followers must be promised not only a more sure path to eternal salvation but a way to achieve more tangible goals as well. Where punishment seems more immediately likely than reward, reformers must be able to turn even that to their advantage.

Most especially, dissenters must be able to manipulate symbols of good and evil so as to define the conflict in cosmic terms. A dissenting group must therefore develop effective means of communicating its ideas and overcoming the counterarguments of the parent body. The emphasis on literacy in schismatic groups nicely serves this purpose.

All of these undertakings require resources of time, money, and skill. Often it is those at the bottom of the social structure who can contribute time, a powerful benefactor who can contribute money, and trained people on the fringes of the parent organization who can contribute skill.

Finally, most schismatic movements need a charismatic leader. One person provides the ideas and inspiration that motivate others to follow.

CONCLUSION. Schism, then, is a division in a religious body in which one or each of the separating groups defines the other as having departed from the true faith. It always involves conflict over what is ultimately true and how that truth should affect human lives. Yet schism also occurs in a social context in which economic divisions and changes, the process of modernization, and political differences impinge on the way people organize themselves into religious bodies. Those structural conditions provide the background and raw materials of schism, and specific organizational conditions provide the means by which a separation is finally accomplished.

SEE ALSO Heresy; Modernity; Orthodoxy and Heterodoxy; Orthopraxy.

BIBLIOGRAPHY

Baker, Derek, ed. *Schism, Heresy and Religious Protest.* Cambridge, U.K., 1972. This collection of papers read at the Ecclesiastical History Society in London illustrates the diverse theological and social sources of the many divisions that have affected the Christian church.

Barrett, David B. *Schism and Renewal in Africa: An Analysis of Six Thousand Contemporary Religious Movements.* Nairobi, 1968. A thorough study of the political, historical, and cultural factors that explain the explosion of new, independent African churches.

Hoge, Dean R. *Division in the Protestant House: The Basic Reasons behind Intra-Church Conflicts.* Philadelphia, 1976. An excellent piece of research from the Presbyterian denomination that examines the intertwining of theological, psychological, and sociological factors in creating two opposing parties in contemporary American Protestantism.

Niebuhr, H. Richard. *The Social Sources of Denominationalism* (1929). New York, 1957. The classic statement of the causes of schism in Protestantism.

Takayama, K. Peter. "Strains, Conflicts, and Schisms in Protestant Denominations." In *American Denominational Organization: A Sociological View,* edited by Ross P. Scherer, pp. 298–329. Pasadena, Calif., 1980. A leading researcher in the sociology of religious organizations proposes hypotheses for predicting schism and examines two recent divisions in light of those propositions.

Wilson, John. "The Sociology of Schism." In *A Sociological Yearbook of Religion in Britain* 4. London, 1971. A little-known article that provides a useful model for understanding the organizational processes involved in schism.

Zald, Mayer N. "Theological Crucibles: Social Movements in and of Religion." *Review of Religious Research* 23 (June 1982): 317–336. A leading proponent of "resource mobilization" theory applies his ideas to religious movements. He first reviews the cultural conditions that make religious change and division more likely and then argues that such movements can happen only if the organizational conditions are also right.

New Sources

Clarke, Peter B. *Mahdism in West Africa: The Ijebu Mahdiyya Movement.* London, 1995.

Hillis, Bryan V. *Can Two Walk Together Unless They Be Agreed?: American Religious Schisms in the 1970s.* Brooklyn, 1991.

McKivigan, John R. *Abolitionism and American Religion.* New York, 1999.

Rochford, E Burke, Jr. "Factionalism, Group Defection, and Schism in the Hare Krishna Movement." *Journal for the Scientific Study of Religion* 28 (June 1989): 162–179.

Walker, Deward E. *Conflict & Schism in Nez Percé Acculturation: A Study of Religion and Politics* (1961). Reprint. Moscow, Id., 1998.

Zuckerman, Phil. "Gender Regulation as a Source of Religious Schism." *Sociology of Religion* 58 (Winter 1997): 353–373.

NANCY T. AMMERMAN (1987)
Revised Bibliography

SCHISM: CHRISTIAN SCHISM

In ecclesiastical contexts, *schism* is both a technical term and a general term referring to a split or division within a segment of the Christian church or between segments of the Christian church. It is a category of ecclesiology that is basic to understanding the history of the Christian church, because the church, in its understanding of itself as an institution, has placed great emphasis on the unity and integrity of structure, order, and dogma.

Schism appeared early in the history of Christianity and took a variety of forms, which makes it difficult to apply any one legal or canonical definition to the phenomenon or the term. Schisms were noted in the earliest documents of the church, including the New Testament. The first and second letters of John note the centrality of ecclesiastical harmony and the danger of heretical distortions of the teaching handed down. The same fear of divisions (*schismata*) is noted in other letters, such as Paul's letters to the Corinthians.

Historically, the notion of schism has been and continues to be important to a large part of the Christian community because of its emphasis on theological and eucharistic unity as fundamental to the nature of the church. But schisms are inherent in any society that claims to have access to the truth and believes that truth is essential to salvation. Schism makes sense only in communities that have the will and the agency—whether pope, council, or Bible—to establish norms of behavior and parameters of belief without excluding the possibility of diversity in theological emphasis.

The foundational nature of this unity was made evident from different perspectives in the writings of Ignatius of Antioch in the first century and Irenaeus in the second century in response to confrontations with heresy. Ignatius emphasized the centrality of the local bishop, and Irenaeus stressed the importance of the canon of scripture and apostolic succession. In addition to the theological affirmation, the birth of the church within the Roman empire and its expansion in the Byzantine milieu heightened this sense of institutional and dogmatic unity within the context of the diversity encouraged by geography and distance. In an empire as multinational as the Byzantine empire, it is easy to understand how schism came to be a political threat and why, as in the example of Constantine and the Donatists, immediate imperial intervention was called for.

While schisms have had a variety of causes, they did exhibit similar sociological dynamics. For instance, they tended to be aggravated as the initial causes and antagonists became lost in the phenomenology of the separation itself. In fact, it is not unusual in Christian history to find that the original factors and personalities causing a schism were forgotten as each party to the dispute forced its own position to a logical extreme in opposition to the other. Hence the very diversity that the early church and even the medieval church demonstrated became perverted as differences in emphasis became dogmas in opposition, as in the cases of monophysitism and Nestorianism.

EARLY SCHISMS. Among the earliest schisms of any significance were those related initially to historical phenomena and ecclesiastical discipline. Such was the case with the Donatists in North Africa and the Meletians in Egypt during the early fourth century. These two cases, as well as the Novatian schism in Rome in the third century, demonstrate the historical conditioning of schism (in these cases persecution) and that questions of order and discipline can and did develop into theological and ecclesiological issues.

The first significant schisms to affect the Christian church were those based on heresy or a one-sided emphasis on a particular, albeit accepted, aspect of Christian belief. These were the withdrawals of Nestorian Christians in Persia in 431 as a result of the Council of Ephesus, and the so-called monophysite Christians in Syria, Egypt, Armenia, and Ethiopia in 451 after the Council of Chalcedon. Political and cultural factors would crystallize these churches in their isolation from the mainstream of Christianity, consisting of Latin and Greek portions of the empire.

Unity was not guaranteed between the two largest geocultural portions of the Christian church—the Latin West and the Greek East. The efforts of Emperor Zeno (474–475; 476–491) to reconcile the monophysites to the official church by publication of the *Henoticon* (482) occasioned the thirty-five-year schism between Rome and Constantinople. The *Henoticon,* compromising the Chalcedonian formulations, was opposed by Felix II, who excommunicated both Zeno and his patriarch, Acacios. The schism lasted from 484 to 519, when it was brought to an end by Emperor Justin I and Pope Hormisdas (514–523). The churches of Rome and Constantinople continued to experience minor and short-lived conflicts based on theological and political issues in the seventh-century Monothelite Controversy and the eighth-century Iconoclastic Controversy.

ROME AND CONSTANTINOPLE. Relations between the churches of Rome and Constantinople continued to degenerate during the eighth century as these churches grew increasingly hostile as well as distant in their ecclesiology and politics. The most notable feature of the ecclesiastical developments of the eighth century was the new alliance that the papacy forged in mid-century with the new Carolingian kings. The logical result of the geographical and cultural isolation to which Rome was subjected was its turn toward the Franks, consummated by Pope Stephen II's alliance with Pépin III in 754. The Franks could give the papacy the military support that the Byzantine emperor could not supply. The crowning of Charlemagne in 800 by Leo III was both a symptom and a cause of the growing ecclesiastical hostility between Rome and Constantinople.

In the ninth century, through the agency of the Carolingians, the issue of the *filioque* was thrust into the already hostile relations between Rome and Constantinople. The *filioque,* Latin for "and the Son" (asserting that the Holy Spirit proceeds from both God the Father and from God the Son) had been inserted into the Nicene Creed in sixth-century Spain to protect the divinity of the Son against residual Arianism and adoptionism. Charlemagne welcomed, endorsed, and adopted the *filioque* officially at the Council of Frankfurt (794) and used its absence among the Byzantines as the basis for charges of heresy. By the mid-ninth century, the two main issues that would characterize East-West ecclesiastical disputes, the *filioque* and papal primacy, were defined.

Photian schism. In 858, Photios assumed the patriarchate of Constantinople on the occasion of the deposition and later resignation of Patriarch Ignatius (847–858). Ignatius's partisans appealed to Rome for his restoration. Their cause was taken up by Nicholas I, who was looking for an opportunity to intervene in Eastern ecclesiastical affairs to enhance his authority. A Roman council in 863 excommunicated Photios as a usurper and called for the restoration of Ignatius, but the council had no way of enforcing its decisions in the East, and the Byzantines bitterly attacked the move as an uncanonical interference in their affairs.

During the same period, the Byzantines had collided with the Frankish missionaries operating in central Europe and Bulgaria over the question of adding the *filioque* to the creed as well as its theological propriety, both of which Photios was to attack in his *Mystagogia.* In 867, Photios held a council and excommunicated Nicholas. In the same year he addressed a letter to the Eastern patriarchs, condemning Frankish errors being propagated in Bulgaria.

The schism, though short-lived, was significant in that it embodied two of the main issues that would poison ecclesiastical relations until the fifteenth century. In 867, Photios was deposed and then, in 877, restored to the patriarchate. The schism ended when the Latin church, through the attendance of three papal legates at the council of 879/880, endorsed by John VIII, confirmed Photios's restoration and the end of the internal schism between the Photians and the Ignatians.

Fourth marriage controversy. The next schism between the churches of Rome and Constantinople concerned the fourth marriage of Emperor Leo VI (886–912). Though married three times, Leo had failed to produce a male heir. When he did sire a son, it was with his mistress, whom he wished to marry so that he could legitimize his son as his successor, Constantine VII. Because Byzantine canonical tradition grudgingly permitted only three marriages, Patriarch Nicholas I refused to permit the emperor to marry a fourth time. Leo appealed to the Eastern patriarchs and to the pope, Sergius III, for a dispensation. In 907 a council approved the fourth marriage, partially on the basis of the dispensation of Sergius. Nicholas I resigned and was replaced by the more cooperative Euthymios. A schism resulted within the Byzantine church between supporters of Nicholas and supporters of Euthymios.

When Leo VI died in 912, his successor, co-emperor Alexander I reappointed Nicholas to the patriarchate. Nicholas addressed a letter to Pope Anastasius III (911–913), optimistically informing him that the schism within the Byzantine church had ended and asking him to condemn the authors of the scandal, but he did not name either Leo or Sergius. The letter was never answered, and Nicholas removed Anastasius's name from the diptychs, the ecclesiastical document maintained by each church that records the names of legitimate and recognized hierarchies, effecting thereby in 912 a formal schism whose significance depends on the value accorded the diptychs.

In 920 a council in Constantinople published a tome of union, which condemned fourth marriages and restored harmony to the two Byzantine factions. By 923, John X sent two legates to assent to the 920 agreement and anathematize fourth marriages. The formal schism between Rome and Constantinople ended in 923 with the restoration of the pope's name to the Constantinopolitan diptychs.

The Great Schism. The issue of the *filioque* was to arise again in the eleventh century. In 1009, Pope Sergius IV (1009–1012) announced his election in a letter containing the interpolated *filioque* clause in the creed. Although there seems to have been no discussion of the matter, another schism was initiated. The addition of the *filioque* was, however, official this time, and the interpolated creed was used at the coronation of Emperor Henry II in 1014.

As the papacy moved into the mid-eleventh century, the reform movement was radically altering its view of the pope's position and authority. This movement, as well as the military threat of the Normans to Byzantine southern Italy, set the stage for the so-called Great Schism of 1054.

The encounter began when Leo IX (1049–1054), at the Synod of Siponto, attempted to impose Latin ecclesiastical customs on the Byzantine churches of southern Italy. Patriarch Michael Cerularios (1043–1058) responded by ordering Latin churches in Constantinople to conform to Byzantine usage or to close. Michael continued this attack on an aggressive reform-minded papacy by criticizing Latin customs, such as the use of azyme (unleavened bread) in the Eucharist and fasting on Saturdays during Lent. The issues of the eleventh-century crisis were almost exclusively those of popular piety and ritual; the *filioque* played a minor part.

Michael's reaction did not suit Emperor Constantine IX (1042–1055), who needed an anti-Norman alliance with the papacy. Michael was forced to write a conciliatory letter to Leo IX offering to clarify the confusion between the churches, restore formal relations, and confirm an alliance against the Normans. Leo sent three legates east. Seeing the legates as part of a plot to achieve a papal-Byzantine alliance at the expense of his position and the Byzantine Italian provinces, Michael broke off discussions.

The attacks of Humbert of Silva Candida (c. 1000–1061), one of the legates, on the Byzantine church made clear for the first time the nature of the reform movement and the changes that had taken place in the Western church. In his anger at Byzantine opposition to papal authority, Humbert issued a decree of excommunication and deposited it on the altar of Hagia Sophia in Constantinople. In it he censured the Byzantines for permitting married clergy, simony, and removing the *filioque* from the creed. The value of the excommunication is questionable, because Leo had died several months earlier. A Constantinopolitan synod, giving up hopes for an alliance, excommunicated the legates.

By the mid-eleventh century, it became clear to the Byzantines that they no longer spoke the same ecclesiological language as the church of Rome. This was to become even more evident during the pontificate of Gregory VII (1073–1085), whose *Dictates of the Pope* could find no resonance in Byzantine ecclesiology.

What is interesting about the mutual excommunications of 1054 is their insignificance. As John Meyendorff notes in his *Living Tradition* (Tuckahoe, N.Y., 1978), "One of the most striking facts about the schism between the East and the West is the fact that it cannot be dated" (p. 69). In fact, when in December 1965 Pope Paul VI and Patriarch Athenagoras lifted the anathemas of 1054, they noted that nothing had actually happened. The anathemas were directed against particular people, not churches, and they were not designed to break ecclesiastical communion. In addition to this, Humbert had exceeded his power when he excommunicated Michael and his supporters in the name of a deceased pope.

The equivocal nature of the events of 1054 was made evident in 1089 when the emperor Alexios I (1081–1118), seeking the West's assistance against the Turks in Anatolia (modern-day Asia Minor) as well as papal support against Norman designs on Byzantine territory, convoked a synod to consider the relations between the two churches. An investigation produced no documentary or synodal evidence to support a formal schism. Patriarch Nicholas III (1084–1111) wrote to Pope Urban II (1088–1099), offering to restore the pope's name to the diptychs on receipt of an acceptable confession of faith. There is no evidence that the pope responded to this offer. What is clear is that what was lacking in the relationship between East and West could have been rectified by a simple confession of faith. The theological issue of the *filioque* was considered by Byzantine theologians to revolve around a misunderstanding stemming from the crudeness of the Latin language.

Effect of the Crusades. If the intensity of the reform movement in the West accelerated the process of schism, the

Crusades were the factor that formalized it on a popular level. Early in the crusading enterprise, Pope Urban II was able to maintain harmonious relations between the Crusaders and the Christians of the East. With his death in 1099, however, relations between Latin and Eastern Christians in the Levant degenerated after the appointment of Latin-rite patriarchs in Jerusalem and Antioch in 1099 and 1100, respectively. It is with the establishment of parallel hierarchies that one can first pinpoint a schism on the structural level. The close contacts between Latin and Greek Christians made differences immediately obvious; not only were they two different peoples, they were also two different churches.

The Fourth Crusade painfully brought the reality of the schism home to the Byzantines with the Latin capture, sack, and occupation of Constantinople and the expulsion of Patriarch John X Kamateros. Pope Innocent III (1198–1216) established a Latin hierarchy and demanded an oath of allegiance from Byzantine clergy. With the Fourth Crusade the central issue of the developing separation of the Eastern and Western churches came to the fore: the nature of the church itself—the universal jurisdiction of the papacy and the locus of authority within the church. The existence of parallel hierarchies in Constantinople, Antioch, and Jerusalem, the centers of Eastern Christendom, marks the fruition of the schism. The dating of the schism, therefore, depends on the locale.

During the thirteenth and fourteenth centuries, both the Latin West and the Greek East formalized their theologies in two radically divergent schools of thought: Thomistic scholasticism and Palamite hesychasm, respectively. Thus, by the fourteenth century the schism was formalized on popular, doctrinal, and methodological planes.

There were several noteworthy efforts to heal the schism between the churches of Rome and of the East, but it is ironic that it was the union efforts of Lyons (1274) and Florence (1439–1441) that formalized the schism, crystallized Byzantine opposition, and provoked schisms within the church of Constantinople itself. Union efforts failed during the thirteenth, fourteenth, and fifteenth centuries because there was no agreement on the locus of authority in the church and because the Eastern and Western churches had developed not only different theologies but also divergent methods of doing theology. Rome sought submission and Byzantine military assistance against the Turks. With the capture of Constantinople by Mohammed II in 1453, all possibility for union was lost.

The Great Western Schism. The church of Rome, for which centralization was essential, underwent one of the most significant schisms in the history of Christianity. Its beginnings lay in the opening of the fourteenth century, when Pope Boniface VIII (1294–1303) lost the battle with Philip IV (1285–1314) over nationalization of the French kingdom. In 1305, the cardinals, divided between Italians and Frenchmen, elected Clement V (1305–1314) to succeed Boniface. Philip pressured Clement, a Frenchman, to move the papal residence from Rome to Avignon in 1309. It remained there, in "Babylonian Captivity," until 1377. The stage for the Great Western Schism was set in the corruption and decadence of an exiled papacy.

The papal thrust for independence from the French kingdom came in the context of the need to protect its Italian holdings. The Romans threatened to elect another pope should Gregory XI (1370–1378) not return. Gregory arrived in Rome in January 1377.

When Gregory died in 1378, the cardinals elected the Italian Urban VI (1378–1389). Although the majority of the cardinals in Rome were French and would have gladly removed the papacy to Avignon, the pressure of the Roman popular demands forced the election. Urban immediately went about reforming the Curia Romana and eliminating French influence. The French cardinals proceeded to elect another pope, Clement VII (1378–1394), who after several months moved to Avignon. The schism within the Western church had become a reality.

This second election would not have been so significant if Urban and Clement had not been elected by the same group of cardinals and had not enjoyed the support of various constellations of national interests. The schism severely compromised papal universalism. The Roman line of the schism was maintained by the succession of Boniface IX (1389–1404), Innocent VII (1404–1406), and Gregory XII (1406–1415). The Avignon line was maintained by Benedict XIII (1394–1423).

In the context of the schism, it was difficult to maintain even the appearance of a unified Western Christendom. The schism produced a sense of frustration as theologians and canonists searched for a solution. In 1408 the cardinals of both parties met in Livorno and, on their own authority, called a council in Pisa for March 1409, composed of bishops, cardinals, abbots, heads of religious orders, and representatives of secular rulers. The council appointed a new pope, Alexander V (1409–1410; succeeded by John XXIII, 1410–1415), replacing the Roman and Avignon popes, who were deposed.

The newly elected Holy Roman Emperor, Sigismund (1410–1437), and Pope Alexander V called a council to meet at Constance in 1414. Voting by nations, the council declared that it represented the Roman Catholic church and held its authority directly from Christ. John XXIII and Benedict XIII were deposed, and Gregory XII resigned. With the election of Martin V (1417–1431), Western Christendom was united once again under one pope. But the papacy had to contend with the challenge of the council that had settled the conflict.

By 1441 the schism between the Latins and the Greeks was declared ended, and conciliarism was effectively eviscerated by the success of Eugenius IV (1431–1447) in uniting the Greeks, who sought union as well as military assistance against the Turks, and other Eastern Christians with Rome.

For many modern historians, however, the tragedy of the period was the failure of the councils and the papacy to face the need for ecclesiastical reform. This failure laid the foundation for the Reformation of the sixteenth century.

THE REFORMATION. The Reformation of the sixteenth century was the second great split to strike Christianity. The same issues that determined the relations between Rome and the East figured in the separation of a large number of the Christians in Germany, Scotland, and Scandinavia. Martin Luther gradually moved from objecting to specific practices of the church of Rome to challenging papal authority as normative. Authority does not reside in the papacy, but rather in scripture; *sola scriptura* became the hallmark of his reforms.

The Reformation was a schism in the Western church and had nothing fundamentally to do with the Orthodox East. It was not, however, uncommon for Western ecclesiastical dissidents to use the Eastern church as an example of an ancient "popeless" Christianity. For many contemporary Eastern Christians, however, the reformers were but another example of the heresy spawned by the schism in the Roman church. As late as the nineteenth century, Eastern Christians, such as Aleksei Khomiakov, noted that all Protestants were but cryptopapists, each Protestant being his own pope.

The history of schism, particularly the schism between the churches of the East and the West, may be considered from the perspective of social, cultural, and political factors. While these are necessary to an adequate understanding of conflict in Christianity, they are not sufficient. Only a consideration of theological and ecclesiological factors allows full appreciation of the roots of schism in Christian history.

SEE ALSO Crusades; Donatism; Heresy, article on Christian Concepts; Iconoclasm; Icons; Monophysitism; Nestorianism; Papacy; Reformation.

BIBLIOGRAPHY

Bouyer, Louis. *The Spirit and Forms of Protestantism.* London, 1956. Offers an excellent introduction to the theological hallmarks of the Reformation and their Roman Catholic sources. Bouyer, a Roman Catholic, considers each Reformation principle as a basis for unity and for schism. The approach is valuable for considering the Reformation as a schism.

Dvornik, Francis. *The Photian Schism: History and Legend* (1948). Reprint, Cambridge, 1970. A brilliant summary of the author's research on the ninth-century patriarch Photios, elucidating the misunderstandings of the complex relationships of the ninth century. The author concludes that Photios was not opposed to Roman primacy and that the idea of a second Photian schism was a fabrication of eleventh-century canonists.

Dvornik, Francis. *Byzantium and the Roman Primacy.* New York, 1966. A historical survey of the relations between the church of Rome and the Byzantine East. Although tendentious in its defense of Roman "primacy," it provides excellent coverage of events from the Acacian schism through the Fourth Crusade. Concludes that the Byzantine church never rejected Roman primacy, but does not define the differing Roman and Byzantine interpretations of primacy.

Every, George. *The Byzantine Patriarchate, 451–1204.* 2d rev. ed. London, 1962. Still the best introduction to the Byzantine church from the fifth to the twelfth centuries; highlights the major conflicts between Rome and Constantinople, including the role of the *filioque,* the Crusades, and papal primacy. Concludes that the progressive estrangement between the two portions of Christendom was not a straight-line process. The timing of the schism, the author notes, depends on the place.

Meyendorff, John. *Byzantine Theology: Historical Trends and Doctrinal Themes.* 2d ed. New York, 1979. A superb presentation of Eastern Christian thought and doctrinal and historical trends that clarifies the roots of the schism. The author considers the process nature of the final separation between the two churches and notes the underlying agenda of authority in the church.

Runciman, Steven. *The Eastern Schism* (1955). Reprint, Oxford, 1963. A highly readable account of the relations between the papacy and the Eastern churches during the eleventh and twelfth centuries. The author maintains that the traditional reasons of doctrinal and liturgical practices for the schism are inadequate; the schism was due to the more fundamental divergence in traditions and ideology that grew up during earlier centuries. He highlights the proximate causes as the Crusades, the Norman invasions of Byzantine Italy, and the reform movement within the papacy.

Sherrard, Philip. *Church, Papacy, and Schism: A Theological Inquiry.* London, 1978. A theological analysis of schism in general. The author focuses on the schism between Rome and the Eastern churches. He argues from the historical perspective that doctrinal issues, which he enumerates, were at the root of the schism and continue to be the reason for separation between the churches of the East and the West.

Ullmann, Walter. *The Origins of the Great Schism: A Study in Fourteenth Century Ecclesiastical History* (1948). Reprint, Hamden, Conn., 1972. Insightful and thorough presentation of the Great Western Schism in the context of fourteenth-century ecclesiastical and political events.

New Sources

Bruce, Steve. *A House Divided: Protestantism, Schism, and Secularization.* London and New York, 1990.

Fahey, Michael Andrew. *Orthodox and Catholic Sister Churches: East Is West and West Is East.* Milwaukee, Wisc., 1996.

Frend, W. H. C. *The Donatist Church: A Movement of Protest in Northern Africa.* Oxford and New York, 1952; reprint, 2000.

Meyendorff, John. *Imperial Unity and Christian Divisions: The Church, 450–680 AD.* Crestwood, N.Y., 1989.

Nicols, Aidan. *Rome and the Eastern Churches: A Study in Schism.* Collegeville, Minn., 1992.

Papadakis, Aristeides, and John Meyendoff. *The Christian East and the Rise of the Papacy: The Church, 1071–1453 A.D.* Crestwood, N.Y., 1994.

Storman, E. J., ed. and trans. *Towards the Healing of Schism: the Sees of Rome and Constantinople: Public Statements and Correspondence between the Holy See and the Ecumenical Patriarch, 1958–1984.* New York, 1987.

Stump, Phillip M. *The Reforms of the Council of Constance, 1414–1418.* Leiden and New York, 1994.

JOHN LAWRENCE BOOJAMRA (1987)
Revised Bibliography

SCHLEGEL, FRIEDRICH

SCHLEGEL, FRIEDRICH (1772–1829), was one of the leading figures of the German Romantic movement. Schlegel's personality was influenced by various poets and thinkers, including Schiller, Goethe, Kant, Fichte, Schleiermacher, Leibniz, and Spinoza. It was not unusual for him first to be attracted by a philosopher or poet and then to turn vehemently against him. Thus Schlegel's personal development was marked by a constant search for new intellectual horizons. He never developed a system of thinking as such, but rather turned ultimately, in 1805, to Roman Catholicism. Hence his concern with general religious history was limited to particular phases of his life.

After studying law, classical philology, and philosophy at Göttingen and Leipzig, Schlegel devoted himself to Greek classicism. In his first publications he propounded the idea that the Greek image of humanity was the most perfect expression of the human ideal of harmony and totality. Yet soon, in turning to Romantic poetry, he rejected the notion that the classical ideal was universally valid, emphasizing instead the necessity for a continuing development of the human spirit.

Of Schlegel's various intellectual activities, the most interesting for the historian of religions is his concern with Indian religion. While at Paris from 1802 to 1804, he studied Sanskrit, for he sought in India the source of human wisdom. The writings of the Indians, which he initially found dignified, sublime, and significant in their reference to God, would point, so he believed, to an original revelation of the true (i.e., Christian) God, one that might be perceived despite the superstition and error that had crept into the Indian tradition. In Schlegel's view, one of the major errors of Indian thinking was the lack of a pronounced ethical conception of the divine; another was the idea of emanation, the idea that God continually unfolds himself to create the world. Feeling a strong aversion to the pantheistic belief that God and the universe are identical in substance, he yet saw pantheism as having a provisional value in that it formed an essential stage in the development of religion, which culminated in Christianity.

Increasingly, however, Schlegel came to believe that the religion of the Indians, whose language he believed to be the world's oldest, did not yield evidence of an original, pure faith. After the publication of *On the Language and Wisdom of the Indians* (1808), which contains a linguistic analysis of Sanskrit, a discussion of various Indian systems of thought, and translations of portions of Indian scriptures, Schlegel abandoned Indian studies. Yet his enthusiasm for things Indian had been communicated to his brother August Wilhelm, who was to become the first professor of Sanskrit in Germany. Despite his prejudices, Friedrich Schlegel can be regarded as a pioneer in the Western study of Indian religions.

BIBLIOGRAPHY

Sedlar, Jean W. *India in the Mind of Germany: Schelling, Schopenhauer and Their Times.* Washington, D.C., 1982. A few pages on Schlegel within a general characterization of German interest in India at the end of the eighteenth century and in the first half of the nineteenth.

Wiese, Benno von. *Friedrich Schlegel: Ein Beitrag zur Geschichte der romantischen Konversionen.* Berlin, 1927. An important study of Schlegel's "conversions" and his place within German romanticism.

Wilson, A. Leslie. *A Mythical Image: The Ideal of India in German Romanticism.* Durham, N.C., 1964. A short presentation of Schlegel's ideal of India in the light of German romanticism.

New Sources

Finlay, Marike. *The Romantic Irony of Semiotics: Friedrich Schlegel and the Crisis of Representation.* Berlin and New York, 1988.

Roche-Mahdi, Sarah. "The Cultural and Intellectual Background of German Orientalism." In *Mapping Islamic Studies,* edited by Azim Narji, pp. 108–127. Berlin, 1997.

HANS J. KLIMKEIT (1987)
Revised Bibliography

SCHLEIERMACHER, FRIEDRICH

SCHLEIERMACHER, FRIEDRICH (1768–1834), German Evangelical theologian, philosopher, and pedagogue. His reappraisal of the task and content not only of Christian dogmatics but also of the whole of Christian life, faith, and theology earned him the title "church father of the nineteenth century." His distinctive approach to Christian doctrine also gave him an importance for the beginnings of nontheological ways of studying religion, and as an eminent figure in church, academy, and society he influenced public life and culture in Germany well beyond the circle of professional theologians.

LIFE AND WORKS. Friedrich Daniel Ernst Schleiermacher was born on November 21, 1768, in Prussian Breslau, Lower Silesia (now, as formerly, Wrocław, in southwestern Poland). His father, Gottlieb Schleiermacher, was a Reformed pastor and a chaplain in the army of Frederick the Great. Previously a thinker of the "enlightened" variety, Gottlieb Schleiermacher encountered the Herrnhutian community (stemming from the Moravian movement) at Gnadenfrei and underwent a spiritual reawakening. Five years later (1783) his fourteen-year-old son Friedrich attended the Herrnhutian Pedagogium at Niesky (1783–1785) and then the community's theological seminary at Barby (1785–1787).

The impress of Herrnhutian Pietism on Schleiermacher was permanent. Many years later (in 1802) he recalled that in the Brethrens' circles he first awoke to humanity's relationship with a higher world, acquiring the religious tendency that carried him through all the storms of skepticism. He professed himself "a Herrnhutian of a higher order" (Schleiermacher, *Kritische Gesamtausgabe,* sec. 5, vol. 5, 1999–, p. 392). But the time of his experience among the Herrnhutians ended in crisis and break. In the seminary he and a group of friends smuggled in forbidden works of Johann Wolfgang von Goethe, Immanuel Kant, Christoph Martin Wieland, and others. Doubts grew about the truth of the dogmatic doctrines of community until Schleiermacher confessed that he could no longer believe in the divinity of Christ and in his vicarious sacrifice (Schleiermacher, *Kritische Gesamtausgabe,* sec. 5, vol. 1, 1985–, p. 50).

Schleiermacher moved on to a period of study at the now rationalist University of Halle (1787–1789), followed by a brief stay (1789–1790) with his maternal uncle Samuel Stubenrauch, who had exchanged a professorship at Halle for a pastorate in Drossen (Osno). Schleiermacher took the first theological examination prescribed by his church, doing well or excellently in all subjects except dogmatics, and he accepted a post as tutor in the family of Count Dohna in Schlobitten, East Prussia (1790–1793). After the second and final examination, in which Schleiermacher's performance in dogmatics was again undistinguished, he assumed an assistant pastorate at Landsberg (Gorzów Wielkopolski, 1794–1796), where he remained until his move to Berlin.

Direct evidence of Schleiermacher's thought in the period between matriculation at Halle and arrival in Berlin (1787–1796) is provided not only by sermons and letters published later, but also by a series of unpublished manuscripts, mainly on ethical subjects. They remained virtually unknown until Wilhelm Dilthey included them in part in an appendix to his life of Schleiermacher, published uin 1863. They subsequently became accessible in the first volume of *Kritische Gesamtausgabe* (1983). They show Schleiermacher above all struggling with Kantian philosophy, discussing key ethical issues as the highest good, freedom, and the value of life. Against Kant he contends that moral experience may ground the ideas of God and immortality. He particularly maintains that "transcendental" (as distinct from merely psychological) freedom is not contained within the requirements of morality. Moreover, through Friedrich Heinrich Jacobi's writings on Barukh Spinoza and the following debate on pantheism, Schleiermacher had become acquainted with the philosophical perspectives of Spinoza. This reflection led him to some of his earliest thoughts on the concept of the "individual," on the notion of feeling or self-consciousness, and to the first shape of the "paradigm of inherence" that joins together Kant's transcendental perspective and Spinoza's ontological view. This philosophical frame increasingly formed the striking features of Schleiermacher's intellectual world.

It is not difficult to trace lines of continuity from these early philosophical beginnings to Schleiermacher's first books. And one must not underestimate the extent to which he was also drawing inspiration, like so many of his contemporaries, from the ancient Greek philosophers. Yet in his *Monologen* (1800) he viewed his intellectual progress after leaving the Herrnhutian community almost as a second conversion brought about by a revelation that did not come to him from any philosophy but from his experiences and views he encountered within the Romantic circle of Berlin. Indeed he had fallen in with the group of intellectuals that gathered around Friedrich Schlegel (1772–1829), with the journal *Athenäum* as the organ of their new Romanticism. "I discovered humanity," Schleiermacher wrote, "and knew that henceforth I should never lose it" (Schleiermacher, *Kritische gesamtausgabe,* sec. 1, vol. 3, 1988, p. 16) His first two major books, written when he was Reformed chaplain at the Charité Hospital in Berlin (1796–1802), were the fruits of this revelation.

The first book, *Über die Religion: Reden an die Gebildeten unter ihren Verächtern* (1799; *On Religion: Speeches to Its Cultured Despisers,* 1988), introduces a radical shift in the comprehension of religion, understood as an indispensable aspect of full humanity. The second one, *Monologen: Eine Neujahrsgabe* (1800; *Soliloquies: A New Year's Gift,* 1926), is its ethical counterpart in the form of the author's deep meditations on the course of his own inner life. Herein the conviction finds expression that each person is meant to represent humanity uniquely in his or her own way. Not the outward, physical world but the free spirit within is the primary reality, and the world is its creation. Those who have learned to look within, to the domain of the eternal and the divine, can even enjoy in imagination what they cannot attain in fact. For those who instead are acquainted with merely looking outside, old age itself is only a self-inflicted evil, and Schleiermacher promises that he at least will remain young until the day he dies.

Because of tensions and personal splits within the Romantic circle, Schleiermacher moved from Berlin and, for two years (1802–1804), served as pastor in the East Pomeranian town of Stolp (Slupsk), in what was then West Prussia. He began to carry out alone the project previously agreed upon with Schlegel of translating Plato's dialogues (the first volume, containing an important programmatic introduction, appeared in 1804), and he published his first strictly philosophical work, *Grundlinien einer Kritik der bisherigen Sittenlehre (Outlines of a Critique of Previous Moral Philosophy)* in 1803. Schleiermacher then received a call for the first, brief stage of his career in the academy. A previous call to the new University of Würzburg, in Bavaria, lost all attractiveness when the Prussian authorities invited him to return as professor and preacher at his own university, Halle. In his lectures at Halle (1804–1806), which ranged widely from philosophical ethics and hermeneutics to theological encyclopedias, New Testament exegesis, church history, dogmatics, and Christian ethics, Schleiermacher's intellectual system began to take shape. His little book *Die Weihnachtsfeier: Ein Gespräch* (1806; *Christmas Eve: A Dialogue,* 1967) gave clear evidence of a fresh approach to traditional Christian beliefs, taking its point of departure neither from dogma nor from the biblical story, but from the fact of the Christian community and its experience of redemption.

The work begun in Halle had to be resumed in Berlin. In 1806 Halle was taken by Napoleon's troops, and its university was closed. Schleiermacher remained for a while, preaching, translating Plato, and writing a commentary on *1 Timothy.* But the next year (1807) he went back to Berlin, where he became active in politics as a German patriot and a constitutional monarchist. In a succession of appointments he became a civil servant in the Department of Education (1808), Reformed pastor at Trinity Church (1809), and finally professor at the new University of Berlin (1810). At various times in the climactic stage of his career (1810–1834) he also served as a member of the commission for organizing the University of Berlin, columnist for *Der preussische Correspondent,* dean of the theological faculty (four times), rector of the university, and secretary of the Prussian Academy of Sciences (of the philosophical section, which then was changed by Schleiermacher into the historical-philological section). In addition, as a leading ecclesiastical statesman, he became embroiled in controversies over the union between the Lutherans and the Reformed, and over the liturgy, constitution, and confession of the union church.

The thirty-three volumes of Schleiermacher's collected works (*Friedrich schleiermacher's sämmtliche Werke,* 1834–1864) disclose the extraordinary breadth of his intellectual activities. In his lectures at Berlin he continued all the subjects he had taken up at Halle and ventured into so many new ones (including dialectics and life of Jesus research) that every branch of theology except Old Testament is represented in the first division of the collected works and every branch of philosophy in the third. Ten volumes of sermons make up the second division. Schleiermacher's correspondence and the incomplete translation of Plato's dialogues (six volumes) were not included, and a great deal of manuscript material remained unpublished, some of which is included in the new edition of his works *(Kritische Gesamtausgabe).* And yet Schleiermacher did not leave a completed system. He died of pneumonia in the midst of his labors on February 12, 1834. Besides, he always felt more at home in speech than in writing. Most of the volumes in the *Sämmtliche Werke* had their origins in the spoken word; many of them represent lectures never revised for publication by Schleiermacher, who neither preached nor lectured from a full manuscript. Of the finished works most important for religious studies, the first book, *Über die Religion,* was cast in the form of addresses, and *Der christliche Glaube* (1821–1822/1830–1831; *The Christian Faith,* 1928), the ripest fruit of the mature period, grew out of his lectures on dogmatics.

INTERPRETATION OF RELIGION. In *On Religion: Speeches to Its Cultured Despisers,* Schleiermacher pursues an anthropological theory of religion, aiming at recognizing the transcendental constitution of religious experience. According to this theory, religion is constituted as a specific region of human experience. Religion is an experience that men and women have; the whole subject takes part in an experiencing that is not enclosed within the circle of subjectivity but is referred to another term (as it were, outside the subject himself or herself), namely to a reality that gives up itself to be experienced. Eighteenth-century debates between deists, skeptics, and rational theists commonly presupposed on all sides that religion is a system of factual beliefs alleged to have immense moral significance. At issue was which beliefs are essential to religion, whether or not the essential beliefs are rationally defensible, and whether or not they really have the beneficial consequences attributed to them. The Christian apologist was expected to show that Christian beliefs were essential and true, or at least could not be refuted, and that civic virtue would collapse without them. Kant's critical philosophy undercut the debate by moving the idea of god out of the domain of theoretical knowledge and giving it the status simply of a moral postulate. But against traditional paradigms for the comprehension of religion (fundamentally, the rationalistic and the supernaturalistic ones), Schleiermacher introduced two theoretical shifts.

The first shift contends the supernaturalistic stance. With this shift Schleiermacher states that religion is essentially an experience; that is, a lived experience. It involves the subject with his or her innermost fibers. Therefore it cannot be brought back to external, extrinsic motives or factors, like news or information (a *notitia Dei),* doctrines or a doctrinal corpus, moral or social patterns, traditions or communities. As experience religion deals with reality, namely with the unique reality an individual is dealt. It has to do primarily neither with the conceptual order nor with projections of one's moral striving. It brings one into direct contact with a peculiar reality; that is, a specific region of reality different from all other regions. Religion then does not endure any other purpose or being in function of other realities than that it brings about. Instead, it owns an inner principle, a proper ground, of which one has to highlight the peculiar constitution. With the second shift, Schleiermacher contends the rationalistic stance. Therewith he states that religion is essentially and ultimately demarcated from any other relationship with reality within human experience. It is a specific, peculiar way to get in touch with reality, a way a person cannot generate out of himself or herself. It is so specific and peculiar that it encloses, carries, and establishes the contact with a "total other" reality. In this alternative understanding one seeks religion within an original connection of existence; that is, within a fundamental, existed connection. In this connection, two existing subjects or terms relate to each other in an asymmetrical relationship. It is then an experience that decentralizes the human subject engaged in it. This originally existing relationship makes up a peculiar experience of reality that is provided with an irreducible intentionality of its own.

Consequently, what the cultured despisers despise, according to Schleiermacher, is not religion but dogmas and usages—only the husks and not the kernel, a mere echo and not the original sound. But what the defenders of religion defend is not religion either, since they make of it a mere prop for morals and social institutions. Religion has a sphere of its own, which it can maintain only if it renounces all claims on anything that belongs either to knowledge or to morality. To make the idea of God the apex of science, for instance, is not the religious way of having God. And to make religion a matter of good behavior is to miss its true, passive nature: it is not human activity but being acted upon by God. If human nature is not to be truncated, religion must be allowed to take its place as an indispensable third alongside knowing and doing.

Two results of great importance stem from this paradigm constructed by Schleiermacher. First, it allows one to overcome the critical judgment; that is, the judgment that affords the suspicion with which rationalism (or the despisers of religion) approaches religion and its manifestations. In this perspective the reality of religion is brought back to what does not actually constitute it. In contrast, Schleiermacher sets to work and enhances a "heuristical reason," one that establishes, or tries to focus on, the genealogical instance that constitutes religious experience and accounts for its peculiar reality and the specific mode of its experiencing as well. It highlights the framework of religion as an actual experience of humans, and thus explains why religion is a decisive, indefeasible component of the human, historical world. Second, it takes into account historical, positive, inidividual religions—religions that are provided with a *principium individuationis* of their own; it distinguishes them from each other and shows them as ethical realities that belong to the lived experience of individuals. This includes two peculiar features of this comprehension of religion. On the one hand, one is engaged in accounting for the historicity and individuality of religions. In other words, it is a question of understanding why the framework of religious experience is contracted into the historical plurality of religions and into a complex phenomenology of the individual religions themselves. According to Schleiermacher they are all entitled to equal dignity insofar as they all fulfill the original structure of religious experience and contract it into a specific historical province of human ethos. On the other hand, one sets up an exercise of critical reason that is able to discriminate, within the complex phenomenology of individual religions, what is authentic in them and what is inauthentic—that is, mixed up in them, substituting or surrogating some of their authentic elements.

In this paradigm for comprehending religion, Schleiermacher points out four main moments or steps. The first step leads to the comprehension of the historical-positive elements that occur at the heart of religious experiences. It includes the exercise of both critical and heuristical reason. The first aims at discriminating authentic from inauthentic elements. It is an inescapable moment of every investigative approach to religions. The second aims at an insight into the individuality and essential features of a given historical form of religious experience. If one does not grasp the proper core, the essence, of an individual historical religion—of a historically lived religion—one cannot get appropriate criteria for testing how its features are shown to be authentic or inauthentic, or even for assessing its historical development. This is the criterion the fifth speech points out as decisive for determining the nature and content of a given religion and, specifically, of Christianity as an historical religion.

The second step consists of a comparative theory of religions. Given the historical-positive individuality of religions, as well as the transcendental structure of religious experience (according to the paradigm established by Schleiermacher with the *Speeches on Religion),* a comparative approach is necessary in understanding religion. Still it gets neither a leveling nor a competitive meaning. Its purpose, rather, is to set out the values (not only in doctrines but also in worships, morals, and experiences of salvation) embodied in the single religions compared. While this approach makes use of analogies between religious phenomena, it does not establish a premier rank or subalternity among religions. It has, rather, at the same time a critical and an evaluating function. The first allows one to recognize specific differences that prelude the highlighting of the individuality of each historical-religious formation. The second is engaged in recognizing the elements that validate the specificity of a religious formation, thus clarifying its essential character that makes up its historical reason for being. The latter accounts for its very historical trajectory or evolution, for the history of a religion is precisely connected with the circumstances of its actual evaluation. Within the third speech such a comparative approach is based upon the effort to tackle the main factors influencing the historical life of religion, namely creativity and free communication of one's own religious life. At the same time it leads to a threefold typology of religions, which anticipates the one worked out in the introduction to *The Christian Faith.*

The third step focuses on the thematization of the essence of religion. This is perhaps the most specifically philosophical feature of this paradigm for understanding religion. It encloses two moments. First is the highlighting of the constituting structure of religious experience (namely the religious a priori) that accounts for such an experience—that is, for the constitution of that region of human experience underlying the historical phenomenology of religious facts. Second is the focusing on the reasons why such a structure is contracted into a plurality of individual formations; they are all constituted by that transcendental structure but still are different from each other as inalienable and untransferable individuals. Uniquely, in this context, religion (as a condition of possibility that warrants such an experience as the one of the relationship with the *Universum*) shows itself to be meaningful for human beings and their history. This is indeed the main argument of the second speech. Here Schleiermacher argues that religion, in its transcendental core (insofar as it is the "function" that brings about and determines the "systems" of religious experience and belief) sets up a relationship with a term (called *Universum*) that withdraws from humans' finite experience and accordingly calls into question what people do and are and experience, even though it is to be apprehended as that which makes sense of the ultimately human condition—as that which fulfills human existence.

The last step unfolds a theory of religious communication. Within this human experience, religion is linguistically set up in a communication. This brings about a community that is shaped by both symbolizing and organizing elements, though with the prevalence of the former. Communication is not an accidental, superfluous, accessory moment of religious experience, but communication belongs to religion's innermost nature and is enclosed within the sources of its concrete constitution. This is the constituting reason of the particular formation of religious experience that is community (church, generally speaking). Community accounts for both the individuality of a religious formation and its historicity. It also accounts for free, responsible, and creative adhesion, or membership, of single individuals who, within community, are linked up by bonds of reciprocal communication. As is well known, community and communication are the main theme of the fourth speech.

Schleiermacher's first book offered much more than a shrewd, ad hominem defense of Christianity; it inaugurated a fresh stage in the critical analysis of religion. The importance of his search for a distinctive religious category is acknowledged even by those who reject his findings. He not only exposed the urgent need to reconceive the task of theology, he also opened the way to more profound and sympathetic treatments of the psychology and history of religion than either traditional theology or freethinking critiques had been able to achieve. Christian theologians and freethinkers had agreed in treating the study of world religions as the anatomy of a sickness (the difference being that the freethinkers were not inclined to make Christianity an exception). Schleiermacher looked at religions as manifestations of human wholeness. Misunderstandings of Schleiermacher's position have sometimes been occasioned by his own language. He did not really mean to move religion out of the domains of knowledge and morals and to confine it within the domain of the emotions. He expressly denied that he intended any such separation. By "intuition and feeling" he meant the immediate, prereflective self-consciousness that cannot be confined to any single department of human selfhood but underlies the whole of it. Neither did he fall into a psychologism that would shut the religious subject up in its own subjectivity. For all his interest in the imagination, his theory of religion is marked by a strong sense of the reality of the transcendent, even though he thought it impossible to have the transcendent as an object.

HERMENEUTICS. The impressive influence of Schleiermacher's hermeneutics was first brought out by Dilthey. Hermeneutics is a twin discipline of criticism, each a sort of technical skill (i.e., they rule a practice). Both are conceived and practiced by Schleiermacher not only in his exegetical work within the field of the New Testament; they rule his whole effort in the field of ancient philosophy, as witnessed by his translation of Plato. That is why hermeneutics falls within the fields of both philosophy and theology. Fundamentally, it understands the spoken or written word as free creative expression of the union between nature and reason (the core of the ethical process). Thus hermeneutics is based upon general principles (that pertain to philosophy) and induces special trends, according to the philological or exegetical treatment of texts handed over by tradition. "Hermeneutics as art of understanding does not exist yet generally, but only in several hermeneutical practices" (Schleiermacher, 1974, p. 75). Schleiermacher's contribution aims at framing a general hermeneutics as ground for special hermeneutical practices. Therefore he puts this general frame into shape through two theses. The negative one states, "Misunderstanding grows out by itself and in every point one must want and strive for understanding" (Schleiermacher, 1974, p. 82). The positive one says we have to "reconstruct *[Nachkonstruiren]* the historical and divinatoric, objective and subjective of a given speech" (Schleiermacher, 1974, p. 83).

Thus Schleiermacher articulates both theses into four canons ruling hermeneutical practice. He distinguishes between grammatical and psychological or technical interpretation (Schleiermacher, 1974, p. 77) that on the other side is open to comparative or divinatory methods (Schleiermacher, 1974, p. 105). Every oral or written witness is a subjective act of speakers, but at the same time is embedded in an over-individual, objective, linguistical context. The grammatical interpretation (Schleiermacher, 1974, pp. 86–103) discloses the objective sphere of language. The psychological interpretation (also called "technical," because a skill is involved) aims at the subjective act and attempts to grasp "the principle that causes the writer to be in motion" (Schleiermacher, 1974, p. 103). This double hermeneutical approach is joined together with another double perspective. One might address a linguistic act in its peculiarity by approaching it through comparative means; that is, in comparison with other similar (semiotic) phenomena. This is a comparative process. Texts might also be grasped from the inside—that is, in a congenial way—inasmuch as they are caught in an immediate act of understanding. Here the divinatory approach is at stake.

These four perspectives of interpretation are connected with each other, even though they show specific affinities. The grammatical interpretation matches to a greater degree the comparative approach, while the psychological matches the divinatory. The ultimate purpose of interpretation is "to better understand an author than he was able to give account of himself" (Schleiermacher, 1974, p. 138). Since, to an author, a lot remains unconscious that must be set out to understand his work, the interpreter brings a surplus of understanding in his or her interpretation. That is why the process of interpretation remains unfinished and is able to achieve its goal only approximatively. Even the hermeneutical "circle" (Schleiermacher, 1974, p. 86) is to be solved only at the initial stages. Indeed the comprehension of a single point always presupposes an understanding of the whole, but this is to be gained only by working through the single points (Schleiermacher, 1974, p. 144).

In connection with general hermeneutics, Schleiermacher constantly gave lectures on criticism. In comparison with hermeneutics, criticism gets its start in the suspicion that what is present does not meet the original state of matter. This disagreement took place either through mechanical errors or through free actions. Consequently, Schleiermacher articulates criticism into two main parts (doctrinal and historical) that echo the traditional distinction of a lower and a higher criticism. Critical endeavors aim at determining the original state of matter both from a historical viewpoint (the historical event witnessed) and through philological means. Both philological and historical criticism make use of external and internal signs to ascertain the congruence with the original state. Schleiermacher held that it is difficult to draw a boundary between higher and lower criticism. The first one determines—largely by approximation, and therein seeks the congruence of internal and external evidence—what pertains to the original fact or state historically witnessed. External evidence probes for the closeness of analyzed elements to its core. Internal evidence probes for their agreement with such a core. The task of lower criticism is to separate out, as accurately and convincingly as possible, the original reading of a text. It is actually an endless task. Exactly the same sort of criteria is to be applied to any kind of text. The critical specialist uses every scrap of available evidence. Even in service of a theological aim, criticism does not rely on dogmatic rules. Exegetical inquiry is comprised of both hermeneutics and criticism. According to Schleiermacher they are thoroughly interdependent. Hermeneutic, as the craft of interpretation, is a historical and philological enterprise, and as such is conditioned by linguistics and criticism. At the same time hermeneutical principles exert a decisive influence both upon the operations of criticism and upon the finer perceptions of linguistics. The effect is on the operations of criticism. In no way does proper hermeneutical effort obviate critical principles. Indeed Schleiermacher suggests that, as a form of historical criticism, while making its own distinctive contributions, hermeneutics relies upon the exact standard of textual criticism.

Schleiermacher's importance within the field of hermeneutics goes back to his conception of a general theory of interpretation. This had considerable influence on philosophical discussion. He constantly thought of New Testament hermeneutics and criticism as a special case of general doctrine and method; within this frame he exercised his manifold exegetical and philological practice concerning both New Testament and ancient philosophy. In the context of the revival of hermeneutical issues in the twentieth century, above all through Martin Heidegger's "hermeneutics of Dasein," Schleiermacher's hermeneutics gained new importance. Schleiermacher was acknowledged as a "classic of hermeneutics," even though more of a philosophical than of a theological sort. Still the influence of his hermeneutical theory and activity persevered, along with some reductive perspectives. Already Dilthey had laid stress on the psychological interpretation. His emphasis brought about misunderstandings, causing the loss of the connection between hermeneutics and criticism, grammatical and psychological interpretation, and the link that united general with special hermeneutics applied to the New Testament. Under the heading of "doubtfulness of Romantic hermeneutics," (Gadamer, 1965, part 2, sec. 1) Hans-Georg Gadamer holds that Schleiermacher lays all the stress on the psychological interpretation, and consequently, gets rid of the objective understanding. On this point the subsequent investigations brought about necessary corrections, pointing to Schleiermacher's contribution in linking up general and special hermeneutics, hermeneutics and criticism, grammatical and psychological interpretation.

Philosophical System. It is worth highlighting Schleiermacher's philosophical thinking, as it provides the framework of his intellectual activities. In his doctrine of science, the *Dialektik* (Schleiermacher, *Kritische Gesamtausgabe,* sec. 2, vol. 10, 2002–, pp. 1–2), Schleiermacher is searching for the highest knowing as a transcendental ground that has to function as the condition of possibility for the unity of thinking and being. The relation of thinking with being has to rely on this transcendental ground. On the other hand, the original unity of thinking and being accounts for the various representations that are different in their content. Here Schleiermacher refers to the immediate self-consciousness (or feeling, in this precise meaning) and understands it as showing an analogy with the transcendent ground. This is the pivotal point of his research, even though it withdraws from every knowing effort. In the second, formal part of his search, Schleiermacher investigates which technical rules are needed to overcome, still only approximately, the difference in thinking toward the unity of knowing. Basing his work upon a theory of construction and combination, he develops the rules of connection from which he derives a system of sciences: ethics, physics, and historical and natural sciences.

Moreover Schleiermacher has addressed ethics, setting out the principles and structures of reason's action upon nature. Here he does not stick to individuals and their faculties but also encompasses the sound forms of ethical process in their framework. In this manner he articulates ethics as a doctrine of goods, virtues, and duties. While the doctrine of goods treats the objectivations of reason that are brought about by ethical subjects, the doctrine of virtues has to show the "forces" on which individual activities rely, and the doctrine of duties treats the resultant modes of human behavior. Schleiermacher understands every unity of reason and nature as "good"; accordingly the variety of goods is formally divided into four spheres: political community (state), social community, science community, and religious community (church). Only the set of all four spheres together makes up the "highest Good," which in its turn is approached in our ethical endeavors as the end of the ethical process.

REINTERPRETATION OF DOGMA. The ethical notion of church, as one of the four "goods," provides the formal framework for Schleiermacher's theology. Religiosity (or piety, *Frömmigkeit*) then gets its natural place within the development of ethical life. Some of the ground traversed in the *Speeches* is covered again in the introduction to his theological masterwork, *Der christliche Glaube (The Christian Faith).* In this work, Schleiermacher began with religiosity as a general human phenomenon and defined the irreducible essence of religion as "the feeling of absolute dependence" (§ 4). A little introspection will show, according to Schleiermacher, that consciousness of self and world are a reciprocal relationship, that is, a mutual or relative dependence. But a second look reveals one's own immediate self-consciousness as coming in its entirety "from somewhere else" (§ 4.4). This deeper consciousness cannot arise from the influence of the world because humans exercise a counterinfluence upon the world and consequently are relatively dependent on it; it is precisely an immediate self-consciousness that encompasses both self and world together as absolutely dependent. God is then the origin (the "out of") of this immediate self-consciousness or feeling. In the feeling of absolute dependence, God is actually experienced in the only possible way, and to be conscious of being absolutely dependent is to be conscious of being in relation to God.

Schleiermacher explained it in a letter on *The Christian Faith* to his friend Friedrich Lücke, "What I understand by 'religious feeling' . . . is the original attestation of an immediate existential relationship" (Schleiermacher, *Kritische Gesamtausgabe,* sec. 1, vol. 10, 1990, p. 318). This feeling, however, simply draws the transcendental frame of religious experience. Actually, it comes about concretely in the manifold elements or "stimulations" *(Erregungen)* of lived experience, which show themselves within the context of objective or sensible consciousness in its ever different features. That is why, among other things, the limits of one's own consciousness of God have to be overcome through a reciprocal communication that forms the base of a religious community (church). The *religious community* is defined as the community in which, within determined limits, an ever-renewed circulation of religious self-consciousness takes place and an orderly, harmonious promotion of religious stimulations is made possible. The task of a philosophy of religion (in Schleiermacher's meaning) is then to set out the individual differences of each single church and each religion. In this frame Schleiermacher understands Christianity as a teleological trend of religiosity that belongs to Monotheismus. *Teleologic* means here that in Christianity the concern with ethical tasks dominates with the idea of the kingdom of God. All the features of Christian religiosity are referred to the impulse originally caused by Christ, the founder, each time linked up with further historical development.

In his *Kurze Darstellung des theologischen Studiums: Zum Behuf einleitender Vorlesungen* (1811/1830; *Brief Outline of Theology as a Field of Study,* 1966), Schleiermacher exemplarily presents his views of what Christian theology is and how the work of theology as science can be seen as a whole. Here *theology* is defined as "positive science" that directly refers to actual historical experience within a set of given social relations (church) and to serve a practical function (the leadership of the Christian Church). Every theological discipline may be regarded as a contribution to the understanding of the essence or distinctive nature of Christianity. The general form of this understanding, as compared with the nature of other religious communities, is supplied through "philosophical theology." Such a discipline points to the features that distinguish community both from outside (apologetics) and within itself (polemics). The norm or the essential core of this understanding is clarified through a series of historical studies, whose whole is called "historical theology," which begins with "exegetical theology," continues with "church history," and ends with "historical knowledge of the present condition of Christianity" (dogmatics and statistics) (Schleiermacher, 1811/1830, § 85, 2: 1, 2, 3). The application of this understanding is contained in "practical theology." The whole of Christian theology is contained in these three overlapping areas.

Dogmatics then is a feature of historical theology focusing on the present state of the Christian community and its actual experience. Thus the object of the knowledge that constitutes *The Christian Faith* is the particular way of being conscious of God that takes its bearing from the central historical fact of the "redemption accomplished by Jesus of Nazareth" (§ 11). Most properly, dogmatics is about religious consciousness, but it is also the theologian's task to develop out of religious consciousness such conceptions of God and the world as are implicit in it and can be understood as representations of it. Schleiermacher executed the task in two parts: the first presents the religious self-consciousness that is presupposed by the specific mode of Christian faith, and thus does not yet set forth the opposition on which pivots the experience of redemption; the second presents such a self-consciousness taking into account the opposition upon which turns the whole experience of redemption. They are respectively the doctrine of creation-preservation and the doctrine of redemption. Here Schleiermacher pioneered a genuinely modern reconstruction of Christian belief immune from the devastating effects of eighteenth-century natural science and historical criticism.

The doctrine of creation, which Schleiermacher takes up in part one of *The Christian Faith,* is reconceived as an attempt to thematize the feeling of absolute dependence. "Creation" is not about a particular divine act (or series of divine acts) in the primeval past, but is instead about the creature consciousness that is a universal phenomenon of human existence in every time and place. The doctrine of creation is therefore indistinguishable in content from the doctrine of preservation: it is concerned with what can be said of the continuous divine activity on the basis of the religious consciousness of absolute dependence. The question of a temporal beginning of the world and humankind is irrelevant to dogmatics. If it nevertheless intrudes, it tends to give rise to misrepresentations of God's activity, as though it were akin to the activity of a human craftsperson. Schleiermacher finds a corresponding misrepresentation in the interventionist view of Providence, which pictures God as one cause or one agent (albeit preeminent) interacting with others, arbitrarily suspending the progress of natural events or undoing the effects of human behavior.

Schleiermacher's God does not intervene in the closed causal system of nature (as viewed by modern natural science) but is identified as its timeless and spaceless ground—this is the meaning of the eternity and omnipresence of the divine causality. That God is "omnipotent" does not mean that he can do whatever he pleases—that he can even interrupt a course of events he did not approve and make things turn out differently than they otherwise would. This would imply that, even if only for one fleeting moment, some chain of events had slipped outside the divine causality, whereas the proper sense of "omnipotence" is exactly that God's power does and effects all—not, however, in the same way finite causes do and effect things. God is omnipotent in the sense that the entire system of nature rests on his timeless and spaceless causality; the world is as it is solely by virtue of "the divine good-pleasure" (§ 120.4). Schleiermacher supplies similar treatment for other divine attributes. One does not call the divine omnipotence "omniscient" or "spiritual" because God has a consciousness like one's own or because he is a kind of sentient world soul, but because the feeling of absolute dependence is unlike a feeling of dependence on blind and dead necessity. There is simply no better way to denote this difference than to contrast the dead and the blind with the living and the conscious, conscious life being the highest thing humans know.

Schleiermacher held that the consciousness of absolute dependence is present in every actual religion and that the doctrine of creation articulates it in a monotheistic form that is not peculiar to Christianity. In Christianity, however, creature consciousness is contained within the consciousness of redemption through Christ: it is as believers in Christ that Christians are aware of themselves as God's creatures. In this experience of redemption, according to Schleiermacher, the purpose of divine omnipotence is made known as the purpose of omnipotent love. The kingdom of God established by Christ must extend its influence throughout the world.

The figure of Christ makes up the core topic of the second part of *The Christian Faith.* He was the second Adam, the completion of the creation of humanity, and there was an actual existence of God in him. To be sure, the way Christ works upon Christians, as Schleiermacher sees it, may be compared to the personal influence of a strong, historical personality—except that his influence is now indirect, mediated through the community he established. But the work of Christ, which is nothing other than the imparting of his own sense of God, is nonetheless unique, because it radiates out from one who possessed a uniquely powerful, indeed perfect, consciousness of God. Only this affirmation answers to the Christian consciousness that dogmatics seeks to describe. And although Schleiermacher did not shirk the historical problems of the New Testament, as his lectures on the life of Jesus demonstrate, he clearly believed that dogmatics could and should deduce its Christological affirmations directly from the Christian consciousness: he asked what Christ must have been like if one is to account for his perceived effects upon the Christian community.

SCHLEIERMACHER'S LEGACY. The historical importance of Schleiermacher is hardly in question, but, from his own day on, it has been hotly disputed whether or not his approach and his positions amount to permanently fruitful gains in the history of religious thought. Theologically he has been assailed from both the left wing and the right. The left-wing critics have been more impressed with his approach to historical science. In his focusing on the Christological problem from the Jesus of history to the Christ of faith, as David Friedrich Strauss pointed out, in *Der Christus des Glaubens und der Jesus der Geschichte. Eine Kritik des schleiermacherschen Lebens Jesu* (1865), Schleiermacher seems to have known in advance what he wanted to find in the Gospels, namely the Savior of his Herrnhutian piety.

The theological right objects that Schleiermacher made the initial methodological blunder of beginning with human experience and then moved on to force the Christian revelation into a preconceived theory of religion. Historians of religion, on the other hand, are more likely to reverse this line of criticism and object that, despite his good intentions, Schleiermacher's treatment of religion remained incorrigibly Christian and dogmatic. All this, of course, would not necessarily imply the unfruitfulness of his approach as a venture in the fields of religious studies, Christian theology, and, last but not least, philosophy. One might sum up his contributions in these areas in the following way: he introduced a new paradigm for understanding religion, made experience into the principle of theology, and settled dialogue as the basic condition of human, truth-productive efforts.

SEE ALSO Empiricism; Hermeneutics; Phenomenology of Religion.

BIBLIOGRAPHY

In the nineteenth century Schleiermacher's works were published in thirty-three volumes in three sections—Theology, Sermons, and Philosophy—as *Friedrich Schleiermacher's sämmtliche Werke* (Berlin, 1834–1864). In the late twentieth century a collection in five sections—Writings and Drafts, Lectures, Sermons, Translations, and Letters—began publication, *Kritische Gesamtausgabe,* edited by Hans-Joachim Birkner et al. (Berlin, 1980–). *Dialektik,* in two tomes, is in sec. 2, vol. 10. Other important editions by Schleiermacher include *Kurze Darstellung des theologischen Studiums: Zum*

Behuf einleitender Vorlesungen (Brief outline of theology as a field of study; Berlin, 1811; 2d ed., Berlin, 1830); *Der christliche Glaube: Nach den Grundsätzen der evangelischen Kirche im Zusammenhange dargestellt* (The Christian faith: Systematically presented according to the principles of the evangelical church; Berlin, 1821–1822; 2d ed., Berlin, 1830–1831); and *Hermeneutik,* edited by Heinz Kimmerle (Heidelberg, Germany, 1974).

The Edwin Mellen Press has undertaken an English edition of Schleiermacher's works with the series Schleiermacher Studies and Translations, including *Brief Outline of Theology as a Field of Study,* translated by Terrence N. Tice (Lewiston, N.Y., 1990); *The Christian Household: A Sermonic Treatise,* translated by Dietrich Seidel and Terrence N. Tice (Lewiston, N.Y., 1991); *On Freedom,* translated by Albert L. Blackwell (Lewiston, N.Y., 1992); *On the Highest Good,* translated by H. Victor Froese (Lewiston, N.Y., 1992); *Luke: A Critical Study,* translated by Connop Thirlwall (Lewiston, N.Y., 1993); *On What Gives Value to Life,* translated by Edwina Lawler and Terrence N. Tice (Lewiston, N.Y., 1995); *Reformed but Ever Reforming: Sermons in Relation to the Celebration of the Handing Over of the Augsburg Confession (1830),* translated by Iain G. Nicol (Lewiston, N.Y., 1997); *Letters on the Occasion of the Political Theological Task and the Sendschreiben (Open Letter) of Jewish Heads of Households,* translated by Gilya G. Schmidt (Lewiston, N.Y., 2001); *Brouillon zur Ethik (1805/1806): Notes on Ethics (1805/1806),* translated by John Wallhauser and Edwina Lawler; *Notes on the Theory of Virtue (1804/1805),* translated by Terrence N. Tice and Edwina Lawler (Lewiston, N.Y., 2003). Other notable translations of Schleiermacher's writings and lectures include *The Life of Jesus,* edited by Jack C. Verheyden, translated by S. Maclean Gilmour (Philadelphia, 1975); *Hermeneutics: The Handwritten Manuscripts,* translated by James Duke and Jack Forstman (Missoula, Mont., 1977); *On the "Glaubenslehre": Two Letters to Dr. Lücke,* translated by James Duke and Francis Fiorenza (Chico, Calif., 1980); *On Religion: Speeches to Its Cultured Despisers,* translated by Richard Crouter (Cambridge, U.K., 1988); *Introduction to Christian Ethics,* translated by John C. Shelley (Nashville, Tenn., 1989); *Christmas Eve: Dialogue on the Incarnation,* translated by Terrence N. Tice (San Francisco, 1990); *Occasional Thoughts on Universities in the German Sense: With an Appendix regarding a University Soon to Be Established (1808),* translated by Terrence N. Tice and Edwina Lawler (San Francisco, 1991); *Dialectic; or, The Art of Doing Philosophy,* translated by Terrence N. Tice (Atlanta, 1996); *Hermeneutics and Criticism and Other Writings,* translated and edited by Andrew Bowie (Cambridge, U.K., 1998). Some important older editions are *The Christian Faith,* edited by H. R. Mackintosh and J. S. Stewart from the second edition (New York, 1963); and *Schleiermacher's Soliloquies,* translated by Horace Leland Friess (Chicago, 1979).

A brief introductory study of Schleiermacher is B. A. Gerrish, *A Prince of the Church: Schleiermacher and the Beginnings of Modern Theology* (Philadelphia, 1984). See also, from the point of view of religious studies, Burkhard Gladigow, "Friedrich Schleiermacher (1768–1834)," in *Klassiker der Religionswissenschaft: Von Friedrich Schleiermacher bis Mircea Eliade* (Munich, 1997). More detailed introductions are Hermann Fischer's accurately updated *Friedrich Daniel Ernst Schleiermacher* (Munich, 2001); Richard R. Niebuhr's *Schleiermacher on Christ and Religion: A New Introduction* (New York, 1964); Kurt Nowak's *Friedrich Schleiermacher: Leben, Werk, und Wirkung* (Göttingen, Germany, 2001); and Martin Redeker's *Schleiermacher: Life and Thought* (Philadelphia, 1973). Studies of particular aspects of Schleiermacher's thought are Christian Albrecht, *Schleiermachers Theorie der Frömmigkeit* (Berlin and New York, 1994); Christian Berner, *La philosophie de Schleiermacher: "Herméneutique," "Dialectique," "Éthique"* (Paris, 1995); Albert L. Blackwell, *Schleiermacher's Early Philosophy of Life: Determinism, Freedom, and Phantasy* (Chico, Calif., 1982); Martin Diederich, *Schleiermachers Geistverständnis* (Göttingen, Germany, 1999); Wilhelm Dilthey, *Aus Schleiermachers leben. In briefen,* vol. 1–4 (Berlin, 1858–1863); Jack Forstman, *A Romantic Triangle: Schleiermacher and Early German Romanticism* (Missoula, Mont., 1977); Hans-Georg Gadamer, *Wahrheit und Methode* (Tübingen, Germany, 1965); Marlin E. Miller, *Der Übergang: Schleiermachers Theologie des Reiches Gottes im Zusammenhang seines Gesamtdenkens* (Gütersloh, Germany, 1970); Giovanni Moretto, *Etica e storia in Schleiermacher* (Naples, Italy, 1979) and *Ispirazione e libertà: Saggi su Schleiermacher* (Naples, Italy, 1986); John Sungmin Park, *Theological Ethics of Friedrich Schleiermacher* (Lewiston, N.Y., 2001); Gunter Scholtz, *Die Philosophie Schleiermachers* (Darmstadt, Germany, 1984) and *Ethik und Hermeneutik: Schleiermachers Grundlegung der Geisteswissenschaften* (Frankfurt am Main, 1995); Markus Schröder, *Die kritische Identität des neuzeitlichen Christentums* (Tübingen, Germany, 1996); Sergio Sorrentino, *Schleiermacher e la filosofia della religione* (Brescia, Italy, 1978) and *Ermeneutica e filosofia trascendentale* (Bologna, Italy, 1986); Craig Stein, *Schleiermacher's Construction of the Subject in the Introduction to "The Christian Faith"* (Lewiston, N.Y., 2001); David Friedrich Strauss, *Der Christus des Glaubens und der Jesus der Geschichte: Ein Kritik des schleiermacherschen Lebens Jesu* (Berlin, 1865); John E. Thiel, *God and World in Schleiermacher's Dialektik and Glaubenslehre: Criticism and the Methodology of Dogmatics* (Bern, Switzerland, and Las Vegas, 1981); and Robert R. Williams, *Schleiermacher the Theologian: The Construction of the Doctrine of God* (Philadelphia, 1978). Important collected works are Hans-Joachim Birkner, ed., *Schleiermacher-Studien* (Berlin and New York, 1996); Günter Meckenstock, ed., *Schleiermacher und die wissenschaftliche Kultur des Christentums* (Berlin and New York, 1991); Ruth Drucilla Richardson, ed., *Schleiermacher in Context* (Lewiston, N.Y., 1991); and Sergio Sorrentino, ed., *Schleiermacher's Philosophy and the Philosophical Tradition* (Lewiston, N.Y., 1992).

B. A. GERRISH (1987)
SERGIO SORRENTINO (2005)

SCHMIDT, WILHELM (1868–1954), German anthropologist and Roman Catholic priest, was born on February 16, 1868, in Hörde (now Dortmund-Hörde) Germany, the son of a factory worker. In 1883 he entered the missionary school in Steyl, Netherlands, that served as the motherhouse of the Societas Verbi Divini (the Society of the Divine Word), which was founded in 1875. There he completed his secondary philosophical and theological studies, and he was ordained a priest in 1892. He studied Semitic languages at the University of Berlin from 1893 to 1895. In 1895 Schmidt was appointed professor of several theological disciplines at the Society of the Divine Word Mission Seminary of Saint Gabriel in Mödling, Austria (established 1889).

Various questions and problems of missionaries (especially from New Guinea) prompted Schmidt to undertake studies in linguistics, ethnology, and comparative religion. In 1906 he founded *Anthropos,* as international review of ethnology and linguistics, and in 1931 he established the Anthropos Institute in Mödling, an organization affiliated to the Society of the Divine Word, and he served as the institute's director until 1950. (In 1962 the institute relocated to Sankt Augustin, near Bonn.) From 1921 until 1938 Schmidt was a professor at the University of Vienna.

Schmidt directed the establishment of the Missionary Ethnological Museum in Rome (1922–1926) under the authorization of Pope Pius XI, and from 1927 to 1939 Schmidt was director of the museum. After the Anschluss of Austria in March 1938, Schmidt resettled with the Anthropos Institute in Switzerland and became a professor at the University of Fribourg (1939–1951). On February 10, 1954, Schmidt died in Fribourg, Switzerland; he was buried at the seminary in Mödling. Schmidt was a member of many scholarly societies and held honorary degrees from six universities.

SCHMIDT'S WORKS. Schmidt began his linguistic studies by examining the native languages of New Guinea, but he soon expanded his field of research to include all of Oceania. He showed the relationships between the Austronesian languages and a certain group of the Southeast Asian mainland that Schmidt called "Austroasiatic" languages. His study *Die Mon-Kmer-Völker: Ein Bindeglied zwischen Völkern Zentralasiens und Austronesiens* (The Mon-Khmer peoples: A link between peoples in central Asia and Austronesia, 1906) was of particular importance.

Schmidt's interest gradually shifted to ethnology. In 1910 he published a book on Pygmy peoples, *Die Stellung der Pygmäenvölker in der Entwicklungsgeschichte Menschen* (The place of Pygmies in the historical development of man), and in 1924 he published *Völker und Kulturen,* which he wrote with Wilhelm Koppers. The latter is an attempt at a worldwide presentation of cultural history based on a system of "culture areas" (*Kultukreise*). Schmidt's interest in this direction came from the work of the anthropogeographer Friedrich Ratzel and the ethnologists Leo Frobenius and Fritz Graebner.

According to Schmidt's system, the oldest culture of humanity (what he called the *Urkultur*) was that of the hunter-gatherers, remnants of which are found among the Pygmies and pygmoids as well as in the Arctic-American area and in southeastern Australia. From this *Urkultur* there arose, independent of one another, the three "primary cultures": (1) a culture based on the cultivation of plants and associated with matriarchy, developing out of the plants-gathering of women; (2) a "higher hunting culture" controlled by men and associated with totemism; (3) a patriarchal pastoral culture based on nomadic animal husbandry.

Each one of the three primary "culture areas" identified by Schmidt arose, in his view, only once in a given geographical area and then spread through migration. This idea forms the basis of his so-called diffusionism.

Through the intermingling of the primary cultures, secondary and tertiary cultures took shape that in turn grew into the high cultures. The aforementioned changes in the economic bases of culture also had an effect on society as well as religion. In his work *Die Sprachfamilien und Sprachenkreise der Erde* (Linguistic families and linguistic circles of the world, 1926) Schmidt attempted an ethnological-linguistic synthesis. Later Schmidt sought to elaborate on Graebner's culture-historical method in his *Handbuch der Methode der kulturhistorischen Ethnologie* (1937; published in translation as *The Culture Historical Method of Ethnology,* 1939) and at the same time to organize his own ideas into a thoroughly systematic form. With his overview of the development of cultures, Schmidt wanted to substitute a historically grounded system for the evolutionist position, which had been influenced by the natural sciences. Schmidt's critics, however, realized that this new approach was too rigid and schematic. Although the cultural forms he identified cannot be considered historical realities, for his followers they were nevertheless valuable as tools for classification.

Soon after 1900 the main objective of Schmidt's research became the elucidation of the development and the origin of religion. This problem has now been abandoned by scholars, because it is not possible to provide an adequate scientific response. Schmidt's interest in this topic was decisively aroused by Andrew Lang. In 1898, in *The Making of Religion,* Lang contradicted the then influential theory of E. B. Tylor that animism was the origin of all religion. Lang pointed out the overt presence of belief in a Supreme Being among Australian Aborigines and other simple peoples. Relying on his own studies, Schmidt published, from 1908 to 1910, a series of articles under the general title "L'origine de l'idée de Dieu" in the journal *Anthropos.* In these articles Schmidt took issue with existing theories of the origin of religion and thoroughly examined the material available on southeastern Australia, disregarding the significant problem of the structure of religious thought, which is now at the center of anthropological considerations, especially cognitivist anthropology (Boyer, 1994). Schmidt wrote this work in French to support the struggle the Catholic Church was then waging against Modernism, a movement particularly prevalent in France.

The German original of "L'origine de l'idée de Dieu" was published in revised form in 1912 as volume one of *Der Ursprung der Gottesidee* (2d ed., 1926). Volumes two through six (1929–1935) of this work deal with the religions of "primeval peoples" (*Urkulturvölker*). Volumes seven through twelve (1940–1955) treat the nomadic peoples of Africa and Asia.

Schmidt arrived at the following conclusions in *Der Ursprung der Gotteidee.* First, he noted that monotheism is the religion of the extant hunter-gatherer peoples investigated by him; their Supreme Being, the creator of the world, is tied to their ethics and is venerated with a cult. Second, he argued that because these peoples represent the oldest accessible form of human culture, it stands to reason that monotheism is the oldest religion of humanity. Third, he declared that because the religions of these peoples, especially their representations of the Supreme Being, display so many characteristic points of agreement, one must concede that they have a single historical origin. Fourth, Schmidt speculated that the image of the Supreme Being held by primitive peoples is so sublime that it could not have been acquired from human experience and therefore it must be traced back to a divine primitive revelation. Finally, he postulated that, in the course of later developments, progress in external culture was achieved by many peoples, yet decadence often occurred in religion and ethics.

According to Schmidt, the original idea of God is conserved with the greatest relative purity in nomadic peoples' belief in a heavenly God; in other cultures the idea lost ground. Sun worship and magic came to prevail in totemistic cultures, and the matriarchal planting cultures made room for earth and fertility cults, lunar mythology, and worship of the dead.

CRITICAL DEBATE CONCERNING SCHMIDT. In the world of anthropologists and religious historians, the work of Schmidt finds particular support among those scholars who, certain criticisms and objections notwithstanding, refer to the historical method, share the same concept of the world as the Austrian anthropologist, and appreciate the wide scope of his scientific undertaking (cf. Demarchi, 1989). Among other scholars, as Alan Barnard writes (2000), the theory of diffusionism, which forms the basis for spatial dislocation and the structure of different cultural environments, is not particularly popular, even if some of its ideas survive in the debate between archaeologists and physical anthropologists on the question of cultural similarity. Notwithstanding this, it is impossible to disagree with Barnard when he states that diffusionism has been important in the development of the idea of "cultural area," an element of modern anthropological thought.

To fully understand the figure of Schmidt and the influence his thinking has retained in some intellectual circles, one should not overlook his association with the cultural and political outlook developed by the Catholic Church in the 1920s and still prevalent in some parts of it. His indefatigable organizational role stemmed from his embodiment of the Catholic political mission, explicitly stated in the encyclical *Maximum Illud* of 1919. This encyclical of Pope Benedict XV had certain important objectives: (1) to reorganize the missions in the Third World that had been weakened by World War I; (2) to win over, once again, colonial peoples, who had often seen the Catholic Church as an instrument of colonial penetration; and (3) to reaffirm the principle of the supranationality and universality of the church, which had been questioned by many (Leone, 1980, p. 124).

Certainly Schmidt was the driving force behind this restructuring process, in which his *Weeks* on religious ethnology (international meetings organized for making known the Catholic idea of this science) also played an important part, but he was more than that. On many issues (the family, nationalism, sex) he represented the viewpoint of the good Catholic. It is no coincidence that, for example, as Ernest Jones (1953) recalls, Sigmund Freud regarded him as an enemy for this reason and held him responsible for the suppression of the *Rivista Italiana di Psicoanalisi.*

Methodologically speaking, one may say that Schmidt's concept of cultural diffusionism harked back to what George W. Stocking (1987) has termed "biblical paradigm." Used by various scholars in different historical contexts, this is a method of interpretation that considers history as the result of a hereditary process, the origins of which are recoverable by applying linguistic methodology to cultural phenomena, finding the roots of different linguistic expressions by comparative means. In this process changes have occurred as a result of degeneration, and human beings, who are placed within it, have become inured to and live in a patriarchal society.

The stress upon the hereditary aspect above all and the failure to examine the system of internal relations between cultural environments have led anthropologists to take little interest in the thinking of Schmidt, especially because functional and structural analysis, which have become established in this discipline, have been so fruitful. This has allowed the development of a productive relationship with natural science, which the followers of the culture-historical method had opposed. The patchy interest in the works of Schmidt has also resulted from a lack of knowledge of German on the part of scholars.

In short, biblical paradigm, characterized by diffusionism, consists of taking the Bible as a tool for the interpretation of human history, the origins of which are identified with the institutions of monogamy and monotheism and are the product of a single source. Such paradigms form the basis of the anti-evolutionism of Schmidt, even if many scholars, such as Marvin Harris (1968), regarding him as a follower of Joseph François de Maistre and thus a reactionary thinker, have emphasized the evolutionary nature of some of his theories.

The belief of Schmidt that involved going back to so-called primordial religion derived from the human tendency to seek out the origins of religion (and to seek it in a probable divine revelation) is the aspect of his thinking that is most discussed. On this topic there was a heated debate (*Man*, 1910) between Schmidt and Alfred R. Radcliffe-Brown, in which Lang also became involved, concerning the figure of the Andaman Island god Puluga. In essence, Radcliffe-Brown accused Schmidt of interpreting Andaman religion in a prejudiced manner by referring it back to his own religious beliefs. Other scholars repeated the charge, against which he was in part defended by Ernest Brandewie (1990), who could not, however, help linking the philosophical outlook of Schmidt to Thomism and the Scholastics, and thus to the traditional view of the Catholic Church regarding the origin of religion and the relation between faith and reason. Brandewie (1990) also recognized in Schmidt's work an objective of apologetics as well as science. Henryk Zimón (1986), on the other hand, holds that Schmidt was not motivated solely by a desire to reconcile Catholic dogma with ethnological research, especially since some Catholic theologians did not support his degenerationist views or his ideas regarding monotheism and primordial revelation.

The critical advance of Raffaele Pettazzoni (1957), in which he held that true monotheism stems from an antipolytheistic revolution instigated by a religious reformer, is also important. The sociological critique developed by Guy E. Swanson (1960) is often neglected. Swanson opposed the Austrian anthropologist by holding that monotheism was not the actual religion of the simplest and most archaic societies. For monotheistic belief to surface required the existence in society of at least three dominant groups, which in his opinion consisted of an organization exercising independent authority in a given social sphere.

Another important methodological problem has been raised by another follower of Schmidt, Joseph Henninger, who wonders whether the similarities between the Supreme Beings of different peoples demonstrates the unique historical origin of belief in a Supreme Being (see first edition of *Encyclopedia of Religion* [1987]). Furthermore, he observes that Schmidt, in claiming that revelation is proved by the presence of a belief in a Supreme Being among such peoples, oversteps the bounds of the historical study of religions and makes philosophical and theological statements. The complex nature of the figure of the Supreme Being in different cultures has been documented by Edward B. Tylor, who thought that in all probability the missionaries themselves had interpreted the religious ideas of the native peoples so as to extract the figure of a monotheistic god from them.

Schmidt has also been criticized for his failure to clearly define the categories he used, such as Supreme Being and monotheism. For this reason even if one accepts his assumptions (which were not been critically evaluated by him), they cannot be easily harmonized with his own theories because they are subject to ambiguous interpretation. Besides, as Zimón stated (1986), when returning to this subject and analyzing the religion of the Bambuti Pygmies, it is always best to make clear in concrete terms the nature of the monotheism of the group being studied. In this case it seems not to have been a clear and unequivocal idea of a Supreme Being called upon under various names and identified as a god of heaven, a god of the forest, or a god of hunting. Contrary to what Schmidt thought, it is a Supreme Being who is dualist in nature, that is, both chthonic and celestial.

One more general aspect of the historical ideas of Graebner and Schmidt, which has even been criticized by those who make reference to the culture-historical method, is the notion of the fixed, permanent nature of cultural elements, which would allow one to go back to primordial cultural forms. For example, Fritz Bornemann (1982), director of the Anthropos Institute from 1950 to 1955, stated that this was an a priori assumption that took for granted what the culture-historical inquiry needed to prove, namely the chronological collocation of the culture being studied. This consideration convinced him to avoid using the term *Urkultur.*

This and other more detailed criticisms of the culture-historical method led some of those who had originally supported Schmidt and Koppers (for example, Josef Haekel) to distance themselves from the theory of "culture areas." If the theory of the origin of monotheism proposed by Schmidt were accepted, it would make meaningless all the research conducted by historians who have sought to reconstruct accurately the course and historical contexts (Mesopotamia, Egypt, ancient Israel) in which—according to Marcel Gauchet (1985), via the influence of a complex series of factors, such as the idea of an absolute Lord as a counterpoint to an earthly ruler—the monotheism that characterizes modern Western civilization emerged.

SEE ALSO Frobenius, Leo; Graebner, Fritz; Kulturkreiselehre; Pettazzoni, Raffaele.

BIBLIOGRAPHY

Barnard, Alan. *History and Theory in Anthropology.* Cambridge, U.K., 2000.

Bornemann, Fritz. "Verzeichnis der Schriften von P. W. Schmidt, S.V.D. (1868–1954)." *Anthropos* 49 (1954): 385–432.

Bornemann, Fritz. *P. Wilhelm Schmidt, S.V.D., 1868–1954.* Analecta Societatis Verbi Divini no. 59. Rome, 1982. Includes additions to Bornemann's 1954 bibliography.

Boyer, Pascal. *The Naturalness of Religious Ideas: A Cognitive Theory of Religion.* Berkeley, Calif., 1994.

Brandewie, Ernest. *Wilhelm Schmidt and the Origin of the Idea of God.* Lanham, Md., 1983. Contains a translation of selections from vols. 1–6 of *Der Ursprung der Gottesidee.*

Brandewie, Ernest. *When Giants Walked the Earth: The Life and Times of Wilhelm Schmidt, SVD.* Fribourg, Switzerland, 1990.

Demarchi, Franco, ed. *Wilhelm Schmidt, un etnologo sempre attuale.* Pubblicazioni dell'Istituto di scienze religiose in Trento 14. Bologna, Italy, 1989.

Gauchet, Marcel. *Le désenchantement du monde.* Paris, 1985.

Harris, Marvin. *The Rise of Anthropological Theory: A History of Theories of Culture.* New York, 1968.

Henninger, Joseph. "P. Wilhelm Schmidt, S.V.D. (1868–1954): Eine biographische Skizze." *Anthropos* 51 (1956): 19–60.

Henninger, Joseph. "Wilhelm Schmidt, S.V.D. (1868–1954)." *Verbum SVD* 20 (1979): 345–362.

Jones, Ernest. *The Life and Work of Sigmund Freud.* Vol. 3. New York, 1953.

Lang, Andrew. "Puluga." *Man* no 30 (1910): 51-53.

Leone, Alba Rosa. "La politica missionaria del Vaticano tra le due guerre." *Studi storici* 21 (1980): 123–156.

Pettazzoni, Raffaele. *L'essere supremo nelle religioni primitive.* Novara, Italy, 1957.

Schmidt, Wilhelm. *Wege der Kulturen: Gesammelte Aufsätze.* Studia Instituti Anthropos, vol. 20. Saint Augustin bei Bonn, Germany, 1964. A memorial volume containing a collection of representative articles.

Radcliffe-Brown, Alfred R. "Puluga: A Reply to Father Schmidt." *Man* 17 (1910): 33–37.

Schmidt, Wilhelm. "Puluga,the Supreme Being of the Andamanese." *Man* 2 (1910): 2–7.

Schmidt, Wilhelm. Nochmals: "Puluga, das höchste Wesen der Andamanesen." *Man* 38 (1910): 66–71.

Schmidt, Wilhelm. Nochmals: "Puluga, das höchste Wesen der Andamanesen." *Man* 47 (1910): 82–86.

Stocking, George W. *Victorian Anthropology.* New York, 1987.

Swanson, Guy E. *The Birth of the Gods: The Origin of Primitive Beliefs.* Ann Arbor, Mich., 1960.

Waardenburg, Jacques. *Classical Approaches to the Study of Religion.* 2 vols. The Hague, 1973–1974. Contains selections from *The Origin and Growth of Religion* and *High Gods in North America.*

Waldenfels, Hans. "Wilhelm Schmidt (1868–1954)." In *Klassiker der Religionswissenschaft: Von Friedrich Schleiermacher bis Mircea Eliade,* edited by Axel Michaels. Munich, 1997.

Zimón, Henryk. "Wilhelm Schmidt's Theory of Primitive Monotheism and Its Critique within the Vienna School of Ethnology." *Anthropos* 81 (1986): 243–260.

Zwernemann, Jürgen. *Culture History and African Anthropology: A Century of Reasearch in Germany and Austria.* Uppsala, Sweden, 1983.

JOSEPH HENNINGER (1987)
ALESSANDRA CIATTINI (2005)
Translated from Italian by Paul Ellis

SCHNEERSON, MENACHEM M. Rabbi Menachem Mendel Schneerson (1902–1994) was the seventh-generation leader of the Habad-Lubavitch Hasidic movement in the period following World War II who played a significant role in the modern Jewish world. He was born in Nikolayev, Ukraine, to Rabbi Levi Yitzhak Schneerson (1878–1944) and Chana Yanowsky (1880–1964). In 1909 the family moved to Yekatrinoslav (Dnepropetrovsk) where Rabbi Levi Yitzhak, a noted Talmudic and qabbalistic scholar, was appointed Hasidic chief rabbi.

Menachem Mendel was named for his paternal ancestor the third Lubavitcher Rebbe (1789–1866), grandson of Rabbi Schne'ur Zalman of Liadi (1745–1812), the founder of the Habad-Lubavitch school of Hasidism. He was given a traditional Jewish education with private tutors and also studied at the Talmudic Academy (*yeshivah*) in Yekatrinoslav, headed for a time by the Vilna Talmudist Rabbi Haim Ozer Grodzinsky (1863–1940). Menachem Mendel was regarded as a brilliant scholar with a wide grasp of languages and general studies as well as of Jewish thought. He came in contact with the leading Talmudist Rabbi Joseph Rozin (1858–1936), the *gaon* (genius) of Rogachov, whose writings he would often quote.

In the 1920s he began to associate closely with his relative Rabbi Joseph Isaac Schneersohn (1880–1950), the sixth Lubavitcher Rebbe, who was endeavouring to preserve traditional Jewish observance in the secularist USSR, and was consequently arrested in 1927 and expelled from Russia. Menachem Mendel married Schneersohn's daughter Chaya Mussya (1901–1988) in 1928.

The couple lived in Berlin and, from 1933, in Paris. In both cities Rabbi Menachem Mendel attended university courses, earning a diploma in electrical engineering from the Ecole Speciale des Travaux Publiques engineering college in Paris. He was also involved in editing the Habad rabbinic journal *HaTamim,* published in Warsaw from 1935 to 1939. This combination of secular study with traditional Torah knowledge was unusual in the Eastern European Hasidic movement, which championed the exclusive study of the Talmud and related literature. The Habad branch of Hasidism had always emphasized rationality. The term *Habad* (popular spelling: *Chabad*) is an acronym of three Hebrew words meaning wisdom, understanding, knowledge. The combination of "worldly" knowledge with intensive religious concern was to characterize Rabbi Menachem Mendel's later work as a religious leader.

When World War II broke out Rabbi Joseph Isaac was trapped in Poland and Menachem Mendel in France. Eventually the U.S. branch of Habad managed to rescue both rabbis and some of the members of their families; other relatives perished in the Holocaust. Rabbi Menachem Mendel and his wife reached New York in 1941.

ASSIMILATION. In the United States, based in Brooklyn, Rabbi Joseph Isaac tried to promote traditional Jewish education and practice among American Jews, with the motto: "America is not different." His older son-in-law Rabbi Samarias Gurary (d.1989) headed an advanced Talmudic Academy (*yeshivah*) and a network of Jewish schools. This endeavour was paralleled by similar work undertaken by other Jewish leaders who had escaped from Europe, although the Lubavitch *yeshivah* included qabbalistic Hasidic teachings in its curriculum.

Rabbi Menachem Mendel, with the support of his father-in-law, embarked on a different course, undertaking the singular task that was to dominate the remainder of his life: the attempt to turn the tide of Jewish assimilation; to regenerate traditional Jewish values and practice; and to find "lost Jews" wherever they might be. His father-in-law created for him, or appointed him to lead, publicist and activist organizations with goals such as promoting religious education for American Jewish children, including those in the public school system; setting up Jewish schools for girls; providing spiritual outreach to Jewish farmers and soldiers; and making contact with Jewish men and women in outlying communities. Thus during the 1940s a number of Lubavitch emissaries were sent from Brooklyn to work as rabbis and teachers in locations around the United States.

In January 1950 Rabbi Joseph Isaac passed away and was succeeded, after a period of uncertainty, by Rabbi Menachem Mendel, who became the seventh Lubavitcher Rebbe. Over the next four decades he became known for his outreach work, which was creating a global phenomenon of unparalleled proportions in the Jewish community. Through his many emissaries (some three thousand before his death) he aimed to address assimilated Jews and also those who felt staunchly Jewish but did not observe all the distinctive *mitsvot* (traditional observances).

OUTREACH. Many traditional Orthodox Jewish immigrants from Eastern Europe tried to protect themselves from the secularization of their new society by living in closed, homogenous communities. Rabbi Schneerson, through his rabbinic teachings, appealed to this group to open its borders to less observant Jews. In 1952 he wrote an open letter addressed to students at all *yeshivot* asking them to befriend and communicate with other Jews less observant than themselves. Over the years he repeatedly claimed that the Jewish people are one, despite apparent differences in observance and belief. A favorite image was the idea that the individual members of the Jewish people are like the letters of a Torah scroll: if one letter is missing, the entire scroll is unfit for use; each individual is essential.

To help foster Jewish religious identity, he established Lubavitch outreach organisations, which made contact with Jews on college campuses and in less-traditional communities. Adult education programs were created, including special *yeshivot* providing supplementary Jewish education for hitherto acculturated Jews. Kfar Chabad, a large village of Chabad followers in Israel, presented itself as a welcoming showcase of tradition for many Israelis.

A key issue for Schneerson was combating the widespread idea that modern science had displaced traditional Jewish belief. In a 1952 letter addressed to a scientist in Israel he employed the concept of axioms to argue that science provides what he called a narrative, but not truth. Science generates a narrative in that if you agree to such-and-such a set of axioms, factors *x* and *y* are likely to result in *z*. However, if you change the axioms, a different result may ensue. He contrasted this relativistic view of science with what he saw as the truth of the Torah. He also claimed that scientific advances and Torah teachings, especially as interpreted in Hasidic thought, were approaching the same goal. He encouraged artists and writers to believe that their creative talent could strengthen Judaism. Through letters and personal contact he maintained close relationships with thousands of individuals in many walks of life, including academics, military figures, politicians, and members of the wider public, as well as prominent rabbis, always endeavouring to increase people's religious observance and, more particularly, to encourage them to become spiritual leaders themselves.

This effort, combined with other factors, such as the moral turbulence of the sixties and the 1967 Six-Day War, which brought the Temple site in Jerusalem back into Jewish hands, contributed to the creation of a Return to Judaism movement. In talks and letters Menahem Mendel presented the outreach ideal as a central facet of Orthodoxy, citing an early Hasidic motif (with strong messianic connotations) of "spreading the wellsprings to the outside" in an effort to combat what he saw as the imminent dissolution of traditional Jewish values and practice among most Jewish people. Traditional Lubavitch values such as love of your fellow and accepting people despite their spiritual failings were important in this process. The Return to Judaism movement eventually grew far beyond Lubavitch and is now a major focus in the work of many other Jewish movements.

Rabbi Schneerson also addressed the non-Jewish world. Controversially, he campaigned to promote a moment of silence for spiritual reflection in the U.S. public schools, and drew attention to a statement by Maimonides that the Jews have the duty to communicate the Seven Noahide Laws—the basic elements of biblical religious morality, including respect for the sanctity of life and traditional sexual ethics—to the larger society around them.

At the same time he campaigned for adherence to the traditional formulation of Jewish identity: one born of a Jewish mother or converted in accordance with strict Jewish law. He thus tried to present the controversial and almost self-contradictory idea that a Jew should be a person who lives according to seemingly exclusivist traditional laws, but at the same time feels a sense of responsibility to Gentile society.

Scholarly work. In Hasidic gatherings Rabbi Schneerson would frequently give scholarly talks which were transcribed by a team of rabbis. His edited writings fill more than a 150 volumes in Hebrew and Yiddish and include commentary on the Pentateuch, discussions of the Talmud and Zohar, qabbalistic Hasidic discourses, and some thirty volumes of letters.

His teachings expound traditional Jewish-Hasidic ideals such as the spiritual virtues of loving one's fellows, Torah study, and prayer and fulfilment of the *mitsvot.* He discusses issues particularly relevant to modernity, such as faith versus reason, the role of the woman, and the significance of the individual. Negative aspects of people ("sins") are viewed as an opportunity for repentance, and this and all other positive values are presented as leading to the redemption of the individual and ultimately of the whole world.

Chabad houses. During the 1980s Rabbi Schneerson developed the concept of Chabad House. This is a house run by a rabbi and his wife sharing the role of spiritual leadership, which aims to combine the hospitality of the home with the sanctity of the synagogue. A Chabad House can be seen as rivaling the more formal synagogue on the one hand and the less religiously rigorous Hillel House or Jewish Center on the other. Rabbi Schneerson's emissaries run Chabad Houses in almost every country where there are Jews. In some cases, his Jewish outreach work had to be more discreet. During the Cold War he maintained secret contact with the Jews of the USSR. After the fall of Communism Lubavitch schools and other institutions have flourished throughout the former Soviet Union.

A central feature of Rabbi Schneerson's teaching was the empowerment of women, claiming that each woman has the ability—in some ways greater than that of a man—to change the world. This contrasts with conventional Jewish Orthodoxy and especially Hasidism, which are often described as casting women in a secondary role. Women continue to have a key place in the Lubavitch movement.

MESSIANISM. The founder of Hasidism, Rabbi Israel Baal Shem Tov (d.1760), had been told in a visionary experience that the Messiah would come when his Hasidic teachings had spread to "the outside." Rabbi Schneerson hoped that the global attempts by his followers to strengthen Jewish observance and spread Hasidic teachings would indeed lead to the messianic Redemption. After the passing of his wife in 1988, Rabbi Schneerson wrote a legal, anticipating his own demise, will but also began to teach that the messianic transformation was imminent. His messianic teachings intensified during his last years. In 1991 he interpreted the Gulf War in messianic terms. He described yearning for the Messiah as a key element in the spirituality of Judaism.

A highly controversial result of these teachings was to generate a movement focused on him as the potential messianic redeemer. Observers are divided as to whether this was his deliberate intention. A faction of his followers initiated a poster campaign depicting him as the Messiah, which still continues, undeterred by his death in 1994. The campaign has been repeatedly condemned by the official leadership of Lubavitch, and, in his lifetime, by Rabbi Schneerson himself. Many voices have been raised against these messianists from various sectors of the Jewish community, some comparing them with Jewish messianists of the past, such as the followers of the seventeenth-century Shabbatai Tzvi. Others point out that unlike the Shabbatians they are in no way antinomian and that the phenomenon underlines the messianic element in Hasidism, of which there are several examples in the nineteenth century. Within the Habad movement the more extreme messianists are seen as negating Menahem Mendel's outreach ideal. They are accused of promoting only the overtly messianic teachings communicated in his talks from 1990 to 1992, and ignoring the main body of his writings.

Despite the internal and external controversies this final messianic thrust produced, since his death the Lubavitch movement has continued to grow. He left no children and no designated successor and, seemingly by unanimous consent among his followers, none has been appointed. His will designated the central committee of the Chabad movement as the trustees of his affairs. That body, based in Brooklyn, provides the centralized focus for the worldwide outreach movement he created.

His life combined contrasts: Talmudic and Jewish mysticism combined with secular education; a miracle-working Hasidic rebbe who reached out to the Reform Jew and the unaffiliated; a practical organizer and activist who was also seen as a mystical Messiah. He sought to bring Jewish spirituality out of its self-imposed ghetto enclave and into the public domain. His voluminous teachings, many recorded on audio-tape and video, remain as evidence of a rare combination of Jewish law, tradition, mysticism, and modernity.

SEE ALSO Hasidim, article on Habad Hasidism; Messianism, article on Jewish Messianism.

BIBLIOGRAPHY

Torah Studies (London, 1986), by British chief rabbi Professor Jonathan Sacks, provides an in-depth view of Rabbi Schneerson's discussions of the Bible and rabbinic sources, combining both spiritual and socially relevant levels of interpretation. *The Letter and the Spirit* (New York, 1998) is an anthology of Rabbi Schneerson's English letters on various topics, edited by Rabbi Dr. Nisan Mindel, his secretary of many years. Simon Jacobson's *Towards a Meaningful Life: The Teachings of the Rebbe* (New York, 1995) extracts his personal, spiritual, and social directives from their rabbinic context and presents them in the form of a universal guide to life. Dr Aryeh Solomon's *The Educational Teachings of Rabbi Menachem M. Schneerson* (Northvale, N.J., 2000) provides an academic investigation of his unusually positive approach as an educationalist. For an informed and scholarly account of the messianic movement that arose around him, see Professor Rachel Elior's "The Lubavitch Messianic Resurgence: The Historical and Mystical Background, 1939–1996" in *Toward the Millenium: Messianic Expectations from the Bible to Waco,* edited by Peter Schafer and Mark R. Cohen (Leiden, Netherlands, 1998).

NAFTALI LOEWENTHAL (2005)

SCHOLARIOS, GENNADIOS (c. 1400–1478),

born Georgios Scholarios and also known as Georgios Kourtesios, was a patriarch of Constantinople (1454–1456; 1463; 1464–1465), educator, philosopher, theologian, and defender of Orthodox Christianity. Born in Constantinople, Scholarios began as a student of Mark Eugenikos, metropolitan of Ephesus, an opponent of the papacy. Later, Gennadios schooled himself in the humanities, philosophy, and theology. Unlike most Greeks of the time, Gennadios also learned Latin and was an admirer of Thomas Aquinas, some of whose works he translated into Greek. While still a layman, he preached regularly at court, taught in his own school, and served the Byzantine emperor John VIII (1425–1448) as imperial secretary and Judge General of the Greeks.

Gennadios has usually been pictured as a supporter of the union of the Latin and Greek churches at the abortive Council of Florence (1438–1439), but he subsequently made an about-face following the death of his teacher, Mark of Ephesus, and became the leader of antipapal forces during the last days of Byzantium. In fact, his complete change in attitude had caused some scholars to believe that there was more than one person named Georgios Scholarios. Recent scholarship, however, has unanimously discarded the latter notion. Moreover, the latest substantive study on Scholarios questions the authenticity of some of the pro-Latin writings attributed to him, so that according to this view, Scholarios was consistent in his opposition to Latin theology, and, therefore, to the union of churches based on the acceptance of Latin doctrines.

Shortly before the fall of Constantinople to the Ottoman Turks (1453), Scholarios became a monk, and according to tradition changed his name from Georgios to Gennadios. Taken captive following the capture of the city, he was released at the instigation of Sultan Mehmed II, who saw in Gennadios, because of his antipapal views, the ideal candidate for the vacant patriarchal throne. Enthroned on January 6, 1454, Patriarch Gennadios maintained a friendly relationship with the sultan, and together they worked out the terms under which Orthodox Christians would live under the Ottomans for the next five centuries.

Despite the friendship of Mehmed II, however, Gennadios's tenure as patriarch was a stormy one. He strove to retain order within the Orthodox church, and in order to prevent conversions to Islam attempted to relax marriage canons; however, he was opposed by those who demanded strict adherence to the letter of the law. Gennadios was successful in reorganizing the Patriarchal Academy in Serres (present-day Serrai, Greece), recognizing the important need of a higher institution of learning for the training of the future leaders of the Greek people and church. After serving as patriarch for three brief terms, he finally abandoned the throne and took up residence in the Monastery of Saint John the Baptist at Serres.

BIBLIOGRAPHY

Joseph Gill's *Personalities of the Council of Florence and Other Essays* (Oxford, 1964) presents the traditional view on Scholarios. The revisionist perspective can be found in Theodore Zissis's *Gennadios II Scholarios: Bios, sungrammata, didaskalia* (Thessalonica, 1980).

NOMIKOS MICHAEL VAPORIS (1987)

SCHOLASTICISM.

An abstract noun formed from the Latin-Greek stem *scholastic-*, pertaining to "school," scholasticism signifies principally the type of training used in the schools, and secondarily, the doctrine given, usually in the universities of the Latin Middle Ages. In a pejorative sense, it connotes dictatorial or authoritarian methods, or a hidebound and unimaginative view, much like the "correct" answer that a schoolmaster would demand from his pupil in the classroom.

METHOD. Principally Scholasticism indicates a method of training and learning that developed in Christian schools between about 1000 and 1650 and reached its peak in the thirteenth century. It arose naturally and spontaneously in the early Middle Ages as teachers lectured on a fixed text, pausing to explain a difficult passage by posing a question and lining up authorities pro and con, *sic et non.* Divergent resolutions of difficulties were often written in the margins of the Bible or lawbook. Abelard's work *Sic et non* is both a collection of seemingly contradictory theological texts and a reasoned methodology for resolving such apparent contradictions. The underlying supposition was the commonly held conviction that truth cannot contradict itself and that all truth is from God. Thus, logic, coupled with a respect for antiquity, was always considered the chief instrument of Scholastic teaching in the Middle Ages.

From its earliest beginnings in the classroom two distinct elements appeared, which developed independently into two Scholastic functions by the thirteenth century: the lecture (*legere*), or explanation of the text, eventually restricted to the morning sessions; and the academic disputation (*disputare*) of a special point, eventually restricted to the afternoon sessions and to special days. In the patristic period only the bishop or a qualified delegate could expound the sacred text or settle disputes; in the Middle Ages these became the formal functions of a "master" (*magister*). Thus a medieval commentary is the master's statement (*sententia*) of the meaning intended in the text; and a medieval "disputed question" is the master's resolution (*determinatio*) of the debate.

When universities (*studium generale,* in the singular) were founded in the late twelfth and early thirteenth centuries, the association of masters established rules for the induction of new masters into the guild. The basic liberal arts studies, prior to theology or other higher faculties and required of all, took about eight years and led to the master of arts degree at the age of twenty-one (minimum), followed by two or more years of teaching the arts. There were three higher faculties: theology (the minimum age for the master being thirty-five), law (civil and canon), and medicine. Each faculty had its own masters with chairs, required textbooks, and agreed upon statutes by which the faculty was governed by a chancellor, dean, or rector. The preferred term for a qualified teacher in the Middle Ages was "master," but by the thirteenth-century Bolognese lawyers preferred to be called "doctor."

By 1230, in the faculty of theology, there were apprentices called "bachelors," who assisted the master in the performance of his duties by reading the text to the younger students in a cursory manner and by responding to questions raised by the students. Soon the subordinate role of the bachelor was subdivided into that of the *cursor biblicus,* who did the preliminary reading of the Bible, and that of the *bachelarius sententiarum,* who lectured on the *Sentences of Peter Lombard* (1100–1160), a collection of patristic texts organized according to doctrinal points.

In all scholastic training the chief instrument of learning was logic, the purpose of which was to acquire scientific knowledge (*scientia*) through definition, division, and argument. For this art the fundamental source was Aristotle, originally in the version of Boethius (d. 524). Before all of Aristotle was known in the late twelfth century, studies preliminary to the study of Bible or any of the higher subjects consisted in studying the seven liberal arts (logic, grammar, rhetoric, arithmetic, geometry, music, and astronomy), with special emphasis given to logic and grammar. Organization of universities at Bologna, Paris, and Oxford took place just as the "new learning" made its appearance in the Latin West from Greek, Arabic, and Hebrew sources in the twelfth century. New works of logic (the rest of Aristotle's *Organon*) and Ptolemaic and Arabic astronomy were simply worked into the known seven arts, but other books—namely those on natural philosophy, moral philosophy, and first philosophy, or metaphysics—could only be added to the arts as "the three philosophies" to make up the faculty of arts and sciences.

The method of teaching these new sciences, although basically the old method, was perfected by these books of "the new logic," especially *Posterior Analytics.* A distinct philosophical content was given to medieval teaching in arts, which inevitably flowed over to theology, thus creating a diversity of scholasticisms.

The Scholastic method, therefore, was universally one and the same throughout the Middle Ages: (1) it was always in Latin, of varying proficiency and elegance on an approved text universally acknowledged as worthy of study; (2) it was structured according to the Aristotelian logic of defining, dividing, and reasoning in its exposition of the text and its resolution of difficulties; and (3) all studies, even the related field of law, led to theology as the "Queen of the Sciences," that is, to the understanding of the Bible. But considering the great diversities that existed among outstanding masters and their followers in terms of loyalties and priorities, it is possible to speak of various schools, movements, and -isms among Scholastics of different periods.

TEACHINGS. Scholasticism as a doctrine is usually divided into three periods: (1) medieval, up to the Reformation; (2) second scholasticism, or the renewed Thomism of the sixteenth century; and (3) a revival of Thomistic philosophy from around 1850 to the Second Vatican Council, or Leonine Thomism. Medieval Scholasticism is also divided into three periods: early medieval, before the introduction of Aristotle to the universities around 1200; high medieval, a vigorous assimilation of Aristotelian thought despite strong opposition in the thirteenth century; and late medieval, usually considered as declining around 1350, after the Black Death.

In early Scholasticism special emphasis was given to grammar and logic during training in arts prior to a long study of the scriptures. Among its outstanding masters were Alcuin at York; Lanfranc and Anselm, first at Bec, then at Canterbury; Anselm and his brother Ralph at Laon; Ive and his successors at Chartres; Peter Abelard in and around Paris; and the canonist Gratian at Bologna. Although the problem of "universals" ranked high, the principal theological problems concerned the Eucharist, the trinity of persons in one God, and the incarnation of the Son of God.

High Scholasticism, incorporating the works of Aristotle in the universities and assimilating his thought, notwithstanding a background of Augustinian Platonism, necessarily includes the vast works of Albertus Magnus, Robert Grosseteste, Bonaventure, Thomas Aquinas, Henry of Ghent, John Duns Scotus, William of Ockham, Thomas Bradwardine, and their contemporaries—with all their philosophical differences and similarities. This was the age of assimilation and of new syntheses of thought, such as Thomism, Scotism, and nominalism (Ockham). Within these syntheses one should note the varying influences of Ibn Sīnā (Avicenna), Ibn Rushd (Averroës), and certain pseudo-Aristotelian works, such as *Liber de causis.*

Late Scholasticism, depending on where one makes the division (some put it at 1277, others around 1315), is generally considered to be a period of intellectual and spiritual decline before the Italian Renaissance (fifteenth century) or the Protestant Reformation (sixteenth century). Wherever its bounds, the period witnessed the rapid spread of universities, a special stirring of popular devotion (Devotio Moderna) in prayer, hymns, and sermons, and a widespread interest in the spoken word of God (the Bible), especially in the vernacular. Heiko Oberman sees this period as the ripening of medieval thought preparatory to Luther's harvest of Christianity. While one must recognize the flowering of art, the spread of printing, the expansion of global exploration, and a growing literacy among the laity, one must nevertheless admit that as far as Scholasticism is concerned, the period yielded a sterile and barbarous formalism performed with perfunctory brevity.

Second scholasticism is a term given to the brief spring of scholastic thought in the sixteenth century, when the *Summa theologiae* of Thomas Aquinas replaced the *Sentences* of Peter Lombard in major Catholic universities. This change was accomplished mainly by Dominicans such as Peter Crokaert in Paris, Thomas de Vio Cajetan at Pavia, Konrad Koellin at Heidelberg and Cologne, and Francisco de Vitoria at Salamanca. All of these men had many disciples with considerable influence later. This revival was given special impetus when the Council of Trent (1545–1563) redefined much of Catholic doctrine, utilizing Thomistic as well as traditional patristic teaching, and when the prestigious Society of Jesus (Jesuits) was founded by Ignatius Loyola in

1534, pledging to follow the teaching of Thomas Aquinas and subsequently renovating Catholicism throughout the world. The revival found expression not only in official documents like the canons and decrees of the Council of Trent, but also in its *Catechism of the Council of Trent,* issued by order of Pius V in 1566, and in the innumerable textbooks of scholastic philosophy and theology (*iuxta mentem S. Thomae*) for use in colleges and seminaries established under the Tridentine reform. The leading Jesuit scholastics of this period were Roberto Bellarmino, Francisco de Toledo, Francisco Suárez, Luis de Molina, professors of the Collegio Romano founded by Ignatius in 1551, and the Complutenses, namely, teachers at the Jesuit college at Alcalá, founded by Cardinal Francisco Ximénes de Cisneros in 1508.

The scholasticism of this period was not simply a repetition of older views, but its theology was substantially invigorated by clashes with the reformers and its philosophy by a renewed interest in the science of nature. Its theology is best seen in the polemical literature and the great number of exceptional commentaries on Thomas's *Summa.* Its philosophy is best seen in treatises on motion and in thoughtful commentaries on Aristotle's *Physics, De caelo,* and other books on nature, notably by Domingo de Soto, Diego de Astudillo, and Juan de Celaya at Paris, and the Jesuit professors, notably Christopher Clavius (1538–1612), at the Collegio Romano. One should distinguish these progressive Artistotelians from the textual type, who were more interested in editing and translating from books than from nature.

Within the context of this revivified philosophy must be seen the astronomy and the two new sciences of Galileo (1564–1642), and to a much lesser extent, the new philosophy of René Descartes (1596–1650). Galileo's early writings depend heavily on the lecture notes of Jesuit professors of philosophy at the Collegio Romano; the butt of his gibes turns out to be the parrots who would not look at the heavens, but only at the text. Descartes, on the other hand, had a less venturesome scholasticism from the Jesuits at La Flèche (1609–1613). While later Descartes sought to replace their teaching with entirely new first principles, their roots, as Étienne Gilson has shown, were medieval and scholastic. Nevertheless both Galileo and Descartes dealt the deathblow to scholasticism and laid the foundation of modern thought.

Meanwhile Catholic theology, which felt the greatest impact from this revival, experienced a second spring. Under Pius V, Thomas Aquinas was declared a doctor of the church, the first so considered since the patristic age; and the first edition of his multivolume *Opera omnia* was published in Rome (1570–1571). Notable commentaries on Thomas's *Summa* began to appear, such as those of Thomas de Vio Cajetan (Lyons, 1540–1541), Conrad Koellin (Cologne, 1512), and Franciscus Silvester Ferrariensis on the *Summa contra gentiles* (Paris, 1552). The original constitution of the Jesuits (1550) obliged its members to study and promote the teaching of Thomas alone. But in the bitter controversy over grace (*De auxiliis,* 1597–1607) that broke out with the Dominicans over the publication of Molina's *Concordia* (1588), a new Thomism emerged in the writings of Francisco de Suárez (1548–1617), that tried to reconcile Thomism with Scotism. After 1607 theology was reduced to repetition and division into diverse specialties, courses, and tractates; and moral theology bogged down over probabilism and, later, Jansenism. For all practical purposes, scholasticism was dead by 1650.

A third appearance of scholasticism occurred in more recent times, when there was a revival of solely the philosophical aspects of Thomism, blessed and fostered by Pope Leo XIII in his encyclical *Aeterni Patris* (1879). Dissatisfaction with the inadequacy of contemporary philosophy to solve pressing problems had been expressed in Italy early in the nineteenth century by teachers of philosophy in Catholic colleges and seminaries. These professors were concerned primarily with future priests and the state of the world vis-à-vis philosophy. Seminary textbooks were often thoroughly Cartesian, and "Christian" only by reason of a few biblical quotations and references to Augustine or Bossuet without a mention of Thomas Aquinas or the Middle Ages. In the Rhineland the distinguished Georg Hermes (1775–1831) sought to adjust Roman Catholic principles to the supposed requirements of Immanuel Kant; his adjustment was condemned in 1835. In Vienna the prolific Anton Günther (1783–1863) sought to do the same for Hegel; his works were placed on the Index of Forbidden Books in 1857. The principal errors of the day were listed in the *Syllabus of Errors* of Pius IX (1864), ranging from pantheism and liberalism to communism and indifferentism. In the eyes of many only the philosophy of Thomas Aquinas could bring humankind back to sanity.

Small beginnings were made by Vincenzo Buzzeti in Piacenza, Joseph and Joachim Pecci (later Pope Leo XIII) in Perugia, and the Sordi brothers and Taparelli among the Jesuits in Naples and Rome. By 1850 the ideas of Thomas were again familiar to readers of *Civiltà Cattholica* and the five-volume *Philosophia Christiana* (Naples, 1853) by Gaetano Sanseverino (1811–1865). These beginnings were augmented in Germany by Josef Kleutgen, in France by Henri Lacordaire, in Spain and the Philippines by Zeferino Gonzales, and in Italy by Tommaso Zigliara. The first major encyclical issued by Leo XIII, *Aeterni Patris,* called for "the restoration in Catholic schools of Christian philosophy according to the mind of St. Thomas, the Angelic Doctor." In all subsequent encyclicals Leo promoted the teaching of Thomas applied to the modern world, with the result that by the time of his death in 1903 Leo had rehabilitated Thomas.

At the beginning of the twentieth century, the Scholastic philosophy of Thomas began to take root in all the main centers of the Catholic world. In this revival, philosophy, not theology, was the central issue, since reason seemed to be common to Christianity and the secular world. In this case scholasticism was identified with Thomistic philosophy, somehow conceived as perennial (*perennis*) and common to all great minds of all ages. For Leo XIII this philosophy was to be found in the *Summa theologiae* of Thomas. When cries were raised about other philosophies, such as those of Bonaventure and Suárez, the reply from Rome (1907–1950) was that all others were to be evaluated by the standard of Thomas. This did not mean that other philosophies were wrong, but rather that only the philosophy of Thomas was to be promoted urgently for the church in the modern world. Throughout this same period there were many Catholics who were unconvinced and impatient, insisting that a more modern and relevant philosophy was needed. These were known as "modernists," eager to secularize Christian principles in order to be accepted.

Before the Second Vatican Council (1962–1965) almost all Catholics were exposed to some shades of Thomistic philosophy, especially through seminaries and colleges, despite the specter of modernism. During the first half of the twentieth century a large number of distinguished Thomists, both Catholic and non-Catholic, addressed important issues in almost every field of human interest: historical, philosophical, sociological, psychological, scientific, and political. Countless journals were founded throughout the world claiming to be scholastic or Thomistic, and the names of Gilson, Maritain, Adler, Grabmann, and Chenu became household names. For many reasons, none of them philosophical, the Second Vatican Council served as a watershed for Leonine scholasticism.

See Also Modernism, article on Christian Modernism; Nominalism; Trent, Council of.

Bibliography

For such a vast subject, it is perhaps best to start with overviews. As such, several entries in *The New Catholic Encyclopedia* (New York, 1967) can be recommended: "Scholasticism," by Ignatius Brady, J. E. Gurr, and me; "Thomism," by me; and "Scotism," by C. Balic and me; each has an extensive bibliography.

On Scholastic method, the standard work by Martin Grabmann, *Die Geschichte der scholastischen Methode,* 2 vols. (1909–1911; reprint, Basel, 1961), can serve as a starting point for the early period, or even Anders Piltz's *The World of Medieval Learning* (Oxford, 1981). For clarification of its technical meaning, one should consult Artur M. Landgraf's "Zum Begriff der Scholastik," *Collectanea Franciscana* 11 (1941): 487–490; M.-D. Chenu's *Toward Understanding Saint Thomas* (Chicago, 1964); and *Les genres littéraires dans les sources théologiques et philosophiques médiévales: Définition, critique et exploitation* (Louvain-la-Neuve, 1982).

As for the various doctrines taught, one must read the primary texts, important secondary sources about each scholastic, or volumes dealing with particular themes. A simple modern manual is useful for philosophy, such as Désiré Mercier's *A Manual of Modern Scholastic Philosophy,* 8th ed., 2 vols. (London, 1917); Gallus Manser's *Das Wesen des Thomismus,* 3d ed. (Freiburg, 1949); Karl Werner's *Die Scholastik des späteren Mittelalters,* 5 vols. (1881; reprint, New York, 1960); Carlo Giacon's *La seconda scolastica,* 3 vols. (Milan, 1944–1950); *I neotomisti italiani del XIX secolo,* 2 vols., edited by Paolo Dezza (Milan, 1942–1944); and *Years of Thomism: Aeterni Patris and Afterwards,* edited by Victor B. Brezik (Houston, 1981).

New Sources

Asselt, William J. van, and Eef Dekker, eds. *Reformation and Scholasticism: An Ecumenical Enterprise.* Grand Rapids, 2001.

Cabezón, José Ignacio, ed. *Scholasticism: Cross-Cultural and Comparative Perspectives.* Albany, 1998.

Colish, Maria L. *Remapping Scholasticism.* Toronto, 2000.

Gallagher, David A., ed. *Thomas Aquinas and His Legacy.* Washington, D.C., 1994.

Kretzmann, Norman, Anthony Kenny, and John Pinberg, eds. *The Cambridge History of Medieval Philosophy.* Cambridge, U.K., and New York, 1982.

McGrath, Alister E. *Reformation Thought: An Introduction.* Oxford and New York, 1988.

Oakley, Francis. *Omnipotence and Promise: The Legacy of the Scholastic Distinction of Powers.* Toronto, 2002.

Rummel, Erika. *The Humanist Scholastic Debate in the Renaissance & Reformation.* Cambridge, Mass., 1995.

Southern, Richard William. *Scholastic Humanism and the Unification of Europe.* Oxford and Cambridge, Mass., 1995.

James A. Weisheipl (1987)
Revised Bibliography

SCHOLEM, GERSHOM (1897–1982), was the founder of a school of rigorous historical and philological study of Jewish mysticism (Qabbalah). Although earlier Jewish historians had treated Qabbalah, they generally regarded it either as disreputable or, at best, as a part of Jewish philosophy. Scholem showed that the mystical tradition was a discipline in its own right, and, by the discovery and dating of hundreds of manuscripts, he established its textual and intellectual history. A prolific writer, he issued his findings in numerous publications.

Scholem was born in Berlin to a family of printers. Although his parents were partly assimilated, Scholem became a passionate Jew and a committed Zionist. He taught himself Hebrew and acquired a Jewish education while still in secondary school. Opposed to World War I on Zionist grounds—that it was against the interests of the Jews—he was expelled from school for circulating a pamphlet against the war.

Scholem was initially influenced by Martin Buber but broke with him over the question of the war. He criticized Buber for using mystical categories to support the German war effort. Later, he developed this criticism of Buber into a polemic against Buber's ahistorical treatment of Jewish sources, especially Hasidism.

In 1919, Scholem decided to write his doctoral dissertation on Qabbalah, and he chose as his subject the early qabbalistic text *Sefer ha-bahir.* Completing this work in Munich in 1922, the following year he emigrated to Palestine, where he found a position as librarian in the emerging Hebrew University. When the university opened in 1925, he was appointed lecturer in Jewish mysticism and was promoted to professor several years later. He served in this capacity until his retirement in 1965.

Scholem's studies of the history of Jewish mysticism can be found in 579 entries in his bibliography. His most important works include *Major Trends in Jewish Mysticism* (first published in 1941), *Sabbatai Sevi: The Mystical Messiah* (Hebrew ed., 1957; rev. English ed., 1973), *Ursprung und Anfänge der Kabbala* (1962), and *The Messianic Idea in Judaism: And Other Essays on Jewish Spirituality* (1971).

At the heart of Scholem's historiography is the belief that myth is crucial to the vitality of a religious tradition, an idea that betrays the influence of German romantic thinkers such as von Baader. Scholem identified the central myth of Qabbalah as Gnostic. He argued that already in late antiquity, Jewish mystics had developed a monotheistic version of Gnostic dualism. This Jewish Gnosticism persisted in underground traditions and made its way from Babylonia via Italy and Germany to southern France, where it surfaced in *Sefer ha-bahir.* In a number of important books and articles, Scholem described how these ideas sparked the development of the qabbalistic movement of Provence and Spain in the thirteenth century. He showed how this movement culminated in *Sefer ha-zohar* (The book of splendor), which he demonstrated to have been the work of Mosheh de León at the end of the thirteenth century.

Scholem traced the history of the Gnostic myth of Qabbalah through sixteenth-century Lurianic Qabbalah to the Shabbatean messianic movement of the seventeenth century. His work on Shabbateanism argued that this heretical movement was not a marginal phenomenon in Jewish history but instead the central event of the seventeenth century. By undermining the hegemony of the rabbis, Shabbateanism became the great watershed between the Middle Ages and modernity and foreshadowed the rise of antinomian secularism. Thus, Scholem argued that the rise of modern Judaism was a consequence of an event within the Jewish religious tradition and not simply the result of outside influences. Secularism, rather than constituting a break from Jewish history, was a product of a dynamic within Jewish history itself.

Scholem's history of Jewish mysticism sweeps from late antiquity to the threshold of modernity, and in his hands, Qabbalah became the key to the history of the Jews during this long period. Scholem argued that Judaism is not a monolithic tradition but consists instead of a dialectical interplay of conflicting forces. Only by understanding this tradition in its anarchistic entirety can one grasp the "essence" of Judaism.

Behind Scholem's historiographical achievement lay a philosophy of modern Judaism that combined Zionism with a kind of religious anarchism. Scholem held that only in a Jewish state could nonapologetic history be written, and only there could the Jews again become the subjects of their own history. He saw the Judaism that would come out of the Zionist movement as something different from either Orthodoxy or the rationalism of the nineteenth century. Similar to his version of historical Judaism as a dynamic conflict between opposing forces, the new Judaism would be pluralistic rather than monolithic.

See Also Qabbalah; Zohar.

Bibliography

Scholem's complete bibliography to 1977 was published by the Magnes Press of the Hebrew University (Jerusalem, 1977). For biographical information, see Scholem's *From Berlin to Jerusalem,* translated by Harry Zohn (New York, 1980). For an analysis of Scholem's thought, see my *Gershom Scholem: Kabbalah and Counter-History* (Cambridge, Mass., 1979).

New Sources

Dan, Joseph. *Gershom Scholem and the Mystical Dimension of Jewish History.* New York, 1987.

Jacobson, Eric. *Metaphysics of the Profane: The Political Theology of Walter Benjamin and Gershom Scholem.* New York, 2003.

Schäfer, Peter. *Gershom Scholem Reconsidered: The Aim and Purpose of Early Jewish Mysticism.* Oxford, 1986.

David Biale (1987)
Revised Bibliography

SCHWEITZER, ALBERT

SCHWEITZER, ALBERT (1875–1965), was philosopher, theologian, musicologist, and humanitarian physician. Schweitzer was born in a Lutheran parsonage in Kaysersberg, Upper Alsace, which was then in Germany. This locale, which included his childhood hometown of Günsbach, and his university city, Strassburg, later became part of France.

In 1899 Schweitzer received a doctorate in philosophy and in 1900 a doctorate in theology from Strassburg. Yet philosophy and theology could not contain all his energies, some of which he directed to music. Between 1905 and 1911 he began making intensive studies and contributions to the literature on Johann Sebastian Bach, whose organ music he also edited. Regarded by his teachers and critics as a man with sufficient talent to be world-renowned as an organ performer, he chose instead to write on the almost mystical spirituality of Bach. Schweitzer later took a zinc-lined organ with him to the damp climate of equatorial Africa and occasionally returned to his Günsbach bench and performed elsewhere in Europe to raise funds for his African ventures.

It was these African endeavors that made a world citizen out of Schweitzer and that led to his winning the Nobel Peace Prize in 1952. After having shown his ability to excel in philosophy, theology, and music, Schweitzer felt a call to become a physician so that he could address human suffering. He recognized a vocation to this role after having been moved by a Strassburg statue of an African, and he chose for his work a site called Lambaréné in Gabon, in French Equatorial Africa. There he went with his wife, physician and researcher Hélène Bresslau, after he received the M.D. degree in 1913, and there he spent most of his remaining fifty years.

Schweitzer became one of the best-known figures in the world, a pioneer in a form of humanitarianism that was to know no boundaries of ideology, nation, or religion. Although the administration of his hospital clinic was often arbitrary, patriarchal, and paternalistic, and although his attitude toward African blacks was so condescending as to be regarded as racist by critics, Schweitzer gained and held credentials because of his ability to serve suffering natives. He attracted volunteers from all over the world, and for decades Lambaréné was a goal for pilgrimages. Visitors ordinarily brought back enthusiastic, almost unrestrained, reports of Schweitzer's motivation and a humane spirituality that emanated from his work and life. Lambaréné was an easy image to grasp, one that left a much bigger stamp on the religious world than did anything Schweitzer was to write or say.

Yet the physician also had much to say in philosophy and religion, and some of his writings on the New Testament found a permanent place in the canons of biblical criticism. It is clear that Schweitzer wanted to make his mark through a multivolume *Kulturphilosophie* (1923), which was translated as *Philosophy of Civilization.* He worked on its third volume for many years between surgical operations in Africa. Its first volume, with its survey of history, has had little impact and would be little read were it not for curiosity about the author.

The second volume, however, includes Schweitzer's personal religious philosophy, identified by his famous phrase "reverence for life." One day in 1915 on a boat on the Ogooué River, Schweitzer had an almost mystical revelatory experience. This led him to concentrate his disparate energies on the notion and ethos of reverence for all life. It was this passion that made the doctor well known, sometimes notorious, because he did not want to kill mosquitoes or bees or any other living things, even though they add to misery by spreading diseases. He felt that reverence for life, for which he presented little philosophical justification but toward which he assembled all his religious energies, made its own claims on humans, whose future depended upon how they regarded all life.

Schweitzer's more vivid theological work concentrated on radical studies of Jesus. Gradually his Lutheranism was transformed into a reverent attention to the "spirit of Christ," and some thought of him as a Unitarian. His *Die Mystik des Apostels Paulus* (1930) elaborated on some of these themes, but *Von Reimarus zu Wrede* (1906), translated as *The Quest of the Historical Jesus* (1910), had epochal significance. The book traces the history of biblical criticism, chiefly in Germany, through a century of liberal efforts to establish a revitalized Christianity around the figure of "the historical Jesus."

Schweitzer devastated the reputation of many predecessors by showing that their search for the historical Jesus was not sufficiently historical. There was no "historical Jesus" to be found, he said, since the biblical records left such figures irretrievable, and he showed that German scholars had usually stopped their quest short, at the point where they found a Jesus who projected their own liberal ideals. The evidence, Schweitzer said, reached instead to a Jesus who turned out to be virtually useless for such purposes. Jesus was an apocalyptic zealot who had thought that God would break into world history and usher in his Kingdom after Jesus began his ministry. When God failed to do this, Jesus by his own sufferings tried to bring on that divine action. There was no way such an eschatologically minded figure could be anything but alien to moderns.

Paradoxically, this did not mean the end of following the spirit of Christ. Schweitzer often wrote in almost mystical terms about following Jesus. In the eyes of many he successfully promoted a search for the divine will in the path of this remote and mysterious Jesus. While Schweitzer's positive theology held limited appeal, serious biblical scholarship has subsequently had to build its New Testament historical research on new foundations.

Bibliography

Taken together, two biographies—*Schweitzer* (New York, 1971), by George N. Marshall and David Poling, and *Albert Schweitzer* (New York, 1975), by James Brabazon—provide a comprehensive portrait of Schweitzer's eclectic talents and undertakings. Jackson Lee Ice restricts himself to a study of a single aspect of Schweitzer's career, namely, his impact on theological and historical studies of Christianity, in *Schweitzer: Prophet of Radical Theology* (Philadelphia, 1971), and Henry Clark probes *The Ethical Mysticism of Albert Schweitzer: A Study of the Sources and Significance of Schweitzer's Philosophy of Civilization* (Boston, 1962). Concise presentations of the highlights of Schweitzer's life and work abound in *Albert Schweitzer: An Anthology,* edited by Charles R. Joy (Boston, 1965), which reprints excerpts, organized by topic, from Schweitzer's prolific writing career, on issues ranging from "Bach's World-View" to "The Cause of the World War," and in *In Albert Schweitzer's Realms,* edited by A. A. Roback (Cambridge, Mass., 1962), a collection of addresses and essays presented at a symposium in his honor. The latter includes articles by Jacques Maritain, Paul Tillich, and Tom Dooley. Many of the themes in these works are discussed in George Seaver's substantial study, *Albert Schweitzer: The Man and His Mind,* 6th ed. (New York, 1969).

New Sources

Bentley, James. *Albert Schweitzer: The Enigma.* New York, 1992.

Berman, Edgar. *In Africa with Schweitzer.* Far Hills, N.J., 1986.

Meyer, Marvin W., and Kurt Bergel. *Reverence for Life: The Ethics of Albert Schweitzer for the Twenty-First Century.* Syracuse, N.Y., 2002.

Schweitzer, Albert. *Out of My Life and Thought: An Autobiography.* Rev. ed. New York, 1990.

Schweitzer, Albert. *The Quest of the Historical Jesus: A Critical Study of Its Progress from Reimarus to Wrede.* (1910) Baltimore, Md., 1998.

Starobeltsev, A. "Life Is Indivisible: Albert Schweitzer's Ethic of Love." *Journal of the Moscow Patriarchate* no. 10 (1989): 37–41.

MARTIN E. MARTY (1987)
Revised Bibliography

SCIENCE AND RELIGION. During the final third of the twentieth century an interdisciplinary field arose that claims the name science and religion. By science it refers to natural sciences such as physics, cosmology, evolutionary biology, genetics, and the neurosciences; and it includes supporting disciplines such as history of science and philosophy of science. Although on occasion scholars in this field will dip into one or another social science, for the most part the field limits itself to the natural sciences. By religion it refers to two regions of religious thought. The first is generically spiritual, wherein research scientists are asked to explore ways in which their understandings of nature emit evidence or lack of evidence of transcendence. The second is doctrinally conceptual, wherein Christian systematic theology, as well as the philosophical or conceptual components to traditions such as Islam, Judaism, Hinduism, Buddhism, and Chinese traditions, are placed in dialogue with the sciences to reconceive God's relation to the world in creation, providence, moral guidance, and related interactions. Science and religion is a field of academic study that invites contributions from a variety of sciences and a variety of religious commitments; it is not itself a religious tradition or homogeneous school of thought.

The science that is relevant here is primarily modern science. Contemporary heirs to ancient religious traditions face upsetting challenges from the revolutionary spirit of the modern world, and science marches as the vanguard of modernity. Its ruthless dedication to empirically derived truth renders science brutal in its disregard for previous beliefs, even sacred beliefs. No appeal to traditional religious authority can stand in the face of repudiation by modern scientific theory or its companion, technology. Awareness of this threat occasionally precipitates defensive religious reactions. Such reactions are frequently temporary, however, and eventually most religious leaders find ways to make peace with the new apprehension of reality heralded by science.

ANCIENT ASIA. Science as the world knows it today was born in western Europe in the sixteenth century and has migrated around the globe challenging traditional societies with a materialistic and humanistic view of reality. However, ancestral examples of quizzing nature to learn its secrets and of ingenious technological innovation can be found in many parts of ancient Asia. For example, the decimal system, including place notation using zero, first appeared in ancient India. As knowledge traveled to central Asia, algebra developed, advancing to second degree equations.

The Chinese were gifted with social organization and, like other ancients, developed sophisticated weapons for war. Other Chinese craft achievements included the compass, gunpowder, ceramics, block printing, and the stirrup. Renaissance Europe imported East Asian porcelain, and even today westerners calls their dishes "china." Yet what the moderns know as the method of scientific discovery and technological innovation seems inimical to the mystical and occult practices of Daoism and Buddhism and to the hierarchical social philosophy of Confucianism. Thus, from the beginning of the twentieth century through the Communist revolution to century's end, many Chinese intellectuals embraced a Chinese form of scientism. Science, it was thought, could do what the previous philosophical and religious traditions had failed to do, namely, restore China to its proper place on the world stage and provide liberation from poverty and backwardness.

Buddhism retains its ancient roots and is showing buds that could flower in contemporary discussions with science. Buddhism is open to three types of relationship with science. First, a supportive relationship is possible where existing science and technology can be employed to support Buddhist projects, such as employment of engineering to construct shrines and statues. Second, a more integral relationship can be found in the five fields of monastic knowledge: linguistics, logic, speculative philosophy, medicine, and creative arts. One of the central philosophical issues has been causality, already raised in Buddhism's four noble truths, where unsatisfied craving is the cause of suffering. This opens Buddhism to integration with physical causality as science investigates it. Third, a consequential relationship obtains when Buddhists, who believe in reincarnation, find themselves fascinated with such sciences as embryology. If an extensive dialogue with science develops among Buddhists, it can be expected to look different from the dialogue between science and Western theists (Richard Payne, "Buddhism and the Sciences," in Peters and Bennett, 2002, pp. 153–172).

ANCIENT GREECE AND ANCIENT ISRAEL. It is widely assumed that for science as a method of discovery to arise three things must be affirmed. First, the natural world must be structured rationally if not mathematically. Second, the rational structure of the human mind must correspond to the structure of nature itself. That is, human beings need the capacity to understand the world of nature. Third, the natural world must be contingent, not eternal or divine or capricious. It must be the case that the world as it is known is not necessary—it could have been different than it is. Hence, the pursuit of knowledge of this world must follow a specific course of research based upon observation of specific phenomena in order to discern specific causal connections.

The correspondence between the rational structure of the world and that of the human mind was discerned in ancient Greece. From the Greek *logos* we derive our concepts of logic and terms ending in *logy,* meaning "study of." Euclid gave us geometry. Pythagoras saw the physical world organized according to number. Hipparchos discovered the precession of equinoxes. Archimedes analyzed the lever. Aristarchos of Samos proposed a heliocentric picture of the universe, while Ptolemy's universe, with the earth at the center, won the day temporarily and dominated Western thought until Nicolaus Copernicus in the sixteenth century. Aristotle set the stage for biology, physics, and metaphysics, all celebrating human rational capacity.

What ancient Israel contributed was reflection on its experience with contingency. The world created by its covenanting God could have been different, but this world exists because the God of Israel freely decided to make it this way. Contingency could be combined with Greek reason. God has "arranged all things by measure and number and weight" (*Wis.* 11:20). The God of eternity and power can be "understood and seen through the things he has made," says Saint Paul (*Rom.* 1:20). Many scholars believe that the fertilization of reason by contingency provided the embryonic beginning of what would eventually gestate into modern Western science.

Stanley L. Jaki theorizes that the role of the incarnation in Christian theology was decisive. Because the incarnation of God in Jesus Christ is a one-time-only event, the created world in general is rendered nondivine. As a result, understanding the world requires direct physical examination rather than indirect idealist speculation. "A created universe had to be rational and consistent, but also contingent, that is, only one of an infinite number of possibilities available to an infinite creator who cannot but be infinitely powerful and rational" (Jaki, 1987, vol. 13, p. 129). This leads to *a posteriori* rather than *a priori* reasoning and, hence, the experimental method of research.

ISLAM AND MEDIEVAL EUROPE. Islam's history is long, covering a broad sweep of civilizational development; therefore, one should expect considerable diversity of approaches to the relationship of science to faith. The root question throughout Islamic history is the relationship between science internal to Islam—that is, within the purview of the Qur'ān or *'ulūm al-'Arab* (science of the Arabs)—and science that is external—that is, deriving from either the natural human capacity to reason or from pre-Muslim traditions. The early Abbasid rulers in the late eight and early ninth centuries vigorously promoted the rational and pre-Islamic sciences. They funded the House of Wisdom (Bayt al-Ḥikmah) to retrieve ancient wisdom and enhance it through translations into Arabic of works in Greek, Syriac, Pahlavi, and Sanskrit. Included in these translation projects were the works of Aristotle and, of course, Ptolemy's *Almagest.* In addition to reading Ptolemy, Muslim scientists engaged in solar and stellar observations and created astronomical tables. Abū Ya'qūb al-Kindi (800–870) articulated the philosophy of the era by affirming an appreciation of the truth wherever it comes from, even if it comes from races distant and nations different from the Arabs.

Without a unifying orthodoxy, a variety of Islamic approaches developed to deal with *'ilm,* or systematized knowledge, that included not only the natural sciences but also philology, lexicography, philosophy, jurisprudence, and theology. The study of nature was pursued on an intellectual soccer field with religious law (*sharī 'ah*) at one end and philosophical theology (*kalām*) at the other. Abū Ḥāmid al-Ghazālī (1058–1111) distinguished *sharī'ah* (sciences derived from divine law and coming from the Qur'ān and the prophets) from the *ghayr sharī'ah* (sciences not having to do with divine law, such as arithmetic, which comes from reason, and medicine, which is produced by experiment). Some proponents of religious law insisted that it should govern all spheres of life, including personal and public conduct; they also argued that religious law should set the parameters for what science can and cannot do.

A significant intellectual development at the *kalām,* or philosophical, end of the field is indirectly relevant for any future dialogue Muslims might take up with modern science. *Kalām* theologians concerned themselves with understanding God (Allāh) as the creator and sustainer of all that is in the material world. The school of Abū al-Ḥasan al-Ash'arī (874–935) contended that God is the only and direct cause of all events in the material world, even human actions. Causal agency is restricted to God. This doctrine, sometimes called *occasionalism,* has the consequence of eliminating reliance upon efficient causation in the physical realm. Without assuming the world to be consistent due to unbreakable causal efficacy or to reliable consistency in divine action, science has nothing to investigate.

Turning to medieval Europe, long before the advent of Islam, Christian theologians had been wrestling with Greek knowledge in the form of natural philosophy. Although Tertullian (160–220) had exclaimed rhetorically, "what has Athens to do with Jerusalem?!" indicating the independence of theology from pagan thought, Augustine of Hippo (354–430), in contrast, absorbed as much Greek learning as possible, declaring science and philosophy to be a welcome handmaid to theology. This affirming attitude prevailed through the Middle Ages with the development of the Two Books doctrine, according to which the book of nature reveals God as creator and the book of Scripture reveals God as redeemer. Medieval Christians read both books, for the scientists and the theologians were typically the same people.

One of the central theological tasks of the early Middle Ages was to reconcile Platonic philosophy, especially the *Timaeus,* with biblical pictures of creation. This task changed sharply in the eleventh and twelfth centuries when, with Islam as the conduit, new translations appeared of the entire corpus of ancient Greek learning. Now, instead of Plato, it became Aristotle who interviewed for the job of theology's handmaid. Islamic scholars such as Ibn Sīnā (Avicenna, 980–1037) and Ibn Rushd (Averroës, 1126–1198) provided texts and commentaries for Latin Christians to examine, reflect on, question, and integrate.

Both Muslim and Christian theologians found problematic Aristotle's assumption that the elements of creation were eternal, thereby challenging biblical notions of creation from nothing (*creatio ex nihilo*), as well as divinely promised eschatological transformation. Aristotle's notion of the soul as the form of the body, which denied the soul's independent existence, seemed incompatible with previously Platonized Muslim and Christian anthropologies. Methodologically, Aristotle's rationalized universe seemed to threaten reliance upon specially revealed knowledge. The exhaustive scope of the causal nexus and sense of determinism seemed to preclude miracles (Peters, Iqbal, and Haq, 2002, pp. 18–27; Ferngren, 2000, p. 263). Initial attempts to exclude Aristotelian philosophy eventually gave way to embrace and intellectual celebration, however, culminating in the synthetic achievements of Albert the Great (1193–1280) and Thomas Aquinas (1225–1274).

Thomas Aquinas's *Summa Theologica* Christianized Aristotle and Aristotlianized Christianity. On the one hand, this synthesis also scientized Christianity, insofar as Aristotle's view of nature amounted to the reigning science of the day. The historian David C. Lindberg reports that "the late-medieval scholar rarely experienced the coercive power of the church and would have regarded himself as free (particularly in the natural sciences) to follow reason and observation wherever they led. There was no warfare between science and the church" (Ferngren, 2000, p. 266). On the other hand, permanent reliance upon this synthesis rendered Christian thought vulnerable to the challenges of what would later become modern science, which replaced much of the Aristotelian cosmology with empirically derived knowledge.

The Copernican Revolution and the Protestant Reformation. The Copernican revolution and the Protestant Reformation were siblings, sharing the same century and exhibiting together a momentary youthful rebellion within the Western Latin church. Nicolaus Copernicus (1473–1543), who was a cathedral canon in Cracow, Poland, surmised that the worldview he had inherited, namely the Ptolemaic worldview of ancient Greece, needed revision. The Ptolemaic or geocentric understanding held that the earth is immovable and that the sun and the other planets orbit the earth. Copernicus, relying upon his own observations (without a telescope), plus his own mathematical calculations, wrote *De revolutionibus orbium coelestium* (On the revolutions of the heavenly bodies) in 1543, advancing the hypothesis that the sun, not the earth, stood at the center of the universe. The Copernican heliocentric view held that the earth—like the other planets—revolves around the sun. The evidence Copernicus raised was not decisive, yet it did provide a hypothetical scheme for calculating what could be observed in the night sky with the unaided human eye.

Copernicus was a devout Roman Catholic; his sixteenth-century counterpart was Protestantism. For the most part, Martin Luther (1483–1546) and John Calvin (1509–1564) paid little attention to the incipient revolution begun in natural science. Luther heard tales of Copernicus's new thought but apparently had no serious engagement. One offhand remark appears in 1539—four years prior to the astronomer's major book—in *Table Talk*, where Luther ponders a rumor that Copernicus believes the earth moves rather than the sun and the sky. Luther is said to have quipped that this would be comparable to somebody riding on a cart or in a ship and imagining that he was standing still while the earth and the trees were moving. Luther added that it was the sun that was commanded to stand still, not the earth, in the biblical description of Joshua fighting at Jericho (*Jos.* 10:12–14). Such remarks did not come from Luther's own authored writings but from students who took notes. Spoken in jest, such items ought not be interpreted as indicating any general opposition to science.

While Luther was attending to the interpretation of scripture and reforming the church, his own Wittenberg Reformation colleagues, a mathematician named Georg Joachim Rheticus and a pastor named Andreas Osiander, in 1543 executed an agreement with Copernicus to publish the first edition his major work, *De revolutionibus.* Twelve hundred copies appeared from a Nuremburg printing press. The anonymous preface, written by Osiander, includes the controversial line: "It is not necessary that these hypotheses should be true, or even probable; but it is enough if they provide a calculus which fits the observations." Significant here are two items: first, the acceptance of hypothesis as a component to developing new ideas; and, second, that this work has scientific value even if not true. What may have motivated such a prefatory statement in anonymous form was most likely a desire to make it easier for Roman Catholics to adopt Copernicus's ideas by softening the conceptual threat and by deleting any references to Lutheranism. Copernicus saw his book and the preface only on his deathbed in 1543 (Owen Gingerich, "The Copernican Revolution," in Ferngren, 2000, pp. 334–339).

Both Luther and Calvin distinguished between astrology and astronomy, and both rejected astrology as idolatry while celebrating astronomy as science. Philip Melanchthon (1497–1560) wrote on astrology, and this annoyed Luther, who trusted the more scientific and less superstitious approach to the stars. For Calvin as well as Luther, sciences such as astronomy and medicine provide valuable knowledge of this world, while human minds are asked to rise beyond this world to appreciate the glory of the God who made it. The historical bridge figure between Copernicus and Galileo, the Lutheran astronomer Johannes Kepler (1571–1630), advanced heliocentrism and suggested that scripture is written for common-sense understanding and should not be taken as a textbook in science.

It is frequently assumed in contemporary discussion that the so-called Copernican revolution consisted of decentering the earth and changing the place of human beings in the hierarchy of the cosmos. Historical evidence does not confirm such an interpretation. That Copernicus's theory led to a significant change in scientific cosmology is indisputable. That his heliocentric view upset a prevailing religious view that allegedly relied upon earth centrism and human centrism is disputable. For the most part, the new cosmology elicited relatively little theological attention and certainly no discernable religious excitement. Some Jesuit scholars in England were working in the 1570s to relocate heaven among the stars in light of Copernicus's new cosmology, but this only testifies to the absence of any initial dismay or disorientation on the part of the church's theologians.

GALILEO'S CONDEMNATION. A modern myth perpetuated by those wishing to see warfare between science and religion is to list martyrs for scientific truth who were allegedly persecuted by an atavistic and dogma-bound ecclesiastical authority (White, 1896, chap. 3). Although this interpretation is exaggerated, a kernel of truth in the condemnations of Galileo Galilei (1564–1642) fuels the fire of scientific-martyr remembrance.

The central issues had to do with interpretations of biblical passages such as *Psalms* 104:4 and *Joshua* 10:12–14, which picture a world with a stable earth and movements by the sun, moon, and other heavenly bodies. Both the authority of the Bible and the authority of the papacy to interpret the Bible seemed to be at stake, not loyalty to Ptolemy per se.

Galileo defended Copernicus against Ptolemy in his *Dialogo sopra i due massimi sistemi del mundo* (Dialogue concerning the two chief world systems) of 1632, buttressing the earlier argument for heliocentrism with telescopic observations as evidence. During nearly two decades of controversy, Galileo argued that biblical allusions to a stationary earth and a moveable sun should be seen as the cosmological frame rather than the theological focus of the Bible's message. Such a principle of interpretation would permit changes in scientific worldview while holding to biblical authority in matters of faith. During the controversies, Cardinal Cesare Baronius (1538–1607) bequeathed to history the famous aphorism, "The Bible tells us how to go to heaven, not how the heavens go."

Such a hermeneutic of Scripture failed to win the day, however, and papal condemnations in both 1616 and 1632 defended a stable earth and a moveable sun on the grounds that the Bible presumes this; that is, heliocentrism would amount to a violation of scriptural authority. Copernicus's *De revolutionibus* was placed on the *Index Expurgatorius* in 1616, and Galileo's *Dialogo* was added in 1632, meaning that Catholics were forbidden to read these works. Curiously, Jesuits in China, who had already begun to teach the Copernican cosmology, had to reverse themselves and begin teaching earth centrism, a pedagogical change that created confusion among their Asian students.

THE NEWTONIAN AND EINSTEINIAN WORLDS. As the story of astronomy winds through Western intellectual history, the advance in Copernicanism was accompanied by a retreat of Aristotelianism, especially a retreat from the sacredness or divinity ascribed to natural objects or forces. Once divine capriciousness was removed from the nexus of natural causation, scientists were ready to plot with confidence the mechanics of the world machine. Thus, the mechanistic model—the model of the natural world as a clock—could establish itself. This is what Newton provided and what became the Western worldview until Einstein.

Sir Isaac Newton (1642–1727) authored influential scientific works such as *Philosophia naturalis principia mathematica* (1687), *Opticks* (1704), and *Arithmetica universalis* (1707). He is remembered and applauded for unifying the heavens with the earth in a single mathematical concept of nature united by the laws of mechanics and the law of gravity. By invoking the idea that all bodies everywhere operate with mutual gravitation, he ascertained that the forces that keep the planets in their orbits must be reciprocally the squares of their distances from their centers. Newton applied what was known about terrestrial mechanics to the heavenly bodies and thereby erased any previously presumed gulf of difference. Arrival at such knowledge is through experiment with mathematical calculations. Scientific knowledge became mundane and objective, liberated from subjective projections of transcendental value or moral bias.

Following fellow English scientist Robert Boyle (1627–1691) in likening the natural world to a well-designed clock, Newton emphasized that the world needs God as the clockmaker—that is, it needs a divine first cause. In addition, the world clock also needs God for frequent adjustment and repair. Newton was a theist with Unitarian rather than Trinitarian leanings, believing in an active God whose *concursus* with nature performed necessary tasks, such as determining the actual paths of planets in their orbits. Historians of science view this as a mistake on Newton's part, as later research would provide a scientific explanation for actions he had thought to be divine. When asked by Napoleon (in an alleged conversation) about God's intervention into planetary orbits, Pierre-Simon, the Marquis de Laplace, answered, "I have no need of that hypothesis." What subsequent scientific history would carry beyond Newton is the image of nature as a universal and mathematizable mechanism, dependable and discernible, with no need for divine intervention (Dillenberger, 1960, p. 125).

Sparked by the publication of five extraordinary scientific papers by Albert Einstein (1879–1955) in 1905, people in the twentieth century began to think of the natural world as much more mysterious than the Newtonian clock model might allow. Einstein's special theory of relativity made both duration and length relative to motion, undercutting the assumption that the universe is framed by a stable or absolute container of time and space. Incorporating gravity into this theory in 1915 to produce his general theory of relativity, Einstein showed that space and matter act on one another so as to deform space itself: space tells matter how to move, and matter tells space how to curve. In Einstein's non-Euclidian world of diverging and intersecting parallel lines, the shortest path from one point to another in the presence of a gravitational field can become a curved line. Thus gravity is said to "bend" light.

Perhaps the most pervasive sense of mystery was introduced with what became known as quantum theory in physics, according to which nature's smallest particles, such as electrons, do not behave mechanistically. Rather, their behavior seems indeterminate and unpredictable; only over the long run, or statistically, do lawlike or mechanical patterns emerge. Still further, the act of observing subatomic behavior influences such behavior, thereby compromising the Newtonian sense of objectivity or nonparticipatory observation in scientific method. Subjectivity seems constitutive of the reality being observed (Ravindra, 1987, 5.72).

One of the implications of Einstein's early work was the concept of an expanding universe, a concept that by the time of its definitive confirmation in 1965 became broadly accepted as Big Bang cosmology—the notion that all of physical reality could be traced back to a singularity 13.7 billion years ago, when time and space began—sent intellectual shock waves through the religious imagination. With the Big Bang, the physical world appears to have an edge, something beyond time and space; with this edge, questions of transcendence arose within physical cosmology. Even Saint Augustine's forbidden question—what was God doing before there was time?—could be re-asked, now by physicists. The mysteries of the quantum world along with the Big Bang led physicists such as Paul Davies to suggest that now "science offers a surer path to God than religion" (Davies, 1983, p. ix).

The Field of Science and Religion. What is known today as the field of science and religion gained its present definition during the 1960s. The American Scientific Affiliation, founded in 1941 by evangelical scientists, set a precedent. Yet the 1960s marked a significant transition in intellectual culture.

Three factors in the intellectual environment of evolutionary adaptation led to the emergence of the new field. First, from within the new science, as reported above, questions of transcendence arose. The confirmation of Big Bang cosmology in 1965 was perhaps the most decisive. Continuing debates over quantum indeterminacy and complementarity began to place physics on the theological agenda. Although the double-helix structure of DNA had been discovered earlier (in 1953) the development of molecular biology in the 1960s, accompanied by startling new prospects in genetic engineering, raised questions of human nature for philosophers and questions of ethics for religious leaders. Science seemed to be asking for religious involvement and interpretation.

The second intellectual factor was the turn taken in the field of philosophy of science. The strict empiricism, positivism, and reductionism that had held sway for the first two thirds of the twentieth century was challenged by a new awareness of historical relativity and the sociology of knowledge. Philosophers such as Michael Polanyi, Norwood Hanson, Thomas Kuhn, Stephen Toulmin, and Imre Lakatos placed scientific knowing into historically conditioned communities of knowing. This challenged alleged scientific objectivity. The result was a new picture of scientific knowledge that began to look like humanistic knowledge, and even like theological knowledge.

The third intellectual factor was a ripening for dialogue within theology. The reign was coming to an end for the giants of neo-orthodox and existentialist Protestant theology—Karl Barth, Emil Brunner, Paul Tillich, Reinhold Niebuhr, H. Richard Niebuhr, Anders Nygren, Gustaf Aulen, and others. This school of thought had immunized theology from science by embracing the Two Language model, according to which science and faith each speak a different language. Science speaks of facts, whereas religion speaks of meaning. Because the languages are untranslatable, so it was assumed, science could have no relevance for matters of faith. Science and faith are allegedly separate realms. One disciple of Paul Tillich and Reinhold Niebuhr, Langdon Gilkey, flooded theological discussion in the 1960s with published works calling attention to the cultural impact of science, making science a theological issue because it is a cultural issue. Science was knocking at the theological door, even if it was not being invited in.

In Roman Catholic theology, the Second Vatican Council (1962–1965) had taken *aggiornamento* as its theme—that is, opening the windows of the church so the winds of the modern world could blow through. The mood of the mid-1960s was one of exuberant openness, and this openness soon included openness to science.

It was in this intellectual environment that a new vision for the interaction of science and religion evolved. For convenience, this emergence is marked with the 1966 publication of *Issues in Science and Religion* by Ian G. Barbour (b. 1923). Barbour grew up in China with a scientist father and theologian mother, and he was present the day in 1929 when Jesuit paleontologist Pierre Teilhard de Chardin arrived with the skull of what would later be called Beijing Man. Educated in both physics and theology, Barbour's first book defined the nascent field for four decades to follow. Barbour's publications, including his Gifford Lectures (1989–1991), have continued to shape it.

Barbour inspired a youthful colleague, Robert John Russell (b. 1946), a United Church of Christ pastor with a Ph.D. in physics, to establish in 1981 the Center for Theology and the Natural Sciences (CTNS) at the Graduate Theological Union in Berkeley, California. CTNS has sought the creative mutual interaction between science and faith. The center also publishes the journal *Theology and Science.* Pope John Paul II exonerated Galileo early in his pontificate, and from 1987 to 2003 the pope sponsored a sustained research program dealing with "scientific perspectives on divine action," conducted cooperatively by the Vatican Observatory and CTNS.

Beginning in the 1970s, centers and societies for the study of science and religion sprang up around the world. At Oxford University the biologist-theologian Arthur Peacocke organized the Society of Ordained Scientists and, followed by historian John Hedley Brooke, nurtured the Ian Ramsey Centre for research in this field. German-language discussions were prompted by the Karl Heim Gesellschaft, founded in 1974, which publishes an annual summary of research. At the Lutheran School of Theology in Chicago, the Zygon Center for Science and Religion, founded by Ralph Wendel Burhoe and supported by the Center for Advanced Study in Religion and Science and the Institute for Religion in an Age of Science, was directed (as of 2004) by Antje Jackelen, with Philip Hefner serving as editor of *Zygon: Journal of Religion and Science.* The European Society for the Study of Science and Theology meets biennially on the European continent. The Association of Science, Society, and Religion in India, the Australian Theological Forum, and the Center for Islam and Science in Islamabad and Edmonton, are examples of centers that draw scientists and religious leaders into academic conversation and generate publications that expand the field.

In the 1990s the John Templeton Foundation of Radnor, Pennsylvania, whose leaders believe interaction with science will facilitate "progress in religion" began funding numerous individuals and organizations. The Templeton Foundation was financial midwife at the 2002 birth of the multi-religious International Society for Science and Religion centered at Cambridge University, with the physicist-theologian John Polkinghorne as its first president. The annual Templeton Prize for contributions to religion are frequently given to scholars in the field of science and religion; recipients have included the physicists Freeman Dyson, Paul Davies, and John Polkinghorne; the philosophers Seyyed Hossein Nasr and Homes Rolston III; as well as Barbour and Peacocke.

WARFARE AND NONWARFARE MODELS OF INTERACTION BETWEEN SCIENCE AND RELIGION. The idea that natural science and Christian faith are locked into perpetual warfare derives from the late-nineteenth-century controversy over Darwinian evolution (Draper, 1874; White, 1896). This reinterpretation of previous history served the agenda of some scientists in England and North America who at that time were seeking to dislodge disciplines such as theology from university accreditation. However, the "warfare thesis," sometimes called the "conflict" model, is but one way to think of the relation of science to religion. The agenda of the field of science and religion is to find a nonwarfare or cooperative pattern of interaction (Peters, 1998, pp. 13–22; Barbour, 1990, pp. 3–30). At the beginning of the twenty-first century, eight patterns of interaction are discernable, four fitting the warfare interpretation and four that embrace peaceful cooperation, if not integration.

Scientism. In the contemporary West, the term *scientism* refers to naturalism, reductionism, or secular humanism—that is, the belief that there exists only one reality, namely, the material world, and that science provides the only trustworthy method for gaining knowledge about this material reality. Science has an exhaustive monopoly on knowledge, rendering all claims by religion about knowledge of supernatural realities as fictions or pseudo-knowledge. All explanations are reducible to secularized material explanations. Religion is defeated in the war by ignoring it.

Here, *scientism* does not mean exactly what it did a century ago in China. Science then appeared as a potential savior, an antireligious and anti-traditional force of revolution that would liberate modern people from their oppressive past. In contemporary intellectual debate, *scientism* still connotes liberation from oppressive religion, but it is restricted to methodology rather than politics and economics.

Scientific imperialism. This is scientism that does not ignore religion; rather, it uses materialist reductionism to explain religious experience and reassess theological claims. Scientific imperialists grant value to religion and religious values, and may even grant the existence of God, yet they claim that science provides a method for discerning religious truth that is superior to that of traditional theology. In contemporary discussion this approach is taken by some physical cosmologists when explaining creation or eschatology, and by sociobiologists or evolutionary psychologists proffering a biological explanation for cultural evolution including religion and ethics. Here religion is defeated in the war by conquering and colonizing it.

Ecclesiastical authoritarianism. According to this model, which defends the reverse of the previous two models, modern science clashes with religious dogma that is authoritatively supported by ecclesiastical fiat, the Bible, or in Islam by the Qurʾān. The 1864 *Syllabus of Errors,* promulgated by the Vatican, asserts that scientific claims must be subject to the authority of divine revelation as the church has discerned it. The Second Vatican Council affirmed academic freedom for natural science and other secular disciplines, removing the Vatican from warfare and placing it in the Two Language model.

The battle over Darwinian evolution. A war is currently being fought between the Darwinian theory of evolution, especially the concept of natural selection, on the one side, and scientific creationists, Intelligent Design advocates, and some factions within Turkish Islam, on the other side. The scientific creationists are heirs to fundamentalist Protestantism; they argue that a fair assessment of the science will show the inadequacy of natural selection to explain what appears to be evolution from one species to another, and this failure to provide a satisfactory scientific explanation indirectly supports the biblical description of creation. Intelligent Design advocates similarly criticize the explanatory adequacy of natural selection, arguing that evolution from one species to another constitutes a leap in complexity, and that advances in complexity require intervention by a transcendent intelligent designer—in other words, materialist explanations are inadequate. Some Muslims in Turkey are showing interest in these two Christian groups because of their desire to combat the secular orientation toward education in a traditionally religious society. That a war is being fought is clear. However, because the actual points at issue deal specifically with the explanatory adequacy of natural selection, it would be misleading to simply dub this a war between science and religion. The evolution battlefield is primarily North America, Australia, and Turkey, with little or no notice in Europe or in other discussions of science and religion.

The Two Languages. The notion that science speaks one language, the language of facts, and religion speaks a different language, the language of values, is the dominant nonwarfare model. The Two Language model—sometimes referred to as the "independence" model—is the prevailing view of both scientists and theologians in Western intellectual life. Science attends to objective knowledge about objects in the penultimate realm, whereas religion attends to subjective knowledge about transcendent dimensions of ultimate concern. Modern persons need both, according to Einstein, who claimed the following: "Science without religion is lame and religion without science is blind" (*Nature* 146 [1940]: 605–607). This Two Language model should not be confused with the classic model of the Two Books, according to which the book of Scripture and the book of nature each provide an avenue of revelation for God. The difference is that the Two Books model sees science as revealing truth about God, whereas the Two Language model sees science as revealing truth solely about the created world.

Hypothetical consonance. Going beyond the Two Language view by assuming an overlap between the subject matter of science and the subject matter of faith, *consonance* directs inquiry toward areas of correspondence between what can be said scientifically about the natural world and what can be said theologically about God's creation. Even though consonance seems to arise in some areas, such as the apparent correspondence of Big Bang cosmology with the doctrine of creation out of nothing, consonance has not been fully confirmed in all relevant shared areas. Hence, the adjective *hypothetical* applies to theology as well as science. The central hypothesis of this model is that there can be only one shared domain of truth regarding the created world, and science at its best and faith at its best both humble themselves before truth; one can therefore trust that consonance will eventually emerge. Hypothetical consonance provides the warrant for what some call "dialogue between science and theology," and others the "creative mutual interaction of science and theology."

Ethical overlap. Building on the Two Language model, wherein mutual respect between scientists and religious leaders is affirmed, some exhibit a strong desire for cooperation on public-policy issues deriving from science and technology. The ecological crisis and human values questions deriving from advances in biotechnology both enlist creative cooperation.

New Age spirituality. Having left the conflict or warfare model behind, synthetic spiritualities, such as those found in the New Age movement, seek to construct a worldview that integrates and harmonizes science with religion. Evolution becomes an overarching concept that incorporates the sense of deep time and imbues the development of a global spiritual consciousness as an evolutionary advance for the cosmos. Many here are prompted by the visionary theology of Teilhard de Chardin (1881–1955), although this Jesuit forerunner could not himself be categorized as New Age. Others in the New Age movement seek to integrate the experience of mystery with advanced discoveries in physics, such as indeterminacy and quantum theory.

Whereas these final four models take us beyond conflict or warfare, the Two Language view presumes independence, while hypothetical consonance, ethical overlap, and New Age spirituality seek a fuller integration. When it comes to research, publication, and conferencing within the field of science and religion, most frequently the assumptions of hypothetical consonance prevail with dialogue pressing toward creative mutual interaction.

The Problem of "Playing God." The two models of hypothetical consonance and ethical overlap provide the framework for assessing one particular pattern of interaction of science with the larger culture, namely, public-policy controversies that invoke abhorrence to "playing God." The phrase "playing God" refers to the power that science confers upon the human race to understand and control the natural world.

When the phrase "playing God" is used, it may connote one of three overlapping meanings. The first meaning is associated with basic scientific research, wherein one may "learn God's awesome secrets." Some research elicits a sense of awe and wonder over the complexity and majesty of the natural world that the human mind is apprehending. Science is like a light shining down into the hitherto dark and secretive caverns of natural mystery, revealing what previously was hidden. It is the revelatory power of science that leads us to think we are gaining godlike powers. Few would ask us to cease our investigation, because "learning for learning's sake" remains the morality of scientific knowledge.

The second meaning of "playing God" belongs to the field of medicine, where doctors seem to have gained power over life and death. In a medical emergency, the patient feels helpless, totally dependent upon the scientific training and personal skill of the physician attending. The surgeon, and the scientific training he or she has been exposed to in medical school, stands between the patient and death. Similarly, large-scale research programs dedicated to finding a cure for cancer or AIDS provide the larger society with hope in the face of helplessness. Here, "playing God" takes on a redemptive or salvific connotation. The genre of jokes about doctors who think of themselves as gods reflects the wider anxiety people have about their helplessness, as well as their dependence upon doctors and their skills.

This medical meaning of "playing God" makes two assumptions. First, that decisions regarding life and death belong to God's prerogative. The second follows from the first: a human being with the power of life and death is thought of in a godlike role. This elicits additional anxiety—namely, worry that the person in the godlike role will succumb to the temptation of pride, of hubris. The concept of hubris articulates the more inchoate fear that we will presume too much, overreach ourselves, violate some divinely appointed limit, and reap destruction. Anxiety over hubris marks the overlapping transition from the second to the third use of the phrase "playing God."

The third use of "playing God" connotes the human ability to alter life and influence human evolution. Here, science and technology team up so that understanding leads to control. Genetic engineering, wherein we alter the DNA and perhaps alter our own essence, is the primary area of science that provokes fears of playing God. Yet such fears also arise in nuclear physics and ecology. The scientific community becomes a microcosm of the entire human community, expressing excessive pride over human powers at the expense of God. Humans substitute their own judgment and powers to determine what nature will be, placing themselves where only God belongs.

The God of "playing God" is not necessarily the God of the Bible. Rather, it is divinized nature. In Western culture, nature has absorbed the qualities of sacredness, and science and technology risk profaning the sacred.

Today's fear of "playing God" is reminiscent of the ancient Greek myth of Prometheus. When the world was being created, according to the myth, the sky god Zeus was in a cranky mood. The Olympian decided to withhold fire from earth's inhabitants, leaving the nascent human race to relentless cold and darkness. The Titan Prometheus, whose name means "to think ahead," could foresee the value of fire for warming homes and providing lamplight for reading late at night. He could anticipate how fire could separate humanity from the beasts, making it possible to forge tools. So Prometheus craftily snuck up into the heavens where the gods dwell and where the sun is kept. He lit his torch from the fires of the sun, and then he carried this heavenly gift back to earth.

On Mount Olympus the gods were outraged that the stronghold of the immortals had been penetrated and robbed. Zeus was particularly angry over Prometheus's impertinence, so he exacted merciless punishment on the rebel. Zeus chained Prometheus to a rock where an eagle could feast all day long on the Titan's liver. The head of the pantheon cursed the future-oriented Prometheus: "Forever shall the intolerable present grind you down." The moral of the story, which is remembered to the present day, is this: human pride or hubris that leads us to overestimate ourselves and enter the realm of the sacred will precipitate vengeful destruction. The Bible provides a variant: "Pride goes before destruction" (*Prv.* 16:18).

For modern people who think scientifically, no longer does Zeus play the role of the sacred. Nature does. It is nature who will strike back in the Frankenstein legend or its more contemporary geneticized version, Michael Crichton's novel *Jurassic Park* (1990) and the subsequent movies. The theme has become a common one: the mad scientist exploits a new discovery, crosses the line between life and death, and then nature strikes back with chaos and destruction.

Some religious leaders have spoken out in theological language to plead for caution in the face of human pride. A 1980 task-force report, *Human Life and the New Genetics*, includes a warning by the U.S. National Council of Churches: "Human beings have an ability to do Godlike things: to exercise creativity, to direct and redirect processes of nature. But the warnings also imply that these powers may be used rashly, that it may be better for people to remember that they are creatures and not gods." A United Methodist Church Genetic Science Task Force report to the 1992 General Conference stated similarly: "The image of God, in which humanity is created, confers both power and responsibility to use power as God does: neither by coercion nor tyranny, but by love. Failure to accept limits by rejecting or ignoring accountability to God and interdependency with the whole of creation is the essence of sin." In sum, humans can sin through science by failing to recognize their limits and, thereby, violate the sacred.

Genetics is the field of research that elicits the most anxiety regarding the threat that scientists will play God. This is because DNA has garnered cultural reverence. The human genome has become tacitly identified with the essence of what is human. A person's individuality, identity, and dignity have become connected to his or her DNA. Therefore, if people have the hubris to intervene in the human genome, they risk violating something sacred. This tacit belief is called by some the "gene myth," by others "the strong genetic principle" or "genetic essentialism." This myth is an interpretive framework that includes both the assumed sacrality of the human genome plus the fear of Promethean pride.

Systematic theologians find themselves questioning the gene myth, doubting the equation of DNA with human essence or human personhood. A person is more than his or her genetic code. The National Council of Churches of Singapore put it this way in *A Christian Response to the Life Sciences* (2002): "It is a fallacy of genetic determinism to equate the genetic makeup of a person with the person" (p. 81). Such a theological anthropology combats the gene myth and opens the door for ethical approval of cautious genetic engineering.

Cautious employment of genetic technology to alter human DNA leads to considerations regarding the distinction between therapy and enhancement. At first glance, therapy seems ethically justifiable, whereas enhancement seems Promethean and dangerous. The term *gene therapy* refers to directed genetic change of human somatic cells to treat a genetic disease or defect in a living person. With four to six thousand human diseases traceable to genetic predispositions—including cystic fibrosis, Huntington's disease, Alzheimer's disease, and many cancers—the prospects of gene-based therapies are raising hopes for dramatic new medical advances. Few if anyone find ethical grounds to prohibit somatic cell therapy via gene manipulation.

The term *human genetic enhancement* refers to the use of genetic knowledge and technology to bring about improvements in the capacities of living persons, in embryos, or in future generations. Enhancement might be accomplished in one of two ways: either through genetic selection during screening or through directed genetic change. Genetic selection may take place at the gamete stage, or more commonly as embryo selection during preimplantation genetic diagnosis (PGD) following in vitro fertilization (IVF). Genetic changes could be introduced into early embryos, thereby influencing a living individual, or by altering the germ line, influencing future generations.

Some forms of enhancement are becoming possible. For example, introduction of the gene for IGF-1 into muscle cells results in increased muscle strength and health. Such a procedure would be valuable as a therapy, to be sure, yet it lends itself to availability for enhancement as well. For those who daydream of so-called designer babies, the list of traits to be enhanced would likely include increased height or intelligence, as well as preferred eye or hair color. Concerns raised by both secular and religious ethicists focus on economic justice—that is, wealthy families are more likely to take advantage of genetic enhancement services, leading to a gap between the "genrich" and the "genpoor."

The most ethical heat to date has been generated over the possibility of germ line intervention, and this applies to both therapy and enhancement. The term *germ line intervention* refers to gene selection or gene change in the gametes, which in turn would influence the genomes of future generations. Because the mutant form of the gene that predisposes for cystic fibrosis has been located on chromosome four, a plan to select out this gene and spare future generations of the suffering caused by this debilitating disease is easily imaginable. This would constitute germ line alteration for therapeutic motives. Similarly, in principle, one could select or even engineer genetic predispositions to favorable traits in the same manor. This would constitute germ line alteration for enhancement motives.

Both of these are risky for the same reason. Too much remains unknown about gene function. It is more than likely that gene expression works in delicate systems, so that it is rare that a single gene is responsible for a single phenotypical expression. If one removes or engineers one or two genes, it might unknowingly upset an entire system of gene interaction that could lead to unfortunate consequences. The prohibition against "playing God" serves here as a warning to avoid rushing in prematurely with what appears to be an improvement but could turn out to be a disaster. Ethicists frequently appeal to the precautionary principle—that is, to refrain from germ line modification until the scope of our knowledge is adequate to cover all possible contingencies.

It is important to note that the precautionary principle does not rely upon the tacit belief in DNA as sacred. Rather, it relies upon a principle of prudence that respects the complexity of the natural world and the finite limits of human knowledge.

The limits of scientific knowledge include two extrascientific yet relevant areas, namely, values and transcendence. The problem of playing God deals primarily with values, ethics, and public policy. Questions of transcendence also appear on the agenda of the growing field of science and religion.

RESEARCH QUESTIONS IN THE DIALOGUE BETWEEN SCIENCE AND RELIGION. Because science raises some questions that only religion can answer, dialogue largely consists of shared exploration of issues emerging from science and treated by both disciplines. Questions regarding the grounding of values, and especially questions of transcendence, set the dialogue agenda.

Physics. In the field of physics, quantum theory affirms contingency and perhaps even indeterminism at the subatomic level, giving rise to questions regarding rationality in the universe and the possibility of noninterventionist divine action in the physical realm. Newtonian physics led to a mechanistic picture of nature wherein the universe appeared like a clockwork, as a closed nexus of cause and effect. The rational structure of a clock provided the model for the rational structure of nature. If the universe is causally closed, then divine action within the world seems forbidden. Divine action would require God to intervene as an outside cause, perhaps in the form of a miracle, and this would upset the nexus. With the advent of quantum theory, natural events are now viewed as contingent. The world no longer looks like a clockwork but more like a history of natural events. For scientists such as Albert Einstein, beyond physical contingency God provides the universe with its rational structure, making it understandable to the human mind. For theologians of science such as Robert John Russell, quantum theory designates a fundamental realm of physical activity where God can act creatively and providentially in an objective yet noninterventionist way (Russell et al., 2001, pp. 293–328). In sum, physics raises philosophical and theological questions that transcend what science alone can address.

Indian Buddhists are finding that their own questions of causality provide a point of contact with both Newtonian and post-Newtonian physics. The classic scholastic system of speculative philosophy and psychology, *abhidharma,* dealt with multiple theories of causality. Discussions of physics among such Buddhists begin with religious questions and move toward possible integration with science.

Scientific cosmology. This field also raises questions that place physics and theological doctrines of creation and providence into dialogue. Two areas are worth special mention: Big Bang cosmology and the anthropic principle.

The standard Big Bang model of the beginning of our universe posits an original singularity and an apparent original moment for the onset of time, $t = 0$ (time equals zero). Physical time seems to have its own beginning. Although debates continue regarding just how old the universe actually is, estimates based upon observations by the Hubble Space Telescope cluster around 13.7 billion years. Before the moment of the Big Bang, before time and space existed, what was the nature of reality? No known physical experiment can test for this, nor can any theory regarding contemporary physical reality be extrapolated backward more than 13.7 billion years. Time and space seem to have an edge, and philosophers and theologians rightly ask what lies beyond the edge. Might we have here scientific confirmation for the classic Jewish and Christian doctrine of *creatio ex nihilo*? (Russell et al., 1987, pp. 273–296; Peters and Bennett, 2002, pp. 55–56).

Since the Big Bang, the universe has been steadily expanding. A key scientific question is this: is the universe open or closed? If it is open—that is, if the amount of mass is insufficient to stop the process, then it will continue to expand until the principle of entropy overtakes it. All the original heat will dissipate, and any remaining matter will fall into a state of equilibrium—in short, it will freeze out of existence. However, if the universe is closed—that is, if the amount of mass is above the relevant threshold, then at some point expansion will stop. Gravity will cause its motion to reverse, and all matter will reconverge on a central point, heating up on the way toward its doom in an unfathomably hot fireball—in short, it will fry. Whether freeze or fry, the future of the cosmos is finite. Might this be scientific disconfirmation of the biblical promise of an eschatological new creation?

The anthropic principle was formulated within physics, not theology. Because of the appearance of complex life forms on planet earth, physicists have been asking the following: what must have been the initial conditions at the moment of the Big Bang to eventually make life possible, or even inevitable? Such factors as the amount of mass, energy, rate of expansion, and so on could not have been different in fractions such as one to a million, or life would have been impossible. The universe seems to be fine-tuned for the appearance of life. Fine-tuning raises questions of intelligent design. The weak anthropic principle asks: Was the universe designed to make life possible? The strong anthropic principle asks: Was the universe designed to make life inevitable? (Peters and Bennett, 2001, p. 57).

Evolutionary biology. In evolutionary biology, scholars in the field of science and religion curiously avoid the public controversy with creationism and Intelligent Design, at least for the most part. Rather, assuming the validity of Darwinian theory, what drives the dialogue are questions regarding discernable purpose or direction within biological processes. The field of sociobiology has prompted widespread discussion regarding the influence of genetic determinism on human culture and religion. Special attention is given to the possible biological origins of human evil and suffering from evil, with a concomitant study of reciprocal altruism in both the animal and human realms.

Even if the evolution controversy is marginal to scholars in the field of science and religion, the controversy looms large in the public debate. Five positions are discernable, making it much more complicated than the image of a simple war between science and religion might connote. The first position would be that of evolutionary biology strictly as science without any attached ideological commitments. The reigning theory is neo-Darwinian, combining Charles Darwin's original nineteenth-century concept of natural selection with the twentieth-century concept of genetic mutation to explain the development of new species over 3.8 billion years. Defenders of quality science education in the public schools most frequently embrace this "science alone" approach.

The second position combines neo-Darwinism with materialist ideology, including repudiation of any divine influence on the course of evolutionary development. Spokespersons for sociobiology, such as E. O. Wilson or Richard Dawkins, are aggressive and vociferous. Evolution here provides apparent scientific justification for scientism, scientific imperialism, and in some cases atheism.

The third position is scientific creationism. During the fundamentalist era of the 1920s, biblical creationists appealed to the authority of the Bible to combat the rise in influence of Darwinism. Since the 1960s, creationists have based their arguments not on biblical authority but rather on counterscience—hence their label, *scientific creationists.* They argue, for example, that the fossil record will contradict standard appeals to natural selection over long periods of time. Those known as "young earth creationists," such as the leaders of the Institute for Creation Research near San Diego, California, hold that the planet earth is less than ten thousand years old and that all species of plants and animals were originally created by God in their present form. They deny macroevolution—that is, they deny that one species has evolved from prior species; although they affirm microevolution—that is, evolution within a species. Key here is that creationists justify their arguments on scientific grounds.

The fourth position is Intelligent Design. Advocates of Intelligent Design sharply attack neo-Darwinian theory for overstating the role of natural selection in species formation. They argue that slow incremental changes due to mutations are insufficient to explain the emergence of new and more complex biological systems. Many of the life forms that have evolved are irreducibly complex, and this counts as evidence that they have been intelligently designed. Intelligent Design scholars such as Michael Behe, Philip Johnson, and William

Dembski posit that appeal to a transcendent designer is necessary for the theory of evolution to successfully explain the development of life forms. Here, scientific questions lead to theological answers.

The fifth position is theistic evolution, according to which God has employed evolutionary processes over deep time to bring about the human race and perhaps even carry the natural world to a redemptive future. Theistic evolution first appeared in the late nineteenth and early twentieth centuries, even in the work of conservative Princeton theologian B. B. Warfield, for whom God's *concursus* with nature brought about the human race, just as God's *concursus* wrote the Scripture with human minds and hands. Teilhard de Chardin is perhaps best known for his evolutionary cosmology directed by God toward a future "Point Omega." Among contemporary scholars at work in the field of science and religion, the roster of theistic evolutionists includes Arthur Peacocke, Philip Hefner, Robert John Russell, Nancey Murphy, Kenneth Miller, John Haught, Martinez Hewlett, and Howard van Til. This school of thought is not occupied with defending evolution against attacks by advocates of scientific creationism or Intelligent Design; rather, it seeks to work through questions raised by randomness and chance in natural selection in light of divine purposes and ends.

Genetics. In genetics, especially molecular biology, new discoveries regarding the life of the early embryo, as well as proposed medical technologies employing cloning (somatic-cell nuclear transfer) and embryonic stem cells, have given rise to intense public-policy debates. Behind these public debates are religious anthropologies. Questions arise regarding the rightness or wrongness of using genetic technology to alter inherited human nature; the question "should we play God?" is asked when contemplating the power of the present generation to influence the future of human evolution. Ethical questions also arise over the use of early embryos for medical research. In sum, genetic science gives rise to questions regarding human nature and the grounding of human dignity.

Public-policy controversies over what is permissible in genetic research have appeared superficially to be warfare between science and religion, although a closer look will find both scientists and theologians lining up on both sides of each debate. The gene patenting controversy of 1995, the cloning controversy of 1997, and the stem-cell controversy at the turn of the twenty-first century led to widespread public-policy debates that incorporated multiple religious considerations. Two specific issues are worth mentioning. One involved the question of playing God. Should scientists receive intellectual property rights (patents) on information gained about the human genome, something nature placed within human beings? Should scientists enter the human genome and alter it, thereby altering essential human nature? Would technological intervention into something so essentially human as DNA be such a mark of Promethean hubris or pride that it might backfire—that is, would nature take out revenge upon us Frankenstein style? Would such scientific activity mark a trespassing of something sacred? Should DNA be treated as sacred?

A second and related issue became the moral status of the human embryo. In both the cloning and the stem-cell controversies, the early embryo would be subject to genetic engineering and, in some experimental situations, destroyed. Does the engineering of the embryo constitute playing God? Does the destruction of an engineered embryo constitute abortion?

The most articulate theological voice and the most forceful ethical voice in the public debate has been that of the Vatican. The way the ethical question gets formulated everywhere on the world scene has been influenced by the formulation of Rome. In its "Declaration on the Production and the Scientific and Therapeutic Use of Human Embryonic Stem Cells" (2000), the Vatican states the issue this way: "Is it morally licit to produce and/or use human embryos for the preparation of ES [embryonic stem] cells? The answer is negative." Further, "the ablation of the inner cell mass of the blastocyst, which critically and irremediably damages the human embryo, curtailing its development, is a gravely immoral act and consequently is gravely illicit." The U.S. National Conference of Catholic Bishops has argued that any intentional destruction of innocent human life at any stage is inherently evil, and that no good consequence can mitigate that evil.

Roman Catholic bioethicists appeal authoritatively to two precedents, *Donum Vitae* (1987) and *Evangelium Vitae* (1995). The central tenet is that morally protectable human personhood becomes applied to the zygote, the egg fertilized by the sperm. These two documents contend that the result of human procreation, from the first moment of its existence, must be guaranteed the unconditional respect that is morally due to the human being in his or her totality and unity in body and spirit: the human being is to be respected and treated as a person from the moment of conception; therefore, from that same moment his or her rights as a person must be recognized, among which in the first place is the inviolable right of every innocent human being to life.

The ethics is supported by metaphysics. Morally protectable dignity is derived from the presence of the immortal soul within the mortal body. In a 1996 elocution on evolution, Pope John Paul II affirmed that it is by virtue of the spiritual soul that the whole person possesses such dignity, even in his or her body. Not reducible to biological evolution, the spiritual soul is immediately created by God. This makes John Paul II an adherent to *creationism*, an ancient view that God creates a new soul for the birth of each new child (not to be confused with scientific creationism described above). What is significant for the controversy is this: the biological sciences cannot on their own discern the presence or absence of an immaterial and immortal soul, only theologically informed philosophy can. Furthermore, belief in the presence of the soul justifies morally protectable human dignity. The ethical implication of this view is that early embryos may not be destroyed for purposes of stem cell research, nor may they be produced through cloning or other artificial means.

Bioethicists do not uniformly agree with the Vatican. Most Jewish ethicists have made their peace with the abortion controversy by dating morally protectable human dignity at birth, relieving them of the pressure to protect the preimplantation embryo in research. Because they argue that God has commissioned the human race to engage in healing, and hence in the practice of medicine, they endorse medical science, including human embryonic stem-cell research.

Some Protestants have drawn upon the distinction between nonmalificence and beneficence. The Vatican proscription depends upon nonmalificence, that is, doing no harm to the embryo. Those countering the Vatican make their appeal to beneficence, that is, the biblical mandate to pursue the good—loving one's neighbor—creatively. Our ethical mandate is to improve human health and well-being, and supporting the advance of medical science, including stem-cell research, treats existing and future suffering people with care as well as dignity.

Neuroscience. The neurosciences raise questions of biological determinism and reductionism. Speculative hypotheses are being asked about the prospect of explaining complex human behavior, including religious experience, in terms of genetic determinism and neural firings in the human brain. As with evolution and genetics, questions are raised: Is religion a form of adaptive behavior that developed when the human brain was expanding in capacity? Is there a "God spot" or region of brain activity in which the potential for religious experience is physically prepared? If so, is it reducible to biological determinism, or does it mark an opening to transcendence? (Herzfeld, 2002; Peterson, 2003; Russell et al., 1999).This is a new field within the sciences, and to date its relevance for religion is the least cultivated.

For the theological or philosophical dimensions of each of the world's religious traditions, the question of truth is a driving force. The theological motivation to engage in dialogue with natural science is an inherent impetus rising out of religious consciousness, out of what Mircea Eliade called "ontological thirst," or thirst for reality. The scientific motivation to engage in dialogue with religion rises out of the realization that questions of transcendence cannot be avoided in physics and cosmology, nor can questions of value and meaning be avoided in genetics and evolutionary biology. The emerging field of science and religion plays host to this dialogue.

BIBLIOGRAPHY

The pioneer of the field now known as *science and religion* is Ian G. Barbour, whose breakthrough book *Issues in Science and Religion* (New York, 1966) provided a reliable history of the interaction between science and faith in the West. This work, along with John Hedley Brooke's *Science and Religion: Some Historical Perspectives* (Cambridge, U.K., 1991), replaced the vitriolic late nineteenth-century accounts by John W. Draper, *History of the Conflict between Religion and Science* (New York, 1874) and A. D. White, *A History of the Warfare of Science with Theology in Christendom* (New York, 1896). See also the predecessor article to this one, Stanley L. Jaki, "Science and Religion," in *The Encyclopedia of Religion*, edited by Mircea Eliade (New York, 1987), vol. 13, pp. 121–133. For an excellent treatment of the Protestant Reformation see John Dillenberger, *Protestant Thought and Natural Science: A Historical Interpretation* (Garden City, N.Y., 1960).

Recommended contemporary anthologies that cover the spectrum of the field within Christianity include *Science and Theology: The New Consonance*, edited by Ted Peters (Boulder, Colo., 1998). Christian and selected non-Christian religious entries are included in *Bridging Science and Religion*, edited by Ted Peters and Gaymon Bennett (London, 2002). Two encyclopedias cover the field: J. Wentzel Vrede van Huyssteen, ed., *Encyclopedia of Science and Religion*, 2 vols. (New York, 2003) and Gary B. Ferngren, ed., *The History of Science and Religion in the Western Tradition: An Encyclopedia* (New York, 2000).

The contemporary discussion of science within Islam is taken up by Seyyed Hossein Nasr, *Religion and the Order of Nature* (Oxford and New York, 1996); Muzaffar Iqbal, *Islam and Science* (Aldershot, U.K., and Burlington, Vt., 2003); and *God, Life, and the Cosmos: Christian and Islamic Perspectives*, edited by Ted Peters, Muzaffar Iqbal, and Seyd Nomanul Haq (Aldershot, U.K., and Burlington, Vt., 2002).

Broad integrations of the various natural sciences with Christian systematic theology are best exemplified by Arthur Peacocke's *Theology for a Scientific Age: Being and Becoming—Natural, Divine, and Human* (Minneapolis, 1993), plus two sets of Gifford Lectures, John Polkinghorne, *The Faith of a Physicist* (Princeton, 1994), and Ian G. Barbour, *Religion in an Age of Science* (San Francisco, 1990), as well as Barbour's *Ethics in an Age of Technology* (San Francisco, 1993).

On epistemological and methodological connections between science and theology, see Nancey Murphy and George F. R. Ellis, *On the Moral Nature of the Universe: Theology, Cosmology, and Ethics* (Minneapolis, 1996); Wolfhart Pannenberg, *Toward a Theology of Nature: Essays on Science and Faith* (Louisville, Ky., 1993); and Niels Henrik Gregersen and J. Wentzel Vrede van Huyssteen, eds., *Rethinking Theology and Science: Six Models for the Current Dialogue* (Grand Rapids, Mich., 1998). On divine action within the physical world, see Paul Davies, *God and the New Physics* (New York, 1983); Philip Clayton, *God and Contemporary Science* (Grand Rapids, Mich., 1997); Robert John Russell, William R. Stoeger, and George V. Coyne, eds., *Physics, Philosophy, and Theology* (Vatican City State and Notre Dame, Ind., 1987); Robert John Russell, Philip Clayton, Kirk Wegter-McNelly, and John Polkinghorne, eds., *Quantum Mechanics: Scientific Perspectives on Divine Action* (Vatican City State and Berkeley, 2001); Hans Schwarz, *Creation* (Grand Rapids, Mich., 2002); and Antje Jackelen, *Zeit und Ewigkeit* (Neukirchen, Germany, 2002). See also Ravi Ravindra, "Einstein, Albert," in *Encyclopedia of Religion* (New York, 1987) vol 5, 71–72.

On genetics, ethics, and social policy, see the National Council of Churches of Singapore, *A Christian Response to the Life Sci-*

ences (Singapore, 2002); Vatican document, "Declaration on the Production and the Scientific and Therapeutic Use of Human Embryonic Stem Cells" (Vatican City State, August 2000; available from http://www.cin.org/docs/stem-cell-research.html); Holmes Rolston III, *Genes, Genesis, and God: Values and Their Origins in Natural and Human History* (Cambridge, U.K., 1999); Celia E. Deane-Drummond, *Biology and Theology Today: Exploring The Boundaries* (London, 2001); and Ted Peters, *Playing God? Genetic Determinism and Human Freedom* (New York, 2002).

On anthropology, see Philip Hefner, *The Human Factor: Evolution, Culture, and Religion* (Minneapolis, 1993); Noreen L. Herzfeld, *In Our Image: Artificial Intelligence and the Human Spirit* (Minneapolis, 2002); Niels Henrik Gregersen, Willem B. Drees, and Ulf Gorman, eds., *The Human Person in Science and Theology* (Edinburgh, 2000); and Warren S. Brown, Nancey Murphy, and H. Newton Malony, eds., *Whatever Happened to the Soul?: Scientific and Theological Portraits of Human Nature* (Minneapolis, 1998). On the evolution controversy, see Ted Peters and Martinez Hewlett, *Evolution from Creation to New Creation* (Nashville, 2003), and Robert John Russell, William R. Stoeger, and Francisco J. Ayala, eds., *Evolutionary and Molecular Biology: Scientific Perspectives on Divine Action* (Vatican City State and Berkeley, 1998). On the relevance of brain research to theology, see Robert John Russell, Nancey Murphy, Theo C. Meyering, and Michael A. Arbib, eds., *Neuroscience and the Person: Scientific Perspectives on Divine Action* (Vatican City State and Berkeley, 1999), and Gregory R. Peterson, *Minding God: Theology and the Cognitive Sciences* (Minneapolis, 2003).

Leading journals include *Islam and Science: Journal of Islamic Perspectives on Science* (Center for Islam and Science, Canada); *Omega: Indian Journal of Science and Religion* (Kerala, India); *Theology and Science* (U.K.); *Zygon: Journal of Religion and Science* (U.K.), *Australian Theological Forum* (Adelaide, Australia); and *Glaube und Denken: Jahrbuch der Karl Heim Gesellschaft* (Tübingen, Germany).

TED PETERS (2005)

SCIENTOLOGY is a spiritual movement that grew out of the ideas and practices advocated by Layfayette Ronald (L. Ron) Hubbard (1911–1986), a writer and former U.S. naval officer. After his discharge from the navy, Hubbard became a writer of popular fiction, but even before he left the service he dedicated himself to determining both the cause of the human situation and the means of correcting it. His efforts led him to author several book-length manuscripts in the late 1940s and to publish several articles. Then in 1950 his book *Dianetics*, released by a small publishing house, jumped onto the *New York Times* best-seller lists.

Dianetics was the name Hubbard gave to the system of thought and practice that grew out of his concentrated exploration of the human mind. He believed humanity's problems were caused by mental aberrations (called *engrams*); he proposed a form of counseling termed *auditing* as the means to rid the self of the engrams. Dianetics teaches that the human mind has a twofold structure: the *analytic mind* and the *reactive mind*. The analytic mind thinks, plans, observes the world, and records memories. However, at particular moments, especially at times of severe distress or pain, the analytic mind recedes, and the reactive mind takes over. The reactive mind simply observes, records, and stores memories at times when the analytic mind is not functional. Such memories are generally not available to the conscious self but may be the source of irrational and dysfunctional behavior. Dianetics was designed to rid people of the effects of the reactive mind and bring them to a state of *clear*.

When Dianetics became a popular movement, Hubbard gathered his most enthusiastic supporters, including a number of physicians, into a board and founded several organizations to structure the movement. He continued to observe people undergoing Dianetic counseling or auditing, which explored individuals' memories. During these processes Hubbard began to encounter memories that seemed to reach to a time prior to birth and even to a previous existence in a different body. This experience and other factors led him to refocus his primary concern from the mind to the human spirit, that permanent part of the self that he believed could continue past death and into reincarnation, a different physical existence in a new body.

Speculation on the human spirit seemed to be suggesting the movement toward religion, a direction that many of Hubbard's associates (including some board members) rejected. Hubbard persisted in developing his thought, however, which as early as 1952 he called Scientology. The first Church of Scientology was founded in Los Angeles in 1954; another opened in Washington, D.C., the following year, with Hubbard serving as its executive director. Other churches soon emerged in New Zealand, South Africa, England, and Ireland.

SCIENTOLOGY BELIEFS. Scientology most closely resembles a Western esoteric-Gnostic system. In the early 1950s Hubbard posited the existence of a spiritual being called a *thetan* that was neither body nor intellect. He hypothesized that the thetan could live apart from the body (a phenomenon he called *exteriorization*) and had existed in other bodies prior to the present one. Further, he concluded, it was the essential nature of the thetan to survive, and it attempted to do so around a set of ever more inclusive concerns that he termed the *eight dynamics*. First, it seeks to survive as an individual—finding expression in creativity, sexuality, and family life. It then seeks to survive by identification with various human groupings, humanity as a whole, all life-forms, and eventually larger concerns—the universe, spirituality, and the infinite or Supreme Being. Hubbard's discussion of the infinite aligns with both Eastern and Western mystical speculations.

Scientology is structured toward grasping the eight dynamics sequentially, beginning with the seemingly mundane issues of individual and social issues, gradually reaching levels at which (in Western eyes) more traditional religious concerns are addressed. The church teaches that until the basic issues of life are set right, the larger issues of spirituality and God are difficult to bring into focus.

Hubbard also set the thetan's path to enlightenment into a fairly familiar myth of entrapment and escape. Thetans are thought to have come into existence billions of years ago. Along the way, they fell into the universe of matter, energy, space, and time (MEST). Although thetans had created MEST, they eventually forgot they were the creators and became imprisoned in their own creation. The thetans as a group also went through several horrendous cosmic events that further stripped them of their abilities and even the conscious memory of what had happened to them. Their various adventures have led them to the present time on earth.

As with other forms of esotericism (alchemy, Qabbalah, hermetics), Scientology proposes an explanation of the human condition, a means of escape, and a way to return to the spiritual world of the pre-MEST thetan. When individuals reach the state of clear, they are no longer bound by the reactive mind and are ready to confront the barriers to complete freedom—those products of the early cosmic events that still affect their lives. Scientology literature describes the cosmic career of the thetans in mythic stories similar to those in ancient Gnostic and Hindu myths. The full content of these myths are revealed only to the church member as they move through the upper levels of church life.

By the time they reach the higher or operating thetan (OT) levels of church membership, members have become intimately familiar with auditing, the basic counseling technique that rids them of engrams and the reactive mind. At the higher levels, auditing is also used to confront additional encumbrances on the thetan produced by its cosmic history. Auditing uses an instrument called an e-meter, a modified whetstone bridge that measures subtle changes in the electrical current moving through the body. In the hands of a trained auditor, it is believed that the e-meter can register changing states in the thetan and greatly assist the process of gaining awareness.

CHURCH ORGANIZATION. The Church of Scientology is organized hierarchically. At the lowest level are the local churches and missions that introduce people to the church and provide members with basic teachings and auditing leading to clear. Local churches are tied together by the Church of Scientology International, which operates similarly to the Mother Church of the Church of Christ, Scientist. Local churches and missions are autonomous but are bound to the international body by a set of licenses that grant the use of Scientology copyrights and trademarks. Local churches also agree to follow the procedures (called the *technology*) laid down in Hubbard's writings in all of the classes and auditing they provide for members. The copyrights and trademarks are held by a unique church structure, the Religious Technology Center, whose chair is considered the true head of the church.

In addition to local churches, there is a set of special church facilities designed to provide the materials, teachings, and services for operating thetans. The basic OT levels (I-V) are provided at the several Advanced Organizations (in Los Angeles, Sydney, Copenhagen, and East Grimstead, United Kingdom). OT VI and VII are delivered through the Flag Service Organization in Clearwater, Florida. OT VIII, the highest level available to church members in the early twenty-first century, is offered aboard an oceangoing vessel, the *Freewinds.* Additional levels are expected to be offered, but their release awaits enough members having attained OT VIII.

Auditors—ministers found in every church facility—are trained at the Saint Hill organizations in Los Angeles, Sydney, and East Grimstead, which function as seminaries. In addition the church has developed a special concern to serve individuals in the arts, many of whom lead public lives. To allow such members the privacy to pursue their own spiritual advancement, the church supports a number of celebrity centers where they may go for auditing and other Scientology course work. A number of Hollywood entertainers have joined the church, and a few, such as Tom Cruise, Isaac Hayes, John Travolta, and Kirstie Alley, have served as spokespersons.

In 1967 Hubbard created a fraternity of dedicated Scientologists to whom he assigned the exacting task of delivering the higher OT levels to the membership. The group, known as the Sea Organization, evolved into an ordered community (analogous to monastic orders) of men and women who committed their lives to working for the spread of Scientology worldwide. Following the reorganization of the church in the early 1980s, the Sea Organization assumed leadership of the church internationally; everyone who holds policy-making and administrative positions at the continental and global levels is a Sea Organization member.

CONTROVERSY. Controversy has plagued Scientology from its earliest days. Many early participants rejected the change from secular Dianetics to religious Scientology. Many early observers, noting the difference between Scientology and the more dominant Western religions, missed the many religious trappings with which they were familiar. Controversy reached a new height in 1963, when U.S. government agents seized the church's e-meters and accused it of practicing medicine without a license. This action had international repercussions. Scientology was banned for a time in parts of Australia, and other governments began to limit the church's activities. The Guardian's Office was established in 1966 to handle attacks on the church.

Controversy peaked in 1979, when members of the Guardian's Office, in their attempt to locate government records about the church, infiltrated government offices and made copies of official documents. After the arrest and conviction of the office's leadership, the church was completely reorganized under the Religious Technology Center and the Church of Scientology International.

Much of the ongoing controversy concerning the church concerns its structure as an esoteric organization (in which teachings are only revealed to the higher-level members) and its finances. The church works on a basis of reciprocity—that is, members give of their time and energy, and the church delivers its services. Most often members donate money for which they receive auditing or classes. This structure, though widely used among esoteric groups, has caused many, including some governments, to question the church's religious nature and brand it a business operation. Before granting the church tax-exempt status in the early 1990s, for example, the U.S. Internal Revenue Service conducted the longest investigation in agency history to that date.

As the anticult movement emerged in the 1970s, critics of Scientology labeled it a cult and published a number of books and shorter writings attacking it. The church fought back in the courts, and while frequently winning, gained a reputation for litigiousness. In subsequent years, critics have contested every aspect of the church's life, while the church has aggressively defended its founder and program.

In spite of ongoing problems with several European countries and its frequent court appearances, the Church of Scientology experienced steady growth through the first half-century of its existence. Since 1954 congregations and missions have opened in more than seventy countries around the world, and the basic text *Dianetics* has been translated into more than fifty languages. The church sponsors a spectrum of social programs to combat illiteracy, drug abuse, crime, and the breakdown of social ethics.

SEE ALSO Anticult Movements; Hubbard, L. Ron.

BIBLIOGRAPHY

Christensen, Dorthe Refslund. *Scientology: Fra terapi til religion.* Copenhagen, 1997.

Church of Scientology International. *Scientology: Theology and Practice of a Contemporary Religion.* Los Angeles, 1998. Includes brief articles by a spectrum of scholars on Scientology.

Church of Scientology International. *What Is Scientology?* Los Angeles, 1998.

Friends of Ron, comp. *L. Ron Hubbard: A Profile.* Los Angeles, 1995. A comprehensive biographical work from the Church of Scientology.

Hubbard, L. Ron. *Dianetics: The Modern Science of Mental Health.* New York, 1950; reprint, Los Angeles, 2000.

Melton, J. Gordon. *The Church of Scientology.* Salt Lake City, Utah, 2001.

Whitehead, Harriet. *Renunciation and Reformulation: A Study of an American Sect.* Ithaca, N.Y., 1987.

J. GORDON MELTON (2005)

SCRIPTURE

SCRIPTURE is the generic concept used in the modern West and, increasingly, worldwide, to designate texts that are revered as especially sacred and authoritative in all of the largest and many smaller religious traditions.

AS A GENERAL CONCEPT. In popular and even in scholarly use today, the term *scripture* is commonly used as though it designated a self-evident and simple religious phenomenon readily identifiable anywhere in the world, namely the idea of a "sacred book." However, as a concept adequate to encompass the functional roles of the great sacred texts of history, *scripture* is a term of considerable ambiguity and complexity.

In the first instance, the specific form and content of scriptural books vary sharply from tradition to tradition and even within a single scriptural corpus. Ritual books, legal maxims and codes, myths and legends, historical accounts, divine revelations, apocalyptic visions, ecstatic poetry, words of teachers and prophets, and hymns or prayers to a deity can all be found in scriptural texts. The love lyrics of the *Song of Songs* in the Hebrew Bible, the talismanic prayers against evil in the last two surahs of the Qurʾān, Kṛṣṇa's self-revelation in chapter 11 of the *Bhagavadgītā,* and the Buddha's parable of the burning house in chapter 3 of the *Lotus Sutra* have had significant roles as scripture, yet they have little or nothing in common in their style, form, subject matter, or intent. Such disparity makes any reasonably comprehensive yet still simple definition of *scripture* as a literary genre impossible.

Second, a major obstacle to delimiting the phenomenon of scripture definitionally is its very medium of expression. The term *scripture* is usually reserved for religious texts that have been committed to the written or printed page, as the word itself and its common equivalents (e.g., "holy writ") suggest. Yet in most religious traditions, sacred texts were transmitted orally in the first place and written down only relatively late. Nor do written sacred books exhaust the full range of texts that function clearly as scripture. The Hindu tradition, for example, presents a major problem for defining "scripture" in terms of the written word. Its holiest texts, the Vedas, have been orally transmitted for three millennia or more—for most of that time in explicit preference to (and even firm rejection of) writing them down. Despite their great length, they were not committed to writing but instead preserved in memory and verbatim recitation until comparatively recent centuries. It may also be argued that nonliterate communities have oral texts that function in similar ways to written sacred texts in literate societies, insofar as these cultures use traditional recitations in cultic practice or hold certain myths or other oral texts sufficiently sacred to be worthy of transmission over generations. For these reasons, a descriptive distinction between oral and written scriptures (or oral and written uses of the same scripture) may on occasion be necessary, even though etymologically "oral scripture" is a contradiction in terms and "written scripture" a redundancy.

A further ambiguity of "scripture" as a conceptual category lies in the wide variety of texts that might be classified as "scriptural." A key problem in this regard involves those "classic" texts in literate cultures that have many cultural, social, and often even religious functions usually associated with more overtly "religious" texts. Examples would be the

Iliad of Homer in later antiquity; the five (or six, nine, twelve, or thirteen) "classics" (*jing*) and the four "books" (*shu*) in traditional Chinese culture; the great Sanskrit epics, the *Mahābhārata* and *Rāmāyana,* in India; and the *Nihongi* (Chronicles of Japan) and *Kojiki* (Records of Ancient Matters) in Shintō tradition. Such texts do have "scriptural" qualities, such as the veneration they inspire and the authority they command, and thus might be treated as "scripture" in certain contexts.

Another problem in delimiting and defining "scripture" is distinguishing the primary sacred text(s) of a religious tradition from others that are also sacred but secondarily so. Such distinction between a community's preeminent scripture(s) and the rest of its sacred texts is helpful in understanding many religious traditions, but others not at all: in some cases, the panoply of texts revered is so great and the relative distinctions of authority and sacrality among them so unclear or unimportant that all have some legitimate claim to the title of scripture. In the Mahāyāna Buddhist tradition as a whole, the number of texts treated as sacred is so vast that it is not possible to single out some as more deserving of the title *scripture* than others, save in particular segments of the tradition where one *sūtra* is given extraordinary status (e.g., Nichiren Buddhist veneration of the *Lotus Sūtra* in Japan). Even in a community with a scriptural book or canon that is clearly more sacred than other revered texts, the decision to reserve the status of "scripture" only for the former can be a debatable one. For example, the Purāṇas function scripturally across a wide spectrum of Indian society even though they are not *śruti;* in rabbinic Jewish tradition, the Mishnah is held to be the oral Torah, also revealed at Sinai; the *ḥadīth* serve in Islam not only to clarify and to explain but to supplement the Qur'ān as a religious authority, especially in matters of practice; and in Therāvada Buddhist traditions, texts such as Buddhaghosa's *Visuddhimagga* are greatly revered even though they do not report the "word of the Buddha" (*buddhavacana*) in the strict sense.

AS A RELATIONAL CONCEPT. As these considerations indicate, neither form nor content can serve to identify or to distinguish scripture as a general phenomenon. It is true that the form, content, or other specific attributes of a text may be perceived by the faithful as the guarantee of the extraordinary character of their major scripture (note, for example, Muslim faith in the literary "matchlessness" *[i'jāz]* of the Qur'anic style). Nevertheless, from the historian's perspective, the sacrality or holiness of a book is not an *a priori* attribute but one that is realized historically in the life of communities who respond to it as something sacred or holy. A text becomes "scripture" in living, subjective relationship to persons and to historical tradition. No text, written, oral, or both, is sacred or authoritative in isolation from a community. A text is only "scripture" insofar as a group of persons perceives it to be sacred or holy, powerful and meaningful, possessed of an exalted authority, and in some fashion transcendent of, and hence distinct from, other speech and writing. That which is scripture for one group may be a meaningless, nonsensical, or even perversely false text for another.

This relational, or contextual, quality is of paramount importance for the study of "scriptural" texts in the history of religion. The "scriptural" characteristics of a text belong not to the text itself but to its role in a community. "Scripture" is not a literary genre but a religio-historical one.

ORIGINS AND DEVELOPMENT OF THE CONCEPT. Whatever the subtleties and difficulties of defining it, scripture is a major phenomenon in the history of religion and thus an important concept in the study of religion. Whence it came and how it has come to serve as a general as well as a culture-specific concept are questions basic to understanding and using it intelligently and adequately as a descriptive term.

The idea of a heavenly book. The development of the concept of a scriptural book is often linked to the notion of a heavenly book. The idea of a heavenly book containing divine knowledge or decrees is an ancient and persistent one found primarily in the ancient Near Eastern and Greco-Roman worlds and in subsequent Jewish, Christian, and Islamic traditions. As Leo Koep points out in *Das himmlische Buch in Antike und Christentum* (Bonn, 1952), it can take one of several forms, typically that of a book of wisdom, book of destinies, book of works, or book of life. References to a celestial book or tablet of divine wisdom appear in ancient Babylonia and ancient Egypt and recur in almost all subsequent Near Eastern traditions, apparently as an expression of divine omniscience. Geo Widengren argues (*The Ascension of the Apostle and the Heavenly Book,* Uppsala, 1950; *Muhhammad, the Apostle of God, and His Ascension,* Uppsala, 1955, esp. pp. 115–139) that such a book was coupled in the ancient Near East, in Judaism, and finally in Islam to a messenger figure to whom the book is given in a personal encounter with God or validated through such an encounter (e.g., Moses at Sinai, Muḥammad on his ascension). The idea of a book of destinies or fates, in which the allotted days and assigned end of human lives are written down, was known, as art and textual evidence show, in ancient Babylonia, Egypt, Greece, Rome, and especially late antiquity. Israel also knew this motif (see *Ps.* 139:16–17), and the sealed book mentioned in *Revelation* 5:1ff. may well be a Christian instance of it. The similar notion of a book of works, in which a heavenly record of human deeds is kept, was also widely known of old. References to the writing down of good and bad deeds, often in connection with a last judgment, are found among the ancient Babylonians, Egyptians, Persians, and Hebrews, as well as Greek, Roman, Jewish, and Christian writers of later antiquity. However, it is in the biblical traditions of Judaism and Christianity (cf. *Ex.* 32:32, *Phil.* 4:3) that the notion of a book of life, in which the names of God's elect are inscribed, finds a special place.

While the precise relationship of these ideas to that of a revealed scriptural book remains to be clarified, elements of all of them do appear in the developed concepts of Jewish and Christian scripture and the Qur'ān, and all of them do reflect the antiquity and strength of the idea of a written book as the repository of divine knowledge or divine decrees.

The idea of a sacred book. The quintessential "book religions" are those that trace their lineage in some fashion to the Hebrews, the prototypical "people of the book." It is not yet fully understood how Judaic ideas of the sacred or heavenly book joined historically with influences from other sectors of the ancient Near Eastern world and the growing status of the book in later antiquity to set in motion the "book religion" that plays so large a role in Christianity, Manichaeism, and, most spectacularly and pronouncedly, in Islam. Wilfred Cantwell Smith has, however, pointed to the gathering strength in the period after Alexander the Great, and especially from the second century CE, of the idea of a sacred book or "classic," a text that carries ultimate authority. Christianity's increasing emphasis on authoritative writings, the point of departure for which was Jewish reverence for the Torah, was especially decisive in this development. Mani's self-conscious effort to produce books of scriptural authority reflects the degree to which by his time (third century CE) a religious movement had to have its own scripture or scriptures to be legitimate. The fourth century in particular seems to have been a time when scriptures, notably the Christian and Manichaean, were coming into their own. But it was the Qur'ān's insistence upon the centrality of the divine book, given now in final form as a recitation of divine speech, that carried the development of book religion to its apogee in the early seventh century. Later developments such as Sikhism's veneration of its "book" (*Granth*) have to be seen as but new variations on a theme already fully articulated in Islam, the book religion *par excellence* (Smith, 1993, ch. 3, pp. 45–64).

Semantic background. The most basic meaning of *scripture,* as of its Indo-European cognates (Ger., *Schrift;* Ital., *scrittura;* Fr., *écriture;* etc.), is "a writing, something written." It is derived from the Latin *scriptura,* "a writing" (pl., *scripturae*). The Latin word translated the Greek *graphē* (pl., *graphai*), which corresponded in Classical and Hellenistic usage to the postexilic Hebrew use of *ketav* (pl., *ketuvim/kitvei*) as a term for a writing: a letter, inscription, written decree, or a holy writing. These terms could even refer to the written law (Plato, *Laws* 11.934)—in the Septuagint, specifically to the Mosaic law, or Torah (*1 Chr.* 15:15). In the Mediterranean world of later antiquity, pagan, Jewish, and Christian writers used these words (or their plurals) to refer to various kinds of written texts in the Hebrew Bible, the Greek Septuagint, and the Old Testament books of the Latin Vulgate (e.g., *Ex.* 32:16, *Tob.* 8:24, *Ps.* 86:6). By the time of the Christian New Testament writers, however, the terms had gradually come to be used especially for sacred books, above all the three divisions of the Hebrew scriptures, the Pentateuch (Torah), Prophets (Nevi'im), and (other) Writings (Ketuvim). In early Christian usage, they were extended also to the Gospels, Pauline epistles, and other texts that eventually formed the New Testament.

In Jewish and Christian usage, the singular forms were applied primarily to a particular passage or particular writing, and the plurals were used in a collective sense for the whole. For example, *Daniel* 10:21 employs *bi-khetav emet* (Septuagint, *en graphē alētheias;* Vulgate, *in scriptura veritatis*), "in a true writing/scripture"; *Luke* 4:21 employs *hē graphē autē* (Vulgate, *haec scriptura*), "this [passage of] scripture" (referring to *Is.* 61:1f.), and *Matthew* 21:42, *Acts of the Apostles* 17:11, and other passages employ *hai graphai* (Vulgate: *scripturae*), "the [Old Testament] scriptures." The Christian fathers used both singular and plural forms collectively to refer to the Old and New Testament books (e.g., *Epistle of Barnabas* 4.7, 5.4; Irenaeus, *Against Heresies* 2.24.3, 2.27.1). Although in the New Testament these terms in singular or plural refer uniformly to scriptural as opposed to other kinds of writings, there is some dispute as to whether the singular *graphē* (*scriptura*) ever refers collectively to the whole of the scriptures or only to one or a part of one of them (as in *Jn.* 10:35 or *Rom.* 11:2).

Other terms, usually also associated with writing or books, were used in like fashion to refer to sacred, authoritative writings. In Greek, *grammata* (sg., *gramma,* "what is written; writing"; Lat., *littera*), used generally for literature or documents (as in the Septuagint, where it usually translates the Hebrew *sefarim/sifrei,* plural of *sefer,* "writing, book"), came in Hellenistic times, in pagan as well as Jewish and Christian contexts, to refer especially to any sacred text (e.g., *2 Tm.* 3.15, *ta hiera grammata;* Vulgate, *sacras litteras*). Scriptural citations in the New Testament and early Christian works are commonly introduced by the formula used in the Septuagint: "(As) it is written," (*Kathōs*) *gegraptai* (*Mt.* 4:4, 4:6, 21:13; *Rom.* l:17, 2:24; *1 Cor.* 2:9, etc.). The Greek *biblos* ("book"), or, more commonly in the Septuagint and New Testament, its diminutive form, *biblion* (pl., *biblia*), referred originally to any type of written document—scroll, codex, book, or letter. In the Septuagint and subsequent Jewish and Christian Greek sources (for example, the Greek preface to *Ben Sira, 1* and *2 Maccabees, 1 Clement,* and the writings of Philo Judaeus, Josephus Flavius, and Origen), although not in New Testament writings, terms like *hiera biblos,* "sacred book," and (*hierai*) *bibloi,* "(sacred) books," were used for the Pentateuch or the entire Hebrew scriptures. From the earliest days of the Christian church, in which "the books" (Heb., *ha-sefarim;* Gk., *ta biblia*) of Hebrew scripture were "the bible of the church" (Hans von Campenhausen, *Aus der Frühzeit des Christentums,* Tübingen, 1963, pp. 152–196), the Greek neuter plural *biblia* or the Latin *biblia* (a neuter plural formed from the Greek) was used in Christian contexts to refer specifically to the Hebrew scriptures. It appears that by the end of the second century, or at least by the end of the fourth, the generally recognized writings of the emerging New Testament were also included in "the books" (Harnack, 1928). In the Middle Ages (certainly from the twelfth century and probably earlier), *biblia* came to be treated commonly as a feminine singular, whence such modern singular forms arose as *the Bible, die Bibel,* and *la Bibbia.*

In the New Testament (e.g., *Rom.* 1:2, *2 Tm.* 3:15) and in the works of the Christian fathers, and as well as in Philo and Josephus, various adjectives were added to the words for "scripture(s)" and "book(s)" to emphasize their special, holy character: for example, *hieros, hagios, sanctus* ("holy"); *theios, divinus* ("divine"); *theopneustos* ("divinely inspired"); *kuriakos* ("of the Lord"). Such usage had much earlier precedents, such as the use in Ptolemaic times of *ta hiera grammata,* "the holy writings," to refer to the sacred Egyptian hieroglyphic literature in contrast to the demotic writings, or the use of the Hebrew equivalents, *kitvei ha-qodesh* ("the Holy Scriptures") in rabbinic writings, or *sifrei ha-qodesh* ("the sacred books") in later, medieval writings, for the sacred scriptures.

Generalization of the concept. In these ways, the Jewish and Christian worlds gradually appropriated the use of such terms as *scripture, holy scripture(s), books, sacred books,* and so forth, primarily as proper-noun designations for their own holy texts. In particular, as Christian culture and religion triumphed in the Mediterranean, especially in southern Europe, *(sacred) scripture* came to mean specifically the Christian Bible. Such limitation of the idea of scripture to a proper noun referring only to the Old and New Testaments continues even today in many Christian circles. Apparently the use of *scriptura(e)* and *scriptura(e) sancta(e)* (or their European-language equivalents) to designate sacred texts in general was until recently, chiefly in the past century or two, unusual at best. *Scriptura* could, of course, always be used as a neutral term for any writing, and it is not a giant step from such usage to a generalized concept of religious writings in other cultures. For example, such a concept may be present when Peter the Venerable (d. 1156) contrasts "sacra scriptura," or Christian scripture, with Muḥammad's "nefaria scriptura," the Qur'ān (*Summa totius haeresis saracenorum,* cited in James Kritzeck, *Peter the Venerable and Islam,* Princeton, 1964, p. 206). A clearer example of the notion of "scripture" as something appearing in many cultures can be found as early as the mid-thirteenth century. In 1254, at the Mongol capital in Inner Asia, the Franciscan traveler William of Rubrouck warned a group of Nestorian Christians about tactics in their coming debate on religion with Buddhists and Muslims before the Great Khan: "They do not have faith in [our] Scriptures; if you recite one [scripture], they will recite another" (in Anastasius van den Wyngaert, *Sinica Franciscana,* Florence, 1929, vol. 1, p. 294).

Such Western generalization of the concept of scripture was, to be sure, hardly novel. In the Muslim world, the concept of sacred "scripture" (*kitāb*) had already been generalized in the Qur'ān, where especially Jews and Christians are spoken of as "people of scripture" (*ahl al-kitāb*). The term designates those communities that have previously received "books" or "scriptures" (*kutub*) sent by God, which were then eclipsed in the perfection of his final "sending" of *the* Scripture [*al-kitāb*], the Qur'ān, through Muḥammad. *Ahl al-kitāb* status was early extended to Zoroastrians and Mandaeans, and later even in some cases to Hindus because of the Veda. There seems, however, to be no evidence of direct influence of the Muslim use of *kutub* on modern Western generic usage. It appears rather that it was the growing Western awareness in the eighteenth century of the Indian Veda in particular, and the Chinese "classics" to some degree, that led to wider acceptance of the idea that there were other scriptures and books of wisdom beyond the Bible that could claim great antiquity as well as importance in their own cultures in much that way the Bible has in the West.

In English, clearly generic use of *scripture* can be found at least as early as the eighteenth century. George Sale wrote in the introduction to his Qur'ān translation of 1734 that the Qur'ān shares things with "other books of scripture" (*pace* the *Oxford English Dictionary,* which can cite no use of *scripture* to refer to non-Christian religious texts before 1764). By the nineteenth century, the generic use of the term or of approximate equivalents like *sacred writings* was much more common. The ambitious series of translations of the great scriptures of the world that was inaugurated in 1879 by Max Müller under the title "The Sacred Books of the East" reflects a clear recognition by this time in the modern West of the worldwide existence of texts that function "scripturally" in ways analogous to those of the Hebrew or Christian Bible.

The extended use of the term *scripture* (or its linguistic equivalent in languages other than English) for any particularly sacred text is now common in modern Western usage and widely current internationally. Even the word *Bible* has been used, albeit less often, in a similarly general sense to refer to any sacred scripture (e.g., Franklin Edgerton's reference to the *Bhagavadgītā* as "India's favorite Bible" in *The Bhagavad Gītā, or Song of the Blessed One,* Chicago, 1925). However, *scripture* is the term that today is most commonly and properly used as the generic term for particularly sacred texts.

CHARACTERISTIC ROLES. Scriptural texts function in a variety of ways in a religious tradition. Some of their major functions can be categorized as follows.

Scripture as Holy Writ. The significance of the written word of scripture is difficult to exaggerate. If the etymology of *scripture* and its common association with the written or printed word have strengthened the tendency in Judeo-Christian culture (and even more in modern, print-dominated society) for Westerners, especially scholars, to treat sacred books primarily or even exclusively as written documents, there is good historical cause for this practice. With the important exception of the Hindu world, the writing down of the major religious text(s) of a community has been typically an epochal event in its history, one often linked to the crystallization of religious organization and systematic theological speculation, as well as to the achievement of a high level of culture. The written scriptural text symbolizes or embodies religious authority in many traditions (often replacing the living authority of a religious founder such as

Muḥammad or the Buddha). Such authority is well expressed in the aforementioned formula, "(As) it is written," which typically prefaces a biblical citation (whereas in the more orally-oriented Islamic and Buddhist worlds, respectively, "God says" introduces a Qur'ānic citation, and "Thus I have heard" is the traditional introduction to a *sūtra*).

Although the fixity and authority of the physical text have been felt particularly strongly in the last two thousand years in the West, the idea of an authoritative sacred writing is not limited to one global region. The "book religion" that Siegfried Morenz contrasted with "cult religion" has flourished notably in the Mediterranean (Morenz, 1950) and, later, the wider Western and Islamic worlds, yet veneration for the sacred word as book has also been important, if not always central, in most of the Buddhist world of Southeast and East Asia. It has been suggested, for example, that there was an early Mahāyāna cult of the book (*sūtra*) that vied with the *stupa* relic cult (G. Schopen, in *Indo-Iranian Journal* 1[1975]: 147–81), and high esteem for the written *sūtras* has been generally prominent in Mahāyāna tradition. Furthermore, it was in India, not the West, that the veneration of the written text reached one of its historical heights in the Sikh movement (the Sikh focus on the sacred book reflects, to be sure, considerable Muslim influence, much as the emphasis of the Mormons on the book reflects Judeo-Christian attitudes to Holy Writ). It is also in Asia that some of the more recent book religions have appeared, as for example, Babism in Iran and Tenrikyō in Japan.

One of the overt ways in which the importance of the written text is evident is in the religious valuation of the act of copying and embellishing a sacred text. Christian, Jewish, and Islamic traditions boast especially strong calligraphic traditions for their scriptures. In the Islamic case, for example, where a considerable iconophobia has held sway in the public sphere, magnificent calligraphic renderings of the Qur'anic word have been not only the favorite expression of the art of the book but also the chief adornment of mosques and most other monuments. Mani (d. 277), the founder of Manichaeism, placed great importance on painting pictures to illustrate his own canon of sacred books, and Manichaean missionary concerns led to the production of beautifully embellished calligraphic texts as well as a picture volume on the teaching. Here holy book and holy image come together (Hans-Joachim Klimkeit, *Manichaean Art and Calligraphy*, Leiden, 1982). Besides furthering fine calligraphy and manuscript illumination, Christians have extensively cultivated rich illustration of the Bible, notably in early medieval Byzantium and late medieval western Europe (Ernst von Dobschütz, *Die Bibel im Leben der Völker*, Witten, 1954, pp. 82f., 123f.). In Tibetan Buddhist monasticism, the zealously careful production of the Bka'-'gur (Kanjur) and Bstan-'gur (Tanjur), whether by hand copying or block printing, is yet another example of the great attention paid to the form of a sacred written text.

Scripture as spoken word. Whatever the central place of the written word, the oral roles of scripture in religious life are equally striking. Morenz (1950) touched upon the oral dimension of every sacred text when he traced the creative genius of "book religion" to the Israelite capacity for "hearing," in contrast to the "seeing" that dominates "cult religion," such as that of ancient Greece. Scripture's importance rests ultimately on the perceived importance of the sacred word that the memorized or written text seeks to fix forever (Heiler, 1979, pp. 339ff.). However much the written text dominates in any form of book religion, its presence in a community is still primarily realized orally and aurally. Historically, all but a small minority of those who have "had" a scripture have been illiterate, and even in highly literate communities the scriptural text is regularly "heard" in worship, teaching, and preaching even more than it is "seen" in silent reading. It is only relatively recently that any kind of reading has become a silent rather than an oral activity (Balogh, 1926–1927; Walter J. Ong, *Orality and Literacy*, London, 1982).

Recitation or reading aloud of scripture is a common feature of piety, whether in Islamic, Sikh, Jewish, or other traditions. Many scriptures have primary or secondary schemes of division according to the needs of recitation or reading aloud in the community (e.g., the 154 divisions of the Torah for synagogal reading over a three-year span). Great esteem is given to the person who knows all of the sacred scripture "by heart"—in the Muslim case, such a person is honored with the special epithet, *ḥāfiẓ*, "keeper, protector, memorizer [of the Word]." In the early synagogue and in the early Christian church, the reading aloud of scripture in worship was fundamental to religious life (Ismar Elbogen, *Der jüdische Gottesdienst*, Leipzig, 1913, chap. 3; Paul Glaue, *Die Vorlesung heiliger Schriften im Gottesdienst*, Berlin, 1907; but cf. Walter Bauer, *Das Wortgottesdienst der ältesten Christen*, Tübingen, 1930), just as it was in pagan cults of the Hellenistic Mediterranean, such as that of Isis (Leipoldt and Morenz, 1953, p. 96). The Jews call both the reading of scripture and the passage read *miqra'* (*Neh.* 8:8), "what is recited, read aloud, a reading." In Talmudic usage, the term came to refer to the Torah (Pentateuch), the Prophets, and the Writings that make up the Tankakh, or Hebrew scriptures. An ancient Greek synogogal inscription in Jerusalem reads, "The synagogue is for the reading aloud (*eis anagnosin*) of the Law" (*Theologischer Begriffslexikon zum Neuen Testament*, ed. L. Coenen et al., Wuppertal, 1967–1971, vol. 1, p. 153). The Greek *anagnosis* or *anagnosma* (Lat., *lectio*) was also used in the same sense in the early Christian context for public scripture reading on the Jewish model. The Arabic word *qur'ān*, which is not attested in pre-Qur'anic sources, probably derives from *qeryānā*, the Syriac equivalent of *miqra'*, and is likewise a verbal noun meaning "reciting, recitation" (Graham, 1984).

In other traditions, notably the Islamic and Buddhist, the recitation of the sacred word is even more central to religious practice, despite the frequently massive importance of veneration of the written text in the same traditions. In

Hindu practice, the oral, recited word completely eclipses the importance of any written form of it and presents the most vivid instance of the all but exclusively oral function of scripture. It appears that until the coming of Islam stimulated the writing down of the Avesta as a book, the most sacred Zoroastrian texts, those in Old Persian, were similarly transmitted and used only orally, in recitation, while the less sacred commentaries *(Zand)* and other religious books in Pahlavi had long been written (Geo Widengren, *Die Religionen Irans,* Stuttgart, 1968, pp. 245–259).

Oral use and even oral transmission of scripture should not be confused with folk oral tradition in which verbatim accuracy is not aspired to (i. e., in which "formulaic composition" predominates: see, for example, Albert B. Lord, *The Singer of Tales,* Cambridge, Mass., 1960). The technical mnemonic methods of oral transmission have sometimes been so highly developed for sacred texts as to render the oral text more reliable than the manuscript tradition—notably in the Islamic and Hindu cases. In any event, few if any scriptural books have the verbatim uniformity popularly associated with the written and especially the printed word. Even the "fixation" of a sacred canon in writing has rarely meant that one definitive documentary text is universally recognized or that variant texts disappear.

Scripture in public ritual. Whether the written or the oral text of a scriptural book predominates, the most visible religious role of a scripture is in public worship. In some instances a scripture is explicitly a ritual text that orders and explains the rite itself, as in the case of the Brāhmaṇas in Vedic tradition. In other cases it is a sacred text either recited in ritual acts (e.g., the Qur'ān, the Zoroastrian *Gāthās,* the Vedic *mantras*, and the Shintō *norito,* or ritual prayers taken from the Engi-shiki) or read aloud from a written copy in communal worship, as in Jewish or Christian practice. Such recitation or reading is often a major, if not the central, element in worship. In some traditions, particularly initiatory sects, the sacred character of a text has led to its being kept secret from the masses and read or recited only by and for initiates. Leipoldt and Morenz (1953, pp. 88ff.) have treated this scriptural "secrecy" in the Mediterranean world in some detail.

Sometimes, perhaps most prominently in the case of the *Ādi Granth* of the Sikhs, a sacred exemplar of the holy scripture even plays a functionally iconic role in the liturgical setting. Ritual veneration of the physical sacred text is also seen in the Tibetan monastic practice of circumambulating the *sūtra* collection of the monastery, the solemn procession of a copy of the Qur'ān in some Muslim funerary rites (Edward W. Lane, *An Account of the Manners and Customs of the Modern Egyptians,* 5th ed., London, 1860, p. 514), and Jewish ritual handling of Torah rolls in the synagogue.

Scripture also characteristically provides the fundamental elements of ritual language, the basic vocabulary as well as texts for hymnody (as in the Christian Psalter), sermon (e.g., the marketplace preaching, or "speaking about *sūtras*" *[shuo-ching],* of Buddhist monks in Sung China; see Overmyer, *Folk Buddhist Religion,* Cambridge, Mass., 1976, p. 179), and especially prayer (as in the Lord's Prayer, the Psalms, the Shema', the Fātiḥah, or the Triratna). Its words frequently form the texts used for recitation in the major rites of passage and other important festival and ritual occasions of a tradition: for example, surah 36 (*Yā Sīn*) is recited especially on 15 Sha'bān (the Muslim "Night of Quittance") and at Muslim funerals, as is the *Lotus Sutra* in mortuary and ancestral ritual in Nichiren Buddhist practice in Japan, or the Gāyātri *mantra* (*Ṛgveda* 3.62.10) at the Upanayana ritual of Hindu initiation.

Ritually important passages of a scriptural text are sometimes pulled together into special anthologies or collections that serve the liturgical needs of the community, as in the Christian breviary, psalter, lectionary, or evangeliarium; the Pāṭimokkha selection from the Vinaya that is recited as a regular part of Buddhist monastic life; or the *Blue Sutra,* an abridgement of the *Lotus Sutra* that is used in the ritual of the modern Reiyūkai Buddhist sect in Japan (Helen Hardacre, *Lay Buddhism in Contemporary Japan,* Princeton, 1984). Whether it is read or recited aloud, given physical prominence as a ritual object, or cited or paraphrased in prayers, homilies, hymns, or litanies, a scriptural text plays one of the most visible and important parts in worship in many traditions.

Scripture in devotional and spiritual life. Closely tied to public ritual, and equally or more important to religious life, is the role of scripture in personal devotion and in mystical, ascetic, and other traditions of spiritual discipline and realization. Aspects of the devotional role of scripture have been treated in the preceding sections, but some further points bear mention.

Recitation and reading aloud are not only central to formal worship (see above), but also to private devotion and the practice of diverse spiritual disciplines. *Meditatio* in the Christian tradition was from the start basically an oral activity of learning the text "by heart" through reciting with concentrated attention and reflection. In turn, as Jean Leclercq has eloquently articulated in *The Love of Learning and the Desire for God* ([1957] 1974), meditation formed the basis of the monastic *lectio divina,* the active, oral reading of and reflecting on scripture upon which the monk's discipline was based in Pachomian, Benedictine, and other rules. Buddhist monastic discipline similarly focuses upon constant meditation upon scripture through reading and recitation, whether in monasteries of Sri Lankan Therāvada, Tibetan Vajrayāna, or Chinese Mahāyāna. Study of the Vedas which centers on recitation and memorization—is said in the *Laws of Manu* (2.166f.) to be the highest austerity, or ascetic discipline. In Islam, Qur'anic recitation (*qirā'ah*) is a public and private form of devotional practice that also demands mindfulness of and meditation on the meaning of the sacred text as well as recitative technique (cf. K. Nelson, *The Art of Reciting the Qur'ān* [Austin, Tex., 1985]).

Closely related to meditative practices involving scriptural texts are the recitation of and meditation upon formulas derived from scripture. The chanting of Hindu and Buddhist *mantras* and of Buddhist *dhāraṇīs*, as well as the recitation of Ṣūfī *dhikr* litanies (many of which are Qur'anic) are major examples of formulaic use of scripture in devotional life.

Other uses of scripture in devotional and spiritual life abound. The setting of scriptural texts to music has been important in diverse traditions of piety. Chant and hymnody are prominent foci for scriptural use in both public and private worship in Jewish, Christian, Muslim, Buddhist, Hindu, Sikh, and other traditions. Similarly, reverence for the physical text of scripture and ritual copying or illumination of it have also been important parts of piety in many scriptual traditions. Nor is it by chance that most reform efforts in religious communities with a scripture mandate a "back to the book" piety that seeks (usually literal) authority in the pages of scripture. Where human beings may prove changeable, the sacred word stands secure for every generation as the unchanging guide to individual as well as group morality and action.

Magical and superstitious use of scripture. All of the previously discussed uses of scripture can tend at times toward bibliolatry—the treatment in an extreme fashion of scripture as an object of worship or a locus of supernatural power. Such treatment of scriptural texts results from the power associated with the written and spoken word. Bibliolatry can take many forms, from doctrinal emphasis on the infallibility of the literal text to overt bibliomancy, the superstitious or magical use of scripture. The answer to a problem or guidance for any occasion is often sought through scripture divination. Thus turning to sometimes random, sometimes specific pages of scripture in times of adversity, uncertainty, bereavement, or the like is a time-honored but little-documented use of scripture in Christian, Jewish, Islamic, Buddhist, and many other traditions. Similar examples of bibliomancy as a protective or empowering device are placing a Bible in the bed of a sick child as a curative, using a tiny Qur'ān or Bible as a protective charm or talisman, seeking omens in scriptural verses, or dissolving slips of paper with words of scripture on them in a drink to make a medicine (Rühle, 1941; Bertholet, 1949).

Quasi-magical notions of scripture can even be seen in "orthoprax" religious life. The proper chanting or reading aloud of scripture is commonly seen as efficacious in a variety of situations. In Theravāda Buddhist practice, collections of scriptural texts known as *parittas* are recited by the monks to ward off the actions of demons and to bring prosperity, health, and other blessings (Lynn de Silva, *Buddhism: Beliefs and Practices in Sri Lanka,* Colombo, 1974, pp. 81–90). In Vedic sacrifice, the efficacy of the rite depends upon the absolutely accurate recitation of the sacred text. Talmudic literature contains many statements about the proper biblical passage to be used for protective or other magical purposes (M. Grunwald and Kaufmann Kohler, "Bibliomancy," *The Jewish Encyclopedia,* 1901–1906). In Nichiren Buddhism, the sacred formula of adoration of the *Lotus Sūtra,* the Daimoku, is said to encapsule the whole of truth in a single invocation. Protestant doctrines of the literal inspiration of every word of the Bible have been used to justify very diverse ideas and practices. Numerology and alphabet mysticism connected with a scriptural text are as prominent in such traditions as those of the qabbalists and the Ṣūfīs and well known in virtually every religious tradition (cf. Bertholet, *op. cit.,* 1949, pp. 14–17, and Schimmel, *The Mystery of Numbers,* 1993).

CHARACTERISTIC ATTRIBUTES OF SCRIPTURE. The scriptures of any given religious tradition possess a number of characteristic attributes. Some of the most important are as follows.

Power. The major functional attributes of scripture are bound up with the power felt to be inherent in scriptural word. Both the written and the spoken word carry a seemingly innate power in human perception. At the most basic level, a word is an action: words do not signify so much as they perform. Hence to speak a name ritually is in some measure to control or to summon the one named. For the faithful, a sacred word is not merely a word, but an operative, salvific word. Its unique, transformative power often rests upon its being spoken (or written) by a god (as in Jewish, Christian, or Muslim tradition). In other cases, the sound itself is primordial and holy (as in India), or the message or teaching embodied in the scriptural word is considered to be salvific truth, with little or no reference to a divine origin (as in many Buddhist traditions).

The power inherent in the spoken word is vividly seen in the idea of a divine, creative word. Many traditions have cosmogonies in which a god creates the world or men or animals through speech: as, for example, the Memphite cosmogony of ancient Egypt (in which the god Ptah creates by thought and speech), *Genesis* 1:3 ("God said, 'Let there be light . . .'"), Qur'ān 40:68 ("[God] said, 'Be,' and it was"), or tribal mythologies, such as those of the African Dogon and South American Witóto peoples, in which the gods create with a spoken word (Marcel Griaule, *Conversations with Ogotemmêli,* London, 1965, pp. 16–40; Konrad T. Preuss, *Religion und Mythologie der Uitoto,* Göttingen, 1921–1923, pp. 633–634).

The power of the spoken word of scripture also appears in a variety of other religious contexts, most prominently in worship (see above; the most extreme case may be that of Veda recitation in Brahmanic ritual). Also noteworthy are the aforementioned practices of *mantra* recitation in Hindu and Tantric traditions, where the sound of the Vedic formula or hymn enables the worshiper or meditator to appropriate the power of a particular divinity *(devatā)*; the *dhikr,* or "remembrance," practiced in Ṣūfī tradition in Islam, in which Qur'anic or other phrases or texts are chanted or sung as a means of focusing consciousness and being upon God; and Buddhist chanting and singing of *sūtras* (and *mantras*) as a meditative practice or act of worship.

The power of the written word has already been touched upon. The Jewish designation of holy books as "that which renders the hands unclean" expresses well the widespread sense of the power latent in every copy of scripture. In most scriptural traditions, such perceived power manifests itself within both "orthoprax" and "popular" spirituality in tendencies towards bibliolatry—the treatment of scripture as an object of worship or as a locus of supernatural power. Magical notions of the power that lies in a copy of a sacred scripture are an extreme extension of religious sensibility to the presence of divine wisdom or ultimate truth in a scriptural text. Even the laying of the hand upon a copy of the Bible in swearing a legal oath of truthfulness echoes such notions.

Authority and sacrality. The power of scripture is clearly expressed in its most common attributes as well as its most common uses. Of all those attributes, the most essential ones are the extraordinary authority and sacrality of scripture vis-à-vis other texts. In both theocratic and nontheocratic religious traditions, scriptural books possess a supramundane authority and degree of holiness for the faithful that no other texts can command.

The authoritative character of scripture is most vivid in those cases in which a sacred text provides the legal basis of communal order. This is especially evident in the Jewish tradition, where the written Torah is the pediment upon which the entire edifice of Jewish life is built, and in the Islamic tradition, where the minimal legal prescriptions and much larger body of moral injunctions found in the Qurʾān are viewed as the ultimate bases of the *sharīʿah.* It is also evident in the role of the Vinaya ("discipline") section of the Tripiṭaka, the "law" of Buddhist monasticism.

The extraordinary sacrality of scripture is seen in almost every facet of its use in communal life. The way in which a scriptural text is handled, the formulas of respect that accompany its mention, citation, recitation, or reading, and the theological doctrines that are developed to set it apart ontologically from all other texts are common evidence of such sacrality. Among many examples that reflect this kind of holiness of scripture are the enshrinement of the ornate Torah scrolls in their special cabinet, the ark, in the synagogue; the tokens of homage paid to the *Ādi Granth* in Sikh worship; the "Little Entrance" procession in Eastern Orthodox churches (or, in Anglican divine service, standing) to honor the reading of the Gospel; the ritual purification required for recitation of the Qurʾān; the merit held to accompany recitation of Buddhist *sūtras*; the virtue attached to copying or memorizing sacred texts such as the Bible or the Qurʾān; the aforementioned folk traditions of the healing power of scripture; and the stress placed upon the eternal, transcendent nature of the Veda, the Torah, the Qurʾān, the Buddhist *sūtras*, and so on.

There is often more than one level or degree of sacred texts in a community. As already noted, it is possible in most traditions to distinguish among various sacred books one text or corpus of texts that is the scripture *par excellence* (e.g., the Qurʾān, Hebrew Bible, Avesta, or Veda). Other texts or groups of texts (e.g., the ḥadīth, Mishnah, Pahlavi books, or Purāṇas) may, however, achieve a quasi-scriptural status as sacred books of nearly or effectively equal importance in the life of the tradition. While, strictly speaking, such texts may be denied fullest scriptural status, they often function in a community in remarkably similar ways to the major scripture of other traditions. Conversely, the supreme scripture in a tradition may play a functionally less important role or less visible role in piety than a theoretically second-order sacred text. India offers the best example of this in the major Vedic Saṃhitās, or collections, which are recognized as the supreme holy texts in all Hindu traditions yet functionally are virtually a *scriptura abscondita* for many Hindus, who make greater active use of non-Vedic or later Vedic texts. In Hindu tradition, an explicit distinction is made between *śruti* ("what is heard," the product of the *ṛṣis*' revelatory experience) and *smṛti* ("what is remembered"), the former applied to the whole of the diverse corpus of Vedic texts, the latter to later sacred texts. Yet in many Hindu sectarian groups, especially those of a devotional (*bhakti*) bent, the most sacred scriptural texts in actual use are *smṛti* texts such as the Bhāgavata Purāṇa. Such popularity of a *smṛti* text takes nothing away from the sacrality of the Veda; rather, it indicates the tendency to elevate ever more texts to the functional status of sacred scripture in everyday piety.

Unicity. A further quality of scripture is its perceived unicity of source, content, and authority in the community involved with it (see especially Leipolt and Morenz, 1953). No matter what the historical origins or textual development of its constituent parts, and no matter how diverse those parts, a scriptural corpus is commonly conceived of as a unified whole, both in its ontological origin as sacred word and its internal consistency and authoritativeness as sacred truth. The many originally separate texts that were collected into the Egyptian *Book of Going Forth by Day,* the diverse "holy scriptures" of the Hebrew or Christian Bible, the myriad *sūtras* of the Chinese Buddhist canon, or the various kinds of Vedic texts revered as *śruti*—these and other bodies of sacred texts are each conceived as an ontological and conceptual unity, whether that unity is one of God's holy word (as in ancient Egypt or Islam), the Buddha-word, or the "sound" (Skt., *śabda;* Chin., *sheng*) of ultimate truth or wisdom heard by the ancient Indian and ancient Chinese sages. If scriptural texts such as the Qurʾān or the *Book of Mormon* can boast a single-source origin with considerable historical justification, the greatest number of scriptures in the world represent collections of material put together not by one person or even one generation but by a gradual process of recognition of sacred texts usually referred to as "canon formation." Nevertheless, once the community has reached general agreement about which texts it accepts as sacred, it is common for it to affirm unity of origin as well as message in its scriptural corpus.

Inspiration and eternality/antiquity. The tendency to see one's own formal or informal canon of scriptures as a unified whole is closely linked to the characteristic development of a theory of inspiration, revelation, or some other kind of suprahuman and primordial origin for its words. All of the prophets and teachers whose words become part of scripture are held to have been inspired in their speech (as with the Hebrew prophets), to have been given God's direct revelation to their fellows (as with Muḥammad and Mani), or to have had an experience in which they transcended the contingent world to grasp ultimate reality (as in the Buddha's enlightenment). Whether the sacred word is vouchsafed to them in a vision or an auditory experience, or given to them as heavenly tablets or books, the earthly bringers of the holy word have been chosen to be, or have become through their own special power, a bridge between the transcendent and the mundane.

The divine word is also commonly held to be eternal, as in the role of Vāc ("speech") as primordial being or goddess in Vedic thought, in the Hindu concept of the eternal Veda (cf. *Laws of Manu* 12.94, 12.99), in the Muslim doctrine of the uncreated, eternal Word of the Qur'ān (which, as God's very Word, is an eternal divine attribute), in the Sikh concept of the *bani* ("word") that preexists and extends beyond the gurus and the *Ādi Granth* (W. Owen Cole and Piara S. Sambhi, *The Sikhs,* London, 1978, p. 44), and in Buddhist ideas of the eternal Dharma or the *buddhavacana* ("Buddha word") in Mahāyāna thought.

A scripture is virtually always conceived to be, if not eternal, at least of great antiquity. The Japanese *Kojiki* and *Nihongi,* the Avesta, the Veda, and the Five Classics of China are all prime examples of sacred texts to which hoary antiquity is ascribed. The authority of a scripture is guaranteed both by its divine or otherwise supramundane origin and by its venerable character as an age-old, if not eternal, word that has been preserved by unbroken and faithful transmission through every generation. These characteristics hold whether the sacred text embodies revelation from a god, preserves the teaching of a master or the wisdom of ancient sages, reports the sacred myths or history of a community, or records the inspired utterances of seers and prophets.

RELATED DEVELOPMENTS. When a scripture emerges in (or helps to create) a religious community, its presence engenders a variety of new phenomena and its influence extends beyond the specifically cultic or confessional sphere into the wider culture as well. A development tied to the emergence of scripture in some traditions is the delineation of an authoritative "canon" of scripture to set it apart from other texts. Traditionally thought of as basic to scripture, the idea of a canon of sacred texts is historically a secondary development in which a community reaches some kind of consensus about the texts that have made it what it is and that loom most important in the tradition and life of that community.

Another development is the growth of traditions of scriptural interpretation by means of which scripture is appropriated as a continuing authority in new circumstances. New circumstances often raise the question of translating the sacred word of scripture, which can pose a dilemma for theories of scripture in the community. Finally, the importance of scripture in religious life has important consequences for culture more broadly. Some of the most evident of these are in the spheres of language, literature, and the arts.

Canon formation. The perceived unicity of scripture leads often to a felt need for an authoritative "canon" (from the Greek *kanōn,* "rule, measure"), or "list," of texts that properly belong to sacred scripture—properly, that is, in the view of those who want to prescribe authoritative as opposed to less authoritative or nonauthoritative texts. Nowhere in the history of religion has the process of canon formation been a clear or unequivocal one, dependent as it usually has been upon the pressure of defining one "orthodoxy" against one or more competing interpretations of faith. In most cases, it is finally not the fiat of a council or individual religious authority seeking to forge a canon in order to delimit orthodoxy, but rather the usage of the majority that determines any canon of sacred and authoritative scripture. This has been especially true of the three traditions in which "canonical" lists of scriptural books have received the most attention: the Christian, Jewish, and Buddhist traditions.

In other cases, such as the Manichaean, Islamic, and Sikh traditions, the early recognition of a single scriptural corpus has meant that the problem of diverse texts eligible for admission or exclusion from a "canon" has hardly arisen. In the Hindu case, the general reverence for the four major Vedic collections, which together with subsequent related texts like the Upaniṣads are given the status of *śruti,* has been complemented by the popular veneration and use of a variety of other texts that strictly rank only as *smṛti* (e.g., the Puraṇas; see Coburn 1984) but whose sacrality and centrality in Hindu religious life is indisputable. In general, the vast array and diversity of functionally sacred texts, as well as the tendency to be inclusive rather than exclusive in defining even *Veda* or *śruti,* have worked against the elaboration of any clear idea of a canon in the Hindu case.

The influence of ideas of a designated canon of scripture such as one finds in Christianity in later antiquity or in classical Therāvada Buddhist thought has been undeniably great. An excellent example is the Chinese Buddhist (as also Daoist) recognition of a *zang,* or "basket," of scriptural texts on the original model of the "Three Baskets" (Tipiṭaka) of Pali scripture. What modern scholarship often rather glibly calls a "canon" in traditions as diverse as the Jain or the classical Chinese (Confucian) would not be recognized uniformly in these traditions—or at least not until relatively recent times, and then often under the influence of Western scholarly conventions—as a body of scripture (or "classics") analogous to a biblical canon.

Interpretation. Every text that achieves scriptural status in a religious community elicits extensive popular and scholarly exegesis and study of its contents. The varied kinds of scriptural interpretation are fundamental elements in a community's relationship to its sacred book, for they provide a bridge between the text and its application to life and between the era in which the text originally arose and all subsequent ages in which it must serve changing needs in new situations. Every application of a scriptural text, from superstitious, talismanic use to use in theological argument, is in some degree an act of interpretation and must be considered a part of scriptural *Rezeptionsgeschichte,* the history of the text as scripture. Even some scriptural books themselves are actually interpretation and elaboration of previous scripture: thus the Abhidhamma segment of the Pali Tipiṭaka is a philosophical expansion on the basic teaching of the Buddha in the Sutta Pitaka, much as the speculation of the Upaniṣads is built upon the earlier Vedic texts.

All scriptural communities boast impressive formal traditions of scholarly interpretation, many of which form the basis of all learning in their respective traditions. The imposing knowledge of a good Talmudic scholar, a learned Therāvada *bhikkhu,* or a first-rate Muslim *ʿalim* is focused upon knowledge of the interpretive tradition tied to the Torah, Tripiṭaka, or Qurʾān, respectively, and its vast oral traditions and written literature. Most esoteric and mystical traditions also rely heavily upon various forms of scriptural exegesis to buttress their ideas. Less formally, the preaching or teaching of a religious message normally relies heavily upon more or less sophisticated and overt forms of exegesis of a scriptural text, just as visual or musical artistic rendering of scriptural themes provide commentary on and interpretation of the meaning of scripture.

Translation and resistance to translation. A common phenomenon related to the role of scripture in changing circumstances is the development of the idea that a scripture cannot be translated from its original, sacred languge: only the original form is felt to carry the inspired and exact meaning or sound. This idea is very old: Ancient Egyptian sacred texts were not translated, even when Nubians ruled Egypt in the eighth and seventh centuries BCE (Leipoldt and Morenz, 1953, pp. 66f.). Resistance to translation of the "Arabic Qurʾān" (surah 12:2, 41:3, et al.) has been especially strong in Islamic tradition. Even when translated by Muslims, the Arabic text is customarily still written or printed beside (or interlinearly with) the translated text of the Persian, Turkish, Swahili, Malay, or other language, since the Arabic text alone is the speech of God *ipsissima verba.* (It should, however, be noted that vernacular translations of the Qurʾān in many of the diverse lands where Muslims abound have long been circulated and used for the necessary business of comprehending the text; this has not diminished appreciably the reverence for the Arabic Qurʾān, but it has facilitated the tranmission of the meanings of the text.) Translation of Vedic texts is unheard of in Hindu tradition, and Jews similarly have placed overwhelming importance upon retaining the original Hebrew text of the Bible in worship (with the major exception of the several centuries in later antiquity when the Septuagint translation was the text used by hellenized Jews).

It is, nevertheless, also the case that translations can come to be viewed as themselves inspired, and their texts as sacred. Salient examples can be found in later antiquity, where the Septuagint was considered an inspired text by hellenized Jews and later by Origen and the other Christian fathers. The Latin translation of Jerome (d. 419) that later developed into the "Vulgate" has been treated as an inspired text by the Roman Catholic church (and was used exclusively for mass until Vatican II), and the major Protestant vernacular translations have been widely held to carry the inspiration of the Holy Spirit. (Resistance to the vernacular mass and resistance to acceptance of the Revised Standard Version of the Bible are recent evidence of just how effectively sacred a translation can be.) Another important example is the Buddhist case, in which the Chinese translations of Sanskrit *sūtras* became the holy texts still used in Chinese and Japanese Buddhist traditions as the scriptural canon.

Some traditions, however, have little or no objection to the translation of scripture into vernaculars accessible to diverse peoples. As one might expect, such an attitude is most often found in explicitly "missionary" and "universalistic" traditions such as the Christian, Buddhist, and Manichaean, and that of the Mormons. The Mormon case is doubly interesting in this regard, as Joseph Smith himself claimed to have translated the *Book of Mormon* from its original "reformed Egyptian" (*Mormon* 32) idiom into English. Here even the earthly "original" of the scriptural "prophet" is a translation of the original golden tablets of the angel.

CULTURAL CONSEQUENCES. The influence and importance of a scriptural text extends far beyond the specifically religious sphere in a culture. One of the most obvious ways that scripture leaves its imprint upon culture and society is through its effect upon language. A scriptural text, whether in its original language or a translation, may provide a major standard for the "classical" grammar and style of an entire language, as in the case of the Qurʾān for Arabic, the "Classics" for Chinese, the Authorized ("King James") Version of the Bible for English, or the *Lutherbibel* for German. In any culture with an important scripture, the linguistic influence of scriptural vocabulary, metaphors, similes, linguistic conventions, and so forth, can be pervasive. Examples from English phrases and images from the Bible alone make this vivid: "hardening of the heart," "a land of milk and honey," "wise as Solomon," "a good Samaritan," "the patience of Job," "the meek shall inherit the earth", or "killing the fatted calf."

Scripture also serves as one of the richest sources for later literature in a cultural tradition. Nowhere is this more evident than in Western Christendom, where one need only think of Dante, Shakespeare, Milton, or Goethe to recognize the generative influence of the Bible upon this tradition's greatest authors. Scripture is, in the first instance, immensely influential as the ultimate proof text in most traditional cultures. This is especialy vivid in Muslim writing and speaking, where the Qurʾān is the final word to be quoted as the seal to any argument, large or small. Western Protestant traditions are also traditionally rife with this kind of use of the Bible. Scripture usually provides the great symbols and lasting images in a culture, whether it is the figure of Abraham in Jewish, Christian, and Muslim cultures (in each case with different emphasis and textual basis), Agni (Fire) in Hindu culture, or the Buddha's great "going forth" to seek enlightenment in Buddhist cultures.

Scripture also has considerable influence upon the arts in most cultures. The most obvious areas of influence are two: the elaborate calligraphy, referred to above, that is commonly developed for the scriptural text itself and manuscript illumination and illustrations that depict scriptural stories and ideas. The massive importance of the calligraphic art in Islam, the scriptural tradition *par excellence,* deserves particular stress. In Islamic culture, calligraphy and abstract (e.g., "arabesque") design associated with calligraphy extend far beyond the scriptural text to provide even the central forms of decoration in Islamic architecture. Prime among the calligraphic subjects used on Islamic buildings is the Qurʾānic word.

In Western culture, traditions of Bible illustration expanded well beyond the biblical text itself to become major strands in all of the visual arts. The stained-glass masterpieces of western and eastern Europe and the Byzantine mosaics of Ravenna and Balkan Europe are major religious examples. The masters of Western art all employed scriptural themes and events in their works, whether explicitly in icons or the Sistine Chapel ceiling, or more subtly in the works of a Chagall or Rouault. In India, iconographic presentation of scriptural figures and stories has always been a vastly important part of the Hindu scene. In the Buddhist world, the most striking example of scriptural representation in the arts is probably the vast stupa of Borobudur, around whose facade stretch hundreds of stone reliefs telling in pictures myriad scriptural stories of the Buddha. The *maṇḍala* in Tibetan and East Asian Buddhism often presents a pictorial condensation of a major event or teaching from the *sūtras*.

The scriptural books of a culture also often provide the themes and even the literal text for musical compositions of all kinds. This is very familiar in the great works of European music, but it is also evident in the music of Hindu, Islamic, and other cultures as well—especially since the line between "secular" and "sacred" music is if anything less clear in most other cultures than it is in the West. "Religious" chant and hymnody (largely drawn from or based on scripture) remain in many of these traditions the most popular forms of musical performance. The Hindu and Islamic worlds provide numerous examples of this.

The cultural consequences and influences of scripture go far beyond these few examples. Even these suggest, however, the immense importance of scripture in human affairs. In and of themselves, scriptures can be forces for good or evil—as Shakespeare noted, "The devil can cite Scripture for his purpose." What is ultimately significant about scripture as a concept and a reality is its role in expressing, focusing, and symbolizing the faith of religious persons and their communities around the globe, both for the faithful themselves and for the outsider who seeks a glimpse into another world of faith and discourse.

SEE ALSO Biblical Exegesis; Biblical Literature; Brāhmaṇas and Āraṇyakas; Buddhist Books and Texts, article on Exegesis and Hermeneutics; Calligraphy; Canon; Epics; Literature, article on Literature and Religion; Qurʾān; Śāstra Literature; Sūtra Literature; Upaniṣads; Vedas.

BIBLIOGRAPHY

Of the surprisingly few comparative or general treatments of scripture, the best, even though limited to the ancient Mediterranean world, are two: most recently, Wilfred Cantwell Smith, *What Is Scripture? A Comparative Approach* (Minneapolis, 1993), and, much earlier, Johannes Leipoldt and Siegfried Morenz, *Heilige Schriften: Betrachtungen zur Religionsgeschichte der antiken Mittelmeerwelt* (Leipzig, 1953). There are substantial phenomenological treatments of holy word, holy writ, and/or scripture in Friedrich Heiler, *Erscheinungsformen und Wesen der Religion* (1961; 2d rev. ed., Stuttgart, 1979), pp. 266–364; in Geo Widengren, *Religionsphänomenologie* (Berlin, 1969), pp. 546–593; and in Gerardus van der Leeuw, *Phänomenologie der Religion* (1933; 2d rev. ed., Tübingen, 1956), translated as *Religion in Essence and Manifestation* (1938; rev. ed., New York, 1963), chaps. 58–64. Another phenomenological study is Gustav Mensching, *Das heilige Wort* (Bonn, 1937). Also of note are the brief articles under the heading "Schriften, heilige" in the second and third editions of *Die Religion in Geschichte und Gegenwart* (Tübingen, 1931, 1961) by Alfred Bertholet and Siegfried Morenz, respectively, and the descriptive survey of major scriptural texts by Günter Lanczkowski: *Heilige Schriften: Inhalt, Textgestalt und Überlieferung* (Stuttgart, 1956). See also Alfred Bertholet, *Die Macht der Schrift in Glauben und Aberglauben* (Berlin, 1949); Siegfried Morenz, "Entstehung und Wesen der Buchreligion," *Theologische Literaturzeitung* 75 (1950): 709–715; Josef Balogh, "'Voces paginarum': Beiträge zur Geschichte des lauten Lesens und Schreibens," *Philogus* 82 (1926–1927): 83–109, 202–240; and William A. Graham's *Beyond the Written Word: Oral Aspects of Scripture in the History of Religion* (Cambridge, U.K., 1987, 1993).

The articles contributed to *Holy Book and Holy Tradition,* edited by Frederick F. Bruce and E. G. Rupp (Grand Rapids, Mich., 1968), vary in quality but provide useful information on particular traditions. Several solid articles can be found in *The Holy Book in Comparative Perspective,* edited by Frederick Mathewson Denny and Rodney L. Taylor (Columbia, S. C., 1985), which contains survey-discussions of some major world scriptural traditions; and a series of more analytic studies are collected in *Rethinking Scripture,* edited by Miriam Levering (Albany, N. Y., 1989), that offer critical reevaluations of scripture as a generic and specific category. A newer, comparative collection of essays is: Hendrik M. Vroom and Jerald D. Gort, eds., *Holy Scriptures in Judaism, Christianity and Islam* (Amsterdam and Atlanta, 1997).

In addition to works cited in the foregoing article under the specific topics treated, several others deserve special mention, especially those that address the problem of the semantic background of the terms *scripture, book,* and so forth found in the West: "Schrift," in *Theologisches Begriffslexikon zum Neuen Testament,* 2 vols. in 3, edited by Lothar Coenen et al. (Wuppertal, 1967–1971); "Bible [Canon]," by Bezalel Narkiss, in *Encyclopaedia Judaica,* vol. 4 (Jerusalem, 1971); and "Écriture sainte [1. Le nom]," by Hildebrand Höpfl, in the *Dictionnaire de la Bible, Supplément,* vol. 2 (Paris, 1926).

Few studies have been devoted to the functional roles of scripture within the various traditions. For the Christian Bible, special note may be made of Ernst von Dobschütz's *Die Bibel im Leben der Völker* (Witten, West Germany, 1934) and his "Bible in the Church," in the *Encyclopaedia of Religion and Ethics,* edited by James Hastings, vol. 2 (Edinburgh, 1909); "Écriture sainte et vie spirituelle," by Jean Kirchmeyer et al., in the *Dictionnaire de spiritualité,* vol. 4 (Paris, 1960); Beryl Smalley's *The Study of the Bible in the Middle Ages,* 2d ed. (Oxford, 1952); Hans Rost's *Die Bibel im Mittelalter* (Augsburg, 1939); *The Cambridge History of the Bible,* 3 vols., edited by Peter R. Ackroyd, C. F. Evans, G. W. H. Lampe, and S. L. Greenslade (Cambridge, 1963–1970). See also the important statement on the problem by Wilfred Cantwell Smith: "The Study of Religion and the Study of the Bible," *Journal of the American Academy of Religion* 39 (June 1971): 131–140. Also useful are Adolf von Harnack's "Über das Alter der Bezeichnung 'die Bücher' ('die Bibel') für die H. Schriften in der Kirche," *Zentralblatt für Bibliothekswesen* 45 (1928): 337–342; Oska Rühle's "Bibel," in *Handwörterbuch des deutschen Aberglaubens* (Berlin, 1927); and Graham, *op. cit.,* pp. 117–154 (concerning Christian oral treatment of the Bible).

On the role of the Qur'ān in Muslim life, see Navid Kermani, *Gott ist schön: Das ästhetische Erleben des Koran* (Munich, 1999); W. A. Graham, "Qur'ān as Spoken Word," in *Approaches to Islam in Religious Studies,* edited by Richard C. Martin (Tuscon, 1985); *idem,* "The Earliest Meaning of 'Qur'ān,'" *Welt des Islams* 23/24 (1984): 361–377; *idem, Beyond the Written Word,* pp. 79–116; Paul Nwyia's *Exégèse coranique et langage mystique* (Beirut, 1970); and Kristina Nelson's *The Art of Reciting the Qur'ān* (Austin, Tex., 1985). On the use of scripture in Indian life, see Frits Staal, *Nambudiri Veda Recitation* (The Hague, 1961); Thomas B. Coburn, "'Scripture' in India: Towards a Typology of the Word in Hindu Life," *Journal of the American Academy of Religion* 52 (1984): 435–459; Graham, *op. cit.,* pp. 67–78.

WILLIAM A. GRAHAM (1987 AND 2005)

SCYTHIAN RELIGION. The Scythians were predominantly nomadic, Iranian-speaking tribes inhabiting the steppes of the northern Black Sea region from the seventh to the third century BCE. Owing to their lack of a written language, what is known of Scythian religion has been reconstructed on the basis of archaeological sources and information from Greek and Roman authors. This reconstruction is partly corroborated by data on the religion of Indo-Iranian peoples kindred to the Scythians.

The basic Scythian pantheon included seven gods. Their functions, which are not always clear, have been determined chiefly on the basis of their identification with Greek gods by Herodotus (4.59) and sometimes on the basis of the etymology of their Scythian names. It is clear, however, that the pantheon was divided into three ranks. In the first rank was Tabiti (the Greek Hestia), in the second were Papaeus (Zeus) and Api (Gaia), and in the third were Oetosyrus or Goetosyrus (Apollo); Artimpasa, or Argimpasa (Aphrodite Ourania); and two gods whose Scythian names are not known but who have been identified with Herakles and Ares. It is possible that the first of these unnamed gods is identical with the primeval figure of Scythian mythology, Targitaus (Herodotus, 4.5–10), who was also identified in the classical tradition with Herakles.

The structure of the Scythian pantheon is not so much a system reflecting the cultic hierarchy of the gods as it is a system mirroring the structure of the universe. The very number of gods reckoned in the Scythian pantheon corresponds to ancient Indo-Iranian tradition. The predominant position of the goddess of fire and the hearth, Tabiti (Iran., Tarayati, "the flaming one, the burning one"), corresponds to the Indo-Iranian concept of fire as the primeval substance and the basis of the universe. The conjugal couple, Papaeus ("father"?) and Api (from the Iranian *ap-*, "water"), personifies the concept, common among the Indo-Iranians, of the marriage of heaven and earth (or water) as a cosmogonical act. From their union was born Targitaus, the forefather of the Scythian people and of the Scythian royal dynasty. His mythological birth may be interpreted as the formation of the middle zone of the cosmos—"the world of people," between the heavenly and chthonic worlds.

The inclusion in the third rank of the pantheon, on a level with this Scythian "Herakles," of three additional gods corresponds to the archaic cosmological conception of the four sides of the world as a structure regulating the universe, and of four gods as their custodians. Of these Scythian gods, Artimpasa (if this reading of her name is accepted) is conjectured to be the Iranian Arti (Ashi), a deity connected with the idea of material abundance, which conforms to her identification with Aphrodite, as proposed by Herodotus. The Scythian "Ares," who was venerated in the form of an ancient iron sword (Herodotus, 4.62), is, evidently, predominantly a war god, corresponding to the Iranian Vere-thragna. The meaning of the figure of Oetosyrus, the Scythian "Apollo," is still highly debatable.

Besides the seven gods of the basic pantheon, other personages of the Scythian religio-mythological system are also known. For example, a myth noted by Herodotus tells of the three sons of Targitaus, in whom, according to the most valid interpretation, can be seen the personification of the three zones of the cosmos and the ancestors of the three strata into which, corresponding to Indo-European tradition, Scythian society was divided: warriors, priests, and agriculturalists. However, in the specific interpretation of each of these personages, there is divergence among scholars. Besides the gods common to all the Scythians, there were also deities that were venerated by separate tribes. For example, the Royal Scyths, the most powerful of the Scythian tribes, worshiped Thagimasadas, identified by Herodotus with Poseidon.

Data on cult leaders among the Scythians are highly fragmentary. The most complete information is on the Enarees, a group of priests connected with the worship of Artimpasa. Divination was among their ritual functions, and sexual transvestism was apparently a feature of their cultic practices. It is not entirely clear whether membership in this group was hereditary; according to some sources, the Enarees came from the Scythian aristocracy. About other Scythian priests there is almost no information. Undoubtedly the Scythian king himself was an important, if not the chief, performer of cultic practices. The most significant evidence of this is the abundance in royal burials of ritual objects, including those having complex cosmological and social symbolism.

Although Scythian religious beliefs, originating in the main in the Common Iranian period, do not specifically express the values of a nomadic people, such values are manifested distinctly in the forms of Scythian cultic life. For example, according to Herodotus—and this has been confirmed archaeologically—the Scythians had neither temples nor monumental images of their gods, a fact connected, apparently, with the mobility of their way of life.

However, certain cultic structures did exist in Scythia. Thus, in the center of each of the districts of Scythia, huge brushwood altars were heaped up in honor of the Scythian "Ares," in the form of square platforms, accessible on one side. At the top of the platform a sword personifying the god was placed vertically, and domestic animals and every hundredth prisoner were sacrificed to it (Herodotus, 4.62). This structure may be interpreted as a cosmogram mirroring the form of the "four-sided universe," and the sword as one of the equivalents of the *axis mundi,* uniting the world of the gods and the world of people. Also known is the existence in the area between the Dnieper and the Southern Bug rivers of a place called Exampaeus, whose name Herodotus translates as "holy ways." Here, according to legend, there was a huge copper caldron cast from arrowheads brought by all the inhabitants of Scythia. This caldron was unquestionably a sacred object for all the Scythians and may be interpreted as one of the symbols of the center of the world.

It is possible that precisely in this Common Scythian cultic center was held the annual Scythian festival connected with the worship of golden sacred objects: a yoked plow, an ax, and a cup that had fallen, according to Scythian myth, from the sky, and that symbolized the cosmic and social order. This festival is one of the few Scythian ritual activities about which relatively detailed information has been preserved. The golden sacred objects, which had a fiery nature and were, perhaps, connected with the goddess Tabiti, were carefully guarded by the Scythian kings and were annually venerated with rich offerings.

According to Herodotus (4.7), during the festival a man would sleep among the golden sacred objects, and he would die less than a year afterward (it is obvious that a violent killing took place); meanwhile, he was allotted as much land as he could cover on horseback in a day. The meaning of this story is not entirely clear, but most probably reference here is to a temporary ritual "deputy king" and his imitation "kingdom." Insofar as the horse in the mythology of the Indo-Iranian peoples is connected with the sun, the method of determining the size of the "kingdom," and also the life span of its "owner," allows one to reconstruct the existence among the Scythians of the concept of the solar nature of the king, and to interpret the festival as calendrical, connected with the yearly cycle of the sun.

Most probably, in the course of this festival was repeated the fate of Targitaus's youngest son, the mythical first king of the Scythians, Colaxais. (The Soviet Iranologist V. I. Abaev has proposed that this name derives etymologically from the Iranian *hvar-xšaya,* "sun king.") The golden sacred objects, obtained, according to the Scythian myth, by this Colaxais, served as proof of the god-given nature of the power of the Scythian kings. This idea also found embodiment in the different investiture ceremonies practiced in Scythia, about which there exists, unfortunately, only highly obscure evidence.

There is information about the methods of sacrifice among the Scythians. Animals (most commonly horses) were asphyxiated while a salutation was made to the god to whom the sacrifice was offered. The flesh was then boiled, and the part intended for the god was thrown on the ground, in front of the sacrificer. There also were ecstatic rituals, in particular purification rituals, during which hemp seeds were burned and wine imported from Greece was used.

The most complete existing information on any aspect of Scythian culture—which has been confirmed, moreover, by archaeological data—is on burial rituals. When a man died, his corpse (apparently embalmed) was carried by cart on a round of visits to the homes of his friends; after forty days the body was buried. The form of the grave (usually a deep chamber-catacomb) and the collection of objects accompanying the dead man were quite uniform and were regulated by tradition. When a king died, his body was carried through the territory of all the tribes subject to him, and this journey was accompanied by various mourning rites. Together with the king were buried retainers of various ranks, and royal horses, and over the grave a monumental burial mound was erected. The graves of ancestors and especially of kings were considered national holy sites and were carefully protected from profanation.

In the early stages of their history, the Scythians (in conformity with the aniconic traditions characteristic of many Indo-Iranians) had virtually no images of gods. During the period of the campaigns in the Near East from the seventh to the early sixth century BCE, they attempted to adapt ancient Eastern iconography for the depiction of personages of their own pantheon. Such depictions were not large-scale monuments but were, rather, decorative elements on ritual objects; however, even these were not widespread in Scythia.

From the sixth to the first half of the fourth century BCE, Scythian art was dominated by the animal style, employing motifs of animals connected to the religio-mythological concepts of the Scythians. The strictly canonical depictions of only certain animals served as a symbolic system for the description of the Scythian mythological model of the world. A definite connection has been established between the repertoire of the animal forms of Scythian art and the archaeological evidence of sacrificial animals found in Scythian monuments. In the fourth century BCE anthropomorphic motifs based on Scythian myths and rituals played an important role in Scythian religious life. These motifs ornamented various ritual objects that were made by Greek artisans from colonies on the northern coast of the Black Sea. In the rich Scythian burials of this time, objects with motifs from Greek mythology have also been found. These most probably reflect not the adoption of Greek cults by the Scythian aristocracy, but yet another attempt to adapt another culture's iconography to embody local religio-mythological concepts.

The religion of the steppe peoples of Asia who were related to or similar in culture to the Scythians was evidently close to that of the Scythians, but data on it are almost completely lacking. The sum of the data on the religious life of the Scythians leads to the conclusion that the overall aim of their ceremonies and rituals was above all to ensure the stability, going back to mythic times, of the cosmic and social order and to guarantee the well-being of the community.

See Also Inner Asian Religions; Prehistoric Religions, article on the Eurasian Steppes and Inner Asia.

Bibliography

The most complete survey of Scythian antiquity is contained in the still-valuable book of Ellis H. Minns, *Scythians and Greeks* (Cambridge, 1913). Important observations on the cultures of the Scythians, including their religion, were made by Mikhail I. Rostovtsev in *Iranians and Greeks in South Russia* (Oxford, 1922). The most recent research devoted exclusively to the religion of the Scythians is S. S. Bessonova's *Religioznye predstavleniia Skifov* (Kiev, 1983). For Scythian mythology and some aspects of Scythian ritual practices, see my book *Ocherki ideologii skifo-sakskikh plemen: Opyt rekonstruktsii skifskoi mifologii* (Moscow, 1977). An interpretation of linguistic data on Scythian mythology and religion is in V. I. Abaev's *Osetinskii iazyk i fol'klor* (Moscow, 1949). A detailed survey of Scythian burials and an analysis of burial rituals has been made by Renate Rolle in *Totenkult der Skythen,* vol. 1 of *Das Steppengebiet,* 2 vols. (Berlin, 1978). For the Scythian religion in the general system of beliefs of the Iranian-speaking peoples of antiquity, see Henrik S. Nyberg's *Die Religionen des alten Iran* (Leipzig, 1938) and Geo Widengren's *Die Religionen Irans* (Stuttgart, 1965). An important landmark in the study of the spiritual legacy of the Scythians is Georges Dumézil's *Romans de Scythie et d'alentour* (Paris, 1978).

New Sources

Dumézil investigated also, from his comparative point of view, social functions and religious customs in Ossetia: see in particular: Georges Dumézil, *Légendes sur les Nartes.* Paris, 1935; *Le livre des héros, légendes ossètes sur les Nartes.* Paris, 1965.

Of the same scholar, who variously dealt with Skythian mythology and heritage, it is worth quoting one of his volumes, where some essays on this subject are collected *La courtisane et les seigneurs colorés et autres essais* (Paris, 1983).

On the same subject see also: L. S. Klejn "The Nartian epos and the legend in Herodotus about the Asiatic origin of the Scythians." *Vestnik Drevnej Istorii* 134 (1975): 14–27.

General monographs on Skythians include: René Grousset, *The Empire of the Steppes,* section I, parts 1, 3, and 4, New Brunswick, 1989) [original French edition, Paris 1939]. Tamara Talbot Rice, *The Scythians* (London, 1957); Boris N. Grakov, *Die Skythen* (Berlin, 1978); Alexej P. Smirnow, *Die Skythen* (Dresden, 1979); D. S. Raevskij, *Model' mira skifskoj kul'tury* (Moskva, 1985); I. V. Kuklina, *Etnogeografija Skifii po antičnym istočnikam* (Leningrad, 1985); Renate Rolle, *Die Welt der Skythen. Stutenmelker und Pferdebogner. Ein antikes Reitervolk in neuer Sicht* (Luzern-Frankfurt, 1980; English Transl. Princeton, 1989); I. N. Chrapunov, *Drevnjaja istorija Kryma. Ucebnoe posobie.* Simferopol, 2003.

For various questions see also: E. A. Grantovsky. *Indo-iranskie kasty u skifov* (Moscow, 1960). Peter Lindegger, *Griechische und römische Quellen zum peripheren Tibet, I: Frühe Zeugnisse bis Herodot: der fernere skythische Nordosten* (Zürich, 1979). Grigorii M. Bongard-Levin, E.A. Grantovskij, translated by Philippe Gignoux, *De la Scythie à l'Inde. Énigmes de l'histoire des anciens Aryens* (Louvain, 1981) (the authors follow Dumezil's perspective). Michail I. Rostowzew, *Skythien und der Bosporus,* German edition by Glen W. Bowersock, translated by Heinz Heinen, et al. (Stuttgart, 1993). Victor Parker, "Bemerkungen zu den Zügen der Kimmerier und der Skythen durch Vorderasien." *Klio* 77 (1995): 7–34. Bruce Lincoln, "On the Scythian Royal Burials." In *Proto-Indo-European. The Archaeology of a Linguistic Problem. Studies in Honour of Marija Gimbutas,* ed. by Susan N. Skomal and Edgar C. Polomé (Washington, D.C., 1987), pp. 267–285. Fridrik Thordarson, "The Scythian Funeral Customs: Some notes on Herodotus IV, 71–75." In *A Green Leaf. Papers in Honour of Professor Jes P. Asmussen,* edited by Werner Sundermann, Jacques Duchesne-Guillemin and Fereydun Vahman (=Acta Iranica 28, Leiden, 1988), pp. 539–547.

Studies specifically devoted to religion are: M. I. Artamonov, "Antropomorfnye bozhestva v religii skifov." In *Archeologitsheskij sbornik. Gosudarstvennyj Ermitazh,* vol. 3, Leningrad, 1961, pp. 57–87. I. I. Tolstoy, *Statyi o folklore* (Moscow and Leningrad, 1966) deals, among other folkloric motifs, with the legend about Heracles and the Snake Maiden. Petro B. T. Bilaniuk, "Die religiöse Lage an der skythischen Schwarzmeerküste und ihr Einfluss auf Westeuropa in der Spätantike und im frühen Mittelalter." In *Die Schwarzmeerküste in der Spätantike und im frühen Mittelalter: Referate des dritten, vom 16 bis 19. Oktober 1990 durch die Antiquarische Abteilung der Balkan-Kommission der österreichischen Akademie der Wissenschaften und das Bulgarische Forschungsinstitut in Österreich veranstalteten Symposions,* edited by Renate Pillinger, Andreas Pülz and Hermann Vetters, Vienna, 1992, pp. 123–135.

The seminal paper by Karl Meuli, "Scythica." *Hermes* 70 (1935): 122–176 deals with Shamanic patterns in Scythian culture, as they were echoed by Greeks. On this subject see also Donat Margreth, *Skythische Schamanen. Die Nachrichten über Enarees-Anarieis bei Herodot und Hippokrates* (Schaffhausen, 1993).

Moreover, Herodotus's account of Skythia has attracted scholarly interest: see, for example: Janós Harmatta, *Forrástamulmányok Herodotos Skythika-jához. Quellenstudien zu den Skythika des Herodot.* Budapest, 1942. O. Kimball Armayor, "Did Herodotus Ever Go to the Black Sea?" *Harvard Studies in Classical Philology* 82 (1978): 45–62. Askold I. Ivantchik, "Une légende sur l'origine des Scythes (Hérodote IV, 5–7) et le problème des sources du Scythikos logos d'Hérodote." *Revue des Études Grecques* 112 (1999): 141–192. Stephanie West, "Hippocrates' Scythian Sketches." *Eirene* 35 (1999): 14–32. Stephanie West, "Herodotus in the North? Reflections on a Colossal Cauldron (4.81)." *Scripta Classica Israelica* 19 (2000): 15–34. Erodoto. *Le storie. Libro IV. La Scizia e la Libia*, ed. by Aldo Corcella and Silvio M. Medaglia (Milano,1993) is important for the rich commentary.

For the later history of Skythia in contact with the Greeks see: Viktor F. Gajdukevic, *Das bosporanische Reich, mit den Ergebnissen der archäologischen Untersuchungen von 1949–1966* (Berlin, 1971); V. I. Kadejev, "Chersonesus, Bosporus and Rome, I–III Centuries A.D." *Vestnik Drevnej Istorii* 148 (1979): 55–76; *Studien zur Geschichte und Kultur des Nordpontos nach antiken Quellen*, edited by Alexandr K. Gavrilov (St. Petersburg, 1992).

The religious aspect is investigated by S. R. Tokhtas'jev, "Apaturum. A History of the Bosporan Shrine of Aphrodite Urania." *Vestnik Drevnej Istorii* 177 (1986): 138–145, and, most of all, in the recent and detailed inquiry by Yulia Ustinova, *The Supreme Gods of the Bosporan Kingdom* (Leiden, 1999).

D. S. Raevskii (1987)
Translated from Russian by Mary Lou Masey
Revised Bibliography

SEASONAL CEREMONIES.

In all parts of the world and in all ages, it has been the custom to mark the beginning of a year, season, or agricultural cycle by a series of public ceremonies. These were designed originally to dramatize the conclusion of one lease on life and to procure, by quasi-magical procedures, fertility, prosperity, sunshine, and rainfall for the next. They fall into a standard pattern. First the rites of mortification, symbolizing the temporary eclipse of the community. Next the rites of purgation, by which all noxious elements that might impair the community's future welfare are eliminated. Then the rites of invigoration, aimed at stimulating the growth of crops, the fecundity of humans and beasts, and the supply of needed sunshine and rainfall throughout the year. Finally, when the new lease is assured, come the rites of jubilation; there is a communal meal at which the members of the community recement their bonds of kinship by breaking bread together, and at which their gods are present. For this occasion, the shades of their ancestors and deceased relatives temporarily rejoin them.

Rites of Mortification. The initial stage of mortification is exemplified principally in the form of fasts, abstinences, and the suspension of public offices and routine business. Thus the Babylonians regarded the first ten or sixteen days of the year in some of their cities as a lenten period, and the Israelites prefaced their autumnal Ḥag ha-Asif ("feast of ingathering") by Yom Kippur ("day of purgation"), on which the sanctuary and its vessels were purified, members of the community ritually aspersed and "cleansed," a fast observed, and all normal activity suspended. In Rome, a fast preceded the feast of Ceres (goddess of crops) in April. In the present day, the Choctaw, Cherokee, and Creek of North America fast at New Year, and among the Mao of Manipur a *genna*, or period of taboo, is observed for four days at the commencement of the harvest. The month of Muḥarram, at the beginning of the year, is a time of abstinence in Morocco, and the Ossets of the Caucasus keep a daily fast during the month before harvest. These examples could be readily multiplied. The Christian Lent and the Islamic Ramaḍān, it may be added, are, in the main, reinterpreted survivals of this usage.

The annual or seasonal eclipse of communal life is exemplified also by the deposition, execution, or temporary humiliation of the king or chieftain, by whom that life is personified and epitomized. In Babylon he was formally degraded on the fifth day of the New Year (Akitu) festival. A major priest stripped him of his robes, slapped his face until he wept, and forced him to his knees. He was then obliged to recite a penitential prayer before he was reinstated. In Cambodia, the king was formerly required to abdicate annually for three days in February, and, in Thailand, he was confined to his palace in late April or early May.

In many cases, the new year did not follow immediately upon the close of the old; there was an intervening "vacant" period, reckoned as outside the calendar. Among the Aztec, for example, it was known as *nemontemi* ("the days unfit for work"); all religious ceremonies and civil activity were then suspended. Similarly, the Maya of Yucatán had a period of *xma kaba kin* ("nameless days") at the end of the year, during which they abstained from all heavy work and even from personal ablutions. In the central provinces of India, this period was actually termed *malmas* ("excreta"), and the institution survives in European popular custom in the abstinences and restrictions imposed during the twelve days between Christmas and Epiphany. During this time, when the real king was temporarily out of office, a substitute was (and is) installed. This was the practice, for instance, in the kingdom of Jambi in Sumatra, among the Kwotto of northern Nigeria, the Kitara of Uganda, and the Bastar of the Central Provinces of India. Such a temporary king, or *interrex* (Gr., *zōganēs*), in the person of a slave, is reported also to have held sway at the ancient Iranian feast of Sacaea, and it has been suggested that the so-called flight of the king (*regifugium*), recognized in ancient Rome as an institution associated with February 24, was a lingering relic of the earlier expulsion of the temporary monarch at the end of his brief term.

Another popular method of symbolizing the expiration of one lease on communal life is to bury a puppet that personifies it and to subsequently disinter it when the succeeding lease begins. Thus, in Romania, a clay doll called *kalojan* (from Gr. *kalos Ioannēs,* "beautiful John") is buried on the Monday preceding Assumption (August 15) and later dug up; in the Abruzzi, the same ceremony is performed with a similar figure named Pietro Pico ("little Peter"). In both cases, these are but Christianized versions of an older pagan usage known to us from the burial and disinterment of the god Attis in Phrygia and of Osiris in Egypt. In parts of Russia, an effigy named Kostrobunko was similarly buried on Saint Peter's day and later disinterred.

The buried spirit of life and fertility is ritually bewailed, usually by women (as regular practice at funerals). Such wailing is attested, on a mythological level, in the cults of Dumuzi in Babylonia, of Attis in Asia Minor, of Osiris in Egypt, and of Adonis in Syria, and in the *iouloi* ("howls") uttered in the cult of Demeter and Persephone in Greece. In this connection, however, it is pertinent to observe that tears are regarded in several cultures as regenerative. The Egyptians are said to have shed them while they sowed the first seeds, and at Great Bessan, in Guinea, oxen are slain and made to weep at an annual ceremony designed to ensure a good harvest. Indeed, it has been suggested that the familiar words of Psalm 126:5, "They that sow in tears shall reap in joy," were inspired by such a custom, and it is significant that the wailing cry, *eleleu,* was a feature of certain Greek seasonal festivals. Hence, it is not impossible that what came eventually to be interpreted as weeping for the slain or buried spirit of fertility was originally functional shedding of tears.

Rites of Purgation. Ceremonies of purgation, or the ritual removal of noxious elements and of the contagion of latent sin, such as might jeopardize the continued life and health of the community or evoke retribution from the gods in the form of blight, drought, plague, war, or other calamities are likewise virtually universal. In Babylon, a ceremony called *kuppuru* (clearance, purgation), involving the cleansing and renovation of the temple, was part of the New Year ceremonies, and as stated above, a similar ceremony, Yom Kippur, was observed among the Israelites before the autumnal harvest. In Rome the month preceding the new year, March, was characterized as the period of *februatio* (whence the month of February), fields and human beings being then lustrated and temples scoured. Such rites of purgation often include a collective confession of sins. Examples of these are the semiannual Japanese ceremony of Ofuharahi ("purification"), at which the Mikado or a member of the Nakatomi order of priests shrives the people, and the Ashanti festival called Odwira. It was similarly a prominent feature of the ancient Israelite Yom Kippur (Day of Atonement), a usage that survives in Jewish ritual to this day.

Latent sins that remain unconfessed are removed in many cases by being loaded symbolically on a scapegoat (either animal or human) who is ceremonially dispatched from the community. This was a prominent feature of the aforementioned Babylonian and Israelite ceremonies, while in Greece it was observed at the feast of Thargelia, in May.

Sometimes the latent evil is removed by expelling an effigy called "Death" or the like. The Inca of Peru, for example, drove out disease before the rainy season in this manner, and in Thailand noxious spirits are ceremonially banished on the last day of the year. In Cambodia the rite is performed in March, and among the Inuit (Eskimo) of Point Barrow, Alaska, the same ceremony is performed as soon as the sun reappears and ushers in a new lease on life. The modern practice of ringing bells, clanging gongs, blowing whistles, and cracking whips on New Year's Eve is a relic of such expulsion of evil and disaster, designed originally to scare away demons—raising, as it were, a pandemonium surpassing theirs.

Finally, evil is often removed by lighting bonfires at such crucial times of the year as New Year, midsummer, and midwinter. This ritual is too familiar to require documentation. It is common not only in most parts of Europe but also among Muslims at the ʿAshūrāʾ festival among the Berbers; and it was observed in antiquity at the Isia (the festival of Isis) in Hellenistic Egypt. Here, however, a word of caution is in order. Fire is also used in popular custom to lustrate fields in order to stimulate crops and also to relume the sun when it reemerges from its winter sojourn underground. Hence, some of the rites that have been interpreted as designed to burn up evil may really be directed toward these alternative purposes.

Rites of Invigoration. The elimination of the old leads naturally to the inauguration of the new, that is, to rites of invigoration. The most widespread of these is the staging of a ritual combat between Fertility and Blight, Rainfall and Drought, Summer and Winter, or simply Life and Death, the positive protagonist (the one who personifies renewal) being always the winner. This seasonal usage is attested among the ancient Hittites of Asia Minor and in reliefs on the walls of an Egyptian temple at Deir al-Bahri. Similarly, among the Iroquoian-speaking tribes of North America, a ritual battle was fought annually in late January or early February between the god of summer or life (Teharoniawagon) and the god of winter or death (Tawiskaron). Often the combat comes eventually to be explained as the commemoration of a historical encounter. The Hittites, for instance, identified the antagonists respectively as themselves and a neighboring people, the Masa, and Plutarch tells of a periodically recurring joust between characters popularly called Alexander and Darius. In the English Mummers' Play, which is really a survival of the same usage, the combatants are sometimes likewise identified as Saint George and the Turkish knight (probably a distortion of Saladin), or as King George and Napoleon, or even (in more recent times) as Churchill and Hitler.

Sexual license is another popular rite of invigoration. Among the Pipils of Central America, it is observed when the first seeds are sown, and in the Ukraine it is (or was) a popular method of stimulating the growth of crops on Saint George's Day (April 23). The Garos encourage sexual intercourse at seasonal festivals, and it is held by several scholars that the familiar stories of the rape of the Sabine women at a festival and of the women of Shiloh (*Jgs.* 21:19–23) reflect the same custom.

The usage was mythified in the "sacred marriage" of god and goddess at the New Year in various ancient Mesopotamian cities and in the marriage of the god Horus and goddess Hathor at an annual celebration at Idfu (Beḥdet) in Egypt; the mating of the god (impersonated by the pharaoh) with a divine bride is portrayed on reliefs at Deir al-Bahri. Similarly, Aristotle tells us that a marriage between Dionysos and the king's consort took place annually in the Bucolicon (*boukolikon*) at Athens. A burlesque of this ritual is a feature of the festival plays still performed in northern Greece. The offspring of the "sacred marriage"—the spirit of the new life—is often introduced as a baby in a crib and thus finds its echo in present-day New Year cards. The famous passage in the *Book of Isaiah* (9:6), "Unto us a child is born, unto us a son is given," is believed by many modern exegetes to have been inspired by this usage.

New members of the tribe or community, especially children, are often initiated at seasonal festivals. This initiation is (or was) carried out, for instance, by Muslim Arabs before the spring harvest and by bedouin at Mecca and at the Nebi Musa (Eastertide) festival at Jericho, as well as by the Haida Indians of the Queen Charlotte Islands at an annual potlatch. Significant in this connection is the statement in the *Book of Joshua* (5:2–8) that when members of the new generation were formally received into the community after the Exodus from Egypt, the initiating rite of circumcision was performed before the festival of Passover. The initiation is sometimes represented as a rebirth. Indeed, among certain people of the lower region of the river Kongo it is termed *kimbasi* ("resurrection"), and the neophytes have first to fall as though dead at the feet of the officiant.

RITES OF JUBILATION. The seasonal program concludes with a communal feast, at which the ancestral dead are also present ("our founders are with us in spirit"). Thus to cite but a few examples, the Greeks supposed that these "ghosts" returned temporarily at the festival of Anthesteria, and the Romans, at the festival of Lemuria; the Mandaeans of Iraq and Iran hold a feast of the dead at the beginning of the year. In the Trobriand Islands, the dead rejoin the living at an annual festival called Milmala; in Thailand, at the New Year festival in April; among the Huzul of the Ukraine, at Easter and Christmas; and among the ancient Celts, at the feast of Samhain. This return of the dead, which survives in the folklore of Halloween, is, of course, the counterpart of the initiation ceremonies; past and future are alike involved in the renewal of corporate life, since both are constituent elements of its continuum. The gods, too, often attend the banquet, either as guests or as hosts, because they too belong to the "kindred."

All of the seasonal rites here described—the initial period of disorder and chaos, the combat, the defeat of the powers of evil and disaster, the installation of the victor as king, the resurrection of the dead, and the inauguration of a new era of the world, sometimes also a "messianic banquet"—are retrojected mythically into cosmogony and projected into eschatology. What happens at the end of each periodic lease on life is held to have happened also at the beginning of the present cycle of the world's existence; the supreme god vanquished a contumacious monster, was installed as king, promulgated a new dispensation, and tendered a banquet to his divided subordinates and sometimes also to ancient heroes. When this era ends, he will do so again. The process is cyclic; as Vergil puts it, "the great order of the centuries is born afresh." Seasonal ceremonies, originally functional means of renewing life from year to year, thus become paradigms of human existence throughout time.

SEE ALSO Agriculture; Fasting; Hieros Gamos; Mortification; Purification; Tears.

BIBLIOGRAPHY

The great quarry for those interested in seasonal rites and customs is James G. Frazer's *The Golden Bough,* 12 vols., 3d ed., rev. & enl. (London, 1911–1915), now available in my abridged and updated edition, *New Golden Bough* (New York, 1959). Much interesting information can also be found in *The Book of Days,* 2 vols., edited by Robert Chambers (London, 1862–1864), and in William S. Walsh's *Curiosities of Popular Customs* (Philadelphia, 1915). A useful source for European customs is Ethel L. Urlin's *Festivals, Holy Days and Saints' Days* (London, 1915), as is, for those who read German, Paul Sartori's *Sitte und Brauch,* 3 vols. (Leipzig, 1910–1914). The "ritual pattern" theory of seasonal festivals is presented in S. H. Hooke's *Myth and Ritual* (Oxford, 1933) and, in somewhat different form, in my *Thespis: Ritual, Myth, and Drama in the Ancient Near East,* 2d ed. (1961; New York, 1977).

New Sources

Aveni, Anthony F. *The Book of the Year: A Brief History of Our Seasonal Holidays.* Oxford and New York, 2003.

Gufler, Hermann. "Cults and Seasonal Dances of the Yamba (Cameroon). " *Anthropos* 92, no. 4–5 (1997): 501–522.

James, E. O. *Seasonal Feasts and Festivals* (1961). Detroit, 1993.

Santino, Jack, ed. *Halloween and Other Festivals of Death and Life.* Knoxville, Tenn., 1994.

Teish, Luisah. *Carnival of the Spirit: Seasonal Celebrations and Rites of Passage.* San Francisco, 1994.

THEODOR H. GASTER (1987)
Revised Bibliography

SECRET SOCIETIES.

The term *secret society* can be used to describe all groups whose membership or very existence is unknown to nonmembers, or that keep certain of their practices or conceptions hidden from nonmembers, no matter how public or recognized they are as a group. Within these broad limits one could include subversive political groups, criminal gangs, and some professional guilds. There may be a religious dimension to these organizations, perhaps in ritual behavior, legends about their origins, or other counterparts to phenomena typical of religious groups. In this article, however, attention will be given to groups that are more clearly religious, as determined by their recognition of supernatural powers or their subscription to certain values and ideals.

It must be admitted, however, that there is no clear border between those secret societies that definitely celebrate religious matters and those that are secular. Of course, secret societies that are both very secret and religious can change into societies that have few secret elements and little specifically religious language. The aura of the past and the persistence of generic or Deistic religious language can nevertheless make such societies seem like rival religions to some people. A prominent indication of this problem is the prohibition of membership in the Freemasons for Roman Catholics and some Lutherans, despite the claim of many Masons that they are not a religion in any way, especially today.

Distinguishing Features. The secret society is characterized first by its being a voluntary or selective group within a natural community. Although there may be times and places in which nearly everyone of a certain gender, age, and status may be included, there is always the theoretical possibility that some otherwise eligible person will not be elected to join the group. The possibility of exclusion is a powerful factor in the sociopsychological dynamics of a secret society. The pool of potential members is also restricted, usually to men beyond puberty. There are few secret societies that include women or children, although secret societies restricted to women are known, such as the Bundu society among the Mende people of Sierra Leone.

Obviously, another primary characteristic of the secret society is secrecy. It is not characteristic of religious secret societies, however, that their very existence or their membership is secret. Instead, it is knowledge of their activities, rituals, texts, doctrines, myths, and offices that is restricted to the group. Some argue that such secrets are new, dangerous, or deep matters that demand the protection of secrecy; in this light it might be said that the secret society is humankind's nursery for new insights and new political or social structures. No matter what the depth or the power of the secrets, however, there is always a measure of artificiality in keeping them secret. Furthermore, at least in some cases, the secrets so carefully guarded are actually trivial and assume importance only because they are shared secrets. At the base of secrecy lies not so much a set of hidden facts as a group of experiences—any group of people that works or performs rites together shares memories that others do not have.

A third major feature of the religious secret society is initiation. There is a logical necessity that entrance into the group be clearly marked so that the group and the individual can be sure exactly who is and who is not included. Many of the initiatory practices can be understood as means by which the simple fact of inclusion in the group is emphasized and reinforced. There are other dimensions to these often elaborate initiation practices, however. In their use of ordeals and trials, the symbolism of death and rebirth can become apparent: one does not merely join an organization, but undergoes a transforming experience and achieves deeper contact with the meaning of life and the world.

Closely related to the phenomenon of initiation is the hierarchical structure of the secret society. Often the society seems to be an outgrowth and extension of puberty-initiation practices. As such, it is based on the notion that human life does not merely grow into maturity, but that a distinctive, new kind of existence or ontology must be attained in the transformation from child to adult. Likewise, then, it is reasonable to recognize still higher stages of life with other initiations. The secret society itself represents such a stage beyond the status of simple adulthood, and within the secret society there may be other stages or levels of advancement. Role differentiation within the society is, from this perspective, not merely a differentiation in function, but a manifestation of degrees of metaphysical weight or height.

Finally, the religious secret society regularly posits a myth concerning its origins that is central to its self-consciousness. Such myths are probably not historically accurate, but should be read as indications of the concerns or mindset of the group. Many primitive secret societies, for example, tell a story in which their secrets were derived from a woman, but subsequently kept from other women. This does not necessarily mean that the male secret society was a device by which the men in a previous age wrested control from the women in a matriarchal society. It does, however, indicate a tension in the men's psychology: they are keeping from the women something in which the women also have, or have had, a stake.

Theories Concerning Origin and Function. Many suggestions concerning the basic motivation for secret societies have been proposed. One theory emphasizes the sexual element. In this view, secret societies constitute an attempt by men to establish a life independent of women, a rejection of feminine power and influence. Secret societies that are not exclusively male are reluctant concessions or counter-reactions to this motive. Other theories on the all-male composition of so many groups include suggestions of homoerotic attraction and the observation that many male animals cultivate activities limited to their gender. This pattern of male bonding can be as casual as the camaraderie incidental to the hunt or the neighborhood bar, or it can take the highly organized form of the secret society. Patterns of gender grouping in work, war, and play also may have their roots in male bonding and thus contribute to the strength of the secret society phenomenon.

A second kind of analysis emphasizes the social and political functions of the societies. On the one hand, the secret society may be consonant with the existing social and political order and may reinforce that order through the fear it inspires. On the other hand, a secret society may be an agency for change, rebellion, or reform. In this situation, it will be opposed by the dominant forces in society, and its need for secrecy will be greater. Its membership and its very existence will be kept secret if possible. Certainly, such groups will be labeled criminal by the dominant society, but they may also be understood as supporting an alternative political or social structure.

In many historical situations, the phenomenon of secrecy has given rise to the attitude that every secret organization is a conspiracy against the welfare of the rest of humankind. The rest of society, if sufficiently distressed, might blame all social ills on a real or even a supposed secret society. It is unlikely that many secret societies have been as powerful or as conspiratorial as public opinion has, on occasion, conceived them to be. Especially pernicious when used as a basis for discrimination and repression is the supposition that subversive secret societies exist among minority populations. The threat, real or imagined, that a secret society represents to the total community is an important factor in the social dynamics of such a group.

A third theory about secret societies stresses more positive social functions. It is argued that secret societies foster a person's sense of identity. In tribal societies they afford some people a sense of privacy in the midst of proximity, and in modern societies they give the individual a special status in the midst of pressures for conformity. It is clear that in some societies the secret group is a primary means of education and socialization. Insofar as the desire to improve oneself or to achieve greater power and status can be considered a beneficial motivation in human life, the secret society has had the positive function of offering people a way to advance their programs of social and financial success.

Such aspiration to greater significance and fuller existence brings us to the religious motivations and functions of the secret society. There is a style of being religious in which the reason and goal of religious activities is the improvement of one's strength or ontological status. By performing certain ritual, ascetic, or ethical acts, or by thinking certain thoughts and controlling the mind, this kind of religion seeks to promote one's career in this or another world. In light of this kind of religious motivation, the secret society is a major arena for structuring, formulating, and traveling a path toward that goal.

The goal, as well as the path, varies from society to society, of course. Among tribal peoples the attempt to progress beyond the stage of adulthood achieved through puberty initiation often takes the form of more and more rigorous physical ordeals. It may involve learning magical techniques. The goal may be conceived in terms of transcending the ordinary human condition, especially by identifying with the dead and the spirits who occupy the next higher rung in the hierarchy of being and power. Many masked dancing rites performed by secret societies are understood to represent the return of the dead to the world of the living. Some of the most shocking practices of secret societies—for example, the eating of raw human flesh in a secret society of the Kwakiutl Indians of North America—can be seen as a way of demonstrating the transhuman (and certainly nonhuman) nature of the life of a secret society member (members of this kind of secret society think of themselves as being something else, superior to humans; the cannibalism demonstrates that they are no longer human because they do something no normal human being would do). The right of secret society members to frighten or steal also derives from this supposed superior existence.

The higher status and power bestowed through the secret society might be conceived as benefiting the fertility of the earth, improving one's health or wealth, giving greater power to the tribe, or enhancing one's interior life. When the secret society is seen as a school for attaining ecstatic states or mystical knowledge, its similarity to monasticism becomes apparent. The element of secrecy is not so prominent in the conventional monastic community, hence the connection between monasticism and secret societies has seldom been recognized. Nevertheless, monastic communities do cultivate religious advancement and identify with a stage of humanity beyond the ordinary, as do many secret societies.

There is also a religious function ascribed to the secret society in those theories that see such societies as the nurseries or nursing homes of religions. The secret of some groups may be a new religious insight that is protected from persecution or ridicule by restricting its rites to believers' eyes. This theory may have been persuasive to those who interpreted the semi-secrecy of early Christian ritual in this way. It has also been argued, however, that secret societies can preserve for a small group some outmoded religious ideas and practices that the rest of a population has abandoned. Through secrecy and mystification, ancient religious patterns might retain some attraction that they would not enjoy in the full light of public scrutiny. Thus, the secret society could embody the first or the last stage in the history of a religious movement.

There is nothing inevitably good or bad in the form of the secret society itself. It is a powerful human phenomenon that can be turned to purposes either beneficial or harmful to its members, the larger society, or both. Of course, many of the factors listed here can be operative at the same time; thus they can strengthen the attraction of a secret society for its members by fulfilling many expectations, both religious and secular.

PROMINENT EXAMPLES. One of the richest areas for research into secret societies in tribal or primitive cultures has been the islands of the South Pacific. The Melanesian Dukduk society and others like it provide classic examples of their type. There is some problem, however, in distinguishing the voluntary secret society from the secret rites performed at puberty on all boys of the tribe, transforming them into men of the tribe. The important distinction lies in the selective nature of membership in the secret society, no matter how similar the society's initiation is to the general puberty initiations. Also, the activities of the secret society tend to take place in special grounds or in buildings away from the village and not in the centrally located "men's houses" that are often found in these cultures.

West Africa has witnessed a proliferation of secret societies. Some of them, such as the Poro society in Sierra Leone, existed among aboriginal cultures, and apparently are unconnected with specific modern religious traditions. Other secret societies in this area are Muslim, or contain a mixture of Muslim and native elements, and may have been influenced by the Ṣūfī orders of North Africa. There are also some women's secret societies and some with members of both sexes, but these are not as old as the all-male groups.

In the history of Kenya, the Mau Mau secret society has figured prominently. It was mainly derived from the large Kikuyu population and emerged in the 1940s as a reaction to the distress this group was experiencing under colonial administration, modernization, and Christian evangelism. The link between nostalgia for the old ways and political aspirations is especially clear in this example.

The secret societies of China are well-known examples of this type of political group, although in many of them the religious factors do not seem to have been prominent. These groups have been known since the first century CE and bear such names as White Lotus, Dragon Flower, and Big Swords. It is thought that they provided those people who did not have a strong family with an alternative affiliation by which to promote their interests. They also provided some authority and order in situations where social and political structures were weak or absent. Where political structures were strong, however, they often constituted the chief form of political opposition or religious dissent. At the beginning of the twentieth century the Boxers, a xenophobic secret society, became known worldwide because of the rebellion that bore their name. More recently, the Triad societies have gained notoriety in Hong Kong and elsewhere for their criminal activities.

In North America, secret societies existed first among Native American groups—for example, the Kwakiutl. Settlers from Europe and Africa brought secret societies to America, or created them after they arrived. An example of an African American secret society was the Moorish Science Temple, established in 1913 in Newark, New Jersey. It provided some unchurched African American men with a semireligious lodge community and presaged the role of Islam in later African American history.

From Italy, the United States inherited another type of secret society, the Mafia. It is unusual in many ways, including its family connections and economic (protection racket) functions. Its specific religious character is not obvious, except in the dedication that it inspires and requires. Ethnic or nationalist secret societies clearly exhibit the role of such organizations in protecting and promoting historical identities in a new world dominated by peoples of other races and religions.

In the Ku Klux Klan the United States saw another kind of motivation for secret-society organization. Founded in the southern states following the Civil War, the Klan was a reaction to the distresses of change experienced by the white population. Again, it is impossible to ascertain to what degree religious factors were used superficially to bolster the organization's strength and to what degree these factors indicated a real religious fervor, however misguided. There was a resurgence of Klan activity during the 1930s when the objects of Klan fear and opposition were expanded beyond blacks and northern white politicians to include Jews and Roman Catholics. The Klan remains in the United States as an organization ready to provide a format for revolt against any social or religious change that some segment of the population does not affirm.

Freemasonry was a prominent example of the secret society in the United States. There are now five million or more Freemasons in the world, about two-thirds of them in the United States. Today their membership is not secret, and the secrecy of the rituals is not a defining factor. The fact that modern U.S. Masonic lodges are often assumed to be primarily social organizations demonstrates that secret societies can dramatically change over time. Mozart's opera *The Magic Flute* (1791) reflects a period, however, in which spiritual aspirations and ideas were more than relics or playful references. Mozart seems to have taken very seriously the humanistic side or interpretation of Masonic symbolism, making his opera into a kind of morality play for serious human aspiration and ideals.

The Masonic orders may not have been founded before the seventeenth century, although in their mythology they claim ancient origins. The same suspicion of a fabricated ancient and medieval past attaches to the Rosicrucians. Many people have taken seriously the idea that ancient religions were preserved in these organizations. In the eighteenth century, Freemasonry was linked to various programs of political and religious reform that emphasized freedom of thought, worship, association, and the press that may have contributed to the French and American revolutions. Insofar as humanistic ideals and deistic beliefs are deemed to be religious, Masonic fraternities constitute at least semisecret, semireligious groups.

Other examples of secret societies include the medieval Knights Templar, the Thugs of India, and the Assassins of Persia. A complete list of secret societies would include many feared groups whose programs were and are condemned by the rest of society. Even in these instances it is nevertheless possible, if not probable, that religious motivation of some sort lay at the foundation of each society and provided it with its major source of dedication and devotion. It is perhaps nowhere clearer, therefore, that a phenomenon worthy of the designation "religious," according to most definitions, need not be good or true in the opinion of most people. The structure of the secret society, with its religious characteristics or dynamics, is in itself a neutral form, but it may embody and promote thoughts or acts deemed wonderful or horrible.

SEE ALSO Assassins; Freemasons; Millenarianism, article on Chinese Millenarian Movements; Rosicrucians.

BIBLIOGRAPHY

Charles William Heckethorn's *The Secret Societies of All Ages and Countries*, 2 vols. (1875–1897; reprint, New York, 1965) examines many groups that might be called "secret societies." Major examples of secret societies are discussed by various authors in *Secret Societies*, edited by Norman MacKenzie (New York, 1967). Theories and analyses are to be found in most of the books mentioned here, but one should note the discussions in Joachim Wach's *Sociology of Religion* (1944; reprint, Chicago, 1962); the article on secrecy and the secret society by Georg Simmel in *The Sociology of Georg Simmel*, translated and edited by Kurt H. Wolff (Glencoe, Ill., 1950); Hugh B. Urban's *Tantra: Sex, Secrecy, Politics, and Power in the Study of Religion* (Berkeley, Calif., 2003); and Lionel Tiger's *Men in Groups* (New York, 1969). See, further, the chapter on secret societies in Sissela Bok's *Secrets: On the Ethics of Concealment and Revelation* (New York, 1983). An older survey of the phenomenon in tribal societies is Hutton Webster's *Primitive Secret Societies: A Study in Early Politics and Religion* (New York, 1932). The following is a sampling of area studies: F. W. Butt-Thompson's *West African Secret Societies* (London, 1929); Jean Chesneaux's *Secret Societies in China in the Nineteenth and Twentieth Centuries* (Ann Arbor, Mich., 1971); Paul Christopher Johnson's *Secrets, Gossip, and the Gods: The Transformation of Brazilian Candomblé* (Oxford, 2002); and Michael R. Allen's *Male Cults and Secret Initiations in Melanesia* (London, 1967). Listings of U.S. groups is to be found in Alvin J. Schmidt's *Fraternal Organizations* (Westport, Conn., 1980) and Alan Axelrod's *The International Encyclopedia of Secret Societies and Fraternal Orders* (New York, 1997). J. M. Roberts's *The Mythology of the Secret Societies* (London, 1972) discusses the reactions to the secret societies in Europe in the eighteenth and nineteenth centuries. The role of the societies in British literature is reviewed in Marie Mulvey Roberts and Hugh Ormsby-Lennon, *Secret Texts, the Literature of Secret Societies* (New York, 1995).

An interpretation of the religious value of specific actions and symbols of secret society rituals is found in Mircea Eliade's *Rites and Symbols of Initiation: The Mysteries of Birth and Rebirth* (New York, 1958), which also includes extensive bibliographical notes (pp. 151–161) dealing with important studies of secret societies in Europe, Asia, Australia, and the Americas.

GEORGE WECKMAN (1987 AND 2005)

SECULARIZATION. The term *secularization* came into use in European languages at the Peace of Westphalia in 1648, where it was used to describe the transfer of territories previously under ecclesiastical control to the dominion of lay political authorities. The term *secularis* was already in use, and the distinction between sacred and secular, roughly equivalent to the differentiation of Christian conceptions of the supernatural from all that was mundane or profane, was widely invoked to assert the superiority of the sacred. Furthermore, the church had long distinguished between those priests called "religious" and those designated as secular priests, that is, between those clergy who functioned within a religious order and those who served the wider society. Later, the term *secularization* was applied in a different, though related, sense, to the dispensation of priests from their vows. The term was applied in even more diverse ways once the concept acquired a more general, sociological connotation in the twentieth century. Sociologists have used this word to indicate a variety of processes in which control of social space, time, facilities, resources, and personnel was lost by religious authorities, and in which empirical procedures and worldly goals and purposes displaced ritual and symbolic patterns of action directed toward otherworldly, or supernatural, ends.

The term was later applied to denote a pattern of social development that earlier sociologists, including Auguste Comte (1798–1857), had already recognized before the term *secularization* was in general sociological use. In the process thus described, the various social institutions become gradually distinct from one another and increasingly free of the matrix of religious assumptions that had earlier informed, and at times had inspired and dominated, their operation. Prior to this change, social action over a very wide field of human activity and organization (including work, decision-making, social and interpersonal relationships, juridical procedures, socialization, play, healing, and life-cycle transitions) is regulated in accordance with supernaturalist preconceptions. The process of structural differentiation in which social institutions (the economy, the polity, morality, justice, education, recreation, health maintenance, and familial organization) become recognized as distinctive concerns operating with considerable autonomy is also a process in which conceptions of the supernatural lose their sovereignty over human affairs, a pattern broadly identified as secularization. Conceptions of the supernatural are gradually displaced from all social institutions except those specifically devoted to cultivating knowledge about, and maintaining relationships with, the posited supernatural order. While those agencies still seek to influence other areas of social life, they become recognized as separate and increasingly circumscribed religious institutions.

DEFINITIONS. This brief discourse already indicates the changing nature of the concept of secularization and the difficulty of providing a fully encompassing definition for it. The concept is distinguishable from secularism, with which it is sometimes confused. Secularization relates essentially to a process of decline in religious activities, beliefs, ways of thinking, and institutions that occurs primarily in association with, or as an unconscious or unintended consequence of, other processes of social structural change. Secularism is an ideology; its proponents consciously denounce all forms of supernaturalism and the agencies devoted to it, advocating nonreligious or antireligious principles as the basis for personal morality and social organization. Secularism may contribute in some degree to processes of secularization, but the evidence, even from officially secularist societies such as those of the former Soviet Union, suggests that it does so only very gradually and much less fundamentally than do broad processes of social structural change such as industrialization and urbanization.

Definitions of secularization are intimately bound to definitions of religion. As long as religion is defined substantively, as beliefs, orientations, attitudes, activities, institutions, and structures pertaining to the supernatural (the definition assumed in this article), it is possible to assess the extent to which religion declines or loses significance for the operation of society. Some sociologists, however, have defined religion in functional terms, that is, as any set of beliefs, ideas, and activities that fulfills certain social functions. (The use of functionalist analysis, which is a standard sociological method, does not, of course, imply commitment to functional definitions; indeed, the combination may produce circular arguments.) Where religion is defined functionally, a wide variety of ideologies and activities that have no reference to the supernatural, to morality, faith, destiny, ultimate meaning, or final purposes, may sometimes be held (by definition) to be religion. Insofar as certain functions are regarded as indispensable for the continuance of society or for its cohesion, it becomes difficult, if not impossible, once functionalist definitions are used, to speak of secularization, since religion is identified by definition with whatever supplies certain indispensable functions. The very discussion of secularization and of the social processes that lead to the decline of supernaturally orientated activities and beliefs implies that a substantive definition of religion is being employed. When reference is made not to religion but to specific religions or religious systems, the definitional problem (itself partly an artifact of the sociological penchant for abstract universalistic concepts) disappears.

The concept of secularization lacks a standard definition. The associated phenomena to which it refers occupy a wide social range. What those phenomena have in common is a pattern of diminishing recourse to supernaturalist explanations, diminishing resources employed for supernatural ends, and diminishing support of agencies or activities that promote relationships with, or dependence on, supernatural forces. Other, somewhat narrower terms that allude to some of the same developments include *desacralization, laicization,* and *dechristianization. Desacralization* refers specifically to the loss of the sense of the sacred as it pertains particularly to places, properties, and activities; it has less relevance to religious organization and is less applicable to thought processes. This essentially negative term fails to specify the character of what replaces the dislodged sense of the sacred once sacrality disappears. As a concept, it allows less gradation than does secularization. *Laïcisation* in French is sometimes used as synonymous with *sécularisation,* but the English term *secularization* has a narrower connotation: It refers specifically to the abrogation of priestly offices and functions or to the transfer of certain functions, such as judicial roles, teaching, and social work, to specialists for whom theological qualifications are no longer deemed necessary or appropriate. *Laicization* refers also to the disavowal of the explicitly sacerdotal claims of religious professionals. *Dechristianization* is clearly more concerned with the decline of only one religious tradition, particularly in its control of institutional activities. As a term it lacks the ethical neutrality of the term *secularization.*

Briefly defined, secularization is the process in which religious consciousness, activities, and institutions lose social significance. It indicates that religion becomes marginal to the operation of the social system, and that the essential functions for the operation of society become rationalized, passing out of the control of agencies devoted to the supernatural.

Indices of Secularization. Analysis of social structure will reveal in broad terms to what extent the order and operation of society depend on conceptions of the supernatural and activities related to it; that is, the extent to which a society is secularized. Short of a complete analysis of the social system, various social facts may serve as indications of secularization, although these vary in specificity and relevance from one social and cultural context to another. Broadly, it may be said that the increasing specialization of function and role entailed in structural differentiation has invariably reduced the influence of religion over other social institutions. Religion in the West has generally become merely a department of the social order rather than the pervasive, or even determinant, influence it once was.

One may say that religious consciousness declines as empirical and matter-of-fact attitudes develop. Depictions of the supernatural become increasingly abstract, and its operation is regarded as remote, while individual convictions concerning obligation, dependence, and remorse appear to be less compelling. Recourse to the supernatural declines, whether as a means for the cognitive understanding of the world or for personal emotional support. There is less allusion to God's will as the guide for attitudes, comportment, and action, and resort to prayers or curses is less frequent. Religious symbols lose their vibrancy and meaning, and charms, rosaries, and crosses become largely decorative items, while magic—for example, in the form of popular astrology—becomes a titillating amusement. Everyday life is negotiated by pragmatic attitudes and cause-and-effect thinking.

As religious action (action directed toward the supernatural) is regarded as less effective in relation to worldly experience, so it diminishes in scope and scale. Religious observances cease to be obligatory to members of society and become entirely voluntary; this indicates, at the least, a diminished regard for such practices by state authorities. While the abandonment of obligatory religious practice may eliminate one set of extraneous motivations for religious action, it does not eradicate others; for example, traditional habits of life, conformity with custom, or the search for social prestige may continue as possible extrareligious inducements for participation in religious rituals and collective performances. The same social act, for instance churchgoing, baptism, or religious marriage or burial, may be prompted by different motives and carry widely different meanings in different cultural contexts. However, despite these considerations, church attendance, church memberships, *rites de passage,* grace at meals, public prayer, pilgrimages, votive offerings, fasting, penances, religious festivals, and church weddings all decline in incidence and in the depth of their sacrality.

To be significant in modern society, religion must be public and organized, a potential resource for all collective and public concerns, influencing the social system to operate in conformity with religious principles and with due regard to the supernatural. In the early evolution of modern societies, religious institutions occupied just such a position, but that influence has waned everywhere throughout the Christian West. This loss of social significance is manifested most explicitly in the diminishing proportion of social resources (taken, for instance, as a proportion of the gross national product) devoted to religion and to the maintenance of the personnel and property that serve supernaturalist goals. Labor, energy, skill, wealth, and time are increasingly employed for other than supernatural ends. Relative to population, the number of churches declines, as does the number of religious functionaries. The monetary remuneration and social status of clergy diminish relative to those of other professions. Ancillary agencies (schools, colleges, hospitals, social welfare facilities) pass from religious to lay, secular, and state control.

The application of the concept of secularization to society at large has an analogue in the process of change occurring within religious institutions per se. Not only is the wider society less influenced by religion, but religious institutions and behavior are themselves increasingly influenced by values and standards that prevail in the secular society. As society increasingly orders its affairs in accordance with technical and scientific criteria, religious institutions themselves are affected. The sacramentalist and sacerdotal orientations of religion become less congruous with the assumptions of everyday life, and the tendency in religious performance is for the distance between sacred and secular to diminish. The special language of liturgy is changed to accommodate secular understanding, organization is increasingly rationalized, economies of scale are sought through ecumenism, and activities necessarily adjust in duration, scheduling, style, and tenor to accommodate external secular constraints and preferences. Church leaders become less certain about the nature of the supernatural, less committed to dogma or the formal creeds to which on induction they subscribe, and increasingly devote themselves to good works, general moral exhortation, community activities within their congregations, fund raising for their churches, and occasional commentary on political issues. This pattern of change has been designated as the internal secularization of the churches.

SECULARIZATION AS A HISTORICAL PROCESS. Secularization has occurred throughout history, unevenly but in a broadly discernible pattern. In preliterate societies, apprehensions that may be considered supernaturalist were both ubiquitous and inextricably intermingled with empirical knowledge and rational techniques. Explanation invoked superempirical entities, social goals were confused with symbolic acts, and magical means were intermixed with pragmatic procedures. Steadily, the process, which Max Weber designated *die Entzauberung der Welt* ("the disenchantment of the world"), drained natural phenomena of their magico-religious meaning as people acquired more matter-of-fact, positivistic orientations.

In this analysis, magic may be subsumed with religion under the general rubric of supernaturalism; indeed, the establishment of a distinction between them may in itself be regarded as one aspect of the process of secularization. The development of monotheistic religions involved the rationalization and systematization of conceptions of the supernatural. This process, very evident in the history of Judaism, steadily extinguished the preexisting plethora of random, local magical ideas and local deities; it introduced a more universalistic spirit, made religious apprehensions ethical, and gradually established a coherent conception of an increasingly transcendent and universal deity. The monotheistic religions were themselves agencies of rationalization, and hence, insofar as they reduced the belief in supernaturalism, they were agencies of secularization. Magical beliefs and practices were not immediately eradicated; they sometimes persisted as subterranean currents reappearing periodically. Judaism and Protestantism were generally more effective secularizing agencies than Roman Catholicism, for although all three formally excoriated magic and folk belief, and sought to disseminate orderly, internally consistent teachings and practices, the Roman Catholic Church sometimes countenanced, absorbed, or accommodated pagan elements.

It is sometimes objected that to regard secularization as a cumulative, long-term historical trend necessarily implies the existence at some unspecified time of an unparalleled age of religious faith. Against this implication, it is argued that Christian history reveals the recurrent complaints of clerical authorities about unbelief, laxness in religious observances, and a variety of contingent derelictions. The historical evidence cannot be denied, but religiosity should not be equated with Christianity. Paganism and heresy were often indicted in the complaints about laxity, but these are manifestations not of the secularity of society but rather of its religiosity. Further, church religion and attendance are only two among many indicators of relative secularity; they intimate nothing either of religious consciousness or of the significance of religion (and its institutions) for the operation of the social system. As long as supernaturalist conceptions (of whatever sort) were effective in everyday life, or as long as religious institutions were sustained by the secular authorities and fulfilled functions as agencies of legitimation, official ideology, and social control, society had not yet experienced any radical modern process of secularization.

In recent Western history, dissociation of religious and political institutions, seen most conspicuously in the separation of church and state (now generally effective despite vestigial links that persist, for example, in England, Scotland, and the Scandinavian countries), implies the secularization of society. At times, ethnic and regional minorities have reinforced their distinctive identity and their political dissent by reasserting religious differences (as in Northern Ireland throughout this century, as in Lebanon in the 1970s and 1980s, or, much less dramatically, as in the Netherlands). In this same manner, societies in which religion has been associated with national independence have found religion to be a conveniently available means of rallying opposition to politically oppressive regimes (as in Communist Poland). Religion may, then, become a form of surrogate politics, but the continuing vigor of religion in such circumstances is artificially sustained by the prevailing political, ethnic, or regional situation. Where no such conditions prevail, the general course of secularization results in the increasing separation of religion from other institutions, most rapidly and markedly from those on which societal arrangements depend (law, politics, economics, and, eventually, education) and more slowly from those rooted in local community life (marriage, the family, and personal morality).

Against the dominant trend, there are occasional revivals of religion. What such movements achieve has not always been contrary to secular tendencies. Reform movements that seek to purge religion of cultural, traditional, or superstitious accretations may be almost explicitly secularizing in their impact. Even religious revivals that seek a return to what are taken to be pristine ideas and single-minded dedication may have the incidental consequences of eliminating elements of folk religiosity, of widening the gap between religion and other social institutions, of more narrowly specifying religion's social role, and of encouraging privatization by emphasizing personal piety. Reform movements such as Renaissance Humanism, Lutheranism, Calvinism, Deism, and Unitarianism were all secularizing forces within Christianity, purging faith and practice of immanentist conceptions of deity, progressively applying the canons of reason to doctrine, and reducing mystical, miraculous, sacramental, and sacerdotal claims. Revivalism, recurrent in eighteenth- and nineteenth-century Christendom (in Methodism, Holiness movements, and Pentecostalism, for example), ostensibly sought to enhance individual emotional commitment and certainly not to put religion to the test of rationality. Yet, expressive religiosity also came to demand discipline and order. When such movements, unencumbered by traditional liturgy and ritual, sought to socialize and organize their followings, they tended to do so by systematic rational procedures, sometimes adapting these from the secular society. Worship assumed forms closer to everyday styles, and the emphasis on subjective awareness, rather than on the supposed objective power of external ritual forms, led to a systematic demand for sustained and calculable performances from individual members. Arcane elements were replaced by goal-oriented methods of propaganda, mission, education, and mobilization. The demand for consistency, methodical regularity, and self-sustained individual responsibility conformed fully to the nature of demands being made in the context of secular employment. Even revivalist religion channeled secularizing tendencies into sections of the population as yet unsocialized.

Contemporary Manifestations. Just as religious institutions have ceased to be central in society, and just as society no longer endorses religious goals as its primary ends, so religious consciousness, although less visible as a phenomenon, appears also to have diminished. These different aspects of religiosity reveal varying degrees of persistence. Thus, the formal civic representation of the church in public life is more evident in societies, such as England, with established national churches than in the United States or Germany. Religious schools are more numerous in France and in Belgium (where state and church institutions are alternatives in many departments of social organization) than in England or the United States. Church attendance is significantly higher in North America than in northern Europe, and church membership in the United States is significantly higher than in England. Such national variations reflect different patterns and degrees of secularization. They do not predicate specific consequences (such as, for instance, a growth of atheism) or a determinate loss in church affiliation or in religious observance, even though these consequences often occur. Nor do they preclude the endurance of enclaves of persisting spirituality or the emergence of new expressions of religious commitment. The patterns vary and, despite other indicators of secularization, spiritual survivals and new religious initiatives do occur.

Even so, none of these manifestations of religiosity refutes the evidence of general secularization. Indeed, as religion loses significance in the public arena, it may expected that it will appear correspondingly more conspicuous in private life, commitment becoming more distinctive as it becomes more exceptional. Again, in some societies, involvement in church life may fulfill cultural or social functions little related to intrinsic religiosity, and its persistence at relatively high levels of participation (for example, in the United States) may relate more to traditions of voluntarism, the need for community identity, or a generalized search for surrogate national ideology than to the societal, or even the personal, significance of religious faith. Numerous new religious movements have emerged in recent decades, and these may even be seen as a response to general secularization: Because they provide meaning, purpose, association, and support for particular sections of the population, their appearance testifies to the inadequacy, irrelevance, or ineffectiveness of the mainstream churches, at least for this particular clientele. Given the traditional exclusivism of Christianity, religious pluralism, to which these new movements are conspicuous testimony, occurs only where secularization is relatively far advanced.

CAUSES. To unravel completely the complex tissue of causal agencies contributing to secularization would be tantamount to reconstructing the entire web of social history. Any trend as pervasive and persistent in the course of human affairs as this one must be extensively related to all other facets of social change. This article has noted the way in which conceptual order was developed and rationalized within the evolution of religion itself. Intellectuals (who themselves were often religious functionaries) were responsible for early secularization, but the initial marginalization of all supernaturalism is attributable to a deepening and more reflective apprehension of the natural order. The beginnings of science and, more generally, the development of empirical inquiry, detachment in observation and experimentation, and the sensed need for ordered, general concepts (incipient universalism) introduced new assumptions about nature and society. The rational and systematic coordination of empirical knowledge led both to the confutation of received supernaturalist conceptions and to an enhanced awareness of humankind's own capacity to harness nature and to organize its own economic and social well-being. Eventually, skepticism became steadily institutionalized in science, providing an implicit challenge to untested and untestable hypotheses, even though many early scientists such as Roger Bacon, Johannes Kepler, Isaac Newton, and Michael Faraday were persons whose thought encompassed both rationalist and mystic concerns.

The application of science, particularly to productive activities, and the evolution of new techniques reduced humans' sense of dependence on the divine. As society became industrialized and urbanized, increasing proportions of the population came to live their lives and make their livelihoods in ways more removed from nature. The possible intervention of the supernatural into everyday life became less plausible except in the interstices of social organization, that is, in marginal pursuits and interests, and even here only for the minority. New ways of thinking evolved as humans came to inhabit an environment that was progressively more and more a product of their own making. Magical, mystical, and metaphysical patterns of thought became steadily less congruous, particularly in all manifestly functional activities, which are governed by well-articulated structures of specific roles. Humanity's increased capacity to assess and supply its own needs led to the assumption that social well-being depended not on God's providence but on social planning. Whereas in earlier epochs the past had dominated the present—a past sacralized by the supposedly timeless truths of religion—modern society was future-oriented, and that future was mundane and material, no longer the future of post-mortem salvation in some supraterrestrial existence.

Social and geographic mobility, which occurred with increasing intensity in order to accommodate the productive demands and distributive rewards of technological society, promoted individualism and detached people from the stable communal contexts and the settled order of past generations in which religious predilections had themselves been rooted. Simultaneously, social organization became less dependent on the local community. The role-articulated social system necessarily made human beings into its calculable parts, while the social environment, following the natural environment before it, became increasingly human-made. Its rational structures elicited, through the role system, rational patterns of instrumental and impersonal action and neutralized, in relations with others, those personal, affective dispositions that religion had traditionally sought to summon and sustain. Eventually, even personal and intimate relationships became invaded by impersonal techniques—for example, in the matter of birth control—so that issues once thought to be very much in the realm of the sacred became matters of rational, calculated planning. Thus, the wider course of social change produced secular contexts and induced patterns of rational social action, as well as changes in individual consciousness that expunged ideas and assumptions about the supernatural and its derivative dispositions.

SECULARIZATION IN OTHER CONTEXTS. Secularization is a Western concept descriptive principally of a process that has occurred in Western society, most conspicuously during this century. Certainly, all the world religions in some degree disciplined and systematized immanentist conceptions and magical apprehensions and practices, but they did so with varying persistence and effectiveness. Hinduism and Buddhism, unlike Judaism and Christianity, absorbed or tolerated more primitive supernaturalism rather than excluding or eradicating it. Islam, although theoretically even more rigorously monotheistic than Christianity, lacked effective centralized organization with which to regulate local magical dispositions, which have widely persisted in Muslim societies into the present day. The long-term historical processes favoring secularization—the extension of rational principles to all areas of social life—were less intense and persistent in the Middle East and in Asia. Nonetheless, as industrialization occurs in developing societies, similar pressures accumulate toward the routinizing and rationalizing of work roles, social relationships, and the framework of social and civic order. Technological development brings similar consequences by reducing the significance of religion for the operation of the social system. Yet, since so many local manifestations of immanentist religiosity persist in these contexts, the paradox of a close juxtaposition of overtly magical practices alongside sophisticated industrial techniques is often found. The course of secularization follows a different path and occurs in different sequence from that familiar in the West.

In Latin America, profound religious changes have occurred with the still incipient process of technologization, and developments that were sequential in Europe have been contemporaneous on that continent. Thus, in recent decades there has been a rapid spread of Protestantism (apparently still carrying many facets of the work ethic); political radicalization has occurred (affecting the Roman Catholic church in significant respects); some separation of the Roman Catholic church from the dominant political structure has been effected; and quasi-magical movements (such as Umbanda and Kardecism in Brazil) have significantly rationalized their teaching and organization. Supernaturalism is being relocated within the social system by diverse patterns of change of a secularizing kind.

Some Islamic countries (e.g., Turkey, Egypt, and Tunisia) have undergone considerable secularization, but in others (e.g., Iran) the resurgence of fundamentalist movements indicates the strains accompanying this process and the extent to which, in the least sophisticated sections of society, religious dispositions can still be mobilized against modernization. A religion in which a specific and concrete system of law occupies so important a place cannot but find itself compromised by the exigencies of modern life. A similar situation, which is a source of conflict between orthodox and liberal (or nonreligious) parties, prevails in Israel, a secular state in which religion retains a unique ideological significance as the locus for a people so often exiled from its mythically promised land. In both Islam and Judaism, religiously enjoined behavior is subject to growing challenge from certain indispensable elements of a modern social system: a rational framework of law (both as an agency of social control and as a regulative instrument for contract); a systematic use of economic incentives and deterrents (whether through a free market or by socialist controls); the use of education to disseminate empirical knowledge, inculcate pragmatic attitudes, and teach rational procedures; and a political system concerned with economic well-being rather than with the implementation of religious principles. Nor is private life exempt from such challenges; for example, a prerequisite of rational social organization, in contradiction of Muslim and Jewish assumptions of male superiority, is equal rights for men and women, an idea that affects such matters as divorce, birth control, custody of children, remuneration for work, and even such customary matters as dress and comportment.

If secularization implied that what had decayed was necessarily a well-integrated and coherent religious tradition, then it might be maintained that this term was inappropriate to Japan, where diverse, loosely related, symbiotic religious traditions never constituted anything remotely equivalent to the "age of faith" of Christian Europe. Nonetheless, it is apparent from the plethora of its traditional magico-religious practices that Japan was eligible for secularization. The Japanese social system operates with only token reference to supernatural assumptions: The emperor is no longer divine. Most Japanese are only loosely attached to Buddhist temples or Shintō shrines. Ancestor worship has sharply declined in recent decades, and in the homes of young people, both the god-shelf (*kamidana*) and the memorial altar (*butsudan*) have become less common. Japan's technological advance has been so rapid, however, that magico-religious dispositions are still far from eclipsed; various magical practices continue in healing, fortune-seeking, and propitiatory acts, some of them institutionalized by the temples or in new religious movements. These phenomena occupy the interstices of institutional life, but they are as little accommodated to the increasingly rational socioeconomic order as is the Confucian precept of filial piety, which, today, is challenged by the premium that modern technology puts, not on age, but on youth.

In the largely village-centered society of India, religious dispositions remain perhaps more powerful than in most other parts of the world, even if they have less hold in the centers of population and industry. In a society with such strong religious and mystical traditions, the secularizing effects of social change are slow. Even so, the state now stands above religious particularism, declares itself to be a secular state, and has acted against religious tradition in official disavowal of the caste implications of Hinduism. Nor is secularization very apparent in Africa, where christianization and islamization are still proceeding and magic is far from displaced. If the term is to be applied to Africa, it must refer to a relatively early stage of a long-term historical process. Even among the dominant social strata in African states, not everyone has renounced magic, but as the echelons of technical and administrative personnel proliferate, education and experience of urban life are likely to make bush witchcraft less common. Christianity is still growing and still plays a significant role in various institutional spheres, particularly education and health, despite secularization of facilities by some states. Churches remain a powerful focus of voluntary allegiance and provide important links between local, poorly organized communal life and the incipient secularized societal system.

See Also Modernism; Modernity; Politics and Religion; Society and Religion.

Bibliography

There is an extensive, chiefly sociological, literature on various aspects of secularization and diffuse and scattered comment in the general literature on contemporary religion and society. For a comprehensive overview, see the "trend report" and bibliography by Karel Dobbelaere, "Secularization: A Multi-Dimensional Concept," constituting the entire issue of *Current Sociology* 29, no. 2 (Summer 1981). For theoretical discussions, see Richard K. Fenn's *Towards a Theory of Secularization* (Storrs, Conn., 1978) and his "The Process of Secularization: A Post-Parsonian View," *Journal for the Scientific Study of Religion* 9 (Summer 1970): 117–136. See also Niklas Luhmann's *Funktion der Religion* (Frankfurt, 1982). An account of secularization in diverse cultural and political contexts is provided in David Martin's *A General Theory of Secularization* (New York, 1978). Various facets are treated in the volume edited by Phillip E. Hammond, *The Sacred in a Secular Age* (Berkeley, Calif., 1985).

Secularization is a subject of controversy. For approaches that challenge the secularization thesis, see Talcott Parsons's

"Christianity and Modern Industrial Society," in *Sociological Theory, Values, and Sociocultural Change,* edited by Edward A. Tiryakian (New York, 1963); and Thomas Luckmann's "Theories of Religion and Social Change," *Annual Review of the Social Sciences of Religion* 1 (1977): 1–28. A range of controversial opinions and a debate is found in *The Culture of Unbelief,* edited by Rocco Caporale and Antonio Grumelli (Berkeley, Calif., 1971); and *La Secolarizzazione,* edited by Sabina S. Acquaviva and Gustavo Guizzardi (Bologna, 1973).

For non-Western countries, see *The Protestant Ethic and Modernization: A Comparative View,* edited by S. N. Eisenstadt (New York, 1968); Ethel Dunn and Stephen P. Dunn's "Religious Behaviour and Socio-Cultural Change in the Soviet Union," in *Religion and Atheism in the U. S. S. R. and Eastern Europe,* edited by Bohdan R. Bociurkiw and John W. Strong (Toronto, 1975); Tamaru Noriyoshi's "The Problem of Secularization: A Preliminary Analysis," *Japanese Journal of Religious Studies* 6 (March–June 1979): 89–114; and *Cultural Identity and Modernization in Asian Countries* (Tokyo, 1983), published by Kokugakuin University.

New Sources

Barker, Eileen, James Beckford, and Karel Dobbelaere, eds. *Secularization, Rationalism, and Sectarianism: Essays in Honor of Bryan R. Wilson.* New York, 1993.

Bruce, Steve. *God Is Dead: Secularization in the West.* Religion in the Modern World series. Malden, Mass., 2002.

Crimmins, James, ed. *Religion, Secularization and Political Thought.* London, 1989.

Dobbelaere, Karel. "Towards an Integrated Perspective of the Processes Related to the Descriptive Content of Secularization." *Sociology of Religion* 60 (1999): 229–247.

Fenn, Richard, ed. *The Blackwell Companion to Sociology of Religion.* Malden, Mass., 2001.

Smith, Christian, ed. *The Secular Revolution: Power, Interests, and Conflicts in the Secularization of American Life.* Berkeley, 2003.

Starck, Rodney. "Secularization, RIP." *Sociology of Religion* 60 (1999): 249–273.

BRYAN R. WILSON (1987)
Revised Bibliography

SEDNA. The concept of an owner, or master, of the animals appears in many hunting and fishing societies. For the Inuit (Eskimo) of Canada and Greenland, for whom sealing was of vital importance, this powerful being was the mistress of seals and other sea animals. Franz Boas, in his monograph about the Inuit on Baffin Island (1888), gave her name as Sedna, which probably means "the one down there." Other Inuit groups referred to the Sea Woman under different names, such as *Nerrivik* (Polar Inuit, "the place of the food") and *Nuliajuk* (Netsilik Inuit, "the lubricious one").

An origin myth tells how Sedna was once a girl who was thrown overboard from a vessel. While she tried to hang on, her fingers were cut off at the joints. She sank to the bottom of the sea, the segments of her fingers turning into sea mammals, and she became the Sea Woman, who was in control of these animals. According to some Iglulik Inuit and Baffin Islanders, she also ruled over the souls of those who had gone to the undersea land of the dead.

Variants of this myth have been recorded from many localities in Greenland and Canada, but from Alaska only a single reference exists. In some variants an orphan girl is thrown overboard, but more often the myth begins with the story of a girl who was fooled into marrying a petrel that had taken on human form. When her father tried to rescue his unhappy daughter and to take her away, the petrel pursued them and stirred up a heavy storm. The father tried to pacify the petrel by throwing his daughter overboard. When she tried to cling to the side of the boat, her father cut off her fingers at the first joint. Her fingertips fell into the sea and became small seals. When she again grasped the side of the boat, her father cut off her fingers at the next joint; these segments fell into the sea and became big, bearded seals. When she still clung to the side of the boat with the stumps of her fingers, her father cut them off at the last joint, and these segments turned into walruses. Sometimes the order of the creation of the sea animals is different, with whales being created first (the girl's nails are associated with baleen), followed by small seals and bearded seals.

In some variants the girl's father forces her to marry a dog because she has refused to marry. Her children become Indians, white people, and so on. In this way the mother of the sea animals is made the mother of men as well; as such, she represents the female principle of the world.

According to Inuit belief, the Sea Woman had the power to withhold the sea animals when certain hunting, birth, and death taboos had been broken. In Greenland it was told that the transgressions would materialize as dirt in the Sea Woman's hair, making her feel uncomfortable; because she had no fingers, she was unable to comb her hair. During a séance, the shaman, whose job it was to rectify this situation, would undertake a journey to the Sea Woman while the others attending the séance would sit silently in the darkness. Before the shaman could comb Sedna's hair he had to fight her. Afterward, she would set the sea animals free, and the shaman would return—that is, wake from his trance—and make the good result known.

In Greenland, ritual wife-exchanges were sometimes held in order to please the Sea Woman and to ensure good hunting, but otherwise the Sea Woman's ritual role was less important there than in Canada, even if myths about shamans' dangerous travels to her undersea house were well known.

In Canada, powerful shamans would draw the Sea Woman up and make her promise to send seals, or the shamans would themselves visit her in the sea. Among the Copper Inuit a shaman might be possessed by the Sea Woman and during a séance tell what caused the lack of seals. Then the participants would quickly admit the taboos they had broken. The dangerous situation was neutralized when its cause was made known.

The Inuit on Baffin Island held great feasts, lasting several days, in which Sedna was ritually killed. These calendar feasts took place in the autumn when sealing was prevented by storms that broke the ice open. Sedna was harpooned through a coiled thong on the floor, which represented a seal's breathing hole. A shaman followed her and stabbed her, thereby cleansing her of the transgressions of taboos that had taken place the previous year (and thereby securing that she no longer would withhold the sea animals). When the lamps were lit again after the séance, blood was seen on the harpoon point and the knife; the blood was an omen of good hunting in the future.

One of the rites that took place as part of the Sedna feast at this change of season was a tug-of-war between those born in the summer and those born in the winter. The result predicted the weather. During the Sedna feast of Baffin Island, normal social bonds were temporarily dissolved when a ritual wife-exchange took place under the leadership of disguised figures representing spirits. These figures were later ritually killed and then revived with a drink of water in the same way as killed seals were given a drink.

Seals and other sea animals were the basis of the existence of nearly all Inuit. The relationship with the Sea Woman was therefore important but very sensitive: she not only controlled these animals, they originated from her.

BIBLIOGRAPHY

The classic description of the Sedna cult on Baffin Island is to be found in Franz Boas's *The Central Eskimo* (1888; reprint, Lincoln, Nebr., 1964). Boas has also published the only reference to the Sea Woman by Inuit from Alaska in his article "Notes on the Eskimo of Port Clarence, Alaska," *Journal of American Folklore* 7 (1894): 205–208. Erik Holtved analyzed the variants of the Sea Woman myth through the use of the historical-geographical method in his article "The Eskimo Myth about the Sea-Woman: A Folkloristic Sketch," *Folk* 8/9 (1966–1967): 145–153. A structural analysis of the myth can be found in Rémi Savard's piece "La déesse sous-marine des Eskimos," in *Échanges et communications: Mélanges offerts à Claude Lévi-Strauss*, vol. 2, edited by Jean Pouillon and Pierre Maranda (The Hague, 1970), pp. 1331–1355. John F. Fisher's article "An Analysis of the Central Eskimo Sedna Myth," *Temenos* (Helsinki) 11 (1975): 27–42, includes a summary of previous analyses of the Sedna myth.

INGE KLEIVAN (1987)

SEFER YETSIRAH (Book of creation) is an ancient Jewish cosmogonical and cosmological treatise that forms part of the literature of Qabbalah; falsely attributed to Abraham the patriarch and to ʿAqivaʾ ben Yosef, a second-century tanna. Composed of six short chapters, it describes God's creation of the world by means of the ten cosmic numbers (*sefirot*) and the twenty-two letters of the Hebrew alphabet.

The date of composition of *Sefer yetsirah* is the subject of controversy among scholars. Gershom Scholem assigns it to the tannaitic period (second to third centuries CE), whereas N. Aloni argued that it is a work of the eighth or ninth century, written under the influence of Arabic linguistics. The treatise is extant in two main versions, one short and one long, without major divergences in ideas between them. It has been translated into several European languages.

A major contribution of *Sefer yetsirah* is its discussion of the magical properties inherent in combinations of letters and the use of these combinations in the creation of the universe. The book's explanation of the proper pronunciation of the letters was the earliest phonetic theory introduced in Judaism. *Sefer yetsirah* also develops a system of correspondence between the Hebrew letters and the limbs of the human body.

The influence of the treatise was felt strongly in several trends in Jewish thought. It affected the development of early Jewish philosophy as in the case of Saʿadyah Gaon (882–942) and his contemporary Dunash ibn Tamim. Avraham ibn ʿEzraʾ wrote a commentary on it, although it has since been lost. Ashkenazic Hasidism, or German Pietists, of the early thirteenth century produced several commentaries, of which three are still extant: the first by Elʿazar of Worms, the second falsely attributed to Saʿadyah Gaon, and the third by Elḥanan ben Yaqar. Almost all the early qabbalists of Provence and Spain wrote commentaries in a theosophic vein; the important ones are those of the thirteenth-century qabbalists Yitsḥaq Sagi Nahor (also known as Yitsḥaq the Blind), ʿAzriʾel of Gerona, and Moses Nahmanides. According to the German pietists and some qabbalists, the permutations of letters and holy names discussed in *Sefer yetsirah* may be used by initiates to create a *golem,* or humanoid creature. The medieval qabbalists also developed elaborate theories of the *sefirot* as divine manifestations.

In the second half of the thirteenth century, *Sefer yetsirah* became the starting point of the ecstatic Qabbalah of Avraham Abulafia, who was influenced by Barukh Togrami's highly esoteric commentary *Maftehot ha-Qabbalah* (Keys of the Qabbalah). The most important of Abulafia's several treatises on *Sefer yetsirah* is *Otsar ʿeden ganuz* (Bodleian Manuscript 1580). The techniques of letter combination described in *Sefer yetsirah* were developed by Abulafia and his school for use in ecstatic practices.

The commentary of the fourteenth-century Spanish qabbalist Yosef ben Shalom Ashkenazi, erroneously attributed in print to Avraham ben David of Posquières, is a classic work that influenced the "practical Qabbalah" of Isaac Luria. Meʾir ibn Avi Sahula compiled in 1331 a lengthy and eclectic commentary (Rome-Angelica Manuscript 45). Since the fifteenth century only a few commentaries have been composed, notably those of Mosheh Cordovero in the sixteenth century and Eliyyahu ben Shelomoh Zalman (known as the Vilna Gaon) in the eighteenth century.

BIBLIOGRAPHY

Aloni, N. "Ha-shiṭah ha-angramatit shel ha-millonut ha-ʿivrit be-sefer yetsirah," and "Sefer yetsirah nusaḥ Rasag be-tsurat megillah mi-genizat Qahir," and "Zeman ḥibbur sefer yetsirah." In *Temirin,* 2 vols., edited by Israel Weinstock. Jerusalem, 1972–1980.

Epstein, Abraham. *Mi-qadmoniyyot ha-Yehudim.* Jerusalem, 1957. See pages 38–46, 179–225.

Gruenwald, Ithamar. "A Preliminary Critical Edition of Sefer Yezira." *Israel Oriental Studies* 1 (1971): 132–177.

Scholem, Gershom. *On the Kabbalah and Its Symbolism.* New York, 1965. See pages 158–204.

Scholem, Gershom. *Les origines de la Kabbale.* Paris, 1966. See pages 33–44.

Séd, Nicolas. "Le Memar samaritain: Le Sefer Yesira et les trente-deux sentiers de la Sagesse." *Revue de l'histoire des religions* 170 (1960): 159–184.

Vajda, Georges. "Nouveaux fragments arabes du commentaire de Dunash B. Tamin." *Revue des études juives* 113 (1954): 37–61.

Vajda, Georges. "Deux nouveaux fragments arabes du commentaire de Dunas B. Tamim." *Revue des études juives* 122 (1963): 149–162.

Vajda, Georges. "Saʿadya commentateur du Livre de la Création." In *Mélanges Georges Vajda,* edited by G. E. Weil, pp. 37–69. Hildesheim, 1982.

Weinstock, Israel. "Le-verur ha-nusah shel sefer yetsirah" and "Le-havharat ofyo shel sefer yetsirah." In *Temirin,* 2 vols., edited by Israel Weinstock. Jerusalem, 1972–1980.

MOSHE IDEL (1987)

SEIDEL, ANNA KATHARINA. Anna K. Seidel (1938–1991) was an eminent sinologist and international authority on Daoism. Seidel was born in Berlin and raised primarily in Munich. Although the family was Roman Catholic, one of Seidel's grandparents was Jewish and her parents sheltered two Jewish friends amid the dangers of Nazi Germany. This made a strong impression on Seidel, shaping a commitment to tolerance and to an international, rather than specifically national, identity. Her family was also the setting for her first, albeit informal, introduction to Chinese culture: a Korean boarder in the Seidel home taught Anna to write Chinese characters and rigorously drilled her on correct forms. Formal sinological training began at the University of Munich (1958–1960) and the University of Hamburg (1960–1961). Seidel was the recipient of a prestigious Studienstiftung des Deutschen Volkes scholarship award, and in 1961 she moved to Paris for graduate studies. She trained from 1961 to 1968 at the École Pratique des Hautes Études at the Collège de France. In 1969 Seidel was made a member of the École Française d'Extrême-Orient in Kyoto, Japan. She moved to Kyoto and lived there until her death twenty-two years later, with interludes in the United States as a visiting professor at the University of Hawai'i in 1978 and at the University of California, Santa Barbara, in 1988.

In Kyoto, Seidel worked at the École Française d'Extrême-Orient's Institut du Hōbōgirin with colleague Hubert Durt, where they continued Paul Demiéville's work redacting the *Hōbōgirin,* a multivolume encyclopedic work of Sino-Japanese Buddhist terms. In addition to her editorial work, Seidel contributed several articles to this encyclopedia, a testament to her expertise and interest in Buddhism. Seidel originally had been attracted to Buddhist studies as a topic for her graduate training. However, when she arrived in Paris she found that the most dynamic and relatively untouched field in Sinology was Daoism, and Paris had become the center of Daoist studies. It is for her work in Daoism that Seidel achieved her international reputation. Seidel's mentors, Max Kaltenmark and Rolf A. Stein, were leaders in this field, and Seidel quickly became a key figure in securing the preeminence of the French school in Daoist studies.

Seidel's contributions were made in conjunction with a radical redefinition of Daoism. In the nineteenth and early twentieth centuries, Daoism was understood to have two forms. One was the much admired, pure "philosophical Daoism" of Laozi and Zhuangzi, consisting of whimsical, engaging stories and a poetic, mystical vision of the cosmos. The other was deemed superstitious, the "religious Daoism" of imperial China, with esoteric ritual and "demon worship," which scholars disdained to study. Frequently this "debased Daoism" was not distinguished from the loosely organized and largely illiterate popular religious tradition. Beginning with the pioneering work of Henri Maspero in the 1920s, which was based on careful study of the hitherto ignored Daoist canon, Daoism came to be seen as a complex, coherent, integrated religion in which both religious and philosophical aspects were intertwined, forming what Seidel later called the "native high religion of China." Seidel's doctoral thesis, "La divinisation de Lao-tseu dans le taoïsme des Han" (The deification of Laozi in Han dynasty Daoism, 1969) is a powerful and influential study based on Han documents that demonstrates this approach. It shows a pivotal development in the history of Daoism: the transformation of the sage Laozi into a god. In addition to revealing the importance and centrality of Laozi as a deity, Seidel wrote seminal articles about another key but unstudied aspect of Daoism, the messianic teachings and millenarian appeal of Daoist schools. Seidel described the elaborate organization of the "Taocracy" of early imperial China that combined Daoism with the workings of state, as well as the important role of Daoism throughout imperial China as a more personal, often salvific religion that provided a means to cope with death and uncertainty.

Seidel's fresh approach was captured in the entry on "Taoism" in the fifteenth edition of the *Encyclopaedia Britannica* (1974). In addition to demonstrating the important developments in Daoism, the article emphasized the complementary, rather than antagonistic, relationship of Confucianism and Daoism. Seidel showed that both drew on an ancient Chinese cosmology and religiosity that posits the harmonious, organic working between the human realm and heaven and earth, mediated by the ruler; the cyclic nature of change and transformation of the cosmos; and the veneration of and protection afforded by ancestors. Other aspects of Daoism, such as the ecstatic states described in the *Zhuangzi* and the meditation and self-perfection exercises of later schools, had roots in ancient shamanic practices and ideas of bodily and mental self-perfection. In her work, Seidel demonstrated the profound but often subtle influence of Daoism on Chinese culture, including Daoism's interaction with the imported Indian tradition of Buddhism. Seidel's work was based on a thorough examination of documents that she analyzed in the appropriate historical and cultural context, occasionally drawing connections to contemporary phenomena.

Seidel not only promoted Sinology, but was passionate about cooperation between colleagues of different nationalities and the formation of a truly international scholarly community. To that end, her residence in Kyoto was famous as a haven and meeting place for young scholars from Europe, North America, and Asia. Seidel would encourage and assist young colleagues, often lending materials from her private library. She participated in the Bellagio conference on Daoism in 1968, and the Tateshina conference in 1972, events that saw a gathering of Daoist experts from around the globe. With Holmes Welch, to whom she was briefly married, Seidel co-edited a volume of essays that grew from the Tateshina conference, *Facets of Taoism* (1979). In 1985, Seidel founded *Cahiers d'Extrême-Asie*, a highly regarded French and English bilingual journal published by École Française d'Extrême-Orient. An express aim of this journal was to bring together the scholarly communities from various continents. Seidel exemplified this in her own work, writing eloquently in German, English, French, and Japanese. She continued making scholarly contributions up until the end of her life, despite serious illness. Her "Chronicle of Taoist Studies in the West 1950–1990" was issued in print weeks before her untimely death in San Francisco in 1991 at age 53; "Mountains and Hells: Religious Geography in Japanese Mandara Paintings" and other articles were published posthumously.

BIBLIOGRAPHY

Seidel, Anna K. *La divinisation de Lao tseu dans le taoïsme des Han.* Paris, 1969; reprinted 1992.

Seidel, Anna K. "A Taoist Immortal of the Ming Dynasty: Chang San-feng." In *Self and Society in Ming Thought*, edited by W. Theodore de Bary, pp. 483–531. New York and London, 1970.

Seidel, Anna K. "The Image of the Perfect Ruler in Early Taoist Messianism: Lao tzu and Li Hung." *History of Religions* 9 (1969/1970): 216–247.

Seidel, Anna K., and Michel Strickmann. "Taoism." In *Encyclopaedia Britannica*, 15th ed., vol. 17, pp. 1034–1044. Chicago, 1974.

Seidel, Anna K. "Buying One's Way to Heaven: The Celestial Treasury in Chinese Religions." *History of Religions* 17 (1978): 419–431.

Seidel, Anna K., and Holmes Welch, eds. *Facets of Taoism: Essays in Chinese Religion.* New Haven, 1979.

Seidel, Anna K. "Taoist Messianism" *Numen* 31, no. 2 (1983): 161–174.

Seidel, Anna K. "Imperial Treasures and Taoist Sacraments" In *Tantric and Taoist Studies in Honor of Rolf A. Stein*, edited by Michel Strickmann, vol. 2, pp. 291–371. Brussels, 1981–1983.

Seidel, Anna K. "Post-mortem Immorality, or the Taoist Resurrection of Body." In *Gilgul: Essays on Transformation, Revolution, and Permanence in the History of Religions*, edited by Shaul Shaked, David Dean Shulman, Gedaliahu A. G. Stroumsa, dedicated to J. Zwi Werblowsky, pp. 223–237. Leiden, 1987.

Seidel, Anna K. "Chronicle of Taoist Studies in the West 1950–1990." *Cahiers d'Extrême-Asie* 5 (1989–1990): 223–347.

Seidel, Anna K. "Mountains and Hells: Religious Geography in Japanese Mandara Paintings." *Studies in Central and East Asian Religions* 5–6 (1992–1993): 122–133.

Seidel, Anna K. *Taoismus, die inoffizielle Hochreligion Chinas.* Tokyo, 1990. Translated into English as "Taoism: The Unofficial High Religion of China." *Taoist Resources* 7, no. 2 (1997): 39–72. Translated into French as "*Taoïsme*, religion non-officielle de la Chine." *Cahiers d'Extrême-Asie* 8 (1995): 1–39.

Seidel, Anna K. "Descente aux enfers et redemption des femmes dans le bouddhisme populaire japonais—le pèlerinage du Mont Tateyama." *Cahiers d'Extrême-Asie* 9 (1996-1997): 1–14.

An extensive bibliography of Seidel's works is found with her obituary by Fabrizio Pregadio in *Taoist Resources* 3, no. 2 (1992): 67–71. Another comprehensive list of her works appears in *Cahiers d'Extrême-Asie* 8 (1995): xix–xxi. Among the twenty obituaries in scholarly journals, those published in *Numen* 38, no. 2 (1991): 283–284 and the *Japanese Journal of Religious Studies* 17, no. 1 (1992): 1–3, are most easily accessible. A more personal account of Seidel's work and life is Phyllis Brook Schafer's "Discovering a Religion," *Taoist Resources* 4, no. 2 (1993): 1–8.

JENNIFER OLDSTONE-MOORE (2005)

SELK'NAM RELIGION. The Selk'nam (also known as the Ona) inhabited the largest island of the Tierra del Fuego archipelago, the Isla Grande. The population of the Selk'nam and their neighbors the Haush (Mánekenka), who lived in the southeastern tip of the island and had a similar culture, was estimated by Martin Gusinde (1931) at approximately four thousand in 1880. During the final decades of the nineteenth century most of the Indians either were slaughtered by the white colonizers or died of diseases brought by them. In 1919 Gusinde (1931) counted 279 Selk'nam and Haush. Fifteen years later, following several epidemics, there were fewer than one hundred. When this author first went to Tierra del Fuego in 1965 there were about fifteen Selk'nam and Haush, including the mestizos. In 1985 there were four, all of whom spoke fluent Spanish and three of whom also had some knowledge of the Selk'nam language. This author had the privilege of working, as an ethnologist, with the last woman shaman, Lola Kiepja, who died October 9, 1966, and during the years that followed with many of the remaining Selk'nam.

The Selk'nam and the Haush were strictly a land-bound people. They were seminomadic hunters. Their most valued game was the guanaco, genetically related to the llama, vicuña, and alpaca. As the Indians were frequently on the move, they used guanaco skins lashed to poles and trees for shelter, though on occasion they built log huts in the form of tipis. They divided their island into a number of territories, called *haruwen,* that were occupied by patrilinear and patrilocal exogamic lineages. Each *haruwen* was associated with one of the four cardinal points, called *shó'on* ("sky"). These were also exogamic units. Although the boundaries of each *haruwen* were well known, they were not always respected. Trespassing was one of the main causes of conflict among the Selk'nam. Another cause for contention was vengeance for the death of a kinsman alleged to have been killed by the supernatural power of a shaman of some other *haruwen.*

The Selk'nam language is related to that of the Tehuelche Indians, former inhabitants of the Patagonian mainland just north of the Strait of Magellan. The language spoken by the Haush has not yet been classified.

The oral tradition of the Selk'nam and Haush was extremely rich and vital. What is termed mythology and shamanism were to them not only explanations or symbolic interpretations of the why and how of "being in the world," but were also inspirations that generated inquiries, stimulated new questions, and revived debate on old ones in the group's constant search for comprehension of the ordering and contradictions of the intangible cosmos and its tangible earthly manifestations.

MYTHOLOGY. It is not surprising that Selk'nam and Haush mythology concerns itself with origins, of which the fountainhead is Pémaulk, or Témaukel, whom Gusinde identified with the supreme being. Unlike the God of the Judeo-Christian tradition, Témaukel is an abstract concept. Though Témaukel is the source of all that exists, it is not an anthropomorphic deity, and therefore it is not accessible to expressions of human aspirations and feelings.

Some of the more tangible subjects of the oral traditions are personages of the previous, prehuman epoch (*hóowin*); these superhuman immortals subsequently became transformed into elements of nature. Moon, as a mighty shaman and incontestable leader of the matriarchy, is the dominant figure of the prehuman epoch; she survives as the actual moon, the symbol of the female threat to the male domination of society, that is, of the dangers of a revival or resurgence of the mythological matriarchy of the *hóowin* epoch.

Because the world has become what it is, Moon has not forgiven the men for provoking her downfall and the destruction of the matriarchy over which she reigned as the all-powerful matron. Even as late as the nineteenth century when the moon entered into an eclipse, the men were wary, frightened, and even fraught with anguish. The reddish tint of the moon was interpreted as a sign of the blood of the men who were to be killed in coming battles and whose deaths were part of her vengeance. The shamans were thought to know by means of their dreams when such an eclipse was to occur. The spirits (*wáiuwen*) of the shamans soared into the heavens to visit her and to discover upon whom her wrath was to fall. Male shamans were in special danger of being "seized by the Moon," for she considered them to have caused her disgrace.

During an eclipse the people who lived nearby gathered to appease Moon's anger. If there were no shaman in camp during an eclipse, the people extinguished the fires in their dwellings and simply huddled under their guanaco capes until the danger passed, remaining silent or speaking only in whispers. When a shaman was present he ordered them to extinguish the domestic fires and to gather around him. The shaman daubed a red circle of paint on each cheek to represent the moon. He also donned a special headdress made of the feathers of a certain hawk. Meanwhile the women painted their bodies red and drew a white stripe across their faces from ear to ear, under the nose. While the women made sweeping movements toward the moon with long sticks or with their guanaco capes to drive away the eclipse, to appease Moon they chanted, "Beautiful heart. Ample face." Then the shaman sang to prepare his spirit to soar to Moon's sanctuary, imitating the call of the hawk as it flies high into the sky, just as the shaman's spirit traveled through the nocturnal heavens to Moon's abode. As he felt his spirit soaring, he repeatedly chanted, "Let us go to the Daughter of the Sky." Moon awaited the arrival of the shamans' spirits. If she disdained a shaman, his spirit would be drawn into her shadow, beneath her knees, and the shaman on earth would know that he was doomed to perish in an approaching combat. He would lament his fate, chanting, "Moon has my headdress beneath her knees." In protest, the women would insult her, singing, "Moon—burnt face. Moon—face full of rage" (Chapman, 1972, chants nos. 5 and 32, and 1982, p. 73).

RITUAL. During the great ceremony called Hain, which sometimes lasted a year or even longer, the young men (*klóketen*) were initiated into adult life. All the men had to be initiated and were obliged to submit to the ordeals and hardships of at least one, or even two or three, separate ceremonies—that is, until the elders were satisfied with their outward and inward signs of maturity. The Hain ceremony also sought to reinforce male dominance over the women. The men's power, the patriarchy, was thought to derive not from legitimacy of any kind, but rather from the fact that the men were in control of the secret that the superhuman men of legendary times (of *hóowin*) had wrested from the women. This had taken place at the time when the formidable male shamans shattered the matriarchy, forcing the great female leader and shaman, Moon, to flee to the heavens and killing all the women in the ceremonial hut, that is, all the females except for the young uninitiated girls and babies who were not in the hut.

The "secret" the men thought they were keeping from the women was that the spirits who appeared in the Hain ceremony were not supernatural, but only men disguised by masks and paints. All the spirits, male and female alike, were impersonated by the men except for the terrifying female from the underworld, Xálpen, a being reputed to be half flesh and half rock, human-eating, voracious, and raging. From within the ceremonial hut the men voiced her cries and the groans she made when she gave birth to a beautiful creature, the baby K'terrnen. Only rarely did Xálpen emerge from the ceremonial hut onto the "stage" in view of the women, and then always as an effigy (constructed of bows tied together to form a large oblong shape that was filled with branches, grass, and weeds to give it body and covered with guanaco hides). The men would push this "monster" onto the stage to overawe the women. But all was not frightening to the women. For instance, they chanted with joy when the baby K'terrnen (in reality a slim *klóketen* disguised with down pasted to his body and to his mask) appeared on the stage. They also were much amused by other frequently repeated scenes, such as that of the faithless wife, the lovely Kula (also a young *klóketen*), who descended from the heavens to be wooed by excited admirers, much to the chagrin of her pitiful husband, Koshmink, whose frenzies of jealousy provoked laughter and derision among the women.

The religious content of this ceremony may not be apparent from this very brief description, nor in the long, minutely detailed account of it provided by Gusinde (1931), but it is implicit in his study and is revealed by the information given the author of this article by some of the last Selk'nam (Chapman, 1982). It consists in the conviction of the women that the Hain spirits were real, even though they may well have known that the men were impersonating them (they were very cautious not to reveal their knowledge to the men). And the men also believed in the spirits. In the case of one very important spirit—Shoort, the husband of Xálpen—the "actor" had to perform certain rituals before disguising himself. That is, the ceremony was not simply an initiation ritual and a hoax to fool the women and justify the patriarchy, it was also an enactment, a representation, of sacred nature, and it was taken very seriously by all the participants, despite its moments of profane hilarity. The Hain ceremony is a beautiful example of the immense range of feelings and sentiments, of ritual and dramatic actions, a symbolic system can create.

The mourning ritual was another expression of religious faith. As the living grieved the loss of a beloved one, they darkened their bodies with black paint made from coals of the fire and chanted laments that each adult inherited from a near kinsman. Moreover, mourners had the right to chant a lament of the "sky" (*shó'on*) with which they were associated. While chanting, mourners at times would lacerate their bodies with sharpened stones or mussel shells until they bled profusely. Another sign of mourning was the shaved crown of the head. Individuals might chant and lacerate themselves for months or even several years following the death of a loved one, especially a son or daughter. When someone well known died, fires would be lit as signals to neighbors to come and participate in the ritual, and if the deceased had been a renowned shaman or hunter, part of the bush or forest would be set on fire to show that his land too was mourning.

The corpse was usually buried near the dwellings, but with no external evidence of the tomb on the surface of the ground. The site was respectfully avoided for some time. Also, the name of the deceased was not pronounced for years following his or her death. Although Gusinde (1931) states that the soul *(kaspi)* of the dead joined the supreme being, Témaukel, beyond the stars, my informants declared that the soul achieved a new being in the realms of the "skies" of infinity, the sky with which the deceased had been associated in life.

The last Selk'nam shaman, Lola Kiepja, sang these words the year she died: "I follow the trail . . . of those who departed. . . . I want to speak of the *cordillera* [Span., "mountain range"]. . . . Those of infinity gave it [power] to me. I receive it. . . . They speak beautifully, they of infinity of Ham-nia [the *cordillera* of infinity of the western sky]" (Chapman, 1972, chants nos. 1 and 3).

SHAMANISM. The shamans (*xo'on*) were held in great esteem for their curing abilities and supernatural power, called *wáiuwen.* But they were also feared, especially those reputed to possess the faculty of throwing a sickness a great distance or provoking instant death simply by staring at a victim. Although all the shamans could cure by drawing sickness out of the body of the patient, not all could "kill" or inflict illnesses. Very few female shamans had such power, and most were exclusively dedicated to curing.

Before beginning to perform, the shamans would don special headgear made of guanaco hide adorned with feathers of certain birds and decorate their faces with painted designs. Supernatural power, *wáiuwen,* took possession of them only when they achieved a trance state, which was induced by self-hypnosis, through chanting and concentration. No stimulants were employed. Once they were in a trance, their singing and body movements would become almost automatic. Experienced shamans would usually require thirty to forty minutes to produce this state of mind. During the séances, they would jump and leap about, pounding their feet and even fists on the ground, vigorously shaking their fur capes to increase the excitement and as a kind of accompaniment to their chants. This sort of extreme tension, however, did not last for the entire period of the trance. In order to cure, the shamans had to pay strict attention to their patients.

Other than provoking death and curing, the shamans were expected to control the weather. Moreover, the male shamans were solicited to predict the outcome of a feud or combat and to aid in the hunt. Certain shamans achieved great fame by attracting whales to shore and killing them with invisible arrows. Others could bewitch guanacos, certain birds, and seals, and even create an abundance of mussels or fish.

The shamans were highly competitive and challenged one another to ordeals, each attempting to demonstrate the superior power of their *wáiuwen.* There were several sorts of ordeals, but only the most expert and daring male shamans would venture to perform the ordeal of the arrow called Kuash-metchen. The shaman, having achieved a trance state, concentrates on his body, more specifically, on "preparing" the canal through which he is to insert the arrow (made entirely of wood and smaller than those used in the hunt). Completely naked, he massages himself as he chants. When he feels ready, he pierces himself with the arrow just below the collar bone and cautiously draws the arrow under his skin, diagonally across his chest, removing it at his waist. Or he might insert the arrow on one side of his waist and move it across his body, extracting it at the opposite side. While performing the feat he chants repeatedly "My body is in darkness. I am myself piercing it with an arrow." (Lola Kiepja recorded this chant; see Chapman, 1972, chant no. 22.) Though the competing shamans would not necessarily meet nor perform at the same time, this feat had to be witnessed by a public. Of the three shamans whom my informants had seen or heard about performing the ordeal, one died from the wounds shortly thereafter.

The shamans, even the most renowned, did not form a privileged sector of society, and neither did the "fathers and mothers of *láiluka*" (the sages) nor the "fathers [*chan-ain*] and mothers [*chan-am*] of the word" (the prophets). The sages were specialists in the tradition called *láiluka,* which consisted of the myths of origin, accounts of supernatural heroes, and of other "events" that took place during the *hóowin* epoch. The prophets had knowledge of the more mystical tradition, which was concerned with the more abstract symbols, such as the "skies" and the "invisible *cordilleras.*" Moreover, they were deemed capable of predicting the future of the local group and of the society as a whole. According to my data, in the last half of the nineteenth century, the prophets were also shamans or sages and some were both. The prophets were at the summit of the prestige hierarchy, but like the shamans and the sages they received little or no material compensations, and they performed the same tasks as others of their sex. The societies of the Selk'nam and the Haush, though highly individualistic and competitive, were, on this level, egalitarian.

The religion (mythology, shamanism, and rituals) can be analyzed in terms of a coherently articulated symbolic system. Though constantly modified, their religious system maintained a traditional structure and also the basic concepts that probably formed part of a millenarian tradition characteristic of other indigenous groups in America, and in Asia as well, and of archaic cultures the world around.

SEE ALSO Tehuelche Religion.

BIBLIOGRAPHY

Beauvoir, José M. *Los shelknam, indígenas de la Tierra del Fuego.* Buenos Aires, 1915.

Bridges, E. Lucas. *Uttermost Part of the Earth.* London, 1948.

Chapman, Anne. "Lola." *Natural History* 53 (1971): 33–41.

Chapman, Anne. Descriptive notes and translations for *Selk'nam (Ona) Chants of Tierra del Fuego, Argentina: Forty-Seven Shaman Chants and Laments.* Folkway Records, FE 4176. Cantometric analysis by Alan Lomax. New York, 1972.

Chapman, Anne. *Drama and Power in a Hunting Society: The Selk'nam of Tierra del Fuego.* Cambridge, 1982.

Cooper, John M. *Analytical and Critical Bibliography of the Tribes of Tierra del Fuego and Adjacent Territory.* Bureau of American Ethnology Bulletin, vol. 63. Washington, D.C., 1917.

Gallardo, Carlos R. *Tierra del Fuego: Los Onas.* Buenos Aires, 1910.

Gusinde, Martin. *Die Feuerland Indianer,* vol. 1, *Die Selk'nam.* Mödling, 1931. Translated as *Los indios de Tierra del Fuego* (Buenos Aires, 1982).

Lothrop, Samuel K. *The Indians of Tierra del Fuego.* New York, 1928.

Wilbert, Johannes. *Folk Literature of the Selknam Indians: Martin Gusinde's Collection of Selknam Narratives.* Berkeley, Calif., 1975.

New Sources

Bierhorst, John. *The Mythology of South America.* New York, 1988.

Borrego, Lius Alberto. "Pristine Archaeologists and the Settlement of the Southern South America." *Antiquity* 66 (September 1992): 768–771.

Borrego, Luis Alberto. *Los Selk'nam (Onas): Evolución Cultural en la Isla Grand Tierro del Fuego.* Buenos Aires, 1991.

ANNE CHAPMAN (1987)
Revised Bibliography

SEMANTICS conveniently divides into two branches, the theory of designation and/or denotation and the theory of meaning. The former constitutes *extensional,* the latter *intensional* semantics. Both branches are thus parts of the modern trivium of syntax, semantics, and pragmatics, which is often called "logical semiotics" for short. Semiotics is in fact modern logic in full dress, and is thought by many, especially perhaps at Oxford University, to occupy a central place in the study of the liberal arts. Syntax is the theory of signs as such and how they are interrelated to form longer signs, phrases, sentences, texts, and so on. In semantics, signs are interrelated in one way or another with the objects for which they stand. And in pragmatics the user of language is brought in fundamentally, as well as the various relations that he or she bears to signs and combinations of signs in particular occasions of use.

Signs are often understood in a broader, nonlinguistic sense to allow for "natural" signs, human artifacts, and the like. Thus a weathercock is a sign that the wind is blowing in a certain direction, smoke is a sign of fire, a stop sign on the highway is a sign to the driver, and so on. The study of nonlinguistic signs harks back to the medieval period and in the nineteenth century was given a considerable boost by the work of the American philosopher C. S. Peirce. Even so, it has not yet achieved the exactitude of logical semiotics and, pending such a development, remains somewhat controversial.

Designation is the fundamental relation between a sign and what it stands for. In the theory of meaning, much more is taken into account. Thus, in Frege's famous example, the phrases "the morning star" and "the evening star" designate the same object, the planet Venus, but differ considerably in meaning. What is meaning? No easy answer is forthcoming. In any adequate theory of it, however, account should surely be taken of the contexts, linguistic and nonlinguistic alike, in which signs or expressions are used, including, where needed, reference to the user.

A detailed history of semantical concepts, and of the broader domain of semiotical concepts, has not yet been written. Especially important here is the material in book 2 of Augustine's *On Christian Doctrine* and book 4 of Peter Lombard's *Book of Sentences* that sustains the doctrine of sacramental theology even to the present day. The contributions of the Scholastic logicians also constitute a rich mine of material that has not yet been sufficiently studied from a modern point of view. Logical semiotics, including semantics, has an important role to play in the study of the languages of theology, both those of fundamental theory and of particular religions.

BIBLIOGRAPHY

Bochenski, Joseph M. *A History of Formal Logic.* Notre Dame, Ind., 1961.

Deely, John. *Introducing Semiotics: Its History and Doctrines.* Bloomington, Ind., 1982.

Martin, R. M. *Truth and Denotation: A Study in Semantical Theory.* Chicago, 1958.

Martin, R. M. *Semiotics and Linguistic Structure.* Albany, N. Y., 1978.

New Sources

Houben, Han, Jac van Wout, and Ineke Sluiter, eds. *The Emergence of Semantics in Four Linguistic Traditions; Hebrew, Sanskrit, Greek, Arabic.* Amsterdam, 1997.

R. M. MARTIN (1987)
Revised Bibliography

SEMIOTICS SEE STRUCTURALISM

SEN, KESHAB CHANDRA

SEN, KESHAB CHANDRA (1838–1884), Indian social and religious reformer. Sen represented for many the prototype of the Indian intellectual who adjusted to the intrusion of the West into Indian society in the second half of the nineteenth century. He graduated from Hindu College, Calcutta, in 1856, and shortly thereafter came under the influence of Debendranath Tagore, the leader of the Brāhmo Samāj. Sen became one of the most ardent advocates of social and religious change, arguing for the eradication of untouchability, the breaking of caste barriers, the education of women, and the ending of child marriage. He was also an advocate of vocational education as a means for improving the economic condition of the people. One of his innovations was the use of cheap, popular literature to spread his ideas; he started at least a dozen journals, including magazines for women, a children's paper, and a daily newspaper. It was, however, as an orator on religious themes and as an organizer of branches of the Brāhmo Samāj throughout India that he was best known.

In 1870 Sen went to England, where he met many of the great figures of the time, including John Stuart Mill, William Gladstone, and Queen Victoria. His popularity in England rested in part on two themes that became central to his preaching and writing. One was an emphasis on Christ as the greatest of religious teachers; the other was his declaration that the British conquest of India was intended by God to help India "in the path of moral, social, and political reformation." He was, however, one of the first to suggest that the West must also learn from India: "Let modern England teach hard science and fact; let ancient India teach sweet poetry and sentiment."

Sen gradually came into conflict with Tagore and the older members of the Samāj, for whereas they insisted that it was a movement within Hinduism and did not involve a break with traditional values and customs, he argued that the Samāj was outside Hinduism and was meant to unite all people in a universal brotherhood. In 1866 he took many of its members into a new organization which he called the Brāhmo Samāj of India. In 1878 the group divided again when Sen, who had preached for years against child marriage, married his thirteen-year-old daughter to the Hindu prince of Cooch Behar, a small princely state. Many of Keshab's followers left him to form a new organization, the Sādhāran Brāhmo Samāj.

For years Sen had been studying the teachings of the world religions, and in 1881 he proclaimed what he called the New Dispensation, which was a synthesis of Hindu Tantrism, *bhakti,* and Christian rituals, with an emphasis on divine revelation. The New Dispensation was the successor, Sen declared, of the earlier revelations—the Hindu, the Jewish, the Christian. Another theme of his preaching during this period was that the image of mother was a better symbol for the divine than the image of father, since a mother is "tenderhearted and indulgent."

After his death in 1884 little remained of Sen's many enterprises, but his importance is to be seen in the enormous appeal of his views to his generation, particularly young people. His vision of a new spirituality that encompassed both Christianity and Hinduism made it possible for Indians to believe, as he put it, that there could be a "European Asia and an Asiatic Europe, a commingling of oriental and occidental ideas and principles" and that he had summoned "ancient India to come into modern India."

SEE ALSO Brāhmo Samāj.

BIBLIOGRAPHY

Collections of Sen's lectures are found in *Keshub Chunder Sen's Lectures in India,* 2 vols., 4th ed. (Calcutta, 1954), and in *Lectures and Tracts,* edited by Sophia Dobson Collett (London, 1870). P. C. Mozoomdar's *The Life and Teachings of Keshub Chunder Sen,* 3d ed. (Calcutta, 1931) is a disciple's account. A modern study of Sen's life and time is to be found in David Kopf's *The Brahmo Samaj and the Shaping of the Modern Indian Mind* (Princeton, 1979). Tapan Raychaudri's *Europe Reconsidered: Perceptions of the West in Nineteenth Century Bengal* (Delhi, 1989) places Sen in the context of social change, as does Kenneth W. Jones in *Socio-Religious Reform Movements in British India* (Cambridge, 1989).

AINSLIE T. EMBREE (1987 AND 2005)

SENG-CHAO SEE SENGZHAO

SENGZHAO (373–414), Chinese Buddhist monk of the Eastern Jin period (317–420) and scholar of the first Chinese Mādhyamika tradition. According to the standard biography in the *Gaoseng zhuan* (Biographies of eminent monks), Sengzhao was born in the vicinity of Chang'an (modern Xi'an) and as a young man earned his living as a transcriber and copyist. Exposed in this way to the Chinese classics, he initially acquired a secular education. He developed a liking for the writings of Daoism, the *Dao de jing* and the *Zhuangzi.* However, his biography states that upon reading the *Vimalakīrtinirdeśa Sūtra,* a text expressing the Buddhist concepts of emptiness (*śūnyatā*) and nonduality, he was converted to Buddhism and became a monk. Although his reputation in the Buddhist community of his day was initially established as a debater, Sengzhao's mark on Chinese Buddhism and his stature as a leading Buddhist literary figure were fixed as a result of his association with the famed Kuchean translator of Indian Mahāyāna Buddhist literature, Kumārajīva (344–413). From 401, when Kumārajīva arrived in Chang'an, Sengzhao served as one of his personal disciples and translating assistants. A gifted stylist, the author of a commentary on the *Vimalakīrti Sūtra* and the writer of prefaces to Indian sūtras and *śāstras,* Sengzhao was one of the most prolific Buddhist writers of his age. His fame as an independent thinker, however, rests primarily on four seminal essays, now collected as the *Zhao lun* (The treatises of Sengzhao): "Wisdom Is Not Knowledge," "Things Are Immutable," "The Emptiness of the Unreal," and "Nirvāṇa Is Nameless." Through these essays Sengzhao interpreted for his contemporaries the Mādhyamika teaching that Kumārajīva brought to China for the first time. Historically, the essays were formative in the thinking of the Perfection of Wisdom (Prajñāpāramitā) tradition during the sixth century, which later came to be known in East Asian Buddhism as the Sanlun (Three-Treatise) tradition. These essays also show that Sengzhao, while remaining true to the core of Buddhist teaching, utilized the insights of Daoism to expand and clarify certain problems in Buddhist texts and, conversely, utilized Buddhist texts to answer fundamental problems posed for him in Daoist writings. His use of a basic Daoist paradigm of "origin and end" (*benmo*) and its variants (*benji,* "root and trace," and its later cousin, *tiyong,* "essence and function") eventually became the basic framework for the analysis of Buddhist doctrine beginning in the Northern and Southern Dynasties period (420–589). Because of his innovative attempts to bridge Indian Buddhist and Chinese concepts and ideals, Sengzhao remains a pivotal figure in the transmission of Indian Buddhism to China as well as in the transformation of Buddhism into its Chinese form.

SEE ALSO Mādhyamika.

BIBLIOGRAPHY

The most comprehensive work on Sengzhao is the two-volume *Jōron kenkyū,* edited by Tsukamoto Zenryū (Kyoto, 1955). See also reviews of this work by Arthur Waley in the *Bulletin of the School of Oriental and African Studies* (University of London) 19 (1957): 195–196, and by Paul Demiéville in *T'oung-pao* 45 (1957): 221–235. Critical analysis of Sengzhao's essays can be found in Richard H. Robinson's *Early Mādhyamika in India and China* (Madison, Wis., 1967). Robinson's work also contains annotated translations of "Wisdom Is Not Knowledge," "Things Are Immutable," and "The Emptiness of the Unreal." Sengzhao's fourth essay, "Nirvāṇa Is Nameless," has been translated by Chang Chung-yüan, *Journal of Chinese Philosophy* 1 (1974): 247–274. Walter Liebenthal's *Book of Chao* (Beijing, 1948) remains a serviceable introduction to the text.

New Sources

Gregory, P. N., and Kuroda Institute. *Sudden and Gradual: Approaches to Enlightenment in Chinese Thought.* Honolulu, 1987.

Ichimura, Shohei. "On the Paradoxical Method of the Chinese Madhyamika: Seng-chao and the Chao-lun treatise." *Journal of Chinese Philosophy* 19, no. 1 (1992): 51–71.

Kuppuram, G., and K. Kumudamani. *Buddhist Heritage in India and Abroad.* Delhi, 1992.

AARON K. KOSEKI (1987)
Revised Bibliography

SEPTUAGINT SEE BIBLICAL LITERATURE, *ARTICLE ON* HEBREW SCRIPTURES

SERAFIM OF SAROV (1759–1833) was a Russian Orthodox priest, monk, mystic, and renowned spiritual elder (starets); born July 19, 1759 in Kursk, central European Russia, and died January 2, 1833 at the Monastery of Sarov in the forests to the north. Serafim is regarded as the preeminent example of Eastern Orthodox spirituality in modern times. In a troubling time of westernization in Russia, he lived during and was himself part of a remarkable flowering of spirituality in Russian Orthodoxy centered around monastic communities such as Sarov and Optina, a spirituality that had deep roots in the Bible, the writings of the Greek fathers, the celebrated *Philokalia* (a collection of ascetic and mystical writings of the fourth to the fifteenth century), and the sacramental life of the Orthodox church. Serafim's impact on his contemporaries and his immense popularity with later generations won him canonization as a saint in 1903.

There is ample information about Serafim's life (including testimonies by eyewitnesses, fellow monks of Sarov, nuns of Diveevo Convent of which he was spiritual patron, and confidants such as N. Motovilov), but no critical edition of the primary sources has been published. Born Prokhor Moshnin, Serafim was attracted to the highly spiritual life of monasticism by virtue of a miraculous healing and other religious experiences in his youth. During a pilgrimage to the Monastery of the Caves at Kiev, he was advised by a starets to enter the Monastery of Sarov, at which he subsequently became a novice (1778), was later tonsured as monk Serafim (1786), and ordained a deacon in the same year. After his ordination to the priesthood (1793), he embraced the life of a hermit in absolute simplicity and spent most of his remaining forty years in various degrees of seclusion both without and within the Monastery of Sarov. However, during the period from 1815 to 1825, he was led by what he regarded as divine revelation to welcome visitors and to give counsel to numerous people, whom he often greeted with the words "My joy!" and "Christ is risen!," and thus himself became an influential starets.

A man of profound prayer and rare spiritual gifts of discernment, healing, and prophecy, Serafim's presence was marked by radiant joy, peace, and love that does not seek its own. He was a child of traditional monasticism and yet "transcended monasticism" (Paul Evdokimoff). His spirituality was thoroughly biblical, trinitarian, and Christocentric, based on the Jesus Prayer and the reading of the Gospels. Although he adopted austere monastic disciplines, he counseled others to practice ascetic labors according to their strength and to make the flesh a friend in performing virtues. He valued devotional practices and good works, but he taught that the essence of the Christian life, which he insisted was one and the same for all, was the experience of the grace of the Holy Spirit enkindling the heart with divine fire.

His brief work, *Instructions*, consisting of notes set down by the monks of Sarov, reflects the traditional teachings of the Eastern church fathers on such subjects as prayer, guarding the heart from evil, solitude, silence, and the active and contemplative life. His most sublime expression of Orthodox spirituality, as the remarkable *Conversation with N. Motovilov* shows, was his own personal testimony to the radiant presence of the Holy Spirit.

BIBLIOGRAPHY

Bolshakoff, Sergius. *Russian Mystics*. Kalamazoo, Mich., 1977. Includes an insightful chapter on Serafim's life, work, and teaching based on unavailable Russian sources.

Evdokimoff, Paul. "Saint Seraphim of Sarov: An Icon of Orthodox Spirituality." *Ecumenical Review* 15 (April 1963): 264–278.

Fedotov, G. P. *A Treasury of Russian Spirituality* (1950). Belmont, Mass., 1975. Includes an interpretive prologue and extensive excerpts from hagiographical accounts of Serafim's life and work, including *Conversation with N. Motovilov*.

Little Russian Philokalia, vol. 1, *St. Seraphim of Sarov*. Platina, Calif., 1980. The most extensive translation of Serafim's teaching available in English.

Zander, Valentine. *St. Seraphim of Sarov*. Crestwood, N. Y., 1975.

THEODORE STYLIANOPOULOS (1987)

SERGII (1867–1944), born Ivan Nikolaevich Stragorodskii, was a Russian Orthodox theologian and patriarch of Moscow, was one of the leading advocates of church reform in tsarist Russia. Among his earlier writings are *The Question of Personal Salvation* (Moscow, 1895), *Eternal Life as the Highest Good* (Moscow, 1895), and contributions to *Meetings of the Religious Philosophical Society* (Saint Petersburg, 1901–1903) and to *Responses of the Diocesan Bishops* (Saint Petersburg, 1905–1906). In 1927 Sergii formally acknowledged the U. S. S. R. as the true motherland of the Orthodox people and was enthroned as patriarch in 1943 with the approval of Joseph Stalin.

Sergii's purpose in accommodating himself to the Soviet regime was to enable the church to achieve at least a minimal visibility during the time of the Soviet holocaust. In signing the controversial Declaration of Loyalty in 1927, he agreed to publish a clear and unambiguous statement of loyalty to the Soviet regime, to exclude from church administration those hierarchs and clergy whom the government deemed unacceptable, as well as those who had emigrated abroad, and to establish defined relations with organs of the Soviet government. His declaration immediately caused confusion and schism within the church in Russia, for millions of the faithful, together with many leading bishops and clergy who were not yet in prison, refused to accept it.

The regime did not repay Sergii with freedom for the church. Instead, the church was subjected to repeated waves of persecution (1929–1930, 1932–1934, and 1936–1939), each more devastating than the last. By 1940, when Russia lay broken and exhausted by the Stalinist revolution, only a few of the prerevolutionary churches remained open and only a fraction of their clergy remained alive and at liberty.

Sergii gambled that the Soviet system would either collapse or moderate enough to permit the church to function as an autonomous institution in accordance with canonical norms. In the meantime, he publicly denied that the church was being persecuted and became a subservient supporter of Soviet propaganda.

Soviet attitudes toward the church softened in 1939 and 1940 for two reasons. In 1939, as a result of the Stalin-Hitler pact of mutual nonaggression, the U.S.S.R. annexed eastern Poland, which contained a substantial Orthodox population. Persecution diminished as the regime sought to utilize the church in integrating the newly acquired population into the U.S.S.R. Further, in 1941, Germany attacked the U.S.S.R. and quickly overran large land masses. In the occupied areas the church speedily revived, and Stalin knew that Sergii was the only one who might be counted upon to defend Moscow's interests behind German lines.

In 1942, Sergii published *The Truth about Religion in Russia* in which he denied that there was any persecution in the U.S.S.R. In September 1943, he was summoned by Stalin and granted permission to formally reestablish the patriarchal administration. Churches were reopened on the Soviet side of the war frontier, and plans were laid to reestablish a network of seminaries and theological academies. Most of the surviving schismatic bishops recognized Sergii's administration before his death in May 1944. Although he died before the details of his agreement with Stalin could be accomplished, Sergii had outwaited the regime and had ensured a period of revival and stabilization for the church that lasted until the outbreak of the persecution by Khrushchev (1959–1964).

BIBLIOGRAPHY

Alexeev, Wassilij, and Theofanis Stavrou. *The Great Revival.* Minneapolis, 1976.

Cunningham, James W. *Vanquished Hope: The Church in Russia on the Eve of the Revolution.* New York, 1981.

Fletcher, William C. *A Study in Survival: The Church in Russia, 1927–1943.* New York, 1965.

Fletcher, William C. *The Russian Orthodox Church Underground, 1917–1970.* Oxford, 1971.

Nichols, Robert Lewis, and Theofanis Stavrou, eds. *Russian Orthodoxy under the Old Regime.* Minneapolis, 1978.

Pospielovsky, Dimitry. *The Russian Church under the Soviet Regime, 1917–1982.* 2 vols. Crestwood, N. Y., 1984.

JAMES W. CUNNINGHAM (1987)

SERGII OF RADONEZH

SERGII OF RADONEZH (1322?–1392) was a Russian Orthodox monastic saint and founder of Holy Trinity-Saint Sergii Monastery (in present-day Sergiyev Posad). The life of Sergii is known largely from two fifteenth-century hagiographical accounts, supplemented by Russian medieval chronicles. Sergii himself wrote nothing.

Sergii (in secular life known as Bartholomew) was born in the principality of Rostov, but early moved with his family to the Muscovite village of Radonezh. In search of the ascetic life, he persuaded his already tonsured brother Stephen to venture with him into the neighboring forests. The severity of their life as hermits caused Stephen to withdraw within the year. For the succeeding two or three years (c. 1345–1348), Sergii tested his vocation alone. However, news of the solitary spread, and he attracted a company of independent monks around the wooden Trinity Church he had erected with his brother. In about 1353 Sergii accepted abbacy and the priesthood.

Soon Sergii received a missive from the patriarch of Constantinople urging him to establish a community rule and thus to transform an essentially idiorrhythmic monastery into a cenobitic one. Although Sergii's monastery may not have been the first Russian monastery of the early Muscovite period to accept such a transformation (c. 1356), it was to be the most influential in so doing. It provided the model (and the founding fathers) for thirty such monasteries in Sergii's lifetime, and perhaps five times that number by the middle of the following century.

The establishment of community life at the Trinity Monastery encouraged not only its spiritual but also its economic development; perhaps for this reason the Muscovite state acted both as Sergii's patron and his client. Sergii's spiritual authority was seen to fit him for several demanding diplomatic tasks. The blessing that he gave Grand Prince Dmitrii (1380) to proceed against the Mongol horde acted as a vital spur to the Muscovite troops and helped to ensure their victory in the battle of Kulikovo, a watershed in Russian history.

But Sergii cannot be described simply as a political saint. When he was offered elevation to a bishop's (and in due course to the metropolitan's) chair he refused it firmly. Regardless of office held or proffered he continued to dress in the roughest of robes and persist with the most menial of tasks. His humility was deep seated: It informed his prayer and predisposed him to visions. These visions were several and various. A number were centered on light or fire, and two of these were linked with the celebration of the Eucharist. But the one most carefully described in the lives of Sergii involved the appearance of the Mother of God, who assured Sergii that his monastery was under her direct protection.

Such visions had no precedent in Russian hagiography, and even elsewhere precise parallels are difficult to find. It may be that they are among the first fruits of that school of mystical (hesychast) prayer that was beginning to make inroads into Russia from Mount Athos in Greece.

Sergii died in 1392. His relics were exposed for veneration in 1422. The monastery (soon to be renamed the Trinity-Saint Sergii Monastery) expanded, and by 1561 it was designated first among all Russian monastic communities. Catherine the Great confiscated much of its great landholdings, but it was the Bolshevik Revolution of 1917 that challenged its very existence. However, the revival of church life during the war years (1941–1945) eventually promoted the reopening of the monastery and the restoration of the relics to the church (1946). The tomb of Saint Sergii once again attracts countless pilgrims year after year.

Bibliography

The hagiographical account of Sergii's life has been translated with care, if not with grace, by Michael Klimenko: *The "Vita" of St. Sergii of Radonezh* (Houston, 1980). See also chapter 6 of G. P. Fedotov's *The Russian Religious Mind,* vol. 2, *The Middle Ages: The Thirteenth to the Fifteenth Centuries,* edited by John Meyendorff (1966; Belmont, Mass., 1975). But the most scholarly studies are in Russian. Noteworthy among these remains Evgenii E. Golubinskii's *Prepodobnyi Sergii Radonezhskii i sozdannaia im Troitskaia Lavra,* 2d ed. (Moscow, 1909).

Sergei Hackel (1987)

SERPENTS See DRAGONS; SNAKES

SERRA, JUNIPERO

SERRA, JUNIPERO (1713–1784), was a Spanish founder of Franciscan missions in California. Educated at the Royal and Pontifical University of Palma in Spain, Serra was a tenured professor of philosophy there when in 1749 he volunteered to go to Mexico as a missionary. There he served his apprenticeship among the Pamé Indians of Sierra Gorda (1750–1758) and in Baja California (1767–1769).

In 1769, when Spain decided to occupy Alta California to prevent Russian or English encroachments, Serra established his first mission there at San Diego, on 16 July. In all, he began nine missions on carefully selected sites after first obtaining the consent of the natives concerned.

After a careful survey of the territory from San Diego to San Francisco, he formed a plan for the development of the whole area. It was a vision not of isolated missions and military presidios but of an interrelated system of ports, presidios, towns, and missions. In 1773 Serra traveled the 1,500 miles to Mexico City to consult with the viceroy, Antonio María Bucareli y Ursúla. In a series of meetings, Serra discussed his plan and his needs with Bucareli and his staff. At their suggestion he wrote a brief in thirty-two sections. Serra's vision was to become the catalyst of the official program.

First, there was a need to regulate relations among the ruling military, the missionaries, the Indians, and the townspeople. This regulation was formulated in the Reglamento Echeveste (July 1773), which was to become the basic law of the state of California. Next, a supply system had to be invented, with the procurement and shipping office in Mexico through the port of San Blas, for a fleet to transport people, animals, and goods to and from California. Such a system was established by the end of the year 1773. Serra also needed mules and oxen to put his California society on wheels. He was granted 150 mules; it was hoped that more animals would be shipped on the hoof via an overland route, then being explored. In January 1776 the first overland expedition arrived at Mission San Gabriel from Tubac, Arizona, bringing 244 people together with provisions and herds of horses and cattle. Later arrivals permitted the founding of four towns, among them San Francisco and Los Angeles.

Above all, Serra needed role models for his neophytes, to train them in the crafts and in Christian living. Five artisans were granted to each mission for this purpose. Only married couples would be accepted as settlers: This set an example of a Christian family as the foundation of a stable society. The money for all these expenditures was to come from the Pious Fund of expelled Jesuits. California remained within the Spanish empire until it became part of the United States in 1850. In 1931, the state of California placed a statue of Serra in Washington, D. C.

Bibliography

Geiger, Maynard. *The Life and Times of Fray Junípero Serra.* 2 vols. Washington, D. C., 1959.

Tibesar, Antonine, ed. *The Writings of Junipero Serra.* 4 vols. Washington, D. C., 1955–1966.

Antoine Tibesar (1987)

SERVETUS, MICHAEL

SERVETUS, MICHAEL (1509?/11?–1553), born Miguel Serveto y Conesa was a Spanish biblical scholar, physician, and theologian. Servetus was born in Villanueva, Spain.

By the time he was fourteen, Servetus had learned Latin, Greek, and Hebrew and was ready to participate in the burgeoning new field of biblical scholarship. Spanish clerics were in the forefront of the movement, Cardinal Ximenes de Cisneros having published an edition of the Bible in three ancient languages, using the oldest available manuscripts, in 1522. Though extreme religious intolerance prevailed, it was still remembered in Spain that at one time Christians, Jews, and Muslims had lived and studied side by side, producing great works of literature, science, and mysticism. As Jews were crowded out of Spanish life, some became Christian. Not fully accepted, they were called *conversos.* According to Roland H. Bainton's *Hunted Heretic: The Life and Death of Michael Servetus, 1511–1553* (1953), it was Bishop Paulus of Burgos, a *converso,* who had secretly and illegally instructed the young Servetus in Hebrew. The dream of a future when religious differences were again tolerated and the vision of a Christianity purified by going back to its roots guided Servetus's work as biblical scholar and theologian. The humanistic style of scholarship, based on observation and argumentation, served not only his theological inquiries but also his study of medicine.

Miguel Serveto y Conesa went to Toulouse at the age of seventeen to study law. Very soon he discovered biblical studies and theology, latinized his name, and began to develop his own ideas about the way Christianity had been before the Council of Nicaea (325). During his studies in Toulouse, he became convinced that the dogma of the Trinity is not based on Scripture.

Another turning point occurred when he traveled with his patron, Juan de Quintana, to the coronation of Charles V as Holy Roman Emperor in 1529. Seeing the splendor and temporal power of the pope, he abruptly left the service of Quintana, going to Basel, Switzerland, where the Reformation was already under way. The toleration he sought, however, did not exist there, either. His first book, *De Trinitatis erroribus* (1531), was written as a coda to a long argument with his host in Basel, Oecolampadius.

***De Trinitatis erroribus* and *Dialogorum de Trinitate*.** In *De Trinitatis erroribus,* he argued that Jesus is the Christ, the Son of God by nature (not by adoption), and that he is God by grace, whereas the Father is God by nature. Servetus emphasized a distinction between the Word and the Son. The Word had existed from eternity as one mode in which God expresses himself. When the Word was completely incarnated in the man Jesus, the Son came into being. The Holy Spirit is another mode in which God expresses himself among humans, but it is not a separate person. Servetus believed that Scripture speaks of the three persons of the Trinity as the varying appearances of God. This heretical view has been called modalistic trinitarianism, with a subordinationist Christology. Both in *De Trinitatis erroribus* and in later works, Servetus drew on passages from the ante-Nicene fathers Irenaeus and Tertullian to support his views.

Servetus's book aroused so much opposition that in 1532 he published *Dialogorum de Trinitate,* in which he made some conciliatory changes without altering his basic conclusions. Pursued by the Inquisition, he assumed the name Michel de Villeneuve and found work as an editor in Lyons, France. In 1538 he began medical studies in Paris, upon completion of which he became physician to the archbishop of Vienne, France, still under his assumed name. Both his editorial and medical careers were distinguished. Among his editorial contributions, the 1535 edition of Claudius Ptolemy's second century *Geography* and the 1540 edition of the Santes Pagnini *Bible* were particularly noteworthy.

***Christianismi Restitutio*.** In 1546 Servetus sent parts of an early draft of *Christianismi restitutio* to John Calvin; the revised book was published anonymously in 1553. In *Christianismi restitutio,* Servetus modifies and supplements the views expressed in his previous works. He adds an emanationist philosophical context, a millenarianist historical view, and a celestial flesh Christology. In his emanationist philosophy, he sees God as above light, above essence, and as describable only in negative terms. According to Servetus, God relates to the world through a continuum progressing from God's hiddenness to his participation in the world. Servetus uses light symbolism to describe this continuum. Everything in this unfolding emanation is part of God, including the Logos (God's internal reason), Wisdom (ideas that are the exemplars of things), and the Word (through which God made the visible world appear). The Word forms a bridge between the invisible world and the visible world, for it is both immaterial and physical. Thus, the essence of God is in everything. This view is not pantheistic, for in it the world is dependent on God for its being; yet God in his being extends beyond the world—God is not dependent on the world.

The millenarian theme appears in the conflict between God's modalistic presence in Christ and Satan's modalistic presence in the Antichrist. This conflict, pursued throughout five ages of world history, began in the garden of Eden when God's creation, including humankind, came under the control of the serpent, and God withdrew. The conflict continued when, after the incarnation, the Antichrist came to the papal throne, whereupon Christ withdrew from the world. All Christian history since the time of Constantine has been under the reign of the Antichrist. In the imminent fifth age, the archangel Michael will destroy Satan, releasing Christ's power.

Prior to the incarnation, Christ was prefigured in the Word. In the incarnation the divine nature mixed with (not united with) Christ's human nature, the mortal body of the man Jesus. Christ came through Mary, but he did not receive Mary's substance, for his divine nature and his human nature or flesh were both of heavenly origin. After the resurrection, Christ was again the Word with a celestial nature, that of God's heavenly substance.

All persons receive a first grace, which comes through the air as the spirit of God (to be distinguished from the Holy Spirit). Receiving the first grace makes it possible to live in accordance with codes of morality but is not sufficient for divinization. Christ's celestial nature makes possible a second grace, by which humanity is regenerated and physically transformed.

Servetus relates these themes to his view of the sacraments. In baptism the soul receives illumination, a wisdom from the Holy Spirit that combats Satan's serpentine wisdom. Baptism is a covenant with God and a commitment on the part of the person; hence, it is not for infants. The Lord's Supper is a sacrament involving the real presence (not only a symbolic presence) of Christ's celestial flesh in the bread and wine. This sacrament effects in the faithful both a spiritual and a physical change. Participants are changed to the nature of God, divinized.

Christianismi restitutio contains Servetus's discovery of the pulmonary circulation of the blood, a result of his medical dissections. This discovery is presented in theological terms to illustrate how each person receives God's spirit just as air circulates through the body. (A thirteenth-century Arab, Ibn al-Nafis, preceded Servetus in his medical discovery, but Servetus's description was more explicit.)

A copy of *Christianismi restitutio* fell into the hands of a Catholic named Guillaume de Trie, who suspected that Servetus was its author. Soon the Inquisition had arrested both Servetus and the printer. Servetus escaped but was apprehended in Geneva. He was tried, condemned for antitrinitarianism and opposition to infant baptism, and burned at the stake on 27 October 1553 at Champel, near Geneva.

Despite the attempts by the publisher and the Roman Catholic Inquisition to destroy every copy of *Christianismi restitutio,* a few copies survived. Servetus's execution gave rise to an important controversy among Protestant church leaders over religious toleration, initiated by the publication in 1554 of *De haereticis, an sint persequendi,* written principally by the French Protestant theologian Sébastien Chateillon under a pseudonym, and by other publications. Servetus's antitrinitarian views influenced prominent leaders in the antitrinitarian movements in Poland and Transylvania, but these leaders did not accept his emanationist philosophy or his celestial flesh Christology. These latter themes were not among the sections of *Christianismi restitutio* that were reprinted in 1569 in *De regno Christi.*

BIBLIOGRAPHY

The original text of *De Trinitatis erroribus* (1531) is available in a facsimile reprint edition (Frankfurt, Germany, 1965). It is more accessible in *The Two Treatises of Servetus on the Trinity,* translated by Earl Morse Wilbur (1932; reprint, New York, 1969). The original text of *Christianismi Restitutio* (1553) is available in a reprint edition (Frankfurt, Germany, 1966). Angel Alcalá and Luis Betes have published the first edited modern translation, *Restitución del cristianismo: Miguel Servet* (Madrid, Spain, 1980).

Roland H. Bainton's reliable biography, *Hunted Heretic: The Life and Death of Michael Servetus, 1511–1553* (Boston, 1953), contains a chronology, detailed notes, and an extensive selected bibliography. Bruno Becker, ed., *Autour de Michel Servet et de Sébastien Castellion* (Haarlem, 1953), contains important essays, including "Michael Servetus and the Trinitarian Speculation of the Middle Ages," by Roland H. Bainton, and "L'influence de Servet sur le mouvement antitrinitarien en Pologne et en Transylvanie," by Stanislas Kot. Mihály Balázs corrected and supplemented Kot's essay in "Die Osteuropäische Rezeption der *Restitutio Christianismi* von Servet," in *Antitrinitarianism in the Second Half of the Sixteenth Century,* edited by Róbert Dán and Antal Pirnát (Leiden, Netherlands, 1982), pp. 13–23. Claudio Manzoni, *Umanesimo ed eresia: Michele Serveto* (Naples, Italy, 1974), and Elisabeth F. Hirsch, "Michael Servetus and the Neoplatonic Tradition: God, Christ and Man," *Bibliothèque d'humanisme et Renaissance* 42 (1980): 561–575, have contributed to an understanding of the Neoplatonic elements in *Christianismi restitutio.* Jerome Friedman, *Michael Servetus: A Case Study in Total Heresy* (Geneva, Switzerland, 1978), contains an informative argument, detailed bibliographical notes, and a glossary that the reader will appreciate.

Earl Morse Wilbur, *A History of Unitarianism: Socinianism and its Antecedents* (Cambridge, Mass., 1945), has a lengthy discussion of Servetus. There is also biographical material in the introduction to *The Two Treatises* (1932; reprint, New York, 1969). Marian Hillar, with Claire S. Allen, *Michael Servetus: Intellectual Giant, Humanist, and Martyr* (Lanham, Md., 2002) is an important addition to scholarly work on Servetus in English. It has a bibliography of Servetus's works and their translations that includes his important editorial and medical contributions. *Out of the Flames* (New York, 2002) by Lawrence and Nancy Goldstone, adds interesting material on the survival of copies of *Christianismi Restitutio.*

Signaled by the publication of *Restitucion del Christianismo* in Spanish in 1980, there has been a flowering of interest in Servetus studies in Spain. These include Angel Acala Galve, *Miguel Servet* (Aragon, Spain, 2000); Jose Luis Cano Rodriguez, *Miguel Servet y el doctor de Velleneufve* (Zaragosa, Spain, 2002); and Manuel de Fuentes Sagaz, *Michael Servetus, 1511–1553* (Barcelona, Spain, 1999). A comprehensive bibliography is maintained by the Servetus International Society at its Web Site, available at http://www.servetus.org.

JOHN C. GODBEY (1987)
MARY WELLEMEYER (2005)

SETH. In Egyptian mythology Seth figures prominently, usually as a villain. He was the son of Geb and brother of Osiris. Jealous of Osiris' rule of the earth, he tricked and slew him, dismembered his body, and scattered the parts. Isis, the sister of both and consort of Osiris, bore Osiris' son, Horus, who had to avenge the death of his father. According to late mythological stories, the case was judged by the tribunal of gods with some contests that showed that the cleverness of Horus was certainly more than a match for the strength of Seth. From earlier mythical allusions in mortuary texts, it is known that Horus emasculated Seth and lost his eye in the conflict. For his role in this drama, Seth became a symbol for evil, trickery, blundering, and blustering. He was identified with the Mesopotamian storm god and was a supporter of Egypt's Asian enemies.

The animal representation of Seth is readily recognizable from its tall, upright, flat-topped ears and long, upright tail divided at the top, but it is not certainly identifiable. It usually appears to be some sort of hound or jackal, but is occasionally more like a hippopotamus, a pig, or an ass. If one single animal were intended, perhaps it would be a feral hog.

From earliest times there seems to have been some connection between Seth and Ash, a Libyan deity. Even before the unification of Upper and Lower Egypt there were probably shrines to Seth in both south and north. Ombos was his principal cult center, but it has provided almost no information about the god or his cult. He is usually associated with the north, and his defeat by Horus represents the conquest of Lower Egypt (the north) by Upper Egypt (the south). The myth of the conflict between Horus and Seth may also have been associated with a struggle over the right of succession, that from father to son winning out over that from brother to brother.

Apparently Seth was not always an evil figure in Egyptian history. During the second dynasty one king identified himself with Seth rather than Horus, and another identified himself with both gods. Later the kings of the fifteenth and sixteenth dynasties were regarded as Sethian, but this is easily explained by their foreign origin. In the New Kingdom Seth was regularly shown as one of the gods accompanying the sun god, Re, on his bark sailing through the day and night skies. In this case Seth clearly assists Re, and the evil being to be opposed by spells or force is Apopis, the serpent who threatens to devour the sun. In the nineteenth dynasty, not only were divisions of the Egyptian army named for Seth, but two kings also took Sety as their throne name.

Bibliography

Hornung, E. "Seth, Geschichte und Bedeutung eines ägyptischen Gottes." *Symbolon* (Cologne), N. F. 2 (1974): 49–63.

Velde, H. te. *Seth, God of Confusion: A Study of His Role in Egyptian Mythology and Religion.* Probleme der Ägyptologie, vol. 6. Leiden, 1967.

Leonard H. Lesko (1987)

SETON, ELIZABETH (1774–1821), was the first American-born Christian saint, and first founder of a sisterhood in the United States. Elizabeth Ann Bayley Seton was born probably in New York City, the second daughter of Richard Bayley by his first wife, Catherine Charlton. Little is known of her formal education save that she attended a school called Mama Pompelion's, learning to play the piano and to speak French.

On January 25, 1794, at the age of nineteen, she married William Magee Seton, a young New York merchant. The union produced five children. In 1797 she cooperated with Isabella Marshall Graham in forming a society to aid destitute widowed mothers. In 1800 she came under the influence of John Henry Hobart, an assistant at Trinity (Episcopal) Church in New York City, and under his guidance her spiritual life deepened perceptibly.

The next nine years tested these spiritual resources to the full. Her husband's business failed, along with his health. He died while on a trip to Italy in 1803. While waiting for passage back to New York, she was befriended by Antonio and Filippo Filicchi and their wives, who introduced her to Roman Catholicism. On her return to New York on June 4, 1804, she entered a period of religious indecision, torn between the entreaties of Hobart and her Protestant friends and relatives, and the urgings of the Filicchis and the American Catholic clergy enlisted by them to sway her. On March 14, 1805, she became a Roman Catholic.

Unable to earn support for herself and her five children in New York, she agreed to the proposal made by William Valentine DuBourg that she come to Baltimore to start a Catholic school for girls. Having already placed her two sons in Georgetown Academy, she embarked for Baltimore with her three daughters on June 9, 1808. Her year there as mistress of the Paca Street School confirmed her vocation to educate girls and found a community, the Sisters of Charity of Saint Joseph. In June–July 1809, she moved both the school and the sisterhood to Emmitsburg, Maryland, where she spent the remainder of her life.

In Emmitsburg, Saint Joseph's School for boarders from more prosperous families soon furnished sufficient income to extend free schooling to needy girls of the local parish, which later earned Seton the title "foundress of the parochial school system in the United States." Adopting a modified rule of the Daughters of Charity of Saint Vincent de Paul in 1812, her sisters rapidly extended their work to include nursing the sick, caring for orphans, and aiding the poor. The community spread to Philadelphia (1814), New York (1817), and Baltimore (1821) under her guidance. Since her death on January 4, 1821, her work has been spread by her spiritual daughters not only at Emmitsburg but also by the New York Sisters of Charity of Mount Saint Vincent-on-the-Hudson, the Cincinnati Sisters of Charity of Mount Saint Joseph, the New Jersey Sisters of Charity of Convent Station, the Pennsylvania Sisters of Charity of Seton Hill at Greensburg, and, in Nova Scotia, the Sisters of Charity of Halifax.

On February 28, 1940, the Roman Congregation of Rites formally introduced her cause for canonization. On December 14, 1961, the validity of two miracles was confirmed, and on March 17, 1963, John XXIII beatified her. On September 14, 1975, Paul VI proclaimed her Saint Elizabeth Ann Seton.

Bibliography

At the time of its first publication my *Elizabeth Bayley Seton, 1774–1821* (1951; reprint, New York, 1976) was judged the definitive biography. Prior to that time Charles I. White's *Life of Mrs. Eliza A. Seton* (New York, 1853) was the chief source of information. Additional published accounts include *Memoir, Letters and Journal of Elizabeth Seton,* 2 vols., edited by Robert Seton (New York, 1869), a not always reliable collection of memorabilia by Mrs. Seton's grandson; Hélène Bailley de Barbery and Joseph B. Code's *Elizabeth Seton* (New York, 1927), first published in French in 1868, which contains many documents; *Letters of Mother Seton to Mrs. Julianna Scott,* edited by Joseph B. Code (1935; 2d ed., New York, 1960), personal glimpses of Mother Seton's friendship with a Protestant friend of Philadelphia; Joseph I. Dirvin's *Mrs. Seton, Foundress of the American Sisters of Charity* (New York, 1962), combining biographical details with an analysis of Mother Seton's spiritual life, particularly as a religious superior; and Sister Mary Agnes McCann's *The History of Mother Seton's Daughters,* 3 vols. (New York, 1917–1923), most useful for the first century of their contributions.

Annabelle M. Melville (1987)

SEVENERS SEE SHIISM, *ARTICLE ON* ISMĀʿĪLĪYAH

SEVENTH-DAY ADVENTISM.

The origins of Seventh-day Adventism run back to the interdenominational Millerite movement in the United States in the early 1840s, when William Miller, a Baptist lay minister and farmer, sought to rekindle a "second awakening" by predicting that Christ would soon return to earth. On the basis of *Daniel* 8:14 ("Unto two thousand and three hundred days; then shall the sanctuary be cleansed"), he calculated that the end would come "about the year 1843"—2,300 years after Artaxerxes of Persia issued a decree to rebuild Jerusalem. Following a series of failed time-settings, Millerites fixed their hopes for the second advent of Christ on October 22, 1844, the Day of Atonement, which, according to the Jewish calendar, fell on the tenth day of the seventh month. The "great disappointment" that resulted from this miscalculation splintered the movement into several factions. The majority, including Miller, admitted their exegetical error but continued to expect Christ's imminent return; eventually they coalesced into the Evangelical Adventist and Advent Christian churches. A much smaller number embraced the suggestion of Hiram Edson, an upstate New York farmer, that only the event, not the date, had been wrong: "that instead of our High Priest *coming out* of the Most Holy of the heavenly sanctuary to come to this earth on the tenth day of the seventh month, at the end of the 2,300 days, he for the first time *entered* on that day the second apartment of that sanctuary and that he had a work to perform in the Most Holy before coming to this earth." Millerites of this persuasion formed the nucleus of what, in the early 1860s, evolved into the Seventh-day Adventist Church.

THE FORMATIVE YEARS: 1844–1863. Edson's sanctuary doctrine, which held that Christ in 1844 inaugurated a new era in the history of salvation, became one of the most distinctive and central tenets of Adventist theology. However, other beliefs—for example, belief in the "shut door," the seventh-day Sabbath, and the gift of prophecy—brought them their greatest notoriety and earned them the name "sabbatarian and shut-door" Adventists.

Early beliefs that October 22 marked the date when God shut the "door of mercy" on all who had rejected the Millerite message gradually gave rise to an open-door theology and to evangelization. The observance of Saturday as the Sabbath, as required by the Ten Commandments and practiced by the Seventh Day Baptists, became the most obvious symbol of Seventh-day Adventist distinctiveness and served as a means by which legalistic members sought to attain the higher morality expected of God's people at the close of history.

Shortly after the "great disappointment," Ellen Gould Harmon, a sickly, introverted adolescent ecstatic from Portland, Maine, began having visionary experiences that validated the sanctuary, shut-door, and Sabbath doctrines. The Millerite movement produced numerous mystics and trance mediums, and the believers in Portland were especially infamous for what Millerite publicist Joshua V. Himes called their "continual introduction of visionary nonsense." Thus, Ellen Harmon would probably have been lost in the crowd of enthusiasts had she not been discovered by James White, a young Adventist preacher and teacher, who became her protector, her promoter, and, in 1846, her husband. Together, James and Ellen White built the Seventh-day Adventist church, James serving as organizer and entrepreneur, Ellen as exhorter and visionary. The Adventist brethren, under James's leadership, functioned as the sect's theologians and biblical exegetes, frequently relying on Ellen's "gift of prophecy" to support their doctrinal positions. Committed to *sola scriptura* biblicism, Adventists regarded Ellen White's charismatic role as confirmatory rather than initiatory; her testimonies related to the Bible as a "lesser light to the greater light." Despite sporadic questioning of her authority, even by her husband, her visions helped to identify Adventists as God's end-time people and thus assured her of a singularly precious place in Adventist history.

In many respects, Seventh-day Adventism developed as a typical nineteenth-century American sect, characterized by millenarianism, biblicism, restorationism, and legalism. Its Old Testament orientation, its self-image as the chosen people, its sabbatarianism, and its sense of cosmic destiny all betrayed the influence of eighteenth-century American Puritanism, while its Arminianism (which rejected Calvinist predestinarianism in favor of free choice of salvation), its doctrine of soul-sleep (asserting that human beings have no separate "spirit" and therefore the dead have no consciousness until the resurrection), its concern for religious liberty, and its adoption of medical and educational reforms also revealed it to be a product of antebellum evangelicalism. Adventists, however, especially during their early years, stressed their distinctiveness and separateness rather than their many points of similarity with the religious landscape of nineteenth-century America.

By 1850, sabbatarian Adventists, still looking for the imminent appearance of Christ, composed a "scattered flock" of about two hundred loosely structured sectarians who sought to restore such primitive Christian practices as foot-washing, greeting with the "holy kiss," and calling each other "brother" and "sister." As time passed uneventfully, their radical millenarianism, which had led some to predict the end in 1845, 1847, and 1851, gave way to a more realistic attitude. As early as 1848 Ellen White had had a vision in which she saw Adventism spreading "like streams of light. . .clear round the world," a scene that implied long-range involvement in earthly affairs. In 1850 her husband began editing *The Advent Review and Sabbath Herald,* which became the official Adventist organ. In 1855 the Whites moved on to the fresher evangelistic pastures of southern Michigan, where the church eventually enjoyed enough material prosperity to elicit, in 1857, a notable jeremiad from the prophetess on its "Laodicean condition," a phrase referring to the "lukewarm" church described in *Revelation* 3:14–18.

By the late 1850s the institutionalization of Seventh-day Adventism was well under way. In 1859 the Adventists adopted a plan of "systematic benevolence" to support a clergy; the next year they selected the name Seventh-day Adventist; by 1863 there were 125 churches with about 3,500 members. That year they organized a General Conference and invited James White to serve as their first president, an honor he temporarily declined. In 1866, in the wake of an epidemic of sickness among church leaders and Ellen White's discovery of the virtues of the "water cure" and vegetarianism, the Adventists established a sanatorium at Battle Creek, Michigan—the Western Health Reform Institute—and began publishing the *Health Reformer,* a monthly magazine. John Harvey Kellogg, who became the leading force in Adventist health reform, developed several new food products, among them ready-to-eat dry cereals. His brother, Will Kellogg, established the company that created a mass market for this new way of eating breakfast.

Years of Transition: 1863–1915. The years following the formal organization of the Adventist Church and its emergence as an established sect saw American Protestantism split into modernist and fundamentalist parties, divided by such issues as evolution and higher criticism. Not surprisingly, Adventists in this period generally, but idiosyncratically, followed the fundamentalists. Because the Adventists observed the seventh-day Sabbath as a memorial of creation, and because Ellen White insisted on a recent six-day creation, they rejected all compromises with evolutionary biology and geology. They also rejected higher criticism in favor of biblical inerrancy, but they displayed less concern about the integrity of the scriptures than about the writings of Ellen White, whose apotheosis occurred during this period. For years Ellen White had lived in the shadow of her husband, providing visionary endorsement for the opinions of the founding fathers of Adventism. But after James's death in 1881 she assumed a more assertive role, directing the activities of a younger generation of male leaders, who quickly learned to clear matters of doctrine, development, and policy with the prophetess. By the time of her death in 1915 she had, despite disclaimers to the contrary, become the real authority for Adventists in matters of behavior as well as belief.

Acceptance of Ellen White's prophetic role set Adventists apart from other fundamentalists, as did their peculiar doctrines regarding the sanctuary and the Sabbath. In fact, nothing distinguished Adventists as a separate religious community as much as their Sabbath-keeping, which led them to distrust not only evolutionists (who undermined belief in a literal Sabbath) but Catholics (whom they blamed for changing the Sabbath from Saturday to Sunday), labor unionists (who, they feared, would force them to work on Saturday), and blue-law-minded evangelical Christians (who, the prophetess said, would pass a national law requiring Sunday observance). Efforts to enact such legislation in the 1880s, coinciding as they did with hard-labor sentences for up to fifty church members who violated blue laws in the South, proved to the Adventists that they were indeed living in the "last days."

Adventist theology shifted in the 1880s, when two West Coast editors, Ellet J. Waggoner and Alonzo T. Jones, both still in their thirties, challenged the legalistic emphasis that had come to characterize the sect. In opposition to General Conference leaders, who maintained that salvation depended upon observing the Ten Commandments (especially the fourth), Waggoner and Jones followed evangelical Christians in arguing that righteousness came by accepting Christ, not by keeping the law. At a pivotal general conference in 1888, Ellen White broke with the Battle Creek administrators—and the view of her late husband—to endorse this controversial "new light," a move that symbolized her "coming out" as the Adventists' matriarch. But despite her pronouncements in favor of "righteousness by faith," the issue of grace versus law remained a sensitive one within Adventism.

For decades Adventists confined their evangelistic efforts almost exclusively to North America. In the early 1870s, however, church leaders became convinced that they had an obligation to carry their message "into all the world" (*Mk.* 16:15), and in 1874 they sent J. N. Andrews, a former General Conference president, to Switzerland as the first Adventist missionary. Other appointments followed in quick succession, first to the large white, Christian populations of Europe, Australia, New Zealand, South Africa, and, later, to the nonwhite peoples of Africa, Asia, and Latin America. By 1900 the Adventists were supporting nearly five hundred foreign missionaries, and over 15 percent of the more than seventy-five thousand Adventists lived outside North America. In part to provide for the growing needs of its foreign missions, as well as to shield its youth from worldly influences, the church developed an extensive educational system. By the second half of the twentieth century, Adventists were operating one of the largest Protestant school systems in the world.

In 1895, in order to train medical personnel for service at home and abroad, Adventists opened the American Medical Missionary College, with campuses in Battle Creek and Chicago. The school's dominant force was Dr. John Harvey Kellogg, a former protégé of the Whites. In his mid-twenties Kellogg became superintendent of the Western Health Reform Institute (later the Battle Creek Sanitarium) and after 1893 headed the Medical Missionary and Benevolent Association, the Adventist body responsible for operating medical institutions around the world. By the early twentieth century the association's two thousand workers considerably outnumbered General Conference employees, an imbalance that aggravated the friction between the imperious and imperialistic Dr. Kellogg and the equally ambitious ministers who ran the General Conference. In 1906 the latter arranged for the doctor and his cohorts to be disfellowshipped for questioning the authority of Ellen White; thus, for the first time, making the acceptance of her testimonies a "test of fellowship." When Kellogg, the most prominent Adventist in the world, left the church, he took the medical college and Battle Creek Sanitarium with him, forcing loyalists in 1909 to open an orthodox medical school, the College of Medical Evangelists (which developed into Loma Linda University), in southern California.

In the years since the Whites moved their fledgling church to Michigan, Battle Creek had grown into the administrative, publishing, medical, and educational center of Adventism. Such centralization and concentration of power concerned Ellen White, who recommended dismantling the Battle Creek colony. As a result, Battle Creek College (now Andrews University) was moved in 1902 to rural southwestern Michigan, and administrative and publishing activities were moved to the outskirts of Washington, D.C., which became the international headquarters.

CONTEMPORARY ADVENTISM. Ellen White died in 1915, leaving a church of more than 136,000 members. By 2001 membership had swelled to over twelve million, roughly 92 percent of whom lived outside of North America. Despite the preponderance of third-world believers, and the fact that recent growth in North America had come to a great extent from Hispanics and blacks, the administrative and economic power of the church remained largely in the hands of white, male leaders. In the mid-1940s the General Conference created segregated black conferences in North America, but it later rejected demands for separate unions that accompanied the civil rights movement of the 1960s. Similarly, as the feminist movement gathered momentum in the 1970s, Adventist women, long relied upon for cheap labor, began demanding equal pay for equal work—but they won their case only after resorting to the courts.

As their church grew and prospered, Adventists felt increasingly uncomfortable with their sectarian identity. Thus, they were greatly cheered in the 1950s when such prominent evangelicals as Donald G. Barnhouse and Walter R. Martin, after studying Adventist beliefs, certified them to be Christians rather than cultists. Many Adventists, nevertheless, continued to live in tension with the church's teachings on the sanctuary and the authority of Ellen White. Dissident voices became increasingly audible in the 1960s, especially after a group of Adventist academics and professionals created the independent Association of Adventist Forums (AAF) in 1967 and began publishing a lively journal, *Spectrum.* During the 1970s and early 1980s, Adventism was torn by claims of Adventist scholars that they had uncovered evidence that the writings of the prophetess not only contained historical and scientific errors but, in many instances, paralleled the prose of other authors—discoveries that forced a rethinking of White's role in the community. During the same period an Australian biblical scholar, Desmond Ford, announced to an AAF group that the church's distinctive view of the sanctuary derived more from White than from the Bible and that it infected Adventism with an unhealthful and unbiblical legalism. Although Ford and a number of his ministerial colleagues were promptly defrocked for their heresy, they still effected a subtle recasting of the sanctuary doctrine, orienting it more toward the atonement than toward last-day events and bringing it more into conformity with evangelical Protestantism. Some sectors of the church, often called "historic Adventists," opposed these developments, but Seventh-day Adventism generally continued to move haltingly along the path from radical millenarian sect to conventional denomination as it entered the twenty-first century.

SEE ALSO White, Ellen Gould.

BIBLIOGRAPHY

There is no standard history of Seventh-day Adventism. Until recently, non-Adventist scholars had tended to ignore Adventists, and Adventist historians have been reticent to examine their heritage critically. Among the several comprehensive histories, the best of the old is M. Ellsworth Olsen's *History of the Origin and Progress of Seventh-day Adventists* (Washington, D.C., 1925), and the best of the new is Richard W. Schwarz and Floyd Greenleaf's *Light Bearers,* rev. ed. (Nampa, Id., 2000), a well-documented survey designed to serve as a college text. *Adventism in America: A History,* edited by Gary Land, rev. ed. (Berrien Springs, Mich., 1998), offers a readable chronological overview written by six Adventist historians. A valuable reference work, filled with historical data, is the *Seventh-day Adventist Encyclopedia,* 2 vols., 2d rev. ed. (Hagerstown, Md., 1996).

The Rise of Adventism: Religion and Society in Mid-Nineteenth-Century America, edited by Edwin S. Gaustad (New York, 1974), though misleadingly titled (most of the essays say nothing about Adventism), does contain a marvelous 111-page bibliography of Millerite and early Adventist publications and an important interpretive essay, "Adventism and the American Experience," by Jonathan M. Butler. The Millerite movement has become the subject of a considerable body of scholarly literature, which Gary Land analyzes in his historiographical introduction to Everett N. Dick's, *William Miller and the Advent Crisis, 1831–1844* (Berrien Springs, Mich., 1994). The best survey of the movement is George R. Knight's popularly written *Millennial Fever and the End of the World* (Boise, Id., 1993). P. Gerard Damsteegt's *Foundations of the Seventh-day Adventist Message and Mission* (Grand Rapids, Mich., 1977) uncritically but microscopically traces the development of Adventist theology to 1874. Ingemar Linden's iconoclastic and unpolished *The Last Trump: An Historico-Genetical Study of Some Important Chapters in the Making and Development of the Seventh-day Adventist Church* (Frankfurt am Main, Germany, 1978) covers roughly the same period in a different style. Douglas Morgan's *Adventism and the American Republic: The Public Involvement of a Major Apocalyptic Movement* (Knoxville, Tenn., 2001) examines the interplay of the denomination's theology with society.

Despite an abundance of inspirational biographies of Adventist leaders, few scholarly studies of individual Adventists have appeared. Notable exceptions include Richard W. Schwarz's

John Harvey Kellogg, M. D. (Nashville, Tenn., 1970), which unfortunately lacks the documentation found in the doctoral dissertation upon which it is based; Ronald L. Numbers's *Prophetess of Health: Ellen G. White and the Origins of Seventh-day Adventist Health Reform,* rev. ed. (Knoxville, Tenn., 1992), a critical analysis of White's health-related activities; Gilbert M. Valentine's *The Shaping of Adventism: The Case of W. W. Prescott* (Berrien Springs, Mich., 1992), a study of a frequently controversial editor and educator; and Calvin W. Edwards and Gary Land, *Seeker After Light: A. F. Ballenger, Adventism, and American Christianity* (Berrien Springs, Mich., 2000), an examination of a minister who was dismissed from the denomination because of his criticisms of the sanctuary doctrine.

JONATHAN M. BUTLER (1987)
RONALD L. NUMBERS (1987)
GARY G. LAND (2005)

SEVERUS OF ANTIOCH

SEVERUS OF ANTIOCH (c. 465–538) was a rhetorician, theologian, and monophysite patriarch of Antioch (512–518). Severus was born in Apollonia, Thrace (modern-day Sozopol, Bulgaria), most likely in 465. He studied philosophy in Alexandria and rhetoric in Berytus (present-day Beirut), where, under the influence of Zacharias the Scholastic, he also acquired an interest in religious questions. After his baptism in Tripoli in 488, Severus became a monk at the monastery of Peter of Oberian, at Maiouma, near Gaza. In an attempt to live a more ascetic life, he left the monastery for the desert. But this soon proved harmful to his health, so he eventually returned to Maiouma.

There he established his own monastery and was ordained presbyter and archimandrite. The monophysite monks sent him to Constantinople in 508 to protest the subversive activities of the Orthodox monk Niphalios, who had managed to turn the Maiouma monks against Severus. Once in Constantinople, Severus gained the favor of the emperor Anastasius I (491–518) for the persecuted monophysite monks. Severus bided his time in Constantinople writing polemical works against the Council of Chalcedon. It was during this period that he wrote his most important work, the *Philalethes.*

In 512 Severus left Constantinople for Antioch where he was subsequently elected patriarch. As patriarch he attempted to strengthen monophysitism through the election of bishops, but his efforts failed. The death of Anastasius I in 518 precipitated a drastic change in ecclesiastical policy. With the ascendancy of the pro-Chalcedonian emperor Justin I (518–527), monophysitism lost favor, and Severus was eventually deposed as patriarch and expelled from Antioch. Severus fled to the Monastery of Ennaton in Egypt and lived for a time with Timothy IV, the monophysite patriarch of Alexandria. He encouraged the Copts at Ennaton to oppose the orthodox patriarchs. Severus also came into conflict with the former follower, Julian of Halicarnassus, whom he had known since his first visit to Constantinople in 508, over his colleague's extreme monophysitism. Severus was an intelligent thinker who sought a middle ground between the orthodox position and monophysitism.

In 535 Severus received (through the ministrations of the empress Theodora) an invitation from the emperor Justinian to come to Constantinople; there he worked with the patriarch Anthimus in an effort to restore monophysitism. Opposition arose to their proposals, and Anthimus was deposed and Severus condemned by the Synod of Constantinople (536).

He was once again forced to flee to Egypt, where he continued to write until his death in Alexandria in 538. Jacobite Syrians and the Copts venerate him as a saint; his feast day is celebrated on February 8.

Severus wrote a great number of works in Greek, but only a small portion of them is extant. A homily is preserved under the name of Gregory of Nyssa (*Patrologia Graeca* 46.627–652). Most of his writings are preserved in Syriac, such as the *Philalethes,* in which Severus refutes 244 chapters from the work of Cyril of Alexandria. He also wrote five treatises against Julian of Halicarnassus; three discourses against the orthodox patriarch Grammaticus; four letters against the extreme monophysite Sergius; and two letters against the orthodox Niphalios. A collection of his letters has been preserved as well as the homilies he delivered on various feasts. He is incorrectly identified as the author of a Syriac anaphora. Many liturgical hymns are also attributed to him, and he is regarded by many as the author of the writings of Dionysius the Areopagite (Pseudo-Dionysius). Many modern scholars have concluded that his teachings approximate those of Cyril of Alexandria. He continues to influence the thought of non-Chalcedonian Syrians and Copts.

BIBLIOGRAPHY

Severus's *Philalethes, Orationes ad Nephalium, Liber contra Impium Grammaticum,* and his writings against Julian of Halicarnassus are available in volumes 4–7, 68–69, 104–105, 124–127, and 136–137 of *Corpus scriptorum Christianorum Orientalum, Scriptores Syri* (Paris, 1929–1971). English translations, by E. W. Brooks, of Severus's letters and hymns can be found in volumes 6, 7, 12, and 14 of *Patrologia Orientalis,* edited by R. Graffin and F. Nau (Paris, 1911–1920).

No English work on Severus is readily available. Secondary sources in other languages include Hans Georg Beck's *Kirche und theologische Literatur in byzantinischen Reich* (Munich, 1977), pp. 387–390, Ioannou Eustratiou's *Sebéros: Ho monophusites patriarches Antiochieas* (Leipzig, 1894), Joseph Lebon's *Le monophysisme sévérien* (Louvain, 1909), and M. Preisker's "Severus von Antiochen" (Ph. D. diss., University of Halle, 1903).

THEODORE ZISSIS (1987)
Translated from Greek by Philip M. McGhee

SEXUALITY

This entry consists of the following articles:

THE TRUE IMAGE

Many religious traditions cherish images surrounded by narratives that tell of the image's origins and its long history as an object of devotion in court and ecclesia. Often these images are *acheiropoetic*, that is, not made by human hands. Their origins are divine. Fashioned by angels or deities, these images descend from heaven and are found by the faithful. They are enshrined and typically prove their peculiar merit by moving, speaking, bleeding, weeping, or performing miracles. In Thai Buddhism, for instance, the Sinhala Buddha floated on a plank when the ship carrying it from Sri Lanka to Thailand was wrecked in a gale. Copies were made of the image and envious rulers were inspired to acquire the original. The statue boasts a long history of migration through theft and conquest. There are different stories about its origin. One says that the image was created by twenty *arhats* (enlightened followers of the Buddha) in order to show the king of Sri Lanka what the Buddha looked like. The likeness proved so authentic that the king spent a week paying homage to the figure and then asked that a replica be made. The resulting sculpture miraculously took on the visual qualities of the Buddha and commanded veneration. Another version states that a dragon turned himself into an apparition of the Buddha to serve as a model for fashioning an authentic likeness. In both accounts the image's production involved a supernatural intervention that served to authorize it and ensure its power to convert the unbelieving. Not surprisingly, these narratives are closely associated with the political identities and ambitions of monasteries, courts, and kings, as well as the spread of Buddhism in new lands or its renewal in Buddhist regions.

The search for the true image is a quest in religious traditions for which cult imagery serves as a means of authorizing sect and court, for focusing and authenticating the power of images to heal, and for devotional practices that center around the cha-

(a) Michael Ostendorfer, *Pilgrimage to the New Church at Regensburg*, 1519, woodcut. *[©Foto Marburg/Art Resource, N.Y.]*

(b) Above. Jan Gossaert, *Saint Luke Painting the Virgin*, 1520, oil on panel. *[Kunsthistorisches Museum, Wien oder KHM, Wien]* **(c)** Opposite. *Mandylion of Edessa with Scenes of the Legend of King Abgar*, unknown artist, eighteenth century, egg tempera and resin glazes on panel. *[The Royal Collection ©2004, Her Majesty Queen Elizabeth II]*

risma of the cult figure. True images are a kind of evidence for the devout, proof of the authenticity of the image's power, and vindication of those who claim it as their own.

Christianity is deeply invested in the practice of the true image. In the eighth and ninth centuries the Eastern Christian world was wracked by violent disagreement over the propriety of images. Successive Eastern emperors forbade the use of icons while many monasteries insisted on their importance. During this time it became common to claim that the image of the Mother and Child had been painted by Saint Luke. The story, which predated the Iconoclastic Controversy, but certainly anticipated anxieties about the status and authority of images in Christianity, strengthened the position of those who argued for icons. The icon associated with this tradition, which first appeared around 600 CE in Rome, showed the Theotokos, or Mother of God, holding the Christ child in one arm and pointing to him with the other. During the Renaissance in Europe, artists produced many examples of the motif, in part because it underwrote their vocation, but no less because the subject enjoyed great popular enthusiasm, sometimes ecstatic. In 1519, the German city of Regensburg was suddenly visited by thousands of pilgrims seeking healing and blessing from an image of the Madonna and Child, which was associated with the miraculous healing of a local man who had been injured during the demolition of a Jewish synagogue. Michael Ostendorfer captured the frenzied tone of the pilgrims in a contemporary print **(a)**. Although medieval artists had depicted Luke painting the Virgin and Child since the twelfth century, none matched the theatrical spectacle of Jan Gossaert's portrayal of the scene **(b)**. The Madonna and Child hover before the artist in a cloud as the artist's hand is guided by an angel. Luke's Gospel appears as a bound volume in the lectern he uses as a drawing table, deftly equating book and image as authorized versions of one another.

The intervention of the angel recalls the legend of the origin of the mandylion **(c)**, the cloth on which Christ's image miraculously appeared when, according to one ver-

ΤΟΝ ΑΓΙΟΝ ΜΑΝΔΗΛΙΟ

sion, an artist attempted to paint his portrait from life at the behest of the king of Edessa. When the artist failed to capture a likeness, angels completed the portrait, thus ensuring its authenticity. Another version states that Christ himself made the image by placing the cloth on his face. Related versions of the story tell of Veronica, a woman who met Christ on his path to Calvary and offered him a cloth to wipe his bloody, soiled face. The result was an image that became especially important among European Christians in the thirteenth century when a papal indulgence was promised to those who uttered a prayer in the presence of a Veronica (a corruption of *vera icon*, or "true image") in Rome. Veronica's Veil multiplied as mementos for pilgrims and as works of fine art by artists during the Baroque period, who seized on the illusionistic possibilities of painting an image of an image of an image (**d** and **e**).

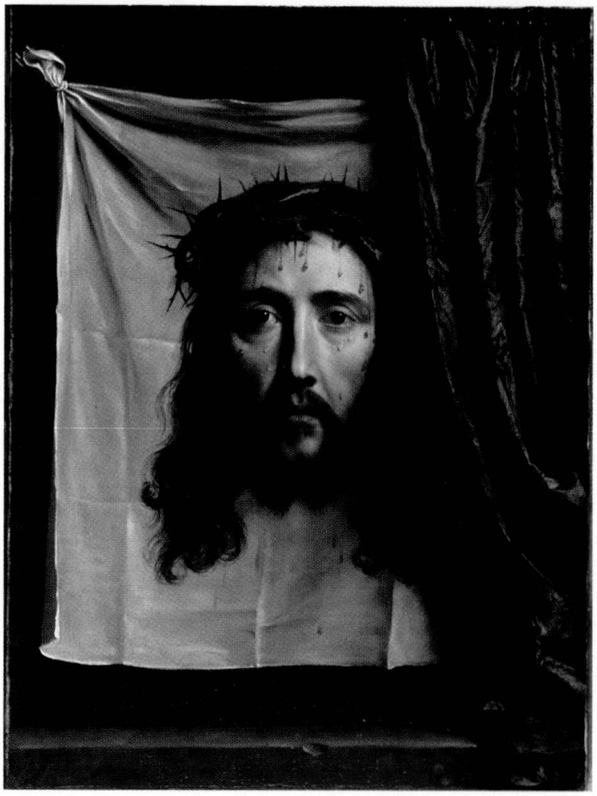

(d) Top. Francisco de Zurbarán, *The Holy Face (Veil of Veronica)*, 1630s, oil on canvas. *[©Art Resource, N.Y.]* **(e) Right.** Philippe de Champaigne, *La Sainte Face*, seventeenth century. ***[Courtesy of the Royal Pavilion, Libraries and Museums, Brighton and Hore]***

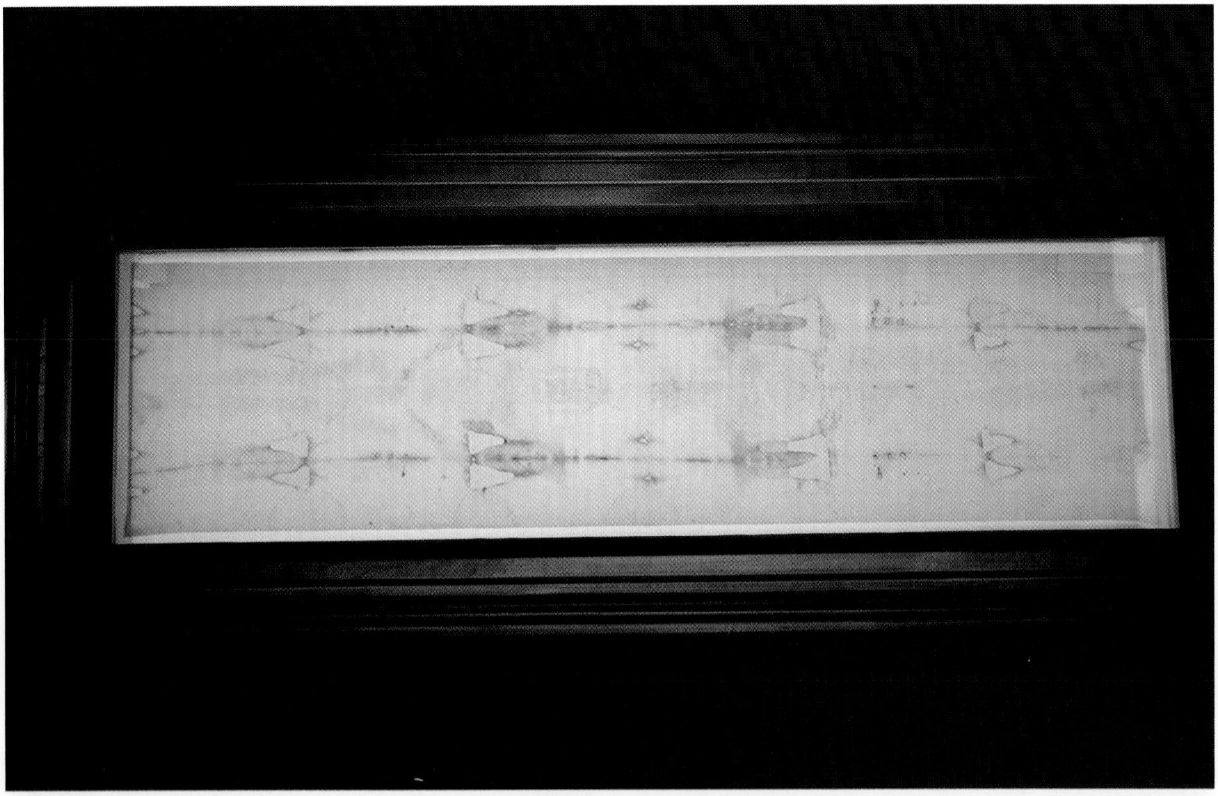

(**f**) The Shroud of Turin, housed at the Cathedral of Turin in Italy. *[©Gaudenti Sergio/Corbis KIPA]*

One of the most striking features of the "true image" is its capacity for replication and the power of copies (of copies of copies) to retain the vitality of the distant, even lost original. In the visual piety of the true image, there is no limit to multiplication. Every copy retains the aura and authenticity of the original. The image of the Virgin and Child appears no less than four times in the print by Ostendorfer (**a**): in the foreground as a sculpture, on the banner waving from the steeple of the church, from a standard fluttering above the crowd on the left of the print, and on the altar inside the church, glimpsed through the open door. Moreover, the image appeared yet again on well over 100,000 clay and silver badges that were produced and avidly acquired by pilgrims to Regensburg during 1520 alone. Images of the Veronica and mandylion were commonly copied and revered across Europe and wherever Catholic missionaries took the faith in the seventeenth and eighteenth centuries. The pattern is recognizable in many kinds of images in Christian practice. The Shroud of Turin (**f**) remains a powerful

(g) *Imagen de la Virgen Maria, Madre de Dios de Guadalupe*, an engraving by Miguel Sánchez depicting an image of Our Lady of Guadalupe on the cloak of Juan Diego, 1648. *[Courtesy of the John Carter Brown Library at Brown University]*

image to this day. Another persistent example is the image of the Virgin of Guadalupe **(g)**, whose origins are likewise miraculous. Images made without human hands may be endlessly copied because the original is devoid of human fabrication. Copies refer to it as faithful relays perhaps because no human is thought to have invented the concept of the image. Seeing the image or a copy of the image connects the devout viewer to the original person—the Virgin or Jesus—with a reliability and a directness that match the viewer's devotion to the person who can satisfy his longing. Acheiropoetic images are representations whose power consists in their promise to destroy the image as artifice and replace it with the very thing to which the image refers. This power of the portrait image is discernible in pre-Christian visual practices that may have informed the earliest conceptions of the Christian icon.

The cult of the saints today remains grounded in the visual piety of selecting an "official" image of the person whom supporters wish to see beatified and then canonized by the church. Supporters of the cause of Mother Teresa have already proffered such an image **(h)**. Since it is based on photographs of the historical person, the image can lay claim to literal accuracy. But the idea of the "true image" does not require the empirical verity of the photograph. Nor is it an idea observed only by Orthodox and Roman Catholic Christians. Warner Sallman, the Protestant painter of the twentieth century's most widely disseminated picture of Jesus **(i)**, stated that this image came to him in a dream or vision, which he quickly

(h) Above. Members of the Sisters of Charity display an image of Mother Teresa in support of her canonization, 2003. *[AP/Wide World Photos]* **(i) Right.** Warner Sallman, *Head of Christ*, oil on canvas. *[©Warner Press, Inc., Anderson, Indiana. Image may not be reproduced without written permission from Warner Press]*

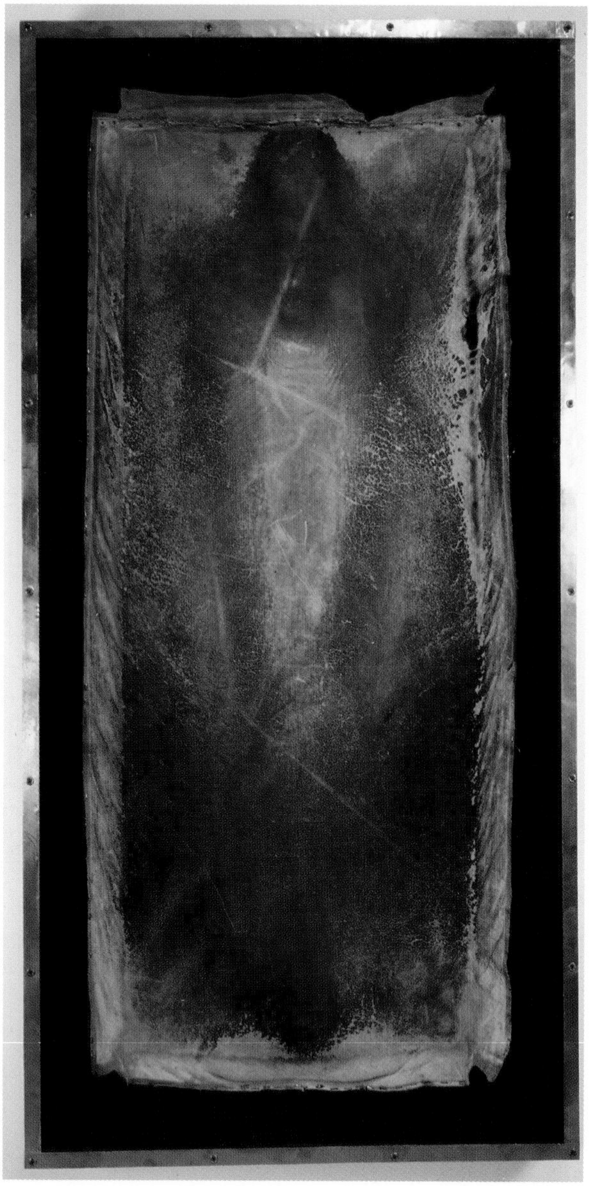

(j) Daniel Goldstein, *Icarian II/Incline*, 1993, leather, sweat, wood, copper, felt, and plexiglass. ***[©1993 Daniel Goldstein; photo credit Benjamin Blackwell; used by permission of the University of California, Berkeley Art Museum]***

transcribed and later painted in a way that suggests the vignette lighting and head-and-shoulders format of portrait photography. And the evocative work of artist Daniel Goldstein **(j)** recalls the mummified figures of Egyptians and the Shroud of Turin **(f)**. Whether fine art or popular devotional imagery, the power of images to endow replicas, even mass-produced replicas, with the presence of the original makes seeing the "true image" a compelling part of religious practice. The search for the original happens by means of the copy.

Bibliography

Belting, Hans. *Likeness and Presence: A History of the Image Before the Era of Art.* Translated by Edmund Jephcott. Chicago, 1994.

Freedberg, David. *The Power of Images: Studies in the History and Theory of Response.* Chicago, 1989.

Kuryluk, Ewa. *Veronica and Her Cloth: History, Symbolism, and Structure of a "True" Image.* Cambridge, Mass., 1991.

MacGregor, Neil, with Erika Langmuir. *Seeing Salvation: Images of Christ in Art.* New Haven, 2000.

Swearer, Donald K. *Becoming the Buddha: The Ritual of Image Consecration in Thailand.* Princeton, 2004.

Tambiah, Stanley Jeyaraja. *The Buddhist Saints of the Forest and the Cult of Amulets: A Study in Charisma, Hagiography, Sectarianism, and Millennial Buddhism.* Cambridge, U.K., 1984.

David Morgan (2005)

AN OVERVIEW [FURTHER CONSIDERATIONS]
SEXUAL RITES IN EUROPE

SEXUALITY: AN OVERVIEW [FIRST EDITION]

In many archaic and traditional societies, sexuality is imbued with religious significance. Myths and rituals exhibiting overt sexual symbolism are often concerned with fertility, both on a cosmic and human level; they are associated with certain religious conceptions, such as divine androgyny, or with the reintegration of the primordial, beatific state that existed before the creation of the world and its social institutions and moral order.

Female sexuality and fertility were important concepts even in the earliest sedentary agricultural societies, which appeared in the Mediterranean region around 7000 BCE. With the development of agriculture, gender roles were differentiated and became more specialized. The question of whether preliterate cultures were aware of the causal relationship between sexual intercourse and pregnancy is still controversial. However, one finds a recurrent identification between woman and furrow (soil), man (phallus) and plow, and intercourse and the act of plowing. Thus human sexuality was associated with the fertility of the natural order.

One can distinguish several general trends in religious attitudes toward sexuality. A "positive" or "naturalistic" attitude may manifest itself in fertility rituals or ritual orgies; a "negative" one, in asceticism and techniques of sexual self-control like those practiced by the Daoists of ancient China. Sexuality may also be perceived as a means for spiritual development, as in the Hindu and Buddhist Tantric tradition.

The sacred character of the ritual orgy is especially evident in some preliterate cultures, where collective rituals followed by intercourse illustrate the religious value of sexual activity. The Aranda and other tribes from central and northwestern Australia practice brief intervals of ritual orgy, during which all sexual proscriptions are suspended. The Aranda believe that they thus return to the freedom and beatitude of their mythical ancestors. Likewise, in Arnhem Land, initiations into the secret cult of the Kunapipi (Gunabibi) emphasize the sacrality of sexual experience and the mystery of feminine fecundity. The final rituals consist of a ceremonial exchange of wives. Ritual license is believed to establish goodwill, friendship, and group cohesiveness.

Also for the Ngaju Dayak of Borneo, sexuality has a sacred character. According to their mythology, the world was created by a godhead conceived as two divine adversaries who engaged each other in violent battle. During the collective annual ceremonies, there is a return to this precosmic sacred time, when as a result of the fighting between the two divinities the world has ceased to exist and social rules and moral interdictions are suspended. While waiting for a new creation, the community lives in the presence of the godhead, which is depicted as the primordial water-snake or the tree of life. Through ritual, its members participate in a sacred orgy, which takes place in accordance with divine commandments (Schärer, 1946, pp. 94ff.).

Another significant sacralization of sexual activity is found in the concept of androgyny. Among the Australian Aborigines, sexual symbolism and activity are considered sacred; only through collective orgies or ritual androgynization can the unity and totality of the primordial time be reenacted. This androgynization is accomplished first through circumcision and then through subincision, an operation that symbolically supplies the initiate with a vulva. The subincised member then represents both the female and male organs. The ritual symbolism of androgyny results in the integration of opposites that constitutes the Australian Aborigines' idea of religious perfection. Ritual practices that transform the male initiate into a "female" are found in societies in Africa, South America, and New Guinea.

In many creation myths, the sexual intercourse or masturbation of a solitary primordial being results in the genesis of the cosmos. In an ancient Egyptian cosmogony, the primeval god is said to have intercourse with his own hand (see Hans Bonnet, *Reallexikon der ägyptischen Religionsgeschichte*, Berlin, 1952, p. 676). This theme is more abstractly stated in a Gnostic myth (Irenaeus, *Against Heresies* 1.30.2) where the "lightdew" emanating from the primordial Father fecundates the Mother and represents a sort of seed. In the myth of the *Śatapatha Brāhmaṇa* (1.7.4), a part of this seed (light) falls below.

Intercourse between gods and mortal women is a common mythological theme. In several cultures, the mythical event is repeated in recurrent rituals that result in the transfer of spiritual "power" from a deity to a human being. During a ceremony of the Cheyenne Indians called "intercourse with the buffalo," married women have intercourse with the elders of the tribe in order to transfer "power" (*xo'pini*) to their own husbands. This rite reenacts the myth of the primordial intercourse between a woman and the Great Spirit, who probably appeared as a buffalo. The Great Spirit's power was further sexually transmitted to the first shaman (see Duerr, 1984).

Horse sacrifices in Ireland and India also reenact a mythical intercourse between a mortal and a god in animal form, through which a transfer of power takes place. According to Gerald de Barri (c. 1146–1223), an Irish king copulated with a mare, after which the mare was killed, cut into pieces, and boiled. The king bathed in this broth, drank it, and ate the boiled meat. This rite is connected with the Celtic equine goddess Epona (from Proto-Indo-European **ekwos*, "horse"). In India, the horse sacrifice (*aśvamedha*) consists of a simulated copulation between the queen and a dead stallion. The queen (*mahiṣī*) lies down beside the stallion and entwines her legs with the hind legs of the horse. The ritual suggests that the force of the white stallion will be received by the queen and transmitted to the king.

One aspect of the sacrality of sexuality is expressed in fertility rites; another, in religious techniques of self-control and asceticism. These techniques, however, are not necessarily based on a dualistic tension between "spirit" and "flesh."

Chinese sex manuals of the Eastern Han dynasty (25–220 CE) hint at a Daoist technique of sexual control. This technique was one of the procedures for "nourishing the vital principle" by which a Daoist would achieve immortality. In addition to this sexual practice, two other procedures ("embryonic respiration" and dao-yin, "gymnastics") have been brilliantly described by Henri Maspero (1937). Essentially, practice was that of *coitus reservatus*: ejaculation was stopped by pressure on the seminal duct, while the seed was supposed to turn back and rise to the brain, which was thus "restored." The "female fluid" (vaginal secretions) was "reabsorbed" and contributed toward prolonging life. During one ritual, it was recommended that the participant change partners as frequently as possible (texts mention as many as one hundred partners, but ten seems to be the standard). Despised by Confucians for being both immoral and ruinous to one's health, this practice nevertheless continued until the seventeenth century.

In India, sexuality has played a significant role in religious life and thought since the Vedic period (cf. Eliade, 1969, pp. 254ff.). But it was not until the emergence of Tantrism that sexual practices were considered a means of obtaining spiritual perfection and absolute freedom or immortality. Ritualized sexual union, *maithuna*, is the last and most important of a series of yogic bodily techniques and meditations. Such a union can be realized either spiritually (i.e., with a divine image mentally constructed and projected in front of the practitioner) or physically with one's wife. In contrast to this "right-hand" Tantrism, the "left-hand" schools require as rite partner a *ḍombī* (lit., "washerwoman"), a girl from a lower class or a courtesan. The more depraved and debauched the woman, the more fit she is for the rite. In accordance with the Tantric doctrines of the identity of opposites, the "noblest and the most precious" is hidden precisely in the "basest and most common."

Tantric texts are often composed in an "intentional language" (*sandhyā-bhāṣā*), a sacred, dark, ambiguous language in which a state of consciousness is expressed by erotic terms and sexual meanings. For example, *bodhicitta* ("thought of awakening") means also *semen virile*; *padma* ("lotus") is interpreted as *bhaga* ("womb"); *vajra* ("thunderbolt") signifies *liṅga* (*membrum virile*). But in certain sectarian movements (such as the Sahajīyā, for example), *vajra* also means *śūnya* "emptiness" and *lalanā* "woman" means *iḍā* (one of the "veins" of the Indian mystical physiology), *abhāva* ("nonbeing"), *candra* ("moon"), *prakṛti* ("nature"), "the Ganges," "vowels," and even *nirvāṇa* (cf. other examples in Eliade, 1969, pp. 253ff.). Thus, a Tantric text is to be read on several different levels. For instance, the verse "The woman and the tongue are immobilized on either side of the sun and the moon" can be understood to refer to the arrest of breath but also the arrest of seminal emission.

Sexual union, *maithuna*, serves to make respiration rhythmical and to aid concentration. The final goal of *maithuna* is the simultaneous "immobilization" of breath, thought, and seminal emission. To lead to this paradoxical state, which surpasses the structure and the limits of the human condition, sexual activity must be radically transformed. The instruction and yogic preparation of the disciple are long and difficult. Even the young female partner is duly instructed by the *guru*; she consecrates her body by *nyāsas* (ritual "projections" of divinities). Thus, sexual union becomes a ritual through which the human couple is changed into the divine pair Śiva and Śakti. The texts emphasize the idea that *maithuna* is above all the integration of the two divine principles: for example, the *Kūlārṇava Tantra* (5.111–112) states that "the true sexual union is the union of the *parāśakti* with the *ātman*; other unions represent only carnal relations with women." The "sacralization" of sexuality through rituals and specific types of meditations is strongly and frequently emphasized. "By the same acts that cause some men to burn in hell for thousands of years, the yogin gains his eternal salvation" (Indrabhuti, *Jñānasiddhi* 15).

According to Vajrayāna mythology, the Buddha himself set the example; by practicing *maithuna*, he succeeded in conquering Māra, and the same technique made him omniscient and the master of magical powers (see Eliade, 1969, pp. 263ff.). The ideal of a final reintegration of opposites is a common goal in both Hindu and Buddhist (Vajrayana) Tantrism. *Mahāsukha*, the "great bliss" (i.e., the beatitude of realizing one's Buddhahood), is the paradoxical state of absolute nonduality (*advaya*); it cannot be known dialectically but can be apprehended only through actual experience. In esoteric Vajrayāna, *mahāsukha* can be obtained by the unification of *prajñā* (wisdom) and *upāya* (the means to attain it), *śūnyatā* (emptiness) and *karuṇā* (compassion), and other pairs of opposites that designate "female" and "male." These terms are often represented iconographically by a couple in sexual embrace. Such a union (*yoga*) is known as *advaya*. Sometimes the two deities are combined into one body. The transcending of sexuality is expressed thus in the form of the androgyne.

The idea that semen contains a vital force is common to the Chinese, Indian, and Greek traditions. For the Chinese, the "vital essence" (*ch'i*) is to be spared and increased; in the Indian tradition, the fire of asceticism (*tapas*) produces supernatural powers (*siddhi*); in Greek medicine, sperm contains "spirit" (*pneuma*), a substance whose loss would diminish the vitality of the whole organism. On the contrary, the accumulation of *pneuma* is an essential requisite for those who perform magic. The Indian follows the same logic: an *apsara*, or heavenly nymph, caused the great ascetic Dadhīca (*Mahābhārata*, *Śalyaparvan* 1) to lose his semen, rendering him powerless (see David N. Lorenzen's *The Kāpālikas and the Kālāmukhas*, New Delhi, 1972, pp. 91–92).

In my article "Spirit, Light, and Seed" (1971), I have analyzed Gnostic evidence within a broad religious context in which semen plays an important role. It has been recently demonstrated that Gnostic experiences are connected with the Greek theories of the *pneuma* (see Giovanni Filoramo's

Luce e Gnosi, Rome, 1980). The original Gnostic testimonies (preserved in Coptic) portray gnosis as a meditative and ritual process in which the strenuous efforts of the adept are intended to achieve a sort of ecstasy. These testimonies belong to ascetic trends of gnosis. They contain polemic undertones directed against the followers of libertine trends. Unfortunately, the original testmonies of the latter have not survived.

SEE ALSO Androgynes; Asceticism; Hierodouleia; Hieros Gamos; Homosexuality; Phallus and Vagina; Tantrism; Virginity; Yoni.

BIBLIOGRAPHY

Several of my own works deal with sexuality in early agricultural societies; see especially *Patterns in Comparative Religion*, translated by Rosemary Sheed (New York, 1958), pp. 125–139, and *A History of Religious Ideas*, vol. 1, *From the Stone Age to the Eleusinian Mysteries*, translated by Willard R. Trask (Chicago, 1978), pp. 11–14.

The mytho-religious associations of sexuality among archaic and traditional societies in Borneo and Australia are treated, respectively, by Hans Schärer in *Ngaju Religion: The Conception of God among a South Borneo People*, translated by Rodney Needham (1946; reprint, The Hague, 1963), and by me in *Australian Religions: An Introduction* (Ithaca, N. Y., 1973) and *Birth and Rebirth: The Religious Meaning of Initiation in Human Culture*, translated by Willard R. Trask (London, 1958). Ritual intercourse among the Cheyenne of North America is described by Hans P. Duerr in *Sedra oder die Liebe zum Leben* (Frankfurt, 1984).

Indo-European sexual rites connected with the horse sacrifice are the focus of Wendy Doniger O'Flaherty's *Women, Androgynes, and Other Mythical Beasts* (Chicago, 1980), which is also published under the title *Sexual Metaphors and Animal Symbolism in Indian Mythology* (Delhi, 1980). Sexual practices associated with the Indian Holī festival are analyzed by Johann Jakob Meyer in his famous *Trilogie altindischer Mächte und Feste der Vegetation*, vol. 1 (Zurich, 1937), although his material must be viewed with caution.

Daoist sexual practices, their origin, means, and aims, have been presented in an excellent essay by Henri Maspero: "Les procédés de 'nourrir le principe vital' dans la religion daoïste ancienne," *Journal asiatique* 229 (1937): 177–252, 353–430. This essay is now readily available in *Le daoïsme et les religions chinoises* (Paris, 1971), pp. 479–589 (see esp. pp. 553–577), and in the English translation by Frank A. Kierman, Jr., *Taoism and Chinese Religion* (Amherst, 1981). The history of Daoist practices is outlined by Robert Hans van Gulik in *Sexual Life in Ancient China* (Leiden, 1961). Here van Gulik develops his earlier treatment of the topic in *Erotic Colour Prints of the Ming Period, with an Essay on Chinese Sex Life from the Han to the Ch'ing Dynasty, B.C. 206–A.D. 1644* 3 vols. (Tokyo, 1951), a rare book.

On Tantric practices, see my *Yoga: Immortality and Freedom*, 2d ed. (Princeton, 1969), Agehananda Bharati's *The Tantric Tradition* (London, 1965), and Wendy Doniger O'Flaherty's *Asceticism and Eroticism in the Mythology of Śiva* (London, 1973). I have described the intellectual pattern underlying several sexual experiences in the religions of the world in "Spirit, Light, and Seed," *History of Religions* 11 (1971): 1–30, now available in my *Occultism, Witchcraft, and Cultural Fashions: Essays in Comparative Religions* (Chicago, 1976).

MIRCEA ELIADE (1987)

SEXUALITY: AN OVERVIEW [FURTHER CONSIDERATIONS]

The theme of human sexuality lies behind much of the most significant, influential, and revolutionary theorizing of the modern study of religion. From Jean-Martin Charcot's early speculations on the remarkable similarities between female hysteria and traditional forms of religious rapture to Sigmund Freud's reflections on the culturally and personally defining mechanisms of Oedipal desire and the sexual dynamics of dreams, literature, and religious phenomena and from the radical ethical critiques of the patriarchal dimensions of these same motifs within nineteenth- and twentieth-century feminist theory to the latest transformations of this ethical-critical discourse within contemporary queer theory, gender studies, and trauma theory, human sexuality, as Michel Foucault so famously observed, has become a central preoccupation of critical thought and is now commonly approached as "the secret" of human identity and behavior, including—and especially—religious identity and behavior.

Certainly such an approach needs to be balanced by other methods and insights, particularly those involving the crucial issues of race and class (themselves inevitably gendered and sexualized), as considerations of the sexual never exhaust the impossibly full semiotic range of religious phenomena. Moreover, sexual motifs in the history of religions hardly signify simple "sexuality" as that category is commonly used today (that is, in a strictly biological, materialistic, or socialized sense), but rather almost always simultaneously connote other specifically transcendent potentialities of the human being and the universe. Despite modern and postmodern doubts about positing ontological meanings, the historical religions have consistently connected human sexuality with cosmic energies and powers that extend far beyond what is meant today by "sexuality." Moreover, they have seen in human sexuality—which they have either repressed, expressed, or, more commonly and complexly, sublimated, symbolized, or displaced—some of the deepest dynamics, even causes, of cosmic creation, community, religious authority, sanctity, aggression, violence, sin, bondage, suffering, salvation, enlightenment, and liberation. The sexual is indeed, even in the religions, one of "the secrets" around which human identity in all its social, political, economic, biological, and religious complexity is constructed (and so also deconstructed).

Ever since Foucault famously reconceptualized "homosexuality" (by asserting that the idea of a stable homosexual identity developed in tandem with modern Western medical and psychological discourses, and that cultures that lacked such linguistic categories could not have produced such identities), it has been tempting to suggest, as many have in fact done, that these allegedly ancient and universal connections between the sacred and sexual are primarily a function of modern language games—that is, that we see such things in history because modern forms of social experience and consciousness, embodied in modern technical vocabularies and economic arrangements, encourage us to do so. This is no doubt partly true. And even if some of the most recent writing on the history of sexuality suggests that such a Foucauldian thesis, at least in its strongest forms, should probably be abandoned now—as it appears that ancient cultures not only knew about what we might call "sexual orientations" but actually created categories of persons and identities to express and classify these, sometimes in an explicitly medical register (see especially the texts of John Boswell and Bernadette J. Brooten for Christianity and the collaborative works of Murray and Roscoe on Islamic homosexualities, Sweet and Zwilling on the early Buddhist and Jain categorizations of sexual identities, and Vanita and Kidwai on same-sex love in Indian literature), this same methodological constructivism has had an immensely creative and positive effect on scholarship since the 1970s, by forcing it to become more self-reflexive about its categories and more critically aware of its histories.

Still, given that every human being throughout history has "had" a body (the English expression is misleading, as it already presumes a questionable dualism) that was presumably created, developed, and defined by the same genetic, hormonal, and developmental processes that largely determine our own, it seems doubtful indeed that one can err too far in positing a broadly construed sexuality as a universal determinative of the history of religions. At the same time, one must recognize that the range of culturally determined sexual expression and identity, along with their attendant religious and metaphysical meanings, probably far exceeds the capacities of imagination, not to mention of analysis.

Sexual Transgressions and Social Utopias. As any number of ancient mythologies and legal systems can show, sexuality has often, if not always, been perceived as a difficult force to control and define. Indeed, much of the religious concern with sexuality boils down to the question of how sexuality can be canalized into the acceptable lineage and inheritance flows of family, clan, tribe, or community.

The inevitable flip side and necessary structural opposite of this social control is found in two phenomena, either as they are actually practiced or as they are imagined: the orgy and the carnival. In both, sexuality is (or is thought to be) ritually used—sometimes symbolically, sometimes quite literally—to break down, at least momentarily, carefully constructed and maintained structures of social control. Such phenomena have played an especially important role in modern theories about religion, particularly via the works of Georges Bataille, Mikhail Bakhtin, and Victor Turner. Bataille's philosophical reflections on taboo and transgression as the psychological keys to the experience of the sacred as personal dissolution into a cosmic continuity, Bakhtin's notion of the carnival and the creative uses of ritual transgression, and Turner's famous reflections on ritual liminality and *communitas* (that unique form of social bonding that is created in moments of ritual transition and transgression) all point to the essentially charismatic power of sexuality and its abilities to transform human religious and social structures, either temporarily or permanently.

Certainly the religions themselves have often considered transgression as a path to a kind of momentary utopia or as a means of social experiment or even revolution. One thinks immediately, for example, of any number of Hindu or Buddhist Tantric traditions, in which the structures of caste, purity, and moral code are systematically violated, often through sexual acts, in an attempt to reveal the illusory nature of all dualisms and expose the deeper nondual or empty nature of reality. One thinks also of the Daoist sexual yoga that was practiced to build up and preserve enough biophysical energy to power spiritual flight toward immortality, a pursuit often in considerable tension with the more mundane Confucian concerns about family and state. Similar patterns can also be seen in Western cultural history. Hence the reports of "deviant" sexual acts so prominently featured in attacks against heresy throughout the history of Christianity, from early claims that Christian Gnostics used sexual fluids as sacramental substances to modern reports of sexual abuse among the Branch Davidians. So too the early modern European concern over witchcraft, which was often expressed through sexual motifs such as the witch's intercourse with the devil, the physical nature of Satan's semen, stolen penises, and the occult orgy—a collective obsession Walter Stephens has read as a late medieval attempt to salvage the supernatural in the face of an early modern skepticism by "proving" it through the physicality of the witch's sex with her "demon lovers." One might also point to another bearer of cultural instability and change, the 1960s American counterculture, which was defined largely by an efflorescence of alternative religious experiments (many of them, interestingly enough, of an Asian, and often Tantric, extraction) and by the triply transgressive mantra, "sex, drugs, and rock and roll."

"Deviant" forms of sexuality and radical social change, in other words, often go hand in hand for the simple reason that social structure (who is who, who is related to whom, who has power over whom) is determined largely by sexual practices and definitions (who penetrates whom and with what meanings). Alter either those practices or those definitions and one alters that structure. In other words, the oft-cited claim that human identity and religious truth are socially constructed, often taken as nihilistic or relativistic, can also be read as implying a kind of golden lining, for what has been constructed can always be reconstructed (after it has been deconstructed). And human sexuality, both because of its ecstatic, emotionally "dissolving" capacities and its dramatic powers to express, violate, or affirm intimate social meanings, is a uniquely powerful site for the realization of these deconstructions and reconstructions.

This socially creative function of religious sexuality is illuminatingly examined in Lawrence Foster's 1984 study of three significant nineteenth-century American religious experiments, each of which arose shortly before the Civil War: the Shakers, the Oneida Perfectionists, and the Mormons. Each of these new religions advanced their utopian visions through alternative sexual practices (interestingly, all based largely on an identical New Testament passage, *Matthew* 22:23–30) that their contemporaries ridiculed, feared, and, in many cases, actively combated. All three traditions, in their responses to the radically new social and economic conditions of an industrializing and individualizing America, shared the conviction that religious life needed to be radically reformed around new theologies, although each community developed a very different sexual embodiment of its respective utopian vision. Thus the Shakers opted for complete celibacy, the Oneida Perfectionists practiced both a kind of "male continence" *(coitus reservatus)* and group marriage in which sexual partners were shared among the community, and the early Mormons turned to polygamy. Sexual experiment, social experiment, and religious revelation were thus all intimately linked.

THE GODDESS, THE ANDROGYNE, AND THE FEMALE MYSTICAL GUIDE: IDEALIZATIONS AND INTERPRETED REALITIES. One of the most oft-noted features of the religions studied in contemporary scholarship is their virtual erasure of the feminine from the divine and, subsequently, from the public social order. It is indeed striking just how absent actual women are in the textual records of the history of religions. This has led, among many other pursuits, to a quarter-century flurry of studies of goddess cults, much of which has been driven by a single question: does the presence of female deities necessarily, or even usually, result in the greater social empowerment of women "on the ground"? The question has been endlessly debated, but one general conclusion, reached around the turn of the twenty-first century, is rather surprising: not only do female deities generally not result in the greater social empowerment of women, there is increasing evidence to suggest that strong goddess cults often correlate negatively with such empowerment; that is, traditions (such as Roman Catholicism or Brahmanic Hinduism) that display dramatic interest in feminine figures tend to disempower women more than traditions that do not display such an interest. There does seem to be some general relationship between symbolism and sociology, then, but that relationship is not always what one might first expect and is by no means stable.

Whatever one chooses to make of such debates, one thing seems beyond question: namely, that women have been generally denied access to scriptural texts and their interpretation, to leadership roles in the community, and to the sacred itself. In recent scholarship, different versions of this thesis have been argued literally thousands of times, in fields ranging from biblical studies to Buddhology. Two very different cases will be sufficient to make our point here: medieval Jewish Qabbalah as studied by Elliot Wolfson in his *Through a Speculum That Shines* (1994), and the *tulku* system of Tibetan Buddhism as analyzed by June Campbell in her *Traveller in Space* (1996).

Much earlier work on the feminine in Qabbalah, focused primarily on the *Shekhinah* or female manifestation of the Godhead, appears to have been driven, implicitly or explicitly, by either a type of Jungian enthusiasm for identifying the *Shekhinah* as the *anima* or "female soul" of Jewish mysticism or by an Eliadean idealization of divine androgyny as a *coincidentia oppositorum,* or "coincidence of opposites." Such readings of androgyny as expressing a kind of spiritual wholeness or gender balance still have much to offer, and no doubt capture part, maybe even much, of the truth, but they need to be deepened and qualified by later, more critical work. More recent scholarship in both Jewish Studies and Indology, for example, has demonstrated that androgyny is often actually a kind of "male androgyny" that admittedly includes but does not grant equal semiotic weight to the feminine, much less to actual women. Ellen Goldberg's 2002 study of the Hindu deity Ardhanārīśvara, the "Lord Who Is Half Woman" (and not, the Goddess Who Is Half Man), is a powerful example of this recent trend, as is Hugh Urban's 2001 study of Tantric rituals in which the female essence is absorbed into the male practitioner, who then stands in for the perfect unity of the god and goddess. One also thinks of Douglas Wile's eloquent and astonishingly detailed studies of Daoist sexual yoga, which show that even though heterosexual intercourse was used by Daoists to reconstitute the primordial "androgyny" of the *dao* as *yin* and *yang,* its primary purpose was to allow the male practitioner to "steal" the mystico-erotic energies of the woman in order to reconstitute that unity in himself.

Wolfson's work on medieval Jewish mysticism has demonstrated something similar, namely, that what the male qabbalists were after finally was a vision of the divine phallus perceived through the cloud-like or amorphous feminine energy, or *Shekhinah,* of God. Jewish mysticism, in other words, employs feminine symbolism and even actual sexual ritual (medieval qabbalists were required to have sex with their wives on the eve of the Sabbath in order to help redeem the divine and human worlds) not in order to establish the centrality, agency, or importance of women or to effect some kind of perfectly symmetrical gender balance, but to arouse the essential and final maleness of God. In structural terms, Qabbalah is both phallocentric (that is, it centers on the phallus of God) and homoerotic (for what we ultimately have are male mystics uniting, through women, with a male God). As in Indian or Chinese sexual yoga, the actual woman is a ritual means toward this end, but her own subjectivity and agency are hardly concerns for the qabbalist, at least as he is represented in the mystical texts themselves.

June Campbell's feminist analysis (itself deeply indebted to the earlier psychoanalytic analyses of Robert A. Paul) of the different institutional, symbolic, and ritual structures of Tibetan Buddhism that work to remove, silence, or literally threaten female agency shows us something similar again. Campbell's intellectual and autobiographical account of her heartfelt search for the *ḍākiṇī*—that female "traveler in space" who mystically guides the spiritual quests of Buddhist meditators by synchronously appearing in their dreams, visions, and scriptural readings—turns out to be both poignant and, ultimately, tragic. Put too simply, Campbell doesn't find her. As part of a wide-ranging analysis, Campbell turns, for example, to the well-known *tulku* system—in which an infant boy is taken away from his mother by an all-male monastery after being identified through ritual and parapsychological means as a dead lama's reincarnation—in order to demonstrate convincingly how "woman" is removed almost entirely from the institutional system in an attempt to create a mythology in which men reproduce and raise themselves independently of women. In the *tulku* mythology, the reincarnated lama's mother is a reproductive organ, but little else; she is a means to an end, not a person in her own right with inalienable rights to her own son and a crucial role to play in his upbringing. Campbell's analysis, moreover, has a personal dimension, as she draws on her experience as a Tantric consort of one of the highest-ranking lamas of contemporary Tibetan Buddhism to demonstrate how secrecy and threats serve to silence women and preserve a false front of celibate authority. Here Tantric ritual practice, far from being a sacralization of human sexuality or a mark of sexual liberation (as it is often presented in apologetic sources) is essentially abusive. By means of secrecy, public denial, and threats, it denies "woman" the very place where Tibetan iconography so dramatically places her: on the lap of the Buddha. Recent work, particularly that of Judith Simmer-Brown, has sought to qualify or soften Campbell's analysis, but the very existence of the debate suggests that the problems of feminine identity and the abusive charismatic guru in Tibetan Buddhism are real ones that will likely not disappear, as the *ḍākiṇī* herself so often does, for a very long time.

GENDER, SPIRITUAL ORIENTATION, AND THE SEXUAL PRODUCTION OF SANCTITY. As historians of religion have studied the feminine since the 1970s, they have grown increasingly aware that the meanings of religious symbols and rituals shift, even reverse, when the gender perspective from which they are observed is switched. In other words, one cannot presume that, say, the experience of animal sacrifice (almost always a male activity), ascetic practice, or even meditation are the same for men and women within a particular religious tradition. Sexual renunciation in early Christianity, for example, no doubt worked very differently for many women—whose lives in Roman society would have been dominated by early and life-long child-rearing and the lack of social opportunities—than it did for most men. And certainly the innumerable misogynistic elements of scriptural and ascetic texts are now read as products of the male psyche and its projections, and not as an accurate representation of "woman" in a particular society. Put simply, we now commonly "read" religion through the lens of gender.

Somewhere around 1980, another major hermeneutical shift occurred within religious studies, this time directing attention toward the category of sexual orientation. In the wake of studies such as John Boswell's magisterial *Christianity, Social Tolerance, and Homosexuality* (1980), it was no longer sufficient to ask about the gender of a particular perspective or phenomena, as if every male ascetic who had "renounced" sexual contact with a woman in order to enter an all-male community or love a male deity was conquering his sexual desires instead of finding a cultural outlet more attuned to his particular sexual-spiritual inclinations. Sexual sublimation, from Plato's *Symposium* to Freud's *Three Essays,* is hardly simply about sex; it is also about the sublime and the mystical, and it is often decidedly homoerotic. Suddenly, everything—from David and Jonathan's intimate friendship and Jesus' "beloved disciple," to Catholic clerical celibacy and Buddhist monasticism—looked different.

Foucault's late work on the history of sexuality (which relies on the earlier pioneering essays of K. J. Dover) is foundational here, particularly as it was picked up, developed, qualified, and corrected by such writers as John Boswell, Daniel Boyarin, Howard Eilberg-Schwartz, Mark Jordan, and Bernadette J. Brooten. Developed and advanced most fully in Greek, Christian, and Jewish contexts, this body of theory eventually was applied to other cultural arenas as well, particularly the Sambia of New Guinea and the Zuni of the American southwest via the pioneering ethnographic work of Gil Herdt and Will Roscoe; Islam through the coedited volumes of J.W. Wright Jr. and Everett K. Rowson and Stephen O. Murray and Will Roscoe; Hinduism via the textual studies of Jeffrey J. Kripal (1995), Giti Thadani, Ruth Vanita and Saleem Kidwai, and Devdutt Pattanaik; and Buddhism through the work of José Cabezón, Michael Sweet and Leonard Zwilling, and Bernard Faure. Recently, moreover, now turning the lens back on itself, a similar erotic hermeneutic has been used to study the psychosexual production of critical theory in the study of religion through an examination of the mystico-erotic experiences of the scholars themselves (see Kripal, *Roads of Excess*).

Certainly one of the most dramatic (and culturally relevant) facets of this scholarly history has been the sexual analysis of Roman Catholicism, particularly as developed in the work of the medieval historian, ethicist, and contemporary cultural critic Mark Jordan. In *The Invention of Sodomy* (1997), Jordan studied the theological origins and rhetorical uses of the category, concept, and term *sodomy.* In his *Silence of Sodom* of a few years later, Jordan demonstrated convincingly (well before the Catholic sex scandals became public in the spring of 2002) that modern Catholicism, despite its vehement public condemnations of homosexuality as a moral and psychosexual "objective disorder," actually produces some stunningly rich and complex homoerotic subcultures within its very heart, in effect defining sanctity as a form of repressed and sublimated (homo)sexuality. Theologically, liturgically, and institutionally, Catholicism privileges an all-male structure whose goal is to encourage and nurture, through a series of male-controlled practices and beliefs, a profound love for another male (deity). In the process, the tradition manages to feature any number of typically "gay" or "queer" practices, from the formation of same-sex communities to liturgical cross-dressing and the adoration and consumption of the male body, all under the normalizing guise of a very large and venerable religion. In effect, the gay Catholic cleric passes as straight in public even as he flaunts his queerness through a series of traditional religious practices that Jordan calls "clerical camp."

This might be a particularly extreme (and so particularly instructive) argument, but the ubiquitousness of celibacy, male imagery, and same-sex communities within religious contexts certainly suggests that the sexual production of sanctity—through the control of theological definition and institutional authority, and through the simultaneous repression and sublimation of erotic energies—is a process very much worth exploring. Here, it seems, one begins to approach one of the secrets of sanctity itself.

TRAUMA AND TRANSCENDENCE. In the broad twentieth-century attempt to understand the altered states of consciousness commonly labeled "mystical"—historically described by the religions themselves in sexual and violent terms (sexual ecstasy and death are arguably the two most common tropes of mystical literature)—scholarly and philosophical discourse eventually had to confront the difficult question of contemporary trauma theory and the related and vexing question of sexual abuse. From the early pioneering speculations of Joseph Breuer, Sigmund Freud, and Jean-Martin Charcot, that "master diagnostician of the supernatural" (Mazzoni, 1996, p. 9), through the literary and philosophical writings of Georges Bataille, Judith Herman, and Judith Butler, to the modern psychiatric studies of Robert Jay Lifton and Bessel A. van der Kolk and the philosophical and textual studies of Amy Hollywood, theorists have consistently read specific types of altered states as psychological responses or symptomatic responses to a previous shattering experience of physical or sexual trauma.

Human beings, these theorists argue in a wide variety of psychological and theological keys, routinely experience life events that are mentally and physically shattering. These may occur in dramatic contexts such as war, political persecution, rape, the death of a loved one, spousal abuse, or a terrorist act, or in the context of less obviously dramatic life events (for example, a divorce, car accident, or witnessed crime) that are nonetheless psychologically damaging. The key is not necessarily the external "objective" nature of the event but the way the human mind responds to it.

A central feature of the conceptualization of trauma is the metaphor of the broken or invaded body-container. In her classic 1966 study *Purity and Danger,* the anthropologist Mary Douglass pointed out the centrality of this metaphor in the construction of purity systems around the world. Purity here is constituted and performed by those substances or acts that preserve both the world order as it is imagined by the community and the body-container of the individual/community—the "social body," as it were. Any substance that oozes or flows from a break in this social(ized) body, or any act that effects such a break, is by definition impure. Tellingly, eating and sex are associated with the classic cases of taboo and impurity, because in each of these activities substances flow in and out of the body-container. Interestingly, trauma theorists have turned to the same symbolism to make sense of what happens when psychic and bodily integrity is lost and boundaries of all sorts are violated, are penetrated, or simply disappear. A specifically traumatic response occurs when something from the outside, something "impure," breaks through the container, denies those boundaries so carefully set up by society in the mind, and possesses the victim as something alien and external. Following such experiences, the mind often returns to the traumatic event through memory, nightmare, obsessive thoughts, or compulsive ritual behavior. Many contemporary theorists and analysts believe that healing can occur only when the traumatized individual is able to recover the event (which he or she may not even remember—forgetfulness or repression are central to trauma) and incorporate it into some sort of narrative or creative response. It is necessary, in other words, to tell a story, to speak the unspeakable, to give witness to the traumatic event, to quite literally re-member the integrity of one's body and soul before the abyss of forgetfulness, denial, and silence.

All of this has profound, and profoundly ambiguous, implications for readings of the trance, ecstatic, and possession phenomena so common in the history of religions. From the account of Jesus' healing ministry recorded in the New Testament (see Davies, 1995), to the repetitive ritual cycle of the Christian liturgy with its meditative focus on a politically tortured man, to the latest scandals involving Catholic priests or charismatic gurus, sexual trauma and altered states of consciousness—and their sacralization—appear repeatedly and seem remarkably ripe for critical analysis and reinterpretation. If there is yet another edge to the "cutting edge" of scholarship on sexuality and the history of religions, this is likely it.

THE ETHICAL AND THE ONTOLOGICAL. Consideration of the relationship between trauma and religion is inherently provocative because it raises very serious questions about many precritical idealizations of religious forms of sexuality, and about the different ways in which religious traditions draw on sexuality and its traumatization to create numinous phenomena. Certainly many early forms of scholarship and most forms of religious belief erased, transformed, or simply did not see such sexual and traumatic dimensions. Happily, such tendencies have been corrected or reversed in recent scholarship. Bernard Faure's examination of Buddhist sexuality, for example, has not hesitated to isolate and question ethically problematic, even abusive, elements of the Buddhist traditions. What to do, for example, with an Indian tantric ritual in which the practitioner has sexual intercourse with a twelve-year-old "maiden" (Faure, 1998, p. 51)? And what should we make of the widespread sexual (ab)use of young boys in Japanese Buddhism that Faure has studied in such detail? Catholic Boston is hardly the exception, it turns out, and might best be understood within a broad comparative study of celibacy, misogyny, sexual sublimation, charisma, secrecy, and altered states of consciousness. Certainly, the *eros* of the mystical as it has been developed and experienced within any number of religious systems appears to be, if we are to believe its many diverse witnesses, ontologically primordial, that is, rooted deeply and blissfully in (human) being, even as its effective access usually requires strategies of sexual repression, moral condemnation, and social suffering that are, by many modern standards, ethically problematic, to say the least. Perhaps it is this same double message, this same mysteriously attractive fear *(mysterium tremendum),* that gives such experiences their enduring numinous power, their conflicted energies, their sacrality.

Although such thoughts certainly honor modern and postmodern discourses about sexuality as the most adequate entry into the topic, it also remains true that, if we are going to remain faithful to our sources, we must be prepared to move beyond our own, perfectly legitimate, ethical, and political concerns to ask the most basic question of all: from the various perspectives of the historical religions, what is sexuality? In the end, this is an ontological question that cannot be answered here, and it may very well have absolutely nothing to do with our or anyone else's ethical concerns. But it is still very much worth asking, as its very asking exposes what will otherwise remain hidden—that is, our own generally naturalistic ontologies of the sexual that can only erase from view what the religions themselves have revealed in so many different ways—namely, that there is something else here, something at once terrific and traumatic, something of mythological proportions that only religious, mythical, poetic, or mystical language can begin to express. The Chinese Daoists ridiculed those who used their sexual yoga merely to increase sexual pleasure or prolong foreplay. This was not what it was ultimately about, at least to the esotericists themselves, who saw their elaborate sexual techniques primarily as a means to effect a mystical alchemy that would transform their physical bodies into a state of winged immortality (remember Plato's *Phaedrus*?). One may or may not share their views on the possibility of such things, but one would do well to at least listen to their hermeneutical complaints and not collapse mystical forms of eroticism—from John Humphrey Noyes's "male continence" to the Daoist's sexual yoga—into modern Western notions of an entirely natural or material sexuality. Sexuality and the sacred are certainly connected, and intimately so, but they do not appear to be the same thing, and their ethical dilemmas are many, at least if one is to take seriously the elaborate sexual witness of the history of religions.

See Also Phallus and Vagina.

Bibliography

Bataille, Georges. *L'Érotisme.* Paris, 1957. Translated by Mary Dalwood as *Death and Sensuality: A Study of Eroticism and the Taboo* (New York, 1962), later reprinted as *Erotism: Death and Sensuality* (San Francisco, 1986).

Boswell, John. *Christianity, Social Tolerance, and Homosexuality: Gay People in Western Europe from the Beginning of the Christian Era to the Fourteenth Century.* Chicago, 1980.

Brooten, Bernadette J. *Love between Women: Early Christian Responses to Female Homoeroticism.* Chicago, 1996.

Campbell, June. *Traveller in Space: In Search of Female Identity in Tibetan Buddhism.* New York, 1996.

Davies, Stevan L. *Possession, Trance, and the Origins of Christianity.* New York, 1995.

Douglas, Mary. *Purity and Danger: An Analysis of the Concepts of Pollution and Taboo.* London, 1966.

Faure, Bernard. *The Red Thread: Buddhist Approaches to Sexuality.* Princeton, N.J., 1998.

Faure, Bernard. *The Power of Denial: Buddhism, Purity, and Gender.* Princeton, N.J., 2003.

Foster, Lawrence. *Religion and Sexuality: The Shakers, the Mormons, and the Oneida Community.* Urbana, Ill., 1984.

Goldberg, Ellen. *The Lord Who Is Half Woman: Ardhanārīśvara in Indian and Feminist Perspectives.* Albany, N.Y., 2002.

Gulik, R. H van. *Sexual Life in Ancient China.* Leiden, Netherlands, 1961.

Herdt, Gilbert H. *Guardians of the Flutes: Idioms of Masculinity.* New York, 1981.

Hollywood, Amy. *Sensible Ecstasy: Mysticism, Sexual Difference, and the Demands of History.* Chicago, 2002.

Jordan, Mark. *The Invention of Sodomy in Christian Theology.* Chicago, 1997.

Jordan, Mark. *The Silence of Sodom: Homosexuality in Modern Catholicism.* Chicago, 2000.

Kripal, Jeffrey J. *Kālī's Child: The Mystical and the Erotic in the Life and Teachings of Ramakrishna.* 2d ed. Chicago, 1998.

Kripal, Jeffrey J. *Roads of Excess, Palaces of Wisdom: Eroticism and Reflexivity in the Study of Mysticism.* Chicago, 2001.

Kvam, Kristen E., Linda S. Schearing, and Valerie H. Ziegler, eds. *Eve and Adam: Jewish, Christian, and Muslim Readings on Genesis and Gender.* Indianapolis, Ind., 1999.

Mazzoni, Cristina. *Saint Hysteria: Neurosis, Mysticism, and Gender in European Culture.* Ithaca, N.Y., 1996.

Murray, Stephen O., and Will Roscoe, eds. *Islamic Homosexualities: Culture, History, and Literature.* New York, 1997.

Pattanaik, Devdutt. *The Man Who Was a Woman and Other Queer Tales from Hindu Lore.* New York, 2002.

Roscoe, Will. *The Zuni Man-Woman.* Albuquerque, N.M., 1991.

Simmer-Brown, Judith. *Dakini's Warm Breath: The Feminine Principle in Tibetan Buddhism.* Boston, 2001.

Stephens, Walter. *Demon Lovers: Witchcraft, Sex, and the Crisis of Belief.* Chicago, 2002.

Sweet, Michael J., and Leonard Zwilling. "The First Medicalization: The Taxonomy and Etiology of Queers in Classical Indian Medicine." *Journal of the History of Sexuality* 3, no. 4 (1993): 590–607.

Sweet, Michael J., and Leonard Zwilling. "Like a City Ablaze: The Third Sex and the Creation of Sexuality in Jain Religious Literature." *Journal of the History of Sexuality* 6, no. 3 (1996): 359–384.

Swidler, Arlene, ed. *Homosexuality and World Religions.* Valley Forge, Penn., 1993.

Thadani, Giti. *Sakhiyani: Lesbian Desire in Ancient and Modern India.* London, 1996.

Urban, Hugh B. *The Economics of Ecstasy: Tantra, Secrecy, and Power in Colonial Bengal.* Oxford and New York, 2001.

Van der Kolk, Bessel A., Alexander C. McFarlane, and Lars Weisaeth, eds. *Traumatic Stress: The Effects of Overwhelming Experience on Mind, Body, and Society.* New York, 1996.

Vanita, Ruth, and Saleem Kidwai, eds. *Same-Sex Love in India: Readings from Literature and History.* New York, 2000.

Wile, Douglas, ed. *Art of the Bedchamber: The Chinese Sexual Yoga Classics, Including Women's Solo Meditation Texts.* Albany, N.Y., 1992.

Wolfson, Elliot R. *Through a Speculum That Shines: Vision and Imagination in Medieval Jewish Mysticism.* Princeton, N.J., 1994.

JEFFREY J. KRIPAL (2005)

SEXUALITY: SEXUAL RITES IN EUROPE

Religiously motivated sexual rites date back to the early years of humanity's existence. Since the beginning of farming, the woman's sacral position shifted into the foreground and her secret fertility has been compared with that of the earth, as the planting of the field has been compared to the sexual act. Orgiastic rites aimed at increasing the earth's fertility, therefore, probably date to humanity's early period as well.

Already historically ascertained, however, are the great feasts in honor of Dionysos, who appears as Bakchos (Bacchus) in his orgiastic-mystic perspective. Their distinguishing characteristic was the frenzy, in which men and women—filled with God—stepped outside of themselves. According to Plutarch, the orgiastic feasts were celebrated at night on mountaintops, accompanied by torchlight and music. The wild flock of maenads (bacchantes), who in their frenzy ripped apart young animals and devoured the raw flesh, was accompanied by nymphs, satyrs, and sirens, who performed openly obscene acts. In the train of the Magna Mater cult, these rites entered Rome in the third century BCE. Followers of this cult not only performed sexually excessive acts, but also criminal deeds, which, according to Titus Livius, caused the Roman Senate to intervene in 186 BCE, and to cease the practice of the cult in the entire empire. This cult already exhibited some of the fundamentals of later sexual rites, up to (or including) modern sexual magic.

GNOSTICISM. These fundamentals can be seen even more clearly and are theoretically better formulated in the first centuries CE in Gnosticism. In various Gnostic systems, as in many ancient mythologies, the highest divine being is androgynous, just as Anthropos, the primal human, is. In order to return to this original wholeness and thereby escape death, which only occurred, according to the *Gospel of Philip,* after the separation of the two sexes, man and woman should sexually unite. In a much broader sense, according to these teachings, with this union other fundamental polarities of the world also become resolved in a *coincidentia oppositorum.* Even the Aeons, as primordial emanations of the supreme being, are said to have come together in sexual intercourse in order to achieve wholeness. For humans, the so-called bridal chamber rite (*thalamos, nymphon*), which was mainly used by the Valentinians, was also a way to reestablish the original divine androgyny; a man as earthly representative of the redeemer (*soter*) and a woman as representative of wisdom (*sophia*) performed the hierogamy (holy wedding), whereupon the present believers copied their actions.

According to an account of Epiphanius from the fourth century (which is not completely above doubt), the Barbelo Gnostics engaged in a prototype of a practice that was also performed in sexual-magical groups of the twentieth century: the ingestion by participants of the rite of the male seed as "body of Christ" and of menstrual blood as "blood of Christ." In this rite, these substances are not used for earthly conception, seen negatively from a Gnostic standpoint, but rather are ingested to achieve self-apotheosis. In Gnosticism as a whole there existed two different ways to achieve this: sexual freedom, but also ascetic tendencies, whose advocates thought to strengthen their spiritual powers by abstaining from sex. A strong proponent was Saturninus, or Satornil, who attempted through strict asceticism (also vegetarianism to a degree) to rescue from Satan's power or influence the part of light in the human being that consisted of light. In a later version, men's sexual proximity to women was permissible, but only in order to strengthen their spiritual power of resistance. This proximity could even extend as far as sexual intercourse, but was not allowed to reach orgasm. This is consistent with ideas that also occur in Indian Tantrism and are similar to the ones ascribed to the medieval Fedeli d'Amore.

CHRISTIANITY. In the first centuries of the Common Era, the repression of sexuality was a common theme within Christianity, contrary to its Jewish origins and the habits of its pagan neighbors. The Desert Fathers were usually converts with a stormy past whose temptations sometimes led them to the brothels in Alexandria. However, the desert standards of asceticism were very repressive, comparable, as far as sexuality was concerned, to the well-known rule of Mount Athos. The sight of a female, even a hen, was regarded as a great spiritual danger. Another example is Macarius, who as a young man was compelled to marry in order to please his parents. By feigning illness, he escaped the marital bed. When his wife died shortly after, he was very relieved and thanked God (see Leloir, 1982). The apostles Andrew and Thomas exhorted rich women to avoid intercourse with their husbands.

A particular importance for the restrictive aspect of sexuality in Christianity is accorded to the influential church father, Augustine of Hippo (354–430). For him, sexual desire was not something "natural," thus being originally willed by God, but rather a punishment for Adam's original sin, which also had sexual connotations for him. Abstinence was thus seen as a path to spiritual freedom from sin.

Sexuality was sometimes even violently repressed by self-mutilation. Castration was practiced by the priests of Cybele, called Galli. It has been suggested that their practice of emasculation could have had an influence on the Christian rejection of sexuality, which is exemplified by Origen's act of self-castration.

FEDELI D'AMORE. When considering the Middle Ages, the so-called Fedeli d'Amore should be mentioned, even if their historical existence as a movement is not firmly established. However, the importance of the movement arises from the fact that Dante Alighieri (1265–1321) is supposed to have been the main proponent of this secret group, which allegedly lasted up to Boccaccio (1313?–1375) and Petrarch (1304–1374). The aim of the Fedeli d'Amore was to free men (and only men) from their earthly limitations and to lead them to divine wisdom through the all-transcending love for a woman (who need not necessarily be a real one, in which case the term *woman* was to be understood as an allegory for the female principle). Dante called this *trasumanar,* which means "going beyond a purely human existence." This practice could lead to erotic trials, whereby the man lay naked next to his "woman" for an entire night, but was not allowed to touch her (*asag*). Through this "love" that transcended all other powers, he lost his "memory" (his usual human individuality), according to Dante, and reached a higher level of awareness. Thereafter, a so-called "exchange of hearts" is said to have occurred, which may suggest the attainment of a kind of androgynous state.

RENAISSANCE MAGIC. In the sixteenth century, in a cultural context in which the ancient theories concerning *pneuma* or *spiritus* were still popular (see Daniel Walker, 1958), the philosopher and magician Giordano Bruno (1548–1600) achieved a spectacular synthesis between the love theories of Marsilio Ficino (1433–1499), the art of memory (see Yates, 1972), and magic. The result, found in two manuscripts probably written in Wittenberg (*De vinculis in genere*), is an erotic magic aimed at the total sexual self-control of the adept. The adept, acquainted with the practices of the art of memory, is instructed to learn to keep his fantasies under control. The images or phantasms produced are under certain circumstances transmitted to the individual or group that is to be magically "bound" (this is the meaning of the verb *vincire,* from which the noun *vinculum,* "bond," is derived). The images consciously produced by the adept are intended to correspond to the erotic expectations of the subjects to be "bound." The magician operates with phantasms that are sometimes sexual, yet he is at the same time completely immune to sexual stimuli. Bruno recommends that the adept never release sperm, for sperm retention represents the correct way to make "bonds" *(vincula).* But Bruno does not seem to have any particular exercise of semen retention in mind. His practices, which are meant to control sexuality through imagination, are similar in principle to Indian Tantric practices.

THE SKOPTSY ("the castrated"), a sect that originated in Russia in the eighteenth century as a dissenting group of the Russian Orthodox Church, resumed the practice of self-mutilation. They still existed in Russia up to 1930, and even later in eastern Romania, where they traditionally exerted a monopoly on coach driving. The Skoptsy are representatives of a view of the world in which the spirit is strongly opposed to the flesh; they believed that only through contempt and mortification of the flesh could the spirit be fully developed. Their efforts to suppress physical lust led in extreme cases to the excision of genitalia. It was said that, in one of their ceremonies, the left breast of a girl aged fifteen or sixteen was excised in a warm bath, after which the assembly took communion by eating the raw flesh that had been cut into fine pieces (Gehring, 1898, pp. 149–150). Even if this story was invented by their detractors, gruesome practices were common among the Skoptsy. Women sometimes had parts of their external genitalia and even one or both breasts cut off. For men, emasculation took place in several stages called *seals:* in the first, the testes were removed; in the second, the penis. In some cases also the pectoral muscles were cut into. And even mutilations on the shoulders, the back and the legs are attested. One could thus become an "angel with five (or six) wings."

THE KHLYSTY. The Skoptsy derived from an earlier sect whose members called themselves *Christy,* that is, "apt to become Christ themselves." They were contemptuously nicknamed the *Khlysty* (whips, or flagellants). Constantly persecuted by the authorities but secretly supported by the fervent nuns of the Ivanovskii cloisters in Moscow and by several merchants, the sect was active until 1762. The Khlysty were ascetic puritans who abstained from meat, alcohol, and tobacco; they fasted, prayed, and performed severe penances. They were said to have practiced infanticide and cannibalism in their secret meetings and to have performed a Black Mass on the naked body of a woman called *bogoroditsa* (bearer of God), whose child had been sacrificed.

The Khlysty were also said to have practiced a kind of *lucerna extincta* rite, in which men and women came together at night and, turning off the lights, had intercourse. They were sometimes alleged to have indulged in incestuous or homosexual intercourse. For the Khlysty, promiscuous intercourse took place after lengthy dances and after forty to fifty strong clashes between groups of men and women gathered in opposite corners of the room (Gehring, 1898, pp. 153–154). Even Grigorij Rasputin (1869–1916), who had great influence at the court of Tzar Nicolas II, propagated individual neo-*khlystic* guidelines. However, he most probably did not belong to such a sect himself.

LUCERNA EXTINCTA. The rite of *lucerna extincta,* as practiced by the Khlysty, has a long history. Livy attributed its origin to the Dionysiac (or Bacchic) groups in Rome. Justin Martyr was the first one (in 150 CE) to accuse heretics of engaging in sexual orgies with the lights extinguished. On the other hand, according to the apologists Minucius Felix and Tertullian, enemies of the church attributed these rites to Christians in the second century CE. Clement of Alexandria mentions them in his description of the Gnostic Carpocratians. In 719 John of Odzun accused an Armenian Adoptionist sect of practicing *lucerna extincta;* in 1050 Michael Psellus accused the Bogomils in Thrace; and in 1090 Paul of Chartres said the heretics of Orléans performed it. In 1180 Walter Map stated that French heretics practiced this rite; Pope Gregory IX, in his bull *Vox in Roma* (1233), attributed it to heretics in Germany and to the Waldensians. Several fifteenth-century sources report that the Franciscan "Fraticelli" were involved in *lucerna extincta* practices.

There are also more recent cases of *lucerna extincta* rites, including those practiced by the followers of the Russian peasant Daniil Filippov (d. 1700). In 1645 Filippov convinced several people that God the Father had come to abide in Filippov's own "pure body." Thenceforth, Filippov called himself Sabaoth and gained several followers. Seven years later, he recruited the peasant Ivan Timofeevich as son and Christ. Suslov was said to have been miraculously born in 1616 (a purely fictitious date) from 100-year-old parents. The trinity was completed by a young girl who bore the titles of "bearer of God" and "daughter of God." Twelve apostles completed the picture. Suslov was repeatedly arrested and tortured, and, though his followers claimed that he was resurrected twice, it seems more probable that he was eventually released. He lived his last thirty years in Moscow and died in 1716 at the age of one hundred, a mythical age attributed to many founders of sects in Russia.

In addition to *lucerna extincta,* fornication and debauchery were also attributed to other heretics of the Middle Ages. The followers of Tanchelm of Antwerp (d. 1115), for instance, were said to have organized revels in which young girls were deflowered in the presence of their mothers; wives and children were offered to Tanchelm's lust (see Russell, 1965, p. 65).

In *Europe's Inner Demons* (1975), Norman R. C. Cohn analyzes the histories of groups that were said to engage in esoteric sexual practices. In dealing with the period from 186 BCE to the end of the fifteenth century, Cohn found that in all allegations of promiscuous intercourse there was a suspicious pattern of uniformity. Promiscuity was frequently associated with more gruesome practices, the most common of which was infanticide. He noted that testimonies of *lucerna extincta* and other practices are directed against groups that seem to form a direct threat to the state or the church and are meant to discredit these groups. These testimonies present a regular pattern, whether they describe Bacchanalia in 186 BCE or witch-hunts in the sixteenth and seventeenth centuries; they belong to a stereotype of detraction used by several power groups against their opponents. Cohn admits that the idea of sexual promiscuity is consistent with the dualistic view of the world held by groups like the Gnostics, Manichaeans, Paulicians, Bogomils, and Cathari. But the first four groups were ascetic, and even the sexual freedom of the Cathari "believers" (in contrast to the asceticism of the "perfect") found its expression in individual deeds, not in collective rites.

WITCHES' SABBATH. Reports of the so-called witches' Sabbath have always been a central theme in the history of sexual rites. What these rites really embody has been answered in different ways by research. As Mircea Eliade wrote, today it is difficult, almost impossible, to determine what was real and what was imaginary when it comes to the witches' confessions. The persecution of witches began in the middle of the fifteenth century, reached its climax in the sixteenth and seventeenth centuries, and subsided around the middle of the eighteenth century. In total, there are said to have been around sixty thousand male and female victims of these witch-hunts; female victims are more numerous, despite extensive regional differences. As Brian Levack states in his book *The Witch-Hunt in Early Modern Europe* (1987), the massive witch-hunt came about because belief in the reality of the witches' Sabbath was widespread. Such a Sabbath was said to involve several witches, who performed blasphemous, obscene rites, which included worship of the devil and which ended in sexual orgies. Therefore, when one witch was condemned, others had to be sought as accomplices.

The English Egyptologist Margaret Murray attempted to prove in *The Witch-Cult in Western Europe* (1921) that the descriptions of the witches' Sabbath given by the witches indicated that they were not torture-induced phantasms, nor drug-induced hallucinatory experiences. The witches' Sabbath was more likely the relic of a pre-Christian peasant fertility cult, which continued to exist into modern times, even supplying the roots of the modern witch movement (Wicca) of the twentieth century. This theory, however, no longer has many followers in scientific circles. On the contrary, the sexual researcher R. E. L. Masters, in his book *Eros und Evil* (1962), argues that the confessions, which contained every imaginable type of sexual debauchery, can be traced to the witch-hunters' morbid erotic fantasies, as well as the victims' hysteria and drug dependency.

Eliade, on the other hand, in *Occultism, Witchcraft, and Cultural Fashions* (1976), emphasizes that the witches' radical protest against the reigning societal and religious circumstances were expressed through the witches' Sabbath. One did not become a witch in order to indulge one's sexual desires, but rather in the hope that these rituals would lead to redemption from the difficulties of everyday life and to bliss as it was once allegedly experienced by humankind in its primeval state in "paradise." Eliade considered it proven that the witches' Sabbath could not have been about sexual desires, because witches often described coitus with the devil as being extraordinarily painful, and this voluntary suffering indicated that the Sabbath was a severe initiation rite.

Carlo Ginzburg in *Ecstasies: Deciphering the Witch's Sabbath* (1989/1992) addresses the witches' sabbath in a particularly comprehensive and well-documented manner. Ginzburg's earlier *The Night Battles* (1966/1985), a groundbreaking work, had attempted to uncover a core of truth in Margaret Murray's unverifiable statements. With the use of court files, he was able to prove the existence of a pagan agrarian cult called *benandanti* among farmers living in northern Italy in the sixteenth and seventeenth centuries. Ginzburg also investigates the true background of the witches' Sabbath. In doing so, he takes the witches' statements during their trials very seriously and does not consider them to be fantasies or torture-induced confessions, in contrast to many authors of mainly feminist bent, who directed their attention almost exclusively to the cruel persecution of women by men. Nevertheless, Ginzburg does not find proof that such events actually took place. Instead, he suspects a more than 1000-year-old residuum of Euro-Asiatic myths and rituals related to shamanism to be the basis of the witches' Sabbath.

In *Demon Lovers* (2002), Walter Stephens delivers a precise investigation, based on early texts on the persecution of witches between 1430 and 1530, describing sexual intercourse between hellish demons and earthly women. The great interest that the inquisitors, judges, and experts at that time had in this question is not considered by Stephens to be based on hostility towards women or on misguided erotic desires on the part of the men. He is convinced, rather, that these men were concerned with serious metaphysical problems. If actual sexual intercourse between supernatural demons and terrestrial women could be proven, then the existence of demons and their interaction with our world would be proven as well. And if there were demons, then there existed also an order beyond our world, and thus a God. In this way, doubts in God, which mainly arose from Aristotle's writings, could be put to rest.

Black Mass. By the end of the seventeenth century, fears of witchcraft were replaced by a more skeptical attitude. Obscene rituals and satanic cults were only being celebrated in very small circles, in which individual moments were more central, as Gerhard Zacharias writes in *Satanskult und Schwarze Messe* (1970, p. 106). In 1682 King Louis XIV of France transferred all responsibility for prosecuting witchcraft from ecclesiastical to secular tribunals, effectively ending the witch-hunts in France. Witches were to be prosecuted only if they had committed crimes against civil law. During such legal proceedings by a special police commission against a group of people accused of poisonings, it was discovered that Black Masses being held in Paris were accompanied by erotic practices and infanticide, and Louis XIV's mistress, the Marquise de Montespan, was involved in the affair. Police reports of the time claim that her naked body served as an altar upon which the Black Mass was performed. Intercourse with the celebrating priest usually followed the profanation of the wafer. The performers of the mass were priests; infant sacrifices seem actually to have been performed.

In the seventeenth century, sexual repression in French nunneries in some cases manifested itself in the form of a sexual frenzy which seized the nuns and spread under the guise of a demonic and diabolic possession inside the convent but also to other nunneries. Several priests, including Louis Gaufridy, Urbain Grandier, and Jean-Baptiste Girard, are connected to these cases. The old Gnostic idea that sin could only be conquered by sin was central to these cases, and the nuns became involved in orgies and peculiar sexual behavior. The most famous cases involved Madelaine de Demandolx de la Palud (Aix-en-Provence, 1611), Jeanne des Anges (Loudun, 1633), Magdelaine Bavent (Louviers, c. 1644), and Catherine Cadière (Aix-en-Provence, 1731). One story of diabolic possession involved Elizabeth de Ranfaing (Nancy, 1618–1625), an attractive woman who subjected herself to self-mortification in an attempt to make herself ugly. In 1617 she succumbed to attacks of uninhibited sexual frenzy that lasted until 1625. After the male doctor who was accused of causing this sexual frenzy was executed, de Ranfaing founded a spurious monastic order noted for its emphasis on iron discipline and sexual repression. This order was, however, condemned by the Holy Office in 1644 and Pope Innocence X in 1649.

Frankists. Sexual rituals were also performed under the leadership of the qabbalist Jakob Leibowicz (1726–1791), known as Frank (Davidowicz, 1998, pp. 343, 354-356). Frank hoped that these rituals would enable him to reach the hidden harmonizing *Sefira Daat* of the qabbalistic tree of life on the terrestrial plane. By performing a "holy wedding," the cosmic harmony would be reestablished. It is not clear how exactly the rituals were performed or how often (probably seldom). At any rate, the sexual acts were performed according to precise directives from Frank, with Frank's followers as witnesses. It is also reported that Frank would suck on women's breasts for "nourishment." Davidowicz advises against judging the Frankists as simple heretics, but rather sees a meaningful link to the latter Qabbala in their teachings. It would be just as misleading to label the Frankists a spin-off of the Shabbateans. In the case of their founder, Shabbetai Tsevi (1626–1676), the practice of sexual rituals is uncertain, even if erotic mysticism and sexual permissiveness were indisputably an aspect of this group after Tsevi's conversion to Islam (Scholem, 1973, pp. 669, 880). In later Shabbatean circles, this sexual permissiveness is much more strongly pronounced.

Magia Sexualis. In the eighteenth and nineteenth centuries, sexual rites became central to the ceremonies of erotic "satanic" clubs. Members of these clubs were usually wealthy young men, such as the English dandy Francis Dashwood of the so-called Knights of Saint Francis of Wycombe, more commonly called the Hell-fire Club. In 1753 Dashwood formed his own sexual brotherhood in Medmenham Abbey, adopting the motto "Fais ce que tu veux" ("Do What Thou

Wilt") from the Thelema Abbey of François Rabelais. In 1763 the English public was shocked to learn that even its prime minister, its chancellor of exchequer, and other cabinet ministers had been masquerading as "monks" and celebrating sexual rites with "nuns."

The founder of modern sexual magic is undoubtedly Pascal Beverly Randolph (1825–1875), an African American writer who rose from poverty to become a trance medium and occultist serving the very high aristocratic, literary, scientific, and occult circles in America, Europe, Asia, and Africa. Randolph became acquainted with the founder of the Theosophical Society, H. P. Blavatsky, though a bitter hostility later arose between the two due to occult rivalry. In his travels Randolph collected vast knowledge of magical mirrors, narcotics, and sexuality as an access to occult knowledge. Around 1870 he founded the Brotherhood of Eulis, through which he published manuscripts on sexual magic. Randolph's teaching reached Europe through the English bookseller Robert H. Fryar, who marketed Randolph's manuscripts in Great Britain. After Randolph's death, the Hermetic Brotherhood of Luxor emerged from among Fryar's friends. The brotherhood expanded Randolph's teachings under the leadership of Max Théon (the pseudonym of Louis Maximilian Bimstein, Binstein, or Beinstein; 1848?–1927), Peter Davidson (1837–1915), and Thomas Henry Dalton (1855?–1895?), better known by the name of Thomas H. Burgoyne.

Sexuality stood at the center of the entire metaphysical system and spiritual experience of the Hermetic Brotherhood of Luxor. Male-female polarity was seen as the original principle of the universe and the primary driving force for evolution. Consequently, the sexual union of a man and woman became a practical path to unity, the divine self, and a state equal to that of an angel. The "vital secretions" or "seminal fluids" that are created by sexual intercourse were seen as fundamental elements for the construction of a "spiritual body." Sexuality was the only thing that could bring the neophytes into contact with higher spiritual spheres and powers of a heavenly hierarchy.

Another important factor for the emergence of modern sexual magic was the fact that Tantric teachings became known in the West. The Victorian pornographic writer and amateur mythologist Edward Sellon (1817/8–1866) is said to have played a key roll with his *Annotations on the Sacred Writings of the Hindus* (1865), which interpreted Tantrism in a one-sided way as purely erotic magical teachings.

Twentieth-century sexual magic. The influence of the Hermetic Brotherhood of Luxor on all subsequent occult groups in Europe and the United States cannot be overestimated; sexual magic became the most intimate central mystery of many of these groups. It is, however, not entirely clear how these ideas were transferred to them. The Hermetic Brotherhood of Light, which was founded in Chicago or Boston in 1895, seems to have played a major role. Seemingly it was from this brotherhood that the irregular German Mason Theodor Reuss (1855–1923) adopted the secret. Reuss in turn initiated the best-known "black magician" of the twentieth century, Aleister Crowley (1875–1947). Reuss was an opera singer and journalist, who founded an entire series of irregular lodges, including the Ordo Templi Orientis (OTO), which he established between 1906 and 1912. Its sexual teachings, which had undergone much further development since Randolph, found expression especially in its seventh, eighth, and ninth degrees, based, respectively, on autoerotic, heterosexual, and homosexual practices. The Austrian chemist Carl Kellner (1850–1905) was an important predecessor to Reuss.

Crowley's OTO rites differed from Reuss's, from which they had emerged. Crowley, whose well-known motto "Do What Thou Wilt" can be traced back to "Fais ce que tu veux" of Rabelais's Thelema Abbey, but which is primarily directed towards discovering the "true will" of one's own personality, expanded his OTO hierarchic structure to twelve degrees. The eighth degree mainly consisted of masturbating on the symbol or sigill of a spirit or demon that was to be called forth. The ninth degree consisted of heterosexual intercourse in which the sexual secretions were consumed or used for evoking a spirit. The eleventh degree was fundamentally homosexual, whereby bleeding caused by anal intercourse was to call up the spirits, whereas the sperm kept them alive.

The basic premise in this form of sexual magic was the fixation of the spirit and will during orgasm solely on some spiritual or material goal, rather than on emotional climax. In this way the spiritual and astral world would be so strongly influenced that this goal would become material reality. Crowley strived for money and success with women through these activities, but he also sought the path to the "conversation with his Holy Guardian Angel," which must be seen as a type of divine self.

The OTO, which still maintains branches in numerous countries, inspired a series of new movements, which also saw themselves as obliged to perform sexual magic in the most varied forms. Examples include the Great Brotherhood of God and the OTOA (A stands for "Antiqua") under Michael Paul Bertiaux, as well as the Typhonian OTO under Kenneth Grant. One might also include the well-known Californian Church of Satan led by Anton LaVey, among whose members was the actress Jane Mansfield, although their beliefs were less esoteric and more directed towards material and social success. The sexual magic of Crowley's OTO also had a major influence on the modern witch movement (Wicca), a fact which can be attributed to Gerald Gardner (1884–1964). Gardner, who met Crowley before his death, founded one of the first modern English covens and propagated the ideas of Margaret Murray, according to which modern witchcraft relates back to an ancient pagan folk religion.

The Russian "Priestess of Satan," Maria de Naglowska (1883–1936), settled in Paris after having spent time in Egypt, Italy, and Switzerland. In Paris, she probably summarized and translated into French several of Randolph's sexual magic manuscripts and books, and published them in his name with the title *Magia Sexualis.* Naglowska also celebrated so-called satanic masses and private séances in Paris; these were actually only preliminaries for *messes d'or* (golden masses) in which seven couples were simultaneously to engage in public sexual intercourse. Self-strangulations in order to enhance the sexual stimulus were practiced in high initiations of men. In her teachings, De Naglowska pleaded for a future matriarchal culture.

In the German-speaking world, the Fraternitas Saturni emerged in 1928 in Berlin from an offshoot of the Panosophic Lodge of Heinrich Tränker (1880–1956), who also led the German branch of Crowley's OTO for a time. The leader of the Fraternitas Saturni was Eugen Grosche (Gregor A. Gregorius 1888–1964). Gregorius, who composed a substantial portion of the lodge's extensive magical material, was mainly interested in creating astral entities with the help of the male and female sexual secretions, which would then be available as spiritual aides when performing other magical operations. The astrological positions of the stars were important for this group—the stars even determined individual coital positions when performing the rites. The famous eighteenth degree of the fraternity's hierarchy, the so-called Gradus Pentalphae, was purely sexual-magical, but most likely it was seldom performed.

Rituals of sexual magic may have also been practiced around 1928 by the Viennese lodge Hekate under the Austrian Orientalist Franz Sättler (1884–c. 1942; fraternal name Dr. Musallam), and by their Berlin branch. Wilhelm Quintscher (1893–1945), who was in contact with Sättler, was also involved with sexual magic in his Orden Mentalischer Bauherren (roughly translates as "Order of Mental Architects"). The Belgian Kymris lodge, which was founded in the 1920s under the Chevalier Clément de Saint-Marcq, was engaged in the ingestion of sexual secretions for purposes of magical rejuvenation. This group considered the devouring of sexual secretions as the actual secret meaning of the Christian last supper.

Italy, too, has witnessed (and is still witnessing) orders that are concerned with sexual magic. The best-known movement is the Fratellanza Terapeutica e Magica di Myriam, which stood under the leadership of Giuliano Kremmerz (the pseudonym of Ciro Formisano, 1861–1930) and based its teachings on an ancient Italic school, to which Count Cagliostro is said to have belonged. The Myriam was connected to a certain Ordine Osirideo Egizio, which allegedly practiced the most secret part of the sexual-magical teachings. However it is not completely clear to what extent the order's manuscripts, first publicly circulated in 1985, contain falsifications. The purpose of the sexual-magical operations described in the manuscripts was to separate a person's solar "spirit" from his physical, astral, and mental bodies in order to autonomize this spirit and to construct around it a body of glory totally independent from earthly constraints, which was supposed to have the ability to survive even physical death. Following exact astrological calculations and long periods of fasting, male and female sexual secretions had to be ingested in a particular order. These procedures were known as *Arcana Arcanorum,* and they formed a type of "internal alchemy," similar to what has been known in India and China for centuries.

Kremmerz' beliefs were also known to the Italian cultural philosopher, Dadaist, and esotericist Julius Evola (1898–1974), who led the magical Group of Ur from 1927 to 1929. This group also espoused teachings from sexual magic. For Evola, sexuality was the only remaining direct path to transcendence for modern humans. According to the order's documents, followers strove to free the spirit from terrestrial constraints by building a body of glory as an instrument for overcoming physical death. This was to happen by conquering the general elementary "principle of life," which reigns over the earthly world and which was said to hide behind the sexual drive. This principle of life, whose flipside is death, was goaded to increasing degrees through sexual encounters, until it would present itself "uncloaked" in a paroxysm. In that moment this spiritual principle had to be permanently overcome in a sudden and dangerous tour de force. Among the practitioners of the Group of Ur (in contrast to Crowley, the OTO, and Kremmerz), the male sexual magician had to resist orgasm at all costs. If he gave in to the elementary powers hidden behind the whipped-up sexuality, they would overwhelm him and he would be driven to death or madness. This path to immortality was, however, only open to men, because women were considered to be the earthly representatives of the previously mentioned principle of life. Evola, who was friends with the reputed Orientalist Giuseppe Tucci, provided probably the most interesting presentation of the connections between religion, esotericism, and sexuality in his book *Metaphysics of Sex* (1958), even if it is marked by his so-called traditional idiosyncrasies.

SUMMARY. What constitutes the power of religiously motivated sexual rituals, which have been in existence since the dawn of humanity? George Bataille (1897–1962) sees excessive eroticism and orgies as a transgression of borders that hit human individuality in its most intimate core. Bataille compares this crossing with death, because the same abyss into transcendence opens up in both cases. Individuality ceases to exist and something deeper comes into being: a *mysterium tremendum,* that which is "holy" in the sense of Rudolf Otto.

For Michel Maffesoli, the orgy and the Dionysic festival satisfy the desire to be together, only on a much larger scale, and they form thereby a necessary counterpart to the ossified rules of everyday life. The arising orgiastic life-emotion becomes then a fundamental structure for society. Maffesoli points out that the orgiastic element is always attributed to darkness, chaos, and night, and thereby it balances out regular daily activities. The divinely social element already represented by community in itself is, according to Maffesoli, celebrated by the chaos of the orgiastic bodies embracing each other in darkness. In the course of this process, one's own body is expanded into a collective body and is thus strengthened.

In conclusion, one must ask whether the term *rite* is even appropriate in this context. *Rite* stems from the Latin term *ritus*, which means "legitimate, regular action." *Ritus* in turn is connected with the Sanskrit *ṛta*, which means "cosmic order" or "truth." Is it not the case that the aim of all the sexual rites discussed in this entry is to question and thwart precisely this general cosmic order and legitimate action?

SEE ALSO Castration; Clitoridectomy.

BIBLIOGRAPHY

General and easily readable surveys on sexuality and religion include Denis de Rougemont, *L'amour et l'occident* (Paris, 1939; rev. ed., 1972), translated by Montgomery Belgion as *Love in the Western World* (New York, 1956; rev. ed., Princeton, 1983), a book that has proven to be very influential; H. Cutner, *A Short History of Sex Worship* (London, 1940), which portrays the history of the phallus cult; Nicolas James Perella, *The Kiss Sacred and Profane: An Interpretative History of Kiss Symbolism and Related Religio-Erotic Themes* (Berkeley, 1969), the contents of which go far beyond the title; the richly illustrated book by Clifford Bishop, *Sex and Spirit* (London, 1996); and Gerhard J. Bellinger, *Im Himmel wie auf Erden: Sexualität in den Religionen der Welt* (Munich, 1993).

Information about the sexual theories and practices among the Gnostics is mainly to be attributed to the church fathers Hippolytus, Ireneaus, and Epiphanius, as well as to writings from Nag Hammadi. As secondary literature see Mircea Eliade, *Occultism, Witchcraft, and Cultural Fashions: Essays in Comparative Religions* (Chicago and London, 1976), pp. 93–119; see pages 85–88 for an important analysis of the *lucerna extincta.* See also Benjamin Walker, *Gnosticism: Its History and Influence* (Wellingborough, U.K., 1983), pp. 107–132 and 147–158; Giovanni Casadio, *Vie gnostiche all'immortalità:* (Brescia, Italy, 1997), pp. 97–117, from which readings were held at the Eranos conference in 1990 in Ascona; Leonhard Fendt, *Gnostische Mysterien* (Munich, 1922); See also L. Leloir. "Infiltrations dualistes chez les Pères du désert," in *Gnosticisme et monde hellénistique*, edited by Julian Ries (Louvain-la-Neuve, Belgium, 1982), pp. 326–336, and Ioan Petru Culianu, *Expériences de l'extase* (Paris, 1984). For the development of sexual teachings in Christianity in the first centuries, Elaine Pagel's *Adam, Eve, and the Serpent* (New York, 1988) is recommended.

There are only a few references dealing with the Fedeli d'Amore in religious scientific literature, including Elemire Zolla, *L'amante invisible* (Venice, 1986), and Mircea Eliade, *Birth and Rebirth: The Religious Meanings of Initiation in Human Culture* (Chicago, 1958). Eliade even attributed a highly probable "initiatic" structure to this movement. See also Henry Corbin's translation of Ruzbehan, *Le jasmin des fideles d'amour* (Lagrasse, France, 1991), and H. T. Hakl's essay "Die Getreuen der Liebe" in *Gnostika* (January 1998): 38–43, (July 1998): 43–50, and (October 1998): 41–50. The entire realm of courtly love is explored in Roger Boase, *Origin and Meaning of Courtly Love* (Manchester, U.K., 1977). With respect to literary historical studies, see the works by Luigi Valli, in particular his *Il linguaggio segreto di Dante e dei "fedeli d'amore,"* (Rome, 1928), and Alfonso Ricolfi, *Studi sui fedeli d'amore* (Foggia, Italy, 1983). Sexual self-control in Renaissance magic is described in Ioan P. Coulianu, *Eros and Magic in the Renaissance* (Chicago, 1987). For the Renaissance see also: Daniel P. Walker, *Spiritual and Demonic Magic from Ficino to Campanela* (London, 1958); Frances A. Yates, *The Art of Memory* (Chicago, 1972);

Promiscuous ritual intercourse is documented in Norman Cohn, *The Pursuit of the Millennium: Revolutionary Millenarians and Mystical Anarchists of the Middle Ages*, 3d ed. (New York, 1970), and in Jeffrey Burton Russell, *Dissent and Reform in the Early Middle Ages* (Berkeley, 1965; reprint, 1982). Gustave Welter provides a useful study of practices among Russian sects in *Histoire des sectes chrétiennes, des origines à nos jours* (Paris, 1950). See also J. Gehring, *Die Sekten der russischen Kirche* (Leipzig, Germany, 1898), as well as the very skeptical Karl Konrad Grass, *Die russischen Sekten*, Vol. 1, *Die Gottesleute oder Chlüsten* (Leipzig, Germany, 1907; reprint, 1966), and Nikolai Volkov, *La secte russe des castrats* (Paris, 1995). Rasputin is the topic of Alexander de Jonge's book *The Life and Times of Grigorii Rasputin* (New York, 1982).

For the history of the Black Mass see H. T. F. Rhodes, *The Satanic Mass* (London, 1954), which is popular but outdated in some areas by newer more detailed studies. Gerhard Zacharias's *Satanskult und Schwarze Messen* (Wiesbaden, Germany, 1970) reproduces numerous original texts, and also contains original material on the witches' Sabbath and the French possession cases. Satanic rites are the subject of Montague Summers's best known book, *Witchcraft and Black Magic* (London, 1946; reprint, New York, 2000).

The best book on the famous possession cases of the seventeenth century is Robert Mandrou, *Magistrats et sorciers en France au dixseptième siècle* (Paris, 1968); short surveys are provided by Jacques Finné in *Érotisme et sorcellerie* (Verviers, Belgium, 1972). For information on qabbalistic sexual rites, see Klaus Samuel Davidowicz, *Jakob Frank, der Messias aus dem Ghetto* (Frankfurt am Main, 1998), and Gershom Scholem, *Sabbatai Sevi: The Mystical Messiah, 1626–1676* (Princeton, 1973). Sir Francis Dashwood and the Hell-fire Club are dealt with in Donald McCormick, *The Hell-Fire Club: The Story of the Amorous Knights of Wycombe* (London, 1958).

On sexual magic, see Joscelyn Godwin, Christian Chanel, and John P. Deveney, *The Hermetic Brotherhood of Luxor: Initiatic and Historical Documents of an Order of Practical Occultism* (York Beach, Me., 1995), which summarizes all known material from this movement and offers an excellent introduction. On the OTO, see Peter R. König, *Das O.T.O. Phänomen* (Munich, 1994), which was partly translated into English and is available online at http://www.cyberlink.ch/~koenig/. See also *O.T.O. Rituals and Sex Magick* by Theodor Reuss and Aleister Crowley, edited by A. R. Naylor (London, 1999). The most comprehensive book on Aleister Crowley is John Symonds, *The Beast 666: The Life of Aleister Crowley* (London, 1997). There is little material available about Maria de Naglowska, the most extensive being the brochures by her pupil Marc Pluquet: *La Sophiale* (Paris, 1993).

For English-language material on the Fraternitas Saturni, see S. Edred Flowers, *Fire and Ice: Magical Teachings of Germany's*

Greatest Secret Occult Order (Saint Paul, Minn., 1990), a short survey work. One can receive insight into the rituals from *Documenta et Ritualia Fraternitatis Saturni*, edited by Adolf Hemberger (Giessen, Germany, 1975–1977). This seventeen-volume work has only been hectographed and has never been offered for sale. On sexual magic in Myriam and the Ordine Osirideo Egizio, see Giuliano Kremmerz, *Corpus philosophorum totius magiae* (Milan, Italy, 1987).

A broad overview of sexuality in esotericism, including Daoist, Tantric, and magical practices, is presented from a traditionalist viewpoint by Julius Evola in his *Metaphysics of Sex* (New York, 1983). The manuscripts of the Group of Ur are presented in *Introduzione alla magia* (Rome, 1987) in three volumes, of which the first has been translated into English as *Introduction to Magic: Rituals and Practical Techniques for the Magus*, edited by Julius Evola and the Ur Group (Rochester, Vt., 2000). See also George Bataille, *Erotism: Death and Sensuality* (San Francisco, 1991); and Michel Maffesoli, *The Shadow of Dionysus: A Contribution to the Sociology of Orgy* (Albany, N.Y., 1993).

IOAN PETRU CULIANU (1987)
HANS THOMAS HAKL (2005)
Translated from German by Marvin C. Sterling

SEYMOUR, WILLIAM. William Joseph Seymour (May 2, 1870–September 28, 1922) is regarded as the founder of Pentecostalism, a movement characterized by the experience of what members refer to as "speaking in tongues." This movement has roots in the Holiness and Perfectionist traditions that emerged in Methodism during the mid-nineteenth century.

Seymour was born in Centerville, Louisiana. In 1900 he moved, via Indianapolis, Indiana, to Cincinnati, Ohio, where he came under the influence of the Holiness minister Martin Wells Knapp. Seymour answered the call to ministry after recovering from a bout of smallpox in which he lost vision in his left eye. He was ordained in 1902 and relocated to Houston, Texas, in 1903, where he became the interim pastor of a Holiness church during the absence of the permanent pastor, Lucy Farrow.

In December 1905, Seymour began attending the Bible school Charles F. Parham had opened in Houston, although racial prejudices forced him to audit classes and sit outside the classroom. Parham taught that Christians needed to be baptized not only with water but also with a second baptism of the Holy Spirit that would be accompanied by speaking in unknown tongues.

Seymour absorbed Parham's doctrines. In 1906 he was invited to either pastor or conduct a revival at a Holiness church in Los Angeles that had broken away from its Baptist affiliation. Although Seymour's Holiness preaching was rejected by those in control of the Holiness congregation, who barred him from the church, several key persons were converted to his view and began meeting with him at a home on Brae Street. Under the influence of Seymour's preaching, people began speaking in tongues at an evening meeting on April 9, 1906. The group grew in numbers and moved to an abandoned building on Azusa Street that formerly was the First African Methodist Episcopal Church. News of the movement spread rapidly through Seymour's periodical, the *Apostolic Faith*, and the street preaching of newly ordained ministers. In 1907 Seymour's ministry was incorporated as the Azusa Street Apostolic Faith Mission of Los Angeles. People from all racial and ethnic affiliations, such as Charles H. Mason, who founded the Church of God in Christ, flocked to Azusa Street from 1907 through 1908.

Three things have been credited with bringing about a decline in Seymour's influence in Pentecostalism after 1908. First, his administrative assistant moved to Portland, Oregon, and joined the ministry of Florence Crawford, who continued publishing the *Apostolic Faith*. Second, one of Seymour's white ministers, William H. Durham, split the movement along racial lines when he parted company with Seymour to found the Apostolic Faith Mission Church of God. Third, Seymour's wing of the movement lost most of its remaining members in 1913 when the Trinity was rejected at a Pentecostal camp meeting.

Seymour traveled around the country preaching to predominately black audiences during the last years of his life. His wife assumed leadership of his branch of the movement—the Apostolic Faith Mission Church of God—after his death in Los Angeles from a heart attack in 1922. Every major form of Pentecostalism must acknowledge its indebtedness to Seymour.

BIBLIOGRAPHY

Murphy, Larry G., J. Gordon Melton, and Gary L. Ward, eds. *Encyclopedia of African American Religions*. New York, 1993.

Nelson, Douglass J. *For Such a Time as This: The Story of Bishop William J. Seymour and the Azusa Street Revival.* Birmingham, U.K., 1981.

Nickel, Thomas R. *Azusa Street Outpouring.* Hanford, Calif., 1979.

Synan, Vinson. *The Holiness-Pentecostal Tradition: Charismatic Movements in the Twentieth Century.* Grand Rapids, Mich., 1997.

Wacker, Grant. *Heaven Below: Early Pentecostals and American Culture.* Cambridge, Mass., 2001.

JAMES ANTHONY NOEL (2005)

SGAM PO PA (GAMPOPA). Sgam po pa Bsod nams rin chen (Gampopa Sönam Rinchen, 1079–1153), also known as Dvags po lha rje, "the doctor from Dvags po," was the figure most responsible for systematizing the doctrines and founding the institutions of the Bka' brgyud (Kagyu) sect of Tibetan Buddhism.

According to traditional biographies, he was born in Gnyal, in south-central Tibet, one of several sons of a local doctor. He became a physician in his teens, and later married; he may have fathered one or more children. When he was barely twenty, however, his immediate family died in an epidemic, and he turned his back on worldly affairs. At twenty-five he joined the Buddhist monastic order under the ordination name Bsod nams rin chen, and went to Central Tibet to study with masters of the Bka' gdams (Kadam) sect, founded a half-century before by the great Indian reformer Atiśa (982–1054). Although Bka' gdams pas taught and practiced the Tantras, they placed special emphasis on the proper observance of monastic discipline and traversing the path to enlightenment in gradually ascending steps that began with a spirit of true renunciation, extended to development of the wisdom and compassion of a *bodhisattva*, and only at the end included Tantric methods. Sgam po pa became an accomplished scholar and meditator, but was not fully satisfied with his experiences.

Hearing of the renowned Tantric yogi and poet Mi la ras pa (Milarepa, 1028/40–1111/23), Sgam po pa traveled to the Mount Everest region to meet him in 1109. He remained with him for eleven months, studying a variety of practices that Mi la ras pa had received from his teacher, the farmer and translator Mar pa (Marpa, 1012–1097), who had studied with the Indian scholar and adept Nāropa (c. 966–1040), himself a disciple of the mysterious Tantric master, Tilopa. The practices included complex Tantric meditations in which enlightenment is approached through visualization of oneself in divine form, as well as manipulation of the physical and mental processes in the subtle body. Of these, Mi la ras pa specially prescribed for Sgam po pa the procedure for generating *gtum mo*, or "inner heat," one of the "Six *Dharmas* of Nāropa." He also learned the "great seal" (*mahāmudrā*; Tib., *phyag rgya chen po*), a perspective on reality and a meditative procedure in which enlightenment is reached by direct contemplation of the empty, luminous, blissful nature of the mind. After leaving Mi la ras pa, Sgam po pa spent a decade in various parts of Central Tibet, mostly engaged in meditative retreat, the outcome of which was realization of the nature of his own mind and attainment of an enlightened state.

In 1121, he went to live on Sgam po mountain, in the Dvags region of south-central Tibet. He built a small temple there, offered instruction, and began to attract disciples. He spent most of his remaining years at Sgam po, lecturing to groups of followers and giving individual advice. In the process, he began to systematize the doctrines and establish the institutional base of what would soon be known as the Bka' brgyud (Oral Lineage) sect. A number of his students, most notably Phag mo gru pa (Pakmo Drupa, 1110–1170), Dus gsum mkhyen pa (Dusum Khyenpa, 1110–1193), and Dvags po sgom tshul (Dakpo Gomtsul, 1116–1169), became themselves (or through their disciples) the founders of nearly all subsequent Bka' brgyud monastic centers and teaching lineages—lineages that, because of their common source in Sgam po pa's center in Dvags, generally are referred to as the Dvags po Bka' brgyud (Dakpo Kagyu).

Sgam po pa's collected works consists of approximately forty texts, most of which appear to be compilations of notes taken by his disciples or compositions by later members of the tradition. Besides three biographies of Sgam po pa written long after his death, his corpus includes lecture series in which he interweaves teachings on Mahāyāna, Tantra, and *mahāmudrā*; dialogues on difficult points with a number of his important disciples; instructions on Tantric deities, rituals, and meditations; discussions of *mahāmudrā* theory and practice; and Bka' gdams pa inspired writings on the ascending stages of the path to enlightenment.

Among the latter are two well-known works probably composed by Sgam po pa himself, the *Lam mchog rin po che'i phreng ba* (Precious garland of the supreme path) and the *Thar pa rin po che'i rgyan* (Jewel ornament of liberation). The former is a collection of numbered lists of things to practice, things to avoid, and things to transcend or understand on the path to enlightenment. The latter is Sgam po pa's longest work and magnum opus, an influential systematic exposition of the entire non-Tantric Buddhist path, from gaining a basic appreciation of our capacity for enlightenment; through developing renunciation by recognizing the perils and vicissitudes of *saṃsāra*; to cultivating the compassion, wisdom, and other virtues of a *bodhisattva*; and finally to achieving perfect buddhahood.

Equally important are Sgam po pa's writings on *mahāmudrā*. There are few texts in which he does not address this crucial term, which connotes the empty nature of reality and of the mind and the perfect, blissful realization of it through meditative insight. He gave systematic analyses of various ways in which *mahāmudrā* might be categorized in relation to the different vehicles of Buddhism; tailored to the needs of gradual or "instantaneous" practitioners; divided along the lines of view, meditation, action, and result; and practiced through such procedures as the four yogas (one-pointedness, nondiscursiveness, single taste, and nonmeditation). Sgam po pa's signal contribution to the discussion of *mahāmudrā*, however, was his insistence that it need not exclusively be associated with complex Tantric practice, but might also be taught as an independent topic, suitable even for those who lacked initiation, but had faith in and the blessings of their lama. Sgam po pa saw *mahāmudrā* as both transcending and pervading all vehicles of Buddhism, and his focus on it helped to establish it as a central concern for all subsequent Bka' brgyud pa masters, as well as a topic of discussion and sometimes debate for scholars in nearly all Tibetan traditions.

Because of his dual focus—on monastic purity and a gradual approach to enlightenment on the one hand, and on *mahāmudrā* as a view, technique, and realization crucial for all practitioners on the other—Sgam po pa was renowned for having "combined the two streams of Bka' gdams and *mahāmudrā*." This dual focus established the doctrinal and institutional ethos for most subsequent developments in the Bka' brgyud sect, setting it apart as a tradition that placed a premium both on Tantric and non-Tantric meditative realization and on adherence to an ascetic—if not always monastic—approach to religious life.

SEE ALSO Mi la ras pa.

BIBLIOGRAPHY

Chang, Garma C. C., trans. and ed., *The Hundred Thousand Songs of Milarepa: The Life-Story and Teaching of the Greatest Poet-Saint Ever to Appear in the History of Buddhism.* 2 vols. New Hyde Park, N.Y., 1962; reprint, Boston, 1989. See vol. 2, pages 463–497. Includes songs and stories stemming from Sgam po pa's discipleship under Mi la ras pa.

'Gos lo tsa ba gzhon nu dpal. *The Blue Annals.* Translated by George N. Roerich. Calcutta, 1949–1953. See pages 451–462. This fifteenth-century classic of Tibetan historiography contains numerous references to Sgam po pa.

Gyaltsen, Khenpo Könchog, trans. *The Great Kagyu Masters: The Golden Lineage Treasury.* Edited by Victoria Huckenpahler. Ithaca, N.Y., 1990. See pages 187–204. Translation of a thirteenth-century collection of hagiographies.

Jackson, David P. *Enlightenment by a Single Means: Tibetan Controversies on the "Self-Sufficient White Remedy."* Vienna, 1994. See pages 9–53, 149–154. Analysis of early Bka' brgyud pa presentations of *mahāmudrā,* and the criticism of them by Sa skya Paṇḍita.

Karthar Rinpoche, Khenpo. *The Instructions of Gampopa: A Precious Garland of the Supreme Path.* Translated by Lama Yeshe Gyamtso. Edited by Laura M. Roth and David N. McCarthy. Ithaca, N.Y., 1996. Primarily a modern commentary on the *Lam mchog rin po che'i phreng ba*; includes the original Tibetan root-text, with English translation.

Kragh, Ulrich. "Culture and Subculture: A Study of the *Mahāmudrā* Teachings of Sgam po pa." M.A. research paper (*speciale*), University of Copenhagen, 1998. Includes excellent summaries of the contents of Sgam po pa's collected works and of his views on *mahāmudrā.*

Nālandā Translation Committee. *The Rain of Wisdom.* Boulder, Colo., 1980. See pages 217–242. Contains a variety of song-poems attributed to Sgam po pa.

Sgam po pa. *The Jewel Ornament of Liberation.* Translated and annotated by Herbert V. Guenther. London, 1959. The first translation of Sgam po pa's great "stages of the doctrine" text; there is an alternative English translation by Khenpo Konchog Gyaltsen Rinpoche (Ithaca, N.Y., 1998).

Stewart, Jampa Mackenzie. *The Life of Gampopa: The Incomparable Dharma Lord of Tibet.* Ithaca, N.Y., 1995. Drawn primarily from previously translated sources, this is an attempt at a "complete" biography of Sgam po pa.

ROGER R. JACKSON (2005)

SHABBAT. The Hebrew word *shabbat* is from a root meaning "to desist" or "to rest," that is, from work and labor. The Sabbath is the day of rest each week after six days of work. The resemblances to the ancient Babylonian *shapattu,* the day of the full moon, as well as the biblical juxtaposition of the Sabbath with the new moon festival (Ro'sh Ḥodesh) in the Bible, have often been noted, and it may well be that originally there was some connection between the Babylonian and the Hebraic institutions. In the biblical narrative (*Gn.* 1:1–2:4), God rests on the seventh day from his creative activity and thereby sanctifies and blesses this day.

The command to keep the Sabbath holy is found in both versions of the Decalogue (*Ex.* 20:8–11, *Dt.* 5:12–15), but the reasons given for Sabbath observance differ. In *Exodus* the creation motif is stressed: "For in six days the Lord made heaven and earth and sea, and all that is in them, and he rested on the seventh day; therefore the Lord blessed the sabbath day and hallowed it." This does not necessarily mean, as Philo of Alexandria understood it, that man must imitate God by resting as he did on the seventh day. It may mean that by resting on the day on which creation was complete, man acknowledges God as creator. In *Deuteronomy* the social motivation is prominent. Man must rest on the Sabbath and allow his slaves to rest with him so that the slaves are released from the burden of unceasing toil. A slave, subordinate to his master, cannot rest when he wishes. Therefore, by resting on the Sabbath, the Israelite demonstrates that he is free to rest because he has been redeemed from bondage.

The nature of the "work" (*mela'khah*) that is forbidden on the Sabbath has received many different interpretations in the course of Jewish history. The only types of forbidden work specified in the Pentateuch are baking and cooking (*Ex.* 16:23), kindling fire (*Ex.* 35:3), and gathering wood (*Nm.* 15:32–36). From the sudden interposition of an injunction to keep the Sabbath into the narrative in which the Israelites are instructed by Moses to build the Tabernacle (*Ex.* 35:1–3), the Talmudic rabbis (B. T., *Shab.* 49b, *B.Q.* 2a) deduced that all the types of work required for the building of the Tabernacle are those forbidden on the Sabbath. This led to a listing (*Shab.* 7.1) of thirty-nine main categories of work, from which many others were derived by analogy.

In addition, various restrictions were introduced by the rabbis, as on the handling of money or of objects normally used for work, and all business activities. According to the rabbis it is forbidden to carry even the smallest object from a private into a public domain. But in cities like Jerusalem and Tel Aviv it is permitted to carry objects within the confines of the city by means of the *'eruv* ("mingling" of domains), an elaborate arrangement of posts and wires encircling the city that, by a legal fiction, converts the whole area into a private domain within which it is permitted to carry.

Reform Judaism largely ignores the rabbinic rules governing acts forbidden on the Sabbath, preferring to understand "work" as gainful occupation alone, and the spiritual atmosphere of the Sabbath as generated chiefly by means of rituals in the home and services in the synagogue. Orthodox Judaism follows the traditional regulations in their entirety. Where new inventions create problems, these are solved by a process of analogy. For instance, Orthodox rabbis have considered whether switching on electric lights falls under the heading of "kindling fire" since there is no combustion of the filament. The consensus today among Orthodox rabbis forbids the use of all electrical appliances on the Sabbath. A rationale for the Orthodox understanding is that work does not mean physical effort as such, but the creative manipulation of the physical world. Moving heavy objects, for example, does involve effort but is not creative, as is writing a letter or lighting a cigarette (since the ability to make fire was man's first great step toward civilization). By refraining on the Sabbath from creative manipulation of the world, people demonstrate that they enjoy their talents as gifts from God, the creator. They are theirs not by right but by permission. People have a stewardship for which they will be called to account by God. Conservative Judaism in the United States follows the traditional view of the Sabbath laws, but Conservative rabbis generally permit switching on electric lights, using a microphone and telephone, and riding in an automobile to the synagogue.

The positive aspects of the Sabbath as a day of spiritual and physical refreshment, as a day of delight (based on *Isaiah* 58:13), are constantly invoked in Jewish literature. In the poetic rabbinic statement (B.T., *Shab.* 119b), man has an additional soul on the Sabbath, and when he comes home to the Sabbath meal he is accompanied by angels. The thirteenth-century Spanish exegete Nahmanides, in his commentary on the *Exodus* version of the Decalogue, sees the prohibition of work on the Sabbath as an instance of the fear of God, whereas the positive injunction to celebrate the Sabbath as a sacred day is an instance of the love of God.

The ideas of honoring the Sabbath and taking delight in it are expressed in the wearing of special clothes, having a well-lit home, forgetting worldly worries and anxieties (for this reason petitionary prayers are not recited on the Sabbath), the study of the Torah, the three meals (instead of the two eaten on weekdays in ancient times) of good food and wine, and the union of husband and wife. This last emphasis would seem to be in reaction against sectarian opinions that sexual congress on the Sabbath is sinful as a creative act. The Karaites have interpreted the prohibition of kindling fire to mean that there must be no fire or light in the home. In all probability the rabbinic emphasis in the Middle Ages on the Sabbath lights is in conscious reaction to this view and an attempt to make the Sabbath a day of joy and tranquillity rather than a day of gloom. At the festive Sabbath meals joyous hymns (*zemirot*) are sung by the family.

Just before the advent of the Sabbath on Friday evening, the mistress of the house prays for her family as she kindles two candles in honor of the day: one candle represents the prohibition of work, the other the positive injunction of Sabbath joy and tranquillity. The festive meal begins with the Qiddush (sanctification), a praise of God in which he is thanked, over a cup of wine, for granting Israel the precious boon that is the Sabbath. The grace before meals is recited over two loaves of bread, covered with a white cloth, representing the manna of which a double portion fell to the Israelites before the Sabbath (*Ex.* 16:22–27).

At the beginning of the synagogue service on Friday night, the Sabbath is welcomed with song. The mystics of Safad in the sixteenth century used to go out into the fields before the Sabbath to welcome the Bride Sabbath. Based on this is the now-universal custom of singing the hymn *Lekhah dodi* (Come My Beloved), composed by Shelomoh Alkabets, a member of the Safad circle. At the termination of the Sabbath the *havdalah* ("distinction") benediction is recited over a cup of wine. In this ceremony God is praised for making a distinction between the holy and the profane, light and darkness, the people of Israel and other peoples, and between the Sabbath and the six working days. He is also thanked for the gift of light over a special candle kindled after the Sabbath. Sweet spices are smelled to restore the soul, which is sad at the departure of the Sabbath.

The central feature of the synagogue service on the Sabbath is the reading of the Torah from a handwritten scroll—the Sefer Torah (Book of the Law). The Torah is divided into portions, one section (*sidrah*) of which is read each Sabbath. The whole Torah is completed in this way each year, and then the cycle begins anew. In ancient times the seven persons called up (to the platform where the reading is done) read from the scroll itself, but nowadays they only recite the benedictions praising God for giving the Torah to his people, and the actual reading is carried out by the rabbi or cantor, who uses a traditional chant. In Reform congregations only a part of the weekly *sidrah* is read, and there is no chanting. Before the reading begins, the Sefer Torah is taken out of the ark that houses it and is borne ceremonially around the synagogue, adorned with a richly embroidered cloth, silver bells, and a silver pointer. After the reading, the Sefer Torah is held aloft with its columns open for all to see while the congregation sings in Hebrew: "This is the Torah which Moses set before the children of Israel by the mouth of God at the hand of Moses." In addition to the Torah reading, a member of the congregation reads from one of the books of the Prophets. This portion is known as the *haftarah* ("conclusion"). The choice of the Prophetic readings was made to coincide in theme with that of the weekly Torah reading.

There are a number of special Sabbaths marked by additions to the standard liturgy and by relevant Prophetic and extra Torah readings. The earliest of these are the four Sabbaths of the weeks before Passover. These are Shabbat Sheqalim (Sabbath of Shekels), a reminder of the practice in Temple times of beginning the annual collection of money for the sacrifices at this period (based on *Exodus* 30:11–16 and 2 *Kings* 11:17–12:17); Shabbat Zakhor (Sabbath of Remembering), a reminder of Amalek (based on *Deuteronomy* 25:17–19 and *1 Samuel* 15:1–34); Shabbat Parah (Sabbath of the Red Heifer), a reminder of the purification rites in Temple times in preparation for Passover (based on *Numbers* 19:1–22 and *Exodus* 36:16–38); and Shabbat ha-Ḥodesh (Sabbath of the New Moon), the declaration that the "first month," Nisan, is the beginning of the new annual cycle for the festivals (based on *Exodus* 12:1–20 and *Ezekiel* 45:16–46:18). The *haftarah* for the Sabbath immediately preceding Passover is from the third chapter of *Malachi*, concluding with a reference to the great (*gadol*) day of the Lord, after which this Sabbath is called Shabbat ha-Gadol (the Great Sabbath).

The Sabbath on which the weekly *sidrah* includes the Song of Moses (*Ex.* 16:1–21) has for the *haftarah* the Song of Deborah (*Jgs.* 4–5) and is known as Shabbat Shirah (Sabbath of Song). On the three Sabbaths preceding the fast of the Ninth of Av, commemorating the destruction of the Temple, the *haftarot* consist of Prophetic readings dealing with calamity, and the seven Sabbaths following the fast have portions from the second part of the *Book of Isaiah*, dealing with the theme of consolation. Since the *haftarah* of the Sabbath preceding the fast begins with the word *ḥazon* ("vision," *Is.* 1), this Sabbath is called Shabbat Hazon; the *haftarah* of the Sabbath immediately after the fast begins with the word *naḥamu* ("comfort ye"), and this Sabbath is called Shabbat Naḥamu. The Sabbath between Ro'sh ha-Shanah and Yom Kippur falls during the penitential season. Its *haftarah* is from *Hosea* 14, beginning with the words "*shuvah Yisra'el*," hence this Sabbath is called Shabbat Shuvah.

BIBLIOGRAPHY

For a discussion of the critical view on the origins of the Sabbath, see U. Cassuto's *A Commentary on the Book of Genesis*, vol. 1, *From Adam to Noah*, translated by Israel Abrahams (Jerusalem, 1961), pp. 65–69. The voluminous tractate Shabbat of the Babylonian Talmud, dealing with every aspect of Sabbath observance in rabbinic times, is now available in English translation by H. Freedman, in the Soncino translation of the Babylonian Talmud, edited by I. Epstein (London, 1938). Solomon Goldman's little book *A Guide to the Sabbath* (London, 1961) is written from the moderately Orthodox point of view. Abraham Joshua Heschel's *The Sabbath: Its Meaning for Modern Man* (New York, 1951) is a fine impressionistic study of the Sabbath as, in the author's words, "a Temple in time." A useful anthology of teachings on the Sabbath is Abraham E. Millgram's *Sabbath: The Day of Delight* (Philadelphia, 1944). The best edition of the Sabbath table hymns, with an introduction and notes in English, is *Zemiroth Sabbath Songs*, edited by Nosson Scherman (New York, 1979).

New Sources

Benyosef, Simya. *Living the Kabbalah: A Guide to the Sabbath and Festivals in the Teaching of Rabbi Rafael Moshe Luria.* New York, 1999.

Dundes, Alan. *The Shabbat Elevator and Other Sabbath Subterfuges: An Unorthodox Essay on Circumventing Custom and Jewish Character.* Lanham, Md., 2002.

Eskenazi, Tamara C., Daniel J. Harrington, and William H. Shea, eds. *The Sabbath in Jewish and Christian Traditions.* New York, 1991.

McKay, Heather A. *Sabbath and Synagogue: The Question of Sabbath Worship in Ancient Judaism.* New York, 1994.

Peli, Pinhas. *The Jewish Sabbath: A Renewed Encounter.* New York, 1991.

LOUIS JACOBS (1987)
Revised Bibliography

SHABBETAI TSEVI [FIRST EDITION] (1626–1676)

SHABBETAI TSEVI [FIRST EDITION] (1626–1676), Jewish messianic pretender (in the definition of those who did not believe in him) and founder of the messianic movement known as Shabbateanism. The Shabbatean movement is in many ways unique, yet it is also representative of the forces at work in Jewish history and of the interaction of external and internal factors.

BACKGROUND. With the expulsion of the Jews at the end of the fifteenth century from Spain and Portugal, a new phase began in Jewish history. The magnitude of the disaster and sufferings seemed to indicate the "birth pangs" of the messianic age as foretold by tradition. Messianic expectations and speculations were rife, and false messiahs arose and disappeared, but still salvation tarried, and new and greater afflictions followed instead, reaching a climax in the Cossack massacres led by Bogdan Khmel'nitskii. Tens of thousands of Jews were slaughtered in these massacres between 1648 and 1658 in Poland and the Ukraine; the decade was a peak of suffering in the postmedieval period, unparalleled until the twentieth century. But now at least every Jew knew that the Messiah was coming, for he had to come. By that time the doctrine of the sixteenth-century qabbalist Isaac Luria had come to dominate Jewish thought and piety, not least because of its profoundly messianic orientation. The qabbalists focused all their religious fervor and asceticism, their power of prayer and meditation, on the imminent advent of redemption. And it was indeed from the circle of qabbalists that the messiah appeared.

LIFE. Shabbetai was born in 1626 into the prosperous Tsevi family of merchants living in Smyrna (Izmir), a city in Asia Minor situated within the Ottoman empire. There, Jews—because of their knowledge of languages, their international connections, and their familiarity with local conditions—were much in demand as agents and brokers by English, Dutch, and other merchants and companies that operated in the Levant. As was customary in Jewish families, Shabbetai, the gifted son, did not go into business but devoted himself to study, first of the Talmud and then of Qabbalah. He seems to have been not only gifted as a scholar but also endowed with a magnetic personality. He soon exhibited eccentric behavior and strange fantasies, which probably also included messianic elements. To avoid scandal, the rabbis and the family made him leave his hometown, and after some wandering through Turkey, he came to Jerusalem. There the winsome young ascetic did not fail to attract attention, not least because of his strange behavior. Nevertheless, he seems to have been sufficiently respected to be sent as emissary of the community to Egypt to collect alms for the Holy City. On his return to Palestine he met in Gaza another young rabbi from Jerusalem, Natan (henceforth known as the prophet Natan of Gaza), who claimed that during the Shavu'ot vigil in May 1665 he had experienced a vision in which it was divinely revealed to him that Shabbetai was the Lord's anointed one, the Messiah of Israel.

Some historians argue that this proclamation was the climax of a messianic plan carefully laid and hatched by Shabbetai and his supporters, who had long cultivated messianic fantasies. Gershom Scholem, on the other hand, maintains that the event was sudden and unpremeditated, that its explosive result was due to a combination of circumstances: the messianic mood of the age, Shabbetai's peculiar character, and Natan's charismatic and prophetic personality. Shabbetai's erratic behavior, diagnosed by Scholem as a manic-depressive condition (an interpretation contested by others), proved to be of theological significance. In his manic states, which would indeed account for his eccentric actions, Shabbetai invented new rituals, at times involving deliberate and highly ritualized transgressions of Jewish law. These instances of messianic antinomianism would occasionally be accompanied by a blasphemous pun. For the traditional liturgical formula "thou who loosenest [*mattir*] those in bonds [*asurim*]," Shabbetai would substitute, when transgressing the law, the benediction "thou who permittest [*mattir*] all prohibitions [*issurim*]." This incipient messianic antinomianism would prove a major factor in the subsequent development of the movement.

After disciplinary floggings had failed to quench Shabbetai's antinomian behavior, he was eventually excommunicated by the rabbis of Jerusalem in 1665. Nevertheless, the glad tidings of his coming quickly spread. Whereas earlier messianic movements had been outbreaks of short duration, leaving no permanent traces, the Shabbatean message spread throughout the Diaspora, and within a short time Shabbetai was venerated as "our lord and king" from Cairo to Hamburg, from Salonika to Amsterdam, from Morocco to Yemen, from Poland to Persia. With few exceptions the skeptics kept their doubts to themselves, not daring to speak out and risk the wrath of popular enthusiasm. Returning triumphantly to his hometown, Smyrna, Shabbetai was riding high on a wave of manic exaltation and messianic enthusiasm that did not shrink from terrorizing his opponents. By then the Turkish authorities felt that things were going too far, and when Shabbetai continued his royal progress from Smyrna to the capital, Constantinople, he was arrested and imprisoned in the fortress of Gallipoli.

Yet the faith continued to spread; after all, everyone knew that the Messiah would have to suffer tribulations before revealing himself with miracles and in all his power and glory. Since the Turkish prison guards were amenable to bribes, Shabbetai lived in captivity like a king, receiving embassies that came to pay him homage and celebrating his bizarre new rituals. The Turkish authorities handled the matter with remarkable restraint. In due course Shabbetai was summoned to the Diwan (the sultan's privy council) and faced with the choice between death under torture and apostasy to Islam. From the palace there emerged shortly afterward not the rabbi Shabbetai Tsevi but a turbaned Mehmet Effendi. But he continued to play a double game: a Muslim in his relations with the Turks (he also persuaded some of his followers to apostatize) and the Messiah to his Jewish believers. This duplicity finally led the authorities to exile him to Albania, where he died in 1676.

AFTERMATH. Now only did the well-nigh incredible happen. Betrayed and disillusioned, Jews had to choose once more. Many of those who had believed—not with an easy faith without works but with great sacrifice, flinging aside their chattels to meet and follow the Messiah—now recognized, shamefacedly and with heavy hearts, that they had been duped. There had been no change in the world and no salvation: they had to go on waiting for the true Messiah.

But not all were ready to submit to the verdict of history. They had experienced salvation and the thrill of renewal within their hearts, and nothing would undo this change. The reality of messianic experience could not be invalidated by outward history, at least for those who saw with eyes of faith. Whereas the majority of those originally gripped by the wave of messianic frenzy slowly returned to the traditional forms of belief and observance, a considerable number, the self-designated *ma'aminim* ("believers"), continued for some time to persevere in the "faith," living outwardly as orthodox Jews but inwardly as believers in the mystico-messianic mission of Shabbetai Tsevi, which in the fullness of time, they trusted, would be fully vindicated. Shabbetai's apostasy was held to be part of the mystery of the Messiah's unique mission and hence not to be imitated. (The prophet Natan, among others, was a forceful spokesman for this view.) A more extreme wing, however, held that the faithful had to follow in the footsteps of the Messiah also in this respect, especially as Shabbetai had occasionally pressured followers to apostatize.

These groups subsequently gave rise to a Shabbatean "heresy" and sectarian theology that first went underground and subsequently partly dissolved and partly left Judaism altogether, thus vanishing as far as Jewish history is concerned. The Shabbatean Dönmeh sect, which adopted the outward guise of Islam, survived clandestinely in Turkey until the twentieth century. A somewhat similar development took place in Poland, where Ya'aqov Frank (1726–1791), an antinomian and megalomaniac nihilist who donned the messianic mantle of Shabbetai Tsevi as his incarnation, having first converted to Islam, subsequently led his followers to conversion to Catholicism, although they remained crypto-Jews. The members of the Frankist movement were gradually assimilated into Polish society and possibly influenced the "messianic" character of nineteenth-century Polish nationalist ideologues such as the poet Adam Mickiewicz (1798–1855), whose mother was descended from a converted Frankist family.

Gershom Scholem has argued that the mystico-theological rationalizations of the messiah's apostasy were in a way prepared and prefigured by Shabbetai's antinomian behavior in his youth and during his messianic heyday. Of interest to the historian of religions is the analogy, in certain respects, with Christianity. Since with the death of Jesus of Nazareth history had proved a disappointment, there developed a theology of paradox that turned the rational and moral stumbling block and *skandalon* into its cornerstone. Both Christianity and Shabbateanism owe part of their emotional appeal to their very paradoxicality. Because the messiah had seemingly failed so shockingly, the belief arose in his divine nature and in his second advent (in later Shabbateanism, also in his reincarnation). Since salvation was not manifest to those who saw with eyes of flesh, a distinction had to be made between an invisible redemption, accessible to the eyes of faith only, and the final consummation when all things, and especially the messianic mystery, would become manifest. Because the messiah had ended his earthly career in disgrace, a theology evolved that explained how and why this disgrace actually constituted the climax of the messianic ministry. In the case of Jesus the paradox took a metaphysical form: by dying he had overcome death. For Shabbatean believers the paradox was of a mystico-moral kind: Shabbetai had had to accept worse than death (after all, Jews were dying a martyr's death in every generation), namely, the most abominable sin, apostasy. By descending into the abyss of impurity, sin, and evil, he had vanquished impurity, sin, and evil. The details of this doctrine were elaborated in the technical terminology of Lurianic qabbalistic theology.

Other aspects of Shabbateanism are of greater relevance to Jewish history. After the Shabbatean outbreak and its ignominious debacle and aftermath (Dönmeh, Frankism), there were no more "automessianic" movements (Martin Buber's term for messianic movements headed by a leader who claims to be the Messiah). The subsequent spiritual disarray prepared the way for the Hasidic revival in eighteenth-century eastern Europe. The collapse of the last great messianic outburst also contributed (according to Scholem) to the process of modernizing assimilation. Brief but violent, the messianic dream had destroyed, for some believers, the traditional structure of faith; the bridges had been burned and there was no way back. Yet, even though the Shabbatean dream had failed in its original form, it had stimulated new dreams: those of redemption as successful entry into modern society.

SEE ALSO Messianism, article on Jewish Messianism; Qabbalah.

BIBLIOGRAPHY

Davies, W. D. "From Schweitzer to Scholem: Reflections on Sabbatai Svi." *Journal of Biblical Literature* 95 (1976): 529ff.

Scholem, Gershom. *Sabbatai Sevi: The Mystical Messiah*, 1626–1676. Translated by R. J. Zwi Werblowsky. Princeton, 1973. Includes a full bibliography.

Scholem, Gershom. *Kabbalah*. Jerusalem, 1974. See especially pages 244ff. on Shabbetai and the movement, 297ff. on Ya'aqov Frank and Frankism, 327ff. on the Dönmeh, 435–436 on Natan of Gaza, 396–397 on Avraham Cardozo, 405–406 and 412–413 on Eybeschutz and Hayun, 441–443 on Yehudah Prosnitz, and 452–453 on Heschel Zoref.

R. J. ZWI WERBLOWSKY (1987)

SHABBETAI TSEVI [FURTHER CONSIDERATIONS].

A number of important new approaches and documents concerning the Shabbatean movement have appeared since the 1970s. Most are concerned with correcting aspects of Gershom Scholem's standard work, *Sabbatai Sevi: The Mystical Messiah* (1973). This supplementary article will follow the structure of R. J. Zwi Werblowsky's entry for the first edition of *The Encyclopedia of Religion* (1987), dealing with new developments in the background, life and movement, and aftermath of the Shabbatean outbreak.

BACKGROUND. Scholem's insistence on the centrality of Isaac Luria's Qabbalah in preparing the ground for Shabbetai's success has been widely criticized. Among the problems raised are Scholem's near monocausal explanatory scheme, the presence of various other factors of obvious importance, and the fact that, whereas Shabbetai was indeed a qabbalist, he was not at all a follower of the Lurianic doctrine. Indeed the very notion that Lurianic Qabbalah was well known in even the major communities of the Jewish world by the 1665 to 1666 period has been questioned.

A broader historical perspective recognizes the importance of motivating forces from outside the Jewish world. Foremost among these, well known to Scholem but given little weight in his story, was the widespread Christian millenarianism and Muslim Mahdism that permeated the early modern world. Events such as the fall of Constantinople to the Ottomans in 1453, the end of the *reconquista* in Spain, European voyages of discovery, the Protestant Reformation, and the scientific revolution all stoked the fires of messianic expectation among Jews, Christians, and Muslims. All three faiths dealt with a plethora of messianic pretenders in the sixteenth and seventeenth centuries. Many Christian millenarians in particular expected the year 1666 (the number of the Beast added to a millennium) to be a date of redemption. The movement that grew up around Shabbetai can hardly have done so in isolation from these larger trends.

Another important factor is the significance to Shabbetai's movement of the *conversos*, descendants of Jews converted in Spain and Portugal during the fifteenth century. The *conversos* and former *conversos* (those who had returned to their ancestral Judaism after escaping Iberia), coming from a strong Christian background, were especially concerned with matters touching on the messiah. They had their own important messianic movements and ideas. Most of the Mediterranean and western European centers of Shabbatean activity, including İzmir, Livorno, Venice, Amsterdam, and

Hamburg, were also centers of former *converso* Jews. Many of Shabbetai's strongest supporters came from this group, including the theologian Abraham Miguel Cardoso. This can help explain the strong strain of Christian ideas and parallels in Shabbatean thought mentioned by Werblowsky.

LIFE AND MOVEMENT. Scholem's views on Shabbetai's personality, which were very controversial early on, have become widely accepted by scholars, including Scholem's diagnosis of Shabbetai as manic-depressive. More has been written about the dynamics of the movement surrounding Shabbetai, especially the social aspects of the movement, relations between Shabbateanism and other contemporary trends, and Shabbatean theology.

The *converso* influences on Shabbateanism include the messianic agitations of Rabbi Menasseh ben Israel of Amsterdam in the previous decade and the reprinting of Menasseh's tract *Hope of Israel* in İzmir in 1659 by a group of former *conversos* who would shortly become major supporters of Shabbetai. Several of the prophets supporting Shabbetai's mission were demonstrably from this background as well, including the aforementioned Cardoso.

Christian and Muslim messianism, and the interest shown by particular Christians in the Shabbatean movement, have come to be seen as critical to Shabbetai's success. The Dutch divine Petrus Serrarius became a major conduit of news about the movement to the curious Christian world. The manifestation of religious ecstasies and popular prophecy among both contemporary Christians and Muslims has been tied to the outbreak of prophecy among ordinary Jews, often women and children, that accompanied Shabbetai's travels in Turkey. Altogether scholars have begun to look at the public phase of Shabbateanism in 1665 and 1666 less as an internal Jewish development, connected strictly with the Spanish expulsion and rise of Lurianic Qabbalah, than as an integral part of the larger European and Ottoman messianic enthusiasm of the time.

The role of women in Shabbateanism has received increased attention. Sarah, the wife of Shabbetai at the height of the movement, is a fascinating figure who may have helped shape aspects of Shabbetai's activities. Many other women were found among the Shabbatean prophets, exerting their influence through the persuasive medium of ecstatic trance states. Women continued in important roles after Shabbetai's apostasy as well.

Though Scholem exploited all the sources available to him, more documents have surfaced. Some of these have influenced debates about Shabbetai's acceptance in various regions. Scholem's contention that most of the Ashkenazi (German- and Yiddish-speaking) world quickly became believers has been questioned, thought not disproved, in light of new evidence. Other sources throw light on the reception of the movement (generally enthusiastic) in Yemen, Morocco, Egypt, and elsewhere. The impact of the printing press and improvements in transportation on the spread of Shabbateanism have also been discussed.

Shabbatean theology has received much attention as well. The influence of astrological ideas, both qabbalistic and more general, centers around the name *Shabbetai*, which also means "the planet Saturn," symbolizing both melancholy and genius. Qabbalistic interpretations of Shabbetai as the "divine androgyne," embodying certain relationships between the mystical *sephirot*, are among many complex ideas scholars have explored concerning Shabbetai's persona, name, and antinomian rituals. Several studies explicate the role of faith in Shabbetai as a redeemer, sometimes considered almost divine, in the theology of Natan of Gaza.

Finally, questions have been asked about the opposition to Shabbetai, both before and after his apostasy. It is unclear why there was not more vocal protest at Shabbetai's many ritual irregularities and why opponents met resistance even after Shabbetai's apostasy. Discussions of these topics have revealed larger rifts in the stability of rabbinic culture at the time.

AFTERMATH. This is perhaps a misnomer, for in the view of Scholem and others interested in the heretical Qabbalah of the movement, Shabbateanism really only becomes important and interesting after Shabbetai's apostasy. Extensive studies have appeared that, while objecting to certain tenet's of Scholem's approach, see the convoluted mystical reasoning of Shabbetai, Natan, Cardoso, and their followers as the "real" significance of the movement.

Shabbetai's apostasy, like the Crucifixion of Jesus, has come to be the most important moment of the messianic drama. Because it is a great paradox, the thing that should never have been able to happen to the messiah, its explanation challenges the theologians to produce their best efforts. Natan explains that the messiah must be reviled and go down into the realm of the evil husks (that is, the Gentile world) in order to mystically redeem the holy souls that are trapped there; only then can the messianic age become manifest. Cardoso purports that the messiah must become a *converso* like himself, just as Queen Esther had to abandon her people and marry King Ahasuerus in order to save the Jews. Later Shabbatean theologians developed a secret mystical language, recognizable almost exclusively to other believers, with which to describe their Shabbatean Qabbalah. Important studies focus on how Shabbetai saw the meaning of his own apostasy and on the instructions he gave his followers after the apostasy.

With the confirmation of Shabbetai's conversion to Islam, some die-hard believers converted to Islam in imitation of Shabbetai's decision. These apostates, the Dönmeh, left considerable records of their beliefs and practices, many of which were published in the years following Scholem's monograph. Perhaps most surprising is the continued existence of a recognizable cast of Dönmeh in modern Turkey. The silence surrounding their identity was broken in the 1990s by Ilgaz Zorlu, a Dönmeh member who wrote a controversial book about what it meant to be part of that group at that time.

A much larger group followed the other possible path for believers, that of secret adherence from within the Jewish world. Studies suggest that the cells of underground Shabbateans were more active, organized, and long-lived than was previously suspected. They existed in Turkey, Greece, Italy, and the Ashkenazic lands. Prophetic conventicles left notebooks and other evidence of their Shabbatean activities. Rabbis of major communities well into the eighteenth century were counted among those who kept faith with Shabbetai (or his memory). Some of these believers committed ritual transgressions of Jewish law, whereas the adherence of others to the sect can be detected only through telltale terms and ideas in their mystical writings. Major crusades were undertaken to uproot these secret Shabbateans, but they often failed to achieve their purpose, partly because the opponents could not convince other Jews that such subtle evidence was meaningful.

In Poland the Frankist movement grew out of Jacob Frank's manipulation of older Shabbatean traditions and his own charismatic personality. Several extremely important new documents from the Frankists turned up in the twentieth century, allowing for a much more complete view of the movement's dynamics. These include fuller versions of Frank's *Dicta*, which suggest that his self-portrayal as a *prostak*, an uneducated Jew whose gifts are strictly divine, is disingenuous. Other studies are slowly unraveling the various groups and layers within Frankism that were often conflated in earlier research.

Finally, Scholem's early suggestion that Shabbatean antinomianism prepared the way for the Jewish Enlightenment (Haskalah) and reform movement by accustoming Jews to nonobservance has continued to be debated. Most scholars appear to discount this thesis because there is not enough evidence. Others have shown that the Shabbateans and *Maskilim* (proponents of Jewish Enlightenment) were hostile to each other. However, certain authors have attempted to recast Scholem's idea in more convincing ways.

SEE ALSO Dönmeh; Frank, Jacob; Messianism, article on Jewish Messianism.

BIBLIOGRAPHY

Many aspects of the Shabbatean movement are discussed in Rachel Elior, ed., *The Sabbatian Movement and Its Aftermath: Messianism, Sabbatianism and Frankism*, 2 vols., with Hebrew and English sections (Jerusalem, 2001). Mystical aspects are central in *Kabbalah*, vol. 8 (2004), dedicated to the Shabbatean movement. Theological aspects are the focus of Yehuda Liebes, *On Sabbaeaism and Its Kabbalah* (in Hebrew; Jerusalem, 1995). Some of these studies are available in English in Yehuda Liebes's *Studies in Jewish Myth and Jewish Messianism*, translated by Batya Stein (Albany, N.Y., 1993). Extremely important work on Natan of Gaza is available in Abraham Elqayam, "The Mystery of Faith in the Writings of Nathan of Gaza" (Ph.D. diss., Hebrew University of Jerusalem, 1993). The theology of the movement is central in Moshe Idel, *Messianic Mystics*, chap. 6 (New Haven, Conn., 1998). Social aspects are the focus in Jacob Barnai, *Sabbateanism: Social Perspectives* (in Hebrew; Jerusalem, 2000), which includes a list of where the chapters were previously published, several in English. Sociological perspectives are the focus of Stephen Sharot, *Messianism, Mysticism, and Magic: A Sociological Analysis of Jewish Religious Movements*, chaps. 7–9 (Chapel Hill, N.C., 1982). Social and historical perspectives are dealt with in Matt Goldish, *The Sabbatean Prophets* (Cambridge, Mass., 2004). Frankism is dealt with in Hillel Levine, *The Kronika—On Jacob Frank* (in Hebrew, Polish, and English; Jerusalem, 1984); and Alexandr Kraushar, *The End of the Sabbataian Heresy*, edited by H. Levy (Boston, 2000). The fight against the movement is the focus of Elisheva Carlebach, *The Pursuit of Heresy: Rabbi Moses Hagiz and the Sabbatian Controversies* (New York, 1990).

MATT GOLDISH (2005)

SHABISTARĪ, AL- (d. AH 720/1320 CE), more fully Sa'd al-Dīn Maḥmūd ibn 'Abd al-Karīm ibn Yaḥyā al-Shabistarī; celebrated Ṣūfī author and Persian poet. He was born in the second half of the thirteenth century at Shabistar (Cabistar), a village near Tabriz in Azerbaijan, but spent the greater part of his life at Tabriz, then capital of the newly established Mongol (Il-khanid) empire. Little is known about him, except that he was married, probably at Kirman, and devotedly attached to one of his disciples named Shaykh Ibrāhīm.

In both the Islamic world and the West, his fame rests on the *Gulshan-i rāz* (Rose Garden of Mystery), a versified compendium of Ṣūfī teachings discovered by European travelers about 1700. In 1838, J. F. von Hammer-Purgstall published a Persian text along with a German verse translation. In 1880, E. H. Whinfield critically edited what has become the standard Persian text with an annotated English translation and an abstract of its contents.

The *Gulshan-i rāz* (in the meter *hazaj*) was al-Shabistarī's reply to fifteen questions posed by Mīr Fakhr al-Sādāt Ḥusayn ibn 'Alī al-Ḥusaynī (1273–1323), a Ṣūfī friend from Herat. Its 1,008 rhyming couplets, cast in the form of questions and lengthy answers on a variety of mystical topics, focus on the unity of being and the perfect human being, the central concepts of Ṣūfī theory after the time of Ibn al-'Arabī (d. 1240).

Many of the same topics are treated in al-Shabistarī's Persian prose works: *Ḥaqq al-yaqin* (Certain Truth), published in little-known miscellanies (see Ma'ārif al-'awārif, Shiraz, 1283/1867, pp. 1–44, and 'Awārif al-ma'ārif, Shiraz, 1317/1938, pp. 4–54); *Mir'āt al-muḥaqqiqīn* (The Mirror of the Mystics), published in the same miscellanies (pp. 44–81 and section 2, pp. 1–46 respectively); *Kanz al-ḥaqā'iq* (The Treasure of Realities), edited by Sayyid Muḥammad 'Alī-i Ṣafīr (Tehran, 1344/1965); and possibly *Risālah-i shāhid* (Epistle of the Witness), apparently no longer extant. Al-Shabistarī is also said to be the author of the

Saʿādat-nāmah, a collection of three thousand couplets, and a Persian translation of the *Minhāj al-ʿābidīn* by Abū Ḥāmid al-Ghazālī (d. 1111).

Al-Shabistarī's *Gulshan-i rāz* became a traditional handbook of instruction in the Niʿmatullāhī Ṣūfī affiliation, and its influence was further enhanced because of the numerous commentaries written on it in Shīʿī Iran for four centuries. One outstanding commentary, *Mafātīḥ al-iʿjāz fī sharḥ-i Gulshan-i rāz* (ed. Kaywān-i Samīʿī, Tehran, 1337/1958), was compiled in 1473 by Shams al-Dīn Muḥammad ibn Yaḥyā al-Lāhījī (d. 1506), a follower of Nūrbakhsh (d. 1465). The best-known nineteenth-century commentaries are the lithograph of Mirzā Ibrāhīm al-Sabzawārī (Tehran 1314/1898 and 1330/1912) and *Sharḥ-i Gulshan-i rāz* (Tabriz 1334/1955) by Mirzā ʿAbd al-Karīm Rāyiḍ al-Dīn al-Zinjānī (d. 1882), a Dhahabī shaykh of Azerbaijan known as ʿĀrif ʿAlī Shāh Uʿjūbah. The anonymous extract of an Ismaʿīlī commentary (*Taʾwīlat*) discovered by W. Ivanow and edited by Henry Corbin (Trilogie ismaelienne, 1961, pp. 131–161, with an introduction, section 3, pp. 1–196), documents a survival of Ismaʿīlī ideas under the mantle of Sufism long after the destruction of Alamut in 1256.

BIBLIOGRAPHY

Corbin, Henry, ed. *Trilogie ismaelienne.* Tehran, 1961.

Corbin, Henry. *The Man of Light in Iranian Sufism.* Translated by Nancy Pearson. Boulder, 1978. See pages 110–120.

Hammer-Purgstall, J. F. von. *Maḥmud Schebisteri's Rosenflor des Geheimnisses.* Leipzig, 1838.

Lahījī, Muḥammad ibn Yahyā. *Miftāḥ al-iʿjāz fī sharḥ Gul-shan-i rāz.* Edited by Kaywān-i Samīʿī. Tehran, 1337/1958.

Whinfield, E. H., trans. *Gulshan i Raz: The Mystic Rose Garden.* London, 1880.

GERHARD BÖWERING (1987)

SHĀFIʿĪ, AL-

SHĀFIʿĪ, AL- (AH 150–208/767–820 CE), more fully Muḥammad ibn Idrīs, was the founder of a school of law and the author of several works of Islamic law (*sharīʿah*). Perhaps more important, he wrote the first treatise of jurisprudence in Islam, in which he discussed the nature and sources of law and developed a legal methodology for the systematic study of the *sharīʿah.*

Al-Shāfiʿī flourished in the early Abbasid period, a time of consolidation for the Islamic empire. Even before the Abbasid dynasty had been established, Muslim jurists were grappling with legal problems resulting from the rapid expansion of the empire and the absorption of new elements of law and local tradition. As a consequence, the Islamic community abounded in legal doctrines, and several schools of law had emerged in response to the new conditions and demands. At this point, the need for a synthesis of divergent legal doctrines became apparent, and in order to derive underlying norms and principles to resolve legal problems, several jurists began to examine the problems that the prophet Muḥammad and his immediate successors had dealt with. It devolved upon al-Shāfiʿī to provide a method of legal reasoning that would make it possible to resolve problems and develop the law into a coherent system. He was the first jurist to examine the *sharīʿah* in accordance with jurisprudential method, and the impact of his method, to which his successors added only refinements, has remained permanent.

LIFE. Little is known of al-Shāfiʿī's childhood and early life. The earliest biographies are very brief, while the detailed accounts given by classical biographers are mixed with legendary stories. The authorities disagree on whether al-Shāfiʿī was born in Gaza, a small town on the coast of Palestine, or in Ashkelon, a larger town not far away. His ancestors belonged to the Banū Hāshim, the clan of the prophet Muḥammad. Some of them, it seems, went with the Arab armies in the early days of the Muslim conquests and stayed in the eastern Mediterranean region. When al-Shāfiʿī was about ten years old, his father died, and his mother took him from Palestine to Mecca. Traditional stories, legendary for the most part, state that he learned the Qurʾān by heart at the age of seven, committed Mālik's *Muwaṭṭaʾ* (a digest of law) to memory at the age of ten, and was declared fit to give legal opinions at the age of fifteen.

After his arrival in Mecca, al-Shāfiʿī studied under several jurists, then went to study in Medina under Mālik ibn Anas (d. 796), the leading jurist of the Hejaz and founder of the school of law bearing his name. Al-Shāfiʿī was then probably twenty years of age. In Medina, he studied Mālik's *Muwaṭṭaʾ* and became a follower of the Mālikī school of law, soon distinguishing himself as a student of the *sharīʿah.* He attracted the attention of the governor of Yemen, who was on a visit to Medina and who helped him to enter government service at the age of thirty. But al-Shāfiʿī was soon to become involved in local controversies, and this led not only to dismissal from his post but also to his deportation in chains to Iraq on the allegation that he was a follower of the Zaydī imam Yaḥyā ibn ʿAbd Allāh, a pretender to the caliphate and an opponent of the Abbasid dynasty in Baghdad. Al-Shāfiʿī appeared before the caliph Hārūn al-Rashid with other conspirators in 803 but was pardoned after eloquently defending his loyalty to the caliph on the grounds that his great-grandfather was related to the great-grandfather of the caliph himself. It is said that al-Shaybānī (d. 804), the leading jurist of the Ḥanafī school and a court counselor, defended him and said that he was a well-known jurist, and this incident brought al-Shāfiʿī into contact with al-Shaybānī, whose books he had studied. Despite the outcome, al-Shāfiʿī was never again to seek government service.

Until his deportation to Iraq, al-Shāfiʿī was known as a follower of Mālik. His study of Ḥanafī doctrines, which filtered to him through al-Shaybānī's works and contacts with Ḥanafī followers, seems to have broadened his knowledge of the law, and he began to see points of strength and weakness in both the Mālikī and Ḥanafī positions. Although he held his own legal opinions, he had not yet emerged as the leader of a new school of law.

In 804 al-Shāfiʿī suddenly left Iraq. The authorities differ on his subsequent travels: Some state that he went to Syria and the Hejaz and returned to Iraq in 810; others do not mention his visit to the Hejaz, reporting that he left Iraq in 814 and went to Egypt after stopping in Syria. But they all seem to agree that he left Iraq for Egypt and that his departure from the Mālikī and Ḥanafī schools had become so pronounced that he preferred to settle in a country where he could discuss his own legal doctrine with greater independence.

In Egypt, al-Shāfiʿī found himself in a congenial position. He was on good terms with the governor, who seems to have encouraged him to leave Baghdad and to develop his teachings in Egypt, far from the center of court intrigues and rival doctrines. During the five years he lived there, al-Shāfiʿī devoted all his time to teaching and dictating his works to his students. But it was still not without difficulty that he preached his own doctrines, and his disagreement with Mālikī teachings brought him into conflict with some Mālikī followers. According to one authority, after a particularly heated controversy al-Shāfiʿī was attacked by an opponent who had lost the argument. Al-Shāfiʿī was already suffering from an intestinal illness that kept him frail and ailing during the later years of his life; seriously injured in the attack, he was taken to his house and died a few days later.

WORKS. Al-Shāfiʿī's legal system is to be found in his collected works, the *Kitāb al-umm* (The Mother Book). It is said that his leading disciples, especially al-Rabīʿ al-Murādī (d. 880), al-Būwayṭī (d. 845), and al-Muzanī (d. 877), were in the habit of transcribing al-Shāfiʿī's lectures, and that al-Shāfiʿī would correct the text when it was read aloud to him. Al-Shāfiʿī's disciples in Egypt, therefore, are responsible for all the books that have survived, whether copied or dictated from his original writings. Doubts have been raised as to whether the *Kitāb al-umm* was not actually composed by a disciple. Even if some words have been changed or rephrased, the book as a whole contains al-Shāfiʿī's own ideas and legal reasoning, and al-Shāfiʿī's biographers agree that his works were handed down to us as recorded by his disciples. Al-Shāfiʿī's book on jurisprudence, *Al-risālah fī uṣūl al-fiqh* (Treatise on the Sources of the Law), was originally written in Iraq, long before he settled in Egypt, but it was revised and rewritten after he left Iraq, and it was also dictated to and put into writing by his disciples. Although al-Shāfiʿī wrote or dictated several other works, including a book on the Qurʾān called *Kitāb aḥkām al-Qurʾān* (Treatise on the Legal Precepts of the Qurʾān), and a compilation of traditions called *Al-musnad* (Collected Traditions), his legal doctrines and methodology are to be found mainly in the *Risālah,* a book on jurisprudence and legal method, and the *Kitāb al-umm,* a book on the law, in which his own system is set forth in accordance with his legal reasoning. The *Risālah,* in particular, is a novel work in the literature of Islamic law, dealing essentially with the sources of the law (*uṣūl al-fiqh*). The *uṣūl* ("roots" or "sources") of the law had been discussed by earlier jurists, each stressing a particular derivative source (in addition to the Qurʾān and traditions, which are agreed upon by all as the primary sources), which distinguished him from other jurists; but none seems to have dealt with the subject in so coherent and systematic a way as al-Shāfiʿī, who discussed the nature and relative significance of each source, and how legal rules are derived from it.

Before al-Shāfiʿī, there were two predominant schools of law: the Mālikī school in the Hejaz and the Ḥanafī in Iraq, each representing local traditions and interests, although they were in agreement on fundamental principles. Both recognized the primacy of the Qurʾān and the traditions as sources of law, but they diverged on other sources, such as custom and local practice (sanctioned by their inclusion in the *sunnah* and the traditions ascribed to the Prophet) as well as the use of personal reasoning *(ijtihād)* and consensus (*ijmāʿ*). In the *Risālah,* al-Shāfiʿī tried to define and set the limits for each source and indicate how it should be used.

According to al-Shāfiʿī, the Qurʾān, as the embodiment of divine revelation, and the traditions, consisting of the Prophet's practices and decisions, are equally binding as sources of law, on the ground that the traditions, though not revelation in the literal sense, are based on divine wisdom inspired in the Prophet. God has imposed on believers the duty of obeying his prophet as they would obey God himself, and he has given evidence that he regards disobedience to the Prophet as disobedience to himself. "When God and his apostle have decreed a matter," says God to the Prophet in a revelation, "it is not for a believing man or woman to exercise a choice in that matter; whoever opposes God and his Apostle has deviated into manifest error" (surah 33:36). In law, therefore, the Prophet's traditions are as valid and binding as the Qurʾān. However, in raising the Prophet's *sunnah* to the level of revelation, al-Shāfiʿī warned that the traditions (consisting of the *sunnah*) must be authentic, since the Prophet's authority had often been invoked by the citation of traditions of doubtful authenticity. In the *Risālah,* al-Shāfiʿī devoted two chapters to a study of the nature and scope of traditions and laid down rules on how to distinguish between authentic and inauthentic traditions. Once a tradition is proved authentic, it must be binding. For this reason, he disagreed with Mālik, who considered the practice *(ʿamal)* of Medina as representing the traditions of the Prophet irrespective of authenticity (on the grounds that the practice of the city of the Prophet was assumed to be equal in validity to the Prophet's traditions). Al-Shāfiʿī also disagreed with Abū Ḥanīfah, representing the Iraqi school of law, who applied *istiḥsān* (juristic preference) to his choice of traditions as a basis for legal decisions without distinguishing between the traditions of the Prophet and those of his companions.

The other sources of the law, based essentially on the exercise of *ijtihād* (legal reasoning), may be called derivative sources because they must have a certain basis in one of the textual sources (Qurʾān and traditions). Al-Shāfiʿī rejected the use of unlimited *ijtihād*, save in the form of *qiyās* (analogy), since this form of legal reasoning presupposes the existence of a general principle in the Qurʾān or a precedent in the traditions. He rejected all other forms of *ijtihād—istiḥsān* (juristic preference), *istiṣlāḥ* (common good), and others—because they permit the use of sources for legal decisions outside the framework laid down in the Qurʾān and traditions. In pursuing this method of legal reasoning, al-Shāfiʿī sought to idealize the law by insisting that it must be derived ultimately from divine revelation and divine wisdom, and to islamize it by confining its sources to the sacred texts of Islam—the Qurʾān and the traditions—and not to other sacred sources (see Khadduri, 1960, pp. 42–45).

Finally, al-Shāfiʿī discussed *ijmāʿ* as another derivative source, one with which he was familiar as a former follower of Mālik. But Mālik's doctrine of *ijmāʿ* was limited to the agreement of the scholars of Medina, because he held that only the scholars of the Prophet's city understood what the Prophet's *sunnah* really meant, and that by their consensus on all matters of law they could make decisions in conformity with precedents set in the *sunnah.* Other jurists outside Hejaz, especially in Iraq, maintained that they were as competent to exercise *ijmāʿ* as the scholars in Medina, and claimed that they were no less familiar with the Prophet's *sunnah* than their peers in Hejaz. But the Iraqi jurists, especially those of the Ḥanafī school, considered *ijmāʿ* to be secondary to *qiyās* as a derivative source. Al-Shāfiʿī went beyond both Mālikī and Ḥanafī jurists by investing *ijmāʿ* with higher authority as an expression of public action. The concept of vox populi vox Dei implied in al-Shāfiʿī's formulation of the *ijmāʿ* of the community is based on the tradition of the Prophet that states: "My people will never agree on an error," although al-Shāfiʿī did not cite the tradition in this form. By investing *ijmāʿ* with high authority, he ranked it higher than *qiyās* as a source of law and second only to the textual sources.

Al-Shāfiʿī's doctrine of the ijmāʿ of the community was opposed by other scholars, including his own followers, but al-Ghazālī (d. 1111) supported the doctrine by confining it to fundamental principles and leaving matters of detail to the agreement of the scholars. Al-Shāfiʿī's doctrine of *ijmāʿ*, though sound in principle, suffers from a procedural weakness in that it provides no adequate method for the community to arrive at an agreement. Some of the jurists offered a corrective measure by proposing that if a few scholars reached an agreement and no objection was raised by others, or if the majority of the scholars agreed and only a few raised an objection, agreement should be binding upon the community. The process remained undefined until modern times, however, when Shaykh Rashīd Riḍā (d. 1935) proposed in his book on the caliphate, *Al-khilāfah aw al-imāmah al-ʿuẓmā* (The Caliphate and the High Imamate; Cairo, 1924), that an elected assembly, composed of members including men knowledgeable in the *sharīʿah*, should exercise *ijmāʿ* on behalf of the community of believers. This device seems to satisfy al-Shāfiʿī's call that on all important matters the action of the community should prevail. At the end of the chapter on *ijmāʿ* in the *Risālah* he stated: "He who holds that which the Muslim community holds shall be regarded as following the community, and he who holds differently shall be regarded as opposing the community he was ordered to follow. So the error comes from separation."

Al-Shāfiʿī probably never intended to found a school bearing his name, for he warned against *taqlīd* (conformity to one school of law) and encouraged independent legal reasoning; but his legal methodology, which laid restrictions on the use of the sources of the law, necessarily limited differences of opinion on legal questions. After he settled in Egypt, his disciples became active in writing down and spreading his teachings, not only there but also in other lands. Within a century after al-Shāfiʿī's death, his doctrine began to spread to the Hejaz, Syria, and Central Asia. Although it was diminished in Egypt under Fatimid rule, it again became predominant under Sultan Ṣalāḥ al-Dīn (known to the West as Saladin, d. 1169). By the time of the Ottoman occupation of Arab lands, the Shāfiʿī school had become the most widespread. Despite the official adoption of the Ḥanafī school by the Ottoman empire and the spread of Shiism in Iran after the rise of the Safavid dynasty at the opening of the sixteenth century, the Shāfiʿī school remains dominant to the present day in Egypt, Syria, the Hejaz, western and southern Arabia, parts of the Persian Gulf, East Africa, the Malay Archipelago, Dagestan, and parts of Central Asia.

BIBLIOGRAPHY

Works by al-Shāfiʿī

The collected works of al-Shāfiʿī are available in *Kitāb al-umm,* 7 vols., edited by Ibn Jamāʿah (Cairo, 1904–1908). I have translated and commented on the *Risālah* in my Islamic Jurisprudence (Baltimore, 1960) and provided a brief introduction to the life and jurisprudence of al-Shāfiʿī on pp. 3–54. There are two published versions of the *Risālah* in Arabic: One is given in Ibn Jamāʿah's edition of *Kitāb al-umm;* the other, a copy from the original edition of al-Shāfiʿī's disciple al-Rabīʿ, has been edited and published separately by Ahmad Shākir (Cairo, 1940). Other works include *Kitāb jumāʿ al-ʿilm* (Treatise on Legal Knowledge; Cairo, 1940); *Al-musnad,* 2 vols., edited by al-Sindī (Cairo, 1950); and *Kitāb aḥkām al-Qurʾān,* 2 vols., edited by al-Kawtharī (Cairo, 1951–1952).

Works about al-Shāfiʿī

In addition to my own work mentioned above, useful works in English include Eric E. F. Bishop's "Al-Shāfiʿī, Founder of a Law School," *Moslem World* 19 (1929): 156–175, and Joseph Schacht's *Origins of Muḥammad Jurisprudence* (Oxford, 1950). Important works in Arabic include al-Khaṭīb al-Baghdādī's *Taʾrīkh Baghdad* (History of Baghdad; Cairo, 1931), vol. 2, pp. 56–73; Abū ʿUmar Yūsuf ibn ʿAbd al-Barr's *Al-intiqāʾ fī faḍāʾil al-thalāthah al-aʾimmah al-fuqahāʾ* (Three Highly Qualified Leaders of Jurisprudence; Cairo,

1932), pp. 66–103; Abū ʿAbd Allāh ibn ʿUmar al-Fakhr al-Rāzi's *Kitāb manāqib al-Shāfiʿī* (Treatise on al-Shāfiʿī's Life Qualities; Cairo, n. d.); Abū Muḥammad ʿAbd al-Raḥmān ibn Abī Ḥātim al-Rāzi's *Kitāb adab al-Shāfiʿī wa-manāqibuh* (Treatise on the Literary and Life Qualities of al-Shāfiʿī), edited by al-Kawtharī (Cairo, 1953); Muṣṭafā ʿAbd al-Rāziq's *Al-Imām al-Shāfiʿī* (The Imam al-Shāfiʿī; Cairo, 1945); Tāj al-Dīn al-Subkī's *Ṭabaqāt al-Shāfiʿīyah al-kubrā* (Treatise on the Life of al-Shāfiʿī's Leading Followers; Cairo, 1907), vol. 1, pp. 100–179; and Muḥammad Abū Zahrah's *Al-Shāfiʿī* (Cairo, 1948).

MAJID KHADDURI (1987)

SHAHĀDAH is a term used in Islam to denote the all-important confession or affirmation of the unity of God and the apostleship of Muḥammad. It derives from the Arabic root *shahida,* meaning "to attest," "to give decisive word," hence "to acknowledge as true," and is used in referring to eyewitness testimony or other dependable evidence. The same root yields one of the names of God in Islam, *al-Shahīd,* "the one whose word is authentic," a term used in the Qurʾān in contrast to *al-Ghāʾib,* "the one in hiddenness" or simply "hiddenness."

For Muslims, the term *shahādah* means giving open, verbal evidence of what is incontestably true. "I bear witness," the phrase runs, "that there is no god but God, and Muḥammad is the messenger of God." The Arabic reads "Ashadu an lā ilāha illā Allāh: Muḥammadun rasūl Allāh." Witness is always in the singular. It is a corporate faith, but the witnessing unit is the person.

These words constitute the vital first "pillar" of Muslim religion; the other four are *ṣalāt* (prayer), *zakāt* (alms), *ṣawm* (fasting), and *ḥajj* (pilgrimage). As with all of the Five Pillars, the *nīyah,* or intention, has to be present in the recitation of the Shahādah if it is to avail as a genuine confession; its casual citation, as, for example, in a classroom discussion, would not amount to confession as faith.

The precise words in the ritual form do not, in fact, occur verbatim in the Qurʾān. But the theme of the sole lordship of Allāh was germinal to Muḥammad's mission, and his prophethood (*rasūlīyah*) was the sole agency entrusted by God with the Qurʾān. Muḥammad's prophethood therefore came to be conjoined inseparably in the Shahādah with the theme of God.

The word *Allāh* is precisely equivalent to the English word *God,* capitalized and without the definite article. *Allāh* is not a happy English usage, though it is sometimes employed in translations of the Shahādah. Care should be taken not to capitalize the word *ilāha* since it is a different term and should be translated as "god" with lowercase *g.* To write "There is no God but God" is without meaning. *Ilāha* is certainly capable of being pluralized ("gods many and lords many"). Not so *Allāh.* The core of Muḥammad's mission was this affirmation of divine unity. The term *Allāh* was already current, and well known to the Meccans, in Muḥammad's day. His own father (who died before his birth) was called ʿAbd Allāh, meaning "servant of God." Thus it was not the existence of Allah that the Prophet proclaimed, but his *sole* existence. All other deities, agencies, or powers intervening between humanity at the base of a hierarchical pyramid and Allāh at its apex, were nonentities, fictions, leaving God and humanity in unmediated relation.

The force of the word *lā* in the Shahādah is, as the grammarians say, that of absolute negation: "There does not exist any deity except . . ." The seven *l*s of the Shahādah (i. e., occurrences of the Arabic letter *lām*) make the recitation lyrical poetry, and serve, in their simple verticals (eleven verticals plus two rounded letters), as a favorite calligraphic device. Numerous passages in the Qurʾān cite the phrase "There is no god except he" (e.g., 2:163, 2:255, 3:2, 3:6, 3:18, 4:84, 6:102). "There is no god but thou" occurs once (21:87), and surah 16:2 reads "There is no god save I." Clearly more than a bare propositional monotheism is meant, as is evident in surah 6:164: "Say: 'Shall I desire as lord any other than God when he is lord of everything?'" Here the confessing "theist" is brought close to Psalm 73:25: "Whom have I in heaven but thee?"

That Muḥammad is the *rasūl,* the "messenger" or "sent one" of God is axiomatic and fundamental in Islam. *Rasūl Allāh,* "apostle of God," is his constant designation in the Qurʾān and in tradition. Indeed, the personal name Muḥammad occurs only four times in the Qurʾān (3:144, 33:40, 47:2, and 48:29). This is indicative of how the personality is absorbed into the vocation. *Rasūl* conveys a higher dignity than does *nabī* ("seer, prophet-seer"), though this term also is sometimes used of Muḥammad. Whereas earlier prophets and apostles had limited messages or areas of meaning and of vocation to particular people or situations, Muḥammad's mandate was final and universal as "a mercy to the worlds."

Within Islam, the brevity and simplicity of the Shahādah are seen as great assets, inasmuch as it avoids the complexities or subtleties attached to the Christian confession of "God in Christ." The theologians in Islam were, of course, involved in subtle issues when they developed their sophisticated *ʿaqidah*s, or creeds. But ordinary believers find ready assurance in what is terse, direct, and uncomplicated. Faith is not so much an exploration of mystery as an acknowledgement of that which warrants submission.

One theological complexity that cannot be avoided, however, is the question whether confession in itself, apart from behavior, constitutes Muslim adherence. In the Umayyad period and beyond, a form of Islam emerged in which Muslims, even caliphs, were utterly ready to recite with intention the confession, or *kalimat al-Shahādāh* (the "words of witness"), even as they lived profligate or negligent lives. Were they, then, true Muslims? Was a measure of ethical attainment and allegiance necessary? Was a faith without works enough? If not, who was to assess the modicum of acceptable conduct? The questions had political implications where rulers were unworthy. Some interpreters insisted that works were vital, that standards were not merely verbal. Others, frightened by the toils of assessment, preferred to leave the question with God and stay hopeful.

It is not clear when the form of the Shahādah was established, but it was certainly well within the Medinese period of Muḥammad's mission, when accessions to Islam used this formula. The formulation probably belongs to a very early period, the time when Muḥammad's status as the sole recipient of the Qur'anic revelation had become assured to his followers. As in the other Semitic faiths, in Islam the concepts of "witness to faith" and "witness unto death" were closely linked by a single cognate term, here *shahīd,* meaning both "testimony giver" and "martyr." During the definitive early expansion of Islam the Shuhadā' (from the plural form of *shahīd)* were warriors in battle.

Ṣūfī, or mystical, Islam has its characteristic dimension for the Shahādah as for the *tawḥīd,* or unity, of God to which the Shahādah witnesses. The formula "Lā ilāha illā Allāh" in Ṣūfī rhythmic recitation, accompanied by bodily swaying and at gradually increasing tempo, serves to induce ecstatic experience of what Ṣūfīs call the unitive state. *Shahādah* in this esoteric sense may be said to contain "all metaphysics. . . . It negates all relativity and multiplicity from the Absolute and returns all positive qualities back to God. . . . Through its repetition this Unity comes to leave its permanent imprint upon the human soul and integrates it into its Center" (Seyyid Hossein Nasr, *Islam and the Plight of Modern Man,* London, 1975).

SEE ALSO Worship and Devotional Life, article on Muslim Worship.

BIBLIOGRAPHY

Carra de Vaux, Bernard. *Les penseurs de l'Islam,* vol. 3, *L'exégèse, la tradition et la jurisprudence.* Paris, 1923. See the chapter on tradition.

Mouradgea d'Ohsson, Ignatius. *Tableau général de l'empire othoman.* 7 vols. in 8. Paris, 1778–1824. See especially volume 1, page 176, and volume 2, pages 319–324 and 348–350.

Schimmel, Annemarie. "The Sufis and the Shahāda." In *Islam's Understanding of Itself,* edited by Richard G. Hovannisian and Speros Vryonis, Jr. Malibu, Calif., 1983.

KENNETH CRAGG (1987)

SHAHRASTĀNĪ, AL-

SHAHRASTĀNĪ, AL- (1086–1153), more fully, Abū al-Fath Muḥammad ibn 'Abd al-Karīm al-Shahrastānī, was a Muslim theologian, heresiographer, and historian of religions. His extant biographical profile, derived from the thirteenth-century biographical dictionary of Ibn Khallikān, remains thin. He was born in 1086 in the town of Shahrastan in Khorasan (Iran). There he obtained his earliest education, studying both jurisprudence (*fiqh*) and theology (*kalām*) under accepted masters. He aligned himself with the dominant Ash'arī school of *kalām,* although his independent intellect led him to declare the shortcomings as well as the benefits of al-Ash'arī's system.

The formative period in his life began at age thirty. On his return from the pilgrimage to Mecca, he stopped in Baghdad for three years to pursue further theological studies. His presence was forceful: By his interaction with some of the finest religious minds of his generation he gained respect as the most articulate exponent of Ash'arī *kalām* at the prestigious Baghdad Niẓāmīyah. After leaving Baghdad he briefly engaged his theological peers in debate at Jurjānīyah and Nishapur then resettled in Shahrastān, where he spent the remainder of his life as a teacher and author until his death in 1153.

Among al-Shahrastānī's several writings, only one, *Kitāb nihāyat al-iqdām fī 'ilm al-kalām* (The height of daring in the science of theology), has been critically edited and translated into English. His most influential work is *Kitāb al-milal wa-al-niḥal* (The book of sects and creeds). In it al-Shahrastānī attempts, as its title implies, an extended investigation into religious sects and philosophical groups. It has been frequently cited, by both Muslim and non-Muslim scholars, as the most significant Muslim heresiography of the premodern period. It surpasses its predecessors—al-Baghdādī's *Farq bayn al-firaq* (Difference among differences), al-Isfarā'inī's *Tabṣīr fī al-dīn* (Clarification in religion), and Ibn Ḥazm's *Fiṣal fī al-milal* (Distinctions among sects)—in objectivity and insight as well as detail and scope.

Al-Shahrastānī's scholarship rests on the shoulders of his Muslim predecessors; he interprets what they only report. Among the novel aspects of his eclectic methodology is his reliance on a group of Neoplatonic spiritualists known as the Sabians, with whom he probably came into contact while in Baghdad and to whom he ascribes both a limited concept of prophecy and a rational system of statutes and ordinances. By upgrading the theological status of the Sabians, he is able to stretch the category of *ahl al-kitāb* ("people of the Book") to accommodate non-Muslims such as the Sabians, including Indian Brahmans, Buddhists, and even some enlightened idolaters, into an ecumenical Muslim worldview.

BIBLIOGRAPHY

Al-Shahrastānī's *Kitāb nihāyat al-iqdām fī 'ilm al-kalām* has been edited and translated into English by Alfred Guillaume as *The Summa Philosophiae of al-Shahrastani* (London, 1931–1934). *Kitāb al-milal wa-al niḥal* has been edited by William Cureton, 2 vols. (London, 1846), and translated into German by T. Haarbrücker as *Schahrastani's Religionspartheien und Philosophen Schulen,* 2 vols. (Halle, 1850–1851).

Beyond these editions and translations, there are few secondary sources to consult. For a comparative view of his thought with reference to *Nihāyat al-iqdām,* see Alfred Guillaume's "Christian and Muslim Theology as Represented by Al-Shahrastānī and St. Thomas Aquinas," *Bulletin of the School of Oriental and African Studies* 13 (1950): 551–580.

A thorough examination of his acquaintance with Greek philosophical categories is set forth in Franz Rosenthal's "Aš-Šayḫ al-Yûnânî and the Arabic Plotinus Source," *Orientalia* 21 (1952): 461–492, 22 (1953): 370–400, and 24 (1955): 42–66. On his evaluation of Indian material, see my "Shahrastānī on Indian Idol Worship," *Studia Islamica* 38 (1973): 61–73, and *Shahrastānī on the Indian Religions* (The Hague, 1976).

BRUCE B. LAWRENCE (1987)

SHĀH WALĪ ALLĀH SEE WALĪ ALLĀH, SHĀH

SHAIVISM SEE ŚAIVISM

SHAKERS. Members of the American religious group the United Society of Believers in Christ's Second Appearing were popularly called Shakers. One of the longest-lived and most influential religious communitarian groups in America, the Shakers originated in 1747 near Manchester, England, in a breakaway from the Quakers led by Jane and James Wardley. The group may also have been influenced by Camisard millenarians who had fled from France to England to escape the persecutions that followed revocation of the Edict of Nantes in 1685. The nickname Shaking Quaker, or Shaker, was applied to the movement because of its unstructured and highly emotional services, during which members sang, shouted, danced, spoke in tongues, and literally shook with emotion. Under the leadership of Ann Lee, a Manchester factory worker who became convinced that celibacy was essential for salvation, the core of the Shakers emigrated to America in 1774 and settled two years later near Albany, New York. Until Lee's death in 1784 the Shakers remained a loosely knit group that adhered to Lee's personal leadership and to what they viewed as a millenarian restoration and fulfillment of the early Christian faith.

During the 1780s and 1790s under the leadership of two of Ann Lee's American converts, Joseph Meacham and Lucy Wright, Shakerism developed from a charismatic movement into a more routinized organization. Meacham and Wright oversaw the establishment of parallel and equal men's and women's orders. Adherents lived together in celibate communities and practiced communal ownership of property inspired by the Christian communism of *Acts* 2:44–45. Supreme authority was vested in the ministry at New Lebanon, New York, usually two men and two women, one of whom headed the entire society. Each settlement was divided into "families"—smaller, relatively self-sufficient communities of thirty to one hundred men and women living together under the same roof but strictly separated in all their activities. By 1800, eleven settlements with sixteen hundred members were functioning in New York, Massachusetts, Connecticut, New Hampshire, and Maine. A second wave of expansion, inspired by the Kentucky Revival and drawing heavily on the indefatigable Richard McNemar, a new light Presbyterian minister who converted to Shakerism, led to the establishment of seven additional settlements, in Ohio, Kentucky, and Indiana, by 1826.

The high point of Shaker membership and the last major effort to revitalize the society came during the decade of spiritual manifestations that began in 1837. Frequently called "Mother Ann's work" because many of the revelations purportedly came from the spirit of Ann Lee and showed her continuing concern for her followers, the period saw a rich outpouring of creativity in new forms of worship, song, and dance, including extreme trance and visionary phenomena. Following the great Millerite disappointments of 1843 and 1844 when the world failed to come to a literal end, hundreds of Millerites joined the Shakers, bringing membership to a peak of some six thousand by the late 1840s. Thereafter the group entered into a long, slow decline. The loss of internal momentum and the changing conditions of external society led the Shakers to be viewed increasingly not as a dynamic religious movement but as a pleasant anachronism in which individuals who could not function in the larger society could find refuge. As late as 1900 there were more than one thousand Shakers, but by the beginning of the twenty-first century, only Sabbathday Lake, Maine, remained as an active community, with very few people living as Shakers there.

As the largest and most successful religious communitarian group in nineteenth-century America, the Shakers attracted the attention of numerous visitors, writers, and creators of more ephemeral communal experiments. The Shakers were known for their neat, well-planned, and successful villages; their functional architecture, simple furniture, and fine crafts; their distinctive songs, dances, and rituals; and their ingenuity in agriculture and mechanical invention. They also were sometimes criticized because of their sophisticated and highly unorthodox theology, which stressed a dual godhead combining male and female elements equally; perfectionism and continuing revelation; and the necessity of celibacy for the highest religious life. They were unique among American religious groups in giving women formal equality with men at every level of religious leadership, and they created a fully integrated subculture that has increasingly come to be viewed with interest and respect.

SEE ALSO Lee, Ann.

BIBLIOGRAPHY

Among the numerous scholarly treatments of the Shakers, the most important are the studies by Edward Deming Andrews, particularly his *The People Called Shakers*, new enl. ed. (New York, 1963). Andrews is excellent on Shaker material culture, especially furniture and crafts, but weaker on religious motivation. Another popular historical overview is Marguerite Fellows Melcher's *The Shaker Adventure* (Princeton, N.J., 1941). For the most incisive analysis of the group, see

Constance Rourke's "The Shakers," in her *The Roots of American Culture and Other Essays,* edited by Van Wyck Brooks (New York, 1942). A provocative but sometimes misleading analysis that attempts to place Shakerism within a larger social and conceptual framework is Henri Desroche's *The American Shakers: From Neo-Christianity to Presocialism* (Amherst, Mass., 1971). Mary L. Richmond has compiled and annotated *Shaker Literature: A Bibliography,* 2 vols. (Hanover, N.H., 1977), a comprehensive bibliography of printed sources by and about the Shakers that supersedes all previous reference works of its kind. Richmond lists the major repositories at which each printed item may be found. She also includes information on collections of manuscripts. The most important of these are at the Western Reserve Historical Society in Cleveland and the Library of Congress in Washington, D.C., and are available on microfilm from their respective libraries.

Benjamin Seth Youngs's *The Testimony of Christ's Second Appearing* (Lebanon, Ohio, 1808) was the first and most comprehensive Shaker theological and historical overview. A shorter and more accessible treatment is Calvin Green and Seth Y. Wells's *A Summary View of the Millennial Church or United Society of Believers (Commonly Called Shakers)* (Albany, N.Y., 1823). The most valuable primary account of Ann Lee and the earliest Shakers is the rare *Testimonies of the Life, Character, Revelations, and Doctrines of Our Ever Blessed Mother Ann Lee and the Elders with Her,* edited by Rufus Bishop and Seth Y. Wells (Hancock, Mass., 1816). Among the many accounts by Shaker seceders and apostates, the most comprehensive and historically oriented is Thomas Brown's *An Account of the People Called Shakers: Their Faith, Doctrine, and Practice* (Troy, N.Y., 1812). Anna White and Leila S. Taylor's *Shakerism: Its Meaning and Message* (Columbus, Ohio, 1904) presents a thorough and insightful history of the Shakers from the perspective of the late nineteenth century.

New Sources

Morgan, John H. *The United Inheritance: The Shaker Adventure in Communal Life.* Bristol, Ind., 2002.

LAWRENCE FOSTER (1987)
Revised Bibliography

SHAMANISM

This entry consists of the following articles:

SHAMANISM: AN OVERVIEW [FIRST EDITION]

Shamanism in the strict sense is preeminently a religious phenomenon of Siberia and Inner Asia. The word comes to us, through the Russian, from the Tunguz *šaman.* Throughout the immense area comprising the central and northern regions of Asia, the magico-religious life of society centers on the shaman. This, of course, does not mean that he is the one and only manipulator of the sacred, nor that religious activity is completely usurped by him. In many tribes the sacrificing priest coexists with the shaman, not to mention the fact that every head of a family is also the head of the domestic cult. Nevertheless, the shaman remains the dominating figure, for throughout the vast area of Asia in which the ecstatic experience is considered the religious experience *par excellence,* the shaman, and he alone, is the great master of ecstasy. A first definition of the complex phenomenon of shamanism—and perhaps the least hazardous—is that it is a technique of ecstasy.

As such, shamanism was documented and described by the earliest travelers in the various regions of Siberia and Inner Asia. Later, similar magico-religious phenomena were observed in North and South America, Indonesia, Oceania, and elsewhere. Because of their shared characteristics, there is every reason to study them together with Siberian and Inner Asian shamanism. But the presence of a shamanic complex in one region or another does not necessarily mean that the magico-religious life of the corresponding people is crystallized around shamanism. This can occur (as, for example, in certain parts of Indonesia), but it is not the most usual state of affairs. Generally, shamanism coexists with other forms of magic and religion. As is well known, magic and magicians are to be found more or less all over the world, whereas shamanism exhibits a particular magical specialty, such as mastery over fire, or magical flight. By virtue of this fact, though the shaman is (among other things) a magician, not every magician can properly be termed a shaman. The same distinction must be applied in regard to shamanic healing; every medicine man is a healer, but the shaman employs a method that is unique to him. As for the shamanic techniques of ecstasy, they do not exhaust all the varieties of ecstatic experience documented in the history of religions and religious ethnology. Hence not every ecstatic can be considered a shaman; the shaman "specializes" in the trance state, during which his soul is believed to leave his body and to ascend to the sky or descend to the underworld.

A similar distinction is also necessary to define the shaman's relation to spirits. All through the primitive and modern worlds we find individuals who profess to maintain relations with spirits, whether they are possessed by them or control them. But the shaman controls his helping spirits, in the sense that he is able to communicate with the dead, demons, and nature spirits without thereby becoming their instrument. To be sure, shamans are sometimes found to be possessed, but these are rather exceptional cases. In Inner and Northeast Asia the chief methods of recruiting shamans are (1) hereditary transmission of the shamanic profession and (2) spontaneous vocation ("call" or "election"). There are also cases of individuals who become shamans of their own free will (as, for example, among the Altaic Turkic peoples) or by the will of the clan (as with the Tunguz), but these self-made shamans are considered less powerful than those who have inherited the profession or who have obeyed the call of the gods and spirits.

However selected, a shaman is not recognized as such until after he has received two kinds of teaching: (1) ecstatic (dreams, trances, etc.) and (2) traditional (shamanic techniques, names and functions of the spirits, mythology and genealogy of the clan, secret language, etc.). This twofold course of instruction, given by the spirits and the old master shamans, is equivalent to an initiation. Sometimes the initiation is public and constitutes an autonomous ritual in itself. But absence of this kind of ritual in no sense implies absence of an initiation; the latter can perfectly well occur in a dream or in the neophyte's ecstatic experience. The syndrome of the shaman's mystical vocation is easily recognized. Among many Siberian and Inner Asian tribes, the youth who is called to be a shaman attracts attention by his strange behavior; for example, he seeks solitude, becomes absentminded, loves to roam in the woods or unfrequented places, has visions, and sings in his sleep. In some instances this period of incubation is marked by quite serious symptoms; among the Yakuts, the young man sometimes has fits of fury and easily loses consciousness, hides in the forest, feeds on the bark of trees, throws himself into water and fire, cuts himself with knives. The future shamans among the Tunguz, as they approach maturity, go through a hysterical or hysteroid crisis, but sometimes their vocation manifests itself at an earlier age—the boy runs away into the mountains and remains there for a week or more, feeding on animals, which he tears to pieces with his teeth. He returns to the village, filthy, bloodstained, his clothes torn and his hair disordered, and it is only after ten or more days have passed that he begins to babble incoherent words.

Even in the case of hereditary shamanism, the future shaman's election is preceded by a change in behavior. The souls of the shaman ancestors of a family choose a young man among their descendants; he becomes absentminded and moody, delights in solitude, has prophetic visions, and sometimes undergoes attacks that make him unconscious. During this period, the Buriats believe, the young man's soul is carried away by spirits; received in the palace of the gods, it is instructed by his shaman ancestors in the secrets of the profession, the forms and names of the gods, the worship and names of the spirits. It is only after this first initiation that the youth's soul returns and resumes control of his body (see the examples quoted in Eliade, 1964, pp. 13ff.). This hereditary form of the transmission of the vocation is also known in other parts of the world (ibid., pp. 21ff.).

A man may also become a shaman following an accident or a highly unusual event—for example, among the Buriats, the Soyot, and the Inuit (Eskimo), after being struck by lightning, or falling from a high tree, or successfully undergoing an ordeal that can be homologized with an initiatory ordeal, as in the case of an Inuit who spent five days in icy water without his clothes becoming wet.

SHAMANISM AND PSYCHOPATHOLOGY. The strange behavior of future shamans has not failed to attract the attention of scholars, and since the middle of the past century several attempts have been made to explain the phenomenon of shamanism as a mental disorder (ibid., pp. 25ff.). But the problem was wrongly put. On the one hand, it is not true that shamans always are, or always have to be, neuropathics; on the other hand, those among them who had been ill became shamans precisely because they had succeeded in healing themselves. Very often in Siberia, when the shamanic vocation manifests itself as some form of illness or as an epileptic seizure, the initiation is equivalent to a cure. To obtain the gift of shamanizing presupposes precisely the solution of the psychic crisis brought on by the first symptoms of election or call.

But if shamanism cannot simply be identified with a psychopathological phenomenon, it is nevertheless true that the shamanic vocation often implies a crisis so deep that it sometimes borders on madness. And since the youth cannot become a shaman until he has resolved this crisis, it is clear that it plays the role of a mystical initiation. The shock provoked in the future shaman by the discovery that he has been chosen by the gods or the spirits is by that very fact valuated as an "initiatory illness." His sufferings are exactly like the tortures of initiation. Just as, in puberty rites or rites for entrance into a secret society, the novice is "killed" by semidivine or demonic beings, so the future shaman sees in dreams his own body dismembered by demons. The initiatory rituals peculiar to Siberian and Inner Asian shamanism include a symbolic ascent to Heaven up a tree or pole; in a dream or a series of waking dreams, the sick man chosen by the gods or spirits undertakes his celestial journey to the world tree. The psychopathology of the shamanic vocation is not profane; it does not belong to ordinary symptomatology. It has an initiatory structure and significance; in short, it reproduces a traditional mystical pattern.

Once healed of his initiatory psychopathological crisis, the new shaman displays a strong and healthy constitution, a powerful intelligence, and more energy than others of the male group. Among the Buriats the shamans are the principal guardians of the rich oral literature. The poetic vocabulary of a Yakut shaman contains twelve thousand words, whereas the ordinary language—the only language known to the rest of the community—has only four thousand. The same observation applies to the shamans of other regions, such as North and South America, Oceania, and Australia (see some examples in Eliade, 1964, pp. 29ff.).

INITIATORY ORDEALS OF SIBERIAN SHAMANS. Relating their ecstatic initiations, the Siberian shamans maintain that they "die" and lie inanimate for from three to seven days in their yurts or in solitary places. During this time, they are cut up by demons or by their ancestral spirits; their bones are cleaned, the flesh scraped off, the body fluids thrown away, and their eyes torn from their sockets. According to a Yakut informant, the spirits carry the future shaman's soul to the underworld and shut him in a house for three years. Here he undergoes his initiation; the spirits cut off his head (which they set to one side, for the novice must watch his own dismemberment with his own eyes) and hack his body to bits, which are later distributed among the spirits of various sicknesses. It is only on this condition that the future shaman will obtain the power of healing. His bones are then covered with new flesh, and in some cases he is also given new blood. According to another Yakut informant, black devils cut up the future shaman's body and throw the pieces in different directions as offerings, then thrust a lance into his head and cut off his jawbone. A Yurak Samoyed shaman told Toivo Lehtisalo that spirits had attacked him and hacked him to pieces, also cutting off his hands. For seven days and nights he lay unconscious on the ground, while his soul was in Heaven.

From a long and eventful autobiography that an Avam Samoyed shaman confided to A. A. Popov, I shall select a few significant episodes. Stricken with smallpox, the future shaman remained unconscious for three days, so nearly dead that on the third day he was almost buried. He saw himself go down to Hell, and after many adventures he was carried to an island, in the middle of which stood a young birch tree, which reached up to Heaven. It was the Tree of the Lord of the Earth, who gave him a branch of it to make himself a drum. Next he came to a mountain. Passing through an opening, he met a naked man plying the bellows at an immense fire on which was a kettle. The man caught him with a hook, cut off his head, chopped his body to bits, and put the pieces into the kettle. There he boiled the body for three years, and then forged him a head on an anvil. Finally he fished out the bones, which were floating in a river, put them together, and covered them with flesh. During his adventures in the otherworld, the future shaman met several semidivine personages, in human or animal form, each of whom instructed him in the secrets of the healing art. When he awoke in his yurt, among his relatives, he was initiated and could begin to shamanize.

A Tunguz shaman relates that, during his initiatory illness, his shaman ancestors pierced him with arrows until he lost consciousness and fell to the ground; then they cut off his flesh, drew out his bones, and counted them before him; if one had been missing, he could not have become a shaman. According to the Buriats the candidate is tortured by his shaman ancestors, who strike him, cut up his body with a knife, and cook his flesh. A Teleut woman became a shamaness after having a vision in which unknown men cut her body to pieces and boiled it in a pot. According to the traditions of the Altaic shamans, their ancestral spirits open their bellies, eat their flesh, and drink their blood (see examples in Eliade, 1964, pp. 42ff.).

The ecstatic experience of the initiatory dismemberment of the body followed by a renewal of organs is also known in other preliterate societies. The Inuit believe that an animal (bear, walrus, etc.) wounds the candidate, tears him to pieces, or devours him; then new flesh grows around his bones. In South America, during the initiation of the Araucanian shaman, the master makes the spectators believe that he exchanges the novice's eyes and tongue for others and puts a stick through his abdomen. At Malekula, in the South Pacific, the initiation of the medicine man includes, among other things, the novice's dismemberment: the master cuts off his arms, feet, and head, and then puts them back in place. Among the Dayak, the *manangs* (shamans) say that they cut off the candidate's head, remove the brain, and wash it, thus giving him a clearer mind. Finally, cutting up the body and the exchange of viscera are essential rites in some initiations of Australian medicine men (ibid., pp. 59ff.).

One of the specific characteristics of shamanic initiations, aside from the candidate's dismemberment, is his reduction to the state of a skeleton. We find this motif not only in the accounts of the crises and sicknesses of those who have been chosen by the spirits to become shamans but also in the experiences of those who have acquired their shamanic powers through their own efforts, after a long and arduous quest. Thus, for example, among the Inuit group known as the Ammasilik, the apprentice spends long hours in his snow hut, meditating. At a certain moment, he falls "dead" and remains lifeless for three days and nights; during this period an enormous polar bear devours all his flesh and reduces him to a skeleton. It is only after his mystical experience that the apprentice receives the gift of shamanizing. The *angakkoqs*, or shamans, of the Iglulik Inuit are able in thought to strip their bodies of flesh and blood and to contemplate their own skeletons for long periods. Visualizing one's own death at the hands of demons and final reduction to the state of a skeleton are favorite meditations in Indo-Tibetan and Mongolian Buddhism. Finally, it is worth noting that the skeleton is quite often represented on the Siberian shaman's costume (ibid., pp. 62ff., 158ff.).

PUBLIC RITES OF SHAMANIC INITIATIONS. Among the public initiation ceremonies of Siberian shamans, those of the Buriats are among the most interesting. The principal rite includes an ascent. A strong birch tree is set up in the yurt, with its roots on the hearth and its crown projecting through the smoke hole. The birch is called *udeśi burkhan*, "the guardian of the door," for it opens the door of Heaven to the shaman. The birch will always remain in his tent, serving as the distinguishing mark of the shaman's residence. On the day of his consecration, the candidate climbs the birch to the top (in some traditions, he carries a sword in one hand) and, emerging through the smoke hole, shouts to summon the aid of the gods. After this, the master shaman, the apprentice, and the entire audience go in procession to a place far from the village, where, on the eve of the ceremony, a large number of birches have been set upright on the ground. The procession halts by a particular birch, a goat is sacrificed, and the candidate, stripped to the waist, has his head, eyes, and ears anointed with blood, while the other shamans play their drums. The master shaman now climbs a birch and cuts nine notches in the top of its trunk. The candidate then climbs it, followed by the other shamans. As they climb they all fall—or pretend to fall—into ecstasy. According to G. N. Potanin, the candidate has to climb nine birches, which, like the nine notches cut by the master shaman, symbolize the nine heavens (*Ocherki severo-zapadnoi Mongolii*, 4 vols., Saint Petersburg, 1881–1883).

In the initiatory rite of the Buriat shaman, the candidate is believed to ascend to Heaven for his consecration. The climb to Heaven by the aid of a tree or pole is also the essential rite in the séances of the Altaic shamans. The birch or pole is likened to the tree or pillar that stands at the center of the world and that connects the three cosmic zones—Earth, Heaven, and Hell. The shaman can also reach the center of the world by beating his drum, for the body of the drum is supposed to be made from a branch taken from the cosmic tree. Listening to the sound of his drum, the shaman falls into ecstasy and flies to the tree, that is, to the center of the world (see Eliade, 1964, pp. 115ff.).

TECHNIQUES OF ECSTASY. Whether he is chosen by superhuman beings or himself seeks to draw their attention and obtain their favors, the shaman is an individual who succeeds in having mystical experiences. In the sphere of shamanism the mystical experience is expressed in the shaman's trance, real or feigned. Shamanistic ecstasy signifies the soul's flight to Heaven, its wanderings about the earth, or its descent to the subterranean world, among the dead. The shaman undertakes these ecstatic journeys for four reasons: first, to meet the celestial god face to face and bring him an offering from the community; second, to seek the soul of a sick man, which has supposedly wandered away from his body or been carried off by demons; third, to guide the soul of a dead man to its new abode; or fourth, to add to his knowledge by frequenting higher nonhuman beings.

Through his initiation, the shaman learns what he must do when his soul abandons the body—and, first of all, how to orient himself in the unknown regions that he enters during his ecstasy. He learns to explore the new planes of existence disclosed by his ecstatic experiences. He knows the road to the center of the world: the hole in the sky through which he can fly up to the highest heaven, or the aperture in the earth through which he can descend to the underworld. He is forewarned of the obstacles that he will meet on his journeys, and knows how to overcome them. In short, he knows the paths that lead to Heaven and Hell. All this he has learned during his training in solitude, or under the guidance of the master shamans.

Because of his ability to leave his body with impunity, the shaman can, if he so wishes, act in the manner of a spirit: he flies through the air, he becomes invisible, he perceives things at great distances; he mounts to Heaven or descends to Hell, sees the souls of the dead and can capture them, and is impervious to fire. The exhibition of certain *faqīr*-like accomplishments during ritual séances, especially the so-called fire tricks, is intended to convince spectators that the shaman has assimilated the mode of being of spirits. The ability to turn into an animal, to kill at a distance, and to foretell the future are also among the powers of spirits; by exhibiting such powers, the shaman proclaims that he shares in the spirits' condition.

CELESTIAL ASCENTS AND DESCENTS TO THE UNDERWORLD. The Buriats, the Yakuts, and other Siberian tribes speak of "white" shamans and "black" shamans, the former having relations with the gods, the latter with the spirits, especially evil spirits. Their costumes differ, being—as among the Buriats—white for the former and blue for the latter. The Altaic "white" shaman himself sacrifices the horse offered to the god of heaven; afterward, in ecstasy, he conducts the animal's soul on its journey to the throne of Bai Ülgen, lord of the upperworld. Putting on his ceremonial costume, the shaman invokes a multitude of spirits, beats his drum, and begins his celestial ascent. He laboriously mimes the difficult passing through heaven after heaven to the ninth and, if he is really powerful, to the twelfth or even higher. When he has gone as high as his powers permit, he stops and humbly addresses Bai Ülgen, imploring his protection and his blessings. The shaman learns from the god if the sacrifice has been accepted and receives predictions concerning the weather and the coming harvest. This episode is the culminating moment of the ecstasy: the shaman collapses, exhausted, and remains motionless and dumb. After a time he rubs his eyes, appears to wake from a deep sleep, and greets those present as if after a long absence.

The Altaic shaman's celestial ascent has its counterpart in his descent to the underworld. This ceremony is far more difficult, and though it can be undertaken by both "white" and "black" shamans, it is naturally the specialty of the latter. The shaman makes a vertical descent down the seven successive subterranean levels, or regions, called *pudak*, "obstacles." He is accompanied by his dead ancestors and his helping spirits. At the seventh "obstacle" he sees the palace of Erlik Khan, lord of the dead, built of stone and black clay and defended in every direction. The shaman utters a long prayer to Erlik, then returns to the yurt and tells the audience the results of his journey.

THE SHAMAN AS PSYCHOPOMP. These descents to the underworld are undertaken especially to find and bring back a sick person's soul, or to escort the soul of the deceased to Erlik's realm. In 1884 V. V. Radlov published the description of a séance organized to escort the soul of a woman to the underworld forty days after her death. The ceremony takes place in the evening. The shaman begins by circling the yurt, beating his drum; then he enters the tent and, going to the fire, invokes the deceased. Suddenly the shaman's voice changes; he begins to speak in a high-pitched falsetto, for it is really the dead woman who is speaking. She complains that she does not know the road, that she is afraid to leave her relatives, and so on, but finally consents to the shaman's leading her, and the two set off together for the subterranean realm. When they arrive, the shaman finds that the dead refuse to permit the newcomer to enter. Prayers proving ineffectual, brandy is offered; the séance gradually becomes more lively, even to the point of the grotesque, for the souls of the dead, through the shaman's voice, begin quarreling and singing together; finally they consent to receive the dead woman. The second part of the ritual represents the return journey; the shaman dances and shouts until he falls to the ground unconscious (*Aus Siberien: Lose Blätter aus dem Tagebuche eines reisenden Linguisten*, Leipzig, 1884).

Medical Cures. The principal function of the shaman in Siberia and Inner Asia is healing. Several conceptions of the cause of illness are found in the area, but that of the "rape of the soul" is by far the most widespread. Disease is attributed to the soul's having strayed away or been stolen, and treatment is in principle reduced to finding it, capturing it, and obliging it to resume its place in the patient's body. The Buriat shaman holds a preliminary séance to determine if the patient's soul has strayed away or if it has been stolen from him and is a captive in Erlik's prison. The shaman begins to search for the soul; if he finds it near the village, its reinstallation in the body is easy. If not, he searches the forests, the steppes, and even the bottom of the sea. Failure to find it indicates that it is a prisoner of Erlik, and the only recourse is to offer costly sacrifices. Erlik sometimes demands another soul in place of the one he has imprisoned; the problem then is to find one that is available. With the patient's consent, the shaman decides who the victim will be. While the latter is asleep, the shaman, taking the form of an eagle, descends on him and, tearing out his soul, goes with it to the realm of the dead and presents it to Erlik, who then allows him to take away the patient's soul. The victim dies soon afterward, and the patient recovers. But he has gained only a respite, for he too will die three, seven, or nine years later.

Survival and Metamorphosis of Some Shamanic Traditions. Shamanic symbolism and practices were well known in Tibet, China, and the Far East (see Eliade, 1964, pp. 428ff.). The Bon shamans were believed to use their drums as vehicles to convey them through the air. Their cure included seeking the patient's soul, a shamanic ceremony popular also with the Tibetan exorcists. In the Tantric rite named Gcod, the practitioner offers his own flesh to be eaten by demons: they decapitate him, hack him to pieces, then devour his flesh and drink the blood. Since sickness is interpreted as the flight of the soul, the Lolo shamans of southern Yunnan, as well as the Karen "doctors" of Burma, read a long litany imploring the patient's soul to return from the distant mountains, forests, or fields. Among the Lolo and the Mea of Indochina, the shamans climb a double "ladder of knives," symbolizing their ascent to Heaven. A great number of shamanic symbols and rituals are to be found among the Tibeto-Burmese Moso (or Na-hsi) inhabiting southwestern China: ascension to Heaven, accompanying the soul of the dead, and so forth. In China, "magical flight" or "journeying in spirit," as well as many ecstatic dances, present a specific shamanic structure (see examples quoted in Eliade, 1964, pp. 447–461). In Japan shamanism is practiced almost exclusively by women. They summon the dead person's soul from the beyond, expel disease and other evil, and ask their god the name of the medicine to be used. According to Charles Haguenaur, the essential functions of a female shaman consist in causing a soul to descend into a house support (a sacred post or any other substitute) and incarnating a soul in order to make it serve as intermediary between the dead and the living, and then sending it back (cited in Eliade, 1964, p. 464).

A number of shamanic conceptions and techniques have been identified in the mythology and folklore of the ancient Germans (ibid., pp. 379ff.). To quote only one example: Óðinn descends on his eight-hoofed horse, Sleipnir, to Hel and bids a long-dead prophetess rise from the grave and answer his questions. In ancient Greece, Abaris flies through the air on his arrow. Hermotimos of Clazomenae had the power of leaving his body "for many years"; in his long ecstasy he journeyed to great distances (see other examples, ibid., pp. 389ff.). Shamanic practices are also to be found in ancient India as well as in the traditions of the Scythians, Caucasians, and Iranians (ibid., pp. 394–421). Among the aboriginal tribes of India, of particular interest is the shamanism of Savara (Saura), characterized by an "initiatory marriage" with a "spirit girl," similar to the practice of the Siberian Nanay (Goldi) and Yakuts (ibid., pp. 72ff., 421ff.).

Some Conclusions. It is as yet impossible to reconstruct the prehistory and earliest history of different shamanisms. But we can appraise the religious and cultural importance of the shamans in those archaic societies dominated by a shamanistic ideology. To begin with, the shamans have played an essential role in the defense of the psychic integrity of the community. They are preeminently the antidemonic champions; they combat not only demons and disease, but also the "black" magicians. In a general way, it can be said that shamanism defends life, health, fertility, and the world of "light," against death, disease, sterility, disasters, and the world of "darkness."

It is as a further result of his ability to travel in the supernatural worlds and to see the superhuman beings (gods, demons, spirits of the dead, etc.) that the shaman has been able to contribute decisively to the knowledge of death. In all probability many features of funerary geography, as well as some themes of the mythology of death, are the result of the ecstatic experiences of shamans. The lands that the shaman sees and the personages that he meets during his ecstatic journeys in the beyond are minutely described by the shaman himself, during or after his trance. The unknown and terrifying world of death assumes form and is organized in accordance with particular patterns; finally, it displays a structure and, in the course of time, becomes familiar and acceptable. In turn, the supernatural inhabitants of the world of death become visible; they show a form, display a personality, even a biography. Little by little the world of the dead becomes knowable, and death itself is evaluated primarily as a rite of passage to a spiritual mode of being. In the last analysis, the accounts of the shamans' ecstatic journeys contribute to a "spiritualizing" of the world of the dead, at the same time that they enrich it with wondrous forms and figures.

There are certain likenesses between the accounts of shamanic ecstasies and certain epic themes in oral literature (see Eliade, 1964, pp. 213ff., 311ff., 368ff.). The shaman's adventures in the otherworld, the ordeals that he undergoes in his ecstatic descents below and ascents to the sky, suggest the adventures of the figures in popular tales and the heroes of epic literature. Probably a large number of epic subjects or motifs, as well as many characters, images, and clichés of epic literature, are, finally, of ecstatic origin, in the sense that they were borrowed from the narratives of shamans describing their journeys and adventures in the superhuman worlds.

It is likewise probable that the preecstatic euphoria constituted one of the universal sources of lyric poetry. In preparing his trance, the shaman drums, summons his spirit helpers, speaks a secret language or the "animal language," imitating the cries of beasts and especially the songs of birds. He ends by attaining a "second state" that provides the impetus for linguistic creation and the rhythms of lyric poetry.

Something must also be said concerning the dramatic structure of the shamanic séance. The sometimes highly elaborate staging of this session obviously exercises a beneficial influence on the patient. In addition, every genuinely shamanic séance ends as a spectacle unequaled in the world of daily experience. The fire tricks, the "miracles" of the rope-trick or mango-trick type, the exhibition of magical feats, reveal another world—the fabulous world of the gods and magicians, the world in which everything seems possible, where the dead return to life and the living die only to live again, where one can disappear and reappear instantaneously, where the laws of nature are abolished and a certain superhuman freedom from such structures is exemplified and made dazzlingly present.

It is difficult for us to imagine the repercussions of such a spectacle in a "primitive" community. The shamanic "miracles" not only confirm and reinforce the patterns of the traditional religion, they also stimulate and feed the imagination, demolish the barriers between dream and present reality, and open windows upon worlds inhabited by the gods, the dead, and the spirits.

See Also Ascension; Buriat Religion; Descent into the Underworld; Dismemberment; Ecstasy; Flight; Spirit Possession.

Bibliography

A general presentation of the shamanistic initiations, mythologies, and practices in Siberia and Inner Asia, North and South America, Southeast Asia, Oceania, and the Far East is found in my book *Shamanism: Archaic Techniques of Ecstasy*, rev. & enl. ed. (New York, 1964). To the bibliography found there, I need add only a few important general works and a number of contributions to the study of shamanism in Southeast Asia, Oceania, and the Far East. The bibliographies related to Inner Asia or South and North America appear in the other articles on shamanism that follow.

Matthias Hermann's *Schamanen, Pseudoschamanen, Erlöser und Heilbringer*, 3 vols. (Wiesbaden, 1970), is useful for its documentation, especially with regard to Indo-Tibetan areas. For a clear presentation, see John A. Grim's *The Shaman: Patterns of Siberian and Ojibway Healing* (Norman, Okla., 1983). Michael J. Harner's *The Way of the Shaman* (New York, 1980), which includes a valuable bibliography, and the volume *Hallucinogens and Shamanism*, which Harner edited (Oxford, 1973), are stimulating and original, as is *Studies in Shamanism*, edited by Carl-Martin Edsman (Stockholm, 1967). Among comparative studies, see Alois Closs's "Interdisziplinäre Schamanismusforschung an der indogermanischen Völkergruppe," *Anthropos* 63/64 (1968–1969): 967–973, and his "Die Ekstase des Shamanen," *Ethnos* (1969): 70–89.

On shamanism in Southeast Asia and Oceania, see my *Shamanism*, pages 337–374. In addition to my bibliography, the reader should consult Rex L. Jones's "Shamanism in South Asia: A Preliminary Survey," *History of Religions* 7 (May 1968): 330–347; Joachim Sterly's *"Heilige Männer" und Medizinmänner in Melanesien* (Cologne, 1965), especially pages 437–553 and the bibliography; Guy Moréchand's "Le chamanisme des Hmong," *Bulletin de l'École Francaise d'Extrême-Orient* (Paris) 54 (1968): 53–294; and Andreas Lommel's *Shamanism: The Beginnings of Art* (New York, 1966) with its rich bibliography. On the shamanistic structure of the Australian medicine man, see my *Australian Religions: An Introduction* (Ithaca, N. Y., 1973), pp. 131–160.

For sources on the shamanic symbolism and techniques in Tibet, China, and the Far East, see, in addition to my Shamanism, Helmut Hoffmann's *Symbolik der tibetischen Religionen und des Schamanismus* (Stuttgart, 1967), especially the bibliography; P. Jos Thiel's "Schamanismus im Alten China," *Sinologica* 10 (1968): 149–204; Ichirō Hori's "Penetration of Shamanic Elements into the History of Japanese Folk Religion," in *Festschrift für Adolf E. Jensen*, edited by Eike Haberland et al. (Munich, 1964), vol. 1, pp. 245–265; Carmen Blacker's *The Catalpa Bow: A Study of Shamanistic Practices in Japan* (London, 1975); H. Byron Earhart's critical review "The Bridge to the Other World", in *Monumenta Nipponica*, 31 (1976): 179–187; and Jung Young Lee's "Concerning the Origin and Formation of Korean Shamanism," *Numen* 20 (1973): 135–160.

On shamanism among the Turks and the Mongols, see the original and learned synthesis of Jean-Paul Roux's *La religion des Turcs et des Mongols* (Paris, 1984), pp. 59ff.

Mircea Eliade (1987)

SHAMANISM: AN OVERVIEW [FURTHER CONSIDERATIONS]

The cross-cultural concept of shamanism promoted by Mircea Eliade (1907–1986) has stood the test of time and has been extended and refined. Eliade's conceptualization of shamanism has promoted the cross-cultural and interdisciplinary application of the term *shaman*. Systematic cross-cultural research has validated a universal (etic) concept of the shaman, illustrating the substantial similarities among spiritual healing practices found in hunter-gatherer societies worldwide. Archaeological research has established a deep prehistorical depth for shamanism, illustrating its central role in the emergence of modern human culture. Perspectives from evolutionary psychology have helped explain the emergence and cross-cultural distribution of shamanism in terms of adaptive psychological, social, and cognitive effects that contributed to human evolution. The worldwide distribution of shamanism reflects its basis in innate brain processes and modules and in biologically based cognitive and representational systems. Modern perspectives reject the earlier pathological characterizations of shamanism, instead recognizing it as a primordial spiritual healing practice that managed psychosocial processes and fundamental aspects of brain function. The role of the hunter-gatherer shamans, with their biological basis in altered states of consciousness, was transformed by sociocultural evolution, producing a universal manifestation of "shamanistic healers" who entered ecstatic states in order to interact with spirits on behalf of the community and clients.

CROSS-CULTURAL CHARACTERISTICS OF SHAMANS. Eliade emphasized shamanism as "preeminently" of Siberia, but he recognized similar practices around the world. Dissension concerning whether shamanism was strictly limited to Siberia or was found worldwide has been resolved through cross-cultural research by Michael Winkelman (1986, 1990, 1992) that illustrates empirically the existence of similar magico-religious practitioners in many hunter-gatherer and simple agricultural and pastoral societies. Michael Harner refers to this worldwide phenomenon as "core shamanism." Shamans were charismatic social leaders who engaged in healing and divination for the local community. In addition to *ecstasy*, or an altered state of consciousness (ASC), spirit world interaction, and community relations, other beliefs and practices associated with shamans include:

- an ASC experience known as *soul journey* or *magical flight;*
- the use of chanting, drumming, and dancing;
- training through deliberately induced ASC, producing visionary experiences;
- an initiatory crises involving a death-and-rebirth experience;
- abilities of divination, diagnosis, and prophecy;
- therapeutic processes focused on *soul loss* and recovery;
- disease caused by spirits, sorcerers, and the intrusion of objects or entities;
- interaction with animals, including control of animal spirits and transformation into animals;
- malevolent acts, or sorcery; and
- hunting magic.

CROSS-CULTURAL DIFFERENCES IN SHAMANISTIC PRACTICES. One characterization of shamanism offered by Eliade was the practice of entering ASC (Eliade used the term *ecstasy*) to interact with spirits on behalf of the community. This characterization led to the extension of the concept of shaman to include many different practices, including those that do not exhibit the other characteristics of the shaman emphasized by Eliade, such as soul flight, animal allies, death-and-rebirth experiences, hunting magic, and the capacity for sorcery. Other practitioners that engage in ASC to interact with spirits on behalf of their communities have some different characteristics that differ from those of the core shamans. Winkelman has suggested the term *shamanistic healers* for this universal manifestation of the shamanic potential involving ASC, community ritual, and spirit interaction.

Differences in shamanic practices were explored by Anna Siikala, who proposed that the breakdown of the clan structure along with stratification of the community led to different types of shamanism, particularly professional shamans. She distinguished between the following:

1. small-group shamans, characteristic of the nomadic northern ethnic groups of Siberia;
2. independent professional shamans, prevalent among paleo-Asian groups, such as the Chukchee;
3. clan shamans, found in Altaic groups; and
4. territorial professional shamans, found in Central Asia and southern Siberia.

Winkelman's cross-cultural research, however, indicates that different types of shamanistic healers developed in different places as a consequence of the effects of sedentary residence and agricultural and political integration. These effects are illustrated in the following characterizations of the distinctive aspects of core shamans, shaman/healers, healers, and mediums.

Core shamanism. Shamans are found worldwide in nomadic or seminomadic hunter-gather, horticultural, and pastoral societies. Shamans were predominantly male, but most societies also had female shamans. In the past, shamans tended to come from shaman families, but anyone could become a shaman if selected by the spirits. Early in life, shamans undertook deliberate activities to enter ASC, undertaking a "vision quest" in which they developed personal relationships with spirits who provided direct training. The developmental experiences of shamans included death-and-rebirth experiences involving dismemberment and reconstruction by the spirits. This provided shamans with powers, especially animal allies that could provide assistance in healing, divination, hunting, and the ability to use sorcery to harm others. A shaman's all-night ceremony involved the entire local community in dancing, drumming, and chanting. A central aspect involved the shaman recounting ASC experiences called *soul journey* or *magical flight,* in which an aspect of the shaman departs the body and travels to other places. Shamans were not normally possessed by spirits; rather they controlled spirits and were believed to be able to fly and transform into animals. Therapeutic processes involved removal of objects or removal of spirits sent by other shamans through sorcery, as well as soul journeys to recover lost souls and engage in relationships with "power animals" (aspects of the shaman's personal essence and powers).

Shaman/healers. Shaman/healers are found in agricultural or pastoral societies at all levels of social complexity. They share characteristics with other types of shamans, but they differ from shamans in important ways. The shaman's direct tutelage by spirits and affirmation by the community is replaced in shaman/healers with instruction by elder practitioners, as well as public ceremonial recognition of the successful initiate, marking their entrance into the profession. In addition, shaman/healers are subordinated to religious practitioners called priests. Shaman/healers also engage in agricultural rituals and often use instruments, such as Tarot cards, with established interpretative systems for divination.

Shaman/healers are generally characterized by extensive role specialization, and the practitioner engages in a limited subset of professional activities associated with the position. For instance, a shaman/healer may perform divination but not healing or agricultural rites. Their ASC experiences are similar to those characteristic of meditators and mystics, although the shamanistic healer's ASC may involve soul journey.

Mediums. Mediums are often referred to as "shamans" (Lewis, 1988), but they were in most respects distinct from core shamans. Historically, Most mediums have been female, and their call to the profession has generally been a possession episode in early adulthood. Possession is interpreted as a "take over" of the person's personality by a spirit. The possession ASC generally involves tremors, convulsions, seizures, and amnesia (these characteristics are often interpreted as evidence of the spirits' control of the medium). Mediums do not usually engage in malevolent acts but instead are called upon to act against sorcerers, witches, and other evil entities. Mediums may worship their possessing spirits, and they often maintain relationships with superior deities to whom they make sacrifices.

Mediums may be more powerful than ordinary women, but, in contrast to the social leadership role of shamans, they tend to appear in complex societies with political hierarchies and religious practitioners, such as priests and healers, who are more powerful than the medium.

Healers. Healers are not usually referred to as shamans. They are almost exclusively male and generally have high economic status and political power. Healers' professional organizations provide training, which is generally expensive, but the profession is remunerative, enabling healers to be full-time specialists. Most healers do not engage in the ASC practices characteristic of shamans, but healers sometimes use rituals and incantations to induce ASC in clients. A principal healing activity is exorcism. Healers also perform life-cycle activities, such as naming ceremonies, marriage rituals, and funerals. Healers often identify sorcerers or witches, and take action against them.

PSYCHOBIOLOGICAL FEATURES OF SHAMANISM. The shamanistic practices found in hunter-gatherer societies around the world, and the universal distribution of shamanistic healers, reflect ecological and social adaptations to human biological potentials. The psychobiological bases of shamanism include basic brain processes, operations of innate representational modules, and neurological structuring of fundamental structures of consciousness (Winkelman, 2000, 2002a, 2002b). Neurological foundations underlie the principal characteristics of shamanism that Eliade emphasized—ecstasy, spirits, and community—as well as other universal characteristics of shamanism (e.g., the visionary journey, the use of music and dance, and animal allies).

Shamanic rituals activate brain structures and processes that elicit integrative psychological and social processes and produce visual and metaphoric representations. This integration of brain functions involves physiologically based brain integration induced by ASC, as well as cognitive synthesis based in integration of specialized representational functions, producing symbolic thought in animism, animal spirits, totemism, and soul flight. The primary neurological features of shamanism are discussed below in terms of the underlying physiological bases and functional dynamics of the following:

- ASC, or operations of consciousness that produce cognitive and personal integration;
- visionary experiences, manifesting a cognitive capacity for presentational symbolism;
- fundamental structures of human consciousness reflected in spirits (animism);
- self-objectification processes reflected in soul journey and death-and-rebirth experiences;
- metaphoric representations using animal and body relations, which is manifested in animism, animal powers, and totemism;
- community bonding processes that elicit attachment dynamics and opioid mechanisms, including mimetic expression, chanting, and dance to produce social coordination; and
- physiological healing processes based in the relaxation response, anxiety management, and elicitation of opioid and serotonergic neurotransmitters.

ASC: THE INTEGRATIVE MODE OF CONSCIOUSNESS The ecstasy, or ASC, that is central to the selection, training, and professional practice of shamans typically involves singing, chanting, drumming, and dancing, followed by collapse and apparent unconsciousness but accompanied by intense visual experiences. This ASC involves a natural brain response that produces physiological, functional, and psychological integration. Arnold Mandell has argued that the physiological dynamics of ASC involve slow-wave discharges from the serotonin circuits of the limbic brain, which produces synchronized waves across the brain. Auditory driving (singing, chanting, drumming, and music) is a primary mechanism for producing ASC and brain-wave synchronization. Dancing, fasting, and other austerities, most psychoactive drugs, and social and sensory isolation reinforce the response. Shamanic ASCs activate the autonomic nervous system to the point of exhaustion, and it collapses into a parasympathetic dominant state that evokes the relaxation response. Skilled shamans may directly enter this state of relaxation through an internal focus of attention, as in meditation. The relaxation response is one of the body's natural healing processes, with adaptive advantages in stress reduction and physiological restoration.

The shaman's ASC elicits the "integrative mode of consciousness" (Winkelman, 2000), a normal brain response to many activities (e.g., chanting, drumming, fasting, meditation) with synchronized brain-wave patterns in the theta and alpha range. These slow-wave patterns are produced by activation of serotonergic linkages between the limbic-brain system (the "emotional brain" or paleomammalian brain) and lower-brain structures. These connections produce coherent theta brain-wave discharges that synchronize the frontal areas of the brain, replacing the normal fast and desynchronized brain-wave activity of the frontal cortex. The integrative mode of consciousness integrates preverbal behavioral and emotional information into the cultural and language mediated processes of the frontal cortex.

Visionary experience as presentational symbolism. An intense visual imagery, what Richard Noll refers to as "mental imagery cultivation," is central to the shamanic ASC experience. These experiences reflect an innate representational system referred to as "presentational symbolism" by Harry Hunt. Visionary experiences provide analysis, analogic synthesis, diagnosis, and planning. Shamanic visions are natural brain phenomena that result from release of suppression of the visual cortex; the visions involve the same brain substrates used for the processing of perceptual information.

Images are a form of psychobiological communication experienced in a preverbal symbol system. Imagery plays a fundamental role in cognition, providing a basis for metaphoric expression and the formation of relations between different levels of information processing. Mental imagery integrates unconscious psychophysiological information with emotional levels, linking somatic and cognitive experience and recruiting and coordinating muscles and organic systems.

Spirits and Human Consciousness. The fundamental features of shamanism—animism, totemism, and animal spirits—are representations of self, intrapsychic dynamics, and social groups. These representations are produced through integration of specialized innate processing modules for natural history intelligence (recognition of animal species) with modules for self-conceptualization and mental attributions regarding social "others" (mind reading). The shamanic role in managing these modules is exemplified in certain characteristics of shamans: (1) social intelligence—being group leader and mediator of intergroup relations; (2) natural history knowledge—being master of animals; and (3) self-conceptualization exemplified in identity shifts developed through animal familiars, soul flight, and death-and-rebirth experiences. These representations reflect preverbal structures of consciousness and the thought processes of lower-brain structures. These specialized forms of knowledge production are combined in metaphoric processes to produce the shamanic features of animism, totemism, and animal spirits. Anthropomorphism and interaction with the spirit world (animism) use the brain's innate representation modules for understanding the self and social others, and for attributing human mental and social characteristics to animals, nature, and the unknown. The phenomena of totemism, animal allies, and animal powers involve the natural history intelligence, employing capacities for distinguishing animal species to understand and mold personal identity and produce differentiation of self and social groups.

Animism and animal allies. Animism involves the use of innate representation modules for understanding self and social others, and for attributing human mental and social capabilities to animals, nature, and the unknown. Stewart Guthrie discusses animism as a human being's use of self-characteristics as a model for the unknown; it is a natural projection of a human being's own qualities in relationship to the environment. Spirit concepts are based in social intelligence, the ability to infer the mental states of others. This intuitive psychology and "theory of mind" attributes mental states to others through the organism's use of its own mental states to model the mind and behaviors of others. This attribution underlies the spirit world.

Animal allies, guardian spirits, and totemism involve a process that is reciprocal to animism and represents humans through the use of the natural-history module's capacity for organizing knowledge about animal species. This universal analogical system for creation and extension of meaning uses natural-history intelligence to differentiate personal and social identities. Animal species provide natural symbol systems for differentiation of self and social groups and have psychosocial functions in empowering people, as illustrated in the guardian spirit quest discussed by Guy Swanson. Spirits are "sacred others," the integration of the spiritual and social worlds in cultural processes, which Jacob Pandian characterizes as the production of the symbolic self. Spirit beliefs exemplify social norms and psychosocial relations, structuring individual psychodynamics and social behavior. Spirit beliefs protect from stress and anxiety through management of emotions and attachments. Spirits provide variable command-control agents for mediating conflict between the different instinctive agents and aspects of self. This facilitates the operation with respect to a hierarchy of goals and the use of problem-solving modules for nonroutine tasks.

Death and rebirth. Transformations of self are also illustrated in a universal feature of shamanic development, the death-and-rebirth experience. This involves illness, suffering, and attacks by spirits, leading to the experience of death and dismemberment, followed by a reconstruction of the body with the help of spirit allies and powers. Roger Walsh characterizes the death-and-rebirth experience as a natural response to overwhelming stress and intrapsychic conflicts. This breakdown of ego structures reflects neurognostic processes of self-transformation, experienced in "autosymbolic images" of bodily destruction. Charles Laughlin, John McManus, and Eugene d'Aquili (1992) discuss these experiences as involving the activation of innate drives toward psychological integration and the restructuring of ego and identity through activation of holistic imperatives to produce a new self-identity and higher levels of psychological integration.

Soul flight as self-objectification. Soul-flight experiences involve natural symbolic systems for self-representation. The shaman's soul journey is structurally similar to ASC found cross-culturally in out-of-body and near-death experiences. The homologies reflect their innate basis in psychophysiological structures as forms of self-representation that are a natural response of the human nervous system. Charles Laughlin (1997) discusses the universality of a body-based metaphor that is manifested in shamanic cosmology and a natural body-based epistemology. Soul flight involves "a view of self from the perspective of other," a form of "taking the role of the other" in presentational symbolism (Hunt, 1995). These self-representations provide forms of self-awareness referenced to the body, but, apart from the body, they produce the altered consciousness and transcendence experienced by shamans.

COMMUNITY RITUALS AND PSYCHOSOCIAL DYNAMICS. Shamanic activity is accomplished on behalf of the community and requires community participation. Soul loss, the most fundamental shamanic illness, is healed by reintegration of the patient into the community. Community rituals produce both psychosocial effects (community cohesion, positive expectation, and social support) and psychobiological effects (the elicitation of attachment and opioid mechanisms).

Opioid-mediated attachment processes. Ede Frecska and Zsuzsanna Kulcsar illustrate how communal rituals elicit attachment bonds and other psycho-socio-physiological mechanisms that release endogenous opiates and produce psychobiological synchrony in a group of people. Shamanic rituals release endogenous opiates through a variety of mechanisms, including austerities, fasting, water restriction, strenuous exercise, and emotional hyperstress (Winkelman, 1997). Shamanic rituals elicit responses from the brain's opioid systems by tapping into social attachment and conditioned cultural symbols (Frecska and Kulcsar, 1989). Emotionally charged symbols elicit the opioid system and permit ritual manipulation of physiological responses in the linking of the psychic, mythological, and somatic spheres. Opioids stimulate the immune system; produce a sense of euphoria, certainty, and belonging; and enhance coping skills, pain reduction, stress tolerance, environmental adaptation, group synchronization, and maintenance of bodily homeostasis (Valle and Prince, 1989).

Mimetic expression and emotional vocalization. Community bonding involves chanting, music, and dance, which can elicit an ancient communicative system that Merlin Donald discusses as mimesis, an imitative communication channel that evolved to enhance social bonding and communication of internal states. Music, chanting, singing, and dancing have origins in mimetic modules that provide rhythm, affective semantics, and melody (see Wallin, Merker, and Brown, 2000). Chanting and music provide a nonlinguistic channel for communication that induces healing states by engaging theta and alpha brain-wave production and by promoting cohesion, coordination, and cooperation among the group. The shamanic practices of drumming, dancing, and ritual imitation are based in operations of this innate mimetic controller and the unique human ability to entrain the body and community to external rhythms.

SHAMANIC THERAPIES. Shamanism is the original psycho-socio-physiological therapy in that it uses rituals and cultural processes to manipulate health from physical through symbolic levels. Therapeutic mechanisms of shamanism include:

- inducing relaxation and the parasympathetic dominant responses that elicit organic healing;
- reducing the physiological effects of stress and anxiety by providing meaning and assurance;
- integrating dissociated aspects of the self and the spiritual-social models into identity;
- enhancing the mammalian bonding-attachment process;
- producing individual psychosocial development and social integration;
- synchronizing and integrating the information processes of the brain's subsystems;
- activating opioid and serotonergic neurotransmitter systems; and
- producing ritual elicitation and cultural programming of neurological processes.

Hypnosis in shamanic healing. James McClenon discusses how an inheritable hypnotizability provided foundations for shamanistic healing. Hypnotic susceptibility provided mechanisms for enhancing recovery from disease, as well as innovations derived from access to the unconscious mind and its creative visions. Hypnotizability produces physiological and psychophysiological responses that facilitated shamanic healing. Hypnotic and ritual behavior among other animals provides mechanisms for adaptation to the social environment by reducing stress and promoting intragroup cohesion, which is experienced by humans as "union" or "oneness." Shamanic healing potentials exploit the co-occurrence of hypnotizability, dissociation, fantasy proneness, temporal lobe lability, and thin cognitive boundaries to enhance connections between the unconscious and conscious mind. This access provided survival advantages by facilitating the development of creative strategies, enhancing suggestibility to symbolically induced physiological changes, and inducing ASC experiences to facilitate psychosomatic healing.

Soul loss. Jeanne Achterberg and Sandra Ingerman discuss soul loss as a central shamanic illness that involves injury to the essence of one's being and damage to crucial aspects of the self, fundamental aspects of personal identity, and the essence of self-emotions. This injury to one's essence is manifested as despair, a loss of meaning in life, and a loss of one's sense of belonging and connection with others. Soul loss results from trauma that causes an aspect of one's self to dissociate, making reintegration of these dissociated aspects of self central to healing. Soul recovery involves regaining the sense of social self that was alienated by trauma. Community participation is central to soul retrieval because social support is vital for the reintegration of the self.

THE EVOLUTIONARY ROOTS OF SHAMANISM. Jean Clottes, David Lewis-Williams, Robert Ryan, and Michael Winkelman have reconstructed the prehistorical emergence of shamanism, which occurred more than forty thousand years ago in the earliest manifestations of modern human culture in the Middle to Upper Paleolithic transition. The similarity in shamanism around the world derives from human nature; it is an aspect of an evolved psychology. Several lines of evidence point to a biogenetic origin for shamanic ritual: (1) continuity with animal ritual and hominid group activities involving vocalizations for interpersonal communication and group coordination, as well as drumming, dancing and mimesis; (2) the direct correspondences of the central features of Paleolithic cave art to the universals of shamanism; and (3) the ability of shamanic ritual processes to provide psychological and social integration processes; that is, the group needs that characterize the changes associated with this period of transition in human history (Winkelman, 2002a).

The central role of shamanic elements in Middle to Upper Paleolithic cave art is seen in the elements and style of these artistic depictions, the nature of the representations of animals and humans, and the ritual use of natural cave features (Winkelman, 2002b; Ryan; Clottes, and Lewis-Williams, 1998; Lewis-Williams, 2002). This art is key evidence for the cultural cognitive revolution, with shamanic ritual, beliefs, practices, and cosmology characterized by cross-modal cognitive integrations that typify the emergent features of Paleolithic thought.

This role of shamanism in the Middle to Upper Paleolithic transition can be understood from psychosocial and psychobiological perspectives that illustrate how shamanic ritual practices and beliefs facilitated adaptations to the ecological and social changes of the Upper Paleolithic, and thus facilitated cognitive evolution. Shamanism produced social bonding mechanisms, self-transformation processes, and analogical thought processes that provided integrative visual and emotional syntheses. Shamanism contributed to cognitive and social evolution through production of visual symbolism and analogical thought processes, and through the ritual activities that promoted group bonding and the identity formation that was central to managing the consequences of the Middle to Upper Paleolithic transition.

The triune brain and shamanic healing. Human evolution produced a fragmentation of consciousness in the modular structure of the brain (Mithen, 1996), the diversification of personal and social identities, and the habitualization of brain processes (Laughlin et al., 1992). Shamanistic activities use ASC, visual symbols, and group rituals to produce psychological, social, and cognitive integration, which serves to manage relationships among behavioral, emotional, and cognitive processes, and between physiological and mental levels of the organism.

One aspect of this shamanic integration involves linkages across the evolutionary strata of the brain. Paul MacLean has proposed that the brain involves three anatomically distinct yet interconnected systems—the reptilian brain, the paleomammalian brain, and the neomammalian brain—that provide the basis for behavioral and emotional "subsymbolic" information. These communication systems employ a visual presentational symbolism (Hunt, 1995) that mediates interactions across levels of the brain and social, affective, and visual symbolic information. The hierarchical management of behavior, emotions, and reason is mediated both physiologically and symbolically. The relationships among innate drives, social attachment, and cultural demands create many different kinds of health problems, including chronic anxiety and fear, behavioral disorders, conflict, excessive emotionality and desire, obsessions and compulsions, dissociations, and repression. The paleomammalian brain mediates many of these processes to promote an integration of the self within the community, thus accommodating the instinctual responses of the reptilian and paleomammalian brain systems to the cultural demands mediated by the frontal brain systems.

CONCLUSIONS. Shamanism is now getting recognition as the original basis of human spiritual and religious practice, a part of human nature that played a significant role in human cognitive and cultural evolution. As a biologically based spiritual and healing system that played a significant role in human survival, social relations, and cosmology, shamanism was humanity's original neurotheology. As human societies became more complex, the original biological basis of shamanism that was manifested in hunter-gatherer societies was substantially modified, eventually emerging in the form of mediumship and possession. Ethnography and cross-cultural studies have, however, helped revive shamanism and have reintroduced it to the modern world, enabling shamanism to re-emerge as a natural religious and spiritual form.

SEE ALSO Healing and Medicine, overview article.

BIBLIOGRAPHY

Achterberg, Jeanne. *Imagery in Healing: Shamanism and Modern Medicine.* Boston, 1985.

Clottes, Jean, and David Lewis-Williams. *The Shamans of Prehistory: Trance and Magic in the Painted Caves.* Translated by Sophie Hawkes. New York, 1998.

Donald, Merlin. *Origins of the Modern Mind: Three Stages in the Evolution of Culture and Cognition.* Cambridge, Mass., 1991.

Frecska, Ede, and Zsuzsanna Kulcsar. "Social Bonding in the Modulation of the Physiology of Ritual Trance." *Ethos* 17, no. 1 (1989): 70–87.

Guthrie, Stewart. *Faces in the Clouds: A New Theory of Religion.* Oxford, 1993.

Harner, Michael. *The Way of the Shaman.* San Francisco, 1980; reprint, 1990.

Hunt, Harry T. *On the Nature of Consciousness: Cognitive, Phenomenological, and Transpersonal Perspectives.* New Haven, Conn., 1995.

Ingerman, Sandra. *Soul Retrieval: Mending the Fragmented Self.* San Francisco, 1991.

Laughlin, Charles. "Body, Brain, and Behavior: The Neuroanthropology of the Body Image." *Anthropology of Consciousness* 8, nos. 2–3 (1997): 49–68.

Laughlin, Charles, John McManus, and Eugene d'Aquili. *Brain, Symbol, and Experience: Toward a Neurophenomenology of Consciousness.* New York, 1992.

Lewis, I. M. *Ecstatic Religion: An Anthropological Study of Spirit Possession and Shamanism.* London, 1971; 2d ed., 1988.

Lewis-Williams, David. *The Mind in the Cave: Consciousness and the Origins of Art.* London, 2002.

Mandell, Arnold. "Toward a Psychobiology of Transcendence: God in the Brain." In *The Psychobiology of Consciousness,* edited by Julian M. Davidson and Richard J. Davidson, pp. 379–464. New York, 1980.

McClenon, James. *Wondrous Healing: Shamanism, Human Evolution, and the Origin of Religion.* DeKalb, Ill., 2002.

McLean, Paul D. *The Triune Brain in Evolution: Role in Paleocerebral Functions.* New York, 1990.

Mithen, Steven J. *The Prehistory of the Mind: A Search for the Origins of Art, Religion, and Science.* London, 1996.

Noll, Richard. "Mental Imagery Cultivation as a Cultural Phenomenon: The Role of Visions in Shamanism." *Current Anthropology* 26 (1985): 443–451.

Pandian, J. "The Sacred Integration of the Cultural Self: An Anthropological Approach to the Study of Religion." In *The Anthropology of Religion: A Handbook,* edited by Steven Glazier, pp. 505–516, Westport, Conn., 1997.

Prince, Raymond. "The Endorphins: A Review for Psychological Anthropologists." *Ethos* 10, no. 4 (1982): 299–302.

Ryan, Robert. *The Strong Eye of Shamanism: A Journey into the Caves of Consciousness.* Rochester, Vt., 1999.

Siikala, Anna-Leena. *The Rite Technique of the Siberian Shaman.* Helsinki, Finland, 1978.

Spilka, Bernard, and Daniel McIntosh, eds. *The Psychology of Religion: Theoretical Approaches.* Boulder, Colo., 1997.

Swanson, Guy. "The Search for a Guardian Spirit: The Process of Empowerment in Simpler Societies." *Ethnology* 12 (1973): 359–378.

Valle, Jacques, and Raymond Prince. "Religious Experiences as Self-Healing Mechanisms." In *Altered States of Consciousness and Mental Health: A Cross Cultural Perspective,* edited by Colleen A. Ward, pp. 149–166. Newbury Park, Calif., 1989.

Wallin, Nils, Bjorn Merker, and Steven Brown, eds. *The Origins of Music.* Cambridge, Mass., 2000.

Walsh, Roger. *The Spirit of Shamanism.* Los Angeles, 1990.

Winkelman, Michael. "Magico-Religious Practitioner Types and Socioeconomic Conditions." *Behavior Science Research* 20, nos. 1–4 (1986): 17–46.

Winkelman, Michael. "Shaman and Other 'Magico-religious Healers': A Cross-cultural Study of Their Origins, Nature, and Social Transformation." *Ethos* 18, no. 3 (1990): 308–352.

Winkelman, Michael. *Shamans, Priests, and Witches: A Cross-cultural Study of Magico-Religious Practitioners.* Tempe, Ariz., 1992.

Winkelman, Michael. "Altered States of Consciousness and Religious Behavior." In *Anthropology of Religion: A Handbook,* edited by Stephen Glazier, pp. 393–428. Westport, Conn., 1997.

Winkelman, Michael. *Shamanism: The Neural Ecology of Consciousness and Healing.* Westport, Conn., 2000.

Winkelman, Michael. "Shamanism and Cognitive Evolution." *Cambridge Archaeological Journal* 12, no. 1 (2002a): 71–101.

Winkelman, Michael. "Shamanism as Neurotheology and Evolutionary Psychology." *American Behavioral Scientist* 45, no. 12 (2002b): 1875–1887.

Winkelman, Michael, and Douglas White. *A Cross-cultural Study of Magico-Religious Practitioners and Trance States: Data Base.* Human Relations Area Files Research Series in Quantitative Cross-cultural Data, vol. 3, edited by David Levinson and Roy Wagner. New Haven, Conn., 1987.

Michael Winkelman (2005)

SHAMANISM: SIBERIAN AND INNER ASIAN SHAMANISM

Shamanism is a fundamental and striking feature of Siberian and Inner Asian cultures. The religions of these regions have therefore been described as shamanistic. Shamanism itself is not, however, a religion, but rather a complex of different rites and beliefs surrounding the activities of the shaman connected with very different religious systems. Shamanism is founded on a special technique for achieving ecstasy by means of which the shaman enters an altered state of consciousness, and on the idea that the shaman is accompanied by helping spirits who assist him in this state. While in a state of trance, the shaman is regarded as capable of direct communication with representatives of the otherworld, either by journeying to the supranormal world or by calling the spirits to the séance. He is thus able to help his fellow men in crises believed to be caused by the spirits and to act as a concrete mediator between this world and the otherworld in accompanying a soul to the otherworld, or fetching it from the domain of the spirits. The shaman acts as a healer and as a patron of hunting and fertility, but also as a diviner, the guardian of livelihoods, and so on.

The Origin of Shamanism. The ecological and cultural differences among the peoples of Siberia and Inner Asia are considerable. The way of life of the Arctic sea-mammal hunters and reindeer breeders differs greatly from that of the nomads of the steppe or the hunters and fishermen of the taiga. It follows that, despite certain basic similarities, the shamanistic complexes are not uniform either. There are variations in the shaman's status in the community, as there are differences, for example, in his ritual accessories or the tradition of beliefs he represents. Tracing the history of shamanism is thus a complicated matter. Shamanism is generally thought to be founded on the animistic concepts of the northern hunting peoples. On the other hand, soul flight, the ability of the shaman to journey to the otherworld, a striking feature of northern and western shamanistic complexes, has led scholars to regard a dualistic concept of the soul as the ideological basis of shamanism. According to this belief, man has one soul confined to the body and a second soul, or part soul, capable of leaving the body freely during sleep, trance, or sickness.

The word *shaman* comes through Russian sources from the Tunguz word *šaman* (*xaman*). There are such varied names for the shaman in Siberia and Inner Asia that these names cannot be used to throw light on the origin of shamanism. A theory was put forward in the nineteenth century that the word derived from the Pali *samaṇa* (Sanskrit, *śramaṇa*) and Chinese *shamen.* Although this theory has been disproved (Németh, 1913–1914; Laufer, 1917), the cultural-historical foundations of shamanism have been sought in Buddhism or others of the great scriptural traditions of the East. It is indeed a fact that Buddhism and Lamaism had a significant effect on the development of shamanism among the Evenki (a Tunguz people), the Mongols, and the Buriats. The wide distribution of the phenomenon of shamanism and the endemicity of certain of its basic ideas—soul flight, soul dualism, the link with animal ceremonialism—in Arctic and sub-Arctic cultures do, however, support the view that the roots of shamanism lie in the Paleolithic hunting cultures. In his fundamental work *Shamanism: Archaic Techniques of Ecstasy* (1964), Mircea Eliade regards the ideas of ecstatic experience and soul flight as the basis of shamanism, and asserts that shamanism grew out of the ancient Paleolithic inheritance, fertilized by Buddhism, Lamaism, and even more ancient East and South Asian influences.

The Shaman in the Community. The small hunting and fishing communities of northern Siberia have provided a setting for shamanism completely different from that of the agrarian cultures of Inner Asia rooted to one locale. Both the status of the shaman in the community and his tasks depend on the supporting culture, its economy, the nature of its social structure, and its practice of religion as a whole. Variations in the status of the shaman and the importance of shamanism as an institution spring from the relationship between the shaman and the group supporting him as well as from the nature of the particular group.

The clan shaman. The Yukagir and the Evenki retained their clan system until relatively recent times, and their shamanism is clearly connected with the organization of the clan. Even at the end of the nineteenth century the Yukagir, a Siberian tribal people, lived off deer hunting and reindeer breeding, the latter having been assimilated from the Evenki. The population, consisting of the remains of formerly larger clans, lived in camps or villages of related families. The shaman, who had to be related to the clan by ties of blood, was one of the leaders of the clan and acted as its general patron. It was also his job to maintain contact between the living and the dead members of the clan and to arrange the shamanizing connected with the calendrical hunting rites. It was during these rites that the shaman would retrieve the souls of the animals to be hunted from the keeper of the species in the otherworld store. The shaman helped individual members of the clan by curing diseases and infertility, by prophesying, and by preventing misfortune threatened by the spirits.

A highly advanced clan system existed among the Evenki, who were spread over a wide area and were divided into different occupational categories: hunters and fishermen, reindeer breeders, and hunters breeding horses and cattle. Their chief social unit was the clan, which had its own area or "river"; the clans were in turn grouped into larger tribes. One of the leaders of the clan was a shaman. Such special status among the Evenki living along the Podkamennaia Tunguska is illustrated by the belief that the shaman's hair may not be cut because it is the dwelling place of the souls of the members of the clan. As the protector and leader of his clan, their shaman set up a *marylya* (a fence made of spirits) around the clan's lands; he also possessed knowledge of the mythical clan river leading to the otherworld. The clan shaman held séances on behalf of his supporters, shamanizing in the course of hunting rites and helping individual members of the clan. At the end of the nineteenth century there also were professional Evenk shamans who would shamanize on behalf of members of a different clan for a fee. These "false" shamans were not accorded the honored and important position of the clan shaman.

The small-group shaman. The shamans in circles of neighbors and relatives among the hunters of northwestern and northern Siberia had a relationship with their supporters comparable to that of the clan shaman. For example, the Nganasani (a Samoyed people) were spread over such a wide area that the clan was of no significance as an economic or local unit. It retained its significance mainly in religious connections, such as in annual rituals. On an occasion such as the clean-tent festival of the Nganasani, held in February when the sun began to rise again, the shaman might act as representative of the clan. He did not, however, achieve a status symbolizing clan unity and the welfare of the clan. He was equipped by his own small community, the tent community or village whose members he assisted as a healer, a bringer of success in hunting, a guardian at difficult births, and so on.

The professional shaman of the north. The relationship between the shaman of the north and his supporters was not as close as that described above in northeastern Siberia.

The Chukchi and the Koriak—small tribal peoples indigenous to Siberia—fell into two occupational categories interacting closely with one another: reindeer breeders and sea-mammal hunters. They showed no signs of a clear clan system, their basic social unit being the hunting communities and nomad camps made up of relatives and neighbors. The annual occupational rites were handled by the family or occupational unit, one typical feature being family shamanism. In this type of shamanism, which cannot be considered shamanism proper, anyone attending a festival could drum and dance in the manner of a shaman. Since the occupational and other important rites were performed among the family or kin, the shaman was not tied to any clearly defined band of supporters. He was a healer and a resolver of various incidental crises. The status of the shaman who was able to choose his clients freely depended on his personal skills. Thus the performance of various tricks played a considerable part in the competition between shamans.

Shamanism in the south. The hierarchical community of the nomads and farmers of southern Siberia and Inner Asia (e.g., the Yakuts, the Buriats, the Tuvin, the southern Altais, the Khakasy, and the horse-breeding Evenki of Transbaikalia) and the rise in status of the area to an administrative unit (called "patriarchal feudalism" by Soviet scholars) above the clan provided a background to shamanism that differed from that of the northern hunting communities. Under the influence of the Lamaism and Buddhism of the south, the ritual aspects of shamanism and the beliefs concerning the supranormal world here developed in a richer and more complex form than shamanism in the north.

While contact with the clan may be significant, regional factors often determine the shaman's sphere of activities. Since becoming a shaman and the passing down of the shamanic tradition is under the strict control of older shamans, shamanism in the south clearly has more institutionalized forms than in the north. Among the Buriats, for example, a large number of initiated shamans join the new candidate in taking part in the shamanic initiation ceremony, thus demonstrating the importance of control from within to the institution of shamanism. In addition to acting as a healer and a diviner and carrying out other conventional tasks, the shaman may also assume the role of sacrificial priest. Practices such as the sacrifice made by the Altaic Tatars of a horse to the god in the sky rely on the ability of the shaman to accompany to the otherworld the soul of the animal sacrificed.

CATEGORIES OF SHAMANS. In addition to the fundamental differences in the status of shamanism as a whole, shamans differ in their nature and prestige from one ethnic group to another. The Hungarian expert on shamanism Vilmos Diószegi observed on interviewing former Tofa shamans in the late 1950s that they fell into different categories according to clan, the color symbolism of their accoutrements, their power, their skill, and ultimately also their own personal characteristics.

The categories of shaman used by different ethnic groups themselves are evident in the names for types of shamans. For example, the most highly respected shaman among the Entsy (a Samoyed people) was the *budtode*, who is in contact with the spirits who live in heaven. The less highly regarded *d'ano* was able to protect humans from evil spirits, and the least respected *sawode* shaman could contact the dead. In the same way the lowest category of shaman among the Nanay (Goldi) was the *siurinka*, shamans who cure the sick. *Nemati* shamans were able both to cure the sick and to perform the shamanizing at the first festival in memory of the dead. Among the shamans with the greatest prestige were the *kasati* shamans, who had command of all shamanic knowledge and who are capable of the most important task of the Nanay shaman, that of accompanying the souls of the dead to the otherworld.

The Yakuts believed that the shaman's prestige was determined by the status of the god who granted him his chief spirit helper, and by the height of the branch on the mythical shaman's tree on which the shaman was instructed by the spirits during his initiation. The division of shamans into black and white, encountered among the Yakuts and elsewhere (e.g., among the Altaic peoples) points to the nature of the spirits with whom the shaman came into contact. White was the color of the sky, black that of the earth. According to the shamanic tradition, the shaman's nature and rank are determined by the spirits initiating him. In practice the distinguishing features were probably the skills and ability to achieve ecstasy of the initiate and the nature of the tradition that he assimilated. A shaman could also rise to a higher category as his knowledge increased. A great shaman often bore the epithet "old."

INITIATION. Gaining command of the shamanic tradition and the ecstatic rite technique called for special training on the part of the beginner. The nature and length of the initiation period depended on the position of the shaman in his community and the importance of shamanism in the culture in question. The length of the apprenticeship, the amount and nature of the tradition to be internalized, the initiate's instruction, the number of initiation rites, and the control of the initiate's abilities varied from one region to another. Two features common to all areas were the shaman's meeting of spirits and winning of spirit helpers while in a state of ecstasy and the recognition of a new shaman by his supporters.

The shaman's disease. A potential shaman could be recognized by an abnormal, often highly nervous, disposition. All over Siberia and Inner Asia, selection was often preceded by the shaman's sickness. The first symptoms might be states of mental unbalance, fits of hysteria, periods of seclusion, unusual visions and the hearing of voices, or states of physical torment. Usually the sickness struck at adolescence, but people stricken as adults might also become shaman initiates. It is impossible to give any specific account of the illness from reports of the symptoms, The point is that shamanizing was the only recognized cure. Often a shaman called in to cure the sufferer would teach him how to shamanize.

Scholars such as Waldemar Jochelson, an expert on the tribal peoples indigenous to Siberian and Inner Asia, have compared the shaman's initiatory sickness to hysteria. The healing effect of shamanizing would then mean that the novice, under the instruction of an older shaman, learned to control his ego functions and the regression of hysteria became an ego-controlled regression during the initiation stage. It is significant that shamans suffering from a preliminary sickness have found that repeated shamanizing is a condition for remaining healthy.

The shaman's sickness was interpreted as the call of the spirits to become a shaman; since the task was so dangerous, shamans say they often resisted the call to the very end. Internal compulsion was not the only reason for selection; there could also be external reasons. A young Chukchi, for example, might choose to become a shaman in the hope of gaining wealth and prestige. Among the Evenki the clan elders or clan shaman might select a child of suitable temperament for training as a shaman.

The position of shaman was handed down within the family, especially in the areas of clan shamanism and the professional shamanism of the south. A. F. Anisimov, an expert on the shamanism of the Podkamennaia Tunguska Evenki, observed that shamans deliberately tried to keep this important position within the family. The inheritance of shamanism is founded on shamanistic ideology. In the northern regions, where selection as shaman was often a matter of incidental vocation, the spirits encountered by the novice were chiefly spirits of nature. The principle of inheritance within the family is a reflection of the notion that the spirits preparing the initiate to become a shaman were ancestor shamans or spirits of nature undertaking the task at the request of the ancestor spirits.

The initiation period. At the start of the initiation period the initiate retired in solitude, learned how to use the drum in seeking ecstatic experiences, and steeped himself in the shamanic tradition. One of his main tasks was to compose his own shaman songs. The songs for calling the spirits sung at séances of Chukchi shamans, for example, were products of the initiation period. In the shamanic view the novice is taught by the spirits; there are, however, reports of situations in which older shamans guide the novice in the art of shamanizing.

The next phase of the initiatory period is one of visions and the hearing of voices, during which the novice undergoes his initiation by the spirits. During these experiences the novice feels that the spirits are actually destroying his old ego, dissecting or boiling it, after which he is to be reassembled as a new shaman, capable of seeing that which is hidden to ordinary men. Thus is repeated the theme of death and rebirth. Despite individual differences the visions follow traditional patterns. For example, among the Samoyeds, the novice is given his spirit helpers by the initiating spirits, and he promises to follow his calling. The handling of his bones, the dismembering and reassembling of his skeleton by the spirits, plays a significant part in the visions describing the shaman's rebirth. In the background here is the idea also found in animal ceremonialism that the bones are the point of attachment for the soul.

Following his initiation by the spirits the shaman still had to prove his powers to his community. He did so at various test shamanizings and through public rites. The small-group shaman of northwestern Siberia acquired his attributes gradually in the course of annual rites. His dress and ritual objects were made by neighbors and relatives who were among his supporters and who also took part in the shamanizings at which these objects were first used. Similarly, great test shamanizings were held in the clan shamanism region and were attended by the entire clan. Through prayers and sacrifices, an ancestor shaman might be asked to indicate a suitable animal for making the shaman's requisites. As we have seen, the rituals surrounding the initiation of the shaman were most richly developed in the shamanism of the southern regions. The Buriat shaman, for example, promised during a great initiation festival to fulfill the obligations of his profession.

The shaman's initiation was less formal among the tribal peoples of Siberian and Inner Asia than elsewhere. The mysteries surrounding the call of the spirits and the experience of meeting them were paramount; as there were few requisites, the ritual announcement of the new status was not of itself significant. The shaman's later actions proved whether or not he was capable and whether he had gained any supporters.

The Shamanistic Belief Tradition. Some indication of the nature of the shamanistic belief tradition is provided by the visions of the initiation period and the shaman songs describing, for example, the shaman's journey to the otherworld. Although the cosmographic concepts vary greatly over Siberia and Inner Asia, and although the influence of Lamaism and Buddhism is very much in evidence among the southern peoples, there are certain structural features shared by all and of wide distribution. Among these are concepts of a multilevel cosmos, the world above, the middle world inhabited by man, and the world below, which is divided into three, seven, or nine levels. The layers are connected either by the world stream (among the Ket, it is by holy water), which begins in heaven and flows through the earth to the underworld, or by a hole at the North Star in the center of the globe through which the Chukchi, among others, believe it is possible to pass from one layer to another. Besides believing in a multilayered cosmos, the northern peoples in particular believe in the concept of a tentlike upper world, the firmaments spanning a round or square world. Supporting it in the center is the cosmic pillar. Phenomena parallel to the cosmic pillar are the cosmic mountain and the cosmic tree. The latter's counterpart in the shamanistic belief tradition is the shaman's tree, by means of which the shaman might travel from one world level to another.

During his initiation period the novice had to study the structure of the cosmos and above all learn the topography of the otherworld: the paths and rivers leading to the otherworld and the dwellings of the various gods, the guardian spirits, the demons of disease, and the dead. The way to the otherworld was usually described as being fraught with difficulties and dangers. The Nanay shaman, for example, was able to list the landmarks along the road to the kingdom of the dead and the dangers in store along the way.

At the séance the shaman turned to various gods and spirits as it became necessary. Linked directly with the shamanistic complex were the spirits of his initiation and his ecstatic experiences. In some cases the shaman enters the service of these spirits; at other times, they are at the shaman's command.

The spirits influencing a shaman's initiation in northeastern Siberia were mainly spirits of nature. One Koriak shaman described how spirits of the wolf, the raven, the bear, the sea gull, and the plover appeared before him in the forest, sometimes in human form, sometimes in the form of an animal, demanding that he enter their service. The Chukchi believed that "everything lives," that even inanimate objects have some sort of soul principle. Thus the shaman's band of spirits might also include various objects, stones, or household utensils. It is significant that there is no difference between the guiding spirits of the initiation period and the spirit helpers proper: the spirits appearing before the novice become his spirit helpers when he is a shaman.

In the small-group shamanism of northwestern Siberia, too, the spirits influencing a shaman's initiation are mainly spirits of nature. The initiation visions of the Nganasani demonstrate that the novice meets a number of spirits who help him in different ways. The selection of a shaman might be made by spirits of nature, such as the spirit of water, who give the novice zoomorphic guides on his journey to the otherworld. The shaman's initiation is performed by special smith spirits, who forge a new shaman on their anvil. The guiding spirits leave the shaman after his ecstatic initiation, by which time he has gotten to know his spirit helpers proper.

The spirits of ancestor shamans play an important part in a shaman's initiation in clan shamanism and the professional shamanism of the south. For example, the Transbaikalia Evenki say that a dead shaman appears before a prospective candidate and orders him to follow. The spirits of ancestor shamans may appear as candidate selectors, as the novice's supranormal teachers, or as initiators carrying out the dissection process, as in the Lower Tunguska region. The spirit of an ancestor shaman usually remains as the shaman's spirit helper proper. Although most of the spirit helpers of, for example, the Evenk shaman are in the form of an animal or a bird, he is usually also supported by shaman's spirits in human form.

Another inherited spirit is the Nanay *ajami*, the tutelary spirit of the novice period, who instructs the novice in matters of the otherworld and provides him with the spirits necessary for shamanizing. The relationship between the *ajami* and the shaman is erotic, the spirit in question being a spirit wife or husband handed down from one shaman to another within the family. Similar marriagelike relationships between spirit and man are also reported elsewhere. The transvestite shamans among the tribal peoples indigenous to Siberia and Inner Asia, for example, might have a spirit lover.

An important part is played in the initiation tales of Yakut shamans by the Animal Mother and the spirits of ancestor shamans, the evil *abaasy* spirits that may perform the novice's initiation mysteries. The Animal Mother, who is the incarnation of the shaman's *kut* soul, his invisible double, was thought to show itself on the birth or death of a shaman and during his supranormal initiation. The Animal Mother, in the form of a bird with iron feathers, was thought to sit on a branch of the shaman's tree, incubating an egg containing the soul of a novice until the soul hatches from the egg.

The nature and number of spirit helpers proper varies from one ethnic group to another. Among the Ob-Ugrians (i. e., the Khanty and Mansi), the shaman might have seven spirit helpers, most of them in the form of an animal, such as a bear, a deer, a wolf, a horse, a snake, a fish, or a bird. Birds common to the northern regions were the eagle and the owl, as well as various waterfowl, in whose form the shaman was said to travel the underwater routes to the otherworld. The beliefs concerning the relationship between the shaman and his spirits are complex. The shaman might travel in the form of the animal accompanying him; the Yakut shaman, for example, fights other shamans in the form of his Animal Mother, as an elk or a deer. On the other hand, the spirit helpers may accompany him as outside assistants. For example, the Evenk shaman of the Podkamennaia Tunguska region had command over a large band of spirits on his journeys to the underworld.

THE SHAMAN'S ACTIVITIES. The shaman's public activities took place at the séance, a ritual performance. While there were many reasons for calling a séance, there was a need to make direct contact with representatives of the spirit world in all cases. All the vital elements of shamanism were present at the séance: the shaman and his assistant, those in need of assistance, an interested audience, and representatives of the spirit world called on by the shaman.

The shaman's attributes. The ritual objects and the shaman's attributes symbolize the shamanistic worldview. The most important item is the drum. Names for the drum are usually connected with the idea of the shaman's journey. For example, the Transbaikalia Evenki call the drum a boat, while the Yakuts, Buriats, and Soyot call it a horse. In this case the drumstick is a "whip." By means of his drum the shaman "rides" or "flies"; in other words, he achieves an altered state of consciousness. The frame of the drum is made from a special tree—a representative of the cosmic tree—

indicated by the spirits, and the membrane from the skin of an animal also chosen by the spirits. The drum-reviving ceremonies in the Altaic regions indicate that the drum animal represents one of the shamanistic spirits: during these ceremonies the animal from whose skin the membrane was made "comes to life again," telling of its life and promising to help the shaman. The motifs carved on the drum frame or drawn on the skin likewise symbolize shamanistic spirits and express cosmological concepts.

Although the shaman's dress, along with the drum, is one of the most striking features of shamanism in northern and Inner Asia, the number and type of attributes varies from one area to another. There is no shaman's dress proper among the Chukchi. While preparing for a séance the shaman was, like the Inuit (Eskimo) shaman, stripped to the waist. Similarly, the only item that identified the shaman among the Nentsy (a Samoyed people) in the northwest of Siberia was the headdress that he wore. The dresses with the greatest number of symbolic ornaments are to be found in central and southern Siberia and in Inner Asia.

The shaman's dress is made of leather or cloth, and onto it are sewn pendants of metal, bone, and cloth depicting spirits in animal or human shape or phenomena associated with the supranormal world. On the back of the Yakut shaman's dress are metal disks, the shaman's sun and moon, providing light on the dark route to the otherworld. Despite the variety of symbolic emblems, the basic idea behind the shaman's dress is clear. The feathers attached to the headdress, the winglike or furry appendages on the sleeves, the antlers or bear's snout on the headdress show that the dress basically represents some kind of animal. The most common type is a bird, found not only in the Altai-Sayan region but also in northern Mongolia and different parts of Siberia. In the Altaic region the dress most often imitates an owl or an eagle, in northern Siberia a deer. The Samoyeds and the Ket also wear a dress reminiscent of a bear.

In addition to the pictures associated with the spirits or the otherworld, the shaman's dress also has iron or bone appendages resembling a human or animal skeleton. These symbolize the death and rebirth experienced by the shaman during the ecstatic visions of his initiation period. The dress represents the mysteries experienced by the shaman and is the dwelling place of the spirits. Thus the dress itself is thought to possess supernormal power. In the areas of clan shamanism the dress could not be sold outside the clan, because the shaman's spirits belonging to the clan were attached to it. A worn-out shaman's dress might be hung on a tree in the forest, so that the spirits could leave it gradually and enter a new dress.

The shamanic séance. The shamanizing séance requires that both the shaman himself and the setting for the rite be meticulously prepared. The séance is often preceded by a period of time during which the shaman goes into seclusion, fasts, meditates, and recalls the details of the rituals he must perform during the séance. He transfers to the role of shaman by putting on the ritual dress and by tuning the drum.

The actual séance is usually held inside after dark, in a dwelling with a fire burning in the center. Because the spirits are thought to be afraid of light, darkness is a prerequisite for shamanizing. The settings for séances varied greatly, depending on the status of the shaman and the importance of his task. In the Podkamennaia Tunguska region the shaman and protector of the clan held his séance in the *sevenčedek*, a tent specially erected for the purpose. Here he acted out the fundamental features of the shamanistic world concept: the middle world inhabited by humans, the upper and lower worlds with their spirits, and the cosmic stream and cosmic tree as landmarks along the shaman's route in the otherworld. The séance was attended by the entire clan, members helping with the preparations. Similar large séance settings are found among the Nanay, whose shaman, being the representative of his clan, transported the souls of the dead to the otherworld. It seems that the higher the status of the shaman and the bigger the group he represented, the richer were the symbolic requisites of the dress and the setting for the séance and the more theatrical the course of shamanizing. The imposing settings of the séance in the southern areas are probably a later development influenced by the great scriptural traditions of the East.

Before the séance, the shaman's assistant, those in need of the shaman's help, and the audience would assemble. At the start of the séance the shaman concentrates on calling his spirit helper by singing and drumming. The themes of the shaman's songs are the calling of the spirit helpers, a description of the spirits' journey, an account of the shaman's own journey to the otherworld, and a description of the topography of the supranormal world. In the songs calling the spirits, during which the shaman might imitate the sounds of his zoomorphic spirit helpers through whistles, shouts, and growls, the shaman invites the spirits to the séance and may also give a step-by-step description of their journey to the séance from their dwelling in the otherworld.

The calling of the spirit helpers is the trance-induction stage. The rhythmic drumming, dancing, and singing gradually become louder and more frenzied as the shaman, while concentrating on the world of the spirits, achieves an altered state of consciousness. This phenomenon, similar to Western hypnosis, is brought about by rhythmical stimulation of the nervous system, growing concentration, motivation on the part of the shaman, and the emotional charge produced by the expectations of the audience. The effect of rhythmical stimulation was further enhanced among the Ob-Ugrians and the tribal peoples indigenous to Siberian Asia by, for example, eating amanita mushrooms. Other common means were the burning of various herbs producing intoxicating smoke, and, more recently, smoking tobacco and consuming alcohol. The use of hallucinogens and other intoxicants is not, however, essential to or even a vital factor in the shaman's trance technique.

The ecstatic climaxes of the séance come at the point where the shaman meets his spirit helpers, journeys with them to the otherworld, or banishes, for example, a disease demon that has taken up residence in a patient. The biggest cultural differences in the shamanistic rite technique are manifest at precisely this stage. The forms of meeting the spirits are based on different belief traditions.

Common to the central and eastern parts of Siberia, for example, among the Yukagir, the Evenki, the Yakuts, the Manchus, the Nanays, and the Orochi is the possession séance, during which the shaman's chief spirit helper enters his body and speaks through him. The shaman fully identifies with the spirit; he in fact turns into the spirit and manifests this change in his gestures, movements, and speech. Another person present at the séance, usually the shaman's assistant, then becomes the shaman, talking to the spirit. In regions where this type of possession-trance is common, the usual explanation for disease is that a demon has entered a person. It is then the shaman's task to banish the demon, and to do this the shaman takes the disease demon upon himself after his spirit helper; in other words, he turns into the demon. There are also complex possession-trance séances at which the shaman, having manifested various spirits, travels with his spirit helpers to the otherworld—when banishing a demon, for example.

The shaman may also create an illusion that the spirit helpers are present at the séance without identifying with them. The Chukchi display great skill in the manifestation of the spirits by the technique of ventriloquism. The shaman brings one spirit after another to the séance, and the audience can hear the spirits speak outside the shaman's body. Meetings of shaman and spirits at séances without possession are also known in western Siberia and Inner Asia. Among the Minusinsk Tatars, for example, the shaman's assistant sprinkles water around for the spirits to drink, so that they will not come too close to the shaman.

If the main idea of the séance is soul flight, or the shaman's journey to the otherworld, the manifestation of the spirits is not as dramatic as at séances of the possession type. Typical séances in the western and northern parts of Siberia—among the Samoyeds and the Ob-Ugrians, for example—are those at which the shaman is imagined as traveling to the otherworld with his spirit helpers. The emphasis is not on role-changing and talking to the spirits but on the description of the shaman's journey. At this type of séance the shaman's trance usually deepens steadily and ends with loss of consciousness. At possession-type and ventriloquist séances the shaman often calls his spirits again after his return, by singing and drumming. In other words, the depth of the trance moves in waves. Since concentration on the spirit world leads to a change in consciousness and focusing his attention on the audience brings the shaman back to his waking state, the depth of shamanic ecstasy depends upon the extent to which he must allow for the audience's wishes during the séance, and thus ultimately on the relationship between the shaman and his supporters.

The séance usually ends with an episode during which the shaman sends his spirit helpers away, answers questions from the audience, and issues instructions on the sacrifices or required propitiations to be made. The basic structure of the séance is thus relatively uniform, regardless of the object of shamanizing, showing variation according to the way in which the spirits are encountered. The various rites, manifestation of the presence of or banishing of spirits, and tricks or demonstrations of skill proving the supranormal abilities of the shaman do, however, vary from one area to another. Despite cultural differences, the basic features of the shaman's technique of ecstasy, his main requisites, the concept of the spirits helping the shaman, and the part played by the audience as a chorus assisting at séances are elements of shamanism common throughout northern and Inner Asia.

SEE ALSO Arctic Religions, overview article; Buriat Religion; Khanty and Mansi Religion; Samoyed Religion; Southern Siberian Religions; Tunguz Religion; Yakut Religion.

BIBLIOGRAPHY

There is a vast amount of literature on shamanism in Siberia and Inner Asia. A list of Russian sources and research literature appearing before 1932 is given in A. A. Popov's *Materialy dlia bibliografi russkoi literatury po izucheniiu shamanstva severoaziatskikh narodov* (Leningrad, 1932). The first widely known general treatise on Siberian shamanism was V. M. Mikhailovskii's "Shamanism in Siberia and European Russia," translated by John Oliver Wardrop, *Journal of the Anthropological Institute of Great Britain and Ireland* 24 (1985): 126–158. Of the general treatises that appeared in the early decades of the twentieth century among the most thorough are M. A. Czaplicka's *Aboriginal Siberia: A Study in Social Anthropology* (Oxford, 1914) and G. K. Nioradze's *Der Schamanismus bei den sibirischen Völkern* (Stuttgart, 1925). Uno Harva's work *Die religiösen Vorstellungen der altaischen Völkern*, "Folklore Fellows Communications," no. 125 (Helsinki, 1938), first published in Finnish in 1933, contains both a survey of shamanism and a systematic account of the main religious features of the peoples of Siberia and Inner Asia. The section on Inner Asian shamanism in the extensive work *Der Ursprung der Gottesidee*, 12 vols. (Münster, 1912–1955), by Wilhelm Schmidt is interesting because of the author's thorough familiarity with the sources.

Later general works dealing with the fundamental idea behind shamanism include Åke Ohlmarks's *Studien zum Problem des Schamanismus* (Lund, 1939), Hans Findeisen's *Schamanentum dargestellt am Beispiel der Besessenheitspriester nordeurasiatischer Völker* (Stuttgart, 1957), Matthias Hermanns's *Schamanen, Pseudoschamanen, Erlöser und Heilbringer*, 3 vols. (Wiesbaden, 1970), and Mircea Eliade's *Shamanism: Archaic Techniques of Ecstasy*, rev. & enl. ed. (New York, 1964). This last work, which first appeared in French as *Le chamanisme et les techniques archaïques de l'extase* (Paris, 1951), examines shamanistic phenomena in different parts of the world and is regarded as a classic in its field.

Material publications and studies on the shamanism of different peoples and ethnic groups have appeared individually and in certain scientific series. One of the most important is *The*

Jesup North Pacific Expedition, edited by Franz Boas (Leiden and New York, 1900–1930), in which the following works give a good account of shamanism in northeastern Siberia: Waldemar Bogoraz's *The Chukchee*, vol. 7 (1904–1909); Waldemar Jochelson's *The Koryak*, vol. 6 (1905–1908); and the latter's *The Yukaghir and the Yukaghirized Tungus*, vol. 9 (1926). The results of Russian and Soviet researchers' field trips to the Altai and to western and central Siberia have been given considerable coverage in the journal *Sbornik Muzeia antropologii i etnografii* (Leningrad, 1900–).

The work *Chernaia vera, ili Shamanstvo u mongolov* (Saint Petersburg, 1891) by Dorzhi Banzarov on Mongolian shamanism is an extensive late-nineteenth-century monograph. Information on shamanism in the Altaic region is covered in A. V. Anokhin's *Materialy po shamanstvu u altaitsev* (Leningrad, 1924). One of the best sources on the Ob-Ugrian peoples is K. F. Karjalainen's *Jugralaisten uskonto* (Porvoo, Finland, 1918). Toivo Lehtisalo describes Nentsy or Yurak shamanism in *Entwurf einer Mythologie der Jurak-Samojeden*, "Mémoires de la Société Finno-ougrienne," vol. 53 (Helsinki, 1924). Some of the most interesting information on Samoyed shamanism is provided by A. A. Popov in, for example, *The Nganson: The Material Culture of the Tavgi Samoyeds* (1949), translated by Elaine K. Ristinen (Bloomington, Ind., 1966). Evenki shamanism is examined by A. F. Anisimov in *Religiia evenkov v istoriko-geneticheskom izuchenii i problemy proiskhozhdeniia pervobytnykh verovanii* (Moscow, 1958) and by S. M. Shirokogoroff in the extensive *Psychomental Complex of the Tungus* (London, 1935), this latter being one of the main sources on research into shamanism. Information on Nanay shamanism is included in P. P. Shimkevich's *Materialy dlia izucheniia shamanstva u gol'dov*, "Zapiski priamurskogo otdela Russkogo geograficheskogo obshchestva," vol. 1 (Khabarovsk, 1896), and Ivan A. Lopatin's *The Cult of the Dead among the Natives of the Amur Basin*, "Central Asiatic Studies," vol. 6 (The Hague, 1960).

Translations of certain extremely interesting articles on shamanism in the U.S.S.R. have been published in *Studies in Siberian Shamanism*, edited by Henry N. Michael (Toronto, 1963). In Hungary, Vilmos Diószegi and Mihály Hoppál have edited anthologies containing general theoretical treatises and a wealth of fresh information produced during field research, and these are also among the main publications on research into shamanism: *Popular Beliefs and Folklore Tradition in Siberia*, edited by Vilmos Diószegi, translated by Stephen P. Dunn (Budapest, 1968); *Shamanism in Siberia*, edited by Vilmos Diószegi and Mihály Hoppál and translated by S. Simon (Budapest, 1978); and *Shamanism in Eurasia*, edited by Mihály Hoppál, "Forum," no. 5 (Göttingen).

Comparative studies of special aspects of shamanism are *The Shaman Costume and Its Significance*, by Uno Holmberg (later Harva), in "Turun suomalaisen yliopiston julkaisuja," series B, vol. 1 (Turku, 1922); my *The Rite Technique of the Siberian Shaman*, "Folklore Fellows Communications," no. 220 (Helsinki, 1978); and E. C. Novik's *Obriad i fol'klor v sibirskom shama-nizme* (Moscow, 1984).

Significant opinions on the fundamental issues of shamanism have been put forward in a number of shorter articles. These include Dominik Schröder's "Zur Struktur des Schamanismus," *Anthropos* 50 (1950), aiming at a definition of shamanism; Ake Hultkrantz's "A Definition of Shamanism," *Temenos* 9 (1973): 25–37; Lauri Honko's "Role-Taking of the Shaman," *Temenos* 4 (1969): 26–55, on the shaman's rite technique; and László Vajda's "Zur phaseologischen Stellung des Schamanismus," *Ural-Altaische Jahrbucher* 31 (1959): 456–485, examining the history of the development of shamanism. Special aspects of shamanism have also been studied by Gisela Bleibtrau-Ehrenberg in "Homosexualität und Transvestition im Schamanismus," *Anthropos* 65 (1970): 189–228; and by H. Nachtigall in "Die Kulturhistorische Wurzel der Schamanen-skelettierung," *Zeitschrift für Ethnologie* 77 (1952): 188–197. Two articles disproving the Pali or Sanskrit origins of the word *shaman* are Julius Németh's "Über den Ursprung des Wortes *Šaman* und einige Bemerkungen zur türkisch-mongolischen Lautgeschichte," *Keleti Szemle* (Budapest) 14 (1913–1914), and Berthold Laufer's "Origin of the Word Shaman," *American Anthropologist* 19 (1917).

ANNA-LEENA SIIKALA (1987)
Translated from Finnish by Susan Sinisalo

SHAMANISM: NORTH AMERICAN SHAMANISM

In the general literature on native North Americans, every sort of priest, healer, ritual specialist, and sorcerer is somewhere called a shaman. Here the term is synonymous with some unarticulated notion of "primitive religious specialist." A clearer understanding of shamanism can be discerned from those scores of descriptions of Native American religions and cultures where romantic and primitivist biases are less influential, although the statement of what distinguishes shamanism from other phenomena is necessarily complicated because of the diversity of shamanism in North America.

In broad terms, North American shamans are individuals with extraordinary access to spiritual power. Shamans must not be simply equated with priests, although they may serve priestly functions. Shamans must not be equated with the recipient of a guardian spirit through vision quest or dream, although they frequently find access to spiritual power in vision and dream experiences. Shamans must not simply be identified with healers, for not all healers are shamans, and further, there are numerous shamanic functions other than healing.

SHAMANIC TRAITS. Given the ambiguity of these broad criteria of North American shamanism, a fuller presentation may take the form of an outline of shamanic traits. This outline is a set of features no one of which is, by itself, distinctive or adequate and no set or single combination of which constitutes an exclusive definition of shamanism. This approach has advantages over the attempt to define North American shamanism in terms of a single necessary distinguishing feature. The outline establishes a framework in which to investigate and study a variety of often complex religious phenomena that may be interrelated around the idea identified by the term *shamanism*.

North American shamans invariably have extraordinary spiritual power, that is, the capacity to influence the world through spiritual forces. Thus a central element of North American shamanism is spiritual power—its nature, acquisition, accession, use, and loss. Native American spiritual concepts are very difficult for the outside observer to comprehend, and herein lies what is both a major obstacle and a challenge to the study of North American shamanism.

Spiritual powers are usually identified in some way that allows them to be humanly conceivable. The spirit forms vary widely; some are identified with animal (or other natural) forms, others with mythological figures and deities. Even the ghost of an ancestor or the soul of some living thing may be identified as a shaman's spirit power.

Individuals initially gain access to spiritual powers in a variety of ways, including inheritance, personal quest, purchase, election by society or by the spiritual power, and extraordinary experience accompanying the suffering of a malevolence. In North America quests for power only rarely involve the use of hallucinogenic drugs; these quests more commonly involve fasting and isolation. The quest for shamanic power and the quest for a guardian spirit are usually distinguishable, although the techniques may not be. In some cultures there is continuity between guardian spirit practices and shamanism. Initiatory experiences, as well as the periods of training that usually follow initiations, may be brief or may extend over a considerable period of time. Initiatory experiences may include images of skeletonization, death, and rebirth or images of magical flight with extended revelatory scenarios, but more often they contain none of these elements.

The acquisition of power is commonly accompanied by the revelation of a power object or other means by which to objectify, display, and make contact with spiritual power. There are endless varieties of power objects held by North American shamans. They are often referred to by native terms commonly translated as "medicine." Power and access to power may also take the form of formulas, charms, and songs. Objects of power and special songs are also commonly held by those who are allied with a guardian spirit. The presence of power is demonstrated by its use in any of the many shamanic functions and, occasionally, in highly dramatized power performances using legerdemain.

Throughout North America, healing is the most central function and use of spiritual power. The most common and widespread theories of disease are those of object intrusion and soul loss. According to the first theory, illness results when a health-obstructing object enters the body. Object intrusion is most commonly believed to be a consequence of malevolent intent and is ascribed to sorcery and witchcraft, but sometimes it is simply an objectification, even personification, of an illness. The corresponding treatment usually involves a technique of sucking, in which the curer, entranced or not, sucks the object from the body using an instrument such as a tube, horn, or his or her mouth directly on the person's body at the place where the object is diagnosed to exist. The object, once removed, may or may not be presented in material form to demonstrate to those present the success of the treatment. Soul loss, the other common theory of disease, is based upon a variety of often complex theories of soul or life forms that may depart the body or be drawn or stolen from the body. Entranced magical flights, dramatized spirit journeys, and prayer recitations are techniques used to retrieve and return the soul or life form, thus restoring health and life.

Several other functions are common among North American shamans: weather control; hunting-related functions, such as game divination, game charming, and intercession with master or mistress of animals; war-related functions; and general clairvoyant and divinatory practices, such as diagnosing disease, foretelling the future, and finding lost objects. These functions are usually, but not always, secondary to healing. While most shamanic actions are clearly understood as having a benevolent intent in societal terms, the shaman is commonly seen within his or her society as potentially, if not actually, malevolent. Shamanic powers may thus be used for sorcery, witchcraft, or revenge, either on the shaman's initiative or at the behest of another.

Shamanic performances occasionally include the use of esoteric languages through which shamans communicate with spirits. In some cultures shamans employ speakers or assistants who interpret shamanic speeches to those present.

The shaman's characteristic attraction to the mystical is often a distinguishing feature of his or her personality. The role of the shaman in society varies widely, from reclusive eccentric on the fringes of society to leader and teacher at the very center of the authority and political structure of the society. Very commonly a community expresses a sense of ambivalence toward its shamans. While they are sought after and held as highly important individuals, they are feared and avoided because of the powers they control. Few North American cultures totally exclude females from shamanic roles, and in some cultures, particularly those found in northern California, females even predominate; nonetheless, throughout the region shamans tend to be more frequently male.

Culture Areas. Shamanism and related beliefs and practices occur widely throughout North America. The following brief review of culture areas presents some of the major religious phenomena in North America that may be considered shamanism or closely related to it.

The Inuit (Eskimo) tribes, both along the coast and in the interior, have figures that most closely resemble Siberian shamans, with whom there is a likely historical connection. Inuit shamans, working individually or in groups, use techniques of ecstasy as well as dramatic performances and clairvoyance to serve individuals in need of curing, and they serve the community by controlling weather and procuring game for the hunt. Magical flights and transformations into spirit beings are characteristic of Inuit shamans; they are also conduits through which the spirits speak. Spiritual power is demonstrated through combats between shamans and the use of legerdemain in dramatic performances.

Tribes along the Northwest Coast have complex shamanic practices. The experience of trance is common to both initiatory experiences and shamanic performances, although techniques of ecstasy are not used everywhere in the region or by all shamans in any one community. While curing is their most important practice, shamans also perform other functions, such as locating food supplies and, in former times when wars were fought, weakening the enemy. The great ceremonial periods in the winter include shamanic festivals during which groups of shamans demonstrate their spiritual powers. Groups of Coast Salish shamans perform dramatizations of canoe journeys into dangerous spirit worlds where they struggle to win back the lost soul of a sufferer. Throughout the area sucking techniques are used to remove malevolent objects. Considerable variation occurs within this area.

The shamanic practices of the Northwest Coast exhibit some continuity with those of the adjacent Basin, Plateau, and northern California areas. Sucking techniques are common, and there is some use of ecstatic techniques. The costume of the shaman is believed to be very powerful, and is a vehicle through which the shamanic tradition is passed from one person to another.

In the Plateau area male and female shamans using song and formula in ritual performances serve a variety of needs. Illness is commonly attributed to witchcraft and ghosts, and shamans act to combat these malevolent forces. The prophetic and millenarian movements that arose in the nineteenth century, which culminated in the Ghost Dance movement of 1890, developed from a shamanic religious heritage. Elements of shamanism also influenced the Indian Shaker religion that arose in this area.

On the Plains and the Prairies, there are many kinds of medicine and holy persons. Fasting and praying in quest of spiritual power is widespread, and while most tribes in this region distinguish between the individual recipient of a guardian spirit and the shamanic figures, there is a continuity between them. Evidence of spiritual power can manifest itself in various forms, such as a public ritual, a tipi or lodge decoration, special garments, and medicine bundles. Medicine bundles are especially important as the residence of spiritual powers; the bundles are kept by a community and passed from generation to generation.

The shamans of these tribes perform many functions, acting either individually or in groups and societies. Besides curing, they were at one time important for success in war, and during the hunt they charmed and called game. Their powers of clairvoyance and prophecy are still widely exercised in various forms of spirit lodges or the Shaking Tent ceremonies. In these ceremonies, the shaman enters a lodge and reads the messages communicated by the spirits through the shaking of the lodge or the appearance of little flashing lights.

The Midewiwin, or Great Medicine Society, is an important part of the religious, social, political, and economic systems of central Algonquin and other tribes in the Great Lakes region. The initiation practices of the Midewiwin call for the ritual shooting and killing of the initiate, who is then revived as a newly born member of the society. The Midewiwin includes graded levels of shamanic figures. The curing performances are complex and involve many in the community.

A variety of shamanic activities are important to the tribes in the Northeast and Southeast Woodlands areas. The earliest records of some of these activities were set down by Jesuit missionaries in the seventeenth century. For some tribes in the eastern portion of this area, shamans served the needs of family groups. Costumes and paraphernalia were elaborate in the shamanic practices of many of these tribes. Shamans tended to specialize according to function: curing, weather control, and hunting. "Societies of affliction," that is, societies composed of all those treated, exist among the Seneca.

The North American Southwest is culturally and historically complex. Among Pueblo cultures there are both shamans and priests, although their roles sometimes overlap. Shamans may either participate in or remain aloof from the dramatic ceremonial performances distinctive among the Pueblo tribes. The integration, yet distinction, of shamanic activities and functions in intensely communal contexts is important to the understanding of these cultures and their religions.

Navajo religion centers on conceptions of health. Extraordinarily complex curing ceremonials that last as long as eight days and nine nights are performed by individuals who learn through apprenticeship the many songs, prayers, and ritual procedures as well as the accompanying story traditions. Many ceremonies are directed toward associated classes of disease etiology.

Among the Pima of the Southwest, shamans treat many kinds of illnesses attributed to spirit forces identified with animals and other natural forms. The treatment is private and includes sucking, blowing, and singing.

In recent decades in Oklahoma and other areas where Native Americans have experienced significant intertribal contact, as well as contact with non-natives, innovative forms of shamanism have resulted that are directed toward the complexities and dangers associated with an acculturative environment.

The development and widespread practice of the peyote religion, legally organized in the twentieth century as the Native American Church, are rooted in an older shamanic tradition. This religious movement commonly serves some of the same needs as does shamanism; its techniques and practices are often similar to those of shamanism.

This brief survey is perhaps adequate only in suggesting the extent, complexity, and importance of shamanism among tribal peoples throughout North America. In many respects the study of shamanism in North America is undeveloped. The publication of Mircea Eliade's *Shamanism: Archaic Techniques of Ecstasy* (1951; Eng. ed., New York, 1964) widely expanded the interest in the study of shamanism as a worldwide religious phenomenon but has had relatively little impact on the study of North American shamanism. Conversely, the consideration of the North American religious practices we have called "shamanism" has had little impact on the broader study of shamanism. North American shamanism therefore raises many important issues that constitute an enriching challenge to the study of the phenomenon worldwide.

SEE ALSO Ghost Dance; North American Indian Religions, article on New Religious Movements; North American Indians, article on Indians of the Plains.

BIBLIOGRAPHY

The principal definitional discussions of shamanism that take North America into consideration are Åke Hultkrantz's "Spirit Lodge, a North American Shamanistic Séance," in *Studies in Shamanism,* edited by Carl-Martin Edsman (Stockholm, 1962), pp. 32–68, and Hultkrantz's "A Definition of Shamanism," *Temenos* 9 (1973): 25–37. In the later article "techniques of ecstasy" is put forward as a necessary criterion, thus leading to the conclusion that most North American practices are pseudoshamanism, since ecstasy is not widespread. Kenneth M. Stewart's "Spirit Possession in Native America," *Southwestern Journal of Anthropology* 2 (1946): 323–339, attempts to show that ecstatic and other entranced states, which the author loosely terms "possession," existed widely throughout North America, but close examination of his data reveals that ecstasy in shamanism occurs rarely beyond the sub-Arctic and the Northwest Coast.

Surprisingly few widely comparative studies of shamanism exist. Leonard L. Leh's "The Shaman in Aboriginal North American Society," *University of Colorado Studies* 21 (1934): 199–263, is a relatively extensive survey by geographic area. Willard Z. Park's study *Shamanism in Western North America* (1938; reprint, New York, 1975) compares Paviotso (Northern Paiute) shamanism with shamanic practices throughout western North America.

The great resource for the study of North American shamanism is the ethnographic record. Although uneven in most respects, it often includes extensive material on shamanism. Exemplary studies that focus on shamanic practices of a single tribe are Park's work on the Paviotso; *Piman Shamanism and Staying Sickness* (Tucson, 1974) by Donald M. Bahr and others; the section on shamanism in Franz Boas's *Religion of Kuakiutl Indians,* vol. 2, *Translations* (New York, 1930); and David E. Jones's *Sanapia, Comanche Medicine Woman* (New York, 1972).

SAM D. GILL (1987)

SHAMANISM: SOUTH AMERICAN SHAMANISM

In particulars of cosmology, ritual, and paraphernalia, shamanism in South America has obviously been shaped by, and has adapted to, local environments and local historical and cultural processes. Nevertheless, in its mental universe and its dialectics and techniques of the sacred, South American shamanism exhibits similarities not only within the subcontinent but to shamanism in North America, the Arctic, and Siberia, indicating historical relationships that must date back to the early peopling of the Americas. This suggests that the basic ideology of shamanism may be sufficiently fundamental to the human condition to have favored its survival over enormous distances in time, space, environment, and social context.

GENERAL MOTIFS OF ECSTASY. Shamanism and religion among the Selk'nam (Ona), Yámana (Yaghan), and Halakwalip (Alacaluf) of the Tierra del Fuego, on the southernmost edge of South America—all presumably descended from the earliest migrants to the subcontinent—appear to represent survivals of archaic ideological systems. But many of the same archaic traits also appear—sometimes attenuated or overlaid with elaborations resulting from outside influences or internal dynamics, often little modified from their ancestral forms—across the whole South American continent, not excluding the high culture areas of the Andes. These common traits include familiar motifs of Siberian and Inuit (Eskimo) shamanism: mystic vocation; initiatory sickness; skeletonization, dismemberment, and contemplation by the shaman of his or her own bones; recruitment of supernatural helpers; rock crystals as manifestations of helping spirits; marriage to spirit wives, or, in the case of female shamans, spirit husbands; "rape" of the soul; sickness through soul loss or intrusion of illness projectiles into the body by magical means, and, conversely, restoration of health, in the first case through retrieval of the patient's strayed or abducted soul by the shaman, and in the second by sucking out the disease-causing foreign object; stratified upperworld and underworld through whose levels the shaman travels in celestial flight or in descent into the chthonic regions; world trees as sky supports with both phallic and uterine associations; great ancestral First Shamans and culture heroes as shaman/transformers; and divination of future events, weather, or favorable hunting conditions.

Of first importance everywhere is the ecstatic trance, mainly attained through the use of botanical hallucinogens, during which the shaman projects his or her soul into otherworlds, and returns with word of the departed, the wishes of the greater powers, and enhanced knowledge and confirmation of the sacred geography and cosmology by which the community orders its social and supernatural environment. This knowledge makes the shaman indispensable to the maintenance of the social and metaphysical equilibrium, and accounts for the shaman's chieflike role in societies that otherwise lack chieftainship. As demonstrated by Johannes Wilbert's work among the Warao, a fishing people of the Orinoco Delta, even among preagricultural peoples and incipient horticulturalists, shamanic cosmologies and cosmic models constructed on the common foundations of a pan-Indian, archaic shamanistic worldview can reach extraordinary heights of complexity. Wilbert's and other recent studies (e.g., Swiss ethnologist Gerhard Baer's work among the Matsigenka of eastern Peru) confirm the shaman's central role across the whole spectrum of indigenous life, from religion, ritual, and curing to social organization and politics.

SPECIFIC FEATURES. Notwithstanding shared motifs in pan-South American shamanism that seem to be survivals of a common archaic substratum, shamanism in the subcontinent exhibits culture-specific tropical New World traits that are at least as significant.

The rattle. Among these distinctive features is the replacement of the drum by the gourd rattle as the indispensable percussion instrument in the shamanic arts over most of South America. Even where the shaman's drum persists, as among the Mapuche, or Araucanians, of Argentina and Chile, it is generally used in combination with the rattle. The symbolism and functions of the rattle are complex and varied. But, in general the rattle's functions parallel the functions of the shamanic drum, including the connection with the world tree as *axis mundi.* Indeed, even more obviously than the iconography of the Siberian shaman's drum, the hollow gourd represents the cosmos; the staff that pierces it and serves as handle symbolizes the world tree as cosmic pathway. The small stones or seeds inside the rattle, in turn, are ancestral souls and spirits whom the shaman activates when he shakes the instrument. The sound of the rattle, in combination with the chants the shaman has been taught by the spirits, enables the shaman to concentrate his or her powers for the flight or descent to otherworlds. Despite the extraordinary prominence and complex ideology of this instrument in South and Central American shamanism, the literature on the subject is poor, with Wilbert's study of the feathered *hebumatarao,* the "spirit rattle" of the Warao shaman (1973), the outstanding exception.

The jaguar. Another trait specific to the American tropics is qualitative identification between the shaman and the jaguar (*Felis onca*). This dominant motif cuts across linguistic, geographical, and cultural boundaries on the subcontinent. In pre-Columbian times it extended into the high cultures of Mexico. Still another leitmotif is the widespread use of one or more potent psychoactive plants as a "technique of ecstasy," not only by shamans but, in specified ritual contexts, a wider adult community under the shaman's direction. Jaguar transformation and the use of plant hallucinogens, in turn, are ideologically and experientially linked.

In the belief systems of many South American Indians, shamans, alone among their fellows, can transform themselves at will into jaguars, whose inherent qualities they share; conversely, jaguars may not actually be animals but transformed shamans, or soul bearers of deceased shamans. Hence, killing a jaguar is fraught with supernatural risk. Reported by early travelers, these beliefs persist to the present day. Thus, the Tacana of eastern Bolivia told the German ethnologist Karin Hissink in 1952 that their *yanaconas* (shamans) regularly transform themselves into their jaguar alter egos through such techniques as somersaulting or taking hallucinogenic snuff. Theodor Koch-Grünberg, who traveled widely among the Indians of northern Brazil and Venezuela (1911–1913) reported that all the shamans he met or heard of identified themselves with the jaguar. All had techniques of jaguar transformation, including the donning of jaguar pelts, claws or teeth as well as intoxication with psychoactive plants. Maquiritaré (Yecuana) shamans believed that specialized benches carved in the likeness of their jaguar counterparts were indispensable to their magic art.

The conceptional identification of shaman and jaguar is confirmed by linguistics. Koch-Grünberg found all Betoi-speaking groups using the same or closely related words for "shaman" and "jaguar." The Dätuana, for example, call the shaman *djaika* and the jaguar *dzaja.* Even though the approximately thirty tribes belonging to theTucanoan language family are separated into a western division and an eastern division, with little contact between the two branches, all identify shamans with jaguars and most use the same or a closely related term for both. Ute Bödiger reported in 1965 that the common term for shaman and jaguar among the Siona was *yái* and among the Coreguaje, *dyái.* Since Siona shamans are themselves jaguars in human form, no jaguar ever attacks them; all they have to do to protect themselves when encountering a jaguar is call out, "My name is Yái!" The Huitoto, whose language is identified by linguists as independent and whose culture is intermediate between Paleo-Indian hunters and Neo-Indian tropical forest cultivators, call their shamans *ikodyai,* a term derived from two Tucanoan words, *dyái* ("jaguar") and *iko* ("soul"). Irving Goldman (1963) reports that the Tucanoan Cubeo differentiate between two kinds of shaman, the *pariékokü,* meaning "man of power," and the *yaví,* meaning "jaguar." The latter has greater prestige: every *yaví* is a *pariékokü,* but not every *pariékokü* is a *yaví.*

Bird symbolism. Several other animal species also play a more or less important symbolic role in shamanism, alongside the great jungle cat. Outstanding among these is the harpy eagle (*Harpia harpyja*) and its close relatives. Its role as shaman's alter ego was first examined in detail in 1962 by the German ethnologist Otto Zerries; in 1977 his student Hildegard Matthäi followed with a study of the general role of raptors among extra-Andean South American Indians, with particular attention to the harpy eagle and the king vulture, *Sarcoramphus papa.* The ecology of these high-flying, carrion-eating birds clearly fits them especially well for a shamanlike role as mediators between the celestial and chthonic spheres. The brilliant plumage of parrots, macaws, and other spectacular tropical forest birds is widely used for feather crowns and wands or prayer sticks, and here the symbolism extends beyond that of shamanic flight to that of "light." Thus, Gerhard Baer (1978) reports that the Matsigenka shaman's feather headdress "gives light and brightness" during the nocturnal séance, just as the feather crowns of the personified sun, moon, star beings, and spirits do. Light, which the shaman can also activate with hallucinogens and chants, in turn, is potentiated communication between the human and extrahuman spheres. The Matsigenka shaman numbers many birds among his or her spirit helpers, and one, the swallow-tailed kite, *Elanoides forficatus*—or, more correctly, its female spirit (*i'nato,* "its Mother")—is the most important tutelary. This bird is nown as *i'vanki,* meaning "his wing." On the other side of the subcontinent the Venezuelan Warao credit the same bird with having established *bahana* shamanism, one of the major orders of shamanism whose main concern is human reproduction and its attendant biological, psychological, and social concerns (Wilbert, 1986).

Still, it is the jaguar that predominates in the imagery of South American shamanism, perhaps because like the shaman, and unlike most other species, it seems not to be confined by its nature to one cosmic realm or one ecological niche. It is nocturnal and inhabits caves, behaviors that associate it with the underworld. It hunts principally on land but is so well adapted to water and so expert a swimmer in pursuit of fish and aquatic game that many Indian mythologies tell of powerful "water jaguars" that spend their lives in the watery underworld to which only shamans have access. Finally, in the manner of the shaman ascending the tree as metaphorical world axis, the jaguar is an agile climber of the great forest trees. Among some tribes it also has powerful, dualistic sexual associations. Like its human counterpart, the jaguar is thus a mediator *par excellence.* The most detailed studies of the shaman-jaguar complex are those of the Colombian anthropologist Gerardo Reichel-Dolmatoff among the Tucanoan Desána of the Vaupés in the northwest Amazon of Colombia. His 1975 work, *The Shaman and the Jaguar,* presents the jaguar-shaman transformation complex and its interrelationship with hallucinogenic plants in a specific social and ideological context.

Plant hallucinogens. Reichel-Dolmatoff found that among the Desána "practically all shamanistic attitudes and practices" are based on the ecstatic trance induced by powerful plant hallucinogens, notably *yagé,* an infusion of the *Banisteriopsis caapi* vine. The same drink is called *ayahuasca* by Quechua-speakers in the Andes. Especially in the Peruvian Amazon, *ayahuasca* is often used in conjunction with one or more species of *Brugmansia* (an arboreal form of the well-known shrublike daturas traditionally used by Indians in Mexico and, in North America, by native peoples in California, Nevada, Virginia, and the Southwest), as well as with thickened tobacco juice. The Matsigenka shaman may use either or all in curing rites. Like *Banisteriopsis,* the different species of *Brugmansia* have their spirit "Mothers," whose "sons" are recruited by the shaman as helpers (Baer, 1978).

Along with *yagé,* South American Indians have discovered the psychoactive properties of many other species that are employed alone or as admixtures to heighten or, otherwise, modify the metaphysical experience. The ethnobotanist Richard Evans Schultes and his collaborators have identified up to two hundred different plant hallucinogens used now or in the past by American Indians, the greater part in South America. Of special interest are several kinds of potent snuffs, including those based on the seeds of *Anadenanthera peregrina* and its sister species *A. colubrina,* and on the inner bark of trees of the genus *Virola,* with admixtures of other plant materials. The former are legumes related to the acacias and mimosas; the latter, like nutmeg, a popular spice of Old World origin, are related to the *Myristicaceae.* Snuffs made from *A. peregrina* were being used in the shamanistic rituals of Arawakan Indians when Columbus first landed in the Antilles; he and his men mistakenly identified the potent powder as tobacco. *Anadenanthera colubrina* was, and is still, employed by Andean Indians as the ritual intoxicant known as *huilca. Huilca* is presumably the snuff used by the ancient preagricultural inhabitants of coastal Peru, where Junius Bird excavated the oldest snuffing paraphernalia thus far known from South America—a whalebone snuff tablet and bird-bone snuffing tube dating from the second millennium BCE.

Such Indian populations as the several subgroups of the Yanoamö of the upper Orinoco, until recently one of the last pure hunting and gathering societies in South America, employ intoxicating snuffs derived mainly from scrapings of the inner bark of *Virola,* whose effects on the central nervous system are activated by the addition of certain other plant materials. Such sophisticated knowledge of the properties of plants suggests long experimentation.

Archaeological and iconographic evidence has also established a time depth of more than three thousand years for the ritual use and deification of yet another important South American plant hallucinogen that remains in use to this day, the mescaline-containing San Pedro cactus, *Trichocereus pachanoi* (Sharon, 1978). Now widely used by a class of mestizo folk healers whose practice includes symbols and techniques inherited from traditional indigenous shamanism, San Pedro is depicted on ancient Peruvian pottery and painted textiles of the Chavin culture, significantly in association with the jaguar, from the late second millennium BCE. Somewhat later the ceramic sculptors of the brilliant Nazca culture of the early first millennium CE personified San Pedro as a supernatural being with the columnar cactus projecting, hornlike, from his forehead and from his shoulders. Like other hallucinogens of Amazonia, the San Pedro beverage is used in conjunction with tobacco juice, which is usually administered through the nostrils. Indeed, tobacco (*Nicotiana,* especially *N. rustica* and *N. tabacum,* both native to South America) plays an important role in ritual intoxication, most often in conjunction with another psychoactive species that is considered of first importance to the ecstatic experience. Less commonly tobacco is *the* consciousness-transforming plant of choice. A prime example is the tobacco shamanism of the Venezuelan Warao, a phenomenon of which Wilbert (1972, 1975, 1987) is the outstanding student. But even where tobacco is not the primary activator of the ecstatic shamanic trance, it is conceptually linked to the shaman. Thus, the Matsigenka term for tobacco is *seri,* and that for the shaman *seripigari* (Baer, 1976).

Hallucinogens and the shamanic vision quest. To the question why the Indians of South America, and also those to the north, should have developed such an extraordinary interest in botanical hallucinogens, the hypothesis of anthropologist Weston La Barre provides an elegant answer: their ancestors, as carriers of an archaic Asiatic shamanistic tradition that valued the ecstatic trance experience, arrived in the New World predisposed toward exploration of the environment for plants capable of triggering that experience. American Indian religions, La Barre proposed in 1970, including those of the great pre-Columbian civilizations of South and Mesoamerica, are or were essentially shamanistic, and so may be seen as extensions into the New World of Mesolithic and even Paleolithic antecedents in northeastern Asia. Shamanism values the ecstatic vision quest.

In some areas of North America the preferred techniques for the vision quest apparently were sensory deprivation, lonely vigil, self-torture, and other nonchemical "techniques of ecstasy." In others, especially the tropics, shamans must have searched their new environments from the start not only for potentially therapeutic flora but for species capable of altering consciousness, and, as among the Colombian Desána, at least temporarily and in strictly structured ritual settings, conferring even upon ordinary persons capabilities otherwise reserved for the religious specialist. Universally the special power of these plants was, and is, attributed not to chemicals but to the divine nature of the species, that is, to the male or female spirit believed to inhabit the individual plant. In a sense the communal use of sacred psychoactive plants represents, like the North American vision quest, a "democratization" of the shamanic experience, akin to the occasional communal ritual consumption by Siberian natives of the fly agaric mushroom, *Amanita muscaria,* under the leadership of the shaman. However, even where a relatively high proportion of adult males lays claim to some shamanic powers, or where, as among the Desána or Yanoama, most men ritually partake of the ritual hallucinogen, those individuals who have been mystically recruited as religious specialists and "technicians of the sacred"—the true shamans—remain uniquely the indispensable mediators between the world of humans and the greater powers of the natural and supernatural environment and of the larger universe.

See Also Jaguars; Tobacco.

Bibliography

Baer, Gerhard. "A Particular Aspect of Matsigenka Shamanism (Eastern Peru): Male-Female Ambivalence." In *Actas del XLI Congreso Internacional de Americanistas,* vol. 3, pp. 114–121. Mexico City, 1976.

Baer, Gerhard. "Religion y Chamanismo de los Matsigenka (Este Peruano)." *Amazonia Peruana* (Lima) 2 (1978): 101–138.

Baer, Gerhard, and Wayne W. Snell. "An Ayahuasca Ceremony among the Matsigenka (Eastern Peru)." *Zeitschrift für Ethnologie* 99 (1974): 63–80.

Bartholomé, Miguel Alberto. "Shamanism among the Avá-Chiripá." In *Spirits, Shamans, and Stars: Perspectives from South America,* edited by David L. Browman and Ronald A. Schwarz, pp. 95–148. New York, 1979.

Bödiger, Ute. *Die Religion der Tukano im nordwestlichen Amazonas.* Kölner Ethnologische Mitteilungen, no. 3. Cologne, 1965.

Dobritzhofer, Martin. *An Account of the Abipones, an Equestrian People of Paraguay* (1784). 3 vols. Translated by Sara Coleridge from the Latin. London, 1822.

Furst, Peter T. *Hallucinogens and Culture.* San Francisco, 1976.

Goldman, Irving. *The Cubeo: Indians of the Northwest Amazon.* Illinois Studies in Anthropology, no. 2. Urbana, Ill., 1963.

Hissink, Karin, and Albert Hahn. *Die Tacana: Ergebnisse der Frobenius-Expedition nach Bolivien 1952 bis 1954,* vol. 1, *Erzählungsgut.* Stuttgart, 1961.

Koch-Grünberg, Theodor. *Vom Roroima zum Orinoco,* vol. 3, *Ethnographie.* Stuttgart, 1923.

La Barre, Weston. "Old and New World Narcotics: A Statistical Question and an Ethnological Reply." *Economic Botany* 24 (1970): 73–80.

Matthäi, Hildegard. *Die Rolle der Greifvögel, insbesondere der Harpyee und des Königsgeiers, bei ausserandinen Indianern Südamerikas.* Hohenschäftlarn, Germany, 1978.

Métraux, Alfred. *Religions et magies indiennes d'Amérique du Sud.* Paris, 1967.

Reichel-Dolmatoff, Gerardo. *The Shaman and the Jaguar: A Study of Narcotic Drugs among the Indians of Colombia.* Philadelphia, 1975.

Schultes, Richard Evans. "An Overview of Hallucinogens in the Western Hemisphere." In *Flesh of the Gods: The Ritual Use of Hallucinogens,* edited by Peter T. Furst, pp. 3–54. New York, 1972.

Schultes, Richard Evans, and Albert Hofmann. *The Botany and Chemistry of Hallucinogens.* Springfield, Ill., 1973.

Sharon, Douglas. *Wizard of the Four Winds: A Shaman's Story.* New York, 1978.

Wilbert, Johannes. "Tobacco and Shamanistic Ecstasy among the Warao Indians of Venezuela." In *Flesh of the Gods: The Ritual Use of Hallucinogens,* edited by Peter T. Furst, pp. 55–83. New York, 1972.

Wilbert, Johannes. "The Calabash of the Ruffled Feathers." *Artscanada* 30 (1973–1974): 90–93.

Wilbert, Johannes. "Magico-Religious Use of Tobacco among South American Indians." In *Cannabis and Culture,* edited by Vera D. Rubin, pp. 439–461. The Hague, 1975.

Wilbert, Johannes. "The House of the Swallow-Tailed Kite: Warao Myth and the Art of Thinking in Images." In *Animal* Myths and Metaphors in South America, edited by Gary Urton, pp. 145–182. Salt Lake City, 1986.

Wilbert, Johannes. *Tobacco and Shamanism in South America.* New Haven, Conn., 1987.

Wilbert, Johannes. "El Significado Cultural del Uso de Tobaco en Sudamèrica." *Acta Americana* 3(2) (1997): 43–57.

Zerries, Otto. "Die Vorstellung zum zweiten Ich und die Rolle der Harpye in der Kultur der Naturvölker Südamerikas." *Anthropos* 57 (1962): 889–914

PETER T. FURST (1987 AND 2005)

SHAMANISM: NEOSHAMANISM

Neoshamanism (also known as urban shamanism) denotes a set of notions and techniques borrowed from traditional peoples and adapted to the life of contemporary urban dwellers. The essence of these techniques lies in attaining a shift of consciousness in which practitioners experience being transported to other worlds—to "non-ordinary reality"—where they interact with spiritual beings, enlisting their help to solve problems of this world. Neoshamanism became a part of urban alternative spirituality during the flower power and the human potential movements of the 1960s and 1970s. This was a period marked by heightened environmental awareness, interest in non-Western religions, and attempts to find alternative ways to organize spirituality and community that were modeled on an idealized image of "traditional peoples."

One basic idea of the counterculture of the 1960s was that alternative realities could be explored in altered states of consciousness, achieved through mind-altering drugs. When the dangers of this approach became evident, and when drugs were delegitimized in Europe and North America, neoshamanism offered drug-free ways of altering consciousness through monotonous percussion (such as that of a drum or rattle), through dancing and chanting, and through the practice of varieties of the Native American vision quest, such as sitting out in the woods without food, or exposure to intense heat, as in a sweat lodge.

These techniques were brought to Western urban spiritual seekers through descriptions by travelers and anthropologists, as well as through lectures and courses by teachers who claimed to be native or partly native—or to have done their apprenticeship with native shamans or medicine men. The anthropologist and writer Carlos Castaneda, who claimed to have done field research with a Yaqui medicine man called Don Juan, described in his books his experiences of shamanic apprenticeship involving explorations of non-ordinary reality under the effect of native mind-altering plants. Castaneda had a strong impact on the broad audience of spiritual seekers by introducing into the popular imagination an archetype of "native shaman," a figure of power and wisdom.

Another founding father of neoshamanism was the American anthropologist Michael Harner. Harner studied shamanic practices in the Americas and Northern Europe (in Saamiland), and he received shamanic training among the Jivaro people of Ecuador, where, under the influence of "teaching plants," he underwent dramatic experiences of alternative reality. Harner brought to fruition the idea of the historian of religions Mircea Eliade (1907–1986) that in the diverse magico-religious practices of traditional cultures there was some common core, which scholars called *shamanism.* Harner devised methods for peeling away cultural garments from these various "techniques of ecstasy" to provide safe and speedy ways for urban dwellers to acquire the experiences that could be called "shamanic," and to achieve altered states of consciousness in which one could enter alternative realities and interact with the spiritual beings encountered there. The main element of these techniques was the *drum journey* (Harner, 1980; Bowie, 2000).

DRUM JOURNEY. A drum journey often serves as a first occasion for spiritual seekers to encounter neoshamanism and to get a taste of what it has to offer. To the monotonous beat of the drum, participants are invited to experience what in the literature on shamanism is known as "a magic flight of the soul," a journey to non-ordinary reality. Drum journeys are performed at courses or lectures, and at New Age fairs, festivals, cafes, and retreat centers. By way of introduction, the aspirants are given instructions as to how to perform their journey, while at the same time they are offered a generalized shamanic worldview. The world of "traditional peoples," it is usually said on these occasions, consists of the lower world, where one meets power animals; the upper world, where one meets spiritual teachers, and the middle world, which is the ordinary world in its non-ordinary aspect. To reach the lower world, the students are asked to imagine a hole in the ground and, to the sound of drumming, enter it, journey through the tunnel that follows, come out in the lower world, and interact with the beings they encounter, engaging with them through all their senses. Some of these beings become their allies or spirit helpers, also known as *power animals.* When the drumming ends and people wake up from the trance-like state they have been in, they are expected to write about their experience, then share it with the teacher and the rest of the group.

Prior to the journey, people are given instructions as to which spirit helpers they are supposed to meet. These are wild animals that in Western popular culture are associated with the desirable "natural" qualities of freedom, body harmony, and physical prowess—such as lions, tigers, pumas, eagles, and dolphins, but not such animals as hens, cows, hyenas, or skunks. There is a high degree of uniformity in the power animals that people meet, even though spirit helpers are supposed to be individual, and even though some people meet idiosyncratic creatures that resemble the aliens in movies or fantasy literature, or even abstract shapes, such as "egg-shaped pyramids." The same is true for the spiritual teachers of the upper world, which may include brave Indian chiefs and warriors, wise medicine women, saints and angels, prophets and spiritual masters, Asa gods (for those engaged with Scandinavian mythology), or even Christ and Buddha. In the words of one neoshamanic teacher, "spirits are chunks of universal energy presented to us in a form that we can understand and accept." The repository of images that people encounter on drum journeys is their shared cultural imagination (Lindquist, 1997, p. 75–77).

This drum journey can be used to meet and address such spiritual beings, in whatever form, and to seek their answers to various questions, from the concrete and practical to the abstract and existential, and to ask their help in accomplishing various tasks, such as quitting smoking, finding a job, or dealing with deep psychological traumas, diseases, and even death and dying. Physical healing modeled on traditional methods of removing foreign intrusions and retrieving a lost or stolen soul are also taught at courses and performed for urban clients by individuals who practice shamanic techniques for physical and psychological healing. Other forms of therapy devised by Harner on the basis of drum journeys include power animal retrieval, wherein a healer makes a journey to meet a power animal on behalf of another person; and shamanic counseling, where a client narrates his or her journey as it unfolds, then analyzes the narrative with the counselor in terms of the client's initial questions. This latter technique closely resembles other types of psychotherapy that are based on mental imagery. Such therapy is used, for example, in transpersonal psychology and psychosynthesis (Assagioli, 1965), in Neuro-Linguistic Programming, in the religious healing of Christian charismatic groups (Csordas, 1997), and in the guided meditation employed in Western high magic (Luhrmann, 1989; Greenwood, 2000).

SEIDR. The seidr ritual is another practice associated with neoshamanism that took root in North America and northern Europe. Seidr was developed by people who were accustomed to working with consciousness-altering techniques of drumming and chanting, and with mental imagery associated with drum journeys, but who were also well acquainted with pre-Christian Scandinavian sources, notably the Edda (a poetic collection of ancient Scandinavian epics) and Icelandic sagas. The Edda describes the outward form of seidr as follows: A sorceress or wise woman, Voelva, is invited to farms to deal with failing harvests. Holding a staff, she climbs onto a platform (or, as modern practitioners call it, a "high seat") and covers her face with a hood. She falls into trance, journeys to the other worlds, meets the spirits, and interacts with them on behalf of the community in order to answer questions and magically secure the desired goals.

The seidr was adopted by Neopagans and neoshamans in North America and northern Europe and developed into several versions of a communal ritual that can be performed for a variety of goals. The ritual always involves the "seiding" individual, who acts as Voelva, and a group of fellow practitioners who play an auxiliary role. The landscapes evoked in the seidr's guided meditation (recited by a member of the group) are based on Scandinavian mythology and on the cosmologies of Asatror. In a trance-like state both the participants and the Voelva make a magical soul flight to non-ordinary reality, but it is only Voelva who enters its innermost realms. The spiritual beings Voelva meets are chiefly the gods and other figures of ancient Nordic cosmology. This form of seidr, practiced extensively by North American and British neo-heathens, can be used for divination; while the Voelva is in a trance, people approach the high seat and ask questions, which the Voelva answers, consulting whatever spirits she or he confronts, or aided by other signs encountered in the otherworld (Blain, 2002; Lindquist, 1997).

The trance state in seidr can also be attained by drumming and chanting performed by the group standing around the platform. The rhythmic songs used on these occasions are special *galdrar.* The drummers are understood to send to the Voelva their "energies," their special intensities or intentionalities, which the Voelva accumulates as if he or she were a sort of battery cell. These energies are then directed toward communal aims, spelled out at the outset of the ritual and dictated by shared normative social morality. The aims might include global or local environmental problems, such as bringing health and strength to the earth and saving rivers, seas, forests, and wild animals. Such local tasks as stopping the cutting down of woods for residential or road construction or healing a local population from disease, may also be set. Alternatively, the goal may be to stop a war, a famine, or a natural calamity in a faraway country, or to offer healing to a specific individual who may or may not be present among the group. In addition to this kind of "instrumental" seidr, the ritual can be performed to receive information on times past or to "see" what a place of historical or archeological significance looked like in ancient times.

Most seidr consist of several runs of the ritual, and several people are given an opportunity to act as Voelva. All those present are welcome to try, and all who do try are duly attended to. As in drum journeys, the ability to journey to non-ordinary reality and meet the inhabitants there is considered to be an innate human quality that is available to all. However, people are endowed with varying abilities to "see," and to convey what they have "seen" to other participants. Individuals gifted in this respect become informal leaders of the community, performing rituals in what becomes an internal tradition, creating new rituals, and inspiring new occasions for rituals that can reinforce community cohesion and the community's normative morality and values.

Both the drum journey and seidr (as well as other methods of entering non-ordinary reality) are methods of consciously working with the mental imagery that one encounters in altered states. This imagery can be used for divination and therapy, but also for creative endeavors in the visual and performance arts, and many neoshamanic practitioners are actively engaged in arts and crafts. Indeed, a person often appropriates the cultural attitude of neoshamanism when he or she starts to use this imagery as a source of creativity, information, and pragmatic action in everyday life. The reality of the journeys becomes integrated into the overall reality of an individual and, sometimes, of a community.

AIMS, IDEOLOGICAL PREMISES, AND WORLDVIEW. Controversy exists among practitioners as to how to regard non-ordinary reality: Is it an independently existing ontological realm (a position that is extremely important for some practitioners), or does it refer to concealed spheres of individual or group consciousness, the realm of imagination and creativity, the subconscious? The drum journey is more geared to the individualistic practice of interacting with the images that make up alternative realities. The cosmology and the pantheon of non-ordinary reality do not need to be shared, although they often are shared. For many, non-ordinary reality becomes most real in interaction with fellow practitioners—through sharing narratives of journeys, through discovering other people's spirits in one's own non-ordinary realities, and through sharing the effects of these interactions in real life.

The ritual of seidr, by contrast, is premised on the community, on shared cosmology, and on the ritual division of labor between people who are willing and capable of "seeing" and conveying the seen, and others who ask questions and direct their intentions toward shared goals. Drum journeys may exist as purely therapeutic, nonembedded practices, anchored in a broadly shared Western cultural imaginary, yet otherwise independent of a specific place and a more narrowly defined communal identity. Seidr, however, can and often does become embedded in the projects of the community.

Both seidr and drum journey are neoshamanic rituals that were devised by Westerners, although both refer to the authentic "other," distant in space and time. Both have a goal that can be conceived as universally shamanic—to connect the non-ordinary reality with the social, lived reality of this world, and to engage the inhabitants of non-ordinary reality, the spirits, as social beings. Seidr, however, is more suitable as a means to reiterate shared values and normative moral premises. Seidr is better for enacting "magical activism" that is focused on furthering the goals that worldly activists pursue, notably environmental and peace activism, activities in which many neoshamans are involved. Magical or shamanic activism is a supplement, or perhaps a substitute, for other, more conventional kinds of activism, mostly because people perceive the latter as lacking in efficiency, as corrupted, or as ensnared in bureaucracy. Seidr thus fits better as a shamanic form for more active political and social engagement, while drum journeys are more suitable as a means of self-realization and self-healing, along with other methods of New Age and human potential therapies.

The goals for which seidr is performed reflect ideas and values that underlie neoshamanism as a coherent cultural system. Internal literature, such as do-it-yourself books, course handouts, and books and articles written by academics who are also practitioners, presents these norms and values with even greater clarity. One of the attractions of neoshamanism is its power to democratize spirituality and broaden the realm of the sacred. Drawing on the animistic worldview of traditional peoples, neoshamanism declares that everything in nature—animals, plants, and even stones—is alive and all life is sacred. This ethos of democratic spirituality, which includes "nature" into the realm of human morality, makes neoshamanism particularly appropriate for spiritual and ideological movements that affirm the sacredness of nature while pursuing the empowerment of subaltern groups (e.g., varieties of feminist spirituality, postcolonial national identity construction).

Shamanism also serves as a metaphor for alternative, nonmainstream modes of creativity, such as those engendered by female and native artists. More generally, shamanism is used as a trope for a visionary mode of creativity in which both artist and shaman are seen as tapping the wellspring of an archaic "mythic imagination" that had previously been suppressed by patriarchal or colonial domination (Orenstein, 1990; Balzer Mandelstam, 1993).

The democratic ethos of neoshamanism is reiterated in the experience of the non-ordinary that is induced primarily by drum journeys, but also by seidr. The tacit understanding among practitioners is that every person has shamanic abilities, everybody has access to non-ordinary reality, and the experiences and narratives of every journeyer are of equal worth. Normative neoshamanic literature often repeats the premise that "shamanism is not a religion; one does not believe in anything in shamanism, not even that it works." There are no dogmas in neoshamanism, no priests; everybody is her or his own priest and everyone is expected to create her or his own cosmology and pantheon through individual experiences of the non-ordinary. Thus, neoshamanism, especially in Scandinavia, is defined as anarchistic spirituality, with no rules to adhere to, no authorities to follow.

The practice, however, sometimes contradicts these ideological premises, especially within more structured religious communities, such as those found in Neopaganism. As in every movement, there are charismatic teachers and leaders who set the tone and formulate the canons. For example, the ontological reality of the non-ordinary and the spirits is treated by some devout practitioners as near dogma, while others prefer to regard the non-ordinary as the Jungian unconscious and the spirits as archetypes. This theoretical discussion, however, is limited to ideologists, who articulate it in written and oral discourse, and often act within and near academic circles. Other practitioners are not concerned with this ontological discussion and continue to engage in neoshamanic practices as long as they work, and as long as they give meaningful answers to their questions. As a rule, practitioners of high engagement are more concerned with these questions than those of low engagement.

Neoshamanism among Shamanisms. The practices that are broadly labeled *shamanic* are highly contextual (Atkinson, 1992), and comparisons between neoshamanism and traditional forms of shamanism can be problematic. Insofar as shamanism comprises a set of practices where the non-ordinary and its inhabitants become relevant for, or even a part of, the this-worldly human community, some highly engaged communities of Western neoshamans become more comparable with so-called traditional societies. The most obvious difference is the democratic appeal of neoshamanism, as compared to the widespread view that traditional shamans are special individuals who are chosen by spirits. In traditional societies, shamanic vocation is often a heavy duty, borne by an individual because she or he cannot avoid it. In addition, traditional shamanic initiations often involve real ordeals, such as the periods of physical and mental suffering that are known in Siberian societies as "shamanic illness." Here, the interaction with spirits resembles combat, and the shaman's victory leads to relationships with spirits that are spelled out in the idiom of mastery and control (Jakobsen, 1999). As a person of power, the shaman in many traditional societies is feared as well as respected; he or she is expected to be able to harm as well as to heal. In most neoshamanic contexts, the process comparable to the traditional shamanic initiation may be an overwhelming experience, but it is rarely reported to be frightening or traumatic, nor is it expected to entail any physical or psychological pain.

In Western neoshamanism, spirits are strict but benevolent allies whose lessons are to be embraced, rather than fierce opponents to be conquered and tamed. This neoshamanic construction of spirits as entirely benevolent beings tends to be associated with low-engagement practice and the use of neoshamanism for therapy and self-enhancement. It should be recalled that neoshamanism organized around drum journeys was originally marketed as a safe alternative to drugs, so it is no wonder that its dangerous aspect was downplayed before it became a major popular movement. The innocuousness of the spirits, however, is contested by the accounts of some high engagement practitioners who act as professional shamans or seidr workers for clients or communities (Blain, 2002).

Native American neoshamanic practices are most widespread in North America, but they are also practiced in northern Europe and Scandinavia and have became a part of the global neoshamanic repertoire. This appropriation of Native American spiritual practices by mainstream spiritual seekers has been controversial and has generated indignation among some Native Americans, who themselves hope to restore their indigenous traditions. Native American spiritual leaders have blacklisted some teachers whom they accused of selling sacred ritual knowledge at courses and lectures. However, such Native American practices as the vision quest, sweat lodge, and Sun Dance are now firmly established as neoshamanic practices.

Whether the revival of local shamanisms in postcolonial and post-Soviet regions should be considered neoshamanism will not be discussed here (but see Vitebski, 1995; Humphrey 2002). The shamanic traditions of many indigenous peoples, especially those of Siberian Russia after the fall of Communism, were rediscovered in the 1990s and have been adopted into local medical practices and the political discourse on new identity construction. These projects have been heavily influenced by global flows of information and people, including Western seekers of shamanic spirituality and exotica, metropolitan neoshamans searching for traditional wisdom, and local shamans traveling abroad and becoming acquainted with Western neoshamanism and with renewed native shamanisms in, for example, North America. Russian metropolitan scholars tend to label new local shamans as *neoshamans.* This labeling implies that such local practitioners are to be explicitly distinguished from (possibly imagined) others who are supposed to have survived hidden away from local urban centers and to represent a putatively authentic local shamanism. Such terminology causes chagrin among local practitioners who claim legitimacy in terms of their belonging to an unbroken tradition of direct initiation. Many Western practitioners are also uncomfortable with the label *neoshaman,* since this term implies that their practices are separate from the "traditional" practices they claim as their prototypes. What in the West can be seen as a struggle for the primacy of representation, however, in postcolonial contexts can have serious consequences for the practitioners' reputations and careers.

See Also Spirituality.

Bibliography

Assagioli, Roberto. *Psychosynthesis: A Manual of Principles and Techniques.* New York, 1965. A normative exposition of theory and practice of the field by one of its founders.

Atkinson, Jane Monning. "Shamanisms Today." *Annual Review of Anthropology* 21 (1992): 307–330. A comprehensive anthropological review of the various uses of the term *shamanism* and shamanic practices all over the world.

Balzer Mandelstam, Marjorie. "Two Urban Shamans: Unmasking Leadership in Fin-de-Soviet Siberia." In *Perilous States: Conversations on Culture, Politics, and Nation,* edited by George E. Marcus, pp. 134–165. Chicago, 1993. An anthropological account of how ideas and metaphors of shamanism are used to legitimize leadership and to shape creativity in post-Soviet Siberia.

Blain, Jenny. *Nine Worlds of Seid-Magic: Ecstasy and Neo-Shamanism in North European Paganism.* London and New York, 2002. An account of historical sources and contemporary practices of seidr by a practitioner who is also an anthropologist. Combines insider advocacy with anthropological analysis.

Bowie, Fiona. *The Anthropology of Religion: An Introduction.* Oxford, 2000. A reader; see pages 190–218.

Csordas, Thomas. *The Sacred Self: A Cultural Phenomenology of Charismatic Healing.* Berkeley, 1997. An anthropological analysis of healing practices among North American Catholic charismatics.

Eliade, Mircea. *Shamanism: Archaic Techniques of Ecstasy.* Translated from the French by Willard R. Trask. London, 1964. A classic review of shamanic practices all over the world by a historian of religions.

Greenwood, Susan. *Magic, Witchcraft, and the Otherworld: An Anthropology.* Oxford and New York, 2000. A historical review and analysis of high magic in England by an anthropologist, based on fieldwork as a participating insider.

Harner, Michael. *The Way of the Shaman: A Guide to Power and Healing.* San Francisco, 1980. A popular how-to book that introduces drum journeys and other neoshamanic practices to broad circles of spiritual seekers.

Humphrey, Caroline. "Shamans in the City." In *The Unmaking of Soviet Life: Everyday Economies after Socialism,* pp. 202–222. Ithaca, N.Y., 2002. An anthropological essay on newly emerged shamanism in a post-Soviet context.

Jakobsen, Merete Demant. *Shamanism: Traditional and Contemporary Approaches to the Mastery of Spirits and Healing.* New York and Oxford, 1999. A critical account of courses in neoshamanism as compared to Inuit shamanic practices; see pages 147–257.

Lindquist, Galina. *Shamanic Performances on the Urban Scene: Neo-Shamanism in Contemporary Sweden.* Stockholm, 1997. An anthropological account based on participant observation.

Luhrmann, Tanya. *Persuasions of the Witch's Craft: Ritual Magic in Contemporary England.* Cambridge, Mass., 1989. A critical anthropological account of high magic in England.

Orenstein Fenman, Gloria. *The Reflowering of the Goddess.* 1990. An ideological manifesto of a founder of eco-feminism who is also a literary critic.

Vitebski, Piers. "From Cosmology to Environmentalism: Shamanism as Local Knowledge in a Global Setting." In *Counterworks: Managing the Diversity of Knowledge,* edited by Richard Fardon, pp. 182–203. London and New York, 1995. An anthropologist's review and analysis of the political and social resurgence of shamanism in post-Soviet Siberia.

GALINA LINDQUIST (2005)

SHAMASH SEE UTU

SHAME SEE SIN AND GUILT

SHANDAO (613–681), eminent Buddhist scholar and major figure in the Chinese Pure Land (Jingtu) movement. Shandao was born in the village of Linzu (Shandong province) and was ordained while still a youth. Eventually, his study of Buddhist scripture led him to the *Guan wuliangshou jing* (Meditation on the Buddha of immeasurable life sūtra), a text that teaches devotion to the Buddha Amitābha as a means of universal salvation. Profoundly impressed by the message of this text, Shandao retired to Mount Zhongnan to pursue his religious career. Later, he became a disciple of the Pure Land scholar Daochuo (562–645) at the latter's monastic home at the Xuanzhong Si. Through him, Shandao became convinced that the deliverance of ordinary sentient beings was possible through the power of the Buddha Amitābha, and thus he gave himself up to the practice and propagation of Pure Land Buddhism. His lifelong practice of recitative *nianfo* (the recitation of the name of the buddha Amitābha) began when he was in his thirties.

In addition to being a learned scholar, Shandao was known as a charismatic preacher. After his conversion to Pure Land belief he devoted his life to propagating *nianfo* practice among clergy and laity alike. Owing to his ardent belief in Amitābha's saving grace and his strict adherence to the Buddhist precepts, Shandao came to be popularly regarded as an incarnation of the Buddha. According to legend, whenever Shandao recited the name of Amitābha a beam of light issued from his mouth. Tradition has it that he copied the "smaller" *Sukhāvatīvyūha Sūtra* (Chin., *Emituo jing*) over ten thousand times and painted some three hundred scenes of Amitābha's Pure Land. Between the years 672 and 675 he supervised, at the insistence of the empress Wu, the construction of a great image of Mahāvairocana Buddha in the caves at the Longmen escarpment, presiding over the inaugural service upon its completion. Among his many writings are a commentary to the *Guan jing,* the *Guan wuliangshou jing shu* (T.D. no. 1753), and four books treating practical rules for devotions to Amitābha.

Like many of his Buddhist contemporaries, Shandao believed that the era of *mofa* (Jpn., *mappō*: the "latter days of the law" or "era of the decadent Dharma"), a degenerate age foretold in scripture in which few devotees would be able to observe Buddhist principles faithfully and attain salvation through their own efforts, was at hand. Shandao's writings are infused with the deep conviction that he was a common mortal, thoroughly immersed in ignorance and delusion and possessing only a minimal capacity to attain enlightenment. Shandao argued that it was precisely for these reasons that one must place faith in Amitābha Buddha, who, in a series of vows made at the beginning of his religious career, had promised to create a Pure Land in which beings might win salvation. One of these vows, number eighteen in the most common Chinese translation of the *Larger Sukhāvatīvyūha Sūtra,* promises birth in the Pure Land for all those who, with undistracted mind, direct their thoughts to Amitābha up to ten successive times. This practice (represented by the Chinese term *nianfo*) was variously interpreted by Buddhist exegetes, but by Shandao's time was held to include the verbal recitation of Amitābha's name.

Shandao's originality lay in his claim that the recitation of the name of Amitābha was the *single* direct cause of the attainment of supreme enlightenment. Prior to Shandao, the tradition of *nianfo* devotion had encompassed a range of practices—meditation on the Buddha's body, circumambulation of his image, and recitation of his name. In most Buddhist sects *nianfo* was done in conjunction with other practices, including the chanting of sūtras, observation of Vinaya precepts, repentance of sins, and praise of the adornments of the Pure Land. But in most cases, the recitation of Amitābha's name was considered an inferior, expedient, or merely provisional method for achieving rebirth in the Pure Land. It was Shandao who first elucidated the notion of recitative *nianfo* as an independent and soteriologically decisive action that would assure birth in the Pure Land in its own right. Shandao attributed the efficacy of recitative *nianfo* to the inconceivable power of Amitābha's vows.

For Shandao, the most important element in *nianfo* devotion, and thus the sole requisite for rebirth in the Pure Land, was a profound faith in Amitābha's saving grace. Acknowledging the frailty of human nature, Shandao taught that the devotee should first become fully convinced he or she has been, from time immemorial, possessed of sinful passions and subject to the cycle of birth and death. He must then believe, with the deepest sincerity, that Amitābha's forty-eight vows embrace him and all other sentient beings, and that such belief assures him of birth in the Pure Land as a *bodhisattva*.

Shandao's reputation spread with the fame of his religious parable known as the "Two Rivers and a White Path." This parable relates the story of a lone traveler who suffers the attacks of bandits and wild animals, successfully crosses a narrow path between the River of Raging Waters (symbolizing greed) and the River of Blazing Flames (symbolizing anger), and finally reaches the safety of the opposite bank (the Pure Land). The traveler finds the White Path by following the instructions of his two teachers, Śākyamuni Buddha and Amitābha Buddha. According to Shandao, the bandits and wild animals represent the human hindrances to enlightenment (e.g., the six sense organs and six corresponding kinds of defilements), while the White Path signifies Amitābha's salvific power as expressed in his vows. The parable, with its ultimate resolution of these obstructions, acts as a guide to Buddhists who desire to faithfully follow Amitābha's teachings.

In general, Shandao's many disciples advocated the practice of recitative *nianfo* as the principal cause of rebirth in the Pure Land. They did, however, endorse a variety of adjunct disciplines, including meditation. Therefore, from the middle of the Tang dynasty (618–907), Pure Land devotion gradually synthesized and unified the three practices of meditation, monastic discipline, and invocation. Shandao's notions of recitative *nianfo* and faith, however, continued to be recognized in later Pure Land Buddhism as the purest and the most essential means to winning rebirth in the Pure Land.

After its introduction to Japan, Shandao's teachings enjoyed wide acceptance. There, the notion of recitative *nianfo* (Jpn., *nenbutsu*) underwent further development and refinement, culminating in doctrines expounded by Hōnen (1133–1212) and Shinran (1173–1263), the founders of the Jōdoshū (Pure Land sect) and Jōdo Shinshū (True Pure Land sect), respectively. Shandao's emphasis on recitation and absolute faith became the hallmarks of Japanese Pure Land devotion.

See Also Daochuo; Hōnen; Jingtu; Nianfo; Shinran; Tanluan.

Bibliography

Fujiwara Ryōsetsu. *The Way to Nirvana.* Tokyo, 1974. A basic study of Shandao's doctrines.

Fujiwara Ryōsetsu. *Zendō jōdokyō no chūshin mondai.* Kyoto, 1977.

New Sources

Chappell, David Wellington. "The Formation of the Pure Land Movement in China: Tao-ch'o and Shandao." In *The Pure Land Tradition: History and Development,* edited by James Foard, Michael Solomon and Richard K. Payne, pp. 139–171. Berkeley, 1996.

Inagaki, Hisao. "Shandao's Exposition of the Method of Contemplation on Amida Buddhism, part 1." *Pacific World: Journal of the Institute of Buddhist Studies* (1999): 77–89.

Inagaki, Hisao. "Shandao's Exposition of the Method of Contemplation on Amida Buddhism, part 2." *Pacific World: Journal of the Institute of Buddhist Studies* (2000): 207–228.

Pas, Julian. "Dimensions in the Life and Thought of Shandao (613–681)." In *Buddhist and Taoist Practice in Medieval Chinese Society,* edited by David W. Chappell, pp. 65–84. Honolulu, 1987.

Pas, Julian F. *Visions of Sukhāvatī, Shandao's Commentary on the Kuan Wu-Liang-Shou- Fo Ching.* Albany, 1995.

Fujiwara Ryōsetsu (1987)
Revised Bibliography

SHANGDI.

During the Shang dynasty (c. 1550–1050 BCE), prayers and sacrifices were offered to a large number of gods, collectively referred to as *di.* Regarded as the deified ancestors (real or putative) of the Shang royal clan and high aristocracy, the *di* were worshiped at regular intervals in accordance with a liturgical calendar. At appropriate times they were also consulted for aid and advice by means of the cracking of oracle bones (i.e., the practice of scapulimancy).

The Shang kings also worshiped a more powerful god, known as Shangdi (High God, or God Above). Owing to the absence of plural forms in Chinese, it is not certain that there was only one god known as Shangdi—the phrase could also mean, collectively, "high gods." But most authorities agree that it was a single deity. Shangdi might also have been regarded in some sense as an ultimate human ancestor; however, the deity was not included in the regular liturgical round of ancestral sacrifices and oracular consultations.

There is no mythic account of Shangdi's origins, nor does he appear in the mythic accounts of the founding personages (whether gods, culture heroes, or sage-emperors) of Chinese high antiquity, such as Yao, Shun, and Yu the Great. There is, however, reason to suppose some correspondence between Shangdi and Huangdi, the Yellow Thearch (a name that first appears in texts long postdating the Shang), the mythic culture hero, patron of metallurgy, and god of the center.

Unlike the lesser *di,* who had authority over such human-centered affairs as the king's health and his fortunes in marriage, warfare, and the hunt, Shangdi had jurisdiction in larger-scale natural and cosmic matters. According to surviving oracle-bone inscriptions, Shangdi had the power to prevent, or put an end to, plagues, drought, floods, violent storms, and other such phenomena. Shangdi apparently was never consulted directly by means of scapulimancy, and only rarely were prayers offered to him directly. Rather, when necessary the lesser gods were consulted to learn his will; they could also be asked to intercede with him on behalf of the king and his people.

While the surviving evidence does not permit a very exact description of Shang theology, it seems probable that Shangdi was thought of as a cosmic god, dwelling in or above the sky at the apex of the rotating heavens. Indeed, Shangdi might have been a deified embodiment of the pole star itself. It is certain that a few centuries after the fall of the Shang dynasty gods were thought of as being, in part, personifications of stars, planets, and astral configurations.

With the conquest of the Shang state by the Zhou dynasty around 1050 BCE, Shangdi's place as the paramount deity of the royal cult was usurped by the Zhou high god, Tian ("heaven"). Tian was not simply Shangdi under another name, but the two high gods were similarly regarded as conscious but relatively impersonal cosmic forces.

The term *Shangdi,* however, survived the fall of the Shang dynasty and continued to appear in religious and cosmological texts for centuries thereafter. In such texts it is not so clear that the reference is always to a unitary high god; in some contexts it seems preferable to construe the term as "high gods." In some texts of the Warring States period (481–221 BCE) a near-synonym, *taidi* ("great god"), is substituted for the term *Shangdi.* Regardless of which term is used, it is clear that the reference is to a celestial god (or gods) dwelling at or around the celestial pole. According to chapter 4 of the *Huainanzi* (139 BCE), "If the height of the Kunlun [cosmic] mountain is doubled . . . [and redoubled, and again redoubled], it reaches up to Heaven itself. If one mounts to there, one will become a demigod. It is called the abode of the Great God [Taidi]." In his commentary to the *Huainanzi,* Gao You (fl. 205–212) states that "the Changhe Gate is the gate [through which] one begins an ascent to Heaven. The Gate of Heaven is the gate of the Purple Fortified Palace [i.e., the circumpolar stars] where Shangdi dwells."

With the development of the organized religion of Daoism around the end of the Latter Han dynasty (third century CE), the term *Shangdi* took on new prominence. As a Daoist term, however, it rarely appears alone; rather it has the general meaning "high god" in the elaborate compound titles given to the numerous divinities in the hierarchical, bureaucratically organized Daoist pantheon. *Yuhuang Shangdi* ("jade sovereign high god") is a characteristic example of such a divine title of nobility.

Meanwhile, the old sense of *Shangdi* was preserved through the officially sponsored study of classical texts by the Confucian bureaucratic elite. Every examination candidate knew by heart such stock phrases from the classics as "[King Wen] brilliantly served Shangdi and secured abundant blessings." With the development of the state cult of Confucianism and the imperial worship of and sacrifice to Heaven (Tian), *Shangdi* came to be regarded as a virtual synonym, perhaps somewhat more concretely conceived, of *Heaven.*

Finally, the term *Shangdi* was adopted by Protestant missionaries, and their Chinese converts, to designate the Judeo-Christian God. More commonly, however, that deity is known in Chinese by a name that was coined by the early Jesuit missionaries, *Tianzhu,* "Lord of Heaven."

SEE ALSO Chinese Religion, article on Mythic Themes; Huangdi; Yuhuang.

BIBLIOGRAPHY

The term *Shangdi* appears many times in the Confucian canon; the standard translation is that of James Legge, *The Chinese Classics,* 5 vols. (Oxford, 1893–1895; 3d ed., Hong Kong, 1960). For the role of Shangdi in the religion of the Shang dynasty, see Chang Tsung-tung's *Der Kult der Shang-Dynastie im Spiegel der Orakelinschriften,* edited by Otto Karow (Weisbaden, 1970); Henri Maspero's *La Chine antique* (1924; Paris, 1965), translated as *China in Antiquity* by Frank A. Kierman, Jr. (Amherst, Mass., 1979) treats the religious role of Shangdi in both Shang and post-Shang classical times.

JOHN S. MAJOR (1987)

SHANGO SEE CARIBBEAN RELIGIONS, *ARTICLE ON* AFRO-CARIBBEAN RELIGIONS

SHANG-TI SEE SHANGDI

SHANKARA SEE ŚAṄKARA

SHAN-TAO SEE SHANDAO

SHAPE SHIFTING can be defined as the alteration in form or substance of any animate object. There seems no limit to the kinds of objects susceptible to such alteration. Examples abound of the shape shifting of plants, animals, humans, and gods. Shape shifting can be caused either by the object changed or by an external force; it can occur for good or for ill and for reasons simple or profound.

Shape shifting is found in essentially every religion and mythological tradition. By no means is it a phenomenon restricted to unsophisticated cultures remote in history and geography from the dominant civilizations. An enduring fascination with shape shifting is easily detected in modern popular culture as well as in the major religions: Comic-book and cartoon characters such as Superman and Spiderman are typical shape-shifters, and shape shifting is certainly an element in the deepest spiritual insights of Christianity, Hinduism, and Buddhism as these religions are currently practiced.

Because of the rich variety of contexts and levels of subtlety in which it is found, it is impossible to assign shape shifting a universal meaning. Zeus's appearance as a swan and Christ's transfiguration are both instances of shape shifting, but they have quite distinct meanings and importance. It is possible, however, in a survey of the phenomenon in its manifold occurrence, to distinguish between types of shape shifting and to find within those types a common meaning and function.

The most frequent type of shape shifting involves strategic deception. Strategic shapeshifters change themselves for reasons of aggression, seduction, or trickery. A second class of shapeshifters are those who use the device for escape from another's aggression or seduction. A third type has the simple function of punishment, and a fourth rewards or compensates the changed object, usually by immortalization. A frequent but often subtle kind of shape shifting seeks liberation from bondage or punishment. A somewhat murkier, though widely found, type may best be described as instances of borderline or confused identity, where one mode of existence is so much like another that the two are repeatedly exchanged. Finally, by far the most profound variety of shape shifting is that which has revelation as its design.

STRATEGIC DECEPTION. Stealth is so essential an ingredient in any conflict that it is in the interest of all contestants to be something or somewhere else than their opponents expect them to be. Kuloscap, for example, the major god of the Micmac Indians of the Maritime Provinces of Canada, overcomes a series of enemies by clever ruses and rapid shape shifting. His power to change himself includes the power to change others, for he will occasionally grant immortality, in the form of a tree or stone, to those who request it. The Maruts, bellicose deities in the service of the Hindu god Indra, can enter undetected into the presence of their enemies by such means as changing themselves into apparently helpless infants. Perhaps the most prodigious of all the shapeshifters of this type is another Hindu god, Viṣṇu, who assumes a great number of incarnations, or avataras, in his battle against evil. The best known of the avataras of Viṣṇu are Rāma and Kṛṣṇa, each of whom is remembered for epic struggles involving shape shifting.

Seduction is probably as usual a reason for shape shifting as is aggression, and it certainly takes more colorful and ingenious forms. At its most basic level seductive shape shifting consists in taking the appearance of another's beloved. Thus the magician Merlin gives Uther Pendragon the form of the duke Gorlois, that he may satisfy his sexual longing for Gorlois's wife. The fruit of this union based on deception is Arthur, king of Britain. So too Zeus, the foremost of the Greeks' Olympian deities, appears to Alcmena in the form of her beloved Amphitryon. But Zeus is usually more inventive, coming to his unsuspecting lovers as a satyr, a shower of gold, a white bull, a swan, and once even as the goddess Artemis. Seductive shape shifting can sometimes be reversed, as commonly happens in Arthurian legend, for example, where the seducer appears as an irresistible young woman but is in fact an agent of evil or death in disguise.

Trickery is the theme of an enormous body of folk tale and myth. Tricksters, displaying remarkably similar characteristics, can be found in a diversity of cultures. They typically take the form of animals but can also be such borderline beings as dwarfs, elves, imps, and trolls. Not always, but frequently, tricksters carry out their mischief through shape shifting. A trickster may, for example, present himself as a person of supernatural powers in order to win a bride or change himself into a snake to steal meat hidden in a skull. A common feature of trickster stories is that these deceptions either are exposed or they backfire on the trickster. The false bridegroom is revealed as a malevolent fox, the trickster finds that his own head has grown onto the snake's body he has assumed, making it impossible for him to draw it out of the skull. Tricksters very often suffer, and even die, for their blundering misdeeds, but they nonetheless return miraculously for more adventure, changing from death back into life—the ultimate feat of the shapeshifter.

The line between trickery and evil is often fuzzy. Satan, for example, has a great supply of tricks, many of which involve shape shifting, but he is certainly no mere trickster. Similarly, the great mischief-maker of Norse mythology, Loki, capable of assuming such diverse forms as bird, flea, milkmaid, or fish, sometimes seems to be the originator of evil itself and not just another divine trickster.

ESCAPE. If stealth is valuable to the aggressor, it is no less valuable to the intended victim. The Greek goddess Daphne is changed into a laurel tree to elude the amorous advances of Apollo. Zeus transforms Io into a heifer to protect her from the wrath of Hera. But such shape shifting is filled with risk. The Celtic god Cian transforms himself into a boar to escape his pursuing enemies. They in turn become greyhounds, hunt down their quarry, and kill him. When Demeter, in the shape of a mare, flees Poseidon, he accomplishes the seduction by taking the shape of a stallion.

PUNISHMENT. Shape shifting has such obvious utility for pursuit and flight that examples of it have little inherent intellectual or religious weight. When it takes the form of punishment it becomes considerably more nuanced. There are, to be sure, numerous simple instances of direct retribution. Thus, Lot's wife is transformed into a pillar of salt for violating the command not to look back at Sodom; in Roman mythology Picus pays for his rejection of Circe's sexual advances when she transforms him into a woodpecker.

In its more refined form shape shifting as punishment emerges in a number of traditions as the transmigration, or reincarnation, of souls. In Hinduism, where the concept is most thoroughly developed, the reincarnated soul has a new shape determined by the quality of its spiritual life in previous existences. There is no end to this serial shape shifting until the soul is able to cleanse itself of all attachment to the changeable. In other words, the soul will be punished by shape shifting until it has no shape left whatsoever. This idea persists in Buddhism, though with much less emphasis. Plato gives the idea considerable authority in the West. In the *Phaedo,* for instance, he has Socrates argue that souls will go through an indefinite number of rebirths but with appropriate transformations. Those who are gluttons in this existence will be asses in the next; the unjust and tyrannical will become wolves and hawks; and those who practice the civil and social virtues will be bees or ants, if they are not changed "back again into the form of man." Elsewhere Plato suggests that humans have fallen into this earthly shape from one more desirable.

LIBERATION. For every tale of punishment by shape shifting there is one of liberation. The princess of one of the tales of the brothers Grimm must weave six shirts out of flower petals and keep silence for six years in order to break the witch's spell that has changed her six brothers into swans. Cinderella must be found by the prince, the café waitress by the movie producer, each thus to be freed from her humiliating bondage.

The shape shifting of liberation, since it must always come from without, grants unusual, often unknown or hidden, powers to the changers. Pygmalion, a Greek sculptor of great skill, innocently shapes a statue, then finds he has fallen in love with it; Aphrodite secretly brings the statue to life as the woman Galatea. Just as innocently a child in another Grimm tale takes a frog to dinner and then to bed, acts of affection that transform him back into the prince he really is.

There is often the assumption in this kind of shape shifting that the change from one state to another is the liberation of a being from its false to its true nature. The water-jar boy of the Indian tale not only springs into human form; he leads his mother into a secret well where she is joined with the supernatural beings who are her true family. The Christian thinker Boethius, tortured to death by the Ostrogoth ruler of Rome Theodoric in 524 CE, wrote that Philosophy, in the shape of a woman, entered his cell to console him with the message that he suffered from his punishment only because "you have forgotten what you are." As long as he could remember that he was in truth pure soul he would be freed from the torment suffered by his earthly shape. The idea that humans are liberated from a false existence to a true one is widely found in mystical literature. Islamic mystics, for example, declare that it is their desire "to be who I am before I was."

A highly sophisticated and extreme form of liberation by shape shifting is found in classical Daoism. For the ancient Daoists the spiritual goal was not a transformation from one kind of being into another, but continuous transformation. All that is, they taught, is in the process of change. Therefore, the path (or dao) of the liberated person does not have a goal; it is a path of endless change. Zhuangzu, a Daoist philosopher who lived several centuries before the common era, wrote that the liberated person "rides on the flow of heaven and earth and the transformation of the six elements and wanders in the infinite" (*Zhuangzsu,* trans. Jane English and Giafu Feng, New York, 1974, p. 9). In other words, the liberated person is an eternal shapeshifter, possessing no shape that is truly his or her own.

IMMORTALIZATION. A relatively small number of shapeshifting tales and beliefs fall into the category of immortalization. At the simplest level are the stories in Greek mythology of Hyacinth, a lover of Apollo who was changed into a lily; of Narcissus, a lover of his own image who also became a flower; and of Echo, a lover of Narcissus, who was cruelly immortalized in the disembodied form of a voice that could never speak for itself.

It has been a common belief in many cultures that gods and heroes have taken permanent places in the night sky. This belief enters into Plato's philosophical speculation, in the *Timaeus,* that the stars are the souls of those liberated from their earthly shapes. The Christian doctrine of the resurrection of the body also shares in the general character of immortalization by shape shifting. "Lo, I tell you a mystery," Paul wrote; "we shall not all sleep but we shall all be changed." It is a change in which "this mortal nature must put on immortality" (*1 Cor.* 15:51–53). This more philosophical, or theological, understanding of shape shifting, it should be noted, is the precise opposite of that of the Daoists, in which all possibility of immortality is rejected.

BORDERLINE AND CONFUSED IDENTITIES. There is a large class of shapeshifters who seem to be existing in two realms at the same time, who seem to be both human and animal, or both deity and natural phenomenon.

The best example of this kind of shape shifting in Greek mythology is Dionysos, a god of multiple origins and traits. There is only one continuous characteristic of Dionysos through all his often contradictory manifestations: He is always closely associated with natural process. His usual dwelling place is in the wild, physically and psychically far from civilized human existence. The natural order from which he is inseparable usually causes social disorder. He is widely known as the god of wine and revelry. Even his birth has a strange ambiguity about it: He was born twice, once prematurely of the goddess Semele, and once from the thigh of Zeus. This double birth may account for the fact that he can sometimes be found in female form. He can assume a great number of shapes, as though the line between his divinity and natural process has no restraining effect. Dionysos is as closely associated with death as he is with life. He was raised in the forest by the satyr Silenus, who was fond of saying that the only happiness in life is to die and leave it as soon as possible. Dionysos dies by being pulled apart by women in an ecstatic ritual and is thus also known by the name Zagreus, the Torn. Once dead, however, he comes back to life, a symbol of the natural process itself, which requires death for the regeneration of life.

Other Greek deities, notably Artemis, Poseidon, and Demeter, have identities bound up with nature, though none so closely as Dionysos, whose origins are, in any case, more Middle Eastern than Greek. The ancient religions of Mesopotamia and Egypt included the worship of a great many gods who changed their shapes in a manner imitative of nature. Ishtar, the Assyro-Babylonian goddess of love and voluptuousness, performs an annual ceremonial killing of her lover Tammuz, "lord of the wood of life," who vanishes into the earth like the threshed and planted grain, only to rise again in the spring into the arms of Ishtar, who then repeats the process. This particular kind of agricultural shape shifting has distant but unmistakable echoes in many other mythological and religious traditions. Note the parallels in the story of Christ: Scourged and crowned in a mock ceremony, he is executed and buried at the time of a spring festival, shortly to rise in the midst of women as a new food for the life of the community.

There are instances of the elusive sort of shape shifting that seem at once to be both divine and natural. Equally elusive is the shape shifting caused by the intimate identity of the human with the animal. Popular Chinese legend commonly has the trickster fox posing as a respected citizen, often without anyone ever seeing his fox form. In Europe werewolf legends are found everywhere. Indeed, until the eighteenth century it was widely believed that some human beings could periodically pass into the form of a wolf; the belief even encouraged a quasi-scientific study of such creatures, thought to be afflicted with a form of insanity called lycanthropy (from the Greek words for "wolf" and "human").

REVELATION. Finally, there is the shape shifting that appears to have as its principal function the awakening or enlightening of observers to an otherwise unnoticed reality.

Þórr (Thor), the hero-god of Norse mythology, was once admitted with his companions to a magical castle where they had to prove themselves by such feats as racing with a giant who seemed to reach the finish line as soon as he started, lifting a cat whose single paw Thor could not raise from the floor, and wrestling with an old woman of frail appearance but astounding strength. When they had lost these contests it was explained to them that they had been competing with thought, the world serpent, and time, as though these were realities about which the heroes needed instruction.

The Greek god Proteus offers an interesting variation on this theme. Because he possessed the gift of prophecy, Proteus was often asked to reveal what the future held for a person. As though to impress his suppliants with the anguish that comes from such revelations, he would change himself into monstrous forms meant to terrify them. To those who refused to be intimidated he offered the requested knowledge.

Revelatory shape shifting does more than simply occur in Christianity; it is its central affirmation. The doctrine of the incarnation is properly to be understood as the revealing self-transformation of God. "In the beginning was the word, and the word was with God, and the word was God. . . . And the word was made flesh and dwelt among us, and we beheld his glory," the *Gospel of John* begins. Only once, however, does one find in the Gospels an event in which something of Jesus' divine form is revealed. Jesus took several of his disciples up a mountain "and was transfigured before them." His face shone as the sun and his raiment was of a brilliant light. The disciples fell on their faces in fear and reverence.

A remarkably similar event can be found in one of the best-known works of Hindu literature, the *Bhagavadgītā*. This text is the account of a conversation between the famed warrior Arjuna and the god Kṛṣṇa, who was in the form of Arjuna's chariot driver. Near the end of this discourse Arjuna begged Kṛṣṇa to show himself in his true divine form. When Kṛṣṇa did so his face shone with the light of a thousand suns, and Arjuna "beheld the universe, in all its multitudinous diversity, lodged as one being within the God of gods." Like the disciples of Jesus, he was both terrified and worshipful before this transformation.

In referring to Jesus and Kṛṣṇa as shapeshifters it may seem that their spiritual importance has been trivialized, that they have been placed in the company of tricksters and seducers. On the contrary, these self-transforming powers of Jesus and Kṛṣṇa show how immensely varied the phenomenon of shape shifting is. What the many shapeshifters have in common is only an external resemblance. When one looks into the inner meaning of each instance of shape shifting and try to understand it in its context, similarities rapidly disappear. Shape shifting is a universal phenomenon to which no universal meaning can be applied. To cite an event as an example of it is not, therefore, to state its meaning, but to encourage inquiry into its meaning.

SEE ALSO Monsters; Therianthropism; Tricksters.

BIBLIOGRAPHY

Because there is no major work on shape shifting as such, the most useful texts for further study are the introductory and classificatory volumes on world mythology. Without question, the most comprehensive classification of mythological themes is Stith Thompson's *Motif-Index of Folk Literature,* 6 vols. (Bloomington, Ind., 1955–1958). *The New Larousse Encyclopedia of Myth* (London, 1973) is a broad and accessible summary of mythological narratives. *Funk and Wagnalls Standard Dictionary of Folklore, Mythology and Legend,* 2 vols. (1949–1950; reprint, New York, 1972), provides brief but useful introductions to the basic terms and categories of mythological study. Joseph Campbell's *The Masks of God,* 4 vols. (New York, 1959–1968), deftly combines an introduction to the world's mythological literature with the author's interpretations of its major themes. The most useful compendium of Greek mythology for the general reader is Robert

Graves's *The Greek Myths,* 2 vols. (Harmondsworth, 1955). For a bibliography of works on the myth and folktale traditions of other cultures see *World Folktales,* edited by Atelia Clarkson and Gilbert B. Cross (New York, 1980).

New Sources

Barkan, Leonard. *Gods Made Flesh: Metamorphosis and the Pursuit of Paganism.* New Haven, 1986.

Forbes Irving, P.M.C. *Metamorphosis in Greek Myths.* Oxford, 1990.

Jackson, Michael. "The Man Who Could Turn into an Elephant: Shape-Shifting Among the Kuranko of Sierra Leone." In *Personhood and Agency: The Experience of Self and Other in African Cultures,* edited by Michael Jackson and Ivan Karp, pp. 59-78. Uppsala, 1990.

Kennett, Frances. "Sor Juana and the Guadelupe." *Feminist Theology: The Journal of the Britain & Ireland School of Feminist Theology* 11/3 (2003): 307-325.

Smith, W. L. "Changing Bodies: The Mechanics of the Metamorphic Curse." *Acta Orientalia* 56 (1995): 125-143.

Steiger, Brad. *Werewolf Book: The Encyclopedia of Shape-Shifting Beings.* Detroit, 1999.

Traini, Renato. "La métamorphose des êtres humains en brutes d'après quelques textes arabes." (The metamorphosis of human beings into monsters according to some Arab texts). In *Miscellanea Arabica et Islamica,* edited by Uitgeverij Peeters, pp. 90–134. Louvain, 1993.

JAMES P. CARSE (1987)
Revised Bibliography

SHARĪʿAH SEE ISLAMIC LAW, *ARTICLE ON* SHARĪʿAH

SHARPE, ERIC J. Eric John Sharpe (1933–2000) was born in Lancashire, England, into a family of straitened circumstances during the Great Depression. The first in his family to undertake tertiary studies, he was fortunate to secure a studentship at the University of Manchester. Sharpe seemed destined for the Methodist ministry, yet, when choosing between two eminent supervisors for his masters thesis, evangelical New Testament specialist F. F. Bruce and the more adventurous liberal scholar of comparative religion S. G. F. Brandon, he chose the latter, researching "the Doctrine of Man" in New Testament and early Vedic thought. Thereafter Sharpe's primary attention was on the business of analyzing and comparing different religions. In 1958 a World Council of Churches award took him to Uppsala, Sweden, where he began doctoral studies within the Faculty of Theology. Interestingly, he did not opt to study under Geo Widengren, a continental equivalent to Brandon, but under the brilliant historian of mission and church in southern Africa—Bengt Sundkler. Sharpe's doctorate, published under the title *Not to Destroy but to Fulfil* (1965), centered on the missiological approach to Indian religions by John Nicol Farquhar (one of Brandon's predecessors). With the rise of the Uppsala school of New Testament criticism at the time, with its stress on oral transmission, young Sharpe also accepted the honor of translating works by such scholars as Birger Gerhardsson (on the remembrance of the *rabbi* Jesus' sayings) and Bertil Gärtner (on the Jesus *logia* in the *Gospel of Thomas*).

By the time he returned to Britain with his Swedish wife Birgitta in 1966, Sharpe had become extremely well-informed in the history of different Western approaches to the critical study of the world's religions. The traditions of particular interest to him were the Hindu and the Germanic, but he kept abreast of studies in the history of ancient and modern Christianity (with special concern for ecumenics). Brandon wanted him back in Manchester, and the Sinologist Howard Smith deferred his retirement until Sharpe returned from a temporary appointment in Indiana. Consolidating his research interests in the encounter between Christianity and Hinduism (and other traditions), Sharpe was eventually enticed into a research and lecture tour to India itself during 1969. The next year he secured a senior lectureship in religious studies at the new University of Lancaster, collaborating with Ninian Smart in the public forum for a better understanding of religious diversity in Britain and for the teaching of world religions. Visiting professorships to North America came his way (Northwestern; Manitoba), and in 1975, serving his last year as the organization's acting general secretary, he and his wife organized the Thirteenth Congress of the International Association for the History of Religions. After Brandon's unexpected death in Egypt, Sharpe reconnected with Manchester. There he kept up a close collegial friendship with John Hinnells, leading to the co-authored book *Hinduism* (1972).

Ambitious for a professorship, Sharpe was forced to look to Commonwealth countries for opportunities, and in 1977 he won the Foundation Chair in religious studies at the University of Sydney, the first of its kind on the Australian continent. This success was mostly due to the publication of his finest book, *Comparative Religion: A History* (1975)—on modern theories and methods in the study of the world's religions. After recovering from ill health, Sharpe settled down at Sydney. While being allowed to test the waters in Sweden, where for a time he held the coveted professorship in the history of religions (within the humanities faculty) at Uppsala, Sharpe committed himself to Australia, and was bent on consolidating a vigorous (if small) department at Sydney until his retirement in 1996. His weakening condition restricted his role in public life during his last years.

Sharpe was one of the world's leading methodologists in the comparative and historical study of religions. If one admits a certain competition between his claims and those of other doyens (e.g., Mircea Eliade, Ninian Smart, and Jacques Waardenburg) at least Sharpe emerged as the world's foremost authority on how one should best orient oneself for understanding other religions. His personal academic experience gave him a distinct advantage in accounting for British evolutionist and diffusionist theories, the myth and ritual school in both English and Scandinavian scholarship, continental phenomenology, and the German *Religionsgeschichtliche Schule* associated with Wilhem Bousset and Richard Reitzenstein. Other books confirming this status were *Understanding Religion* (1983) and *Nathan Söderblom and the Study of Religion* (1990), even if both exposed his flanks to theorists of a different bent.

Although Sharpe primarily self-inscribed as a historian of religions (and religious ideas), and remained loyal to the historically rooted agenda followed in Manchester and Uppsala, he was always intrigued by Christian and Western images of the East (thus *Faith meets Faith* [1977] and *The Universal Gita* [1985]), and he was concerned with understanding Christian missionary interpretations of the "other" (e.g., *Karl Ludwig Reichelt* [1984]). These missiological interests could be misunderstood, and, in the last stages of his career, Sharpe fell subject to criticism by younger methodologists that his work carried a hidden theological agenda. In *Understanding Religion*, admittedly, he appeared strident in separating the new discipline of religious studies from divinity (because at Sydney his department was initially launched through the Board of Studies in Divinity). Yet in his critics' eyes he looked to be a man with plenty of theological proclivities himself. Had he not received a doctorate in theology from Uppsala? And had not he occasionally engaged in Christian theology?

These questions were brewing at the so-called Sharpe Symposium, hosted by the American Academy of Religion in Chicago in 1988. If some wanted to accuse him of "closet theology," however, Sharpe could maintain against his detractors that only a warped methodological orientation would arise if a theorist had rejected his own natal tradition. In any case, Sharpe's approach to theology was more nuanced than met the eye. Certainly, he denied the possibility of eluding theological values. The phenomenology of religion, in his view, could never be an act of pure objectivism per se; it inevitably involved "charity," or the concession of goodwill that gave someone else the chance to voice their commitments. He also held that studies in religion should not be willfully secularized, and that the scholar of religion did best with a "dual citizenship" between his or her own and another's tradition. In private notes, however, Sharpe recognized how, "professionally speaking, [theology] may be one of the narrowest and most inbred [disciplines]." Only when one's attitudes were broadened, "Faith could best meet Faith" in generous interreligious dialogue; yet dialoguers would lack integrity and demean the other if they did not represent their own faith (or faith background) existentially, so that believers, including willing theologians, are essential in the dialogical process.

BIBLIOGRAPHY

Eric Sharpe's most important theoretical works are *Comparative Religion: A History*, 2d ed. (London, 1986), and *Understanding Religion* (London, 1983). For reflection on his work, see Annette Aronowicz et al., "Doing the History of Religion" (the Sharpe Symposium), *Method and Theory in the Study of Religion* 1, no. 1 (1989): 40–114; followed by Sharpe, "On the Sharpe Symposium," *Method and Theory in the Study of Religion* 1, no. 2 (1989): 213–226. See also Arvind Sharma, ed., *The Sum of Our Choices: Essays in Honour of Eric J. Sharpe* (Atlanta, 1996), which includes a portrait (p. v) and a curriculum vitae with a full list of publications (pp. 409–417), and Sharma's "Portrait: Eric J. Sharpe," *Religion* 31 (2001): 63–66; Carole M. Cusack and Peter Oldmeadow, eds., *This Immense Panorama: Studies in Honour of Eric Sharpe* (Sydney, 1999); and Garry W. Trompf, "Eric John Sharpe," *Svensk Missions Tidskrift* 89, no. 2 (2001): 176–182.

GARRY W. TROMPF (2005)

SHAVU'OT, or Pentecost, is the Jewish festival that falls on the sixth day of the month of Sivan (and also on the seventh day, outside Israel). In the Pentateuch (*Ex.* 34:22, *Dt.* 16:10) the festival is called Shavu'ot ("weeks") because it falls after seven weeks (forty-nine days) have been counted from the "morrow of the Sabbath" (*Lv.* 23:15) of Passover. In the Talmudic literature a debate is recorded between the Sadducees and the Pharisees: the former understood the word *Sabbath* in the verse to mean literally the Sabbath of Passover (so that, for them, Shavu'ot always fell on Sunday), while the latter, whose view is accepted, understood "the Sabbath" to be the first day of Passover. It is difficult to know what doctrinal issues really lie behind these two opinions, since, if the report is accurate, it is unlikely that the debate was purely exegetical.

In the Pentateuch the festival appears to have been a purely agricultural one. The rabbinic name for the festival, 'Atseret ("assembly"), the term used in *Numbers* 29:35 for the additional festival of Sukkot, suggests that originally the festival was no more than an adjunct to Passover. But beginning no later than the second century CE a vast transformation of the festival took place. The arrival at Mount Sinai of the people coming from slavery in Egypt (*Ex.* 19:1) occurred in the third month from the Exodus (the month of Sivan, as it came to be called). Through examination of the texts, a view developed that the theophany at Sinai had taken place on the sixth of Sivan, and Shavu'ot was then celebrated as the anniversary of the giving of the Torah. (Although the passage speaks only of the Decalogue being given at Sinai, later Jewish tradition held that the whole of the Torah was given to Moses at that time.)

The liturgy of the day contains references to the Torah and the 613 commandments (the rabbinic figure for the sum total of positive precepts and negative injunctions of the law). A feature found only on this festival is the recital of an Aramaic hymn on the first day in praise of the Torah. It is generally held that these hymns are vestiges of introductions in Aramaic to the Targum, the Aramaic translations of the texts that, in ancient times, were always read in the synagogue. The Pentateuchal reading is from the Sinai narrative (*Ex.* 19–20), and the Prophetic reading from *Ezekiel* 1, the vision of the heavenly chariot. The link between the two is that of revelation, to the people as whole and to the individual prophet. The *Book of Ruth* as well is read in the synagogue. Ruth, the prototype of the righteous proselyte, took upon herself the observance of God's laws, as did the Israelites at Sinai.

There are no special Shavuʿot rituals, in view of the late origin of the festival in the form in which it is now celebrated. However, there are a number of customs, such as decorating the synagogue with plants and flowers (because beautiful plants are said to have flowered on the barren mountain when the Torah was given) and eating dairy dishes at the festive meal (because, like milk, the Torah nourishes young and old). The sixteenth-century mystics of Safad introduced the all-night vigil on Shavuʿot night, a practice that has been widely adopted by all Jews. During this night an anthology of readings from all the classical sources of Judaism is studied.

Bibliography

The little book by Chaim Pearl, *A Guide to Shavuoth* (London, 1959), is an adequate statement of the laws and customs of the festival.

Louis Jacobs (1987)

SHAYKH AL-ISLĀM (Turk., *şeyhülislam*) is a title associated with Islamic religious figures; it was used most commonly in the period of the Ottoman empire, when it denoted the chief jurisconsult, or *muftī*, of Istanbul, who was the supreme religious authority in the empire and the administrative head of the Ottoman hierarchy of religious scholars (*ʿulamāʾ*). The title seems to have come into use in the Islamic east in the late tenth century. From that time it served to distinguish individuals who had achieved prominence in some branch of the faith. Although pre-Ottoman biographical literature mentions the title in connection with Ṣūfī notables, it was even then more commonly, and later almost exclusively, applied to specialists in Islamic holy law, the *sharīʿah*.

The transition of the term form an honorific to an actual office defies charting. However, from the tenth century certain local religious officials are known to have held office under the title (although not necessarily performing the same functions) in such disparate lands as Seljuk Iran and Anatolia, Mamluk Egypt and Syria, the Delhi sultanate of India, Safavid Iran, Timurid Transoxiana, and the Muslim regions of China. It was under the Ottomans, however, that the office achieved both its full definition and its preeminence.

According to Ottoman tradition, the first shaykh al-Islām was Şemseddin al-Fenari (d. 1431), a celebrated *sharīʿah* scholar and *qāḍī* ("judge") appointed by Sultan Murād II (1421–1451). With the conquest of Constantinople (Istanbul) in 1453, the *shaykh al-Islām*, always chosen from among the noted jurists of the day, thereafter resided in the capital city as its chief *muftī*.

Like any *muftī*, the *shaykh al-Islām* was responsible for issuing written opinions (*fatwās*), based on established *sharīʿah* authorities, in response to legal questions submitted for his expert interpretation of the law. Such opinions were not binding. The petitioner was under no legal obligation to follow a *muftī*'s findings, or even those of a *shaykh al-Islām*. Nonetheless, a *fatwā* delivered by the *shaykh al-Islām* possessed compelling moral authority. A *shaykh al-Islām* presumably earned his post as much through a reputation for integrity as for scholarship. Moreover, he was the only officer in the realm entitled to pronounce on the sultan's fitness to rule. The subordination of the worldly to the spiritual was more in theory than in practice, but many *shaykh al-Islāms* did not hesitate to issue opinions at odds with their sovereign's wishes. In any case, for the entire span of the empire, the *shaykh al-Islām*'s *fatwā* was the emblem of legitimation, required for the deposition of the sultan as well as for the undertaking of any major imperial policy.

During the tenure of the post's most renowned incumbent, Mehmed Ebussüud (d. 1574), the *shaykh al-Islām* came to control the examination and appointment of the major judges and professors in the empire. As a result, the independence of the office was further compromised, and subsequent holders of the past became increasingly subject to political pressures, including summary dismissal.

With the secularizing reforms of the nineteenth century, the *shaykh al-Islām*, with the entire body of Ottoman *ʿulamāʾ*, was systematically deprived of authority and importance. In November 1922, the last *shaykh al-Islām* left office when the nationalist Turks under Mustafa Kemal Atatürk (d. 1938), founder of the Turkish Republic, abolished the Ottoman sultanate. The post was never reconstituted, but local officials in Muslim countries outside Turkey have occasionally used the title in the modern era.

Bibliography

The history of the important Ottoman office of *shaykh al-Islām*, making use of still largely unmined and untranslated Ottoman sources, remains to be written. The standard work in Turkish on the entire Ottoman religious hierarchy, Ismail Hakki Uzunçarşılı's *Osmanlı Devletinin İlmiye Teşkilâtı* (Ankara, 1965), should be supplemented by relevant chapters in Halil İnalcık's *The Ottoman Empire: The Classical Age, 1300–1600*, translated by Norman Itzkowitz and Colin Imber (New York, 1973), along with R. C. Repp's Ph.D. dissertation, "An Examination of the Origins and Development of the Office of Shaikh al-Islam in the Ottoman Empire" (Oxford University, 1966), and my own Ph.D. dissertation, "The Ottoman Ulema 1703–1839 and the Route to Great Mollaship" (University of Chicago, 1976), J. H. Kramers's "Shaikh al-Islām," in *The Encyclopaedia of Islam* (Leiden, 1913–1934), while somewhat dated, can be read alongside Richard W. Bulliet's "The Shaikh al-Islām and the Evolution of Islamic Society," *Studia Islamica* 35 (1972): 53–67, for the general history of the office in the Islamic world.

MADELINE C. ZILFI (1987)

SHAYKHĪYAH. Shaykhīyah was a controversial school of theology within Twelver or Imāmī Shiism, originally inspired by the teachings of Shaykh Aḥmad al-Ahsāʾī (1753–1826), a leading scholar of the early Qājār period, and his immediate followers. His thought is a creative synthesis of considerable merit and complexity, selectively drawing from the mystical philosophy (*ḥikmat-i ilāhī*) of Mullā Ṣadrā Shīrāzī (1579–1641) and other famous Shīʿī heretics, from certain elements of the Akhbārī school of Shīʿī scholarship with its emphasis on the exclusive authority of the words of the *imāms,* and apparently from Ismāʿīlī eschatological theories. Though advancing several criticisms of the *ḥikmat* tradition and of Sufism, the Shaykhīyah may be regarded as the most powerful expression of spiritual dissent from the theology and claims to authority of the dominant Uṣūlī *ʿulamāʾ* of Iran and Iraq during the eighteenth century and early nineteenth century. As a strong movement toward the charismatic individual and his or her access to direct inner revelation from the *imāms,* the early movement was originally called the Kashfīyah. The condemnation of their doctrines as heretical and splits within the movement alongside the development of Bābism from its midst led to a variety of responses, most of which led to the two main branches of the Shaykhīyah reconciling themselves to the dominant theology and jurisprudence of Twelver Shiism.

SHAYKH AḤMAD: LIFE AND THOUGHT. Shaykh Aḥmad was born in the eastern Arabian province of al-Aḥsāʾ in 1753. From an early age he showed an inclination toward learning and an ascetic form of spirituality. In his autobiography he relates how as a child and a young man he experienced a series of initiatory dreams and visions in which certain of the twelve Shīʿī *imāms* and the Prophet Muḥammad taught him esoteric knowledge. These visionary experiences later became central in the formation of his philosophical and religious teachings on the nature and functions of the *imāms* in creation (al-Aḥsāʾī, 1957).

In the early 1790s Shaykh Aḥmad left his native country for Iraq. There he came into close contact with the controversies then stirring among the Twelver *ʿulamāʾ*. In religious debates dominated by questions of juristic authority, the *ʿulamāʾ* were largely divided into two camps: Uṣūlīyah and Akhbārīyah. The Uṣūlī triumph of the eighteenth century (the result of a mixture of power politics, rational argument, and intimidation) successfully raised the Uṣūlī *mujtahids* (the preeminent jurists) to a dominant position within Shiism through their doctrine of *taqlīd,* which dictated that the Shīʿah must follow the rulings of a living *mujtahid* on all matters of ritual practice. For their part the Akhbārīyah held that only the now-hidden twelfth *imām* is infallible, immune from sins, and therefore worthy to be followed; all persons, including learned scholars, are to follow the *imām.* Consequently they held that the Qurʾān and traditions reveal the will of God and provide sufficient guidance for the practice of Shiism; in the absence of explicit proof texts, the believer must forgo judgment on a ruling.

Shaykh Aḥmad remained uncommitted to either party. In Iraq he studied under leading representatives of both schools, but his philosophical worldview kept him aloof from identification with either Uṣūlī rationalism or Akhbārī conservatism. He quickly established a reputation for piety and learning and attracted a large following of students and admirers. In 1806 he ventured to Iran, where he gained increasing fame not only among the clerics but also with a large number of Qājār royalty, including Fatḥ ʿAlī Shāh, and powerful merchants.

In Iran Shaykh Aḥmad wrote his most important works dealing with the spiritual exegesis of Shīʿī traditions, discussing *al-Ziyārah al-Jāmiʿah* (1861), and critiques of the philosophical systems of Mullā Ṣadrā Shīrāzī, *al-Mashāʾir* and *al-ʿArshīyah* (1861), and of Muḥsin Fayḍ Kāshānī, *al-Risālah al-ʿilmīyah* (1856). His writings appear to have been widely circulated and commented on. Although he expressed his views cautiously and frequently resorted to *taqīyah* (pious dissimulation of one's true beliefs), his growing popularity and seeming unorthodox beliefs soon made him the target of fierce attacks from certain *mujtahids.*

Al-Aḥsāʾī was accused of holding that the *imāms* are the creators and sustainers of the cosmos (the notion of delegation, or *tafwīḍ*), a charge that arose from his understanding of certain traditions of the *imāms* dealing with ontology and the mystery of the emergence of being. Shaykh Aḥmad advanced a strict apophatic theology in which God remains forever beyond human comprehension and indeed beyond being as the essential divine ground (*kunh al-dhāt*). Yet other traditions and Qurʾanic verses indicate that the very purpose of human existence is to know and love a God who is closer to one than one's life vein. The bridge between the transcendence and immanence of God is the primordial Muḥammadan reality (*ḥaqīqah muḥammadīyah*), which is, for Shaykh Aḥmad, none other than the pleroma of the Fourteen Immaculate Ones (*chahārdah-i maʿṣūm,* namely Muḥammad, Fāṭimah, and the twelve Shīʿī *imāms*). Here the *imāms* are held to be eternal spiritual realities who, in their unity, are the creative primal will of God and the means through which God is known to persons. In Shaykh Aḥmad's hierarchy of being, the Fourteen Immaculate Ones are also designated as the "Light of Lights" (*nūr al-anwār*). It is only through the *imāms* in their reality as the primal will that a manifestation (*maẓhar*) of God occurs. On this point al-Aḥsāʾī differs with the Ishrāqī school of Shīʿī Neoplatonism, which sees the Light of Lights as the originating source of being.

Shaykh Aḥmad maintains that the *imāms*' nature as spiritual beings demands, in contrast to the dominant theology of Shiism, that the *imāms* exist within spiritual bodies situated in the visionary, mediate realm of Hūrqalyā, an intermediate world of archetypal figures (*ʿālam al-mithāl).* Within this imaginal world, the soul encounters the *imāms* and is transformed through a divine anthropomorphosis designated as a second or spiritual birth (*al-walādah al-rūḥānīyah*). It is in this archetypal region of being that the night journey (*miʿrāj*) of the Prophet and the final resurrection occur, a belief that undermines the insistence upon the physicality of these experiences in the dominant theology of Shiism (see Corbin, 1977, chaps. 9–11, for translations of Shaykhī texts on this theme).

Shaykh Aḥmad's rejection of the *mujtahids*' claims to authority also caused conflicts. As with the Akhbārīyah, Shaykh Aḥmad denies that believers must submit to the rulings of some *mujtahid.* Instead, he advances his doctrine of the Fourth Support (*al-rukn al-rābiʿ*). Shaykh Aḥmad logically reduces the traditional five bases of Shiism to three: the unity of God, prophethood, and the imamate. In addition there must always exist the "perfect Shīʿah": Shīʿī saints who serve as intermediaries between the *imāms* and believers. The perfect Shīʿah partake of the grace of the *imāms* through spiritual vision and not through the fallible discursive reasoning of the *mujtahids*. Consequently their knowledge of religious truths is immune from error by virtue of their intimacy with the *imāms.* Although Shaykh Aḥmad did not specifically claim to be the "bearer" of this Fourth Support, his description of the attributes of the perfect Shīʿī appears to be a self-portrait. Thus he distinguishes himself from earlier philosophers and theologians by asserting that he is at variance with both these groups because of his unique spiritual relationship with the *imāms.* Unlike the former, he "does not speak without being guided by the *imāms*" (al-Aḥsāʾī, 1957, p. 14).

In about 1822 an undistinguished *mujtahid* from Qazvin, Mullā Muḥammad Taqī Baraghānī, accused him of the heresies of *tafwīḍ* and the denial of bodily resurrection. Most of the leading *ʿulamāʾ* and philosophers remained sympathetic or neutral toward Shaykh Aḥmad, and it was not at this point that his close followers were considered to be heretics outside Shiism. Nevertheless this controversy prompted the *shaykh* to leave Iran for Iraq. There too Shaykh Aḥmad found himself at the center of debate with many *ʿulamāʾ* antagonistic to his views. Deciding that it was wiser to move once more, he set out for Mecca but died in 1826 at the age of seventy-three before he reached the holy city.

The Shaykhī School. Al-Aḥsāʾī designated Sayyid Qāʿim Rashtī (d. 1843) as his successor. Under Rashtī's leadership, the Shaykhī school emerged as a separate and organized movement within Shiism. Rashtī clearly formulated the Shaykhī doctrine of salvation history and the evolutionary cycles of revelation that had been ambiguously expressed by his master (al-Aḥsāʾī, 1956, vol. 1, p. 103). Possibly influenced by Ismāʿīlī ideas, Rashtī held that there are two ages of the dispensation of Muḥammad: the period of outward observances (*ẓawāhir*) and perfection of the *shariʿah*, followed by the period of inward realities (*bawāṭin*) and the disclosure of esoteric truths. The first age ended at the close of the twelfth Islamic century (eighteenth century CE), and Shaykh Aḥmad is held to be the first promulgator of the new age of inward realities. These views, not widely circulated but well known among Rashtī's closest followers, heightened a sense of millenarian hope among some Shaykhīyah for the full disclosure of the new age through the guidance of the perfect Shīʿah or possibly even the long-expected return of the Hidden *Imām.*

Despite opposition, the Shaykhīyah attained its greatest successes under Rashtī's leadership. Indeed the Shīʿah in Karbala became divided into Shaykhī and Uṣūlī factions. When Rashtī died without designating a successor, the movement splintered into several antagonistic parties, of which the three most important were the conservative Tabrīzī Shaykhīyah led by Mīrzā Ḥasan Gawhar (d. 1849), the Kirmānī Shaykhīyah led by the powerful Qājār notable Ḥājj Muḥammad Karīm Khān Kirmānī (1810–1870), and the Bābī movement led by Sayyid ʿAlī Muḥammad Shīrāzī (1819–1844), known as the Bāb.

The Tabrīzī Shaykhīyah later led by the Māmaqānī family played a central role in the trial and execution of the Bāb and reached a reconciliation with the Uṣūlīs. Henceforth they remained undistinguishable in outward practice and appearance from the rest of the Shīʿī community. Their only distinguishing feature was their championing of the character and thought of Shaykh Aḥmad.

The Bābī movement's millenarian fervor and eventual rejection of Shīʿī orthodoxy forced Karīm Khān to adjust Shaykhī teachings in order to distance himself and his party from the Bābīs. In contrast to the Bābīs, he emphasized the continuing role of the *imāms* and accepted the Uṣūlī legal method. Karīm Khān denied that either Shaykh Aḥmad or Sayyid Kāẓim was to be regarded as the Fourth Support of their day, for this is a general category of guides consisting of all Imāmī *ʿulamāʾ* (Kirmānī, Al-rukn al-rābiʿ, Kirman, 1949). Eventually the Kirmānī Shaykhīyah returned to the more mystical position that the Fourth Support is an unnamed spiritual hierarchy of saints who, like the Hidden *Imām,* remain unknown to the general populace. The Kirmānī Shaykhīyah came to regard themselves as an elite minority within Shiism, preserving and deepening the esoteric dimensions of Shiism through the guidance of their *shaykhs* (see Corbin, 1972). The leadership of the school remained in the Ibrāhīmī family, descendents of Karīm Khān. After the assassination of Shaykh ʿAbd al-Riḍā Khān Ibrāhīmī in the aftermath of the Iranian revolution of 1979, the school moved to Basra, where it is led by Sayyid ʿAlī al-Mūsawī. Kirmānī Shaykhī groups are found in the early twenty-first century in Iran and Iraq (particularly in Basra). Tabrīzī Shaykhīs (although unlike the Kirmānīs they never use the term) relocated to Karbala at the beginning of the twentieth century to rekindle the original Shaykhī community there under Rashtī. They are well integrated in the Twelver scholarly community (their leader is described as a *marja'*, a source of emulation using the Uṣūlī term) and are based in Kuwait, Saudi Arabia, Karbala, and Damascus, led in the early twenty-first century by Mīrzā ʿAbd Allāh Íā'irī Iḥqāqī.

SEE ALSO Bābīs.

BIBLIOGRAPHY

A useful summary of Shaykhī teachings is in chapter 2 of Mangol Bayat's *Mysticism and Dissent* (Syracuse, N.Y., 1982), which attempts to link the Shīʿī traditions of philosophical dissent to late-nineteenth-century and early-twentieth-century anticlerical, secular nationalists. On the relationship between the Shaykhīyah and the Bābīs, see Abbas Amanat's *Resurrection and Renewal* (Ithaca, N.Y., 1989); and Denis MacEoin's "Early Shaykhī Reactions to Babism," in *Studies in Babi and Baha'i History*, vol. 1, edited by Moojan Momen (Los Angeles, 1982) and "Orthodoxy and Heterodoxy in Nineteenth Century Shiism: The Cases of Shaykhism and Babism," *Journal of the American Oriental Society* 110 (1990): 323–329. Both Bayat and Amanat suffer from a Whiggish approach to Shaykhī history as a moment in the historical development of the Baha'i faith. A number of studies have appeared on Shaykh Aḥmad, including Juan Cole's "Shaykh Aḥmad al-Aḥsā'ī and the Sources of Religious Authority," in *The Most Learned of the Shīʿa*, edited by Linda Walbridge, pp. 82–93 (New York, 2001), and "The World as Text: Cosmologies of Shaykh Aḥmad al-Aḥsā'ī," *Studia Islamica* 80 (1994): 145–163. Idris S. Hamid's "The Metaphysics and Cosmology of Process" (Ph.D. diss., State University of New York, Buffalo, 1998) is a valuable study of the philosophical method and system of Shaykh Aḥmad. A useful modern biography is Muḥammad Isbir, *al-'Allāma al-Jalīl Shaykh Aḥmad ibn Zayn al-Dīn al-Aḥsā'ī fī dā'irat al-ḍaw'* (Beirut, Lebanon, 1993).

Garcia Scarcia's "Kirmān 1905: La 'Guerra' tra Seihī e Bālasarī," *Annali del Instituto Universitario di Napoli* 13 (1963): 186–203, discusses the Shaykhī-Uṣūlī division in Twelver Shiism. Denis MacEoin's "From Shaykhism to Babism" (Ph.D. diss., University of Cambridge, 1979) is an excellent study on the role of authority claims and the interplay of charismatic versus legal authority in the rise of the Shaykhī and Bābī movements. Moojan Momen's "Uṣūlī, Akhbārī, Shaykhī, Bābī: The Tribulations of a Qazwin Family," *Iranian Studies* 36 (2003): 317–337, is a masterful microhistorical study of relations between these differing groups.

Henry Corbin presents a concise study of the Kirmānī Shaykhī school, with emphasis on philosophical issues, in *L'école shaykhie en théologie shi'ite* (Tehran, Iran, 1967), an expanded version of which appears in his *En Islam iranien*, vol. 4, bk. 6 (Paris, 1972). M. A. Amir-Moezzi's "An Absence Filled with Presences," *BSOAS* 64 (2001): 1–18, is a useful study of Shaykhī hermeneutics. Shaykhī ontology and eschatology are treated in Vahid Rafati's "The Development of Shaykhī Thought in Shīʿī Islam" (Ph.D. diss., University of California, Los Angeles, 1979). A. L. M. Nicolas's *Essai sur le cheikisme*, 4 vols. (Paris, 1910–1914), is outdated but contains some valuable biographical information.

There are many primary sources for the history and teachings of the Shaykhīyah, including more than one hundred tracts by Shaykh Aḥmad. For a comprehensive catalog of Shaykhī primary sources, see Abū al-Qāsim Khān Ibrāhīmī's *Fihrist-i kutub-i Shaykh Aḥmad Aḥsā'ī va sā'ir mashāyikh-i ʿiẓām*, 3d ed. (Kirman, Iran, 1977); now abridged and translated by Moojan Momen as a Bulletin of Baha'i Studies Monograph (Newcastle, U.K., 1991). Among Shaykh Aḥmad's published works are his autobiography, *Sīrat al-Shaykh Aḥmad al-Aḥsā'ī* (Baghdad, 1957); *Jawāmi' al-kalim*, 2 vols. (Tabrīz, Iran, 1856–1860), a general collection; *Sharḥ al-Ziyārah al-Jāmi'ah al-kabīrah*, 4 vols. (Tehran, 1850–1851), a vast commentary that provides a veritable *summa* of Shīʿī philosophy as a commentary on a famous supplication and visitation recitation of the tenth *imām*, ʿAlī al-Hādī; and other commentaries on the writings of Mullā Ṣadrā (Tabrīz, Iran, 1861–1862). Most of these works have been reprinted in Beirut since the late 1990s and are available on Shaykhī websites. A new institute, Mu'assasat al-Fikr al-Awḥad, based in Damascus and founded by the Tabrīzī and Karbalā'ī Shaykhīs, has been producing studies and editions of the works of Shaykh Aḥmad since 2001. Shaykhī texts on the theme of spiritual bodies are translated in Henry Corbin's *Spiritual Body and Celestial Earth* (Princeton, N.J., 1977), chaps. 9–11.

The World Wide Web has become a major resource for Arabic texts and academic studies. A descriptive bibliography of the Shaykhīyah by Stephen Lambden is at http://www.hurqalya.pwp.blueyonder.co.uk/SHAYKHISM/shaykhism-bib1.htm. Two academic sites affiliated with H-Net, with primary source materials in translation and studies, are "Occasional Papers in Shaykhi, Babi and Baha'i Studies" at http://www.h-net.org/~bahai/bhpapers.htm and "Translations of Shaykhi, Babi and Baha'i Texts" at http://www.h-net.org/~bahai/trans.htm. The Kirmānī Shaykhīs have a site with an extensive library of texts at http://www.alabrar.info. There are also a number of Tabrīzī and Karbalā'ī Shaykhī sites, including http://www.awhad.com.

STEVEN SCHOLL (1987)
SAJJAD H. RIZVI (2005)

SHCHERBATSKII, FEDOR SEE STCHERBATSKY, THEODORE

SHEEP AND GOATS appear frequently in the history of religions, from prehistoric times down to the present, and across a wide geographic area. Both appear most commonly as animals of sacrifice, but the ram and especially the goat have also served as symbols of sexual virility and so are often associated with fertility cults.

PREHISTORIC TIMES. Evidence of the symbolic importance of sheep and goats in prehistoric times comes primarily from their representation in art. Their importance as totemic animals among some contemporary tribal peoples also presumably reflects much more ancient beliefs.

Prior to their domestication in the Neolithic period, wild sheep and goats were hunted as game and seem to have become cult objects quite early. In Upper Paleolithic art, for instance, 7 percent of the animal representations consist of images of rams. From the Neolithic period to the Bronze Age, depictions of both goats and rams (most commonly the former) are encountered quite often in the art of Mesopotamia, Iran, Afghanistan, and Central Asia. It may be assumed that beliefs and myths connected with these animals underwent a considerable development at this time.

On a diadem from Hissar III (Iran, first half of the second millennium BCE) images of rams and goats are arranged in mirrorlike symmetry. In Çatal Hüyük (Asia Minor, seventh and sixth millennia BCE) ram heads are depicted on the walls of sanctuaries. Rams seem to have been associated with the goddess who is also depicted there as a kind of proprietress of human beings and of both wild and domestic animals. On a wall of the Leopard Sanctuary, also at Çatal Hüyük, there is a depiction of a stylized tree with a goatlike animal on either side. This general motif, a tree or a plant with flanking sheep or goats, is very common in pottery decoration and glyptic art from this period. Symbolic representations of water (perhaps rain) and of snakes are also found in connection with it. These mythologems became very widespread and existed up to modern times in Central Asia.

More indirect evidence for the religious importance of sheep and goats in Neolithic times comes from the practices of various tribal peoples. Their survivals of worship of sheep as totemic animals up to the modern period may represent a practice that goes back to very ancient times. One such practice was the prohibition against eating mutton among some tribes of Madagascar, who believed that tribal members were descended from sheep. The sheep was also a totemic animal for the Kharia of Bengal, the Kalanga of South Africa, the Batoro of Uganda, and the tribes of the Altaic region, among others. The fact that the word for "ram" is contained in the Greek family name Krioid (from the Greek *krios*) may hint at an earlier totemic belief in Greece as well. Finally, it should be noted that the goat has served as a totemic animal among some San (Bushmen) tribes of southern Africa.

HISTORICAL TIMES. In historical times one begins to find more differentiated notions of the symbolic importance of sheep and goats and are thus able to discuss each in more detail.

Sheep. Because of the innate traits and behavior of sheep, such qualities as gentleness, timidity, inoffensiveness, and passivity have been consistently attributed to them. These qualities have also been interpreted as expressions of innocence, mildness, simplicity, and love, and, consequently, as a willingness to be sacrificed. The sheep's defenselessness against predators (some animals are actually called "sheep eaters") also made a deep cultural impression. Considering such perceptions of sheep, and taking into account their relatively high fecundity (and hence their availability and expendability), it becomes easy to understand how the idea of the sheep as a sacrificial animal came into being and became widespread in Judaism, ancient Greece, ancient China, and elsewhere.

Numerous examples of sheep as sacrificial animals can be found in the Judeo-Christian tradition. A lamb was slaughtered in the Israelite Passover rite (*Ex.* 12:21–24, *Nm.* 8:8–12). In the New Testament, in both the *Gospel of John* and the *Book of Revelation,* Christ is referred to as the Lamb of God who redeems the sins of the world (*Jn.* 1:29, 1:36; *Rv.* 5:6–14, 6:1): that is, the killing of Christ is directly compared to the slaughtering of a sacrificial sheep in order to take away sins (compare the motif of the scapegoat). Lamb is the traditional meal during Christian celebrations of Easter; marzipan and chocolate lambs holding flags—to represent Christ victorious—are also popular at Easter time.

Sheep have been sacrificial animals among many other peoples as well. In the Islamic world, the ritual slaughter of a sheep is called for during the feast of the pilgrimage. Just as in the Judeo-Christian tradition a ram is sacrificed in the place of Isaac, in the Islamic tradition a ram is substituted for Ishmael.

Among the ancient Greeks sheep were sacrificed to Aphrodite and Zeus, and also to the chthonic gods. For sacrifice to the last a black sheep or ram was used and was allowed to be completely consumed by fire, whereas when sacrifices were made to other gods most of the animal's flesh was reserved to be eaten. The most important sacrifice was the Kriobolion ("slaughter of sheep"), an orgiastic and mystical event associated with the cult of Attis.

In addition to their use in sacrifice, sheep have also been associated with weddings and thus with fertility. In ancient Athens, for instance, the fleece of a sacred sheep (*aegis*) was brought by a priestess to newly married women. The ram, viewed primarily as a symbol of sexual power, played an even more important role in Classical Greece. It was associated mainly with the cult of Hermes but also with the cults of Aphrodite, Zeus, Poseidon, Cybele, Hera, Hephaistos, the sileni, and the satyrs. Although Hermes was often depicted next to sheep or riding a sheep, particular emphasis was placed on the ram and especially on its connection with virility. The size and weight of the ram's sexual organ were commented upon, and it was believed that a good ram could cover fifty ewes. Such beliefs are reflected in mythology: Hermes, burning with love for Persephone, decided to approach her in the form of a ram. It was thought that a god could have much more amorous enjoyment in the form of a ram than as a human. The ram was also connected with gold and the sun, both symbols of vital power.

In Rome there were similar beliefs and practices. Sheep were favored as sacrificial animals and were offered to Mars, Faunus (the protector of sheep and flocks), Pales, and Dea Dia. They were also associated, as in Greece, with weddings: A bridegroom and his bride were required to sit on a sheepskin that was specially sanctified for the occasion. Finally, sheep also seem to have acquired a chthonic meaning in

Rome: They were used in the cult of the *lares* and *manes,* sacrificed to the dead, and depicted on tombs.

In ancient Egypt the cult of the ram was widespread. On the island of Elephantine the ram was believed to embody the local god Khnum. Excavations there have revealed the burial ground of the sacred rams of Khnum's temple, and actual mummies of sacred rams have been found. In Mendes (which means "ram"), the ram embodied Osiris, the Egyptian god of the underworld, and in Thebes the sun god Amun was depicted as a ram.

Various Hindu deities are associated with the ram as well. Indra, the warrior god, is called a ram in the *Ṛgveda* (1.10.2, 1.51.1), and one of the forms of the god of fire, Agni, was that of a ram.

The ancient and modern peoples of Iran and Central Asia have many beliefs concerning sheep. Among the Pamiri of Central Asia, sheep are believed to have a divine nature and are associated with the sun. A story is told of a sacred sheep, illumined by a sacred flame, descending from the mountains. In the Islamic version of this story, the sheep is said to have been sent by the Prophet. In the Pahlavi-Sasanid work *Karnamag* (eleventh century), an enormous ram symbolizes the happiness (*farr*) of the king and his dynasty, and more broadly the happiness and well-being of any man. In Iranian Sasanid art, rams are depicted with ceremonial ribbons around their necks, for sheep were believed to bring happiness and health; if one walked through a flock of sheep one would free oneself of disease. There is a striking parallel to these Iranian themes in the Chinese tradition, where the term for happiness consists of the graphs for "man" and "ram." For the Kalmuks, a Mongolian people, the ram is a symbol of fertility and abundance, and a white ram is believed to be a creature from heaven. The connection of the ram with fertility is found in Hittite and Russian rituals as well. The mountain Tajiks annually attach drawings of a ram's horn to the front walls of their houses in order to increase fertility.

Many ancient beliefs and practices were connected with the chthonic nature of the ram. The late Bronze Age cemeteries of northern Afghanistan and southern Uzbekistan contain separate burials of goats and rams isolated from the human graves and supplied with a large number of vessels and even funeral food—part of the carcass of a ram! Evidently the animals were substituted for human corpses that for some reason could not be buried here. Much later, in graves in Ferghana (Central Asia) dating from the seventh and eighth centuries CE, rams were buried equipped with saddles and bridles, evidently as substitutes for horses. The mountain people of the Iagnob River valley in Tajikistan held a funeral feast for a dead sheep as though it were human. The Tajiks believed that if a person killed a ram for a purpose pleasing to God, a ram would meet that person in the next world to carry him or her across the bridge leading to paradise; similiar beliefs are found in Islamic culture generally and among the Turkmens, who thought it necessary to slaughter a ram at the moment when a corpse was brought out of the house for burial. Zoroastrians have also believed that one could be helped to cross the Chinvat Bridge leading to Heaven by the ritualistic sacrifice of a ram.

Goats. In religious practice and mythology, goats have been important as symbols of extraordinary virility and fecundity and as animals associated with the profane. Like the sheep, the goat has also long been a favorite animal of sacrifice.

Many references to goats can be found in the ancient Near East. A Babylonian hymn compares Ishtar to a goat and Tammuz to a kid. Also in Babylonia, a goat was sacrificed in order to rid a person of disease. The goat was killed while a tamarisk knife was drawn across the person's throat, and the goat was then buried as if it were a person. Among the Hittites, the parts of the body of a newborn child were homologized to the body of a sacrificed goat. In a Sumerian tradition the goat was linked with the god Enki, who had the form of a goat in front and a fish's tail in back and who was crowned with the head of a ram. This bizarre combination reflects Enki's nature as ruler of both water and plants.

In the Israelite religion the goat was the preferred sacrifice to Yahveh. Here is also found the institution of the "scapegoat." A goat was brought before a priest, who placed his hands upon its head while enumerating the sins of the people. A special envoy then took the goat into an impassable wilderness and let it go. Upon return the envoy had to undergo a ritual purification (*Lv.* 16:3–28). The practice was not limited to the Israelites alone, however, but was common to many peoples, although the expelled animal was not always a goat.

The goat was less important to the Greeks. Nevertheless, depictions of goat-demons appeared at a very early period in Greek art. In Classical Greece this was Pan, with hooves and horns but with a man's body and head. His Roman analogue was Faunus, who was called the "goat god," although he was originally worshiped as a wolf god.

The Olympian god most closely associated with the goat was Dionysos. According to one legend, Zeus changed the young Dionysos into a kid, which Hermes brought to the nymphs at Mount Nysa. Dionysos was able to assume the form of a goat and was sometimes regarded as a goat. His progeny were often seen as goatlike; goats were offered to him in sacrifice, and the goat was his attribute. Such beliefs and practices were doubtless connected with the cult of vegetation and fertility, which is also the link between the goat and the cult of Aphrodite. The goat was her sacred animal, which she was often portrayed as riding. The goat also played a role in the cults of Zeus, Hera, Apollo, Artemis, and Hermes, and the Greeks had the institution of the scapegoat as well. In Rome, goats were sacrificed during the Lupercalia and were also associated with the storm deities.

Goats appear in ancient Indian religion in several connections. The god Agni sometimes had a goat as his mount.

The Asvins were compared to two goats (*Ṛgveda* 2.39.2–3). The deity Pusan, who was associated with the sun and with roads, rode on a chariot harnessed to goats (*Ṛgveda* 6.58.2), and during the Asvamedha (the horse sacrifice) a goat was sacrificed to him. The goat's connection with fertility is also apparent in ancient India; a woman wanting a child had to eat the ritually cooked flesh of a red goat (*Kausitaki Sankhayana* 35.17ff.). The milk of a red goat was believed to protect one from misfortune.

In Zoroastrianism, Verethraghna, the god of victory, is sometimes described as a "beautiful wild goat with sharp horns" (*Yasht* 14.8.25). In Mithraic reliefs the goat symbolizes a mortal being at the peak of vitality and power.

A cult of the goat was widespread from ancient times in Central Asia. The depiction of a goat on a figurine dating from the beginning of the third millennium BCE establishes the existence at that period of a goddess in whose cult a goat figured importantly. Traces of this cult can still be found among the inhabitants of the Pamir and among the Nuristani, inhabitants of the Hindu Kush. The latter have even retained the altars of this goddess, Markum, to whom women annually sacrifice a goat. For the Pamiri this goddess has become a peri, or fairy, who is recognized as the sole owner and proprietress of the mountain goats. When a hunter kills a goat, his kill is believed to be the gift of the heavenly owner of goats, the peri.

Ancient beliefs about goats have survived in the folklore of various modern peoples. The sacrifice of a goat figures in the Russian fairy tale about Alenushka and her brother Ivanushka, for instance, and the goat Schmierbock appears in Norwegian folk tales as the owner of a treasure of gold. Goats are often described as sources of light and milk and are associated with the Milky Way. The goat Heiðrún gives mead in Valhǫll, while in Indian stories the goat gives neither milk nor mead but coins. An Estonian folktale features a serpent king with a golden cup that contains the milk of a heavenly goat and has the properties of a magic mirror. Modern-day mummers continue to link the goat with the ancient cult of fertility when they sing "Where the goat goes, there the wheat grows" and when they portray the mock death of a goat and its subsequent resurrection.

As in ancient times, the goat continues to be associated in various traditions with the netherworld and with chthonic power. In this respect the goat is opposed to the "pure" lamb. A Slavic popular belief holds that a water sprite can be appeased with the pelt of a black goat; among the Slavs a black goat was sometimes sacrificed to a deceased person. In Slavic and Germanic folklore the Devil has the hooves of a goat.

Finally, it should be noted that the goat figures importantly in astrological symbolism (Capricorn the Goat is a sign of the zodiac, as is Aries the Ram), folk medicine, heraldry, and the interpretation of dreams.

See Also Scapegoat.

Bibliography

The literature on beliefs connected with the ram and the goat is extensive. A general compilation of information on animals, although partly outdated, is Angelo de Gubernatis's *Zoological Mythology, or Legends of Animals,* vol. 1 (London, 1872). See also Jean-Pierre Dones's *Des animaux dans la mythologie* (Lyons, 1956), a very useful survey, and *Mify narodov mira,* 2 vols. (Moscow, 1980–1982), an excellent compilation of mythological and religious information. Ancient beliefs are analyzed in depth in E. V. Antonova's *Ocherki kul'tury drevnikh zemledel'tsev Perednei i Srednei Azii: Opyt rekonstruktsii mirovospriiatiia* (Moscow, 1984). The best compilation of the beliefs of antiquity is Otto Keller's *Die antike Tierwelt,* vol. 1 (Leipzig, 1909). A basic study is *The Scapegoat,* vol. 9 of James G. Frazer's *The Golden Bough,* 3d ed., rev. & enl. (London, 1913). For Central Asia and adjacent areas, see my *Kangiuisko-sarmatskii farn (k istoriko-kul'turnym sviaziam plemen iuzhnoi Rossii i Srednei Azii)* (Dushanbe, 1968), translated into German as "Das Kangzhu-Sarmatische Farnah," *Central Asiatic Journal* 16 (1972): 241–289 and 20 (1976): 47–74; and my *Sredniaia Aziia v drevnosti i srednevekov'e* (Moscow, 1977).

New Sources

Bonney, Meta. *The World of Sheep and Goats.* Carmarthen, U.K., 1993.

Edwards, Jeanette. "Why Dolly Matters: Kinship, Culture, and Cloning." *Ethnos: Journal of Anthropology* 63 (November 1999): 301–325.

Shoemaker, H. Stephen. "Sheep and Goats." *Christian Century* 117 (July 5–12, 2002): 714.

B. A. Litvinskii (1987)
Translated from Russian by Sylvia Juran
Revised Bibliography

SHEKHINAH. The term *Shekhinah,* generally translated as "presence," was coined by rabbinic sages in the formative period (first through sixth centuries) to denote the manifestation of a transcendent God in the world of space and time. On balance, there is little evidence in classical rabbinic literature that *Shekhinah* denotes a hypostatic entity ontically distinct from God, a secondary or demiurgical being akin to the Logos in the writings of Philo or in the prologue to the *Gospel of John.* As a number of scholars have noted, in most instances, *Shekhinah* is used interchangeably for the supreme divine being, though it is evident that the reference is, more specifically, to the appearance of God in history and nature, a mythopoeic expression of divine providence related especially to Israel. This theme is epitomized in a dictum that has instilled hope in the hearts of pious Jews through many a dark moment, *Shekhinah* accompanies the Jewish nation into exile (Babylonian Talmud, *Megillah* 29a). The implication of this promise is clearly that the deliverance of Israel from exile heralds the redemption of God, a bold mythical idea that a number of rabbis insist must be accepted since Scripture sanctions it explicitly.

The word *shekhinah* is derived from the root *shkn,* which means to dwell, to abide, and thus it is functionally synonymous with *kavod*, the scriptural expression used to designate the divine glory, the revelatory aspect of God that assumes material form—most often of a luminous nature—in relation to the people of Israel. Related to *shkn* is *mishkan*, the priestly designation of the Tabernacle, the temporary abode of God's indwelling that accompanied the Israelites on the sojourn through the desert (*Ex.* 40:34-38), the prototype of the Jerusalem Temple built in the time of Solomon, which is described in similar language as the place where God shall abide if the Israelites uphold the covenant and obey the commandments (*1 Kgs* 6:13). In the Solomonic account, a paradox that has plagued the religious sensibility of Jews from time immemorial is made explicit: on one hand, God describes himself as dwelling in the darkness of the thick cloud, *lishkon ba-arafel* (*1 Kgs.* 8:12; cf. *Ex.* 20:18; *Dt.* 5:19; *2 Sm.* 22:10; *Ps.* 18:10, 97:2; *Jb.* 38:9; *2 Chr.* 6:1), an image that conveys the inherent inscrutability and hiddenness of the divine, and yet, on the other hand, it is the will of God that summons Solomon to build a "stately house" *(beit zevul)* to serve as a place for his dwelling eternally (*1 Kgs.* 8:13), a domicile to give shelter to the name (*1 Kgs.* 20), a locution that resonates with the Deuteronomistic emphasis on the abiding of the divine name (*shem*) in the sanctuary (*Dt.* 12:5, 11; 14:23-24; 16:11). The glory inhabits the earthly temple through the agency of the name, presumably the tetragrammaton, a conception that is related to the widespread belief in the ancient Near East concerning the magical power of divine or angelic names. The query placed in the mouth of Solomon when he addresses God as he stands before the altar reflects the anxiety that lies at the core of this paradox: "But will God really dwell on earth? Even the heavens and the heaven of heavens cannot contain You, how much less this house that I have built" (*1 Kgs.* 8:28). In the continuation of Solomon's remarks, the reader confronts one of the axiomatic principles of theistic faith that persists to this very day:

> Turn, O Lord my God, to the prayer and supplication of Your servant, and heed the song and prayer that Your servant offers before You this day. May your eyes be open night and day toward this House, to the place of which you have said "Let My name be there," to heed the prayer that your servant prays toward this place. And You will listen to the supplications of Your servant and Your people Israel that they pray toward this place, and You will give heed in Your place of dwelling in heaven (*el meqom shivttekha el ha-shamayim*), You will listen and pardon (*1 Kgs* 8:28-30).

This archaic text captures the insight that the possibility of prayer within a theisitic context, that is, a religious setting that presumes a personal deity attentive to human needs, is dependent on the representation of God in embodied form, which, in turn, necessitates the construction of a physical place where this form will reside—even though it is forbidden to depict it iconically—and become accessible to the worshipper. From the aforecited verses readers learn, moreover, that the sacred space below corresponds to the imaginal construct of the heavenly Temple, an idea well attested in ancient Near Eastern mythologies and reaffirmed in different cultural settings throughout Jewish history; it is precisely the offering of prayer in the former that activates God's forgiveness in the latter. Solomon cannot logically resolve the paradox of how a God so vast that he cannot be contained by the heavens will reside in the earthly Temple. Interestingly, there is a rabbinic text, transmitted in the name of Rabbi Yoḥanan by Rabbi Judah bar Simon, that expands on Solomon's wonder by placing an analogous question in the mouth of Moses. Perhaps the theological significance of the midrashic text lies in the fact that it deepens the scriptural mystery and comes close to offering the rabbinic version of a kenotic incarnation: When Moses is commanded to build the Tabernacle, he trembles and asks God how the presence can reside in the Tabernacle when all the heavens cannot contain him, recalling that when Solomon built the Temple, a physical space larger than the Tabernacle, he posed a similar question to God. The divine response is instructive: "Moses, it is not as you think, rather twenty planks on the north, twenty planks on the south, eight on the west (*Ex.* 26:18-25), and I will descend and constrict my presence in your midst below (*ered u-metsamtsem shekhinati beineikhem lematan*)" (*Pesiqta' Rabbati* 2:10; compare *Exodus Rabbah* 34:1). Paradoxical though it may be, God has the capacity to delimit his presence to a constricted physical space, whether the Tabernacle, the Temple, or the Synagogue; the spiritual calling of liturgical worship within a theistic framework demands this very possibility. Lest there be any misunderstanding, it must be stated emphatically that the rabbinic text does not employ the language of emptying and suffering the humility of death, hallmark features of the kenotic orientation, scripturally anchored in *Philippians* 2:7-8. This use of the term "kenosis" to depict the midrashic theme is limited to the theme of God constricting his presence to a space with distinctive and measurable boundaries, an occurrence that would necessitate self-limitation on the part of the seemingly limitless divine being.

A crucial verse that doubtlessly informed the rabbinic conception is the command uttered by God to the Israelites through Moses, "They should make a sanctuary (*miqdash*) for me and I will dwell (*shakhanti*) in their midst" (*Ex.* 25:8). This surmise regarding the rabbis is supported by the rendering of the verse in Targum Onkelos, one of the ancient Aramaic interpretative translations of the Torah: "And they shall make a sanctuary before Me and I shall cause My *Shekhinah* to dwell among them (*asherei shekhinetti beineihon*)." The disclosure of the divine presence requires an enclosure—the root of the word *miqdash*, "sanctuary," is *qdsh*, which means, primarily, "to set aside" and, secondarily, "to consecrate," to separate holy from mundane—initially the transient Tent of Meeting *(ohel mo'ed)* and later the stationary Temple (*beit miqdash*). In accord with some of the Jerusalem priests responsible for the section of Torah demarcated by biblical scholars as P, the priestly stratum, identified more recently by Israel Knohl as the "Holiness School," a distinct layer within this stratum, the theological rationale for the narrative of Israel's sacred history is linked especially to the *mishkan*, the edifice that provided an enclosure to both shelter the glory and facilitate its disclosure in the community of the holy people (*Lv.* 15:31, 28:11): "I will dwell (*shakhanti*) amidst the children of Israel, and I will be their God. And they will know that I am the Lord their God who brought them out of Egypt that I might dwell (*leshokhni*) in their midst, I am the Lord their God" (*Ex.* 29:45-46). The demand for ritual purity contained in the priestly interdictions, particularly salient in the holiness code (*Lv.* 18), which had a profound impact on the religious sensibility promulgated by the rabbis in their construction of a halakhic framework, was in no small measure dependent on the mythopoeic belief in the material abiding of the divine presence in the midst of the Israelites (*Nm.* 5:3, 16:3).

In general terms, the rabbinic conception of *Shekhinah* is phenomenologically on a par with the priestly notion. To be sure, the rabbis formulated their ideas after the destruction of the Second Temple in 70 CE, and thus, in contrast to the priests whose views are preserved in Scripture, the abiding of *Shekhinah* is not restricted to the physical space where the sacrificial cult is performed. The Temple, tellingly referred to by Onkelos as the "house of His presence," *beit shekhintteih* (*Dt* 12:5), is replaced by the rabbinic institutions of the schoolroom (*beit midrash*), the synagogue (*beit keneset*), and the domestic space of the family, as these are the main locations wherein one can access the indwelling of the divine presence through the cultivation of a life of holiness by means of the performance of ritual. Rabbinically, the two primary ways of worshipping God in the absence of the sacrificial cult were Torah study and prayer. Concerning the former, a classic formulation of this sentiment is found in the respective dicta of Rabbi Hananyah ben Teradyon and Rabbi Halafta from the village of Hananyah. According to the former, if two men sit down together to study Torah, *Shekhinah* resides with them (Mishnah, *Pirqei Avot* 3:2); according to the latter, *Shekhinah* dwells amidst ten men who sit together, occupied with Torah, though he eventually acknowledges that *Shekhinah* is found even with the solitary individual engaged in study (Mishnah, *Pirqei Avot,* 3:6; compare Babylonian Talmud, *Berakhot* 6a).

The rabbinic emphasis on the indwelling of *Shekhinah* should not be taken as a mere figurative expression, or as a circumlocution to avoid an anthropomorphic conception of the deity, but rather as signifying an encounter that approximates the intensity of mystical experience. The view that *Shekhinah* dwells with the man who studies Torah by himself is supported by the prooftext "In every place where I cause my name to be mentioned I will come to you and bless you" (*Ex.* 20:21). Implicit in the homiletical use of this verse is the presumption that the name of God is symbolically interchangeable with Torah, an idea that became a cornerstone for various forms of medieval Jewish esotericism. It is reasonable to suppose, moreover, that underlying the rabbinic belief that study of Torah facilitates the indwelling of *Shekhinah* is a presumption regarding the congruence of the hermeneutical enterprise and religious experience that may even be on the level of prophetic revelation. Such an interpretative possibility is supported by a Talmudic pericope that begins with a comment attributed to the third-century Palestinian Amora, Avdimi of Haifa: "From the day the Temple was destroyed, prophecy was taken from the prophets (*nevi'im*) and given to the sages (*ḥakhamim*)." The anonymous redactor interposes the rhetoric query, "Is it not the case that a sage (*ḥakham*) is a prophet (*navi*)? Thus it is said even though it is taken from the prophets it is not taken from the sages." At this juncture the redactor transmits the teaching of Ameimar, a fifth-century Babylonian Amora, "The sage is preferable to the prophet (*ḥakham adif mi-navi*), as it says 'and the prophet wise of heart' (*Ps.* 90:12). Who is dependent upon whom? I would say the lesser one is dependent on the greater" (Babylonian Talmud, *Baba Batra* 12a). Ameimar's exegetical proof rests on an intentional misreading of the Masoretic text from *Psalms* 90:12 (also attested in the Targum to the verse), *we-navi levav hohkmah*, part of the psalmist's appeal to God, *limnot yamenu ken hoda we-navi lev hokhmah*, "Instruct us to number our days that we might gain wisdom of the heart." Ameimar reads *wenavi* (*nun-bet-alef*), "and we might gain," as *we-navi (nun-bet-yod-alef)* "and the prophet," a textual change—and not simply an eisegetical interpretation masked as exegesis—that lends support to his claim that the sage is more worthy than the prophet. The strategy reflected in the dictum of Avdimi is not to deny the efficacy of prophecy nor is it based on the supposition that the institution of prophecy ended at a certain period in the past. On the contrary, prophecy endures, but since the destruction of the Temple it has been entrusted to the sages, an insight that affirms not only that prophetic vision serves scholastic wisdom, but also that scholastic wisdom is inherently visionary. This, one suggests, is the intent of Ameimar's dictum "The sage is preferable to the prophet"—textual study, the principle task of the sage, is not merely on a par with prophecy, but it is itself a prophetic undertaking.

The juxtaposition of Torah study and the indwelling of *Shekhinah* points to the influential role assigned by rabbinic authorities to the imagination in actively configuring the semiotic body of God. The key source that articulates the contemplative practice of visualization is a passage wherein the dictum "It matters not whether one augments or one diminishes if only one orients one's heart to heaven" (Babylonian Talmud, *Berakhot* 5b) is applied to Torah study. The proper intention, *kawwanah*, required by study entails that one direct one's heart to God, *she-yekhawwen libbo la-shamayim.* The word *kawwanah* is derived from *kiwwen* (from the root *kwn*), to turn or to face a particular direction, to orient oneself, to find one's spatial bearings. Despite the many embellishments and transformations of this critical term through the course of the history of Jewish thought and religious philosophy, something of its etymological foundation is retained, for *kawwanah* involves an orientation in space, an intentional facing, a directing of the heart to the other. But what is it to face the other when the face of the other is not visible, to turn one's gaze upon that which cannot be seen? Here one arrives at the phenomenological mystery of the rabbinic notion of incarnation: By directing the heart through study heavenward, the celestial habitation of the transcendent other (the word *shamayim*, which literally means "heaven," is one of God's appellations in rabbinic thought), the individual provides the mental space wherein the incorporeal God is embodied. The body of *Shekhinah* is composed of the letters of Torah, which is the name, but that body is apprehended only when Torah is contemplated with the appropriate intention.

In a similar manner, the rabbinic conception of *kawwanah* in prayer, at least according to one trajectory discernible in the landscape of rabbinic texts, entailed the visual apprehension of the divine presence in the imagination. In this context, the term *kawwanah* refers to an internal state of consciousness by means of which the worshiper creates a mental icon of God. Although one must speak of this as an "internal" state, the phenomenal boundaries of inside and outside dissolve, for only by means of the internal image does the worshiper experience the divine as external. The conception of mental imaging is epitomized in the teaching attributed to Simeon the Pious, reported by Hana ben Bizna: "The one who prays must see himself as if *Shekhinah* were opposite him, as it says, 'I have set the Lord always before me' (*Ps.* 16:8)" (Babylonian Talmud, *Sanhedrin* 22a). Prayer requires a visualization of that which cannot be visualized, a process predicated on the assumption that God can assume incarnate form. The word "incarnate" refers to the ontic presencing of God in a theophanic image, a form that should be distinguished from both the embodiment of God in human flesh and the metaphorical representation of that which cannot be represented in a rhetorical trope. The specific form that this image assumes is suggested by the prooftext cited by Simeon the Pious, *shiwwiti yhwh lenegddi tamid*, "I shall place the tetragrammaton before me constantly." The image that the worshiper must set in his mind is that of the ineffable name, the sign of that which cannot be signified, for only through the name is the invisible rendered visible. Rabbinic discussions on the intention in prayer are based on the notion of an imaginal body attributed to God. The form that the body of *Shekhinah* assumes, which inheres in human imagination, is constituted by the letters of the unutterable name (un)spoken in the sacred space of prayer.

The symbol of *Shekhinah* continued to play a decisive role in the various genres of medieval Jewish religious creativity, to wit, rabbinic homilies, biblical commentaries, philosophical treatises, mystical compositions, and liturgical poetry. In the minds of qabbalists, in particular, *Shekhinah* is accorded a significance, both quantative and qualitative, unparalleled in earlier texts. As the theosophic system of the qabbalah crystallized in the twelfth and thirteenth centuries, *Shekhinah* routinely was associated with the last of the ten *sefirot*, the luminous attributes that constitute the revealed aspect of the hidden God, although one also finds evidence in some sources, including *Sefer ha-Bahir*, one of the earliest documents that expounds a theosophic conception, a distinction (which can be traced terminologically to pre-qabbalistic texts) between *Shekhinah* above and *Shekhinah* below; interpreted qabbalistically, the former is associated with the third *sefirah*, *binah*, and the latter with the tenth, *malkhut*. Needless to say, qabbalists absorb many of the older rabbinic portrayals of *Shekhinah*, but what is most distinctive about their approach is the explicit representation of the divine presence in a litany of female images, to wit, matronae, bride, daughter, sister, mother, community of Israel, heavenly Jerusalem, throne, temple, tabernacle, moon, sea, and earth, just to mention a few of the salient examples.

To appreciate the gender valence associated with *Shekhinah*, it is necessary to contextualize the matter in a broader hermeneutical and cultural perspective. Undeniably, one of the great contributions of qabbalists to the history of Judaism is the explicit utilization of gender images to depict the nature of God and the consequent application of erotic symbolism to characterize the divine-human relationship. In line with earlier rabbinic tradition regarding the two main attributes of God, but explicating the sexual implications far more openly, qabbalists envisage the unity of God in androgynous terms as the coupling of male and female, which are respectively aligned with the attributes of lovingkindness and judgment, the right and left side of the divine economy. Gender symbolism in traditional qabbalistic literature is dynamic, presupposing, as it does, crossing of boundaries and intermingling of identity, male in female and female in male, one containing the other within which the other is contained. In spite of the flexibility of gender transformation, however, the process is determined by an inflexible structure, and hence while one may legitimately speak of variability in qabbalistic gender symbolism, it is not helpful to introduce the notion of ambiguity. Male and female are correlated consistently with the activity of projection and the passivity of restriction: the potency to overflow is masculine, the capacity to withhold feminine. The religious obligation imposed traditionally on the Jewish man to unify God is interpreted as the harnessing of male and female, a pairing of right and left, the will to bestow and the desire to contain. But, just as the entirety of the Godhead is androgynous, so each of the *sefirot* exemplifies the dual capacity to overflow and to receive, and *Shekhinah* is no exception. In relation to the *sefirot* above her, *Shekhinah* receives the divine efflux and is thus engendered as feminine; in relation to the worlds below her, *Shekhinah* overflows and is thus engendered as masculine. The sovereignty or governance over this world—in virtue of which the name *malkhut*, "kingship," is attributed to *Shekhinah*—is not indicative of a positive valorization of the feminine, as some have maintained, but rather it marks the capacity of *Shekhinah* to be transformed into a demiurgic being, which is masculine in relation to the worlds beneath the realm of divine emanations.

In spite of the symbolic representation of God as male and female, the gender orientation of medieval qabbalists was androcentric in nature, and, consequently, both the male and female elements, active bestowal and passive reception, were interpreted as features of the male. The simplest way to express the matter is to note that qabbalists read the account of God having created Adam male (*zakhar*) and female (*neqevah*) in the first chapter in Genesis in light of the second account wherein the derivative ontic status of woman (*ishshah*) from man (*ish*) is made explicit, the woman having been constructed from the body of man. Accordingly, the proto-human, *adam*, is conceived as a male androgyne, the single gender that contains its other as part of itself, a typical patriarchal construction. For qabbalists, therefore, one can speak properly of an Edenic state of the androgynous prelapsarian man, a condition to be retrieved in the end of time. In the *conjunctio oppositorum*, two sexes are unified and woman is restored to man, the ideal unification that tolerates no difference. Representations of *Shekhinah* as feminine, and especially as the erotic object of male desire, bespeak the sexual dimorphism characteristic of a state of exile wherein the unity of the male androgyne has been severed, and as a consequence the male seeks his other, to restore the part of his self that has been taken and rendered independent. Redemption entails the overcoming of this dimorphic condition, the reconstitution of the androgynous male, expressed by the image of the ascent of *Shekhinah* as the diadem (*atarah*) that rises to the head of *keter*, the first of the *sefirot*. By virtue of this ascent *Shekhinah* is transformed into the crown of the male and the unity that was rendered asunder in the beginning of creation is repaired.

See Also Attributes of God, article on Jewish Concepts; Qabbalah.

Bibliography

Green, Arthur. "Shekhinah, the Virgin Mary, and the Song of Songs: Reflections on a Kabbalistic Symbol in Historical Context." *AJS Review* 26 (2002): 1-52.

Liebes, Yehuda. *Studies in the Zohar.* Translated by Arnold Schwartz, Stephanie Nakache, and Penina Peli. Albany, N.Y., 1993.

Mopsik, Charles. "The Body of Engenderment in the Hebrew Bible, the Rabbinic Tradition, and the Kabbalah." In *Fragments for a History of the Human Body,* edited by Michel Feher with Ramona Naddaff and Nadia Tazi, pp. 49-73. New York, 1989.

Pattai, Raphael. *The Hebrew Goddess.* New York, 1967.

Schäfer, Peter. *Mirror of His Beauty: Feminine Images of God from the Bible to the Early Kabbalah.* Princeton, N.J., 2002.

Scholem, Gershom. *On the Mystical Shape of the Godhead: Basic Concepts in the Kabbalah.* Translated by Joachim Neugroschel, edited and revised by Jonathan Chipman. New York, 1991.

Tishby, Isaiah. *The Wisdom of the Zohar.* Translated by David Goldstein. Oxford, 1989.

Urbach, Ephraim E. *The Sages: Their Concepts and Beliefs.* Translated by Israel Abrahams. Jerusalem, 1975.

Wolfson, Elliot R. *Through a Speculum that Shines: Vision and Imagination in Medieval Jewish Mysticism.* Princeton, N.J., 1994.

Wolfson, Elliot R. *Circle in the Square: Studies in the Use of Gender in Kabbalistic Symbolism.* Albany, N.Y., 1995.

Wolfson, Elliot R. "Coronation of the Sabbath Bride: Kabbalistic Myth and the Ritual of Androgynisation." *Journal of Jewish Thought and Philosophy* 6 (1997): 301-344.

Wolfson, Elliot R. "Occultation of the Feminine and the Body of Secrecy in Medieval Kabbalah." In *Rending the Veil: Concealment and Secrecy in the History of Religions,* edited by Elliot R. Wolfson, pp. 113-154. New York and London, 1999.

Elliot R. Wolfson (2005)

SHEMBE, ISAIAH (c. 1870–1935), was the founder of the Zulu amaNazaretha church and the most outstanding figure in the independent church movement in South Africa. The large majority of the three thousand African independent churches are either "Ethiopian" or "Zionist." The Ethiopian churches are carbon copies of mission-related churches (mainly of a Methodist or Congregational type) that have seceded from white mission churches over the issue of apartheid in the church. The Zionist churches, whose name implies an identification with the holy mountain of Zion in the Old Testament, are largely charismatic prophet-led healing groups. Worship in the Zionist churches is an African variant of Pentecostal spirituality. Shembe is the outstanding personality associated with a very small group of churches, often referred to as African "messianic" churches, where the leader is ascribed by his followers with supernatural powers.

Fountains and mountains are the holy places where these prophets generally receive their calling. Shembe was told by a voice to climb a mountain, and it directed him to a cave where he had a dream. From this lofty position he was invited by the voice to survey the earth, and he there discovered his own putrefying corpse. The voice warned him against sexual sins, and he woke up exclaiming, "I have seen Jehovah." This experience on the mountain was to remain with him as a determinative factor throughout his life. By a divine call he had been set apart for a prophetic task on behalf of the Zulu.

These were turbulent times in Zulu society and South African politics, and Shembe was closely related to Meseni Qwabe, one of the militant leaders of the Zulu "reluctant rebellion" of 1906. At the same time he met W. M. Leshega, a leader of a newly formed African Baptist church, who was also one of the leaders of the "Ethiopian" movement. In 1911 Shembe founded his own organization, the amaNazaretha Baptist Church, which differed from Leshega's organization on one elementary point: Saturday rather than Sunday was observed as the holy day of the week.

In 1912, Shembe once again had a revelation and was compelled to climb a particular mountain, called Inhlangakazi, located inland from the city of Durban. This mountain retreat lasted twelve days. During that time Shembe felt that he was being challenged by mysterious and supernatural powers, but he met all their temptations with the answer, "No, I am waiting for Jehovah." Angels then brought him heavenly food in the form of bread and wine; having received these gifts, he knew that he had acquired a new identity and was now a new man. When he returned to his people he also discovered that he had received a new and surprising power, one which he interpreted as the characteristic gift of Jesus of Nazareth: that of driving out demons and healing the sick. To Shembe, these were fundamental experiences: the pilgrimage to the mountain with its asceticism and its nearness to God, the identification with Moses who had climbed another mountain and was then received as the liberator of his people, and the acquisition of the power of healing. He was now ready for his task as a prophet to his people.

Compared with other African charismatic church leaders, Shembe's originality stands out on a number of points. Especially noteworthy is his creative use of traditional Zulu culture in the life of worship within the church. During church festivals the whole congregation, divided into different gender and age-groups and arrayed in traditional Zulu dress, expresses its collective religious experience in a slow-moving, dignified, and solemn dance. The annual pilgrimage to the Inhlangakazi mountain provided an opportunity for intense group cohesion of the multitude arriving from near and far.

Hymns in other independent and mission-related churches are sometimes just mechanical translations of Anglo-Saxon revival songs or ancient ecclesiastical rhymes. Shembe's hymns, on the other hand, convey the very heartbeat of Zulu religious experience from birth to death. Shembe was highly auditive; new hymns—both lyrics and melodies combined—often came to him while he was sleeping. This was, indeed, his strongest motive for learning the art of writing. Having remained illiterate until he was roughly forty years of age, Shembe acquired this new ability in order to commit to writing these irresistible songs that would well up from his unconscious: solemn, simple, and searching. His congregation—probably without exception—shared the feeling of being healed by the prophet, by his incisive exorcism, and his healing hand, mesmerizing the expectant crowd with his mystical black veil.

Shembe's Zulu hymn book, John L. Dube's biography of Shembe in Zulu, and Absalom Vilakazi's recent work (1986) are the main sources for a study of Shembe's faith and spirituality, and they remain a unique testimony that provides insight into the mind and spirit of an independent church leader of that period. The title Shembe claimed for himself was that of "the Servant," sent by the Lord to his deprived and despised Zulu people: "But I alone come from afar, / Sent by the Lord among you."

Just as Moses and Jesus had been sent to the Jews, so the Servant was sent to the Zulu. What once was biblical experience had now become a Zulu reality. "So it is also today / on the hilltops of Ohlange" (Ohlange being the place where Shembe built his church center called Ekuphakameni). In a manner that can easily be misinterpreted, he draws a comparison between himself and the biblical archetypes Moses and Jesus. One of his hymns comes close to being a creed for the amaNazaretha church. It begins "I believe in the Father and the Holy Spirit / and the communion of saints of the Nazaretha." Here the Son is omitted so as to provide room for the Servant of the Spirit. But it is important to emphasize that while referring to his own role as a servant, healer, and helper, he is at the same time aware of Christ on the throne in heaven. Shembe knew that he himself, "having come with nothing and leaving with nothing," would stand before the judgment seat of God.

In order to understand Shembe's relationship to Jesus the Christ one must recall that in hierarchial Zulu society, a visitor could not directly approach the king but first had to turn to junior chiefs whose task it was to introduce the visitor to the ultimate authority. According to Nazaretha belief, this is the task of Servant Shembe in heaven, concerning the approach to the King of Kings on the throne. The Zulu prophet is seen as having a mediating role. In the words of Shembe's hymns there is ambiguity and richness of meaning. And those words, no less than the totality of Shembe's religious practice, must of course be understood in the context from which they emerged: in the worship and struggle of the Nazaretha community.

Bibliography

Becken, Hans J. *Theologie der Heilung: Das Heilen in den afrikanischen unabhängigen Kirchen.* Hermannsburg, 1972.

Dube, John L. *uShembe.* Durban, 1936. A biography of Shembe, in Zulu.

Kiernan, J. P. "Prophet and Preacher: An Essential Partnership in the Work of Zion." *Man* 11 (November 1976): 356–366.

Marks, Shula. *Reluctant Rebellion: The 1906–8 Disturbances in Natal.* Oxford, 1970.

Oosthuizen, Gerhardus C. *The Theology of a South African Messiah: An Analysis of the Hymnal of "The Church of the Nazarenes."* Leiden, 1967.

Schlosser, Katesa. *Eingeborenenkirchen in Süd- und Südwest Afrika.* Kiel, 1958.

Shembe, J. G., ed. *Izihlabelelo zamaNazaretha.* Durban, 1940. A hymn book, in Zulu, by Shembe's son, Johannes Galilee, who succeeded him as leader of the church.

Sundkler, Bengt. *Bantu Prophets in South Africa.* 2d. ed. Oxford, 1961.

Sundkler, Bengt. *Zulu Zion and Some Swazi Zionists.* Lund and Oxford, 1976.

Vilakazi, Absalom. *Shembe: The Revitalization of African Society.* Johannesburg, 1986.

BENGT SUNDKLER (1987)

SHEMINI ʿATSERET See SUKKOT

SHEMUʾEL THE AMORA (c. 180–c. 263), called

Mar Shemuʾel, was a first-generation Babylonian amora, son of Abbaʾ bar Abbaʾ. With his contemporary, Rav, Shemuʾel spread the Mishnah—edited in Palestine—and thus laid the foundation for the rabbinic movement outside the Land of Israel. He learned the Palestinian tradition primarily from masters who had been in Palestine and combined it with the native Persian Jewish heritage.

Shemuʾel's influence as a teacher was enhanced by his authority as a judge in the Jewish court of Nehardea, a city on the Euphrates River. He probably functioned not as a head of an actual academy but rather as a rabbi with a circle of disciples. The prestige he enjoyed is reflected in the portrayal of him as a master devoted to Torah study, extremely honest, enjoying divine protection, friendly with the exilarch and the Sasanid king Shāpūr, an expert in monetary law, and unusually well versed in dreams, medicine, astronomy, and other natural sciences (B.T., *Ber.* 18b, 19a, 56a, 58b; *Shab.* 129a; Goodblatt, 1975).

Shemuʾel played a pivotal role in the history of Judaism in that he enabled the Mishnah to become not only a central work of study but also a source of guidance in the actual life of Jews. The present arrangement of his and Rav's dicta in the *gemaraʾ* is probably the result of a decision to use them as a literary framework for post-Shemuʾel traditions. Many of Shemuʾel's teachings in their original, oral form may have consisted of brief explanatory glosses to individual *mishnayyot.* Longer traditions of Shemuʾel used the Mishnah as a point of departure for extending its teachings. Although Shemuʾel comprehensively treated the Mishnah, including those laws inapplicable in the Diaspora, he especially responded to topics relevant to a third-century Babylonian audience.

Following the rise of the new Sasanid empire in 226 and the disruption of the existing relationship between the Persians and the Jews, Shemuʾel worked out a *modus vivendi* with King Shāpūr I (r. 241–272?) and thereby provided guidelines for a Diaspora Jewish life. He declared that for certain matters, "the law of the kingdom is the law" (B.T., *Giṭ.* 10b), and he offered a "realistic" definition of the messianic age as entailing the end of political subjugation for the people of Israel and not a supernatural transformation of the world (B.T., *Ber.* 34b). He drew from the *Book of Esther* the message that Jews can live peacefully in the Diaspora.

He was concerned with establishing the proper prayer texts and, especially, with the need for the right intention in praying (e.g., J.T., *Ber.* 2.4). By asserting that the divine presence is found in the whole world, he made traditional liturgical and other religious language applicable in the Diaspora.

Shemuʾel believed that learning the Mishnah lengthens one's life, that explicating one's Mishnaic learning gives one peace of mind (B.T., *ʿEruv.* 54a, *Hag.* 10a), and as seen in his formulation of a blessing that is to be said before Torah study (B.T., *Ber.* 11b) that studying enables a person to achieve an experience of the sacred.

See Also Amoraim; Mishnah and Tosefta.

Bibliography

Shemuʾel's traditions are discussed from a literary perspective in Abraham Weiss's *Hithavut ha-Talmud bi-shelemuto* (New York, 1943) and Jacob N. Epstein's *Mavoʾ le-nusaḥ ha-Mishnah,* 2 vols. (1948; reprint, Jerusalem, 1964), pp. 211–234. Jacob Neusner's *A History of the Jews in Babylonia,* 5 vols. (Leiden, 1966–1970), esp. vol. 2, and David M. Goodblatt's *Rabbinic Instruction in Sasanian Babylonia* (Leiden, 1975) address historical questions. See also my books *Samuel's Commentary on the Mishnah* (Leiden, 1975) and *Post Mishnaic Judaism in Transition* (Chico, Calif., 1980), which, after raising the methodological problems in studying Shemuʾel and his teachings, comprehensively treat his traditons and attempt to place his work within an intellectual history of Judaism.

Baruch M. Bokser (1987)

SHENOUTE.

This early Christian monastic leader and outstanding Coptic author is often referred to as "the Great" or "the Archimandrite," a title equivalent to "abbot" and given to him by Cyril of Alexandria (412–444) in order to distinguish him from later namesakes in the Coptic Church. Born in southern Egypt c. 347 CE, Shenoute became a monk while still in his youth and was chosen c. 385 to head his monastery. His death is commemorated on July 14 (Coptic Epēp 7 = Julian July 1), and probably he died on that date in 465. The tradition that Shenoute lived to be 118 years old can be at least approximately confirmed from statements in his own and his immediate successor's writings. Unknown in the West until the late seventeenth century, Shenoute has emerged only gradually as a significant historical figure. His writings provide invaluable glimpses into the development of Egyptian monasticism during its second and third generations, as well as information about Christianity during the period when it became the dominant, state-sanctioned religion of the Roman Empire.

Shenoute was the third head of his monastery, which was founded by his uncle, across the Nile from Panopolis (modern Akhmīm), on the model of Pachomius's monastic system, although it was never formally a part of that system. Shenoute's native language was Coptic (the Egyptian language during the centuries after the rise of Christianity), but he learned Greek while he was still an ordinary monk, when he also acquired a profound knowledge of the Bible in both languages. His earliest writings are two long open letters to his community (written c. 380) exposing sin and hypocrisy in the monastery, criticizing its leadership, and announcing his intention to depart and live as a hermit. Subsequent events revealed Shenoute as gifted with penetrating insight, for which reason he was made head of the monastery when his disgraced predecessor died.

Shenoute was the ultimate authority over two men's communities and one for women. He himself spent most of his time in isolation in the nearby desert, communicating with the three communities through trusted, older male monks, who carried letters back and forth. Over the years of his leadership, Shenoute compiled his own letters into a set of nine volumes of "canons," which served as a set of rules for the monastery during Shenoute's lifetime and then for centuries afterwards. Shenoute's *Canons* provide detailed information about the carefully regulated life of the male and female monastics (covering nearly every aspect of life, from prayer to defecation), as well as insight into the personality of this remarkable late antique monastic figure.

Despite living as a hermit, Shenoute visited the monastery regularly to worship with his fellow monks (typically perhaps only four times each year). On these occasions he might also preach, and his appearance could attract large crowds of laypeople. The predominant theme of Shenoute's preaching was the urgent need for repentance, but his sermons often provide fascinating vignettes from the everyday world of late antique Egypt. This information is supplemented by Shenoute's treatises and letters, the latter addressed either to specific individuals, including local authorities from the provincial governor on down, or to entire communities, including Panopolis and nearby villages.

This part of Shenoute's corpus is particularly illuminating of the conflict between Christianity and paganism in the late Roman Empire. Shenoute was among those fanatic Christians who were willing to use every means, including violence, to destroy the physical basis of pagan worship (temples, images) and to convert nonbelievers. The relevant dossier of texts from Shenoute is without parallel elsewhere and throws extraordinary light on events and people in and near Panopolis around the end of the fourth century, especially a confrontation between Shenoute and a former governor (Flavius Aelius Gessius) who apparently was trying to disguise his pagan sympathies in a world that was becoming overwhelmingly Christian.

Shenoute's writings also provide information about socioeconomic circumstances (he championed the poor against oppressive landowners), ecclesiastical politics (he was an unquestioning supporter of Alexandrian theology and church politics, although refusing to be made a bishop; in 431 he accompanied Archbishop Cyril to the Council of Ephesus), efforts to establish a unified orthodoxy and orthopraxy (he opposed Arians, Melitians, Origenists, magicians, and Manichaeans, among others), and Christian spirituality (particularly interesting themes in Shenoute's works are demonology, proper interpretation of the Bible, appropriate forms of worship, and the role of prophetic insight and visions).

Near the end of his life, Shenoute took up residence again within the monastery walls. After his death, "our holy and prophetic father Apa Shenoute" quickly became a revered saint in the Coptic Church. His sermons, treatises, and letters were assembled in volumes alongside his *Canons* and served as a source of liturgical readings, at least in his own monastery. Later, some of these lections were added to the standard Coptic Holy Week liturgy.

Although Shenoute's name and reputation were known all over Egypt during his lifetime, the Arab Conquest (641) heralded the end of the transmission of his writings. In subsequent centuries very little of his corpus was translated into Arabic, so that when his monastery collapsed in the fourteenth century, little remained of Shenoute's writings except a large heap of deteriorating parchment books within the monastery's spectacular mid-fifth-century church (the only monastery building that remained standing, whose brilliant white limestone walls gained it the designation "White Monastery"). Shenoute's continuing fame and veneration in the Coptic Church has depended almost entirely on the liturgical tradition, based on a hagiographic "Life of Shenoute," with roots in an ancient encomiastic tradition, but to which legends continued to accrue even after it was translated into Arabic.

Although Shenoute's great literary achievement marks the high point of Coptic literature, his corpus must now be reconstructed from thousands of manuscript fragments that in modern times became scattered in dozens of museums and libraries from Egypt across Europe to North America. Recent progress in this task of reconstruction has led to a renewed effort to edit and translate his works systematically.

SEE ALSO Coptic Church; Monasticism, overview article; Pachomius.

BIBLIOGRAPHY

Behlmer, Heike. *Schenute von Atripe, De iudicio* (Torino, Museo Egizio, Cat. 63000, Cod. IV). Turin, 1996. An edition and translation (German) of one major work by Shenoute, with commentary.

Emmel, Stephen. "From the Other Side of the Nile: Shenute and Panopolis." In *Perspectives on Panopolis: An Egyptian Town from Alexander the Great to the Arab Conquest,* edited by Arno Egberts et al., pp. 95–113. Leiden, 2002. An analysis of crucial aspects of Shenoute's antipagan activities.

Emmel, Stephen. "Shenoute the Monk: The Early Monastic Career of Shenoute the Archimandrite." In *Il monachesimo tra eredità e aperture. Atti del simposio "Testi e temi nella tradizione del monachesimo cristiano" per il 50° anniversario dell'Istituto Monastico di Sant'Anselmo, Roma, 28 maggio–10 giugno 2002,* edited by M. Bielawski and D. Hombergen, pp. 151–174. Rome, 2004. An analysis of Shenoute's earliest letters, from the first volume of his *Canons.*

Emmel, Stephen. *Shenoute's Literary Corpus.* 2 vols. Louvain, 2004. A summation of two centuries of scholarship on Shenoute, laying the groundwork for future research by means of a reconstruction of nearly one hundred manuscripts of Shenoute's works; a fundamental guide to what was published of Shenoute's corpus up to 2004, with complete bibliography.

Krawiec, Rebecca. *Shenoute and the Women of the White Monastery: Egyptian Monasticism in Late Antiquity.* Oxford, 2002. A study of Shenoute's letters to female monastics, especially the letters in the second volume of his *Canons* (as reconstructed by Emmel, 2004).

Layton, Bentley. "Social Structure and Food Consumption in an Early Christian Monastery: The Evidence of Shenoute's *Canons* and the White Monastery Federation AD 385–465." *Muséon* 115 (2002): 25–55. The first systematic study of all nine volumes of Shenoute's *Canons* (as reconstructed by Emmel, 2004).

Leipoldt, Johannes. *Schenute von Atripe und die Entstehung des national ägyptischen Christentums.* Leipzig, 1903. The first fundamental study of Shenoute, not yet entirely superseded (although sooner or later it must be replaced).

Young, Dwight W. *Coptic Manuscripts from the White Monastery: Works of Shenute.* Vienna, 1993. An assortment (rather arbitrary than systematic or thematic) of fragments of Shenoute's works, with English translations and notes.

STEPHEN EMMEL (2005)

SHERIRAʾ GAON

SHERIRAʾ GAON (c. 906–1006), Babylonian halakhist and head of the academy at Pumbedita for some thirty years. Sheriraʾ was a major league authority whose many *responsa* circulated throughout the whole Jewish Diaspora. He combined his legal preeminence with a rational attitude toward Talmudic legend, thus setting the pattern that was followed by his son and successor, Hʾai.

The single most influential work by Sheriraʾ is the book-length *Iggeret* (Epistle), sent as a response to the community of Kairouan in North Africa. Yaʿaqov bar Nissim had asked on behalf of his co-religionists that the gaon explain how the oral law had reached its present form in the Talmud, how and when the various rabbinic works had been compiled and edited, and what was the import of the frequent disagreements among the Talmudic rabbis. This series of questions doubtless reflected the anxiety felt among rabbinites confronted by the Karaite claim that the Talmud was a human product anchored in history rather than a divine oral law. In the *Epistle,* which Salo Baron has called the "outstanding historiographic contribution of the geonic era," Sheriraʾ provided indispensable literary and historical data on the process by which the Talmud evolved; indeed, he defined the terms of much future discussion of this topic, both medieval and modern. The *Epistle* divides into two parts: the first traces the history of Talmudic literature through the pioneering inductive use of selected source materials, while the second is a history of exilarchic and geonic leadership probably based on the academy's archives. The basic ideological position of Sheriraʾ is that the oral law had a literary history but did not substantively develop through the Mishnaic and Talmudic periods. The Mishnah and the Talmud are authoritative crystallizations of the law possessed by the earlier generations, and even Talmudic discussion simply recaptures, on the whole, the knowledge of the ancients. This conservative theory of Talmudic law, much of it based on statements and materials found in the Talmud itself, has remained the ideological basis of Orthodox Judaism until present times.

SEE ALSO Hʾai Gaon; Halakhah, article on History of Halakhah; Judaism, article on Judaism in the Middle East and North Africa to 1492.

BIBLIOGRAPHY

Isaac Hirsch Weiss's *Dor dor ve-dorshav,* vol. 4 (New York, 1924), pp. 106–174, remains the best overall treatment of the career and achievement of Sheriraʾ. Salo W. Baron's *A Social and Religious History of the Jews,* vol. 6, 2d ed., rev. & enl. (New York, 1958), pp. 204–206, 425–427, provides ample bibliographic and comparative data on the *Epistle.* In my article "Raʿayon Torah she-beʿal peh beiggeret Rav Sheriraʾ Gaʾon," *Daʿat* 4 (1980): 5–17, I discuss the ideological import of the *Epistle.*

GERALD J. BLIDSTEIN (1987)

SHIISM

This entry consists of the following articles:

AN OVERVIEW
ISMĀʿĪLĪYAH
ITHNĀ ʿASHARĪYAH

SHIISM: AN OVERVIEW

Shiism is a major branch of Islam with numerous subdivisions, all upholding the rights of the family of the Prophet (*ahl al-bayt*) to the religious and political leadership of the Muslim community. The name is derived from *shīʿat ʿAlī,* the Arabic term for the "party" of ʿAlī ibn Abī Ṭālib, cousin of the prophet Muḥammad and husband of Muḥammad's daughter Fāṭimah.

ORIGINS AND EARLY DEVELOPMENT. Historically, the Shīʿah emerged in support of the caliphate of ʿAlī (AH 35–40/656–661 CE) during the First Civil War, which followed the murder of the third caliph, ʿUthmān. The Shīʿah see the foundation of Shiism, however, in Muḥammad's appointment of ʿAlī as his successor, a choice that the Prophet is claimed to have made at Ghadīr Khumm not long before his death, and one that the Muslim community ignored in recognizing Abū Bakr as the first caliph. After the murder of ʿAlī and the abdication of his eldest son, Ḥasan, in 661, the Shīʿah continued a latent opposition to the Umayyad caliphate from their center in ʿAlī's former capital of Kufa in Iraq. Their attachment to the family of the Prophet, and especially to ʿAlī's sons and descendants, reflected local resentment of both the loss of the caliphate to Damascus and the Umayyad denigration of ʿAlī and his caliphate. Reports about the activity of one ʿAbd Allāh ibn Sabaʾ, who in some anti-Shīʿī sources is described as the founder of Shiism and as having denied ʿAlī's death and taught his divinity, are legendary. If such beliefs arose at this early stage, they remained marginal.

Kufan revolts. The violent death of ʿAlī's second son, Ḥusayn, at Karbala, Iraq, in 680 led to the formation of a radical wing within the Shīʿah. After the death of the caliph Muʿāwiyah, the Kufan Shīʿah invited Ḥusayn from Medina, promising to back his claim to the caliphate. The Umayyad governor gained control of the situation, however, and it was a Kufan army that met Ḥusayn and killed him together with many of his relatives. A Penitents movement arose in Kufa; they lamented the death of the Prophet's grandson at his grave in Karbala and sought revenge from those responsible. In 685 the leadership of the Penitents was taken over by al-Mukhtār ibn Abi ʿUbayd, who revolted in Kufa and proclaimed another son of ʿAlī, Muḥammad, to be the imam and Mahdi, the messianic Restorer of Islam. Unlike Ḥasan and Ḥusayn, Muḥammad was not the son of Fāṭimah, and he was known, after his own mother, as Ibn al-Ḥanafīyah. The movement backing him was called the Kaysānīyah after Abū ʿAmrah Kaysān, chief of al-Mukhtār's guard and leader of the non-Arab clients (*mawālī*) in Kufa. These clients, local Semites and Persians, now joined the Shīʿah in large numbers for the first time, although the leading role in the movement was still played by Arabs.

The Kaysānīyah movement, which survived the collapse of al-Mukhtār's revolt and the death of Muḥammad ibn al-Ḥanafīyah in 700, elaborated some of the beliefs and doctrines that came to distinguish the radical wing of the Shīʿah. They condemned the first three caliphs before ʿAlī as illegitimate usurpers and considered ʿAlī and his three sons, Ḥasan, Ḥusayn, and Muḥammad, as successive, divinely appointed imams endowed with supernatural qualities. Many of them denied the death of Muḥammad ibn al-Ḥanafīyah, the Mahdi, in the belief that he was hiding and would return in glory to rule the world. They taught *rajʿah,* the return of many of the dead at the time of the coming of the Mahdi for retribution before the Resurrection, and *badāʾ,* the possibility of a change in the decisions of God.

Abbasid revolution. A branch of the Kaysānīyah known as the Hāshimīyah continued the line of imams to Muḥammad ibn al-Ḥanafīyah's son Abū Hāshim, who, in contrast to his father, took an active part in the leadership and organization of the movement. After his death in about 717/8 the Hāshimīyah split into several groups over the succession. The majority recognized Muḥammad ibn ʿAlī, a descendant of the Prophet's uncle ʿAbbās, as the imam after Abū Hāshim; they became historically important as the core of the revolutionary movement in Khorasan that overthrew the Umayyad dynasty and established the Abbasid caliphate in 750. The Abbasids initially espoused the Shīʿī cause, establishing the reign of the family of the Prophet and demanding revenge for ʿAlī and his wronged descendants. Soon, however, they distanced themselves from their mostly extremist Shīʿī followers to seek broader support in the Muslim community, while the Shīʿah increasingly confined their backing to the descendants of ʿAlī and Fāṭimah. After the collapse of a widely supported Shīʿī rebellion in favor of the ʿAlid Muḥammad al-Nafs al-Zakīyah, Caliph al-Mahdī (775–785) pressed the Abbasid Shīʿah to trace the line of divinely invested imams back to ʿAbbās through his own ancestors, thus denying that the Abbasids had inherited their title from Abū Hāshim and ʿAlī. The Abbasid Shīʿah disintegrated soon afterward.

Extremists and moderates. Other minor offshoots of the Hashimīyah were notable for their extremist doctrine. Bayān ibn Samʿān (killed 936) taught in Kufa that Abū Hāshim, who had conferred prophethood on him, would return as the Mahdi. ʿAbd Allāh ibn Muʿāwīyah (d. 748/9), a descendant of ʿAlī's brother Jaʿfar and recognized by some as the successor of Abū Hāshim, claimed that the Divine Spirit had devolved upon him through the prophets and imams and that he was able to revive the dead. To ʿAbd Allāh ibn al-Ḥārith, one of his followers in al-Madāʾin (Ctesiphon), Iraq, is ascribed a major role in the elaboration of key doctrines including metempsychosis, the preexistence of human souls as shadows (*aẓillah*), metaphorical interpretation of the resurrection, judgment, paradise, and hell, and a cyclical history of eras (*adwār*) and aeons (*akwār*) initiated by seven Adams. Such teaching became characteristic of many groups of extremists (*ghulāt*) excommunicated by the mainstream Shīʿah in the following centuries. The Kaysānīyah as a whole was repudiated by the more conservative, moderate Shīʿah in Kufa. All of its branches rapidly disintegrated after the rise of the Abbasid caliphate and virtually disappeared by the end of the second century AH. Its place in the radical wing of the Shīʿah was taken by the Imāmīyah, who traced the line of imams after ʿAlī through Ḥasan, Ḥusayn, and the latter's descendants.

The increasing prominence of the Husaynid imams within the Shīʿah was connected with a shift in the function of the imam. With the rise of legal and theological schools espousing conflicting doctrines in the late Umayyad period, many of the Shīʿah sought the guidance of the imam as an authoritative, divinely inspired teacher rather than as a charismatic leader. The first to perform this new role was Muḥammad al-Bāqir (d. 735?), a grandson of Ḥusayn who was widely respected for his learning among both the Shīʿah and non-Shīʿah. His teaching of religious law and Qurʾān exegesis attracted a large number of the Kufan Shīʿah. Keeping aloof from revolutionary activity, he laid the foundations of Imāmī Shīʿī law. A few years after his death his brother Zayd ibn ʿAlī came to Kufa and was persuaded to lead an anti-Umayyad revolt. Although he was widely supported by the Kufan Shīʿah, including some prominent former followers of his brother, the more radical followers of al-Bāqir refused to back Zayd ibn ʿAlī after he declined to condemn the first two caliphs unequivocally as unjust usurpers. They turned instead to al-Bāqir's son Jaʿfar al-Ṣādiq, who, like his father, strictly refused any involvement in armed rebellion. Zayd's revolt ended quickly in failure, and he was killed in 740. The movement backing him survived, however, and formed a Shīʿī sect known as the Zaydīyah. They were moderate both in defining the religious rank of their imams and in condemning the rest of the Muslim community for its failure to do so, yet they were militant advocates of armed uprising against the illegitimate rulers. In contrast to the Zaydīyah, the Imāmīyah exalted the rank of the imams and broke radically with the Muslim community at large, accusing it of apostasy for failing to accord the imams their proper rank and rights. Politically, however, they remained quietist. They were called Rāfiḍah, "rejectors," by the followers of Zayd because of their refusal to support his revolt. The term became a pejorative nickname among Sunnī Muslims, who used it, however, to refer to the Imāmīyah's repudiation of the three caliphs preceding ʿAlī. Those Shīʿī moderates of Kufa who shrank back from the Zaydī commitment to revolt were soon absorbed into Sunnīsm as ʿAlī came to be accepted generally as the fourth of the "Rightly Guided" (Rāshidūn) successors of Muḥammad.

THE IMĀMĪYAH AND TWELVER SHĪʿAH. The Imāmīyah became a significant religious community with a distinctive law, ritual, and religious doctrine under Jaʿfar al-Ṣādiq (d. 765), the foremost scholar and teacher among their imams. Jaʿfar elaborated the legal pronouncements of his father into a comprehensive doctrine; in recognition of his role, Imāmī law is sometimes called the Jaʿfarī legal school. In theology, some of his statements upheld intermediate positions on controversial questions such as human free will versus predestination, and the nature of the Qurʾān. These were developed into systematic theological thought by certain contemporary Imāmī scholars who took a prominent part in the intercommunal theological debates of his time. Jaʿfar enjoyed a high reputation as a teacher of esoteric and mystical thought, though his actual role in this field is obscure.

The imamate. The constitutive element of the Imāmī community is its doctrine of the imamate, which was definitely formulated in this age. It was based on the belief that humanity is at all times in need of a divinely appointed and guided leader and authoritative teacher in all religious matters. Without such a leader, according to Imam Jaʿfar, the world could never exist for a moment. In order to fulfill his divine mission, this leader must be endowed with full immunity (*ʿiṣmah*) from sin and error. Following the age of the prophets, which came to a close with Muḥammad, the imams continue their prophetic mission in every respect except that they do not bring a new scripture. The imamate is thus raised to the rank of prophethood. Rejection, disobedience, or ignorance of any of the divinely invested imams constitutes infidelity equal to rejection of the Prophet. The great mass of the companions of Muḥammad had thus apostatized from Islam when they accepted the caliphate of Abū Bakr and ignored the Prophet's divinely inspired designation of ʿAlī as his legatee *(waṣī)*, and the majority of the Muslim community continued to live in a state of apostasy. After ʿAlī, Ḥasan, and Ḥusayn, the line of legitimate imams had passed through Ḥusayn's descendants to Jaʿfar al-Ṣādiq, the sixth imam. It would continue to be handed down by designation from father to son until the end of time. Although the imam was the only legitimate ruler of the Muslim community, his imamate did not depend on his actual reign or an active attempt to gain it. Imam Jaʿfar did not aspire to rule and forbade his followers from engaging in revolutionary activity on his behalf. He predicted that the imams would not regain their rightful position until the emergence of the Qāʾim (lit. "riser," i.e., the *mahdī)* from among them to rule the world.

The succession to Jaʿfar al-Ṣādiq was disputed and led to a schism among the Imāmīyah. His eldest son and designated successor, Ismāʿīl, had died before him. A group of his followers considered the designation as irreversible, however, and either denied Ismāʿīl's death or recognized Ismāʿīl's son Muḥammad as the imam. They became the founders of the Ismāʿīlīyah. In the absence of a new designation, the majority of Jaʿfar's followers at first recognized his eldest surviving son, ʿAbd Allāh al-Afṭaḥ. When ʿAbd Allāh died a few months later without sons, they turned to his brother Mūsā al-Kāẓim, the seventh imam of the Twelver Shīʿah. Some of them, however, continued to recognize ʿAbd Allāh as the rightful imam before Mūsā. They were known as the Faṭḥīyah and constituted a sizable sect in Kufa until the late fourth century AH (tenth century CE). Mūsā was arrested later in his life by Caliph Hārūn al-Rashīd and died in prison in Baghdad in 799. His death was denied by many of his followers, who considered his position as seventh imam to be of momentous significance and expected his return as the Mahdi. They did not recognize ʿAlī al-Riḍā, the eighth imam of the Twelver Shīʿah, although some of them considered him and his successors as lieutenants (*khulafāʾ*) of the Mahdi until his return. They also formed a sizable sect known as the Wāqifah and competed with the group that was to become the Twelver Shīʿah. In the Sus region of southwestern Morocco they gained a following among Berber tribes that survived until the sixth century AH (twelfth century CE).

The Abbasid caliph al-Maʾmūn attempted to bring about a reconciliation between the ʿAlid and Abbasid branches of the family of the Prophet by appointing ʿAlī al-Riḍā as his successor in 817, but this move ended in failure. ʿAlī al-Riḍā died two years later, and the caliph was widely accused of having poisoned him. The succession after al-Riḍā down to the eleventh imam, Ḥasan al-ʿAskarī, produced only minor schisms, but the death of the latter in 874, apparently without a son, left his followers in disarray. The main body, henceforth known as the Twelver Shīʿah (the Ithnā ʿAsharīyah in Arabic), eventually came to affirm that a son had been born to him before his death but had been hidden. This son had become the twelfth imam and continued to live in concealment. Identified with the Qāʾim and the Mahdi, he was expected to reappear in glory to rule the world and make the cause of the Shīʿah triumphant. The time of his absence (*ghaybah*) falls into two parts. In the age of the lesser *ghaybah* he was in regular contact with four successive agents (sg., *wakīl* or *safīr*) who represented him among the community of his followers, communicating their questions and requests to him and his answers and instructions to them. In 941, the fourth intermediary died without appointing a successor, and the greater *ghaybah* began. During this *ghaybah* no one can claim to be in regular contact with the Hidden Imam. He continues to live unrecognized on earth, however, and may occasionally identify himself to one of his followers or otherwise intervene in the fortunes of his community.

Intellectual currents. The absence of the imam strengthened the position of the scholars (*'ulamā'*) in the Shī'ī community as transmitters and guardians of the teaching of the imams. They now undertook to gather, examine, and systematize this teaching. For the most part, the first transmitters of the statements of the imams had been Kufans, while the compilation and sifting of the traditions into more comprehensive collections was the work of the school of Qom in northwestern Iran. Some Kufan Shī'ī families had settled early in this town, and it became a bastion of Imāmī Shiism, adhering to the imamate of 'Alī al-Riḍā and his descendants in the ninth century even though the Imāmīyah had been eclipsed in Kufa by the predominance of the Zaydīyah, Wāqifah, and Faṭḥīyah. The traditionist school of Qom reached its peak in the works of Abū Ja'far al-Kulaynī of Rayy (d. 941) and Ibn Bābawayhi al-Ṣadūq of Qom (d. 991/2).

A rival school in Baghdad progressively adopted the rationalist theology of the Mu'tazilah, who espoused human free will and an anti-anthropomorphist, abstract concept of God in sharp conflict with the predominant theology of Sunnī Islam. The Baghdad school rejected Mu'tazilī doctrine, however, where it clashed with the basic Imāmī beliefs about the imamate; thus it repudiated the Mu'tazilī thesis of the unconditional, eternal punishment of the unrepentant sinner in the hereafter, affirming the effectiveness of the intercession of the imams for sinners among their faithful followers. In fact, faith in the power of the imams' intercessions was a vital motive for the visits to their shrines that have always been a major aspect of popular Shī'ī piety. Twelver Shī'ī theologians also maintained, against the Mu'tazilī position, that the opponents of the imams occupied the status of infidels and that the imamate was, like prophecy, a rational necessity, not merely a revealed legal requirement. The leading figures of the theological school of Baghdad were Shaykh al-Mufīd (d. 1022) and Sharif al-Murtaḍā 'Alam al-Hudā (d. 1044). Their student, Shaykh Abū Ja'far al-Ṭūsī (d. 1067), became the most important early systematizer of Twelver Shī'ī law; his work has remained fundamental for all later developments.

The Twelver Shī'ah today constitute the great majority of the Shī'ah and are often referred to simply by the latter name. Most of the people of Iran and southern Iraq are Twelvers. There are sizable Twelver Shī'ī communities in Bahrein, in al-Ḥaṣā and Qaṭif in eastern Saudi Arabia, in southern Lebanon, in Aleppo in northern Syria, and in parts of Afghanistan. On the Indian subcontinent Twelver Shī'ah are widespread, especially in Punjab, Delhi, and Baroda, as well as in the Deccan, where the first Shī'ī missionaries appeared in the fifteenth century, and where the majority of the Quṭbshāhīs of Golconda and the 'Adil-shāhīs of Bijapur were Shī'ī. In recent years, a considerable number of Pakistani families have also joined the Twelvers.

EXTREMIST SECTS. On the fringe of the Imāmīyah and the Twelver Shī'ah there arose numerous minor sects of varying nature classed generically as *ghulāt* ("extremists") and frequently excommunicated by the mainstream. Common grounds for the charge of extremism were deification of the imams and antinomianism.

Imāmī *ghulāt*. The most prominent figure among the early Imāmī *ghulāt* in Kufa was Abū al-Khaṭṭāb al-Asadī, who was excommunicated by imam Ja'far and killed together with seventy of his followers, the Khaṭṭābīyah, about 755. The Khaṭṭābīyah recognized Abū al-Khaṭṭāb as a prophet sent by Ja'far, whom they viewed as God. Al-Mufaḍḍal ibn 'Umar al-Ju'fī, who is sometimes described as the head of an offshoot of the Khaṭṭābīyah, but who became a trusted agent of Imam Mūsā al-Kāzīm, appears to have played a major role in the transmission of gnostic teaching about the preexistence and transmigration of souls and the cyclical history earlier associated with the Kaysānī 'Abd Allāh ibn al-Ḥārith.

The heresiographers speak of two complementary currents among the *ghulāt* in the second half of the eighth century. The Mukhammisah (Pentadists) believed in a divine pentad consisting of Muḥammad, 'Alī, Fāṭimah, Ḥasan, and Ḥusayn. The five were united in meaning (*ma'nā*) but distinct in name (*ism*) and had manifested themselves throughout history in the form of prophets and imams. The Mufawwiḍah (Delegationists) taught that the Eternal One, whose name is unknowable, had delegated the creation of the world to the divine pentad. At the beginning of the *ghaybah*, the *ghulāt* of this tradition coalesced into two rival sects, the Isḥāqīyah and the Nuṣayrīyah. The Isḥāqīyah was founded by the Basran Isḥāq al-Aḥmar (d. 899), who disputed the position of the second *safīr* of the twelfth imam. The sect spread from Iraq to Aleppo and the Syrian coast. In Syria it was wiped out by its Nuṣayrī rivals in the thirteenth century and disappeared in Iraq about the same time.

Nuṣayrīyah and 'Alawīyūn. The Nuṣayrīyah took their name from Muḥammad ibn Nuṣayr al-Namīrī, a companion of the ninth and tenth imams. They became a fully constituted sect under his successors, especially al-Ḥusayn ibn Ḥamdān al-Khaṣībī (d. 957 or 969), who carried the sect's teaching to northern Syria and was buried in Aleppo. It was extinguished in Iraq after the Mongol invasion but has survived to the present in Syria, especially in Latakia and the Jabal al-Anṣārīyah region to the east and in the regions of Alexandretta and Cilicia (Adana and Tarsus). In modern times the Nuṣayrīyah are commonly referred to as 'Alawīs or Alawites.

The name *ʿAlawī* (Turk., *Alevi*) is frequently also applied to other extremist Shīʿī communities in Anatolia. Similar groups in Iran are often pejoratively called ʿAlī-Ilāhī ("ʿAlī deifiers"). Such groups generally have their roots in the late Mongol age (fourteenth and fifteenth centuries) and represent a mixture of popular extremist Shiism and Sufism. Strong pro-ʿAlid sentiments on a popular level were already widespread among Türkmen tribes during the great Turkish expansion into Iran and western Asia in the Seljuk period. These sentiments were reinforced during the Mongol period by the Sufism spread by some of the great religious orders that were themselves moving toward Shīʿī beliefs. In the fifteenth century the Kizilbash Türkmen federation and religious order adopted such extremist Shīʿī doctrine under the leadership of the Safavids, who now claimed ʿAlid descent. After the foundation of the Safavid state, however, the rulers furthered orthodox Twelver Shiism as the official religion and gradually divested themselves of the religious veneration and backing of the Kizilbash. Under the Ottomans, the Bektāshi dervish order, which became closely associated with the Janissaries, embraced a similar mixture of Ṣūfī and extremist Shīʿī beliefs.

A major sect among the so-called ʿAlī-Ilāhīs are the Ahl-i Ḥaqq ("people of the truth"), whose origins apparently go back to the fifteenth century and whose main centers are in the Kurdish regions of western Iran and eastern Iraq and in Azerbaijan. They represent a syncretism of popular Ṣūfī rites, legends, and folklore superimposed on an extremist Shīʿī foundation. While ʿAlī is recognized as one of the seven avatars of the divinity, he is completely overshadowed by the figure of Sultan Seḥāk (Isḥāq).

Shaykhīyah. In modern times Shaykh Aḥmad al-Ahsaʾī (d. 1826), the author of a Twelver Shīʿī theosophical doctrine, has been charged with extremist views and excommunicated by the *mujtahids* in Iran. He was specifically accused of denying the physical resurrection and the physical nature of the ascension of the prophet Muḥammad. He thus became the founder of the Shaykhī sect, which, besides espousing his theosophical teaching, also opposes the authority of the *mujtahids*, in accordance with the Akhbārī position. The sect is scattered throughout Iran and Iraq, with its center in Kirman. Out of it also developed the Bābī and, indirectly, the Bahāʾī religions, but these fall outside the pale of Shiism.

THE ISMĀʿĪLĪYAH. An offshoot of the Imāmīyah, the Ismāʿīlīyah first became historically important after the middle of the ninth century as a secret revolutionary movement promising the impending advent of Muḥammad ibn Ismāʿīl, grandson of Jaʿfar al-Ṣādiq, as the Mahdi. The movement soon split into two. One of its branches recognized the hidden leaders of the movement as imams descended from Muḥammad ibn Ismāʿīl. With backing of this branch, the leaders rose to rule as the Fatimid caliphate (909–1171). The other branch, commonly known as the Qarāmiṭah, broke with the leadership and refused to recognize the imamate of the Fatimid caliphs. Their most conspicuous success was the establishment of a Qarmaṭī state in eastern Arabia that lasted from 899 until 1076.

The Fatimid branch was rent by a schism during the caliphate of al-Ḥākim (996–1021), whose divinity was proclaimed by a group of enthusiastic followers. The sect arising from this deviation is known as the Druze. After the death of the caliph al-Mustanṣir in 1094 the Persian Ismāʿīlī communities recognized his eldest son, Nizār, who did not succeed to the caliphate, as their imam. Known as the Nizārīyah, they established their headquarters, and later the seat of their imams, in the mountain stronghold of Alamūt in the Elburz mountains. In Syria, where they also occupied some mountain fortresses, they became known to the Crusaders as *ḥashīshīyīn* ("hashish addicts"), a name that was then deformed to "Assassins." The main line of Nizārī imams has continued down to the Aga Khans in modern times. A second line, which split off soon after the Mongol conquest of Alamūt in 1256, came to an end in 1796. The branch continuing to recognize the Fatimid caliphs was further split after the death of al-Amir in 1130. The majority of the Ismāʿīlīyah in Yemen and India now recognized as their imam al-Ṭayyib, the caliph's infant son, about whose fate nothing is known. In his absence the spiritual leadership of these sectarians, known as Ṭayyibīyah, became vested in their *dāʿī muṭlaq*. As the line of these spiritual leaders became divided in 1591, the Ṭayyibīyah split into two communities, the Dāʾūdīyah and the Sulaymānīyah. That part of the Ismāʿīlī community adhering to the Fatimid caliphate until its fall disintegrated thereafter.

THE ZAYDĪYAH. Retaining the politically militant and religiously moderate attitude predominant among the early Kufan Shīʿah, the Zaydīyah developed a doctrine of the imamate distinctly at variance with Imāmī beliefs. They neither accepted a hereditary line of imams nor considered the imam as divinely protected from sin and error. Rather they held that any descendant of Ḥasan or Ḥusayn qualified by religious learning could claim the imamate by armed rising against the illegitimate rulers and would then be entitled to the allegiance and backing of the faithful. Thus there were often long periods without legitimate Zaydī imams. The list of recognized Zaydī imams itself has never been entirely fixed although there is general agreement on many of them. In the absence of any claimant possessing the high qualifications of religious learning, the Zaydīyah often supported ʿAlid rulers as mere *dāʿīs* ("summoners," i.e., imams with restricted competence). Although they, like the Imāmīyah, generally affirmed that ʿAlī, Ḥasan, and Ḥusayn had been invested as imams by Muḥammad's designation (*naṣṣ*), they maintained that the designation had been obscure so that its meaning could be discovered only by investigation. Thus they minimized the offense of the companions of the Prophet and the Muslim community in ignoring that designation and in backing the early caliphs. In theology, the Zaydīyah from the tenth century on mostly accepted Muʿtazilī doctrine.

For more than a century after the revolt of Zayd, the Zaydī movement remained based in Kufa near the center of Abbasid power, where various ʿAlid rebellions backed by it were quickly suppressed. In the second half of the ninth century, however, two Zaydī reigns were founded in remote regions protected by mountain ranges. In Ṭabaristān (modern Mazandarān) on the southern coast of the Caspian Sea, the Hasanid Ḥasan ibn Zayd rose to power in 864. This first Zaydī state lapsed in 900 but was restored in 914 by the Husaynid imam al-Nāṣir al-Uṭrūsh, who had converted to Islam many of the natives of Daylam and Gīlān living west of Ṭabaristān. He was also the founder of a legal school doctrine to which his converts adhered, although the older Zaydī community in the region followed the legal doctrine of the Ḥasanid imam al-Qāsim ibn Ibrāhīm (d. 860). The two communities, known as the Naṣirīyah and the Qāsimīyah, were often at odds, and, although eventually recognizing each other's doctrine as equally valid, for long periods supported different ʿAlid imams or *dāʿīs*. They survived until the sixteenth century, when the Caspian Zaydīyah converted to Twelver Shiism under pressure from the Safavid shah Ṭahmāsp.

In Yemen the imam Yaḥyā al-Hādī ila al-Ḥaqq, a grandson of al-Qāsim ibn Ibrāhīm, established Zaydī rule in 897. He introduced the legal and theological doctrine of his grandfather, which he elaborated and modified in his own writings. The unity of the Zaydī community in Yemen was rent in the eleventh century by the rise of two heterodox sects, the Muṭarrifīyah and the Ḥusaynīyah. The former was opposed to some aspects of the Muʿtazilī doctrine espoused by the Caspian Zaydī imams and elaborated a distinctive theory of nature that it attributed to al-Hādī and his sons. The Ḥusaynīyah denied the death of the imam al-Ḥusayn al-Mahdī in 1013 and expected his return as the Mahdi. Both sects disappeared by the fourteenth century. Relations with the Caspian community were intermittently close for some centuries, and much of its religious literature was transferred to Yemen in the twelfth century. Only exceptionally, however, was an imam ruling in either region able to extend his control to the other. The Zaydī community in Yemen, living mostly in the northern highlands, has survived to the present, although the last imam, Muḥammad al-Badr, was overthrown by the revolution of 1962.

SEE ALSO Aga Khan; ʿAlawīyūn; Assassins; Druze; Ghaybah; Imamate; ʿIṣmah; Qarāmiṭah; Shaykhīyah.

BIBLIOGRAPHY

Scholarly literature on Shiism is still limited and uneven. There is no comprehensive survey of Shiism in its full range. In the wider context of schisms in Islam, the development of the various branches of Shiism is outlined by Henri Laoust in *Les schismes dans l'Islam* (Paris, 1965). There are brief chapters on Twelver Shiism, the Zaydīyah, and Ismāʿīlīyah in *Islam,* edited by C. F. Beckingham, volume 2 of *Religion in the Middle East,* edited by Arthur J. Arberry (Cambridge, 1969).

The origins and early history of the Shīʿah and the Khārijīs in the Umayyad age was classically described, chiefly on the basis of the early Kufan historian Abū Mikhnaf, in Julius Wellhausen's *Die religiös-politischen Oppositionsparteien im alten Islam* (Göttingen, 1901), translated by R. C. Ostle and S. M. Walker as *The Religio-Political Factions in Early Islam* (Amsterdam, 1975). A recent study, taking into account later Shīʿī sources, is S. Husain M. Jafri's *Origins and Early Development of Shīʿa Islam* (London, 1979).

Twelver Shiism is treated in Dwight Donaldson's *The Shīʿite Religion* (London, 1933) and, from a Shīʿī perspective, in ʿAllāmah Sayyid Muḥammad Ḥusayn Ṭabaṭabāʾī's *Shi'ite Islam,* translated from the Persian by Seyyed Hossein Nasr (Albany, 1975). Ṭabaṭabāʾī has also gathered significant Twelver Shīʿī texts, sermons, and sayings of imams in *A Shīʿite Anthology,* translated with explanatory notes by William C. Chittick (Albany, N.Y., 1981). The papers of the 1968 Colloque de Strasbourg, published as *Le Shîisme imâmite* (Paris, 1970), offer scholarly contributions on various aspects of the history of Twelver Shiism. John Norman Hollister's *The Shīʿa of India* (London, 1953) deals with the Twelvers, Ismāʿīlīyah, Bohoras, and Khojas on the Indian subcontinent. A well-informed survey of the role of Shiism in Iran, especially in recent history, is provided by Yann Richard's *Le Shīʿisme en Iran* (Paris, 1980).

On contemporary Shīʿī *ghulāt* sects, much material has been gathered in Klaus Müller's *Kulturhistorische Studien zur Genese pseudo-islamischer Sektengebilde in Vorderasien* (Wiesbaden, 1967), whose conclusions about the genesis of these sects are, however, open to question.

A sketch of the history of the Ismāʿīlīyah is given by W. Ivanow in *Brief Survey of the Evolution of Ismaʿilism* (Leiden, 1952). The genesis of Ismāʿīli gnostic doctrine has been reexamined in H. Halm's *Kosmologie und Heilslehre der frühen Ismāʿīlīya* (Wiesbaden, 1978).

Cornelis van Arendonk's *De Opkomst van het Zaidietische Imamaat in Yemen* (Leiden, 1919), translated into French by Jacques Ryckmans as *Les débuts de l'imamat Zaidite au Yémen* (Leiden, 1960), offers a history of the Zaydīyah until the foundation of the Zaydī state in Yemen. I have studied the development of Zaydī doctrine up to the twelfth century in *Der Imam al-Qāsim ibn Ibrāhīm und die Glaubenslehre der Zaiditen* (Berlin, 1965).

New Sources

Dinault, David. *The Shiites: Ritual and Popular Piety in a Muslim Community.* New York, 1992.

Kohlberg, Etan. *Belief and Law in Imām; Shīʿīsm.* Aldershot, U.K., 1991.

Kohlberg, Etan, ed. *Shiʿism.* Aldershot, U.K., 2003.

WILFERD MADELUNG (1987)
Revised Bibliography

SHIISM: ISMĀʿĪLĪYAH

A major branch of the Shīʿah, the Ismāʿīlīyah traces the line of imams through Ismāʿīl, son of Imam Jaʿfar al-Ṣādiq (d. AH 148/765 CE). Ismāʿīl was initially designated by Jaʿfar as his successor but predeceased him. Some of Jaʿfar's followers who considered the designation irreversible either denied the death of Ismāʿīl or accepted Ismāʿīl's son Muḥammad as the rightful imam after Jaʿfar.

The Pre-Fatimid Age. The communal and doctrinal history of the Ismaʿilīyah in this period poses major problems that are still unresolved for lack of reliable sources. The Muslim heresiographers mostly speak of two Ismāʿīlī groups after the death of Imam Jaʿfar: The "pure Ismāʿīlīyah" held that Ismāʿīl had not died and would return as the Qāʾim *(mahdī)*, while the Mubārakīyah recognized Muḥammad ibn Ismāʿīl as their imam. According to the heresiographers, al-Mubārak was the name of their chief, a freedman of Ismāʿīl. It seems, however, that the name (meaning "the blessed"), was applied to Ismāʿīl by his followers, and thus the name Mubārakīyah must at first have referred to them. After the death of Jaʿfar most of them evidently accepted Muḥammad ibn Ismāʿīl as their imam in the absence of Ismāʿīl. Twelver Shīʿī reports attribute a major role among the early backers of Ismāʿīl to the Khaṭṭābīyah, the followers of the extremist Shīʿī heresiarch Abū al-Khaṭṭāb (d. 755?). Whatever the reliability of such reports, later Ismāʿīlī teaching generally shows few traces of Khaṭṭābī doctrine and repudiates Abū al-Khaṭṭāb. An eccentric work reflecting a Khaṭṭābī tradition, the *Umm al-kitāb* (Mother of the book) transmitted by the Ismāʿīlīyah of Badakhshān, is clearly a late adaptation of non-Ismāʿīlī material.

Nothing is known about the fate of these Ismāʿīlī splinter sects arising in Kufa in Iraq on the death of Imam Jaʿfar, and it can be surmised that they were numerically insignificant. But about a hundred years later, after the middle of the third century AH (ninth century CE), the Ismāʿīlīyah reappeared in history, now as a well-organized, secret revolutionary movement with an elaborate doctrinal system spread by missionaries called *dāʿīs* ("summoners") throughout much of the Islamic world. The movement was centrally directed, at first apparently from Ahwaz in southwestern Iran. Recognizing Muḥammad ibn Ismāʿīl as its *imām*, it held that he had disappeared and would return in the near future as the Qāʾim to fill the world with justice.

Early doctrines. The religious doctrine of this period, which is largely reconstructed from later Ismāʿīlī sources and anti-Ismāʿīlī accounts, distinguished between the outer, exoteric (*ẓāhir*) and the inner, esoteric (*bāṭin*) aspects of religion. Because of this belief in a *bāṭin* aspect, fundamental also to most later Ismāʿīlī thought, the Ismāʿīlīyah were often called Bāṭinīyah, a name that sometimes has a wider application, however. The *ẓāhir* aspect consists of the apparent, directly accessible meaning of the scriptures brought by the prophets and the religious laws contained in them; it differs in each scripture. The *bāṭin* consists of the esoteric, unchangeable truths (*ḥaqāʾiq*) hidden in all scriptures and laws behind the apparent sense and revealed by the method of esoteric interpretation called *taʾwīl*, which often relied on qabbalistic manipulation of the mystical significance of letters and their numerical equivalents. The esoteric truths embody a gnostic cosmology and a cyclical, yet teleological history of revelation.

The supreme God is the Absolute One, who is beyond cognizance. Through his intention (*irādah*) and will (*mashīʾah*) he created a light which he addressed with the Qurʾanic creative imperative, *kun* ("Be!"), consisting of the letters *kāf* and *nūn*. Through duplication, the first, preceding (*sābiq*) principle, Kūnī ("be," fem.) proceeded from them and in turn was ordered by God to create the second, following *(tālī)* principle, Qadar ("measure, decree"). Kūnī represented the female principle and Qadar, the male; together they were comprised of seven letters (the short vowels of Qadar are not considered letters in Arabic), which were called the seven higher letters (*ḥurūf ʿulwīyah*) and were interpreted as the archetypes of the seven messenger prophets and their scriptures. In the spiritual world, Kūnī created seven cherubs (*karūbīyah*) and Qadar, on Kuni's order, twelve spiritual ranks (*ḥudūd rūḥānīyah*). Another six ranks emanated from Kūnī when she initially failed to recognize the existence of the creator above her. The fact that these six originated without her will through the power of the creator then moved her to recognize him with the testimony that "There is no god but God," and to deny her own divinity. Three of these ranks were above her and three below; among the latter was Iblīs, who refused Kunī's order to submit to Qadar, the heavenly Adam, and thus became the chief devil. Kūnī and Qadar also formed a pentad together with three spiritual forces, Jadd, Fatḥ, and Khayāl, which were often identified with the archangels Jibrāʾīl, Mīkhāʾīl, and Isrāfīl and mediated between the spiritual world and the religious hierarchy in the physical world.

The lower, physical world was created through the mediation of Kūnī and Qadar, with the ranks of the religious teaching hierarchy corresponding closely to the ranks of the higher, spiritual world. The history of revelation proceeded through seven prophetic eras or cycles, each inaugurated by a speaker (*nāṭiq*) prophet bringing a fresh divine message. The first six speaker-prophets, Adam, Noah, Abraham, Moses, Jesus, and Muḥammad, were each succeeded by a legatee *(waṣī)* or silent one *(ṣāmit)* who revealed the esoteric meaning hidden in their messages. Each legatee was succeeded by seven imams, the last of whom would rise in rank to become the speaker of the next cycle and bring a new scripture and law abrogating the previous one. In the era of Muḥammad, ʿAlī was the legatee and Muḥammad ibn Ismāʿīl the seventh imam. Upon his return Muḥammad ibn Ismāʿīl would become the seventh speaker prophet and abrogate the law of Islam. His divine message would not entail a new law, however, but consist in the full revelation of the previously hidden esoteric truths. As the eschatological Qāʾim and *mahdī*, he would rule the world and consummate it. During his absence, the teaching hierarchy was headed by twelve *ḥujjahs* residing in the twelve provinces (*jazāʾir*). Below them were several ranks of *dāʿīs*. The number and names of these ranks given in early Ismāʿīlī texts vary widely and reflect speculative concerns rather than the actual organization of the hierarchy, about which little is known for either the pre-Fatimid or Fatimid age. Before the advent of the Qāʾim, the teaching of the esoteric truths must be kept secret. The neophyte had to swear an oath of initiation vowing strict secrecy and to pay a fee. Initiation was clearly gradual, but there is no evidence of a number of strictly defined grades; the accounts of anti-Ismāʿīlī sources that name and describe seven or nine such grades leading to the final stage of pure atheism and libertinism deserve no credit.

Emergence of the movement. The sudden appearance of a widespread, centrally organized Ismāʿīlī movement with an elaborate doctrine after the middle of the ninth century suggests that its founder was active at that time. The Sunnī anti-Ismāʿīlī polemicists of the following century name as this founder one ʿAbd Allāh ibn Maymūn al-Qaddāḥ. They describe his father, Maymūn al-Qaddāḥ, as a Bardesanian who became a follower of Abū al-Khaṭṭāb and founded an extremist sect called the Maymūnīyah. According to this account, ʿAbd Allāh conspired to subvert Islam from the inside by pretending to be a Shīʿī working on behalf of Muḥammad ibn Ismāʿīl. He founded the movement in the latter's name with its seven grades of initiation leading to atheism and sent his *dāʿīs* abroad. At first he was active near Ahwāz and later moved to Basra and to Salāmīyah in Syria; the later leaders of the movement and the Fatimid caliphs were his descendants. This story is obviously anachronistic in placing ʿAbd Allāh's activity over a century later than that of his father. Moreover, Twelver Shīʿī sources mention Maymūn al-Qaddāḥ and his son ʿAbd Allāh as faithful companions of Imams Muḥammad al-Bāqir (d. 735?) and Jaʿfar al-Ṣādiq respectively. They do not suggest that either of them was inclined to extremism. It is thus unlikely that ʿAbd Allāh ibn Maymūn played any role in the original Ismāʿīlī sect and impossible that he is the founder of the ninth-century movement. The Sunnī polemicists' story about ʿAbd Allāh ibn Maymūn is, however, based on Ismāʿīlī sources. At least some early Ismāʿīlī communities believed that the leaders of the movement including the first Fatimid caliph, al-Mahdī, were not ʿAlids but descendants of Maymūn al-Qaddāḥ. The Fatimids tried to counter such beliefs by maintaining that their ʿAlid ancestors had used names such as al-Mubarak, Maymūn, and Saʿīd in order to hide their identity. While such a use of cover names is not implausible, it does not explain how Maymūn, allegedly the cover name of Muḥammad ibn Ismāʿīl, could have become identified with Maymūn al-Qaddāḥ. It has, on the other hand, been suggested that some descendants of ʿAbd Allāh ibn Maymūn may have played a leading part in the ninth-century movement. The matter evidently cannot be resolved at present. It is certain, however, that the leaders of the movement, the ancestors of the Fatimids, claimed neither descent from Muḥammad ibn Ismāʿīl nor the status of imams, even among their closest *dāʿīs*, but described themselves as *ḥujjahs* of the absent imam Muḥammad ibn Ismāʿīl.

The esoteric doctrine of the movement was of a distinctly gnostic nature. Many structural elements, themes, and concepts have parallels in various earlier gnostic systems, although no specific sources or models can be discerned. Rather, the basic system gives the impression of an entirely fresh, essentially Islamic and Shīʿī adaptation of various widespread gnostic motives. Clearly without foundation are the assertions of the anti-Ismāʿīlī polemicists and heresiographers that the Ismāʿīlīyah was derived from various dualist religions, such as Zoroastrianism, Manichaeism, Bardesanism, Mazdakism, and the Khurramdīnīyah.

The movement was rent by a schism about 899 after ʿAbd Allāh (ʿUbayd Allāh), the future Fatimid caliph al-Mahdī, succeeded to the leadership. Repudiating the belief in the imamate of Muḥammad ibn Ismāʿīl and his return as the *mahdī*, al-Mahdī claimed the imamate for himself. He explained to the *dāʿīs* that his predecessors in the leadership had been legitimate imams but had concealed their rank and identity out of caution. They were descendants of Imam Jaʿfar's son ʿAbd Allāh, who had been the rightful successor to the imamate rather than Ismāʿīl; the names of Ismāʿīl and his son Muḥammad had merely been used to cover up their identity as the imams.

This apparently radical change of doctrine was not accepted by some of the leading *dāʿīs*. In the region of Kufa, Ḥamdān Qarmaṭ and ʿAbdan broke with al-Mahdī and discontinued their missionary activity. Qarmaṭ's followers were called the Qarāmiṭah, and the name was often extended to other communities that broke with the Fatimid leadership, and sometimes to the Ismāʿīlīyah in general; it will be used here for those Ismāʿīlīyah who did not recognize the Fatimid imamate. ʿAbdān was the first author of the movement's books. He was murdered by a *dāʿī* initially loyal to al-Mahdī, and Ḥamdan Qarmaṭ disappeared. On the west coast of the Persian Gulf, the *dāʿī* Abū Saʿid al-Jannabi followed the lead of Qarmaṭ and ʿAbdan, who had invested him with his mission. He had already seized a number of towns, including al-Qaṭīf and al-Aḥsā, and had thus laid the foundation of the Qarmaṭī state of Bahrein. Other communities that repudiated al-Mahdī's claim to the imamate were in the region of Rayy in northwestern Iran, in Khorasan, and in Transoxiana. Most prominent among the *dāʿīs* who remained loyal to al-Mahdī was Ibn Ḥawshab, known as Manṣūr al-Yaman, the senior missionary in the Yemen. He had brought the region of Jabal Maswar under his control, while his younger colleague and rival, ʿAlī ibn al-Faḍl, was active in the Bilād Yāfiʿ further southwest. The *dāʿī* Abū ʿAbd Allāh al-Shīʿī, whom Manṣūr al-Yaman had sent to the Kutāmah Berber tribe in the mountains of eastern Algeria, and probably also the *dāʿī* al-Haytham, whom he had dispatched to Sind, remained loyal to al-Mahdī. Some of the Ismāʿīlīyah in Khorasan also accepted his claim to the imamate. Residing at this time in Salāmīyah, al-Mahdī then left for Egypt together with his son, the later caliph al-Qāʾim, as his safety was threatened because of the disaffection of the leading Syrian *dāʿī*. At first he intended to proclaim himself as the *mahdī* in the Yemen. Increasing doubts about the loyalty of ʿAlī ibn al-Faḍl, who later openly defected, seem to have influenced his decision to go to the Maghreb, where Abū ʿAbd Allāh al-Shīʿī, having overthrown the Aghlabids and seized Tunisia, proclaimed him caliph and *mahdī* in 910.

THE FATIMID AGE (910–1171). With the establishment of the Fatimid countercaliphate, the Ismāʿīlī challenge to Sunnī Islam reached its peak and provoked a vehement political and intellectual reaction. The Ismāʿīlīyah came to be condemned by orthodox theologians as the archheresy of Islam. The Fatimid Ismāʿīlīyah was weakened by serious splits, first that of the Qarāmiṭah and later those of the Druzes, the Nizārīyah, and the Ṭayyibīyah.

The Qarāmiṭah. The Ismāʿīlī communities that repudiated the claim of the Fatimid al-Mahdī to the imamate were initially left without united leadership and in doctrinal disarray. Soon after the rise of the Fatimid caliphate they recovered some organizational and doctrinal unity on the basis of a reaffirmation of the belief in the imamate of Muḥammad ibn Ismāʿīl and in his expected return as the Qāʾim. This belief was also espoused by the Transoxianan *dāʿī* Muḥammad ibn Ah-mad al-Nasafī in his *Kitāb al-maḥṣūl* (Book of the yield), which gained wide authority among the Qarmaṭī Ismāʿīlīyah. The book itself is lost, but numerous quotations from it and discussions in later works attest to its importance and make it possible to reconstruct its contents. Al-Nasafī introduced in it a Neoplatonic cosmology that superseded and partly replaced the earlier cosmolgy and became basic to much of Ismāʿīlī esoteric doctrine throughout the Fatimid age.

In this cosmology Kūnī and Qadar were replaced by the Neoplatonic Universal Intellect and Soul. God, who is beyond any attribute and name and even beyond being and non-being, has originated (*abdaʿa*) the Intellect through his divine order or volition (*amr*). The Intellect is described as the first originated being *(al-mubdaʿ al-awwal)* since the *amr* has become united with it in existence. The Universal Soul emanated from the Intellect, and from the Soul in turn issued the seven spheres of the heavens with their stars. These spheres revolve with the Soul's movement, producing the mixture of the four single natures—dryness, humidity, cold, and warmth—to form the composites of earth, water, air, and ether. Out of the mingling of the composites arise the plants with a vegetative soul, which in turn give rise to the animals endowed with a sensitive soul. Out of the animal realm arises the human being with a rational soul that seeks to ascend through the spiritual hierarchy and to rejoin its origin in the Intellect.

Proclamation of the mahdī. The *dāʿī* of Rayy, Abū Hatim al-Rāzī (d. 934), claimed superior authority among the Qarmaṭī *dāʿīs* as the lieutenant of the absent *imām.* He succeeded in converting a number of powerful men in the region, sent his *dāʿīs* throughout northwestern Iran, and maintained a correspondance with Abū Ṭāhir al-Jannābī, who had succeeded his father, Abū Saʿīd, in the leadership of the Qarmaṭī state in Bahrein. The Qarmaṭī *dāʿīs* were at this time predicting the advent of the *mahdī* after the conjunction of Jupiter and Saturn in the year 928, an occurrence that they believed would bring the era of Islam to an end and usher in the seventh and final era. As the date approached, Abū Ṭāhir carried out daring attacks ever farther into southern Iraq and finally threatened the Abbasid capital of Baghdad itself. In 930 he sacked Mecca during the pilgrimage season, slaughtered pilgrims and inhabitants, and carried off the Black Stone of the Kaʿbah as a sign for the end of the era of Islam. In 932 he proclaimed a young Persian from Isfahan as the expected *mahdī.*

Events now took a different course than had commonly been predicted by the Ismāʿīlīyah for the coming of the *mahdī.* According to the erudite expert of the chronology of nations, al-Bīrūnī (d. 1050?), the date was chosen to coincide with the passing of fifteen hundred years after Zoroaster, the end of the year 1242 of the era of Alexander, for which prophecies ascribed to Zoroaster and Jāmāsp had predicted the restoration of the reign of the Magians. The Persian was said to be a Magian and a descendant of the Persian kings. His hometown of Isfahan had long been associated by the astrologers with the rise of a Persian dynasty which would conquer the Arab caliphate. The Persian is reported to have ordered the worship of fire and the cursing of all the prophets and to have licensed the most outrageous abominations. After the Persian put some Qarmaṭī leaders to death, Abū Ṭāhir felt compelled to kill him and to avow that he had been duped by an impostor.

The significance of this episode must be judged with caution. The Persian, anti-Arab aspect was evidently a spontaneous development among the leaders of the Qarmaṭī community of Bahrein. It does not confirm the assertions of the Sunnī polemicists that the Ismāʿīlī movement originated in an anti-Islamic and anti-Arab plot of Persian dualists, but it may have given rise to them. More deeply rooted in the movement were the antinomian sentiments radically expressed in the cursing of the prophets, the founders of the religious laws. Antinomian tendencies were naturally inherent in religious thought which looked for an esoteric spiritual meaning concealed behind the exoteric surface of scripture and law. Though sometimes latent for a long time, they manifested themselves powerfully at various stages in the history of the Ismāʿīlīyah.

The ignominious course and outcome of the affair led to massive defections of adherents and shocked the leading *dāʿīs.* Abū Ḥātim al-Rāzī's *Kitāb al-iṣlāḥ* (Book of correction), in which he criticized and "corrected" various points of al-Nasafī's *Kitāb al-maḥṣūl,* appears to have been written in reaction to the events. Abū Ḥātim in particular objected to the antinomian tendencies apparent in some of the teaching of al-Nasafī. Arguing that all esoteric truth inevitably requires an exoteric revealed law, he affirmed against al-Nasafī that both Adam, the first speaker prophet, and Jesus had brought a religious law. While admitting that the seventh speaker prophet, Muḥammad ibn Ismāʿīl, would not bring a law but reveal the spiritual truths, he insisted that the era of Muḥammad had not come to an end with the first presence and disappearance of the seventh imam. There was in each prophetic cycle an interval (*fatrah*) between the presence of the seventh imam and the advent of the speaker prophet who would inaugurate the new era, during which time the seventh imam was represented by his lieutenants (*khulafaʾā*).

Abū Ḥātim's ideas failed to rally the Qarmaṭī communities around his leadership as the lieutenant of the imam. In his *Kitāb al-nuṣrah* (Book of support), the younger *dāʿī* Abū Yaʿqūb al-Sijistānī consistently upheld al-Nasafī's views against Abū Ḥātim's criticism and categorically rejected Abū Hatim's thesis that esoteric truths could be attained only through the religious law. In Khorasan and Transoxiana in particular the authority of al-Nasafī's *Kitāb al-maḥṣūl* seems to have remained paramount after the author's death in 944. The *dāʿīs* in Iraq continued to recognize the authority of ʿAbdān, in whose name they composed numerous treatises tinged with popular philosophy. After repudiating their pseudo-*mahdī*, the Qarāmiṭah of Bahrein again claimed to be acting on the orders of the hidden *mahdī*. Abū Ṭāhir soon reached an agreement with the Abbasid government under which he guaranteed the safety of the pilgrimage to Mecca in return for an annual tribute and a protection fee paid by the pilgrims. The Black Stone of the Kaʿbah was returned to Mecca in 951 after payment of a high ransom.

Decline of the movement. In preparation for his conquest of Egypt and the East, the fourth Fatimid caliph, al-Muʿizz (953–975) strove to win the dissident eastern Ismāʿīlī communities for the Fatimid cause and to this end made some ideological concessions to them (see below). His efforts were partly successful, and he gained the allegiance of Abū Yaʿqūb al-Sijistānī, who in his later works fully backed the Fatimid imamate. Other *dāʿīs*, however, resisted his overtures. Most important, he failed to persuade the Qarāmiṭah of Bahrein, who even allied themselves with the Abbasid caliphate and fought the Fatimid conquerors in Syria and Egypt. Although they later concluded a truce with the Fatimids and at times officially recognized the Fatimid caliphate, they never accepted its religious authority. In the later tenth century they lost their military prowess and were reduced to a local, self-contained power while the Qarmaṭī communities elsewhere either were absorbed into the Fatimid Ismāʿīlīyah or disintegrated. The Qarmaṭī state in Bahrein survived until 1077/8. Little is known about the specific religious beliefs of the sectarians there. Muslim law and rites such as prayer and fasting were not practiced, and all mosques were closed. Much property was owned communally, and some of the revenue from tributes and imposts on sea trades was distributed among the members of the community. Such institutions were, however, not directly founded on the religious teaching, which promised a rule of justice and fairness but did not develop a social program.

The Brethren of Purity. Much discussed and still unresolved is the question of the relationship of the *Rasāʾil Ikhwān al-Ṣafāʾ* (Epistles of the Brethren of Purity) and their anonymous authors to the Ismāʿīlīyah. This encyclopedia of fifty-two treatises on all sciences of the ancients pervaded by an esoteric religious message was, according to two authors of the later tenth century, composed by a group of secretaries and scholars in Basra about the middle of the century. Later Ismāʿīlī tradition, however, claims that it was written by one of the hidden *imāms* and his *dāʿīs* a century earlier. The treatises speak of the *imām* as in hiding, though accessible, and foresee his appearance. Some modern scholars have argued that a part or most of the encyclopedia was composed in the pre-Fatimid Ismāʿīlī community and that quotations and references in the text that belong to the tenth century are later additions. Others consider it as essentially non-Ismāʿīlī though influenced by Ismāʿīlī thought; this judgment is usually based on a comparison with Fatimid Ismāʿīlī literature. It is evident that the authors, if they did live in the tenth century, could not have been adherents of the Fatimid imamate. Yet the thought and terminology of the treatises are pervasively Ismāʿīlī and must have originated in an Ismāʿīlī environment. In the middle of the tenth century Basra was dominated by the Qarāmiṭah of Bahrein. It is not unlikely that the authors undertook their project with the approval of the Qarmaṭī leaders, but nothing definite is known about their relationship and the attitude of the later Qarāmiṭah to the encyclopedia.

The Fatimid Ismāʿīlīyah. The first Fatimid caliph rose with the claim of being not only the imam but also the expected *mahdī*. This claim inevitably raised questions concerning the acts and the eschatological role ascribed to the *mahdī* in apocalyptic traditions. Al-Mahdī answered such questions by maintaining that the prophecies concerning the *mahdī* would be gradually fulfilled by himself and by the *imāms* succeeding him. He gave his son and successor the caliphal title al-Qāʾim, another eschatological name that usually had been considered to refer to the *mahdī*. In one basic respect he uncompromisingly countered the Ismāʿīlī expectations for the advent of the *mahdī*: While the pre-Fatimid teaching affirmed that the *mahdī* as the seventh speaker prophet would abrogate the law of Islam and make the esoteric spiritual truths public, al-Mahdī insisted on strict observation of the religious law of Islam and severely punished some *dāʿīs* who ignored it and published esoteric teaching. Official Fatimid doctrine always emphasized the equal validity and necessity of the *zahir* and the *bātīn*, of religious work (*ʿamal*) in accordance with the law and esoteric knowledge (*ʿilm*).

Ismāʿīlī law. Under al-Mahdī began the career of Qāḍi al-Nuʿmān (d. 974), the founder of Ismāʿīlī law and author of its most authoritative compendium, the *Kitāb daʿāʾim al-Islām* (Book of the buttresses of Islam). In the absence of an Ismāʿīlī legal tradition, Qāḍi al-Nuʿmān relied primarily on the legal teaching of Imāms Muḥammad al-Bāqir and Jaʿfar al-Ṣādiq, transmitted by Twelver Shīʿī traditionists, and secondarily on Zaydi traditions. As a former Mālikī jurist, he was evidently also influenced by Mālikī legal concepts. In substance Ismāʿīlī law naturally agrees closely with Twelver Shīʿī law, it prohibits, however, the temporary marriage (*mutʿah*) allowed in the latter and nullifies bequests to a legal heir except when consent of the other legal heirs is obtained. It gives the imam authority for determining the beginning of the month without regard to the sighting of the new moon as required by all other Muslim legal schools. Since the early Fatimid period the beginning of the months was generally established in practice on the basis of astronomical calculation and thus often fell one or two days earlier than for other Muslims; this discrepancy often caused intercommunal quarrels about the beginning and end of the fasting month of Ramaḍān.

Esoteric doctrines. The Ismāʿīlī law codified by Qāḍi al-Nuʿmān was adopted by the fourth Fatimid caliph, al-Muʿizz, as the official law of the Fatimid empire to be applied to all its Muslim subjects. Al-Muʿizz also substantially reformed the Fatimid esoteric doctrine with the clear aim of making it more acceptable to the dissident Qarmaṭī communities in order to gain their backing for the Fatimid imamate. Thus he reaffirmed the early belief that Muḥammad ibn Ismāʿīl as the seventh imam was the seventh speaker prophet and the Qāʾim and ignored al-Mahdī's claim that ʿAbd Allāh rather than Ismāʿīl had been the legitimate imam after Jaʿfar al-Ṣādiq. In his view, the acts of the Qāʾim in the physical world would, however, be carried out by his lieutenants (*khulafāʾ*)—a term familiar to the Qarāmiṭah, who also spoke of the lieutenants of the Qāʾim who were to head the hierarchy during his absence. For al-Muʿizz, however, these lieutenants were *imāms* and descendants of Muḥammad ibn Ismāʿīl, who would not return to the physical world but would head the spiritual hierarchy at the end of the world. The lieutenants of the Qāʾim formed a second heptad of imams in the sixth era, which the prophet Muḥammad had been granted as a special privilege. Following the earlier Fatimid caliphs and three hidden imams descended from Muḥammad ibn Ismāʿīl, al-Muʿizz was the seventh *imām* of this heptad. He seems to have envisaged an early end of the physical world and is quoted to have affirmed that there would not be another heptad of imams after him.

Al-Muʿizz also opened the door to the Neoplatonic cosmology of al-Nasafī, which so far had been rejected by the Fatimid Ismāʿīlīyah. Abū Yaʿqūb al-Sijistānī, who was converted to the Fatimid Ismāʿīlīyah, became their main representative of Neoplatonic thought. Many of his books and treatises are extant. The esoteric teaching, severely restricted under al-Mahdī, was now organized in formal lecture sessions (*majālis*) held twice weekly. The lectures were prepared by the official chief *dāʿī* and submitted to the imam for approval. Attendance at the lectures was restricted to the initiates, who were required to pay religious dues. The Ismāʿīlī communities remained a small minority throughout the Fatimid reign.

The Druze. During the later reign of the sixth Fatimid caliph, al-Ḥākim (996–1021), the eschatological expectations that al-Muʿizz had incited gave rise to a new schismatic movement. Encouraged by al-Ḥākim's abnormal conduct, some of the Ismāʿīlīyah came to speculate that he might be the expected Qāʾim. While the official teaching hierarchy strove to counter these speculations, an enthusiastic follower, Ḥasan al-Akhram, publicly proclaimed al-Ḥākim's divinity in 1017. He told his Ismāʿīlī audience that their resurrection (*qiyamah*) had occurred and that the era of their concealment had come to an end. In spite of the favor shown him by the caliph, Ḥasan was murdered a few months later. In 1019 the movement reemerged, now led by Ḥamzah ibn ʿAlī, the true founder of its doctrine.

Its adherents were called *durūz* (Druze) after al-Dar(a)zī, an early rival of Ḥamzah who caught the eye of the public. Ḥamzah claimed to be the imam, the Qāʾim of the Age (*qāʾim al-zamān*), and the embodiment of the Universal Intellect. He identified some of his assistants with the Universal Soul and other ranks of the spiritual hierarchy of the Ismāʿīlīyah: Al-Ḥākim and his ancestors back to the second Fatimid caliph, al-Qāʾim, were held to be manifestations of the transcendent godhead. Ḥamzah proclaimed the abrogation not only of the exoteric religious law but also of the esoteric teaching of the Ismāʿīlīyah through the appearance of God on earth in royal dignity. He defined his own message as the pure doctrine of unity (*tawḥīd*) that renewed the message of the Adam of Purity (*Ādam al-ṣafāʾ*), who had opened the cycle of humanity. The six prophets of the following eras from Noah to Muḥammad ibn Ismāʿīl had each brought a blameworthy law ordering the worship of nonbeing and the unity of the idol (*ʿibādat al-ʿadam wa-tawḥīd al-ṣanam*). Ḥamzah thus employed many Ismāʿīlī concepts but transformed them so radically that the Druze religion is usually considered to be outside the Ismāʿīlīyah. After the death of al-Ḥākim the new sect was persecuted and quickly suppressed in Egypt. It has survived to the present, however, in the mountains of Syria and Lebanon.

Leading figures. A prominent part in the initial fight of the official Fatimid teaching hierarchy against the founders of the Ḥākim cult was played by the *dāʿī* Ḥamid al-Dīn al-Kirmānī. Active in Baghdad and Basra, he came to Cairo about 1015, presumably invited to assist in the struggle against the heretics. Recognizing that the heresy was essentially rooted in the fervent hopes for the advent of the Qāʾim with its antinomian implications raised by traditional Ismāʿīlī teaching, al-Kirmānī reacted sharply against them. In a letter addressed to Ḥasan al-Akhram he scornfully repudiated the idea that the resurrection had occurred with the appearance of al-Ḥākim and that the era of the prophet Muḥammad had come to an end. The resurrection would not occur before the signs predicted by Muḥammad had appeared. The era of Muḥammad and the validity of the law of Islam would continue under the reign of al-Ḥākim's successors. Ignoring the traditional Ismāʿīlī theories about a limited number of heptads of *imāms*, al- Kirmānī envisaged the triumphant rule of the hundredth imam in the era of Muḥammad.

In one of his larger works, the *Kitāb al-riyāḍ* (Book of meadows), he critically reviewed the controversy between Abū Ḥātim al-Rāzī and Abū Yaʿqūb al-Sijistānī over al-Nasafī's *Kitāb al-maḥṣūl.* Almost invariably he backed the position of Abū Ḥātim but went even further in his affirmation of the indispensibility of the law. The belief that the Qāʾim would abrogate the law was faulty, for spiritual knowledge could never be based on anything but the prophetic laws and their rules for worship. Rather the Qāʾim would restore the laws in their original form and abolish the teaching hierarchy, which would no longer be needed because knowledge would become actual and general while ignorance would be reduced to potentiality. Abū Yaʿqūb, he argued, was mistaken in asserting that after the Qāʾim a time of pure spiritual knowledge without work and law would begin like the great era before Adam. Rather, before Adam pure ignorance had reigned among the creatures since they did not know the hierarchy, and likewise, after the Qāʾim ignorance would be gradually actualized again and knowledge would become potential because of the abolition of the hierarchy.

Although al-Kirmānī thus maintained, against Abū Yaʿqūb, the absolute priority of the law over spiritual knowledge, he also made a major contribution to the esoteric teaching. In his most famous work, the *Kitāb rāḥat al-ʿaql* (Peace of mind), he propounded a new cosmology evidently influenced by the Muslim philosophers of al-Fārābī's school. He replaced the pair of the Intellect and the Soul ruling the spiritual world by a hierarchy of ten Intellects. The place of the Soul thus was taken by the Second Intellect or First Emanation *(al-munbaʿith al-awwal),* which proceeded from the higher relation of the First Intellect. From the lower relation of the First Intellect proceeded the Third Intellect, or Second Emanation, which is the first potential being, equated with matter and form and thus the basis of the physical world. Seven further Intellects originated jointly from the First and Second Intellects. The tenth one is the Active Intellect *(al-ʿaql al-faʿʿal),* the demiurge governing the lower world. The structure of the astral world and of the religious hierarchy was described by al-Kirmānī as closely paralleling that of the spiritual world. Al-Kirmānī's cosmology had little impact on Fatimid doctrine, which mostly preferred the older cosmology of al-Nasafī and Abū Yaʿqūb. It was later adopted by the Ṭayyibi Ismāʿīlīyah in the Yemen.

A prominent *dāʿī* during the long caliphate of the Fatimid al-Mustanṣir (1036–1094) was Nāṣir-i Khusraw, well known as a Persian poet and as the author of a travel narrative. Because of his activity as a Fatimid *dāʿī,* he was forced to leave Balkh and found refuge in a Badakhshān mountain village in the upper Oxus valley, where he wrote and taught until his death about 1088/9. He became the patron saint of the Ismāʿīlī community of Badakhshān, which has preserved many of his Ismāʿīlī works. Some of these are Persian translations and adaptations of earlier books in Arabic; most important is his *Kitāb jāmiʿ al-ḥikmatayn* (Book joining the two wisdoms), in which he analyzed agreement and disagreement between the views of the Muslim philosophers and the prophetic wisdom of Ismāʿīlī gnosis.

Another leading figure in the contemporary Fatimid teaching hierarchy was al-Muʾayyad fī al-Dīn of Shiraz, the son of an Ismāʿīlī *dāʿī* active at the Buyid court. Al-Muʾayyad succeeded his father and converted the Buyid emir Abū Kālījār and some of his Daylamī troops to the Ismāʿīlīyah but was forced to leave because of pressure on Abū Kālījār from the Abbasid court. He fled to Cairo where he was appointed chief *dāʿī* in 1058. Although he was soon dismissed and exiled for a time, he regained wide influence as a *dāʿī* before his death in 1077. His early career is described in his autobiography. His poetry, gathered in a *dīwān,* is strictly doctrinal. The most massive of his numerous works is an eight-volume collection of eight hundred of his teaching sessions (*majālis*). His doctrine was later considered highly authoritative, especially among the Ṭayyibi Ismāʿīlīyah in the Yemen and India.

Later schisms. During the latter part of the caliphate of al-Mustanṣir the Ismāʿīlī movement in Iran was spurred to revolutionary activity by the teaching and leadership of Ḥasan-i Ṣābbāḥ, who in 1090 seized the mountain stronghold of Alamūt northwest of Qazvin and made it his headquarters. He had earlier visited Cairo when Nizār, al-Mustanṣir's eldest son, was the designated heir. After the death of al-Mustanṣir, the powerful vizier al-Afḍal put the youngest son, Ahmad, on the throne with the caliphal name al-Mustaʿlī and captured and immured Nizār, who had resisted. Ḥasan-i Ṣābbāḥ, however, continued to recognize Nizār as the legitimate imam and claimed that Nizār had escaped and broken with the Ismāʿīlī leadership in Cairo. He gained general support among the Ismāʿīlīyah in Iran and northern Syria and thus became the founder of the Nizārī branch. Al-Mustaʿlī was recognized by most of the Ismāʿīlīyah in Egypt, the Yemen, India, and by many in Syria and Palestine.

A further split among the Ismāʿīlīyah still backing the imamate of the Fatimid caliphs occurred after the assassination of al-Mustaʿlī's son and successor, al-Āmir, by a Nizārī in 1130. Eight months earlier al-Āmir's newborn son, al-Ṭayyib, had officially been proclaimed his prospective heir, but a cousin of al-Āmir, ʿAbd al-Majīd al-Ḥāfiẓ, was now put on the throne. First merely appointed regent, he was later proclaimed caliph and *imām.* Some Ismāʿīlī communities, especially in the Yemen and India, repudiated his claim and continued to recognize al-Ṭayyib, about whose fate nothing is known, as the rightful successor of al-Āmir. They were led by the Sulayhid queen al-Sayyidah residing in Dhū Jiblah in central Yemen. Most of the Ismāʿīlīyah in Egypt, southern Syria, and southern Yemen, where they were led by the Zurayʿid rulers of Aden, accepted the imamate of al-Ḥāfiẓ in spite of the irregularity of the succession of a cousin. They were known as the Ḥāfiẓīyah or Majīdīyah. The Fatimid caliphate was now in full decline and was overthrown in 1171 by the Ayyubid Ṣālaḥ al-Dīn (Saladin), who restored Sunnism as the official religion in Egypt. Ḥāfiẓī communities survived chiefly in Upper Egypt and continued to recognize as their *imāms* certain descendants of the last Fatimid caliph, al-ʿAdid, who were kept prisoners in Cairo. Under official persecution the Ḥāfiẓī communities gradually disintegrated; the last mention of them occurs in the late thirteenth century.

THE POST-FATIMID ISMĀʿĪLĪYAH. With the disintegration of the Ḥāfiẓī branch, only the Nizārī and Ṭayyibī communities, which had separated from the official Fatimid Ismāʿīlīyah before the fall of the Fatimid dynasty, remained. Both branches, though further divided by schisms, have survived to the present.

The Nizārīyah. With the seizure of Alamūt, Ḥasan-i Ṣābbāḥ initiated a policy of armed revolt against the seljuk sultanate. The Nizārīyah captured and fortified numerous mountain castles in the Elburz range, towns in Quhistān in northwestern Iran, and later also mountain strongholds such as Qadmūs and Masyāf in northern Syria. In the face of the overwhelming military superiority of their opponents they relied on intimidation through the spectacular assassination of prominent leaders by *fidāʾīs*, self-sacrificing devotees. Because of their apparently irrational conduct they were commonly called *ḥashīshīyīn*, hashish addicts. Stories that the *fidāʾīs* were in fact conditioned for their task by the use of hashish are legendary. Their designation as *ḥashīshīyīn* was taken over by the Crusaders in Syria and entered European languages as "assassins."

Ḥasan-i Ṣābbāḥ also elaborated an apologetic missionary doctrine that became known as the "new preaching" (*daʿwah jadīdah*) of the Ismāʿīlīyah. At its core was the thesis of humanity's permanent need for *taʿlīm,* divinely inspired and authoritative teaching, which was basic in much of Shīʿī thought. Ḥasan-i Ṣābbāḥ developed it in a series of arguments establishing the inadequacy of human reason in gaining knowledge of God and then went on to demonstrate that only the Ismāʿīlī *imām* was such a divinely guided teacher. The Nizārīyah came to be commonly called the Taʿlīmīyah after this doctrine, and Sunnī opponents such as al-Ghazālī concentrated their efforts on refuting it. Ḥasan-i Ṣābbāḥ further stressed the autonomous teaching authority of each imam in his time, independent of his predecessors, thus paving the way for the Nizārī radicalization of the doctrine of the imamate as compared with Fatimid doctrine.

Among the Sunnīs apparently attracted by the "new preaching" was the heresiographer and Ashʿarī theologian al-Shahrastānī (d. 1143). Although he kept his relations with the Nizārīyah secret, they were revealed by his student al-Samʿāni. Among his extant writings are some crypto-Ismāʿīlī works including an incomplete Qurʾān commentary in which he used Ismāʿīlī terminology and hinted at his conversion by a "pious servant of God" who had taught him the esoteric principles of Qurʾanic exegesis. Most notable, however, is his refutation of the theological doctrine of the philosopher Ibn Sīnā (Avicenna) from a concealed Ismāʿīlī point of view, entitled *Kitāb al-muṣāraʿah* (Book of the wrestling match). Here he defended the Ismāʿīlī thesis that God, as the giver of being, is beyond being and nonbeing, rejected Avicenna's description of God as the involuntary necessitating cause of the world, and suggested that the Active Intellect which brings the human intellect from potentiality to actuality is the prophetic intellect rather than the intellect of the lunar sphere as held by the followers of Avicenna.

Qiyāmah doctrine. After his death in 1124, Ḥasan-i Ṣābbāḥ was succeeded as lord of Alamūt and chief of the Nizārī community by his assistant Buzurgummīd. On Ramaḍān 17, 599 (August 8, 1164) the latter's grandson, known as Ḥasan ʿalā Dhikrihi al-Salām, solemnly proclaimed the resurrection (*qiyāmah*) in the name of the absent imam and declared the law of Islam abrogated. He interpreted the spiritual meaning of the resurrection as a manifestation of the unveiled truth in the imam, which actualized paradise for the faithful capable of grasping it while condemning the opponents to the hell of spiritual nonexistence. Two years later Ḥasan was murdered by a brother-in-law who objected to the abolition of the Islamic law. His son Muḥammad (1166–1210) further elaborated the *qiyāmah* doctrine. While Ḥasan seems to have indicated that as the *ḥujjah* of the imam he was spiritually identical with him, Muḥammad maintained that his father had been the imam by physical descent; apparently he claimed that Ḥasan was the son of a descendant of Nizār who had secretly found refuge in Alamūt.

According to the *qiyāmah* doctrine, the resurrection consisted in recognizing the divine truth in the present imam, who was the manifestation of the order to create (*amr*) or word (*kalimah*) and, in his revelatory aspect the Qāʾim. The *imām* thus was raised in rank above the prophets. There had been *imām*-Qāʾims also in the earlier prophetic cycles: Mechizedek (Malik al-Salām), Dhū al-Qarnayn, Khiḍr, Maʿadd, and, in the era of Muḥammad, ʿAlī. They were recognized by the prophets of their time as the manifestation of the divine. In the *qiyāmah,* the spiritual reality of the *imām*-Qāʾim manifests itself openly and directly to the faithful. The teaching hierarchy intervening between them and the imam thus had faded away as unnecessary in accordance with the earlier predictions about the advent of the Qāʾim. There remained only three categories of humanity: the opponents of the imam adhering to the law of Islam, his ordinary followers known as the "people of graduation" (*ahl al-tarattub*), who had advanced beyond the law to the esoteric (*bāṭīn*) and thus had attained partial truth, and "the people of union" (*ahl al-waḥdah*), who see the imam plainly in his spirtual reality discarding outward appearances and have therefore reached the realm of pure truth.

Muḥammad's son Jalāl al-Dīn Ḥasan (1210–1221) repudiated the *qiyāmah* doctrine and proclaimed his adherence to Sunnī Islam. He publicly cursed his predecessors as infidels, recognized the suzerainty of the Abbasid caliph, ordered his subjects to follow the law in its Sunnī form, and invited Sunnī scholars for their instruction. Thus he became commonly known as the New Muslim (*naw-muṣūlmān*). His followers mostly obeyed his orders as those of the infallible imam. Under his son ʿAlāʾ al-Dīn Muḥammad (1221–1255) the application of the law was again relaxed, though it was not abolished.

During, ʿAlaʾ al-Dīn's reign the philospher and astronomer Naṣir al-Dīn Ṭūsī (d. 1274), originally a Twelver Shīʿī, joined the Ismāʿīlīyah and actively supported the Nizārī cause, though he later turned away from them and wrote some theological works backing Twelver Shīʿī belief. In a spiritual autobiography written for his Ismāʿīlī patrons he described his upbringing as a strict adherent of the law and his subsequent study of scholastic theology and philosophy. While he found philosophy intellectually most satisfying, he discovered that its principles were shaky when the discourse reached its ultimate goal, the knowledge of God and the origins and destiny of humanity, and recognized the need for an infallible teacher to guide reason to its perfection. He then chanced upon a copy of the sacred articles (*fuṣūl-i muqaddas*) of Imam Ḥasan ʿalā Dhikrihi al-Salām and decided to join the Ismāʿīlīyah. While some of Ṭūsī's works written in this period, such as his widely read Nasirean Ethics (*akhlāq-i Nāṣīrī*), show traces of Nizārī thought, he also composed some religious treatises specifically addressed to the Nizārīyah. The contemporary Nizārī teaching is primarily known through them, particularly his *Rawḍat al-taslīm* (Meadow of submission) or *Taṣawwurāt* (Representations).

Return to concealment. The restoration of the law by Jalāl al-Dīn Ḥasan was now interpreted as a return to a period of precautionary dissimulation (*taqīyah*) and concealment (*satr*) in which the truth is hidden in the *bāṭīn*. The resurrection proclaimed by Ḥasan ʿalā Dhikrihi al-Salām had come at about the middle of the millennium of the era of the prophet Muḥammad and had set the pattern for the final resurrection at the end of it. In the era of Muḥammad, the times of concealment and of resurrection might alternate according to the decision of each *imām*, since every *imām* was potentially a Qāʾim. The contradictions in the conduct of the imams were merely in appearance, since in their spiritual reality they were identical and all acted in accordance with the requirements of their time. In the time of concealment the state of union with the *imām* was confined to his *ḥujjah*, who was consubstantial with him. His other followers, the "people of gradation," were divided into the strong (*aqwiyāʾ*) and the weak (*ḍuʿafāʾ*) according to their closeness to the truth.

Post-Alamūt developments. In 1256 ʿAlāʾ al-Dīn Muḥammad's son and successor Khūrshāh surrendered Alamūt to the Mongol conquerors and was killed soon afterward. The Nizārī state was thus destroyed, and the Persian Ismāʿīlī communities were decimated by massacres. Thereafter the *imāms* lived mostly in concealment, and there is considerable uncertainty about their names, number, and sequence. Following a disputed succession their line soon divided into two branches, one continuing with Muḥammad-shāh, the other with Qāsim-shāh. Of the Muḥammad-shāhī imams, Shāh Ṭāhir Dakanī (d. 1549?) achieved fame as a religious scholar and leader. The popularity of his teaching aroused the suspicion of the Safavid shah Ismāʿīl, who exiled him to Kashan. Later he was forced to leave Iran and eventually found refuge in Ahmadnagar in the Deccan, where he became an adviser of the ruler Burhān Niẓām Shāh, whom he encouraged to proclaim Shiism as the official religion. His writings consisted mainly of commentaries on Twelver Shīʿī and philosophical treatises, although he also maintained relations with his Ismāʿīlī followers. The last known *imām* of the Muḥammad-shāhī line was Amīr Muḥammad Baqīr, with whom his Syrian Ismāʿīlī followers lost all contact after 1796. After a vain search for a descendant of his, a section of the Syrian community changed allegiance in 1887 to the Qāsim-shāhī line represented by the Aga Khans. A smaller section, known as the Jaʿfarīyah, is at present the only community that continues to adhere to the Muḥammad-shāhī line.

Imāms of the Qāsim-shāhī branch are known to have lived in the later fifteenth and again in the seventeenth century in the village of Anjudān near Maḥallāt in Iran, where their tombs have been found. They were in this period, and until the ninteenth century, commonly associated with the Niʿmatullāhī Ṣūfī order. With the appointment of Imam Abū al-Ḥasan Shāh as governor of Kerman in 1756 they rose to political prominence. His grandson Ḥasan ʿAlī Shāh Maḥallātī married a daughter of the Qajar king of Persia, Fatḥ ʿ Alī Shāh, who gave him the title of Aga Khan, which has since been borne hereditarily by his successors. Ḥasan ʿAlī Shāh moved to India in 1843 and after 1848 resided in Bombay. Opposition to his authority in the Ismāʿīlī Khoja community led to court litigation ending in 1886 in the judgment of Sir Joseph Arnould in his favor. It recognized the Khojas as part of the wider Nizārī Ismāʿīlī community. The fourth Aga Khan, Karīm Khān, succeeded his grandfather in 1957.

Religious literature. The wide dispersal of the Nizārī communities, language barriers among them, and their often tenuous relations with the concealed imams led to largely independent organization and literary traditions. In Persia conditions after the fall of Alamūt encouraged the imams and their followers to adopt Ṣūfī forms of religious life. Ṣūfī ideas and terminology had already influenced the *qiyāmah* and late Alamūt doctrine; now Ismāʿīlī ideas were often camouflaged in apparently Ṣūfī poetry, the *imām* being revered as the Ṣūfī saint. Doctrinal works, written again from the sixteenth century on, essentially reflect the teaching of the late Alamūt age with its emphasis on the role of the *ḥujjah* of the imam as the only gate to his spiritual essence and truth. Interest in the traditional Ismāʿīlī cosmology and cyclical prophetic history waned as the religious literature of the Fatimid age was no longer available.

The community of Badakhshān, which accepted the Nizārī imamate probably before the fall of Alamūt, remained attached to the writings, both genuine and spurious, of Nāṣir-i Khusraw, although many Persian Nizārī works of the Alamūt and post-Alamūt age also found their way there. It also transmitted and revered the *Umm al-Kitāb,* the anonymous Persian work sometimes erroneously described as proto-Ismāʿīlī. It reflects some of the gnostic thought of the Kufan Shīʿī *ghulāt* of the eighth century, but its final redaction may be as late as the twelfth century.

The literature of the Nizārī community in Syria, written in Arabic, developed independently of the Persian literature even in the Alamūt period. There is no evidence that Persian works were translated into Arabic. Although the resurrection was proclaimed in Syria, apparently with some delay, the *qiyāmah* and post-*qiyāmah* doctrine of the Persian Nizārīyah with its exaltation of the imam as the manifestation of the divine word made practically no impact there. The Syrian community preserved a substantial portion of Fatimid and Qarmaṭī literature, and scholarly tradition continued to concentrate on the traditional cosmolgy and cyclical prophetic history. In some religious texts of a more popular character, Rashīd al-Dīn Sinān (d. 1193?) the leader of the Syrian Ismāʿīlīyah, known to the crusaders as the "Old Man of the Mountain," is celebrated as a popular hero and assigned a cosmic rank usually reserved for the imam.

The Indian subcontinent. The origins and early history of the Nizārī community on the Indian subcontinent are largely obscure. The Nizārīyah there are often collectively referred to as Khojas, although there are other, smaller Nizārī groups such as the Shamsīyah and Momnas, while some Sunnī and Twelver Shīʿī Khoja groups have split from the main body of the Nizārīyah. According to their legendary history, the Nizārī faith was first spread by pir Shams al-Dīn, whose father is said to have been sent as a *dāʿī* from Alamūt. The community was ruled thereafter by pirs descended from Shams al-Dīn. Pir Ṣadr al-Dīn, who can be dated with some likelihood in the later fourteenth century, is credited with the conversion of the Khojas from the Hindu caste of the Lohanas and to have laid the foundation of their communal organization, building their first *jamāʿat-khānah*s (assembly and prayer halls) and appointing their *mukhi*s (community leaders). The center of his activity was in Ucch in Sind. A substantial section of the community seceded in the sixteenth century under the pir Nar (Nūr) Muḥammad Shāh, who broke with the *imām*s in Iran claiming that his father, Imam Shāh, had been the imam and that he had succeeded him. This community, known as Imam-Shāhīs or Satpanthis, has further split on the issue of leadership and lives chiefly in Gujarat and Khandesh. It has tended to revert to Hinduism but shares much of its traditional religious literature with the Nizārī Khojas.

This literature, which is known as Sat Panth (True Path), consists of *ginān*s or *gnān*s, religious poems composed in, or translated into, several Indian languages and meant to be sung to specific melodies in worship. Most of them are attributed to the early pirs but cannot be dated accurately and may have undergone substantial changes in the transmission. They include hymns, religious and moral exhortation, and legendary history of the pirs and their miracles, but contain no creed or theology. Islamic and Hindu beliefs, especially popular Tantric ones, are freely mixed. While idol worship is rejected, Hindu mythology is accepted. ʿAlī is considered the tenth avatar (incarnation of the deity), and the imams are identical with him. The Qurʾān is described as the last of the Vedas, which are recognized as sacred scriptures whose true interpretation is known to the pirs. Faith in the true religion will free believers from further rebirths and open paradise, which is described in Islamic terms, to them, while those failing to recognize the *imām*s must go through another cycle of rebirths. The Arabic and Persian Ismāʿīlī literature has been virtually unknown among the Khojas except for the Persian *Pandiyāt-i jawānmardī,* a collection of religious and moral exhortations of the late fifteenth-century Nizārī imam al-Mustanṣir which was adopted as a sacred book. Khojas live chiefly in lower Sind, Cutch, Gujarat, Bombay, and in wide diaspora, particularly in East and South Africa, Arabia, Ceylon, and Burma.

Further Nizārī communities are found in the mountains of Chitral, Gilgit, and Hunza in Pakistan, in parts of Afghanistan, and in the region of Yarkand and Kashgar in Chinese Turkistan. Organization, religious practices, and observance of *sharīʿah* rules vary among the scattered communities. The recent Aga Khans have stressed the rootedness of the Nizārī Ismāʿīlīyah in Shīʿī Islam and its continued bonds with the world of Islam.

The Ṭayyibīyah. After breaking with the Fatimid teaching hierarchy, the Ṭayyibīyah in the Yemen recognized the Sulayhid queen as the *ḥujjah* of the concealed *imām* al-Ṭayyib; with her backing they set up an independent teaching hierarchy headed by a *dāʿī muṭlaq* ("unrestricted summoner") whose spiritual authority since her death in 1138 has been supreme. The second *dāʿī muṭlaq,* Ibrāhīm al-Ḥamidī (1151–1162), became the real founder of the Ṭayyib i esoteric doctrine, which he elaborated especially in his *Kitāb kanz al-walad* (Book of the child's treasure). The position remained in his family until 1209, when it passed to ʿAlī ibn Muḥammad of the Banū al-Walīd al-Anf family, which held it for more than three centuries with only two interruptions. The political power of the Yemenite *dāʿī*s reached a peak during the long incumbency of Idris ʿImād al-Dīn ibn al-Ḥasan, the nineteenth *dāʿī muṭlaq* (1428–1468). He is also the author of a seven-volume history of the Ismāʿīlī imams, *Kitāb ʿuyūn al-akhbār* (Book of choice stories) and of a two-volume history of the Yemenite *dāʿī*s, *Kitāb nuzhat al-akhbār* (Book of story and entertainment), as well as works of esoteric doctrine and religious controversy. While the Yemenite *dāʿī*s had been able to act relatively freely with the backing or protection of various rulers during the early centuries, they usually faced hostility from the

Zaydī *imāms* and in the sixteenth century suffered relentless persecution. In 1539 the twenty-third *dāʿī muṭlaq* appointed an Indian, Yūsuf ibn Sulaymān, as his successor, evidently in recognition of the growing importance of the Indian Ṭayyiī community. Yūsuf came to reside in the Yemen, but after his death in 1566 his successor, also Indian, transferred the headquarters to Gujarat in India.

Doctrines. The Ṭayyibīyah preserved a large portion of the Fatimid religious literature and generally maintained the traditions of Fatimid doctrine more closely than the Nizārīyah. Thus the Ṭayyibī *dāʿīs* always insisted on the equal importance of the *ẓāhir* and *bātīn* aspects of religion, strict compliance with the religious law and esoteric teaching. Qāḍi al-Nuʿmān's *Daʿāʾim al-Islām* has remained the authoritative codex of Ṭayyibī law and ritual to the present. In the esoteric doctrine, however, there were some innovations which gave the Ṭayyibī gnosis its distinctive character. The *Rasāʾil Ikhwān al-Ṣafā* were accepted as the work of one of the pre-Fatimid hidden imams and were frequently quoted and interpreted.

The cosmological system of al-Kirmānī with its ten higher Intellects replaced that of al-Nasafī predominant in the Fatimid age. Ibrāhīm al-Ḥāmidī changed its abstract rational nature by introducing a myth that Henry Corbin has called the Ismāʿīlī "drama in heaven." According to it, the Second and Third Intellects emanating from the First Intellect became rivals for the second rank. When the Second Intellect attained his rightful position by his superior effort, the Third Intellect failed to recognize his precedence; in punishment for his haughty insubordination he fell from the third rank behind the remaining seven Intellects and, after repenting, became stabilized as the Tenth Intellect and demiurge (*mudabbir*). The lower world was produced out of the spiritual forms (*ṣuwar*) that had also refused to recognize the superior rank of the Second Intellect, and out of the darkness generated by this sin. The Tenth Intellect, who is also called the spiritual Adam, strives to regain his original rank by summoning the fallen spiritual forms to repentance.

The first representative of his summons (*daʿwah*) on earth was the first and universal Adam, the owner of the body of the world of origination (*ṣāḥib al-juththah al-ibdaʿīyah*), or higher spiritual world. He is distinguished from the partial Adam who opened the present age of concealment (*satr*), in which the truth is hidden under the exterior of the prophetic messages and laws. After his passing the first Adam rose to the horizon of the Tenth Intellect and took his place, while the Tenth Intellect rose in rank. Likewise after the passing of the Qāʾim of each prophetic cycle, that being rises and takes the place of the Tenth Intellect, who thus gradually reaches the Second Intellect.

Countless cycles of manifestation *(kashf)* and concealment alternate in succession until the great resurrection (*qiyāmat al-qiyāmāt*) that consummates the megacycle (*al-kawr al-aʿẓam*) lasting 360,000 times 360,000 years. The soul of every believer is joined on the initiation to the esoteric truth by a point of light; this is the believer's spiritual soul, which grows as the believer advances in knowledge. After physical death the light rises to join the soul of the holder of the rank *(ḥadd)* above the believer in the hierarchy. Jointly they continue to rise until the souls of all the faithful are gathered in the light temple (*haykal nūrānī*) in the shape of a human being which constitutes the form of the Qāʾim (*surah qāʾimīyah*) of the cycle, which then rises to the horizon of the Tenth Intellect. The souls of the unbelievers remain joined to their bodies, which are dissolved into inorganic matter and further transformed into descending orders of harmful creatures and substances. Depending on the gravity of their sins they may eventually rise again through ascending forms of life and as human beings may accept the summons to repentance or end up in torment lasting the duration of the megacycle.

Indian communities. The Ṭayyibīyah in India are commonly known as the Bohoras. There are, however, also Sunnī and some Hindu Bohoras; they are mostly engaged in agriculture, while the Ismāʿīlī Bohoras are generally merchants. The origins of the Ṭayyib i community in Gujarat go back to the time before the Ṭayyibī schism. According to the traditional account an Arab *dāʿī* sent from the Yemen arrived in the region of Cambay with two Indian assistants in 1068. The Ismāʿīlī community founded by him, though led by local *walīs*, always maintained close commercial as well as religious ties with the Yemen and was controlled by the Yemenite teaching hierarchy. It naturally followed the Yemenite community at the time of the schism. From Cambay the community spread to other cities, in particular Patan, Sidhpur, and Ahmadabad. In the first half of the fifteenth century the Ismāʿīlīyah were repeatedly exposed to persecution by the Sunnī sultans of Gujarat, and after a contested succession to the leadership of the Bohora community, a large section, known as the Jaʿfarīyah, seceded and converted to Sunnīsm.

After its transfer from the Yemen in 1566, the residence of the *dāʿī muṭlaq* remained in India. The succession to the twenty-sixth *dāʿī muṭlaq*, Dāʾūd ibn ʿAjabshāh (d. 1591), was disputed. In India Dāʾūd Burhān al-Dīn ibn Quṭbshāh was recognized by the great majority as the twenty-seventh *dāʿī muṭlaq*. However, Dāʾūd ibn ʿAjabshāh's deputy in the Yemen, Sulaymān ibn Ḥasan, a grandson of the first Indian *dāʿī muṭlaq* Yūsuf ibn Sulaymān, also claimed to have been the designated successor and after a few years he came to India to press his case. Although he found little support, the dispute was not resolved and resulted in the permanent split of the Dāʾūdī and Sulaymānī factions recognizing separate lines of *dāʿīs*.

The leadership of the Sulaymanīyah, whose Indian community was small, reverted back to the Yemen with the succession of the thirtieth *dāʿī muṭlaq*, Ibrahim ibn Muḥammad ibn Fahd al-Makramī, in 1677. Since then the position of *dāʿī muṭlaq* has remained in various branches of the Makrami family except for the time of the forty-sixth *dāʿī,* an Indian. The Makramī *dāʿīs* usually resided in Badr in Najrān. With the backing of the tribe of the Banū Yām they ruled Najrān independently and at times extended their sway over other parts of the Yemen and Arabia until the incorporation of Najrān into Saudi Arabia in 1934. The peak of their power was in the time of the thirty-third *dāʿī muṭlaq,* Ismāʿīl ibn Hibat Allāh (1747–1770), who defeated the Wahhābīyah in Najd and invaded Ḥaḍramawt. He is also known as the author of an esoteric Qurʾān commentary, virtually the only religious work of a Sulaymānī author published so far. Since Najrān came under Saudi rule, the religious activity of the *dāʿīs* and their followers has been severely restricted. In the Yemen the Sulaymānīyah are found chiefly in the region of Manakha and the Ḥarāz mountains. In India they live mainly in Baroda, Ahmadabad, and Hyderabad and are guided by a representative (*manṣūb*) of the *dāʿī muṭlaq* residing in Baroda.

The *dāʿīs* of the Dāʾūdīyah, who constitute the great majority of the Ṭayyibīyah in India, have continued to reside there. All of them have been Indians except the thirtieth *dāʿī muṭlaq,* ʿAlī Shams al-Dīn (1621–1631), a descendant of the Yemenite *dāʿī* Idrīs ʿImād al-Dīn. The community was generally allowed to develop freely although there was another wave of persecution under the emperor Awrangzīb (1635–1707), who put the thirty-second *dāʿī muṭlaq,* Quṭb al-Dīn ibn Dāʾūd, to death in 1646 and imprisoned his successor. The residence of the Dāʾūdī *dāʿī muṭlaq* is now in Bombay, where the largest concentration of Bohoras is found. Outside Gujarat, Dāʾūdī Bohoras live in Maharashtra, Rajasthan, in many of the big cities of India, Pakistan, Sri Lanka, and Burma, and the East Africa. In the Yemen the Dāʾūdī community is concentrated in the Haraz mountains.

After the death of the twenty-eighth *dāʿī muṭlaq,* Adam Ṣafī al-Dīn, in 1621, a small faction recognized his grandson ʿAlī ibn Ibrāhīm as his successor and seceded from the majority recognizing ʿAbd al-Ṭayyib Zakī al-Dīn. The minority became known as ʿAlia Bohoras and have followed a separate line of *dāʿīs* residing in Baroda. Holding that the era of the prophet Muḥammad had come to an end, a group of ʿAlias seceded in 1204/1789. Because of their abstention from eating meat they are called Nagoshias (not meat eaters). In 1761 a distinguished Dāʾūdī scholar, Hibat Allāh ibn Ismāʿīl, claimed that he was in contact with the hidden *imām,* who had appointed him his *ḥujjah* and thus made his rank superior to that of *dāʿī muṭlaq.* He and his followers, known as Hibtias, were excommunicated and persecuted by the Dāʾūdīyah. Only a few Hibtia families are left in Ujjain. Since the turn of the century a Bohora reform movement has been active. While recognizing the spiritual authority of the *dāʿī muṭlaq* it has sought through court action to restrict his powers of excommunication and his absolute control over community endowments and alms. All of these groups are numerically insignificant.

SEE ALSO Aga Khan; Assassins; Druze; Ginān; Ikhwān al-Ṣafāʾ; Nāṣir-i Khusraw; Qarāmiṭah.

BIBLIOGRAPHY

The study of the Ismāʿīlīyah has been transformed since the 1930s, when the existence of a secret and extensive Ismāʿīlī religious literature became known, particularly through the efforts of W. Ivanow. The results of Ivanow's research were published in his *A Guide to Ismaili Literature* (London 1933), revised and enlarged in *Ismaili Literature: A Bibliographical Survey* (Tehran, 1963). These works are now superseded by Ismail K. Poonawala's *Biobibliography of Ismāʿīlī Literature* (Malibu, Calif., 1977). A general survey of the Ismāʿīlīyah is lacking; W. Ivanow's *Brief Survey of the Evolution of Ismailism* (Leiden, 1952) is inadequate.

Pre-Fatimid Ismāʿīlī doctrine and its sources are studied in Heinz Halm's *Kosmologie und Heilslehre der frühen Ismāʿīlīya* (Wiesbaden, 1978). The historical origins of the Ismāʿīlī movement and the relationship of the Qarāmiṭah and the Fatimids were first examined in M. J. de Goeje's *Mémoire sur les Carmathes du Bahraiʾn et les Fatimides,* vol. 1 of *Mémoires de l'histoire et de géographie orientales,* 2d ed. (Leiden, 1886), which is still of interest for the history of the Qarāmiṭah but obsolete in its conclusions. A new approach to some of the problems was taken by Bernard Lewis in *The Origins of Ismāʿīlīsm: A Study of the Historical Background of the Fatimid Caliphate* (1940; reprint, New York, 1975). His conclusions were criticized by W. Ivanow through a broader assembly of Ismāʿīlī sources; most relevant among Ivanow's numerous works are his *Ismaili Tradition Concerning the Rise of the Fatimids* (London, 1942), containing Arabic texts and some English translations; *The Alleged Founder of Ismaʿilism* 2d ed. (Bombay, 1957), and *Studies in Early Persian Ismailism,* 2d ed. (Bombay, 1955). Penetrating articles on various aspects of early Ismāʿīlīyah were thereafter published by S. M. Stern, most of which have been republished together with some previously unpublished papers in his posthumous *Studies in Early Ismaʿilism* (Jerusalem, 1983). See further Wilferd Madelung's "Fatimiden und Baḥrainqarmaṭen," *Der Islam* 34 (1958): 34–88, and "Das Imamat in der frühen ismailitischen Lehre," *Der Islam* 37 (1961): 43–135.

The basic study of the history and doctrine of the Nizārīyah in the Alamūt period is Marshall G. S. Hodgson's *The Order of Assassins* (1955; reprints, New York, 1980). A more recent, briefer historical survey is offered by Bernard Lewis, *The Assassins: A Radical Sect in Islam* (London, 1968). The modern Nizārī Ismāʿīlī followers of the Aga Khans is treated with a historical background by Sami N. Makarem in *The Doctrine of the Ismailis* (Beirut, 1972). Azim Nanji's *The Nizārī Ismāʿīlī Tradition in the Indo-Pakistan Subcontinent* (Delmar, N.Y., 1978) deals with the history and the religious literature (*ginans*) of the Khojas. J. N. Hollister's *The Shiʿa of India* (London, 1953), chapters 13–26, deals with the history, beliefs, and religious practices of the Bohora and Khoja communities on the Indian subcontinent. A history of the Bohora community and of its modern reform movement by a Bohora modernist is Asghar Ali Engineer's *The Bohras* (New Delhi, 1980).

The studies of Ismāʿīlī esoteric thought on a comparative basis by Henry Corbin deserve special mention; see for instance his "De la gnose antique à la gnose ismaélienne," in *Convegno di scienze morali, storiche e filologiche, 27 Maggio–1 Giugno 1956* (Rome, 1957), and his *Histoire de la philosophie islamique,* vol. 1 (Paris, 1964), pp. 110–151. The volume

Ismaʿili Contributions to Islamic Culture, edited by Seyyed Hossein Nasr (Tehran, 1977), contains articles by various scholars on aspects of Ismāʿīlī thought.

WILFERD MADELUNG (1987)

SHIISM: ITHNĀ ʿASHARĪYAH

The Twelver Shīʿah, known also by their Arabic name, Ithna ʿAshariyah (and also Imaniyah), constitute the largest group within Shī ʿī Islam, and their moderate juridical and theological doctrine has always placed them at the center of the entire Shī ʿī spectrum, to the extent that they are often identified with Shiism as such.

CENTRALITY OF THE IMAM. For all the Shīʿah, the being of the imam is necessary for the continuation of the world and of human history; according to a famous Shīʿī *ḥadīth,* "The earth shall never be destitute of the proof (*ḥujjah*) of God," namely the imam. In the words of Jaʿfar al-Ṣādiq, the sixth imam in the line of ʿAlī ibn Abī Ṭālib, the imams are God's witnesses on earth, his "signs" (*ʿalāmāt*), and those who are "firm in knowledge" (*al-rāsikhūn fī'l ʿilm*) according to the Qurʾanic dictum. They are the gates (*abwāb*) toward God and his vicegerents (*khulafāʾ Allāh*) on earth. They possess perfect knowledge not only of the Qurʾān but of all revealed books in both their outward (*ẓāhir*) and inward (*bāṭin*) aspects. They also possess knowledge of God's supreme name (*al-ism al-aʿẓam*) as well as the "books" containing all esoteric knowledge, including the science of the symbolic meaning of the letters of the Arabic alphabet (*al-jafr*). On the Night of Power (*laylat al-qadr*), commemorating when the Qurʾān was first revealed, God revealed to them knowledge of all events of the year to come. The imam is chosen by God and the Prophet or by the previous imam through clear designation (*naṣṣ jalī*) and possesses "initiatory" power (*walāyah/wilāyah*), while the Prophet possesses the powers of both prophecy (*nubūwah*) and "initiation" (*walayāh*).

The twelve imams. The various branches among the Shīʿah separated from each other on the question of the number of imams that they accepted; the Ithnā ʿAsharīyah are so called because for them the twelfth imam is that last in the chain that goes back to ʿAlī and Fāṭimah. (For the general evolution of the different Shīʿī subdivisions, see the overview article, above.)

The twelve imams of the Ithnā ʿAsharīyah are as follows:

1. ʿAl ibn Abī Tālib (d. AH 40/661 CE)
2. al-Ḥasan ibn ʿAlī (d. AH 49/669 CE)
3. al-Ḥusayn ibn ʿAlī (d. AH 60/680 CE)
4. ʿAlī ibn al-Ḥusayn, Zayn al-ʿAbidīn (d. AH 95/714 CE)
5. Muḥammad al-Bāqir (d. AH 115/733 CE)
6. Jaʿfar al-Ṣādiq (d. AH 148/765 CE)
7. Mūsa al-Kāẓim (d. AH 183/799 CE)
8. ʿAlī al-Riḍā (d. AH 203/818 CE)
9. Muḥammad Jawād al-Taqi (d. AH 220/835 CE)
10. ʿAlī al-Naqī (d. AH 254/868 CE)
11. al-Hasan al-ʿAskari (d. AH 260/874 CE)
12. Muḥammad al-Mahdi, al-Qaʾim al-Hujjah (entered major occultation in AH 329/941 CE)

The Shīʿī emphasis upon the imam is to be seen not only in the central role accorded to esoteric hermeneutics (*taʾwīl*) in relation to the power of *walāyah* possessed by the imam, but also in the central function of the imam in daily religious life and his eschatological significance. Shīʿī Muslims must know their imams in order to be saved, and the imams, as well as the Prophet, of course, can and do intercede for believers before God at the hour of judgment. The imam continues to be a living presence in religious life, a link between believer and God, the source of grace and the fountain of knowledge. Endowed with a transhistorical reality, he is not experienced simply as a figure belonging to religious history.

The Hidden Imam. The ever-present reality of the imam is felt especially in the case of the twelfth imam or the Mahdi who is, according to the Twelvers, in occultation (*ghaybah*). The imam went into minor occultation (*al-ghaybah al-ṣughrā*) in 872, during which time he had direct representatives (*bāb*) among his followers; beginning in 941 he went into the major occultation (*al-ghaybah al-kubrā*), which has lasted until today and during which the institutionalized channels to him are no longer accessible. The major occultation is not simply a state of being hidden. Rather, it signifies the miraculous mode of life of the imam, who, while being alive and participating in the worldly experience, also resides in the higher planes of existence. He is real the ruler of the word and the Lord of the Hour (*ṣaḥib al-zamān*). He is the pole upon which religion stands (*qāʾim*) and the guarantee for the preservation and perpetuation of the tradition. He is also the guide to the spiritual world and appears in person to those possessing the necessary spiritual qualifications to see him. Devout Twelvers pray continuously for a vision of him, and sites where such visions have taken place have often become sanctuaries and sacred precincts to which the faithful make pilgrimage in the same way that they visit the tombs of the other imams.

The twelfth imam is also the Mahdi who will come out of occultation at the time when oppression and inequity in the world reach their peak. He will destroy evil, establish the rule of justice according to the divine law, and reveal the inner unity of religions. He will prepare the second coming of Christ with which the history of present-day humanity will come to an end. All Twelvers pray for his coming, and as a result of this belief, there exists a strong messianic view in Shiism, a current which has manifested itself in many political and nonpolitical forms over the centuries. While most Sunnīs also believe in the coming of the Mahdi, such a belief is not a necessity for Sunnī Islam, while among the Twelvers the identity of the Mahdi is known, and the expectation of his coming colors the whole ethos of the religion and influences all its manifestations from the theological to the political.

HISTORICAL DEVELOPMENT. The historical development of Twelver Shiism can be envisaged both from the viewpoint of its involvement in sociopolitical events of history and from that of the development of Shīʿī thought. The two are certainly interrelated but not identical. In either case, however, the period during which the imams were alive and functioning as living leaders of the community provides the model which different forces and groups among the Twelvers have sought to emulate in one way or another in all later ages.

Twelver Shiism in Islamic History. The participation of the imams in Islamic history was certainly not uniform, nor was it based on a single pattern. The imams all acted on the basis of the same principles but, in accordance with the circumstances and situations confronting them, sometimes followed the path of quietism and other times that of activism.

Origins. Two events in the formative period, however, stand out as crucial to the later history of the Twelvers and in fact all of Islam: the Battle of Ṣiffīn at the end of the caliphate of ʿAlī (661) and the uprising of Imam Ḥusayn against the Umayyad caliph Yazīd (680). The nearly five and a half years of ʿAlī's rule remain of course an ideal to which the Shīʿah have referred over the centuries, for these years constitute the only period during which a Shīʿī imam actually held political power. The Battle of Ṣiffīn, which marked the first open breech in the Muslim community (*ummah*), was fought between ʿAlī and Muʿāwiyah, the governor of Syria who had refused to pay allegiance to ʿAlī as caliph on the pretext that the death of the third caliph, ʿUthmān, had not been avenged. That ʿAlī was murdered by the Khārijīs after the battle, that Muʿāwiyah survived to found the Umayyad caliphate with its capital in Damascus, and that henceforth the followers of ʿAlī were persecuted all helped to consolidate the Shīʿah and cement them together as a distinct group within the Muslim community.

It was the death of ʿAlī's son, Imam Ḥusayn, that made this cleavage definite and final and helped to crystallize the distinctive ethos of Shiism. Imam Ḥusayn had refused to pay allegiance to Muʿāwiyah's son Yazīd and, rather than suffer humiliation, decided to move from Medina to Kufa, where he had been promised help to confront the mighty Umayyad military power against overwhelming odds. Surrounded in the desert of southern Iraq, he and his family—all the nearest descendants of the Prophet—were killed after a valiant fight, while the female members, along with Imam Ḥusayn's son, the fourth imam, Zayn al-ʿĀbidin, who was then ill, were taken prisoner and brought to Damascus. The severed head of Ḥusayn was sent to Yazīd in Damascus where Ḥusayn's sister, Zaynab, protested violently before the general public and spread the news of the tragedy that had befallen the Prophet's favorite grandson. The event shook the conscience of the community at large, but it was especially effective in consolidating the Shīʿah, and it resulted in many proto-Shīʿī political movements that finally brought about the downfall of the Umayyads and made possible the coming of their political successors, the Abbasids. Yazid himself had been aware of the danger that Zaynab posed for the Umayads and exiled her to Cairo where she buried the head of her brother in a site known to this day as Ra's al-Ḥusayn (the Head of Ḥusayn). The whole city of Cairo grew around this holy site. From the purely religious point of view, the event at Karbala was all-important in providing the element of suffering and "redemption" through participation in the tragedy of the imams so characteristic of Shīʿī piety.

Political quietism. Imam Zayn al-ʿ Ābidin, witness to the indescribable tragedy that befell his father and other members of his family, withdrew from active life to devote himself to the dissemination of inner knowledge as had his uncle Ḥasan, the second imam. The events of Karbala had a special effect upon Imam Zayn al-ʿĀbidin in that they brought out an exceptional poetic eloquence in his words and sayings; his *Ṣaḥīfah,* a collection of prayers and litanies in exquisite Arabic, is called the "psalm of the Family of the Prophet."

With the weakening of Umayyad power, the Shīʿī imams received a greater degree of freedom to dissemminate their teachings; thus, the great majority of Shīʿī traditions come from the fifth, sixth, and seventh imams. The fifth imam, Muḥammad al-Bāqir, was in fact called Bāqir al-ʿUlūm, "garden of knowledge," and his sayings are a major source of both the law and the esoteric sciences, while the sixth imam, Jaʿfar al-Ṣādiq, played such an important role in the formulation of Shīʿī law that as a school of law it is known as the Jaʿfarī school. He influenced Sunnī jurisprudence as well, and the great Sunnī jurist Abū Hanīfah is said to have studied with him. Imam Jaʿfar was not only a master of the Islamic esoteric sciences and the author of the first extant esoteric commentary upon the Qurʾān, but also knowledgeable in the natural and occult sciences. Many treatises in these fields, especially in alchemy, are attributed to him. Imam Jaʿfar trained a vast number of students and is the father of formal Shīʿī religious education and of the *Sharīʿah,* the Shīʿī school of law being known to this day as Jaʿfarī. In fact he must be considered as the founder of the first "circle of learning" (*ḥawzah-yi ʿilmīyah*), which was to develop later into the well-known medieval universities.

Imam Riḍā, the one imam who was close to the Abbasid court, was especially important as a source of Ṣūfī teachings in both Shīʿī and Sunnī Islam but also had a particularly royal aspect to him. To this day he is referred to as the Shah of Khorasan, and throughout history the Persian rulers have been custodians of the vast endowments which manage the architectural complex of his mausoleum in Mashhad.

After the death of Imam Riḍā, the Abbasids resumed a close watch on the activities of his successors, who mostly remained imprisoned or under heavy surveillance until the disappearance of the twelfth imam, Muḥammad al-Mahdī. During his minor occulation he continued to discourse with the Shīʿī community through his "gates" (*abwāb,* sg., *bāb*), four revered men who were highly respected by the community, but with the death of the last *bāb* the major occultation began and Twelver Shiism entered into a new phase.

During the next six centuries Shiism remained a quietist movement from the political point of view, but its influence and numbers continued to grow in Persia and India, and it waxed and waned in Syria. During the later tenth century, with most of Persia and Syria ruled by the Twelver Shīʿī Buyids and Egypt and North Africa controlled by the Ismāʿīlī Fatimids, Sunnī Islam seemed to be fighting a defensive battle. It was only with the help of Sunnī Turks, supported by the weakened Abbasid caliphate, and with the defeat of the Fatimids by the Crusaders that the political power of Shiism began to wane.

Although the Shīʿī Buyids were Persian, the Sunnī Ghaznavids and Seljuks were Turks, and the Abbasids were Arabs, it is wrong to conclude simply that the Persians were Shīʿī and the Arabs and Turks Sunnī. The situation is much more complex. While it is true that most of the great Twelver Shīʿī scholars have been Persian and that with the Safavids Persia became mostly Shīʿī, it is also a fact of Islamic history that during the tenth and eleventh centuries the intellectual defense of Sunnī Islam also came from the Persian province of Khorasan with such figures as al-Juwaynī and al-Ghazalī. Moreover, while the Turks of Sunnī persuasion helped to prevent the spread of Shiism in the eleventh century, five centuries later Shīʿī Turkish tribes brought Shah Ismāʿīl to power in Persia and helped make Twelver Shiism the state religion of Safavid Persia.

In any case, with the destruction of both Seljuk and Abbasid power by the Mongols, Shiism began to gain ground once again. The period following the Mongol invasions of the thirteenth century marks a rapid spread of Twelver Shiism thanks to both the appearance of such outstanding Shīʿī statesmen and scholars as Naṣir al-Dīn Ṭūsī and ʿAllāmah Ḥillī and the spread of certain Ṣūfī orders such as the Nūrbakhshī, which prepared the ground for the consolidation of Safavid power in Persia through the spread of their Twelver tendencies.

The Safavid state. With the advent of the Safavids in the sixteenth century, Twelver Shiism identified itself for the first time with a distinct political power, as the Ismaʿiliyah had done centuries before with the establishment of the Fatimid caliphate in Cairo and the Zaydiyah with their own imamate in Yemen. (On a lesser scale the same event was taking place in India with the establishment of small Twelver kingdoms in the South.) Paradoxically enough, the Twelvers, who were the most numerous among the Shīʿah, were the last to enter the political arena.

Ruling with the help of Twelver Shiism, the Safavids in turn helped it spread within Persia while supporting Shīʿī communities outside their borders. An alliance was created between the Persian monarchy and the Twelver *ʿulamāʾ* (sg., *ʿālim:* "scholar"). While the central authority of the kings remained strong, an equilibrium was maintained between the state and the Twelver establishment, and in fact, certain religious offices, such as those of the *ṣadr* (chief religious authority) and *imām jumʿah* (Friday prayer leader) were filled by the monarch. However, as the power of the state began to wane, the class of Shīʿī *ʿulamāy,* led by such figures as Mullā Muḥammad Bāqir Majlisī (d. 1700), sought to assert greater power and authority as representatives of the Hidden Imam, to whom all real authority, political as well as religious, belonged. Still, when the Safavid state was destroyed as a result of the Afghan invasion in 1722, far from taking power into their hands and fighting for the preservation of a Shīʿī state, nearly all of the outstanding Twelver *ʿulama'* chose the path of quietism, with many retiring to Najaf in Iraq and devoting themselves to purely religious concerns.

Renewed activism. For several decades from the rule of Nadir Shāh (r. 1736–1747) and Karim Khān Zand (r. 1750–1779) to the establishment of the Qajars in 1779, Twelver Shiism remained politically quiet and somewhat peripheral. It was only during the long reign of Fatḥ ʿAlī Shāh in the beginning of the nineteenth century that the power of the Twelver *ʿulamāʾ* began to rise again. The king favored and even encouraged religious courts and ceased to appoint judges as had been done in the Safavid period. The religious scholars came to be favored directly while the privileged position of the descendants of the Prophet (the *sādāt*) so emphasized by the Safavids weakened.

This new period of ascendancy of Twelver political power resulted in the participation of the *ʿulamāʾ* in many major political events, culminating in the Tobacco Rebellion of 1891–1892 and finally the Constitutional Revolution of 1906, in which the role of the *ʿulamāʾ* was central. Despite the direct participation of the Twelver establishment in political power, however, at no time during the Qajar or, for that matter, the Safavid, period does one see a widely accepted Twelver doctrine of the illegitimacy of the government or the state. Occasionally one does see a figure such as Mullā Aḥmad Narāqi, who in his *ʿAwāʾid al-ayyām* (Benefits of the Times) argues for the strengthening of the juridical power of the jurisprudent (*faqīh*), a view that some scholars have interpreted as the historical antecedent of Ayatollah Khomeini's thesis of the "rule of the jurisprudent" (*vilāyat-i faqīh*). But even if such a doubtful interpretation is accepted, such views remained rare and indeed anomalous. The almost unanimously held position was that of perhaps the most celebrated Twelver juridical scholar of the age, Shaykh Murtaḍā Anṣāri, who continued to the end of his life to remain piously opposed to all activity in the political order, even to the administering of justice according to the *sharīʿah.*

During the Constitutional Revolution the Twelver *ʿulamāʾ* were leaders on both sides of the debate about a parliamentary system and constitutional monarchy. While those who opposed such a system rallied behind Shaykh Faḍl Allāh Nūrī, the leading Twelver *ʿālim* of the day, the pro-

Constitution forces, although often partly secularized and imbued with Western, liberal ideas, also rallied behind and were supported by leading figures among the class of *ʿulamāʾ*, such as Sayyid Muḥammad Ṭabāṭabāʾī and Sayyid ʿAbd Allāh Bihbahānī. As a result of this participation, with the final victory of the pro-Constitution forces the power of the "liberal wing" of the *ʿulamāʾ* grew even more than before, and they remained, despite the modernization which was to follow during the next seven decades, the most politically powerful body of *ʿulamāʾ* in the whole of the Islamic world.

Pahlavi rule. From the time of the Constitutional Revolution through the Pahlavi period, the power of the *ʿulamāʾ* decreased in relation to what had existed in the Qajar era but nevertheless remained considerable. As the state became more powerful during the reign of Riḍa Shāh Pahlavi (1925–1941), juridical power was taken out of the hands of the *ʿulamāʾ* and bestowed on the government once again. Education was taken out of their hands as well, but the traditional educational institutions were allowed to survive and Qom was made a major center for Shīʿī studies. Shīʿī centers of learning were in fact strengthened during the rule of Muḥammad Riḍa Shāh (1941–1979), who had a more lenient attitude toward the *ʿulamāʾ* than had his father.

During this period the erosion of the power of the *ʿulamāʾ* did not, however, come so much from direct government action (although such measures as land reform did affect the *ʿulamāʾ* adversely) as from the general process of modernization. But because the government did not oppose religious activity in any way, religious reaction to secularization and modernization also thrived. It manifested itself first and foremost in a veritable revival of Shīʿī learning and religious thought and finally by sociopolitical action seeking to oppose the process of modernization. In this domain not all the voices of Twelver Shiism were by any means in accord nor were all the voices of dissent of a religious character. The majority of Twelver authorities continued to preach the traditional doctrine of abstention from direct involvement in politics, while those who spearheaded political opposition in the beginning were often forces of the secular left, although they used images, symbols, and slogans of a Shīʿī coloring. In the end, however, the minority Shīʿī voice that preached direct political control and rule of society won the day, destroying its secular partners and silencing at least for now and at least within Iran those Twelver voices which preached the traditional political doctrine of quietism and withdrawal from worldly activity.

Islamic Revolution. Twelver Shiism thus entered another new phase of its history with the Revolution of 1978–1979 in Iran. While the nature, direction, and outcome of that history cannot as yet be judged or evaluated from a religious point of view (whatever one might be able to say of its immediate political, economic, and social consequences), the one fact that is certain is that this event will have a deep effect not only upon the future role of Twelver Shiism within Iran but also upon the destiny of Shiism in those countries with Shīʿī majorities (such as Iraq) or minorities. It will also bear upon the question of the preservation of unity or the possibility of further segmentation within Shiism itself.

The development of Shīʿī thought. Although intertwined with the development of Islamic thought in general, Twelver Shīʿī thought possesses a distinct historical development of its own. For the sake of convenience in this analysis it is possible to divide that development into five periods.

First period: the era of the imams. The first period, which is unique in that it contains at once the root and inner content of all later Twelver thought, spans the life of the Prophet and the imams to the occultation of the twelfth imam. This seminal period of three centuries saw not only the sayings of the Prophet and the imams (*aḥādīth*), which, along with the Qurʾān, serve as the source for all Shīʿī thought from law to theology and philosophy, collected and assembled, but also the earliest distinct schools of Shīʿī thought became crystallized, especially around the fifth and sixth imams. By the ninth century Jaʿfarī law was already formulated, theological and theosophical thought received their earliest formulations, and other intellectual and occult sciences began to be cultivated within the Twelver worldview.

Second period: ninth to eleventh centuries. This period, which coincides with the rise of the Buyids in Persia and Iraq, produced the first group of important Twelver scholars who codified the teachings of the imams and brought Shīʿī learning to its first golden age. Especially noteworthy is Muḥammad al-Kulaynī (d. 941), the author of *Kitāb al-kāfī* (The sufficient book), perhaps the most influential of the four canonical collections of Shīʿī *ḥadīth.* Al-Kulaynī, born and educated near Qom, taught in Baghdad, where he lies buried. The *Kitāb al-kāfī* consists of three major parts: the *uṣūl,* dealing with theology, prophetology, theodicy, and similar subjects; the *furūʿ*, dealing with jurisprudence; and the miscellaneous articles at the end.

Al-Kulaynī was followed successively by the other two major Shīʿī scholars of tradition, Ibn Bābūyah (or Ibn Bābawayhal, known also as Ṣadūq, d. 991/2) and Muḥammad al-Tūsī (d. 1067/8), who was also the founder of the Twelver university at Najaf, which survives to this day as the most important and ancient Shīʿī center of learning. Another eminent Twelver scholar of the period was Sayyid Sharīf al-Raḍī (d. 1016), who assembled the sayings of ʿAlī in the *Nahj al-balāghah* (The path of eloquence), which many Western scholars, in contrast to traditional and contemporary Twelver views, believe to have been written by Sayyid Sharīf al-Raḍī himself.

A student of Ibn Bābūyah and Sayyid Sharīf, Shaykh al-Mufīd, marks the beginning of rational Twelver theology. Although the Nawbakhti family had begun employing certain Muʿtazili theses in ninth-century Twelver thought, it remained for Shaykh Muḥammad al-Mufīd (d. 1022) to inaugurate the full employment of rational arguments in religious debates.

Third period: eleventh to thirteenth centuries. The third period of Twelver thought stretches from the fall of the Buyids and the temporary eclipse of Shiism to the Mongol invasion. By and large the Seljuk opposition to Shiism had the direct effect of diminishing the intense Twelver intellectual activity of the two previous centuries. Nonetheless, there were some notable figures in this period, including Abū Jaʿfar al-Ṭūsī (d. 1068), the author of the famous *Kitāb al-istibṣār* (Book of examination) and *Tahdhib al-aḥkām* (Purification of principles), and Abū ʿAlī Ṭabarsī (d. 1153/4), well known for his Qurʾān commentary, *Majmaʿ al-bayān* (Compendium of discourse).

Fourth period: thirteenth to sixteenth centuries. The Mongol invasion, despite its ravaging effects, also marked the beginning of a new phase of widespread Islamic intellectual activity. This fourth period of Twelver thought begins with the towering figure of Naṣīr al-Dīn Ṭūsī (d. 1274), who not only revived Avicennian philosophy in the matrix of Twelver thought but also wrote the *Kitāb al-tajrīd* (The book of catharsis), which is considered as the first systematic work of Twelver theology and which is without doubt the most widely read work on the subject. Naṣīr al-Dīn was also responsible for the revival of Twelver learning, the consequences of which stretched over the centuries into the Safavid and even later periods. His contemporary Najm al-Dīn Muḥaqqiq al-Ḥillī (d. 1277) was an expert on the principles of Twelver jurisprudence *(uṣūl),* for which he wrote the authoritative work, *Kitāb al-maʿārij* (Book of scales), while also developing the science of the application of these principles (*furūʿ*) in his equally famous *Sharāʿiʾ al-islām* (Laws of Islam).

Ṭūsī's successor and student, Jamāl al- Dīn ʿAllāmah al- Ḥillī (d. 1325), was one of the most prolific and many-faceted intellectual figures of Twelver Shiism, at once a theologian, jurisprudent, philosopher, and political thinker. He also acted directly upon the political scene by being instrumental in the conversion of the Il-khanid ruler Öljeitu to Twelver Shiism and participated in religious polemics by answering Sunnī criticisms against Shiism and attacking Sunnīsm himself. His polemical *Minhāj al-kirāmah* (Ways of munificence) was in turn refuted by Ibn Taymīyah. Al-Ḥillī is also especially known in the annals of Twelver thought for his *Kashf al-murād* (Discovery of the desired end), a commentary upon Ṭūsī's *Tajrīd* and the first of a long list of commentaries and glosses written upon this work over the next seven centuries.

This period is also marked by the continuation of Islamic philosophy in a specifically Twelver climate in the hands of such figures as Ṣaʾin al- Dīn ibn Turkah Iṣ-fahānī (d. 1427), the Dashtakī family, and Jalāl al-Dīn Dawānī (d. 1502/3), the theologian and philosopher who began as a Sunnī Muslim but was later converted to Shiism. Most of these philosophers were at once followers of the Peripatetic school of Ibn Sīnā as revived by Ṭūsī and Qutb al-Dīn Shīrazī (d. 1310/11 or 1316/7) and the Illuminationist or *Ishrāqī* school of Suhrawardī (d. 1191).

The gnostic teachings of the Andalusian Ṣūfī Muḥyi al-Dīn ibn ʿArabī (d. 1240), who was himself a Sunnī, also began to penetrate Twelver circles and to become integrated with Shīʿī gnosis (*ʿirfān-i Shīʿī*) during this period. Such Twelver gnostics as Sayyid Ḥaydar Āmulī (fourteenth century), author of *Jāmiʿ al-asrār* (Sum of secrets), one of the *summas* of Shīʿī gnosis, and Ibn Abī Jumhūr al-Aḥsaʾi, author of *Kitāb al-mujlī* (The book of that which makes manifest) (d. after 1496), were disciples of both the school of Ibn ʿArabī and the gnosis that issued from the teachings of the Twelver imams. Other figures of Twelver Sufism during this period include Ibn Ṭāʾūs (fifteenth century), Sayyid Muḥammad Nūrbakhsh (d. 1464), and Muḥsin Kāshifī (d. 1500/1 or 1504/5), all of whom were of considerable importance for the subsequent conversion of Persia to Twelver Shiism. In this process the Kubrawīyah order played an important role, but more significant still was that of the Ṣafavīyah. This Ṣūfī order, founded by Safi al-Dīn Ardibīlī, which was to become specifically Shīʿī, was to inaugurate a new phase in the history of Shiism with the conquest of Persia by Shah Ismāʿīl Ṣafavī in 1499.

Fifth period: sixteenth to twentieth centuries. The fifth and final phase of the history of Twelver thought begins with the Safavid declaration of Twelver Shiism as the state religion of Persia and lasts to this day. The state support of Shiism naturally caused a major revival of Twelver thought in nearly every field. Jurisprudence and theology began to thrive with such scholars as ʿAlī ibn Ḥusayn Karakī, who was already well known before the advent of the Safavids. Other jurisprudents and theologians were brought by the rulers to Isfahan and other major Persian cities from Jabal ʿĀmil, Bahrayn, and Ḥillah in Iraq.

Among the most colorful of these figures was Shaykh Bahāʾ al-Dīn ʿĀmilī, the religious leader (*shaykh al-islām*) of Isfahan, who was at once jurisprudent, theologian, Ṣūfī, mathematician, architect, and poet. He helped popularize Twelver jurisprudence by writing the *Jāmiʿ-i ʿabbāsi* (The ʿAbbāsī summa) on jurisprudence in Persian while composing several Ṣūfī poems in simple Persian that could be understood by people in the streets and bazaars. His friend and contemporary, Mīr Dāmād (d. 1630) was the founder of the new school of Islamic philosophy that has come to be known as the "School of Isfahan"; he wrote numerous works in Arabic and Persian, of which the *Qabasāt* (Sparks of fire) is perhaps the most important. His student Ṣadr al-Dīn Shīrāzī (Mullā Ṣadrā, 1640) is certainly the greatest of the later Islamic philosophers; he wielded immense influence not only upon Persia but also in India, where his monumental *Al-asfār al-arbaʿah* (Four journeys), which summarizes his theosophical teachings, was translated into Urdu only during the nineteenth and twentieth centuries. Although his most famous immediate students, Mullā Muḥsin Fayḍ Kāshānī (d. 1680) and ʿAbd al-Razzāq Lahījī (d. 1661/2), turned mostly to the religious sciences, *kalām,* and Sufism, the "transcendent theosophy" (*al-ḥikmah al-mutaʿāliyah*) of Mullā Ṣadrā began to gather followers from near and far and soon became the central intellectual school of Twelver Shiism.

Toward the end of the Safavid period the onset of an antiphilosophical and anti-Ṣūfī trend caused Sufism to go underground and partially eclipsed the school of Mullā Ṣadrā. This was the age of Muḥammad Bāqir Majlisī, the author of the monumental Twelver encyclopedia *Biḥar al-anwār* (Seas of light) and many other juridical and theological works. This period was also witness to treatises on popular piety.

After an interim period of uncertainty and chaos marked by the Afghan invasion, the conquest of Persia by Nādir Shāh, and the rule of Karīm Khān Zand, the establishment of the Qajars in 1779 marked once again a revival of Twelver thought. The nineteenth century was witness not only to the major jurisprudents and theologians already mentioned, but also to several notable philosophers such as Mullā 'Alī Nūrī (d. 1831), Mullā'Alī Zunūzī (d. 1889), Āqā Muḥammad Riḍā Qumsha'ī (d. 1888), and the most famous of the Qajar philosophers, Ḥājjī Mullā Hādī Sabziwārī (d. 1871), whose *Sharḥ al-manẓūmah* (Commentary on the bean) remains a favorite philosophical text to this date. These men revived the teachings of Mullā Ṣadrā as well as those of Ibn 'Arabī in its Twelver form. Their disciples were in turn the direct teachers of the outstanding Twelver philosophers of the late Qajar and Pahlavi periods such as Sayyid Abū al-Ḥasan Rafī'ī Qazwinī, Sayyid Muḥammad Kāẓim 'Aṣṣar, and 'Allāmah Sayyid Muḥammad Ḥusayn Tabāṭabā'i, all of whom died in the second half of the twentieth century. This period marks in fact a most active and fecund era during which the Twelver intellectual tradition encountered the challenges of the modern West for the first time, traditional Twelver thought was revived, and Islamic modernism began to penetrate into certain strands of Twelver Shiism. The last few decades have been marked by as strong interest and renewal of this tradition.

Twelver Shī'ī Doctrines in Relation to Sunnism. Twelver Shiism shares with Sunnī Islam the acceptance of the unity of God, the text of the Qur'ān, and the prophetic function of the Prophet, including the finality of his prophetic function and belief in eschatological events described in the Qur'ān and the *ḥadīth*. It differs from Sunnīsm in its emphases upon the quality of justice *('adl)* as innate and intrinsic to the divine nature and upon the significance of the imam with all the consequences this doctrine entails as far as esoteric knowledge, the role of *'aql* or intellect, and attitude toward intellectual sciences are concerned. Also in contrast to Sunnīsm, for which *ḥadīth* means the sayings of the Prophet, Shiism also includes in its *ḥadīth* collections the sayings of the imams, although it does distinguish clearly between prophetic traditions *(al-ḥadīth al-nabawī)* and the traditions of the imams *(al-ḥadīth al-walawī)*. As far as the prophetic traditions are concerned, the lines of transmission are usually different for Sunnī and Shī'ī Muslims, but the content of most of the sayings are the same.

Twelver Shiism possesses the same sacred law (*sharī'ah*) as Sunnī Islam, with small differences in the ritual aspects which are practically no greater than differences between the four Sunnī schools themselves. Injunctions concerning transactions are also similar in most instances, the most important exceptions being the Shī'ī acceptance of temporary marriage (*mut'ah*), certain aspects of the laws of inheritance, and also a religious tax (*khums*) in addition to the general religious tax (*zakāh*) accepted by Sunnīs. Altogether, despite many polemics with Sunnīsm, over the ages, Shiism represents an essential aspect of Islamic orthodoxy and has its roots in the Qur'anic revelation and the soul of the Prophet as does Sunnīsm.

The doctrines of the Twelvers are summarized in the "principles of religion" (*uṣūl al-dīn*) as stated in the sayings of the imams. These principles include *tawḥīd* (attesting to God's unity); *'adl* (accepting that God is just by nature); *nubūwwah* (prophecy or accepting the prophetic function of all the prophets beginning with Adam and ending with the prophet of Islam); *imāmah* (accepting the twelve imams from 'Alī to the Mahdī); and *ma'ād* (accepting the immortality of the soul, the responsibility of human beings for their actions, divine judgment and the paradisal, purgatorial, or infernal states that humans experience in accordance with the fruits of their actions and divine mercy).

The Twelvers understand these principles, as well as the whole Qur'ān and *ḥadīth,* according to not only their outward meaning but also their inner sense and reality. Thus *ta'wīl,* this process of going from the outward to the inward, is emphasized in every aspect of Twelver Shiism, whether it be the Qur'anic sciences or the interpretation of religious rites. Through the Twelver understanding of the meaning of the imam and the power of *walāyah/wilāyah,* there exists an esoteric character even within the exoteric aspects of the religion. It might in fact be said that whereas in Sunnī Islam the exoteric and the esoteric are clearly separated (and the latter identified with Sufism), among the Twelvers, in addition to the presence of Sufism in its Shī'ī form, esoterism flows into the exoteric domain and bestows a mystical aspect on the whole manifestation of Shiism, including popular piety.

Jurisprudence. Twelver Shiism, like Sunnī Islam, emphasizes the importance of the divine law (*sharī'ah*) and the necessity of following its injunctions, most of which are in fact like those of Sunnī Islam. Twelver jurisprudence, or *fiqh,* although related to the Sunnī schools of *fiqh* in accepting the Qur'ān and *ḥadīth* as the two basic sources of law, also differs from them in certain important ways. Most of the four Sunnī schools of law accept with different degrees of emphasis the use of *ijmā'* (consensus of the community) and *qiyās* (analogy) as sources for drawing legal injunctions where the Qur'ān and *ḥadīth* and *sunnah* do not provide direct guidance.

Divine injunction. For the Twelvers, however, every event that occurs in the world comes as a result of divine injunction (*ḥukm*), which includes for them the sayings and actions of the imams. Basing themselves on the famous saying of the Prophet (the *ḥadīth al-thaqalayn*) according to which the Prophet mentioned to his companions that after his death he would leave Muslims the Qurʾān and his family, the Twelvers base their *fiqh* completely on the Qurʾān injunctions issued by the Prophet and the imams and consider both *ijmāʿ* and *qiyās* to be inadmissible for juridical decision-making. For them there are but two sources for juridical injunctions: the Qurʾān and the *ḥadīth* and *sunnah* understood in their Shīʿī sense. *Ḥadīth,* in fact, is also seen by the Twelvers as being nothing but commentaries upon the Qurʾān and the extension of Qurʾanic teachings by the Prophet and the imams so that the Qurʾān becomes ultimately the sole source of the *sharīʿah.*

Juridical authority belongs exclusively to the Prophet and the imams, and ultimately to God. According to the *Furūʿ al-kāfī* of al-Kulaynī, this authority was transferred by Imam Jaʿfar al-Ṣādiq to the jurisprudents (*fuqahāʾ*), who, in the absence of the imams, receive their authority from the Hidden Imam, or the Mahdī. Judges, in fact, should be chosen by the imam and according to Twelver belief, one should not accept judges chosen by political authorities unless it is necessary and under conditions that necessitate *taqīyah* "dissimulation."

Ijtihād. The Twelver concept of *ijtihād* (use of legal reasoning) implies, therefore, not drawing conclusions from and on the basis of the Qurʾān, *ḥadīth, ijmāʿ,* and *qiyās,* but seeking answers to problems facing the community or the individual from the Qurʾān and *ḥadīth* (including the sayings of the imams) alone, and relying completely on the emulation of the Prophet and the imams and their understanding of the teachings of the Qurʾān. In this sense the range of *ijtihād* among the Twelvers is more limited than among the Sunnīs, but from the point of view of the actual practice of *ijtihād,* it can be said that it occupies a more central and living role in Twelver Shiism. In Sunnī Islam the gates of *ijtihād* are said to have been closed since the establishment of the widely accepted schools of law a thousand years ago, whereas for the Twelvers, the gate of *ijtihād* has always remained open. In fact, a Twelver is supposed to imitate and follow a living *mujtahid,* the person who has the qualifications to practice *ijtihād.* Each person who reaches the degree of *ijtihād* must derive the injunctions of the law afresh from the traditional sources, and the *mujtahids* have always exercised greater power and influence in Twelver Shiism than *multīs* in Sunnī Islam, especially since the late Safavid period.

Another unique feature of Twelver jurisprudence is the institution of the "source of imitation" or *marjaʿi taqlīd.* In the middle of the nineteenth century, as the power of the *mujtahids* grew, there came into being the office of the supreme *mujtahid* whom all Twelvers were to imitate. This transformation was brought about by Shaykh Murtaḍa Anṣārī (d. 1864), who formulated the doctrine in his *Farāʾiḍ al-uṣūl* (Precious Pearls of Uūl). The institution continued for more than a century until 1962, the year of the death of Ayatollah Burūjirdī, who was the last *mujtahid* to be universally accepted as the supreme head of the Twelver hierarchy and who was imitated by all Twelvers.

The importance of *ijtihād* as used currently by Twelvers has not, however, been always the same for all segments of the community. During the Safavid period there existed a fierce struggle between the Akhbārīyah, who relied solely upon the sayings (*akhbār*) of the Prophet and the imams as incorporated in the four canonical collections of Shīʿī *ḥadīth,* and the Uṣūlīyah, who relied upon the use of reason in the understanding of the principles *(uṣūl)* of jurisprudence and their application on the basis of the Qurʾān and *ḥadīth.* The founder of the Akhbārī school was Muḥammad Amīn Astrābādī (d. 1623/4), who, in his *al-Fawāʾid al-madanīyah* (Civil Benefits), attacked the *mujtahids* strongly and accused them of destroying Islam. During the early Qajar period, when the Russians were fighting against Persia, an Akhbārī religious leader named Mīrzā Muḥammad Akhbārī of Bahrein promised the ruler Fatḥ ʿAlī Shāh the head of the Russian general if he were to ban the Uṣūlīyah. When Mīrzā Muḥammad kept his promise and brought the head, Fatḥ ʿAlī Shāh, fearing his power, exiled him to Iraq. Henceforth Akhbārī influence, which had been paramount in the Zand period, began to wane, and soon they were totally eclipsed as a result of the works of the Uṣūlī Muḥammad Bāqir Waḥīd Bihbahānī (d. 1792). The nineteenth century became, as a result, the golden period for the science of principles of jurisprudence, *uṣūl al-fiqh,* and the period when the *mujtahids* rose to power.

The Akhbārī-Uṣūlī debate that has characterized much of Twelver thought during the past few centuries resembles in many ways the earlier Muʿtazilī-Ashʿarī debate in Sunnī Islam, but of course in the context of elements and factors that are typical of Twelver Shiism. The Uṣūlīyah emphasize the competence of reason in interpreting the Qurʾān and *ḥadīth* and the necessity of *ijtihād.* They do not accept uncritically the four canonical codices of Shīʿī *ḥadīth* and rely heavily upon the ever-renewed and living interpretation of these sources of law to the extent of forbidding the imitation of a decreased *mujtahid.* The Akhbārīyah oppose the Uṣūlīyah on all these counts, criticizing them especially on the role they allot to reason in the interpretation of the injunctions of the divine law.

Philosophy and theosophy. The Twelver attitude toward the so-called intellectual sciences (*al-ʿulūm al-ʿaqlīyah*) was from the beginning more positive than that of the school of theology (*kalām*) that came to dominate Sunnī Islam from the fourth century AH (tenth century CE). This more open attitude can be found in some of the sayings of the sixth and eighth imams, not to speak of the metaphysical discourses of ʿAlī contained in the *Nahj al-balāghah.* As a result, philosophy or theosophy (*al-ḥikmah al-ilāhīyah*) also constitutes an important aspect of Twelver religious thought and is far from being only Greek philosophy in Arabic or Persian dress.

Philosophy. While many of the early Islamic philosophers, such as al-Fārābī and Ibn Sīnā (Avicenna), were either Twelvers or had Twelver tendencies, from the Mongol invasion and the advent of Naṣīr al-Dīn Ṭūsī onward, Islamic philosophy took refuge for the most part in the Shīʿī world (although it also had a long life among some Sunnīs), and some of the greatest of the later Islamic philosophers following Ṭūsī, such as Ibn Turkah Iṣfahāni, Mīr Dāmād, and Mullā Ṣādra, were also Twelver thinkers.

Later Islamic philosophy following Suhrawardi and Ṭūsī also drew directly from specifically Twelver sources, especially the *Nahj al-balāghah* and the *Uṣūl al-kāfī* of al-Kulaynī. One cannot study a work such as the *Asfār* of Mullā Ṣādra without becoming aware of the central significance of the teachings of the Qurʾān as interpreted by the Prophet and the imams and the Shīʿī *ḥadīth* corpus in the development of later Islamic philosophy. Some of the most significant pages of Shīʿī theological and religious thought as ordinarily understood are to be found in such late works.

Religious sciences and theology (kalām). From the beginning Shiism emphasized the importance of religious knowledge. While cut off from worldly power, the early Shīʿah, including of course the imams, devoted most of their energy to the dissemination of religious knowledge as transmitted by the Prophet through the chain of the imams. This knowledge included Qurʾānic commentary, *ḥadīth,* and law as well as the esoteric sciences. Gradually there developed a sizable body of specifically Twelver religious works in nearly every field. After the *Nahj al-balāghah* and the *Ṣaḥīfah al-sājjadīyah* (Scroll of Sajjād) of Imam Zayn al-ʿAbidīn, the most important specifically Shīʿī religious works are the four codices of the sayings of the Prophet and the imams assembled in the tenth and eleventh centuries: the *Kitāb al-kafī* of al-Kulaynī, *Manā yaḥḍuruhu al-faqīh* (Everyone his own jurist) of Ibn Bābūyah, and *Kitāb al-tahdhīb* (The book of refinement) and *Kitāb al-istibṣār* (The book of scrutinization) of Muḥammad al- Ṭūsī. Henceforth all Twelver religious thought from the philosophical and theological to the juridical and political drew from these four canonical collections or *al-kutub al-arbaʿah.*

Kalām, as the discipline dealing with the rational defense of the tenets of the faith, developed much later in Twelver Shiism than it did in either Sunnī Islam or Ismaʿīlī Shiism. The Twelvers began to develop *kalām* in a systematic sense with Nasir al-Din Ṭūsī, whose *Kitāb al-tajrīd* is the first and most important Twelver *kalām* work, commented upon by generations of theologians starting with the author's own celebrated student ʿAllāmah al-Ḥillī. Shīʿī *kalām* was rejuvenated during the Safavid period when such figures as ʿAbd al-Razzāq Lāhījī wrote major works devoted to this discipline. During this period, however, the philosophers (*ḥukamā-yi ilāhī* in Persian) strongly opposed the whole discipline of *kalām* and claimed that the "science of God" or theology in its universal sense was the subject of their discipline rather than the science of the *mutakallimūn,* those who followed the field of study known technically as *kalām.*

Political and social thought. During most of its history Twelver Shiism has followed the example of Imam Ḥasan and most other Imams in remaining aloof from the everyday world and its political entanglements, shunning even the ministering of justice and turning temporal defeat into spiritual victory by placing before itself a political ideal identified with the rule of the Hidden Imam and the *parousia* he will bring about. The imams themselves shied away from direct political activity even when the opportunity arose, as in the case of Imam Jaʿfar al-Ṣādiq who was offered the caliphate by Abū Muslim, or else they were prevented from doing so, as in the case of Imam Riḍā who was poisoned after being chosen successor of the Abbasid caliph al-Maʾmūn.

Relation to power. Nonetheless, the case of Imam Ḥusayn, who arose against the Umayyad caliph Yazīd, presents the other strand in Shiism, which is that of political protest against iniquity and injustice. After the occultation of the twelfth imam, practically all the major Twelver jurists and scholars reiterated the political theory according to which the Sunnī caliphate was illegitimate, the real ruler of the world was the Hidden Imam, and in his absence the ruler or sultan who was just and who supported or at least permitted the practice of Shiism should be conditionally supported, although there were also occasional Shīʿī revolts against established authority. With the Safavids' establishment of a Shīʿī Twelver kingdom of Persia, or on a smaller scale with the establishment of Twelver states in Bijapur and other states in the Deccan in India, this agreement between the Shīʿī authorities and the state in a sense became formalized and served as the basis of a pact between religion and the state upon which the sociopolitical order functioned. In Qajar Persia this theory was on one or two occasions repudiated in favor of the theory of direct rule of the jurisprudents as in the case of Mullā Aḥmad Narāqī (d. 1828/9) as he has been interpreted by certain later figures, while others such as Sayyid Muḥammad Bāqir Shaftī (d. 1844) took the administration of justice into their hands. But it was not until the declaration of the rule of the jurisprudent (*vilāyat-i faqīh*) by Ayatollah Khomeini that the classical Shīʿī theory was rejected in Iran in the name of the direct rule of the jurisprudent and the latter view was put into practice. This view has, however, been contested by many Shīʿī authorities even within Iran as can be seen in Mahd ī Hāʾirī Yazdī's *Hikmat wa ḥukūmat.*

Socioeconomic issues. As far as social thought is concerned, Twelver ideas are not very different from those of the Sunnīs, with the emphasis upon the family as the most important social unit. Twelver Shiism permits temporary marriage (*mutʿah*), which, although definitely practiced at the time of the Prophet, was banned in Sunnī Islam under the caliphate of ʿUmar. It also emphasizes inheritance for the female members of the family and the children rather than brothers and sisters more than do Sunnī schools of law.

As far as the economic order is concerned, although the craft guilds and orders of chivalry have existed throughout the Islamic world, because these orders traced their origin to ʿAlī, they were easily integrated into the Twelver religious world and its piety and possessed a more open and organic link with the formal, exoteric aspects of the religion than was the case among the Sunnīs. In fact, even in the Sunnī world the religious ambience of the orders of guilds *(aṣnāf)* and those of chivalry (*futūwāt*) have resembled that of Shiism, since these organizations have been linked to the Ṣūfī orders, most of which trace their chains of transmission (*silsilahs*) back to ʿAlī. (Even in Shiism, however, where these organizations have been linked to the formal and exoteric dimension of the religion, there have been important Ṣūfī orders such as the Khāksār that have linked the guilds and the chivalric associations to the general religious framework.)

Religious practices. The Twelvers share with the Sunnīs the belief in the performance of the obligatory rites of canonical prayer (*ṣalāh* or *namāz*), fasting (*ṣawm*), and pilgrimage *(ḥājj)*, although in each case there are small differences with the four schools of Sunnī law. In the case of the prayers, for example, the postures, numbers, and times are the same, but the Twelvers add two formulas to the call to prayers (*adhān*) and usually group together the noon and afternoon prayers, as well as the evening and night prayers, rather than waiting for an hour or two between them. Again, the fast is usually begun a few minutes earlier and terminated a few minutes later than in Sunnī practice, and there are likewise minor differences in the *ḥājj* ceremonies, the most important of which is an extra circumambulation of the Kaʿbah performed by the Shīʿah.

Special rites. What is more distinctive of Twelver religious practices, however, is the performance of certain rites in addition to the obligatory ones. In the case of prayer, the Twelvers invoke many long litanies and chant many prayers derived totally from the sayings of the imams, a practice that occurs in the Sunnī world only in the climate of Sufism. Among the most famous of these prayers are the *Duʿaʾ* (Supplication) *of Kumayl* and the *Duʿāʾ of Ṣabaḥ* by ʿAlī, the *Scroll of Sajjād* by Imam Zayn al-ʿĀbidīn, and the *Jawshan-i kabīr* (Great Armor), attributed to the Prophet and usually recited during the nights of Ramaḍān. There are also numerous other prayers by the imams that are recorded in al-Ku-laynī's *Uṣūl al-kāfī* and Majlisī's *Biḥār al-anwār* and form part of Twelver devotional life; these range from the most contemplative and metaphysical statements on the doctrine of the divine nature to intimate yearnings of the soul for the love of God. Twentieth-century compilations such as the *Mafātīḥ al-jinān* (Keys of paradise) of ʿAbbās Qummī assemble prayers that, woven around the cardinal rites of canonical prayer, fasting, and pilgrimage, punctuate the whole calendar of the life of the Twelver community.

Pilgrimages. The tombs of all the imams are considered extensions of the supreme centers of Mecca and Medina, and thus, pilgrimage to these sites, not to speak of the authentic *imām-zādahs*, or tombs of the imams' descendants, are strongly encouraged by the jurists and the official religious hierarchy and play a very important role in Shīʿī religious life. The most important of these holy places are Najaf, where ʿAlī is buried (although Mazār-i Sharīf in Afghanistan is claimed by some to be his tomb); Karbalāʾ, where Imam Ḥusayn and his family are interred; Kāẓimayn, the tombs of the fifth and ninth imams; Mashhad, the mausoleum of Imam ʿAlī al-Riḍā; and Samarrāʾ, where the tenth and eleventh imams are buried and where the twelfth imam went into occultation.

Some of these major sites, such as Mashhad, feature distinguished monuments of Islamic art; others, including Najaf and Qom, have become important university centers over the centuries, and pilgrimages there have also involved the dissemination of religious knowledge through both oral transmission and written works.

In addition to the major sites, other important Shīʿī pilgrimage centers include the tomb of Sayyidah Zaynab, the sister of Imam Ḥusayn, outside of Damascus (she is also honored with a *maqām,* or "station," in Cairo, which many consider to be her tomb), and that of Hazrat-i Maʿṣūmah, the sister of the eighth imam, in Qom. A unique pilgrimage site sacred to both Shīʿī and Sunnī Muslims is the Raʾs al-Ḥusayn in Cairo, where the head of Imam Ḥusayn lies buried; the mausoleum remains to this day the spiritual pole of the city of Cairo.

Popular practices. Among the many popular Shīʿī observances, the commemoration of the martyrdom of Imam Ḥusayn at Karbalāʾ on the tenth day of the month of Muḥarram marks the peak of the religious calendar in terms of emotional intensity and commitment. Outside of the annual pilgrimage to Mecca, there is no more impressive religious ceremony in the Islamic world than the vast ʿĀshūrāʾ processions in Persia and the Indian subcontinent. From the fifteenth century on, there developed the practice of *rawzah-khvānī,* the chanting of the story of Karbalāʾ, and soon after, the *taʿziyah,* or passion play in which the same tragedy is acted out. There are many other Shīʿī observances, ranging from such religiously commendable acts as sacrificing animals to ward off evil, paying a sum of money (*ṣadaqah*) to the poor for the same reason, or serving a religious meal (*sufrah*), the remains of which are given to the poor, to different forms of magic and popularized occult sciences that are given a religious garb and have become part of popular religious tradition despite official religious opposition to them.

SEE ALSO ʿAlī Ibn Abī Ṭālib; ʿĀshūrāʾ; Domestic Observances, article on Muslim Practices; Falsafah; Folk Religion, article on Folk Islam; Ghaybah; Ḥadīth; Ḥusayn ibn ʿAlī; Imamate; Ishrāqīyah; Ijtihād; Islamic Law; Jaʿfar al-Ṣādiq; Kalām; Rāwzah-Khvānī; Taqīyah; Taʿziyah; Walāyah; Worship and Devotional Life, article on Muslim Worship.

BIBLIOGRAPHY

Algar, Hamid. *Religion and the State in Iran, 1785–1906.* Berkeley, 1969.

Arjomand, Said Amir. *The Shadow of God and the Hidden Imam.* Chicago, 1984.

Aṣ–Saduq, ash-Shaykh. *A Shi'ite Creed.* Translated by Asif A. A. Fyzee. Tehran, 1982.

Bausani, Alessandro. *Persia religiosa da Zaratustra a Bahâ'u'llah.* Milan, 1959.

Bayat, Mangol. *Mysticism and Dissent.* Syracuse, 1982.

Chittick, William C., trans. and ed. *A Shi'ite Anthology.* Albany, N.Y., 1981.

Corbin, Henry. *En Islam iranien.* 4 vols. Paris, 1971–1972.

Corbin, Henry. *History of Islamic Philosophy.* Translated by L. and Ph. Sherrarot. New York and London, 1993.

Corbin, Henry, with S. H. Nasr and Osman Yahia. *Histoire de la philosophie islamique,* vol. 1. Paris, 1964.

Donaldson, D. M. *The Shi'ite Religion.* London, 1933.

Enayat, Hamid. *Modern Islamic Political Thought.* London, 1982.

Gobineau, Joseph Arthur (Comte de). *Les religions et philosophies dans l'Asie centrale.* 2d ed. 1863. Reprint, Paris, 1957.

Ḥillī, Ibn al-Muṭahhar al-. *Al-Bāb al-Hādī 'Ashar.* Translated by William M. Miller. London, 1928.

Hollister, John Norman. *The Shi'a of India.* London, 1953.

Jafri, S. Husain M. *Origins and Early Development of Shi'a Islam.* London, 1979.

Kazemi Moussavi, Ahmad. *Religious Authority in Shi'ite Islam.* Kuala Lumpur, 1996.

Keddie, Nikki R., ed. *Religion and Politics in Iran: Shi'ism from Quietism to Revolution.* New Haven, 1983.

Mazzaoui, Michel M. *The Origins of the Safawids: Śi'ism, Śūfism, and the Gulāt.* Wiesbaden, 1972.

McDermott, Martin J. *The Theology of al-Shaikh al-Mufīd.* Beirut, 1978.

Modaressi, Tabātabā'ī. *An Introduction to Śhi'i Law.* London, 1984.

Momen, Moojan. *An Introduction to Shi'i Islam: The History and Doctrine of Twelver Shi'ism.* New Haven, Conn., and London, 1985.

Mufīd, Shaykh al-. *Kitāb al-irshād.* Translated by I. K. A. Howard. London, 1981.

Nasr, Seyyed Hossein. "Ithnā 'ashariyya." In *The Encyclopaedia of Islam,* new ed. Leiden, 1960–.

Nasr, Seyyed Hossein. *Ideals and Realities of Islam.* 2d ed. London, 1975.

Nasr, Seyyed Hossein, Hamid Dabashi, and Seyyed Vali Reza Nasr, eds. *Expectation Millenium—Shi'ism in History.* Albany, N.Y., 1989.

Nasr, Seyyed Hossein, Hamid Dabashi, and Seyyed Vali Reza Nasr, eds. *Shi'ism—Doctrine, Thought and Spirituality.* Albany, N.Y., 1988.

Richard, Yann. *Le Shi'isme en Iran.* Paris, 1980.

Rizvi, Saiyad Athar Abbas. *Socio-Intellectual History of the Isnā 'Asharī Shī'īs in India.* 2 vols. Canberra, 1986.

Sachedina, Abdelaziz Abdulhussein. *Islamic Messianism: The Idea of Mahdi in Twelver Shi'ism.* Albany, N.Y., 1981.

Savory, Roger. *Iran under the Safavids.* Cambridge, 1980.

Le shî'isme imâmite. Colloque de Strasbourg. Paris, 1970.

Strothmann, Rudolf. *Die Zwölfer Schī'a.* Leipzig, 1926.

Ṭabaṭabā'ī, 'Allāmah Sayyid Muḥammad Ḥusayn. *Shi'ite Islam.* Edited and translated by Seyyed Hossein Nasr. Albany, N.Y., 1975.

SEYYED HOSSEIN NASR (1987 AND 2005)

SHIM'ON BAR YOḤ'AI (second century CE) was a Palestinian tanna, rabbinic leader, mystic, and ascetic. Shim'on was one of the two most prominent students of 'Aqiva' ben Yosef (the other was Me'ir); he was the student who provoked the deposition of Gamli'el from the position of *nasi'* of Israel (cf. B.T., *Ber.* 28a). Shim'on was one of the five rabbis ordained by Yehudah ben Bava' during the Hadrianic persecutions that followed the Bar Kokhba Revolt. After the Sanhedrin was reestablished in the Galilean city of Usha, Shim'on taught in nearby Tiberias and Meron. According to several legends, he was responsible for locating many lost tombs and removing these sources of ritual uncleanness from Tiberias, thereby restoring its prominence in the region.

Shim'on is the subject of many rabbinic legends. The best known of these recounts how he and his son hid in a cave after he was sentenced to death by the Romans; according to some versions, when he emerged from the cave after twelve years and saw people who were engaged in farming rather than in the study of Torah, he set their fields afire by only a glance in their direction (B.T., *Shab.* 33b). As a punishment Shim'on and his son were sent back to the cave by God for another year. Shim'on demonstrated magical powers in other stories as well: He filled a valley with gold coins (J.T., *Ber.* 9.2, 13d) and exorcised a demon from the daughter of the Roman emperor (B.T., *Me'il.* 17b).

Shim'on is one of the most frequently mentioned authorities in the Mishnah, where he is referred to without patronymic; his rulings cover most of the major topics taken up in rabbinic sources. One of the more famous sayings attributed to him declares that if the Jews properly observed two consecutive Sabbaths, they would be redeemed immediately (B.T., *Shab.* 118b). There is no systematic critical study of his traditions. Jacob Epstein believes that the corpus of his traditions was one of the primary documents used in the redaction of the Mishnah.

The Talmud considers Shim'on to be the paradigm of the scholar who is totally immersed in the study of the Torah. A rabbi of his caliber was not required to interrupt his study even for the important daily recitation of the Shema' (J.T., *Ber.* 1.2, 3b). Concerning the study of Torah, he said: "If I had been at Mount Sinai at the time the Torah was given to Israel, I would have asked God to endow man with two mouths, one to talk of the Torah and one to attend to his other needs. . . . But the world can barely withstand the slander of [persons with] one [mouth]. It would be all the worse if [each individual] had two" (J.T., *Ber.* 1.2, 3b).

Shim'on himself believed that he was the holiest person ever to have lived: If one individual were to merit entering heaven, he said, it would be Shim'on (J.T., *Ber.* 9.2, 13d).

Shim'on is assigned authorship of several Midrashic compilations: the *Sifrei* on *Numbers* and *Deuteronomy* (B.T., *San.* 86a) and the *Mekhilta' de-Rabbi Shim'on bar Yoh'ai,* a midrash on the Book of Exodus. Several short apocalyptic mystical compilations are also linked with his name. Medieval mystics credited him with the authorship of the *Zohar,* one of the most important texts of the Qabbalah (an attribution still considered valid by many contemporary mystics despite evidence to the contrary).

The holiday of Lag ba-'Omer, on the eighteenth of Iyyar, is thought to be the anniversary of his death; it is celebrated at his traditional place of burial in Meron.

See Also Tannaim; Zohar.

BIBLIOGRAPHY

Jacob N. Epstein's *Mavo' le-sifrut ha-tanna'im* (Jerusalem, 1957) discusses the place of Shim'on's traditions in the development of the Mishnah. In *Rabbi Shim'on ben Yoḥ'ai* (in Hebrew; Jerusalem, 1966) Israel Konovitz collects all the references to Shim'on in rabbinic literature.

New Sources

Chernick, Michael L. "'Turn It and Turn It Again': Culture and Talmud Interpretation." *Exemplaria* 12 (2000): 63–103.

Rosenfeld, Ben-Zion R. "Simeon b. Yohai—Wonder Worker and Magician Scholar, 'saddiq' and 'hasid.'" *REJ* 158 (1999): 349–384.

Tzvee Zahavy (1987)
Revised Bibliography

SHIM'ON BEN GAMLI'EL II

SHIM'ON BEN GAMLI'EL II (second century CE) was a Palestinian tanna. He held the hereditary office of *nasi',* or president, of the Sanhedrin. It is said that he studied Greek and that he supported a policy of peace with Rome.

According to a Talmudic source, two of his rabbinic colleagues—Me'ir, the *ḥakham* of the Sanhedrin, and Natan, its *av beit din*—sought to oust Shim'on from his position as *nasi'* during a power struggle within the ranks of rabbinic leadership. In the Talmudic account, the two masters became angry when Shim'on decreed that the students in the academy at Usha should not stand in their honor when they entered. Me'ir and Natan then conspired to test Shim'on on an obscure tractate of the law in order to bring him to disgrace. Shim'on was coached by one of his supporters, passed the test, and banished Me'ir and Natan from the academy. Nonetheless, they continued to send the scholars advice about problems in the interpretation of the law and they were eventually readmitted (B.T., *Hor.* 13b).

On the basis of a reference in this story to a ceremonial sash worn by Natan, Jacob Neusner (1969) suggests that Natan was the head of the Jewish community in Babylonia, son of an official in the Parthian government, and that he had come to Palestine to advance the influence of the Parthians in preparation for their struggle against Roman authority. Shim'on's sympathy to Roman interests, Neusner says, may have made him the primary target of a conspiracy by Natan. It is equally plausible, however, that the events were part of a struggle within the Palestinian community as Shim'on tried to restore authority to the office of *nasi'* after some of its powers were usurped by the scholars.

Many legal rulings in Shim'on's name appear throughout the major rabbinic compilations, and his views are almost always decisive: The Talmud declares that the law follows Shim'on ben Gamli'el in all but three instances (B. T., *Ket.* 77a). His statement that not all who wish to recite God's name in the prayers may do so (*Ber.* 4.8) is an example of his restrictive views regarding the use of divine names for liturgical purposes. Shim'on sometimes cites precedents for religious prescriptions and rulings; for example, he refers to several customs for fellowship meals in Jerusalem (Tosefta, *Ber.* 4.9). He also serves as a transmitter of teachings by his contemporaries Yehudah, Me'ir, and Yose.

See Also Tannaim.

BIBLIOGRAPHY

No full critical analysis of the corpus of Shim'on's tradition has been undertaken. In Volume 3 of *Tannaitic Symposia* (in Hebrew; Jerusalem, 1969), pp. 159–228, Israel Konovitz collects all the references to Shim'on in rabbinic literature. Jacob Neusner's *A History of the Jews in Babylonia,* vol. 1 (Leiden, 1969), pp. 79–85, proposes a historical approach to the analysis of one major tradition.

New Sources

Schwartz, Seth. "Gamaliel in Aphrodite's Bath: Palestinian Judaism and Urban Culture in the Third and Fourth Centuries." In *The Talmud Yerushalmi and Graeco-Roman Culture,* vol. 1, edited by Peter Schäfer, pp. 203–217. Tübingen, 1998.

Tzvee Zahavy (1987)
Revised Bibliography

SHIM'ON BEN LAQISH

SHIM'ON BEN LAQISH was a third-century amora, generally known in the Jerusalem Talmud by his full name and in the Babylonian Talmud by the acronymic form ReSH (Rabbi Shim'on) Laqish. Although Shim'on may have had some early training in rabbinic learning (see J.T., *Kil.* 9.4, 32b), he eventually became a circus gladiator, perhaps out of financial distress (see J.T., *Git.* 4.9, 46a–b; *Ter.* 8.5, 45d). Later, a chance encounter with Yoḥanan (bar Nappaḥa') led him to marry that sage's sister and enter the world of the rabbinate. He settled in Tiberias, the site of Yoḥanan's academy, and there became his colleague and close companion. The Talmud refers to them as the "two great[est] men of the world," that is, of their time (J.T., *Ber.* 8.6, 12c; and see B.T., *Ket.* 54b).

As a scholar Shimʿon was noted for the encyclopedic breadth of his learning, his faithful loyalty to received tradition, and his dialectical acuity (J.T., *Git.* 3.1, 44d; B.T., *San.* 24a). In his teaching he emphasized the importance of regular study of Torah (J.T., *Ber.* 9.5, 14d) and was reputed to review each day's lesson forty times in advance of presenting it before his teacher (B.T., *Taʿan.* 8a). Shimʿon defended the honor and privileges of the learned elite against patriarchal pressures for a more monarchial structure in rabbinic leadership (J.T., *San.* 2.1, 19d–20a; *Gn. Rab.* 78.12). While he condemned the Romans as more cruel than all previous oppressors combined (*Lv. Rab.* 13.5), he also praised them for enforcing justice in the land (*Gn. Rab.* 9.13; to be sure, he also spoke in defense of flattery, B.T., *Sot.* 41b). He was noted for his custom of avoiding anyone whose personal honesty was subject to question and, perhaps as a result of his earlier career, he was noted for his personal bravery.

Some of Shimʿon's aggadic opinions are interesting for their counter-traditional stand. For example, he is said to have claimed that the Jews borrowed the names of the angels from the Babylonians during their enforced stay in that land and that the events described in the *Book of Job* never took place (J.T., *Sot.* 5.6, 20d).

Shimʿon is said to have died of grief after his dear friend Yoḥanan made mocking reference to his martial skill during a halakhic argument (B.T., *B.M.* 84a). Yoḥanan himself, it is said, thereupon wasted away of remorse.

SEE ALSO Amoraim; Yoḥanan bar Nappaḥaʾ.

BIBLIOGRAPHY

Aaron Hyman's *Toledot tannaʾim ve-amoraʾim* (1910; reprint, Jerusalem, 1964) is an uncritical compendium of traditional lore concerning Shimʿon. It is almost useless as a tool for modern, critical biography, but it remains valuable as an encyclopedic gathering of information. Avraham Wasserman's "Resh Laqish bein ha-lisṭim," *Tarbiz* 49 (1980): 197–198, deals with one aspect of Shimʿon's career.

New Sources

Brettler, Marc Zvi. "Rabbi Simeon ben Lakish at the Gladiator's Banquet: Rabbinic Observations on the Roman Arena." *HTR* 83 (1990): 93–98.

ROBERT GOLDENBERG (1987)
Revised Bibliography

SHINGONSHŪ.

SHINGONSHŪ. The Japanese esoteric Buddhist tradition of Shingon takes its name from the Chinese term *zhenyan*, which literally means "true word" and is the Chinese translation of the Sanskrit term *mantra*, meaning spoken phrases taken to have extraordinary powers. The practice of reciting *mantras* is taken as characteristic of this tradition and points to the continuity of the tradition's practices from its Indic origins through to its modern Japanese instantiation. The centrality of *mantra* recitation is evidenced by two early names for the tradition, *Mantranaya* (path of *mantras*), and *Mantrayāna* (vehicle of *mantras*). Shingon is an esoteric tradition, meaning that its practices are only to be transmitted by a qualified teacher (Jpn., *ajari;* Skt., *ācārya*) to a student who has undergone the appropriate initiations. When speaking of the Shingon tradition, it refers primarily to a lineage of ritual practice.

Other key terms that amplify the character of the Shingon tradition include *tantra*, which originates as a bibliographic category but which is now used as a synonym for the esoteric tradition within Buddhism, and *Vajrayāna,* which means the thunderbolt vehicle, referring to the speed of attaining full awakening. In some systems of classification, Mantranaya and Pāramitānaya (path of perfections) are paired as two parts of Mahāyāna, while other systems consider Vajrayāna to be a third vehicle superceding Hīnayāna and Mahāyāna. *Mikkyō* is also often used in association with Shingon and means esoteric teachings. While Shingon is predominantly esoteric in character, an esoteric element is also found in the Tendai tradition. This latter is often referred to as *Tendai mikkyō* (usually abbreviated as *Taimitsu*), and is contrasted with *Tōji mikkyō* (usually abbreviated as *Tōmitsu*), named for one of the earliest Shingon temples, Tōji (Eastern Temple) in Kyoto.

INDIAN ORIGINS. The Tantric tradition of Buddhism originated in medieval India following the demise of the Gupta empire, around 550 CE. While there are a variety of theories about the origins of esoteric Buddhism and its relations to other Indian religious traditions, it seems clear that there was no one particular origin. Rather, a wide variety of reinterpreted practices and doctrinal developments went into the making of what only later took on an identity as a movement, school, or tradition.

The two main texts for the Shingon tradition are the *Mahāvairocana Sūtra* (Jpn., Dainichikyō, T.D. no. 848) and the *Sarvatathāgata-Tattvasamgraha Sūtra* (T.D. no. 865, a portion of the *Vajraśekhara Sūtra*, Jpn., *Kongochogyō*, by which name it is commonly known in contemporary Shingon), and are thought to have been composed in Northwest India early in the eighth century. Others have suggested, however, that the *Sarvatathāgata-Tattvasamgraha* was composed in Southern India in the late seventh century, while the *Mahāvairocana* was composed in Western India in the middle of the seventh century.

CHINESE TRANSMISSION. While Tantric texts and practices were known in China from as early as the third century CE, the Shingon lineage itself traces its origins to the rise in the Tang dynasty (618–907) of an esoteric Buddhist school. This school is taken to have originated in the work of three figures: Śubhākarasiṃha (637–735), Vajrabodhi (671–741) and Amoghavajra (705–774). Also important was Śubhākarasiṃha's disciple Yixing (683–727), who not only assisted Śubhākarasiṃha in the translation of the *Mahāvairocana Sūtra*, but also wrote an important commentary on it.

There are three Chinese translations of the *Sarvatathāgata-Tattvasaṃgraha Sūtra.* Vajrabodhi's (T.D. no. 866), Amoghavajra's (T.D. no. 865), and Shihu's (T.D. 882). Of these, it is Amoghavajra's that is most widely used in the Shingon tradition. This version, completed circa 754, is based on a text that Amoghavajra brought back to China from Sri Lanka or South India, where he travelled and studied in 744–746 CE.

Although these two texts—the *Mahāvairocana* and *Sarvatathāgata-Tattvasaṃgraha*—are considered to be foundational for Shingon, other texts are also important. The *Adhyardhaśatikāprajñāpāramitā Sūtra* (Jpn., Rishukyō, *Prajñāpāramitā Sūtra in One Hundred Fifty Verses*) is part of the Tantric Prajñāpāramitā literature, and is frequently recited as part of daily services in Shingon temples. The version used is the Chinese translation by Amoghavajra (T.D. no. 243), another of the texts he acquired during his travels in Sri Lanka and South India. The other important works are the *Yugikyō* (T.D. no. 867, reconstructed Sanskrit title: *Vajraśekhara vimāna sarvayogayogi Sūtra,* translator indeterminate), and the *Sussidhikara-Sūtra* (T.D. no. 893, Jpn., *Soshitsuji kyō*), translated by Śubhākarasiṃha in 726 CE.

TRADITIONAL LINEAGE OF PATRIARCHS. The Shingon tradition traces its teachings back to the Buddha Mahāvairocana (Jpn., Dainichi), who is considered to be the Dharmakāya Buddha. In Mahāyāna thought there developed a theory of three Buddha bodies. These are the nirmāṇakāya (form, or manifestation body), saṃbhogakāya (reward, or celestial body), and dharmakāya (dharma, or actual body). In contrast with most of the Buddhist tradition, Shingon holds that the Dharmakāya actively teaches.

According to an early lineage of patriarchs given by Kūkai, Mahāvairocana transmitted the teachings to Vajrasattva, who was then succeeded by Nāgārjuna, Nāgabodhi, Vajrabodhi, Amoghavajra, Huiguo, and finally by Kūkai himself. There are, however, several variations in the lineages recorded by different masters. These variations result from differing interpretations of who had received which of the main two ritual transmissions, the Vajradhātu and Garbhakośadhātu. For example, the lineage recorded by Shūkaku (1150–1202) only has seven patriarchs. He removes Vajrabodhi, asserting instead that Amoghavajra had received transmission directly from Nāgabodhi when Amoghavajra travelled to India. Other lineage records also add and delete various figures, including Samantahadra, Mañjuśrī, Vajrapāṇi, Dharmagupta, Śubhākarasiṃha (637–735), and Xuanchao.

KŪKAI, THE FOUNDER. Kūkai (774–835, posthumously titled Kōbō Daishi, commonly referred to in honorific form as O Daishi sama) is considered to be the founder of Japanese Shingon. He was born on the island of Shikoku, into an aristocratic family, the Saeki, a branch of the Ōtomo clan. At fifteen, in 788, he went to the capital, Nara, where he began to study the Confucian classics under the guidance of a maternal uncle. Three years later, he entered the Confucian College (Jpn., *daigaku*) that served to recruit and train court officials. Within the next few years, however, he showed increasing interest in Buddhism, and at some point left the college.

He is known to have engaged in various ascetic practices during this period. For example, on Mt. Kinbu he practiced the Kokūzō Gumonji hō, a ritual dedicated to Kokūzō bosatsu (Skt., Ākāśagarbha bodhisattva), intended to improve the practitioner's memory. This practice involves reciting the *mantra* of Ākāśagarbha one million times over a period of one hundred days. This indicates an early contact with esoteric Buddhism, as the Gumonji hō practice is based on the *Kokuzōgumonjinohō* (T.D. no. 1145) translated by Śubhākarasiṃha. It appears that this work was brought to Japan by Dōji (d. 744 CE) of the Nara temple Daianji, and that Kūkai received transmission of the practice from Gonzō (758–827), a leading cleric of the times.

Although it is unclear who recommended him, Kūkai was chosen as a state-sponsored student to accompany the envoy Fujiwara Kadonomaro to China in the years 804 to 805. After some difficulties, Kūkai eventually reached the Green Dragon Monastery (Qing-long si) in the Chinese capital of Chang'an. He reports having been initiated into the dual lineage of ritual practice by his master Huiguo (746–805, Jpn., Keika). Kūkai portrays this very dramatically, explaining that Huiguo was only clinging to life in order to transmit the teachings to a worthy disciple. Shortly after Kūkai's initiation, Huiguo encourages Kūkai to return to Japan, and then dies.

By 806 Kūkai had returned to Kyushu, the southern island of Japan, but he had to wait an additional three years until he was given permission to proceed to the capital, Heian (today's Kyoto), by the new emperor, Saga. He was directed to reside at Takaosanji, a temple in the suburbs of the capital. This would be the center of his activities until 823, when he was given authority over Tōji, one of the two temples built to flank the entrance to the city. In 816 he was granted permission to establish a training center specifically for Shingon Mikkyō on Kōyasan (High, Wild Mountain), where he eventually retired due to illness in 831. Still active in the promotion of Shingon within the court, he received permission to establish the Shingon chapel (Jpn., Shingon-in) on the grounds of the palace, providing a base for Shingon to play a part in services for the court, such as the Buddha Relics Offering. Early in 835 he died while residing on Kōyasan. Tradition has it, however, that he did not die, but rather passed into an unbroken meditation (Skt., *samādhi*).

In contemporary Shingon the difference between the Tantric texts and practices already extant in Japan during the Nara period (known as Nara Mikkyō) and the dual system introduced by Kūkai is taken for granted. The tradition itself describes Nara Mikkyō as incomplete, unsystematic, and impure, categorizing it as zōmitsu (mixed or heterogenous esotericism). Kūkai's form is said to be mature, systematic, and pure, and it is categorized as junmitsu (pure esotericism).

The zōmitsu/junmitsu distinction, however, appears to be relatively late, dating perhaps only from the late seventeenth or early eighteenth century. Like all such scholastic categories it simultaneously serves both organizing and polemic ends.

RELATION BETWEEN KŪKAI AND SAICHŌ. The other major figure of Heian Japan is Kūkai's elder contemporary Saichō (767–822). Saichō also travelled to China in the same ambassadorial entourage as Kūkai. Saicho's main interest was Tiantai (Jpn., Tendai), but after his studies on Mt. Tiantai, he did receive initiation into an esoteric Buddhist lineage. This was shortly before his return to Japan, however, so he did not have any opportunity to pursue this further. Following Saichō's return to Japan, in 806 he was directed by Emperor Kanmu, Saga's predecessor, to establish the Tendai tradition at Enryakuji on Mt. Hiei, still the main center of Japanese Tendai today. The imperial edict establishing the Saichō's new school specified the two dimensions of training. One portion of the curriculum was centered on the Mo-ho chih-kuan, the foundational Tendai work by the Tiantai patriarch Chih-i (538–597), and is known as *shikangō* (from the Japanese pronunciation of *chih-kuan* as *shikan*). The second portion of the curriculum was to be esoteric in character, focusing on the Mahāvairocana Sūtra. This track was known as *shanagō* (*shana* being an abbreviated form of *Birushana*, the Japanese pronunciation of *Vairocana*).

Initially relations between Saichō and Kūkai went smoothly. While Saichō worked to establish a Mikkyō element within his Lotus Sūtra based Tendai, he needed Kūkai's assistance, having himself only received the most rudimentary introduction to esoteric Buddhism while in China. Saichō regularly borrowed texts from Kūkai, until finally in 816 a breach occurred between the two. The schism resulted from a fundamental difference in the way the two understood the place of mikkyō. Saichō wanted to integrate Mikkyō into his Tendai Lotus school. Saichō saw Tendai as foundational to, and therefore encompassing of all forms of, East Asian Buddhism, including Shingon. Kūkai, on the other hand, understood Shingon to embody the highest, most effective teachings of Buddhism, and therefore to supercede all other forms, including Tendai.

SHINGON DEVELOPMENTS IN THE MEDIEVAL PERIOD. Kakuban (Kōgyō Daishi, 1095–1144) played a key role in the medieval development of Shingonshū, being involved both in a revivalist movement, known as "shingi shingonshū," and in articulating Shingon conceptions with Amidist ones. Devotion to the Buddha Amida (Skt., Amitābha) became increasingly popular during the medieval period of Japanese Buddhist history. While Amida played an important role in the Tantric Buddhism transmitted from India through China to Japan, this new popularity stimulated Shingon practitioners to draw on those resources, giving greater prominence to Amida and his Pure Land of Bliss (Skt., Sukhāvatī; Jpn., Gokuraku Jōdo), described in the Larger *Sukhāvatīvyuha Sūtra* (Skt *Sukhāvatīvyūha Sūtra;* Jpn., *Daimuryōju kyō*, T.D. nos. 360–364). Kakuban also gave great emphasis to the buddha realm of Mahāvairocana Buddha, the Pure Land of Esoteric Grandeur (Jpn., Mitsugon Jōdo), described in the Mahāyāna Sūtra of Mystic Grandeur (Skt., *Ghanavyūha Sūtra;* Jpn., *Daijō mitsugongyō;* T.D. nos. 681, 682). Mahāvairocana's Pure Land of Esoteric Grandeur became identified not only with Amida's Pure Land of Bliss, but also with Vairocana Buddha's Lotus Womb World (Jpn., Kezōkai, also Garland World, Jpn., Kegon sekai), described in the *Garland Sūtra* (Skt., *Avataṃsaka Sūtra*, Jpn., *Kegon gyō*, T.D. nos. 278, 279, 293).

Kakukai (Nanshōbō, 1142–1223) was the thirty-seventh superintendent of Kongōbuji, the main temple of the Chuin ryū on Mt. Kōya. Like Kakuban, Kakukai also responded to the rising popularity of Amida, arguing that the Pure Land was to be realized in this world rather than after death. This extended the idea of becoming awakened in this incarnation formulated by Kūkai. This immanentist interpretation is seen in the identification of Mt. Kōya with the Pure Land of Bliss. Today, the last train station before entering the mountain is called Gokurakubashi—Bridge to the Land of Bliss.

In medieval Japan, self-identified Shintō lineages began to develop. The Watarai clan, which served the Ise shrine, assimilated many esoteric elements into its interpretation of the Shintō tradition. Drawing Shingon's dual *maṇḍala* (Jpn., *ryōbu mandara*), this became known as Ryōbu Shintō. Similarly, Yuiitsu Shintō ("one and only Shintō," also Yoshida Shintō after its founder Yoshida Kanetomo, 1435–1511) drew on Shingon symbolism, ideology, and practice. The latter includes a Yuiitsu Shintō *goma* (votive fire) clearly modeled on the Shingon *goma*. A late medieval Japanese development within Shingon was another reform movement known as Shingon ritsu, which emphasized adherence to the rules of the order (Skt., *vinaya*, Jpn., *ritsu*). This sect was established by Eizon (Shiembō, 1201–1290), and was centered at the Saidaiji temple in Nara.

KEY DOCTRINES. Shingon teaches that one can achieve complete, full awakening in the present through esoteric practice. *Sokushin jōbutsu* (being awakened in this body) is a key doctrine of Shingon. Although later interpretations in light of the idea of inherent awakening (Jpn., *hongaku*) have tended to conflate the two ideas, the Shingon doctrine predated the idea of inherent awakening in Japan.

The path to awakening in Shingon is based on the idea that the practitioner is already identical with the Buddha. Ritual practice in which the practitioner actively identifies with the Buddha, experiencing the world as a buddha, actualizes the inherent bodhicitta. An exposition of this is found in the *Ihon Sokushin jōbutsu-gi* attributed to Kūkai, which presents three perspectives on the nature of the relation between the practitioner and the Buddha. In principle (ri) a person is already identical with the Buddha. This is called *rigu jōbutsu*. Although already inherently awakened, because of obscurations (Skt., *kleśa*, Jpn., *bonnō*), it is necessary to engage in practice to actualize one's awakening. This is called *kaji jōbutsu.* Buddhahood is actualized in a two-fold pattern of revealing (Jpn., *ken*) and acquiring (Jpn., *doku*), called *kendoku jōbutsu.* Thus, the idea of already being inherently awakened as understood in Shingon does not preclude the necessity for practice, as some antinomian interpretations of the inherent awakening doctrine developed in medieval Japan would suggest.

The role of ritual practice is to realise the three-fold identity of the practitioner and the buddha. This identity is between the three mysteries (Skt., *triguhya,* Jpn., *sanmitsu*), referring to the body (Skt., *kāya-guhya*), speech (Skt., *vāg-guhya*) and mind (Skt., *mano-guhya*) of the Buddha, and the three actions (Skt., *trikarma*) of ritual practice, the bodily (Skt., *kāya-karma*), oral (Skt., *vāk-karma*) and mental (Skt., *manaḥ-karma*) of the practitioner. The formation of hand gestures (Skr. *mudrā*) manifests the unity of the practitioner's body with that of the Buddha. The recitation of *dhāraṇī* and *mantra* manifests the unity of the practitioner's speech with that of the Buddha. And, the visualizations prescribed in ritual texts constitute the unity of the practitioner's mind with that of the Buddha.

Two strains of ritual practice were introduced to China by Śubhākarasiṃha and Vajrabodhi, the Garbhakośadhātu based on the Mahāvairocana and the Vajradhātu based on the *Sarvatathāgata-Tattvasaṃgraha,* respectively. The Shingon tradition considers these two to have been unified by Kūkai's teacher, Huiguo. Each of the two sūtras describes a set of buddhas, *bodhisattvas,* and other deities, organized in various assemblies and portrayed in *maṇḍala.* The Diamond World *maṇḍala* (Skt., *Vajradhātu maṇḍala;* Jpn., *Kongōkai mandara*) represents the assemblies described in the *Sarvatathāgata-Tattvasaṃgraha,* while the Womb World *maṇḍala* (Skt., *Garbhakośadhātu maṇḍala,* Jpn., *Taizōkai mandara*) represents those of the *Mahāvairocana* (specifically the second chapter). Thus the two strains of ritual practice relate to the different assemblies described in the two sūtras, and portrayed in the two *maṇḍalas.*

SHINGON PRACTICES: KŌMYŌ SHINGON, AJIKAN, AND THE TRAINING IN FOUR PARTS. Kōmyō Shingon, or Clear Light Mantra, is one of the most common contemporary practices, being promoted for lay practitioners and found not only among Shingon adherents but also among adherents of other Japanese Buddhist traditions as well. Recitation of the *mantra* was promoted particularly by Myōe Kōben (1173–1232) at the beginning of the thirteenth century, perhaps in response to other simplified practices, such as *nembutsu* recitation. The *mantra* is "*on abogya beiroshanō makabotara mani handoma jimbara harabaritaya un*" (Skt., *oṃ amogha vairocana mahāmudrā maṇi padma jvāla pravarttaya hūṃ,* "Praise be to the flawless, all-pervasive illumination of the great *mudrā,* turn over to me the wish-fulfilling jewel, lotus, and radiant light"). Traditionally, it was believed that recitation of this *mantra* over pure sand would empower it, so that it spread over an ill person or corpse, and that person would be healed or reborn in Amitābha's Pure Land.

There are three preliminaries to the training sequence to become a Shingon priest. These are Susokukan (breath counting meditation), *Gachirin kan* (visualization of the full moon), and Ajikan (visualization of the syllable A in the Siddham script). In contemporary Shingon, Ajikan has become an independent practice in itself. It takes the form of a short ritual (Skt., *sādhana*), structured like other Shingon rituals. The symbolism of the syllable A is rooted in Indian theories of language. As the first letter of the Sanskrit syllabery, it is creative. At least implicitly present within each syllable of the syllabery, it is omnipresent. And, as the negative prefix, it is destructive.

The training sequence (Jpn., *shidō kegyō,* "training in four parts") involves performance of four different rituals over a hundred day period. It begins with a relatively simple ritual called the Juhachidō, or Eighteen Paths. Originally this involved the recitation of eighteen *mantras* with their accompanying *mudrās,* though the contemporary form is more complicated, involving more *mantras* and *mudrās.* This practice establishes a karmic connection between the practitioner and the five central buddhas of the Karma Assembly of the *Vajradhātu maṇḍala:* Mahāvairocana (Jpn., Dainichi, center), Akṣobhya (Jpn., Ashuku, East), Ratnasambhava (Jpn., Hōshō, South), Amitāyus (Jpn., Amida, West), and Amoghasiddhi (Jpn., Fukūjōju, North).

The second ritual is the Kongōkai, which continues to develop the relation to the *Vajradhātu maṇḍala,* expanding now beyond the five central buddhas to include an additional thirty-two deities. Each of the four buddhas who form Mahāvairocana's retinue have their own retinue of four attendant *bodhisattvas,* known collectively as the Sixteen Great Bodhisattvas. There are then an additional four groups of four: the Four Pāramitās, the Four Inner Goddesses of Offering, the Four Outer Goddesses of Offering, and the Four Gatekeepers.

The *Taizōkai* is the third ritual in the training sequence, and it is focused on the eleven assemblies of the *Garbhakośadhātu maṇḍala.* These eleven are the Mind of All Buddhas (or Universal Knowledge, Jpn., *henchi*), All Bodhisattvas (or Mantra Holders, Jpn., *jimyō*), Avalokiteśvara (Jpn., Kannon), Vajrapaṇi (Jpn., Kongōshu), Acalanātha (Jpn., Fudō), Mañjuśrī (Jpn., Monjushiri), Sarvanīvaraṇa-viṣkambhin (Jpn., Jokaishō), Kṣitigarbha (Jpn., Jizō), Ākāśagarbha (Jpn., Kokūzō), Śākyamuni (Jpn., Shakamuni), and the External Vajras (Jpn., Gekongōbu). Indicative of the Indian roots of Shingon is the *Taizōkai's* evocation of one group of the Exterior Vajras, the Worldly Deities. These are twelve deities known from the Vedic and Brahmanic traditions, ten of whom have directional associations: Īśāna (or Maheśvara; Jpn., Ishanaten, or Daijizaiten, Northeast), Indra (Jpn., Indara, also Taishakuten, East), Āditya (or Sūrya; Jpn., Nitten), Brahmā (Jpn., Bonten, Zenith), Agni (Jpn., Katen, Southeast), Yama (Jpn., Emma, South), Rākṣasa (or Nirṛti; Jpn., Rasetsu, or Niritei, Southwest), Varuṇa (Jpn., Suiten, West) Pṛthivi (Jpn., Jiten, Nadir),

Candra (Jpn., Gatten), Vāyu (Jpn., Fū, Northwest) and Vaiśravaṇa (Jpn., Bishamon, also Tamon, North).

The fourth and final ritual is the Fudō Myōō Sokusai Goma, or Fire Offering to Acalanātha Vidyārāja for Pacification. Although largely structured like the Kongōkai ritual, the goma integrates deities from both *maṇḍalas* in its performance. Within the standard format of the ritual, the goma adds five sets of fire offerings. These are to Agni (Jpn., Katen); the Lord of the Assembly (i.e., Prajñā Bodhisattva); the Chief Deity (Jpn., honzon—i.e., Acalanātha Vidyārāja; Jpn., Fudō Myōō); the thirty-seven deities of the Karma Assembly of the *Vajradhātu maṇḍala* (discussed above); and, finally, the Twelve Worldly Deities, the Seven Astral Lights (sun, moon, and five visible planets), and the Twenty-Eight Lunar Mansions (the twenty-eight days of a complete lunar cycle).

KŌYASAN. The most prominent contemporary center of Shingon in Japan is Mount Kōya (Jpn., Kōyasan), located in a valley between eight mountain peaks, representing an eight-petalled lotus flower expressing the compassionate nature of the Garbhakośadhātu. Originally established as a training center, it also serves today as the administrative center for the most prominent Shingon lineage, the Chūin ryū. The main temple of the lineage is called Kongōbuji.

On Mount Kōya there are two complexes that today attract the most attention. The first of these is known as the Garan, which serves as the main ritual center for the Chuin ryū sect. The Garan includes the Kondō, or Golden Hall; the Western and Eastern (or Great) Pagodas; shrines to the *kami* of the mountain; and various other halls and temples. The interior decoration of the two pagodas represents the interpenetration of the Vajradhātu and Garbhakośadhātu. The Eastern Pagoda, for example, has Mahāvairocana of the Garbhakośadhātu in the center, surrounded by the four buddhas that form his retinue in the Vajradhātu.

Okunoin is a cemetery where the remains of Kūkai are entombed. According to legend, when the posthumous title of Kōbō Daishi was awarded, an entourage from the court came to the mountain to read the Imperial proclamation at the tomb. The tomb was opened at that time and it was discovered that Kūkai's hair and nails had continued to grow. It was declared that he had not died, but rather had entered into a state of perpetual meditation. The ashes of many of Japan's most important historical figures have been entombed along the pathways leading to the tomb of Kūkai. The form of the majority of these tombs is the five-element stupa (Jpn., *gorinhoto*). The five elements are earth (represented by a cube inscribed with the Siddham script syllable A), water (a sphere with the syllable VA), fire (a four-sided pyramid with the syllable RA), wind (a demilune with the syllable HA), and space (represented by a maṇi-jewel with the syllable KHA). These five elements constitute the world of the known, the objective. A sixth element, consciousness, represents the knower, the subjective, which has the known as its object. The five elements are identified with the Garbhakośadhātu, while consciousness is identified with the Vajradhātu, and the unity of knower and known is identified with the Dharmakāya Buddha, Mahāvairocana.

RELATION WITH SHUGENDŌ AND THE NEW RELIGIONS. The indigenous tradition of Shugendō (also, Yamabushi) involves the practice of austerities in the mountains of Japan. Kūkai is thought to have associated with groups of mountain ascetics, as exemplified by his practice of the Kōkūzo Gumonji ho at Mount Kinbu, one of the main centers of Shugendō. It is also thought that he was already familiar with Mount Kōya from his period before travelling to China, and it was on the basis of this prior familiarity that he chose it for his training center.

Shugendō, with its open syncretism of Buddhist (particularly Tantric) and Shintō elements, was abolished by the Meiji government in 1872 as part of the government's efforts to purify Shintō. Because of the existing connection between Tantric Buddhism and Shugendō, Shugendō sects chose to affiliate themselves with either Shingon or Tendai. With the return of religious freedom under the postwar constitution, the institutional affiliations between Shugendō sects and either Shingon or Tendai have lapsed. This has been accompanied by a decline in the use of Buddhist interpretations for Shugendō practices. In contemporary Japan, Shugendō practitioners often conduct large, outdoor fire rituals (Jpn., *saitō goma*). The *saitō goma* is a Shugendō adaptation of the Tantric fire ritual (Skt., *homa;* Jpn., *goma*). Evidencing perhaps a return to traditional syncretic practices, *saitō goma* conducted by Shugendō practitioners are performed today not only at specifically Shugendō sites, but also at Shintō shrines and Buddhist temples.

In contemporary times various of the "new religions," such as Agonshū, Shinnyoen, and Gedatsukai, have based their teachings or practice on various aspects of Shingon. Agonshū, for example, on the one hand claims to be a return to the original teachings of the Buddha Śākyamuni as found in the *agamas* (Jpn., *agon*), but draws heavily on esoteric Buddhist symbolism and practice, particularly as mediated by the Shugendō tradition. Agonshū conducts goma performances on the first day of each month (Jpn., *tsuitachi goma*) at its center in Tokyo. Agonshū also draws on Shugendō symbolism, for example, sponsoring large-scale *saitō goma* in celebration of the Hoshi Matsuri (Star Festival) in February of each year.

SHINGON IN THE WEST. Like other forms of Japanese Buddhism, Shingon was brought to the West by Japanese nationals in search of work during the late nineteenth and early twentieth centuries. In 1909 Reverend Shutai Aoyama came to San Francisco intending to provide religious services to the immigrant Japanese community. Due to illness and lack of funds, his mission did not actually start until 1912, when a temporary temple was established in Los Angeles. In the Hawaiian islands, lay practitioners began as early as 1902 to establish informal temples, particularly devoted to miraculous cures attributed to the power of Kūkai. These came under the scrutiny of Shingon officials in Japan, who then dispatched Reverend Eikaku Seki to establish an official branch of Kongōbuji in Honolulu. In 1940 a new, permanent temple was completed to house the mission in Los Angeles, but within a year war broke out between Japan and the United States. As leaders of the Japanese community, ministers were among the first to be arrested and imprisoned for the duration of the war. The new temple building came to be used as a storehouse for the belongings of the Japanese families interned in the relocation camps scattered throughout the western United States. After the end of the war, the temple community was able to reestablish itself, with the temple building serving as housing for returning families. The Shingon Mission of Hawai'i in Honolulu held its centennial celebration in 2002, and the Kōyasan Buddhist Temple in Los Angeles celebrates its centennial in 2012.

SEE ALSO Buddhism, article on Buddhism in Japan; Buddhism, Schools of, article on Japanese Buddhism; Mahāvairocana; Nirvāṇa.

BIBLIOGRAPHY

Abé, Ryūichi. "Saichō and Kūkai: A Conflict of Interpretations." *Japanese Journal of Religious Studies,* 22, nos. 1–2 (1995): 103–137.

Abé, Ryūichi. *The Weaving of Mantra: Kūkai and the Construction of Esoteric Buddhist Discourse.* New York, 1999.

Astley-Kristensen, Ian, tr. *The Rishukyō: The Sino-Japanese Tantric Prajñāpāramita in 150 Verses (Amoghavajra's Version).* Buddhica Britannica, series continua, III. Tring, U.K., 1991.

Berger, Patricia. "Preserving the Nation: The Political Uses of Tantric Art in China." In *Latter Days of the Law: Images of Chinese Buddhism, 850–1850,* edited by Marsha Weidner. Lawrence, Kans., 1994.

Davidson, Ronald M. *Indian Esoteric Buddhism: A Social History of the Tantric Movement.* New York, 2002.

Gardiner, David Lion. "Kūkai and the beginnings of Shingon Buddhism in Japan." Ph.D. dissertation, Stanford University, 1995.

Giebel, Rolf W., trans. *Two Esoteric Sutras: The Adamantine Pinnacle Sutra, The Susiddhikara Sutra.* Berkeley, Calif., 2001.

Gieble, Rolf W., and Dale A. Todaro, trans. *Shingon Texts.* Berkeley, Calif., 2004.

Hakeda, Yoshito S. *Kūkai: Major Works.* New York, 1972.

Hitoshi, Miyake. *Shugendō: Essays on the Structure of Japanese Folk Religion.* H. Byron Earhart, ed. Ann Arbor, Mich., 2001.

Hodge, Stephen. *The Mahā-Vairocana-Abhisaṃbodhi Tantra, With Buddhaguhya's Commentary.* London and New York, 2003.

Kiyota, Minoru. *Shingon Buddhism: Theory and Practice.* Los Angeles, 1978.

Klein, Susan Blakely. *Allegories of Desire: Esoteric Literary Commentaries of Medievel Japan.* Cambridge, Mass., 2002.

Klimburg-Salter, Deborah E. *The Silk Route and The Diamond Path: Esoteric Buddhist Art on the Trans-Himalayan Trade Routes.* Los Angeles, 1982.

Mammitzsch, Ulrich. *The Evolution of the Garbhadhātu Maṇḍala.* Śata-Piṭaka Series, no. 363. New Delhi, 1991.

Morrell, Robert E. "Shingon's Kakukai on the Immanence of the Pure Land," *Japanese Journal of Religious Studies,* 11. nos. 2–3 (1984): 195–220.

Orzech, Charles D. "Seeing Chen-yen Buddhism: Traditional Scholarship and the Vajrayāna in China." *History of Religions* 29, no. 2 (1989): 87–114.

Orzech, Charles D. *Politics and Transcendent Wisdom: The Scripture for Humane Kings in the Creation of Chinese Buddhism.* University Park, Pa., 1998.

Payne, Richard. *The Tantric Ritual of Japan: Feeding the Gods, The Shingon Fire Ritual.* Śata-Piṭaka Series, vol. 365. Delhi, 1991.

Payne, Richard. "The Shingon Ajikan: Diagrammatic Analysis of Ritual Syntax." *Religion* (1999).

Payne, Richard. "Romantic Mimesis and the Invisibility of Shingon Buddhism: The Japanese Vajrayāna Tradition in the United States." In *Buddhist Missionaries in the Era of Globalization,* Linda Learman, ed. Honolulu, 2004.

Rambelli, Fabio. "True Words, Silence, and the Adamantine Dance: On Japanese Mikkyō and the Formation of the Shingon Discourse." *Japanese Journal of Religious Studies,* 21, no. 4 (1994): 373–405.

Reader, Ian. "The Rise of a Japanese 'New New Religion': Themes in the Development of Agonshū." *Japanese Journal of Religious Studies* 15, no. 4 (1988): 235–261.

Sanford, James. "Wind, Waters, Stupas, Mandalas: Fetal Buddhahood in Shingon." *Japanese Journal of Religious Studies* 24, no. 1–2 (1997): 1–38.

Scheid, Bernhard. *Der Eine und Einzige Weg der Götter: Yoshida Kanetomo und die Erfindung des Shinto.* Vienna, 2001.

Sharf, Robert H. "Visualization and Mandala in Shingon Buddhism." In *Living Images: Japanese Buddhist Icons in Context,* edited by Robert H. Sharf and Elizabeth Horton Sharf. Stanford, Calif., 2001.

Sharf, Robert H. "On Esoteric Buddhism in China." Appendix 1 in *Coming to Terms with Chinese Buddhism: A Reading of the Treasure Store Treatise.* Kuroda Institute Studies in East Asian Buddhism, no. 14. Honolulu, 2002.

Snodgrass, Adrian. *The Matrix and Diamond World Mandalas in Shingon Buddhism.* 2 vols. Śata-Piṭaka Series, nos. 354, 355. New Delhi, 1988.

Strickmann, Michel. *Mantras et mandarins: Le bouddhisme tantrique en Chine.* Paris, 1996.

Strickmann, Michel. "Homa in East Asia." In *Agni: The Vedic Ritual of the Fire Altar, vol. II,* edited by Frits Staal. Berkeley, Calif., 1983.

ten Grotenhuis, Elizabeth. *Japanese Mandalas: Representations of Sacred Geography.* Honolulu, 1999.

Tsuda Shin'ichi. "A Critical Tantrism." *Memoirs of the Research Department of the Toyo Bunko,* no. 36 (1978): 167–231.

Unno, Mark. *Shingon Refractions: Myoe and the Mantra of Light.* Boston, 2004.

Vanden Broucke, Pol. "On the Title and the Translator of the Yugikyō (T. XVIII no. 867)." *Bulletin of the Research Institute of Esoteric Buddhist Culture,* Kōyasan University (Kōyasan Daigaku Mikkyō Bunka Kenkyūsho Kiyō), no. 7 (1994): 212–184.

van der Veere, Henny. *A Study in the Thought of Kōgyō Daishi Kakuban, with a Translation of his Gorin kuji myō himitsushaku.* Leiden, 2000.

RICHARD K. PAYNE (2005)

SHINKŌ-SHŪKYŌ SEE NEW RELIGIOUS MOVEMENTS, *ARTICLE ON* NEW RELIGIOUS MOVEMENTS IN JAPAN

SHINRAN (1173–1262) was the founder of the Jōdo Shinshu, or True Pure Land school, of Mahāyāna Buddhism. Born in Japan during a period of social turmoil and religious change, Shinran became a Tendai monk at age nine and followed that discipline on Mount Hiei. At age twenty-nine, moved by a deep spiritual disquiet, he meditated for one hundred days in the Rokkakudō Temple in Kyoto, where he had a vision that led him to become a disciple of the Pure Land teacher Hōnen in 1201. He later received Hōnen's permission to copy his central work, the *Senchaku hongan nembutsu shū* (Treatise on the Nembutsu of the select primal vow), and to make a portrait of the master. Because of strong criticism voiced by the monks of Mount Hiei and Kōfukuji in Nara and the indiscretions of certain of his disciples, Hōnen and his leading disciples were exiled. Shinran went to Echigo (now Niigata prefecture) in 1207 under the criminal name of Fujii Yoshizane.

During the next period of approximately seven years of exile and residence at Kokubu in Echigo, Shinran married Eshin-ni and fathered six children. Shinran is particularly noted for establishing marriage among the clergy and abandoning monastic precepts as a religiously justified act. He was inspired by a dream vision of the *bodhisattva* Kannon (Skt., Avalokiteśvara, Bodhisattva of Compassion), who promised to take the form of a woman to be his helpmate in his mission to spread Pure Land teachings to the masses.

Pardoned in 1211, Shinran left Echigo in 1213 bound for the Kantō. There he gradually created a sizable community by establishing small *dōjō* (meeting places) in followers' homes throughout the region. Upon his return to Kyoto in 1235 or 1236, Shinran engaged in correspondence with his disciples, answering questions on doctrine and giving advice about various issues raised by the nascent community. Among his literary efforts, he completed and revised the *Kyōgyōshinshō,* wrote various commentarial texts such as the *Yuishinshō-mon'i* and *Ichinentannenmon'i,* and composed collections of *wasan* (hymns) expressing basic themes of his teaching or praising the texts and masters of the Pure Land tradition. For the most part, Shinran wrote in the language of the common people.

Variant interpretations of Shinran's teachings inevitably led to conflicts among his followers. These issues were a persistent theme of Shinran's later letters, and continued to plague the community after he died. However, in Shinran's last years, Zenran, his eldest son, created conflict and misunderstanding among the disciples by claiming to have received a special teaching and authority from Shinran. After Shinran dispelled these misunderstandings by disowning his son, peace returned to the community. Shinran expressed some of his deepest insights in his final letters and writings. Among these are his assertion that believers are "equal to the Tathagata" and his expression of faith in the absolute "other power" (*tariki*) of Amida (Skt., Amitabha) Buddha. In 1262 Shinran died peacefully at the home of a brother.

Shinran's spiritual disillusionment with monastic discipline and his experience of faith in Amida Buddha's Primal Vows (*hongan*) under the guidance of Hōnen became the basis and inspiration for the development of the Jōdo Shinshū as a major and distinctive expression of Pure Land teaching in Japanese history. Influenced by *hongaku* ("primordial enlightenment") thought in Tendai philosophy, as well as by contemporary Chinese Pure Land scholarship, Shinran expanded the vision of the meaning of Amida Buddha's compassion stressed in the Pure Land tradition.

Shinran maintains that there are two stages in the salvation process established by the virtue of Amida Buddha. These are *ōsō,* "going to the Pure Land," and *gensō,* "returning." *Ōsō* refers to the elements of religious experience that lead to rebirth in the Pure Land. *Gensō* indicates the altruistic end of salvation whereby we become part of the salvation process guiding all beings to enlightenment. Shinran analyzes the first stage, that of going to the Pure Land, into four dimensions, discussed in the four sections of the *Kyōgyōshinshō.* These are Teaching, Practice, Faith, and Enlightenment.

The section on teaching refers to the *Daimuryōjukyō* (Larger Pure Land Sūtra), which narrates the story of how, ten *kalpas* ago, the *bodhisattva* Hōzō (Dharmākara) completed five *kalpas* of religious training and became Amida Buddha in the Western Pure Land through the fulfillment of his forty-eight Primal Vows.

The section on practice establishes that the recitation of Amida's name (the Nembutsu, from Chin., *nianfo*) is the way provided by the eighteenth vow for the salvation of all beings. Shinran maintained that the Nembutsu is the great practice praised by all Buddhas, for the name itself is the embodiment of Amida's virtue.

The section on faith reveals Shinran's most distinctive understanding of Pure Land teaching. Here he shows that faith is the true and real mind of Amida Buddha expressed in human consciousness. Against the background of the Mahayana tradition, he asserts that faith itself is the realization of Buddha nature *(shinbusshō).*

In developing this interpretation, Shinran went beyond the limited conception of Amida portrayed in the *sūtra* myth narrative. He understood Amida as the sole reality of the cosmos, joining Pure Land teachings to the concept of Primordial Enlightenment (Jpn., *hongaku*) of the Tendai philosophy. Amida Buddha was no longer merely one Buddha among others, limited in time to his Enlightenment ten *kalpas* ago. Rather, he is the eternal Buddha (*Jōdo wasan* no. 55). According to the *Jinenhōnishō,* Amida, as the ultimate, formless body of Dharma (Skt., *dharmakāya*), takes form in order to manifest his essential nature, which is beyond all comprehension and definition. Amida Buddha is the symbol for eternal life and light, the compassion and wisdom that makes salvation possible for every human being, no matter how evil and corrupt. The power of his vow is manifest in human history through the name, formulaically expressed in the words "Namu Amida Butsu" ("Hail to Amida Buddha"), which serve as the external cause of salvation.

The Light (*kōmyō*) is the inner condition of salvation experienced as undoubting faith in the name and vow and the simultaneous exclamation of the Nembutsu. Faith is not a human act but ultimately the bestowal of Amida's true and real mind within the human consciousness as the immediate awareness both of one's own spiritual incapacity and of the unfailing embrace of Amida's compassion. In that moment, the assurance of salvation is attained as a deep inner movement of total reliance on the vow. It is for this reason that Shinran emphasized the "power of the other" (*tariki*), that is, the salvific power of Amida, rather than one's own effort (*jiriki*), as essential to salvation. The awareness received in that moment indicates that the disciple has attained the level of the truly assured (*shōjōjū*). All the causes, and therefore also the fruit, of salvation have been perfected. The believer's spiritual status in the life is "equal to the Tathagāta," although his actual enlightenment awaits him in the future as the causal basis for this final attainment has been established through his presently experienced faith in Amida's vow.

According to Shinran, the recitation of the Nembutsu is not performed as a means to gain rebirth in the Pure Land through one's own merit. Rather, it is a spontaneous outflow of gratitude for the assurance of salvation received. The section designated Enlightenment teaches that the final destiny of beings is birth in the Pure Land, which is identified with *nirvāṇa.* It is also to become a Buddha and, after the manner of the *bodhisattva,* to return to this defiled realm to save all beings.

The community initiated through Shinran's efforts and teaching eventually differentiated into several branches. Among them, the most significant have been the Takada Senjūji and the Honganji, which latter would later divide into East and West branches. At first a relatively minor movement within Japanese Buddhism, Jōdo Shinshū was transformed into a powerful religious and social institution through the eloquence, simplicity, and determination of the eighth patriarch, Rennyo (1415–1499). Despite internal divisions, it has remained a major popular religious force in Japan.

See Also Amitābha; Hōnen; Jōdo Shinshū; Mappō; Nianfo; Pure and Impure Lands; Rennyo.

Bibliography

Akamatsu Toshihide. *Shinran.* Tokyo, 1969. A detailed survey of Shinran's life.

Akamatsu Toshihide and Kasahara Kazuo, eds. *Shinshushi gaisetsu.* Kyoto, 1963. A collection of essays on Kamakura Buddhism, the life of Shinran, and the development of Shinshu institutions.

Bloom, Alfred. *Shinran's Gospel of Pure Grace.* Tucson, Ariz., 1965. A systematic study of Shinran's teaching.

Bloom, Alfred. *The Life of Shinran Shonin: The Journey to Self-Acceptance.* Leiden, 1968. A critical examination of issues of Shinran's biography.

Futaba Kenko. *Shinran no kenkyu.* Kyoto, 1962. An analysis of social and religious issues related to the life of Shinran.

Ienaga Saburo. *Shinran Shonin gyojitsu.* Kyoto, 1948. A chronological outline of Shinran's life and activities with important textual references.

Ingram, Paul O. *The Dharma of Faith: An Introduction to Classical Pure Land Buddhism.* Washington, D. C., 1977. A study of Shinran's teaching set in the context of Buddhist tradition; includes a study of Rennyo.

Kasahara Kazuo. *Shinran to togoku nomin.* Tokyo, 1957. A study of Shinran's life in the context of the social development of the Kanto area.

The Kyo Gyo Shin Sho. Translated by Hisao Inagaka et al. Abridged ed. Kyoto, 1966. A translation of Shinran's comments in the *Kyogyoshinsho.*

Matsunaga, Daigan, and Alicia Matsunaga. *Foundation of Japanese Buddhism,* vol. 2. Los Angeles, 1976. A detailed historical survey of major Buddhist schools of the Kamakura period.

Matsuno Junko. *Shinran.* Tokyo, 1959. A detailed study of Shinran's life.

Shigefuji, Shinei. *Nembutsu in Shinran and His Teachers: A Comparison.* Toronto, 1980. A detailed examination of Shinran's teachings in relation to the Pure Land tradition.

Shinshu Seiten: Jodo Shin Buddhist Teaching. San Francisco, 1978. An anthology of translations from Shinran and Rennyo with supplementary explanatory materials, assembled by Buddhist Churches of America.

Suzuki, D. T. *Collected Writings on Shin Buddhism.* Edited by the Eastern Buddhist Society. Kyoto, 1973. Essays on Mahayana and Pure Land Buddhism.

Suzuki, D. T., trans. *The Kyogyoshinsho by Gutoku Shaku Shinran.* Edited by the Eastern Buddhist Society. Kyoto, 1973.

Ueda Yoshifumi, ed. and trans. *The Letters of Shinran: A Translation of Mattosho.* Kyoto, 1978. A translation of Shinran's major letters, with explanatory introduction.

New Sources

Chilson, Clark. "Born-Again Buddhists: Twentieth-Century Initiation Rites of Secretive Shinshu Societies in Central Japan." *Studies in Central and East Asian Religions* 11 (1999): 18–36.

Dobbins, James C. *Jodo Shinsu: Shin Buddhism in Medieval Japan.* Bloomington, 1989.

Smith, Joel R. "Human Insufficiency in Shinran and Kierkegaard." *Asian Philosophy* 6 (July 1996): 117–128.

Ueda, Yoshifumi, and Dennis Hiroto. *Shinran: An Introduction to His Thought.* Kyoto, 1989.

ALFRED BLOOM (1987)
Revised Bibliography

SHINTŌ.

Shintō is a Japanese term often translated as "the way of the gods." Broadly, it refers to the worship of the multifarious Japanese *kami* (gods). In modern Japan, it signifies forms of ritual practice and belief focusing on Shintō shrines (*jinja,* literally "*kami*-places") which are institutionally separate from Buddhist temples. However, the worship of *kami* in Japan is not restricted to Shintō, and those who worship the *kami* at Shintō shrines are nearly all Buddhists and/or members of Japanese new religions. A narrow definition of Shintō might restrict it to only those elements in Japanese religious history that have explicitly identified themselves by the term *Shintō,* while broad definitions of the term sometimes see Shintō as coterminous with the entirety of Japanese culture, past and present.

The meaning of the term *Shintō* has undergone many changes in the course of Japan's history. The most radical took place as recently as the mid-nineteenth century, when Japan resumed full contact with the outside world after two and a half centuries of seclusion. Immediately after taking office in 1868, the modernizing Meiji government issued decrees dissociating *kami* from buddhas. Up to this time, *kami*-worship throughout Japan had largely taken place at shrine-temple complexes run by Buddhist clergy. Buddhas, *kami,* and other well-known divinities were understood to form part of a common pantheon also revered by numerous Shūgendō (mountain ascetic) practitioners and other specialized religious groups and movements. In the years following 1868, a nationwide system of shrines, priests, and doctrines relating only to non-Buddhist divinities (mainly these were *kami* stripped of their Buddhist titles) was developed with government support. At the apex of this system was the shrine of Amaterasu the sun goddess, deity of the shrine of Ise and divine ancestress of the imperial line now back in power following the collapse of the shogunate. Until the end of World War II, this new, dissociated form of Shintō was regarded under Japanese law as "nonreligious." The divinity of the emperor and the unique status and mission of the land of Japan since the Age of the Gods were not religious ideas preached by shrine priests but historical facts transmitted by schoolteachers. Generations of Japanese children were taught that Shintō represented an ancient, unchanging tradition; an idea also promulgated quite successfully outside Japan, where modern Shintō is often believed to be a survival of Japan's "primal" religion. Since 1946, under postwar laws guaranteeing personal religious freedom and the separation of religion and state, this understanding of Shintō is no longer sponsored by the government nor taught in schools, and Shintō teachings and practices are now regarded in law as "religious." Nevertheless, what is usually meant by Shintō today is essentially the same nationwide system of shrines, priests, and *kami*-rituals that was dissociated from Buddhism in the mid-nineteenth century and for the first eighty years of its existence regarded as nonreligious. The study of Shintō as religion therefore raises many interesting questions.

RECENT DEVELOPMENTS IN THE STUDY OF SHINTŌ. The study of Shintō underwent radical changes in the late twentieth century as modern critical methods were brought to bear on a subject that had been neglected for many years. Until the 1980s, serious modern scholarship on Shintō hardly existed inside or outside Japan. In the minds of most academics, the term *Shintō* evoked a discredited system of state-sponsored emperor worship, heavily implicated in the ultranationalism that had culminated in Japan's defeat in 1945. Japanese scholars with impressive but possibly compromising expertise in prewar Shintō studies were out of favour, and few postwar scholars were interested in studying customs and traditions relating to *kami* performed mainly by the older generation at decaying local shrines. Within Japan, the study of Shintō as a system of religious meaning was largely the preserve of conservative scholar-priests connected with shrines and seminaries whose view of Shintō had changed little since 1945, and in some cases since the nineteenth century. While some major shrines prospered as the Japanese economy expanded, no intellectually respectable Shintō worldview emerged in the decades following World War II that could compete for international scholarly attention with the new-found appeal of Zen and other forms of Japanese Buddhism or the shifting fortunes of the dynamic, self-promoting new religions.

In the 1980s, however, new questions about Shintō and new understandings of Shintō began to emerge among both Japanese and non-Japanese academics. The critical study of Shintō rapidly developed as a field of vibrant international scholarship, and the question of Shintō became highly significant, indeed central, within the study of Japanese religions. Because new understandings of Shintō developed so quickly, books and articles published at different times present widely varying views of Shintō. Readers who consult different works may be confused about whom and what to believe on the topic. Before embarking on the study of Shintō in more detail, it is thus necessary to understand what the main views of Shintō are and why the study of Shintō is now such a contested, problematic, and interesting area of enquiry.

TWO VIEWS OF SHINTŌ. Broadly speaking, there are two extreme views of what Shintō is, as well as an emerging middle ground within which increasingly sophisticated debates are taking place. At one extreme is a view of Shintō that holds that it is Japan's ancient and enduring indigenous religion. This view dominated understandings of Shintō inside and outside Japan throughout the late nineteenth and twentieth centuries. It was succinctly stated, for example, in the opening sentence of the scholar-priest Hirai Naofusa's 1987 article on Shintō in the first edition of the *Encyclopedia of Religion.* "Shintō," wrote Hirai, "is the name given to the traditional religion of Japan, a religion that has existed continuously from before the founding of the Japanese nation until the present." This view, which might best be described as neo-traditionalist, celebrates Shintō both as a religion and as something quintessentially Japanese, implicitly contrasting an ancient, native Shintō spiritual heritage with later "foreign" religions and ideologies such as Buddhism or Western thought. This presentation of Shintō as a kind of Japanese natural phenomenon is consistent with the prewar understanding of Shintō as a unique and enduring attribute of the Japanese "race," and hence the Japanese nation-state. It also fit well with popular postwar *nihonjin-ron,* or "theory of Japaneseness," literature, which claimed a unique character and identity for the Japanese as opposed to other human beings. This understanding of Shintō is essentialist and ahistorical. Historical transformations in *kami*-worship are read as temporary departures from a pure Shintō core, while to account for the plethora of contradictory beliefs and practices related to *kami,* types or subdivisions of Shintō are proposed, such as Imperial Household Shintō, Shrine Shintō, Sect Shintō, or Folk Shintō, although Shintō means something different in each case. Because the national morality doctrines of pre-1945 Shintō were jettisoned at the end of the war, neo-traditionalists have tended to present Shintō ideas as matters mysteriously beyond the realm of doctrine. Thus the Shintō scholar Ono Sōkyō declared of the notion of *kami* in *Shintō: The Kami Way* (1960), "it is impossible to make explicit and clear that which fundamentally by its very nature is vague" (p. 8). Above all, the neo-traditionalist construction of Shintō as a separate, self-contained religious tradition comprehensively marginalizes the role of Buddhism, which was officially introduced from Korea in the sixth century and in one way or another has dominated Japanese religious life, including *kami*-worship, ever since.

At the other extreme is the radical view of Shintō associated with the Japanese historian Kuroda Toshio, who in his 1981 article "Shintō in the History of Japanese Religion" threw down a major and controversial challenge to the prevailing neo-traditionalist understanding of Shintō. Kuroda declared that the idea of an ancient, enduring, indigenous tradition of Shintō was "no more than a ghost image produced by a word linking together unrelated phenomena" (Mullins et al., p. 27). Kuroda's argument, stated simply but based on detailed research into early and medieval Buddhism, was that throughout most of Japan's history the shrines, shrine rituals, priests, concepts of *kami,* and other key elements of what are now called Shintō were really Buddhist through and through. The idea of an ancient Shintō tradition, native to Japan and separate from Buddhism, Kuroda argued, is nothing but a modern invention, a supporting pillar of nineteenth-century nationalism meant to sustain the ideology of emperor worship. The notion of Shintō as an ancient, unchanging tradition was designed by Meiji bureaucrats to persuade Japanese people to comply with the will of their divine emperor in pursuit of rapid industrialization at home and imperial expansion abroad. Kuroda preferred to reserve the term *Shintō* for those relatively rare occasions from the late Heian period onward when the term was actually used. Instead, he referred to pre-Meiji Japanese *kami* beliefs and practices as elements in what he called the *kenmitsu taisei,* or exoteric-esoteric system, a complex and variegated worldview founded on prevailing esoteric Buddhist patterns of belief and ritual practice that incorporated *kami* alongside other Buddhist divinities. Kuroda's claim that "ancient Shintō" was entirely a Meiji period invention, if correct, has profound implications for the modern study of Shintō. Above all, it means that *kami*-worship, at least before 1868, can only properly be understood within the context of Japanese Buddhism; Shintō would thus become a nonsubject.

EMERGING ISSUES. Following Kuroda's radical challenge, the study of Shintō gained a new lease of life as scholars debated the key question of whether Shintō has existed uninterruptedly throughout Japanese history or, conversely, emerged as an independent religion only in modern times. Some critics of the Shintō establishment took the opportunity to dismiss today's Shintō as "merely" a nineteenth-century invented tradition. This was not a new charge; the Victorian Japanologist Basil Hall Chamberlain, who witnessed the process at first hand, described it in an essay titled "The Invention of a New Religion" (reprinted in *Japanese Things,* Tokyo, 1971). Others have pointed out that all successful traditions require periodic reinvention, and Shintō may be no exception. Even if Shintō as it is known today was invented at the time of the Meiji restoration in 1868, all scholars agree that there have been systems of shrines dedicated to *kami* in Japan throughout recorded history and perhaps before, so an ancient, continuous tradition of *kami*-worship, whether it be called Shintō or not, must surely be acknowledged in any analysis of Shintō past and present. Moreover, the Japanese imperial line is undeniably ancient, continuous, and bound up with *kami* beliefs. Thus, the debate has shifted from a simple either/or issue (either Shintō is a modern invention or it is an ancient enduring tradition) to detailed enquiries into such topics as the past and present use of the term *Shintō;* ways of discerning and discussing continuity and change in *kami* worship within an overarching Buddhist context; the relations between the imperial institution, *kami,* and shrines over long periods of time; and the role of Shintō within contemporary Japanese religion and society.

As a result of Kuroda's work, the term *Shintō* is now used with great caution by scholars, especially when dealing with premodern eras. Studies of Japanese religion now consciously seek to avoid making false distinctions between Shintō and Buddhism as if these have always represented separate spheres of life. Even in contemporary Japan, where Shintō shrines and Buddhist temples have been institutionally separate since 1868 and it might seem to make sense to speak of Shintō and Buddhism as different religions, most people who visit shrines to the *kami* also visit Buddhist temples, and often for similar purposes, namely to seek "practical benefits" (*genze riyaku, kubosa*) such as easy childbirth, safe travel, true love, or success in examinations. Many, though not all, of the successful new religions of Japan also incorporate both Shintō and Buddhist themes into their rituals and beliefs. Shintō and Buddhist discourses, therefore, continue to be integrated in various ways within the lived experience of Japanese people. Kuroda's dismissal of an imagined past in which a distinctive, indigenous Shintō tradition persisted separately from Buddhism has thus highlighted continuities, as well as discontinuities, between pre- and post-Meiji Japanese religion.

SHINTŌ IN JAPANESE HISTORY. Since Shintō has meant different things at different times, it makes sense to approach the study of Shintō historically, so that themes which emerge can be treated within their historical context rather than as features of a timeless Shintō. The major systems of belief and practices relating to *kami* and shrines can then be considered without prejudging the issue of whether in a particular time and place these are best described as *Shintō*. For convenience, Japanese history will be divided into five periods, approximately as follows:

- Early Japan (prehistory–ninth century CE).
- Medieval Japan (tenth–sixteenth centuries).
- Edo period (1600–1868).
- Meiji restoration to World War II (1868–1945).
- Contemporary Japan (1945–present).

Early Japan. Neo-traditionalists assert that there was an unnamed, indigenous religion in Japan focusing on the worship of *kami,* and that this tradition was obliged to name itself Shintō in order to distinguish itself from the Buddhism later introduced from China and Korea. In practice, it is very difficult to disentangle different strands of ritual and belief and to identify one element as indigenous and another as imported. Archaeological evidence suggests that in prehistoric Japan (before 400 CE), spiritual powers related to water supplies, agriculture, seafaring, and other precarious undertakings were worshipped at various sites. The introduction of rice culture from the mainland encouraged hierarchical forms of community, whose leaders' authority was reinforced by rituals for the *kami.* Chinese accounts provide the earliest written information on Japan, reporting among other things that spiritual forces could be deployed by powerful women. The *Weizhi,* a Chinese text from the late third century CE, famously describes a Queen Pimiko who maintained her rule by what the Chinese called "magic and sorcery." Fifth-century Chinese histories tell of five Japanese kings who, like their Korean counterparts, sent tributes to China and received mirrors, ceremonial swords, and other gifts from the Chinese emperor in return. Such prized items evidently came to be used widely for ritual purposes.

The "kings" known to the Chinese were probably the rulers of the Yamato clan, which by the late fourth century had already achieved political dominance over other powerful clans in eastern, central, and western Japan. The main site of the Yamato court was at Mount Miwa in central Japan, where Ōmononushi, the protective deity of the Yamato, was worshipped as "the spirit of the land." Around the fifth century, Chinese-style notions of an all-embracing imperial rule meant that the competing clans progressively converged under a central authority, adopting common myths of origin. Huge burial tombs constructed for the Yamato rulers at this time attested to their military and political dominance. Royal funeral and succession rites were developed that involved pacification of the deceased king's spirit through a recitation of his genealogy and accomplishments. Members of immigrant clans with expertise in writing were in charge of these rituals. They developed methods of recording names and other Japanese terms using Chinese characters phonetically. The two earliest such writings, the *Kojiki* (Record of ancient matters, 712 CE) and *Nihonshoki* (Chronicle of Japan, 720 CE) affirm the divine ancestry of the Yamato line and provide detailed accounts of "the age of the gods," including the creation of the world and the descent of certain *kami* to the land. Sub-narratives chronicling the subordination of descendants of "earthly *kami*" appear to symbolize the conquest of previously independent clans. The founding myths (*engi*) of great seafaring shrines such as the Sumiyoshi Taisha (in modern Osaka) are also retold, locating established sites of ritual power within the Yamato story.

Through such narratives, influenced heavily by Chinese themes and first written down almost two centuries after Buddhism came to Japan, the Yamato claimed the sun deity Amaterasu as their ancestor, enshrining this important *kami* at Ise in the direction of the sunrise and dedicating a succession of imperial princesses to officiate at the Ise shrines. While the cult of Amaterasu became increasingly important to the preservation of the emperor's mystique, the removal of Amaterasu's shrine from the Yamato court and the delegation of worship at Ise to female members of the imperial family at this time suggest that female ritualists who, like Queen Pimiko, had previously played an important ritual-political role at the center, were now to be marginalized.

Court offerings and the registering of shrines. Under Yamato rule, regular offerings of "divine treasures" made to the court symbolized the fealty of subordinate clans. Archaeological findings show that certain ancient ritual sites of strategic importance to Yamato rule attracted thousands of offerings from the Yamato court over many centuries. An example is Oki no shima, a small island off the coast of northwest Kyushu dedicated to the deity Munakata, a *kami* revered by local clans with important links to the continent. The implication is that the Yamato made ritual offerings to raise the status of selected shrines in order to secure relations with important subordinate clans. Such exchanges, and subsequent systems of registering and ranking important shrines by the central authority served to reinforce the Chinese-style notion of the Japanese emperor as absolute lord of "all under heaven." Under the Ritsuryō system of Chinese law, introduced in the seventh century, the notion of Japan as a single realm controlled by the emperor was reinforced by the propagation of Buddhism from the center and the appropriation of local *kami* cults by the central government. Imperial rites such as the mysterious *daijōsai* ritual of imperial succession involved offerings from representative shrines, while seasonal court rituals following the agricultural cycle, such as the *niiname* (ritual of new rice), and official *norito* prayers to the *kami* were replicated in major shrines throughout Japan.

The management of these ritual activities was the province of several lineages of court ritualists, including the influential Nakatomi clan, who in 669 divided into two branches. One branch retained the Nakatomi name and responsibility for ritual affairs, while the members of the Fujiwara branch rose to an unparalleled position as the controlling political family of Japan in their roles as ministers, advisers, regents, and heirs to the imperial line. Like other leading clans based in the capital, the Fujiwara now sought to affirm a continuing inherited right to political power by developing a cult of their own clan deity (*ujigami),* a powerful ancestral *kami* to be worshipped exclusively by their own clan. Since the Fujiwara had no such deity, the thunderbolt *kami,* Takemikazuchi, originally enshrined at Kashima in the east, was ritually "invited" to the court capital, along with the divine ancestor *kami* of the Nakatomi. From the eighth century these deities occupied the Kasuga shrine, which thus became the tutelary shrine of the Fujiwara clan, part of the Kofukuji-Kasuga temple-shrine complex around which the Nara capital developed. Subsequently, the Fujiwara's clan rites at Kasuga became part of the official ritual calendar, thus blurring the distinction between public, Ritsuryō-style state ritual at recognized shrines and "private" observances at important independent shrines.

While court histories and chronicles provide a wealth of data about the view from the center, there is scant information from this period about nonregulated cults and practices pursued at provincial shrines and no evidence that these shrines shared a common theology or ritual practice that could be called Shintō. Local records (*fudoki*) indicate that rites were performed by local clan chiefs doubling as ritual specialists—to propitiate angry *kami,* for example. These rites were normally held in *yashiro,* open places of assembly, rather than in shrine buildings. The growing influence of Buddhist and Daoist ideas gave shape to some local rites, while the increase in offerings to and from the court and registered shrines required more permanent shrine buildings to provide storage. The court policy of making grants of money, land, and official rank to local communities through officially registered shrines encouraged the creation of such shrines in virtually every community. Most major shrines developed from the eighth century as *jingūji,* or shrine-temples. These were sites of veneration of buddhas and *kami* which acquired considerable economic and political power as well as religious significance. The Ritsuryō understanding of power as something distributed from the center and transmitted by heredity fostered claims by leading provincial clans for recognition as branches of the major clans already established at court. Applications for shrines to be registered and ranked ever higher on the basis of the power or miracles of their *kami* proliferated. By the tenth century the *Engishiki* (Procedures of the Engi era) recorded nearly three thousand officially recognized shrines throughout Japan, far too many for the Ministry of Kami Affairs (Jingikan) to cope with. In practice, a few hundred "national official shrines" in the central provinces and some shrines of particularly powerful deities throughout the country remained under the aegis of the ministry, while the majority of local shrines developed in their own ways, increasingly under the influence of Buddhism. The ambitious project of regulating shrines and temples according to the Ritsuryō system did not achieve its goal, but more than a thousand years later, in 1868, it was to provide a reference point for the "restoration" of supposedly Shintō institutions such as the Jingikan.

Early references to the term Shintō. Most early references to the *kami* connected with the Yamato court and the imperial line allude to them as *jingi,* a high-status term for the heavenly deities drawn from Chinese Confucian vocabulary. Thus laws relating to *kami,* called *jingi-ryo,* were administered by the Jingikan. However the *Nihonshoki* also contains the earliest rare occurrences of the word *Shintō*. At the time, this term was pronounced "*jindō*" (equivalent to the term *shen-dao* in Chinese, meaning "spirits"). The *Nihonshoki* records that Emperor Yomei "had faith in the *buddhadharma* and 'revered' *jindō*" while Emperor Kotoku "revered the *buddhadharma* but 'scorned' *jindō*" (he is said to have cut down the trees at a shrine). Interpretations of these brief references to *Shintō* vary; some scholars find in them evidence that Shintō was recognized at this early stage as a religion separate from Buddhism; others have proposed the meaning "Daoism." Because these references relate to the two emperors' contribution to the establishment of Buddhism in Japan, *jindō* most probably just means "spirits" and refers to individual, potentially troublesome, local *kami* who could be pacified by Buddhist rites (a usage of the term *shen-dao* well-attested in Chinese Buddhist sources) rather than to a system of religious thought and practice regarded as an alternative to Buddhism.

Medieval Japan. The medieval period witnessed a variety of developments in systems of *kami*-worship, stimulated by social and political changes and the spread of Buddhism and other Chinese religious influences. It is often said that an "amalgamation of *kami* and buddhas" (*shinbutsu shūgō*) took place in the medieval period or earlier. The phrase *shinbutsu shūgō* is regularly encountered in modern writing; it is the antonym of *shinbutsu bunri* or "dissociation of *kami* and buddhas." This dissociation did occur (though it was not at the time called *shinbutsu bunri*) and can be dated to a specific point in time, 1868. However, there is no comparable moment in early Japan where *kami* and buddhas came together fully formed; rather, the various notions of *kami* encountered in Japanese history were developed through interaction with continental modes of thought, including Buddhism, itself susceptible to a degree of adaptation in the new context. As we have seen, early representations of the imperial *kami* as *jingi* owed something to Chinese ideas, while the notion of *jindō* construed *kami* as spirits within a Chinese-style Buddhist worldview. An example of amalgamation is the god Hachiman, in some respects the greatest divinity in Japan. Hachiman was already strongly identified with the propagation of Buddhism before he rose to prominence at court in the early eighth century, having been ceremonially transported from western Japan to Nara to endorse the building of the Great Eastern Temple (the Todaiji). Until 1868 this divinity was normally referred to as Great Bodhisattva Hachiman; after the dissociation of 1868 he became, and still is now, Great Kami Hachiman.

Buddhism has a long history of assimilating local spirits into its own cosmology and soteriology. Already in China there existed well-developed theories of "temporary appearance" (in Japanese: *keshin*) and "original source–trace manifestation" (*honji-suijaku*; the idea that local divinities emanate from the original Buddha). These theories accounted for the various outward forms manifested by cosmic, ultimately formless, buddhas and *bodhisattvas* to accomplish the liberation of all beings from this world of illusion. By the medieval period a richly articulated international Buddhist worldview, fifteen hundred years in the making and transmitted through esoteric lineages of monastic masters and disciples, predominated in Japan. The key question was how a particular shrine or *kami* was to be incorporated within a religious discourse that was overwhelmingly Buddhist. There was no single answer to this question, and we find shrine and temple priests offered a wide range of explanations, from the view that *kami*, like other sentient beings, need to receive Buddhist teaching in order to attain salvation (these were referred to as "real" *kami* or *jisshin*, literally "they are merely what they seem"), through the notion favored particularly at court that the *kami* are the special guardians of Buddhism (and therefore of Japan as a Buddhist kingdom), to declarations by the new Shintō medieval cults that the *kami* are not only fully enlightened but, in a reversal of the Buddhist formula, are really the foundational entities underlying the temporary forms of the buddhas and *bodhisattvas* worshipped in India, China, and Japan. Some *kami* were also identified as angry spirits (*goryō*) of notable historical figures who had been unfairly disgraced or died in tragic circumstances. They expressed their anguish through curses (*tatari*) which took the form of epidemics, and cults were developed for their pacification; once appeased they could evolve into benign and powerful *kami*. Even *jisshin*, or "real" *kami*, could actually be buddhas who had temporarily "dimmed their light and mingled with the dust" (*wakō dōjin*), the more effectively to teach the *buddhadharma* in human or animal forms. In general, the status of miscellaneous *kami* rose within the Buddhist hierarchical cosmos during the early and medieval periods to the point where identifying either a buddha or a major *kami* as the focus of worship became a matter of style rather than substance; a situation which still prevails today.

The twenty-two shrines. Attempts under the Ritsuryō system to establish central control of local shrines through registration, award of ranks, reciprocal offerings, and unification of rites had come to an end by the eleventh century. Only a small elite group known as "the twenty-two shrines," with close ties to the emperor and the Fujiwara, now received court offerings and shrine visits from members of the court. These great shrines, more accurately shrine-temple complexes, came to possess significant economic and political power. Through donation of lands they developed extensive, tax-free estates able to support a full-time clergy. The priests developed intricate and often secret rationales and rituals designed to conserve and reinforce the close associations between the shrine-temple complex, its various deities, and the ruling elite. Such associations involved systems of equivalences, identifying local divinities with named buddhas and *bodhisattvas*. This precious knowledge, which coupled the fortunes of the ruler to the well-being of the cultic site, was recorded in documents which came to acquire the status of sacred texts, comparable to Buddhist esoteric manuals.

The secret teachings of the shrine-temple complexes incorporated yin and yang theory, Confucianism, and other elements derived from continental thought, and they provided a point of departure for new "Shintō" theories about the sacred sites and their divinities. This in turn fostered popular devotion to the shrine-temples in the form of worship, pilgrimage, and donations. Pilgrimage became increasingly popular as a religious practice among the court aristocracy of the late Heian period. In the Kamakura period (1185–1333), the practice spread to lower orders of society, with a consequent increase in both the numbers of pilgrims and their economic importance to the shrine-temple complexes. The teachings available to devotees underlined the importance of visiting the shrines, which came to be understood as reservoirs of spiritual purity, endowed with the power to enlighten. The teachings also identified the combinatory divinities at each shrine. At Ise, for example, the sun goddess Tenshōdaijin (Amaterasu) was the Buddha Vairochana (Jap., Rushana, Dainichi-nyorai) or according to another source the Bodhisattva Avalokiteshvara (Jap., Kannon bosatsu). These divinities, endowed with magical and healing powers, offered advantages to all who came within their ambit in quest of miracles, religious merit, or enlightenment.

Late medieval developments. Most shrines throughout the country were obliged to seek new supporters from near or far, and the steady decline of the court meant that by the fifteenth century even the twenty-two shrines were receiving negligible imperial support, though their reputation as top shrines persisted. Provincial governors, meanwhile, founded civic shrines in local capitals to host public rituals for the landowning elite, featuring military, theatrical, and agricultural rites and displays. In a context of political instability, military clans originally formed by warring landowners rose to power, eventually eclipsing the resources and ritual status of the court and promulgating their own forms of religiosity. The Minamoto military clan, which provided Japan's first shogun in 1192, adopted as their ancestral and tutelary deity Hachiman, the *bodhisattva-kami* long associated with both military conquest and Buddhist merit.

The new combinatory cults, based at shrine-temple complexes but propagating their teachings to a wider audience, therefore viewed both *kami* and Buddhist divinities as enlightened beings. They offered specific means of salvation to individuals, in the manner of esoteric Buddhist lineages. The combinatory cults drew in different proportions on Buddhist, Daoist, Confucian, and *kami* beliefs, and during the Kamakura period came to dominate the medieval religious landscape. Although some of these combinatory cults may be described as Shintō and others as Buddhist, this is not a particularly helpful way of understanding their nature and role in the medieval context. From the perspective of a modern Shintōist, movements such as Watarai Shintō or Yoshida Shintō might be construed as the first tentative shoots of a later revival of "pure" Shintō, but in the context of their time they were creative religious movements that, like the "new Buddhisms" of the Kamakura period, drew inspiration from images, rituals, and doctrine selected from a variety of sources. Their founders and systematizers added new elements and interpretations, sometimes presenting these as ancient truths, to provide a meaningful and authoritative path to salvation for contemporary worshipers faced with a range of religious possibilities.

The leadership of these combinatory cults was exclusively male, as was the perspective of their writings. Where a public religious role relied on heredity this was patrilineal, with adoption of a suitable male heir where necessary. Religious institutions and movements in medieval Japan, whether interpreting native, Chinese, or Buddhist strands of thought, shared and thereby reinforced a long-established view of women as lesser beings, subject to various "hindrances" such as blood pollution and turbulent emotions that rendered them unfit for any responsible public role within a religious hierarchy, or indeed any other field of governance. Although women were encouraged to participate in the expanding popular cults as ordinary pilgrims, supplicants, or worshipers, and some of the new Buddhist movements such as Pure Land and Nichiren asserted their theoretical spiritual equality, the contributions that women undoubtedly made to the development of the medieval combinatory cults remain largely invisible to history.

Ryōbu, Watarai, and Sannō Shintō. Among the most successful cults developed by the twenty-two shrines were Ryōbu Shintō and Watarai Shintō, both focusing on the Ise shrines; and Sannō Shintō, based at Mount Hiei. As imperial support declined, popular ritual activities based on these teachings provided significant economic support for the major complexes. The success of these cultic centers formed the popular and enduring conception of *kami* as enlightened beings at least equal to buddhas, and they redefined pilgrimage and other shrine rituals as techniques of individual purification and enlightenment.

Ryōbu (Dual) Shintō developed as an aspect of Shingon Buddhist thought, both to account for the existence of two shrines at Ise (one dedicated to Amaterasu, the other to the food deity Toyouke) and to explain the place of these important imperial *kami* within esoteric Buddhist cosmology and ritual practice. Buddhism had been taboo within the Ise shrine ever since a notorious bid in 768 by the priest Dōkyō to succeed his protégée, the nun-empress Shōtoku, as emperor. Had he been successful, Dōkyō's accession to the throne would have destroyed the principle of heredity on which not only the imperial succession but also the power and status of the Fujiwara and other major clans at court relied. Once Dōkyō had been thwarted, thanks to an oracle from the *bodhisattva-kami* Hachiman at Usa, which rejected Dōkyō's claim to the throne, Ise was reconstituted as an inviolable symbol of the hereditary imperial line, out of bounds to Buddhist priests, Buddhist raiment, and even Buddhist vocabulary. Nevertheless, Buddhism thrived at Ise, and it was priest-monks associated with the Ise estates who produced the medieval texts underpinning Ryōbu Shintō. *Dual,* in the context of Ryōbu Shintō, refers to the two *maṇḍalas* of Shingon esoteric Buddhism and their correspondence to the two Ise shrines. Texts such as the *Nakatomi Harae Kunge* (Exegesis of the Nakatomi Purification Formula) produced by Ise monks explained that the taboo on signs of Buddhism within the precincts of the shrine resulted from a pact made in the Age of the Gods between Amaterasu and the demon king, who feared that Japan, once created, would become a Buddhist country. Amaterasu cleverly offered to ban Buddhism at her shrine if the demon king promised not to destroy the land. Thus the Ise taboo existed to guarantee, not to oppose, the spread of Buddhism in Japan.

On the basis of such theories and other "secret" texts, which later became known as the Five Books of Shintō (*Shintō gobusho*), priests of the Watarai lineage in charge of the Ise Outer Shrine argued, on the basis of Chinese yin-yang theory, quotations from the *Nihonshoki,* and other sources, that the shrine of Toyouke was equal, and in fact superior, to that of Amaterasu, deity of the Inner Shrine. These debates, which on occasion generated bitter lawsuits between the two shrines, had more than scholastic implications; the success of the Watarai pilgrimage trade depended on pilgrims' confidence that to visit the Outer Shrine of Toyouke was to visit the real Ise shrine. Although the Watarai declined in influence after supporting the losing Southern side in the contest of the Northern and Southern courts (1336–1392), Ise Shintō theories were subsequently taken up by the Arakida family of Inner Shrine priests and by various Buddhist sects, while elements of these Ise Shintō teachings, such as the notion of a God of Great Origin, were also disseminated through Yoshida Shintō.

While Ise Shintō was closely though not exclusively derived from Shingon Buddhist theories, Sannō Shintō (Shintō of the Mountain King) was a complex tradition of cosmology, ritual, and art flowing from the great Tendai temple-shrine complex on Mount Hiei outside Kyoto, originally founded in the ninth century by Saichō. Worship of seven indigenous and invited deities, including the combinatory deity Hie Sannō, formed the focus of the Sannō cult, whose intricate theoretical basis was developed by specialist monastic chroniclers (*kike*) drawing on a great variety of Buddhist and other sources. The wealth of equivalences, correspondences, and cross-references in the theoretical systems underpinning the cultic complexes meant significant overlap and integration between the different systems; so, for example, Sannō was also Amaterasu, deity of Ise, and an emanation (*gongen*) of the Buddha Shakyamuni.

Japan as a land of the gods (shinkoku). The period from the eleventh to thirteenth centuries saw a post-Ritsuryō structure emerge in which Japan was conceived not as a reflection of the ideal Chinese state but as a separate Buddhist land, and indeed as a center for the spread of Buddhism. The imperial line secured its future by defending Buddhism and the power of Buddhism protected the country. Esoteric Buddhism reached the peak of its ritual influence at court, while the "new Buddhisms" of the Kamakura period, emphasizing the perils of *mappō* (the degenerate age of the *dharma*) and the corresponding need for "easy" methods of liberation, vied to offer techniques of salvation designed by the buddhas for the special time and circumstances of Japan. Nichiren (1222–1282), for example, argued that the *kami* who protected Buddhism (and hence the country) had abandoned Japan because of neglect of the *Lotus Sūtra.* The popular notion of Japan as a *shinkoku,* or land of the *kami,* at this time relied on the *honji-suijaku* understanding of *kami* as emanations, traces, or local appearances of the cosmic buddhas and *bodhisattvas,* or as guardians of the *dharma.* The existence of these pro-Buddhist divinities throughout the country provided conclusive evidence that Japan, as a *shinkoku,* or divine land, was, along with India and China, one of the three great centers of the Buddhist world. This notion reinforced the legitimacy of the emperor as protector of Buddhism and validated the activities of numerous cults performing religious rituals and maintaining sacred sites. Subsequently, following the abortive Mongol invasions of the late thirteenth century, the notion of *shinkoku* began to change, implying Japan's superiority to her neighbors, a tendency later encouraged in the Edo period by the rise of National Learning. By the Meiji period, under the influence of nationalist thought and the dissociation of *kami* and buddhas, the Buddhist significance of *shinkoku* was entirely lost, so that to the modern ear the phrase can mean nothing more profound than "the *kami* are on our side."

Yoshida Shintō. Following the catastrophic Ōnin War of 1467–1477 and the final collapse of the system of imperial support for the twenty-two shrines, a new religious movement known, among other names, as Yui-itsu Shintō (the one and only Shintō) emerged in Kyoto. Its founder was the religious entrepreneur Yoshida Kanetomo, a priest at the Yoshida shrine originally founded by the Fujiwara as the Heian branch of their tutelary Kasuga shrine. Kanetomo ostensibly rejected Buddhism in favor of his Yui-itsu Shintō, though the new teachings that he promulgated about the *kami* of the Yoshida shrine struck a chord with his audience precisely because they offered an attractive synthesis of the prevailing forms of religious knowledge, arranging Buddhist, Confucian, and Daoist or yin-yang ideas according to principles of Chinese numerology. Kanetomo secured the endorsement of the emperor for his interpretation of Shintō, even for the bold claim that all the major divinities of Japan, including the deities of Ise, had migrated to the Yoshida shrine, so that a pilgrimage or offering to the Yoshida shrine was now the only effective way to benefit from the power and blessings of these deities. Although the rise of Yoshida Shintō inevitably provoked opposition from other cultic sites, Kanetomo's version of Shintō was outstandingly successful. It grew to the status of a nationwide cult, spreading elements of Ryōbu and Watarai Shintō along with Kanetomo's ideas.

Yoshida Shintō used for its own propagation an image known as "the oracles of the three shrines" (*sanja takusen*). This took the form of a scroll inscribed with the names of the top three shrines in Japan (Ise, Kasuga, and Iwashimizu Hachiman; these three were seen as representing all shrines) and three brief oracular statements affirming the virtues of honesty, purity, and compassion. These three shrines also represented, according to Fujiwara tradition, a covenant made in the Age of the Gods between the Fujiwara (Kasuga), the shogunate (Hachiman), and the imperial house (Ise) to cooperate in the rule of Japan. Copies of the scroll formed a kind of virtual shrine at which the deities of the Yoshida shrine could be revered. By such means, followers of Yoshida Shintō were encouraged to identify all shrines as signifiers of the parent Yoshida shrine in Kyoto.

Edo Period (1600–1868). Following many decades of civil war and the sudden appearance, and almost as sudden disappearance after a century, of Catholic Westerners, the Edo period saw the growth of cities and the rise of a prosperous merchant class, the government's incorporation of all Buddhist sects, regardless of religious differences, into a single nationwide system of local temple registration, and the favoring of neo-Confucianism as a political philosophy for the military elite. A massive expansion of popular pilgrimage to cultic sites founded on local religious associations, or *kō,* was accompanied by the spread of syncretic religious movements involving *kami* worship. This period witnessed several developments that turned out to be crucial to the formation of modern Shintō. These included the establishment of a viable national system of shrine ranking and registration under the Yoshida and Shirakawa houses; the increasing conceptualization of Shintō as an anti-Buddhist, or at least non-Buddhist, native tradition; the association of Shintō with Confucian ethical thought; and the rise of the most important intellectual tradition behind modern Shintō, that of *Kokugaku,* or National Learning.

Neo-Confucianism. The military leaders who emerged to unite Japan during the sixteenth century following the Warring States period were unable to claim ancestral legitimacy as the rulers of Japan, and they therefore adopted the neo-Confucian notion of *tendō* (the way of heaven) to legitimise their violent appropriation of power. In addition, the first Tokugawa shogun, Ieyasu, was enshrined after his death in the magnificent purpose-built mausoleum of Nikkō, where he was venerated according to Sannō Shintō rites as a *daigongen,* or great emanation of the Buddha. Successive Tokugawa shoguns made official pilgrimages to the Nikkō shrine, symbolically affirming that the enshrined spirit of their ancestor Ieyasu was equivalent in status to the imperial deity of Ise, and a Buddhist divinity.

Under the Tokugawa *bakufu* (government) the influence of Confucian ideas expanded—in particular the neo-Confucianism of Zhu Xi (1130–1200), and to a lesser extent that of Wang Yangming (1472–1529). Neo-Confucianism encouraged "the investigation of things"; an activity which could take the form of rational enquiry or Zen-like methods of contemplation. Confucianism encouraged the study of the ancient past, the days of Confucius, as the template for an ideal society. Originally this meant China's past, but among Japanese scholars interest shifted towards that which was specifically Japanese: the Age of the Gods as documented in native Japanese literature. Neo-Confucianism in China already had an anti-Buddhist character, and this too was transferred to Japan. The combination of anti-Buddhist sentiment and interest in ancient Japanese texts led some thinkers in the Tokugawa period to distinguish Buddhism as a separate category from Japan's indigenous tradition, which some identified as Shintō.

Attempts to separate out a form of Shintō that would be independent of Buddhism required a radical rethinking of key Shintō concepts in non-Buddhist terms. Here again, Confucianism provided an alternative philosophical legitimation, in this case for Shintō notions such as *kami.* A number of influential theorists of the early Edo period sought an intellectual rapprochement between Confucianism and Shintō. Hayashi Razan (1583–1657) was an independent scholar and advisor to the *bakufu* who developed a theory of *kami* as *ri* (principle). He undertook extensive studies of major shrines and their cults with the aim of showing that they were, or should have been, distinct from Buddhism. Yamaga Sokō (1622–1685) argued that the ethical ideals exemplified in ancient Shintō predated Chinese ethics, and therefore Japan, not China, should be regarded as the Middle Kingdom, an idea later taken up by proponents of National Learning. Yoshikawa Koretari (1616–1694) modernized Yoshida Shintō teachings by linking them to neo-Confucianism, focusing on the virtue of self-denial (*tsutsushimi*) to be achieved by purification (*harae*). Yamazaki Ansai (1616–1682) developed an extremely influential system which he called Suika Shintō, based on a reference to an oracle in a thirteenth-century Ise Shintō text which declares: "To receive divine beneficence (*sui*), give priority to prayer; to obtain divine protection (*ka*), make uprightness your basis." In Ansai's Confucian reading of the Shintō scriptures, *kami* were again identified with the principle (*ri*) that unites heaven and man. *Kami* inheres in the human heart or mind (*kokoro*) and should be united and venerated there through sincerity and prayer. Elaborating on Confucian notions of respect and self-denial, Ansai interpreted the *Nihonshoki* and *Kojiki* narratives as documenting eternal relations between imperial line, lord, and vassal. The intellectual and esoteric aspects of Suika Shintō came to influence the imperial court, to the extent that some ancient court rites were revived in the late seventeenth and eighteenth centuries. Ansai's ideas were subsequently developed in different ways by his numerous disciples and their schools. The idea that Confucian ethics and Shintō rites are natural bedfellows continued into the modern period in the post-Meiji emperor system (exemplified, for example, in the 1890 Imperial Rescript on Education) and in prewar teachings on national morality.

Shrines and temples in the Edo period. In order to control the shrines, the Tokugawa *bakufu* restricted the land holdings of the twenty-two shrine complexes and placed them under the control of local *daimyō* (feudal lords). In 1665 they granted to the Yoshida family and to certain court families, notably the Shirakawa, the power to grant licenses (ranks) to shrine priests. The intention was to give the Yoshida, as servants of the *bakufu,* an effective monopoly over licensing. Although disputes continued well into the Edo period between the Yoshida and Shirakawa over the boundaries of their respective influence, the system provided the government for the first time with meaningful central control over the activities of virtually all shrines and their priests in Japan. Meanwhile, as one of the measures designed to expel Christianity, Buddhist temples throughout Japan had been organized into parishes where local families, including those of shrine priests, were required to register and to conduct their family's funeral rites. As the economy grew during the Edo period, the family system that required the eldest son to perform ancestral rituals spread to all levels of society and led to an increasing need for the services of Buddhist temples. Many Buddhist temples prospered, but their position as administrative agencies of the *bakufu* and their monopoly over funeral rites became a cause for resentment, not least among the rising class of professional shrine priests licensed by the Yoshida and Shirakawa, some of whom wished to conduct funerals of their own. These factors contributed to anti-Buddhist feeling, which in some cases took the form of a pro-Shintō movement. As early as 1666, for example, the government of the Mito domain closed more than a thousand Buddhist temples, ordered all Buddhist objects to be removed from shrines, and ordered a shrine to be built for each village. Overall, however, throughout the Edo period the popular view remained that Shintō and Buddhist institutions, rites, and practices complemented rather than competed with each other.

Increasingly, shrines and temples in prosperous urban areas competed to attract visitors with festivals, entertainments, food, and cultural activities, while popular preachers connected with the Yoshida school, such as the renowned Masuho Zankō (1655–1742), drew large crowds with down-to-earth sermons on Shintō topics. Many festivals developed into their modern forms during the Edo period. The annual calendar was standardized by the Edo *bakufu*, the *gosekku* (five seasonal days) were declared national holidays, and festivals were celebrated on these numerologically significant days. For example, the third day of the third month was *jōshi*—rites of purification in which impurity was transferred to dolls, which were then cast into the water (the origin of today's *hina matsuri,* or doll's festival)—while on the seventh day of the seventh month the *tanabata* star festival was celebrated. From their origins as communal agricultural rites for the *kami,* annual festivals increasingly became spectacles in urban areas, drawing large crowds to view the rituals and processions rather than to participate directly in them.

Religious confraternities. Many local or more widespread religious confraternities (*kō*) developed in this period, some independently of any religious establishment and most often with the goal of pooling funds to enable representative members to travel on pilgrimage to great shrines or sacred mountains. Some of these groups evolved into the Sect Shintō organizations of the Meiji period. The focus of devotion might be pilgrimage (to Ise, the Shikoku circuit, or a host of other venues), or religious practices relating to particular divinities such as Inari, Konjin, or Jizō. Pilgrimage, a predominantly urban phenomenon in the Edo period, offered one of the few legitimate grounds for travel under the Tokugawa regime and provided an essential source of income for major religious institutions. Encouraging and enabling groups and individuals to undertake pilgrimage became a preoccupation of all the important cultic sites. This was particularly true of the Ise complex, which hosted a constant round of regular pilgrimages organized by the shrine's countrywide network of enterprising *oshi* (pilgrim-masters). A popular jingle ran, "You should visit Ise at least once in your life," while another, mindful of the many worldly distractions available to wide-eyed pilgrims, advised "When you go to Ise, don't forget to visit the shrine!" Remarkably, several apparently spontaneous mass nationwide pilgrimages to Ise, some involving millions of people, occurred at intervals of about seventy years throughout the Edo period. Reflecting the changing meaning of the shrine and the requirements of the pilgrimage trade, the oracles of the three shrines (*sanja takusen*) scroll, which in the late medieval period had signified the enshrinement of the top three deities at the Yoshida shrine in Kyoto, now displayed personified images of the gods as combinatory divinities. With Amaterasu at its center (in male Buddhist garb; the gender of Amaterasu became fixed only after the Meiji period) the scroll came to be regarded primarily as a souvenir of pilgrimage to Ise. According to the beliefs and values of the particular *kō* involved, and the nature of the shrines and temples visited *en route,* the pilgrimage itself might be conceived as embodying acts of religious merit-making, purification, expiation, petition, intercession, or healing.

Prominent among mountain-worship *kō* were those focusing on Mount Fuji. Mountains in Japan represent "otherness" for agricultural communities and have often been the site of encounters with buddhas, *kami,* and other spiritual beings. Agricultural rites commonly celebrated the descent of *kami* to the rice fields and their return to the mountains. Shūgendō religious specialists conducted elaborate combinatory rituals in which participation in the ascent of the mountain represented a spiritual birth, death, purification, and enlightenment. Edo-period mountain cults became eclectic and adapted to the interests of the common people. *Fuji-kō,* religious associations focusing on Mount Fuji, were inaugurated in the early seventeenth century by Hasegawa Takematsu, or Kakugyō, whose spiritual powers derived from ascetic practices performed at the mountain. Around eight hundred Fuji sects developed, attracting worshippers mainly from Edo and the surrounding area. To follow just one thread: in 1688 after an ascent of Mount Fuji inspired by Kakugyo's teachings, Ito Jikigyō (1671–1733) revealed himself to be an emanation of the Bodhisattva Miroku (Maitreya, the coming Buddha). Jikigyō's *Miroku-ha* (Maitreyism) teachings emphasizing faith in Mount Fuji attracted a wide following. They were subsequently reinterpreted, first by Kotani Sanshi Rokugyō (d. 1841) who taught that the whole world was under the care of the *kami* "mother and father of all" (*moto no chichi-haha*) who resided on Mount Fuji, and again after the Meiji restoration by Shibata Hamamori (1809–1890), who erased Buddhist elements, emphasized emperor worship, and is now regarded as the founder of the modern Jikkyō-kyō. The movement was recognized as a Shintō sect and named Shintō Jikkyō-kyō in 1882. Shibata's son attended the 1893 World Parliament of Religions in Chicago. The teachings today emphasize cheerfulness and sincerity; thousands of members dressed in white ascend Mount Fuji in August shouting "*rokkon shōjō*" ("purification of the six sense-organs") originally a phrase found in the *Lotus Sūtra,* though the group maintains a strong Shintō identity. The ascent of sacred mountains was normally denied to women before the Meiji restoration.

National Learning (Kokugaku). From the early eighteenth century, as economic growth, increasing literacy, and the spread of printed literature extended opportunities for scholarly study among the lower levels of society, Confucian interpretations of Shintō began to be overtaken by rationalist and philological studies of native literature. Rather than seeking arcane correspondences between Shintō and Chinese systems of thought, scholars interested in Japanese ancient customs began to approach the study of Japanese literature in a critical and empirical manner, examining in painstaking detail different recensions of texts and the forms of writing used in different periods of Japanese history. These researches led, among other things, to the debunking of much of the literature produced by medieval Shintō. Yoshimi Yoshikazu, for example, compared the Watarai's *Shintō gobusho* (the Five Books of Shintō) with texts of the Nara period to prove that the Watarai "ancient" texts were in fact the product of medieval minds. Similar devastating critiques were aimed at the Yoshida and Suika Shintō sacred books.

These methodological advances underpinned the development of what came to be known as *Kokugaku* (National Learning or Japanese Studies). Initially this was an academic discipline that sought to uncover the forms of Japanese culture that existed before any influence from outside, in particular before the introduction of Buddhism and Chinese thought. Favorite topics were early Japanese collections of poetry such as the *Man'yōshū* and *Kokinshū* and the narratives relating to *kami* in the *Nihonshoki* and *Kojiki.* Kada Azumamaro (1669–1736) was perhaps the first writer to offer a nonliteral account of the Age of the Gods in the *Nihonshoki,* arguing that the myths depicted an ethical ideal to which humans should aspire. His disciple Kamo no Mabuchi (1697–1769) took a similar approach to the *Man'yōshū,* identifying desirable "Japanese" qualities of masculine vigor and spontaneity which, he argued, were later obscured by the introduction of undesirable "feminine" literary and aesthetic values imported from the continent.

In the late eighteenth century, National Learning developed from an academic discipline into a significant sociereligious movement made up of scholars with large followings whose goal became the "restoration" (*fukko*) of Shintō. The major figure in this movement and a towering figure in Japanese intellectual history was Motoori Norinaga (1730–1801). Inspired by Kamo no Mabuchi to turn his attention to ancient Japanese literature in search of the original Japanese "way," Norinaga's remarkable critical scholarship and relentless schedule of lecture tours gained him hundreds of dedicated disciples and nationwide recognition. His major commentary on the *Kojiki* remains an authoritative work. In terms of literary theory, Norinaga argued that the truth of things was set out in the ancient texts; though obscure it could be grasped by the sincere Japanese heart. He elevated unmediated feeling and the "movement of the heart" over Confucian and Buddhist scholastic moralizing and identified these suprarational qualities as unique to the Japanese way, thus providing his contemporaries with a new nativist lens through which to view the classics of Japanese literature. In the narratives of the Age of the Gods he found both a literal account and an ideal of ethical behavior manifested in the inviolable imperial line.

Hirata Atsutane and restoration Shintō. Norinaga's approach was thoroughly Japanocentric, and it is this aspect of his thought that became most prominent in the teachings of Hirata Atsutane (1776–1843). Atsutane was inspired by Norinaga's writings and later came to be regarded as Norinaga's successor in *Kokugaku,* though the two never actually met. Atsutane's approach was more religious than literary, and as a scholar he proved eclectic and populist, without the intellectual rigor of Norinaga. Drawing on the notion of an original "Japanese way" superior to the continental philosophies, Atsutane developed the theory that Shintō was a universal religion that lay at the root of all religious truth, wherever found. This enabled Atsutane to incorporate popular Buddhist ideas such as karma, ancestor worship, geomancy, and the spirit world into his teaching on the grounds that these were elements of original Shintō that had also found their way into lesser, foreign religions. His approach was actually not very different from that of the medieval Shintō theorists who sought correspondences between the Age of the Gods, Buddhism, and yin and yang. Perhaps because of this, and the fact that he had acquired a large following in several areas of Japan, Atsutane was commissioned first by the Yoshida and then by the Shirakawa to teach Shintō to shrine priests. Atsutane's adopted son Kanetane successfully expanded the movement after his father's death and in the 1850s, as Japan reopened to the West, the Hirata school's pro-Japanese and antiforeign views attracted new followers from all classes, including influential samurai concerned about Japan's fragile international position. To secure the "Japanese way" in the face of the foreign threat, the Hirata faction envisaged a restored Shintō in which the Yoshida and Shirakawa would play a prominent role.

The influential restoration ideologue Ōkuni Takamasa (1792–1871) held Atsutane in high esteem and used some of Atsutane's ideas on comparative religion in his own attempts to accommodate Christianity, speculating that Adam, Eve, and Cain were *kami* sent from Japan to open up the Western world, while the Virgin who bore Jesus may have been the *kami* Hiruko. However, despite the Hirata school's passion for the restoration of Shintō and Ōkuni's regard for Atsutane's theories, it was not the Hirata vision of Shintō that was "restored" when the emperor came to power in 1868. Instead, a refurbished system of imperial ritual was introduced, controlled from the court. Devised by Ōkuni and colleagues from the Tsuwano fief, it offered no role to the Yoshida and Shirakawa families, nor to any other schools of Edo-period Shintō. In one major respect, however, it fulfilled a major aim of the Hirata school by instituting a form of Shintō that was regarded as both unique to the Japanese race and separate from Buddhism.

Meiji restoration to World War II. The Meiji restoration of 1868 led to profound changes in every aspect of Japanese life, and the transformation of Shintō has to be understood in this context. The new Meiji government's broad aim was to create as rapidly as possible a modern state out of what had been a feudal society. While the ultimate goal of modernization—a rich, powerful, industrialized empire at least equal to those of the European powers—was hardly in dispute, there was less consensus over the means of achieving the goal and, in particular, the price to be paid for it in terms of loss of meaning and cultural identity. Debates on these topics occupied some of the best minds of the early Meiji period. The first objective of the new Meiji government was to make a break from Tokugawa traditions and to mobilize an unprepared populace to pull in one new direction rather than many. Like other emerging European nations, the Japanese regime sought to build public confidence and cohesion by wrapping radical new ventures in symbols of the past. In the case of Japan, the process perhaps went further than in any other modern nation and was, arguably, more successful.

In the realm of religion, developments in the first few years of the Meiji period were propelled principally by ideology, but also by bureaucratic, political, and economic considerations. With hindsight, a process of trial and error is evident. In regard to local shrines, one of the first acts of the new government, heavily influenced by National Learning ideologues, was to restore the Jingikan (Ministry of Kami Affairs) and assign to it, instead of to the Yoshida and Shirakawa houses, responsibility for all shrines. In an edict of 1871 the shrines were designated as sites for state ritual, abandoning completely any association with the Edo-period schools and theories of Shintō that the authorities regarded as unsuited to the new age. As early as March and April 1868, *shinbutsu hanzen* (clarification of *kami* and buddhas) decrees were issued requesting accounts of the identity of *kami* worshipped at shrines, temples, and festivals nationwide. Priests serving *kami* within Buddhist temples (many such priests combined Buddhist and Shintō clerical roles) had to choose either to become dedicated shrine priests or remain Buddhists; they could not be both. This ruling was particularly damaging to Shūgendō ritualists who occupied the middle ground, even before Shūgendō was banned altogether in 1873. The Buddhist names and identities of *kami* were no longer to be used, which meant that legions of *kami* required new or amended names. *Kami* shrines could no longer contain Buddhist symbols, so statues, paintings, inscriptions, sacred texts, vestments, and other ritual items all had to be removed. This was in many cases a destructive process, marked by hooliganism toward both shrines and Buddhist temples under the slogan "*Haibutsu kishaku!*" ("Expel the Buddha; destroy Shakyamuni!"). Many priceless shrine treasures were destroyed or discarded. The process also entailed the closure of Buddhist temples; between 1868 and 1874, perhaps thirty thousand temples disappeared, and more than fifty thousand Buddhist clerics were returned to lay life.

Meiji Shintō and the Great Teaching. The intention of these initial reforms was not to destroy Buddhism but to redefine Shintō from the center as a state cult, and the consequences of this radical bureaucratic process for local shrines and for those who remained their priests in the early years of Meiji were almost as severe as for Buddhists. During 1869–1870, bitter disputes among Shintō factions in the new Jingikan over the proper rituals to be conducted at shrines paralyzed decisions about the instructions to be issued to shrine priests. Meanwhile, government bureaucrats issued orders for the wholesale rationalization (the merging and closing) of thousands of lesser shrines, in order to leave only one shrine for each administrative area. This shrine would become the focus of a new system of shrine registration (*ujiko shirabe*) intended to supplant the Tokugawa Buddhist temple registration system. Both the notion of shrines as the private property of priests and the principle of heredity for shrine priests were abolished, so that the livelihood of priests hung in the balance. Shrines were first asked to perform funerals, widely regarded as defiling and formerly the preserve of Buddhism, then following the so-called pantheon dispute of 1875 they were forbidden from doing so. These rapid developments left many shrine priests in a state of disarray, justifiably fearful for their own careers, unsure of the nature and status of their shrines, and unclear too about the appropriate teachings they should give and rituals they should perform.

Meanwhile, initiatives were afoot in Tokyo to spread a National Teaching suitable for the new era. This new unified teaching was intended to underpin the concept of shrines as sites reserved exclusively for imperial state rites and not, as had been the case in the Edo period, ritual centers offering a multiplicity of Buddhist and Shintō teachings. Underpinning the promulgation of the National Teaching was a logic that equated the National Teaching with Shintō, and Shintō with the uniquely Japanese "way of humanity" exemplified in the narratives of the Age of the Gods, preserved eternally in the traditions of the imperial house and manifest in codes of government. Shintō, according to this way of thinking, was explicitly distinguished from mere "religions" (such as Christianity, Buddhism, Edo forms of Shintō, and sectarian teachings) which rested on the theories of fallible human founders. The new national creed, referred to as the Great Teaching (*taikyō*) formed the substance of the Great Promulgation Campaign (*taikyō senpu undō*) launched in 1869. Initially the Jingikan sought to employ exemplary individuals as *senkyōshi,* Shintō missionaries, to spread the "three great teachings" (*sanjō no kyōsoku*) to the people at large. *Senkyōshi* of the right calibre, however, proved extremely hard to find, and in 1872 the failing project was transferred to the new (and short-lived) Ministry of Religion, which recruited and trained, though it did not itself finance, a new army of "national evangelists" (*kyōdōshoku*) drawn from many different walks of life to propagate the national creed. These evangelists included Buddhist and Shintō priests, actors, comedians, storytellers, and clergy of new religious movements such as Konkōkyō and Kurozumikyō. The Great Teaching comprised a threefold instruction to the people:

1. Revere the deities and love your country.
2. Make clear the principles of heaven and the way of man.
3. Reverence the emperor and abide by the will of the court.

Inevitably, the various *kyōdōshoku* gave their own slant to the Great Teaching. Experienced Buddhist teachers took the opportunity to integrate the ideas and practices of their own sects, while clergy of semiofficial religious movements welcomed the opportunity to become *kyōdōshoku,* in part to shield their group from possible persecution. Shrine priests, though restricted in that role to the performance of approved state rituals, could earn extra revenue by conducting funerals and other religious functions in the role of national evangelist; such work also financed their evangelism. The three great teachings were of course capable of different interpretations. Official commentaries on the teachings issued to the *kyōdōshoku* encouraged activities such as payment of taxes, the development of a "rich country, strong army," the importation of Western science and culture, and compulsory education.

Shrine Shintō and Sect Shintō. The difficulties of spreading the National Teaching using unpaid intermediaries and problems with persistent doctrinal disputes among shrine factions convinced the Meiji government that the dissemination of national doctrines should not be entrusted to shrine priests, who held many different views on the meanings and purposes of their shrines. Shrine priests were therefore prevented from evangelizing and increasingly confined their activities to state-approved ritual matters, while also maintaining the cults of local tutelary deities on behalf of their parishioners. A new calendar of rites was introduced early in the Meiji period that emphasized rituals for emperors in the "unbroken lineage" and for the first time synchronized the annual ritual cycle of shrines throughout the country with that of the imperial household, thus ascribing to the emperor the role of priest of the nation. Increasingly, Shrine Shintō came to be seen as nonreligious, in the elevated sense of being supra-religious or nondenominational. Some Shintō priests had created independent religious fraternities supportive of the National Teaching while acting as national evangelists, and from the late 1870s these groups were awarded the new status of Shintō sect, a category falling somewhere between Shintō and religion that recognized both their popular religious appeal and their affinities with the national cult. The Shintō sects also included revelatory new religions such as Kurozumikyō and pre-Meiji confraternities such as Shintō Jikkyō-kyō. Up until 1945, the number of Shintō sects was restricted to thirteen, with additional groups such as Ōmoto classed for administrative reasons as sub-sects.

By the first half of the nineteenth century, several new independent religious movements had emerged, each founded by a charismatic shamanic figure spontaneously possessed by a deity that revealed itself to be the parent or universal *kami*: God. These movements, which have been termed "vitalistic," included Tenrikyō, Konkōkyō, and Kurozumikyō. None of these movements initially saw itself as a Shintō movement, but each was eventually recognized by the Meiji authorities as a Shintō sect. The survival of these large and widespread religious movements indicates that they were able to adapt successfully to prevailing sociopolitical circumstances, including the radical changes of the Meiji restoration. Kurozumikyō adapted relatively easily to the National Teaching, and Kurozumikyō clergy took a full part in the great promulgation campaign. In order to evade persecution under the shogunate, Konkō Daijin (1814–1883), the founder of Konkōkyō, obtained a shrine licence in 1864 from the Shirakawa, but after the Meiji restoration in 1873 he renounced any association with Shintō, refusing to take any part in the great promulgation campaign. Fearing for the future of the organization, his close disciple and successor, Satō Norio, studied the National Learning and became a national evangelist, along with more than a hundred other Konkōkyō ministers. He developed a creed for Konkōkyō that presented the movement as a form of national Shintō. By the 1880's Satō had became an avid proponent of the three great teachings and the "spirit of the national polity" (*kokutai seishin*). Tenrikyō's redoubtable female founder, Nakayama Miki (1798–1887), also courted persecution and imprisonment by rejecting national Shintō, and recognition of Tenrikyō as a Shintō sect was granted only in 1906 under the leadership of her grandson. Tenrikyō formally rejected its Shintō identity in the 1970s and remains uneasy about this apparent compromise with the Shintō establishment.

The emperor system. With Shrine Shintō broadly distinguished from religion, Meiji bureaucrats turned their attention to the promulgation of Shintō imperial mythology as historical fact. The Meiji Constitution of 1889 resulted from seventeen years of secret debates and drafts over such issues as the relations between religion and state and freedom of religion, with full awareness of European models. The constitution affirmed the "sacred and inviolable" person of the emperor and made a key distinction between private religious belief and public activity. Article 28 stated that "Japanese subjects shall, within limits not prejudicial to peace and order, and not antagonistic to their duties as subjects, enjoy freedom of religious belief." After 1889 it therefore became unconstitutional to withdraw from emperor-centered Shintō rites, since these were civic duties rather than religious ritual. The constitution was swiftly followed in 1890 by the Imperial Rescript on Education (*Kyōiku chokugo*), which became, in effect, a sacred text, enshrined in schools alongside a picture of the emperor and reverently recited. It set out the basic tenets of the emperor system as well as the Confucian five relationships, exhorting loyalty and filial piety to the emperor as the divine descendant of the imperial *kami* Amaterasu. As an expression of National Teaching, the issuing of the rescript to schools signaled that schoolteachers would henceforth be responsible for conveying the doctrinal aspects of the state cult, while shrine priests contributed the shrine-based ritual dimension; after the Russo-Japanese War of 1904–1905 rites were introduced in schools too. The binding relationship established at this point between, on the one hand, the ideology of the emperor system transmitted through schools and other organs of the state such as local government and the armed forces and, on the other hand, the emperor-worshipping rites performed at Shintō shrines, formed the heart of the prewar "national faith" of Japan.

Between 1906 and 1929 the number of shrines throughout Japan was once again radically reduced by a generally unpopular program of shrine mergers *(jinja gappei)* designed to streamline shrine parishes and match the remaining major shrines with local administrative areas. The policy resulted in the destruction of more than eighty thousand shrines, about half the national total. Many were small unrecognized shrines but some were venerable *shikinai-sha* (shrines registered in the *Engishiki*).

The question of State Shintō. In 1945, the nexus of state, shrine, and emperor-worship relationships built up over nearly eighty years by various means was referred to by the postwar Occupation authorities as State Shintō. This neologism (in Japanese *kokka shintō)* first appeared in the Directive for the Disestablishment of State Shintō issued by the Supreme Commander of Allied Powers (SCAP) in December of 1945, and it subsequently shaped debates about whether Shintō should be seen as the main architect or an innocent casualty of prewar imperialistic nationalism. State Shintō was defined in the 1945 directive as "that branch of Shintō (*kokka shintō* or *jinja shintō*) which by official acts of the Japanese government has been differentiated from the religion of Sect Shintō (*shūha shintō* or *kyōha shintō*) and has been classified a non-religious cult commonly known as State Shintō, National Shintō, or Shrine Shintō." SCAP staff found the precise referent of the term "State Shintō" difficult to pin down. The focus on Shintō diverted attention somewhat from the fact that by this time the ideology and values of the emperor system were embraced by virtually all religious groups: Buddhist, Christian, and sectarian. Devotion to the emperor was by no means an exclusively Shintō phenomenon; it was, after all, instilled into every Japanese child in school. The term "State Shintō" subsequently came to be interpreted in a number of very different and incompatible ways. As a concept, it captures a historical moment rather than providing a useful analytical category. Debates continue about the extent to which Shintō, more than other religions, was implicated in the discredited emperor cult and "national ethics" teaching which demanded subjugation to the *kokutai* (body of the state). Clearly, much depends on the definition of Shintō.

Shintō in contemporary Japan. The Occupation authorities certainly did not believe that state-sponsored teachings and rites relating to a divine emperor and the age of the gods could be nonreligious. They felt the need to distinguish what was religious from what was not so that a clear line could be drawn between religion and state in the new constitution. It was because Shintō was religious, not because it was Shintō, that it had to be separated from the state. From the SCAP perspective, separation of religion and state was axiomatic. The relationship between religion and state is, of course, a cultural variable and there are as many ways in which the two are related in the modern world as there are states and religions. However, the fact is that in 1945 an eighty-year relationship between Shrine Shintō and the Japanese state apparatus ended overnight. Under the 1947 constitution, religion and state were separated and individual religious freedom guaranteed. Shrine Shintō therefore entered the postwar period as a voluntaristic religion (strictly speaking Shintō is a multitude of such religions, since under the Religious Juridical Persons Law of 1951 each Shintō shrine is registered as a separate religious body). Under the new constitution, Shintō's formal relationship with the state could be no closer than that enjoyed by Christianity, Buddhism, the Shintō sects, Jehovah's Witnesses, or indeed any other of the hundreds of religious organizations, new and old, native and foreign, to be found in contemporary Japan. The repositioning of Shintō as one religion among many presented a serious challenge to the shrines and their priests and put the very survival of Shrine Shintō in question.

Change and continuity. The changes wrought to Shrine Shintō by the Occupation administration were significant but limited in scope. A review of the continuities and discontinuities between prewar and postwar Shintō shows that the concept of Shintō established in the Meiji period survived more or less intact. The emperor remained monarch, though belief in his divine ancestry was now unnecessary. Very little destruction of Shintō resources occurred. The Shintō Directive removed war memorials, which had attracted ultranationalist sentiments, but these were not Shintō shrines as such. Devotional images of the emperor, copies of the Imperial Rescript on Education, and ultranationalist ethics textbooks such as *Cardinal Principles of the National Entity (kokutai no hongi)* were removed from schools, but shrines built since the Meiji restoration of 1868 to promote the emperor system were untouched. The single most important element of Meiji Shintō, the 1868 dissociation of *kami* and buddhas, went unchallenged as far as Shintō shrines, Buddhist temples, and their respective priests were concerned, though new syncretic religions were now free to develop. In place of central government, the independent *jinja honchō* (literally "Shrines HQ" though the official name in English is "The Association of Shinto Shrines") was established to administer the nationwide network of shrines under "the spiritual leadership of the Ise shrine." Though some major shrines opted for independence, and others may yet follow, the *jinja honchō* oversees virtually all shrines in Japan, managing shrine ranks and priestly qualifications and providing modern-day equivalents of Meiji court messengers and imperial offerings to shrines.

A residual notion of the Meiji shrine parishes remains, reflected in the expectation that shrines should receive financial support from local residents. Shintō priests still overwhelmingly carry out rites rather than preach doctrine, and very few of the tens of thousands of shrines destroyed by shrine merger have been restored, so the current shrine (and temple) landscape of Japan remains characteristic of the Meiji period rather than previous eras. The Yasukuni shrine to the war dead, chief of the provincial *gokoku* (nation-protecting) shrines, stands as a powerful symbol of Meiji values. It is controversial in Japan and among Japan's neighbors since it, more than any other Shintō institution, appears to challenge the boundary constructed in 1945 between religion and state. The imperial family's rites remain exclusively Shintō in style, with no reversion to former Buddhist practices. Finally, and despite the postwar legal status of Shintō as religion, the Meiji idea of Shintō as nonreligious still prevails, at least to the extent that Shintō practices are widely regarded as custom or tradition rather than religion. As a consequence, legal battles have been fought over the propriety of participation by government officials in Shintō rituals such as the blessing of new buildings. For most Japanese, seasonal shrine visits, rituals, and festivals relating to particular shrines and *kami* are seen as part of a broad spectrum of "given" customary practices.

Shintō has changed in some ways since 1945. After a difficult postwar period of austerity, increased spending power resulting from the Japanese "economic miracle" from the 1970s onward helped restore the fortunes of many shrines. Shrines with a nationwide reputation continue to attract substantial numbers of pilgrims and tourists, particularly at the New Year, when some 80 percent of the population makes a shrine visit. Many major shrines have survived and some have prospered by effectively marketing the benefits of their *kami* (traffic safety, examination success, business success, safety at work, and many others) or the beauty and tranquillity of their surroundings. Most shrines have their own annual ritual calendar with special purification ceremonies and festivals at key points in the year. Family rituals such as "seven-five-three" (*shichi-go-san*) when children of three, five, and seven visit the shrine with their parents, have increased in popularity with the rise of modern family units. Travel companies and shrines have cooperated to attract participants to new or revived pilgrimage routes. While the constitution prevents public funds from being spent on religious events, local authorities in many areas have been keen to support colorful festivals that attract visitors and benefit the local economy. Consequently, many festivals have come to be seen as cultural rather than religious events. While rural depopulation led to the decline of many agricultural traditions in the postwar period, some have been revived as a result of city dwellers returning to rural areas. However, Shrine Shintō lacks a strong sense of identity and purpose in modern Japan, and there are real concerns within the Shintō establishment that, as communities become increasingly fragmented and lifestyles more individualistic, many shrines will fade away. Some observers have suggested that Shrine Shintō will continue to decline until it can offer women real opportunities to achieve leadership within the priesthood and in other important roles currently occupied only by men. This represents a considerable challenge since Shintō is, among other things, a powerful symbol of conservatism in a society where seniority in many occupational fields is still a male preserve.

Shintō new religions. While some shrines may be struggling, an area of growth throughout most of the postwar period has been that of new religions with a Shintō identity. Shintō-related new religious movements in Japan account for a significant proportion of religious activity, with the largest groups counting their adherents in hundreds of thousands. However, the many different groups involved have their own histories and disparate aims. They seldom if ever act in concert, and do not regard themselves as parts of a greater Shintō whole. On the contrary, members of new religious movements are often encouraged to think of their own group as possessing the special truth of Shintō. Beliefs and practices of the Shintō-style new religions vary considerably. To take just a few examples: Tenshō kōtai jingū kyō (literally "the religion of the imperial shrine of Amaterasu," known also as the dancing religion) connects with Shintō mainly through its name. The movement was founded in 1945 by a remarkable woman, Kitamura Sayo (1900–1967). She endured marriage as the sixth bride of a man who, on the orders of his stingy mother, divorced each wife after using her as cheap labor for a season. Kitamura experienced possession (*kami-gakari*) by a spirit snake who then revealed itself as the god Tenshō kōtai jingū and commissioned Kitamura to save the world. Dressed as a man, performing the "dance of no-self" in streets, parks, and railway stations, and denouncing Japan's rulers as "maggots and traitors," Kitamura traveled widely in Japan and overseas, attracting many devoted followers. Known to her disciples as Ōgami-sama, or great goddess, she taught that passions and attachment were the cause of suffering and was credited with numerous miracles and healings.

Sekai kyūsei-kyō ("religion for the salvation of the world," known also as M.O.A.) was founded by Okada Mokichi (1882–1955), a member of the prewar Ōmoto Great Origin sect, following a revelation by the Bodhisattva Kannon. In 1928 Okada set up the Great Japan Association for the Worship of Bodhisattva Kannon, which practised healing and communion with spirits. Forced by the government to focus on the healing aspect, the movement was renamed Japan Association for Healing through Purification. After the war the revived movement split and Okada formed the group now called Sekai kyūsei-kyō. His followers see Okada as a living *kami* (*ikigami*) and combine Shintō-style rites and symbolism with a reverence for fine art, both Western and Japanese. Members are wary of modern medicinal drugs and promote an organic diet and "light-healing" (*jōrei*), in which healing rays are transmitted from the palm of the hand towards the patient. Several major evangelical Shintō-style healing movements that use similar methods trace their origin to (and regard themselves as the real heirs of) Okada's teaching, the best-known being Sūkyo Mahikari, founded in 1978. Many other smaller groups embracing Shintō symbolism have been founded by men and women offering healing, prophecy, revelation, or psychic powers and adopting a Shintō or Shintō-Buddhist idiom. Worldmate (originally known as Cosmomate) is a New Age Shintō movement whose success has been founded on the best-selling publications of its energetic creator, the business guru Fukami Toshū. Worldmate teaches that a proper relationship with the right *kami* is the key to worldly success.

Through his International Shintō Foundation however, Fukami has also provided significant philanthropic support for academic research in the field of Japanese religions, including the critical study of Shintō in all its forms.

CONCLUDING REMARKS. It is relatively easy to ask questions about Shinto, less easy to summarize it. By adopting a wider definition of Shintō, as *kami* belief, for example, the scope of discussion could be extended to include a multitude of Japanese folk traditions and miscellaneous practices relating to *kami*. Alternatively, one could adopt an aesthetic approach and explore Shintō readings of Japanese literature in the manner of the pioneers of National Learning. An ethnographic approach would illumine the infinitely varied details of festivals and shrine rituals in many places and eras. Here, Shintō has been considered in terms of systems of *kami* worship over time. Shintō has been construed in many different ways in the course of Japan's history, and this process will no doubt continue. In the late twentieth century, new directions in Shintō theology emerged, some adopting a robust response to the charge that Meiji Shintō is an invention and asserting that yes, Shintō is a modern religion, it regards both the emperor and the land of Japan as sacred, and this is its strength. Others have argued for an environmentalist reading of Shintō as a forest tradition or a nature religion. Yet others have drawn comparisons with Western Neopaganism.

The approach adopted in this survey to the study of Shintō has been historical, since it is the changing, historically conditioned aspect of Shintō that is most often and most obviously neglected in textbook presentations of Shintō as an ageless, unchanging, primal tradition. It has also been well argued, however, that while Shintō may not be "primal" in the ordinary sense, it should nevertheless be seen an "adjusted" primal religion; that is, the deliberately rough archaism of contemporary Shintō rituals reflects choices made by sophisticated religious actors who are well aware of their historical positioning and of alternative ways of being religious. This approach perhaps best captures the worshiper's point of view, which should never be forgotten.

SEE ALSO Amaterasu Ōmikami; Buddhism, article on Buddhism in Japan; Kami; Priesthood, article on Shintō Priesthood.

BIBLIOGRAPHY

Ashkenazi, Michael. *Matsuri.* Honolulu, 1993.

Blacker, Carmen. *The Catalpa Bow: A Study of Shamanistic Practices in Japan.* London, 1992. A classic work on shamanism in Buddhist, Shintō, and folk contexts.

Bocking, Brian. *A Popular Dictionary of Shintō.* Richmond, U.K., 1995.

Bocking, Brian. *The Oracles of the Three Shrines: Windows on Japanese Religion.* Richmond, U.K., 2001.

Breen, John, and Mark Teeuwen, eds. *Shintō in History: Ways of the Kami.* A substantial edited collection of recent Japanese and Western scholarship on Shintō, with extensive bibliography; articles range from Daoism in early Japan to twentieth-century Shintō studies.

Chamberlain, Basil Hall. *Japanese Things: Being Notes on Various Subjects Connected with Japan.* Rutland,Vt. and Tokyo, 1971 (reprint of the 1905 edition).

Grapard, Allan. *The Protocol of the Gods: A Study of the Kasuga Cult in Japanese History.* Berkeley, 1992.

Hardacre, Helen. *Shintō and the State, 1868–1988.* Princeton, N.J., 1989. Addresses the changes in Shintō at the Meiji restoration.

Havens, Norman, and Inoue Nobutaka, eds. *Encyclopedia of Shintō,* vol. 1. Tokyo, 2001.

Inoue Nobutaka, ed. *Shinshūkyō Kyōdan jinbutsu jiten.* Tokyo, 1996.

Inoue Nobutaka, Itō Satoshi, Endō Jun, and Mori Mizue. *Shintō: A Short History.* Edited by Inoue Nobutaka; translated and adapted by Mark Teeuwen and John Breen. London, 2003. A succinct and comprehensive critical introduction to the history of Shintō.

Itō Satoshi, Endo Jun, Matsuo Kooichi, and Mori Mizue. *Nihonshi shōhyakka: Shintō.* Tokyo, 2002.

Japanese Journal of Religious Studies (Nanzan University, Japan). The major English-language journal for the study of Japanese religions. An index of articles, many available online, is available from http://www.ic.nanzan-u.ac.jp/SHUBUNKEN/publications/publications.htm. Themed issues of *JJRS* particularly relevant to Shintō, each issue bringing together articles by leading scholars, include *Tracing Shintō in the History of Kami Worship* (2002, vol. 29, nos. 3–4); *Local Religion in Tokugawa History* (2001, vol. 28, nos. 3–4); *Pilgrimage in Japan* (1997, vol. 24, nos. 3–4); *The Legacy of Kuroda Toshio* (1996, vol. 23, nos. 3–4); *The New Age in Japan* (1995, vol. 22, nos. 3–4); and *The Emperor System and Religion in Japan* (1990, vol. 17, nos. 2–3).

Kokugakuin Daigaku Nihon Bunka Kenkyūjo, ed. *Shintō jiten.* Tokyo, 1994.

Kuroda Toshio. *Jisha Seiryoku.* Tokyo, 1980. See also Kuroda's article "Shintō in the History of Japanese Religion," published in the *Journal of Japanese Studies* 7, no. 1 (1981): 1–21 and reprinted in Mullins et al., *Religion and Society in Modern Japan* (see below).

Miyachi Masato. *Tennōsei no seijishiteki kenkyū.* Tokyo, 1981.

Mullins, Mark R., Shimazono Susumu, and Paul L. Swanson, eds. *Religion and Society in Modern Japan: Selected Readings.* Berkeley, 1993. This anthology includes Kuroda's "Shintō in the History of Japanese Religion," articles on Shūgendō, Yasukuni Jinja, and other aspects of contemporary religion, and documents including the 1890 Imperial Rescript on Education, the 1945 Shintō Directive, and extracts from the 1889 and 1947 constitutions.

Nelson, John. *A Year in the Life of a Shintō Shrine.* Seattle, 1996.

Ono Sōkyō. *Shinto: The Kami Way.* Rutland, Vt., and Tokyo, 1962.

Reader, Ian. *Religion in Contemporary Japan.* London, 1991.

Sakamoto Koremaru. *Kokka shintō keisei katei no kenkyū.* Tokyo, 1994.

Satō Hiroo. *Kami, hotoke, ōken no chūsei.* Tokyo, 1998.

Smyers, Karen A. *The Fox and the Jewel: Shared and Private Meanings in Contemporary Japanese Inari Worship.* Honolulu, 1999.

Teeuwen, Mark. *Watarai Shintō: An Intellectual History of the Outer Shrine in Ise.* Leiden, the Netherlands, 1996.

Teeuwen, Mark, and Fabio Rambelli. *Buddhas and Kami in Japan: Honji Suijaku as a Combinatory Paradigm.* London, 2002.

Yasumaru Yoshio. *Kamigami no meiji ishin.* Tokyo, 1979.

Yasumaru Yoshio, and Miyachi Masato, eds. *Nihon kindai shisō taikei 5: shūkyō to kokka.* Tokyo, 1988.

Yoshie, Akio. *Shinbutsu shūgō.* Tokyo, 1996.

BRIAN BOCKING (2005)

SHIPS SEE BOATS

SHĪRĀZĪ, MUḤAMMAD ṢADRĀ SEE MULLĀ ṢADRĀ

SHIVAISM SEE ŚAIVISM

SHNE'UR ZALMAN OF LYADY (1745–1813)

was the founder of the Habad school of Hasidism. Born into a prominent Jewish family in Liozno, Belorussia, Shne'ur Zalman had an extensive rabbinic education before he became associated with the Hasidic movement. At the age of twenty he joined the circle of students around Dov Ber of Mezhirich (Międzyrzecz, Poland) and was immediately recognized as a person of unusual intellectual abilities. Dov Ber encouraged him to continue with his legal studies as well as to cultivate his developing mastery of the *Zohar* and the Lurianic mystical writings. Legend has it that he was the teacher of Dov Ber's son, Avraham "the Angel" (1739/40–1777), in exoteric matters while the latter initiated him into the secrets of Qabbalah. Shne'ur Zalman's profound legal knowledge is reflected in the *Shulhan 'arukh shel ha-Rav* (1814), an updating of the code of Jewish law.

As the major theoretician of the Hasidic movement, Shne'ur Zalman is author of a number of works that are classics of the movement's thought. His popular *Liqquṭei Amarim* (*Tanya'*), published anonymously in 1797, is the most important systematic theological treatise that Hasidism produced. His collected homilies (*Torah Or,* 1836; *Liqquṭei Torah,* 1848) detail the system first laid out in that work, deftly reinterpreting the entire prior corpus of qabbalistic writings.

Shne'ur Zalman was also an important political figure in the spreading Hasidic "empire." After the emigration of Menahem Mendel of Vitebsk, the leading Hasidic figure in Belorussia, to the Holy Land in 1777, Shne'ur Zalman became, de facto, the leader of Hasidism in that area. This authority was formally recognized in 1788 when he was appointed leader of *kolel Reisin,* the institution responsible for that district's support of the Hasidic efforts in the Land of Israel.

As leader in the district closest to the anti-Hasidic stronghold of Lithuania, Shne'ur Zalman undeservedly bore the brunt of the sharp anti-Hasidic polemics of the 1780s and 1790s. A moderate who certainly believed in Torah study, respect for sages, and other matters that concerned the *mitnaggedim* ("opponents" of Hasidism), his efforts at peacemaking between the warring camps ended in failure. In 1798 he was arrested and imprisoned in Saint Petersburg, after leaders of the *mitnaggedim,* including the rabbi of Pinsk, accused him of disloyalty to the tsar and of leading a dissenting sect. He was released on the nineteenth of the Jewish month of Kislev in that year, a day still celebrated by Habad Ḥasidim as a festival. Imprisoned again in 1801, it seems likely that his notoriety in the eyes of the Russian authorities increased his popularity as a leader among the Ḥasidim.

After settling in Lyady in 1801, Shne'ur Zalman was established as a major figure in the Hasidic world. His distinctive personal style, combining rigorous intellectuality and a detached, self-negating mysticism, cast its stamp on the religious life of his disciples and made Habad a unique subculture within Hasidism. He devoted himself fully to the education of these disciples, and Lyady became the major center of study in the Hasidic world.

Shne'ur Zalman left two disciples who continued to develop a mystical theology along the lines of his thought. These were his son Dov Ber of Lubavitch (1773–1827), who became the leader of the Habad community upon his father's death, and Aharon Horwitz of Starosielce (1766–1828), a profound scholar whose previously little known work has recently been the object of much scholarly interest.

SEE ALSO Hasidism, article on Habad Hasidism.

BIBLIOGRAPHY

A biography of the traditional hagiographic type in English is that by Nissan Mindel, *Rabbi Schneur Zalman* (New York, 1969), based largely on Hayyim Meir Heilman's *Bet Rabbi* (1900; reprint, Jerusalem, 1965). Greater historical awareness is shown in Mordecai Teitelbaum's *Ha-rav mi-Liadi u-mifleget ḤaBaD* (1910; reprint, Jerusalem, 1970).

New Sources

Foxbrunner, Roman A. *Habad: The Hasidism of R. Shneur Zalman of Lyady.* Tuscaloosa, Ala., 1992.

Schachter-Shalomi, Zalman. *Wrapped in a Holy Flame: Teachings and Tales of the Hasidic Masters.* Edited by Nataniel M. Miles-Yepez. San Francisco, 2003.

Steinsaltz, Adin. *Opening the Tanya: Discovering the Moral and Mystical Teachings of a Classic Work of Kabbalah.* Edited by Meir Hanegbi. Translated by Yaacov Tauber. San Francisco, 2003.

ARTHUR GREEN (1987)
Revised Bibliography

SHONA RELIGION.

Bantu-speaking peoples first moved into the central area between the Limpopo and Zambezi rivers (what is now Zimbabwe) some two millennia ago. Over the centuries, small polities formed and combined into a number of complex states, which in turn divided in the face of internal and external pressures. The term *Shona* is relatively new and is applied to the indigenous inhabitants of this region, excluding only the small ethnic groups at the northern and southern peripheries and the nineteenth-century Nguni invaders from the south, namely, the Ndebele, who now occupy southwest Zimbabwe, and the Shangane in the southeast. The Shona peoples are often classified according to four main dialect groups: the Zezuru in the center, the Korekore to the north, the Manyika to the east, and the Karanga to the south. The Shona are the dominant ethnic group in contemporary Zimbabwe, comprising about eight million people, or four-fifths of the population of the country.

At the time of colonization at the end of the nineteenth century, the Shona comprised a large number of independent petty chiefdoms. They lived in scattered villages based on patrilineages. They subsisted primarily on agriculture and kept some livestock—especially cattle, which had significance in marriage payments and for religious purposes. There was considerable internal trade in such goods as agricultural products, ironwork, and tobacco; the earlier external trade in gold and ivory had fallen to a mere trickle by this stage. Now, a century later, even rural Shona benefit from the technology and consumer comforts bought from the proceeds of wage labor and cash cropping. At least a quarter of the Shona population now claim affiliation to some Christian denomination, and Christian beliefs have infiltrated the thinking of professing traditionalists. Traditional beliefs and practices are, however, still dominant, even among many professed Christians.

TRADITIONAL RELIGION. Shona religion traditionally focused on relations with spirits of the dead. These include spirits of strangers, spirits of deceased ancestors, spirits of the land, and spirits of ancient heroes. Most Shona also acknowledge a high god (known by a variety of names) who is too remote to be concerned with the affairs of humans; he was, however, accessible through the cult in southern Shona country and is becoming more widely accessible through the influence of Christianity.

Superficially, the Shona believe in a clear hierarchy of spirits, with the high god at the top, followed by spirits of heroes, of the land, of ancestors, and finally of strangers. Indeed, to many Shona, the spiritual world appears fixed in a permanent and ancient hierarchy. In practice, however, the relative status of different spirits often varies with locality and changes over time. The relative importance of different spirits often depends on the activities of their mediums.

Spirits of all levels may be associated with mediums or hosts. When a man or woman is about to become a medium, the first sign is usually sickness, often accompanied by mental disturbances, which a diviner interprets as a call by a spirit for the sick person to become its host. The patient is initiated as a medium and from time to time is possessed by the spirit. In the state of possession, the medium goes into a kind of trance during which he or she is supposed to lose consciousness, and the spirit is believed to speak and act through the medium. Mediums of the more important spirits are the major religious specialists in traditional Shona society.

Divination is most frequently performed by a possessed medium, although certain mechanical means, especially the use of various types of dice, are also used. Most ritual activity takes place in response to illness or other misfortunes, and mediums who have been through similar sufferings themselves are often best able to help others to cope with their problems. Misfortune is usually explained in terms of the influence of spirits, although occasionally it may also be explained in terms of the evil machinations of a witch.

Shona maintain that certain persons, aided by evil spirits, have perverted values and delight in their esoteric powers to do harm. This belief is likely to come into practice only when there are severe social tensions, and accusations of witchcraft may be used to justify rifts in a formerly close-knit community.

The ancestral cult. When illness or other misfortune is sufficiently worrying for a diviner to be consulted, the most common result of divination is that the trouble is attributed to the spirit of a deceased ancestor who wishes to be honored. The deceased head of a family is believed to be responsible for the well-being of all his descendants. A deceased mother or maternal grandmother may also be considered influential, especially in matters concerning the fertility of girls. It is said that not even a witch can attack a member of a family without the cooperation of aggrieved ancestral spirits.

When a man dies, his spirit is believed to wander around restlessly until it is settled in the family homestead by a ritual normally performed a year or more after death. After this, his spirit is frequently invoked in the homestead, particularly when any important event takes place within the family. He may have a bull dedicated to him from the family herd of cattle, which may be sacrificed in his honor should divination reveal this to be his wish. At any ritual in his honor, descendants must gather together with their spouses to reaffirm their unity as a group and the necessity of cooperation between them. The same is true for a female ancestor. The spirits of family ancestors are seen as spirit elders who continue to control and to care for the family groups for which they were responsible during their lives. Many such ancestral spirits are believed to preside over important family gatherings through a possessed medium, who is a member of the family. As the extended kinship system weakens, especially in urban areas, the ancestral cult becomes a more private affair, providing a means of explaining and coping with personal misfortune.

Spirits of the land. Ancestors of chiefly lineages are responsible for all the people living in their territorial domains.

The domain for which any chiefly spirit is responsible may be the chiefdom as a whole or a section of the chiefdom particularly associated with the spirit. Such a spirit is, in most of Shona country, called *mhondoro* ("lion") and frequently will have a medium who has high status in the community as a whole.

Where there is a history of invasion of one people by another, a differentiation of function has often developed between the cult of the chiefly spirits, which is concerned with political power, and the cult of the defeated autochthonous spirits, which concerns rainfall and the fertility of the land. In such cases, the autochthonous spirit might be considered equal to, or even more powerful than, the chiefly lion spirits.

Rituals are held in honor of territorial spirits to request good rains before a harvest and to give thanks after the harvest. Such rituals principally involve the brewing of millet beer, to which all families in the spirit's domain should contribute, and singing and dancing over a couple of days in honor of the spirit, often at a tree shrine in the veld. At the directions of the possessed medium, rites may also be held to avert threats to crops through drought or pests. Certain days are considered holy to the spirit guardians of the land, and on these days no traditional work may be done in the fields.

Mediums of territorial spirits preside at all rituals in honor of their spirits. They may also preside at the trial of someone accused of a crime against the spirit, such as incest or working on a holy day. In many parts of Shona country, the possessed mediums of chiefly spirits are responsible for electing a new chief, who is to be their representative in the government of the country. Chief and mediums are subsequently expected to consult with one another and to cooperate on important issues. Since the territorial spirits are responsible for all people in their land, a possessed medium may be consulted over the private difficulties of residents and may acquire a reputation for divining and healing beyond the territorial limits of the domain.

A medium's reputation depends on the ability to convince people at séances and to acquire a large clientele. In practice, if the medium is to acquire and maintain a position of influence, the medium's oracular pronouncements, whether in private divination or concerning the election of a chief, must accord with public opinion. In many situations, therefore, mediums serve to crystalize and to voice public opinion. More generally, spirit mediums represent great figures of the Shona past and have frequently become symbols of rejection of white dominance.

Regional cults. Certain spirits spread their influence beyond the territorial domain of any political authority. Such spirits may be associated with powerful political figures of the past, symbolizing conglomerations of chiefdoms that for a period may have been subject to a single ruling dynasty. Or they may be conceived as spirits of ancient heroes who lived before the establishment of any present dynasties. The mediums of such spirits are consulted by clients from a number of neighboring chiefdoms on private problems and on public issues such as drought and chiefly inheritance. Some of these spirits, such as Chaminuka and Nehanda, have become national figures on account of the activities of their mediums in successive wars against the Ndebele and against white settlers.

The most widespread regional cult is that of the high god, Mwari, which is centered on a number of shrines in southern Shona country. In the past, this was the dominant religious cult among most Karanga and Kalanga peoples, and it received some attention from the invading Ndebele. The main shrines in the Matopo Hills are maintained by a hereditary priesthood. There, sacrifices for rain are offered and a voice from a cave utters oracles for those who wish to consult Mwari. Selected young boys and girls dedicated to Mwari live for a time at the center to help maintain the shrine and dance at rituals; often they become important spirit mediums when they return home on reaching maturity, thus maintaining close contacts between the cult center and outlying traditional cults. Mwari was accepted as the Shona name for God by early Christian missionaries, and through Christian influence it has now been accepted far beyond the sphere of influence of the traditional cult centers.

Peripheral cults. Throughout Shona country, certain spirits are believed to be the concern of their hosts only. These are usually conceived as spirits of aliens, or occasionally of animals, who died away from home and so wander about, unsettled and restless, until they find a human host they can possess. Such a spirit may confer special powers on the host, particularly those of divining and healing, as well as such skills as hunting or playing music. Often, however, alien spirits are said only to want to dance, and they possess their hosts only at dances held in honor of such spirits, when a number of hosts of similar spirits are likely to be present and to become possessed simultaneously. These séances, usually held in response to illness in one of the hosts, allow persons who are undergoing some kind of strain to find relief in the attention they receive and in the dramatic dancing they perform.

CHRISTIANITY AMONG THE SHONA. Christian missionaries, active in Shona country for nearly a hundred years, have strongly influenced contemporary Shona religion. Initially, conversion to Christianity was largely associated with the acquisition of wealth, mainly through education and consequent employment but also through access to improved agricultural techniques. For many, Christianity was a symbol of the new ways of life that colonization introduced and, in particular, of the comforts that the new technology made possible; for others it became a symbol of white oppression.

Different mission churches were located in different rural areas; branches of these churches in the cities were able to provide places where migrants could meet others from their home areas. They also established accessible means of communication with the rural areas. With its emphasis on the high god rather than on local cults, Christianity was better adapted than traditional religion to cope with the new situation of high mobility and intermingling of people from different regions, especially in the urban centers.

Christianity does not, however, incorporate mechanisms for coping with tension at the family and local level, and as presented by missionaries it retains an impersonal approach to illness. Consequently, professed Christians still frequently revert to ancestral and local cults when faced with persistent illness and other personal problems, particularly when these reflect social tensions.

Since the early 1930s, many Shona have joined the new independent churches, which have adopted forms of Christianity but are free from foreign control. These pay more attention to traditional cosmologies, and particularly to the belief in afflicting spirits and in witchcraft as causes of misfortune, but like the mission churches they provide a means of overcoming the boundaries of family and local cults. These churches tend to attract many disparate peoples, although most of their followers are relatively uneducated. Faith healing, a central activity in most of them, is a major means for attracting converts. Afflicting spirits are exorcised, rather than being accommodated as in traditional religion or simply dismissed as in the mission churches.

Although in ritual and belief independent churches are much closer to traditional religion than are the mission churches, the antagonism between them and traditional cults is much greater than in the case of mission churches because their adherents are drawn largely from a common body of people. For those outside positions of leadership, however, there is an easy intermingling of religious systems. Individuals may move in and out of the various religious groups depending on the circumstances of the moment, and most Shona see nothing wrong in such religious mobility. For most Shona, the various forms of Christianity together with the various traditional cults all provide a pool of religious responses from which an individual can choose, depending on his or her needs of the moment.

BIBLIOGRAPHY

The most comprehensive ethnography of the Shona, which gives special emphasis to religion, is my own *Shona Peoples,* 2d ed. (Gweru, 1982). This book contains a full bibliography. Michael Gelfand has written a number of works on the religion of different Shona groups, which, despite flaws in research methodology and presentation, provide useful material: The best of these are *Shona Ritual* (Cape Town, 1959), which describes the religion of the central Shona (Zezuru), and *African Crucible* (Cape Town, 1968), which looks at the changing situation. Peter Fry's *Spirits of Protest* (Cambridge, 1976) provides insights into the political and social roles of Zezuru spirit mediums. Hubert Bucher's *Spirits and Power* (Cape Town, 1980) analyzes Shona cosmology from secondary sources. On issues closely related to religion, G. L. Chavunduka's *Traditional Healers and the Shona Patient* (Gwelo, 1978) includes information on the relationship between Shona religion and illness; Gelfand's *Witchdoctor* (London, 1964) is a good account of Shona diviner-healers and their practices; and his *The African Witch* (Edinburgh, 1967) provides the best available description of Shona witchcraft beliefs and practices. On the introduction of Christianity into Shona society, Marshall W. Murphree's *Christianity and the Shona* (London, 1969) gives a concise analysis of the interrelationships of different religious groups (including traditionalists) in a Shona community. M. L. Daneel provides a thorough coverage of the most important independent churches in *Old and New in Southern Shona Independent Churches,* 2 vols. (The Hague, 1971–1974).

M. F. C. BOURDILLON (1987)

SHOTOKU TAISHI (574–622), or Prince Shotoku, was a member of the Japanese imperial family during the sixth and seventh centuries CE. He was responsible for Japan's first constitution as well as the spread of Buddhism in Japan. He is also known as Umayado no Miko, Toyotomimi, and Kamitsu Miya. The name Umayado is derived from the legend that Shotoku was born to Princess Anahobe no Hashihito when she was walking in front of the door of a stable (*umayado*). According to Kume Kunitake, this legend might have been influenced by the story of Jesus' birth, which had been brought to China by Nestorian Christians during the Tang dynasty (618–907). The name Toyotomimi, or "wise ears," refers to the fact that Shotoku was considered to be so learned that he could listen to ten lawsuits simultaneously and decide them without error. The name Kamitsu Miya is derived from the location of his palace. The name Shotoku (saintly virtue) was given to him after his death to honor him for his contribution to the prosperity of Buddhism in Japan.

YOUNG SHOTOKU AND HIS ERA. Shotoku was born in 574 (572 or 573 according to some scholars) as the second son of Prince Tachibana no Toyohi, who ascended the throne as Emperor Yomei in 585. Yomei, whose short reign ended when he died of natural causes in 587, is also known as the first Japanese emperor to declare his faith in Buddhism, which had been officially introduced into Japan from Korea in 538—or 552, according to the *Nihonshoki* (*Chronicle of Japan*), which was compiled in 720. The emperor's official acceptance of Buddhism caused a division among the imperial courtiers, so that the Mononobe family, which was opposed to the new religion, and the Soga family, which supported Buddhism, fought over the succession after Yomei's death. Young Shotoku, whose grandmothers both came from the Soga family, followed their loyalty to Buddhism. According to one legend, he carved a statue of Shitenno, or the four heavenly kings regarded as protectors of Buddhism, to pray for victory. After the Soga family defeated the Mononobe family in 587, Shotoku constructed the Shitennōji temple in Osaka, which later became the first official Buddhist temple in Japan.

Emperor Sushun, who ascended the throne in 587, plotted to murder Soga no Umako, the head of the Soga family, which had become tyrannical after their defeat of the Mononobe clan; however, Umako succeeded in assassinating Sushun. It was under these unstable conditions that Empress Suiko, the first female ruler of Japan, ascended the throne in 593. Suiko, who was the sister of Emperor Yomei, designated Shotoku as her regent shortly after she became empress, and she delegated secular authority to him.

SHOTOKU AS REGENT. Shotoku governed as prince regent on behalf of Empress Suiko from 593 until his death in 621 or 622. His administration was conspicuous for instituting many of the policies that became foundational for the Japanese state and culture. In 604 Shotoku instituted the *kan'i junikai*, literally "twelve grades of cap rank," which was the first system of courtly ranks in Japan. The *kan'i junikai* designated twelve grades of courtiers, each with a distinctive colored cap. The ranks were named after the six Confucian virtues, each of which was subdivided to make twelve ranks in all. Instead of the former ranking system, which had been based on hereditary clan membership, Shotoku's system was intended to reward talented individuals and promote loyalty to the court.

In the following year, Shotoku promulgated the Seventeen-Article Constitution, which was really a set of moral precepts and service regulations for public servants rather than a constitution in the modern sense of the term. The contents of the constitution were based primarily on Confucian and Buddhist thought. For example, the high praise of harmony, solidarity, and cooperation in Article 1 reflects Confucian influence, while the respect for the Three Treasures—Buddha, Buddha's teaching, and the Buddhist community—expressed in Article 2 honors the new faith that Shotoku wished to encourage. Although some scholars doubt that the document was actually composed by Shotoku, this first constitution has had a significant influence on later Japanese legal codes.

Shotoku had three aides from three rival kingdoms in what is now Korea: Eji came from Koguryŏ, Kakuka is thought to have come from Paekche, and Hata no Kawakatsu came from a family from Silla. Although the three kingdoms fought among themselves during Shotoku's lifetime, the three advisers cooperated in supporting the prince regent, who was eager to introduce the political systems, art, and religions of the Asian mainland into Japan. Shotoku also sent ambassadors, scholar-monks, and students in the years 600, 607, 608, and 614 to the rulers of the Sui dynasty, which had unified China in 589. One of the main purposes of these diplomatic embassies was to collect writing materials, commentaries, and other reference works to bring back to Japan.

In 601 Shotoku began the construction of a new palace in Ikaruga, which lies halfway between Asuka (the residence of Suiko as well as the stronghold of Umako) and Naniwa (Osaka), where an international port was located. In 605 Shotoku moved into Ikaruga no miya (the palace at Ikaruga). There he built a famous Buddhist temple, the Hōryūji, to pray for the repose of his father's soul.

SHOTOKU'S ATTITUDE TOWARD RELIGION. With the penetration of Sino-Korean civilization and Buddhism into Japan from the fifth century onward, the country was destined to undergo a series of social, political, and cultural changes. In addition to the cosmological theories of the Yin-Yang school, two universal principles—Dao and *dharma*—were introduced by Confucianism and Buddhism, respectively. These principles stood in tension with the indigenous Japanese religious worldview, which was later called Shintō. The first serious attempt to deal with this tension was made by Shotoku, attempting to affirm Shinto, Confucianism, and Buddhism simultaneously by holding them in balance, as it were, in the Seventeen-Article Constitution.

Regardless of Shotoku's devotion to Buddhism and his advocacy of Confucian virtues, however, the *Nihonshoki* indicates that he was dedicated above all to unifying the Japanese nation by upholding the divine prerogatives of the throne through appropriation of the teachings of Buddhism and Confucianism. On the other hand, he was eager to continue the tradition of his imperial ancestors who had venerated the *kami*. In short, what Shotoku envisaged was the establishment of a multireligious policy that harmonized Shintō, Confucian tradition, and Buddhism. This synthesis was to serve as the bulwark of a strongly centralized nation ruled by the imperial family.

Shotoku himself, however, was a Buddhist. In the early days of Japanese Buddhism, some powerful clan leaders looked for salvation in this world from the newly-introduced foreign religion, as well as protection for their country. In contrast to this line of thought, Shotoku accepted the internal and spiritual dimensions of Buddhism. According to the *Nihonshoki*, he lectured to Empress Suiko on the *Shomangyo*, or *Śrīmālā Sūtra*, and the *Hokekyo*, or *Saddharmapuṇḍarīka Sūtra*, in 606. He also wrote commentaries or *gisho* on three sutras: the *Shomangyo gisho*, the *Yuimagyo* (the *Vimalakīrti Nirdeśa Sūtra*) *gisho* and the *Hokekyo gisho*, all of which are estimated to be the oldest written documents in Japan. Scholars disagree, however, about whether they were written by Shotoku himself, and if so, to what extent they originated with Shotoku.

POPULAR VENERATION OF SHOTOKU. According to Tamura Encho, more than a hundred biographies were written about Shotokụ by the end of the Tokugawa era (1600–1868), most of which were based on, or at least influenced by, the *Shotoku-taishi-denryaku*, or *Denryaku*, which was supposedly written in the early tenth century. This text became increasingly popular among the Japanese people as the founders of Japanese Buddhist sects, particularly Shinran (1173–1262), venerated Shotoku as the founder of Japanese Buddhism. The *Denryaku* is full of legendary or mythological episodes, one of which introduces Princess Anahobe's strange dream of a golden monk (who introduces himself as *kuse no bosatsu* [bodhisattva of salvation]), which caused her to become pregnant. Shotoku came to be regarded as an incarnation of Kannon, the god or goddess of mercy (Avalokiteśvara in Sanskrit) on the basis of this story. During the two centuries between the *Nihonshoki* and the *Denryaku*, Shotoku was transformed in the popular imagination from a hero to a savior.

What is significant is that Shotoku was not only a historically important person but also a paradigmatic figure. That is to say, Shotoku was stereotyped, and as such, his personality and career were interpreted by later tradition as embodiments of attributes and qualities that later Japanese Buddhists admired. Once Shotoku was idealized in this way, he was further glorified in pious legends and popular literature. The various attributes of buddhas and bodhisattvas as well as the virtues of King Aśoka and the ideal Buddhist layman Yuima (Vimalakīrti) were incorporated into the sacred traditions about Shotoku. It is not surprising, therefore, that very shortly after his death Shotoku became the object of the Taishi (Prince) cult, which was in effect similar to the veneration of Sakyamuni (Prince Siddhārtha) and Maitreya (Prince Ajita).

See Also Buddhism, article on Buddhism in Japan; Japanese Religions, overview article.

Bibliography

Gamaike Seishi, ed. *Taishi Shinko.* Tokyo, 1999.
Hayashi Mikiya. *Taishi Shinko no Kenkyu.* Tokyo, 1980.
Iida Mizuho. *Shotoku Taishi Den no Kenkyu.* Tokyo, 2000.
Miyamoto Youtaro. *Seiden no Kozo ni Kansuru Shukyogaku teki Kenkyu.* Okayama, Japan, 2003.
Oyama Seiichi, ed. *Shotoku Taishi no Shinjitsu.* Tokyo, 2003.
Sakamoto Taro. *Shotoku Taishi.* Tokyo, 1985.
Sakamoto Taro, et al., eds. *Shotoku Taishi Zenshu.* 4 vols. Kyoto, Japan, 1988.
Tamura Encho. *Shotoku Taishi.* Tokyo, 1964.
Tanaka Tsuguhito. *Shotoku Taishi Shinko no Seiritsu.* Tokyo, 1983.
Yoshimura Takehiko. *Shotoku Taishi.* Tokyo, 2002.

Miyamoto Youtaro (2005)

SHRINES are places or containers of religious presence. One of the distinctive features of religion is that its objects do not "exist" in the ordinary sense of the word. Deity, spirit, soul, afterlife, and other familiar categories of religion lie outside the realms of everyday objects in time and space. However, human beings across multiple cultures experience the presence of these religious realities at particular times and places and in relation to material objects. Much of the work of shrines is to provide habitations for sacred presences within the everyday world. As places having a particular shape and materiality, shrines give particular density to complex sets of religious associations, memories, moods, expectations, and communities. Shrines may be seen as sites of condensation of more dispersed religious realities, places where meanings take on specific, tangible, and tactile presence.

The English word *shrine* is derived from the Latin *scrinium*, meaning a box or receptacle. The shrine is the receptacle within the material world for the religious association that believers experience when they come into the presence of these receptacles. Many shrines are unambiguously religious, linking events, persons, and places central to religious traditions. Mecca (Saudi Arabia), Jerusalem (Israel), Canterbury (United Kingdom), Nara (Japan), and Varanasi (or Benares, India) are sites that immediately come to mind as centers of religious density, hosting many places of sacred value to various religious communities. Other shrines may be more open-ended, not tied to particular religious traditions but linked strongly to a particular regional or national identity. In the United States, for example, sites such as Niagara Falls or the Vietnam Veterans Memorial draw pilgrim-tourists out of motivations and meanings that may be closely tied to religious ones.

Shrines and Sacred Persons. Shrines are often associated with the physical remains of persons understood to have been exemplary in spiritual attainment. The bones and teeth of the body of the Buddha that remained after his cremation have become objects of great veneration because they enable the devotee to link the meaning of the Buddha's message (*dharma*) with the trace of his physical presence in the world. In medieval Europe, fragments of wood believed to have been part of the cross on which Jesus was crucified took on a similar status of veneration. In South Asia the graves (*dargahs*) of Muslim saints serve as centers of access to spiritual presence for Muslims and non-Muslims because they are understood to be magnets for transformative power from which the devotee may draw for various life-enhancing purposes such as health, wealth, and success in the ordinary world. Across much of the landscape of Europe, Christian shrines from the medieval and early modern periods located within or near churches contain the graves of saints and martyrs, persons who exemplified the highest achievement of religious values.

In Durham Cathedral in the north of England, the body of Saint Cuthbert (635?–687), a preacher, healer, and leader, lies behind the altar. When the cathedral was completed in 1104 and Saint Cuthbert's body was exhumed, it was reported that the body had not decomposed. Hence, the deceased but intact body, located in close proximity to the altar, reinforces the Christian belief in the resurrection of the exemplary leader of the church, whose body remains suspended between a natural deceased state and a transformed resurrected state. The cathedral, and the shrine to Saint Cuthbert within it, marks a place for Christians where the religious configuration of reality overtakes ordinary experience. A visit to the site reinforces the pilgrims' hopes and confidence in their religious commitments.

A secular version of a shrine and sacred persons may be seen in the Vietnam Veterans Memorial in Washington, D.C. Located on the Mall (the open corridor that extends from the Capitol to the Lincoln Memorial) the Vietnam Veterans Memorial is a simple, black marble, V-shaped wall that gradually extends down from ground level to a depth of six feet. Visitors file past the wall, descending to grave depth and then ascending back to ground level as they see the names of the 58,000 American men and women who died in the Vietnam War. The polished black marble serves as a mirror to those who gaze at the wall reading the names even as they see their own reflections. The Vietnam Memorial carries no explicitly religious symbolism. Instead, its minimalist aesthetic creates an open space for grief and awe into which visitors may bring their own religious understandings. While the shrine is not located on the site of the events commemorated, it is located on the site of the nation's center, symbolized by the markers of its progenitors: George Washington, Abraham Lincoln, and Thomas Jefferson. In this way the particular meanings of the Vietnam War's history reside surrounded by the associations of national identity and the collective sense of the "soul" of America.

Shrines as Thresholds between Nature and Culture. In some religious traditions, shrines may be located at important intersections of nature and culture. In the north of India, for example, shrines at Yamunotri and Gangotri mark the places where the two sacred rivers, the Yamuna and the Ganga (Ganges) emerge from the Himalayan glacier and begin their descent to the sea. These temples house the images of the goddesses and link them to the rivers that are their embodied forms in the world. Hence, pilgrims make the arduous journey to the sources of these rivers in order to fulfill vows of devotion and to be in the presence of the goddesses at their most primordial moments of appearance in the ordinary world. At the temples, Hindu priests provide a variety of ritual services and record the visits of pilgrims in temple archives.

In the United States, some extraordinary geological sites have taken on a religious or quasi-religious significance for visitors. Niagara Falls, the Grand Canyon, and Yellowstone and Yosemite National Parks offer sites that fit into an American sensibility about nature that endows it with religious meaning. The National Park Service, an administrative unit of the federal government, maintains access to these natural sites. While no specific religious meaning within a particular tradition is referred to, the pamphlets and brochures published for visitors evoke the language of awe and reverence that resembles more traditional religion.

Shrines as Markers of Historical Significance. Events occur in particular places, and events that later take on meaning for religious communities become important sites for shrines. For Jews the remaining wall of the Temple in Jerusalem, destroyed by the Romans in 70 CE, remains a sacred place of pilgrimage. To stand at the wall, facing the temple, for prayer and meditation brings additional intensity for Jews as they remember the sacred history and the hope for the coming of the Messiah. Visitors write prayers on small pieces of paper, roll them up, and place them in the cracks between the stones. It is said that all prayers placed there will be answered. Close by is the Muslim shrine called "The Dome of the Rock," an octagonal structure built by the Umayyad Caliph Abd al-Malik in 691. The site marks the place where the Prophet Muḥammad ascended into heaven. For Muslims, visiting and praying at the shrine connects them to the person of the Prophet. A bit farther away is the Church of the Holy Sepulcher, which marks the site of Jesus' burial and resurrection. Pilgrims often walk the streets through Jerusalem that are said to be the route Jesus walked on his way to his crucifixion, the Via Dolorosa, and end their journey at this church. Such a journey enables the pilgrims to take the story of Jesus into a temporal and spatial intensity by being in the places where these events that have become formational for Christian religious identity occurred.

Shrines may also mark places where one religious history displaces another. In the town of Chimayó in northern New Mexico, there is a small church, El Sanctuario de Chimayó, which has become an important pilgrimage center for Spanish-speaking Americans and Native Americans. The foundational story is that in the early nineteenth century a Spanish peasant, Bernardo Abeyta, came across a healing site used by the local Tewa Indians. The site consisted of a hole within a rock surface that was filled with dirt. As he passed by, a white light that came out of the hole blinded Abeyta. Then there appeared a crucifix of Christ that resembled one that was venerated in Guatemala. Abeyta took the crucifix to the nearest church, but miraculously the cross returned to the site where Abeyta had found it. Subsequently, Abeyta and a group of Catholic laymen established a shrine there. Over the following two centuries, El Sanctuario has become an important pilgrimage and healing center. During Holy Week, the week preceding Easter, thousands of pilgrims walk the road to Chimayó, many fulfilling vows for having been healed. In a room next to the sanctuary there is a display of prosthetic devices, photographs, letters, and works of art presented by grateful devotees. The hole that contains the sacred healing dirt, El Posito, remains an important part of the pilgrims' journey, for pilgrims gather a handful of the dirt to carry back home. The site combines Catholic traditions of saint veneration and pilgrimage with a Native American emphasis on healing power that comes from the earth itself.

A site of a very different sort that has taken on characteristics of a shrine is the Nazi death camp at Auschwitz, in Poland. During World War II the Nazi regime set up many sites for mass extermination of Jews and others by applying the modern technology of gas chambers and crematoria. Many Jews and others have made visits to Auschwitz, the most notorious of the camps, to come face-to-face with the place of horror that took so many lives. Many groups of Jewish young adults make pilgrimage visits to Auschwitz and other sites of Jewish life in eastern Europe that were destroyed during the Holocaust and complete their journey in Israel. In this way the groups move together through the historical nightmare of the recent past and enter into the place of present and future hope for the Jewish people as a community bound together by religiously shaped memory and anticipation.

SHRINES AS CENTERS OF SERVICE AND COMMERCE. Because shrines anchor the worlds of religious belief and material location, they frequently double as centers that provide various services and commodities. Shrines associated with sacred substances may offer medical and therapeutic as well as spiritual services. In the southwest of France, a healing center grew up around the site of a natural spring where a young woman had visions of the Virgin Mary in 1858. The shrine at Lourdes has become a major center in which religious and medical services are provided for pilgrims.

Indeed, stalls and shops surround many shrines, with vendors offering ritual supplies, food, and memorabilia that enable the visitor to perform important ceremonial obligations and take away mementos of the experience. In India, family descendants of a saint whose shrine has become a center of pilgrimage are frequently the heirs to the income from donations and sales of commodities at the site. In this way the shrine provides for both the religious and material benefit of the descendants.

SHRINES AS DESTINATIONS. An important function shrines serve is to provide points of destination to groups of pilgrims who join together on the road and forge temporary bonds of solidarity under the umbrella of shared beliefs and attitudes. The shrine may be located at the end of the road, or a network of shrines may serve as nodal points along the way, but often the migration of the pilgrims is as important, or more so, than the shrine itself. Pilgrims may walk for several days to reach a shrine, only to stay just a few hours. The journey may be more important than the destination, yet without the destination and what lies waiting for the pilgrims' arrival the journey would have no compelling rationale.

The examples discussed here suggest some of the ways in which shrines occupy the location between the worlds of religious belief and understanding and the material, spatial, and economic aspects of life. As places grounded solidly in the natural and constructed world of material objects, the shrine also grounds the more elusive and other-worldly dimensions of religion, the dimensions that lie beyond, in the realms of belief, longing, and wonder.

SEE ALSO Center of the World; Jerusalem, overview article; Pilgrimage; Relics.

BIBLIOGRAPHY

Martin Robinson, *Sacred Places, Pilgrim Paths: An Anthology of Pilgrimage* (London, 1997) provides a general overview of shrines and pilgrimages. Studies of shrines are often located within the frameworks of presentations of particular religions. For India, see Surindrer Bhardwaj, *Hindu Places of Pilgrimage in India: A Study in Cultural Geography* (Berkeley, Calif., 1973), and Roy Burmah, *The Hindu-Muslim Syncretic Shrines and Communities.* (New Delhi, 2002). For Christian shrines, Linda Lehrhaupt, *Pilgrimage in Modern Ireland* (New York, 1990); National Conference of Catholic Bishops, *Catholic Shrines and Places of Pilgrimage in the United States* (Washington, D.C., 1992); and Sidney Nolan, *Christian Pilgrimage in Modern Western Europe* (Chapel Hill, N.C., 1989). For Jewish tradition, there is Sidra Ezrahi, *Booking Passage: Exile and Homecoming in the Modern Jewish Imagination* (Berkeley, Calif., 2000). For natural objects as shrines, see Patrick V. McGreevy, *Imagining Niagara: The Meaning and Making of Niagara Falls* (Amherst, Mass., 1994). A detailed consideration of theories of shrines can be found in Jonathan Z. Smith, *To Take Place: Toward Theory in Ritual* (Chicago, 1987). For useful collections of essays on shrines in popular culture, see Ian Reader, ed., *Pilgrimage in Popular Culture.* (Houndmills, U.K., 1993). An excellent treatment of the Vietnam Memorial in Washington, D.C. as a pilgrimage site, see Raymond Michalowski and Jill Dubisch *Run for the Wall: Remembering Vietnam on a Motorcycle Pilgrimage* (New Brunswick, N.J., 2001).

PAUL B. COURTRIGHT (1987 AND 2005)

SHUGENDŌ

SHUGENDŌ is a distinctive Japanese tradition combining both indigenous and imported traditions, particularly Buddhism, and featuring the mastery of magical and ritual techniques to be practiced in and around sacred mountains. The name *Shugendō* means literally "the way [*dō*] of mastering [*shu*] extraordinary religious power [*gen*]"; the connection with sacred mountains is not included in the term but is implicit. Practitioners were called *shugenja,* "persons [*ja*] who master extraordinary religious power," but the more common name by which they have been known is *yamabushi,* "those who sleep [or lie down, *bushi*] in the mountains [*yama*]"—in other words, those who make mountains their home. Shugendō arose in part out of the ancient Japanese tradition of sacred mountains, but also features some Taoist influence, and especially ritual, divinities, symbolism, and doctrine from Buddhism.

Although Shugendō groups trace their origin to the late seventh- and early eighth-century tradition of En no Ozunu, the institutional organization of Shugendō did not take place until about the eleventh century. Eventually more than a hundred mountains were headquarters for a number of main traditions and many local variations of Shugendō, which was never unified on a national basis by a single teaching or a single authority. *Shugendō* is the general term referring to all aspects of this way—the mountain headquarters, the ecclesiastical organization, the teachings and practices, and the overall ethos of gaining magico-religious power through special training in sacred mountains.

This pervasive movement, which spread rapidly throughout all areas of Japan except the island of Hokkaido (which was developed later), was one of the main channels for disseminating religious teachings (such as elements of Buddhism) to the common people. It flourished until shortly after the feudal period, when in 1872 the government abolished Shugendō (partly in the attempt to "purify" Shintō and separate Buddhism from Shintō). With complete religious freedom in 1945 after World War II, some Shugendō groups have been able to reorganize, but they do not compare in size or vigor to the flourishing movement that existed from the eleventh through the nineteenth century.

FORMATION. The two main formative elements for Shugendō are the prehistoric Japanese heritage of sacred mountains, and imported traditions (from Korea and China) of religious realization. Although these two sets of elements eventually became almost imperceptibly intertwined, it is important to distinguish them in order to understand the emergence of Shugendō.

Sacred mountains—including particular beliefs and practices associated with them—have been so important in Japanese religious history that scholars have used the terms *sangaku shinkō* (mountain beliefs or cult) and *sangaku shukyō* (mountain religion) to refer to this nationwide but unorganized, highly localized phenomenon. Prehistoric practices surrounding sacred mountains were shaped by the character of the *kami* associated with a site and the type of worship accorded that spirit.

The claim has been made that in prehistoric times, before rice agriculture was introduced to Japan, there was a "pure hunting culture" and that the "original" mountain *kami* was a hunting divinity worshiped on the summit of the mountain. The significance of this theory is that, if substantiated, it would point to a hunting culture and a mountain *kami* related to hunting as the first Japanese precedent of religious practices on the mountain peak. However, there is insufficient evidence to support the claim, and because prehistoric conditions are so poorly documented, it is unlikely that such evidence will be found.

The earliest form of religious practices at Japanese sacred mountains for which there is archaeological evidence is related to the ptotohistorical period just before and after the common era, and closely associated with agriculture. These archaeological finds occur at the foot of mountains (rather than at the peak), often in conjunction with large boulders. Some of the finds are the stone representations of jewels, mirrors, and swords—the so-called imperial regalia, important to the imperial family and in Shintō. The ritual bowls and mortars also found there have led some scholars to conclude that the boulders (often venerated even today as the temporary dwelling place of *kami)* were the altars on which offerings were made. The mortars and ritual bowls may well have been for brewing and offering a special "overnight" sake (rice wine) that is mentioned in the *Kojiki* and *Nihongi,* early chronicles of Japan. The protohistorical evidence for sacred mountains shows that *kami* were believed to dwell within the mountains and that they were worshiped at the foot of mountains, probably in connection with fertility (offering of rice wine in connection with the rice harvest, a venerable tradition still honored in Shintō).

The second set of formative elements for Shugendō was the host of beliefs, symbolism, and ritual imported to Japan from the Asian continent. Especially Buddhist—but also some Taoist—notions and techniques of religious realization interacted with the indigenous Japanese phenomenon of sacred mountains to create the peculiar blend of traditions that coalesced into Shugendō. One of the major changes brought about by the imported traditions is that it shifted interest in sacred mountains from the foothills to the peak. The primary influence for this change seems to have been Buddhism, whose practitioners viewed sacred mountains as ideal locations for practicing Buddhist austerities and mastering ritual and magical techniques. Taoist notions were added to the mystique of Japan's sacred mountains, so that they came to be viewed as the dwelling place of "mountain wizards" (*xian* in Chinese, *sen* or *sennin* in Japanese).

The legendary figure En no Ozunu is viewed by Shugendō followers as having established the precedent of practicing Buddhist austerities, overlaid with a Taoist mystique, in Japanese mountains. He is first mentioned in the *Shoku nihongi* record of 699, when he was banished on the charge of misusing his magical powers to control people. This simple notice connects his practice of magic with a sacred mountain, Katsuragi. The ninth-century account of the *Nihon ryōiki* contains the full-blown tradition of En no Ozunu used by Shugendō leaders to glorify their legendary founder: here he is treated as a miraculous figure who exemplified the ideals of Buddhist asceticism and Taoistic mysticism, in the context of sacred mountains. Following these ideals, En no Ozunu withdrew into a mountain cave and practiced the Buddhist magical formula of the Peacock King (Kujaku-ō), thereby gaining magical powers such as the ability to fly through the air. After competition with a jealous *kami,* he became a Daoist wizard and ascended to Heaven. In this account he is called En no Ubasoku (*ubasoku* is the Japanese rendering of the Sanskrit term *upāsaka,* "unordained Buddhist practitioner"); in Shugendō he is honored as En no Gyōja, in other words, En the Ascetic. Legends developed proclaiming that En no Gyōja had opened up the mountains of Yoshino, Ōmine, and Kumano, some of the earliest institutional centers of Shugendō.

There is no substantial record of the life and activities of En no Ozunu, but his tradition of gaining special religious powers by practicing Buddhist and Daoist techniques of religious realization within the precincts of sacred mountains became the precedent for a host of practitioners on many sacred mountains. Especially during the Heian period (794–1185), unorganized wandering ascetics developed such practices. There were various names for these practitioners: *ubasoku* (Skt., *upāsaka*) drew heavily on Buddhism; *hijiri* ("wise man, holy man") and *onmyōji* ("master of *yin* and *yang,*" fortuneteller) utilized especially the techniques derived from Onmyōdō ("the way of *yin* and *yang*"); *genja* ("person of extraordinary religious power") used various techniques. These practitioners conducted austerities and pilgrimages within sacred mountains while practicing specific techniques (such as reciting Buddhist *sutras* and magical formulas) to gain special religious powers; some of them used this power to provide rituals of blessing and healing to laypeople. Gradually some sacred mountains became centers for organizing these practitioners into institutional groups. One of the foremost was Kumano, which from about the eleventh century had become popular as a pilgrimage site for the imperial family and, increasingly, for the nobility and other people as well.

Shugendō was a major channel for unifying and continuing such diverse practices. Prominent sacred mountains became Shugendō centers that attracted large numbers of practitioners and molded their beliefs and practices into distinctive blends of doctrine and action. While revering En no Gyōja as the founder of Shugendō and generally accepting all the diverse elements within this tradition, local centers revered a specific person who founded practice at that mountain (usually called the one who "opened the mountain") and developed a particular pattern of holy sites, symbolism, doctrine, and ritual.

Dynamics and Significance. By about the thirteenth century, Shugendō had become a highly organized tradition with many well-established local variations. Although each center emphasized its own particular blend of teachings and practices, some features were common to most groups. Distinctive forms of dress and ritual tools were arranged in sets of twelve or sixteen items: several characteristic items by which Shugendō practitioners were recognized are the small black cap (of Buddhist origin), the seashell or conch, the priest's staff, and a portable altar. The set of twelve or sixteen items had its own symbolism, as did each aspect and measurement of a particular item. For example, the portable altar, which contained a few Buddhist scriptures, tools, and maybe a small statue (such as Fudō) for worship while the practitioner was on pilgrimage in the mountains, symbolized the cosmos from which the initiate was reborn as a result of his mountain practice.

Such complex symbolism could also occur on a grander scale. For example, worship at Kumano featured a pattern of three sacred mountains viewed as three interrelated cosmic worlds (*mandara,* from Skt. *maṇḍala*): one mountain represented the Womb World Mandala (*taizōkai*), a second mountain represented the Diamond World Mandala (*kongōkai*), and the third represented the higher union of these opposites in a Womb and Diamond World Mandala. In doctrinal terms, the three *maṇḍalas* express the teaching of Esoteric Buddhism of a higher reality; in practical terms, the *maṇḍalas* and Japanese sacred mountains became permanently interrelated, so that the pilgrim who visited these sacred mountains and followed prescribed rules of purity and training was sure to realize the attainment of Buddhahood. Similar patterns of three sacred mountains, with local variations, are found at other Shugendō headquarters throughout Japan.

The most conspicuous religious performances within Shugendō are the ascetic procedures followed by pilgrims during periodic retreats on sacred mountains, tracing a Buddhist pattern of ten stages from hell and beastly existence to heaven and the enlightened status of Buddhahood. The formal pattern of ten stages is common to Buddhism generally, but Shugendō centers gave dramatic turns to such doctrinal teachings. For example, the first stage of hell, which meant weighing one's *karman,* or past (here, evil) conduct, was acted out in some Shugendō traditions by lowering a *yamabushi* over a precipice with a rope, in which position he was required to confess all his sins. This is typical of the Shugendō emphasis on asceticism in concrete and experiential terms. Perhaps the outstanding ritual performance of Shugendō is the fire rite called Saitogōma, which may derive in part from indigenous Japanese fire rites. (The word *goma* is related linguistically to the Indian terms *soma* or *homa.*) The immediate precedent of Saitogōma is the heritage of fire rituals in Esoteric Buddhism, but the Shugendō rite, an outdoor night ceremony performed as the culmination of a period of religious realization, combines the notion of attainment of Buddhahood with the general sense of gaining power from ritual association with sacred mountains.

By participating in successive mountain retreats (often called "peaks"), a Shugendō initiate acquired the ability to minister to laypeople, and the veteran *yamabushi* increased in rank in the local organization. Each center had its own complex rules of training and sets of ranks. As Shugendō became more highly institutionalized, especially from about the thirteenth century, the older tradition of wandering, unorganized practitioners gave way to the establishment of a central headquarters that trained and controlled individual *yamabushi.* These *yamabushi* lost their status as individual wandering ascetics, and although they continued to be viewed as possessing the mystique and power of sacred mountains, they spent more of their time in an itinerant ministry, dispensing charms and blessings from the sacred mountain to common people. There emerged complex networks of parish relationships between Shugendō headquarters and many families in the surrounding area, with itinerant *yamabushi* both carrying blessings from the mountain to the people and also guiding individual believers on pilgrimages to the mountain. As *yamabushi* leaders called *sendatsu* guided their parishioners on the pilgrimage, walking from outlying areas to the sacred mountain, they stayed each night at specially designated lodging houses.

At times the competition between rival Shugendō groups erupted into violence and disputes that had to be settled by secular authorities. In their role as itinerant ministers, sometimes accompanied by wives who assisted in rites of possession and exorcism, *yamabushi* were very influential in spreading religious traditions to the populace; they taught practical versions of Esoteric Buddhism, and disseminated the Kōshin cult (derived in part from Daoist tradition). As they mingled with the people, *yamabushi* came to be associated with the long-nosed mountain goblin called *tengu;* they were also suspected of abusing their right of free travel by acting as military spies. By Tokugawa times (1600–1867), people viewed *yamabushi* more as popular exorcisers than as mountain ascetics, and *yamabushi* frequently appeared in plays as pseudoreligious or comical characters. In short, the institutionalization of the *yamabushi* career led to their popularization at the expense of their ascetic and religious character.

The proscription of Shugendō by the Meiji government in 1872 was due primarily to the desire of the new rulers to "restore" Shintō to a pure state, free from foreign—that is, Buddhist—influence, in order to support the notion of the emperor as head of the nation and its indigenous religion (Shintō). Shugendō, being a patent amalgam of Shintō and Buddhism, was an obvious obstacle to such a program. The moral and financial corruption that had plagued Shugendō since the late Tokugawa period was another possible reason for the proscription, which resulted in the splitting of Shugendō centers into independent Buddhist and Shintō elements. With the enactment of freedom of religion in 1945, however, some Shugendō traditions surviving in Buddhism and Shintō were revived and new Shugendō organizations appeared.

Shugendō is significant as a good example of the emergence of Japanese religion from the interaction of indigenous and imported traditions. Most of the elements that make up Shugendō are found throughout Japanese religious history, even to the present day: indeed, several founders of Japanese new religions have been connected with Shugendō, or have displayed similar patterns of religious behavior, such as retreat on sacred mountains for the practice of austerities and the attainment of sacred power.

SEE ALSO En no Gyōja; Onmyōdō.

BIBLIOGRAPHY

The original research on Shugendō is found in Japanese publications, which include many compilations of original documents, as well as detailed studies of particular Shugendō organizations. Three major studies especially valuable for their synthetic interpretation are Wakamori Tarō's *Shugendōshi kenkyū* (Tokyo, 1943); Hori Ichirō's *Wagakuni minkan shinkōshi no kenkyū*, 2 vols. (Tokyo, 1953); and Miyake Hitoshi's *Shugendō girei no kenkyū* (Tokyo, 1971). Miyake has also written a shorter, convenient overview in *Shugendō: Yamabushi no rekishi to shisō* (Tokyo, 1978). Representative of the resurgence of interest in Shugendō and the publication of many specialized studies is the series "Sangaku shūkyōshi kenkyū sōsho" (Tokyo, 1975–).

Western-language publications on Shugendō are still relatively few. The first modern work on Shugendō is Gaston Renondeau's *Le Shugendō: Histoire, doctrine et rites des anachorètes dits Yamabushi* (Paris, 1965), which emphasizes historical documents and treats Shugendō mainly in terms of doctrinal developments out of Tendai and Shingon. Hartmut O. Rotermund has written two major works on Shugendō. His earlier work, *Die Yamabushi: Aspekte ihres Glaubens, Lebens und ihrer sozialen Funktion im japanischen Mittelalter* (Hamburg, 1968), traces Shugendō as viewed in Japanese literature. His later work, *Pèlerinage aux neuf sommets: Carnet de route d'un religieux itinérant dans le Japon du dix-neuvième siècle* (Paris, 1983), is a detailed study of the travels and experiences of one *yamabushi* through his writings. In *A Religious Study of the Mount Haguro Sect of Shugendō: An Example of Japanese Mountain Religion* (Tokyo, 1970) I have utilized my fieldwork with a contemporary Shugendō group to interpret its religious worldview.

New Sources

Hitoshi, Miyake. *Shugendo: Essays on the Structure of Japanese Folk Religion.* Edited by H. Byron Earhart. Ann Arbor, 2001.

H. BYRON EARHART (1987)
Revised Bibliography

SHUGS LDAN (SHUGDEN).

In modern times, Tibetan Buddhism, and the Dge lugs (Geluk) school in particular, has been agitated by an intense dispute concerning a controversial deity, Rdo rje shugs ldan (Dorje Shugden). Some of the questions raised by this dispute are common to many Buddhist traditions, where the integration of local deities within a normative Buddhist framework is often delicate. This dispute also raises more particular questions concerning competing conceptions of the Dge lugs tradition.

Buddhists understand themselves to be bound by taking refuge in the Buddha, *dharma*, and *saṃgha*. As such they are not supposed to worship other deities. But this restriction creates difficulties—particularly, but not only, for those involved in the world. What are they to do with the deities who have, they believe, a large influence on their welfare, health, and prosperity? The standard answer has been that Buddhists may propitiate these lesser mundane deities (asking them respectfully for help) but may not entrust them with their long-term spiritual welfare, an attitude they can adopt only toward supramundane beings, buddhas, *bodhisattvas*, or *arhats*. This normative line, however, is often blurred in practice, where respectful propitiation shades into worship. As a result some of the most popular mundane deities have tended to rise toward the supramundane status, at times leading to protracted conflicts.

Tibetan Buddhism has had to deal extensively with such problems. One of the ways various deities (often but not always the indigenous non-Buddhist gods and goddesses) have been integrated in the Tibetan Buddhist pantheon is through the notion of *dharma* protector, a deity who has taken an oath to protect the Buddhist teachings. This type of deity, already known in India, has often been used in Tibet to integrate local deities into the Buddhist pantheon. Based on the model of Padmasamabhava's activities, many of the local gods are understood to be bound by an oath to protect the *dharma* and are propitiated as such. But this activity has also tended to elevate the status of these gods, leading to controversies. This scenario is quite clear in the case of Shugs ldan.

Shugs ldan's Dge lugs followers claim that their tradition goes back to a rather obscure and bloody episode of Tibetan history, the violent death of Grags pa rgyal mtshan (Drakba Gyeltsen; 1618–1655), an important Dge lugs lama rival of the fifth Dalai Lama (1617–1682). Because of his premature death, Grags pa rgyal mtshan is said to have transformed into a wrathful spirit bent on the protection of the doctrinal purity of the Dge lugs tradition. He is also said to have been particularly irked at the Dge lugs lamas, such as the fifth Dalai Lama, who studied and practiced the teachings of other traditions. It is even suggested that the deaths of several of these less orthodox lamas can be attributed to this spirit.

As often occurs, however, historical realities are somewhat different. It was only during the early part of the twentieth century that the systematic connection between Shugs ldan and Grags pa rgyal mtshan appears to have been clearly established. This seems to have been due to Pabongka (1878–1941), a charismatic teacher who spearheaded a revival movement within the Dge lugs tradition, a movement in part motivated by the success of the nonsectarian revival among the other schools. The connection with Grags pa rgyal mtshan seems to have been a way for Pabongka to justify the adoption of Shugs ldan, originally a non-Dge lugs deity, as the main protector of his movement. In this way Pabongka created a new understanding of the Dge lugs tradition focused on three elements: Vajrayogini as the main meditational deity, Shugs ldan as the protector, and Pabongka as the *gūru.* Pabongka's vision was also strongly exclusivist. Not only was the Dge lugs tradition considered supreme, its followers were warned of dire consequences in case they had any interest in other traditions. Shugs ldan would take care of them, as illustrated by the story of several eclectic Dge lugs lamas who died prematurely at Shugs ldan's hands.

Shugs ldan appears to have originally been a local deity associated with a small pond in Dol, an area near the junction of the Zangbo and Yarlung Valleys. This deity seems to have been adopted first by the Sagya tradition, where he was considered a minor and yet powerful protector who could be dangerous. He appeared in the Dge lugs tradition as early as the first half of the eighteenth century, when he was propitiated by several important lamas, but they do not seem to have made any connection with Grags pa rgyal mtshan. Moreover, there was no claim for Shugs ldan to be anything but a minor worldly protector used for his power to help in matters of wealth, disease, and protection from spirits. This changed with Pabongka, who made him into one of the main protectors of the tradition. Pabongka's disciple Trijang (1901–1983), the fourteenth Dalai Lama's charismatic teacher, stressed this practice among his disciples and pushed the glorification of Shugs ldan even further, insisting that this deity is ultimately a fully enlightened buddha who merely appears as a mundane deity.

The novelty of this deity and his exclusive character could not but irritate some Dge lugs teachers, particularly the Dalai Lamas, who have often presented their rule as inclusive of other schools. There was already some tension between Pabongka and the thirteenth Dalai Lama, but the conflict came to the fore only in the 1970s, when the fourteenth Dalai Lama started to make pronouncements against this deity and the accompanying practice. The Dalai Lama seems to have been particularly irritated by a small book about Shugs ldan published by Dzemay, a learned Dge lugs lama. But the main source of opposition seems to have been the Dalai Lama's perception that the Shugs ldan practice undermined the ritual basis legitimizing his rule.

The Dalai Lama institution is not just political. It also rests on an elaborate ritual system that is not limited to Dge lugs practices but includes the deities of other schools, particularly those associated with the early Tibetan Empire. Hence, this ritual system has close ties with the Rnying ma (Nyingma), the Buddhist school most closely associated with the early Empire. This link is particularly visible in the role played in this ritual system by Padmasambhava and by Dorje drakden (Nechung), a Tibetan god who is said to protect the Dalai Lama and his government. The propitiation of Shugs ldan threatened this eclectic system. By presenting Shugs ldan as an exclusive deity in charge of visiting retribution upon those Dge lugs pa who have adopted practices from other traditions, the cult of Shugs ldan undermines the ritual system underlying the Dalai Lama institution as conceived by the present incumbent (the fourteenth Dalai Lama).

Shugs ldan's followers would protest that their practice is primarily not directed at anyone in particular but stems from their religious commitments, particularly their devotion to their teachers Pabongka and Trijang. Nevertheless, the threatening tone of this tradition and its divisiveness are hard to ignore.

BIBLIOGRAPHY

Dreyfus, Georges. "The Shuk-den Affair: Origins of a Controversy." *Journal of the International Association of Buddhist Studies* 21, no. 2 (1998): 227–270.

Mumford, Stan. *Himalayan Dialogue.* Madison, Wis., 1989.

Nebesky-Wojkowitz, René de. *Oracles and Demons of Tibet.* The Hague, 1956.

GEORGES DREYFUS (2005)

SHUN SEE YAO AND SHUN

SHUNNING SEE EXCOMMUNICATION; EXPULSION

SIBERIAN RELIGIONS SEE ARCTIC RELIGIONS; PREHISTORIC RELIGIONS, *ARTICLE ON* THE EURASIAN STEPPES AND INNER ASIA; SHAMANISM, *ARTICLE ON* SIBERIAN AND INNER ASIAN SHAMANISM; SOUTHERN SIBERIAN RELIGIONS

SIBYLLINE ORACLES. In Greek tradition (accepted by the Romans not later than the fourth century BCE and by the Jews not later than the second) a sibyl is an old woman who utters ecstatic predictions of woe. The etymology of the name is unknown. In Greece the earliest mention of the term is found in the writings of the philosopher Heraclitus about

500 BCE, though the figure of the sibyl and perhaps some kind of oracles attributed to her were probably known from the eighth century BCE on. In the following years the tradition of sibylline oracles became well established (and was caricatured by Aristophanes in late-fifth-century BCE Athens).

The sibyls were thought to wander through the world and to attain an extraordinary age—as much as a thousand years. But Delphi, Samos, Erythrae in Ionia, Marpessus in Troas, and Cumae and Tibur in Italy each had its own resident sibyl. Other individual sibyls were known respectively as Persian, Chaldean, Phrygian, and Egyptian, and there were less-famous sibyls elsewhere. According to the Christian apologist Lactantius, the Roman Varro (first century BCE) gives a list of the ten aforementioned sibyls, which became the canon in the Middle Ages, enlarged to twelve in the Renaissance. The first mention of the Hebrew Sibyl in classical sources is in Pausanias (10.12.9) in the second century CE, but such a figure was associated with oracles long before then. Like other sibyls, she had a personal name, which Pausanias gives as Sabba (a variant is Sambethe). She is referred to in extant oracles as a pagan daughter-in-law of Noah.

Places in which sibyls were supposed to deliver their oracles, such as the cave in Cumae, were revered and visited by pilgrims. Few people, however, claimed to have seen a living sibyl. In Petronius's *Satyricon* (chap. 48), Trimalchio does, but he is not meant to be believed. In reality people were primarily acquainted with collections of ancient (or allegedly ancient) oracles that were attributed to individual sibyls and that seemed to be relevant or could be applied to given situations. In fact the origin of the Greek figure of the sibyl is more literary than real, based on the influence of the oriental tradition of ecstatic prophecy intermingled with the old epic characters of inspired women, such as Cassandra (a kind of prototype of the sibyls).

The oracles were written in Greek hexameters, and their content was often protected by acrostics. Latin sibylline oracles appear only late (for instance, in Procopius, concerning the Goths of the sixth century CE). The oracles of the Cumaean Sibyl were supposed to have been originally inscribed on palm leaves.

THE NATURE OF SIBYLLINE INSPIRATION. In Greece and Rome inspired (or natural) prophecy was considered the attribute of women, whereas technical and induced divination was a man's territory. Of course both were considered of divine origin (either from the god Apollo or the God of Jews or Christians), but the division is an interesting testimony of the assessment of gender roles.

Not all inspired women were reducible to a unique type, but sometimes the differences were blurred. So the first testimony of the performance of the sibyl (Heraclitus) describes her in a clear state of possession and domination by the god, uttering prophecies "with maddened mouth" in a rough and not embellished way (as opposed to elaborated inspired poetry). However, one must differentiate three types of inspired women: the Pythia, the sibyl, and other heroines whose characteristics are assimilated to the two first. The Pythia (and generally speaking all the priests and priestesses of Apollonean sanctuaries), as a mortal, is supposed to utter divine messages and be a mere voice of the god, responding to questions concerning the future. The sibyl (who sometimes introduces herself as half divine, half mortal) has a universal and omnitemporal knowledge, historical as well as eschatological, though she speaks as urged by divine pressure and even violence. Paradoxically, despite the frequent allusion to a verbal message, these prophecies are always transmitted as written poetical texts. As for the mantic heroines, they share some traits with the two former but are often amplified or even overdone.

There is no precise description of the way the sibylline inspiration was conceived. The discussions in Plutarch's Pythian dialogues concerning the inspiration of the Delphic prophetess are only partially appropriate for the sibylline predictions because of the different kind of prophetic performance. The most interesting coincidence would be the definition of the sibyl's role as an instrument (Greek, *organon*) of Apollo and later of the God of Jews and Christians. As noted above, in some ancient descriptions the sibyl is assimilated to some mythical figures, Daphne, Manto, Cassandra, who are linked to Apollo and who suffered the violence of the god for having refused his sexual pursuits. In all theses cases the punishment is a transformation that implies either aphasia or the incredibility of the prophecies or, conversely, the transformation into a mere voice after her physical extinction. In the collection of *Sibylline Oracles* the sibyl complains of being incessantly urged by God to utter prophecies. Later, in the most genuinely Christian tradition, she is assimilated to the biblical prophets, and the theme of divine violence disappears.

HISTORY OF THE ORACULAR TEXTS. The Romans claimed to have received a partial collection of the prophecies of the Cumaean Sibyl under one of the two Tarquinian kings in the sixth century BCE. What is certain is that a collection of such books (the so-called *Libri sibyllini*) existed in Rome and was preserved in the temple of Jupiter Capitolinus during the Republic. These books were entrusted to a special priestly commission, composed first of two, then of ten, then of fifteen members, who could consult them only when ordered to do so by the senate in times of recognized emergency. When the temple of Jupiter burned in 83 BCE, the Sibylline Books were destroyed and were ultimately replaced by a new collection. Augustus transferred these oracles to the newly built temple of Apollo on the Palatine and ordered a severe pruning of the texts.

Rome seems to have been unique in making the sibylline oracles a monopoly of the state. However, though the text of these *Libri* is not known exactly, the references given by the sources indicate that they were mostly prescriptions regarding cultic practices and expiations in time of crisis and not properly prophecies of the kind known from other texts.

Only the oldest examples cited by the historians contain a formulation similar to the ordinary sibylline prophecies. Most probably then the legend of the arrival of these books in Rome in the time of the Tarquinian kings, despite its (seemingly) late and fictitious nature, points to an influence in origin of the Greek tradition (via the contacts with the Greek settlers) but modified and amplified by important Etruscan ritual elements and finally mixed with their own Roman religious traditions and institutions.

Elsewhere sibylline books seem to have circulated openly. Being authoritative everywhere, the sibylline texts were of course controversial and often suspected to be forgeries. Unfortunately only scattered examples of pagan sibylline oracles exist. The most famous are perhaps those preserved by Phlegon of Tralles (early second century CE). One seems to belong to 125 BCE, another perhaps to Sulla's time, and a third certainly refers to the celebration of the Secular Games under Augustus, though it may incorporate older texts. Roman tradition attributes, perhaps correctly, to sibylline oracles the initiative for building the first temple to Ceres, Liber, and Libera in Rome, for introducing the cult of Asklepios from Epidaurus, for the human sacrifices of 226 BCE, for the consultation of Apollo at Delphi in 216 BCE, and for the introduction of the cult of Magna Mater in 205 BCE. In Rome there seems to have been steady collaboration between Apollo and the Cumaean Sibyl; elsewhere Apollonian divination and sibylline prophecy did not always agree.

A Roman law against reading Sibylline Books is mentioned in an obscure context by Justin Martyr in his first *Apology* (44.12) from the middle of the second century CE. The sibylline texts remained authoritative in Rome until the fourth century CE, when they were still consulted by Julian. According to the contemporary account of Rutilius Namatianus, these texts were destroyed by Stilicho not later than 408 CE. But the authority of Vergil, who had given such prominence to the Cumaean Sibyl in his fourth *Eclogue* and in the *Aeneid*, saved the prestige of the sibyls among the Christians, as one can clearly see in the writings of Lactantius, Eusebius, and Emperor Constantine. The Christians found in Vergil and in other sibylline texts prophecies of the annunciation of Christ. Independently of the Christians, and in fact before Christianity existed, the Jews produced sibylline texts that purported to convey divine expectations and reactions from a Jewish point of view and invited recognition of the true God. The Christians accepted these Jewish texts, occasionally interpolated them, and added to them other texts of unequivocally Christian character. The collection of Sibylline Books that has reached survived is thus of mixed Jewish and Christian authorship, but the extant manuscripts are all of Christian origin. Collectively they are known as the *Sibylline Oracles.*

These manuscripts can be roughly divided into two groups. Some, published as early as the sixteenth century, contain the first eight books. Others, made known chiefly by Cardinal Angelo Mai in the early nineteenth century, include books numbered from nine to fourteen, but books nine and ten contain material already included in the first eight books, whereas books eleven to fourteen add new material. In modern editions, beginning with that by Charles Alexandre (1841–1856), the two series are conflated, and therefore books nine and ten are not present. Books three, four, and five were already known in some form to Clement of Alexandria; books six, seven, and eight were known to Lactantius in about 300 CE. Some Christian fragments of sibylline oracles are to be found outside the present collection in quotations by ancient writers.

CONTENT OF THE SIBYLLINE ORACLES. As is evident from Vergil's reference to the "final age" in his fourth *Eclogue,* the division of world history into periods was a feature of pagan sibylline prophecies. This is confirmed by a pagan literary test, Lycophron's *Alexandra* (third or second century BCE), which is influenced by pagan sibylline texts. The authors of the Jewish and Christian Sibylline Books developed the universal aspect that distinguished them. The influence of the *Book of Daniel* is unmistakable. Like the *Book of Daniel,* the sibylline authors embraced the theory of the four monarchies. They combined with it the division of history into ten "generations." The note of hostility toward Rome (and toward the Hellenistic rulers as long as they existed) is quite clear but not ubiquitous. As such, these texts belong to the resistance literature of the Near East against foreign domination. As in the *Book of Revelation,* the return of Nero at the head of the Parthian army figures prominently in books four, five, and eight. The fate of people after death is reflected in the Christian texts of books two, seven, and eight but not in the Jewish texts. Given the poor knowledge of the Greek-speaking Jews in the Diaspora after the first century CE, these sibylline oracles are perhaps altogether more important for the history of the Jewish Diaspora than for early Christianity.

The order in which the *Sibyllin Oracles* have been preserved was established by a late compiler, and therefore it does not fit the chronology of each book. The oldest core of the collection is in book three, roughly dated between 163 and 145 (or 140) BCE, but it was reworked and enlarged after 31 BCE (and perhaps also in the first century CE).

The first two books (not clearly separated in the manuscripts) are Jewish in origin but were elaborated and reworked by Christians. The present text assumes the fall of Jerusalem in 70 CE, and its curious interest in Phrygia may point to its place of origin. A Christian origin has been proposed for these books, because they are not mentioned before the speech attributed to Emperor Constantine entitled *Oratio ad sanctorum coetum.* Nevertheless a Jewish origin for some parts is unquestionable. Their position in the whole collection is based on the fact that book one describes the creation of the world and the succession of human generations, whereas book two has more apocalyptic and eschatological elements.

Book three, perhaps the most important historically, contains texts of ideological orientations dating from various periods. Lines 1–96 seem to be later than Cleopatra and the Battle of Actium (31 BCE) and perhaps even later than Nero; lines 350–380 seem to refer to anti-Roman movements of the first century BCE; and lines 466–469 seem to refer to the era of Sulla. The main corpus is a messianic prophecy involving Jews and Greeks with special attention given to Egypt. Three allusions to a seventh king of Egypt (ll. 193, 318, 608) in all likelihood refer to Ptolemy Philometor (180–145 BCE). There is a reference to the *Book of Daniel* in line 396, but its implications are doubtful. In lines 194–195 there is a reference to the resurgence of the Jews after some catastrophe, possibly the reign of Antiochus IV. In lines 388–400 and following a strange oracle about a king of Asia presents problems. Finally, in lines 653–656 and following there is a prophecy about a savior from the East or from the sun. It is by no means obvious that this king should be identified with the seventh king of Egypt. The book as a whole, though at certain points strongly anti-Roman and anti-Macedonian, is not radical in its hostility and seems to hope for and to wish to foster good relations between Jews and Egyptian Greeks.

Book four seems to be based on pagan sibylline oracles of the end of the fourth century BCE. The text (ll. 49–101) knows of four empires and ten generations and identifies the tenth generation and the fourth empire with Macedon. This part, it has been suggested, belonged to an ancient chronological level (prior to the collection), perhaps the fourth century BCE. The Jewish elaboration presupposes the rise of Rome and the end of the Temple of Jerusalem, the legend of Nero's flight to the Parthians, and the eruption of Vesuvius in 79 CE. It insists on baptism as a prerequisite of salvation and on the rejection of the Temple cult. This points to some Jewish sectarian groups, not necessarily to a Judeo-Christian sect.

Book five, which has a Christian allusion in lines 256–259, knows of the destruction of the Temple and the legend of Nero, and Hadrian is still favorable to the Jews. A date before 132 CE seems probable, but line 51, with its reference to Marcus Aurelius, must be treated as a later interpolation. The text is strongly hostile to Rome and Egypt and contains a mysterious allusion to a temple in Egypt destroyed by the Ethiopians (ll. 501 and following).

Book six is a short Christian text known to Lactantius in the form of a hymn. Book seven is Christian in its present form, with possible but puzzling Jewish, Gnostic, and even Neoplatonic traits. Book eight seems to be a combination of Jewish and Christian texts with a puzzling reference to an eschatological queen (l. 194) in the Jewish section (ll. 1–216), which is hostile to Rome and was probably written before 195 CE. The Christian part is, at any rate, earlier than 300 CE. It includes a famous acrostic (ll. 217–243, with a later addition in ll. 244–250), whose Latin translation is frequently quoted by Christian authors and was adopted into liturgical texts of the Middle Ages.

Books eleven through fourteen, taken together, are an apocalyptic outline of world history since the Flood. Book eleven is Jewish and may not be much later than Vergil's death in 19 CE, alluded to in line 171. Lines 160–161, however, seem to point to a later date and are perhaps interpolations. It is not an anti-Roman book. Moreover the author seems to be familiar with the Augustan laudatory ideology. Book twelve is Jewish with Christian interpolations and was written not long after 235 CE (though it could also have been composed with the following book). It reflects a time and milieu (Egypt) in which Jews were inclined to accept the Roman Empire. Book thirteen is Jewish with Christian interpolations, is dated around 265 CE, and contains propaganda for Odenathus of Palmyra. Both books twelve and thirteen probably circulated independently, alongside book eleven, as a kind of imperial chronicle. Book fourteen, a confused text of Jewish origin that awaits satisfactory interpretation, seems to end with the Arab conquest of Alexandria and with Jewish collaboration in it in the middle of the seventh century CE. If this is correct, it shows Jews composing sibylline texts in Greek at a late date.

Christians maintained an interest in sibylline oracles and composed new ones throughout the Middle Ages. The queen of Sheba was sometimes identified with the sibyl Sabba. The Tiburtine Sibyl became especially popular both in the West and in the East. Some of her texts, though now in medieval redactions, probably go back to the fourth century CE. As late as the thirteenth century Thomas of Celano alludes to her in his *Dies irae*.

SEE ALSO Oracles.

BIBLIOGRAPHY

There is no satisfactory modern collection of the scattered pagan sibylline texts, although Hermann Diels's *Sibyllinische Blätter* (Berlin, 1890) can still be profitably consulted. The standard texts of the Jewish-Christian books are Charles Alexandre's *Oracula sibyllina,* 2 vols. (Paris, 1841–1856; 2d ed., Paris, 1869, which does not replace the first); Aloisius Rzach's *Oracula sibyllina* (Vienna, 1891); and Johannes Geffcken's *Die Oracula sibyllina* (Leipzig, Germany, 1902). The text of books 1–11 with a German translation and some parallel texts are in Alfons Kurfess, ed. and trans., *Sibyllinische Weissagungen* (Munich, 1951); and Jörg-Dieter Gauger, *Sibyllinische Weissagungen* (Düsseldorf and Zürich, 1998), which includes the most important texts illustrating the Nachleben of these oracles and a useful introduction and commentary. David S. Potter, *Prophecy and History in the Crisis of the Roman Empire* (Oxford, U.K., 1990), is a thorough study of book 13.

An English translation is James H. Charlesworth, ed., *The Old Testament Pseudepigrapha,* vol. 1, *Apocalyptic Literature and Testaments* (Garden City, N.Y., 1983), pp. 317–472. Paolo Sacchi, ed., *Apocrifi dell'Antico Testamento,* vol. 3, includes an annotated translation of books 3, 4, and 5 by Liliana Rosso Ubigli (Brescia, Italy, 1999), pp. 383–535. Alejandro Díez Macho, ed., *Apócrifos del Antiguo Testamento,* vol. 3, *Oráculos Sibilinos* (Madrid, 2002), pp. 329–612, includes a translation of the *Sibylline Oracles* by Emilio Suárez de la Torre and an exhaustive introduction. A good annotated French translation of some parts of the Christian books is Jean-Michel Roessli, "Les Oracles Sibyllins," in *Écrits apochryphes chrétiens* (Paris, 2004).

The following works, listed in chronological order, include discussions of both pagan and Jewish-Christian texts: Ernst Sackur, *Sybillinische Texte und Forschungen Pseudomethodius* (Halle, Germany, 1898; reprint, Turin, Italy, 1963); Johannes Geffcken, *Komposition und Entstehungszeit der Oracula Sibyllina* (Leipzig, Germany, 1902); Aloisius Rzach, "Sibyllen" and "Sibyllinische Orakel," in *Real-encyclopädie der classischen Altertumswissenschaft,* vol. 2A, cols. 2073–2183 (Stuttgart, Germany, 1923); Wilhelm Hoffmann, *Wandel und Herkunft der sibyllinischen Bücher in Rom* (Leipzig, Germany, 1933); Harald Fuchs, *Der geistige Widerstand gegen Rom in der antiken Welt* (Berlin, 1938); Henri Jeanmaire, *La sibylle et le retour de l'âge d'or* (Paris, 1939); Aurelio Peretti, *La sibilla babilonese nella propaganda ellenistica* (Florence, 1943); Samuel Kennedy Eddy, *The King Is Dead* (Lincoln, Nebr., 1961); Raymond Bloch, "L'origine des livres sibyllins à Rome," *Neue Beiträge zur Geschichte der Alten Welt* 11 (1965): 281–292; Paul J. Alexander, *The Oracle of Baalbek: The Tiburtine Sibyl in Greek Dress* (Washington, D.C., 1967); Valentin Nikiprowetzky, *La troisième sibylle* (Paris, 1970); Valentin Nikiprowetzky, "Ré-flexions sur quelques problèmes du quatrième et du cinquième livre," *HUCA* 43 (1972): 29–76; John J. Collins, *The Sibylline Oracles of Egyptian Judaism* (Missoula, Mont., 1974); John J. Collins, "The Place of the Fourth Sibyl in the Development of the Jewish Sibyllina," *Journal of Jewish Studies* 25 (Winter 1974): 365–380; Arnaldo Momigliano, "La portata storica dei vaticini sul Settimo Re nel Terzo Libro degli Oracoli Sibillini" (1975), in *Sesto Contributo,* vol. 2 (Rome, 1980), pp. 551–559; Paul J. Alexander, "The Diffusion of Byzantine Apocalypses in the Medieval West and the Beginnings of Joachimism," in *Prophecy and Millenarianism,* edited by Ann Williams (Essex, U.K., 1980), pp. 53–106; John J. Collins, *Between Athens and Jerusalem* (New York, 1983), pp. 61–72, 148–155; Luisa Breglia Pulci Doria, *Oracoli Sibillini tra rituali e propaganda* (Naples, Italy, 1983); John J. Collins, "The Sibylline Oracles," in *Jewish Writings of the Second Temple Period,* edited by Michael E. Stone (Assen, Netherlands, 1984), pp. 357–381; John R. Bartlett, *Jews in the Hellenistic World* (Cambridge, U.K., 1985), pp. 35–55; Emil Schürer, *A History of the Jewish People in the Age of Jesus Christ,* vol. 3.1 (Edinburgh, U.K., 1986), pp. 618–653; Nazarena Valenza Mele, "Hera ed Apollo a Cuma e la mantica sibillina," *Rivista dell'Istituto Nazionale d'Archeologia e Storia dell'Arte,* ser. 3, 14–15 (1991–1992): 5–72; Jesús-María Nieto Ibáñez, *El hexámetro de los Oráculos Sibilinos* (Amsterdam, 1992); David S. Potter, *Prophets and Emperors* (Cambridge, Mass., and London, 1994); Emilio Suárez de la Torre, "Sibylles, mantique inspirée et collections oraculaires," *Kernos* 7 (1994): 179–205; John J. Collins, *Seers, Sibyls, and Sages in Hellenistic-Roman Judaism* (Leiden, Netherlands, 1997); Ileana Chirassi Colombo and Tullio Seppilli, eds., *Sibille e Linguaggio Oracolare: Mito, Storia, Tradizione* (Pisa, Italy, 1998); Emilio Suárez de la Torre, "La sibila de Eritras: análisis de fuentes hasta el siglo II d. C.," in *Epieikeia: Homenaje al Profesor Jesús Lens Tuero* (Granada, 2000), pp. 439–467; Giulia Sfameni Gasparro, "La sibilla, voce del dio per pagani, ebrei e cristiani: un modulo profetico al crocevia delle fedi," in *Oracoli Profeti Sibille: Rivelazione e salvezza nel mondo antico* (Rome, 2002), pp. 61–112; Jean-Michel Roessli, "Augustin, les sibylles et les *Oracles Sibyllins,*" in *Augustinus Afer: Saint Augustin: africanité et universalité,* edited by Pierre-Yves Fux, Jean-Michel Roessli, Otto Wermelinger (Fribourg, Switzerland, 2003), pp. 263–286; Mariangela Monaca, *La Sibilla a Roma: I Libri Sibillini tra religione e politica* (Cosenza, Italy, 2004); Monique Bouquet and Françoise Morzadec, *La Sibylle: Parole et représentation* (Rennes, France, 2004).

Arnaldo Momigliano (1987)
Emilio Suárez de la Torre (2005)

SIDDHĀRTHA See BUDDHA

SIDDHAS See MAHĀSIDDHAS

SIDDUR AND MAḤZOR.

The *siddur* and the *maḥzor* (pl., *siddurim* and *maḥzorim*) are the prayer books used in Jewish public worship. The term *siddur* ("order"; from the Hebrew root *sdr,* "order, arrange") signifies an order of prayer and generally denotes weekday and Sabbath liturgy. The term *maḥzor* ("cycle"; from the root *ḥzr,* "return, come around again") denotes the annual cycle of prayer for holidays that come but once a year; the *maḥzor* is therefore usually subdivided nowadays into separate volumes for each holiday: that is, the *maḥzor* for Passover, Sukkot, or Shavuʿot (the Pilgrimage Festivals) or for Roʾsh ha-Shanah or Yom Kippur (the Days of Awe, or High Holy Days). Surprisingly, the determination of a standardized text for these volumes is a relatively late phenomenon and, in fact, is still open to editorial discretion. Even though there now exists authorized wording for all standard prayers, and even though one can anticipate generally what basic prayers each *siddur* or *maḥzor* will contain, many *siddurim* published today also contain selections drawn from the *maḥzor,* and different editions vie with each other to be more comprehensive.

History. No comprehensive textual standardization seems to predate the ninth century. Until then, and particularly before the promulgation of the Mishnah (c. 200 CE), the very nature of early rabbinic liturgy militated against prescribed texts for prayer, in that a single authorized set of fixed wording was avoided. Instead, prayer leaders were given a certain order of mandated themes that they were encouraged to express creatively as worship proceeded; they thus combined the complementary principles of structural fixity (*qevaʿ*) and linguistic spontaneity (*kavvanah*). After the close of the tannaitic era (c. 200), there are isolated individual orders of prayer (called *seder tefillot*), and the very act of saying prayers is often described by the verb meaning "to order" them, as if an official "order," or *siddur,* were in existence; but except for specific prayers attributed to the personal taste of individual rabbis, there is evidence against the existence of authoritative, generally accepted, inalterable sets of wording such as are found in the *siddur* or *maḥzor* of today.

This principle of freedom within structure is particularly evident in the prayers of Palestinian Jewry where it continued in force even beyond the amoraic (or Talmudic) age (after c. 500), at least until that community's partial destruction by the Crusades, at which time Palestinian spiritual independence was interrupted. True, there are Palestinian orders of service from that time with their own typical linguistic preferences, but these are marked by enormous poetic variation, both within the basic prayers themselves and in the insertions or additions for special occasions.

Babylonian Jewry, on the other hand, favored ever-increasing linguistic fixity, particularly after the middle of the eighth century, under the leadership of its newest scholarly elite, the geonim. In their attempt to standardize worldwide Jewish practice, these authorities initiated the practice of sending *responsa* to outlying Jewish communities, in which they described their own liturgical preferences and declared them as universally binding. By the middle of the eleventh century, they had penned at least two complete orders of prayer, and it is from these compositions (especially the first one) that today's *siddur* and *maḥzor* eventually evolved. Later sources mention a third prayer book, compiled by H'ai Gaon (d. 1038), but it has not survived.

The first of these comprehensive compendiums of prayer, and the most influential to this day, is *Seder Rav Amram,* sent by Amram Gaon (d. 871) to a Jewish community in Spain, whence it circulated widely to become the model for all western European rites. In content, it is Amram's prescribed wording for a comprehensive set of prayers—both *siddur* and *maḥzor* combined—along with detailed legal instructions regarding how worship is to proceed. Extant manuscripts of *Seder Rav Amram* are somewhat undependable with regard to the text of the prayers, which scribes did not always copy accurately, but the accompanying legal commentary is preserved faithfully enough to ascertain that Amram relied on Babylonian precedent and was motivated, in fact, by the desire to universalize its practice at the expense of Palestinian alternatives that were vying for cultural influence in newly established Jewish settlements of North Africa and western Europe. So Amram sought to demonstrate a clear chain of authority going back to the Babylonian Talmud, via Geonic interpreters, such as his predecessor in office, Natronai (d. 858), who had tried to accomplish the same goal by recording a list of daily blessings incumbent on every Jew, and whose list Amram now borrowed for inclusion in his *Seder.*

The second Geonic prayer book is *Siddur Saʿadyah,* the work of Saʿadyah Gaon (d. 942). In an introduction thereto, Saʿadyah states his intention: to help the average worshiper differentiate the proper from the improper in the baffling array of liturgical customs then extant. Like *Seder Rav Amram, Siddur Saʿadyah* is comprehensive, being at once both *siddur* and *maḥzor.* But it differs from *Seder Rav Amram* in at least five ways: (1) it contains only short, uncomplicated instructions on the conduct of worship, rather than lengthy excurses; (2) these are recorded in Arabic, not Aramaic; (3) Saʿadyah incorporates Palestinian material; (4) he favors *piyyuṭim* (poetic insertions in the standard body of prayers); and (5) in general, he displays a mastery of the Islamic liturgical aesthetic typical of his day, particularly in his preference for logical order, grammatical purity, linguistic precision rooted in scripture, and philosophy (see his two *baashot,* petitions, following the Tefillah, for example).

By the tenth century, the center of the Jewish world had shifted to western Europe. There, each nascent community proceeded to define its own liturgical identity, paying special heed to Amram's paradigmatic *Seder,* but in some cases showing familiarity also with *Siddur Saʿadyah* or other independent Geonic precedents, and also with decisions reached by earlier authorities in North Africa (especially in Kairouan) and in Palestine itself. Thus every community developed its own liturgical rite, which amounted in each case to a local modification of Geonic prototype, in which Amram's prayer book predominated. All such European variations eventually became classified as rites common either to Ashkenaz (Franco-Germany) or to Sefarad (the Iberian Peninsula), but in either case, the resulting liturgical corpus did not yet differentiate its material calendrically, so that daily, Sabbath, and holy day prayers were all combined indiscriminately in one volume called variously *maḥzor* or *siddur* (or even *seder,* as in *Seder Rav Amram*). By the fourteenth century, however, the liturgy had expanded to the point where its unmanageable bulk resulted in a subdivision into several works. In Ashkenaz, these were the *siddur,* for daily and Sabbath prayers; the *maḥzor,* for holiday liturgy; and a further subdivision of the *maḥzor,* which more and more frequently appeared as a separate work, the Haggadah, a Passover Eve home devotional "order," or *seder.*

By the 1520s both the *siddur* and the *maḥzor* appeared in printed form, with the result that mass-produced standardized texts began to whittle away at long-standing local points of diversity. These texts, however, were often the work of printers whose competence lay in the new technology and its business-related affairs, not in rabbinic scholarship relevant to the rigorous reproduction of authentic texts. Consequently, texts from the seventeenth to the nineteenth century featured efforts to emend their errors. Especially noteworthy in this regard is Shabbetai Sofer, a prominent Polish grammarian and qabbalist, who (from 1613 to 1618) attempted to fix a scientifically accurate rite. Wolf Heidenheim (1757–1832) extended his critical spirit into the modern age by printing scientifically annotated editions; and in 1868, Heidenheim's disciple, Seligman Baer, summarized critical opinion up to his time in *Seder ʿavodat Yisraʾel.*

By then, the Sephardic rite had been carried throughout the Mediterranean, Holland, England, and even the New World by Spanish émigrés and their descendants, where it evolved further according to liturgical canons of these lands. The Ashkenazic rite was carried eastward across northern Europe to Poland and Russia, and then to North America where it now predominates. Qabbalists after the sixteenth century and their spiritual descendants, Polish Ḥasidim, combined the two rites.

In the 1800s, liturgical reform based on theological, academic, political, and aesthetic considerations was the norm for much of European Jewry, particularly in Germany, but increasingly also in America. The most significant works, perhaps, are the 1819 *Hamburg Prayer Book,* which first introduced comprehensive and theologically based liturgical reform to Germany, and David Einhorn's *ʿOlat tamid* (1858), which became the model for the Reform movement in the United States and Canada, where a standardized *Union Prayer Book* has existed since 1894/5.

Alongside those of the Reform movement, the most numerically significant liberal prayer books in America are those of the Conservative movement. The original series emerged in the 1940s as the Conservative movement sought to delineate its own ideological specificity. But the appearance of its *Maḥzor for Rosh Hashanah and Yom Kippur* in 1972 heralded a major liturgical renaissance, in which all Jewish communities now find themselves, and the older books are being replaced.

Since the work of Leopold Zunz (1794–1886), prayer books have been studied according to geographic provenance, so that rites are assumed to correlate with the rise and fall of Jewish communities around the world. Actually, the determining factor is not geographic, but social, distance; prayer books today reflect ideological positioning of specific Jewish groups and their consequent social distance from each other. Prayer book preference derives from a prior communal self-definition—as British Reform, or Hasidic (according to this or that sect), or American Conservative, and so on. A few years after publication of the American Conservative movement's new *maḥzor* in 1972, a new Reform *siddur, Gates of Prayer,* appeared in 1975, and its companion *maḥzor, Gates of Repentance,* was published in 1978. These were patterned to some extent after *Service of the Heart* (1967) and *Gate of Repentance* (1973), the twin volumes issued by Great Britain's Union of Liberal and Progressive Synagogues. Clearly, world Jewry is in the process of defining a new post–World War II identity, replete with remarkable liturgical creativity, including a proliferation of alternative prayer books that replicate on the level of whole books the very principle of "freedom within structure" that has marked rabbinic liturgy from its earliest days.

STRUCTURE AND CONTENTS. Every *siddur* and *maḥzor* is identical in that the public liturgy consists of a specified core of daily prayers, which are elaborated on holy days so as to reflect their relevant calendrical themes and moods. This normal daily structure calls for three services: morning (Shaḥarit), afternoon (Minḥaht), and evening (ʿArvit, or Maʿariv); the latter two are generally combined, in practice, and recited together just before and just after nightfall. On holy days, an additional service (Musaf) is appended to the morning one. On Yom Kippur (originally, on all fast days) a concluding service (Neʿillah) is recited.

Daily service. Traceable in part to pre-70 days, before the destruction of the Temple, are two central rubrics: (1) the Shemaʿ (*Dt.* 6:4–9, 11:13–21; *Nm.* 15:37–41) and its blessings and (2) the Tefillah (lit., "the prayer"), also known as the ʿAmidah (The Standing Prayer) and as the Shemoneh ʿEsreh (The Eighteen Benedictions). Derived from *Deuteronomy* 6:7, "You shall speak of them . . . when you lie down and when you rise up," the Shemaʿ approximates an evening and morning creed that asserts the unity of God. Its accompanying blessings further define God as creator of light; loving revealer of Torah to the convenanted chosen people, Israel; and redeemer in history (at the paradigmatic salvific event, the Exodus from Egypt, and by analogy, ultimately, for final redemption at the end of days).

The subsequent Tefillah presents nineteen benedictions of which the middle thirteen constitute the basic liturgical petitions. Gamliʾel of Yavneh (c. 90 CE) is credited with arranging eighteen of them. Until then, numerous alternative sets of benedictions—"proto-*tefillot,*" so to speak—were the norm, and these varied in both number and content. Those who accept the authenticity of chapter 51 of the *Book of Ben Sira* consider it the earliest known example of such a proto-*tefillah* (c. 280 or 180 BCE). But Gamliʾel's standardized formulation superseded local usage, and (perhaps a century or two later, in Babylonia) the single petition for a messianic rebuilding of Zion was divided into two separate requests, so that the "Eighteen Benedictions" now number nineteen.

Theologically speaking, the Tefillah's first three benedictions assert (1) the continuity of Israel's covenant with God, in that the merit of the biblical patriarchs is said to warrant messianic deliverance to their descendants ever after; (2) God's power, particularly, to resurrect the dead; and (3) God's sanctity. The last three blessings may have originated in the Temple cult, as they (1) anticipate a restoration of that cult (in messianic times), (2) offer God thanksgiving, and (3) pray for peace. Some scholars see a further theological message in Gamliʾel's arrangement of the middle blessings, which are said to reflect the classical Jewish doctrine of salvation, beginning with knowledge of God, repentance, and divine forgiveness; and culminating in the ingathering of the exiles, establishing a system of justice for the appropriate meting out of reward and punishment, and rebuilding Zion under messianic rule.

Not every current liturgy includes all these classical theological statements. Since the *Hamburg Prayer Book,* Reform Jews in particular have modified some of these positions in one way or another, and even Orthodox prayer books that hew faithfully to the received texts have often emended their literal message by the inclusion of running commentaries that accompany the prayers in question.

In time, other rubrics were added to the Shemaʿ and the Tefillah. Personal prayer within the context of public worship, for example, originally followed the final blessing of the Shemaʿ; but with Gamliʾel's mandate to say the Tefillah in that place, it was postponed until the Tefillah's conclusion. The current *siddur* includes an ideal example of personal prayer attributed to one of the rabbis of the Babylonian Talmud, instead of calling for personal devotion from individual worshipers upon conclusion of the Tefillah. Similarly, a Talmudic tradition that as much as an entire confession is appropriate after the recitation of the Tefillah led, by the Middle Ages, to a series of fixed supplications called Taḥanun, which beg God to act graciously despite humankind's paucity of good works. So today's *siddur* appends to the Tefillah first the "private prayer" from the Talmud and then the Taḥanun. On Mondays and Thursdays a scriptural reading then precedes the conclusion of the service (a practice ascribed by tradition to Ezra).

Concluding prayers include the ʿAleinu and the Qaddish. The ʿAleinu is a second-century composition intended for Roʾsh ha-Shanah, but by the fourteenth century it was recited here too, where it provides a daily reminder of two polar attitudes in Judaism: universalism (in that God is sovereign over all), and particularism (in that God selected Israel as the chosen people). The Qaddish resembles Christianity's "Our Father" (the Lord's Prayer), in that both it and the Qaddish date from the first century and request "the coming of the Kingdom." Originally, the Qaddish was intended as the conclusion to a daily study session that culminated in a sermonic exposition on the theme of God's promise, but by the eighth century it had become associated with death; it was known in Austria, some five hundred years later, expressly as a mourners' prayer. It is said as such today, though it appears elsewhere in various forms to divide the sections of the service.

These expansions—"private prayer," Taḥanun, reading of scripture, the ʿAleinu, and the Qaddish—after the second major rubric, the Tefillah, are balanced by comparable additions before the first one, the Shemaʿ. A second-century practice of preparing for formal prayer by the informal recitation of psalms, grew by the ninth century (at least) to become an entire rubric called Pesuqei de-Zimraʾ (Verses of Song). Its essence is *Psalms* 145–150, followed by a benediction known as Birkat ha-Shir (Blessing of Song). These psalms are known as the Daily Hallel, and thus form one of three *hallels* in the *siddur* and *maḥzor,* the other two being the Great Hallel (*Ps.* 136) and the Egyptian Hallel (*Ps.* 113–118), which, in general, characterize holy day worship.

Even these introductory Verses of Song are now prefaced by another lengthy unit known as Birkhot ha-Shaḥar (Morning Benedictions). It arose as private home devotion but was included as public worship in Amram's *Seder,* and it has remained so despite centuries of debate. Birkhot ha-Shaḥar contains (1) several blessings, generally predating 200 CE, relevant to awakening and preparing for the new day and (2) study material devoted in the main to recalling the Temple cult.

The afternoon service consists primarily of a Tefillah. The evening service presents the nightly Shemaʿ with, however, an additional blessing requesting divine protection at night (the Hashkivenu). There then follows a Tefillah, which was originally optional but has been treated as obligatory since at least the twelfth century. Both services conclude wtih the ʿAleinu and the Qaddish.

Sabbath prayers. The basic core just outlined is altered for special days, by (1) a variety of linguistic changes in standard prayers and (2) the inclusion of new material befitting the Sabbath theme. For example, the Sabbath is treated as a foretaste of the perfect messianic age, so the thirteen intermediary Tefillah petitions, which imply a lack, and therefore imperfection, drop out. Instead, one finds a single benediction affirming the day's holiness, "Qedushat ha-Yom" ("Sanctification of the Day"). The morning Torah reading is supplemented by a correlated reading from the Prophets called the *haftarah,* and the Torah alone is read again on Sabbath afternoon.

The *siddur* calls also for introducing the Sabbath at home by another Qedushat ha-Yom (known as Qiddush) that accompanies the drinking of wine and the lighting of candles; these practices date from the first century, if not earlier, though the benediction accompanying the Sabbath lights is a later addition (c. ninth century). At Sabbath's end, the Havdalah prayer asserts Judaism's fundamental binary dichotomy of reality into opposite realms of sacred and profane.

In the sixteenth century, a service of welcoming the Sabbath (Qabbalat Shabbat) was added to the *siddur* for Friday evening. Rooted in qabbalistic theology, it portrays creation as a series of continually advancing stages of divine emanation, so that creation and creator are one and the same entity seen from two different perspectives, both of which eventuate in the Sabbath. *Sabbath* (Heb., *shabbat*) thus signifies not only the last day of creation but also the final emanation of the godhead, the female part, so to speak, of an androgynous God who is pictured as if its masculine and feminine aspects are in exile from each other, paralleling the fragmentation of this, the unredeemed world. Accordingly the Qabbalat Shabbat service welcomes the Sabbath not only as the seventh day of creation but also as the female aspect of the creator, God, personified as the Sabbath bride. The service progresses through the recitation of six psalms, representing the first six days of creation, after which the Sabbath arrives and is greeted with the sixteenth-century poem *Lekhah dodi* (Come, my beloved), in which the masculine aspect of God is invited to greet his feminine counterpart, or bride, in preparation for divine union.

Holy day liturgy. Like the Sabbath prayers of the *siddur,* the holy day *maḥzor* demonstrates the principle of relevant thematic expansion of a basic liturgical core. But it differs in that it is rich in *piyyuṭim* (sg., *piyyuṭ*). These are highly stylized poems initiated in Byzantine-ruled Palestine from the fourth or fifth to the seventh century and composed continually thereafter elsewhere, until the dawn of modernity. Scholars do not agree on an explanation of the phenomenon: Some see *piyyuṭim* as a form of natural creativity, akin to surrounding Byzantine church hymnody; others follow medieval etiology and explain this poetry as a Jewish response to persecution. Whatever the case, some *piyyuṭim* were somehow selected for retention in the versions of the *maḥzor* that survived history to become the extant rites actually practiced, and thousands more are still being uncovered in manuscript caches. *Piyyuṭim* are categorized and named according to their poetic form and function, and the liturgical place they occupy. The most important *piyyuṭim*, for example, are *qerovot*, by which one designates those interwoven in the benedictions of the Tefillah.

The mood and message of specific holy days are implicitly imparted by their *piyyuṭim*. Sukkot *piyyuṭim*, for example, focus on the booths (*sukkot*) and the taking of the *lulav* and the *etrog* (the "four species" commanded in *Leviticus* 23:40); and, following rabbinic interpretation of Sukkot as a day of judgment, the Sukkot *maḥzor* features *piyyuṭim* called *hoshanot* that implore God to save. Shavu'ot, the holiday that celebrates revelation on Sinai, includes *piyyuṭim* called *azharot*, which list commandments. Passover is recognizable from *piyyuṭim* regarding the Exodus and related traditions, such as the law and lore pertinent to the making of *matsah* (unleavened bread). Passover has also a home Seder with its accompanying liturgical Haggadah. Its contents and structure are largely recognizable by the first or second century, though many passages now in use are medieval, and some reach back only a few hundred years.

The two minor festivals of Purim and Ḥanukkah, which celebrate divine redemption as reported in the *Book of Esther* and in *Maccabees*, respectively, are marked liturgically by a special Tefillah insertion acknowledging thanksgiving "for the miracle." Purim also features public liturgical recitation of the scroll of *Esther*, a practice paralleled since the Middle Ages by the reading of four other biblical "scrolls": *Lamentations*, on Tish'a be-Av; *Ecclesiastes*, on Sukkot; *Song of Songs*, on Passover; and *Ruth*, on Shavu'ot. The Ḥanukkah home ritual of kindling lights for eight days contains two blessings, one that interprets the practice as being derived from divine command and another that affirms the Ḥanukkah miracle. Both blessings are Talmudic, and the second one is used by later authorities as a paradigm for the benediction over the Sabbath lights.

Like the other holy days, Ro'sh ha-Shanah and Yom Kippur present their own *maḥzorim*. The former is marked by a service for the blowing of the shofar (ram's horn) on two separate occasions. The more important of the two asserts the trifold doctrine of *malkhuyot, zikhronot*, and *shofarot*, that is, (1) God's sovereignty, (2) God's abiding remembrance of the covenant with Israel, and (3) the significance of the shofar sound as, first, an evocation of the covenant at Sinai and, second, its role in foreshadowing the messianic era. *Malkhuyot* ("sovereignty") seems to have been added only in the second century; the other two elements are observable in pre-70 fast-day liturgy.

Two of the many Ro'sh ha-Shanah *piyyuṭim* deserve mention. First, *Unetanneh toqef* posits the grand imagery of judgment before God, and a book of life in which human deeds are recorded, such that one's fate is written down on Ro'sh ha-Shanah and sealed on Yom Kippur; but (it concludes) penitence, prayer, and charity affect atonement. Legend ascribes this poem to an era of persecution in medieval Germany, but its actual origin lies in Byzantine Jewish hymnody centuries earlier. Second, *Avinu malkenu* begs for grace despite one's lack of works. It began as a brief prayer for rain by 'Aqiva' ben Yosef (second century), but it is today a much expanded litany, each line beginning with "Avinu malkenu" (lit., "Our father and king"; today often rendered "Our parent and ruler").

The *maḥzor* for Yom Kippur, the climax of the penitential season, contains a suitably day-long compilation of prayer, which begins with the famous Kol Nidrei, an Aramaic liturgical legal formula, deriving either from post-Talmudic Palestine or from Babylonian magical folk-traditions. It became popular despite the condemnation of authorities, and in Ashkenazic worship it became known for its chant, which bears traces of the oldest stratum of synagogue music (called *mi-sinai*, "from Sinai"), traceable to twelfth- or thirteenth-century northern Europe. The Yom Kippur *maḥzor* repeats some Ro'sh ha-Shanah liturgy too, notably *Avinu malkenu*, certain alterations in the Tefillah that emphasize the themes of divine judgment in the year ahead and the inscription of one's fate in the book of life, and *Unetanneh toqef*.

A short and a long form of communal confession are embedded in the services for Yom Kippur Day. The rabbinic concept of *con*fession *(viddui)*, implied originally *pro*fession as well, that is, recognition of human failure and virtue alike. Thus, for example, pilgrims bringing their second tithe (*Ma'as. Sh.* 5.10–13) *pro*fess their successful fulfillment of covenantal responsibility and call on God to respond in appropriate measure. But *con*fession of shortcomings was emphasized on Yom Kippur, as can be seen from the formula recited by the high priest in the Temple then (*Yoma'* 3.8, 4.2, 6.2). That formula later entered the synagogue service, along with spontaneous personal confessions, a format favored at least until the sixth century (B.T., *Yoma'* 87b). But by the eighth century, standardized communal confessions had become the norm.

The Yom Kippur *maḥzor* is known also for the 'Avodah and for Yizkor. The 'Avodah is a lengthy poetic saga detailing sacred history from creation to the appointment of Aaron and his descendants as hereditary priests. The Temple cult is then portrayed in loving detail, drawing heavily on rabbinic recollection of what once transpired there on Yom Kippur

Day. Yizkor (more properly, Hazkarat Neshamot) is a memorial rubric consisting largely of prayers composed in the wake of massacres by Crusaders in central Europe, and the Khmel'nitskii persecutions in seventeenth-century Poland. Liberal liturgies have expanded these two rubrics, so that their ʿAvodah sometimes extends sacred history up to the present and anticipates the future; their memorial services regularly include explicit reference to the Holocaust. (Indeed, the Holocaust and the subsequent birth of the modern state of Israel have emerged as newly celebrated holy days—Yom ha-Sho'ah and Yom ha-ʿAtsma'ut—with their own liturgical insertions in some *siddurim* printed today.)

Finally, it should be noted that both the *siddur* and the *maḥzor,* even though they are intended primarily for public worship, contain home prayers as well. In addition to those already mentioned—Sabbath lights, Qiddush, and Havdalah; Ḥanukkah lights; Passover Seder; the *sukkah* and waving the *lulav* and *etrog*—the *siddur* contains regular table liturgy—blessings over diverse foods and grace after meals—which go back to first-century strata, if not earlier.

SEE ALSO Shabbat.

BIBLIOGRAPHY

The tannaitic and amoraic periods (i.e., until c. 500 CE) are best surveyed in Richard S. Sarason's translation of Joseph Heinemann's *Prayer in the Talmud* (Berlin, 1977). The period thereafter, including the Geonic standardization process, and Geonic prayer books, is analyzed in detail in my book *The Canonization of the Synagogue Service* (Notre Dame, Ind., 1979). For further evidence of tannaitic linguistic variety (i. e., before 200 CE), dealt with by Heinemann, see my essay "Censoring In and Censoring Out: A Function of Liturgical Language," in *Ancient Synagogues,* edited by Joseph Guttman (Chico, Calif., 1981), pp. 19–37.

The earliest relatively complete compilations of prayer texts come from the post-Talmudic period, either from Palestine or Babylonia. Many Palestinian texts have been published, and a good sampling of them is listed in the bibliography of *genizah* fragments given by Heinemann in *Prayer in the Talmud,* p. 302. Of the two extant *siddurim* composed by Babylonian Geonim, only *Seder R. Amram Gaon* exists in English translation: part 1, translated by David Hedegord (Lund, 1951), and part 2, translated by Tryggve Kronholm (Lund, 1974). An illustration of the critical discussion surrounding the veracity of Amram's textual recension can be found in volume 1 of Louis Ginzberg's *Geonica* (1909; reprint, New York, 1968), pp. 119–154. Though *Siddur Saʿadyah* is not in English translation, a classical discussion thereof can be found in Ismar Elbogen's "Saadiah's Siddur," in *Saadia Anniversary Volume of the American Academy for Jewish Research,* edited by B. Cohen (New York, 1943), pp. 247–261. A treatment of some of the problems in reconstructing that *siddur* is available in Naphtali Wieder's "Fourteen New Genizah Fragments of Saadiah's Siddur Together with a Reproduction of a Missing Part," in *Saadya Studies,* edited by E. I. J. Rosenthal (Manchester, 1943).

For a sampling of studies on individual rites and prayer books, see Abraham I. Schechter's treatment of the early Italian rite, *Studies in Jewish Liturgy* (Philadelphia, 1930), and D. Kaufman's "The Prayer Book according to the Ritual of England before 1290," *Jewish Quarterly Review* 4 (1892): 20–63.

Because they are Hebrew poems of considerable linguistic complexity, most *piyyuṭim* remain untranslated. An exception is Ismar Elbogen's excellent "Kalir Studies," *Hebrew Union College Annual* 3 (1926): 215–224, and 4 (1927): 405–431. Several *piyyuṭim* have also been translated and annotated by Jakob J. Petuchowski. See especially the chapter entitled "Cult Entertainment and Worship" in his *Understanding Jewish Prayer* (New York, 1972), pp. 26–34, which discusses the perspective adopted by Elʿazar Kalir, the author of the poetry investigated by Elbogen, and the single person whose primacy among authors of *piyyuṭim* is rarely questioned; and *Theology and Poetry* (London, 1978), which discusses the origin of *piyyuṭim* only briefly but then translates and annotates a variety of these poems with theological consequence. Petuchowski also collaborated with Joseph Heinemann in producing a popular translation of basic prayers and some *piyyuṭim,* along with short but reliable introductions, in *Literature of the Synagogue* (New York, 1974).

The later European era in which the "authorized" shape of the current rites was determined deserves much more research than has been conducted to date. Lacking are liturgically oriented investigations of the influence of specific personalities and movements from the beginnings of the early western European literature until the printing press and the advent of the Enlightenment, particularly in English. A summary of some attitudes typical of the later period of Hasidic prayer books can be encountered in Louis Jacobs's *Hasidic Prayer* (New York, 1972); and for a theory regarding qabbalistic influence generally on the standardization of prayer texts, see my review of Stefan C. Reif's *Shabbethai Sofer and His Prayer Book* (Cambridge, 1979) in the *Journal of Reform Judaism* 29 (1982): 61–67. Reif is excellent on the seventeenth century and the process of standardizing prayer books that it brought.

Treatments of individual prayers are too numerous to be listed here, but many are referred to in the notes to Heinemann's *Prayer in the Talmud* and my *Canonization of the Synagogue Service,* mentioned above. In addition, many pioneer studies of lasting value, including descriptions of the Palestinian order of service, and theories on the origins of the major rubrics in the *siddur* have been collected by Jakob J. Petuchowski in *Contributions to the Scientific Study of Jewish Liturgy* (New York, 1970). For the early lectionary, one should consult Ben Zion Wacholder's "Prolegomenon" to Jacob Mann's *The Bible as Read and Preached in the Old Synagogue,* vol. 1, rev. ed. (New York, 1971).

The *siddurim* and *maḥzorim* resulting from modern-day prayer book reform have attracted much attention. The issues facing German reformers are beautifully summarized, albeit with considerable bias, by an early American Reform rabbi, David Philipson, in his classic account *The Reform Movement in Judaism* (1907; rev. ed., reprint, New York, 1967). A more scientific account is Petuchowski's *Prayerbook Reform in Europe* (New York, 1968) and his essay "Abraham Geiger, the Reform Jewish Liturgist," in his *New Perspectives on Abraham Geiger: An HUC-JIR Symposium* (New York, 1975), pp. 42–55. American alterations in the *siddur* and the *maḥzor* can be traced by looking first at Eric L. Friedland's "'*Olath tamid* by David Einhorn," *Hebrew Union College Annual* 45 (1974): 307–332, and "The Atonement Memorial Service in the American Maḥzor," *Hebrew Union College Annual* 55 (1984): 243–282. The former details the influence and style of Einhorn's epochal *'Olat tamid,* and the latter treats the memorial service from its origins to date. The *Union Prayer Book* is treated in Lou H. Silberman's essay "The *Union Prayer Book:* A Study of Liturgical Development," in *Retrospect and Prospect,* edited by Bertram Wallace Korn (New York, 1965), pp. 46–80, and in my article "The Language of Survival in American Reform Liturgy," *CCAR Journal* 24 (1977): 87–106. The prayer books that defined Conservative Judaism in the 1940s can be approached through a reading of Robert Gordis's candid account of the *siddur* he himself directed, "A Jewish Prayer Book for the Modern Age," *Conservative Judaism* 2 (October 1945): 1–20.

The liturgical renaissance of today arises out of the initial, somewhat inchoate, strivings of a "creative liturgy" movement that I surveyed in "Creative Liturgy," *Jewish Spectator* 40 (Winter 1975): 42–50. The Conservative movement's new *Maḥzor for Rosh Hashanah and Yom Kippur,* edited by Jules Harlow (New York, 1972), is reviewed in Petuchowski's "Conservative Liturgy Come of Age," *Conservative Judaism* 27 (1972): 3–11. The Reform movement's current *siddur, Gates of Prayer,* and its *maḥzor, Gates of Repentance,* both edited by Chaim Stern (New York, 1975–1978), are accompanied by companion volumes, prepared under my editorial supervision, that discuss the purpose and philosophy behind them: *Gates of Understanding,* 2 vols. (New York, 1977–1983), in which see especially vol. 1, pp. 131–168. Finally, my own thought has most recently been published in *Beyond the Text: A Wholistic Interpretation of Liturgy* (Bloomington, Ind., 1986).

New Sources

Brisman, Leslie. "'As It Is Written' in the New Conservative Prayerbook ['Siddur Sim Shalom']." *Orim* 1–2 (1986): 6–22.

Ellenson, David Harry. "A New Rite from Israel: Reflections on 'Siddur Va'ani Tefillati' of the Masorati (Conservative) Movement." *Studies in Contemporary Jewry* 15 (1999): 151–168.

Falk, Marcia. *The Book of Blessings: New Jewish Prayers for Daily Life, the Sabbath, and the New Moon Festival.* San Francisco, 1996.

Gelbard, Shmuel Pinhas. "Prayer and the 'Siddur.'" *Journal of Jewish Music and Liturgy* 24 (2001–2002): 8–18.

Hammer, Reuven. *Entering the High Holy Days: A Guide to the Origins, Themes, and Prayers.* Philadelphia, 1998.

Newman, Judith Hood. *Praying by the Book: The Scripturalization of Prayer in Second Temple Judaism.* Atlanta, 1999.

Silverman, Morris. "Further Comments on the Text of the Siddur." *Journal of Jewish Music and Liturgy* 13 (1990–1991): 33–42.

Weissler, Chava. *Voices of the Matriarchs: Listening to the Prayers of Early Modern Jewish Women.* Boston, 1998.

LAWRENCE A. HOFFMAN (1987)
Revised Bibliography

SÍDH.

SÍDH. Various occasional titles are used to designate the otherworld in early Irish, but the normal generic term for it is *sídh* (pl. *sídhe*). Its common currency in this sense is confirmed, if that were necessary, by the fact that it was borrowed by the author of the Old Welsh poem *Preideu Annwn* (The spoils of Annwn). The poem tells of a raid by Arthur and three shiploads of his followers on the otherworld stronghold of Kaer Sidi (from the Old Irish genitive *sídhe*) with the aim of carrying off the magic caldron of abundance which belonged to the lord of the otherworld. *Annwn* is a common term in Welsh for the otherworld, conceived in this instance as somewhere reached after a journey by boat but more generally described as somewhere beneath the ground. Similarly the Irish otherworld, whether designated by *sídh* or by another word, is occasionally envisaged as being overseas but much more frequently as being underground.

It is said that when the Gaels (the Irish Celts) came to Ireland and defeated the divine Tuatha Dé Danann, their poet and judge Amhairghin decreed that Ireland be divided in two and that the underground half be given to the Tuatha Dé Danann and the other half to the Gaels. So it was done, and the Daghdha, the senior of the gods, assigned to each of the chiefs of the Tuatha Dé his own fairy dwelling. As Marie-Louise Sjoestedt has commented, this division "marks the end of the mythical period when the supernatural was undisputed master of the earth, and the beginning of a new period in which men and gods inhabit the earth together. From that moment the great problem of religion becomes important, the problem of the relationship between man and the gods" (*Gods and Heroes of the Celts,* London, 1949, p. 47).

But while the otherworld was generally associated with the subterranean regions, it was not confined to them. Transcending as it did the limitations of human space as well as time, its location was perceived with considerable flexibility: it could be under the sea as well as under the ground, in nearby or distant islands, in houses which may disappear as suddenly as they first appeared, or it could be coextensive with the secular world. It could be reached through a cave, the waters of a lake, a magic mist, or simply through the acquisition of heightened insight. But it was not merely a spiritual world, which is presumably why the creators of Celtic mythic narrative sought in many instances to give it a clear geographic identity: Lucan in his *Pharsalia* (5.452) wrote that the continental Celts had no fear of death since it was for them only the middle of a long life. According to him, their druids taught them that after death human souls continued to control their bodies in another world (*alio orbe*); *mutatis mutandis,* this would also be a fair summary of the view of the afterlife implicit in early Irish and Welsh tradition.

Very frequently in Irish tradition the subterranean location of the otherworld is identified with certain hills and mounds, whether natural or manmade—so much so, in fact, that the word *sídh* commonly means simply "fairy or otherworld hill," in other words, an ordinary hill, usually modest in size, within which a whole world of supernatural beings live their own varied lives. Sometimes the *sídh* is a megalithic burial mound, as in the case of the great tumulus of Newgrange at Bruigh na Bóinne, which was pre-Celtic but was assimilated to Gaelic mythology and considered to be the home of the god Mac ind Óg, the Irish equivalent of British and continental Celtic Maponos. The related Welsh term, *gorsedd* ("mound"), had similar supernatural associations, though these are less fully or clearly documented. But evidently this denotation of "hill" was not the primary meaning of **sedos*, the Celtic form from which Irish *sídh* derived. Based on the Indo-European root *sed-* ("sit"), its semantic evolution seems to have moved from "residence in general" to "residence of the gods," that is, the otherworld, and then to those hills within which the gods were believed to reside. Nor does its evolution end there, for by semantic transference Irish *sídh* came to refer also to the supernatural beings who inhabit the *sídh* residence, and in modern spoken Irish the generic term for an otherworldly being or fairy is *sídheog*, the diminutive of *sídh*.

See Also Annwn.

BIBLIOGRAPHY

Carey, John. "The Location of the Otherworld in Irish Tradition." *Éigse* 19 (1982): 36–43. Seeks to demonstrate that the overseas location of the otherworld was not part of the indigenous tradition. The point is well argued, if not wholly proven.

Nutt, Alfred. "The Happy Otherworld in the Mythico-Romantic Literature of the Irish." In *The Voyage of Bran, Son of Febal, to the Land of the Living*, edited by Kuno Meyer and Alfred Nutt, vol. 1, pp. 101–332. London, 1895.

Ó Cathasaigh, Tomás. "The Semantics of 'síd.'" *Éigse* 17 (1977–1978): 137–155. Examines the generally accepted identity of *sídh* ("otherworld [hill]") and *sídh* ("peace") and explores its implications in terms of the relationship between sacral kingship and the supernatural powers.

PROINSIAS MAC CANA (1987 AND 2005)

SIḤR SEE MAGIC, *ARTICLE ON* MAGIC IN ISLAM

SIKHISM.

The word *Sikh* means disciple or student (from Sanskrit *śiṣya*, Pali *sikha*). Sikhism is traced to the person and ideology of Gurū Nānak, who was born in the Punjab in 1469. The religion developed through Nānak's nine successor *gurūs* within the historical and geographical parameters of Hinduism and Islam. In the early twenty-first century there are twenty million Sikhs. The vast majority lives in the fertile plains of the Punjab, with agriculture as a major occupation. But with their spirit of adventure and entrepreneurship skills, many have migrated to other parts of India and around the globe. Sikhs follow the teachings of their ten gurūs—from Nānak to Gobind Singh. They believe in the oneness of reality. They revere their sacred text, the *Gurū Granth*. They conduct public worship in a *gurdwara*, with the *Gurū Granth* as the center of all their rites and ceremonies. Both Sikh men and women keep their hair unshorn and identify themselves in the code given by their tenth gurū.

HERITAGE: GURŪ NĀNAK AND THE ORIGINS OF SIKHISM. Sikhism began with the religious experience of Nānak. When he was twenty-nine years old, he had a divine revelation. Thereafter Nānak traveled extensively, spreading his message of the singularity of the ultimate reality and the consequent unity of humanity. Poetry was his medium of expression. At the end of his travels, he settled on the banks of the river Ravi, where a community of Sikhs gathered. Several institutions that are vital to Sikh spirituality and morality in the twenty-first century had their genesis in this first community established by Nānak.

Sevā, voluntary service, was for Nānak an essential condition of moral discipline. Through service to their community, Sikh believers cultivate humility, overcome egotism, and purify their body and mind. *Sevā* may take the form of attending to the holy book, sweeping and dusting Sikh shrines, or preparing and serving food. It also includes helping the larger community by building schools, hospitals, orphanages, and charity homes.

Langar is both the community meal and the kitchen in which it is prepared. In Gurū Nānak's time, the idea of different castes eating together was revolutionary. It has evolved into a central practice of Sikhism. Eating together in a *gurdwara* complex means a lot to Sikhs, especially in diasporic communities. So long as they cover their heads, non-Sikhs are welcomed too. *Langar* testifies to the social equality and familyhood of all people.

Sangat is a sacred gathering of Sikhs. Gurū Nānak welcomed everyone who wished to follow his teachings. It is an egalitarian community without priests or ordained ministers. Members of a Sikh congregation sit on the floor as they sing hymns, listen to scriptural readings, and pray together without restrictions of gender, race, creed, or caste. According to Sikh scripture, *sangat* has transformative powers: "Just as iron rubbed against the philosopher's stone turns into gold, so does dark ignorance transform into brilliant light in company of the good" (*Gurū Granth* 303).

A gurū, for Nānak, is someone who reveals the divine. The role of the gurū is to apply the eyeliner of knowledge (*gyān anjan*) to enhance vision so one can see the transcendent One (*Gurū Granth* 610). Before Gurū Nānak passed away, he appointed Angad as his successor, bequeathing him his inspired utterances.

The second gurū continued the tradition of sacred poetry, which he felt was important for the knowledge it brought to human life. The transference of guruship from Nānak to Angad was repeated successively until the installation of the tenth gurū, Gobind Singh. The ten gurūs are:

Gurū Nānak (1469–1539)
Gurū Angad (1504–1552)

Gurū Amar Das (1479–1574)

Gurū Ram Das (1534–1581)

Gurū Arjan (1563–1606)

Gurū Hargobind (1595–1644)

Gurū Har Rai (1630–1661)

Gurū Har Kishen (1656–1664)

Gurū Tegh Bahadur (1621–1675)

Gurū Gobind Singh (1666–1708)

For the Sikhs the same light is reflected in these ten different bodies, and the same voice speaks through all ten.

Before his death in 1708, the tenth gurū ended the line of personal gurūs by investing the *Granth* with guruship. From that time on, Sikhs have revered the *Granth* as their ever present gurū and derived their guidance and inspiration from this sacred book. There is no other gurū. Thus the message and the mission begun by Gurū Nānak continued through nine more gurūs and culminated in the *Gurū Granth.* Sikhs celebrate the identity between their gurūs and their poetic utterances: "Bani [voice] is the *gurū*, the *gurū* is Bani, within Bani lie all elixirs" (*Gurū Granth* 982).

Gurū Arjan and the Crystallization of Sikh Religion. Gurū Arjan, the fifth gurū, was the son of Bibi Bhani (daughter of Gurū Amar Das, the third gurū) and Gurū Ram Das (the fourth gurū). During his guruship, Sikhism acquired strong scriptural, doctrinal, and organizational foundations. Gurū Arjan gave Sikhism its scripture, the *Gurū Granth*, and its sacred space, the Golden Temple (Harī Mandir). He encouraged agriculture and trade and organized a system of financial support for the Sikh religion. During this period Sikhs traded in Afghanistan, Persia, and Turkey. Gurū Arjan articulated a distinct Sikh identity that was clearly different from Hinduism and Islam: "I do not make the *ḥājj* nor any Hindu pilgrimage, I serve the One and no other. I neither perform Hindu worship nor do I offer Muslim prayers, I have taken the formless One into my heart. I am neither Hindu nor Muslim" (*Gurū Granth* 1136). Arjan's compilation of the *Granth* and his building of the Harī Mandir were both vital phenomena for the construction of Sikh psyche and Sikh identity.

The *Gurū Granth*. With Bhai Gurdas as his scribe, Arjan compiled the *Gurū Granth* in 1604. He gathered together the passionate expressions of the Sikh gurūs, Hindu *bhaktas*, and Muslim saints. The Sikh gurū's editorial lens did not demarcate boundaries between Sikh, Hindu, or Muslim: the spiritual language was common to them all. Whatever resonated philosophically and artistically with the verse of the founding gurū, he included it in the *Granth.* But Arjan did not model the Sikh text on either Muslim or Hindu scriptures, nor did he include passages from either of their revered scriptures. Against a divisive backdrop in which God was either *Rām* or *Rahim*, the worship was either *namaz* or *puja*, the place of worship *mandir* or *masjid*, and the language of scripture either Sanskrit or Arabic, the Sikh gurū brought together voices that expressed a common spiritual quest. What governed Gurū Arjan's choice was not a syncretism or synthesis of concepts and doctrines from prevailing religious traditions but rather his penetrating insight into the divine. Like his predecessors, Gurū Arjan believed that knowledge of the transcendent is attained neither through servitude to a god of the Hindu pantheon (*sevai gosain*) nor through worship to Allah (*sevai allāh*). It is received through an active recognition of, and participation in, the divine will (*hukam*):

> Some address Rām, some Khuda, Some worship Gosain, some Allah . . . . Says Nānak, those who recognize the divine will It is they who know the secret of the transcendent One. (*Gurū Granth* 885)

Arjan was a prolific poet and reiterated Nānak's metaphysical formulation, *"Ik Oaṅkār"* (literally, "1 Being Is") in vivid imagery and from a variety of perspectives. The *Granth* contains 2,218 hymns by him, including his popular hymn *Sukhmani* (The pearl of peace).

Once the *Granth* was complete, Gurū Arjan set most of its hymns to thirty-one classical Indian *rāgas.* In this way he harmonized the verses with the natural rhythm of the day, season, region, and inner moods and emotions. But he did not limit the musical measures to the classical *rāga* system; he also utilized folk musical patterns with elemental beats as well as regional *bhakti* and *kafi* forms with their own primal rhythms and other musical styles extending from Afghanistan to the south of the Indian Peninsula. Rather than construct theological treatises or list ethical injunctions, he gave the Sikhs a body of literature, which he wanted them to eat (*khavai*) and savor (*bhunchai*). In his epilogue to the *Granth*, Arjan offers the *Granth* as a platter: "they who eat this, they who relish it / they are liberated."

The *Gurū Granth* is a *thal* (large metal dish) on which lies truth (*sat*), contentment (*santokh*), and contemplation (*vicaru*). The epistemological value of these dishes is savored and absorbed by the body. The fifth gurū made Nānak's aesthetic experience the quintessential practice for the growing Sikh community.

The Harī Mandir. On August 16, 1604, Gurū Arjan ceremoniously put the *Granth* in the inner sanctuary of the Harī Mandir in Amritsar. He had built the *gurdwara* in the center of a pool his father had begun. The gurū-architect's structural plans and designs concretized the philosophical message and the literary patterns of the sacred verse. Later patrons, including Māhārājā Ranjit Singh, employed Muslim, Hindu, and Sikh craftspeople to build upon and embellish the unique Sikh ideals cherished by Gurū Arjan. Emerging from the shimmering waters, Gurū Arjan's structure appears to stand without any solid borders or boundaries. The innumerable abstract patterns on its walls set the imagination in motion. The panoramic view of the building merging at once with transparent waters and radiant sunlight sweeps the visitor into a sensory swirl. Here the Sikhs visually encounter Gurū Nānak's perception of the infinite One.

The entry into the Golden Temple complex requires a downward motion. The physical descent ensures that the precincts are entered with a sense of humility. Gurū Nānak had said, "Getting rid of ego, we receive the word" (*Gurū Granth* 228). In order to absorb the divine, the selfish, egotistical "I" must be emptied. Gurū Arjan reiterated the pathogenic effects of egocentricity: "By getting rid of arrogance we become devoid of hatred" (*Gurū Granth* 183). The poison of arrogance and egocentricity fills arteries with hostility toward the human family and the mind with inertia and ignorance.

The four doors of the Harī Mandir were Arjan's architectural translation of his ethical injunction: "*kṣatriya, brahman, śūdra,* and *vaiśya,* all four classes have the same mandate" (*Gurū Granth* 747). Rejecting societal distinctions, the *Granth* declares that religion succeeds "when the entire earth becomes one color" (*Gurū Granth* 663). "Color" (*varna*) is the standard Indian word for the four classes, so by calling for the world to be of "one color," it is demanding an end to class discrimination. The four doors opened up to welcome people from all castes and complexions. Walking through the doors, Sikhs could understand what Nānak meant: "accept all humans as your equals, and let them be your only sect" (*Japu* 28).

Gurū Gobind Singh and the Cultivation of Sikh Identity. The tenth gurū, Gobind Singh, created the Khālsā (Community of the Pure) in 1699 and translated Nānak's metaphysical ideal of the singular divine into an effective social reality. Gurū Tegh Bahadur (the ninth gurū and father of Gurū Gobind Singh) gave up his life for religious freedom. The tenth gurū was barely nine at that time. His mother, Mata Gujari, brought him up courageously. Sikhs pay homage at the two shrines dedicated to her near the town of Sirhind: Gurdwara Mata Gujari, where she spent the last four days of her life and, just a mile away, Gurdwara Joti Sarup, where she was cremated.

The Khālsā was born when Gurū Gobind Singh invited the first five initiates to sip *amrit,* the sacred nectar, from the same bowl. By sipping from the same bowl, these five people from different castes boldly denounced the divisions of caste, class, and hereditary profession. Gurū Gobind Singh had prepared the drink by stirring water in a steel bowl with his double-edged sword while sacred hymns were recited. His wife, Mata Jitoji, added sugar puffs, intermingling the strength of steel with the sweetness of sugar. The drink nourished the initiates physically and psychologically to fight against oppressive and unjust leaders and uphold the values of liberty and equality.

The *amrit* initiation is open to both Sikh men and women, and both are equally enjoined to wear the emblems of the Khālsā, popularly known as the "five K's":

1. *kesha,* uncut hair,
2. *kangha,* a comb tucked in the hair to keep it tidy,
3. *kara,* a steel bracelet worn around the right wrist,
4. *kacha,* long underwear,
5. *kirpan,* a sword.

These five K's have become an essential part of their individual and communal identity. Furthermore all Sikh men have the surname Singh, meaning "lion," and all women have the surname Kaur, meaning "princess." Thus Sikh men and women abandon their former castes, hereditary occupations, belief systems, and rituals and join the new family. Women are liberated from tracing their lineage to their father or adopting a husband's name after marriage.

Gurū Gobind Singh was also a superb poet. He composed heroic and martial poetry to inspire bravery and infuse the hearts of men and women with self-confidence and love for the divine. His verses are included in the collection known as the *Dasam Granth* (Tenth book).

Māharājā Ranjit Singh (1780–1839) and the Sikh Kingdom. By the middle of the eighteenth century Sikhs had become a major political force, and at the end of the century they established a state of their own. In 1799 Ranjit Singh, the nineteen-year-old leader of a Khālsā band, seized power peacefully in the city of Lahore. Guided by Sada Kaur (1762–1832), his mother-in-law, Ranjit Singh integrated twelve warring Sikh bands into a sovereign state. In 1801 the Sikhs crowned him māharājā of the Punjab. Known as the "Lion of the Punjab," Ranjit Singh ruled for forty years. He created a formidable army and added Multan, Kashmir, and Peshawar to his kingdom. His court represented unparalleled pageantry and brilliance. He wore the world's largest diamond (the Kohinoor) on his right arm.

The māharājā remained a devout Sikh who built and renovated many shrines. Even his foreign employees had to live by the Sikh code: they had to wear their beards long and refrain from eating beef and from smoking tobacco. A decade after his death, Sikhs lost their enormous and splendid kingdom to the British in 1849. Ranjit Singh's wife, Maharani Jindan (1817–1863), was famous for her sharp intelligence, and the British referred to her as the only courageous "man" in the area. The Sikh māharājā's Kohinoor diamond was cut down to fit Queen Victoria's crown, and his young son Dalip (1838–1893) was converted to Christianity and exiled to England. Generations of heroic Sikhs began to serve the British army, valorously fighting in Europe, Africa, and Asia. Sikhs formed a major part of the imperial army in World War I.

Singh Sabha and the Rediscovery of Sikh Identity. Māharājā Ranjit Singh loved pomp and ceremony, and at his court he reintroduced many of the Brahmanic rites that had been discarded by the Sikh gurūs. Later, under colonial rule, Christian missionaries started to make conversions among the Sikhs. In response to this loss of Sikh identity, the Singh Sabha movement was founded in Amritsar in 1873. Its goal was to reform and renew Sikh philosophy and culture. Similar movements were founded by Hindus and Muslims to counteract Christian missionary activity. The Singh Sabha promoted the building of Sikh schools and colleges; one of its greatest achievements was the founding of the Khālsā College at Amritsar in 1892. The Singh Sabha also encouraged the production of books and newspapers to help bring Sikhs back to the teachings of their ten gurūs. Bhai Vir Singh, the most prolific and inspiring Singh Sabha author, created vivid female characters like Sundari, Rani Raj Kaur, and Subhag Kaur as paradigms for Sikh morality.

The Shiromani Gurdwara Prabandhak Committee, established in 1920, continues to be the highest Sikh executive committee. With its headquarters in Amritsar, the Shiromani Gurdwara Prabandhak Committee sets up rules and regulations for Sikhs to follow throughout the world.

In an attempt to formalize the message of the gurūs, the *Sikh Rahit Maryada* (Sikh code of conduct) was published in 1950. This thirty-seven-page document was produced after years of deliberation and consultation amongst eminent Sikhs both in India and abroad. It is used as the standard guide by Sikhs in their performance of personal (*shakhsī*) and organizational (*panthak*) duties. The *Sikh Rahit Maryada* forbids both men and women to cut or trim their hair. It also forbids them to eat meat from an animal that has been slowly bled to death in the *ḥalāl* method (Sikhs may only eat *jhatka* meat—from an animal killed in one stroke). It prohibits adultery and the use of tobacco and narcotics. This important Sikh manual also tries to combat female oppression. Sikh women should not veil their faces; female infanticide is forbidden; and widows are free to remarry. It also abolishes the old Punjabi custom whereby a widow was shamefully wrapped in a sheet and carried away to the brother of her dead husband.

WORSHIP: *GURŪ GRANTH*. Reading their sacred verse, hearing it, singing it, or sitting in its presence constitute the core of Sikh ritual. To have a room in their homes enshrining the *Gurū Granth* is the aspiration of most Sikhs. Both at home and in public places of worship, the *Gurū Granth* is treated with the highest respect and veneration. It is draped in cloth (called *rumala*), placed on quilted mats, and supported by cushions. A canopy hangs over it for protection, and a whisk is waved over it as a sign of respect. Sikhs everywhere bow before the *Gurū Granth* and seat themselves on the floor. They remove their shoes and cover their heads in the presence of their holy book. The *Gurū Granth* is opened at dawn. This act of opening the holy book is called *prakash*, "making the light manifest." *Vak*, or "the order of the day," is obtained by opening the book at random and reading the passage on the top of the left-hand page. After dusk, the *Gurū Granth* is closed. The closing ritual is called *sukhasan*, which means "to place at rest." The *Gurū Granth* is read for all rites of passage, for any family celebration (e.g., a new house, a new job, an engagement), and for all times of uncertainty and difficulty (e.g., sickness or death). The reading at these events may be *saptah*, a seven-day reading, or it may be *akhand*, a forty-eight hour, nonstop reading of its 1,430 portfolio pages, during which several readers take turns. Any Sikh, male or female, who can read Gurmukhi script may read the *Gurū Granth*. *Kīrtan* is the singing of the scriptural verses. Harmonium and *tabla* (a set of drums) are the most common musical accompaniments.

Special social functions and rites of passage are marked by the *bhog* ceremony. The word *bhog* literally means "pleasure." In Sikhism it signifies the gratification attained by having concluded a reading of the scriptures. It has similar connotations to the Greek word *eucharist*, which means "thanksgiving" and refers specifically the Christian sacrament of Holy Communion. *Bhog* involves reading the concluding pages of the *Gurū Granth*, saying *ardas* (the Sikh counterpart of the Lord's Prayer in Christianity), and partaking of the Sikh sacrament of *karahprashad*, which concludes every religious ceremony. *Karahprashad* is a sweet sacrament consisting of equal portions of butter, flour, sugar, and water. During its preparation, Sikh men and women keep their heads covered and their feet bare and recite the verses of the gurūs. When the *karahprashad* is ready, it is put in a large flat dish and placed on the right side of the *Gurū Granth*. After scriptural readings, the warm and aromatic sacrament is distributed to the entire congregation.

***GURDWARA*.** In public, Sikh worship is conducted in a *gurdwara*; literally, the doorway (*dwara*) to the gurū. The shrines serve as a central point for the local Sikh community: they are its source of information, assistance, food, shelter, and fellowship. The *gurdwaras* are designed on the open and inclusive architectural patterns of the Harī Mandir. There is no central chamber from which any male or female is excluded, for the *Gurū Granth* is the focal point to which everyone has equal access.

Besides the Harī Mandir, there are five places that are particularly important for the Sikhs. They are called the five *takhts*, the five seats of temporal authority. The Akal Takht in Amritsar faces the Golden Temple and is regarded as the supreme seat of religious and temporal authority. The other four are associated with the tenth gurū: Patna Sāhib in Bihar, where he was born; Keshgarh, in Anandpur, where he created the Khālsā; Hazur Sāhib in Nander, where he died; and Damdama, near Bhatinda, which later developed into a center of Sikh learning.

CELEBRATIONS. True living for Sikhs involves remembering the one reality as often and as intimately as possible. The daily spiritual routine (*nit nem*) consists of recitations of hymns from the various gurūs, including Gurū Nānak's *Japu*, which is read, recited, or heard on tape in the morning.

Annually Sikhs celebrate *gurpurabs* (the days of the gurū). These days commemorate the birthdays of their gurūs, important historical events, and the martyrdom of their heroes. All over the world Sikhs joyously celebrate the birth of Gurū Nānak, the installation of the *Gurū Granth* in the Harī Mandir, and the birth of the Khālsā. *Baisakhi*, which is also the first day of the Sikh calendar and commemorates Gurū Gobind Singh's creation of the Khālsā. During *gurpurabs*, uninterrupted readings of scripture take place, intellectual symposiums are held, and musical performances are organized. *Gurpurab* celebrations also include huge Sikh processions with colorful floats carrying the *Gurū Granth* and depicting different aspects of Sikh life. Throughout the *gurpurab*, Sikhs will stop fast-moving cars and buses on the road and offer langar (food and snacks) to the travelers.

The Punjabi folk dances, *gidda* and *bhangra*, are popular performances during Sikh celebrations. *Gidda* is choreographed by women in gentle and lithesome movement. Together they celebrate nature and its bountiful gifts through the seasons of spring, summer, monsoon, autumn, and winter. Amid sparkling agrarian scenes, *gidda* captures simple activities: how they milk cows, cook mustard seeds, do needlework, fan in the summer, buy glass bangles, churn milk in the morning, carry water in earthenware pitchers sturdily balanced on their heads, and help with plowing and harvesting. *Bhangra* is traditionally performed by a group of men. It dates back to the fourteenth century, originating in West Punjab (now a part of Pakistan). But in modern times *bhangra* has become extremely popular with both Sikh men and women. Dressed in bright colors, the group dances in an elemental rhythm to the beat of a large drum, and everybody joins in songs celebrating Punjabi village life. With the migration of Sikh communities to the West, this Punjabi folk dance has become popular with young music lovers in Britain, Europe, and North America. The modern form of *bhangra* combines North Indian folk music with a kaleidoscope of contemporary styles, including reggae and Western pop.

RITES OF PASSAGE. In Sikhism there are four rites of passage: name giving, *amrit* initiation, marriage, and death.

Name Giving. Sikh children are named in consultation with the holy book. While the spine of the book rests on the cushions, a reader (a family member if the rite is held at the home, an official reader if it is at the *gurdwara*) holds the *Gurū Granth* closed with both hands and then gently lets it open at random. The child is given a name that begins with the first letter appearing at the top of the left-hand page where the *Gurū Granth* opens. Sikhs do not have different names for boys and girls. The addition of the name *Kaur* or *Singh* indicates the gender of the child. The child also receives his or her first *kara* or steel bracelet. The recitation of *kirtan* (hymns of praise) readings from the *Gurū Granth*, the recitation of *ardas* (the daily prayer), and the partaking of *langar* are the central activities, just as they are for all Sikh rites of passage.

***Amrit* initiation.** No particular age is prescribed for *amrit* initiation. It may be as soon as a boy or a girl is old enough to be able to read the scripture and comprehend the articles of the Sikh faith. The initiation is open to all. According to the *Rahit Maryada*, "Any man or woman of whatever nationality, race, or social standing, who is prepared to accept the rules governing the Sikh community, has the right to receive *amrit* initiation." It follows the pattern established by Gurū Gobind Singh on Baiskahi 1699. Sikhs firmly believe that during Baisakhi (the first day of the Indian New Year) festivities in Anand pur that year, the guru and his wife prepared amrit and five men from different castes sipped it from the same bowl. The drink purified them of all mental constraints, ending centuries of hereditary oppressions of caste, class, and profession. Zealous proselytization is alien to Sikhs.

Weddings. Anand Karaj (from *anand*, "bliss," and *karaj*, "event") is the Sikh rite of marriage. No words or gestures are directly exchanged between the bride and groom, nor are any legal formalities performed between their families. The wedding takes place either in a *gurdwara* or in the home of the bride, with everyone seated on the floor in front of the *Gurū Granth*. Anand Karaj begins with the father of the bride handing one end of a scarf (about two and a quarter yards in length) to the groom and the other to his daughter. Through the auspiciously colored scarf (pink, saffron, or red), the couple is bonded together. Each holding one end of the scarf, the groom and the bride then walk around the holy book four times. The four circumambulations by the couple correspond to the four *lavan* (circle) passages read by the official reader of the *Gurū Granth*. After each circling of the book, the bride and the groom touch their foreheads to the ground and rejoin the congregation by seating themselves on the floor in front. Bowing together to the *Gurū Granth* marks their acceptance of each other. They are solely—and equally—bound to the sacred word rather than to any legal or social authority. The rite concludes with Gurū Amar Das's rapturous hymn *Anand*, the name of the wedding ceremony itself. This popular scriptural hymn by the third gurū is liturgically recited at the conclusion of all Sikh congregational services and joyful ceremonies. But with its focus on the bliss that results from the union of the individual with the divine, *Anand* is particularly appropriate for the wedding ceremony.

Death. Life and death are regarded as natural processes, and just as each day that dawns must set, so must all people depart. The dead body is carried on a stretcher by the closest male relatives and friends of the family to the funeral grounds, where it is cremated. As customary from ancient times, the pyre is lighted by the oldest son. The body returns to the elements it is made up of: the fire of the person merges with the crematory flames, his or her breath merges with the air, his or her body merges with the body of the earth, and his or her ashes and bones (*phul*; literally, "flowers") are immersed in the flowing waters of a river or stream. Death in the family is marked by a reading of the *Gurū Granth*. A *bhog* ceremony takes place on the tenth day, with the final prayers recited for peace to the deceased. At the death anniversary, the family will supply *langar* to the community.

POPULAR MORALITY. Sikhism validates normal activities: "While laughing, playing, dressing up, and eating we attain liberation" (*Gurū Granth* 522). Its strong work ethic is summed up in a popular maxim: "Work hard [*kirat karni*], remember the divine [*nām japna*], and share your enjoyment with others [*vand chhakna*]." Sikhs bring the divine into the daily rhythms of their lives, and they even exalt the divine in their everyday greetings: whenever they want to say hello or goodbye, they join their hands and say *"sat sri akal"* (truth is timeless). Their frequent exclamation—*waheguru*—surges with a sense of wonder and echoes Gurū Nānak's awe (*wah*) when he first experienced the transcendent One.

SEE ALSO Ādi Granth; Dasam Granth; Hindi Religious Traditions; Nānak; Singh, Gobind.

BIBLIOGRAPHY

For a basic introduction to Sikhism, see Harbans Singh, *The Heritage of the Sikhs*, 2d rev. ed. (New Delhi, 1994); Hew McLeod, *Sikhism* (London, 1997); Khushwant Singh, *A History of the Sikhs*, 2d ed. (Delhi, 1991); Max Arthur Macauliffe, *The Sikh Religion: Its Gurus, Sacred Writings, and Authors* (Oxford, 1909); Owen Cole and Piara Singh Sambhi, *The Sikhs: Their Religious Beliefs and Practices*, 2d ed. (Brighton, U.K., 1995); J. S. Grewal, *From Guru Nanak to Maharaja Ranjit Singh: Essays in Sikh History* (Amritsar, India, 1972); and Nikky-Guninder Kaur Singh, *Sikhism* (New York, 1993). For an introduction to Sikh sacred literature, see Hew McLeod, *Textual Sources for the Study of Sikhism* (Manchester, U.K., 1984; reprint, Chicago, 1990); and Nikky-Guninder Kaur Singh, trans., *The Name of My Beloved: Verses of the Sikh Gurus* (San Francisco, 1995). The standard reference is Harbans Singh, *The Encyclopaedia of Sikhism* (Patiala, India, 1992).

For studies on the development of the *Gurū Granth*, see Pashaura Singh, *The Guru Granth: Canon, Meaning, and Authority* (Delhi, 2000); Gurinder Singh Mann, *The Making of Sikh Scripture* (New York, 2001); and S. S. Kohli, *A Critical Study of the Ādi Granth*, 2d ed. (Delhi, 1976).

Scholars have studied Sikhism from a variety of perspectives. See Surjit Hans, *A Reconstruction of Sikh History from Sikh Literature* (Jalandhar, India, 1988); Nripinder Singh, *The Sikh Moral Tradition* (New Delhi, 1990); Harjot Oberoi, *The Construction of Religious Boundaries: Culture, Identity, and Diversity in the Sikh Tradition* (Chicago, 1994); Cynthia Mahmood, *Fighting for Faith and Nation: Dialogues with Sikh Militants* (Philadelphia, 1997); Louis Fenech, *Martyrdrom in the Sikh Tradition* (Delhi, 2000); and Brian Axel, *The Nation's Tortured Body: Violence, Representation, and the Formation of a Sikh Diaspora* (Durham, N.C., 2001).

Also see Mark Juergensmeyer and Gerry Barrier, eds., *Sikh Studies: Comparative Perspectives on a Changing Tradition* (Berkeley, 1979); Gurdev Singh, ed., *Perspectives on the Sikh Tradition* (Chandigarh, India, 1986); Joseph T. O'Connell, Milton Israel, and Willard G. Oxtoby, eds., *Sikh History and Religion in the Twentieth Century* (Toronto, 1988); Jasbir Singh Mann and Kharak Singh, eds., *Recent Researches in Sikhism* (Patiala, India, 1992); Christopher Shackle, Gurharpal Singh, and Arvind-Pal Singh Mandair, eds., *Sikh Religion, Culture, and Ethnicity* (Richmond, U.K., 2001); and Pashaura Singh and N. Gerald Barrier, eds., *Sikhism and History* (New Delhi, 2004).

For feminist perspectives, see Nikky-Guninder Kaur Singh, *Feminine Principle in the Sikh Vision of the Transcendent* (Cambridge, U.K., 1993); and Doris Jakobsh, *Relocating Gender in Sikh History: Transformation, Meaning, and Identity* (Delhi, 2003). For Sikh art and literature, see Madanjit Kaur, *The Golden Temple: Past and Present* (Amritsar, India, 1983); Patwant Singh, *The Golden Temple* (Hong Kong, 1988); Susan Stronge, ed., *The Arts of the Sikh Kingdoms* (London, 1999); Kerry Brown, ed., *Sikh Art and Literature* (London, 1999); and B. N. Goswamy, *Piety and Splendour: Sikh Heritage in Art* (New Delhi, 2000).

For studies on the Sikh diaspora, see Parminder Bhachu, *Twice Migrants: East African Sikh Settlers in Britain* (New York, 1985); Bruce La Brack, *The Sikhs of Northern California, 1904–1975* (New York, 1988); Gerry Barrier and Verne A. Dusenbery, eds., *The Sikh Diaspora: Migration and the Experience Beyond Punjab* (Delhi, 1989); D. S. Tatla, *Sikhs in North America: An Annotated Bibliography* (New York, 1991); Pashaura Singh and Gerry Barrier, eds., *Sikh Identity: Continuity and Change* (Delhi, 1999); Harold Coward, ed., *The South Asian Religious Diaspora in Britain, Canada, and the United States* (Albany, N.Y., 2000); and Cynthia Mahmood and Stacy Brady, *Guru's Gift: An Ethnography Exploring Gender Equality with North American Sikh Women* (Mountain View, Calif., 2000).

NIKKY-GUNINDER KAUR SINGH (2005)

SIKKIMESE RELIGION

SEE BUDDHISM, SCHOOLS OF, *ARTICLE ON* HIMALAYAN BUDDHISM

ŚĪLABHADRA (c. 529–645; Tib., Ngang tshul bzan po; Chin., Jiexian; Jpn., Kaiken) was an Indian Buddhist dialectician belonging to the Yogācāra-Vijñānavāda school, a master of the Nālandā monastic university, a disciple of Dharmapāla, and the teacher of Xuanzang. Several accounts of Śīlabhadra's life are extant. The Tibetan sources are fragmentary, but, owing to the fact that Xuanzang gives an account of him in his writings, those in Chinese are more informative. From the Tibetan biographers, such as Taranatha and Sum pa mkhan po, one learns only that Śīlabhadra was contemporary with Śākyamati, Yaśomitra, and Sa'i rtsa lag. But Chinese biographies such as those found in Xuanzang's *Xiyu ji* (viz. T.D. 51.914c–915a) and Yiqing's *Nanhai jikgui neifa juan* (T.D. 54.229b) enable one to construct an outline of his religious career.

Śīlabhadra belonged to the royal family of Samatata in East India and was a member of the brahman caste. Fond of study even as a child, he traveled through several countries of India in search of religious teachers and arrived finally at the monastic university at Nālandā. There he studied under, and was ordained by, the Yogācāra master Dharmapāla, attaining the highest level of scholarship under his guidance.

During this period, a non-Buddhist teacher from South India, jealous of Dharmapāla's scholarly and religious attainments, wished to challenge him to a doctrinal debate. At the request of the local king, Dharmapāla accepted this challenge. When Śīlabhadra heard of this he volunteered to debate in his master's place. Although only thirty years old, Śīlabhadra was victorious in the debate and was rewarded with a town, where he then built a monastery. He succeeded Dharmapāla as head of the Nālandā monastic university and became known by the respectful epithet Zhengfa Zang ("treasury of the good law").

The Vijñānavāda theory of Dharmapāla insisted on distinguishing among five categories of people: (1) those destined to be *bodhisattvas*, (2) those destined to be *pratyekabuddhas*, (3) those destined to be *śrāvakas*, (4) those of undetermined spiritual destination, and (5) those who can never be emancipated (*icchantika*). His theory that there exist people who will never attain Buddhahood is in clear contrast to the One Vehicle teachings (*ekayāna*), according to which everyone has a Buddha nature and will eventually become emancipated. It was Śīlabhadra who transmitted the Vijñānavāda theory of Dharmapāla to Xuanzang. Although Śīlabhadra was 106 years old when Xuanzang met him, he taught the Vijñānavāda theories to Xuanzang for about five years. Xuanzang in turn transmitted Dharmapāla's theory to Kuiji (632–682), who founded the Faxiang sect in China.

A notable doctrinal disputation between Śīlabhadra and Jñānaprabha (unattested; Chin., Zhiguang; Jpn., Chiko) was held at Nālandā. Fazang (643–712) gives an account of this conflict in his works *Huayan jing tanxuan ji* (T. D. 35.111c–112a), *Shiermen lun zongzhi yiji* (T.D. 42.213a, b), and *Dasheng qixin lun yiji* (T.D. 44.242a–c). This account was related to him by Divakara, an Indian Dharma master and translator, at the Dayuan Si in Chang'an.

The topic of the debate was the "three times," or "three steps," of the Buddha's teaching. Śīlabhadra, who was of the Vijñanavadin line based on the *Saṃdhinirmocana Sūtra* and the *Yogācārabhūmi,* expounded the Three Steps as follows: (1) the teaching of the Hīnayāna principles regarding the Four Noble Truths and the emptiness of the self (*pudgalanairātmya*), (2) the teaching of the imaginary nature of things (*parikalpitasvabhāva*) and the emptiness of things (*dharmanairātmya*), and (3) the teaching of "consciousness only" (*cittamātra*). On the other hand, Jñānaprabha, who was of the Mādhaymika (Madhyamaka) line based on the *Prajñāpāramitā Sūtra* and the Mādhyamika *śāstras,* interpreted the Three Steps as (1) the teaching of the Lesser Vehicle (Hīnayāna), (2) the teaching that the external world does not exist but that the mind does, and (3) the teaching that neither the external world nor the mind exists. Each thinker regarded the third step as the highest. It is interesting that this ideological difference was stated so clearly by the seventh century, because the same kind of hermeneutical discussion is found later in Tibetan Buddhism, in the *Drang nges legs bshad snying po* of Tsong kha pa, for example. Unfortunately, as there are no sources other than Fazang's report regarding this conflict between Śīlabhadra and Jñānaprabha, its historical credibility remains uncertain. In Xuanzang's biography, for example (T. D. 50.261a, b), Jñānaprabha appears as a disciple of Śīlabhadra, and there is no mention of this doctrinal dispute.

The only extant work by Śīlabhadra is the *Buddhabhūmivyākhyāna* (a commentary on the *Buddhabhūmi Sūtra*). This work is preserved in the Tibetan canon (Derge edition no. 3997; Beijing edition no. 5498).

SEE ALSO Dharmapāla; Xuanzang; Yogācāra.

BIBLIOGRAPHY

Beal, Samuel, trans. *Si-yu-ki, Buddhist Records of the Western World* (1884). 2 vols. Reprint, Delhi, 1981.

Beal, Samuel, trans. *The Life of Xuanzang* (1888). Rev. ed., London, 1911.

Joshi, Lal Mani. *Studies in the Buddhistic Culture of India* (1967). 2d rev. ed. Delhi, 1977.

Nishio Kyoo, *Butsuji kyoron no kenkyu* (1940), 2 vols. Reprint, Tokyo, 1982. Contains an edited Tibetan text of the *Buddhabhumivyakhyana* with Japanese translation.

Takakusu Junjiro, trans. *A Record of the Buddhist Religion as Practised in India and the Malay Archipelago (A.D. 671–695)* (1896). Reprint, Delhi, 1966.

MIMAKI KATSUMI (1987)

SILVER SEE GOLD AND SILVER

SIMA CHENGZHEN (647–735; adult style, Ziwei; name in religion, Daoyin) was an eminent court Daoist and Shangqing patriarch of the Tang period (618–907). A native of Wen County in modern Henan province, Sima Chengzhen was a descendant of the Sima ruling family of the Jin dynasty (265–420) and of high regional officials under the Sui (581–618) and early Tang. Sima Chengzhen received his Daoist initiation from the Shangqing patriarch Pan Shizheng (587–684) at Mount Songshan, the Central Peak, in Henan. Pan, a counselor on Daoist doctrine to Emperor Gaozong (r. 650–684), transmitted to Sima the inspired fourth-century writings of the Shangqing scriptural corpus, as well as meditational and physiological techniques practiced by that movement. Sima Chengzhen succeeded his master as the twelfth patriarch of the Shangqing lineage. After a period of wandering, he lived in seclusion on Mount Tiantai in Zhejiang, where he assumed the epithet Boyun zi, Master White Cloud.

Sima Chengzhen was successively summoned to the court by three sovereigns: the empress Wu Zetian (r. 684–704) and the emperors Ruizong (r. 710–712) and Xuanzong (r. 712–756). Ruizong, who engaged in discussions on cosmology and governance with the Daoist, in 711 founded the temple Tongbo guan for Sima Chengzhen near the master's earlier retreat on Mount Tiantai. Among Sima's surviving writings is a richly illustrated hagiography of Wangzi Jin, the resident saint of the Tongbo temple site, titled *Shangqing shi dichen Tongbo zhenren zhen tuzan* (*Daozang* 612). Responding to Emperor Xuanzong's invitation in 721, Sima once again undertook the journey to the capital Chang'an. The patriarch conferred a Daoist ordination on the emperor and was in turn granted numerous honors and court titles. Xuanzong adopted Sima's counsel regarding the reform of China's principle mountain cults and commissioned the Daoist, a renowned calligrapher, to establish a standard text of Laozi's classic "The Way and Its Power" (*Dao de jing*) to be engraved in stone. Sima also presented Xuanzong with designs for Daoist swords and mirrors, of which an illustrated description has come down in the *Shangqing hanxiang jianjian tu* (*Daozang* 431). Xuanzong finally ordered the construction of a new temple as a retreat for Sima. It was situated on Mount Wangwu, on the border between Shanxi and Henan provinces, where the emperor's sister Princess Yuzhen, an ordained Daoist nun, was also active. According to the commemorative inscription *Tang Wangwu shan Zhongyan tai Zhengyi* [read *Zhenyi*] *xiansheng miaojie* (*Daozang* 970), Sima Chengzhen settled on Mount Wangwu in 724 and died there in 735. His posthumous title, bestowed by Emperor Xuanzong, was Master Zhenyi. Among his more than seventy disciples were Li Hanguang (683–769), the thirteenth Shangqing patriarch, and Xue Jichang (d. 759), who became a prominent master of the Southern Peak (Mount Heng in Hunan) and Tiantai (Zhejiang) lineages.

Although the subject of continuous official attentions, Sima was drawn to a life of seclusion. His best-known works are concerned with Shangqing methods of personal cultivation and meditation, elucidating the Daoist stages of transcendence. The meditation guide "On Sitting in Forgetfulness" (*Zuowang lun* [*Daozang* 1036]), attributed to Sima Chengzhen, outlines a program in seven steps identified as faith, detachment, renunciation through mental concentration, stoicism, discernment, oblivion, and finally, attainment of the Dao. The title of this guide features again as one of five stages (purification, seclusion, contemplation, sitting in forgetfulness, liberation) in "The Master Concealed in Heaven" (*Tianyin zi* [*Daozang* 1026]), commentated by Sima Chengzhen. Sima's program and precepts for adepts affirm that the goals of deliverance and physical immortality were attainable through sheer application. This belief was famously advocated by Sima's younger Daoist contemporary, Wu Yun (d. 778), who has also been credited with a work titled "Sitting in Forgetfulness." Sima's essay on "The Quintessence of Swallowing Breath" (*Fuqi jingyi lun* [*Daozang* 830]) discusses the absorption of *qi*-energy, dietary regimens, and physical exercises for prolonging life and curing diseases.

Highly appreciated by leading literati and statesmen of his time, including Zhang Yue (667–731), Sima contributed to the esteem in which Shangqing writings were held in literary circles under the Tang. In addition to ancient Daoist concepts of meditation (especially in the *Zhuangzi*), Sima's teachings on purification, quietude, and the universal attainability of transcendence assimilated doctrines current in Confucianism and Buddhism on the subject of inborn human nature, the rectification of an individual's moral purpose, and mental discipline and tranquility. In these areas, Sima Chengzhen in turn exercised an influence on the subsequent development of Daoist inner alchemy and neo-Confucian thought and practices under the Song (960–1279).

SEE ALSO Daoism, article on The Daoist Religious Community.

BIBLIOGRAPHY

Engelhardt, Ute. *Die klassische Tradition der Qi-Übungen (Qigong). Eine Darstellung anhand des Tang-zeitlichen Textes* Fuqi jingyi lun *von Sima Chengzhen.* Wiesbaden, Germany, 1987.

Kohn, Livia. *Seven Steps to the Tao: Sima Chengzhen's Zuowanglun.* Nettetal, Germany, 1987.

Kohn, Livia. "The teaching of *T'ien-yin-tzu.*" *Journal of Chinese Religions* 15 (1987): 1–28.

Kroll, Paul W. "Szu-ma Ch'eng-chen in T'ang verse." *Society for the Study of Chinese Religion Bulletin* 6 (1978): 16–30.

Xu Kangsheng. "Lüelun Sima Chengzhen de daojiao sixiang." In *Daojia yu daojiao: di er jie guoji xueshu yantao hui lunwen,* vol. 2, edited by Chen Guying and Feng Dawen, pp. 254–263. Quangzhou, People's Republic of China, 2001.

FRANCISCUS VERELLEN (2005)

SIMEON BAR YOHAI SEE SHIM'ON BAR YOḤ'AI

SIMEON BEN GAMALIEL II SEE SHIM'ON BEN GAMLI'EL II

SIMEON BEN LAKISH SEE SHIM'ON BEN LAQISH

SIMONS, MENNO (1496–1561). Dutch priest, the major northern European leader of an Anabaptist group that later came to be known as the Mennonite church. His firm leadership and numerous writings helped to consolidate the pacifist wing of early Dutch Anabaptism and to make it normative, after the ill-fated attempt of some to establish the kingdom of God by force in the northern German city of Münster in 1534–1535.

Simons was born of peasant stock in Witmarsum, in the province of Friesland, in 1496 and was enrolled in a monastic school at an early age. Since Friesland was dominated by the Premonstratensian Order at that time, and since Simons was installed in 1524 by that order as a priest in Pingjum as well as in his home parish of Witmarsum in 1531, it may be assumed that he was a member of that order and received his training in it, perhaps in the nearby monastery of Vinea Domini. The order was known for its excellent libraries and the emphasis it placed upon education.

Simons's religious struggle began early in his career as a priest, in connection with his celebration of the Mass. His doubts about the real presence of Christ in the bread and wine indicate that Reformation ideas had reached Friesland. He wrote later that he had searched the writings of the reformers in vain for answers to the question of infant baptism, which became his second concern. His problem with the Mass was most likely inspired by the antisacramental movement in the Netherlands, as well as by Erasmian humanism and the teachings of the Brethren of the Common Life. Questions about the validity of infant baptism may have arisen when Simons heard that an Anabaptist tailor named Sicke Freerks had been publicly executed in nearby Leeuwarden for having himself baptized a second time, but it appears also that Simons had already encountered literature on the subject before this event.

In his search for answers Simons eventually turned to the scriptures, which he had apparently not read during his days as a student at the monastery. Yet he must have held the scriptures to be a significant authority, for he expressed deep disappointment at not finding in them the kind of support he felt necessary for the practice of the Mass and infant baptism. He continued to serve in his priestly office, but his new studies must have begun to change his emphasis, for by 1528 he had become known as an "evangelical preacher." According to Simons's own account, his spiritual pilgrimage was a gradual transition, lasting eleven years, from a routine reliance on tradition to a deep personal faith in Christ and reliance on the scriptures as final authority in matters of faith. Gradually his views became known, and by January 1536 he had found it prudent to go into hiding. He used this time for spiritual exercises and writing. After nearly a year had elapsed he accepted a call from a representative Anabaptist delegation to be the spiritual leader of the scattered groups of believers. He was baptized and ordained by Obbe Philips. Sometime during this interim period Simons also married a woman about whom little more than her name, Gertrude, is known.

Simons's personal and theological point of departure was the new birth. His first major treatise, entitled *The Spiritual Resurrection* (1536), was followed a year later by a restatement of this theme under the title *The New Birth* (1537). This emphasis on conversion occurs centrally in his subsequent writings, particularly when he refers to his own spiritual struggle before 1536.

Intimately related to this theme was his emphasis on the nature of the church. Simons was convinced that the church had fallen from its apostolic purity in both doctrine and life. Reformation of the present structures was no longer possible; a new beginning patterned after the church in the Bible was called for. This was, in large part, the content of his three writings of 1539: *Foundation of Christian Doctrine, Christian Baptism,* and *Why I Do Not Cease Teaching and Writing.* Grace and ethics were to go hand in hand. The true church is the bride of Christ and must, therefore, be without spot or wrinkle (*Eph.* 5:27). Simons did not believe in sinless perfection, but rather that Christians must help each other achieve the fullness of life in Christ through both faith and obedience.

This vision of the church, as well as cultural acceptance and economic prosperity, led to a dynamic witness at all social levels. But it also led to numerous divisions that were to trouble the later years of Simons's work. Because of these tensions, many of his writings came to be unduly defensive and polemical. Circumstances, and his co-workers, forced him into a harsher stand on excommunication and the ban (exclusion from membership) than he had taught earlier.

The doctrine of a pure church also forced him into polemical exchanges with Reformed theologians and others on his view of the incarnation. A pure church required a pure Savior. Hence Simons believed that Jesus had received both his divine and his human nature directly from God, and that Mary was as passive as a glass of water through which a ray of sun passes. Although this Christology of heavenly flesh was not new by that time, and was also taught by others, it brought ridicule to Simons as he tried, with increasing bitterness, to defend the doctrine.

Simons led a harried and persecuted life. In 1542 a bounty of one hundred guilders was offered by Holy Roman Emperor Charles V (1500–1558) for his capture; this did not seriously disrupt his travels, even though some who had given him lodging and food were executed. His journeys extended from Friesland to the Cologne area, and east to Danzig (present-day Gdansk). He was eventually permitted to settle in Holstein, northeast of Hamburg, perhaps because he had broken with earlier Anabaptists in expressing his belief that a Christian could also be a magistrate, provided that he lives in obedience to Christ. Extensive writings continued to flow from his pen and press in Holstein until his death on January 31, 1561.

Bibliography

The Complete Writings of Menno Simons, c. 1496–1561, edited by J. C. Wenger (Scottdale, Pa., 1956), remains the standard English sourcebook. Irvin B. Horst has prepared a scholar's research guide entitled *A Bibliography of Menno Simons* (The Hague, 1962). The most comprehensive recent biography has been written by Christoph Bornhäuser, *Leben und Lehre Menno Simons'* (Neukirchen, 1973). Cornelius Krahn's *Dutch Anabaptism: Origin, Spread, Life and Thought, 1450–1600* (The Hague, 1968) places Simons's work into the broader context of Dutch and Anabaptist history.

Cornelius J. Dyck (1987)

SIMON THE NEW THEOLOGIAN SEE SYMEON THE NEW THEOLOGIAN

SIN SEE NANNA

SIN AND GUILT.

The human being, as *homo religiosus,* is a creature that worries. This worrying is both a burden and a distinction. In the dark age of mutation to *Homo sapiens,* at the turning point between animality and humanity, the human intuition of the presence of the surrounding numinous tipped the balance toward humanness. As soon as this ape could stand on its feet, its glance could lift itself from the earth, the source of food, and direct itself toward the stars, that is, to a sphere higher—not only spatially—than that of the satisfaction of its bodily needs and functions. In this way humans discovered the universe and, concomitantly, the existential problem of their place in the cosmos, assigned to them by some power, for some particular reason, toward some goal. They thus invented an entire mythical universe in answer to the questions evoked by this fundamental anxiety.

Mircea Eliade has shown time and again that the central characteristic of myth is a narrative of origins. If one knows how things started and why they went awry, one finds some kind of solace, as does the patient upon learning from a physician the name of his or her disease. This reassurance is, however, partial at best: The essentials for living are the most precarious for humans among all the creatures of the earth. Reflecting on the origins of his human condition, humans came inevitably and universally to the conclusion that this present life is not what it was meant to be by the god(s) *in illo tempore.* In short, from being anxious, humans became unhappy, stricken with guilt feelings about an initial accident that is repeated endlessly throughout human existence and can be called "sin."

Sin and guilt, however, come in a great variety of shades, according to the various sensitivities represented by the great number of religious and philosophical feelings and systems. In this article the classification of the different approaches to the issue is of primordial importance. The article shall attempt to distribute the material from a phenomenological point of view, starting with the cosmological apprehension of humans as surrounded by taboos and continuing with the tragic conception that to live at all is a sin. In a second major section, the transition from such a naturalistic understanding to an ethical conception will be assessed. The third area of investigation concerns the Judeo-Christian tradition and its antitaboo, antideterministic, antinaturistic notion of sin as a breach of a personal covenant with God and humanity. A brief excursus discusses the very different notions of sin and guilt among the ancient Greeks. Finally, a particular case is made of Islam as another branch of the monotheistic tradition.

THE COSMOLOGICAL VISION. Martin Heidegger in his *Sein und Zeit* (1929) speaks of the "fall" of humans into the world. This is a felicitous rendering of the basic feeling that developed as soon as humans became aware of being part of the vast cosmos. From the dawn of consciousness, humans felt impotent, an unbearable condition. That is why they resorted to magic. When all rational response to reality becomes pent up and frustrated, the only alternative to passive inaction is the biological function of magic. Magic is the manipulation of occult forces in nature; it is a way of participating in cosmic functions. Here specific acts are wrought as mimesis of their archetypal models; they deal with objects that are never indifferent, although some are of common use and, so to speak, tolerated by the gods, while others are taboos, that is, reserved by the gods for themselves. Humanity's manipulation of a taboo is a dangerous business and demands ritual reparation. But it is not *sensu stricto* a sin, and there is here no true guilt. The violation of a taboo is often absolutely unavoidable, like everything pertaining to sexuality or the return home of the victorious warrior. Making reparation to the numinous consists in magically purging the offender through specific magical acts, sometimes through death. It is not a punishment however, for that would imply personal culpability, that is, violation of a commandment expressing a divine will. What is dreaded by the "primitive" is not offending a transcendent being but upsetting the cosmological order. Thanks to myth, the primitive knows what is taboo, and thanks to magical rites, knows what to do and how to do it: the primitive confesses and expiates.

If one follows Raffaele Pettazzoni (*La confessione dei peccati,* 1929–1936) and picks up the one conception of sin that he calls magical (in contrast to theistic), one is struck by the biological aspect of what is called sin in confessions. They tend to focus, for example, upon sexuality, but more generally, in agrarian cultures, they are clearly oriented toward a cosmobiology. The appropriate expiation transfers to another object the threat of biological evil. It is so little a matter of guilt on the part of the confessant that he lists sins that he obviously never committed. Sin, in this context, is not a personal but a material object.

One must therefore complement what has been said above about purgation of the offender with a more objective aspect of the ritual. As Robert Hertz has noted, more often than not the point is not only to purge the transgressor of the mystical substance he unduly appropriated, but to bring it back to its original focus. The personal participation in upsetting the cosmos is, of course, not ignored. But it is not the center of concern, for humanity finds itself living after a cosmic catastrophe whose "culprit" is anonymous. Death is no punishment but belongs to life structure and to world order. Everything is here determined before the anthropogony occurs. Later, when humans discovered agriculture, they applied to themselves its cyclical resurgence, the "eternal return," and so were born the initiation rites whose center is the symbolic death of the initiate followed by the symbolic return to life. Again on this score, death does not imply any consciousness of a guilt to be atoned for.

At this point, one can discern two variants in the treatment of the presence of evil in the world according to the cosmological view. The second variant will be reviewed below in the section on Mesopotamia. This first division may be concluded with the mention of the first variant, namely, the conception of individual life as being by itself already an offense, an injustice, an arrogance, to be atoned for. Such a view is found in geographical areas as remote from one another as Central America and Greece. According to the Maya and Aztec myth, this world is the last extant in a series of creations destroyed by cataclysms. This one endures only on account of the sacrifices of human hearts offered to the gods, who themselves made the first oblation (see K. Garbay, *Historia de los Mexicanos por sus pinturas,* 2d ed., Mexico City, 1973).

Thus, the most archaic form of fault is defilement, that is, "a strain or blemish that infects from without" (Ricoeur, 1967, p. 8). The focus is on the world rather than humanity, and the ethical sin is confused with the material evil, for all failure upsets the cosmological order and brings with it defilement, thus drawing between sacred and profane a dividing line that often makes no sense to modern humans. This, however, constitutes what Ricoeur calls "our oldest memory," for which the concept of retribution is central. That is why it took no less than the questioning of this foundational myth to dissociate ethical sin from physical evil and suffering.

Mesopotamian Religion. This second variant to the cosmological conception mentioned earlier is found in Mesopotamia. There for the first time, the anonymity of evil was felt intolerable. The phenomenology of evil had to find a language by which a responsible agent could be incriminated as the bearer of guilt. Two ways were open: either through demonizing powers and forces manipulating humans as pawns on a chessboard or through designating human culprits, thus making them the bearers of guilt. Both solutions are found in Mesopotamian mythologies. The former, however, is fundamental. It gives expression to the all-important human sentiment that evil was already present before the anthropogony. Before becoming guilty through participation, the human is a victim. This tragic conception found expression in the text *Ludlul bel nemeqi,* where the so-called Babylonian Job cannot make sense of his misfortune. Similarly, in *A Dialogue about Human Misery,* the so-called Babylonian Qohelet concludes that one cannot know the divine intentions. But already a Sumerian confessional says, "Whether man has acted shamefully, whether he has acted well, he knows not at all."

One is struck by the pessimism of the Mesopotamian myths. The cosmological myth *Enuma elish,* for example, resembles a Greek tragedy. Humanity falls into sin as it falls into existence. In the background of all Babylonian and Assyrian penitential psalms, the free will of humans is never up to the demands of the divine standards of purity: "Mankind as many as there be [commit] sin . . . the food that belongs to God I have eaten." So people are naturally sinful, and this can be explained by a kind of generative transmission of that status. "The penalty of my father, of my grandfather, of my mother, of my grandmother, of my family, of relations through brothers and sisters, may it not come nigh me" (Langdon, 1927).

If the defilement of sin is "our oldest memory," the inexorability of sin is also very much present today, to the extent that people have maintained a dualistic view of reality. This finds expression in phylogenetic laws (Darwin), in the psychological fabric of humanity (Freud), and in societal structures (Marx). But until now the word *sin* has been used here only by approximation, for it is only when the fault is put in the context of a covenantal relation with God that one can speak, *sensu stricto,* of sin (against an expressed divine will). Here, taboos and magic have no role to play. If they are still found in the documents, they are reduced to the state of traces. This article thus turns to the next religious venture; it has been characterized by some as a process of demythologization.

The Religions of Israel. Starting with those remnants of the fault as defilement, one may observe with Ricoeur (1967, p. 70f.) the customary positive character of the stain; purity's characteristic, on the other hand, is negative. When, as in the Bible, sin becomes a breach in the living relation with God, there is conversion of the positive to the negative. Sin is "the loss of a bond, of a root, of an ontological ground" counterbalanced by the positive "fundamental symbolism of the return." One has entered another world, but not one isolated from the rest of the universe.

One central characteristic of the Hebrew scriptures is that they are polemical in reaction to the ways of thinking of the neighboring world. It is clear that such documents cannot be read in isolation from their environment. Taking issue, for example, with the ontological dualism present everywhere, Israel understands the profane as being in analogy with the sacred. Humans have been created in the image of God (*Gn.* 1:26f.). Something of the kind existed in Mesopotamia, where the king was the image of the divine, in contradistinction to all other human beings. Israel "demythologized" this notion through a process of democratization. Not the king only, but human *qua* human is *imago Dei.* The creator has granted humans creative faculties: speech, sexuality, conscience. Conscience is here no intrinsic human quality but a gift of God; it is the Hebrew *lev* (*Ex.* 35:21–22, 29). It makes the individual an ethical being. For the first time, one meets a vivid consciousness of sin: Abel's blood cries out from the ground (*Gn.* 4:10); Joseph's brothers acknowledge their guilt (*Gn.* 42:21ff.); the psalmist laments "my sin is ever before me" (*Ps.* 51:5). Sin is now assessed within a context of interrelationship between God and man, that is, of the covenant. It is thus no longer just an ethical fault. Neither is it a juridical offense only. Being in covenant with God entails an existence in holiness; sin therefore is deviation (*'avon*), a straying from the norms of holiness, understood as the very dynamism of life. It is a crime against God's sanctity, and it is only to be expected that it would occasion the far-ranging disturbance of life. For God's holiness and the holy human response to it keep the cosmos and humanity in *shalom* (peace, integrality, wholeness, sanity.) Far from the face of God, there can be only disease and catastrophe (*Lv.* 26:1ff.; *Dt.* 28:1ff.).

Thus is the notion of sin oriented toward a liturgical understanding. To the microcosmic concentration of the liturgy in the Temple of Jerusalem corresponds the macrocosmic liturgy of the world with humans at its center. This, which is especially true of the Priestly source, is also fundamental for Yahvism in general (*Is.* 6:3, 6:5). Pushed to the extreme, sin becomes a *pesha'*, that is, an apostasy, an abandonment of rectitude, of justice, of fidelity—in brief, of Torah. Thus there is in the Bible no theory of sinfulness, but, very practically, there are sins, a thousand and one ways to go astray from an existence whose whole *raison d'être* is to be holy. Here the realism is such that sins corrupt the whole "heart," which therefore must be replaced by a pure heart, and not only on the individual level but, eschatologically and actually, on the communal level when all Israel is made "new," "whole," "holy."

Thus, for Israel, since humanity is created coresponsible for the governance of creation and indeed is high priest in the cosmic temple (*Gn.* l:26ff. and the whole literary Priestly "layer" in the Pentateuch), it is also ultimately responsible for the presence of evil in the universe and in history. The known world is a perverted "garden" where even the generative and the creative powers of humans are twisted in their process and their aim, and diverted from their natural bliss. In sorrow are people to produce their food amid a plantation that is the reverse of the one of Eden, as it is full of thorns and thistles. Ultimately everyone returns, not to "paradise," but to dust (*Gn.* 3:16–19).

That deviation is the product of both the human "heart" (internal) and an external power, personified in *Genesis* 3 as the "serpent," which is an evil spirit according to other texts. There is between the two a correspondence. The serpent's discourse is immediately intelligible to humans, evoking in them favorable echoes. For humanity is inclined to do evil (*Gn.* 6:5). Later this inclination is conceptualized in the Apocrypha and rabbinism as the *yetser ha-ra'* (*4 Esd.* 7:118, *2 Bar.* 40:42f.). Thus there is present here a trace of a tragic anthropology, insisting upon the passivity and the alienation of humanity. The point these texts want to make is that by birth, the status of humanity is to be separated from God. Before any human act, sin is already there. It follows from this that the divine covenant is a gracious gift, undeserved and productive of a second birth, the birth of a "circumcised" life (i. e., marked by the intimate relationship with God).

As, however, the *yetser ha-ra'* is no radical evil but a permanent temptation, there is here no *servum arbitrium* or original sin in the sense of an inherited corrupt nature. Sin is a kind of second nature in humans (*Jer.* 13:23); it is human obstinacy to alienate oneself. Ezekiel speaks of the human *niddah* (impurity), and Paul, later, uses the Greek term *hamartia* in the singular.

From the pragmatic concern with sins one has now passed to the reflective elaboration of a theory of sin that underscores humanity's congenital weakness. Humans are "flesh"; they are born sinners (*Ps.* 51:7). They are capable of only relative justice (*Is.* 51:1). Sinning has become an attitude connatural to humans, a permanent blemish (*Is.* 6:5). This realism leads the New Testament to the conclusion that the world is ruled by evil (*Rom.* 3:9, *Col.* 1:13, *1 Jn.* 5:19), because humans have enthroned it.

Sin is not only a fault before God, it is also an act wronging one's neighbor. David claims that he did not sin against King Saul (*1 Sm.* 19:4; 24:12); in return, Saul would be committing a sin against David in attempting to kill him, something Saul acknowledges later (*1 Sm.* 26:21). Time and again the prophets, in particular, equate the one aspect of humanity's sin with the other. No one denounces more forcefully than Amos social ills as sins against humans and against God. When, later, Jesus is asked which is the greatest commandment, he replies by equating the commitment to love God with that to love one's neighbor, i.e., one's fellow human beings (*Mt.* 22:36–40; cf. *Dt.* 6:5, *Lv.* 19:18).

Sin entails the curse. A classic description of the latter is found in *Deuteronomy* 28 (cf. *Lv.* 26). As Johannes Pedersen writes, "Sin breeds the curse, and the curse breeds sin" (1959, vol. 1, p. 441). "The sinner is charged with a curse, for the curse is a dissolution which takes place in the soul of the sinner" (ibid., p. 437). This is why there is an intimate relation between sin and disease or other misfortunes. In the first case as in the second, one "is stricken in the soul" (*1 Kgs.* 8:38). Human-made evil includes military defeat, drought, famine, and so forth (8:33–40). There are thus three possible causes of illness: one's own sin, the curse of others, or the sinfulness of humanity in general (cf., *Ps.* 32:1ff., 38:3ff., etc.; *Sir.* 38:1–15).

The Israelites did not distinguish between performance and performer, sin and sinner. Sin is the doing of the sinner; the sinner sins. There cannot be a judgment of the deed that would not be a judgment of the doer. Beyond illness and disease, death is the ultimate punishment of sin. But death is not just the final accident ending human existence. As has been seen, sin is the dissolution of the soul; life is torn apart by sin (*Dt.* 27:15–26). It is really the presence of death in the midst of life, and suffering is its foretaste. As Paul is later to proclaim, "death is the wages of sin" (*Rom.* 6:23).

Being phenomenologically a movement of radical reform within Judaism, one deeply influenced by apocalypticism, early Christianity crystallized the notion of sinfulness into a state of universal corruption (*Mt.* 7:11). In contrast to the rabbis, Paul emphasized the unavoidability of sin. It is due to Adam's "fall" (*Rom.* 5:12ff.), on the one hand, and to an equation made between weakness of the flesh and its antagonism to God (*Rom.* 8:3, "the flesh of sin"), on the other. Moreover the law has brought human sinfulness to a paroxysm, for the law makes sin real and sanctionable (*Rom.* 4:15). It is this very paroxysm that expresses itself in the crucifixion of the just *par excellence,* its total reversal by the grace of God making Christ's death atone for humankind's sins. Paul writes, "Christ died for our sin" (*1 Cor.* 15:3), and further, "Christ was innocent of sin, and yet for our sake God made him one with the sinfulness of men, so that in him we might be made one with the goodness of God himself" (*2 Cor.* 5:21). Thus "in Christ" (a favorite expression of Paul) it has become possible to lead a saintly life, which as was seen above is, according to the Hebrew Bible, the goal of creation. In summary, the final answer to humanity's guilt, according to the New Testament, is given by the death of Christ which overcomes the human state of sin and guilt and thereby inaugurates the kingdom of God on earth.

The Greeks. For the sixth-century philosopher Anaximander, being itself is already evil. One finds in Greece other echoes of such pessimism. Tragedy is, after all, a Greek invention. According to this conception of existence, humanity's fault (not sin) is a blindness sent by the gods, a fatal error that the Greeks called *hamartia.* In Sophocles' *Oedipus at Colonus,* the hero says, "In me personally you would not find a fault *[hamartias]* to reproach me with to having thus committed these crimes against myself and against my kin" (ll. 967f.). One may observe that Oedipus is the ambivalent symbol of crime and excusable fault. For Aristotle, *hamartia* is the terrible and tragic fault made by distinguished individuals, by heroes. He insists on their nobility. In sum, there is more fascination in Greece with hero worship than with hamartology. As E. R. Dodds has shown, in the Greek tradition one is dealing more with a "shame culture" than with real guilt. The Homeric hero "loses face"; his public reputation (*timē*) means everything to him. Although with time there occurred a moralization process whereby shame became guilt, the ground for feeling guilty remained murky. It is tied with *hubris;* still, the sixth-century poet Theognis says, "No man . . . is responsible for his own ruin or his own success: of both these things the gods are the givers. No man can perform an action and know whether its outcome will be good or bad" (ll. 133–136). So, despite the protest of the fifth-century philosopher Heraclitus that "character *is* destiny" (frag. 119), one's *daemon* was in general more important, for an ancient Greek, than one's character.

Plato adopts the opinion of Socrates that "no one sins willingly," for wrongdoing is an error of judgment. No one who knows what is good (which is also happiness), would choose not to imitate it. *Ananke* (necessity) exists, but it operates within the kind of life freely chosen by the soul. "He who chooses is responsible, not God" (*Republic* 10.617e). The only sin is to shift from the voluntary to the involuntary. When this is avoided, the soul can be assimilated to God by contemplating the world of the Forms, which is divine and well ordered. By imitating such a world the soul becomes divine and well ordered as well.

Aristotle takes issue with Socrates' optimism that no one sins voluntarily. For, in the first place, people are responsible for the way they figure out what is good for them. Second, once a goal is set, human reflection decides what are the appropriate means to reach it, and the means selected makes one guilty or innocent. The human soul disposes of a power of choice (*proairesis*); it is the root of liberty, but the passions can overcome intellection. There is indeed a guilty *lack* of knowledge, which, for an alcoholic, for instance, is self-inflicted. Euripides has Medea say, "I do realize how terrible is the crime I am about, but passion overrules my resolutions, passion that causes most of the misery in the world" (*Medea* 1078–1080). Happiness, however, is submission to intellection (*nous*), that is, to what is most divine in humans. There is a veritable rational determinism concerning the ends of such submission. To obey *nous* assures contact with the immortal. But there is no notion here of sin in the sense of a breach in a personal relationship with God. For God is a Thought thinking itself and is totally indifferent to humanity and the world.

The Stoa puts the emphasis on individual autonomy within a human communion *(koinonia, philia, oikeiosis)* whose cement is Reason which permeates the whole. In the second century CE, Marcus Aurelius wrote:

> All things are implicated with one another, and the bond is holy; and there is hardly anything unconnected with any other thing. For things have been coordinated, and they combine to form the same universe [order]. For there is one universe made up of all things, and one God who pervades all things, and one substance, and one law, one common reason in all intelligent animals, and one truth; if indeed there is also one perfection for all animals which are of the same stock and participate in the same reason. (*Meditations* 7.9)

Here universal laws are identical with divine laws, so that human life is conceived by the Stoic thinker Epictetus (c. 55–c. 135) as a divine service (*huperesia* or *diakonia*). The ideal is to live according to nature, for the world order is totally rational and anything that happens must therefore be accepted. Providence is another name for necessity. Sin is error, the violation of the cosmic laws.

Finally, a more clearly religious solution is proposed by Orphism. In Orphic thought, the root of evil is the body; it is a prison for the soul. The soul is punished in the body for earlier sins. If these sins are not expiated during one incarnation, the soul transmigrates to another body. This doctrine of reincarnation provided an elegant solution to the moral dilemma of divine justice and human suffering. The way to purify the soul of sin is to emancipate the individual from group solidarity and its corollary, vicarious suffering for another's fault. The goal is to escape from the wheel of deaths and rebirths through rituals that bring *katharsis,* that is, a cleansing from the old taint of carnality.

THE CHRISTIAN CHURCH. This article will deal here—all too briefly, to be sure—with three Christian theologians chosen for their towering stature in the history of the Eastern and the Western churches and for their lasting influence on Christian thinking and philosophy until the present day. Irenaeus (c. 120–202), with whom this discussion shall start for reasons of chronology, has a conception of humanity before the Fall that Augustine found himself incapable of sharing. For Irenaeus, the time before the Fall is that of Adam's immaturity. He has been created in the "image of God" but is still to be brought to the stage of the "likeness of God." The Fall delayed the process of maturation, but on the other hand, it also marked a kind of human weaning from the parental God. Only a relatively independent being can enter a meaningful relationship with the creator. Human history consists of the vicissitudes of that relationship. It would however end in total failure were it not for the incarnation. Christ is his father's manifestation *(manifestatio, phanerōsis),* thus making God visible. To see God in Christ is the way for humans to be divinized. God came down to humans, and humans climb up to God.

When turning to Origen (c. 185–c. 254), one finds humanity at the crossroads of two diverging theologies: the theology of Justin and Clement, "Greek" and indifferent to the role of the flesh, and the theology of Irenaeus, deeply biblical and christological. In *On First Principles (Peri archōn),* there is no mention of an original sin committed by Adam. Rather Origen emphasizes the fall of souls. These are preexisting pure spirits that strayed from their creator and fell into human bodies. They are in pilgrimage back to God. This process of salvation is also a process of restoration, of mending, of putting the world back in order. This is possible because there is between God and the world a kinship the trace of which in humans is the *nous.* There is here no autonomous existence of darkness. Evil is simply a turning away from God.

It is thus with no surprise that one finds Origen focusing upon Christ's work rather than on his person. Christ is the great educator who brings humanity from deficiency to perfection. The goal (*teleiōsis*) is the perfection of human nature by the Logos, the divinization of humanity. The means is obedience to God, which Christ teaches by his word and by his death: "The Son . . . made himself obedient unto death to teach obedience to those who could reach salvation only by way of obedience." Salvation is *apokatastasis pantōn* (a restitution of all things and a definite achievement). Even Satan will be saved. But until the eschaton, the movement of drawing near to God is endless. All has been revealed; but all is to be discovered. Christ has come; but he ceaselessly comes.

The church father Augustine (354–430) is without rival as regards the theology of the West. Augustine inaugurates a "new type of discourse, that of onto-theology," says Ricoeur. The question *unde malum* would be legitimate only if evil were substantial, as the Manichaeans teach. But it is not so. Already Basil of Caesarea (330–379) had stated that there is no ontological reality to evil (*Hexaemeron* 2.5). Augustine follows suit and says that the problem is rather *unde malum faciamus,* stressing more forcefully still that evil is no substance, no creature. All creatures participate in being and are therefore good. It is only through his free choice that humans bring sin from potential to real, from nothingness to an act. Evil is negative. It is *amissio boni* or *privatio boni.* It is a deficiency of the created that makes freedom possible and hence human history.

Augustine had the opportunity to underscore this theologoumenon of the gratuitousness of God's grace in his polemics against Pelagius (fl. c. 400–418). This British monk taught that humanity can reach perfection in holiness by the practice of virtues and asceticism. Humans therefore bear the sole guilt for their sins, as they are endowed with free will. "If sin is innate, it is not voluntary, if it is voluntary, it is not innate." Pelagius of course chooses the second proposition. Children are in the situation of Adam before the Fall. Some of them imitate Adam; others become perfectly washed of all sin.

In response to Pelagius, Augustine considerably hardened his stance. He developed the "original sin" theory (inaugurated by Cyprian, 200–258, and by Ambrose, c. 330–397) and stated that all humans are born sinful and guilty, meriting eternal damnation. With the Fall, the human spirit has been victimized by the rebellion of the body, which should have been its servant. (By contrast, the animal, although under the dictum of nature, is not guilty, because it has no reason, no spirit.) Originally nature was *natura sana,* but it has become *natura vitiata.* This explains why sin is transmitted from one generation to another, making sin as unavoidable as life itself. This inherent nothingness in humans impairs their liberty. Evil is an act; it has an existential character and can be described as a *defectus,* an *aversio a Deo, conversio ad creaturas* (*Against Secundinus the Manichaean* 17). For this, which is a perversion, God is not responsible. He is responsible for the musical instrument, not for its discord.

Augustine's theories are not exempt from ambiguities. They have remained so in the church for sixteen centuries (Tresmontant, 1961, p. 611). For the freedom and the culpability of humans is on the other hand predestined by God. Augustine developed the doctrine of double predestination, which had such a powerful impact on Calvin and on so many Christian theologians. The seminal transmission of sin and guilt was Augustine's way of counterbalancing the culpability of the individual. Humanity finds evil already present before actualizing it itself. But the fact that perverted nature is inherited considerably relativizes humanity's ultimate responsibility, for Augustine attributed to evil a quasi-nature through a continuous contingency.

ISLAM. In the Qur'ān, sin is essentially pride and opposition to God. The model of such misbehavior is given by Iblīs (Satan), who refused to prostrate himself before Adam.

Human sin is minimized to the level of a weakness that has become a kind of habit: "the heart is prone to evil" (12:53). In fact, the original mistake of Adam proved beneficial for humanity, for through this mistake the world became populated and God worshiped by a great number of people. Besides, the forgiveness of sin is within easy reach for all (57:28 and passim). Repentance does not require atonement, and the pilgrim on the *ḥājj* to Mecca returns home as innocent as a newborn child. Prophets and saints are delivered in this life from moral and physical evils. Believers are further delivered from eternal punishment. However, good works as well as faith are necessary for salvation.

The power of God stands at the center of Muslim faith. That power is such that it can even be arbitrary. For example, God commands reprehensible acts from Muḥammad. The Qur'ān (35:9) declares that God leads astray those he chooses (cf. 42:12, 40:36). If God willed, everyone in the land would believe. But God does not impose his will on humans so that they may be responsible for themselves (10:99f., 18:28). This does not detract from the fact that all has been decreed beforehand by God, including humanity's failings.

See Also Confession of Sins; Evil; Magic.

Bibliography

Mircea Eliade's *A History of Religious Ideas,* 3 vols. (Chicago, 1978–1986), has become an instant classic. Its synthesis of religious thought and the extent of its bibliographic data are without parallel elsewhere. From a philosophical and phenomenological point of view, Paul Ricoeur has written two remarkable books, *The Symbolism of Evil* (Boston, 1967) and *The Conflict of Interpretations* (Evanston, Ill., 1974). He is also the author of a study on Augustine, which, although as yet unpublished, I have used here with his permission.

On ancient Near Eastern religions, the irreplaceable *Ancient Near Eastern Texts relating to the Old Testament,* 3d ed., edited by J. B. Pritchard (Princeton, 1969), needs no commendation. It is an inexhaustible source of reliable, often firsthand, information. Stephen Langdon's *Babylonian Penitential Psalms* (Paris, 1927) remains the indispensable book on that question. Although in need of updating, the admirable synthesis of Israel's psyche and culture by Johannes Pedersen, *Israel: Its Life and Culture,* 2 vols. (1926–1947; reprint, Oxford, 1959), remains unmatched, except, on the institutions, by Roland de Vaux's *Ancient Israel: Its Life and Institutions,* 2d ed. (London, 1965). One should add to these two works the excellent systematic studies of Old Testament theology by Walther Eichrodt, *Theology of the Old Testament,* 2 vols. (Philadelphia, 1961–1967), and by Gerhard von Rad, *Old Testament Theology,* 2 vols. (New York, 1962–1965).

There are many monographs on "sin and guilt" according to the Jewish and Christian understanding, written in several languages. Few of them, however, have the scope and soberness of expression of the French collective work *Théologie du péché* (Tournai, 1960), by Philippe Delhaye et al. Here one finds invaluable information on the notion of sin in "primitive" religions, in the Bible, among the Greeks, in Roman Catholic theology, and to a lesser extent in Eastern Christianity and Protestantism. On Protestantism, one should, of course, turn to Karl Barth's *Church Dogmatics,* vol. 3.1, *The Doctrine of Creation* (New York, 1958), and to Paul Tillich's *Systematic Theology,* vol. 2, *Existence and the Christ* (Chicago, 1960). Another synoptic treatment of sin in the history of religions is provided by the collective work *Man and His Salvation,* edited by Eric J. Sharpe and John R. Hinnells (Totowa, N. J., 1973), which explores aspects of Buddhism, Islam, Hinduism, early Christianity, Jewish Hasidism, Zoroastrianism, and so on.

The French theologian A.-M. Dubarle has written extensively on the problem of sin in the Bible and in church doctrine. Especially deserving notice here is his *Le péché originel: Perspectives théologiques* (Paris, 1983). Claude Tresmontant, another French theologian, gives an excellent presentation of the problem of creation and anthropology from the origins of Christianity to the time of Augustine in *La métaphysique du christianisme* (Paris, 1961), which is particularly important for its treatment of Origen and Augustine. Pierre Nautin's *Origène, sa vie et son œuvre* (Paris, 1977) reconstructs with great care Origen's biography and the tenets of his thinking.

The best treatment of Greek thought about sin and guilt is E. R. Dodds's *The Greeks and the Irrational* (Berkeley, Calif., 1951), especially his chapter on shame. On the Buddhist conception of sin, offense, and illusion, Henri de Lubac's *Aspects of Buddhism* (New York, 1963) has the merit of being a reliable translation for Western readers of Eastern concepts that are not easily understood by noninitiates.

New Sources

Blocher, Henri. *Original Sin: Illuminating the Riddle.* New Studies in Biblical Theology. Downers Grove, Ill., 2001.

Buruma, Ian. *The Wages of Guilt: Memories of War in Germany and Japan.* New York, 1995.

Carrasco, Davíd. "Uttered from the Heart: Guilty Rhetoric among the Aztecs." *History of Religions* 39 (August 1999): 1–31.

Connor, Peter. *Georges Bataille and the Mysticism of Guilt.* Baltimore, Md., 2000.

Delumeau, Jean. Eric Nicholson, trans. *Sin and Fear: the Emergence of the Western Guilt Culture, 13th–18th Centuries.* New York, 1991.

Enright, Robert and Joanna North, eds. *Exploring Forgiveness.* Madison, Wisc., 1998.

Tavuchis, Nicholas. *Mea Culpa: A Sociology of Apology and Recrimination.* Stanford, 1991.

West, Angela. *Deadly Innocence: Feminist Theology and the Mythology of Sin.* New York, 1995.

André LaCocque (1987)
Revised Bibliography

SINGH, GOBIND (1666–1708), the last of the ten *gurūs* ("teachers") of Sikhism. After his death the Sikh *gurū* was understood to be the *Ādi Granth,* the sacred book. Until Gobind Singh, the Sikh community, whose religious ideals and practices were a North Indian combination of Vaiṣṇava devotional movements from South India and elements of Islamic Sufism, had been led by a series of *gurūs* beginning with Nānak (1469–1539) and passing through to Gobind Singh's father, the ninth *gurū*, Tegh Bahādur.

Gobind Singh (originally Gobind Rāi) is known as the paradigm of the chivalrous, proud, martial, and loyal religious ideal to which members of the Sikh Khālsā, "the community of pure ones," aspire. In fact, it was Gobind Singh who established the Khālsā, and gave all male Sikhs the surname Singh ("lion") and Sikh women the name Kaur ("lioness"). Gobind Singh is further known as the reported author of the *Dasam Granth* (Tenth Volume), an epic work that stands second only to the *Ādi Granth* in prestige in the Sikh community. Under Gobind Singh's rule (1675–1708) Sikhism was transformed from a persecuted sect to a powerful religious community that has stood as the political and economic mainstay of the Punjab ever since.

Gobind Singh was born at Patna (in the Indian state of Bihar) on December 26, 1666, the only child of Tegh Bahādur and his wife Gujari. He spent the first few years of his life in Bihar before returning to his ancestral home, Anandpur, in the foothills of the Himalayas. He was nine years old when his father was summoned by the Mughal emperor to answer charges of extortion, and was executed in Delhi on November 11, 1675. Before he died, he proclaimed Gobind as his successor. Fearing further reprisals, the young *gurū* and his entourage moved farther back into the mountains and set up their camp at Paonta, on the banks of the Yamuna River. Here Gobind was taught Sanskrit and Persian (in addition to the Punjabi and Braj he had learned at Patna) and the arts of war. He spent much time hunting and composing poetry. His favorite themes were based on Hindu mythology, notably the exploits of the goddess Caṇḍī, the destroyer of demons.

In his autobiography, *Bicitra nātak* (The wonderful drama), Gobind wrote, "I came into the world charged with the duty to uphold the right in every place, to destroy sin and evil . . . that righteousness may flourish: that the good may live and tyrants be torn out by their roots." As he grew into manhood Gobind decided to organize his followers into a fighting force. Soon he raised a small army that came into conflict with neighboring Rajput chiefs. Gobind defeated their combined forces at Bhangani in 1686 and those of the Mughal governor of Punjab at Nadaun a year later. His increasing strength alarmed the Mughals, and the emperor Aurangzeb sent his eldest son, Prince Moazzam, against him. The prince discreetly decided to leave Gobind alone and directed his generals to reduce the hill chieftains. Gobind utilized these years to fortify Anandpur by building a chain of fortresses. He married three wives, who bore him four sons.

Gobind gave religious sanction to practices introduced by his father, Tegh Bahādur, and his grandfather, the sixth *gurū*, Hargobind. Early in 1699 Gobind sent out *hukumnāmahs* (orders) to the Sikhs to present themselves at Anandpur on the Hindu New Year's day with their hair and beards unshorn, as was customary among certain ascetic sects.

On April 13, 1699, after the morning service, Gobind drew his sword and asked for five men to offer their heads for sacrifice. He took them behind a tent and reappeared before the congregation, his sword dripping with blood, but then revealed that instead of the men he had slaughtered five goats. He addressed the volunteers as the "five beloved," *panj piyāre*, who were destined to become the nucleus of a new community, the Khālsā (from the Persian *khālis*, "the pure ones"). He baptized the five men (who came from different Hindu castes) by making them drink, from a single bowl, *amrit* (nectar) he had churned with a double-edged dagger. He gave them a new family name, Singh ("lion"), and after his own baptism changed his name from Gobind Rāi to Gobind Singh. Five emblems (*kakkār* or the "five *ks*") were prescribed for the Khālsā: to wear their hair and beards unshorn (*kais*); to carry a comb (*kanghā*) in their hair to keep it tidy; to wear the knee-length breeches (*kachhā*) then worn by soldiers; to wear a steel bracelet (*karā*) on their right wrist as a symbol of poverty and pledge to their *gurūs*; and always to carry a saber (*kirpān*) to defend their faith. In addition to these five emblems, the converts were forbidden to smoke or chew tobacco, to consume alcoholic drinks, to eat the flesh of animals slaughtered by being bled to death (as was customary among Jews and Muslims); they were permitted only *jhatkā* meat, that of an animal dispatched with one blow. Because their adversaries were largely Muslims, the Khālsā were forbidden to molest their women. The idea, in short, was to raise an army of *sant sipāhis* (soldier-saints).

The vast majority of the *gurū*'s followers underwent baptism and became hirsute Kesādhāri Khālsā, as distinct from the Sahajdhari Sikhs ("those who take time to adopt"). The eruption of this militant force alarmed the neighboring Hindu chieftains as well as the Muslim Mughals. Gobind was compelled to evacuate Anandpur. No sooner had he left than his two youngest sons were captured and executed. The *gurū* was left with forty men who stockaded themselves at Chamkaur. In the skirmishes that ensued the *gurū* was able to escape, but his two elder sons fell in battle. Tradition holds that despite these adversities Gobind sent the emperor a defiant poem entitled *Zafarnāmā* (The Epistle of victory). There he wrote, "What use is it to put out a few sparks when you raise a mighty flame instead?"

Gobind eluded his pursuers and found safe refuge at Muktsar. He spent a year in the region baptizing large segments of the Hindu peasantry, including those of the Phulkian States: Patiala, Nabha, Jind, and Faridkot. With the assistance of a disciple, Manī Singh, he prepared a definitive edition of the Sikh scripture, the *Ādi Granth*, compiled by the fifth *gurū*, Arjun, in which he inserted compositions of his father, Tegh Bahādur. He also collected his own writings in the *Dasam Granth*.

It is not clear whether or not Gobind intended to complain to the emperor against Wazir Khan, governor of the

Punjab, about the murder of his infant sons, but he was on his way to the Mughal capital when he received news of the emperor's death and the conflict over succession between his sons. The *gurū* decided to back Prince Moazzam, and a detachment of Sikh soldiers fought a victorious battle on his side at Jajau on June 8, 1707. Later Gobind visited the new emperor at Agra and stayed on for several months. The emperor did not take any action against his governor of the Punjab, and when he marched to his southern domains against his rebellious brother, Kam Baksh, the *gurū* followed him as far as Nander (now in Maharashtra). At Nander two young Pathans who were in his entourage entered his tent and stabbed him. It is most likely that the assassins were hirelings of the Punjab governor. Before he succumbed to his wounds on October 7, 1708, Gobind proclaimed an end to the succession of *gurūs* and exhorted the Sikhs to look upon the *Ādi Granth* as the symbolic representation of their ten *gurūs*.

Gobind Singh remains the *beau ideal* of the Khālsā Sikhs, the paradigm of chivalry combined with valor, poetic sophistication, and generosity. He is referred to as *dasam padshāh* ("tenth emperor"), *nīle ghorey dā asvār* ("rider of the roan stallion"), *citiān bājān vālā* ("lord of white hawks"), and *kalgi dhar* ("wearer of plumes").

See Also Ādi Granth; Dasam Granth; Nānak; Sikhism.

Bibliography

Whereas few English-language sources deal exclusively with Gobind Singh, a number of general works on the Sikh religion contain sections dealing with his life and writings, based on his own work and contemporary records in Persian and Gurmukhi. Gokul Chand Narang's *Transformation of Sikhism*, 5th ed. (New Delhi, 1960) deals with the gradual rise of Sikh militancy that culminated with Gobind Singh. The volume *Poetry of the Dasam Granth* (Delhi, 1959), compiled by Dharmapal Asta, is the only attempt to present the *gurū*'s own compositions and others traditionally ascribed to him. Unfortunately, the translations do not do justice to the original.

New Sources

Gajrani, Shiv. *Guru Gobind Singh: Personality and Vision.* Patiala, 2000.

Kapoor, Sukhbir Singh. *The Ideal Man: The Concept of Guru Gobind Singh, the Tenth Prophet of the Sikhs.* London, 1988.

Singh, Balbir. *Message of Guru Gobind Singh and Other Essays.* Patiala, 1997.

Singh, Dalib. *Guru Gobind Singh and Khalsa Discipline.* Amritsar, 1992.

Singh, Dharam. *Dynamics of the Social Thought of Guru Gobind Singh.* Patiala, 1998.

Khushwant Singh (1987)
Revised Bibliography

SINHALA RELIGION.

The Sinhala of Sri Lanka are for the most part Buddhists, yet their practical religion is a composite system derived from a variety of sources, including pre-Buddhist indigenous beliefs, Indic astrology, popular Hinduism, Brahmanism, and Dravidian religion, especially that of South India. Over many years these seemingly non-Buddhist beliefs have been incorporated into a Buddhist framework and ethos. The religious beliefs that have derived from non-Buddhist sources have been labeled "spirit cults." This is a heuristically useful label if one does not make the mistake of defining them as non-Buddhist or anti-Buddhist. Some aspects of the spirit cults, such as the beliefs in *pretas*, or the malevolent spirits of departed ancestors, are very ancient popular beliefs that have been assimilated by Buddhism. Furthermore, Buddhist canonical texts are full of references to pious laypersons who on death have become reborn as gods, which means that, as Marasinghe puts it in *Gods in Early Buddhism* (Colombo, 1974), the *karman* theory is a kind of machine that can create its own gods. The theory of *karman* can, at the very least, easily justify the creation or continuing existence of the many kinds of supernatural beings that inhabit the behavioral universe of Buddhist nations in South and Southeast Asia. The crux of the issue is not whether these beliefs are Buddhist or non-Buddhist: It is that one can remain a Buddhist, and a citizen of Sri Lanka or Burma or Thailand, *without* subscribing to a belief in the spirit cults. The latter is not a necessary condition to being a Buddhist. Being a Buddhist is necessary for one's ethnic and national identity in the Theravāda societies of South and Southeast Asia, whereas the spirit cults have little or no bearing on one's larger identity. One is not a "heretic" if one rejects the popular religions; indeed, in some instances it may indicate affirmation of Buddhist orthodoxy and the ideal cultural values of the group.

To place the Sinhala spirit cults in a larger perspective it is useful to begin with a consideration of Vädda religion as described by C. G. Seligmann and Z. Seligmann in *The Veddas* (Cambridge, 1911). These aboriginal inhabitants of Sri Lanka speak a Sinhala dialect and were at least peripherally part of the traditional political system, owing allegiance to the king of Kandy. Although they were Sinhala-speaking, and their spirit cults showed considerable overlap with that of Sinhala Buddhists, most Väddas never converted to Buddhism. An examination of Vädda religion will help us understand more fully the nature of the Sinhala spirit cults and their relationship with Buddhism.

Cult of the Nä Yakku. The Väddas, unlike the Sinhala Buddhists, had as the basis of their religion a system of ancestor worship. Väddas who die are said to become deities known as *nä yakku* (sg., *yakā*), literally "kinsmen deities"; the transformation of a person's spirit to a *yakā* occurs a few days after his or her death. Ancestral spirits help the living but show wrath if neglected.

Complementing the spirits of the recently dead is a pantheon of major Vädda deities. This pantheon is headed by Kandē Yakā ("lord of the mountain"). Ancestral spirits are considered to be feudal attendants of Kandē Yakā and have his warrant to assist or punish the living. The concept of permission or warrant (*varan*) and the system whereby the higher gods engage lower deities as attendants are identical with Sinhala beliefs.

Kandē Yakā then is a benevolent deity who brings prosperity and wealth to Vädda society. He is sometimes propitiated as Kandē Vanniya (Lord Kandē). Several other major deities are propitiated in Vädda collective rituals. There is Bam̆bura Yakā, a grim spirit who presides over yams, and for whom a mimetic ritual of the boar hunt is performed; In̆digolle Yakā, also called Galē Yakā ("lord of the rock"), who is often propitiated with his spouse In̆digolle Kiri Ammā; and Bilin̆di Yakā, an infant deity also widely propitiated in Vädda country (nowadays in parts of the Eastern and Uva provinces). In addition there is a whole class of female deities called *kiri ammā* ("milk mother, grandmother"). These *kiri ammā* are the spirits of eminent Vädda women, generally the wives of Vädda headmen or chiefs, many of whom are thought to haunt mountain springs and rocky hillsides. A few of these *kiri ammā* are prominent enough to have individual names. These named *kiri ammā* are often invoked for curing children's diseases and for sickness in general. In addition to these major deities are minor deities, all of whom are the spirits of prominent deceased Väddas. Thus, the Vädda religion recognizes a pantheon that is comprised of individual ancestors as well as a special class of deities who are deified heroes. Although these deified ancestors and heroes are an important element in Vädda worship there are also Vädda deities such as In̆digolle Yakā, who are believed to have come from across the oceans. These latter beliefs—those of deified ancestors and foreign deities—directly link Vädda religion with that of their Sinhala neighbors, at least in parts of the Northwestern and North Central Provinces, and in Uva and in the Central Province (the Kandyan region).

The Sinhala Buddhists have no system of ancestor worship like that of the *nä yakku,* but they do believe in a cult of deified ancestors and foreign deities, which Parker, in his *Ancient Ceylon* (London, 1904), has labeled the *baṇḍāra* cult. *Baṇḍāra* means "chief," and this cult is that of a group of deities who are viewed as "lords" or "chiefs." Parker has called this a form of ancestor worship, but this is an erroneous identification, for the Sinhala do not deify their immediate ancestors. Rather, deified heroes or leaders of a local area or region constitute a major part of the cult. The striking feature of the *baṇḍāra* cult, however, is that all deities, both local and foreign, were originally human beings who have been deified. Many of them have the title *baṇḍāra* ("lord"); all of them are viewed as lords or chiefs and are subordinate to the great gods or *devas* of the Sinhala Buddhist pantheon, who are viewed as kings or world rulers (*cakravartins*).

The Baṇḍāra Cult among the Sinhala. The *baṇḍāra* cult has been formalized in many parts of the Kandyan region into a cult of the Dolaha Deviyo ("twelve gods"). The Twelve Gods are individually and collectively propitiated in group rituals. The operative pantheon in most parts of the Kandyan region thus consisted of the *baṇḍāra* cult, formalized into a numerological category of the Twelve Gods. Many of these gods have in fact demonic attributes and are often referred to in rituals as *devatā* ("godling"), a composite of the demonic and the divine. The Twelve Gods are associated with most of the social, economic, and personal needs of the worshiper—hunting, animal husbandry, and rice cultivation, as well as individual afflictions such as illnesses due to demonic incursions.

There is, then, a striking similarity between the Vädda gods and the Sinhala pantheon of the *baṇḍāra.* The deities in both pantheons are chiefs or lords (but not kings); they are euhemerized beings, often ancestral heroes. In collective rituals the Väddas propitiate their gods with meat offerings; among the Sinhala, however, only some of these deities (those possessing demonic qualities, like Gange Baṇḍāra) are offered meat (impure) offerings. Furthermore, and this is of crucial significance, both Vädda and Sinhala pantheons show considerable overlap. Thus, Kiri Ammā is the operative female deity among both the Vädda and the Kandyan Sinhala. The Vädda god Kandē Yakā, the benevolent deity of the hunt, is perhaps none other than Kandē Deviyō of the Kandyans. In Kandyan rituals Kandē Deviyō also appears as the god of the hunt. The Vädda term *yakā* appears to have been transformed into *dēviyō* ("god") by the Sinhala, since *yakā* clearly means "demon" in Sinhala. Several other deities are shared by both Vädda and Sinhala. In addition, many ritual terms are common to both cultures: *han̆gala* (priest's robe), *ayuda* (arms, ornaments of the deity), *kapurāla* (priest), *aḍukku* (meal served to the deity), *doḷa* (offering to demons), and *puda* (offering to gods). These terms, as well as the *baṇḍāra* cult itself, are not confined to the Kandyan area exclusively but constitute (or historically constituted) a series of overlapping circles covering most of Sinhala-speaking Sri Lanka. Even when the numerological category of twelve was not used (as in the North Central Province), there was throughout Sri Lanka a system of local village worship of *baṇḍāras*, or lords, who constituted a pantheon of euhemerized ancestors or heroes.

Both Vädda religion and the *baṇḍāra* cult of the Kandyan Sinhala show striking resemblances to the *nat* cultus of the Burmese and the Thai cult of the *phī.* Worship of both *nats* and *phī* constitutes an indigenous cult of ancestors, having a role similar to the cult of the Kandyan *baṇḍāra.* Note that *baṇḍāra* means "lord," which is exactly what *nat* (from the Sanskrit *nātha*) means. Furthermore, the *nats* are associated with natural phenomena, as are many Kandyan and Vädda deities. It is indeed likely that a form of euhemerism was the old indigenous, pre-Buddhist religion, not only of Sri Lanka, but of other Theravāda nations of this region. The full significance of *nat* or *baṇḍāra* comes out clearly in relation to the great, often Brahmanic-derived *devas*, who constitute the upper level of the pantheon. These *devas* are kings or *cakravartins*; the *baṇḍāras* are lesser beings and thus are chieftains or lords who owe formal suzerainty to the "god-kings."

As institutionalized at the village and tribal level, the form of village religion described above is intrinsically associated with that of the inspired priest acting as a medium or mouthpiece of the apotheosized ancestor or hero. The Seligmanns and other anthropologists writing on tribal India refer to him as "shaman." This designation is somewhat misleading since "shamanism" in South and Southeast Asia is different from the classic Siberian type. In the latter the soul of the shaman leaves the body. In the South Asian type this rarely happens; the deity possesses the priest and the god is thus physically "present" in the human community. Furthermore, the extreme individualism of classic shamanism is not found here. The possessed priest activates a formal, publicly accepted pantheon of deities; he rarely has personal guardian gods or individual spirits as in classic shamanism.

Traditional Sinhala religion probably coexisted, as it does today, with other forms of religious belief and practice, such as witchcraft, sorcery, and divination. When the great historical religions like Buddhism were introduced into this region the older religion had to adapt itself to the new situation. The basic mechanism whereby non-Buddhist beliefs were incorporated into Buddhism was the theory of *karman.* Deified ancestors could easily be incorporated through the theory of *karman* so that the death of the ancestor and his subsequent rebirth as a deity could be explained in terms of his good and bad actions in previous births. Over and beyond this, the older system of spirit cults had to be integrated with those of the great traditions, which included the great Brahmanic *devas* and the Buddha himself. This relationship between the older spirits and the *devas* and Buddha was expressed in the political idiom of the secular state.

The Baṇḍāra Cult and the Worship of Devas. The *baṇḍāra* cult, or the cult of the Twelve Gods, was the operative folk religion of many villages in the Kandyan kingdom for many centuries. But the cult of the *baṇḍāras* was in turn enveloped in the cult of the *devas*, the superordinate god-kings of the pantheon. What then is the relationship between the *baṇḍāra* cult and the great *devas*, most of whom derived historically from Brahmanism? To appreciate the full significance of this relationship one must shift one's ground from the narrow perspective of Vädda or Kandyan religion to the larger perspective of a Sinhala Buddhist nation. The *baṇḍāras* were local or regional deities, and although some of them, such as Maṅgara and Devatā Baṇḍāra, were widely dispersed they were viewed as chieftains, not kings. The *devas* by contrast were national deities, viewed as kings, holding jurisdictional sway over Sri Lanka; they were protectors of that Sinhala Buddhist nation. The *baṇḍāras* are subservient to the *devas*, and the latter, according to popular religion, are in turn subordinate to the Buddha. The *devas* have a warrant (*varan*) from the Buddha himself, whereas the lesser *baṇḍāras* generally exercise their authority with permission from the *devas*.

The concept of divine protectors of the secular and sacred realm is an ancient one in Sri Lanka. First, there was the ancient Buddhist doctrinal notion of the guardians of the four quarters of the universe. In addition to this there developed in Sri Lanka the idea of four guardians of the state. If the Buddhist guardians protected the cosmos the *devas* were protectors of the nation, and therefore were of great significance in the practical religion. The concept of the four gods *(hatara dēviyō)* and the four shrines *(hatara dēvāle)* were clearly established in the kingdoms of Kōṭṭe (fifteenth century) and in Kandy. In popular usage the term *hatara varan dēviyō* ("gods of four warrants"), which should in theory have referred to the four Buddhist guardians of the universe, came to be synonymous with the concept of the Four Gods—the guardians of the kingdom.

In relation to the concept of the Four Gods, numerology is once again very important. There have always been four guardian gods, but the deities occupying these positions show considerable variation. In general one would say that the positions of the Four Gods from the fifteenth century onward were filled from the following list of *devas*: Viṣṇu, Nātha, Vibhiṣaṇa, Saman (Lakṣmaṇa), Skanda, and the goddess Pattinī. If the *baṇḍāras* were part of the operative village religion, the *devas*, in particular the Four Gods, were part of the state cultus. In the Kandyan kingdom, for example, the Four Gods were paraded in the annual state procession along with the tooth relic. The king, the chiefs, and their retinue also participated in this event. The procession reflected in microcosm the larger macrocosmic structure of the Kandyan state.

Underlying the organization of the pantheon is a political idiom, very much like that found in the *nat* cultus in Burma as described by Melford Spiro in *Burmese Supernaturalism* (Englewood Cliffs, N. J., 1967): The Four Gods are the kings and guardians of Buddhism and the secular state and the Twelve Gods are the chiefs, attendants, or ministers or the god-kings. The order in the pantheon is based on the idea of order in the political state. Crucial to the feudal idiom underlying the pantheon is the notion of *sīmā* ("limit, boundary"), which has several meanings in the political sphere. First, in relation to territory, it indicates the boundary or border of a kingdom, province, or village; second, in relation to authority and control, it is the limit of a political domain, for example, the king has *sīmā* over the kingdom, the chief over a province, and the headman over a village; third, in relation to time, it means a "time limit" (*kāla sīmāva*) on the exercise of political authority, that is, the *kāla sīmāva* for the king is the king's lifetime, for a chief only a year. All these meanings of *sīmā*, so important in the political idiom, are transferred intact to the religious context. Thus, the deities in the pantheon all have their *sīmā* in terms of territory, authority, and time. The *baṇḍāras* have the village, region, or province as their *sīmā*. However, these boundaries are not permanently fixed: A regional deity may eventually come to have a national reputation and worship, as in the case of Kiri Ammā and Maṅgara, and more recently of Dēvatā Baṇḍāra. Nevertheless the ideology that the *baṇḍāras* are regional chiefs is important in that it defines their status in the overall religious system of the Sinhala. The Four Gods by contrast have as their *sīmā* the whole of Sri Lanka, but they also have their special *sīmā* over which they have more direct control. These generally are the regions surrounding the pilgrimage center(s) of each deity.

DEMONS, GODS, AND THE BUDDHA. At the lowest level of Sinhala religion are such demons and evil spirits as *pretas*, who are viewed as the malevolent spirits of dead kinsmen. All these evil spirits embody Buddhist notions of spiritual and ethical hindrances, such as craving *(taṇhā)*, hatred *(krodha)*, greed *(lobha)*, defilements *(kleśa)*, and enmity *(vaira)*. Evil beings, like good beings, are *karman*-bound creatures who, because of their propensity to cause harm, are caught in a situation where salvation is difficult if not impossible. They cause illness, both physical and psychic, and may possess people, especially women. They are born in blood and violence, and they must be propitiated with meat and other impure substances. In the western and southern parts of Sri Lanka they are propitiated in elaborate ritual dramas, described by Paul Wirz (1954) and more recently by Bruce Kapferer (1983).

The demons are under the authority of the *devas* (i.e., the great gods of the pantheon), who must control them to ensure a just social order. The *devas* are essentially rational and just deities, viewed by Sinhala Buddhists as future Buddhas or *bodhisattvas*. These *devas* (as well as the lesser *baṇḍāras*) are bound to the worshiper in a nexus of mutual obligation: The god protects humans, their cattle, and their crops, and ensures the common weal; humans in turn expresses their gratitude by transferring the merit they have earned to the gods and thus hastening the *nirvāṇa* and Buddha-aspiration of the latter. These transactions are formally expressed in the annual post-harvest thanksgiving rituals where the myths of the gods are sung, where ritual dramas celebrating their lives are enacted, and where thanks are offered to them by the village community.

Over and above the cults of the gods and demons is the worship of the Buddha. The Buddha himself is viewed as the supreme deity and totally benevolent, reigning over the rest of the pantheon. In his role as overlord of the pantheon he is referred to as "king"; in his role as the teacher of salvation he is "monk." In public parades known as *perahära,* the Buddha's role as king is predominant; in the rituals and prayers addressed to him inside the *vihāra,* his role as monk comes to the fore. These latter prayers and rituals in the Buddhist temple are standard throughout the nation, whereas there exist regional variations in the cult practices associated with the gods and demons. If the rituals to the gods and demons have to do with this world (health, wealth, fertility), the Buddhist rituals have to do with the next world, or with one's rebirth and the eventual realization of *nirvāṇa.* The unity of the Sinhala Buddhists as a moral community is expressed in *Buddhist* symbolism. The omnipresence of the Buddha in Sri Lanka is expressed in the symbolism of his sacred footprint embedded at Srī Pada Mountain (known also as Adam's Peak), the visible presence everywhere of monks and *dagobas* or *stūpas* containing relics of the Buddha or the saints of the early Buddhist church, and the sacred places of Buddhist pilgrimage where people from different regions come together to celebrate their collective unity as Buddhists. Sinhala religion as a totality has been adapted, through its long history, into a Buddhist framework.

CHANGE IN SINHALA RELIGION. Changes in the religious beliefs of the Sinhala have occurred in a variety of ways without radically affecting the formal structure of the pantheon, which has the Buddha at the apex, followed by four guardian gods of the realm, followed by the regional and village gods and godlings (*baṇḍāras*), followed by the malevolent demons, spirits, and ghosts. The most common forms of change are as follows.

(1) Migrations of peoples and cults from South India are a common phenomenon to this day. Hindu gods and deities are, however, incorporated into the Buddhist pantheon and given Buddhist legitimation. For example, Hindu gods like Viṣṇu and Saman (Laksmana) appear with their consorts in early Sinhala iconography. When they are converted into *bodhisattvas* in Sinhala religion they lose their consorts as befits good Buddhist salvation aspirants.

(2) Sociopolitical and economic conditions may favor the rise or decline of a god. This the cult of the god Nātha, who was in charge of the sovereignity of the Kandyan kings, dramatically declined after the British conquest of Kandy in 1815. Similarly, a god may rise into prominence and eclipse others in terms of public popularity.

(3) The external changes mentioned above are rationalized in terms of a dialectic of internal change in the pantheon. The more popular a deity, the more favors he grants his devotee; this in turn means that the devotee transfers merit to him, thereby bringing the god closer to his goal of Buddhahood. But the closer the god is to the Buddha model the less he is interested in the affaris of the world. Consequently, he must eventually become otiose, and more world-involved—even demonic—beings from the lower reaches of the pantheon move up to take his place. Thus, the logic of *karman* and the transfer of merit govern internal mobility in the pantheon.

(4) Finally, social changes may produce radical changes in the formal structure of the pantheon. In *The Cult of the Goddess Pattini* by the author of this aritcle (pp. 290–291), it is noted that the politcal conditions of the Kōṭṭe Kingdom (1410–1544) in Sri Lanka resulted in the extension of the jurisdictional sway of the major guardian gods into the *baṇḍāras*. Similarly, modern sociopolitical conditions, including the centraliza-

tion and democratization of the state and the development of modern communications, have tended to erode the spheres of influence of minor gods and demons. Today, some gods are coming into especial prominence, while other gods and their cults are declining.

It is likely that modern socioeconomic and political conditions may produce radical changes in the formal structure of the pantheon as sketched above. Nevertheless, Sinhala religion will retain its basic core. The pantheon headed by the Buddha and the system of worship associated with him are not likely to change. Even if the cult of the Four Gods and the Twelve Gods should collapse, some deities will continue to preside over humanity's "this-worldly" destiny—and so will the belief in named demons and *pretas*, the spirits of dead ancestors. All deities will continue to embody Buddhist values and remain bound to each other and to humans by the ethics of *karman* and the transfer of merit.

SEE ALSO Folk Religion, article on Folk Buddhism; Merit, article on Buddhist Concepts; Nāgas and Yakṣas; Nats; Saṃgha; Tamil Religions.

BIBLIOGRAPHY

The two most comprehensive books on Sinhala religion dealing with the demon and *deva* cults are Bruce Kapferer's *A Celebration of Demons* (Bloomington, Ind., 1983) and my *The Cult of the Goddess Pattini* (Chicago, 1984). Paul Wirz's *Exorcism and the Art of Healing in Ceylon* (Leiden, 1954), written in the thirties, is still a useful reference work, but better still is the excellent and little-known article by Dandris De Silva Gooneratne, "On Demonology and Witchcraft in Ceylon," *Journal of the Royal Asiatic Society, Ceylon Branch* 4 (1865–1866): 1–117, both dealing with the demon and astrological cults. Michael M. Ames's article "Magical-Animism and Buddhism: A Structural Analysis of the Sinhalese Religious System," in *Religion in South Asia*, edited by Edward B. Harper (Seattle, 1964), and Richard F. Gombrich's *Precept and Practice* (Oxford, 1971) deal with the *deva* cults in the southern province and the Kandyan villages respectively and also discuss the articulation of the spirit cults and astrological beliefs with Buddhism. H. L. Seneviratne's excellent *Rituals of the Kandyan State* (Cambridge, 1978) is a comprehensive study of the state cultus of the sacred tooth relic and the worship of the Four Gods. For recent socioeconomic changes in Sinhala religion, read my "Social Change and the Deities," *Man* 12 (1977): 377–396, and *Medusa's Hair* (Chicago, 1981).

New Sources

Gombrich, Richard Francis, and Gananath Obeyesekere. *Buddhism Transformed: Religious Change in Sri Lanka.* Princeton, N.J., 1988.

Scott, David. *Formations of Ritual: Colonial and Anthropological Discourses on the Sinhalayaktovil.* Minneapolis, 1994.

GANANATH OBEYESEKERE (1987)
Revised Bibliography

SIOUX RELIGION SEE LAKOTA RELIGIOUS TRADITIONS

SIRHINDĪ, AHMAD (AH 971–1034/1564–1624 CE),

an eminent Indian Muslim Ṣūfī, known also as *mujad-did-i alf-i thānī* "renewer of the second millennium [of the Islamic era]"). He was a prolific writer on Islamic mysticism and theology. His celebrated collection of letters, addressed to his fellow Ṣūfīs as well as to a few officials of the state, was repeatedly hailed as a landmark in the development of Muslim religious thought in India.

Sirhindī's religious activities were conducted within the Naqshbandī order of the Ṣūfīs, which was introduced into the subcontinent bySirhindī's spiritual mentor, Muḥammad al-Bāqī Billah. Sirhindī became a prominent personality in the order, brought about an expansion of its influence in India and elsewhere, and attracted numerous disciples, whom he instructed in the Naqshbandī mystical doctrine. He devoted a great deal of attention to the spiritual progress of the believer toward perfection. His works reflect an unrelenting effort to integrate the basic concepts of Islam into a comprehensive Ṣūfī outlook. True to the classical Ṣūfī tradition, he endeavored to analyze Islamic concepts in a two-fold fashion in order to discover in each of them the inner and secret (*bātin*) aspect in addition to the outward (*ẓāhir*) one. In other words, all things have form (*ṣūrah*) and essence (*ḥaqīqah*), and the highest achievement lies in understanding the inner, essential aspect of commandments and articles of faith.

The most original contribution of Sirhindī to mystical thought seems to be his description of the spiritual transformation that occurred at the end of the first millennium of the Islamic era, following intricate changes in the structure of the mystical "realities" (*ḥaqā'iq*), the spiritual condition of the Muslim community improved in a substantial manner. Prophetic perfections, which had been fading away since the death of Muḥammad, regained their splendor. The person in possession of these perfections was the *mujaddid*, the renewer or revivifier of the second millennium. It is likely that Sirhindī considered himself to be fulfilling this religiously crucial role; his disciples certainly saw him in this light.

Most scholars of medieval Muslim India maintain that Sirhindī performed a crucial role in the history of Indian Islam. Indian Muslims have always faced a dilemma concerning the attitude that they should adopt toward Hindu civilization, and two streams of thought developed among them: some held that Indian Muslims should take into account the sensibilities of the Hindus and seek a common ground for the two civilizations, while others maintained that the Muslim minority, in constant danger of assimilation into the polytheistic Hindu environment, must preserve the pristine purity of Islam and reject any local influence. Sirhindī appeared on the Indian scene during the reign of the Mughal emperor Akbar (1556–1605), who systematically attempted to make Islam and the ruling dynasty more acceptable to the non-Muslim Indians. The most conspicuous step in this direction was his abolition of the *jizyah,* a tax that Islamic law imposes on the non-Muslim inhabitants of a Muslim state. Sirhindī strongly opposed Akbar's conciliatory policy toward the Hindus. He made devastating attacks on Hinduism and maintained that the honor of Islam required the humiliation of the infidels and the resolute imposition of Islamic law upon them. Because Sirhindī expressed these views in letters to officials of the Mughal court, numerous scholars have credited him with reversing the heretical trends of Akbar's era and with restoring pristine purity to Indian Islam.

Recent research has shown, however, that this interpretation is far from certain. It is true that Sirhindī wrote to state officials and suggested changes in the imperial policy, but there is no evidence that the Mughal empire changed its attitude toward the Hindus as a result of his activities. Sirhindī was first and foremost a seeker after religious truth. The overwhelming majority of his epistles deal with typically Ṣūfī issues. The concepts of prophecy (*nubūwah*) and sainthood (*wilāyah*), the relationship between religious law (*sharīʿah*) and the mystical path (*tarīqah*), the theories of unity of being *(waḥdat al-wujūd)* and unity of appearance (*waḥdat al-shuhūd*)—these command Sirhindī's attention in most of his works. In dealing with these matters, Sirhindī belongs to the stream of mystical thought established by Ibn al-ʿArabī, though they differ in certain aspects. Questions of the relationship between the Islamic state and its Hindu population, which have acquired tremendous importance in the modern period and have therefore been central in numerous modern interpretations of Sirhindī's thought, do not seem to have been in the forefront of his interests.

Bibliography

Sirhindi's *magnum opus* is the collection of his Persian letters, *Maktūbāt-i imām-i rabbānī* (1899; reprint, Istanbul, 1973). See also *Selected Letters of Shaykh Aḥmad Sirhindī* (Karachi, 1968), translated and edited by Fazlur Rahman. A more recent work is J. G. J. ter Harr's *Follower and Heir of the Prophet: Shaykh Aḥmad Sirhindī (1564–1624) as Mystic* (Leiden, 1992). Sirhindī's theology is the main topic in Burhan Ahmad Faruqi's *The Mujaddid's Conception of Tawḥīd* (1943; reprint, Lahore, 1970). My own study, *Shaykh Aḥmad Sirhindī: An Outline of His Thought and a Study of His Image in the Eyes of Posterity* (London, 1971), deals with the central concepts of Sirhindī's thought, reviews the development of his image in later literature, and includes an extensive bibliography.

Yohanan Friedmann (1987 and 2005)

SISTERS OF CHARITY See SETON, ELIZABETH

ŚIVA [FIRST EDITION]. The ancient name of Śiva is *Rudra*, the Wild God. His seminal myth is told in the most sacred, most ancient Indian text, the *Ṛgveda* (c. 1200–1000 BCE; hymns 10.61 and 1.71). When time was about to begin he appeared as a wild hunter, aflame, his arrow directed against the Creator making love with his virgin daughter, the Dawn. They had the shape of two antelopes. Some of the Creator's seed fell on the earth. Rudra himself as Fire (Agni) had prepared the seed, from which mankind was to be born. From a rupture of the undifferentiated plenum of the Absolute some of the seed fell on the earth. Rudra's shot failed to prevent its fall; time, which was about to begin, came in between, in the shape of the flight of his arrow. The Creator, Prajāpati, terribly frightened, made Rudra Lord of Animals (Paśupati) for sparing his life (*Maitrāyaṇī Saṃhitā* 4.2.12; after 1000 BCE). The gods, as they witnessed the primordial scene, made it into a *mantra,* an incantation, and out of this *mantra* they fashioned Vāstoṣpati, "lord of the residue (*vāstu*)," "lord of the site (*vāstu*)," or "lord of what is left over on the sacrificial site." However, Paśupati—"lord of animals," "lord of creatures," "lord of the soul of man"—is Rudra-Śiva's most significant name.

Fundamental pairs of antitheses inhere in the primordial Ṛgvedic myth of Rudra Paśupati and Rudra Vāstoṣpati. As Fire he incites Prajāpati toward creation; as the formidable hunter he aims at the act of creation, meaning to prevent the "incontinence" of the Creator, the shedding of the seed. Rudra acts as hunter and yogin in one. The scene has for its background the plenum of the uncreated or the Absolute that was and is before the mythical moment of the inception of the life.

In the Vedic sacrificial ritual, Vāstoṣpati receives as an oblation the remainder of the sacrifice. The power of the completed sacrifice is left in the remainder and magically ensures the continuity of the rites, of the entire tradition—and of the order and rhythms of art. Vāstoṣpati is the guardian and protector of the site, the buildings and their content, in later Hinduism.

Jan Gonda, in his article "The Śatarudriya," in the festschrift *Sanskrit and Indian Studies* (Dordrecht, 1980, p. 75), considers Rudra "the representative of the dangerous, unreliable and hence to be feared nature." Looking at Śiva from another angle, Daniel H. H. Ingalls, in "Kālidāsa and the Attitudes of the Golden Age" in the *Journal of the American Oriental Society* (1976), sees that "Śiva represents the reconciliation of good and evil, of beauty and ugliness, of life and death—the vision solved all problems and could transmute a man's suffering into joy." Neither of these views refers to the primordial and central myth of Rudra, in which Rudra acts as consciousness of metaphysical reality or the Absolute in its relation to life on earth.

In Vedic times, the fierce hunter had the power over life and death, to afflict a mortal wound or to heal it. He was worshiped with the words "Do not hurt me" and also invoked as "lord of songs, lord of sacrifice, bringing cooling remedy, radiant like the sun, like gold" (*Ṛgveda* 1.43.4–5). He was praised as the lord of the high and the low, of robbers, of the ill-formed, but also of craftsmen working in wood, metal, and clay. Praise went to him in the flux of waves, in young grass and the desert, in soil and air, house and palace. This is how the *Śatarudriya* hymn of the *Yajurveda* (after 1000 BCE) invokes him, an omnipresent power whose shape reverberates in uncounted Rudras like him who are his retinue. Rudra's color is copper red, his throat deep blue; one of his names is the Blue-Red One. His home is everywhere, but particularly in the North, in Himalayan caves but also on crossroads, cremation grounds, and the battlefield.

The gods meant to exclude Rudra from the Vedic sacrifice. This is mythically accounted for by the primordial flight of his arrow. Rudra, though he had been made lord of animals, was not himself born yet as a god. The story of Rudra's birth has several versions. The *Śatapatha Brāhmaṇa* (9.1.1.6; c. mid-first millennium BCE) tells of Prajāpati, from whom all the gods departed except Manyu (Anger). Prajāpati cried. His tears fell on Manyu, who became thousand-headed, thousand-eyed, hundred-quivered Rudra. Rudra was hungry. Prajāpati asked the gods to gather food for Rudra, who stood there flaming. The gods appeased Agni-Rudra. By the *Śatarudriya* offering and hymn they drove out his pain, his evil. The *Śatarudriya* sacrifice was the first to be performed on completion of the Vedic sacrificial altar. Rudra, as soon as he was born from Prajāpati, was given this place in the Vedic sacrifice. To this day the *Śatarudriya* hymn is recited in Śaiva temples every morning.

On being born, Rudra was invested with the cosmos by Prajāpati. His eightfold domain consisted of the five elements—earth, water, fire, air, and space—together with sun and moon, the measurers of time, and the sacrificer, or initiate. Rudra is the totality of manifestation. He did not create the cosmos. He became and is the cosmos. God and the world are one. As the cosmos is a product of Śiva's eight forms, so is the human being, the microcosm.

The *Śvetāśvatara Upaniṣad* (c. late first millennium BCE), like the *Ṛgveda*, implores Rudra not to injure man or beast. The formidable hunter is everywhere, he merges with the ogdoad and transcends it, he rules over all the worlds, makes them appear and withdraws them at the end of time. In him at the beginning and at the end the universe is gathered. The dweller in the mountain resides in the cave of the heart of man. He is immanent and transcendent, the one supreme God. Though he has a face, a hand, a foot on every side, no one can see him; he is seen only with the mind and heart. Those who know the Lord by introspection, yoga, and loving devotion (*bhakti*) are freed from the fetter (*pāśa*) of worldly existence, for he is the cause of worldly existence and of liberation. In his auspicious, unterrifying form he is the Lord, the omnipresent Śiva, hidden in all beings.

Rudra, the "wild god," is one with Śiva, the auspicious, supreme god whose splendor encompasses his primordial form. His being in manifestation is to be meditated upon as a river of five streams from five sources (*Śvetāśvatara Upaniṣad* 1.5). They are the five senses with their objects "an impetuous flood of five pains." If Rudra as the ogdoad is the cosmos, as the pentad he is the five senses, the sense perception and experience of the cosmos. Five is Śiva's sacred number in particular. His *mantra*, "Namaḥ Śivāya," has five syllables, and his "body" is said to be constituted of five *mantras* (*Taittirīya Āraṇyaka* 10.43–47; c. third century BCE). They evoke the body of God in the five directions of space, in the five elements, in the five senses.

Vedic Rudra, the fierce hunter, is clad in the skins of wild animals. In the *Mahābhārata* (c. 400 BCE–400 CE), Śiva is seen by the hero Arjuna, in a vision, as an archer and an ascetic. A hymn of the *Ṛgveda* (10.136), on the other hand, celebrates Rudra drinking from one cup with an ascetic. The *Mahābhārata* sums up the relation of Śiva to yoga, saying that "Śiva is yoga and the lord of yogins; he can be approached by yoga only."

In post-Vedic times Prajāpati's role as creator was taken over by Brahmā. Rudra decapitates his father, Brahmā. Various reasons are given in the Puranas (fourth through fourteenth centuries CE); one of them, the lusting of Brahmā for his daughter, recalls the primordial scene. The head of Brahmā clings to Śiva's hand. Śiva as a penitent beggar, the skull his begging bowl, goes on a pilgrimage of expiation. After twelve years the skull falls from Śiva's hand in Banaras, and Śiva is released from his sin. His pilgrimage takes the god to a hermitage in a forest of deodar trees. The hermits believe that the young, naked beggar has come to seduce their women—and Śiva's phallus (*liṅga*) falls from his body, by his own will or by a curse of the sages; it then arises as a flaming pillar. These events are part of the play (*līlā*) of Śiva in this world to enable his devotee to recognize God in the guises he assumed. The sages apparently fail to identify the begging bowl, Brahmā's head or skull (*brahmaśiras*), in the beggar's hand. Brahmaśiras is also the name of Śiva's most formidable weapon, the Pasupata weapon.

Most of Śiva's myths are known to the *Mahābhārata*. The myth of Śiva the ascetic, paradoxically, is the theme of his marriage to Pārvatī, daughter of Parvatarāja, "Lord Mountain." In it is included the story of the destruction—and resurrection—of Kāma, the god Desire, an archer who aimed his arrow at Śiva but was reduced to ashes by a glance from Śiva's third eye. Fire and ashes belong to Śiva as much as serpents and the moon's crescent, for Śiva's nature is twofold: he is fierce as fire, yet cool and calm as the moon. He is the reluctant bridegroom, the indefatigable lover, and the ascetic. He is the savior of the world; he swallowed its poison, and it left a dark blue mark on his throat. He destroys demons or shows them his grace. He defeats death; he is the death of death, for he is time and transcends time as eternity. He is the teacher who in silence expounds to the sages music, yoga, gnosis, and all the arts and sciences. He is a dancer, Lord of Dancers, who dances the world in and out of existence. He is a male god inseparably united with his female power (*śakti*). One image shows him half male, half female. His theriomorphic form is the bull called Nandin (Joy). His main attributes are trident, skull, and antelope. His symbol is the *liṅga*, the (phallic) pillar, the most sacred object of worship—although none is known in India prior to the third to second century BCE. The *liṅga* stands erect in its double significance; full of creative power, and also of the yogic power to withhold the seed. Its symbolism is akin to the meaning of the primordial scene.

Whereas the relation of Śiva to Brahmā-Prajāpati is crucial, that of Śiva to Viṣṇu is one of coexistence or subordination but also of amalgamation and interchange. Viṣṇu sometimes carries the name of Śiva or Rudra; Viṣṇu is conjoint in one type of image with Śiva as Harihara; in one painting Viṣṇu-Kṛṣṇa carries Śiva's insignia, trident and serpent, whereas Śiva holds Kṛṣṇa's flute. Śaivism and Vaiṣṇavism are complementary, although sectarian rivalry led to the conception of the gruesome Śarabheśa. To each of the three great Hindu gods is assigned one of the three tendencies (*guṇa*) of cosmic substance (*prakṛti*), that of Śiva being *tamas* (darkness), the disruptive tendency that precedes every new creation.

In the darkness of the flood between the dissolution of the universe and the beginning of a new world, the flaming pillar of Śiva's *liṅga* arose and was worshiped by Brahmā and Viṣṇu. This is celebrated by vigil, vows, fast, and worship on Mahāśivarātri, the Great Night of Śiva, the climax of the religious year, on the fourteenth lunar day of the dark half of the last month of the lunar year. The last night of each month is Śiva's Night (Śivarātri) and the evening of each day throughout the year is the time for his worship.

SEE ALSO Indian Religions, article on Mythic Themes; Rudra; Śaivism; Tantrism.

BIBLIOGRAPHY

Eliade, Mircea. *Yoga: Immortality and Freedom.* Translated by Williard R. Trask. 2d ed. Princeton, 1969. The basic work on yoga clarifies the conception of God (Īśvara) in the yoga system and that of Śiva the Great God and Great Yogin.

Gonda, Jan. *Die Religionen Indiens.* 2 vols. Vol. 1, *Veda und älterer Hinduismus,* 2d rev. ed. Stuttgart, 1978. Vol. 2, *Der jüngere Hinduismus.* Stuttgart, 1963. A most thorough and judicious presentation of the religions of India, including a survey of the character and history of Śaivism.

Gonda, Jan. *Viṣṇuism and Śivaism: A Comparison.* London, 1970. In their juxtaposition the two views of the world define one another. Copious, detailed notes enrich the scope of the book.

Kramrisch, Stella. *The Presence of Śiva.* Princeton, 1981. A presentation focused on the ontological and cosmogonic implications of the mythology of Śiva and the persistent themes within its network.

O'Flaherty, Wendy Doniger. *Śiva: The Erotic Ascetic.* London, 1981. Reprint of *Asceticism and Eroticism in the Mythology of Śiva* (1973). A monograph that structurally and masterfully analyzes one fundamental aspect, the erotic-ascetic polarity within Śiva; based on hitherto mostly unpublished textual sources.

Rao, T. A. Gopinatha. *Elements of Hindu Iconography,* vol. 2, parts 1 & 2 (1916). Reprint, New York, 1968. Although first published in 1916, this work remains a comprehensive and valid support of Śaiva studies.

Scheuer, Jacques. *Śiva dans le Mahābhārata.* Paris, 1982. This book fills a gap in the present knowledge about Śiva by establishing Śiva's position in the central theme of the Mahābhārata.

STELLA KRAMRISCH (1987)

ŚIVA [FURTHER CONSIDERATIONS].

Classical Sanskrit images of Śiva found in Vedic texts and epic mythology influentially inform, but do not encompass, Hindus' imagination of the great god Śiva in both the past and present. Certainly the classical Sanskrit texts contribute images of the authority and majesty of the Lord, as well as his divine play (*līlā*). They provide a sacred rationale for his worship, but it is other kinds of texts in Sanskrit and in the regional languages of India that foreground the practice of his worship, especially those focusing on the accessibility of the Lord to humankind. These other texts illustrate how Śiva is imagined and embraced in ritual, devotional, philosophical, and political communities in India, and in Hindu communities abroad; how he is given a home in the practices, hearts, and minds of his devotees.

RITUAL DIMENSIONS. Granite temples across India, striking in their majestic size and antiquity, are homes of Śiva. Many of the temples were built according to the Āgamas, philosophical and ritual manuals from medieval times written in Sanskrit. *Śaiva* temples were constructed according to a philosophy of emission (*sṛṣṭi*) and reabsorption (*saṃhāra*). The main enclosed sanctum in the temple, where only priests can normally enter, contains the most subtle image of Śiva, the *liṅga.* It is considered to be the most subtle because it does not have any distinguishing marks; as such, it is the source of the emission of Śiva's divine substance. As his divine emission radiates outward, it undergoes a process of densification. Thus, the images of Śiva around the outside of the temple walls and visible to all are personified, with distinctive iconographies related to the Sanskritic mythologies; for example, popular images on temple walls are those of Ardhanārīśvara (the Lord who is half woman), Dakṣīṇāmurti (the Teacher), and Naṭarāja (the Lord of the dance).

The philosophy of emission and reabsorption also applies to the rituals performed in the temple. According to the Āgamas, worshippers are classified into two main groups: those who seek liberation (*mokṣa*), such as priests and renouncers, and those who seek worldly enjoyments (*bhoga*), such as householders. The focus of the former is on reabsorption; the latter, emission. Priests undertake elaborate rituals to spiritualize their bodies by placing *mantras* on their body parts; thus they become subtle like Śiva and are fit to perform his worship. Laypeople, who stand outside the sanctum, make offerings of material gifts (*pūjā*) and mental and devotional prayers to Śiva.

One of the most important ritual festivals held at the temple is Mahāśivarātri, the Great Night of Śiva, which occurs on the fourteenth lunar day (*tithi*) of the dark half of the lunar month of January/February or February/March, according to classical texts. The fourteenth *tithi* of the dark half of the lunar month is the last day of the moon's waning cycle, or the new moon, just prior to the commencement of its waxing period, which culminates in the full moon. Thus, there is actually a Śivarātri every lunar month; however, Mahāśivarātri is especially important because it is said to be favored by Śiva himself, because it comes at the end of the lunar calendar, and because of its status as a major *vrat* (vow) in the Hindu calendar. Devotees fast all day, then go to the temple at night to view the ritual bathing of the Śiva *liṅga* and to hear religious discourses and engage in singing devotional songs; the most devout stay awake all night in contemplative devotion to the Lord.

DEVOTIONAL DIMENSIONS. The heart is the most important home of Śiva in the devotional traditions of Śiva-*bhakti*. To a great extent, *bhakti* traditions are a response to the formality of temple worship: They validate laypeople's direct participation in the worship of the Lord by insisting that a committed, loving attitude towards God is all that is needed to maintain a good relationship with God. *Bhakti*'s thesis provided a justification for laypeople to worship images of God themselves, without priestly mediation. For example, villagers who are not in the priestly caste can conduct their own *pūjā*s at village shrines. Families in villages and cities can worship at home in special *pūjā* rooms, where one can offer traditional prayers and *mantras* or else just offer one's own prayers to God. In contrast to temple worship, where by tradition the priests are all male, at home the worship is most often offered by the mother of the household. *Bhakti* also provided a way for laypeople to characterize their role in temple worship as essential, direct, and meaningful.

Medieval *bhakti* poetry exists in all the major regional languages of India. Some of the most famous poetry that is dedicated to Śiva was written by the three male leaders (*nāyaṉmār*) of Tamil Śiva-*bhakti*—Campantar, Appar, and Cuntarar (seventh to ninth centuries CE); a female poet from Karnataka, Mahādēviyakka, who wrote in Kannada (twelfth century CE); and a female poet from Kashmir, Lallā Dēd (also known as Lal Ded, Lalli, and Lalleshwari; c. 1320–1391 CE), who wrote in Kashmiri. Their *bhakti* poetry was not simply a humanizing of God; that had already been done in mythology and iconography. It was the human response to God in all vicissitudes, from awe to love, that the *bhakti* poets foregrounded. *Bhakti* validated the relationship possible through embodiment.

Consider this stanza from Appar, as translated by Indira V. Peterson:

> If you could see the arch of his brow, the budding smile on lips red as the *kovvai* fruit, cool matted hair, the milk-white ash on coral skin, and the sweet golden foot raised up in dance, then even human birth on this wide earth would become a thing worth having.

In Appar's vision, God is alive; his lips are red, emerging into a smile, and the colors of his body are vivid. His dance has cosmic significance, as per the classical mythology, but it is also personally meaningful. The poet addresses his fellow humans with "if you could see," and he assures them that their unmediated vision of the living Lord is worth the price of birth in this world. Drawing on the powerful mythological image of the cosmic dance of the Lord, the poet foregrounds the live encounter with the Lord.

Even though Mahādēviyakka and Lallā Dēd lived centuries apart in very different regions of the subcontinent and are claimed by distinctive traditions (the former by Vīraśaivism, the latter by Kashmir Śaivism), a pattern emerges in what is understood to be their life stories. With some support from their poetry, the hagiographies of Mahādēviyakka and Lallā Dēd present the saints as having been married, but problematically so, since they were both determined to follow a spiritual, and not a worldly, path. Both of them eventually extricated themselves from this overdetermined social path, and each set out on her own, eschewing even clothing. The way they imagined their spiritual path, as revealed in their poetry, is distinctive. Mahādēviyakka was completely in love with "the lord white as jasmine" (a form of Śiva), and imagined herself married to him. Lallā Dēd tended to refer to Śiva in more abstract terms, such as "Supreme Principle" and "Consciousness," and expressed her desire to experience unity with him through identification with his divine essence.

PHILOSOPHICAL DIMENSIONS. The mind is also a home of Śiva. In many Indian languages, there are no separate terms for *mind* and *heart*; they are inextricably tied together in the same word. Both *bhakti* and philosophy involve emotional commitment to, and intellectual engagement with, God. However, the earliest Hindu philosophical texts, the Upaniṣads, and then medieval and later philosophies that drew on them, tended to frame the path of spiritual liberation in epistemological terms, emphasizing knowledge and experiences of the mind. On the occasions when these texts do suggest that the true self resides in the heart, they convey the notion that true knowledge is not necessarily rational according to common understanding, for a critique of ordinary dualistic knowledge is in the fore of these influential philosophical sources.

Philosophies of Śiva are embedded in both mythology and iconography. The classical story of Śiva's game of dice, which pervades Sanskrit-language mythology, regional-language epics, and major sculptural traditions (such as the caves at Ellorā and Elephanta), provides an intriguing image of Śiva's power of creation. As Śiva plays, his nature as a subtle yet dense unity increasingly devolves into fragments of externalized form, pushed into shape by gaps created by the uncertainty of the game; these fragments become elements of the known world, including humankind. This basic pattern informs the dynamics of the temple, as discussed earlier, but the story highlights the role of chance, and it dwells on the plurality of possible outcomes and then paths to restore Śiva's wholeness, so the dicing can begin again.

Gender is a key symbol of the process, as Śiva devolves from self-containment to the androgyne (Ardhanārīśvara, the Lord who is half woman), to an independent, iconic Śiva and his wife Pārvatī. The androgyne thus stands as a mediating term, important because it instantiates gender while simultaneously offering a critique of it. Through spiritual practices such as *haṭhayoga,* one can access the critique to transcend the duality of gender and of consciousness.

These philosophical ideas were codified in one of the most important medieval schools of Śaiva philosophy, Kashmir Śaivism. The major classical exponent of this school, which claimed Lallā Dēd, was the philosopher Abhinavagupta (c. 975–1025 CE). Emphasizing nondualism (*advaita*), this school maintains that the ultimate (*paramārtha*) and ordinary (*vyavahāra*) levels of reality are both real and true simultaneously. Śiva is the oneness of reality that appears as the manifest universe through his power of *śakti,* and he is thus the origin of all apparent distinctions. The yogi participates in true Śiva-nature by the experience of the relationships among God's unified essence and multiple forms. Through the vibration (*spanda*) of awareness, the yogi is attuned to three simultaneous levels of consciousness: division (separation among objects), unity-in-division (the link between the unity of the subject and diversity of the objects), and undivided unity (of all things in the divine subject).

The other important classical Śaiva school of philosophy is the medieval Tamil Śaiva Siddhānta school (originated twelfth to fourteenth centuries CE), which sought to locate itself as the culmination of Tamil Śiva-*bhakti* by characterizing the poets' hymns as emotional and spontaneous, a preliminary stage leading towards the knowledge revealed in its own philosophical canon. This school views the world as composed of three irreducible realities, Lord (*pati*), soul (Tamil, *uyir,* Skt., *paśu*), and bond (Tamil, *iruḷmala;* Skt., *pāśa*). The soul is located between Lord (Śiva) and bond. Through knowledge and devotional action, the soul loosens the grip of the aspects of the bond that are *karma* and *māyā;* then, through the Lord's grace, the soul achieves the attainment of the Lord and experiences bliss and pure knowledge in a relationship where "the two are as one."

POLITICAL DIMENSIONS. Through ideology and practice, Śaivas construct a home for Śiva as a ruler. In its extended sense, politics is the attempt to gain authoritative power, and the staking of one's claim involves defining oneself in opposition to others. This dynamic is found in Tamil Śiva-*bhakti* and Kannada Vīraśaiva hymns, many of which contain explicit invectives against Buddhists and Jains, and implicit claims to superiority among the many streams of Hinduism, especially Vaiṣṇavism. The sectarian impulse also informs the medieval philosophical schools, the texts of which include detailed discussion of and argumentation with perspectives of other schools, towards demonstrating the preeminence of their own teachings.

In terms of practices, in addition to family-oriented worship services, Śaivism has a side in which a masculine, militant identity is promoted. Robert Gardner and Ákos Östör's film, *Sons of Shiva* (1985), captures a celebration of the Śaiva folk festival Gajan by village male householders, who join together for three days to perform rituals of penance to the Lord. The Naga Sadhus, nude male ascetics who organize themselves into regiments (*akharas*) as in an army and carry the weapon-like trident, embody this form of Śaivism, as do other secretive male sects, including the Nath Babas (Gorakhnathis) and the Aghoris.

Since the late 1960s, this masculine, militant side of Śaivism has been used to define a political party that has sought and intermittently achieved governmental authority, the Shiv Sena, whose name translates to "army of Śiva." This party, which is based in Mumbai (Bombay), was founded by Bal Thackeray and promotes an extreme Hindu nationalist (Hindutva) agenda, which links it to the Bharatiya Janata Party and Rashtriya Swayamseval Sangh. A potent symbol for the party is the historical figure of Shivaji (1627–1680), a Maratha king who is understood in many contrasting ways; the Shiv Sena understands him to have been an incarnation of Śiva and a warrior defender of Hindus against Muslims. The party has been definitively identified as an instigator of the violence that rocked Mumbai in 1992 and 1993.

ŚAIVISM ABROAD. Śiva is at home in many Western countries, including the United States. As Vasudha Narayanan once wittily remarked, Śiva and other major Hindu gods and goddesses received visas to come to the United States from India, whereas many of the more local deities did not. The pan-Indian gods have been favored in terms of the public Hindu temple culture that has been emerging in the United States since the late 1970s, for that realm, especially in the immigrant context, demands negotiation and consensus. In contrast, home shrines (*pūjā* rooms), which are a central part of Hindu practice and exist in Hindu homes across the United States, have considerably more flexibility according to personal tastes and resources.

In the United States, Śiva usually shares a temple with Viṣṇu, with both being central deities therein; this is not common in India, where temples were and are constructed along sectarian lines. Lacking a dominant Hindu context, the temples in the United States have had to be more inclusive to attract the kind of attendance and material resources required for their construction and maintenance. Daily and major festivals are held at the temples, with Mahāśivarātri being a popular annual festival.

Two temples in Hawai'i are especially devoted to Śiva, and their central images are viewed as manifestations of the god: the Iraivan/Kadavul temple at Kauai, Hawai'i, and the Viswanatha temple at Wahiawa (Oahu). Śiva is said to have appeared to the founder of the Kauai temple, Swami Sivaya Subramuniyaswami, who was born in the United States and initiated in Sri Lanka, and in 1987 a crystal Śiva-*liṅga* was found in Arkansas and brought to the Kauai temple. The Wahiawa temple has a "Sacred Healing Stone" as its Śiva-*liṅga*, a manifestation of Śiva that is also understood with respect to local mythologies such that it is also said to be an embodiment of the Hawaiian god Lono, as well as an embodiment of two sisters from Kauai who were turned into rocks. The adaptability of Śaivism is demonstrated in the historical and ongoing relationship between tradition and creativity.

BIBLIOGRAPHY

Ritual Dimensions

Clothey, Fred W., and J. Bruce Long. *Experiencing Śiva: Encounters with a Hindu Deity.* Columbia, Mo., 1983. This collection of essays explores the relationships between Śiva and his devotees through literature and ritual.

Davis, Richard H. *Ritual in an Oscillating Universe: Worshipping Śiva in Medieval India.* Princeton, 1991. Important study of the contemporary worship of Śiva in temples according to the medieval philosophical and ritual Āgama texts.

Huyler, Stephen P. *Meeting God: Elements of Hindu Devotion.* New Haven, 1999. Engaging introductory discussion of general patterns in Hindu worship of the gods, from village to temple; includes a section on Śiva. Beautifully illustrated with over 150 color photographs.

Kannikeswaran, Kanniks. "Abodes of Shiva." 1999. Available from Templenet at: www.templenet.com/abode.html. Provides photographic illustrations and historical and ritual descriptions of Śaiva temples all over India, with a special focus on temples in Tamil Nadu, South India.

Younger, Paul. *The Home of the Dancing Śivan.* New York, 1995. In an engaging, story-like narrative, the author discusses the history of the famous Chidambaram temple to the Dancing Śiva in Tamil Nadu, South India, and describes contemporary worship there.

Devotional Dimensions

Cutler, Norman J. *Songs of Experience: The Poetics of Tamil Devotion.* Bloomington, Ind., 1987. An important literary study of the way Tamil *bhakti* poetry simultaneously embodies the spiritual experience of the poets, the praise of God, and the engagement of the audience. Includes translations from Tamil Śiva-*bhakti* and Viṣṇu-*bhakti* traditions.

Peterson, Indira V. *Poems to Śiva: The Hymns of the Tamil Saints.* Princeton, 1989. Engaging introduction to hymns of the three most famous and prolific Tamil Śiva-*bhakti* saints, including analysis of the hymns and the manner in which they are sung today, as well as translations of many of their most popular stanzas.

Prentiss, Karen Pechilis. *The Embodiment of Bhakti.* New York, 1999. An interpretive history of Tamil Śiva-*bhakti* through analysis of the hymns of the three most famous saints, the inclusion of the hymns in medieval temple worship and their contextualization in biographies, and their interpretation by a medieval philosopher. Includes translations of the hymns and a philosophical text (Umāpati's *Tiruvarutpayan̲*).

Ramanujan, A. K., trans. *Speaking of Śiva.* Baltimore, 1973; reprint, New York, 1985. Presents translations from four medieval Śiva-*bhakti* saints in the Vīraśaiva tradition who wrote poems in the Kannada language, preceded by an illuminating introduction to Vīraśaivism.

Philosophical Dimensions

Dhavamony, Maraisusai. *Love of God according to Śaiva Siddhānta.* Oxford, 1971. Classic reference source on a variety of Tamil texts to Śiva, including *bhakti* and philosophy, with discussion and partial translations of texts.

Dyczkowski, Mark S. G. *The Doctrine of Vibration: An Analysis of the Doctrines and Practices of Kashmir Śaivism.* Albany, N.Y., 1987. Lucid exposition of key doctrines and developments in Kashmir Śaivism.

Goldberg, Ellen. *The Lord Who Is Half Woman: Ardhanārīśvara in Indian and Feminist Perspective.* Albany, N.Y., 2002. Important feminist analysis of the classical mythological and iconographical form of Śiva as the Lord who is half woman, highlighting the vital role of the feminine principle.

Handleman, Don, and David Shulman. *God Inside Out: Śiva's Game of Dice.* New York, 1997. Engaging discussion of philosophy in the classical Sanskrit mythology of Śiva, arguing that Śiva's game of dice is the divine play that creates the universe.

Prentiss, Karen Pechilis. "On the Making of a Canon: Historicity and Experience in the Tamil Śiva-*bhakti* Canon." *International Journal of Hindu Studies* 5, no. 1 (2001): 1–26. Discussion of how the Tamil Śaiva Siddhānta school located itself as the culmination of Tamil Śiva-*bhakti* by emotionalizing the *bhakti* hymns through an analysis of the *Tirumuṟaikaṇṭapurāṉ am* (a translation of which follows the article on pages 27–44).

Political Dimensions

Banerjee, Sikata. *Warriors in Politics: Hindu Nationalism, Violence, and the Shiv Sena in India.* Boulder, Colo., 2000. Lucid analysis of the violent strategies of the Shiv Sena in the political, economic, and social contexts. Includes an important analysis of "masculine Hinduism."

Gardner, Robert, and Ákos Östör, directors. *Sons of Shiva.* Cambridge, Mass, 1985. This half-hour film documents the participation of male devotees in a festival to Śiva in the town of Vishnupur, West Bengal, including rituals of the sacred thread, firewalking, and trance.

Hansen, Thomas Blom. *The Saffron Wave: Democracy and Hindu Nationalism in Modern India.* Princeton, 1999. Provides an accessible overview of the rise of Hindu nationalism in the 1980s and 1990s.

Śaivism Abroad

Mazumdar, Shampa, and Sanjoy Mazumdar. "Creating the Sacred: Altars in the Hindu American Home." In *Revealing the Sacred in Asian and Pacific America,* edited by Jane Naomi Iwamura and Paul Spickard, pp. 143–157. New York, 2003. The authors argue that Hindu home shrines are underrepresented in scholarship, though they are central to Hindu tradition and play an important role in a new cultural context.

Narayanan, Vasudha. "Creating the South Indian 'Hindu' Experience in the United States." In *A Sacred Thread: Modern Transmission of Hindu Traditions in India and Abroad*, edited by Raymond Brady Williams, pp. 147–176. New York, 1992. An important discussion of syncretism and identity in Hindu temple worship in the United States; includes information on the two Śiva temples in Hawai'i.

Subramuniyaswami, Satguru Sivaya. *Dancing with Śiva: Hinduism's Contemporary Catechism*. 5th ed. Kappa, Hawai'i, 1997. Faith-based question-and-answer discussion of all aspects of Śaivism.

Tamil Electronic Library. "A List of Hindu Temples in USA and Canada." Available from: www.geocities.com/kalyan.geo/temple1.html. Provides addresses, phone numbers, and websites of Hindu temples by state and by province.

Waghorne, Joanne Punzo. "The Hindu Gods in a Split-Level World: The Sri-Siva-Vishnu Temple in Suburban Washington, D.C." In *Gods of the City: Religion and the American Urban Landscape*, edited by Robert A. Orsi, pp. 103–130. Bloomington, Ind., 1999. Engaging discussion of the economic, social, and religious aspects of constructing a house for God in the American suburbs.

KAREN PECHILIS (2005)

SKANDHAS SEE SOUL, *ARTICLE ON* BUDDHIST CONCEPTS

SKEPTICS AND SKEPTICISM. The term *skeptic* comes from the Greek words *skeptikos* ("an inquirer, one who reflects") and *skeptesthai* ("to view, to consider"). Philosophical skepticism arose from some of the observations made by early Greek philosophers. Heraclitus said that the world is in such flux that "one cannot step twice in the same river." The only truth, he asserted, was that everything changes. Cratylus went further and said that, since everything changes, people change, and their language changes, so that knowledge and communication are not really possible. The Sophists Protagoras and Gorgias asserted additional skeptical views. Protagoras argued that humanity is the measure of all things; by implication, each person measures the world individually, so there are no general human truths. Gorgias is said to have argued that nothing exists, but even if it did one could not know it, and even if one did know it one could not communicate it. The culmination of these early skeptical comments was Socrates' remark, at his trial, that all he knew was that he knew nothing.

Systematic accounts of human inability to gain accurate knowledge about the world were first rendered by Arcesilas (c. 315–241 BCE) and Carneades (213–129 BCE). They developed arguments, directed primarily against Stoic and Epicurean opponents, to undermine any claims of knowledge and to establish that nothing can be known. This view, termed "Academic skepticism," presented a series of arguments against the truth of purported sense and rational knowledge, and against any standard that could be employed to distinguish between truth and falsity. Cicero presented this view in his *De Academica* and *De natura deoreum.*

A more skeptical group claimed that the Academic skeptics were really negative dogmatists, as they indeed asserted that nothing can be known and that "all assertions are merely probable." Following the legendary Pyrrho of Elis (360–275 BCE), who would not make any judgment, a movement called Pyrrhonism developed about 100 BCE. Its theoretician, Aenesidemus (100–40 BCE), and his successors set forth a series of "tropes," or ways of suspending judgment on all questions, scientific, mathematical, metaphysical, theological, and ethical. The Pyrrhonian materials were gathered together by Sextus Empiricus in his *Outlines of Pyrrhonism* and *Against the Dogmatists* (c. 200 CE) and were to play a most important role in the rise of modern skepticism.

Both the Academic and Pyrrhonian skeptics offered their doubts as ways of finding peace of mind and of conforming with popular religion. Their opponents claimed to know what the world was like, and to base their way of life on such knowledge. However, if these opponents were to find they were mistaken in their knowledge they would become mentally disturbed and uncertain as to how to live. The skeptics, however, by suspending judgment, would attain peace of mind. They would live undogmatically, doing what was natural and/or conventional. They would behave normally and accept the laws of their society and its customs, including religious ones. Others might scoff at popular religion because it did not conform to their "knowledge" of the world. The Academics and Pyrrhonians suspended judgment on such questions as "Do the gods exist?" and simply followed the religious customs of their communities undogmatically, without committing themselves to any theological claims. The skeptics thus could say that they were no threat to accepted religion.

The Greek skeptics, from Arcesilaus to Sextus, had apparently little effect on Judaism or Christianity (although Pyrrhonism flourished principally in Alexandria, Athens, and Rome). In Jewish postbiblical writing, the word for "skeptic" is *aipikuros.* Obviously derived from the name *Epicurus,* the term denotes both a general doubter and one who doubts crucial features of Judaism. Criticisms of *aipikurosim* indicate some awareness of skepticism in the Jewish community.

Church fathers occasionally comment on skeptical views, although only Augustine appears to have taken them very seriously. He had read Cicero's account. When he became a Christian, he wrote various dialogues about the status of religious knowledge; one of them, *Contra Academicos,* showed how faith and grace aided in overcoming problems of skepticism.

During the Middle Ages ancient skeptical views were little known or discussed, except through Augustine's rebuttal. Some Muslim and Jewish philosophers, however, pointed to basic skeptical problems in the acceptance of revealed religion. Ibn Rushd (Averroës) had shown that Aristotle's philosophy conflicted with certain revealed claims, such as the statement that the world was created and the individual soul is immortal. Maimonides argued that some religious claims could be proved and also disproved by reason and therefore had to be accepted on faith. The Muslim mystic al-Ghazālī sought to show that science and reason could not lead to satisfactory knowledge about the world and that God's omnipotence prevents people from being able to know God or God's handiwork. The skeptical implications of these Jewish and Muslim views appeared in discussions in the late Middle Ages, especially among the Latin Averroists and in the writings of Nicholas of Cusa.

In the sixteenth century a new period in skepticism began, partly as a result of the humanist revival of the classics (including the rediscovery of Cicero's accounts of Academic skepticism and the writings of Sextus Empiricus), partly as a result of new data about the geographical, human, and astronomical world that contradicted previously accepted theories, and partly because skeptical arguments were employed in theological conflicts between Roman Catholics and reformers. Erasmus, disputing Luther, appealed to ancient skeptical arguments to deny that one could tell if people had free will. Erasmus suspended judgment on theological issues while accepting on faith the views of his church. Montaigne, after reading Sextus Empiricus, modernized the ancient skeptical arguments into a thorough attack on the science and theology of his time. He showed how attempts to know the world led to contradictions and absurdities. He also introduced a fideistic note, that humans should turn to God and accept on faith whatever knowledge God gives humans. In view of all the doubts about religious claims to knowledge (of such subjects as the nature of God, God's relationship to humanity, and humanity's spiritual nature and religious destiny), one should accept the faith into which one is born. Changing faiths would require knowledge of the merits of various faiths, whether they are true, or truer than one's own.

Whether or not Montaigne was sincere in his fideism, his position was adopted by various Counter-Reformers in France who sought to show that the Calvinists made indefensible claims about the source of religious knowledge and the nature of such knowledge. These Catholics sought to reduce the Calvinists to complete skeptics. The Calvinists, in turn, tried in a similar way to reduce the Catholics, by arguing that it was uncertain who the pope was, what he and church councils had said, and so on.

Montaigne's presentation of the new Pyrrhonism brought about a general skeptical crisis among many intellectuals in the seventeenth century. Descartes's philosophy was designed to overcome all doubts by pushing skepticism even further than Sextus or Montaigne. By finding one fundamental truth ("I think, therefore I am"), one could then establish a general criterion of truth and discover truth in mathematics, physics, and theology. Others, faced with the same skeptical crisis, sought a solution in the interpretation of biblical prophecies (Joseph Mede and Henry More), in a desperate appeal to faith (Pascal), or in moderating one's quest for knowledge to a kind of probabilism (Gassendi, Chillingworth, and the English latitudinarian theologians).

Many sought to undermine Descartes's optimistic answer to skepticism, and to cast doubts on any metaphysical foundation to modern science and any rational basis to theology. This attempt was coupled with skeptical criticism of scripture as a collection of books containing special indubitable knowledge—criticism launched by La Peyrère in his *Men before Adam* and by Spinoza in his *Tractatus Theologico-Politicus.* The French Protestant philosopher, historian, and theologian Pierre Bayle joined these skeptical strands together in his massive *Historical and Critical Dictionary* (1697–1702), casting doubts on the new philosophies of the seventeenth century, from Descartes to Locke and Leibniz, as well as on older philosophies. Bayle's only advice to his readers was to abandon reason for faith. Voltaire and Hume developed the more irreligious implications of Bayle's attacks. Voltaire called Bayle's work "the arsenal of the Enlightenment," and used it to undermine any confidence in the Judeo-Christian tradition. Hume used Bayle's skepticism to show that one has no rational basis for one's beliefs in any area whatsoever. One's beliefs in science or religion are based on natural factors, on animal faith. Kant developed Hume's skeptical criticism of arguments about the nature of God, contending that knowledge of the nature and existence of God is beyond the capabilities of pure reason and that all theological arguments about the existence and nature of God are faulty.

Hume's naturalistic skepticism and the limitations placed on human reason by Kant's analysis would seem to have led modern thought into an unconquerable skepticism. Many more recent philosophies have suggested ways of avoiding, overcoming, or living with skepticism: ways that others, in turn, have shown to be impracticable. Hume and Kant ended a tradition of seeking rational knowledge about the existence and nature of God. This skepticism about theological knowledge produced a vital form of fideism. J. G. Hamann, a religious friend of Kant's, argued that Hume was actually the greatest voice of orthodoxy. By eliminating any appeal to reason or evidence in religion, he showed it rested on faith. Hume had said skepticism is the first step toward becoming a true and believing Christian. It is doubtful, however, that Hume was any kind of Christian but, rather, was a deist or an agnostic. Hamann, however, used Hume's writings to urge Kant to turn to faith. Kierkegaard found the basis of his fideism in Hamann's interpretation of Hume and developed the total skepticism that he regarded as inherent to religious belief.

Modern skepticism from Montaigne onward eroded confidence in traditional metaphysical and theological systems, a process that is reflected in the accommodation of its tenets in pragmatism, positivism, and existentialism. This process also led to radical expressions of fideism as the basis for religious belief, such as those of Pascal and Kierkegaard, and to various forms of Neo-orthodoxy in the twentieth century.

SEE ALSO Doubt and Belief; Existentialism; Neoorthodoxy; Positivism.

BIBLIOGRAPHY

Burnyeat, Myles, ed. *The Skeptical Tradition.* Berkeley, 1983. Studies by various European and American scholars on skepticism from ancient times to the nineteenth century.

Penelhum, Terence. *God and Skepticism: A Study of Skepticism and Fideism.* Boston, 1983. An examination of whether fideism is justified by skepticism.

Popkin, Richard H. *The History of Scepticism from Erasmus to Spinoza.* Berkeley, 1979. A study of the revival of skepticism in the Renaissance and the Reformation and its import for the development of modern philosophy.

Popkin, Richard H. *The High Road to Pyrrhonism.* San Diego, Calif., 1980. A collection of essays dealing with skepticism in the late seventeenth and the eighteenth century.

Popkin, Richard H. "The Third Force in Seventeenth Century Philosophy: Skepticism, Science and Biblical Prophecy." *Nouvelles de la republique des lettres* 3 (1983): 35–63. On the role played by interpretations of biblical prophecies as a way of dealing with skepticism, from Joseph Mede to Henry More and Newton.

Richter, Rauol. *Der Skeptizismus in der Philosophie.* 2 vols. Leipzig, 1904–1908. Important survey of the history of skepticism from the perspective of nineteenth-century German thought. Covers the material up to Nietzsche.

Robin, Léon. *Pyrrhon et le scepticisme grec.* Paris, 1944. A standard study of Greek skepticism.

Russell, Bertrand. *Sceptical Essays.* London, 1928. An expression of skepticism by one of the twentieth century's leading philosophers.

Santayana, George. *Scepticism and Animal Faith.* London, 1923. A powerful statement by a leading naturalist philosopher of the force of skepticism.

Schmitt, Charles B. *Cicero Scepticus: A Study of the Influence of the Academica in the Renaissance.* The Hague, 1972. A study of the development of skeptical influences in the late Middle Ages and the Renaissance as a result of the rediscovery of Cicero's statement of ancient skepticism.

New Sources

Brooke, John Hedley. *Science and Religion: Some Historical Perspectives* New York, 1991.

Kitcher, Philip. *The Advancement of Science without Legend: Objectivity without Illusions.* New York, 1993.

Howard-Snyder, Daniel, and Paul Moser, eds. *Divine Hiddenness: New Essays.* New York, 2002.

Wilson, A. N. *God's Funeral: The Decline of Faith in Western Civilization.* New York, 1999.

Wilson, David Sloan. *Darwin's Cathedral: Evolution, Religion, and the Nature of Society.* Chicago, 2002.

RICHARD H. POPKIN (1987)
Revised Bibliography

SKOBTSOVA, MARIA.

Mother Maria Skobtsova (1891–1945) became a very unusual sort of Russian Orthodox nun in 1932. She did not join a monastic community or withdraw from her secular milieu, the Russian émigré community of France. Instead, she defined her way as "monasticism in the world."

For a nun, this lifestyle had little precedent in modern Orthodoxy and Mother Maria did not intend to set a new trend for others to follow. She needed and demonstrated a great deal of dedication, responding pragmatically to people's suffering rather than simply accepting a convent rule. As she put it, she saw "the true image of God in the human being [. . .] the very icon of God incarnate in this world" in each of the individuals she helped.

Mother Maria often criticized traditional Russian convents as inward-looking and defensive. This criticism provided the basis for her mystery play, *Anna,* composed in the late 1930s.

Mother Maria believed that monasticism should be reconsidered as a part of the revival of the Russian Church abroad, newly liberated from its former state-imposed constraints. She wrote, "we have no enormous cathedrals, no encrusted gospels or monastery walls." Rather, her Church had been granted "awe-inspiring freedom,'" which could compensate for every kind of earthly deprivation.

She addressed this topic in vivid lectures, many of which were published. One 1937 discourse, not published until sixty years later, provoked much comment, both among Russian émigrés as well as among residents of the former Soviet Union.

Mother Maria's disdain for tradition appears all the more curious, however, considering that her childhood friend K. P. Pobedonostev (1827–1907) promoted conservative values in his role as the Over-Procurator of the Church's synod. Mother's Maria's relationship with Pobedonostev resulted from her family's elevated social position. But her social standing did not cause her to value her lifestyle and privileges of which the Russian revolution, as well as her impending exile, would eventually deprive her. Early in 1917, even before the state required it, she had donated a significant proportion of her lands to meet her former tenants' needs. This action supported her membership in the Socialist Revolutionary Party, which she had joined that year. In 1918 she was elected mayor of Anapa, a tribute to her respect in the community. Although the Russian civil war of 1919 ended this appointment, her moderate socialism and her Christian concern for the needy survived. Both those attitudes comprised "Orthodox Action," the movement that she founded and led in 1936 and that later sustained her work in France.

Mother Maria was always concerned with individuals. She feared the most efficient organizations might lose that emphasis: "I would say that we should not give away a single hunk of bread unless the recipient means something as a person for us." Although she was consistently compassionate, she eschewed sentimentality.

Throughout the 1930s, Mother Maria housed and supported people who were "restless, orphaned, poor, drunk, despairing, useless, lost whichever way they went, homeless, naked, [and] lacking bread." She founded a series of homes to provide food and shelter. Perhaps her principal achievement, however, was to counteract despair. As she noted, such endeavors required her to experience what the other feels, "to become all things to all people," to work long hours, and to maintain a rich reserve of good cheer.

In this way, Mother Maria became "a mother for all, for all who need maternal care, assistance or protection." She had expressed this intention after the youngest of her three children died in infancy in 1926.

She was married twice, in 1910 and in 1919. During her first marriage, Mother Maria aspired to a literary career. Her poetry became popular in the literary world of St Petersburg, and her poems that were published in 1912 and 1916 are again in print. She continued to write poetry during the Russian emigration. From 1916 on, her concerns were largely religious, yet after she became a nun, she did not want her poems to be published. The death of her elder daughter in 1936, however, prompted the publication of her later verse, much of which contains revealing statements of devotion that are convincingly her own. She continued writing in this vein, on stray scraps of paper, for years afterwards.

In addition to writing poetry, she also created art using canvas and wood, furnishing the chapels she founded with her unconventional embroideries and icons. The German occupation of France (1940) exacerbated past social problems and imposed unprecedented limitations on the Jewish population. Mother Maria and her colleagues sheltered Jews at her homes and safeguarded many of them by listing them as members of her parish. She also arranged to transport them to safer destinations.

The Nazis arrested Mother Maria and her colleagues in February 1943. But her confinement to the Ravensbrück concentration camp enabled her to minister to companions in distress. Her work was unalloyed by any fear of death. On Good Friday, 1945, although she was not chosen for extermination, she volunteered to take a fellow prisoner's place and was executed.

BIBLIOGRAPHY

A collection of Mother Maria's Russian writings is given in Elizaveta Kuz'mina-Karavaeva and Mat' Mariia's, *Ravnina russkaia,* edited by A.N. Shustov and E.A. Polikashin (St. Petersburg, Russia, 2001), but all her theological prose is omitted. As of 2004, a critical and comprehensive edition of her Russian works in five volumes was being compiled and edited by T. Emel'ianova (Moscow, Russia). A selection of her theological articles is available in English as *Mother Maria Skobtsova: Essential Writings,* translated by R. Pevear, L.Volokhonsky, and others (Maryknoll, New York, 2003).

Sergei Hackel's biography of Mother Maria was first published in 1965, and it later appeared in a revised edition as *Pearl of Great Price: The Life of Mother Maria Skobtsova, 1891–1945* (London and Crestwood, N. Y., 1981). The book includes extracts from her writings and has been published in German, Russian, Italian, Greek, and Finnish.

SERGEI HACKEL (2005)

SKY

This entry consists of the following articles:

THE HEAVENS AS HIEROPHANY
MYTHS AND SYMBOLISM

SKY: THE HEAVENS AS HIEROPHANY

The concept of a close relationship between the starry heavens and human beings is ancient, multifaceted, and widespread. The changing colors of the sky, the alternation between night and day, different weather patterns and seasons, eclipses, the appearance and disappearance of the sun, moon, and stars, all contribute to the interest, awe, and attraction humans feel for the sky and sky-related phenomena. Throughout human history, this fascination with the celestial world has given rise to a great many myths, rituals, and monuments. For heuristic purposes this association between the cosmic and the human may be divided into two categories: technomorphic representations and anthropomorphic representations. Anthropomorphic representations may be further divided into two classifications: heavenly divinities, often considered to be personifications of the sky and/or the heavenly bodies, and human beings of celestial essence or those who have been transferred to the heavens.

TECHNOMORPHIC REPRESENTATIONS. Since very ancient times, people have tended to construct cosmologies based on an analogy between the structure of the heavens and human activies. Such cosmologies are sometimes called technomorphic representations (from the Greek *technē,* "craft"). The sky was often imagined as a solid object (vault, bucket, etc.) made of iron, stone, wood, or other material. The stars might be simply holes or windows in the solid sky, or they might be torches, flames, lights, nails, flowers, plants, or animals. Naive ideas were not infrequent, such as the notion that stars are shards of the old sun and moon broken off by the spirits and continually polished by them.

The shapes formed by an arbitrarily selected number of stars give rise to the constellations. The free play of imagination made one great cluster of stars into the Milky Way and another group into an animal (the Great Bear) or a wagon: the first wagon made by a human, the wagon of Óðinn (Odin), Icarus, Jason, Philomelus, Abraham, David, Elijah, Peter, Mary, or Jesus, a wagon whose wheels creak at midnight and whose tremblings produce snow.

In these naive cosmologies, the North Star often plays an important role, being one extremity of the *axis mundi* on which the heavenly vault turns. Thus Estonians call the

North Star, "nail of the firmament" (*pōhja nael*), around which the heavenly dome turns. The Saami (Lapps) have similar representations. They also believe that if the nail is not in place, the sky would fall to earth; this will happen at the end of the world when everything will be consumed by fire. The Finns say that the sky is the lid of the earth. In contrast, the Buriats see it as a big turning bucket. The Yakuts thought it was made of several animal skins spread over one another. The Buriats added to this that the Milky Way was the place where the skins were sewn together. A great number of representations relating to the "cosmic mantle" and to the "heavenly tent" have been analyzed by Robert Eisler in his *Weltenmantel und Himmelszelt* (1910). Influenced by the Religionsgeschichtliche Schule, Eisler looked for Oriental prototypes for all Mediterranean astral beliefs. At the same time, he related sacred kingship to the idea of a cosmic ruler whose attribute was usually a starry mantle, and showed that this tradition was carried over by Christianity down to the present times.

The idea that the stars are the signs of a mysterious heavenly writing is related to the shapes of the constellations. The "heavenly book," or the celestial vault in its entirety, may be a register kept by a specific deity (e.g., the Babylonian god Nabu). This register contained the past, present, and future of the entire universe. In all probability, this concept forms the background of astrology.

The sun and the moon, the largest heavenly bodies, are also the object of technomorphic representations. In Manichaeism, for instance, they are simply two boats navigating in the sky, whose role is to aid in the transfer of the light kept prisoner into the material world.

ANTHROPOMORPHIC REPRESENTATIONS. Personifications of objects and natural phenomena have allowed people in all times and cultures to explain and understand the world around them. In this context, the personification of the heavens has been an essential element of human concepts as projected in myths, legends, and theologies. The personification of the heavens is expressed essentially as divinities or as purified people who have been translated there.

Heavenly deities. In many cultures the sky, the sun, the moon, and the known planets were conceived as personal gods. These gods were responsible for all or some aspects of existence. Prayers were addressed to them, offerings were made to them, and their opinions on important matters were sought through divination.

It is known that many world mythologies—including some of those considered the most ancient from a historico-cultural viewpoint—make a distinction between a primordial divinity of the sky (such as the Greek Ouranos) and an active divinity (such as Zeus), head of a pantheon of gods. The sky divinity usually tends to become remote and otiose. E. O. James has shown that a sky god was known among various groups of both Indo-European and Semitic people. This sky god ranged from a tribal supreme being, often remote and ineffectual, to an active creator and ruler of the universe.

Among the astral gods, the sun god is one of the most important. He was very prominent in the Nile Valley as Re-Atum but less prominent both in Mesopotamia (where Shamash had a subordinate position) and among the Indo-Europeans. The sun divinity may also be female.

A moon goddess (or god, usually in those cultures where the sun god is female) is also very important in several cultures. In Mediterranean religions, the moon goddess could be featured as a Great Mother responsible for fertility. The Iranian Anāhitā had a moon crescent as her attribute. Artemis of Ephesos was a lunar divinity. Later on, the Greek Artemis and the Roman Diana were definitely identified with the moon.

On the other hand, Anāhitā's own name was related to the name of the planet Venus. In Pahlavi, *Anāhid* is Venus's name. Other Venus goddesses are the Babylonian Ishtar, the Phoenician Astarte, Aramean ʿAttar-ʿatteh, and the Arabian ʿAttar or Astar. Venus as morning and evening star often may be represented as a male god.

In late Babylonian religion, the planetary gods had precise identities. They were divided into two groups: the beneficent (Marduk, Ishtar-Sarpanïtu, and Nabu) and the maleficent (Ninib and Nergal). Marduk was Jupiter and together with Venus/Ishtar, the principle of creation, he gave life to Mercury/Nabu, the representative of the happy destiny of humanity. Mars/Nergal, the war god, and Saturn/Nergal, the death god, were destructive powers. Among the Babylonians, the moon god—Enzu of Lagash, Sin of Akkad, or Nanna of Ur—was more important than the solar god, Shamash, Babbar, or Nigirsu.

The relationship between humanity and the stars. Catasterism, the transfer of human beings to heaven, usually in the shape of a constellation, is related to the very ancient beliefs that dead children become stars, that a falling star foretells the death of a relative, and that even the human soul is a star. Less naively expressed, the last statement is attributed to Heraclitus by the fourth-century Neoplatonist Macrobius: "Anima scintilla stellaris essentiae."

As early as the fifth century BCE, the playwright Aristophanes mocked catasterism in his comedy *Freedom*. Alcmaeon of Croton, a physician, thought that the soul was immortal like the endless movement of the divine stars. The playwright Euripides reported that Helen of Troy was translated to the "palace of Zeus" beyond the starry sky. Even according to the "materialists," Leucippus and Democritus, the fiery soul was cognate with the sun and the moon.

Catasterism was also attested to in Egypt in the third century BCE. According to the Pyramid Texts, the king follows Orion and Sirius to the sky. During his heavenly ascent, Sothis/Sirius is his sister. According to Wilhelm Gundel, the idea that humans continue to live after death in the stars (and were stars in heaven even before their birth) is Egyptian in origin. Walter Burkert also emphasizes the differences between Babylonian and Egyptian astral religion: Whereas the divinity of the astral bodies is particularly important in Babylonia, the Egyptians stress the idea of a correspondence between humans and the stars. The belief in an astral immortality, already featured by Plato as a possibility of posthumous reward, became commonplace among his disciples Xenocrates, Crantor, and Heracleides Ponticus. Later, mythology and science converged toward impressive representations such as those of the eschatological myths of Plutarch (c. 46–c. 119 CE). These representations cannot be ascribed to an uninterrupted Pythagorean tradition, as the French scholar A. Delatte and his school suggest. The most prominent representative of this school was L. Rougier, who defended the Pythagorean thesis against Franz Cumont, defender of the Oriental thesis of the German Religionsgeschichtliche Schule. During the Hellenistic period and late antiquity, the underground hell of the platonic myths was transferred to a place in heaven.

In no religious tradition except gnosticism did all the astral gods become evil demons. A strong polemic against astrology is implicit in gnostic mythology. Astrology, based on an ancient Babylonian and Egyptian inheritance, took shape in the third century BCE. In astrology, a particular relationship between human destiny and the heavenly bodies is expressed. This relationship takes on complicated forms, which can often be retraced to basic representations such as the "heavenly book" and the heavenly figures, or constellations. Astrology also put into mathematical language some methods of divination, which probably were based on the idea of the influence of the planets upon human individual and collective history.

SEE ALSO Astrology; Cosmology; Moon; Stars; Sun; Supreme Beings.

BIBLIOGRAPHY

Ancient astral beliefs are surveyed by Robert Eisler in *Weltenmantel und Himmelszelt: Religionsgeschichtliche Untersuchungen zur Urgeschichte des antiken Weltbildes,* 2 vols. (Munich, 1910). Valuable information is also contained in Uno Harva Holmberg's *Der Baum des Lebens* (Helsinki, 1923) and, above all, in Wilhelm Gundel's *Sternglaube, Sternreligion und Sternorakel: Aus der Geschichte der Astrologie,* 2d ed. (Heidelberg, 1959).

Babylonian astral religion is the object of the second volume of Franz Xaver Kugler's *Sternkunde und Sterndienst in Babel: Assyriologische, astronomische und astralmythologische Untersuchungen,* 3 vols. in 2 (Münster, 1907–1924).

On the sky god among the Semites and the Indo-Europeans, the standard work is E. O. James's *The Worship of the Sky-God: A Comparative Study in Semitic and Indo-European Religion* (London, 1963).

Theories concerning astral religion have been recently discussed in my own work, *Psychanodia I: A Survey of the Evidence concerning the Ascension of the Soul and Its Relevance,* "Études préliminaires aux religions orientales dans l'empire romaine," vol. 99 (Leiden, 1983).

New Sources

Aveni, Anthony F. *Conversing with the Planets: How Science and Myth Invented the Cosmos.* New York, 1992.

Barton, Tamsyn S. *Ancient Astrology.* New York, 1994.

Grant, Edward. *Planets, Stars, and Orbs: The Medieval Cosmos, 1200–1687.* New York, 1996.

Krupp, E. C. *Beyond the Blue Horizon: Myths and Legends of the Sun, Moons, Stars, and Planets.* New York, 1991.

Wright, M. R. *Cosmology in Antiquity.* New York, 1995.

IOAN PETRU CULIANU (1987)
Revised Bibliography

SKY: MYTHS AND SYMBOLISM

> But when the stars of Orion and Seirios have climbed up into midheaven and rosy-fingered Dawn is facing Arkturos, then, Perses, pluck and bring home all your clusters of grapes. Set them to dry in the heat of the sun for ten days and nights, and in the shade for five days, and then on the sixth day draw off the blessings of glad Dionysus into your jars. (Hesiod, *Works and Days* 609–617)

> Moctezuma, having observed the comet since midnight, went the next day to Netzahualpilli to seek its meaning. Replied the king of Texcoco, "Your vassals, the astrologers, soothsayers and diviners have been careless! That sign in the heavens has been there for some time and yet you describe it to me now as if it were a new thing. I thought you had already discovered it and that your astrologers had explained it to you. Since you now tell me you have seen it I will answer you that that brilliant star appeared in the heavens many days ago. (Durán, 1964, pp. 247–248)

Diverse as they are both in interpretation and cultural origin, these epigraphs capture the essence of why ancient people turned to the sky for direction and meaning. Their queries were immediate: "When shall I plant?" "When shall I hunt?" And they were deeper: "Will the child I am about to bear be born healthy?" "Will the gods repay my offering to them by sending gentle rain and a good crop?" But why look upward and outward to commune with the transcendent? Of all the numinous forces in nature's domain that can serve as paragons of order in the world—cycles of plants, animals, the running of the stream, the first rain, the last frost—only what happens in heaven offers the precise predictive power that enables people to cast their eyes around the corner of time into the future.

Sunrise, sunset, the phases of the moon, the annual appearance and disappearance of the constellations—all occur with undeviating regularity. Harness the power of the sky and one opens the doorway of time to come.

When Greek poet Hesiod spoke the *Works and Days* (the first quotation), he was using the sky as a rational guide for how to run a farm. If one desires the optimum vintage, pick the grapes only when the brightest star in the constellation of Böotes, the Ploughman, makes its first annual predawn appearance. People have been aware of the clockwork sky since Paleolithic times. Alongside cave drawings of antelope and bison, one finds tally marks indicating the direction of the light of the moon and the course of the sun. Such practical concerns involved in the making of calendars constitute the earliest forms of exact science.

The second quotation offers a somewhat less rational perspective on the sky. The early seventeenth-century chronicler Torquemada's account of the celestial omens cast by Netzahualpilli, king of Texcoco, a rival state of the Aztecs, pertains to the appearance of a comet in the skies over ancient Mexico in the early fifteenth century. He tells of King Moctezuma's retort, in which the ruler boasts of his prior knowledge of the same phenomenon. Torquemada goes on to give details of the frightful omens concerning disasters that indeed later befell the unfortunate monarch. If it seems odd to find the occult art of astrology attached to scientific comet watching, one should keep in mind that until well after the Western European Renaissance the principal reason for charting the heavens was to interpret messages sent by celestial spirits. As the Babylonian cuneiform tablets in the Old World and the Maya codices in the New World demonstrate, mathematical predictions about the positions of celestial bodies have long been strongly wedded to religious concerns.

"As above, so below." The logic of the credo of astrology, a form of divination, developed quite naturally out of the realization that the movement and position of the sun could be closely correlated with seasonal cycles of life and that the moon governed both the tides and the menstrual cycle. Might not other celestial forces influence tides in the affairs of men and women? Sky objects became deified. They were worshipped, revered, even compensated for the good that they brought, and they were offered sacrifice as a means of averting misfortune. We may not think of Hesiod's poetry as science, nor of Moctezuma's astrological ruminations as religion, but both pursuits are foundational in worldviews undivided by Enlightenment thinking. In the symbolic sphere of sky-meaning dealt with in this entry one confronts the unfragmented world of an alien *other* open to dialog with tangible cosmic forces that constitute a living, breathing reality.

The Structure of the Upper World. Early records from the Middle East offer a common if not universal concept of the arrangement of things in the firmament (literally a "thin plate"). Consider these Old and New Testament cosmological speculations: "He set a circle upon the face of the deep" (*Prv.* 8:27); "He sitteth upon the circle of the earth" (*Is.* 40:22). Both suggest a god in heaven who looks down upon the edge (horizon) of a flat disk. But the earth rests on pillars: "For the pillars of the earth are the Lord's and He hath set the world upon them" (1 *Sm.* 2–8). Above the disk lies the water than makes rainfall and below the water that wells up from artesian springs: "God spread forth the earth above the waters" (*Ps.* 36:6); "Above the earth is the solid firmament supporting the upper waters" (*Gn.* 1:6–7).

Elsewhere, *Exodus* 20:4 speaks of a tripartite universe: the heavens, the earth, and the watery abyss beneath the earth; or, as in *Psalms* 115:16, the heavens, the earth, and She'ol. As a rule the Bible imagines the physical sky to be a vast hemisphere, sometimes, as in *Psalms* 104:2, stretched out over the earth. In the *Book of Job* the sky is a building supported by columns (26:11), a storehouse for snow and hail (38:22), the winds (37:9), and water (38:37). In *Genesis* 7:11 the sky has windows through which rain falls to the earth.

The Egyptian cosmos depicted in tomb paintings consists of a rectangular box with Egypt at the center. A flat sky was supported by columns on high mountains. The Nile surrounded all and continued its course into the heavens as a celestial river—the Milky Way. The stars were lamps hung by ropes or painted on the body of Nut, the feminine sky deity. For the Inca the Milky Way is also a sky river, for the Maya it is a road; both are extensions of terrestrial parallels. Among the Egyptian sky lamps roamed deities and spirits. The sun god Ra traveled the sky in a boat. Reference is made to a ladder connecting heaven and earth whereby spirits could ascend to heaven upon death.

Diné Bahane, the Navajo story of creation, describes the smooth hard shell of the sky overhead. There is a hole on its eastern side through which ancient ancestor spirits could enter into a second world. Other entries led to successive upper worlds, each of a different color, in a layered universe. Each layer is inhabited by different kinds of animal deities.

In some cosmologies, the layer-cake concept continues in the world below. In the Western tradition, it offers the spatial polar opposite to the good found in heaven above. The first mention of hell in Western history appears in Hesiod's *Theogony*, where it is called Tartaros, the lower deck of a three-story cosmos. Influenced by the Greeks and the New Testament, the Italian poet Dante (1265–1321) would later tell of a hell that came equipped with nine decks, each of which offered inverse luxury accommodations commensurate with the sin in which one indulged. Gluttonous, lustful, and slothful people sat near the top; murderers, blasphemers, and self-robbers (those who committed suicide) resided in the middle; and grafters, simonists (those who committed fraud), soothsayers, and a variety of traitors occupied the upside-down penthouse at the lowest level of hell.

While Maya heaven consisted of thirteen layers, the lower was composed of nine. Like the Dantean lower realm, it was populated with evildoers: the Lords of the Underworld, each in charge of his own particular pestilence. In most instances then, unknown transcendent space seems to be modeled after terrestrial parallels.

Why Sky Gods Behave as They Do. Myths are stories that try to give answers to life's big questions: Where did I come from? Why must I die? What will happen to me when

I die? This section will attempt to convey how some of the celestial metaphors that lie behind particular asterisms derive from the discovery of perceived likenesses between the actions of celestial bodies and particular aspects of life for which people sought meaning.

Designating the planets by name and seeking omens from their behavior lay at the foundation of astrally based religions practiced by nearly all our cultural predecessors. The drama overhead constituted a parallel plane of existence—a stage on which people here on earth could reflect and examine human behavior. The gods of the ancient Near East, for example, were not personages who guided nature's forces or programmed its laws. These "attribution deities" began with the actual properties of the material elements that gave them their names. Thus, Esharra, an earth god, was the manifest fruitfulness of the land that made for a bountiful harvest and fat cattle. The rubescent sky god Nergal (Mars) was the red feverishness of the summer sun that destroyed crops; Merodach the youthfulness of the spring equinox sun; Dumuzi the sun at the beginning of summer; and Ishtar (Venus) the returning greenness of the grass after winter's frost and summer's scorching heat.

Venus. Venus, for example, was given a host of names. She was called Ishtar in Chaldea, Nabu in Babylonia, Anāhīta by the Persians, Benu by the Sumerians, Astarte and then Aphrodite by the Greeks—all feminine appellations. The Greeks recognized Venus's dual aspect, referring to the planet as Phosphoros in the morning and Hesperos in the evening. Later the Romans named these aspects Lucifer and Vesper. In ancient Mesoamerica, Venus was a male, Quetzalcoatl (feathered serpent); to the Maya he was Kukulcan. Hawaiians named the planet Hokuloa, the Tahitians Ta'urua. Wasp Star, Red Star, Great Star, Lone Star, Lord of the Dawn, Home of the Love Goddess, Proclaimer, Companion to the Royal Inebriate, Bringer of Light, Satan himself—all these titles were given this single celestial source of light by imaginative people from various epochs and corners of the world.

What did these names mean? Bringer of Light and Lord of the Dawn are understandable enough, for Venus always precedes the rising sun. But why has Venus variously been linked with the highest ideal of feminine beauty, love, and sexuality, as in the Western tradition, or with death and resurrection, as in the Mesoamerican tradition? In the ancient Middle East, where Venus was called Ishtar, there is a long history of worship of the goddess who evoked the power of the dawn. The first syllable of Ishtar's name is probably derived from the Sanskrit *ush*, meaning "a burning" or "fire." *Ush* also came to mean "east," the direction to which worshipers turned their faces in order to feel the rays of the bright sun god, both powerful and nurturing. Later, east became the cardinal axis about which most early Old World maps were constructed. It marked where the sun rose on the equinoxes, the first days of autumn and spring. The English word *orientation* means "easting," and most old European cathedrals face that direction. Concerning Ishtar, the pre-Christian worshipers upon whose pagan temples these edifices now stand needed to be sure that every time they faced the cosmic axis and uttered her name they would soon feel within their breasts the power of dawn, of fire, of creation and fertility. When the Sumerians spoke to Ishtar they drew out her feminine sensuousness:

> Ishtar is clothed with pleasure and love
> She is laden with vitality, charm and voluptuousness
> In lips she is sweet; life is in her mouth.
> At her appearance rejoicing becomes full.
> She is glorious; veils are thrown over her head.
> Her figure is beautiful; her eyes are brilliant.
> (Pritchard, 1955, p. 383)

Unlike the other planets, Venus always remains close to the sun, close to the surface of the earth. Thus Ishtar descends into the underworld with the sun at night, only to return the morning after her lustful affair with Shamash, bringing with her omens related to the fertility of the land and of women.

Like Ishtar's descent and return, the death and resurrection of Quetzalcoatl are visibly manifest every time Venus disappears in the western sky in the evening and reappears in the eastern sky in the morning. According to the *Annals of Cuauhtitlan,* a colonial document from Central Mexico, after an eight day disappearance into the underworld, Venus is resurrected in the eastern sky as Lord of the Dawn.

For the ocean-bound people of ancient Hawai'i, the planets were sustainers, supporters or pillars of a giant celestial round house built on the model of the houses in which they once lived. They were placed in the sky to help people—to warn them of coming events. To learn the warning system, one needed to pay close attention and follow the movement of the planets among the stars from year to year. Some planetary deities paid special attention to fishermen, others to tattoo artists—one cannot explain why in every case. Like the stars, the planets could intermarry and breed children. Bright Venus, as one might expect, was by far the most prominent. It was variously known as Dog of the Morning, Star of Day, and Forerunner of the Morning, a status similar to that of the Greco-Roman Phosphoros-Lucifer.

When Hawaiian Venus was the Great Star, its name was Hokuloa, which placed it in the same class as the sun and moon, but when it dodged unsteadily from side to side, like Mercury, it was dubbed the Royal Inebriate. For seafarers like the Hawaiians, weather prediction ranked high in importance alongside astrological affairs of war and state. Naholoholo, literally "swift-moving," like the storms in this region, is one old Hawaiian name given to Venus. In one tale, the Great Guide Star of the Evening deviates from his course to suppress the fury of a hurricane and, as a result, loses his balance and falls out of his canoe.

Venus's habit of dogging the rising and setting sun also had its effect on Chinese celestial imagery. In eighth-century China, for example, white was the color of ghosts, and the brilliance of Venus also mocked the flash of swordly metal. This is probably why the Chinese called the planet the Grand White and the Executioner's Star—a planet that portended deadly plots and cutting edges. When Venus crossed the constellation of the Battle Ax (part of Gemini), it foretold the clash of weapons; when it entered the Ghost constellation, it was time to execute the vassals. Warriors once stood on the Great Wall following the movements of the Grand White, even at the expense of neglecting to observe the maneuvers of their enemies. When the planet was especially bright—for example, if it could be seen in the daytime—its spotlight aspect indicated an omen of special importance. Perhaps the yin principle would strongly override the yang so that a lower-order vassal could rise up against the Emperor of the Sun.

Other attribution deities. Other planets exacted their own metaphors. For example, the red planet Mars—planet of blood and fire for the Tang of sixth-century China—was regarded as the punishment star. It was especially potent when it passed its namesake constellations of Virgo and Scorpio. Curiously, Antares, the bright red star in Scorpio, also means "rival of Mars" in the Western tradition. Its hot, rosy radiation also warned of drought.

Because they once were earth gods, all the planets in the Sumerian pantheon had terrestrial dwelling places. The dwelling place of Mars (Nergal) was a violent domicile that generated the malevolence associated with the war god. The names the Assyrians gave to Mars suggest anything but beneficence and dependability. He was the pestilential one, hostile and rebellious. War was another of the aspects of Mars, which, some Assyriologists contend, may have been associated with the planet's blood red color, especially when it lies low over the land. Or is it the erratic motion Mars exhibits, well beyond that of the other planets?

Slowest moving of all the planets, Saturn was Ninib to the Sumerians, a phlegmatic old man who lumbered ever so slowly across the celestial vault. Saturn also received the designation Lu-Bat, the steady one, for it could be counted upon, more than any other so-called wanderer (the Sumerians likened the planets to errant sheep who strayed from the flock) to be present in the night sky just as the sun ruled the day. Because it moves thoughtfully, steadily, and deliberately, Saturn's character reflects wisdom and intelligence more than speed and vigorous activity. By inhibiting the uppermost realm, a result of the extreme length of time it takes the planet to complete its cycle around the zodiac, Saturn occupied the biggest sphere and was therefore accorded the highest power in divinatory astrology.

Nearer to the sun than the cold, remote location of Saturn, yet farther than fiery Mars, lies Jupiter—Greek Zeus. Jupiter is commonly associated with justice. He became a moderator and, consequently, most fit to rule the celestial gods. He alone held the power to create storms, floods, and earthquakes. As Marduk he was elevated to the position of tutelary, or protective, deity of the city of Babylon. He also rose to the godhead position in the later Babylonian astral religions as a consequence of that city having gained prominence over its rivals.

To fleeting Mercury, ancient people applied terms such as *burner* or *sparkler*, terms that visually depict the way the planet twinkles at the horizon. Animals associated with Mercury, the stealthy fox and the leopard, characterize its aspect as a trickster, for Mercury would always foil one who tried to follow him by hiding and disappearing frequently.

CELESTIAL IMAGERY. Conditioned to believe that myth can have no basis in observed fact, the modern mind might seem content to sweep such detail under the rug of superstition and irrational mysticism. But by appealing to natural phenomena that actually took place in land and sky—by paying attention to qualities peculiar to each planet—one can begin to piece together an empirical side of the mythic coin that complements and enriches the seemingly strange logic behind sky myths. Moreover, if the listener to whom the story is being told knows the celestial imagery that goes with each chapter, the greater its efficacy. The tale truly begins to come to life in the real world.

Culture structures nature. And so people order the stars as well as the planets into patterns in the sky. The most common set is the zodiac, literally a circle of animals, usually twelve or thirteen in number, that circumscribe the sky. The Egyptian zodiac consisted of twelve constellations, the Maya thirteen, the Chinese twenty-eight. The zodiac constitutes the roadway along which the sun, moon, and stars pass. Its stars play a major role in acquiring astrological predictions.

Among the Desána of Colombia, hexagonal shapes and outlines (e.g., a number of bright stars centered on the Belt of Orion rather than a sky band) provided the ordering principle. Hexagons indicate life's creative-transformative energies concentrated and at work. The Desána see these recurring shapes in the structure of rock crystals, which are common shamanic power objects. They see them in honeycombs, wasps' nests, the womb, ritual enclosures, and the plates on the back of a tortoise.

The Aztecs viewed in their star patterns the sustainers of life—the gods they sought to repay with the blood of sacrifice for bringing favorable rains, for keeping the earth from quaking, for spurring them on in battle. Among the gods was Black Tezcatlipoca, who ruled the night from his abode in the north, with its wheel (the Big Dipper). He presided over the cosmic ballcourt (Gemini), where the gods played a game to set the fate of humankind. He lit the fire sticks (Orion's belt) that brought warmth to the hearth. And at the end of every 52-year calendrical cycle, Black Tezcatlipoca timed the rattlesnake's tail (the Pleiades) so that it passed overhead at midnight—a guarantee that the world would not come to an end and that humanity would be granted another epoch of life. The priests in Tenochtitlan, the Aztec capital, climbed to the top of their sky watchers' temple on the Hill of the Star to witness this auspicious sign. These indigenous cultures lived their sky, knowing that everything that happened on earth was destined in the cosmos.

THE SKY IN CREATION NARRATIVES. *Genesis* means "origination," and every genesis myth begins with a sense of time. The modern scientific genesis began more than thirteen billion years ago in a Big Bang from which all events and things have spun. But this, unlike all other cosmologies, is decidedly nonparticipatory—a story without a purpose as one modern cosmologist has characterized it.

In the Old Testament *Genesis*, the purpose seems to be to demonstrate that all things were intended to be good. Perhaps all people need to believe in a world that can be conceived as orderly, intentional, purposeful, and, above all, created specifically with them in mind—a good world. The orderly creation by word in *Genesis* stands in stark contrast to the early Greek *Theogony* and the earlier Babylonian *Enuma Elish* from which it undoubtedly derived. These militaristic states portray a present world that emerges in the aftermath of a battle among cosmic forces. In the *Theogony*, the history of the world is characterized as the history of the descent of the orderly government of Zeus by succession from his godly predecessors.

The Babylonian creation myth, also acted out in heaven, follows a similar might-is-right storyline with Marduk, the analog of Zeus and Jupiter, battling Tiamat (Typhoeus in the *Theogony*), the raging force of the untamed waters. Out of Marduk's victory in battle comes a common motif in stories of creation, the raising of the sky:

> He shot off an arrow, and it tore her interior. It cut through her inward parts, it split her heart. When he had subdued her, he destroyed her life. He split her open like a mussel in two parts; Half of her he set in place and formed the sky therewith as a roof. He fixed the crossbar and posted guards; He commanded them not to let her waters escape. (Heidel, 1942, p. 42)

The idea behind this fantastic imagery is that divine kingship lies at the root of the state, and it must be established authoritatively once and for all through compulsive force. In like manner, a violent process also was necessary to create an orderly universe.

The concept of raising the sky is especially prominent in the cosmogonies of Polynesia and Micronesia, as well as in Nigeria and the Malay Peninsula. One story conceives of the sky as a vessel suspended over the earth by a cord. Once it hung so low to the earth that one of the first humans accidentally bumped against it while raising his pestle to grind rice. He raised the sky higher up with his hands to its present position.

The further back one traces creation myths, the more hazy they become on the issue of whether man or woman came first in the genealogy. Perhaps this only reflects the magnitude of the problem about where the principle of sexual union originates. For example, in the Babylonian *Enuma Elish*, the blending of the male and female principle is manifested in the commingling of fresh and salt waters where the Tigris and Euphrates meet the Persian Gulf. Before this time the universe was a watery chaos not unlike that in the biblical *Genesis*. Likewise Ometecuhtli, the creation deity of the Aztecs who resides in the uppermost layer of heaven, is bisexual.

The *Popol Vuh*, the Quiché Maya story of the creation of "all the sky earth," features twin heroes (usually depicted as the sun and moon, or the sun and Venus) who go into the underworld to battle the lords of pestilence. One brother defeats the evil lords by tricking them into offering themselves for sacrifice. He demonstrates his power over time by sacrificing his twin brother, tearing out his heart; then, by voice command, he reverses time and brings him back to life. So ecstatic are the lords with such legerdemain that they plead to Venus: "Do it to us!" Venus indulges them, but, cleverly, only completes the first half of the process. Were it not for Venus's cunning actions in the netherworld before the dawn of history, the Maya say, the world would be far worse off with disease than it is today. Cunning and trickery are qualities of sky gods in many Native American narratives.

The Chinese think about their past in terms of three ages: the mythological, the ancient, and the modern. The first two are of special concern. Creation was an event that, by most accounts, took place close to half a million years ago. It began just as the sages in many other cultures tell it: by the opening of heaven and earth. This was not a creation *ex nihilo* (out of nothing), but rather a stepwise fabrication fired up by the Dao, an unknowable principle that resulted in the sorting out of an originally undifferentiated chaos.

First there was a One, and out of that One, the Two was produced, the yin-yang principle that constitutes the makeup of everything conceivable. As in the biblical *Genesis*, there is also an anthropic version of the fabrication of the universe. Pangu, a creator god, goes about his work with hammer and chisel as he sculpts masses of chaotic matter into the correct shape. They say his labors lasted eighteen thousand years; day by day as he worked along, he increased in stature, and the heavens rose and the earth expanded around him. Once he made the stage ready, he died. But even his death benefited humans directly, for his body parts became the entities that fill up earth's basin: his head became the mountains; his left eye, the sun; his right eye, the moon; his beard, the stars; his limbs, the four quarters; his blood, the rivers; his flesh, the soil; his breath, the wind and clouds; his voice, the thunder. His limbs were the four directions; metals, rocks, and precious stones were made from his teeth, bones, and marrow. His sweat became the rain, and the insects that stuck to his body were the people.

Sky gods usually appear to be both unique religious creations and products of history. At one end of a broad continuum lie deities who display characteristics related to rulership of the world and moral oversight (e.g., the Indian Varuṇa and Iranian Ahura Mazdā); at the other end are deities whose chief traits mark them as creators, bringers of rain and fecundity, and likely to develop into more specialized storm gods (e.g., Zeus, Jupiter, Thor, and possibly the Inca Viracocha and the Teotihuacan storm god). In the middle of the array would stand the figure of a cosmocrat like Mahāvairocana, the cosmic buddha of the Shingon school in Japan.

Making Sacred Space on Earth. As the Roman *urbs* was the place of assembly, *civitas* was the religious and political association of tribal families. Both translate as "city." The Etruscans founded the city all at once rather than by gradual degrees. A white bull drew a plough in one direction, a black bull in the other as circular furrows were plowed to circumscribe the intended location of the heart of the city: the *templum*, whence the modern English word *temple*.

Knowing which way to face lies at the basis of rules of communication between people and their gods. Which way must a priest or worshippers turn in order to perform correctly a private or public ceremony, a consecration or sacrifice? For the Etruscans the setting of directions was not according to humans but rather to the world itself. There was a front and a back to Etruscan ritual space, a left and a right in the early *templum*—this human-built representation of the celestial *templum*, the home of the gods who lived in the sky. "Four parts did it have: that toward the east *antica*, *positca* that toward the west: the northern part on the left, the southern on the right," wrote the Roman historian Isidorus. Thus, gates to the city were placed at four cardinal interruptions in the furrow. A foundation sacrificial ritual honoring the ancestors, ancient gods, and heroes, then took place at the center. "There is no place in the city not impregnated with religion and not occupied by some divinity," wrote Livy.

Historians of religions have sorted out a number of reasons that motivated ancient cultures around the world to seek divine plans for the arrangement and orientation of ceremonial architecture. Paul Wheatley, in discussing the spatial arrangement of buildings in the Chinese city, suggests that those religions that specifically associated the creation of the universe with the origin of humanity tend to dramatize the cosmogony by attempting to reproduce on earth a miniaturized version of the cosmos. On the other hand, those that relate divine revelation to the meaning of human existence often abstract their gods from the landscape; the attendant rituals appear to bear little connection to the environment. Thus, in eastern Asia and particularly in Mesoamerica, where creation hypotheses are heavily mythologized, one can expect religion to have played a decisive role in the planning of ceremonial space.

Historian of religions Mircea Eliade gave an account of cosmic hierophanies, which he considers to be sacred phenomena revealed at different cosmic levels. His discussion of architectural hierophanies emphasizes the cohesive bond between ancient religion and cosmology. The use of ceremonial architecture to convey celestial messages to a throng celebrating a ritual seems to have flowered in the classic Maya world (200–900 CE). There are numerous examples of important events—inaugurations, celebrations of victories in battle, great royal turning points—being commemorated on days when some important celestial event occurred. Such elaborate theatrical stagings reveal Maya beliefs about the essence of heavenly power in a direct and forceful way. The goal of specialized Maya ceremonial architecture seems to have been to instill in the viewer-participant the same sort of passion that might have welled up in the breast of the medieval Christian pilgrim who for the first time saw the sun shine through the stained glass windows of, say, the cathedral of Chartres. For the ancient Maya, the cosmos carried powerful messages and their delivery occurred, as one might expect in the tropics, in the open outdoor space of the royal court.

Among the cosmo-magical principles of place-making cited by Wheatley are the location of major ceremonial structures over caves or springs, natural openings to the underworld, and the orientation of such structures to prominent points in the land and skyscape. Thus, the great pyramid of Cholula, Mexico, the largest Native American structure, faces the sunset at the summer solstice between the twin volcanoes Popocatepetl and Ixtaccíhuatl. Likewise, Teotihuacán's Pyramid of the Sun, built over a cave, is oriented to a mountain on the north, as well as toward the west to the setting point of the Pleiades star group, the first annual appearance of which marks New Year's day, when the sun passes directly overhead.

Shrines often mark connection points with the sky-earth. For example, a small chapel on the side of Cholula's pyramid is positioned over a natural spring that connects to the underworld. The radial *ceque* system of the Inca capital of Cuzco is delineated by *huacas*, sacred places (many of them natural springs) where worshippers feed the earth mother, Pachamama. The Hopi marked the solstices, which the elders referred to as "houses" where the sun stops in its travels along the horizon. At these places along the high mesa, the priests erected small shrines. There a sun priest in charge of the calendar would deposit prayer sticks, an offering to welcome the sun and to encourage it on its celestial journey. Some of these shrines have special openings that allow shafts of sunlight to penetrate particular directions, thus serving as another way to mark the appropriate time. Sometimes the sun priest would gesture to the sun, whirling a shield decorated with sun designs to imitate the sun's turning motion, hastening away any malevolent spirits who might impede the great luminary.

Celestially motivated structures might be classified as theaters, as well as observatories. The modern preoccupation with precision and exactitude in assessing ancient building alignments often undervalues the symbolic significance of sky phenomena. (A modern example is the proposed design of the new World Trade Center complex in New York, which incorporates a colossal shadow casting device to mark the precise moment of the September 11, 2001, event.) Cosmic hierophanies often translate into light and shadow phenomena in architectural space dedicated to worshipping the ancestor creator gods. One example of a hierophany involving the subtle influence of light and shadow on Mesoamerican Maya architecture occurs at the ruins of Chichén Itzá. About an hour before sunset on the vernal equinox, the nine platforms that make up the pyramidal base of the Temple of Kukulcan cast thin shadows on the balustrade wall of the north stairway in such a way as to form an undulating line. The union of this line with the large serpent head at the base of the northern staircase presents a striking picture of a serpent of light. Here was an appropriate event to take place on a temple dedicated to Quetzalcoatl-Kukulcan, the feathered serpent god of creativity and reservation—and it seems to have been designed to take place at the right time.

Toward the end of the last millennium, the Chichén hierophany was appropriated by the government as a national holiday when it was realized that the event also takes place on the birthday of the nineteenth-century Mexican liberator Benito Juárez. Today, the world New Age community descends on the serpent on equinox day to find salvation and renewal by seeking the ancient truths and lost wisdom of the Maya, which they believe are revealed on this special day. Thousands of people attend the annual event, which has its European parallel in the Stonehenge pilgrimage on the summer solstice. Thus, the ruins of antiquity become the contested ground for the ownership of sacred time and place—between native and foreigner, between scientific expert and New Ager, between local commoner and national bureaucracy.

Like all seasonal rituals in the round of cyclic time, the serpent hierophany is really about hope—the return of a desired past that elevates the present above the mundane. The descending serpent offers food for a spiritually starved society possessed by a longing to recreate a glorious past superior to an unfulfilling present. Whether a descending serpent, a wandering planet, or a conspicuous star group that calls to mind a parallel in the earthly realm, whatever emerges out of the sky seems ever-present, all-powerful and, above all, stable and reliable. The heavens are the hallmark of a collection of living entities that command reverence, exude wisdom, and, with an aura of mystery and wonderment, offer the prospect of human salvation.

See Also Ascension; Cosmology; Heaven and Hell; Moon; Stars; Sun.

Bibliography

An astronomical tour of ancient sacred places as sources of transcendent power is given in Edwin C. Krupp, *Skywatchers, Shamans, and Kings: Astronomy and the Archaeology of Power* (New York, 1997). Krupp's earlier *Echoes of the Ancient Skies: The Astronomy of Lost Civilizations* (New York, 1983) focuses further on archaeological manifestations of celestial symbolism. *Skywatchers: A Revised Version of Skywatchers of Ancient Mexico* by Anthony Aveni (Austin, Tex., 2001) focuses mostly on Mesoamerica (see esp. chap. 5). Aveni's *Conversing with the Planets: How Science and Myth Invented the Cosmos*, rev. ed. (Boulder, Colo., 2003) offers a chapter (3) on sky mythology that includes how early Christianity transformed the pagan sky gods. Chapter 2 of *Maya Cosmos: Three Thousand Years on the Shaman's Path* by David Freidel, Linda Schele, and Joy Parker (New York, 1993) gives an excellent overview of ancient and contemporary Maya celestial mythology. Also of a regional nature, historian of religion Lawrence Sullivan's *Icanchu's Drum: An Orientation to Meaning in South American Religions* (New York, 1988) discusses celestial beings, world planes, and the transcendent as manifested in sky myth.

Most relevant among the many works of Mircea Eliade are *The Sacred and the Profane: The Nature of Religion* (New York, 1959) and *Patterns in Comparative Religion* (New York, 1958), especially chapter 2: "The Sky and Sky Gods." Chapter 1 in Eliade's *Cosmos and History: The Myth of the Eternal Return* (New York, 1954) develops several themes, such as the symbolism of the center and the celestial archetypes of human space. *From Primitives to Zen: A Thematic Sourcebook of the History of Religions*, edited by Mircea Eliade (New York, 1967), is an excellent sourcebook. Also see W. Brede Kristensen's *The Meaning of Religion: Lectures in the Phenomenology of Religion* (The Hague, 1960); see especially chapter 3, "The Worship of the Sky and of Celestial Bodies," which takes an approach very different from Eliade's. Also useful is George B. Foucart's excellent article "Sky and Sky Gods" in the *Encyclopaedia of Religion and Ethics*, edited by James Hastings, vol. 11 (Edinburgh, 1920). Further, on sky gods see the brief essay "The Supreme Being: Phenomenological Structure and Historical Development" in *The History of Religions: Essays in Methodology*, edited by Mircea Eliade and Joseph M. Kitagawa (Chicago, 1959), pp. 59–66. A classic English-language work on the sky gods is E. O. James's *The Worship of the Sky-God: A Comparative Study in Semitic and Indo-European Religion* (London, 1963). In addition, although methodologically outdated, James G. Frazer's *Worship of Nature*, vol. 1 (London, 1926), remains an excellent source for data (see pp. 1–315 on "the worship of the sky"). See also Charles H. Long's concise work *Alpha: The Myths of Creation* (New York, 1963); Alexander Heidel's *The Babylonian Genesis: The Story of Creation* (Chicago, 1942); James Bennett Pritchard, *Ancient Near Eastern Texts Relating to the Old Testament*, 2d ed., corr. and enl. (Princeton, 1955); and Diego Durán, *The Aztecs: The History of the Indies of New Spain* (New York, 1964).

Lindsay Jones's *Monumental Occasions: Reflections on the Eventfulness of Religious Architecture* (Cambridge, Mass., 2000) and *Twin City Tales: A Hermeneutical Reassessment of Tula and Chichén Itzá* (Niwot, Colo., 1995) deal with broader theoretical questions and the historical interpretation of cosmically related architecture. In the art historical realm the image of the sky dome in art and architecture is dealt with in Ananda K. Coomaraswamy's "The Symbolism of the Dome" in *Selected Papers*, vol. 1: *Traditional Art and Symbolism*, edited by Roger Lipsey (Princeton, 1977), pp. 415–458. See also Alexander C. Soper's "The 'Dome of Heaven' in Asia," *Art Bulletin* 29 (1947): 225–248; and Karl Lehmann's "The Dome of Heaven," *Art Bulletin* 27 (1945): 1–27.

Cosmogony and Ethical Order: New Studies in Comparative Ethics, edited by Robin Lovin and Frank Reynolds (Chicago, 1985) offers a series of essays on creation stories from around the world. David Carrasco's edited volumes *To Change Place: Aztec Ceremonial Landscapes* (Niwot, Colo., 1991); *The Imagination of Matter: Religion and Ecology in Mesoamerican*

Traditions (Oxford, 1989); and *Mesoamerica's Classical Heritage: From Teotihuacan to the Aztecs* (Boulder, Colo., 2000) have revolutionized the approaches of cultural anthropology and the history of religion to the subject of Mesoamerican cosmologies. Lastly, the author acknowledges Peter Chemery's essay from the first edition of *The Encyclopedia of Religion* (New York, 1987) both for guidance and for information in the preparation of this updated contribution.

ANTHONY F. AVENI (2005)

SLAVIC RELIGION. The exact origin of the Slavs, an indigenous European people, is not known, but by about 800 BCE pockets of Slavs were scattered in a region east of the Vistula and the Carpathians and west of the Don. Some six hundred years later the Slavs inhabited a large area in central and eastern Europe. Over the centuries they were driven north, south, and east by successive migrations of Germanic and Asiatic tribes.

Around the sixth century CE the Slavs began separating into three groups, the West, South, and East Slavs. Proto-Slavic, an Indo-European language, was spoken in an area extending from the north of Russia to the south of Greece, and from the Elbe and the Adriatic coast to the Volga. By about the tenth century, Proto-Slavic had separated into three subgroups, the ancestors of the West Slavic, South Slavic, and East Slavic language groups.

The West Slavs lived in a region reaching beyond the Elbe and were bounded on the west by Germanic tribes. The language they spoke developed into modern Polish, Czech, Slovak, and Wendish. (The Wends settled between the Elbe and the Oder, in what is now Germany, and their descendants today are entirely surrounded by Germans.) The South Slavs, covering the area east of the Adriatic, south of the Danube, and west of the Black Sea, had the Magyars and Vlachs as their northern and eastern neighbors. Their language was the forerunner of Slovenian, Serbo-Croatian, Macedonian, and Bulgarian. The ancestors of today's Russians, Belorussians, and Ukrainians, the East Slavs lived in an area bounded by Lake Ladoga, the upper Volga and Don, and the Dnieper. To the southeast were the Khazars and Pechenegs, Asiatic steppe dwellers; to the north and east were Finno-Ugric peoples; and to the northwest were Balts.

FORMATION OF SLAVIC RELIGION. The term *Slavic religion* can be used to refer to the mythology and cultic life common to all Slavs from the sixth to the tenth century. The basic structure of Slavic mythology, composed of Old Euopean and Indo-European elements, stems from the proto-Slavic culture in the Slavic homeland. Strong affinities with the mythology and religious nomenclature of the early Slavs have been found among their close neighbors, the Balts, the Iranians, and the Thracians.

Three important factors must be borne in mind in regard to Slavic religion. First, literacy came to the Slavs in the aftermath of Christianization. As a consequence, there is no pagan literature as such. However, songs, fairy tales, and oral epics such as the Russian *byliny*, which survived among peasants, are representative of pagan religious traditions.

The worship of pagan gods did not disappear immediately with the arrival of Christianity. Descriptions of pagan temples, idols, and practices can be found in early church chronicles. Later, with the advance of Christianity, many pagan practices found new manifestations that were compatible with the new religion. This was especially true in the Byzantine sphere of influence, and, in fact, the best examples of pagan prototypes that merged with Christian figures are found in Russia.

The second important factor in the formation of the Slavic religion was the close contact of the Slavs with neighboring peoples, especially the Balts and Indo-Iranians. This contact is attested by some common Slavic words pertaining to religion that have clear affinities with Iranian.

The third and most essential factor is the heritage of mythological images. In the tradition of Celtic, Baltic, Greek, and other related mythologies of Europe, Slavic beliefs strongly preserved very ancient pre-Indo-European images typical of an agricultural, matrifocal, and matrilinear culture. (This oldest substratum is called Old European.) Slavic paganism as described by Christian missionaries, however, was clearly dominated by male gods of Indo-European origin. Their names and functions can be reconstructed by means of comparative Indo-European mythology and linguistics. These gods belonged to a pastoral, patriarchal, and warlike people of the Eurasian steppes who superimposed their social system and religion upon the Old European culture about 3000 BCE.

The stratigraphy of Slavic religion and mythology thus contains the following levels: (1) Old European, rooted in a local Neolithic culture; (2) Indo-European, derived from the pastoral; patriarchal culture of the Eurasian steppes; and (3) Christian, in which pagan prototypes fused with Christian figures, producing a "double faith." (Christianity was introduced into Moravia in 863, Bulgaria in 885, Poland in 966, and Russia in 988.)

SOURCES. Written sources begin with the sixth-century Byzantine historian Procopius, who wrote that the Slavic Sclavenian and Antes tribes worshiped a thunder god as "lord of the whole world." They sacrificed bulls and other animals to him, and they made other offerings at times of death, illness, or war to ensure salvation. They also venerated and made sacrifices to rivers, nymphs, and "other demons." Divination and sacrifice were carried out together.

Scarcely any other reliable written information is available for the sixth through the tenth century. In the East Slavic area, the only Slavic pantheon on record is that set up by Vladimir I in 980. Eight years later he cast down the pagan deities and forcibly baptized the population of Kiev. The Russian *Primary Chronicle* (compiled c. 1111) says: "And Vladimir began to rule Kiev alone, and he set up idols on a hill outside the palace court—a wooden figure of Perun, and his head was of silver and his mouth was of gold; Khors and Dazhbog and Stribog and Simargl and Mokosh—and he and his people made sacrifice to the idols." Simultaneously, "Vladimir also placed Dobrynja, his uncle, in Novgorod, and after Dobrynja came to Novgorod, he set up an idol of Perun above the river Volkhov, and the people of Novgorod revered him as a god."

The descriptions that we have of Slavic idols and temples, it must be remembered, come from the writings of the very people who destroyed them. The most reliable sources on the religion of the West Slavs are provided by Otto, a twelfth-century bishop of Bamberg, whose war with the pagan gods of the Slavs in northern Germany was recorded by this three biographers, Ebbo, Herbord, and Monachus Prieflingensis, as well as by Thietmar, bishop of Merseburg, who wrote firsthand accounts of eleventh-century Wendish paganism (see Palm, 1937). Early sources on the pre-Christian religion in Poland, Bohemia, Moravia, Bulgaria, Serbia, Croatia, and Slovenia are either biased or very scant. Slavic religion and mythology cannot be reconstructed on the basis of written records alone. Of utmost importance are archaic motifs in folklore, linguisitic reconstructions, and archaeological monuments. In the past, very few scholars drew upon all these sources; in this respect, much research is yet to be done.

Temples and Idols. The most precise descriptions of temples and idols come from the eleventh through the thirteenth century in the area of the northwestern Slavs, present-day Germany. The best-documented site is Arkona, a citadel-temple of the god Sventovit, which was destroyed in 1168 by Christian Danes when they stormed the island of Rügen. According to Saxo Grammaticus (*Gesta Danoraum* 14), Arkona was a red-roofed log structure of consummate workmanship, encircled by a yard and protected by a splendidly carved wooden fence bearing various symbols painted in "heathen" style. The fence had a single entrance. In the inner chamber of the temple loomed the awe-inspiring statue of Sventovit, larger than life and with four heads that faced the cardinal directions. Carl Schuchhardt's excavation in 1921 proved the existence of the temple. Repeated excavations in 1969 and 1970 revealed an earlier layer of the sanctuary dating to the tenth century, and possibly to the ninth.

After conquering Arkona, the Danish armies took Garz (Karentia), also on the island of Rügen, which Saxo describes as a castle hill with swamps on all sides. Of its three temples, the largest had an inner room consisting of roof, posts, and purple hangings. In the middle of this room stood an oaken statue of Rugievit—whose name, according to Saxo, meant "god of Rügen [Rugia]"—having seven heads, with seven swords hanging from his girdle and an eighth sword held in his hand. Saxo says the other temples belonged to "Porevit" and "Potenut," respectively.

The earliest source, Thietmar (1014), describes a similar temple on the castle hill of Riedegost or Radigast (Rethra). It was made of timber, and the exterior was adorned with sculptures to which animal horns were attached. It contained several hand-sculpted idols dressed in helmets and armor and each dedicated to a god, the most important being that of Zuarasici (Svarozhich).

Carl Schuchhardt, who excavated Rethra in 1922, concluded that the temple, presumably built about 1000 CE, was destroyed by fire about 1068, but that its floor plan was square. Thietmar said that Riedegost was principal among all the local temples. People came to it with homage before going to war, and with offerings on their return. The priests determined reconciliation offerings by means of dice and horse oracles. it was apparently the sanctuary for the entire Lutici confederation, of which the Retharii were one tribe.

Bishop Otto of Bamberg went twice to Szczecin (Stettin), where there were two temples (according to Ebbo) or four (according to Herbord). The most important of these temples stood upon one of the three hills and was dedicated to Triglav, the three-headed "summus deus" (Ebbo, 3.1). It was richly sculptured inside and out, and its interiors were decorated with war booty. On his first trip there (about 1124), Otto cut off the idol's three heads and sent them to Pope Calixtus II. Another idol of Triglav was destroyed in Brandenburg, probably by Albrecht the Bear (Albert I), sometime between 1150 and 1157.

At Wolin, according to Monarchus Prieflingensis, Otto found a temple with a sacred spear that, as legend had it, had been placed there in memory of Julius Caesar. According to Ebbo, there was also an outdoor cultic center with idols, which became the site of the new Adalbert Church. The practice of building a church on the site of a pagan sanctuary was one of the most effective, and most commonly employed, methods of combating paganism all over the Slavic area. It attracted the people to whom the place itself was still holy, and it removed all traces of the worship previously performed there.

Otto's mission of 1128 destroyed the temple at Wolgast. According to Ebbo, when Otto's men entered the temple in search of idols, they found only a gigantic shield hanging on the wall. Fearing the crowd that had gathered outside, they carried the shield with them for protection, whereupon the crowd fell to the ground, thinking it was an appearance of the war god Gerovit (Iarovit). Herbord describes the shield as covered with gold leaf, and he equates Gerovit with Mars.

Helmold of Bosau, writing of the pagan revival among the Wends in 1134, mentions "Prove deus Aldenburgensis terrae." On his trip with the bishop Gerald to Oldenburg and to the interior between that city and Lubeck in 1156, he saw a grove where an oak tree was enclosed within a courtyard surrounded by a fence of stakes. It was dedicated to the god of that land, Proven, for whom no idol was present. The monk Herbertus describes a sacred grove where a large tar-covered idol stood leaning against a tree (presumably an oak). Most likely, the name *Proven* is a distortion or variant of *Perun,* the name of the Slavic thunder god.

According to the Russian *Primary Chronicle,* when Prince Igor made a peace treaty with Byzantium at Kiev in 945, he and his men went to a hill where there was a statue of Perun. There they laid down their arms and swore to keep the treaty. In his treaty with Byzantium in 971, Prince Sviatoslav made a similar oath, stating that those who would not respect the treaty would be cursed by Perun and Volos and that they would become as yellow as the gold of their ornaments and be destroyed by their own weapons.

A ruined temple, perhaps of Perun, was discovered in 1951 near Novgorod in a place called Peryn. The wooden structure itself was not preserved, but the floor plan, an octagonal rosette shape, was clearly evident. In the center was charcoal, indicating where the idol and a place for fire had probably been located. Nearby was a flat stone, apparently a part of an altar. In 1958, at Staraia Ladoga, a wooden effigy of a god with mustache and beard and wearing a conical helmet was found in a layer dated to the ninth or tenth century.

From all that is presently known of East Slavic temples, wooden idols stood on hills within temples for which there are no descriptions. On the analogy of the excavated temples of the Balts in the Smolensk area dating from the fifth to the seventh century, such hills were fortified and had wooden structures on the inner side of the ramparts. A round temple containing a wooden idol stood in the center or at the end of the hill fort.

A tradition going back millennia is evidenced by carved images of gods, produced throughout proto-Slavic periods and later times, that are similar to those of early history. A number of stone statues, some with three or four heads, others holding a drinking horn, wearing a conical cap, and decorated with incised horse figures or sun symbols, are known from excavations. Similar idols from Stavchany in the upper Dniester Valley date from the fourth century CE (see Gimbutas, *The Slavs,* 1971, fig. 61).

Idols were dedicated to various gods. In the West Slavic area, the richest temples belonged to the warrior god of "heavenly light" in his various aspects (Svarozhich, Iarovit, Sventovit), whereas the thunder god (Perun) was worshiped outdoors, in a grove where an oak tree stood. The East Slavs also erected temples for Perun.

It is clear that at the time when Christianity arrived, the official religion was dominated by warrior gods of Indo-European heritage. Following the destruction of their temples, these gods sank into the subculture so that only vestiges of their earlier glory survived.

GODS OF INDO-EUROPEAN HERITAGE. Three divine archetypes of the Indo-European religious tradition are clearly represented in the Slavic pantheon: the god of heavenly light, the god of death and the underworld, and the thunder god. The first two stand in opposition to each other, but the relationship of the three deities is triangular, not hierarchical.

The god of heavenly light, also known as the white god, and the god of death and the underworld, also known as the black god, form a fundamental polarity in the Slavic religious tradition. This opposition of mythological figures is reflected in the semiotic system of Slavic languages, based on the arrangement of oppositions such as day and night, light and dark, life and death, good and evil. The white and black gods are mentioned in Helmold's twelfth-century *Chronica Slavorum,* pertaining to the West Slavs: "They expect a fortunate lot from the good god and from the evil one an unfortunate [lot]; for this reason is the evil god called devil in their language, or 'black god.'" The *Gustinskii Chronicle* of 1070 reports that ancient sorcerers were convinced that "there be two gods: one heavenly and the other in hell." The white god is the deity of daylight while the black god is the god of night. Both have close analogies in the Vedic Mitra-Varuna and the Baltic Dievas-Velinas oppositions.

The Slavic thunder god, Perun, deity of justice and fecundity, stands close to the god of heavenly light; he was the chief adversary of the black god. Although described as the "lord of the whole world" by Procopius and listed first in Vladimir's pantheon, Perun was never addressed as "summus deus" ("highest god") as was the god of heavenly light (Sventovit).

The god of heavenly light. Many different names identify the god of heavenly light: the forms *Belobog, Belbog,* and *Belun* (all meaning "white god") are common in Slavic place-names and folklore. Close relatives in the Kievan pantheon are the sun gods Dazhbog, Khors (an obvious borrowing of the Iranian name for the personified sun, *Khursīd*), and possibly Stribog (whose name is perhaps related to the Iranian *srira,* "beautiful"). The personified sun appears throughout Slavic folklore: each morning he rides out from his golden palace in the east in a two-wheeled chariot drawn by horses. He begins the day as a youth and dies each night as an old man. He is attended by two lovely virgins (the morning and evening stars), seven judges (the planets), and seven messengers (the comets). As a "year god," this deity ages with each season. The polycephalic images, three- or four-faced gods, known as Triglav or as Chetyregod, represent different faces of the year god.

Among the West Slavs, Iarovit, Porovit, Sventovit, and Svarozhich, described in the eleventh and twelfth centuries, repesent various aspects of the year god: spring, summer, autumn, and winter. Several of these names had calendrical significance. *Iaro* was connected with *iaru,* meaning "young, ardent, bright," and *Porovit* may have been related to *pora,* "midsummner." Sventovit, whose name is from *svent-,* "light" and "holy," was worshiped in October, during the harvest. Svarozhich was worshiped in the temple at Radigast. Judging from his name (a diminutive of *Svarog,* signifying that he was a son of Svarog, the heavenly smith), Svarozhich probably represented the aspect of the newborn winter sun. However, Svarog (glossed as Hephaistos in thirteenth-century records) and Svarozhich could also be a single god, since the diminutive form of addressing deities is a characteristic Slavic phenomenon. (For instance, *bozhich,* "little god," is a form frequently used instead of *bog,* "god.") As in all other Indo-European religions, this deity was portrayed as a warrior, dressed in armor and a helmet, carrying a sword and shield, and accompanied always by a horse. Weapons and horses were manifestations of his powers.

In Christian times, the god of heavenly light fused with the Christian God and Saint John (Ivan). Up to the beginning of the twentieth century, the spring aspect of the god survived in Belorussia and Russia in the image of Iarilo, who was worshiped in the week following Whitsuntide. Folklore preserves the image of Iarilo riding upon a white horse: he wears a white cloak, is crowned with wildflowers, and carries a sheaf of wheat. Girls honored Iarilo by performing choral dances upon newly sown fields. In the eighteenth century, the Orthodox bishop of Voronezh is central Russia proscribed a pagan festival and "satanic" games centered on an idol called Iarilo. In Kostroma, until 1771, people buried an idol with exaggerated male attributes. The burial of a phallic idol typifies the year god's cycle. The death of the year god, symbolized by submerging his image in water or by burning a birch tree, was commemorated in Belorussia until the early twentieth century.

Reminiscent of the Indo-European archetype of the divine twins—the Dioscuri of Greek myth, the Asvins of the Vedas, the Dievo Suneliai of Lithuanian folk songs—are the saints Boris and Gleb, Cosmas and Damian, and Flor and Lavr. The emblem of Boris and Gleb, the youthful martyrs, was a young shoot. They sometimes appear as *bogatyri* ("knights") who have vanquished a dragon and harnessed him to a plow, and on Serbian icons they are depicted as doctors holding the tools of their trade. In Russia, Flor and Lavr were the protectors of horses. Their holiday was August 18, at which time animals were sacrificed to them and the flesh cooked for a feast in their honor.

The cult of the dawn was common among all Slavs. The Slavic deity Zoria, or Zaria, is the heavenly bride, the goddess of beauty, the dawn. At daybreak she is greeted, like Usas of India, as "the brightest maiden, pure, sublime, and honorable."

Certain Slavic myths give an anthropomorphic interpretation to the relationship between the sun and the moon. The Russian word for "moon," *mesiats,* is masculine, but many legends portray the moon as a beautiful young woman whom the sun marries at the beginning of summer, abandons in winter, and returns to in spring. In other myths, the moon is the husband and the sun is his wife, as in Baltic mythology. In folk beliefs, Mesiats is addressed as *kniaz'* ("prince") and is believed to have powers over the growth of plants. In Polish, the word for "moon," *księżyc,* is the diminutive form of the word meaning "prince" or "lord."

The god of death and the underworld. The names *Veles* and *Volos* apparently represent two aspects of the same god: (1) a sorcerer god of death, related to music and poetry, and (2) a god of cattle, wealth, and commerce. The etymology suggests ancient functions: *vel-* is connected with "death," "the dead," and "giant" on one hand and with "sight, foresight, insight" on the other. *Volos* has connections with "hair, fur" and with "disease, evil spirit." The original name of the god must have been *Veles,* not *Volos.*

Veles was degraded to a devil at the beginning of Christian times. All that remains of this god are such expressions as *k Velesu za more* ("to Veles in the otherworld") and the formula "*Velesov vnuk*" ("grandson of Veles"), apostrophizing the musician and prophetic poet Boian of the Old Russian epic *Slovo o polku Igoreve.* Place-names incorporating *Veles* imply sites where this god was worshiped, such as Titov Veles in Macedonia.

Volos was merged with the image of Saint Blasius (Vlasii) and also partly with that of Saint Nicholas (Nikola), the patrons of flocks and crops. He was honored as such up to the twentieth century on his holiday, 11 February. Such forms as *Volosovo* and *Volosovskii* were frequently used as names for monasteries and churches in Russia. According to legend, they were founded on the spots where the idols of Volos stood in pre-Christian times.

Idols and places of Volos worship are mentioned as late as the eighteenth century. Of utmost importance is the description of the sacrifice of the priest Volkhv in *Skazanii o postroenii grada Yaroslavlia* (Legends about the Founding of Yaroslavl), published in 1876 and based on a manuscript of 1781. Having burned the sacrificial victim and prophesied in the name of Volos, the priest was himself sacrificed to the god. This is a parallel to the self-sacrifice of the Germanic god Óðinn (Odin).

The thunder god. Overseer of justice and order, purifier and fructifier, and adversary of the devil, Perun is feared to this day in some Slavic areas. His presence and actions are perceived in lightning and thunder. His animals (the bull and the he-goat), his birds (the dove and the cuckoo), and his weapons (the ax and the arrow) are pervasive symbolic motifs in Slavic folk beliefs and songs.

Parallels in other Indo-European mythologies, such as the Baltic Pērkons and Perkūnas and the Germanic Þórr (Thor), attest to the antiquity of this god. The root *per-/perk-* ("to strike, to splinter," "oak, oak forest," "mountaintop") is common to Indo-European languages. The oak was Perun's sacred tree. Oak forests and mountaintops—where a god of storms might easily alight—are attested by literary sources as places of veneration. The name *Peryn,* known from Russia and the Balkans, must have preceded the name *Perun.* The original name of the god is likely to have been **Perkyn,* which conforms to the Baltic *Perkūnas* and to Indo-European words for "oak" (Latin *quercus,* from **perkus*) and "oak forest" (Slavic **pergynja,* Celtic *hercynia*); hence the origin of the designation "oak god" (Brückner, 1980, p. 106).

With the onset of Christianity, Perun gradually merged with Saint Elijah (Il'ia), who is portrayed in Russian icons crossing the heavens in a chariot. Bull sacrifice and a communal feast on Saint Il'ia's Day, July 20, were recorded in northern Russia in 1907. Saint Il'ia's Day was most reverently celebrated into the mid-twentieth century in the Rhodope Mountains of Bulgaria. The festival, during which a bull was sacrificed and prepared for the communal feast, took place on a hill or summit.

Household guardians. Slavic names for household guardians—Russian *ded*, *dedushka* (dim.), and *domovoi*; Ukrainian *did*, *didko*, and *domovyk*; Czech *dedek*; and Bulgarian *stopan*—have the meaning "grandfather" or "house lord," suggesting their origins in ancestor worship within a patrilineal culture. The guardian is commonly represented as an old man wearing a fur coat, or as an animal (a dog, bear, or snake). He was believed to live behind or beneath the oven. He cared for animal herds and protected the entire home and its occupants from misfortune. If not honored, Domovoi might leave the house, his departure bringing on illness or the death of householders or cattle. There is a related belief among the Slavs that well-being cannot establish itself in a newly built house until after the death of the head of the family, who then becomes its guardian. If the family moves into a new home, it takes its guardian with it.

The Russian forest spirit, Leshii or Lesovik (from *les*, "forest"), also appears as an old man or an animal. His principal function is to guard forests and animals.

Ancestor worship, a prominent practice among all pre-Christian Slavs, is evidenced in gifts presented to the dead. A strong belief in life after death is indicated by prehistoric and even modern burial rites. Food offerings are made in cemeteries to this day. Everything deemed necessary for the afterlife—weapons, tools, clothing, wives, slaves, horses, hunting dogs, food—was buried in the grave or was burned if the deceased was cremated. The richer one was in life, the more pompous the burial. Slavic royal tombs of prehistory and early history are as elaborate as those of other Indo-European groups: Phrygian, Thracian, Baltic, or Germanic.

The Arab traveler Ibn Faḍlān stated (922) that when a Slavic nobleman died, his body was laid provisionally in a grave for ten days while his property was divided. The deceased, who was dressed in rich garments and equipped with weapons, food, and drink, was seated in a boat. His wife (who chose death voluntarily in order to enter the afterworld with her husband) was killed by stabbing and seated next to him. Then all was consumed by fire. A funeral banquet (*trizna*) continued for days and nights.

Thereafter, the deceased was commemorated and offered food on the third, seventh, twentieth, and fortieth days after death. Similar observances took place six and twelve months after death. In addition to these family observances, general festivals commemorating the dead occurred three or four times a year. These feasts, called "holy *dziady*," were offered in the home and in cemeteries. The holy *dziady*—the word literally means "ancestors"—show that the Slavs looked upon their forefathers as guardians.

Mythic Images Rooted in Old European Religion.

The primary figures of the oldest stratum of Slavic culture are predominantly female: Fates, Death, Baba Yaga, Moist Mother Earth, and a host of nymphs and goblins (water, mountain, and forest spirits) largely preserved in folklore and attested by written records. In all these feminine figures may be discerned features of the goddesses of Old Europe: the life-giving and life-taking goddess, the goddess of death and regeneration, and the pregnant earth goddess.

Life-giving and life-taking goddesses and their associates. Mokosh is the only female deity mentioned in the Kievan pantheon of 980. In folk beliefs, Mokysha, or Mokusha, has a large head and long arms; at night she spins flax and shears sheep. Her name is related to spinning and plaiting and to moisture. The life-giving and life-taking goddess, or Fate, was the spinner of the thread of life and the dispenser of the water of life. Mokosh was later transformed into the East Slavic goddess Paraskeva-Piatnitsa, who was associated with spinning, water, fertility, health, and marriage.

Up to the twentieth century, it was believed that fate took the form of birth fairies who appeared at the bedside of a newborn baby on the third or the seventh day after birth. In anticipation of the fairies, the baby was washed and dressed in new clothes while a special dinner was prepared. Bread, salt, and wine were put out for the fairies. Three Fates of different ages were believed to appear. They determined the infant's destiny and invisibly inscribed it upon his or her forehead. If the parents feared the Fates, they hid the infant outside the home, a practice common among the South Slavs.

Fate was given various names by the Slavs. To Russians she was Rozhenitsa or Rozhdenitsa ("birth giver"); to Czechs she was Sudička; to Serbs and Croats she was Sudjenica or, earlier, Sudbina (cf. Russian *sud'ba*, "fate"); and to Bulgarians she was Narechnitsa (from *narok*, "destiny"). Both Rozhenitsa and the male Rod, to whom offerings were made, are mentioned in a thirteenth-century Russian text, *Slovo Isaia proroka*.

The Russian *dolia* and the Serbian *sreča* represent the fate of a person's material life. There were good and bad *dolia*s and *sreča*s. The benevolent spirit protected her favorites and served them faithfully from birth to death. The malevolent spirit, *nedolia* or *nesreča*, usually personified as a poor and ugly woman, capable of transforming herself into various shapes, bestowed bad luck. The person who attracted an evil *dolia* would never succeed, and all efforts to shake bad fortune would be in vain.

Fate could also appear as two sisters, Life and Death. Her deathly aspect was known as Mora, Marà, or Smert' ("death"). She was perceived as a tall white woman who could change her shape. When chased by dogs, she turned into a stick, a block, a bat, or a basket. The plague was personified as a slim black woman with long breasts who sometimes had the legs of a cow or horse and the eyes of a snake.

To Slovenes, Croats, and Serbs she was known as Kuga; to Bulgarians and Russians she was Chuma.

Associates of the life-giving and life-taking goddesses were female spirits filled with passionate sensuality, who mingled with humans and dwelt in forests or in mountain caves. They helped with household chores, spun hemp, and reaped grain and tied it into sheaves. They worked rapidly and produced crops that never diminished. The Bohemians called them *divoženky*, the Poles *dziwożony*, the Slovaks *divja davojke*, and the Bulgarians *divi-te zheny* ("wild women"). Tall and naked, they had long breasts and long hair, which they flung over their shoulders. They were distinguished by short feet or chicken legs. They yearned for motherhood, and they often took care of neglected babies and punished bad mothers. Sometimes they substituted their own ugly offspring for handsome human children. In response to an injury or malicious joke, they could kill by touch or tickle. Being half human, they could marry and become model wives and housekeepers, but if their true identity became known, they disappeared instantly.

Another related spirit, Paludnitsa ("midday spirit"), had the appearance of an airy white lady or of an old woman who wandered at noon in the fields during harvesttime. She also floated upon violent gusts of wind. Whomever she touched died a sudden death. Her most common victims were young women who either already had children or were in childbed.

Baba Yaga and Ved'ma. The Old European goddess of death and regeneration is reflected in the Slavic deity Baba Yaga, who has been preserved in folk tales as a witch. She was said to live in darkness and to devour humans, but she was also believed to have a gift for prophecy. She was usually old and ugly, with bony legs, a long nose, and disheveled hair, but she might also appear as a young woman, or as two sisters. Baba Yaga was represented as a bird or a snake, and she could turn herself into an animal or even into an inanimate object. The first half of her compound name, *baba*, suggests "grandmother" and "pelican"; the second, *yaga*, from Proto-Slavic *(*y*)*ęga*, means "disease" or "fright." The word *baba* can also mean "block," or "woodpile," which connotes destruction, death, and decay.

In East Slavic tradition, Baba Yaga has a male counterpart: Koshchei Bessmertnyi, "Koshchei the Immortal." His name, from *kost'* ("bone"), suggests the notion of the dying and rising god, that is, a deity who cyclically dies and is reborn. In folk tales, Baba Yaga is either the mother or the aunt of Koshchei. Another male equivalent of Baba Yaga in her role of the "mother of the winds" is Morozko ("frost").

Ved'ma ("witch") is a demonized goddess. She can be seen flying beneath the clouds and over the mountains and valleys on a broom or a rake. She departs from the house through the chimney as a bird or a fiery snake. She can produce rain or cause a storm simply by touching an object with her broom. She possesses a magical ointment, the source of water, which she sprinkles on herself before flying. Ved'ma can be old and ugly or very beautiful. She can make herself invisible, turn into a ball of yarn, and move rapidly. She knows the magical properties of plants and is the keeper of the water of life and death.

Moist Mother Earth and Corn Mother. The sacred deity known as Moist Mother Earth (Mati Syra Zemlia) was perceived as pure, powerful, and pregnant. Up to the twentieth century peasants believed that in springtime it was a grave sin to strike the earth with anything before March 25, because during that time the earth was pregnant. Plowing and digging were forbidden on the holidays of this deity. For centuries, peasants settle disputes over property by calling upon Mother Earth to witness the justice of their claims. Marriages were confirmed by the participants' swallowing lumps of earth (a tradition recorded in nineteenth-century northern Russia). Oaths were taken in a similar manner (attested as late as 1870 in the Orel district of central Russia) or by putting earth on one's head.

The corn (i.e., grain) spirit was personified as the Corn Mother or as the Old Rye (Barley, Wheat, or Oat) Woman. She made crops grow. At harvest, it was believed that she was present in the last stalks of grain left standing in the field. In Pomerania, the person who cut the last stalks of grain fashioned them into a doll, which was called Corn Mother or Old Woman and was brought home on the last wagon. In some areas, the Corn Mother, in the form of a doll or a wreath, was symbolically drenched with water (drowned) and was kept until the following spring, when some of its grain was mixed with the new seed grain at planting time. The agricultural cycle of death (harvest) and rebirth (planting) was thus ensured, life-taking and life-giving in turn.

Nymphs. Two types of nymph were known to the Slavs: *vilas* and *rusalkas*. Both are usually depicted as beautiful young women, although *rusalkas* are also described as children or as old women.

Vilas. Many Slavs believed that *vilas* originated like blossoms with the morning dew or that they were born when the sun shone through the rain. Others said that *vilas* were born from meadow grasses whose roots resembled garlic bulbs; still others believed that they were born of the mountains.

The *vila* is depicted as a very beautiful young girl who wears a thin white dress and whose long, loose, red or gold tresses fall over her back and breasts. She is distinguished from a human maiden by her feet, which resemble the hooves of a donkey or a goat. She can turn into a horse, a swan, or a falcon. Because she is so beautiful, she cannot tolerate the presence of anyone more beautiful than she or anyone who laughs at the sight of her feet. Possessed of supernatural strength, she can, with a single glance, kill anyone who displeases her.

There are three kinds of *vila*, associated with mountains, with water, and with clouds. The mountain *vila* helps care for children and orphans, the water *vila* can poison springs, and the cloud *vila*, who has wings, can fly. Well known throughout the South Slavic area is the story of the Swan Maiden: she was a cloud *vila* forced to become the wife of a mortal when he stole her wings; later she finds her wings and flies off to the clouds. The water *vila* lives near water, either by mountain lakes and springs or on the seacoast, sometimes in caves or pits in the earth. All the *vilas* can understand the languages of fish and birds. They often gather near water where they dance in a *kolo* ("circle"). If a human interrupts their *kolo*, they may blind him or make him dance until he drops dead. Sometimes, the *vilas* dance their *kolo* in the clouds.

In Slavic folklore *vilas* are associated with diseases and injuries. Nevertheless, they can also heal wounds with herbs and can cure grave afflictions, especially blindness and barrenness.

Rusalkas. Descriptions of *rusalkas* vary from region to region. They are sometimes said to live in the forest, but in most accounts they are reported to live at the bottom of lakes and rivers, in the deepest water. The *rusalka* is seen as the mistress of water, the female counterpart of the male spirit of water, the *vodianoi*. In early Russian religion, water itself was personified and venerated, often in the form of a female spirit.

The *rusalka* is depicted as a beautiful young woman with a white body and long, loose, green or gold hair that she combs while sitting on a riverbank. Always naked, she loves to swing on branches and to play, sing, and dance. She entices men off forest paths or lures them into her dance so as to tickle them to death and carry them into the water. In some accounts, the *rusalka* is said to have a tail like a fish; in other accounts, she is a seven-year-old girl. In northern Russia, the *rusalka* was believed to be an ugly, hairy old woman with long, sagging breasts.

Many narratives attest to the human origin of *rusalkas*. They were believed to be the spirits of drowned or strangled women, young female suicides, or the souls of unbaptized dead children (sometimes drowned by their mothers); in other words, they originated from unclean deaths.

Goblins. In the West and South Slavic areas, goblins were perceived as little men (dwarfs) who, if they were fed and cared for, brought good harvests and money. The Bohemian *šetek* or *šotek* stayed in sheep sheds or hid in pea patches or wild pear trees. The Slovak *škratak*, Polish *skrzat* or *skrzatek*, and Slovene *škrat* (cf. German *Schrat*) appeared as a small bird emitting sparks. The Polish *latawiec* ("flying goblin") took the shape of a bird or a snake. A close parallel is the Lithuanian *aitvaras*, who usually appeared as a bird (rooster) or a fiery snake and who brought forth milk products and grain. It was generally thought that goblins could be hatched from an egg carried for a certain length of time in one's armpit.

CONCLUSION. Except in the northwestern Slavic area (present-day Germany), Slavic religion can today be studied only at the folkloristic level. In the northwestern Slavic area, eleventh- and twelfth-century records describe temples housing warrior idols of Indo-European heritage and religious ceremonies presided over by a priestly order. Enough evidence has been preserved to give a fairly clear picture of Slavic religion in that area.

In Christian times, peasants amalgamated Old European and Indo-European goddesses and gods with Christian figures and saints into a typically Slavic folk religion. They preserved those heathen images that were best suited to their agrarian way of life. Strongly preserved are Mother Earth and Corn Mother; Iarilo, the stimulator of crops; Perun, a stimulator of slumbering vegetation and purifier of evil powers; and personifications of the moon and the dawn. Of these, Mother Earth was revered most of all; even in the field of law her powers were great. The thunder god, Perun, remains influential to this very day, appearing in the battle with cosmic chaos in the shape of a serpent or dragon hiding in whirlwinds.

SEE ALSO Baltic Religion; Germanic Religion; Indo-European Religions.

BIBLIOGRAPHY

Afanas'ev, A. N., ed. *Poeticheskie vozzreniia slavian na prirodu* (1865–1869). 3 vols. Reprint, The Hague, 1969–1970.

Brückner, Alexander. *Mitologia slowianska i polska* (1918). Reprint, Warsaw, 1980.

Dordević, T. "Veštica i vila u našem narodnom verovanju i predanju." *Srpski etnografski zbornik* 66 (1953).

Gasparini, Evel. *Il matriarcato slavo: Antropologia culturale dei protoslavi.* Florence, 1973.

Gimbutas, Marija. "Ancient Slavic Religion: A Synopsis." In *To Honor Roman Jakobson: Essays on the Occasion of His Seventieth Birthday*, vol. 1, pp. 738–759. The Hague, 1967.

Ivanov, Viacheslav V., and Vladimir N. Toporov. *Slavianskie iazykovye modeliruiushchie semioticheskie sistemy: Drevnii period.* Moscow, 1965.

Jakobson, Roman. "Slavic Mythology." In *Funk and Wagnalls Standard Dictionary of Folklore, Mythology, and Legend* (1949–1950), edited by Maria Leach, vol. 2, pp. 1025–1028. Reprint, 2 vols. in 1, New York, 1972.

Krauss, F. S. *Volksglaube und religiöser Brauch der Südslaven.* Münster, 1890.

Kulišić, Špiro. *Srpski mitološki rečnik.* Belgrade, 1970.

Machek, Václav. "Essai comparatif sur la mythologie slave." *Revue des études slaves* 23 (1947): 48ff.

Mansikka, Viljo Johannes. *Die Religion der Ostslaven.* Helsinki, 1922.

Meyer, Karl Heinrich. *Fontes historiae religionis Slavicae.* Berlin, 1931.

Moszyński, Kazimierz. *Kultura ludowa slowian*, vol. 2, *Kultura duchowa.* Cracow, 1939.

Niederle, Lubor. *Manuel de l'antiquité slave*, vol. 2, *La civilisation.* Paris, 1926. See chapter 6, pages 126–168.

Palm, Thede. *Wendische Kultstatten: Quellenkritische Untersuchungen zu den letzten Jahrhunderten slavischen Heidentums.* Lund, 1937.

Perkowski, Jan L., ed. *Vampires of the Slavs.* Cambridge, Mass., 1976.

Pettazzoni, Raffaele. "Osservazioni sul paganesimo degli Slavi Occidentali." *Studi e materiali di storia delle religioni* 19–20 (1943–1946): 157–169.

Propp, Vladimir Iakovlevich. *Istoricheskie korni volshebnoi skazki.* Leningrad, 1946.

Propp, Vladimir Iakovlevich. "The Historical Roots of Some Russian Religious Festivals." In *Introduction to Soviet Ethnography,* edited by Stephen P. Dunn and Ethel Dunn, vol. 2, pp. 367–410. Berkeley, 1974.

Reiter, Norbert. "Mythologie der alten Slaven." In *Wörterbuch der Mythologie,* edited by Hans W. Haussig, vol. 2, pp. 165–208. Stuttgart, 1973.

Rybakov. B. A. "Drevnie elementy v russkom narodnom tvorchestve (Zhenskoe bozhestvo i vsadniki)." *Sovetskaia etnografiia* 1 (1948): 90–106.

Shapiro, Michael. "Baba-Jaga: A Search for Mythopoeic Origins and Affinities." *International Journal of Slavic Linguistics and Poetics* 27 (1983): 109–135.

Tokarev, Sergei A. *Religioznye verovaniia vostochnoslavianskikh narodov XIX-nachala XX veka.* Moscow, 1957.

Yankovitch, Nénad. "Le soleil dans l'antiquité serbe." *Antiquités nationales et internationales* (Paris) 4, no. 14–16 (April–December 1963): 70–80.

Zelenin, Dimitri K. *Ocherki slavianskoi mifologii.* Saint Petersburg, 1916.

Znayenko, Myroslava T. *The Gods of the Ancient Slavs: Tatishchev and the Beginnings of Slavic Mythology.* Columbus, Ohio, 1980.

New Sources

Afanasyev, A. N. *Poeticheskiye vozzrenija slavyan na prirodu* [Poetical views of Slavs on Nature], vol.1–3, Moscow, 1995.

Belyakova, G. S. *Slavyanskaja mifologija* [Slavic mythology]. Moscow, 1995.

Haney, Jack V. *Russian Legends.* Armonk, N.Y., 2003.

Ivanits, Linda. *Russian Folk Belief.* Armonk, N.Y., 1992.

Johnson, Kenneth. *Slavic Sorcery: Shamanic Journey of Initiation.* St. Paul, Minn., 1998.

Kapica, F. S. *Slavyanskije tradicionnije verovanija, prazdniki i rituali* [Slavic traditional beliefs, festivities and rituals]. Moscow, 2001.

Kulikowski, Mark. *A Bibliography of Slavic Mythology.* Columbus, Ohio, 1989.

Lofstedt, Torsten M. *Russian Legends about Forest Spirits in the Context of Northern European Mythology.* Berkeley, 1993.

Perkowski, Jan L. *The Darkling: A Treatise on Slavic Vampirism.* Columbus, Ohio, 1989.

Petruhin, A.Y., T. A. Arapkina, L. N. Vinogradova, and S. M. Tolstaya, eds. *Slavyanskaja mifologija* [Slavic mythology]. Moscow, 1995.

Ryan, W. F. *The Bathhouse at Midnight: A Historical Survey of Magic and Divination in Russia.* University Park, Pa. 1999.

Shaparova, N. S. *Kratkaya enciklopedija slavyanskoj mifologii* [A short dictionary of Slavic mythology]. Moscow, 2001.

Siminov, Pyotr. *Essential Russian Mythology: Stories that Change the World.* London, 1997.

Tokarev, S. A., ed. "Mifi narodov mira [World myths]." *Bolshaya Rossijskaya Enciklopedija,* vol.1–2. Moscow, 1998.

Tolstoy, N. I., ed. *Slavyanskije drevnosti* [Slavic antiquity]. vol.1. Moscow, 1995.

Warren, Elizabeth. *Russian Myths.* Austin, 2002.

Yovino-Young, Marjorie. *Pagan Ritual and Myth in Russian Magic Tales: A Study in Patterns.* Lewiston, N.Y., 1993.

MARIJA GIMBUTAS (1987)
Revised Bibliography

SLEEP, as a periodic, recurrent state of inactivity and altered consciousness, marks a boundary line in human experience. However sleep is culturally evaluated and understood, it is a state quite different from ordinary, waking life. As such, it has been a universal object of religious interest and imagination. The various traditions, symbolisms and rituals of sleep are closely related to religious understanding of night and the role of dreams, to assessments of death, and to themes associated with its apparent opposites: dawn and awakening.

MYTHOLOGIES OF SLEEP. Figures and notions associated with sleep appear in numerous mythologies and folk traditions.

Personifications of sleep. While personified figures of sleep appear in mythology, poetry, and artistic representations, they are rarely themselves the focus of cultic activity. The personifications often reveal the ambiguous assessment of sleep: it is peaceful and restorative, and it is like death. For example, while the early Iranian *Vispe Ratavo* (7.4) can enjoin the worship of sleep, sleep is more usually understood within that tradition to be a negative force controlled by the demon Bushyasta; in India, the ambivalent deities Rudra (*Kaivalya Upaniṣad* 6–9) and Śiva (*Uṇādi Sūtra* 1.153) are identified as lords of sleep.

The most developed personification of sleep occurs within the Greco-Roman tradition with the archaic figure of Hypnos (Lat., Somnus). Schematically, the poet Hesiod (eighth century BCE) located Hypnos and his brother, Death (Thanatos), along with the race of Dreams, as the asexually produced children of Night. Sleep is the friend of man; Death, his pitiless adversary (*Theogony* 211–213, 756–766). In other poetic and artistic materials, the fraternal relations of Sleep and Death are further developed; they are twin brothers (*Iliad* 14.231). Hypnos or Somnus is personified as a small winged bird, an infant, or a young warrior. In some traditions, Sleep carries a horn or a poppy-stalk from which he drips a liquid that causes slumber. The only recorded instance of a regular cult of sacrifice to Hypnos is at Triozen (Pausanius, 2.31.3); rather it is Hermes, in his role as conductor of dreams, who was the object of nightly libations and petitions for a good sleep.

Sleeping gods. At its most complex level, the notion of sleeping gods is tied to cosmic cyclical patterns of the periodic dissolution and recreation of the world. Thus Viṣṇu falls asleep on the back of the cosmic serpent (Śeṣa or Ananta) at the end of each world-age. In late Puranic texts, Nidrā, the personified goddess of sleep, is depicted as entering Viṣṇu's body. Visnu sleeps until Brahmā commands Nidrā to depart so that Viṣṇu might awake and recreate the cosmos (*Mārkaṇḍeya Puraṇā* 81.53–70). Viṣṇu also is represented as undergoing an annual period of sleep. During the monsoon months, beginning in June and July, Viṣṇu—and therefore the world—sleeps (*Padma Purāṇā* 63, 125). In late traditions, Indra is thought to perform Viṣṇu's functions during this period (*Harivaṃsá* 50.26).

The notion of a deity undergoing periodic durations of sleep is not uncommon and may be expressed in ritual as well as myth. Thus there was an annual Syrian ritual of the "awakening" of Melqart-Herakles (Josephus Flavius, *Jewish Antiquities* 8.146), while, from earliest times through the Roman period, the daily Egyptian temple service began with a hymn awakening the sun (Pyramid Text 573).

However, gods are most commonly celebrated for being sleepless and hence all-seeing. YHVH (Psalm 121:3–4), the Adityas (*Ṛgveda* 2.27.9), Mitra (*Ṛgveda* 3.59.1), Ahura Mazdā (*Vidēvdāt* 19.20), Sraosha (*Yasht* 11.10–12), and others are praised for never sleeping. A special motif is that of a god with multiple eyes, some of which are always open, while others are asleep, thereby guaranteeing their omniscience (for example, Argos and El-Kronos in the account of Philo of Byblus). The opposite motif, that of the sleeping and therefore powerless deity, is represented by Elijah's taunts to the priests of Baal (*1 Kgs.* 18.27–28) and east European Christian dualistic creation myths that have the Devil working while God sleeps during the sabbath that followed creation.

Sleep in heroic tales and folklore. One of the more persistent folkloristic themes is that of a lengthy sleep, a Rip Van Winkle motif in which sleep serves as a sort of suspended animation for a period of years. While occasionally the emphasis is on perpetual sleep, conferred as either a punishment or a boon (both are claimed in different accounts of the Greek hero Endymion), there is, more frequently, a terminus. Best known is the widely distributed eschatological tale of the Sleeping Emperor, asleep within a cave or mountain. Frederick Barbarossa is held to be asleep within the Kyffhäuser, seated at a marble table surrounded by his knights, awaiting his awakening, when he will lead Germany in a glorious battle and usher in a golden age. The same sort of claim is made for Charlemagne asleep in a hill near Paderborn, Wittekind in Westphalia, Siegfried in Geroldseck, Henry I in Goslar, Thomas of Erceldoune in the Eildon Hills, and others. These beliefs may at times fuel apocalyptic movements, as in the case of the flagellants of Thuringia, led by Konrad Schmid in the fourteenth century. The same motif occurs in the hagiography of wise men: Epimenides sleeping fifty-seven years in the Dictaean cave near Knossus, Shimʿon bar Yoḥ'ai in Palestine for twelve, Zalmoxis in Thrace for three.

The widespread legend of the Seven Sleepers of Ephesus, first recorded in a Western language by Gregory of Tours in the sixth century, has also found its way into the Qur'ān (18.8–25); the legend narrates how the seven Christian anti-idolators slept in a cave for 367 years before being awakened during the reign of Theodosius II. Subsequently, they returned to sleep, not to be awakened again until the general resurrection. Related, but different from this motif of cave hibernation, are the Jewish legends of two figures who sleep during a period of tribulation: Abimelech the Ethiopian, who slept for sixty-six years from the destruction of the Temple by the Babylonians; Ḥoni ha-Meʿaggel ("the circle maker"), who slept for seventy years, in one account from the destruction of the Temple, in another, from the period of the conflict between Aristobulus II and Hyrcanus II.

Equally persistent, although not well organized into a narrative scheme, is the motif of magical sleep most familiar from tales such as that of Sleeping Beauty, wherein a potion, a spell, or an object causes unnatural sleep that either cannot be undone or must be undone by countermagic or by an act of accidental or innocent intervention.

In heroic quest-sagas, the hero is often put to a test, one of which is that sleep is forbidden until the quest is accomplished. The best known instance is a negative example: Gilgamesh's failure to stay awake. In such sagas, the hero frequently confronts a sleepless adversary, such as the dragon in the *Argonautica* who guards the Golden Fleece until it is overcome by Jason through the intercession of Medea and her magic song invoking "Sleep, highest of gods" (Apollonius Rhodius, 4.146).

Soul loss and transformation. A tradition of exceedingly wide distribution is that the soul becomes separated from the body during sleep and that death will result if the individual is awakened or the body moved before it returns. So ubiquitous is this belief that E. B. Tylor thought it one of the basic human experiences that gave rise to religion and James G. Frazer devoted the third volume of *The Golden Bough* to its ramifications.

Closely related to the theme of the separable soul is the notion that sleep is a time of shape-changing (often expressed in folklore in accounts of were-animals). These traditions are most fully elaborated in shamanism. The shaman is, among other things, an expert in the retrieval of lost souls by being able to achieve a sleeplike trance and pursuing them. In South America, one of the tests for shamanic abilities is that the candidate frequently experiences lengthy periods of deep sleep. Throughout shamanism, the return of the shaman from an ecstatic journey is most commonly described as an "awakening." During his journey, the shaman will frequently change shape. Snorri Sturlson's description of the shamanic attributes of the Norse god Óðinn (Odin) is representative of this related set of elements: while his body lay "as if sleeping or dead," he assumed the form of a bird, animal, fish, or snake and traveled to far lands "on his own or other men's errands" (*Ynglingasaga* 7).

RITUALS OF SLEEP. Religious practices related to sleep or the interruption of sleep are characteristic of many traditions.

Social location. Who sleeps with whom is a central question of religious etiquette. This is not only a matter of sanctioned sexuality. Within many societies, a mark of male adulthood is residential segregation in the men's house, a location of secret rituals forbidden to women. Elements of rituals of initiatory separation focus on this shift in social location. In other societies, the blueprint of a domestic house represents a map of such social and sexual relations. For example, in central Thailand, only certain members of the family sleep in the bedroom; other close relations may enter the room but may not sleep there; guests are restricted to an entrance room, separated from the sleeping room by a clearly demarcated threshold.

Incubation. Going to a particular sacred place to sleep in order to gain a religious end is common. Most frequently such incubation is for the purpose of gaining a revelation or a cure. The former is to be related to similar phenomena such as the American Indian dream quest; the latter, to the general ideology of shrines. Perhaps the most extensive record of incubation is that by Aelius Aristides in the second century who has left, in his *Sacred Teachings,* a report of his experiences in a variety of Asklepian shrines over a twenty-seven year period.

Sleep interruption or deprivation. The regular interruption of sleep is a common practice in religious asceticism, especially in monastic communities. Thus the Christian "canonical hours" in which monks would be aroused at either midnight or 2:00 AM for prayer. Similar interruptions figure in other spiritual regimens such as the Daoist practice of the "expulsion of the breath" that must be undertaken at least five times during the period of midnight to noon.

Sleeplessness is an often recurring feature of religious asceticism and vision quests. In the lists of five sins that must be "cut off" by a yogin, sleep appears (*Mahābhārata* 12.241.3). Like the sleeplessness of the hero, sleep deprivation is the mark of a spiritual athlete. The hagiographies of holy persons frequently celebrate either their ability to sleep far less than ordinary people or to do without sleep entirely. For example, the pre-Christian Syrian Stylites were said to resist sleep for seven days while perched on columns. According to legend, if they fell asleep, a scorpion would sting them awake (Lucian, *Syrian Goddess* 29). In the traditions of the Christian Desert Fathers, preserved in texts such as Palladius's *Lausiac History,* monks such as Doretheus, Macarius of Alexandria and Pachomius are praised for never sleeping. All-night vigils, spending days and nights immersed in cold water, and sleeping only in a sitting position were frequent ritual means for achieving sleep deprivation. Sleeplessness is also a feature of initiatory ordeals. In Australia, novices are prevented from sleeping for periods of up to three days. The goal in these varied practices appears to be twofold: to transcend the normal bodily processes and to achieve heightened consciousness.

METAPHORS OF SLEEP IN RELIGIOUS SPEECH. References to sleep in myth and religious literature reflect its metaphorical significance as the state of death, ignorance, or enlightenment.

Sleep as death. In many languages, sleep is a metaphor for death. While this may serve as a euphemism, the connection, as the Greek myth of Death and Sleep as twin brothers suggests, is deeper. At one level, there is the physical resemblance of a sleeping body to a corpse. This association is heightened by burial ceremonies that treat the grave or receptacle as a bed and place the corpse in a position of repose (either prone or sitting). The parallel is stronger in cultures that hold that the soul escapes from the sleeper's body just as it does from the corpse at death. Finally, there is the view that the land of the dead is a land of sleep. To return from the dead is to be awakened.

Some myths of the origin of death lay emphasis on the sleep motif. For example, the Selk'nam of Tierra del Fuego tell of the repeated attempts of the ancestors, who were tired of life, to achieve a deep sleep. After many failures, another group of ancestors wrap them in blankets and teach them the way of "transformation sleep." After a few days of such sleep (i. e., death), they will either be reborn on earth or, if they do not wish to return, they will be reborn as another kind of being or take up a celestial existence.

Sleep as ignorance. The understanding of sleep as a cessation of consciousness leads readily to the use of sleep as a metaphor for ignorance. In gnostic traditions within a diversity of religions, sleep, forgetfulness and oblivion have become characteristics of earthly existence. Salvation consists of awakening and recollection. In these traditions, the archaic language of the darkness and sleep of the land of the dead has been transferred to ordinary, mundane existence. The waking world of light and consciousness has been transferred to the "beyond."

Sleep as enlightenment. While enlightenment is most frequently expressed in terms of awakening (as in the root *budh,* "to wake, be awake," which has given rise to such words as *Buddha, bodhisattva,* and *bodhi,* "perfect knowledge," all reflecting the sense "to be awake from the slumber of ignorance and delusion"), it can, at times, be expressed in the language of sleep. This is especially the case in mystical systems where lack of consciousness of the world and contact with the supramundane is emphasized. In her various writings, Teresa of Ávila uses terms such as *sleep, falling asleep, being numb, repose, languishing,* and *stupor* to describe ecstasy. This builds on the Augustinian tradition that ecstasy is a state midway between sleep and death, more than sleep, less than death, where the soul is withdrawn from the bodily senses (Augustine, *De Genesi ad litteram* 12.26.53). In the Indic Upaniṣadic tradition, the language of sleep in relation to enlightenment is further developed. The brief *Mandukya Upaniṣad* presents the common fourfold schematization: (1) waking consciousness, (2) dream consciousness, that is, ordinary sleep, (3) deep sleep (*susupti*), a sleep without consciousness or dreams, and, the goal, (4) pure consciousness. Deep sleep is the realm of the "Knower"; the only danger is to confuse this penultimate stage with the true gnosis of the fourth state.

See Also Asklepios; Consciousness, States of; Dreams; Shamanism; Shape Shifting.

Bibliography

Material on sleep can be gleaned from monographs on related topics—for example, the classic study of incubation by Ludwig Deubner, *De incubatione* (Leipzig, 1900)—and from the large body of literature on dreams, of which Ernesto de Martino's *Il sogno e le civiltà umane* (Bari, 1966) is most useful. Still, there is no reliable cross-cultural overview of sleep. The chapter on the interrelationships of sleep, death, and the erotic titled "On the Wings of the Morning: The Pornography of Death" in Emily Townsend Vermeule's *Aspects of Death in Early Greek Art and Poetry* (Berkeley, 1979) is an exemplary study that needs to be matched for other cultures.

Jonathan Z. Smith (1987)

SMART, NINIAN.

SMART, NINIAN. Roderick Ninian Smart (1927–2001)—usually cited without his first name—was one of the most influential religion scholars of the twentieth century. Combining academic and personal leadership with a generosity of spirit and gracious personality, he was loved and cherished by many people all over the world. Praised by colleagues and students as an imaginative, inspiring teacher who possessed both lightness of touch and depth of learning, he enjoyed a high academic profile and wide international influence, especially in the English-speaking world. His prolific output established his worldwide reputation, based on an immense range of knowledge and a compassionate concern for humane and universal values. His careful attention to the intricate details of different religions, philosophies, and cultures was always set within a larger global vision transcending narrow tribal and national boundaries. Intent upon promoting personal and social well-being, he authored, edited and co-edited more than forty books (which were translated into many other languages) and over 250 articles, essays, chapters, and encyclopedia entries. His writings on the study of religion have influenced generations of students and scholars and also a wide general readership eager to learn about world religions and philosophies.

Biography and Scholarly Achievements. Born in Cambridge, England, to Scottish parents on May 6, 1927, Smart was educated at Glasgow Academy after his father had become Regius Professor of Astronomy at the University of Glasgow. Both his father and mother, a published poet and woman of means, deeply influenced him. Ninian and his two brothers all grew up to become professors in different disciplines. After school, Smart joined the British Army Intelligence Corps (1945–1948) and after infantry training was sent to learn Cantonese at the School of Oriental and African Studies, University of London. Postings to Singapore and then Sri Lanka provided his first extended contact with Buddhism. After demobilization, he joined Queen's College, Oxford, in 1948 to study classics, ancient history, and philosophy, while continuing his interest in Chinese and Asian studies, later supplemented by Sanskrit and Pali at Yale. Graduate studies at Oxford in the philosophy of religion were combined with the comparative study of religions. Working with J. L. Austin and R. C. Zaehner, Smart presented the first postwar dissertation in philosophy of religion at Oxford, later published as *Reasons and Faiths: An Investigation of Religious Discourse, Christian and Non-Christian* (1958).

At Oxford he met Libushka Baruffaldi, and they were married in 1954, Libushka providing loving support that sustained him and their four children throughout his long career. Smart's first post was a lectureship in philosophy at University College of Wales, Aberystwyth (1952–1956), followed by appointments in the history and philosophy of religion at King's College, London University (1956–1961), and then as first H. G. Wood Professor of Theology at Birmingham University (1961–1967). In 1967, Lancaster University appointed Smart as founding professor of religious studies, a position he held till 1982. Together with his colleagues, Smart brought the Lancaster Religious Studies Department to great international renown, promoting the historical, phenomenological, and social-scientific study of religion. During his time there, more than twenty Sri Lankan students obtained a doctorate in religious studies at Lancaster, and more than one hundred Lancaster religion graduates later held posts in higher education worldwide. He also served as pro-vice-chancellor of Lancaster University (1969–1972). Later, Lancaster University awarded him its highest honor as honorary professor of religious studies, and he became emeritus in 1989.

From 1976 on, Smart was also professor of religious studies at the University of California, Santa Barbara, dividing his time for some years between Lancaster and California. In 1986 he became the first J. F. Rowny Professor in the Comparative Study of Religion, a position he held until his retirement in 1998. In 1996 he was named the Academic Senate's research professor, the highest academic honor of the University of California for its faculty. Smart chaired departments at the Universities of London, Birmingham, Lancaster, and at Santa Barbara. He was elected president of the major learned societies in his field, the British Association for the History of Religion (1981–1985), the American Society for the Study of Religion (1984–1987), and the American Academy of Religion (1998–2000). He was awarded seven honorary doctorates, including degrees from Loyola University, Chicago, and the Universities of Glasgow, Stirling, Kelaniya (Sri Lanka), Lancaster, and Middlesex. In 1999, Queen's College, Oxford, where he had studied, made him an honorary fellow.

Smart was frequently invited as guest lecturer and visiting professor at, among other institutions, Yale, Wisconsin, Princeton, Banaras, Queensland, Otago, Cape Town, Bangalore, and Hong Kong. His Heslington Lectures at the University of York (1966) were published as *Secular Education and the Logic of Religion* (1968). His Gifford Lectures at the University of Edinburgh (1979–1980) appeared as *Beyond Ideology: Religion and the Future of Western Civilization* (1981/1982), and his Drummond Lectures at the University of Stirling (1985) as *Religion and the Western Mind* (1987). Other prestigious lectures included the Stewart Seminars at Princeton University (1971), resulting in a major theoretical work, *The Science of Religion and the Sociology of Knowledge* (1973/1978); the Chavara Lectures at the Center for Indian and Inter-Religious Studies, Rome (1993); and the Dharma Endowment Lectures at Dharmaram College, Bangalore (1997).

Smart was strongly committed to wider issues in religious education. He was prominent in setting up the Shap Working Party on World Religions in Education (1969), aimed at helping teachers in English schools to introduce the study of world religions into the curriculum. As one of its founding co-chairs and a subsequent president, Smart provided significant leadership and, in 1969, was appointed director of the Schools Council Project on Religious Education in Secondary Schools, which he was instrumental in establishing in Lancaster. The related Project on Religious Education in Primary Schools was set up under his direction in 1973. Through his close collaboration with the acclaimed BBC television series *The Long Search* (1974–1977), dealing with the religions of the world (though not those of Africa), and through his association with the popular Open University religious studies program in Britain he exercised extensive public influence. With several British colleagues Smart was also, in 1971, cofounder of the internationally known journal *Religion: A Journal of Religion and Religions*, now edited in Lancaster and California.

An extensive traveler, Smart attended innumerable conferences and meetings, always encouraging younger scholars. His friends knew him as a keen cricket and tennis player who greatly enjoyed family life, conviviality, and good conversation; and as someone who doodled, wrote limericks and poems (some published as *Smart Verse*, 1996), drew cartoons, and painted with water colors. Smart was looking forward to a long, active retirement but, soon after his permanent return to Lancaster, he died unexpectedly on January, 29, 2001. This tragic loss occasioned warm tributes from former colleagues, friends, and students around the world. The many memorial celebrations and colloquia honoring this eminent scholar seem already to have moved his life and work into the realm of legend.

APPROACHES TO THE STUDY OF RELIGIONS. Smart wrote extensively—and, in the eyes of certain critics, sometimes too superficially—on most religious traditions in the modern world. He became well known through the five editions of his widely used textbook, *The Religious Experience* (first published as *The Religious Experience of Mankind*, 1969), later superseded by *The World's Religions: Old Traditions and Modern Transformations* (1989). His early work in the philosophy of religion dealt with questions of truth and dialogue, combined with an interest in the study of Buddhism and Hinduism. Smart went on to develop a phenomenologically grounded, multidisciplinary, cross-cultural approach to the comparative study of religious traditions ancient and modern, what he later called the study of "worldviews" and "ideologies." He also spoke of religious studies as "aspectual," "dealing with a vital aspect of human institutions and experience," exploring the power that religion exercised over the human mind, imagination, societies, and cultures. Without denying the necessity of philology, he emphasized the need for clear conceptual analysis and attention to "religion on the ground," requiring a social-science approach.

Smart's work has made important contributions to theory and method in the study of religion, comparative ethics, religious education, sociology of religion, and studies in politics and religion. Much of the theoretical orientation of his vast program is lucidly summarized in his two inaugural addresses, "The Principles and Meaning of the Study of Religion" (1968) and, twenty years later, "The Study of Religion as a Multidisciplinary and Cross-cultural Presence among the Human Sciences" (1989), where he also announced his intention to undertake a future study of a universal human "grammar of symbolism," once he had completed his work on world philosophies. Unfortunately, his early demise prevented this promising plan from coming to fruition.

His second book, *A Dialogue of Religions* (1960/1981) presents an imaginary dialogue between six different people (a Christian, a Jew, a Muslim, a Hindu, a Sri Lankan Buddhist, and a Japanese Buddhist), covering topics from rebirth and salvation to the worship of God, incarnation and history, Buddhism, and the Trinity. The book reflects Smart's sympathetic imagination and his capacity to understand the dialogical process. Many consider his early *Doctrine and Argument in Indian Philosophy* (1964/1992) to be his finest and technically most accomplished work. It showed an excellent grasp of complex issues in Indian philosophy and was innovative in not using Sanskrit or Pali words in the text, but instead giving their English translation, supplemented by an annotated glossary explaining the original Pali and Sanskrit words. Another helpful but less well-known study on Indian thought is *The Yogi and the Devotee: The Interplay between the Upanishads and Catholic Theology* (1968), based on his Teape Lectures given in Delhi and Calcutta in 1964.

Smart's writings on education date mainly from the late 1960s to the mid-1970s. *Secular Education and the Logic of Religion* (1968) was influential in shaping the form and content of British religious education by arguing: (1) the pluralist nature of society; (2) the neutrality of the state with regard to religious matters; and (3) the need for a disinterested, rather than confessional, study of religion at all levels of education. This book championed a nondogmatic, multi-faith approach through the use of a phenomenological method that promoted empathetic understanding and objectivity. It also first introduced Smart's account of the multidimensional character of religion, later widely diffused through *The Religious Experience* and subsequent publications, such as *Worldviews: Crosscultural Explorations of Human Beliefs* (1995/2000) and *Dimensions of the Sacred: An Anatomy of the World's Beliefs* (1996). These dimensions are the doctrinal or philosophical, mythic or narrative, ethical or legal, ritual or practical, experiential or emotional, and social or organizational, to which he later added the artistic or material and the political or economic. These describe religions as they exist rather than reducing them to their origins and functions. It is wholly appropriate to speak, as some do, of a Smartian six- (or eight-) dimensional approach to the study of religion, which many have found illuminating in reaching conceptual clarity and empathetic understanding of religious traditions and secular ideologies.

Among Smart's last books were an *Atlas of the World's Religions* (1999) and *World Philosophies* (1999), which begins with the "one world" theme and shows his continuing exploration of philosophical diversity, including that of African philosophies, within a new worldview of global pluralism. Described as "the heaviest book he has written," its impressively wide sweep and inclusiveness are its great strengths, reflecting immense learning, though it has been judged as "too ambitious and too reductive," pleasing neither the specialist nor the general reader. Others assess it more positively, for it shows Smart's continuing preoccupation with important philosophical issues, his clarity of perception and acuity of mind, and an astute observation of a fast-changing global scene.

Significance and Legacy. Smart was a great pragmatist, but also a pioneer, prophet, and visionary. The newly emerging global civilization was for him "an age of opportunity" requiring a balance between personalism and pluralism. Speaking of "a creative critical pluralism" arising out of the interactive encounter of different cultures, and a new "transcendental humanism," he affirmed: "It is the mutual interpenetration of cultures through empathy that the comparative study of religion offers as a major ingredient in the formation of a peaceful global city" (*Beyond Ideology*, 1981, p. 312). He strongly opposed the ghettoization of religious studies and dispassionately pleaded for treating all symbolic systems or worldviews together, calling for a deeper conversation between the different religions through the creation of a new umbrella organization, a global academy of religion.

It is too early for a full critical assessment of Smart's contribution to the study of religion. Only time will tell which of his numerous works and ideas will be of lasting influence in the comparative study of religion, in philosophy of religion, or in education. His writings can be seen as mirroring some of the important developments in the modern study of religion without including more recent theoretical issues developed by poststructuralist, postcolonial, and feminist critics. Although sometimes criticized as too broad-ranging, Smart's work advocates a strong pluralist position and possesses a genuine inclusiveness, reflecting the ability to represent "the other" through a deep empathy that is rare among scholars. Although one might not always agree with a particular thesis, his ideas throw light on many different problems in the study of religion.

Smart carried his brilliance and learning lightly, advocating that "the understanding of religion is not only important in itself, but it can be fun." He also maintained that being religious is more important than studying religion. His scholarly achievements and the wide diffusion of his work owe much to his effective use of the media. Described as a peripatetic scholar of religion, philosopher, comparative theologian, poet, and global citizen, Smart's personality was in many ways as important as his approaches to the study of religion. He once wrote, "the study of religion is a science that requires a sensitive and artistic heart," and he embodied this more than most. A more nuanced interpretation of his achievements and the historical significance of his oeuvre is still to come, but it is imperative that all that is most original, innovative, and best in his work will be carried on by others for whom his legacy remains both inspiring and challenging.

Bibliography

Extensive bibliographical references to Smart's works, though not complete, can be found in the two *Festschrift* publications that appeared during his lifetime (giving him great pleasure): *Aspects of Religion: Essays in Honour of Ninian Smart*, edited by Peter Masefield and Don Wiebe (New York, 1994), and *The Future of Religion: Postmodern Perspectives, Essays in Honour of Ninian Smart*, edited by Christopher Lamb and Dan Cohn-Sherbok (London, 1999). Lancaster University is developing the Ninian Smart Archive and a bibliography, which will list all of Smart's publications, from the strictly academic to the merely flippant and entertaining. A good overview of Smart's wide research can be gained from John J. Shepherd, ed., *Ninian Smart on World Religions: Collected Works*, 2 vols. (Aldershot, UK, 2005), which brings together key articles in the theory and method of the study of religion, religious education, philosophy of religion, interfaith dialogue, comparative ethics, Buddhism and Hinduism, religious traditions in the modern world, and religions and worldview analysis. Smart himself published two collections of selected articles: *Concept and Empathy: Essays in the Study of Religion*, edited by Donald Wiebe (London and New York, 1986), a compilation of previously published articles that contains his Lancaster University inaugural address, "The Principles and Meaning in the Study of Religion"; and *Reflections in the Mirror of Religion*, edited by John Burris (London and New York, 1997). Smart's approach to religious experience has been analyzed by Jose Kuruvachira, *Religious Experience Buddhist, Christian, Hindu: A Critical Study of*

Ninian Smart's Interpretation of the Numinous and the Mystical (New Delhi, 2003).

Smart's work was referred to several times in the first edition of *The Encyclopedia of Religion*, edited by Mircea Eliade (New York, 1987), to which he contributed the articles on "Soteriology" (vol. 13, pp. 418–423) and "Comparative-Historical Method" (vol. 3, pp. 571–574), themes that are also discussed in his *The Science of Religion and the Sociology of Knowledge* (Princeton, 1973).

In addition to the publications cited in the entry above, other books by Smart include *Philosophers and Religious Truth* (London, 1964/1969); *The Philosophy of Religion* (New York, 1970/1979); *The Phenomenon of Religion* (London, 1973/1978); *New Movements in Religious Education*, co-edited with Donald Horder (London, 1975); *The Phenomenon of Christianity* (London, 1979), also published as *In Search of Christianity: Discovering the Diverse Vitality of Christian Life* (San Francisco, 1979); and *Sacred Texts of the World: A Universal Anthology*, co-edited with Richard D. Hecht (New York, 1982), wherein Smart's different dimensions of religion are used for the arrangement of selected texts, including passages from new religions and secular worldviews. Smart's interests in comparative theology and what some call his "theological intentions," are evident from *The Concept of Worship* (London and New York, 1972); his *Christian Systematic Theology in a World Context*, coauthored with Steven Konstantine (London and Minneapolis, 1991); and *Buddhism and Christianity: Rivals and Allies* (London and Honolulu, 1993). Smart's Gifford Lectures were published as *Beyond Ideology: Religion and the Future of Western Civilization* (London, 1981; San Francisco, 1982). His own religious beliefs are perhaps most clearly delineated in "An Ultimate Vision" in *Ultimate Visions: Reflections on the Religions We Choose*, edited by Martin Forward, pp. 257–265 (Oxford, 1995).

Themes relating to religion, politics, and nationalism are taken up in many of Smart's writings, but are especially focused on in *Mao* (London, 1974); *Religion and Politics in the Modern World*, co-edited with Peter H. Merkl (New York and London, 1983/1985); and in *Religion and Nationalism: The Urgency of Transnational Spirituality and Toleration* (Rome, 1994). Personal appreciations of Ninian Smart as a colleague, scholar, teacher, and friend are found in "Tributes to Ninian Smart (1927–2001)" in *Religion* 31, no. 4 (2001): 315–386.

URSULA KING (2005)

SMITH, HANNAH WHITALL

SMITH, HANNAH WHITALL (1832–1911), author, evangelist, and social activist, was born to birthright Quaker parents in Philadelphia, Pennsylvania on February 7, 1832. Frustrations with her slow spiritual progress as a young Quaker girl immersed in the troubled Quakerism of her time cast the only shadows over what she otherwise describes as her "sunshine years." Her early journals give strong intimations of the concepts that later became the central themes of her ministry as a spiritual guide. The unfailing provision of loving— even doting— parents shaped her understanding of the "unselfishness" of the loving God of the Bible, whose unfailing care for humankind she portrayed in both its fatherly and motherly expressions. The love and bounty of her childhood milieu later defined the pivotal point of her understanding of the mature Christian's experience of God: "God is enough!" With these givens, early in her life as an evangelical believer, Smith also concluded that God's infinite love and power would ultimately bring all errant humankind back into his family. The heretical tones of this "restitutionism" sometimes threatened Smith's standing within the evangelical community. However, her adherence to an early promise she had made to a group of English evangelicals to never promote her "heresy" publicly allowed her to develop and maintain the spiritual authority she came to command in these circles.

Smith married Philadelphia Quaker Robert Pearsall Smith (1827–1898) in 1851. Her plans to pursue higher education came to an abrupt end with the birth of the first of their six children (only three survived into adulthood). The rise of spiritual renewal movements within American and British Protestantism in 1859 led the Smiths to embrace the evangelical understanding of the authority of the Christian scriptures over the priority the Friends traditionally had given to the more mystical guidance of each individual's "inner light." The Smiths both professed evangelical conversion and resigned from the Society. After rejecting the rigid biblicism of the Plymouth Brethren, Smith turned to the Wesleyan Holiness revivalism sponsored by a group of Methodist ministers called the National Holiness Association, which shaped her theology and message for the next twenty years. The openness of Wesleyan churches and camp meetings to women's public ministry allowed Smith to quickly become a favored teacher and evangelist. The nonsectarian nature of the revival opened up similar engagements for Smith within the parallel Calvinist-oriented Holiness movement, which was rising in many Presbyterian and other Reformed churches.

European sales of Smith's brief account of the life of her son Frank (1854–1872), who died while a student at Princeton, introduced her to the Protestant communities of England and Europe. The enthusiastic reception of the 1875 publication of her spiritual manual *The Christian's Secret of a Happy Life* assured her a prominent role in the European revival. (The devotional classic became one of the best-sellers of all nineteenth century publications and remains one of the most widely read guides to evangelical spirituality.) Smith became known as "The Angel of the Churches." She played the central role in an eclectic group of participants at the annual holiness camp meetings held at the Broadlands estate of Lord and Lady Mount-Temple, along with author George Macdonald (1824–1905), African American evangelist Amanda Smith (1837–1915), who had accompanied Hannah to England, and hundreds of Oxford and Cambridge students caught up in the continuing holiness renewal movement. At the Brighton Convention for the promotion of Christian holiness in May 1875, where more than 8,000 English and Continental clergy and lay persons gathered to discuss the theology and life advocated by the Smiths, her teaching sessions on the higher Christian life regularly attracted 5000 attendees.

At the height of the revival's influence, questions arose as to her husband Robert's moral and doctrinal integrity, and Hannah and he abruptly returned to the United States. The work of the previous two years, however, left a formative and lasting imprint on world Protestantism. In Germany, Scandinavia and Switzerland the old pietistic "Fellowship Movements" in the established Lutheran and Reformed churches were revived. In Germany, the Inner City Movement was activated to urban social reform. The Wesleyan free churches on the continent were strengthened and new non-denominational holiness associations were formed, which by the turn of the twentieth century became the source of new European holiness and Pentecostal bodies. The most influential of all such associations was the Keswick Convention, through which missionary and student volunteer programs spread the Holiness/Higher-Life message throughout evangelical Protestantism.

After their return to America Smith and her husband both turned their energies to new interests: he to a position with her family's glass business, and she to raising her children, her writing, and active involvement in social reform while still maintaining a lifetime ministry as counselor to the constant stream of inquirers who contacted her. She was the first president of the Pennsylvania chapter of the Woman's Christian Temperance Union in 1874 and was influential in electing her friend Frances Willard (both women had deep roots within the Holiness revival movement) as president of the Union in 1879 on a reform platform which supported women's suffrage as well as temperance. Smith later became the director of the evangelism division of the WCTU, a training ground for women evangelists who were denied a public platform by their denominations. She also introduced Frances Willard to the leaders of the British temperance movement, leading to the organization of the World Christian Temperance Union.

The Smiths moved to England in 1888 to be near their daughter Mary (1864–1945) and her children. Hannah quickly became a featured speaker on behalf of various reform causes in Anglican Churches, free churches, public festivals, and even at Westminster Abbey. The Smiths previous contacts with William and Henry James, Walt Whitman, family members closely connected with Johns Hopkins and other American colleges and universities, along with a circle of social contacts associated with the marriages of her children, placed the Smith family in regular contact with a celebrated circle of artists and intelligentsia. Mary's first husband was Frank Costello (1855–1899), a member of Parliament. Her second husband was Bernard Berenson (1865–1959) celebrated art historian. Her daughter Alys (1867–1951) was the first wife of Bertrand Russell (1872–1970). Hannah negotiated Russell's first American lectureship through her brother-in-law, a director of Johns Hopkins. Her views on women's higher education strongly influenced her niece Martha Carey Thomas, the first dean and second president of Bryn Mawr College, who became Hannah's surrogate in fulfillment of the educational ambitions that had been denied her. Both of Mary's children whom Hannah reared, Ray Strachey (1887–1940) a social activist, and Karin Stephen (1887–1953), one of the first Freudian psychoanalysts, married into the Bloomsbury circle. William Lloyd Tennyson, George Bernard Shaw, Sydney Webb, Lytton Strachey (1880–1932), Vanessa Bell (1879–1961) and Virginia Woolf (1882 –1941) among many others, were frequent visitors at Smith's home. Her children and their spouses and guests didn't hesitate to talk with Smith about her rigid adherence to her Quaker and evangelical mores. An invalid for the last seven years of her life, she remained alert and involved. Her granddaughter Ray Strachey took her in her wheel chair to demonstrate at the Parliament building before a critical vote on women's suffrage. Ray also published Hannah's last work: *Group Movements of the Past and Experiments in Guidance* (1934), which presented her views and concerns for the numerous religious renewal movements she has participated in or observed for over half a century.

Smith's son Logan (1865–1946), Oxford professor of literature and author of the trivia genre in English literature, shared his home with Smith until her death in 1911.

BIBLIOGRAPHY

Dieter, Melvin. "The Smiths: A Biographical Sketch with Selected Items from the Collection." *Asbury Seminarian* 38, no. 2 (spring 1983): 6–42.

Dieter, Melvin E. *The Holiness Revival of the Nineteenth Century.* 2d ed. Lanham, Md., 1996.

Parker, Robert Allerton. *The Transatlantic Smiths.* New York, 1959.

Smith, Hannah Whitall. *The Christian's Secret of a Happy Life.* Old Tappan, N.J., 1875.

Smith, Hanna Whitall. *The Unselfishness of God and How I Discovered It: My Spiritual Autobiography.* New York, 1903.

Smith, Hannah Whitall. *Living in the Sunshine.* Chicago, 1906.

Smith, Logan Pearsall, ed. *A Religious Rebel: The Letters of "H.W.S." (Mrs. Pearsall Smith).* London, 1949. Published in the United States as *Philadelphia Quaker: The Letters of Hannah Whitall Smith.* New York, 1950.

Strachey, Barbara. *Remarkable Relations: The Story of the Pearsall Smith Family.* New York and London, 1980.

Strachey, Ray, ed. *Religious Fanaticism: Extracts from the Papers of Hannah Whitall Smith.* London, 1928.

MELVIN E. DIETER (2005)

SMITH, JOSEPH (1805–1844), the founder of the Church of Jesus Christ of Latter-day Saints, popularly known as the Mormons. Joseph Smith, Jr. was perhaps the most original, most successful, and most controversial of several religious innovators—including Ellen Gould White (Seventh-day Adventists), Mary Baker Eddy (Christian Science), and Charles Taze Russell (Jehovah's Witnesses)—who created important religious movements in nineteenth-century America.

Born in Sharon, Vermont, on December 23, 1805, Smith was the third of the nine children of Joseph and Lucy Mack Smith. He grew up in the unchurched and dissenting, but God-fearing, tradition of a New England Protestant biblical culture, which attracted many of those whose economic standing in established society had been eroded. In 1816, plagued by hard times and misfortune, the sturdy, self-reliant, and closely-knit Smith family left New England for western New York in search of economic betterment; they settled in the village of Palmyra, along the route of the Erie Canal.

During the 1820s, as the Smiths continued to struggle against economic reversals, the religiously inclined young man had a number of visions and revelations. These convinced him that he was to be the divinely appointed instrument for the restoration of the gospel, which in the opinion of many of his contemporaries had been corrupted. Under the guidance of an angel he unearthed a set of golden plates from a hill near his parents' farm. He translated these golden plates with divine aid and published the result in 1830 as the *Book of Mormon.* Smith claimed that this book, named after its ancient American author and compiler, was the sacred history of the pre-Columbian inhabitants of America, migrants from the Near East, some of whom were the ancestors of the American Indians. In 1829 divine messengers had conferred the priesthood—the authority to baptize and act in the name of God—on Smith and his associate Oliver Cowdery. Shortly after the publication of the *Book of Mormon,* Smith and Cowdery officially organized the Church of Christ in Fayette, New York, on April 6, 1830. In 1838 the name was changed to the Church of Jesus Christ of Latter-day Saints.

Prominent among those attracted to Smith's teachings was Sidney Rigdon, erstwhile associate of Alexander Campbell. Rigdon invited Smith and his New York followers to establish a Mormon settlement in Kirtland, Ohio. It was there that Smith greatly amplified and broadened his theological and organizational principles in a series of revelations (first published in 1833 as the *Book of Commandments,* and later enlarged into the current, canonical *Doctrine and Covenants*). The Saints were enjoined to gather in communities as God's chosen people under an egalitarian economic system called the Law of Consecration and Stewardship. They were also directed to build a temple as the sacred center of the community. These revelations initiated a patriarchal order that harkened back to Old Testament traditions. Another ancient source was Smith's translation of some Egyptian papyri published as *The Book of Abraham* in 1842. This work became a source of some controversy when a modern translation published in 1968 suggested that these papyri were ordinary funerary documents—though the Church has continued to accept *The Book of Abraham* as canonical.

In the meantime, Smith also established settlements in Missouri, which he regarded as the center of a future Zion. In 1838 economic difficulties and internal dissension forced Smith to give up the Kirtland settlement. His intention of gathering all the Saints in Missouri, however, had to be deferred after the Mormons were ruthlessly driven from the state in 1839. It was in Nauvoo, a settlement founded in 1839 on the Mississippi River, that Smith further expanded his ambitious vision of a Mormon empire that was to be both spiritual and temporal. By 1844 Nauvoo had become the largest city in Illinois, with a population of about eleven thousand. This city was under the full religious, social, economic, and political control of the Mormon kingdom, with Joseph Smith as its charismatic leader.

Some historians suggest that he may have become touched by megalomania; he assumed leadership of the Mormon militia in the resplendent uniform of a lieutenant general and announced his candidacy for the presidency of the United States. Smith ostensibly made his gesture toward the presidency in order to avoid making a politically difficult choice between the two major parties, but he was also imbued with the millennial belief that if God wanted him to be president and establish Mormon dominion in the United States, no one could hinder him. Innovative ordinances, such as baptism for the dead, and especially plural marriage—with Smith and his closest associates secretly taking numerous wives—offended the religious sensibilities of some Mormons. Likewise, controversial doctrines such as preexistence, metaphysical materialism, eternal progression, the plurality of gods, and the ability of humans to become divine through the principles of Mormonism, failed to gain universal acceptance among the Saints. A group of alarmed anti-Mormons effectively capitalized on internal dissent and were able to organize a mob that killed Smith and his brother Hyrum on June 27, 1844.

History has shown the killers of the Mormon prophet wrong in thinking that they had delivered a mortal blow to Mormonism, although their crime was an implicit recognition of Smith's crucial role in creating and sustaining the new religion. It was his spirituality, imagination, ego, drive, and charisma that not only started Mormonism but kept it going in the face of nearly insurmountable internal and external opposition. At the same time, these were the very characteristics that had generated much of that opposition. Smith's was a multifaceted and contradictory personality. Reports of encounters with him by both non-Mormons and believers give the impression of a tall, well-built, handsome man whose visionary side was tempered by Yankee practicality, geniality, and a sense of humor that engendered loyalty in willing followers. Though after his death his followers could not all agree on precisely what he had taught and split into several factions, they all accepted Smith's central messages of the restoration of the gospel and the divine status of the *Book of*

Mormon, continuing revelation by prophets, and the establishment of the kingdom of God with Christ as its head.

See Also Mormonism.

Bibliography

The literature on Joseph Smith is as controversial as his life. Most of the anti-Smith polemics are based on affidavits collected by Mormon apostate Philastus Hurlbut and published by Eber D. Howe as *Mormonism Unvailed* (Painesville, Ohio, 1834). Smith's mother, Lucy Mack Smith, presented the other side in *Biographical Sketches of Joseph Smith the Prophet* (1853; reprint, New York, 1969). *History of the Church of Jesus Christ of Latter-day Saints,* by Joseph Smith, Jr., 2d rev. ed., 6 vols., edited by B. H. Roberts (Salt Lake City, 1950) is an indispensable source collection. The most authoritative account of Smith's family background and early career is Richard L. Bushman's *Joseph Smith and the Beginnings of Mormonism* (Urbana, Ill., 1984).

The nineteenth-century theory that the *Book of Mormon* was Sidney Rigdon's plagiarized version of a novel by Solomon Spaulding was first demolished by I. Woodbridge Riley in *The Founder of Mormonism: A Psychological Study of Joseph Smith, Jr.* (New York, 1902). David Persuitte has revived the argument that the *Book of Mormon,* especially its claim for the Israelite origins of the American Indians, was influenced by Ethan Smith's *View of the Hebrews* (Poultney, Vt., 1823) in *Joseph Smith and the Origins of the Book of Mormon* (Jefferson, N.C., 2000). The first modern interpretation is Fawn M. Brodie's *No Man Knows My History: The Life of Joseph Smith, the Mormon Prophet* (1945; 2d ed., rev. & enl., New York, 1971), which advances a psychoanalytic interpretation and sees him as a product of his cultural environment. Mormons prefer Donna Hill's less critical *Joseph Smith, the First Mormon* (Garden City, N. Y., 1977), though scholars cannot afford to bypass Brodie. The most successful attempt to avoid the prophet-fraud dichotomy is Jan Shipps's *Mormonism: The Story of a New Religious Tradition* (Urbana, Ill., 1984). A short biography in the *Penguin* series by the distinguished Jacksonian scholar Robert V. Remini, *Joseph Smith* (New York, 2000), is essentially a PR job, skirting controversial issues. There is no reliable up-to-date biography of Smith.

Klaus J. Hansen (1987 and 2005)

SMITH, MORTON. Robert Morton Smith was born in Philadelphia on May 28, 1915, the son of the physician Rupert Henry Smith and his wife Mary (Funk). He received a B.A. from Harvard in 1936, with a major in English. Thereafter he continued at Harvard Divinity School (S.T.B. 1940), where he studied the New Testament (NT) under Henry Cadbury, Judaism under Harry A. Wolfson, and Greco-Roman religions under Arthur D. Nock. At Wolfson's urging he learned rabbinic Hebrew as background to NT studies. He was awarded a travel fellowship for study at the Hebrew University in Jerusalem, where he was stranded by the outbreak of World War II, but he used the time to complete a doctoral dissertation, written in Hebrew, submitted in 1945, accepted in 1948, and published in English translation as *Tannaitic Parallels to the Gospels* (1951). From 1948 to 1950 he returned to Harvard Divinity School, where he eventually earned a Th.D. in 1957 with a controversial thesis, eventually published in 1971 as *Palestinian Parties and Politics That Shaped the Old Testament.* His first teaching appointments were as instructor and then assistant professor in biblical literature at Brown University (1950–1955), followed by a year as visiting professor in the history of religions at Drew University (1956–1957). In 1957 he was appointed successor to Elias J. Bickerman as professor of ancient history at Columbia University. He held this chair until his retirement in 1985, though he continued to teach at Columbia, in the Department of Religion, until shortly before his death on July 11, 1991.

Smith was ordained an Episcopal priest in 1946 and served in parishes in Baltimore (1946–1948) and Boston (1949–1950). Though he never officially left the priesthood—he continued to be listed in the *Episcopal Clerical Directory* until the end of his life—he held no subsequent church-related positions. During his later life many considered him an atheist, but it would probably be more accurate to call him an agnostic.

Throughout his life, one of Smith's principal scholarly interests remained the question of boundaries between disciplines, groups, and religions. On the one hand, he endeavored to show the inadequacies of commonly accepted boundaries. On the other hand, he undertook with equal passion to highlight the overlooked distinctions between separate groups within ancient Judaism and early Christianity. He was equally at ease in Hebrew, Greek, and Latin, and his work frequently involved more than one discipline from among biblical studies, classics, rabbinics, and patristics. Several of his articles, even early in his career, were devoted to breaking down conceptual barriers between Israelite and other ancient Near Eastern religions, such as his 1952 essay "The Common Theology of the Ancient Near East" in *Studies in the Cult of Yahweh* (vol.1, pp.15–27). In his works on Second Temple Judaism, too, he castigated those who, in his opinion, lacked due regard for context as well as due precision in terminology ("Terminological Boobytraps," in *Studies in the Cult of Yahweh* [vol. 1, pp. 95–103]). Smith emphasized affinities across disciplines but also the distinctive character of groups: the "syncretists" and the "Yahweh-alone party" in the biblical period, the Pharisees as a less-than-dominant "sect" in first-century Judaism, the Zealots and the Sicarii as two distinct groups, Pauline Christianity as a minority phenomenon.

Smith is probably remembered most for his publication of a letter attributed to Clement of Alexandria (c. 150–before 216 CE). In 1958 he discovered what appears to be an eighteenth-century copy of this heretofore unknown letter in the library of the desert monastery of Mar Saba, about twelve miles southeast of Jerusalem. This letter contains substantial quotes from a "secret gospel" (*mustikon euangelion*) of Mark, which combines elements of the raising of Lazarus in *John* 11:1–44 with the story of Jesus' encounter with a rich young man (*Lk.* 18:23 and parallels in *Mk.* 10:22; *Mt.* 19:22) inserted in the context of *Mark* 10:34. The most controversial part of the secret gospel—and of Smith's interpretation of it—is an allusion to nocturnal teaching, interpreted by Smith as an initiation rite with baptismal and sexual implications (*Clement of Alexandria,* 1973, pp. 91, 167–188; *Secret Gospel,* 1973, p. 113). It was suggested or insinuated that the letter was a modern forgery, or even that Smith himself was responsible for such a forgery. The most explicit accusations were brought by Quentin Quesnell in "The Mar Saba Clementine: A Question of Evidence" (*Catholic Biblical Quarterly* 37, no. 1 [1975]: 48–67), to which Smith responded in the same journal (38, no. 2 [1976]: 196–199). No tests have been carried out on the manuscript, which has been available to most researchers only through the photographs taken by Smith. The manuscript was seen in Mar Saba in 1976 by several scholars, including David Flusser and Guy G. Stroumsa, in the context described by Smith. On that occasion it was taken from Mar Saba to the Orthodox patriarchate in Jerusalem. Since then, it has not been made available to scholars.

Stroumsa (2003) notes that a perusal of the extensive correspondence between Smith and Gershom Scholem, the foremost scholar of his generation in the field of Jewish mysticism, reveals the gradual development of Smith's thought about the letter and the gospel as his studies progressed. Although it took Smith fifteen years between discovery and full publication, he had described his Mar Saba manuscript finds in the patriarchate's journal, *Nea Sion,* as early as 1960. His interpretation of the gospel and the letter have not found wide acceptance, and even the discovery itself remains highly controversial (Ehrman, 2003). The continued popular as well as scholarly interest in Smith's discovery is evidenced by the space devoted to it on the internet (see http://www.earlychristianwritings.com/secretmark.html) and by a special issue of the *Journal of Early Christian Studies* (11, no. 2 [2003]) devoted to "The Secret Gospel of Mark: A Discussion." The work on the Mar Saba manuscript strengthened Smith's interest in magic, which led to his equally provocative and controversial book *Jesus the Magician* (1978). This interest had been stimulated by his early contacts with Gershom Scholem's work on Jewish mysticism and magic. It is evident already in Smith's seminal 1956 essay "Palestinian Judaism in the First Century" (*Studies in the Cult of Yahweh,* vol. 1, p. 108), which highlights the diversity of Jewish groups, the Pharisees being only one among many. His continued interest in magic found expression in several articles on the subject (*Studies in the Cult of Yahweh,* vol. 2, pp. 208–256). His catalogue of the British Museum's collection of magical gems remained unfinished at his death but has since been published by Simone Michel, Peter Zazoff, and Hilde Zazoff (*Magische Gemmen im British Museum,* 2001).

While Smith's fame (or notoriety) was based on his unconventional and, to many, uncomfortable ideas, the questions he raised—if not the answers he proposed—have profoundly influenced scholarship in the fields he dealt with.

See Also Jesus; Judaism; Magic; Pharisees; Scholem, Gershom.

Bibliography

Calder, William M., III. "Morton Smith." *Gnomon* 64, no. 4 (1992): 382–384. This obituary contains concise but detailed biographical information.

Ehrman, Bart D. "Response to Charles Hedrick's Stalemate." *Journal of Early Christian Studies* 11, no. 2 (2003): 155–163. In his critique of Hedrick and Stroumsa, Ehrman argues that homoerotic elements in Secret Mark are central to Smith's interpretation and that the correspondence between Smith and Scholem (to be published by Stroumsa) does not prove the authenticity of Smith's manuscript find.

Hedrick, Charles W. "The Secret Gospel of Mark: Stalemate in the Academy." *Journal of Early Christian Studies* 11, no. 2 (2003): 133–145. Encourages scholars to integrate the study of the Secret Gospel of Mark into their reconstruction of early Christianity.

Meyer, Marvin. "Secret Gospel of Mark." In *Secret Gospels: Essays on Thomas and the Secret Gospel of Mark,* pp. 107–178. Harrisburg, 2003.

Smith, Morton. *Tannaitic Parallels to the Gospels.* Philadelphia, 1951; corrected reprint 1968. This dissertation received a book-length reply in Jacob Neusner, *Are There Really Tannaitic Parallels to the Gospels? A Refutation of Morton Smith* (Atlanta, 1993). Some of the shortcomings of Neusner's argumentative and personal attack on the person he still calls "the sole really important teacher I ever had" (p. x and *passim*) have been exposed by Shaye J. D. Cohen, "Are There Tannaitic Parallels to the Gospels?" *Journal of the American Oriental Society* 116, no. 1 (1996): 85–89.

Smith, Morton. *Palestinian Parties and Politics That Shaped the Old Testament.* New York, 1971; 2nd rev. ed. London, 1987. A brilliant attempt to identify diverse ideologies behind different parts of the Hebrew Bible.

Smith, Morton. *Clement of Alexandria and a Secret Gospel of Mark.* Cambridge, Mass., 1973. The voluminous scholarly edition and commentary on the Letter of Clement of Alexandria from the Mar Saba library.

Smith, Morton. *The Secret Gospel: The Discovery and Interpretation of the Secret Gospel According to Mark.* New York, 1973. A description of the discovery of the Letter of Clement and a popular commentary on its contents.

Smith, Morton. *Jesus the Magician.* New York, 1978. Smith's controversial comparison of Jesus with magicians of late antiquity.

Smith, Morton. *Studies in the Cult of Yahweh.* Edited by Shaye J. D. Cohen. 2 vols. Leiden, 1996. Contains forty of Smith's more important articles, many not easily accessible in their original publications, plus a full bibliography (283 items) of his writings (vol. 2, pp. 257–277) as well as "In Memoriam Morton Smith" (vol. 2, pp. 279–285) by the editor.

Stroumsa, Guy G. "Comments on Charles Hedrick's Article: A Testimony." *Journal of Early Christian Studies* 11, no. 2

(2003): 147–153. Stroumsa reports on his visit to Mar Saba, during which the manuscript published by Smith was located and transferred to Jerusalem. Stroumsa is also preparing the first edition of Smith's correspondence with Scholem, in which the issue of the Secret Gospel of Mark and its implications for the study of Jesus and early Christianity was raised on a number of occasions beginning in 1959.

JOSEPH SIEVERS (2005)

SMITH, WILFRED CANTWELL. Wilfred Cantwell Smith (1916–2000) was a historian of religion, a comparative theologian, and an ordained minister of the United Church of Canada. In 1949 Smith founded the Institute of Islamic Studies at McGill University in Montreal, where he matched Muslim and Christian appointments. He later succeeded R. L. Slater as director of the Center for the Study of World Religions at Harvard University (1964–1985), quitting Harvard for Dalhousie University in Halifax, Nova Scotia, to dissociate himself from U.S. militarism during the Vietnam War years. While at Harvard, Smith coordinated the university's first undergraduate concentration in religious studies.

After majoring in oriental languages at the University of Toronto, Smith studied theology under H. H. Farmer and Islamics under H. A. R. Gibb in Great Britain. In 1941 he joined the faculty of Forman Christian College in Lahore (in present-day Pakistan), then a center of multireligious dialogue. An admirer of Jawaharlal Nehru more than Mohandas Gandhi, Smith deplored the 1947 partition of India because he considered nationalism to be morally bankrupt.

As president of the Student Christian movement in Canada following the Depression era, Smith embraced John Macmurray's personalist philosophy and the Social Gospel movement. Smith's first book (rejected for a doctorate by Cambridge University) stressed class-based socioeconomic determinants in religion and politics. Stalinism, however, cured his enthusiasm for Marxist immanentism. Concluding that self-criticism requires a transhistorical referent, Smith linked issues of justice to a prophetic sense of transcendence. Thereafter, he vehemently challenged the practice of restricting the humanities and religious studies to a social science orientation.

A Princeton University doctorate (1948) led to publications on Islamic modernism, in which Smith juxtaposed "objective" cultural history and "subjective" faith. He noted the conflict in Islam between secularly educated professionals, who are needed to run a state, and traditionalists, who define statehood according to conservative interpretations of *sharī'ah* (theocratic law).

Islamic insistence on divine transcendence and its ban on idolatry reinforced Smith's polemic against reifying conceptions in and of religion. He gained international attention with a call to abandon the word *religion* as an academic category. This proposal was rejected, but his terms for construing the data—cumulative tradition and personal faith—were widely adopted. The former can be studied by any observer; the latter requires participation in the evolution of a tradition.

Smith's typical method was to analyze the changing meanings of key words, illustrating lost nuances by citing original senses in other languages (e.g., Arabic words for *truth*) and ruminating on shifts from verb to noun and singular to plural forms. To him, singular usage of *religion* and *scripture* resists reifying phenomena. From failures to adduce universally accepted definitions of such terms, Smith concluded not that linguistic essentialism is wrong but that misconstruals show insensitivity to necessarily tentative, metaphorical references to transcendence. A liberal, Smith's fundamentalist Calvinist upbringing was apparent in his assumption that earlier meanings are truer, later meanings being distorted by rationalization.

A major trilogy on faith, comparative history of religion, and world theology (published in 1977, 1979, and 1981) linked early *believing* to *beloving*, denied that belief (in the sense of hypothetical opinion) is what religion is about, and argued that existential trust is what relates human beings to the transcendent, however named. Among Ernst Troeltsch's categories, Smith emphasized the mystical-poetic.

Smith rejected as positivistic contemporary faith in pseudoscience and condemned the technocrats who dismissed humanizing concerns as irrelevant for decisions leading to the bombing of Hiroshima. Without sacrificing the scholarly rigor of historians of religion (often criticized for antiquarian fixation on texts), he emphasized living religion and dialogue, not just for gathering information, but as essential to becoming true to others and oneself in plural affirmations of transcendence.

Unrepentant over using Christian theological categories, Smith insisted that religious studies are about people responding to God Buddhistically, Christianly, secularly, and so on, focusing on different paradigmatic symbols. He pointed out that the Muslim homologue to Jesus is not Muḥammad but the Qur'ān. His final major work, written with his wife Muriel, was a study of scriptural dialogue through texts.

Dubbed an "experiential-expressivist," Smith considered himself primarily a historian in the global tradition of Arnold Joseph Toynbee, appealing to knowable but not fully describable "facts" of human relationship. In Smith's view, comparative, personal data are intuitively grasped and cogent if expressible in terms derived from two or more starkly contrasting traditions, such as Hinduism and Islam in India. Against academic fragmentation, he essayed a world history of religion as the cultural product of humanizing faith, of which the faithful are the final arbiters. According to Smith, true relationships are only validated by participant observers through "colloquy." Beyond both objective and subjective approximations is the truth and goodness, which the "critical corporate self-consciousness" (Smith, 1997, p.123) of spiritual and intellectual peers discerns.

Critics among philosophers of religion (e.g., John Hick, Ninian Smart) and later deconstructionists challenged the insider-outsider dichotomy intrinsic to Smith's conception of faith and tradition and his privileging of insiders. His hermeneutic of recovery rather than suspicion obscured how radical his insistence was that truth is dialogical. In global politics, Smith expected Muslims, Christians, humanistic atheists, and others to converge on the truth that matters. Mark Heim argues that, theologically, this was not pluralism, as Hick and Smith supposed, but ecumenical inclusivism, which wrongly assumes that religious ends are the same for all. In theology, Smith was more Muslim-Methodist than Trinitarian, foregrounding Jesus' humanity, not claims concerning his divinity.

Bibliography

Bae, Kuk-Won. *Homo Fidei: A Critical Understanding of Faith in the Writings of Wilfred Cantwell Smith and Its Implications for the Study of Religion.* New York, 2003.

Cracknell, Kenneth, comp. *William Cantwell Smith: A Reader.* Oxford, 2001.

Smith, Wilfred Cantwell. *Islam in Modern History.* Princeton, 1957.

Smith, Wilfred Cantwell. *The Meaning and End of Religion: A New Approach to the Religious Traditions of Mankind.* New York, 1963.

Smith, Wilfred Cantwell. *Religious Diversity,* edited by Willard G. Oxtoby. New York, 1976.

Smith, Wilfred Cantwell. *Belief and History.* Charlottesville, Va., 1977.

Smith, Wilfred Cantwell. *Faith and Belief.* Princeton, 1979.

Smith, Wilfred Cantwell. *Towards a World Theology: Faith and the Comparative History of Religion.* Philadelphia, 1981.

Smith, Wilfred Cantwell. *What Is Scripture? A Comparative Approach.* Minneapolis, 1993.

Smith, Wilfred Cantwell. *Modern Culture from a Comparative Perspective,* edited by John W. Burbidge. Albany, N.Y., 1997.

Whaling, Frank, ed. *The World's Religious Traditions: Current Perspectives in Religious Studies, Essays in Honour of Wilfred Cantwell Smith.* New York, 1984.

Peter Slater (2005)

SMITH, W. ROBERTSON. William Robertson Smith (1846–1894) was a celebrated Scottish biblical critic and a theorist of both religion and myth. Smith's accomplishments were multiple. He brought higher biblical criticism from Germany to the English-speaking world and then developed it far beyond its continental origins. Although his German mentors reconstructed the history of Israelite religion from the Bible itself, Smith ventured beyond the Bible to Semitic religion and thereby pioneered the comparative study of religion. Whereas others viewed ancient religion from the standpoint of the individual, Smith approached it from the standpoint of the group and thereby helped pioneer the sociology of religion.

As an original theorist of religion, Smith asserted that ancient religion was centrally a matter of ritual, not creed. Practice, not belief, counted most. Religion was initially communion between god and humans, not a prescientific explanation of the world. As an equally original theorist of myth, Smith similarly maintained that myth was initially an explanation of ritual, not of the world. Since Smith's time, the ritualist theory of myth has found adherents not only in biblical studies but also in classics, anthropology, and literature.

Smith was educated at home by his father, a minister of the breakaway Free Church of Scotland. Intellectually precocious, Smith was as brilliant in science and mathematics as in classics and Hebrew. He studied divinity at the University of Edinburgh, where he excelled. In 1870, at the young age of twenty-three, he was appointed to the professorship of Old Testament at the College of the Free Church in Aberdeen. He began teaching a day after his ordination as a minister in the Free Church.

Smith's professional troubles began with the publication in 1875 of the article "Bible" for the ninth edition of the *Encyclopaedia Britannica,* then published in Scotland. On the basis of that article, he was in 1876 formally charged with heresy. The main issue concerned the authorship of the *Book of Deuteronomy,* which Smith, following the older, continental scholars with whom he had become acquainted, deemed not Moses' farewell address to Israel but instead a work composed long after Moses' time. Smith's Free Church critics assumed that in denying Mosaic authorship, Smith was denying the divine authority of the Bible. On the contrary, argued Smith, revelation itself was gradual and progressive, so that the denial of Mosaic authorship was simply the denial that the advanced, prophetic views expressed in *Deuteronomy* had been revealed to Moses himself. After four years, during which Smith was suspended from his chair, he won his case and was reinstated. But the appearance of subsequent articles reopened the charge, and though never convicted of heresy, he was in 1881 removed from his professorship.

Embittered but undeterred, Smith had already begun to offer public lectures on his views to huge audiences in Edinburgh and Glasgow. From these lectures came his first two books, *The Old Testament in the Jewish Church* (1881) and *The Prophets of Israel and Their Place in History to the Close of the Eighth Century* (1882).

While still a minister (as he had not been convicted of heresy), Smith sought no pastoral post. Instead, to support himself he became coeditor and eventually sole editor of the same edition of the *Britannica* that had caused his undoing. He enlisted J. G. Frazer (1854–1941) to write the entries that began the transformation of Frazer from stuffy classicist to pioneering anthropologist.

In 1883 Smith was appointed lord's almoner reader in Arabic at Cambridge University. In 1885 he was elected a fellow of Christ's College. In 1889 he became Sir Thomas Adams Professor of Arabic at Cambridge. He utilized his knowledge of Arabic to root Israelite religion in the religion and culture of ancient Arabia, where for him lay the origin of Semitic culture. His studies culminated in his final and fullest work, *Lectures on the Religion of the Semites*, which was delivered as three series of Burnett Lectures at the University of Aberdeen from 1888 to 1891.

Smith had been a sickly child, but in adulthood he became remarkably fit for prolonged periods. Still, like other family members, he eventually succumbed to tuberculosis. He died in Cambridge at the age of forty-seven. He proved well enough to publish only the first series of the Burnett Lectures (in 1889). Only in the last decade of the twentieth century were the notes of the second and third series of lectures discovered and published.

Whereas Émile Durkheim (1858–1917), in *The Elementary Forms of the Religious Life* (1912), focused on Australian Aborigines as the most primitive and therefore presumably clearest case of religion per se, Smith in the *Lectures* turned to "heathen Arabia" as the earliest and therefore presumably clearest case of Semitic religion. Smith's fundamental assumption is that the Semites were initially at a "primitive" stage of culture, so that the key to understanding them is to see them as akin to primitives worldwide. He thus uses the terms *primitive* and *ancient* (or *antique*) almost interchangeably. Unlike Frazer, who was concerned with only the similarities among primitives the world over, Smith was concerned with the differences as well as the similarities between early Semites and other primitives, just as he was concerned with the differences as well as the similarities between early Semites and later ones. But it was his focus on the similarities that was revolutionary and controversial.

The basic religious divide for Smith is that between primitives and moderns. Whereas the heart of modern religion is its beliefs, the heart of primitive religion is its rituals. Smith's focus on practice rather than belief as the core of primitive and ancient religion was revolutionary. Yet on ritual, as on other aspects of religion, his revolution stops abruptly short. He does not propose that modern religion likewise be looked at from the side of ritual foremost. He draws a rigid hiatus between primitive and modern religion. Modern religion he approaches no differently from others of his day. It is creedal first and ritualistic second—no doubt a reflection of Smith's antiritualistic, Protestant viewpoint. Whereas twentieth-century theorists of religion tend to stress the similarities between primitive and modern religion, Smith stresses the differences. If on the one hand Smith gives equal attention to the differences and the similarities between primitives and early Semites, on the other hand he emphasizes the differences between both of them and modern Christianity.

In place of creed in ancient and primitive religion there was myth. Whereas in modern religion creed prescribes ritual, in ancient religion myth explained ritual. Unlike the practice of ritual, the belief in myth was not obligatory. In connecting myth to ritual, Smith was again revolutionary. Whereas others viewed myth as an explanation of the world, he proposed myth as an explanation of ritual. But here too he stops short. Myth for him plays a minor role, arising only after the original reason for a ritual has somehow been lost. The importance wrongly attributed to mythology is for him part of the importance that is wrongly accorded to belief. Since Smith's time other myth-ritualists have given myth far more significance. For Frazer, myth is indispensable to ritual from the start, providing the script for the magical ritual.

To drive home the point that in primitive and ancient religion ritual precedes belief, Smith compares religion with politics and indeed makes religion a part of politics. Religious duty was civic duty. But "so long as the prescribed forms [of practice] were duly observed, a man was recognised as truly pious, and no one asked how his religion was rooted in his heart or affected his reason" (Smith, 1894, p. 21). Practice alone counted.

Once again Smith was revolutionary—here in seeing ancient and primitive religion as collective rather than individual. Because Smith takes for granted that modern religion really is a matter of the individual, his bold approach once again stops abruptly. Where notably Durkheim argues that religion by definition is collective, Smith's "sociologizing" is confined to ancient and primitive religion.

Another equally fundamental difference for Smith is that whereas modern religion is spiritual, primitive and ancient religion is materialist. God is conceived of as the biological father of worshippers. That conception of God has moral consequences as well, with "the parent protecting and nourishing the child, while the child owes obedience and service to his parents" (Smith, 1894, p. 41). Yet again Smith was original—this time in placing morality within rather than outside primitive religion.

For Smith, the key relationship between god and his or her worshippers in any religion is that of communication. Therefore the key function of the key ritual, sacrifice, is as a "means of converse between God and man" (Smith, 1894, p. 216). Sacrifice constitutes not "a gift made over to the god"—the conventional view of his time—but "an act of communion, in which the god and his worshippers unite by partaking together of the flesh and blood of a sacred victim" (Smith, 1894, pp. 226–227). Sacrifice as gift comes only later. A gift is intended to alleviate guilt and to secure forgiveness, but originally there is no guilt to be alleviated or forgiveness to be secured, for worshippers have in no way fallen short.

In primitive religion misfortunes like plague and famine were initially attributed to the weakening of the bond between god and the community. Sacrifice served to restore the bond. Only eventually was the weakening attributed to sin. Sacrifice then came to be taken as atonement. Nevertheless the ultimate aim of even atonement was the restoration of the bond between god and community.

In its fullest, Christian form, God sacrifices himself to atone for the sins of the worldwide community, though Jesus' death still serves primarily to restore the fellowship between God and humanity. Indeed Smith increasingly downplays the atoning aspect of Jesus' death, for which he never found a satisfactory place in his irenic characterization of Christianity. The ineluctable link between atonement and fear, in contrast to that between communion and love, could not but push religion based on fear in the direction of, by Smith's own criteria, magic rather than religion. Frazer attributed Smith's reluctance to acknowledge the place of fear in religion to his own belief in a God of love rather than of fear.

Despite Smith's insistence on the presence of both communion and atonement in primitive and higher religion alike, the gulf between these stages of religion remains wide because primitive religion still conceives of both materially, whereas higher religion conceives of both spiritually. In primitive religion the goal is physical contact with god—achieved through the shared eating of a sacrifice, which in its earliest form is the eating of the totemic god itself. At first little attention is paid to the cause of the separation from god or to the justification for it. The materialist conception of religion clouds the recognition of spiritual concepts like ethics, sin, and atonement.

Consequently "to free the spiritual truth from the husk was the great task that lay before the ancient religions" (Smith, 1894, p. 439). The Prophets were the first to sever communion from material sacrifice—Smith taking the Prophets as uniformly antiritualistic. Once communion with God came to be conceived of spiritually, separation from God came to be conceived of ethically, as a matter of the justification for the separation and of the amends needed for overcoming it. But the subsequent, postexilic restoration of material sacrifice conflated anew the spiritual with the material. Only with Christianity was the spiritual fully disentangled from the material.

To explain the evolution of sacrifice, Smith appeals to God. Israelites and Christians on their own could never have made the leap from a material conception of sacrifice to a spiritual one. Only God's intercession, undertaken indirectly through inspiration, can account for the jump.

Smith is rightly viewed as a pioneering, perhaps even the pioneering sociologist of religion. He shifted the focus of the study of primitive and ancient religion from beliefs to institutions and from the individual to the group. For him, the function of primitive and ancient religion is the preservation of the group, even if he does not, like the more relentlessly sociological Durkheim, make group experience the origin of religion, let alone make the group the object of worship.

BIBLIOGRAPHY

Bediako, Gillian M. *Primal Religion and the Bible: William Robertson Smith and His Heritage.* Sheffield, U.K., 1995.

Beidelman, T. O. *W. Robertson Smith and the Sociological Study of Religion.* Chicago, 1974.

Black, John Sutherland, and George Chrystal. *The Life of William Robertson Smith.* London, 1912.

Durkheim, Émile. *The Elementary Forms of the Religious Life.* Translated by Joseph Ward Swain. New York, 1965. Original publication of this translation was in 1915.

Johnstone, William, ed. *William Robertson Smith: Essays in Reassessment.* Sheffield, U.K., 1995.

Jones, Robert Alun. "Robertson Smith, Durkheim, and Sacrifice: An Historical Context for *The Elementary Forms of the Religious Life.*" *Journal of the History of the Behavioral Sciences* 17 (1981): 184–205.

Jones, Robert Alun. "Robertson Smith and James Frazer on Religion: Two Traditions in British Social Anthropology." In *Functionalism Historicized,* edited by George W. Stocking Jr., pp. 31–58. Madison, Wis., 1984.

Riesen, Richard A. *Criticism and Faith in Late Victorian Scotland.* Lanham, Md., 1985.

Rogerson, John. *Old Testament Criticism in the Nineteenth Century.* London, 1984. See particularly chap. 20.

Rogerson, John. *The Bible and Criticism in Victorian Britain.* Sheffield, U.K., 1995. See particularly chaps. 4–10.

Smith, William Robertson. "Bible." In *Encyclopaedia Britannica,* 9th ed., vol. 3. Edinburgh, 1875.

Smith, William Robertson. *The Old Testament in the Jewish Church.* London, 1881.

Smith, William Robertson. *The Prophets of Israel and Their Place in History to the Close of the Eighth Century.* 1st ed. London, 1882; 2d ed., London, 1892; reprint of 2d ed. with new introduction by Robert Alun Jones, New Brunswick, N.J., 2002.

Smith, William Robertson. *Lectures on the Religion of the Semites.* 1st ser. Edinburgh, 1889; 2d ed., London, 1894; reprint of 2d ed. with new introduction by Robert A. Segal, New Brunswick, N.J., 2002.

Smith, William Robertson. *Lectures on the Religion of the Semites.* 2d and 3d ser. Edited by John Day. Sheffield, U.K., 1995.

T. O. BEIDELMAN (1987)
ROBERT A. SEGAL (2005)

SMOKING. Plants whose properties when consumed place the user in an unusual state have always been looked upon as being endowed with supernatural power. Such plants play an important part in both religious ceremonies and in healing. In such a context, these plants have been either used as symbols or consumed in different forms, including smoking. The one plant that has consistently maintained such religious association is tobacco, a New World contribution to the world's flora. Other plant products that can be smoked, such as hashish and opium, both of which originated in the Near East, have never had significant functions in religious ritual, although most recently some midwestern sects in the United States claim hashish smoking as part of their religious rituals.

The genus *Nicotiana* (tobacco) consists of seventy-four species, all but two of which are native to the North American continent. The latter two, *N. fragrans* and *N. suaveolens,* grow wild in Australia but were not used for smoking before the arrival of the white people. The most popular species are *N. rustica* and *N. tabacum.* Several others, such as *N. bigelovii* and *N. attenuata,* grow wild in the western Unites States. Indian tribes of California, the northern Plains, and the Northwest Coast are known to have planted these as their only agricultural effort.

Ancient Native American and European reports describe tobacco as a strong and addictive herb smoked with apparent hallucinogenic effects. Tobacco as it is known today produces no such effects. The indigenous people of the American continent may have been using more potent admixtures, or tobacco may have only induced a state that allowed its user to ease into altered states of consciousness.

It is possible that the use of tobacco was at first confined to shamans, priests, and medicine men. Data indicate that the tobacco plant and products derived from it were held in high esteem and those who grew or could obtain the plant used it as a precious offering to both worldly and supernatural rulers. Later, due to the interchange of ritual customs, the abundance of tobacco in some areas, and European influence, tobacco smoking became a worldwide custom; but its sacrosanct character among the natives of the Americas survived.

NORTH AMERICA. Tobacco initially grew wild. Gathered as a cultivated plant, it made its appearance with maize in North America. The two primary modes of tobacco consumption were smoking pipes and cigarettes and chewing. Tobacco pipes have been found in archaeological excavations of basket making culture sites (some as early as 2500 BCE) in the Southwest.

The Plains Indians developed considerable skill and ingenuity, as well as aesthetic sensitivity and care in making pipes. As Peter T. Furst points out,

> No object, no matter how splendidly proportioned or complex in iconography, can convey the enormous depth of feeling, ritual and belief, the very conception of the universe and how it came to be, the mutuality and interdependence of the sexes, and, indeed the whole relationship of human beings to the holy earth and sky, which are embodied in these traditional Native American smoking instruments. (Furst, 1982)

The famous Plains pipes are made of catlinite, thought to represent the flesh and blood of dead ancestors and dead buffalo, poured together and turned to stone. Catlinite had been mined in southwestern Minnesota by the Oto and Iowa tribes, who were replaced in the seventeenth century by Siouan-speaking groups, who became sole owners of the sacred material and compelled all other tribes to buy the stone from them.

Bowl and stem of the ritual pipe were carried separately when not in use. Apart, the instruments had no supernatural power. In many tribes women carved or decorated the stems, which had male attributes, and men fashioned the bowls, which were considered to have female attributes. The Plains Indians undertook no ceremony or ritual act without smoking pipes, which were kept in their medicine bundles. When an Indian died, his tobacco and pipe were placed with him in his burial place.

Kinnikinnick was the native name for the smoked material. This term means "mixture" to the Algonquin. They mixed their tobacco with different plant materials, such as sumac, bearberry, manzanilla, and dogwood bark. Though they used plants other than tobacco for smoking, none had the sacred nature attributed to tobacco.

The Indians of the Northwest Coast were introduced to smoking by Western explorers, who found them chewing their tobacco with lime. These tribes limited tobacco to important rituals, especially to commemorative feasts for the dead. Their pipes were carved out of wood or ivory and decorated with pictures of animals or mythological scenes. The shamans smoked pipes primarily to communicate with their guardian spirits and also during healing ceremonies. For them, tobacco was the symbol of the equilibrium of the universe and of divine benevolence from generation to generation.

SOUTH AMERICA. Both *N. tabacum* and *N. rustica* were modified by selection or by hybridization in South America, probably in Peru, Ecuador, Bolivia, and northern Argentina. Even today, tobacco is used by many native tribes, but is rarely smoked by them. The preferable form of consumption is chewing or drinking in the form of a syrupy juice. Tobacco juice is taken either by mouth or through the nostrils, or administered as an enema. The last method has been documented for the Inca and Tihuanaco of the pre-Conquest periods.

Smoking tobacco for the purpose of divination was practiced by Venezuelan tribes, who also offered tobacco as a gift to their gods. The Guajiro of Colombia, the Kumaná of the Orinoco River, and the Warao and the Shipibo-Conibo on the Ucayali River also celebrate healing ceremonies by smoking, or smoke in preparation for other drug use. The Piro and the Machiganga of Peru inhale tobacco snuff through tubes made of bird bones as medicine against colds. This old remedy was adopted by Europeans in the sixteenth century.

MESOAMERICA. The most extensive depictions of smoking and the oldest and most abundant data on the pre-Columbian use of tobacco (mostly in the form of cigars) are found in Maya art. The word *cigar* is Maya in origin; the word *tobacco* might be derived from an Arawak word for "cigar." The Maya also depicted cigarette smoking, for which there are no early records elsewhere. Pipe smoking did not appear in Maya art, and it is doubtful that it was a custom. Early Spanish reports describe the coating of cigars with a varnish of clay, which was then decorated, and the stuffing of small tubes of cane, clay, and other materials with shredded tobacco, which was either smoked or used to blow smoke.

Besides smoking, the Maya also chewed, licked, ate, and drank tobacco, social customs reported frequently from Conquest times to the present day. Tobacco as a form of incense, however, had an exclusive and important role in ceremonial healing. The Maya attributed most diseases to supernatural intervention, and native healing was, and still is, a predominantly religious act of communication with supernatural forces in which religion and medicine remain inseparable.

The pre-Columbian Maya often depicted their divine rulers, nobles, and gods smoking. Among the deities, god L appears to be a heavy smoker; the death god, the rain god, god D of the creation, and the ancestral god N could be characterized as only occasional indulgers. God K not only smokes on occasion but he is shown with a smoking cigar stuck through his forehead. Some of the mythological animals, usually representing gods, are also shown smoking: Monkeys have a strong lead, with jaguars second, and frogs or toads third. All of these animals are also patron deities of days or months.

Noble Maya lords were also frequently shown smoking or handling cigars or cigarettes either alone or in the company of others. Apparently no women participated in these rituals, although they are sometimes shown on ancient paintings and monuments in proximity to smokers. The context of these scenes is varied and not always clear. There are processional scenes with supernaturals and their impersonators, and there are scenes with offerings of human victims or other sacrifices. Other smoking scenes commemorate ancestors and still others show smoking to be one of several ways to achieve a state of trance.

The Lacandon, a few hundred Maya Indians still living in the Chiapas rain forest, continue to cultivate tobacco in the ancient ways. They believe that the Nohoch Yum Chacob, the white-haired, bearded servants of the god of rain and thunder, live in the second highest level of the heavens and smoke cigars. Comets or meteorites are thought to be the glowing butts they throw away. Until recently the Lacandon placed cigars as offering to their gods in the holy area. There is a special ceremony of thanksgiving during their tobacco harvest: Thanksgiving is offered to the deity depicted on a "god pot," who is usually smoking, seated on the hieroglyph for "earth."

The Maya of Yucatán believe that the Balams, the gods of wind and the four directions, are heavy cigar smokers. When the gods light the cigars by pounding heavy rocks together to create a spark, there is thunder and lightning on earth. Tobacco smoking also has an important role in a number of milpa (corn patch) ceremonies.

The Tzeltal Maya of Oxchuc offer thirteen calabashes of tobacco in their celebration of the New Year. The Tzotzil tribe attributes magical power to tobacco and uses it as a defense against evil forces, such as Pucuh, the demon of death. Tobacco in all its forms is considered by most Maya tribes as the most effective agent against the numerous underworld threats, evil spirits, demons, and any form of witchcraft that may cause illness or death. The healing shaman uses tobacco to divine the exact cause of the illness and to find out how to help the patient. Maya travelers protect themselves from evil influences by chewing tobacco and by carrying gourds filled with tobacco. In many of the Mesoamerican areas, tobacco and smoking paraphernalia are placed in graves to accompany the spirit of the dead as a protection during the journey to the underworld and as a gift the dead can offer to the gods.

The main body of data on tobacco use among the Aztec comes from observations and reports by Europeans. Torquemada (1615) wrote that the old earth goddess, Cihuacoatl, female warrior and creator of humankind, had a body composed of tobacco, and she was the incarnation of the plant. Hernando Ruiz de Alarcón (1629) described rites to honor the war god, Huitzilopochtli, to whom an offering of tobacco is as pleasing as one composed of other drugs. Fray Diego Durán (c. 1581) reported that the fire god, Xiuhtecuhtli, received tobacco, incense, and pulque daily, sprinkled onto the fire in his temple. The priests who prepared victims for sacrifice to the goddess Toci (old earth or moon goddess, patron of the day named Jaguar) wore small tobacco gourds on their backs, as did the priests serving Tezcatlipoca, the counterpart to the Maya god K. Both in the Codex Mendoza and in the Codex Florentine several of the figures participating in sacrificial rites are pictured carrying tobacco gourds *(yetecomatl)* and pouches (*yequachtli*) or incense ladles *(tlemaitl)*, the insignia of Aztec priesthood. Tobacco was carried in powder form or shaped into balls and used as a form of incense. When actually smoked it was mixed with other herbs, among them jimsonweed (*Datura stramonium*). During a beautiful ceremony called Dance of Flowers, the vegetation goddess Xochiquetzal invited other gods to sit with her; they smoked together and were entertained by her court.

Among the Mexicans tobacco was a protection against witchcraft or wild animals, but it could also be used to cast spells. Fray Bernardino de Sahagún (1569–1582) described a hunt for snakes, which were enfeebled and stunned when powdered tobacco was hurled at them.

The Totonac of Papantla de Olarte believed that tobacco protected them not only against snakes but also against the dead, and they offered it to the supernatural rulers of the forest. The Cuicatec used wild tobacco in rituals conducted on hilltops or in caves. Among the Mazatec the healer used a paste of powdered tobacco and lime to render pregnant women invulnerable to witchcraft. The Tlaxcalan offered tobacco to their war god Camaxtli. Bowls of tobacco, eagle feathers, and two bloodstained arrows were sent to the enemy camp by the cacique of Michoacán to announce the outbreak of war. The Huichol regarded tobacco as a prized possession of Grandfather Fire. They made small tobacco balls, touched them with feathers, and wrapped them in corn husks. During pilgrimages, these "cigarettes" were carried in small gourds tied to their quivers to symbolize the birth of tobacco. After completion of the pilgrimage, they burned and smoked tobacco in honor of Grandfather Fire.

These ancient and recent reports show that tobacco was used by the Aztec and numerous tribes living between the Maya and North American Indians in the form of incense, as a drink, or by smoking. Smoking of the sacred herb was also practiced by the gods. Tobacco in all its forms and modes of consumption was regarded as a substance of pervading holiness, a gift from the gods, an offering to the supernatural forces of the heavens and the underworld, and a means to communicate with them.

SEE ALSO Tobacco.

BIBLIOGRAPHY

Arents, George. *Tobacco.* 5 vols. Edited by Jerome E. Brooks. New York, 1937–1952.

Durán, Diego. *Los dioses y ritos* and *El calendario* (c. 1581). Translated by Fernando Horcasitas and Doris Heyden as *Book of the Gods and The Ancient Calendar.* Norman, Okla., 1971.

Furst, Peter T. *Hallucinogens and Culture.* San Francisco, 1976.

Furst, Peter T., and Jill L. Furst. *North American Indian Art.* New York, 1982.

Harner, Michael J., ed. *Hallucinogens and Shamanism.* Oxford, 1973.

Robicsek, Francis. *The Smoking Gods.* Norman, Okla., 1978.

Ruiz de Alarcón, Hernando. *Tratado de las supersticiones de naturales de esta Neuve España* (1629). Translated and edited by J. Richard Andrews and Ross Hassig as *Treatise on the Heathen Superstitions That Today Live among the Indians Native to This New Spain, 1629.* Norman, Okla., 1985.

Sahagún, Bernardino de. *Historia general de las cosas de la Nueva España* (compiled 1569–1582; first published 1820). Translated by Arthur J. O. Anderson and Charles E. Dibble as *Florentine Codex: General History of the Things of New Spain,* 13 vols. (Santa Fe, N. Mex., 1950–1982).

Torquemada, Juan de. *De los veinte y un libros rituales y monarquía indiana* (1615). 3d ed. Mexico City, 1975.

Tozzer, A. M. *A Comparative Study of the Mayas and the Lacandones.* New York, 1907.

FRANCIS ROBICSEK (1987)

SNAKES. Because of their shape and their relation to the environment, snakes play an important role in the beliefs of various peoples. Their swiftness and peculiar locomotion, along with the periodical sloughing of their skin, their glistening beauty, and the venom of some species have given them a place apart in the animal world. Their supposedly sinister character and dangerousness cause fear; their enigmatic and ambivalent nature has led human beings to contradictory assessments of them: On the one hand, they are thought of as evil and as a cause of death; on the other, they are believed to embody beneficial and even divine powers. As a result, in some religions they may be both accursed and worshiped. The serpent Apophis was regarded by the ancient Egyptians as the worst enemy of Re, the sun god; yet Re is also protected by the serpent Mehen on his journey through the underworld. In the Bible the scaly reptile can be a symbol both of death (the fall of humanity, *Gn.* 3) and of life (the brazen serpent, *Nm.* 21:6–8). In Indian mythology Kāliya, the prince of serpents, is the embodiment of evil and is overcome by Kṛṣṇa; yet the serpent Śeṣa is companion and couch for Viṣṇu.

THE SERPENT AND ORIGINS. In the mythology of many peoples a serpent is linked to the origin of the world and to creation; it is the primordial material or the primordial being. According to an ancient tradition of the druids (priests among the Celtic peoples) the world originated from an egg that came from the mouth of a serpent. Various of the oldest Egyptian gods were thought of as serpents: as, for example, Atum before he ascended from the primeval ocean, and Amun of Thebes, who was also called Kematef ("he who has fulfilled his time"). In the philosophical speculations of the ancient Near East on creation, serpents and dragons symbolized that which had not yet been made manifest: the still undivided unity that held sway before the creation of the world. Only after the Babylonian god Marduk had overcome the dragonlike monster Tiamat could he form heaven and earth from the latter's body. In the Old Testament one frequently finds the motif of God's struggle against the serpentlike or dragonlike monster of chaos that lives in the water; it is with the victory over Rahab that the mighty waters of the primeval deep are dried up (*Is.* 51:9–10). Indra's victory over the monster Vṛtra, who has neither feet nor hands, is a cosmogonic act by which water and light are liberated from the embrace of the forces of chaos. Also among the Indian sagas of creation is the story of Vāsuki, the world serpent, who is pulled this way and that by the gods and demons (*asuras*) so that Mandara, the world mountain that stands in the ocean of milk, is set in motion like a creative whisk. According to a myth of the Nahuatl (ancient Mexico), in primordial times there existed a formless mass of water in which a great female monster lived; the gods Quetzalcoatl and Tezcatlipoca transformed themselves into serpents, tore the monster into two parts, and from these formed heaven and earth. Ceremonies carried out by American Indian tribes of the Northwest Coast (Kwakiutl, Haida) in the winter, when there is little sunlight, commemorate the primordial time when the sun was imprisoned by the powers of darkness and water, which are symbolized by the serpent Sisiul. The inhabitants of Rossel Island (Louisiade archipelago, Melanesia) used to believe that Wonajö, who had the form of a serpent, created their island and the stars. Among the Ungarinyin (Aborigines of northwestern Australia), the primeval serpent Ungud is linked to the origin of the earth; from its eggs emerged the Wandjina, the ancestors of humans.

The Serpent, Ancestors, and Souls. It is likely that representations of serpents on monoliths from the Neolithic age in France were connected with the veneration of ancestors. A belief in the Mediterranean world is that a snake that lives in the house embodies the soul of the family's first ancestor; among the Romans, the serpent embodied the *paterfamilias.* Thus the Roman poet Vergil (*Aeneid* 5.83ff.) tells how Aeneas visits the tomb of his father, Anchises, and how the sacrificial foods offered to Anchises are accepted by a speckled serpent. Many murals at Pompeii show vipers protectively surrounding an altar as symbols of the *genius loci,* or tutelary deity of the place. In Greece, ancestors such as Kekrops and Erechtheus, who had been transformed into heroes, were venerated in the form of serpents. A serpent and a vessel on ancient Greek tombstones depicts a libation to the dead. The ancient Scythians who lived north of the Black Sea regarded themselves as descendants of Targitaus, a son of the god of heaven and of the half-human, half-snakelike daughter of Dnieper, the river god. In some gnostic writings of the Hellenistic period there is the notion that the first human beings crawled on the ground like snakes. In New Guinea and the Admiralty Islands there is a legend that the first human beings were born of a serpent. Among the Australian Aborigines the moon is regarded as ancestor of the tribe; his totem is a serpent. Many chieftains among the Paiwan (east coast of Taiwan) claim descent from the "hundred-step serpent." The Zulu (South Africa) look upon certain snakes as divinized ancestors who have the power to return to earth in this form. In Southwest Asia a serpent-princess is supposed to have been the founder of particular dynasties.

In Africa, Asia, and Oceania the snake is often associated with the soul. According to the beliefs of the Maasai (East Africa) the souls of chieftains and medicine men turn into snakes after death and live on in this form. The Melanesians identify their ancestors with this reptile, and it is frequently found as a totem, in New Britain and New Ireland, for example. In Chinese fairy tales the dead may reappear as serpents. In Europe, too, one finds the idea that the soul can leave the body in the form of a serpent, not only after death but even in dreams (cf. the saga of Guntram, the Frankish king). Various Slavic peoples believe that the souls of deceased ancestors dwell in snakes, which guard the homes of their human descendants.

Protector of the House and Bestower of Happiness. According to widespread popular belief, snakes should not be killed, because they protect the house and bring good fortune; if they are supplied with milk, they bring health and prosperity. In fairy tales the toad may replace the serpent in this role; both animals are accounted to be of chthonic origin and are numbered among the life-giving powers that contribute to the welfare of those who maintain contact with the earth and its forces. In the Alpine regions, for example, there is a familiar tale of a serpent with a golden crown; as long as the serpent is treated well, it brings happiness to the house and its inhabitants. Finns regard the ring snake as a sacred domestic animal and give it food; they believe that if it should be killed, the death of the family's best cow or even of the stockbreeder himself will follow. In Sweden a white snake is treated as a beneficent protector of the home and cared for with reverent awe. Among the ancient Prussians (a Baltic people), at a certain season of the year, food was set out for serpents living in the house; it was a bad omen if they did not take the food. In India even poisonous snakes were fed as protective spirits; there are areas even in modern times where every house has had a protective serpent (*vāstusarpa*). Among the Suk and Bari of East Africa, who live as nomadic shepherds, the serpent is called "child of God," fed with milk, and looked upon as a bringer of good fortune. Serpents, dragons, and toads are widely considered to be protectors and bearers of treasures and riches. In central Europe there are still place-names (e.g., Drachenfels, "dragon-rock") that allude to local sagas built around the idea of a Lindwurm (from the Old Norse *linn-ormr,* "serpent-dragon") who protects a treasure; Fáfnir, who guarded the treasure of the Nibelungs, was such a dragon. In the cultural orbit of India the *nāgas* are the guardians and givers of the vital forces stored up in springs and wells and of the coral and pearls deposited in the sea. The Buddhist Jātaka tales tell of a Nāga prince who possesses a pearl that grants his every wish. The charitable Chinese dragon that brings good fortune is said to have the head of a horse or a camel and the body of a serpent, while his beard often contains a pearl. In the cults and customs of the Ivory Coast (West Africa) the snake is regarded as a bringer of wealth and fame; in Benin the python in particular is a symbol of happiness and prosperity. In Melanesia the snake plays the part of culture hero; in many sagas he gives human beings the edible plants, fire, and frequently simple tools like the shell knife and stone ax as well.

Wisdom and Power. The serpent knows all mysteries; if a person eats its flesh (or the heart of a dragon, as the Germanic hero Siegfried did), many things are revealed to him; in particular, he can understand the speech of the birds. In Greek myths if a serpent licks the ears of a human being, the human will understand the languages of animals (cf., e.g., the story of Melampus and the sons of Laocoön). The children of Hecuba, queen of Troy, were licked by a serpent and received the gift of prophecy. Snakes were associated with Athena, the Greek goddess of wisdom, and in the Middle Ages with Prudentia, the personification of prudence or practical wisdom. Then there is the well-known saying of Jesus: "Be wise as serpents" (*Mt.* 10:16). The serpent represented on the croziers of Coptic and Byzantine bishops symbolizes the prudence with which the faithful are to be guided. The Aztec god Quetzalcoatl ("feathered serpent") was the founder of the body of priestly wisdom; high priests bore the title "Prince of Serpents." Animals that were superior to human beings in certain abilities became symbols of power: Thus the prophet Isaiah (*Is.* 27:1) describes the great powers threatening the people of God as a leviathan (Babylon?) and a dragon (Egypt?). The representation of an asp known as the uraeus that the pharaohs wore on their foreheads was a symbol of their sovereignty; the uraeus was also worn by Horus, the royal god; the serpent on the brow of Re, the sun god, was said to annihilate all enemies. The horned serpent on the seals of scrolls from ancient Mesopotamia is probably a sign of divine power; it is sacred to the god Ningishzida, the guardian at the door of heaven. Among more primitive peoples, too, the serpent can be a symbol of power and sovereignty; thus it is part of the decoration on the festive garb of the Paiwan chieftains of Taiwan. Iconographically related to the serpent is the dragon—it was the emperor's sign in China, and the Anglo-Saxons painted it on royal banners. The power inherent in the serpent was also thought to be apotropaic; thus the serpent protected temples (Egypt), tombs (classical antiquity), and the thresholds of homes (Sweden).

Representatives of Cosmic Powers. In classical antiquity the serpent Uroboros, which swallows its own tail, is able to embrace the entire universe. Various Indian paintings and sculptures show the dancing god Siva inside a cosmic ring that is clearly recognizable as the body of a serpent with a head at each end. In Germanic mythology the Miðgarðsormr ("world serpent"), with which Þórr (Thor) does battle, is wound like a belt around the world. In some mythologies, the struggle between the storm god and a serpent symbolizes the antagonism between the uranian powers above and the chthonic powers below; this is true, for instance, of the battle between the Hittite storm god and Illuyanka. In the conflict between the two principles of being (between good and evil at the ethical level) the place of the divinity may be taken by an eagle. The enmity between the divine bird and the snake is a theme in the mythology and art of many peoples: It is found on seals from ancient Mesopotamia; in Homer's *Iliad;* in India, where the bird Garuda is known as "the serpent-slayer" (*nāgāntaka*); and in Christian contexts, where the eagle is a symbol of Christ and the serpent, dragon, and basilisk are demonic animals.

The serpent belongs not only to the water and the earth; it can also be associated with the heavens. In Melanesian, Finnic, and Aztec mythologies, snakes represent the lightning; among the Babylonians, in India, and in ancient Mexico the Milky Way was associated with a serpent. The motif of the rainbow as a snake is found in Oceania and tropical Africa; the Dogon of West Africa, for example, think of the rainbow as the serpent of the water god Nommo. Australian tribes regard the rainbow snake, under the name of Yulunggul, as a creative divinity and bestower of culture. Above all, however, the serpent has a lunar significance; Mircea Eliade speaks of it as "an epiphany of the moon" (*Patterns in Comparative Religion,* New York, 1958, p. 165). Like the moon that is gradually diminished and then gradually renews itself, so the serpent sheds and renews its skin and becomes a symbol of death and resurrection. The Ngala tribe (central Kongo) believes that the moon at one time lived on earth as a python. Also to be interpreted in lunar terms is the horned serpent of the pre-Columbian Nazca culture (Peru); the horn is a widespread symbol of power. The double serpent—one with a head at each end—can simultaneously symbolize both moon and sun, as among the Kwakiutl tribe of Indians. In addition to Quetzalcoatl, the serpent of the nocturnal sky, the Aztec believed in a turquoise serpent of the diurnal sky, which was associated with the solar god Huitzilopochtli. The Egyptian uraeus, like the serpent that is equated with Helios in Greek magical papyri, was certainly solar in character.

Death and the Underworld. Serpents frequently play an important role in religious conceptions about the origins of sin. A striking parallel to the story in the *Book of Genesis* of the fall of Adam and Eve is to be found in a myth of the Basari (northern Togo); here the serpent misleads the first human beings into eating certain fruits that until then only God (Unumbotte) had eaten. According to a story of the Dusun (northern Borneo), Kenharingen, the creator, said that those who shed their skins would not die; human beings paid no heed and are therefore snatched away by death, but snakes remain alive forever because they listened to God and shed their skins. After the Babylonian hero Gilgamesh at last found the plant of immortality, he was robbed of it by a serpent while he was bathing, thus forfeiting eternal life to the snake. Persian tradition tells of a plant called *haoma* that bestowed immortality; but Ahura Mazdā's adversary, Ahriman, created a serpent to harm the miraculous plant.

The figure of the serpent also stands for the threatening forces that bring death. In the Finnic concept of the next world, the traveler into the realm of the dead is threatened by an ever-vigilant serpent. The Norse Edda tells of a hall in the kingdom of the dead that has walls made of the bodies of serpents; poison drips from its roof. Etruscan iconography displays various demons of the underworld accompanied by serpents. Bronze Age statuettes found in Crete show a female figure with a serpent in each elevated hand and two serpents rearing up at her breasts; these statuettes are probably connected with the chthonic cult of the goddess of the earth and of the dead. The Erinyes (Furies) of Greek mythology are subterranean goddesses of vengeance; heads covered with writhing snakes, they pursue all evildoers. The Hindu goddess Kālī, the great "devourer" who destroys life, has as her attributes skulls and serpents. In Aztec lore the earth goddess Coatlicue, the "Lady with the Skirt of Serpents," is also the goddess of death; in Mictlen (the realm of the dead) poisonous snakes serve as food. The Egyptians believed the underworld to be inhabited by, among other things, fire-breathing serpents armed with knives; some sayings in the *Book of Going Forth by Day* are meant as protection against them (7.33–35). In Christianity the serpent is often associated with sin, death, and the Prince of Darkness who rules over the damned.

Life and Immortality. The serpent has possession of the plant of immortal life (*Epic of Gilgamesh*); in various fairy tales and in some Greek sagas (Glaucus, Tylon) snakes restore the dead to life by means of a plant known only to them. In Melanesian and South American traditions the snake gives human beings the knowledge of edible plants; in ancient Egypt, Renenutet, "mistress of the fertile land" (the goddess of agriculture), was worshiped in the form of a serpent. The serpent is closely associated with the fruit of life and the water of life; in Southwest Asia and in China it is considered to be the giver of rain. Among the Hopi Indians (Arizona) a feast of serpents is celebrated in August in order to obtain rain; during the dancing at this celebration the participants carry live rattlesnakes between their teeth. The (East) Indian *nāgas* are givers of fertility; sacrifices associated with the *nāgakal* (a cobra idol of stone) erected in Indian villages are supplications for the birth of children. Snakes have phallic significance in the most varied of cultures: classical antiquity, the ancient Near East, India, and Melanesia; some American Indian cultures employ the double symbol of the serpent (phallus) and the rhombus (vulva); according to an association made in ancient Mexico (Codex Borgia) the penis is controlled by a serpent-demon. The snake thrown into a cave in the worship of the Greek goddess Demeter also had a phallic significance: The snake was expected to promote the powers of growth present in the earth. Many peoples have believed that the snake obtained long life and even immortality by shedding its skin; as a result the serpent became an attribute of Shadrapa (ancient Syria) and Asklepios (Greece), who were gods of healing; the latter was taken over by the Romans as Aesculapius, and the staff of Aesculapius with snakes wound around it is still the symbol of the medical profession (the caduceus). In the Egyptian *Book of Going Forth by Day* transformation into a serpent will give new life to the dead person (chap. 87). The snake that in the mysteries of the Thracian-Phrygian god Sabazios was drawn across the bosom of the initiate, gave hope for the attainment of immortality. The bronze serpent that Moses displayed on a standard became a prefiguration of the Savior's death on the cross and of redemption (*Jn.* 3:14f.).

The Demonic and the Divine. Because of the ambivalence with which they are regarded, serpents may be associated either with devils or with gods. On cylinder seals from ancient Mesopotamia multiheaded serpents embody the forces hostile to the gods. Even as a small child, Apollo, the Greek god of light, killed the python of Delphi, which was persecuting his mother, Leto. In a similar manner the apocalyptic serpent threatens the celestial virgin (*Rv.* 12:1–5). Among the more generally known demonic serpents are Apophis (Egypt), the Miðgarðsormr (Germany), Kulshedra (Albania), and the numerous *kaia* (Melanesia).

In the belief of the ancient Greeks the Agathos Daimon, frequently thought of as a winged serpent, played the role of a good spirit. As bringer of salvation and giver of life the serpent became a divine animal; it was associated with Anat, the goddess of war venerated at Ugarit (modern-day Shamra, Syria), and, in the form of a dragon, with Marduk, the principal Babylonian god. The figure depicted by worshipers of Mithra as having the head of a wolf and a body entwined by serpents is usually interpreted as representing Aion, the god of time. The cobra was sacred to Uto, the regional goddess of Lower Egypt. The Hindu snake goddess Manasa is invoked even today against snakebite. One of the terrifying divinities of Buddhism is Bhutadamara, who combats demons: His adornment consists of eight serpents. In the Kalderash gypsy tribe (France) there are still traces of a cult of serpents that reaches back to ancient India; thus in the spring the tribe celebrates the day of the snake or divine serpent. An explicit worship of snakes was practiced by the Lombards (sixth to eighth centuries in Italy) and by the Lithuanians; but in this context mention must be made of various sects of gnostics in late antiquity generally grouped together under the name of Ophites: They adored the godhead in the form of a serpent. The cult of snakes indigenous to West Africa (especially Dahomey) came to America with the slaves and acquired a new form in the magical and religious Voodoo of Haiti.

See Also Dragons.

Bibliography

Important older presentations of the religious significance of serpents were for the most part devoted to particular cultures. See, for example, Erich Küster's *Die Schlange in der griechischen Kunst und Religion* (Giessen, 1933), Jean Philippe Vogel's *Indian Serpent Lore or the Nagas in Hindu Legend and Art* (London, 1926), Gottfried Wilhelm Locher's *The Serpent in Kwakiutl Religion: A Study in Primitive Culture* (Leiden, 1932), and Hans Ritter's *Die Schlange in der Religion der Melanesier* (Basel, 1945). Two more recent publications treating the African world may be mentioned: John Snook's *African Snake Stories* (New York, 1973) and Alfred Hauenstein's "Le serpent dans les rites, cultes et coutumes de certaines ethnies de Côte d'Ivoire," *Anthropos* 73 (1978): 525–560. *The Rainbow Serpent: A Chromatic Piece,* edited by Ira R. Buchler and Kenneth Maddock (The Hague, 1978), treats Australian material before bringing in other mythologies. In *Serpent Symbolism in the Old Testament: A Linguistic, Archaeological, and Literary Study* (Haddonfield, N.J., 1974), Karen Randolph Joines discusses biblical treatments of the theme and their influence on Christianity. C. F. Oldham supplies good basic material on the astral significance of the serpent in *The Sun and the Serpent: A Contribution to the History of Serpent-Worship* (London, 1905), but some interpretations need correcting. The importance of the serpent in the Greek mystery cults and their influence on the Christian world is the subject of Hans Leisegang's "Das Mysterium der Schlange," *Eranos-Jahrbuch* 7 (1939): 151–250. Two comprehensive treatments are Balaji Mundkur's *The Cult of the Serpent: An Interdisciplinary Survey of Its Manifestations and Origins* (Albany, N. Y., 1983) and my *Adler und Schlange: Tiersymbolik im Glauben und Weltbild der Völker* (Tübingen, 1983).

New Sources

Loibl, Elisabeth. *Deuses animais.* São Paulo, 1984.

Martinek, Manuela. *Wie die Schlange zum Teufel wurde: die Symbolik in der Paradiesgeschichte von der hebräischen Bibel bis zum Koran.* Wiesbaden, 1996.

Wilson, Leslie S. *The Serpent Symbol in the Ancient Near East: Nahash and Asherah: Death, Life, and Healing.* Lanham, Md., 2001.

MANFRED LURKER (1987)
Translated from German by Matthew J. O'Connell
Revised Bibliography

SNORRI STURLUSON (1179–1241) is Iceland's greatest historian. His writings include the *Prose Edda* and the *Heimskringla*, which along with the *Poetic Edda* are the major primary sources for Germanic mythology and religion. Snorri was sent at a young age to a settlement in southern Iceland called Oddi to be fostered by Jón Loptsson, grandson of Sæmund Sigfússon and of Magnus III of Norway. Jón Loptsson was the most powerful chieftain in Iceland at the time, and his farm was a center of learning without equal. Snorri received the best education possible; his power and stature increased, and he was elected law speaker in 1215. After one term, ending in 1218, he journeyed to Norway to visit its rulers, the regent Earl Skúli and the young King Hákon. For several years Snorri traveled widely throughout Norway and Sweden. He thwarted a scheme to force Iceland to submit to Norwegian rule and left Norway in great honor, promising to work for Norway's cause in Iceland. Snorri was re-elected law speaker for three terms (1222–1232), and it was during this period that he found the time to produce his greatest writings. Ever a ruthless and opportunistic leader, Snorri was involved in many disputes, even with his own relatives, and in 1241 he was murdered by one of his enemies.

Upon his return from Norway, Snorri composed the *Háttatál* (List of Verse Forms), a poem in praise of Earl Skúli and King Hákon that became the final section of a three-part handbook for skaldic poets now known as the *Prose Edda.* The *Háttatál* consisted of three poems in 102 stanzas demonstrating possible verse forms for Old Norse skaldic poetry. By itself it would have been difficult for Snorri's contemporaries to understand, despite its explanatory prose commentary, for there were many complicated metaphors with allusions to long-forgotten mythological material. Snorri therefore went on to write a second part (the *Skáldskaparmál*) on poetic diction that supplied the rules for the formation of kennings (compound metaphors) and *heiti* (poetical nouns). Many of the examples of kennings contain mythological information not found elsewhere. Moreover, there is an extensive introduction (the *Bragarœður*), according to which the god Ægir, during a visit to Valhǫll, entertained his table companion Bragi with old tales of the gods, including important myths, such as the theft of Iðun's apples, the adventures of Þjazi, and the story of how Óðinn (Odin) obtained the poetic mead.

Since much of this mythological material, too, would have been unfamiliar to the readers of his time (who, like Snorri, were Christians in a country that two centuries earlier had accepted the Christian faith), he prefaced it with an introduction to Norse mythology, the *Gylfaginning* (The deluding of Gylfi). In this section he presents Gylfi, a fictional Swedish king who, disguised as an old wanderer, travels to Ásgarðr to find out about the ancient pagan gods and meets Óðinn, also in disguise, who answers his questions. Óðinn describes the Norse mythological world from its beginning to its end in the Ragnarǫk (the destruction of the cosmos and its rebirth), noting important facts about the various gods, Valhǫll, Yggdrasill (the cosmic tree), and more. It was presumably Snorri who also wrote a prologue with a euhemeristic derivation of the Norse gods as kings descended from King Priam of Troy. As sources, Snorri used Eddic and skaldic poetry and oral tradition.

Snorri then proceeded to compose the *Heimskringla* (Orb of the world), his monumental history of the Norwegian kings from their mythical origins through Magnús V Erlingsson (r. 1162–1184). The first part, the *Ynglingasaga,* traces the origins of the kings back to their mythical ancestor Yngvifreyr, and before him to Njǫrðr and ultimately Óðinn. The purpose of the *Ynglingasaga* was to provide a meaningful connection between the traditional and Christian periods and to provide the Norwegian kings with an illustrious ancestry that confirmed their sacred right and ability to govern. As a source on Norse mythology, the *Ynglingasaga* is the most important of the *Heimskringla* sagas, though others contain mythological material as well.

SEE ALSO Eddas; Loki; Óðinn; Sagas; Saxo Grammaticus.

BIBLIOGRAPHY

Snorri's *Prose Edda* is available in full in *The Prose Edda of Snorri Sturluson: Tales from the Norse Mythology* (Berkeley, Calif., 1992), translated by Jean I. Young. See also *Edda: Prolog of Gylfaginning* (Oxford, U.K., 1982), edited by Anthony Faulkes; *Edda: Skáldskaparmál* (2 vols., London, 1988), edited by Anthony Faulkes; *Edda: Háttartál* (Oxford, U.K., 1991), edited by Anthony Faulkes; and Snorri Sturluson, *Edda* (London, 1987), translated by Anthony Faulkes. *Heimskringla: History of the Kings of Norway* (Austin, Tex., 1964), by Snorri Sturluson, translated with introduction and notes by Lee M. Hollander, is an excellent English translation of Snorri's work on Norwegian kings. Secondary literature includes Hans Fix, ed. *Snorri Sturluson: Beiträge zu Werk und Rezeption* (Berlin, 1998); Stefanie von Schnurbein "The Function of Loki in Snorri Sturluson's *Edda,*" *History of Religions* 40 (November 2000), 109–124; John Lindow, "Loki and Skaði," in *Snorrastefna* (Reykjavík, 1990), edited by Úlfar Bragason; Thomas A. DuBois, *Nordic Religions in the Viking Age* (Philadelphia, 1999); and Frederic Amory, review of *Skáldskaparmál: Snorri Sturluson's Ars Poetica and Medieval Theories of Language,* by Margaret Clunies Ross, *Scandinavian Studies* 62 (Summer, 1990), 331–339. In addition, Marlene Ciklamini has published two useful works on Snorri: *Snorri Sturluson* (Boston, 1978), and "Ynglinga Saga: Its Function and Its Appeal," *Mediaeval Scandinavia* 8 (1975): 86–99.

JOHN WEINSTOCK (1987 AND 2005)

SNOUCK HURGRONJE, CHRISTIAAN (1857–1936), was a Dutch Islamicist and colonial adviser. At the University of Leiden, Christiaan Snouck Hurgronje studied theology and initially intended to become a minister. His early interest in literary and historical criticism of the Bible, a field then still regarded as suspect by some conservative Christians, contributed to his decision in 1878 to renounce the ministry and pursue a scholarly career in Arabic and Islamic studies. In 1880 he defended a doctoral thesis on the origins of the traditional pilgrimage to Mecca. In August 1884 he traveled to Jidda, where he was invited by Meccan religious scholars and notables to visit Mecca. Although he dressed as a Muslim and adopted a Muslim name, ʿAbd al-Ghaffār, Snouck Hurgronje did not conceal his identity as a non-Muslim from his hosts; he remained in Mecca from February to August 1884. In 1889 he published, with photographs, a detailed ethnographic account of contemporary Meccan social and intellectual life, translated as *Mecca in the Latter Part of the Nineteenth Century* (1931). A chapter of this work is devoted to Mecca's Javanese colony.

Snouck Hurgronje's interests as a historian of religions were strongly informed by ethnography. For Snouck Hurgronje, both historical and contemporary religious beliefs and movements had to be understood in terms of the social and political contexts in which they occurred. After his return to Europe from Mecca, he continued to lecture and write on general themes in Islam and Islamic jurisprudence but he became increasingly interested in the Dutch East Indies (present-day Indonesia). In 1889 he was sent to Batavia (present-day Djakarta), where he served as a colonial adviser while remaining an ethnographer and a religious scholar. In 1892 he was posted at Aceh, a region of Sumatra in frequent rebellion against Dutch rule since 1873. Living like a Muslim (though again not concealing his European identity) and reestablishing ties with Acehnese he had first met in Mecca, his comprehensive reporting on Islamic political and religious movements began to shape colonial policy. He recommended that the government co-opt the secular chieftains, while suppressing the Islamic leaders who were the instigators of the rebellion. His advice was informed by his view of the Islamic leadership as alien agitators intent upon imposing norms and values contrary to local customs. Snouck Hurgronje continued his role as Islamicist and colonial adviser to the Dutch government from his return to Leiden in 1906 until his retirement in 1927.

SEE ALSO Acehnese Religion.

BIBLIOGRAPHY

Snouck Hurgronje's ethnography, *The Acehnese,* 2 vols., translated by A. W. S. O'Sullivan (Leiden, 1906), remains a classic. For an analysis of his scholarship on Islam, see Jacques Waardenburg's *L'Islam dans le miroir de l'occident* (The Hague, 1970), which contains an extensive bibliography. James T. Siegal's *The Rope of God* (Berkeley, Calif., 1969) contains an extensive discussion of Snouck Hurgronje's views on Islam and Acehnese society.

New Sources

Snouk Hurgronje, C., and P. Sj. Van Koningsveld. *Minor German Correspondences of C. Snouck Hurgronje: From Libraries in France, Germany, Sweden, and the Netherlands.* Leiden, 1987.

DALE F. EICKELMAN (1987)
Revised Bibliography

SOCIALLY ENGAGED BUDDHISM SEE ENGAGED BUDDHISM

SOCIETY AND RELIGION [FIRST EDITION]. Relations between religion and society are fundamental to the nature of religion and, according to long-standing intellectual claims, are intrinsic to the nature of society. Indeed, societies are characterized by the values they embody, the individual and collective motivations they encourage, the incentives they inspire and sanction, and the ideals by which belief, attitude, and behavior are established and secured. Accordingly, religion can hardly be identified or defined except in terms of human social relations. Religion offers prescriptions for social order, individual behavior, and collective action. Thus, all religious traditions give expression to the relationship between what are acknowledged and understood to be the most compelling objectives of human life and day-to-day conduct. To a remarkable extent, the religions of the world can be distinguished from each other on the basis of their selective interpretations of this fundamental relationship and in terms of the attitudes toward society that they prescribe and honor. And yet, while the religious traditions of the world can be distinguished from each other on these grounds, they also share some common convictions about this fundamental relationship and what it entails.

RELATIONS BETWEEN SOCIETY AND VARIOUS RELIGIOUS TRADITIONS. All religious traditions seek a measure of congruence between the ideals they espouse and the societal ordering of life in which such ideals are meant to be expressed. As a consequence, a society is known by its collective aspirations—aspirations to which religion attributes sanction. Similarly, all religious traditions have mechanisms to inspire their adherents toward objectives that their societies have not yet attained. The relationship between these ideals and the collective behavior that religion sanctions is always subject to correction and modification, given the more comprehensive sense of the world's well-being to which the teaching of the world's religions attest. All religious traditions provide some means by which individuals and communities can establish (or reestablish) their lives on a basis that is distinct from the social and cultural status quo. That is, all religious traditions sanction forms of withdrawal from the world or release from the social status quo. In so doing, they certify that religious ideals and the day-to-day ordering of common life are not fully congruent, but rather are characterized by conflict and tension. The effective resolution or mediation of such conflicts requires deliberate spiritual and practical strategies.

Given the complex nature of their relationship to society, religious traditions often find it useful to invoke a distinction between sacred and secular, and to apply this distinction in establishing the status of society. While there is an inviolable tendency within religious consciousness to affirm that all of life is sacred, there is also the recognition that what is sacred is determined in relation to what is reckoned to be profane. Sacred and secular are dichotomous terms that can only be defined in relationship to each other. Thus, the intrinsic dynamism of each religious tradition issues from its comprehension of how all can be sacred when sacred is known and perceived only in contrast to the profane. The teachings of the religious traditions are drawn from knowledge and experience of how individual and collective human life ought to be ordered, and how human aspirations are to be accorded privilege, in light of the complexities of this fundamental relationship between the sacred and the profane. Consequently, the religious traditions offer tested formulas by which the boundaries and contours of the sacred can be discerned in relation to the boundaries and contours of the profane. But all of them seek to affirm that life itself is sacred, and that its societal forms and expressions can and must be infused by such perceptions and convictions.

Confucianism. Confucius (552?–479 BCE) traveled from state to state throughout China in order to awaken the social responsibility of the populace and to generate social and political reforms. Indeed, the teachings of Confucius are designed to create the moral context sufficient to encourage a harmonious family life, a state that is governed equitably, and a world with sufficient spiritual resourcefulness to allow its inhabitants to live in peace. In Confucius's eyes, individual character and a just social and political order are both consequences of moral cultivation. His emphasis upon the cultivation of individual moral character as well as a harmonious social order prompted his followers to point his teachings in two directions. The first, represented by the *Great Learning* (*Daxue*), from the fifth century BCE, emphasized the social implications of Confucian teaching. The second, represented by the *Doctrine of the Mean* (*Zhong yong*), attributed to Zisi (483–402 BCE), Confucius's grandson, lays stress on the harmonization of emotion, temperament, and intelligence, as the means of achieving full realization of one's individual nature. The *Doctrine of the Mean* affirms that it is through the realization of individual natures that more comprehensive forms of social and political harmony can occur. Because Confucian teaching carried this twofold capacity, to provide individual moral incentive while prescribing the bases for harmonious social and political order, it became the prevailing school of thought in China, and, in 136 BCE, was proclaimed official state doctrine. Through the centuries, Confucianism has exercised a fundamental formative role throughout Chinese social and cultural life, and particularly in the spheres of government, jurisprudence, education, music, and the ritual life of the people. While both Daoism and Buddhism have had enormous impact on Chinese religion and philosophy, the fundamental cohesiveness of traditional Chinese society can be attributed to the capacity of Confucian teaching to identify compatibilities between individual moral imperatives and the dictates of social order.

Islam. The Islamic religion offers a clear example of societal order that is prescribed by religious doctrine. Indeed, within regions where Islam dominates, it is just as appropriate to refer to Islamic states as to Islamic religion. The Islamic ideal is meant to be developed into community-states; the individual's relationship with God is interdependent with relationships among human beings in social settings. Thus, there are Islamic peoples, a Muslim empire, and indeed an Islamic civilization, all of which originated from the insights and teachings of the prophet Muḥammad in Arabia in the seventh century CE. Understanding that a Muslim is identified as one who "surrenders" to the will of God and who confesses "There is no god but God and Muḥammad is his prophet" establishes a strong basis for social and political cohesiveness. Islamic doctrine and Islamic law are conceived as aspects of the same will. The characteristic Islamic ethos blends the spiritual with the temporal, the public with the private, and individual religious aspiration with the affairs of the state. Because there can be no fundamental distinction between the religious and temporal spheres of life, Muslims understand Islamic states to have come into being in accordance with the divine will. Thus, from the beginning, the Muslim world has been populated by theocratic states. Indeed, much of the tension that exists within that world today derives from the power of modern educational and social reform and of increasing political democratization to upset the religious and social harmony that was explicit in traditional Islamic law.

Shintō. The indigenous culture and ethos of Japan, Shintō offers an example of interdependency between spiritual and temporal elements that are virtually impossible to distinguish. Having come to expression through the ancient folk tales, myths, and rites of the Japanese people, Shintō developed in close correspondence to the emerging and ongoing Japanese collective identity. Thus, Shintō came to describe those beliefs and practices that were distinctively and inherently Japanese. It has no single founder, no authorized sacred scripture, and no set of prescribed doctrines. The myths to which it lays claim are in many respects similar to those that have been found among the peoples of Southeast Asia. Yet, the attitude to life that Shintō espouses is distinctively Japanese, and its influences are to be felt in myriad ways throughout Japanese social and cultural life. In its encounter with religious and cultural traditions whose origins lie elsewhere—Confucianism, Daoism, and Buddhism, in particular—Shintō has displayed both its adaptive and resistive sides. Its presence among the people always has been associated with respect for ancestors that through the centuries has translated into respect for the emperor and the imperial line. This connotes a devotion to the power (*kami*) from which life flows, by which human conduct must be guided, and by means of which the people are united.

Hinduism. The religion (as well as civilization) of India presents a more complicated picture. Within Hindu civilization, religion functions much less in correspondence with national objectives, and much more as a way of life or mode of consciousness. The Hindu perception that human life consists of an endless series of births and rebirths, together with Hindu belief in *karman*—namely, that previous acts are factors that determine present and future circumstances—leads to a stratification of social classes as well as to a hierarchical ordering of religious values. Individuals are enjoined to perform the laws and duties (*dharma*) that are expected and required of the class, or caste, to which he or she belongs. Indeed, the distinctions between classes correspond to the fundamentally distinguishable estates of human beings. *Brahmāṇas* (brahmans), judged to be in the preeminent positions, are understood to be the guardians of the divine power. *Kṣatriyas*, the nobility, exist to protect the people. *Vaiśyas*, members of the third estate, are obliged to do the necessary work, that is, to tend farmland, to conduct trade, to care for cattle, and so on. The fourth estate, that of the *śūdras*, a kind of servant class, is supposed "to serve meekly." Hindu teaching justifies social stratification insofar as it understands such stratification to be sanctioned by cosmic action. The social system is a necessary complement to the power of *karman*, and it is through *karman* that individuals can hope for an eventual release from the perpetual cycle of birth and rebirth. Thus, in Hindu understanding, there is a strong duality between spirit and matter. And while the existing social matrix is acknowledged and upheld, it sustains conditions that are deplorable. But such interpretation occurs within perceptions and convictions that affirm the world to be a single reality, and thus affirm religion and society to be complementary.

Buddhism. Originating from a keen perception of the pervasiveness of suffering and spiritual ignorance in human life, Buddhism gives expression to the relationship between religion and society via the conviction that worldly life cannot ensure lasting or final happiness. Its founder, Siddhārtha Gautama (c. 563?–483? BCE), counseled his hearers and followers to resist a life of indulgence in sensual pleasure as well as a life of perpetual self-mortification. The "middle path" between these two extremes was designed to encourage true knowledge, tranquility, and enlightenment, pursued via a process that, as in Hinduism, works through a succession of lives toward an ultimate goal, *nirvāṇa*. This final goal is conceived as a transcendent state in which the individual is free from craving and sorrow and over which suffering has no effective control.

The deliberate character of spiritual formation, under Buddhism's auspices, has required a strong monastic movement. The purpose of monastic life is to provide the context and spiritual nurture so that aspirants, guided by the dictates of the famous Eightfold Path, might progress toward *nirvāṇa*. Within the monastic order (*saṃgha*), life was to be lived simply; however, extreme ascetic practices were not condoned. Indeed, Buddhism can be described as a monastic religion, to be supported as well as followed by the laity. Thus, Buddhism has come to influence, but not to define, the societies within which it has become prevalent. In India, China, Japan, Tibet, Burma, Sri Lanka, and indeed, throughout Southeast and Southwest Asia, and even within the United States, it has been pliable and adaptive. It teaches a way of life that is exemplified by the monks, who are regarded as moral leaders, and is both respected and practiced by the laity. Buddhism specifically teaches that the response to suffering humanity should be active compassion, and the direct result of this has been the formation of social service ministries (i.e., hospitals, schools, orphanages, and other benevolent institutions). Compassion also dictates such individual virtues as generosity, morality, patience, vigor, concentration in meditation, and wisdom. But these virtues belong to a fundamental emphasis upon the primacy of individual consciousness; this is understood in stricter Theravāda Buddhism as communion with the Buddha and in Mahāyāna Buddhism as the vow of the human spirit to become a Buddha.

Daoism. Rooted in a response to the transition from feudalism toward a new social order in sixth-century BCE China, Daoism has had a formative influence on Chinese culture in all of its aspects. Associated with Lao-tzu, the reputed author of the *Dao de jing*, Daoism teaches a practical way of life (the natural way) as well as an attitude that enables its adherents to dispose themselves peacefully in the presence of the unity of the universe. It counsels harmony, simplicity, and peacefulness, which are expressed in artistic and cultural forms, such as landscape painting, tea drinking, and so on. Although it was never raised to official governmental status, as was Shintō in Japan, it has been the source of a collective attitude toward life in traditional Chinese society and was influential up to 1949, when the Communist government came to power.

Judaism. Within Judaism, complexities in the basic relationship of religion to society are mediated in a variety of ways. The Hebrew scriptures attest, for example, that creation (the world that was made by the one true God) is good and is intended for enjoyment. At the same time, the goodness and sanctity of life are interpreted in light of strong and abiding convictions regarding the special status and character of a people whose way of life is ordered according to precise and specific covenantal sanctions. In Jewish understanding, the covenant promise, "If you hear my words and obey my commands, I will be your god and you shall be my people" (*Ex.* 19:5), is not given to everyone. Thus, while Judaism affirms the propriety of all of life, it is particularly attentive to what has been properly consecrated and sanctified. Understanding the relation between God and his people to be delineated through the convenant, Judaism also places great emphasis upon the conditions—through laws and ritual practices—by which the covenant is honored and protected. The primacy of the covenant insures that those who are bound to a sovereign deity according to its dictates possess a collective identity. It also implies that this identity will distinguish them from all other peoples who are not so bound. Thus, the relationship between religion and society, in Jewish thought and understanding, must be depicted from two standpoints, that is, from outside and from within the covenantal relationship. In the more comprehensive sense, God established the pattern for harmonious existence between himself and all peoples when the world was created. And in establishing the covenant, God chose a people through which the redemption of that same world was to be carried out. From either vantage point, Judaism understands the world, and thus society, to be the environment in which divine activity occurs. From both vantage points, salvation involves the realization of the creator's purpose for his creation. Thus, Judaism affirms a basic compatibility between religious ideals and social reality, a compatibility that through the centuries has been invested in the idea of the nation of Israel, a nation of both religious and political circumscription.

Christianity. Beginning as a movement within Judaism, Christianity has inherited its predecessor's emphasis upon the primacy of the covenant as well as its singularly monotheistic understanding of the nature of deity. However, informed by the life of Jesus Christ and giving a triune formulation to its belief in the one true God, Christianity, even in its initial stages of development, made appeals not only to Jews but to all inhabitants of the Greco-Roman world. As a consequence, adherence to the covenant was reinterpreted in terms more spiritual and less juridical than otherwise prevails in Judaism.

Indeed, the Christian revision of the understanding of the covenant required the formulation of a new covenant, which would be the basis of a revised collective identity. This new covenant made it possible to conceive of Christianity in universal terms and to identify followers of Jesus Christ. Thus, basic convictions about the goodness of the created order as well as the need for redemption—convictions Christianity shares with Judaism—have to be applied and understood contextually. It is possible to apply such convictions to mean that there should be a Christian state and to cite the same convictions as providing a rationale for conceiving of Christians as "the salt of the earth," whose task it is to bring and/or discover the presence of God wherever they find themselves. And when these basic religious convictions are combined with insights derived in large part from Greek and Hellenistic influence, it is also possible to approach society both in transcendent and ideal terms, as in the Christian understanding of the kingdom of God.

Thus, it can be demonstrated that particular prescriptions regarding the relationships between religion and society are inherent in the basic and formative dispositions by which each of the religious traditions is motivated. Indeed, in every instance, one can anticipate the attitude that a religion will take toward society by knowing how that religion portrays the human condition, what value it places on human community, and how it delineates what is expected of the individual in light of its more comprehensive understanding of the cosmic order.

The Study of Society and Religion. Though the relationship between religion and society did not become an object of concentrated study in the West until the nineteenth century, the subject has formed the basis for perennial intellectual exposition from the time that questions arose concerning the ingredients of an ideal society, as, for example, in Plato's *Republic*. The way in which ethical and moral ideals contribute to effective social and community life are also explored in the writings of Aristotle (particularly in his *Nicomachean Ethics*), Epictetus, Marcus Aurelius, and other Epicureans and Stoics. The subject also appears in medieval Christian literature, wherein Greek contentions and categories of thought are utilized to lend expression to biblical affirmations. Syntheses were formed through a combination of Greek formulations of the relationships of permanence to change and of being to becoming with the Judeo-Christian understanding of the relationships between the creator and creation. Plato's question in *Timaeus*, "What is that which always is and has no becoming, and what is that which is always becoming and never is?" was answered in classical Christian theology in terms that described the relation between God and the world. Under such formulas, the world—and, by extension, society—was accorded a secondary, subordinate, and derivative reality in contrast to God, the seat of all permanence, or of "that which always is and has no becoming." And the theological task for the medieval writers, under dictates of the relationship between sacred and profane, was to affirm the intrinsic goodness and propriety of the subordinate reality in full recognition of the fact that its status could only be conceived in contrast to what was acknowledged to be primary.

The normative exposition of this relationship was offered by Augustine (354–430), in his *City of God*, in which the temporal order was conceived in the likeness of the eternal order and yet accorded an intrinsic positive status. Whereas Augustine utilized Platonic philosophical categories to spell out these interdependencies, Thomas Aquinas (1225–1274) employed an Aristotelian mode to affirm compatibilities between heavenly and earthly realms as well as between ecclesiastical and civil orders. At the time of the Protestant Reformation, Martin Luther (1483–1546) developed a doctrine of "two kingdoms," as, for example, in his *Christian Liberty*, so that both temporary and permanent obligations and services could be distinguished and rightly ordered. And there are many examples within Christian theological literature of attempts to create earthly or civil societies in close approximation to the heavenly or permanent ideal. John Calvin (1509–1564), the author of *Institutes of the*

Christian Religion, wished this for his city of Geneva. The Cambridge Platform of 1648 outlines the plan of the Massachusetts Bay Puritans to order their community life on biblical principles, supported by both divine and natural law. All of these formulations conceived of the relationship of religion to society to be modeled according to the interdependencies between the ideal and the actual and sought to mediate the distance between such states by exploring the relationships between theory and practice.

Comte and Saint-Simon. The subject became an object of analytical (as distinct from theological) scholarly interest in the nineteenth century, with the birth of the science of sociology. Auguste Comte (1798–1857), the acknowledged founder of sociology, built upon the influence of Claude-Henri de Rouvroy, Comte de Saint-Simon (1760–1825) in developing an evolutionary conception of the growth of intellectual consciousness. In Saint-Simon's view, human sensitivity had already passed through the religious stages of polytheism and monotheism, as well as through the philosophical stage of metaphysics, and had just embarked upon the era of positive science. Having come to this new stage, it was man's task to identify the conditions necessary to create an effective rapprochement between intellectuals and the society as a whole. Comte, sharing Saint-Simon's aspiration to improve social and political conditions, also approached theology as an antecedent and provisional mode of human intelligence that had been superseded by both philosophy and science. Each held that the theological mode identifies humankind's first way of coming to terms with experience. But as human knowledge became more exact and progressively more certain, all previous stages or forms of understanding became obsolete.

Lévy-Bruhl and Durkheim. Comte's views were highly respected within nineteenth and early twentieth-century French thought, specifically by Lucien Lévy-Bruhl (1857–1939) and Émile Durkheim (1858–1917). Lévy-Bruhl, sharing the widespread enthusiasm for "the law of three stages," worked particularly to distinguish the mental reasoning processes of archaic (first stage) and more civilized (third stage) human beings. In his *How Natives Think* (1910) and *Primitive Mentality* (1922), which he described as "one and the same work in two volumes," he concentrated on the distinctive mental habits of primitive (or rudimentary) peoples in order to characterize religious consciousness. He contended that the mode of intelligence that is exercised among archaic human beings can be described as being mystical, prelogical, and pervaded by a sense of "affectational participation." To call it mystical is to recognize that it is "at all times oriented to occult forces." To call it prelogical is to describe it as being "indifferent to the laws of contradiction." "Affectational participation" is the phrase Lévy-Bruhl used to describe the way in which, in rudimentary apprehension, the data of experience tend to flow together and associate with each other in complex ways. His intention was to isolate fundamental differences between human beings of contemporary scientific disposition and those of a previous religious stage of intellectual development by comparing and contrasting the mental habits that lend form to knowledge in the two instances.

It is clear, however, that the same analytical strategy can be employed for alternative purposes. Instead of simply focusing on the coordinated mental habits of so-called rudimentary peoples for purposes of sketching a possible primitive world of thought and experience, the scholar can decipher and describe the prevailing mental habits ("collective representations") wherever they occur. This, in brief, describes the analytical intentions of Durkheim, whose work illustrates a methodological shift from evolutionary to organic conceptions of the relationships between religion and society. Indeed, it was Durkheim who first defined religion as "something eminently social." His *The Elementary Forms of the Religious Life* (1912) stands as a landmark in the development of both sociological theory and the academic study of religion. The study registers in both contexts because Durkheim's intention to identify "the religious nature of man" by seeking to explain "the most primitive and simple religion" was a part of his preoccupation with man's relation to society. He contended that "religious representations are collective representations." That is, they give expression to the manner in which intellectual life is formed and constituted. To be sure, knowledge is shaped by the intellect, which bestows order, offers pattern, lends arrangement, and seeks coherence. And yet order, pattern, arrangement, and coherence do not derive from an isolated intellect, but from intellects in social association. The collective ideal is always socially conceived and formulated. Thus religion becomes associated with the collective social vision, apart from which the social context cannot be understood.

Weber. It was left to Max Weber (1864–1920) to break with the evolutionist model, and to place an analysis of the interdependencies between religion and society within a cross-cultural framework. Weber's primary intention was to understand how cultures are formed. Noting the self-evident compatibilities between Protestant-religious and capitalist-economic incentives in those nations and societies that have been influenced by the Reformation, Weber worked to identify the interrelationships between motivations and intentions, on the one hand, and acts and events, on the other, within whatever society came under his analytical scrutiny. He observed that religious ideas possess independent causal significance in all systems of social action or processes of social change. The interdependence of Protestant theology (motive) and capitalist economics (action) is Weber's chief example of the dynamics of social integration. But the same principles will apply to the place, status, and function of all religious traditions within their respective sociocultural environments. In general terms, religion, standing as ideology and as conceptual system, supplies motivation within a society. In more specific terms, the prevailing conception of deity within a society influences individual and collective actions as well as the significance that is attributed to social relationships. For example, conception of deity in Hindu religion both affects and is in keeping with the socioeconomic situation of Indian culture. So, too, the way in which the cosmos is depicted in Hindu scriptures bears causal relevance to the socioeconomic theory of those peoples whose life has been influenced by Hindu religious principles. Similarly, there is sanction within the Judeo-Christian doctrine of creation to make the world acceptable; this doctrine is implicit in the economic theory sanctioned in Judeo-Christian theology. In all of these instances, religion can be seen to lend constitutionality to the social order.

Weber's influence. The method Weber devised was intended to be used on a cross-cultural basis and, where possible, comparatively. He himself was eager to test his methods and theories on as many traditions as he had time and energy to study. Weber left the way clear for others to inquire into the social characteristics of individual religions, whether or not they wished to insert their findings into comparative cultural contexts.

Indeed, one would expect that significant sociocultural analyses of the major religious traditions would be inspired by Weber's pioneering work and would approach religion and society as formative cultural elements, to be described and defined in relation to one another. In this regard, the work of Gustave von Grunebaum, Wilfred Cantwell Smith, and Clifford Geertz on Islam should be cited. Notable, too, are the studies of William Theodore de Bary, James B. Pratt, and Charles Norton Eliot on the religions of India. Also significant are the more specialized analyses of Melford E. Spiro, Edward Conze, and Richard F. Gombrich on Buddhism; Oscar Lewis's *Life in a Mexican Village* (1963); Ch'ing-K'un Yang's *Religion in Chinese Society* (1961); Henri Frankfort's work on the religions of Egyptian antiquity; W. E. H. Stanner's portrayal of Aboriginal life in Australia; Vittorio Lanternari's *The Religions of the Oppressed* (1963), which analyzed religion functioning as protest movement; and Gerhard Lenski's *The Religious Factor* (1961), a comprehensive analysis of modern American socioreligious interaction.

Weber's interest in comparative cultural analysis was forwarded by Joachim Wach (1898–1955), a German-born scholar who taught at the University of Chicago from 1944 until his death. Wach is probably the first prominent historian of religion to approach the major religious traditions of the world as instances of organic coordination, for which the societal element is both formative and constitutive. It was Wach's conviction that religion could be studied properly only if ideational, cultic, and social components were approached as interdependent. He contended that it is through the instrumentation of religion that such elements become integrated within a culture. The comparative history of culture, as Weber had recommended, is the context within which these integrative processes are best studied.

Perhaps the most straightforward of attempts to approach the major religious traditions of the world as examples of organic coordination has been provided by Ninian Smart in his book *The Religious Experience of Mankind* (1969). Unlike Weber, however, Smart does not arrive at the religious traditions after engaging in complex theoretical analyses of the components of more comprehensive sociocultural ideological stances. Nor does he treat the religious as a testing ground for more extensive methodological or cultural issues. Instead, without flourish or methodological brocade, Smart contends that religions consist of strands of dimensions (John Henry Newman might have called them "notes") that are present in various degrees of emphasis in the religious traditions. Although Smart does not insist that the list be taken as exhaustive, there are six strands or dimensions: doctrine, mythology, ethics, ritual, social institutions, and religious experience. As noted, not all dimensions are present to the same degree in all religions. Indeed, not all of the dimensions are present in every religion. But some are present in all religions, and the way in which they are present and interact with society gives a religion its internal dynamism as well as its morphology. In *The Phenomenon of Religion* (London, 1973), Smart writes:

> For instance, the shape of a particular myth may be in part determined by the exigencies of the kinship-system in the society in which it is recited. More sweepingly, the dominance of mother-goddesses in certain phases of religion might be at least partially ascribed to the emergence of agriculture. Conversely, some features of a society may be heavily influenced by religion itself, in which case the direction of the explanation runs the other way. (p. 44)

In Smart's view, such examples illustrate the "mutual dynamic," that is, the ongoing "dialectic in which a religion and its society help and shape one another." It is on this basis that Smart subsequently referred prominently to religion, in its social setting, as being "worldview," and the study of religion "worldview analysis" (see Smart, *Worldviews: Crosscultural Exploration of Human Beliefs*, New York, 1983).

Other contributions. The methods and insights of Durkheim and Weber were instrumental in establishing the dominant theoretical framework to identify and clarify relationships between religion and society. Yet, along the way, there were numerous additional contributions that became accepted as belonging to the subject's permanent intellectual legacy. In 1864, for example, N. D. Fustel de Coulanges (1830–1889) published his seminal study, *The Ancient City*, which traced the impact of religious beliefs and customs upon the social institutions of classical Western civilization. At approximately the same time, Herbert Spencer (1820–1903) utilized a theory of evolution to describe the processes by which religious ideas develop in correspondence with the development of social institutions. In 1889, W. Robertson Smith, in his *Lectures on the Religion of the Semites*, portrayed Jewish worship and belief against the background of the customs and folkways of Semitic nomads. In 1887, Ferdinand Tönnies (1855–1936) published his *Gemeinschaft und Gesellschaft* (translated as *Community and Society*, 1957), which traced the shift from a "communal, status-based concentric society of the Middle Ages to the more individualistic, impersonal and large-scale society of the democratic-industrial period." In so doing, Tönnies illustrated the intricate relations that religion and society have had in selected historical periods.

Focusing his Weberian sensitivities on the influence the Christian religion has had on Western culture, Ernst Troeltsch (1865–1923) identified two prominent forms of social organization, church and sect, in correspondence with two formative dispositional factors. In his *The Social Teaching of the Christian Churches* (1912), Troeltsch argued that the two forms of social organization have been dominant within Christianity because the religion has fostered two distinctive and not always congruent attitudes toward the world. Churches reflect an intention to accept the social order and lend credibility to its status; sects are motivated by the desire to disassociate from the societal status quo. Troeltsch's analyses, illustrating an application of Weberian inquiry to a specific religious tradition, also fostered linkages between sociological study and theological reflection. Bernhard Groethuysen, in his study of the development of the middle class (*Die Entstehung der bürgerlichen Welt- und Lebensanschauung in Frankreich*, 1927), illustrated that the bourgeois outlook developed in eighteenth-century France when the traditional dogma of the Roman Catholic church, removed from the formative environment of religious ritual and practice, had become "abstract." Gustav Mensching, who trained under Rudolf Otto at Marburg and became professor of the history of religions at Bonn, developed an approach that treated religions as instances of social coordination, motivated along the two distinctive dispositional lines of folk religion and universal religion (see his *Die Religion*, 1959).

The field of anthropology contributed several studies that are basic to an understanding of the relations between religion and society. A. R. Radcliffe-Brown (1881–1955), for example, portrayed religion as belonging to the complex social machinery that enables human beings to live harmoniously and collectively. Paul Radin (1883–1959) investigated the beliefs and attitudes of primitive societies in light of his theory that religion has roots in fear and that the basis of fear is insecurity; Radin's intention was to isolate the psychological origins of religious sensitivity. Bronislaw Malinowski (1884–1942), drawing much of his evidence from analyses of the collective behavior of the Trobriand Islanders, approached religion as one of the primary social institutions that is produced and shaped in response to the need for cultural survival. Durkheim's nephew Marcel Mauss (1872–1950) saw religion as belonging to that range of entities that deserved to be classified as "total social pheonomena." Such analyses provided corroboration of the contention that religion and society could be approached, described, and defined in relation to one another.

Contemporary research. One direct line of succession from Weber to present-day sociology of religion is an extended commentary on social-action theory as modified, tempered, and extended in the work of Thorstein Veblen (1857–1929); John R. Commons (1862–1945); Robert M. MacIver (1882–1970); Karl Mannheim (1893–1947), who is important for his treatment of the influence of utopian ideas within selected societies; Alfred Marshall (1842–1924); Vilfredo Pareto (1848–1923); and, perhaps most significantly, Talcott Parsons (1902–1979). Parsons is important not only because of his own contributions to the field—his translation of Weber's *Protestant Ethic* (1930) may have been the single most important event in bringing the work of the German sociologist to the attention of the English-speaking world—but, in addition, because of the remarkable influence he has had on other scholars who have become leaders in the field. Because of his translation of Weber's book, Parsons is associated with the legacy of Weber, but he must also be given credit for reviving interest in Durkheim's view and for making Durkheim into something more than an analyst of primitive societies. In exploring the congruences between Weber's and Durkheim's interests, Parsons was influential, too, in establishing associations between the German and French schools of social theory. By combining Durkheim's insight regarding the influence of social constraints with Weber's interest in discerning the way in which religious values are translated as social sanctions, Parsons was led to a new view of the structure of social action. He contended that the social milieu possesses a set of conditions that are beyond the control of each individual, but not outside the mastery of collective human agency. Interweaving Durkheim's and Weber's insights and working to give due respect to both scholars, Parsons offered this summary in *The Structure of Social Action* (New York, 1937):

> Durkheim called attention to the importance of the relation of symbolism as distinguished from that of intrinsic causality in cognitive patterns. . . . Weber integrated the various aspects of the role of non-empirical cognitive patterns in social action in terms of his theory of the significance of the problems of meaning and the corresponding cognitive structures, in a way which preclude, for analytical purposes, their being assimilated to the patterns of science. (p. 715)

Parsons worked to give due respect to both scholars.

Parsons was a nestor. His reworking and fusing of Weberian and Durkheimian themes was so comprehensive and detailed that he inspired a host of students to take up the same or related investigatory causes. Indeed, one of the most significant paths of intellectual influence within religious studies is that initiated by Talcott Parsons and his associates at Harvard. They insisted that social thought be pursued in a methodologically sophisticated cross-cultural and interdisciplinary manner.

The anthropologist Clifford Geertz, one of the most influential of Parsons's students, is known not only for his studies of Islamic religion and culture but also for his proposal that religion should be viewed as a "cultural system." In his highly regarded article "Religion as Cultural System," first published in *Anthropological Approaches to the Study of Religion*, edited by Michael Banton (New York, 1966), Geertz defined religion in organic terms:

> Religion is (1) a system of symbols which acts to (2) establish powerful, pervasive, and long-lasting moods and motivations in men by (3) formulating conceptions of a general order of existence and (4) clothing these conceptions with such an aura of factuality that (5) the moods and motivations seem uniquely realistic.

The role assigned to religion befits Geertz's conception of culture as "an historically transmitted pattern of meaning."

Similar combinations of interests are reflected in the work of Thomas Luckmann and Peter L. Berger, who were influenced by Karl Mannheim, Robert Merton, continental philosophical phenomenology, and, in particular, the work of Alfred Schutz (1899–1959). Luckmann and Berger share concerns about the fate of the individual within a "socially construed" context. In *The Invisible Religion* (New York, 1967), Luckmann identifies religion as "symbolic self-transcendence," and he sketches the process by which the human organism transcends its particularities by constructive objective, all-embracing, and morally binding universes of meaning. In describing the way in which this process is effected, Luckmann wrote of "the social construction of reality." For Berger, all religious propositions are "projections grounded in specific infrastructures," and religion itself is that "human enterprise by which a sacred cosmos is established." Without an awareness of the presence of the sacred in human consciousness, according to Berger, it would likely not have been possible "to conceive of a cosmos in the first place." Berger writes:

> It can thus be said that religion has played a strategic part in the human enterprise of world-building. Religion implies the farthest reach of man's self-externalization, of his infusion of reality with his own meanings. Religion implies that human order is projected into the totality of being. Put differently, religion is the audacious attempt to conceive of the entire universe as being humanly significant. (Berger, 1967, pp. 27–28)

Both Luckmann and Berger acknowledge that religion is present in institutions, that is, in readily identifiable religious organizations such as churches, synagogues, and temples. But they are unwilling to restrict the social reality of religion to these institutional forms. They observe that a sociology of religion that deals only with such organizations is a sociology of churches that may be concentrating upon already "frozen" forms of religion. In the larger sense, religion (Luckmann's "invisible religion") legitimates the fundamental values of a society by constructing symbolic universes of meaning. Berger understands the process of legitimation to require two important steps: first, "religion legitimates social institutions by bestowing upon them an ultimately valid ontological status, that is, by locating them within a sacred and cosmic frame of reference" (Berger, 1967, p. 33); and, second, "religion . . . serves to maintain the reality of that socially constructed world within which men exist in their everyday lives" (ibid., p. 42).

What Berger and Luckmann divined in theory, namely, the dynamics of the interdependence of religious patterns of meaning and the social construction of reality, Robert N. Bellah has disclosed as a certifiable American fact under the concept of *civil religion.* In so doing, Bellah discerns a systematic, organic form of religious understanding in the collective American consciousness that he believes has existed since the founding of the nation:

> What we have, then, from the earliest years of the republic is a collection of beliefs, symbols and rituals with respect to sacred things and institutionalized in a collectivity. This religion—there seems no other word for it—while not antithetical to and indeed sharing much in common with Christianity, was neither sectarian nor in any specific sense Christian. At a time when the society was overwhelmingly Christian, it seems unlikely that this lack of Christian reference was meant to spare the feelings of the tiny non-Christian minority. Rather, the civil religion expressed what those who set the precedents felt was appropriate under the circumstances. It reflected their private as well as their public views. Nor was the civil religion simply "religion in general." . . . because of its specificity, the civil religion was saved from empty formalism and served as a genuine vehicle of national religious self-understanding. (Bellah, 1967, p. 9)

So far I have traced a line of inquiry, from Durkheim and Weber forward, that attests that religion gains concrete expression and possesses meaning within the context of social reality. This conviction can be interpreted as a refinement and extension of Weber's analyses of the interrelationships between motives and acts in the constitution of a culture. It belongs to Durkheim's more comprehensive observation that religious conceptions always reflect prescribed patterns of social organization. But how do scholars respond when the interrelationships are not clear or when expected correlations between motivation and action are in a state of disarray? Their recourse is to study the lack of correspondence as well as the dysfunctions that have become apparent. The term used to denote the ineffectiveness of religious meaning (because such meaning no longer corresponds with one's experience within the social reality) is *secularization.* Secularization means that some prior prevailing pattern of religious and ideological order is no longer functioning characteristically as a viable source of motivation or behavior. The work of Bryan Wilson, Thomas F. O'Dea, Charles Y. Glock, Rodney Stark, Guy Swanson, and Harvey Cox, among others, was directed toward making sociological and religious sense of this pervasive development. As a consequence, scholarly analyses of the relation between religion and society that appeared in the mid-1980s focused increasingly on the function and status of the sacred in a secular society. I refer specifically to two anthologies: Mary Douglas and Steven

Tipton's *Religion and America: Spiritual Life in a Secular Age* (1982) and Phillip E. Hammond's *The Sacred in a Secular Society* (1985). The ingredients are the same as they were when Durkheim, Weber, and the others constructed the dominant paradigm. But there have been significant shifts, and necessary conceptual readjustments, in every chronicle that has attempted to correlate analyses of the relationship between religion and society with a more extensive portrayal of the evolution or development of Western intellectual history.

RELIGION AND SOCIETY IN THE CONTEMPORARY ERA. Contemporary discussion of the relationship between religion and society is framed by widespread social and cultural change. Societies affected by complex processes of modernization are having difficulty deciding whether, under the new circumstances, traditional religion exercises benevolent or malevolent social influence.

In many quarters, the fundamental issue has to do with whether traditional religious aspirations are congruent or compatible with Marxist political theory and practice. In those areas of the world where Christianity has been the dominant religious tradition—and where, historically, it has been identified with the interests of colonial powers—there is a fascination with liberation theologies that sometimes advocate social and political revolution. Within these settings, the relations between religion and society are being shaped by the responses that the traditions are making to new formulations of faith that are tailored to facilitate transitional or revolutionary activity. The dominant responses have been of two contrasting kinds. One of these kinds of responses condones (sometimes radical) change and appears to its enemies to be in league with the very secularizing forces that traditional religions oppose. The other, fundamentalist, response calls for a return to the purity of the tradition at its origins and has shown itself willing at times to adopt a militant, antirevolutionary stance. Within the United States, in particular, this conflict is implicit in the controversy surrounding the rise of a radical religious right. It has found expression, too, in court cases and legislative debate concerning abortion, prayer in schools, and the status of public religious observance.

Yet even in the present situation, perennial ingredients have been made explicit. In its social manifestations, religion still presents itself as the guardian of sensitivities concerning distinctions between the sacred and the profane. And in its religious dimensions, society continues to be known by the collective aspirations to which its sanctioned activity lends expression.

SEE ALSO Comte, Auguste; Durkheim, Émile; Fustel de Coulanges, N. D.; Law and Religion; Lévy-Bruhl, Lucien; Malinowski, Bronislaw; Marxism; Marx, Karl; Mauss, Marcel; Otto, Rudolf; Political Theology; Radcliffe-Brown, A. R.; Radin, Paul; Revolution; Smith, W. Robertson; Sociology; Spencer, Herbert; Tönnies, Ferdinand; Troeltsch, Ernst; Varṇa and Jāti; Wach, Joachim; Weber, Max.

BIBLIOGRAPHY

Bellah, Robert N. "Religious Evolution." *American Sociological Review* 29 (June 1964): 358–374.

Bellah, Robert N. "Civil Religion in American." *Daedalus* 96 (Winter 1967): 1–21.

Bellah, Robert N., and Phillip E. Hammond. *Varieties of Civil Religion.* San Francisco, 1980.

Berger, Peter L. *The Sacred Canopy: Elements of a Sociological Theory of Religion.* Garden City, N. Y., 1967.

Cohn, Norman R. C. *The Pursuit of the Millennium.* 3d ed. New York, 1970.

Ch'en, Kenneth. *Buddhism in China.* Princeton, 1964.

Conze, Edward. *Buddhism: Its Essence and Development.* Oxford, 1951.

Douglas, Mary. *Natural Symbols: Explorations in Cosmology.* New York, 1970.

Douglas, Mary. "The Effects of Modernization on Religious Change." In *Religion and America: Spiritual Life in a Secular Age,* edited by Mary Douglas and Steven Tipton, pp. 25–43. Boston, 1982.

Eisenstadt, Shmuel N. *The Political Systems of Empires.* New York, 1963.

Evans-Pritchard, E. E. *Nuer Religion.* Oxford, 1956.

Frankfort, Henri. *Kingship and the Gods* (1948). Reprint, Chicago, 1978.

Geertz, Clifford. *Islam Observed.* New Haven, 1968.

Hammond, Phillip E., ed. *The Sacred in a Secular Age: Toward Revision in the Scientific Study of Religion.* Berkeley, 1985.

Kitagawa, Joseph M. *Religion in Japanese History.* New York, 1966.

Lanternari, Vittorio. *The Religions of the* Oppressed. New York, 1963.

Leach, Edmund. *Dialectic in Practical Religion.* Cambridge, 1968.

Lewis, Oscar. *Life in a Mexican Village.* Urbana, Ill., 1963.

Lee, Robert, and Martin E. Marty, eds. *Religion and Social Conflict.* New York, 1964.

O'Dea, Thomas F. *Sociology and the Study of Religion: Theory, Research, Interpretation.* New York, 1970.

Pareto, Vilfredo. *The Mind and Society.* 4 vols. New York, 1935.

Parsons, Talcott. *Essays in Sociological Theory.* 2d rev. ed. Glencoe, Ill., 1954.

Parsons, Talcott. *Structure and Process in Modern Society.* Glencoe, Ill., 1960.

Radcliffe-Brown, A. R. *Structure and Function in Primitive Society.* London, 1952.

Schneider, Louis. *Sociological Approach to Religion.* New York, 1970.

Smith, Wilfred Cantwell. *Islam in Modern History.* Princeton, 1957.

Spiro, Melford E. *Buddhism and Society: A Great Tradition and its Burmese Vicissitudes.* 2d ed. Berkeley, 1982.

Stark, Rodney, and William S. Bainbridge. *The Future of Religion: Secularization, Revival and Cult Formation.* Berkeley, 1985.

Swanson, Guy E. *Religion and Regime: A Sociological Account of the Reformation.* Ann Arbor, 1967.

Swanson, Guy E. *Social Change.* Glenview, Ill., 1971.

Wach, Joachim. *Sociology of Religion* (1944). Reprint, Chicago, 1962.

Walzer, Michael. *The Revolution of the Saints.* New York, 1965.

Weber, Max. *The Protestant Ethic and the Spirit of Capitalism.* London, 1930.

Weber, Max. *The Sociology of Religion.* Boston, 1963.

Wilson, Bryan R. *Religion in Secular Society.* London, 1966.

Yinger, J. Milton. *Religion, Society, and the Individual.* New York, 1957.

Yinger, J. Milton. *The Scientific Study of Religion.* New York, 1970.

Yinger, J. Milton. *Sociology Looks at Religion.* New York, 1963.

WALTER H. CAPPS (1987)

SOCIETY AND RELIGION [FURTHER CONSIDERATIONS]. As Walter Capps observed in his essay on this subject, "relations between religion and society are fundamental to the nature of religion and, according to long-standing intellectual claims, are intrinsic to the nature of society." There is a great deal of support for this general assumption, but defining its basic terms—*society* and *religion*—can be problematic. Contemporary theorists think of both as constructed realities and therefore privilege the role of symbols, ritual, and discourse in their analyses. Religion tends to be defined in terms of its relation to collective life, yet how and in what ways religion fulfills its classical task of binding people into a common universe of meaning, as was articulated early in the twentieth century in the sociologist Emile Durkheim's study of the totemic system in Australia, are issues of continuing debate and discussion.

TOWARD CULTURAL ANALYSIS. At the end of the twentieth century and into the twenty-first theorists moved away from conceptions of culture as a simple set of vague and broad value orientations. Today culture is viewed less as a coherent system of signs and meanings, and more focus is placed on its fragmented, malleable, and internally contradictory features. Anthropologists, sociologists, and social historians have lost some of their earlier confidence in explanations that focus narrowly on social class or social structure and have attempted instead to explore more deeply the meanings that underlie those categories. Commentators recognize that no consistent meanings can be attributed to the effects of social position and social relationships; instead, meanings are grounded in the acts of individuals and groups in a particular time and place. Victoria E. Bonnell and Lynn Hunt underscore this fundamental insight when they write: "Social categories—artisans, merchants, women, Jews—turned out to vary from place to place and from epoch to epoch, sometimes from year to year" (Bonnell and Hunt, 1999, p. 7).

A forerunner of this so-called cultural turn was the work on linguistics of the French anthropologist Claude Lévi-Strauss. His attention to systems of signs and symbols contributed to the rise of semiotics, with the implication that culture can be analyzed much like a language, with its own distinctive codes of meaning embedded within it. Other French scholars made significant contributions that advanced a "poststructuralist" mode of analysis, especially Michel Foucault, Roland Barthes, and Jacques Derrida, all of whom emphasized a lack of fixed structures of meaning and the ways in which language shapes conceptions of reality. Bonnell and Hunt summarize the intellectual impact of those contributions as follows:

> In the poststructuralist view, language or discourse did not mirror some prior social understanding or positioning and it could never penetrate to the truth of existence; it itself configured the expression of social meaning and functioned as a kind of veil between humans and the world around them. Despite their differences, structuralism and poststructuralism both contributed to the general displacement of the social in favor of culture viewed as linguistic and representational. Social categories were to be imagined not as preceding consciousness or culture or language but as depending upon them. Social categories only came into being through their expressions or representations. (Bonnell and Hunt, 1999, p. 9)

In the United States, several scholars have made more recent contributions to the cultural analysis of religion. Jonathan Z. Smith's work on ritual (1987) merits mention in this respect. Rather than examine ritual in terms of its legitimating function within a collectivity, Smith proposed another function of ritual that often is overlooked: provoking thoughtful reflection about the nature of the social order and its maintenance. Ritual in this sense implies not just expressive but also communicative processes involving moral obligations and the ways they form and re-form society. Robert N. Bellah, another major contributor to the study of religion, put forth a very general argument about the constitutive power of ritual, as suggested by the title of his essay, "The Ritual Roots of Society and Culture" (2003). He traced the beginnings of human solidarity in language and music, arguing that they are a product of ritual. In keeping with the work of Erving Goffman (1967) and Randall Collins (1998), Bellah regards ritual as fundamental to understanding social action in a general sense throughout society; he quotes Roy A. Rappaport as saying that ritual is "humanity's basic social act" (Rappaport, 1999, p. 107).

More generally, others have emphasized the importance of viewing culture as an expression of social behavior. Ann Swidler (1986, pp. 276–277) views culture as a "toolkit" with a "repertoire" of "strategies of action." Robert Wuthnow (1987) and Pierre Bourdieu (1990) both privilege "practice" as a key component. Trying to establish some balance between culture as system and culture as practice, William H. Sewell conceives culture as a "dialectic between system and practice" (1999, p. 47). Viewed in this manner, culture (and ritual in particular) is a means of organizing social action.

Along the same lines, Bruce Lincoln (2000) proposed a polythetic model of religion with four components:

1. A discourse that claims that its concerns transcend the human, temporal, and contingent while claiming for itself a similarly transcendent status.
2. A set of practices informed and structured by that discourse.
3. A community whose members construct their identity with reference to the discourse and its attendant practices.
4. An institution that regulates discourse, practices, and community, reproducing and modifying them over time while asserting their eternal validity and transcendent value.

Reminiscent of Durkheim's classic definition, Lincoln looks upon all four elements—discourse, practice, community, and institution—as interdependent and thus constituting a system, though one that is always malleable and in process. Rather than seeing religion as a fixed form, he emphasizes its variability with respect to its relationship to ethics and aesthetics. He makes use of the philosopher Søren Kierkegaard's three categories of aesthetics, ethics, and religion yet interprets them not in a personal, subjective sense but as an integrated triad of interpersonal social relations. In his view culture necessarily involves the domains of aesthetics and ethics, but religion as a third domain is more variable in its form and its relationship to the other two. "Of particular interest," he writes, "is the way religion connects to the other domains of culture: specifically, the capacity of religious discourse to articulate ethical and aesthetic positions in a uniquely stabilizing fashion. What religion does—and this, I submit, is its defining characteristic—is to invest specific human preferences with transcendent status by misrepresenting them as revealed truth, primordial traditions, divine commandments, and so forth. In this way, it insulates them against most forms of debate and critique, assisting their transmission from one generation to another as part of a sacred canon" (Lincoln, 2000, p. 416).

Noteworthy in this conceptualization is the lack of attention to personal religious experience or the response of individuals to manifestations of the sacred; also, there is no mention of psychological needs or drives. Instead, the focus is on religion in its social formation and the way it gives transcendent status to other domains of culture. Thinking along similar lines, Burton L. Mack (2000, p. 289) poses a crucial question when he asks, "What might a theory of religion look like when fully integrated into the human enterprise of social construction?"

A comprehensive theory of religion would presuppose that at least since the Enlightenment the power of religion to maintain hegemony over the ethical and the aesthetic has been reduced considerably. There is indeed considerable contestation between religion and the latter two domains in contemporary Western societies, yet the religious element in the construction of social formations has not disappeared. This is true partly because as contemporary theorists such as Collins (1998) emphasize, ritual is at the core of any kind of social action; hence, as Bellah says, there is "an element of the sacred" at the very basis of social life whether or not it is defined explicitly as such (Bellah, 2003, p. 32). Drawing on Goffman's notion of interaction ritual, Bellah elaborates further:

> In this process of ritual interaction the members of the group, through their shared experience, feel a sense of membership, however fleeting, with a sense of boundary between those sharing the experience and those outside it; they feel some sense of moral obligation to each other, which is symbolized by whatever they focused on during the interaction; and, finally, they are charged with what Collins calls emotional energy but which he identifies with what Durkheim called moral force. (Bellah, 2003, p. 32)

Thus at every level of social formation, from the smallest group to total societies, ritual operates, varying only in its degree of complexity. Whether ritual will become infused with religious symbolization and therefore give rise to a full-blown religious discourse is an open question. If one accepts Smith's argument that ritual functions to inspire reflection on what people regard as common social practice, chances are that a more explicit religious ritual will evolve. Its capacity for transcending the human, temporal, and contingent meshes with fundamental human efforts implicit in elementary ritual to bring order and legitimacy to life. However, in the Enlightenment tradition, in which the aesthetic and ethical domains have come to be removed from the religious, efforts at restructuring culture in religion's favor often face serious challenges. Under these circumstances religion certainly exists and often flourishes but does so largely in a state of contestation with other cultural domains.

The persisting presence of religion in relation to other aspects of culture lies in the power of myth and ritual to stretch the human imagination in the direction of creating and maintaining a social formation. Myth and ritual function in human life by placing ordinary experience in an extraordinary perspective and thus generate a larger narrative that transcends time and space. Religion is critical if for no other reason than that, as Mack says, "the process of social formation creates and draws upon interests in and agreements about forces and features of social experience that are difficult to name and locate in the daily round of activity" (Mack, 2000, p. 290).

Precisely because the mythic world is more encompassing and expands the horizons of human imagination, it encourages creative and unlimited responses that can be employed for the symbolic restructuring of everyday life. Mack explains this when he says, "The gap between the social world and the mythic panoply, and the fact that the imaginary world is so richly disordered, may be thought of as creating a space for play, experimentation, thoughtful meditation, cheating, winking, and/or calling one another to task" (Mack, 2000, p. 291).

Religion and Institutional Differentation. In light of the fact that the creative capacity of religious symbols, discourse, and practice is coordinated through social institutions, it is necessary to consider the general process of social differentiation. This process often is viewed as being peculiar to the West, yet the sociologist Peter Beyer (2003) cautions that it would be a mistake to assume that the word *religion* has always had a distinct meaning for Europeans or that people other parts of the world have not adopted a somewhat similar meaning of that term. Differentiated religion as it is known today is largely a product of seventeenth- and eighteenth-century Europe, brought on in part by the Protestant Reformation but also by the political conditions that gave rise to nationalism.

Nation-states within Europe came to be closely associated with distinctive religious traditions, Catholic or Protestant, and thus incorporated religion as a significant component of their identity. With increased global expansion in the colonizing era, Europeans encountered other peoples elsewhere in the world whose religions and cultures were strikingly different and, by the nineteenth century, had formed totalizing conceptions for those entities, such as Hinduism, Buddhism, Confucianism, and Islam. Also important in that period was the growing awareness of the distinction between religion and nonreligion. Hence, societal identities not only are enmeshed in religious traditions but involve juxtapositions of one religion against another and against whatever is presumed to be nonreligion.

In this differentiated state religion takes on a more specified set of social functions in relation to society and to other institutions within society. It is driven by a logic that applies to all institutions; that is, it is driven toward greater rationalization of its procedures, elaboration of its distinctive teachings, and clarity about its spheres of authority and influence. Religion becomes more of a symbolic world unto itself as it loses control over some of the historical functions it once served. Social theorists have interpreted this trajectory of religious change in varying and opposing ways, such as the upgrading of levels of autonomous personal responsibility in keeping with religious values (Parsons, 1963), "secularization" (Wilson, 1985), and religious privatization (Berger, 1967). Simply put, Parsons sees religious values as increasingly diffused within society through a process of transformation, Wilson points to the loss of significance of beliefs and values in the public arena and the resulting marginalization of religious organizations, and Berger argues for a shift in the social location of religion away from the society as a whole and toward smaller, more limited worlds of social experience.

However viewed, religion's boundaries in the modern world are very much at issue. Privatized religion implies a continuing subjective world of meaning cut off from broader institutional sectors, such as the economy and politics, or a reduced space in which the mythic imagination can operate. Commentators generally agree that religious privatization is discernible particularly in Europe and the United States. At the same time there are countermovements that attempt to infuse religious and spiritual meaning into the so-called secular spheres. This process of dedifferentiation, or attempts at reenchanting the public sphere, is evident in the holistic health movement, the search for spirituality in the workplace, and the significance attached to meditation and prayer in healing within the medical establishment. The extent to which these efforts have succeeded in achieving a unity of public and private experience or even in fulfilling what might be called a traditional religious function is a matter of debate.

Important in understanding the interplay between society and religion are the differing social forms of religion. Those forms define the boundaries of religion's mythic space and the locus of its social formations. Among those social formations are organized religion, state religion, and movement religion (Beyer, 2003). Individualistic, communal, popular, and transnational forms of religion are equally important but are not germane to this discussion.

Organized religion functions, at least in modern democratic societies, in a pluralistic environment of competing alternatives. Rational-choice theorists applaud the absence of a religious monopoly with authority over society and underscore the role of competition as a source of organizational innovation. They argue that these conditions encourage a higher level of religious mobilization and societal engagement because religious organizations have a clearer notion of their purpose: what they are and what they have to offer to recruits. It seems reasonable to assume that energies arising out of a religiously pluralistic context offer some reinforcement of broader societal values, particularly competition and innovation, but rational-choice theory is limited in explaining religious dynamics in relation to society. There are differing types of rationality, as the sociologist Max Weber understood; moreover, the way in which rationality functions within religion is not uniform across societal contexts, an observation that led the comparative sociologist David Martin to conclude that "it is probably worth putting a question mark over the presumed effects of rationalization" (Martin, 1996, p. 42). In keeping with the preceding analysis, any comprehensive analysis of religion and society must allow for the nonutilitarian aspects of social formation, that is, the constitutive power of ritual, symbol, and discourse.

State religion refers to a form of religion in which the state plays a critical role in defining or enforcing its dogma, its practice, or both. The rise of militant religious nationalism in Muslim countries and elsewhere early in the twenty-first century signals a fusion of state identities with particular religions, or what has come to be called religious nationalism with its highly charged symbols and mythic formulations (Friedland, 2001). Milder forms of state religion are found elsewhere and in varying degrees of vitality, such as in the United Kingdom and the Scandinavian countries. What all these religions have in common is that they are "top-down," much in the sense of Jean-Jacques Rousseau's "civil religion" imposed by the state with an emphasis on presumably unifying dogmas. In contrast, as N. J. Demerath observes, civil religion in the United States is more a "bottom-up" phenomenon in the Durkheimian sense; in his words, "our civil religion is a kind of religious common denominator that bubbles forth from our long-standing 'Judeo-Christian tradition' and underscores the religious significance of the nation as a whole and its government. It is more of a passive cultural legacy than the result of an activist political decision" (Demerath, 2003, p. 354). The role of civil religion in integrating society is complicated, especially when, as often happens, there are competing interpretations of its meaning.

Social movement religion, as the name implies, is the most fluid and malleable of the three social forms. Religiously based movements are common in modern societies, addressing a broad spectrum of issues across the liberal-to-conservative ideological spectrum. They funnel energies and galvanize commitments to a variety of causes by selectively appropriating religious symbols and teachings that serve their particular interests. Many are special-purpose organizations that attempt to convince people of the significance of a singular moral or ethical cause in what amounts to an effort to raise levels of social consciousness. Others are more truly sectarian movements in the classical sense, aimed at reforming established religious bodies or advancing an explicit religious concern. Because all such movements typically seek to bring about social change through persuasion, they must strike a delicate balance between religious and ideological purity and sensitivity to public values and interests. Thus, religion of this type takes on a populist, negotiated quality, and society is likened to an arena of continuously competing movements trying to reshape it.

Bibliography

Bellah, Robert N. "The Ritual Roots of Society and Culture." In *Handbook of the Sociology of Religion,* edited by Michele Dillon, pp. 31–44. Cambridge, U.K., 2003.

Berger, Peter. *The Sacred Canopy: Elements of a Sociological Theory of Religion.* Garden City, N.Y., 1967.

Beyer, Peter. "Social Forms of Religion and Religions in Contemporary Global Society." In *Handbook of the Sociology of Religion,* edited by Michele Dillon, pp. 45–60. Cambridge, U.K., 2003.

Bonnell, Victoria E., and Lynn Hunt, eds. *Beyond the Cultural Turn: New Directions in the Study of Society and Culture.* Berkeley, Calif., 1999.

Bourdieu, Pierre. *The Logic of Practice.* Translated by Richard R. Nice. Cambridge, U.K., 1990.

Collins, Randall. *The Sociology of Philosophies: A Global Theory of Intellectual Change.* Cambridge, Mass., 1998.

Demerath, N. J. III. "Civil Society and Civil Religion as Mutually Dependent." In *Handbook of the Sociology of Religion,* edited by Michele Dillon, pp. 348–358. Cambridge, U.K., 2003.

Friedland, Roger. "Religious Nationalism and the Problem of Collective Representation." *Annual Review of Sociology* 27 (2001): 125–152.

Goffman, Erving. *Interaction Ritual: Essays on Face-to-Face Behavior.* New York, 1967.

Lincoln, Bruce. "Culture." In *Guide to the Study of Religion,* edited by Willi Braun and Russell T. McCutcheon, pp. 409–422. London and New York, 2000.

Mack, Burton L. "Social Formation." In *Guide to the Study of Religion,* edited by Willi Braun and Russell T. McCutcheon, pp. 283–296. London and New York, 2000.

Martin, David. "Religion, Secularization, and Post-Modernity." In *Religion and Modernity: Modes of Co-Existence,* edited by Pal Repstad, pp. 35–43. Stockholm, 1996.

Parsons, Talcott. "Christianity and Modern Industrial Society." In *Sociological Theory and Modern Society,* edited by Talcott Parsons, pp. 385–421. New York, 1967.

Rappaport, Roy A. *Ritual and Religion in the Making of Humanity.* Cambridge, U.K., 1999.

Roof, Wade Clark. *Spiritual Marketplace: Baby Boomers and the Remaking of American Religion.* Princeton, 1999.

Sewell, William H., Jr. "The Concept(s) of Culture." In *Beyond the Cultural Turn: New Directions in the Study of Society and Culture,* edited by Victoria A. Bonnel and Lynn Hunt, pp. 35–61. Berkeley, Calif., 1999.

Smith, Jonathan Z. *To Take Place: Toward Theory in Ritual.* Chicago, 1987.

Swidler, Ann. "Culture in Action: Symbols and Strategies." *American Sociological Review* 51 (April 1986): 273–286.

Wilson, Bryan. "Secularization: The Inherited Model." In *The Sacred in a Secular Age,* edited by Phillip E. Hammond, pp. 9–20. Berkeley, Calif., 1985.

Wuthnow, Robert. *Meaning and Moral Order: Explorations in Cultural Analysis.* Berkeley, Calif., 1987.

Wade Clark Roof (2005)

SOCIETY OF FRIENDS See QUAKERS

SOCIETY OF JESUS See JESUITS

SOCINUS See SOZZINI, FAUSTO PAVOLO

SOCIOBIOLOGY AND EVOLUTIONARY PSYCHOLOGY

This entry consists of the following articles:

SOCIOBIOLOGY AND EVOLUTIONARY PSYCHOLOGY: AN OVERVIEW

Sociobiology and evolutionary psychology are related fields, both of which claim that biology is the principal determinant in human affairs. Sociobiology was initially, and by some accounts is entirely, the study of the genetic bases of animal behavior. Sociobiologists regularly also attempt to explain human behavior. Sociobiology is, as the term suggests, the biology of animal *and* human society. Sociobiology preceded and developed into evolutionary psychology, which features mental dispositions more than genes as the evolutionary determinants. The relationship of the two disciplines is both congenial and contested.

Even more contested, by biologists, social scientists, and humanists alike, is how far either discipline succeeds. Edward O. Wilson, the founder of sociobiology, calls it a "new holism," even, with capitals, "the Modern Synthesis" (1975, pp. 7, 4). But critics see it as genetic reductionism. Evolutionary psychologists claim that humans have what Jerome H. Barkow, Leda Cosmides, and John Tooby call an "adapted mind," and call for a "conceptual integration" of all the diverse academic disciplines studying humans, their behaviors, minds, cultures under this biological "view of a single, universal panhuman design" (1992, pp. 4–5). Critics see this too as biological imperialism.

SOCIOLOBIOLOGY. Wilson opened his 1975 *Sociobiology* with auspicious claims: "Sociobiology is defined as the systematic study of the biological basis of all social behavior. It may not be too much to say that sociology and the other social sciences, as well as the humanities, are the last branches of biology waiting to be included in the Modern Synthesis" (p. 7). He concludes his massive study: "Scientists and humanists should consider together the possibility that the time has come for ethics to be removed temporarily from the hands of the philosophers and biologicized" (p. 562). A quarter century later, the "temporary" is becoming more permanent. Only in a biologically based "consilience" is there any hope of "the unity of knowledge" (Wilson, 1992).

A frequent motif in the claims of both sociobiology and evolutionary psychology is that the basic thrust of all life is "selfish." Richard Dawkins titles an influential book *The Selfish Gene*, and opens: "We are survival machines—robot vehicles blindly programmed to preserve the selfish molecules known as genes" (1989, p. v). Philosophers, especially ethicists, object that biologists are labeling genes with a word borrowed from the cultural phenomenon of morality. A less pejorative theory could avoid reading back objectional features from culture into nature, and avoid speaking as though animals and genes were ethical agents in conditions of only superficial similarity.

Sociobiologists reply that the words *selfish* and *altruistic* as they use them in genetic biology have nothing to do with motivation, only with behavior. These replies are not always convincing, because Wilson does propose to "biologicize" ethics, and Dawkins does begin his *Selfish Gene* with the injunction: "Let us try to *teach* generosity and altruism, because we are born selfish" (1989, p. 3).

Critics of this selfishness at the root of sociobiology claim that there is, even in biology, more than one way of framing this behavior. After all, biologists claim that organisms are quite interrelated, living in communities, ecosystems, with myriad coactions, cooperations, interdependencies. Genes are spread around; that is the only way they can be conserved. Organisms are selected for their capacities to leave more of their genes in the next generation, which, if it can be thought of as the survival of the "selfish," can as easily be thought of as the survival of the "senders." Organisms are tested for their capacities to bequeath what they know genetically to their offspring. Sociobiology needs also to be about shared identity, kinship. William D. Hamilton in a founding paper develops the idea of "inclusive fitness" (Hamilton, 1964).

Biologists could be committing what Alfred North Whitehead called the fallacy of misplaced concreteness (Whitehead, 1967, p. 51). Selecting out one feature of a situation, one forgets the degree of abstraction involved from the real world, and mistakenly portrays the whole by overenlarging a factor of only limited relevance. An even more insistent criticism is that sociobiology fails to recognize the novel, nonbiological dimensions of human culture. Culture "denotes an historically transmitted pattern of meanings embodied in symbols, a system of inherited conceptions expressed in symbolic forms, by means of which men communicate, perpetuate, and develop their knowledge about and attitudes toward life" (Geertz, 1973, p. 89). Although animal ethologists use the word *culture* in reference to animals with capacities for communication and imitated behaviors, culture in the sense of ideas passing from mind to mind is peculiarly human. Human language is elevated remarkably above anything known in nonhuman nature; the capacities for symbolization, abstraction, grammar, vocabulary development, teaching, literary expression, and argument are quite advanced. The determinants of animal and plant behavior are never anthropological, political, economic, technological, scientific, philosophical, ethical, or religious.

Humans have lived in cultures for perhaps a million years, reproducing across thousands of generations. There is every reason to expect that those humans will do best reproductively who do best culturally, and, vice versa, that a genotype will be selected to produce a culturally congenial phenotype. But the question remains whether this emergence of culture introduces behaviors that, however much they continue to require biology, also transcend it with a distinctive human genius.

Sociobiologists insist that biology is dominant in human culture. Wilson puts this in a bold, if somewhat loose, metaphor: "The genes hold culture on a leash. The leash is very long, but inevitably values will be constrained in accordance with their effects on the human gene pool" (1978, p. 167). This is "the general sociobiological view of human nature, namely that the most diagnostic features of human behavior evolved by natural selection and are today constrained throughout the species by particular sets of genes" (1978, p. 43). Michael Ruse agrees: "I argue that Darwinian factors inform and infuse the whole of human experience, most particularly our cultural dimension. . . . Human culture, meaning human thought and action, is informed and structured by biological factors. Natural selection and adaptive advantage reach through to the very core of our being" (1986, pp. 140; 147).

Earlier versions of sociobiology supposed that the genetic shaping of beliefs was rather direct and one way. In later versions, more attention is given to gene-culture coevolution. The genes are still in control, however; cultural variations are selected and persist only when the genes can use them the better to reproduce, although the detail of such innovative practices will be transmitted to the next generation culturally and nongenetically.

The genes build what is called an epigenetic mind. *Epigenesis* conveys the idea of a secondary genesis, ancillary to the primary genetic determinants, a sort of epiphenomenon. Ruse and Wilson put it this way: "Human thinking is under the influence of 'epigenetic rules,' genetically based processes of development that predispose the individual to adopt one or a few forms of behaviours as opposed to others" (1986, p. 180). Humans have innate mental dispositions, such as to avoid incest, or fear strangers.

Critics reply that human beliefs can differ radically. The ancient Scythian nomads in southern Siberia believed that when their chieftains die they should bury their concubines with them, along with their horses and other necessities for the next life; modern Americans believe in women's rights, and doubt that horses ought to be treated this way. Which of these beliefs one comes to hold depends more on one's education than on genes. If the new ideas are contagious enough culturally they can spread indefinitely through the population.

Significant cultural changes can occur within a century, even a decade. Genetic changes can only be transmitted to offspring, which disseminate slowly through a population. Entire cultures rise and fall in less than a thousand years, the minimum period of time in which biologists estimate there might be significant changes in the genetic pool of a human population. The millenarian genes cannot track the ephemeral cultural changes. Individual persons can gain new information constantly throughout a lifetime. Cultural practices get borrowed, traded, adapted; they intermingle across genetic lines. When oral cultures evolve to become literate cultures, people can transmit ideas to thousands who read books a thousand miles away or a thousand years later. This accelerates the pace of cultural information transfer by orders of magnitude over that of genetic information transfer. It is difficult to yoke horses and jet planes in coevolution and have them travel anywhere together.

Cultural options can operate without modifying the genetics. In computer imagery, the same "hardware" (biology) supports diverse programs of "software" (culture). Sociobiologists may reply that the hardware does limit what sorts of software can run on it. Critics counter that the metaphor overlooks how the infant brain is synaptically unfinished and is to a considerable extent "wired up" during the child's education into its culture. The evolved brain allows many sets of mind: one does not have to have Plato's genes to be a Platonist, Darwin's genes to be a Darwinian, or Jesus' genes to be a Christian. The system of inheritance of ideas is independent of the system of inheritance of genes.

EVOLUTIONARY PSYCHOLOGY. *Evolutionary psychology* is a descendent of sociobiology, with more attention to mind and its cultural capacities, but retaining the underlying biological determinants. Jerome H. Barkow realizes that there is a "complex psychology" in humans, with genes and culture interacting, sometimes working together, sometimes pulling in opposite directions. Nevertheless, it remains basically correct "to speak of the genes anchoring the psychological predispositions that tend to pull our cultures back to fitness-enhancing orbits" (Barkow, 1989, p. 8).

Humans have what John Tooby and Leda Cosmides call an "adapted mind" made up of a set of "complex adaptations" that, over our evolutionary history, have promoted survival (Barkow, Cosmides, and Tooby, 1992, p. 69). These form a set of behavioral subroutines, selected for coping in culture, by which humans maximize their offspring. The mind is more like a Swiss army knife, with tools for this and that, rather than a general-purpose learning device. Humans have needed teachability, but they have also needed channeled reaction patterns. The adapted mind evolved a complex of behavior-disposition modules, each dedicated to task-specific, survival-specific functions such as obeying parents, or being suspicious of strangers, or ostracizing noncooperators. In picking mates, men are disposed to select younger women, who are likely to be fertile. Women are disposed to select men of social status, who are likely to be good providers.

Critics find that some more or less "automatic" behavior is desirable. Subroutines to which we are genetically inclined are shortcuts to survival, reliable modes of operating whether or not persons have made much rational reflection over these behaviors. Nevertheless, the mind is not overly compartmentalized, because behaviors interconnect. If women are prone to choose men of status, that requires considerable capacity to make judgments about what counts as status economically, politically, and religiously. They will have to judge which one of their suitors, who often are still relatively young, is most likely to attain status in the decades of their child rearing. Behavioral modules seem unlikely for the detail of such decisions under changing cultural conditions. Capacities to select such a mate are perhaps somewhat "instinctive," but they are unlikely to be an adaptive mechanism isolated from general intelligence and moral sensitivity.

Any such articulated behavioral modes need to be figured back into a more generalized intelligence. Those who advocate evolutionary psychology need to integrate many disciplines: evolutionary biology, cognitive science, behavioral ecology, psychology, hunter-gatherer studies, social anthropology, biological anthropology, primatology, and neurobiology. These are not disciplines in which one becomes expert by behavioral mechanisms using a Swiss-army-knife mind. Educators, whether scientists or humanists, need broadly analytical and synoptic minds. Evolutionary psychologists seem to be arguing that we can and ought be able to re-adapt by critical thought these adapted minds we inherit.

In overall assessment, many conclude that humans live under what Robert Boyd and Peter J. Richerson call "a dual inheritance system" (1985). Humans have some dispositions to which they are genetically disposed, and other dispositions into which they are culturally educated. Their actual behavior is an interactive resultant. Human behaviors fall within an ellipse with two foci, one genetic and one cultural, and, depending on where one is within the ellipse, behaviors may be dominantly under the pull of genes, or culture, or various hybrids with components of both. In the "leashing" analogy, the leashing can be of culture by nature, or nature by culture, or each keeping the other leashed with various lengths of leash.

How individuals behave in fact is often determined by their learning experiences, or by social trends. Choices depend on parents, teachers, peers, advertising pressures, fads and fashions, social policies and institutions. Even in behaviors regarding biological reproduction, cultural beliefs can override any genetic dispositions to maximize offspring. L. L. Cavalli-Sforza and M. W. Feldman (1981) show that fertility has declined in Europe in the last century, and that Italian women, for example, do not maximize their offspring, differing in their beliefs and behavior from their mothers and grandmothers. The fertility rate per woman in the United States fell from 7 in 1800 to 2.1 in 1990, in a period in which resources rose at a rate matching the fall in fertility. The reasons for the changes must be cultural, not genetic.

Richard C. Lewontin, a Harvard biologist, concludes: "The genes, in making possible the development of human consciousness, have surrendered their power both to determine the individual and its environment. They have been replaced by an entirely new level of causation, that of social interaction with its own laws and its own nature" (1991, p. 123). Marshall Sahlins, an anthropologist, concludes: "Biology, while it is an absolutely necessary condition for culture, is equally and absolutely insufficient: it is completely unable to specify the cultural properties of human behavior or their variations from one human group to another" (1976, p. xi). Biology determines some outcomes but underdetermines many others.

Sociobiologists claim to give a scientific account of the "human qualities . . . insofar as they appear to be general traits of the species," the human "biogram" (Wilson, 1975, p. 548). Likewise, the evolutionary psychologists, though distancing themselves from too simplistic a genetic determination of culture, are hoping for "universal mechanisms" in the plural behavioral routines of their "adapted mind." Explanations should be based on "the underlying level of universal evolved architecture. . . . One observes variable manifest psychologies or behaviors between individuals and across cultures and views them as the product of a common, underlying evolved psychology, operating under different circumstances" (Barkow, Cosmides, and Tooby, 1992, p. 45).

Kenneth Bock complains: "Human culture histories here emerge as fortuitous meanderings of people within bounds set by a human nature produced by organic evolution" (Bock, 1980, p. 118). Blacks were slaves in the southern United States and freed in 1863 during the Civil War. Long segregated, in the second half of the twentieth century they became quite integrated into American life, and the great-grandchildren of slaves became legislators, mayors, college presidents, and military generals. A generic theory common to all *Homo sapiens* cannot explain the struggle from slavery to freedom by applying a universal theory to variant initial cultural conditions. The allegedly universal explanation is not robust enough to tell the particular critical stories of the exodus from slavery to freedom. The critical difference lies in the historically emergent ethical conviction that slavery is wrong and freedom is right, and that blacks are, in morally relevant respects, to be given equal opportunities and responsibilities with whites.

These newfound convictions have little to do with selfish genes or instinctive adaptive mechanisms. Persons with essentially the same genetic makeup are being converted from one ethic to the other. The biological theory is not explaining this cultural development.

BIBLIOGRAPHY

Barkow, Jerome H. "Evolved Constraints on Cultural Evolution." *Ethology and Sociobiology* 10 (1989): 1–10.

Barkow, Jerome H., Leda Cosmides, and John Tooby, eds. *The Adapted Mind: Evolutionary Psychology and the Generation of Culture.* New York, 1992.

Bock, Kenneth. *Human Nature and History: A Response to Sociobiology.* New York, 1980.

Boyd, Robert, and Peter J. Richerson. *Culture and the Evolutionary Process.* Chicago, 1985.

Cavalli-Sforza, Luigi Luca, and Marcus W. Feldman. *Cultural Transmission and Evolution: A Quantitative Approach.* Princeton, N.J., 1981.

Dawkins, Richard. *The Selfish Gene.* New edition. New York, 1989.

Geertz, Clifford. *The Interpretation of Cultures.* New York, 1973.

Hamilton, William D. "The Genetical Evolution of Social Behavior. Parts I and II." *Journal of Theoretical Biology* 7 (1964): 1–52.

Lewontin, Richard C. *Biology as Ideology: The Doctrine of DNA.* New York, 1991.

Rolston, Holmes, III. *Genes, Genesis, and God.* Cambridge, UK, 1999.

Ruse, Michael. *Taking Darwin Seriously.* Oxford, UK, 1986.

Ruse, Michael, and Edward O. Wilson. "Moral Philosophy as Applied Science." *Philosophy: Journal of the Royal Institute of Philosophy* 61 (1986): 173–192.

Sahlins, Marshall. *The Use and Abuse of Biology: An Anthropological Critique of Sociobiology.* Ann Arbor, Mich., 1976.

Whitehead, Alfred North. *Science and the Modern World.* New York, 1967.

Wilson, Edward O. *Sociobiology: The New Synthesis.* Cambridge, Mass., 1975.

Wilson, Edward O. *On Human Nature.* Cambridge, Mass., 1978.

Wilson, Edward O. *Consilience: The Unity of Knowledge.* New York, 1992.

HOLMES ROLSTON III (2005)

SOCIOBIOLOGY AND EVOLUTIONARY PSYCHOLOGY: DARWINISM AND RELIGION

A number of scientists argue that biology has much greater scope of application than previously thought, and they are ready to apply evolutionary theory (and other theories of biology) to all aspects of human existence, and to develop a new Darwinian social and human science. They hold that evolutionary biology can yield profound consequences for our understanding of human thought and behavior. This research program used to be called *sociobiology* but since the 1980s it often has been called *evolutionary psychology.* It is a disputed question whether sociobiology and evolutionary psychology are basically the same, or two different research programs in biology. What they do have in common is that both attempt to demonstrate the impact of biological evolution on the human mind, behavior, and culture, including the phenomena of religion.

Evolutionary psychology seeks to apply theories of evolutionary biology in order to understand human psychology. The basic strategy is to link evolutionary biology to psychology and psychology to culture. The working hypothesis is that operating beneath the surface of cultural variation is a human mind which contains universal, psychological mechanisms or species-typical information-processing programs which evolved in the Pleistocene period to solve adaptive problems regularly faced by our hunter-gatherer ancestors—problems that directly or indirectly affected reproduction, such as finding mates, or problems of protecting offspring, fleeing predators, communicating, and cooperating. The core idea is that if we want to understand culture, including religion, the best way to do this is to understand first that humans are not born with empty minds, a tabula rasa, or blank slate, which can be inscribed at will by society or individuals, but creatures whose minds are partly hardwired at birth. This hardwiring probably underlies many human universals, that is, forms of behavior and psychological characteristics shared by people in all cultures, such as incest avoidance, feelings of guilt, sex-role differences, and religious mythmaking. There is an inherent human nature driving human events, but it is shaped to cope with Pleistocene conditions rather than modern conditions.

THE SCOPE OF BIOLOGICAL EXPLANATIONS OF HUMAN AFFAIRS. Few scholars would dispute that human beings have evolved out of nature. It is also very probable that the main cause of evolutionary change is natural selection. But how much and how far natural selection has affected and shaped human thinking, behavior, and institutions is the subject of a very heated debate. The defenders of evolutionary psychology say that people have seriously underestimated the extent to which natural selection has shaped human thought and behavior; the critics claim that it is easy to overstate the extent to which evolutionary theory can give us detailed insights into human nature.

It might therefore be helpful to think about a scale of views about the appropriate application of evolutionary theory to humans, or about how much that can successfully be explained in Darwinian terms. We could then at least distinguish between:

1. *Anti-Darwinists* who maintain that evolutionary explanations are invalid when it comes to explaining both nature and culture.
2. *Non-Darwinists* who maintain that evolutionary—in contrast to cultural—explanations can tell us very little or perhaps nothing about human thought, behavior, and society.
3. *Moderate Darwinists* who maintain that evolutionary explanations can tell us important things about human thought, behavior, and society, and must therefore be treated as a supplement to and a possible correction to cultural explanations.
4. *Ultra-Darwinists* who maintain that evolutionary—in contrast to cultural—explanations can tell us very much or perhaps everything we need to know about human thought, behavior, and society.

We here have a continuum, and thus there are no clear lines of demarcation between these four views. Creationists exemplify the first extreme, and at the other end of the scale are people such as Daniel C. Dennett, who in *Darwin's Dangerous Idea* (1995) maintains that Darwin's dangerous idea (evolution by natural selection) bears "an unmistakable likeness to universal acid: it eats through just about every traditional concept, and leaves in its wake a revolutionized worldview, with most of the old landmarks still recognizable, but transformed in fundamental ways" (p. 63). Evolutionary psychologists belong more or less to the ultra-Darwinian camp. Anthropologists, sociologists, and scholars of religion, on the other hand, typically could be classified as non-Darwinians. Evolutionary psychologists have called their view the "standard social science model" and maintained that the understanding of the human mind present in this model—as basically passive, as a basin into which the local culture is gradually poured—has distorted the study of human beings and culture.

The crucial difference is that non-Darwinists (or standard social scientists) believe that we have now evolved to a state of being so much creatures of our culture that our evolutionary origins can tell us little or nothing about what we are now, whereas ultra-Darwinists (or Darwinian social scientists) think that an understanding of the evolutionary process that made us what we are is essential—it provides the key—for understanding who we are and why we behave and think the way we do.

This difference can be illustrated by focusing on, for instance, male polygynous behavior—men wanting to have sex with a lot of women. A non-Darwinian explanation of male philandering understands it as rooted in particular cultural backgrounds, which implies that in a different kind of cultural situation the behavior would not exist. A Darwinian explanation understands this kind of predisposition as hardwired into the male psyche, which implies that male polygynous behavior would likely manifest itself no matter what the cultural environment was like: it is genetically hardwired because such behavior increased the reproductive success of males (but not of females) in the environment in which the male psyche evolved.

How strong this male polygynous predisposition (or any other human psychological trait) is supposed to be is a point on which evolutionary psychologists disagree. Although they predict that most men would have a predisposition to philander, they might hold different views about whether males could control this desire fairly easily, or whether it is like hunger—something that must be fulfilled. Moreover, the strength of the psychological mechanisms in males for philandering does not have to be the same for all males. Various aspects of our character are deep in our genes, but they can vary between individuals. The extent to which a male philanders depends not only on the strength of this predispostion in the individual, but also on the social environment he inhabits, the prevailing social conventions, his attachment to his partner, and his religious beliefs.

Evolutionary psychologists, consequently, do not deny that the environment or culture as well as genetic factors play roles in determining human thought and behavior. The weaker the psychological trait is, the more space there is for cultural influence to shape human thought and behavior. But changes in society and human behavior could be very difficult and take a very long time if Darwinians are right. Given that (1) human genes change very slowly, and (2) the human brain is genetically hardwired to have a certain content, that is, particular species-specific psychological mechanisms that cause thought and behavior, it follows that (3) humans are actually adapted for living a life of the late Stone Age, because that is the historical period in which our genes and psychological mechanisms were formed, and consequently (4) we cannot with great success change certain things in human society, because in general, biological forces cannot be manipulated as easily as cultural forces. The last implication provides the breeding ground for the politically sensitive debate about any biological explanation of human behavior. Evolutionary psychology can have profound social, political, and religious implications.

Evolutionary Psychology of Religion. Religion constitutes a great challenge to evolutionary biology, because religion is one of the major categories of behavior undeniably unique to the human species. Whereas in morality we can find some similarities between animal behavior and moral behavior (for instance, in respect to reciprocal cooperation), this is not true when it comes to religious behavior. There exist no prayers, religious rituals, or beliefs in God or gods among members of other species living on this planet.

The standard Darwinian explanation of the existence of religion is that religion emerged and spread because it secured the reproductive success of those of our distant ancestors who embraced it. Tribes who developed religious beliefs, myths, and rituals had a better chance of surviving and reproducing than those tribes who failed to do so. Above all they congeal identity. Religious practice provided these individuals living in a harsh and dangerous environment with unquestioned membership in a group claiming great powers, and by this means gave them a driving purpose in life compatible with their self-interest. The beliefs, myths, rituals, and the institutional structures of different religions may differ greatly, but this is not crucial, because the function of all religions is ultimately the same—to protect the genes and secure the fitness of the individuals. The standard explanation of why religion is selectively advantageous is because it justifies and reinforces moral precepts. Religion indirectly, and morality directly, secured the genetic fitness of our distant ancestors, and for *Homo sapiens,* it continues to do so today. In fact, the most radical ultra-Darwinians hold that everything in culture serves the reproductive success of individuals and, ultimately, the success of their genes. Natural selection regulates everything of any importance in both nature and culture.

Some scientists such as Edward O. Wilson have concluded from the fact that religion is selectively advantageous that religion is probably an ineradicable part of human nature whose sources run much deeper than those of ordinary habits. Therefore, if people want to abandon traditional religions, they need to find a replacement. Wilson's controversial suggestion is that perhaps science can become our new religion—a secular religion he calls "scientific naturalism." Others, such as Scott Atran, deny the existence of a genetic religious inclination and maintain that humans merely have the capacity to become religious. This difference of opinion arises from the fact that Atran claims that religiosity is not an adaptation and has no evolutionary function as such. Another alternative evolutionary explanation of religion holds that religions are a byproduct of natural selection rather than a direct adaptation. Religion is not directly promoted by natural selection, but merely made possible by other features of the human organism, which gives it a survival advantage. Human intelligence, for instance, is an adaptation, but science is not; science is rather a byproduct of a big brain.

This second explanation of religion (and of other cultural phenomena) is of course something non-Darwinians also accept. The crucial difference, however, is that evolutionary psychologists maintain moreover that natural selection has framed universal human psychological mechanisms, stemming from our long-enduring existence as hunter-gatherers, which impose a particular substantive content on culture, or in this case, on religious representation. Consequently, evolutionary psychologists use evolutionary theory not only to explain why and when religion arises but also to explain recurrent patterns in religious thought and behavior. For instance, Pascal Boyer maintains that ideas about gods, spirits, and ghosts pervade religions because humans are endowed with species-typical psychological mechanisms which evolved in the Stone Age for reasoning about the behavior of human agents. It is because of these structural developments of the brain that ideas about supernatural agencies became and continue to be culturally widespread. Evolution by natural selection gave us a particular kind of mind so that only particular kinds of religious notions can be acquired.

Criticism of Evolutionary Psychology. Evolutionary psychology is still in its early phase, and any well-grounded verdict about its fruitfulness and adequacy when it comes to understanding religion will have to wait for its further development. Nevertheless, a variety of critical responses against evolutionary psychology have emerged from biologists such as Stephen Jay Gould and Richard Lewontin, philosophers such as Holmes Rolston and Mikael Stenmark, and religionists such as John Bowker and Keith Ward. Their charges include that evolutionary psychology—in some or all of its versions—contains a naturalist-atheistic bias; that it presupposes scientism (the idea that all genuine knowledge is to be found through science and science alone); that it is self-refuting; that it is unrigorous (data are skimpy); that it neglects alternative hypotheses; that it does not take seriously the fact that there are many alternative evolutionary forces besides direct adaptation that affect the establishment of characters; and that it fails to explain religious missionary activity, which helps to ensure the replication of genes unlike the missionaries' own.

Although it would be undeniably interesting to reach a general verdict about the prospect of evolutionary psychology, it is important to consider its merits and demerits on a case-by-case basis. Perhaps some elements of religious thought and behavior can best be explained in Darwinian terms, whereas others require instead cultural explanations. We should not accept evolutionary psychology because it is sometimes correct, nor should we reject it because it is sometimes mistaken. The future will tell whether evolutionary psychology will be of great or minor importance for the study of religion.

Bibliography

Atran, Scott. *In Gods We Trust: The Evolutionary Landscape of Religion.* Oxford, 2002. A provocative evolutionary account of the so-called counterintuitive and factually impossible world of religions.

Barkow, Jerome H.; Leda Cosmides; and John Tooby, eds. *The Adapted Mind: Evolutionary Psychology and the Generation of Culture.* Oxford, 1992. A highly influential book in which the research program of evolutionary psychology is presented.

Bowker, John. *Is God a Virus? Genes, Culture, and Religion.* London, 1995. A critical response to Lumsden and Wilson's *Genes, Mind, and Culture* by a religionist.

Boyer, Pascal. *Religion Explained: The Evolutionary Origins of Religious Thought.* New York, 2001.

Broom, Donald M. *The Evolution of Morality and Religion.* Cambridge, U.K., 2003. An evolutionary account of the close ties between morality and religion.

Dawkins, Richard. *River Out of Eden: A Darwinian View of Life.* New York, 1995. A controversial speculation from a Darwinian and naturalist perspective about "God's utility function."

Dennett, Daniel C. *Darwin's Dangerous Idea: Evolution and the Meanings of Life.* London, 1995. The ultra-Darwinian manifesto.

Gould, Stephen, and Richard Lewontin. "The Spandrels of San Marco and the Panglossian Paradigm—A Critique of the Adaptationist Programme." *Proceedings of the Royal Society of London B* 205 (1979): 581–598. The classic argument presented against the idea that natural selection regulates everything of any importance in evolution.

Hinde, Robert A. *Why Gods Persist: A Scientific Approach to Religion.* London, 1999. A defense of the idea that religious observance results from pan-cultural human characteristics which have shaped religious systems in all their diversity.

Lumsden, Charles, J., and Edward O. Wilson. *Genes, Mind, and Culture.* Cambridge, Mass., 1981. Presents an early version of evolutionary psychology, though it still was called sociobiology.

Mithen, Steven. *The Prehistory of the Mind: A Search for the Origins of Art, Religion, and Science.* London, 1996. An attempt to explain the connection between the development of the brain and the origins of religion.

Pinker, Steven. *The Blank Slate: The Modern Denial of Human Nature.* London, 2002. An influential criticism of the contemporary social sciences and the idea of an empty mind.

Pyysiäinen, Ilka, and Veikko Anttonen, eds. *Current Approaches in the Cognitive Science of Religion.* London, 2002. A collection of articles written by evolutionary psychologists of religion and scholars holding similar views.

Rolston, Holmes. *Genes, Genesis, and God: Values and Their Origins in Natural and Human History.* Cambridge, U.K., 1999. A critical but also sympathetic response to the biologization of religion.

Stenmark, Mikael. *Scientism: Science, Ethics, and Religion.* Aldershot, U.K., 2001. A critical philosophical discussion of evolutionary theories of morality and religion.

Stenmark, Mikael. "Contemporary Darwinism and Religion" In *Darwinian Heresies,* edited by Abigail Lustig, Robert J. Richards, and Michael Ruse, pp. 173–191. Cambridge, U.K., 2004. A presentation and analysis of different attitudes towards religion found among biologists.

Ward, Keith. *God, Chance, and Necessity.* Oxford, 1996. Contains a response by a religionist and theologian to some of the exaggerated claims of biologists about religion.

Wilson, David Sloan. *Darwin's Cathedral: Evolution, Religion, and the Nature of Society.* Chicago, 2002. Wilson explores the relevance of group selection for understanding religion and society.

Wilson, Edward O. *On Human Nature.* Cambridge, Mass., 1978. The classic attempt to develop and defend a Darwinian social and human science.

Wright, Robert. *The Moral Animal: The New Science of Evolutionary Psychology.* London, 1994. A well-written presentation of the theories of evolutionary psychology for the general public.

MIKAEL STENMARK (2005)

SOCIOLOGY

This entry consists of the following articles:

SOCIOLOGY AND RELIGION [FIRST EDITION]
SOCIOLOGY AND RELIGION [FURTHER CONSIDERATIONS]
SOCIOLOGY OF RELIGION [FIRST EDITION]
SOCIOLOGY OF RELIGION [FURTHER CONSIDERATIONS]

SOCIOLOGY: SOCIOLOGY AND RELIGION [FIRST EDITION]

The discipline of sociology has been closely associated with the study of religion ever since sociology emerged as a distinct field in the mid-nineteenth century; only psychology is similarly close. Indeed, Auguste Comte, the social philosopher who coined the word *sociology,* saw his new science equally as religion and as science. In his *Positive Philosophy* (1830–1842), and again in *Positive Polity* (1851–1854), Comte envisioned sociology (which he first named social physics) not only as the queen of the sciences but also as the scientific basis of the new religion of Positivism, which would gradually push all existing religions out of sight. There were some excellent thinkers of the nineteenth century—among them Harriet Martineau and Frederick Harrison in England—who took Comte's religion very seriously. But the real and enduring relationship between sociology and religion was established by those, including Comte, who saw religion as one of the vital constituents of the social bond and thus necessarily a matter for careful study by sociologists.

DEVELOPMENT OF THE DISCIPLINE. A significant change in attitude toward religion took place from that adopted by the eighteenth-century French *philosophes* to that represented by the nineteenth-century founders of sociology. The critical rationalists of the Enlightenment in the eighteenth century had seen religion essentially as a mental or intellectual phenomenon, for the most part a tissue of superstitions, and therefore capable of eradication once the truth was told the people; but the sociologists from the beginning saw religion as a nearly inseparable aspect of social organization, a necessary window to understanding the past and present. Karl Marx, no lover of religion in any form, was not denigrating religion when, in a famous phrase, he declared it the "opium of the people." What he meant, as the context of his essay on Hegel's *Philosophy of Right* shows, is that in a world of human exploitation, religion is necessary to man; it is at once "the expression of real distress and the protest against real distress." Religion would not be banished, Marx stressed, until all of the social conditions of religion had been removed by revolution. Friedrich Engels, after Marx's death, went even further. He found many analogies between the infant socialism of his day and the infant Christianity of imperial Rome. Those who wished to understand the foundations of Christianity, Engels advised, needed only to look at "a local section of the International Workingmen's Association." He even advanced the idea that socialism, when it eventually drove out Christianity, would itself take on some of the attributes of religion. In this prophecy he has been proved largely right. As socialism became a mass movement in Europe in the nineteenth and early twentieth centuries, a prominent element was the apostasy of socialists from Judaism or Christianity and their turning to a surrogate. The longer socialism lasts in the Soviet Union, the more intense the reverence for Lenin and the more numerous the festivals and ceremonies in honor of great personages and events of the past.

Ludwig Feuerbach's *The Essence of Christianity* (1841) must be seen (despite Marx's assault on it) as a profoundly sociological work in its dominant theme of religion as alienation and etherealization of powers belonging in man alone, and also in the structural character of his treatment of dogma, liturgy, and symbol. Too often the political purpose of Alexis de Tocqueville's classic *Democracy in America* (2 vols., 1835–1840) leads us to overlook the cultural and social content of the work, especially in the second volume. Religion fascinated Tocqueville, and along with analyses of Protestantism and Roman Catholicism based upon the social-status groups to be found in each, there are treatments of the patterns that spiritual fanaticism and of pantheism tend to take in democratic society. Frédéric Le Play's monumental work *The European Workers* (1855), although directed primarily to family structures, contains a significant amount of insight into religion and the worker.

The attention these early sociologists gave religion in their studies of the social order was magnified in the works of the European sociologists at the end of the nineteenth century who are the true founders of contemporary sociological theory. Max Weber, Émile Durkheim, Ferdinand Tönnies, Georg Simmel, and Ernst Troeltsch all made the study of religion a crucial aspect of their systematic theories of society and of a human's relation to society. We shall come back to these seminal theorists, for they are still very much a part of current sociology. For the moment suffice it to say that in the aggregate they subjected religion to precisely the same kind of study that went into their explorations of politics, morality, science, and other major phenomena of modern society. Durkheim's *Elementary Forms of the Religious Life* (1912), without question his greatest book, richly represents the application to religion of the modern sociological concepts of community, role, social interaction, and hierarchy. Weber's *The Protestant Ethic and the Spirit of Capitalism* (1904–1905) and, above all, his *Sociology of Religion* (1920–1921) demonstrated the functional role of Calvinist belief in the seventeenth-century rise of the Protestant work ethic and illuminated the interaction throughout history of major forms of religion and the prevailing currents of social hierarchy and of bureaucracy. In his *Gemeinschaft und Gesellschaft* (Community and Society; 1887) Tönnies stressed religion as well as family as crucial elements of the "community" that he counterposed to "society," the former close and cohesive, the latter tending toward impersonality and anonymity. It was Troeltsch who, in his *Social Teachings of the Christian Church* (1912), made the fundamental distinction between "churches" and "sects" a fertile basis for insight into the effects of structural characteristics in religion upon matters of faith and dogma. Simmel, primarily interested in the social elements of capitalism and also of human personality and its intimate recesses, chose to make what he called "autonomous religious values" central elements of all forms of social interaction. Whether it is the tie between child and parent or that between citizen and nation, there is, Simmel declared, an ineradicable "religious key" to be found.

A kind of symbiotic relationship existed in the nineteenth century between sociology and religion. It should not be overlooked that in many areas religion, quite independently of currents in the social sciences, took on a strong social consciousness, manifest in the Social Catholic tradition in France and Germany and in the Social Gospel of some of the Protestant churches, especially in England and the United States. Interest in the study as well as the possible relief of social problems—delinquency, family breakdown, alcoholism, and poverty—is first manifest in the United States, not in the colleges and universities, but in religious seminaries; the study was thought by seminary leaders to be vital to any clergyman's pastoral work. Many of the sociologists active in the early part of the twentieth century began their careers as clergymen or seminarians. It is not at all surprising that, during its first half-century, American sociology, lacking the kind of strong philosophical and historical influences that guided sociology in Europe, chose social problems as its primary subject matter. The American public may thus be forgiven for sometimes confusing sociology with socialism. From the beginning, the character of sociology in America was, and in some measure still is, more pragmatic, problem-oriented, and policy-directed than in Europe.

This close and reciprocal relationship between religion and sociology calls attention to another important aspect of their common history. Both areas of thought, sociology and the distinctively social cast of religion in the West, may be profitably seen as intellectual responses to the two great revolutions of modern times: the industrial and the democratic. Beginning in England and France in the eighteenth century, these massive disturbances of the social landscape spread in the nineteenth century to all of Europe and in the twentieth to the whole world. The growth and mechanization of the factory system, the mushrooming of villages into cities, the multiplication of population, the development of more egalitarian democracies and wider electorates—all of these, together with some of their by-products such as science and technology, the spirit of secularism, and an ever growing political bureaucracy, were bound to have profound impact upon the traditional social structure of Western nations. Everywhere the forces of political and economic modernism resulted in the fragmentation of ancient loyalties—of nation, community, kin, and religion. In sum, the rise and spread of sociology in the nineteenth and the twentieth centuries are part and parcel of the dual revolution that overcame first the West, then the world.

SOCIOLOGICAL ANTINOMIES. More than any other social science, sociology is the almost immediate intellectual result of the two revolutions. This fact is abundantly illustrated by the broad antinomies of the new discipline, which either encompass or loom over its more concrete concepts. In the sociological tradition five major antinomies arose in response to the great social changes of the past two centuries; each embodies a perspective that focuses upon a particular dialectic.

1. *Community versus Society* is the first of these antinomies, the opposition that Tönnies referred to as that between *Gemeinschaft* and *Gesellschaft:* the smaller, more cohesive, communal, and durable social relationships contrasted to the larger, looser, and more impersonal relationships of the marketplace and to the equally large and impersonal ties inherent in the national state. From the beginning, sociologists tended to see conflict between the two types of relationship. This conflict increasingly is resolved in modern society by the triumph of the latter over the former, with consequent reduction in the necessary nurturing conditions of personality, morality, and social order.

2. *Authority versus Power* is the second antinomy. Authority is the natural accompaniment of any kind of organization, whether small and informal or large and impersonal. Authority inheres in the very roles of the members of such groups; in some degree it is natural to the very fabric of social life. Power, however, as the term is used by the pioneering sociologists, is characteristically perceived through its manifestations in the state and in large, corporate industry. Power tends to be more coercive than authority; more important, it is impersonal, rule-bound, office-centered, and expansive. In modern sociological writing, *bureaucracy,* whether in government, large industry, or profession, is most commonly made the focus of power, rather than authority. Here too an intrinsic conflict is perceived, and there is a wide conviction that in modern history the forces of bureaucratic power are winning out against traditional types of social and moral authority.

3. *Status versus Class,* the third antinomy, is a dichotomy emphasized in the work of Max Weber. But, like the other antinomies, it is found almost everywhere in sociology. Here

traditional systems of hierarchy such as those spawned by Western feudalism, systems characterized by an almost universally perceived and accepted structuring of populations into upper, middle, and lower classes, are sharply distinguished from the diverse, variegated, and highly specialized statuses held by individuals in modern society as the result of the atomization of traditional classes under the blows of the two great revolutions. This antinomy, too, reflects a contrast between modern society and the whole social order devastated or made largely obsolete by industrialism and democracy.

4. *Sacred versus Secular,* the fourth antinomy, is where religion as the subject of sociological study most obviously comes to mind. From the sociological point of view, the large trends in modern history—impersonalization of social relationships, bureaucratization of authority, and the fragmentation of traditional classes—are accompanied by the secularization of society: the replacement of sacred values by others based upon utility, pragmatism, and hedonism.

5. *Membership versus Alienation* is the fifth and final member of my list of sociological antinomies. Throughout sociology, especially among the pioneers from Comte to Durkheim, there is the clear sense that modern society reflects a widespread alienation of individuals from their accustomed memberships in family, community, religion, and social class. More than any other social science, sociology is responsible for the image of "the masses," of large aggregates of people wrenched from their traditional roles and made into a standardized, homogenized, and faceless multitude. For sociology, the very essence of alienation is the estrangement of individuals from community and other primary forms of association—estrangement even from self.

CENTRAL CONCEPTS. With this historical background in mind, it is possible to understand more clearly the patterning of central concepts in contemporary sociology. We shall confine ourselves to those that have virtually universal acceptance by sociologists and that, taken together, constitute the theoretical structure of sociology today. All have been widely useful in understanding religion and the other major institutions of society. The concepts are primarily analytical, but they also take on significance as tools in social synthesis and the making of social policy. Although these concepts originated in the several great moral perspectives outlined above, their value to sociology and the other social sciences lies solely in their scientific utility in the study of human behavior.

Social interaction. All social structures are compounds of certain fundamental, universal patterns of social interaction. Social interaction among human beings differs from all other types of interaction in nature in that it is *symbolic:* that is, organized around signs and symbols that carry distinct meanings to those involved in the interaction. Animals interact; so do atoms and molecules; but symbolic interaction is limited to human beings. They alone fashion arbitrary symbols, reflected in language, thought, morality, religion, and other spheres—all of which constitute human culture, which has its own paths of evolution through time. Human thought is purposive, searching for meanings, responding to nature only through the acquired "filters" of values, norms, and meanings passed on from generation to generation. Our interactions are all influenced by the "pictures in our heads" (Walter Lippman), by our "definition of the situation" (W. I. Thomas). We never react to others or to the environment at large in a direct, unfiltered way. No matter who or what is before us, we perceive it as part of a larger context of meaning, one that we usually have experienced before. The really crucial episodes of symbolic interaction with other people take place during infancy and childhood. That is when, precisely through such interactions, the individual's self begins to take shape. The early American sociologist Charles H. Cooley referred to the self as "the looking-glass self," meaning that the reflection of ourselves we see in the responses of others to us has a strong influence upon what kinds of selves—passive, aggressive, diffident, demonstrative, inward- or outward-turning—we are likely to be throughout our lives.

Social aggregates. When we look out on the world, we do not see masses of discrete individuals. We see social groups, associations, and organizations—or rather, we see individuals who are nearly inseparable from such aggregates. Man, as Aristotle wrote, is a social animal. What I have noted in the paragraph above about social interaction supports this claim. Interaction not only takes place in terms of meanings ascribed by the individuals concerned; it also tends to fix these meanings through symbols as elements of the culture that is transmitted through social mechanisms from one generation to the next. Social groups are composites of basic types of social interaction: cooperation, conflict, conformity, coercion, exchange, and so forth.

A great deal of contemporary sociological theory deals with analyses of social groups and organizations of all kinds and sizes. The reason for such analysis is not only the intrinsic interest of the structures themselves but the variable effects different types of groups have upon individual behavior. One of the most famous and by now deeply rooted typologies of social aggregates was referred to above: Tönnies's *Gemeinschaft-Gesellschaft,* or what Cooley called *primary* and *secondary groups.*

The sociological theory of groups, communities, and associations has been widely applied to religion in the literature of sociology. Émile Durkheim declared that religion originated in primitive man's absolute dependence upon his community and therefore his worship of it. Durkheim demonstrated through examples how the primitive worship of tribe and totem has become transmuted into many of the more ethereal symbols of the advanced and universal religions. Troeltsch and Simmel showed the close correlation between the size of a religious organization and the type of doctrine held: in small sects it is easier to insist upon a strict, undeviating dogma and code of conduct than in the larger, more cosmopolitan, and relatively impersonal churches. Every belief that is in any way tinged by religious passion suffers in strictness and purity as the number of its adherents grows. As Simmel pointed out, the history of socialism illustrates this as well as does that of Christianity.

Sociologists have recently given much attention to the *reference group*. This may be family, school class, church group, or neighborhood, or it may be a street gang or other manifestation of deviant or delinquent behavior. Whatever its nature, the group is by definition the social entity—complete with values, symbols, and role models—to which one tends chiefly to refer in self-appraisals. One's assessments of one's own actual or potential bravery, cowardice, honesty, loyalty, team play, or betrayal are formed by observation and experience with one's dominant reference group. At any given time we may, especially in complex modern society, have not one or two but many reference groups of varying importance. But generally one group is supreme at any given time: in civil life it may be one's professional group; in war, however, it is likely to be composed of other, comparable, soldiers.

Social authority. The study of authority follows from the study of groups. No group, however small and informal, is without some degree of authority. It may proceed from the dominant personality in the group, from ready consensus, from cooperation necessary to the achievement of some end, or from mere custom and tradition. But no form of social life exists without authority, from the mother's domination of infant to the state's sovereignty over its citizens.

The most famous theorist of authority is Max Weber, who identifies three types: the *charismatic*, the *traditional*, and the *rational-bureaucratic*. The first is the kind of authority that emanates directly from the great individual, whether a Jesus in religion, a Caesar in warfare, or a Napoleon in war and government. Such authority is inseparable from that individual. Often, as in Judaism, Christianity, and Buddhism, the charismatic authority of the founder becomes "routinized," as Weber put it, through disciples and followers. Words spoken by the founder become writ, tradition, dogma, and liturgy. Most traditional authority is the result of cumulation through the centuries of certain injunctions or admonitions or simple ways of doing things originally prescribed by some leader of charismatic power. The third great type of authority for Weber was bureaucracy—a rationalized, calculated, designed structure in which the office or function rather than the individual is crucial. Weber and his followers see a large part of history as involving the passage of authority from the charismatic to the traditional to, finally, especially in the modern Western world, the rational-bureaucratic. Weber saw educational, charitable, military, and political organizations, as well as churches, undergoing this development in time.

Some sociologists, such as Robert K. Merton, building on Weber's base, have studied the impacts upon personality of these types of authority, especially the traditional and the bureaucratic. When Weber, citing the poet Schiller, wrote of "the disenchantment of the world," he had in mind the relentless supplanting of the purely spontaneous and the traditional or customary by the forces of bureaucracy in the modern world. A bureaucratization of the spirit as well as of organizations takes place; sociologists following Weber have brought insights into the sheer power of bureaucracy—power to bend men's wills, power to alter the very ends of an organization. Thus the church, the hospital, the university, or the army may grow so large that the organization becomes its own reason for being, where devotion to organizational processes may crowd out many of the original motivating goals.

The structure of authority has played an immense role in the histories of religions. The authority of Hinduism lies chiefly in the Indian caste system, and it was revolt against caste and its forms of punishments for infractions of caste inviolability that as much as anything inspired the Buddha's renunciation of Hinduism and his founding of a new religion flowing directly from his charismatic being. Struggles over the legitimacy of priestly and ecclesiastical authority have been the substance of a great deal of Christian history: Indeed, the Reformation was largely a challenge to the legitimacy of the authority wielded by the pope and the Curia Romana. It would be difficult to find any religion in which boundless authority is not attributed to some divine being or principle, but as to the mediation by men on earth of that authority, religious sects and churches, like political and economic organizations, differ vastly, ranging from the self-immured anchorite to an organization as huge and complex as the Roman Catholic church.

Social roles. "All the world's a stage," wrote Shakespeare, "and all the men and women merely players. / They have their exits and their entrances; / and one man in his time plays many parts." Natural man is a myth, although that fact has not prevented people through the ages from wondering what an individual would be were he totally isolated from all the social and cultural forces that shape our lives and assign us our varied roles. It is as true to say that human beings are roles as it is to say that all roles are human beings. We do not know people except in their near infinity of roles, but on the other hand any study of roles must be of individual persons.

Roles are, at bottom, ways of behavior, most of which have been handed down through the ages. There is no recognized role that is without norms from the social order to give it direction and meaning; nor can there be a social role that is not a part of some social union or interaction. Even Simeon Stylites occupied a role in the desert that, although physically isolated, was nevertheless part of a religious organization. Very strong in any role is the element of legitimacy. We will accept from individuals in their role capacities as police, physicians, clergy, teachers, and parents obligations we might be loath to accept from others. We do not consider the most intimate examination of our bodies offensive or immoral if done by a physician, nor do we think the close observation of our minds disturbing if it is carried out by a priest or psychiatrist. Role, in short, confers legitimacy. Killing other human beings is widely deemed immoral, but most people do not hold the same act as immoral when done by a soldier in fulfillment of his legitimate role.

There is also a strong element of duty inherent in every recognized role. To occupy the role of mother or father, teacher or lawyer, cleric or police officer, or any other of the multitude of roles in society means to accept the various values and norms that define or identify these roles. When we find ourselves saying "It is my duty to" perform certain acts of social character, we are only acceding to the implicit demands inherent in every social role. To assume the role of parent is to assume certain duties and obligations, starting with the care and feeding of the infant. Roles are often reciprocal and complementary. Obviously there cannot be a teacher without a student, a physician without a patient. Our culture, drawn from the ages, is the source of the diverse prescriptions for what we think of as normal role-behavior. Illness may be physical in origin, but the actual *roles* of the sick—self-regard and regard by others—are cultural and vary from people to people, age to age.

We must not overlook the phenomenon of *role conflicts.* In simple societies these are few, but they are numerous in a society that is as filled with specializations and alternatives as modern Western society. Essentially the feminist revolution of the past century in the West has been a series of assaults upon previously unchallenged roles of women. Much social history is in essence the history of roles—their persistence, their alterations, their conflicts, and their erasure by negative forces.

Nor should we overlook the history of the *prestige* of given roles. Roles are statuses: any role can be evaluated by its rank in a social order's scale of values. Whenever we ask about anyone's status, we are asking about his position in a social hierarchy. When one is born to or achieves a given role in society, he also, willy-nilly, has the status of that role. A given role—for example, physician, businessman, scholar, or leather worker—can be of very high or low status, depending upon the social order or age in history. But despite the relativity and diversity of status rankings of roles, there are certain universal criteria of the kind of status of a given role—namely, gender, age, wealth, power, education, job, ethnicity, and kinship. Thus, in Western society, a middle-aged, economically or politically powerful, Caucasian, college-educated, professional man of "good family" has historically been accorded high status.

Social classes are coalescences of people who have low, medium, or high "amounts" of the various kinds of status by which a society ranks its members. Karl Marx declared social class to be the dominant key to the understanding of history, and further believed that in due time the lower class—the proletariat or working class—would overthrow the upper class by revolution, thus inaugurating socialism and a classless society. For Marx, social class, whether low or high, was the crucial determinant of social behavior. But Max Weber, the principal architect of the contemporary sociological theory of status and stratification, realized that in modern, developed Western society, the single concept of class was inadequate to define the complexity of social life. He thus distinguished between power (chiefly political), economic level, and status—the last meaning the ranking an individual may receive in society by factors independent of power and wealth—for example, ancestry, family, breeding, schooling, mental acuity, talent, and so forth. Sociologists have come to realize that, in Western society, social classes are not the distinct, homogeneous entities they once were. The forces of modernization have fragmented social classes as they have kinship systems and certain religions. It is much more accurate today in the West to refer to *minorities* and *elites,* all of highly variable status, all dependent upon numerous spheres of values in our complex society. The number of elites is almost beyond count, and they are to be found in sports, theater, movies, television, and even crime as well as in politics, industry, professional groups, and universities. The large number of roles generated by liberal democracy, a highly technological society, and an increasingly secularized and relativist moral order carry with them the inevitable prestige-ranking that results in their being statuses, ascribed and achieved, as well as roles.

Deviance and change. From its beginnings in the nineteenth century, sociology has been closely concerned with the phenomena of deviance and change in human behavior. Few human beings live their lives in perfect accord with the rules and norms governing social interaction, social groups, social authorities, and social roles. Always there is at least an infinitesimal variance between role perfection, ideally defined, and actual role performance. When such variance becomes pronounced, we refer to it as deviant behavior, that is, behavior that violates the normative rules, codes, and stereotypes of a given social order. From a universal point of view, relativity is the very essence of moral behavior; behavior that would be regarded as deviant in a middle-class U. S. suburb might be acceptable in an urban ghetto or in an utterly foreign culture. Headhunting would be regarded as deviant, to say the least, in America and most parts of the world, but it is far from being perceived as deviant in certain primitive cultures. The same holds for cannibalism and a host of other practices. What defines deviant behavior is the flouting or bypassing of rules and norms in a specific social order or system. Killing, robbing, arson, mutilation, and assault are almost universally regarded as deviant *within* the social order, but they are not so regarded when they are the acts of legitimate soldiers at war with external enemies.

Émile Durkheim is probably the preeminent pioneer in the study of social deviance, and his most basic principles continue to undergird its study and conceptualization. From Durkheim, especially his famous *Suicide* (1896), we have learned that deviance is at one and the same time abnormal and normal. Suicide, crime, desertion of family, arson, and the like are all abnormal in that they are recognized as violations of a given moral and social code and are punished or deplored accordingly. But, Durkheim continued, certain incidences of these acts of deviance are to be expected—are to be considered *sociologically* normal—when certain social, economic, and political conditions are present. Thus, sudden and high rates of urbanization, industrialization, and secularization in a population are almost certain to induce processes of community disorganization that in turn lead to erosions of social authority and of traditional social roles. Deviant behavior almost always increases in such circumstances. Durkheim concluded that the high rates of suicide he observed in the Western nations resulted from the alienation of people from traditional moral values and from the ties of close social cohesion—family, church, village, neighborhood, and so on.

When we consider change, we often find that it is the continuation and cumulation of deviant acts that will in time lead to changes in the social groups and roles by which deviant behavior is identified. One need think only of the changes that have occurred in the last century in the public definition of what is proper behavior in a "lady." There is no need to list the behavior patterns now almost universally accepted as respectable in women that even a half century ago would have raised the eyebrows of the conventional. It suffices to say that in very large degree the change in the criteria of female respectability over many decades is the cumulative consequence of a multitude of at first minor, then major deviances from the norm.

Religion is, of course, a fertile field for the study of deviance in the strict sociological sense. Many of the mainline religions have undergone extraordinary changes in creed and liturgy during the last century, and although we cannot ignore the calculated, planned nature of many of these changes, we are obliged to note the small but increasingly significant deviations of religious people from the strict codes of their forebears.

But not all social change is gradual, continuous, and cumulative. When we turn to the more notable historical changes in social systems and social organizations, we are forced to deal with the discontinuous—with the major conflict, the sporadic event, and the sudden, unforeseeable intrusion of an alien system. Nor can we overlook the immense force of charismatic human beings in religion, politics, science, or other social systems. Most change is slow and incremental, often so slow as to be more nearly persistence and fixity than change. But there are periods when changes are great, sudden, and explosive, inducing myriad consequences in thought and action in the population. Wars such as the two great ones of the twentieth century, spectacular revolutions such as the French and the Russian, spiritual awakenings such as that associated with John XXIII and the Second Vatican Council, major epidemics, rapid scientific and technological advance—these and other great interruptions of the normal have to be taken into consideration when we deal with social change.

There is one more preoccupation with change that has sociological as well as ethnological or anthropological aspects: *social evolution.* At the same time that anthropologists such as E. B. Tylor, Lewis Morgan, and James G. Frazer were constructing their patterns of social and cultural evolution, such sociologists as Auguste Comte, Herbert Spencer, and Lester Ward were engaged in almost identical pursuits. Inevitably religion figured large in social-evolutionary schemes. There was search for, and wide disagreement about, the natural origin of religion: some found it in psychic states such as animism, others in ritual acts like totemism, still others in awe of celestial bodies and terrestrial phenomena such as the changes of seasons. There was similarly universal interest among anthropologists and sociologists, and again wide disagreement, about the natural stages of development that religion has gone through from its origins to the development of the great world religions such as Christianity and Islam. For the most part, contemporary sociology has dismissed the kind of interest in social and religious evolution that was rife in the nineteenth century. Both unilinear and multilinear patterns of the supposed development of religion in the human race have come under wide attack as being more nearly philosophical and speculative than scientific. Unlike their forebears, today's sociologists do not foresee the demise of religion and its succession by the scientific and secular. Religion, it is now generally believed by sociologists, answers certain psychosocial needs in human beings, and until or unless these needs become casualties of biological evolution of the human species, religion in one or another form will remain a persisting reality of human culture.

Sociological interest in religion is as great today as it ever has been during the past two centuries. Once the orientation toward universalist schemes of religious evolution faded, much more concrete, empirical, and scientific studies of religious behavior began to proliferate in all Western countries. Numerous sociological studies are to be found on such topics as the relation of religious thought and behavior to social class, to ethnicity, and to wealth and poverty; the systems of authority, stratification, and role formations in religion; religion and political ideology; and religion as a mainspring of social integration, but also of social change and revolution. These are but a few of the problems concerning religion that present-day sociologists consider significant. The general development and refinement of sociological methods of investigation—survey, case history, statistical, and mathematical, among others—have occurred as often in inquiries into religious behavior as in studies of other dimensions of human existence. There is no reason to suppose that the close relation between religion and sociology, now close to two centuries old, will dissolve soon.

SEE ALSO Comte, Auguste; Durkheim, Émile; Evolution, article on Evolutionism; Marxism; Modernity; Society and Religion; Study of Religion; Tönnies, Ferdinand; Troeltsch, Ernst; Weber, Max.

BIBLIOGRAPHY

The *International Encyclopedia of the Social Sciences* (New York, 1968–1979) is indispensable as a reference work for further inquiries into the nature of sociology as a discipline, its principal concepts and methods, and its varied studies of religious life. For general histories of sociology, the following are recommended: Howard S. Becker and Harry Elmer Barnes's *Social Thought from Lore to Science,* 3 vols., 3d ed. (New York, 1961); Lewis A. Coser's *Masters of Sociological Thought* (New York, 1971), and my own *The Sociological Tradition* (New York, 1966), which is concerned at length with the relation between the rise of sociology and the two great revolutions of the modern world.

Robert K. Merton's *Social Theory and Social Structure,* rev. ed. (New York, 1968) offers an incisive and comprehensive conspectus of contemporary sociological theory. George C. Homans's *The Nature of Social Science* (New York, 1967) is a compact and penetrating statement of the conceptual apparatus of sociology; James A. Black and Dean J. Champion's *Methods and Issues in Social Research* (New York, 1976) and Gideon Sjoberg and Roger Nett's *A Methodology for Social Research* (New York, 1968) provide lucid surveys of the most significant methods today employed in sociological research. C. Wright Mills's *The Sociological Imagination* (Oxford, 1959) and Talcott Parsons's *The Social System* (Glencoe, Ill., 1951) offer spectacularly contrasting formulations of the ultimate goals of a scientific sociology. Each has proved to be seminal in subsequent sociological thought, the first for its emphasis upon the concrete, personal, and nonsystematic, the second for its stress upon sociology as a grand and unified structure of systematic theory.

On social and symbolic interaction, the classic work is George H. Mead's *Mind, Self, and Society* (1934; reprint, Chicago, 1963). All of the concepts of interaction through symbols and of the directive force of these upon the development of individual personality are to be found in this work. More recent studies of social interaction are *The Self in Social Interaction,* edited by Chad Gordon and Kenneth J. Gergen (New York, 1968), and George C. Homans's *Social Behavior: Its Elementary Forms* (New York, 1974).

Two works are fundamental historically in the sociological theory of communities and associations. First, Ferdinand Tönnies's *Community and Society* (1887), translated by Charles P. Loomis (New York, 1963), wherein the contrast between traditional, communal society and large-scale, impersonal society is made central, and Charles H. Cooley's *Social Organization* (1909; reprint, New York, 1962) in which the concepts of the primary and the secondary groups in the social order are advanced systematically. More recent works along this line are David Riesman's *The Lonely Crowd: A Study in the Changing American Character* (New Haven, 1950), and my own work, *The Quest for Community: A Study in the Ethics of Order and Freedom* (Oxford, 1953). George C. Homans's *The Human Group* (New York, 1950) is also valuable.

In the study of authority and power, the classic sociological writings are those of Max Weber at the turn of the century in which he distinguished charismatic, traditional, and rational-bureaucratic authority. His *The Theory of Social and Economic Organization* (1922), translated by Alexander Morell Hamilton and Talcott Parsons (Oxford, 1947), is probably the most complete source of Weber's theory of authority, though *Politics as a Vocation* (1919), translated by H. H. Gerth and C. Wright Mills (Philadelphia, 1965), is also valuable. Georg Simmel's study of superordination and subordination, found in *The Sociology of Georg Simmel,* translated and edited by Kurt Wolff (Glencoe, Ill., 1964), is also highly important. See also Seymour Martin Lipset's *Political Man* (Garden City, N.Y., 1960), Robert Bierstedt's *Power and Progress* (New York, 1974), and my own *Twilight of Authority* (Oxford, 1975).

In the identification of social roles and statuses in society, the writings of Simmel, Weber, Cooley, and Mead are fundamental. Robert K. Merton, as cited above, is invaluable for synthesis and summary of recent work done with respect to roles and role sets. David Riesman's *The Lonely Crowd,* also cited above, is notable for its differentiation of inner-directed, tradition-directed, and other-directed personalities in the light of the modern variegation of roles in society. Florian Znaniecki's *Social Relations and Social Roles* (San Francisco, 1965) is highly illuminating in its uniting of classic and contemporary studies. On social class and social status, we should not overlook Karl Marx's works, commencing with *The Manifesto of the Communist Party* and reaching culmination in *Capital.* The writings of Max Weber, already cited, are eminently pertinent here for their criticism of Marx and their shaping of the contemporary theory of class and status. See also Thomas B. Bottomore's *Elites and Society* (New York, 1965), John Dollard's *Caste and Class in a Southern Town,* 3d ed. (Garden City, N.Y., 1957), Nathan Glazer and Daniel P. Moynihan's *Beyond the Melting Pot* (Cambridge, Mass., 1963), Peter I. Rose's *They and We,* 2d ed. (New York, 1974), and Richard Sennett and Jonathan Cobb's *The Hidden Injuries of Class* (New York, 1973) for diverse and sensitive insights into status and class.

On deviant behavior, Albert K. Cohen's *Delinquent Boys: The Culture of the Gang* (Glencoe, Ill., 1955), Howard S. Becker's *Outsiders: Studies in the Sociology of Deviance* (New York, 1963), and Marshall B. Clinard's *Sociology of Deviant Behavior,* 4th ed. (New York, 1974), are all notable in the field. Ralph Ellison's novel *The Invisible Man* (New York, 1952) is a recognized masterpiece in the interpretation of individual alienation. David Riesman's *The Lonely Crowd* should be mentioned again in this context. *Contemporary Social Problems,* 4th ed., edited by Robert K. Merton and me (New York, 1976), is probably the most sweeping and comprehensive study of the various forms of deviance.

An excellent beginning in the sociology of social change is Wilbert E. Moore's *Social Change,* 2d. ed. (Englewood Cliffs, N.J., 1974). Cyril E. Black's *The Dynamics of Modernization* (New York, 1966) details the patterns of change found in developing countries, and Bryce F. Ryan's *Social and Cultural Change* (New York, 1969) presents a comparative picture of social change in Western and non-Western societies. For contrasting views on the relevance of social evolutionism to the study of change in time, see Talcott Parsons's *The Evolution of Societies,* edited by Toby Jackson (Englewood Cliffs, N.J., 1977), and my own *Social Change and History* (Oxford, 1969).

Following are a few of the more notable sociological studies of religion not mentioned above in the text. Joachim Wach's *Soci-*

ology of Religion (1944; reprint, Chicago, 1962) and J. Milton Yinger's *The Scientific Study of Religion* (New York, 1970) are excellent presentations of the broad perspectives of the subject. Peter L. Berger's *The Sacred Canopy: Elements of a Sociological Theory of Religion* (Garden City, N.Y., 1967) is distinctive in its command of both the theoretical and empirical aspects of the sociological study of religion. Close to it in importance, and giving greater scope to the methodologies involved, is Charles Y. Glock and Rodney Stark's *Religion and Society in Tension* (Chicago, 1965). Gerhard Lenski's *The Religious Factor: A Sociological Study of Religion's Impact on Politics, Economics, and Family Life* (Garden City, N.Y., 1961) is valuable for the author's own inquiry and also for his wide coverage of other scholarly works. Books on religion as an integrative and stabilizing force are legion; Guenter Lewy, in *Religion and Revolution* (Oxford, 1974), emphasizes the immense role of religion as a force for social change since ancient times. Finally, the monumental work of Werner Stark, *The Sociology of Religion: A Study of Christendom*, 5 vols. (New York, 1966–1972), must be recommended strongly.

ROBERT NISBET (1987)

SOCIOLOGY: SOCIOLOGY AND RELIGION [FURTHER CONSIDERATIONS]

Robert Nisbet's article is a summary of his lifelong views, expressed most fully in *The Sociological Tradition* (1966). According to Nisbet, the core of classical sociology—evinced in the work of Karl Marx (1818–1883), Alexis de Tocqueville (1805–1859), Émile Durkheim (1858–1917), Max Weber (1864–1920), Ferdinand Tönnies (1855–1936), and Georg Simmel (1858–1918)—is a set of five polarities or "antitheses." Together the antitheses spell out the difference between traditional and modern societies: community versus society, authority versus power, status versus class, sacred versus secular, and membership versus alienation. Sociology, for Nisbet, arose in response to the two great revolutions that brought about the change from tradition to modernity: the industrial revolution, beginning in England, and the democratic revolution, beginning in France.

It would be simplistic to say that for Nisbet classical sociology preaches conservativism. Nisbet is aware, for example, of Durkheim's liberalism and of his concern for the rights of individuals. Nisbet notes that Engels compares modern socialism with early Christianity and with recurrent millenarian movements. Still Nisbet's main concern is to show how religion was seen by classical sociologists as a conservative force, the loss of which, combined with the loss of the other bulwarks of tradition, led to the travails posed by modernity.

CONTEMPORARY SOCIOLOGICAL INTEREST IN RELIGION. Nisbet's article prompts three questions. First, is it truly the case that "sociological interest in religion is as great today as it ever has been since the past two centuries?" The question is not whether there are prominent sociologists of religion in the early twenty-first century but whether religion itself is still as central a topic for sociologists generally as it once was. Surely it is not, and surely the course of secularization that Nisbet stresses as a preoccupation of classical sociologists would lead one to expect a decline in interest.

CLASSICAL AND CONTEMPORARY SOCIOLOGY OF RELIGION. Second, while Nisbet emphasizes the continued influence of classical sociology, he acknowledges differences between it and contemporary sociology of religion. He notes that

> unlike their forebears, today's sociologists of religion do not foresee the demise of religion and its succession by the scientific and the secular. Religion, it is now generally believed by sociologists, answers certain psychological needs in human beings, and until or unless these needs become casualties of biological evolution of the human species, religion in one form or another will remain a persisting reality of human culture.

But is it true that contemporary sociologists, in contrast to classical ones, do not predict the end of religion? Surely there is scant census. If sociologists like Grace Davie deny the end of religion, sociologists like Steve Bruce (2002) predict it. Some critics of what is called "the secularization thesis" maintain that religion has taken new, less institutionalized forms—itself a challenge to the sociology of religion. Often it is said that religion, which is thereby defined as organized, is being replaced by a more free-floating "spirituality." Durkheim himself defined religion as organized and on that ground contrasted it to magic. But Durkheim, unlike Weber, argued that religion would never die out. There was then no consensus among classical sociologists either.

Is it true that contemporary sociologists deem religion eternal because they attribute it to "psychosocial needs"? If so, has there been a shift from religion seen as serving society to religion seen as serving the individual?

The classical sociologist who best fits Nisbet's characterization is indisputably Durkheim, for whom religion grandly serves society. For Durkheim, the function, or effect, of religion is the instillment or intensification of a sense of dependence on society. Members of society are beholden to it for everything, not least for their morality, language, tools, values, thoughts, categories of thought, and concept of objectivity. Knowing that none of these phenomena is their individual creation, members ascribe them to something external, on which they are therefore dependent. Everyday life confirms their dependence, but religion, which for Durkheim means above all religious gatherings, confirms it most intensely. Members feel "effervescent," as if possessed. The state they attribute to God in fact comes from the experience of the group. From dependence on God, and therefore on society, comes loyalty and therefore unity—the ultimate effect of religion. The society that prays together stays together.

However much religion shapes society, it itself is a social product. The origin of religion is not individual because there is no individual—more precisely no innate one. In primitive society members are occupationally alike and therefore have no distinctive identity and so no individuality. This relationship of members to one another Durkheim calls "mechanical solidarity." Only in modern society is there a division of labor and therefore the specialization that constitutes individuality. This relationship of members to one another Durkheim labels "organic solidarity." But even individuality is a social phenomenon: its cause is the division of labor, and its operation requires formal recognition of the individual by society.

Durkheim denies individuality any place in traditional religion, which deals entirely with the mechanical, preindividualistic side of social life. In modern society that side, and so traditional religion, will continue to diminish as organic solidarity grows. But Durkheim proposes the creation of a religion worshiping not God but the individual. Yet by the individual he means the nonegoistic individual, who reveres rather than violates the rights of others and who thereby promotes rather than threatens the group. Coinciding with the harmonious individuality of organic solidarity, Durkheim's new, secular religion would thus serve society no less fully than traditional religion has done. In short, no variety of sociology of religion could be more directed to the need of the group than Durkheim's.

By contrast, the need religion serves for Max Weber, Durkheim's fellow great classical sociologist of religion, is that of the individual. In "primitive" religion, which for Weber amounts to magic, the needs served are immediate and physical, such as food and clothing. In "higher" religion the need served is existential: a desire for "meaning" or "meaningfulness." Whether or not this need, which for Weber is the key one fulfilled by religion, qualifies as "psychosocial," it is conspicuously the need of an individual, not of a group.

Yet for Weber the group remains indispensable not only to the fulfillment of the need for meaning but to the very existence of it. A magician is like a plumber. He or she is self-employed and is hired anew each time. Not until there emerges a stable clientele of worshipers—a congregation or cult—do full-time religious officials or priests come into being. Not until priests succeed magicians does metaphysics (a comprehensive explanation of the world) emerge in place of mere techniques. Likewise not until priests arise do ethics (ends achieved through obedience) emerge in place of coercion (ends achieved through techniques). The combination of metaphysics and ethics makes religion "rational" and constitutes the stage of religion after magic. Finally, not until a cult emerges does the concept of a fixed god (singular, powerful, named, personal, and involved) emerge in place of the magical concept of multiple, weak, nameless, impersonal, and uninvolved fleeting gods. Only with the development of rational religion—a comprehensive explanation of the world, a prescribed means of securing long-term rewards, and a universal god permanently involved in human affairs—does there develop not so much a discrepancy between expectation and experience (there is a discrepancy whenever magic fails) as a desire to resolve that discrepancy systematically. That desire is for meaning.

A sufficient explanation for the failure of magic is that the technique has been misapplied. But rational religion must explain the failure of the gods to respond to the behavior they themselves have dictated. The gods have failed to prevent or withhold suffering, so the explanation sought is a theodicy. Since all human beings for Weber recognize the discrepancy between their expectations and their experiences, all harbor the potential desire for meaning. But its emergence depends on rational religion, the emergence of which itself depends on a particular kind of religious leader (a priest) whose emergence depends in turn on a particular kind of social organization (a cult). In short, the group provides the indispensable means to individual ends.

Undeniably Weber, like Durkheim, is also concerned with the impact of religion on society. For him, that impact, or effect, is unintentional. To cite Weber's most celebrated case, the role of ascetic Protestantism in creating capitalism was wholly coincidental.

For the contemporary sociologist of religion Peter Berger, as for Weber, a meaningful experience is a justified experience, and the experiences most requiring justification are suffering—death above all. But in contrast to Weber, for whom the need for meaning is implanted, for Berger the need is innate: "Men are congenitally compelled to impose a meaningful order upon reality" (Berger, 1969/1967, p. 22). If the need is innate, then society, hence sociology, plays no part in accounting for it. Berger epitomizes the shift, called "de-sociologizing," that Nisbet observes (Segal, 1989, pp. 109–135). Contemporary sociologists see religion as much less of a social phenomenon, and therefore much less of a subject for sociology, than classical ones did. If the need for meaning is innate and if in addition religion either best fulfills or even alone fulfills that need, then religion for contemporary sociologists is indeed eternal, as Nisbet declares.

Because religion for Berger justifies suffering, the meaning it provides constitutes, as for Weber, a theodicy. The justifications, or "legitimations," provided by religion are the staunchest possible ones because they carry the unassailable authority of divinity. In Berger's pet terms, religion confers on experience a "sacred canopy" or "plausibility structure."

Berger grants that religion serves not only the individual function of giving meaning but also the social function of securing obedience. Here he is like Durkheim. But he concentrates on the individual function and, more, deems the social one a consequence of it. Unjustified suffering threatens to trivialize even the most firmly sanctioned social life.

For Berger, as for both Durkheim and Weber, society is indispensable to the establishment and perpetuation of religion—no matter what the function of religion is. No Robinson Crusoe could either invent or sustain the legitimations that religion provides. Social support is, as for Durkheim, mandatory for validating those legitimations.

In his earlier writings Robert Bellah, like Durkheim, is primarily concerned with the effect of religion on society, not on the individual. Like Berger, he is concerned with how religion provides meaning as a way of securing obedience rather than as an end in itself.

Dealing with changing societies, Bellah investigates specifically how religion either spurs or retards modernization. Tokugawa religion, he argues, constitutes the Japanese counterpart to Weber's Protestant ethic:

> Japanese religion never tires of stressing the importance of diligence and frugality and of attributing religious significance to them, both in terms of carrying out one's obligations to the sacred and in terms of purifying the self of evil impulses and desires. That such an ethic is profoundly favorable to economic rationalization was the major point of Weber's study of Protestantism and we must say that it seems similarly favorable in Japan. (Bellah, 1957, p. 196)

Bellah calls his later approach to religion "symbolic realism" and distinguishes it from various other approaches. In so doing he is seemingly shifting the issue from the origin and function of religion to the truth of religion. As he declares: "If we define religion as that symbol system that serves to evoke . . . the totality that includes subject and object and provides the context in which life and action finally have meaning, then I am prepared to claim that as Durkheim said of society, religion is a reality *sui generis.* To put it bluntly, religion is true" (Bellah, 1970, pp. 252–253). But the truth of religion for Bellah is in fact its accordance with human experience of the world, not necessarily with the nature of the world itself. Because religion for Bellah makes no truth claims about the world itself, it is "beyond belief." Though Bellah refers to the "expressive" function of religion, religion for him functions to instill, not merely to articulate, attitudes toward the world. Religion functions primarily to give humans a secure, clear place in the world.

Later Bellah is asserting that religion functions primarily to serve not society but the individual. Because he, unlike Weber, makes the meaning-giving function of religion the function of religion from the start, he may, like Berger, be deeming the need for meaning innate. In that event he too would be "de-sociologizing" religion. He simply never says. Even so his focus on the bestowal of meaning as the chief function of religion at any stage makes him akin not only to Berger but also to other contemporary social scientists, notably the anthropologists Mary Douglas, Clifford Geertz, and Victor Turner and the psychoanalyst Erik Erikson.

SOCIOLOGY AND RELIGIOUS STUDIES. Third, the "close relation between religion and sociology" that Nisbet claims continues into the present is different from the relation between religious studies and sociology. Certainly it is often argued that contemporary sociologists of religion like Berger and Bellah are even closer to "religionists" in their approach to religion than their classical predecessors were. But are they in fact? Are the individual needs stressed by Berger and Bellah the same as those touted by religionists like Mircea Eliade (1907–1986)? For Berger and Bellah, the need for meaning, even if innate, is not a need for religious meaning itself. The need is more general and is itself secular. Even if for Berger and Bellah religion is the best way of securing meaning, religion is still a means to an end, where for Eliade it is the end itself. For Eliade, human beings need contact with God because they need contact with God. By contrast, for Berger and Bellah, humans need meaning that at most contact with God best provides. The need would remain secular even if contact with God were the sole way of fulfilling it. In the lingo of the field, even contemporary sociology of religion remains reductionistic. Nisbet notes that classical sociologists "all made the study a crucial aspect of their systematic studies of society and of man's relation to society. . . . [T]hey subjected religion to precisely the same kind of study that went into their explorations of politics, morality, science, and other major phenomena of modern society." In so doing they and their contemporary successors have approached religion antithetically from the way that it has—or had—traditionally been approached within religious studies.

Yet in the past few decades most scholars within religious studies have abandoned the rigidly antireductionistic, antisocial scientific stance of Eliade. Within religious studies, not just outside it, religion has come to be recognized as a multifaceted phenomenon to be accounted for by an array of disciplines. The defensiveness toward sociology and the other social sciences has diminished. One can therefore say that religious studies and sociology have become even closer—not merely because of changes on the part of sociology, as Nisbet would stress, but equally because of changes on the part of religious studies.

BIBLIOGRAPHY

Bellah, Robert N. *Tokugawa Religion.* Glencoe, Ill., 1957.

Bellah, Robert N. *Beyond Belief.* New York, 1970.

Bellah, Robert N. *The Broken Covenant.* New York, 1975.

Bellah, Robert N. "The Revolution and Symbolic Realism." In *Religion and the American Revolution,* edited by Jerald C. Brauer, pp. 55–73. Philadelphia, 1976.

Berger, Peter L. *The Noise of Solemn Assemblies.* Garden City, N.Y., 1961.

Berger, Peter L. *The Precarious Vision.* Garden City, N.Y., 1961.

Berger, Peter L. *The Sacred Canopy* (1967). Garden City, N.Y., 1969.

Berger, Peter L. *A Rumor of Angels* (1969). Garden City, N.Y., 1970.

Berger, Peter L. *The Heretical Imperative* (1979). Garden City, N.Y., 1981.

Bruce, Steve. *God Is Dead.* Oxford, 2002.

Bruce, Steve, ed. *Religion and Modernization.* Oxford, 1992.

Durkheim, Émile. *The Division of Labor in Society.* Translated by George Simpson. New York, 1933.

Durkheim, Émile. *The Elementary Forms of the Religious Life.* Translated by Joseph Ward Swain. New York, 1965. Translation originally published in 1915.

Durkheim, Émile. "Individualism and the Intellectuals." In *Durkheim on Religion*, edited by W. S. F. Pickering, pp. 59–73. Translated by Jacqueline Redding and W. S. F. Pickering. London and Boston, 1975.

Nisbet, Robert. *The Sociological Tradition.* New York, 1966.

Segal, Robert A. *Religion and the Social Sciences.* Atlanta, 1989.

Weber, Max. *The Protestant Ethic and the Spirit of Capitalism.* Translated by Talcott Parsons. New York, 1958.

Weber, Max. *The Sociology of Religion.* Translated by Ephraim Fischoff. Boston, 1963.

ROBERT A. SEGAL (2005)

SOCIOLOGY: SOCIOLOGY OF RELIGION [FIRST EDITION]

The systematic and objective study of the relations between religion and society existed long before Auguste Comte (1798–1857) coined the word *sociologie.* Xenophanes (c. 560–c. 478 BCE) was already dabbling in the discipline of sociology when he noted that the gods of the Ethiopians were black and had snub noses, while those of the Thracians had light blue eyes and red hair. Similarly, the Muslim philosopher Ibn Khaldūn (1332–1406 CE), in the *Muqaddimah*, or introduction (1377), to his *Kitāb al-ʿibar* (History of the world), displayed a keen understanding of the concept of social solidarity (*ʿaṣabīyah*) in his analysis of the role of religion in the rise and fall of the kingdoms of North Africa. In modern times, classicists, historians of religion, and "secular" historians have undoubtedly written more, and probably better, studies of religion than have professional sociologists. The true strength of sociology as a discipline seems to lie in its more explicit use of models, theories, and, more recently, statistical methods, that collectively make for a coherent approach of broad, or even universal significance. In contrast to more idiographic modes of scholarship, the sociology of religion makes its mark by treating religion and society nomothetically, that is, by searching for their regularities as interrelated networks, or systems, of thought, feeling, and behavior.

The appearance of the sociological study of religion in modern times is closely related to the rise of capitalism, cultural pluralism, religious tolerance, and the liberal state. The discipline therefore cannot claim to be a "natural" way of looking at religion and society. On the contrary, it is a cultural artifact produced by unique historical developments in Western social thought that enabled, or compelled, researchers to distance themselves from the normative claims made by the religions and societies they studied. In effect, the sociology of religion is the product of one of its own seminal concerns, that is, the secularization of religious thought and institutions. In contrast to the sociology of religion, the related discipline of religious sociology has sought closer ties with theology and institutional religion, primarily with the Roman Catholic Church in France and Belgium.

The history of the sociology of religion can be roughly divided into four periods: traditional social thought, skepticism and speculation, conservative and romantic reaction, and modern social theory.

TRADITIONAL SOCIAL THOUGHT. The body of thought that was first transformed and secularized as modern sociology began to take shape can be called traditional social thought. Far from being a unified system of ideas, it included divergent and even contradictory elements: Platonic idealism, Aristotelian teleology, Stoic natural law, Augustinian social realism, and the various social theories of the medieval Schoolmen. What especially characterized traditional social thought was its synthesis of social and ethical analysis. Because society, like nature, was thought to have a goal or purpose, the "is" of social analysis was not separated from the "ought" of values in the era of traditional social thought. In Christian hands, the study of social institutions was ultimately subordinated to soteriological ends. Traditional social thought stressed the cosmological and divine provenience of all rightly established social values and institutions. Regarding man as a social and political creature, it taught the existence of an objectively real "common good" that could be known by "right reason" and realized by goodwill. As do other religions, Christianity defined this common good in terms of a transcendent order of things that included society and the universe alike. The mainstream of traditional social thought expressed the organic unity of society in the language of natural law. According to this theory, institutions could be philosophically justified or condemned—and not only legitimated mythologically—to the degree they reflected the law that God had given to nature itself.

Traditional social thought bequeathed to the sociology of religion some of its basic concepts: society, religion, obligation, and the basic regularity or lawfulness of existence. Transformed as a secular concept, its notion of natural law would become the foundation of the early natural and social sciences.

SKEPTICISM AND SPECULATION. The lawful order of society that theorists in the Middle Ages and the Renaissance sought was one that invited the spiritual perfection of the human race. During the seventeenth and eighteenth centuries, thinkers continued their search for order. But the order that now seemed to concern them was one that would explain the diversity of languages, mores, and religions in terms of some simple, natural uniformities. The role played by reason in all of this was magnified by some, including the rationalists, while it was minimized by others, especially the empiricists.

During the seventeenth and eighteenth centuries, traditional social thought came under intellectual attack and—after the publication of Richard Hooker's *Of the Laws of Ecclesiastical Polity* in 1600—was increasingly on the defensive. The challengers, who were no more united than the defenders of tradition, included many Renaissance and Enlightenment thinkers: political critics such as Niccoló Machiavelli and Thomas Hobbes, satirists such as Bernard Mandeville, the Italian jurist Giovanni Battista Vico, and the *philosophes* (better called *sociologues* according to Crane Brinton) of the

French and Scottish Enlightenments. The intellectual inspiration behind this criticism of traditional social thought was also quite diverse. It included Isaac Newton's mechanical philosophy, the anthropocentric epistemology of René Descartes, Francis Bacon's empiricism (and his attack on teleology), and various speculative systems of thought that aimed at putting both society and the economy on more "realistic" foundations, that is, less religious or moral ones. Equally important was the rise of the nation-state and the appearance of the commercial or middle classes, a new element in society that would take over the writing of social and economic theory from the clergy.

Attack on Natural Law. Speaking for the bourgeoisie and proclaiming the triumph of the commercial revolution, a number of seventeenth-century thinkers launched an attack on the traditional concept of natural law. Hugo Grotius and Samuel Pufendorf, both Protestant laymen, showed that natural law could be divorced from God. Thomas Hobbes went much further and reduced natural law to "convenient Articles of Peace," that is, to a simple, utilitarian device. The "nature" that interested him was not a reflection of a divine order, but the psychobiological nature of insecure, "masterless men" living in a world no longer held together by traditional bonds of loyalty and deference. Even John Locke, who seemed to have boundless respect for Hooker's traditionalism, conceded that the law of nature was merely "a creature of the understanding." These philosophical efforts, which often were undertaken to sanctify property rights, secularized the idea of natural law and extended it from jurisprudence (where the Schoolmen had left it) to moral philosophy, which laid the foundation for the emerging social sciences.

Throughout the eighteenth century, writers of a secular or "enlightened" persuasion blamed religion and superstition for many of society's ills. Anticlericalism became a routine feature of nearly all social criticism. Convinced that religion had failed to curtail the endemic chaos of European life, a search was launched for new sources of social order. As a result, the traditional idea that society should be constructed according to the preordained blueprints of divine and natural law was replaced by the notion that society was, or could be, constructed by man's own "artifice" or "contrivance." A secular, social humanism thus came into being that, in turn, would beget most of the philosophical and sociological theories of the modern world. In order to create a richer and safer society, thinkers such as Hobbes, Mandeville, d'Holbach, Helvétius, Spinoza, and Hume sought to harness or manipulate self-interest and other passions formerly repressed or held in check by traditional social thought.

One of the most important results of this speculation was the discovery of what today would be called social systems. What fascinated thinkers of this period was the possibility of developing impersonal networks of interaction that—without the intervention of religion, morality, or the state—would "naturally" generate order and prosperity. The idea of social systems owed much to literary irony and social satire. It was broached early in the eighteenth century by Bernard Mandeville, who fondly commented on the "publick Benefits" that result from the proper cultivation of "private Vices." Later in that century, Adam Ferguson developed the concept still further when he described institutions that are "the result of human activity, but not the execution of any human design." Adam Smith explained the idea in terms that would soon dominate Western social thought when he said that "systems in many respects resemble machines." As time went on, each of the "systems" developed by social thought—mechanical, organic, cybernetic, and, finally, semiotic—would be used, one after the other, in the sociological analysis of religion.

Unlike his more skeptical colleagues, Smith based his idea of economic and moral systems firmly on natural law and divine providence (i.e., his famous and influential "invisible hand"). Together with Locke's political philosophy, Smith's economics provided a groundwork for the unique synthesis of religious piety, political liberalism, and capitalism that would flourish in the Anglo-Saxon world through the twentieth century. The success of this cultural synthesis probably accounts for the fact that religious scholarship in the United Kingdom and North America has been less anticlerical and antireligious than the social thought of the continent.

Birth of sociology of religion. It was perhaps at this juncture, when "laical social science"—as twentieth-century economist Joseph A. Schumpeter terms it—began to apply the idea of natural law to social and economic phenomena, that the sociology of religion was born. While professing to take an empirical approach, most studies of religion during this period concentrated on the historical or the psychological origins of religious belief, raising questions that could be answered only by speculation. Generally, the effect was to reduce religion to a dependent variable of some more obvious reality such as climate, fear, ignorance, or ecclesiastical legerdemain. One of the most brilliant, but still speculative, essays in the early sociology (and social psychology) of religion was written by Adam Smith himself in the *Wealth of Nations* (5.1.3). There the great economist, applying his notions of economic competition and psychological approbation to the problem of sectarian rivalry, produced one of the earliest theories of denominational pluralism.

Among the more valuable contributions made by the scholarship of this period to the sociology of religion was the analysis of religion's role in social control. Pioneers in this area included figures as diverse as Montesquieu (Charles-Louis de Secondat), who studied the relation between religion and law, and Mandeville, who was interested in religion and social values. The most important contribution of the age of skepticism and speculation was probably its elaboration of the idea of secularization itself. For many eighteenth-century writers, the decline of religion was simply a corollary of the idea of progress. Most were convinced that as science and enlightenment advanced, religion and superstition would inevitably succumb to the forces of reason. Because changes in religion, social institutions, science, and technology were thought to be closely related, it seemed only natural that changes in one area would bring about automatic improvements in others. Furthermore, because of the alleged universality of the laws of development (denied only by J. G. Herder, Jean-Jacques Rousseau, and a few others), the historical progress and secularization of one nation could be taken as a paradigm for the transformation of any other. These assumptions conspired to make the process of secularization appear to be as indubitable as the laws of nature itself.

The thinkers of the age of skepticism and speculation challenged some of the deepest convictions of traditional social thought. In place of the divine origin that tradition had assigned to law, morality, and institutions, these thinkers stressed society's conventional nature. Whereas tradition had given "right reason" the task of conforming society to its natural or sacred patterns, David Hume argued that "reason is and ought to be the slave of the passions." The teleology of the common good taught by traditional thinkers was discarded as a "wild goose chase" (as Mandeville put it), and was finally replaced by utilitarian self-interest, Kantian individualism, and the faith that social and economic systems could operate "naturally"—that is, without direct governmental, religious, or moral support. Skeptical philosophers of the age therefore sought to undo the classical synthesis of the sacred and the social. Their various attempts to design an autonomous, secular morality seemed to leave religion with only a minor—or a negative—role to play in the affairs of humankind. For the first time, the office of the moralist was separated from that of the *moraliste*, that is, the detached observer of social mores. The *moraliste's* disengagement from religious belief and commitment would later become a hallmark of the social-scientific approach to religion.

CONSERVATIVE AND ROMANTIC REACTION. Speculation ultimately ran afoul of the empiricism of the age, especially when it resulted in futile discussions about the origin of religion, or about man's essential instincts in the "state of nature." The havoc caused by the industrial revolution and the French Revolution (and the reign of terror that followed in its wake) brought into question the Enlightenment's optimistic belief that man could make or improve his society simply through his own artifice or contrivance. The conservative and romantic reactions that ensued significantly altered attitudes toward society and religion alike.

Romantics bewailed the dehumanizing effects of the industrial revolution and the French Revolution on individuals and communities. They also taught that religion—which played a large role in their discussions of *Volksgeist* and *Volksseele* ("the spirit and soul of the nation or folk")—could no longer be arrogantly dismissed as a vulgar superstition of the past. Conservatives, on the other hand, insisted that society was not merely the artificial creation of individual contractors, but that, on the contrary, the individual was formed by society, and society by God. In effect, they had rediscovered the organic interrelations between community, religion, tradition, authority, and the individual. For conservative thinkers like Louis de Bonald (1754–1840) and François René de Chateaubriand (1768–1848), religion was no longer just a matter of dogma or faith; it was a social phenomenon. As monarchists and spokesmen for the aristocracy, they rejected the idea that self-interest, once it had been set free in the marketplace, would automatically produce social order. Bonald, along with Friedrich Karl von Savigny (1779–1861) and Justus Möser (1720–1794), attacked the abstract universalism of contemporary theories of natural law and the individualism implied by the eighteenth century's doctrine of natural rights. In their eyes, these teachings were the philosophical offspring of the political and industrial revolutions that had deformed European civilization.

Through their influence on Saint-Simon and Durkheim, the conservatives deeply influenced later discussions about religion and its role in the formation of institutions and individual life. Their work provided an inspiration for later sociologists who stressed the integrating or stabilizing function of religion. Their analysis of religion as a *corps intermediaire* standing between the individual and the state was a topic that would emerge again in the discussions of intermediate associations, mediating structures, and guilds in the writings of sociologists from Durkheim to Peter L. Berger.

MODERN SOCIAL THEORY. The development of modern social theory has been characterized by a clearer understanding of the secular foundations of sociology, a determination to move research beyond mere speculation, a professionally cultivated tension between empathy and detachment in fieldwork, sophisticated efforts to relate religious studies to the models and theory-building of the social sciences in general, and ongoing debates over materialism, reductionism, behaviorism, positivism, evolutionism, and the hermeneutics of religious symbols. The anticlerical diatribes of the *philosophes* yielded to a more or less dispassionate analysis of the role of religion in the maintenance of social solidarity and in the promotion of social change.

Although modern social theory really begins in the eighteenth century with David Hume, Adam Ferguson, Adam Smith, and the Scottish Enlightenment, most sociologists today trace the founding of their discipline to Claude-Henri de Rouvroy, Comte de Saint-Simon (1760–1825) and his onetime secretary, Auguste Comte (1798–1857). Sociology does indeed owe much to these two Frenchmen. In Auguste Comte's work, especially in his evolutionary schema purporting to trace history through its religious, metaphysical, and scientific stages, sociology discovered its own mythological charter. For both Marxist and liberal thinkers after Comte, the demise of religion would be taken as the prerequisite of progress and as an axiom of the social and natural sciences. Herbert Spencer dogmatically proclaimed that since moral injunctions were losing their sacred origins, a deliberate secularization of morals was imperative. From the beginning, the controversy over secularization was couched in extreme terms. Some—including Weber, Marx, and later Sorokin—argued that the decline of religion was inevitable. More recently, Talcott Parsons, Robert N. Bellah, Mary Douglas, Thomas Luckmann, and others have maintained that secularization is ultimately impossible. Arguing on empirical grounds, more cautious scholars have suggested that while religion may decline or disappear in specific areas of society, "the secularization process" is not necessarily universal, inevitable, or irreversible.

Contributions of Émile Durkheim. There have been only two truly great figures in the sociology of religion in the modern period, Émile Durkheim and Max Weber. Between them, they set the problems and parameters of the field, leaving the theoretical integration of their insights to others. Durkheim was influenced not only by Saint-Simon and Comte, but by W. Robertson Smith's writings on Semitic religion and by his own teacher, the classicist N. D. Fustel de Coulanges. Durkheim's primary contribution to the sociology of religion was his analysis of the role played by religion in the generation of the *conscience collective*, the collective moral conscience and consciousness of society. Although he shared the common assumption of his time that religion was bound to play an ever-smaller role in modern life, he focused not on the demise of religion but on its transformation. He called the religion of modern societies the "cult of the individual."

Durkheim's analysis of this concept paved the way for modern sociology's interest in diffuse or parainstitutional forms of religiousness, for example, Thomas Luckmann's "invisible religion," Talcott Parsons's "privatization of religion," and Robert Bellah's "civil religion." As a "theologian of civil religion," as Bellah once called him, Durkheim was vitally interested in using sociology to heal the wounds of the acquisitive individualism he found in modern industrial society. While his moralism, his naive faith in altruism, and his interest in guilds seem rooted in the concerns of traditional social thought, the core of Durkheim's doctrine was thoroughly secular. Although he held that there are no false religions, divinity for him was never more than "society transfigured and symbolically expressed." His analysis of religion rested on a basic confusion between the meaning or content of religious symbols (their sacrality) and one of the functions of religion (the unifying of society). This confusion caused him to underestimate the dysfunctional or disruptive capacity of religion, and to overemphasize its role in the generation of social solidarity.

The strengths and the weaknesses of Durkheim's sociology of religion were inherited by the functionalist school. As it developed in the hands of A. R. Radcliffe-Brown, Bronislaw Malinowski, and others, functionalism sought to interpret religion in terms of its contribution to the total social system, or to the psychobiological well-being and integration of the individual. Some functionalists speculated as freely about the psychosocial functions of religion (e.g., about its fear-reducing function) as did their skeptical predecessors in the eighteenth century. Although widely criticized for the tautological vacuousness of its implicit teleology, whereby religion is nearly reduced to its own consolidating function, functionalism continues to pervade the sociology of religion today as received wisdom, if not as explicit theory.

Influences of German scholarship. German scholarship in the history of religions (*Religionsgeschichte*) and the cultural sciences (*Geisteswissenschaften*) evolved ways of conceptualizing religion that went far beyond the narrow, cognitive approach of Comte, Spencer, and E. B. Tylor. Friedrich Schleiermacher (1768–1834) had insisted that religion was grounded in feeling *(Gefühl)* rather than in the intellect. Consequently, religion must be more than a primitive attempt to "figure out" the world. Wilhelm Dilthey (1833–1911), working under the influence of Schleiermacher, pointed out the unique nature of religion and the need to understand it sympathetically, or from within (*Verstehen*), a point that would be developed in a significant way in the sociology of religion by Max Weber.

In 1917, Rudolf Otto, in his epochal book *The Idea of the Holy*, made a frontal attack on Protestant liberalism that, since Kant, tended to reduce the religious experience to ethics. Otto showed, quite to the contrary, that the essence of religion was the experience of standing before the holy in dread, awe, and fascination. The holy, far from being a way of "figuring out" the world, was a mysterious experience that both attracts and repels. Otto called it the *mysterium tremendum et fascinosum*. These developments in German theology and religious studies paved the way for a much more sophisticated and sympathetic understanding of religion than was common in most parts of Europe at that time.

In Germany, the scholars who influenced the sociology of religion most decisively were Ernst Troeltsch (1865–1923) and Max Weber (1864–1920). Working in philosophical and theological traditions dominated by Immanuel Kant, G. W. F. Hegel, J. G. Fichte, Friedrich Schleiermacher, and Albrecht Ritschl, Troeltsch emphasized the interaction of spiritual and material forces in religious history. He saw in the history of Christianity a continuous dialectic between movements and institutions that are willing to compromise with the world, and ones that refuse to do so. This became the basis for his typology of church (the compromising religious institution), sect (the rejectionist position), and mysticism (the religious outlook of individuals concerned more about the experience of religious ecstasy than about religious institutions per se).

This simple scheme, modified by the subsequent work of others on denominations, cults, and parainstitutional religions, became the basis for the taxonomy of religious affiliations in the West. Although he finally concluded that Protestantism had been more deeply affected by the modern world than vice versa, Troeltsch seemed to hold—with his friend Weber—that there was a significant relationship between ascetic Calvinism and the rise of capitalism. What primarily set apart the writings of these distinguished scholars was Troeltsch's historicism and Weber's ideal-typical, sociological approach to religion.

Contributions of Max Weber. While Troeltsch was deeply perplexed by the theological implications of his own historicism, Weber described himself as a "religiously unmusical" individual primarily concerned about facing up to reality "like a man." His methodological divorce of facts and values (i.e., "value-free social science") seemed to be a secular transformation of the relationship between the Creator and the creation, which Weber described in his study of ancient Israel. Likewise, his emphasis on the "ethical personality" seems to have been deeply influenced by the disenchanted Calvinism of his own family. Both the existentialism of his political commitments and his social hermeneutics call to mind the voluntarism of the Calvinist tradition. In short, he was, in many ways, a religious thinker in spite of himself. In the sociology of religion he is known primarily for his thesis that ascetic Protestantism decisively influenced the rationalization of the world in general, and the rise of capitalism in particular.

While others before him had pointed out that modern capitalism developed primarily in the Protestant countries of northern Europe, Weber provided a sociopsychological explanation for the correlation. According to Weber, the Calvinist doctrine of predestination generated a deep anxiety among Protestants—English Puritans in particular—over their own salvation. Believing that wealth was a sign of their election, the Puritans turned to work "in their callings" as though their souls depended on it. In other words, the Puritans' religious anxiety was the irrational goad behind their rationalization and disenchantment of the world. Believing that his thesis could be proven or confirmed by comparative research, Weber wrote a series of detailed studies on ancient Israel, India, and China. While his basic contentions have been severely criticized by historians, Weber's thesis continues to be widely debated. Even now, it continues to inspire sociological and historical research. Mastery of the conceptual tools he fashioned is still part of apprenticeship in the sociology of religion (e.g., legitimation, theodicy, charisma, routinization, and so on).

Working as contemporaries, Durkheim and Weber made contributions to the sociology of religion that were as different as they were monumental. While Durkheim stressed the role of religion in the consolidation of society, Weber was interested primarily in the part it played in social change. For Durkheim, collective "effervescence" was the *fons et origo* of religious concepts and power; for Weber the concepts and power of religious systems originated in the charisma of individual founders and prophets. Durkheim believed that sociological analysis began with "social facts"; Weber held that the interpretation of social action ultimately rested on an understanding of the intentionality of individual actors. Durkheim sought to reunite sociology and philosophy; Weber insisted on their separation. The divorce of the "is" and the "ought to be" that runs throughout Weber's work on religion grew out of a conviction that there could be no philosophical justification of values. Beneath values he finds nothing but sheer will, prejudice and tradition. Later twentieth-century thinkers as diverse as Herbert Marcuse, on the left, and Leo Strauss, on the right, have sensed in Weber's work a deeply entrenched nihilism. This nihilism seems to be rooted in his romantic conviction that the secularization and disenchantment of the world are the fate of Western civilization.

Contributions of Karl Marx. Although he is remembered for his pithy and often insightful remarks on religion, Karl Marx's own contributions to the sociology of religion were negligible. His real impact on the discipline has been made indirectly through the diffusion of his theory of the interaction of the superstructure and infrastructure of society. Marx drew attention to the cultural and functional similarities between religion, law, politics, and ideology—all aspects of the superstructure. While insisting that superstructures are ultimately determined by the "relations of production" at work below, Marx did seem to recognize the relative autonomy of religious concepts, and their ability to function as independent variables. He sought to abolish religion by actualizing its eschatological hopes in this world with revolutionary praxis. Nevertheless, he held that the real secularizing force in modern society is not the revolutionary proletariat, but a bourgeoisie that had "drowned the most heavenly ecstasies of religious fervor . . . in the icy waters of egotistical calculation."

Since the Enlightenment, many thinkers have tried to develop a general "sociology of history," that is, a nomothetic alternative to the historian's idiographic approach to social change. Vico, Turgot, Adam Smith, Adam Ferguson, Lord Kames (Henry Home), John Millar, Hegel, Herder, Tönnies, and many others sought to explain the complex transition from traditional society to enlightened civilization in terms of some basic dynamics or all-encompassing *Weltplan.*

Applied to religious studies, most of these schemes were highly conjectural. This was especially true of the evolutionary theories of nineteenth-century writers like Herbert Spencer, John Lubbock, and E. B. Tylor. Speculative as their ideas were, the evolutionists soon became enormously influential. Men like Durkheim, Weber, and Tönnies, who did not openly align themselves with evolutionism, nevertheless conceived developmental typologies that were clearly evolutionistic. Marx's analysis of history was couched in terms of a "dialectical" process, a materialistic variation on Hegelianism that turned history itself into a set of unfolding internal relations.

A number of bourgeois theorists sought to discuss social change without falling prey to the determinism of the Marxists or the positivism of the historicists. Weber had an "approach-avoidance" reaction to the rationalization process that, for him, was the key to historical development. While Weber did not share the naive optimism of most nineteenth-century evolutionists, behind his complex, ideal-typical analysis of the rise of capitalism, one senses a kind of subtle, evolutionary movement at work. In a deliberate attempt to counter Tönnies's treatment of modern society *(Gesellschaft)* as characterized by a weakening of social bonds, Durkheim insisted that the "organic solidarity" that holds modern society together is just as effective as the "mechanical solidarity" of the past. Applied to the study of religion, the nineteenth century's preoccupation with conjectural schemes of development had the unfortunate effect of reducing all questions about religion to the question of its place in evolution or history.

Contributions of Talcott Parsons. In the twentieth century, Talcott Parsons (1902–1979) directed the attention of sociology to the place of religion in the general system of social action. In order to solve the "Hobbesian problem of social order," Parsons devised a number of encompassing systems that combined the insights of Durkheim, Weber, Freud, the Cambridge economist Alfred Marshall, and the Harvard biochemist L. J. Henderson (a disciple of Vilfredo Pareto). Parsons granted to culture, and *a fortiori* to religion, a place of "cybernetic" sovereignty. From its exalted place in the system of action, religion could create values, shape norms, inform social roles, and provide overall guidance to the "systems" of society, personality, and behavior. Among his more important contributions to the sociology of religion and culture were his discussions of "value-generalization," "denominational pluralism," "the privatization of religion," "liberalism," "fundamentalism," and the "instrumental activism" of the neo-Calvinist tradition. In his later work, Parsons gave more attention to the structure of systems and less to "action" as such. Objective factors influencing action received more attention, and the subjectivity of the actor received less. Under his aegis, a revised form of evolutionism enjoyed a brief recrudescence in the social sciences. Although "neoevolutionism," as it was called, sought to avoid the excesses and ethnocentrism of social Darwinism, its basic categories and dynamics were quite similar: adaptation, sociocultural differentiation, and integration. Out of this period of Parsons's work came the widely read essay by his student, Robert N. Bellah, entitled "Religious Evolution."

Because of the ascendancy of religion, ideas, and values in Parsons's "pattern maintenance," many criticized him as an idealist, or even as an ideological defender of the status quo. Ironically, some criticized his later work for its "behaviorism" and "positivism." Whatever the case, toward the end of his life Parsons began to speculate more freely about the "ends of man," the "telic environment," and the "human condition." These interests prompted some to wonder whether, like Bellah, Parsons was trying to go beyond the social sciences, or whether he was about to turn into a theologian himself. For all of his scientific (or scientistic) rigor, Parsons—like Durkheim and Bellah—was deeply concerned about the perennial issues of classical social thought.

Contemporary influences. The sociology of religion has received considerable stimulation from literary criticism (Kenneth Burke), contemporary studies in semiotics and hermeneutics (Hans-Georg Gadamer and Paul Ricoeur) and phenomenology (Alfred Schutz). Edmund Husserl's advice to go back "to the things themselves" has been broadly interpreted by some sociologists as a challenge to take the reported experience of informants more seriously. Thus, phenomenology seems to have inspired in some quarters a renewed interest in a qualitative, humanistic sociology. In religious studies, the term *phenomenology* has come to be applied quite diversely (1) to a nonconfessional, value-free approach to religion; (2) to cross-cultural, comparative studies; and (3) to a descriptive, nonexplanatory orientation toward the sacred that "brackets" both the ultimate reality "behind" it and all influences of this world on its manifestation in society. The phenomenological approach has often encouraged a secular orientation to the study of religion that, in turn, has facilitated the development of religious studies in nontheological circles. It has shown itself antithetical to a sociological orientation only when its "bracketing" puts the investigation of the secular and social influences on religion off-limits.

One of the sociologists responsible for introducing phenomenology into religious studies is Peter L. Berger. Berger's work has been influenced by the sociological phenomenology of Alfred Schutz and by the work of such figures as Durkheim, Weber, Marx, George Herbert Mead, and W. I. Thomas. Holding with other social scientists (such as Talcott Parsons, Robert N. Bellah, Clifford Geertz, Thomas Luckmann, and Arnold Gehlen) that humankind creates culture—and religion—in order to compensate for the limitations of its genetic patterns, Berger treats religious symbols as psychosocial projections generated by a process of objectification, reification, and internalization. Religion functions primarily as a "plausibility structure," legitimating human existence and providing a theodicy to explain its misery. In exceptional cases, such as biblical prophecy, religion may even serve to delegitimate social structures. While Berger's theory of religion rests upon a philosophical anthropology that may be more graphic than real, he has managed to put together a theoretical vocabulary that many sociologists of religion find useful.

In American sociology, community studies conducted by William Lloyd Warner, Liston Pope, Robert and Helen Lynd, and others have taught us a great deal about the relationships between religion and society. Until the 1940s, the guiding lights of the sociology of religion in the United States were not Durkheim and Weber, but Herbert Spencer, Lester Frank Ward, William Graham Sumner, and W. Robertson Smith; the theory that these thinkers applied to religion was remote from a theological approach. While James H. Leuba in his book *The Belief in God and Immortality* (1916) found that only 19 percent of the "greater sociologists" believed in religion, most of the practitioners of the sociology of religion continued to be believers. Many of these scholars were liberal followers of the Social Gospel movement. Later on, when this movement came under attack by fundamentalism, neoorthodoxy, and the secular academic world, interest in the sociology of religion itself began to wane. (Significantly, this took place at about the same time "value-free" sociology was divesting itself of social work.) H. Richard Niebuhr's *The Social Sources of Denominationalism* (1929) went nearly unnoticed by the major sociological journals. By the 1940s, the sociological study of religion in North America had largely passed into the hands of the newly formed Catholic Sociological Society. By the mid-1980s, the Association for the Sociology of Religion had absorbed the Catholic group in a wider, ecumenical organization. Another professional organization called the Society for the Scientific Study of Religion is associated with a more statistical, and sometimes with a more positivistic, approach to the subject.

CONCLUSIONS. By about 1920, the sociology and anthropology of religion had generated the concept of culture as it is known in modern social science. Because interest in this field has subsequently shifted from religion to culture itself, the study of religion currently plays a minor part in the sociological curriculum. Although religion made vital contributions to modern social theory (providing even Karl Marx with clues for the demythologizing of exchange value), religious data are now often used merely as illustrations of general theories. Students of the subject spend a great deal of their energy on correlational research ("religion-and- . . ."), that is, studying the interrelations between religion, social mobility, racial prejudice, voting patterns, divorce, family planning and so on. While these studies have greatly expanded our knowledge of the relations between society and religion, they have seldom contributed to the building of theories as such.

Sociologists of religion have "revisited" Troeltsch, Weber, and the other notable theorists, refining the work of these writers into typologies that seldom have the vigor or the historical perspective of earlier formations. Another indication of the impoverishment of the field is the neglect of comparative, cross-cultural studies. By default, the sociology of religion has become an adjunct to the study of the Christian religion, and not only in the hands of the "Christian sociologists." Although the discipline came to its maturity in the richly comparative work of Durkheim, Weber, and others (who were perfectly at home in philosophy and the humanities in general), historicism, positivism, and the exigencies of academic careers have conspired to reduce comparative studies in the field to a cautious manipulation of easily quantified variables. Because of this lack of historical and comparative depth, few sociologists working on religion have been able to make contributions that are of interest to the rest of sociology or religious studies. The few sociologists who have made their mark in this field (e.g., Bellah, Berger, David A. Martin, and Bryan R. Wilson) have made abundant use of comparative and historical materials. While the study of religion owes much to the social sciences in general, currently anthropology—represented by the work of such writers as Clifford Geertz, Mary Douglas, Claude Lévi-Strauss, and Victor Turner—seems to have had a greater impact than sociology itself.

In the modern period, a number of scholars have tried to rebuild the bridges traditional social thought had built between facts and values, namely, the religious engineering of Saint-Simon and Comte, the secular moralism of Durkheim, and various practical studies of the Christian sociologists in North America or the followers of *la sociologie religieuse* in France and Belgium. Nevertheless, because of the limited cultural significance of the sociology of religion today, only a few alienated theologians would say, with Marx, that the critique of society begins with the critique of religion.

In order to alleviate the cynicism that seemed to attend the analysis of religion in conventional sociology, Bellah has called for a more liberal suspension of disbelief ("symbolic realism"). This, in effect, would mark a return to Durkheim's idea that no religion is false. Unfortunately, symbolic realism seems to have led only to an uneasy and inauthentic reconciliation of the social sciences and religious faith. It is rather ironic that the prestige of the sociology of religion has never been higher among the theological disciplines than it is currently. Theologians, biblical scholars, and church historians are turning to a sociological approach to their fields, though sometimes without fully digesting it or realizing its theoretical costs.

Because its roots lie in such far-flung places as idealism, materialism, skepticism, literary satire, and romantic and conservative protest, the sociology of religion appears to be all things to all people. To put the best face on the fact, some methodologists refer to the discipline as a "multiparadigm" field that, unlike the natural sciences, does not advance by sequentially isolating and falsifying disjunctive paradigms. It does not confront its subject matter head-on with a proud phalanx of unified theory, but from all sides with scattered guerrilla bands armed only with piecemeal models and "polymethodic" tactics. Since the sociology of religion has failed to realize the nomothetic goals it once set for itself, some have legitimately wondered how it differs from the humanities and their idiographic approach.

Today, widespread criticism of the positivism of conventional social science, new interest in semiotics and the cybernetic control of shared cultural symbols, and ongoing investigations into the intentionality of the individual social actor may be paving the way for some interesting changes in the sociology of religion. These changes may bring the discipline into closer and more fruitful relations with the humanities and with the history of religions. The work of Parsons, Bellah, Berger, and others has generated a more sophisticated, less dogmatic attitude toward the theory of secularization itself. A growing number of researchers would probably agree with Saint-Simon that "religion cannot disappear; it can only be transformed."

SEE ALSO Anthropology, Ethnology, and Religion; Christian Social Movements; Civil Religion; Durkheim, Émile; Functionalism; Modernity; Political Theology; Politics and Religion; Psychology; Secularization; Society and Religion; Structuralism; Study of Religion; Weber, Max.

Bibliography

There are several good introductory textbooks that deal with the sociology of religion, including Roland Robertson's *The Sociological Interpretation of Religion* (New York, 1970) and Thomas F. O'Dea's *The Sociology of Religion* (Englewood Cliffs, N.J., 1966). Joachim Wach's *Sociology of Religion* (1944; Chicago, 1962) lays out the field in an encyclopedic, but helpful, way. Among the numerous volumes dealing with the development of classical social thought and speculation on religion and society in the early modern period are Leo Strauss's *Natural Right and History* (Chicago, 1953), Jacob Viner's *The Role of Providence in the Social Order* (Princeton, 1972), and the essays by Robert Bierstedt, Kenneth Bock, and Robert A. Nisbet in *A History of Sociological Analysis*, edited by Thomas B. Bottomore and Robert A. Nisbet (New York, 1978). Compared with these works, Jan de Vries's *The Study of Religion: A Historical Approach* (New York, 1967) deals more specifically with the analysis of religion itself.

Nearly all of the major "classical" texts in the field are available in English. These include Émile Durkheim's *The Elementary Forms of the Religious Life* (1915; reprint, New York, 1965) and three works by Max Weber: *The Protestant Ethic and the Spirit of Capitalism* (1930; reprint, London, 1974); *The Sociology of Religion* (Boston, 1963); and *From Max Weber: Essays in Sociology* (1946; Oxford, 1967). An accurate and accessible introduction to Weber's thought is Reinhard Bendix's *Max Weber: An Intellectual Portrait* (1960; Berkeley, 1977). Ernst Troeltsch's *The Social Teaching of the Christian Churches*, 2 vols. (1931; Chicago, 1981) is still one of the finest sociological treatments of historical Christianity. Many of the concerns raised by Weber and Troeltsch were further developed and modified by three American classics: H. Richard Niebuhr's *The Social Sources of Denominationalism* (New York, 1929), Liston Pope's *Millhands and Preachers: A Study of Gastonia* (1942; New Haven, 1965), and Gerhard Lenski's *The Religious Factor: A Sociological Study of Religion's Impact on Politics, Economics, and Family Life* (Garden City, N.Y., 1961). The general development of the sociology of religion in the United States has been discussed by Myer S. Reed, Jr., in "An Alliance for Progress: The Early Years of the Sociology of Religion in the United States," *Sociological Analysis* 42 (Spring 1981): 27–46, and in "After the Alliance: The Sociology of Religion in the United States from 1925 to 1949," *Sociological Analysis* 43 (Fall 1982): 189–204. Robert N. Bellah's *Beyond Belief: Essays on Religion in a Post-Traditional World* (New York, 1970) is an example of the post-Parsonian trend in contemporary American sociology of religion.

Winston Davis (1987)

SOCIOLOGY: SOCIOLOGY OF RELIGION [FURTHER CONSIDERATIONS]

In the late twentieth century sociology of religion has been marked by three trends, all of which represent a broadening of the field. The standard focus on the origin and function of religion has been broadened into a concern as well with, first, the propriety of religion and, second, the truth of religion. Peter Berger and Robert Bellah best represent these dual trends. The third trend has been the supplementing of an explanatory approach to religion with a hermeneutical, or interpretive, one. This trend is best represented by Clifford Geertz. Though Geertz is, formally, an anthropologist, he has been more influential than any sociologist in pioneering this approach to religion and to culture as a whole. By no coincidence his key work, *The Interpretation of Cultures* (1973), won the Sorokin Award of the American Sociological Association.

The Propriety of Religion. In his earlier writings, Berger rails against the life made easy by religion (see, for example, 1961a, 1961b, 1967 [with Luckmann], and 1969). He denounces religion for accepting rather than challenging seculardom. He denounces his own Christianity for supporting rather than questioning such American values, processes, and institutions as financial success, class and racial divisions, the Cold War, capital punishment, and the family unit: "We are saying nothing new. We would refer the reader to Kierkegaard's attack on the 'Christendom' of his time or to Barth's assault on a later model of which theological liberalism was the expression. . . . In the American religious-secular continuum of values, Christianity appears embedded in taken-for-granted reality. It does not stand out from the rest of the culture, at least not in its middle-class Protestant forms. Consequently, it can offer no challenge to all that is taken for granted. As we have seen, commitment to Christianity thus undergoes a fatal identification with commitment to society, to respectability, to the American way of life. Under these conditions, the encounter with the [true] Christian message is rendered extremely difficult, to say the least" (1961a, p. 116). Religion that seeks to justify society constitutes what Berger, employing Jean-Paul Sartre's famous phrase, calls "bad faith."

The earlier Berger considers as bad faith not only the use of religion to sanction seculardom but also, reciprocally, the use of seculardom to justify religion. He denounces as improper what Geertz, in his own analysis of religion, ironically applauds as effective: the meshing of a conception of reality with a way of life. For Berger, when religion fits society snugly, the affirmation of it requires no effort. Everybody accepts it as conventional wisdom: "The religious institution does not (perhaps one should say 'not any longer') generate its own values; instead, it ratifies and sanctions the values prevalent in the general community. There is little if any difference between the values propagated by the religious institution and those of any secular institution of equivalent status in the community (such as the school)" (1961a, pp. 40–41).

In his later writings, Berger stresses the shaky rather than solid foundation of modern religion in particular (see, for example, 1970, 1973 [with Berger and Kellner], and 1980). Whereas the earlier Berger emphasizes the ease with which religion is affirmed, the later Berger stresses the difficulty involved. The source of the difficulty is the existence of competing religions, themselves in competition with secular worldviews. Competing claims to certainty render any claim tenuous. Bereft of certainty, one must leap unto faith: "Faith is no longer socially given, but must be individually achieved—be it by a wrenching act of decision along the lines of Pascal's 'wager' or Kierkegaard's 'leap'—or more trivially acquired as a 'religious preference.' Faith, in other words, is much harder to come by in the pluralistic situation" (Berger, Berger, and Kellner, 1973, p. 81). Put more mundanely, "It is relatively easy, sociologically speaking, to be a Catholic in a social situation where one can readily limit one's significant others to fellow Catholics, where indeed one has little choice in the matter, and where all the major institutional forces are geared to support and confirm a Catholic world. The story is quite different in a situation where one is compelled to rub shoulders with every conceivable variety of 'those others,' [where one] is bombarded with communications that deny or ignore one's Catholic idea, and where one has a terrible time even finding some quiet Catholic corners to withdraw into. It is very, very difficult to be cognitively *entre nous* in modern society, especially in the area of religion" (Berger, 1970, p. 44). Having come to accept as legitimate the subjective basis of religion, Berger also comes to see the legitimacy of the use to which religion is put: giving meaning to life.

When, in his later writings, Robert Bellah turns from Japan and the rest of the world to America, he changes his focus from analyzing religion to preaching it. His claim that there exists a "civil religion" in America seems a mere restatement of Émile Durkheim's fundamental claim that every society worships itself (see Bellah, 1975, 1976). Yet Bellah is interested less in the social function of civil religion than in the obligation that civil religion imposes. He is not concerned, as Durkheim is, with the dependence on society that religion instills. Instead, he is concerned with the sense of duty that religion inculcates. That duty is not to society but to God. Whereas for Durkheim duty to God means duty to society, for Bellah duty to society means duty to God. For Bellah, religion does not, as it does for Durkheim, serve to weld people into a nation, at least as an end in itself. Rather, it welds them as a means of fulfilling the nation's ideals—for example, of peace and equality. The fulfillment of these ideals constitutes a duty not only to the nation but even more to God, whose chosen nation America believes itself to be. This duty is therefore less social than truly religious: serving one's country in order to serve God, who is the inspiration of society rather than, as for Durkheim, the projection of society.

Whereas for Berger the normative question is whether a religion that sanctions the proverbial status quo is proper, for Bellah the normative question is whether a religion that serves society alone is proper. Put another way, for the earlier Bellah (1957) the question is what religion *does* do. For the later Bellah, the question is what religion *should* do.

THE TRUTH OF RELIGION. The earlier Berger views sociology and, in general, the social sciences as unable either to deny or affirm the truth of religion. The later Berger, beginning with *A Rumor of Angels* (1970), reverses this position and comes to view the social sciences as able to affirm the truth of religion. The earlier as well as the later Berger is intent on reconciling the social sciences with religious truth, but the earlier Berger does so by declaring the issue of truth beyond the social scientific ken: "[I]t is impossible within the frame of reference of scientific theorizing to make any affirmations, positive *or* negative, about the ultimate ontological status of this alleged reality. Within this frame of reference, the religious projections can be dealt with only as such, as products of human activity and human consciousness, and rigorous brackets have to be placed around the question as to whether these projections may not also . . . *refer to* something else than the human world in which they empirically originate. . . . In other words, every inquiry into religious matters that limits itself to the empirically available must necessarily be based on a '*methodological* atheism'" (1969, p. 100).

The later Berger reconciles the social sciences with religious truth in the opposite fashion: by arguing that the social sciences can establish the existence of god, or of the transcendent. Berger has come to oppose the view that he had formerly espoused: that the truth of religion is beyond the social scientific ken. He thus has come to believe that the social sciences can catalogue "signals of transcendence": those experiences of hope, humor, and above all order that entail, because they presuppose, the existence of the transcendent. "Thus man's ordering propensity implies a transcendent order, and each ordering gesture is a signal of this transcendence" (1970, p. 57). "Man's propensity for order is grounded in a faith or trust that, ultimately, reality is 'in order,' all right, 'as it should be'" (1970, p. 54). Whereas the earlier Berger spurns any evidence for belief as bad faith, the later Berger solicits evidence for belief.

Bellah calls his later approach to religion "symbolic realism" and distinguishes it from three other approaches: "historical realism," "consequential reductionism," and "symbolic reductionism." Historical realism deems religion cognitive, literal, and true: religion is a true explanation of the physical world. Historical realists are, presumably, fundamentalists. Consequential reductionism considers religion cognitive, literal, but false: religion is superstition. But consequential reductionists are concerned less with the falsity of religion than with the effect of religion on society when it is believed true. Consequential reductionists include social functionalists like Bronislaw Malinowski and A. R. Radcliffe-Brown.

Symbolic reductionism also considers religion false when taken cognitively and literally but considers it true when taken noncognitively and symbolically: as the disguised expression of something real within individuals, society, or the physical world. The ranks of symbolic reductionists include many nineteenth- and early twentieth-century social scientists—among them E. B. Tylor, J. G. Frazer, Karl

Marx, Durkheim, and Sigmund Freud. One exception is Max Weber, who for Bellah is rather a consequential reductionist because he is interested less in the reduction of religion to something underlying it than in the effect of religion on society. Bellah would presumably classify his own earlier self as a consequentialist, as he would at least partly his then-mentor, Talcott Parsons.

In contrast to historical realism, which also seeks the meaning of religion for believers, symbolic realism deems that meaning symbolic rather than literal, and deems it experiential rather than explanatory. Religion for believers is not a scientific-like account of the world but an encounter with it: "For religion is not really a kind of pseudogeology or pseudohistory but an imaginative statement about the truth of the totality of human experience" (Bellah, 1970, p. 244). "These [religious] symbols are not 'made up' by the human ego or deduced by rational reflection. They are born out of the tragedy and the suffering, the joy and the victory of men struggling to make sense out of their world. They tell us nothing at all about the universe except insofar as the universe is involved in human experience" (Bellah, 1970, p. 95).

Because religion for Bellah expresses humans' experience of the world rather than explaining the world itself, it is true: "If we define religion as that symbol system that serves to evoke . . . the totality that includes subject and object and provides the context in which life and action finally have meaning, then I am prepared to claim that as Durkheim said of society, religion is a reality *sui generis.* To put it bluntly, religion is true" (Bellah 1970, pp. 252–253). In this respect Bellah, just like Berger, goes beyond the issue of origin and function to that of truth.

THE HERMENEUTICAL APPROACH TO RELIGION. Like that of both Berger and Bellah, Clifford Geertz's focus has shifted over time. Beginning with his first collection of essays, *The Interpretation of Cultures* (1973), he has turned from an explanatory approach to religion to an interpretive one. Inspired by the philosopher Paul Ricoeur, he has come to view all of culture, including religion, as akin to a literary text, which therefore requires the equivalent of exegesis.

All interpretivists equate explanation with cause and interpretation with meaning. They differ over how they distinguish causes from meanings. Geertz adopts not only the distinction but also the example drawn by the philosopher Gilbert Ryle, who contrasts twitching to winking. Writes Geertz: "The two movements are, as movements, identical; from an I-am-a-camera, 'phenomenalistic' observation of them alone, one could not tell which was twitch and which was wink, or indeed whether both or either was twitch or wink. Yet the difference, however unphotographable, between a twitch and a wink is vast; as anyone unfortunate enough to have had the first taken for the second knows. The winker is communicating, and indeed communicating in a quite precise and special way: (1) deliberately, (2) to someone in particular, (3) to impart a particular message, (4) according to a socially established code, and (5) without cognizance of the rest of the company" (Geertz, 1973, p. 6).

In the familiar senses of the terms "cause" and "meaning," a twitch is causal, or meaningless, because it has no purpose. It is involuntary and therefore unintentional. It is not inexplicable, for its cause explains it, but it is purposeless. A wink is meaningful because it has a purpose as well as a cause—more accurately, a purpose rather than a cause. It is voluntary and therefore intentional.

In the more technical sense of the terms, following the usage that Geertz adopts from Ryle, a wink is meaningful rather than causal not just because it is purposeful, or intentional, but also because the purpose is inseparable from the behavior: Winking is not caused by a prior contraction of the eyelids; it *is* the intentional contraction of the eyelids. The purpose cannot therefore be the cause of the behavior, for a cause must be separate from its effect. The purpose and the behavior are two aspects of a single action rather than, as in causal explanation, two actions: the cause and the effect. If the contraction were the effect of winking, winking would be the cause. But because the contraction is the expression of winking, winking is the meaning.

To describe only the behavior would be to give what Geertz, following Ryle, calls a "thin description." To describe the meaning expressed by the behavior is to give what Geertz, again following Ryle, calls a "thick description." By a thick description Geertz means an interpretation.

When the earlier Geertz asserts that humans strive to make sense of life, he is arguing that that striving causes them to engage in religious and other sense-making activities. When the later Geertz makes the same assertion, he is simply saying that humans engage in religious and other sense-making activities, which express rather than effect humanity's sense-making character.

If the later Geertz's concern with the meaning rather than the cause of human behavior puts him within the interpretive, or hermeneutical, tradition, his concern with the public rather than private nature of that meaning puts him within the Wittgensteinian branch of that tradition: "The generalized attack on privacy theories of meaning is, since early Husserl and late Wittgenstein, so much a part of modern thought that it need not be developed once more here. What is necessary is to see to it that the news of it reaches anthropology" (Geertz, 1973, p. 12).

While Geertz never cites him, he is closest to the Wittgensteinian philosopher Peter Winch. Where other interpretivists, such as the philosophers R. G. Collingwood and William Dray, use empathy alongside evidence to reconstruct the meanings of actors' behavior, Winch uses a knowledge of the rules of the public activities, or "forms of life," in which actors participate to decipher the meanings of their behavior. For Winch, behavior has meaning because the activities in which actors participate have rules, which they follow in order to achieve their ends. Rules are like the grammar of a language. Because Winch seeks meanings through public rules rather than private deliberations, he employs, or would employ, fieldwork far more than empathy. His approach is far more anthropological than that of either Collingwood or Dray and so is closer to Geertz's.

For Geertz, as for Winch, the meaning of culture is public and is expressed in the rules of public activities: "culture is best seen not as complexes of concrete behavior patterns—customs, usages, traditions, habit clusters—. . . but as a set of control mechanisms—plans, recipes, rules, instructions . . . for the governing of behavior" (Geertz, 1973, p. 44). "Cultural forms . . . draw their meaning from the role they play (Wittgenstein would say their 'use') in an ongoing pattern of life" (Geertz, 1973, p. 17). Practice rather than belief, ritual rather than myth, "ethos" rather than "world view" is the key to the meaning of culture, and fieldwork, not empathy, is the key to unraveling that meaning.

Despite the later Geertz's insistence on interpretation rather than explanation, Geertz can be read as offering either an explanation or an interpretation. When, in an essay in *The Interpretation of Cultures* that originally appeared in1957, he writes that "the drive to make sense out of experience, to give it form and order, is evidently as real and as pressing as the more familiar biological needs" (Geertz, 1973, p. 140), that drive can be taken not only as the definition of religious and other cultural expressions but, alternatively, as the cause of religious and other cultural effects. Religion would thereby be, as for Max Weber, the fulfillment of a need to make sense of life rather than, as for interpretivists like Collingwood, Dray, and Winch, one possible expression of humanity's sense-making nature.

Indeed, even in "Thick Description," the one new essay in *The Interpretation of Cultures* and the programmatic interpretive statement (1973, ch. 1), Geertz declares that anthropology should no more be exclusively interpretive than exclusively explanatory. Interpretation should supplement, not supplant, explanation. Anthropology should be an "interpretive science."

Just as Geertz's model of pure interpretation is literary criticism, so his model of interpretive science is medicine. According to Geertz, interpretation in medicine merely classifies behavior: A medical diagnosis identifies a set of symptoms as belonging to, say, the category *measles*. By contrast, according to Geertz, explanation goes beyond interpretation to account for both the source and the effect of behavior: While symptoms themselves are part of the definition of a disease rather than either its origin or even its consequence, a diagnosis also gives or suggests both the origin and the consequences of the disease. Diagnosis combines interpretation with explanation, as otherwise in "Thick Description" interpretation by itself does.

Applied to anthropology, categories identified by Geertz have included *revolution, kinship, ethos, worldview, myth, ritual, religion, art,* and *cultural system.* In the category *revolution,* for instance, one "symptom" of revolution might be political protests. One source might be inequality. One consequence might be equality. The "double task" in "diagnosing" revolution would therefore be both "to uncover the conceptual structures [i.e., interpretive categories] that inform our subjects' acts, the 'said' of social discourse, and to construct a system of analysis [i.e., explanation] in whose terms what is generic to those structures, what belongs to them because they are what they are, will stand out against the other determinants [i.e., causes] of human behavior" (Geertz, 1973, p. 27). One would fully have deciphered an instance of revolution—or of religion—only by having first identified the phenomenon as a case of the category and then having accounted for it.

When Geertz follows the model of medical diagnosis, interpretive science is generalized: The doctor seeks the category into which the patient's symptoms fall. But when otherwise in "Thick Description" Geertz pits interpretation against scientific explanation, by *interpretation* he means the primacy of the particular over the general. Geertz opposes generalizations on multiple grounds. They invariably prove inaccurate or tendentious. They are somehow inseparable from the particulars that yield them and, when separated, turn out to be banal or empty: "Theoretical formulations [i.e., generalizations] hover so low over the [particularistic] interpretations they govern that they don't make much sense or hold much interest apart from them. . . . [S]tated independently of their [particularistic] applications, they seem either commonplace or vacant" (Geertz, 1973, p. 25).

Above all for Geertz, generalizations miss the distinctiveness of the particulars they are derived from: "Within the bloated categories of regime description, Feudalism or Colonialism, Late Capitalism or The World System, Neo-Monarchy or Parliamentary Militarism, there is a resident suchness, deep Moroccanicity, inner Indonesianness, struggling to get out. Such a conception of things is usually called nationalism. That is certainly not wrong, but, another bloated category, grouping the ungroupable and blurring distinctions internally felt, it is less definite than it seems. Every quiddity has its own form of suchness, and no one who comes to Morocco or Indonesia to find out what goes on there is likely to confuse them with each other or to be satisfied with elevated banalities about common humanity or a universal need for self-expression" (Geertz, 1995, p. 23).

For Geertz, it is in the particular and not in the general that the significance of any cultural phenomenon lies: "The notion that the essence of what it means to be human is most clearly revealed in those features of human culture that are universal rather than in those that are distinctive to this people or that is a prejudice we are not necessarily obliged to share. Is it in grasping such general facts—that man has everywhere some sort of 'religion'—or in grasping the richness of this religious phenomenon or that—Balinese trance or Indian ritualism, Aztec human sacrifice or Zuñi raindancing—that we grasp him? Is the fact that 'marriage' is universal (if it is) as penetrating a comment on what we are as the facts concerning Himalayan polyandry, or those fantastic Australian marriage rules, or the elaborate bride-price systems of Bantu Africa?" (Geertz, 1973, p. 43).

Geertz's insistence on the superiority of the particular to the general helped pioneer the postmodern approach to culture, including religion, throughout the social sciences. Yet Geertz himself has never gone as far as his avowedly postmodernist successors, who reject generalizations as but one part of their rejection of a scientific approach to religion and the rest of culture. Geertz continues to employ general categories and continues to account for them. Furthermore, he does not dismiss the possibility of an objective analysis of religion and culture. Most important, he does not set an interpretive, or hermeneutical, approach to religion against a scientific one. His advocacy of an interpretive social science akin to medical diagnosis evinces the middle ground that he seeks. He strives to make social science interpretive, not to replace social science with interpretation.

BIBLIOGRAPHY

Bellah, Robert N. *Tokugawa Religion: The Values of Pre-Industrial Japan.* Glencoe, Ill., 1957.

Bellah, Robert N. *Beyond Belief: Essays on Religion in a Post-Traditional World.* New York, 1970.

Bellah, Robert N. *The Broken Covenant: American Civil Religion in a Time of Trial.* 2d ed. Chicago, 1992.

Bellah, Robert N. "The Revolution and Symbolic Realism." In *Religion and the American Revolution,* edited by Jerald C. Brauer, pp. 55–73. Philadelphia, 1976.

Berger, Peter L. *The Noise of Solemn Assemblies: Christian Commitment and the Religious Establishment in America.* Garden City, N.Y., 1961a.

Berger, Peter L. *The Precarious Vision: A Sociologist Looks at Social Fictions and Christian Faith.* Garden City, N.Y., 1961b.

Berger, Peter L. *The Sacred Canopy: Elements of a Sociological Theory of Religion.* Garden City, N.Y., 1967.

Berger, Peter L. *A Rumor of Angels: Modern Society and the Rediscovery of the Supernatural.* Garden City, N.Y., 1969.

Berger, Peter L. *The Heretical Imperative: Contemporary Possibilities of Religious Affirmation.* Garden City, N.Y., 1979.

Berger, Peter L., and Thomas Luckmann. *The Social Construction of Reality: A Treatise in the Sociology of Knowledge.* Garden City, N.Y., 1966.

Berger, Peter L., Brigitte Berger, and Hansfried Kellner. *The Homeless Mind: Modernization and Consciousness.* New York, 1973.

Collingwood, R. G. *The Idea of History,* ed. T. M. Knox. New York, 1946.

Dray, William. *Laws and Explanation in History.* London, 1957.

Geertz, Clifford. *The Interpretation of Cultures: Selected Essays.* New York, 1973.

Geertz, Clifford. *Local Knowledge: Further Essays in Interpretive Anthropology.* New York, 1983.

Geertz, Clifford. *After the Fact: Two Countries, Four Decades, One Anthropologist.* Cambridge, Mass., 1995.

Ryle, Gilbert. *Collected Papers.* 2 vols. New York, 1971.

Winch, Peter. *The Idea of a Social Science and Its Relation to Philosophy.* London, 1958; rev. 2d ed., London, 1990.

ROBERT A. SEGAL (2005)

SOCRATES (c. 469–399 BCE) was a Greek philosopher. Commonly regarded as the father of philosophy, Socrates' influence on Western thought has been huge throughout history. Almost every epoch saw in him a precursor of its own ideas and values, and a model of wisdom and morality.

SOURCES. Socrates is the only Western philosopher who wrote nothing. Hence all first-hand information on his life, personality, and thought derives from reports by those who knew him personally. Among those, a special role is played by his friends and associates who, in a series of dialogues commonly referred to as the *Sokratikoi logoi,* portray him in discussion with prominent intellectuals and politicians. These writings spread immediately after Socrates' death, becoming a popular literary genre in the first half of the fourth century BCE. Unfortunately, from a *corpus* of hundreds of conversations only those reported by Plato (428/427–348/347 BCE) and Xenophon (430–355 BCE) survive complete; the Socratic dialogues of other authors are lost except for some fragments. The most substantial of these fragments are from Aeschines of Sphettus; the fragments of Antisthenes, Aristippos, Euclides of Megara, and Phaedo of Elis are scarce.

Plato, the most important among Socrates' associates, wrote almost solely dialogues in which Socrates is the main speaker. Although in these writings Plato seems to present his own philosophy, this happens often under the strong influence of his master. Especially in Plato's earlier dialogues, written soon after 399 BCE, it is possible to make out many traits of Socrates' own philosophical thoughts. These dialogues include *Apology, Crito, Laches, Charmides, Euthyphro, Hippias Minor, Ion, Republic I,* and *Protagoras* from Plato's first period; and *Lysis, Euthydemus, Hippias Major, Menexenus, Meno,* and *Gorgias* from his second period. The middle dialogues (*Symposium, Cratylus, Phaedo, Republic II–X, Phaedrus, Parmenides,* and *Theaetetus*) and the late ones (*Timaeus, Critias, Sophist, Statesman, Philebus,* and *Laws*) are much closer to Plato's own than to his master's philosophy. Unlike Plato, Xenophon was not present at Socrates' trial and death and wrote his *logoi* many years after 399. His Socratic works are *Apology, Symposium, Oeconomicus,* and *Memorabilia.*

Other primary sources outside the Socratic circle are supplied by the Attic comedy. Socrates was used as a comic character in Ameipsias' *Connus* and Aristophanes' *Clouds,* two of the three comedies performed for the first time in Athens in 423 BCE. Of these dramatic works only *Clouds* survives complete, though in a revised edition. This version, like most of the evidence coming from the comedians after 423 BCE, gives a caricature of Socrates as an atheistic natural philosopher who is both an ascetic moral teacher and a sophist (for instance, in Aristophanes' *Birds* and *Frogs*).

Among the writings of authors who were not personally acquainted with Socrates, most important are those of Aristotle (384–322 BCE), who probably learned of him from Plato and others while attending the Athenian Academy. Aristotle's interest in Socrates was aimed at assigning to him a precise place in the history of philosophy, distinguishing the elements in Plato's oeuvre actually belonging to Socrates from those constituting Platonic interpretations of Socratic thought. Major evidence of this is to be found in several passages of *Metaphysics*, *Nicomachean* and *Eudemean Ethics*, and *Magna Moralia.*

Since all of the later Socratic sources of antiquity rely on the writings of the mentioned authors or on works which were lost, they are far less able to convey the real philosophical thoughts of Socrates. But since in some cases these testimonies contain information that is not elsewhere preserved, they should nevertheless be taken into account. The major Socratic texts occur within a variety of literary genres:

1. the philosophers (Cicero, Plutarch, and others);
2. Diogenes Laertius;
3. the apologetic writers (Aelius Aristides, Libanius, and others);
4. the antiquarian writers (Aulus Gellius, Aelian, Athenaeus, and others);
5. the anthologists, the lexicographers, and the *Suda;*
6. the early Christian writers.

LIFE The only certain fact about Socrates' life is the year in which he was condemned and put to death, in 399 BCE. All other circumstances reported about him have no historical reliability, although in many cases their symbolic and philosophic meanings are of great interest.

Some sources report that Socrates, of the Antiochid tribe and the deme of Alopeke, was born on the birthday of the goddess of midwives, Artemis, the sixth Tragelion. He was the son of the midwife Phaenarete and the statuary Sophroniscus, with whom he worked during his youth. His family was likely wealthy, since he served several times in the heavy infantry, where he had to provide himself weapons and armor. During his later life, however, it seems that he became extremely poor, probably due to his absorption in philosophy, which left him no time for attending to his personal affairs. It is reported that he married Xanthippe, famous for her bad temper. His three sons Lamprocles, Sophroniscus, and Menexenus were still young at the time of his death, and were probably sons of another wife named Myrto, whose marriage to Socrates is variously described as preceding, following, or bigamously coinciding with his union to Xanthippe.

Throughout the literary and the iconographic sources of antiquity Socrates is renowned for the ugliness of his physiognomy. He had a snub nose, broad nostrils, protruding eyes, and an overly-dimensioned mouth, with extremely thick lips. Furthermore, he was bald, his neck was short and thick, and his belly was huge. His appearance was thus compared to that of a satyr or silenus. His physical toughness and endurance were known to be exceptional: he was able to practice extreme continence or abstemiousness as well as to outdrink anyone without ever getting drunk himself. He bathed infrequently and wore ostentatiously simple clothing, always went barefoot, and never became ill; he could go without sleep for days and sustain prolonged, trance-like spells of intense mental concentration. During the Peloponnesian War (431–404 BCE) he gave proof of his bravery in the campaigns of Potidaea (432–429 BCE), where he saved the life of Alcibiades (432 BCE); Daelium (424 BCE); and Amphipolis (422 BCE).

Except for these military campaigns and two other trips to Samos and the Isthmian games, Socrates stayed always in Athens. Due to his extraordinary charisma he gathered around him a circle of friends and associates, who saw in him a "truly divine and marvelous man" (Plato, *Symposium* 219c). In 423 BCE he was a well-known personality in Athens, portrayed in Aristophanes' *Clouds* as a leading representative of a new kind of education. His fame reached even Archelaus of Macedonia, Scopas of Krannon, and Eurylochus of Larisa, whose invitations to their courts he declined.

In 406 BCE Socrates belonged to the Athenian Council of Five Hundred when the so-called trial of the Arginusae took place. In it, the generals of the Athenian fleet faced charges of neglect of duty following the naval battle of the Arginusae Islands during the Peloponnesian War. Athens won, but a storm wrecked several ships afterward, and the officers failed to rescue the survivors. In Socrates' tribe the assembly made the illegal proposal to condemn the generals to death collectively instead of individually, as required by law. Whereas the other members all accepted the proposal, Socrates refused, thus demonstrating loyalty to the laws of his city. Two years later, when the Thirty Tyrants attempted to involve him in criminal political activities by securing his complicity in the arrest of Leon of Salamis, he refused, for which he would have been put to death, if the Thirty had not been overthrown in time (Plato, *Apology* 32d and Xenophon, *Memorabilia* IV, 4, 3).

Five years later Anytus, a prominent politician of the restored democracy, together with the obscure Lycus and Meletus, brought the following indictment against Socrates: "Socrates is guilty of not recognizing the gods which the city recognizes, and of introducing other, new divinities. Further, he is guilty of corrupting the young. The penalty is death" (Favorinus, in Diogenes Laertius II, 40). Found guilty on both counts (by votes of 280-220 and 360-140), he was sentenced to death by hemlock. Having declined the alternative penalty of exile, and the opportunity to escape from prison (as his associates urged him to do), he was executed in 399 BCE.

PHILOSOPHY AND RELIGION. As was common in Athenian wealthy families, Socrates was educated in the traditional disciplines of *mousike* ("education of the spirit") and *gumnastike* ("education of the body") and in Ionian natural sciences. The sources report that he became a disciple of the physicist Archelaus, through whom he was introduced to the theories of Anaximenes and Anaxagoras. Though he was apparently fascinated by them, the more he deepened his studies, the more he became aware of the limits of natural philosophy. He noticed that this discipline was not able to obtain any certain knowledge of the natural phenomena because of its mechanistic character—that is, its habit to explain one cause with another—without ever finding a supreme principle of being capable of "holding together any other thing" (Plato, *Phaedo* 99c). Disappointed, he left his studies in Ionian science and started looking for a "second sailing" in research (Plato, *Phaedo* 99c).

The direction of this new approach was indicated to Socrates by a religious experience which marked a turning point in his life. According to Plato's account, around 430 BCE Socrates' friend Chaerephon went to the oracle of Apollo in Delphi and posed the question whether anyone was wiser than Socrates. The oracle answered that no one was. When Chaerephon went back to Athens and told his friend of this response, Socrates was puzzled, since he thought that he possessed no expertise at all. In order to decipher the oracle's meaning, he set about to find someone wiser than himself among people with reputations for their wisdom. Upon questioning them systematically he realized that they in fact lacked the knowledge they claimed, and were therefore less wise than he, who at least *knew* that he knew nothing. He thus understood that the wisdom meant by the oracle consisted exactly of this peculiar knowledge, the awareness of ignorance. He came also to understand that the oracle had chosen him to propagate this knowledge by showing every human being that his claims to substantive wisdom were unfounded. From that moment until the last day of his life Socrates felt compelled to fulfill this "divine mission" in honor of Apollo, the god who praises the virtues of humility and restraint (as is evident in the famous Delphic inscription, "Know thyself!").

This enterprise of questioning, examining, and refuting other people in order to make them aware of their ignorance is commonly known as the Socratic *elenchus*. Its most important achievement consists of understanding and in making others understand the fallible, that is the human nature of wisdom (*anthropine sophia*), juxtaposed to the absolute wisdom of the gods (*theia sophia*), which is altogether unreachable for humankind. To this philosophical acknowledgment everyone is compelled, since "the unexamined life is not worth living for a human being" (Plato, *Apology* 38a). Elenchus is the only possible source of intellectual and moral well-being, since it improves the most valuable part of man, the seat of all his virtue and knowledge: the soul (*psuche*). Unlike the traditional conceptions of the Orphics, the Pythagoreans and the Ionians, Socrates is the first to identify the *psuche* both with the entire and real self and the "Igo" of consciousness and personality. The supreme duty of a human being is to "care for it" (Plato, *Apology* 29e and Xenophon, *Memorabilia* I, 2, 4–5), a task best accomplished by "purifying" it through intellectual training and elenchtic testing.

Though aimed at improving the soul, the practice of elenchus is not merely destructive. Socrates' disavowal of scientific knowledge implies that from a practical point of view he knows exactly what knowledge is. As Aristotle points out, this knowledge is of a "different kind" if compared to that of the experts or the physiologists (*Eudemean Ethics* 1246b 36). It has a non-epistemic character, since it is confined to make out what is good (*agathon*) for the soul in an immediate, concrete, and practical sense. Both in Plato and Xenophon, Socrates identifies this good with what is beneficial (*ophelimon, chresimon*). Virtue, as the real application of this good, is thus founded on knowledge that is the goodness of the soul. Once the soul knows what is good in a given situation, it has the correct focus for its actions, a focus that eventually turns out to be beneficial as well.

Major evidence for Socrates' firm faith in the practical effects of the knowledge of the good is provided by his theodicy. As shown by Xenophon, Socrates believes in unwritten laws that have a divine origin (*Memorabilia* IV, 4, 19–25). Unlike the human laws, which can be violated without necessarily incurring punishment, the unwritten laws contain the punishment within themselves. They are a cosmic rule, deeply rooted into the profundity of reality. This conception occurs also in Plato's *Apology*, when Socrates replies to the menaces of his accusers by saying that "the goddess Themis will not allow that a good man will be hurt by a worse one" (30c), or when, immediately after he has been sentenced to death, he declares that "a good man cannot suffer any harm, neither in his life nor after his death, because the gods take care of him" (41d).

Socrates' conception of the divine is closely linked to his search for the goodness of the soul. This becomes clear in the teleological proof of God's existence reported by Xenophon (*Memorabilia* I, 4, 1–19 and IV, 3, 1–18; cf. Plato, *Gorgias* 507e–508a): since everything that is good is beneficial, it has to be necessarily the product of intelligent design; this entails the existence of one or more intelligent designer-creators possessing the wisdom and the power necessary for producing the orderly and beautiful universe; therefore, these beings must have an entirely benevolent and caring attitude toward the world they created, ruling it in a fashion analogous to the way the human soul rules the body. And because of its intrinsic theoretical capacities this very soul "partakes of the divine" more than any other thing in the universe (*Memorabilia*, IV, 3, 14), and the man who practices its capacities through philosophy is at the same time "virtuous" and "pious" (*Memorabilia* IV, 3, 16–18). Piety itself is strongly connected to morality, since it is a service to the gods that helps them to promulgate goodness in the universe (Plato, *Euthyphro* 14b). For Socrates there is no split between philosophy, ethics, and religion; they all call for acts directed to improve both the human soul and the universe.

The interdependence between the human and the divine sphere in Socrates' teleology was thus eminently practical and non-epistemic. With it Socrates tried to reform religion from an ethical point of view. This meant rejecting the moral imperfections of the Homeric gods, foremost their enmities and lies. The chasm between human and divine ethics had to be eliminated, in order to restore the lost faith in the nobility of the gods and to make them thus more believable. Socrates' anthropocentric teleology was perhaps the last attempt in Greek history to achieve this. In an epoch characterized by an increasing number of particular cults often in open conflict with each other, he gave a new impulse to Greek religion, establishing homogeneous criteria for mortals and gods. He did this while remaining on the solid ground of tradition: his "moralized" gods were still the gods of the city, whom he called to witness his oaths and worshipped with prayers and sacrifices, communicating with them through dreams, divination, and even poetic inspiration. Despite the orthodoxy of Socrates' religious behavior, however, in 399 he was tried, convicted, and condemned to death for impiety.

Socrates was first accused of not recognizing the gods of the city. According to Socrates' own account of the reason he was charged, this indictment was not for having moralized the gods, but mainly because the accusers assimilated these gods to the natural elements which were studied by the Ionian physiologists during those years (Plato, *Apology* 18b–c, 19a–d, 23c–d, 26d, and Aristophanes' *Clouds*). Since few years earlier Anaxagoras had already been declared guilty of the same charge due to his affiliation with the Periclean circle, it is likely that the accusers against Socrates also had a political rather than a religious background.

The second charge was that of introducing "new divinities" (*hetera daimonia kaina*: Plato, *Apology* 24c, and others). It is probable that the target was the *daimonion* of Socrates, although the use of the generic plural form *daimonia* may indicate that the accusers wanted to include in the charge also other divinities, or that they themselves did not have a clear idea of which gods exactly were worshipped by Socrates. The *daimonion ti* (literally: the "daemonic something") was one of the most peculiar traits of Socratic religion. According to the sources, Socrates regarded it as a divine "sign" or an "interior voice" which had been his companion since childhood. It gave him advice which was merely dissuasive, particular, personal, and practical (according to Xenophon the *daimonion* also prescribed advice to Socrates' friends). Since Socrates considered the counsel of the *daimonion* unfailingly correct, he always followed it, even if it urged him against something of which he was fully convinced. This particular circumstance showed that in Socrates' view the *daimonion* could be stronger than discursive thinking, but was perfectly compatible with it: Although its advice sometimes seemed to contradict the elenchus, eventually it turned out to be perfectly rational. The privilege of Socrates' exclusive relationship with the *daimonion* was likely considered suspect by his accusers; still, in the religious context of ancient Athens, which was extremely tolerant towards the introduction of new or even foreign divinities, this alone could hardly have led to a prosecution.

It seems therefore probable that the reason for Socrates' conviction was merely political, since the religious accusations were unfounded. In fact, the most serious charge brought against Socrates was that of corruption of the youth. The practice of elenchus entailed a new education, which could subvert social morality. This was evident in the Socratic circle, where men like Critias and Alcibiades were famous for their antidemocratic political attitude. To the newly restored democracy Socrates and his circle were a danger to be eliminated as soon as possible. This may have been the reason why the pious Socrates, who believed in the goodness of the gods, was eventually condemned for impiety.

SEE ALSO Apollo; Aristotle; Atheism; Delphi; Plato; Theodicy.

BIBLIOGRAPHY

A complete bibliography of the Socratic literature from antiquity until 1988 is to be found in Andreas Patzer, *Bibliographia Socratica* (Freiburg, Germany, 1985), and Luis E. Navia and Ellen L. Katz, *Socrates: An Annotated Bibliography* (New York, 1988).

A comprehensive survey on the most important Socratic testimonies in English translation is delivered by John Ferguson, *Socrates: A Source Book* (London, 1970); see also the complete editions of Xenophon, Aristophanes, and Aristotle in the Loeb Classical Library (Cambridge, Mass.). The ancient sources can be divided into primary (A), that is the texts of authors who knew Socrates personally or could hear from him indirectly, and secondary (B), which consist of later writings, mostly founded upon the primary sources.

(A) The major primary source are Plato's dialogues, edited in Greek by John Burnet (*Platonis Opera*, Oxford, 1900–1917; reprinted 1976). The English translations are numerous, one of the most recent being the *Complete Works* edited by John M. Cooper and D. S. Hutchinson (Indianapolis, Ind., 1997). The most accessible English translation of Xenophon's Socratic writings is that of Hugh Treddenick and Robin Waterfield, *Conversations of Socrates* (London, 1990). For a scholarly edition of Aristophanes' *Clouds* see Kenneth J. Dover, Oxford, 1968. Aristotle's references to Socrates have been collected by Thomas Déman, *Le témoignage d'Aristote sur Socrate* (Paris, 1942).

(B) The Greek and Latin texts of all the Socratic sources except Plato, Xenophon, and Aristophanes are to be found in the *Socratis et Socraticorum Reliquiae*, edited by Gabriele Giannantoni (Naples, 1990).

Modern scholarship on Socrates starts with Friedrich Schleiermacher's "The Worth of Socrates as a Philosopher" (1815), translated by Connop Thirlwall, *The Philological Museum* 2 (1833): 538–555. In this essay arises for the first time the question of which sources, if any, can be reliable for a reconstruction of Socrates' thought. This question, commonly referred to as the "Socratic problem," has been answered in many different ways, spawning a vast amount of literature. Useful guides to it are: *Der historische Sokrates*, edited by Andreas Patzer (Darmstadt, Germany, 1987), and Mario Montuori, *The Socratic Problem* (Amsterdam, 1992). For a survey on the reception of Socrates throughout history see Herbert Spiegelberg, *The Socratic Enigma* (New York, 1964).

Classical works on Socrates are: Georg Wilhelm Friedrich Hegel, *Lectures on the History of Philosophy* (1833), translated by Elizabeth Sanderson Haldane (London, 1963), vol. 1: pp. 384–448; Søren Kierkegaard, *The Concept of Irony, with Constant Reference to Socrates* (1841), translated by Lee M. Capel (New York, 1965); George Grote, *Life, Teachings, and Death of Socrates* (1850, reprinted, New York, 1859); Friedrich Nietzsche, *The Birth of Tragedy from the Spirit of Music* (1872), translated by Clifton P. Fadiman (New York, 1954); Eduard Zeller, *Socrates and the Socratic Schools* (1889), translated by Oswald J. Reichel (New York, 1962); Karl Joël, *Der echte und der xenophontische Sokrates* (Berlin, 1893–1901); Heinrich Maier, *Sokrates. Sein Werk und seine geschichtliche Stellung* (Tübingen, Germany, 1913); Guy C. Field, *Socrates and Plato* (London, 1913); John Burnet, *Greek Philosophy. From Thales to Plato* (London, 1913), pp. 102–156; Frances M. Cornford, *Before and after Socrates* (Cambridge, 1932); Alfred E. Taylor, *Varia Socratica* (Oxford, 1911), and *Socrates* (Edinburgh, 1933); Werner Jaeger, *Paideia* (1933), translated by Gilbert Highet (New York, 1939), vol. 2: pp. 13–75; Olof Gigon, *Sokrates. Sein Bild in Dichtung und Geschichte* (Bern, Switzerland, 1947); Vasco de Magalhães-Vilhena, *Le problème de Socrate. Le Socrate historique et le Socrate de Platon*, and *Socrate et la légende Platonicienne* (Paris, 1952); Norman Gulley, *The Philosophy of Socrates* (London, 1968); William Keith Chambers Guthrie, *Socrates* (London, 1971); Mario Montuori, *Socrates. Physiology of a Myth* (1974), translated by J. M. P. Langdale and M. Langdale (Amsterdam, 1981); Gerasimos Santas, *Socrates' Philosophy in Plato's Early Dialogues* (Boston, 1979); Luis E. Navia, *Socrates, the Man and His Philosophy* (New York, 1985); Richard B. Rutherford, *The Art of Plato* (London, 1995), and Christopher Charles Whiston Taylor, *Socrates* (New York, 1998).

Important essays have been collected in the following volumes: *The Philosophy of Socrates: A Collection of Critical Essays*, edited by Gregory Vlastos (Garden City, N.Y., 1971); *The Socratic Movement*, edited by Paul A. Van der Waerdt (Ithaca, N.Y., 1994); *Socrates: Critical Assessments*, edited by William J. Prior (New York, 1996), 4 vols. More essays are to be found in *Der fragende Sokrates*, edited by Karl Pestalozzi (Stuttgart, Germany, 1999), and *Sokrates*, edited by Herbert Kessler (Kusterdingen, Germany, 1993–2001), 5 vols.

A turning point in Socratic studies was settled by Gregory Vlastos (*Socrates: Ironist and Moral Philosopher* [Ithaca, N.Y., 1991], and *Socratic Studies*, edited by Myles Burnyeat [New York, 1994]). The Socrates renaissance that began in North America in 1990 owes much both to his scholarship and teaching: Charles H. Kahn, *Plato and the Socratic Dialogue* (New York, 1996); George Rudebusch, *Socrates, Pleasure and Value* (New York, 1999); Alexander Nehamas, *Virtues of Authenticity: Essays on Plato and Socrates* (Princeton, N.J., 1999); Hugh H. Benson, *Socratic Wisdom: The Model of Knowledge in Plato's Early Dialogues* (New York, 2000); Gary A. Scott, *Plato's Socrates as Educator* (Albany, N.Y., 2000); Thomas C. Brickhouse and Nicholas D. Smith, *Socrates on Trial* (Oxford, 1989), *Plato's Socrates* (New York, 1994), *The Philosophy of Socrates* (Boulder, Colo., 2000), and *The Trial and Execution of Socrates: Sources and Controversies* (New York, 2002).

See also the collections of articles: *Essays on the Philosophy of Socrates*, edited by Hugh H. Benson (New York, 1992); *Socratic Questions: New Essays on the Philosophy of Socrates and Its Significance*, edited by Barry S. Gower and Michael C. Stokes (New York, 1992), and *Does Socrates Have a Method? Rethinking the Elenchus in Plato's Dialogues and Beyond*, edited by Gary Alan Scott (University Park, Pa., 2002).

Studies especially dedicated to the topic of Socrates and religion are: Robert M. Wenley, *Socrates and Christ* (1889, reprinted, London, 2002); John Burnet, "The Socratic Doctrine of the Soul," *Proceedings of the British Academy* 7 (1915–1916): 235–259; *Greek Religious Thought*, edited by Frances M. Cornford (New York, 1923): pp. 158–187; James Beckman, *The Religious Dimension of Socrates' Thought* (1943, reprinted Waterloo, Ont., 1979); Ehrland Ehnmark, "Socrates and the Immortality of the Soul," *Eranos* 14 (1946): 105–122; Antonio Tovar, *Vida de Sócrate* (Madrid, 1947); Wilhelm Nestle, "Sokrates und Delphi," in Wilhelm Nestle, *Griechische Studien* (Stuttgart, Germany, 1948): pp. 173–185; Francesco Sarri, *Socrate e la genesi storica dell'idea occidentale di anima* (Rome, 1975); *Socratic Piety and the Power of Reason. New Essays on Socrates*, edited by Eugene Kelly (Lanham, Md., 1984); Hans-Georg Gadamer, "Sokrates' Frömmigkeit des Nichtwissens" (1990) in Hans-Georg Gadamer, *Gesammelte Werke*, vol. 7 (Tübingen, Germany, 1991): pp. 83–117; Michelle Gellrich, "Socratic Magic: Enchantment, Irony, and Persuasion in Plato's Dialogues," *Classical World* 87 (1994): 275–307; Mark. L. McPherran, *The Religion of Socrates* (University Park, Pa., 1996); Robert Parker, *Athenian Religion* (Oxford, 1997): pp. 152–217; Paul W. Gooch, *Reflections on Jesus and Socrates* (New Haven, Conn., 1997); Jean-Joël Duhot, *Socrate ou l'éveil de la conscience* (Paris, 1999): pp. 73–163; Silvia Lanzi, *Theos Anaitios. Storia della teodicea da Omero ad Agostino* (Rome, 2000): pp. 97–101; *Reason and Religion in Socratic Philosophy*, edited by Nicholas D. Smith and Paul B. Woodruff (New York, 2000); Ernst R. Sandvoss, *Sokrates und Jesus* (Munich, 2001); and Minoura Eryō, "Ein Aspekt der griechischen Religion. Źberlegungen zur Methode der religionsgeschichtlichen Forschung nach Sokrates," in *Unterwegs. Neue Pfade in der Religionswissenschaft*, edited by Christoph Kleine, Monika Schrimpf, and Katja Triplett (Munich, 2004): pp. 197–205.

ALESSANDRO STAVRU (2005)

SÖDERBLOM, NATHAN (1866–1931). Swedish churchman, theologian, Luther scholar, ecumenical pioneer, and historian of religions. Lars Olaf Johnathan Söderblom was born into a deeply religious family in Trönö, Hälsingland Province, Sweden. His father, a fervent evangelical preacher, was pastor of the Trönö parish and led his family in a life of devotion, study, discipline, and hard work. In 1883 young Nathan entered the university at Uppsala as a candidate in classical and Oriental languages but later changed to work for a degree in divinity. The theological faculty in Uppsala at the time was immovably conservative and literalist; it had been little touched by the German theology reigning on the European continent. Söderblom in consequence was disappointed with his divinity studies.

The outstanding events of the university years for him were the discovery of biblical criticism, his acquaintance with the theology of Albrecht Ritschl, and his participation in the Student Missionary Society. The new biblical criticism posed an acute crisis for Söderblom; while he enthusiastically welcomed its methods and insights, it threatened the conservative Swedish view of the Bible as a literal revelation. Söderblom resolved his difficulties through Ritschl's broad view of a dynamic revelation not confined to the literal words of the book. His attitudes in these matters earned him a reputation as a dangerous liberal, an accusation that would plague him all his life and that probably accounts for his failure to become a docent upon graduation. It was his participation in the Student Missionary Society and a consuming concern for Christian missions that first stimulated Söderblom's interest in non-Christian religious experience and laid the basis for his work as historian of religions.

In 1893 Söderblom was ordained and served for a time as chaplain in the Uppsala mental hospital, but in 1894 he accepted an appointment as pastor to the Swedish legation in Paris. In addition to pastoral duties, Söderblom cemented a close relationship with the Protestant Theological Faculty of the Sorbonne. Auguste Sabatier, A. and J. Réville, and Léon Marillier in particular exerted strong influence on his thinking, and he continued the study of Iranian languages that he had begun earlier. In 1899 he published in Paris *Les fravashis,* a short but erudite study of a type of spiritual beings in ancient Iranian religion; his Sorbonne doctoral dissertation, *La vie future d'après le Mazdéisme,* followed in 1901, establishing him among the leading Iranologists of Europe.

In 1901 Söderblom was invited to a professorship in Uppsala. The chair was in theology, but under Söderblom it became, practically speaking, one in the history of religions. The strong Swedish tradition in history of religions had its beginning with this appointment. Söderblom was a popular teacher who also rapidly became a decisive influence in the church as a leader of a general revival of religion and theology in Sweden. In 1912 he was appointed to the new chair of the history of religions in Leipzig which he held jointly with that of Uppsala. His most important contribution to the theory of the nature of religion, *Gudstrons Uppkomst* (2d ed., Stockholm, 1914), and his books *The Nature of Revelation,* translated by Frederic C. Pamp (Oxford, 1933), and *Natürliche Theologie und allgemeine Religionsgeschichte* (Stockholm, 1913) belong to these years. The German connections also enabled him to carry out his work of reconciliation among Christians of the belligerent nations during World War I.

In 1914 the Swedish king chose Söderblom to replace J. A. Ekman as archbishop of Sweden. The first four years of his tenure coincided with World War I, and even while the fighting continued, Söderblom pleaded for a conference between Christians of the two sides. His interest in ecumenical matters had begun in his student days, and it continued through the Lambeth Conference of 1905 and the agreement between Anglicans and Swedish Lutherans concluded in 1922. The culmination for Söderblom was the great Stockholm conference of 1925 on life and work, of which he was a principal mover. His work among the combatants in World War I and his efforts toward Christian unity were the principal bases for the award of the Nobel Peace Prize that he received in 1930. The last of many honors bestowed on him was the Gifford lectureship for 1931–1932. He delivered the lectures for 1931, published as *The Living God* (1933; reprint, 1962), but he died before he could complete the series.

The central element in Söderblom's thought, as apparent in his work both as theologian and as historian of religions, was the concept of revelation. He held that revelation is dynamic, not confined to the words of the Bible but also to be seen in nature, history, and genius. Neither is it the exclusive possession of Christianity, for he believed there to be revelation wherever genuine religion is found. Nevertheless, he also held to the inherent religious superiority of Christianity over other traditions and believed that he could prove this superiority through purely disinterested and scientific study of the history of religions. His effort was thus to gain a concrete grasp of the world's religions in all their historical diversity and richness but also to demonstrate the merits of Christianity as the climax of the revelation of the living God to human beings.

BIBLIOGRAPHY

There is a full-scale biography of Söderblom by his most famous student, Tor Andrae, *Nathan Söderblom* (Uppsala, 1932). A short biographical account, as well as a preliminary bibliography of Söderblom's writings, is to be found in *Nathan Söderblom in Memoriam,* edited by Nils Karlström (Stockholm, 1931). Söderblom's theological thought is ably expounded in Charles J. Curtis's *Nathan Söderblom, Theologian of Revelation* (Chicago, 1966).

New Sources

Bråkenhielm, C.R., and G.W. Hollman. *The Relevance of Theology: Nathan Söderblom and the Development of an Academic Discipline: Proceedings from a Conference held in Uppsala, April 14–16, 2002.* Uppsala, 2002.

Hallencreutz, Carl F. "The American Influence on Nathan Soderblom and the Legacy of His Ecumenical Strategy" *Svensk Missionstidskrift* 85, no. 1 (1997): 16–23.

Sharpe, E.J. *Nathan Söderblom and the Study of Religion.* Chapel Hill, N.C., 1990.

CHARLES J. ADAMS (1987)
Revised Bibliography

SOFER, MOSHEH (1762–1839), a Jewish religious leader, was known as the Ḥatam Sofer (Ḥasam Soyfer in

Ashkenazic pronunciation) and as Moses Schreiber in governmental documents. Born in Frankfurt, Mosheh Sofer studied there under the chief rabbi, Pinḥas Horovitz, and under Natan Adler, a qabbalist known for his strict and unusual ritual practices. When in 1782 Adler became the rabbi of Boskowitz, Moravia (now in the Czech Republic), Sofer left with him. He married in Prossnitz, Moravia, in 1787 and later served as rabbi of Dresnitz, Moravia (1794–1798), and of Mattersdorf, Hungary (1798–1806). From 1806 until his death he was the chief rabbi of Pressburg (now Bratislava, Slovakia), then one of the chief cities of Hungary, where he established a large and influential *yeshivah* (Talmudic academy). After the death of his first wife he married the daughter of ʿAqivaʾ Eger, one of the leading Talmudists of the age. His descendants (all by his second marriage) include a number of important Talmudic scholars and Orthodox leaders.

The Ḥatam Sofer is generally viewed as the intellectual leader of the "Old Orthodox" opposition to Reform Judaism. One of the last great Talmudic scholars educated in Germany, he differed from later German Orthodoxy in that he opposed not only all ritual and liturgical innovations but also any changes in traditional education and style of life. Coining the slogan "The Torah forbids what is new," he vehemently fought the Mendelssohnian Enlightenment (Haskalah), the use of German in sermons, and even the slightest innovation in custom. He wished to retain Jewish national and cultural separateness and to strengthen the moral and coercive powers of the rabbinate and Jewish community to prevent innovation. He viewed the legal emancipation of the Jews as a poor substitute for messianic redemption and a return to Zion.

A charismatic and energetic leader, the Ḥatam Sofer aroused both intense admiration and violent opposition. His influence in western Hungary on Orthodoxy, especially non-Hasidic Orthodoxy, remained intense into the twentieth century; his example helped give Hungarian Orthodoxy its zealous, uncompromising imprint. Outside the Hungarian cultural area, his influence was felt mainly in the realm of traditional Talmudic and halakhic (religious-legal) scholarship. Though the Ḥatam Sofer published very little during his lifetime, the immense corpus of his posthumous works includes almost twelve hundred *responsa* (legal opinions), *novellae* on the Talmud, sermons, biblical and liturgical commentaries, and religious poetry.

SEE ALSO Orthodox Judaism.

BIBLIOGRAPHY

Relatively little has been written on Mosheh Sofer in English, and some of this work is marred by a polemical bent. A great deal more is available in Hebrew, including the corpus of his own works. Probably the most balanced assessment is Jacob Katz's "Contributions toward a Biography of R. Moses Sofer" (in Hebrew), in *Studies in Mysticism and Religion Presented to Gershom G. Scholem* (Jerusalem, 1967), edited by E. E. Urbach and others, pp. 115–148.

New Sources

Schreiber, Aaron M. "The Hatam Sofer's Nuanced Attitude towards Secular Learning, Maskilim, and Reformers." *Torah U-Madda Journal* 11 (2002–2003): 123–173.

STEVEN M. LOWENSTEIN (1987)
Revised Bibliography

SOHM, RUDOLF

SOHM, RUDOLF (1841–1917), was a German Lutheran jurist and church historian. Rudolf Sohm was a member of the law faculties at Göttingen, Freiburg, Strassburg, and Leipzig universities and published in the fields of Roman and Germanic law and of canon law and church history. As a renowned jurist he entered into the controversy regarding the character of authority and organization in the primitive Christian community. In 1892 he published the first volume of his masterwork, *Kirchenrecht* (Canon law); the second volume was published posthumously in 1923. Sohm was politically active and in 1896 he helped Friedrich Naumann found the National-Sozial Partei (not to be confused with the later Nazi Party).

In *Kirchenrecht,* Sohm argued that the early church had no legal constitution. He claimed that "ecclesiastical law stands in contradiction to the nature of Ecclesia." Legal concepts, he believed, are completely inappropriate when considering the early church, which was informed by a power of a different order. This power he called "charisma" (from Gr., *charis*), which is "a gift of grace" imparted by the Holy Spirit. In Paul's view (*1 Cor.* 12:4–28), the gifts of grace are manifest in the congregation as well as in apostles, prophets, and teachers. The congregation had the "gift" of acknowledging charismatic leaders; the community was not a democracy but rather a "pneumatocracy." In his interpretation Sohm found that the community gave special status to the teacher whose charismatic gifts were exercised in conjunction with scripture and sacraments.

The development of a legal order within the church was a "fall" away from authenticity. This "fall" brought about the heresy, or apostasy, of Roman Catholicism and of bureaucratized Lutheranism. The fall away from the authentic church appeared in the development from the charismatic power of the individual Christian leader to the authority of the Christian official (in possession of legal and tenure rights), thence to a Christian corporation with legal and coercive control over individual salvation. This "fall" occurs because the unregenerate "natural man" is a "born Catholic" who seeks legal authenticity and a guarantee of salvation and who desires what is tangible and visible, providing pomp and circumstance that appeal to the senses. This "natural man" relies upon "small faith" bound to ecclesiastical law, that is, bound to the past. The true church is invisible and, as Martin Luther asserts, is oriented to the believers' life with God through Christ and the Holy Spirit, a regenerating power. Faith in the invisible church is a protection of the freedom of the gospel and against the absolutizing of the authority of the visible church.

Sohm has been severely criticized for having no concept of church order, for example, by his admirer Ernst Troeltsch in *Die Soziallehren der christlichen Kirchen und Gruppen* (1912). On the other hand, Emil Brunner was considered Sohm's disciple (see Brunner's *Missverständnis der Kirche,* 1951); Karl Barth spoke scornfully of Brunner as "only a follower of Sohm." Sohm's work has exercised a significant influence on biblical studies and on studies in ecclesiology and in the critique of tradition. Max Weber appropriated, generalized, and secularized Sohm's concept of charisma, thus almost entirely transforming it.

SEE ALSO Leadership.

BIBLIOGRAPHY

Adams, James Luther. "Rudolf Sohm's Theology of Law and the Spirit." In *Religion and Culture: Essays in Honor of Paul Tillich,* edited by Walter Leibrecht, pp. 219–235. New York, 1959.

Haley, Peter. "Rudolf Sohm on Charisma." *Journal of Religion* 60 (1980): 185–197.

Sohm, Rudolf. *Outlines of Church History* (1888). Boston, 1958.

New Sources

Köhler, Wiebke. *Rezeption in der Kirche: begriffsgeschichtliche Studien bei Sohm, Afanas'ev, Dombois und Congar.* Göttingen, 1998.

JAMES LUTHER ADAMS (1987)
Revised Bibliography

SŌKA GAKKAI

SŌKA GAKKAI is a large religious organization that rapidly increased its strength after World War II. Official membership figures in December 2003 included approximately 8,210,000 households in Japan and 1,502,000 individuals in other countries. Makiguchi Tsunesaburo (1871–1944), the founder of Sōka Gakkai, was a primary school teacher who sought to establish an educational movement based on a new educational method. In 1928 Makiguchi became a follower of an exclusive subsect of the Nichiren sect of Buddhism, which promoted the merger of his educational and religious movements. In 1930 Makiguchi and Toda Jōsei (1900–1958), his chief disciple, published *Sōka Kyoikugaku Taikei* (The system of value-creating pedagogy). By 1941 the number of sympathizers had increased to approximately two thousand; at this time the activities of the Sōka Kyoiku Gakkai were inseparable from the activities of lay groups belonging to the Nichiren Shōshū sect. The movement was disbanded in 1943 by the government, but in 1945 it resumed activities under a new name: Sōka Gakkai. The decade of the 1930s was a period of consolidation; 1945 marked the resumption of previous activities; and the 1950s and 1960s were decades of explosive growth.

Makiguchi Tsunesaburo, while serving as a primary school teacher and principal, sought a type of education that would lead his pupils to voluntarily make efforts to develop their abilities and live a better life. After his efforts failed in a public school setting, he began to search for religious values upon which he could realize his ideal form of education. The deaths of family members led him to Nichiren Shōshū Buddhism, a lay-oriented and people-centered subsect of Nichiren Buddhism. Makiguchi embraced the idea that the nation would be saved by true Buddhism and that every person could be a bearer of belief and could guide others to salvation. Sōka Gakkai succeeded in developing a modern Nichiren Buddhism with the goal of enhancing the well-being of people in this world through their self-reforming efforts.

Before its explosive expansion period, its predecessor Sōka Kyoiku Gakkai suffered severe persecution. Makiguchi was jailed in 1943 for refusing to venerate the symbol of the Ise Shrine. He died in prison in 1944. Only twenty or so persons attended the service for the one-year memorial of his death in November 1945.

In 1951 Toda Jōsei reactivated the movement under the new name Sōka Gakkai and became its second president. The membership soon increased to five thousand. By 1956, Toda's long-cherished desire to obtain 750,000 households as followers had been achieved. Toda died in 1958 and was succeeded in 1960 by Ikeda Daisaku (b. 1928). Sōka Gakkai reported that its membership had reached three million households in 1962, and 7.5 million households in 1970. This period marked the peak of its growth.

The main religious practice of Sōka Gakkai followers is the chanting of the Daimoku, a repetition of "*Nam-Myōhō-renge-kyō*" ("the *Lotus Sūtra* is the important and superb sūtra"), chanted while facing a holy *maṇḍala* chart upon which this phrase is written. Called *Gohonzon* (the sacred object for worship), it is believed that Nichiren designated this chart as the sacred image of the *dharma.* Through this practice, followers can become united with the Buddha and live a happy life in which the eternal life of the Buddha is embodied. Sōka Gakkai changed the focus of traditional Buddhism from enlightenment and salvation in another world to a focus that is more oriented toward this world.

Sōka Gakkai emphasizes group activities and meetings ranging from small neighborhood gatherings to mass assemblies. During Sōka Gakkai's initial development period, small gatherings called roundtable meetings were held at followers' homes. At a meeting, members study the teachings of the leaders, report on their religiously interpreted daily practices, and mutually encourage one another's efforts. Reports that an individual has succeeded in his or her life thanks to Sōka Gakkai practices are praised by other members with a clapping of hands. Members discuss personal problems and comment on their experience of having participated in a joint program. A sense of community is nurtured in this way. Sōka Gakkai seeks to effect a human revolution by enhancing individual and societal well-being.

Having begun as an educational movement, Sōka Gakkai became a religious organization heavily engaged in society. Utilizing the democratic representative system of government in Japan, Sōka Gakkai members stood for election at all levels. The traditional doctrine of Nichiren Buddhism included a mission to save the state and the world through the wisdom of Buddhist Dharma. This tradition was lost during the Edo period (1603–1867), but it was revived in Japan's modernization process and was later united with nationalism.

The various movements for national salvation initiated by Nichiren Buddhists in modern Japan can be summarized as *Nichirenism.* Sōka Gakkai developed the mission of modern Nichirenism most effectively in postwar Japan. Sōka Gakkai leaders believed that one way to save Japan would be to increase Sōka Gakkai's influence gradually in the national parliament and local assemblies by winning many seats and by advocating policies based on such concepts as Buddhist democracy, Buddhist neutralism, the Third Civilization, and so on. By 1955, Sōka Gakkai had won several seats in local assemblies; three members were elected to the House of Councilors in 1956. Initially, the goal was to make Nichiren Shōshū the national religion. However, in 1964, the Kōmei Party (Kōmeitō) was established to separate the political activities from the religious activities of Sōka Gakkai. In 1970 it was disclosed that Sōka Gakkai had prevented the proposed publication of a book criticizing the movement. As a result the group was exposed to fierce public criticism. Sōka Gakkai was forced to make a public commitment to follow the rule of "separation of politics and religion" by structurally separating the Kōmei Party from the Sōka Gakkai religious organization and forbidding a person from holding office in both organizations.

As membership peaked in Japan, Sōka Gakkai made inroads into other countries and saw remarkable growth outside Japan. In the United States, an initial group was formed in 1960; it developed rapidly, reporting a membership of 200,000 in 1970. After the 1970s, as the Sōka Gakkai expanded in many regions of the world, it began to place its weight behind peace movements and United Nations activities. Sōka Gakkai was authorized as an NGO (nongovernmental organization) with advisory status to the Office of the United Nations High Commissioner for Refugees in 1981 and to the United Nations Information Office in 1982. The third president, Ikeda Daisaku (honorary president since 1979), impressed the public with his activities on the global level. He held numerous dialogues with prominent figures in various countries, and, utilizing various media, emerged as a charismatic spiritual leader in the contemporary world. Through this process, the nationalistic tendencies observed in Sōka Gakkai during the 1960s have gradually waned.

One of the more difficult problems for Sōka Gakkai after the latter half of the 1970s was its relations with the Nichiren Shōshū sect, its parent group. Nichiren Shōshū, as one of the traditional Buddhist sects in Japan, had a body of followers amounting to around fifty thousand. Sōka Gakkai, though an affiliated organization, grew in strength under the Nichiren Shōshū umbrella until its membership was more than one hundred times the membership of the parent organization. There had earlier been serious conflicts with Nichiren Shōshū over traditional doctrine and the authority of monks after Sōka Gakkai emphasized new styles of lay religiosity and the authority of the Sōka Gakkai president. Nichiren Shōshū and Sōka Gakkai finally split from each other in 1991.

Another difficult problem involved strong criticism from political rivals. The Liberal Democratic Party had kept its position as the ruling party in Japan for many years and sensed a potential threat from the Kōmei Party. Relations between the Kōmei Party and Sōka Gakkai provoked controversy over whether this was a violation of the principle of separation between politics and religion. Over time, however, the Liberal Democratic Party and the Kōmei Party strengthened ties, and in 1998 they formed a coalition government.

Sōka Gakkai has been characterized by its aggressive propaganda asserting that its teachings alone are correct and criticizing other religions and other Buddhist sects. The *Shakubuku Kyoten* (Manual for forcible persuasion), first published in 1951, clearly demonstrated Sōka Gakkai's exclusiveness, and few religious organizations have had a long-term friendly relationship with Sōka Gakkai. Since the 1980s, however, when Ikeda Daisaku began to place value on dialogue with prominent leaders of the world, more organizations have shown an interest in establishing friendly relations with Sōka Gakkai. The founder, Makiguchi Tsunesaburo, had valued people's sense of voluntarism and self-initiative, and Sōka Gakkai promoted democracy as one of its primary values after the 1960s, directing its policy toward strengthening international cooperative activities. As such, the organization has strengthened its capacity to adapt to a pluralistic democracy.

Sōka Gakkai is representative of new religious organizations that developed rapidly from the 1920s to the 1960s. In particular, the history of religions in the 1950s and 1960s in Japan cannot be told without referring to Sōka Gakkai. Many factors contributed to this new religious organization's rapid growth. Most important was perhaps the creation of a Buddhist belief system with a modern code of behavior in a time when traditional Buddhist organizations and new religious groups were competing with one another. The Sōka Gakkai thought system encouraged people to act on their own initiative, to participate in community activities, and to pursue happiness in this world.

SEE ALSO New Religious Movements, article on New Religious Movements in Japan; Nichiren; Nichirenshū; Nikkō.

BIBLIOGRAPHY

Dawson, Lorne L. "The Cultural Significance of New Religious Movements: The Case of Soka Gakkai." *Sociology of Religion* 62, no. 3 (2001): 337–364.

Hammond, Phillip, and David Machacek. *Soka Gakkai in America: Accommodation and Conversion.* Oxford, 1999.

Metraux, Daniel. *The History and Theology of Soka Gakkai: A Japanese New Religion.* Lewiston, N.Y., 1988.

Shimazono Susumu. "The Expansion of Japan's New Religions into Foreign Cultures." *Japanese Journal of Religious Studies* 18, nos. 2–3 (1991): 105–132.

Shimazono Susumu. "Sōka Gakkai and the Modern Reformation of Buddhism." In *Buddhist Spirituality: Later China, Korea, Japan and the Modern World,* edited by Takeuchi Yosinori, pp. 435–454. New York, 1999.

White, James. *The Sōka Gakkai and Mass Society.* Stanford, Calif., 1970.

Williams, George M. *Freedom and Influence: The Role of Religion in American Society (An NSA Perspective).* Santa Monica, Calif., 1985.

Wilson, Brian, and Karel Dobbelaere. *A Time to Chant: The Sōka Gakkai Buddhists in Britain.* Oxford, 1994.

SHIMAZONO SUSUMU (2005)

SŎ KYŎNGDŎK (1489–1546), was a leading neo-Confucian philosopher of Yi-dynasty Korea (1392–1910). In Korea he is best known by his honorific name, Hwadam. During the Yi dynasty, neo-Confucianism supplanted Buddhism as Korea's main spiritual and intellectual tradition. Among the many neo-Confucian thinkers in Korea during this five-hundred-year period, three are honored above all others: Hwadam, Yi Hwang (T'oegye, 1501–1570), and Yi I (Yulgok, 1536–1584). These three philosophers are credited with bringing the Korean assimilation of the complex neo-confucian system of thought to complete maturity and with developing a characteristic Korean problematic.

Hwadam, the earliest of the three, is renowned as an original and seminal thinker. He came from a relatively poor gentry family and was largely self-educated. Although he was repeatedly offered posts in government, he never accepted, choosing instead to lead an impoverished life in the mountains or countryside, where he devoted himself entirely to study and teaching. There are many anecdotes concerning his inquisitiveness regarding natural phenomena, but his most serious work was devoted to fundamental metaphysical questions and to the complex system of the *Book of Changes* (Kor., *Yŏkgyŏng;* Chin., *Yi jing*).

Hwadam strongly proclaimed his independence of judgment and his originality; the small body of his writings that have come down to us, however, bear a marked resemblance to the monistic metaphysics of material force (Kor., *ki;* Chin., *qi)* developed by the early Chinese Neo-Confucian, Zhang Zai (1020–1077). Like Zhang, he taught that material force was the sole component of all existence. In its ultimate, formless, pure condition, material force is without beginning or end; this he referred to as the Supreme Vacuity (Kor., *t'ae ho;* Chin., *tai xu*). By a process of condensation the distinct forms of the beings of the phenomenal world emerge from the Supreme Vacuity, and to it their stuff returns at death. Thus he argued that in the strict sense there is no death, only transformation.

Korean neo-Confucianism is especially known for its exclusive adherence to the orthodox tradition of Chinese neo-Confucianism derived from the thought of Zhu Xi (1130–1200). Hwadam lived at the end of Korea's fluid appropriation period. However, his thought is bold and deviant in a tradition that soon after became both more judicious and more authoritarian. Most later scholars followed the apparent dualism of the Zhu Xi school, but, among them, one school of thought tended to emphasize the role of material force; this school traces its immediate ancestry to Yi I, and ultimately to Hwadam. A distinctive characteristic of Korean neo-Confucian thought is its thorough exploration of the implications and tensions in Zhu Xi's dualism of principle (Kor., *i;* Chin., *li)* and material force. Hwadam's philosophy expressed a pure polar position that permanently established one of the extreme parameters of Korean neo-Confucian thought. As such it became a constant reference point for later generations of thinkers.

SEE ALSO Confucianism in Korea.

BIBLIOGRAPHY

The first book-length treatment of Korean neo-Confucianism is *The Rise of Neo-Confucianism in Korea,* edited by Wm. Theodore de Bary and JaHyun Haboush (New York, 1985). It contains a range of articles on the major figures and facets of the Korean neo-Confucian tradition by leading scholars in the field. The best general history of Korea in English is Ki-baik Lee's *A New History of Korea,* translated by Edward W. Wagner and Edward J. Schultz (Cambridge, Mass., 1984).

MICHAEL C. KALTON (1987)

SOL INVICTUS. Worship of the sun god, Sol, was known in republican Rome, but it was of minor importance. In imperial Rome, however, in the third century CE (the last century of pagan Rome), the cult of the sun god became a major and, at times, dominant force in Roman religion. The cult of the Syrian sun god from Emesa, installed at Rome under the emperor Elagabalus (218–222), was short-lived, but in 274 the emperor Aurelian began a vigorous campaign of propaganda celebrating the sun god as the exclusive protector of Rome's imperial might. Under the epithets *oriens* ("the rising one"), *invictus* ("the invincible one"), and *comes Augusti* ("comrade of Augustus"), Sol was hailed as "the rising sun who dispels the forces of evil," as "invincible conqueror of Rome's enemies," and as the "companion and guardian deity of the emperor."

Numismatic iconography, the primary source for this propaganda campaign, portrayed Sol wearing the radiate crown and holding the globe, symbol of world rule, in his hand, while the vanquished enemy cowered at his feet. This campaign was continued with particular force by the emperors Probus (276–282) and Constantine (306–337). As late as 324, coins of Constantine celebrated Sol as the grantor of imperial power to the emperor. Only thereafter, in the last thirteen years of Constantine's reign, did references to Sol and to all other pagan divinities disappear from the coins.

A variety of influences contributed to the importance of Sol Invictus, the Invincible Sun, in imperial ideology of the third century CE. It was an age of religious syncretism and growing monotheism, when philosophers and common people alike increasingly viewed all divinities as emanations of one supreme divine force. Sol was equated with Mithra, and as Sol Invictus Mithra was regarded as the most powerful and most immediate divine mediator between humans and the invisible majesty of the supreme god. Thus Sol Invictus was the natural associate of the emperor, who ruled the earth as the vicegerent of the supreme god. The symbolism of the Pantheon built by the emperor Hadrian (117–138) had already intimately linked the emperor and Sol as the visible manifestations of the beneficent and omnipotent supreme god. The cult title *Invictus* was a natural outgrowth of this relationship. First attested for Sol in 158 CE, it was almost certainly borrowed by the god from the emperor's own panoply of titles.

The pervasive influence of imperial propaganda, together with the popularity of Mithraism in the third century, assured Sol Invictus an influence upon other divine formulations, Christian as well as pagan. A vault mosaic of the third century in the tomb of the Julii under Saint Peter's portrays Christ as Sol, rising in his chariot. The words of the Christmas Mass in the *Missale Gothicum* hail Christ as Sol Iustitiae ("sun of justice"), while the traditional date of Christmas, first attested in the fourth century, is hardly unrelated to the fact that December 25 was celebrated as the birthday of Sol Invictus Mithra.

BIBLIOGRAPHY

Gaston H. Halsberghe's *Cult of Sol Invictus* (Leiden, 1972), edited by Maarten J. Vermaseren as volume 23 of "Études préliminaires aux religions orientales dans l'empire romain," is an uncritical collection of evidence and is to be used with caution. See my review in *Byzantine Studies* 2 (1975): 81–82. The significance of the cult of Sol Invictus in imperial ideology is treated with great insight by Ernst H. Kantorowicz in his article "Oriens Augusti: Lever du Roi," *Dumbarton Oaks Papers* 17 (1963): 117–177. For a more recent discussion, see my *Princeps a Diis Electus: The Divine Election of the Emperor as a Political Concept at Rome* (Rome, 1977), pp. 238–243, 281–315, and my article "The Theology of Victory at Rome," in *Aufstieg und Niedergang der römischen Welt,* vol. 2.17.2 (Berlin and New York, 1981), pp. 804–825.

New Sources

Chirassi Colombo, Ileana. "Sol invictus o Mithra. (Per una rilettura in chiave ideologica della teologia solare del mitraismo nell'ambito del politeismo romano)." In *Mysteria Mithrae. Atti del Seminario Internazionale su La specificità storico-religiosa dei misteri di Mithra, con particolare riferimento alle fonti documentarie di Roma e Ostia, Roma e Ostia, 28–31 marzo 1978,* ed. by Ugo Bianchi, pp. 649–672. Leiden, 1979.

Clauss, Manfred. "Sol invictus Mithras." *Athenaeum* 58 (1990): 423–450.

Fauth, Wolfgang. *Helios Megistos: Zur synkretistischen Theologie der Spätantike.* Leiden, 1995.

Halsberghe, Gaston H. "Le culte de Deus Sol Invictus à Rome au III siècle après J.C." In *Aufstieg und Niedergang der Römischen Welt* 2.17.4, pp. 2181–2201. Berlin and New York, 1984.

MacDowall, David W. "Sol invictus and Mithra. Some Evidence from the Mint of Rome." In *Mysteria Mithrae. Atti del Seminario Internazionale su La specificità storico-religiosa dei misteri di Mithra, con particolare riferimento alle fonti documentarie di Roma e Ostia, Roma e Ostia, 28–31 marzo 1978,* edited by Ugo Bianchi, pp. 557–569. Leiden, 1979.

Turcan, Robert. *Héliogabale et la sacre du soleil.* Paris, 1985.

Wallraff, Martin. *Christus verus sol. Sonnenverehrung und Christentum in der Spätantike.* Münster, 2001.

J. RUFUS FEARS (1987)
Revised Bibliography

SÖLLE, DOROTHEE. Dorothee Nipperdey Sölle (1929–2003) was born in Cologne, Germany, to a bourgeois family whose religious attitudes were formed by liberal Protestantism. She was a Lutheran and remained a member of the Lutheran Church throughout her life. In her family, culture was defined by familiarity with German philosophers and poets such as Immanuel Kant and Johann Wolfgang von Goethe. Until the last year of World War II, when food became scarce, Dorothee was preserved from the ugliness of the war. As an idealistic adolescent her deep sense of patriotism was overwhelmed by Germany's defeat. Following the war, she began to read the existentialists, especially Martin Heidegger and Jean Paul Sartre and entered into a period of nihilism. At university she studied post-Enlightenment philosophy. The works of Blaise Pascal, Søren Kierkegaard, and Simone Weil led her to the study of theology, which became the basis of her life's work. In 1954 she married Dietrich Sölle. That marriage produced two children, a son and a daughter. After ten years, the marriage ended in divorce. In 1969 she married a former Benedictine priest, Fulbert Steffensky. That marriage produced a daughter and lasted until her death in 2003.

Sölle states that Kierkegaard seduced her into religion, but that she found her entrance into faith through studying with Rudolf Bultmann and Friedrich Gogarten. Intellectually, she was unable to leave behind the tenets of the Enlightenment to embrace faith, and through these two teachers she discovered this was not required. From this time onward she began her personal theological development. Characteristic of her theology was the conviction that the reading and writing of theology should make a practical difference not only in an individual's life, but also in the life of the nation, the hemisphere, and the planet. Symbolic of this belief was the formation of an ecumenical group in Cologne (1968–1972) named Political Evensong. Built upon the conviction that every robust theology has political implications, each meeting was marked by information, meditation, and action. The marriage of theology and political activism that was to become a hallmark of Sölle's theology was ill-received by both Catholics and more conventional Protestants.

Initially, Sölle's theology was deeply Christocentric. She regarded Christ as God's clearest voice. Although she never left behind this personal conviction, her later theology became more theocentric. In this way, she felt she was better able to embrace and include in her theology all the peoples of the earth. In the mid-1970s, Sölle began the move from designating her theology as *political* to designating it as *liberation theology*. She did this for several reasons, the primary one being her conviction that political theology had ambiguous beginnings in the works of some German ideologues. Her espousal of liberation theology, however, grew from her firm belief that its methodology was accurate. Theological reflection upon praxis became the basic characteristic of all of her subsequent writing.

As Sölle continued her practice of liberation theology, she concerned herself with various forms of praxis that reinforced the subjugation of women, that saw value in war, and that led to the ecological destruction of the planet. Subsequently, her reflection upon these practices in the light of the Gospel led her to become a feminist, a pacifist, and an ecological theologian. These interests led to her involvement in the conciliar process, the goal of which was to work for reconciliation in the areas of justice, peace, and the integrity of creation.

Sölle's allegiance to the church did not blind her to its moral inadequacies nor to the sometime ineptness of its doctrinal proclamations. In a conversation with the Jesuit Daniel Berrigan, she concurred with his image of the church as an umbrella. It provided protection against the elements, sometimes better protection than at other times. She argued that the proper stance toward the church was one of affirmation and critique. In attempting to live a radical Christianity and in the endeavor to love God above all things, it was at times necessary, she contended, to distance oneself from the church and to break with certain traditional teachings, at least as they were commonly presented. Still, the church played an important role in her development: it passed on the tradition of Jesus and his "political" invitation to establish the kingdom. Sölle considered it a mistake of contemporaries who proposed that without tradition people are freer.

Sölle's entire life was marked by teaching and writing. She was a prolific writer. Her first book, *Stellvertretung: ein Kapitel Theologie nach dem 'Tode Gotles' (Christ the Representative)*, was published in 1965. Her final book, *Gegenwind (Against the Wind: Memoir of a Radical Christian)* was published in 1999. In between, she wrote over twenty books, some of which included poetry, that addressed her liberation concerns. Among the most significant is *Gott Denken (1990; Thinking about God)*. In this book, Sölle reveals her command of classical theology. She explains how theology is done within a certain paradigm or set of presuppositions and subsequently explicates the orthodox, liberal, and liberation theological paradigms. Then, she demonstrates how each of the basic tenets of Christian faith is understood within each paradigm. Finally, she concludes with two chapters on her approach to an understanding of God. In her mind, the question "Do you believe in God?" was superficial and close to meaningless. Instead, she insisted, the question is "Do you live out God?" According to her, the answer could only be derived from one's involvement in the works of justice demanded by the kingdom of God.

Sölle taught religion and theology at longer or shorter intervals throughout her life, beginning with a six-year period teaching at the Gymnasium for Girls in Cologne-Mulheim. Her longest engagement was as professor of systematic theology at Union Theological Seminary in New York (1975–1987).

Sölle died of a heart attack in 2003 in southern Germany at a conference at which she and her husband were keynote speakers.

BIBLIOGRAPHY

Sölle, Dorothee. *Christ the Representative: An Essay in Theology after the Death of God.* Translated by David Lewis. Philadelphia, 1967. Sölle's first published work describes Christ as representing humankind before God, as well as representing God among humankind. It is a response to the "God is dead" theology prominent in that decade.

Sölle, Dorothee. *Thinking about God: An Introduction to Theology.* Translated by John Bowden. Philadelphia and London, 1990. This work describes three theological paradigms: orthodox, liberal, and liberation. Within that context, Sölle demonstrates how the basic tenets of Christianity are understood within each paradigm. She concludes the books with her understanding of the meaning of God.

Sölle, Dorothee. *Against the Wind: Memoir of a Radical Christian.* Translated by Barbara Rumscheidt and Martin Rumscheidt. Minneapolis, 1999. This memoir is an account of Sölle's personal and theological journey. In it, she notes the people and events that most influenced her development. It concludes with a poignant message to her children.

NANCY C. RING (2005)

SOLOMON, or, in Hebrew, Shelomoh, was the son of David and third king of Israel and Judah (c. 960–920 BCE). During Solomon's reign the united kingdom reached its greatest extent and height of prosperity. The account of this reign, in *1 Kings* 1–11, is in its present form a collage of various historical and literary sources. Solomon's accession to the throne (*1 Kgs.* 1–2), portrayed as the result of palace intrigue and a struggle for power between two sons of David and their supporters, is part of the so-called court history of David. The hand of the Deuteronomistic historian, the author of the larger history of the monarchy in *Kings,* may be seen in his treatment of the theophany in *1 Kings* 3:1–15 and its parallel in 9:1–9, in the account of the building of the Temple and its dedication (chapters 5–8), and in Solomon's failures and God's rejection of his rule over the northern state of Israel (*1 Kgs.* 11). This historian did make use of an earlier source, the "book of the deeds of Solomon" (*1 Kgs.* 11:41), which probably contained information on building activities and other royal undertakings gleaned from royal inscriptions. The basic history by the Deuteronomist was also embellished by later additions having to do with the greatness of Solomon's reign. The treatment of Solomon in *2 Chronicles* 1–9 depends upon *Kings,* with some omissions and additions. The sources cited by the Chronicler, however, namely books by the prophets Nathan, Ahijah, and Iddo, are most likely fictitious.

Solomon's greatest achievement, according to the historian of *Kings,* was his building of the Temple and palace in Jerusalem (*1 Kgs.* 5–8). Originally the Temple was built as a royal sanctuary, one of many temples throughout the realm, but through the centralization reform of King Josiah (*2 Kgs.* 22–23) it became the only legitimate cult place in the kingdom, and it is from this perspective that the Temple's significance is treated in *Kings.* Solomon is also credited with the construction of major fortifications at Hazor, Megiddo, and Gezer for the consolidation of his realm, and this building activity seems to be confirmed by archaeology. The Bible also suggests that the state prospered greatly from various commercial ventures, a fact attested by a marked rise in the level of the material culture of the land as evidenced by archaeological finds. Nevertheless, one must be cautious in accepting all that is attributed to Solomon's reign, for it is unlikely that he had political control over the whole region from the Euphrates to the border of Egypt or that his court and military force were as large as *1 Kings* 5:1–8 (EV 4:21–28) states.

The biblical tradition celebrates Solomon's wisdom. The historian of *Kings* tells the story (*1 Kgs.* 3) of how Solomon experienced a dream theophany at Gibeon in which God granted him his request for wisdom in order to govern his people aright and, along with wisdom, gave him long life and prosperity. This gift of wisdom is then illustrated by a folktale in which Solomon makes a successful judgment between two mothers who claim the same infant. This theme of Solomon's wisdom is greatly expanded by later additions, including the story of the queen of Sheba's visit and other remarks about Solomon's great wisdom and wealth (*1 Kgs.* 10).

The Deuteronomist regards the decline of Solomon's realm and the ultimate division of the kingdom as the result of Solomon's marriages to many foreign wives. While these may have been diplomatic marriages made as a matter of state, the historian viewed them as encouraging the importation of foreign deities into the kingdom, thereby compromising the exclusive worship of Yahveh. A more immediate cause of political unrest and division of the kingdom is attributed to Solomon's heavy taxation of the Israelites, from which no relief was given by his successor, Rehoboam, a condition that led to Israel's revolt (*1 Kgs.* 12). The Chronicler refrains from any criticism of Solomon's reign.

On the basis of the statement about Solomon's composition of many proverbs and songs (*1 Kgs.* 5:12 [EV 4:32]), later editors of the Bible attributed to Solomon much of the *Book of Proverbs* as well as the *Song of Songs.* It also led to the composition of works in Solomon's name. The author of *Ecclesiastes* calls himself "the son of David," thereby suggesting his identity with Solomon. Two later Jewish works using Solomon's name are the *Wisdom of Solomon,* written in Greek in Alexandria, and the *Psalms of Solomon,* probably written in Hebrew in Roman Palestine. An early Christian work ascribed to Solomon is the *Testament of Solomon.*

Both the New Testament and the Qur'ān (*sūrah* 21:78–81) make reference to Solomon's wisdom, but it is especially in Jewish *aggadah* (Ginzberg, 1956) that his wisdom and career receive the fullest amplification. Solomon is made an expert in many fields of science as well as in occult and hidden wisdom. Many additional stories are told in the *aggadah* to illustrate Solomon's ability to judge wisely. Special attention is given to the building of the Temple and to Solomon's throne, which later becomes a prize of war transmitted from one invading kingdom to another down to Roman times. The aggadic tradition also tells about a period of humiliation that Solomon endured for his sins against the Law. During this time he was an outcast, and an impostor reigned in his stead until he eventually regained the throne.

The Solomonic tradition embraces the whole wisdom tradition, both in its worldly aspect and in its piety, and embodies all the fantasies about the past glory of the united kingdom of Israel and Judah at the height of its power.

SEE ALSO Biblical Temple.

BIBLIOGRAPHY

Treatments of the history of Solomon's reign can be found in John Bright's *A History of Israel,* 3d ed. (Philadelphia, 1981), and in the contribution by J. Alberto Soggin, "The Davidic-Solomonic Kingdom," to *Israelite and Judean History,* edited by John H. Hayes and J. Maxwell Miller (Philadelphia, 1977). A discussion of the literary tradition can be found in Burke O. Long's *1 Kings with an Introduction to Old Testament Historical Literature* (Grand Rapids, Mich., 1984). This also contains an extensive bibliography. For the aggadic traditions, see Louis Ginzberg's *The Legends of the Bible* (New York, 1956), pp. 553–578.

New Sources

Cazeaux, Jacques. *Saül, David, Salomon: la royauté et le destin d'Israël.* Paris, 2003.

Knoppers, Gary N. *Two Nations under God: The Deuteronomistic History of Solomon and the Dual Monarchies.* Atlanta, 1993.

Torijano, Pablo A. *Solomon, the Esoteric King: From King to Magus, Development of a Tradition.* Leiden and Boston, 2002.

JOHN VAN SETERS (1987)
Revised Bibliography

SOLOMON ISLANDS RELIGIONS.

Peoples of the Solomon Islands have been somewhat arbitrarily divided by convention into "Melanesian" (Guadalcanal, Malaita, Isabel, San Cristobal or Makira, Gela, New Georgia, Choiseul, Shortlands, Santa Cruz) and "Polynesian" (Rennell, Bellona, Tikopia, Anuta, Sikaiana, Ontong Java). The Melanesians of Bougainville and Buka, in the northern Solomons chain, are often included, although they are separated by a political border and by gulfs of language (because Papuan languages, as opposed to Oceanic- Austronesian languages, are mainly spoken in the northern Solomons). Solomons religions may be mapped for convenience onto "Melanesian" and "Polynesian" features, despite modern linguistic and ethnographic evidence showing close relationships between the Oceanic languages and cultures of the Solomons and those of eastern Melanesia, Micronesia, and Polynesia.

The so-called Polynesian Outliers in the Solomons have religions of the western Polynesian type, of which Raymond Firth, Richard E. Feinberg, Ian Hogbin, and Torben Monberg have given good descriptions. Firth's detailed studies of Tikopia ritual and belief provide some of the best evidence on traditional Polynesian religion.

The Melanesian religions of the Solomons were preeminently concerned with mediating relations with ancestral ghosts and nonhuman spirit beings, soliciting and manipulating their support (*mana*) and deploying powers of magic for success in fighting, feasting, gardening, fishing, curing, and other pursuits. Through human sacrifice, sacrifice of pigs and other offerings, elaborate rituals, and prayer, the living sought the support and potentiation without which human efforts alone could not succeed.

For most parts of the Solomons there is limited evidence on the pre-Christian past: Christianity took early hold on Gela, Isabel, the New Georgia group, Choiseul, the Shortlands, and most areas of Guadalcanal and San Cristobal. Douglas L. Oliver's important prewar study (published in 1955) of the Siuai of Bougainville gives good evidence on the religion of a Papuan-speaking people, and A. M. Hocart's early texts from Simbo (Eddystone) as well as C. G. Wheeler (Mono-Alu, northwest Salomon) are useful in reconstructing a western Solomons religious system. Some modern ethnographers of Malaita (among others, Roger Keesing, Pierre Maranda and Elli Köngäs Maranda, Ben Burt, Sandra Revolon, and Christine Jourdan) have worked in areas where the ancestral religions are still practiced. The more recent studies shed new light on old problems of the Solomon Islands religion.

GHOSTS, GODS, AND SPIRITS. The pioneer student of Melanesian religions, R. H. Codrington, observed that Solomon Islanders and New Hebrideans worshiped two broad categories of invisible beings: ancestral ghosts and spirits that were never human. Whereas New Hebrides (Vanuatu) religions focused on spirits, according to Codrington, those of the Solomons focused on ghosts.

If we look at the western and northern Solomons as well as the southeastern islands that Codrington knew best, this generalization fades. In the New Georgia group and Choiseul, ancient beings, which Hocart (1922) and Harold Scheffler (1965) refer to as "gods," were accorded a central place. These gods differed in their powers, nature, and mythic origins; they were often ranked hierarchically as more or less powerful, as intervening in different ways and degrees in human affairs, and as having introduced different customs and skills. The *bangara* of Choiseul and the *tamasa* of Simbo are relatively well documented. From Papuan-speaking Bougainville, we have Oliver's account of the Siuai *kupuna* spirits, some of which affected the lives of all, while others affected only local descent groups.

In all parts of the Solomons, including the areas where higher spirit beings were believed to exercise the greatest powers, ancestral ghosts were thought to be ever-present participants in daily life, propitiated by, watching over, and occasionally chastising their living kin. The *manuru* ghosts of Choiseul and the *tomate* of Simbo are counterparts of the *tindalo* of Gela and the *akalo* of Malaita.

Other classes of spirits, of forest and sea and sky, were recognized by Solomon Islanders. These spirits were of nonhuman origin. Some were malevolent, others, especially female spirits, were benevolent, and others merely capricious. Some were involved in human life; others were distant. Snakes, birds, sharks, and other animals were often seen as messengers from or manifestations of these spirits. Representations in folk art and in drawings collected by early ethnologists suggest that the spirits were often conceived as having (invisible) forms that combined animal and human features. Food taboos prevented the members of a clan from eating the "totemic" plants or animals in which they grounded their identities

SHADES, SOULS, AND ABODES OF THE DEAD. Most Melanesians of the Solomons recognized two or more nonphysical components of a human being. Commonly a distinction was made between "breath" and "shadow" (or "reflection") as component souls. Souls of the dead were generally believed to go to an afterlife, a land of the dead where souls lived in villages and gardened and fished in an existence parallel to corporeal life. These abodes of the dead were usually associated with particular islands. Marapa in Marau Sound, Guadalcanal, and Ramos Island, between Malaita and Isabel, were commonly thought by peoples in surrounding areas to be abodes of the dead. But whereas one soul component went off to the village of the dead, an ancestral shade, all-seeing though usually invisible, remained around the living.

A number of Malaitan myths have to do with the resurrection of dead culture heroes, others belong to the Orpheus myth category (a culture hero accessing the land of the dead to bring his wife back to life and losing her irremediably through his own fault upon their return home), and several are variants of a "Myth of the Original Sin" (see below), widespread in the south Pacific, staging a snake, a woman, and a man, in which an end is put to the "Golden Age" by the failure of the man to understand the true—chtonian—nature of his wife.

Dream experiences were and still are taken as the wanderings of one's shade among the shades of the dead and of the living: reports by those who recovered from coma were taken as experiential evidence on the fate of the dead (in Oceanic languages, the term *mate* commonly refers to states of unconsciousness, coma, and death). Communication with the dead, in the form of dreams, divination, omens, and prayer, infused daily life with religious significance.

Yet although many Solomonese were deeply religious in the sense that they saw everywhere the signs of ghosts, deities, and spirits, their concerns were pragmatic rather than theological, focused on this world rather than on the invisible world lying behind it. Thus, most peoples of the Solomons had relatively undeveloped ideas, other than those expressed in myths of origin or of ancient times, about the nature of the spirit world and about how spirits intervened in human life. Ghosts, according to the Kwaio of Malaita, are "like the wind" in manifesting their effects in many places at once and in going beyond the constraints of time, space, and agency that bind the living. But how these spirits do whatever it is they do is beyond human ken and even beyond human interest. The living are concerned not with explaining unseen forces but with using them to practical ends: with interpreting and manipulating the will of spirit beings, propitiating them after the infringment of a taboo, enlisting their support, and deploying their magical powers (*mana*). Whether the ghosts or spirits have done their part can be discovered by divination, read in omens, or known retrospectively in the outcomes of human effort: success or failure in fighting, feasting, and other enterprises.

***MANA* AND TABOO.** Retrospective pragmatism and relative unconcern with theological explanation and all-embracing cosmology are manifest in the ancient Oceanic concept of *mana*. Interpretations from Codrington's time onward have viewed *mana* as an invisible medium of supernaturally conferred power, manifest in sacred objects. Chiefs or warriors "had" *mana* by virtue of supernatural support; others gained it temporarily through sacrifice or magic. Thus C. E. Fox in his *The Threshold of the Pacific* (1924), writing of San Cristobal, likened *mana* (there *mena*) to a liquid in which weapons or sacred objects were immersed; E. S. Craighill Handy in his *Polynesian Religion* (1927) likened *mana* to electricity.

According to Roger Keesing (this encyclopedia, previous edition),

> contemporary ethnographic studies and reexamination of linguistic evidence suggest that *mana* as an invisible medium or substance or energy may be more a creation of European than of indigenous imagination. *Mana* in the religions of the Solomons referred to a process, retrospectively interpreted, and to a state or quality manifest in results, rather than to an invisible spiritual medium of power.

However, in north Malaita at least, many landscape features are considered to have *mana* (*mamana*) by their very nature: imposing rocks, some majestic trees that are honored by hanging shell-money spans on their branches, and the like. In Malaita, *mamana* also means "truth" as well as "power." In Ben Burt's words, "Kwara'ae translate *mamana* as 'true,' which is quite appropriate since it entails not only reality and veracity but also 'true' in the archaic English sense of effective and faithful. For Kwara'ae traditionalists, ghosts are 'true' in that they can and will actually do what is expected of them" (1993, p. 54).

Evidence that *mana* was conceived primarily as a process and quality, and not as a "substance," comes both from modern ethnographic accounts, especially in Keesing's studies of the Kwaio of Malaita, and from linguistic evidence. In the Malaita languages and in Roviana in the western Solomons, *mana,* when used as a noun, is marked with a nominalizing affix that shows that it is an abstract verbal noun: "*mana*-ness" or "*mana*-ization." In all the Solomons languages where cognates of *mana* occur, we find the word used as a verb (the ghosts—and female spirits or female "gods" as well—"*mana* for" or "*mana*-ize" the living) and as a verbal adjective (magic is *mana,* that is, potent or effective), in addition to its uses as a noun. Comparative evidence suggests that these uses of *mana* as a verb are ancient and basic in Oceanic-Austronesian languages. Although more evidence is needed, it at least seems clear that in the religions of the Solomons, ideas about *mana* were not expressed in systematic theological interpretations but were concerned with controlling and retrospectively interpreting the interventions of spirits or gods in human life. Ian Hogbin noted, of his research on *mana* (there *nanama*) on Guadalcanal, that "nobody knows how *nanama* works, and I gathered that the thought had never occurred to anyone before I made inquiries" (1936, pp. 241–274).

In contrast to Hogbin's view, it should be pointed out that many Malaitans other than those he wrote about do know how *mana* works and how to to acquire it. According to them *mana* validates a good life, prosperity, and the like, and one obtains it through proper social behavior and adequate ritual practices. Although it has been ignored by many if not most anthropologists who have worked in the Solomons—a notable exception being Ben Burt's documentation of women priests (1993, pp. 58, 138, 145, 271)—it is noteworthy that the traditional religion recognized beneficient female spirits, like the *'ai ni asi* or *'ai la matekwa,* the "woman" (or "goddess" as some Solomonese have it) "of the sea" can bestow *mana* on people. And the same obtains with the *geo* (brush turkey, megapod), a female deity worshipped in the Maliata hills, in Guadalcanal, and generally in the central province of the Solomons (Gabriel Maelaasi, from Funafou, Lau Lagoon, north Malaita, Personal Communication, April 2004). Furthermore, in connection with the power of women, it is significant that when possessed by a spirit, a woman may very effectively counter the decision of a chief and cancel all his plans.

On the other hand, *mana* is closely asssociated with what could be called its mirror image, *taboo* (or *abu*). Actually, someone infringing a taboo will not only lose whatever *mana* one has but one will also incur severe punishment unless offering a generally momentous neutralizing compensation to the spirits. In that way taboo functions as inverted or negative *mana,* depriving the person at fault of all dignity and "social truth." In the words of Burt, who sharpens up the converging interpretations of Keesing and of the Marandas, "For tabu is ultimately about the control of power [*mana*], a way of socializing the 'strength' of both spiritual and human beings and controlling it by the rules which should govern relationships in society" (1993. pp. 64–66).

An important source of taboo relates to the ontological power of women, frightening to men (Maranda and Köngäs Maranda, 1970; Burt 1993; Maranda 2001; see also www.oceanie.org, which has multimedia data on *mana,* taboo, sacrifices, ancestor worship, the position of men and women, and other topics). As a matter of fact, the life-giving power of women fragilizes the cosmological status of men in the Solomons as well as in many other societies of the South Pacific. Consequently, men have invented elaborate mythical and ritual scripts to try to override their culturally characterized inferiority as regards procreation. Among such stratagems figures the role of high priests who, on behalf of all the men of their clans, act as "mothers," giving funeral birth to the dead—a mimicry of biological reproduction.

The ontological power of women—their *mana*—stems from their association with Mother Earth, embodied in the snake (worshiped by women priests; Burt, 1993, p. 145) of which woman is a daughter. And since, in Oceania, everything connected with the earth (stability, fecundity, and the like) is female and "low," while "high" (instability, barrenness, and the like) is male, and since vaginal blood flows from the lower part of the female torso, that fluid becomes lethal if it gets in contact with men. Hence the stringent taboo that surrounds the areas where women menstruate and give birth (Maranda and Köngäs Maranda, 1970; Keesing, 1982; Burt, 1993; Maranda, 2001). Thus, whereas men strive to acquire *mana* from the spirits and not to lose it, women are *naturally* endowed with a similar but extremely dangerous power, that of *faasua,* of "defiling."

Social Structure and Religion. In tribal societies, we can discern close structural relationships between sociopolitical organization and the nature, scope, and powers of supernatural beings. For Malaita, Keesing's (1982) account of the religion of the Kwaio and the Marandas' (1970, 2001) publications on the Lau illustrate the close fit between hierarchies of ancestors, the structure of descent groups, and rituals focused on ancestral shrines. For the western Solomons, Scheffler (1965) analyzes a similar close relationship between the propitiation of gods and spirits by descent-group congregations and the social structure of the living.

Peoples of the mountainous interiors (like the Kwaio) generally had small, autonomous descent groups and relatively egalitarian social systems. Correspondingly, ritual was localized in small congregations, and cosmologies and myths were relatively undeveloped. Peoples with maritime orientations tended to have more hierarchical sociopolitical systems (with hereditary chiefs in some areas), more centralized and elaborate ritual systems, and more fully elaborated cosmological beliefs and myths. Thus, the Lau of the northern Malaita lagoon, with an elaborate cosmology positing a series of heavens and an extensive body of myths, contrast somewhat with the Baegu of the nearby mountains, despite the cultural heritage they clearly share.

In none of these Melanesian societies of the Solomons were there full-time ritual specialists. The priests referred to in the literature served as ritual officiants on behalf of their groups. Succession to such duties was in some places hereditary; but in everyday respects, these officiants lived and worked as other men did.

Cults and Indigenous Churches in the Colonial Period. Cargo cults of classic Melanesian type apparently emerged in the Solomons only in parts of Bougainville and Buka, in the sphere of German and Australian influence. Thus, the Lontis movement of southern Bougainville, in 1913–1914, and cargo movements in the 1930s show continuity through to the anticolonialist cultism of the Hahalis Welfare Society of Buka in the 1960s. More politically oriented movements with millenarian overtones (Keesing, 1982) have continued into the 1980s.

On Small Malaita an early syncretic religious cult was reported in 1896, and there is some evidence of a prophetic cult in north-central Malaita somewhat earlier. In the 1920s syncretic movements that combined elements of traditional and Christian theology and ritual were reported from the same area; sporadic cult activity with anticolonial overtones continued in the 1930s. European reports of millenarian fantasy notwithstanding, the Maasina Rule movement, which took shape in the aftermath of the Guadalcanal campaign of World War II, was solidly political—a challenge to colonial rule—although it had religious trappings.

Since the 1960s two strong indigenous movements have commanded widespread allegiance. On New Georgia a leader named Silas Eto, called the Holy Mama, created an indigenous religious movement combining elements of Methodism and folk belief and ritual. The movement remained strong into the 1980s. On Guadalcanal, the Moro movement has institutionalized a synthesis of traditional custom, Christianity, and capitalism that has adapted successfully to political and economic changes. The Remnant Church has experienced fluctuation since the 1970s in Malaita.

Figures compiled from different sources from 1997 to 1999 (see www.adherents.com) provide an approximate distribution of Solomon Islanders according to religion: Christians would number some 93 percent; pagans (traditional) some 4 to 6 percent; individuals with no religion, some 3 percent. The film *The Lau of Malaita* (Granada Television, "Disappearing World" series, 1987) presents a lively account of the endeavors by pagans to keep their traditions and culture alive despite the unquestionable impact of Christianity.

The Christians are mostly only nominally so, which Terry Brown, the Anglican bishop of Malaita recently deplored in his Bishop's Address to the Diocese of Malaita Diocesan Council in Auki (the capital of Malaita Province) on May 22, 2003:

> Another emerging problem in ministry in the Diocese seems to be an increase in various questionable and uncritical syncretistical practices. Examples include the Melanesian Brothers' blessing of piles of stones to protect villages from evil influences, persons' revealing through dreams and visions those causing sickness through sorcery, cargo-cult-like movements involving stones and walking sticks, neo-Israelite movements of discovering the ancient sites of the Lost Tribe of Israel in the Malaita bush, inappropriate *aenimoni* payments to control God's grace, "sucking out" of evil ancestral blood, special holy water combinations including special ingredients such as kerosene—the list goes on. Unfortunately, some clergy and Melanesian Brothers seem to be involved in a lot of these activities. Generally I am quite open to the integration of Christianity and Melanesian culture (and syncretism generally) but some of these practices seem to go well over the line. They are dividing communities and causing people to relapse into magic and superstition. Unfortunately, many people seem to need these magical rites and visions and are unable to trust simply in God's loving grace.

See Also Cargo Cults; Mana; Tikopia Religion.

BIBLIOGRAPHY

There are six detailed accounts of religions in the Solomons: besides Raymond Firth's masterful studies of Tikopia culture and religion, Charles E. Fox, *The Threshold of the Pacific: An Account of the Social Organization, Magic and Religion of the People of San Cristoval in the Solomon Islands* (London, 1924), Richard E. Feinberg's *Anuta: Social Structure of a Polynesian Island* (Laie, Hawai'i, 1981), Torben Monberg's *The Concepts of Supernaturals*, part 1 of *The Religion of Bellona Island* (Copenhagen, 1966), Roger Keesing's *Kwaio Religion: The Living and the Dead in a Solomon Island Society* (New York, 1982), Ben Burt's comprehensive survey of both traditional and Christianized Kwara'ae (Malaita), *Tradition and Christianity: The Colonial Transformation of a Solomon Island Society* (Harwood Academic Publishers, 1993), and Denis Monnerie, *Nitu. Les Vivants, les morts et le cosmos selon la société de Mono-Alu (Iles Salomon)* (Leyde, 1996), a monograph on the northwest Solomons based on G. C Wheeler's *Mono-Alu Folklore* (London, 1926) and on an unfinished and unpublished manuscript by the latter.

Briefer modern accounts of the Solomon islands religions are given in Ian Hogbin's *Experiments in Civilization* (London, 1939); *Guadalcanal Society: The Kaoka Speakers* (New York, 1964); and "Mana," *Oceania* 6 (1936): 241–274; Douglas L. Oliver's *Solomon Islands Society* (Cambridge, Mass., 1955); Harold Scheffler's *Choiseul Island Social Structure* (Berkeley, 1965); Pierre Maranda and Elli Köngäs Maranda, "Le Crâne et l'utérus: Deux Théorèmes nord-malaïtains," in *Echanges et communications*, vol. 2, edited by J. Pouillon and Pierre Maranda. pp. 829–861 (Paris and The Hague, 1970); Matthew Cooper's "Langalanga Religion," *Oceania* 43 (1972): 113–122; Harold M. Ross's *Baegu: Social and Ecological Organization in Malaita, Solomon Islands* (Urbana, Ill., 1973); Pierre Maranda, "Mapping Historical Transformation Through the Canonical Formula: The Pagan vs. Christian Ontological Status of Women in Malaita, Solomon Islands," in *The Double Twist: From Ethnography to Morphodynamics*, edited by P. Maranda, pp. 97–120 (Toronto, 2001) and his "Mythe, métaphore, métamorphose et marchés: l'igname chez les Lau de Malaita, îles Salomon," *Journal de la Société des Océanistes* 114–115 (2002): 91–114. Illustrative of earlier work is A. M. Hocart's "The Cult of the Dead in Eddystone of the Solomons," *Journal of the Royal Anthropological Institute of Great Britain and Ireland* 52 (1922): 71–112.

Solomon Islands theologian Esau Tuza gives an account of his ancestral religion in "Spirits and Powers in Melanesia," in *Powers, Plumes and Piglets: Phenomena of Melanesian Religion*, edited by N. Habel (Bedford, Australia, 1979). A reinterpretation of *mana* (see E. S. Craighill Handy *Polynesian Religion* (Honolulu, Bernice P. Bishop Museum Bulletin 34, 1927) is given in Keesing's "Rethinking Mana," *Journal of Anthropological Research* 40 (Spring 1984): 137–156. Anticolonialist cultism is treated in the following of his articles: "Politico-Religious Movements and Anticolonialism on Malaita: Maasina Rule in Historical Perspective," published in two parts in *Oceania* 48 (1978): 241–261 and 49 (1978): 46–73; and "Kastom and Anticolonialism on Malaita: Culture as a Political Symbol," *Mankind* 13 (1982): 357–373.

Roger M. Keesing (1987)
Pierre Maranda (2005)

SOLOVEITCHIK, JOSEPH BAER. Joseph Soloveitchik (1903–1993) was the most widely influential Orthodox Jewish theologian of the twentieth century and one of Orthodox Judaism's key American religious leaders. Alone among the handful of major Jewish theologians of that period, Orthodox or otherwise, he combined extraordinary erudition in the vast corpus of Talmudic literature with broad and deep knowledge of Western philosophy and theology. This gave him an unparalleled opportunity to interpret the world of Jewish law, rabbinic scholars, and scholarship—so central to Judaism throughout its history—to outsiders, at the same time giving him the ability to interpret to insiders the sophisticated elements of modern theology and religious life.

Life and Era. Soloveitchik was born in Pruzhan, Poland, on February 27, 1903 to one of the most prominent rabbinic families in eastern Europe. Reversing family tradition, he left home and rabbinical studies in 1925 to enroll at the University of Berlin, receiving a doctorate in philosophy six years later, with a dissertation on the neo-Kantian philosopher Hermann Cohen. Soloveitchik immigrated to the United States in 1932, assuming the position of Chief Rabbi of Boston, his home until his death in 1993. In 1941 he succeeded his father as the senior Talmudist at Yeshiva University, where he remained until disabled by illness in 1985. During those years he taught and ordained more rabbis than any other Talmudist in the United States, deeply influencing American Orthodoxy in the process.

In this period, leaders of American Orthodoxy were concerned that large numbers of Jewish immigrants were abandoning their European roots in Orthodoxy and assimilating into American society. Modern Orthodoxy saw its great challenge in adapting to the conditions of American modernity while remaining loyal to the traditions of Orthodoxy. Soloveitchik played a crucial role in making this possible by virtue of the force of his ideas, and the thousands of practicing rabbis he ordained who looked to him for ongoing guidance.

His admirers saw in him a combination of three personas: traditional halakhic authority, charismatic teacher, and theologian. Paradoxically perhaps, traditional halakhic authority was especially important to his success in helping Orthodoxy adapt to America's modernity, for authority in that community rests in no small measure in the hands of its rabbinic scholars. The traditionalist elements in Soloveitchik's ideology and life included his vigorous and influential opposition to mixed pews in synagogues; his traditional rabbinic garb and demeanor; his daily schedule revolving almost entirely around the study and teaching of rabbinic texts; and his distinguished eastern European heritage—about which he often told nostalgic and moving stories.

The more modern elements of Soloveitchik's ideology and life included his positive orientation to secular education and aspects of Western culture; his spiritual leadership of American religious Zionism; his progressive attitude towards women's education (he founded a coeducational Jewish school in Boston in which male and female students studied Talmud together); and his approval of interdenominational cooperation. Many of Soloveitchik's most distinguished traditionalist Orthodox rabbinic colleagues vigorously opposed some or all of these positions, and they remain controversial in Orthodox circles to this day. Soloveitchik's progressivism in these areas shaped what has come to be called "Modern Orthodoxy," helping prevent what some feared would become the complete decline and marginalization of Orthodoxy in America.

Writings. Soloveitchik's writings fall into two categories: the halakhic and the theological. Although he spent most of his daily schedule in the study and teaching of Talmud, he wrote relatively few works in this field. In these halakhic works Soloveitchik applies and expands the innovative and rigorous method of Talmudic analysis first developed by his distinguished grandfather, Rabbi Haim Soloveitchik. However, the younger Soloveitchik did apply this methodology far more fully and systematically than any of his predecessors or contemporaries to Jewish law governing the spiritual life, such as laws concerning repentance and prayer. This is an emphasis thought to be reflective of his particularly deep spiritual and theological nature.

Beyond illuminating the world of halakha and of the Talmudist, as mentioned above, Soloveitchik's theological works are important for their sheer creativity and theological insight, as well as for their insight into Soloveitchik's inner spiritual and intellectual world. Many of his writings are highly personal and reveal the inner struggles of a man caught between the cerebral life of the Talmud scholar and the passionate life of the spirit, between the traditionalism of his eastern European rabbinic heritage and the claims of modernity.

Throughout his theological oeuvre, Soloveitchik uses a typological method whereby different ideal types of persons contend within each individual in dialectical tension. This method, derived in part from Eduard Spranger and Karl Barth (1886–1968), is consistent with the method of Talmudic analysis developed most fully by Soloveitchik's grandfather. There is thus an interesting methodological similarity between the two domains of Soloveitchik's intellectual pursuits, the halakhic and the theological.

***Halakhic Man* and *Lonely Man of Faith*.** Soloveitchik's reputation as a Jewish thinker was first established in 1944 with the publication of his first major work, *Halakhic Man*, which explicates the inner world of the Talmudist. Soloveitchik distinguishes here between two ideal types of humans, which he calls "Cognitive Man" and "Religious Man." Drawing heavily on neo-Kantian philosophy, Soloveitchik states that Cognitive Man is best exemplified by the mathematician-scientist who constructs abstract, mathematically formulated models to explain and thereby demystify the cosmos. Religious Man, in contrast, cultivates that mystery, and seeks to transcend the physical bonds of the universe in search of God. "Halakhic Man"—the Talmudic virtuoso—combines elements of both and is thus portrayed as the ideal type. In the key turn of this argument—and a surprising one it is—Halakhic Man is most similar to the neo-Kantian hero Cognitive Man, for Halakhic Man also constructs abstract theoretical models. But these models are normative, representing halakhic concepts governing human behavior. Thus, through the Law, Halakhic Man brings God into a world in need of repair, whereas Religious Man travels in the opposite direction, seeking refuge in God, away from this troubled world.

Whereas *Halakhic Man* draws from rationalist neo-Kantian thought and focuses on the world of the Talmudist, *Lonely Man of Faith* (1965), Soloveitchik's second major published work, speaks in the language of existentialism and focuses on the inner world of the religious person living in the conditions of modernity. The monograph is hauntingly personal as well. Once again Soloveitchik—now working with the two creation stories in *Genesis*—distinguishes between two ideal types, Adam I, or "Majestic Man," and Adam II, or "Covenantal Man." Adam I, created in the image of God, carries out the mandate to rule the world and is functionally oriented and outer-directed, seeking to master the universe through science and technology. Adam II, on the other hand, is submissive, inner-directed and nonutilitarian. Most importantly, Adam II is, in Soloveitchik's terms, "ontologically lonely": he experiences radical uniqueness as a human being and seeks to redeem that loneliness in a covenantal community with God and fellow humans. Soloveitchik argues this can only be achieved through a Kierkegaardian sacrificial gesture to God that redeems Adam II from loneliness. Although Soloveitchik clearly identifies with Adam II, one of the central points of the work is that both Adams are biblically mandated modes of existence. Each individual must live both these lives, oscillating dialectically between the submissive covenantal life of Adam II and the practical, dominating life of Adam I, between the life of prayer and the life of technological and scientific majesty.

Halakha, Soloveitchik maintains, sustains this dialectic by ensuring that the prayerful person lives the practical life so characteristic of halakha, while also ensuring the practical life always yields to prayer and sacrificial gesture when it must.

The modern condition is dominated by individuals Soloveitchik has labeled as Adam I types. The "Man of Faith" is thus doubly lonely, not only for ontological reasons, but because Adam I fails to understand the sacrificial gesture and covenantal community so central to the Man of Faith's life. Soloveitchik stresses that even modern Adam I can be religious in the decorous, synagogue- or church-going sense. But this aesthetic religiosity fails to attain the in-depth existence of true faith. Thus Soloveitchik not only affirms some of the key values of modernity, including its emphasis on science and technology, but also attempts to provide a trenchant, even postmodern critique of modernity and its religious experience.

Other writings. Two other important works, *U-Vikashtem Mi-Sham* ("But if you seek from there") and *Halakhic Mind,* appear to date back to the 1940s, although the former was first published in 1978 and the latter in 1985. In *U-Vikashtem Mi-Sham,* Soloveitchik traces phenomenologically the odyssey of the "Man of God," from the first natural stirrings in contemplating the glories of universe and reflecting upon philosophical and spiritual experiences to the Man of God's ultimate attachment to God, or *devekut.* Although this quest begins with a deep feeling of human freedom and competence, the seeker confronts obstacles as human initiative reaches its limits. Eventually, the seeker is overcome by the sheer power of God's unexpected self-revelation through the Law. The seeker oscillates between awe and love of God, between the experience of God's commanding presence as overwhelming necessity and the experience of God's presence as autonomously chosen, which can be fully realized only with the ultimate goal of *devekut.* Crucial to resolving these tensions is the halakha and the community of its observers.

Halakhic Mind, the most purely philosophical of Soloveitchik's works, offers a sustained argument for the autonomy of religion as a cognitive domain. Soloveitchik argues that the task of philosophy of religion is to reconstruct subjective inner experiences from religion's objectified expressions, which in the case of Judaism would be through analysis of its halakhic material—hence the title, *Halakhic Mind.* This work is especially noteworthy not only for its early advocacy of a form of cognitive pluralism, but also for its explicit dissociation from influential medieval and modern Jewish philosophers, on the grounds that they failed to take the full measure of halakha's autonomy.

The Voice of My Beloved Knocks (1971) is a classic essay of religious Zionism, wherein Soloveitchik first treats the problem of evil and human suffering as it emerges from reflection about the Holocaust. He then argues that the true Jewish response to all tragedy is not passive speculation but vigorous action, the betterment of the human moral and religious self, and the amelioration of Jewish suffering. To Soloveitchik, the establishment of the State of Israel represents exactly such a response.

SEE ALSO Jewish Thought and Philosophy, article on Modern Thought; Orthodox Judaism.

BIBLIOGRAPHY

A comprehensive multilingual bibliography of works published by and about Soloveitchik, listing many hundreds of items, together with a topical index, appear in Eli Turkel and Hayim Turkel's *Mekorot Ha-Rav* (Jerusalem, 2001), although more primary and secondary material continues to be published. An English translation of *Halakhic Man* by Lawrence Kaplan was published in 1983 (Philadelphia), and *Halakhic Mind* was published in 1986 (New York). *Lonely Man of Faith* first appeared in *Tradition* 7, no. 2 (summer 1965): 5–67, and was later republished in book form (New York, 1992). No English translation of *U-Vikashtem Mi-Sham* has been published to date. It is widely available in *Ish Halakha Galui Ve-Nistar* (Jerusalem, 1979).

Two collections of essays about Soloveitchik are worthy of note: *Exploring the Thought of Rabbi Joseph B. Soloveitchik,* edited by Marc Angel (Hoboken, N.J., 1997); and *Emunah Be-Zemanim Mishtanim* (Faith in times of change), edited by Avi Sagi (Jerusalem, 1997). Aaron Rakeffet-Rothkoff has published a two-volume biography of Soloveitchik, *The Rav: The World of Rabbi Joseph B. Soloveitchik* (Hoboken, N.J., 1999). One of the more comprehensive critical overviews of Soloveitchik's thought and the cultural context of his life remains that of Singer and Sokol, "Joseph B. Soloveitchik:

Lonely Man of Faith" in *Modern Judaism* 2, no. 3 (fall 1982): 227–272.

MOSHE SOKOL (2005)

SOLOV'EV, VLADIMIR

SOLOV'EV, VLADIMIR (1853–1900), Russian mystical philosopher. Born in Moscow, Solov'ev was educated at the University of Moscow and the Moscow Theological Academy where, in 1873, his master's thesis, "The Crisis of Western Philosophy," earned him immediate repute. Solov'ev's lifelong concerns were to demonstrate rationally the truth of Christianity and to inspire an activist Christianity that would transform the world. His dedication to the philosophical goal of synthesizing religion, philosophy, science, and art in a comprehensive system that he called "total-unity" (*vse-1edinstvo*) precluded his ever marrying. He is considered Russia's first systematic philosopher.

Solov'ev conceived of God as an all-inclusive being: that is, as absolute reality, which is progressively united with its creation through the interaction of the Logos and Sophia. The Logos is the word, reason, the active principle of creation. Sophia is the passive principle. More a symbol than a metaphysical concept, Sophia, whom Solov'ev experienced in three visions as a beautiful woman, also denotes, ambiguously, divine wisdom, the body of God, the universal church, the bride of Christ, and active love for the world and humanity. Although Solov'ev stated explicitly that his concept of Sophia was not intended to introduce a new god into the Trinity, he wrote poems to her that contain marked gnostic and erotic elements and in which she emerges almost as a female principle of divinity.

Solov'ev regarded the incarnation of the Logos in Jesus Christ as the central event in history and Jesus Christ as a "second Adam," a God-man, the prototype of the transfiguration of all humankind through love. His concept of God, not purely Christian, is somewhat pantheistic. His theology, moreover, was influenced by gnosticism; qabbalistic literature; writers such as Jakob Boehme, Paracelsus, and Franz Xaver von Baader; and by philosophical Idealism, as well as by the Slavophiles, Dostoevskii, and Nikolai Fedorov. Catholics regard him as a convert; Russian Orthodox writers argue that he remained in their faith.

Solov'ev's life and works are customarily divided into three periods. These periods are characterized by philosophical, theocratic, and ethical and apocalyptic concerns. In the first period, the 1870s, he opposed abstract philosophy, criticized Western empiricism and rationalism as inadequate for the discovery of truth, maintained the identity of being and knowing, and advocated mystical intuition and integral knowledge as the path to God.

In the second period, the 1880s, hoping to realize his ideal of a "free theocracy"—a Christian society united by internal and voluntary bonds—Solov'ev tried to reunite the Russian Orthodox and the Roman Catholic churches. Believing that it was Russia's mission to incarnate the ideal of theocracy, in 1881 he appealed to Alexander III to spare the lives of the assassins of Alexander II, the tsar's father. The tsar's refusal convinced Solov'ev that Russia was not yet a Christian state. He resigned his teaching post, declared Russian Orthodoxy to be dead, and turned to the pope to realize his ecumenical goal—a new church that would incorporate the spirituality of the East with the activism of the West and that would encompass all aspects of life, action, and thought, as well as faith. The pope did not accept Solov'ev's ideas on Sophia, nor his program for a theocratic union administered by tsar and pope. Solov'ev, for his part, could not accept Roman Catholic emphasis on obedience.

With the collapse of his theocratic hopes, Solev'ev, in his third period, turned his attention to the practical problems of building a Christian society. In *Justification of the Good* (1895; English translation, 1918) he criticized the "abstract moralism" of Tolstoi, the amoralism of Nietzsche, and the "collective immoralism" implicit in nationalism and socialism. In *The Meaning of Love* (1892–1894; English translation, 1947) he argued that the purpose of sex was not procreation but the overcoming of egoism through love for the other.

In the last decade of his life, Solov'ev became preoccupied with the power of evil and had apocalyptic premonitions. His *Three Conversations concerning War, Progress, and the End of History,* also translated as *War and Christianity from the Christian Point of View* (1900; both English translations, 1915), is a discussion of the morality of militarism, power politics, and pacifism. Appended to it is "A Tale of Antichrist." The Antichrist, depicted by Solov'ev as a godless benefactor of humanity, is overcome by a revolt led by the Jews. Evil is, at last, vanquished and the churches reunited.

Solov'ev's influence was enormous. The saintliness of his personal life led Dostoevskii to model Aliosha in *The Brothers Karamazov* after him. His works were the fountainhead of the new spiritual, philosophical, and artistic currents of the Russian Silver Age (c. 1898–1917), and the Christian idealism and political liberalism of Sergei and Evgenii Trubetskoi, Pavel Novgorodtsev, and others stemmed in part from his thought and example. His sophiology helped shape the theology of Sergei Bulgakov and Pavel Florenskii, and it inspired the poetry and prose of the Russian Symbolists. Also important to Russian Symbolism was Solov'ev's view of art as a theurgy and of beauty as an incarnation of the divine. His apocalypticism and vision of pan-Mongolism (the rule of the "yellow" races over the "white") influenced Symbolist political thought, especially after 1904.

BIBLIOGRAPHY

The collected works of Solov'ev are *Sobranie sochinenii Vladimira Sergeevicha Solov'eva,* 10 vols., edited by S. M. Solov'ev and E. L. Radkov (Saint Petersburg, 1911–1914), reprinted with two supplementary volumes (Brussels, 1966–1969). *Pis'ma Vladimira Sergeevicha Solov'eva,* 3 vols., a collection of letters, was edited by E. L. Radkov (Saint Petersburg, 1908–

1911). His poems are published as *Stikhotvoreniia S. Solov'eva* (Moscow, 1915). In addition to the several English translations of Solov'ev's works cited in this entry, others are available in *A Solo'vyov Anthology*, compiled by S. L. Frank and translated by Nathalie A. Duddington (New York, 1950), and *V. S. Soloviev: Politics, Law, and Morality*, edited and translated by Vladimir Woznick (New Haven, Conn., 2000). Translations of "Lectures on Godmanhood" and "Foundations of Theoretical Philosophy" are included in *Russian Philosophy*, vol. 3, edited by James M. Edie and others (Chicago, 1965).

Secondary works on Solov'ev include Samuel D. Cioran's *Vladimir Solov'ev and the Knighthood of the Divine Sophia* (Waterloo, Ont., 1977); Helmut Dahm's *Vladimir Solovyev and Max Scheler* (Dordrecht and Boston, 1975), especially chapter 8, which contains translations of Soviet criticism and judgment of Solov'ev; Konstantin Mochul'skii's *Vladimir Solovev* (Paris, 1936); Egbert Munzer's *Solovyev: Prophet of Russian-Western Unity* (London, 1956); Dmitri Strémooukhoff's *Vladimir Soloviev and His Messianic Work* (Belmont, Mass., 1980); V. V. Zenkovsky's *A History of Russian Philosophy*, 2 vols. (New York, 1953), pp. 469–531; *Vladimir Solov'ev: Reconciler and Polemicist*, edited by Wil van den Bercken, Manon de Courten, and Evert van der Sweer (Paris, 2000); and *Vladimir Solov'ev: pro et contra*, 2 vols., edited by V. F. Boikov (Saint Petersburg, 2000, 2002).

BERNICE GLATZER ROSENTHAL (1987 AND 2005)

SOMA is a Vedic god; a drink offered to the gods and shared among ritual participants; and the plant that yields the juice for this drink. Middle and late Vedic literature describe the classical Vedic rituals in detail, and among these rituals, the *soma* rites are among the most prestigious and complex. In these rites, stalks of the *soma* plant are soaked in water and then crushed. The extracted liquid is poured through a filter into vessels. Left plain, or mixed with milk and various oblations, it is then offered into the fire for the gods and drunk by the priests and by the sacrificer of the rite. During the principal day of a *soma* sacrifice, there are three rounds of *soma* preparation and offering, one each in the morning, midday, and evening.

The later Vedic literature and the rites they describe often continue traditions already well established in the *Ṛgveda*. Indeed, although it contains hymns created for various rites, the core *Ṛgveda* is primarily a liturgical collection for *soma* rites. The principal collection of hymns dedicated to Soma in the *Ṛgveda* is book 9, which contains 114 hymns to the Soma Pavamāna ("Soma purifying himself"). These hymns were chanted as the *soma* was pressed and poured through the filter into vessels.

In the early tradition, participation in the *soma* rite was essential for both gods and men—Goddesses and women were both excluded from drinking the liquid. Among the gods, the principal recipient, Indra, is the dominant divinity in the *soma* rite and therefore in the *Ṛgveda* itself. Receiving the *soma* strengthens Indra and enables him to perform the deeds that have made, and continue to make, life possible. Indra drinks the *soma*—three lakes of *soma* according to *Ṛgveda* 5.29.7—in order to strike down Vṛtra, the paragon and paradigm of all obstacles. "Sharpened by *soma*" (*Ṛgveda* 10.108.8), Indra, together with a band of priests, releases the cattle, the symbol of dawn and substance of prosperity in Vedic India, by breaking open the cave in which they had been imprisoned. Offered *soma*, Indra defeats the human and semi-demonic enemies of his worshippers.

Because men participate in the *soma* rite as both offerers and drinkers of *soma*, they too are transformed by it. A family lord, clanlord, or king legitimately rules because he possesses the *soma*, and together with Indra, he too overcomes obstacles and gains cattle and other forms of wealth. By performing the *soma* rite he becomes truly an Ārya, a full participant in the elite culture of Vedic India, and he enlists the help of the gods in overcoming all those who do not sacrifice, those who are not Āryas. By drinking *soma*, he extends his lifetime. Soma "knots me together in my joints," says the poet of *Ṛgveda* 8.48.5. "Let the *soma*-drops guard me from my foot slipping, and let them keep me from lameness." Soma himself is the "deathless" (*amṛta*), and therefore those who drink the liquid become "deathless." In the core *Ṛgveda*, this "deathlessness" is the prevention of premature death, although, in later hymns and in the succeeding tradition, deathlessness becomes "immortality," and *soma* becomes the drink that sustains the life of ancestors in heaven.

Soma the god is a warrior who is victorious in battle. The Pavamāna hymns describe Soma's descent through the filter as an assault or a raid. Soma overcomes all obstacles and thereby wins freedom of movement. Mixing *soma* with milk signifies the capture of cattle, and after Soma has won all such good things, he becomes the generous king who distributes them. In another image of a victorious *soma*, these hymns depict *soma* as a racehorse, which wins rich stakes for those who prepare the drink.

In the *Ṛgveda*, *soma* is also compared to the sun or even kindles it. According to various descriptions, Soma illuminates the sun (*Ṛgveda* 9.37.4), begets the sun in the waters (9.42.1), stands above like the sun (9.54.3), makes the sun shine (9.63.7), and harnesses the steed of the sun (9.63.8). *Soma*'s association with the sun reinforces its connection with kingship and with life, for the sun rules in heaven and represents life and freedom. At the end of the Ṛgvedic period, this association of *soma* and the sun began to shift in favor of an identification of *soma* and the moon. According to the later Veda, as the moon fills with *soma*, it waxes; and as the *soma* is depleted, it wanes. The *soma* in the moon sustains gods and ancestors, and even drips down to earth where it gives birth to plants and animals.

The roots of Vedic *soma* and the *soma* rite extend beyond the Veda itself. Like Indian *soma*, the *haoma*—its equivalent in the Zoroastrian ritual—is both a drink and a deity associated with well-being and deathlessness. Beyond the Indo-Iranian tradition, *soma* likely inherits Indo-European traditions of the drink of deathlessness—"ambrosia," a word etymologically corresponding to *amṛta* "deathless"—and replaces Indo-European rit/es of offering and drinking mead. In the *Ṛgveda, soma* is termed *madhu* (honey), which is etymologically equivalent to "mead." There may be a mythological link between mead and *soma* as well. According to one Ṛgvedic narrative, the *soma* plant grew on a mountain, protected by a hundred concentric fortress walls and guarded by an archer. Manu, the first sacrificer, sends a falcon to steal the *soma* and bring it back to him, so that he can offer it to Indra. The story evolved in the later Vedic and Epic traditions, according to which the eagle Garuḍa steals the *soma* from heaven and from Indra, although he eventually returns it to Indra. This narrative of the theft of *soma* may share a common ancestor with a myth of the *Snorra Edda,* according to which Odin, taking the form of an eagle, flies away with the mead of Suttung, hidden in the mountain Hnitbjorg.

One of the perennial questions in the study of *soma* has been the identity of the Ṛgvedic and Indo-Iranian *soma* plant. Already in the later Vedic period, sacrificers were using various plants to perform the *soma* rite. Such substitutions were possible because *soma* is as much the product of the words, chants, and acts of the ritual as it is the juice of a plant. The *Ṛgveda,* however, does mention a particular *soma* plant (perhaps called *aṃśu*) that grows on mountains. Of the various identifications of this *soma* plant, ephedra has been an enduring candidate and has dominated much of the recent discussion. It is a stimulant, whose effect might be suggested by the description of *soma* as *jāgṛvi* (wakeful). Other scholars, however, have argued that *soma* was a hallucinogen in part because of *soma*'s connection with light and possibly with visionary experience. Numerous other possibilities have also been suggested. Fortunately, the precise identification of the *soma* plant, while interesting and significant, is not critical for the interpretation of most *soma* hymns and of the *soma* rite.

See Also Haoma.

Bibliography

Essential to the study of *soma* is Thomas Oberlies, *Die Religion des Ṛgveda* (Vienna, 1999), which focuses particularly on the role of *soma* in Vedic religion. Two volumes have appeared, with one more yet to come. Volume 2 is a compositional analysis of *soma* hymns. A very helpful study of the meaning of *soma* is Tat'iana Elizarenkova, "The Problem of Soma in the Light of Language and Style of the *Ṛgveda* " in *Langue, style et structure dans le monde indien: Centenaire de Louis Renou,* edited by Nalini Balbir and Georges-Jean Pinault (Paris, 1996): 13–31. There is much of value in older discussions of *soma,* and, in particular, apart from an implausible interpretation of Ṛgvedic *soma* as the moon, in Alfred Hillebrandt, *Vedic Mythology,* vol. 1 (Delhi, 1980): 121–266 (a translation of the second revised edition of *Vedische Mythologie* [Breslau, 1927]). On the narrative of the theft of *soma,* see Ulrich Schneider, *Der Somaraub des Manu* (Wiesbaden, 1971), and on the later development of the story, Jarl Charpentier, *Die Suparṇasage* (Uppsala, 1920).

S. S. Bhawe has published an English translation of more than half the hymns of the Soma Pavamāna book in *The Soma-Hymns of the Ṛgveda,* parts 1-3 (Baroda, 1957–1962). Karl F. Geldner, *Der Rig-Veda,* 4 volumes (Harvard Oriental Series, vols. 33–36: Cambridge, 1951-1957) gives German translations of all the *soma* hymns, and Louis Renou, *Études védiques et pāṇinéennes,* vols. 8–9 (Paris, 1961), gives French translations.

For the *soma* ritual, Willem Caland and Victor Henry, *L'Agniṣṭoma: Description complète de la forme normale du sacrifice de Soma dans le culte védique,* 2 vols. (Paris, 1906–1907), details the model Vedic *soma* rite, and Ramachandra Narayan Dandekar, *Śrautakośa,* vol. 2 (English section), parts 1 and 2 (Poona, 1973–1982), provides translations of Vedic ritual texts' descriptions of that rite. For recent performances of the Agnicayana, an elaborate form of the *soma* ritual, see Frits Staal, *Agni: The Vedic Ritual of the Fire Altar,* 2 vols. (Berkeley, 1983) and T. M. P. Mahadevan and Frits Staal, "The Turning-Point in a Living Tradition: Somayāgam 2003" in the *Electronic Journal of Vedic Studies* 10, no. 1 (2003), available from http://users.primushost.com/~india/ejvs/.

On the various possibilities for the identification of the *soma* plant, a good analysis is Jan E. M. Houben, "The Soma-Haoma Problem: Introductory Overview and Observations on the Discussions," in the *Electronic Journal of Vedic Studies* 9, no. 1 (2003). A judicious botanical appraisal of various possibilities is Harri Nyberg, "The Problem of the Aryans and the Soma: The Botanical Evidence," in *The Indo-Aryans of Ancient South Asia, edited by George Erdosy* (Berlin, 1995): 382–406.

Joel P. Brereton (2005)

SOPHIA is a Greek word that means "wisdom." In the Greek translation of the Hebrew scriptures (Old Testament), the name *Sophia* is given as a translation of *Ḥokhmah* (also meaning "wisdom"), the name of a figure with feminine features. In the Greek version of the apocryphal book the *Wisdom of Solomon* (written in Alexandria at the beginning of the common era), Sophia is said to be the emanation of God's glory, the Holy Spirit, the immaculate mirror of his energy, nay, even the spouse of the Lord (Septuagint 8:3). In the Greek rendering of *Ben Sira,* or *Sirach,* she is depicted as a woman: To the wise man she is both a tender mother, who spoils him as if he were her favorite child, and his young mistress, who surprises him with unexpected wildness (15:2). In *Proverbs* (c. 300), Wisdom "standeth at the top of high places and cries at the gates" (8:2–3; what Oriental woman would thus expose herself?) to proclaim that the Lord had brought her forth (not "created") before he began the creation. After he had created the world, she stood before him as his daily delight (8:30). This image was inspired by the pagan belief, represented on many excavated objects, that a goddess (either the Egyptian Maat or a Canaanite figure) stands before the godhead to please and entertain him.

In *The Thunder, Whole Mind,* one of the writings found at Nag Hammadi in 1945 and written probably during the first pre-Christian century by an Alexandrian Jew, Sophia manifests herself through a series of impressive paradoxes: as both the wisdom of the Greeks and the *gnōsis* of the barbarians, as both the saint and the whore, as the "All-Mother."

The ideas that God is female or that he has a feminine spouse lie further back still. Recently, in the Israeli Negev and near Hebron, Hebrew inscriptions have been found dating back to the eighth century that speak about "the Lord and his Asherah" (Asherah, or Athirat, was a Canaanite goddess of love, war, and fertility). On one jar bearing such an inscription, YHVH seems to be represented by the Egyptian god Bes (possessing an enormous phallus) together with a feminine figure (Athirat?). In Elephantine (near Aswan, Egypt) the Jews venerated Anat Jahu, another Canaanite deity, possibly as the spouse of the Lord. Ḥokhmah (Sophia) is the positive offprint of this photographic negative, the great goddess of the pre-Greek and pre-Hebrew Mediterranean, who, variously called Anat, Athirat, or Astarte (comparable to the later Greek Aphrodite), was considered to be a sacred prostitute, as were her devotees, and was still venerated as *dea meretrix* (goddess/whore) during classical times in the Near East.

Gnosticism integrated this Jewish myth. Simon the Magician, a first-century Samaritan (i. e., heterodox Jew), taught that the spouse of the Lord, called Sophia or the Holy Spirit, was actually "the first Idea of God" and had descended in order to produce the angels and powers that created the world. These tyrannical powers then overwhelmed her and forced her reincarnation again and again. (A contemporary version of this story is *She* by Rider Haggard.) At last she became one Helena, a prostitute in a brothel at Tyre (Phoenicia), whence Simon redeemed her. Here the cosmogonic Sophia of Hebrew lore has been combined with the Neo-Pythagorean concept of Helena as a symbol of the fallen and reascending heavenly soul.

In another Gnostic text, the *Apocryphon of John* (Alexandria, first century), Sophia is the last of the spiritual entities to come into existence. She falls into the cosmos because of her wantonness, but there she fights against the demiurge in her struggle to make man spiritually conscious. The same theme is Christianized by the greatest Gnostic, Valentinus, according to whom Sophia desires to penetrate the mystery of ultimate being, then falls through hubris (*tolma*) but is saved by Christ.

In the modern *gnōsis,* initiated around 1600 by Jakob Boehme, a similar mythology has developed. In addition to Christ, the German pietists discern the feminine Sophia, a goddess (the Holy Spirit?) and bride to the wise man. To become like Adam before the birth of Eve from his side, man must unite with his inner Sophia and become androgynous. English representatives of this tradition were John Pordage (1607–1681) and Jane Leade (1623–1704). Franz von Baader (1764–1841), a Bohemian philosopher, regarded androgyny and Sophianology as the aim and purpose of marriage. At the time of the Holy Alliance, these ideas were exported to Russia, where they were accepted by the Freemasons and such brilliant Orthodox theologians as Vladimir Solov'ev and Sergei Bulgakov.

See Also Gnosticism; Hierodouleia; Ḥokhmah.

Bibliography

Benz, Ernst. *Der Mythus vom Urmenschen.* Munich, 1955.

Bulgakov, Sergei. *The Wisdom of God.* New York, 1937.

Winter, Urs. *Frau und Göttin.* Fribourg, 1982.

New Sources

Casadio, Giovanni. "Donna e simboli femminili nella gnosi del secondo secolo." In *La donna nel pensiero cristiano antico,* pp. 305–329. Genoa, 1992.

Orbe, Antonio S.J., "Sophia Soror: apuntes para la teología del Espíritu Santo." In *Mélanges d'histoire des religions offerts à Henri-Charles Puech,* pp. 355–363. Paris, 1974.

Stead, G. C. "The Valentinian Myth of Sophia." *Journal of Theological Studies* 20 (1969): 75–104 (reprinted in *Substance and Illusion in the Christian Fathers,* London 1985).

Sfameni Gasparro, Giulia. "Il personaggio di Sophia nel Vangelo secondo Filippo." *Vigiliae Christianae* 31 (1977): 244–281 (reprinted in *Gnostica et Hermetica. Saggi sullo gnosticismo e sull'ermetismo,* Rome, 1982, pp. 73–119).

Tommasi Moreschini, Chiara O. "L'androginia di Cristo-Logos: Mario Vittorino tra platonismo e gnosi." *Cassiodorus* 4 (1998): 11–46.

Zandee, Jan. "Die Person der Sophia in der Vierten Schrift des Codex Jung." In *Le Origini dello, Gnosticismo,* edited by Ugo Bianchi, pp. 203–214. Leiden, 1967.

Gilles Quispel (1987)
Revised Bibliography

SORCERY See MAGIC; WITCHCRAFT

SOROKIN, PITIRIM ALEKSANDROVICH

(1889–1968), became controversial among his fellow sociologists after it became clear in the late 1930s that his heuristic key into social-cultural dynamics was a metaphysical distinction between a "sensate" materialism and "ideational" supernaturalism. His denunciation of the sensate materialism of Western culture emerged from spiritual commitments forged in his youth.

Born in the Vologda province of northern Russia, Sorokin was the son of a craftsman who restored icons in Orthodox churches while struggling with alcoholism, and of a mother who died three years after his birth. His early years were spent helping his artisan father, who died when Sorokin was ten. Sorokin then supported himself making icons, read widely in Russian literature and theology, and was influenced by nature mysticism.

These spiritual commitments were not explicit, however, when he arrived at Harvard University in 1929 and became founding chair of the Department of Sociology two years later. Early in his career, Sorokin was identified chiefly for his political activities. In December 1906, he was sentenced to spend four months in a czarist prison. Released in early 1907, he became a revolutionary organizer, first in the Volga region and then in Saint Petersburg. Admitted to the University of Saint Petersburg in 1910, he studied sociology and law, and graduated in 1914. In 1917 Sorokin became personal secretary to Prime Minister Alexander Kerensky and was a cabinet minister in the short-lived 1917 Russian government. With the triumph of V. I. Lenin in 1918, Sorokin, at the request of Kerensky, organized the brief effort to liberate Russia from the Bolshevik Communists. Lenin and the Bolsheviks prevailed, and after months of hiding in the forests, Sorokin turned himself over to the police. He was sentenced to death, only to be saved after several highly placed supporters appealed directly to Lenin on his behalf. Sorokin was freed on December 16, 1918, convinced that czarist jails were more humane than those of the Bolsheviks. Between 1919 and 1922 he was a professor of sociology at the University of Saint Petersburg.

In late 1922, Sorokin and his wife Elena left Russia under political persecution. They arrived in New York in 1923. Sorokin was now an émigré scholar with growing scientific credentials and an ever-deepening appreciation for the nonmaterial aspects of reality that Marxist-Leninism denied. Sorokin published *The Sociology of Revolution* (1925), after which he was able to gain speaking opportunities based on a growing academic reputation and his political experiences highlighting the coercive aspects of the Russian revolution.

In 1924 Sorokin was invited to join the University of Minnesota, where he spent six years. At age forty, he accepted a position at Harvard at the personal request of its president. In 1937 he published the first three volumes of his defining work, *Social and Cultural Dynamics*, the most widely reviewed sociological work in the United States between 1937 and 1942. Sorokin met with criticism from most social scientists for his critique of materialist cultures. He distinguished *ideational cultures*, in which ultimate reality is deemed a spiritual presence and in which the sociocultural world is centered on the supernatural, from *sensate cultures*, in which reality is deemed to be strictly material and the sociocultural world centers itself accordingly. He asserted that the sensate culture of the West was dying, and that ideational culture would emerge. A *New York Times* review by one leading sociologist described Sorokin as "a Tarter who has struck an alliance with neo-Thomism" (quoted in Johnston, 1995, p. 114). He was condemned by others for attacking progress and empiricism, for doing philosophy of history under the guise of pseudoscience, and for being prejudiced and superficial. In these pivotal years at Harvard, Sorokin's prophetic style and his sweeping sociology of history constituted an unwelcome deviation from disciplinary focus. In 1946, after a divisive battle with the American sociologist Talcott Parsons, he was forced to step down as chair of the Department of Sociology through its incorporation into the new Department of Social Relations.

CREATIVE ALTRUISM AND *THE WAYS AND POWER OF LOVE*. A new career phase began for Sorokin in 1942, with an appreciative letter from the American businessman Eli Lilly. Sorokin's critique of materialism and his writings on the sociology of war (1938–1944) were leading him to the study of what he termed "creative altruism." He was convinced that love as captured in the sermon on the mount and the Golden Rule, and understood scientifically, could serve as a means toward a better human future. With Lilly's support, he opened the Harvard Research Center in Creative Altruism in 1946. He became increasingly interested in investigating scientifically the energy of love, which he understood both metaphysically and practically.

In 1954 Sorokin published *The Ways and Power of Love*, a creative study at the interface of science, religion, and other-regarding love. Here he developed a five-dimensional measure of love. Low *intensity* love makes possible minor actions, while high intensity love requires much time, energy, and resources. Sorokin's second dimension of love is *extensivity*: "The extensivity of love ranges from the zero point of love of oneself only, up to the love of all mankind, all living creatures, and the whole universe" (Sorokin, 2002, p. 16). Sorokin added the dimension of *duration*, which "may range from the shortest possible moment to years or throughout the whole life of an individual or of a group" (2002, p. 16). The fourth dimension of love is *purity*, or freedom from egoistic motivation. Pure love—that is, love that is truly disinterested and asks for no return—represents the highest form of emotion (2002, p. 17). Finally, Sorokin included the *adequacy* of love. Adequate love achieves ennobling purposes, and is, therefore, anything but blind or unwise. Sorokin argued that the greatest lives of love and altruism approximate or achieve "the highest possible place, denoted by 100 in all five dimensions" (2002, p. 19), while persons "neither loving nor hating would occupy a position near zero" (2002, p. 19). He was impressed by the love of figures such as al-Ḥallāj, Damien the Leper, Mohandas Gandhi, Jesus of Nazareth, Dorothy Day, Simone Weil, and Teresa of Ávila. Because these individuals were able to maintain a love at high levels in all five dimensions, Sorokin posited their participation in a love energy that defines God, or is related to what he termed "the Supraconscious." Ingroup exclusivism, argued Sorokin, "has brought upon mankind more suffering than any other catastrophe" (2002, p. 461).

THE LEGACY OF SOROKIN. Sorokin rose quickly in the ranks of American sociology, and fell out of favor just as dramatically. But in the early 1960s, his work on altruism was receiving considerable attention. His lasting significance for religious studies and the global community lies in his pioneering efforts to develop a deep dialogue between science, religion, and altruistic love. His thoughts parallel those of Pierre Teilhard de Chardin with regard to love as the highest energy for personal and social transformation (King, 2004). Although his center at Harvard faded in the early 1960s, his work shaped the founding of the Institute for Research on Unlimited Love in 2001.

SEE ALSO Russian Orthodox Church; Sociology.

BIBLIOGRAPHY

Johnston, Barry V. *Pitirim A. Sorokin: An Intellectual Biography.* Lawrence, Kans., 1995. A complete summary of Sorokin's writings and career.

King, Ursula. "Love—A Higher Form of Human Energy in the Work of Teilhard de Chardin and Sorokin." *Zygon* 39, no. 1 (2004): 77–102. An insightful comparison of Teilhard de Chardin and Sorokin.

Post, Stephen G. *Unlimited Love—Altruism, Compassion, Service.* Philadelphia, 2003. Builds extensively on Sorokin's writings on love.

Sorokin, Pitirim A. *The Sociology of Revolution.* Philadelphia, 1925. A sociology of the causes and nature of revolution.

Sorokin, Pitirim A. *Contemporary Sociological Theories: Through the First Quarter of the Twentieth Century.* New York, 1928. A useful overview of the great sociologists.

Sorokin, Pitirim A. *Social and Cultural Dynamics.* 3 vols. New York, 1937. Sorokin's great work on sensate and ideational cultures.

Sorokin, Pitirim A. *Social and Cultural Dynamics*; Vol. 4: *Basic Problems, Principles, and Methods.* New York, 1941.

Sorokin, Pitirim A. *The Crisis of Our Age: The Social and Cultural Outlook.* New York, 1941; 2d ed., 1992. Focuses on sensate culture and its adverse implications.

Sorokin, Pitirim A. *Society, Culture, and Personality: Their Structure and Dynamics, a System of General Sociology.* New York, 1947. A further analysis of sensate and ideation cultural dynamics.

Sorokin, Pitirim A. *The Reconstruction of Humanity.* Boston, 1948. The human future requires more extensive "altruization."

Sorokin, Pitirim A. *Altruistic Love: A Study of American "Good Neighbors" and Christian Saints.* Boston, 1950; reprint 1968. A study of local "good neighbors" with regard to demographics and other variables.

Sorokin, Pitirim A. *A Long Journey: The Autobiography of Pitirim A. Sorokin.* New Haven, Conn., 1963. This is Sorokin's mature retrospect on his life, and on his contributions to sociology.

Sorokin, Pitirim A. *The Ways and Power of Love: Types, Factors, and Techniques of Moral Transformation.* Philadelphia, 2002. Originally published in 1954, this is Sorokin's greatest work on religion, love, and science.

STEPHEN G. POST (2005)

SORSKII, NIL (1433–1508), also known as Nilus of Sora. Russian hesychast and saint. Nil became a monk early in life and served his novitiate at the important northern monastery of Saint Cyril at Beloye Ozero. After a journey to the monastic communities of Mount Athos and Constantinople, he returned to Beloye Ozero with a commitment to hesychast spirituality. In the 1470s or 1480s Nil made his way to the deserted banks of the river Sora. His intention was to establish a monastic community that differed from the strict and complex pattern of life at his monastery of origin and was based, instead, on the pattern of the Athonite skete: loosely structured, sparsely populated, with silence at its core, and with no one superior.

In Nil's community the flexibility of the monastics' everyday arrangements corresponded to the flexibility with which their inner life was to be regulated. Hours of weekday prayer were left to the discretion of the individual, although all were cautioned against unrelieved prayer beyond certain limits. The goal was that silence (Gr., *hesuchia*) by which communion with God would be fostered.

Nil wrote at some length about the temptations that impede prayer: avarice, anger, sadness, spiritual torpor, vanity, and pride. To counteract these, one must infuse the mind and heart with the awareness of God. To this end Nil commends the Jesus Prayer. With the constant use of such prayer the monk may even anticipate what the Greek fathers had described as *theōsis*—divinization, or union with God by grace. Regarding his own experience, Nil's retention of the first person singular in his (unattributed) quotation of Symeon the New Theologian suggests that, at the very least, it corresponds to his own aspirations. "As I sit in the midst of my cell," he wrote, "I see a light which is not of this world. Within me I see the maker of the world. I converse with him and love him. . . . God loves me, he has received me into his very being, and he hides me in his embrace" (Mariia S. Maikova, 1912, pp. 28–29).

Nil's intention was to provide authentic teaching, and for this purpose he borrowed from hesychast masters such as John Cassian, John Climacus, Isaac the Syrian, Gregory of Sinai, and Symeon the New Theologian. Nil, who knew Greek, was the first to communicate the essence of their teachings to the Russian reader.

Nil's integrity as editor and spiritual guide gained him a reputation throughout the land. In 1490 he was invited to Moscow to debate the question of the Judaizers, the followers of the contemporary Novgorod-Moscow heresy. He was certainly opposed to the persecution, still more the execution, of the heretics. Nil's followers were to be accused of sheltering, if not actually favoring, heretics in the years to follow.

But the most noteworthy appearance of Nil in public concerned the question of the secularization of monastic lands. At a council convened in 1503 by Ivan III (who favored secularization), Nil apparently rose to place before it an unexpected proposal: that monasteries should own no villages, and that monastics should live in deserted places and should gain their sustenance by the work of their own hands. The proposal was to be defeated, and Russian monasteries continued virtually unchecked as ever more prosperous landowners until the age of Catherine the Great (1729–1796). A prerequisite for Nil's type of spirituality was that monks should neither own property nor even yearn for it.

Nil's followers, the "Trans-Volgan" elders, peripheralized by the Possessor establishment of the succeeding age (for church and state alike were to follow in the footsteps of Ivan Sanin [Joseph of Volokolamsk] and to favor monastic ritualism as well as land ownership), were to live out their lives in obscurity. In the latter half of the eighteenth century, Nil acquired a remarkable heir in Paisii Velichkovskii (1722–1794), who influenced, among others, the Russian elders of the Optino Hermitage and through them the Russian world beyond. The nineteenth century thus revived the reputation of Nil and confirmed, unobtrusively, his cult as saint.

Bibliography

Nil's basic texts are edited by Mariia S. Maikova as *Nila Sorskago predanie i ustav (s vstupitel'noi stat'ei),* "Pamiatniki drevnei pis'mennosti," no. 179 (Saint Petersburg, 1912). Selections are translated in G. P. Fedotov's *A Treasury of Russian Spirituality* (1950; reprint, Belmont, Mass., 1975), pp. 90–113. Full translations into German are provided by Fairy von Lilienfeld in *Nil Sorskij und seiner Schriften: Die Krise der Tradition im Russland Ivans III* (Berlin, 1963), pp. 195–284. The latter also contains a judicious discussion of Nil's life and writings. A sound general study of Nil's career is George A. Maloney's *Russian Hesychasm: The Spirituality of Nil Sorskij* (The Hague, 1973). Both the latter works will need to be checked against more recent publications by such Soviet scholars as S. Ia. Lur'e and N. A. Kazakova.

Sergei Hackel (1987)

SOTERIOLOGY The term *soteriology* means "doctrine of salvation" or, more concretely, the "way of salvation," and derives from the Greek *sōtēria,* which in turn is built on *sōtēr,* or "savior." The term is usually used to refer to the salvation of individuals, but it can also relate to the salvation of a group. The implication of the idea is that human beings are in some kind of unfortunate condition and may achieve an ultimately good state either by their own efforts or through the intervention of some divine power. Very commonly, there is belief in a savior God, that is, a God whose special concern is with the welfare of the human race. Examples of this idea are, in the ancient world, Isis, Mithra, and Christ; in the Far East, Amida Buddha in Japan and Guanyin in China; and Kṛṣṇa and Rāma in the Hindu tradition.

The notion that people need to be saved implies that a defective condition is normally prevalent, and the major religions have differing views as to the root of this problem. Thus many Indian systems ascribe a humanity's ultimate troubles to ignorance (*avidyā*). By contrast there is the Christian doctrine of original sin in which the human race is implicated through the primordial acts of Adam and Eve. Additionally, there are varying conceptions of how human life works: For instance, in Judaism, Christianity, and Islam, as well as in indigenous Chinese religion and in various others, life stretches essentially from birth or conception to death, and then the question arises about the status of postmortem existence, if any. But in the South Asian framework, the condition of living beings is *saṃsāra,* which implies a potentially endless round of rebirth or reincarnation from which one escapes only through ultimate liberation, or *mokṣa.* In Western monotheisms the question is often whether there is an afterlife; in the Indian tradition the afterlife is a given, and the question is whether one can get out of it.

The conception of salvation relates most clearly to the idea of some ultimate value or being, *nirvāṇa,* God, *brahman,* and so on. It may be thought of as an identity with such an ultimate state or being, or more frequently as a kind of communion with a personal Lord in a heavenly place, that is, "the place of God." Various means may be used to gain liberation or final communion. Where God is a personal object of worship typically salvation has to be effected by the deity, and this is where doctrines of grace and their analogues come in. Even here it is assumed in some way that the human being cooperates even if only by calling on the divine name for help. Where there is no such personal God, the individual must prepare himself, often through rigorous methods, in order to be in a position to gain eternal freedom. Consequently there are typically "self-help" and "other-help" kinds of religion. There are also different emphases as to whether salvation is something that ultimately occurs after death, for instance, by one's being transferred to a heavenly state, or is something attainable in this life. Thus in a number of Indian systems there is the ideal of the *jīvanmukta,* that is, one who has gained liberation (*mukti*) while still living (*jīvan*). It is typical of "self-help" systems to postulate this kind of liberation, but even in "other-help" systems there is a prefiguring of final salvation, as indicated typically by the question asked by some Christians, Are you saved? (not, Will you be saved?).

The usual scheme of the major religions that take the idea of individual salvation seriously is to pose the question in terms of a finite series of alternatives: One either attains heaven or one doesn't. At death one is either simply destroyed, or one goes to a state that is the opposite of salvation, namely damnation, in hell. There may also be an intermediate state, such as purgatory. In the Indian scheme of things, with the doctrine of reincarnation, many variations become possible. Usually (though not in the Dvaita school of Madhva) hells are in effect purgatories, for ultimately the individual rises out of them and resumes wandering through other regions and states of the cosmos. Again, the rewards for meritorious conduct in this life are varied, because there are many levels of superior social or ontological status. Thus, there is in some systems of belief, notably in Buddhism, a system of gradations of heavens, which correspond to differing levels of moral and spiritual attainment. Generally, though there may be places of punishment, the choice is between being liberated from rebirth or not being so liberated and carrying on. The choice in Western religions tends to be starker, so that the alternative to heaven is often seen as hopeless: "Abandon hope all ye who enter here" was written above the entrance to Dante's Hell.

In addition to the major religious traditions, there are secular ideologies that have analogues to religious doctrines of salvation. This is partly because some religions hold out hopes of a renewed blessed state that is community-oriented and located on this earth: the notion, for instance, of the millennium when humans will live in harmony and glory on the earth. Such a concept is easily secularized into utopian ideals considered as practical goals, such as the truly communist society in the Marxist picture, which is thought of as a social and economic system in which class contradictions and alienation have been overcome. What is lacking from the Marxist view, however, is a precise analogue of individual salvation that has been such a prominent idea in the religious systems. Hitler's thousand-year Reich was also modeled after millenarian expectations but was essentially tribal in orientation. Democratic capitalism has had a vaguer notion of progress without any clear idea of an ultimate state of human satisfaction. On the individual level, there is no real soteriology in scientific humanism, except that a person may find satisfaction retrospectively in thinking that he or she has done his or her duty in this life and has made a contribution to the welfare of the human race. More analogous to religious ideas are those of existentialism: In Heidegger's thought individuals can live authentically in the face of, and conscious of, their own deaths and thus in a sense overcome death from within a finite existence.

The concept of "living liberation" introduces a more general way of looking at soteriology, namely seeing it as concerned with the ultimate goal of the religious or spiritual life. In addition to the achievement of certain states, such as liberation from rebirth or life in heaven, there are central experiences, such as enlightenment and gnosis, that have ultimate significance. Sometimes it is the attainment of such experiences that gives people a sense of having attained living liberation. It is possible to have such experiences (e.g., Zen *satori*) without thinking that they guarantee anything about life after death. Such a soteriology is analogous to the secular existentialist type.

A religious act that has some relation to soteriology is the act of healing. Indeed, the etymology of the word *salvation* suggests "making whole," and there are indications of the close connection between physical and spiritual health in the New Testament (e.g., the emphasis on Jesus' healing miracles), and in many small-scale societies (e.g., in African classical religions, and in the new religious movements in Africa and elsewhere). Often disease is seen as arising from some deep alienation from society as a whole, or as the result of harmful religious practices (e.g., witchcraft). Healing is thus simultaneously the restoration of the individual's right relationship with the group.

The various dimensions of religion serve to illustrate differing means of salvation. Here it is perhaps a little misleading to use the word *means*, in that according to a number of religions, salvation arises from God's act rather than from human acts, and therefore there is no way of interpreting religion as itself an instrument causing salvation. Still one can look to a number of themes. Note first of all that the nature of the salvation envisaged will depend on the way the religious ultimate is viewed. In classical China the emphasis on both Heaven and the dao as underlying cosmic and social harmony suggests that the elimination of disharmony is important; the Mahayana Buddhist emphasis on "emptiness" suggests the importance of a kind of intellectual vision, paralleling the Buddha's own enlightenment; theism of various kinds suggests the centrality of the right relationship to a personal creator, and so forth. Given the differing goals, what are the various means?

Beginning with the ritual dimension of religion, one may note that the right performance of ritual may be central to soteriology. Thus the early Christian view of the sacrament of baptism implied that the neophyte, on entering the Christian community, dies like Christ and is resurrected with Christ. Provided there are no problems in the rest of the person's life, he or she is assured of ultimate salvation because of the ritual or sacramental union with Christ as victor over sin and death. This is repeated and reinforced by the eucharistic sacrament wherein Christ's eternal life is imparted to the faithful person in the bread and wine. There are similar motifs in the old mystery religions, for example the direct participation in the ritual reenactment of the myth of Persephone at Eleusis, and in the rites of Isis.

Ritual of a rather different sort is found in ancestral cults. Here the members of the deceased's family employ ritual means (e.g., proper feeding of the deceased, the right performance of funeral rites, etc.) to ensure that the departed are sent on their way serenely, or at least treated with propriety so that their afterlives are not scenes of misery and displacement.

The most important soteriological function of ritual is to open up lines of communication with the god. These allow those who participate in the rite to tap into the living substance of the divine and so to gain some kind of blessed or eternal life. Christian sacraments, for instance, allow the faithful to participate in Christ's resurrection. Such participation remains the main motif of Christian soteriology, although many other themes are also important. These include the ideas of Christ's victory over death and Satan, his expiatory sacrifice on behalf of humanity and in recognition of human sin, and his moral example.

As well as the use of ritual means of gaining salvation, there is the importance of the mythic "score" that the ritual plays out. Christians, for instance, see their own lives as possibly reflecting the life of Christ, and more generally the life of Israel. Understanding the mythic narrative means sharing the power of the mythic dimension of the faith. This lends a special importance to scriptures and other works, both literary and oral, that expound the stories of religious founders, gods, and heroes. So the *ḥadīth* and the Qurʾān itself throw light on the life of the Prophet Muḥammad and become exemplars of the kind of actions and attitudes expected of the Muslim if he is to please God. But apart from making possible the imitation of great heroes, mythic narratives also provide assurance of the divine being's care and concern for those who worship him. The revelation to Muḥammad provides the matrix for Islamic life and so gives assurance that from within this life the faithful will gain salvation. Similarly the story of the people of Israel and of the Jewish people since biblical times gives the Jew a sense of his election by God as part of an ongoing drama of history in which both God and the Jewish people will be vindicated. The *Bhagavadgītā* gives a special view of Viṣṇu's salvific power and assures his devotees of his desire to save those who turn to him in love and *bhakti.* The *Lotus Sūtra* tells the story of the loving guardianship of Avalokiteśvara, who acts to save those Buddhists who turn to him (or her, in China) in faith and imitation.

Both ritual and the enactment or contemplation of myth help to nurture experience, and often it is a striking experience that gives people a sense of being saved. In Christianity, especially in the less sacramentally oriented forms of Protestantism, there is emphasis upon conversion-experiences, being "born again," and attaining an inner illumination concerning one's own salvation. In the Indian tradition there is much emphasis here also. In *jñāna,* or knowledge, one experiences an encounter with the ultimate, whether this be the discrimination (*viveka*) of the eternal from the noneternal in Sāṃkhya-Yoga, the attainment of the higher *dhyānas* in Buddhism, or the realization of the identity of *ātman* and *brahman* in Advaita. While the doctrine of a personal God will suggest the spontaneity of such a being "born again," however, the more contemplative forms of Indian and East Asian religion, from Chan and Neo-Confucianism to Theravāda Buddhism and Hindu yoga, stress the greater importance of technique (methods of meditation, breathing exercises, etc.).

The institutional dimension of religion can have a double relevance to soteriology. On the one hand, organizations may claim some kind of privilege or monopoly in relation to salvation. In the Christian tradition this view has received the familiar tag, *"Extra ecclesiam nulla salus"* ("There is no salvation outside the church"), which stems from exclusivist interpretations of the sacred myth (echoing Jesus' "I am the Way"). In Islam membership in the sacred community is vital. In Buddhism one "takes refuge" in the Buddha, the *dharma,* and the *saṃgha,* the latter being the monastic community, with which the laity are closely connected. Such a doctrine of institutional exclusivity can be moderated by other doctrines, however, for instance the "baptism of desire" in Christianity, the initiation into the church in the wider sense of those non-Christians who, not having heard the gospel, yet lead a moral and holy life and so implicitly exhibit a "desire for Christ." One can compare this traditional idea with Karl Rahner's concept of the "anonymous Christian."

On the other hand, the conception of soteriology itself may be collective. Here the idea of God's saving work is applied primarily to the group as a whole—for instance, the people of Israel, who have a special destiny and a crucial role in the providential unfolding of history. In Judaism and its offshoot, Christianity, millenarian and eschatological thinking is important, though it may take on a very provisional and concrete character, for example, the coming of the Messiah in traditional Judaism, leading to the restoration of Israel. In Shīʿah Islam there is the analogous figure of the *mahdi* and the whole eschatology of the Hidden Imām. While such mythic themes help to maintain the communitarian aspect of future hope, they do not always blend well with other aspects of soteriology, such as the concept of the resurrection of the body and of the immortality of the soul. Sometimes resurrection is seen as supplying the disembodied soul with a "body," a kind of personal clothing that is in heavenly terms to what the physical body is in earthly terms. At other times it is seen as something earthly. Likewise the communal aspect of faith can be pictured in heavenly terms as in the Christian doctrine of the communion of saints, which is a kind of transcendent continuation of the church on earth.

The ethical dimension of soteriology is sometimes underplayed insofar as it is by the grace of God rather than through ethical (or ritual) efforts that one is saved. Morality may thus have an oblique relationship to soteriology: The good person in the Calvinist tradition, for example, may show some symptoms of being saved, but his or her salvation is not because of good works. Likewise in Pure Land Buddhism, especially in the teaching of Shinran, there is stress upon simple faith and calling on the name of Amida: If the virtuous person can be saved, how much more the sinner. By contrast religions of self-help give more importance to moral action as part of the means of gaining liberation or salvation. Thus virtue may at least be a precondition of study of the Ultimate, as in Advaita Vedanta or it may be integral to the Path, as in Buddhism.

Ethics may be combined with participation in the mythic career of one's exemplar. In general, the Mahayana Buddhists follow the path of the *bodhisattva:* They model their conduct on the self-sacrificial and compassionate life of the great Avalokiteśvara, or one of the other salvation-bringing *bodhisattvas.* It is not that following the path will bring salvation by itself, for it is rather by the transfer of merit from the limitless store of the *bodhisattva* that the otherwise unworthy person reaches ultimate liberation. But the mythic conception holds up an ethical and religious ideal that determines the follower's ethical perceptions. The path of the imitation of Christ in the Christian tradition has an analogous function. Similar motifs can be found elsewhere. In Hinduism, Rāma, Kṛṣṇa, and other avatars serve as alternative models of conduct. In Judaism, the reading of the Hebrew Bible provides the pious Jew with the model of Abraham or one of the other great figures of the past. In Islam there is the imitation of the Prophet Muḥammad, and so on. In the Jewish case there is also a very close integration between ritual and ethical rules through the written and oral Torah. Such an integration stresses the importance of obedience to the will of God, though ultimately it is God's action that ensures the final welfare of the individual Jew.

The means of salvation may be closely tied to the figure of the spiritual leader. Thus, even in self-help religious traditions or subtraditions it may be important for the individual to receive guidance from a specialist. Meditation and yoga, for example, must be guided by a guru. In Buddhism the Buddha himself is important as the one who brings the knowledge of the Way to humans, while the Saṃgha provides the institutional framework for leading the holy life. In small-scale societies the figure of the shaman is often important in serving as the expert who provides healing and reenacts the death and resurrection of the person who has suffered evil. In ancient Greek religion there were mystagogues and leaders, such as Pythagoras and Plotinus, who served as authorities and exemplars for their followers. Such figures, whether shaman or mystic, serve as a bridge to the mythic idea of the savior God who helps humans by himself taking on human form. Thus in Zoroastrianism can be seen the theme of the future savior Saoshyant, the figure of Christ in the Christian tradition, the various mediating figures in the Hindu tradition, and the saving *bodhisattvas* of the Mahāyāna. Since such conceptions may be held to infringe on the purity of monotheism (some, of course, do not arise from a theistic background in any case) this savior-god concept cannot strictly speaking play a part in Judaism and Islam. As mediators of salvation such figures can be surrounded by other personages who have a role in helping human beings towards their ultimate welfare—for instance, the saints of the Christian tradition, above all the Virgin Mary in the Catholic and Orthodox traditions, and the lesser deities of the Hindu tradition.

In addition to the other dimensions of religion, the doctrinal too can play a role in liberation, given that a faith may stress the philosophical aspect, so that thinking about the world along certain lines may be conducive to a kind of knowledge that saves. Thus in Mahāyāna Buddhism the analysis of causation and the impermanence of things may be instrumental in attaining a new way of seeing the world that recognizes its existential "emptiness." There is a certain analogue in ancient Greek conceptions of philosophy as culminating in a sort of vision, as, for instance, in Plato. Likewise in neo-Confucianism the investigation of things has a certain meditative role that yields vital, even salvific, knowledge. Doctrine and philosophy have of course, other nonsoteriological functions. They may, for instance, help define the community. But they are also ways of depicting reality as it is, and the vision thereof can thus be facilitated by practicing philosophical argumentation. Sometimes philosophy is used in a dialectical and critical way, to uproot entrenched concepts and to subvert habitual ways of looking at the world through the screen of language. In this way it can prepare for *satori* or other direct experiences of the "way things are." On the whole, Indian philosophy has stressed (admittedly in a rather theoretical way) the importance of this practice of philosophy for *mokṣa,* or liberation.

The belief in rebirth makes some difference to soteriology. It may involve a certain elitism. In Theravāda Buddhism or Jainism, for instance, there are only a few saints at any given time, but this does not preclude a much wider group from hoping for ultimate literation in a future life. It also raises issues about identity, especially since the concept of the person in some systems is tied to the concept of rebirth. That is to say, if liberation is defined as ultimate escape from the round of reincarnation, then a kind of negative theology (or more strictly negative anthropology) is applied to the liberated "self." Thus in Buddhism various ways of speaking of the enlightened or liberated person after death are denied. Similarly, in Advaita, realization of oneness with *brahman* implies no more rebirth, since in that identity beyond final death there is no longer any individuality as it is understood in the empirical world. Even in Sāṃkhya-Yoga, where there is in theory a plurality of souls or *puruṣas* surviving in a state of isolated freedom, there is doubt as to whether one can speak of individuality in any meaningful sense. Moreover the ultimate state, which is one of absence of pain, does not seem to differ essentially from unconsciousness. By contrast the state of liberation according to Advaita is blissful, and such a positive evaluation of postmortem *nirvāṇa* is also made.

Where God is believed to govern the cosmos, rebirth becomes an expression of his will. So in Rāmānuja's theism, for instance, a person's destiny is worked out over many, many lives, but in accord with God's will. If he saves the individual it happens in one lifetime, but the fact that an individual has reached a state where he or she calls on God is itself a sign of previous deeds. Followers of Rāmānuja split over the question of whether salvation was solely by God's grace, or whether surrender (*prapatti*) was necessary. In the latter case, a measure of human effort was necessary for salvation. Although Rāmānuja did not fully work out his doctrine of grace, he seems to have inclined more to the former view. Later, the dualist Madhva held to a doctrine akin to predestination, namely that God's sole task was to guide the cosmos in working out the results of the *karman* that already flowed from the inner nature of the individual.

Traditional cosmologies have assigned different "places" for salvation or damnation. Although heaven is conceived in theistic systems as the dwelling place of God (and vivid descriptions are given, such as in the *Book of Revelation* in the New Testament and in the Qurʾān), there are also heavens that are more fully devoted to the well-being and pleasure of the individual. Examples include the Buddhist and (to some extent) the Hindu heavens, which are attainable by the individual through rebirth but remain ultimately impermanent. The person goes thither as a reward for virtuous conduct, but however long he dwells, this is not final salvation. Some theistic forms of Hinduism postulate heavens that reflect the desires of the devotees in their longing for and adoration of God. A somewhat similar idea is found in Pure Land Buddhism. But such a heaven or paradise, though reflecting the joy of God's presence, may also incorporate many analogues to worldly pleasures. By contrast, hells reflect the deep pains of alienation from God and his love. Some systems postulate differing levels of salvation or heavenly existence in order to register the variety of possible human fates. The *Bhagavadgītā,* for instance, suggests that those who seek identity with *brahman* will attain it, but that it is a lower level than personal coexistence with Viṣṇu in Vaikuṇṭha Heaven.

Many religions conceive of release or salvation as the ultimate destiny of all humans (or of all living beings). In principle this is the case with Indian religious systems, with the exception of Madhva's dualism, which conceives of some souls as destined by their very nature for eternal punishment. But elsewhere in Buddhism and Hinduism hells are not everlasting places of punishment but in effect function as purgatories. A similar idea is found in Zoroastrianism, where the sins of the unsaved are finally burned away and all can rejoice in the victory of Ahura Mazda. But Christianity and the other Western theisms conceive of eternal punishment as the fate of some (though some Christians have believed in an empty hell and the ultimate salvation of everyone). The emphasis on divine judgment suggests the radical differentiation of the saved from the sinners. Much recent Christian theology, however, has emphasized a psychological or existential interpretation of the old pictures of heaven and hell, and stresses the sense of alienation from God or closeness to him in the events and vicissitudes of this life. There has been a corresponding decline in belief in hell, partly through the fading of the retributive view of justice. Modern cosmology has also weakened older ways of thinking of a succession of heavens above and purgatories or hells below, or of a Pure Land or other paradise "to the West." Hence there is greater emphasis upon salvation and its opposite as states of relationship to the Ultimate, or as states of mind. It has always been a characteristic of most Indian views of ultimate release, however, that such a condition is "beyond the heavens" and so not to be figured in a primarily spatial way (though there have also been disputes as to whether a soul is atomic or all-pervasive).

Finally it may be noted that some phases of traditions show a lack of interest in any radical notion of soteriology. Classical Confucianism has a picture of the ideal person or sage but not a doctrine of being saved from some pervasive evil or ignorance. In ancient Israel there was little concern with individual salvation until later on. Some modern secular worldviews such as scientific humanism do not possess the idea, and others such as Marxism do so only in an analogous sense. Classic small-scale religions, such as those in Africa, are typically more concerned with group welfare than with ultimate judgment about individuals. Nevertheless, the growth of modern individualism has highlighted the importance of thinking about how traditional patterns of soteriology might throw light on the symbols of judgment and ultimate meaning that remain vital in understanding the human condition.

SEE ALSO Atonement; Enlightenment; Millenarianism; Mokṣa; Redemption.

BIBLIOGRAPHY

Brandon, S. G. F. *Man and His Destiny in the Great Religions.* Manchester, 1962.

Brandon, S. G. F., ed. *The Saviour God: Comparative Studies in the Concept of Salvation Presented to Edwin Oliver James* (1963). Reprint, Westport, Conn., 1980.

Leeuw, Gerardus van der. *Phänomenologie der Religion.* Tübingen, 1933. Translated as *Religion in Essence and Manifestation: A Study in Phenomenology* (1938; 2d ed., 2 vols., New York, 1963).

O'Flaherty, Wendy Doniger, ed. *Karma and Rebirth in Classical Indian Traditions.* Berkeley, Calif., 1980.

Toynbee, Arnold, et. al. *Man's Concern with Death.* London, 1968.

New Sources

Bianchi, Ugo, and Marten J. Vermaseren, ed. *La soteriologia dei culti orientali nell'Impero romano.* Leiden, 1982. Proceedings of an epoch-making conference which has given impetus to the historical location of the notion of salvation. See the important review by Robert Turcan, *Revue de l'histoire des religions* 201, 2 (1984): 188–191.

Doré, Josef. "Salut-Rédemption." In *Dictionnaire des religions* pp. 1799–1807. Paris, 1993. Theological.

Doré, Josef. "Salvifique (dans le christianisme)." In *Dictionnaire des religions,* pp.1809–1812. Paris, 1993. Christian (Catholic) conception vis-à-vis Buddhism.

Flasche, Rainer. "Heil." In *Handbuch religionswissenschaftlicher Grundbegriffe,* vol. 3, edited by H. Cancik, B. Gladigow, and K.-H. Kohl, pp. 66–74. Stuttgart, 1993. Phenomenological.

Massein, Pierre. "Salvifique (dans le boudhisme)." In *Dictionnaire des religions,* pp.1808–1809. Paris, 1993.

NINIAN SMART (1987)
Revised Bibliography

SOUL

This entry consists of the following articles:

CONCEPTS IN INDIGENOUS RELIGIONS
ANCIENT NEAR EASTERN CONCEPTS
GREEK AND HELLENISTIC CONCEPTS
INDIAN CONCEPTS
BUDDHIST CONCEPTS
CHINESE CONCEPTS
JEWISH CONCEPT
CHRISTIAN CONCEPTS
ISLAMIC CONCEPTS

SOUL: CONCEPTS IN INDIGENOUS RELIGIONS

Whereas in a Christian context the human soul is thought about and overvalued in relation to the body, in the traditional thinking of so-called archaic societies an immanent power, a vital principle, an individualized dynamism, is usually recognized to exist not only in humans but in certain other material and biological beings as well. Whatever moves, whatever lives, is supposed to be the abode of one or many souls.

This article shall essentially deal with what is conceived of as the spiritual principle of the human being, the prototype of the "beings-forces" of nature, and not with the more or less anthropomorphized spirits, gods, or genies, nor with powers that are supposed to have a mineral, an animal, or a vegetable as a continuous substratum.

The essence of the soul is power, to the extent that power, soul, and life become interchangeable categories. But with regard to traditional societies one can really speak neither of the uniqueness of the soul nor of homogenous and always precise concepts. The linguistic equivalents in use remain very approximate. Since the idea of the soul is rarely the object of metaphysical discussion in these societies, it is difficult to really know if what is designated by the aborigines as "spirit of the man," or "spirit in the man," corresponds to separate realities, to distinct functions of the same reality, or to inherent potentialities of a determined substance. Nevertheless, the fact that primitive humans think of themselves as unlimited with regard to their physical potentialities shows that they examines themselves in order to seize their hidden essence, which extends far beyond their bodies.

In the explanations relating to the subject, one observes a constant concern about concrete detail and the rejection of abstractions, which results in a correspondence between ontological pluralism and a plurality of phenomena; but nothing is represented as either purely material or purely spiritual. The quantitative character of the power of the soul is accentuated by this plurality of personal souls and by the identification of the degree of force that each individual disposes of in their relation to evil spirits, in their generative power, and in the influence they has on their fellow citizens, for example. Each of these individual powers tends to free itself and to exert itself in an independent way: for example, through the heart in courageous deeds of battle or through the mind in the wisdom of a palaver. The soul never appears as a pure essence but is identified through props and manifestations. Its power can vary from individual to individual, and even in the same individual in the course of his or her life.

Theoretical Elaborations. While most of the ethnologists of religion have been interested in problems relating to the soul, E. B. Tylor (*Primitive Culture,* 1871) and Lucien Lévy-Bruhl (*L'âme primitive,* 1927) were among those who formulated the principal theories regarding this subject. In *The Golden Bough,* James Frazer remained close to Tylor's concepts. R. R. Marett, criticizing both Tylor and Frazer, coined the word *animatism* to describe the tendency of the mind to consider inanimate objects as living and endowed with feelings and a will of their own.

According to Tylor, who was one of the first to propose a theory of primitive religion, the evolution of religious systems had its origin in a primitive animism, defined as a belief in spiritual beings. The notion of the soul arose from the fusion of the idea of a life principle with a double, or an impalpable phantom that could separate itself from the body it resembled. Belief in a phantom double originated in the experience of the independent double of distant or deceased individuals appearing in nocturnal dreams and diurnal fantasies.

But studies in the history of religions have not validated Tylor's hypotheses. His sequential interpretation (belief in a double, attribution of a soul to animals and then to objects, ancestor and spirit cults, fetishism, idolatry, polytheism, monotheism) has been shown to be incorrect; the importance that he gave to dream-inspired revelations in the origin of myth and religion has been contested; and the historical evidence proves that monotheism appeared much earlier than Tylor thought.

According to Lévy-Bruhl, the primitive soul must be seen as participating in a unique principle. All beings function as the vehicles, and the diversely specified incarnations, of an anonymous and impersonal force that sociology has popularized under its Melanesian name, *mana.* Participation in *mana,* which is at one and the same time substance, essence, force, and a unity of qualities, confers on things and beings a sacred and mysterious character that animates nature and maintains an interaction between all its parts. Belief in an essence common to certain beings and objects has been defined as totemism. But Lévy-Bruhl also viewed souls as variable and multiple powers, unequally located in the universe. Next to emanations-forces and powers of nature are placed the beings-forces, the personified souls, endowed both with intelligence and will.

It is, however, to be emphasized that both Lévy-Bruhl and Marett erred in concluding that the primitive conceives of everything in nature as being animated, even if there is a belief that anything can serve as a prop for an animation under specific circumstances. The idea that all is soul is a theoretical construction. The idea that the individual soul does not exist and that it fuses either with the cosmos or with the group is also erroneous, because, on the one hand, the individuals's identification with the vegetable, animal, or divine world does not exclude the differentiation of powers and, on the other hand, among many African peoples (the Kikuyu of Kenya, for example), the collective soul (or family spirit) is entirely different from the soul of the individual.

The idea that primitive thought ignores any dualism separating the body and soul also lacks validation. Numerous examples show that there exists a quite noticeable distinction between the body element and the diversity of spiritual entities that one may call "souls" for the sake of convenience, entities that may have the body as a prop or that, as the double of ego, constitute what Frazer called the "external soul."

VARIETIES OF THE SOUL. Owing to a lack of better and more varied terms, term *soul* is used here, in the singular, to refer to conceptions with greater differences than those existing between Shintō and Christianity; *soul* often designates, for a single living being, plural entities, distinguished by the autochthonous peoples themselves to account for what they judge to be independent spiritual forces. As beliefs can and do contradict each other from one ethnic group to another, it is hardly possible to imagine a typology that could be valid for a single continent or even for a large cultural area; consequently, it seems more appropriate to illustrate the diversity of souls—the complexity and ambiguity of these beliefs—with some examples.

The Fang of Gabon name seven types of souls: (1) *eba,* a vital principle located in the brain, which disappears after death; (2) *nlem,* the heart, the seat of conscience, which inspires the acts of men and also disappears at the time of death; (3) *edzii,* an individual name that retains a sort of individuality after death; (4) *ki* (or *ndem*) the sign of the individual and at the same time his or her force that perpetuates itself after disincarnation; (5) *ngzel,* the active principle of the soul as long as it is in the body; (6) *nsissim,* both shadow and soul; and (7) *khun,* the disincarnated spirit, which can appear as a ghost.

From this example, one can see that the soul is never conceived of as an amorphous substance; rather, it is represented through functional props (brain, heart), through images (shadow, ghost), through symbols (name, character sign), or by its activities. The differentiation of souls may also occur in relation to ethical or sexual criteria or their modalities of action.

The Mbua of the Rio Branco territory in Brazil (the São Paulo littoral) believe that there exists in each individual both a beneficial soul and a dangerous soul, which manifest themselves through communication, that is to say, through speech and an impulsive process comparable to telepathy. Moreover, there is a third type of soul called *ñee,* which is the initial core of the personality and plays the part of the protective spirit. This soul stands guard while humans sleep in the forest; but unlike the guardian angel, it is not a being distinct from a human. If the three souls simultaneously abandon the body, the person dies. The Mossi of Burkina Faso (Upper Volta) believe that death comes from the disunion in the soul (*siga*) of two invisible principles, one male (*hirma*) and the other female (*tule*).

Mircea Eliade has noted that the Aborigines of Australia recognize a distinction between two souls: the real ego, which preexists individuals and survives them, perhaps through reincarnation, as certain tribes believe; and the trickster-soul, which manifests itself in dreams, resists its definitive separation from the body, and may remain in the body of another person after the death of its owner. Humans have to perform special rites to defend themselves against the trickster-soul.

This last example suggests what is to many theoreticians of primitive culture a fundamental distinction: that is, the distinction between soul-substance, which animates the body and which temporarily locates itself in the vital centers or in the products relating to its force (saliva, sweat, blood, sperm, tears), and the external soul, which is also plural and whose different aspects correspond to various particular functions.

Internal soul. Wilhelm Wundt called the potentialities of particular parts of the body (head, heart, liver, eye) "organic souls." But if the soul is designated by the places where it shows its power, it is in the whole body that one finds the substance of the soul.

Among the corporal expressions of vital dynamism, a privileged place is assigned to blood and to respiration. In one of the myths of the Iurak of Central Asia, the world perishes from a fire caused by the death of a sacred tree; as it tumbles down, the tree sheds its blood, which streams over the earth, changing itself into fire as it flows. Thus, the disanimation of the center of the world produces (as a consequence) the disanimation of all beings. Respiration is conceived of as both the sign of life and its principle. Such was the power of breath among the Celts that during the Battle of Druin Damghaire the druid Mog Ruith, using only his breath, transformed his enemies into rocks.

A vital spiritual force is also supposed to reside in sperm. Sexual relations are the symbol and the means of the continuity of the vital force in humans. To say to an old African man that he does not have any more "force" is to tell him to his face that, on the one hand, he is impotent, and that, on the other, he is no longer capable of creation. Finally, it is to be noted that certain extraordinary potentialities of the body may be present as the result of its being possessed by a superior power.

External soul. This term designates the powers of the soul located outside the body. Frazer spoke at length about this in *The Golden Bough.* Discovering in themselves potentialities that appear to them to be superior to those shown by their ordinary physical performance, individuals have a tendency to conceptualize this superiority more readily outside than inside their own bodies.

Thus, what may be called external soul can leave the body during a dream or sometimes two or three years before physical death (Dogon, Serer, Kongo of Africa); habitually lives in an animal double (totem), in a human double, in the shadow; and expresses itself through speech and rhythm in relation to the "non-me" (the soul of communication).

Thus, the indigenous peoples of the Bank's Islands in Vanuatu fear that death will come to them if they see their reflection in the water of a cave. If a deceased person does not have a shadow, he or she may a shadow themself and may frighten the person who sees them as ghosts. An individual can attack another using a shadow acting as an intermediary.

The Sotho of southern Africa believe that a crocodile can seize a passerby if it catches hold of the person's shadow at the surface of the water. But in this context the word *shadow* is used figuratively to designate some inner aspect that is *like* a shadow—clearly individual and separable from the person, but at the same time immaterial despite being represented by way of material substance. This is an example of the conceptual expressing itself through objects accessible to the senses.

The "double" (which is identified with the shadow in some cultures, distinguished from it in others) is a second self, mysteriously united to an individual. It can die with the individual, or it can be seized and consumed by a witch, which action, in turn, causes a mortal sickness in the victim (a general belief in West Africa). On the island of Mota in Melanesia, the term *tamaniu* refers to a kind of double, referring to any animal that is mystically connected to human. People are forbidden to eat the *tamaniu.* Human and animal protect and influence each other in profound solidarity, but here the double does not have the exact same traits as the original.

The fact that some human powers are represented by the hair and nails that continue to grow for a short time after death, and that they are symbolically transported and buried and become the objects around which family funerals are celebrated in the case of the death of a loved one in a foreign land or of an untransportable corpse (e.g., in Benin civilization), does not mean that a soul is held to live in the hair and the nails. Rather, they are viewed in very much the same way as the placenta, which, like them, is buried in most parts of Africa—which is to say, they are thought to be relics of life and power.

The souls of animals, like the souls of things (e.g., a statuette), may also enter into symbolic and participative relationship with the human soul, but an animal—for example, a bird that flies away, a fly that enters a person's ear, a snake that kills—may also temporarily become the prop of a person's external soul. Sorcerers and witches are supposed to possess, to varying degrees, this liberty to transport themselves, to live in a double, to metamorphose in order to reach the people on whom they wish to act. Sometimes, the double (e.g., the *aklama* of the Ewe of Togo) is thought of as a sort of tutelary spirit, an adviser on matters related to the luck of the individual, one that suggests a good deed or the way to avoid an accident.

ORIGIN OF THE SOUL. The soul can originate from an almighty spirit, from Mother Earth, or from special genies; it can also be obtained as a gift, by conquest, or by choice.

Among the Ewe of Togo—who use the terms *luvo* (the "substance of the soul") and *gbogbo* (the "breath of life")—the individual, before incarnation, exists as a spirit, and together with the supreme creator Mawu-Lisa he or she chooses their own destiny. This choice is supposed to take place in the field called *bome,* the place of prenatal existence, a kind of reservoir of stagnant and infantile lives where the primordial mother, Bomeno, cuts clay from which to fashion the newborn, which she then sends into women's wombs. The myths relating to the origin of each individual introduce the notions of initial choice of their life (*gbetsi*), of reproduction of a character type (*kpoli*), and of reincarnation of an ancestor (*dzoto*).

The Bambara of Mali believe that humans possess twin souls called *ni* and *dya,* which are given by the deity Faro. The *tere,* which represents character, conscience, and force, is given to humanity by the deity Pemba. Finally, it is from the deity Mousso Koroni Koundyé that each individual obtains their *waso,* a malignant force that lives in the foreskin or in the clitoris and disappears at the moment of circumcision or clitoridectomy.

Among some peoples the generation of the soul is not the action of a divinity external to humans; rather it is through traditional methods that a soul can be obtained as a power. Thus, during their lifetime the Jivaroan people of Ecuador try to obtain a soul they call *arutam wakani,* which cannot be killed by physical violence, poisoning, or sympathetic magic. The search for this soul, which takes place around the age of six, involves a pilgrimage to a sacred waterfall, fasting, and the capture of a wandering soul during a vision of large animals in combat. The individual then feels an irrepressible desire to kill. The act of killing leads to the acquisition of the victims' souls and thus confers cumulative supernatural power. Those who have an *arutam* soul and are killed by either natural or supernatural means can, at the moment of death, form a revengeful soul called *muisak,* which leaves the corpse through the mouth in order to kill the murderer. Each individual, regardless of sex, is supposed also to possess an ordinary soul (*nekas wakan*) that is relatively passive; this soul is represented by blood, and bleeding is even believed to be a hemorrhage of the soul. But the *nekas wakan* is only of secondary interest in relation to the *arutam wakani* and the *muisak.*

The Yoruba of Nigeria believe that force can be ingested and that this food possesses the quality of a soul. Thus the new king of Ife had to consume the heart of his predecessor, once that organ had been reduced to powder, in order to incorporate in himself the substance of royalty.

DESTINY OF THE SOUL. The migration of the soul is the extreme consequence of the freedom of movement attributed to spiritual entities. Indeed, most primitive peoples believe that a form of soul becomes detached from the body in dreams, but there are some who also hope to reach a stage of personal weightlessness through ecstasy.

Thus the Tupi-Guaraní of Brazil believe that incessant dancing associated with strict fasting will make them become so light that they will reach the "land of no evil" beyond the seas, where they will remain eternally young and be free from work and life's trials.

The majority of the so-called primitive societies believe that after death their ancestors live in another world that either parallels the world of the living or is similar to it. The voluntary burial of weapons and food in tombs can be traced as far back as the Mousterian epoch, to the Neanderthals, and during the Upper Paleolithic period the dead were usually covered with red ochre, a sign of life and perhaps resurrection.

Many African peoples believe that an ancestor identified either by divination or by some distinguishing traits, although living in the country of spirits, can be reincarnated in a newborn child, and sometimes even in several newborns, especially twins.

When detached from the body after death, certain souls can disappear, and others can reach various worlds beyond. For example, one soul makes its way to the place where its ancestors live; another is transmitted as a vital force to its descendants, usually to its grandsons. The ghost remains as a double next to the corpse or appears to the living while they sleep.

Regarding forms of life after death, an example from the Dakota is illustrative. The sky god Skan attributes to each person at birth four types of souls. (1) *Nagi,* the spirit that controls the actions of human beings until their death, when it leaves the body to await Skan's judgment. If *nagi* is deserving, it joins the world of spirits (*wanagi tamakoce*); if not, it is condemned to wander endlessly. (2) *Niya,* the vital breath, which though immaterial, is visible whenever it wills. It gives vitality to the body, making it understand what is good and bad, and it helps the body to influence people. The *niya* can leave the body of the human being, and if the *nagi* abandons the body at the same time, it means death. After death, the *niya* gives testimony on the role of the *nagi,* which helps in the judgment of the latter. (3) *Nagiya,* the shadow, the external double, responsible for supernatural actions. A man possessed by the *nagiya* of a bear, for example, will have the nature of a bear. The *nagiya* also allows communication between animals and humans. (4) *Sicun,* the guardian spirit. It is never visible and is sent forth by the *wakan kin* ("superior spirits") to make humans react differently from animals. After death, it goes back to where it came from.

Almost everywhere, the voyage of the soul after death implies a gradual purification through a series of trials (e.g., crossing a stream, climbing to the sky by means of a rope). The ultimate destination is the land of the soul, depicted as a celestial space or an underground place, a glade or a desert, or a place devoid of all tangible character. In the Solomon Islands, the beyond is said to be both a distant country and a nearby cave. The idea of the dead resting in the west where the sun sets, or underground, or in marshes does not contradict the idea of their close invisible presence.

That the individual continues to exist in a new condition does not mean that the soul is conceived of as being immortal. Life can have a circular and cyclical movement that death does not interrupt, provided that the correct rites relating to burial (cremation in the Solomon Islands), lamentation, prayer for the dead, and sacrificial offerings are carried out. Primitive peoples speak not of an eternal life but of a very long life, a kind of existence resembling the one the dead have had on earth. Behavior, good or bad, as well as the manner of death, largely determines the posthumous power. Among the Fon of Dahomey, the individual whose death was caused by lightning, drowning, or leprosy can never achieve ancestorhood, and among the Tongans of Polynesia only the nobles are totally immortal. Among other peoples, some ancestors can ascend to the heights of divinity.

Here, mutilation prevents the soul of a dead human from performing harmful acts (Bering Inuit); there, the noxious powers of a sorcerer's soul are destroyed through the burning of the body (Ganda of Uganda). While continuing a life in the other world, the dead person can be present elsewhere; as a specter or a ghost (Raketta of New Guinea) or in the form of an animal (lizard among the Samoans, python among the Kamba of East Africa). Although invisible, the souls of the dead can appear in dreams or to those specialists who know their desires and so can intercept their messages.

SUMMARY. In the religions of primitive societies, the soul is not necessarily the particularized form of a general and undifferentiated supernatural force; it is neither the genie living in a material reality nor the unique prototype of the ego or of the person considered as a moral and judicial entity. Many societies believe in the existence of several souls in the same individual, each of them having a distinct function. Generally, greater importance is given to the power of animation (*anima*) than to the faculty of representation (*animus*). And the notion that some spiritual element of the person survives after death is quasi-general.

SEE ALSO Afterlife; Animism and Animatism; Blood; Breath and Breathing; Cannibalism; Death; Preanimism; Spittle and Spitting; Tears.

BIBLIOGRAPHY

Centre National de la Recherche Scientifique. *La notion de personne en Afrique noire.* 2d ed. Paris, 1981.

Crawley, A. E. *The Idea of the Soul.* London, 1909.

Frazer, James G. *The Golden Bough.* 12 vols. 3d ed., rev. & enl. London, 1911–1915. Abridged and edited by Theodor H. Gaster as *The New Golden Bough* (New York, 1959).

Hamayon, Roberte. *Le chasse à l'âme. Esquisse d'une théorie du chamanisme sibérien.* Nanterre, 1990.

Leeuw, Gerardus van der. *Phänomenologie der Religion.* Tübingen, 1933. Translated as *Religion in Essence and Manifestation* (1938; 2d ed., 2 vols., New York, 1963).

Lévy-Bruhl, Lucien. *L'âme primitive.* Paris, 1927. Translated as *The "Soul" of the Primitive* (New York, 1928).

Marett, R. R. *The Threshold of Religion.* 3d ed. London, 1915.

Tylor, E. B. *Primitive Culture* (1871). 2 vols. New York, 1970.

CLAUDE RIVIÈRE (1987 AND 2005)
Translated from French by G. P. Silverman-Proust

SOUL: ANCIENT NEAR EASTERN CONCEPTS

Neither Sumerian nor Assyro-Babylonian cuneiform sources have left any account, however incomplete, of their psychological ideas, probably because, for these ancient peoples, such ideas were considered self-evident and did not need to be set down in writing. Scholars are thus faced with a difficult situation, which is made still more difficult by the scholars themselves projecting their own cultures onto the subject they are studying, namely their own ideas concerning the body and the soul (in this context see, for example, the title of this article, which is not particularly appropriate to deal with the cultural attitudes of the ancient peoples described here).

Using the meager information provided by the texts, the issue was initially dealt with by Oppenheim and—albeit in a less general manner—by von Soden, both in 1964 (Oppenheim, 1964; revised 1977, pp. 198–206; von Soden, 1964) but it remained a peripheral research subject for a long period, with the notable exception of Saggs (1974) and Jacobsen (1976, pp. 155–164). In the 1980s important studies finally appeared that dealt with the key aspects of the question and formed the basis for the subsequent systematic treatment (Klein, 1982; Groneberg, 1985; Jacobsen, 1989) in the years that followed.

MESOPOTAMIA. There are three obvious sources of information on Mesopotamian psychological ideas: (1) the anthropogeny of the *Atrahasis* poem and an analysis of this compared to other myths of the same sort; (2) details from exorcist rituals to banish or remove evil spirits or funerary rites; (3) the "personal god" and the literature dealing with this.

The *Atrahasis* poem draws upon traditional themes dealt with elsewhere (Kikawada, 1983) and may be dated to the Old Babylonian period (twentieth–sixteenth centuries BCE). It tells the story of the revolt of the lesser gods, who are tired of the heavy burden of work, and the resulting creation of the human race to take their place in performing this task, leaving them free to remain with the greater gods. The rapid growth of this new creature, which—like the gods—could not die from old age or sickness, resulted in a disruption of the order of the cosmos and provoked the anger of the king of the gods, Enlil, who tried to wipe out the human race with the universal flood. Ziusudra/Utanapishtim, the archetype of the biblical Noah, is saved in the ark, which floated upon the waters. The growth of the new human race, his descendants, was kept in check by old age and sickness.

The poem's composition centers upon puns, which are of fundamental importance in the anthropogenic story (Bottéro, 1982; Abusch, 1998; Alster, 2002). It should be borne in mind that the pun was a favorite device used by the schools of scribes to develop the hermeneutics of the texts, which the apprentice scribes and their teachers studied and copied (Bottéro, 1992, p. 100). This is the only literary source to deal extensively with the origin and nature of the human being, yet for a long time (the poem was published by W. G. Lambert and A. R. Millard at Oxford in 1969: *Atram-hasis. The Babylonian Story of the Flood)* this source of information was not used because of its hermeneutic wordplay technique, which added to the difficulty inherent in such a poetic text and which was therefore only more clearly explained years later.

In order to create humankind, the gods killed a god with whose flesh and blood they mixed clay to form the new creature. Henceforth, as Bottéro has shown (1982), all the terms employed allow extensive wordplay, providing an interpretative key to the nature of humankind.

The ghost. Abusch (1998), developing these initial ideas, has shown a relationship between the flesh of the god and the ghost (*eṭemmu*), which remained in the underworld for a certain time after the death of an individual. This was the period of time for which the ghost retained its individual identity and that corresponded to the memory those who were still alive had of the dead person. It would clearly be difficult for this to last for more than three generations, that is, to concern older relatives known personally (*cf.* van der Toorn, 1996, p. 54; Abusch, 1995, revised 2002, p. 272; more generally Abusch, 1998, pp. 372–373); other than grandparents (or in exceptional cases, great-grandparents), there remained only the vague memory of ancestors perceived as an indistinguishable single group. The *eṭemmu* has been the subject of various articles: see Abusch, *Etemmu*, in van der Toorn, Becking, and van der Horst, 1999, pp. 309–312. It should be pointed out that many scholars, by imposing their own cultural experiences and philosophy, have identified in the *eṭemmu* an idea very like the European one of the "soul," disregarding the whole range of beings described to scholars since 1964 by Oppenheim (1964). Finally, in this line of thinking, European in outlook, for the sake of completeness we should mention the work of Chiodi (1994), a work that is inadequate in terms of the conclusions it draws as well as limited in terms of the selective nature of the sources it uses, and the work of Spronk (1986, pp. 96–125), wider in scope but with critical weaknesses.

Other terms occur repeatedly in the anthropogeny, always linked by puns: the human intellect (*ṭēmu*, *cf.* puns with *damu* and *eṭemmu*), which stems from the blood (*damu*) of the god, while the bodily element comes from the clay. Thus, the flesh of the god (*šīru*) does not produce the human body. Developing the ideas of Abusch further, we can understand the Babylonian conception of a divine being, "a high ontological density being," as Bottéro has stated (2001, p. 38), a being that, via this "density," was thought of as a luminous splendor (*melammu*). This component acted as a support (just as the human physical body, *zumru*, acted as a support for those elements making up psyche) drawn from the instincts and emotions, linked to the vital forces (and this is the nature of the *eṭemmu* ghost). The body of a god thus corresponded to part of the human psyche. This particular part of the psyche may also be found empirically in the "higher" animals (for example, dogs, donkeys), and it is perhaps in this light that an obscure passage of commentary should be interpreted ("commentaries" are notes by the scribal schools, which provide extremely concise explanations, mostly via puns, of myths, rituals, and divinatory or exorcistic texts), in which it is stated that the *eṭemmu* of some gods are animals (Livingstone, 1986, pp. 82–83, 88–89). In the human being too this element represents the individual "animal nature." We know that the ghosts of those who have not had the chance to progress in life, to attain success and maturity, the vital drives and fulfillment of those qualities belonging to an adult, those desires, loves, and emotions linked to manhood and motherhood (children, adolescents), are among the most restless and dangerous ghosts, since this part of the human psyche—whether because of inertia or unused energy—would wander and haunt the world of the living, generally seeking the fulfillment that premature death had made impossible. The dangerous nature of a ghost that had not been given proper funeral rites was probably consistent with this idea, since these would permit the ghost to pass to the underworld: the ultimate aim of this element of the psyche consisted in reaching the appropriate place, the underworld, after death.

The ability to reason: Human intelligence. Abusch (1998, p. 371) points out that the blood of the murdered god had provided human beings not only with intelligence (*ṭēmu*) but also with their life force (expressed in the poem as the heartbeat, *uppu*, symbolized by the beating of drums). Both the ego and the self, the origin of which, according to Abusch (1998, p. 378 ff.) is again passed on to mankind from the blood of the god, complete the psychological profile, fitting in with the interpretations that can be inferred from consideration of the personal god. The ego and the self are thus parallel to the flesh of the god, which for its part provides both the physical form and the ghost (that is the "animal" element), making up the death soul. Both parts of the murdered god, flesh and blood (respectively *širu* and *damu*), thus have a part to play, within the context of his divine parentage, in passing on to the new being, created by the mixing of clay, his essential characteristics. It is known that the expression *širu u* (*u* = and) *damu* was commonly used to indicate racial or family origins (van den Toorn, 1996, p. 42; Abusch, 1998, p. 370, fn. 15; Stol, 2000, p. 9), thus making even more clear to the contemporary listener the idea of the divine origin of mankind.

The anthropogeny of the *Atrahasis*—even if restricted only to certain elements, namely those that were of interest to its anonymous author—opens up the possibility of interpreting other human psychological features as well, which appear in other texts. Thanks to the information provided here, the systematic treatment of those elements that the modern Western world would define as relating to the soul or the psychological has recently become possible.

Abusch (1998, pp. 378–383) maintains, not without good reason, that the "personal god" (*ilu*) corresponds with intelligence (*ṭému*), thought of as that unique ability to think and plan, bestowed upon humans alone among all living creatures. He refers in passing to the Babylonian proverb "when you plan ahead your god is yours, when you do not plan ahead your god is not yours" (1998, p. 379).

Multiple external souls. Yet the personal god represents an even more complex set of realities. On the one hand this includes features beyond intellectual ability, while on the other it goes back to a system of male and female beings (with which it is contrasted, thus explaining its true significance), which symbolize, in the guise of discrete divine figures, fundamental human characteristics (Oppenheim, 1964; revised 1977). On a higher plane, there is the couple *ilu* ("god": male) and *lamassu* (female); they can be compared with another couple, *ishtaru* (female: translated as "goddess," a name that derives from the goddess Ishtar) and *šédu* (male).

To provide an explanation for the characteristics of these beings, Oppenheim recalls the anthropolgical theory of "multiple external souls" through which the individual finds fulfilment and relates to the outside world. In this respect he gives examples taken from the classical world, the Bible, and the Gospels in order to show how, albeit using different formulae, other cultures have managed to express psychological ideas of multiple external souls, ideas no more unusual in the Western than in the Mesopotamian world (Oppenheim, 1977, pp. 199–201). He compares the Greek *eudaimon* with the *ilu*, whose effect can be seen in a stroke of luck, in the unwitting avoidance of danger, thus leading to the adjective *ilānû* (*ilu* + adjectival indicator *ān*, + adjectival genitive ending *û*) being coined to describe a lucky person. This particular quality is linked to the reason, although from a Western perspective it is completely different in character. The *lamassu*, which is harder to relate to a specific aspect of the ego, may be compared to the Greek *eidolon*, the power that allows individual characteristics of every kind, including physical, to be displayed. *Šēdu*, the male equivalent of *lamassu*, is connected with the life force and the sexual, procreative drive of the individual. In this sense it may be compared with the Latin *genius*. *Ishtaru*, the counterpart of *ilu*, should be linked to *šimtu*, a word normally rendered as "destiny, fortune, fate," all of which are in fact only rough translations. Its meaning may be better understood by translating the word as "destiny," in the sense of the determination of a power (possibly, but not exclusively divine) to act and exert power in the surrounding world; it involves the allocation of personality, necessary in order to find personal fulfillment, completed only with death. We should think of the *daimon*, as described by James Hillmann in *The Soul's Code* (New York, 1996, chapter 1). Once again a parallel may be advanced with the Greek *moira*, but also *physis*, that is, "nature," "inherent quality"; *ištaru* is thus the external soul in relation to fate, in terms of the whole range of daily events, of gifts and capabilities, tasks and duties. It is this that grants a human being the *šimtu* that he will attain in his personal life (Oppenheim, 1977, pp. 201–205).

Arnaud (1996) has shown that the ancient Mesopotamians thought that the fetus was formed by epigenesis (that is by the successive accretion of different parts) rather than by germination. The soul should probably be regarded as being formed in the same way as the fetus. Along with the instinctive and emotional element, which is centered in the ghost (*eṭemmu*) after death, there is also the *zaqīqu* (dream soul: Abusch, 1998, p. 372, fn. 21; Sculock, 2002, p. 1 ff.), which, like the ghost, resides in the physical body. Two other substances should also be mentioned: *bāštu* and *dūtu*, the "life force" (*bāštu* comes from the verb *bāšu*, "to feel ashamed") and "the ability to plan," respectively (Groneberg, 1985; Saggs, 1974, p. 7).

Finally we should mention the *kūbu*, "fetus," which, despite being physical, has certain similarities with the *eṭemmu*. The *kūbu* as an unborn child lives in the underworld and individually in its mother's womb. *Kūbu* was also an underworld deity, a dangerous demon, although it could also be benign and is linked to growth (Stol, 2000, pp. 9, 29–33). The world below, acting as a womb or as Mother Earth, accepts the dead and provides energy to those who are coming into being (Abusch, 1995; revised 2002, p. 217). In a certain sense *kūbu* and *eṭemmu* may be regarded as the beginning and end of this process. In this respect the existence of necromantic rites should be noted, showing that, for witches at any rate, ghosts could be used for advantage (Finkel, 1983–1984; Tropper, 1989), since, like the *kūbu*, they also possessed certain powers.

The manner in which names are assigned to these things, these "multiple external souls," should not be regarded as an inflexible system of classification that did not change over the millennia. In popular thinking some traits and characteristics may have been understood differently, with certain features emphasized or played down, so that in considering Mesopotamian psychology, we should always allow a certain leeway within the elaborate structure set out here.

The *melammu*. The divine splendor (*melammu*) means that the gods are not only similar to, but of the same nature as, the stars (Reiner, 1995, pp. 1–24). This particular detail is significant when considering the most important divine element within the human being. The key to interpreting this lies in the *maqlû*, a complex ritual remedy against magic, by which a man who had been fallen under a witch's spell could be purified. Abusch (1995, reprinted 2002), who has provided the most complete and detailed interpretation of the nature, origin, and extent of this ritual, has pointed out that the witch's spell takes place during a dream and that the affected individual ascends to heaven and becomes one of the stars while taking part in the celebration of the ritual (which may perhaps also have ecstatic significance: Abusch, 1995, reprinted 2002, p. 285). The nature of *melammu* should be considered in this context (Cassin, 1968). The word, along with others related to it (*puluhtu*, "fear [aroused by the sight of the *melammu*]," *namirtu*, "brightness, light [that is the visible nature of the *melammu*]," *rašubbatu*, "awesomeness," *šalummatu*, "radiance"), even if reflecting different shades of meaning, has been compared with the Hebrew *kābōd*, the Greek *charis*, and the Iranian *xvarenâh*. *Melammu* is the splendor that illuminates a god or a temple (although Gilgamesh is also lit up in this way in the Sumerian poem *Gilgamesh and Agga*) and that envelops the person or object from which it emanates: in this sense it is a manifestation not only of divine power but also of life energy, understood in terms of charm, beauty, and attraction.

The nature of the Sumerian world. While it is correct that the Sumerian and Akkadian worlds may be regarded as parts of the same single civilization, it is, however, beyond question that the two peoples differ in certain respects, not just synchronically but also diachronically. The ghost, *eṭemmu*, is called *gidim* in Sumerian (from the Semitic *qādīm*, "ancestor": the Akkadian *eṭemmu* is also probably derived from *gidim*: Abusch, 1998, p. 373). It is not mentioned in the anthropogeny of the Sumerian myth *Enki and Ninmah*, which is directly related to the anthropogeny of the *Atrahasis* poem—this has been studied in detail by Kikawada (1983)—nor in the bilingual anthropogenic myth "KAR 4," in which the motif of killing of divine beings in order to create the human race appears (Abusch, 1998, p. 369 ff.). While there may be an exact semantic overlap between *eṭemmu* and *gidim*, in contrast we should examine the word *lil₂*, where the similarity with Akkadian terminology is more complicated. In general terms it may be stated that *lil*, discussed in detail by Jacobsen (1989), is a translation of the Akkadian *zaqīqu*, which, as well as signifying dream soul, also means "breeze." The term also reappears in the name of the king of the gods, *En- lil₂*, translated as "Lord wind." His realm is the atmosphere, the intermediate element of the cosmos, which at one extreme touches heaven (the home of his father, An), while at its other edge touches the surface of the earth (it is not by chance that the god is called a "trader"). It permits all living beings to exist, and it is indeed the presence of a special kind of wind, the breath, that distinguishes the living from the dead. Enlil is thus closely connected with the movement of air, with the wind, with gusts, and with the breath. The god is regarded as having given life to the universe (life being considered as a breath, *napištum*, Sumerian *zi*). In addition, a specific exhalation of breath consists of a word, and it is no mere chance that this is also a feature of the medium, where the spoken word makes clear to the listener the otherwise unattainable thought of the one with whom he is speaking. This idea relates directly to the sacred nature of the word, both spoken and written, and this is what is behind the use of puns by the scribal tradition when commenting on the texts.

The Sumerian and Akkadian languages both use the same term for "word" as for "matter, affair" (Sumerian *inim* = Akkadian *awātu*), and this is relevant to an analysis of the meaning of the term *lil₂*. The comparison with tempests and blasts of wind, even those that bring destruction (signs of the power of Enlil), and less obvious features, such as life and the word, show clearly how objectification matches subjectification and vice versa, an idea which both Oppenheim

(1964; revised 1977) and Abusch (1998, pp. 379–380) have taken as the basis for their interpretation of personal gods as objectifications of psychological realities, confirming what Eliade (1975, vol. 1, p. 96) had stated in his description of the characteristic features of Mesopotamian religion. *Lil₂* is also a demon, the wind that brings sickness, developed in two demon figures, *Lilû* (male) and *Lilîtu* (female), respectively, *incubus* and *succuba.* These are two specters that emanate from those who have died before having the chance to enjoy sex and procreation (Wiggermann, in Stol, 2000, p. 227), but, in a purely internal sense, it is the mind of the sleeper, who moves in the dream while his body lies still and comes into contact with the divine world (Jacobsen, 1989, p. 274), where the name of the god of dreams, Sigsig, is mentioned (the name Sig[s]ig comes from the Akkadian Ziqīqu/Zaqīqu, the god of the "dream soul, zephyr, breeze"; Oppenheim, 1964, pp. 232–237: "the winds" or "the ever blowing one"). The dream state, like the atmosphere, has an intermediary nature, if another name of the god of dreams in a text may be interpreted as "Enlil with regards to dreams" (Oppenheim, 1964, p. 233). An evil demon lurking in the night or a benign god, which externalizes a state of mind, the dream illustrates the ambivalent nature that is also characteristic of other beings.

The literature and glyptics provide further descriptions of two protective beings, the goddess *Lama* and the god *Utug.* These went in front of and behind the individual, guiding him toward sure contact with higher divine realities, namely toward purification and health (one example taken from an exorcism: *ᵈUdug-sig₅-ga ᵈLama-sig₅-ga he₂-en-da-sug₃- sug₃-ge-eš*, "May the good [*sig₅-ga*] *Utukku* [Akkadian for *Udug*] and the good [*sig₅-ga*] *šedu* [= *Lama*: this identification is made in bilingual texts] go with him [the patient])." The goddess *Lama* was not simply restricted to human beings alone but others also, such as, for example, cities and higher gods (Foxvog, Heimpel, and Kilmer, 1980–1983). As regards the *Udug*, this indicates a demonic, not necessarily benign, being: indeed part of the exorcistic texts clearly deals with the casting out of the *Udug-hul* (*hul*, "evil"), although it should be remembered that there is also a *dingir-hul* (*dingir* = Akkadian *ilu*, "god").

Particular attention should be paid to the personal god and goddess who are portrayed as divine parents. Klein (1982) has shown how the choice of words clearly distinguishes these two beings from natural parents. The "personal god" (Klein correctly expresses reservations as to whether this is a suitable term to use for the situation to which it refers) is the principle from which humanity originates, to whom he should refer during the course of life. This being should not be thought of as clearly defined, if, as Klein demonstrates (1982, p. 303, fn. 3), the same ruler can call upon different gods as his "parents." Even allowing for the fact that the position of rulers may represent a very special case, that of a king, it should be pointed out that the whole idea may not have been so very different as regards the ordinary individual. The expressions generally used are: (Sumerian) *dingir-sag-du₃-ni* = (Akkadian) *ilum bānišu*, "his (= the individual human being's) creator god (= the one who begat him) = the god who created him"; (Sumerian) *ama-dim₂-ma-ni* = (Akkadian) *ummu bānītišu*, "the mother (here a goddess) who produced him"; and (Sumerian) *lu₂-ulu₃ dumu-dingir-ra-na* = (Akkadian) *awīlu māri ilišu*, "man, the son of his god." These external objectifications provide evidence for the existence of a divine principle (albeit divided into two male and female opposites) essential to the human being, evidence that is confirmed by the information in the anthropogenic mythology.

SYRIA-PALESTINE, ANATOLIA. The epigraphic evidence for this region is much less abundant and much more fragmented than that found in Mesopotamia. Even literary evidence is scarcer and less widespread, and it is therefore impossible to provide a similar picture. However, both the fact that Akkadian belonged to the group of Semitic languages spoken in the region, and the geographical proximity of this region to Mesopotamia, which tended to encourage links, lead to the conclusion that the picture was not radically different. It is still not possible, given the nature of the sources, to paint a picture showing the corresponding relationship between the "multiple external souls," as there are only vague references to these. These relate to the word *nbš*, used in the sense of "soul" (van der Toorn, 1996, p. 232), referring to the soul of a Neo-Hittite king (in the eighth century BCE; del Olmo Lete, 1996, pp. 74–77), who wants to ascend to heaven and feast with the gods. *Nbš* is from the same root as the Akkadian *napištum* (see above), which Saggs (1974, p. 8) had previously linked with the Hebrew *nepeš*, taken to mean "external soul." Even a quite well-documented term, such as the Hebrew *'ob* (usually taken to mean "spirit of the dead," comparable to the Akkadian *eṭemmu*), which could be compared with Western Semitic material, contains ambiguities that make it impossible to provide a consistent interpretation (Tropper, *Spirit of the Dead*, in van der Toorn, Becking, and van der Horst, 1999, pp. 806–809). In the silence of the sources it is nonetheless possible to discern a change in the relation between body and soul (meaning by this simply the part of the human being that is not the physical body). During the second and third millennium BCE the distinction between these two elements was emphasized. In Mesopotamia this was clearly illustrated by the *Atrahasis* poem, when the two elements are mixed together, the divine ingredient, that is, the flesh and blood of the god, with the clay. This distinction is part of the common cultural heritage of the Near East region. The theory concerning this has been stated by del Olmo Lete (1996, pp. 53–80) in the context of a study investigating the continuity between Syrian culture of the second millennium and the Western Semitic world of the first millennium. In this study the particular features of the Western Semitic world of the second millennium, as set out in the texts from Ugarit, are compared with the psychological ideas of the Syria-Palestinian culture (and its Punic offshoot in the Mediterranean) in the first millennium.

To identify its distinctive important features, we should examine the Ugaritic mythological series "Baal and Anat" (del Olmo Lete, 1995). This is the broad story of the struggle between life and chaos (considered as death), which has echoes in Mesopotamian mythology, even if they are very distinct and distant, such as the poems concerning the conflict of the god Ninurta against the demon Asakku in Sumerian (called *lugal-e*) and Akkadian, and the Akkadian poem, which is derived from this, on the apotheosis of Marduk, the *Enuma elish.* It consists of three poems: "The Battle of the God Baal with the God Yam," "The Palace of Baal," and "The Battle between the god Baal and the God Mot." The mythological series as a whole is the story of the changing rule of the universe. In the first instance the three sons of the supreme god El, Baal, Yam, and Mot, divide up the three tiers of the cosmos, namely the earth, the sea, and the underworld. But the peace is short-lived. The first poem describes the victory of Baal over the god of the sea, Yam, who represents primordial chaos, like the goddess Tiamat in the *Enuma elish.* The second poem concerns the challenge of Baal, who has become the king of the gods, against his enemy Mot, following the construction of the palace that Baal has had the god of craft, Kothar, build for him as the seat of his rule of the cosmos. Baal is defeated in battle, goes down to the underworld, and is eaten by Morte (Mot). The gods all planned the disappearance of Baal, who on this occasion acts as a symbol of life of which he is patron—confined between the two extremes of birth and death. Since life on earth is struggling under the oppressive heat, his "sister" Anath goes off to look for her "brother"; he has the powers of a weather god and can make life thrive once more. The goddess, enraged, confronts and defeats Mot, tearing him to pieces. Baal is thus freed and able to escape from the stomach of his enemy. But Mot also comes back to life and the two gods confront each other once more. Finally the conflict is resolved by a judgment, handed down by the god El, that persuades Mot to return to his own realms.

This outline of the myth clearly shows, on two levels, the way that life alternates, both in an abstract sense, in contrast with death, and in terms of the cycle of the seasons, the alternating fertility of plant and animal life (W. Herrmann, *Baal,* in van der Toorn, Becking, and van der Horst, 1999, pp. 134–136). Yet the most dramatic adventure of the god Baal goes even further. He is given the epithet *rpu* ("healer"), not only because he has overcome death (Mot) but also because (it should not be forgotten that the word *baal* means "lord") he is the first of the *rpum,* the dead kings who are the ancestors of the sovereign (W. Herrmann, *Baal,* and H. Rouillard, *Rephaim,* in van der Toorn, Becking, and van der Horst, 1999, respectively pp. 135 and 692–700; see "Kingship in the Ancient Mediterranean World, Syria and Palestine. Including Israel"). These characteristics of the god Baal are clear in the texts from Ugarit (fourteenth and thirteenth centuries BCE), but their origins may be much older: some of the soteriological features of Baal can be traced back to texts from Ebla (twenty-fifth century BCE), in which Fronzaroli has managed to find the forerunner of Saint George confronting the dragon (Fronzaroli, 1997a, 1997b; on the closeness of the two divine figures, Hadda, main character in the texts examined by Fronzaroli, and Baal, see W. Hermann, *Baal,* in van der Toorn, Becking, and van der Horst, 1999, p. 132). Besides, Baal is also a *mlk* (Ugaritic = *malik*) chief "adviser" (del Olmo Lete, 1996, p. 56), leader of a group of chthonic beings called the *mlkm* (= Akkadian *mālikū,* plural). When the king dies, he becomes a *mlk* and, as such, becomes one of the group of *mlkm.* The Old Babylonian ritual *kispu* from Mari, a city on the Euphrates, refers to the *mālikū* and is consistent with the Ugaritic cultural passages in this regard. The mythological pattern in the story of the descent to the underworld and resurrection of Baal, the relationship of this god with both the kings and the *rpum* and *mlkm* too, when the kings themselves are also included in these last two groups, provides the outline of a Western Semitic idea that is clearly apparent in the Ugarit texts and with which similar information from subsequent periods should be compared. Nor should we disregard the Hittite concept of the kingship, summarized in the euphemistic expression *DINGIR^LIM-iš kišari,* "he has become a god," to indicate the death of the king. In the west, therefore, both in Syria and in Anatolia, the deification of the sovereign after his death was a distinctive cultural feature, which is only partially paralleled in Mesopotamia. In the first millennium the textual evidence becomes even more scarce; however, it is possible to employ both the archeological evidence as regards funerary rites, paying particular attention to the *tophet* of Punic cities in the west, as well as the biblical and classical sources dealing with the *molk* sacrifice and the alleged sacrifice of children (del Olmo Gete, 1996, pp. 53–61). The *tophet,* a graveyard area where the cremated remains of dead children were buried, shows that passage through fire had acquired the ability to convey to eternal life those who had not had the time to become a part of the normal life of society. The apotheosis and beatific vision of the dead kings, both the kings of Ugarit (who were not cremated in the second millennium) and those of the Hittites (who have handed down to us texts concerning funerary cremation rites in the second millennium) and Neo-Hittites (in the first millennium), were extended in the first millennium to dead children: a socially downward shift that changed eschatology, increasing the division between the physical body (which was to be destroyed by burning) and the incorporeal part of the individual, which was to be dispatched to its proper divine place (del Olmo Gete, 1996, p. 61). Yet the funeral pyres both of Melqart (Sergio Ribichini, *Melqart,* in van der Toorn, Becking, and van der Horst, 1999, pp. 563–565) in particular (Melqart, whose name, *mlk qrt,* means "king of the city," is called "Baal of Tyre"), as well as those of Dido and Hannibal, show that the fire constituted a ritual life-giving moment (Melqart is called the "Herakles of Tyre" and, like the Greek hero, he passes into the fire). One of the most important differences related to cremation: in Mesopotamia destroying the body did serious harm and could deprive the dead person of his identity (Abusch, 1998, pp. 372–378; but del Olmo Gete, 1996, pp. 68–69, interprets part of the same evidence in precisely the opposite way). The Hebrew world too developed differently. The Old Testament condemnation of these ideas, which were considered an abomination, show how the Hebrew cultural environment, consistent with its monotheist creed, did not develop in the same way as, starting from the Canaan cultural beginnings, was typical of the other peoples of the region.

See Also Baal; Canaanite Religion, overview article.

Bibliography

Since Oppenheim (1964) provided a general outline of this, the subject has not been comprehensively dealt with and scholarly research has been restricted to specialist publications. An extensive bibliography is therefore necessary for the reader who wishes to assess and thoroughly examine the topics discussed here. In order to show the way in which the study of the subject has developed, the bibliography is given in chronological order.

A. L. Oppenheim, *Ancient Mesopotamia: Portrait of a Dead Civilization* (Chicago and London, 1964); rev. ed. completed by E. Reiner 1977, pp. 198–206. W. von Soden, "Die Schutzgenien Lamassu und Schedu in der babylonisch-assyrischen Literatur," *Baghdader Mitteilungen* 3 (1964): 148–156. Elena Cassin, *La splendeur divine: Introduction à l'étude de la mentalité mésopotamienne* (Paris, 1968). H. W. F. Saggs, "'External Souls' in the Old Testament," *Journal of Semitic Studies* 19 (1974): 1–12. Mircea Eliade, *Storia delle credenze religiose*, vol. 1 (Florence, 1979); originally *Histoire des croyances et des idées religieuses* (Paris, 1975). Thorkild Jacobsen, *The Treasures of Darkness* (New Haven, Conn., and London, 1976). D. Foxvog, W. Heimpel, and A. D. Kilmer, *"Lamma/Lamassu,"* in *Reallexicon der Assyriologie*, vol. 6, pp. 446–453 (Berlin and New York, 1980–1983). Irving L. Finkel, "Necromancy in Ancient Mesopotamia," *Archiv für Orientforschung* 29/30 (1983–1984): 1–17. Jacob Klein, "'Personal God' and Individual Prayer in Sumerian Religion," *Archiv für Orientforschungen* 19 (1982): 295–306. Jean Bottéro, "La création de l'homme et sa nature dans le Poème d'Atrahasîs," in *Societies and Languages of the Ancient Near East—Studies in Honour of I. M. Diakonoff*, edited by M. A. Dandemayev et al., pp. 24–32 (Warminster, U.K., 1982). I. M. Kikawada, "The Double Creation of Mankind," in *Enki and Ninmah, Atrahasis I 1–351*, and *Genesis* 1–2, *Iraq* 45 (1983): 43–45. Brigitte Groneberg, "Eine Einführungsszenze in der altbabylonischen Literatur: Bemerkungen zum persönlichen Gott," in *Keilschriftlichen Literaturen*, edited by K. Hecker and W. Sommerfeld (= XXXII Rencontre Assyriologique Innternationale) (Berlin, 1985), pp. 93–108. Aldasir Livingstone, *Mystical and Mythological Explanatory Works of Assyrian and Babylonian Scholars* (Oxford, 1986). Klaas Spronk, *Beatific Afterlife in Ancient Israel and in the Ancient Near East* (= Alter Orient und Altes Testament 219) (Neukirchen-Vluyn, Germany, 1986). J. Tropper, *Totenbefragung im Altrn Orient und im Alten Testament* (=Alter Orient und Altes Testament 223) (Neukirche-Vluyn, Germany, 1989) pp. 47–109. Jean Bottéro, *Mesopotamia: Writing, Reasoning, and the Gods* (English translation, Chicago and London, 1992).Tzvi Abusch, "Ascent to the Stars in Mesopotamian Ritual: Social Metaphor and Religious Experience," in *Death, Ecstasy, and the Other Worldly Journeys*, edited by J. J. Collins and M. Fishbane, pp. 15–38 (Albany, N.Y., 1995) (= T. Abusch, ed., *Mesopotamian Witchcraft* [Leiden, 2002], pp. 271–286). Silvia Maria Chiodi, *Le concezioni dell'oltretomba presso i sumeri* (Rome, 1994). Erica Reiner, *Astral Magic in Babylonia* (Philadelphia, 1995). Gregorio del Olmo Lete, "Semitas occidentales," in *Mitología y Religión del Oriente Antiguo*, vol. 2/2: 45–222, edited by Gregorio del Olmo Lete (Barcelona, Spain, 1995). Karel van der Toorn, *Family Religion in Babylonia, Syria and Israel* (Leiden, 1996). Arnaud, D., "Le fœtus et les dieux au Proche-Orient sémitique ancien," *Revue de l'histoire des religions* 213 (1996): 123–142. Gregorio del Olmo Lete, "El continuum cultural cananeo," *Aula Orientalis Supplementa* 14, Sabadell (Barcelona, 1996). Pelio Fronzaroli, "Il serpente dalle sette teste a Ebla," in *Alle soglie della classicità il Mediterraneo tra tradizione e innovazione. Studi in onore di Sabatino Moscati*, edited by E. Acquaro et al., pp. 1135–1144 (Pisa and Rome, 1997) (= 1997a). Pelio Fronzaroli, "Les combats de Hadda à Ebla," *MARI* 8 (1997): 283–290 (= 1997b). Tzvi Abusch, "Ghost and God: Some Observations on a Babylonian Understanding of Human Nature," in *Self, Soul and Body in Religious Experience*, edited by A. I. Baumgarten, J. Assmann, and G. G. Stroumsa, pp. 363–383 (Leiden, 1998). K. van der Toorn, B. Becking, and P. W. van der Horst, eds., *Dictionary of Deities and Demons in the Bible*, 2d ed. (Leiden, 1999). Marten Stol, *Birth in Babylonia and the Bible. Its Mediterranean Setting* (Groningen, Netherlands, 2000). Jean Bottéro, *Religion in Ancient Mesopotamia*, translated by T. L. Fagan (Chicago and London, 2001). Bent Alster, "*ilu awilum: we-e i-la*, 'Gods: Men' versus 'Man: God'—Punning and the Reversal of Patterns in the *Atrahasis* Epic," in *Riches Hidden in Secret Places: Ancient Near Eastern Studies in Memory of Thorkild Jacobsen*, edited by T. Abusch, pp. 35–40 (Winona Lake, Ind., 2002). J. Scurlock, "Soul Emplacements in Ancient Mesopotamian Funerary Rituals," in *Magic and Divination in the Ancient World*, edited by L. Ciraolo and J. Seidel, pp. 1–6 (Leiden, 2002).

Pietro Mander (2005)
Translated from Italian by Paul Ellis

SOUL: GREEK AND HELLENISTIC CONCEPTS

The modern Western idea of the soul has both eschatological and psychological attributes, and the presence of the Greek word *psuchē*, or "soul," in concepts such as psychiatry and psychology suggests that the Greeks viewed the soul in the modern way. Yet the absence of any psychological connotations in the earliest extant usages of *psuchē* shows that at least the early Greek concept of the soul was different from later beliefs. Taking this difference as my point of departure, I shall first trace the development of the conception of the soul of the living, then look at the conception of the soul of the dead, and, finally, analyze the fate of the soul according to Hellenistic religions.

Soul of the Living. The Greek conception of the soul in the Archaic age (800–500 BCE) might best be characterized as multiple. Following the widely accepted terminology developed by the Scandinavian Ernst Arbman (1926, 1927), we can distinguish in the oldest literary texts—Homer's *Iliad* and *Odyssey* (commonly dated to the eighth and seventh century, respectively)—two types of soul. On the one hand, there is the free soul, or *psuchē*, an unencumbered soul representing the individual personality. This soul is inactive (and unmentioned) when the body is active; it is located in an unspecified part of the body. Its presence is the precondition for the continuation of life, but it has no connections with the physical or psychological aspects of the body. *Psuchē* manifests itself only during swoons or at death, when it leaves the body never to return again. On the other hand, there are a number of body-souls, which endow the body with life and consciousness. The most frequently occurring form of body-soul in Homer's epics is *thumos*. It is this soul that both urges people on and is the seat of emotions. There is also *menos*, which is a more momentary impulse directed at specific activities. At one time, *menos* seems to have meant "mind, disposition," as appears from related verbs and the fact that the Vedic *manas* has all the functions of the Homeric *thumos*. As is indicated by the related Sanskrit *dhūmah* and the Latin *fumus*, *thumos* probably once meant "smoke"; it later usurped most of the connotations of *menos*. A word emphasizing the intellect more than *thumos* and *menos* is *nous*, which is the mind or an act of mind, a thought or a purpose. In addition, there are a number of organs, such as the heart and the lungs, which have both physical and psychological attributes.

In Homer, then, the soul of the living does not yet constitute a unity. The resemblance of this kind of belief in the soul to that of most "primitive" peoples strongly suggests that it belongs to a type of society in which the individual is not yet in need of a center of consciousness. Studies that relate the structural elements of Archaic Greek society to the emotional realities of that society, however, are sorely missing; in fact, studies of belief in the soul never seem to investigate this question.

In the course of the Archaic age, we hear of journeys of the soul—an important capability of the free soul that is not mentioned in Homer. Fascinating accounts tell of persons whose souls were reputed to wander away during a trance. It was told, for example, about one Hermotimos of Clazomenae, a city on the western coast of present-day Turkey, that his soul "wandering apart from the body, was absent for many years, and in different places foretold events such as great floods . . . while his stiff body was lying inert, and that the soul, after certain periods reentering the body as into a sheath, aroused it" (Apollonius, *Mirabilia* 3). Here we have a clear case of a person lying in trance whose soul is supposed to have left the body.

A similar case is reported of Aristeas of Proconnesus, an island in the Sea of Marmara. Herodotus (4.14) tells the following local legend. Aristeas entered a fuller's shop in Proconnesus and dropped dead. But, after the story of his death had spread, someone said that he had just met Aristeas outside the town. And when the relatives came to fetch the dead body from the fuller's shop, they did not find it. After six years Aristeas reappeared and composed a poem, the *Arimaspea*, in which he related a journey to the far North. A later account relates that the soul of Aristeas was seen flying from his mouth in the shape of a raven.

Aristeas's disappearance from the shop suggests that his "death" was in fact a deep trance during which his soul was believed to leave his body. The bilocation at the moment of his supposed death fits into a general pattern according to which bilocation always takes place when the free soul leaves the body—that is to say, during sleep, trance, or death. Aristeas's poem apparently used the first person to describe his journey to the Rhipaean Mountains in the North, as do the Siberian shamans when recounting their adventures during trances. Those who knew Aristeas personally would have known that he experienced his adventures only in a trance; others who knew only his poem must have concluded that he had experienced his adventures while awake. These and similar reports have been interpreted as manifestations of a shamanistic influence due to trade and colonization that had brought the Greeks in contact with the shamanistic culture of the Black Sea Scythians in the seventh century. Yet, the shamanistic parallels that have been adduced are either too general—ecstasy and the journey of the soul occur in too many places to be distinguishing traits—or cannot withstand close scrutiny. It seems more acceptable to claim these legends as valid testimonies for the existence of the free soul in Archaic Greece.

Toward the end of the Archaic age, two important developments took place. First, the gradual breakdown of the aristocratic hegemony in the later Archaic age had promoted a certain degree of individualization, and thus the idea of ending up in the unattractive and impersonal beyond that was the Homeric underworld became less and less acceptable. These changes promoted an "upgrading" of the *psuchē*, which in the middle of the fifth century even came to be called "immortal." The philosopher Pythagoras, who lived in the second half of the sixth century, introduced the speculative doctrine of metempsychosis—a doctrine probably influenced by Indo-Iranian sources. Initially, the concept of metempsychosis did not enter the mainstream of Classical Greek religion and remained restricted to marginal religious movements such as Pythagoreanism and Orphism. It was not above ridicule: a contemporary satirist relates that when Pythagoras saw a dog being beaten, he exclaimed: "Stop! Do not beat him. It is the *psuchē* of a dead friend. I recognized him when I heard his whine." However, the doctrine became very popular in post-Classical times.

The second development of the late Archaic age was the gradual incorporation by *psuchē* of *thumos*, which made the *psuchē* the center of consciousness. This transformation has not yet been satisfactorily explained, but it was most likely related to the growing differentiation of Greek society. Because of our limited sources, we can trace the course of this process only in Athens, whence, through the work of the tragedians of the second half of the fifth century, we acquire a detailed look at the changing nature of *psuchē*. Dramatic situations present persons, especially women, whose *psuchē* sighs or melts in despair, suffers pangs, or is "bitten" by misfortune—emotions never associated with *psuchē* in Homer. Characters even address their own *psuchē*, and a particular personality is referred to as, for example, a "mighty *psuchē*" or a "sweet *psuchē*." This development evidently reflects the growth of the private sphere in Athenian society, which promoted a more delicate sensibility and a greater capacity for tender feelings, such as we find more fully in the fourth century.

The culmination of the *psuchē* as the center of man's inner life was the necessary precondition for the Socratic view that a man's most important task was to take care of his *psuchē*. This view of the soul was taken up by Plato, throughout whose work concern about the *psuchē* remains axiomatic. As Friedrich Solmsen observes, "The *psyche* which he holds to be immortal and for whose fate after life reincarnation offered some meaningful answer, is now the central organ whose vibrations respond to the individual's sufferings and emotional experiences and whose decisions initiate his activities" (Solmsen, 1982, p. 474). Plato even goes so far as to include all intellectual functions in the *psuchē* as well.

Aristotle, on the other hand, almost completely discarded *psuchē*, but "care for the soul" and "cure of the soul" remained important topics for the philosophical schools of the Epicureans, the Stoics, and the Cynics. Pursuing the concept of *psuchē* in these schools, however, belongs more to the area of the history of philosophy than to that of religion.

So far, we have been concerned only with *psuchē* as the soul of the living. However, in the second half of the sixth century, the philosopher Anaximenes seems to have used the term *pneuma*, the purely biological breath, to denote the soul of the cosmos in analogy to the soul of man (the testimony is debated, however). The Pythagoreans also believed in an "infinite breath" (*apeiron pneuma*) that was "breathed in" by the cosmos. And in the course of the fifth century, various passages appear in which *pneuma* is used where we would have expected *psuchē*. Yet *pneuma* never completely lost its biological connection and it did not replace *psuchē* in designating the eschatological soul. In Hellenistic times, *pneuma* figures notably in various philosophies, but it rises to religious prominence only among Hellenistic Jewry and in early Christianity.

Souls of the Dead and the Afterlife. The Greeks, like many other peoples, considered the soul of the dead to be a continuation of the free soul of the living. In the Homeric epic it is always *psuchē* that leaves for the underworld; the dead in the afterlife are indeed often called *psuchai*. The body-souls *thumos*, *menos*, and *nous* end their activity at the moment of death—their connection with the body is the cause of their disappearance. The *psuchē*, however, was not the only mode of existence after death; the deceased was also compared to a shadow or presented as an *eidōlon* ("image"), a word that stresses the fact that for the ancient Greeks the dead looked exactly like the living.

The physical actions of the souls of the dead were described in two opposite ways. On the one hand, the Greeks believed that the dead souls moved and spoke like the living; the image of the deceased in the memory of the living play a major part in this activity. There is a corollary of this idea in the *Odyssey* (book 11) where Orion and Herakles are depicted as continuing their earthly activities. On the other hand, the souls of the dead are depicted as being unable to move or to speak properly: when the soul of Patroclus left Achilles, he disappeared squeaking (*Iliad* 23.101). The circumstance of death was also of some importance in the formation of ideas about the soul of the deceased. Homer (*Odyssey* 11.41) describes the warriors at the entrance to Hades still dressed in their bloody armor. Aeschylus (*Eumenides* 1.103) has the *eidōlon* of Clytemnestra display her death wounds, and Plato elaborately explains this idea, refining it in a way by adding that the soul also retains the scars of its former existence. On vases, the souls of the dead are even regularly shown with their wounds, sometimes still bandaged.

The idea of the soul of the dead in ancient Greece appears, then, to be influenced by the image of the deceased in the memory of the living, by the circumstances of death, and by the brute fact of the actual corpse. These ideas were never completely systematized and could occur in one and the same description. Just after his death, for example, Patroclus can be described as appearing to Achilles exactly as he was during his life. And as long as he has contact with Achilles he speaks like a normal mortal; only when the contact is over does he leave squeaking. With the passing of time the precise memories of a specific person fade away, and it is understandable that the more personal traits gradually recede behind a more general idea of the dead as the opposite of the living. In time, the individual soul becomes just a member of the countless number of "all souls." The souls move in "swarms" in the Homeric underworld and in the tragedies; the idea of the underworld found its way even into the famous description in book 6 of Vergil's *Aeneid*.

Earlier generations of scholars freely made inferences of belief in the soul from funeral rites. Nowadays we have become much more careful, but the evidence from Homer and other sources suggests that a proper funeral functioned as a rite of passage into afterlife for the dead. This seems to be reflected, for example, in the myth of Sisyphus, who instructed his wife not to perform the proper funeral rites after death so that he could persuade the queen of the underworld, Persephone, to let him return to the land of the living.

After a proper funeral the soul went to murky Hades, (the name is perhaps best translated as "house of invisibility"), which is ruled by the king of the same name and his wife Persephone, the daughter of the goddess Demeter. The comfortless picture of Hades as "the land of no return" can hardly be separated from Babylonian and Semitic ideas as they appear in the Hebrew scriptures (Old Testament). The exact location of Hades remained vague; in the *Iliad* it was situated under the earth, in the *Odyssey* at the edge of the world. In the Homeric epics, the underworld was still reached by just crossing the river Acheron, but in the course of the Archaic age the transition between life and death became less "automatic" than in Homer. The new concern for the soul reflected itself now in the introduction of the ferryman Charon and the idea of guidance by the god Hermes Chthonios.

Not everyone, though, went to Hades. In the *Odyssey*, various heroes, such as Menelaus, went to the Elysian Fields. Others, such as Achilles, went to the so-called Isles of the Blessed, where the poet Hesiod, who lived somewhat later than Homer, also situated part of the "heroic" race, which included all the Homeric heroes. From the seventh century on, initiation into the mysteries of Eleusis becomes one of the means for the common man to share in the happiness the heroes enjoyed. As the Homeric *Hymn to Demeter* (1.480ff.) says of those who have seen the secret rites: "Prosperous is that one of men upon earth who has seen them; but he who is uninitiated and has no share in the rites never has a portion of like happiness when he is dead and under the murky gloom." Any ethical requirements are still notably absent from this promise of the life eternal. At the end of the sixth century, however, clear indications of a more ethical view of the afterlife appeared, according to which the just were rewarded and the bad penalized, views especially connected with the Pythagorean and Orphic movements. These views also influenced ideas about the fate of Eleusinian initiates. However, despite the great interest in the afterlife that can be found in the literature connected with the mysteries, there is no specific mention of the soul or metempsychosis; the initiates apparently expected to arrive in the underworld in person.

On the whole, however, it must be stated that the ancient Greeks displayed only a limited interest in the life hereafter. It is in keeping with this limited interest that they did not worship their ancestors. The one festival that commemorated them had probably already ceased to be celebrated at the end of the Classical age. It is also part of this lack of interest in the afterlife that the Greeks of the Archaic and earlier Classical age rarely ever mentioned souls of the dead returning to the upperworld. Only the philosopher Plato, in the fourth century, mentions the existence of ghosts wandering around tombs and graveyards. It is true that during the Athenian festival of the Anthesteria the *kēres* were believed to appear on earth, but is is unlikely that these were the souls of the dead as earlier generations of scholars, who were strongly influenced by animistic views of Greek religion, liked to believe.

HELLENISTIC RELIGIONS. Toward the end of the fifth century the idea developed that the body remained behind on earth but the soul disappeared into the air. The celestial eschatology became highly important in the dialogues of Plato, who introduced the idea that the soul, or at least its immortal part, returned to its original abode in the heavenly area. The large-scale loss of Hellenistic writings makes it difficult to trace the idea of the soul in detail. However, a late oracle of Apollo at Claros, which contains Hellenistic views, declares:

> When someone asked Apollo whether the soul remained after death or was dissolved, he answered, "The soul, so long as it is subject to its bonds with the destructible body, while being immune to feelings, resembles the pains of that [the body]; but when it finds freedom after the mortal body dies, it is borne entire to the aether, being then forever ageless, and abides entirely untroubled; and this the First-born Divine Providence enjoined." (translated in MacMullen, 1981, p. 13)

In various of his writings, the philosopher Plutarch (c. 40–120 CE) also described the flight of the soul to the heavens, in particular to the moon, which became increasingly popular as the final abode of the soul. These views, like metempsychosis, remained popular among philosophers and the educated classes, but it is virtually impossible to establish to what extent they were shared by the lower classes.

As regards the mystery religions, which consisted of a mixture of Greek and native elements, it seems highly unlikely that the cults of Isis, the Syrian Goddess (Dea Syria), and Cybele had any specific teachings about the fate of the soul; at least there are no such indications within the considerable evidence we have regarding these cults. Rather late sources relate that the mysteries of Dionysos and Sabazios were directed to the purification of the soul, but the information is not very specific. Even the so-called Orphic Hymns do not display the otherworldly interest we might expect from hymns carrying the name of Orpheus. Mithraism is the only cult about which anything more detailed is known, that being only that the soul was supposed to pass through the seven spheres of planets after death.

When the rhetorician Menander (third century CE) composed a small handbook on oratory for such customary occasions as birth, marriage, and funerals, he also included some directions on how to speak about the afterlife: "for it is not unsuitable," he notes, "on these topics also to philosophize." He refers to Elysium,

> where Rhadamanthus, Menelaus, Achilles, and Memnon, reside. And perhaps, better, he [the deceased] now lives among the gods, traversing the heavens and looking down on life below. Perhaps even, he is reproaching those who mourn for him; for the soul is related to the divine, descends thence, but longs again to mount to its kind—as Helen, the Dioscuri, and Heracles, they say, belong to the gods' community (translated in MacMullen, 1984, p. 11).

The ambivalent view of the afterlife reflected in this passage is typical of Hellenistic religions. The gods of the Hellenistic period were generally thought of as gods effective in this life, just as the more traditional gods had been. Earlier generations of scholars have often considered the mystery cults competitors with Christianity in regard to the life hereafter, but it now appears more and more clear that the interest of most people in Hellenistic times rested firmly with this life. The inscriptions that have given us innumerable epitaphs display only a negligible interest in the soul or the life eternal. It was only with Christianity that there developed a new interest in the soul and the life hereafter, but its doctrine of the resurrection of the flesh always remained repugnant to the pagan world.

BIBLIOGRAPHY

The standard study, still well worth reading, has long been Erwin Rohde's *Psyche: The Cult of Souls and Belief in Immortality among the Greeks*, translated from the original German edition (1894) by W. B. Hillis (London, 1925). Ernst Arbman's fundamental study is "Untersuchungen zur primitiven Seelenvorstellung mit besonderer Rucksicht auf Indien," pts. 1–2, *Le monde oriental* 20 (1926): 85–222 and 21 (1927): 1–185. My book *The Early Greek Concept of the Soul* (Princeton, 1983) confronts the Greek material with the latest insights from social anthropology and folklore. David B. Claus's *Toward the Soul* (New Haven, 1981) is a detailed, if conceptually limited, investigation of all the passages in Greek literature in which the term *psuchē* appears. Valuable studies of the development of the concept of *psuchē* are three by Friedrich Solmsen: "*Phren, Kardia, Psyche* in Greek Tragedy," in *Greek Poetry and Philosophy*, edited by Douglas E. Gerber (Chico, Calif., 1984), pp. 265–274; "Plato and the Concept of the Soul (*Psyche*): Some Historical Perspectives," *Journal of the History of Ideas* 44 (July-September 1983): 355–367; and *Kleine Schriften*, vol. 3 (Hildesheim, 1982), pp. 464–494. Fritz Graf discusses in detail the ideas of the hereafter connected with the Eleusinian mysteries in *Eleusis und die orphische Dichtung Athens in vorhellenistischer Zeit* (Berlin, 1974). Helmut Saake's "Pneuma," in *Paulys Realencyclopädie der classischen Altertumswissenschaft*, suppl. vol. 14 (Munich, 1974), is an up-to-date survey of notions of *pneuma*. Arthur Darby Nock's *Essays on Religion and the Ancient World*, vol. 1 (Cambridge, Mass., 1972), pp. 296–305, and Ramsey MacMullen's *Paganism in the Roman Empire* (New Haven, 1981) and *Christianizing the Roman Empire* (New Haven, 1984) demonstrate the lack of interest in the afterlife in the Hellenistic religions.

New Sources

Adamson, Peter. "Aristotelianism and the Soul in the Arabic Plotinus." *Journal of the History of Ideas* 62 (January 2001): 211–232.

Blumenthal, H. J. *Aristotle and Neoplatonism in Late Antiquity: Interpretations of the 'De Anima.* London, 1996.

Durrant, Michael, ed. *Aristotle's De Anima in Focus.* New York, 1993.

Levison, John R. *The Spirit in First Century Judaism.* New York, 1997.

Schibli, Hermann S. "Xenocrates' Daemons and the Irrational Soul." *Classical Quarterly* 43 (1993): 143–168.

Steiner, Peter M. *Psyche bei Platon.* Göttingen, 1992.

Wagner, Ellen, ed. *Essays on Plato's Psychology.* Lanham, Md., 2001.

Yengoyan, Aram A. "Whatever Happened to the Soul? A Review Essay." *Comparative Studies in Society and History* 46 (April 2004): 411–418.

JAN N. BREMMER (1987)
Revised Bibliography

SOUL: INDIAN CONCEPTS

The scripturally based historical religions that originated in India, including Buddhism, Hinduism, Jainism, and Sikhism, hold nuanced and distinctive perspectives on the concept of the soul. In a shared cultural environment, each tradition sought to relate itself to influential and established religious ideals, yet to distinguish its own position with respect to that ideal. The soul is one such concept. All of the traditions accept the fundamental ontological premise that there is an animating and vital incorporeal aspect of human beings, the presence of which distinguishes life from death. The status of the soul with respect to bodily life and death is a key issue, and in the Indian traditions this implicates the law of *karma*, which holds that actions have a residual force that has influence over an individual beyond the present lifetime and is thus the driving force behind the cycle of birth and death (*saṃsāra*). Notably, this residual force of *karma* is never equated with the soul in Indian traditions. Liberation from this cycle, which all the traditions define as the ultimate goal, is achieved by spiritual knowledge and practice as defined by each tradition.

It is necessary to keep strictly to the notion of the soul as an animating and vital principle when discussing Indian traditions generally, for the spiritual meanings of the term from Western classical traditions, including the immortality of the soul and its participation in an eternal afterlife, which are commonly understood as a functional definition of *soul* in the contemporary Western context, are not found in Indian traditions. Indian religions invest the concept of the soul as a life-force with their own distinctive meanings. For example, a major difference between classical Indian and Western traditions is the Indian traditions' critique of the individuated state in their visions of spiritual liberation. In Indian religions, ordinary bodily embodiment is the individuated state that acts and thus gives rise to *karma*. Since spiritual liberation is defined as the cessation of *karma*, and thus release from the cycle of birth and rebirth, the individuated state in which one produces *karma* is dissolved when spiritual liberation is achieved. This means not only that the body is dissolved, but also the individuated state of the life-force or soul. There is no philosophically developed idea of a personified, individually identifiable soul that continues to exist in an eternal afterlife in Indian religions. How the residual force of *karma* can influence successive lifetimes is a problem that the Indian traditions address and will be discussed with respect to each tradition in the sections that follow. Their common ground is that in their imagining of the achievement of spiritual liberation, which is freedom from *karma* and the cycle of birth and rebirth, the individuation characteristic of ordinary embodiment is dissolved.

The Indian traditions tend to envision the path of spiritual liberation in epistemological and devotional terms. However, there is an exception to the general rule in Indian traditions that individuality is incompatible with the achievement of spiritual liberation, and this approach adds an ontological dimension. There is a special category of the embodied, perfected being who is spiritually liberated; this category also contrasts with Western notions, which tend to view embodiment as indicative of an imperfect state. In Indian traditions, one can be perfectly spiritually realized and yet remain in the body, though it is understood that this is a rare occurrence. This is not an ordinary instance of embodiment, since perfected beings do not create *karma* and its effects, although they do act in the world. Each Indian tradition has its own nuance in describing the nature of the perfected being, but they have in common the assertion that the perfected being has a holistic vision of truth beyond the ordinary limitations of humankind. This special category of perfected, embodied being generally describes categories of religious leaders in the Indian religious traditions, including the *gurū* in Hinduism, the Buddha in Buddhism, the Jina in Jainism, and the ten *gurūs* in Sikhism.

In addition to these major differences with Western notions of the soul, the Indian traditions pose distinctive philosophical questions with respect to the concept, including whether the soul is temporary or permanent; whether it is autonomous; whether it is real or not; whether it is subject to *karma* or not; and whether it is personal or universal. The overwhelming evidence of profound differences between Indian and Western ideas of the soul has led many to question the applicability of the term to Indian traditions, to the extent that the influential classical Sanskrit term *ātman*, which is most commonly believed to correspond to the Western notion of the soul, is no longer translated as *soul* by modern translators of the Upaniṣad philosophical texts; they instead translate *ātman* as "self." The advantages of using "self" are as a marker of difference from Western notions, and as an indicator of the Indian traditions' concern with personality, *karma*, and self-awareness in defining the nature of humankind. The main drawback is the Western tendency to equate self with ego, which is unfortunate because Indian traditions offer a profound and consistent critique of the ego as a limited and materialistic obstacle to true spiritual knowledge. In this light, it seems that the connotations of the available English terms are either too transcendent or too materialistic to represent the Indian positions, which revel in explorations of the gray area in between, toward developing ideas on this mediating concept.

VEDIC CONCEPTS OF THE SOUL. The Vedas, which include the Vedic hymns (c. 1500–1000 BCE), the liturgical and mythological Brāhmaṇas and Āraṇyakas (c. 1000–800 BCE), and the philosophical Upaniṣads (the earliest texts date to circa 700–400 BCE, the middle texts to circa 400 BCE–100 CE, with later texts written up till the sixteenth century), are some of the earliest oral and written texts in Indian religious tradition. Hinduism claims all of these texts as its own revealed canon. Buddhism, Jainism, and Sikhism reject the Vedas as a foundational scripture, but maintain dialogue with formative concepts, especially those articulated in the Upaniṣads.

In the ritualistic world of the Vedic hymns, the main concern is with transformations, especially those effected by the performance of sacrifice. An influential hymn (*Ṛgveda* 10.90) portrays the creation of the universe by the primordial, bloodless sacrifice of a Cosmic Man. This hymn may have provided a cosmic precedent for the Vedic people's central ritual practice of blood sacrifice with animals, primarily goats and horses, as represented in many Vedic hymns. The hymns preserve the sense of gravity and care with which the people approached the taking of a life, and their rationale for the ritual involved speculation on the soul. For example, a hymn on the horse sacrifice (*Ṛgveda* 1.162) proclaims that the horse is not really harmed by the slaughterer's axe; instead, the horse goes on pleasant paths to the realm of the gods as an offering, bearing the prayers of the community.

Other hymns deal with the subject of natural death outside of the ritual context of sacrifice; in these cases the body is also burned to effect a transition (*Ṛgveda* 10.14, 10.16, 10.56). The biological body (*śarīra*) is burned, but again it is asserted that the fire in a sense makes the body whole, unharmed, or "cooked fully" so that the dead person or beloved (nonsacrificial) horse can "go forth to the fathers." The hymns seem to suggest that there is then a brief, disembodied stage, in which the spirit has no body, breath, or senses, before joining with another body. This stage, which is only very briefly represented in the hymns, involves the concept of *tanū*. The *tanū* is perhaps a subtle structure that attracts various cosmic forces, such as *manas* (mind, heart, life-force; see *Ṛgveda* 10.58), *asu* (animating power), *prāṇa* (breath), and mental forces to intersect and facilitate the creation of a new body. Thus it makes individual the cosmic universal forces that are unborn (*aja*) and thus transcendental. These forces that are unborn are represented in another famous creation hymn, the *Nāsadīya* (*Ṛgveda* 10.129), in which creation is a "stirring" of vital forces such as heat and breath, presenting an important universal homology to the human microcosm. Another way that this universal dimension is expressed in the Vedic hymns is through the concept of *ṛta* (*Ṛgveda* 7.66.12–13, 1.105.12), which has been translated as "truth" and "cosmic order"; more recently, it is translated as "harmony." *Ṛta* is the subtle foundation of the universe that is distinct from, yet harmonizes, all of the elements within it, thus connecting the potentially chaotic parts into a related whole.

These ideas concerning the levels of human and cosmic reality and their intersection, which were suggested but not philosophically developed in the Vedic hymns, provided material for the central focus on metaphysical and cosmological issues in the subsequent yet connected texts, the Upaniṣads.

Interpretation of the Vedic hymns was initiated in the Brāhmaṇas and the Āraṇyakas, but it was the Upaniṣads that took up the question of knowing the knower in a sustained fashion, to the extent that the Upaniṣads were considered to be the branch of the Vedas that contained salvific knowledge (*jñānakāṇḍa*), in contradistinction to the other branches, which were considered to contain information about rites (*karmakāṇḍa*).

Upaniṣad means "hidden connection"; the texts by this name purport to describe the unseen vital forces operative in the universe, their connection to things that can be seen, including humankind, and humankind's ability to know them through a mystical as opposed to a rational knowledge. The texts' thesis is that through self-knowledge one can break through ordinary consciousness, which is most often represented in the texts as dualistic perception, and in so doing achieve the ultimate experience of unity with the foundational essence of the universe.

The Upaniṣads use the term *brahman* to indicate this foundational essence, which is a synthesis of the Vedic hymns' ideas of *aja* (unborn) and *ṛta* (harmony), yet points beyond them, since *brahman* is understood to be an ontological absolute, an unchanging ground of being that supports and pervades all things in the universe. As the primary entity, *brahman* is an undifferentiated, subtle unity; in gradual acts of self-transformation, this subtle unity experiences a densification that creates aspects of the universe. Humankind is understood to be a densification of *brahman.* In terms of ordinary perception, one cannot see the essence of *brahman* within humankind, but one can infer its presence from the necessities of living, including breath (*prāṇa*), as well as the fact that one "eats food and sees what is pleasing" (*Chāndogya Upaniṣad* 5.12–18); these are the specificities of name and form (*nāmarūpa*) and distinguishing marks (*liṅga*) of personal identity, and they point toward, but are not identified with, the essence of *brahman* within.

The essence of *brahman* as it relates to humankind is known as the *ātman*, or self. The *ātman* is humankind's "hidden connection" to *brahman.* While the *ātman* is seemingly individualized, since it exists in every human being, it is not stamped with the individual personality of a given person; rather, it is the agent that holds together the individual's personality, and as such it is identical in everyone. Thus it is possible to see a relationship between the concept of *ātman* and that of *tanū* from the Vedic hymns.

The *ātman* can be thought of as a "central instance of cognition" in humankind, indicating its special connection to mind, for the ordinary personality is subject to *karma* and transmigration until one achieves knowledge of the *ātman*'s identity with *brahman.* At death, "a person consisting of mind only" (that is, one who knows *brahman*) merges with *brahman*, never to return; in contrast, those who perform actions, such as sacrifices, pass into elements such as sky and wind before taking birth on earth again; and at a still lower level, "those who do not know these two paths become worms, insects, or snakes" (*Bṛhadāraṇyaka Upaniṣad* 6.2.15–16). The *ātman* holds together the phenomenological personality, but it has no distinguishing marks characteristic of individuality. It is thus an agent of continuity, not a mark of personal identity. When spiritual liberation is achieved, the *ātman* merges with *brahman*; the individual marks of a person are dissolved, both in terms of the body and personality structure, and in terms of the mind, as individual self-reflective consciousness dissolves into pure, nondualistic consciousness.

Hindu Concepts of the Soul. As many scholars have noted, the Upaniṣads are the most influential texts in terms of subsequent developments in Hinduism. Drawing on them, several prominent philosophical schools in medieval India developed distinctive perspectives on the nature of the self, including the possibility that one could achieve spiritual liberation while in the state of embodiment.

The Advaita Vedānta school of Śaṅkara (c. 788–820 CE) posits that the phenomenal world is illusory (*māyā*), and is made up of layers or sheaths (*kośas*). The subtle body (*sūkṣma śarīra* or *liṅga śarīra*), which preserves personal identity and is subject to *karma* and transmigration, is made up of three sheaths; breath (*prāṇamāyā*), mind (*manomāyā*), and cognition (*vijñānamāyā*). In contrast, the only reality is *brahman* and *ātman*; however, humankind does not know this due to the ignorance (*avidyā*) of reliance on sense perception. Since ignorance is the source of humankind's bondage, knowledge (*jñāna*) is the path to liberation; specifically, knowledge of the nonduality (*advaita*) of reality.

While the Advaita perspective has been understood to be uncompromisingly world-rejecting, the viewpoint does permit the thesis that one can be liberated while embodied. The *Bṛhadāraṇyaka Upaniṣad* states that "He attains *brahman* even here" (4.4.7); Śaṅkara's commentary on this verse understands it to mean that "He attains *brahman*, identity with *brahman*, liberation, living in this very body." Thus, liberation is epistemological, not ontological; it requires one to transcend bodily consciousness by dissociating with the physical and psychological aspects of the body. A modern illustration of this approach would be the world famous female *gurū*, Ānandamayī Mā (1896–1982), who referred to her physical body only as "this body," and who would not feed herself, but was instead fed by her devotees.

Later medieval philosophers responded to Śaṅkara's position on the nature of humankind's relationship to *brahman* as well as the possibility of living liberation. These philosophers all have a theistic component to their philosophies. Rāmānuja (1017–1137 CE) was the chief proponent of the Viśiṣṭādvaita or Modified Nondualist school of Vedānta. In his view, the *ātman* (or *jīva*) is literally bound to the body and its psychological modalities; this is not illusory as in the Advaita system. Though the self remains untouched by the faults of humankind, it is still bound up with them, and must be liberated by exhausting the negative effects of *karma.* Thus, while Śaṅkara tended to put the emphasis on knowledge, Rāmānuja put it on action. One is to perform duties of a devotional, moral, and ritualistic nature with complete detachment (*karma yoga*) towards the results or benefits of the action. God is the focus of these activities. In Rāmānuja's thought, dedicated and unselfish action devoted to God burns off bad *karma* and increases knowledge, so that one can achieve equanimity in this life and achieve liberation when one leaves the body upon death (*videhamukti*). In this liberated state, the self reaches God's (Viṣṇu's) heaven (Vaikuṇṭha), where it resides in a *brahman*-like state in intimate association with God but not identical with God; thus the modified nondualism of this school's perspective.

Madhva (1238–1317) was the chief proponent of the Dvaita or Dualist school of Vedānta. In his philosophy, God (Viṣṇu) is the only independent, self-existent (*svatantra*) reality; all other aspects of existence are dependent (*paratantra*) on God. This is a relational, not absolute, dualism; the individualized self of humankind is a reflection of God, but this knowledge is obscured by an ignorance that is metaphysically derived from God. The self becomes deluded into identifying itself as the ego, and this creates the bond of *karma*. The will of God drives the system. In an argument that was subsequently controversial, Madhva suggested that it was God's will to liberate some selves but not others, an idea that resembles a theory of predestination. The path to liberation is through action, including (in ascending stages) detachment from the body, devotion to God, study and critical reflection on the scriptures, and meditation on the attributes of God as presented in the scriptures; all of these represent indirect knowledge of God. The final stage is the direct and immediate vision of God, which is permitted by God's grace. This is living liberation, but it is not the final state of spiritual liberation, for the body continues to exist through a special category of residual *karma* (*prārabdha-karma*). Ultimate liberation takes place when the self leaves the body at death and travels through the worlds of the gods, at last arriving at the enjoyment (*bhoga*) of God, in which the liberated self communes with God in full and blissful consciousness.

The Tamil-language Śaiva Siddhānta school, which tradition views as founded by Meykaṇṭār (thirteenth century) and whose canonical texts date from the mid-twelfth to the fourteenth centuries, shares many of its central concepts with the Sanskrit school of the same name. Śaiva Siddhānta views the world as composed of three irreducible realities, Lord (*pati*), soul (Tamil, *uyir*; Skt., *paśu*), and bond (Tamil, *iruḷmala*; Skt., *pāśa*). As described by the most prolific author in the tradition, Umāpati Civācāryār (c. 1290–1340), in his canonical text, *Tiruvaruṭpayaṉ* (The fruit of divine grace), the soul is located between Lord and bond. Through knowledge and devotional action, the soul loosens the grip of the aspects of the bond that are *karma* and *māyā*; then, through the Lord's grace, the soul achieves the attainment of the Lord and experiences bliss and pure knowledge in a relationship where "the two are as one," which is this school's distinctive take on the *advaita* theory.

Hindu Śākta Tantric tradition centralizes the Goddess in its path to spiritual liberation, understanding her to be *brahman*. While accepting the monism of *advaita*, this form of Tantrism emphasizes the relationship between one and many; *brahman* is one but is embodied in many forms, including the *ātman* in humankind. A distinctive ritual practice is to "interidentify" (*nyāsa*) aspects of the microcosm (many) with the macrocosm (one) through physical, mental, and verbal practices, creating a set of relations between them. The adept then dissolves the distinctions, creating a reunification of both the spiritual and material aspects of reality.

Buddhist Ideas of the Self. In early texts, the Buddha (c. 563–486 BCE) is represented as a teacher who places the greatest emphasis on the human condition as it is experienced here and now. A famous example is the metaphor of the wounded man from a middle-length discourse attributed to the Buddha, by which he contrasts the immediacy of the situation with the misguided posing of contextual questions that cannot be answered: "It is as if. . . a man who had been wounded by an arrow thickly smeared with poison . . . would say, 'I will not have this arrow removed until I have learned the name of the man [who shot him]. . .the clan to which he belongs . . . whether he is tall or short. . . .'" (*Majjhima Nikāya* 1, 428). It is this emphasis that informs a current stream of discussion in Buddhist studies, with some practitioners and scholars questioning the relevance of ideas of metaphysical import, including *karma* and rebirth, to the Buddha's original teachings. These proponents themselves acknowledge, however, that, historically, Buddhism has been understood by practitioners to involve these ideas, as evidenced by the traditional assertion that the Buddha saw his own past lives at the time of his enlightenment, and that his foster-mother saw her past lives as she passed into *nirvāṇa* (Pali, *nibbāna*), as well as the influential image of the "wheel of becoming," which pictures both pleasant and painful realms of rebirth.

The Buddha used the same lexicon of religious terms in use during his time, including those in the Upaniṣads, to distinguish his thought from others. His insistence on *anātman* (Pali, *anattā*), meaning "no *ātman*," is an example of this. There is no unchanging subtle essence to humanity, for everything arises and exists in a codependent, mutable fashion to become material phenomena, including humankind, which is composed of the five aggregates: body (*rūpa*), sensation (*vedanā*), perception (Skt., *saṃjñā*; Pali, *saññā*), mental formations (*saṃskāra*; *samkhāra*), and consciousness (*vijñāna*; *viññāṇa*). Yet with humankind, *karma* is implicated, as the following saying attributed to the Buddha suggests: "There is no 'being' found here [within oneself], only a heap of karmic constituents. Just as the word 'chariot' is used when we come across a combination of parts, so we speak conventionally of a [human] being when the Five Aggregates are present" (*Saṃyutta Nikāya* 1, 135).

What, then, is the continuity that carries forth the influence of *karma* incurred on either an individual or a social basis? Drawing on the early Buddhist text, the *Sutta Piṭaka*, Karel Werner (1988) has argued that there are several terms that suggest an idea of a personality structure in the early Pali texts that is rather like the *tanū* in the Vedic hymns. All of them are mental, not bodily, as we saw with the *ātman* of the Upaniṣads and Vedānta. One term is the "mental body" (*nāmakāya*), which controls the mental aggregates and is opposed to the body; another is the mind (*manas*), the sixth sense within the perception aggregate that controls the other senses; another is consciousness (*viññāṇa*), one of the aggregates and the one that is understood to give rise to the whole person in the chain of dependent origination; and another is the "collection of one's characteristics or habits" (*citta*). Drawing on the *abhidamma* philosophy of early Buddhism, Rupert Gethin (1994) has suggested that *bhavaṅga*, a form of consciousness that defines who one is, is determined for the next birth by the last full consciousness process of the present life. Each of these concepts denotes a way to imagine the continuity of constantly changing elements through death and into rebirth, as required by the *karma* theory. However, any confusion of these terms with an unchanging essence such as *ātman* was understood to represent ignorance, which was suffering (*dukkha*). Later texts in the Mahāyāna school emphasized the doctrine of *śūnyatā* (emptiness), that everything was empty of own-being, amplifying the message of the earliest texts that there is no unchanging essence.

JAIN CONCEPTS OF THE SOUL. Discourses attributed to the spiritual leader (Jina) Mahāvīra (c. 599–467) demonstrate his profound concern with instructing disciples in self-discipline, which is primarily understood to involve the liberation of the soul (*ātman* or *jīva*) from the bondage of *karma*. In the *Uttarādhyayana Sūtra*, which is believed to record the final lectures of Mahāvīra prior to his liberation and is thus one of the most important texts in the Śvetāmbar sect's canon, he lists nine eternal verities that define the universe and provide the context for humankind's striving for liberation (*Uttarādhyayana Sūtra* 28.14): sentient soul (*jīva*), insentient nonsoul or matter (*ajīva*), contact of *karma* with the soul (*āsrava*), bondage of the soul by *karma* (*bandha*), meritorious forms of *karma* (*puṇya*), demeritorious forms of *karma* (*pāpa*), blockage of the contact of *karma* with the soul (*saṃvara*), dissociation of the soul from *karma* (*nirjarā*), and liberation (*mokṣa*, *nirvāṇa*).

A dualism exists at the center of Jain ontology and soteriology. Sentient souls are nonsubstantial and innumerable; they are characterized by consciousness, bliss, and energy. Insentient nonsouls are characterized by physical matter, space, motion, rest, and time. Together they make up the universe, in a connection that is constituted by *karma*. Improper karmic actions are imagined to be a fine dust that sticks to the soul. The path of liberation (*mokṣa-mārg*) is in essence the sundering of this connection; thoughts and practices that result in detachment are encouraged, so that the soul is "dry" and will not attract the dust of *karma* as would a "wet" or passionate soul. The soul is coterminous with the body in its current state of bondage (*svadehaparimāṇa*), and experiences the joys and sorrows of *karma*. For those who seriously pursue the path of purification, ultimately the soul completely releases itself from connection to matter. In the final state of liberation the soul is *kevalin* (possessing infinite knowledge), alone and autonomous, residing immobile for eternity at the highest point of the universe in Jainism's traditional cosmology. Yet even here there is a reminder of the soul's journey from the body, for the soul retains the outline shape of the body, yet it is featureless.

There are several conditions Jainism sets in terms of the possibility of achieving spiritual liberation. First, it is crucial that one has a human birth. Jains believe that animals are in the process of advancing through *karma*, which informs the Jains' cardinal practice of *ahiṃsā* (nonviolence), but only human beings can achieve spiritual liberation. Further, it is understood that mendicants, rather than laypeople, are in a position to achieve *mokṣa*. On the macrocosmic level, Jain cosmology suggests that there are only certain places and times when *mokṣa* is possible; thus, one can be born and live at a time when spiritual liberation is not possible. In this case, making progress towards *mokṣa* remains ethically enjoined. Mendicants engage in rigorous practices in order to obliterate voluntary *karma* and even involuntary bodily actions, in keeping with ideal Jain figures; for example, celebrated monks have fasted to death, and Jinas are popularly understood to have adamantine bodies. Jain laypeople focus not so much on the ideology of *mokṣa-mārg*, though they do practice five vows similar to the monks', but on devotional activities that produce good *karma* or merit, including providing material support for the mendicants, endowing temples, performing pilgrimages, celebrating festivals, and singing praises to the Jinas; these activities foster the well-being of individuals and the community of Jains.

SIKH CONCEPTS OF THE SOUL. Sikhism considers the soul (*ātman* or *jīva*) embodied in humankind to be a divine spark (*joti*): "The body belongs to the material world, but the spirit or soul in it is the essence of God" (*Ādi Granth* 695). God is known by several names in the *Ādi Granth* scripture (*Akāl Purakh*, the Timeless One; *Ik Oaṅkār*, One Being Is; *Sat Kartār*, the True Creator); God is formless and never incarnates, but is spiritually manifest in all the aspects of creation. The problem for humankind is the state of *haumai*, in which the person believes that he or she is independent and self-reliant, and is thus ignorant of God's nature and the connection between God and soul. A corollary of *haumai* is *māyā*, by which humankind is unable to see the oneness and reality of God through the veil of seemingly individualized aspects of the world. These fundamental misunderstandings influence one's *karma*, which in turn leads to rebirth.

The goal of spiritual liberation is to replace the sense of "I-am-ness" with identification with the divine will of God. A key practice is *nām-simran* or remembrance of the divine name, which as a practice is an individual or group recitation of scriptural verses. It is understood to be more than this, however, because the word (*bāṇī*) of God is the one true *gurū* subsequent to the passing on of the tenth *gurū*, and as such is what leads humankind toward God-consciousness on a daily basis, permitting humankind to experience unity with God through meditation on God's word.

According to Gurū Nānak's *Japujī*, which opens the Sikh scriptures, there are five realms of consciousness in humankind's progression towards spiritual liberation: *Dharam khaṇḍ*, awareness of the world and one's actions; *Jñāna khaṇḍ*, knowledge of the greatness of God's creation; *Saram khaṇḍ*, spiritual illumination; *Karam khaṇḍ*, innate performance of moral action; and *Sac khaṇḍ*, realization of the truth of oneness with God. The emphasis in the Sikh tradition is for all Sikhs to strive to become a *jīvanmukti*, one who experiences the fullness of God consciousness in the here and now.

Bibliography

Vedism and Hinduism

Brooks, Douglas Renfrew. *The Secret of the Three Cities: An Introduction to Hindu Śākta Tantrism.* Chicago, 1990. Beautifully written introductory yet comprehensive discussion of Hindu Tantric worship of the Goddess; includes translation of the influential *Tripurā Upaniṣad.*

Deutsch, Eliot. *Advaita Vedānta: A Philosophical Reconstruction.* Honolulu, 1980. A short, lucid presentation of the fundamental concepts of a philosophical school whose teachings have been influential from medieval times until the present day.

Fort, Andrew O., and Patricia Y. Mumme, eds. *Living Liberation in Hindu Thought.* Albany, N.Y., 1996. A meticulous and accessible edited volume exploring classical Hindu philosophical and theological discussions of the soul through embodied spiritual liberation in Vedānta, Yoga, and Śaivism, with a comparative concluding essay.

Hallstrom, Lisa Lassell. *Mother of Bliss: Ānandamayī Mā (1896–1982).* New York, 1999. Very engaging scholarly discussion of a beloved and internationally famous female *gurū.*

Harper, Katherine Anne, and Robert L. Brown, eds. *The Roots of Tantra.* Albany, N.Y., 2002. This important volume takes up the issue of defining Tantra and explores its meanings and practices in history, art and archaeology, and texts, including comparison with the Vedas.

Mahony, William K. *The Artful Universe: An Introduction to the Vedic Religious Imagination.* Albany, N.Y., 1998. Very accessible discussion of the philosophical and artistic imagination as revealed in Vedic hymns and the Upaniṣads.

O'Flaherty, Wendy Doniger, ed. *The Rig Veda: An Anthology.* New York, 1984. Remains the most accessible and interesting translation of key selections from this famous collection of hymns.

Olivelle, Patrick. *Upaniṣads.* New York, 1996. Classic translation of twelve principle Upaniṣads, including a lucid introduction to the texts' literary history, composition, cosmology, and theories of humanity.

Pechilis, Karen, ed. *The Graceful Guru: Hindu Female Gurus in India and the United States.* New York, 2004. An accessible discussion of historical, philosophical, cultural, and gender issues on female *gurūs* through an introduction, biographical articles on ten *gurūs*, and an afterword.

Prentiss, Karen Pechilis. *The Embodiment of Bhakti.* New York, 1999. Includes an introduction to the Tamil Śaiva Siddhānta school, along with an analysis and translation of *Tiruvaruṭpayaṉ*, one of its fourteen canonical texts.

Roebuck, Valerie J, trans. and ed. *The Upaniṣads.* New York, 2003. A new translation of thirteen principle Upaniṣads, including the *Maitrī Upaniṣad.* Includes a short, lucid introduction to the texts' history, authorship, and key concepts.

Slaje, Walter. "Water and Salt (III): An Analysis and New Translation of the Yājñavalkya-Maitreyī Dialogue." *Indo-Iranian Journal* 45, no. 3 (2002): 205–220. Important and interesting discussion of the *ātman* as a "central instance of cognition" that represents the highest concentration of the "distilled essence" of *brahman.*

Werner, Karel. "Indian Concepts of Human Personality in Relation to the Doctrine of the Soul." *Journal of the Royal Asiatic Society of Great Britain and Ireland* 1 (1988): 73–97. Werner has argued forcefully and convincingly that *soul* as it is commonly understood in Western tradition is not a category that applies to Indian traditions. This article, which is a substantially revised version of an earlier essay ("Personal Identity in the Upaniṣads and Buddhism," in Victor B. Hayes, ed., *Identity Issues and World Religions* [Bedford Park, South Australia, 1986], pp. 24–33), addresses the philosophy of human personality in the Vedic hymns, the Upaniṣads, and the Sutta Piṭaka in the Pali canon of early Buddhism.

Buddhism

Anderson, Carol. *Pain and Its Ending: The Four Noble Truths in the Theravāda Buddhist Canon.* London, 1999. Revisions the historicity of the four noble truths, arguing that they may not have been a central teaching originally, but emerged as such around the middle of the first millennium.

Egge, James R. *Religious Giving and the Invention of Karma in Theravāda Buddhism.* London, 2002. This study provides an important historical contextualization of the development of the *karma* theory in early India, including comparison with Brahmanical and Jain theories.

Gethin, Rupert. "Bhavaṅga and Rebirth According to the Abhidamma." In *The Buddhist Forum*, vol. 3 (1991–1993), edited by Tadeusz Skorupski and Ulrich Pagel, pp. 11–35. London, 1994. Argues that a special form of consciousness provides the link between birth and rebirth.

McDermott, James P. "Karma and Rebirth in Early Buddhism." In *Karma and Rebirth in Classical Indian Traditions*, edited by Wendy Doniger O'Flaherty, pp. 165–192. Berkeley, Calif., 1980. This article provides an important review of several early Buddhist perspectives on reconciling the doctrine of impermanence with the theory of *karma* and rebirth.

Mitchell, Donald W. *Buddhism: Introducing the Buddhist Experience.* New York, 2002. An accessible and interesting single-volume scholarly introduction to early Buddhism; Buddhism in India, Tibet, and East Asia; Buddhism in Asia today; and Buddhism in the West.

Ñāṇamoli, Bhikku, and Bhikku Bohdi, trans. *The Middle-Length Discourses of the Buddha: A Translation of the Majjhima

Nikāya (Teachings of the Buddha). Somerville, Mass., 1995; 2d ed., 2001. Well-received translation of early sayings attributed to the Buddha on *nirvāṇa* and the four noble truths. Includes introductory discussion and summaries of the discourses.

Omvelt, Gail. *Buddhism in India: Challenging Brahmanism and Caste.* New Delhi, India, 2003. An accessible new reading of Buddhism in India through the lens of B. R. Ambedkar's (1891–1956) strong emphasis on the ethical and egalitarian nature of the Buddha's thought in his critique of Hindu metaphysics and social structure.

Walters, Jonathan S. "Gotamī's Story." In *Buddhsim in Practice,* edited by Donald S. Lopez, pp. 113–138. Princeton, N.J., 1995. Translation of a popular story on the Buddha's foster-mother's *nirvāṇa,* with a lucid introduction that explains the significance of her recollection of her past lives for Buddhists.

Walters, Jonathan S. "Communal Karma and Karmic Community in Theravāda Buddhist History." In *Constituting Communities: Theravāda Buddhism and the Religious Cultures of South and Southeast Asia,* edited by John Clifford Holt, Jacob N. Kinnard, and Jonathan S. Walters, pp. 9–39. Albany, N.Y., 2003. Convincingly argues that "sociokarma" is an underrepresented topic in scholarship on Theravāda Buddhism, and provides a seven item typology, from social *karma* to the *karma* of institutions. The other articles in this volume offer diverse, relevant reflections.

Werner, Karel. "Indian Concepts of Human Personality in Relation to the Doctrine of the Soul." *Journal of the Royal Asiatic Society of Great Britain and Ireland* 1 (1988): 73–97. See annotation in Vedism and Hinduism section.

Jainism

Cort, John E., ed. *Open Boundaries: Jain Communities and Cultures in Indian History.* Albany, N.Y., 1998. Eleven fascinating articles, the majority discussing textual materials, though a couple of articles discuss sacred space and ritual. In the introduction the editor intriguingly notes a parallel between Jain soteriological and social meanings of "other."

Cort, John E. *Jains in the World: Religious Values and Ideology in India.* New York, 2001. Drawing on texts and fieldwork, the author discusses relationships between the prescriptive ideology of the path of liberation and the experience of worldly well-being in the lives of Jain people in Gujarat, India.

Granoff, Phyllis. "Life as Ritual Process: Remembrance of Past Births in Jain Religious Narratives." In *Other Selves: Autobiography and Biography in Cross-Cultural Perspective,* edited by Phyllis Granoff and Koichi Shinohara. Oakville, Ontario, 1994. (Reprinted as "Jain Stories Inspiring Renunciation," in Donald S. Lopez, ed., Religions of India in Practice, pp. 412–417 [Princeton, N.J., 1995].) Provides a translation of Jain didactic stories illustrating humankind's inability to recognize former kin in new births, and the karmic consequences.

Jaini, Padmanabh S. *The Jaina Path of Purification.* Delhi, 1979. Classic account of Jain beliefs from an analysis of authoritative textual materials, providing distinction between the two major sects in Jainism. Includes very detailed discussion of types of *karma* and stages of the soul's path towards liberation. Also includes many illustrative diagrams and photographs, one an image of a liberated soul in the shape of a body.

Jaini, Padmanabh S. "Karma and the Problem of Rebirth in Jainism." In *Karma and Rebirth in Classical Indian Traditions,* edited by Wendy Doniger O'Flaherty, pp. 217–238. Berkeley, Calif., 1980. The author discusses the topics with reference to classical texts. Includes two appendixes, one a diagram and discussion of Jain cosmology, and the other a speculative discussion of how the effects of *karma* are transferred at rebirth.

Kelting, M. Whitney. *Singing to the Jinas: Jain Laywomen, Maṇḍaḷ Singing, and the Negotiations of Jain Devotion.* New York, 2001. Important fieldwork-based discussion of the participation of laywomen today in Jain devotional practices and their teaching activities therein.

Sikhism

Cole, W. Owen, and Piara Singh Sambhi. *The Sikhs: Their Religious Beliefs and Practices.* London, 1978. Remains the most accessible and comprehensive single volume that covers the history, beliefs, and practices of the Sikhs. Includes appendixes on the Sikh code of conduct, translations of key prayers, and the structure of the *Ādi Granth* scripture.

McLeod, Hew. *Textual Sources for the Study of Sikkhism.* Chicago, 1990. Provides translations of key texts in an accessible volume, including hymns to the divine name, stories of the *gurūs,* and the Sikh Code of Conduct.

Singh, Dharam. *Sikh Theology of Liberation.* New Delhi, 1991. Concise, engaging account of Sikh beliefs concerning the soul.

Singh, Nikky-Guninder Kaur. *The Feminine Principle in the Sikh Vision of the Transcendent.* Cambridge, U.K., 1993. Important feminist study of pervasive images of the feminine in Sikh scripture, including the image of the bride as a symbol of the beauty of both soul and body.

Thursby, Gene R. *The Sikhs.* Leiden, 1992. Concise and accessible volume focusing on the history and community of the Sikhs. Illustrated with beautifully reproduced black-and-white photographs with explanative captions.

KAREN PECHILIS (2005)

SOUL: BUDDHIST CONCEPTS

It is only slightly paradoxical to say that Buddhism has no concepts of the soul: Its most fundamental doctrine teaches that no such thing exists and that the realization of this truth is enlightenment. In *The Buddha and His Teachings* (Colombo, 1957), G. P. Malalasekera, a Sinhala statesman and lay Buddhist, states this position forcefully:

> In its denial of any real permanent Soul or Self, Buddhism stands alone. This teaching presents the utmost difficulty to many people and often provokes even violent antagonism towards the whole religion. Yet this doctrine of No-soul or Anatta, is the bedrock of Buddhism and all the other teachings of the Buddha are intimately connected with it. The Buddha is quite categorical in its exposition and would have no compromise. In a famous passage He declares, "Whether Buddhas arise in this world or not, it always remains a fact that the constituent parts of a being are lacking in a Soul," the Pali word used for "Soul" being Atta. (pp. 33–34)

Of course, one must be careful about what exactly is being denied here. The closest direct equivalent to "soul" in Sanskrit or Pali is *jīva,* from the verbal root *jīv,* meaning "to live." In Jainism, it denotes an individual, transmigrating, and eternal entity; and in the Vedānta school of Hinduism, the related term *jīvātman* denotes the individual (but not universal) form of the world soul, called *ātman* or *brahman.* In one context, Buddhism uses this term to deny the existence of the soul. The questions whether such a *jīva* is identical to, or different from, the body are two of a list of "unanswerable questions"—unanswerable for the clear epistemological reason that since no *jīva* really exists, it cannot be identical to or different from anything. But in other contexts the word *jīva* and the closely related term *jīvita* are used uncontroversially to refer to animate life in contrast to inanimate objects or dead beings. One of the "constituent parts of a being," as Malalasekara called them, is termed *jīvitendriya* ("life faculty"), which has both physical and mental forms; its presence in a collection of such constituents is essential for that collection to be alive, or loosely for that "being" to "exist." What is denied by Buddhism is that any such collection contains or is equivalent to a permanent independent entity, whether individual or universal. The word standardly used in Buddhism to refer to such a (nonexistent) entity is *ātman,* or in Pali, *attan* (nominatives ātmā and *attā* respectively). In Indo-Aryan languages this (or related forms) often functions simply as the ordinary reflexive pronoun, used in the masculine singular for all numbers and genders. But since at least the time of the Upaniṣads it has also been used in religious and philosophical writing to refer to an eternal essence of humanity. By contrast, Buddhism is referred to as *anātmavāda* ("the teaching of not-self, or no-soul"). Other terms are used to refer to that whose ultimate reality Buddhism denies, but they can all, like *jīva* and *ātman,* also be used uncontroversially in other contexts. Examples are *pudgala* (*puggala*) or their synonyms *puruṣa* (*purisa*), usually translated "person," and *sattva (satta),* "being." (*Puruṣa* is the term for "soul" in the Sāṃkhya school of Hinduism.) If Buddhism denies, then, the existence of any ultimately real self, soul, person, or being, how does it account for the existence of human beings, their identity, continuity, and ultimate religious goal?

It is never denied that at the level of "conventional truth," in the everyday transactional world, there are more or less stable persons, namable and humanly recognizable. At the level of "ultimate truth," however, this unity and stability of personhood is seen to be merely a matter of appearances. Ultimately (or in some schools of Buddhism, in fact, only penultimately) there exist only collections of impersonal and impermanent elements (*dharma;* Pali, *dhamma*) arranged into temporary configurations by the moral force of past deeds (*karman*) and by self-fulfilling but self-ruinous desire and selfishness (both cognitive and affective). There are different ways of analyzing the person in terms of these elements. One of the most ancient and frequent methods used is a list of five categories, aggregates, or constituents of personality (*skandhas*; Pali, *khandhas*), which are body, or material form, and the four mental categories, namely feelings, perceptions (or ideas), mental formations (a heterogeneous class, most of which are volitional or dispositional), and consciousness. Common also is a list of twelve sense-bases (*yatanās*), comprising the six senses (the usual five plus mind, always regarded as a sense in Buddhism) and their six corresponding subjects or fields. There are also eighteen elements (*dhātus*), which are the six senses, their objects, and the six resultant sense-consciousnesses. The various schools of Buddhism went on to produce many other lists, some involving quite large numbers, which develop and elaborate this basic idea. Whatever the list, the idea behind it is explained by this excerpt from the Pali commentary to a passage in the canon in which the Buddha speaks of "an ignorant person":

> [The Buddha] uses conventional language [here]. Buddhas have two types of speech, conventional and ultimate. Thus "being," "man," "person," [the proper names] "Tissa," "Naga" are used as conventional speech. "Categories," "elements," and "sense-bases" are used as ultimate speech. . . . The fully enlightened one, the best of speakers, declared two truths, the conventional and the ultimate; there is no third. Words [used by] mutual agreement are true because of worldly convention; words of ultimate meaning are true because of the existence of elements. (*Saratthappakāsinī,* vol. 2, p. 77)

This analysis of personhood is nontemporal; personal continuity is accounted for by a theory of temporal atomism in which what appears to be a continuing and identical person or self is held to be in fact a series of discrete elements in an objectively given time sequence. Each discrete temporal particle in the succession of mental and physical elements is called a "moment" (*kṣaṇa;* Pali, *khaṇa*). Each of these moments is divided into phases or submoments, usually those of "arising," "presence," and "cessation." There is a frequent and conscious parallel in the texts between the ordinary, "conventional" events of birth, life, and death and the "ultimate" phases of each moment. The Buddha is alleged to have said, "Ultimately, as the constituents of personality are born and grow old, moment by moment, so you, monk, are born, grow old and die." Estimates of the length of these moments varied, some assuming a subliminal, even infinitesimal length, others seeing a moment as roughly the length of a perception or thought (and so resembling the notion of a sense-datum in Western philosophy). Whatever the postulated length, these moments are seen as discrete entities that are nevertheless held together in individual "streams" (a common Buddhist metaphor). This individuation is effected in two ways. First, it is effected by the simple fact of the body. Mental moments are necessarily associated in any one human lifetime with a material body (though there are in Buddhist mythology some nonhuman, nonmaterial worlds), and the body is assumed to be necessarily numerically self-identical. Second, there are held to be certain kinds of conditioning relations (loosely, "causal laws") in the process of *kar-*

man, which explain mental continuity both within one lifetime and over a series of rebirths. Among these conditioning relations are such things as contiguity between adjacent moments in a successive series and qualitative similarity between earlier and later parts of one "stream."

The two closely related problems of how karmic streams are held together and of how an act and its result are connected in one (and only one) series of rebirths, given the instantaneous arising and ceasing of momentary elements, led to a great deal of debate among Buddhist thinkers and to a great deal of new theory. One school, for example, thought that a special element, called possession or acquisition (*prāpti*), came into existence with each act in order to bind it to the stream in which it occurred, while another element, nonpossession or nonacquisition (*aprāpti*), served to keep away elements and acts not belonging to the stream. Two metaphorical terms were used by most schools to depict the process of act and retribution: *vāsanā* ("perfuming, trace") and *bīja* ("seed"). These traces or seeds were deposited in the mind by actions and remained there until their karmic result occurred. This process was called *vipāka* ("maturation, ripening"), and the result was *phala* ("fruit"); indeed, in Indian thought, *bīja* and *phala* commonly mean simply cause and effect. Sometimes particular kinds of mind, or forms of consciousness, were designated as the locus or vehicle of these traces or seeds. One school spoke of a subtle mind (*sūkṣma-citta*), another of a root-consciousness (*mūla-vijñāna*), in which the seeds of *karman* were stored. From these sorts of speculation arose a notion that was to have great importance in the Mahāyāna tradition: that of the store- or receptacle-consciousness (*ālaya-vijñāna*). Like all forms of consciousness, this was thought to be impermanent, momentary, and characterized as not-self, but it was also thought to be the place from which there arose not only the karmic results of past acts but also, in the more idealist versions, the (illusory) experience of an objective world. Many opponents of this idea, both within and without the Buddhist fold, saw this idea as amounting to a soul-in-disguise. One tradition, which seems at one point to have been very widespread in India but for which scarcely any reliable sources remain (it is known only, with one exception, through the distorting lens of others' refutations), was called the Pudgalavāda, the Personalist school, since it actually used the taboo word *pudgala* to denote what continues through the process of rebirth.

In the Māyāyana tradition, particularly in Tibet and China, another very important idea, which was often associated with the concept of the store-consciousness, was the *tathāgata-garbha* ("embryo of the Enlightened One"). This concept provided a solution not to the problem of connecting acts and their results but to that of how a conditioned, unenlightened phenomenon (or rather, a collection of phenomena) such as a human could attain the unconditioned enlightenment of *nirvāṇa.* The embryo of the Enlightened One was said to exist, pure and untarnished, in all beings; the task was to discover it. Insofar as "soul" is taken to mean something like "that which is spiritually most valuable in human beings and which makes it possible for them to transcend their ordinary psychophysical conditions and attain the religiously ultimate goal," this may be called a Buddhist notion of the soul. Certainly, in some of the developments of the idea, particularly in China and Japan, where one reads (in English) of the "Buddha mind" or "Buddha nature" inherent in all beings, one seems—although only at first sight—to have returned to the universal-essence view of *ātman* in the Upaniṣads, which the Buddha so trenchantly rejected.

Many of these ideas are technical, even scholastic, details, in the elaboration of basic Buddhist doctrine. But how does Buddhism address the question of self-consciousness, the linguistic and reflexive awareness of oneself that has led so many traditions of thought to see humans as possessing a "soul" different from the rudimentary consciousness of animals? (In Western philosophy the classic exposition of this is by Descartes.) In the philosophical schools of Mahāyāna, the conscept of *svasaṃvedanā* was developed; this may be translated "self consciousness" or "reflexivity," but Buddhist thinkers held that it was not consciousness of *a* self, or *the* self, but merely the capacity of consciousness *itself.* That is, the internatl structure of consciousness is self-refelxive, but it cannot be concluded from this that it reflects a real self or soul that exists outside the momentary arising and cessation of the mind. Another kind of account of this, which gives more of a sense of the dynamics of Buddhist thought and practice than do the details of scholasticism or the abstract arguments of philosophy, can be seen in the way in which Buddhism supposes that one's sense of self develops—and disappears—in the progression from ordinary unenlightened human to enlightened saint. The teaching of no-soul takes effet in two major ways, as one loses gradually the "fetters" that bind one to the wheel of truth.

First, on "entering the stream" bound for enlightenment, one of the fetters lost is *satkāyadṛṣṭi* (Pali, *sakkayadiṭṭhi*). Often translated as "personality belief," literally it means "the view of a really existing body," although "body" here does not denote simply the physical body but all the five constituents of personality seen as a group. "Personality belief" is the explicit view, or assumption, that what appears to be an individual person, the psychophysical conglomerate, represents or implies a real, permanent self or soul. It does not refer to the phenomenological or experiential sense of being a self, but to the use of this sense, however vaguely, as actual or potential evidence for a metaphysical theory. Losing this fetter thus constitutes a conscious allegiance to the Buddhist denial of self as a doctrine, without any immediate disappearance of the underlying subjective or "self-ish" pattern of experience.

Second, there is this underlying sense of self as the continuing subject of experience and agent of action, referred to in Buddhist thought by the term *asmimāna,* "the conceit 'I am.'" This fetter, which is necessarily part of consciousness for the unenlightened, is an experiential datum or reaction pattern that is lost at the time of enlightenment; indeed, its loss is precisely what enlightenment is. The term is made up of two parts: *asmi* is the first-person singular of the verb to be, thus "I am"; *māna* comes from a verbal root meaning to think, but it regularly has the connotations of proud or conceited thought. For this reason the translation "the conceit 'I am'" is useful, since not only can it point to the fact that the experiential datum of an "I" is taken in Buddhism to be a conception, something made up by a mental act, but also it suggests that this artificial mental construction is necessarily regarded with "conceited" pride and attachment. Thus not only is "the conceit 'I am'" a cognitive fact, or aspect of consciousness (for the unenlightened); it is also a moral (or rather immoral) event. The idea that the experiential datum of an "I" is in fact the result of an act of utterance—an act performed automatically and unconsciously, but still an act because it is operative in the process of *karman*—is embodied in the term *ahaṃkāra.* This is most often explained, by Indian tradition as well as by Western scholarship, as I-making or I-construction—from *aham,* "I," and *kāra* (from the verbal root *kṛ*), "making." It can also, complementarily, be taken as "the utterance of 'I.'" Along with *mamankāra,* "the utterance of 'mine,'" the term describes one of the seven underlying tendencies operative in unenlightened consciousness. Thus, the Buddhist view is that through the act of uttering "I" or "I am," explicitly or implicitly, a self-positing and self-creating subjectivity is constructed, to which inevitably the person in whom it occurs is attached, and through which all his forms of "selfishness" (conceptual and moral) arise.

Two stories in the ancient texts illustrate this attitude and show both the conceptual and the psychological relation between the ideas or utterances "I" and "I am" and the impersonal elements that are the "ultimate" constituents of the human person. A king, enticed by the mellifluous sound of a lute, asks his servant to bring him the sound. They bring the lute, but the king exclaims, "Away with the lute, I want the sound!" The servants explain, "This thing called a lute is made up of a great number of parts. . . . It makes a sound [the verb is *vadati,* literally, 'speaks'] because it is composed of a number of parts—that is, the box, strings. . . ." The king then takes the lute, breaks it up into smaller and smaller pieces, and finally throws it away. The moral is drawn: "In this way, monks, a monk investigates the constituents of personality. . . . But for him there is no 'I,' 'mine,' or 'I am.'"

The story of the elder Khemaka is similar. On hearing that he "does not consider there to be a self or anything belonging to a self" in the five constituents of personality, some other monks exclaim, "Is he not then an *arhat* [an enlightened saint]?" Khemaka hears of this but tells them that he is not an *arhat,* because "with regard to the five constituents, I have a sense of 'I am,' but I do not see '*this* is what I am'!" He explains by analogy with the scent of a flower: The smell is there, but it is impossible to say exactly from where it originates (whether from petals, colors, pollen or some other source). "Although, friends, a noble disciple has put away the five lower fetters (including personality belief), still there is a residue in the constituents of personality of the conceit of 'I am,' of the desire for 'I am,' of the underlying tendency to 'I am,' which is not finally destroyed." If one practices the life of meditation to the full, he says, these things (and with them all the higher fetters) will eventually disappear. When this happens, *nirvāṇa* is attained, and the teaching of no-soul has served its purpose.

SEE ALSO Ālaya-vijñāna; Buddhist Philosophy; Dharma, article on Buddhist Dharma and Dharmas; Karman, article on Buddhist Concepts; Nirvāṇa; Pratītya-samutpāda; Sarvāstivāda; Sautrāntika; Tathāgata-garbha.

BIBLIOGRAPHY

Translations of Buddhist texts directly relevant to this issue were mainly made into French in the first half of the century. These will be available in specialized libraries and remain by far the best source, since the translators provide many references to other texts and other useful information as well as giving direct access to the primary materials. Titles include Étienne Lamotte's *Le traité de l'acte de Vasubandhu, Karma*-siddhiprakaraṇa (Brussels, 1936); his translation of the Chinese text *Dazhidulun,* traditionally attributed to Nāgārjuna, as *Le traité de la grande vertu de sagesse,* 5 vols. (Louvain, 1944–1980), is a treasury of scholarship on almost every aspect of Buddhism. Louis de La Vallée Poussin translated the Chinese version of the most important work of Buddhist scholasticism, *L'Abhidharmakosa de Vasubandhu,* 6 vols. (1923–1931; Brussels, 1971). The last section of this work, a discussion of the concept of the person between an "orthodox" Buddhist and a member of the Personalist school, was translated from the Sanskrit and Tibetan versions by Theodore Stcherbatsky, as *The Soul Theory of the Buddhists* (1920; Vāranāsi, 1970). The Pali version of this debate is included in the *Kathīvatthu,* translated by Shwe Zan Aung and Caroline Rhys Davids as *Points of Controversy* (London, 1915). Important texts of the Sanskrit and Tibetan traditions have been translated and discussed by Joe Wilson *in Chandrakīrti's Sevenfold Reasoning: Meditation on the Selflessness of Persons* (Dharamsala, 1980), and by Jeffrey Hopkins in *Meditation on Emptiness* (London, 1983).

Secondary sources include my *Selfless Persons: Imagery and Thought in Theravada Buddhism* (London, 1982), which discusses the doctrine of *anattā* as presented in the Pali texts; David S. Ruegg's *La théorie du Tathāgatagarbha et du Gotra* (Paris, 1969), which discusses the *tathāgata-garbha* theory, as presented in Sanskrit and Tibetan texts; and Paul Williams's *Mahāyāna Buddhism: The Doctrinal Foundations* (London and New York, 1989), which treats these and other aspects of the Mahāyāna tradition in its entirety. Three older works, dated in some ways perhaps but still valuable, are Edward Conze's *Buddhist Thought in India* (1962; Ann Arbor, 1970), Arthur Berriedale Keith's *Buddhist Philosophy in India and Ceylon* (Oxford, 1923), and E. J. Thomas's *The History of Buddhist Thought,* 2d ed. (1951; New York, 1967). Buddhist notions of the soul, along with those from a number of different religious traditions, are discussed by the Christian theologian John Hick in *Death and Eternal Life* (London, 1976).

New Sources

Brown, B.E. *The Buddha Nature: A Study of the Tathagatagarbha and Alayavijñana.* Delhi, 1991.

Forman, R.K.C. *The Problem of Pure Consciousness: Mysticism and Philosophy.* New York, 1990.

Hamilton, S. *Early Buddhism: A New Approach: the I of the Beholder.* Richmond, 2000.

Lopez, D. S. *Buddhism in Practice.* Princeton, 1995.

Vasubandhu, and S. Anacker. *Seven Works of Vasubandhu, The Buddhist Psychological Doctor.* Delhi, 1984.

Williams, P. *Altruism and Reality: Studies in the Philosophy of the Bodhicaryavatara.* Richmond, 1998.

Williams, P. *Mahayana Buddhism: The Doctrinal Foundations.* New York, 1989.

STEVEN COLLINS (1987)
Revised Bibliography

SOUL: CHINESE CONCEPTS

An early reference to the Chinese theory of the "soul" records an explanation on human life offered by a learned statesman in 535 BCE: the earthly aspect of the soul (*po*) first comes into existence as the human life begins; after *po* has been produced, the heavenly aspect of the soul (*hun*) emerges. As generally understood, *hun* is the spirit of a person's vital force that is expressed in consciousness and intelligence, and *po* is the spirit of a person's physical nature that is expressed in bodily strength and movements. Both *hun* and *po* require the nourishment of the essences of the vital forces of the cosmos to stay healthy. When a person dies a natural death, his or her *hun* gradually disperses in heaven, and the *po*, perhaps in a similar manner, returns to earth. A violent death may cause the *hun* and *po* to linger in the human world and perform evil and malicious acts.

Underlying this theory of the two souls is the *yinyang* dichotomy, which is often associated with the *Book of Changes*, one of the most ancient and philosophically sophisticated wisdom books in human civilization. *Yin* and *yang* symbolize the two primordial forces of the cosmos. *Yin*, the receptive, consolidating, and conserving female element, and *yang*, the active, creative, and expanding male element, give rise to the multiplicity of things through their continuous and dynamic interactions. The relationship between *yin* and *yang* is competitive, complementary, and dialectic. Furthermore, there is always a *yang* element in the *yin* and a *yin* element in the *yang;* the *yang* element in the *yin* also contains *yin* and the *yin* element in the *yang* also contains *yang*. This infinite process of mutual penetration makes an exclusivistic dichotomy (such as a dichotomy between creator and creature, spirit and matter, mind and body, secular and sacred, consciousness and existence, or soul and flesh) inoperative as a conceptual apparatus in Chinese cosmological thinking.

A natural consequence of the nonexclusivistic *yinyang* dichotomy is what may be referred to as the thesis of the "continuity of being." F. W. Mote (1971) has characterized the uniqueness of the indigenous Chinese cosmological thinking as the lack of a creation myth. As Mote points out, the idea of a god who creates the cosmos *ex nihilo* is alien to the ancient Chinese mode of thought about the universe. Since there is no notion of God as a creator, let alone a notion of the "wholly other" that can never be comprehended by human rationality even though it is the ultimate reason of human existence, the Chinese take the world as given, as always in the process of becoming. This becoming process, known as the "great transformation" (*dahua*), makes every modality of being in the universe a dynamic change rather than a static structure. A piece of stone, a blade of grass, a horse, a human being, a spirit, and Heaven all form a continuum. They are all interconnected by the pervasive *qi* (vital force, material force) that penetrates every dimension of existence and functions as the constitutive element for each modality of being.

Qi, which means both energy and matter, denotes, in classical Chinese medicine, the psychophysiological strength and power associated with blood and breath. Like the Greek idea of *pneuma*, or its more intriguing Platonic formulation of *psuchē*, *qi* is the air-breath that binds the world together. Indeed, its expansion (*yang*) and contraction (*yin*), two simple movements each containing infinite varieties of complexity, generate the multiplicity of the universe. This distinctively biological and specifically sexual interpretation makes the Chinese explanatory model significantly different from any cosmology based on physics or mechanics. To the Chinese, the cosmos came into being not because of the willful act of an external creator or the initial push of a prime mover. Rather, it is through the continuous interaction of Heaven and Earth, or the mutual penetration of *yin* and *yang*, that the cosmos (*youzhou*), an integration of time and space, emerged out of chaos, an undifferentiated wholeness. Implicit in the differentiating act of chaos itself are the two primary movements of *qi*—*yin* and *yang*. Since the cosmos is not fixed, there has been continuous creativity. Thus change and transformation are the defining characteristics of the cosmos, which is not a static structure but a dynamic process.

The "continuity of being" that exists because of the nature of *qi*, the cosmic energy that animates the whole universe from stone to Heaven, makes it impossible to imagine a clear separation between spirit and matter and, by implication, flesh and soul. Understandably, a form of animism and its corollary, panpsychism, are taken for granted by the Chinese. To the Chinese, there is *anima*, *mana*, *pneuma*, or *psuchē* in stones, trees, animals, human beings, spiritual beings, and Heaven. Precious stones, such as jade; rare trees, such as pines more than a thousand years old; unusual animals, such as the phoenix, the unicorn, and the dragon, are all, in a sense, spiritual beings. There is no matter devoid of spirituality. Human beings, spiritual beings, and Heaven are, in a sense, material. Totally disembodied spirit is also difficult to envision.

The *Problematik* of soul, in the Chinese context, must be approached by a cluster of key concepts centered around the idea of *qi* mentioned above. If we try to find the closest approximation of a functional equivalent of the notion of soul in Chinese, the word *ling* seems to work in some cases. After all, the modern Chinese translation of the English word *soul* is *ling-hun,* a compound made of *ling* and *hun,* earlier referred to as "the heavenly aspect of the soul." *Ling* is a spiritual force; the term especially refers to the inspirational content of a spiritual force. *Ling* is often joined with the word *shen,* which is commonly rendered as "spirit." In both classical and modern Chinese, the two words are, in most cases, interchangeable. Strictly speaking, however, *ling* is more localized and suggests a more specific content. *Shen* can be mysterious to the extent that its functioning in the world is totally beyond human comprehension, but the presence of *ling* is likely to be sensed and felt by those around. Soul, in the Chinese sense, can perhaps be understood as a refined vital force that mediates between the human world and the spiritual realm.

From the perspective of *qi,* the uniqueness of being human lies in the fact that we are endowed with the finest of the vital forces in the cosmos. Human beings are therefore the embodiments of soul. One manifestation of the human soul is human sensitivity. Even though the idea that man is made in the image of God is not applicable to the Chinese perception of humanity, the Christian notion that humanity is a form of circumscribed divinity may find a sympathetic echo in the Chinese concept that human beings mediate and harmonize the myriad things between Heaven and Earth. In an anthropocosmic sense, human beings are guardians, indeed co-creators, of the universe. The reason why man forms a trinity with Heaven and Earth is that his soul enables him to bring himself into a spiritual accord with the creative transformation of the cosmos. Strictly speaking, man is not the measure of all things; if he should become so, it is because he has earned the right to speak and judge on behalf of Heaven and Earth. Man's ultimate concern, then, is to harmonize with nature and enter into a spiritual communion with the cosmos.

In the spiritual realm, the idea of soul is closely associated with two related concepts, *gui* and *shen* (rendered by Wing-tsit Chan as positive and negative spiritual forces). *Shen,* commonly translated as "spirit" in modern Chinese, etymologically conveys the sense of expansion; *gui,* on the other hand, means contraction. The soul that expands belongs to the *yang* force and is associated with heaven; the soul that contracts belongs to the *yin* force and is associated with earth. In popular religion, *shen* refers to gods that are good and *gui* refers to demons (or ghosts) that are harmful. When the two words are joined together, they may simply refer to spiritual beings in general. In sacrifices, *guishen* may refer to ancestors. The flexible use of these concepts suggests the complexity of the spiritual realm in Chinese religiosity. It should not prevent us from noticing an underlying pattern that is applicable to virtually all situations.

Obviously, the negative spirit *(gui)* and positive spirit (*shen*) are manifestations of the two vital forces, *yin* and *yang.* It may not be farfetched to suggest that the negative spirit is the bodily soul (*po*) and the positive spirit is the heavenly aspect of the soul (*hun*) in us. We as human beings, according to the thesis of the continuity of being, are integral parts of Heaven and Earth and the myriad things. The two souls that are in us are microcosms of the cosmic forces. We are thus intimately connected with nature on the one hand and heaven on the other. In actuality, a person is not an isolated individuality, but a center of relationships. It is not our own souls that constitute what we are. There are numerous souls, individual and communal, that make humans active participants of the cosmic process. We, the living, are not separated (or indeed separable) from the dead, especially from our ancestors, those to whom we owe our lives. The biological nature of our existence is such that we do not exist as discrete temporal and spatial entities. Rather, we are part of the cosmic flow that makes us inevitably and fruitfully linked to an ever-expanding network of relationships. Human selfhood is not an isolated system; on the contrary, it is always open to the world beyond. The more we are capable of establishing a spiritual communion with other modalities of being, the more we are enriched as human beings.

Nevertheless, the power and potency of the human soul is determined by a variety of factors, especially political factors. For example, the soul of the emperor is the most exalted among the human souls; because of his high status he alone may offer sacrifices to Heaven and to the most sacred mountains and rivers. The soul of an ordinary person is such that he can only establish an intimate spiritual communion with his deceased parents and grandparents. However, this bureaucratic differentiation of the social functions of souls is not rigidly fixed. It is possible for people from the lowest echelons of society to cultivate themselves so that the quality of their souls can match the genuineness of Heaven, an accomplishment no worldly power, wealth, or reputation can approximate.

Before the introduction of Buddhism to China, both the Confucians and the Daoists had already developed indigenous traditions of immortality. For the Confucian, one achieves immortality by establishing one's moral excellence, by performing unusual meritorious political deeds or by writing books of enduring value. These three forms of immortality are deeply rooted in the historical consciousness of the Chinese, but they also point to a transcending dimension that makes morality, politics, and literature spiritual (or soulful) in the Confucian tradition. The individual soul achieves immortality through active participation in the collective communal soul of the moral, political, and literary heritage. Soul is not only inherent in natural objects; it is also present in cultural accomplishments.

In the Daoist tradition, immortality is attained through inner spiritual transformation. In a strict sense, what the Daoist advocates is not the immortality of the soul but longevity of the body. Yet the reason why the body can age gracefully (or elevate itself to a state of agelessness) is that it has become translucent like the soul without desires or thoughts.

The Indian notion of the transmigration of the soul that entered East Asia with the introduction of Buddhism has provoked heated debates in China since the fourth century. Partly because of the Buddhist influence, the notions of *karman*, previous lives, hells, and journeys of souls are pervasive in Chinese folk religions. Fan Chen's essay "On the Mortality of the Soul," viewed in this perspective, may have been a successful Confucian refutation of the Buddhist belief in the separation of body and soul; but as a rationalist-utilitarian interpretation of the soul, its persuasive power was greatly undermined both by sophisticated Buddhists who denied the permanence of the phenomenal self and by lay people who were under the influence of Buddhist devotional schools.

Since there has been continuous interaction between the great traditions and folk traditions in China, the folk belief that souls are spiritual beings that float around the human world, on the one hand, and the naturalistic, organicist interpretation of souls as expressions of the vital force, on the other, are not conflicting perceptions of the same reality. In fact, there are enough points of convergence between them that they can well be understood as belonging to the same religious discourse. To the Chinese, souls are neither figments of the mind nor wishful thoughts of the heart. They have a right to exist, like stones, plants, and animals, in the creative transformation of the cosmos. The malevolent, negative souls can harm people, haunting the weak and upsetting the harmonious state of the human community. However, by and large, human beings benefit from the positive aspects of the soul, for through the "soul force" they are in touch with the dead and with the highest spiritual realm, Heaven.

See Also Qi.

BIBLIOGRAPHY

Balazs, Étienne. "The First Chinese Materialist." In his *Chinese Civilization and Bureaucracy: Variations on a Theme*, edited by Arthur F. Wright and translated by H. M. Wright, pp. 255–276. New Haven, 1964.

Bodde, Derk. "The Chinese View of Immortality: Its Expression by Chu Hsi and Its Relationship to Buddhist Thought." *Review of Religion* 6 (May 1942): 369–383.

Chan, Wing-tsit, ed. and trans. *A Source Book in Chinese Philosophy*. Princeton, 1963. See pages 11–13 and 299–383.

Fung Yu-lan. *A History of Chinese Philosophy*, vol. 2, *The Period of Classical Learning* (1953). 2d ed. Translated by Derk Bodde. Princeton, 1973. For a discussion of Fan Chen's "On the Mortality of the Soul," see pages 289–292.

Liebenthal, Walter. "The Immortality of the Soul in Chinese Thought." *Monumenta Nipponica* 8 (1952): 327–397.

Loewe, Michael. *Ways to Paradise: The Chinese Quest for Immortality*. London, 1979.

Loewe, Michael. *Chinese Ideas of Life and Death*. London, 1982.

Maspero, Henri. "Daoism in Chinese Religious Beliefs of the Six Dynasties Period." In his *Daoism and Chinese Religion*, translated by Frank A. Kierman, pp. 265–298. Amherst, 1981. A Daoist approach to immortality.

Mote, F. W. *Intellectual Foundations of China*. New York, 1971.

Needham, Joseph. *Science and Civilisation in China*, vol. 5, pt. 2, *Chemistry and Chemical Technology*. Cambridge, 1974. See pages 71–126.

Tsuda Sayukichi. "Shinmetsu fumetsu no ronso ni tsuite." *Toyogakuho* 24, no. 1 (1942): 1–52 and 24, no. 2 (1942): 33–80.

Tu Wei-ming, "The Continuity of Being: Chinese Visions of Nature." In his *Confucian Thought: Selfhood as Creative Transformation*, pp. 35–50. Albany, N.Y., 1985.

Yü Ying-shih. "Views of Life and Death in Later Han China, A.D. 25–220." Thesis, Harvard University, 1962.

Tu Wei-ming (1987)

SOUL: JEWISH CONCEPT

Unlike the Egyptian and Akkadian terms that have been translated as "soul" (e.g., *ba, ka, khu, shimtu, shedu, ishtaru*), the most important Hebrew words for this concept (*nefesh, neshamah* or *nishmah*, and *ruaḥ*) do not primarily refer to appearance, destiny, power, or supernatural influences, but to respiration—the inner, animating element of life. While the Hebrew Bible distinguishes between spirit and flesh, it does not accept the type of dualism of body and soul characteristic of Greek thought. Hebrew terms for the soul usually refer to an activity or characteristic of the body or to an entire living being. To "afflict the soul" means to practice physical self-denial (*Lv.* 16:29ff.).

Hebrew *nefesh*, usually translated as "soul," refers to the breath, as does the term *neshamah* (or *nishmah*), which became the most common word for the soul in postbiblical Hebrew. The verbs formed from the roots of these words (*nafash* and *nasham*) mean "to breathe." The two words are found together in *Genesis* 2:7, which narrates how the first human (*adam*) received the breath of life (*nishmat ḥayyim*) from God and became a living soul (*nefesh ḥayyah*). Another meaning of *nefesh* is "life," particularly animal life. Here the soul is a kind of material principle of vitality, which is separable from the inert substance (*basar*) of the body. *Neshamah*, on the other hand, sometimes refers particularly to conscious life or intelligence. *Nefesh* also may refer to mental states, in particular to strong emotions or physical cravings. At times *nefesh* refers to human capabilities, such as the capacity for eloquent speech.

The word *ruaḥ*, which is often rendered as "spirit," refers to powers or actions outside the body and often has the meaning of "wind." *Ruaḥ* is the mysterious vitality in the material body, which is considered a divine gift. *Ruaḥ* sometimes denotes forces external to the body that operate in or through the body or the mental faculties. These forces are states of exaltation and depression beyond normal experience that come and go "like the wind." (The clearest example of the various meanings of *ruaḥ* in a single passage is *Ezekiel* 37:1–14, the vision of the valley of dry bones.)

According to the Hebrew Bible, a dead human being remains in possession of the soul upon entering She'ol, a shadowy place sometimes synonymous with the grave, where the vitality and energy associated with worldly life are drastically decreased. Since both the body and the soul enter She'ol, the later doctrine of the resurrection (as expressed in *Isaiah* 24–27 and *Daniel* 12) indicates a reentry into life in both aspects. The first definite appearance in Jewish thought of a doctrine of personal survival of death in a general resurrection of the dead comes in the literature associated with the Hasmonean Revolt (166–164 BCE), from which time it increases in importance to become a central dogma, later a part of the basic doctrine of Christianity.

The work in the Hebrew canon that expresses the idea of resurrection most explicitly is the *Book of Daniel.* The final chapter of this Hebrew-Aramaic text of the second century BCE expands some details of the divine judgment of the nations with a "secret" revelation wherein it is made known that at some future time many of the dead will wake to everlasting life, while some will wake only to eternal suffering. References to the concept of resurrection are also found in *Isaiah* 26, which modern scholars regard as part of a late addition to the book. It alludes to personal resurrection, which, it suggests, will be restricted to certain categories of the dead and to the shades or *refa'im.* The original nature of the *refa'im* in Canaanite mythology is the subject of continuing debate, but in biblical contexts they are usually understood as impotent ghosts.

The "dew of light" mentioned in *Isaiah* 26, as well as in the Pseudepigrapha (e.g., *1 Bar.* 29:7, 73:2; *1 Enoch* 60:7), suggests ideas of restored fertility, and is associated in the Jewish tradition with individual resurrections as well as a general resurrection. However, the passages in *Daniel* and *Isaiah* concerning the role of the soul in resurrection are ambiguous and have allowed for extensive and often contradictory speculation. The Sadducees, in the first century CE, followed a literal reading of the accepted scriptures and denied that the idea of a general resurrection was found there. But the Pharisees and their successors, the tannaim (first and second centuries CE) and the amoraim (third through fifth centuries CE) were convinced that the scriptures, properly understood in the light of an oral instruction passed down through Moses and the later prophets, were filled with hints and allusions concerning the world to come.

RABBINIC VIEWS. A synopsis of concepts of the soul in rabbinic literature may give an overly uniform appearance to this material, which developed over many generations. Statements scattered through this vast literature may appear when cited in isolation to be pure speculation or assertions of dogma, but they often have a primarily polemic point in context. With explicit and implicit contradictions so abundant in the Talmud, no fully articulated system (or systems) can be found, but it is possible to summarize majority views and influential positions.

The close connection between soul and body characteristic of the biblical worldview is continued in the rabbinic literature. The Palestinian Talmud (J.T., *Kil.* 8.4, 31c) attributes the origin of different portions of the physical body to human parents, while the spirit, life, and soul are attributed to God. This admits a greater duality than is acknowledged in the Hebrew Bible, but the soul is regarded as the active element, and so is responsible for sin, while the body is only its vehicle. Such an attitude is contrary to Greek views known in Hellenistic Judaea whereby the body is seen as a trap that debases or hinders the soul. According to Kaufmann Kohler and Ephraim Urbach (see, respectively, *Jewish Theology* and *The Sages,*) this view of the body as the source of sin and impurity is not found in rabbinic Judaism. Urbach also concluded that neither the concept of the soul's immortality, separate from the body, nor the idea of its transmigration into other bodies, is rabbinic. The absence of early, authoritative pronouncements on such points allowed for widely variant speculations within later orthodox and heterodox thought. Talmudic Judaism, as Urbach indicates, found moral duality existing within the soul, which contains both good and evil impulses, the latter including the ambitious, self-centered, and envious impulses in human beings that must be controlled rather than extirpated. The Talmud presents the soul as a supernatural entity created and bestowed by God and joined to a terrestrial body (B.T., *Ber.* 60a). God takes back the soul at death, but later restores it to the dead body. Similar views of the soul are elaborated elsewhere in the Talmud and early *midrashim,* although not without opposing voices. Among these is the concept of the soul's preexistence, which, Urbach argues, appears in rabbinic sayings only after the third century centuries CE. According to some, all human souls came into existence during creation as parts of the "wind of God," understood here as "spirit" (B.T., *'A. Z.* 5a, *Yev.* 62a; *Gn. Rab.* 8.1, 24.4). Unborn souls abide in a *guf* ("a body"; commentators suggest "promptuary") among the treasures of the *'aravot,* the seventh heaven, where also are found the souls of the righteous and the "dew of light" with which God will resurrect the dead (B.T., *Ḥag.* 12b, *Yev.* 62a, *Shab.* 152b). The Messiah will come when the supply of souls in the *guf* is exhausted, or, according to others, when God has created those souls he has held in his intention from the beginning (B.T., *'A. Z.* 5a, *Yev.* 62a, *Nid.* 136; *Gn. Rab.* 24.4; cf. also *Apocalypse of Ezra* 4:35).

According to one view, God compels the selected or newly created soul to enter the womb at the time of conception. Even after the soul has entered this world, it is not entirely forgetful of its origins and is not without divine care.

It is accompanied by angels (B.T., *Ber.* 60b, end; B.T., *Shab.* 119a), and nightly, while the body sleeps, the soul ascends to heaven, from which it returns with renewed life for the body *(Gn. Rab.* 14.9; probably implied in B.T., *Ber.* 60a). On the Sabbath the body enjoys an "additional soul," which is sent forth by and returns to God, as Shimʿon ben Laqish discovered by an ingenious rendering of the word *va-yinafash* in *Exodus* 31:17 (B.T., *Beits.* 16a, *Taʿan.* 27b).

Although the soul had protested at its embodiment and its birth into the world, it also protests at the death of the body. The soul hovers about the dead body for three days, hoping that life will return (*Tanḥuma'*, Miqets 4, Pequdei 3; cf. B.T., *Shab.* 152a). Ultimately the soul leaves the body and awaits the resurrection, when they will reunited and judged together (B.T., *San.* 91). Concerning the fate of the soul in the meantime, one view is that the souls of the righteous will remain with God, while the souls of the wicked wander in the air or are hurled from one end of the world to the other by angels (B.T., *Shab.* 152b).

Not everyone will be resurrected. The generation destroyed in the Flood, the men of Sodom (*San.* 10.3) who were punished by complete annihilation, and, with ironic appropriateness, those who denied the doctrine of resurrection will not return to life. Attempts have been made as well to relate doctrines of the soul or of the resurrection to Jewish concepts of religious duty and piety (e.g., B.T., *Ket.* 111b), a problem that was to be taken up at length by philosophers and mystics in later centuries.

Philosophical Views. Philosophical speculation in Judaism arose through the desire to reconcile the Jewish tradition with contemporary intellectual discourse. In medieval Jewish philosophy, the effort at reconciliation was directed at two rival forms of thought, Platonism and Aristotelianism, both of which were read under the influence of Neoplatonic commentaries and misattributed texts, such as the excerpts from Plotinus that circulated as the *Theology of Aristotle.* Isaac Husik noted (1916) that as a group, Jewish philosophers hesitated between (1) the Platonic view of the soul as a distinct entity that enters the body from a spiritual world and acts by using the body as its instrument and (2) the Aristotelian view that, as far as the lower faculties such as sense, memory, and imagination are concerned, the soul is merely a form of the physical body and perishes with it. They found biblical references to support both views, although the latter provided a clearer division between the human and the divine.

Philo Judaeus (d. 45–50 CE) sought to reconcile Greek, predominantly Platonic and Stoic, philosophy with scripture, particularly the Pentateuch. He accomplished this through a device he borrowed from the Greeks, the allegorical method of interpretation, which the Stoics had used for the Homeric epics. Philo accepted most of the Greek distinction between body and soul, including the belief that the body and its desires were the cause of the pollution of the soul, the body being a prison from which the soul must escape. Humans are related to the world of the senses through the body and the lower parts (or functions) of the soul, but through reason a human being is related to the suprasensual, or divine, realm, to which the higher portion of the soul seeks to be reunited. For Philo, the religious task is to bring about the union of the individual soul with the divine Logos, transcending both the material world and the limits of the rational soul.

In Philo's adaptation of Plato, there is a transcendent, preexistent, incorporeal Logos, a direct projection of the ideas in the mind of God, and there is also an immanent Logos, the totality of God's powers existing in the material world. The intelligible world of the transcendent Logos is the model for the human world, in which all things, including individual souls, or minds, are reflections of the ideas, or images, as these are mediated through the immanent Logos. Directly below the immanent Logos in the descent from God are the rational, unbodied souls, which have the nature of living beings. Some of these were, or will be, incarnate in human bodies; others have not and never will be so embodied. These latter beings are ranked according to their inherent level of likeness to the divine. They are found in the heavens and in the air, and are known to the Greeks as *daimones,* that is (following the etymology in Plato's *Cratylus* 398b), "knowers," but in Hebrew they are called *mal'akhim,* "messengers," because they are God's messengers in his dealings with the created world. Translators of scripture have called them "angels," that is, "heralds."

The rational, human soul, a fragment of the Logos in human form, is capable of achieving a separate existence at a new level; the angels cannot. Without the support of God, however, the rational soul would perish by dissolving into its original, undifferentiated state. This is the fate of personal obliteration awaiting the wicked. The souls of the righteous, the wise and virtuous, will be brought close to God in proportion to their merits. Not only can some reach the level of the highest angels beneath the immanent Logos, as did Elijah, but some can attain the level of the ideas of the intelligible world, as did Enoch. Moses, the most perfect man, who delivered the most perfect law by which souls are disciplined and improved, stands above all created species and genera, before God himself. Philo thus attempts to link the Platonic ascent of the soul to the Platonic ideas, using the biblical concepts of prophecy and election. No place is made for a resurrection of the body reunited with the soul.

Philosophical and systematic theological writings from Jewish sources appear again later in the ninth and tenth centuries in response to the philosophical schools of Islam. The work of Yitsḥaq Yisra'eli (c. 850–950) is largely Platonic in origin. Yisra'eli believed in the substantiality and immortality of the soul, of which he distinguished three kinds in every human being. The first is the rational soul, which receives wisdom, discriminates between good and evil, and is subject to punishment for wrongdoing. The second is the animal soul, which humans share with beasts. It consists of sense perception, and it controls motion, but has no connection with reality and can judge only from appearances. The third is the vegetative soul, which is responsible for nutrition, growth, and reproduction; it has no sense perception or capacity to move. These distinctions, with major and minor variations, were to become common in Jewish as well as in Muslim and Christian writings.

Yitsḥaq Yisra'eli's younger contemporary, Sa'adyah ben Yosef, or Sa'adyah Gaon (c. 882–942), summarized his ideas about the soul in the sixth treatise of his *Book of Beliefs and Opinions* (Arabic version, *Kitāb al-amānāt wa-al-I'tiqādāt,* completed about 933; Hebrew paraphrases and full translation as *Sefer ha-emunot ve-ha-de'ot*). Sa'adyah follows the less widely accepted of the Talmudic and Midrashic views that the soul is formed with the completion of the body and that there is a continuous creation of souls. He accepts, however, the predetermined limit of the total number of souls. He defends the localization of the soul in the heart with a demonstration of synonymous uses of the words in biblical texts, as well as with ancient and medieval physiological theories locating consciousness in the heart. Like the celestial spheres, the soul is perfectly transparent, so that although it permeates the body through vessels leading from the heart, it is too fine to be seen. When the soul leaves the body it is stored up until the time of general retribution, when it is restored to its own body to face God's judgment. Because of their pure, celestial nature, the souls of the wise and just rise to the heavenly spheres. The souls of the wicked, however, become turbid from the impurities of their earthly lives, and after death they drift aimlessly among the lower elements. When it first leaves the body, the soul is troubled by the thought of the disintegration of its former abode. The earthbound souls of the wicked are greatly distressed by this corruption, while pure souls are much less concerned by it and soon begin their ascent.

Sa'adyah used the resources of Arabic philosophical teachings to construct a rationalized exposition of some Talmudic views of the soul. The majority of his successors were content with more general resemblances, preferring to concentrate on the assurance of personal immortality and retribution when they discussed the soul. Shelomoh ibn Gabirol (c. 1021–1058), one of the great Jewish liturgical poets of medieval Spain, connected the soul with the nature of the universe. For Ibn Gabirol, a Neoplatonist, the individual human soul is part of the world soul and contains a higher faculty than that of the rational soul, which is that of immediate intellectual intuition. The soul contains all the forms of existence in its essence and can intuit these forms. Ibn Gabirol separates the soul from God through an intricate series of emanations, but to many his views seemed to attribute too much of the divine to the human soul.

Elaboration of the concept of soul in terms of Jewish thought was attempted by another Spanish poet-philosopher, Yehudah ha-Levi (c. 1058–1141), in his Arabic dialogue *Al-Khazarī* (The book of argument and proof in defense of the despised faith). Ha-Levi argues that philosophy, which has been presented as an eclectic Neoplatonism, is not absolutely wrong in teaching men to seek communion with the divine by subduing the organic and emotional, or vegetative and animal, elements of the soul to the rational. He states that there is another faculty of the soul, the religious faculty, which is capable of grasping truths and experiences beyond the reach of reason alone, so that the immaterial substance of the higher faculties of the soul becomes indestructible and immortal by assimilating universal and eternal concepts. According to ha-Levi, rabbinic Judaism is uniquely able to foster this higher, religious faculty of the soul. By leading a temperate and moral life the soul attains immortality and closeness to God.

The Neoplatonic approach of Shelomoh ibn Gabirol was resumed in later decades by another Spanish poet, Mosheh ibn 'Ezra' (1070–1138), who was influenced, it is thought, by the Ṣūfīs. Ibn 'Ezra' believed in the preexistence of the individual soul and in the transmigration of souls until they gain sufficient wisdom to be reunited with their source in the world soul. Markedly Aristotelian, in contrast, is the work of Avraham ibn Daud (1100–1180), a Spanish historian and astronomer who argued that the soul is the form of the body, that it can grasp universal ideas and discriminate between good and evil, and that it can survive the body. Ibn Daud criticized the idea of the preexistence of the soul as illogical, arguing that if a preexistent soul died with the body their union was without purpose, while if it survived the body their temporary union was also pointless.

In the twelfth century the dominant influence was not that of Ibn Daud, however, but of Moses Maimonides (Mosheh ben Maimon, 1135/8–1204). In his major philosophical work, *The Guide of the Perplexed* (c. 1190), he bases his theory of the soul on Aristotelian thought as he understood it through the great Arabic commentaries of Ibn Sīnā (Avicenna) and Al-Fārābī and on biblical texts interpreted by an elaborate theory of the meaning of scriptural language. For Maimonides, the complete soul, or *nefesh,* is coextensive with the physical body and is not separable from it. It has five functions, namely, (1) the nutritive, (2) the sensitive, which consists of the five senses, (3) the imaginative, (4) the appetitive, which manifests itself in desires and emotions, and (5) the rational. The rational function itself consists of (1) the reflective aspect, which acquires knowledge and makes ethical judgments, (2) the practical aspect, and (3) the theoretical aspect, which consists of knowledge of unchanging realities.

The rational faculty is twofold. The material intellect latent in all human beings can be developed into the acquired intellect by the proper use of the mind. The acquired intellect is a disposition of the soul and perishes with the body. The acquired intellect can realize correct general concepts about the world, and when these are realized the rational soul assimilates the corresponding thoughts of the Active Intellect, which is the emanation through which God governs the material world. In this manner elements of divinity enter into the acquired intellect. If the soul has been directed toward contemplation of the nature of God and the world, the acquired intellect is replaced by the actualized intellect, which consists of these general concepts received from the active intellect. When the body dies the lower faculties of the soul are destroyed, but the actualized intellect, being of divine origin, is reunited with God through the Active Intellect. Through rational contemplation, such souls are rewarded by immortality. The souls of those who indulged the senses and emotions will perish with their bodies. According to the *Treatise on Resurrection,* although Maimonides believed in resurrection, he considered it a temporary condition wherein the souls of the righteous remain before they depart from the physical world entirely.

The threat to traditional religious beliefs presented by Maimonidean intellectualism was not met successfully until the late fourteenth century, in the *Or Adonai* (Light of the Lord) of Hasdai Crescas. Crescas attacked the theory of the soul as being a form coextensive with the physical body. He also rejected the assumption that reason is the characteristic feature of the human soul. He argued that the will and the emotions are basic parts of human nature and not merely bodily distractions to be discarded with the flesh, which survive the death of the body and play a part in determining the ultimate condition and fate of the soul. He contended that religious teaching and practice are correctly directed at shaping the will and the emotions, rather than the reason.

Qabbalistic Views. According to Qabbalah, a person is a spiritual being whose body is merely an external wrapping. There are three essentially different parts of the soul in qabbalistic thought, designated by the Hebrew terms *nefesh, ruaḥ,* and *neshamah.* The *nefesh* is the vital element and enters the body at birth; it dominates the physical and psychological aspects of the self. In contrast, the *ruaḥ* and *neshamah* must be developed through spiritual discipline. The *ruaḥ* comes into being when a person can overcome the body and its desires and it is thus associated with the ethical aspects of life. The *neshamah* is the highest part of the soul and is produced through study of the Torah and observation of the commandments. Torah study awakens the higher centers, through which the individual attains the capacity to apprehend God and the secrets of creation.

According to Gershom Scholem, Qabbalah took this division of the soul primarily from Jewish Neoplatonism and introduced theosophic and mythic elaborations. In Qabbalah the *neshamah* is that part of the soul that consists of the spark of the divine and is exclusively concerned with the knowledge of God. According to the fundamental text of thirteenth-century qabbalistic literature, the *Zohar,* each part of the soul originates in the world of the *sefirot* (the emanations of God). *Nefesh* originates in the *sefirah* Malkhut ("kingdom"), the lowest emanation, which corresponds to the Congregation of Israel. *Ruaḥ* originates in Tif'eret ("grandeur"), the central *sefirah,* also known as Rahamim ("mercies"). *Neshamah* emerges from the third *sefirah,* Binah ("understanding"). The *sefirot* are assigned male and female aspects, and the soul has its origins in a union of these male and female archetypes and takes on masculine and feminine forms only in its emanations downward.

After the compilation of the *Zohar,* two additional parts of the soul were introduced, the *ḥayyah* and *ye-ḥidah* ("life" and "only one"; cf. *Psalms* 22:21). These were assigned higher levels than the *neshamah* and could be acquired only by spiritually evolved individuals. The soul of the Messiah, which was on the level of *yehidah,* had its source in the *sefirah* Keter ("crown"), the highest of the emanations.

According to Qabbalah, the *nefesh, ruaḥ,* and *neshamah* have different destinies after death. The *nefesh* hovers over the body for a time; the *ruaḥ* goes to a terrestrial realm assigned according to its virtue, and the *neshamah* returns to its home with the divine. Only the *nefesh* and *ruaḥ* are subject to punishment.

In the thought of Isaac Luria (1534–1572) and his disciples, the doctrine of metempsychosis was incorporated into concepts of the nature and destiny of creation and the mission of the Jewish people. The task of *tiun,* that is, the restoration or reintegration into the divine pattern of existence of the flawed material universe, is entrusted to human souls, who seek out and redeem the scattered sparks of divinity in the world. Most souls are given repeated chances to achieve this task, thus constituting a kind of reincarnation, which earlier Jewish mystics had considered primarily a form of punishment or expiation for sins. In the Lurianic system, ritual commandments are important for achieving *tiun,* both for the individual soul and for the whole world.

See Also Ascension; Jewish Thought and Philosophy, article on Premodern Philosophy.

Bibliography

For a brief discussion of the historical and theoretical background of Jewish views of the soul, see Louis Jacobs's *A Jewish Theology* New York, 1973). Walther Eichrodt provides a useful treatment of Israelite views of the human personality and the problem of death in *Theology of the Old Testament,* 2 vols. (Philadelphia, 1961–1967); see pages 118–150 and 210–228 in volume 2. Louis Ginzberg offers an incomparable survey of the entire postbiblical period in *The Legends of the Jews,* 7 vols. (1909–1938; Philadelphia, 1937–1966). His survey includes the intertestamental literature and the writings of the church fathers on biblical events, as well as Jewish sources through the nineteenth century.

Although dated, George Foot Moore's *Judaism in the First Centuries of the Christian Era; The Age of Tannaim,* 3 vols. (1927–1930; Cambridge, Mass., 1970), remains a classic treatment of postbiblical sectarian Jewish literature, particularly the pseudopigrapha and the other Talmudic and Midrashic literature. On concepts involving the soul, see especially pages 368–371, 404, and 486–489 in volume 1; pages 279–322 ("Retribution after Death"), 353, and 377–395 ("Eschatology") in volume 2; and pages 148 (note 206), 196–197, and 204–205 in volume 3. A more advanced and detailed work then Moore's, and one covering a longer period, is E. E. Urbach's *The Sages: Their Concepts and Beliefs,* 2 vols. (1969; Jerusalem, 1975). The chapter titled "Man" in volume 1 covers in great detail the Talmudic and Midrashic views on ensoulment, preexistence, and embryonic consciousness, as well as related concepts, and attempts to determine the relative and absolute chronologies of statements and their attribution in the sources. Notes on pages 784–800 in volume 2 and the bibliography, pages 1061–1062, cite many earlier secondary studies. A specialized work is Shalom Spiegel's *The Last Trial: On the Legends and Lore of the Command to Abraham to Offer Issac as a Sacrifice; The Akedah* (1950; Philadelphia, 1967), which includes a chapter on the soul's flight from the body and the dew of resurrection in Midrashic literature.

A comprehensive survey from the perspective of philosophy is Julius Guttman's *Philosophies of Judaism: The History of Jewish Philosophy from Biblical Times to Franz Rosenzweig* (1933; New York, 1964). Articles on the Jewish concept of the soul from the *Encyclopedia Judaica* (Jerusalem, 1971) have been collected together with new material, in a single volume; *Jewish Philosophers,* edited by Steven T. Katz (New York, 1975). On the philosophy of Philo, see Harry A. Wolfson's *Philo: Foundations of Religious Philosophy in Judaism, Christianity and Islam,* 2 vols. (Cambridge, Mass., 1947); see especially chapter 7, "Souls, Angels, Immortality," in volume 1. Issac Husik's *A History of Medieval Jewish Philosophy* (1916); New York, 1969) remains a standard, detailed survey of Jewish philosophies in the Middle Ages. For the concept of the soul during this period, a useful but rather narrowly focused volume is Philip David Bookstaber's *The Idea of Development of the Soul in Medieval Jewish Philosophy* (Philadelphia, 1950).

Articles by Gershom Scholem written for the *Encyclopedia Judaica* have been collected in *Kabbalah* (New York, 1974); see especially "Man and His Soul (Psychology and Anthropology of the Kabbalah)" and "Gilgul," on the transmigration of souls.

New Sources

Arbel, Daphna V. "Forms of Spirit and Soul: Transcendent Anthropomorphism in the 'Shi'ur Komah' Traditions." *Studies in Spirituality* 12 (2002): 5–22.

Baumgarten, A. I., J. Assmann, and G. G. Strousma. *Self, Soul, and Body in Religious Experience.* Leiden and Boston, 1998,

Blau, Yitzchak. "Body and Soul: 'tehiyyat ha-metim' and 'gilgulim' in Medieval and Modern Philosophy." *Torah U-Madda Journal* 10 (2001): 1–19.

Eylon, Dina Ripsman. *Reincarnation in Jewish Mysticism and Gnosticism.* Jewish Studies, no. 25. Lewiston, N.Y., 2003.

Kallus, Menachem. "Pneumatic Mystical Possession and the Eschatology of the Soul in Lurianic Kabbalah." In *Spirit Possession in Judaism: Cases and Contexts from the Middle Ages to the Present,* edited by Matt Goldish, pp. 159–185, 385–413. Detroit, 2003.

Newmyer, Stephen T. "Antoninus and Rabbi on the Soul: Stoic Elements of a Puzzling Encounter." *Koroth* 9 (1988): 108–123.

Rubin, Nissan. "Body and Soul in Talmudic and Mishnaic Sources." *Koroth* 9 (1988): 151–164.

Tucker, Gordon. "Body and Soul in Jewish Tradition." *Proceedings of the Rabbinical Assembly of America* 45 (1984): 141–156.

JACK BEMPORAD (1987)
Revised Bibliography

SOUL: CHRISTIAN CONCEPTS

The concept of the soul in Christian literature and tradition has a complex history. Moreover, Christian thought about its destiny is by no means uniform, nor is it always even clear.

TERMINOLOGY. The New Testament word *psuchē* is rooted in the Hebrew *nefesh,* and in English both are generally translated "soul." In primitive Semitic thought *nefesh* (Arabic, *nafs*) is a fine, diminutive replica of the body. As such it can be contrasted with *ruaḥ,* an onomatopoeic word that mimics the sound of breathing and is used to designate the spirit or principle of life that in such thought is seen in the breath, which stands in contrast to the flesh. The New Testament word *psuchē,* however, has complex overtones associated with the concept of life, sometimes also signifying what today would be called the self and often assuming a special connotation as the seat of the supernatural or eternal life, the life that cannot be destroyed by the malice of humans as can the body, yet can be destroyed by God (*Mt.* 10:39). So valuable is the *psuchē* that not even the whole of the material universe could compensate for its loss (*Mt.* 16:26, *Mk.* 8:36ff.).

When the *psuchē* is fully dedicated to God it acquires a special character (*1 Pt.* 1:22, 4:19), and in this dedication it can be anchored in God and be aware of possessing eternal life, assured of salvation from all that could alienate it from that inheritance (*Heb.* 6:19). Such is the "soul" or "self" that is under the care of Christ. Yet since the *psuchē* is spiritual, not material, it is not to be guarded as one guards an earthly mansion, nor to be placed like a precious heirloom in a safe deposit box, nor tended as one tends a delicate plant. On the contrary, Jesus urges his disciples to let go of it, abandoning it to God's care (*Mt.* 16:25, *Mk.* 8:35, *Lk.* 9:24, *Jn.* 12:25). Such is the paradox of self-giving, a concept that finds expression also in Hindu and Buddhist thought.

In the New Testament then, the *psuchē,* although fundamentally rooted in a Hebrew concept, encompasses so much of what is today understood as the "self" that it confronts one with many of the very complex problems to be found in modern discussions of selfhood. Yet the term carries also other connotations, as shall be seen later. Furthermore, in its adjectival form, *psuchikos,* it can be used to designate the natural, biological life of humans, as distinguished from the spiritual life, which is called *pneumatikos* (*1 Cor.* 2:14, 15:46; *Jude* 19). The dualistic distinction implied in this usage echoes one that is familiar to readers of gnostic literature. *Psuchē,* however, always refers to that dimension of humanity that is of eternal value and therefore contrasted with the human carnal embodiment.

In *Ezekiel* (13:17ff.) there is an echo of the primitivistic belief that the *nefesh* can slip out of the nostrils or another orifice during sleep (hence the old superstition against sleeping with one's mouth open) or, in the case of violent death, at the point of the assassin's sword. Ezekiel warns his bearers against women who sew frilly sleeves around their wrists, "the better to ensnare lives." This passage reflects both the old material concept of the *nefesh* and the ancient fear of witches, who made a profitable business out of nocturnal exploits in which they stole the *nefashot* of unwary sleepers, catching their souls like moths in handkerchiefs and then selling them to families with a member who, as one might say today, had "lost his mind." The Arabs entertained similar views about the vulnerability of the *nafs* to such evil agencies.

SOUL AND SPIRIT. The English words *soul* and *spirit* are attempts to represent the two sets of ideas found in the Bible: *Soul* is continuous with the Hebrew *nefesh* and the Greek *psuchē,* while *spirit* is continuous with the Hebrew *ruaḥ* and the Greek *pneuma.* The one set of ideas, however, cannot be entirely dissociated from the other. For example, when one thinks of the ideas of wind, breath, or spirit, one would probably attach any of them to *pneuma* rather than to *psuchē;* nevertheless, one should bear in mind that the word *psuchē* has an etymological connection with the verb *psuchein* ("to breathe"), as does the Latin *animus* with *anemos,* the Greek word meaning "wind." So some study of the concept of spirit is not only relevant to but necessary for any study of the Christian concept of the soul.

Ruaḥ, which the New Testament writers translate as *pneuma* and which is traditionally rendered "spirit" in English, does not have the quasi-physical connotation that *nefesh* has. For although *ruaḥ* is sometimes used to signify "wind" or "breath" (e.g., in *Job* 15:30), it is not accurately described as ambiguous in meaning since in Hebrew it refers simply to the principle of vital activity, however manifested. The Hebrews did not make the sharp distinction, as does Western tradition, between the physical connotations of "wind" and the spiritual connotations of "spirit" or "mind." So the effects of *ruaḥ* may be heard as one hears a hurricane, or seen as one might see breath on a mirror or the dancing of branches of trees on a windy day. Or it may be perceived in more complex ways, as one perceives the resutls of God's action in human events. Since the ancients saw in breathing the evidence of life and in its absence the lack of life, breath would seem an obvious locus for *ruaḥ.* Nevertheless, they would so see it only as they see in the brain an obvious locus for mental activity, although not even the most positivistic of contemporary analytical philosophers would identify mental activity simply with the three pounds of pinkish-gray tissue people carry in their heads. *Ruaḥ* is also the inner strength of a man or woman, which is weakened in times of despondency and is revived in times of exhilaration. Short-tempered people are short of *ruaḥ* (*Ex.* 6:9). The *ruaḥ* of God (Elohim) is uniquely powerful in its effects on humans, affecting them in all sorts of ways, not all of them benevolent. Since the Hebrews had no special word for nature as did the Greeks (*phusis*), one word had to do service for all seemingly superhuman activity. God sends plagues and earthquakes as well as gentle rain and sunshine. The *ruaḥ* of the Lord, however, is that of righteousness and love, of justice and mercy, inspiring the utterances of the prophets upon whom it falls.

Behind the New Testament use of *pneuma* lie these earlier uses of *ruaḥ.* The spirit of God is given to Jesus in baptism (*Mt.* 3:13ff.) and from Jesus to the disciples. John the Baptist distinguishes the baptism he gives from the one Jesus is to give, which is to be by the Holy Spirit (*en pneumati hagiō*) and by fire (*Mt.* 3:11). Here John is represented as anticipating the experience of the disciples on the day of Pentecost, described in *Acts* 2 as the descent of the Spirit on the assembly as if in "tongues of fire." The extent to which the New Testament writers accounted the Holy Spirit of God a separate entity, as in the trinitarian doctrine developed in later Christian thought, is, to say the least, obscure and need not be of concern here. *Pneuma,* however, is very frequently used, both in a somewhat pedestrian way (e.g., the disciples are afraid, thinking they are seeing a ghost, *Lk.* 24:37) and in more reverential senses having the full range of Hebrew meanings along with special meanings arising out of the pentecostal experience. Both Paul and John make notable use of the antinomy of flesh (*sarx*) and spirit (*pneuma*). What makes one righteous is circumcision not of the flesh but of the spirit (*Rom.* 2:29). Had not the psalmist noted that the Lord was less pleased by burnt offerings than by a humble and contrite heart (*Ps.* 51)? Christians do not walk according to the flesh but according to the spirit (*Rom.* 8:13).

Although Paul follows traditional usage in such matters, he also uses *pneuma* in several less expected ways, for example, as if he were alluding to the soul (*2 Cor.* 2:13) and as if referring to the mind as the seat of human consciousness (*1 Cor.* 7:34). He also writes as if mystically identifying the soul or conscious self of the Christian with the spiritual realm or dimension to which it has been introduced through Christ; he writes as if the Christian were so absorbed into Christ that everything he or she thought or said or did issued thence. Paul has a tendency to express his dominant sense of mystical union with Christ by coalescing all such distinctions as might lie between *psuchē* and *pneuma,* focusing upon what today would more readily be called a spiritual dimension of being, one in which the human participates in the divine.

John pointedly contrasts *sarx* ("flesh") with *pneuma* ("spirit"), as in *John* 3:5–8. Because God is a spirit, all dealings with him are in the spiritual, not the carnal, dimension (*Jn.* 4:24). The words of Jesus are the revelation of God, and as such they are to be recognized as spirit (*pneuma*) and life (*zōē*). Spirit is symbolized by the physical act of breathing: In *John* 20:22 Jesus breathes on the apostles as a symbol of his bestowal of the Holy Spirit (*pneuma hagion*). Alluding to the Holy Spirit, John uses the term *paraklētos:* the one who helps or pleads one's cause. This term had been used in classical Greek in much the same way as the Latin *advocatus* ("advocate," or the English *counsel*). As used by John, it seems to recall the notion of the spirit of truth as used in the

Qumran literature in the sense of "helper," where the typically gnostic contrast between the spirit of light and the spirit of darkness is also notable. Jesus, as God pitching his tent awhile in the carnal world of humankind, is he who can mediate between humans, in their mixed, carnal-spiritual state, and God, who is pure spirit. In the light of such modes of conceptualizing, the distinction between soul and spirit tends to evanesce. The contrast is between the carnal realm and the spiritual realm. The characteristics of the spirit (coming "like the rushing of a mighty wind" and "blowing where it listeth") become, then, descriptions of the way in which the spiritual dimension behaves; that is, it behaves otherwise than according to the "laws" of physics or biology.

To sum up: With the translation of *nefesh* as *psuchē* in the Greek version of the Bible (Septuagint), which the New Testament writers used, the ground is laid for the tendency toward the coalescence of the ideas suggested by the terms *psuchē* and *pneuma.* For both words focus on the traditional Semitic preoccupation with the idea of life. What matters to the spiritual person is not the life measured in days or years (*bios*) but the spiritual energy, the inner life of a person, his or her *zōē,* which has the capacity to become everlasting. It is to this that the soul is to be resurrected, so that resurrection then entails an ongoing, everlasting state, which Christ has made possible even for sinful men and women. Thus the struggle in this life is not so much against flesh (*sarx*) as "against the spiritual army of evil agencies" (*pros ta pneumatika tes ponerias; Eph.* 6:12). By extension, then, the soul, as the higher part of a human, becomes indistinguishable from the spiritual dimension of the human's being.

Still, one cannot easily overemphasize the fact that the New Testament Christians were heirs of a classical Hebrew view in which a human does not *have* a body or *have* a soul; he or she *is* a soul-body unity. Flesh and spirit, however, are opposed as evil and good aspects of humanity. Recognition of this may have opened the way to a later accommodation to the Greek soul-body dualism. In Hebrew thought the soul was sometimes conceived as if it were a sort of liquid in the jar of the body, one that can be diminished and also replenished. In *Genesis* 2:7 God breathed his Spirit into the very dust out of which he made humans, and the human being then "became a living soul." This imagery haunts Hebrew thought and the New Testament writers inherit the model it fostered.

ORIGIN OF THE SOUL. Within the development of Christian thought on the origin of the individual soul, three views have been maintained: (1) creationism, (2) traducianism, and (3) reincarnationism.

Creationism is the doctrine that God creates a new soul for each human being at conception. Upheld by Jerome, Hilary, and Peter Lombard, it was by far the most widely accepted view on the subject in the Middle Ages. Thomas Aquinas insisted upon it (*Summa theologiae* 1.118), and in the Reformed tradition the Calvinists generally taught it. Its consequences for certain moral questions, notably that of abortion, are clear.

Traducianism is the theory that the soul is transmitted along with the body by the parents. Forms of this view were proposed by some of the Fathers (such as Gregory of Nyssa and, notably, Tertullian), but in the Middle Ages it found little if any favor. Lutherans, however, tended to accept it, and in the early nineteenth century a modified form of it was proposed within the Roman Catholic tradition by the founder of the Rosminians, Antonio Rosmini-Serbati.

It is widely supposed that reincarnationism (a form of resurrection belief) is alien to Christian thought, but this supposition is not warranted by the evidence. The doctrine of the preexistence of the soul was certainly held by Origen and others in the tradition of Christian Platonism. Reincarnationism (not of course in its crude, primitivistic form, but in an ethical one, such as is found in Plato and in Indian philosophy) has a long and interesting, albeit partly underground, tradition in Christian thought and literature from early times down to the present day. Christian reincarnationists hold that the soul passes through many embodiments in the process of its development and spiritual growth and is judged accordingly, not on the basis of only one life of indeterminate duration. The soul, in this view, has a very long history, with origins antedating humanity itself.

DESTINY OF THE SOUL. Paul taught that because "the wages of sin is death" (*Rom.* 6:23), humans have no more entitlement to immortality than has any other form of life. Thanks, however, to the power of Christ's resurrection, every man and woman of the Christian way who truly believes in the power of Christ will rise with him (*Phil.* 3:21) in a body that will be like Christ's "glorious" body (*tō sōmati tēs doxēs autou*). The resurrection of Christ makes humans capable of personal resurrection, yet they can attain their own resurrection only insofar as they appropriate the power of Christ, which they can do through believing in its efficacy and accepting his divine gift of salvation from death and victory over the grave.

Indeed, although notions of immortality are inextricably woven into New Testament thought alongside the central resurrection theme, they are dependent on the latter in the thought of Paul and other New Testament writers. For all human beings, death has always been the supreme terror, the "final enemy"; now, Paul proclaims, it has been conquered, making possible the immortal life of the soul.

Yet one must not expect to find in the first century any clearly formulated universal doctrine of the afterlife. The expectation of the end of the age and the imminent return of Christ (the Parousia) so governed the Christian outlook during that period as to discourage speculation about the nature of the soul or whatever it is in humans that survives the physical body. Paul himself pointedly discouraged idle speculation on the precise nature of the resurrected body (*1 Cor.* 15:35–58). As, however, the hope of the Parousia gradually lost much of its urgency, the need for formulation of an answer to such questions pressed itself on theological minds. Since the biblical writers had left these questions so open, and since a variety of beliefs from throughout the Mediterranean world had consciously or otherwise affected those who were thinking seriously about such matters, different and sometimes incompatible views were brought together. Even before the Christian era the Jews had been entertaining beliefs about the afterlife that had not been in the general mold of their classical thought but had been picked up from foreign sources after the Exile (587/6 BCE). In the time of Jesus, for instance, some (such as the Pharisees) believed in a resurrection from the dead which others (for example, the Sadducees) repudiated.

In classical Hebrew thought the souls of the dead went to She'ol, the counterpart of the Hades of Greek mythology, a sort of nonworld, an underground place of darkness and dust so dreary that, as Homer remarked, one would rather be a poor beggar in the land of the living than a king in the land of the dead. Yet in later Hebrew thought *sophia* ("wisdom") is seen as delivering human beings from She'ol (*Prov.* 15:24). Unlike souls in the hell of later Christian theology, who have put themselves beyond God's benevolent power, those in She'ol could be the objects of God's care, for his power extends even there (*Dt.* 32:22, *Ps.* 139:8). In the New Testament, the concept of She'ol is sometimes replaced by that of death, for example in Paul's use of the Greek *thanatos* in *1 Corinthians* 15:55, quoting *Hosea* 13:14. However, in *Acts* 2:27, quoting *Psalms* 16:10, the term *haides* is retained.

In the rabbinical thought of the century before the advent of Christianity, *she'ol* came to mean a place exclusively for the wicked. The righteous go to *pardes* ("paradise," or, more strictly, "garden"), a late Hebrew term derived from the Greek *paradeisos,* the Septuagint translation for "Garden of Eden." *Pardes* was understood as a celestial restoration of the original, unfallen state of humanity. Sometimes, however, it represented an intermediate state between the death of the righteous and the final judgment—hence Jesus' promise to the penitent thief that they would meet that same day in "paradise" (a passage that would otherwise present grave interpretative difficulties), and other similar usages in the New Testament.

Along with such developments comes the notion of Gehenna as a pit of fire into which the wicked are to be thrown to be burned like trash. The symbolism of this transitional, intertestamental period is, however, by no means consistent; and the confusion is carried over into the New Testament, where both *haidēs* and *geenna* (*Mt.* 18:9 and *Mk.* 9:43) have been traditionally rendered "hell" in English, although they have different connotations in the Greek text. Hades, although it can function as a storehouse for the dead who await judgment (as in *Rv.* 20:13–14) and as a destructive power like death (as in *Mt.* 16:18), can also be (as in *Lk.* 16:23) a place of punishment indistinguishable from Gehenna.

The concept of Gehenna as a dumping ground for the incineration of the wicked originates with the "Valley of the son of Hinnom," the place on the boundary between Judah and Benjamin that in later Hebrew literature had an unsavory reputation as the site of a cultic shrine where human sacrifice was offered (*2 Kgs.* 23:10; *2 Chr.* 28:3, 33:6). When reference is made in *Isaiah* 66:24 to the place where the dead bodies of those who have rebelled against the Lord shall lie, this valley is the place being alluded to. In *2 Esdras* 7:6 Gehenna has become a furnace within sight of paradise. In Jewish apocalyptic literature it was often seen as a pit of unquenchable fire in which the wicked are destroyed, body and soul, a notion echoed in *Matthew* 10:28. The writer of *Revelation* calls this destination of the wicked "the second death" (21:8). In this Gehenna imagery lies the origin of the popular medieval concept of hell, in which, however, the soul, being indestructible, cannot be extinguished by the fire but is tormented everlastingly.

In early Christian thought, such a background for the concept of the soul and its destiny resulted in a confusion that no appeal to scripture could possibly clear, since the confusion was already embedded in the Bible itself. So one finds that Tertullian, writing in his *De anima* (c. 210), assigns to the soul a sort of corporality. This tendency is to be found in other anti-gnostic writers of the period, including his contemporary Irenaeus. By contrast, Origen (c. 185–c. 254) and his influential Christian school at Alexandria taught that the soul preexisted in an incorporeal state and was imprisoned in a physical body as a result of its former waywardness. Origen probably also taught a form of reincarnationism. Gregory of Nyssa (c. 330–c. 395), Nemesius (who was bishop of Emesa toward the end of the fourth century), and the Greek theologian Maximos the Confessor (c. 580–662), all interpreted the biblical concepts of the soul along Platonic lines and in the general tradition of Origen and his school.

In the thirteenth century, Thomas Aquinas follows the doctrine of the soul presented in Aristotle's *Eudemus,* teaching that, while body and soul together constitute a unity, the soul, as the "form" of the body, is an individual "spiritual substance" and as such is capable of leading a separate existence after the death of the body. This medieval doctrine of the soul, while largely determining the official teaching of the Roman Catholic church on the nature of the soul and its destiny, also indelibly imprinted itself on the theology of the Reformation. For the classical reformers, although contemporaneous with the great Renaissance movement in Europe, were thoroughly medieval in the mold of their theological thinking. The fact that Thomas described the essence of the pain of hell as the loss of the vision of God did little to mitigate the horror of hell in the popular mind.

In popular preaching during the Middle Ages and for centuries thereafter, hell was invariably depicted as a physical fire in which the souls of the damned, being somehow endowed with temporary bodies equipped to suffer physical pain, are eventually summoned on the Last Day to have their original bodies returned and enabled to suffer everlasting torture under the same conditions. The angels, however, according to Thomas, have no physical bodies; therefore Satan and the other denizens of hell must be equipped in some other way to undergo, as they certainly must, the punishment superabundantly due to them in the place of torment over which they reign. Nor could Dante's obviously symbolic treatment and allegorical vision of hell in the *Commedia* have assuaged the horror of hell in the popular mind. After all, much of Dante's genius lay in his ability to invest his great epic with an extraordinary realism that fixed itself on the minds of even those readers whose literary education had accustomed them to the allegorical methods so dear to the medieval mind.

Out of confusion in the concept of the soul, then, had sprung an increasing confusion in the Christian view of its destiny, making eschatology the least coherent aspect of the Christian theological tradition. For example, the soul has an independent existence and is sometimes envisioned, in Platonic fashion, as well rid of the burden of its physical encumbrance. Yet in the end the whole person, body and soul, must be restored in order to enjoy the fruits of Christ's redemption. In the first century, on account of the imminent expectation of the Parousia, Christians could plausibly see the separation of soul from body as a very temporary state of affairs, as represented in the catacombs by such inscriptions as "Dormit in pace" ("He sleeps in peace") and "Dormit in Christo" ("He sleeps in Christ"). As time went on, however, such a notion, although persisting to this day in pious epitaphs, could no longer serve as a theologically satisfactory account of what happens to the soul during a waiting period between death and the general resurrection of the dead. For it would suggest, if not entail, the view that heaven and hell are uninhabited until that general resurrection shall occur. Such a view is not conformable to the standard vision of Christian piety on this subject—least of all where, as in Roman Catholic tradition, the saints are already in heaven (the Church Triumphant) interceding for and otherwise helping their fellow Christians in the Church Militant on earth. Moreover, both the words of Jesus to the penitent thief (*Lk.* 23:43) and the parable of the rich man and Lazarus (*Lk.* 16:19), with their implication of a paradisial, Garden-of-Eden bliss, surely exclude the notion of a sleep till the Day of Judgment.

Furthermore, out of the doctrine of the intermediate state, which is at least foreshadowed in late Judaism and found in early Christian thought in a rudimentary form, was gradually developed the doctrine of purgatory. The concept of purgatory is of singular importance in the Christian doctrine of the life of the soul. Abused though the doctrine of purgatory was by legalistic distortions and ecclesiastical corruption in late medieval practice, purgatory has gradually come to be seen, through the influence of developments in English Tractarian thought in the nineteenth century, as a state not so much of punishment as of purification, refreshment, and growth. This theological development is adumbrated in some medieval Christian literature, notably the *Trattato* (*Dicchiarazione*) of Catherine of Genoa (1447–1510).

The souls in purgatory have generally been regarded as disembodied (or at least lacking earthly embodiment), yet capable of the peculiar kind of pain that purgatory entails: a pain of waiting and longing. The duration of purgatory is indeterminate; but it is always assumed that some who enter it may be released comparatively soon and certainly that multitudes are to be released long before the Day of Judgment. What then happens to them on their release? Speculative theologians have made various proposals. According to Roman Catholic theology, each soul on its separation from the body is subjected to a "particular" judgment, as distinguished from the final or "general" judgment. In 1336, Pope Benedict XII, in his bull *Benedictus Deus,* specifically declared that souls, having been subjected to this particular judgment, are admitted at once to the beatific vision, which is heaven, or proceed at once to purgatory to be cleansed and readied for the heavenly state, or are consigned to hell. This teaching does not merely exclude explicitly the primitive Christian view represented by the *dormit in pace* type of epitaph; it makes nonsense of traditional Roman Catholic piety. For if purgatory be considered in any sense a state of punishment, hell a state of both torment and hopelessness, and heaven one of that joyful activity that comes with the full knowledge of God that is the reward of the righteous, then the traditional prayer for the dead ("Requiescant in pace"; "May they rest in peace") seems to express an inapposite wish for any of the three categories.

That ancient prayer echoes the primitive wish that the souls of the dead may not be inclined, because of their troubled state, to haunt the living but may instead pursue their business in peace and tranquillity and have no such harassing inclination. This primitive wish is, of course, transfigured in Catholic thought and sentiment, where it is illumined by the response "Et lux perpetua luceat eis" ("May perpetual light shine upon them"), expressing a loving concern for the progress of the souls of the dead and the belief that they are advancing toward the fulfillment of their destiny. Nevertheless, at the regular Roman Catholic burial service a beautiful prayer beckons the angels to come forth to meet the deceased and conduct him or her "into the heavenly city, Jerusalem."

BIBLIOGRAPHY

For the Hebrew background of the New Testament view, a reliable source is the brief article "Soul" by Norman Porteous in *The Interpreter's Dictionary of the Bible* (New York, 1962). Rudolf Bultmann provides abundant background for an understanding of the New Testament writers' general outlook in his *Theology of the New Testament,* vol. 1 (New York, 1951). Oscar Cullmann has written an important essay on this topic, which was published in *Immortality and Resurrection,* edited by Krister Stendahl (New York, 1965). The other essays in this collection, by Harry A. Wolfson, Werner

Yaeger, and Henry J. Cadbury, also merit attention. Augustine's view, articulated in his *On the Immortality of the Soul,* greatly influenced both the medieval schoolmen and the reformers. *Saint Thomas and the Problem of the Soul in the Thirteenth Century* (Toronto, 1934), by Anton C. Pegis, provides a useful introduction to the view of Thomas Aquinas as set forth in the first volume of his *Summa theologiae.* Étienne Gilson treats the subject in his study *The Spirit of Mediaeval Philosophy* (London, 1936), and John Calvin discusses the origin, immortal nature, and other aspects of the soul in his *Institutes of the Christian Religion,* 2 vols. (Philadelphia, 1960). For the Renaissance view of Pietro Pomponazzi, see Clement C. J. Webb's *Studies in the History of Natural Theology* (Oxford, 1915).

The soul plays a central role in the various forms of Christian mysticism. The notion of the "fine point" of the soul, a cell remaining sensitive to God despite the fall and consequent corruption of humankind, is a common topic of such literature: For example, see *The Living Flame of Love* by John of the Cross. For the Salesian tradition, see Henri Bremond's treatment in his *Histoire littéraire du sentiment religieux en France* (1915–1932), 2d ed. (Paris, 1967–1968), edited by René Taveneaux, especially vol. 7. Whether any form of reincarnationism is reconcilable to Christian faith is specifically considered in two books of mine: *Reincarnation in Christianity* (Wheaton, Ill., 1978) and *Reincarnation as a Christian Hope* (London, 1982).

New Sources

Armstrong, A. H. *Expectations of Immortality in Late Antiquity.* Milwaukee, Wis., 1987.

Brown, Warren S., Nancy Murphy, and H. Newton Maloney, eds. *Whatever Happened to the Soul? Scientific and Theological Portraits of Human Nature.* Minneapolis, 1998.

Chirban, John T., ed. *Personhood: Orthodox Christianity and the Connection between Body, Mind, and Soul.* Westport, Conn., 1996.

Cary, Phillip. *Augustine's Invention of the Inner Self.* Oxford and New York, 2000.

Crabbe, M. James C., ed. *From Soul to Self.* London and New York, 1999.

O'Connell, Robert J. *The Origin of the Soul in St. Augustine's Later Works.* New York, 1987.

Oguejiofor, J. Obi. *The Philosophical Experience of Immortality in Thomas Aquinas.* Lanham, Md., 2001.

Perrett, Roy W., ed. *Death and Immortality.* Dordrecht and Boston, 1987.

Sherry, Patrick. *Spirit, Saints, and Immortality.* Albany, 1984.

GEDDES MACGREGOR (1987)
Revised Bibliography

SOUL: ISLAMIC CONCEPTS

Islamic concepts of the soul vary, ranging from the traditional (and most prevalent) to the mystical. They include doctrines formulated by individual schools of Islamic dialectical theology (*kalām*) and theories developed within Islamic philosophy (*falsafah*). It is possible to classify very broadly the different types of such concepts under four categories: traditional, theological, philosophical, and mystical (Ṣufī). Differences (as well as overlappings) abound, not only between these categories, but also within them. Nonetheless, the various Islamic concepts of the soul all seek or claim a Qur'anic base. Hence, the proper starting point of any discussion of such concepts is the Qur'ān. Before turning to the Qur'ān, however, a few preliminary remarks on the use of the Arabic terms *rūḥ* ("spirit") and *nafs* ("soul") are in order.

As in other languages, these terms relate to the ideas of breath and wind. In pre-Islamic Arabic poetry, *rūḥ* can mean "wind," "breath," or "that which one blows" (as when kindling a fire). In post-Qur'anic Arabic, the two terms are often used interchangeably when referring to the human soul, but distinctions between them are also maintained within certain conceptual schemes. In the Qur'ān, in addition to the grammatical reflexive use of *nafs* as "self," the term is used to refer to the human soul, whereas *rūḥ* normally refers to the spirit that proceeds from God. In pre-Islamic Arabic poetry, these two terms do not have a religious or supernatural connotation. Thus *rūḥ* refers to the physical breath or wind, while *nafs* (when not used reflexively) refers to the blood, sometimes to the living body. This usage is consistent with the secular nature of this poetry, whose themes revolve around the poet's mundane loves, sorrows, heroic exploits, and concept of tribal honor. The poetry is also noted for its vivid descriptions of nature—desert scenery and animal life, wild and domestic—that convey a sense of the splendor, power (sometimes harshness), and vitality of nature, but never anything that can be construed as either teleological or mystical. There are also affirmations in this poetry that, with death, everything ends, that there is nothing beyond the grave. A seeming exception to this consists of references to the *hāmah*, a birdlike apparition resembling a small owl, which, according to pre-Islamic Arab belief, departs from the head of a slaughtered man, perches by his grave, and continues to shriek, "give me to drink," until the death is avenged. The association of this belief with the tribal law of avenging the death of a kinsman is obvious.

***RŪḤ* AND *NAFS* IN THE QUR'ĀN.** As indicated earlier, *rūḥ* ("spirit") in the Qur'ān refers normally to God's spirit. The term appears in different contexts. It is the divine creative breath: God creates man (Adam) from clay, animating him by blowing into the clay of his spirit (15:29; 32:9; 38:72). Again, God blew of his spirit into Mary, causing the conception of Jesus (21:91; 66:12). Spirit is sent by God as a messenger: it is *al-rūḥ al-amīn* ("the faithful spirit") that comes to Muḥammad's heart (26:193)—hence the Qur'anic commentators' identification of "the faithful spirit" with the angelic messenger Gabriel. Mary conceives when God sends his spirit to her in the form of a perfect man (19:17). Spirit is also *rūḥ al-qudūs* ("the holy spirit") which God sends to help Jesus (2:87, 2:253). Jesus himself is referred to as a spirit from God, but it is also made clear that this does not mean that he is the son of God (4:171).

Spirit relates also to the *amr* of God (16:2; 17:85; 40:15; 42:52), a term that can mean either "command" or "affair." Muslim scholars have disagreed on the interpretation of this term as well as on the referent of *rūḥ* ("spirit") in surah 17:85: "They ask thee [Muḥammad] about the spirit. Say: 'The spirit is of my Lord's *amr*, of knowledge ye have been given but little.'" Some have understood *amr* here as "affair," not "command," and *rūḥ* as referring to the human spirit. If this interpretation is correct, then the verse provides an exception to the normal Qurʾanic use of the term *rūḥ*.

The term *nafs*, when not used in the grammatical reflexive sense of "self," refers to the human soul, not God's spirit. The human soul, however, relates to the divine spirit, since, as indicated earlier, God brings life to man by breathing into him of his spirit. The equivalence of life and soul in the Qurʾān, however, is not explicitly stated. Nor is there any explicit statement as to whether the soul is immaterial or material. The Qurʾān is primarily concerned with the moral and religious orientation of the human soul, with its conduct, and with the consequences of such conduct in terms of reward and punishment in the hereafter. This concern with the moral and religious disposition of the soul is reflected in the Qurʾanic characterization of the soul as either *ammārah*, *lawwāmah*, or *muṭmaʾinnah*. The *ammārah* (12:53) is the soul that by nature incites or commands what is evil. Qurʾanic commentators have identified this with the carnal self. The *lawwāmah* (75:2) is the soul that constantly blames itself, interpreted by some commentators as upbraiding itself in the quest of goodness. The *muṭmaʾinnah* (89:27) is the tranquil soul of the virtuous believer that will return to its lord.

With death, the soul leaves the body, to rejoin it on the Day of Judgment. Thereafter the righteous go to Paradise, the wicked dwell in Hell. Two questions in particular that relate to the resurrection were to occupy Islamic religious thinkers. The first is whether or not it is the remains of the same body that is resurrected. To this the Qurʾān gives no detailed answer, only an affirmation that God has the power to bring back to life what has been decayed: "Who will revive these bones when they are decayed? Say: 'He who created them the first time will revive them'" (36:78–79). The second is the question of what happens to the soul between the time of death and the day of resurrection. There are Qurʾanic statements (8:49; 9:101; 32:21; 47:27) that suggest that wicked souls will be punished even before the resurrection and that the souls of martyrs will be in paradise: "Do not reckon that those killed in battle are dead; they are living with their Lord, provided for" (3:169). Such statements become a basis for traditional doctrines regarding the soul's fate in the interim between death and the final day of judgment.

Traditional Concepts. In Islam, the most prevalent concepts of the soul can perhaps best be termed "traditional." Their immediate inspiration is the Qurʾān, interpreted literally, and the *ḥadīth*, or "tradition." A chief source for our knowledge of the traditional concepts of the soul in Islam is *Kitāb al-rūḥ* (The Book of the Spirit), by the Damascene Ibn Qayyim al-Jawzīyah (d. 1350), a celebrated Ḥanbalī theologian and jurisconsult.

The term *rūḥ*, Ibn Qayyim maintains, is applicable in Arabic usage to both the spirit that comes from God and the human spirit. In the Qurʾān, however, it is used to refer to the spirit that comes from God. This spirit proceeds from the *amr* of God. The term *amr* in the Qurʾān, Ibn Qayyim insists, always means "command." Since the spirit proceeds from the command of God, it is a created being, although its creation antedates the creation of the human soul. The human body is created before the human soul. The latter, though created, is everlasting. Death means the separation of this soul from the body, to rejoin it permanently when the resurrection takes place. When the Qurʾān speaks of the soul that incites to evil, the soul that upbraids, and the tranquil soul, this does not mean that a human has three souls. These, Ibn Qayyim argues, are characteristics of one and the same human soul.

Ibn Qayyim gives a lengthy critique of the philosophical doctrine of an immaterial soul, incorporating in his criticism the arguments the theologian al-Ghazālī (d. 1111) had used in showing that Ibn Sīnā (Avicenna; d. 1037) had failed to demonstrate the immateriality of the human soul. Ibn Qayyim rejects the concept of an immaterial soul. An immaterial spirit or soul would be totally unrelated to what is spatial. What is unrelated to the spatial and the bodily cannot be spoken of as being in a body or outside it, or as traveling away from the body or returning to it. But this is the scriptural language expressing the activities of the soul. The human soul is hence material but "differs in quiddity [*al-māhiyyah*] from the sensible body, being a body that is luminous, elevated, light, alive, and in motion. It penetrates the substance of the body organs, flowing therein in the way water flows in roses, oil in olives, and fire in charcoal" (*Kitāb al-rūḥ*, Hyderabad, 1963, p. 310). The body, in fact, is the mold (*qālib*) of the soul. Body and soul interact, helping to shape each other's individual characteristics. Thus, when death takes place, souls leaving their bodies have their individuality and are hence differentiated one from another.

During sleep, souls leave their bodies temporarily, sometimes communicating with other souls, whether of the living or of the dead. With death, the soul leaves the body but can very swiftly return to it. The souls of the virtuous can communicate with each other, the wicked souls being too preoccupied in their torments for this. For in the interim between death and the resurrection, most souls rejoin their bodies in the grave to be questioned by the two angels of death, Munkar and Nakir. The wicked, unbelieving souls suffer punishment and torment in the grave, while the virtuous believers enjoy a measure of bliss. Ibn Qayyim equates the period of the grave with the *barzakh*, a Qurʾanic term (23:100; 25:53; 55:20) that originally meant "hindrance" or "separation." The souls of prophets are in paradise, as are those of martyrs, although there are disagreements among traditional Muslims as to whether this applies to all martyrs. These disagreements, Ibn Qayyim maintains, are reconcilable once the legal conditions governing the fate of the soul are known. To cite but one of his examples, a martyr who dies before paying a debt is excluded from entry into paradise during this interim but does not suffer torment.

The prayers of the living over the souls of the dead are heard by the latter, who are helped by them. Ibn Qayyim devotes a long section of his book to this topic. The length of this chapter indicates the importance to Muslims of the visiting of graves and the offering of prayers over the dead, for these visits are very much part of traditional Muslim piety and a source of consolation to the bereaved.

THEOLOGICAL (KALĀM) CONCEPTS. Islam's dialectical theologians, the *mutakallimūn,* no less than the more traditional Muslims, sought to uphold a Qurʾanic concept of the soul. They sought to uphold it, however, within scripturally rooted perspectives of the world that they formulated and rationally defended. Their concepts of the human soul were governed largely by two questions, one metaphysical, the other eschatological. The metaphysical question pertained to the ultimate constituents of the created world: Do these consist of indivisible atoms or of what is potentially infinitely divisible? The eschatological question arose out of their doctrine of bodily resurrection: if, in the ages between the world's beginning and its end, dead human bodies decompose to become parts of other physical entities (organic or inorganic), how can there be a real resurrection, that is, a return to life of the actual individuals who once lived and died, and not the mere creation anew of replicas of them?

Regarding the metaphysical question, most of the *mutakallimūn* were atomists. Their concepts of the soul were for the most part materialist: they regarded it either as a body, or identified it with life, which they maintained is a transient quality, an accident, that occurs to a body. But there were disagreements among them, particularly among members of the "rationalist" Muʿtazilī school of *kalām,* which attained the height of its power and influence in the first part of the ninth century. Thus, one of its leading theologians, al-Naẓẓām (d. 845), rejected atomism. Moreover, he conceived of the soul (which he identified with life) as a subtle body that is diffused in all parts of the physical body. His concept of the soul is substantially the same as that of the traditional concept defended by Ibn Qayyim. Another exception of a different type was the view of the Muʿtazilī Muʿammar (d. 835). He was an atomist and espoused a concept of the soul as an immaterial atom. Other theologians held the soul to be an atom, but not immaterial. But if it is a material atom, is life identical with it? If life is not identical with it, then could life be an accident that inheres in the single atom? The Muʿtazilah disagreed as to whether the accidents could inhere in the single atom or only in atoms that are interrelated, forming a body. They also disagreed as to whether spirit, soul, and life are identical. But the prevalent Muʿtazilī view was that the soul is material and that life, whether or not identical with soul, is a transient accident.

It is in terms of this prevalent view that the eschatological question mentioned earlier must be understood. If life is a transient accident and the dead body's atoms separate to combine differently forming other physical entities, where is the continuity that would guarantee the identity of the individual to be resurrected? Without this continuity, what appears to be the resurrected individual is only a similar being, a *mithl.* To resolve this difficulty, some of the Muʿtazilah resorted to the doctrine that nonexistence (*al*ʿ*adam*) is "a thing" (*shay*ʾ) or "an entity," "an essence" (*dhāt*), to which existence is a state that occurs. Thus a nonexistent entity *A* acquires existence for a span of time, loses it during another span, and regains it eternally at the resurrection, *A* remaining *A* throughout all these stages.

The doctrine that nonexistence is an entity, a thing, was rejected by the Ashʿarī school of *kalām.* This school was founded by al-Ashʿarī (d. 935), originally a Muʿtazilī who rebelled against his school. (Ashʿarism gradually gained ascendancy to become the dominant school of *kalām* in Islam.) But while the Ashʿarīyah opposed fundamental Muʿtazilī doctrines, they were also atomists. Their atomism formed part of their occasionalist metaphysics according to which all events are the direct creation of God. Accidents are transient and do not endure for more than one moment of time and are hence constantly recreated. Life, the Ashʿarīyah held, is a transient accident created and recreated while the individual lives. It is hence not difficult to see that the eschatological problem regarding the soul that the Muʿtazilah tried to solve persisted.

For an Ashʿarī answer to this difficulty, I will turn to al-Ghazālī. His main arguments for the possibility of bodily resurrection are found in two works. The first is his criticism of the Islamic philosophers, particularly Ibn Sīnā, the *Tahāfut al-falāsifah* (The Incoherence of the Philosophers). In this work he argues in great detail to show that Ibn Sīnā has failed to demonstrate his theory that the human soul is an immaterial, immortal substance. At the same time, he argues for the possibility of bodily resurrection in terms of a theory of an immaterial, immortal soul, maintaining that God at the resurrection creates for such a soul a new body. The second work, *Al-iqtiṣād fī al-lʿtiqād* (Moderation in Belief), written shortly after the *Tahāfut,* gives a different explanation. Significantly, in this work al-Ghazālī repudiates the theory he advocated in the *Tahāfut,* maintaining that he had advanced it only for the sake of argument, to show that bodily resurrection is possible even if one adopts a doctrine of an immaterial soul. The true doctrine, he then continues, is the Ashʿarī, namely that life is a transient accident constantly created and recreated in the living body. Resurrection is the return to life and existence of what was originally a first creation by God. God is able to recreate what he had previously created. A copy is simply a copy, never the recreation of what was actually a new creation. Al-Ghazālī does not discuss how one can differentiate between the resurrected, recreated original being, and the copy, the *mithl,* but the implication of his argument is that this is knowable to God, who is the creator of all things.

Al-Ghazālī follows substantially the line of reasoning of his predecessor and teacher, the Ashʿarī al-Juwaynī (d. 1085). Unlike al-Juwaynī, however, al-Ghazālī does not discuss whether spirit or soul is the same as life. Al-Juwaynī is more explicit on this. Spirit is a body that pervades the physical body, animating it. Life, however, is a transient accident that inheres in spirit. With the exception of this distinction between life and spirit, al-Juwaynī's concept of the soul is in harmony with the traditional concept defended by Ibn Qayyim.

Philosophical Concepts. The theories of the soul formulated by Islam's philosophers, the *falāsifah* (sg., *faylasūf*), derive largely from Plato, Aristotle, and Plotinus. But there are other influences—Greek medicine and Stoic thought, for example. An influential short Arabic treatise on the difference between spirit (*rūḥ*; Gr., *pneuma*), and soul (*nafs*; Gr., *psuchē*) by the Christian translator, Qusṭā Ibn Lūqā (d. 912), is of interest, not only for its ideas, but also for its listing of the sources of these ideas—Plato (his *Phaedo* and *Timaeus*), Aristotle, Theophrastus, and Galen. Spirit, according to this treatise, is a subtle body. Its less refined form spreads in the body, from the heart through the veins, causing animation, breathing, and pulsation. The more refined spirit spreads from the brain through the nervous system to cause sensation and movement. Spirit, however, is only the proximate intermediary cause of these activities; its efficacy is caused by the soul, which is an immaterial, immortal substance. With death, spirit ceases, but not soul.

It was, however, in its Neoplatonic form that the doctrine of the soul's immateriality and immortality left its greatest impact on Islamic thought. This impact was not confined to philosophy proper but is discernible in the religious thought of various Islamic sectarian groups—the Ismāʿīlīyah, for example. The other most important source for the *falāsifah*'s concepts of the soul was Aristotle. The majority accepted Aristotle's definition of the soul as the entelechy of the body, his idea of its division into vegetative, sensitive, and rational and of the latter into theoretical and practical, and his description of the states of its various parts as these change from potentiality to actuality. Within the Platonic, Aristotelian, and Neoplatonic frameworks, however, there were differences in the *falāsifah*'s conceptions of the soul. An idea of these differences can be obtained by considering the conceptions offered by some representative philosophers.

Al-Kindī (d. c. 870), the first Islamic philosopher, for example, subscribes to the doctrine of the soul as an immaterial, immortal substance and at the same time defends the Qurʾanic doctrine of bodily resurrection. His surviving treatises, however, do not include anything that shows the manner in which he synthesized these two doctrines. The physician-philosopher al-Rāzī (d. 926), on the other hand, offers a theory of the human soul inspired largely by Plato's *Timaeus.* Soul is one of the five eternal principles; the others are God, atomic (disorganized) matter, absolute space, and absolute time. At a moment in time, God imposes order on matter, rendering it receptive of soul. When soul unites with matter, it becomes individuated, forming the particular living creatures. Man alone among these creatures is endowed with reason, an emanation from God. There is a lengthy but finite span of time, in which soul remains conjoined with matter and individuated. During this period there is transmigration of souls within animal and human life. The finite period ends when reason in men prevails. The individual souls then disengage from matter, returning to their original state of one soul. The initial state of the four other eternal principles resumes, continuing into the infinite future.

With al-Fārābī (d. 950) and Ibn Sīnā, we encounter two highly developed psychological theories. Both presupposed a Neoplatonic emanative scheme. The celestial world, for al-Fārābī, consists of a succession from God of dyads, intelligences, and bodily spheres; for Ibn Sīnā, it consists of a succession of triads, intelligences, souls, and bodily spheres. For both, the last successive celestial intelligence is the Active Intellect, after which our terrestrial world comes into existence. The entire process of successive emanations from God exists eternally.

According to al-Fārābī, the human rational soul is at first a potentiality in the material body. In some individuals, the objects of sensory perception, the material images, are transformed by the illuminary action of the Active Intellect into abstract concepts. These human souls that achieve abstract conceptual thought attain an immaterial status. (There are higher levels of conceptual thought, culminating with rare individuals, the philosopher-prophets, in the human soul's periodic union with the Active Intellect.) Only those souls that have attained an immaterial status are immortal. Good souls, those that have continued to live according to the dictates of reason, shunning the lower passions, live in eternal happiness, contemplating the celestial intelligences and God. Those rational souls that have betrayed their calling, surrendering to the lower passions, live in eternal misery, seeking contemplation of the celestial intelligences but unable to achieve it. The souls of the majority of mankind, however, never attain an immaterial status and, with death, cease to exist.

Ibn Sīnā, on the other hand, insists on the individual immortality of all souls. The rational soul, an emanation from the Active Intellect, joins the human body and becomes individuated by it. It is an immaterial, individual substance that exists with the body but is not imprinted in it. Souls that have lived the rational life, controlling the lower passions and remaining untarnished by vice, are rewarded in the hereafter. They live in eternal bliss, contemplating the celestial beings and God. This applies to nonphilosophical virtuous souls that have lived in accordance with the divine law, for this law is an expression of philosophical truth in the language of imagery and symbol, which the nonphilosopher can understand. Souls that have not lived the rational, virtuous life or have not adhered to the commands of the religious law are punished in the hereafter. They live eternally in torment, seeking contemplation of the celestial beings and God, but are unable to achieve this. The Qurʾanic language describing the afterlife in physical terms is symbolic. Ibn Sīnā's theory of the soul culminates in mysticism. But this is intellectual mysticism. God, for Ibn Sīnā, is pure mind. The soul's journey to God includes the inundation of the souls of exceptional individuals with all of the intelligibles from the Active Intellect. This experience is intuitive, occurring all at once.

Ibn Rushd (Averroës; d. 1198) was the most Aristotelian of the *falāsifah.* In those writings addressed to the general Islamic reader, he affirms the doctrine of reward and punishment in the hereafter, insisting, however, that the scriptural language describing the hereafter should be understood on different levels, depending on one's intellectual capacity. His more technical psychological writings, notably his commentaries on Aristotle, leave no room for a doctrine of individual immortality. These writings, however, left a much greater impact on medieval and Renaissance Europe than they did on Islam. In the Islamic world, it was Ibn Sīnā's theory of the soul that had the greater influence on subsequent *falsafah* and religious thought.

ṢUFĪ CONCEPTS. In considering this very vast subject, it is well to differentiate between three of its aspects: (1) what Ṣufīs conceived the human soul to be, (2) the soul's purification and the path of holiness it must follow as it seeks God, (3) the relation of the soul to God, particularly in its intimate experiencing of the divine. These aspects are related, but the third represents a central issue on which Ṣufīs were divided and which caused controversy in the general history of Islamic religious thought.

According to some, the Ṣufī (and Ashʿarī theologian) al-Qushayrī (d. 1074) observes, the term "soul" refers to those of man's characteristics that are afflicted with illness and to his blameworthy actions. It is possible, he maintains, "that the soul is a subtle entity [*laṭīfah*] placed in this [bodily] mold [*qālib*], being the receptacle of ill dispositions, just as spirit [*al-rūḥ*] is placed in this mold, being the receptacle of praiseworthy dispositions" (*Al-risālah al-Qushayrīyah*, Cairo, 1966, vol. 1, p. 249). The earlier Ṣufī al-Tirmidhī (fl. 894) also gives expression to the view that the soul is evil. Both, moreover, reflect traditional and *kalām* concepts of the soul as material.

Al-Ghazālī, on the other hand, often uses Avicennian language in his discussions of the soul. (This fact need not necessarily commit him to Avicennian ontology, since he frequently suggests that Ibn Sīnā's philosophical language can be interpreted in occasionalist, Ashʿarī terms.) At the beginning of his *Mīzān al-ʿAmal* (The Criterion for Action), al-Ghazālī also indicates that Ṣufīs subscribe to the doctrine of the soul's immateriality as they reject the concept of physical reward and punishment in the hereafter. Thus, within Sufism there are differences in belief as to whether the soul is material or immaterial. There is less difference (and greater emphasis), however, on the subject of its purification and the ascetic devotional course it must pursue. (Differences between Ṣufī orders here are largely a matter of ritual, not substance.)

It is, however, the relation of the human soul—the self, the "I"—to God that is at the heart of Sufism, and it was this issue that caused conflict. The mystical experience itself is both overwhelming and ineffable. Utterances attempting to convey it are symbolic, sometimes prone to overstatement, and hence prone to being misunderstood. Central to this issue is the interpretation of the mystical experience of *fanāʾ*, the "passing away" or "annihilation" of the self in the divine essence, the latter representing *baqāʾ*, "permanence."

Ṣufīs like al-Ghazālī interpreted *fanāʾ* as "closeness" (*qurb*) to God and thus helped to reconcile Sufism with the generally accepted tenets of Islam. The issue, however, remained a sensitive one, as reflected, for example, in the philosophical tale, *Ḥayy Ibn Yaqẓān*, by the Andalusian philosopher Ibn Ṭufayl (d. 1185). Ḥayy, the story's hero, who grows up on an uninhabited tropical island, undergoes a process of self-education that culminates in the mystical experience. At first he falls into the error of thinking that his soul becomes one with the divine essence; he is delivered from this mistake through God's mercy as he realizes that such concepts as unity and plurality and union and disjunction are applicable only to bodies, not to immaterial selves that have experiential knowledge of God.

The relation of the soul to God in Ṣufī thought takes on a highly metaphysical turn in the complex theosophy of the great mystic Ibn al-ʿArabī (d. 1240) and his followers, particularly ʿAbd al-Karīm al-Jīlī (d. 1408?). Ibn al-ʿArabī is noted for his doctrine of the unity of being (*waḥdat al-wujūd*) wherein creation (*al-khalq*) is a mirroring of the Truth (*al-ḥaqq*), the Creator. Perfect souls are reflections of the perfection of the divine essence. The prophets are the archetypes of these perfect souls: each prophet is a word (*kalimah*) of God. The perfect soul is a microcosm of reality. The idea of man as a microcosm did not originate with Ibn al-ʿArabī; it was utilized by the *falāsifah* and by al-Ghazālī. But with Ibn al-ʿArabī and those who followed him it acquires a spiritual and metaphysical dimension all its own, representing a high point in the development of the concept of soul in the history of Islamic religious thought.

BIBLIOGRAPHY

For a comprehensive study, see D. B. Macdonald's "The Development of the Idea of Spirit in Islam," *Acta Orientalia* (1931): 307–351, reprinted in *The Moslem World* 22 (January and April 1932): 25–42, 153–168. For Qurʾanic, traditional, and *kalām* concepts, see Régis Blachère's "Note sur le substantif 'nafs' dans le Coran," *Semitica* 1 (1948): 69–77; F. T. Cooke's "Ibn al-Quiyim's Kitab al-Rūḥ," *The Moslem World* 25 (April 1935): 129–144; and Albert N. Nader's *Le système philosophique des muʿtazila* (Beirut, 1956); see also the work by Majid Fakhry cited below. For philosophical concepts, see

Avicenna's "On the Proof of Prophecies," translated by me in *Medieval Political Philosophy: A Sourcebook*, edited by Ralph Lerner and Muhsin Mahdi (New York, 1963), pp. 112–121; Majid Fakhry's *A History of Islamic Philosophy*, 2d ed. (New York, 1983); Lenn E. Goodman's "Rasi's Myth of the Fall of the Soul," in *Essays on Islamic Philosophy and Science*, edited by George F. Hourani (Albany, N. Y., 1975), pp. 25–40; my article "Avicenna and the Problem of the Infinite Number of Souls," *Mediaeval Studies* 22 (1960); 232–239; and *Avicenna's Psychology*, edited and translated by Fazlur Rahman (London, 1952). For Ṣūfī concepts, see A. E. Affifi's *The Mystical Philosophy of Muḥyid Dīn Ibnul ʿArabī* (Cambridge, 1939); A. J. Arberry's *Sufism* (1950; reprint, London, 1979); Ibn al-ʿArabī's *The Bezels of Wisdom*, translated with an introduction and notes by R. W. J. Austin (London, 1980); Reynold A. Nicholson's *Studies in Islamic Mysticism* (1921; reprint, Cambridge, 1976); Annemarie Schimmel's *Mystical Dimensions of Islam* (Chapel Hill, N.C., 1975); and Fadlou Shehadi's *Ghazālī's Unique Unknowable God* (Leiden, 1964).

MICHAEL E. MARMURA (1987)

SOUND SEE MUSIC; PERCUSSION AND NOISE